ST/ESA/STAT/SER.R/49

Department of Economic and Social Affairs
Département des affaires économiques et sociales

2019
Demographic Yearbook
Annuaire démographique

Seventieth issue/Soixante-dixième édition

United Nations
New York, 2020

The Department of Economic and Social Affairs of the United Nations Secretariat is a vital interface between global policies in the economic, social and environmental spheres and national action. The Department works in three main interlinked areas: (i) it compiles, generates and analyses a wide range of economic, social and environmental data and information on which Member States of the United Nations draw to review common problems and to take stock of policy options; (ii) it facilitates the negotiations of Member States in many intergovernmental bodies on joint courses of action to address ongoing or emerging global challenges; and (iii) it advises interested Governments on the ways and means of translating policy frameworks developed in United Nations conferences and summits into programmes at the country level and, through technical assistance, helps build national capacities.

Le Département des affaires économiques et sociales du Secrétariat de l'Organisation des Nations Unies sert de relais entre les orientations arrêtées au niveau international dans les domaines économiques, sociaux et environnementaux et les politiques exécutées à l'échelon national. Il intervient dans trois grands domaines liés les uns aux autres : i) il compile, produit et analyse une vaste gamme de données et d'éléments d'information sur des questions économiques, sociales et environnementales dont les États Membres de l'Organisation se servent pour examiner des problèmes communs et évaluer les options qui s'offrent à eux; ii) il facilite les négociations entre les États Membres dans de nombreux organes intergouvernementaux sur les orientations à suivre de façon collective afin de faire face aux problèmes mondiaux existants ou en voie d'apparition; iii) il conseille les gouvernements intéressés sur la façon de transposer les orientations politiques arrêtées à l'occasion des conférences et sommets des Nations Unies en programmes exécutables au niveau national et aide à renforcer les capacités nationales au moyen de programmes d'assistance technique.

NOTE

Symbols of United Nations documents are composed of capital letters combined with figures. Mention of such a symbol indicates reference to a United Nations document.

The designations employed and the presentation of material in this publication do not imply the expression of any opinion whatsoever on the part of the Secretariat of the United Nations concerning the legal status of any country, territory, city or area, or of its authorities, or concerning the delimitation of its frontiers or boundaries.

Where the designation "country or area" appears in the headings of tables, it covers countries, territories, or areas.

NOTE

Les cotes des documents de l'Organisation des Nations Unies se composent de lettres majuscules et de chiffres. La simple mention d'une cote dans un texte signifie qu'il s'agit d'un document de l'Organisation.

Les appellations employées dans cette publication et la présentation des données qui y figurent n'impliquent de la part du Secrétariat de l'Organisation des Nations Unies aucune prise de position quant au statut juridique des pays, territoires, villes ou zones, ou de leurs autorités, ni quant au tracé de leurs frontières ou limites.

L'appellation "pays ou zone" figurant dans les titres des rubriques des tableaux désigne des pays, des territoires, ou des zones.

ST/ESA/STAT/SER.R/49

UNITED NATIONS PUBLICATION
Sales number: B.20.XIII.22

PUBLICATION DES NATIONS UNIES
Numéro de vente: B.20.XIII.22

ISBN 978-92-1-148351-2
eISBN 978-92-1-005249-8
Print ISSN: 0082-8041
Online ISSN: 2412-0006

Topics of the Demographic Yearbook series: 1948 - 2019

Sujets des diverses éditions de l'Annuaire démographique : 1948 - 2019

Year Année	Sales No. - Numéro de vente	Issue - Edition	Special topic - Sujet spécial
1948	49.XIII.1	First-Première	General demography-Démographie générale
1949-50	51.XIII.1	Second-Deuxième	Natality statistics-Statistiques de la natalité
1951	52.XIII.1	Third-Trosième	Mortality statistics-Statistiques de la mortalité
1952	53.XIII.1	Fourth-Quatrième	Population distribution-Répartition de la population
1953	54.XIII.1	Fifth-Cinquième	General demography-Démographie générale
1954	55.XIII.1	Sixth-Sixième	Natality statistics -Statistiques de la natalité
1955	56.XIII.1	Seventh-Septième	Population censuses-Recensement de population
1956	57.XIII.1	Eighth-Huitième	Ethnic and economic characteristics of population-Caractéristiques ethniques et économiques de la population
1957	58.XIII.1	Ninth-Neuvième	Mortality statistics- Statistiques de la mortalité
1958	59.XIII.1	Tenth-Dixième	Marriage and divorce statistics- Statistiques de la nuptialitè et de la divortialité
1959	60.XIII.1	Eleventh-Onzième	Natality statistics- Statistiques de la natalité
1960	61.XIII.1	Twelfth-Douzième	Population trends- l' évolution de la population
1961	62.XIII.1	Thirteenth-Treizième	Mortality Statistics- Statistiques de la mortalité
1962	63.XIII.1	Fourteenth-Quatorzième	Population census statistics I- Statistiques des recensements de population I
1963	64.XIII.1	Fifteenth-Quinzième	Population census statistics II- Statistiques des recensements de population II
1964	65.XIII.1	Sixteenth-Seizième	Population census statistics III- Statistiques des recensements de population III
1965	66.XIII.1	Seventeenth-Dix-septième	Natality statistics- Statistiques de la natalité
1966	67.XIII.1	Eighteenth-Dix-huitième	Mortality statistics I- Statistiques de la mortalité I
1967	E/F.68.XIII.1	Nineteenth-Dix-neuvième	Mortality statistics II - Statistiques de la mortalité II
1968	E/F.69.XIII.1	Twentieth-Vingtième	Marriage and divorce statistics-Statistiques de la nuptialité et de la divortialité
1969	E/F.70.XIII.1	Twenty-first-Vingt et unième	Natality statistics-Statistiques de la natalité
1970	E/F.71.XIII.1	Twenty-second-Vingt-deuxième	Population trends-l' évolution de la population
1971	E/F.72.XIII.1	Twenty-third-Vingt-troisième	Population census statistics I- Statistiques de recensements de population I
1972	E/F.73.XIII.1	Twenty-fourth-Vingt-quatrième	Population census statistics II- Statistiques des recensements de population II
1973	E/F.74.XIII.1	Twenty-fifth-Vingt-cinquième	Population census statistics III- Statistiques des recensements de population III
1974	E/F.75.XIII.1	Twenty-sixth-Vingt-sixième	Mortality statistics - Statistiques de la mortalité
1975	E/F.76.XIII.1	Twenty-seventh-Vingt-septième	Natality statistics- Statistiques de la natalité
1976	E/F.77.XIII.1	Twenty-eighth-Vingt-huitième	Marriage and divorce statistics- Statistiques de la nuptialité et de la divortialité
1977	E/F.78.XIII.1	Twenty-ninth-Vingt-neuvième	International Migration Statistics- internationales
1978	E/F.79.XIII.1	Thirtieth-Trentième	General tables- Tableaux de caractère général
1978	E/F.79.XIII.8	Special issue-Edition spéciale	Historical supplement-Supplément rétrospectif
1979	E/F.80.XIII.1	Thirty-first-Trente et unième	Population census statistics-Statistiques des recensements de population
1980	E/F.81.XIII.1	Thirty-second-Trente-deuxième	Mortality statistics- Statistiques de la mortalité
1981	E/F.82.XIII.1	Thirty-third-Trente-troisième	Natality statistics-Statistiques de la natalité
1982	E/F.83.XIII.1	Thirty-fourth-Trente-quatrième	Marriage and divorce statistics-Statistiques de la nuptialité et de la divortialité
1983	E/F.84.XIII.1	Thirty fifth-Trente-cinquième	Population census statistics I-Statistiques des recensements de population I
1984	E/F.85.XIII.1	Thirty-sixth-	Population census statistics II-

Topics of the Demographic Yearbook series: 1948 - 2019

Sujets des diverses éditions de l'Annuaire démographique : 1948 - 2019

Year Année	Sales No. - Numéro de vente	Issue - Edition	Special topic - Sujet spécial
		Trente-sixième	Statistiques des recensements de population II
1985	E/F.86.XIII.1	Thirty-seventh- Trente-septième	Mortality statistics- Statistiques de la mortalité
1986	E/F.87.XIII.1	Thirty-eighth- Trente-huitième	Natality statistics- Statistiques de la natalité
1987	E/F.88.XIII.1	Thirty-ninth- Trente-neuvième	Household composition- Les éléments du ménage
1988	E/F.89.XIII.1	Fortieth- Quarantième	Population census statistics- Statistiques des recensements de population
1989	E/F.90.XIII.1	Forty-first- Quarante-et-unième	International Migration Statistics- Statistiques des migration internationales
1990	E/F.91.XIII.1	Forty-second- Quarante-deuxième	Marriage and divorce statistics- Statistiques de la nuptialité et de la divortialité
1991	E/F.92.XIII.1	Forty-third- Quarante-troisième	General tables- Tableaux de caractère général
1991	E/F.92.XIII.9	Special Issue	Population Ageing and the Situation of Elderly Persons Vieillissement de la population et situation des personnes âgées
1992	E/F.94.XIII.1	Forty-fourth- Quarante-quatrième	Fertility and mortality statistics- Statistiques de la fecondité et de la mortalité
1993	E/F.95.XIII.1	Forty-fifth- Quarante-cinquième	Population census statistics I- Statistiques des recensements de population I
1994	E/F.96.XIII.1	Forty-sixth- Quarante-sixième	Population census statistics II- Statistiques des recensements de population II
1995	E/F.97.XIII.1	Forty-seventh- Quarante-septième	Household composition-Les éléments du ménage
1996	E/F.98.XIII.1	Forty-eighth- Quarante-huitième	Mortality statistics- Statistiques de la mortalité
1997	E/F.99.XIII.1	Forty-ninth- Quarante-neuvième	General tables- Tableaux de caractère général
1997	E/F.99.XIII.12	Special issue- Edition spéciale (CD)	Historical supplement- Supplément rétrospectif
1998	E/F.00.XIII.1	Fiftieth- Cinquantième	General tables- Tableaux de caractère général
1999	E/F.01.XIII.1	Fifty-first- Cinquante-et-unième	General tables- Tableaux de caractère général
1999	E/F.02.XIII.6	Special issue- Edition spéciale (CD)	Natality Statistics- Statistiques de la natalité
2000	E/F.02.XIII.1	Fifty-second- Cinquante-deuxième	General tables- Tableaux de caractère général
2001	E/F.03.XIII.1	Fifty-third- Cinquante- troisième	General tables- Tableaux de caractère général
2002	E/F.05.XIII.1	Fifty-fourth- Cinquante-quatrième	General tables- Tableaux de caractère général
2003	E/F.06.XIII.1	Fifty-fifth- Cinquante-cinquième	General tables- Tableaux de caractère général
2004	E/F.07.XIII.1	Fifty-sixth- Cinquante-sixième	General tables- Tableaux de caractère général
2005	E/F.08.XIII.1	Fifty-seventh- Cinquante-septième	General tables- Tableaux de caractère général
2006	E/F.09.XIII.1	Fifty-eighth- Cinquante-huitième	General tables- Tableaux de caractère général
2007	E/F.10.XIII.1	Fifty-ninth- Cinquante-neuvième	General tables- Tableaux de caractère général
2008	E/F.11.XIII.1	Sixtieth- Soixantième	General tables- Tableaux de caractère général
2009 - 2010	B.12.XIII.1 H	Sixty-first Soixante-et-unième	General tables- Tableaux de caractère général
2011	B.13.XIII.1 H	Sixty-second Soixante- deuxième	General tables- Tableaux de caractère général
2012	B.14.XIII.1 H	Sixty-third Soixante- troisième	General tables- Tableaux de caractère général

Topics of the Demographic Yearbook series: 1948 - 2019

Sujets des diverses éditions de l'Annuaire démographique : 1948 - 2019

Year Année	Sales No. - Numéro de vente	Issue - Edition	Special topic - Sujet spécial
2013	B.15.XIII.1 H	Sixty-fourth Soixante- quatrième	General tables- Tableaux de caractère général
2014	B.16.XIII.1 H	Sixty-fifth Soixante- cinquième	General tables and Whipple's Index, censuses,1985-2014 - Tableaux de caractère général et l'indice de Whipple, recensements, 1985-2014
2015	B.17.XIII.1 H	Sixty-sixth Soixante- sixième	General tables and Whipple's Index, censuses,1985-2015 - Tableaux de caractère général et l'indice de Whipple, recensements, 1985-2015
2016	B.18.XIII.1 H	Sixty-seventh Soixante- septième	General tables and Whipple's Index, censuses,1985-2016 - Tableaux de caractère général et l'indice de Whipple, recensements, 1985-2016
2017	B.19.XIII.1 H	Sixty-eighth Soixante- huitième	General tables and Whipple's Index, censuses,1985-2017 - Tableaux de caractère général et l'indice de Whipple, recensements, 1985-2017
2018	B.20.XIII.1 H	Sixty-ninth Soixante- neuvième	General tables and Whipple's Index, censuses,1985-2018 - Tableaux de caractère général et l'indice de Whipple, recensements, 1985-2018
2019	B.20.XIII.22	Seventieth Soixante- dixième	General tables and Whipple's Index, censuses,1985-2019 - Tableaux de caractère général et l'indice de Whipple, recensements, 1985-2019

CONTENTS - TABLE DES MATIERES

FERTILITY

FOETAL MORTALITY

INFANT AND MATERNAL MORTALITY

GENERAL MORTALITY

NATALITÉ

MORTALITÉ FŒTALES

MORTALITÉ INFANTILE ET MORTALITÉ LIÉE À LA MATERNITÉ

MORTALITÉ GÉNÉRALE

NUPTIALITY

DIVORCE

ANNEX

INDEX

NUPTIALITÉ

DIVORTIALITÉ

ANNEX

INDEX

EXPLANATIONS OF SYMBOLS

Category not applicable	..
Data not available	...
Magnitude zero or less than half of unit employed	-
Provisional	*
Data tabulated by year of registration rather than occurrence	+
Based on less than specified minimum	◆
Relatively reliable data	Roman type
Data of lesser reliability	*Italics*

EXPLICATION DES SIGNES

Sans objet	..
Données non disponibles	...
Néant ou chiffre inférieur à la moitié de l'unité employée	-
Données provisoires	*
Donnée exploitées selon l'année de l'enregistrement et non l'année de l'événement	+
Rapport fondé sur un nombre inférieur à celui spécifié	◆
Données relativement sûres	Caractères romains
Données dont l'exactitude est moindre	*Italiques*

INTRODUCTION

The *Demographic Yearbook* is an international compendium of national demographic statistics provided by national statistical authorities to the Statistics Division of the United Nations Department of Economic and Social Affairs. The *Demographic Yearbook* is part of the set of coordinated and interrelated publications issued by the United Nations and its specialized agencies, designed to supply statistical data for such users as demographers, economists, public-health workers and sociologists. Through the co-operation of national statistical services, available official demographic statistics are compiled in the *Demographic Yearbook* for more than 230 countries or areas throughout the world.

The *Demographic Yearbook 2019* is the seventieth issue in a series published by the United Nations since 1948. It contains tables on a wide range of demographic statistics, including a world summary of selected demographic statistics, statistics on the size, distribution and trends in national populations, fertility, foetal mortality, infant and maternal mortality, general mortality, nuptiality and divorce. Data are shown by urban/rural residence, as available. The volume provides Technical Notes, a synoptic table, a historical index and a listing of the issues of the *Demographic Yearbook* published to date. This issue of *Demographic Yearbook* contains data as available including reference year 2019.

This edition of the *Demographic Yearbook* features also table 3a with Whipple's index by sex and urban/rural residence for the population censuses conducted worldwide since 1985. Whipple's index is an index of age preference in age reporting and can therefore serve to highlight some of the problems related to age distribution.

The Technical Notes on the Statistical Tables are provided to assist the reader in using the tables. Table A, the synoptic table, provides an overview of the completeness of data coverage of the current *Demographic Yearbook*. The cumulative historical index is a guide on content and coverage of all seventy issues, and indicates, for each of the topics that have been published, the issues in which they are presented and the years covered. It also contains a list of tables published online through UNdata[1] (http://data.un.org/Explorer.aspx?d=POP). A list of the *Demographic Yearbook* issues, with their corresponding sales numbers and the special topics featured in each issue are shown on pages iii, iv and v. Additionally, all issues of the *Demographic Yearbook* are available online at the Statistics Division's website: https://unstats.un.org/unsd/demographic-social/products/dyb/index.cshtml.

Until the fourty-eighth issue (1996), each issue consisted of two parts, the general tables and special topic tables, published in the same volume[2]. Beginning with the fourty-ninth issue (1997), the special topic tables were being disseminated in digital format as supplements to the regular issues. Two CD-ROMs have been issued: the *Demographic Yearbook Historical Supplement*, which presents a wide panorama of basic demographic statistics for the period 1948 to 1997, and the *Demographic Yearbook*: *Natality Statistics*, which contains a series of detailed tables dedicated to natality and covering the period from 1980 to 1998. Later on, three volumes of *Demographic Yearbook* Special Census Topics for the 2000 round of censuses, covering the period from 1995 to 2004, were published on-line at http://unstats.un.org/unsd/demographic/products/dyb/dybcens.htm. Current *Demographic Yearbook* population and housing censuses data for the 2000, 2010 and 2020 rounds (1995 to the present) are presented at https://unstats.un.org/unsd/demographic-social/products/dyb/index.cshtml#censusdatasets. These datasets cover basic population characteristics, educational, household, ethnocultural and economic characteristics, and also foreign-born and foreign population. Special tabulations on household and economic characteristics with data based on population censuses since 1995 are available respectively at https://unstats.un.org/unsd/demographic-social/products/dyb/dyb_household/ and https://unstats.un.org/unsd/demographic-social/products/dyb/dyb_eco/.

Population statistics are not available for all countries or areas, for a variety of reasons. In an effort to provide estimates of mid-year population and of selected vital statistics for all countries and areas, two annexes are presented. Annex I presents United Nations population estimates for the period 2009-2018 and Annex II presents the medium variant estimates of crude birth and death rates, infant mortality and total fertility rates, as well as life expectancy at birth over the period 2015-2020. These data were produced by the United Nations Population Division and are published in the *2019 Revision of World Population Prospects*[3].

Demographic statistics shown in this issue of the *Demographic Yearbook* are available online at the *Demographic Yearbook* website https://unstats.un.org/unsd/demographic-social/products/dyb/index.cshtml#overview.

Information about the Statistics Division's data collection and dissemination programme is also available on the same website. Additional information can be made available by contacting the Statistics Division of the United Nations Department of Economic and Social Affairs at demostat@un.org.

TECHNICAL NOTES ON THE STATISTICAL TABLES

1. GENERAL REMARKS

1.1 Arrangement of Technical Notes

These Technical Notes are designed to provide the reader with relevant information related to the statistical tables. Information pertaining to the *Demographic Yearbook* in general is presented in the sections dealing with geographical aspects, population and vital statistics. In addition, preceding each table are notes describing the variables, remarks on the reliability and limitation of the data, countries and areas covered, and information on the presentation of earlier data. When appropriate, details on computation of rates, ratios or percentages are presented.

1.2 Arrangement of tables

The numbering of tables from one issue of *Demographic Yearbook* to the next is preserved to the extent possible. However, since for some of the tables the numbering may not correspond exactly to those in previous issues, the reader is advised to use the historical index that appears at the end of this book to find the reference to data in earlier issues.

1.3 Source of data

The statistics presented in the *Demographic Yearbook* are national data provided by official statistical authorities unless otherwise indicated. The primary source of data for the *Demographic Yearbook* is a set of questionnaires sent annually by the United Nations Statistics Division to over 230 national statistical services. Data reported on these questionnaires are supplemented, to the extent possible, with data taken from official national publications, official websites and through correspondence with national statistical services. In the interest of comparability, rates, ratios and percentages have been calculated by the Statistics Division of the United Nations, except for the life table functions, the total fertility rate, and also crude birth rate and crude death rate for some countries or areas as appropriately noted. The methods used by the Statistics Division to calculate these rates and ratios are described in the Technical Notes for each table. The population figures used for these computations are those pertaining to the corresponding years published in this or previous issues of the *Demographic Yearbook.*

In cases when data in this issue of the *Demographic Yearbook* differ from those published in earlier issues or related publications, statistics in this issue may be assumed to reflect revisions to the data received by June 2020.

2. GEOGRAPHICAL ASPECTS

2.1 Coverage

Data are shown for all individual countries or areas that provided information. Table 3 is the most comprehensive in geographical coverage, presenting data on population and surface area for all countries or areas with a population of at least 50 persons. Not all of these countries or areas appear in subsequent tables. In many cases the data required for a particular table are not available. In general, the more detailed the data required for a table, the fewer the number of countries or areas that can provide them.

In addition, rates and ratios are presented only for countries or areas reporting at least a minimum number of relevant events. The minimums are stated in the Technical Notes to individual tables.

Except for summary data shown for the world and by major areas and regions in tables 1 and 2 and data shown for capital cities and cities with a population of 100 000 or more in table 8, all data are presented at the national level. The number of countries or areas shown in each table is provided in table A, the synoptic table.

2.2 Territorial composition

To the extent possible, all data, including time series data, relate to the territory within 2018 boundaries. Exceptions are footnoted in individual tables. Relevant clarifications are specified below.

Data relating to **Denmark** exclude Faeroe Islands and Greenland, which are shown separately.

Data relating to **Finland** include Åland Islands, unless otherwise indicated by a footnote.

Data relating to **France** exclude Overseas Departments, which are shown separately, unless otherwise indicated by a footnote.

Data relating to **United Kingdom of Great Britain and Northern Ireland** exclude Guernsey, Isle of Man and Jersey which are shown separately.

Data relating to **Western Sahara** comprise the Northern Region (former Saguia el Hamra) and Southern Region (former Rio de Oro).

2.3 Nomenclature

Because of space limitations, the country or area names listed in the tables are generally the commonly employed short titles currently in use[4] in the United Nations, the full titles being used only when a short form is not available. The latest version of the *Standard Country or Area Codes for Statistics Use* can be accessed at https://unstats.un.org/unsd/methodology/m49/.

2.3.1 Order of presentation

Countries or areas are listed in English alphabetical order within the following continents: Africa, North America, South America, Asia, Europe and Oceania.

The designations and presentation of the material in this publication were adopted solely for the purpose of providing a convenient geographical basis for the accompanying statistical series. The same qualification applies to all notes and explanations concerning the geographical units for which data are presented.

2.4 Surface area data

Surface area data shown in table 1 represent the land area, whereas in table 3 the total surface area unless otherwise indicated. The total surface area comprises land area and inland waters (assumed to consist of major rivers and lakes) and excluding only Polar Regions and uninhabited islands. The surface area given is the most recent estimate available. They are presented in square kilometres; a conversion factor of 2.589988 having been applied to surface areas originally reported in square miles.

2.4.1 Comparability over time

Comparability over time in surface area estimates for any given country or area may be affected by changes in the surface area estimation procedures, increases in actual land surface by reclamation, boundary changes, changes in the concept of "land surface area" used or a change in the unit of measurement used. In most cases it was possible to ascertain the reason for a revision; otherwise, the latest figures have generally been accepted as correct.

2.4.2 International comparability

Lack of international comparability between surface area estimates arises primarily from differences in definition. In particular, there is considerable variation in the treatment of coastal bays, inlets and gulfs, rivers and lakes. International comparability is also impaired by the variation in methods employed to estimate surface area. These range from surveys based on modern scientific methods to conjectures based on diverse types of information. Some estimates are recent while others may not be. Since neither the exact method of determining the surface area nor the precise definition of its composition and time reference is known for all countries or areas, the estimates in table 3 should not be considered strictly comparable from one country or area to another.

3. POPULATION

Population statistics, that is, those pertaining to the size, geographical distribution and demographic characteristics of the population, are presented in a number of tables of the *Demographic Yearbook*.

Summary estimates of the mid-year population of the world, major areas and regions for selected years and of its age and sex distribution in 2019 are set forth in tables 1 and 2, respectively.

Data for countries or areas include population census figures, estimates based on results of sample surveys (in the absence of a census), postcensal or intercensal estimates and those derived from continuous population registers. In the present issue of the *Demographic Yearbook*, the latest available census figure of the total population of each country or area and mid-year estimates for 2010 and 2019 are presented in table 3. Mid-year estimates of total population for ten years (2010-2019) are shown in table 5 and mid-year estimates of urban and total population by sex for ten years (2010-2019) are shown in table 6. The latest available data on population by age, sex and urban/rural residence are given in table 7. The latest available figures on the population of capital cities and of cities or urban agglomerations of 100 000 or more inhabitants are presented in table 8.

The statistics on total population, population by age, sex, or urban/rural distribution are used for the calculation of rates in the *Demographic Yearbook*. Vital rates by residence (urban/rural), age or sex were calculated using data presented in tables 6 or 7 in this issue or the corresponding tables of previous issues of the *Demographic Yearbook*.

3.1 Sources of variation of data

The comparability of data is affected by several factors, including (1) the definition of total population; (2) the definition used to classify the population into its urban/rural components; (3) the accuracy of age reporting; (4) the extent of over-enumeration or under-enumeration in the most recent census or other source of benchmark population statistics; and (5) the quality of population estimates. These five factors will be discussed in some detail in sections 3.1.1 to 3.1.3 below. Other relevant problems are discussed in the technical notes to the individual tables. Readers interested in more detail, relating in particular to the basic concepts of population size, distribution and characteristics as elaborated by the United Nations, should consult the *Principles and Recommendations for Population and Housing Censuses, Revision 3*[5].

3.1.1 Total population

The most important impediment to comparability of total populations is the difference between the concept of a *de facto* and *de jure* population. A *de facto* population includes all persons physically present in the country or area at the reference date. The *de jure* population, by contrast, includes all usual residents of the given country or area, whether or not they were physically present in the area at the reference date. By definition, therefore, a *de facto* total and a *de jure* total are not entirely comparable.

Comparability of even two *de facto* or *de jure* totals is often affected by the fact that strict conformity to either of these concepts is rare. For example, some so-called *de facto* counts do not include foreign military, naval and diplomatic personnel present in the country or area on official duty, and their accompanying family and household members; some do not include foreign visitors in transit through the country or area or transients on ships in harbours. On the other hand, they may include such persons as merchant seamen and fishermen who are temporarily out of the country or area working at their trade.

The *de jure* population figure presents even greater variations in comparability, in part because it depends in the first place on the concept of "usual residence", which varies from one country or area to another and is difficult to apply consistently in a census or survey enumeration. For example, non-national civilians temporarily in a country or area as short-term workers may officially be considered residents after a stay of a specified period of time or they may be considered as non-residents throughout the duration of their stay; at the same time, these individuals may be officially considered as residents or non-residents of the country or area from which they came, depending on the duration and/or purpose of their absence. Furthermore, regardless of the official treatment, individual respondents may apply their own interpretation of residence in responding to the inquiry. In addition, there may be considerable differences in the accuracy with which countries or areas are informed about the number of their residents temporarily out of the country or area.

The population statistics presented in the tables of the *Demographic Yearbook* refer to the *de facto* population or to the *de jure* population. In an effort to overcome, to the extent possible, the effect of the lack of strict conformity to either the *de facto* or the *de jure* concept given above, significant exceptions with respect to inclusions and exclusions of specific population groups, are footnoted when they are known.

A possible source of variation within the statistics of a single country or area may arise from the fact that some countries or areas collect information on both the *de facto* and the *de jure* population in, for example, a census, but prepare detailed tabulations for only the *de jure* population. Hence, even though the total population shown in table 3 is de facto, the figures shown in the tables presenting various characteristics of the population, for example, urban/rural distribution, age and sex distribution, may be on the *de jure* concept.

3.1.2 Urban/rural classification

International comparability of urban/rural distributions is seriously impaired by the wide variation among national definitions of the concept of "urban". The definitions used by individual countries or areas and their implications are shown at the end of technical notes for table 6.

3.1.3 Age distribution

The classification of population by age is a core element of most analyses, estimation and projection of population statistics. Unfortunately, age data are subject to a number of sources of error and non-comparability. Accordingly, the reliability of age data should be of concern to users of these statistics.

3.1.3.1 Collection and compilation of age data

Age is the estimated or calculated interval of time between the date of birth and the date of the census or survey, expressed in completed solar years[6]. There are two methods of collecting information on age. The first is to obtain the date of birth for each member of the population in a census or survey and then to calculate the completed age of the individual by subtracting the date of birth from the date of enumeration[7]. The second method is to record the individual's completed age at the time of the census or survey, that is to say, age at last birthday.

The recommended method is to calculate age at last birthday by subtracting the exact date of birth from the date of the census. Some practices, however, do not use this method but instead calculate the difference between the year of birth and the year of the census. Classifications of this type are footnoted whenever possible. They can be identified to a certain extent by a smaller than expected population under one year of age. However, an irregular number of births from one year to the next or age selective omission of infants may also obscure the expected population under one year of age.

3.1.3.2 Errors in age data

Errors in age data may be due to a variety of causes, including ignorance of the correct age; reporting years of age in terms of a calendar concept other than completed solar years since birth[8]; carelessness in reporting and recording age; a general tendency to state age in figures ending in certain digits (such as zero, two, five and eight); a tendency to exaggerate length of life at advanced ages; a subconscious aversion to certain numbers; and wilful misrepresentations.

These reasons for errors in reported age data are common to most investigations of age and to most countries or areas, and they may significantly impair comparability of the data.

As a result of the above-mentioned difficulties, the age-sex distribution of population in many countries or areas shows irregularities which may be summarized as follows: (1) a deficiency in the number of infants and young children; (2) a concentration at ages ending with zero and five (that is, 5, 10, 15, 20, ...); (3) heaping at even ages (for example, 10, 12, 14, ...) relative to odd ages (for example, 11, 13, 15, ...); (4) unexpectedly large differences between the frequency of males and females at certain ages; and (5) unaccountably large differences between the frequencies in adjacent age groups. Comparing of identical age-sex cohorts from successive censuses, as well as studying the age-sex composition of each census, may reveal these and other inconsistencies, some of which in varying degree are characteristic of even the most modern censuses.

This edition of the *Demographic Yearbook* features a tabulation (table 3a) with Whipple's index by sex and urban/ rural residence for the population censuses conducted worldwide since 1985. Whipple's index is an index of age preference in age reporting and can therefore serve to highlight some of the problems related to age distribution.

4. VITAL STATISTICS

For purposes of the *Demographic Yearbook*, vital statistics of concern are those of live birth, death, foetal death, marriage and divorce.

This volume of the *Demographic Yearbook* presents tables on fertility, nuptiality and divorce as well as tables on mortality referring to foetal mortality, infant and maternal mortality and general mortality.

4.1 Sources of variation of data

Most of the vital statistics data published in this *Demographic Yearbook* are sourced from national civil registration systems. The completeness and the accuracy of the data that these systems produce vary from one country or area to another.

National civil registration systems may not exist in all countries, and in some cases, the registration system covers only certain vital events. For example, in some countries or areas only births and deaths are registered. There are also differences in the effectiveness with which national laws pertaining to civil registration operate in the various countries or areas. The manner in which the law is implemented and the degree to which the public complies with the legislation determine the reliability of vital statistics obtained from the civil registers.

It should be noted that some statistics on marriage and divorce are obtained from sources other than civil registers. For example, in some countries or areas, the only source for data on marriages is church registers. Divorce statistics, on the other hand, are obtained from court records and/or civil registers according to national practice. The actual compilation of these statistics may be the responsibility of the civil registrar, the national statistical office or other government offices.

Other factors affecting international comparability of vital statistics are much the same as those that must be considered in evaluating the variations in other population statistics. Differences in statistical definitions of vital events, differences in geographical and ethnic coverage of the data and diverse tabulation procedures may also influence comparability.

In addition to vital statistics from civil registers, some vital statistics published in the *Demographic Yearbook* are official estimates. These estimates are frequently from population censuses and sample surveys. As such, their comparability may be affected by the national completeness of reporting in population censuses and household surveys, whether a *de facto* or *de jure* based census, non-sampling and sampling errors and other sources of bias.

Readers interested in more detailed information on standards for vital statistics should consult the *Principles and Recommendations for a Vital Statistics System Revision 3*[9]; *Guidelines on the Legislative Framework for Civil Registration, Vital Statistics and Identity Management*[10]; *Handbook on Civil Registration and Vital Statistics Systems: Management, Operation and Maintenance, Revision 1*[11]; *Handbook on civil registration, vital statistics and identity management systems: Communication for development*[12]; *Handbook on Civil Registration and Vital Statistics Systems: Policies and Protocols for the Release and Archiving of Individual Records*[13]; and *Handbook on Civil Registration and Vital Statistics Systems: Computerization*[14]. The *Handbook on the Collection of Fertility and Mortality Data*[15] provides information in collection and evaluation of data on fertility and mortality collected in population censuses and household surveys. These publications are also available on the website at https://unstats.un.org/unsd/demographic-social/Standards-and-Methods/index.cshtml.

4.1.1 Statistical definition of events

An important source of variation lies in the statistical definition of each vital event. The *Demographic Yearbook* attempts to collect data on vital events, using the standard definitions put forth in Chapter I of *Principles and Recommendations for a Vital Statistics System Revision 3*. These definitions are as follows:

LIVE BIRTH is the complete expulsion or extraction from its mother of a product of conception, irrespective of the duration of pregnancy, which after such separation breathes or shows any other evidence of life such as beating of the heart, pulsation of the umbilical cord, or definite movement of voluntary muscles, whether or not the umbilical cord has been cut or the placenta is attached; each product of such a birth is considered live-born.

DEATH is the permanent disappearance of all evidence of life at any time after the occurrence of live birth, i.e., the postnatal cessation of vital functions without capability of resuscitation. This definition excludes foetal deaths.

FOETAL DEATH is death prior to the complete expulsion or extraction from its mother of a product of conception, irrespective of the duration of the period of gestation. Death is indicated by the fact that after such separation, the foetus does not breathe or show any other evidence of life, such as beating of the heart, pulsation of the umbilical cord, or definite movement of voluntary muscles.

MARRIAGE is an act, ceremony or process by which the legal relationship of spouses is constituted. The legality of the union may be established by civil, religious or other means as recognized by the laws of each country. Countries may wish to expand the definition to cover civil unions if they are registered. In that case, registered partnership usually refers to a legal construct, entailing registration with the public authorities according to the laws of each country, that becomes the basis for legal conjugal obligations between two persons.

DIVORCE is a final legal dissolution of a marriage, that is, the separation of spouses that confers on the parties the right to remarriage under civil, religious and/or other provisions, according to the laws of each country. In the case where a country recognizes registered partnerships, a legal dissolution of a registered partnership constitutes the legal final dissolution of such a partnership, according to national laws, which confers on the parties the right to enter into another partnership or marriage.

In addition to these internationally recommended definitions, the *Demographic Yearbook* collects and presents data on abortions, defined as:

ABORTION is defined, with reference to the woman, as any interruption of pregnancy before 28 weeks of gestation with a dead foetus. There are two major categories of abortion: spontaneous and induced. Induced abortions are those initiated by deliberate action undertaken with the intention of terminating pregnancy; all other abortions are considered spontaneous.

4.1.2 Problems relating to standard definitions

A basic problem affecting international comparability of vital statistics is deviations from the standard definitions of vital events. An example of this can be seen in the cases of live births and foetal deaths. In some countries or areas, an infant must survive for at least 24 hours, to be inscribed in the live-birth register. Infants who die before the expiration of the 24-hour period are classified as late foetal deaths and, barring special tabulation procedures, they would not be counted either as live births or as deaths. Similarly, in several other countries or areas, those infants who are born alive but die before registration of their birth, are also considered late foetal deaths.

Unless special tabulation procedures are adopted in such cases, the live-birth and death statistics will both be deficient by the number of these infants, while the incidence of late foetal deaths will be increased by the same amount. Hence the infant mortality rate is underestimated. Although both components (infant deaths and live births) are deficient by the same absolute amount, the deficiency is proportionately greater in relation to the infant deaths, causing greater errors in the infant mortality rate than in the birth rate.

Moreover, the practice exaggerates the late foetal death ratios. Some countries or areas make provision for correcting this deficiency (at least in the total frequencies) at the tabulation stage. Data for which the correction has not been made are indicated by a footnote whenever possible.

The definitions used for marriage and divorce also present problems for international comparability. Unlike birth and death, which are biological events, marriage and divorce are defined only in terms of law and custom and as such are less amenable to universally applicable statistical definitions. They have therefore been defined for statistical purposes in general terms referring to the laws of individual countries or areas. Laws pertaining to marriage and particularly to divorce, vary from one country or area to another. With respect to marriage, the most widespread requirement relates to the minimum age at which persons may marry but frequently other requirements are specified.

When known the minimum legal age of men and women at which marriage can occur with or without parental consent is presented in table 24-1. Laws and regulations relating to the dissolution of marriage by divorce range from total prohibition, through a wide range of grounds upon which divorces may be granted, to the granting of divorce in response to a simple statement of desire or intention by spouses.

4.1.3 Fragmentary geographical or ethnic coverage

As per the international standards, vital statistics for any given country or area should cover the entire geographical area and include all ethnic groups. Fragmentary coverage is, however, not uncommon. In some countries or areas, registration is compulsory for only a small part of the population, limited to certain ethnic groups, for example. In other places there is no national provision for compulsory registration, but only municipal or state ordinances that do not cover the entire geographical area. Still others have developed a registration area that comprises only a part of the country or area, the remainder being excluded because of inaccessibility or for economic and cultural considerations that make regular registration practically impossible.

4.1.4 Tabulation procedures

4.1.4.1 By place of occurrence

Vital statistics presented at the national level relate to the de facto, that is, the present-in-area population. Thus, unless otherwise noted, vital statistics for a given country or area cover all the events that occur within its present boundaries and among all segments of the population therein. They may be presumed to include events among nomadic tribes and indigenous peoples, and among nationals and foreigners. When known, deviations from the *de facto* concept are footnoted.

Urban/rural differentials in vital rates for some countries may vary considerably depending on whether the relevant vital events were tabulated on the basis of place of occurrence or place of usual residence. For example, if a substantial number of women residing in rural areas near major urban centres travel to hospitals or maternity homes located in a city to give birth, urban fertility and neo-natal and infant mortality rates will usually be higher (and the corresponding rural rates will usually be lower) if the events are tabulated on the basis of place of occurrence rather than on the basis of place of usual residence. A similar process will affect general mortality differentials if substantial numbers of persons residing in rural areas use urban health facilities when seriously ill.

4.1.4.2 By date of occurrence versus by date of registration

To the extent possible, the vital statistics presented in the *Demographic Yearbook* refer to events that occurred during the specified year, rather than to those that were registered during that period. However, a considerable number of countries or areas tabulate their vital statistics not by date of occurrence, but by date of registration. Because such statistics can be misleading, the countries or areas known to tabulate vital statistics by date of registration are identified in the tables by a plus sign "+". Since information on the method of tabulating vital statistics is not available for all countries and areas, tabulation by date of registration may be more prevalent than the symbols on the vital statistics tables would indicate.

Because quality of data is inextricably related to the timeliness of registration, this must always be considered in conjunction with the quality code description in section 4.2.1 below. If registration of births is complete and timely (code "C"), the ill effects of tabulating by date of registration, are, for all practical purposes, nullified. Similarly, with respect to death statistics, the effect of tabulating events by date of registration may be minimized in many countries or areas in which the sanitary code requires that a death must be registered before a burial permit can be issued, and this regulation tends to make registration prompt. With respect to foetal death, registration is usually done right away or not at all. Therefore, if registration is prompt, the difference between statistics tabulated by date of occurrence and those tabulated by date of registration may be negligible. In many cases, the length of the statutory time period allowed for registering various vital events plays an important part in determining the effects of tabulation by date of registration on the comparability of data.

With respect to marriage and divorce, the practice of tabulating data by date of registration does not generally pose serious problems. In many countries or areas marriage is a civil legal contract which, to establish its legality, must be celebrated before a civil officer. It follows that for these countries or areas registration would tend to be almost automatic at the time of, or immediately following, the marriage ceremony. Because the registration of a divorce in many countries or areas is the responsibility solely of the court or the authority which granted it, and since the registration record in such cases is part of the records of the court proceedings, it follows that divorces are likely to be registered soon after the decree is granted.

On the other hand, if registration is not prompt, vital statistics by date of registration will not produce internationally comparable data. Under the best circumstances, statistics by date of registration will include primarily events that occurred in the immediately preceding year; in countries or areas with less developed systems, tabulations will include some events that occurred many years in the past. Examination of available information reveals that delays of many years are not uncommon for birth registration, though the majority is recorded between two to four years after birth.

As long as registration is not prompt, statistics by date of registration will not be internationally comparable either among themselves or with statistics by date of occurrence.

It should also be mentioned that lack of international comparability is not the only limitation introduced by date-of-registration tabulation. Even within the same country or area, comparability over time may be lost by the practice of counting registrations rather than occurrences. If the number of events registered from year to year fluctuates because of *ad hoc* incentives to stimulate registration, or to the sudden need, for example, for proof of (unregistered) birth or death to meet certain requirements, vital statistics tabulated by date of registration are not useful in measuring and analyzing demographic levels and trends. All they can give is an indication of the fluctuations in the need for a birth, death or marriage certificate and the work-load of the registrars. Therefore, statistics tabulated by date of registration may be of very limited use for either national or international studies.

4.2 Quality of published vital statistics

The quality of vital statistics can be assessed in terms of a number of factors. Most fundamental is the completeness of the civil registration system on which these statistics are based.

4.2.1 Quality code for vital statistics from registers.

In the *Demographic Yearbook* annual "Questionnaire on Vital Statistics" national statistical offices are asked to provide their own estimates of the completeness of the births, deaths, late foetal deaths, marriages and divorces recorded in their civil registers.

On the basis of information from the questionnaires, from direct correspondence and from relevant official publications, it has been possible to classify current national statistics from civil registers of birth, death, infant death, late foetal death, marriage and divorce into three broad quality categories, as follows:

C: Data estimated to be virtually complete, that is, representing at least 90 per cent of the events occurring each year.

U: Data estimated to be incomplete, that is representing less than 90 per cent of the events occurring each year.

|: Data not derived from civil registration systems but considered reliable, such as estimates derived from population and housing censuses.

...: Data for which no specific information is available regarding completeness.

These quality codes appear in the first column of the tables which show total frequencies and crude rates (or ratios) over a period of years for all tables on live births, late foetal deaths, infant deaths, deaths, marriages, and divorces. Reliability of maternal mortality statistics is provided by the World Health Organisation.

The classification of countries and areas in terms of these quality codes may not be uniform. Nevertheless, it was felt that national statistical offices were in the best position to judge the quality of their data. It was considered that even the very broad categories that could be established on the basis of the available information would provide useful indicators of the quality of the vital statistics presented in the *Demographic Yearbook*.

Among the countries or areas indicating that the registration of live births was estimated to be 90 per cent or more complete (and hence classified as "C" or "+C" in table 9), the following countries or areas provided information on the method used to evaluate the completeness estimate:

(a) Demographic analysis – Argentina, Australia, Austria, Brazil, Bulgaria, Chile, China - Hong Kong SAR, Croatia, Dominican Republic, Egypt, Estonia, Italy, Kazakhstan, Kenya. Latvia, Luxemburg, Lithuania, Malaysia, Malta, Mauritius, New Zealand, Papua New Guinea, Panama, Peru, Romania, Republic of Moldova, San Marino, Saudi Arabia, Seychelles, South Africa, State of Palestine, Trinidad and Tobago and Venezuela (Bolivarian Republic of).

(b) Dual record check – Australia, Austria, Belgium, Brazil, Brunei Darussalam, Cuba, Cyprus, Estonia, Faeroe Islands, Fiji, Greenland, Hungary, Iraq, Israel, Italy, Jamaica, Kuwait, Latvia, Malaysia, Mongolia, Montserrat, New Zealand, Norway, Oman, Qatar, Republic of Korea, Romania, Saint Vincent and the Grenadines, Uruguay and Venezuela (Bolivarian Republic of).

(c) Other specified methods – Albania, Argentina, Armenia, Aruba, Australia, Bahrain, Bolivia (Plurinational State of), Botswana, Brazil, Burundi, Canada, Curaçao, Denmark, Ecuador, France, Germany, Guatemala, Guinea, India, Ireland, Jordan, Kazakhstan, Kyrgyzstan, Lebanon, Liechtenstein, Malaysia, Myanmar, Papua New Guinea, Poland, Puerto Rico, Russian Federation, Singapore, Slovenia, Spain, Sweden, Tajikistan, Uzbekistan and Venezuela (Bolivarian Republic of).

Among the countries or areas indicating that the registration of late foetal-deaths was estimated to be 90 per cent or more complete (and hence classified as "C" or "+C" in table 12), the following countries or areas provided information on the method used to evaluate the completeness estimate:

(a) Demographic analysis – Argentina, Armenia, Austria, Bulgaria, Burundi, Chile, Croatia, Egypt, Estonia, Italy, Kazakhstan, Latvia, Lithuania, Luxemburg, Malta, Mauritius, Oman, Papua New Guinea, Republic of Korea, Romania, San Marino, Saudi Arabia, Seychelles, Trinidad and Tobago and Venezuela (Bolivarian Republic of).

(b) Dual record check – Austria, Bahamas, Belgium, Cuba, Estonia, Greenland, Hungary, Iraq, Israel, Italy, Kuwait, Latvia, Lithuania, Montserrat, New Zealand, Norway, Qatar and Romania.

(c) Other specified methods – Bahrain, Burundi, Canada, Denmark, France, Germany, Kyrgyzstan, Papua New Guinea, Poland, Puerto Rico, Slovenia, Spain, Sweden, Russian Federation and Uzbekistan.

Among the countries or areas indicating that the registration of infant deaths was estimated to be 90 per cent or more complete (and hence classified as "C" or "+C" in table 15), the following countries or areas provided information on the method used to evaluate the completeness estimate:

(a) Demographic analysis – Argentina, Armenia, Australia, Austria, Brazil, Bulgaria, Burundi, Chile, China - Hong Kong SAR, Croatia, Egypt, Estonia, Israel, Italy, Kazakhstan, Kenya, Latvia, Lithuania, Luxemburg, Malta, Mauritius, New Zealand, Oman, Panama, Papua New Guinea, Republic of Korea, Republic of Moldova, Romania, San Marino, Saudi Arabia, Seychelles and Trinidad and Tobago.

(b) Dual record check – Australia, Austria, Bahamas, Belgium, Brazil, Brunei Darussalam, Cuba, Cyprus, Estonia, Faeroe Islands, Greenland, Hungary, Iraq, Ireland, Israel, Italy, Jamaica, Kuwait Latvia, Lithuania, Mongolia, Montserrat, New Zealand, Norway, Qatar, Romania, Saint Vincent and the Grenadines.

(c) Other specified methods – Aruba, Australia, Bahrain, Botswana, Brazil, Burundi, Canada, Curaçao, Cayman Islands, Denmark, Ecuador, France, Germany, Guinea, Jordan, Kyrgyzstan, Lebanon, Liechtenstein, Papua New Guinea, Poland, Puerto Rico, Russian Federation, Singapore, Slovenia, Spain, Sweden, Tajikistan and Uzbekistan.

Among the countries or areas indicating that the registration of deaths was estimated to be 90 per cent or more complete (and hence classified as "C" or "+C" in table 18), the following countries or areas provided information on the method used to evaluate the completeness estimate:

(a) Demographic analysis – Argentina, Australia, Austria, Brazil, Bulgaria, Chile, China - Hong Kong SAR, Croatia, Dominican Republic, Egypt, Estonia, Israel, Italy, Jordan, Kazakhstan, Kenya, Latvia, Lithuania, Luxemburg, Malaysia, Malta, Mauritius, New Zealand, Oman, Papua New Guinea, Panama, Peru, Republic of Korea, Republic of Moldova, Romania, San Marino, Saudi Arabia, Seychelles, South Africa, State of Palestine, United States of America and Venezuela (Bolivarian Republic of).

(b) Dual record check – Australia, Austria, Bahamas, Belgium, Brazil, Brunei Darussalam, Cuba, Cyprus, Estonia, Faeroe Islands, Greenland, Hungary, Iraq, Israel, Italy, Jamaica, Kuwait, Latvia, Lithuania, Malaysia, Mongolia, Montserrat, New Zealand, Norway, Qatar, Romania, Saint Vincent and the Grenadines and Venezuela (Bolivarian Republic of).

(c) Other specified methods – Armenia, Aruba, Australia, Bahrain, Botswana, Brazil, Canada, Curaçao, Denmark, Ecuador, France, Germany, Guinea, India, Jordan, Kyrgyzstan, Liechtenstein, Myanmar, Papua New Guinea, Poland, Puerto Rico, Russian Federation, Singapore, Slovenia, Spain, Sweden, United States of America and Uzbekistan.

Among the countries or areas indicating that the registration of marriages was estimated to be 90 per cent or more complete (and hence classified as "C" or "+C" in table 23), the following countries or areas provided information on the method used to evaluate the completeness estimate:

(a) Demographic analysis – Argentina, Australia, Austria, Bulgaria, Burundi, Chile, China - Hong Kong SAR, Croatia, Egypt, Estonia, Italy, Latvia, Lithuania, Luxemburg, Malta, Mauritius, Republic of Moldova, Romania, San Marino, Saudi Arabia, Seychelles, Trinidad and Tobago and Venezuela (Bolivarian Republic of).

(b) Dual record check – Australia, Austria, Bahamas, Belgium, Brunei Darussalam, Cuba, Estonia, Faeroe Islands, Hungary, Iraq, Israel, Italy, Kazakhstan, Kuwait, Latvia, New Zealand, Norway, Oman, Qatar, Republic of Korea, Romania and State of Palestine.

(c) Other specified methods – Aruba, Australia, Burundi, Curaçao, Denmark, Dominican Republic, France, Germany, Jordan, Kyrgyzstan, Lebanon, Liechtenstein, Papua New Guinea, Poland, Puerto Rico, Russian Federation, Slovenia, Spain, Sweden, Tajikistan and Uzbekistan.

Among the countries or areas indicating that the registration of divorces was estimated to be 90 per cent or more complete (and hence classified as "C" or "+C" in table 25), the following countries or areas provided information on the method used to evaluate the completeness estimate:

(a) Demographic analysis – Australia, Austria, Bulgaria, Burundi, Croatia, Egypt, Estonia, Italy, Latvia, Lithuania, Luxemburg, Republic of Moldova, Romania, San Marino, Saudi Arabia, Seychelles, Trinidad and Tobago and Venezuela (Bolivarian Republic of).

(b) Dual record check – Austria, Belgium, Brunei Darussalam, Cuba, Estonia, Faeroe Islands, Hungary, Iraq, Israel, Italy, Kazakhstan, Kuwait, Latvia, New Zealand, Norway, Oman, Qatar, Republic of Korea, Romania and State of Palestine.

(c) Other specified methods – Aruba, Burundi, Curaçao, Denmark, Germany, Jordan, Kyrgyzstan, Lebanon, Liechtenstein, Mauritius, Papua New Guinea, Poland, Puerto Rico, Russian Federation, Slovenia, Sweden, Tajikistan and Uzbekistan.

4.2.2 Treatment of vital statistics from registers

On the basis of the quality code described above, the vital statistics shown in all tables of the *Demographic Yearbook* are treated as either reliable or unreliable. Data coded "C" are considered reliable and appear in roman type. Data coded "U" or "..." are considered unreliable and appear in *italics*.

It should be noted that the indications of reliability used for infant mortality rates, maternal mortality ratios and late foetal death ratios (all of which are calculated using the number of live births in the denominator) are determined on the basis of the quality codes for infant deaths, deaths and late foetal deaths respectively. To evaluate these rates and ratios more precisely, one would have to take into account the quality of the live-birth data used in the denominator of these rates and ratios. The quality codes for live births are shown in table 9 and described more fully in the text of the technical notes for that table.

4.2.3 Treatment of estimated vital statistics

In addition to data from vital registration systems, estimated frequencies and rates of the events, usually *ad hoc* official estimates that have been derived either from the results of a population census or sample survey or by demographic analyses, also appear in the *Demographic Yearbook*. Estimated frequencies and rates have been included in the tables because it is assumed that they provide information that is more accurate than that from existing civil registration systems. By implication, they are assumed to be reliable and as such they are set in roman type.

Estimated data are denoted by the symbol "|".

4.3 Cause of death

World Health Organization (WHO) Member States are bound by the International Nomenclature Regulations to provide the Organization with cause of death data coded in accordance with the current revision of the International Statistical Classification of Diseases and Related Health Problems (ICD). In order to promote international comparability of cause of death statistics, the World Health Organization organizes and conducts an international conference for the revision of the ICD on a regular basis in order to ensure that the Classification is kept current with the most recent clinical and statistical concepts. The data are now usually submitted to WHO at the full four-character level of detail provided by the ICD and are compiled and stored in the WHO Mortality Database at the level of detail as provided by the country. Data from the WHO Mortality Database are available in electronic format at http://www3.who.int/whosis/menu.cfm.

Although revisions provide an up-to-date version of the ICD, such revisions create several problems related to the comparability of cause of death statistics. The first is the lack of comparability over time that inevitably accompanies the use of a new classification. The second problem affects comparability between countries and areas because they may adopt a new classification at different times. The more refined the classification becomes the greater is the need for expert clinical diagnosis of cause of death. In many countries or areas, few of the deaths occur in the presence of an attendant who is medically trained, i.e., most deaths are certified by a non-medically trained attendant. Because the ICD contains many diagnoses that cannot be identified by a non-medically trained person, the ICD is not always accurately or precisely used, which affects international comparability particularly between countries and areas where the level of medical services differs widely.

The chapters of the tenth revision[16], consist of an alphanumeric coding scheme of one letter followed by three numbers at the four-character level. Chapter one contains infectious and parasitic diseases, chapter two refers to all neoplasms, chapter three to disorders of the immune mechanism including diseases of the blood and blood-forming organs; and chapter four to endocrine, nutritional and metabolic diseases. The remaining chapters group diseases according to the anatomical site affected, except for chapters that refer to mental disorders; complications of pregnancy, childbirth and the puerperium; congenital malformations; and conditions originating in the perinatal period. Finally, an entire chapter is devoted to symptoms, signs, and abnormal findings. The eleventh revision is released in 2018 and is available online at https://www.who.int/classifications/icd/en/.

4.3.1 Maternal mortality

According to the tenth revision of the ICD, "Maternal death" is defined as the death of a woman while pregnant or within 42 days of termination of pregnancy, irrespective of the duration and the site of the pregnancy, from any cause related to or aggravated by the pregnancy or its management but not from accidental or incidental causes.

"Maternal deaths" should be subdivided into direct and indirect obstetric deaths. Direct obstetric deaths are those resulting from obstetric complications of the pregnant state (pregnancy, labour and puerperium), from interventions, omissions, incorrect treatment, or from a chain of events resulting from any of the above. Indirect obstetric deaths are those resulting from previous existing disease or disease that developed during pregnancy and which was not due to direct obstetric causes, but which was aggravated by physiologic effects of pregnancy.

While the denominator for the maternal mortality ratio theoretically should be the number of pregnant women, it is impossible to determine the number of pregnant women. A further recommendation by the tenth revision is therefore that maternal mortality ratios be expressed per 100,000 live births or per 100,000 total births (live births and foetal deaths). The maternal mortality ratio calculated here is expressed per 100,000 live births. Although live births do not represent an unbiased estimate of pregnant women, this figure is more reliable than other estimates. In particular, live births are more accurately registered than live births plus foetal deaths.

---

1 UNdata is an Internet based data service maintained by the Statistics Division of the United Nations Department of Economic and Social Affairs.

2 There are two exceptions – the 1978 and 1991 issues, which were disseminated in separate volumes from the respective regular issues.

3 United Nations, Department of Economic and Social Affairs, Population Division (2019), *2019 Revision of World Population Prospects* (https://population.un.org/wpp/).

4 ST/ESA/STAT/SER.M/49/Rev.4/WWW; https://unstats.un.org/unsd/methodology/m49/; see also Standard Country or Area Codes for Statistical Use, Sales No. M.98.XVII.9, United Nations, New York, 1999.

5 Sales No. E.15.XVII.10, United Nations, New York, 2015.

6 Ibid, para. 4.151.

7 Alternatively, if a population register is used, completed ages are calculated by subtracting the date of birth of individuals listed in the register from a reference date to which the age data pertain.

8 A source of non-comparability may result from differences in the method of reckoning age, for example, the Western versus the Eastern or, as it is usually known, the English versus the Chinese system. By the latter, a child is considered one year old at birth and advances an additional year at each Chinese New Year. The effect of this system is most obvious at the beginning of the age span, where the frequencies in the under-one-year category are markedly understated. The effect on higher age groups is not so apparent. Distributions constructed on this basis are often adjusted before publication, but the possibility of such aberrations should not be excluded when census data by age are compared.

9 Sales No. E.13.XVII.10, United Nations, New York, 2014.

10 https://unstats.un.org/unsd/demographic-social/Standards-and-Methods/files/Handbooks/crvs/CRVS_GOLF_Final_Draft-E.pdf United Nations, New York, 2019.

11 https://unstats.un.org/unsd/demographic-social/Standards-and-Methods/files/Handbooks/crvs/crvs-mgt-E.pdf

United Nations, New York, 2018.

12 https://unstats.un.org/unsd/demographic-social/Standards-and-Methods/files/Handbooks/crvs/CRVS-IdM-E.pdf United Nations, New York, 2019.

13 Sales No. E.98.XVII.6, United Nations, New York, 1998.

14 Sales No. E.98.XVII.10, United Nations, New York, 1998.

15 Sales No. E.03.XVII.11, United Nations, New York, 2004.

16 *International Statistical Classification of Diseases and Related Health Problems*, Tenth Revision, Volume 2, World Health Organization, Geneva, 1992.

INTRODUCTION

L'Annuaire démographique est un recueil de statistiques démographiques internationales qui est établi par la Division de statistique du Département des affaires économiques et sociales de l'Organisation des Nations Unies. Il fait partie d'un ensemble de publications complémentaires publiées par l'Organisation des Nations Unies et les institutions spécialisées, qui ont pour objet de fournir des statistiques aux démographes, aux économistes, aux spécialistes de la santé publique et aux sociologues. Grâce à la coopération des services nationaux de statistique, il a été possible de faire figurer dans la présente édition de *l'Annuaire démographique* les statistiques officielles disponibles pour plus de 230 pays ou zones du monde entier.

L'Annuaire démographique 2019 est la soixante-dixième édition d'une série que publie l'ONU depuis 1948. Le présent volume comprend un aperçu mondial des statistiques démographiques de base et des tableaux qui regroupent des statistiques sur la dimension, la répartition et les tendances de la population, la natalité, la mortalité fœtale, la mortalité infantile et la mortalité liée à la maternité, la mortalité générale, la nuptialité et la divortialité. Des données classées selon le lieu de résidence (zone urbaine ou rurale) sont présentées dans un grand nombre de tableaux. L'*Annuaire démographique* contient des notes techniques, un tableau synoptique, un index historique et une liste des éditions de *l'Annuaire démographique* publiées jusqu'à présent. Cette édition de l'*Annuaire démographique* contient les données disponibles couvrant les années de référence jusqu'à 2019.

La présente édition de l'*Annuaire démographique* comprend aussi le tableau 3a avec l'indice de Whipple selon le sexe et la résidence urbaine/rurale pour les recensements de la population effectués dans le monde entier depuis 1985. L'indice de Whipple est un indice de préférence pour certains âges dans la déclaration de l'âge et peut donc servir à mettre en évidence certaines des difficultés liées à la répartition par âge.

Les notes techniques sur les tableaux statistiques sont destinées à aider le lecteur. Le tableau A, qui correspond au tableau synoptique, donne un aperçu de l''exhaustivité des données publiées dans la présente édition de l'*Annuaire démographique*. Un index cumulatif donne des renseignements sur les matières traitées dans chacune des 70 éditions et sur les années sur lesquelles portent les données. L'index contient aussi une liste des tableaux publiés en ligne à travers le portal UNdata[1] (http://data.un.org/Explorer.aspx?d=POP). Les numéros de vente des éditions antérieures et une liste des sujets spéciaux traités dans les différentes éditions sont indiqués aux pages iii, iv, et v. En plus, toutes les éditions de l'*Annuaire démographique* sont disponibles en ligne sur le site web de la Division des Statistiques : https://unstats.un.org/unsd/demographic-social/products/dyb/index.cshtml

Jusqu'à la quarante-huitième édition (1996), chaque édition se composait de deux parties : les tableaux de caractère général et ceux sur des sujets spéciaux, publiés dans le même volume[2]. À partir de quarante-neuvième édition (1997), les tableaux sur les sujets spéciaux ont été publiés dans un format numérique en tant que suppléments à l'*Annuaire démographique*. Deux CD-ROM ont été produits : l'*Annuaire démographique : Supplément historique*, qui présente un grand nombre de statistiques démographiques pour la période allant de 1948 à 1997, et l'*Annuaire démographique : Statistiques de la natalité*, qui contient des tableaux détaillés sur la natalité pour la période allant de 1980 à 1998. Par la suite, trois volumes concernant *l'Annuaire démographique* consacrés à des thèmes de recensement spéciaux pour le cycle de recensements de 2000 ont été publiés en ligne à l'adresse suivante : http://unstats.un.org/unsd/demographic/products/dyb/dybcens.htm. Les données actuelles sur les thèmes du recensement de l'*Annuaire démographique* pour les années de référence entre 1995 et aujourd'hui, lorsqu'elles sont disponibles, sont présentées sur https://unstats.un.org/unsd/demographic-social/products/dyb/index.cshtml#censusdatasets. Ils comprennent des données sur la population selon les principales caractéristiques démographiques, scolaires, ethnoculturelles et économiques, les caractéristiques des ménages ainsi que des données sur les étrangers dans le pays ou les personnes nées à l'étranger. Particulièrement, on a présenté sous forme de table aux adresses suivantes, les données des recensements pour les années de référence entre 1995 et aujourd'hui, qui portent sur les thèmes des caractéristiques des ménages et des caractéristiques économiques : https://unstats.un.org/unsd/demographic-social/products/dyb/dyb_household/ et https://unstats.un.org/unsd/demographic-social/products/dyb/dyb_eco/.

Les statistiques sur la population ne sont pas disponibles pour tous les pays et zones pour plusieurs raisons. Deux annexes sont présentées afin d'offrir des estimations sur la population en milieu d'année et un aperçu des statistiques de l'état civil pour chaque pays ou zone. La première porte sur des estimations concernant la population pour la période 2009-2018. La seconde présente les estimations des variantes moyennes concernant les taux bruts de natalité et de mortalité, la mortalité infantile, les indicateurs synthétiques de fécondité et l'espérance de vie à la naissance pour la période 2015-2020. Ces données ont été établies par la Division de la population de l'ONU et publiées dans les *Perspectives de la population mondiale : La révision de 2019*[3].

Les statistiques démographiques figurant dans la présente édition de l'*Annuaire démographique* sont disponibles en ligne sur les pages Web consacrées à *l'Annuaire démographique* : https://unstats.un.org/unsd/demographic-social/products/dyb/index.cshtml#overview. On trouvera également des renseignements sur le programme de collecte et de diffusion des données de la Division de statistique sur le même site. Il est possible de se procurer d'autres données en contactant la Division de statistique du Département des affaires économiques et sociales de l'Organisation des Nations Unies à l'adresse suivante : demostat@un.org.

NOTES TECHNIQUES SUR LES TABLEAUX STATISTIQUES

1. REMARQUES D'ORDRE GÉNÉRAL

1.1 Notes techniques

Les notes techniques ont pour but de donner au lecteur des informations pertinentes en lien avec les tableaux statistiques. Les renseignements qui concernent l'*Annuaire démographique* en général sont présentés dans des sections portant sur diverses considérations géographiques, sur la population et sur les statistiques de natalité et de mortalité. Les tableaux sont ensuite commentés séparément et l'on trouvera pour chacun une description des variables et des observations sur la fiabilité et les lacunes des données ainsi que sur les pays et zones visés et sur les données publiées antérieurement. Des détails sont également donnés, le cas échéant, sur le mode de calcul des taux, quotients et pourcentages.

1.2 Tableaux

Dans la mesure du possible, la numérotation des tableaux dans les éditions successives de *l'Annuaire démographique* est préservée. Comme la numérotation des tableaux ne correspond pas exactement à celle des éditions précédentes, il est recommandé de se reporter à l'index qui figure à la fin du présent ouvrage pour trouver les données publiées dans les précédentes éditions.

1.3 Origine des données

Sauf indication contraire, les statistiques présentées dans *l'Annuaire démographique* sont des données nationales fournies par les organismes de statistique officiels. Elles sont recueillies essentiellement au moyen de questionnaires qui sont envoyés tous les ans à plus de 230 services nationaux de statistique. Les données communiquées en réponse à ces questionnaires sont complétées, dans toute la mesure possible, par des données tirées de publications nationales officielles et des sites web d'organismes officiels et des renseignements communiqués par les services nationaux de statistique à la demande de l'ONU. Pour que les données soient comparables, les taux, rapports et pourcentages ont été calculés par la Division de statistique de l'ONU, à l'exception des paramètres des tables de mortalité et des indicateurs synthétiques de fécondité ainsi que des taux bruts de natalité et de mortalité pour certains pays et zones, qui ont été dûment signalés en note. Les méthodes suivies par la Division pour le calcul des taux et rapports sont décrites dans les notes techniques relatives à chaque tableau. Les chiffres de population utilisés pour ces calculs sont ceux qui figurent dans la présente édition de *l'Annuaire démographique* ou qui ont paru dans des éditions antérieures.

Chaque fois que l'on constatera des différences entre les données du présent volume et celles des éditions antérieures de *l'Annuaire démographique*, ou de certaines publications apparentées, on pourra en conclure que les statistiques publiées cette année sont des chiffres révisés communiqués à la Division de statistique avant juin 2020.

2. CONSIDÉRATIONS GÉOGRAPHIQUES

2.1 Portée

Des données sont présentées sur tous les pays ou zones qui en ont communiquées. Le tableau 3, le plus complet, contient des données sur la population et la superficie de chaque pays ou zone ayant une population d'au moins 50 habitants. Ces pays ou zones ne figurent pas tous dans les tableaux qui suivent. Dans bien des cas, les données requises pour un tableau particulier n'étaient pas disponibles. En général, les pays ou zones qui peuvent fournir des données sont d'autant moins nombreux que les données demandées sont plus détaillées.

De plus, les taux et rapports ne sont présentés que pour les pays ou zones ayant communiqué des chiffres correspondant à un nombre minimal de faits considérés. Les minimums sont indiqués dans les notes techniques relatives à chacun des tableaux.

À l'exception des données récapitulatives présentées dans les tableaux 1 et 2 pour l'ensemble du monde et les grandes zones et régions et des données relatives aux capitales et aux villes de 100 000 habitants ou plus dans le tableau 8, toutes les données se rapportent aux pays. Le nombre de pays sur lequel porte chacun des tableaux est indiqué dans le tableau A.

2.2 Composition territoriale

Autant que possible, toutes les données, y compris les séries chronologiques, se rapportent au territoire de 2018. Les exceptions à cette règle sont signalées en note à la fin des tableaux. Des clarifications importantes sont présentées ci-dessous.

Les données relatives au **Danemark** ne comprennent pas les Iles Féroé et le Groenland, qui font l'objet de rubriques distinctes.

Les données relatives à la **Finlande** comprennent les Îles d'Åland, sauf indication contraire en note de bas de page.

Les données relatives à la **France** ne comprennent pas les départements d'outre-mer, qui font l'objet de rubriques distinctes, sauf indication contraire en note de bas de page.

Les données relatives au **Royaume-Uni de Grande-Bretagne et d'Irlande du Nord** ne comprennent pas la Guernesey, l'île de Man et Jersey, qui font l'objet de rubriques distinctes.

Les données relatives au **Sahara Occidental** comprennent la région septentrionale (ancien Saguia-el-Hamra) et la région méridionale (ancien Rio de Oro).

2.3 Nomenclature

En règle générale, pour gagner de la place, on a jugé commode de désigner dans les tableaux les pays ou zones par les noms abrégés couramment utilisés par l'Organisation des Nations Unies[4], les désignations complètes n'étant utilisées que lorsqu'il n'existait pas de forme abrégée. La liste des désignations des pays ou zones est disponible à l'adresse suivante : https://unstats.un.org/unsd/methodology/m49/ .

2.3.1 Ordre de présentation

Les pays ou zones sont classés dans l'ordre alphabétique anglais et regroupés par continent comme ci-après : Afrique, Amérique du Nord, Amérique du Sud, Asie, Europe et Océanie.

Les appellations employées dans la présente édition et la présentation des données qui y figurent n'ont d'autre objet que de donner un cadre géographique commode aux séries statistiques. La même observation vaut pour toutes les notes et précisions concernant les unités géographiques pour lesquelles des données sont présentées.

2.4 Superficie

Les données relatives à la superficie qui figurent dans le tableaux 1 représentent la superficie des terres alors que les données relatives à la superficie qui figurent dans le tableaux 3 représentent la superficie totale, sauf indication contraire par une note. La superficie totale englobe les terres émergées (la superficie des terres) et les eaux intérieures qui sont censées comprendre les principaux lacs et cours d'eau, mais excluent les régions polaires et les îles inhabitées. Les données relatives à la superficie correspondent aux chiffres estimatifs les plus récents. Les superficies sont toutes exprimées en kilomètres carrés ; les chiffres qui avaient été communiqués en miles carrés ont été convertis au moyen d'un coefficient de 2,589988.

2.4.1 Comparabilité dans le temps

La révision des estimations antérieures de la superficie, des augmentations effectives de la superficie terrestre due par exemple à des travaux d'assèchement, à des rectifications de frontières, à des changements d'interprétation du concept de « terres émergées » ou à l'utilisation de nouvelles unités de mesure peut avoir des incidences sur la comparabilité dans le temps des estimations relatives à la superficie d'un pays ou d'une zone donnés. Dans la plupart des cas, il a été possible de déterminer la raison de ces révisions ; toutefois, même lorsque la raison n'était pas connue, on a généralement admis que ces derniers sont exacts.

2.4.2 Comparabilité internationale

Le manque de comparabilité internationale entre les données relatives à la superficie est dû principalement à des différences de définition. En particulier, la définition des golfes, baies et criques, lacs et cours d'eau varie sensiblement d'un pays à l'autre. La diversité des méthodes employées pour estimer les superficies nuit elle aussi à la comparabilité internationale. Certaines données proviennent de levés effectués selon des méthodes scientifiques modernes ; d'autres ne représentent que des conjectures reposant sur diverses catégories de renseignements. Certains chiffres sont récents, d'autres pas. Étant donné que ni la méthode de calcul de la superficie ni la composition du territoire et la date à laquelle se rapportent les données ne sont connues avec précision pour tous les pays ou zones, les estimations figurant dans le tableau 3 ne doivent pas être considérées comme rigoureusement comparables d'un pays ou d'une zone à une autre.

3. POPULATION

Les statistiques de la population, c'est-à-dire celles qui se rapportent à la dimension, à la répartition géographique et aux caractéristiques démographiques de la population, sont présentées dans un certain nombre de tableaux de *l'Annuaire démographique*.

Les tableaux 1 et 2 présentent respectivement des estimations récapitulatives de milieu d'année de la population du monde, des grandes zones et régions, pour certaines années présélectionnées, ainsi que de sa répartition selon l'âge et le sexe pour l'année 2019.

Les données concernant les pays ou les zones représentent les résultats de recensements de population, des estimations fondées sur les résultats d'enquêtes par sondage (s'il n'y a pas eu recensement), des estimations postcensitaires ou intercensitaires, ou des estimations établies à partir de données provenant des registres permanents de population. Dans la présente édition, le tableau 3 indique pour chaque pays ou zone le chiffre le plus récent de la population totale issu du dernier recensement et des estimations établies au milieu de l'année 2010 et de l'année2019. Le tableau 5 contient des estimations de la population totale au milieu de chaque année pendant 10 ans (2010-2019), et le tableau 6 des estimations de la population urbaine et de la population totale, par sexe, au milieu de chaque année pendant 10 ans (2010-2019). Les dernières données disponibles sur la répartition de la population selon l'âge, le sexe et le lieu de résidence (zone urbaine ou rurale) sont présentées dans le tableau 7. Les derniers chiffres disponibles sur la population des capitales et des villes de 100 000 habitants ou plus sont regroupés dans le tableau 8.

On a utilisé pour le calcul des taux les statistiques de la population totale et de la population répartie selon l'âge, le sexe ou le lieu de résidence (zone urbaine ou rurale). Les taux démographiques selon la résidence (urbaine/rurale), l'âge ou le sexe ont été calculés à partir des données présentées dans les tableaux 6 ou 7 de la présente édition ou dans les tableaux correspondants d'éditions précédentes de *l'Annuaire démographique*.

3.1 Sources de variation des données

Plusieurs facteurs influent sur la comparabilité des données : 1) la définition de la population totale ; 2) les définitions utilisées pour faire la distinction entre population urbaine et population rurale ; 3) les difficultés liées aux déclarations d'âge ; 4) l'étendue du surdénombrement ou du sous-dénombrement dans le recensement le plus récent ou dans une autre source de statistiques de référence sur la population ; 5) la qualité des estimations relatives à la population. Ces cinq facteurs sont analysés en détail aux sections 3.1.1 à 3.1.3 ci-après. D'autres questions seront traitées dans les notes techniques relatives à chaque tableau. Pour plus de précisions concernant, notamment, les notions fondamentales de dimension, de répartition et de caractéristiques de la population qui ont été élaborées par l'Organisation des Nations Unies, le lecteur est invité à se reporter aux *Principes et recommandations concernant les recensements de la population et de l'habitat, Révision 3*[5].

3.1.1 Population totale

Le principal obstacle à la comparabilité des données relatives à la population totale est la différence qui existe entre population de fait et population de droit. La population de fait comprend toutes les personnes présentes dans le pays ou la zone à la date de référence, tandis que la population de droit comprend toutes celles qui résident habituellement dans le pays ou la zone, qu'elles y aient été ou non présentes à la date de référence. Par définition, la population totale de fait et la population totale de droit ne sont donc pas rigoureusement comparables entre elles.

Même lorsque l'on veut comparer deux totaux qui se rapportent à des populations de fait ou deux totaux qui se rapportent à des populations de droit, on risque souvent de faire des erreurs pour cette raison qu'il est rare que l'une et l'autre notions soient appliquées strictement. Pour citer quelques exemples, certains chiffres qui sont censés porter sur la population de fait ne tiennent pas compte du personnel militaire, naval et diplomatique étranger en fonction dans le pays ou la zone, ni des membres de leurs familles et de leurs ménages ; d'autres ne comprennent pas les visiteurs étrangers de passage dans le pays ou la zone ni les personnes à bord de navires ancrés dans des ports. En revanche, il arrive que l'on compte des personnes, inscrits maritimes et marins pêcheurs par exemple, qui, en raison de leur activité professionnelle, se trouvent hors du pays ou de la zone de recensement.

Les risques de disparités sont encore plus grands quand il s'agit de comparer des populations de droit, car les comparaisons dépendent au premier chef de la définition que l'on donne à l'expression « lieu de résidence habituel », qui varie d'un pays ou d'une zone à l'autre et qu'il est, de toute façon, difficile d'appliquer uniformément pour le dénombrement lors d'un recensement ou d'une enquête. Par exemple, les civils étrangers qui se trouvent temporairement dans un pays ou une zone comme travailleurs à court terme peuvent officiellement être considérés comme résidents après un séjour d'une durée déterminée, mais ils peuvent aussi être considérés comme non-résidents pendant toute la durée de leur séjour ; ailleurs, ces mêmes personnes peuvent être considérées officiellement comme résidents ou comme non-résidents du pays ou de la zone d'où elles viennent, selon la durée et, éventuellement, la raison de leur absence. En plus, quel que soit son statut officiel, chacun des recensés peut, au moment de l'enquête, interpréter à sa façon la notion de résidence. De plus, les autorités nationales ou les entités responsables des zones ne savent pas toutes avec la même précision combien de leurs résidents se trouvent temporairement à l'étranger.

Les chiffres de population présentés dans les tableaux de l'*Annuaire démographique* représentent la population de fait ou la population de droit. Lorsque l'on savait que les données avaient été recueillies selon une définition de la population de fait ou de la population de droit qui s'écartait sensiblement de celle exposée plus haut, on l'a signalé en note, de manière à compenser dans toute la mesure possible les conséquences des divergences.

Il peut y avoir hétérogénéité dans les statistiques d'un même pays ou d'une même zone dans le cas des pays ou zones qui ne font une exploitation statistique détaillée des données que pour la population de droit alors qu'ils recueillent des données sur la population de droit et sur la population de fait à l'occasion d'un recensement, par exemple. Ainsi, tandis que les chiffres relatifs à la population totale qui figurent au tableau 3 se rapportent à la population de fait, ceux des tableaux qui présentent des données sur diverses caractéristiques de la population, par exemple le lieu de résidence (zone urbaine ou rurale), l'âge et le sexe, peuvent être basés sur le concept de la population de droit.

3.1.2 Lieu de résidence (zone urbaine ou rurale)

L'hétérogénéité des définitions nationales du terme « urbain » nuit considérablement à la comparabilité internationale des données concernant la répartition selon le lieu de résidence. Les définitions utilisées par les différents pays ou zones et leurs implications sont exposées à la fin des notes techniques correspondant au tableau 6.

3.1.3 Répartition par âge

La répartition de la population selon l'âge est un paramètre fondamental de la plupart des analyses, estimations et projections relatives aux statistiques de la population. Malheureusement, ces données sont sujettes à un certain nombre d'erreurs et difficilement comparables. C'est pourquoi pratiquement tous les utilisateurs de ces statistiques doivent considérer ces répartitions avec la plus grande circonspection.

3.1.3.1 Collecte et exploitation des données sur l'âge

L'âge est l'intervalle de temps déterminé par calcul ou par estimation qui sépare la date de naissance de la date du recensement et qui est exprimé en années solaires révolues[6]. Les données sur l'âge peuvent être recueillies selon deux méthodes : la première consiste à obtenir la date de naissance de chaque personne à l'occasion d'un recensement ou d'un sondage, puis à calculer l'âge en années révolues en soustrayant la date de naissance de celle du dénombrement[7]. La seconde consiste à enregistrer l'âge en années révolues au moment du recensement, c'est-à-dire l'âge au dernier anniversaire.

La méthode recommandée consiste à calculer l'âge au dernier anniversaire en soustrayant la date exacte de la naissance de la date du recensement. Toutefois, on n'a pas toujours recours à cette méthode ; certains pays ou zones calculent l'âge en faisant la différence entre l'année du recensement et l'année de la naissance. Lorsque les données sur l'âge ont été établies de cette façon, on l'a signalé chaque fois que possible par une note. On peut d'ailleurs s'en rendre compte dans une certaine mesure, car les chiffres dans la catégorie des moins d'un an sont plus faibles qu'ils ne devraient l'être. Cependant, un nombre irrégulier de naissances d'une année à l'autre ou l'omission de certains âges parmi les moins d'un an peut aussi fausser les chiffres de la population de moins d'un an.

3.1.3.2 Erreurs dans les données sur l'âge

Les causes d'erreurs dans les données sur l'âge sont diverses : on peut citer notamment l'ignorance de l'âge exact, la déclaration d'années d'âge correspondant à un calendrier différent de celui des années solaires révolues depuis la naissance[8], la négligence dans les déclarations et dans la façon dont elles sont consignées, la tendance générale à déclarer des âges se terminant par certains chiffres tels que 0, 2, 5 ou 8, la tendance pour les personnes âgées à exagérer leur âge, une aversion subconsciente pour certains nombres, et les fausses déclarations faites délibérément.

Les causes d'erreurs mentionnées ci-dessus, communes à la plupart des enquêtes sur l'âge et à la plupart des pays ou zones, peuvent nuire sensiblement à la comparabilité.

À cause des difficultés indiquées ci-dessus, les répartitions par âge et par sexe de la population d'un grand nombre de pays ou de zones font apparaître les irrégularités suivantes : 1) sous-estimation des groupes d'âge correspondant aux enfants de moins d'un an et aux jeunes enfants ; 2) polarisation des déclarations sur les âges se terminant par les chiffres 0 ou 5 (c'est-à-dire 5, 10,15, 20...) ; 3) prépondérance des âges pairs (par exemple 10, 12, 14...) au détriment des âges impairs (par exemple 11, 13, 15...) ; 4) écart considérable et surprenant entre le rapport masculin/féminin à certains âges ; 5) différences importantes et difficilement explicables entre les données concernant des groupes d'âge voisins. En comparant les statistiques provenant de recensements successifs pour des cohortes identiques sur le plan de l'âge et de la répartition par sexe et en étudiant la répartition par âge et par sexe de la population à chaque recensement, on peut déceler l'existence de ces incohérences et de quelques autres, un certain nombre d'entre elles se retrouvant à des degrés divers même dans les recensements les plus modernes.

La présente édition de l'*Annuaire démographique* comprend le tableau 3a avec l'indice de Whipple selon le sexe et la résidence urbaine/rurale pour les recensements de la population effectués dans le monde entier depuis 1985. L'indice de Whipple est un indice de préférence pour certains âges dans la déclaration de l'âge et peut donc servir à mettre en évidence certaines des difficultés liées à la répartition par âge.

4. STATISTIQUES DE L'ÉTAT CIVIL

Aux fins de *l'Annuaire démographique*, on entend par statistiques de l'état civil les statistiques des naissances vivantes, des décès, des morts fœtales, des mariages et des divorces.

Dans le présent volume de l'*Annuaire démographique*, on a présenté des tableaux sur la natalité, la mortalité, la nuptialité et la divortialité. Les tableaux consacrés à la mortalité sont groupés sous les rubriques suivantes : mortalité fœtale, mortalité infantile, mortalité liée à la maternité et mortalité générale.

4.1 Sources de variations des données

La plupart des statistiques de l'état civil publiées dans le présent volume de l'*Annuaire démographique* émanent des systèmes nationaux d'enregistrement des faits d'état civil. Le degré d'exhaustivité et d'exactitude de ces données varie d'un pays ou d'une zone à l'autre.

Il n'existe pas partout de système national d'enregistrement des faits d'état civil et, dans quelques cas, seuls certains faits sont enregistrés. Par exemple, dans certains pays ou zones, seuls les naissances et les décès sont enregistrés. Il existe également des différences quant au degré d'efficacité avec lequel les lois relatives à l'enregistrement des faits d'état civil sont appliquées dans les divers pays ou zones. La fiabilité des statistiques provenant des registres d'état civil dépend des modalités d'application de la loi et de la mesure dans laquelle le public s'y soumet.

Il est à signaler que dans certains cas les statistiques de la nuptialité et de la divortialité sont tirées d'autres sources que les registres d'état civil. Dans certains pays ou zones, par exemple, les seules données disponibles sur la nuptialité proviennent des registres des églises. Selon la pratique suivie par chaque pays, les statistiques de la divortialité sont tirées des actes des tribunaux et/ou des registres d'état civil. L'officier de l'état civil, le service national de statistique ou d'autres services administratifs peuvent être chargés d'établir ces statistiques.

Les autres facteurs qui influent sur la comparabilité internationale des statistiques de l'état civil sont à peu près les mêmes que ceux qu'il convient de prendre en considération pour interpréter les variations observées dans les statistiques de la population. La définition des faits d'état civil aux fins de statistique, la portée des données du point de vue géographique et ethnique ainsi que les méthodes d'exploitation des données sont autant d'éléments qui peuvent influer sur la comparabilité.

En plus des statistiques tirées des registres d'état civil, l'*Annuaire démographique* présente des statistiques de l'état civil qui sont des estimations officielles nationales, fondées souvent sur les résultats de sondages ou des recensements de la population. Aussi leur comparabilité varie-t-elle en fonction du degré d'exhaustivité des déclarations recueillies lors des recensements de la population ou d'enquêtes sur les ménages, des erreurs d'échantillonnage ou autres, et des distorsions d'origines diverses.

Pour plus de détails sur les normes d'établissement des statistiques d'état civil, le lecteur pourra se reporter aux : *Principes et recommandations pour un système de statistiques de l'état civil, troisième révision*[9] ; *Guidelines on the Legislative Framework for Civil Registration, Vital Statistics and Identity Management*[10] ; *Manuel des systèmes d'enregistrement des faits d'état civil et de statistiques de l'état civil : Gestion, fonctionnement et tenue, Révision 1*[11]; *Handbook on civil registration, vital statistics and identity management systems: Communication for development*[12]; *Manuel des systèmes d'enregistrement des faits d'état civil et de statistiques de l'état civil : Principes et protocoles concernant la communication et l'archivage des documents individuels*[13]; *Manuel des systèmes d'enregistrement des faits d'état civil et de statistiques de l'état civil : Informatisation*[14]. Le *Manuel de collecte de données sur la fécondité et la mortalité*[15] fournit des informations ayant trait à la collecte et à l'évaluation des données sur la fécondité, sur la mortalité et sur d'autres faits d'état civil, qui ont été recueillies au cours des enquêtes sur les ménages. Ces publications sont également disponibles sur le Web à partir des adresses suivantes : https://unstats.un.org/unsd/demographic-social/Standards-and-Methods/index.cshtml

4.1.1 Définition des faits d'état civil aux fins de la statistique

Une cause importante d'hétérogénéité dans les données est le manque d'uniformité des définitions des différents faits d'état civil. Aux fins de *l'Annuaire démographique*, il est recommandé de recueillir les données relatives aux faits d'état civil en utilisant les définitions établies au Chapitre I des *Principes et recommandations pour un système de statistiques de l'état civil, troisième révision*. Ces définitions sont les suivantes :

La NAISSANCE VIVANTE est l'expulsion ou l'extraction complète du corps de la mère, indépendamment de la durée de la gestation, d'un produit de la conception qui, après cette séparation, respire ou manifeste tout autre signe de vie, tel que battement de cœur, pulsation du cordon ombilical ou contraction effective d'un muscle soumis à l'action de la volonté, que le cordon ombilical ait été coupé ou non et que le placenta soit ou non demeuré attaché ; tout produit d'une telle naissance est considéré comme « enfant né vivant ».

Le DÉCÈS est la disparition permanente de tout signe de vie à un moment quelconque postérieur à la naissance vivante (cessation des fonctions vitales après la naissance sans possibilité de réanimation). Cette définition ne comprend pas les morts fœtales.

La MORT FŒTALE est le décès d'un produit de la conception lorsque ce décès est survenu avant l'expulsion ou l'extraction complète du corps de la mère, indépendamment de la durée de la gestation. Le décès est indiqué par le fait qu'après cette séparation le fœtus ne respire ni ne manifeste aucun signe de vie, tel que battement de cœur, pulsation du cordon ombilical ou contraction effective d'un muscle soumis à l'action de la volonté.

Le MARIAGE est l'acte, la cérémonie ou la procédure qui établit un rapport légal entre les époux. L'union peut être rendue légale par une procédure civile ou religieuse, ou par toute autre procédure, conformément à la législation du pays.

Le DIVORCE est la dissolution légale et définitive des liens du mariage, c'est-à-dire la séparation des époux qui confère aux parties le droit de se remarier civilement ou religieusement, ou selon toute autre procédure, conformément à la législation du pays.

En plus de ces notions définies internationalement, l'*Annuaire démographique* recueille et met à disposition ces données sur les avortements :

Par référence à la femme, l'AVORTEMENT se définit comme toute interruption de grossesse qui est survenue avant 28 semaines de gestation et dont le produit est un fœtus mort. Il existe deux grandes catégories d'avortement : l'avortement spontané et l'avortement provoqué. L'avortement provoqué a pour origine une action délibérée entreprise en vue d'interrompre une grossesse. Tout autre avortement est considéré comme spontané.

4.1.2 Problèmes posés par les définitions établies

Les variations par rapport aux définitions établies des faits d'état civil sont le principal obstacle à la comparabilité internationale des statistiques de l'état civil. Un exemple en est fourni par le cas des naissances vivantes et celui des morts fœtales. Dans certains pays ou zones, il faut que le nouveau-né ait vécu 24 heures pour pouvoir être inscrit sur le registre des naissances vivantes. Les décès d'enfants qui surviennent avant l'expiration du délai de 24 heures sont classés parmi les morts fœtales tardives et, en l'absence de méthodes spéciales d'exploitation des données, ne sont comptés ni dans les naissances vivantes ni dans les décès. De même, dans plusieurs autres pays ou zones, les décès d'enfants nés vivants et décédés avant l'enregistrement de leur naissance sont également comptés parmi les morts fœtales tardives.

À moins que des méthodes spéciales n'aient été adoptées pour l'exploitation de ces données, les statistiques des naissances vivantes et des décès ne tiendront pas compte de ces cas, qui viendront en revanche accroître d'autant le nombre des morts fœtales tardives. Le taux de mortalité infantile sera donc sous-estimé. Bien que les éléments constitutifs du taux (décès d'enfants de moins d'un an et naissances vivantes) accusent exactement la même insuffisance en valeur absolue, les lacunes sont proportionnellement plus fortes pour les décès de moins d'un an, ce qui cause des erreurs plus importantes dans les taux de mortalité infantile.

De plus, cette pratique augmente les rapports de mortinatalité. Quelques pays ou zones effectuent les ajustements nécessaires pour corriger cette anomalie (du moins dans les fréquences totales) au moment de l'établissement des tableaux. Si aucun ajustement n'a été effectué, cela est indiqué dans les notes chaque fois que possible.

Les définitions du mariage et du divorce posent aussi un problème du point de vue de la comparabilité internationale. Contrairement à la naissance et au décès, qui sont des faits biologiques, le mariage et le divorce sont uniquement déterminés par la législation et la coutume et, de ce fait, il est moins facile d'en donner une définition statistique qui ait une application universelle. À des fins statistiques, ces notions ont donc été définies de manière générale par référence à la législation de chaque pays ou zone. La législation relative au mariage et plus particulièrement au divorce varie d'un pays ou d'une zone à l'autre. En ce qui concerne le mariage, l'âge de nubilité est la condition la plus fréquemment requise, mais il arrive souvent que d'autres conditions soient exigées.

Lorsqu'il est connu, l'âge minimum auquel le mariage peut avoir lieu avec le consentement des parents (et dans certains cas sans le consentement des parents) est indiqué au tableau 24-1. Les lois et règlements relatifs à la dissolution du mariage par le divorce vont de l'interdiction absolue, en passant par diverses conditions requises pour l'obtention du divorce, jusqu'à la simple déclaration, par l'épouse, de son désir ou de son intention de divorcer.

4.1.3 Couverture géographique ou ethnique fragmentaire

Selon les standards internationaux, les statistiques de l'état civil devraient s'étendre à l'ensemble du pays ou de la zone auxquels elles se rapportent et englober tous les groupes ethniques. En fait, il n'est pas rare que les données soient fragmentaires. Dans certains pays ou zones, l'enregistrement n'est obligatoire que pour une petite partie de la population, par exemple pour certains groupes ethniques. Dans d'autres, il n'existe pas de disposition qui prescrive l'enregistrement obligatoire sur le plan national, mais seulement des règlements ou décrets des municipalités ou des États, qui ne s'appliquent pas à l'ensemble du territoire. Il en est encore autrement dans d'autres pays ou zones où les autorités ont institué une zone d'enregistrement comprenant seulement une partie du territoire, le reste étant exclu en raison des difficultés d'accès ou parce qu'il est pratiquement impossible, pour des raisons d'ordre économique ou culturel, d'y procéder à un enregistrement régulier.

4.1.4 Méthodes de présentation des données

4.1.4.1 Selon le lieu de l'événement

Les statistiques de l'état civil qui sont présentées pour l'ensemble du territoire national se rapportent à la population de fait ou la population présente. En conséquence, sauf indication contraire, les statistiques de l'état civil relatives à une zone ou à un pays donné portent sur tous les faits survenus dans l'ensemble de la population, à l'intérieur des frontières actuelles de la zone ou du pays considéré. On peut donc estimer qu'elles englobent les faits d'état civil survenus dans les tribus nomades et parmi les populations autochtones ainsi que parmi les ressortissants du pays et les étrangers. Des notes signalent les exceptions lorsque celles-ci sont connues.

Pour certains pays, les écarts entre les taux démographiques pour les zones urbaines et pour les zones rurales peuvent varier notablement selon que les faits d'état civil ont été exploités sur la base du lieu de l'événement ou du lieu de résidence habituel. Par exemple, si un nombre appréciable de femmes résidant dans des zones rurales proches de grands centres urbains accouchent dans les hôpitaux ou maternités d'une ville, les taux de fécondité ainsi que les taux de mortalité néo-natale et infantile seront généralement plus élevés dans les zones urbaines (et par conséquent plus faibles dans les zones rurales) si les faits sont exploités en se fondant sur le lieu de l'événement et non sur le lieu de résidence habituel. Le phénomène sera le même dans le cas de la mortalité générale si un bon nombre de personnes résidant dans des zones rurales font appel aux services de santé des villes lorsqu'elles sont gravement malades.

4.1.4.2 Selon la date de l'événement ou la date de l'enregistrement

Autant que possible, les statistiques de l'état civil figurant dans *l'Annuaire démographique* se rapportent aux faits survenus pendant l'année considérée et non aux faits enregistrés au cours de ladite année. Bon nombre de pays ou zones, toutefois, exploitent leurs statistiques de l'état civil selon la date de l'enregistrement et non selon la date de l'événement. Comme ces statistiques risquent d'induire en erreur, les pays ou zones dont on sait qu'ils établissent leurs statistiques d'après la date de l'enregistrement sont signalés dans les tableaux par un signe plus « + ». On ne dispose toutefois pas pour tous les pays ou zones de renseignements complets sur la méthode d'exploitation des statistiques de l'état civil et les données sont peut-être exploitées selon la date de l'enregistrement plus souvent que ne le laisserait supposer l'emploi des signes.

Étant donné que la qualité des données est inextricablement liée aux retards dans l'enregistrement, il faudra toujours considérer en même temps le code de qualité qui est décrit à la section 4.2.1 ci-après. Évidemment, si l'enregistrement des naissances est complet et effectué en temps voulu (code « C »), les effets perturbateurs de la méthode consistant à exploiter les données selon la date de l'enregistrement seront pratiquement annulés. De même, s'agissant des statistiques des décès, les effets pourront bien souvent être réduits au minimum dans les pays ou zones où le code sanitaire subordonne la délivrance du permis d'inhumer à l'enregistrement du décès, ce qui tend à hâter l'enregistrement. Quant aux morts fœtales, elles sont généralement déclarées immédiatement ou ne sont pas déclarées du tout. En conséquence, si l'enregistrement se fait dans un délai très court, la différence entre les statistiques établies selon la date de l'événement et celles qui sont établies selon la date de l'enregistrement peut être négligeable. Dans bien des cas, la durée des délais légaux accordés pour l'enregistrement des faits d'état civil est un facteur dont dépend dans une large mesure l'incidence sur la comparabilité de l'exploitation des données selon la date de l'enregistrement.

En ce qui concerne le mariage et le divorce, la pratique consistant à exploiter les statistiques selon la date de l'enregistrement ne pose généralement pas de graves problèmes. Le mariage étant, dans de nombreux pays ou zones, un contrat juridique civil qui, pour être légal, doit être conclu devant un officier de l'état civil, il s'ensuit que dans ces pays ou zones l'enregistrement a lieu presque systématiquement au moment de la cérémonie ou immédiatement après. De même, dans de nombreux pays ou zones, le tribunal ou l'autorité qui a prononcé le divorce est le seul habilité à enregistrer cet acte, et comme l'acte d'enregistrement figure alors sur les registres du tribunal l'enregistrement suit généralement de peu le jugement.

En revanche, si l'enregistrement n'a lieu qu'avec un certain retard, les statistiques de l'état civil établies selon la date de l'enregistrement ne sont pas comparables sur le plan international. Au mieux, les statistiques par date de l'enregistrement prendront surtout en considération des faits survenus au cours de l'année précédente ; dans les pays ou zones où le système d'enregistrement n'est pas très développé, il y entrera des faits datant de plusieurs années. Il ressort des documents dont on dispose que des retards de plusieurs années dans l'enregistrement des naissances ne sont pas rares, encore que, dans la majorité des cas, les retards ne dépassent pas deux à quatre ans.

Tant que l'enregistrement se fera avec retard, les statistiques fondées sur la date d'enregistrement ne seront comparables sur le plan international ni entre elles ni avec les statistiques établies selon la date de fait d'état civil.

Il convient également de noter que l'exploitation des données selon la date de l'enregistrement ne nuit pas seulement à la comparabilité internationale des statistiques. Même à l'intérieur d'un pays ou d'une zone, le procédé qui consiste à compter les enregistrements et non les faits peut compromettre la comparabilité des chiffres sur une longue période. Si le nombre des faits d'état civil enregistrés varie d'une année à l'autre (par suite de l'application de mesures visant tout particulièrement à encourager l'enregistrement ou parce qu'il est subitement devenu nécessaire de produire le certificat d'une naissance ou d'un décès non enregistré pour l'accomplissement de certaines formalités), les statistiques de l'état civil établies d'après la date de l'enregistrement ne permettent pas de quantifier ni d'analyser l'état et l'évolution de la population. Tout au plus peuvent-elles révéler l'évolution des conditions d'exigibilité de l'acte de naissance, de décès ou de mariage et les fluctuations du volume de travail des bureaux d'état civil. Les statistiques établies selon la date de l'enregistrement peuvent donc ne présenter qu'une utilité très réduite pour des études nationales ou internationales.

4.2 La qualité des statistiques de l'état civil qui sont publiées

La qualité des statistiques de l'état civil peut être évaluée en se fondant sur plusieurs facteurs. Le facteur essentiel est la complétude du système d'enregistrement des faits d'état civil d'après lequel ces statistiques sont établies.

4.2.1 Codage qualitatif des statistiques provenant des registres de l'état civil

Dans le questionnaire relatif au mouvement de la population qui leur est envoyé chaque année dans le cadre de l'établissement de *l'Annuaire démographique*, les services nationaux de statistique sont invités à donner leur propre évaluation du degré de complétude des données sur les naissances, les décès, les décès d'enfants de moins d'un an, les morts fœtales tardives, les mariages et les divorces figurant dans leurs registres d'état civil.

D'après les renseignements directement communiqués par les gouvernements ou extraits des questionnaires ou de publications officielles pertinentes, il a été possible de classer les statistiques de l'enregistrement des faits d'état civil (naissances, décès, décès d'enfants de moins d'un an, morts fœtales tardives, mariages et divorces) en trois grandes catégories, selon leur qualité :

C : Données jugées pratiquement complètes, c'est-à-dire représentant au moins 90 % des faits d'état civil survenant chaque année.

U : Données jugées incomplètes, c'est-à-dire représentant moins de 90 % des faits survenant chaque année.

| : Données ne provenant pas des systèmes nationaux d'enregistrement des faits d'état civil, mais jugées fiables, telles que les estimations dérivées des recensements de population ou du logement.

... : Données dont le degré de complétude ne fait pas l'objet de renseignements précis.

Ces codes de qualité figurent dans la première colonne des tableaux qui présentent, pour un nombre d'années déterminé les chiffres absolus et les taux (ou rapports) bruts concernant les naissances vivantes, les morts fœtales tardives, les décès d'enfants de moins d'un an, les décès, les mariages et les divorces. Les niveaux de fiabilité des statistiques de mortalité maternelle sont transmis par l'Organisation mondiale de la santé.

La classification des pays ou zones selon ces codes de qualité peut ne pas être uniforme. On a estimé néanmoins que les services nationaux de statistique étaient les mieux placés pour juger de la qualité de leurs données. On a pensé que les catégories que l'on pouvait distinguer sur la base des renseignements disponibles, bien que très larges, permettaient cependant de se faire une idée de la qualité des statistiques de l'état civil publiées dans l'*Annuaire démographique*.

Sur les pays ou zones qui ont estimé à 90 % ou plus le degré d'exhaustivité de leur enregistrement des naissances vivantes (classé « C » ou « +C » dans le tableau 9), les pays ou zones suivants ont communiqué des renseignements concernant les bases sur lesquelles leur estimation reposait :

(a) Analyse démographique : Afrique du Sud, Arabie saoudite, Argentine, Australie, Autriche, Brésil, Bulgarie, Chili, Chine - Hong Kong RAS, Croatie, Égypte, Estonie, État de Palestine, Italie, Kazakhstan, Kenya, Lettonie, Lituanie, Luxemburg, Malaisie, Malte, Maurice, Nouvelle-Zélande, Panama, Papouasie-Nouvelle-Guinée, Pérou, République de Moldova, République dominicaine, Roumanie, Saint-Marin, Seychelles, Trinité-et-Tobago et Venezuela (République bolivarienne du).

(b) Double contrôle des registres : Australie, Autriche, Belgique, Brésil, Brunéi Darussalam, Chypre, Cuba, Estonie, Fidji, Groenland, Hongrie, Îles Féroé, Iraq, Israël, Italie, Jamaïque, Koweït, Lettonie, Malaisie, Mongolie, Montserrat, Norvège, Nouvelle-Zélande, Oman, Qatar, République de Corée, Roumanie, Saint Vincent et les Grenadines, Uruguay et Venezuela (République bolivarienne du).

(c) Autre méthode : Albanie, Allemagne, Argentine, Arménie, Aruba, Australie, Bahreïn, Bolivie (État plurinational de), Botswana, Brésil, Burundi, Canada, Curaçao, Danemark, Espagne, Équateur, Fédération de Russie, France, Guatemala, Guinée, Inde, Irlande, Jordanie, Kazakhstan, Kirghizstan, Liban, Liechtenstein, Malaisie, Mexique, Myanmar, Ouzbékistan, Papouasie-Nouvelle-Guinée, Pologne, Porto Rico, Singapour, Slovénie, Suède, Tadjikistan et Venezuela (République bolivarienne du).

Sur les pays ou zones qui ont estimé à 90 % ou plus le degré d'exhaustivité de leur enregistrement des morts fœtales tardives (classé « C » ou « +C » dans le tableau 12), les pays ou zones suivants ont communiqué des renseignements concernant les bases sur lesquelles leur estimation reposait :

(a) Analyse démographique : Arabie saoudite, Argentine, Arménie, Autriche, Bulgarie, Burundi, Chili, Croatie, Égypte, Estonie, Italie, Kazakhstan, Lettonie, Lituanie, Luxemburg, Malte, Maurice, Mexique, Oman, Papouasie-Nouvelle-Guinée, République de Corée, Roumanie, Saint-Marin, Seychelles, Trinité-et-Tobago et Venezuela (République bolivarienne du).

(b) Double contrôle des registres : Autriche, Bahamas, Belgique, Cuba, Estonie, Groenland, Hongrie, Iraq, Israël, Italie, Koweït, Lettonie, Lituanie, Montserrat, Norvège, Nouvelle-Zélande, Qatar et Roumanie.

(c) Autre méthode : Allemagne, Bahreïn, Burundi, Canada, Danemark, Espagne, Fédération de Russie, France, Kirghizstan, Ouzbékistan, Papouasie-Nouvelle-Guinée, Pologne, Porto Rico, Slovénie et Suède.

Sur les pays ou zones qui ont estimé à 90 % ou plus le degré d'exhaustivité de leur enregistrement des décès à moins d'un an (classé « C » ou « +C » dans le tableau 15), les pays ou zones suivants ont donné des indications touchant la base de cette estimation :

(a) Analyse démographique : Arabie saoudite, Argentine, Arménie, Australie, Autriche, Brésil, Bulgarie, Burundi, Chili, Chine - Hong Kong RAS, Croatie, Égypte, Estonie, État de Palestine, Israël, Italie, Kazakhstan, Kenya, Lettonie, Lituanie, Luxemburg, Malte, Maurice, Nouvelle-Zélande, Oman, Panama, Papouasie-Nouvelle-Guinée, République de Corée, République de Moldova, Roumanie, Saint-Marin, Seychelles et Trinité-et-Tobago.

(b) Double contrôle des registres : Australie, Autriche, Bahamas, Belgique, Brésil, Brunéi Darussalam, Cuba, Chypre, Estonie, Groenland, Hongrie, Îles Féroé, Iraq, Irlande, Israël, Italie, Jamaïque, Koweït, Lettonie, Lituanie, Mongolie, Montserrat, Norvège, Nouvelle-Zélande, Qatar, Roumanie et Saint-Vincent-et-les-Grenadines.

(c) Autre méthode : Allemagne, Aruba, Australie, Bahreïn, Botswana, Brésil, Burundi, Canada, Curaçao, Danemark, Espagne, Équateur, Fédération de Russie, France, Guinée, Îles Caïmans, Jordanie, Kirghizstan, Liban, Liechtenstein, Ouzbékistan, Papouasie-Nouvelle-Guinée, Pologne, Porto Rico, Singapour, Slovénie, Suède et Tadjikistan.

Sur les pays ou zones qui ont estimé à 90 % ou plus le degré d'exhaustivité de leur enregistrement des décès (classé « C » ou « +C » dans le tableau 18), les pays ou zones suivants ont donné des indications touchant la base de cette estimation :

(a) Analyse démographique : Arabie saoudite, Afrique du Sud, Argentine, Australie, Autriche, Brésil, Bulgarie, Chili, Chine - Hong Kong RAS, Croatie, Égypte, Estonie, État de Palestine, États-Unis d'Amérique, Israël, Italie, Jordanie, Kazakhstan, Kenya, Lettonie, Lituanie, Luxemburg, Malaisie, Malte, Maurice, Nouvelle-Zélande, Oman, Panama, Papouasie-Nouvelle-Guinée, Pérou, République de Corée, République de Moldova, République dominicaine, Roumanie, Saint-Marin, Seychelles, et Venezuela (République bolivarienne du).

(b) Double contrôle des registres : Australie, Autriche, Bahamas, Belgique, Brésil, Brunéi Darussalam, Cuba, Chypre, Estonie, Groenland, Hongrie, Îles Féroé, Iraq, Israël, Italie, Jamaïque, Koweït, Lettonie, Lituanie, Malaisie, Mongolie, Montserrat, Norvège, Nouvelle-Zélande, Qatar, Roumanie, Saint-Vincent-et-les-Grenadines et Venezuela (République bolivarienne du).

(c) Autre méthode : Allemagne, Arménie, Aruba, Australie, Bahreïn, Botswana, Brésil, Canada, Curaçao, Danemark, Espagne, États-Unis d'Amérique, Équateur, Fédération de Russie, France, Guinée, Inde, Jordanie, Kirghizstan, Liechtenstein, Myanmar, Ouzbékistan, Papouasie-Nouvelle-Guinée, Pologne, Porto Rico, Singapour, Slovénie et Suède.

Sur les pays ou zones qui ont estimé à 90 % ou plus le degré d'exhaustivité de leur enregistrement des mariages (classé « C » ou « +C «» dans le tableau 23), les pays ou zones suivants ont communiqué des renseignements concernant les bases sur lesquelles leur estimation reposait :

(a) Analyse démographique : Arabie saoudite, Argentine, Australie, Autriche, Bulgarie, Burundi, Chili, Chine - Hong Kong RAS, Croatie, Égypte, Estonie, Italie, Lettonie, Lituanie, Luxemburg, Malte, Maurice, République de Moldova, Roumanie, Saint-Marin, Seychelles, Trinité-et-Tobago et Venezuela (République bolivarienne du).

(b) Double contrôle des registres : Australie, Autriche, Bahamas, Belgique, Brunéi Darussalam, Cuba,

Estonie, État de Palestine, Hongrie, Îles Féroé, Iraq, Israël, Italie, Kazakhstan, Koweït, Lettonie, Norvège, Nouvelle-Zélande, Oman, Qatar, République de Corée et Roumanie.

(c) Autre méthode : Allemagne, Aruba, Australie, Burundi, Curaçao, Danemark, Espagne, Fédération de Russie, France, Kirghizstan, Jordanie, Liban, Liechtenstein, Ouzbékistan, Papouasie-Nouvelle-Guinée, Pologne, Porto Rico, République dominicaine, Roumanie, Slovénie, Suède et Tadjikistan.

Sur les pays ou zones qui ont estimé à 90 % ou plus le degré d'exhaustivité de leur enregistrement des divorces (classé « C » ou « +C » dans le tableau 25), les pays ou zones suivants ont communiqué des renseignements concernant les bases sur lesquelles leur estimation reposait :

(a) Analyse démographique : Arabie saoudite, Australie, Autriche, Bulgarie, Burundi, Croatie, Égypte, Estonie, Italie, Lettonie, Lituanie, Luxemburg, République de Moldova, Roumanie, Saint-Marin, Seychelles, Suède, Trinité-et-Tobago et Venezuela (République bolivarienne du).

(b) Double contrôle des registres : Autriche, Belgique, Brunéi Darussalam, Cuba, Estonie, État de Palestine, Hongrie, Îles Féroé, Iraq, Israël, Italie, Kazakhstan, Koweït, Lettonie, Norvège, Nouvelle-Zélande, Oman, Qatar, République de Corée et Roumanie.

(c) Autre méthode : Allemagne, Aruba, Burundi, Curaçao, Danemark, Fédération de Russie, Jordanie, Kirghizstan, Liban, Liechtenstein, Maurice, Ouzbékistan, Papouasie-Nouvelle-Guinée, Pologne, Porto Rico, Slovénie, Suède, et Tadjikistan.

4.2.2 Traitement des statistiques tirées des registres d'état civil

Dans tous les tableaux de l'*Annuaire démographique*, on a indiqué le degré de fiabilité des statistiques de l'état civil en se fondant sur le codage qualitatif décrit ci-dessus. Les statistiques codées « C », jugées sûres, sont imprimées en caractères romains. Celles qui sont codées « U » ou « ... », jugées douteuses, sont reproduites en *italique*.

Il convient de noter que, pour les taux de mortalité infantile, les taux de mortalité maternelle et les rapports de morts fœtales tardives (calculées en utilisant au dénominateur le nombre de naissances vivantes), les indications relatives à la fiabilité sont déterminées sur la base des codes de qualité utilisés pour les décès d'enfants de moins d'un an, les décès totaux et les morts fœtales tardives, respectivement. Pour évaluer ces taux et rapports de façon plus précise, il faudrait tenir compte de la qualité des données relatives aux naissances vivantes, utilisées au dénominateur dans leur calcul. Les codes de qualité pour les naissances vivantes figurent au tableau 9 et sont décrits plus en détail dans les notes techniques se rapportant à ce tableau.

4.2.3 Traitement des estimations fondées sur les statistiques de l'état civil

En plus des données provenant des systèmes d'enregistrement des faits d'état civil, *l'Annuaire démographique* contient aussi des estimations relatives aux fréquences et aux taux. Il s'agit d'estimations officielles, généralement calculées à partir des résultats d'un recensement de la population ou d'un sondage ou par analyse démographique. Si des estimations concernant les fréquences et les taux figurent dans les tableaux, c'est parce que l'on considère qu'elles fournissent des renseignements plus exacts que les systèmes existants d'enregistrement des faits d'état civil. En conséquence, elles sont également jugées sûres et sont donc imprimées en caractères romains.

Les données estimatives sont dénotées par le «|».

4.3 Causes de décès

Les États membres de l'Organisation mondiale de la santé (OMS) sont tenus de communiquer à celle-ci les données sur les causes de décès codifiées selon la révision en vigueur de la Classification internationale des maladies et des problèmes de santé connexes (CIM). Pour assurer la comparabilité internationale des statistiques des causes de décès, l'OMS organise régulièrement des conférences internationales de révision de la Classification internationale des maladies afin de suivre, au fur et à mesure, les progrès les plus récents de la médecine clinique et de la statistique. Les données sont généralement présentées à l'OMS selon le degré de détail à tous les quatre caractères requis par la CIM et sont compilées et archivées dans la Base de données sur la mortalité de l'OMS au degré de détail présenté par le pays. Les données de la Base de données sur la mortalité de l'OMS sont disponibles sur le site Internet suivant : http://www3.who.int/whosis/menu.cfm.

Les révisions de la CIM permettent certes de disposer d'une version actualisée, mais elles posent plusieurs problèmes de comparabilité des statistiques des causes de décès. Le premier tient au manque de comparabilité dans le temps, qui accompagne inévitablement la mise en œuvre d'une classification nouvelle. Le deuxième est celui de la comparabilité entre pays ou zones, car les différents pays peuvent adopter la nouvelle classification à des époques différentes. Établir la cause des décès exige des compétences de plus en plus poussées à mesure que la classification devient plus précise. Or, dans beaucoup de pays ou zones, il est rare que les décès se produisent en présence d'un témoin possédant une formation médicale et le certificat de décès est le plus souvent établi par quelqu'un qui n'est pas qualifié sur le plan médical. Étant donné que la CIM répertorie de nombreux diagnostics qu'il est impossible d'établir si l'on n'a pas de formation en médecine, la CIM n'est pas toujours exactement ou précisément utilisée ce qui affecte la comparabilité internationale, notamment entre pays ou zones où la qualité des services médicaux est très disparate.

Les chapitres de la dixième révision[16] se fondent sur un système de codification alphanumérique à une lettre suivie de trois chiffres pour les catégories à quatre caractères. Le chapitre 1 concerne les maladies infectieuses et parasitaires et le chapitre 2 l'ensemble des néoplasmes. Le chapitre 3 a trait aux troubles du système immunitaire, aux maladies du sang et aux organes hématopoïétiques. Le chapitre 4 porte sur les maladies du système endocrinien, de la nutrition et du métabolisme. Les autres chapitres groupent les maladies selon leur site anatomique, à l'exception de ceux qui concernent les affections mentales, les complications de la grossesse, de l'accouchement et des suites de couches, les malformations congénitales et les affections de la période périnatale. Enfin, un chapitre entier est consacré aux symptômes, manifestations et résultats anormaux. La onzième révision a été lancée en 2018 et est disponible en ligne : https://www.who.int/classifications/icd/en/.

4.3.1 Mortalité liée à la maternité

D'après la dixième révision de la CIM, la « mortalité liée à la maternité » est définie comme le décès d'une femme survenu au cours de la grossesse ou dans un délai de 42 jours après sa terminaison, quelle qu'en soit la durée et la localisation, pour une cause quelconque déterminée ou aggravée par la grossesse ou les soins qu'elle a motivés, mais ni accidentelle ni fortuite.

Les « décès liés à la maternité » doivent se répartir en décès par cause obstétricale directe et indirecte. Les décès par cause obstétricale directe sont ceux qui résultent de complications obstétricales de l'état de grossesse (grossesse, travail et suites de couches), d'interventions, d'omissions, d'un traitement incorrect ou d'un enchaînement d'événements de l'un quelconque des facteurs ci-dessus. Les décès par cause obstétricale indirecte sont ceux qui résultent d'une maladie préexistante ou d'une affection apparue au cours de la grossesse, sans qu'elle soit due à des causes obstétricales directes, mais qui a été aggravée par les effets physiologiques de la grossesse.

En théorie, le nombre de femmes enceintes aurait dû être pris comme dénominateur pour le taux de mortalité maternelle, mais il est impossible de déterminer ce nombre. En conséquence, il est en outre recommandé dans la dixième révision d'exprimer les taux de mortalité maternelle sur la base de 100 000 naissances vivantes ou 100 000 naissances totales (naissances vivantes et morts fœtales). Le taux de mortalité maternelle est ici calculé par 100 000 naissances vivantes. Bien que les naissances vivantes ne permettent pas d'évaluer sans distorsion le nombre des femmes enceintes, leur nombre est plus fiable que d'autres estimations car le nombre des naissances vivantes est plus exactement enregistré que celui des naissances vivantes et des morts fœtales.

---

[1] UNdata est un service de données en ligne géré par la Division de statistique du Département des affaires économiques et sociales de l'Organisation des Nations Unies.

[2] Les éditions de 1978 et de 1991 font exception à la règle, puisque les tableaux sur des sujets spéciaux ont été publiés séparément.

[3] Organisation des Nations Unies, Département des affaires économiques et sociales, Division de la population (2019). Perspectives de la population mondiale : La révision de 2019 (https://population.un.org/wpp/).

[4] ST/ESA/STAT/SER.M/49/Rev.4/WWW ; https://unstats.un.org/unsd/methodology/m49/ ; voir également Code standard des pays et des zones à usage statistique, numéro de vente : M.98.XVII.9, Nations Unies, New York, 1999.

[5] Numéro de vente : E.15.XVII.10, Nations Unies, New York, 2015.

[6] Ibid., par. 4.151.

[7] Lorsque l'on utilise un registre de la population, on peut également calculer l'âge en années révolues en soustrayant la date de naissance de chaque personne inscrite sur le registre de la date de référence à laquelle se rapportent les données sur l'âge.

[8] L'emploi de méthodes différentes de calcul de l'âge, par exemple la méthode occidentale et la méthode orientale, ou, comme on les désigne plus communément, la méthode anglaise et la méthode chinoise, représente une cause de non-comparabilité. Selon la méthode chinoise, on considère que l'enfant est âgé d'un an à sa naissance et qu'il avance d'un an à chaque nouvelle année chinoise. Les répercussions de cette méthode sont particulièrement apparentes dans les données pour le premier âge : les données concernant les enfants de moins d'un an sont nettement inférieures à la réalité. Les effets sur les chiffres relatifs aux groupes d'âge suivants sont moins visibles. Les séries ainsi établies sont souvent ajustées avant d'être publiées, mais il ne faut pas exclure la possibilité d'aberrations de ce genre lorsque l'on compare des données censitaires sur l'âge.

[9] Numéro de vente : E.13.XVII.10, publication des Nations Unies, New York, 2014.

[10] https://unstats.un.org/unsd/demographic-social/Standards-and-Methods/files/Handbooks/crvs/CRVS_GOLF_Final_Draft-E.pdf United Nations, New York, 2019.

[11] https://unstats.un.org/unsd/demographic-social/Standards-and-Methods/files/Handbooks/crvs/crvs-mgt-E.pdf United Nations, New York, 2018.

[12] https://unstats.un.org/unsd/demographic-social/Standards-and-Methods/files/Handbooks/crvs/CRVS-IdM-E.pdf United Nations, New York, 2019

[13] Numéro de vente : F.98.XVII.6, publication des Nations Unies, New York, 1998.

[14] Numéro de vente : F.98.XVII.10, publication des Nations Unies, New York, 1998.

[15] Numéro de vente : F.03.XVII.11, United Nations, New York, 2004.

[16] Organisation mondiale de la santé, Classification statistique internationale des maladies et problèmes de santé connexes, dixième révision, vol. 2, Genève, 1992.

Table A. Demographic Yearbook 2019 synoptic table: Availability of data by country/area, table and sex, where applicable
Tableau A. Tableau synoptique de l'Annuaire démographique 2019 : Disponibilité des données par pays ou zone, tableau et le sexe, si disponible

Continent and country or area Continent et pays ou zone	Table totals	General topic and table number - Sujet général et numéro de tableau																
		Summary - Apercu			Population							Fertility - Natalité				Foetal mortality - Mortalité foetale		
		3		4	5	6		7		8		9	10		11	12	13	14
		Total	M/F			Total[1]	M/F	Total	M/F	Total	M/F		Total	M/F				
Total number of countries or areas - Total des pays ou zones	..	240	228	188	224	228	228	222	217	208	170	174	156	131	88	94	63	48
AFRICA - AFRIQUE																		
Algeria - Algérie	18	•	•	•	•	•	•	•	•	•	…	•	…	…	…	•	…	…
Angola	11	•	•	•	•	•	•	•	•	•	•	…	…	…	…	…	…	…
Benin - Bénin	10	•	•	…	•	•	•	•	•	•	•	…	…	…	…	…	…	…
Botswana	22	•	•	•	•	•	•	•	•	•	…	•	•	•	…	•	…	…
Burkina Faso	10	•	•	…	•	•	•	•	•	•	•	…	…	…	…	…	…	…
Burundi	13	•	•	•	•	•	•	•	•	•	•	•	…	…	…	…	•	…
Cabo Verde	25	•	•	•	•	•	•	•	•	•	•	•	•	•	…	•	•	…
Cameroon - Cameroun	10	•	•	•	•	•	•	•	•	•	•	…	…	…	…	…	…	…
Central African Republic - République centrafricaine	2	•	•	…	…	…	…	…	…	…	…	…	…	…	…	…	…	…
Chad - Tchad	9	•	•	…	•	•	•	•	•	•	•	…	…	…	…	…	…	…
Comoros - Comores	2	•	•	…	…	…	…	…	…	…	…	…	…	…	…	…	…	…
Congo	11	•	•	…	•	•	•	…	…	…	…	…	•	•	…	…	…	…
Côte d'Ivoire	17	•	•	•	•	•	•	•	•	•	•	•	•	•	…	…	…	…
Democratic Republic of the Congo - République démocratique du Congo	2	•	•	…	…	…	…	…	…	…	…	…	…	…	…	…	…	…
Djibouti	5	•	•	…	•	…	…	…	…	•	…	…	…	…	…	…	…	…
Egypt - Égypte	25	•	•	•	•	•	•	•	•	•	•	•	•	•	•	…	…	…
Equatorial Guinea - Guinée équatoriale	9	•	•	…	•	•	•	•	…	•	•	…	…	…	…	…	…	…
Eritrea - Érythrée	10	•	•	…	•	•	•	•	•	•	•	…	…	…	…	…	…	…
Eswatini	16	•	•	•	•	•	•	•	•	•	…	•	…	…	…	•	…	…
Ethiopia - Éthiopie	9	•	•	…	•	•	•	•	•	•	•	…	…	…	…	…	…	…
Gabon	6	•	•	…	…	•	•	…	…	•	•	…	…	…	…	…	…	…
Gambia - Gambie	7	•	•	…	•	•	•	•	•	…	…	…	…	…	…	…	…	…
Ghana	14	•	•	…	•	•	•	•	•	•	•	…	•	•	…	…	…	…
Guinea - Guinée	16	•	•	•	•	•	•	•	•	•	•	…	•	•	…	…	…	…
Guinea-Bissau - Guinée-Bissau	9	•	•	…	•	•	•	•	•	•	…	…	…	…	…	…	…	…
Kenya	18	•	•	•	•	•	•	•	•	•	•	•	•	…	…	•	…	…
Lesotho	19	•	•	•	•	•	•	•	•	•	…	•	•	…	…	…	…	…
Liberia - Libéria	7	•	•	…	•	•	•	…	…	•	•	…	…	…	…	…	…	…
Libya - Libye	7	•	•	…	•	•	•	•	•	…	…	…	…	…	…	…	…	…
Madagascar	11	•	•	•	•	•	•	•	•	•	•	…	…	…	…	…	…	…
Malawi	16	•	•	•	•	•	•	•	•	•	•	•	•	…	…	…	…	…
Mali	11	•	•	•	•	•	•	•	•	•	•	…	…	…	…	…	…	…
Mauritania - Mauritanie	8	•	…	…	•	•	•	•	…	•	…	…	•	…	…	…	…	…
Mauritius - Maurice	27	•	•	•	•	•	•	•	•	•	•	•	•	•	•	•	…	…
Mayotte	22	•	•	•	•	•	•	•	•	…	…	•	•	•	…	…	…	…
Morocco - Maroc	10	•	…	…	•	•	•	•	•	•	…	…	…	…	…	…	…	…
Mozambique	12	•	•	•	•	•	•	•	•	•	•	•	…	…	…	…	…	…
Namibia - Namibie	14	•	•	…	•	•	•	•	•	•	•	…	•	•	…	…	…	…
Niger	13	•	•	•	•	•	•	•	•	•	•	•	…	…	…	…	…	…
Nigeria - Nigéria	6	•	•	…	•	•	•	•	…	…	…	…	…	…	…	…	…	…
Republic of South Sudan - République de Soudan du Sud	11	•	•	…	•	•	•	•	•	•	•	…	…	…	…	…	…	…
Reunion - Réunion	24	•	•	•	•	•	•	•	•	•	•	•	•	…	…	…	•	…
Rwanda	11	•	•	•	•	•	•	•	•	•	•	…	…	…	…	…	…	…
Saint Helena ex. dep. - Sainte-Hélène sans dép.	23	•	…	•	•	•	•	•	•	•	•	•	•	•	•	…	…	…
Saint Helena: Ascension - Sainte-Hélène: Ascension	1	•	…	…	…	…	…	…	…	…	…	…	…	…	…	…	…	…
Saint Helena: Tristan da Cunha - Sainte-Hélène: Tristan da Cunha	1	•	…	…	…	…	…	…	…	…	…	…	…	…	…	…	…	…
Sao Tome and Principe - Sao Tomé-et-Principe	16	•	•	•	•	•	•	•	•	•	•	•	…	…	…	…	…	…
Senegal - Sénégal	11	•	•	•	•	•	•	•	•	•	•	…	…	…	…	…	…	…
Seychelles	24	•	•	•	•	•	•	•	•	•	…	•	•	•	…	…	•	•
Sierra Leone	14	•	•	•	•	•	•	•	•	•	•	•	…	…	…	…	…	…
Somalia - Somalie	3	•	•	…	…	…	…	…	…	•	…	…	…	…	…	…	…	…
South Africa - Afrique du Sud	27	•	•	•	•	•	•	•	•	•	•	•	•	•	•	•	…	…
Sudan - Soudan	10	•	•	…	•	•	•	•	•	…	…	…	…	…	…	…	…	…
Togo	8	•	•	…	•	•	•	•	•	•	…	…	…	…	…	…	…	…
Tunisia - Tunisie	19	•	•	•	•	•	•	•	•	•	•	•	•	…	…	•	…	…

Table A. Demographic Yearbook 2019 synoptic table: Availability of data by country/area, table and sex, where applicable
Tableau A. Tableau synoptique de l'Annuaire démographique 2019 : Disponibilité des données par pays ou zone, tableau et le sexe, si disponible

Continent and country or area Continent et pays ou zone	General topic and table number - Sujet général et numéro de tableau												
	Infant and maternal mortality - Mortalité infantile et mortalité liée à la maternité				General mortality - Mortalité générale						Nuptiality and divorces - Nuptialité et divortialité		
	15	16		17	18	19		20	21	22	23	24	25
		Total	M/F			Total	M/F						
Total number of countries or areas - Total des pays ou zones	140	112	107	129	169	159	158	115	72	196	146	112	120
AFRICA - AFRIQUE													
Algeria - Algérie	•	...	...	...	•	•	•	...	...	•	•	...	•
Angola	...	...	...	...	...	...	...	...	...	•	...	...	...
Benin - Bénin	...	...	...	...	...	...	...	...	...	•	...	...	...
Botswana	•	•	•	...	•	•	•	...	...	•	•	•	...
Burkina Faso	...	...	...	...	...	...	...	...	...	•	...	...	...
Burundi	...	...	...	...	...	...	...	...	...	•	...	...	...
Cabo Verde	•	•	•	•	•	•	•	...	...	•	•	•	...
Cameroon - Cameroun	...	...	...	...	...	...	...	...	...	...	...	...	...
Central African Republic - République centrafricaine	...	...	...	...	...	...	...	...	...	...	...	...	...
Chad - Tchad	...	...	...	...	...	...	...	...	...	...	...	...	...
Comoros - Comores	...	...	...	...	...	...	...	...	...	...	...	...	...
Congo	...	...	...	...	...	•	•	...	...	•	...	•	...
Côte d'Ivoire	...	...	...	...	•	...	...	...	...	•	•	...	•
Democratic Republic of the Congo - République démocratique du Congo	...	...	...	...	...	...	...	...	...	...	...	...	...
Djibouti	...	...	...	...	...	...	...	...	...	•	...	...	...
Egypt - Égypte	•	•	...	•	•	•	•	•	...	•	•	•	•
Equatorial Guinea - Guinée équatoriale	...	...	...	...	...	...	...	...	...	•	...	...	...
Eritrea - Érythrée	...	...	...	...	...	...	...	...	...	•	...	...	...
Eswatini	•	...	...	...	•	•	•	...	...	•	...	...	...
Ethiopia - Éthiopie	...	...	...	...	...	...	...	...	...	...	...	...	...
Gabon	...	...	...	...	...	...	...	...	...	...	...	...	...
Gambia - Gambie	...	...	...	...	...	...	...	...	...	...	...	...	...
Ghana	...	...	...	...	...	•	•	...	...	•	...	...	...
Guinea - Guinée	...	...	...	...	...	•	•	...	...	•	•	...	...
Guinea-Bissau - Guinée-Bissau	...	...	...	...	...	...	...	...	...	•	...	...	...
Kenya	•	...	...	...	•	•	•	...	...	•	...	...	...
Lesotho	•	...	...	...	•	•	•	...	...	•	•	•	•
Liberia - Libéria	...	...	...	...	...	...	...	...	...	...	...	...	...
Libya - Libye	...	...	...	...	...	...	...	...	...	...	...	...	...
Madagascar	...	...	...	...	...	...	...	...	...	•	...	...	...
Malawi	...	...	...	...	•	•	•	...	...	•	...	...	...
Mali	...	...	...	...	...	...	...	...	...	•	...	...	...
Mauritania - Mauritanie	...	...	...	...	...	...	...	...	...	•	...	...	...
Mauritius - Maurice	•	•	•	•	•	•	•	•	...	•	•	•	•
Mayotte	•	•	...	•	•	•	•	•	...	•	•	•	•
Morocco - Maroc	...	...	...	•	...	...	...	•	...	•	...	...	...
Mozambique	...	...	...	...	...	...	...	...	...	•	...	...	...
Namibia - Namibie	...	...	...	...	...	•	•	...	...	•	...	...	...
Niger	...	...	...	...	...	•	•	...	...	...	...	...	...
Nigeria - Nigéria	...	...	...	...	...	...	...	...	...	...	...	...	...
Republic of South Sudan - République de Soudan du Sud	...	...	...	...	...	...	...	...	•	•	...	...	...
Reunion - Réunion	•	•	...	•	•	•	•	•	...	•	•	•	•
Rwanda	...	...	...	...	...	...	...	...	...	•	...	...	...
Saint Helena ex. dep. - Sainte-Hélène sans dép.	•	•	•	...	•	•	•	...	...	•	•	•	•
Saint Helena: Ascension - Sainte-Hélène: Ascension	...	...	...	...	...	...	...	...	...	...	...	...	...
Saint Helena: Tristan da Cunha - Sainte-Hélène: Tristan da Cunha	...	...	...	...	...	...	...	...	...	...	...	...	...
Sao Tome and Principe - Sao Tomé-et-Principe	...	...	...	...	•	•	•	...	...	•	•	...	...
Senegal - Sénégal	...	...	...	...	...	...	...	...	...	•	...	...	...
Seychelles	•	...	...	•	•	•	•	•	...	•	•	•	•
Sierra Leone	...	...	...	...	...	•	•	...	...	•	...	...	...
Somalia - Somalie	...	...	...	...	...	...	...	...	...	...	...	...	...
South Africa - Afrique du Sud	•	•	•	•	•	•	•	•	...	•	•	•	•
Sudan - Soudan	...	...	...	...	...	...	...	...	...	•	•	...	•
Togo	...	...	...	...	...	...	...	...	...	...	...	...	...
Tunisia - Tunisie	...	...	...	•	•	...	...	...	...	•	•	•	•

Table A. Demographic Yearbook 2019 synoptic table: Availability of data by country/area, table and sex, where applicable
Tableau A. Tableau synoptique de l'Annuaire démographique 2019 : Disponibilité des données par pays ou zone, tableau et le sexe, si disponible (continued - suite)

Continent and country or area Continent et pays ou zone	Table totals	Summary - Apercu			Population							Fertility - Natalité				Foetal mortality - Mortalité foetale		
		3		4	5	6		7		8		9	10		11	12	13	14
		Total	M/F			Total[1]	M/F	Total	M/F	Total	M/F		Total	M/F				
AFRICA - AFRIQUE																		
Uganda - Ouganda	11	•	•	•	•	•	•	•	•	•	•	...	...	...	...	...	...	...
United Republic of Tanzania - République Unie de Tanzanie	10	•	•	•	•	•	•	•	•	•	•	...	...	...	...	...	...	...
Western Sahara - Sahara occidental	2	•	•	...	...	...	...	...	...	...	...	...	...	...	...	...	...	...
Zambia - Zambie	16	•	•	•	•	•	•	•	•	•	•	•	•	•	...	...	...	...
Zimbabwe	10	•	•	...	•	•	•	•	•	•	•	...	...	...	...	...	...	...
AMERICA, NORTH - AMÉRIQUE DU NORD																		
Anguilla	18	•	•	•	•	•	•	•	•	•	...	•	...	...	...	...	...	...
Antigua and Barbuda - Antigua-et-Barbuda	15	•	...	•	•	•	•	•	•	...	...	•	•	...	...	...	...	...
Aruba	25	•	•	•	•	•	•	•	•	•	•	•	•	•	...	...	...	...
Bahamas	25	•	•	•	•	•	•	•	•	•	•	•	•	•	•	...	...	...
Barbados - Barbade	8	•	•	...	•	•	•	•	•	...	...	...	...	...	...	...	...	...
Belize	23	•	•	•	•	•	•	•	•	•	•	•	•	•	...	•	...	...
Bermuda - Bermudes	28	•	•	•	•	•	•	•	•	•	•	•	•	•	...	•	•	•
British Virgin Islands - Îles Vierges britanniques	19	•	•	•	•	•	•	•	•	...	...	•	•	...	...	•	...	...
Canada	25	•	•	•	•	•	•	•	•	•	•	•	•	•	•	•	...	...
Cayman Islands - Îles Caïmanes	18	•	•	•	•	•	•	•	•	•	•	•	•	...	...	...	...	...
Costa Rica	29	•	•	•	•	•	•	•	•	•	•	•	•	•	•	•	•	...
Cuba	29	•	•	•	•	•	•	•	•	•	...	•	•	•	•	•	•	•
Curaçao	22	•	•	•	•	•	•	•	•	...	...	•	•	•	...	...	...	...
Dominica - Dominique	15	•	•	•	•	•	•	•	•	...	...	•	...	...	...	...	...	...
Dominican Republic - République dominicaine	28	•	•	•	•	•	•	•	•	•	•	•	•	•	•	•	•	...
El Salvador	22	•	•	•	•	•	•	•	•	•	•	•	•	•	•	...	...	...
Greenland - Groenland	20	•	•	•	•	•	•	•	•	•	•	•	•	•	...	...	•	...
Grenada - Grenade	24	•	•	•	•	•	•	•	•	•	•	•	•	•	...	...	...	...
Guadeloupe	21	•	•	•	•	•	•	•	•	...	...	•	•	...	...	...	...	...
Guatemala	27	•	•	•	•	•	•	•	•	•	•	•	•	•	•	•	...	...
Haiti - Haïti	7	•	•	...	•	•	•	•	•	...	...	...	...	...	...	...	...	...
Honduras	11	•	•	...	•	•	•	•	•	•	•	...	•	...	...	...	...	...
Jamaica - Jamaïque	22	•	•	•	•	•	•	•	•	•	•	•	•	•	...	...	...	...
Martinique	22	•	•	•	•	•	•	•	•	•	•	•	•	...	...	...	...	...
Mexico - Mexique	30	•	•	•	•	•	•	•	•	•	•	•	•	•	•	•	•	•
Montserrat	22	•	•	•	•	•	•	•	•	...	...	•	•	•	...	•	...	...
Nicaragua	20	•	•	•	•	•	•	•	•	•	...	•	•	•	...	...	...	...
Panama	28	•	•	•	•	•	•	•	•	•	•	•	•	•	•	•	...	...
Puerto Rico - Porto Rico	28	•	•	•	•	•	•	•	•	•	•	•	•	•	•	•	...	...
Saint Barthélemy - Saint-Barthélemy	16	•	•	•	•	•	•	•	•	...	...	•	•	•	...	...	...	...
Saint Kitts and Nevis - Saint-Kitts-et-Nevis	11	•	•	•	•	•	•	•	•	...	...	•	...	...	...	...	...	...
Saint Lucia - Sainte-Lucie	13	•	•	...	•	•	•	•	•	•	•	...	•	...	...	...	...	...
Saint Pierre and Miquelon - Saint Pierre-et-Miquelon	19	•	•	•	•	•	•	•	•	•	•	•	•	•	...	...	...	...
Saint Vincent and the Grenadines - Saint-Vincent-et-les Grenadines	23	•	•	•	•	•	•	•	•	...	...	•	•	•	...	...	...	...
Saint-Martin (French part) - Saint-Martin (partie française)	16	•	•	•	•	•	•	•	•	...	...	•	•	•	...	...	...	...
Sint Maarten (Dutch part) - Saint-Martin (partie néerlandaise)	13	•	•	•	•	•	•	•	•	...	...	•	...	...	...	...	...	...
Trinidad and Tobago - Trinité-et-Tobago	20	•	...	•	•	•	•	•	•	•	•	•	...	...	...	...	...	...
Turks and Caicos Islands - Îles Turques et Caïques	23	•	•	•	•	•	•	•	•	•	•	•	•	•	...	...	...	...
United States of America - États-Unis d'Amérique	25	•	•	•	•	•	•	•	•	•	...	•	•	•	•	•	...	...
United States Virgin Islands - Îles Vierges américaines	14	•	•	•	•	•	•	•	•	•	...	•	...	...	...	...	...	...

Table A. Demographic Yearbook 2019 synoptic table: Availability of data by country/area, table and sex, where applicable
Tableau A. Tableau synoptique de l'Annuaire démographique 2019 : Disponibilité des données par pays ou zone, tableau et le sexe, si disponible (continued - suite)

General topic and table number - Sujet général et numéro de tableau

Continent and country or area Continent et pays ou zone	Infant and maternal mortality - Mortalité infantile et mortalité liée à la maternité				General mortality - Mortalité générale						Nuptiality and divorces - Nuptialité et divortialité		
	15	16		17	18	19		20	21	22	23	24	25
		Total	M/F			Total	M/F						
AFRICA - AFRIQUE													
Uganda - Ouganda	...	...	...	...	...	...	...	...	...	•	...	...	...
United Republic of Tanzania - République Unie de Tanzanie	...	...	...	...	...	...	...	...	...	...	...	...	...
Western Sahara - Sahara occidental	...	...	...	...	...	...	...	...	...	...	...	...	...
Zambia - Zambie	...	...	...	...	•	•	•	...	...	...	...	...	...
Zimbabwe	...	...	...	...	...	...	...	...	...	•	...	...	...
AMERICA, NORTH - AMÉRIQUE DU NORD													
Anguilla	...	...	...	•	•	•	•	•	...	•	•	•	...
Antigua and Barbuda - Antigua-et-Barbuda	•	...	...	•	•	•	...	•	...	•	...	...	...
Aruba	•	•	•	•	•	•	•	•	...	•	•	•	•
Bahamas	•	•	•	•	•	•	•	•	...	•	•	•	...
Barbados - Barbade	...	...	...	•	...	...	...	...	...	...	...	...	...
Belize	•	•	•	•	•	•	•	•	...	•	...	...	...
Bermuda - Bermudes	•	•	•	•	•	•	•	•	...	•	•	•	•
British Virgin Islands - Îles Vierges britanniques	•	...	...	•	•	•	•	...	...	•	•	...	•
Canada	•	•	•	•	•	•	•	•	•	•	...	...	...
Cayman Islands - Îles Caïmanes	...	...	...	•	•	•	•	...	...	•	•	...	...
Costa Rica	•	•	•	•	•	•	•	•	•	•	•	•	•
Cuba	•	•	•	•	•	•	•	•	•	•	•	•	•
Curaçao	•	•	•	...	•	•	•	...	•	•	•	•	•
Dominica - Dominique	...	...	...	•	•	...	...	•	...	•	•	...	•
Dominican Republic - République dominicaine	•	•	•	•	•	•	•	...	•	•	•	•	•
El Salvador	...	•	•	•	...	•	•	•	...	•	...	•	...
Greenland - Groenland	•	...	...	...	•	•	•	...	•	•	...	...	...
Grenada - Grenade	•	•	•	•	•	•	•	•	...	...	•	•	•
Guadeloupe	•	•	...	•	•	•	•	•	...	•	•	•	•
Guatemala	•	•	•	•	•	•	•	•	...	•	•	•	•
Haiti - Haïti	...	...	...	...	...	...	...	...	...	...	...	...	...
Honduras	...	...	...	•	...	...	...	...	...	...	...	...	...
Jamaica - Jamaïque	...	...	...	•	•	•	•	•	•	•	•	...	•
Martinique	•	...	...	•	•	•	•	•	•	•	•	...	•
Mexico - Mexique	•	•	•	•	•	•	•	•	•	•	•	•	•
Montserrat	•	•	•	•	•	•	•	•	...	...	•	•	...
Nicaragua	...	...	...	•	•	•	•	•	...	•	•	...	•
Panama	•	•	•	•	•	•	•	•	•	•	•	•	•
Puerto Rico - Porto Rico	•	•	•	•	•	•	•	•	•	•	•	•	•
Saint Barthélemy - Saint-Barthélemy	•	...	...	...	•	•	•	...	...	...	•	...	...
Saint Kitts and Nevis - Saint-Kitts-et-Nevis	...	...	...	•	...	...	...	•	...	...	...	...	...
Saint Lucia - Sainte-Lucie	...	...	...	•	...	...	...	•	...	•	...	...	...
Saint Pierre and Miquelon - Saint Pierre-et-Miquelon	•	...	...	•	•	•	•	...	...	...	•	...	...
Saint Vincent and the Grenadines - Saint-Vincent-et-les Grenadines	•	•	•	•	•	•	•	•	...	•	•	•	•
Saint-Martin (French part) - Saint-Martin (partie française)	•	...	...	...	•	•	•	...	...	...	•	...	...
Sint Maarten (Dutch part) - Saint-Martin (partie néerlandaise)	...	...	...	...	•	...	...	...	...	•	•	...	•
Trinidad and Tobago - Trinité-et-Tobago	•	•	•	...	•	•	•	...	...	•	•	•	•
Turks and Caicos Islands - Îles Turques et Caïques	•	...	...	•	•	•	•	•	...	•	•	•	•
United States of America - États-Unis d'Amérique	•	•	...	•	•	•	•	•	•	•	•	...	•
United States Virgin Islands - Îles Vierges américaines	•	...	...	•	•	...	...	•	...	...	...	...	...

Table A. Demographic Yearbook 2019 synoptic table: Availability of data by country/area, table and sex, where applicable
Tableau A. Tableau synoptique de l'Annuaire démographique 2019 : Disponibilité des données par pays ou zone, tableau et le sexe, si disponible (continued - suite)

General topic and table number - Sujet général et numéro de tableau

Continent and country or area Continent et pays ou zone	Table totals	Summary - Apercu			Population							Fertility - Natalité				Foetal mortality - Mortalité foetale		
		3		4	5	6		7		8		9	10		11	12	13	14
		Total	M/F			Total[1]	M/F	Total	M/F	Total	M/F		Total	M/F				
AMERICA, SOUTH - AMÉRIQUE DU SUD																		
Argentina - Argentine	25	•	•	•	•	•	•	•	•	•	•	•	•	•	...	•	...	...
Bolivia (Plurinational State of) - Bolivie (État plurinational de)	17	•	•	•	•	•	•	•	•	•	•	•	...	...	...	...	...	...
Brazil - Brésil	26	•	•	•	•	•	•	•	•	•	...	•	•	•	...	•	...	...
Chile - Chili	27	•	•	•	•	•	•	•	•	•	•	•	•	•	•	•	...	...
Colombia - Colombie	26	•	•	•	•	•	•	•	•	•	•	•	•	•	•	•	•	•
Ecuador - Équateur	29	•	•	•	•	•	•	•	•	•	...	•	•	•	•	•	•	•
Falkland Islands (Malvinas) - Îles Falkland (Malvinas)	9	•	•	...	...	•	•	•	•	•	•	...	...	...	...	...	...	...
French Guiana - Guyane française	21	•	•	•	•	•	•	•	•	•	•	•	•	...	...	...	...	...
Guyana	17	•	•	•	•	•	•	•	•	•	...	•	•	...	...	...	...	...
Paraguay	22	•	•	•	•	•	•	•	•	•	•	•	•	...	...	...	•	...
Peru - Pérou	25	•	•	•	•	•	•	•	•	•	•	•	•	•	...	...	...	...
Suriname	22	•	•	•	•	•	•	•	•	•	•	•	•	•	...	...	...	...
Uruguay	26	•	•	•	•	•	•	•	•	•	•	•	•	•	•	•	...	...
Venezuela (Bolivarian Republic of) - Venezuela (République bolivarienne du)	26	•	•	•	•	•	•	•	•	•	...	•	•	•	•	•	...	...
ASIA - ASIE																		
Afghanistan	11	•	•	•	•	•	•	•	•	•	•	...	...	...	...	...	...	...
Armenia - Arménie	30	•	•	•	•	•	•	•	•	•	•	•	•	•	•	•	•	•
Azerbaijan - Azerbaïdjan	28	•	•	•	•	•	•	•	•	•	•	•	•	•	•	•	•	•
Bahrain - Bahreïn	28	•	•	•	•	•	•	•	•	•	•	•	•	•	•	•	•	...
Bangladesh	20	•	•	•	•	•	•	•	•	•	•	•	•	•	...	...	...	...
Bhutan - Bhoutan	13	•	•	•	•	•	•	•	•	•	•	•	...	...	...	...	...	...
Brunei Darussalam - Brunéi Darussalam	24	•	•	•	•	•	•	•	•	•	•	•	•	•	•	...	...	...
Cambodia - Cambodge	9	•	•	...	•	•	•	•	•	•	•	...	...	...	...	...	...	...
China - Chine[2]	14	•	•	•	•	•	•	•	•	•	...	•	...	...	...	...	...	...
China, Hong Kong SAR - Chine, Hong Kong RAS	30	•	•	•	•	•	•	•	•	•	•	•	•	•	•	•	•	•
China, Macao SAR - Chine, Macao RAS	26	•	•	•	•	•	•	•	•	•	•	•	•	•	•	•	...	...
Cyprus - Chypre	25	•	•	•	•	•	•	•	•	•	...	•	•	•	•	...	...	...
Democratic People's Republic of Korea - République populaire démocratique de Corée	5	•	•	...	...	...	...	...	...	•	•	...	...	...	...	...	...	...
Georgia - Géorgie	28	•	•	•	•	•	•	•	•	•	...	•	•	•	•	•	•	•
India - Inde[3]	14	•	•	•	•	•	•	•	•	•	•	•	...	...	...	...	...	...
Indonesia - Indonésie	16	•	•	•	•	•	•	•	•	•	•	...	•	...	...	...	...	...
Iran (Islamic Republic of) - Iran (République islamique d')	23	•	•	•	•	•	•	•	•	•	•	•	•	•	...	...	...	...
Iraq	16	•	•	•	•	•	•	•	•	•	•	•	...	...	...	...	...	...
Israel - Israël[4]	30	•	•	•	•	•	•	•	•	•	•	•	•	•	•	•	•	•
Japan - Japon	30	•	•	•	•	•	•	•	•	•	•	•	•	•	•	•	•	•
Jordan - Jordanie	18	•	•	•	•	•	•	•	•	•	•	•	...	...	...	...	...	...
Kazakhstan	29	•	•	•	•	•	•	•	•	•	•	•	•	•	•	•	•	...
Kuwait - Koweït	26	•	•	•	•	•	•	•	•	•	•	•	•	•	...	•	...	...
Kyrgyzstan - Kirghizstan	30	•	•	•	•	•	•	•	•	•	•	•	•	•	•	•	•	•
Lao People's Democratic Republic - République démocratique populaire lao	18	•	•	•	•	•	•	•	•	•	•	•	•	•	...	...	...	...
Lebanon - Liban	8	•	•	...	...	•	•	...	...	•	•	...	...	...	...	...	...	...
Malaysia - Malaisie	24	•	•	•	•	•	•	•	•	•	...	•	•	•	•	•	...	...
Maldives	26	•	•	•	•	•	•	•	•	•	•	•	•	•	•	•	...	...
Mongolia - Mongolie	29	•	•	•	•	•	•	•	•	•	•	•	•	•	•	•	•	•
Myanmar	21	•	•	•	•	•	•	•	•	•	•	•	•	•	...	•	...	...
Nepal - Népal	12	•	•	...	•	•	•	•	•	•	•	...	...	...	...	...	...	...
Oman	26	•	•	•	•	•	•	•	•	•	•	•	•	•	•	•	...	...
Pakistan[5]	8	•	•	•	•	•	•	...	...	•	...	...	...	...	...	...	...	...
Philippines	25	•	•	•	•	•	•	•	•	•	...	•	•	•	•	•	...	...
Qatar	27	•	•	•	•	•	•	•	•	•	•	•	•	•	•	...	...	...
Republic of Korea - République de Corée	28	•	•	•	•	•	•	•	•	•	•	•	•	•	•	•	...	...
Saudi Arabia - Arabie saoudite	19	•	•	•	•	•	•	•	•	•	•	•	•	•	...	...	...	...
Singapore - Singapour	28	•	•	•	•	•	•	•	•	•	...	•	•	•	•	•	•	...

Table A. Demographic Yearbook 2019 synoptic table: Availability of data by country/area, table and sex, where applicable
Tableau A. Tableau synoptique de l'Annuaire démographique 2019 : Disponibilité des données par pays ou zone, tableau et le sexe, si disponible (continued - suite)

Continent and country or area Continent et pays ou zone	General topic and table number - Sujet général et numéro de tableau												
	Infant and maternal mortality - Mortalité infantile et mortalité liée à la maternité				General mortality - Mortalité générale						Nuptiality and divorces - Nuptialité et divortialité		
	15	16		17	18	19		20	21	22	23	24	25
		Total	M/F			Total	M/F						
AMERICA, SOUTH - AMÉRIQUE DU SUD													
Argentina - Argentine	•	•	•	•	•	•	•	•	•	•	•	...	...
Bolivia (Plurinational State of) - Bolivie (État plurinational de)	...	...	...	...	...	•	•	...	•	•	•	•	...
Brazil - Brésil	•	•	•	•	•	•	•	•	•	•	•	•	•
Chile - Chili	•	•	•	•	•	•	•	•	•	•	•	•	...
Colombia - Colombie	•	•	•	•	•	•	•	•	...	•	...	...	...
Ecuador - Équateur	•	•	•	•	•	•	•	•	•	•	•	•	•
Falkland Islands (Malvinas) - Îles Falkland (Malvinas)	...	...	...	...	...	...	...	...	...	•	...	...	...
French Guiana - Guyane française	...	...	...	•	•	•	•	•	•	•	•	...	•
Guyana	...	...	...	•	•	...	...	•	•	•	•	...	...
Paraguay	•	...	...	•	•	•	•	•	...	•	•	•	...
Peru - Pérou	•	•	•	•	•	•	•	•	...	•	•	•	•
Suriname	•	...	...	•	•	•	•	•	...	•	•	...	•
Uruguay	•	•	•	•	•	•	•	•	...	•	•	...	•
Venezuela (Bolivarian Republic of) - Venezuela (République bolivarienne du)	•	•	•	•	•	•	•	•	...	•	•	•	•
ASIA - ASIE													
Afghanistan	...	...	...	...	...	...	...	...	...	•	...	...	...
Armenia - Arménie	•	•	•	•	•	•	•	•	•	•	•	•	•
Azerbaijan - Azerbaïdjan	•	•	•	...	•	•	•	...	•	•	•	•	•
Bahrain - Bahreïn	•	•	•	•	•	•	•	•	...	•	•	•	•
Bangladesh	•	•	•	...	•	...	...	...	...	•	•	...	•
Bhutan - Bhoutan	...	...	...	...	•	...	...	...	...	•	...	...	...
Brunei Darussalam - Brunéi Darussalam	•	...	...	•	•	•	•	•	...	•	•	•	•
Cambodia - Cambodge	...	...	...	...	...	...	...	...	...	...	...	...	...
China - Chine[2]	...	...	...	...	•	•	•	...	...	•	...	...	...
China, Hong Kong SAR - Chine, Hong Kong RAS	•	•	•	•	•	•	•	•	•	•	•	•	•
China, Macao SAR - Chine, Macao RAS	•	•	•	...	•	•	•	...	•	•	•	•	•
Cyprus - Chypre	•	•	•	•	•	•	•	•	...	•	•	•	•
Democratic People's Republic of Korea - République populaire démocratique de Corée	...	...	...	...	...	...	...	...	...	•	...	...	...
Georgia - Géorgie	•	•	•	•	•	•	•	•	...	•	•	•	•
India - Inde[3]	•	...	...	...	•	...	...	...	...	•	...	...	...
Indonesia - Indonésie	...	...	...	...	...	•	•	...	...	•	•	...	•
Iran (Islamic Republic of) - Iran (République islamique d')	•	...	...	•	•	•	•	•	...	•	•	•	•
Iraq	•	...	...	•	•	...	...	•	...	•	...	...	...
Israel - Israël[4]	•	•	•	•	•	•	•	•	•	•	•	•	•
Japan - Japon	•	•	•	•	•	•	•	•	•	•	•	•	•
Jordan - Jordanie	...	...	...	•	•	...	...	•	...	•	•	•	•
Kazakhstan	•	•	•	•	•	•	•	•	•	•	•	•	•
Kuwait - Koweït	•	•	•	•	•	•	•	•	...	•	•	•	•
Kyrgyzstan - Kirghizstan	•	•	•	•	•	•	•	•	•	•	•	•	•
Lao People's Democratic Republic - République démocratique populaire lao	•	...	...	...	•	•	•	...	...	•	...	...	...
Lebanon - Liban	...	...	...	•	...	...	...	•	...	...	...	...	...
Malaysia - Malaisie	•	...	...	•	•	•	•	•	...	•	•	•	•
Maldives	•	•	•	•	•	•	•	•	...	•	•	...	•
Mongolia - Mongolie	•	•	•	•	•	•	•	•	...	•	•	•	•
Myanmar	•	•	•	...	•	•	•	...	...	•	...	...	...
Nepal - Népal	...	...	...	...	...	•	•	...	...	•	...	...	...
Oman	•	•	•	•	•	•	•	•	...	•	•	...	•
Pakistan[5]	...	...	...	...	...	...	...	...	...	•	...	...	...
Philippines	•	•	•	•	•	•	•	•	...	•	•	•	...
Qatar	•	•	•	•	•	•	•	•	•	•	•	•	•
Republic of Korea - République de Corée	•	•	•	•	•	•	•	•	•	•	•	•	•
Saudi Arabia - Arabie saoudite	•	...	...	•	•	•	•	...	...	•	...	...	...
Singapore - Singapour	•	•	•	•	•	•	•	•	•	•	•	•	•

Table A. Demographic Yearbook 2019 synoptic table: Availability of data by country/area, table and sex, where applicable
Tableau A. Tableau synoptique de l'Annuaire démographique 2019 : Disponibilité des données par pays ou zone, tableau et le sexe, si disponible (continued - suite)

Continent and country or area Continent et pays ou zone	Table totals	General topic and table number - Sujet général et numéro de tableau																
		Summary - Apercu		Population								Fertility - Natalité				Foetal mortality - Mortalité foetale		
		3		4	5	6		7		8		9	10		11	12	13	14
		Total	M/F			Total[1]	M/F	Total	M/F	Total	M/F		Total	M/F				
ASIA - ASIE																		
Sri Lanka	23	•	•	•	•	•	•	•	•	•	•	•	•	•	...	•	...	...
State of Palestine - État de Palestine	18	•	•	•	•	•	•	•	•	•	...	•	...	...	...	...	...	...
Syrian Arab Republic - République arabe syrienne	10	•	•	...	•	•	•	•	•	•	•	...	...	...	...	...	...	...
Tajikistan - Tadjikistan	28	•	•	•	•	•	•	•	•	•	•	•	•	...	•	•	•	•
Thailand - Thaïlande	24	•	•	•	•	•	•	•	•	•	•	•	•	•	...	...	...	...
Timor-Leste	13	•	•	•	•	•	•	•	•	•	•	•	...	...	...	...	...	...
Turkey - Turquie	27	•	•	•	•	•	•	•	•	•	•	•	•	•	•	...	...	...
Turkmenistan - Turkménistan	4	•	•	...	...	...	...	...	...	...	...	...	...	...	...	...	...	...
United Arab Emirates - Émirats arabes unis	23	•	•	•	•	•	•	...	...	•	•	•	•	•	...	•	...	...
Uzbekistan - Ouzbékistan	29	•	•	•	•	•	•	•	•	•	•	•	•	•	•	•	•	•
Viet Nam	12	•	•	•	•	•	•	•	•	...	...	...	...	...	...	...	...	...
Yemen - Yémen	12	•	•	•	•	•	•	•	•	•	...	•	...	...	...	...	...	...
EUROPE																		
Åland Islands - Îles d'Åland	27	•	•	•	•	•	•	•	•	•	•	•	•	•	•	•	•	•
Albania - Albanie	27	•	•	•	•	•	•	•	•	•	•	•	•	•	•	•	•	•
Andorra - Andorre	25	•	•	•	•	•	•	•	•	•	•	•	•	•	•	•	...	...
Austria - Autriche	28	•	•	•	•	•	•	•	•	•	•	•	•	•	•	•	...	...
Belarus - Bélarus	29	•	•	•	•	•	•	•	•	•	•	•	•	...	•	•	•	•
Belgium - Belgique	30	•	•	•	•	•	•	•	•	•	•	•	•	•	•	•	•	•
Bosnia and Herzegovina - Bosnie-Herzégovine	25	•	•	•	•	•	•	•	•	...	...	•	•	•	•	•	...	...
Bulgaria - Bulgarie	30	•	•	•	•	•	•	•	•	•	•	•	•	•	•	•	•	•
Croatia - Croatie	29	•	•	•	•	•	•	•	•	•	•	•	•	•	•	•	•	•
Czechia - Tchéquie	30	•	•	•	•	•	•	•	•	•	•	•	•	•	•	•	•	•
Denmark - Danemark	30	•	•	•	•	•	•	•	•	•	•	•	•	•	•	•	•	•
Estonia - Estonie	30	•	•	•	•	•	•	•	•	•	•	•	•	•	•	•	•	•
Faroe Islands - Îles Féroé	28	•	•	•	•	•	•	•	•	•	•	•	•	•	•	•	•	•
Finland - Finlande	30	•	•	•	•	•	•	•	•	•	•	•	•	•	•	•	•	•
France	28	•	•	•	•	•	•	•	•	•	•	•	•	•	•	...	•	...
Germany - Allemagne	30	•	•	•	•	•	•	•	•	•	•	•	•	•	•	•	•	•
Gibraltar	17	•	•	•	•	•	•	•	•	•	•	•	•	•	...	...	...	...
Greece - Grèce	28	•	•	•	•	•	•	•	•	•	•	•	•	•	•	•	...	...
Guernsey - Guernesey	12	•	•	•	•	•	•	•	•	•	...	•	...	...	...	...	...	...
Holy See - Saint-Siège	4	•	•	...	•	...	...	...	...	•	...	...	...	...	...	...	...	...
Hungary - Hongrie	30	•	•	•	•	•	•	•	•	•	•	•	•	•	•	•	•	•
Iceland - Islande	28	•	•	•	•	•	•	•	•	•	•	•	•	•	•	•	•	•
Ireland - Irlande	27	•	•	•	•	•	•	•	•	•	•	•	•	•	...	•	...	...
Isle of Man - Île de Man	16	•	...	•	•	•	•	•	•	•	•	•	•	...	...	...	...	...
Italy - Italie	30	•	•	•	•	•	•	•	•	•	•	•	•	•	•	•	•	•
Jersey	13	•	•	•	•	•	•	•	•	•	•	•	...	...	...	...	•	...
Latvia - Lettonie	30	•	•	•	•	•	•	•	•	•	•	•	•	•	•	•	•	•
Liechtenstein	22	•	•	•	•	•	•	•	•	•	•	•	•	•	...	...	...	...
Lithuania - Lituanie	30	•	•	•	•	•	•	•	•	•	•	•	•	•	•	•	•	•
Luxembourg	28	•	•	•	•	•	•	•	•	•	•	•	•	•	•	•	...	...
Malta - Malte	27	•	•	•	•	•	•	•	•	•	•	•	•	•	•	...	...	...
Monaco	14	•	•	•	•	•	•	•	•	•	•	•	...	...	...	...	...	...
Montenegro - Monténégro	23	•	•	•	•	•	•	•	•	•	•	•	•	•	...	...	•	...
Netherlands - Pays-Bas	28	•	•	•	•	•	•	•	•	•	•	•	•	•	•	•	...	...
North Macedonia - Macédoine du Nord	28	•	•	•	•	•	•	•	•	•	•	•	•	•	•	•	•	...
Norway - Norvège	29	•	•	•	•	•	•	•	•	•	•	•	•	•	•	•	•	...
Poland - Pologne	30	•	•	•	•	•	•	•	•	•	•	•	•	•	•	•	•	•
Portugal	30	•	•	•	•	•	•	•	•	•	•	•	•	•	•	•	•	•
Republic of Moldova - République de Moldova	29	•	•	•	•	•	•	•	•	•	•	•	•	•	•	...	•	•
Romania - Roumanie	30	•	•	•	•	•	•	•	•	•	•	•	•	•	•	•	•	•
Russian Federation - Fédération de Russie	23	•	•	...	•	•	•	•	•	•	•	...	•	•	•	...	•	•
San Marino - Saint-Marin	28	•	•	•	•	•	•	•	•	•	•	•	•	•	•	•	...	...
Serbia - Serbie	30	•	•	•	•	•	•	•	•	•	•	•	•	•	•	•	•	•
Slovakia - Slovaquie	30	•	•	•	•	•	•	•	•	•	•	•	•	•	•	•	•	•
Slovenia - Slovénie	30	•	•	•	•	•	•	•	•	•	•	•	•	•	•	•	•	•
Spain - Espagne	30	•	•	•	•	•	•	•	•	•	•	•	•	•	•	•	•	•

Table A. Demographic Yearbook 2019 synoptic table: Availability of data by country/area, table and sex, where applicable
Tableau A. Tableau synoptique de l'Annuaire démographique 2019 : Disponibilité des données par pays ou zone, tableau et le sexe, si disponible (continued - suite)

Continent and country or area / Continent et pays ou zone	General topic and table number - Sujet général et numéro de tableau: Infant and maternal mortality - Mortalité infantile et mortalité liée à la maternité				General mortality - Mortalité générale						Nuptiality and divorces - Nuptialité et divortialité		
	15	16 Total	16 M/F	17	18	19 Total	19 M/F	20	21	22	23	24	25
ASIA - ASIE													
Sri Lanka	•	•	•	...	•	•	•	...	...	•	•	•	...
State of Palestine - État de Palestine	•	...	...	...	•	•	•	...	...	•	•	•	•
Syrian Arab Republic - République arabe syrienne	...	...	...	•	...	...	...	...	...	...	...	...	...
Tajikistan - Tadjikistan	•	•	•	•	•	•	•	•	...	•	•	•	•
Thailand - Thaïlande	•	•	•	•	•	•	•	•	...	•	•	...	•
Timor-Leste	...	...	...	...	•	...	...	...	...	•	...	...	...
Turkey - Turquie	•	•	•	•	•	•	•	•	•	•	•	•	•
Turkmenistan - Turkménistan	...	...	...	•	...	...	...	•	...	...	...	...	...
United Arab Emirates - Émirats arabes unis	•	•	•	•	•	•	•	...	...	•	•	•	•
Uzbekistan - Ouzbékistan	•	•	•	•	•	•	•	•	...	•	•	•	•
Viet Nam	...	...	...	...	•	...	...	...	...	•	•	...	•
Yemen - Yémen	...	...	...	...	•	...	...	...	...	•	...	...	...
EUROPE													
Åland Islands - Îles d'Åland	•	•	•	...	•	•	•	...	...	•	•	•	•
Albania - Albanie	•	•	•	...	•	•	•	...	...	•	•	•	•
Andorra - Andorre	•	•	•	•	•	•	•	•	...	...	•	•	...
Austria - Autriche	•	•	•	•	•	•	•	•	•	•	•	•	•
Belarus - Bélarus	•	•	•	•	•	•	•	•	•	•	•	•	•
Belgium - Belgique	•	•	•	•	•	•	•	•	•	•	•	•	•
Bosnia and Herzegovina - Bosnie-Herzégovine	•	•	•	•	•	•	•	•	...	•	•	•	•
Bulgaria - Bulgarie	•	•	•	•	•	•	•	•	•	•	•	•	•
Croatia - Croatie	•	•	•	•	•	•	•	•	...	•	•	•	•
Czechia - Tchéquie	•	•	•	•	•	•	•	•	•	•	•	•	•
Denmark - Danemark	•	•	•	•	•	•	•	•	•	•	•	•	•
Estonia - Estonie	•	•	•	•	•	•	•	•	•	•	•	•	•
Faroe Islands - Îles Féroé	•	•	•	...	•	•	•	...	•	•	•	•	•
Finland - Finlande	•	•	•	•	•	•	•	•	•	•	•	•	•
France	•	•	•	•	•	•	•	•	•	•	•	•	•
Germany - Allemagne	•	•	•	•	•	•	•	•	•	•	•	•	•
Gibraltar	...	...	...	...	•	...	...	...	...	•	•	...	•
Greece - Grèce	•	•	•	•	•	•	•	•	•	•	•	•	•
Guernsey - Guernesey	...	...	...	...	•	...	...	...	...	•	...	...	...
Holy See - Saint-Siège	...	...	...	...	...	...	...	...	...	...	...	...	...
Hungary - Hongrie	•	•	•	•	•	•	•	•	•	•	•	•	•
Iceland - Islande	•	•	•	•	•	•	•	•	•	•	...	•	...
Ireland - Irlande	•	•	•	•	•	•	•	•	•	•	•	•	•
Isle of Man - Île de Man	•	...	...	...	•	•	•	...	...	...	•	...	...
Italy - Italie	•	•	•	•	•	•	•	•	•	•	•	•	•
Jersey	...	...	...	...	•	...	...	...	...	...	...	...	...
Latvia - Lettonie	•	•	•	•	•	•	•	•	•	•	•	•	•
Liechtenstein	•	•	•	...	•	•	•	...	...	...	•	•	•
Lithuania - Lituanie	•	•	•	•	•	•	•	•	•	•	•	•	•
Luxembourg	•	•	•	•	•	•	•	•	•	•	•	•	•
Malta - Malte	•	•	•	•	•	•	•	•	•	•	•	•	•
Monaco	...	...	...	...	•	...	...	...	...	...	•	...	•
Montenegro - Monténégro	•	•	•	•	•	•	•	...	...	...	•	...	•
Netherlands - Pays-Bas	•	•	•	•	•	•	•	•	•	•	•	•	•
North Macedonia - Macédoine du Nord	•	•	•	•	•	•	•	...	•	•	•	•	•
Norway - Norvège	•	•	•	•	•	•	•	•	•	•	•	•	•
Poland - Pologne	•	•	•	•	•	•	•	•	•	•	•	•	•
Portugal	•	•	•	•	•	•	•	•	•	•	•	•	•
Republic of Moldova - République de Moldova	•	•	•	•	•	•	•	•	•	•	•	•	•
Romania - Roumanie	•	•	•	•	•	•	•	•	•	•	•	•	•
Russian Federation - Fédération de Russie	...	•	•	•	...	•	•	•	•	•	...	•	...
San Marino - Saint-Marin	•	•	•	•	•	•	•	•	•	•	•	•	•
Serbia - Serbie	•	•	•	•	•	•	•	•	•	•	•	•	•
Slovakia - Slovaquie	•	•	•	•	•	•	•	•	•	•	•	•	•
Slovenia - Slovénie	•	•	•	•	•	•	•	•	•	•	•	•	•
Spain - Espagne	•	•	•	•	•	•	•	•	•	•	•	•	•

Table A. Demographic Yearbook 2019 synoptic table: Availability of data by country/area, table and sex, where applicable
Tableau A. Tableau synoptique de l'Annuaire démographique 2019 : Disponibilité des données par pays ou zone, tableau et le sexe, si disponible (continued - suite)

Continent and country or area Continent et pays ou zone	Table totals	Summary - Apercu: 3 Total	3 M/F	4	Population: 5	6 Total[1]	6 M/F	7 Total	7 M/F	8 Total	8 M/F	Fertility - Natalité: 9	10 Total	10 M/F	11	Foetal mortality - Mortalité foetale: 12	13	14
EUROPE																		
Svalbard and Jan Mayen Islands - Îles Svalbard et Jan Mayen	2	•	•	...	...	...	...	...	...	...	...	...	...	...	...	...	...	...
Sweden - Suède	30	•	•	•	•	•	•	•	•	•	•	•	•	•	•	•	•	•
Switzerland - Suisse	30	•	•	•	•	•	•	•	•	•	•	•	•	•	•	•	•	•
Ukraine	29	•	•	•	•	•	•	•	•	•	•	•	•	...	•	•	•	•
United Kingdom of Great Britain and Northern Ireland - Royaume-Uni de Grande-Bretagne et d'Irlande du Nord	30	•	•	•	•	•	•	•	•	•	•	•	•	•	•	•	•	•
OCEANIA - OCÉANIE																		
American Samoa - Samoas américaines	19	•	•	•	•	•	•	•	•	•	...	•	•	•	...	...	...	...
Australia - Australie	28	•	•	•	•	•	•	•	•	•	•	•	•	•	•	•	...	...
Cook Islands - Îles Cook	16	•	•	•	•	•	•	•	•	•	•	•	•	...	...	...	...	...
Fiji - Fidji	19	•	•	•	•	•	•	•	•	•	•	•	•	•	...	...	...	...
French Polynesia - Polynésie française	24	•	...	•	•	•	•	•	•	•	•	•	•	•	•	•	...	...
Guam	25	•	•	•	•	•	•	•	•	•	•	•	•	•	...	•	•	•
Kiribati	15	•	•	•	•	•	•	•	•	•	•	•	...	...	...	...	...	...
Marshall Islands - Îles Marshall	9	•	•	...	•	•	•	•	•	•	...	...	...	...	...	...	...	...
Micronesia (Federated States of) - Micronésie (États fédérés de)	9	•	•	...	•	•	•	•	•	•	...	...	...	...	...	...	...	...
Nauru	15	•	•	•	•	•	•	•	•	...	...	•	•	•	...	...	...	...
New Caledonia - Nouvelle-Calédonie	22	•	•	•	•	•	•	•	•	•	•	•	•	...	•	...	...	...
New Zealand - Nouvelle-Zélande	30	•	•	•	•	•	•	•	•	•	•	•	•	•	•	•	•	•
Niue - Nioué	14	•	•	•	•	•	•	•	•	•	•	•	...	...	...	...	...	...
Norfolk Island - Île Norfolk	9	•	•	•	...	•	•	•	•	...	...	...	...	...	...	...	...	...
Northern Mariana Islands - Îles Mariannes septentrionales	10	•	•	...	•	•	•	•	•	•	•	...	...	...	...	...	...	...
Palau - Palaos	18	•	•	•	•	•	•	•	•	•	...	•	•	•	...	•	...	...
Papua New Guinea - Papouasie-Nouvelle-Guinée	9	•	•	...	•	•	•	•	...	•	•	...	...	...	...	...	...	...
Pitcairn	12	•	...	•	...	•	•	•	•	•	•	•	...	...	...	...	...	...
Samoa	19	•	•	•	•	•	•	•	•	•	•	•	•	•	...	...	...	...
Solomon Islands - Îles Salomon	11	•	•	...	•	•	•	•	•	•	...	...	...	...	...	...	...	...
Tokelau - Tokélaou	8	•	•	...	•	•	•	•	•	...	...	...	•	...	...	...	...	...
Tonga	9	•	•	...	...	•	•	•	•	•	•	...	...	...	...	...	...	...
Tuvalu	13	•	...	•	•	•	•	•	...	•	...	•	•	...	...	...	...	...
Vanuatu	12	•	•	...	•	•	•	•	•	•	•	...	...	...	...	...	...	...
Wallis and Futuna Islands - Îles Wallis et Futuna	8	•	...	...	•	•	•	•	•	•	...	...	...	...	...	...	...	...

General topic and table number - Sujet général et numéro de tableau

Table A. Demographic Yearbook 2019 synoptic table: Availability of data by country/area, table and sex, where applicable
Tableau A. Tableau synoptique de l'Annuaire démographique 2019 : Disponibilité des données par pays ou zone, tableau et le sexe, si disponible (continued - suite)

Continent and country or area Continent et pays ou zone	General topic and table number - Sujet général et numéro de tableau: Infant and maternal mortality - Mortalité infantile et mortalité liée à la maternité				General mortality - Mortalité générale						Nuptiality and divorces - Nuptialité et divortialité		
	15	16 Total	16 M/F	17	18	19 Total	19 M/F	20	21	22	23	24	25
EUROPE													
Svalbard and Jan Mayen Islands - Îles Svalbard et Jan Mayen	...	...	...	...	...	...	...	...	...	...	...	...	...
Sweden - Suède	•	•	•	•	•	•	•	•	•	•	•	•	•
Switzerland - Suisse	•	•	•	•	•	•	•	•	•	•	•	•	•
Ukraine	•	•	•	•	•	•	•	•	•	•	•	•	•
United Kingdom of Great Britain and Northern Ireland - Royaume-Uni de Grande-Bretagne et d'Irlande du Nord	•	•	•	•	•	•	•	•	•	•	•	•	•
OCEANIA - OCÉANIE													
American Samoa - Samoas américaines	•	...	...	...	•	•	•	...	...	•	•	...	•
Australia - Australie	•	•	•	•	•	•	•	•	•	•	•	•	•
Cook Islands - Îles Cook	•	...	...	...	•	...	...	...	...	•	•	...	...
Fiji - Fidji	•	...	...	•	•	•	•	...	...	•	...	...	...
French Polynesia - Polynésie française	•	•	•	...	•	•	•	...	•	•	•	•	...
Guam	•	•	•	...	•	•	•	...	...	•	•	...	•
Kiribati	...	...	...	...	•	•	•	...	...	•	...	...	...
Marshall Islands - Îles Marshall	...	...	...	...	...	...	...	...	...	•	...	...	...
Micronesia (Federated States of) - Micronésie (États fédérés de)	...	...	...	...	...	...	...	...	...	•	...	...	...
Nauru	...	...	...	...	•	•	•	...	...	•	...	...	...
New Caledonia - Nouvelle-Calédonie	•	•	•	...	•	•	•	...	...	•	•	•	...
New Zealand - Nouvelle-Zélande	•	•	•	•	•	•	•	•	•	•	•	•	•
Niue - Nioué	...	...	...	...	•	...	...	...	...	•	•	...	...
Norfolk Island - Île Norfolk	...	...	...	...	•	...	...	...	...	...	•	...	...
Northern Mariana Islands - Îles Mariannes septentrionales	...	...	...	...	...	...	...	...	...	•	...	...	...
Palau - Palaos	•	...	...	...	•	•	•	...	...	•	...	...	...
Papua New Guinea - Papouasie-Nouvelle-Guinée	...	...	...	...	...	...	...	...	...	•	...	...	...
Pitcairn	...	...	...	...	•	...	...	...	...	...	•	...	•
Samoa	•	...	...	...	•	•	•	...	...	•	•	...	...
Solomon Islands - Îles Salomon	...	...	...	•	...	...	...	•	...	•	...	...	...
Tokelau - Tokélaou	...	...	...	...	...	...	...	...	...	...	...	...	...
Tonga	...	...	...	...	...	...	...	...	...	•	...	...	...
Tuvalu	...	...	...	...	•	•	•	...	...	•	...	...	...
Vanuatu	...	...	...	...	...	•	•	...	...	•	...	...	...
Wallis and Futuna Islands - Îles Wallis et Futuna	...	...	...	...	...	...	...	...	...	•	...	...	...

FOOTNOTES - NOTES

• Data presented in the table. - Les données présentées dans le tableau.

... Data not available. - Données non disponibles.

1 Including countries with data on total population by sex but without data on urban population. - Y compris les pays avec des données sur la population totale selon le sexe mais pas sur la population urbaine.

2 For statistical purposes, the data for China do not include those for the Hong Kong Special Administrative Region (Hong Kong SAR), Macao special Administrative Region (Macao SAR) and Taiwan province of China. - Pour la présentation des statistiques, les données pour Chine ne comprennent pas la Région Administrative Spéciale de Hong Kong (Hong Kong RAS), la Région Administrative Spéciale de Macao (Macao RAS) et Taïwan province de Chine.

3 Including data for the Indian-held part of Jammu and Kashmir, the final status of which has not yet been determined. - Y compris les données pour la partie du Jammu et du Cachemire occupée par l'Inde dont le statut définitif n'a pas encore été déterminé.

4 Including data for East Jerusalem and Israeli residents in certain other territories under occupation by Israeli military forces since June 1967. - Y compris les données pour Jérusalem-Est et les résidents israéliens dans certains autres territoires occupés depuis 1967 par les forces armées israéliennes.

5 Excluding data for the Pakistan-held part of Jammu and Kashmir, the final status of which has not yet been determined. - Non compris les données concernant la partie du Jammu et Cachemire occupée par le Pakistan dont le statut définitif n'a pas été déterminé.

Table 1 – *Demographic Yearbook 2019*

Table 1 presents for the world and major areas and regions estimates of the order of magnitude of population size, rates of population increase, crude birth and death rates, land area as well as population density.

Description of variables: Estimates of world population by major areas and by regions are presented for 1960, 1970, 1980, 1990, 2000, 2010 and 2019. Average annual percentage rates of population growth, crude birth and crude death rates are shown for the period from 2015 to 2020. Land area in square kilometers and population density estimates relate to 2019.

All population estimates and rates presented in this table were prepared by the Population Division of the United Nations Department of Economic and Social Affairs, and have been published in the *2019 Revision of World Population Prospects*[1].

The scheme of regionalization used for these estimates is described below. Although some continental totals are given, this table presents six major areas that are so drawn as to obtain greater homogeneity in sizes of population, types of demographic circumstances and accuracy of demographic statistics. Five of the major areas are subdivided into a total of 20 regions, which are arranged within the major areas; these regions together with Northern America, which is not subdivided, make a total of 21 regions.

The major areas of Northern America and Latin America and the Caribbean are distinguished, rather than the conventional continents of North America and South America, because population trends in the middle American mainland and the Caribbean region more closely resemble those of South America than those of America north of Mexico. Data for the traditional continents of North and South America can be obtained by adding Central America and Caribbean region to Northern America and deducting from Latin America. Latin America, as defined here, has somewhat wider limits than it would be if defined only to include the Spanish-speaking, French-speaking and Portuguese-speaking countries.

The average annual percentage rates of population growth are calculated by the Population Division of the United Nations using an exponential rate of increase.

Crude birth and crude death rates are expressed in terms of the average annual number of births and deaths, respectively, per 1 000 mid-year population. These rates are estimated.

The land areas of regions are estimated by the Population Division of the United Nations.

Computation: Density, calculated by the Statistics Division of the United Nations, is the number of persons in the total population of 2019 per square kilometer of the respective land area.

Reliability of data: With the exception of land area, all data are set in *italic* type to indicate their conjectural quality.

Limitations: The estimated orders of magnitude of population and land area are subject to all the basic limitations set forth in connection with table 3, and to the same qualifications set forth for population and surface area statistics in sections 3 and 2.4 of the Technical Notes, respectively.

Likewise, rates of population increase and population density are affected by the limitations of the original figures. However, it may be noted that, in compiling data for regional and major areas totals, errors in the components may tend to compensate each other and the resulting aggregates may be more reliable than the quality of the individual components would imply.

Because of their estimated character, many of the birth and death rates shown should also be considered only as orders of magnitude, and not as measures of the true level of fertility or mortality.

In interpreting the population densities, one should consider that some of the regions include large segments of land that are uninhabitable or barely habitable, and density values calculated as described make no allowance for this, nor for differences in patterns of land settlement.

Composition of major areas and regions

AFRICA

Eastern Africa
Burundi
Comoros
Djibouti
Eritrea
Ethiopia
Kenya
Madagascar
Malawi
Mauritius
Mayotte
Mozambique
Réunion
Rwanda
Seychelles
Somalia
South Sudan
Uganda
United Republic of Tanzania
Zambia
Zimbabwe

Middle Africa
Angola
Cameroon
Central African Republic
Chad
Congo
Democratic Republic of the Congo
Equatorial Guinea
Gabon
Sao Tome and Principe

Northern Africa
Algeria
Egypt
Libyan Arab Jamahiriya
Morocco
Sudan
Tunisia
Western Sahara

Southern Africa
Botswana
Eswatini
Lesotho
Namibia
South Africa

Western Africa
Benin
Burkina Faso
Cabo Verde
Côte d'Ivoire
Gambia
Ghana
Guinea
Guinea-Bissau
Liberia
Mali
Mauritania
Niger
Nigeria
Saint Helena
Senegal
Sierra Leone
Togo

ASIA

Eastern Asia
China
China, Hong Kong SAR
China, Macao SAR
Democratic People's Republic of Korea
Japan
Mongolia
Republic of Korea

South-Central Asia
Afghanistan
Bangladesh
Bhutan
India
Iran (Islamic Republic of)
Kazakhstan
Kyrgyzstan
Maldives
Nepal
Pakistan
Sri Lanka
Tajikistan
Turkmenistan
Uzbekistan

South-Eastern Asia
Brunei Darussalam
Cambodia
Indonesia
Lao People's Democratic Republic
Malaysia
Myanmar
Philippines
Singapore
Thailand
Timor Leste
Viet Nam

Western Asia
Armenia
Azerbaijan
Bahrain
Cyprus
Georgia
Iraq
Israel
Jordan
Kuwait
Lebanon
Oman
Qatar
Saudi Arabia
State of Palestine
Syrian Arab Republic
Turkey
United Arab Emirates
Yemen

EUROPE

Eastern Europe
Belarus
Bulgaria
Czech Republic
Hungary
Poland
Republic of Moldova
Romania
Russian Federation
Slovakia
Ukraine

Northern Europe
Åland Islands
Denmark
Estonia
Faeroe Islands
Finland
Guernsey
Iceland
Ireland
Isle of Man
Jersey
Latvia
Lithuania
Norway
Sweden
United Kingdom of Great Britain and Northern Ireland

Southern Europe
Albania
Andorra
Bosnia and Herzegovina

Croatia
Gibraltar
Greece
Holy See
Italy
Malta
Montenegro
North Macedonia
Portugal
San Marino
Serbia
Slovenia
Spain

Western Europe
Austria
Belgium
France
Germany
Liechtenstein
Luxembourg
Monaco
Netherlands
Switzerland

LATIN AMERICA and the CARIBBEAN

Caribbean
Anguilla
Antigua and Barbuda
Aruba
Bahamas
Barbados
Bonaire, Saba and Sint Eustatius
British Virgin Islands
Cayman Islands
Cuba
Curaçao
Dominica
Dominican Republic
Grenada
Guadaloupe
Haiti
Jamaica
Martinique
Montserrat
Puerto Rico
Saint Kitts and Nevis
Saint Lucia
Saint Vincent and the Grenadines
Sint Maarten (Dutch part)
Trinidad and Tobago
Turks and Caicos Islands
United States Virgin Islands

Central America
Belize
Costa Rica
El Salvador
Guatemala
Honduras
Mexico
Nicaragua
Panama

South America
Argentina
Bolivia (Plurinational State of)
Brazil
Chile
Colombia
Ecuador
Falkland Islands (Malvinas)
French Guiana
Guyana
Paraguay
Peru
Suriname
Uruguay
Venezuela (Bolivarian Republic of)

NORTHERN AMERICA

Bermuda
Canada
Greenland
Saint Pierre and Miquelon
United States of America

OCEANIA

Australia and New Zealand
Australia
New Zealand
Norfolk Island

Melanesia
Fiji
New Caledonia
Papua New Guinea
Solomon Islands
Vanuatu

Micronesia
Guam
Kiribati
Marshall Islands
Micronesia (Federated States of)
Nauru
Northern Mariana Islands
Palau

Polynesia
American Samoa
Cook Islands
French Polynesia
Niue
Pitcairn
Samoa
Tokelau
Tonga
Tuvalu
Wallis and Futuna Islands

---

[1] *United Nations, Department of Economic and Social Affairs, Population Division (2019). World Population Prospects: The 2019 Revision* (https://population.un.org/wpp/

Tableau 1 – *Annuaire démographique 2019*

Le tableau 1 présente, pour l'ensemble du monde et les grandes zones et régions, des estimations concernant l'ordre de grandeur de la population, les taux d'accroissement démographique, les taux bruts de natalité et de mortalité, la superficie des terres et la densité de peuplement.

Description des variables : des estimations de la population mondiale par grandes zones et régions sont présentées pour 1960, 1970, 1980, 1990, 2000 et 2010 ainsi que pour 2019. Les taux annuels moyens d'accroissement de la population et les taux bruts de natalité et de mortalité portent sur la période allant de 2015 à 2020. Les indications concernant la superficie des terres exprimée en kilomètres carrés et les estimations de la densité de population se rapportent à 2019.

Toutes les estimations de population et les taux de natalité, taux de mortalité et taux annuels d'accroissement de la population qui sont présentés dans le tableau 1 ont été établis par la Division de la population du Département des affaires économiques et sociales de l'Organisation des Nations Unies, et ont été publiés dans les *Perspectives de la population mondiale : La révision de 2019* [1].

Bien que l'on ait donné certains totaux pour les continents (tous les autres pouvant être calculés), on a réparti le monde en six grandes zones qui ont été découpées de manière à obtenir une plus grande homogénéité du point de vue des dimensions de population, des types de situations démographiques et de l'exactitude des statistiques démographiques. Cinq de ces six grandes zones ont été subdivisées en 20 régions. Avec l'Amérique septentrionale, qui n'est pas subdivisée, on arrive à un total de 21 régions.

Au lieu de faire la distinction classique entre l'Amérique du Nord et l'Amérique du Sud, on a choisi d'opérer une comparaison entre l'Amérique septentrionale et l'Amérique latine et Caraïbes, parce que les tendances démographiques dans la partie continentale de l'Amérique centrale et dans la région des Caraïbes se rapprochent davantage de celles de l'Amérique du Sud que de celles de l'Amérique au nord du Mexique. On obtient les données pour les continents traditionnels de l'Amérique du Nord et de l'Amérique du Sud en extrayant les données concernant l'Amérique centrale et les Caraïbes de celles relatives à l'Amérique latine et en les regroupant avec celles relatives à l'Amérique septentrionale. L'Amérique latine ainsi définie a par conséquent des limites plus larges que celles des pays ou zones de langues espagnole, portugaise et française qui constituent l'Amérique latine au sens le plus strict du terme.

Les taux annuels moyens d'accroissement de la population sont calculés par la Division de la population de l'Organisation des Nations Unies en appliquant un taux d'accroissement exponentiel.

Les taux bruts de natalité et de mortalité représentent respectivement le nombre annuel moyen de naissances et de décès par millier d'habitants en milieu d'année. Ces taux sont estimatifs.

La superficie des terres pour les régions a été estimée par la Division de la population de l'Organisation des Nations Unies.

Calculs : la densité, calculée par la Division de statistique de l'Organisation des Nations Unies, est égale au rapport entre l'effectif total de la population en 2019 et la superficie des terres exprimée en kilomètres carrés.

Fiabilité des données : á l'exception des données concernant la superficie des terres, toutes les données sont reproduites en *italique* pour en faire ressortir le caractère conjectural.

Insuffisance des données : les estimations concernant l'ordre de grandeur de la population et la superficie des terres reposent en partie sur les données du tableau 3 ; elles appellent donc toutes les réserves fondamentales formulées à propos de ce tableau, et celles qui ont été respectivement formulées aux sections 3 et 2.4 des Notes techniques en ce qui concerne les statistiques relatives à la population et à la superficie.

Les taux d'accroissement et les indices de densité de la population se ressentent eux aussi des insuffisances inhérentes aux données de base. Toutefois, il est à noter que, lorsque l'on additionne des données par territoire pour obtenir des totaux régionaux et par grandes zones, les erreurs qu'elles comportent arrivent parfois à s'équilibrer, de sorte que les agrégats obtenus peuvent être un peu plus exacts que chacun des éléments dont on est parti.

Vu leur caractère estimatif, nombre des taux de natalité et de mortalité du tableau 1 doivent être considérés uniquement comme des ordres de grandeur et ne sont pas censés mesurer exactement le niveau de la natalité ou de la mortalité.

Pour interpréter les valeurs de la densité de population, on se souviendra qu'il existe dans certaines des régions de vastes étendues de terres inhabitables ou à peine habitables et que les chiffres calculés selon la méthode indiquée ne tiennent compte ni de ce fait ni des différences de dispersion de la population selon le mode d'habitat.

Composition des grandes zones et régions

AFRIQUE

Afrique orientale
Burundi
Comores
Djibouti
Érythrée
Éthiopie
Kenya
Madagascar
Malawi
Maurice
Mayotte
Mozambique
Ouganda
République-Unie de Tanzanie
Réunion
Rwanda
Seychelles
Somalie
Soudan du Sud
Zambie
Zimbabwe

Afrique centrale
Angola
Cameroun
Congo
Gabon
Guinée équatoriale
République centrafricaine
République démocratique du Congo
Sao Tomé-et-Principe
Tchad

Afrique septentrionale
Algérie
Égypte
Jamahiriya arabe libyenne
Maroc
Sahara occidental
Soudan
Tunisie

Afrique australe
Afrique du Sud
Botswana
Eswatini
Lesotho
Namibie

Afrique occidentale
Bénin
Burkina Faso
Cabo Verde
Côte d'Ivoire
Gambie
Ghana
Guinée
Guinée-Bissau
Libéria
Mali
Mauritanie
Niger
Nigéria
Sainte-Hélène
Sénégal
Sierra Leone
Togo

AMÉRIQUE LATINE ET CARAÏBES

Caraïbes
Anguilla
Antigua-et-Barbuda
Aruba
Bahamas
Barbade
Bonaire, Saint-Eustache et Saba
Cuba
Curaçao
Dominique
Grenade
Guadeloupe
Haïti
Îles Caïmanes
Îles Turques et Caïques
Îles Vierges américaines
Îles Vierges britanniques
Jamaïque
Martinique
Montserrat
Porto Rico
République dominicaine
Saint-Kitts-et-Nevis
Sainte-Lucie
Saint-Martin (partie néerlandaise)
Saint-Vincent-et-les Grenadines
Trinité-et-Tobago

Amérique centrale
Belize
Costa Rica
El Salvador
Guatemala
Honduras
Mexique
Nicaragua
Panama

Amérique du Sud
Argentine
Bolivie (État plurinational de)
Brésil
Chili
Colombie
Équateur
Guyana
Guyane française
Îles Falkland (Malvinas)
Paraguay
Pérou
Suriname
Uruguay
Venezuela (République bolivarienne du)

AMÉRIQUE SEPTENTRIONALE

Bermudes
Canada
États-Unis d'Amérique
Groenland
Saint-Pierre-et-Miquelon

ASIE

Asie orientale
Chine
Chine, Région administrative spéciale de Hong Kong
Chine, Région administrative spéciale de Macao
Japon
Mongolie
République de Corée
République populaire démocratique de Corée

Asie centrale et Asie du Sud
Afghanistan
Bangladesh
Bhoutan
Inde
Iran (République Islamique d')
Kazakhstan
Kirghizistan
Maldives
Népal
Ouzbékistan

Pakistan
Sri Lanka
Tadjikistan
Turkménistan

Asie du Sud-Est
Brunéi Darussalam
Cambodge
Indonésie
Malaisie
Myanmar
Philippines
République démocratique populaire lao
Singapour
Thaïlande
Timor-Leste
Viet Nam

Asie occidentale
Arabie saoudite
Arménie
Azerbaïdjan
Bahreïn
Chypre
Émirats arabes unis
État de Palestine
Géorgie
Iraq
Israël
Jordanie
Koweït
Liban
Oman
Qatar
République arabe syrienne
Turquie
Yémen

EUROPE

Europe orientale
Bélarus
Bulgarie
Fédération de Russie
Hongrie
Pologne
République de Moldova
République tchèque
Roumanie
Slovaquie
Ukraine

Europe septentrionale
Danemark
Estonie
Finlande
Guernesey
Île de Man
Îles d'Åland
Îles Féroé
Îles Svalbard et Jan Mayen
Irlande
Islande
Jersey
Lettonie
Lituanie
Norvège
Royaume-Uni de Grande-Bretagne et d'Irlande du Nord
Suède

Europe méridionale
Albanie
Andorre
Bosnie-Herzégovine
Croatie
Espagne
Gibraltar
Grèce
Italie
Macédoine du Nord
Malte
Monténégro
Portugal
Saint-Marin
Saint-Siège
Serbie
Slovénie

Europe occidentale
Allemagne
Autriche
Belgique
France
Liechtenstein
Luxembourg
Monaco
Pays-Bas
Suisse

OCÉANIE

Australie et Nouvelle-Zélande
Australie
Île Norfolk
Nouvelle-Zélande

Mélanésie
Fidji
Îles Salomon
Nouvelle-Calédonie
Papouasie-Nouvelle-Guinée
Vanuatu

Micronésie
Guam
Îles Mariannes septentrionales
Îles Marshall
Kiribati
Micronésie (États fédérés de)
Nauru
Palaos

Polynésie
Îles Cook
Îles Wallis et Futuna
Nioué
Pitcairn
Polynésie française
Samoa
Samoa américaines
Tokélaou
Tonga
Tuvalu

---

[1] *Organisation des Nations Unies, Département des affaires économiques et sociales, Division de la population (2019). Perspectives de la population mondiale : La révision de 2019* (https://population.un.org/wpp/)

1. Population, rate of increase, birth and death rates, land area and density for the world, major areas and regions: selected years
Population, taux d'accroissement, taux de natalité et taux de mortalité, superficie des terres et densité pour l'ensemble du monde, les régions macro géographiques et les composantes géographiques : diverses années

Major areas and regions Régions macro géographiques et composantes	Mid-year population estimates - Estimations de population au milieu de l'année (millions)							Annual rate of increase - Taux d'accroissement annuel (%)	Crude birth rate - Taux bruts de natalité	Crude death rate - Taux bruts de mortalité	Land area (km2) - Superficie des terres (km2) (000s)	Density - Densité[1]
	1960	1970	1980	1990	2000	2010	2019	2015-2020			2019	
WORLD TOTAL - ENSEMBLE DU MONDE	3 034.9	3 700.4	4 458.0	5 327.2	6 143.5	6 956.8	7 713.5	1.1	18	8	130 094	59
AFRICA - AFRIQUE	283.4	363.4	476.4	630.3	811.0	1 039.3	1 308.1	2.5	34	8	29 648	44
Eastern Africa - Afrique orientale	83.6	109.7	146.5	197.2	257.4	339.3	433.9	2.7	34	7	6 667	65
Middle Africa - Afrique centrale	32.2	40.2	52.9	70.9	96.1	131.6	174.3	3.0	40	10	6 497	27
Northern Africa - Afrique septentrionale	63.2	82.5	106.8	139.7	171.3	202.9	241.8	1.9	25	6	7 769	31
Southern Africa - Afrique méridionale	19.4	25.0	32.4	42.0	51.4	58.4	66.6	1.4	21	9	2 651	25
Western Africa - Afrique occidentale	84.9	106.1	137.8	180.5	234.7	307.0	391.4	2.7	37	10	6 064	65
LATIN AMERICA AND CARIBBEAN - AMÉRIQUE LATIN ET CARAÏBES	220.5	286.7	361.3	442.8	521.8	591.4	648.1	0.9	17	6	20 139	32
Caribbean - Caraïbes	20.7	25.2	29.6	34.1	38.1	41.2	43.3	0.4	17	8	226	192
Central America - Amérique centrale	51.1	69.4	91.1	113.4	135.3	157.6	177.6	1.2	19	6	2 452	72
South America - Amérique méridionale	148.7	192.1	240.5	295.4	348.4	392.5	427.2	0.9	16	6	17 461	24
NORTHERN AMERICA - AMÉRIQUE SEPTENTRIONALE	204.6	231.0	254.0	279.8	312.4	343.3	366.6	0.7	12	9	18 652	20
ASIA - ASIE	1 705.0	2 142.5	2 649.6	3 226.1	3 741.3	4 209.6	4 601.4	0.9	16	7	31 033	148
Eastern Asia - Asie orientale	805.9	999.4	1 198.1	1 393.3	1 519.8	1 604.9	1 672.6	0.4	11	7	11 560	145
South Central Asia - Asie centrale méridionale	619.1	775.4	980.4	1 240.0	1 511.9	1 775.4	1 991.4	1.2	20	7	10 327	193
South Eastern Asia - Asie méridionale orientale	214.0	281.4	357.6	444.5	525.0	596.9	662.0	1.1	18	6	4 341	153
Western Asia - Asie occidentale	66.1	86.2	113.5	148.3	184.6	232.4	275.3	1.6	21	5	4 805	57
EUROPE	605.4	656.9	693.6	720.9	725.6	736.4	747.2	0.1	10	11	22 135	34
Eastern Europe - Europe orientale	253.5	276.2	294.7	309.8	303.9	294.9	293.4	-0.1	11	13	18 053	16
Northern Europe - Europe septentrionale	81.7	87.3	89.8	92.0	94.5	100.4	105.8	0.5	11	9	1 702	62
Southern Europe - Europe méridionale	117.8	127.5	138.6	143.5	144.8	153.0	152.4	-0.1	8	10	1 295	118
Western Europe - Europe occidentale	152.4	166.0	170.5	175.5	182.3	188.1	195.5	0.4	10	10	1 085	180
OCEANIA - OCÉANIA	16.0	19.9	23.2	27.3	31.4	36.9	42.1	1.4	17	7	8 486	5
Australia and New Zealand - Australie et Nouvelle Zélande	12.6	15.6	17.7	20.4	22.9	26.5	30.0	1.2	13	7	7 946	4
Melanesia - Melanésie	2.9	3.7	4.7	6.0	7.5	9.2	10.9	1.9	27	7	530	21
Micronesia	0.2	0.2	0.3	0.4	0.5	0.5	0.5	1.0	21	6	3	171
Polynesia - Polynésie	0.3	0.4	0.5	0.5	0.6	0.7	0.7	0.5	20	6	8	84

FOOTNOTES - NOTES

1 Population per square kilometre of land area. Figures are estimates of population divided by land area and are not to be considered as either reflecting density in the urban sense or as indicating the supporting power of a territory's land and resources. - Habitants par kilomètre carré. Il s'agit simplement du quotient calculé en divisant la population par la superficie des terres et n'est par considéré comme indiquant la densité au sens urbain du terme ni l'effectif de population que les terres et les ressources du territoire sont capables de nourrir.

Table 2 - *Demographic Yearbook 2019*

Table 2 presents estimates of population and the percentage distribution by age group and sex as well as the sex ratio for all ages; data are presented for the world, the six major areas and the twenty regions for 2019.

Description of variables: All population estimates presented in this table are prepared by the Population Division of the United Nations Department of Economic and Social Affairs. These estimates are published (using more detailed age groups) in the *2019 Revision of World Population Prospects*[1].

The scheme of regionalization used for these estimates is discussed in detail in the technical notes for table 1. Age groups presented in this table are: 0-14 years, 15-64 years, and 65 years or over. Sex ratio refers to the number of males per 100 females of all ages.

The percentage distributions and the sex ratios that appear in this table were calculated by the Statistics Division of the United Nations Department of Economic and Social Affairs using the estimates prepared by the Population Division of the United Nations Department of Economic and Social Affairs.

Reliability of data: All data are set in *italic* type to indicate their conjectural quality.

Limitations: The data presented in this table are from the same series of estimates, prepared by the Population Division of the United Nations, presented in table 1. The estimated orders of magnitude of population are subject to all the basic limitations set forth for population statistics in section 3 of the Technical Notes. In brief, because they are estimates, these distributions by broad age groups and sex should be considered only as orders of magnitude. However, in compiling data for regional and major areas' totals, errors in the components tend to compensate each other and the resulting aggregates may be somewhat more reliable than the quality of the individual components would imply.

In addition, data in this table are limited by factors affecting data by age. These factors are described in the technical notes for table 7. Because the age groups presented in this table are broad, these problems are minimized.

---

[1] *United Nations, Department of Economic and Social Affairs, Population Division (2019). World Population Prospects: The 2019 Revision* (https://population.un.org/wpp/)

Tableau 2 – *Annuaire démographique 2019*

Le tableau 2 présente, pour l'ensemble du monde, les six grandes zones et les vingt régions, des estimations concernant la population en 2019 ainsi que sa répartition en pourcentage selon des tranches d' âge et le sexe, et le rapport de masculinité pour tous les âges.

Description des variables : toutes les données figurant dans le tableau 2 ont été établies par la Division de la population du Département des affaires économiques et sociales de l'Organisation des Nations Unies, et ont été publiés dans les *Perspectives de la population mondiale : La révision de 2019*[1].

La classification géographique utilisée pour établir ces estimations est exposée en détail dans les notes techniques relatives au tableau 1. Les groupes d'âge présentés dans ce tableau sont définis comme suit : de 0 à 14 ans, de 15 à 64 ans et 65 ans ou plus. Le rapport de masculinité correspond au nombre d'individus de sexe masculin pour 100 individus de sexe féminin sans considération d'âge.

Les pourcentages et les rapports de masculinité qui sont présentés dans le tableau 2 ont été calculés par la Division de statistique du Département des affaires économiques et sociales de l'Organisation des Nations Unies à partir des estimations établies par la Division de la population de l'Organisation des Nations Unies.

Fiabilité des données : toutes les données figurant dans ce tableau sont reproduites en *italique* pour en faire ressortir le caractère conjectural.

Insuffisance des données : les données de ce tableau appartiennent à la même série d'estimations, établie par la Division de la population de l'Organisation des Nations Unies, que celles qui figurent au tableau 1. Les estimations concernant l'ordre de grandeur de la population appellent donc toutes les réserves fondamentales qui ont été formulées à la section 3 des Notes techniques à propos des statistiques relatives à la population. Sans entrer dans le détail, il convient de préciser que les données relatives à la répartition par grand groupe d'âge et par sexe doivent être considérées uniquement comme des ordres de grandeur en raison de leur caractère estimatif. Toutefois, il est à noter que, lorsque l'on additionne des données par territoire pour obtenir des totaux régionaux et par grandes zones, les erreurs qu'elles comportent arrivent parfois à s'équilibrer, de sorte que les agrégats obtenus peuvent être un peu plus exacts que chacun des éléments dont on est parti.

En outre, les donnés figurant dans le tableau 2 comportent certaines imprécisions en raison des facteurs influant sur les données par âge (voir à ce propos les notes techniques relatives au tableau 7). Ces imprécisions sont cependant atténuées du fait de l'étendue des groupes d'âge présentés dans le tableau 2.

---

[1] *Organisation des Nations Unies, Département des affaires économiques et sociales, Division de la population (2019). Perspectives de la population mondiale : La révision de 2019* (https://population.un.org/wpp//)

2. Estimates of population and its percentage distribution by age group and sex, and sex ratio, for the world, major areas and regions: 2019

Estimations de la population et pourcentage de répartition selon les tranches d'âge et le sexe, et le rapport de masculinité, pour l'ensemble du monde, les grandes régions et les régions géographiques : 2019

Major areas and regions / Grandes régions et régions	Population (millions)												Sex ratio - Rapport de masculinité[1]
	Both sexes - Les deux sexes				Male - Masculin				Female - Féminin				
	All ages - Tous âges	0-14	15-64	65+	All ages - Tous âges	0-14	15-64	65+	All ages - Tous âges	0-14	15-64	65+	
WORLD TOTAL - ENSEMBLE DU MONDE													
Number - Nombre	*7 713*	*1 975*	*5 035*	*703*	*3 889*	*1 020*	*2 554*	*316*	*3 824*	*955*	*2 482*	*387*	
Percent - Pourcentage	*100.0*	*25.6*	*65.3*	*9.1*	*100.0*	*26.2*	*65.7*	*8.1*	*100.0*	*25.0*	*64.9*	*10.1*	*101.7*
AFRICA - AFRIQUE													
Number - Nombre	*1 308*	*530*	*732*	*46*	*654*	*269*	*364*	*20*	*655*	*262*	*368*	*25*	
Percent - Pourcentage	*100.0*	*40.6*	*56.0*	*3.5*	*100.0*	*41.2*	*55.7*	*3.1*	*100.0*	*40.0*	*56.2*	*3.8*	*99.8*
Eastern Africa - Afrique orientale													
Number - Nombre	*434*	*183*	*238*	*13*	*215*	*92*	*117*	*5*	*219*	*91*	*121*	*7*	
Percent - Pourcentage	*100.0*	*42.2*	*54.9*	*2.9*	*100.0*	*42.9*	*54.6*	*2.5*	*100.0*	*41.5*	*55.3*	*3.3*	*98.5*
Middle Africa - Afrique centrale													
Number - Nombre	*174*	*79*	*91*	*5*	*87*	*40*	*45*	*2*	*87*	*39*	*46*	*3*	
Percent - Pourcentage	*100.0*	*45.3*	*52.0*	*2.8*	*100.0*	*45.7*	*51.8*	*2.5*	*100.0*	*44.8*	*52.1*	*3.0*	*99.6*
Northern Africa - Afrique septentrionale													
Number - Nombre	*242*	*79*	*149*	*14*	*121*	*40*	*75*	*6*	*120*	*39*	*74*	*7*	
Percent - Pourcentage	*100.0*	*32.7*	*61.7*	*5.6*	*100.0*	*33.3*	*61.5*	*5.2*	*100.0*	*32.1*	*61.9*	*6.1*	*101.0*
Southern Africa - Afrique méridionale													
Number - Nombre	*67*	*20*	*43*	*4*	*33*	*10*	*21*	*1*	*34*	*10*	*22*	*2*	
Percent - Pourcentage	*100.0*	*29.7*	*65.0*	*5.3*	*100.0*	*30.5*	*65.3*	*4.2*	*100.0*	*28.9*	*64.8*	*6.3*	*96.9*
Western Africa - Afrique occidentale													
Number - Nombre	*391*	*170*	*211*	*11*	*197*	*86*	*106*	*5*	*194*	*83*	*105*	*6*	
Percent - Pourcentage	*100.0*	*43.4*	*53.8*	*2.8*	*100.0*	*43.9*	*53.6*	*2.6*	*100.0*	*42.8*	*54.1*	*3.0*	*101.3*
LATIN AMERICA AND CARIBBEAN - AMÉRIQUE LATIN ET CARAÏBES													
Number - Nombre	*648*	*157*	*435*	*56*	*319*	*80*	*214*	*25*	*329*	*77*	*221*	*32*	
Percent - Pourcentage	*100.0*	*24.2*	*67.1*	*8.7*	*100.0*	*25.1*	*67.1*	*7.8*	*100.0*	*23.3*	*67.1*	*9.6*	*96.8*
Caribbean - Caraïbes													
Number - Nombre	*43*	*10*	*28*	*4*	*21*	*5*	*14*	*2*	*22*	*5*	*14*	*2*	
Percent - Pourcentage	*100.0*	*24.2*	*65.5*	*10.4*	*100.0*	*25.0*	*65.6*	*9.5*	*100.0*	*23.4*	*65.4*	*11.2*	*97.6*
Central America - Amérique centrale													
Number - Nombre	*178*	*48*	*117*	*13*	*87*	*25*	*57*	*6*	*91*	*24*	*60*	*7*	
Percent - Pourcentage	*100.0*	*27.3*	*65.7*	*7.1*	*100.0*	*28.4*	*65.1*	*6.5*	*100.0*	*26.1*	*66.2*	*7.7*	*96.1*
South America - Amérique méridionale													
Number - Nombre	*427*	*98*	*290*	*39*	*210*	*50*	*143*	*17*	*217*	*48*	*147*	*22*	
Percent - Pourcentage	*100.0*	*22.9*	*67.8*	*9.2*	*100.0*	*23.8*	*68.1*	*8.1*	*100.0*	*22.2*	*67.6*	*10.3*	*97.0*
NORTHERN AMERICA - AMÉRIQUE SEPTENTRIONALE													
Number - Nombre	*367*	*67*	*240*	*60*	*181*	*34*	*120*	*27*	*185*	*33*	*119*	*33*	
Percent - Pourcentage	*100.0*	*18.3*	*65.4*	*16.4*	*100.0*	*18.9*	*66.3*	*14.8*	*100.0*	*17.7*	*64.5*	*17.8*	*98.0*
ASIA - ASIE													
Number - Nombre	*4 601*	*1 091*	*3 115*	*395*	*2 353*	*570*	*1 600*	*183*	*2 248*	*521*	*1 515*	*212*	
Percent - Pourcentage	*100.0*	*23.7*	*67.7*	*8.6*	*100.0*	*24.2*	*68.0*	*7.8*	*100.0*	*23.2*	*67.4*	*9.4*	*104.7*
Eastern Asia - Asie orientale													
Number - Nombre	*1 673*	*288*	*1 169*	*215*	*853*	*153*	*600*	*99*	*820*	*135*	*569*	*116*	
Percent - Pourcentage	*100.0*	*17.2*	*69.9*	*12.9*	*100.0*	*18.0*	*70.4*	*11.6*	*100.0*	*16.4*	*69.4*	*14.2*	*104.1*
South Central Asia - Asie centrale méridionale													
Number - Nombre	*1 991*	*557*	*1 316*	*119*	*1 026*	*290*	*678*	*58*	*966*	*267*	*638*	*62*	
Percent - Pourcentage	*100.0*	*28.0*	*66.1*	*6.0*	*100.0*	*28.3*	*66.1*	*5.6*	*100.0*	*27.6*	*66.0*	*6.4*	*106.2*
South Eastern Asia - Asie méridionale orientale													
Number - Nombre	*662*	*168*	*448*	*45*	*331*	*86*	*225*	*20*	*331*	*82*	*224*	*26*	
Percent - Pourcentage	*100.0*	*25.4*	*67.7*	*6.9*	*100.0*	*26.1*	*67.9*	*6.0*	*100.0*	*24.7*	*67.5*	*7.7*	*99.8*
Western Asia - Asie occidentale													
Number - Nombre	*275*	*78*	*182*	*16*	*144*	*40*	*97*	*7*	*131*	*38*	*84*	*9*	
Percent - Pourcentage	*100.0*	*28.3*	*65.9*	*5.7*	*100.0*	*27.7*	*67.4*	*4.8*	*100.0*	*29.0*	*64.3*	*6.7*	*109.9*
EUROPE													
Number - Nombre	*747*	*120*	*487*	*140*	*361*	*62*	*241*	*58*	*386*	*58*	*245*	*83*	
Percent - Pourcentage	*100.0*	*16.1*	*65.2*	*18.8*	*100.0*	*17.1*	*66.9*	*16.0*	*100.0*	*15.1*	*63.5*	*21.4*	*93.3*
Eastern Europe - Europe orientale													
Number - Nombre	*293*	*49*	*196*	*48*	*138*	*25*	*96*	*17*	*155*	*24*	*100*	*31*	
Percent - Pourcentage	*100.0*	*16.9*	*66.7*	*16.4*	*100.0*	*18.4*	*69.2*	*12.4*	*100.0*	*15.5*	*64.5*	*20.0*	*88.8*
Northern Europe - Europe septentrionale													
Number - Nombre	*106*	*19*	*67*	*20*	*52*	*10*	*34*	*9*	*54*	*9*	*34*	*11*	
Percent - Pourcentage	*100.0*	*17.6*	*63.7*	*18.8*	*100.0*	*18.2*	*64.6*	*17.2*	*100.0*	*16.9*	*62.8*	*20.3*	*97.5*
Southern Europe - Europe méridionale													
Number - Nombre	*152*	*21*	*99*	*32*	*74*	*11*	*49*	*14*	*78*	*10*	*49*	*18*	
Percent - Pourcentage	*100.0*	*14.0*	*64.9*	*21.1*	*100.0*	*14.8*	*66.5*	*18.7*	*100.0*	*13.3*	*63.4*	*23.3*	*95.5*

2. Estimates of population and its percentage distribution by age group and sex, and sex ratio, for the world, major areas and regions: 2019

Estimations de la population et pourcentage de répartition selon les tranches d'âge et le sexe, et le rapport de masculinité, pour l'ensemble du monde, les grandes régions et les régions géographiques : 2019 (continued - suite)

Major areas and regions / Grandes régions et régions	Population (millions)												Sex ratio - Rapport de masculinité[1]
	Both sexes - Les deux sexes				Male - Masculin				Female - Féminin				
	All ages - Tous âges	0-14	15-64	65+	All ages - Tous âges	0-14	15-64	65+	All ages - Tous âges	0-14	15-64	65+	
Western Europe - Europe occidentale													
Number - Nombre	*196*	*30*	*125*	*40*	*96*	*16*	*63*	*18*	*100*	*15*	*62*	*23*	
Percent - Pourcentage	*100.0*	*15.6*	*63.8*	*20.6*	*100.0*	*16.3*	*65.3*	*18.4*	*100.0*	*14.9*	*62.4*	*22.7*	*96.5*
OCEANIA - OCÉANIA													
Number - Nombre	*42.13*	*9.98*	*26.87*	*5.28*	*21.09*	*5.13*	*13.48*	*2.48*	*21.04*	*4.85*	*13.39*	*2.80*	
Percent - Pourcentage	*100.0*	*23.7*	*63.8*	*12.5*	*100.0*	*24.3*	*63.9*	*11.7*	*100.0*	*23.0*	*63.6*	*13.3*	*100.2*
Australia and New Zealand - Australie et Nouvelle Zélande													
Number - Nombre	*29.99*	*5.79*	*19.41*	*4.78*	*14.90*	*2.97*	*9.69*	*2.24*	*15.08*	*2.82*	*9.73*	*2.54*	
Percent - Pourcentage	*100.0*	*19.3*	*64.7*	*15.9*	*100.0*	*20.0*	*65.0*	*15.0*	*100.0*	*18.7*	*64.5*	*16.8*	*98.8*
Melanesia - Melanésie													
Number - Nombre	*10.92*	*3.82*	*6.68*	*0.42*	*5.57*	*1.97*	*3.40*	*0.20*	*5.35*	*1.85*	*3.28*	*0.22*	
Percent - Pourcentage	*100.0*	*35.0*	*61.1*	*3.8*	*100.0*	*35.5*	*61.0*	*3.5*	*100.0*	*34.6*	*61.3*	*4.2*	*104.0*
Micronesia													
Number - Nombre	*0.54*	*0.16*	*0.35*	*0.04*	*0.27*	*0.08*	*0.18*	*0.02*	*0.27*	*0.08*	*0.17*	*0.02*	
Percent - Pourcentage	*100.0*	*29.6*	*63.8*	*6.6*	*100.0*	*30.1*	*64.0*	*5.9*	*100.0*	*29.0*	*63.6*	*7.4*	*102.1*
Polynesia - Polynésie													
Number - Nombre	*0.68*	*0.20*	*0.43*	*0.05*	*0.34*	*0.10*	*0.22*	*0.02*	*0.34*	*0.10*	*0.21*	*0.03*	
Percent - Pourcentage	*100.0*	*29.6*	*63.3*	*7.1*	*100.0*	*30.2*	*63.2*	*6.6*	*100.0*	*29.0*	*63.3*	*7.6*	*102.9*

FOOTNOTES - NOTES

[1] Males per 100 females of all ages - Hommes pour 100 femmes de tous âges

Table 3 - *Demographic Yearbook 2019*

Table 3 presents for each country or area of the world the total, male and female population enumerated at the latest population census, estimates of the mid-year total population for 2010 and 2019, the average annual exponential rate of population increase (or decrease) for the period 2010 to 2019, the surface area and the population density for 2019.

Description of variables: The total, male and female population is the population enumerated at the most recent census for which data are available. The date of this census is given. Population census data are usually the results of a nation-wide gathering of individual information through full field enumeration. Alternatively, other approaches for generating reliable statistics on population and housing can be used by countries, such as the use of population registers. Data that are the result of such an alternative approach are also coded as census and are footnoted accordingly. Also, the results of sample surveys, essentially national in character, may be presented showing the appropriate code.

Mid-year population estimates refer to the population on 1 July. Otherwise, a footnote is appended. Mid-year estimates of the total population are those provided by national statistical offices.

Surface area, expressed in square kilometres, refers to the total surface area, comprising land area and inland waters (assumed to consist of major rivers and lakes) and excluding polar regions as well as uninhabited islands. Exceptions to this are noted. Surface areas, originally reported in square miles by the country or area, have been converted to square kilometres using a conversion factor of 2.589988.

Computation: The annual rate of population increase is the average annual exponential rate of population growth between 2010 and 2019, computed by the Statistics Division of the United Nations Department of Economic and Social Affairs using the unrounded mid-year estimates of 2010 and2019. This rate is expressed as percentage.

Density is the number of persons in the 2019 total population per square kilometre of total surface area.

Reliability of data: Reliable mid-year population estimates are those that are based on a complete census (or a sample survey) and have been adjusted by a continuous population register or on the basis of the calculated balance of births, deaths and migration. Mid-year estimates of this type are considered reliable and appear in roman type. Mid-year estimates not calculated on this basis are considered less reliable and are shown in italics.

Census data and sample survey results are considered reliable and, therefore, appear in roman type.

Rates of population increase that were calculated using population estimates considered less reliable, as described above, are set in italics rather than roman type.

All surface area data are assumed to be reliable and therefore appear in roman type.

Population density data, however, are considered reliable or less reliable on the basis of the reliability of the 2019 population estimates used as the numerator.

Limitations: Statistics on the total population enumerated at the time of the census, surface area data and estimates of the mid-year total population are subject to the same qualifications as have been set forth for surface area and population data in sections 2.4 and 3 of the Technical Notes, respectively.

Regarding the limitations of census data, it should be noted that although census data are considered reliable, and therefore appear in roman type, the actual quality of census data varies widely from one country or area to another. When known, an estimate of the extent of over-enumeration or under-enumeration is given in footnotes.

Rates of population increase are subject to all the qualifications of the population estimates mentioned above. In some cases, they simply reflect the rate calculated or assumed in constructing the estimates themselves when adequate measures of natural increase and net migration were not available. Despite their shortcomings, these rates provide a useful index for studying population change and can be also useful in evaluating the accuracy of vital and migration statistics.

Population density data as shown in this table give only an indication of actual population density as they do not take account of the dispersion or concentration of population within countries or areas nor the proportion of habitable land. They should not be interpreted as reflecting density in the urban sense or as indicating the supporting power of a territory's land and resources.

Tableau 3 – *Annuaire démographique 2019*

Le tableau 3 indique pour chaque pays ou zone du monde la population totale selon le sexe d'après les derniers recensements effectués, les estimations concernant la population totale au milieu de l'année 2010 et de l'année 2019, le taux moyen d'accroissement annuel exponentiel positif ou négatif de la population pour la période allant de 2010 à 2019, ainsi que la superficie et la densité de population en 2019.

Description des variables : la population masculine et féminine totale est, la population enregistrée lors du recensement le plus récent sur lequel on dispose de données. La date de ce recensement est indiquée. Les données des recensements de la population sont habituellement le résultat d'un collecte à l'échelle nationale des données individuelles obtenues au moyen d'un dénombrement complet. Les pays peuvent recourir à d'autres moyens pour établir des statistiques fiables sur la population et le logement, tels que des registres de la population. Les données obtenues par ce moyen sont présentées comme celles d'un recensement et sont annotées en conséquence. Par ailleurs, les résultats des enquêtes par sondage, réalisées habituellement à l'échelle nationale, peuvent être présentés à l'aide du code correspondant.

Les estimations de la population en milieu d'année sont celles de la population au 1er juillet. Lorsque la date est différente, cela est signalé par une note. Les estimations de la population totale en milieu d'année sont celles qui ont été communiquées par les services nationaux de statistique.

La superficie - exprimée en kilomètres carrés - représente la superficie totale, c'est-à-dire qu'elle englobe les terres émergées et les eaux intérieures (qui sont censées comprendre les principaux lacs et cours d'eau) mais exclut les régions polaires et certaines îles inhabitées. Les exceptions à cette règle sont signalées en note. Les superficies initialement exprimées en miles carrés par les pays ou les zones ont été transformées en kilomètres carrés au moyen d'un coefficient de conversion de 2,589988.

Calculs : le taux d'accroissement annuel est le taux exponentiel annuel moyen de variation (en pourcentage) de la population entre 2010 et 2019, calculé par la Division de statistique du Département des affaires économiques et sociales de l'Organisation des Nations Unies à partir des estimations en milieu d'année non arrondies pour les années 2010 et 2019.

La densité est égale au rapport de l'effectif total de la population en 2019 à la superficie totale, exprimée en kilomètres carrés.

Fiabilité des données : les estimations en milieu d'année qui sont considérées sûres sont fondées sur un recensement complet (ou sur une enquête par sondage) et ont été ajustées en fonction des données provenant d'un registre permanent de population ou en fonction de la balance établie par le calcul des naissances, des décès et des migrations. Les estimations de ce type sont considérées comme sûres et apparaissent en caractères romains. Les estimations en milieu d'année dont le calcul n'a pas été effectué sur cette base sont considérées comme moins sûres et apparaissent en italique.

Les données de recensements ou les résultats d'enquêtes par sondage sont considérés comme sûrs et apparaissent par conséquent en caractères romains.

Les taux d'accroissement de la population, calculés à partir d'estimations jugées moins sûres d'après les normes décrites ci-dessus, sont indiqués en italique plutôt qu'en caractères romains.

Toutes les données de superficie sont présumées sûres et apparaissent par conséquent en caractères romains. En revanche, les données relatives à la densité de la population sont considérées plus ou moins sûres en fonction de la fiabilité des estimations de la population en 2019 ayant servi de numérateur.

Insuffisance des données : les statistiques portant sur la population totale dénombrée lors d'un recensement, les données de superficie et les estimations de la population totale en milieu d'année appellent les mêmes réserves que celles formulées aux sections 2.4 et 3 des Notes techniques à propos des statistiques relatives à la superficie et à la population.

S'agissant de l'insuffisance des données obtenues par recensement, il convient d'indiquer que, bien que ces données soient considérées comme sûres et apparaissent par conséquent en caractères romains, leur qualité réelle varie considérablement d'un pays ou d'une région à l'autre. Lorsque l'on possédait les renseignements voulus, on a donné une estimation du degré de sur-dénombrement ou de sous-dénombrement.

Les taux d'accroissement appellent toutes les réserves formulées plus haut à propos des estimations concernant la population. Dans certains cas, ils représentent seulement le taux calculé ou que l'on a pris pour base pour établir les estimations elles-mêmes lorsque l'on ne disposait pas de mesures appropriées de l'accroissement naturel et des migrations nettes. Malgré leurs imperfections, ces taux fournissent des indications intéressantes pour l'étude du mouvement de la population et, utilisés avec les précautions nécessaires, ils peuvent également servir à évaluer l'exactitude des statistiques de l'état civil et des migrations.

Les données relatives à la densité de population figurant dans le tableau 3 n'ont qu'une valeur indicative en ce qui concerne la densité de population effective, car elles ne tiennent compte ni de la dispersion ou de la concentration de la population à l'intérieur des pays ou zones, ni de la proportion du territoire qui est habitable. Il ne faut donc y voir d'indication ni de la densité au sens urbain du terme ni du nombre d'habitants qui pourraient vivre sur les terres et avec les ressources naturelles du territoire considéré.

3. Population by sex, annual rate of population change, surface area and density
Population selon le sexe, taux de changement annuel de la population, superficie et densité

Continent, country or area and census date / Continent, pays ou zone et date du recensement	Census type[a]	Population at the latest available census / Population d'après le dernier recensement disponible (in units — en unités)			Estimate type[a]	Mid-year estimates / Estimations au milieu de l'année (in thousands — en milliers)		Annual rate of change / Taux de changement annuel 2010-19	Surface area / Superficie (km²) 2019	Density / Densité 2019[b]
		Both sexes / Les deux sexes	Male / Masculin	Female / Feminin		2010	2019			
AFRICA - AFRIQUE										
Algeria - Algérie										
16 IV 2008	DF	34 452 759[1]	17 428 500[1]	17 024 259[1]	DJ	35 978	43 413[2]	2.1	2 381 741	18
Angola										
16 V 2014	DF	25 789 024	12 499 041	13 289 983	DF	17 430[3]	30 176[4]	6.1	1 246 700	24
Benin - Bénin										
11 V 2013	DF	10 008 749	4 887 820	5 120 929	DF	8 779[2]	...	...	114 763	...
Botswana										
9 VIII 2011	DF	2 024 904	988 957	1 035 947	DJ	1 823	2 339[5]	2.8	582 000	4
Burkina Faso										
9 XII 2006	DF	14 196 259	6 842 560	7 353 699	DJ	15 731[2]	20 870[2]	3.1	272 967	76
Burundi										
16 VIII 2008	DF	7 877 728	3 838 045	4 039 683	DF	9 461	12 044	2.7	27 834	433
Cabo Verde										
16 VI 2010	DJ	491 683	243 403	248 280	DJ	494[2]	550[2]	1.2	4 033	136
Cameroon - Cameroun										
11 XI 2005	DF	17 052 134	8 408 495	8 643 639	DJ	20 127[6]	25 492[6]	2.6	475 650	54
Central African Republic - République centrafricaine										
8 XII 2003	DF	3 151 072	1 569 446	1 581 626		...	...	...	622 984	...
Chad - Tchad										
20 V 2009	DJ	11 039 873	5 452 483	5 587 390	DJ	11 470	15 693	3.5	1 284 000	12
Comoros - Comores										
1 IX 2003	DF	575 660[7]	285 590[7]	290 070[7]		...	...	...	2 235	...
Congo										
28 IV 2007	DF	3 697 490	1 821 357	1 876 133	DJ	4 119	5 336	2.9	342 000	16
Côte d'Ivoire										
15 V 2014	DF	22 224 509	11 441 896	10 782 613	DF	20 845[8]	25 822[8]	2.4	322 462	80
Democratic Republic of the Congo - République démocratique du Congo										
1 VII 1984	DF	29 916 800	14 543 800	15 373 000		...	...	...	2 344 858	...
Djibouti										
29 V 2009	DF	818 159	440 067	378 092	DF	841[9]	...	...	23 200	...
Egypt - Égypte										
18 IV 2017	DJ	94 798 827[10]	48 891 518[10]	45 907 309[10]	DF	78 685	*98 902	2.5	1 002 000	99
Equatorial Guinea - Guinée équatoriale										
20 VI 2015	DF	*1 222 442	*651 820	*570 622	DF	1 622[11]	1 406[12]	-1.6	28 051	50
Eritrea - Érythrée										
9 V 1984	DF	2 621 566[13]	1 309 736[13]	1 311 830[13]	DF	2 691[14]	3 379[14]	2.5	121 144	28
Eswatini										
29 IV 2017	DJ	1 093 238	531 111	562 127	DJ	1 056[15]	1 172[15]	1.2	17 363	68
Ethiopia - Éthiopie										
29 V 2007	DF	73 750 932	37 217 130	36 533 802	DF	79 634[16]	98 537[16]	2.4	1 104 300	89
Gabon										
22 V 2013	DF	1 811 079	934 072	877 007		...	...	...	267 668	...
Gambia - Gambie										
15 IV 2013	DF	*1 882 450	*930 699	*951 751	DF	1 731	2 213	2.7	11 295	196
Ghana										
26 IX 2010	DF	24 658 823	12 024 845	12 633 978	DF	...	30 281[17]	...	238 537	127
Guinea - Guinée										
15 III 2014	DJ	10 523 261	5 084 306	5 438 955	DJ	9 557[18]	12 218[19]	2.7	245 836	50
Guinea-Bissau - Guinée-Bissau										
15 III 2009	DF	1 497 859	725 956	771 903	DF	1 460[2]	1 605[2]	1.0	36 125	44
Kenya										
24 VIII 2019	DF	47 562 772[20]	23 548 056	24 014 716	DF	38 474[21]	...	...	591 958	...
Lesotho										
10 IV 2016	DJ	2 007 201	982 133	1 025 068	DF	1 892[22]	...	...	30 355	...
Liberia - Libéria										
21 III 2008	DF	3 476 608	1 739 945	1 736 663	DF	3 627	...	...	111 369	...
Libya - Libye										
15 IV 2006	DF	*5 298 152[23]	*2 687 513[23]	*2 610 639[23]	DF	5 689[23]	...	...	1 676 198	...

3. Population by sex, annual rate of population change, surface area and density
Population selon le sexe, taux de changement annuel de la population, superficie et densité (continued - suite)

Continent, country or area and census date / Continent, pays ou zone et date du recensement	Census type[a]	Population at the latest available census / Population d'après le dernier recensement disponible (in units — en unités): Both sexes / Les deux sexes	Male / Masculin	Female / Feminin	Estimate type[a]	Mid-year estimates / Estimations au milieu de l'année (in thousands — en milliers): 2010	2019	Annual rate of change / Taux de changement annuel 2010-19	Surface area / Superficie (km²) 2019	Density / Densité 2019[b]
AFRICA - AFRIQUE										
Madagascar 18 V 2018	DJ	*25 833 588	*12 738 948	*13 094 640	DF	*20 142*[24]	*26 620*[24]	*3.1*	587 041	*45*
Malawi 3 IX 2018	DJ	17 563 749	8 521 460	9 042 289	DF	*13 948*[2]	...	...	117 726	...
Mali 1 IV 2009	DF	14 528 662	7 204 990	7 323 672	DF	*15 370*[25]	...	...	1 240 192	...
Mauritania - Mauritanie 24 III 2013	DF	3 460 388[26]	...	...	DF	*3 341*[2]	...	...	1 030 700	...
Mauritius - Maurice[27] 4 VII 2011	DF	1 237 000	611 053	625 947	DJ	1 281[28]	1 266[5]	-0.1	1 979	640
Mayotte 5 IX 2017	DJ	256 518[29]	122 261[29]	134 257[29]	DJ	...	269[30]	...	368	732
Morocco - Maroc 1 IX 2014	DJ	33 848 242	...	...	...	*31 894*[31]	*35 587*[32]	...	446 550	*80*
Mozambique 1 VIII 2017	DF	*28 861 863	*13 800 857	*15 061 006	DF	*22 417*[15]	*29 318*[15]	*3.0*	799 380	*37*
Namibia - Namibie 28 VIII 2011	DF	2 113 077	1 021 912	1 091 165	DF	*2 143*[2]	*2 459*[5]	*1.5*	824 116	*3*
Niger 10 XII 2012	DF	16 734 935	8 183 513	8 551 422	DJ	*15 204*[2]	...	...	1 267 000	...
Nigeria - Nigéria 21 III 2006	DF	140 431 790	71 345 488	69 086 302	DF	*159 608*[22]	...	...	923 768	...
Republic of South Sudan - République de Soudan du Sud 21 IV 2008	DF	8 260 490	4 287 300	3 973 190	DF	9 005[33]	...	...	658 841	...
Reunion - Réunion 1 I 2015	DJ	850 727	411 435	439 292	DJ	821[30]	858[30]	0.5	2 510	342
Rwanda 15 VIII 2012	DF	10 393 542	4 981 197	5 412 345	DF	*10 413*[2]	*12 374*[34]	*1.9*	26 338	*470*
Saint Helena ex. dep. - Sainte-Hélène sans dép. 7 II 2016	DF	4 802	...	...	DF	4	4	0.6	123[35]	36
Saint Helena: Ascension - Sainte-Hélène: Ascension 7 II 2016	DF	556[36]	...	...		...	...	...	88	...
Saint Helena: Tristan da Cunha - Sainte-Hélène: Tristan da Cunha 9 II 2016	DJ	271[36]	...	...		...	...	...	98	...
Sao Tome and Principe - Sao Tomé-et-Principe 13 V 2012	DJ	178 739	88 867	89 872	...	*164*	*206*[34]	...	964	*214*
Senegal - Sénégal 19 XI 2013	DF	13 357 492	6 658 089	6 699 403	DJ	12 509[37]	*16 209*[2]	*2.9*	196 712[38]	*82*
Seychelles 26 VIII 2010	DF	90 945	46 912	44 033	DF	90	98	0.9	457	214
Sierra Leone 5 XII 2015	DF	7 092 113[39]	3 490 978[39]	3 601 135[39]	DF	*6 131*[40]	*7 901*[12]	*2.8*	72 300	*109*
Somalia - Somalie 15 II 1987	DF	7 114 431	3 741 664	3 372 767		...	...	...	637 657	...
South Africa - Afrique du Sud 10 X 2011	DF	51 770 560	25 188 791	26 581 769	DF	*51 329*[40]	*58 775*[4]	*1.5*	1 221 037	*48*
Sudan - Soudan 21 IV 2008	DF	30 504 166	15 413 282	15 090 883	DF	32 491[2]	40 204[2]	2.4	...	...
Togo 6 XI 2010	DJ	6 191 155	3 009 095	3 182 060	DJ	*6 191*[2]	*7 617*[4]	*2.3*	56 785	*134*
Tunisia - Tunisie 23 IV 2014	DF	10 982 754	5 472 338	5 510 416	DF	*10 566*	*11 722*	*1.2*	163 610	*72*
Uganda - Ouganda 27 VIII 2014	DF	34 634 650	16 897 849	17 736 801	DF	*31 785*	*40 308*[8]	*2.6*	241 550	*167*

3. Population by sex, annual rate of population change, surface area and density
Population selon le sexe, taux de changement annuel de la population, superficie et densité (continued - suite)

Continent, country or area and census date / Continent, pays ou zone et date du recensement	Census type[a]	Population at the latest available census / Population d'après le dernier recensement disponible (in units — en unités)			Estimate type[a]	Mid-year estimates / Estimations au milieu de l'année (in thousands — en milliers)		Annual rate of change / Taux de changement annuel 2010-19	Surface area / Superficie (km²) 2019	Density / Densité 2019[b]
		Both sexes / Les deux sexes	Male / Masculin	Female / Feminin		2010	2019			
AFRICA - AFRIQUE										
United Republic of Tanzania - République Unie de Tanzanie										
26 VIII 2012	DF	44 928 923[41]	21 869 990[41]	23 058 933[41]	DF	*43 188[42]*	*55 891[34]*	*2.9*	947 303	*59*
Western Sahara - Sahara occidental[43]										
31 XII 1970	DF	76 425	43 981	32 444		...	...	...	266 000	...
Zambia - Zambie										
16 X 2010	DF	12 526 314	6 117 253	6 409 061	DJ	...	*17 381[17]*	...	752 612	*23*
Zimbabwe										
17 VIII 2012	DF	13 061 239	6 280 539	6 780 700		...	...	...	390 757	...
AMERICA, NORTH - AMÉRIQUE DU NORD										
Anguilla										
11 V 2011	DF	13 572	6 707	6 865	DF	16	*16[37]	-0.5	91	171
Antigua and Barbuda - Antigua-et-Barbuda										
27 V 2011	DF	88 566	...	...	...	91	96[5]	...	442	218
Aruba										
29 IX 2010	DJ	101 484	48 241	53 243	DJ	102	112	1.1	180	622
Bahamas										
3 V 2010	DJ	351 461	170 257	181 204	DJ	352[17]	385[17]	1.0	13 940	28
Barbados - Barbade										
1 V 2010	DJ	277 821[44]	133 018[44]	144 803[44]	DJ	278	...	...	431	...
Belize										
12 V 2010	DJ	322 453	161 227	161 226	DJ	*324*	*408*	*2.6*	22 965	*18*
Bermuda - Bermudes[45]										
20 V 2016	DJ	63 779	30 690	33 089	DJ	64[17]	64[46]	0.0	54	1 186
British Virgin Islands - Îles Vierges britanniques										
12 VII 2010	DF	28 054	13 820	14 234	DF	28	...	...	151	...
Canada										
10 V 2016	DJ	35 151 730[47]	17 264 200[47]	17 887 530[47]	DJ	34 005[48]	*37 589[49]	1.1	9 984 670	4
Cayman Islands - Îles Caïmanes										
10 X 2010	DJ	55 036[50]	27 218[50]	27 818[50]	DJ	56	68	2.2	264	257
Costa Rica										
30 V 2011	DJ	4 301 712	2 106 063	2 195 649	DJ	4 538[51]	5 060[52]	1.2	51 100	99
Cuba										
14 IX 2012	DJ	11 167 325	5 570 825	5 596 500	DJ	11 171	11 202	0.0	109 884	102
Curaçao										
26 III 2011	DJ	150 563	68 848	81 715	DJ	149[40]	157[4]	0.6	444	355
Dominica - Dominique										
14 V 2011	DF	68 913	34 973	33 940	DF	71	...	...	750	...
Dominican Republic - République dominicaine										
1 XII 2010	DJ	9 445 281	4 739 038	4 706 243	DJ	*9 479[2]*	*10 358[2]*	*1.0*	48 671	*213*
El Salvador										
12 V 2007	DJ	5 744 113	2 719 371	3 024 742	DJ	6 183[15]	...	...	21 041	...
Greenland - Groenland										
1 I 2008	DJ	56 462[53]	29 885[53]	26 577[53]	DJ	57[53]	56[53]	-0.1	2 166 086	0
Grenada - Grenade										
12 V 2011	DF	106 667	53 898	52 769	DF	105	...	...	345	...
Guadeloupe										
1 I 2015	DJ	397 990[54]	183 479[54]	214 511[54]	DJ	404[54]	...	...	1 639	...
Guatemala										
24 XI 2002	DJ	11 237 196	5 496 839	5 740 357	DJ	14 362[42]	...	...	108 889	...
Haiti - Haïti										
11 I 2003	DJ	8 373 750	4 039 272	4 334 478	DJ	*10 085[55]*	*11 578[55]*	*1.5*	27 750	*417*
Honduras										
10 VIII 2013	DJ	8 303 771	4 052 316	4 251 456	...	*8 046[56]*	*9 158[57]*	...	112 492	*81*

3. Population by sex, annual rate of population change, surface area and density
Population selon le sexe, taux de changement annuel de la population, superficie et densité (continued - suite)

Continent, country or area and census date / Continent, pays ou zone et date du recensement	Census type[a]	Population at the latest available census / Population d'après le dernier recensement disponible (in units — en unités): Both sexes / Les deux sexes	Male / Masculin	Female / Feminin	Estimate type[a]	Mid-year estimates / Estimations au milieu de l'année (in thousands — en milliers): 2010	2019	Annual rate of change / Taux de changement annuel 2010-19	Surface area / Superficie (km²) 2019	Density / Densité 2019[b]
AMERICA, NORTH - AMÉRIQUE DU NORD										
Jamaica - Jamaïque										
4 IV 2011	DJ	2 697 983[58]	1 334 533[58]	1 363 450[58]	DJ	2 702	2 733	0.1	10 991	249
Martinique										
1 I 2015	DJ	380 877	176 328	204 549	DJ	394[30]	...	...	1 090	...
Mexico - Mexique										
12 VI 2010	DF	112 336 538[59]	54 855 231[59]	57 481 307[59]	DJ	*113 749*[60]	126 578[61]	*1.2*	1 964 375	64
Montserrat										
12 V 2011	DJ	4 922	2 546	2 376	DF	5	...	...	103	...
Nicaragua										
4 VI 2005	DJ	5 142 098	2 534 491	2 607 607	DJ	*5 816*	*6 528*	*1.3*	130 373	*50*
Panama										
16 V 2010	DF	3 405 813	1 712 584	1 693 229	DF	*3 662*[17]	4 219[17]	*1.6*	75 320	56
Puerto Rico - Porto Rico										
1 IV 2010	DJ	3 725 789[62]	1 785 171[62]	1 940 618[62]	DJ	3 721[63]	3 194[62]	-1.7	8 868	360
Saint Barthélemy - Saint-Barthélemy										
1 I 2015	DJ	9 625	5 117	4 508		...	...	...	22	...
Saint Kitts and Nevis - Saint-Kitts-et-Nevis										
15 V 2011	DF	47 195	23 012	24 183	DF	*53	...	...	261	...
Saint Lucia - Sainte-Lucie										
10 V 2010	DJ	165 770	82 268	83 502		...	...	...	539[64]	...
Saint Pierre and Miquelon - Saint Pierre-et-Miquelon										
1 I 2015	DJ	6 021	2 940	3 081		...	...	...	242	...
Saint Vincent and the Grenadines - Saint-Vincent-et-les Grenadines										
12 VI 2012	DJ	109 991	56 419	53 572	DJ	110	111	0.1	389	284
Saint-Martin (French part) - Saint-Martin (partie française)										
1 I 2015	DJ	35 684	16 884	18 800		...	...	...	53	...
Sint Maarten (Dutch part) - Saint-Martin (partie néerlandaise)										
9 IV 2011	DF	33 609	15 868	17 741	DF	36	...	...	34	...
Trinidad and Tobago - Trinité-et-Tobago										
9 I 2011	DF	1 332 901	...	...	...	1 318[28]	1 364[5]	...	5 127	266
Turks and Caicos Islands - Îles Turques et Caïques										
25 I 2012	DJ	*31 458[50]	*16 037[50]	*15 421[50]	DJ	*35*	*43	*2.4*	948[65]	*45*
United States of America - États-Unis d'Amérique										
1 IV 2010	DJ	308 745 538	151 781 326	156 964 212	DJ	309 348[66]	328 240[66]	0.7	9 833 517	33
United States Virgin Islands - Îles Vierges américaines										
1 IV 2010	DJ	106 405[62]	50 854[62]	55 551[62]	DJ	106[67]	...	...	347	...
AMERICA, SOUTH - AMÉRIQUE DU SUD										
Argentina - Argentine										
27 X 2010	DF	40 117 096	19 523 766	20 593 330	DF	40 788[17]	44 939[17]	1.1	2 796 427[68]	16
Bolivia (Plurinational State of) - Bolivie (État plurinational de)										
21 XI 2012	DF	10 059 856	5 019 447	5 040 409	DF	*10 031*[40]	*11 470*[4]	*1.5*	1 098 581[69]	*10*
Brazil - Brésil										
31 VII 2010	DJ	190 755 799	93 406 990	97 348 809	DJ	*195 498*[70]	*210 147*[70]	*0.8*	8 515 767	*25*

Continent, country or area and census date Continent, pays ou zone et date du recensement	Census type[a]	Population at the latest available census Population d'après le dernier recensement disponible (in units — en unités)			Estimate type[a]	Mid-year estimates Estimations au milieu de l'année (in thousands — en milliers)		Annual rate of change Taux de changement annuel 2010-19	Surface area Superficie (km²) 2019	Density Densité 2019[b]
		Both sexes Les deux sexes	Male Masculin	Female Feminin		2010	2019			
AMERICA, SOUTH - AMÉRIQUE DU SUD										
Chile - Chili 24 IV 2002	DF	15 116 435	7 447 695	7 668 740	DF	17 064[71]	19 107[71]	1.3	756 102	25
Colombia - Colombie 18 IV 2018	DJ	44 164 417	21 570 493	22 593 924	DJ	*44 350*[72]	*49 396*[72]	*1.2*	1 141 748	*43*
Ecuador - Équateur 28 XI 2010	DF	14 483 499	7 177 683	7 305 816	DF	*15 012*[73]	*17 268*[73]	*1.6*	257 217[74]	*67*
Falkland Islands (Malvinas) - Îles Falkland (Malvinas)[75] 9 X 2016	DF	3 354	1 820[76]	1 532[76]		...	...	...	12 173	...
French Guiana - Guyane française 1 I 2015	DJ	259 865	128 973	130 892	DJ	229[30]	...	...	83 534	...
Guyana 15 IX 2012	DF	746 955	371 805	375 150	DF	752[77]	744[77]	-0.1	214 969	3
Paraguay 28 VIII 2002	DF	5 163 198	2 603 242	2 559 956	DF	*6 266*[78]	*7 153*[78]	*1.5*	406 752	*18*
Peru - Pérou 22 VIII 2017	DF	29 381 884[79]	14 450 757[79]	14 931 127[79]	DF	*28 693*[80]	*32 131*[80]	*1.3*	1 285 216	*25*
Suriname 13 VIII 2012	DJ	541 638	270 629	271 009	DJ	531	...	...	163 820	...
Uruguay 4 X 2011	DJ	3 286 314	1 577 725[81]	1 708 481[81]	DJ	3 397	3 519[2]	0.4	173 626	20
Venezuela (Bolivarian Republic of) - Venezuela (République bolivarienne du) 1 IX 2011	DJ	27 227 930	13 549 752	13 678 178	DF	28 396[82]	32 065	1.3	929 690	34
ASIA - ASIE										
Afghanistan 23 VI 1979	DF	13 051 358[83]	6 712 377[83]	6 338 981[83]	DF	*24 486*[84]	*30 726*[84]	*2.5*	652 864	*47*
Armenia - Arménie 12 X 2011	DF	2 871 771	1 346 729	1 525 042	DJ	3 045	2 965[30]	-0.3	29 743	100
Azerbaijan - Azerbaïdjan 13 IV 2009	DJ	8 922 447	4 414 398	4 508 049	DJ	9 054	10 020	1.1	86 600	116
Bahrain - Bahreïn 27 IV 2010	DJ	1 234 571	768 414	466 157	DJ	1 229	1 484	2.1	778	1 906
Bangladesh 15 III 2011	DF	144 043 697	72 109 796	71 933 901	DF	*148 620*	*166 500*	*1.3*	148 460	*1 122*
Bhutan - Bhoutan 30 V 2017	DF	727 145[85]	380 453[85]	346 692[85]	DF	*696*[86]	*742*[87]	*0.7*	38 394	*19*
Brunei Darussalam - Brunéi Darussalam 20 VI 2011	DJ	393 372	203 144	190 228	...	*387*[40]	*460*	...	5 765	*80*
Cambodia - Cambodge 3 III 2019	DF	*15 288 489[88]	*7 418 577[88]	*7 869 912[88]	DF	*14 303*[89]	...	...	181 035	...
China - Chine 1 XI 2010	DJ	1 339 724 852[90]	686 852 572[90]	652 872 280[90]	DF	*1 337 700*[91]	*1 397 715*[91]	*0.5*	9 600 000	*146*
China, Hong Kong SAR - Chine, Hong Kong RAS 30 VI 2016	DJ	7 336 585[92]	3 375 362[92]	3 961 223[92]	DJ	7 024	7 507	0.7	1 107	6 782
China, Macao SAR - Chine, Macao RAS 12 VIII 2011	DF	625 674	305 398	320 276	DJ	537	672	2.5	33[93]	20 364
Cyprus - Chypre 1 X 2011	DJ	840 407[94]	408 780[94]	431 627[94]	DJ	*829*[95]	*876*[96]	*0.6*	9 251	*95*
Democratic People's Republic of Korea - République populaire démocratique de Corée 1 X 2008	DJ	24 052 231	11 721 838	12 330 393		...	...	...	120 538	...

3. Population by sex, annual rate of population change, surface area and density
Population selon le sexe, taux de changement annuel de la population, superficie et densité (continued - suite)

Continent, country or area and census date Continent, pays ou zone et date du recensement	Census type[a]	Population at the latest available census Population d'après le dernier recensement disponible (in units — en unités)			Estimate type[a]	Mid-year estimates Estimations au milieu de l'année (in thousands — en milliers)		Annual rate of change Taux de changement annuel 2010-19	Surface area Superficie (km²) 2019	Density Densité 2019[b]
		Both sexes Les deux sexes	Male Masculin	Female Feminin		2010	2019			
ASIA - ASIE										
Georgia - Géorgie										
5 XI 2014	DJ	3 713 804	1 772 864	1 940 940	...	4 453	3 723[97]	...	69 700	53
India - Inde										
9 II 2011	DF	1 210 854 977[98]	623 270 258[98]	587 584 719[98]	DF	1 176 742[99]	1 312 240[99]	1.2	3 287 263	399
Indonesia - Indonésie										
1 V 2010	DJ	237 641 326	119 630 913	118 010 413	DJ	238 519[100]	266 912[101]	1.2	1 910 931	140
Iran (Islamic Republic of) - Iran (République islamique d')										
24 IX 2016	DJ	79 926 270	40 498 442	39 427 828	DJ	74 340[102]	83 075[102]	1.2	1 628 777	51
Iraq										
16 X 1997	DF	19 184 543[103]	9 536 570[103]	9 647 973[103]	DF	32 211	38 836	2.1	435 052	89
Israel - Israël										
27 XII 2008	DF	7 412 180[104]	3 663 910[104]	3 748 270[104]	DJ	7 624[105]	*9 053[105]	1.9	22 072	410
Japan - Japon										
1 X 2015	DJ	127 094 745[106]	61 841 738[106]	65 253 007[106]	DJ	128 070[106]	126 265[107]	-0.2	377 930[108]	334
Jordan - Jordanie										
30 XI 2015	DF	9 531 712[109]	5 046 824[109]	4 484 888[109]	DF	6 699[110]	10 554[110]	5.1	89 318	118
Kazakhstan										
25 II 2009	DF	16 009 597	7 712 224	8 297 373	DF	16 322[111]	18 514[112]	1.4	2 724 902	7
Kuwait - Koweït										
21 IV 2011	DF	3 065 850	1 738 372	1 327 478	DF	2 933	4 420[30]	4.6	17 818	248
Kyrgyzstan - Kirghizstan										
24 III 2009	DJ	5 362 793	2 645 921	2 716 872	DJ	5 448[113]	6 390[30]	1.8	199 949	32
Lao People's Democratic Republic - République démocratique populaire lao										
1 III 2015	DJ	6 492 228	3 254 770	3 237 458	DJ	6 230[12]	7 123[12]	1.5	236 800	30
Lebanon - Liban										
1 X 2011	SDF	3 779 859[114]	1 840 940[114]	1 938 919[114]		...	...	...	10 452	...
Malaysia - Malaisie										
6 VII 2010	DJ	28 334 135[115]	14 562 638[115]	13 771 497[115]	DJ	28 589[116]	32 581[116]	1.5	330 621	99
Maldives										
20 IX 2014	DF	402 071[117]	227 749[117]	174 322[117]	DF	320	534[118]	5.7	300	1 780
Mongolia - Mongolie										
11 XI 2010	DF	2 647 199	1 314 246	1 332 953	DF	2 739	3 268	2.0	1 564 116	2
Myanmar										
29 III 2014	DF	51 486 253[119]	24 824 586[119]	26 661 667[119]	DF	59 780[120]	54 340[121]	-1.1	676 577	80
Nepal - Népal										
22 VI 2011	DJ	26 494 504	12 849 041	13 645 463	DJ	28 044	29 610[5]	0.6	147 181	201
Oman										
12 XII 2010	DF	2 773 479	1 612 408	1 161 071	DF	...	4 618[122]	...	309 980	15
Pakistan										
15 III 2017	DF	*207 774 520[123]	*106 449 322[124]	*101 314 780[124]	DF	173 510[123]	...	...	796 095	...
Philippines										
1 VIII 2015	DJ	100 979 303[125]	51 069 962[125]	49 909 341[125]	DJ	93 135[17]	107 288[12]	1.6	300 000	358
Qatar										
20 IV 2015	DF	2 404 776	1 816 981	587 795	DF	1 715	2 799	5.4	11 627	241
Republic of Korea - République de Corée										
1 XI 2015	DJ	51 069 375	25 608 502	25 460 873	DJ	49 554	51 337[126]	0.4	100 339	512
Saudi Arabia - Arabie saoudite										
27 IV 2010	DF	27 236 156	15 531 471	11 704 685	DF	27 411	34 218	2.5	2 206 714	16
Singapore - Singapour										
30 VI 2010	DJ	3 771 721[127]	1 861 133[127]	1 910 588[127]	DJ	5 077[128]	5 704[128]	1.3	725[129]	7 867
Sri Lanka										
20 III 2012	DJ	20 359 439	9 856 634	10 502 805	...	20 675	*21 803	...	65 610	332
State of Palestine - État de Palestine										
1 XII 2017	DF	4 705 855	2 394 359	2 311 496	DF	4 023	4 977	2.4	6 025	826
Syrian Arab Republic - République arabe syrienne										
22 IX 2004	DF	*17 921 000[130]	*9 161 000[130]	*8 760 000[130]	DF	20 619[130]	...	...	185 180	...

3. Population by sex, annual rate of population change, surface area and density
Population selon le sexe, taux de changement annuel de la population, superficie et densité (continued - suite)

Continent, country or area and census date / Continent, pays ou zone et date du recensement	Census type[a]	Population at the latest available census / Population d'après le dernier recensement disponible (in units — en unités): Both sexes / Les deux sexes	Male / Masculin	Female / Feminin	Estimate type[a]	Mid-year estimates / Estimations au milieu de l'année (in thousands — en milliers): 2010	2019	Annual rate of change / Taux de changement annuel 2010-19	Surface area / Superficie (km²) 2019	Density / Densité 2019[b]
ASIA - ASIE										
Tajikistan - Tadjikistan 21 IX 2010	DF	7 564 502	3 817 004	3 747 498	DF	7 519	9 127	2.2	142 600	64
Thailand - Thaïlande 1 IX 2010	DJ	65 981 659	32 355 032	33 626 627	DJ	63 878	66 374[2]	0.4	513 140	129
Timor-Leste 11 VII 2015	DF	1 183 643	601 112	582 531	DF	1 089[2]	1 281[2]	1.8	14 919	86
Turkey - Turquie 3 X 2011	DJ	74 526 000[131]	37 431 000[131]	37 095 000[131]	DJ	73 723[132]	82 377[133]	1.2	783 562	105
Turkmenistan - Turkménistan 10 I 1995	DF	4 483 251	2 225 331	2 257 920		...	...	...	488 100	...
United Arab Emirates - Émirats arabes unis 5 XII 2005	DF	4 106 427[134]	2 806 141[134]	1 300 286[134]	DF	8 264[134]	...	...	71 024[135]	...
Uzbekistan - Ouzbékistan 12 I 1989	DJ	19 810 077	9 784 156	10 025 921	DJ	28 562[112]	33 256[136]	1.7	448 969	74
Viet Nam 1 IV 2019	DJ	96 208 984	47 881 061	48 327 923	DJ	86 947[137]	*96 484[138]	1.2	331 236	291
Yemen - Yémen 16 XII 2004	DF	19 685 161	10 036 953	9 648 208	DJ	23 154[2]	...	...	527 968	...
EUROPE										
Åland Islands - Îles d'Åland 31 XII 2000	DJ	25 776[139]	12 700[139]	13 076[139]	DJ	28[53]	30[53]	0.8	1 583	19
Albania - Albanie 1 X 2011	DJ	2 800 138	1 403 059	1 397 079	...	2 913	2 862[30]	...	28 748	100
Andorra - Andorre 31 XII 2011	DJ	69 758[53]	35 147[53]	34 611[53]	DJ	70[140]	76[141]	0.9	468	163
Austria - Autriche 31 X 2011	DJ	8 401 940	4 093 938	4 308 002	DJ	8 361	8 859[30]	0.6	83 878	106
Belarus - Bélarus 14 X 2009	DJ	9 503 807	4 420 039	5 083 768	DJ	9 491	9 475[30]	0.0	207 600	46
Belgium - Belgique 1 I 2011	DJ	11 000 638	5 401 718	5 598 920	DJ	10 896	11 456[30]	0.6	30 528	375
Bosnia and Herzegovina - Bosnie-Herzégovine 30 IX 2013	DJ	3 531 159	1 732 270	1 798 889	...	3 843	*3 492[30]	...	51 209	68
Bulgaria - Bulgarie 1 II 2011	DJ	7 364 570	3 586 571	3 777 999	DJ	7 534	7 000[30]	-0.8	110 372	63
Croatia - Croatie 1 IV 2011	DJ	4 284 889	2 066 335	2 218 554	DJ	4 295	4 076[30]	-0.6	56 594	72
Czechia - Tchéquie 25 III 2011	DJ	10 436 560	5 109 766	5 326 794	DJ	10 474	10 669	0.2	78 871	135
Denmark - Danemark[142] 1 I 2011	DJ	5 560 628[53]	2 756 582[53]	2 804 046[53]	DJ	5 545[53]	5 814[53]	0.5	42 934	135
Estonia - Estonie 31 XII 2011	DJ	1 294 455	600 526	693 929	DJ	1 331	1 325[30]	-0.1	45 261	29
Faroe Islands - Îles Féroé 11 XI 2011	DJ	48 346	25 125	23 221	DJ	49	52	0.7	1 393	37
Finland - Finlande 31 XII 2010	DJ	5 375 276	2 638 416	2 736 860	DJ	5 335[143]	5 518[141]	0.4	336 872[144]	16
France 1 I 2015	DJ	64 300 821	31 138 550	33 162 271	DJ	62 918[145]	64 822[146]	0.3	551 500	118
Germany - Allemagne 9 V 2011	DJ	80 219 695	39 145 941	41 073 754	DJ	81 757	83 019[147]	0.2	357 582	232
Gibraltar 12 XI 2012	DJ	32 194[148]	16 061[148]	16 133[148]	DF	31[149]	...	...	6	...
Greece - Grèce 9 V 2011	DF	10 816 286	5 303 223	5 513 063	DF	11 121	10 725[30]	-0.4	131 957	81
Guernsey - Guernesey 31 III 2015	DJ	62 234	30 819	31 415	DJ	62[150]	63[150]	0.1	64	981

3. Population by sex, annual rate of population change, surface area and density
Population selon le sexe, taux de changement annuel de la population, superficie et densité (continued - suite)

Continent, country or area and census date / Continent, pays ou zone et date du recensement	Census type[a]	Population at the latest available census / Population d'après le dernier recensement disponible (in units — en unités)			Estimate type[a]	Mid-year estimates / Estimations au milieu de l'année (in thousands — en milliers)		Annual rate of change / Taux de changement annuel 2010-19	Surface area / Superficie (km²) 2019	Density / Densité 2019[b]
		Both sexes / Les deux sexes	Male / Masculin	Female / Feminin		2010	2019			
EUROPE										
Holy See - Saint-Siège[151]										
1 VII 2009	DF	466[152]	320	146	DF	0[153]	...	...	0[154]	...
Hungary - Hongrie										
1 X 2011	DF	9 937 628	4 718 479	5 219 149	DJ	10 000	9 773[155]	-0.3	93 023	105
Iceland - Islande										
31 XII 2011	DJ	315 556[126]	158 151[126]	157 405[126]	DJ	318[126]	357[156]	1.3	103 000	3
Ireland - Irlande										
24 IV 2016	DJ	4 761 865	2 354 428	2 407 437	...	4 560	4 904[155]	...	69 825	70
Isle of Man - Île de Man										
24 IV 2016	DF	78 560	...	...	DJ	83[157]	...	...	572	...
Italy - Italie										
9 X 2011	DJ	59 433 744	28 745 507	30 688 237	DJ	59 277	...	...	302 069	...
Jersey										
27 III 2011	DJ	97 857	48 296	49 561	DJ	96[30]	107[30]	1.2	116	921
Latvia - Lettonie										
1 III 2011	DJ	2 070 371	946 102	1 124 269	DJ	2 098	1 920[30]	-1.0	64 573	30
Liechtenstein										
31 XII 2015	DJ	37 622	18 660	18 962	DJ	36	39	0.8	160	241
Lithuania - Lituanie										
1 III 2011	DJ	3 043 429	1 402 604	1 640 825	DJ	3 097	2 794[155]	-1.1	65 286	43
Luxembourg										
1 II 2011	DJ	512 353	254 967	257 386	DJ	507	614[30]	2.1	2 586	237
Malta - Malte										
20 XI 2011	DF	417 432	207 625	209 807	DJ	415[158]	494[159]	1.9	315	1 565
Monaco										
7 VI 2016	DJ	37 308[160]	18 240[160]	19 068[160]	DJ	36[160]	...	...	2	...
Montenegro - Monténégro										
1 IV 2011	DJ	620 029	306 236	313 793	DJ	619	622[155]	0.0	13 812	45
Netherlands - Pays-Bas										
1 I 2011	DJ	16 655 799	8 243 482	8 412 317	DJ	16 615	17 282[30]	0.4	41 543	416
North Macedonia - Macédoine du Nord										
31 X 2002	DJ	2 022 547	1 015 377	1 007 170	DJ	2 055	2 077[30]	0.1	25 713	81
Norway - Norvège										
19 XI 2011	DJ	4 979 955[161]	2 495 777[161]	2 484 178[161]	DJ	4 889[10]	5 328[155]	1.0	323 772	16
Poland - Pologne										
31 III 2011	DJ	38 044 565	18 420 389	19 624 176	DJ	38 042[10]	37 973[155]	0.0	312 679	121
Portugal										
21 III 2011	DF	10 282 306	4 868 755	5 413 551	DJ	10 573	10 277[30]	-0.3	92 226	111
Republic of Moldova - République de Moldova										
12 V 2014	DF	2 805 194[162]	1 352 353[162]	1 452 841[162]	DJ	3 562[163]	*2 682[164]	-3.2	33 846	79
Romania - Roumanie										
20 X 2011	DF	20 121 641[10]	9 788 577[10]	10 333 064[10]	...	20 247[10]	19 414[155]	...	238 391	81
Russian Federation - Fédération de Russie										
14 X 2010	DF	143 436 145	66 457 074	76 979 071	DJ	142 849	...	...	17 098 246	...
San Marino - Saint-Marin										
7 XI 2010	DF	*30 652	*14 791[76]	*15 818[76]	DF	33[53]	...	...	61	...
Serbia - Serbie										
1 X 2011	DJ	7 186 862[165]	3 499 176[165]	3 687 686[165]	DJ	7 291[165]	6 964[166]	-0.5	88 444	79
Slovakia - Slovaquie										
21 V 2011	DJ	5 397 036	2 627 772	2 769 264	DJ	5 431	5 450[30]	0.0	49 035	111
Slovenia - Slovénie										
1 I 2015	DJ	2 062 874	1 022 229	1 040 645	DJ	2 049	2 081[30]	0.2	20 273	103
Spain - Espagne										
1 XI 2011	DJ	46 815 915	23 104 350	23 711 560	DJ	46 562	46 937[156]	0.1	505 969	93
Svalbard and Jan Mayen Islands - Îles Svalbard et Jan Mayen										
1 XI 1960	DF	3 431[167]	2 545[167]	886[167]		...	...	...	62 422	...
Sweden - Suède										
31 XII 2011	DJ	9 482 855[53]	4 726 834[53]	4 756 021[53]	DJ	9 378[53]	10 230[168]	1.0	438 574	23

3. Population by sex, annual rate of population change, surface area and density
Population selon le sexe, taux de changement annuel de la population, superficie et densité (continued - suite)

Continent, country or area and census date Continent, pays ou zone et date du recensement	Census type[a]	Population at the latest available census Population d'après le dernier recensement disponible (in units — en unités) Both sexes Les deux sexes	Male Masculin	Female Feminin	Estimate type[a]	Mid-year estimates Estimations au milieu de l'année (in thousands — en milliers) 2010	2019	Annual rate of change Taux de changement annuel 2010-19	Surface area Superficie (km²) 2019	Density Densité 2019[b]
EUROPE										
Switzerland - Suisse 31 XII 2011	DF	8 035 391	3 973 280	4 062 111	DJ	7 825	*8 514[169]	0.9	41 291	206
Ukraine 5 XII 2001	DF	48 240 902	22 316 317	25 924 585	DF	45 871	*42 153[170]	-0.9	603 500	70
United Kingdom of Great Britain and Northern Ireland - Royaume-Uni de Grande-Bretagne et d'Irlande du Nord[171] 27 III 2011	DF	63 379 787	31 126 054	32 253 733	DJ	62 759	*66 797[10]	0.7	242 495	275
OCEANIA - OCÉANIE										
American Samoa - Samoas américaines 1 IV 2010	DJ	55 519[62]	28 164[62]	27 355[62]	DJ	67[62]	...	...	199	...
Australia - Australie 9 VIII 2016	DF	23 717 421[172]	11 686 665[172]	12 030 751[172]	DJ	22 032[46]	*25 366[46]	1.6	7 692 024	3
Cook Islands - Îles Cook 1 XII 2016	DF	17 434	8 520	8 914	DF	24	*20	-1.8	236[173]	86
Fiji - Fidji 17 IX 2017	DF	884 887	448 595	436 292	DF	849[174]	889[174]	0.5	18 272	49
French Polynesia - Polynésie française 17 VIII 2017	DF	281 674	...	...	DJ	265[40]	...	...	3 687[175]	...
Guam 1 IV 2010	DJ	159 358	81 552	77 806	DJ	...	168[62]	...	541	311
Kiribati 7 XI 2015	DF	110 136	54 096	56 040		...	...	...	726[176]	...
Marshall Islands - Îles Marshall 3 IV 2011	DF	53 158	27 243	25 915	DF	*54*[177]	...	...	181	...
Micronesia (Federated States of) - Micronésie (États fédérés de) 1 IV 2010	DJ	102 843	52 193	50 650	DJ	*108*[2]	*104*[178]	*-0.4*	702	*149*
Nauru 31 X 2011	DF	10 084	5 105	4 979		...	...	...	21	...
New Caledonia - Nouvelle-Calédonie 26 VIII 2014	DF	268 767	135 542	133 225	DF	250	...	...	19 100	...
New Zealand - Nouvelle-Zélande 5 III 2013	DF	4 353 198[179]	2 119 464[179]	2 233 734[179]	DJ	4 351[180]	4 917[180]	1.4	268 107	18
Niue - Nioué 9 III 2017	DF	1 719	831	888	DJ	1	...	...	260	...
Norfolk Island - Île Norfolk 9 VIII 2011	DF	2 302	1 082	1 220		...	...	...	36	...
Northern Mariana Islands - Îles Mariannes septentrionales 1 IV 2010	DF	53 883	27 746	26 137	DF	*48*	...	...	457	...
Palau - Palaos 13 IV 2015	DJ	17 661	9 433	8 228	DJ	21	...	...	459	...
Papua New Guinea - Papouasie-Nouvelle-Guinée 10 VII 2011	DF	7 275 324	3 772 864	3 502 460		...	...	...	462 840	...
Pitcairn 19 II 2020	DF	45	...	...		...	...	...	5	...
Samoa 7 XI 2016	DF	195 979	100 892	95 087	DF	*186*	*201*	*0.8*	2 842	*71*

3. Population by sex, annual rate of population change, surface area and density
Population selon le sexe, taux de changement annuel de la population, superficie et densité (continued - suite)

Continent, country or area and census date / Continent, pays ou zone et date du recensement	Census type[a]	Population at the latest available census / Population d'après le dernier recensement disponible (in units — en unités)			Estimate type[a]	Mid-year estimates / Estimations au milieu de l'année (in thousands — en milliers)		Annual rate of change / Taux de changement annuel 2010-19	Surface area / Superficie (km²) 2019	Density / Densité 2019[b]
		Both sexes / Les deux sexes	Male / Masculin	Female / Feminin		2010	2019			
OCEANIA - OCÉANIE										
Solomon Islands - Îles Salomon										
22 XI 2009	DF	515 870[181]	264 455[181]	251 415[181]	DF	*555*[182]	*681*[182]	*2.3*	28 896	*24*
Tokelau - Tokélaou										
18 X 2016	DF	1 285	652	633	DF	...	2[183]	...	12	137
Tonga										
30 XI 2016	DF	100 651	50 255	50 396		...	...	...	747	...
Tuvalu										
4 XI 2012	DF	10 782	...	...		...	...	...	26	...
Vanuatu										
7 XI 2016	DF	272 459[184]	138 265[184]	134 194[184]	DF	*239*[185]	*290*[186]	*2.1*	12 189	*24*
Wallis and Futuna Islands - Îles Wallis et Futuna										
23 VII 2018	DF	11 562	...	...		...	...	...	142	...

FOOTNOTES - NOTES

Italics: estimates which are less reliable. - Italiques : estimations moins sûres.

* Provisional. - Données provisoires.

a 'Code' indicates the source of data, as follows:
DF - De facto
DJ - De jure
SDF - Sample survey, de facto
SDJ - Sample survey, de jure

Le 'Code' indique la source des données, comme suit :
DF - Population de fait
DJ - Population de droit
SDF - Enquête par sondage, population de fait
SDJ - Enquête par sondage, Population de droit

b Population per square kilometre of surface area. Figures are estimates of population divided by surface area and are not to be considered either as reflecting density in the urban sense or as indicating the supporting power of a territory's land and resources. - Nombre d'habitants au kilomètre carré. Il s'agit simplement d'éstimations de la population divisé par celui de la superficie: il ne faut pas y voir d'indication de la densité au sens urbain du terme ni de l'effectif de population que les terres et les ressources du territoire sont capables de nourrir.

1 Total resident population including common and collective households of nomadic population, and population counted separately. - Population résidente totale y compris les ménages ordinaires et collectifs de la population nomade, et la population comptée à part.
2 Data refer to national projections. - Les données se réfèrent aux projections nationales.
3 Unrevised data that do not take into account the results of the 2014 population census. - Ces données n'ont pas été revisées et elles ne prennent pas en compte les résultats du recensement de la population de 2014.
4 Postcensal estimates. - Estimations post censitaires.
5 Based on the results of the 2011 Population Census. - Basé sur les résultats du recencement de la population de 2011.
6 Source: Population projections and estimates of priority targets for the various health programs and interventions, National Institute of Statistics (2016). - Source : Projections démographiques et estimations des cibles prioritaires des différents programmes et interventions de sante, Institut National de la Statistique (2016).
7 Excluding Mayotte. - Non compris Mayotte.
8 Based on the results of the 2014 Population Census. - D'après les résultats du recensement de la population de 2014.
9 Data are calculated from the results of the Population and Housing Census of 2009. - Les données sont calculées à partir des résultats du recensement de la population et de l'habitat de 2009.
10 Data refer to usual resident population. - Les données se réfèrent à la population résidente habituelle.
11 Data refer to projections based on the 1983 Population Census. - Les données se réfèrent aux projections basées sur le recensement de la population de 1983.
12 Estimates or projections based on the 2015 population census. - Estimations ou projections fondées sur les résultats du recensement de la population de 2015.
13 Source: The 1984 Population and Housing Census of Ethiopia (Analytical Report at National Level). - Source : Recensement de la population et des logements de l'Éthiopie en 1984 (rapport analytique au niveau national).
14 Estimates based on the 2000 quick population count results and 1995, 2002 and 2010 Eritrea Demographic and Health Surveys. - Des estimations fondées sur le dénombrement rapide de la population de 2000 et sur les enquêtes érythréennes de la démographie et de la santé de 1995, 2002 et 2010.
15 Data refer to national projections based on 2007 census. - Les données sont des projections nationales d'après les résultats du recensement de la population de 2007.
16 Estimates considering also the results of the 2007 Population Census. - Estimations en prennant en considération les résultats du recensement de la population de 2007.
17 Data based on the 2010 Population Census. - Les données sont fondées sur le recensement de la population de 2010.
18 Intercensal estimates. Population in households only. - Estimations inter-censitaires. Population dans les ménages seulement.
19 Population in households only. Postcensal estimates. - Population dans les ménages seulement. Estimations post censitaires.
20 The figure for both sexes excludes a total of 1524 intersex persons (841 in Rural and 683 in urban). - Le chiffre pour les deux sexes exclut un total de 1 524 personnes intersexes (841 pour le milieu rural et 683 pour le milieu urbain).
21 Post-censal estimates based on the 2009 Population Census. - Les estimations post-censitaire fondées sur le recensement de la population de 2009.
22 Data are projections based on the 2006 Population Census. - Projections fondées sur le recensement de la population de 2006.
23 Data refer to Libyan nationals only. - Les données se raportent aux nationaux libyens seulement.
24 Data refer to projections based on the 1993 Population Census. - Les données se réfèrent aux projections basées sur le recensement de la population de 1993.
25 Projections considering also the results of the 2009 Population Census. - Projections en prennant en considération les résultats du recensement de la population de 2009.
26 Including nomadic population. - Y compris la population nomade.
27 Excludes the islands of St. Brandon and Agalega. - Non compris les îles St. Brandon et Agalega.

[28] Based on the results of the 2000 Population Census. - Basé sur les résultats du recencement de la population de 2000.
[29] Data from the main operation. - Données de l'opération principale.
[30] Data refer to 1 January. - Données se raportent au 1 janvier.
[31] Based on the results of the 2004 Population Census. - D'après des résultats du recensement de la population de 2004.
[32] Projections based on the results of national survey on population and health conducted between 2010 and 2011, and especially population and housing census 2014. - Des projections de la population fondées sur les résultats de l'enquête nationale de la population et de la santé réalisée entre 2010 et 2011 et, surtout, du recensement général de la population et de l'habitat de 2014.
[33] Data are projections based on the 2008 Population and Housing Census. - Projection basée sur le recensement 2008 de la population et des logements.
[34] Projections based on the 2012 Population Census. - Projections fondées sur le recensement de la population de 2012.
[35] St. Helena Island has no substantial natural inland waters however there are 15 reservoirs and similar open water storage features on island. - L'île de Sainte-Hélène ne dispose d'aucune grande étendue d'eau intérieure naturelle, mais on y trouve 15 réservoirs et autres installations similaires.
[36] Data refer to Saint Helenian resident population. - Pour la population résidante de Sainte-Hélène.
[37] Data refer to 31 December. - Données se raportent au 31 décembre.
[38] Surface area is based on the 2002 population and housing census. - La superficie est fondée sur les données provenant du recensement de la population et du logement de 2002.
[39] Data are de facto Census counts that have been adjusted for age and sex errors. - Les données correspondent aux valeurs du recensement de facto corrigées pour tenir compte des erreurs d'âge et de sexe.
[40] Intercensal estimates. - Estimations inter-censitaires.
[41] Data have not been adjusted for underenumeration, estimated at 7 per cent. - Les données n'ont pas été ajustées pour compenser les lacunes du dénombrement, estimées à 7 p. 100.
[42] Projections based on the 2002 Population Census. - Projections fondées sur le recensement de la population de 2002.
[43] Comprising the Northern Region (former Saguia el Hamra) and Southern Region (former Rio de Oro). - Comprend la région septentrionale (ancien Saguia-el-Hamra) et la région méridionale (ancien Rio de Oro).
[44] Data refers to resident population adjusted for the undercount of 18 per cent and including the institutional population. - Les données concernent la population résidente, y compris la population des institutions, et ont été ajustées pour tenir compte du sous-dénombrement estimé à 18 p. 100.
[45] Bermuda is 100 per cent urban. - 100 pour cent de la population des Bermudes est urbaine.
[46] Based on the results of the 2016 Population Census. - Basé sur les résultats du recencement de la population de 2016.
[47] To ensure confidentiality, the values, including totals are randomly rounded either up or down to a multiple of '5' or '10.' As a result, when these data are summed or grouped, the total value may not match the individual values since totals and sub-totals are independently rounded. Similarly, percentages, which are calculated on rounded data, may not necessarily add up to 100%. - À des fins de confidentialité, les chiffres, y compris les totaux, sont aléatoirement arrondis au multiple de 5 ou de 10 inférieur ou supérieur. Par conséquent, lorsque ces chiffres sont additionnés, le total peut ne pas correspondre à la somme des valeurs individuelles, dans la mesure où les totaux et les totaux partiels sont arrondis indépendamment. De même, la somme des pourcentages, qui sont calculés à partir des données arrondies, peut ne pas correspondre à 100 %.
[48] Adjusted for census net undercoverage (including adjustment for incompletely enumerated Indian reserves). Final intercensal estimates. - Ajusté pour la sous-estimation du recensement (y compris les réservations en Inde incomplètement énumérées). Estimations inter-censitaires definitives.
[49] Adjusted for census net undercoverage (including adjustment for incompletely enumerated Indian reserves). Postcensal estimates. - Ajusté pour la sous-estimation du recensement (y compris les réservations en Inde incomplètement énumérées). Estimations post censitaires.
[50] Excluding the institutional population. - Non compris la population dans les institutions.
[51] Based on the national household surveys 2010-2014 and the 2011 population census. - D'après les données de l'enquête nationale des ménages 2010-2014 et les résultats du recensement de la population de 2011.
[52] Based on the national household survey of 2019. - D'après l'enquête nationale auprès des ménages de 2019.
[53] Population statistics are compiled from registers. - Les statistiques de la population sont compilées à partir des registres.
[54] Excluding data for Saint Barthélémy and Saint Martin. - Non compris les données pour Saint Barthélémy et Saint Martin.
[55] Projections produced by l'Institut Haïtien de Statistique et d'Informatique (IHSI) and the Latin American and Caribbean Demographic Centre (CELADE) - Population Division of ECLAC. - Les données sont projections produits par l'Institut Haïtien de Statistique et d'Informatique (IHSI) et le centre démographique de l'Amérique latine et les Caraïbes - Division de la population de la CEPALC.
[56] Data refer to projections based on the 2001 Population Census. - Les données se réfèrent aux projections basées sur le recensement de la population de 2001.
[57] Projections based on the 2013 Population Census. - Projections fondées sur le recensement de la population de 2013.
[58] The figures represent the census counts adjusted for under-coverage. Adjustments are done by applying weights calculated (to 4 decimal places) for each sex and age group to the enumerated population when the tabulations are produced. Minor discrepancies between totals and the sum of the component parts of a table and minor discrepancies between the totals across tables are due to rounding after weights are applied. - Les chiffres représentent le dénombrement résultant du recensement ajusté pour tenir compte du sous-dénombrement. Les ajustements sont effectués en appliquant un coefficient de pondération calculé (à la quatrième décimale) pour chaque sexe et groupe d'âges de la population dénombrée lors de l'établissement des tableaux. Les écarts mineurs entre les totaux et la somme des éléments constitutifs d'un tableau ainsi qu'entre les totaux figurant dans différents tableaux sont dus au fait que les chiffres sont arrondis après la pondération.
[59] Including an estimation of 1 334 585 persons corresponding to 448 195 housing units without information of the occupants. - Y compris une estimation de 1 334 585 personnes correspondant aux 448 195 unités d'habitation sans information sur les occupants.
[60] Data revised by CONAPO (National Population Council). - Données révisées par CONAPO (Conseil national de la population).
[61] The population projections of CONAPO (National Population Council). - Les projections démographiques de la CONAPO (Conseil national de la population).
[62] Including armed forces stationed in the area. - Y compris les militaires en garnison sur le territoire.
[63] Including armed forces stationed in the area. Based on the results of the 2010 Population Census. - Y compris les militaires en garnison sur le territoire. D'après le résultats du recensement de la population de 2010.
[64] Refers to habitable area. Excludes St. Lucia's Forest Reserve. - S'applique à la zone habitable. Exclut la réserve forestière de Sainte-Lucie.
[65] Including low water level for all islands (area to shoreline). - Incluent le niveau de basses eaux pour toutes les îles.
[66] Excluding U.S. Armed Forces overseas and civilian U.S. citizens whose usual place of residence is outside the United States. Postcensal estimates. - Non compris les militaires américains à l'étranger et les civils américains dont le lieu de résidence habituel est en dehors des États-Unis. Estimations post censitaires.
[67] Including armed forces stationed in the area. Source: U.S. National Center for Health Statistics, National Vital Statistics Reports (NVSR). - Y compris les militaires en garnison sur le territoire. Source : US National Center for Health Statistics, National Vital Statistics Reports (NVSR).
[68] The total area includes continental areas and islands, and excludes Antarctic area. - La superficie totale comprend les zones continentales et les îles, mais n'inclut pas la région de l'Antarctique.
[69] Data updated according to "Superintendencia Agraria". Interior waters correspond to natural or artificial bodies of water or snow. - Données actualisées d'après la « Superintendencia Agraria ». Les eaux intérieures correspondent aux étendues d'eau naturelles ou artificielles et aux étendues neigeuses.
[70] Data refer to national projections. Data include persons in remote areas, military personnel outside the country, merchant seamen at sea, civilian seasonal workers outside the country, and other civilians outside the country, and exclude nomads, foreign military, civilian aliens temporarily in the country, transients on ships and Indian jungle population. - Les données se réfèrent aux projections nationales. Y compris les personnes vivant dans des régions éloignées, le personel militaire en dehors du pays, les marins marchands, les ouvriers saisonniers en dehors du pays, et autres civils en dehors du pays, et non compris les nomades, les militaires étrangers, les étrangers civils temporairement dans le pays, les transiteurs sur des bateaux et les Indiens de la jungle.
[71] Estimates or projections based on the 2017 Population Census. - Estimations ou projections fondées sur le recensement de la population de 2017.
[72] Data are revised projections taking into consideration also the results of the 2018 census. - Les données sont des projections révisées tenant compte également des résultats du recensement de 2018.
[73] Excludes nomadic Indian tribes. Data based on the 2010 Population Census. - Non compris les tribus d'Indiens nomades. Les données sont fondées sur le recensement de la population de 2010.
[74] Excludes nomadic Indian tribes. - Non compris les tribus d'Indiens nomades.

75 A dispute exists between the governments of Argentina and the United Kingdom of Great Britain and Northern Ireland concerning sovereignty over the Falkland Islands (Malvinas). - La souveraineté sur les îles Falkland (Malvinas) fait l'objet d'un différend entre le Gouvernement argentin et le Gouvernement du Royaume-Uni de Grande-Bretagne et d'Irlande du Nord.

76 Figures for male and female may not add up to the total, since they do not include the category "Unknown". - La somme des chiffres indiqués pour les sexes masculin et féminin peut n'être pas égale au total parce qu'elle n'inclut pas la catégorie " inconnue ".

77 Estimates based on low variant projections. - Des estimations fondées sur des projections de variante basse.

78 Estimates or projections considering also the results of the 2012 Population Census. - Estimations ou projections en prennant en considération les résultats du recensement de la population de 2012.

79 Data have not been adjusted for underenumeration and exclude an estimated population of 1,855,501 at the national level. - Les données n'ont pas été ajustées pour compenser les lacunes du dénombrement. Les données excluent un nombre de personnes estimé à 1,855,501 à l'échelle nationale.

80 Source: INEI – National population estimates and projections from bulletin No. 24 published in July 2019. Data refer to 30 June. - Source : INEI - Estimations et projections nationales de la population, publiées dans le bulletin numéro 24 , juillet 2019. Données se raportent au 30 juin.

81 Figures for male and female population do not add up to the figure for total population, because they exclude 108 homeless people of unknown sex. - Les chiffres relatifs à la population masculine et féminine ne correspondent pas au chiffre de la population totale, parce que l'on en a exclu 108 personnes sans toit dont le sexe n'est pas connu.

82 Revised data. - Données révisées.

83 Excluding nomad population. Data refer to the settled population based on the 1979 Population Census and the latest household prelisting. The refugees of Afghanistan in Iran, Pakistan, and an estimated 1.5 million nomads, are not included. - Non compris les nomades. Les données se rapportent à la population stationnaire sur la base du recensement de 1979 et du recensement préliminaire des logements le plus récent. Sont exclus les réfugiés d'Afghanistan en Iran et au Pakistan et les nomades estimés à 1,5 million.

84 Data refer to the settled population based on the 1979 Population Census and the latest household prelisting. The refugees of Afghanistan in Iran, Pakistan, and an estimated 1.5 million nomads, are not included. - Les données se rapportent à la population stationnaire sur la base du recensement de 1979 et du recensement préliminaire des logements le plus récent. Sont exclus les réfugiés d'Afghanistan en Iran et au Pakistan et les nomades estimés à 1,5 million.

85 Excluding 8408 tourists and foreigners. - À l'exclusion de 8 408 touristes et étrangers.

86 Data refer to projected figures based on the Population and Housing Census 2005 (district projection). - Les données se réfèrent aux projections basées sur le recensement de la population et de l'habitat de 2005 (projections locales).

87 Estimates or projections based on the 2017 Population Census. Data refer to 30 May. - Estimations ou projections fondées sur le recensement de la population de 2017. Données se raportent au 30 mai.

88 Excluding migrants working abroad. - Non compris les migrants qui travaillent à l'étranger.

89 Excluding foreign diplomatic personnel and their dependants. Data based on the 2008 Population Census. - Non compris le personnel diplomatique étranger et les membres de leur famille les accompagnant. Données fondées sur le recensement de population de 2008.

90 For statistical purposes, the data for China do not include those for the Hong Kong Special Administrative Region (Hong Kong SAR), Macao Special Administrative Region (Macao SAR) and Taiwan province of China. Data are from Communique of the National Bureau of Statistics of the People's Republic of China on Major Figures of the 2010 Population Census (No.1). - Pour la présentation des statistiques, les données pour la Chine ne comprennent pas la Région Administrative Spéciale de Hong Kong (Hong Kong RAS), la Région Administrative Spéciale de Macao (Macao RAS) et Taïwan province de Chine. Données issues du communiqué du Bureau national de la statistique de la République populaire de Chine sur les chiffres importants du recensement de 2010 (n° 1).

91 For statistical purposes, the data for China do not include those for the Hong Kong Special Administrative Region (Hong Kong SAR), Macao Special Administrative Region (Macao SAR) and Taiwan province of China. Data have been estimated on the basis of the annual National Sample Survey on Population Changes. - Pour la présentation des statistiques, les données pour la Chine ne comprennent pas la Région Administrative Spéciale de Hong Kong (Hong Kong RAS), la Région Administrative Spéciale de Macao (Macao RAS) et Taïwan province de Chine. Les données ont été estimées sur la base de l'enquête annuelle "National Sample Survey on Population Changes".

92 Data refer to Hong Kong resident population at the census moment, which covers usual residents and mobile residents. Usual residents refer to two categories of people: (1) Hong Kong permanent residents who had stayed in Hong Kong for at least three months during the six months before or for at least three months during the six months after the census moment, regardless of whether they were in Hong Kong or not at the census moment; and (2) Hong Kong non-permanent residents who were in Hong Kong at the census moment. Mobile Residents, they are Hong Kong permanent residents who had stayed in Hong Kong for at least one month but less than three months during the six months before or for at least one month but less than three months during the six months after the census moment, regardless of whether they were in Hong Kong or not at the census moment. Data are estimates from sample enquiry. - Les données se rapportent à la population résidente à Hong Kong au moment du recensement. Cette population est composée des résidants habituels et des résidants mobiles. La population résidente est partagée en deux catégories: (1) les résidents permanents qui ont habité à Hong Kong au moins trois mois pendant les six mois précédents ou les six mois suivants le recensement; (2) les habitants non-permanents de Hong Kong qui étaient à Hong Kong au moment du recensement. La population mobile se rapporte aux résidents permanents de Hong Kong qui ont habité à Hong Kong pendant les six mois après le recensement pour une période comprise entre un mois et trois mois, indépendamment du fait qu'ils étaient à Hong Kong au moment du recensement au pays. Les données sont des chiffres estimatifs dérivés d'une enquête par sondage.

93 Inland waters include the reservoirs. - Les eaux intérieures comprennent les réservoirs.

94 Data refer to government controlled areas. - Les données se rapportent aux zones contrôlées par le Gouvernement.

95 Data refer to government controlled areas. Data refer to annual average population. - Les données se rapportent aux zones contrôlées par le Gouvernement. Les données correspondent à la population annuelle moyenne.

96 Data refer to government controlled areas. Data refer to 1 January. - Les données se rapportent aux zones contrôlées par le Gouvernement. Données se raportent au 1 janvier.

97 Data refer to 1 January. Based on the results of the 2014 Population Census. - Données se raportent au 1 janvier. D'après les résultats du recensement de la population de 2014.

98 Includes data for the Indian-held part of Jammu and Kashmir, the final status of which has not yet been determined. - Y compris les données pour la partie du Jammu et du Cachemire occupée par l'Inde dont le statut définitif n'a pas encore été déterminé.

99 Includes data for the Indian-held part of Jammu and Kashmir, the final status of which has not yet been determined. Data refer to 1 March. Data refer to projections based on the 2001 Population Census. - Y compris les données pour la partie du Jammu et du Cachemire occupée par l'Inde dont le statut définitif n'a pas encore été déterminé. Données se raportent au 1 mars. Les données se réfèrent aux projections basées sur le recensement de la population de 2001.

100 Data are based on the publication: "Indonesia Population Projection 2010-2035" - Les données sont basées sur la publication : << Indonesia Population Projection 2010-2035 >>

101 Data are based on the publication: "Indonesia Population Projection 2015-2045" - Les données sont basées sur la publication : << Indonesia Population Projection 2015-2045 >>

102 Data refer to the Iranian Year which begins on 21 March and ends on 20 March of the following year. - Les données concernent l'année iranienne, qui commence le 21 mars et se termine le 20 mars de l'année suivante.

103 Excluding the population in three autonomous provinces in the north of the country. - La population des trois provinces autonomes dans le nord du pays est exclue.

104 Data are rounded for confidentiality reasons. Includes data for East Jerusalem and Israeli residents in certain other territories under occupation by Israeli military forces since June 1967. - Chiffres arrondis pour des raisons de confidentialité. Y compris les données pour Jérusalem-Est et les résidents israéliens dans certains autres territoires occupés depuis 1967 par les forces armées israéliennes.

105 Includes data for East Jerusalem and Israeli residents in certain other territories under occupation by Israeli military forces since June 1967. Data refer to Israeli citizens and permanent residents who are listed in the Population Register. - Y compris les données pour Jérusalem-Est et les résidents israéliens dans certains autres territoires occupés depuis 1967 par les forces armées israéliennes. Les données se rapportent aux citoyens israéliens et aux résidents permanents qui sont répertoriés dans le registre de la population.

106 Excluding diplomatic personnel outside the country and foreign military and civilian personnel and their dependants stationed in the area. - Non compris le personnel diplomatique hors du pays ni les militaires et agents civils étrangers en poste sur le territoire et les membres de leur famille les accompagnant.

[107] Excluding diplomatic personnel outside the country and foreign military and civilian personnel and their dependants stationed in the area. Because of rounding, totals are not in all cases the sum of the respective components. Estimates or projections based on the 2015 population census. - Non compris le personnel diplomatique hors du pays ni les militaires et agents civils étrangers en poste sur le territoire et les membres de leur famille les accompagnant. Les chiffres étant arrondis, les totaux ne correspondent pas toujours rigoureusement à la somme des composants respectifs. Estimations ou projections fondées sur les résultats du recensement de la population de 2015.

[108] Data refer to 1 October 2007. - Les données se réfèrent au 1er octobre 2007.

[109] Excluding data for Jordanian territory under occupation since June 1967 by Israeli military forces. - Non compris les données pour le territoire jordanien occupé depuis juin 1967 par les forces armées israéliennes.

[110] Excluding data for Jordanian territory under occupation since June 1967 by Israeli military forces. Data refer to 31 December. - Non compris les données pour le territoire jordanien occupé depuis juin 1967 par les forces armées israéliennes. Données se raportent au 31 décembre.

[111] Data refer to resident population. Recalculated population estimates taking into account late registration of births and deaths until May 2017. - Les données concernent la population résidente. Réestimation du nombre d'habitants compte tenu de l'enregistrement tardif des naissances et des décès jusqu'en mai 2017.

[112] Data refer to resident population. - Les données concernent la population résidente.

[113] Data refer to annual average population. - Les données correspondent à la population annuelle moyenne.

[114] Source: Living conditions of household survey, October 2011 to September 2012. - Source: Enquête sur les conditions de vie des ménages, octobre 2011 à septembre 2012.

[115] Data have been adjusted for underenumeration. - Les données ont été ajustées pour compenser les lacunes du dénombrement.

[116] Estimates based on the adjusted results of the Population and Housing Census of 2010. - Les estimations sont fondée sur les résultats ajustées du recensement de la population et de l'habitat de 2010.

[117] Data refer to resident population which includes resident Maldivians and resident foreigners. - Les données concernent la population résidente, qui comprend les Maldiviens et les étrangers.

[118] Data refer to resident population which includes resident Maldivians and resident foreigners. Based on the results of the 2014 Population Census. - Les données concernent la population résidente, qui comprend les Maldiviens et les étrangers. D'après les résultats du recensement de la population de 2014.

[119] The total for the whole country includes 1,206,353 persons estimated not to have been counted in parts of States of Rakhine, Kachin and Kayin. - Le total pour l'ensemble du pays s'élève à 1 206 353 personnes qui ne vivraient pas dans les États rakhine, kachin et kayin.

[120] Data refer to 1 October. - Données se raportent au 1 octobre.

[121] Data refer to 1 October. Based on the results of the 2014 Population Census. - Données se raportent au 1 octobre. D'après les résultats du recensement de la population de 2014.

[122] Data refer to registered population data from Royal Oman Police. - Les données portent sur la population enregistrée par la police royale de l'Oman.

[123] Excluding data for the Pakistan-held part of Jammu and Kashmir, the final status of which has not yet been determined. - Non compris les données concernant la partie du Jammu et Cachemire occupée par le Pakistan dont le statut définitif n'a pas été déterminé.

[124] Excluding data for the Pakistan-held part of Jammu and Kashmir, the final status of which has not yet been determined. Figures for male and female may not add up to the total, since they do not include the category "Unknown". - Non compris les données concernant la partie du Jammu et Cachemire occupée par le Pakistan dont le statut définitif n'a pas été déterminé. La somme des chiffres indiqués pour les sexes masculin et féminin peut n'être pas égale au total parce qu'elle n'inclut pas la catégorie " inconnue ".

[125] Excluding 2134 Filipinos in Philippine Embassies, Consulates and Missions Abroad. - Excepté 2134 Philippins travaillant dans les ambassades, les consulats et les missions des Philippines à l'étranger.

[126] Data refer to registered resident population. - Les données concernent la population enregistrée résidente.

[127] Data are based on the latest register-based population estimates for 2010. Data refer to resident population which comprises Singapore citizens and permanent residents. - Données basées sur les estimations démographiques les plus récentes fondées sur les registres de 2010. Les données se rapportent à la population résidente composé des citoyens de Singapour et des résidents permanents.

[128] Data refer to total population, which comprises Singapore residents and non-residents. Data refer to 30 June. Data exclude residents who have been away from Singapore for a continuous period of 12 months or longer as at the reference date. - Les données se rapportent à la population totale composé des résidents de Singapour et les non résidents. Données se raportent au 30 juin. Non compris les résidents hors de Singapour pour une période ininterrompue de 12 mois ou plus avant de la date de référence.

[129] The land area of Singapore comprises the mainland and other islands. - La superficie terrestre de Singapour comprend l'île principale et les autres îles.

[130] Including Palestinian refugees. - Y compris les réfugiés de Palestine.

[131] Based on a sample taken at the time of census. Because of rounding, totals are not in all cases the sum of the respective components. - D'après un échantillon obtenu au moment du recensement. Les chiffres étant arrondis, les totaux ne correspondent pas toujours rigoureusement à la somme des composants respectifs.

[132] Data refer to 31 December. Data based on Address Based Population Registration System. - Données se raportent au 31 décembre. Les données sont basées sur le registre national de la population basé sur l'adresse.

[133] Data based on Address Based Population Registration System. - Les données sont basées sur le registre national de la population basé sur l'adresse.

[134] Data include non-national population. - Les données comprennent les non-nationaux.

[135] Land area only. - La superficie des terres seulement.

[136] Data refer to 1 January. Data refer to resident population. - Données se raportent au 1 janvier. Les données concernent la population résidente.

[137] Data are adjusted according to the results of the 2009 census and 2014 intercensus. - Les données ont été ajustées à partir des résultats du recensement de la population de 2009 et des données intercensitaires de 2014.

[138] Average population adjusted according to Population and Housing Census on 1 April 2019. - Population moyenne ajustée selon le recensement de la population et de l'habitat du 1er avril 2019.

[139] Statistics are compiled from registers. - Les statistiques sont compilées à partir des registres.

[140] Decrease in population due to revision in administrative registers. Population statistics are compiled from registers. Data refer to 1 January. - Diminution de la population due à la révision des registres administratifs. Les statistiques de la population sont compilées à partir des registres. Données se raportent au 1 janvier.

[141] Data refer to 1 January. Population statistics are compiled from registers. - Données se raportent au 1 janvier. Les statistiques de la population sont compilées à partir des registres.

[142] Excluding Faeroe Islands and Greenland shown separately, if available. - Non compris les Iles Féroé et le Groenland, qui font l'objet de rubriques distinctes, si disponible.

[143] Population statistics are compiled from registers. Excluding Åland Islands. - Les statistiques de la population sont compilées à partir des registres. Non compris les Îles d'Åland.

[144] Excluding Åland Islands. - Non compris les Îles d'Åland.

[145] Excluding diplomatic personnel outside the country and including members of alien armed forces not living in military camps and foreign diplomatic personnel not living in embassies or consulates. - Non compris le personnel diplomatique hors du pays et y compris les militaires étrangers ne vivant pas dans des camps militaires et le personnel diplomatique étranger ne vivant pas dans les ambassades ou les consulats.

[146] Excluding diplomatic personnel outside the country and including members of alien armed forces not living in military camps and foreign diplomatic personnel not living in embassies or consulates. Data refer to 1 January. - Non compris le personnel diplomatique hors du pays et y compris les militaires étrangers ne vivant pas dans des camps militaires et le personnel diplomatique étranger ne vivant pas dans les ambassades ou les consulats. Données se raportent au 1 janvier.

[147] Data refer to 1 January. Based on the results of the 2011 Population Census. - Données se raportent au 1 janvier. Basé sur les résultats du recencement de la population de 2011.

[148] Excluding military personnel, visitors and transients. - Non compris les militaires, ni les visiteurs et transients.

[149] Excluding military personnel, visitors and transients. Data refer to 31 December. - Non compris les militaires, ni les visiteurs et transients. Données se raportent au 31 décembre.

[150] Data refer to 31 March. - Données se raportent au 31 mars.

[151] Data refer to the Vatican City State. - Les données se rapportent à l'Etat de la Cité du Vatican.

[152] The population figure is 466 persons. - La population est égale à 466 personnes.

[153] The population figure is 466 persons. Data refer to 6 December. - La population est égale à 466 personnes. Données se raportent au 6 décembre.

[154] Surface area is 0.44 km^2. - Superficie: 0,44 km^2.

[155] Data refer to 1 January. Data refer to usual resident population. - Données se raportent au 1 janvier. Les données se réfèrent à la population résidente habituelle.

[156] Data refer to registered resident population. Data refer to 1 January. - Les données concernent la population enregistrée résidente. Données se raportent au 1 janvier.
[157] Data refer to 30 April. - Données se raportent au 30 avril.
[158] Including civilian nationals temporarily outside the country. - Y compris les civils nationaux temporairement hors du pays.
[159] Including civilian nationals temporarily outside the country. Data refer to 1 January. - Y compris les civils nationaux temporairement hors du pays. Données se raportent au 1 janvier.
[160] Data refer to resident population only. - Pour la population résidante seulement.
[161] Including residents temporarily outside the country. Population statistics are compiled from registers. - Y compris les résidents se trouvant temporairement hors du pays. Les statistiques de la population sont compilées à partir des registres.
[162] Tiraspol, Bender, Slobozia, Ribnita, Camenca Yrigoricpol/Grigoriopol are districts from Transnistria where the census was not conducted. - Tiraspol, Bender, Slobozia, Ribnita, Camenca, Yrigoricpol/Grigoriopol sont des districts de la Transnistrie où le recensement n'a pas eu lieu.
[163] Excluding Transnistria and the municipality of Bender. - Les données ne tiennent pas compte de l'information sur la Transnistria et la municipalité de Bender.
[164] Excluding Transnistria and the municipality of Bender. Data refer to usual resident population based on the 2014 Census. Tiraspol, Bender, Slobozia, Ribnita, Camenca Yrigoricpol/Grigoriopol are districts from Transnistria where the 2014 census was not conducted. - Les données ne tiennent pas compte de l'information sur la Transnistria et la municipalité de Bender. Les données se rapportent à la population habituellement résidente et sont fondées sur le recensement de 2014. Tiraspol, Bender, Slobozia, Ribnita, Camenca, Yrigoricpol/Grigoriopol sont des districts de la Transnistrie où le recensement n'a pas eu lieu.
[165] Excludes data for Kosovo and Metohia. - Sans les données pour le Kosovo et Metohie.
[166] Excludes data for Kosovo and Metohia. Data refer to 1 January. Based on the results of the 2011 Population Census. - Sans les données pour le Kosovo et Metohie. Données se raportent au 1 janvier. Basé sur les résultats du recencement de la population de 2011.
[167] Inhabited only during the winter season. The Norwegian population of these islands is included also in the de jure population of Norway. - N'est habitée que pendant la saison d'hiver. La population norvégienne de ces îles est comprise également dans la population de droit de la Norvège.
[168] Data refer to 1 January. Population statistics are compiled from registers. Data refer to registered resident population. - Données se raportent au 1 janvier. Les statistiques de la population sont compilées à partir des registres. Les données concernent la population enregistrée résidente.
[169] Data refer to legal resident population. Data refer to 1 January. - Les données concernent la population légalement résidente. Données se raportent au 1 janvier.
[170] Data refer to 1 January. The Government of Ukraine has informed the United Nations that it is not in a position to provide statistical data concerning the Autonomous Republic of Crimea and the city of Sevastopol. - Données se raportent au 1 janvier. Le gouvernement Ukrainien a informé l'ONU qu'il n'est pas en mesure de fournir des données statistiques concernant la République autonome de Crimée et la ville de Sébastopol.
[171] Excluding Channel Islands (Guernsey and Jersey) and Isle of Man, shown separately, if available. - Non compris les îles Anglo-Normandes (Guernesey et Jersey) et l'île de Man, qui font l'objet de rubriques distinctes, si disponible.
[172] These data have been randomly rounded to protect confidentiality. Individual figures may not add up to totals, and values for the same data may vary in different tables. Including population in off-shore, migratory and shipping. - Ces données ont été arrondies de façon aléatoire afin d'en préserver la confidentialité. La somme de certains chiffres peut ne pas correspondre aux totaux indiqués et les valeurs des mêmes données peuvent varier d'un tableau à un autre. Y compris les populations extraterritoriales, les populations nomades et les populations maritimes.
[173] Excluding Niue, shown separately, which is part of Cook Islands, but because of remoteness is administered separately. - Non compris Nioué, qui fait l'objet d'une rubrique distincte et qui fait partie des îles Cook, mais qui, en raison de son éloignement, est administrée séparément.
[174] Data refer to 17 September. - Données se raportent au 17 septembre.
[175] Including water bodies of lake Vaihiria, lake Temae and the Maiao lagoons, but not lake Maeva and the lagoons of Raiatea and Tahaa from the upper islands. No lagoons from lower islands are included. - Y compris les étendues d'eau des îles haute : le lac Vaihiria, le lac de Temae et les lagunes de Maiao. Le lac de Maeva et les lagunes de Raiatea et de Tahaa ne sont pas inclus. Concernant les îles basses, les lagons ne sont pas inclus dans le calcul de la superficie.
[176] Excluding 84 square km of uninhabited islands. Land area only. - Exclut des îles inhabitées d'une superficie de 84 kilomètres carrés. La superficie des terres seulement.
[177] Projections are prepared by the Secretariat of the Pacific Community based on the 1999 census of population and housing. - Les projections sont preparées par le Secrétariat de la Communauté du Pacifique à partir des résultats du recensement de la population et de l'habitat de 1999.
[178] Based on the 2010 Population and Housing Census and 2013/2014 Household Income and Expenditure Survey. - Données fondées sur les résultat du recensement de la population et de l'habitat de 2010, et ceux de l'enquête auprès des ménages sur des revenus et des dépenses de 2013/2014.
[179] Data include overseas visitors in New Zealand on census night. These data have been randomly rounded to protect confidentiality. Individual figures may not add up to totals, and values for the same data may vary in different tables. - Y compris les visiteurs étrangers qui se trouvaient en Nouvelle-Zélande le soir du recensement. Ces données ont été arrondies de façon aléatoire afin d'en préserver la confidentialité. La somme de certains chiffres peut ne pas correspondre aux totaux indiqués et les valeurs des mêmes données peuvent varier d'un tableau à un autre.
[180] Because of rounding, totals are not in all cases the sum of the respective components. - Les chiffres étant arrondis, les totaux ne correspondent pas toujours rigoureusement à la somme des composants respectifs.
[181] Data have not been adjusted for underenumeration. - Les données n'ont pas été ajustées pour compenser les lacunes du dénombrement.
[182] Projections based on adjusted 2009 census counts. - Projections fondées à partir des comptes rajustés du recensement de 2009.
[183] Data refers to 2019 Tokelau population count. Data refer to 12 December. - Les données se rapportent au dénombrement de la population tokélaouane de 2019. Données se raportent au 12 décembre.
[184] Data is based on mini-census taken in 2016. - Selon le mini-recensement de 2016.
[185] Estimates based on the results of 1999 and in 2009 censuses. - Estimations fondées sur les résultats des recensement de la population de 1999 and 2009.
[186] Estimates based on the results of 2009 census and 2016 mini-census. - Estimaions fondées sur les résultats du recensement de 2009 et du mini-recensement de 2016.

Table 3a – *Demographic Yearbook 2019*

Table 3a presents the values of the Whipple's index by sex, urban or rural residence, for total area and both sexes combined, according to the availability of the underlying data in the *Demographic Yearbook* database.

The data used to compile these indices are the datasets of population by single years of age, sex, and urban or rural residence, of the population censuses conducted worldwide since 1985. These datasets have been reported by the National Statistical Offices to the United Nations Statistics Division via the *Demographic Yearbook* questionnaires.

The footnotes that appear at the end of this table are notes that refer to the respective dataset of population by single years of age, sex, and urban or rural residence.

Whipple's index is an index of age preference in age reporting. The way it is calculated for this table, it is meant to indicate preference or avoidance of ages ending in digits "0" (zero) or "5" (five) during age reporting for a population census.

The formula used to calculate the values of the Whipple's index for this table is:

$$\frac{P25+P30+P35+P40+P45+P50+P55+P60}{\frac{1}{5}(P23+P24+P25+\cdots+P58+P59+P60+P61+P62)}*100$$

where Px refers to the number of persons of age x in completed years. The sum in brackets in the denominator is the sum of the number of persons of every single age from 23 to 62.

The values of the Whipple's index generally vary between 100, indicating no preference for "0" or "5" (in other words no heaping in ages ending in "0" or "5"), and 500, indicating that age reporting was entirely concentrated in ages ending in digits "0" or "5". The higher than 100 the value of the index, the higher is the heaping of age reporting in ages ending in "0" or "5".

For more information about the measurement of age and digit preference, please refer to *The Methods and Materials of Demography, Second Edition* (2004), Edited by Jacob S. Siegel and David A. Swanson.

Tableau 3a – *Annuaire démographique 2019*

Le tableau 3a présente les valeurs de l'indice de Whipple par sexe, résidence urbaine ou rurale, pour la superficie totale et les sexes combinés, selon la disponibilité des données sous-jacentes dans la base de données de l'*Annuaire démographique*.

Les données utilisées pour établir ces indices sont les séries de données de la population par âge simple, sexe et résidence urbaine ou rurale, pour les recensements de la population effectués dans le monde entier depuis 1985. Ces séries de données sont communiquées par les services nationaux de statistique à la Division de statistique de l'Organisation des Nations Unies par le biais des questionnaires de l'*Annuaire démographique*.

Les notes qui figurent à la fin de ce tableau sont des notes renvoyant aux différentes séries de données de la population par âge simple, sexe et résidence urbaine ou rurale.

L'indice de Whipple est un indice de préférence de certains âges dans les déclarations de l'âge. La manière dont il est calculé pour ce tableau permet d'indiquer l'attraction ou la répulsion pour des âges se terminant par les chiffres « 0 » (zéro) ou « 5 » (cinq) lors de la déclaration de l'âge effectuée dans le cadre d'un recensement de population.

La formule utilisée pour calculer les valeurs de l'indice de Whipple pour ce tableau est la suivante:

$$\frac{P25+P30+P35+P40+P45+P50+P55+P60}{\frac{1}{5}(P23+P24+P25+\cdots+P58+P59+P60+P61+P62)}*100$$

Px étant le nombre de personnes d'âge x en années révolues. La somme entre parenthèses en dénominateur est la somme du nombre de personnes selon l'âge simple de 23 à 62 ans.

Les valeurs de l'indice de Whipple varient généralement entre 100, indication d'absence de préférence pour « 0 » ou « 5 » (en d'autres termes pas de prépondérance des âges se terminant par « 0 » ou « 5 »), et 500, indiquant que les déclarations de l'âge étaient entièrement polarisées sur les âges se terminant par les chiffres « 0 » ou « 5 ». Plus la valeur de l'indice est supérieure à 100, plus les déclarations de l'âge sont polarisées sur les âges se terminant par « 0 » ou « 5 ».

Pour en savoir plus sur la mesure de l'âge et la préférence pour les chiffres, prière de consulter l'ouvrage intitulé *The Methods and Materials of Demography, Second Edition (2004),* publié sous la direction de Jacob S. Siegel et David A. Swanson.

3a. Whipple's Index by sex and urban/rural residence, 1985 - 2019
L'indice de Whipple par le sexe et la résidence urbaine/rurale, 1985 - 2019

Continent, country or area, date and code[a] / Continent, pays ou zone, date et code[a]	Total			Urban - Urbaine			Rural - Rurale		
	Both sexes Les deux sexes	Male Masculin	Female Féminin	Both sexes Les deux sexes	Male Masculin	Female Féminin	Both sexes Les deux sexes	Male Masculin	Female Féminin
AFRICA - AFRIQUE									
Algeria - Algérie[1]									
16 IV 2008 (CDJC)	100.7	100.5	100.9	100.7	100.5	100.9	100.7	100.6	100.8
Angola									
16 V 2014 (CDFC)	106.1	105.3	106.8	104.9	104.5	105.4	108.2	107.1	109.1
Benin - Bénin									
15 II 1992 (CDFC)	216.1	205.6	224.6	185.4	171.6	197.9	234.6	228	239.6
11 II 2002 (CDJC)	229.1	218.9	237.8	190.4	180.1	200	257.5	250	263.5
Botswana									
21 VIII 1991 (CDFC)	104.8	106.6	103.3	102.4	103.6	101.4	107.7	110.8	105.3
17 VIII 2001 (CDFC)	100.9	101.8	100.2	...	...	...	...	...	...
9 VIII 2011 (CDFC)	100.8	101.3	100.3	101.7	101.8	101.6	99	100.5	97.5
Burkina Faso									
10 XII 1985 (CDJC)	193	173.8	208.4	153.1	140.9	166.7	198.6	179.4	213.2
10 XII 1996 (CDJC)	162.6[2]	144[2]	177.5[2]	99.5[3]	99.6[3]	99.5[3]	99.6[3]	99.7[3]	99.5[3]
9 XII 2006 (CDJC)	145.1	133.8	154.5	131.1	130.5	131.8	150.2	135.3	161.5
Burundi									
16 VIII 1990 (CDJC)	152.9	141.7	163	...	...	...	...	...	...
16 VIII 2008 (CDJC)	156.8	149.4	164.4	137.2	136.5	138.3	159.4	151.5	167.1
Cabo Verde									
23 VI 1990 (CDFC)	111.9	110.7	112.8	108	107.7	108.3	115.3	113.7	116.4
16 VI 2010 (CDJC)	105.8	105.7	105.9	105.3	105.1	105.6	106.7	106.8	106.5
Cameroon - Cameroun									
11 XI 2005 (CDJC)	173.5	165.1	181.4	...	...	...	...	...	...
Central African Republic - République centrafricaine									
8 XII 1988 (CDFC)	139.4	132	146.1	129.9	125.2	134.3	144.5	135.8	152.3
Chad - Tchad									
20 V 2009 (CDJC)	231.3	216.3	245.2	...	...	...	...	...	...
Congo									
1 I 1985 (CDJC)	107.3	107.5	107.1	...	...	...	...	...	...
28 IV 2007 (CDFC)	103.5	103.1	103.8	...	...	...	...	...	...
Côte d'Ivoire									
1 III 1988 (CDFC)	126.3	117.3	136.2	116.4	112.7	121	132.7	120.5	145
15 V 2014 (CDJC)	116.5	114.3	118.9	112.3	111.8	112.9	121.2	117.1	125.6
Egypt - Égypte									
21 XI 2006 (CDFC)	196.5	175.3	218.2	177.1	162.7	191.9	213.5	186.4	241.4
18 IV 2017 (CDJC)[4]	196	184.3	208.3	193.1	186.1	200.3	198.5	182.8	215
Eswatini									
25 VIII 1986 (CDFC)	125.9	125.4	126.3	118.3	118.2	118.5	129.3	130.1	128.8
11 V 1997 (CDFC)	120.6	121.5	119.7	116.9	117.9	115.8	122.3	123.7	121.2
11 V 2007 (CDJC)	99.8	101.2	98.6	99	100.7	97.4	100.1	101.5	99.1
29 IV 2017 (CDJC)	100.6	101.4	99.8	...	...	...	...	...	...
Ethiopia - Éthiopie									
11 X 1994 (CDFC)	272.3	258.9	285	248.7	232.6	264	276.5	263.7	288.7
29 V 2007 (CDFC)	252.1	241	262.9	232.3	222.5	242.4	256.7	245.4	267.5
Gabon									
31 VII 1993 (CDFC)	116.6	115.9	117.4	...	...	...	...	...	...
Gambia - Gambie									
15 IV 1993 (CDFC)	229.8	215.2	244.5	191.2	183.2	201.2	256.2	241.6	268.9
Ghana									
26 III 2000 (CDFC)	184	175.8	191.6	159.7	154.7	164.5	205.6	195.2	215.3
26 IX 2010 (CDFC)	159.1	155.2	162.5	138.3	136.6	139.8	184.7	178.2	190.6
Guinea - Guinée									
15 III 2014 (CDJC)	200.7	185	214	166.2	160.8	171.9	221.1	202.1	235.4
Guinea-Bissau - Guinée-Bissau[5]									
15 III 2009 (CDJC)	137.8	128.9	145.7	...	...	...	...	...	...
Kenya									
24 VIII 1989 (CDJC)	147.8	142.6	152.8	144.1	140.8	149.4	148.9	143.3	153.5
24 VIII 1999 (CDFC)	148.3	143.2	153.2	...	...	...	...	...	...
24 VIII 2009 (CDFC)	146.4	144.6	148.2	141.1	141.1	141.2	149.8	147.1	152.2
Lesotho									
13 IV 2006 (CDJC)	105.3	105.8	104.9	...	...	...	...	...	...
Liberia - Libéria									
21 III 2008 (CDFC)	142.2	136.3	148.1	...	...	...	...	...	...
Malawi									
1 IX 1987 (CDFC)	138.5	137.9	139.1	...	...	...	...	...	...
1 IX 1998 (CDFC)	147.7	149.2	146.4	142.6	146.5	137.3	148.7	149.7	147.7

3a. Whipple's Index by sex and urban/rural residence, 1985 - 2019
L'indice de Whipple par le sexe et la résidence urbaine/rurale, 1985 - 2019 (continued - suite)

Continent, country or area, date and code[a] / Continent, pays ou zone, date et code[a]	Total			Urban - Urbaine			Rural - Rurale		
	Both sexes Les deux sexes	Male Masculin	Female Féminin	Both sexes Les deux sexes	Male Masculin	Female Féminin	Both sexes Les deux sexes	Male Masculin	Female Féminin
AFRICA - AFRIQUE									
8 VI 2008 (CDFC)	120.6	121	120.2	113	114.7	111	122.2	122.5	121.9
3 IX 2018 (CDJC)	106.2	105.7	106.6	104.7	104.6	104.8	106.5	106	107
Mali									
1 IV 1987 (CDJC)	184.5	171.4	195.9	163.7	154.1	173	190.4	176.7	202
1 IV 1998 (CDJC)	180.1	166.8	192.3	166.5	158	175.2	185.6	170.7	198.6
1 IV 2009 (CDFC)	156.5	145.7	166.6	142.7	139.1	146.8	161.1	148.2	172.5
Mauritius - Maurice[6]									
1 VII 1990 (CDFC)	103.4	102.4	104.3	...	...	...	...	...	...
2 VII 2000 (CDJC)	102.4	102.1	102.7	102.3	102	102.7	102.5	102.2	102.7
4 VII 2011 (CDJC)	100.6	101	100.3	100.8	101.2	100.3	100.5	100.9	100.2
Mayotte									
31 VII 2007 (CDJC)	124.4	126.9	122.3	...	...	...	...	...	...
21 VIII 2012 (CDJC)	101.1	102.9	99.6	...	...	...	...	...	...
5 IX 2017 (CDJC)[7]	97.9	99	96.9	97.9	98.8	97	98.2	102.2	94.8
Morocco - Maroc									
1 IX 2004 (CDFC)	113.4	108.4	118	110.1	107.5	112.5	118.2	109.8	126.2
Mozambique									
1 VIII 1997 (CDJC)	118.6	117.9	119.3	111.7	110.9	112.4	121.5	121	121.9
1 VIII 2007 (CDFC)	126	126.2	125.9	...	...	...	...	...	...
Namibia - Namibie									
21 X 1991 (CDFC)	105.8	104.9	106.5	103.5	102.9	104.2	107.1	106.4	107.6
27 VIII 2001 (CDFC)	103.9	103.2	104.5	103.6	102.9	104.4	104.1	103.5	104.6
28 VIII 2011 (CDFC)	103.9	103.8	104	104.3	103.6	105	103.4	104.1	102.9
Niger									
20 V 2001 (CDJC)	270.1	254.7	285.2	...	...	...	...	...	...
10 XII 2012 (CDJC)	105.1	104.7	105.4	...	...	...	...	...	...
Nigeria - Nigéria									
26 XI 1991 (CDFC)	293.5	279.8	307.1	...	...	...	...	...	...
Republic of South Sudan - République de Soudan du Sud									
21 IV 2008 (CDFC)	183.1	178.4	187.9	...	...	...	...	...	...
Reunion - Réunion									
15 III 1990 (CDFC)	99.9	99.8	100.1	...	...	...	...	...	...
8 III 1999 (CDJC)	100	100.3	99.7	...	...	...	...	...	...
1 I 2015 (CDJC)	99.2	98.7	99.6	99.1	98.6	99.6	104.3	103.4	105.1
Rwanda									
16 VIII 2002 (CDJC)	106.3	106.6	106.1	107.4	108.3	106.2	106	106	106.1
15 VIII 2012 (CDJC)	110.2	110.4	109.9	108.3	109.3	107.1	110.6	110.7	110.5
Saint Helena ex. dep. - Sainte-Hélène sans dép.									
8 III 1998 (CDJC)	101	98.8	103.3	...	...	...	...	...	...
10 II 2008 (CDJC)[8]	98.8	99.9	97.8	...	...	...	...	...	...
7 II 2016 (CDJC)[9]	103.9	99.4	109	...	...	...	...	...	...
Saint Helena: Ascension - Sainte-Hélène: Ascension									
8 III 1998 (CDJC)	117.5	111	130.7	...	...	...	...	...	...
Saint Helena: Tristan da Cunha - Sainte-Hélène: Tristan da Cunha									
22 II 1987 (CDFC)	55.2	48.6	61	...	...	...	...	...	...
Sao Tome and Principe - Sao Tomé-et-Principe									
4 VIII 1991 (CDFC)	102.7	101.5	103.8	...	...	...	...	...	...
25 VIII 2001 (CDJC)	105.7	106.2	105.3	...	...	...	...	...	...
13 V 2012 (CDJC)	104.1	103.2	105	...	...	...	...	...	...
Seychelles									
17 VIII 1987 (CDFC)	100.9	102.8	99	...	...	...	...	...	...
26 VIII 1994 (CDFC)	100.9	99.9	102	...	...	...	...	...	...
29 VIII 1997 (CDFC)	101.6	100.8	102.5	...	...	...	...	...	...
26 VIII 2002 (CDJC)	100.8	99.2	102.5	...	...	...	...	...	...
26 VIII 2010 (CDFC)	101.3	101.7	101	...	...	...	...	...	...
South Africa - Afrique du Sud									
5 III 1985 (CDFC)	124.3	120.9	127.7	...	...	...	...	...	...
7 III 1991 (CDFC)	113.1	111.5	114.7	...	...	...	...	...	...
10 X 1996 (CDFC)[10]	100.5	100.3	100.7	99.3	99.5	99.1	102.5	101.7	103.1
10 X 2001 (CDFC)	97.1	97	97.2	...	...	...	...	...	...
10 X 2011 (CDFC)	97.6	97.8	97.4	...	...	...	...	...	...

3a. Whipple's Index by sex and urban/rural residence, 1985 - 2019
L'indice de Whipple par le sexe et la résidence urbaine/rurale, 1985 - 2019 (continued - suite)

Continent, country or area, date and code[a] / Continent, pays ou zone, date et code[a]	Total			Urban - Urbaine			Rural - Rurale		
	Both sexes Les deux sexes	Male Masculin	Female Féminin	Both sexes Les deux sexes	Male Masculin	Female Féminin	Both sexes Les deux sexes	Male Masculin	Female Féminin
AFRICA - AFRIQUE									
Tunisia - Tunisie									
20 IV 1994 (CDFC)	102.4	102.4	102.4	102.4	102.4	102.4	102.4	102.3	102.4
Uganda - Ouganda									
12 I 1991 (CDFC)	168	154.8	180.5	158.6	150.8	167.3	169.4	155.5	182.2
12 IX 2002 (CDFC)	134.2	129.6	138.4	128.2	128.5	128	135.2	129.7	140
27 VIII 2014 (CDFC)	131.5	129	133.7	130.6	132.2	129	131.8	127.7	135.4
United Republic of Tanzania - République Unie de Tanzanie									
28 VIII 1988 (CDFC)	189.2	175.1	201.8	173.7	167.3	180.7	193.3	177.4	206.7
26 VIII 2012 (CDFC)	154.4	152.6	156.1	139.5	141.5	137.7	162.3	158.8	165.5
Zambia - Zambie									
20 VIII 1990 (CDFC)	120.7	121.9	119.6	117.2	119.8	114.2	123.1	123.5	122.7
25 X 2000 (CDFC)	127.6	128.9	126.3	123.9	125.3	122.4	129.9	131.4	128.5
16 X 2010 (CDJC)	123.8	126.8	120.7	122.3	125.2	119.3	124.9	128.2	121.8
Zimbabwe									
18 VIII 1992 (CDFC)	120.6	122.2	119.2	115.9	119.5	111.4	123.7	124.6	123
17 VIII 2002 (CDFC)	115.1	115.2	115	109.7	110.9	108.4	119	119	119.1
17 VIII 2012 (CDFC)	110.8	110.8	110.8	...	...	...	...	...	...
AMERICA, NORTH - AMÉRIQUE DU NORD									
Anguilla									
13 IV 1992 (CDFC)	104.8	109	100.4	...	...	...	...	...	...
9 V 2001 (CDFC)	104.4	105.6	103.2	...	...	...	...	...	...
Antigua and Barbuda - Antigua-et-Barbuda									
28 V 2001 (CDJC)	104.3	103.1	105.4	...	...	...	...	...	...
Aruba									
6 X 1991 (CDJC)	99.3	99.4	99.3	...	...	...	...	...	...
14 X 2000 (CDJC)	103.9[11]	103.3	104.5	...	...	...	...	...	...
29 IX 2010 (CDJC)[11]	103.4	103.6	103.3	...	...	...	...	...	...
Bahamas									
1 V 1990 (CDFC)	103.4	102.3	104.5	...	...	...	...	...	...
1 V 2000 (CDFC)	101.5	100.4	102.5	...	...	...	...	...	...
3 V 2010 (CDJC)	101.3	101.6	101.1	...	...	...	...	...	...
Barbados - Barbade									
1 V 2000 (CDFC)	103.8	104.4	103.3	...	...	...	...	...	...
Belize									
12 V 1991 (CDFC)	103.5	103.2	103.8	...	...	...	...	...	...
12 V 2010 (CDJC)	104.2	103.9	104.5	...	...	...	...	...	...
Bermuda - Bermudes									
20 V 1991 (CDJC)	99	97.9	100	...	...	...	...	...	...
20 V 2000 (CDJC)[12]	100.2	100	100.3	...	...	...	...	...	...
20 V 2010 (CDJC)[13]	100.9	101.1	100.8	100.9	101.1	100.8	...	...	...
20 V 2016 (CDJC)[13]	101.2	100.5	101.8	101.2	100.5	101.8	...	...	...
British Virgin Islands - Îles Vierges britanniques									
12 V 1991 (CDJC)	102.6	104.5	100.5	...	...	...	...	...	...
Canada									
4 VI 1991 (CDJC)	99.6	99.6	99.6	99.6	99.6	99.7	99.6	99.6	99.5
14 V 1996 (CDJC)	99.7	99.7	99.7	...	...	...	...	...	...
15 V 2001 (CDJC)	99.7	99.7	99.8	99.8	99.8	99.8	99.6	99.5	99.8
16 V 2006 (CDJC)[11]	99.9	100	99.9	100	100	100	99.6	99.6	99.7
2 V 2011 (CDJC)	100.8	101	100.7	100.9	101.1	100.8	100.4	100.6	100.3
10 V 2016 (CDJC)[14]	100.8	101	100.7	100.9	101	100.7	100.7	100.7	100.7
Cayman Islands - Îles Caïmanes									
15 X 1989 (CDFC)	104.1	102.7	105.5	...	...	...	...	...	...
10 X 2010 (CDJC)[12]	102.3	102.8	101.8	102.3	102.8	101.8	...	...	...
Costa Rica									
26 VI 2000 (CDJC)	109.1	109.8	108.4	108.6	108.9	108.3	109.9	111.1	108.6
30 V 2011 (CDJC)	104	104.2	103.9	103.8	103.8	103.9	104.6	105.2	103.9
Cuba									
7 IX 2002 (CDJC)	102.2	102.5	101.9	102.5	102.7	102.2	101.5	102	100.9
14 IX 2012 (CDJC)	101.5	101.6	101.3	...	...	...	...	...	...

Continent, country or area, date and code[a] / Continent, pays ou zone, date et code[a]	Total			Urban - Urbaine			Rural - Rurale		
	Both sexes Les deux sexes	Male Masculin	Female Féminin	Both sexes Les deux sexes	Male Masculin	Female Féminin	Both sexes Les deux sexes	Male Masculin	Female Féminin
AMERICA, NORTH - AMÉRIQUE DU NORD									
Dominican Republic - République dominicaine									
24 IX 1993 (CDJC)	116.5	114.9	118	111.5	109.9	113	123.5	121.4	125.5
18 X 2002 (CDJC)	108	108.9	107.1	105.8	106.3	105.4	112.1	113.5	110.7
1 XII 2010 (CDJC)	111.5	113.8	109.2	109.9	111.9	108.1	116.5	119.3	113.1
El Salvador									
27 IX 1992 (CDFC)	126	127.5	124.6	119.9	119.7	120	133.5	136.6	130.7
12 V 2007 (CDJC)	105.9	107.1	105	105.3	106.3	104.5	107.3	108.7	106.2
Guadeloupe									
8 III 1999 (CDJC)	100.5	100.5	100.4	...	...	...	...	...	...
1 I 2015 (CDJC)[15]	100.2	99.8	100.4	100.2	99.8	100.5	99.3	102.4	96.2
Honduras									
11 V 1988 (CDFC)	104.1	104.5	103.6	102.4	102.5	102.3	105.3	105.9	104.8
28 VII 2001 (CDJC)	121.8	123.3	120.4	118.5	118.8	118.3	125.1	127.5	122.7
10 VIII 2013 (CDJC)	119.7	121.6	118.1	120	120.9	119.1	119.4	122.4	116.6
Jamaica - Jamaïque									
7 IV 1991 (CDJC)	107.6	108.8	106.5	...	...	...	...	...	...
10 IX 2001 (CDJC)[16]	107.4	108.7	106.1	106.9	107.5	106.4	107.9	110	105.7
4 IV 2011 (CDJC)	103.3	103.4	103.1	103.6	103.6	103.6	102.8	103.2	102.5
Martinique									
15 III 1990 (CDJC)	104.4	104.1	104.6	...	...	...	...	...	...
1 I 2015 (CDJC)	99.4	100.7	98.4	99.5	100.7	98.5	97.1	100	94.5
Mexico - Mexique									
12 III 1990 (CDJC)	125.2	123.5	126.8	...	...	...	...	...	...
14 II 2000 (CDJC)	116.7	116.5	116.9	114.8	114.3	115.3	123.4	124.3	122.7
17 X 2005 (CDJC)	118.8	118.7	118.9	117.5	117	117.9	123.8	124.8	122.8
12 VI 2010 (CDFC)[17]	114	114.1	113.9	113.7	113.6	113.9	115.1	116.2	114.1
Montserrat									
12 V 2011 (CDJC)	101.9	95.9	108.4	...	...	...	...	...	...
Nicaragua									
4 VI 2005 (CDJC)	111.6	112.8	110.5	108.5	109.2	107.8	116.4	117.8	115.1
Panama									
13 V 1990 (CDFC)	109.3	109.2	109.3	104.6	104.5	104.8	115.6	115	116.3
14 V 2000 (CDFC)	103.2	103.3	103.2	...	...	...	...	...	...
Puerto Rico - Porto Rico									
1 IV 1990 (CDJC)	105.6	106.1	105.1	...	...	...	...	...	...
1 IV 2000 (CDJC)	101.7	102	101.6	...	...	...	...	...	...
1 IV 2010 (CDJC)[18]	102	102	102	...	...	...	...	...	...
Saint Barthélemy - Saint-Barthélemy									
1 I 2015 (CDJC)	102.3	99.3	105.8	...	...	...	...	...	...
Saint Lucia - Sainte-Lucie									
12 V 1991 (CDFC)	110.5	110.5	110.4	...	...	...	...	...	...
22 V 2001 (CDFC)	105.5	105.8	105.2	104	100.5	107.3	106.2	108	104.4
Saint Pierre and Miquelon - Saint Pierre-et-Miquelon									
8 III 1999 (CDFC)	100.5	104.6	96.1	...	...	...	...	...	...
1 I 2015 (CDJC)	100	96.6	103.5	...	...	...	...	...	...
Saint Vincent and the Grenadines - Saint-Vincent-et-les Grenadines									
12 V 1991 (CDFC)	106.6	105.2	107.9	...	...	...	...	...	...
12 VI 2001 (CDFC)	105.3	105.3	105.3	105.6	106.8	104.4	105.1	104.1	106.1
Saint-Martin (French part) - Saint-Martin (partie française)									
1 I 2015 (CDJC)	97.3	102.2	93.5	...	...	...	...	...	...
Sint Maarten (Dutch part) - Saint-Martin (partie néerlandaise)									
9 IV 2011 (CDFC)	100.7	100.2	101.2	...	...	...	...	...	...
Trinidad and Tobago - Trinité-et-Tobago									
9 I 2011 (CDJC)	106.6	107.2	105.9	...	...	...	...	...	...
Turks and Caicos Islands - Îles Turques et Caïques									
10 IX 2001 (CDFC)	104.2	100.1	108.6	...	...	...	...	...	...
United States of America - États-Unis d'Amérique									
1 IV 1990 (CDJC)	104.5	104.8	104.2	...	...	...	...	...	...

3a. Whipple's Index by sex and urban/rural residence, 1985 - 2019
L'indice de Whipple par le sexe et la résidence urbaine/rurale, 1985 - 2019 (continued - suite)

Continent, country or area, date and code[a] / Continent, pays ou zone, date et code[a]	Total			Urban - Urbaine			Rural - Rurale		
	Both sexes Les deux sexes	Male Masculin	Female Féminin	Both sexes Les deux sexes	Male Masculin	Female Féminin	Both sexes Les deux sexes	Male Masculin	Female Féminin
1 IV 2000 (CDJC)[19]	101.8	102.1	101.5	102.1	102.4	101.7	100.8	101	100.5
1 IV 2010 (CDJC)	102.2	102.5	102	102.4	102.7	102.2	101.5	101.7	101.2
AMERICA, SOUTH - AMÉRIQUE DU SUD									
Argentina - Argentine									
15 V 1991 (CDFC)	104.2	103.3	105.2	...	...	...	...	...	...
18 XI 2001 (CDFC)	102.4	101.8	103	...	...	...	...	...	...
27 X 2010 (CDFC)	102.6	102.5	102.7	102.6	102.5	102.7	102.5	102.9	102
Bolivia (Plurinational State of) - Bolivie (État plurinational de)									
3 VI 1992 (CDFC)	125.4	121.1	129.5	111.4	108	114.4	146.1	139.4	152.7
5 IX 2001 (CDFC)	114.6	113.1	116	109.1	108	110.2	124.6	121.9	127.6
21 XI 2012 (CDFC)	110.4	110.5	110.3	108	108.1	108	115.7	115.4	116.1
Brazil - Brésil									
1 IX 1991 (CDJC)	103.3	103.3	103.3	102.3	102.3	102.2	107.2	106.9	107.4
1 VIII 2000 (CDJC)[20]	104.2	104.3	104	103.6	103.7	103.5	107.1	107.3	107
31 VII 2010 (CDJC)	104.8	105.6	104.1	104.7	105.4	104	105.6	106.6	104.4
Chile - Chili									
22 IV 1992 (CDFC)	100.3	98.9	101.7	100.2	98.6	101.7	101	100.2	101.9
24 IV 2002 (CDFC)	99.5	98.5	100.5	99.4	98.2	100.5	100.2	100	100.4
Colombia - Colombie									
15 X 1985 (CDFC)	147.9	146.5	149.2	139.8	136.8	142.4	166.9	166.5	167.3
24 X 1993 (CDFC)	118.9	117.7	120	111.7	108.9	114.1	139.6	139.9	139.4
22 V 2005 (CDFC)	103.5	104.2	102.9	102.1	102.4	101.8	108.6	109.8	107.3
22 V 2005 (CDJC)	103.5	104.2	102.9	102.1	102.4	101.8	108.7	109.9	107.3
18 IV 2018 (CDJC)	100.8	101.1	100.6	100.5	100.7	100.3	102.2	102.8	101.6
Ecuador - Équateur									
25 XI 1990 (CDFC)[21]	132.5	131.2	133.8	122.9	121	124.7	146.6	145.4	147.9
25 XI 2001 (CDFC)[21]	112.1	111.8	112.4	107.9	107	108.7	119.9	120.4	119.4
28 XI 2010 (CDFC)	103.7	104.1	103.3	103	103.4	102.7	104.9	105.4	104.4
French Guiana - Guyane française									
15 III 1990 (CDJC)	106.2	105.7	106.7	...	...	...	...	...	...
8 III 1999 (CDJC)	101.1	100.9	101.3	...	...	...	...	...	...
1 I 2015 (CDJC)	101.6	101.5	101.6	102.2	102.5	102	97	95.9	98.5
Paraguay									
26 VIII 1992 (CDFC)	108.6	107.9	109.3	105.7	104.3	107	112	111.8	112.3
28 VIII 2002 (CDFC)	104.8	104.3	105.2	103.2	102.6	103.7	107.1	106.5	107.8
Peru - Pérou									
21 X 2007 (CDFC)[22]	109.4	109.1	109.6	106.9	106.5	107.3	118.8	118.5	119.1
22 VIII 2017 (CDFC)[23]	101.3	101.2	101.5	101.4	101.3	101.6	100.9	100.8	101
Suriname									
2 VIII 2004 (CDJC)	101.1	100.4	102	102.4[24]	101.4[24]	103.5[24]	98.3[24]	98.2[24]	98.4[24]
13 VIII 2012 (CDJC)	101.7	101.8	101.7	...	...	...	...	...	...
Uruguay									
23 X 1985 (CDFC)	106.2	104.9	107.4	106.2	104.7	107.5	106.3	106.1	106.5
22 V 1996 (CDFC)	103.3	102.8	103.8	103.2	102.5	103.8	104	104.5	103.3
1 VI 2004 (CDFC)[25]	106	105.9	106.2	106.1	105.9	106.3	105.4	105.7	105
4 X 2011 (CDJC)	101.8	101.9	101.7	101.8	101.9	101.7	101.8	101.6	102
Venezuela (Bolivarian Republic of) - Venezuela (République bolivarienne du)									
20 X 1990 (CDFC)[26]	106.4	106.5	106.3	105	104.8	105.3	114.9	116.1	113.4
1 IX 2011 (CDJC)	101.3	101.6	101	101.3[27]	101.6[27]	101[27]	101.4[27]	102[27]	100.7[27]
ASIA - ASIE									
Armenia - Arménie									
10 X 2001 (CDJC)	103	102.8	103.3	103.7	103.7	103.8	101.6	101.1	102.1
12 X 2011 (CDJC)	101.8	101.5	102	102.4	102.3	102.6	100.6	100.2	101
Azerbaijan - Azerbaïdjan									
27 I 1999 (CDJC)	100.4	99.8	101	100.3	99.8	100.8	100.5	99.7	101.2
13 IV 2009 (CDJC)	100.4	100.1	100.7	100.8	100.3	101.3	99.9	99.7	100.1
Bahrain - Bahreïn									
16 XI 1991 (CDFC)	96.6	98.3	93.6	...	...	...	...	...	...
7 IV 2001 (CDJC)	100.2	99.9	100.9	...	...	...	...	...	...
27 IV 2010 (CDJC)	100.2	99.3	101.9	...	...	...	...	...	...

3a. Whipple's Index by sex and urban/rural residence, 1985 - 2019
L'indice de Whipple par le sexe et la résidence urbaine/rurale, 1985 - 2019 (continued - suite)

Continent, country or area, date and code[a] / Continent, pays ou zone, date et code[a]	Total			Urban - Urbaine			Rural - Rurale		
	Both sexes Les deux sexes	Male Masculin	Female Féminin	Both sexes Les deux sexes	Male Masculin	Female Féminin	Both sexes Les deux sexes	Male Masculin	Female Féminin
ASIA - ASIE									
Bangladesh[28]									
22 I 2001 (CDFC)	299.5	295.8	303.4	283.1	277.9	289.8	305	302.6	307.4
Bhutan - Bhoutan									
30 V 2005 (CDFC)	116.4	117.7	114.9	118.7	119.6	117.4	115.4	116.8	113.9
30 V 2017 (CDFC)[29]	108.1	110.4	105.4	...	...	...	...	...	...
Brunei Darussalam - Brunéi Darussalam									
7 VIII 1991 (CDFC)	98.8	98.7	98.8	...	...	...	...	...	...
20 VI 2011 (CDJC)	100.9	101.6	100.2	100.6	101.3	99.8	102	102.3	101.6
Cambodia - Cambodge									
3 III 1998 (CDFC)	118.1	116.2	119.6	119.8	117.6	121.8	117.6	115.9	119.1
3 III 2008 (CDFC)[30]	109.9	108.2	111.3	109.7	108.5	110.8	109.9	108.1	111.5
China - Chine									
1 VII 1990 (CDFC)	101	101.1	100.9	101.9	102	101.8	100.6	100.7	100.5
1 XI 2000 (CDJC)	101.7	101.7	101.6	101.6	101.8	101.4	101.7	101.7	101.7
1 XI 2010 (CDJC)[31]	98.8	98.9	98.8	98.7	98.9	98.6	98.9	98.9	99
China, Hong Kong SAR - Chine, Hong Kong RAS									
11 III 1986 (CDFC)	101.7	101.4	102.1	101.7	101.3	102.1	102.1	102.5	101.7
15 III 1996 (CDJC)	99.7	99.8	99.7	...	...	...	...	...	...
14 III 2001 (CDJC)[32]	100.2	100.3	100.1	...	...	...	...	...	...
14 VII 2006 (CDJC)[33]	98.3	98.4	98.3	...	...	...	...	...	...
30 VI 2011 (CDJC)[32]	99.4	100	98.9	...	...	...	...	...	...
30 VI 2016 (CDJC)[33]	99.9	99.9	99.8	...	...	...	...	...	...
China, Macao SAR - Chine, Macao RAS									
30 VIII 1991 (CDJC)	100.8	101.4	100.3	...	...	...	...	...	...
23 VIII 2001 (CDJC)	95.5	94.7	96.2	...	...	...	...	...	...
12 VIII 2011 (CDJC)	98.9	97.6	100	...	...	...	...	...	...
Cyprus - Chypre									
1 X 1992 (CDJC)	98.7	98.3	99	98.8	98.4	99.3	98.4	98.3	98.5
1 X 2001 (CDJC)[34]	100.7	100.7	100.6	100.9	101.4	100.4	100.1	99.1	101.1
1 X 2011 (CDJC)[34]	105.4	106.6	104.4	...	...	...	...	...	...
Democratic People's Republic of Korea - République populaire démocratique de Corée									
31 XII 1993 (CDJC)	105	105.2	104.7	104.4	104.6	104.2	105.8	106.2	105.5
1 X 2008 (CDJC)	101	100.6	101.3	...	...	...	...	...	...
Georgia - Géorgie									
17 I 2002 (CDJC)	101.4	101.7	101.1	101.6	102	101.3	101.1	101.4	100.8
5 XI 2014 (CDJC)	99.9	99.9	99.8	99.8	99.6	99.9	100	100.4	99.7
India - Inde									
1 III 1991 (CDFC)[35]	290.3	292.6	287.9	258.7	253.8	264.3	302.1	307.7	296.2
1 III 2001 (CDFC)[36]	230	241	218.4	217.2	216.8	217.8	235.5	252	218.7
9 II 2011 (CDFC)[37]	171	174.6	167.4	152.9	151	154.9	180.5	187.1	173.8
Indonesia - Indonésie									
31 X 1990 (CDFC)	163.3	160.2	166.3	139.7	135.8	143.7	174.2	171.7	176.5
30 VI 2000 (CDJC)[38]	152.2	151.3	153.1	136.8	136.4	137.2	164.2	163.1	165.2
1 V 2010 (CDJC)	114.5	114.2	114.9	110.2	110.2	110.2	119	118.4	119.7
Iran (Islamic Republic of) - Iran (République islamique d')									
22 IX 1986 (CDFC)	122.6	121.1	124.1	114.4	113.4	115.5	133.1	131.3	134.8
11 IX 1991 (CDJC)	128.7	127	130.4	122.5	121.3	123.9	138.5	136.4	140.6
11 IX 1994 (CDJC)	107.4	106.8	108.1	107.1	108	106.2	107.8	104.5	111.2
23 X 1996 (CDJC)	108.8	108.6	109	105.7	105.6	105.8	114.1	114	114.3
28 X 2006 (CDJC)[39]	111.6	110.4	112.8	109.3	108.5	110.1	117.2	115.2	119.2
24 X 2011 (CDJC)	103.7	103.8	103.5	103.6	103.8	103.5	103.7[40]	103.8[40]	103.6[40]
24 IX 2016 (CDJC)	104.1	104.2	104	104[39]	104.1[39]	103.9[39]	104.5[39]	104.6[39]	104.3[39]
Iraq									
16 X 1997 (CDFC)	106.2	105.6	106.8	105.5	104.9	106.1	108	107.6	108.5
Israel - Israël									
4 XI 1995 (CDFC)[41]	101.4	101.8	101	101.3	101.8	100.9	101.9	101.5	102.3
4 XI 1995 (CDJC)	101.1	101.1	101.1	101	101	101	101.5	101.6	101.4
27 XII 2008 (CDFC)[42]	98.9	99	98.9	99	99.1	98.9	98.6	98.3	99
Japan - Japon									
1 X 1985 (CDFC)	98.4	98.4	98.3	98.3	98.4	98.2	98.7	98.5	98.8
1 X 1990 (CDFC)	98.9	98.9	98.9	98.9	99	98.8	98.8	98.6	99

3a. Whipple's Index by sex and urban/rural residence, 1985 - 2019
L'indice de Whipple par le sexe et la résidence urbaine/rurale, 1985 - 2019 (continued - suite)

Continent, country or area, date and code[a] Continent, pays ou zone, date et code[a]	Total			Urban - Urbaine			Rural - Rurale		
	Both sexes Les deux sexes	Male Masculin	Female Féminin	Both sexes Les deux sexes	Male Masculin	Female Féminin	Both sexes Les deux sexes	Male Masculin	Female Féminin
ASIA - ASIE									
1 X 1995 (CDFC)	99	99	99	99	99.1	99	98.8	98.6	98.9
1 X 2000 (CDJC)	99.1	99.1	99	99.1	99.2	99	99	98.8	99.2
1 X 2005 (CDJC)[43]	99.1	99.2	99.1	99.2	99.2	99.1	99	98.8	99.1
1 X 2010 (CDJC)[43]	100.9	100.9	100.9	100.9	100.9	100.8	101	100.9	101.1
1 X 2015 (CDJC)[43]	100.8	100.7	100.8	100.8	100.7	100.8	100.8	100.7	100.9
Jordan - Jordanie									
1 X 2004 (CDFC)[44]	100.8	100.4	101.3	...	...	...	...	...	...
30 XI 2015 (CDFC)[45]	111.4	112.3	110.3	...	...	...	...	...	...
Kazakhstan									
12 I 1989 (CDFC)	98.9	98.8	99	98.7	98.6	98.8	99.2	99	99.4
26 II 1999 (CDJC)[46]	99.9	99.8	99.9	100.1	100	100.2	99.5	99.5	99.4
Kuwait - Koweït									
20 IV 1985 (CDFC)	139.5	142.6	133.9	...	...	...	...	...	...
21 IV 2011 (CDFC)	102.2	102.6	101.7	102.2	102.6	101.7	...	...	...
Kyrgyzstan - Kirghizstan									
12 I 1989 (CDJC)	99.3	99.1	99.5	98.4	98	98.8	99.9	99.8	100.1
24 III 1999 (CDJC)	99.4	99.2	99.6	99.2	98.9	99.5	99.5	99.3	99.7
24 III 2009 (CDJC)	100.6	100.5	100.8	...	...	...	...	...	...
Lao People's Democratic Republic - République démocratique populaire lao									
1 III 2005 (CDJC)	138.3	136.4	140.2	120.8[47]	120.9[47]	120.6[47]	146[47]	143.3[47]	148.5[47]
1 III 2015 (CDJC)	129.3	128.4	130.2	120	119.8	120.3	134.8	133.5	136
Malaysia - Malaisie									
14 VIII 1991 (CDFC)	114.2	113.8	114.6	110.3	110.2	110.3	118.8	117.9	119.7
6 VII 2010 (CDJC)	120.4	120.7	120	120.6	120.7	120.5	119.7	120.6	118.7
6 VII 2010 (CDJC)[48]	120.7	121.1	120.3	...	...	...	...	...	...
Maldives									
25 III 1985 (CDFC)	176.7	175.3	178.4	166.3	170.9	159.4	180.7	177.2	184.2
8 III 1990 (CDFC)	156.4	159.9	152.7	149.3	154.5	142.6	159.2	162.4	156.1
25 III 1995 (CDFC)	143.1	144.5	141.7	137.3	137.9	136.7	145.5	147.5	143.5
31 III 2000 (CDFC)	106.9	109.5	104.3	...	...	...	...	...	...
21 III 2006 (CDFC)[49]	103.8	104.9	102.8	104	105.5	102.5	103.7	104.5	102.9
20 IX 2014 (CDFC)[50]	105.4	109.8	99.1	106.1	110.5	100.1	105	109.4	98.3
Mongolia - Mongolie									
5 I 2000 (CDFC)	99.9	99.6	100.2	99.9	99.7	100.1	99.9	99.5	100.2
11 XI 2010 (CDJC)	101.6	101.3	101.9	101.7	101.4	102	101.5	101.3	101.7
Myanmar[51]									
29 III 2014 (CDFC)	123.3	124	122.6	115.8	116	115.6	126.7	127.6	125.8
Nepal - Népal									
22 VI 1991 (CDJC)	202.4	195.6	209	186.2	179.2	193.9	204.2	197.6	210.5
22 VI 2001 (CDJC)	206.1	205.7	206.6	...	...	...	...	...	...
22 VI 2011 (CDJC)	188.6	191.3	186.2	169.9	167.8	172	193.1	197.5	189.3
Oman									
7 XII 2003 (CDFC)	158.5	165.6	146.9	154.9	163.1	141.1	170.2	174.1	164.4
Philippines									
1 IX 1995 (CDJC)	115.7	116.5	114.9	...	...	...	...	...	...
1 V 2000 (CDJC)	110.8	111.6	110	...	...	...	...	...	...
1 VIII 2007 (CDJC)	104.8	104.9	104.7	...	...	...	...	...	...
1 V 2010 (CDJC)[52]	108.5	109.1	107.9	...	...	...	...	...	...
1 VIII 2015 (CDJC)[53]	106.8	107.2	106.3	107.5	108	107	105.9	106.4	105.4
Qatar									
16 III 1986 (CDFC)	149.1	151.9	140.2	...	...	...	...	...	...
20 IV 2015 (CDFC)	100.7	100.7	100.9	...	...	...	...	...	...
Republic of Korea - République de Corée									
1 XI 1985 (CDFC)	99.4	98.9	99.8	99.6	99.4	99.8	98.8	97.9	99.6
1 XI 1990 (CDFC)	99.5	99.2	99.8	99.6	99.4	99.8	99.1	98.5	99.7
1 XI 1995 (CDJC)	99.9	99.7	100.1	100	99.8	100.2	99.4	99.2	99.6
1 XI 2000 (CDJC)[54]	100	99.8	100.2	100.2	100	100.4	99.2	98.9	99.4
1 XI 2005 (CDJC)[54]	100.4	100.2	100.6	100.6	100.4	100.8	99.4	99.2	99.7
1 XI 2015 (CDJC)	101.8	101.3	102.3	101.8	101.3	102.2	101.8	101.2	102.5
Singapore - Singapour									
30 VI 2000 (CDJC)	98.2	98.1	98.3	...	...	...	...	...	...
30 VI 2010 (CDJC)[55]	99.7	99.7	99.7	...	...	...	...	...	...
Sri Lanka									
17 VII 2001 (CDFC)[56]	97	97.5	96.4	98.2	98.5	97.8	96.8[57]	97.3[57]	96.2[57]

3a. Whipple's Index by sex and urban/rural residence, 1985 - 2019
L'indice de Whipple par le sexe et la résidence urbaine/rurale, 1985 - 2019 (continued - suite)

Continent, country or area, date and code[a] / Continent, pays ou zone, date et code[a]	Total			Urban - Urbaine			Rural - Rurale		
	Both sexes Les deux sexes	Male Masculin	Female Féminin	Both sexes Les deux sexes	Male Masculin	Female Féminin	Both sexes Les deux sexes	Male Masculin	Female Féminin
ASIA - ASIE									
20 III 2012 (CDJC)	100.2	100.3	100	100.3	100.7	100	100.1	100.2	100.1
State of Palestine - État de Palestine									
9 XII 1997 (CDFC)[58]	109.1	103	115.3	...	...	...	...	...	...
1 XII 2007 (CDFC)[38]	103.8	102.6	104.9	104.4[59]	103.2[59]	105.7[59]	100.8	100	101.6
Syrian Arab Republic - République arabe syrienne[60]									
3 IX 1994 (CDFC)	111.8	109.9	113.8	111.9	110.4	113.5	111.7	109.2	114.1
Tajikistan - Tadjikistan									
12 I 1989 (CDJC)	99	98.9	99.1	97.6	97.1	98	99.9	100	99.9
20 I 2000 (CDFC)	99.3	99.2	99.4	100.1	100	100.1	99	98.9	99.1
21 IX 2010 (CDFC)	103.6	103.9	103.4	105.8	106.6	105	102.8	102.9	102.7
Thailand - Thaïlande									
1 IV 2000 (CDJC)[61]	104.7	104.7	104.8	108.1	108.1	108.1	103	103	103
1 IX 2010 (CDJC)	110.6	111.1	110.1	115.6	116.2	115	106.3	106.8	105.8
Timor-Leste									
11 VII 2010 (CDFC)	130.3	128.9	131.7	126	125.6	126.5	132.3	130.6	134
11 VII 2015 (CDFC)	125	125.1	125	119.4	119.3	119.5	127.8	128.1	127.5
Turkey - Turquie									
20 X 1985 (CDFC)	149.4	133.8	165.3	...	...	...	...	...	...
21 X 1990 (CDFC)	139.7	128.9	150.8	...	...	...	...	...	...
22 X 2000 (CDFC)	125.7	123.2	128.3	122.7	121.3	124.2	131.7	127.2	136.4
3 X 2011 (CDJC)[62]	101.2	101.7	100.8	101.4	101.7	101.1	100.8	101.5	99.9
Viet Nam									
1 IV 1989 (CDJC)	98.5	98.1	98.8	98.3	97.8	98.8	98.4	98	98.7
1 IV 1999 (CDJC)	99.2	98.8	99.6	99.1	98.6	99.6	99.3	98.8	99.7
1 IV 2009 (CDJC)	100.4	99.8	100.9	100.6	100	101.1	100.3	99.8	100.8
Yemen - Yémen									
16 XII 1994 (CDFC)	293.9	282.6	304.9	245	229.6	265	311.7	305.8	316.8
EUROPE									
Åland Islands - Îles d'Åland[63]									
31 XII 2000 (CDJC)	100.7	101.5	99.8	102.9	101.9	103.8	99	101.2	96.7
Austria - Autriche									
15 V 1991 (CDJC)	97.9	97.9	97.9	97.8	97.9	97.7	98.2	98.1	98.2
15 V 2001 (CDJC)	97.4	97.5	97.3	97.3	97.5	97.2	97.5	97.3	97.6
31 X 2011 (CDJC)	100	100.1	100	100.2	100.2	100.2	99.7	99.8	99.7
Belarus - Bélarus									
12 I 1989 (CDJC)	99.4	99.3	99.5	98.9	98.8	99.1	100.3	100.3	100.2
16 II 1999 (CDJC)	99.6	99.4	99.8	99.7	99.6	99.9	99.2	98.9	99.5
14 X 2009 (CDJC)	101.5	101.6	101.5	101.7	101.6	101.7	101	101.3	100.7
Belgium - Belgique									
1 X 2001 (CDJC)	99.5	99.4	99.7	99.5	99.4	99.7	99.2	98.9	99.4
1 I 2011 (CDJC)	100	99.9	100.1	100	99.9	100.1	100.3	99.1	101.6
Bosnia and Herzegovina - Bosnie-Herzégovine									
31 III 1991 (CDJC)	100.4	100.5	100.2	...	...	...	...	...	...
30 IX 2013 (CDJC)	100.1	99.8	100.3	...	...	...	...	...	...
Bulgaria - Bulgarie									
1 II 2011 (CDJC)	101.2	101	101.4	101.1	100.9	101.3	101.4	101.4	101.4
Croatia - Croatie									
31 III 1991 (CDFC)	99.1	99.2	99.1	99	99.3	98.8	99.2	99.1	99.4
31 III 2001 (CDJC)	98.2	98.4	98.1	98.3	98.6	98.1	98.1	98.1	98.2
1 IV 2011 (CDJC)	100.3	100.5	100.2	100.3	100.4	100.2	100.4	100.5	100.2
Czechia - Tchéquie									
3 III 1991 (CDJC)	99	98.8	99.1	...	...	...	...	...	...
1 III 2001 (CDJC)	99.2	99.1	99.3	99	98.9	99.1	99.8	99.8	99.9
25 III 2011 (CDJC)	99.6	99.6	99.7	99.5	99.4	99.6	99.9	100.1	99.8
Denmark - Danemark[64]									
1 I 1991 (CDJC)	100.5	100.6	100.5	...	...	...	...	...	...
Estonia - Estonie									
31 III 2000 (CDJC)	100	99.7	100.3	100.2	100	100.4	99.7	99.1	100.2
31 XII 2011 (CDJC)	100	100	100.1	100.1	100	100.1	100	99.9	100.2
Finland - Finlande									
17 XI 1985 (CDJC)	99.8	99.9	99.6	...	...	...	...	...	...
31 XII 1990 (CDJC)	99.5	99.6	99.5	...	...	...	...	...	...

3a. Whipple's Index by sex and urban/rural residence, 1985 - 2019
L'indice de Whipple par le sexe et la résidence urbaine/rurale, 1985 - 2019 (continued - suite)

Continent, country or area, date and code[a] / Continent, pays ou zone, date et code[a]	Total			Urban - Urbaine			Rural - Rurale		
	Both sexes Les deux sexes	Male Masculin	Female Féminin	Both sexes Les deux sexes	Male Masculin	Female Féminin	Both sexes Les deux sexes	Male Masculin	Female Féminin
EUROPE									
31 XII 2000 (CDJC)	99.5	99.6	99.4	99.9	100.1	99.7	98.9	98.9	98.8
31 XII 2010 (CDJC)	100.1	100.1	100	100	100.1	99.8	100.3	100	100.5
France									
5 III 1990 (CDJC)	99.2	99	99.3	99.5	99.4	99.6	98.2	98.1	98.4
8 III 1999 (CDJC)[65]	100.5	100.5	100.5	100.5	100.5	100.5	100.8	100.7	100.8
1 I 2015 (CDJC)	100	100	100.1	100	100	100.1	100	100.1	99.9
Germany - Allemagne									
9 V 2011 (CDJC)	100	100	100.1	100	100	100.1	100.1	100.1	100.1
Gibraltar									
14 X 1991 (CDFC)	105.7	104.9	106.6	...	...	...	...	...	...
12 XI 2001 (CDFC)[66]	98	98.6	97.5	...	...	...	...	...	...
12 XI 2012 (CDJC)[67]	99.5	100.3	98.7	...	...	...	...	...	...
Greece - Grèce									
17 III 1991 (CDFC)	108.8	107.4	110.1	108.5	107.3	109.7	109.1	107.6	110.7
18 III 2001 (CDJC)[68]	105	104.9	105.1	104.8	104.6	104.9	105.8	105.7	106
9 V 2011 (CDFC)	101.4	101.8	101.1	101.3	101.6	101.1	101.8	102.3	101.2
Guernsey - Guernesey									
23 III 1986 (CDJC)	96.1	96.1	96	...	...	...	...	...	...
13 III 1996 (CDJC)	97.5	98.5	96.6	...	...	...	...	...	...
29 IV 2001 (CDJC)	97.2	97.4	96.9	...	...	...	...	...	...
31 III 2015 (CDJC)[46]	101.4	102.4	100.3	...	...	...	...	...	...
Hungary - Hongrie									
1 I 1990 (CDFC)	102.1	102.5	101.8	102.4	102.8	102	101.7	101.9	101.5
1 II 2001 (CDFC)	101.6	101.8	101.5	101.9	102.2	101.6	101.2	101.2	101.2
1 X 2011 (CDFC)	100.2	100.2	100.2	100.1	100.2	100.1	100.4	100.3	100.5
Ireland - Irlande									
21 IV 1991 (CDFC)	100.5	100.5	100.4	...	...	...	...	...	...
28 IV 1996 (CDFC)	100.2	100.2	100.1	100.3	100.5	100.2	99.9	99.7	100
28 IV 2002 (CDFC)	99.5	99.8	99.2	99.7	99.9	99.4	99.3	99.5	99
23 IV 2006 (CDFC)	100.9	101	100.8	101	101.2	100.8	100.8	100.7	100.8
10 IV 2011 (CDFC)	100.7	101	100.5	100.9	101.2	100.5	100.5	100.5	100.4
Isle of Man - Île de Man									
6 IV 1986 (CDJC)	99.2	98.6	99.8	...	...	...	...	...	...
14 IV 1991 (CDJC)	97.7	98.1	97.3	...	...	...	...	...	...
14 IV 1996 (CDJC)	97.9	98.9	97	...	...	...	...	...	...
29 IV 2001 (CDJC)	97.8	98	97.5	...	...	...	...	...	...
23 IV 2006 (CDJC)	98.3	98.4	98.3	...	...	...	...	...	...
27 III 2011 (CDJC)	99.3	100.4	98.2	...	...	...	...	...	...
24 IV 2016 (CDJC)	99	99.3	98.7	...	...	...	...	...	...
Italy - Italie									
21 X 2001 (CDJC)	101.1	101	101.1	...	...	...	...	...	...
9 X 2011 (CDJC)	99.8	99.8	99.8	...	...	...	...	...	...
Jersey									
23 III 1986 (CDFC)	98	98	98	...	...	...	...	...	...
10 III 1991 (CDJC)	99.2	100.6	97.8	...	...	...	...	...	...
10 III 1996 (CDJC)	99.4	100.7	98.1	...	...	...	...	...	...
11 III 2001 (CDJC)	98.9	99.6	98.3	...	...	...	...	...	...
27 III 2011 (CDJC)	100	100.7	99.3	...	...	...	...	...	...
Latvia - Lettonie									
31 III 2000 (CDJC)[69]	100.5	100.2	100.7	100.4	100.4	100.4	100.6	99.8	101.5
1 III 2011 (CDJC)	99.4	99.6	99.3	99.5	99.7	99.3	99.3	99.3	99.4
Liechtenstein									
31 XII 2010 (CDJC)	100.5	102.1	99	...	...	...	...	...	...
31 XII 2015 (CDJC)	100.4	101.3	99.5	...	...	...	...	...	...
Lithuania - Lituanie									
12 I 1989 (CDJC)	100.6	100.5	100.7	100.7	100.6	100.8	100.3	100.2	100.4
6 IV 2001 (CDJC)	99.8	99.7	99.9	99.4	99	99.7	100.8	101.1	100.5
1 III 2011 (CDJC)	100	100.1	99.9	100	100.2	99.8	100	99.9	100
Luxembourg									
15 II 2001 (CDJC)	99.2	98.9	99.6	...	...	...	...	...	...
1 II 2011 (CDJC)	99.7	99	100.4	...	...	...	...	...	...
Malta - Malte									
26 XI 1995 (CDJC)	101.2	101.2	101.2	101.2	101.2	101.2	125.7	107.6	138.4
27 XI 2005 (CDJC)	101.3	101.9	100.6	101.2	102	100.5	114.3	100	127.3
20 XI 2011 (CDFC)	99.4	100	98.9	99.4	99.9	98.9	100.3	102.3	98.1
Monaco									
21 VI 2000 (CDJC)	100.9	99.9	101.9	...	...	...	...	...	...

3a. Whipple's Index by sex and urban/rural residence, 1985 - 2019
L'indice de Whipple par le sexe et la résidence urbaine/rurale, 1985 - 2019 (continued - suite)

Continent, country or area, date and code[a] Continent, pays ou zone, date et code[a]	Total			Urban - Urbaine			Rural - Rurale		
	Both sexes Les deux sexes	Male Masculin	Female Féminin	Both sexes Les deux sexes	Male Masculin	Female Féminin	Both sexes Les deux sexes	Male Masculin	Female Féminin
EUROPE									
Montenegro - Monténégro									
31 X 2003 (CDJC)	100.2	99.9	100.5	100.2	99.6	100.8	100.2	100.3	100
1 IV 2011 (CDJC)	100	99.7	100.3	99.9	99.3	100.5	100.1	100.2	99.9
Netherlands - Pays-Bas									
1 I 2002 (CDJC)	101.2	101.3	101	101.3	101.5	101.1	101	101.1	101
1 I 2011 (CDJC)	100.2	100.2	100.2	...	...	...	...	...	...
North Macedonia - Macédoine du Nord									
20 VI 1994 (CDJC)	100.2	100.2	100.2	100	100.1	99.8	100.6	100.5	100.8
31 X 2002 (CDJC)	100.3	100.3	100.3	...	...	...	...	...	...
Norway - Norvège									
3 XI 1990 (CDJC)	99.9	99.9	99.9	99.9	99.9	100	99.9	100	99.8
3 XI 2001 (CDJC)[70]	100.1	100.1	100.1	100.1	100.1	100.2	99.7	99.9	99.6
19 XI 2011 (CDJC)[70]	99.8	99.8	99.7	99.7[71]	99.6[71]	99.7[71]	100.1[71]	100.4[71]	99.8[71]
Poland - Pologne									
6 XII 1988 (CDFC)	100.5	100.6	100.4	100.5	100.6	100.4	100.5	100.6	100.5
20 V 2002 (CDJC)[72]	100.7	100.7	100.7	100.9	100.8	100.9	100.4	100.5	100.2
31 III 2011 (CDJC)	100.1	100.1	100.1	100.1	100.1	100.1	100.1	100.1	100
Portugal									
15 IV 1991 (CDFC)	101.4	101.7	101.1	101.4	101.7	101.2	101.3	101.6	101.1
21 III 2011 (CDJC)	100.7	100.8	100.5	100.8	101	100.7	100.4	100.4	100.3
Republic of Moldova - République de Moldova									
12 I 1989 (CDJC)	100.5	100.4	100.5	100.2	99.9	100.4	100.7	100.8	100.6
5 X 2004 (CDFC)[73]	103.2	103.3	103.2	102.9	102.9	102.9	103.5	103.5	103.5
12 V 2014 (CDFC)[74]	100.5	100.3	100.6	100.3	100	100.7	100.5	100.4	100.6
Romania - Roumanie									
7 I 1992 (CDJC)	96.2	96.2	96.2	95.6	95.8	95.4	97.1	96.8	97.4
18 III 2002 (CDJC)	95.8	95.9	95.8	95.3	95.5	95.2	96.5	96.3	96.7
20 X 2011 (CDFC)[4]	96.6	96.6	96.6	96.4	96.5	96.3	96.8	96.7	96.9
Russian Federation - Fédération de Russie									
12 I 1989 (CDJC)	97.8	97.7	97.9	97.7	97.6	97.7	98.3	98.2	98.4
14 X 2010 (CDJC)	103	103	103	103.5	103.5	103.5	101.7	101.6	101.7
Serbia - Serbie[75]									
31 III 2002 (CDJC)	99.9	99.9	100	100.4	100.4	100.5	99.2	99.3	99.2
1 X 2011 (CDJC)	99.4	99.2	99.5	99.7	99.3	100	98.9	99.1	98.7
Slovakia - Slovaquie									
3 III 1991 (CDJC)	100	99.8	100.2	...	...	...	...	...	...
25 V 2001 (CDJC)	99.5	99.5	99.6	99.7	99.6	99.8	99.3	99.3	99.3
21 V 2011 (CDJC)	100.2	100.2	100.3	100.3	100.2	100.4	100.2	100.2	100.1
Slovenia - Slovénie									
31 III 1991 (CDJC)	99	99.1	98.9	99.7	99.7	99.6	98.4	98.6	98.1
31 III 2002 (CDJC)	101.9	102.1	101.8	102.2	102.3	102.2	101.6	101.9	101.3
1 I 2011 (CDJC)	100.6	100.1	101.3	100.7	100.1	101.3	100.6	100	101.3
1 I 2015 (CDJC)	99.3	99.5	99	99.3	99.6	99.1	99.2	99.4	99
Spain - Espagne									
1 III 1991 (CDJC)	102.4	102.4	102.3	...	...	...	...	...	...
1 XI 2001 (CDFC)[76]	99	99	99	99	99	98.9	99.1	99	99.1
1 XI 2011 (CDJC)	98.3	98.6	98.1	...	...	...	...	...	...
Sweden - Suède									
1 XI 1990 (CDJC)	99.7	99.8	99.6	...	...	...	...	...	...
31 XII 2003 (CDJC)	100	100	100.1	...	...	...	...	...	...
31 XII 2011 (CDJC)	99.7	99.8	99.6	...	...	...	...	...	...
Switzerland - Suisse									
4 XII 1990 (CDJC)	100.6	100.9	100.2	100.7	100.9	100.5	100.2	100.7	99.7
5 XII 2000 (CDFC)	99.7	99.9	99.5	99.7	99.9	99.6	99.5	99.9	99.1
31 XII 2011 (CDJC)	99.9	99.9	99.9	99.9	99.9	99.8	100	99.9	100.1
Ukraine									
5 XII 2001 (CDFC)	102.7	102.7	102.7	103.1	103.1	103.2	101.7	101.8	101.5
United Kingdom of Great Britain and Northern Ireland - Royaume-Uni de Grande-Bretagne et d'Irlande du Nord[77]									
21 IV 1991 (CDFC)[78]	98	98	98	...	...	...	...	...	...
29 IV 2001 (CDFC)[79]	98.1	98	98.1	98.2	98.2	98.2	97.6	97.5	97.7
27 III 2011 (CDJC)	100.2	100.3	100.2	100.3	100.3	100.3	99.8	99.8	99.8

3a. Whipple's Index by sex and urban/rural residence, 1985 - 2019
L'indice de Whipple par le sexe et la résidence urbaine/rurale, 1985 - 2019 (continued - suite)

Continent, country or area, date and code[a] / Continent, pays ou zone, date et code[a]	Total			Urban - Urbaine			Rural - Rurale		
	Both sexes Les deux sexes	Male Masculin	Female Féminin	Both sexes Les deux sexes	Male Masculin	Female Féminin	Both sexes Les deux sexes	Male Masculin	Female Féminin
OCEANIA - OCÉANIE									
Australia - Australie									
30 VI 1986 (CDFC)	101.6	101.7	101.5	101.6	101.6	101.5	101.8	102	101.6
6 VIII 1991 (CDFC)	101.7	101.4	102.1	...	...	...	...	...	...
9 VIII 1996 (CDFC)	101.6	101.5	101.7	...	...	...	...	...	...
7 VIII 2001 (CDJC)	101.4	101.3	101.5	101.4	101.3	101.5	101.3	101.4	101.3
8 VIII 2006 (CDJC)[80]	100.2[81]	100.3[81]	100.2[81]	100.2	100.2	100.1	100.4	100.5	100.3
9 VIII 2011 (CDJC)[80]	100.8[81]	100.8[81]	100.7[81]	100.7	100.7	100.7	101.3	101.3	101.3
9 VIII 2016 (CDJC)[80]	101.1[81]	101.1[81]	101[81]	101	101	101	101.8	102	101.6
Cook Islands - Îles Cook									
1 XII 1996 (CDJC)	99.1	97.2	101.1	...	...	...	...	...	...
Fiji - Fidji									
31 VIII 1986 (CDFC)	105.4	105	105.7	...	...	...	...	...	...
25 VIII 1996 (CDFC)	100.2	100.6	99.8	99.8	99.9	99.7	100.6	101.3	99.9
French Polynesia - Polynésie française									
3 IX 1996 (CDFC)	98.6	97.8	99.5	...	...	...	...	...	...
20 VIII 2007 (CDFC)	102.8	103.2	102.4	...	...	...	...	...	...
Guam									
1 IV 1990 (CDJC)	107.1	106.2	108.2	107	105.5	108.7	107.2	106.6	107.8
1 IV 2000 (CDJC)[18]	100.3	100.4	100.3	...	...	...	...	...	...
Kiribati									
10 X 2010 (CDFC)	104.7	103.3	105.9	106	106	106.1	103.3	100.7	105.7
7 XI 2015 (CDFC)	105.8	107.1	104.5	107.5	110.9	104.5	103.9	103.1	104.6
Marshall Islands - Îles Marshall									
13 XI 1988 (CDFC)	101.2	103.3	98.9	...	...	...	...	...	...
1 VI 1999 (CDFC)	104	106.2	101.7	...	...	...	...	...	...
3 IV 2011 (CDFC)	103.7	102	105.3	103.1	102.9	103.3	105.4	99.4	111.9
Micronesia (Federated States of) - Micronésie (États fédérés de)									
1 IV 2010 (CDJC)	102.5	102.3	102.7	...	...	...	...	...	...
New Caledonia - Nouvelle-Calédonie									
4 IV 1989 (CDFC)	99.5	99.4	99.6	...	...	...	...	...	...
New Zealand - Nouvelle-Zélande									
4 III 1986 (CDJC)	100.7	100.6	100.7	100.7	100.7	100.8	100.2	99.9	100.6
5 III 1991 (CDFC)	100.3	100.4	100.3	100.5	100.6	100.4	99.7	99.3	100
5 III 1996 (CDJC)	100	100	100	100.1	100.1	100.1	99.5	99.5	99.5
6 III 2001 (CDJC)[80]	100	99.9	100	100.2	100.1	100.2	99	99	99.1
7 III 2006 (CDFC)[80]	99.7	...	...	...	...	...	...	...	...
7 III 2006 (CDJC)[80]	99.6	99.7	99.6	99.7	99.8	99.7	99.1	99.3	98.9
5 III 2013 (CDJC)[80]	100.3	100	100.5	100.3	100.1	100.5	100.2	100	100.4
Niue - Nioué									
29 IX 1986 (CDFC)	105.8	106	105.6	...	...	...	...	...	...
7 IX 2001 (CDFC)	98.5	93.8	103.4	...	...	...	...	...	...
Northern Mariana Islands - Îles Mariannes septentrionales									
1 IV 1990 (CDFC)	108	108.4	107.4	111.7	111.2	112.1	106.6	107.5	105.3
Palau - Palaos									
15 IV 2000 (CDJC)	103.4	105.5	100.5	...	...	...	...	...	...
Papua New Guinea - Papouasie-Nouvelle-Guinée									
11 VII 1990 (CDFC)	139	140.1	137.7	...	...	...	...	...	...
9 VII 2000 (CDFC)	134	134.2	133.8	131	133.4	128	134.5	134.4	134.7
Pitcairn									
31 XII 1991 (CDFC)	96.2	90.9	100	...	...	...	...	...	...
Samoa									
5 XI 2001 (CDFC)	96.4	95.9	97	...	...	...	...	...	...
7 XI 2011 (CDFC)	97.5	96	99.1	...	...	...	...	...	...
7 XI 2016 (CDFC)	97.5	96.6	98.4	97.5	97.2	97.9	97.5	96.5	98.6
Tokelau - Tokélaou									
18 X 2011 (CDFC)	102.7	104.3	101.2	...	...	...	...	...	...
18 X 2011 (CDJC)[82]	105.7	109.6	102	...	...	...	...	...	...
Tonga									
28 XI 1986 (CDJC)	98.2	99	97.4	...	...	...	...	...	...
30 XI 1996 (CDFC)[83]	100.7	101.7	99.6	...	...	...	...	...	...
30 XI 2006 (CDJC)	98.6	97.8	99.4	95.2	93.3	97.2	99.7	99.3	100.1
30 XI 2016 (CDFC)	99.6	99.7	99.4	96	97.1	95	100.7	100.6	100.9

3a. Whipple's Index by sex and urban/rural residence, 1985 - 2019
L'indice de Whipple par le sexe et la résidence urbaine/rurale, 1985 - 2019 (continued - suite)

Continent, country or area, date and code[a] / Continent, pays ou zone, date et code[a]	Total			Urban - Urbaine			Rural - Rurale		
	Both sexes Les deux sexes	Male Masculin	Female Féminin	Both sexes Les deux sexes	Male Masculin	Female Féminin	Both sexes Les deux sexes	Male Masculin	Female Féminin
OCEANIA - OCÉANIE									
Tuvalu									
1 XI 2002 (CDFC)	98.5	100.8	96.4	...	...	...	...	...	...
Vanuatu									
16 V 1989 (CDJC)	106.9	104.8	109	102.4	98.1	107.8	108.1	106.8	109.3
16 XI 2009 (CDFC)	110.5	111.3	109.7	...	...	...	...	...	...
7 XI 2016 (CDFC)[84]	112.2	112.9	111.6	...	...	...	...	...	...
Wallis and Futuna Islands - Îles Wallis et Futuna									
3 X 1996 (CDFC)	96	97.8	94.3	...	...	...	...	...	...

FOOTNOTES - NOTES

Italics: estimates which are less reliable. - Italiques : estimations moins sûres.

* Provisional. - Données provisoires.

a 'Code' indicates the source of data, as follows:
CDFC - Census, de facto, complete tabulation
CDJC - Census, de jure, complete tabulation

Le 'Code' indique la source des données, comme suit :
CDFC - Recensement, population de fait, tabulation complète
CDJC - Recensement, population de droit, tabulation complète

1 Data refer to population in housing units and collective living quarters only. - Correspond aux personnes qui vivent dans des unités d'habitation et dans des logements collectifs seulement.

2 Data for urban and rural do not add up to the total; reason for discrepancy not ascertained. - La somme des données pour la résidence urbaine et rurale n'est pas égale au total; on ne sait pas comment s'explique la divergence.

3 Urban and rural data were reported in different years and do not add up to the total. - Les données concernant la population urbaine et la population rurale portent sur des années différentes et leur somme ne correspond pas au total cité.

4 Data refer to usual resident population. - Les données se réfèrent à la population résidente habituelle.

5 Excludes collective living quarters. - Exclut les logements collectifs.

6 Excludes the islands of St. Brandon and Agalega. - Non compris les îles St. Brandon et Agalega.

7 Data from the main operation. - Données de l'opération principale.

8 Data refer to Saint Helenian resident population. - Pour la population résidante de Sainte-Hélène.

9 Data refer to total resident population, Saint Helenian and other nationalities. - Les données concernent la population résidente totale, originaire de Sainte-Hélène ou possédant une autre nationalité.

10 Data have been adjusted for underenumeration, estimated at 10.69 per cent. - Les données ont été ajustées pour compenser les lacunes du dénombrement estimées à 10,69 p. 100.

11 Because of rounding, totals are not in all cases the sum of the respective components. - Les chiffres étant arrondis, les totaux ne correspondent pas toujours rigoureusement à la somme des composants respectifs.

12 Excluding the institutional population. - Non compris la population dans les institutions.

13 Bermuda is 100 per cent urban. - 100 pour cent de la population des Bermudes est urbaine.

14 To ensure confidentiality, the values, including totals are randomly rounded either up or down to a multiple of '5' or '10.' As a result, when these data are summed or grouped, the total value may not match the individual values since totals and sub-totals are independently rounded. Similarly, percentages, which are calculated on rounded data, may not necessarily add up to 100%. - À des fins de confidentialité, les chiffres, y compris les totaux, sont aléatoirement arrondis au multiple de 5 ou de 10 inférieur ou supérieur. Par conséquent, lorsque ces chiffres sont additionnés, le total peut ne pas correspondre à la somme des valeurs individuelles, dans la mesure où les totaux et les totaux partiels sont arrondis indépendamment. De même, la somme des pourcentages, qui sont calculés à partir des données arrondies, peut ne pas correspondre à 100 %.

15 Excluding data for Saint Barthélémy and Saint Martin. - Non compris les données pour Saint Barthélémy et Saint Martin.

16 Total represents population in private dwellings, the non-institutional population and persons found on the streets between the hours of 5am and 7am on September 26, 2001; the figures represent the census counts adjusted for under-coverage. - Le total représente la population vivant dans des logements privés et les personnes trouvées dans la rue entre 5 et 7 heures du matin le 26 septembre 2001, mais ne tient pas compte des personnes vivant dans des établissements; les chiffres sont ceux du recensement corrigés pour tenir compte du sous-dénombrement.

17 Including an estimation of 1 334 585 persons corresponding to 448 195 housing units without information of the occupants. - Y compris une estimation de 1 334 585 personnes correspondant aux 448 195 unités d'habitation sans information sur les occupants.

18 Including armed forces stationed in the area. - Y compris les militaires en garnison sur le territoire.

19 Excluding U.S. Armed Forces overseas and civilian U.S. citizens whose usual place of residence is outside the United States. - Non compris les militaires américains à l'étranger et les civils américains dont le lieu de résidence habituel est en dehors des États-Unis.

20 Data include persons in remote areas, military personnel outside the country, merchant seamen at sea, civilian seasonal workers outside the country, and other civilians outside the country, and exclude nomads, foreign military, civilian aliens temporarily in the country, transients on ships and Indian jungle population. - Y compris les personnes vivant dans des régions éloignées, le personel militaire en dehors du pays, les marins marchands, les ouvriers saisonniers en dehors du pays, et autres civils en dehors du pays, et non compris les nomades, les militaires étrangers, les étrangers civils temporairement dans le pays, les transiteurs sur des bateaux et les Indiens de la jungle.

21 Excludes nomadic Indian tribes. - Non compris les tribus d'Indiens nomades.

22 Excluding population in the Carmen Alto district, Huamanga province and Ayacucho department. - À l'exclusion de la population du district de Carmen Alto, de la province de Huamanga et du département d'Ayacucho.

23 Data have not been adjusted for underenumeration and exclude an estimated population of 1,855,501 at the national level. - Les données n'ont pas été ajustées pour compenser les lacunes du dénombrement. Les données excluent un nombre de personnes estimé à 1,855,501 à l'échelle nationale.

24 The districts of Paramaribo and Wanica are considered urban areas, whereas all other districts are considered more or less rural areas. - Les districts de Paramaribo et de Wanica sont considérés comme des zones urbaines, les autres districts étant considérés comme des zones rurales à divers degrés.

25 Unrevised data. Data refer to resident population in Uruguay according to Census Phase 1, carried out between the months of June and July 2004. - Les données n'ont pas été révisées. Les données se rapportent à la population résidente en Uruguay d'après la phase 1 du recensement, qui a eu lieu entre juin et juillet 2004.

26 Excluding Indian jungle population. - Non compris les Indiens de la jungle.

27 For operational purposes, population centers with 2,500 and more inhabitants are considered as urban area and less than 2,500 are considered as rural area. - À des fins opérationnelles, les centres de population comptant 2 500 habitants ou plus sont considérés comme zones urbaines, ceux qui en comptent moins de 2 500 comme zones rurales.

28 Data have not been adjusted for underenumeration, estimated at 4.96 per cent. - Les données n'ont pas été ajustées pour compenser les lacunes du dénombrement, estimées à 4,96 p.100.

29 Excluding 8408 tourists and foreigners. - À l'exclusion de 8 408 touristes et étrangers.

30 Excluding foreign diplomatic personnel and their dependants. - Non compris le personnel diplomatique étranger et les membres de leur famille les accompagnant.

31 For statistical purposes, the data for China do not include those for the Hong Kong Special Administrative Region (Hong Kong SAR), Macao Special Administrative Region (Macao SAR) and Taiwan province of China. Data exclude 2.3 million servicemen, 4.65 million persons with permanent resident status difficult to define, and 0.12 per cent undercount based on the post enumeration survey. - Pour la présentation des statistiques, les données pour la Chine ne comprennent pas la Région Administrative Spéciale de Hong Kong (Hong Kong RAS), la Région Administrative Spéciale de Macao (Macao RAS) et Taïwan province de Chine. Les données ne comprennent pas 2,3 millions de militaires, 4,65 millions de personnes ayant le statut de résident permanent mais difficiles à définir, et des lacunes estimées à 0,12 pour cent sur la base de l'enquête de vérification du recensement.

32 Data refer to Hong Kong resident population at the census moment, which covers usual residents and mobile residents. Usual residents refer to two categories of people: (1) Hong Kong permanent residents who had stayed in Hong Kong for at least three months during the six months before or for at least three months during the six months after the census moment, regardless of whether they were in Hong Kong or not at the census moment; and (2) Hong Kong non-permanent residents who were in Hong Kong at the census moment. Mobile Residents, they are Hong Kong permanent residents who had stayed in Hong Kong for at least one month but less than three months during the six months before or for at least one month but less than three months during the six months after the census moment, regardless of whether they were in Hong Kong or not at the census moment. - Les données se rapportent à la population résidente à Hong Kong au moment du recensement. Cette population est composée des résidants habituels et des résidants mobiles. La population résidente est partagée en deux catégories: (1) les résidents permanents qui ont habité à Hong Kong au moins trois mois pendant les six mois précédents ou les six mois suivants le recensement; (2) les habitants non-permanents de Hong Kong qui étaient à Hong Kong au moment du recensement. La population mobile se rapporte aux résidents permanents de Hong Kong qui ont habité à Hong Kong pendant les six mois après le recensement pour une période comprise entre un mois et trois mois, indépendamment du fait qu'ils étaient à Hong Kong au moment du recensement au pays.

33 Data refer to Hong Kong resident population at the census moment, which covers usual residents and mobile residents. Usual residents refer to two categories of people: (1) Hong Kong permanent residents who had stayed in Hong Kong for at least three months during the six months before or for at least three months during the six months after the census moment, regardless of whether they were in Hong Kong or not at the census moment; and (2) Hong Kong non-permanent residents who were in Hong Kong at the census moment. Mobile Residents, they are Hong Kong permanent residents who had stayed in Hong Kong for at least one month but less than three months during the six months before or for at least one month but less than three months during the six months after the census moment, regardless of whether they were in Hong Kong or not at the census moment. Data are estimates from sample enquiry. - Les données se rapportent à la population résidente à Hong Kong au moment du recensement. Cette population est composée des résidants habituels et des résidants mobiles. La population résidente est partagée en deux catégories: (1) les résidents permanents qui ont habité à Hong Kong au moins trois mois pendant les six mois précédents ou les six mois suivants le recensement; (2) les habitants non-permanents de Hong Kong qui étaient à Hong Kong au moment du recensement. La population mobile se rapporte aux résidents permanents de Hong Kong qui ont habité à Hong Kong pendant les six mois après le recensement pour une période comprise entre un mois et trois mois, indépendamment du fait qu'ils étaient à Hong Kong au moment du recensement au pays. Les données sont des chiffres estimatifs dérivés d'une enquête par sondage.

34 Data refer to government controlled areas. - Les données se rapportent aux zones contrôlées par le Gouvernement.

35 Excluding data for Jammu and Kashmir. - Non compris les données concernant la partie du Jammu et Cachemire.

36 Includes data for the Indian-held part of Jammu and Kashmir, the final status of which has not yet been determined. Excluding Mao-Maram, Paomata and Purul sub-divisions of Senapati district of Manipur. The population of Manipur including the estimated population of the three sub-divisions of Senapati district is 2,291,125 (Males 1,161,173 and females 1,129,952). - Y compris les données pour la partie du Jammu et du Cachemire occupée par l'Inde dont le statut définitif n'a pas encore été déterminé. Non compris les subdivisions Mao-Maram Paomata et Purul du district de Senapati dans l'État du Manipur. Cet État compte 2 291 125 habitants (1 161 173 hommes et 1 129 952 femmes), y compris la population estimative des trois subdivisions du district de Senapati.

37 Includes data for the Indian-held part of Jammu and Kashmir, the final status of which has not yet been determined. - Y compris les données pour la partie du Jammu et du Cachemire occupée par l'Inde dont le statut définitif n'a pas encore été déterminé.

38 Data have not been adjusted for underenumeration. - Les données n'ont pas été ajustées pour compenser les lacunes du dénombrement.

39 Differences between the total country figures and sum of urban and rural areas are due to the inclusion of unsettled population. - Les différences entre les chiffres pour l'ensemble du pays et la somme des zones urbaines et rurales s'expliquent par l'inclusion de la population non sédentaire.

40 Including unsettled population. - Y compris la population non sédentaire.

41 The data is from the census sample. - Données extraites de l'échantillon de recensement.

42 Because of rounding, totals are not in all cases the sum of the respective components. Includes data for East Jerusalem and Israeli residents in certain other territories under occupation by Israeli military forces since June 1967. Data are rounded for confidentiality reasons. - Les chiffres étant arrondis, les totaux ne correspondent pas toujours rigoureusement à la somme des composants respectifs. Y compris les données pour Jérusalem-Est et les résidents israéliens dans certains autres territoires occupés depuis 1967 par les forces armées israéliennes. Chiffres arrondis pour des raisons de confidentialité.

43 Excluding diplomatic personnel outside the country and foreign military and civilian personnel and their dependants stationed in the area. - Non compris le personnel diplomatique hors du pays ni les militaires et agents civils étrangers en poste sur le territoire et les membres de leur famille les accompagnant.

44 Excluding data for Jordanian territory under occupation since June 1967 by Israeli military forces. Including registered Palestinian refugees and Jordanians abroad. - Non compris les données pour le territoire jordanien occupé depuis juin 1967 par les forces armées israéliennes. Y compris les réfugiés palestiniens enregistrés et les Jordaniens à l'étranger.

45 Excluding data for Jordanian territory under occupation since June 1967 by Israeli military forces. - Non compris les données pour le territoire jordanien occupé depuis juin 1967 par les forces armées israéliennes.

46 Unrevised data. - Les données n'ont pas été révisées.

47 Excluding usual residents not in the country at the time of census. - À l'exclusion des résidents habituels qui ne sont pas dans le pays au moment du recensement.

48 Data have been adjusted for underenumeration. - Les données ont été ajustées pour compenser les lacunes du dénombrement.

49 Total population is taken as de facto and de jure together. - Population totale considérée comme de fait et de droit.

50 Data refer to resident population which includes resident Maldivians and resident foreigners. - Les données concernent la population résidente, qui comprend les Maldiviens et les étrangers.

51 Data refer to enumerated population. The total for the whole country excludes 1,206,353 persons estimated not to have been counted in parts of States of Rakhine, Kachin and Kayin. - Les données se rapportent à la population dénombrée. L' effectif de la population pour le pays ne comprend pas les personnes qui ne sont pas dénombrées dans certaines régions des États de Rakhine, Kachin et Kayin estimées à un chiffre de 1 206 353 personnes.

52 Excluding 2739 Filipinos in Philippine Embassies, Consulates and Missions Abroad. - Excepté 2739 Philippins travaillant dans les ambassades, les consulats et les missions des Philippines à l'étranger.

53 Excluding 2134 Filipinos in Philippine Embassies, Consulates and Missions Abroad. - Excepté 2134 Philippins travaillant dans les ambassades, les consulats et les missions des Philippines à l'étranger.

54 Excluding foreigners. - Non compris les étrangers.

55 Data are based on the latest register-based population estimates for 2010. Data refer to resident population which comprises Singapore citizens and permanent residents. - Données basées sur les estimations démographiques les plus récentes fondées sur les registres de 2010. Les données se rapportent à la population résidente composé des citoyens de Singapour et des résidents permanents.

56 The Population and Housing Census 2001 did not cover the whole area of the country due to the security problems; data refer to the 18 districts for which the census was completed only (in three districts it was not possible to conduct the census at all and in four districts it was partially conducted). Unrevised data. - Le recensement de la population et du logement de 2001 n'a pas été réalisé sur la superficie totale du pays à cause de problèmes de sécurité; les données ne concernent que les 18 districts entièrement recensés (3 districts n'ont pas été recensés du tout, et 4 ont été recensés en partie). Les données n'ont pas été révisées.

[57] Data for rural areas include data of estate sectors consisting of all plantations which are 20 acres or more in extent and with ten or more resident labourers. - Les données pour les zones rurales comprennent celles pour les domaines, dont l'ensemble des plantations de plus de 10 hectares comptant au moins 10 travailleurs résidents.
[58] Total population does not include Palestinian population living in those parts of Jerusalem governorate which were annexed by Israel in 1967, amounting to 210 209 persons. Likewise, the results does not include the estimates of not enumerated population based on the findings of the post enumeration study, i.e 83 805 persons. - Les données relatives à la population totale ne comprennent pas la population palestinienne -équivalent à 210 209 personnes - habitant dans les territoires du gouvernorat de Jérusalem qui ont été annexés par Israël en 1967. Egalement, les données ne tiennent pas compte des estimations de la population calculée sur la base des résultats de l'enquête postcensitaire, équivalent à 83 805 personnes.
[59] Data for urban include population in refugee camps. - Les données pour la population urbaine comprennent la population dans les camps réfugiés.
[60] Including Palestinian refugees. - Y compris les réfugiés de Palestine.
[61] All persons falling within the scope of the census were enumerated on a de jure basis, except students who were enumerated on a de facto basis. - Toutes les personnes englobées dans le recensement ont été dénombrées comme population de droit, à l'exception des étudiants qui ont été dénombrés comme population de fait.
[62] Based on a sample taken at the time of census. Because of rounding, totals are not in all cases the sum of the respective components. The figures were calculated by dividing and rounding to thousand. Therefore, "0" may indicate value of less than 500. - D'après un échantillon obtenu au moment du recensement. Les chiffres étant arrondis, les totaux ne correspondent pas toujours rigoureusement à la somme des composants respectifs. Les chiffres ont été calculés en divisant et en arrondissant au millier. Par conséquent, "0" peut indiquer une valeur inférieure à 500.
[63] Statistics are compiled from registers. - Les statistiques sont compilées à partir des registres.
[64] Excluding Faeroe Islands and Greenland shown separately, if available. - Non compris les Iles Féroé et le Groenland, qui font l'objet de rubriques distinctes, si disponible.
[65] Data include Overseas Departments. - Y compris les données des départements d'outre-mer.
[66] Excluding families of military personnel, visitors and transients. - Non compris les familles des militaires, ni les visiteurs et transients.
[67] Excluding military personnel, visitors and transients. - Non compris les militaires, ni les visiteurs et transients.
[68] Including armed forces stationed outside the country and alien armed forces in the area. - Y compris les militaires nationaux hors du pays et les militaires étrangers en garnison sur le territoire.
[69] Age classification is based on the difference between the year of birth and the year of the census, rather than on completed years of age. - La classification par âge est fondée sur la difference entre l'année de naissance et l'année de recensement,et non sur l'âge en années révolues.
[70] Including residents temporarily outside the country. Population statistics are compiled from registers. - Y compris les résidents se trouvant temporairement hors du pays. Les statistiques de la population sont compilées à partir des registres.
[71] The total number may include 'Unknown residence', but the categories urban and rural do not. - Le nombre total peut inclure les personnes dont la résidence n'est pas connue, à l'inverse des catégories de population urbaine et rurale.
[72] Excluding civilian aliens within the country, but including civilian nationals temporarily outside the country. - Non compris les civils étrangers dans le pays, mais y compris les civils nationaux temporairement hors du pays.
[73] Excluding Transnistria and the municipality of Bender. Excluding non-residents present in country at time of census. - Les données ne tiennent pas compte de l'information sur la Transnistria et la municipalité de Bender. Non compris les non-résidents présents dans le pays au moment du recensement.
[74] Excludes non-residents present in country at time of census (visitors, foreigners temporarily residing in country, etc.). Tiraspol, Bender, Slobozia, Ribnita, Camenca Yrigoricpol/Grigoriopol are districts from Transnistria where the census was not conducted. - Exclue les non-résidents présents dans le pays au moment du recensement (visiteurs, étrangers résidant temporairement dans le pays, etc.). Tiraspol, Bender, Slobozia, Ribnita, Camenca, Yrigoricpol/Grigoriopol sont des districts de la Transnistrie où le recensement n'a pas eu lieu.
[75] Excludes data for Kosovo and Metohia. - Sans les données pour le Kosovo et Metohie.
[76] Excluding transients visitors. - Non compris les visiteurs en transit.
[77] Excluding Channel Islands (Guernsey and Jersey) and Isle of Man, shown separately, if available. - Non compris les îles Anglo-Normandes (Guernesey et Jersey) et l'île de Man, qui font l'objet de rubriques distinctes, si disponible.
[78] Counts for the 1991 Census are taken from 'Key Statistics for Urban and Rural Areas: Great Britain 1991' published volume based on the usually resident population. - Les chiffres du recensement de 1991 sont extraits de l'ouvrage « Key Statistics for Urban Areas: Great Britain 1991 » et sont fondés sur la notion de résidence habituelle.
[79] Counts for the 2001 Census are taken from 'Key Statistics table 1 for the Urban/Rural classification: England and Wales' available on CD based on the usually resident population. - Les chiffres du recensement de 2001 proviennent du tableau intitulé « Key Statistics table 1 for the Urban/Rural classification: England and Wales » disponible sur CD-ROM et sont fondés sur la notion de résidence habituelle.
[80] These data have been randomly rounded to protect confidentiality. Individual figures may not add up to totals, and values for the same data may vary in different tables. - Ces données ont été arrondies de façon aléatoire afin d'en préserver la confidentialité. La somme de certains chiffres peut ne pas correspondre aux totaux indiqués et les valeurs des mêmes données peuvent varier d'un tableau à un autre.
[81] Including population in off-shore, migratory and shipping. - Y compris les populations extraterritoriales, les populations nomades et les populations maritimes.
[82] Data includes Tokelaun Public Service employees and their immediate families based in Apia but excludes non-residents present at the time of the census. - Les données comprennent les agents de la fonction publique des Tokélaou et leur famille directe basés à Apia mais excluent les non-résidents présents au moment du recensement.
[83] Data refer to Tongans and part-Tongans only. - Les données ne concernent que la population tongane et partie-Tongans seulement.
[84] Data is based on mini-census taken in 2016. - Selon le mini-recensement de 2016.

Table 4 - *Demographic Yearbook 2019*

Table 4 presents, for each country or area of the world, basic vital statistics for the period 2015 - 2019: live births, crude birth rate, deaths, crude death rate, rate of natural increase, infant deaths, infant mortality rate, life expectancy at birth by sex and total fertility rate.

Description of variables: The vital events and rates shown in this table are defined as follows[1]:

Live birth is the complete expulsion or extraction from its mother of a product of conception, irrespective of the duration of pregnancy, which after such separation breathes or shows any other evidence of life such as beating of the heart, pulsation of the umbilical cord, definite movement of voluntary muscles, whether or not the umbilical cord has been cut or the placenta is attached; each product of such a birth is considered live born.

Death is the permanent disappearance of all evidence of life at any time after live birth has taken place (post-natal cessation of vital functions without capability of resuscitation).

Infant deaths are deaths of live born infants under one year of age.

Life expectancy at birth is defined as the average number of years of life for males and females if they continued to be subject to the same mortality experienced in the year(s) to which these life expectancies refer.

The total fertility rate is the average number of children that would be born alive to a hypothetical cohort of women if, throughout their reproductive years, the age-specific fertility rates remained unchanged. The standard method of calculating the total fertility rate is the sum of the age-specific fertility rates.

Crude birth rates and crude death rates presented in this table are calculated using the number of live births and the number of deaths obtained from civil registers. These civil registration data are used only if they are considered reliable (estimated completeness of 90 per cent or more).

Similarly, infant mortality rates presented in this table are calculated using the number of live births and the number of infant deaths obtained from civil registers. If, however, the registration of births or infant deaths for any given country or area is estimated to be less than 90 per cent complete, the rates are not calculated.

For some countries, the data and rates presented in this table are based on vital statistics data sourced from censuses or demographic surveys.

Rate computation: The crude birth and death rates are the annual number of each of these vital events per 1 000 mid-year population. Infant mortality rate is the annual number of deaths of infants under one year of age per 1 000 live births in the same year.

Rates of natural increase are the difference between the crude birth rate and the crude death rate. It should be noted that the rates of natural increase presented here may differ from the population growth rates presented in table 3 as rates of natural increase do not take net international migration into account while the population growth rates do.

Crude birth rates, crude death rates and infant mortality rates that appear in this table have been calculated by the United Nations Statistics Division, unless otherwise noted. Exceptions include official estimated rates for India, which were based on the sample registration system. Rates calculated by the United Nations Statistics Division presented in this table have been limited to those countries or areas having a minimum number of 30 events (for live births, deaths or infant deaths) in a given year.

Reliability of data: Rates calculated on the basis of registered vital statistics which are considered unreliable (estimated to be less than 90 per cent complete) are not calculated. Estimated rates, prepared by individual countries or areas, are presented whenever applicable.

The designation of vital statistics as being either reliable or unreliable is discussed in general in section 4.2 of the Technical Notes. The technical notes for tables 9, 15 and 18 provide specific information on reliability of statistics on live births, infant deaths, and deaths, respectively.

The values shown for life expectancy in this table come from official life tables. It is assumed that, if necessary, the basic data (population and deaths classified by age and sex) have been adjusted for deficiencies before their use in constructing the life tables.

Limitations: Statistics on births, deaths and infant deaths are subject to the same qualifications as have been set forth for vital statistics, in general, in section 4 of the Technical Notes and in the technical notes for individual tables presenting detailed data on these events (table 9, live births; table 15, infant deaths; table 18, deaths).

In assessing comparability, it is important to take into account the reliability of the data used to calculate the rates, as discussed above.

The problem of obtaining precise correspondence between numerator (births and deaths) and denominator (population for crude birth and death rates) as regards the inclusion or exclusion of armed forces, refugees, displaced persons and other special groups is particularly difficult where vital rates are concerned.

It should also be noted that crude rates are particularly affected by the age-sex structure of the population. Infant mortality rates, and to a much lesser extent crude birth rates and crude death rates, are affected by the variation in the definition of a live birth and tabulation procedures.

NOTES

[1] *Principles and Recommendations for a Vital Statistics System Revision 3,* Sales No. E.13.XVII.10, United Nations, New York, 2014.

Tableau 4 – *Annuaire démographique 2019*

Le tableau 4 présente, pour chaque pays ou zone du monde, des statistiques de base de l'état civil pour les années 2015 – 2019 : les naissances vivantes, le taux brut de natalité, les décès, le taux brut de mortalité et le taux d'accroissement naturel de la population, les décès d'enfants de moins d'un an et le taux de mortalité infantile, l'espérance de vie à la naissance par sexe et l'indice synthétique de fécondité.

Description des variables : les faits d'état civil utilisés aux fins du calcul des taux présentés dans le tableau 4 sont définis comme suit[1] :

La naissance vivante est l'expulsion ou l'extraction complète du corps de la mère, indépendamment de la duré de la gestation, d'un produit de la conception qui après cette séparation, respire ou manifeste tout autre signe de vie, tel que battement de cœur, pulsation du cordon ombilical ou contraction effective d'un muscle soumis à l'action de la volonté, que le cordon ombilical ait été coupé ou non et que le placenta soit ou non demeuré attaché ; tout produit d'une telle naissance est considéré comme « enfant né vivant ».

Le décès est la disparition permanente de tout signe de vie à un moment quelconque postérieur à la naissance vivante (cessation des fonctions vitales après la naissance sans possibilité de réanimation).

Il convient de préciser que les chiffres relatifs aux décès d'enfants de moins d'un an se rapportent aux naissances vivantes.

L'espérance de vie à la naissance est le nombre moyen d'années que vivraient les individus de sexe masculin et de sexe féminin s'ils continuaient d'être soumis aux mêmes conditions de mortalité que celles qui existaient pendant les années auxquelles se rapportent les valeurs indiquées.

L'indice synthétique de fécondité représente le nombre moyen d'enfants que mettrait au monde une cohorte hypothétique de femmes qui seraient soumises, tout au long de leur vie, aux mêmes conditions de fécondité par âge que celles auxquelles sont soumises les femmes, dans chaque groupe d'âge, au cours d'une année ou d'une période donnée. La méthode standard pour calculer l'indice synthétique de fécondité consiste à additionner les taux de fécondité par âge simple.

Les taux bruts de natalité et de mortalité ont été établis sur la base du nombre de naissances vivantes et du nombre de décès inscrits sur les registres de l'état civil. Ces données n'ont été utilisées que lorsqu'elles étaient considérées comme sûres (degré estimatif de complétude égal ou supérieur à 90 p. 100).

De même, les taux de mortalité infantile présentés dans le tableau 4 ont été établis à partir du nombre de naissances vivantes et du nombre de décès d'enfants de moins d'un an inscrits sur les registres de l'état civil. Toutefois, lorsque les données relatives aux naissances ou aux décès d'enfants de moins d'un an pour un pays ou zone quelconque n'étaient pas considérées complètes à 90 p. 100 au moins, les indices n'ont pas été calculés.

Pour quelques pays, les données et les taux présentés dans ce tableau ont été extraites des recensements de la population ou des enquêtes démographiques.

Calcul des taux : les taux bruts de natalité et de mortalité, représentent le nombre annuel de chacun de ces faits d'état civil pour 1 000 habitants au milieu de l'année considérée. Les taux de mortalité infantile correspondent au nombre annuel de décès d'enfants de moins d'un an pour 1 000 naissances vivantes survenues pendant la même année.

Le taux d'accroissement naturel est égal à la différence entre le taux brut de natalité et le taux brut de mortalité. Il y a lieu de noter que les taux d'accroissement naturel indiqués dans le tableau 4 peuvent différer des taux d'accroissement de la population figurant dans le tableau 3, les taux d'accroissement naturel ne tenant pas compte des taux nets de migration internationale, alors que ceux-ci sont inclus dans les taux d'accroissement de la population.

Sauf indication contraire, les taux bruts de natalité et de mortalité, et les taux de mortalité infantile figurant dans le tableau 4, ont été calculés par la Division des statistiques de l'Organisation des Nations Unies. Les exceptions comprennent l'Inde, pour laquelle les taux estimatifs officiels ont été fournis sur la base d'un système d'enregistrement par échantillonnage. Les taux calculés par la Division des statistiques de l'Organisation des Nations Unies qui sont présentés dans le tableau 4 se rapportent aux pays ou zones où l'on a enregistré au moins 30 événements (pour les naissances vivantes, les décès ou pour les décès d'enfants de moins d'un an) au cours d'une année donnée.

Fiabilité des données : les taux n'ont pas été calculés lorsque les statistiques de l'état civil issues de systèmes d'enregistrement d'état civil étaient jugées douteuses (degré estimatif de complétude inférieur à 90 p.100) et des taux estimatifs, calculés par les pays ou zones, ont été présentés lorsqu'ils étaient disponibles.

On trouve à la section 4.2 des Notes techniques des explications générales concernant la façon dont les statistiques de l'état civil ont été classées selon leur degré de fiabilité. Les notes techniques relatives aux tableaux 9, 15 et 18 ont trait respectivement à la fiabilité des statistiques des naissances vivantes, des décès d'enfants de moins d'un an et des décès.

Les valeurs relatives à l'espérance de vie figurant dans le tableau 4 proviennent de tables officielles de mortalité. On présume que les données de base (la population et les décès par sexe et âge) ont été rectifiées d'éventuelles insuffisances avant d'être utilisées pour construire les tables de mortalité.

Insuffisance des données : les statistiques des naissances, décès et décès d'enfants de moins d'un an appellent toutes les réserves qui ont été formulées à propos des statistiques de l'état civil en général à la section 4 des Notes techniques et dans les notes techniques relatives aux différents tableaux présentant des données détaillées sur ces événements [tableau 9 (naissances vivantes), tableau 15 (décès d'enfants de moins d'un an) et tableau 18 (décès)].

Pour évaluer la comparabilité des divers taux, il importe de tenir compte de la fiabilité des données utilisées pour calculer ces taux, comme il a été indiqué précédemment.

Le calcul des taux est particulièrement affecté par la difficulté à obtenir une correspondance parfaite entre le numérateur (naissances et décès) et le dénominateur (population, pour les taux bruts de natalité et de mortalité) en raison de l'inclusion ou non dans la population des forces armées, des réfugiés, des personnes déplacées ou d'autres groupes sociaux.

Il y a lieu de noter que la structure par âge et par sexe de la population influe de façon particulière sur les taux bruts. Le manque d'uniformité dans la définition des naissances vivantes et dans les procédures de mise en tableaux a une incidence sur les taux de mortalité infantile et, à un moindre degré, sur les taux bruts de natalité et les taux bruts de mortalité.

NOTE

[1] *Principles and Recommendations for a Vital Statistics System Revision 3,* Sales No. E.13.XVII.10, United Nations, New York, 2014

4. Vital statistics summary and life expectancy at birth: 2015 - 2019
Aperçu des statistiques de l'état civil et de l'espérance de vie à la naissance : 2015 - 2019

Continent, country or area and year Continent, pays ou zone et année	Live births / Naissances vivantes: Code[a]	Live births: Number / Nombre	Live births: Crude birth rate / Taux brut de natalité	Deaths / Décès: Code[a]	Deaths: Number / Nombre	Deaths: Crude death rate / Taux brut de mortalité	Rate of natural increase / Taux d'accroissement naturel	Infant deaths / Décès d'enfants de moins d'un an: Code[a]	Infant deaths: Number / Nombre	Infant deaths: Rate (per 1000 births) / Taux (par 1000 naissances)	Life expectancy at birth / Espérance de vie à la naissance: Male[b] / Masculin[b]	Life expectancy at birth: Female[b] / Féminin[b]	Total fertility rate / L'indice synthétique de fécondité
AFRICA - AFRIQUE													
Algeria - Algérie													
2015	C	1 040 285[1]	26.0	U	*182 570*[1]	...	...	U	*23 150*[1]	...	76.4[2]	77.8[2]	3.100
2016	C	1 066 823[1]	26.1	U	*180 404*[1]	...	...	U	*22 271*[1]	...	77.1[2]	78.2[2]	3.100
2017	C	1 059 514[1]	25.4	U	*174 168*[1]	...	...	U	*21 416*[1]	...	76.9[2]	78.2[2]	...
2018		...	...		...	...	...	U	*21 846*[1]	...	77.1[2]	78.4[2]	...
2019		...	...		...	...	...	U	*21 030*[1]	...	77.2[2]	78.6[2]	...
Angola													
2018		...	...		...	...	...		...	...	60.6	63.4	...
2019		...	...		...	...	...		...	...	60.8	63.7	...
Botswana													
2015	U	*46 765*[3]	...	U	*13 030*[3]	...	...	U	*1 012*[3]	...	...	...	...
2016	U	*49 984*[3]	...	U	*12 825*[3]	...	...	U	*1 041*[3]	...	64.9[4]	65.9[4]	2.300[4]
2017	C	43 290[3]	19.1	U	*12 386*[3]	...	...	U	*985*[3]	...	...	...	...
2018	C	54 023[3]	23.5	U	*12 609*[3]	...	...	U	*891*[3]	...	...	...	...
Burundi													
2015	+U	*266 820*[5]	...		...	...	...		...	...	...	...	5.700
2016		...	...		...	...	...		...	...	56.3	60.5	5.500[6]
2017		...	...		...	...	...		...	...	56.9	61.3	4.340
Cabo Verde													
2015	+C*	9 740[7]	18.6	C	2 744[8]	5.2	13.3	C	163[8]	16.7	71.5[9]	79.9[9]	2.320[10]
2016	+C*	9 907[7]	18.6	C	2 580[8]	4.9	13.8	C	164[8]	16.6	71.8[9]	80.0[9]	2.310[10]
2017	+C*	9 831[7]	18.3	C	2 497[8]	4.6	13.6	C	167[8]	17.0	72.2[9]	80.2[9]	2.290[10]
2018	+C*	9 231[7]	17.0		...	...	...		...	...	72.6[9]	80.4[9]	2.280[10]
2019		...	...		...	...	...		...	...	...	...	2.260[10]
Cameroon - Cameroun[11]													
2018		...	...		...	...	...		...	...	...	...	4.800
Côte d'Ivoire													
2015	+U	*626 783*	...	+U	*47 065*[12]	...	...		...	...	54.7	57.3	...
2016	+U	*659 247*	...	+U	*45 995*[12]	...	...		...	...	54.9	57.5	...
2017	+U	*619 181*	...	+U	*44 813*[12]	...	...		...	...	55.1	57.7	...
2018	+U	*635 924*	...	+U	*46 385*[12]	...	...		...	...	55.3	57.9	...
2019		...	...		...	...	...		...	...	55.5	58.0	...
Egypt - Égypte													
2015	+C	2 685 276	30.2	C	573 879	6.5	23.7	C	42 050	15.7	...	...	3.500
2016	+C	2 600 173	28.6	C	556 148	6.1	22.5	C	39 301	15.1	70.5	73.3	3.500
2017	+C	2 557 440	26.9	C	547 208	5.7	21.1	C	38 685	15.1	70.8	73.6	...
2018		...	...		...	...	...		...	...	71.2	74.0	...
2019		...	...		...	...	...		...	...	72.7	75.1	...
Eswatini													
2015		...	...		...	...	...		...	...	...	...	3.500
2016	U	*28 556*[13]	...	+U	*5 309*[14]	...	...	+U	*162*[14]	...	...	...	...
2017	U	*26 915*[13]	...	+U	*5 073*[14]	...	...	+U	*123*[14]	...	...	...	3.200
2018	U	*23 174*[13]	...	+U	*5 032*[14]	...	...	+U	*156*[14]	...	44.1[15]	48.1[15]	...
Guinea - Guinée													
2015		...	...		...	...	...		...	...	...	...	5.000[16]
2016		...	...		...	...	...		...	...	...	...	4.800[16]
2017		...	...		...	...	...		...	...	58.4	61.4	4.740[16]
2018		...	...		...	...	...		...	...	...	...	4.800[16]
2019		...	...		...	...	...		...	...	...	...	4.630[16]
Kenya													
2015	+U	*950 224*	...	+U	*200 205*	...	...	+U	*23 123*	...	...	...	3.900[17]
2016	+U	*948 351*	...	+U	*189 930*	...	...	+U	*21 475*	...	...	...	3.900[17]
2017	+U	*923 487*	...	+U	*190 877*	...	...	+U	*19 895*	...	...	...	3.900[17]
2018	+U	*1 138 654*	...	+U	*192 019*	...	...	+U	*20 350*	...	...	...	3.900[17]
2019	+U	*1 178 260*	...	+U	*190 696*	...	...		...	...	...	...	...
Lesotho													
2015	+U	*10 800*[18]	...	+U	*17 929*	...	...	+U	*218*	...	...	...	...
2016	+U	*9 655*	...	+U	*13 768*	...	...	+U	*17*	...	51.7[19]	59.6[19]	...

4. Vital statistics summary and life expectancy at birth: 2015 - 2019
Aperçu des statistiques de l'état civil et de l'espérance de vie à la naissance : 2015 - 2019 (continued - suite)

Continent, country or area and year / Continent, pays ou zone et année	Live births / Naissances vivantes			Deaths / Décès			Rate of natural increase / Taux d'accroissement naturel	Infant deaths / Décès d'enfants de moins d'un an			Life expectancy at birth / Espérance de vie à la naissance		Total fertility rate / L'indice synthétique de fécondité
	Code[a]	Number / Nombre	Crude birth rate / Taux brut de natalité	Code[a]	Number / Nombre	Crude death rate / Taux brut de mortalité		Code[a]	Number / Nombre	Rate (per 1000 births) / Taux (par 1000 naissances)	Male[b] / Masculin[b]	Female[b] / Féminin[b]	
AFRICA - AFRIQUE													
Lesotho													
2017	+U	*9 463*	...	+U	*13 671*	...	...	+U	*158*	...	...	...	...
2018	+U	*7 902*	...	+U	*13 406*	...	...	+U	*150*	...	...	...	...
2019	+U	*7 515*	...	+U	*13 494*	...	...	+U	*180*	...	...	...	...
Madagascar[20]													
2018		...	...		...	...	...		...	...	63.3	65.2	...
Malawi[21]													
2018	I	576 525	32.8	I	110 776	6.3	26.5		...	...	...	...	...
Mali													
2017		...	...		...	...	...		...	...	65.7	68.2	...
Mauritius - Maurice[22]													
2015	+C	12 640	10.0	+C	9 747	7.7	2.3	+C	173	13.7	[III]71.1	77.8	1.362
2016	+C	12 948	10.2	+C	10 174	8.1	2.2	+C	154	11.9	[III]71.2	77.8	1.399
2017	+C	13 385	10.6	+C	10 140	8.0	2.6	+C	164	12.3	[III]71.3	77.9	1.449
2018	+C	12 980	10.3	+C	10 787	8.5	1.7	+C	181	13.9	[III]71.3	77.7	1.407
2019	+C	12 846	10.1	+C	11 174	8.8	1.3	+C	187	14.6	[III]71.1	77.6	1.395
Mayotte													
2015	C	8 997	38.3	C	636	2.7	35.6	C	71	7.9	75.7	77.4	4.880
2016	C	9 496	38.9	C	705	2.9	36.0	C	96	10.1	74.1	76.8	4.950
2017	C	9 762	38.2	C	735	2.9	35.3	C	86	8.8	75.3[23]	75.7[23]	4.910
2018	C	9 590	36.1	C	758	2.9	33.3	C	94	9.8	74.8[23]	76.9[23]	...
Mozambique													
2015		...	...		...	...	...		...	...	51.7	55.9	...
2016		...	...		...	...	...		...	...	52.0	56.2	...
2017		...	...		...	...	...		...	...	51.0[4]	56.5[4]	...
2018	U	*1 086 425*[24]	...		...	...	...		...	...	51.4[4]	56.9[4]	...
2019	U	*1 111 038*[24]	...		...	...	...		...	...	51.7[4]	57.4[4]	...
Niger[25]													
2015	+U	*320 643*	...		...	...	...		...	...	...	...	...
2016	+U	*315 317*	...		...	...	...		...	...	...	...	...
Reunion - Réunion													
2015	C	14 011[26]	16.4	C	4 531	5.3	11.1	C	93	6.6	77.1	83.6	2.460
2016	C	13 742[26]	16.0	C	4 689	5.5	10.5	C	98	7.1	77.5	84.2	2.440
2017	C	13 708[26]	15.9	C	4 673	5.4	10.5	C	87	6.3	78.1	84.5	2.460
2018	C	13 364[26]	15.5	C	5 011	5.8	9.7	C	82	6.1	...	...	...
Rwanda													
2015		...	...		...	...	...		...	...	63.7	67.5	...
2017		...	...		...	...	...		...	...	64.6	68.4	...
Saint Helena ex. dep. - Sainte-Hélène sans dép.													
2015	C	40	8.9	C	55	12.3	-3.4	C	1	...	...	...	...
2016	C	35	7.5	C	45	9.7	-2.1	C	1	...	...	...	...
2017	C	36	7.9	C	58	12.7	-4.8	C	-	...	...	...	...
2018	C	26	...	C	52	11.3	...	C	-	...	[X]74.3[27]	80.4[27]	...
2019	C	31	6.9	C	38	8.5	-1.6		...	...	...	...	...
Sao Tome and Principe - Sao Tomé-et-Principe													
2015	C	5 022	26.5	C	1 226	6.5	20.0		...	...	63.2	69.7	...
2016	C	5 105	26.4	C	1 212	6.3	20.1		...	...	63.6	70.1	...
2017	C	5 190	26.3	C	1 202	6.1	20.2		...	...	64.0	70.5	...
Senegal - Sénégal[4]													
2015		...	...		...	...	...		...	...	64.4	66.8	4.900
2016		...	...		...	...	...		...	...	64.8	67.2	4.700
2017		...	...		...	...	...		...	...	65.3	67.7	4.600
2018		...	...		...	...	...		...	...	65.8	68.1	...
2019		...	...		...	...	...		...	...	66.2	68.5	...
Seychelles													
2015	+C	1 592	17.0	+C	703	7.5	9.5	+C	17	...	70.1	78.7	2.310
2016	+C	1 645	17.4	+C	747	7.9	9.5	+C	22	...	68.7	80.2	2.390
2017	+C	1 651	17.2	+C	748	7.8	9.4	+C	18	...	70.3	78.5	2.410

4. Vital statistics summary and life expectancy at birth: 2015 - 2019
Aperçu des statistiques de l'état civil et de l'espérance de vie à la naissance : 2015 - 2019 (continued - suite)

Continent, country or area and year Continent, pays ou zone et année	Live births Naissances vivantes Code[a]	 Number Nombre	 Crude birth rate Taux brut de natalité	Deaths Décès Code[a]	 Number Nombre	 Crude death rate Taux brut de mortalité	Rate of natural increase Taux d'accroissement naturel	Infant deaths Décès d'enfants de moins d'un an Code[a]	 Number Nombre	 Rate (per 1000 births) Taux (par 1000 naissances)	Life expectancy at birth Espérance de vie à la naissance Male[b] Masculin[b]	 Female[b] Féminin[b]	Total fertility rate L'indice synthétique de fécondité
AFRICA - AFRIQUE													
Seychelles													
2018	+C	1 650	17.1	+C	818	8.5	8.6	+C	31	18.8	68.5	77.4	2.410
2019	+C	1 605	16.4	+C	795	8.1	8.3	+C	27	...	69.7	78.4	2.340
Sierra Leone													
2015	+U	*353 187*	...		...	...	...		...	...	48.3[28]	50.8[28]	...
South Africa - Afrique du Sud													
2015	U	*966 162*	...	U	*473 266*	...	...	U	*24 994*	...	...	...	2.470
2016	C	906 375	16.1	U	*456 612*	...	...	U	*20 649*	...	...	...	2.450
2017	C	913 499	16.0		...	...	...		...	...	...	...	2.420
2018		...	...		...	...	...		...	...	...	...	2.400
Tunisia - Tunisie													
2015	C	222 534	19.9	U	*65 743*	...	...		...	...	74.5	77.8	2.302
2016	C	219 441	19.4	U	*62 601*	...	...		...	...	74.5	78.1	2.314
2017	C	208 000	18.2	U	*68 846*	...	...		...	...	74.5	78.1	2.210
Uganda - Ouganda													
2015		...	...		...	...	...		...	...	...	...	5.800
2016		...	...		...	...	...		...	...	...	...	5.400
2017		...	...		...	...	...		...	...	...	...	5.400
2018		...	...		...	...	...		...	...	...	...	5.400
2019		...	...		...	...	...		...	...	...	...	5.400
United Republic of Tanzania - République Unie de Tanzanie[29]													
2015		...	...		...	...	...		...	...	...	...	5.200
2016		...	...		...	...	...		...	...	...	...	5.200
2017		...	...		...	...	...		...	...	...	...	5.100
2018		...	...		...	...	...		...	...	...	...	5.100
2019		...	...		...	...	...		...	...	...	...	5.000
Zambia - Zambie													
2017	U	*104 816*[30]	...	U	*39 150*[31]	...	...		...	...	...	...	...
AMERICA, NORTH - AMÉRIQUE DU NORD													
Anguilla													
2015	+C	165	11.2	+C	61[32]	4.1	7.1		...	...	...	...	...
2016	+C	135	9.0	+C*	83[32]	5.5	3.4		...	...	...	...	...
2017	+C	145	...		...	...	...		...	...	...	...	...
2019	+C	130	8.3		...	...	...		...	...	...	...	...
Antigua and Barbuda - Antigua-et-Barbuda													
2015	+C	1 159	12.8	+C	527	5.8	7.0	+C	10	...	80.5	75.2	...
2016	+C	1 063	11.5	+C	542	5.9	5.7	+C	13	...	80.1	75.2	...
2017	+C	1 108	11.8	+C	599	6.4	5.4		...	...	74.4	80.5	...
2018	+C	1 015	10.7	+C	581	6.1	4.6		...	...	...	...	...
Aruba													
2015	C	1 244	11.4	C	679	6.2	5.2	+C	6	...	...	...	1.821
2016	C	1 259	11.4	C	781	7.1	4.3	+C	5	...	...	...	1.821
2017	C	1 202	10.8	C	707	6.4	4.5	+C	6	...	...	...	1.746
2018	C	1 028	9.2	C	717	6.4	2.8	+C	9	...	...	...	1.485
2019	C	1 029	9.2	C	665	5.9	3.2	+C	5	...	...	...	1.485
Bahamas													
2015	+U*	*4 253*	...	+C*	2 243	6.1	...	+C*	82	...	...	...	...
2016	+U*	*4 093*	...	+C*	2 288	6.1	...	+C*	70	...	...	...	...
2017	+U*	*4 017*	...	+C*	2 372	6.3	...	+C*	72	...	...	...	...
Belize													
2015	U	*7 459*	...	U	*1 792*	...	...	U	*129*	...	...	...	2.600
2016	U	*7 226*	...	U	*1 805*	...	...	U	*100*	...	...	...	2.195

4. Vital statistics summary and life expectancy at birth: 2015 - 2019
Aperçu des statistiques de l'état civil et de l'espérance de vie à la naissance : 2015 - 2019 (continued - suite)

Continent, country or area and year Continent, pays ou zone et année	Live births Naissances vivantes Co-de[a]	 Number Nombre	 Crude birth rate Taux brut de natalité	Deaths Décès Co-de[a]	 Number Nombre	 Crude death rate Taux brut de mortalité	Rate of natural increase Taux d'accroissement naturel	Infant deaths Décès d'enfants de moins d'un an Co-de[a]	 Number Nombre	 Rate (per 1000 births) Taux (par 1000 naissances)	Life expectancy at birth Espérance de vie à la naissance Male[b] Masculin[b]	 Female[b] Féminin[b]	Total fertility rate L'indice synthétique de fécondité
AMERICA, NORTH - AMÉRIQUE DU NORD													
Belize													
2017	U	*7 252*	...	U	*1 872*	...	...	U	*104*	...	...	...	...
2018	U	*7 775*	...	U	*1 886*	...	...	U	*98*	...	...	...	...
Bermuda - Bermudes													
2015	C	583[33]	9.4	C	478[33]	7.7	1.7	C	2[34]	...	77.3	84.9	1.443
2016	C	591[33]	9.3	C	492[33]	7.7	1.6	C	2[34]	...	77.5	85.1	1.435
2017	C	576[33]	9.0	C	481[33]	7.5	1.5	C	-[34]	...	77.7	85.4	1.400
2018	C	530[33]	8.3	C	533[33]	8.3	0.0	C	1[34]	...	79.5	85.7	1.343[35]
2019		...	...		...	...	...		...	...	79.6	85.8	...
British Virgin Islands - Îles Vierges britanniques													
2015	C	266	9.1	C	136	4.7	4.5	C	4	...	72.9	80.8	...
2016	C	269	...	C	120	...	...	C	4	...	...	...	...
2017	C	248	...	C	155	...	...	C	7	...	...	...	...
Canada													
2015	C	382 392[36]	10.7	C	264 333[36]	7.4	3.3	C	1 737[36]	4.5	[III]79.9	84.0	1.563[36]
2016	C	383 102[36]	10.6	C	267 213[36]	7.4	3.2	C	1 741[36]	4.5	[III]80.0	84.1	1.543[36]
2017	C	376 291[36]	10.3	C	276 689[36]	7.6	2.7	C	1 699[36]	4.5	...	...	1.496[36]
2018	C	372 329[36]	10.0	C	283 706[36]	7.7	2.4	C	1 750[36]	4.7	[III]80.0	84.1	1.499[36]
Cayman Islands - Îles Caïmanes													
2015	C	649	11.0	C	170[37]	2.9	8.1		...	...	...	...	...
2016	C	660	10.8	C	193[37]	3.1	7.6		...	...	...	...	...
2017	C	625	9.9	C	216[37]	3.4	6.5		...	...	...	...	...
2018	C	640	9.9	C	214[37]	3.3	6.6		...	...	...	...	...
2019	C	646	9.5	C	250[37]	3.7	5.8		...	...	...	...	...
Costa Rica													
2015	C	71 819	14.9	C	21 039	4.4	10.5	C	557	7.8	77.4	82.4	1.750
2016	C	70 004	14.3	C	22 603	4.6	9.7	C	555	7.9	...	...	1.700
2017	C	68 816	13.9	C	23 251	4.7	9.2	C	548	8.0	77.6	82.7	1.671
2018	C	68 479	13.7	C	23 786	4.8	8.9	C	573	8.4	77.8	82.9	1.662
2019	C*	64 287	12.7	C*	24 237	4.8	7.9	C*	533	8.3	77.7	82.7	1.557*
Cuba													
2015	C	125 064	11.1	C	99 691	8.9	2.3	C	535	4.3	...	...	1.721
2016	C	116 872	10.4	C	99 388	8.8	1.6	C	497	4.3	...	...	1.626
2017	C	114 971	10.2	C	106 949	9.5	0.7	C	465	4.0	...	...	1.610
2018	C	116 333	10.4	C	106 196	9.5	0.9	C	461	4.0	...	...	1.647
Curaçao													
2015	C	1 877	11.9	C	1 398	8.8	3.0	C	20	...	...	...	1.900
2016	C	1 789	11.2	C	1 482	9.3	1.9	C	20	...	74.9	81.0	1.700
2017	C	1 548	9.7	C	1 420	8.9	0.8	C	16	...	[III]74.7	81.5	1.500
2018	C	1 680	10.5	C	1 399	8.8	1.8	C	14	...	...	...	1.700
2019	C	1 583	10.1	C	1 387	8.8	1.2	C	9	...	...	...	...
Dominica - Dominique													
2015	+C	861	12.1	+C	664	9.3	2.8		...	...	...	...	...
2016	+C	796	11.2	+C	686	9.6	1.5		...	...	...	...	...
2017	+C	647	9.6		...	...	...		...	...	...	...	...
Dominican Republic - République dominicaine													
2015	U	*167 178*	...	U	*41 598*	...	...	U	*937*	...	[VI]70.0	74.8	2.336
2016	U	*158 252*	...	U	*43 843*	...	...	U	*811*	...	...	...	2.310
2017	U	*165 550*	...	U	*42 862*	...	...	U	*685*	...	...	...	2.286
2018	U	*171 249*	...	U	*41 997*	...	...	U	*247*	...	...	...	2.263
2019	U	*167 686*	...	U	*42 811*	...	...	U	*748*	...	...	...	2.241
El Salvador[38]													
2015	C	109 617	17.0		...	...	...		...	...	...	...	...
Greenland - Groenland													
2015	C	854	15.2	C	472	8.4	6.8	C	9	...	...	...	2.112
2016	C	830	14.8	C	487	8.7	6.1	C	6	...	...	...	2.047

4. Vital statistics summary and life expectancy at birth: 2015 - 2019
Aperçu des statistiques de l'état civil et de l'espérance de vie à la naissance : 2015 - 2019 (continued - suite)

Continent, country or area and year Continent, pays ou zone et année	Live births / Naissances vivantes: Code[a]	Live births: Number / Nombre	Live births: Crude birth rate / Taux brut de natalité	Deaths / Décès: Code[a]	Deaths: Number / Nombre	Deaths: Crude death rate / Taux brut de mortalité	Rate of natural increase / Taux d'accroissement naturel	Infant deaths / Décès d'enfants de moins d'un an: Code[a]	Infant deaths: Number / Nombre	Infant deaths: Rate (per 1000 births) / Taux (par 1000 naissances)	Life expectancy at birth / Espérance de vie à la naissance: Male[b] / Masculin[b]	Life expectancy at birth: Female[b] / Féminin[b]	Total fertility rate / L'indice synthétique de fécondité
AMERICA, NORTH - AMÉRIQUE DU NORD													
Greenland - Groenland													
2017	C	853	15.2	C	499	8.9	6.3	C	6	...	...	...	2.096
2018	C	819	14.6	C	487	8.7	5.9	C	6	...	[II]69.4	72.5	1.997
2019	C	849	15.1	C	548	9.7	5.4	C	10	...	[V]68.3	73.0	2.054
Grenada - Grenade													
2015	+C	1 694	15.4	+C	869	7.9	7.5	+C	28	...	...	...	...
2016	+C	1 577	14.2	+C	898	8.1	6.1	+C	31	19.7	...	...	...
2017	+C	1 398	12.5	+C	885	7.9	4.6	+C	34	24.3	...	...	...
Guadeloupe													
2015	C	5 368[26]	13.5	C	3 052[26]	7.7	5.8	C	43[26]	8.0	77.0	84.8	2.180
2016	C	5 276[26]	13.4	C	3 383[26]	8.6	4.8	C	41[26]	7.8	...	...	2.200
2017	C	4 626[26]	11.8	C	3 273[26]	8.3	3.5	C	40[26]	8.6	...	...	1.980
2018	C	4 249[26]	10.1	C	3 258[26]	7.7	2.3	C	32[26]	7.5	...	...	...
Guatemala													
2015	C	391 425	24.2	C	80 876	5.0	19.2	C	8 202	21.0	[VI]67.9	75.0	...
2016	C	390 382	23.6	C	82 565	5.0	18.6	C	8 366	21.4	...	...	...
2017	C	381 664	22.5	C	81 726	4.8	17.7	C	7 626	20.0	...	...	...
2018	C	383 263	22.1	C	83 071	4.8	17.3	C	7 564	19.7	...	...	...
Jamaica - Jamaïque													
2015	C	37 900	13.9	U	*19 249*	...	...		...	...	...	...	...
2016	C	36 160	13.3	U	*19 761*	...	...		...	...	...	...	...
2017	C	34 423	12.6	U	*19 661*	...	...		...	...	...	...	...
2018	C	34 209	12.5	U	*19 762*	...	...		...	...	...	...	...
2019	C	34 632	12.7	U	*18 233*	...	...		...	...	...	...	...
Martinique													
2015	C	3 972[26]	10.5	C	3 058[26]	8.1	2.4		...	...	79.4	84.7	...
2016	C	3 782[26]	10.0	C	3 284[26]	8.7	1.3		...	...	...	...	...
2017	C	3 640[26]	9.8	C	3 217[26]	8.7	1.1	C	40	11.0	...	...	...
Mexico - Mexique													
2015	C	2 096 274[39]	17.3	+C	654 593[40]	5.4	11.9	+C	26 045[40]	12.4	72.3	77.7	...
2016	C	2 028 358[39]	16.5	+C	684 437[40]	5.6	11.0	+C	24 722[40]	12.2	...	...	...
2017	C	2 000 591[39]	16.1	+C	693 848[40]	5.6	10.5	+C	25 180[40]	12.6	...	...	...
2018	C*	2 162 535	17.3	+C	704 803[40]	5.6	11.6	+C	23 142[40]	10.7	72.2	77.9	...
Montserrat													
2015	C	48	9.6	C	49	9.8	-0.2	C	3	...	...	...	...
2016	C	46	9.1	C	43	8.5	0.6	C	-	...	...	...	...
2017	C	55	...	C	39	...	...		...	...	...	...	...
2018	C	45	9.7	C	38	8.2	1.5		...	...	...	...	...
2019	C	47	...	C	59	...	...		...	...	...	...	...
Nicaragua													
2016	+U	*137 772*	...	+U	*23 205*	...	...		...	...	...	...	...
2017	+U	*136 724*	...	+U	*23 826*	...	...		...	...	...	...	...
2018	+U	*136 361*	...	+U	*23 818*	...	...		...	...	...	...	...
Panama													
2015	C	75 901	19.1	C	18 182	4.6	14.5	C	935	12.3	74.8[41]	80.9[41]	2.400
2016	C	75 184	18.6	C	18 882	4.7	13.9	C	1 046	13.9	75.0[41]	81.1[41]	2.400
2017	C	76 166	18.6	C	19 482	4.8	13.8	C	1 063	14.0	75.2[41]	81.2[41]	2.400
2018	C	76 863	18.5	C	19 720	4.7	13.7	C	1 092	14.2	75.3[41]	81.4[41]	2.400
2019	C*	72 256	17.1	C*	18 591	4.4	12.7	C*	1 005	13.9	...	...	...
Puerto Rico - Porto Rico													
2015	C	31 241	9.0	C	28 409	8.2	0.8	C	222	7.1	[III]76.4	84.0	1.339
2016	C	28 344	8.3	C	29 649	8.7	-0.4	C	222	7.8	[III]76.6	84.1	1.246
2017	C	24 395	7.3	C	31 140	9.4	-2.0	C	172	7.1	[III]76.6	84.4	1.105
2018	C	21 492	6.7	C	29 284	9.2	-2.4	C	142	6.6	[III]76.5	84.7	1.038
2019	C	20 409	6.4	C	29 638	9.3	-2.9	C	135	6.6	[III]76.3	84.8	...

4. Vital statistics summary and life expectancy at birth: 2015 - 2019
Aperçu des statistiques de l'état civil et de l'espérance de vie à la naissance : 2015 - 2019 (continued - suite)

Continent, country or area and year Continent, pays ou zone et année	Live births Naissances vivantes Code[a]	 Number Nombre	 Crude birth rate Taux brut de natalité	Deaths Décès Code[a]	 Number Nombre	 Crude death rate Taux brut de mortalité	Rate of natural increase Taux d'accroissement naturel	Infant deaths Décès d'enfants de moins d'un an Code[a]	 Number Nombre	 Rate (per 1000 births) Taux (par 1000 naissances)	Life expectancy at birth Espérance de vie à la naissance Male[b] Masculin[b]	 Female[b] Féminin[b]	Total fertility rate L'indice synthétique de fécondité
AMERICA, NORTH - AMÉRIQUE DU NORD													
Saint Barthélemy - Saint-Barthélemy													
2017	C	72	...	C	40	...	...	C	-	...	...	...	...
Saint Kitts and Nevis - Saint-Kitts-et-Nevis													
2015	+C	632	...		...	...	...		...	...	...	...	...
2016	+C	676	...		...	...	...		...	...	...	...	...
2017	+C	648	...		...	...	...		...	...	...	...	...
2018	+C	593	...		...	...	...		...	...	...	...	...
2019	+C	594	...		...	...	...		...	...	...	...	...
Saint Pierre and Miquelon - Saint Pierre-et-Miquelon													
2017	C	30	4.8	C	65	10.4	-5.6	C	-	...	...	...	...
Saint Vincent and the Grenadines - Saint-Vincent-et-les Grenadines													
2015	C	1 813	16.4	C	885[42]	8.0	8.4	C	26	...	70.6	76.3	2.188
2016	C	1 729	15.7	C	934[42]	8.5	7.2	C	25	...	71.0	75.2	2.102
2017	C	1 539	13.9	C	917[42]	8.3	5.6	C	17	...	71.1	75.1	1.900
Saint-Martin (French part) - Saint-Martin (partie française)													
2017	C	500	14.0	C	152	4.3	9.8	C	5	...	...	...	...
Sint Maarten (Dutch part) - Saint-Martin (partie néerlandaise)													
2015	+C	500	13.1	+C	197	5.2	7.9		...	...	[III]73.8	80.5	...
2016	+C	458	11.6	+C	160	4.1	7.6		...	...	[III]74.0	80.6	...
2017	+C	363	9.0	+C	172	4.2	4.7		...	...	[III]74.0	82.8	...
Trinidad and Tobago - Trinité-et-Tobago													
2015	C*	18 062	13.4	C*	10 651	7.9	5.5	C*	182	10.1	...	...	...
2016	C*	18 142[43]	13.4	C*	11 460	8.5	4.9	C*	223	12.3	...	...	...
2017	C*	16 569[43]	12.2	C*	11 410	8.4	3.8	C*	190	11.5	...	...	...
2018	C*	16 217[43]	11.9	C*	11 564	8.5	3.4	C*	172	10.6	...	...	...
2019	C*	16 058[44]	11.8	C*	11 266[44]	8.3	3.5		...	...	...	...	...
Turks and Caicos Islands - Îles Turques et Caïques													
2015	C	437	11.9	C	97[45]	2.6	9.3	C	1	...	...	...	...
2016	C	518	13.7	C	89[45]	2.3	11.3		...	...	...	...	...
2017	C	555	13.9	C	122[45]	3.1	10.9	C	3	...	...	...	...
2018	C	454	11.0	C	102[45]	2.5	8.5	C*	-	...	...	...	...
2019	C*	487	11.3	C*	126[45]	2.9	8.4		...	...	...	...	...
United States of America - États-Unis d'Amérique													
2015	C	3 978 497	12.4	C	2 712 630	8.5	3.9	C	23 455	5.9	76.3	81.1	1.844
2016	C	3 945 875	12.2	C	2 744 248	8.5	3.7	C	23 161	5.9	76.2	81.1	...
2017	C	3 855 500	11.9	C	2 813 503	8.7	3.2	C	22 341	5.8	76.1	81.1	...
2018	C	3 791 712	11.6		...	...	...	C	21 498	5.7	...	...	...
United States Virgin Islands - Îles Vierges américaines[46]													
2015	C	1 325	12.8	C	673	6.5	6.3	C	4	...	...	...	...
2016	C	1 187	11.0	C	632	5.9	5.2	C	3	...	...	...	...
2017		...	...	C	707	6.6	...	C	10	...	...	...	...
2018	C*	1 197	...		...	...	...		...	...	...	...	...

4. Vital statistics summary and life expectancy at birth: 2015 - 2019
Aperçu des statistiques de l'état civil et de l'espérance de vie à la naissance : 2015 - 2019 (continued - suite)

Continent, country or area and year Continent, pays ou zone et année	Live births Naissances vivantes Code[a]	 Number Nombre	 Crude birth rate Taux brut de natalité	Deaths Décès Code[a]	 Number Nombre	 Crude death rate Taux brut de mortalité	Rate of natural increase Taux d'accroissement naturel	Infant deaths Décès d'enfants de moins d'un an Code[a]	 Number Nombre	 Rate (per 1000 births) Taux (par 1000 naissances)	Life expectancy at birth Espérance de vie à la naissance Male[b] Masculin[b]	 Female[b] Féminin[b]	Total fertility rate L'indice synthétique de fécondité
AMERICA, SOUTH - AMÉRIQUE DU SUD													
Argentina - Argentine													
2015	C	770 040	17.9	C	333 407	7.7	10.1	C	7 445	9.7	73.7[9]	80.3[9]	2.321
2016	C	728 035	16.7	C	352 992	8.1	8.6	C	7 093	9.7	...	...	2.183
2017	C	704 609	16.0	C	341 688	7.8	8.2	C	6 579	9.3	...	...	2.100
2018	C	685 394	15.4	C	336 823	7.6	7.8	C	6 048	8.8	...	...	...
Bolivia (Plurinational State of) - Bolivie (État plurinational de)													
2015	U	*209 154*[47]	...		...	...	...		...	...	[VI]65.0	69.4	...
2016	U	*199 574*[47]	...		...	...	...		...	...	[II]68.6[48]	75.3[48]	...
2017	U	*197 348*[47]	...		...	...	...		...	...	[II]69.1[49]	75.9[49]	...
2018	U*	*178 710*[47]	...		...	...	...		...	...	[II]69.6[50]	76.5[50]	...
2019		...	...		...	...	...		...	...	[II]70.0[51]	77.0[51]	...
Brazil - Brésil													
2015	C	3 058 783	15.0	+C	1 231 400[52]	6.0	8.9	+C	31 238[53]	10.2	71.9	79.1	1.716[54]
2016	C	2 903 933	14.1	+C	1 274 630[52]	6.2	7.9	+C	30 541[53]	10.5	...	...	1.692[54]
2017	C	2 962 815	14.3	+C	1 277 579[52]	6.2	8.1	+C	30 636[53]	10.3	...	...	...
Chile - Chili													
2015	C	244 670	13.6	C	103 327	5.7	7.9	C	1 683	6.9	77.1	82.7	1.790
2016	C	231 749	12.8	C	104 026	5.7	7.0	C	1 629	7.0	76.7	81.8	1.690
2017	C	219 186	11.9	C	106 388	5.8	6.1	C	1 557	7.1	77.4[55]	83.0[55]	1.570
2018	C*	221 724	11.8	C*	106 786	5.7	6.1	C*	1 235	5.6	...	...	...
2019		...	...		...	...	...		...	...	[II]77.7	83.2	...
Colombia - Colombie													
2015	U	*660 999*	...	U	*219 472*	...	...	U	*7 244*	...	[VI]72.1	78.5	2.020[56]
2016	U	*647 521*	...	U	*223 078*	...	...	U	*7 220*	...	...	...	1.997[56]
2017	U	*656 704*	...	U	*227 624*	...	...	U	*7 044*	...	...	...	1.976[56]
2018	U	*649 115*	...	U	*236 932*	...	...	U	*7 329*	...	...	...	1.953[56]
2019	U*	*638 516*	...	U*	*242 609*	...	...	U*	*7 166*	...	...	...	1.928[56]
Ecuador - Équateur[57]													
2015	U	*283 313*	...	U	*65 391*	...	...	U	*3 011*	...	[VI]73.2[9]	78.8[9]	2.542[9]
2016	U	*272 090*	...	U	*68 304*	...	...	U	*3 078*	...	73.7[9]	79.3[9]	2.499[9]
2017	U	*291 397*	...	U	*70 144*	...	...	U	*3 298*	...	73.9[9]	79.5[9]	2.459[9]
2018	U*	*293 139*	...	U*	*71 007*	...	...	U*	*3 350*	...	74.1[9]	79.7[9]	2.421[9]
French Guiana - Guyane française													
2015	C	6 806[26]	26.7	C	834[26]	3.3	23.5		...	...	76.4	82.0	...
2016	C	7 270[26]	27.7	C	901[26]	3.4	24.3		...	...	...	...	...
2017	C	8 057[26]	29.4	C	964[26]	3.5	25.9		...	...	...	...	...
Guyana[58]													
2015	+U	*16 202*[59]	...	+C	4 922	6.6	...		...	...	...	...	...
2016	+U	*14 907*[59]	...	+C	5 109	6.9	...		...	...	...	...	...
2017	+U	*13 608*[59]	...	+U*	*5 637*[59]	...	...		...	...	...	...	...
2018		...	...	+U*	*4 949*[59]	...	...		...	...	...	...	...
2019		...	...	+U*	*5 766*[59]	...	...		...	...	...	...	...
Paraguay													
2015	+U	*132 241*	...	+U	*24 885*	...	...		...	...	...	...	...
2016	+U	*128 117*	...	+U	*27 243*	...	...	+U	*485*	...	...	...	...
2017	+U	*129 903*	...	+U	*26 404*	...	...		...	...	...	...	...
2018	+U	*123 187*	...	+U	*29 139*	...	...	+U	*490*	...	71.4	77.2	...
Peru - Pérou													
2015	+U	*529 029*[60]	...	+U	*96 240*[60]	...	...	+U	*3 852*[60]	...	[VI]71.5	76.8	2.325[61]
2016	+U	*522 269*[60]	...	+U	*97 241*[60]	...	...	+U	*3 756*[60]	...	...	...	2.303[61]
2017	+U	*511 867*[60]	...	+U	*121 024*[60]	...	...	+U	*5 224*[60]	...	...	...	2.281[61]
2018	+U	*511 960*[60]	...	+U	*126 291*[60]	...	...	+U	*5 739*[60]	...	...	...	2.258[61]
2019	+U*	*485 269*[62]	...	+U*	*114 945*[60]	...	...	+U*	*4 758*[60]	...	...	...	2.233[61]

Continent, country or area and year Continent, pays ou zone et année	Live births / Naissances vivantes: Code[a]	Live births: Number / Nombre	Live births: Crude birth rate / Taux brut de natalité	Deaths / Décès: Code[a]	Deaths: Number / Nombre	Deaths: Crude death rate / Taux brut de mortalité	Rate of natural increase / Taux d'accroissement naturel	Infant deaths / Décès d'enfants de moins d'un an: Code[a]	Infant deaths: Number / Nombre	Infant deaths: Rate (per 1000 births) / Taux (par 1000 naissances)	Life expectancy at birth / Espérance de vie à la naissance: Male[b] / Masculin[b]	Life expectancy: Female[b] / Féminin[b]	Total fertility rate / L'indice synthétique de fécondité
AMERICA, SOUTH - AMÉRIQUE DU SUD													
Suriname													
2015	C	10 148	17.9	C	3 663	6.5	11.4	C	149	14.7	[III]70.1	75.3	2.330
2016	C	9 910	17.2	C	3 591	6.2	11.0	C	170	17.2	...	...	2.230
2017	C	9 785	16.8	C	3 508	6.0	10.8	C	199	20.3	...	...	2.119
2018	C	9 809	16.6	C	3 763	6.4	10.2	C	190	19.4	[III]71.0	75.9	2.170
Uruguay													
2015	C	48 926	14.1	C	32 967	9.5	4.6	C	367	7.5	...	...	1.837[4]
2016	C	47 058	13.5	C	34 273	9.8	3.7	C	376	8.0	73.8	80.6	1.825[4]
2017	C	43 036	12.3	C	33 173	9.5	2.8	C	280	6.5	...	...	1.814[4]
2018	C	40 139	11.4	C	34 412	9.8	1.6	C	273	6.8	...	...	1.804[4]
2019		...	...		...	...	...		...	...	...	...	1.794[4]
Venezuela (Bolivarian Republic of) - Venezuela (République bolivarienne du)													
2015	U	*600 875*	...	C	163 712	5.4	...	C	9 276	...	...	...	...
2016	U	*642 644*	...	C	188 725	6.1	...	C	11 783	...	72.3[63]	78.4[63]	...
2017	U	*579 349*	...	C	190 236	6.1	...	C	11 671	...	72.4[63]	78.5[63]	...
2018		...	...		...	...	...		...	...	72.6[63]	78.7[63]	...
ASIA - ASIE													
Afghanistan[64]													
2015		...	...		...	...	...		...	...	...	...	5.300
Armenia - Arménie													
2015	C	41 763	13.9	C	27 878[65]	9.3	4.6	C	370[65]	8.9	[II]71.7	78.2	1.600
2016	C	40 592	13.6	C	28 226[65]	9.4	4.1	C	352[65]	8.7	[II]71.6	78.3	...
2017	C	37 700	12.7	C	27 157[65]	9.1	3.5	C	311[65]	8.2	[II]71.9	78.7	...
2018	C	36 574	12.3	C	25 751[65]	8.7	3.6	C	261[65]	7.1	[II]72.4	79.0	...
2019	C	36 041	12.2	C	26 286[65]	8.9	3.3		...	...	...	...	...
Azerbaijan - Azerbaïdjan													
2015	+C	166 210[65]	17.2	+C	54 697[65]	5.7	11.6	+C	2 033[65]	12.2	72.7	77.6	2.100
2016	+C	159 464[65]	16.3	+C	56 648[65]	5.8	10.5	+C	1 666[65]	10.4	72.8	77.5	2.000
2017	+C	144 041[65]	14.6	+C	57 109[65]	5.8	8.8	+C	1 700[65]	11.8	73.1	77.8	...
2018	+C	138 982[65]	14.0	+C	57 250[65]	5.8	8.2	+C	1 547[65]	11.1	73.3	78.2	...
2019	+C	141 179[65]	14.1	+C	55 916[65]	5.6	8.5		...	...	...	...	...
Bahrain - Bahreïn													
2015	C	20 983[66]	15.3	C	2 787[67]	2.0	13.3	C	156[67]	7.4	[VI]75.8	77.4	2.093
2016	C	20 714[66]	14.5	C	2 858[67]	2.0	12.5	C	109[67]	5.3	...	...	1.984
2017	C	20 581[66]	13.7	C	2 902[67]	1.9	11.8	C	133[67]	6.5	...	...	1.945
2018	C	19 740[66]	13.1	C	3 052[67]	2.0	11.1	C	129[67]	6.5	...	...	1.838
2019	C	20 245[66]	13.6	C	3 016[67]	2.0	11.6		...	...	...	...	...
Bangladesh													
2015	U	*2 987 320*	...	U	*810 390*	...	...	U	*86 632*	...	...	...	2.100
2016	U	*3 006 960*	...	U	*820 080*	...	...	U	*84 195*	...	70.3[68]	72.9[68]	2.100
2017	U	*3 009 950*	...	U	*829 770*	...	...	U	*72 239*	...	70.6	73.5	2.050
2018	U	*3 012 180*	...	U	*823 000*	...	...	U	*66 268*	...	...	...	2.050
2019	U	*3 013 650*	...	U	*815 850*	...	...	U	*63 287*	...	71.1	74.2	2.040
Bhutan - Bhoutan[69]													
2017	|	11 239	15.5	|	4 894	6.7	8.7		...	...	...	...	...
Brunei Darussalam - Brunéi Darussalam													
2015	+C	6 699	16.2	+C	1 547	3.8	12.5	+C	58	8.7	...	...	1.800
2016	+C	6 437	15.4	+C	1 632	3.9	11.5	+C	52	8.1	76.9	78.7	1.800
2017	+C	6 452	15.0	+C	1 696	3.9	11.1	+C	60	9.3	76.3	78.3	1.800
2018	+C	6 199	14.0	+C	1 612	3.6	10.4	+C	56	9.0	76.4	78.5	1.700

4. Vital statistics summary and life expectancy at birth: 2015 - 2019
Aperçu des statistiques de l'état civil et de l'espérance de vie à la naissance : 2015 - 2019 (continued - suite)

Continent, country or area and year Continent, pays ou zone et année	Live births / Naissances vivantes: Co-de[a]	Live births: Number / Nombre	Live births: Crude birth rate / Taux brut de natalité	Deaths / Décès: Co-de[a]	Deaths: Number / Nombre	Deaths: Crude death rate / Taux brut de mortalité	Rate of natural increase / Taux d'accroissement naturel	Infant deaths / Décès d'enfants de moins d'un an: Co-de[a]	Infant deaths: Number / Nombre	Infant deaths: Rate (per 1000 births) / Taux (par 1000 naissances)	Life expectancy at birth / Espérance de vie à la naissance: Male[b] / Masculin[b]	Life expectancy: Female[b] / Féminin[b]	Total fertility rate / L'indice synthétique de fécondité
ASIA - ASIE													
China - Chine[70]													
2015	I	16 550 000	12.1	I	9 750 000	7.1	5.0		...	...	...	...	...
2016	I	17 860 000	13.0	I	9 770 000	7.1	5.9		...	...	...	...	...
2017	I	17 230 000	12.4	I	9 860 000	7.1	5.3		...	...	...	...	...
2018	I	15 230 000	10.9	I	9 930 000	7.1	3.8		...	...	...	...	...
2019	I	14 650 000	10.5	I	9 980 000	7.1	3.3		...	...	...	...	...
China, Hong Kong SAR - Chine, Hong Kong RAS													
2015	C	59 878	8.2	C	46 108	6.3	1.9	C	85	1.4	81.4	87.3	1.196[71]
2016	C	60 856	8.3	C	46 905	6.4	1.9	C	109	1.8	81.3	87.3	1.205[71]
2017	C	56 548	7.7	C	46 829	6.3	1.3	C	97	1.7	81.9	87.6	1.125[71]
2018	C	53 716	7.2	C	47 400	6.4	0.8	C	80	1.5	82.3	87.7	1.072[71]
2019	C	52 856	7.0	C	48 957	6.5	0.5	C	78	1.5	82.2	88.1	1.051[71]
China, Macao SAR - Chine, Macao RAS													
2015	C	7 055	11.0	C	2 002	3.1	7.9	C	11	...	[IV]79.9	86.3	1.142
2016	C	7 146	11.0	C	2 248	3.4	7.5	C	12	...	[IV]80.2	86.4	1.138
2017	C	6 529	10.1	C	2 120	3.3	6.8	C	15	...	[IV]80.3	86.4	1.019
2018	C	5 925	9.0	C	2 069	3.1	5.9	C	20	...	[IV]80.6	86.6	0.924
2019	C	5 979	8.9	C	2 282	3.4	5.5	C	9	...	[IV]80.8	86.7	0.932
Cyprus - Chypre[72]													
2015	C	9 170	10.8	C	5 859[73]	6.9	3.9	C	25	...	79.8	83.5	1.320
2016	C	9 455	11.1	C	5 471[73]	6.4	4.7	C	25	...	80.3	84.7	...
2017	C	9 229	10.7	C	5 996[73]	7.0	3.8		...	...	80.0	84.1	...
2018	C	9 329	10.7	C	5 768[73]	6.6	4.1	C	22	...	...	...	...
2019	C*	9 625	11.0	C*	6 020[73]	6.9	4.1		...	...	...	...	...
Georgia - Géorgie													
2015	C	59 249	15.9	C	49 121[65]	13.2	2.7	C	507[65]	8.6	68.6	77.2	2.300
2016	C	56 569	15.2	C	50 771[65]	13.7	1.6	C	507[65]	9.0	68.2	77.1	2.200
2017	C	53 293	14.3	C	47 822[65]	12.8	1.5	C	512[65]	9.6	...	...	...
2018	C	51 138	13.7	C	46 524[65]	12.5	1.2	C	416[65]	8.1	...	...	...
2019	C	48 296	13.0	C	46 659[65]	12.5	0.4		...	...	...	...	...
India - Inde[74]													
2015	I	...	20.8[75]	I	...	6.5[75]	...	I	...	37.0[75]	...	...	2.300
2016	I	...	20.4[75]	I	...	6.4[75]	...	I	...	34.0[75]	[V]67.4[76]	70.2[76]	2.300[76]
2017	I	...	20.2[75]	I	...	6.3[75]	...	I	...	33.0[75]	...	...	2.200[76]
2018	I	...	20.0[75]	I	...	6.2[75]	...	I	...	32.0[75]	[V]68.2[76]	70.7[76]	2.200[76]
Indonesia - Indonésie													
2015		...	...		...	...	...		...	...	...	...	2.170[77]
2016		...	...		...	...	...		...	...	...	...	2.156[77]
2017		...	...		...	...	...		...	...	...	...	2.142[77]
2018		...	...		...	...	...		...	...	69.3	73.2	2.128[77]
2019		...	...		...	...	...		...	...	71.3[77]	75.1[77]	2.114[77]
Iran (Islamic Republic of) - Iran (République islamique d')													
2015	+C	1 570 219[78]	19.9	+C	374 827[78]	4.8	15.2		...	...	...	...	...
2016	+C	1 528 053[78]	19.1	+C	369 751[78]	4.6	14.5	+C	8 261[78]	5.4	72.5[78]	75.5[78]	2.113
2017	+C	1 487 913[78]	18.4	+C	376 678[78]	4.6	13.7	+C	8 304[78]	5.6	...	...	...
2018	+C	1 366 519[78]	16.6	+C	377 193[78]	4.6	12.1	+C	7 530[78]	5.5	...	...	...
2019		...	...	+C*	395 392[78]	4.8	...		...	...	...	...	...
Iraq													
2016	U	*777 823*	...	U	*140 111*	...	...		...	...	...	...	4.020
2017	U	*803 010*	...	U	*142 766*	...	...	U	*18 611*	...	...	...	3.960
2018		...	...		...	...	...		...	...	71.7	75.6	3.600[79]
Israel - Israël[80]													
2015	C	178 723	21.3	C	44 507[81]	5.3	16.0	C	563[81]	3.2	80.1	84.1	3.093
2016	C	181 405	21.2	C	44 244[81]	5.2	16.0	C	570[81]	3.1	80.7	84.2	3.108

4. Vital statistics summary and life expectancy at birth: 2015 - 2019
Aperçu des statistiques de l'état civil et de l'espérance de vie à la naissance : 2015 - 2019 (continued - suite)

Continent, country or area and year Continent, pays ou zone et année	Live births Naissances vivantes			Deaths Décès			Rate of natural increase Taux d'accrois-sement naturel	Infant deaths Décès d'enfants de moins d'un an			Life expectancy at birth Espérance de vie à la naissance		Total fertility rate L'indice synthétique de fécondité
	Co-de[a]	Number Nombre	Crude birth rate Taux brut de natalité	Co-de[a]	Number Nombre	Crude death rate Taux brut de mortalité		Co-de[a]	Number Nombre	Rate (per 1000 births) Taux (par 1000 naiss-ances)	Male[b] Masculin[b]	Female[b] Féminin[b]	
ASIA - ASIE													
Israel - Israël[80]													
2017	C	183 648	21.1	C	44 923[81]	5.2	15.9	C	564[81]	3.1	80.6	84.6	3.112
2018	C	184 370	20.8	C	44 802[81]	5.0	15.7	C	550[81]	3.0	80.9	84.8	3.088
2019	C*	181 709	20.1	C	45 961[81]	5.1	15.0	C	534[81]	2.9	...	...	...
Japan - Japon[82]													
2015	C	1 005 677[83]	7.9	C	1 290 444[83]	10.1	-2.2	C	1 916[83]	1.9	80.8	87.1	1.451[84]
2016	C	976 978[83]	7.7	C	1 307 748[83]	10.3	-2.6	C	1 928[83]	2.0	81.0	87.1	1.442[84]
2017	C	946 065[83]	7.5	C	1 340 397[83]	10.6	-3.1	C	1 761[83]	1.9	81.1	87.3	1.428[84]
2018	C	918 400[83]	7.3	C	1 362 470[83]	10.8	-3.5	C	1 748[83]	1.9	81.3	87.3	1.416[84]
2019	C*	865 234	6.9	C*	1 381 098	10.9	-4.1		...	...	...	...	...
Jordan - Jordanie[85]													
2015	C	198 018	20.7	U	*26 640*	...	...		...	...	...	...	...
2016	C	197 789	20.2	U	*27 608*	...	...		...	...	72.8	74.2	3.380
2017	C	211 441	21.0	U	*27 516*	...	...		...	...	72.4	74.6	...
Kazakhstan													
2015	C	398 458	22.7	U	*130 811*	...	...	C	3 751	9.4	67.5	76.3	2.739
2016	C	400 694	22.5	U	*131 231*	...	...	C	3 438	8.6	68.0	76.6	2.775
2017	C	390 262	21.6	U	*129 009*	...	...	C	3 109	8.0	68.7	76.9	2.732
2018	C	397 799	21.8	U	*130 448*	...	...	C	3 184	8.0	68.9	77.2	2.837
2019	C	402 310	21.7	U	*133 128*	...	...	C	3 360	8.4	68.8	77.3	2.905
Kuwait - Koweït													
2015	C	59 271	14.9	C	6 481	1.6	13.3	C	456	7.7	79.1	80.0	...
2016	C	58 797	14.4	C	6 338	1.6	12.9	C	448	7.6	81.0	80.5	...
2017	C	59 172	14.7	C	6 679	1.7	13.1	C	413	7.0	79.7	82.7	...
2018	C	56 121	13.6	C	6 807	1.7	12.0	C	417	7.4	80.1	83.3	...
Kyrgyzstan - Kirghizstan													
2015	C	163 452	27.4	C	34 808	5.8	21.6	C	2 945	18.0	66.8	74.8	3.189
2016	C	158 160	26.0	C	33 475	5.5	20.5	C	2 621	16.6	67.0	75.1	3.059
2017	C	153 620	24.8	C	33 166	5.4	19.4	C	2 401	15.6	67.2	75.4	2.953
2018	C	171 149	27.1	C	32 989	5.2	21.8	C	2 535	14.8	67.4	75.6	3.284
Lao People's Democratic Republic - République démocratique populaire lao													
2015	|	125 614[86]	18.8	|	27 083[86]	4.1	14.8	|	3 164[86]	25.2	61.8[87]	65.2[87]	3.200
2016		...	...		...	...	...		...	...	63.0[87]	67.0[87]	...
2017		...	...		...	...	...		...	...	64.0[87]	67.0[87]	...
2018		...	...		...	...	...		...	...	64.0[87]	68.0[87]	...
Malaysia - Malaisie													
2015	C	521 136	16.7	C	155 786	5.0	11.7	C	3 582	6.9	...	...	2.002
2016	C	508 203	16.1	C	162 201	5.1	10.9	C	3 390	6.7	72.6	77.2	1.918
2017	C	508 685	15.9	C	168 168	5.3	10.6	C	3 496	6.9	72.7	77.4	1.890
2018	C	501 945	15.5	C	172 031	5.3	10.2	C	3 622	7.2	72.7	77.6	1.841
2019		...	...		...	...	...		...	...	72.2	77.3	...
Maldives													
2015	C	6 986[88]	20.3	C	1 130[88]	3.3	17.0	C	63[88]	9.0	73.1	74.6	...
2016	C	6 756[88]	19.3	C	1 226[88]	3.5	15.8	C	53[88]	7.8	73.0	74.7	...
2017	C	6 723[88]	18.8	C	1 241[88]	3.5	15.4	C	64[88]	9.5	...	...	...
Mongolia - Mongolie													
2015	+C	82 130	27.1	+C	17 620	5.8	21.3	+C	1 234	15.0	[x]65.3	74.8	3.100
2016	+C	79 920	25.9	+C	17 763	5.8	20.1	+C	1 315	16.5	...	...	3.000
2017	+C	75 321	23.9	+C	17 357	5.5	18.4	+C	1 009	13.4	65.9	75.4	2.800
2018	+C	78 444	24.5	+C	17 864	5.6	18.9	+C	1 037	13.2	66.1	75.8	2.900
2019	+C	79 580	24.4	+C	18 403	5.6	18.7	+C	1 041	13.1	66.4	76.0	3.000
Myanmar													
2015	+U	*739 152*[89]	...	+U	*225 526*[89]	...	...	+U	*9 849*[89]	...	59.7[90]	69.3[90]	2.483
2016	+U	*765 844*[89]	...	+U	*213 187*[89]	...	...	+U	*9 476*[89]	...	60.3[90]	69.8[90]	2.459
2017	+U	*787 172*[89]	...	+U	*231 210*[89]	...	...	+U	*9 761*[89]	...	60.8[90]	70.2[90]	2.440

4. Vital statistics summary and life expectancy at birth: 2015 - 2019
Aperçu des statistiques de l'état civil et de l'espérance de vie à la naissance : 2015 - 2019 (continued - suite)

Continent, country or area and year Continent, pays ou zone et année	Live births Naissances vivantes Code[a]	 Number Nombre	 Crude birth rate Taux brut de natalité	Deaths Décès Code[a]	 Number Nombre	 Crude death rate Taux brut de mortalité	Rate of natural increase Taux d'accroissement naturel	Infant deaths Décès d'enfants de moins d'un an Code[a]	 Number Nombre	 Rate (per 1000 births) Taux (par 1000 naissances)	Life expectancy at birth Espérance de vie à la naissance Male[b] Masculin[b]	 Female[b] Féminin[b]	Total fertility rate L'indice synthétique de fécondité
ASIA - ASIE													
Oman													
2015	U	*86 286*[91]	...	U	*8 167*[91]	...	...	U	*818*[91]	...	74.2[92]	78.8[92]	2.900
2016	U	*88 346*[91]	...	U	*8 196*[91]	...	...	U	*816*[91]	...	...	...	2.900
2017	C	90 371	19.8	U	*8 861*	...	...	C	850	9.4	74.8[92]	79.2[92]	2.896
2018	C	89 071	19.4	U	*8 979*	...	...	C	762	8.6	75.0[92]	79.1[92]	2.858
2019	C	86 819	18.8	U	*8 581*	...	...	C	686	7.9	75.2[92]	79.2[92]	2.700
Pakistan													
2018		...	...		...	...	...		...	...	...	...	3.600[93]
2019		...	...		...	...	...		...	...	...	...	3.700[94]
Philippines													
2015	C	1 744 767	17.3	C	560 605	5.6	11.7	C	20 750	11.9	...	...	...
2016	C	1 731 289	16.9	C	582 183	5.7	11.2	C	21 874	12.6	...	...	...
2017	C	1 700 618	16.3	C	579 237	5.6	10.8	C	20 311	11.9	...	...	...
2018	C	1 668 120	15.8	C	590 709	5.6	10.2	C	21 019	12.6	...	...	1.977[95]
Qatar													
2015	C	26 622	10.9	C	2 317	1.0	10.0	C	197	7.4	77.5	82.1	2.000
2016	C	26 816	10.2	C	2 347	0.9	9.3	C	161	6.0	78.9	82.3	1.850
2017	C	27 906	10.2	C	2 294	0.8	9.4	C	151	5.4	79.0	82.5	1.833
2018	C	28 069	10.2	C	2 385	0.9	9.3	C	172	6.1	79.1	82.4	...
2019	C	28 412	10.2	C	2 200	0.8	9.4		...	...	...	...	...
Republic of Korea - République de Corée													
2015	C	438 420[96]	8.6	C	275 895[97]	5.4	3.2	C	1 190[97]	2.7	79.0	85.2	1.239[97]
2016	C	406 243[96]	7.9	C	280 827[97]	5.5	2.5	C	1 154[97]	2.8	79.3	85.4	1.172[97]
2017	C	357 771[96]	7.0	C	285 534[97]	5.6	1.4	C	1 000[97]	2.8	79.7	85.7	1.052[97]
2018	C	326 822[96]	6.4	C	298 820[97]	5.8	0.5	C	931[97]	2.8	79.7	85.7	0.977[97]
Saudi Arabia - Arabie saoudite													
2015	I	449 149[98]	14.5	I	69 206[99]	2.2	12.2		...	...	73.1[9]	75.7[9]	2.690[9]
2016	I	447 040[98]	14.1	I	58 097[99]	1.8	12.2	I	5 084[98]	11.4	73.5[100]	74.8[100]	2.360[98]
2017	I	488 130[101]	15.0	I	58 915[98]	1.8	13.2	I	6 608[101]	13.5	...	...	2.000[102]
2018		...	...		...	...	...		...	...	73.7[100]	76.4[100]	1.900[102]
Singapore - Singapour													
2015	C	42 185	10.8	+C	19 862	5.1	5.7	+C	84	2.0	80.5[103]	85.1[103]	1.240[104]
2016	C	41 251	10.5	+C	20 017	5.1	5.4	+C	101	2.4	80.7[103]	85.1[103]	1.200[104]
2017	C	39 615	10.0	+C	20 905	5.3	4.7	+C	94	2.4	80.9[103]	85.4[103]	1.160[104]
2018	C	39 039	9.8	+C	21 282	5.3	4.4	+C	88	2.3	81.2[103]	85.5[103]	1.140[104]
2019	C	39 279	9.8	+C	21 446	5.3	4.4	+C	75	1.9	81.4[105]	85.7[105]	1.140[104]
Sri Lanka													
2015	+C	336 097	16.0	+C*	131 614	6.3	9.8	+C*	2 845	8.5	...	...	...
2016	+C*	331 073	15.6	+C*	130 765	6.2	9.4		...	...	...	...	...
2017	+C*	326 052	15.2	+C*	139 822	6.5	8.7		...	...	...	...	...
2018	+C*	328 112	15.1	+C*	139 498	6.4	8.7		...	...	...	...	...
2019	+C*	319 010	14.6	+C*	146 053	6.7	7.9		...	...	...	...	...
State of Palestine - État de Palestine													
2015	U	*133 185*[106]	...	U	*12 075*[106]	...	...	U	*871*[106]	...	72.0	75.0	...
2016	U	*138 238*[106]	...	U	*12 202*[106]	...	...	U	*880*[106]	...	72.1	75.2	...
2017	U	*140 441*[106]	...	U	*11 778*[106]	...	...	U	*821*[106]	...	72.8	75.1	...
2018	U	*141 407*[106]	...	U	*12 296*[106]	...	...	U	*897*[106]	...	72.9	75.2	...
Tajikistan - Tadjikistan													
2015	U	*237 541*[107]	...	U	*33 563*[65]	...	...	U	*3 082*[65]	...	...	...	3.064
2016	U	*230 044*[107]	...	U	*34 134*[65]	...	...	U	*2 725*[65]	...	71.9	75.7	2.930
2017	U	*224 057*[107]	...	U	*32 027*[65]	...	...	U	*2 405*[65]	...	73.0	76.9	2.830
2018	U	*231 020*[107]	...	U	*32 699*[65]	...	...		...	...	...	...	...
Thailand - Thaïlande													
2015	+U	*738 930*	...	+U	*445 964*[108]	...	...	+U	*4 221*[108]	...	71.6	78.4	...
2016	+U	*666 207*[108]	...	+U	*469 085*[108]	...	...	+U	*4 233*[108]	...	71.8	78.6	...

4. Vital statistics summary and life expectancy at birth: 2015 - 2019
Aperçu des statistiques de l'état civil et de l'espérance de vie à la naissance : 2015 - 2019 (continued - suite)

Continent, country or area and year / Continent, pays ou zone et année	Live births / Naissances vivantes: Co-de[a]	Live births: Number / Nombre	Crude birth rate / Taux brut de natalité	Deaths / Décès: Co-de[a]	Deaths: Number / Nombre	Crude death rate / Taux brut de mortalité	Rate of natural increase / Taux d'accroissement naturel	Infant deaths / Décès d'enfants de moins d'un an: Co-de[a]	Infant deaths: Number / Nombre	Rate (per 1000 births) / Taux (par 1000 naissances)	Life expectancy at birth / Espérance de vie à la naissance: Male[b] / Masculin[b]	Female[b] / Féminin[b]	Total fertility rate / L'indice synthétique de fécondité
ASIA - ASIE													
Thailand - Thaïlande													
2017	+U	*656 570*[108]	...	+U	*458 010*[108]	...	...	+U	*3 861*[108]	...	72.0	78.8	...
2018	+U	*628 450*[108]	...	+U	*461 818*[108]	...	...	+U	*3 800*[108]	...	72.2	78.9	...
2019	+U*	*596 736*	...	+U*	*494 339*	...	...		...	...	73.0	80.1	...
Timor-Leste													
2015	I	36 202[109]	30.2	I	9 209[109]	7.7	22.5		...	...	...	...	4.290[4]
2016		...	...		...	...	...		...	...	...	...	4.090[4]
2017		...	...		...	...	...		...	...	...	...	3.900[4]
2018		...	...		...	...	...		...	...	66.3[4]	68.8[4]	3.703[4]
Turkey - Turquie													
2015	C	1 335 564	17.0	C	405 528[110]	5.2	11.8	C	13 677[110]	10.2	[III]75.3	80.7	2.151
2016	C	1 313 615	16.5	C	422 827[110]	5.3	11.2	C	12 915[110]	9.8	[III]75.3	80.7	2.105
2017	C	1 295 784	16.1	C	426 504[110]	5.3	10.8	C	12 118[110]	9.4	[III]75.3	80.8	...
2018	C	1 248 847	15.4	C	426 106[110]	5.2	10.1	C	11 629[110]	9.3	[III]75.6	81.0	...
2019	C*	1 183 652	14.4	C*	435 941[110]	5.3	9.1		...	...	...	...	...
United Arab Emirates - Émirats arabes unis													
2015	...	*97 328*[111]	...	...	*8 755*[111]	...	...	...	*640*[111]	...	...	...	...
2016	...	*98 299*[111]	...	...	*8 988*[111]	...	...	...	*597*[111]	...	...	...	...
2017	C	97 738	10.5	C	8 826	0.9	9.6	C	607	6.2	...	...	...
2018	C	95 309	10.2	C	8 794	0.9	9.2	C	500	5.2	78.4	81.8	...
Uzbekistan - Ouzbékistan													
2015	+C	734 141	23.5	+C	152 035[65]	4.9	18.6	+C	8 320[65]	11.3	71.2	76.0	2.491
2016	+C	726 170	22.8	+C	154 791[65]	4.9	17.9	+C	7 764[65]	10.7	71.4	76.2	2.455
2017	+C	715 519	22.1	+C	160 723[65]	5.0	17.1	+C	8 235[65]	11.5	71.3	76.1	2.419
2018	+C	768 520	23.3	+C	154 913[65]	4.7	18.6	+C	7 557[65]	9.8	72.3	77.0	2.604
2019	+C	814 960	24.5	+C	154 570[65]	4.6	19.9		...	...	72.8	77.4	...
Viet Nam													
2015		...	...		...	...	...		...	...	70.7	76.1	2.100
2016		...	...		...	...	...		...	...	70.8	76.1	2.090
2017		...	...		...	...	...		...	...	...	...	2.041
2018		...	...	C	569 338	6.0	...		...	...	70.9	76.2	2.050
2019		...	...	C	556 015	5.8	...		...	...	71.0[19]	76.3[19]	2.090[19]
Yemen - Yémen													
2016	U	*575 556*[112]	...	U	*25 927*[113]	...	...		...	...	...	...	...
2017	U	*645 833*[112]	...	U	*31 999*[113]	...	...		...	...	...	...	...
EUROPE													
Åland Islands - Îles d'Åland													
2015	C	275	9.5	C	285	9.8	-0.3	C	-	...	80.6	84.0	1.689
2016	C	293	10.1	C	297	10.2	-0.1	C	1	...	78.5	83.6	1.792
2017	C	279	9.5	C	235	8.0	1.5	C	-	...	81.2	85.9	1.684
2018	C	280	9.4	C	272	9.2	0.3	C	-	...	80.9	85.0	1.636
2019	C*	266	8.9	C*	265	8.9	0.0		...	...	...	...	...
Albania - Albanie													
2015	C	32 715	11.4	C	22 418	7.8	3.6	C	233	7.1	...	...	...
2016	C	31 733	11.0	C	21 388	7.4	3.6	C	277	8.7	77.0	80.1	...
2017	C	30 869	10.7	C	22 232	7.7	3.0	C	248	8.0	77.1	80.0	...
2018	C	28 934	10.1	C	21 804	7.6	2.5	C	257	8.9	77.4	80.5	...
2019	C	28 561	10.0	C	21 937	7.7	2.3		...	...	...	...	...
Andorra - Andorre													
2015	C	659	9.3	C	282	4.0	5.3	C	-	...	...	...	...
2016	C	634	8.8	C	310	4.3	4.5		...	...	...	...	...
2017	C	588	8.0	C	323	4.4	3.6		...	...	...	...	...
2018	C	543	7.3	C	335	4.5	2.8	C	1	...	...	...	...
2019	C	539	7.1	C	301	4.0	3.1		...	...	...	...	...

4. Vital statistics summary and life expectancy at birth: 2015 - 2019
Aperçu des statistiques de l'état civil et de l'espérance de vie à la naissance : 2015 - 2019 (continued - suite)

Continent, country or area and year Continent, pays ou zone et année	Live births / Naissances vivantes Co-de[a]	Number Nombre	Crude birth rate Taux brut de natalité	Deaths / Décès Co-de[a]	Number Nombre	Crude death rate Taux brut de mortalité	Rate of natural increase Taux d'accrois-sement naturel	Infant deaths / Décès d'enfants de moins d'un an Co-de[a]	Number Nombre	Rate (per 1000 births) Taux (par 1000 naiss-ances)	Life expectancy at birth / Espérance de vie à la naissance Male[b] Masculin[b]	Female[b] Féminin[b]	Total fertility rate L'indice synthétique de fécondité
EUROPE													
Austria - Autriche													
2015	C	84 381[114]	9.8	C	83 073[115]	9.6	0.2	C	259	3.1	78.6	83.6	1.494
2016	C	87 675[114]	10.0	C	80 669[115]	9.2	0.8	C	269	3.1	79.1	84.0	1.529
2017	C	87 633[114]	10.0	C	83 270[115]	9.5	0.5	C	256	2.9	79.3	83.9	...
2018	C	85 535[114]	9.7	C	83 975[115]	9.5	0.2	C	231	2.7	79.3	83.9	...
2019	C*	84 952	9.6	C*	83 386[115]	9.4	0.2		...	...	...	...	...
Belarus - Bélarus													
2015	C	119 028	12.5	C	120 026	12.6	-0.1	C	352	3.0	68.6	78.9	...
2016	C	117 779	12.4	C	119 379	12.6	-0.2	C	373	3.2	68.9	79.0	...
2017	C	102 556	10.8	C	119 311	12.6	-1.8	C	332	3.2	69.3	79.2	...
2018	C	94 042	9.9	C	120 053	12.7	-2.7	C	238	2.5	69.3	79.5	...
2019	C*	87 851	9.3	C*	120 913	12.8	-3.5		...	...	...	...	...
Belgium - Belgique													
2015	C	122 274[116]	10.8	C	110 541[116]	9.8	1.0	C	400[116]	3.3	78.5[23]	83.1[23]	...
2016	C	121 896[116]	10.8	C	108 097[116]	9.5	1.2	C	387[116]	3.2	...	...	...
2017	C	119 690[116]	10.5	C	109 666[116]	9.6	0.9	C	429[116]	3.6	...	...	...
2018	C	118 319[116]	10.4	C	110 693[116]	9.7	0.7	C	444[116]	3.8	79.2	83.7	...
2019	C*	116 128[116]	10.1	C*	108 783[116]	9.5	0.6		...	...	...	...	...
Bosnia and Herzegovina - Bosnie-Herzégovine													
2015	C	28 906	8.2	C	37 070	10.5	-2.3	C	174	6.0	...	...	...
2016	C	29 276	8.3	C	35 530	10.1	-1.8	C	152	5.2	...	...	...
2017	C	29 158	8.3	C	36 336	10.4	-2.0	C	183	6.3	...	...	...
2018	C	29 467	8.4	C	37 744	10.8	-2.4	C	183	6.2	...	...	...
Bulgaria - Bulgarie													
2015	C	65 950	9.2	C	110 117	15.3	-6.2	C	434	6.6	[III]71.1	78.0	1.529
2016	C	64 984	9.1	C	107 580	15.1	-6.0	C	423	6.5	[III]71.2	78.2	1.542
2017	C	63 955	9.0	C	109 791	15.5	-6.5	C	408	6.4	[III]71.3	78.4	...
2018	C	62 197	8.9	C	108 526	15.4	-6.6	C	358	5.8	[III]71.4	78.4	...
2019	C	61 538	8.8	C	108 083	15.4	-6.6		...	...	...	...	...
Croatia - Croatie													
2015	C	37 503	8.9	C	54 205	12.9	-4.0	C	154	4.1	...	...	...
2016	C	37 537	9.0	C	51 542	12.3	-3.4	C	161	4.3	...	...	...
2017	C	36 556	8.9	C	53 477	13.0	-4.1	C	148	4.0	74.9	81.0	...
2018	C	36 945	9.0	C	52 706	12.9	-3.9	C	157	4.2	74.9	81.5	...
2019	C*	36 135	8.9	C*	51 794	12.7	-3.8		...	...	...	...	...
Czechia - Tchéquie													
2015	C	110 764	10.5	C	111 173	10.5	0.0	C	272	2.5	75.8	81.4	1.570
2016	C	112 663	10.7	C	107 750	10.2	0.5	C	317	2.8	76.2	82.1	1.630
2017	C	114 405	10.8	C	111 443	10.5	0.3	C	304	2.7	76.0	81.8	...
2018	C	114 036	10.7	C	112 920	10.6	0.1	C	292	2.6	76.1	81.9	...
2019	C*	112 231	10.5	C*	112 362	10.5	0.0		...	...	...	...	...
Denmark - Danemark[117]													
2015	C	58 205	10.3	C	52 555	9.3	1.0	C	216	3.7	[II]78.6	82.5	1.714
2016	C	61 614	10.8	C	52 824	9.2	1.5	C	194	3.1	[II]78.8	82.8	1.785
2017	C	61 397	10.7	C	53 261	9.2	1.4	C	231	3.8	[II]79.0	82.9	...
2018	C	61 476	10.6	C	55 232	9.5	1.1	C	226	3.7	[II]79.0	82.9	...
2019	C	61 167	10.5	C	53 958	9.3	1.2		...	...	...	...	...
Estonia - Estonie													
2015	C	13 907	10.6	C	15 243	11.6	-1.0	C	35	2.5	73.1	81.8	1.580
2016	C	14 053	10.7	C	15 392	11.7	-1.0	C	33	2.3	73.2	81.9	1.600
2017	C	13 784	10.5	C	15 543	11.8	-1.3	C	32	2.3	73.7	82.3	...
2018	C	14 367	10.9	C	15 751	11.9	-1.0	C	23	...	73.9	82.4	...
2019	C	14 099	10.6	C	15 401	11.6	-1.0		...	...	...	...	...
Faroe Islands - Îles Féroé													
2015	C	605	12.4	C	377	7.7	4.7	C	-	...	[II]78.3	84.5	2.427
2016	C	674	13.6	C	379	7.7	6.0	C	3	...	...	...	2.625
2017	C	656	13.1	C	447	8.9	4.2	C	6	...	[II]80.9	83.7	2.479
2018	C	684	13.4	C	394	7.7	5.7	C	-	...	[II]80.1	84.8	2.501
2019	C	683	13.2	C	411	7.9	5.2	C	3	...	[II]80.4	85.3	2.394

4. Vital statistics summary and life expectancy at birth: 2015 - 2019
Aperçu des statistiques de l'état civil et de l'espérance de vie à la naissance : 2015 - 2019 (continued - suite)

Continent, country or area and year Continent, pays ou zone et année	Live births Naissances vivantes			Deaths Décès			Rate of natural increase Taux d'accroissement naturel	Infant deaths Décès d'enfants de moins d'un an			Life expectancy at birth Espérance de vie à la naissance		Total fertility rate L'indice synthétique de fécondité
	Code[a]	Number Nombre	Crude birth rate Taux brut de natalité	Code[a]	Number Nombre	Crude death rate Taux brut de mortalité		Code[a]	Number Nombre	Rate (per 1000 births) Taux (par 1000 naissances)	Male[b] Masculin[b]	Female[b] Féminin[b]	
EUROPE													
Finland - Finlande													
2015	C	55 197[118]	10.1	C	52 207[118]	9.6	0.5	C	97[118]	1.8	78.5[118]	84.1[118]	1.650
2016	C	52 521[118]	9.6	C	53 626[118]	9.8	-0.2	C	99[118]	1.9	78.4[118]	84.1[118]	1.570
2017	C	50 042[118]	9.1	C	53 487[118]	9.8	-0.6	C	102[118]	2.0	78.7[118]	84.2[118]	...
2018	C	47 297[118]	8.6	C	54 255[118]	9.9	-1.3	C	101[118]	2.1	78.9[118]	84.3[118]	...
2019	C*	45 597	8.3	C*	53 559	9.7	-1.4		...	...	...	...	...
France													
2015	C	760 421	11.8	C	581 770	9.0	2.8	C	2 655	3.5	[IV]79.1[23]	85.1[23]	1.924[23]
2016	C	744 697	11.5	C	581 073	9.0	2.5	C	2 577	3.5	[III]79.2	85.3	1.894[23]
2017	C	730 242	11.3	C	593 606	9.2	2.1	C	2 639	3.6	...	...	...
2018	C	719 737	11.1	C	596 422	9.2	1.9	C	2 600	3.6	...	...	...
Germany - Allemagne													
2015	C	737 575	9.0	C	925 200	11.3	-2.3	C	2 405	3.3	[III]78.2	83.1	1.500
2016	C	792 131	9.6	C	910 899	11.1	-1.4	C	2 698	3.4	...	...	...
2017	C	784 884	9.5	C	932 263	11.3	-1.8	C	2 566	3.3	78.7	83.4	...
2018	C	787 523	9.5	C	954 874	11.5	-2.0	C	2 505	3.2	[III]78.5	83.3	...
2019	C*	778 129	9.4	C*	939 536	11.3	-1.9		...	...	...	...	...
Gibraltar													
2015	+C	492[119]	14.7	+C	235[120]	7.0	7.7		...	...	...	...	...
2016	+C	424[119]	12.5	+C	249[120]	7.3	5.1		...	...	...	...	...
Greece - Grèce													
2015	C	91 847	8.5	C	121 183	11.2	-2.7	C	364	4.0	78.1	83.2	...
2016	C	92 898	8.6	C	118 788	11.0	-2.4	C	387	4.2	78.4	83.4	...
2017	C	88 553	8.2	C	124 495	11.6	-3.3	C	306	3.5	78.8	83.9	...
2018	C	86 440	8.1	C	120 296	11.2	-3.2	C	300	3.5	78.9	83.5	...
2019	C*	83 746	7.8	C*	125 016	11.7	-3.8		...	...	...	...	...
Guernsey - Guernesey													
2015	C	580[121]	9.3	C	557[121]	9.0	0.4		...	...	...	...	...
2016	C	595[121]	9.6	C	536[121]	8.6	0.9		...	...	...	...	...
2017	C	571[121]	9.2	C	586[121]	9.4	-0.2		...	...	...	...	...
2018	C	542[121]	8.7	C	574[121]	9.2	-0.5		...	...	[III]80.2[122]	84.4[122]	...
2019	C	497[121]	7.9	C	539[121]	8.6	-0.7		...	...	...	...	...
Hungary - Hongrie													
2015	C	92 135[123]	9.4	C	131 575[124]	13.4	-4.0	C	383[125]	4.2	72.1	78.6	1.440
2016	C	95 361[123]	9.7	C	127 098[124]	13.0	-3.2	C	368[125]	3.9	72.4	79.2	1.490
2017	C	94 646[123]	9.7	C	131 877[124]	13.5	-3.8	C	328[125]	3.5	72.4	79.0	1.490
2018	C	93 467[123]	9.6	C	131 247[124]	13.4	-3.9	C	304[125]	3.3	72.6	79.2	1.490
2019	C	93 100[126]	9.5	C	129 892[124]	13.3	-3.8		...	...	...	...	...
Iceland - Islande													
2015	C	4 129	12.5	C	2 178	6.6	5.9	C	9	...	[II]81.0	83.6	1.805
2016	C	4 034	12.0	C	2 309	6.9	5.1	C	3	...	[II]80.7	83.7	1.745
2017	C	4 071	11.9	C	2 238	6.5	5.3	C	11	...	[II]80.6	83.9	...
2018	C	4 228	12.0	C	2 254	6.4	5.6	C	7	...	[II]81.0	84.1	...
Ireland - Irlande													
2015	+C	65 537	13.9	+C	30 064	6.4	7.5	+C	225	3.4	...	...	1.940
2016	+C	63 836	13.4	+C	30 390	6.4	7.0	+C	208	3.3	...	...	...
2017	+C	61 824	12.9	+C	30 317	6.3	6.6	+C	174	2.8	80.4	84.0	...
2018	+C	61 022	12.5	+C	31 009	6.4	6.2	+C	174	2.9	80.5	84.1	...
2019	+C	59 796	12.2	+C	31 134	6.3	5.8		...	...	...	...	...
Isle of Man - Île de Man													
2015	+C	785	9.0		...	...	...		...	...	...	...	...
2016	+C	758	9.1	+C	852	10.2	-1.1	|	2[19]	...	...	...	1.683
2017	+C	753	9.0	+C	837	10.0	-1.0		...	...	...	...	...
2018	+C	717	...	+C	876	...	...		...	...	...	...	...
2019	+C	710	...	+C	850	...	...		...	...	...	...	1.683
Italy - Italie													
2015	C	485 780	8.0	C	647 571	10.7	-2.7	C	1 398	2.9	...	...	1.350
2016	C	473 438	7.8	C	615 261	10.1	-2.3	C	1 427	3.0	80.6	85.0	...
2017	C	458 151	7.6	C	649 061	10.7	-3.2	C	1 347	2.9	80.6	84.9	...

4. Vital statistics summary and life expectancy at birth: 2015 - 2019
Aperçu des statistiques de l'état civil et de l'espérance de vie à la naissance : 2015 - 2019 (continued - suite)

Continent, country or area and year Continent, pays ou zone et année	Live births Naissances vivantes			Deaths Décès			Rate of natural increase Taux d'accroissement naturel	Infant deaths Décès d'enfants de moins d'un an			Life expectancy at birth Espérance de vie à la naissance		Total fertility rate L'indice synthétique de fécondité
	Code[a]	Number Nombre	Crude birth rate Taux brut de natalité	Code[a]	Number Nombre	Crude death rate Taux brut de mortalité		Code[a]	Number Nombre	Rate (per 1000 births) Taux (par 1000 naissances)	Male[b] Masculin[b]	Female[b] Féminin[b]	
EUROPE													
Italy - Italie													
2018	C	439 747	7.3	C	633 133	10.5	-3.2	C	1 228	2.8	80.9	85.2	...
2019	C*	420 170	...	C*	634 432	...	...		...	...	...	...	...
Jersey													
2015	+C	1 021[39]	10.1	+C	762	7.5	2.6		...	...	...	...	...
2016	+C	1 020[39]	9.9	+C	831	8.1	1.8		...	...	...	...	...
2017	+C	954[39]	9.2	+C	803	7.7	1.4		...	...	...	...	...
2018	+C	942[39]	8.9	+C	820	7.8	1.2		...	...	...	...	...
Latvia - Lettonie													
2015	C	21 979	11.1	C	28 478	14.4	-3.3	C	90	4.1	69.7	79.3	1.707
2016	C	21 968	11.2	C	28 580	14.6	-3.4	C	81	3.7	69.8	79.4	1.743
2017	C	20 828	10.7	C	28 757	14.8	-4.1	C	86	4.1	69.8	79.6	...
2018	C	19 314	10.0	C	28 820	15.0	-4.9	C	61	3.2	70.0	79.6	...
2019	C	18 786	9.8	C	27 719	14.4	-4.7		...	...	...	...	...
Liechtenstein													
2015	C	325	8.7	C	252	6.7	1.9	C	2	...	...	...	...
2016	C	378	10.0	C	271	7.2	2.8	C	1	...	...	...	1.610
2017	C	338	8.9	C	249	6.6	2.3	C	-	...	...	...	...
2018	C	378	9.9	C	274	7.2	2.7	C	-	...	...	...	...
Lithuania - Lituanie													
2015	C	31 475	10.8	C	41 776	14.4	-3.5	C	132	4.2	69.1	79.6	...
2016	C	30 623	10.7	C	41 106	14.3	-3.7	C	139	4.5	69.5	80.0	...
2017	C	28 696	10.1	C	40 142	14.2	-4.0	C	85	3.0	70.7	80.4	...
2018	C	28 149	10.0	C	39 574	14.1	-4.1	C	96	3.4	70.9	80.6	...
2019	C	27 393	9.8	C	38 281	13.7	-3.9		...	...	...	...	...
Luxembourg													
2015	C	6 115	10.7	C	3 983	7.0	3.7	C	17	...	...	...	...
2016	C	6 050	10.4	C	3 967	6.8	3.6	C	23	...	[III]80.7	85.4	...
2017	C	6 174	10.4	C	4 263	7.1	3.2	C	20	...	[III]79.9	84.4	1.390
2018	C	6 274	10.3	C	4 318	7.1	3.2	C	27	...	[III]80.0	84.5	1.380
2019	C	6 230	10.1	C	4 283	7.0	3.2		...	...	...	...	...
Malta - Malte													
2015	C	4 325	9.7	C	3 442	7.7	2.0	C	25	...	79.7	84.0	1.370
2016	C	4 476	9.8	C	3 342	7.3	2.5	C	33	7.4	80.6	84.4	1.370
2017	C	4 319	9.2	C	3 571	7.6	1.6	C	30	6.9	80.2	84.6	1.260
2018	C	4 444	9.2	C	3 688	7.6	1.6	C	25	...	80.4	84.6	1.230
2019	C	4 350	8.8	C	3 688	7.5	1.3		...	...	...	...	...
Monaco													
2015	C	1 067[127]	28.4	C	595[128]	15.8	12.6		...	...	...	...	...
2016	C	938[127]	24.6	C	503[129]	13.2	11.4		...	...	...	...	...
2017	C	958[127]	25.5	C	490[128]	13.0	12.5		...	...	...	...	...
2018	C	983[127]	25.7	C	528[128]	13.8	11.9		...	...	...	...	...
Montenegro - Monténégro													
2015	C	7 386	11.9	C	6 329	10.2	1.7	C	16	...	...	...	...
2016	C	7 569	12.2	C	6 464	10.4	1.8	C	26	...	...	...	...
2017	C	7 432	11.9	C	6 523	10.5	1.5	C	10	...	...	...	...
2018	C	7 264	11.7	C	6 504	10.5	1.2	C	12	...	...	...	...
2019	C	7 223	11.6	C	6 595	10.6	1.0	C	17	...	...	...	...
Netherlands - Pays-Bas													
2015	C	170 510[130]	10.1	C	147 134[130]	8.7	1.4	C	561[130]	3.3	...	...	...
2016	C	172 520[130]	10.1	C	148 997[130]	8.7	1.4	C	597[130]	3.5	...	...	...
2017	C	169 836[130]	9.9	C	150 214[130]	8.8	1.1	C	607[130]	3.6	80.2	83.4	...
2018	C	168 525[130]	9.8	C	153 363[130]	8.9	0.9	C	582[130]	3.5	80.3	83.4	...
2019	C	169 680[130]	9.8	C	151 885[130]	8.8	1.0		...	...	...	...	...
North Macedonia - Macédoine du Nord													
2015	C	23 075	11.1	C	20 461	9.9	1.3	C	198	8.6	73.4	77.4	1.500
2016	C	23 002	11.1	C	20 417	9.9	1.2	C	273	11.9	73.7	77.5	1.500
2017	C	21 754	10.5	C	20 318	9.8	0.7	C	201	9.2	74.0	77.9	...

4. Vital statistics summary and life expectancy at birth: 2015 - 2019
Aperçu des statistiques de l'état civil et de l'espérance de vie à la naissance : 2015 - 2019 (continued - suite)

Continent, country or area and year Continent, pays ou zone et année	Live births Naissances vivantes Co-de[a]	 Number Nombre	 Crude birth rate Taux brut de natalité	Deaths Décès Co-de[a]	 Number Nombre	 Crude death rate Taux brut de mortalité	Rate of natural increase Taux d'accrois-sement naturel	Infant deaths Décès d'enfants de moins d'un an Co-de[a]	 Number Nombre	 Rate (per 1000 births) Taux (par 1000 naiss-ances)	Life expectancy at birth Espérance de vie à la naissance Male[b] Masculin[b]	 Female[b] Féminin[b]	Total fertility rate L'indice synthétique de fécondité
EUROPE													
North Macedonia - Macédoine du Nord													
2018	C	21 333	10.3	C	19 727	9.5	0.8	C	122	5.7	74.6	78.8	...
2019	C*	19 725	9.5	C*	20 412	9.8	-0.3		...	...	...	...	...
Norway - Norvège													
2015	C	58 815	11.3	C	40 676[131]	7.8	3.5	C	133[131]	2.3	...	...	1.730
2016	C	58 890	11.3	C	40 726[131]	7.8	3.5	C	128[131]	2.2	...	...	1.710
2017	C	56 633	10.7	C	40 774[131]	7.7	3.0	C	130[131]	2.3	...	...	1.620
2018	C	55 120	10.4	C	40 840[131]	7.7	2.7	C	129[131]	2.3	81.0	84.5	1.560
2019	C*	54 496	10.2	C*	40 727[131]	7.6	2.6		...	...	...	...	...
Poland - Pologne													
2015	C	369 308	9.7	C	394 921	10.4	-0.7	C	1 476	4.0	73.6	81.6	1.289
2016	C	382 257	10.1	C	388 009	10.2	-0.2	C	1 522	4.0	73.9	81.9	1.357
2017	C	401 982	10.6	C	402 852	10.6	0.0	C	1 604	4.0	74.0	81.8	...
2018	C	388 178	10.2	C	414 200	10.9	-0.7	C	1 494	3.8	73.9	81.7	...
2019	C	374 954	9.8	C	409 709	10.7	-0.9		...	...	...	...	...
Portugal													
2015	C	85 500[39]	8.3	C	108 539[132]	10.5	-2.2	C	250[132]	2.9	[III]77.4	83.2	1.300
2016	C	87 126[39]	8.4	C	110 573[132]	10.7	-2.3	C	282[132]	3.2	[III]77.6	83.3	1.360
2017	C	86 154[39]	8.4	C	109 758[132]	10.7	-2.3	C	229[132]	2.7	[III]77.7	83.4	...
2018	C	87 020[39]	8.5	C	113 051[132]	11.0	-2.5	C	287[132]	3.3	[III]77.8	83.4	...
2019	C*	87 019[39]	8.5	C*	112 278[132]	10.9	-2.5		...	...	...	...	...
Republic of Moldova - République de Moldova[133]													
2015	C	38 610	13.6	C	39 906	14.1	-0.5	C	375	9.7	67.5	75.5	1.300
2016	C	37 394	13.3	C	38 489	13.7	-0.4	C	353	9.4	68.1	76.2	1.280
2017	C	34 060	12.4	C	36 768	13.3	-1.0	C	330	9.7	69.4	77.0	1.190
2018	C	32 606	12.0	C	37 200	13.7	-1.7	C	326	10.0	...	...	1.166
2019	C*	29 682	11.1	C*	36 794	13.7	-2.7		...	...	...	...	...
Romania - Roumanie													
2015	C	197 491	10.0	C	261 294	13.2	-3.2	C	1 500	7.6	[III]71.9	78.9	...
2016	C	205 773	10.4	C	258 404	13.1	-2.7	C	1 399	6.8	[III]72.0	79.0	...
2017	C	202 151	10.3	C	261 402	13.3	-3.0	C	1 364	6.7	[III]72.3	79.2	...
2018	C	202 744	10.4	C	263 911	13.6	-3.1	C	1 226	6.0	[III]72.4	79.4	...
2019	C*	185 733	9.6	C*	259 506	13.4	-3.8		...	...	...	...	...
San Marino - Saint-Marin													
2015	C	269	8.0	C	235	6.9	1.0	C	-	...	...	...	...
2016	C	262	7.7	C	253	7.4	0.3	C	1	...	...	...	...
2017	C	228	6.6	C	278	8.1	-1.5	C	-	...	82.7	86.8	...
2018	C	235	6.8	C	244	7.1	-0.3	C	1	...	...	...	...
Serbia - Serbie[134]													
2015	+C	65 657	9.3	+C	103 678	14.6	-5.4	+C	346	5.3	72.6	77.7	1.464
2016	+C	64 734	9.2	+C	100 834	14.3	-5.1	+C	348	5.4	72.7	77.8	1.460
2017	+C	64 894	9.2	+C	103 722	14.8	-5.5	+C	305	4.7	73.0	77.9	...
2018	+C	63 975	9.2	+C	101 655	14.6	-5.4	+C	311	4.9	73.2	78.1	...
2019	+C*	63 723	9.2	+C*	102 131	14.7	-5.5		...	...	...	...	...
Slovakia - Slovaquie													
2015	C	55 602	10.3	C	53 826	9.9	0.3	C	285	5.1	73.0	79.7	1.400
2016	C	57 557	10.6	C	52 351	9.6	1.0	C	311	5.4	73.7	80.4	...
2017	C	57 969	10.7	C	53 914	9.9	0.7	C	263	4.5	73.8	80.3	...
2018	C	57 639	10.6	C	54 293	10.0	0.6	C	288	5.0	73.7	80.4	...
2019	C	57 054	10.5	C	53 234	9.8	0.7		...	...	...	...	...
Slovenia - Slovénie													
2015	C	20 641	10.0	C	19 834	9.6	0.4	C	33	1.6	...	...	1.570
2016	C	20 345	9.9	C	19 689	9.5	0.3	C	41	2.0	[II]77.6	83.5	...
2017	C	20 241	9.8	C	20 509	9.9	-0.1	C	42	2.1	78.1	83.7	1.620
2018	C	19 585	9.5	C	20 485	9.9	-0.4	C	33	1.7	78.3	84.0	1.610
2019	C*	19 328	9.3	C*	20 588	9.9	-0.6		...	...	...	...	...

4. Vital statistics summary and life expectancy at birth: 2015 - 2019
Aperçu des statistiques de l'état civil et de l'espérance de vie à la naissance : 2015 - 2019 (continued - suite)

Continent, country or area and year / Continent, pays ou zone et année	Live births / Naissances vivantes			Deaths / Décès			Rate of natural increase / Taux d'accroissement naturel	Infant deaths / Décès d'enfants de moins d'un an			Life expectancy at birth / Espérance de vie à la naissance		Total fertility rate / L'indice synthétique de fécondité
	Code[a]	Number / Nombre	Crude birth rate / Taux brut de natalité	Code[a]	Number / Nombre	Crude death rate / Taux brut de mortalité		Code[a]	Number / Nombre	Rate (per 1000 births) / Taux (par 1000 naissances)	Male[b] / Masculin[b]	Female[b] / Féminin[b]	
EUROPE													
Spain - Espagne													
2015	C	418 432	9.0	C	420 408	9.1	0.0	C	1 117	2.7	...	...	1.330
2016	C	408 734	8.8	C	408 231	8.8	0.0	C	1 097	2.7	80.3	85.8	1.330
2017	C	391 265	8.4	C	422 037	9.1	-0.7	C	1 064	2.7	80.4	85.7	...
2018	C	370 827	7.9	C	425 153	9.1	-1.2	C	998	2.7	80.5	85.8	...
2019	C*	357 924	7.6	C*	415 070	8.8	-1.2		...	...	...	...	...
Sweden - Suède													
2015	C	114 870	11.7	C	90 907	9.3	2.4	C	282	2.5	...	...	1.850
2016	C	117 425	11.8	C	90 982	9.2	2.7	C	292	2.5	...	...	1.850
2017	C	115 416	11.5	C	91 972	9.1	2.3	C	278	2.4	80.8	84.1	...
2018	C	115 832	11.4	C	92 185	9.1	2.3	C	235	2.0	80.9	84.3	...
Switzerland - Suisse													
2015	C	86 559	10.5	C	67 606	8.2	2.3	C	340	3.9	[II]80.8	85.0	1.540
2016	C	87 883	10.5	C	64 964	7.8	2.7	C	316	3.6	[II]81.1	85.0	1.550
2017	C	87 381	10.3	C	66 971	7.9	2.4	C	310	3.5	[II]81.4	85.3	...
2018	C	87 851	10.3	C	67 088	7.9	2.4	C	287	3.3	81.7	85.4	...
2019	C*	81 564	9.6	C*	66 315	7.8	1.8		...	...	...	...	...
Ukraine[135]													
2015	+C	411 781[136]	9.6	+C	594 796[137]	13.9	-4.3	+C	3 318[137]	8.1	...	...	...
2016	+C	397 037[136]	9.3	+C	583 631[137]	13.7	-4.4	+C	2 955[137]	7.4	66.7	76.5	...
2017	+C	363 987[136]	8.6	+C	574 123[137]	13.5	-4.9	+C	2 786[137]	7.7	67.0	76.8	...
2018	+C*	335 874[136]	7.9	+C*	587 665[137]	13.9	-6.0	+C	2 397[137]	7.1	...	...	...
2019	+C*	308 817[136]	7.3	+C*	581 114[137]	13.8	-6.5		...	...	...	...	...
United Kingdom of Great Britain and Northern Ireland - Royaume-Uni de Grande-Bretagne et d'Irlande du Nord[138]													
2015	C	776 746[139]	11.9	+C	601 272	9.2	2.7	+C	3 004	3.9	...	...	...
2016	C	774 386[139]	11.8	+C	595 655	9.1	2.7	+C	2 976	3.8	[III]79.2	82.9	...
2017	C	754 754[139]	11.4	+C	605 748	9.2	2.3	+C	2 947	3.9	[III]79.2	82.9	...
2018	C	730 918[139]	11.0	+C	614 313	9.2	1.8	+C	2 818	3.9	[III]79.3	82.9	...
2019	C*	712 550[139]	10.7	+C*	603 419	9.0	1.6		...	...	...	...	...
OCEANIA - OCÉANIE													
American Samoa - Samoas américaines													
2015	C	1 096	18.0	C	314	5.2	12.8	C	11	...	...	...	...
2016	C	1 013	16.8	C	280	4.7	12.2	C	14	...	...	...	...
2017	C	1 001	16.6	C	310	5.1	11.5	C	14	...	...	...	...
Australia - Australie													
2015	C	305 377	12.8	C	159 052	6.7	6.1	C	991	3.2	[III]80.4	84.5	1.796
2016	C	311 104	12.9	C	158 504	6.6	6.3	C	970	3.1	[III]80.5	84.6	1.792
2017	C	309 142	12.6	C	160 909	6.5	6.0	C	1 019	3.3	[III]80.5	84.6	1.741
2018	C	315 147	12.6	C	158 493	6.3	6.3	C	988	3.1	[III]80.7	84.9	1.740
Cook Islands - Îles Cook													
2015	+C	205	11.1	+C	102	5.5	5.6	+C	-	...	...	...	...
2016	+C	242	12.5	+C	87	4.5	8.0	+C	-	...	...	...	...
2017	+C	222	11.4	+C	93	4.8	6.6	+C	1	...	...	...	...
2018	+C*	232	12.5	+C*	121	6.5	6.0	+C*	4	...	...	...	...
2019	+C*	225	11.1	+C*	105	5.2	5.9	+C*	2	...	...	...	...
Fiji - Fidji													
2015	+C	17 882	20.6	+C	6 672	7.7	12.9	+C	226[140]	12.6	66.8	70.1	2.910
2016	+C	15 620	17.9	+C	7 476[140]	8.6	9.4	+C	216[140]	13.8	...	...	...
2017	+C	14 023	15.8	+C	6 992[140]	7.9	7.9	+C	300[140]	21.4	[III]65.4	68.5	...

4. Vital statistics summary and life expectancy at birth: 2015 - 2019
Aperçu des statistiques de l'état civil et de l'espérance de vie à la naissance : 2015 - 2019 (continued - suite)

Continent, country or area and year Continent, pays ou zone et année	Live births Naissances vivantes			Deaths Décès			Rate of natural increase Taux d'accrois-sement naturel	Infant deaths Décès d'enfants de moins d'un an			Life expectancy at birth Espérance de vie à la naissance		Total fertility rate L'indice synthétique de fécondité
	Co-de[a]	Number Nombre	Crude birth rate Taux brut de natalité	Co-de[a]	Number Nombre	Crude death rate Taux brut de mortalité		Co-de[a]	Number Nombre	Rate (per 1000 births) Taux (par 1000 naiss-ances)	Male[b] Masculin[b]	Female[b] Féminin[b]	
OCEANIA - OCÉANIE													
French Polynesia - Polynésie française													
2015	C	3 888	14.2	C	1 409	5.2	9.1	C	27	...	74.4	78.1	1.827
2016	C	3 969	14.5	C	1 394	5.1	9.4	C	25	...	74.5	78.6	1.865
2017	C	3 821	13.9	C	1 608	5.8	8.0	C	29	...	74.0	77.7	1.802
2018	C	3 776	13.6	C	1 616	5.8	7.8	C	38	10.1	73.2	78.8	1.793
Guam													
2015	C	3 367[141]	20.8	C	1 009[141]	6.2	14.6	C	47[141]	14.0	75.9	82.2	...
2016	C	3 433[141]	21.1	C	1 022[141]	6.3	14.8	C	37[141]	10.8	...	...	...
2017	C	3 292[141]	20.1	C	1 008[141]	6.2	13.9	C	28[141]	...	73.6	78.6	2.800
2018	C	3 175[141]	18.9	C	1 056[141]	6.3	12.6	C	37[141]	11.7	...	...	2.678
2019	C*	3 059[141]	18.2	C*	1 037[141]	6.2	12.0		...	...	...	...	...
Kiribati[142]													
2015	+U	*2 368*	...	+U	*709*	...	...		...	...	...	...	...
Nauru													
2015	C	360	31.9	C	90	8.0	23.9		...	...	...	...	...
2016	C	358	32.5	C	100	9.1	23.4		...	...	...	...	...
2017	C	304	...	C	94	...	...		...	...	...	...	...
New Caledonia - Nouvelle-Calédonie													
2015	C	4 191	15.4	C	1 465	5.4	10.0	C	25	...	...	...	...
2016	C	4 271	15.6	C	1 569	5.7	9.8	C	16	...	...	...	...
2017	C	4 059	14.6	C	1 529	5.5	9.1	C	20	...	75.1	80.1	...
New Zealand - Nouvelle-Zélande													
2015	+C	61 038[143]	13.3	+C	31 608[143]	6.9	6.4	+C	249[144]	4.1	...	...	1.994
2016	+C	59 427[145]	12.7	+C	31 179[144]	6.6	6.0	+C	213[144]	3.6	...	...	1.875
2017	+C	59 610[145]	12.4	+C	33 339[144]	7.0	5.5	+C	228[144]	3.8	...	...	1.839
2018	+C	58 020[145]	12.0	+C	33 216[144]	6.9	5.1	+C	219[144]	3.8	...	...	1.744
2019	+C	59 637[145]	12.1	+C	34 242[144]	7.0	5.2	+C	267[144]	4.5	...	...	1.754
Niue - Nioué													
2015	C	26	...	C	16	...	...		...	...	...	...	...
2016	C	27	...	C	7	...	...		...	...	...	...	...
Norfolk Island - Île Norfolk[146]													
2015		...	...	+C	11	...	...		...	...	...	...	...
Palau - Palaos													
2015	C	242	13.7	C	136	7.7	6.0	C	4	...	...	...	...
2016	C	213	12.0	C	175	9.9	2.1	C	-	...	...	...	...
2017	C	221	12.4	C	183	10.3	2.1	C	5	...	...	...	...
2018	C	256	14.0	C	143	7.8	6.2	C	3	...	...	...	...
Pitcairn													
2019	C	-	...	C	3	...	...		...	...	...	...	...
Samoa													
2015	+U	*8 210*[147]	...	+U	*1 112*[147]	...	...	+U	*5*[147]	...	...	...	...
2016	+U	*9 378*[147]	...	+U	*2 020*[147]	...	...	+U	*10*[147]	...	73.7	76.0	3.769[148]
2017	+U	*9 278*[147]	...	+U	*1 037*[147]	...	...	+U	*10*[147]	...	...	...	...
2018	+U	*13 392*[149]	...	+U	*1 114*[147]	...	...	+U	*2*[147]	...	...	...	...
2019	+U	*9 604*[147]	...		...	...	...	+U	*7*[147]	...	...	...	...
Tuvalu													
2015	+U	*208*	...	+U	*66*	...	...		...	...	...	...	...
2016	+U	*210*	...	+U	*90*	...	...		...	...	...	...	...

FOOTNOTES - NOTES

Italics: data from civil registers which are incomplete or of unknown completeness. - Italiques : données incomplètes ou dont le degré d'exactitude n'est pas connu, provenant des registres de l'état civil.

* Provisional. - Données provisoires.

a 'Code' indicates the source of data, as follows:
C - Civil registration, estimated over 90% complete
U - Civil registration, estimated less than 90% complete
| - Other source, estimated reliable
+ - Data tabulated by date of registration rather than occurence

... - Information not available

Le 'Code' indique la source des données, comme suit :
C - Registres de l'état civil considérés complets à 90 p. 100 au moins
U - Registres de l'état civil qui ne sont pas considérés complets à 90 p. 100 au moins
| - Autre source, considérée fiable
+ - Données exploitées selon la date de l'enregistrement et non la date de l'événement
... - Information non disponible

b A Roman number in front of the data for males specifies the range of the reference period of life expectancy for males and females presented on the row. For example, a reference year of 2005 and a range of V years means that the reference period for the life expectancy is 2001 - 2005. The absence of a Roman number means the reference period is one year and the reference period therefore coincides with the reference year. - Un chiffre romain devant la donnée relative aux hommes indique l'étendue de la période de référence concernant l'espérance de vie des hommes et des femmes présentée dans la ligne. Par exemple, une année de référence 2005 et une étendue de V signifie que la période de référence pour l'espérance de vie est 2001-2005. L'absence de chiffre romain signifie que la période de référence est d'un an et donc coïncide avec l'année de référence.

1 Excluding live-born infants who died before their birth was registered. Data refer to Algerian population only. - Non compris les enfants nés vivants décédés avant l'enregistrement de leur naissance. Les données ne concernent que la population algérienne.
2 Data refer to Algerian population only. - Les données ne concernent que la population algérienne.
3 Source: Vital Statistics Report. - Source: Vital Statistics Report.
4 Data refer to national projections. - Les données se réfèrent aux projections nationales.
5 Data refer only to events recorded in hospitals and health centres. - Ces données ne concernent que les faits d'état civil enregistrés dans les hôpitaux et les centres de santé uniquement.
6 The calculation of the total fertility rate is based on the number of live births during the three year period prior to the survey. - L' indice synthétique de fécondité a été calculé sur bases des enfants nés sur la période des trois années précédant l'enquête.
7 Source: Vital Statistics Report, National Statistics Institute. Registered births only. - Source: Rapport sur les statistiques de l'état civil, Institut national de la statistique. Naissances enregistrées seulement.
8 Source: Statistical Report, Ministry of Health and Social Security. - Source: Rapport statistique, ministère de la Santé et de la Sécurité sociale.
9 Data based on the 2010 Population Census. - Les données sont fondées sur le recensement de la population de 2010.
10 Source: Demographic Projection, National Statistics Institute. - Source: Projection démographique, Institut national de la statistique.
11 Source: Demographic and Health Survey (ESDC-V) 2018. - Source : Enquête Démographique et de Santé (EDSC-V) 2018.
12 The rate of registration of deaths is less than 20 per cent at the national level. - Le taux d'enregistrement des décès est inférieur à 20 p. 100 au niveau national.
13 Source: Reports of the Ministry of Health. Data refers to births in health institution. - Source : Rapports du Ministère de la Santé. Les données se rapportent aux naissances dans les établissements de santé.
14 Source: Ministry of Home Affairs. - Source : Ministère de l'intérieur.
15 Data refer to projections based on the 2007 Population Census. - Les données se réfèrent aux projections basées sur le recensement de la population de 2007.
16 Based on underlying data of the Population and Housing Census 2014 and Multiple Indicator Cluster Survey 2016. - Estimations basées sur le Récensement Général de la Population et de l'Habitation 2014 et Enquête par Grappes à Indicateurs Multiples 2016.
17 Source: Kenya Demographic and Health Survey data. - Source: Données de l'enquête du Kenya sur la démographie et la santé.
18 The marked increase is due to the improvement in birth registration. - L'augmentation sensible s'explique par l'amélioration d'enregistrement des naissances.
19 Data refer to the 12 months preceding the census in April. - Les données se rapportent aux douze mois précédant le recensement d'avril.
20 Data refer to projections based on the 1993 Population Census. - Les données se réfèrent aux projections basées sur le recensement de la population de 1993.
21 Data refer to the 12 months preceding the census in September. - Les données se rapportent aux 12 mois précédant le recensement de septembre.
22 Excludes the islands of St. Brandon and Agalega. - Non compris les îles St. Brandon et Agalega.
23 Provisional data. - Données provisoires.
24 Source: Ministry of Health - Source : Ministère de la santé
25 Source: Ministry of Public Health, Department of Statistics. - Source: Ministère de la Santé Publique, Direction des Statistiques.
26 Excluding live-born infants who died before their birth was registered. - Non compris les enfants nés vivants décédés avant l'enregistrement de leur naissance.
27 Data refer to Saint Helenian resident population. - Pour la population résidante de Sainte-Hélène.
28 Data refer to the 12 months preceding the census in December. - Les données se rapportent aux 12 mois précédant le recensement de décembre.
29 Source: Demographic and Health Survey. - Source : Demographic and Health Survey (enquête démographique et sanitaire).
30 Completeness estimated at 15.3%. - Degré de complétude évalué à 15.3 pour cent.
31 Completeness estimated at 19%. - Degré de complétude évalué à 19 pour cent.
32 Excluding visitors. - Ne comprend pas les visiteurs.
33 Bermuda is 100 per cent urban. Excluding non-residents and foreign service personnel and their dependants. - 100 pour cent de la population des Bermudes est urbaine. À l'exclusion des non-résidents et du personnel diplomatique et de leurs charges de famille.
34 Bermuda is 100 per cent urban. - 100 pour cent de la population des Bermudes est urbaine.
35 Excluding non-residents and foreign service personnel and their dependants. - À l'exclusion des non-résidents et du personnel diplomatique et de leurs charges de famille.
36 Including Canadian residents temporarily in the United States, but excluding United States residents temporarily in Canada. - Y compris les résidents canadiens se trouvant temporairement aux Etats-Unis, mais ne comprenant pas les résidents des Etats-Unis se trouvant temporairement au Canada.
37 Including resident deaths outside of the islands but buried in the islands. - Y compris les décès de résidents hors des îles mais inhumés dans les îles.
38 Excluding children born in the country of non-resident mothers. - Exceptés les enfants nés dans le pays des mères non-résidentes.
39 Data refer to births to resident mothers. - Ces données concernent les enfants nés de mères résidentes.
40 Data refer to resident population only. - Pour la population résidante seulement.
41 Excluding Indian jungle population. - Non compris les Indiens de la jungle.
42 Data refer to resident and non resident deaths that occurred in Saint Vincent and the Grenadines. - Les données concernent les décès de résidents et de non-résidents survenus à St Vincent-et-les-Grenadines.
43 Source: Ministry of Legal Affairs. - Source : Ministère des affaires juridiques.
44 Source: National Statistical Office. - Source : Service national de statistique.
45 Excluding deaths of persons living abroad. - Exception faite des personnes décédées à l'étranger.
46 Source: U.S. National Center for Health Statistics, National Vital Statistics Reports (NVSR). - Source : US National Center for Health Statistics, National Vital Statistics Reports (NVSR).
47 Data refer to the number of less than one year olds registered in the year. - Les données se rapportent au nombre d'enfants de moins d'un an enregistrés dans l'année.
48 Data refer to the 12 months from 30 June 2015 to 30 June 2016. - Les données font référence aux douze mois de 30 juin 2015 à 30 juin 2016.
49 Data refer to the 12 months from 30 June 2016 to 30 June 2017. - Les données font référence aux douze mois de 30 juin 2016 à 30 juin 2017.
50 Data refer to the 12 months from 30 June 2017 to 30 June 2018. Data refer to national projections. - Les données font référence aux douze mois de 30 juin 2017 à 30 juin 2018. Les données se réfèrent aux projections nationales.
51 Data refer to national projections. Data refer to the 12 months from 30 June 2018 to 30 June 2019. - Les donnés se réfèrent aux projections nationales. Les données font référence aux douze mois de 30 juin 2018 à 30 juin 2019.
52 Including deaths abroad and deaths of unknown place of residence. - Y compris décès à l'étranger et décès dont le lieu de résidence n'est pas connu.
53 Including deaths abroad and deaths of unknown residence of mother. - Y compris décès à l'étranger et décès de nourrissons nés de mères dont le lieu de résidence n'est pas connu.
54 Projected value based on the results of 2000 and 2010 censuses, statistics from civil registration and reporting of live births in the ministry of health system. - Projection basée sur les résultats des recensements de 2000 et 2010, des statistiques d'état civil et les registres des naissances vivantes du Ministère de la santé.

[55] Estimates or projections based on the 2017 Population Census. - Estimations ou projections fondées sur le recensement de la population de 2017.
[56] Data are revised projections taking into consideration also the results of the 2018 census. - Les données sont des projections révisées tenant compte également des résultats du recensement de 2018.
[57] Excludes nomadic Indian tribes. - Non compris les tribus d'Indiens nomades.
[58] Source: General Registrar Office. - Source : Bureau général de l'État civil.
[59] Estimated completeness of registration is within 80-89 per cent. - Degré de complétude de l'enregistrement est évalué à 80-89 pour cent.
[60] Source: Reports of the Ministry of Health. - Source : Rapports du Ministère de la Santé.
[61] Source: INEI – National population estimates and projections from bulletin No. 24 published in July 2019. - Source : INEI - Estimations et projections nationales de la population, publiées dans le bulletin numéro 24 , juillet 2019.
[62] Source: Reports of the Ministry of Health. Data extracted from online system representing only 85.6 per cent of estimated births. - Source : Rapports du Ministère de la Santé. Données extraites du système en ligne, qui ne représentent que 85.6 % du nombre total estimé de naissances.
[63] Based on the results of the 2011 Population Census. - Basé sur les résultats du recencement de la population de 2011.
[64] Rates are for the period 1-36 months prior to the interview and "Source: 2015 Afghanistan Demographic and Health Survey". - Ces taux se rapportent à la période de 1 à 36 mois précédant l'entretien et « Source : Enquête démographique et sanitaire de 2015, Afghanistan ».
[65] Excluding infants born alive of less than 28 weeks' gestation, of less than 1 000 g in weight and 35 cm in length, who die within seven days of birth. - Non compris les enfants nés vivants après moins de 28 semaines de gestations, pesant moins de 1 000 g, mesurant moins de 35 cm et décédés dans les sept jours qui ont suivi leur naissance.
[66] Sources: Births and Deaths National Registration System database, and medical records of government hospitals. Data refer to Bahraini and non-Bahraini births including some visitors, and Bahraini births abroad. - Les sources: Les bases de données des << Births and Deaths National Registration System >> et les dossiers médicaux des hôpitaux du gouvernement. Les données se rapportent aux naissances de Bahreïniens et de non-Bahreïniens, y compris d'enfants non résidents, ainsi que de Bahreïniens résidant à l'étranger.
[67] Data refer to Bahraini and non-Bahraini deaths including some visitors, and Bahraini deaths abroad. Sources: Births and Deaths National Registration System database, and medical records of government hospitals. - Les données se rapportent aux décès de Bahreïniens et de non-Bahreïniens, y compris de non-résidents, ainsi que de Bahreïniens résidant à l'étranger. Les sources: Les bases de données des << Births and Deaths National Registration System >> et les dossiers médicaux des hôpitaux du gouvernement.
[68] Source: Sample vital registration system of Bangladesh - Source : << Sample Vital Registration System >> du Bangladesh.
[69] Data refer to the 12 months preceding the census in May. - Les données se rapportent aux 12 mois précédant le recensement de mai.
[70] For statistical purposes, the data for China do not include those for the Hong Kong Special Administrative Region (Hong Kong SAR), Macao Special Administrative Region (Macao SAR) and Taiwan province of China. Data have been estimated on the basis of the annual National Sample Survey on Population Changes. - Pour la présentation des statistiques, les données pour la Chine ne comprennent pas la Région Administrative Spéciale de Hong Kong (Hong Kong RAS), la Région Administrative Spéciale de Macao (Macao RAS) et Taïwan province de Chine. Les données ont été estimées sur la base de l'enquête annuelle "National Sample Survey on Population Changes".
[71] The fertility rates have been compiled using a population denominator which has excluded female foreign domestic helpers. - Les taux de fécondité ont été compilés pour une population (en dénominateur) ne comprenant pas les domestiques étrangères.
[72] Data refer to government controlled areas. - Les données se rapportent aux zones contrôlées par le Gouvernement.
[73] Data refer to deaths of residents only. - Les données renvoient aux décès de résidents uniquement.
[74] Includes data for the Indian-held part of Jammu and Kashmir, the final status of which has not yet been determined. - Y compris les données pour la partie du Jammu et du Cachemire occupée par l'Inde dont le statut définitif n'a pas encore été déterminé.
[75] Rates were obtained by the Sample Registration System of India, which is a large demographic survey. - Les taux ont été obtenus par le Système de l'enregistrement par échantillon de l'Inde qui est une large enquête démographique.
[76] Based on the Sample Registration System of India, which is a large demographic survey. - Les données sont fondées sur le Système de l'enregistrement par échantillon de l'Inde qui est une large enquête démographique.
[77] Data are based on the publication: "Indonesia Population Projection 2015-2045" - Les données sont basées sur la publication : << Indonesia Population Projection 2015-2045 >>
[78] Data refer to the Iranian Year which begins on 21 March and ends on 20 March of the following year. - Les données concernent l'année iranienne, qui commence le 21 mars et se termine le 20 mars de l'année suivante.
[79] Based on Multiple Indicators Cluster Survey. - D'après l'Enquête par Grappes à Indicateurs Multiples.
[80] Includes data for East Jerusalem and Israeli residents in certain other territories under occupation by Israeli military forces since June 1967. - Y compris les données pour Jérusalem-Est et les résidents israéliens dans certains autres territoires occupés depuis 1967 par les forces armées israéliennes.
[81] Including deaths abroad of Israeli residents who were out of the country for less than a year. - Y compris les décès à l'étranger de résidents israéliens qui ont quitté le pays depuis moins d'un an.
[82] Data refer to Japanese nationals in Japan only. - Les données se raportent aux nationaux japonais au Japon seulement.
[83] The total number may include 'Unknown residence', but the categories urban and rural do not. - Le nombre total peut inclure les personnes dont la résidence n'est pas connue, à l'inverse des catégories de population urbaine et rurale.
[84] Total fertility rate computed as the sum of the age-specific fertility rates from age 15 to 49 years old. - Le taux de fécondité cumulé est calculé comme somme des taux de fécondité par âge de 15 à 49 ans.
[85] Excluding data for Jordanian territory under occupation since June 1967 by Israeli military forces. Excluding foreigners, including registered Palestinian refugees. - Non compris les données pour le territoire jordanien occupé depuis juin 1967 par les forces armées israéliennes. Non compris les étrangers, mais y compris les réfugiés de Palestine enregistrés.
[86] Data refer to the 12 months preceding the census in March. - Les données se rapportent aux 12 mois précédant le recensement de mars.
[87] Based on underlying data of the 2015 census. - Données fondées sur celles extraites du recensement de 2015.
[88] Data do not include foreigners. - Les données sur les etrangers ne sont pas inclus.
[89] Data are from Vital Registration System (VRS). - Les données proviennent du système d'enregistrement des faits d'état civil.
[90] Based on Vital Registration System (VRS). - Système d'enregistrement des faits d'état civil.
[91] Data from Births and Deaths Notification System (Ministry of Health and all health care providers). - Les données proviennent du système de notification des naissances et des décès (Ministère de la santé et tous prestataires de soins de santé).
[92] Data refer to Omani citizen only. - Les données concernent les citoyens d'Oman uniquement.
[93] Based on the results of the Pakistan Demographic and Health Survey (PDHS). - D'après les résultats de l'étude sur la santé et la démographie du Pakistan.
[94] Based on the results of the Pakistan Demographic Survey. - Données extraites de l'enquête démographique effectuée par le Pakistan.
[95] Data have not been adjusted for under-registration. Data based on the 2015 census-based population projection. Official data on total fertility rates are based on survey data (National Demographic and Health Survey) and not on vital statistics. - Non compris d'un ajustement pour sous-enregistrement. Données fondées sur la projection démographique établie à partir du recensement de 2015. Les données officielles sur les taux globaux de fécondité sont tirées d'une enquête (enquête démographique et sanitaire nationale) et non des statistiques de l'état civil.
[96] Excluding alien armed forces, civilian aliens employed by armed forces, and foreign diplomatic personnel and their dependants. Data refer to residence of child. - Non compris les militaires étrangers, les civils étrangers employés par les forces armées ni le personnel diplomatique étranger et les membres de leur famille les accompagnant. Les données correspondent à la résidence de l'enfant.
[97] Excluding alien armed forces, civilian aliens employed by armed forces, and foreign diplomatic personnel and their dependants. - Non compris les militaires étrangers, les civils étrangers employés par les forces armées ni le personnel diplomatique étranger et les membres de leur famille les accompagnant.
[98] Data refer to Saudi Arabian nationals only. Survey based estimates. - Les données ne concernent que les ressortissants saoudiens. Estimations basées sur des enquêtes.
[99] Data refer to Saudi Arabian nationals only. Based on 2010 population census and 2016 demographic survey. - Les données ne concernent que les ressortissants saoudiens. D'après le recensement de la population de 2010 et l'enquête démographique de 2016.
[100] Data refer to Saudi Arabian nationals only. - Les données ne concernent que les ressortissants saoudiens.
[101] Survey based estimates. - Estimations basées sur des enquêtes.

[102] Source: Family Health survey. - Source : Enquête sur la santé familiale.
[103] Data refer to resident population which comprises Singapore citizens and permanent residents. - Les données se rapportent à la population résidente composé des citoyens de Singapour et des résidents permanents.
[104] Data refer to resident total fertility rate. - Les données se rapportent aux indices synthétique de fécondité de la population résidante.
[105] Provisional data. Data refer to resident population which comprises Singapore citizens and permanent residents. - Données provisoires. Les données se rapportent à la population résidente composé des citoyens de Singapour et des résidents permanents.
[106] Source: Palestinian Central Bureau of Statistics, Population Register, updated version 2019. Data exclude Jerusalem ID holders. - Source: Bureau central de statistique palestinien, registre de la population, version actualisée jusqu'au 2019. Les données ne tiennent pas compte des détenteurs de carte d'identité de Jérusalem.
[107] Excluding infants born alive of less than 28 weeks' gestation, of less than 1 000 g in weight and 35 cm in length, who die within seven days of birth. Data have been adjusted for under-registration. - Non compris les enfants nés vivants après moins de 28 semaines de gestations, pesant moins de 1 000 g, mesurant moins de 35 cm et décédés dans les sept jours qui ont suivi leur naissance. Y compris un ajustement pour sous-enregistrement.
[108] Source: Strategy and Planning Division, Ministry of Public Health. - Source : Division de la stratégie et de la planification, Ministère de la Santé publique.
[109] Data refer to the 12 months preceding the census in July. - Les données se rapportent aux 12 mois précédant le recensement de juillet.
[110] Data from MERNIS (Central Population Administrative System). - Données de MERNIS (Système central de données démographiques).
[111] The registration of births and deaths is conducted by the Ministry of Health. An estimate of completeness is not provided. - L'enregistrement des naissances et des décès est mené par le Ministère de la Santé. Le degré estimatif de complétude n'est pas fourni.
[112] Including Non-Yemeni births. - Y compris les naissances non-yéménites.
[113] Including Non-Yemeni deaths. - Y compris les décès non-yéménites.
[114] Including births occurring abroad of mothers with residence in Austria. - Y compris les naissances survenues à l'étranger des mères avec résidence en Autriche.
[115] Including deaths of nationals abroad. - Y compris les décès des nationaux survenus à l'étranger.
[116] Including armed forces stationed outside the country, but excluding alien armed forces stationed in the area. - Y compris les militaires nationaux hors du pays, mais non compris les militaires étrangers en garnison sur le territoire.
[117] Excluding Faeroe Islands and Greenland shown separately, if available. - Non compris les Iles Féroé et le Groenland, qui font l'objet de rubriques distinctes, si disponible.
[118] Excluding Åland Islands. - Non compris les Îles d'Åland.
[119] Including live births by military personnel and their dependants. - Y compris les naissances vivantes parmi les membres du personnel militaire et leurs personnes à charge.
[120] Excluding armed forces. - Non compris les militaires en garnison.
[121] For year ending 31 March. - Période annuelle se terminant le 31 mars.
[122] Data is a three year average for the years 2016-2018. - Les données correspondent à une moyenne de trois ans couvrant les années 2016 à 2018.
[123] Data include the live births of women with unknown residence and homeless. Data include the live births of women with Hungarian usual residence regardless of whether the live birth occurred in Hungary or in a foreign country, and do not include the live births of women with foreign country usual residence. - Les données incluent les enfants nés vivants de femmes dont la résidence n'est pas connue et de femmes sans domicile fixe. Les données concernent les enfants nés vivants de femmes dont la résidence habituelle est en Hongrie, que la naissance vivante ait eu lieu en Hongrie ou dans un pays étranger, et ne comprennent pas les enfants nés vivants de femmes dont la résidence habituelle est dans un pays étranger.
[124] Data include the deceased persons with Hungarian usual residence regardless of whether the death occurred in Hungary or in a foreign country, and do not include the deceased persons with foreign country usual residence. - Les données comprennent tous les décès survenus alors que leur résidence habituelle était en Hongrie, que le décès ait eu lieu en Hongrie ou dans un pays étranger, et ne comprennent pas les décès des personnes dont la residence habituelle était dans un pays étranger.
[125] Data include the deceased infants with Hungarian usual residence regardless of whether the death occurred in Hungary or in a foreign country, and do not include the deceased infants with foreign country usual residence. - Les données comprennent les nourrissons décédés alors que leur résidence habituelle était en Hongrie, que le décès ait eu lieu en Hongrie ou dans un pays étranger, et ne comprennent pas les nourrissons décédés dont la residence habituelle était dans un pays étranger.
[126] Data include the live births of women with Hungarian usual residence regardless of whether the live birth occurred in Hungary or in a foreign country, and do not include the live births of women with foreign country usual residence. - Les données concernent les enfants nés vivants de femmes dont la résidence habituelle est en Hongrie, que la naissance vivante ait eu lieu en Hongrie ou dans un pays étranger, et ne comprennent pas les enfants nés vivants de femmes dont la résidence habituelle est dans un pays étranger.
[127] Source: City Hall, Civil Status Registry Office, resident and non-resident births. - Source : La mairie, Bureau de l'État Civil, toutes les naissances.
[128] Source: City Hall, Civil Status Registry Office, resident and non-resident deaths. - Source : La mairie, Bureau de l'État Civil, toutes les décès.
[129] Source: City Hall, Civil Status Registry Office, resident and non-resident deaths. Including still births. - Source : La mairie, Bureau de l'État Civil, toutes les décès. Les données comprennent les mortinaissances.
[130] Including residents outside the country if listed in a Netherlands population register. - Englobe les résidents se trouvant à l'étranger à condition qu'ils soient inscrits sur le registre de population des Pays-Bas.
[131] Including residents temporarily outside the country. - Y compris les résidents se trouvant temporairement hors du pays.
[132] Data refer to usual resident population. - Les données se réfèrent à la population résidente habituelle.
[133] Excluding Transnistria and the municipality of Bender. - Les données ne tiennent pas compte de l'information sur la Transnistria et la municipalité de Bender.
[134] Excludes data for Kosovo and Metohia. - Sans les données pour le Kosovo et Metohie.
[135] The Government of Ukraine has informed the United Nations that it is not in a position to provide statistical data concerning the Autonomous Republic of Crimea and the city of Sevastopol. - Le gouvernement Ukrainien a informé l'ONU qu'il n'est pas en mesure de fournir des données statistiques concernant la République autonome de Crimée et la ville de Sébastopol.
[136] Data refer to births with weight 500g and more (if weight is unknown - with length 25 centimeters and more, or with gestation during 22 weeks or more). - Données concernant les nouveau-nés de 500 grammes ou plus (si le poids est inconnu – de 25 centimètres de long ou plus, ou après une grossesse de 22 semaines ou plus).
[137] Data includes deaths resulting from births with weight 500 g and more (if weight is unknown - with length 25 cm and more, or with gestation during 22 weeks or more). - Y compris les décès de nouveau-nés de 500 g ou plus (si le poids est inconnu – de 25 cm de long ou plus, ou après une grossesse de 22 semaines ou plus).
[138] Excluding Channel Islands (Guernsey and Jersey) and Isle of Man, shown separately, if available. - Non compris les îles Anglo-Normandes (Guernesey et Jersey) et l'île de Man, qui font l'objet de rubriques distinctes, si disponible.
[139] Data tabulated by date of occurrence for England and Wales, and by date of registration for Northern Ireland and Scotland. - Données exploitées selon la date de l'événement pour l'Angleterre et le pays de Galles, et selon la date de l'enregistrement pour l'Irlande du Nord et l'Ecosse.
[140] Data recorded by Ministry of Health and Medical Services (MoHMS). - Données enregistrées par le Ministère de la santé et des services médicaux (MoHMS).
[141] Including United States military personnel, their dependants and contract employees. - Y compris les militaires des Etats-Unis, les membres de leur famille les accompagnant et les agents contractuels des Etats-Unis.
[142] Data refer to registered events only within island councils and civil registration office. - Correspond aux événements enregistrés par les conseils des îles et par les services de l'état civil.
[143] Random rounding to base 3 is applied in this table as a confidentiality measure. - Les chiffres sont arrondis à la base 3 de manière aléatoire, pour des raisons de confidentialité.
[144] Random rounding to base 3 is applied in this table as a confidentiality measure. Data refer to deaths of residents only. - Les chiffres sont arrondis à la base 3 de manière aléatoire, pour des raisons de confidentialité. Les données renvoient aux décès de résidents uniquement.
[145] Random rounding to base 3 is applied in this table as a confidentiality measure. Data refers to births registered in the country to mothers resident in the country. - Les chiffres sont arrondis à la base 3 de manière aléatoire, pour des raisons de confidentialité. Les données se rapportent aux naissances enregistrées dans le pays pour lesquelles la mère réside dans le pays.
[146] Data cover the period from 1 July of the previous year to 30 June of the present year. - Pour la période allant du 1er juillet de l'année précédente au 30 juin de l'année en cours.
[147] Source: Births, Deaths, and Marriages Registration Division, Samoa Bureau of Statistics. - Source : Division de l'enregistrement des naissances, des décès et des mariages du Bureau de statistique du Samoa.
[148] Based on the result of Census report 2016. Method: Direct calculation. - D'après les résultats du recensement de 2016. Méthode directe.

[149] Source: Births, Deaths, and Marriages Registration Division, Samoa Bureau of Statistics. The huge increase in 2018 is due to late registrations of all unregistered persons regardless of their age conducted mid-February to June. - Source : Division de l'enregistrement des naissances, des décès et des mariages du Bureau de statistique du Samoa. La forte augmentation constatée en 2018 s'explique par l'organisation, de la mi-février au mois de juin, d'une campagne de déclaration tardive pour toutes les personnes qui n'étaient pas encore déclarées, quel que soit leur âge.

Table 5 - *Demographic Yearbook 2019*

Table 5 presents national estimates of mid-year population for all available years between 2010 and 2019.

Description of variables: Mid-year estimates of the total population are those provided by national statistical offices. They refer to the *de facto* or *de jure* population on 1 July of the reference year. Exceptions to this are footnoted accordingly. The data are presented in thousands, rounded by the Statistics Division of the United Nations Department of Economic and Social Affairs.

For some countries or areas the figures presented in this table and the figures used to calculate rates in subsequent tables are not the same, as these countries have provided a reference population for vital events that is different than the total population.

Unless otherwise indicated, all estimates relate to the population within present geographical boundaries. Major exceptions to this principle are explained in footnotes.

Reliability of data: Reliable mid-year population estimates are those that are based on a complete census (or on a sample survey) and have been adjusted on a basis of a continuous population register or on the balance of births, deaths and migration. Reliable mid-year estimates appear in roman type. Mid-year estimates that are not calculated on this basis are considered less reliable and are shown in *italics.*

Limitations: Statistics on estimates of the mid-year total population are subject to the same qualifications as have been set forth for population statistics in general in section 3 of the Technical Notes.

International comparability of mid-year population estimates is also affected by the fact that some of these estimates refer to the *de jure*, and not the *de facto*, population. These are indicated in the column titled "Code". The difference between the *de facto* and the *de jure* population is discussed in section 3.1.1 of the Technical Notes.

Earlier data: Estimates of mid-year population have been shown in previous issues of the *Demographic Yearbook*. Information on the years and specific topics covered is presented in the Historical Index.

Tableau 5 – *Annuaire démographique 2019*

Le tableau 5 présente des estimations nationales de la population en milieu d'année pour le plus grand nombre possible d'années entre 2010 et 2019.

Description des variables : les estimations de la population totale en milieu d'année sont celles qui ont été communiquées par les services nationaux de statistique. Elles correspondent à la population de fait ou se réfèrent à la population de droit, au 1er juillet de l'année de référence. Lorsque la date est différente, cela est signalé par une note. Sauf indication contraire, tous les chiffres sont exprimés en milliers. Les données ont été arrondies par la Division de statistique du Département des affaires économiques et sociales de l'Organisation des Nations Unies.

Pour certains pays ou territoires, les données présentées dans ce tableau sont différentes des données utilisées pour calculer les taux dans les tableaux suivants, parce que ces pays ont fourni une population de référence pour les événements démographiques différente de la population totale.

Sauf indication contraire, toutes les estimations se rapportent à la population présente sur le territoire actuel des pays ou zones considérés. Les principales exceptions à cette règle sont expliquées en note.

Fiabilité des données : les estimations de la population en milieu d'année sont considérées sûres quand elles sont fondées sur un recensement complet (ou sur une enquête par sondage) et ont été ajustées en fonction des données provenant d'un registre permanent de population ou en fonction des naissances, décès et mouvements migratoires qui ont eu lieu pendant la période. Les estimations considérées comme sûres apparaissent en caractères romains. Les estimations dont le calcul n'a pas été effectué sur cette base sont considérées comme moins sûres et apparaissent en italique.

Insuffisance des données : les statistiques concernant les estimations de la population totale en milieu d'année appellent toutes les réserves qui ont été formulées à la section 3 des Notes techniques à propos des statistiques de la population en général.

Le fait que certaines des estimations concernant la population en milieu d'année se réfèrent à la population de droit et non à la population de fait influe sur la comparabilité internationale. Ces cas ont été signalés dans la colonne « Code ». La différence entre la population de fait et la population de droit est expliquée à la section 3.1.1 des Notes techniques.

Données publiées antérieurement : des estimations de la population en milieu d'année ont été publiées dans des éditions antérieures de l'*Annuaire démographique*. Pour plus de précisions concernant les années et les sujets pour lesquels des données ont été publiées, se reporter à l'index.

5. Estimates of mid-year population: 2010 - 2019
Estimations de la population au milieu de l'année : 2010 - 2019

Continent and country or area / Continent et pays ou zone	Code[a]	2010	2011	2012	2013	2014	2015	2016	2017	2018	2019
		Population estimates (in thousands) - Estimations (en milliers)									
AFRICA - AFRIQUE											
Algeria - Algérie	DJ	35 978	36 717	37 495	38 297	39 114	39 963	40 836	41 696	42 578	43 413[1]
Angola	DF	17 430[2]	17 992[2]	18 577[2]	19 184[2]	25 901[3]	26 682[3]	27 504[3]	28 360[3]	29 250[3]	30 176[3]
Benin - Bénin	DF	8 779[1]	9 067[1]	9 365[1]	...	10 293[4]	10 585[4]	10 883[4]	11 187[4]	11 496[4]	...
Botswana	DJ	1 823	1 850	2 071[5]	2 115[5]	2 156[5]	2 195[5]	2 231[5]	2 267[5]	2 303[5]	2 339[5]
Burkina Faso[1]	DJ	15 731	16 249	16 779	17 323	17 880	18 450	19 034	19 632	20 244	20 870
Burundi	DF	9 461	9 771	10 073	10 367	10 654	10 933	11 215	11 495	11 772	12 044
Cabo Verde[1]	DJ	494	500	506	512	518	525	531	538	544	550
Cameroon - Cameroun[6]	DJ	20 127	20 710	21 277	21 848	22 454	23 050	23 642	24 254	24 863	25 492
Chad - Tchad	DJ	11 470	11 881	12 307	12 747	13 201	13 670	14 152	14 649	15 162	15 693
Congo	DF	...	...	...	4 278	...	...	...	4 709	...	...
	DJ	4 119	4 257	4 394	...	4 666	4 802	4 934	...	5 203	5 336
Côte d'Ivoire[7]	DF	20 845	21 302	21 758	22 215	22 723	23 334	23 950	24 571	25 194	25 822
Djibouti[8]	DF	841	865	...	...	...	...	...	...	...	...
Egypt - Égypte	DF	78 685	80 530	82 550	84 629	86 811	88 958	91 023	95 203	97 147	*98 902
Equatorial Guinea - Guinée équatoriale	DF	1 622[9]	...	...	...	...	1 225[10]	1 268[10]	1 312[10]	1 358[10]	1 406[10]
Eritrea - Érythrée[11]	DF	2 691	2 759	2 829	2 901	2 976	3 052	3 131	3 212	3 295	3 379
Eswatini[12]	DJ	1 056	1 068	1 080	1 093	1 106	1 119	1 133	1 146	1 159	1 172
Ethiopia - Éthiopie[13]	DF	79 634	81 668	83 741	85 837	87 952	90 075	92 205	94 352	96 503	98 537
Gambia - Gambie	DF	1 731	1 790	1 850	1 857	1 898	1 959	2 020	2 083	2 148	2 213
Ghana[14]	DF	...	25 235	25 825	26 428	27 043	27 670	28 308	28 957	29 614	30 281
Guinea - Guinée[15]	DJ	9 557[16]	9 812[16]	10 071[16]	10 334[16]	10 600[3]	10 918[3]	11 233[3]	11 555[3]	11 884[3]	12 218[3]
Guinea-Bissau - Guinée-Bissau[1]	DF	1 460	1 472	1 485	1 499	1 514	1 531	1 548	1 566	1 585	1 605
Kenya[17]	DF	38 474	39 545	40 657	41 788	42 961	44 157	45 389	46 595	47 849	...
Lesotho[18]	DF	1 892	1 897	1 903	1 909	1 917	1 924	...	...	...	...
Liberia - Libéria	DF	3 627	3 705	3 784	3 865	3 946	...	...	...	...	...
Libya - Libye[19]	DF	5 689	5 791	5 892	5 994	6 096	6 162	...	...	...	...
Madagascar[20]	DF	20 142	20 696	21 263	21 842	22 434	23 040	23 658	24 290	24 934	26 620
Malawi[1]	DF	13 948	14 389	14 845	15 317	15 805	16 310	16 833	...	...	...
	DJ	...	...	...	...	...	...	...	17 373	...	...
Mali[21]	DF	15 370	15 843	16 312	16 808	17 319	17 819	18 341	18 874	19 418	...
Mauritania - Mauritanie[1]	DF	3 341	3 297	3 378	3 537	3 637	3 720	3 783	3 894	3 984	...
Mauritius - Maurice[22]	DJ	1 281[23]	1 252[5]	1 256[5]	1 259[5]	1 261[5]	1 263[5]	1 263[5]	1 265[5]	1 265[5]	1 266[5]
Mayotte	DJ	...	...	...	...	228[24]	232[25]	241[25]	250[25]	*265[24]	269[25]
Morocco - Maroc	DF	31 894[26]	32 245[26]	32 597[26]	32 950[26]	...	...	...	...	...	...
	DJ	...	...	...	...	33 770[27]	34 125[27]	34 487[27]	34 852[27]	35 220[27]	35 587[27]
Mozambique[12]	DF	22 417	23 050	23 701	24 366	25 042	25 728	26 424	27 129	27 844	29 318
Namibia - Namibie	DF	2 143[1]	2 116[5]	2 155[5]	2 196[5]	2 238[5]	2 281[5]	2 324[5]	2 369[5]	2 414[5]	2 459[5]
Niger	DJ	15 204[1]	15 731[1]	16 994[28]	17 680[28]	18 389[28]	19 125[28]	19 865[28]	20 651[28]	...	...
Nigeria - Nigéria[18]	DF	159 608	164 798	170 157	175 690	181 403	187 302	193 393	...	...	...
Republic of South Sudan - République de Soudan du Sud[29]	DF	9 005	9 389	9 783	10 182	10 585	11 000	11 425	11 868	12 323	...
Reunion - Réunion	DJ	821[25]	829[25]	834[25]	839[24]	847[24]	851[25]	853[25]	854[25]	*864[24]	858[25]
Rwanda	DF	10 413[1]	10 718[1]	10 483[28]	10 737[28]	10 997[28]	11 263[28]	11 533[28]	11 809[28]	12 090[28]	12 374[28]
Saint Helena ex. dep. - Sainte-Hélène sans dép.	DF	4	4	4	4[30]	4	4	5	5	5	4
Sao Tome and Principe - Sao Tomé-et-Principe	DF	164	167	...	...	...	...	...	...	...	...
	DJ	...	...	...	182[28]	186[28]	190[28]	194[28]	198[28]	202[28]	206[28]
Senegal - Sénégal	DJ	12 509[30]	12 842[30]	13 208[1]	13 509[1]	13 926[1]	14 357[1]	14 800[1]	15 256[1]	15 726[1]	16 209[1]
Seychelles	DF	90	87	88	90	91	93	95	96	97	98
Sierra Leone	DF	6 131[16]	6 323[16]	6 515[16]	6 708[16]	6 900[16]	...	7 296[10]	7 499[10]	7 701[10]	7 901[10]
South Africa - Afrique du Sud	DF	51 329[16]	52 129[16]	52 930[3]	53 751[3]	54 574[3]	55 407[3]	56 252[3]	57 098[3]	57 939[3]	58 775[3]
Sudan - Soudan[1]	DF	32 491	33 284	34 093	34 918	35 733	36 602	37 489	38 378	39 280	40 204
Togo	DJ	6 191[1]	6 278[3]	6 431[3]	6 589[3]	6 752[3]	6 921[3]	7 092[3]	7 265[3]	7 440[3]	7 617[3]
Tunisia - Tunisie	DF	10 566	10 674	10 784	10 895	11 012	11 163	11 304	11 435	11 551	11 722
Uganda - Ouganda	DF	31 785	32 940	34 131	...	34 141[7]	35 502[7]	36 653[7]	37 839[7]	39 059[7]	40 308[7]
United Republic of Tanzania - République Unie de Tanzanie	DF	43 188[31]	44 485[31]	45 798[31]	46 356[28]	47 831[28]	49 359[28]	50 942[28]	52 555[28]	54 199[28]	55 891[28]
Zambia - Zambie[14]	DJ	...	13 719	14 145	14 580	15 023	15 474	15 934	16 405	16 888	17 381
Zimbabwe[28]	DF	...	...	...	13 369	13 652	13 943	14 240	14 542	14 849	...

5. Estimates of mid-year population: 2010 - 2019
Estimations de la population au milieu de l'année : 2010 - 2019 (continued - suite)

Continent and country or area / Continent et pays ou zone	Code[a]	Population estimates (in thousands) - Estimations (en milliers)									
		2010	2011	2012	2013	2014	2015	2016	2017	2018	2019
AMERICA, NORTH - AMÉRIQUE DU NORD											
Anguilla	DF	16	...	14	14	14	15	15	...	...	*16[30]
Antigua and Barbuda -	DF	91	...	...	...	...	...	...	...	...	...
Antigua-et-Barbuda	DJ	...	86[5]	87[5]	88[5]	89[5]	91[5]	92[5]	94[5]	95[5]	96[5]
Aruba	DJ	102	103	105	106	108	109	110	111	111	112
Bahamas[14]	DJ	352	355	359	362	366	370	373	377	381	385
Barbados - Barbade	DJ	278	278	278	277	277	275	...	...	...	...
Belize	DJ	*324*	*332*	*341*	*350*	*359*	*368*	*378*	*388*	*398*	*408*
Bermuda - Bermudes[32]	DJ	64[14]	63[14]	62[14]	62[14]	62[14]	62[14]	64[33]	64[33]	64[33]	64[33]
British Virgin Islands - Îles Vierges britanniques	DF	28	28	28	29	...	29	...	...	...	...
Canada[34]	DJ	34 005[35]	34 339[35]	34 714[35]	35 083[35]	35 437[35]	35 703[35]	36 109[36]	36 543[37]	37 058[37]	*37 589[3]
Cayman Islands - Îles Caïmanes	DJ	56	55	56	56	57	59	61	63	64	68
Costa Rica	DJ	4 538[38]	4 592[38]	4 651[38]	4 712[38]	4 772[38]	4 834[39]	4 890[40]	4 947[41]	5 004[42]	5 060[43]
Cuba	DJ	11 171	11 172	11 174	11 192	11 224	11 239	11 239	11 230	11 215	11 202
Curaçao	DJ	149[16]	151[16]	152[3]	154[3]	156[3]	158[3]	160[3]	160[3]	159[3]	157[3]
Dominica - Dominique	DF	71	71	71	71	72	71[30]	71[30]	*67[30]	...	...
Dominican Republic - République dominicaine[1]	DJ	*9 479*	*9 580*	*9 681*	*9 785*	*9 883*	*9 980*	*10 075*	*10 169*	*10 266*	*10 358*
El Salvador[12]	DJ	6 183	6 216	6 251	6 289	6 328	6 460	6 521	6 582	6 643	...
Greenland - Groenland[44]	DJ	57	57	57	56	56	56	56	56	56	56
Grenada - Grenade	DF	105	...	108	109	109	110	111	111	...	...
Guadeloupe[45]	DJ	404	404	403	401	399	397	395	429[25]	422[25]	...
Guatemala[31]	DJ	14 362	14 714	15 073	15 438	15 807	16 183	16 556	16 932	17 311	...
Haiti - Haïti[46]	DJ	*10 085*	*10 248*	*10 413*	*10 579*	*10 746*	*10 912*	*11 078*	*11 245*	*11 412*	*11 578*
Honduras	DF	*8 046[47]*	*8 215[47]*	*8 385[47]*	...	...	...	...	...	...	...
	DJ	...	...	...	*8 287[4]*	*8 432[4]*	*8 577[4]*	*8 721[4]*	*8 866[4]*	*9 012[4]*	*9 158[4]*
Jamaica - Jamaïque	DJ	2 702	2 700	2 708	2 715	2 721	2 725	2 728	2 729	2 728	2 733
Martinique	DJ	394[25]	392[25]	388[25]	386[25]	382	378[25]	377[25]	375[25]	369[25]	...
Mexico - Mexique	DJ	*113 749[48]*	115 367[48]	116 936[48]	118 454[48]	119 936[48]	121 348[48]	122 715[49]	124 042[49]	125 328[49]	126 578[49]
Montserrat	DF	5	...	...	...	...	...	...	...	...	...
	DJ	...	5	5	5	5	5	5	...	5[50]	...
Nicaragua	DJ	*5 816*	*5 997*	*6 071*	*6 134*	*6 198*	*6 263*	*6 328*	*6 394*	*6 460*	*6 528*
Panama[14]	DF	*3 662*	*3 724*	*3 788*	*3 851*	3 913	3 975	4 037	4 098	4 159	4 219
Puerto Rico - Porto Rico[51]	DJ	3 721[52]	3 679[3]	3 634[3]	3 593[3]	3 535[3]	3 473[3]	3 407[3]	3 325[3]	3 195[3]	3 194
Saint Barthélemy - Saint-Barthélemy[25]	DJ	...	...	...	9	10	...	...	...	...	...
Saint Kitts and Nevis - Saint-Kitts-et-Nevis	DF	*53	...	...	...	...	...	...	...	...	...
Saint Lucia - Sainte-Lucie	DF	...	167	169	171	173	174	176	177	179	...
Saint Pierre and Miquelon - Saint Pierre-et-Miquelon	DJ	...	6[25]	6[25]	...	...	6	6[25]	6[25]	...	...
Saint Vincent and the Grenadines - Saint-Vincent-et-les Grenadines	DJ	110	110	110	110	110	110	110	110	111	111
Saint-Martin (French part) - Saint-Martin (partie française)	DJ	...	...	...	...	35	...	37[25]	36	35	...
Sint Maarten (Dutch part) - Saint-Martin (partie néerlandaise)	DF	36	33	35	37	37[25]	38[25]	39[25]	41[25]	41[25]	...
Trinidad and Tobago -	DF	1 318[23]	...	...	...	...	...	...	...	...	...
Trinité-et-Tobago	DJ	...	...	1 335[5]	1 341[5]	1 345[5]	1 350[5]	1 354[5]	1 357[5]	1 359[5]	1 364[5]
Turks and Caicos Islands - Îles Turques et Caïques	DJ	*35*	*34*	*32*	*34*	*35*	*37*	*38*	*40*	**41*	**43*
United States of America - États-Unis d'Amérique[53]	DJ	309 348	311 663	313 998	316 205	318 563	320 897	323 128	325 147	327 167	328 240
United States Virgin Islands - Îles Vierges américaines[54]	DJ	106	106	105	105	104	104	108	107	...	...

5. Estimates of mid-year population: 2010 - 2019
Estimations de la population au milieu de l'année : 2010 - 2019 (continued - suite)

Continent and country or area / Continent et pays ou zone	Code[a]	Population estimates (in thousands) - Estimations (en milliers)									
		2010	2011	2012	2013	2014	2015	2016	2017	2018	2019
AMERICA, SOUTH - AMÉRIQUE DU SUD											
Argentina - Argentine[14]	DF	40 788	41 261	41 733	42 203	42 670	43 132	43 590	44 045	44 495	44 939
Bolivia (Plurinational State of) - Bolivie (État plurinational de)	DF	10 031[16]	10 191[16]	10 351[3]	10 508[3]	10 666[3]	10 825[3]	10 985[3]	11 146[3]	11 307[3]	11 470[3]
Brazil - Brésil[55]	DJ	195 498	197 397	199 242	201 033	202 769	204 451	206 081	207 661	208 495	210 147
Chile - Chili[56]	DF	17 064	17 254	17 443	17 612	17 788	17 971	18 167	18 419	18 751	19 107
Colombia - Colombie[57]	DJ	44 350	44 796	45 218	45 623	46 021	46 431	46 900	47 408	48 258	49 396
Ecuador - Équateur[58]	DF	15 012	15 266	15 521	15 775	16 027	16 279	16 529	16 777	17 023	17 268
French Guiana - Guyane française[25]	DJ	229	238	240	244	252	255	263	274	282	...
Guyana[59]	DF	752	751	747	746	746	745	743	741	745	744
Paraguay[60]	DF	6 266	6 363	6 461	6 559	6 657	6 756	6 855	6 954	7 053	7 153
Peru - Pérou[61]	DF	28 693	28 906	29 113	29 341	29 616	29 964	30 423	30 974	31 562	32 131
Suriname	DJ	531	540	...	550	559	567	576	583	590	...
Uruguay	DJ	3 397	3 413	3 426[1]	3 440[1]	3 454[1]	3 467[1]	3 480[1]	3 493[1]	3 506[1]	3 519[1]
Venezuela (Bolivarian Republic of) - Venezuela (République bolivarienne du)	DF	28 396[62]	28 811	29 231	29 650	30 070	30 489	30 883	31 277	31 671	32 065
ASIA - ASIE											
Afghanistan[63]	DF	24 486	24 988	25 500	26 023	26 557	27 101	27 657	28 224	30 075	30 726
Armenia - Arménie	DJ	3 045	3 028	3 024	3 022	3 014	3 005	2 992	2 979	2 969	2 965[25]
Azerbaijan - Azerbaïdjan	DJ	9 054	9 173	9 296	9 417	9 535	9 649	9 758	9 854	9 940	10 020
Bahrain - Bahreïn	DJ	1 229	1 195	1 209	1 253	1 315	1 370	1 424	1 501	1 503	1 484
Bangladesh	DF	148 620	150 611	152 700	154 790	156 880	158 900	160 800	162 700	164 600	166 500
Bhutan - Bhoutan	DF	696[64]	708[64]	721[64]	733[64]	745[64]	757[64]	769[64]	...	734[65]	742[65]
Brunei Darussalam - Brunéi Darussalam	DF	387[16]	...	...	...	...	...	...	...	...	...
	DJ	...	...	399	403	408	412	417[66]	430	442	460
Cambodia - Cambodge[67]	DF	14 303	14 521	14 741	14 963	15 184	15 405	...	...	...	...
China - Chine[68]	DF	1 337 700[69]	1 344 100[70]	1 350 695[70]	1 357 380[69]	1 364 270[69]	1 371 220[69]	1 378 665[69]	1 386 395[69]	1 392 730[69]	1 397 715[69]
China, Hong Kong SAR - Chine, Hong Kong RAS	DJ	7 024	7 072	7 150	7 179	7 230	7 291	7 337	7 392	7 451	7 507
China, Macao SAR - Chine, Macao RAS	DJ	537	550	568	592	622	643	653	648	659	672
Cyprus - Chypre[71]	DJ	829[24]	851[24]	864[24]	862[24]	853[24]	848[24]	852[24]	860[24]	870[24]	876[25]
Georgia - Géorgie	DF	4 453	4 483	4 491	4 487	...	...	...	...	...	...
	DJ	...	...	...	...	3 727[7]	3 717[7]	3 719[7]	3 724[72]	3 727[72]	3 723[73]
India - Inde[74]	DF	1 176 742	1 192 506	1 208 116	1 223 581	1 238 887	1 254 019	1 268 961	1 283 600	1 298 041	1 312 240
Indonesia - Indonésie	DJ	238 519[75]	241 991[75]	245 425[75]	248 818[75]	252 165[75]	255 588[76]	258 497[76]	261 355[76]	264 162[76]	266 912[76]
Iran (Islamic Republic of) - Iran (République islamique d')[77]	DJ	74 340	...	76 038	76 942	77 856	78 773	80 038	81 070	82 084	83 075
Iraq	DF	32 211	33 052	33 913	34 794	35 736	36 659	...	...	*37 842	38 836
Israel - Israël[78]	DJ	7 624	7 766	7 911	8 059	8 216	8 380	8 546	8 713	8 883	*9 053
Japan - Japon[79]	DJ	128 070	127 833[10]	127 629[10]	127 445[10]	127 276[10]	127 141[80]	126 995[80]	126 786[10]	126 529[80]	126 265[80]
Jordan - Jordanie[81]	DF	6 699	6 993	7 427	8 114	8 804	9 559	9 798	10 053	10 309	10 554
Kazakhstan[82]	DF	16 322[83]	16 557[83]	16 792[83]	17 036[83]	17 288[83]	17 543[83]	17 794[83]	18 038[83]	18 276	18 514
Kuwait - Koweït	DF	2 933	3 107	3 247	3 428	3 767	3 971	4 079	4 022	4 125	4 420[25]
Kyrgyzstan - Kirghizstan	DJ	5 448[24]	5 515[24]	5 608[24]	5 720[24]	5 836[24]	5 957[24]	6 080[24]	6 198[24]	6 323[24]	6 390[25]
Lao People's Democratic Republic - République démocratique populaire lao[10]	DJ	6 230	6 349	6 466	6 581	6 693	6 672	6 787	6 901	7 013	7 123
Malaysia - Malaisie[84]	DJ	28 589	29 062	29 510	30 214	30 709	31 186	31 634	32 023	32 382	32 581
Maldives	DF	320	325	331	336	438[85]	454[85]	472[85]	492[85]	512[85]	534[85]
Mongolia - Mongolie	DF	2 739	2 786	2 840	2 899	2 963	3 027	3 089	3 149	3 208	3 268
Myanmar[86]	DF	59 780	50 149[7]	50 667[7]	51 184[7]	51 991[7]	52 451[7]	52 917[7]	53 388[7]	53 863[7]	54 340[7]
Nepal - Népal	DJ	28 044	28 585	26 873[5]	27 257[5]	27 646[5]	28 038[5]	28 431[5]	28 826[5]	29 219[5]	29 610[5]
Oman[87]	DF	...	3 295	3 623	3 855	3 993	4 159	4 414	4 560	4 602	4 618
Pakistan[88]	DF	173 510	177 100	...	184 350	188 020	191 710	...	...	...	...
Philippines	DJ	93 135[14]	94 824[14]	96 511[14]	98 197[14]	99 880[14]	100 833[10]	102 530[10]	104 169[10]	105 755[10]	107 288[10]
Qatar	DF	1 715	1 733	1 833	2 004	2 216	2 438	2 618	2 725	2 760	2 799
Republic of Korea - République de Corée	DJ	49 554	49 937	50 200	50 429	50 747	51 015	51 218	51 362	51 607	51 337[89]
Saudi Arabia - Arabie saoudite	DF	27 411	28 173	28 897	29 613	30 340	31 062	31 788	32 613	33 414	34 218
Singapore - Singapour[90]	DJ	5 077	5 184	5 312	5 399	5 470	5 535	5 607	5 612	5 639	5 704

5. Estimates of mid-year population: 2010 - 2019
Estimations de la population au milieu de l'année : 2010 - 2019 (continued - suite)

Continent and country or area Continent et pays ou zone	Code[a]	2010	2011	2012	2013	2014	2015	2016	2017	2018	2019
		Population estimates (in thousands) - Estimations (en milliers)									
ASIA - ASIE											
Sri Lanka	DF	20 675	20 892	...	...	...	...	...	...	...	...
	DJ	...	...	20 425	20 585	20 778	20 970	*21 203	*21 444	*21 670	*21 803
State of Palestine - État de Palestine	DF	4 023	4 125	4 226	4 328	4 429	4 530	4 632	4 733	4 854	4 977
Syrian Arab Republic - République arabe syrienne[91]	DF	20 619	21 124	...	...	...	...	...	...	...	...
Tajikistan - Tadjikistan	DF	7 519	7 714	7 897	8 074	8 257	8 452	8 647	8 837	*8 931	9 127
Thailand - Thaïlande	DJ	63 878	64 076	64 266	64 621	64 955	65 027	65 013	65 522	66 200[1]	66 374[1]
Timor-Leste[1]	DF	1 089	1 120	1 152	1 180	1 212	1 200	1 221	1 242	1 261	1 281
Turkey - Turquie[92]	DJ	73 723[30]	74 724[30]	75 627[30]	76 668[30]	77 696[30]	78 741[30]	79 815[30]	80 313	81 339	82 377
United Arab Emirates - Émirats arabes unis[93]	DF	8 264	8 394[30]	8 526[30]	8 661[30]	8 799[30]	8 939[30]	9 121[30]	9 304[30]	9 367[30]	...
Uzbekistan - Ouzbékistan[82]	DJ	28 562	29 339	29 774	30 243	30 758	31 299	31 848	32 389	32 956	33 256[25]
Viet Nam	DJ	86 947[94]	87 860[94]	88 809[94]	89 760[94]	90 729[94]	91 710[94]	92 695[94]	*93 678[94]	*94 666[94]	*96 484[95]
Yemen - Yémen[1]	DJ	23 154	23 833	24 527	25 235	25 956	26 687	27 426	28 170	...	...
EUROPE											
Åland Islands - Îles d'Åland[44]	DJ	28	28	28	29	29	29	29	29	30	30
Albania - Albanie	DF	2 913	...	...	...	...	...	...	...	...	...
	DJ	...	2 905	2 900	2 895	2 889	2 881	2 876	2 873	2 866	2 862[25]
Andorra - Andorre[44]	DJ	70[96]	70[25]	70[25]	70	70	71	72	73[25]	75[25]	76[25]
Austria - Autriche	DJ	8 361	8 389	8 426	8 477	8 544	8 629	8 740	8 795	8 838	8 859[25]
Belarus - Bélarus	DJ	9 491	9 473	9 464	9 466	9 475	9 490	9 502[24]	9 498[24]	9 483[24]	9 475[25]
Belgium - Belgique	DJ	10 896	11 044	11 128	11 183	11 231	11 285[24]	11 331[24]	11 375[24]	11 427[24]	11 456[25]
Bosnia and Herzegovina - Bosnie-Herzégovine	DF	3 843	3 841	3 837	...	...	...	...	...	...	...
	DJ	...	...	...	3 531	3 526	3 518	3 511	3 510[25]	3 500[25]	*3 492[25]
Bulgaria - Bulgarie	DJ	7 534	7 348	7 306	7 264	7 224	7 178	7 128[24]	7 076[24]	7 025[24]	7 000[25]
Croatia - Croatie	DJ	4 295	4 281	4 268	4 256	4 238	4 204	4 174	4 125	4 088	4 076[25]
Czechia - Tchéquie	DJ	10 474	10 496	10 511	10 511	10 525	10 543	10 565	10 590	10 626	10 669
Denmark - Danemark[97]	DJ	5 545	5 567	5 587	5 609	5 640	5 678	5 724	5 761	5 790	5 814
Estonia - Estonie	DJ	1 331	1 327	1 323	1 318	1 315	1 315	1 316[24]	1 317	1 322[24]	1 325[25]
Faroe Islands - Îles Féroé	DJ	49	49	48	48	48	49	49	50	51	52
Finland - Finlande[44]	DJ	5 335[98]	5 360[98]	5 386[98]	5 410[98]	5 433[98]	5 451[98]	5 466[98]	5 479[98]	5 486[98]	5 518[25]
France[99]	DJ	62 918	63 223	63 537	63 863	64 164	64 385	*64 544	*64 672	*64 769	64 822[25]
Germany - Allemagne	DJ	81 757	80 275[5]	80 426[5]	80 646[5]	80 983[5]	81 687[5]	82 349[100]	82 657[100]	82 906[100]	83 019[101]
Gibraltar[102]	DF	31	32	33	33	33	34	34	...	...	...
Greece - Grèce	DF	11 121	11 105	11 045	10 965	10 892	10 821	10 776	10 761	10 733	10 725[25]
Guernsey - Guernesey[103]	DJ	62	63	63	63	62	62	62	62	62	63
Holy See - Saint-Siège[104]	DF	0[105]	...	0[106]	...	...	...	...	...	...	...
Hungary - Hongrie	DJ	10 000	9 972	9 920	9 893	9 866[107]	9 843[107]	9 814[107]	9 788[107]	9 776[107]	9 773[108]
Iceland - Islande[89]	DJ	318	319	321	324	327	331	335	343	353	357[25]
Ireland - Irlande	DF	4 560	4 580	4 600	4 624	4 658	4 702	...	...	...	...
	DJ	...	...	...	...	...	...	4 755[107]	4 807[107]	4 867[107]	4 904[108]
Isle of Man - Île de Man[109]	DJ	83	...	85	86	86	87	83	84	...	...
Italy - Italie	DJ	59 277	59 379	59 540	60 234	60 789	60 731	60 627	60 537	60 422	...
Jersey[25]	DJ	96	97	98	99	100	101	103	104	106	107
Latvia - Lettonie	DJ	2 098	2 060	2 034	2 013	1 994	1 978	1 960	1 942	1 927	1 920[25]
Liechtenstein	DJ	36	36	37	37	37	37	38	38	38	39
Lithuania - Lituanie	DJ	3 097	3 028	2 988	2 958	2 932[107]	2 905[107]	2 868[107]	2 828[107]	2 802[107]	2 794[108]
Luxembourg	DJ	507	518	531	543	556	570	583	596	608	614[25]
Malta - Malte[110]	DJ	415	416	420	426	435	445	455	468	485	494[25]
Monaco[111]	DJ	36	36	36	37	37[25]	38[25]	38[25]	38[25]	38[25]	...
Montenegro - Monténégro	DJ	619	620	621	621	622[107]	622[107]	622[107]	622[107]	622[107]	622[108]
Netherlands - Pays-Bas	DJ	16 615	16 693	16 755	16 804	16 865	16 940	17 030	17 100	17 232	17 282[25]
North Macedonia - Macédoine du Nord	DJ	2 055	2 059	2 061	2 064	2 067	2 070	2 072	2 075	2 076	2 077[25]
Norway - Norvège[107]	DJ	4 889	4 953	5 019	5 080	5 137	5 189	5 235[24]	5 277[24]	5 296[25]	5 328[25]
Poland - Pologne[107]	DJ	38 042	38 051	38 059	38 032	38 006	37 982	37 957	37 962	37 956	37 973[25]
Portugal	DJ	10 573	10 558	10 515	10 457	10 401	10 358	10 325	10 300	10 284	10 277[25]
Republic of Moldova - République de Moldova[112]	DJ	3 562	3 560	3 560	3 559	2 857[113]	2 835[113]	2 802[113]	2 755[113]	2 706[113]	*2 682[113]
Romania - Roumanie[107]	DF	...	...	...	...	19 916	19 822	19 706	19 592	19 477	19 414[25]
	DJ	20 247	20 148	20 060	19 989	...	...	...	...	...	...

5. Estimates of mid-year population: 2010 - 2019
Estimations de la population au milieu de l'année : 2010 - 2019 (continued - suite)

Continent and country or area Continent et pays ou zone	Code[a]	Population estimates (in thousands) - Estimations (en milliers)									
		2010	2011	2012	2013	2014	2015	2016	2017	2018	2019
EUROPE											
Russian Federation - Fédération de Russie	DJ	142 849	142 961	143 202	143 507	...	...	...	...	...	...
San Marino - Saint-Marin[44]	DF	33	33	34	33	34	34[25]	34[25]	34[25]	...	...
	DJ	...	...	...	...	...	...	...	...	35	...
Serbia - Serbie[114]	DJ	7 291	7 237[5]	7 201[5]	7 167[5]	7 132[5]	7 095[5]	7 058[5]	7 021[5]	6 983[5]	6 964[101]
Slovakia - Slovaquie	DJ	5 431	5 398	5 408	5 413	5 419	5 424	5 431	5 439	5 447	5 450[25]
Slovenia - Slovénie	DJ	2 049	2 052	2 056	2 059	2 062	2 063	2 064	2 066	2 070	2 081[25]
Spain - Espagne	DJ	46 562	46 736	46 766	46 593	46 481[89]	46 448[89]	46 450[89]	46 533[89]	46 729[89]	46 937[115]
Sweden - Suède[44]	DJ	9 378	9 449	9 519	9 600[89]	9 696[89]	9 799[89]	9 923[116]	10 058[116]	10 120[115]	10 230[115]
Switzerland - Suisse	DJ	7 825	7 912	7 997	8 089	8 189[117]	8 282[117]	8 373[117]	8 452[118]	8 507[117]	*8 514[119]
Ukraine	DF	45 871	45 706	45 593	45 553[25]	45 426[25]	42 845[120]	42 673[120]	42 485[120]	42 386[121]	*42 153[121]
United Kingdom of Great Britain and Northern Ireland - Royaume-Uni de Grande-Bretagne et d'Irlande du Nord[122]	DJ	62 759	63 285	63 705	64 106[107]	64 597[107]	65 110[107]	65 648[107]	66 041[123]	66 436[108]	*66 797[107]
OCEANIA - OCÉANIE											
American Samoa - Samoas américaines[51]	DJ	67	64	64	63	62	61	60	60	...	...
Australia - Australie[33]	DJ	22 032	22 340	22 733	23 128	23 476	23 816	24 191	24 602	*24 993	*25 366
Cook Islands - Îles Cook	DF	24	19	20	*19	*19	*18	*19	*20	*19	*20
Fiji - Fidji[124]	DF	849	854	858	862	866	869	871	...	887	889
French Polynesia - Polynésie française	DJ	265[16]	267[16]	268[16]	270[16]	271[16]	273[16]	275[16]	276[16]	277[3]	...
Guam[51]	DJ	...	160	160	160	161	162	163	164	168	168
Kiribati[125]	DF	...	...	...	*109*	...	...	...	...	...	...
Marshall Islands - Îles Marshall	DF	*54*[126]	...	...	*54*[125]	...	*55*[125]	...	...	...	...
Micronesia (Federated States of) - Micronésie (États fédérés de)	DJ	*108*[1]	*103*[127]	*103*[127]	*103*[127]	*104*[127]	*104*[127]	*104*[127]	*104*[127]	*104*[127]	*104*[127]
Nauru[1]	DF	...	...	*10*	...	...	*11*	*11*	...	...	...
New Caledonia - Nouvelle-Calédonie	DF	250	254	259	264	268	272	275[25]	279[25]	...	...
New Zealand - Nouvelle-Zélande[128]	DJ	4 351	4 384	4 408	4 442	4 510	4 596	4 693	4 794	4 841	4 917
Niue - Nioué	DJ	1	1	1[129]	2[129]	2[129]	2[129]	2[129]	...	...	...
Northern Mariana Islands - Îles Mariannes septentrionales	DF	*48*	*46*	*51*[130]	*51*[130]	*51*[130]	...	...	...	...	...
Palau - Palaos	DJ	21	21	21	18	18	...	18	18	18	...
Papua New Guinea - Papouasie-Nouvelle-Guinée[131]	DF	...	...	...	...	...	...	*8 151*	...	...	...
Samoa	DF	*186*	...	*189*	*191*	*192*	*193*	...	*198*	*199*	*201*
Solomon Islands - Îles Salomon[132]	DF	*555*	*570*	*584*	*598*	*612*	*625*	*639*	*653*	*667*	*681*
Tokelau - Tokélaou	DF	...	...	...	*1*[133]	...	...	...	...	...	2[134]
Tuvalu	DF	...	*11*	*11*	*11*	*11*	*11*	*11*	...	...	...
Vanuatu	DF	*239*[135]	*244*[135]	*250*[135]	*255*[135]	*261*[135]	*266*[135]	...	*278*[136]	*284*[136]	*290*[136]
Wallis and Futuna Islands - Îles Wallis et Futuna[131]	DF	...	...	...	...	...	...	*12*	...	...	...

FOOTNOTES - NOTES

Italics: estimates which are less reliable. - Italiques : estimations moins sûres.

* Provisional. - Données provisoires.

[a] 'Code' indicates source of data, as follows: - Le 'Code' indique la source des données, comme suit :
DF: Population de facto - Population de fait
DJ : Population de jure - Population de droit

[1] Data refer to national projections. - Les données se réfèrent aux projections nationales.

[2] Unrevised data that do not take into account the results of the 2014 population census. - Ces données n'ont pas été revisées et elles ne prennent pas en compte les résultats du recensement de la population de 2014.

[3] Postcensal estimates. - Estimations post censitaires.

[4] Projections based on the 2013 Population Census. - Projections fondées sur le recensement de la population de 2013.

[5] Based on the results of the 2011 Population Census. - Basé sur les résultats du recencement de la population de 2011.

[6] Source: Population projections and estimates of priority targets for the various health programs and interventions, National Institute of Statistics (2016). -

Source : Projections démographiques et estimations des cibles prioritaires des différents programmes et interventions de sante, Institut National de la Statistique (2016).

[7] Based on the results of the 2014 Population Census. - D'après les résultats du recensement de la population de 2014.

[8] Data are calculated from the results of the Population and Housing Census of 2009. - Les données sont calculées à partir des résultats du recensement de la population et de l'habitat de 2009.

[9] Data refer to projections based on the 1983 Population Census. - Les données se réfèrent aux projections basées sur le recensement de la population de 1983.

[10] Estimates or projections based on the 2015 population census. - Estimations ou projections fondées sur les résultats du recensement de la population de 2015.

[11] Estimates based on the 2000 quick population count results and 1995, 2002 and 2010 Eritrea Demographic and Health Surveys. - Des estimations fondées sur le dénombrement rapide de la population de 2000 et sur les enquêtes érythréennes de la démographie et de la santé de 1995, 2002 et 2010.

[12] Data refer to national projections based on 2007 census. - Les données sont des projections nationales d'après les résultats du recensement de la population de 2007.

[13] Estimates considering also the results of the 2007 Population Census. - Estimations en prennant en considération les résultats du recensement de la population de 2007.

[14] Data based on the 2010 Population Census. - Les données sont fondées sur le recensement de la population de 2010.

[15] Population in households only. - Population dans les ménages seulement.

[16] Intercensal estimates. - Estimations inter-censitaires.

[17] Post-censal estimates based on the 2009 Population Census. - Les estimations post-censitaire fondées sur le recensement de la population de 2009.

[18] Data are projections based on the 2006 Population Census. - Projections fondées sur le recensement de la population de 2006.

[19] Data refer to Libyan nationals only. - Les données se raportent aux nationaux libyens seulement.

[20] Data refer to projections based on the 1993 Population Census. - Les données se réfèrent aux projections basées sur le recensement de la population de 1993.

[21] Projections considering also the results of the 2009 Population Census. - Projections en prennant en considération les résultats du recensement de la population de 2009.

[22] Excludes the islands of St. Brandon and Agalega. - Non compris les îles St. Brandon et Agalega.

[23] Based on the results of the 2000 Population Census. - Basé sur les résultats du recencement de la population de 2000.

[24] Data refer to annual average population. - Les données correspondent à la population annuelle moyenne.

[25] Data refer to 1 January. - Données se raportent au 1 janvier.

[26] Based on the results of the 2004 Population Census. - D'après des résultats du recensement de la population de 2004.

[27] Projections based on the results of national survey on population and health conducted between 2010 and 2011, and especially population and housing census 2014. - Des projections de la population fondées sur les résultats de l'enquête nationale de la population et de la santé réalisée entre 2010 et 2011 et, surtout, du recensement général de la population et de l'habitat de 2014.

[28] Projections based on the 2012 Population Census. - Projections fondées sur le recensement de la population de 2012.

[29] Data are projections based on the 2008 Population and Housing Census. - Projection basée sur le recensement 2008 de la population et des logements.

[30] Data refer to 31 December. - Données se raportent au 31 décembre.

[31] Projections based on the 2002 Population Census. - Projections fondées sur le recensement de la population de 2002.

[32] Bermuda is 100 per cent urban. - 100 pour cent de la population des Bermudes est urbaine.

[33] Based on the results of the 2016 Population Census. - Basé sur les résultats du recencement de la population de 2016.

[34] Adjusted for census net undercoverage (including adjustment for incompletely enumerated Indian reserves). - Ajusté pour la sous-estimation du recensement (y compris les réservations en Inde incomplètement énumérées).

[35] Final intercensal estimates. - Estimations inter-censitaires definitives.

[36] Final postcensal estimates. - Estimations postcensitaires definitives.

[37] Updated postcensal estimates. - Estimations post censitaires mises à jour.

[38] Based on the national household surveys 2010-2014 and the 2011 population census. - D'après les données de l'enquête nationale des ménages 2010-2014 et les résultats du recensement de la population de 2011.

[39] Based on the national household survey of 2015. - Basée sur l' enquête nationale auprès des ménages de 2015.

[40] Based on the national household survey of 2016. - D'après l'enquête nationale auprès des ménages de 2016.

[41] Based on the national household survey of 2017. - D'après l'enquête nationale auprès des ménages de 2017.

[42] Based on the national household survey of 2018. - D'après l'enquête nationale auprès des ménages de 2018.

[43] Based on the national household survey of 2019. - D'après l'enquête nationale auprès des ménages de 2019.

[44] Population statistics are compiled from registers. - Les statistiques de la population sont compilées à partir des registres.

[45] Excluding data for Saint Barthélémy and Saint Martin. - Non compris les données pour Saint Barthélémy et Saint Martin.

[46] Projections produced by l'Institut Haïtien de Statistique et d'Informatique (IHSI) and the Latin American and Caribbean Demographic Centre (CELADE) - Population Division of ECLAC. - Les données sont projections produits par l'Institut Haïtien de Statistique et d'Informatique (IHSI) et le centre démographique de l'Amérique latine et les Caraïbes - Division de la population de la CEPALC.

[47] Data refer to projections based on the 2001 Population Census. - Les données se réfèrent aux projections basées sur le recensement de la population de 2001.

[48] Data revised by CONAPO (National Population Council). - Données révisées par CONAPO (Conseil national de la population).

[49] The population projections of CONAPO (National Population Council). - Les projections démographiques de la CONAPO (Conseil national de la population).

[50] Data refer to 22 September. Data refer to the intercensal population count. - Données se raportent au 22 septembre. Les données se réfèrent au dénombrement intercensitaire de la population.

[51] Including armed forces stationed in the area. - Y compris les militaires en garnison sur le territoire.

[52] Based on the results of the 2010 Population Census. - D'après le résultats du recensement de la population de 2010.

[53] Excluding U.S. Armed Forces overseas and civilian U.S. citizens whose usual place of residence is outside the United States. Postcensal estimates. - Non compris les militaires américains à l'étranger et les civils américains dont le lieu de résidence habituel est en dehors des États-Unis. Estimations post censitaires.

[54] Including armed forces stationed in the area. Source: U.S. National Center for Health Statistics, National Vital Statistics Reports (NVSR). - Y compris les militaires en garnison sur le territoire. Source : US National Center for Health Statistics, National Vital Statistics Reports (NVSR).

[55] Data include persons in remote areas, military personnel outside the country, merchant seamen at sea, civilian seasonal workers outside the country, and other civilians outside the country, and exclude nomads, foreign military, civilian aliens temporarily in the country, transients on ships and Indian jungle population. Data refer to national projections. - Y compris les personnes vivant dans des régions éloignées, le personel militaire en dehors du pays, les marins marchands, les ouvriers saisonniers en dehors du pays, et autres civils en dehors du pays, et non compris les nomades, les militaires étrangers, les étrangers civils temporairement dans le pays, les transiteurs sur des bateaux et les Indiens de la jungle. Les données se réfèrent aux projections nationales.

[56] Estimates or projections based on the 2017 Population Census. - Estimations ou projections fondées sur le recensement de la population de 2017.

[57] Data are revised projections taking into consideration also the results of the 2018 census. - Les données sont des projections révisées tenant compte également des résultats du recensement de 2018.

[58] Excludes nomadic Indian tribes. Data based on the 2010 Population Census. - Non compris les tribus d'Indiens nomades. Les données sont fondées sur le recensement de la population de 2010.

[59] Estimates based on low variant projections. - Des estimations fondées sur des projections de variante basse.

[60] Estimates or projections considering also the results of the 2012 Population Census. - Estimations ou projections en prennant en considération les résultats du recensement de la population de 2012.

[61] Data refer to 30 June. Source: INEI – National population estimates and projections from bulletin No. 24 published in July 2019. - Données se raportent au 30 juin. Source : INEI - Estimations et projections nationales de la population, publiées dans le bulletin numéro 24 , juillet 2019.

[62] Revised data. - Données révisées.

[63] Data refer to the settled population based on the 1979 Population Census and the latest household prelisting. The refugees of Afghanistan in Iran, Pakistan, and an estimated 1.5 million nomads, are not included. - Les données se rapportent à la population stationnaire sur la base du recensement de 1979 et du recensement préliminaire des logements le plus récent. Sont exclus les réfugiés d'Afghanistan en Iran et au Pakistan et les nomades estimés à 1,5 million.

[64] Data refer to projected figures based on the Population and Housing Census 2005 (district projection). - Les données se réfèrent aux projections basées sur le recensement de la population et de l'habitat de 2005 (projections locales).
[65] Data refer to 30 May. Estimates or projections based on the 2017 Population Census. - Données se raportent au 30 mai. Estimations ou projections fondées sur le recensement de la population de 2017.
[66] Source: 2016 Population and Housing Census Update. - Source : Révision des chiffres du recensement de la population et des logements de 2016.
[67] Excluding foreign diplomatic personnel and their dependants. Data based on the 2008 Population Census. - Non compris le personnel diplomatique étranger et les membres de leur famille les accompagnant. Données fondées sur le recensement de population de 2008.
[68] For statistical purposes, the data for China do not include those for the Hong Kong Special Administrative Region (Hong Kong SAR), Macao Special Administrative Region (Macao SAR) and Taiwan province of China. - Pour la présentation des statistiques, les données pour la Chine ne comprennent pas la Région Administrative Spéciale de Hong Kong (Hong Kong RAS), la Région Administrative Spéciale de Macao (Macao RAS) et Taïwan province de Chine.
[69] Data have been estimated on the basis of the annual National Sample Survey on Population Changes. - Les données ont été estimées sur la base de l'enquête annuelle "National Sample Survey on Population Changes".
[70] Data have been adjusted on the basis of the Population Census of 2010. - Les données ont été ajustées à partir des résultats du recensement de la population de 2010.
[71] Data refer to government controlled areas. - Les données se rapportent aux zones contrôlées par le Gouvernement.
[72] Data refer to annual average population. Based on the results of the 2014 Population Census. - Les données correspondent à la population annuelle moyenne. D'après les résultats du recensement de la population de 2014.
[73] Data refer to 1 January. Based on the results of the 2014 Population Census. - Données se raportent au 1 janvier. D'après les résultats du recensement de la population de 2014.
[74] Data refer to 1 March. Includes data for the Indian-held part of Jammu and Kashmir, the final status of which has not yet been determined. Data refer to projections based on the 2001 Population Census. - Données se raportent au 1 mars. Y compris les données pour la partie du Jammu et du Cachemire occupée par l'Inde dont le statut définitif n'a pas encore été déterminé. Les données se réfèrent aux projections basées sur le recensement de la population de 2001.
[75] Data are based on the publication: "Indonesia Population Projection 2010-2035" - Les données sont basées sur la publication : << Indonesia Population Projection 2010-2035 >>
[76] Data are based on the publication: "Indonesia Population Projection 2015-2045" - Les données sont basées sur la publication : << Indonesia Population Projection 2015-2045 >>
[77] Data refer to the Iranian Year which begins on 21 March and ends on 20 March of the following year. - Les données concernent l'année iranienne, qui commence le 21 mars et se termine le 20 mars de l'année suivante.
[78] Includes data for East Jerusalem and Israeli residents in certain other territories under occupation by Israeli military forces since June 1967. Data refer to Israeli citizens and permanent residents who are listed in the Population Register. - Y compris les données pour Jérusalem-Est et les résidents israéliens dans certains autres territoires occupés depuis 1967 par les forces armées israéliennes. Les données se rapportent aux citoyens israéliens et aux résidents permanents qui sont répertoriés dans le registre de la population.
[79] Excluding diplomatic personnel outside the country and foreign military and civilian personnel and their dependants stationed in the area. - Non compris le personnel diplomatique hors du pays ni les militaires et agents civils étrangers en poste sur le territoire et les membres de leur famille les accompagnant.
[80] Because of rounding, totals are not in all cases the sum of the respective components. Estimates or projections based on the 2015 population census. - Les chiffres étant arrondis, les totaux ne correspondent pas toujours rigoureusement à la somme des composants respectifs. Estimations ou projections fondées sur les résultats du recensement de la population de 2015.
[81] Data refer to 31 December. Excluding data for Jordanian territory under occupation since June 1967 by Israeli military forces. - Données se raportent au 31 décembre. Non compris les données pour le territoire jordanien occupé depuis juin 1967 par les forces armées israéliennes.
[82] Data refer to resident population. - Les données concernent la population résidente.
[83] Recalculated population estimates taking into account late registration of births and deaths until May 2017. - Réestimation du nombre d'habitants compte tenu de l'enregistrement tardif des naissances et des décès jusqu'en mai 2017.
[84] Estimates based on the adjusted results of the Population and Housing Census of 2010. - Les estimations sont fondée sur les résultats ajustées du recensement de la population et de l'habitat de 2010.
[85] Based on the results of the 2014 Population Census. Data refer to resident population which includes resident Maldivians and resident foreigners. - D'après les résultats du recensement de la population de 2014. Les données concernent la population résidente, qui comprend les Maldiviens et les étrangers.
[86] Data refer to 1 October. - Données se raportent au 1 octobre.
[87] Data refer to registered population data from Royal Oman Police. - Les données portent sur la population enregistrée par la police royale de l'Oman.
[88] Excluding data for the Pakistan-held part of Jammu and Kashmir, the final status of which has not yet been determined. - Non compris les données concernant la partie du Jammu et Cachemire occupée par le Pakistan dont le statut définitif n'a pas été déterminé.
[89] Data refer to registered resident population. - Les données concernent la population enregistrée résidente.
[90] Data refer to 30 June. Data refer to total population, which comprises Singapore residents and non-residents. Data exclude residents who have been away from Singapore for a continuous period of 12 months or longer as at the reference date. - Données se raportent au 30 juin. Les données se rapportent à la population totale composé des résidents de Singapour et les non résidents. Non compris les résidents hors de Singapour pour une période ininterrompue de 12 mois ou plus avant de la date de référence.
[91] Including Palestinian refugees. - Y compris les réfugiés de Palestine.
[92] Data based on Address Based Population Registration System. - Les données sont basées sur le registre national de la population basé sur l'adresse.
[93] Data include non-national population. - Les données comprennent les non-nationaux.
[94] Data are adjusted according to the results of the 2009 census and 2014 intercensus. - Les données ont été ajustées à partir des résultats du recensement de la population de 2009 et des données intercensitaires de 2014.
[95] Average population adjusted according to Population and Housing Census on 1 April 2019. - Population moyenne ajustée selon le recensement de la population et de l'habitat du 1er avril 2019.
[96] Data refer to 1 January. Decrease in population due to revision in administrative registers. - Données se raportent au 1 janvier. Diminution de la population due à la révision des registres administratifs.
[97] Excluding Faeroe Islands and Greenland shown separately, if available. Population statistics are compiled from registers. - Non compris les Iles Féroé et le Groenland, qui font l'objet de rubriques distinctes, si disponible. Les statistiques de la population sont compilées à partir des registres.
[98] Excluding Åland Islands. - Non compris les Îles d'Åland.
[99] Excluding diplomatic personnel outside the country and including members of alien armed forces not living in military camps and foreign diplomatic personnel not living in embassies or consulates. - Non compris le personnel diplomatique hors du pays et y compris les militaires étrangers ne vivant pas dans des camps militaires et le personnel diplomatique étranger ne vivant pas dans les ambassades ou les consulats.
[100] Data refer to annual average population. Based on the results of the 2011 Population Census. - Les données correspondent à la population annuelle moyenne. Basé sur les résultats du recencement de la population de 2011.
[101] Data refer to 1 January. Based on the results of the 2011 Population Census. - Données se raportent au 1 janvier. Basé sur les résultats du recencement de la population de 2011.
[102] Data refer to 31 December. Excluding military personnel, visitors and transients. - Données se raportent au 31 décembre. Non compris les militaires, ni les visiteurs et transients.
[103] Data refer to 31 March. - Données se raportent au 31 mars.
[104] Data refer to the Vatican City State. - Les données se rapportent à l'Etat de la Cité du Vatican.
[105] Data refer to 26 February. The population figure is 460 persons. - Données se raportent au 26 février. La population est égale à 460 personnes.
[106] Data refer to 21 June. The population figure is 451 persons. - Données se raportent au 21 juin. La population est égale à 451 personnes.
[107] Data refer to usual resident population. - Les données se réfèrent à la population résidente habituelle.
[108] Data refer to 1 January. Data refer to usual resident population. - Données se raportent au 1 janvier. Les données se réfèrent à la population résidente habituelle.
[109] Data refer to 30 April. - Données se raportent au 30 avril.
[110] Including civilian nationals temporarily outside the country. - Y compris les civils nationaux temporairement hors du pays.
[111] Data refer to resident population only. - Pour la population résidante seulement.
[112] Excluding Transnistria and the municipality of Bender. - Les données ne tiennent pas compte de l'information sur la Transnistria et la municipalité de Bender.
[113] Data refer to usual resident population based on the 2014 Census. Tiraspol, Bender, Slobozia, Ribnita, Camenca Yrigoricpol/Grigoriopol are districts from Transnistria where the 2014 census was not conducted. - Les données se

rapportent à la population habituellement résidente et sont fondées sur le recensement de 2014. Tiraspol, Bender, Slobozia, Ribnita, Camenca, Yrigoricpol/Grigoriopol sont des districts de la Transnistrie où le recensement n'a pas eu lieu.

114 Excludes data for Kosovo and Metohia. - Sans les données pour le Kosovo et Metohie.

115 Data refer to 1 January. Data refer to registered resident population. - Données se raportent au 1 janvier. Les données concernent la population enregistrée résidente.

116 Data refer to annual average population. Data refer to registered resident population. - Les données correspondent à la population annuelle moyenne. Les données concernent la population enregistrée résidente.

117 Data refer to legal resident population. - Les données concernent la population légalement résidente.

118 Data refer to annual average population. Data refer to legal resident population. - Les données correspondent à la population annuelle moyenne. Les données concernent la population légalement résidente.

119 Data refer to 1 January. Data refer to legal resident population. - Données se raportent au 1 janvier. Les données concernent la population légalement résidente.

120 Data refer to annual average population. The Government of Ukraine has informed the United Nations that it is not in a position to provide statistical data concerning the Autonomous Republic of Crimea and the city of Sevastopol. - Les données correspondent à la population annuelle moyenne. Le gouvernement Ukrainien a informé l'ONU qu'il n'est pas en mesure de fournir des données statistiques concernant la République autonome de Crimée et la ville de Sébastopol.

121 Data refer to 1 January. The Government of Ukraine has informed the United Nations that it is not in a position to provide statistical data concerning the Autonomous Republic of Crimea and the city of Sevastopol. - Données se raportent au 1 janvier. Le gouvernement Ukrainien a informé l'ONU qu'il n'est pas en mesure de fournir des données statistiques concernant la République autonome de Crimée et la ville de Sébastopol.

122 Excluding Channel Islands (Guernsey and Jersey) and Isle of Man, shown separately, if available. - Non compris les îles Anglo-Normandes (Guernesey et Jersey) et l'île de Man, qui font l'objet de rubriques distinctes, si disponible.

123 Data refer to annual average population. Data refer to usual resident population. - Les données correspondent à la population annuelle moyenne. Les données se réfèrent à la population résidente habituelle.

124 Data refer to 17 September. - Données se raportent au 17 septembre.

125 Projections are prepared by the Secretariat of the Pacific Community based on the 2011 census of population and housing. - Les projections sont preparées par le Secrétariat de la Communauté du Pacifique à partir des résultats du recensement de la population et de l'habitat de 2011.

126 Projections are prepared by the Secretariat of the Pacific Community based on the 1999 census of population and housing. - Les projections sont preparées par le Secrétariat de la Communauté du Pacifique à partir des résultats du recensement de la population et de l'habitat de 1999.

127 Based on the 2010 Population and Housing Census and 2013/2014 Household Income and Expenditure Survey. - Données fondées sur les résultat du recensement de la population et de l'habitat de 2010, et ceux de l'enquête auprès des ménages sur des revenus et des dépenses de 2013/2014.

128 Because of rounding, totals are not in all cases the sum of the respective components. - Les chiffres étant arrondis, les totaux ne correspondent pas toujours rigoureusement à la somme des composants respectifs.

129 Intercensal estimates. Data refer to usual resident population. - Estimations inter-censitaires. Les données se réfèrent à la population résidente habituelle.

130 Source: U.S. National Center for Health Statistics, National Vital Statistics Reports (NVSR). - Source : US National Center for Health Statistics, National Vital Statistics Reports (NVSR).

131 Estimates are prepared by the Secretariat of the Pacific Community based on the last population and housing census. - Les estimations sont preparées par le Secrétariat de la Communauté du Pacifique à partir des résultats du dernier recensement de la population et de l'habitat.

132 Projections based on adjusted 2009 census counts. - Projections fondées à partir des comptes rajustés du recensement de 2009.

133 Data refer to 1 December. - Données se raportent au 1 décembre.

134 Data refer to 12 December. Data refers to 2019 Tokelau population count. - Données se raportent au 12 décembre. Les données se rapportent au dénombrement de la population tokélaouane de 2019.

135 Estimates based on the results of 1999 and in 2009 censuses. - Estimations fondées sur les résultats des recensement de la population de 1999 and 2009.

136 Estimates based on the results of 2009 census and 2016 mini-census. - Estimaions fondées sur les résultats du recensement de 2009 et du mini-recensement de 2016.

Table 6 - *Demographic Yearbook 2019*

Table 6 presents total population by sex for as many years as possible between 2010 and 2019, as well as urban population as available.

Description of variables: Data are from nation-wide population censuses or are estimates, some of which are based on sample surveys of population carried out among all segments of the population. This characteristic of the data is indicated in the column "Code". The codes used are explained at the end of the table.

Urban is defined according to the national census definition. The definitions for each country, as available, are provided as part of this technical note.

Percentage computation: Urban percentages are the number of persons residing in an area defined as "urban" per 100 total population. They are calculated by the Statistics Division of the United Nations Department of Economic and Social Affairs. In very few cases the data for total population have been revised whereas the data for the urban and rural population have not been revised. These data are footnoted accordingly. In these cases, particular caution should be used in interpreting the figures for the percentages urban.

Reliability of data: Estimates that are believed to be less reliable are set in *italics* rather than in roman type. Classification in terms of reliability is based on the method of construction of the total population estimate discussed in the technical notes for table 3.

Limitations: Statistics on urban population by sex are subject to the same qualifications as have been set forth for population statistics in general, as discussed in section 3 of the Technical Notes.

The basic limitations imposed by variations in the definition of the total population and in the degree of under-enumeration are perhaps more important in relation to urban/rural than to any other distributions. The classification by urban and rural is affected by variations in defining usual residence for purposes of sub-national tabulations. Likewise, the geographical differentials in the degree of under-enumeration in censuses affect the comparability of these categories throughout the table. The distinction between *de facto* and *de jure* population is also very important with respect to urban/rural distributions. The difference between the *de facto* and the *de jure* population is discussed at length in section 3.1.1 of the Technical Notes.

A most important and specific limitation, however, lies in the national differences in the definition of urban. Because the distinction between urban and rural areas is made in so many different ways, the definitions have been included at the end of this table. The definitions are necessarily brief and, where the classification of urban involves administrative civil divisions, they are often given in the terminology of the particular country or area. As a result of variations in terminology, it may appear that differences between countries or areas are greater than they actually are. On the other hand, similar or identical terms (for example, town, village, district) as used in different countries or areas may have quite different meanings.

The definition of urban/rural areas is based on both qualitative and quantitative criteria that may include any combination of the following: size of population, population density, distance between built-up areas, predominant type of economic activity, conformity to legal or administrative status and urban characteristics such as specific services and facilities[1]. Although statistics classified by urban/rural areas are widely available, no international standard definition appears to be possible at this time since the meaning differs from one country or area to another. The urban/rural classification of population used here is reported according to the national definition.

Earlier data: Urban and total population by sex have been shown in previous issues of the Demographic Yearbook. For information on specific years covered, readers should consult the Historical Index.

DEFINITION OF "URBAN"

AFRICA

Algeria: The urban/rural delimitation is performed after the census operation based on the classification of built-up areas. Groupings of 100 or more constructions, distant less than 200 metres from one another are considered urban.
Botswana: Agglomeration of 5 000 or more inhabitants where 75 per cent of the economic activity is non-agricultural.

Burkina Faso: All administrative centres of provinces (total of 45) plus 4 medium-sized towns are considered as urban areas.
Burundi: Commune of Bujumbura.
Comoros: Every locality or administrative centre of an island, region or prefecture that has the following facilities: asphalted roads, electricity, a medical centre, telephone services, etc.
Egypt: Governorates of Cairo, Alexandria, Port Said, Ismailia, Suez, frontier governorates and capitals of other governorates, as well as district capitals (Markaz). The definition of urban areas for the 2006 Census is "shiakha", a part of a district.
Equatorial Guinea: District centres and localities with 300 dwellings and/or 1 500 inhabitants or more.
Ethiopia: Localities of 2 000 or more inhabitants.
Eswatini: A geographical area constituting of a city or town, characterized by higher population density and vast human features in comparison to areas surrounding it.
Guinea: Administrative centres of prefectures and the capital city (Conakry).
Kenya: Areas having a population of 2 000 or more inhabitants that have transport systems, build-up areas, industrial/manufacturing structures and other developed structures.
Lesotho: All administrative headquarters and settlements of rapid growth.
Liberia: Localities of 2 000 or more inhabitants.
Malawi: All townships and town planning areas and all district centres.
Mauritius: The five Municipal Council Areas which are subdivided into twenty Municipal Wards defined according to proclaimed boundaries.
Namibia: Proclaimed urban areas for which cadastral data is available and other unplanned squatter areas.
Niger: Capital city, capitals of the departments and districts.
Reunion: A commune or a group of communes with more than 2,000 inhabitants in a continuous building area (no more than 200 meters between two buildings).
Rwanda: All administrative areas recognized as urban by the law. These are all administrative centres of provinces, and the cities of Kigali, Nyanza, Ruhango and Rwamagana.
Senegal: Agglomerations of 10 000 or more inhabitants.
South Africa: Places with some form of local authority.
Sudan: Localities of administrative and/or commercial importance or with population of 5 000 or more inhabitants.
Tunisia: Population living in communes.
Uganda: Gazettes, cities, municipalities and towns.
United Republic of Tanzania: Areas legally recognized (gazetted) as urban and all areas recognized by local government authorities as urban.
Zambia: Localities of 5 000 or more inhabitants, the majority of whom all depend on non-agricultural activities.

AMERICA, NORTH

Bermuda: The country is considered 100 per cent urban.
Canada: Areas with 1 000 or more inhabitants and a population density of 400 or more persons per square kilometre, based on population counts from the recent population census.
Costa Rica: Administrative centres of cantons.
Cuba: Localities with 2 000 or more inhabitants; or localities with more than 1 000 inhabitants having half or more of economically active population engaged in non-agricultural activities.
Dominican Republic: Administrative centres of municipalities and municipal districts, some of which include suburban zones of rural character.
El Salvador: Administrative centres of municipalities.
Greenland: Localities of 200 or more inhabitants.
Guadeloupe: A commune or a group of communes with more than 2,000 inhabitants in a continuous building area (no more than 200 meters between two buildings).
Guatemala: Municipality of Guatemala Department and officially recognized centres of other departments and municipalities.
Haiti: Administrative centres of communes.
Honduras: Localities of 2 000 or more inhabitants, having essentially urban characteristics.
Jamaica: Localities of 2 000 or more inhabitants, having urban characteristics.
Martinique: A commune or a group of communes with more than 2 000 inhabitants in a continuous building area (no more than 200 meters between two buildings).
Mexico: Localities of 2 500 or more inhabitants.
Nicaragua: Administrative centres of municipalities and localities of 1 000 or more inhabitants or with more than 150 dwellings, with streets, electric light, water service, school and health centre.
Panama: Localities of 1 500 or more inhabitants having essentially urban characteristics. Beginning 1970, localities of 1 500 or more inhabitants with such urban characteristics as streets, water supply systems, sewerage systems and electric light.

Puerto Rico: Agglomerations of 2 500 or more inhabitants, generally having population densities of 1 000 persons per square mile or more. Two types of urban areas: urbanized areas of 50 000 or more inhabitants and urban clusters of at least 2 500 and less than 50 000 inhabitants.
Saint-Barthélemy: A commune or a group of communes with more than 2 000 inhabitants in a continuous building area (no more than 200 meters between two buildings).
Saint-Martin (French part): A commune or a group of communes with more than 2 000 inhabitants in a continuous building area (no more than 200 meters between two buildings).
Saint Pierre and Miquelon: A commune or a group of communes with more than 2 000 inhabitants in a continuous building area (no more than 200 meters between two buildings).
United States of America: Agglomerations of 2 500 or more inhabitants, generally having population densities of 1 000 persons per square mile or more. Two types of urban areas: urbanized areas of 50 000 or more inhabitants and urban clusters of at least 2 500 and less than 50 000 inhabitants.
United States Virgin Islands: Agglomerations of 2 500 or more inhabitants, generally having population densities of 1 000 persons per square mile or more. Two types of urban areas: urbanized areas of 50 000 or more inhabitants and urban clusters of at least 2 500 and less than 50 000 inhabitants. (As of the 2000 Census, no urbanized areas are identified in the United States Virgin Islands.)

AMERICA, SOUTH

Argentina: Populated centres with 2 000 or more inhabitants.
Bolivia: Localities of 2 000 or more inhabitants.
Brazil: Area inside the urban perimeter of a city or town, defined by municipal law.
Chile: Areas of concentrated housing units with more than 2 000 inhabitants, or between 1 001 and 2 000 inhabitants having 50 per cent or more of its economically active population doing secondary or tertiary activities. As an exception, centres of tourism and recreation with more than 250 housing units that do not satisfy the population requirement are nevertheless considered urban.
Colombia: Urban census area, defined by Departamento Administrativo Nacional de Estadistica (DANE) for statistical purposes, corresponding to the areas delimited by the census perimeter.
Ecuador: Capitals of provinces and cantons.
Falkland Islands (Malvinas): Town of Stanley.
French Guiana: A commune or a group of communes with more than 2 000 inhabitants in a continuous building area (no more than 200 meters between two buildings).
Paraguay: Cities, towns and administrative centres of departments and districts.
Peru: Populated centres with more than 5 000 inhabitants, which have public services, educational institutions and health facilities.
Suriname: The districts of Paramaribo and Wanica.
Uruguay: Cities, villages, towns and other populated areas as defined by the Law of Population Centers.
Venezuela (Bolivarian Republic of): Centres with a population of 2 500 or more inhabitants.

ASIA

Armenia: Cities and urban-type localities, officially designated as such, usually according to the criteria of number of inhabitants and predominance of agricultural, or number of non-agricultural workers and their families.
Azerbaijan: An administrative division which covers more than 15 000 population, engaging mainly in industrial and other economic and social activities and which include administrative and cultural centers.
Bahrain: Communes or villages of 2 500 or more inhabitants.
Brunei Darussalam: Municipality areas of Bandar Seri Begawan, Kuala Belait, Seria, Pekan Tutong and Pekan Bangar; and heavily populated areas with urban characteristics.
Cambodia: Areas at the commune level satisfying the following three conditions: (1) Population Density exceeding 200 per square Km, (2) Percentage of male employed in agriculture below 50 per cent, (3) Total population of the commune exceeds 2 000 inhabitants.
China: According to the Regulation on the Classification of Urban/Rural Residence for Statistical Purposes.
Cyprus: As determined by the Department of Town Planning and Housing of the Ministry of Interior.
Georgia: Cities and urban-type localities, officially designated as such, usually according to the criteria of number of inhabitants and predominance of agricultural, or number of non-agricultural workers and their families.
India: Towns (places with municipal corporation, municipal area committee, town committee, notified area committee or cantonment board); also, all places having 5 000 or more inhabitants, a density of not less than 1 000 persons per square mile or 400 per square kilometre, pronounced urban characteristics and at least three fourths of the adult male population employed in pursuits other than agriculture.
Indonesia: Area which satisfies certain criteria in terms of population density, percentage of agricultural households, access to urban facilities, existence of additional facilities, and percentage of built up area not for housing.
Iran (Islamic Republic of): Every district with a municipality.

Israel: Localities with 2 000 or more residents.
Japan: City (shi) having 50 000 or more inhabitants with 60 per cent or more of the houses located in the main built-up areas and 60 per cent or more of the population (including their dependants) engaged in manufacturing, trade or other urban type of business.
Jordan: Localities of 5 000 or more inhabitants.
Kazakhstan: Cities of Republican status (population centres of special national importance or with a population of usually more than one million), Oblast status (population centres that are major economic and cultural centres with developed industrial and social infrastructure and a population of more than 50,000, the country has 40 Oblast status cities), Raion status and settlements located under their administrative jurisdiction.
Kuwait: All localities in Kuwait are urban.
Kyrgyzstan: Cities and urban-type localities, officially designated as such, usually according to the criteria of number of inhabitants and predominance of agricultural, or number of non-agricultural workers and their families.
Lao People's Democratic Republic: Areas or villages that satisfy at least three of the following five conditions: located in metropolitan areas of district or province, there is access to road in dry and rainy seasons, more than 70 per cent of the population has access to piped water, more than 70 per cent of the population has access to public electricity, there is a permanent market operating every day.
Malaysia: Gazetted areas with their adjoining built-up areas which have a combined population of 10 000 or more. Built-up areas are defined as areas contiguous to a gazetted area and have at least 60 per cent of their population (aged 15 years and over) engaged in non-agricultural activities. The definition of urban areas also takes into account the special development area which is not gazetted and can be indentified and separated from the gazetted area or built-up area of more than 5km and a population of at least 10 000 with 60 per cent of the population (aged 15 years and over) engaged in non-agricultural activities.
Maldives: Malé, the capital.
Mongolia: Capital (Ulaanbaatar), provincial centers and towns.
Myanmar: Areas classified by the General Administration Department as wards. Generally, these areas have an increased density of building structures, population and better infrastructure development.
Nepal: As declared by the government municipalities.
Pakistan: Places with metropolitan corporation, municipal corporation, municipal committee, town committee or cantonment at the time of the census. .
Philippines:
Areas (barangays) with more than 5 000 inhabitants, at least one establishment with a minimum of 100 employees, or five or more small establishments with 10 to 99 employees and five or more facilities within the two-kilometre radius from the barangay hall, as per *Philippine Statistics Authority (PSA) Board Resolution No. 01, Series of 2017-098 – Adoption of the Operational Definition of Urban Areas in the Philippines*. In addition, all barangays in the National Capital Region are automatically classified as urban.
Republic of Korea: For estimates: Localities with 50 000 or more inhabitants. For census: the figures are composed in the basis of the minor administrative divisions such as Dongs (mostly urban areas) and Eups or Myeons (rural areas).
Saudi Arabia: Localities with more than 5 000 inhabitants.
Singapore: Singapore is a city-state.
Sri Lanka: All areas administered by municipal and urban councils.
State of Palestine: Any locality where the population amounts to 10 000 persons or more. This applies to all governorates/districts regardless of their size, and to all localities whose populations vary from 4 000 to 9 999 persons provided they have at least four of the following elements: public electricity network, public water network, post office, health center with a full time physician and a school offering a general secondary education certificate.
Syrian Arab Republic: Cities, Mohafaza centres and Mantika centres, and communities with 20 000 or more inhabitants.
Tajikistan: Cities and urban-type localities, officially designated as such, usually according to the criteria of number of inhabitants and predominance of agricultural, or number of non-agricultural workers and their families.
Thailand: Municipal areas.
Turkey: Localities with 20 000 inhabitants or more.
Turkmenistan: Cities and urban-type localities, officially designated as such, usually according to the criteria of number of inhabitants and predominance of agricultural, or number of non-agricultural workers and their families.
Uzbekistan: Cities and urban-type localities, officially designated as such, usually according to the criteria of number of inhabitants and predominance of agricultural, or number of non-agricultural workers and their families.
Viet Nam: Urban areas include inside urban districts of cities, urban quarters and towns. All other local administrative units (communes) belong to rural areas.

EUROPE

Albania: Towns and other industrial centres of more than 400 inhabitants.
Austria: Urban areas are localities with 2 000 or more inhabitants. The delineation of localities goes back to 1991.
Belarus: Urban settlements are settlements authorized under the law as towns, urban-type settlements, workers settlements and health resort areas.

Belgium: All the communes which are not part of the list of rural communes are considered as urban communes. There are 33 communes which are considered rural: Alveringem, Amblève, Bertogne, Bièvre, Bullange, Burg-Reuland, Clavier, Erezée, Fauvillers, Frasnes-lez-Anvaing, Froidchapelle, Gedinne, Gouvy, Havelange, Herstappe, Heuvelland, Houffalize, Houyet, Langemark-Poelkapelle, Léglise, Lierneux, Lo-Reninge, Manhay, Momignies, Ravels, Sainte-Ode, Sint-Laureins, Sivry-Rance, Stoumont, Tenneville, Vaux-sur-Sûre, Vleteren and Vresse-sur-Semois.
Bulgaria: All towns and cities according to the Territorial and Administrative-Territorial Division of the country.
Czech Republic: Localities with 2 000 or more inhabitants.
Estonia: Urban settlements include cities, cities without municipal status and towns.
Finland: Urban communes including those municipalities in which at least 90 per cent of the population lives in urban settlements or in which the population of the largest urban settlement is at least 15 000.
France: A commune or a group of communes with more than 2 000 inhabitants in a continuous building area (no more than 200 meters between two buildings).
Greece: Urban is considered every municipal or communal department of which the largest locality has 2 000 inhabitants and over.
Hungary: Localities recognized by the President of the Republic with the title of town, on the basis of specific (economic, commercial, institutional, cultural etc.) criteria.
Iceland: Localities of 200 or more inhabitants.
Ireland: Cities and towns including suburbs of 1 500 or more inhabitants.
Latvia: Cities and urban-type localities, officially designated as such, usually according to the criteria of number of inhabitants and predominance of agricultural, or number of non-agricultural workers and their families.
Liechtenstein: Communes with 10 000 inhabitants or more.
Lithuania: Urban population refers to persons who live in cities and towns, i.e., the population areas with closely built permanent dwellings and with the resident population of more than 3 000 of which 2/3 of employees work in industry, social infrastructure and business. In a number of towns the population may be less than 3 000 since these areas had already the status of "town" before the law was enforced (July 1994).
Malta: Grid cells of 1 square km with a density of at least 300 inhabitants per square km and a minimum population of 5 000, and densely populated areas (i.e. areas with a density superior to 500 inhabitants per square km).
Montenegro: According to the current law of territorial division of Montenegro, which conveys to each local community the obligation to decide which settlements are urban and which are rural.
Netherlands: Urban: Municipalities with a population of 2 000 and more inhabitants. Semi-urban: Municipalities with a population of less than 2 000 but with not more than 20 per cent of their economically active male population engaged in agriculture, and specific residential municipalities of commuters.
Norway: A hub of buildings inhabited by at least 200 people and where the distance between the buildings does not exceed 50 metres. The boundaries are dynamic and may be changed due to developments and population changes.
North Macedonia: A city is a populated place that has more than 3000 inhabitants, has a developed industrial and social infrastructure, and over 51% of employees work outside the primary activities.
Poland: All areas which have town rights or the status of a town with provisions of separate laws.
Portugal: Localities with 2 000 or more inhabitants.
Republic of Moldova: Cities and urban-type localities, officially designated as such, usually according to the criteria of number of inhabitants and predominance of agricultural, or number of non-agricultural workers and their families.
Romania: Localities in which the majority of the resources are employed in non-agricultural activities with a diversified level of endowment, having a constant and significant socio-economic influence on the whole area.
Russian Federation: Cities and urban-type localities, officially designated as such, usually according to the criteria of number of inhabitants and predominance of agricultural, or number of non-agricultural workers and their families.
Serbia: Municipalities, cities and the city of Belgrade.
Slovakia: Municipalities with the status of towns, according to the following criteria: 1) it is an economic, administrative, cultural or tourism centre; 2) provides services for other municipalities; 3) has urban character (at least partly); and 4) has 5 000 inhabitants or more.
Slovenia: Settlements of 3 000 or more inhabitants, settlements that serve as seats of municipalities with at least 1 400 inhabitants, and sub-urban areas that are being gradually integrated with an urban settlement of 5 000 or more inhabitants
Switzerland: Agglomerations and isolated towns (towns not attached to a cluster with at least 10,000 inhabitants) are the urban space.
Ukraine: Cities and urban-type localities officially designated as such, usually according to the criteria of number of inhabitants and predominance of agricultural, or number of non-agricultural workers and their families.
United Kingdom of Great Britain and Northern Ireland: For England and Wales, the built-up areas of 10 000 or more inhabitants; for Scotland, the settlements of 3 000 or more inhabitants; and for Northern Ireland, the settlements of 5 000 or more inhabitants.

OCEANIA

Australia: Areas of concentrated urban development with populations of 200 people or more, primarily identified using objective dwelling and population density criteria using data from the 2016 Census.
American Samoa: Agglomerations of 2 500 or more inhabitants, generally having population densities of 1 000 persons per square mile or more. Two types of urban areas: urbanized areas of 50 000 or more inhabitants and urban clusters of at least 2 500 and less than 50 000 inhabitants. (As of Census 2000, no urbanized areas are identified in American Samoa.)
Cook Islands: Raratonga, the most populous island.
Guam: Agglomerations of 2 500 or more inhabitants, generally having population densities of 1 000 persons per square mile or more, referred to as "urban clusters".
New Caledonia: Nouméa and communes of Païta, Nouvel Dumbéa and Mont-Dore.
New Zealand: All cities, plus boroughs, town districts, townships and country towns with a population of 1 000 or more usual residents.
Northern Mariana Islands: Agglomerations of 2 500 or more inhabitants, generally having population densities of 1 000 persons per square mile or more. Two types of urban areas: urbanized areas of 50 000 or more inhabitants and urban clusters of at least 2 500 and less than 50 000 inhabitants.
Palau: States with 2 500 inhabitants or more (the only state which satisfies this condition is Koror state).
Samoa: Only Apia Urban Area (AUA) region.
Tokelau: All of Tokelau's population is considered to be rural.
Tonga: Nuku'alofa.
Vanuatu: Luganville centre and Port Vila.

NOTES

[1] For further information, see *Social and Demographic Statistics: Classifications of Size and Type of Locality and Urban/Rural Areas.* E/CN.3/551, United Nations, New York, 1980.

Tableau 6 – *Annuaire démographique 2019*

Le tableau 6 présente des données sur la population totale selon le sexe pour le plus grand nombre possible d'années entre 2010 et 2019, ainsi que la population urbaine si disponible.

Description des variables : les données proviennent de recensements de la population ou sont des estimations fondées, dans certains cas, sur des enquêtes par sondage portant sur toute la population. Le code qui figure dans la colonne « Code » du tableau indique comment les données ont été obtenues. Les codes utilisés sont expliqués à la fin du tableau.

Le sens donné au terme « urbain » est conforme aux définitions utilisées dans les recensements nationaux. Les définitions pour chaque pays, si disponible, font partie de ce note technique.

Calcul des pourcentages : les pourcentages de la population urbaine sont calculés par la Division de statistique du Département des affaires économiques et sociales de l'Organisation des Nations Unies et représentent le nombre de personnes qui vivent dans des régions considérées comme urbaines pour 100 personnes de la population totale. Dans de très rares cas, les données pour la population totale ont été révisées mais les données pour la population urbaine et la population rurale ne l'ont pas été. Ces données sont indiquées en note. Dans ces cas, les proportions de population urbaine ou rurale sont à interpréter avec précaution.

Fiabilité des données : les estimations considérées comme moins sûres sont indiquées en italique plutôt qu'en caractères romains. Le classement du point de vue de la fiabilité est fondé sur la méthode utilisée pour établir l'estimation de la population totale qui figure au tableau 3 (voir les explications dans les notes techniques relatives à ce même tableau).

Insuffisance des données : les statistiques de la population urbaine selon le sexe appellent toutes les réserves qui ont été formulées à la section 3 des Notes techniques à propos des statistiques de la population en général.

Les limitations fondamentales imposées par les variations de la définition de la population totale et par les lacunes du recensement se font peut-être sentir davantage dans la répartition de la population en population urbaine et population rurale que dans sa répartition suivant toute autre caractéristique. De fait, des différences dans la définition du lieu de résidence habituel utilisée pour l'exploitation des données à l'échelon sous-national influent sur la classification en population urbaine et en population rurale. De même, les différences de degré de sous-dénombrement suivant la zone, à l'occasion des recensements, ont une incidence sur la comparabilité de ces deux catégories dans l'ensemble du tableau. La distinction entre population de fait et population de droit est également très importante du point de vue de la répartition de la population en population urbaine et en population rurale. Cette distinction est expliquée en détail à la section 3.1.1 des Notes techniques.

Toutefois, la difficulté la plus importante tient aux différences de définition du terme « urbain » selon le pays. Les distinctions faites entre « zone urbaine » et « zone rurale » varient tellement que les définitions utilisées ont été reproduites à la fin de ces notes techniques. Les définitions sont forcément brèves et, lorsque le classement en « zone urbaine » repose sur des divisions administratives, on a souvent désigné celles-ci par le nom qu'elles portent dans la zone ou le pays considéré. Par suite des variations dans la terminologie, les différences entre pays ou zones peuvent sembler plus grandes qu'elles ne le sont réellement. Il se peut aussi que des termes similaires ou identiques, tels que ville, village ou district, aient des significations très différentes selon les pays ou zones.

La distinction entre « zone urbaine » et « zone rurale » repose sur une série de critères qualitatifs aussi bien que quantitatifs, notamment l'effectif de la population, la densité de peuplement, la distance entre îlots d'habitations, le type prédominant d'activité économique, le statut juridique ou administratif, et les caractéristiques d'une agglomération urbaine, c'est-à-dire l'existence de services publics et d'équipements collectifs[1]. Bien que les statistiques différenciant les zones urbaines des zones rurales soient très répandues, il ne paraît pas possible pour le moment d'adopter une classification internationale type de ces zones, vu la diversité des interprétations nationales. La classification de la population en population urbaine et population rurale retenue ici est celle qui correspond aux définitions nationales.

Données publiées antérieurement : des statistiques concernant la population urbaine et la population totale selon le sexe ont été publiées dans des éditions antérieures de l'*Annuaire démographique*. Pour plus de précisions concernant les années pour lesquelles ces données ont été publiées, se reporter à l'index historique.

DÉFINITIONS DU TERME « URBAIN »

AFRIQUE

Algérie : La délimitation des zones urbaines et rurales se font après l'opération du recensement sur la base de la classification des agglomérations. Regroupement de 100 constructions ou plus distantes l'une à l'autre de moins de 200m ont été considérées comme zones urbaines.
Afrique du Sud : Zones dotées d'une administration locale.
Botswana : Agglomération de 5 000 habitants ou plus dont 75 p. 100 de l'activité économique n'est pas de type agricole.
Burkina Faso : Tous les chefs-lieux de province (45 au total) plus 4 villes moyennes ont été considérées comme zones urbaines.
Burundi : Commune de Bujumbura.
Comores : Toute localité ou chef-lieu d'une île, région/préfecture disposant des infrastructures suivantes : route bitumée, électricité, centre hospitalier, téléphone, etc.
Égypte : Chefs-lieux des gouvernorats du Caire, d'Alexandrie, de Port Saïd, d'Ismaïlia, de Suez ; chefs-lieux des gouvernorats frontaliers, autres chefs-lieux de gouvernorat et chefs-lieux de district (Markaz). La définition des zones urbaines pour le recensement de 2006 est celle de « shiakha », une partie d'un district.
Éthiopie : Localités de 2 000 habitants ou plus.
Eswatini : Zone géographique qui constitue une ville et se caractérise par une densité de population et de constructions humaines plus élevée que dans les zones qui l'entourent.**Guinée :** Centres administratifs des préfectures et la ville capitale (Conakry).
Guinée équatoriale : Chefs-lieux de district et localités comprenant 300 habitations et/ou 1 500 habitants ou plus.
Kenya : Zone ayant une population de 2 000 habitants ou plus qui dispose de réseaux de transport, comporte des zones bâties, des structures industrielles ou manufacturières et d'autres équipements modernes.
Lesotho : Tous les chefs-lieux administratifs et établissements en forte croissance.
Libéria : Localités de 2 000 habitants ou plus.
Malawi : Toutes les villes et zones urbanisées et tous les chefs-lieux de district.
Maurice : Les cinq circonscriptions municipales, divisées en vingt arrondissements municipaux dont les limites ont été officiellement définies.
Namibie : Zones urbaines déclarées pour lesquelles il existe des données cadastrales et autres zones d'habitat non planifié.
Niger : Ville capital, villes capitales de départements ou de districts.
Ouganda : « Gazettes », villes, municipalités et bourgs.
République-Unie de Tanzanie : Toutes les zones érigées en communes et les zones reconnues par les autorités gouvernementales comme urbaines.
Réunion : Une commune ou un ensemble de communes présentant une zone de bâti continu (pas de coupure de plus de 200 mètres entre deux constructions) qui compte au moins 2 000 habitants.
Rwanda : Toutes les zones administratives reconnues comme urbaines par la loi. Il s'agit de tous les chefs - lieux des provinces, de la ville de Kigali ainsi que des villes de Nyanza, Ruhango et Rwamagana.
Sénégal : Agglomérations de 10 000 habitants ou plus.
Soudan : Centres administratifs et/ou commerciaux ou localités ayant une population de 5 000 habitants ou plus.
Tunisie : Population vivant dans les communes.
Zambie : Localités de 5 000 habitants ou plus dont l'activité économique prédominante n'est pas de type agricole.

AMÉRIQUE DU NORD

Bermudes : Le pays est considéré entièrement urbain.
Canada : Agglomérations de 1 000 habitants ou plus ayant une densité de population d'au moins 400 habitants au kilomètre carré, basé sur les chiffres de population du dernier recensement de la population.
Costa Rica : Chefs-lieux de canton.
Cuba : Localités ayant une population supérieure à 2 000 habitants ; ou une population supérieure à 1 000 habitants dont la moitié de la population économiquement active s'occupe des activités non-agricoles.
El Salvador : Chefs-lieux des municipalités.
États-Unis d'Amérique : Agglomérations de 2 500 habitants ou plus ayant généralement une densité de population d'au moins 1 000 habitants au mile carré. Deux types de zones urbaines : zones urbanisées de 50 000 habitants ou plus et groupements urbains comptant au moins 2 500 habitants mais moins de 50 000.
Groenland : Localités d'au moins 200 habitants.
Guadeloupe : Une commune ou un ensemble de communes présentant une zone de bâti continu (pas de coupure de plus de 200 mètres entre deux constructions) qui compte au moins 2 000 habitants.
Guatemala : Municipalité du département de Guatemala et centres administratifs officiels d'autres départements et municipalités.
Haïti : Chefs-lieux de communes.
Honduras : Localités d'au moins 2 000 habitants ayant des caractéristiques essentiellement urbaines.
Îles Vierges américaines : Agglomérations de 2 500 habitants ou plus ayant généralement une densité de population d'au moins 1 000 habitants au mile carré. Deux types de zones urbaines : zones urbanisées de 50 000 habitants ou plus et groupements urbains comptant au moins 2 500 habitants mais moins de 50 000. (D'après les résultats du recensement de 2 000, les Îles Vierges américaines ne comptent aucune zone urbanisée.)
Jamaïque : Localités de 2 000 habitants ou plus ayant des caractéristiques urbaines.
Martinique : Une commune ou un ensemble de communes présentant une zone de bâti continu (pas de coupure de plus de 200 mètres entre deux constructions) qui compte au moins 2 000 habitants.
Mexique : Localités d'au moins 2 500 habitants.
Nicaragua : Centres administratifs des municipalités et localités d'au moins 1 000 habitants ou d'au moins 150 logements, possédant des rues, un éclairage électrique, un réseau de distribution d'eau, une école et un dispensaire.
Panama : Localités d'au moins 1 500 habitants ayant des caractéristiques essentiellement urbaines. À partir de 1970, localités de 1 500 habitants ou plus présentant des caractéristiques urbaines, telles que rues, éclairage électrique, systèmes d'approvisionnement en eau et réseaux d'égouts.
Porto Rico : Agglomérations de 2 500 habitants ou plus ayant généralement une densité de population d'au moins 1 000 habitants au mile carré. Deux types de zones urbaines : zones urbanisées de 50 000 habitants ou plus et groupements urbains comptant au moins 2 500 habitants mais moins de 50 000.
République dominicaine : Chefs-lieux des municipalités et districts municipaux, dont certains comprennent des zones suburbaines ayant des caractéristiques rurales.
Saint-Barthélemy : Une commune ou un ensemble de communes présentant une zone de bâti continu (pas de coupure de plus de 200 mètres entre deux constructions) qui compte au moins 2 000 habitants.
Saint-Martin (Partie française) : Une commune ou un ensemble de communes présentant une zone de bâti continu (pas de coupure de plus de 200 mètres entre deux constructions) qui compte au moins 2 000 habitants.
Saint-Pierre-et-Miquelon : Une commune ou un ensemble de communes présentant une zone de bâti continu (pas de coupure de plus de 200 mètres entre deux constructions) qui compte au moins 2 000 habitants.

AMÉRIQUE DU SUD

Argentine : Centres comptant au moins 2 000 habitants.
Bolivie : Localités de 2 000 habitants ou plus.
Brésil : Zone à l'intérieur du périmètre urbain d'une ville, définie par la législation municipale.
Chili : Zones d'habitat concentré comptant 2 000 habitants ou plus, ou comptant entre 1 001 et 2 000 habitants dont 50 pour cent au moins de la population active s'occupe d'une activité secondaire ou tertiaire. Par dérogation, les centres qui ont une fonction touristique ou récréative et plus de 250 unités de logement mais n'atteignent pas le critère de population sont néanmoins considérés comme zones urbaines.

Colombie : Zone urbaine de recensement, définie par le Département administratif national d'État (DANE) à des fins statistiques, correspondant aux zones délimitées par le périmètre de recensement.
Équateur : Capitales des provinces et chefs-lieux de canton.
Guinée française : Une commune ou un ensemble de communes présentant une zone de bâti continu (pas de coupure de plus de 200 mètres entre deux constructions) qui compte au moins 2 000 habitants.
Îles Falkland (Malvinas) : Ville de Stanley.
Paraguay : Grandes villes, villes et chefs-lieux des départements et des districts.
Pérou : Centres peuplés de plus de 5 000 habitants, dotés de services publics, d'établissements d'enseignement et d'établissements de santé.
Suriname : Les districts de Paramaribo et de Wanica.
Uruguay : Les villes, villages et autres zones habitées répondant aux définitions de la loi sur les agglomérations.
Venezuela (République bolivarienne du) : Centres de 2 500 habitants ou plus.

ASIE

Arabie saoudite : Localités de plus de 5 000 habitants.
Arménie : Grandes villes et localités de type urbain, officiellement désignées comme telles, généralement sur la base du nombre d'habitants et de la prédominance des travailleurs agricoles ou non agricoles avec leur famille.
Azerbaïdjan : Division administrative regroupant plus de 15 000 habitants se livrant principalement à des activités industrielles et autres activités économiques et sociales et comprennant des centres administratifs et culturels.
Bahreïn : Communes ou villages comptant au moins 2 500 habitants.
Brunéi Darussalam : Les communes de Bandar, Seri Begawan, Kuala Belait, Seria, Pekan Tutong and Pekan Bangar; et les zones densement peuplé qui possèdent des caractéristiques urbaines.
Cambodge : Zones au niveau de la commune répondant aux trois conditions suivantes : 1) Densité démographique supérieure à 200 habitants au km carré, 2) pourcentage d'hommes travaillant dans l'agriculture inférieur à 50 pour cent, 3) population totale de la commune supérieure à 2 000 habitants.
Chine : Suivant la Réglementation sur la classification de la résidence urbaine/rurale à des fins de statistiques.
Chypre : Selon la définition du Département de l'urbanisme et du logement du Ministère de l'intérieur.
État de Palestine : Localités peuplées de plus de 10 000 personnes. L'expression désigne tous les gouvernorats (districts), quelle qu'en soit la taille, ainsi que toutes les villes dont la population est comprise entre 4 000 et 9 999 personnes qui disposent d'au moins quatre des éléments suivants : réseau public de distribution d'électricité, réseau public de distribution d'eau, bureau de poste, centre médical doté d'un médecin à temps plein et école préparant les élèves au certificat général de l'enseignement secondaire.
Géorgie : Grandes villes et localités de type urbain, officiellement désignées comme telles, généralement sur la base du nombre d'habitants et de la prédominance des travailleurs agricoles ou non agricoles avec leur famille.
Inde : Villes [localités dotées d'une charte municipale, d'un comité de zone municipale, d'un comité de zone déclarée urbaine ou d'un comité de zone de regroupement (cantonnement)] ; également toutes les localités qui ont une population de 5 000 habitants au moins, une densité de population d'au moins 1 000 habitants au mile carré ou 400 au kilomètre carré, des caractéristiques urbaines prononcées et où les trois quarts au moins des adultes de sexe masculin ont une occupation non agricole.
Indonésie : Les zones urbaines sont celles qui répondent à certains critères : densité de population, pourcentage de ménages agricoles, accès aux équipements urbains, existence d'équipements supplémentaires, et pourcentage de superficie bâtie à usage autre que l'habitation.
Iran (République islamique d') : Tous les districts comptant une municipalité.
Israël : Tous les lieux comptant au moins 2 000 résidents.
Japon : Villes (shi), comptant au moins 50 000 habitants, où 60 p. 100 au moins des logements sont situés dans les principales zones bâties, et dont 60 p. 100 au moins de population (y compris les personnes à charge) exercent un métier dans l'industrie, le commerce et d'autres branches d'activités essentiellement urbaines.
Jordanie : Localités comptant 5 000 habitants ou plus.
Kazakhstan : Villes ayant statut républicain (centres de population présentant une importance nationale spéciale ou comptant une population généralement de plus d'un million d'habitants), statut régional (Oblast')

(centres de population qui sont de grands centres économiques et culturels, dotés d'une infrastructure industrielle et sociale développée et comptant une population de plus 50 000 habitants, le pays compte 40 villes ayant statut régional), statut départemental, et agglomérations relevant de leur juridiction administrative.

Kirghizistan : Grandes villes et localités de type urbain, officiellement désignées comme telles, généralement sur la base du nombre d'habitants et de la prédominance des travailleurs agricoles ou non agricoles avec leur famille.

Koweït : Toutes les localités sont urbaines au Koweït.

Malaisie : Zone ayant le statut de centre urbain et dont la population totale dépasse 10 000 habitants. On nomme périphérie toute zone contiguë à un centre urbain dont au moins 60 % de la population (âgée de 15 ans et plus) a une activité non agricole. La définition des zones urbaines couvre également les zones spéciales de développement qui n'ont pas officiellement le statut de centre urbain, se trouvent à 5 kilomètres ou plus d'un tel centre ou de sa périphérie et comptent au moins 10 000 habitants dont 60 % (parmi les plus de 15 ans) ont une activité non agricole.

Maldives : Malé (la capitale).

Mongolie : Ulaanbaatar (la capitale), les chefs-lieux des provinces et les villes.

Myanmar : Les zones reconnues par les autorités gouvernementales comme urbaines. Ces zones se caractérisent par une densité de population et de constructions humaines plus élevée et disposent de meilleures infrastructures.

Népal : Zones déclarées telles par les municipalités.

Ouzbékistan : Grandes villes et localités de type urbain, officiellement désignées comme telles, généralement sur la base du nombre d'habitants et de la prédominance des travailleurs agricoles ou non agricoles avec leur famille.

Pakistan : Lieux avec une corporation métropolitaine, une corporation municipale, un comité municipal, un comité municipal ou un cantonnement au moment du recensement.

Philippines : Zones (barangays) de plus de 5 000 habitants, au moins un établissement d'au moins 100 employés, ou au moins cinq petits établissements comptant de 10 à 99 employés et cinq installations ou plus dans un rayon de deux kilomètres du barangay, comme Résolution no. 01 du Conseil de la Philippine Statistics Authority (PSA), série du 2017-098 - Adoption de la définition opérationnelle des zones urbaines aux Philippines. En outre, tous les barangays de la région de la capitale nationale sont automatiquement classés en zones urbaines.

République arabe syrienne : Villes, chefs-lieux de district (Mohafaza) et chefs-lieux de sous district (Mantika), et communes d'au moins 20 000 habitants.

République de Corée : Pour les estimations : localités de 50 000 habitants ou plus. Pour recensements, les données sont établies sont la base des divisions administratives mineures comme les Dongs (principalement en zone urbaines) et des Eups ou Myeons (en zones rurales).

République démocratique populaire lao : Zones ou villages répondant à au moins trois des cinq conditions suivantes: situés dans l'aire métropolitaine du district ou de la province, accessibles par la route en toute saison, plus de 70 pour cent de la population ayant accès à de l'eau distribuée par canalisation, plus de 70 pour cent de la population ayant accès au réseau d'électricité et existence d'un marché ouvert tous les jours.

Singapour : Le pays consiste seulement d'une ville.

Sri Lanka : Toutes les zones administrées par les conseils municipaux et urbains.

Tadjikistan : Grandes villes et localités de type urbain, officiellement désignées comme telles, généralement sur la base du nombre d'habitants et de la prédominance des travailleurs agricoles ou non agricoles avec leur famille.

Thaïlande : Zones municipales.

Turkménistan : Grandes villes et localités de type urbain, officiellement désignées comme telles, généralement sur la base du nombre d'habitants et de la prédominance des travailleurs agricoles ou non agricoles avec leur famille.

Turquie : Localités comptant 20 000 habitants ou plus.

Viet Nam : Zones urbaines comprises à l'intérieur des districts urbains des villes ainsi que des quartiers urbains et des localités. Toutes les autres unités administratives locales (communes) sont considérées comme zones rurales.

EUROPE

Albanie : Villes et autres centres industriels de plus de 400 habitants.

Autriche : Les zones urbaines sont les localités comptant 2 000 habitants ou plus. Leur délimitation remonte à 1991.
Bélarus : Les établissements urbains sont des établissements autorisés en vertu de la loi comme les villes, les agglomérations de type urbain, les cités ouvrières et les zones de villégiature de santé.
Belgique : Toutes les communes qui ne sont pas dans la liste des communes rurales sont considérées comme des communes urbaines. Il y a 33 communes qui sont considérées comme rurales: Alveringem, Amblève, Bertogne, Bièvre, Bullange, Burg-Reuland, Clavier, Erezée, Fauvillers, Frasnes-lez-Anvaing, Froidchapelle, Gedinne, Gouvy, Havelange, Herstappe, Heuvelland, Houffalize, Houyet, Langemark-Poelkapelle, Léglise, Lierneux, Lo-Reninge, Manhay, Momignies, Ravels, Sainte-Ode, Sint-Laureins, Sivry-Rance, Stoumont, Tenneville, Vaux-sur-Sûre, Vleteren et Vresse-sur-Semois.
Bulgarie : Toutes les zones considérées comme villes et bourgs selon la Division territoriale et administrative du pays.
Estonie : Les établissements urbains comprennent les villes et les agglomérations n'ayant pas de statut municipal.
Fédération de Russie : Grandes villes et localités de type urbain, officiellement désignées comme telles, généralement sur la base du nombre d'habitants et de la prédominance des travailleurs agricoles ou non agricoles avec leur famille.
Finlande : Communes urbaines (communes où au moins 90 % de la population vit en milieu urbain ou dont le plus grand centre urbain compte au moins 15 000 habitants).
France : Une commune ou un ensemble de communes présentant une zone de bâti continu (pas de coupure de plus de 200 mètres entre deux constructions) qui compte au moins 2 000 habitants.
Grèce : Est considérée comme zone urbaine toute municipalité ou commune dont la plus grande localité compte 2 000 habitants ou plus.
Hongrie : Localités dont le statut de ville a été reconnu par le Président de la République compte tenu de critères spécifiques (économiques, commerciaux, institutionnels, culturels, etc.).
Irlande : Localités, y compris leur banlieues, comptant 1 500 habitants ou plus.
Islande : Localités de 200 habitants ou plus.
Lettonie : Grandes villes et localités de type urbain, officiellement désignées comme telles, généralement sur la base du nombre d'habitants et de la prédominance des travailleurs agricoles ou non agricoles avec leur famille.
Liechtenstein : Les communes comptant 10 000 habitants ou plus.
Lituanie : Par population urbaine, on entend les personnes qui vivent dans des villes ou des localités, à savoir les zones habitées comportant des logements permanents proches les uns des autres et dont la population est d'au moins 3 000 habitants, les deux tiers desquels étant employés dans le secteur industriel, l'infrastructure sociale ou le commerce. Un certain nombre de villes peuvent compter moins de 3 000 habitants dans la mesure où elles avaient acquis le statut de ville avant l'entrée en vigueur de la nouvelle loi en juillet 1994.
Macédoine du Nord : Villes sont les localités comptant au moins 3 000 habitants, dotés d'une infrastructure industrielle et sociale développée, dont plus de 51 pour cent de la population active s'occupe des activités qui ne sont pas primaires.
Malte : Zones de 1 kilomètre carré avec une densité minimum de 300 au kilomètre carré et un minimum de 5 000 habitants, et zones à forte densité de population (supérieure à 500 habitants au kilomètre carré).
Monténégro : D'après la législation actuelle relative à l'organisation territoriale du Monténégro, qui oblige chaque collectivité à déterminer quelles sont ses zones urbaines et rurales.
Norvège : Ensemble construit habité par au moins 200 personnes, où les bâtiments ne sont pas éloignés de plus de 50 mètres les uns des autres. Les limites en sont évolutives et peuvent être redéfinies pour tenir compte de l'urbanisation et de l'évolution de la population.
Pays Bas : Zones urbaines : municipalités comptant au moins 2 000 habitants. Zones semi-urbaines : municipalités comptant moins de 2 000 habitants, mais où 20 p. 100 au maximum de la population active de sexe masculin pratiquent l'agriculture, et certaines municipalités de caractère résidentiel dont les habitants travaillent ailleurs.
Pologne : Toutes les zones qui ont les droits d'une ville ou le statut d'une ville avec dispositions de lois distinctes.
Portugal : Localités comptant 2 000 habitants ou davantage.
République de Moldova : Grandes villes et localités de type urbain, officiellement désignées comme telles, généralement sur la base du nombre d'habitants et de la prédominance des travailleurs agricoles ou non agricoles avec leur famille.
République tchèque : Localités d'au moins 2 000 habitants.
Roumanie : Localités où la majorité des ressources en main-d'œuvre est employée dans des activités non agricoles avec un niveau diversifié de ressources, exerçant une influence socioéconomique constante et importante sur l'ensemble de la zone.

Royaume-Uni de Grande-Bretagne et d'Irlande du Nord : Pour l'Angleterre et le Pays de Galles, les zones bâties comptant 10 000 habitants ou plus ; pour l'Écosse, les établissements humains comptant 3 000 habitants ou davantage et pour l'Irlande du Nord, les établissements comptant 5 000 habitants.
Serbie : Municipalités, villes et Belgrade.
Slovaquie : Municipalités avec statut de ville, conformément aux critères : 1) est un centre économique, administratif, culturel ou touristique ; 2) fournit des services pour d'autres municipalités ; 3) a un caractère urbain, au moins en partie ; et 4) compte 5 000 habitants ou plus.
Slovénie : Établissements de 3 000 habitants ou plus, chefs-lieux de municipalités comptant au moins 1 400 habitants, et quartiers suburbains qui s'intègrent progressivement dans une ville de 5 000 habitants ou plus.
Suisse : L'espace urbain comprend les agglomérations et les villes isolées (n'appartenant pas à une agglomération et comptant au moins 10 000 habitants à elles seules).
Ukraine : Grandes villes et localités de type urbain, officiellement désignées comme telles, généralement sur la base du nombre d'habitants et de la prédominance des travailleurs agricoles ou non agricoles avec leur famille.

OCÉANIE

Australie : Zones de développement urbain concentré comptant 200 habitants ou plus, identifiées principalement à l'aide de critères objectifs en matière de logement et de densité de population, à l'aide des données du recensement de 2016.
Guam : Agglomérations de 2 500 habitants ou plus ayant généralement une densité de population d'au moins 1 000 habitants au mile carré et considérées comme étant des groupements urbains.
Îles Cook : Rarotonga, île la plus peuplée.
Îles Mariannes septentrionales : Agglomérations de 2 500 habitants ou plus ayant généralement une densité de population d'au moins 1 000 habitants au mile carré. Deux types de zones urbaines : zones urbanisées de 50 000 habitants ou plus et groupements urbains comptant au moins 2 500 habitants mais moins de 50 000.
Nouvelle-Calédonie : Nouméa et communes de Païta, Dumbéa et Mont-Dore.
Nouvelle-Zélande : Toutes les villes et les quartiers, districts et bourgs ayant 1 000 habitants permanents ou plus.
Palaos : États comptant 2 500 habitants ou plus (le seul État qui remplit cette condition est l'État de Koror).
Samoa : Seule la région urbaine d'Apia (AUA).
Samoa américaines : Agglomérations de 2 500 habitants ou plus ayant généralement une densité de population d'au moins 1 000 habitants au mile carré. Deux types de zones urbaines : zones urbanisées de 50 000 habitants ou plus et groupements urbains comptant au moins 2 500 habitants mais moins de 50 000. (D'après les résultats du recensement de 2000, les Samoa américaines ne comptent aucune zone urbanisée.)
Tokélaou : L'ensemble de la population est considéré comme vivant en milieu rural.
Tonga : Nuku'alofa.
Vanuatu : Centre de Luganville et Port-Vila.

NOTES

[1] Pour plus de précisions, voir *Social and Demographic Statistics : Classifications of Size and Type of Locality and Urban/Rural Areas*, E/CN.3/551, publication des Nations Unies, New York, 1980.

6. Total and urban population by sex: 2010 - 2019
Population totale et population urbaine selon le sexe : 2010 - 2019

Continent, country or area, and date / Continent, pays ou zone et date	Code[a]	Both sexes - Les deux sexes			Male - Masculin			Female - Féminin		
		Total	Urban - Urbaine		Total	Urban - Urbaine		Total	Urban - Urbaine	
			Number Nombre	Percent P.100		Number Nombre	Percent P.100		Number Nombre	Percent P.100
AFRICA - AFRIQUE										
Algeria - Algérie										
1 VII 2010	ESDJ	*35 978 000*	...	...	*18 205 000*	...	...	*17 773 000*	...	...
1 VII 2011	ESDJ	*36 717 000*	...	...	*18 579 000*	...	...	*18 138 000*	...	...
1 VII 2012	ESDJ	*37 495 000*	...	...	*18 976 000*	...	...	*18 519 000*	...	...
1 VII 2013	ESDJ	*38 297 000*	...	...	*19 383 000*	...	...	*18 914 000*	...	...
1 VII 2014	ESDJ	*39 114 275*	...	...	*19 801 163*	...	...	*19 313 112*	...	...
1 VII 2015	ESDJ	*39 963 249*	...	...	*20 235 204*	...	...	*19 728 045*	...	...
1 VII 2016	ESDJ	*40 835 602*	...	...	*20 680 271*	...	...	*20 155 331*	...	...
1 VII 2017	ESDJ	*41 695 626*	...	...	*21 118 894*	...	...	*20 576 732*	...	...
1 VII 2018	ESDJ	*42 577 723*	...	...	*21 570 556*	...	...	*21 007 167*	...	...
1 VII 2019[1]	ESDJ	*43 413 000*	...	...	*21 993 000*	...	...	*21 420 000*	...	...
Angola										
1 VII 2010[2]	ESDF	*17 429 637*	...	...	*8 427 802*	...	...	*9 001 835*	...	...
1 VII 2011[2]	ESDF	*17 992 033*	...	...	*8 707 868*	...	...	*9 284 165*	...	...
1 VII 2012[2]	ESDF	*18 576 568*	...	...	*8 999 074*	...	...	*9 577 494*	...	...
1 VII 2013[2]	ESDF	*19 183 590*	...	...	*9 301 632*	...	...	*9 881 958*	...	...
16 V 2014	CDFC	25 789 024	16 153 987	62.6	12 499 041	7 860 614	62.9	13 289 983	8 293 373	62.4
1 VII 2014[3]	ESDF	*25 901 182*	*16 235 542*	*62.7*	*12 553 707*	*7 900 523*	*62.9*	*13 347 475*	*8 335 019*	*62.4*
1 VII 2015[3]	ESDF	*26 681 590*	*16 761 094*	*62.8*	*12 943 812*	*8 165 438*	*63.1*	*13 737 778*	*8 595 656*	*62.6*
1 VII 2016[3]	ESDF	*27 503 526*	*17 310 474*	*62.9*	*13 355 101*	*8 442 190*	*63.2*	*14 148 425*	*8 868 284*	*62.7*
1 VII 2017[3]	ESDF	*28 359 634*	*17 881 283*	*63.1*	*13 783 460*	*8 729 543*	*63.3*	*14 576 174*	*9 151 740*	*62.8*
1 VII 2018[3]	ESDF	*29 250 009*	*18 473 609*	*63.2*	*14 228 926*	*9 027 566*	*63.4*	*15 021 083*	*9 446 043*	*62.9*
1 VII 2019[3]	ESDF	*30 175 553*	*19 087 816*	*63.3*	*14 691 938*	*9 336 450*	*63.5*	*15 483 615*	*9 751 366*	*63.0*
Benin - Bénin										
1 VII 2010[1]	ESDF	*8 778 648*	*3 873 462*	*44.1*	*4 301 224*	*1 903 683*	*44.3*	*4 477 424*	*1 969 779*	*44.0*
1 VII 2011[1]	ESDF	*9 067 076*	*4 072 574*	*44.9*	*4 446 877*	*2 003 366*	*45.1*	*4 620 199*	*2 069 208*	*44.8*
1 VII 2012[1]	ESDF	*9 364 619*	*4 280 693*	*45.7*	*4 597 122*	...	...	*4 767 497*	...	...
11 V 2013	CDFC	10 008 749	4 460 503	44.6	4 887 820	...	...	5 120 929	...	...
1 VII 2014[4]	ESDF	*10 293 235*	...	...	*5 033 372*	...	...	*5 259 863*	...	...
1 VII 2015[4]	ESDF	*10 584 935*	...	...	*5 182 478*	...	...	*5 402 457*	...	...
1 VII 2016[4]	ESDF	*10 882 953*	...	...	*5 334 603*	...	...	*5 548 350*	...	...
1 VII 2017[4]	ESDF	*11 186 785*	...	...	*5 489 507*	...	...	*5 697 278*	...	...
1 VII 2018[4]	ESDF	*11 496 140*	...	...	*5 647 059*	...	...	*5 849 081*	...	...
Botswana										
1 VII 2010	ESDJ	*1 822 859*	...	...	*895 007*	...	...	*927 852*	...	...
1 VII 2011	ESDJ	*1 849 692*	...	...	*910 404*	...	...	*939 288*	...	...
9 VIII 2011	CDFC	2 024 904	1 297 287	64.1	988 957	619 472	62.6	1 035 947	677 815	65.4
1 VII 2012[5]	ESDJ	*2 070 984*	*1 361 699*	*65.8*	*1 010 236*	*664 243*	*65.8*	*1 060 748*	*697 456*	*65.8*
1 VII 2013[5]	ESDJ	*2 114 890*	*1 411 436*	*66.7*	*1 031 654*	*688 505*	*66.7*	*1 083 236*	*722 931*	*66.7*
1 VII 2014[5]	ESDJ	*2 156 366*	*1 460 383*	*67.7*	*1 051 886*	*712 382*	*67.7*	*1 104 480*	*748 001*	*67.7*
1 VII 2015[5]	ESDJ	*2 195 134*	*1 508 277*	*68.7*	*1 070 797*	*735 745*	*68.7*	*1 124 337*	*772 532*	*68.7*
1 VII 2016[5]	ESDJ	*2 230 905*	*1 554 836*	*69.7*	*1 088 246*	*758 457*	*69.7*	*1 142 659*	*796 379*	*69.7*
1 VII 2017[5]	ESDJ	*2 266 857*	*1 602 216*	*70.7*	*1 110 760*	*785 086*	*70.7*	*1 156 097*	*817 130*	*70.7*
1 VII 2018[5]	ESDJ	*2 302 878*	...	...	*1 134 505*	...	...	*1 168 373*	...	...
1 VII 2019[5]	ESDJ	*2 338 851*	...	...	*1 153 123*	...	...	*1 185 728*	...	...
Burkina Faso[1]										
1 VII 2010	ESDJ	*15 730 977*	...	...	*7 590 133*	...	...	*8 140 844*	...	...
1 VII 2011	ESDJ	*16 248 558*	...	...	*7 839 350*	...	...	*8 409 208*	...	...
1 VII 2012	ESDJ	*16 779 206*	...	...	*8 095 324*	...	...	*8 683 882*	...	...
1 VII 2013	ESDJ	*17 322 796*	...	...	*8 357 967*	...	...	*8 964 829*	...	...
1 VII 2014	ESDJ	*17 880 386*	...	...	*8 627 830*	...	...	*9 252 556*	...	...
1 VII 2015	ESDJ	*18 450 494*	...	...	*8 904 256*	...	...	*9 546 238*	...	...
1 VII 2016	ESDJ	*19 034 397*	...	...	*9 187 904*	...	...	*9 846 493*	...	...
1 VII 2017	ESDJ	*19 632 147*	...	...	*9 478 805*	...	...	*10 153 342*	...	...
1 VII 2018	ESDJ	*20 244 080*	...	...	*9 777 136*	...	...	*10 466 944*	...	...
1 VII 2019	ESDJ	*20 870 060*	...	...	*10 082 776*	...	...	*10 787 284*	...	...
Burundi										
1 VII 2010	ESDF	*9 461 117*	...	...	*4 667 414*	...	...	*4 793 703*	...	...
1 VII 2011	ESDF	*9 770 966*	...	...	*4 821 919*	...	...	*4 949 047*	...	...
1 VII 2012	ESDF	*10 072 586*	...	...	*4 972 342*	...	...	*5 100 244*	...	...
1 VII 2013	ESDF	*10 367 166*	...	...	*5 119 077*	...	...	*5 248 090*	...	...
1 VII 2014	ESDF	*10 654 129*	...	...	*5 261 796*	...	...	*5 392 333*	...	...
1 VII 2015	ESDF	*10 933 352*	...	...	*5 400 270*	...	...	*5 533 083*	...	...
1 VII 2016	ESDF	*11 215 024*	...	...	*5 539 816*	...	...	*5 675 209*	...	...
1 VII 2017	ESDF	*11 495 438*	...	...	*5 678 570*	...	...	*5 816 869*	...	...

6. Total and urban population by sex: 2010 - 2019
Population totale et population urbaine selon le sexe : 2010 - 2019 (continued - suite)

Continent, country or area, and date / Continent, pays ou zone et date	Code[a]	Both sexes - Les deux sexes: Total	Both sexes: Urban - Urbaine: Number Nombre	Both sexes: Urban - Urbaine: Percent P.100	Male - Masculin: Total	Male: Urban - Urbaine: Number Nombre	Male: Urban - Urbaine: Percent P.100	Female - Féminin: Total	Female: Urban - Urbaine: Number Nombre	Female: Urban - Urbaine: Percent P.100
AFRICA - AFRIQUE										
Burundi										
1 VII 2018	ESDF	11 772 322	...	...	5 815 408	...	...	5 956 914	...	...
1 VII 2019	ESDF	12 044 164	...	...	5 949 575	...	...	6 094 589	...	...
Cabo Verde										
16 VI 2010	CDJC	491 683	303 673	61.8	243 403	151 219	62.1	248 280	152 454	61.4
1 VII 2010[1]	ESDJ	494 040	...	...	244 338	...	...	249 702	...	...
1 VII 2011[1]	ESDJ	499 929	...	...	247 814	...	...	252 115	...	...
1 VII 2012[1]	ESDJ	505 983	...	...	251 384	...	...	254 599	...	...
1 VII 2013[1]	ESDJ	512 173	...	...	255 033	...	...	257 140	...	...
1 VII 2014[1]	ESDJ	518 467	...	...	258 744	...	...	259 723	...	...
1 VII 2015[1]	ESDJ	524 833	...	...	262 501	...	...	262 331	...	...
1 VII 2016[1]	ESDJ	531 239	...	...	266 287	...	...	264 951	...	...
1 VII 2017[1]	ESDJ	537 661	...	...	270 091	...	...	267 570	...	...
1 VII 2018[1]	ESDJ	544 081	...	...	273 904	...	...	270 177	...	...
1 VII 2019[1]	ESDJ	550 483	...	...	277 720	...	...	272 764	...	...
Cameroon - Cameroun[6]										
1 VII 2010	ESDJ	20 127 358	...	...	9 975 947	...	...	10 151 411	...	...
1 VII 2011	ESDJ	20 709 658	...	...	10 271 305	...	...	10 438 353	...	...
1 VII 2012	ESDJ	21 277 400	...	...	10 548 982	...	...	10 728 418	...	...
1 VII 2013	ESDJ	21 848 088	...	...	10 825 833	...	...	11 022 255	...	...
1 VII 2014	ESDJ	22 454 094	...	...	11 134 230	...	...	11 319 864	...	...
1 VII 2015	ESDJ	23 050 282	...	...	11 417 323	...	...	11 632 959	...	...
1 VII 2016	ESDJ	23 642 400	...	...	11 706 438	...	...	11 935 962	...	...
1 VII 2017	ESDJ	24 253 757	...	...	12 008 210	...	...	12 245 547	...	...
1 VII 2018	ESDJ	24 863 335	...	...	12 302 528	...	...	12 560 807	...	...
1 VII 2019	ESDJ	25 492 354	...	...	12 609 256	...	...	12 883 098	...	...
Chad - Tchad										
1 VII 2010	ESDJ	11 469 500	2 542 406	22.2	5 668 049	1 256 418	22.2	5 801 451	1 285 988	22.2
1 VII 2011	ESDJ	11 880 614	2 665 217	22.4	5 876 234	1 318 235	22.4	6 004 379	1 346 982	22.4
1 VII 2012	ESDJ	12 306 561	2 793 589	22.7	6 092 153	1 382 919	22.7	6 214 408	1 410 671	22.7
1 VII 2013	ESDJ	12 746 650	2 927 481	23.0	6 315 618	1 450 487	23.0	6 431 033	1 476 994	23.0
1 VII 2014	ESDJ	13 200 844	3 066 996	23.2	6 546 755	1 521 029	23.2	6 654 089	1 545 966	23.2
1 VII 2015	ESDJ	13 670 084	3 212 470	23.5	6 786 021	1 594 715	23.5	6 884 063	1 617 755	23.5
1 VII 2016	ESDJ	14 152 314	3 363 534	23.8	7 032 311	1 671 346	23.8	7 120 003	1 692 188	23.8
1 VII 2017	ESDJ	14 649 076	3 520 661	24.0	7 286 344	1 751 151	24.0	7 362 731	1 769 510	24.0
1 VII 2018	ESDJ	15 162 044	3 684 377	24.3	7 548 902	1 834 383	24.3	7 613 141	1 849 993	24.3
1 VII 2019	ESDJ	15 692 969	3 855 240	24.6	7 820 817	1 921 314	24.6	7 872 152	1 933 926	24.6
Congo										
1 VII 2010	ESDJ	4 118 775	2 299 393	55.8	2 025 613	1 134 755	56.0	2 093 162	1 164 638	55.6
1 VII 2011	ESDJ	4 257 195	2 383 630	56.0	2 102 229	1 176 896	56.0	2 154 966	1 206 734	56.0
1 VII 2012	ESDJ	4 394 327	2 460 535	56.0	2 170 749	1 215 331	56.0	2 223 578	1 245 204	56.0
1 VII 2013	ESDJ	4 530 366	2 537 004	56.0	2 238 395	1 253 501	56.0	2 291 971	1 283 503	56.0
1 VII 2014	ESDJ	4 666 379	2 613 169	56.0	2 306 196	1 291 468	56.0	2 360 183	1 321 701	56.0
1 VII 2015	ESDJ	4 801 684	2 688 943	56.0	2 373 559	1 329 192	56.0	2 428 125	1 359 751	56.0
1 VII 2016	ESDJ	4 934 312	2 764 263	56.0	2 438 566	1 366 645	56.0	2 495 746	1 397 618	56.0
1 VII 2017	ESDJ	5 069 800	2 839 087	56.0	2 506 780	1 403 795	56.0	2 563 020	1 435 292	56.0
1 VII 2018	ESDJ	5 203 073	2 913 720	56.0	2 572 865	1 440 803	56.0	2 630 208	1 472 917	56.0
1 VII 2019	ESDJ	5 336 074	3 298 418	61.8	2 628 512	1 634 394	62.2	2 707 562	1 664 024	61.5
Côte d'Ivoire										
1 VII 2010[7]	ESDF	20 845 167	...	...	10 742 336	...	...	10 102 831	...	...
1 VII 2011[7]	ESDF	21 301 704	...	...	10 983 811	...	...	10 317 893	...	...
1 VII 2012[7]	ESDF	21 758 244	...	...	11 225 286	...	...	10 532 958	...	...
1 VII 2013[7]	ESDF	22 214 787	...	...	11 466 762	...	...	10 748 025	...	...
15 V 2014	CDFC	22 224 509	10 881 387	49.0	11 441 896	5 495 438	48.0	10 782 613	5 385 949	50.0
1 VII 2014[7]	ESDF	22 723 460	11 444 572	50.4	11 734 076	5 834 493	49.7	10 989 384	5 610 079	51.0
1 VII 2015[7]	ESDF	23 334 439	11 830 560	50.7	12 036 040	6 102 272	50.7	11 298 398	5 728 288	50.7
1 VII 2016[7]	ESDF	23 950 475	12 262 643	51.2	12 340 861	6 318 521	51.2	11 609 614	5 944 122	51.2
1 VII 2017[7]	ESDF	24 571 044	12 678 659	51.6	12 648 124	6 526 432	51.6	11 922 920	6 152 227	51.6
1 VII 2018[7]	ESDF	25 194 402	13 126 283	52.1	12 956 707	6 750 444	52.1	12 237 695	6 375 839	52.1
1 VII 2019[7]	ESDF	25 821 956	13 556 527	52.5	13 267 837	6 965 615	52.5	12 554 119	6 590 912	52.5
Egypt - Égypte										
1 VII 2010	ESDF	78 684 622	33 804 181	43.0	40 228 119	17 255 735	42.9	38 456 503	16 548 446	43.0
1 VII 2011	ESDF	80 529 566	34 495 468	42.8	41 152 525	17 596 284	42.8	39 377 041	16 899 184	42.9
1 VII 2012	ESDF	82 549 976	35 372 982	42.9	42 167 660	18 031 407	42.8	40 382 316	17 341 575	42.9
1 VII 2013	ESDF	84 628 982	36 213 473	42.8	43 217 105	18 470 748	42.7	41 411 877	17 742 725	42.8

6. Total and urban population by sex: 2010 - 2019
Population totale et population urbaine selon le sexe : 2010 - 2019 (continued - suite)

Continent, country or area, and date / Continent, pays ou zone et date	Code[a]	Both sexes - Les deux sexes			Male - Masculin			Female - Féminin		
		Total	Urban - Urbaine		Total	Urban - Urbaine		Total	Urban - Urbaine	
			Number Nombre	Percent P.100		Number Nombre	Percent P.100		Number Nombre	Percent P.100
AFRICA - AFRIQUE										
Egypt - Égypte										
1 VII 2014	ESDF	86 811 192	37 098 131	42.7	44 300 565	18 894 134	42.6	42 510 627	18 203 997	42.8
1 VII 2015	ESDF	88 957 833	37 999 018	42.7	45 378 728	19 347 041	42.6	43 579 105	18 651 977	42.8
1 VII 2016	ESDF	91 023 393	38 895 815	42.7	46 413 993	19 787 083	42.6	44 609 400	19 108 732	42.8
18 IV 2017[8]	CDJC	94 798 827	40 240 407	42.4	48 891 518	20 723 472	42.4	45 907 309	19 516 935	42.5
1 VII 2017	ESDF	95 202 532	40 432 110	42.5	49 095 021	20 818 309	42.4	46 107 511	19 613 801	42.5
1 VII 2018	ESDF	97 147 368	41 398 653	42.6	50 070 213	21 293 773	42.5	47 077 155	20 104 880	42.7
Equatorial Guinea - Guinée équatoriale										
20 VI 2015*	CDFC	1 222 442	863 313	70.6	651 820	...	...	570 622	...	...
1 VII 2015[9]	ESDF	1 225 377	932 512	76.1	642 098	...	...	583 279	...	...
1 VII 2016[9]	ESDF	1 268 165	965 074	76.1	664 519	...	...	603 646	...	...
1 VII 2017[9]	ESDF	1 312 447	998 772	76.1	687 723	...	...	624 724	...	...
1 VII 2018[9]	ESDF	1 358 276	1 033 648	76.1	711 737	...	...	646 539	...	...
1 VII 2019[9]	ESDF	1 405 704	1 069 741	76.1	736 590	...	...	669 115	...	...
Eritrea - Érythrée[10]										
1 VII 2010	ESDF	2 691 414	959 076	35.6	1 328 220	458 920	34.6	1 363 194	500 156	36.7
1 VII 2011	ESDF	2 758 710	984 049	35.7	1 360 721	470 508	34.6	1 397 989	513 542	36.7
1 VII 2012	ESDF	2 828 680	1 009 342	35.7	1 394 589	482 248	34.6	1 434 091	527 093	36.8
1 VII 2013	ESDF	2 901 138	1 034 874	35.7	1 429 730	494 104	34.6	1 471 407	540 771	36.8
1 VII 2014	ESDF	2 975 851	1 060 585	35.6	1 466 026	506 044	34.5	1 509 825	554 541	36.7
1 VII 2015	ESDF	3 052 498	1 086 415	35.6	1 503 313	518 040	34.5	1 549 185	568 375	36.7
1 VII 2016	ESDF	3 131 148	1 112 354	35.5	1 541 625	530 088	34.4	1 589 523	582 266	36.6
1 VII 2017	ESDF	3 211 946	1 138 401	35.4	1 581 036	542 187	34.3	1 630 910	596 213	36.6
1 VII 2018	ESDF	3 294 680	1 164 508	35.3	1 621 437	554 316	34.2	1 673 242	610 192	36.5
1 VII 2019	ESDF	3 379 039	1 190 612	35.2	1 662 675	566 445	34.1	1 716 364	624 168	36.4
Eswatini										
1 VII 2010[11]	ESDJ	1 055 506	237 641	22.5	500 070	113 554	22.7	555 436	124 087	22.3
1 VII 2011[11]	ESDJ	1 067 773	241 947	22.7	506 186	115 493	22.8	561 587	126 454	22.5
1 VII 2012[11]	ESDJ	1 080 337	246 441	22.8	512 432	117 528	22.9	567 905	128 913	22.7
1 VII 2013[11]	ESDJ	1 093 158	251 122	23.0	518 788	119 658	23.1	574 370	131 464	22.9
1 VII 2014[11]	ESDJ	1 106 189	255 986	23.1	525 232	121 881	23.2	580 957	134 105	23.1
1 VII 2015[11]	ESDJ	1 119 375	261 028	23.3	531 737	124 195	23.4	587 638	136 833	23.3
1 VII 2016[11]	ESDJ	1 132 657	266 230	23.5	538 274	126 593	23.5	594 383	139 637	23.5
29 IV 2017	CDJC	1 093 238	259 766	23.8	531 111	128 701	24.2	562 127	131 065	23.3
1 VII 2017[11]	ESDJ	1 145 970	271 573	23.7	544 811	129 068	23.7	601 159	142 505	23.7
1 VII 2018[11]	ESDJ	1 159 250	277 042	23.9	551 317	131 612	23.9	607 933	145 430	23.9
1 VII 2019[11]	ESDJ	1 172 433	282 622	24.1	557 760	134 217	24.1	614 673	148 405	24.1
Ethiopia - Éthiopie[12]										
1 VII 2010	ESDF	79 634 000	13 931 000	17.5	40 123 000	6 950 000	17.3	39 511 000	6 981 000	17.7
1 VII 2011	ESDF	81 668 000	14 589 000	17.9	41 119 000	7 274 000	17.7	40 549 000	7 315 000	18.0
1 VII 2012	ESDF	83 741 000	15 246 000	18.2	42 135 000	7 598 000	18.0	41 606 000	7 648 000	18.4
1 VII 2013	ESDF	85 837 000	15 979 000	18.6	43 164 000	7 960 000	18.4	42 673 000	8 019 000	18.8
1 VII 2014	ESDF	87 952 000	16 734 000	19.0	44 204 000	8 332 000	18.8	43 748 000	8 402 000	19.2
1 VII 2015	ESDF	90 075 000	17 521 000	19.5	45 250 000	8 721 000	19.3	44 825 000	8 800 000	19.6
1 VII 2016	ESDF	92 205 000	18 327 000	19.9	46 303 000	9 120 000	19.7	45 902 000	9 207 000	20.1
1 VII 2017	ESDF	94 352 138	19 161 490	20.3	47 364 992	9 534 811	20.1	46 987 146	9 626 679	20.5
1 VII 2018	ESDF	96 503 000	20 057 000	20.8	48 430 000	9 977 000	20.6	48 073 000	10 080 000	21.0
1 VII 2019	ESDF	98 536 550	20 776 812	21.1	49 430 939	10 326 225	20.9	49 105 606	10 450 593	21.3
Gabon										
22 V 2013	CDFC	1 811 079	1 577 646	87.1	934 072	813 098	87.0	877 007	764 548	87.2
Gambia - Gambie										
15 IV 2013*	CDFC	1 882 450	...	...	930 699	...	...	951 751	...	...
31 XII 2015[13]	SSDF	1 922 950	1 057 467	55.0	915 357	503 304	55.0	1 007 593	554 163	55.0
Ghana										
26 IX 2010	CDFC	24 658 823	12 545 229	50.9	12 024 845	6 016 059	50.0	12 633 978	6 529 170	51.7
1 VII 2011[14]	ESDF	25 235 268	12 844 745	50.9	12 319 770	6 270 758	50.9	12 915 498	6 573 987	50.9
1 VII 2012[14]	ESDF	25 824 920	13 144 879	50.9	12 621 125	6 424 150	50.9	13 203 795	6 720 729	50.9
1 VII 2013[14]	ESDF	26 427 760	13 451 714	50.9	12 928 916	6 580 808	50.9	13 498 844	6 870 906	50.9
1 VII 2014[14]	ESDF	27 043 093	13 764 931	50.9	13 242 709	6 740 539	50.9	13 800 384	7 024 392	50.9
1 VII 2015[14]	ESDF	27 670 174	13 817 894	49.9	13 562 093	6 903 107	50.9	14 108 081	6 914 787	49.0
1 VII 2016[14]	ESDF	28 308 301	...	...	13 886 734	...	...	14 421 567	...	...
1 VII 2017[14]	ESDF	28 956 587	...	...	14 216 288	...	...	14 740 299	...	...
1 VII 2018[14]	ESDF	29 614 337	...	...	14 550 431	...	...	15 063 906	...	...
1 VII 2019[14]	ESDF	30 280 811	...	...	14 888 808	...	...	15 392 003	...	...

6. Total and urban population by sex: 2010 - 2019
Population totale et population urbaine selon le sexe : 2010 - 2019 (continued - suite)

Continent, country or area, and date / Continent, pays ou zone et date	Code[a]	Both sexes - Les deux sexes: Total	Both sexes - Urban - Urbaine: Number Nombre	Both sexes - Urban - Urbaine: Percent P.100	Male - Masculin: Total	Male - Urban - Urbaine: Number Nombre	Male - Urban - Urbaine: Percent P.100	Female - Féminin: Total	Female - Urban - Urbaine: Number Nombre	Female - Urban - Urbaine: Percent P.100
AFRICA - AFRIQUE										
Guinea - Guinée										
1 VII 2010[15]	ESDJ	9 557 125	...	...	4 612 159	...	...	4 944 966	...	...
1 VII 2011[15]	ESDJ	9 812 181	...	...	4 735 246	...	...	5 076 935	...	...
1 VII 2012[15]	ESDJ	10 071 008	...	...	4 860 153	...	...	5 210 855	...	...
1 VII 2013[15]	ESDJ	10 333 576	...	...	4 986 865	...	...	5 346 711	...	...
15 III 2014	CDJC	10 523 261	3 657 122	34.8	5 084 306	1 821 369	35.8	5 438 955	1 835 753	33.8
1 VII 2014[16]	ESDJ	10 599 848	3 684 996	34.8	5 115 365	1 832 976	35.8	5 484 483	1 852 020	33.8
1 VII 2015[16]	ESDJ	10 917 711	3 825 273	35.0	5 273 425	1 847 667	35.0	5 644 286	1 977 606	35.0
1 VII 2016[16]	ESDJ	11 233 038	3 966 389	35.3	5 430 371	1 917 466	35.3	5 802 667	2 048 923	35.3
1 VII 2017[16]	ESDJ	11 555 062	4 111 607	35.6	5 590 797	1 989 359	35.6	5 964 265	2 122 248	35.6
1 VII 2018[16]	ESDJ	11 883 517	4 260 887	35.9	5 754 536	2 063 314	35.9	6 128 981	2 197 573	35.9
1 VII 2019[16]	ESDJ	12 218 357	4 414 267	36.1	5 921 548	2 139 346	36.1	6 296 809	2 274 921	36.1
Guinea-Bissau - Guinée-Bissau[1]										
1 VII 2010	ESDF	1 460 221	584 228	40.0	709 482	283 859	40.0	750 739	300 369	40.0
1 VII 2011	ESDF	1 472 233	595 358	40.4	716 622	289 796	40.4	755 611	305 562	40.4
1 VII 2012	ESDF	1 485 189	606 976	40.9	724 208	295 974	40.9	760 981	311 002	40.9
1 VII 2013	ESDF	1 499 277	619 166	41.3	732 337	302 438	41.3	766 940	316 728	41.3
1 VII 2014	ESDF	1 514 451	631 938	41.7	740 981	309 191	41.7	773 470	322 747	41.7
1 VII 2015	ESDF	1 530 673	645 283	42.2	750 119	316 226	42.2	780 554	329 057	42.2
1 VII 2016	ESDF	1 547 777	659 138	42.6	759 666	323 512	42.6	788 111	335 626	42.6
1 VII 2017	ESDF	1 565 842	673 556	43.0	769 659	331 072	43.0	796 183	342 484	43.0
1 VII 2018	ESDF	1 584 791	688 511	43.4	780 070	338 902	43.4	804 721	349 609	43.4
1 VII 2019	ESDF	1 604 561	703 994	43.9	790 873	346 992	43.9	813 688	357 002	43.9
Kenya										
1 VII 2010[17]	ESDF	38 473 893	...	...	19 047 448	...	...	19 426 445	...	...
1 VII 2011[17]	ESDF	39 545 118	...	...	19 583 833	...	...	19 961 285	...	...
1 VII 2012[17]	ESDF	40 656 572	...	...	20 137 201	...	...	20 519 371	...	...
1 VII 2013[17]	ESDF	41 787 735	...	...	20 707 136	...	...	21 080 599	...	...
1 VII 2014[17]	ESDF	42 961 187	...	...	21 289 752	...	...	21 671 435	...	...
1 VII 2015[17]	ESDF	44 156 577	14 280 766	32.3	21 886 677	7 160 225	32.7	22 269 900	7 120 541	32.0
1 VII 2016[17]	ESDF	45 389 112	14 679 464	32.3	22 508 628	7 363 696	32.7	22 880 484	7 315 769	32.0
1 VII 2017[17]	ESDF	46 595 199	15 069 937	32.3	23 117 881	...	...	23 477 319	...	...
1 VII 2018[17]	ESDF	47 848 953	15 475 429	32.3	23 750 828	...	...	24 098 124	...	...
24 VIII 2019	CDFC	47 562 772[18]	14 831 017[18]	31.2	23 548 056	7 352 137	31.2	24 014 716	7 478 880	31.1
Lesotho										
1 VII 2010[19]	ESDF	1 891 830	...	...	913 030	...	...	978 800	...	...
1 VII 2011[19]	ESDF	1 896 833	...	...	913 701	...	...	983 132	...	...
1 VII 2012[19]	ESDF	1 902 707	...	...	914 954	...	...	987 753	...	...
1 VII 2013[19]	ESDF	1 909 321	...	...	916 722	...	...	992 599	...	...
1 VII 2014[19]	ESDF	1 916 573	...	...	918 944	...	...	997 629	...	...
1 VII 2015[19]	ESDF	1 924 381	...	...	921 565	...	...	1 002 816	...	...
10 IV 2016	CDJC	2 007 201	685 938	34.2	982 133	...	...	1 025 068	...	...
Liberia - Libéria										
1 VII 2010	ESDF	3 627 144	1 732 457	47.8	1 813 631	846 461	46.7	1 813 513	885 996	48.9
1 VII 2011	ESDF	3 704 838	1 784 042	48.2	1 851 636	869 557	47.0	1 853 202	914 485	49.3
1 VII 2012	ESDF	3 784 197	1 837 163	48.5	1 890 438	893 283	47.3	1 893 759	943 880	49.8
1 VII 2013	ESDF	3 865 256	1 891 865	48.9	1 930 053	917 657	47.5	1 935 203	974 208	50.3
1 VII 2014	ESDF	3 946 311	1 946 567	49.3	1 969 668	942 031	47.8	1 976 643	1 004 536	50.8
Libya - Libye[20]										
1 VII 2010	ESDF	5 689 419	5 013 386	88.1	2 883 880	2 544 388	88.2	2 805 538	2 468 998	88.0
1 VII 2011	ESDF	5 790 518	5 101 275	88.1	2 934 512	2 588 402	88.2	2 856 006	2 512 874	88.0
1 VII 2012	ESDF	5 892 239	5 189 460	88.1	2 985 408	2 632 510	88.2	2 906 831	2 556 950	88.0
1 VII 2013	ESDF	5 994 241	5 277 638	88.0	3 036 393	2 676 558	88.1	2 957 849	2 601 081	87.9
1 VII 2014	ESDF	6 096 208	5 365 529	88.0	3 087 301	2 720 398	88.1	3 008 907	2 645 131	87.9
1 VII 2015	ESDF	6 162 356	5 411 529	87.8	3 129 260	2 707 215	86.5	3 033 156	2 704 314	89.2
Madagascar										
1 VII 2010[21]	ESDF	20 142 015	...	...	9 972 090	...	...	10 169 925	...	...
1 VII 2011[21]	ESDF	20 696 070	...	...	10 246 397	...	...	10 449 673	...	...
1 VII 2012[21]	ESDF	21 263 403	...	...	10 527 277	...	...	10 736 126	...	...
1 VII 2013[21]	ESDF	21 842 167	...	...	10 813 817	...	...	11 028 350	...	...
1 VII 2014[21]	ESDF	22 434 363	...	...	11 107 006	...	...	11 327 357	...	...
1 VII 2015[21]	ESDF	23 040 065	...	...	11 406 883	...	...	11 633 182	...	...
1 VII 2016[21]	ESDF	23 657 964	...	...	11 712 798	...	...	11 945 166	...	...
1 VII 2017[21]	ESDF	24 289 542	...	...	12 025 485	...	...	12 264 057	...	...

6. Total and urban population by sex: 2010 - 2019
Population totale et population urbaine selon le sexe : 2010 - 2019 (continued - suite)

Continent, country or area, and date / Continent, pays ou zone et date	Code[a]	Both sexes - Les deux sexes: Total	Both sexes - Urban - Urbaine: Number Nombre	Both sexes - Urban - Urbaine: Percent P.100	Male - Masculin: Total	Male - Urban - Urbaine: Number Nombre	Male - Urban - Urbaine: Percent P.100	Female - Féminin: Total	Female - Urban - Urbaine: Number Nombre	Female - Urban - Urbaine: Percent P.100
AFRICA - AFRIQUE										
Madagascar										
18 V 2018*	CDJC	25 833 588	5 033 775	19.5	12 738 948	2 482 233	19.5	13 094 640	2 551 542	19.5
1 VII 2018[21]	ESDF	24 933 879	...	...	12 344 489	...	...	12 589 390	...	...
1 VII 2019[21]	ESDF	26 619 734	5 186 958	19.5	13 126 609	2 557 770	19.5	13 493 125	2 629 188	19.5
Malawi										
1 VII 2010[1]	ESDF	13 947 592	...	...	6 804 310	...	...	7 143 282	...	...
1 VII 2011[1]	ESDF	14 388 550	...	...	7 029 149	...	...	7 359 401	...	...
1 VII 2012[1]	ESDF	14 844 822	...	...	7 261 499	...	...	7 583 323	...	...
1 VII 2013[1]	ESDF	15 316 860	...	...	7 501 653	...	...	7 815 207	...	...
1 VII 2014[1]	ESDF	15 805 239	...	...	7 749 963	...	...	8 055 276	...	...
1 VII 2015[1]	ESDF	16 310 431	...	...	8 006 715	...	...	8 303 716	...	...
1 VII 2016[1]	ESDF	16 832 910	...	...	8 272 152	...	...	8 560 758	...	...
1 VII 2017[1]	ESDJ	17 373 200	...	...	8 546 500	...	...	8 826 700	...	...
3 IX 2018	CDJC	17 563 749	2 816 492	16.0	8 521 460	1 401 373	16.4	9 042 289	1 415 119	15.7
Mali[22]										
1 VII 2010	ESDF	15 370 000	...	...	7 679 000	...	...	7 691 000	...	...
1 VII 2011	ESDF	15 843 000	...	...	7 919 000	...	...	7 924 000	...	...
1 VII 2012	ESDF	16 312 000	...	...	8 159 000	...	...	8 153 000	...	...
1 VII 2013	ESDF	16 808 000	...	...	8 411 000	...	...	8 397 000	...	...
1 VII 2014	ESDF	17 319 000	...	...	8 671 000	...	...	8 648 000	...	...
1 VII 2015	ESDF	17 819 000	...	...	8 838 000	...	...	8 981 000	...	...
1 VII 2016	ESDF	18 341 000	...	...	9 244 000	...	...	9 097 000	...	...
1 VII 2017	ESDF	18 874 286	...	...	9 361 646	...	...	9 512 640	...	...
1 VII 2018	ESDF	19 418 097	...	...	9 631 376	...	...	9 786 721	...	...
Mauritania - Mauritanie										
1 VII 2010[1]	ESDF	3 340 627	...	...	1 678 324	...	...	1 662 303	...	...
1 VII 2011[1]	ESDF	3 296 958	...	...	1 644 572	...	...	1 652 386	...	...
24 III 2013	CDFC	3 460 388[23]	1 697 792	49.1	...	...	...	...	...	...
1 VII 2013[1]	ESDF	3 537 368	...	...	1 743 074	...	...	1 794 294	...	...
1 VII 2015[1]	ESDF	3 720 125	...	...	1 834 735	...	...	1 885 390	...	...
1 VII 2016[1]	ESDF	3 782 701	...	...	1 864 664	...	...	1 918 037	...	...
Mauritius - Maurice[24]										
1 VII 2010[25]	ESDJ	1 280 924	533 771	41.7	631 692	261 489	41.4	649 232	272 282	41.9
1 VII 2011[5]	ESDJ	1 252 404	509 229	40.7	619 591	249 439	40.3	632 813	259 790	41.1
4 VII 2011	CDFC	1 237 000	496 841	40.2	611 053	243 629	39.9	625 947	253 212	40.5
1 VII 2012[5]	ESDJ	1 255 882	509 177	40.5	621 297	249 422	40.1	634 585	259 755	40.9
1 VII 2013[5]	ESDJ	1 258 653	519 306	41.3	622 861	254 605	40.9	635 792	264 701	41.6
1 VII 2014[5]	ESDJ	1 260 934	518 370	41.1	624 002	254 204	40.7	636 932	264 166	41.5
1 VII 2015[5]	ESDJ	1 262 605	517 482	41.0	624 769	253 796	40.6	637 836	263 686	41.3
1 VII 2016[5]	ESDJ	1 263 473	516 160	40.9	625 206	253 181	40.5	638 267	262 979	41.2
1 VII 2017[5]	ESDJ	1 264 613	514 937	40.7	625 727	252 588	40.4	638 886	262 349	41.1
1 VII 2018[5]	ESDJ	1 265 303	513 556	40.6	626 030	251 972	40.2	639 273	261 584	40.9
1 VII 2019[5]	ESDJ	1 265 711	512 128	40.5	626 167	251 243	40.1	639 544	260 885	40.8
Mayotte										
21 VIII 2012	CDJC	212 645	...	...	103 173	...	...	109 471	...	...
1 VII 2014[26]	ESDJ	227 961	...	...	109 603	...	...	118 358	...	...
1 I 2015	ESDJ	232 189	...	...	110 666	...	...	121 523	...	...
1 I 2016	ESDJ	240 987	...	...	114 859	...	...	126 128	...	...
1 I 2017	ESDJ	250 143	...	...	119 219	...	...	130 924	...	...
5 IX 2017[27]	CDJC	256 518	242 091	94.4	122 261	115 314	94.3	134 257	126 777	94.4
1 VII 2018*[26]	ESDJ	265 425	...	...	126 521	...	...	138 904	...	...
1 I 2019	ESDJ	269 471	...	...	128 431	...	...	141 040	...	...
Morocco - Maroc										
1 VII 2010[28]	ESDF	31 894 046	18 446 241	57.8	15 831 463	9 051 145	57.2	16 062 583	9 395 096	58.5
1 VII 2011[28]	ESDF	32 245 120	18 802 208	58.3	16 010 979	9 212 763	57.5	16 234 141	9 589 444	59.1
1 VII 2012[28]	ESDF	32 596 997	19 157 539	58.8	16 190 815	9 373 546	57.9	16 406 182	9 783 993	59.6
1 VII 2013[28]	ESDF	32 950 445	19 512 904	59.2	16 371 475	9 533 742	58.2	16 578 971	9 979 162	60.2
1 VII 2014[29]	ESDJ	33 769 512	20 352 799	60.3	16 825 793	10 068 187	59.8	16 943 719	10 284 612	60.7
1 IX 2014	CDJC	33 848 242	20 432 439	60.4	...	...	...	...	...	...
1 VII 2015[29]	ESDJ	34 124 870	20 751 800	60.8	17 001 717	10 255 722	60.3	17 123 153	10 496 078	61.3
1 VII 2016[29]	ESDJ	34 486 536	21 154 782	61.3	17 180 879	10 445 229	60.8	17 305 657	10 709 553	61.9
1 VII 2017[29]	ESDJ	34 852 121	21 560 585	61.9	17 361 992	10 636 101	61.3	17 490 129	10 924 484	62.5
1 VII 2018[29]	ESDJ	35 219 547	21 968 101	62.4	17 544 027	10 827 825	61.7	17 675 520	11 140 276	63.0
1 VII 2019[29]	ESDJ	35 586 616	22 376 115	62.9	17 725 947	11 019 826	62.2	17 860 669	11 356 289	63.6

6. Total and urban population by sex: 2010 - 2019
Population totale et population urbaine selon le sexe : 2010 - 2019 (continued - suite)

Continent, country or area, and date / Continent, pays ou zone et date	Code[a]	Both sexes - Les deux sexes			Male - Masculin			Female - Féminin		
		Total	Urban - Urbaine		Total	Urban - Urbaine		Total	Urban - Urbaine	
			Number Nombre	Percent P.100		Number Nombre	Percent P.100		Number Nombre	Percent P.100
AFRICA - AFRIQUE										
Mozambique										
1 VII 2010[11]	ESDF	22 416 881	6 908 291	30.8	10 799 284	3 384 605	31.3	11 617 597	3 523 686	30.3
1 VII 2011[11]	ESDF	23 049 621	7 141 715	31.0	11 108 128	3 496 582	31.5	11 941 493	3 645 133	30.5
1 VII 2012[11]	ESDF	23 700 715	7 385 294	31.2	11 426 321	3 613 684	31.6	12 274 394	3 771 610	30.7
1 VII 2013[11]	ESDF	24 366 112	7 639 557	31.4	11 751 849	3 736 166	31.8	12 614 263	3 903 391	30.9
1 VII 2014[11]	ESDF	25 041 922	7 905 004	31.6	12 082 782	3 864 267	32.0	12 959 140	4 040 737	31.2
1 VII 2015[11]	ESDF	25 727 911	8 181 475	31.8	12 419 014	3 997 895	32.2	13 308 897	4 183 580	31.4
1 VII 2016[11]	ESDF	26 423 623	8 468 799	32.1	12 760 324	4 136 950	32.4	13 663 299	4 331 849	31.7
1 VII 2017[11]	ESDF	27 128 530	8 766 777	32.3	13 106 447	4 281 319	32.7	14 022 083	4 485 458	32.0
1 VIII 2017*	CDFC	28 861 863	...	...	13 800 857	...	...	15 061 006	...	...
1 VII 2018[11]	ESDF	27 843 933	9 076 397	32.6	13 458 078	4 431 557	32.9	14 385 855	4 644 840	32.3
1 VII 2019[11]	ESDF	29 318 301	9 910 835	33.8	14 125 393	4 810 297	34.1	15 192 908	5 100 538	33.6
Namibia - Namibie										
1 VII 2010[1]	ESDF	2 143 410	...	...	1 047 900	...	...	1 095 510	...	...
1 VII 2011[5]	ESDF	2 116 077	900 163	42.5	1 026 911	439 993	42.8	1 089 166	460 170	42.2
28 VIII 2011	CDFC	2 113 077	903 434	42.8	1 021 912	440 334	43.1	1 091 165	463 100	42.4
1 VII 2012[5]	ESDF	2 155 440	940 825	43.6	1 046 434	459 668	43.9	1 109 006	481 157	43.4
1 VII 2013[5]	ESDF	2 196 086	982 519	44.7	1 066 541	479 844	45.0	1 129 545	502 675	44.5
1 VII 2014[5]	ESDF	2 237 894	1 025 147	45.8	1 087 178	500 469	46.0	1 150 716	524 678	45.6
1 VII 2015[5]	ESDF	2 280 716	1 068 625	46.9	1 108 276	521 496	47.1	1 172 440	547 129	46.7
1 VII 2016[5]	ESDF	2 324 388	1 112 868	47.9	1 129 754	542 893	48.1	1 194 634	569 975	47.7
1 VII 2017[5]	ESDF	2 368 747	1 157 806	48.9	1 151 533	564 615	49.0	1 217 214	593 191	48.7
1 VII 2018[5]	ESDF	2 413 643	1 203 340	49.9	1 173 540	586 616	50.0	1 240 103	616 724	49.7
1 VII 2019[5]	ESDF	2 458 936	1 249 372	50.8	1 195 708	608 851	50.9	1 263 228	640 521	50.7
Niger										
1 VII 2010[1]	ESDJ	15 203 820	3 104 574	20.4	7 594 624	1 555 201	20.5	7 609 198	1 549 372	20.4
1 VII 2011[1]	ESDJ	15 730 756	3 309 954	21.0	7 859 534	1 658 395	21.1	7 871 221	1 651 559	21.0
1 VII 2012[30]	ESDJ	16 993 563	2 750 279	16.2	8 446 540	1 366 889	16.2	8 547 023	1 383 390	16.2
10 XII 2012	CDFC	16 734 935	...	...	8 183 513	...	...	8 551 422	...	...
1 VII 2013[30]	ESDJ	17 679 758	2 899 523	16.4	8 792 478	1 441 063	16.4	8 887 281	1 458 460	16.4
1 VII 2014[30]	ESDJ	18 389 162	3 010 567	16.4	9 150 266	1 496 252	16.4	9 238 897	1 514 315	16.4
1 VII 2015[30]	ESDJ	19 124 882	3 125 234	16.3	9 521 427	1 553 241	16.3	9 603 456	1 571 993	16.4
1 VII 2016[30]	ESDJ	19 865 066	3 242 161	16.3	9 898 628	1 611 354	16.3	9 966 438	1 630 807	16.4
1 VII 2017[30]	ESDJ	20 651 070	3 390 443	16.4	10 296 314	...	...	10 354 756	...	...
Nigeria - Nigéria[19]										
1 VII 2010	ESDF	159 608 173	...	...	81 400 168	...	...	78 208 005	...	...
1 VII 2011	ESDF	164 798 232	...	...	84 047 098	...	...	80 751 134	...	...
1 VII 2012	ESDF	170 157 060	...	...	86 780 100	...	...	83 376 959	...	...
1 VII 2013	ESDF	175 690 143	...	...	89 601 973	...	...	86 088 170	...	...
1 VII 2014	ESDF	181 403 148	...	...	92 515 605	...	...	88 887 542	...	...
1 VII 2015	ESDF	187 301 926	...	...	95 523 982	...	...	91 777 944	...	...
1 VII 2016	ESDF	193 392 517	...	...	98 630 184	...	...	94 762 333	...	...
Republic of South Sudan - République de Soudan du Sud[31]										
1 VII 2010	ESDF	9 005 261	...	...	4 652 459	...	...	4 352 803	...	...
1 VII 2011	ESDF	9 389 376	...	...	4 844 597	...	...	4 544 780	...	...
1 VII 2012	ESDF	9 782 927	...	...	5 041 284	...	...	4 741 642	...	...
1 VII 2013	ESDF	10 182 291	...	...	5 240 881	...	...	4 941 410	...	...
1 VII 2014	ESDF	10 585 044	...	...	5 442 151	...	...	5 142 892	...	...
1 VII 2015	ESDF	11 000 128	...	...	5 649 689	...	...	5 350 439	...	...
1 VII 2016	ESDF	11 425 377	...	...	5 862 347	...	...	5 563 030	...	...
1 VII 2017	ESDF	11 868 209	...	...	6 083 876	...	...	5 784 333	...	...
1 VII 2018	ESDF	12 323 419	...	...	6 311 618	...	...	6 011 801	...	...
Reunion - Réunion										
1 I 2010	CDJC	821 136	808 540	98.5	398 006	391 623	98.4	423 130	416 917	98.5
1 I 2010	ESDJ	821 136	...	...	397 953	...	...	423 183	...	...
1 I 2011	ESDJ	828 581	...	...	401 139	...	...	427 442	...	...
1 I 2012	ESDJ	833 944	...	...	403 504	...	...	430 440	...	...
1 VII 2013[26]	ESDJ	838 935	...	...	405 519	...	...	433 416	...	...
1 VII 2014[26]	ESDJ	846 747	816 334	96.4	409 549	394 281	96.3	437 198	422 052	96.5
1 I 2015	CDJC	850 727	838 228	98.5	411 435	405 123	98.5	439 292	433 105	98.6
1 I 2015	ESDJ	850 727	...	...	410 762	...	...	439 965	...	...
1 I 2016	ESDJ	852 924	...	...	410 558	...	...	442 366	...	...
1 I 2017	ESDJ	853 659	...	...	408 957	...	...	444 702	...	...

6. Total and urban population by sex: 2010 - 2019
Population totale et population urbaine selon le sexe : 2010 - 2019 (continued - suite)

Continent, country or area, and date / Continent, pays ou zone et date	Code[a]	Both sexes - Les deux sexes: Total	Both sexes - Urban - Urbaine: Number / Nombre	Both sexes - Urban - Urbaine: Percent / P.100	Male - Masculin: Total	Male - Urban - Urbaine: Number / Nombre	Male - Urban - Urbaine: Percent / P.100	Female - Féminin: Total	Female - Urban - Urbaine: Number / Nombre	Female - Urban - Urbaine: Percent / P.100
AFRICA - AFRIQUE										
Reunion - Réunion										
1 VII 2018*[26]	ESDJ	864 459	...	...	414 304	...	...	450 155	...	...
1 I 2019	ESDJ	857 961	...	...	408 736	...	...	449 225	...	...
Rwanda										
1 VII 2010[1]	ESDF	10 412 820	1 541 097	14.8	5 029 450	...	...	5 383 371	...	...
1 VII 2011[1]	ESDF	10 718 379	1 564 883	14.6	5 183 505	...	...	5 534 874	...	...
1 VII 2012[30]	ESDF	10 482 641	1 732 175	16.5	5 049 164	889 118	17.6	5 433 477	843 057	15.5
15 VIII 2012	CDFC	10 393 542	1 760 994	16.9	4 981 197	902 501	18.1	5 412 345	858 493	15.9
1 VII 2013[30]	ESDF	10 736 771	1 844 040	17.2	5 178 354	889 382	17.2	5 558 417	954 658	17.2
1 VII 2014[30]	ESDF	10 996 891	1 962 945	17.8	5 310 430	947 912	17.9	5 686 461	1 015 033	17.8
1 VII 2015[30]	ESDF	11 262 564	2 086 390	18.5	5 445 206	1 008 724	18.5	5 817 359	1 077 666	18.5
1 VII 2016[30]	ESDF	11 533 445	2 214 421	19.2	5 582 519	1 071 844	19.2	5 950 925	1 142 578	19.2
1 VII 2017[30]	ESDF	11 809 300	2 347 098	19.9	5 722 258	1 137 299	19.9	6 087 041	1 209 799	19.9
1 VII 2018[30]	ESDF	12 089 721	2 484 438	20.6	5 864 287	1 205 111	20.6	6 225 434	1 279 327	20.6
1 VII 2019[30]	ESDF	12 374 397	...	...	6 008 384	...	...	6 366 013	...	...
Saint Helena ex. dep. - Sainte-Hélène sans dép.										
1 VII 2012	ESDF	4 123	...	...	2 094	...	...	2 029	...	...
31 XII 2013	ESDF	4 211	...	...	2 139	...	...	2 072	...	...
7 II 2016[32]	CDJC	4 534	...	...	2 396	...	...	2 138	...	...
Sao Tome and Principe - Sao Tomé-et-Principe										
1 VII 2010	ESDF	163 783	...	...	80 409	...	...	83 375	...	...
1 VII 2011	ESDF	166 728	...	...	81 783	...	...	84 945	...	...
13 V 2012	CDJC	178 739	119 781	67.0	88 867	58 710	66.1	89 872	61 071	68.0
1 VII 2013[30]	ESDJ	182 328	122 398	67.1	90 577	60 805	67.1	91 751	61 593	67.1
1 VII 2014[30]	ESDJ	186 024	125 121	67.3	92 347	62 113	67.3	93 677	63 008	67.3
1 VII 2015[30]	ESDJ	189 819	127 922	67.4	94 173	63 464	67.4	95 646	64 457	67.4
1 VII 2016[30]	ESDJ	193 712	130 798	67.5	96 053	64 857	67.5	97 659	65 941	67.5
1 VII 2017[30]	ESDJ	197 700	133 748	67.7	97 988	66 291	67.7	99 712	67 457	67.7
1 VII 2018[30]	ESDJ	201 784	136 775	67.8	99 978	...	...	101 806	...	...
1 VII 2019[30]	ESDJ	205 965	139 877	67.9	102 023	...	...	103 943	...	...
Senegal - Sénégal										
31 XII 2010	ESDJ	12 509 434	5 086 978	40.7	6 157 675	2 521 940	41.0	6 351 759	2 565 038	40.4
31 XII 2011	ESDJ	12 841 702	6 086 966	47.4	6 350 673	3 010 218	47.4	6 491 029	3 076 748	47.4
1 VII 2013[1]	ESDJ	13 508 715	...	...	6 735 420	...	...	6 773 295	...	...
19 XI 2013	CDFC	13 357 492	...	...	6 658 089	...	...	6 699 403	...	...
1 VII 2014[1]	ESDJ	13 926 253	...	...	6 941 357	...	...	6 961 847	...	...
1 VII 2015[1]	ESDJ	14 356 575	...	...	7 153 656	...	...	7 202 919	...	...
1 VII 2016[1]	ESDJ	14 799 859	...	...	7 372 487	...	...	7 427 372	...	...
1 VII 2017[1]	ESDJ	15 256 346	7 089 780	46.5	7 597 938	3 537 982	46.6	7 658 408	3 551 798	46.4
1 VII 2018[1]	ESDJ	15 726 037	7 344 567	46.7	7 829 997	3 661 872	46.8	7 896 040	3 682 695	46.6
1 VII 2019[1]	ESDJ	16 209 125	...	...	8 140 343	...	...	8 068 782	...	...
Seychelles										
1 VII 2010	ESDF	89 770	...	...	45 907	...	...	43 863	...	...
26 VIII 2010	CDFC	90 945	...	...	46 912	...	...	44 033	...	...
1 VII 2011	ESDF	87 441	...	...	43 127	...	...	44 314	...	...
1 VII 2012	ESDF	88 303	...	...	43 313	...	...	44 990	...	...
1 VII 2013	ESDF	89 949	...	...	44 735	...	...	45 214	...	...
1 VII 2014	ESDF	91 359	...	...	45 278	...	...	46 081	...	...
1 VII 2015	ESDF	93 419	...	...	46 322	...	...	47 097	...	...
1 VII 2016	ESDF	94 677	...	...	47 343	...	...	47 334	...	...
1 VII 2017	ESDF	95 843	...	...	48 793	...	...	47 050	...	...
1 VII 2018	ESDF	96 762	...	...	49 259	...	...	47 503	...	...
1 VII 2019	ESDF	97 625	...	...	49 665	...	...	47 960	...	...
Sierra Leone										
1 VII 2010[33]	ESDF	6 130 640	2 414 256	39.4	3 004 269	...	...	3 126 371	...	...
1 VII 2011[33]	ESDF	6 322 934	2 512 424	39.7	3 101 611	...	...	3 221 323	...	...
1 VII 2012[33]	ESDF	6 515 229	2 610 592	40.1	3 198 953	...	...	3 316 276	...	...
1 VII 2013[33]	ESDF	6 707 523	2 708 760	40.4	3 296 294	...	...	3 411 229	...	...
1 VII 2014[33]	ESDF	6 899 819	2 806 929	40.7	3 393 636	...	...	3 506 183	...	...
5 XII 2015[34]	CDFC	7 092 113	2 905 097	41.0	3 490 978	1 438 636	41.2	3 601 135	1 466 461	40.7
1 VII 2016[9]	ESDF	7 296 402	2 990 394	41.0	3 591 542	1 480 877	41.2	3 704 860	1 509 517	40.7
1 VII 2017[9]	ESDF	7 499 486	3 073 627	41.0	3 691 506	1 522 096	41.2	3 807 980	1 551 531	40.7

6. Total and urban population by sex: 2010 - 2019
Population totale et population urbaine selon le sexe : 2010 - 2019 (continued - suite)

Continent, country or area, and date / Continent, pays ou zone et date	Code[a]	Both sexes - Les deux sexes			Male - Masculin			Female - Féminin		
		Total	Urban - Urbaine		Total	Urban - Urbaine		Total	Urban - Urbaine	
			Number Nombre	Percent P.100		Number Nombre	Percent P.100		Number Nombre	Percent P.100
AFRICA - AFRIQUE										
Sierra Leone										
1 VII 2018[9]	ESDF	7 701 185	3 156 293	41.0	3 790 791	1 563 032	41.2	3 910 394	1 593 261	40.7
1 VII 2019[9]	ESDF	7 901 454	3 238 372	41.0	3 889 366	1 603 675	41.2	4 012 088	1 634 697	40.7
South Africa - Afrique du Sud										
1 VII 2010[33]	ESDF	51 328 662	...	...	24 872 137	...	...	26 456 526	...	...
1 VII 2011[33]	ESDF	52 129 117	...	...	25 284 863	...	...	26 844 254	...	...
10 X 2011	CDFC	51 770 560	32 559 331	62.9	25 188 791	...	...	26 581 769	...	...
1 VII 2012[3]	ESDF	52 930 356	...	...	25 697 905	...	...	27 232 452	...	...
1 VII 2013[3]	ESDF	53 751 096	...	...	26 117 346	...	...	27 633 750	...	...
1 VII 2014[3]	ESDF	54 574 401	...	...	26 537 411	...	...	28 036 989	...	...
1 VII 2015[3]	ESDF	55 406 634	...	...	26 961 734	...	...	28 444 900	...	...
1 VII 2016[3]	ESDF	56 252 336	...	...	27 390 632	...	...	28 861 703	...	...
1 VII 2017[3]	ESDF	57 097 857	...	...	27 819 944	...	...	29 277 913	...	...
1 VII 2018[3]	ESDF	57 939 226	...	...	28 247 177	...	...	29 692 049	...	...
1 VII 2019[3]	ESDF	58 775 022	...	...	28 672 747	...	...	30 102 275	...	...
Sudan - Soudan										
1 VII 2010	ESDF	32 491 081[1]	11 296 966[35]	34.8	16 438 874[1]	5 749 007[35]	35.0	15 809 330[1]	5 547 959[35]	35.1
1 VII 2011	ESDF	33 284 049[1]	11 749 240[35]	35.3	16 958 637[1]	5 974 957[35]	35.2	16 325 402[1]	5 774 283[35]	35.4
1 VII 2012	ESDF	34 092 831[1]	12 218 313[35]	35.8	17 359 311[1]	6 209 462[35]	35.8	16 733 503[1]	6 008 851[35]	35.9
1 VII 2013	ESDF	34 917 504[1]	12 704 550[35]	36.4	17 768 098[1]	6 452 691[35]	36.3	17 149 419[1]	6 251 858[35]	36.5
1 VII 2014	ESDF	35 732 543[1]	13 208 281[35]	37.0	18 171 717[1]	6 704 798[35]	36.9	17 560 839[1]	6 503 483[35]	37.0
1 VII 2015	ESDF	36 601 618[1]	13 729 842[35]	37.5	18 603 671[1]	6 965 944[35]	37.4	17 997 958[1]	6 763 898[35]	37.6
1 VII 2016	ESDF	37 489 029[1]	14 269 540[35]	38.1	19 044 018[1]	7 236 276[35]	38.0	18 444 995[1]	7 033 264[35]	38.1
1 VII 2017[1]	ESDF	38 378 441	...	...	19 485 705	...	...	18 892 734	...	...
1 VII 2018[1]	ESDF	39 279 651	...	...	19 933 446	...	...	19 346 211	...	...
1 VII 2019[1]	ESDF	40 204 167	...	...	20 392 770	...	...	19 811 397	...	...
Togo										
6 XI 2010	CDJC	6 191 155	2 334 495	37.7	3 009 095	1 131 533	37.6	3 182 060	1 202 962	37.8
1 VII 2011[3]	ESDJ	6 277 718	2 498 763[36]	39.8	3 051 882	1 219 982[36]	40.0	3 225 836	1 278 782[36]	39.6
1 VII 2012[3]	ESDJ	6 430 825	2 580 788[36]	40.1	3 127 501	1 257 830[36]	40.2	3 303 324	1 322 958[36]	40.0
1 VII 2013[3]	ESDJ	6 589 095	2 663 899[36]	40.4	3 205 772	1 296 177[36]	40.4	3 383 324	1 367 722[36]	40.4
1 VII 2014[3]	ESDJ	6 752 334	2 748 039[36]	40.7	3 286 603	1 335 012[36]	40.6	3 465 731	1 413 028[36]	40.8
1 VII 2015[3]	ESDJ	6 920 514	2 833 093[36]	40.9	3 369 994	1 374 280[36]	40.8	3 550 520	1 458 814[36]	41.1
1 VII 2016[3]	ESDJ	7 092 022	2 918 932[36]	41.2	3 455 135	1 413 914[36]	40.9	3 636 888	1 505 018[36]	41.4
1 VII 2017[3]	ESDJ	7 265 286	3 005 419[36]	41.4	3 541 238	1 453 848[36]	41.1	3 724 048	1 551 572[36]	41.7
1 VII 2018[3]	ESDJ	7 440 364	3 092 420[36]	41.6	3 628 345	1 494 021[36]	41.2	3 812 019	1 598 399[36]	41.9
1 VII 2019[3]	ESDJ	7 617 279	3 179 804[36]	41.7	3 716 473	1 534 373[36]	41.3	3 900 807	1 645 432[36]	42.2
Tunisia - Tunisie										
1 VII 2010	ESDF	10 565 704	7 039 718	66.6	5 275 893	...	...	5 289 811	...	...
1 VII 2011	ESDF	10 674 420	7 084 742	66.4	5 327 337	...	...	5 347 083	...	...
1 VII 2012	ESDF	10 784 255	7 248 086	67.2	5 379 282	...	...	5 404 972	...	...
1 VII 2013	ESDF	10 895 219	7 354 268	67.5	5 431 735	...	...	5 463 485	...	...
23 IV 2014	CDFC	10 982 754	7 437 671	67.7	5 472 338	3 713 527	67.9	5 510 416	3 724 144	67.6
1 VII 2014	ESDF	11 012 486	7 461 796[37]	67.8	5 487 152	...	...	5 525 333	...	...
1 VII 2015	ESDF	11 162 666	7 574 564[37]	67.9	5 562 100	...	...	5 600 566	...	...
1 VII 2016	ESDF	11 304 482	7 671 696[37]	67.9	5 620 629	...	...	5 683 853	...	...
1 VII 2017	ESDF	11 434 994	7 797 248[37]	68.2	5 679 737	...	...	5 755 256	...	...
Uganda - Ouganda										
1 VII 2010	ESDF	31 784 600	...	...	15 516 600	...	...	16 268 000	...	...
1 VII 2011	ESDF	32 939 800	...	...	16 118 600	...	...	16 821 200	...	...
1 VII 2012	ESDF	34 131 400	...	...	16 741 400	...	...	17 390 000	...	...
1 VII 2014[7]	ESDF	34 141 299	...	...	16 594 490	...	...	17 546 809	...	...
27 VIII 2014	CDFC	34 634 650	8 438 009	24.4	16 897 849	4 042 324	23.9	17 736 801	4 395 685	24.8
1 VII 2015[7]	ESDF	35 502 100	...	...	17 344 000	...	...	18 158 100	...	...
1 VII 2016[7]	ESDF	36 652 700	...	...	17 926 900	...	...	18 725 800	...	...
1 VII 2017[7]	ESDF	37 838 900	...	...	18 527 900	...	...	19 311 000	...	...
1 VII 2018[7]	ESDF	39 059 000	...	...	19 146 800	...	...	19 912 200	...	...
1 VII 2019[7]	ESDF	40 308 000	...	...	19 780 500	...	...	20 527 500	...	...
United Republic of Tanzania - République Unie de Tanzanie										
1 VII 2010[38]	ESDF	43 187 823	11 378 015	26.3	21 252 423	5 618 133	26.4	21 935 400	5 759 882	26.3
1 VII 2011[38]	ESDF	44 484 857	11 875 395	26.7	21 914 229	5 867 287	26.8	22 570 628	6 008 108	26.6

6. Total and urban population by sex: 2010 - 2019
Population totale et population urbaine selon le sexe : 2010 - 2019 (continued - suite)

Continent, country or area, and date / Continent, pays ou zone et date	Code[a]	Both sexes - Les deux sexes			Male - Masculin			Female - Féminin		
		Total	Urban - Urbaine		Total	Urban - Urbaine		Total	Urban - Urbaine	
			Number Nombre	Percent P.100		Number Nombre	Percent P.100		Number Nombre	Percent P.100
AFRICA - AFRIQUE										
United Republic of Tanzania - République Unie de Tanzanie										
1 VII 2012[38]	ESDF	*45 798 475*	*12 386 841*	*27.0*	*22 585 634*	*6 123 839*	*27.1*	*23 212 841*	*6 263 002*	*27.0*
26 VIII 2012[39]	CDFC	44 928 923	13 305 004	29.6	21 869 990	6 407 396	29.3	23 058 933	6 897 608	29.9
1 VII 2013[30]	ESDF	*46 356 279*	...	...	*22 585 059*	...	...	*23 771 220*	...	...
1 VII 2014[30]	ESDF	*47 831 361*	...	...	*23 323 466*	...	...	*24 507 895*	...	...
1 VII 2015[30]	ESDF	*49 359 408*	...	...	*24 088 086*	...	...	*25 271 322*	...	...
1 VII 2016[30]	ESDF	*50 941 672*	...	...	*24 879 894*	...	...	*26 061 778*	...	...
1 VII 2017[30]	ESDF	*52 554 628*	...	...	*25 687 154*	...	...	*26 867 474*	...	...
1 VII 2018[30]	ESDF	*54 199 163*	...	...	*26 510 095*	...	...	*27 689 068*	...	...
1 VII 2019[30]	ESDF	*55 890 747*	...	...	*27 356 189*	...	...	*28 534 558*	...	...
Zambia - Zambie										
16 X 2010	CDFC	12 526 314	5 021 022	40.1	6 117 253	2 452 904	40.1	6 409 061	2 568 118	40.1
1 VII 2011[14]	ESDJ	*13 718 722*	*5 563 212*	*40.6*	*6 786 799*	*2 757 061*	*40.6*	*6 931 923*	*2 806 151*	*40.5*
1 VII 2012[14]	ESDJ	*14 145 327*	*5 780 936*	*40.9*	*6 997 492*	*2 863 581*	*40.9*	*7 147 835*	*2 917 355*	*40.8*
1 VII 2013[14]	ESDJ	*14 580 290*	*6 005 218*	*41.2*	*7 212 648*	*2 973 485*	*41.2*	*7 367 642*	*3 031 733*	*41.1*
1 VII 2014[14]	ESDJ	*15 023 315*	*6 235 786*	*41.5*	*7 432 123*	*3 086 651*	*41.5*	*7 591 192*	*3 149 135*	*41.5*
1 VII 2015[14]	ESDJ	*15 473 905*	*6 472 258*	*41.8*	*7 655 669*	*3 202 882*	*41.8*	*7 818 236*	*3 269 376*	*41.8*
1 VII 2016[14]	ESDJ	*15 933 883*	*6 715 149*	*42.1*	*7 884 009*	*3 322 364*	*42.1*	*8 049 874*	*3 392 785*	*42.1*
1 VII 2017[14]	ESDJ	*16 405 229*	*6 964 965*	*42.5*	*8 117 939*	*3 445 261*	*42.4*	*8 287 290*	*3 519 704*	*42.5*
1 VII 2018[14]	ESDJ	*16 887 720*	*7 221 318*	*42.8*	*8 357 340*	*3 571 368*	*42.7*	*8 530 380*	*3 649 950*	*42.8*
1 VII 2019[14]	ESDJ	*17 381 168*	*7 483 937*	*43.1*	*8 602 112*	*3 700 550*	*43.0*	*8 779 056*	*3 783 387*	*43.1*
Zimbabwe										
17 VIII 2012	CDFC	13 061 239	4 284 145	32.8	6 280 539	2 039 224	32.5	6 780 700	2 244 921	33.1
1 VII 2013[30]	ESDF	*13 368 620*	*4 424 783*[37]	*33.1*	*6 428 233*	*2 108 204*[37]	*32.8*	*6 940 389*	*2 316 578*[37]	*33.4*
1 VII 2014[30]	ESDF	*13 652 297*	*4 535 793*[37]	*33.2*	*6 564 085*	*2 162 369*[37]	*32.9*	*7 088 214*	*2 373 427*[37]	*33.5*
1 VII 2015[30]	ESDF	*13 943 242*	*4 648 970*[37]	*33.3*	*6 703 559*	*2 217 591*[37]	*33.1*	*7 239 681*	*2 431 379*[37]	*33.6*
1 VII 2016[30]	ESDF	*14 240 168*	*4 763 408*[37]	*33.5*	*6 846 020*	*2 273 413*[37]	*33.2*	*7 394 149*	*2 489 990*[37]	*33.7*
1 VII 2017[30]	ESDF	*14 542 235*	*4 878 395*[37]	*33.5*	*6 991 066*	*2 329 497*[37]	*33.3*	*7 551 172*	*2 548 898*[37]	*33.8*
1 VII 2018[30]	ESDF	*14 848 905*	*4 993 375*[37]	*33.6*	*7 138 445*	*2 385 567*[37]	*33.4*	*7 710 459*	*2 607 811*[37]	*33.8*
AMERICA, NORTH - AMÉRIQUE DU NORD										
Anguilla										
11 V 2011	CDFC	13 572	...	...	6 707	...	...	6 865	...	...
Antigua and Barbuda - Antigua-et-Barbuda										
27 V 2011	CDJC	85 567	...	...	40 986	...	...	44 581	...	...
1 VII 2011[5]	ESDJ	85 567	...	...	40 988	...	...	44 579	...	...
1 VII 2012[5]	ESDJ	86 793	...	...	41 572	...	...	45 221	...	...
1 VII 2013[5]	ESDJ	88 069	...	...	42 180	...	...	45 889	...	...
1 VII 2014[5]	ESDJ	89 391	...	...	42 810	...	...	46 581	...	...
1 VII 2015[5]	ESDJ	90 755	...	...	43 460	...	...	47 295	...	...
1 VII 2016[5]	ESDJ	92 157	...	...	44 129	...	...	48 028	...	...
1 VII 2017[5]	ESDJ	93 581	...	...	44 809	...	...	48 772	...	...
1 VII 2018[5]	ESDJ	95 014	...	...	45 493	...	...	49 521	...	...
1 VII 2019[5]	ESDJ	96 453	...	...	46 180	...	...	50 273	...	...
Aruba										
1 VII 2010	ESDJ	101 873	...	...	48 419	...	...	53 454	...	...
29 IX 2010	CDJC	101 484	...	...	48 241	...	...	53 243	...	...
1 VII 2011	ESDJ	102 809	...	...	48 801	...	...	54 008	...	...
1 VII 2012	ESDJ	104 577	...	...	49 557	...	...	55 020	...	...
1 VII 2013	ESDJ	106 383	...	...	50 329	...	...	56 054	...	...
1 VII 2014	ESDJ	107 823	...	...	50 990	...	...	56 833	...	...
1 VII 2015	ESDJ	109 225	...	...	51 681	...	...	57 544	...	...
1 VII 2016	ESDJ	110 354	...	...	52 250	...	...	58 104	...	...
1 VII 2017	ESDJ	110 850	...	...	52 543	...	...	58 307	...	...
1 VII 2018	ESDJ	111 466	...	...	52 798	...	...	58 668	...	...
1 VII 2019	ESDJ	112 019	...	...	52 998	...	...	59 022	...	...

6. Total and urban population by sex: 2010 - 2019
Population totale et population urbaine selon le sexe : 2010 - 2019 (continued - suite)

Continent, country or area, and date / Continent, pays ou zone et date	Code[a]	Both sexes - Les deux sexes: Total	Both sexes: Urban - Urbaine: Number Nombre	Both sexes: Urban - Urbaine: Percent P.100	Male - Masculin: Total	Male: Urban - Urbaine: Number Nombre	Male: Urban - Urbaine: Percent P.100	Female - Féminin: Total	Female: Urban - Urbaine: Number Nombre	Female: Urban - Urbaine: Percent P.100
AMERICA, NORTH - AMÉRIQUE DU NORD										
Bahamas										
3 V 2010	CDJC	351 461	...	...	170 257	...	...	181 204	...	...
1 VII 2010[14]	ESDJ	351 500	...	...	170 200	...	...	181 300	...	...
1 VII 2011[14]	ESDJ	355 020	...	...	171 810	...	...	183 210	...	...
1 VII 2012[14]	ESDJ	358 600	...	...	173 460	...	...	185 140	...	...
1 VII 2013[14]	ESDJ	362 230	...	...	175 120	...	...	187 110	...	...
1 VII 2014[14]	ESDJ	365 920	...	...	176 810	...	...	189 110	...	...
1 VII 2015[14]	ESDJ	369 670	...	...	178 530	...	...	191 140	...	...
1 VII 2016[14]	ESDJ	373 480	...	...	180 280	...	...	193 200	...	...
1 VII 2017[14]	ESDJ	377 360	...	...	182 300	...	...	195 060	...	...
1 VII 2018[14]	ESDJ	381 320	...	...	184 380	...	...	196 940	...	...
1 VII 2019[14]	ESDJ	385 340	...	...	186 480	...	...	198 860	...	...
Barbados - Barbade										
1 V 2010[40]	CDJC	277 821	...	...	133 018	...	...	144 803	...	...
1 VII 2010	ESDJ	277 758	...	...	133 018	...	...	144 740	...	...
1 VII 2011	ESDJ	277 622	...	...	133 119	...	...	144 503	...	...
1 VII 2012	ESDJ	277 668	...	...	133 355	...	...	144 313	...	...
1 VII 2013	ESDJ	277 492	...	...	133 369	...	...	144 123	...	...
1 VII 2014	ESDJ	277 199	...	...	133 343	...	...	143 856	...	...
1 VII 2015	ESDJ	274 633	...	...	131 146	...	...	143 487	...	...
Belize										
12 V 2010	CDJC	322 453	145 832	45.2	161 227	71 087	44.1	161 226	74 745	46.4
1 VII 2010	ESDJ	*323 598*	*146 323*	*45.2*	*161 800*	*71 328*	*44.1*	*161 798*	*74 995*	*46.4*
1 VII 2011	ESDJ	*332 084*	*149 955*	*45.2*	*166 043*	*73 110*	*44.0*	*166 041*	*76 845*	*46.3*
1 VII 2012	ESDJ	*340 792*	*153 683*	*45.1*	*170 397*	*74 938*	*44.0*	*170 395*	*78 745*	*46.2*
1 VII 2013	ESDJ	*349 728*	*157 508*	*45.0*	*174 865*	*76 815*	*43.9*	*174 863*	*80 693*	*46.1*
1 VII 2014	ESDJ	*358 899*	*161 434*	*45.0*	*179 451*	*78 740*	*43.9*	*179 448*	*82 694*	*46.1*
1 VII 2015	ESDJ	*368 310*	*165 463*	*44.9*	*184 157*	*80 717*	*43.8*	*184 153*	*84 746*	*46.0*
1 VII 2016	ESDJ	*377 968*	*169 598*	*44.9*	*188 986*	*82 746*	*43.8*	*188 982*	*86 852*	*46.0*
1 VII 2017	ESDJ	*387 879*	*173 841*	*44.8*	*193 942*	*84 827*	*43.7*	*193 937*	*89 014*	*45.9*
1 VII 2018	ESDJ	*398 050*	*178 195*	*44.8*	*199 028*	*86 963*	*43.7*	*199 022*	*91 232*	*45.8*
1 VII 2019	ESDJ	*408 487*	*182 663*	*44.7*	*204 247*	*89 155*	*43.7*	*204 240*	*93 508*	*45.8*
Bermuda - Bermudes[41]										
20 V 2010	CDJC	64 237	64 237	100.0	30 858	30 858	100.0	33 379	33 379	100.0
1 VII 2010[14]	ESDJ	64 129	...	...	30 792	...	...	33 337	...	...
1 VII 2011[14]	ESDJ	63 193	...	...	30 218	...	...	32 975	...	...
1 VII 2012[14]	ESDJ	62 408	...	...	29 819	...	...	32 589	...	...
1 VII 2013[14]	ESDJ	61 954	...	...	29 587	...	...	32 367	...	...
1 VII 2014[14]	ESDJ	61 777	...	...	29 499	...	...	32 278	...	...
1 VII 2015[14]	ESDJ	61 735	...	...	29 480	...	...	32 255	...	...
20 V 2016	CDJC	63 779	63 779	100.0	30 690	30 690	100.0	33 089	33 089	100.0
1 VII 2016[42]	ESDJ	63 791	...	...	30 695	...	...	33 096	...	...
1 VII 2017[42]	ESDJ	63 892	...	...	30 737	...	...	33 155	...	...
1 VII 2018[42]	ESDJ	63 973	...	...	30 768	...	...	33 205	...	...
1 VII 2019[42]	ESDJ	64 027	...	...	30 786	...	...	33 241	...	...
British Virgin Islands - Îles Vierges britanniques										
12 VII 2010	CDFC	28 054	...	...	13 820	...	...	14 234	...	...
Canada										
1 VII 2010[43]	ESDJ	34 004 889	...	...	16 847 823	...	...	17 157 066	...	...
2 V 2011	CDJC	33 476 690	27 147 190	81.1	16 414 225	13 190 225	80.4	17 062 455	13 956 960	81.8
1 VII 2011[43]	ESDJ	34 339 328	...	...	17 014 528	...	...	17 324 800	...	...
1 VII 2012[43]	ESDJ	34 714 222	...	...	17 209 900	...	...	17 504 322	...	...
1 VII 2013[43]	ESDJ	35 082 954	...	...	17 401 165	...	...	17 681 789	...	...
1 VII 2014[43]	ESDJ	35 437 435	...	...	17 581 697	...	...	17 855 738	...	...
1 VII 2015[43]	ESDJ	35 702 908	...	...	17 712 801	...	...	17 990 107	...	...
10 V 2016[44]	CDJC	35 151 730	28 575 665	81.3	17 264 200	13 912 045	80.6	17 887 530	14 663 615	82.0
1 VII 2016[45]	ESDJ	36 109 487	...	...	17 916 496	...	...	18 192 991	...	...
1 VII 2017[46]	ESDJ	36 543 321	...	...	18 135 268	...	...	18 408 053	...	...
1 VII 2018[46]	ESDJ	37 057 765	...	...	18 402 681	...	...	18 655 084	...	...
1 VII 2019*[47]	ESDJ	37 589 262	...	...	18 678 085	...	...	18 911 177	...	...

6. Total and urban population by sex: 2010 - 2019
Population totale et population urbaine selon le sexe : 2010 - 2019 (continued - suite)

Continent, country or area, and date / Continent, pays ou zone et date	Code[a]	Both sexes - Les deux sexes: Total	Both sexes - Urban - Urbaine: Number Nombre	Both sexes - Urban - Urbaine: Percent P.100	Male - Masculin: Total	Male - Urban - Urbaine: Number Nombre	Male - Urban - Urbaine: Percent P.100	Female - Féminin: Total	Female - Urban - Urbaine: Number Nombre	Female - Urban - Urbaine: Percent P.100
AMERICA, NORTH - AMÉRIQUE DU NORD										
Cayman Islands - Îles Caïmanes										
10 X 2010[48]	CDJC	55 036	55 036	100.0	27 218	27 218	100.0	27 818	27 818	100.0
31 XII 2010	ESDJ	55 036	55 036	100.0	27 219	27 219	100.0	27 817	27 817	100.0
31 XII 2011	ESDJ	55 517	55 517	100.0	27 454	27 454	100.0	28 063	28 063	100.0
31 XII 2012	ESDJ	56 732	56 732	100.0	27 753	27 753	100.0	28 979	28 979	100.0
31 XII 2013	ESDJ	55 747	55 747	100.0	27 133	27 133	100.0	28 614	28 614	100.0
31 XII 2014	ESDJ	58 238	58 238	100.0	28 322	28 322	100.0	29 916	29 916	100.0
31 XII 2015	ESDJ	60 413	60 413	100.0	30 264	30 264	100.0	30 149	30 149	100.0
31 XII 2016	ESDJ	61 361	61 361	100.0	29 422	29 422	100.0	31 939	31 939	100.0
31 XII 2017	ESDJ	63 415	63 415	100.0	32 212	32 212	100.0	31 203	31 203	100.0
31 XII 2018	ESDJ	65 813	65 813	100.0	31 875	31 875	100.0	33 938	33 938	100.0
31 XII 2019	ESDJ	69 914	69 914	100.0	34 539	34 539	100.0	35 375	35 375	100.0
Costa Rica										
1 VII 2010[49]	ESDJ	4 538 307	3 304 248[50]	72.8	2 206 526	1 579 816[50]	71.6	2 331 781	1 724 432[50]	74.0
30 V 2011	CDJC	4 301 712	3 130 871	72.8	2 106 063	1 509 161	71.7	2 195 649	1 621 710	73.9
1 VII 2011[49]	ESDJ	4 592 346	3 343 241	72.8	2 238 615	1 603 354	71.6	2 353 731	1 739 887	73.9
1 VII 2012[49]	ESDJ	4 651 166	3 384 925	72.8	2 266 220	1 621 617	71.6	2 384 946	1 763 308	73.9
1 VII 2013[49]	ESDJ	4 711 986	3 427 548	72.7	2 276 708	1 624 941	71.4	2 435 278	1 802 607	74.0
1 VII 2014[49]	ESDJ	4 772 098	3 469 802	72.7	2 325 438	1 662 288	71.5	2 446 660	1 807 514	73.9
1 VII 2015[51]	ESDJ	4 833 752	3 512 683	72.7	2 350 223	1 683 770	71.6	2 483 529	1 828 913	73.6
1 VII 2016[52]	ESDJ	4 889 762	3 551 728	72.6	2 373 531	1 703 473	71.8	2 516 231	1 848 255	73.5
1 VII 2017[53]	ESDJ	4 946 700	3 592 070	72.6	2 405 636	1 722 499	71.6	2 541 064	1 869 571	73.6
1 VII 2018[54]	ESDJ	5 003 673	3 630 938	72.6	2 431 983	1 742 776	71.7	2 571 690	1 888 162	73.4
1 VII 2019[55]	ESDJ	5 059 730	3 670 174	72.5	2 452 241	1 758 286	71.7	2 607 489	1 911 888	73.3
Cuba										
1 VII 2010	ESDJ	11 171 443	8 416 524	75.3	5 592 729	4 143 388	74.1	5 578 714	4 273 136	76.6
1 VII 2011	ESDJ	11 171 679	8 409 543	75.3	5 592 332	4 140 377	74.0	5 579 347	4 269 166	76.5
1 VII 2012	ESDJ	11 174 287	8 494 128	76.0	5 583 306	4 159 342	74.5	5 590 981	4 334 786	77.5
14 IX 2012	CDJC	11 167 325	8 575 189	76.8	5 570 825	4 177 485	75.0	5 596 500	4 397 704	78.6
1 VII 2013	ESDJ	11 191 608	8 596 991	76.8	5 580 810	4 186 436	75.0	5 610 798	4 410 555	78.6
1 VII 2014	ESDJ	11 224 190	8 625 144	76.8	5 595 379	4 199 578	75.1	5 628 811	4 425 566	78.6
1 VII 2015	ESDJ	11 238 661	8 639 191	76.9	5 600 904	4 205 871	75.1	5 637 757	4 433 320	78.6
1 VII 2016	ESDJ	11 239 114	8 644 181	76.9	5 599 279	4 207 382	75.1	5 639 835	4 436 798	78.7
1 VII 2017	ESDJ	11 230 142	8 642 754	77.0	5 591 525	4 204 316	75.2	5 638 617	4 438 438	78.7
1 VII 2018	ESDJ	11 215 344	8 637 568	77.0	5 580 437	4 199 163	75.2	5 634 908	4 438 406	78.8
1 VII 2019	ESDJ	11 201 549	8 633 350	77.1	5 570 081	4 194 838	75.3	5 631 469	4 438 512	78.8
Curaçao										
1 VII 2010[33]	ESDJ	148 703	...	...	68 065	...	...	80 639	...	...
26 III 2011	CDJC	150 563	...	...	68 848	...	...	81 715	...	...
1 VII 2011[33]	ESDJ	150 831	...	...	68 910	...	...	81 921	...	...
1 VII 2012[3]	ESDJ	152 088	...	...	69 490	...	...	82 598	...	...
1 VII 2013[3]	ESDJ	153 822	...	...	70 342	...	...	83 480	...	...
1 VII 2014[3]	ESDJ	155 909	...	...	71 269	...	...	84 640	...	...
1 VII 2015[3]	ESDJ	157 980	...	...	72 187	...	...	85 794	...	...
1 VII 2016[3]	ESDJ	159 663	...	...	72 990	...	...	86 674	...	...
1 VII 2017[3]	ESDJ	160 175	...	...	73 246	...	...	86 929	...	...
1 I 2018[3]	ESDJ	160 012	...	...	73 172	...	...	86 840	...	...
1 I 2019[3]	ESDJ	158 659	...	...	72 538	...	...	86 121	...	...
Dominica - Dominique										
1 VII 2010	ESDF	70 730	...	...	35 604	...	...	35 126	...	...
14 V 2011	CDFC	68 913	...	...	34 973	...	...	33 940	...	...
1 VII 2011	ESDF	70 755	...	...	35 762	...	...	34 992	...	...
1 VII 2012	ESDF	71 042	...	...	36 053	...	...	34 989	...	...
1 VII 2013	ESDF	71 221	...	...	36 144	...	...	35 077	...	...
1 VII 2014	ESDF	71 575	...	...	36 324	...	...	35 251	...	...
31 XII 2015	ESDF	71 089	...	...	36 325	...	...	34 764	...	...
31 XII 2016	ESDF	71 379	...	...	36 473	...	...	34 906	...	...
31 XII 2017*	ESDF	67 408	...	...	34 444	...	...	32 964	...	...
Dominican Republic - République dominicaine										
1 VII 2010[1]	ESDJ	*9 478 612*	*6 992 189*	*73.8*	*4 747 103*	*3 431 480*	*72.3*	*4 731 509*	*3 560 709*	*75.3*
1 XII 2010	CDJC	9 445 281	7 013 575	74.3	4 739 038	3 449 122	72.8	4 706 243	3 564 453	75.7

6. Total and urban population by sex: 2010 - 2019
Population totale et population urbaine selon le sexe : 2010 - 2019 (continued - suite)

Continent, country or area, and date / Continent, pays ou zone et date	Code[a]	Both sexes - Les deux sexes: Total	Both sexes - Urban - Urbaine: Number / Nombre	Both sexes - Urban - Urbaine: Percent / P.100	Male - Masculin: Total	Male - Urban - Urbaine: Number / Nombre	Male - Urban - Urbaine: Percent / P.100	Female - Féminin: Total	Female - Urban - Urbaine: Number / Nombre	Female - Urban - Urbaine: Percent / P.100
AMERICA, NORTH - AMÉRIQUE DU NORD										
Dominican Republic - République dominicaine										
1 VII 2011[1]	ESDJ	9 580 139	7 172 502	74.9	4 796 628	3 520 702	73.4	4 783 511	3 651 800	76.3
1 VII 2012[1]	ESDJ	9 680 963	7 348 975	75.9	4 845 755	3 608 025	74.5	4 835 208	3 740 950	77.4
1 VII 2013[1]	ESDJ	9 784 680	7 524 149	76.9	4 896 319	3 694 713	75.5	4 888 361	3 829 436	78.3
1 VII 2014[1]	ESDJ	9 883 486	7 691 885	77.8	4 944 386	3 777 718	76.4	4 939 100	3 914 167	79.2
1 VII 2015[1]	ESDJ	9 980 243	7 854 203	78.7	4 991 398	3 858 029	77.3	4 988 845	3 996 174	80.1
1 VII 2016[1]	ESDJ	10 075 045	8 011 084	79.5	5 037 329	3 935 569	78.1	5 037 716	4 075 515	80.9
1 VII 2017[1]	ESDJ	10 169 172	8 163 504	80.3	5 082 876	4 010 852	78.9	5 086 296	4 152 652	81.6
1 VII 2018[1]	ESDJ	10 266 149	8 314 335	81.0	5 129 824	4 085 301	79.6	5 136 325	4 229 034	82.3
1 VII 2019[1]	ESDJ	10 358 320	8 457 450	81.6	5 174 343	4 155 896	80.3	5 183 977	4 301 554	83.0
El Salvador[11]										
1 VII 2010	ESDJ	6 183 002	3 954 803	64.0	2 913 743	1 834 400	63.0	3 269 259	2 120 404	64.9
1 VII 2011	ESDJ	6 216 143	4 019 742	64.7	2 925 284	1 862 924	63.7	3 290 858	2 156 818	65.5
1 VII 2012	ESDJ	6 251 495	4 086 880	65.4	2 938 123	1 892 642	64.4	3 313 372	2 194 238	66.2
1 VII 2013	ESDJ	6 288 899	4 156 007	66.1	2 952 174	1 923 447	65.2	3 336 726	2 232 560	66.9
1 VII 2014	ESDJ	6 328 196	...	...	2 967 351	...	...	3 360 845	...	...
1 VII 2015	ESDJ	6 460 271	4 502 693	69.7	3 042 036	2 119 867	69.7	3 418 235	2 382 826	69.7
1 VII 2016	ESDJ	6 520 675	4 590 491	70.4	3 070 065	2 161 168	70.4	3 450 610	2 429 323	70.4
1 VII 2017	ESDJ	6 581 940	4 678 816	71.1	3 098 633	2 202 778	71.1	3 483 307	2 476 038	71.1
Greenland - Groenland[56]										
1 VII 2010	ESDJ	56 534	47 646	84.3	29 939	25 045	83.7	26 595	22 601	85.0
1 VII 2011	ESDJ	56 682	48 045	84.8	29 992	25 233	84.1	26 690	22 812	85.5
1 VII 2012	ESDJ	56 810	48 224	84.9	30 105	25 331	84.1	26 705	22 893	85.7
1 VII 2013	ESDJ	56 483	48 221	85.4	29 867	25 333	84.8	26 616	22 888	86.0
1 VII 2014	ESDJ	56 295	48 232	85.7	29 742	25 320	85.1	26 553	22 912	86.3
1 VII 2015	ESDJ	56 114	48 284	86.0	29 634	25 329	85.5	26 480	22 955	86.7
1 VII 2016	ESDJ	56 186	48 447	86.2	29 701	25 436	85.6	26 485	23 011	86.9
1 VII 2017	ESDJ	56 171	48 527	86.4	29 651	25 435	85.8	26 520	23 092	87.1
1 VII 2018	ESDJ	56 023	48 586	86.7	29 536	25 461	86.2	26 487	23 125	87.3
1 VII 2019	ESDJ	56 225	48 928	87.0	29 654	25 648	86.5	26 571	23 280	87.6
Grenada - Grenade										
1 VII 2010	ESDF	105 038	...	...	52 788	...	...	52 250	...	...
12 V 2011	CDFC	106 667	...	...	53 898	...	...	52 769	...	...
1 VII 2012	ESDF	107 599	...	...	54 435	...	...	53 164	...	...
1 VII 2013	ESDF	108 580	...	...	54 926	...	...	53 654	...	...
1 VII 2014	ESDF	109 374	...	...	55 185	...	...	54 189	...	...
1 VII 2015	ESDF	110 096	...	...	55 543	...	...	54 553	...	...
1 VII 2016	ESDF	110 910	...	...	55 955	...	...	54 955	...	...
1 VII 2017	ESDF	111 467	...	...	56 222	...	...	55 245	...	...
Guadeloupe[57]										
1 I 2010	CDJC	403 355	397 070	98.4	187 932	184 752	98.3	215 423	212 318	98.6
1 VII 2010	ESDJ	403 995	...	...	187 847	...	...	216 148	...	...
1 VII 2011	ESDJ	403 975	...	...	187 410	...	...	216 565	...	...
1 VII 2012	ESDJ	402 717	...	...	186 558	...	...	216 159	...	...
1 VII 2013	ESDJ	401 153	...	...	185 375	...	...	215 778	...	...
1 VII 2014	ESDJ	399 102	...	...	184 152	...	...	214 950	...	...
1 I 2015	CDJC	397 990	391 984	98.5	183 479	180 438	98.3	214 511	211 546	98.6
1 VII 2015	ESDJ	397 001	...	...	182 561	...	...	214 440	...	...
1 VII 2016	ESDJ	394 826	...	...	181 161	...	...	213 666	...	...
1 I 2017	ESDJ	429 085	...	...	197 571	...	...	231 514	...	...
1 I 2018	ESDJ	422 290	...	...	194 321	...	...	227 969	...	...
Guatemala[38]										
1 VII 2010	ESDJ	14 361 666	...	...	7 003 337	...	...	7 358 328	...	...
1 VII 2011	ESDJ	14 713 763	...	...	7 173 966	...	...	7 539 797	...	...
1 VII 2012	ESDJ	15 073 375	...	...	7 352 869	...	...	7 720 506	...	...
1 VII 2013	ESDJ	15 438 384	...	...	7 903 145	...	...	7 535 238	...	...
1 VII 2014	ESDJ	15 806 675	...	...	8 087 279	...	...	7 719 396	...	...
1 VII 2015	ESDJ	16 182 732	...	...	7 906 856	...	...	8 275 876	...	...
1 VII 2016	ESDJ	16 555 556	...	...	8 092 768	...	...	8 462 788	...	...
1 VII 2017	ESDJ	16 932 440	...	...	8 281 066	...	...	8 651 374	...	...
1 VII 2018	ESDJ	17 311 086	...	...	8 469 989	...	...	8 841 097	...	...

6. Total and urban population by sex: 2010 - 2019
Population totale et population urbaine selon le sexe : 2010 - 2019 (continued - suite)

Continent, country or area, and date / Continent, pays ou zone et date	Code[a]	Both sexes - Les deux sexes: Total	Both sexes: Urban - Urbaine: Number Nombre	Both sexes: Urban - Urbaine: Percent P.100	Male - Masculin: Total	Male: Urban - Urbaine: Number Nombre	Male: Urban - Urbaine: Percent P.100	Female - Féminin: Total	Female: Urban - Urbaine: Number Nombre	Female: Urban - Urbaine: Percent P.100
AMERICA, NORTH - AMÉRIQUE DU NORD										
Haiti - Haïti[58]										
1 VII 2010	ESDJ	*10 085 214*	*4 817 666*	*47.8*	*4 993 731*	*2 321 608*	*46.5*	*5 091 483*	*2 496 059*	*49.0*
1 VII 2011	ESDJ	*10 248 306*	...	...	*5 075 517*	...	...	*5 172 789*	...	...
1 VII 2012	ESDJ	*10 413 211*	*5 154 940*	*49.5*	*5 158 254*	*2 495 108*	*48.4*	*5 254 957*	*2 659 832*	*50.6*
1 VII 2013	ESDJ	*10 579 230*	...	...	*5 241 572*	...	...	*5 337 658*	...	...
1 VII 2014	ESDJ	*10 745 665*	...	...	*5 325 099*	...	...	*5 420 566*	...	...
1 VII 2015	ESDJ	*10 911 819*	...	...	*5 408 465*	...	...	*5 503 354*	...	...
1 VII 2016	ESDJ	*11 078 033*	...	...	*5 491 848*	...	...	*5 586 185*	...	...
1 VII 2017	ESDJ	*11 244 774*	...	...	*5 575 496*	...	...	*5 669 278*	...	...
1 VII 2018	ESDJ	*11 411 527*	...	...	*5 659 140*	...	...	*5 752 387*	...	...
1 VII 2019	ESDJ	*11 577 779*	...	...	*5 742 515*	...	...	*5 835 264*	...	...
Honduras										
1 VII 2010[59]	ESDF	*8 045 990*	...	...	*3 965 430*	...	...	*4 080 560*	...	...
1 VII 2013[4]	ESDJ	*8 287 178*	*4 427 308*	*53.4*	*4 044 225*	*2 091 200*	*51.7*	*4 242 953*	*2 336 108*	*55.1*
10 VIII 2013	CDJC	8 303 771	4 480 746	54.0	4 052 316	2 116 113	52.2	4 251 456	2 364 633	55.6
1 VII 2014[4]	ESDJ	*8 432 153*	*4 524 482*	*53.7*	*4 113 061*	*2 130 193*	*51.8*	*4 319 092*	*2 394 289*	*55.4*
1 VII 2015[4]	ESDJ	*8 576 532*	*4 622 076*	*53.9*	*4 181 657*	*2 169 691*	*51.9*	*4 394 875*	*2 452 385*	*55.8*
1 VII 2016[4]	ESDJ	*8 721 014*	*4 720 178*	*54.1*	*4 250 392*	*2 209 764*	*52.0*	*4 470 622*	*2 510 414*	*56.2*
1 VII 2017[4]	ESDJ	*8 866 351*	*4 818 912*	*54.4*	*4 319 664*	*2 250 493*	*52.1*	*4 546 687*	*2 568 419*	*56.5*
1 VII 2018[4]	ESDJ	*9 012 229*	*4 918 132*	*54.6*	*4 389 313*	*2 291 803*	*52.2*	*4 622 916*	*2 626 329*	*56.8*
1 VII 2019[4]	ESDJ	*9 158 345*	*5 017 687*	*54.8*	*4 459 196*	*2 333 620*	*52.3*	*4 699 149*	*2 684 067*	*57.1*
Jamaica - Jamaïque										
1 VII 2010	ESDJ	2 702 314	...	...	1 324 134	...	...	1 378 180	...	...
4 IV 2011[60]	CDJC	2 697 983	1 454 153	53.9	1 334 533	700 957	52.5	1 363 450	753 196	55.2
1 VII 2011	ESDJ	2 699 838	...	...	1 335 466	...	...	1 364 372	...	...
1 VII 2012	ESDJ	2 707 805	...	...	1 339 740	...	...	1 368 065	...	...
1 VII 2013	ESDJ	2 714 669	...	...	1 343 798	...	...	1 370 871	...	...
1 VII 2014	ESDJ	2 720 554	...	...	1 346 711	...	...	1 373 843	...	...
1 VII 2015	ESDJ	2 725 288	...	...	1 349 294	...	...	1 375 994	...	...
1 VII 2016	ESDJ	2 728 151	...	...	1 350 950	...	...	1 377 201	...	...
1 VII 2017	ESDJ	2 728 915	...	...	1 351 375	...	...	1 377 540	...	...
1 VII 2018	ESDJ	2 728 432	...	...	1 349 868	...	...	1 378 564	...	...
1 VII 2019	ESDJ	2 732 539	...	...	1 351 515	...	...	1 381 024	...	...
Martinique										
1 I 2010	CDJC	394 173	380 973	96.7	182 073	175 573	96.4	212 100	205 400	96.8
1 I 2010	ESDJ	394 173	...	...	182 110	...	...	212 063	...	...
1 I 2011	ESDJ	392 291	...	...	180 676	...	...	211 615	...	...
1 I 2012	ESDJ	388 364	...	...	178 824	...	...	209 540	...	...
1 I 2013	ESDJ	385 551	...	...	177 955	...	...	207 596	...	...
1 VII 2014	ESDJ	382 392	316 323	82.7	177 001	145 508	82.2	205 391	170 815	83.2
1 I 2015	CDJC	380 877	367 749	96.6	176 328	169 911	96.4	204 549	197 838	96.7
1 I 2015	ESDJ	378 243	...	...	174 193	...	...	204 050	...	...
1 I 2016	ESDJ	376 847	...	...	174 200	...	...	202 647	...	...
1 I 2017	ESDJ	374 780	...	...	173 293	...	...	201 487	...	...
1 I 2018	ESDJ	368 640	...	...	169 594	...	...	199 046	...	...
Mexico - Mexique										
12 VI 2010[61]	CDFC	112 336 538	86 287 410[35]	76.8	54 855 231	41 946 540[35]	76.5	57 481 307	44 340 870[35]	77.1
1 VII 2010	ESDJ	*113 748 671[62]*	*82 629 456[35]*	*72.6*	*55 671 595[62]*	...	...	*58 077 076[62]*	...	...
1 VII 2011	ESDJ	115 367 452[62]	83 726 767[35]	72.6	56 472 858[62]	...	...	58 894 594[62]	...	...
1 VII 2012	ESDJ	116 935 670[62]	84 776 446[35]	72.5	57 246 931[62]	...	...	59 688 739[62]	...	...
1 VII 2013	ESDJ	118 453 929[62]	85 792 843[35]	72.4	57 992 814[62]	...	...	60 461 115[62]	...	...
1 VII 2014	ESDJ	119 936 411[62]	86 782 031[35]	72.4	58 721 525[62]	...	...	61 214 886[62]	...	...
1 VII 2015	ESDJ	121 347 800[62]	87 743 091[35]	72.3	59 416 305[62]	...	...	61 931 495[62]	...	...
1 VII 2016	ESDJ	122 715 165[63]	88 677 252[35]	72.3	60 090 244[63]	...	...	62 624 921[63]	...	...
1 VII 2017	ESDJ	124 041 731[63]	89 586 802[35]	72.2	60 740 740[63]	...	...	63 300 991[63]	...	...
1 VII 2018	ESDJ	125 327 797[63]	92 297 621[35]	73.6	61 368 864[63]	...	...	63 958 933[63]	...	...
1 VII 2019[63]	ESDJ	126 577 691	...	...	61 977 632	...	...	64 600 059	...	...
Montserrat										
12 V 2011	CDJC	4 922	...	...	2 546	...	...	2 376	...	...
1 VII 2016	ESDJ	5 045	...	...	2 596	...	...	2 449	...	...
22 IX 2018[64]	ESDJ	4 649	...	...	2 306	...	...	2 343	...	...
Nicaragua										
1 VII 2010	ESDJ	*5 815 524*	...	...	*2 878 523*	...	...	*2 937 001*	...	...
1 VII 2011	ESDJ	*5 996 619*	...	...	*2 966 111*	...	...	*3 030 508*	...	...

6. Total and urban population by sex: 2010 - 2019
Population totale et population urbaine selon le sexe : 2010 - 2019 (continued - suite)

Continent, country or area, and date / Continent, pays ou zone et date	Code[a]	Both sexes - Les deux sexes: Total	Both sexes: Urban - Urbaine: Number Nombre	Both sexes: Urban - Urbaine: Percent P.100	Male - Masculin: Total	Male: Urban - Urbaine: Number Nombre	Male: Urban - Urbaine: Percent P.100	Female - Féminin: Total	Female: Urban - Urbaine: Number Nombre	Female: Urban - Urbaine: Percent P.100
AMERICA, NORTH - AMÉRIQUE DU NORD										
Nicaragua										
1 VII 2012	ESDJ	6 071 045	...	...	3 000 778	...	...	3 070 267	...	...
1 VII 2013	ESDJ	6 134 270	...	...	3 029 990	...	...	3 104 280	...	...
1 VII 2014	ESDJ	6 198 154	...	...	3 059 810	...	...	3 138 344	...	...
1 VII 2015	ESDJ	6 262 703	3 630 420	58.0	3 090 448	1 755 776	56.8	3 172 255	1 874 644	59.1
1 VII 2016	ESDJ	6 327 927	3 676 119	58.1	3 122 048	1 776 327	56.9	3 205 879	1 899 792	59.3
1 VII 2017	ESDJ	6 393 824	3 722 549	58.2	3 154 465	1 797 179	57.0	3 239 359	1 925 370	59.4
1 VII 2018	ESDJ	6 460 411	3 769 803	58.4	3 187 500	1 818 380	57.0	3 272 911	1 951 423	59.6
1 VII 2019	ESDJ	6 527 691	3 817 763	58.5	3 220 940	1 839 908	57.1	3 306 751	1 977 855	59.8
Panama										
16 V 2010	CDFC	3 405 813	...	...	1 712 584	...	...	1 693 229	...	...
1 VII 2010[14]	ESDF	3 661 835	2 385 445	65.1	1 841 305	1 171 489	63.6	1 820 530	1 213 956	66.7
1 VII 2011[14]	ESDF	3 723 821	2 449 917	65.8	1 871 749	1 203 430	64.3	1 852 072	1 246 487	67.3
1 VII 2012[14]	ESDF	3 787 511	2 514 402	66.4	1 903 085	1 235 377	64.9	1 884 426	1 279 025	67.9
1 VII 2013[14]	ESDF	3 850 735	2 578 868	67.0	1 934 264	1 267 319	65.5	1 916 471	1 311 549	68.4
1 VII 2014[14]	ESDF	3 913 275	2 643 353	67.5	1 965 087	1 299 262	66.1	1 948 188	1 344 091	69.0
1 VII 2015[14]	ESDF	3 975 404	2 707 838	68.1	1 995 695	1 331 207	66.7	1 979 709	1 376 631	69.5
1 VII 2016[14]	ESDF	4 037 043	2 772 324	68.7	2 026 044	1 363 153	67.3	2 010 999	1 409 171	70.1
1 VII 2017[14]	ESDF	4 098 135	2 836 794	69.2	2 056 085	1 395 090	67.9	2 042 050	1 441 704	70.6
1 VII 2018[14]	ESDF	4 158 783	2 901 275	69.8	2 085 950	1 427 378	68.4	2 072 833	1 473 897	71.1
1 VII 2019[14]	ESDF	4 218 808	2 965 759	70.3	2 115 458	1 459 649	69.0	2 103 350	1 506 110	71.6
Puerto Rico - Porto Rico[65]										
1 IV 2010	CDJC	3 725 789	3 493 256	93.8	1 785 171	...	...	1 940 618	...	...
1 VII 2010[66]	ESDJ	3 721 208	...	...	1 782 619	...	...	1 938 589	...	...
1 VII 2011[3]	ESDJ	3 678 732	...	...	1 763 441	...	...	1 915 291	...	...
1 VII 2012[3]	ESDJ	3 634 488	...	...	1 739 072	...	...	1 895 416	...	...
1 VII 2013[3]	ESDJ	3 593 077	...	...	1 720 280	...	...	1 872 797	...	...
1 VII 2014[3]	ESDJ	3 534 874	...	...	1 688 886	...	...	1 845 988	...	...
1 VII 2015[3]	ESDJ	3 473 177	...	...	1 656 336	...	...	1 816 841	...	...
1 VII 2016[3]	ESDJ	3 406 520	...	...	1 620 193	...	...	1 786 327	...	...
1 VII 2017[3]	ESDJ	3 325 001	...	...	1 580 651	...	...	1 744 350	...	...
1 VII 2018[3]	ESDJ	3 195 153	...	...	1 518 043	...	...	1 677 110	...	...
Saint Barthélemy - Saint-Barthélemy										
1 I 2015	CDJC	9 625	...	...	5 117	...	...	4 508	...	...
Saint Kitts and Nevis - Saint-Kitts-et-Nevis										
1 VII 2010*	ESDF	52 650	...	...	25 750	...	...	26 900	...	...
15 V 2011	CDFC	47 195	...	...	23 012	...	...	24 183	...	...
Saint Lucia - Sainte-Lucie										
10 V 2010	CDJC	165 770	...	...	82 268	...	...	83 502	...	...
1 VII 2011	ESDF	167 366	...	...	82 925	...	...	84 441	...	...
1 VII 2012	ESDF	169 115	...	...	83 669	...	...	85 446	...	...
1 VII 2013	ESDF	170 745	...	...	84 368	...	...	86 377	...	...
1 VII 2014	ESDF	172 623	...	...	85 639	...	...	86 984	...	...
1 VII 2015	ESDF	174 257	...	...	86 472	...	...	87 786	...	...
1 VII 2016	ESDF	175 819	...	...	87 261	...	...	88 558	...	...
1 VII 2017	ESDF	177 301	...	...	88 003	...	...	89 298	...	...
1 VII 2018	ESDF	178 696	...	...	88 693	...	...	90 002	...	...
Saint Pierre and Miquelon - Saint Pierre-et-Miquelon										
1 I 2015	CDJC	6 021	...	...	2 940	...	...	3 081	...	...
1 VII 2015	ESDJ	6 021	...	...	2 940	...	...	3 081	...	...
Saint Vincent and the Grenadines - Saint-Vincent-et-les Grenadines										
1 VII 2010	ESDJ	109 815	49 951	45.5	55 859	...	...	53 956	...	...
1 VII 2011	ESDJ	109 903	49 991	45.5	55 904	...	...	53 999	...	...
12 VI 2012	CDJC	109 991	50 926	46.3	56 419	...	...	53 572	...	...
1 VII 2013	ESDJ	110 079	50 967	46.3	56 464	...	...	53 615	...	...

6. Total and urban population by sex: 2010 - 2019
Population totale et population urbaine selon le sexe : 2010 - 2019 (continued - suite)

Continent, country or area, and date / Continent, pays ou zone et date	Code[a]	Both sexes - Les deux sexes			Male - Masculin			Female - Féminin		
		Total	Urban - Urbaine		Total	Urban - Urbaine		Total	Urban - Urbaine	
			Number Nombre	Percent P.100		Number Nombre	Percent P.100		Number Nombre	Percent P.100
AMERICA, NORTH - AMÉRIQUE DU NORD										
Saint Vincent and the Grenadines - Saint-Vincent-et-les Grenadines										
1 VII 2014	ESDJ	110 167	51 008	46.3	56 509	...	...	53 658	...	...
1 VII 2015	ESDJ	110 255	51 048	46.3	56 555	...	...	53 701	...	...
1 VII 2016	ESDJ	110 343	...	...	56 600	...	...	53 744	...	...
1 VII 2017	ESDJ	110 431	...	...	56 645	...	...	53 787	...	...
1 VII 2018	ESDJ	110 520	...	...	56 690	...	...	53 829	...	...
1 VII 2019	ESDJ	110 608	...	...	56 735	...	...	53 872	...	...
Saint-Martin (French part) - Saint-Martin (partie française)										
1 VII 2014	ESDJ	35 405	...	...	17 144	...	...	18 261	...	...
1 I 2015	CDJC	35 684	...	...	16 884	...	...	18 800	...	...
1 VII 2017	ESDJ	35 640	...	...	17 244	...	...	18 396	...	...
1 VII 2018	ESDJ	35 457	...	...	17 151	...	...	18 306	...	...
Sint Maarten (Dutch part) - Saint-Martin (partie néerlandaise)										
1 VII 2010	ESDF	35 526	...	...	16 927	...	...	18 600	...	...
9 IV 2011	CDFC	33 609	...	...	15 868	...	...	17 741	...	...
1 VII 2011	ESDF	33 436	...	...	15 772	...	...	17 656	...	...
1 VII 2012	ESDF	34 670	...	...	16 656	...	...	18 005	...	...
1 VII 2013	ESDF	36 611	...	...	17 910	...	...	18 701	...	...
1 I 2014	ESDF	37 132	...	...	18 159	...	...	18 973	...	...
1 I 2015	ESDF	38 247	...	...	18 694	...	...	19 553	...	...
1 I 2016	ESDF	39 410	...	...	19 256	...	...	20 155	...	...
1 I 2017	ESDF	40 535	...	...	19 769	...	...	20 766	...	...
1 I 2018	ESDF	40 614	...	...	19 759	...	...	20 855	...	...
Trinidad and Tobago - Trinité-et-Tobago										
1 VII 2010[25]	ESDF	1 317 714	...	...	660 822	...	...	656 892	...	...
9 I 2011	CDJC	1 328 019	...	...	666 305	...	...	661 714	...	...
1 VII 2012[5]	ESDJ	1 335 194	...	...	669 905	...	...	665 289	...	...
1 VII 2013[5]	ESDJ	1 340 557	...	...	672 596	...	...	667 961	...	...
1 VII 2014[5]	ESDJ	1 345 343	...	...	674 997	...	...	670 346	...	...
1 VII 2015[5]	ESDJ	1 349 667	...	...	677 166	...	...	672 501	...	...
1 VII 2016[5]	ESDJ	1 353 895	...	...	679 288	...	...	674 607	...	...
1 VII 2017[5]	ESDJ	1 356 633	...	...	680 661	...	...	675 972	...	...
1 VII 2018[5]	ESDJ	1 359 193	...	...	681 946	...	...	677 247	...	...
1 VII 2019[5]	ESDJ	1 363 985	...	...	684 350	...	...	679 635	...	...
Turks and Caicos Islands - Îles Turques et Caïques										
1 VII 2010	ESDJ	*34 500*	...	...	*17 810*	...	...	*16 690*	...	...
1 VII 2011	ESDJ	*33 500*	...	...	*17 160*	...	...	*16 340*	...	...
25 I 2012*[48]	CDJC	31 458	...	...	16 037	...	...	15 421	...	...
1 VII 2012	ESDJ	*32 199*	...	...	*16 365*	...	...	*15 834*	...	...
1 VII 2013	ESDJ	*33 677*	...	...	*17 132*	...	...	*16 545*	...	...
1 VII 2014	ESDJ	*35 168*	...	...	*17 907*	...	...	*17 261*	...	...
1 VII 2015	ESDJ	*36 689*	...	...	*18 689*	...	...	*18 000*	...	...
1 VII 2016	ESDJ	*37 910*	...	...	*19 169*	...	...	*18 741*	...	...
1 VII 2017	ESDJ	*39 790*	...	...	*20 296*	...	...	*19 494*	...	...
1 VII 2018*	ESDJ	*41 360*	...	...	*21 104*	...	...	*20 256*	...	...
1 VII 2019*	ESDJ	*42 953*	...	...	*21 928*	...	...	*21 029*	...	...
United States of America - États-Unis d'Amérique										
1 IV 2010	CDJC	308 745 538	249 253 271	80.7	151 781 326	121 698 595	80.2	156 964 212	127 554 676	81.3
1 VII 2010[67]	ESDJ	309 348 193	...	...	152 088 743	...	...	157 259 450	...	...
1 VII 2011[67]	ESDJ	311 663 358	...	...	153 263 360	...	...	158 399 998	...	...
1 VII 2012[67]	ESDJ	313 998 379	...	...	154 467 180	...	...	159 531 199	...	...
1 VII 2013[67]	ESDJ	316 204 908	...	...	155 589 564	...	...	160 615 344	...	...
1 VII 2014[67]	ESDJ	318 563 456	...	...	156 780 062	...	...	161 783 394	...	...

6. Total and urban population by sex: 2010 - 2019
Population totale et population urbaine selon le sexe : 2010 - 2019 (continued - suite)

Continent, country or area, and date / Continent, pays ou zone et date	Code[a]	Both sexes - Les deux sexes			Male - Masculin			Female - Féminin		
		Total	Urban - Urbaine		Total	Urban - Urbaine		Total	Urban - Urbaine	
			Number Nombre	Percent P.100		Number Nombre	Percent P.100		Number Nombre	Percent P.100
AMERICA, NORTH - AMÉRIQUE DU NORD										
United States of America - États-Unis d'Amérique										
1 VII 2015[67]	ESDJ	320 896 618	...	...	157 960 035	...	...	162 936 583	...	...
1 VII 2016[67]	ESDJ	323 127 513	...	...	159 078 923	...	...	164 048 590	...	...
1 VII 2017[67]	ESDJ	325 147 121	...	...	160 125 630	...	...	165 021 491	...	...
1 VII 2018[67]	ESDJ	327 167 434	...	...	161 128 679	...	...	166 038 755	...	...
United States Virgin Islands - Îles Vierges américaines[65]										
1 IV 2010	CDJC	106 405	...	...	50 854	...	...	55 551	...	...
AMERICA, SOUTH - AMÉRIQUE DU SUD										
Argentina - Argentine										
1 VII 2010[14]	ESDF	40 788 453	37 126 653	91.0	19 940 704	17 996 224	90.2	20 847 749	19 130 429	91.8
27 X 2010	CDFC	40 117 096	36 467 245	90.9	19 523 766	17 596 022	90.1	20 593 330	18 871 223	91.6
1 VII 2011[14]	ESDF	41 261 490	37 600 508	91.1	20 180 791	18 236 611	90.4	21 080 699	19 363 897	91.9
1 VII 2012[14]	ESDF	41 733 271	38 073 305	91.2	20 420 391	18 476 577	90.5	21 312 880	19 596 728	91.9
1 VII 2013[14]	ESDF	42 202 935	38 544 203	91.3	20 659 037	18 715 667	90.6	21 543 898	19 828 536	92.0
1 VII 2014[14]	ESDF	42 669 500	39 021 268	91.5	20 896 203	18 958 322	90.7	21 773 297	20 062 946	92.1
1 VII 2015[14]	ESDF	43 131 966	39 487 935	91.6	21 131 346	19 195 446	90.8	22 000 620	20 292 489	92.2
1 VII 2016[14]	ESDF	43 590 368	39 951 022	91.7	21 364 470	19 430 772	90.9	22 225 898	20 520 250	92.3
1 VII 2017[14]	ESDF	44 044 811	40 410 715	91.7	21 595 623	19 664 392	91.1	22 449 188	20 746 323	92.4
1 VII 2018[14]	ESDF	44 494 502	40 866 408	91.8	21 824 372	19 895 973	91.2	22 670 130	20 970 435	92.5
1 VII 2019[14]	ESDF	44 938 712	41 317 551	91.9	22 050 332	20 125 215	91.3	22 888 380	21 192 336	92.6
Bolivia (Plurinational State of) - Bolivie (État plurinational de)										
1 VII 2010[33]	ESDF	10 030 501	...	...	5 056 056	...	...	4 974 445	...	...
1 VII 2011[33]	ESDF	10 190 775	...	...	5 138 206	...	...	5 052 569	...	...
1 VII 2012[3]	ESDF	10 351 118	6 965 568	67.3	5 219 006	3 437 451	65.9	5 132 112	3 528 117	68.7
21 XI 2012	CDFC	10 059 856	6 788 962	67.5	5 019 447	3 314 824	66.0	5 040 409	3 474 138	68.9
1 VII 2013[3]	ESDF	10 507 789	7 110 575	67.7	5 297 727	3 511 796	66.3	5 210 062	3 598 779	69.1
1 VII 2014[3]	ESDF	10 665 841	7 256 749	68.0	5 376 880	3 586 449	66.7	5 288 961	3 670 300	69.4
1 VII 2015[3]	ESDF	10 825 013	7 403 841	68.4	5 456 332	3 661 290	67.1	5 368 681	3 742 551	69.7
1 VII 2016[3]	ESDF	10 985 059	7 551 625	68.7	5 535 975	3 736 216	67.5	5 449 084	3 815 409	70.0
1 VII 2017[3]	ESDF	11 145 770	7 699 908	69.1	5 615 713	3 811 135	67.9	5 530 057	3 888 773	70.3
1 VII 2018[3]	ESDF	11 307 314	7 848 776	69.4	5 695 665	3 886 115	68.2	5 611 649	3 962 661	70.6
1 VII 2019[3]	ESDF	11 469 896	7 998 346	69.7	5 775 959	3 961 231	68.6	5 693 937	4 037 115	70.9
Brazil - Brésil										
1 VII 2010[68]	ESDJ	195 497 797	164 920 459	84.4	96 706 703	...	...	98 791 094	...	...
31 VII 2010	CDJC	190 755 799	160 925 804	84.4	93 406 990	77 710 179	83.2	97 348 809	83 215 625	85.5
1 VII 2011[68]	ESDJ	197 397 018	167 096 245	84.6	97 610 297	...	...	99 786 721	...	...
1 VII 2012[68]	ESDJ	199 242 462	169 230 105	84.9	98 487 258	...	...	100 755 204	...	...
1 VII 2013[68]	ESDJ	201 032 714	171 317 079	85.2	99 336 858	...	...	101 695 856	...	...
1 VII 2014[68]	ESDJ	202 768 562	173 358 764	85.5	100 159 507	...	...	102 609 055	...	...
1 VII 2015[68]	ESDJ	204 450 649	175 355 103	85.8	100 955 522	...	...	103 495 127	...	...
1 VII 2016[68]	ESDJ	206 081 432	177 309 126	86.0	101 726 102	...	...	104 355 330	...	...
1 VII 2017[68]	ESDJ	207 660 929	179 217 279	86.3	102 471 274	...	...	105 189 655	...	...
1 VII 2018[68]	ESDJ	208 494 900	...	...	101 971 173	...	...	106 523 727	...	...
1 VII 2019[68]	ESDJ	210 147 125	...	...	102 760 295	...	...	107 386 830	...	...
Chile - Chili[69]										
1 VII 2010	ESDF	17 063 927	14 925 790	87.5	8 397 402	7 264 399	86.5	8 666 525	7 661 391	88.4
1 VII 2011	ESDF	17 254 159	15 107 423	87.6	8 491 323	7 355 442	86.6	8 762 836	7 751 981	88.5
1 VII 2012	ESDF	17 443 491	15 287 861	87.6	8 584 706	7 446 073	86.7	8 858 785	7 841 788	88.5
1 VII 2013	ESDF	17 611 902	15 449 360	87.7	8 667 644	7 527 165	86.8	8 944 258	7 922 195	88.6
1 VII 2014	ESDF	17 787 617	15 618 271	87.8	8 754 428	7 611 719	86.9	9 033 189	8 006 552	88.6
1 VII 2015	ESDF	17 971 423	15 795 077	87.9	8 845 449	7 700 039	87.1	9 125 974	8 095 038	88.7
1 VII 2016	ESDF	18 167 147	15 983 549	88.0	8 943 482	7 794 843	87.2	9 223 665	8 188 706	88.8
1 VII 2017	ESDF	18 419 192	16 225 460	88.1	9 074 217	7 920 315	87.3	9 344 975	8 305 145	88.9

6. Total and urban population by sex: 2010 - 2019
Population totale et population urbaine selon le sexe : 2010 - 2019 (continued - suite)

Continent, country or area, and date / Continent, pays ou zone et date	Code[a]	Both sexes - Les deux sexes			Male - Masculin			Female - Féminin		
		Total	Urban - Urbaine		Total	Urban - Urbaine		Total	Urban - Urbaine	
			Number Nombre	Percent P.100		Number Nombre	Percent P.100		Number Nombre	Percent P.100
AMERICA, SOUTH - AMÉRIQUE DU SUD										
Chile - Chili[69]										
1 VII 2018	ESDF	18 751 405	16 543 423	88.2	9 244 484	8 082 847	87.4	9 506 921	8 460 576	89.0
1 VII 2019	ESDF	19 107 216	16 883 696	88.4	9 424 139	8 254 179	87.6	9 683 077	8 629 517	89.1
Colombia - Colombie										
1 VII 2010[70]	ESDJ	44 349 775	33 493 392	75.5	21 697 042	16 011 517	73.8	22 652 733	17 481 875	77.2
1 VII 2011[70]	ESDJ	44 796 093	33 806 267	75.5	21 909 973	16 163 670	73.8	22 886 120	17 642 597	77.1
1 VII 2012[70]	ESDJ	45 217 714	34 103 474	75.4	22 110 083	16 307 377	73.8	23 107 631	17 796 097	77.0
1 VII 2013[70]	ESDJ	45 622 930	34 393 141	75.4	22 301 809	16 446 952	73.7	23 321 121	17 946 189	77.0
1 VII 2014[70]	ESDJ	46 021 270	34 684 615	75.4	22 490 228	16 587 368	73.8	23 531 042	18 097 247	76.9
1 VII 2015[70]	ESDJ	46 431 100	34 995 033	75.4	22 684 088	16 736 793	73.8	23 747 012	18 258 240	76.9
1 VII 2016[70]	ESDJ	46 900 058	35 367 438	75.4	22 906 987	16 916 346	73.8	23 993 071	18 451 092	76.9
1 VII 2017[70]	ESDJ	47 407 570	35 788 089	75.5	23 148 221	17 118 866	74.0	24 259 349	18 669 223	77.0
18 IV 2018	CDJC	44 164 417	34 107 027	77.2	21 570 493	16 324 552	75.7	22 593 924	17 782 475	78.7
1 VII 2018[70]	ESDJ	48 258 494	36 424 653	75.5	23 573 287	17 430 958	73.9	24 685 207	18 993 695	76.9
1 VII 2019[70]	ESDJ	49 395 678	37 425 856	75.8	24 123 683	17 914 385	74.3	25 271 995	19 511 471	77.2
Ecuador - Équateur										
1 VII 2010[71]	ESDF	15 012 228	9 412 612	62.7	7 443 875	4 611 039	61.9	7 568 353	4 801 573	63.4
28 XI 2010	CDFC	14 483 499	9 090 786	62.8	7 177 683	4 451 434	62.0	7 305 816	4 639 352	63.5
1 VII 2011[71]	ESDF	15 266 431	9 596 628	62.9	7 567 676	4 700 620	62.1	7 698 755	4 896 008	63.6
1 VII 2012[71]	ESDF	15 520 973	9 780 650	63.0	7 691 912	4 790 437	62.3	7 829 061	4 990 213	63.7
1 VII 2013[71]	ESDF	15 774 749	9 963 884	63.2	7 815 935	4 880 045	62.4	7 958 814	5 083 839	63.9
1 VII 2014[71]	ESDF	16 027 466	10 145 875	63.3	7 939 552	4 969 197	62.6	8 087 914	5 176 678	64.0
1 VII 2015[71]	ESDF	16 278 844	10 326 384	63.4	8 062 610	5 057 750	62.7	8 216 234	5 268 634	64.1
1 VII 2016[71]	ESDF	16 528 730	10 505 180	63.6	8 184 970	5 145 594	62.9	8 343 760	5 359 586	64.2
1 VII 2017[71]	ESDF	16 776 977	10 682 148	63.7	8 306 557	5 232 565	63.0	8 470 420	5 449 583	64.3
1 VII 2018[71]	ESDF	17 023 408	10 857 208	63.8	8 427 261	5 318 564	63.1	8 596 147	5 538 644	64.4
1 VII 2019[71]	ESDF	17 267 986	11 030 216	63.9	8 547 067	5 403 496	63.2	8 720 919	5 626 720	64.5
Falkland Islands (Malvinas) - Îles Falkland (Malvinas)[72]										
15 IV 2012[73]	CDFC	2 840	...	...	1 491	...	...	1 349	...	...
9 X 2016	CDFC	3 354	...	...	1 820[74]	...	...	1 532[74]	...	...
French Guiana - Guyane française										
1 I 2010	CDJC	229 040	201 042	87.8	113 599	98 933	87.1	115 441	102 109	88.5
1 I 2010	ESDJ	229 040	201 042	87.8	113 599	98 933	87.1	115 441	102 109	88.5
1 I 2011	ESDJ	237 549	...	...	117 732	...	...	119 817	...	...
1 I 2012	ESDJ	239 648	...	...	119 538	...	...	120 110	...	...
1 I 2013	CDJC	244 118	...	...	121 653	...	...	122 465	...	...
1 I 2013	ESDJ	244 118	...	...	121 653	...	...	122 465	...	...
1 I 2014	ESDJ	252 338	...	...	125 189	...	...	127 149	...	...
1 I 2015	CDJC	259 865	224 631	86.4	128 973	110 366	85.6	130 892	114 265	87.3
1 I 2015	ESDJ	254 541	...	...	127 237	...	...	127 304	...	...
1 I 2016	ESDJ	262 527	...	...	130 596	...	...	131 931	...	...
1 I 2017	ESDJ	274 153	...	...	136 093	...	...	138 060	...	...
1 I 2018	ESDJ	281 612	...	...	139 842	...	...	141 770	...	...
Guyana										
1 VII 2010[75]	ESDF	752 113	...	...	377 267	...	...	374 846	...	...
1 VII 2011[75]	ESDF	750 663	...	...	376 596	...	...	374 067	...	...
1 VII 2012[75]	ESDF	746 724	...	...	371 731	...	...	374 993	...	...
15 IX 2012	CDFC	746 955	...	...	371 805	...	...	375 150	...	...
1 VII 2013[75]	ESDF	746 263	...	...	371 609	...	...	374 654	...	...
1 VII 2014[75]	ESDF	745 873	...	...	371 519	...	...	374 355	...	...
1 VII 2015[75]	ESDF	744 945	...	...	371 149	...	...	373 796	...	...
1 VII 2016[75]	ESDF	743 458	...	...	370 491	...	...	372 967	...	...
1 VII 2017[75]	ESDF	741 365	...	...	369 520	...	...	371 845	...	...
1 VII 2018[75]	ESDF	744 962	...	...	372 995	...	...	371 967	...	...
1 VII 2019[75]	ESDF	743 699	...	...	372 733	...	...	370 966	...	...
Paraguay[76]										
1 VII 2010	ESDF	6 265 877	3 652 713	58.3	3 165 316	1 785 556	56.4	3 100 561	1 867 157	60.2
1 VII 2011	ESDF	6 363 276	3 738 905	58.8	3 213 839	1 827 856	56.9	3 149 438	1 911 049	60.7
1 VII 2012	ESDF	6 461 041	3 825 311	59.2	3 262 466	1 870 215	57.3	3 198 575	1 955 096	61.1
1 VII 2013	ESDF	6 559 027	3 911 850	59.6	3 311 123	1 912 591	57.8	3 247 904	1 999 259	61.6
1 VII 2014	ESDF	6 657 232	3 998 524	60.1	3 359 806	1 954 982	58.2	3 297 426	2 043 541	62.0

6. Total and urban population by sex: 2010 - 2019
Population totale et population urbaine selon le sexe : 2010 - 2019 (continued - suite)

Continent, country or area, and date / Continent, pays ou zone et date	Code[a]	Both sexes - Les deux sexes: Total	Both sexes - Urban - Urbaine: Number Nombre	Both sexes - Urban - Urbaine: Percent P.100	Male - Masculin: Total	Male - Urban - Urbaine: Number Nombre	Male - Urban - Urbaine: Percent P.100	Female - Féminin: Total	Female - Urban - Urbaine: Number Nombre	Female - Urban - Urbaine: Percent P.100
AMERICA, SOUTH - AMÉRIQUE DU SUD										
Paraguay[76]										
1 VII 2015	ESDF	*6 755 756*	*4 085 396*	*60.5*	*3 408 566*	*1 997 419*	*58.6*	*3 347 190*	*2 087 977*	*62.4*
1 VII 2016	ESDF	*6 854 536*	*4 174 834*	*60.9*	*3 457 365*	*2 041 139*	*59.0*	*3 397 170*	*2 133 695*	*62.8*
1 VII 2017	ESDF	*6 953 646*	*4 264 473*	*61.3*	*3 506 242*	*2 084 904*	*59.5*	*3 447 404*	*2 179 568*	*63.2*
1 VII 2018	ESDF	*7 052 983*	*4 354 253*	*61.7*	*3 555 140*	*2 128 682*	*59.9*	*3 497 843*	*2 225 571*	*63.6*
1 VII 2019	ESDF	*7 152 703*	*4 444 274*	*62.1*	*3 604 135*	*2 172 518*	*60.3*	*3 548 568*	*2 271 757*	*64.0*
Peru - Pérou										
30 VI 2010[77]	ESDF	*28 692 915*	...	...	*14 266 452*	...	...	*14 426 463*	...	...
30 VI 2011[77]	ESDF	*28 905 725*	...	...	*14 359 189*	...	...	*14 546 536*	...	...
30 VI 2012[77]	ESDF	*29 113 162*	...	...	*14 443 547*	...	...	*14 669 615*	...	...
30 VI 2013[77]	ESDF	*29 341 346*	...	...	*14 537 066*	...	...	*14 804 280*	...	...
30 VI 2014[77]	ESDF	*29 616 414*	...	...	*14 657 288*	...	...	*14 959 126*	...	...
30 VI 2015[77]	ESDF	*29 964 499*	...	...	*14 821 760*	...	...	*15 142 739*	...	...
30 VI 2016[77]	ESDF	*30 422 831*	...	...	*15 052 061*	...	...	*15 370 770*	...	...
30 VI 2017[77]	ESDF	*30 973 992*	...	...	*15 336 495*	...	...	*15 637 497*	...	...
22 VIII 2017[78]	CDFC	29 381 884	23 311 893	79.3	14 450 757	11 377 486	78.7	14 931 127	11 934 407	79.9
30 VI 2018[77]	ESDF	*31 562 130*	...	...	*15 642 691*	...	...	*15 919 439*	...	...
30 VI 2019[77]	ESDF	*32 131 400*	...	...	*15 938 284*	...	...	*16 193 116*	...	...
Suriname										
13 VIII 2012	CDJC	541 638	359 146	66.3	270 629	177 215	65.5	271 009	181 931	67.1
1 VII 2013	ESDJ	550 222	...	...	274 859	...	...	275 363	...	...
1 VII 2014	ESDJ	558 773	...	...	279 071	...	...	279 702	...	...
1 VII 2015	ESDJ	567 291	...	...	283 259	...	...	284 032	...	...
1 VII 2016	ESDJ	575 763	...	...	287 422	...	...	288 341	...	...
1 VII 2017	ESDJ	583 200	386 500	66.3	290 800	190 700	65.6	292 400	195 800	67.0
1 VII 2018	ESDJ	590 100	391 200	66.3	294 200	193 100	65.6	295 900	198 100	66.9
Uruguay										
1 VII 2010	ESDJ	3 396 706	3 216 519	94.7	1 640 886	1 539 959	93.8	1 755 820	1 676 560	95.5
1 VII 2011	ESDJ	3 412 636	3 238 644	94.9	1 648 466	1 551 366	94.1	1 764 170	1 687 279	95.6
4 X 2011	CDJC	3 286 314	3 110 701	94.7	1 577 725[79]	1 478 967[79]	93.7	1 708 481[79]	1 631 626[79]	95.5
1 VII 2012[1]	ESDJ	3 426 466	3 253 370	94.9	1 655 693	1 559 292	94.2	1 770 774	1 694 078	95.7
1 VII 2013[1]	ESDJ	3 440 157	3 268 281	95.0	1 662 884	1 567 325	94.3	1 777 273	1 700 956	95.7
1 VII 2014[1]	ESDJ	3 453 691	3 283 177	95.1	1 670 026	1 575 363	94.3	1 783 665	1 707 813	95.7
1 VII 2015[1]	ESDJ	3 467 054	3 297 948	95.1	1 677 118	1 583 363	94.4	1 789 936	1 714 585	95.8
1 VII 2016[1]	ESDJ	3 480 222	3 312 523	95.2	1 684 140	1 591 280	94.5	1 796 082	1 721 243	95.8
1 VII 2017[1]	ESDJ	3 493 205	3 326 886	95.2	1 691 102	1 599 115	94.6	1 802 103	1 727 772	95.9
1 VII 2018[1]	ESDJ	3 505 985	3 341 003	95.3	1 697 985	1 606 843	94.6	1 808 000	1 734 160	95.9
1 VII 2019[1]	ESDJ	3 518 552	3 354 867	95.3	1 704 782	1 614 457	94.7	1 813 771	1 740 410	96.0
Venezuela (Bolivarian Republic of) - Venezuela (République bolivarienne du)										
1 VII 2011	ESDF	28 810 899	...	...	14 443 172	...	...	14 367 727	...	...
1 IX 2011	CDJC	27 227 930	24 182 998[80]	88.8	13 549 752	11 902 155[80]	87.8	13 678 178	12 280 843[80]	89.8
1 VII 2012	ESDF	29 230 592	...	...	14 654 181	...	...	14 576 411	...	...
1 VII 2013	ESDF	29 650 188	...	...	14 865 265	...	...	14 784 923	...	...
1 VII 2014	ESDF	30 069 829	...	...	15 075 999	...	...	14 993 830	...	...
1 VII 2015	ESDF	30 489 354	...	...	15 283 762	...	...	15 205 592	...	...
1 VII 2016	ESDF	30 883 254	...	...	15 488 512	...	...	15 394 742	...	...
1 VII 2017	ESDF	31 277 130	...	...	15 690 386	...	...	15 586 744	...	...
1 VII 2018	ESDF	31 670 952	...	...	15 889 454	...	...	15 781 498	...	...
1 VII 2019	ESDF	32 064 741	...	...	16 085 704	...	...	15 979 037	...	...
ASIA - ASIE										
Afghanistan[81]										
1 VII 2010	ESDF	*24 485 600*	*5 690 300*	*23.2*	*12 524 700*	*2 929 900*	*23.4*	*11 960 900*	*2 760 400*	*23.1*
1 VII 2011	ESDF	*24 987 700*	*5 879 200*	*23.5*	*12 782 000*	*3 027 400*	*23.7*	*12 205 700*	*2 851 800*	*23.4*
1 VII 2012	ESDF	*25 500 100*	*6 074 200*	*23.8*	*13 044 400*	*3 127 700*	*24.0*	*12 455 700*	*2 946 500*	*23.7*
1 VII 2013	ESDF	*26 023 100*	*6 275 600*	*24.1*	*13 312 400*	*3 231 600*	*24.3*	*12 710 700*	*3 044 000*	*23.9*
1 VII 2014	ESDF	*26 556 754*	*6 483 434*	*24.4*	*13 585 933*	*3 338 764*	*24.6*	*12 970 821*	*3 144 670*	*24.2*
1 VII 2015	ESDF	*27 101 365*	*6 698 033*	*24.7*	*13 865 015*	*3 449 379*	*24.9*	*13 236 350*	*3 248 654*	*24.5*
1 VII 2016	ESDF	*27 657 145*	*6 919 560*	*25.0*	*14 149 838*	*3 563 570*	*25.2*	*13 507 307*	*3 355 990*	*24.8*

6. Total and urban population by sex: 2010 - 2019
Population totale et population urbaine selon le sexe : 2010 - 2019 (continued - suite)

Continent, country or area, and date / Continent, pays ou zone et date	Code[a]	Both sexes - Les deux sexes			Male - Masculin			Female - Féminin		
		Total	Urban - Urbaine		Total	Urban - Urbaine		Total	Urban - Urbaine	
			Number Nombre	Percent P.100		Number Nombre	Percent P.100		Number Nombre	Percent P.100
ASIA - ASIE										
Afghanistan[81]										
1 VII 2017	ESDF	28 224 323	7 148 224	25.3	14 438 456	3 631 353	25.2	13 785 867	3 516 871	25.5
1 VII 2018	ESDF	30 075 018	7 507 953	25.0	15 312 423	3 792 857	24.8	14 762 595	3 715 096	25.2
1 VII 2019	ESDF	30 725 560	7 761 765	25.3	15 643 288	3 921 208	25.1	15 082 272	3 840 557	25.5
Armenia - Arménie										
1 VII 2010	ESDJ	3 044 868	1 933 144	63.5	1 460 773	906 766	62.1	1 584 095	1 026 378	64.8
1 VII 2011	ESDJ	3 027 938	1 918 721	63.4	1 452 588	899 253	61.9	1 575 350	1 019 468	64.7
12 X 2011	CDFC	2 871 771	1 847 124	64.3	1 346 729	851 475	63.2	1 525 042	995 649	65.3
1 VII 2012	ESDJ	3 024 127	1 915 060	63.3	1 450 560	897 133	61.8	1 573 567	1 017 927	64.7
1 VII 2013	ESDJ	3 021 979	1 915 758	63.4	1 447 572	896 463	61.9	1 574 407	1 019 295	64.7
1 VII 2014	ESDJ	3 013 839	1 913 481	63.5	1 441 323	894 594	62.1	1 572 516	1 018 887	64.8
1 VII 2015	ESDJ	3 004 588	1 909 960	63.6	1 434 095	891 769	62.2	1 570 493	1 018 191	64.8
1 VII 2016	ESDJ	2 992 364	1 904 230	63.6	1 423 906	886 581	62.3	1 568 458	1 017 649	64.9
1 VII 2017	ESDJ	2 979 442	1 898 630	63.7	1 413 485	881 506	62.4	1 565 957	1 017 124	65.0
1 VII 2018	ESDJ	2 969 001	1 895 362	63.8	1 404 965	878 143	62.5	1 564 036	1 017 219	65.0
1 I 2019	ESDJ	2 965 269	...	...	1 401 731	...	...	1 563 538	...	...
Azerbaijan - Azerbaïdjan										
1 VII 2010	ESDJ	9 054 300	4 802 200	53.0	4 486 300	2 364 400	52.7	4 568 000	2 437 800	53.4
1 VII 2011	ESDJ	9 173 100	4 859 100	53.0	4 550 300	2 394 700	52.6	4 622 800	2 464 400	53.3
1 VII 2012	ESDJ	9 295 800	4 936 900	53.1	4 616 200	2 435 200	52.8	4 679 600	2 501 700	53.5
1 VII 2013	ESDJ	9 416 800	5 016 000	53.3	4 681 200	2 476 300	52.9	4 735 600	2 539 700	53.6
1 VII 2014	ESDJ	9 535 100	5 072 100	53.2	4 744 700	2 505 700	52.8	4 790 400	2 566 400	53.6
1 VII 2015	ESDJ	9 649 300	5 126 300	53.1	4 805 700	2 534 000	52.7	4 843 600	2 592 300	53.5
1 VII 2016	ESDJ	9 757 800	5 175 700	53.0	4 863 400	2 559 600	52.6	4 894 400	2 616 100	53.5
1 VII 2017	ESDJ	9 854 000	5 218 400	53.0	4 914 600	2 581 600	52.5	4 939 400	2 636 800	53.4
1 VII 2018	ESDJ	9 939 800	5 255 900	52.9	4 960 200	2 600 800	52.4	4 979 600	2 655 100	53.3
1 VII 2019	ESDJ	10 019 600	5 298 100	52.9	5 000 000	2 621 700	52.4	5 019 600	2 676 400	53.3
Bahrain - Bahreïn										
27 IV 2010	CDJC	1 234 571	1 234 571	100.0	768 414	768 414	100.0	466 157	466 157	100.0
1 VII 2010	ESDJ	1 228 543	...	...	764 357	...	...	464 186	...	...
1 VII 2011	ESDJ	1 195 020	...	...	741 483	...	...	453 537	...	...
1 VII 2012	ESDJ	1 208 964	...	...	760 449	...	...	448 515	...	...
1 VII 2013	ESDJ	1 253 191	...	...	788 381	...	...	464 810	...	...
1 VII 2014	ESDJ	1 314 562	...	...	806 487	...	...	508 075	...	...
1 VII 2015	ESDJ	1 370 322	...	...	846 365	...	...	523 957	...	...
1 VII 2016	ESDJ	1 423 726	...	...	888 389	...	...	535 337	...	...
1 VII 2017	ESDJ	1 501 116	...	...	951 312	...	...	549 804	...	...
1 VII 2018	ESDJ	1 503 091	...	...	946 864	...	...	556 227	...	...
1 VII 2019	ESDJ	1 483 756	...	...	920 564	...	...	563 192	...	...
Bangladesh										
1 VII 2010	ESDF	148 620 000	38 540 000	25.9	76 120 000	20 427 000	26.8	72 500 000	18 113 000	25.0
15 III 2011[82]	CDFC	149 772 364	...	...	74 980 386	...	...	74 791 978	...	...
1 VII 2011	ESDF	150 611 000	39 000 000	25.9	77 101 062	20 560 587	26.7	73 509 938	18 439 413	25.1
1 VII 2012	ESDF	152 700 000	41 100 000	26.9	78 200 000	...	...	74 500 000	...	...
1 VII 2013	ESDF	154 790 000	42 580 000	27.5	77 510 000	...	...	77 280 000	...	...
1 VII 2014	ESDF	156 880 000	44 110 000	28.1	78 560 000	22 068 556	28.1	78 320 000	22 041 444	28.1
1 VII 2015	ESDF	158 900 000	45 700 000	28.8	79 600 000	22 864 044	28.7	79 300 000	22 835 956	28.8
1 VII 2016	ESDF	160 800 000	47 400 000	29.5	80 500 000	23 714 567	29.5	80 300 000	23 685 433	29.5
1 VII 2017	ESDF	162 700 000	49 216 750	30.3	81 400 000	24 623 500	30.3	81 300 000	24 593 250	30.3
1 VII 2018	ESDF	164 600 000	49 791 500	30.3	82 400 000	24 911 052	30.2	82 200 000	24 880 448	30.3
1 VII 2019	ESDF	166 500 000	50 366 250	30.3	83 330 000	25 198 603	30.2	83 170 000	25 167 647	30.3
Bhutan - Bhoutan										
1 VII 2010[83]	ESDF	695 823	242 001	34.8	363 384	129 298	35.6	332 439	112 703	33.9
1 VII 2011[83]	ESDF	708 265	252 038	35.6	369 476	134 484	36.4	338 789	117 554	34.7
1 VII 2012[83]	ESDF	720 679	262 325	36.4	375 554	139 798	37.2	345 125	122 530	35.5
1 VII 2013[83]	ESDF	733 004	272 839	37.2	381 582	145 219	38.1	351 421	127 619	36.3
1 VII 2014[83]	ESDF	745 153	283 543	38.1	387 520	150 737	38.9	357 633	132 806	37.1
1 VII 2015[83]	ESDF	757 042	294 402	38.9	393 324	156 328	39.7	363 718	138 074	38.0
1 VII 2016[83]	ESDF	768 577	...	...	398 948	...	...	369 629	...	...
30 V 2017[84]	CDFC	727 145	274 316	37.7	380 453	143 313	37.7	346 692	131 003	37.8
30 V 2018[69]	ESDF	734 374	...	...	383 909	...	...	350 465	...	...
30 V 2019[69]	ESDF	741 672	...	...	387 402	...	...	354 270	...	...

6. Total and urban population by sex: 2010 - 2019
Population totale et population urbaine selon le sexe : 2010 - 2019 (continued - suite)

Continent, country or area, and date / Continent, pays ou zone et date	Code[a]	Both sexes - Les deux sexes			Male - Masculin			Female - Féminin		
		Total	Urban - Urbaine		Total	Urban - Urbaine		Total	Urban - Urbaine	
			Number Nombre	Percent P.100		Number Nombre	Percent P.100		Number Nombre	Percent P.100
ASIA - ASIE										
Brunei Darussalam - Brunéi Darussalam										
1 VII 2010[33]	ESDF	386 800	...	...	199 800	...	...	187 000	...	...
20 VI 2011	CDJC	393 372	296 257	75.3	203 144	151 663	74.7	190 228	144 594	76.0
1 VII 2012	ESDJ	398 700	...	...	205 800	...	...	192 900	...	...
1 VII 2013	ESDJ	403 300	...	...	207 900	...	...	195 400	...	...
1 VII 2014	ESDJ	407 600	...	...	209 700	...	...	197 900	...	...
1 VII 2015	ESDJ	412 400	...	...	211 900	...	...	200 500	...	...
1 VII 2016[85]	ESDJ	417 256	312 448	74.9	214 104	160 061	74.8	203 152	152 387	75.0
1 VII 2017	ESDJ	429 500	...	...	223 400	...	...	206 100	...	...
1 VII 2018	ESDJ	442 400	...	...	233 400	...	...	209 000	...	...
1 VII 2019	ESDJ	459 500	...	...	244 500	...	...	215 000	...	...
Cambodia - Cambodge										
1 VII 2010[86]	ESDF	14 302 779	2 926 810	20.5	6 973 994	1 406 183	20.2	7 328 785	1 520 627	20.7
1 VII 2011[86]	ESDF	14 521 275	3 042 794	21.0	7 088 691	1 462 518	20.6	7 432 584	1 580 276	21.3
1 VII 2012[86]	ESDF	14 741 414	3 165 683	21.5	7 204 166	1 520 722	21.1	7 537 248	1 644 961	21.8
3 III 2013[87]	SSDF	14 676 591	3 146 212	21.4	7 121 508	1 527 479	21.4	7 555 083	1 618 734	21.4
1 VII 2013[86]	ESDF	14 962 591	3 285 951	22.0	7 320 112	1 580 866	21.6	7 642 479	1 705 085	22.3
1 VII 2014[86]	ESDF	15 184 116	3 412 183	22.5	7 436 178	1 642 397	22.1	7 747 938	1 769 786	22.8
1 VII 2015[86]	ESDF	15 405 157	3 540 575	23.0	7 551 944	1 705 018	22.6	7 853 213	1 835 557	23.4
3 III 2019*[88]	CDFC	15 288 489	...	...	7 418 577	...	...	7 869 912	...	...
China - Chine[89]										
1 VII 2010[90]	ESDF	1 337 700 000	669 780 000[92]	50.1	687 480 000[91]	...	...	653 430 000[91]	...	...
1 XI 2010[93]	CDJC	1 339 724 852	665 575 306	49.7	686 852 572	...	...	652 872 280	...	...
1 VII 2011[94]	ESDF	1 344 100 000	691 000 000[92]	51.4	691 000 000[91]	...	...	657 000 000[91]	...	...
1 VII 2012[94]	ESDF	1 350 695 000	701 305 000[95]	51.9	692 315 000	...	...	658 380 000	...	...
1 VII 2013[90]	ESDF	1 357 380 000	721 465 000[95]	53.2	695 615 000	...	...	661 765 000	...	...
1 VII 2014[90]	ESDF	1 364 270 000	740 135 000[95]	54.3	699 035 000	...	...	665 235 000	...	...
1 VII 2015[90]	ESDF	1 371 220 000	760 160 000[95]	55.4	702 465 000	...	...	668 755 000	...	...
1 VII 2016[90]	ESDF	1 378 665 000	782 070 000[95]	56.7	706 145 000	...	...	672 520 000	...	...
1 VII 2017[90]	ESDF	1 386 395 000	803 225 000[95]	57.9	709 760 000	...	...	676 635 000	...	...
1 VII 2018[90]	ESDF	1 392 730 000	822 420 000[95]	59.1	712 440 000	...	...	680 290 000	...	...
1 VII 2019[90]	ESDF	1 397 715 000	839 900 000[95]	60.1	714 390 000	...	...	683 325 000	...	...
China, Hong Kong SAR - Chine, Hong Kong RAS										
1 VII 2010	ESDJ	7 024 200	...	...	3 294 300	...	...	3 729 900	...	...
30 VI 2011[96]	CDJC	7 071 576	...	...	3 303 015	...	...	3 768 561	...	...
1 VII 2011	ESDJ	7 071 600	...	...	3 303 000	...	...	3 768 600	...	...
1 VII 2012	ESDJ	7 150 100	...	...	3 327 300	...	...	3 822 800	...	...
1 VII 2013	ESDJ	7 178 900	...	...	3 329 900	...	...	3 849 000	...	...
1 VII 2014	ESDJ	7 229 500	...	...	3 344 500	...	...	3 885 000	...	...
1 VII 2015	ESDJ	7 291 300	...	...	3 365 600	...	...	3 925 700	...	...
30 VI 2016[97]	CDJC	7 336 585	...	...	3 375 362	...	...	3 961 223	...	...
1 VII 2016	ESDJ	7 336 600	...	...	3 375 400	...	...	3 961 200	...	...
1 VII 2017	ESDJ	7 391 700	...	...	3 392 500	...	...	3 999 200	...	...
1 VII 2018	ESDJ	7 451 000	...	...	3 410 300	...	...	4 040 700	...	...
1 VII 2019	ESDJ	7 507 400	...	...	3 423 000	...	...	4 084 400	...	...
China, Macao SAR - Chine, Macao RAS										
1 VII 2010	ESDJ	537 000	...	...	257 200[91]	...	...	279 700[91]	...	...
1 VII 2011	ESDJ	549 600	...	...	263 500	...	...	286 100	...	...
12 VIII 2011	CDFC	625 674	...	...	305 398	...	...	320 276	...	...
1 VII 2012	ESDJ	567 900	...	...	274 300	...	...	293 600	...	...
1 VII 2013	ESDJ	591 900	...	...	285 700	...	...	306 200	...	...
1 VII 2014	ESDJ	621 700	...	...	305 500	...	...	316 200	...	...
1 VII 2015	ESDJ	642 900	...	...	317 500	...	...	325 400	...	...
1 VII 2016	ESDJ	652 500	...	...	319 900	...	...	332 600	...	...
7 VIII 2016[98]	SSDJ	650 834	...	...	314 018	...	...	336 816	...	...
1 VII 2017	ESDJ	648 400	...	...	305 900	...	...	342 500	...	...
1 VII 2018	ESDJ	658 900	...	...	309 300	...	...	349 600	...	...
1 VII 2019	ESDJ	672 000	...	...	314 500	...	...	357 500	...	...
Cyprus - Chypre[99]										
1 VII 2010[26]	ESDJ	829 446	...	...	404 182	...	...	425 264	...	...
1 VII 2011[26]	ESDJ	850 881	...	...	413 876	...	...	437 006	...	...

6. Total and urban population by sex: 2010 - 2019
Population totale et population urbaine selon le sexe : 2010 - 2019 (continued - suite)

Continent, country or area, and date / Continent, pays ou zone et date	Code[a]	Both sexes - Les deux sexes: Total	Both sexes: Urban - Urbaine: Number Nombre	Both sexes: Urban - Urbaine: Percent P.100	Male - Masculin: Total	Male: Urban - Urbaine: Number Nombre	Male: Urban - Urbaine: Percent P.100	Female - Féminin: Total	Female: Urban - Urbaine: Number Nombre	Female: Urban - Urbaine: Percent P.100
ASIA - ASIE										
Cyprus - Chypre[99]										
1 X 2011	CDJC	840 407	566 191	67.4	408 780	273 065	66.8	431 627	293 126	67.9
1 VII 2012[26]	ESDJ	863 945	...	...	420 015	...	...	443 930	...	...
1 VII 2013[26]	ESDJ	861 930	...	...	419 183	...	...	442 747	...	...
1 VII 2014[26]	ESDJ	852 504	...	...	414 682	...	...	437 823	...	...
1 VII 2015[26]	ESDJ	847 700	...	...	412 300	...	...	435 400	...	...
1 VII 2016[26]	ESDJ	851 600	...	...	414 700	...	...	436 900	...	...
1 VII 2017[26]	ESDJ	859 519	...	...	419 086	...	...	440 434	...	...
1 VII 2018[26]	ESDJ	870 068	...	...	424 670	...	...	445 398	...	...
1 I 2019	ESDJ	875 899	...	...	427 831	...	...	448 068	...	...
Georgia - Géorgie										
1 VII 2010	ESDF	4 452 800	2 360 900	53.0	2 118 100	...	...	2 334 700	...	...
1 VII 2011	ESDF	4 483 400	2 381 500	53.1	2 135 600	...	...	2 347 800	...	...
1 VII 2012	ESDF	4 490 700	...	...	2 141 300	...	...	2 349 400	...	...
1 VII 2013	ESDF	4 487 150	...	...	2 140 100	...	...	2 347 050	...	...
5 XI 2014	CDJC	3 713 804	2 122 623	57.2	1 772 864	980 985	55.3	1 940 940	1 141 638	58.8
1 VII 2015[7]	ESDJ	3 717 100	2 125 700	57.2	1 776 300	...	...	1 940 800	...	...
1 VII 2016[7]	ESDJ	3 719 300	2 128 500	57.2	1 780 500	...	...	1 938 800	...	...
1 VII 2017[100]	ESDJ	3 723 917	...	...	1 786 530	...	...	1 937 387	...	...
1 VII 2018[100]	ESDJ	3 726 549	...	...	1 791 229	...	...	1 935 320	...	...
1 I 2019[7]	ESDJ	3 723 464	...	...	1 790 899	...	...	1 932 565	...	...
India - Inde[101]										
1 III 2010[59]	ESDF	1 176 742 000	...	...	609 107 000	...	...	567 634 000	...	...
9 II 2011	CDFC	1 210 854 977	377 106 125	31.1	623 270 258	195 489 200	31.4	587 584 719	181 616 925	30.9
1 III 2011[59]	ESDF	1 192 506 000	...	...	617 316 000	...	...	575 191 000	...	...
1 III 2012[59]	ESDF	1 208 116 000	...	...	625 446 000	...	...	582 670 000	...	...
1 III 2013[59]	ESDF	1 223 581 000	...	...	633 505 000	...	...	590 076 000	...	...
1 III 2014[59]	ESDF	1 238 887 000	...	...	641 484 000	...	...	597 403 000	...	...
1 III 2015[59]	ESDF	1 254 019 000	...	...	649 374 000	...	...	604 644 000	...	...
1 III 2016[59]	ESDF	1 268 961 000	...	...	657 168 000	...	...	611 793 000	...	...
1 III 2017[59]	ESDF	1 283 600 000	...	...	664 802 000	...	...	618 799 000	...	...
1 III 2018[59]	ESDF	1 298 041 000	...	...	672 334 000	...	...	625 707 000	...	...
1 III 2019[59]	ESDF	1 312 240 000	...	...	679 741 000	...	...	632 500 000	...	...
Indonesia - Indonésie										
1 V 2010	CDJC	237 641 326	118 320 256	49.8	119 630 913	59 559 622	49.8	118 010 413	58 760 634	49.8
1 VII 2010[102]	ESDJ	238 518 787	118 803 981	49.8	119 852 718	59 698 817	49.8	118 666 069	59 105 164	49.8
1 VII 2011[102]	ESDJ	241 990 736	122 164 186	50.5	121 602 475	61 382 741	50.5	120 388 261	60 781 445	50.5
1 VII 2012[102]	ESDJ	245 425 244	125 558 071	51.2	123 331 006	63 081 616	51.1	122 094 238	62 476 455	51.2
1 VII 2013[102]	ESDJ	248 818 090	128 964 283	51.8	125 036 002	64 785 519	51.8	123 782 088	64 178 764	51.8
1 VII 2014[102]	ESDJ	252 164 786	132 387 038	52.5	126 715 188	66 493 813	52.5	125 449 598	65 893 225	52.5
1 VII 2015[103]	ESDJ	255 587 921	135 901 402	53.2	128 483 450	68 279 703	53.1	127 104 471	67 621 699	53.2
1 VII 2016[103]	ESDJ	258 496 505	139 103 578	53.8	129 910 159	69 868 278	53.8	128 586 346	69 235 300	53.8
1 VII 2017[103]	ESDJ	261 355 475	142 318 766	54.5	131 310 606	71 462 134	54.4	130 044 869	70 856 632	54.5
1 VII 2018[103]	ESDJ	264 161 642	145 541 658	55.1	132 682 955	73 058 747	55.1	131 478 687	72 482 911	55.1
1 VII 2019[103]	ESDJ	266 911 905	148 771 903	55.7	134 025 583	74 658 523	55.7	132 886 322	74 113 380	55.8
Iran (Islamic Republic of) - Iran (République islamique d')										
1 VII 2010[104]	ESDJ	74 339 576	51 242 546	68.9	37 767 220	26 114 342	69.1	36 572 356	25 128 204	68.7
24 X 2011	CDJC	75 149 669	53 646 661	71.4	37 905 669	27 023 638	71.3	37 244 000	26 623 023	71.5
1 VII 2012[104]	ESDJ	76 037 535	54 611 776[105]	71.8	38 336 983	27 547 622[105]	71.9	37 700 552	27 064 154[105]	71.8
1 VII 2013[104]	ESDJ	76 942 276	55 506 192[105]	72.1	38 777 566	27 988 342[105]	72.2	38 164 710	27 517 850[105]	72.1
1 VII 2014[104]	ESDJ	77 856 411	56 412 837	72.5	39 224 036	28 435 933	72.5	38 632 375	27 976 904	72.4
1 VII 2015[104]	ESDJ	78 773 093	57 326 841	72.8	39 672 171	28 887 379	72.8	39 100 922	28 439 462	72.7
1 VII 2016[104]	ESDJ	80 038 166	59 226 231	74.0	40 551 419	29 880 878	73.7	39 486 747	29 345 353	74.3
24 IX 2016	CDJC	79 926 270	59 146 847[106]	74.0	40 498 442	29 841 414[106]	73.7	39 427 828	29 305 433[106]	74.3
1 VII 2017[104]	ESDJ	81 070 480	60 281 499	74.4	41 048 740	30 517 645	74.3	40 021 740	29 763 854	74.4
1 VII 2018[104]	ESDJ	82 083 918	61 329 440	74.7	41 538 139	31 030 645	74.7	40 545 779	30 298 795	74.7
1 VII 2019[104]	ESDJ	83 075 062	62 367 382	75.1	42 017 710	31 539 435	75.1	41 057 352	30 827 947	75.1
Iraq										
1 VII 2010	ESDF	32 210 813	...	...	16 418 691	...	...	15 792 122	...	...
1 VII 2011	ESDF	33 051 526	...	...	16 839 048	...	...	16 212 479	...	...
1 VII 2012	ESDF	33 913 305	23 475 543	69.2	17 270 036	11 954 703	69.2	16 643 269	11 520 840	69.2
1 VII 2013	ESDF	34 794 194	24 162 634	69.4	17 710 750	12 299 131	69.4	17 083 444	11 863 502	69.4

6. Total and urban population by sex: 2010 - 2019
Population totale et population urbaine selon le sexe : 2010 - 2019 (continued - suite)

Continent, country or area, and date Continent, pays ou zone et date	Code[a]	Both sexes - Les deux sexes			Male - Masculin			Female - Féminin		
		Total	Urban - Urbaine		Total	Urban - Urbaine		Total	Urban - Urbaine	
			Number Nombre	Percent P.100		Number Nombre	Percent P.100		Number Nombre	Percent P.100
ASIA - ASIE										
Iraq										
1 VII 2014	ESDF	*35 736 260*	*24 896 261*	*69.7*	*18 182 503*	*12 667 144*	*69.7*	*17 553 757*	*12 229 117*	*69.7*
1 VII 2015	ESDF	*36 658 503*	*25 631 821*	*69.9*	*18 520 532*	*12 935 587*	*69.8*	*18 137 971*	*12 696 234*	*70.0*
1 VII 2019	ESDF	*38 836 326*	*27 134 294*	*69.9*	*19 621 019*	*13 693 935*	*69.8*	*19 215 306*	*13 440 360*	*69.9*
Israel - Israël[107]										
1 VII 2010	ESDJ	7 623 561	6 987 615[91]	91.7	3 771 020	3 446 730[91]	91.4	3 852 541	3 540 885[91]	91.9
1 VII 2011	ESDJ	7 765 832	7 111 015[91]	91.6	3 843 068	3 509 308[91]	91.3	3 922 764	3 601 706[91]	91.8
1 VII 2012	ESDJ	7 910 525	7 235 231[91]	91.5	3 916 125	3 572 531[91]	91.2	3 994 400	3 662 700[91]	91.7
1 VII 2013	ESDJ	8 059 456	7 369 053[91]	91.4	3 991 347	3 640 471[91]	91.2	4 068 109	3 728 581[91]	91.7
1 VII 2014	ESDJ	8 215 668	7 502 325[91]	91.3	4 070 269	3 707 183[91]	91.1	4 145 398	3 795 142[91]	91.6
1 VII 2015	ESDJ	8 380 149	7 643 990[91]	91.2	4 153 233	3 778 276[91]	91.0	4 226 916	3 865 714[91]	91.5
1 VII 2016	ESDJ	8 546 009	7 795 761[91]	91.2	4 237 229	3 855 306[91]	91.0	4 308 780	3 940 455[91]	91.5
1 VII 2017	ESDJ	8 713 268	7 950 920[91]	91.3	4 321 810	3 933 949[91]	91.0	4 391 458	4 016 970[91]	91.5
1 VII 2018	ESDJ	8 882 764	8 114 294[91]	91.3	4 407 285	4 016 793[91]	91.1	4 475 480	4 097 502[91]	91.6
Japan - Japon[108]										
1 VII 2010	ESDJ	128 070 000	...	...	62 330 000	...	...	65 740 000	...	...
1 X 2010	CDJC	128 057 352	116 156 631	90.7	62 327 737	56 569 051	90.8	65 729 615	59 587 580	90.7
1 VII 2011[9]	ESDJ	127 833 000	...	...	62 202 000	...	...	65 631 000	...	...
1 VII 2012[9]	ESDJ	127 629 000	...	...	62 085 000	...	...	65 544 000	...	...
1 VII 2013[9]	ESDJ	127 445 000	...	...	61 987 000	...	...	65 458 000	...	...
1 VII 2014[9]	ESDJ	127 276 000	...	...	61 906 000	...	...	65 370 000	...	...
1 VII 2015[109]	ESDJ	127 141 000	...	...	61 848 000	...	...	65 294 000	...	...
1 X 2015	CDJC	127 094 745	116 137 232	91.4	61 841 738	56 532 149	91.4	65 253 007	59 605 083	91.3
1 VII 2016[109]	ESDJ	126 995 000	...	...	61 781 000	...	...	65 213 000	...	...
1 VII 2017[9]	ESDJ	126 786 000	...	...	61 681 000	...	...	65 105 000	...	...
1 VII 2018[109]	ESDJ	126 529 000	...	...	61 558 000	...	...	64 972 000	...	...
1 VII 2019[109]	ESDJ	126 265 000	...	...	61 441 000	...	...	64 823 000	...	...
Jordan - Jordanie[110]										
31 XII 2010	ESDF	*6 699 000*	*6 051 000*	*90.3*	*3 448 000*	...	...	*3 250 000*	...	...
31 XII 2011	ESDF	*6 993 000*	*6 318 000*	*90.3*	*3 704 852*	...	...	*3 288 148*	...	...
31 XII 2012	ESDF	*7 427 000*	*6 710 000*	*90.3*	*3 934 783*	...	...	*3 492 217*	...	...
31 XII 2013	ESDF	*8 114 000*	*7 331 000*	*90.4*	*4 298 752*	...	...	*3 815 248*	...	...
31 XII 2014	ESDF	*8 804 000*	*7 954 000*	*90.3*	*4 664 310*	...	...	*4 139 690*	...	...
30 XI 2015	CDFC	9 531 712	8 611 323	90.3	5 046 824	4 561 944	90.4	4 484 888	4 049 379	90.3
31 XII 2015	ESDF	*9 559 000*	*8 636 000*	*90.3*	*5 061 000*	...	...	*4 498 000*	...	...
31 XII 2016	ESDF	*9 798 000*	*8 852 000*	*90.3*	*5 188 000*	...	...	*4 610 000*	...	...
31 XII 2017	ESDF	*10 053 000*	*9 082 000*	*90.3*	*5 323 000*	...	...	*4 730 000*	...	...
31 XII 2018	ESDF	*10 309 000*	*9 313 600*	*90.3*	*5 458 000*	...	...	*4 851 000*	...	...
Kazakhstan[111]										
1 VII 2010[112]	ESDF	16 321 872	8 896 771	54.5	7 866 461	4 165 677	53.0	8 455 411	4 731 094	56.0
1 VII 2011[112]	ESDF	16 557 201	9 050 732	54.7	7 983 365	4 237 915	53.1	8 573 836	4 812 817	56.1
1 VII 2012[112]	ESDF	16 792 089	9 202 707	54.8	8 100 335	4 309 949	53.2	8 691 754	4 892 758	56.3
1 VII 2013[112]	ESDF	17 035 550	9 355 723	54.9	8 221 757	4 383 901	53.3	8 813 793	4 971 822	56.4
1 VII 2014[112]	ESDF	17 288 285	9 635 300	55.7	8 348 857	4 523 126	54.2	8 939 428	5 112 174	57.2
1 VII 2015[112]	ESDF	17 542 806	9 936 301	56.6	8 477 451	4 672 945	55.1	9 065 355	5 263 356	58.1
1 VII 2016[112]	ESDF	17 794 055	10 142 840	57.0	8 605 139	4 774 020	55.5	9 188 916	5 368 820	58.4
1 VII 2017[112]	ESDF	18 037 776	10 336 836	57.3	8 729 888	4 868 292	55.8	9 307 888	5 468 544	58.8
1 VII 2018	ESDF	18 276 452	10 604 004	58.0	8 852 247	4 998 115	56.5	9 424 205	5 605 890	59.5
1 VII 2019	ESDF	18 513 673	10 818 430	58.4	8 973 665	5 103 920	56.9	9 540 008	5 714 510	59.9
Kuwait - Koweït										
1 VII 2010	ESDF	*2 933 268*	...	...	*1 674 156*	...	...	*1 259 112*	...	...
21 IV 2011	CDFC	3 065 850	3 065 850	100.0	1 738 372	1 738 372	100.0	1 327 478	1 327 478	100.0
1 VII 2011	ESDF	*3 106 676*	...	...	*1 767 685*	...	...	*1 338 991*	...	...
1 VII 2012	ESDF	*3 246 622*	...	...	*1 856 265*	...	...	*1 390 357*	...	...
1 VII 2013	ESDF	*3 427 595*	...	...	*1 968 382*	...	...	*1 459 213*	...	...
1 VII 2014	ESDF	*3 767 415*	...	...	*2 161 594*	...	...	*1 605 821*	...	...
1 I 2015	ESDF	*3 743 660*	...	...	*2 185 298*	...	...	*1 558 362*	...	...
1 VII 2016	ESDF	*4 079 305*	...	...	*2 505 012*	...	...	*1 574 293*	...	...
1 VII 2017	ESDF	*4 022 255*	...	...	*2 428 774*	...	...	*1 593 481*	...	...
1 VII 2018	ESDF	*4 124 606*	...	...	*2 548 919*	...	...	*1 575 687*	...	...
1 I 2019	ESDF	*4 420 110*	...	...	*2 736 531*	...	...	*1 683 579*	...	...
Kyrgyzstan - Kirghizstan										
1 VII 2010[26]	ESDJ	5 447 960	1 854 245	34.0	2 689 231	876 120	32.6	2 758 729	978 125	35.5
1 VII 2011[26]	ESDJ	5 514 754	1 873 047	34.0	2 722 714	885 117	32.5	2 792 040	987 930	35.4

6. Total and urban population by sex: 2010 - 2019
Population totale et population urbaine selon le sexe : 2010 - 2019 (continued - suite)

Continent, country or area, and date / Continent, pays ou zone et date	Code[a]	Both sexes - Les deux sexes: Total	Both sexes - Les deux sexes: Urban - Urbaine: Number Nombre	Both sexes - Les deux sexes: Urban - Urbaine: Percent P.100	Male - Masculin: Total	Male - Masculin: Urban - Urbaine: Number Nombre	Male - Masculin: Urban - Urbaine: Percent P.100	Female - Féminin: Total	Female - Féminin: Urban - Urbaine: Number Nombre	Female - Féminin: Urban - Urbaine: Percent P.100
ASIA - ASIE										
Kyrgyzstan - Kirghizstan										
1 VII 2012[26]	ESDJ	5 607 511	1 878 643	33.5	2 770 269	887 727	32.0	2 837 242	990 916	34.9
1 VII 2013[26]	ESDJ	5 719 852	1 921 936	33.6	2 827 672	909 216	32.2	2 892 180	1 012 720	35.0
1 VII 2014[26]	ESDJ	5 835 816	1 965 159	33.7	2 886 758	930 751	32.2	2 949 058	1 034 408	35.1
1 VII 2015[26]	ESDJ	5 957 271	2 008 148	33.7	2 948 932	952 329	32.3	3 008 339	1 055 819	35.1
1 VII 2016[26]	ESDJ	6 079 840	2 051 748	33.7	3 011 702	973 955	32.3	3 068 138	1 077 793	35.1
1 VII 2017[26]	ESDJ	6 198 465	2 097 487	33.8	3 072 164	996 210	32.4	3 126 301	1 101 277	35.2
1 VII 2018[26]	ESDJ	6 323 115	2 147 343	34.0	3 135 725	1 020 851	32.6	3 187 390	1 126 492	35.3
1 I 2019	ESDJ	6 389 500	...	...	3 169 634	...	...	3 219 866	...	...
Lao People's Democratic Republic - République démocratique populaire lao										
1 VII 2010[9]	ESDJ	*6 230 200*	...	...	*3 106 600*	...	...	*3 123 700*	...	...
1 VII 2011[9]	ESDJ	*6 348 800*	...	...	*3 166 300*	...	...	*3 182 500*	...	...
1 VII 2012[9]	ESDJ	*6 465 800*	...	...	*3 225 200*	...	...	*3 240 600*	...	...
1 VII 2013[9]	ESDJ	*6 580 800*	...	...	*3 283 200*	...	...	*3 297 600*	...	...
1 VII 2014[9]	ESDJ	*6 693 300*	...	...	*3 339 800*	...	...	*3 353 400*	...	...
1 III 2015	CDJC	6 492 228	2 137 831	32.9	3 254 770	1 076 928	33.1	3 237 458	1 060 903	32.8
1 VII 2015[9]	ESDJ	*6 671 680*	...	...	*3 342 462*	...	...	*3 329 218*	...	...
1 VII 2016[9]	ESDJ	*6 787 007*	...	...	*3 400 453*	...	...	*3 386 554*	...	...
1 VII 2017[9]	ESDJ	*6 900 846*	...	...	*3 457 542*	...	...	*3 443 304*	...	...
1 VII 2018[9]	ESDJ	*7 012 994*	...	...	*3 513 775*	...	...	*3 499 219*	...	...
1 VII 2019[9]	ESDJ	*7 123 205*	...	...	*3 569 021*	...	...	*3 554 184*	...	...
Lebanon - Liban[113]										
1 X 2011	SSDF	3 779 859	...	...	1 840 940	...	...	1 938 919	...	...
Malaysia - Malaisie										
1 VII 2010[114]	ESDJ	28 588 637	20 290 864	71.0	14 730 542	10 404 757	70.6	13 858 095	9 886 107	71.3
6 VII 2010[82]	CDJC	28 334 135	20 124 970	71.0	14 562 638	10 298 698	70.7	13 771 497	9 826 272	71.4
1 VII 2011[114]	ESDJ	29 062 036	20 826 580	71.7	14 980 010	10 684 359	71.3	14 082 026	10 142 221	72.0
1 VII 2012[114]	ESDJ	29 510 022	21 355 255	72.4	15 215 309	10 965 006	72.1	14 294 713	10 390 249	72.7
1 VII 2013[114]	ESDJ	30 213 664	22 041 500	73.0	15 604 813	11 330 984	72.6	14 608 851	10 710 516	73.3
1 VII 2014[114]	ESDJ	30 708 527	22 597 286	73.6	15 867 796	11 624 061	73.3	14 840 731	10 973 225	73.9
1 VII 2015[114]	ESDJ	31 186 135	23 173 701	74.3	16 112 125	11 925 089	74.0	15 074 010	11 248 612	74.6
1 VII 2016[114]	ESDJ	31 633 518	23 677 030	74.8	16 346 281	12 186 777	74.6	15 287 237	11 490 253	75.2
1 VII 2017[114]	ESDJ	32 022 575	24 080 382	75.2	16 542 746	12 392 317	74.9	15 479 829	11 688 065	75.5
1 VII 2018[114]	ESDJ	32 382 275	24 495 697	75.6	16 721 439	12 606 055	75.4	15 660 836	11 889 642	75.9
1 VII 2019[114]	ESDJ	32 581 387	24 817 031	76.2	16 830 551	12 780 768	75.9	15 750 836	12 036 263	76.4
Maldives										
1 VII 2010	ESDF	319 738	...	...	161 708	...	...	158 030	...	...
1 VII 2011	ESDF	325 135	...	...	164 349	...	...	160 786	...	...
1 VII 2012	ESDF	330 655	...	...	167 058	...	...	163 597	...	...
1 VII 2013	ESDF	336 224	...	...	169 800	...	...	166 424	...	...
1 VII 2014[115]	ESDF	437 535	171 165	39.1	261 709	101 744	38.9	175 826	69 422	39.5
20 IX 2014[116]	CDFC	402 071	153 904	38.3	227 749	85 438	37.5	174 322	68 466	39.3
1 VII 2015[115]	ESDF	454 434	180 019	39.6	274 607	107 894	39.3	179 827	72 125	40.1
1 VII 2016[115]	ESDF	472 426	189 458	40.1	288 502	114 514	39.7	183 924	74 944	40.7
1 VII 2017[115]	ESDF	491 589	199 523	40.6	303 478	121 647	40.1	188 111	77 876	41.4
1 VII 2018[115]	ESDF	512 038	210 248	41.1	319 663	129 334	40.5	192 375	80 914	42.1
1 VII 2019[115]	ESDF	533 941	221 678	41.5	337 167	137 614	40.8	196 774	84 064	42.7
Mongolia - Mongolie										
1 VII 2010	ESDF	2 738 622	1 799 648	65.7	1 335 111	863 536	64.7	1 403 511	936 112	66.7
11 XI 2010	CDFC	2 647 199	1 797 338	67.9	1 314 246	869 827	66.2	1 332 953	927 511	69.6
1 VII 2011	ESDF	2 786 322	1 856 224	66.6	1 354 472	886 139	65.4	1 431 850	970 085	67.8
1 VII 2012	ESDF	2 839 711	1 911 462	67.3	1 379 091	910 746	66.0	1 460 620	1 000 716	68.5
1 VII 2013	ESDF	2 899 011	1 961 169	67.6	1 409 648	936 682	66.4	1 489 363	1 024 487	68.8
1 VII 2014	ESDF	2 963 113	1 993 017	67.3	1 446 149	955 833	66.1	1 516 964	1 037 184	68.4
1 VII 2015	ESDF	3 026 864	2 043 251	67.5	1 485 034	985 919	66.4	1 541 830	1 057 332	68.6
1 VII 2016	ESDF	3 088 856	2 122 131	68.7	1 518 797	1 027 311	67.6	1 570 059	1 094 820	69.7
1 VII 2017	ESDF	3 148 917	2 139 269	67.9	1 548 177	1 034 384	66.8	1 600 740	1 104 885	69.0
1 VII 2018	ESDF	3 208 189	2 172 343	67.7	1 577 109	1 049 578	66.6	1 631 080	1 122 765	68.8
1 VII 2019	ESDF	3 267 673	2 228 476	68.2	1 605 711	1 076 449	67.0	1 661 962	1 152 027	69.3
Myanmar										
1 X 2010	ESDF	*59 780 329*	*18 342 824*[117]	*30.7*	*29 723 184*	*8 992 226*[117]	*30.3*	*30 057 145*	*9 350 598*[117]	*31.1*
1 X 2011[7]	ESDF	*50 149 496*	*14 650 579*[117]	*29.2*	*24 185 705*	*7 009 280*[117]	*29.0*	*25 963 791*	*7 641 299*[117]	*29.4*

6. Total and urban population by sex: 2010 - 2019
Population totale et population urbaine selon le sexe : 2010 - 2019 (continued - suite)

Continent, country or area, and date / Continent, pays ou zone et date	Code[a]	Both sexes - Les deux sexes: Total	Both sexes: Urban - Urbaine: Number Nombre	Both sexes: Urban - Urbaine: Percent P.100	Male - Masculin: Total	Male: Urban - Urbaine: Number Nombre	Male: Urban - Urbaine: Percent P.100	Female - Féminin: Total	Female: Urban - Urbaine: Number Nombre	Female: Urban - Urbaine: Percent P.100
ASIA - ASIE										
Myanmar										
1 X 2012[7]	ESDF	50 666 887	14 824 883[117]	29.3	24 435 871	7 092 798[117]	29.0	26 231 016	7 732 085[117]	29.5
1 X 2013[7]	ESDF	51 184 273	14 999 184[117]	29.3	24 686 034	7 176 313[117]	29.1	26 498 239	7 822 871[117]	29.5
29 III 2014[118]	CDFC	50 279 900	14 877 943	29.6	24 228 714	7 114 224	29.4	26 051 186	7 763 719	29.8
1 X 2014[7]	ESDF	51 991 031	15 173 838[117]	29.2	25 066 439	7 256 002[117]	28.9	26 924 592	7 917 836[117]	29.4
1 X 2015[7]	ESDF	52 450 516	15 363 901[117]	29.3	25 256 187	7 331 696[117]	29.0	27 194 329	8 032 205[117]	29.5
1 X 2016[7]	ESDF	52 916 691	15 560 352[117]	29.4	25 450 309	7 411 120[117]	29.1	27 466 382	8 149 232[117]	29.7
1 X 2017[7]	ESDF	53 387 948	15 762 776[117]	29.5	25 647 847	7 494 003[117]	29.2	27 740 101	8 268 773[117]	29.8
1 X 2018[7]	ESDF	53 862 731	15 970 715[117]	29.7	25 847 922	7 580 078[117]	29.3	28 014 809	8 390 637[117]	30.0
1 X 2019[7]	ESDF	54 339 766	16 183 650[117]	29.8	26 049 847	7 669 067[117]	29.4	28 289 919	8 514 583[117]	30.1
Nepal - Népal										
1 VII 2010	ESDJ	28 043 744	...	...	14 066 638	...	...	13 977 106	...	...
22 VI 2011	CDJC	26 494 504	4 523 820	17.1	12 849 041	2 306 049	17.9	13 645 463	2 217 771	16.3
1 VII 2011	ESDJ	28 584 975	...	...	14 343 343	...	...	14 241 632	...	...
1 VII 2012[5]	ESDJ	26 873 066	...	...	13 030 795	...	...	13 842 271	...	...
1 VII 2013[5]	ESDJ	27 257 347	...	...	13 215 791	...	...	14 041 556	...	...
1 VII 2014[5]	ESDJ	27 646 053	...	...	13 403 432	...	...	14 242 621	...	...
1 VII 2015[5]	ESDJ	28 037 904	...	...	13 593 069	...	...	14 444 835	...	...
1 VII 2016[5]	ESDJ	28 431 494	5 552 712	19.5	13 784 009	2 825 721	20.5	14 647 486	2 726 992	18.6
1 VII 2017[5]	ESDJ	28 825 709	...	...	13 975 678	...	...	14 850 032	...	...
1 VII 2018[5]	ESDJ	29 218 867	...	...	14 167 241	...	...	15 051 626	...	...
1 VII 2019[5]	ESDJ	29 609 623	...	...	14 358 034	...	...	15 251 589	...	...
Oman										
12 XII 2010	CDFC	2 773 479	2 091 320	75.4	1 612 408	1 227 680	76.1	1 161 071	863 640	74.4
1 VII 2011	ESDF	3 295 298[119]	2 484 794[120]	75.4	2 090 883[119]	1 591 989[120]	76.1	1 204 415[119]	895 881[120]	74.4
1 VII 2012	ESDF	3 623 001[119]	2 731 895[120]	75.4	2 332 687[119]	1 776 097[120]	76.1	1 290 314[119]	959 775[120]	74.4
1 VII 2013	ESDF	3 855 206[119]	2 906 988[120]	75.4	2 502 235[119]	1 905 190[120]	76.1	1 352 971[119]	1 006 381[120]	74.4
1 VII 2014	ESDF	3 992 893[119]	3 010 810[120]	75.4	2 579 811[119]	1 964 256[120]	76.1	1 413 082[119]	1 051 093[120]	74.4
1 VII 2015	ESDF	4 159 102[119]	3 136 138[120]	75.4	2 684 844[119]	2 044 228[120]	76.1	1 474 258[119]	1 096 598[120]	74.4
1 VII 2016	ESDF	4 414 051[119]	3 432 019[121]	77.8	2 886 083[119]	2 296 140[121]	79.6	1 527 968[119]	1 133 279[121]	74.2
1 VII 2017	ESDF	4 559 963[119]	3 542 940[121]	77.7	2 984 404[119]	2 374 363[121]	79.6	1 575 559[119]	1 168 577[121]	74.2
1 VII 2018[119]	ESDF	4 601 706	...	...	2 990 103	...	...	1 611 603	...	...
1 VII 2019[119]	ESDF	4 617 927	...	...	2 945 254	...	...	1 672 673	...	...
Pakistan[122]										
1 VII 2010	ESDF	173 510 000	...	...	89 760 000	...	...	83 750 000	...	...
1 VII 2011	ESDF	177 100 000	...	...	91 590 000	...	...	85 510 000	...	...
15 III 2017*	CDFC	207 774 520	75 584 989	36.4	106 449 322[74]	39 149 151[74]	36.8	101 314 780[74]	36 428 187[74]	36.0
Philippines										
1 V 2010[123]	CDJC	92 335 113	41 855 571	45.3	46 634 257	20 840 798	44.7	45 700 856	21 014 773	46.0
1 VII 2010[14]	ESDJ	93 135 100	...	...	46 980 200	...	...	46 154 900	...	...
1 VII 2011[14]	ESDJ	94 823 800	...	...	47 832 400	...	...	46 991 400	...	...
1 VII 2012[14]	ESDJ	96 510 900	...	...	48 684 200	...	...	47 826 700	...	...
1 VII 2013[14]	ESDJ	98 196 500	...	...	49 535 100	...	...	48 661 400	...	...
1 VII 2014[14]	ESDJ	99 880 300	...	...	50 385 100	...	...	49 495 200	...	...
1 VII 2015[9]	ESDJ	100 833 371	...	...	50 996 187	...	...	49 837 184	...	...
1 VIII 2015[124]	CDJC	100 979 303	51 728 697	51.2	51 069 962	25 884 921	50.7	49 909 341	25 843 776	51.8
1 VII 2016[9]	ESDJ	102 530 196	...	...	51 840 147	...	...	50 690 049	...	...
1 VII 2017[9]	ESDJ	104 169 230	...	...	52 654 442	...	...	51 514 788	...	...
1 VII 2018[9]	ESDJ	105 755 180	...	...	53 441 468	...	...	52 313 712	...	...
1 VII 2019[9]	ESDJ	107 288 150	...	...	54 201 305	...	...	53 086 845	...	...
Qatar										
21 IV 2010	CDFC	1 699 435	...	...	1 284 739	...	...	414 696	...	...
1 VII 2010	ESDF	1 715 098	1 715 098	100.0	1 296 110	1 296 110	100.0	418 988	418 988	100.0
1 VII 2011	ESDF	1 732 717	1 732 717	100.0	1 288 590	1 288 590	100.0	444 127	444 127	100.0
1 VII 2012	ESDF	1 832 903	1 832 903	100.0	1 355 199	1 355 199	100.0	477 704	477 704	100.0
1 VII 2013	ESDF	2 003 700	2 003 700	100.0	1 477 632	1 477 632	100.0	526 068	526 068	100.0
1 VII 2014	ESDF	2 216 180	2 216 180	100.0	1 652 037	1 652 037	100.0	564 143	564 143	100.0
20 IV 2015	CDFC	2 404 776	2 404 776	100.0	1 816 981	1 816 981	100.0	587 795	587 795	100.0
1 VII 2015	ESDF	2 437 790	2 437 790	100.0	1 840 643	1 840 643	100.0	597 147	597 147	100.0
1 VII 2016	ESDF	2 617 634	2 617 634	100.0	1 975 536	1 975 536	100.0	642 098	642 098	100.0
1 VII 2017	ESDF	2 724 606	2 724 606	100.0	2 046 047	2 046 047	100.0	678 559	678 559	100.0
1 VII 2018	ESDF	2 760 170	2 760 170	100.0	2 048 206	2 048 206	100.0	711 964	711 964	100.0
1 VII 2019	ESDF	2 799 202	2 799 202	100.0	2 064 276	2 064 276	100.0	734 926	734 926	100.0

6. Total and urban population by sex: 2010 - 2019
Population totale et population urbaine selon le sexe : 2010 - 2019 (continued - suite)

Continent, country or area, and date Continent, pays ou zone et date	Code[a]	Both sexes - Les deux sexes: Total	Both sexes - Urban - Urbaine: Number Nombre	Both sexes - Urban - Urbaine: Percent P.100	Male - Masculin: Total	Male - Urban - Urbaine: Number Nombre	Male - Urban - Urbaine: Percent P.100	Female - Féminin: Total	Female - Urban - Urbaine: Number Nombre	Female - Urban - Urbaine: Percent P.100
ASIA - ASIE										
Republic of Korea - République de Corée										
1 VII 2010	ESDJ	49 554 112	...	...	24 881 114	...	...	24 672 998	...	...
1 XI 2010[125]	CDJC	48 580 293	39 822 647	82.0	24 167 098	19 798 739	81.9	24 413 195	20 023 908	82.0
1 VII 2011	ESDJ	49 936 638	...	...	25 069 867	...	...	24 866 771	...	...
1 VII 2012	ESDJ	50 199 853	...	...	25 187 380	...	...	25 012 473	...	...
1 VII 2013	ESDJ	50 428 893	...	...	25 285 319	...	...	25 143 574	...	...
1 VII 2014	ESDJ	50 746 659	...	...	25 445 077	...	...	25 301 582	...	...
1 VII 2015	ESDJ	51 014 947	...	...	25 585 894	...	...	25 429 053	...	...
1 XI 2015	CDJC	51 069 375	41 677 695	81.6	25 608 502	20 791 896	81.2	25 460 873	20 885 799	82.0
1 VII 2016	ESDJ	51 217 803	...	...	25 670 949	...	...	25 546 854	...	...
1 VII 2017	ESDJ	51 361 911	...	...	25 736 793	...	...	25 625 118	...	...
1 VII 2018	ESDJ	51 606 633	...	...	25 863 502	...	...	25 743 131	...	...
1 VII 2019[126]	ESDJ	51 337 424	41 685 860	81.2	25 609 342	20 686 743	80.8	25 728 082	20 999 117	81.6
Saudi Arabia - Arabie saoudite										
27 IV 2010	CDFC	27 236 156	...	...	15 531 471	...	...	11 704 685	...	...
1 VII 2010	ESDF	27 410 508	...	...	15 643 804	...	...	11 766 704	...	...
1 VII 2011	ESDF	28 173 195	...	...	16 124 760	...	...	12 048 435	...	...
1 VII 2012	ESDF	28 896 840	...	...	16 566 096	...	...	12 330 744	...	...
1 VII 2013	ESDF	29 613 064	...	...	16 974 234	...	...	12 638 830	...	...
1 VII 2014	ESDF	30 339 795	...	...	17 393 435	...	...	12 946 360	...	...
1 VII 2015	ESDF	31 062 069	...	...	17 818 656	...	...	13 243 413	...	...
1 VII 2016	ESDF	31 787 580	...	...	18 259 719	...	...	13 527 861	...	...
1 VII 2017	ESDF	32 612 846	...	...	18 746 422	...	...	13 866 424	...	...
1 VII 2018	ESDF	33 413 660	...	...	19 240 956	...	...	14 172 704	...	...
1 VII 2019	ESDF	34 218 169	...	...	19 739 056	...	...	14 479 113	...	...
Singapore - Singapour										
30 VI 2010[127]	CDJC	3 771 721	...	...	1 861 133	...	...	1 910 588	...	...
30 VI 2010[128]	ESDJ	5 076 732	...	...	2 641 339	...	...	2 435 393	...	...
30 VI 2011[128]	ESDJ	5 183 688	...	...	2 690 534	...	...	2 493 154	...	...
30 VI 2012[128]	ESDJ	5 312 437	...	...	2 765 614	...	...	2 546 823	...	...
30 VI 2013[128]	ESDJ	5 399 162	...	...	2 824 655	...	...	2 574 507	...	...
30 VI 2014[128]	ESDJ	5 469 724	...	...	2 864 408	...	...	2 605 316	...	...
30 VI 2015[128]	ESDJ	5 535 002	...	...	2 891 101	...	...	2 643 901	...	...
30 VI 2016[128]	ESDJ	5 607 283	...	...	2 920 951	...	...	2 686 332	...	...
30 VI 2017[128]	ESDJ	5 612 253	...	...	2 897 264	...	...	2 714 989	...	...
30 VI 2018[128]	ESDJ	5 638 676	...	...	2 893 284	...	...	2 745 392	...	...
30 VI 2019[128]	ESDJ	5 703 569	...	...	2 926 359	...	...	2 777 210	...	...
Sri Lanka										
1 VII 2010	ESDF	*20 675 000*	...	...	*10 273 000*	...	...	*10 402 000*	...	...
1 VII 2011	ESDF	*20 892 000*	...	...	*10 381 000*	...	...	*10 511 000*	...	...
20 III 2012	CDJC	20 359 439	3 704 470	18.2	9 856 634	1 800 327	18.3	10 502 805	1 904 143	18.1
1 VII 2012	ESDJ	*20 425 000*	...	...	*9 888 000*	...	...	*10 537 000*	...	...
1 VII 2013	ESDJ	*20 585 000*	...	...	*9 966 000*	...	...	*10 619 000*	...	...
1 VII 2014	ESDJ	*20 778 000*	...	...	*10 059 000*	...	...	*10 719 000*	...	...
1 VII 2015	ESDJ	*20 970 000*	...	...	*10 153 000*	...	...	*10 817 000*	...	...
1 VII 2016*	ESDJ	*21 203 000*	...	...	*10 265 460*	...	...	*10 937 540*	...	...
1 VII 2017*	ESDJ	*21 444 350*	...	...	*10 382 372*	...	...	*11 061 978*	...	...
1 VII 2018*	ESDJ	*21 670 000*	...	...	*10 492 000*	...	...	*11 178 000*	...	...
1 VII 2019*	ESDJ	*21 803 000*	...	...	*10 556 000*	...	...	*11 247 000*	...	...
State of Palestine - État de Palestine										
1 VII 2010	ESDF	*4 023 462*	...	...	*2 043 857*	...	...	*1 979 605*	...	...
1 VII 2011	ESDF	*4 124 795*	...	...	*2 095 887*	...	...	*2 028 908*	...	...
1 VII 2012	ESDF	*4 226 410*	...	...	*2 148 060*	...	...	*2 078 350*	...	...
1 VII 2013	ESDF	*4 327 751*	...	...	*2 200 092*	...	...	*2 127 659*	...	...
1 VII 2014	ESDF	*4 429 084*	...	...	*2 252 122*	...	...	*2 176 962*	...	...
1 VII 2015	ESDF	*4 530 416*	...	...	*2 304 151*	...	...	*2 226 265*	...	...
1 VII 2016	ESDF	*4 632 025*	...	...	*2 356 322*	...	...	*2 275 703*	...	...
1 VII 2017	ESDF	*4 733 357*	...	...	*2 408 351*	...	...	*2 325 006*	...	...
1 XII 2017	CDFC	4 705 855	4 018 942[129]	85.4	2 394 359	2 043 943[129]	85.4	2 311 496	1 974 999[129]	85.4
1 VII 2018	ESDF	*4 854 013*	...	...	*2 469 162*	...	...	*2 384 851*	...	...
1 VII 2019	ESDF	*4 976 684*	...	...	*2 530 966*	...	...	*2 445 718*	...	...

6. Total and urban population by sex: 2010 - 2019
Population totale et population urbaine selon le sexe : 2010 - 2019 (continued - suite)

Continent, country or area, and date / Continent, pays ou zone et date	Code[a]	Both sexes - Les deux sexes: Total	Both sexes: Urban - Urbaine: Number Nombre	Both sexes: Urban - Urbaine: Percent P.100	Male - Masculin: Total	Male: Urban - Urbaine: Number Nombre	Male: Urban - Urbaine: Percent P.100	Female - Féminin: Total	Female: Urban - Urbaine: Number Nombre	Female: Urban - Urbaine: Percent P.100
ASIA - ASIE										
Syrian Arab Republic - République arabe syrienne[130]										
1 VII 2010	ESDF	20 619 000	11 033 000	53.5	10 539 000	5 661 000	53.7	10 080 000	5 372 000	53.3
1 VII 2011	ESDF	21 124 000	11 297 000	53.5	10 794 000	5 795 000	53.7	10 330 000	5 502 000	53.3
Tajikistan - Tadjikistan										
1 VII 2010	ESDF	7 519 280	1 996 961	26.6	3 794 467	1 007 796	26.6	3 724 813	989 165	26.6
21 IX 2010	CDFC	7 564 502	2 006 605	26.5	3 817 004	1 012 642	26.5	3 747 498	993 963	26.5
1 VII 2011	ESDF	7 714 198	2 042 660	26.5	3 893 798	1 032 106	26.5	3 820 401	1 010 554	26.5
1 VII 2012	ESDF	7 897 313	2 085 698	26.4	3 987 517	1 054 904	26.5	3 909 796	1 030 794	26.4
1 VII 2013	ESDF	8 074 266	2 138 737	26.5	4 078 857	1 083 119	26.6	3 995 409	1 055 618	26.4
1 VII 2014	ESDF	8 256 572	2 193 224	26.6	4 174 269	1 112 352	26.6	4 082 303	1 080 873	26.5
1 VII 2015	ESDF	8 451 630	2 237 893	26.5	4 276 777	1 136 493	26.6	4 174 854	1 101 401	26.4
1 VII 2016	ESDF	8 646 973	2 280 367	26.4	4 379 342	1 159 476	26.5	4 267 631	1 120 891	26.3
1 VII 2017	ESDF	8 837 002	2 321 759	26.3	4 479 048	1 182 016	26.4	4 357 954	1 139 743	26.2
1 VII 2018*	ESDF	8 931 200	2 343 000	26.2	4 528 600	1 193 600	26.4	4 402 600	1 149 400	26.1
1 VII 2019	ESDF	9 126 560	2 384 777	26.1	4 627 300	1 216 680	26.3	4 499 260	1 168 097	26.0
Thailand - Thaïlande										
1 VII 2010	ESDJ	63 878 267	...	...	31 451 801	...	...	32 426 466	...	...
1 IX 2010	CDJC	65 981 659	29 133 829	44.2	32 355 032	14 120 842	43.6	33 626 627	15 012 987	44.6
1 VII 2011	ESDJ	64 076 033	...	...	31 529 148	...	...	32 546 885	...	...
1 VII 2012	ESDJ	64 266 365	...	...	31 614 938	...	...	32 651 427	...	...
1 VII 2013	ESDJ	64 621 302	...	...	31 773 349	...	...	32 847 953	...	...
1 VII 2014	ESDJ	64 955 313	...	...	31 922 490	...	...	33 032 823	...	...
1 VII 2015	ESDJ	65 027 401	...	...	31 932 092	...	...	33 095 309	...	...
1 VII 2016	ESDJ	65 013 495	...	...	31 894 480	...	...	33 119 015	...	...
1 VII 2017	ESDJ	65 521 660	32 257 097	49.2	31 807 391	15 626 525	49.1	33 714 269	16 630 572	49.3
1 VII 2018[1]	ESDJ	66 199 900	36 134 800	54.6	32 013 600	17 452 600	54.5	34 186 300	18 682 200	54.6
1 VII 2019[1]	ESDJ	66 374 300	37 120 900	55.9	32 073 900	17 917 800	55.9	34 300 400	19 203 100	56.0
Timor-Leste										
11 VII 2010	CDFC	1 066 409	316 086	29.6	544 198	166 163	30.5	522 211	149 923	28.7
1 VII 2013[1]	ESDF	1 180 069	...	...	602 526	...	...	577 544	...	...
1 VII 2014[1]	ESDF	1 212 107	...	...	618 789	...	...	593 318	...	...
1 VII 2015[1]	ESDF	1 200 379	...	...	613 386	...	...	586 993	...	...
11 VII 2015	CDFC	1 183 643	349 208	29.5	601 112	179 565	29.9	582 531	169 643	29.1
1 VII 2016[1]	ESDF	1 221 133	...	...	623 430	...	...	597 703	...	...
1 VII 2017[1]	ESDF	1 241 506	...	...	633 197	...	...	608 309	...	...
1 VII 2018[1]	ESDF	1 261 407	...	...	642 639	...	...	618 768	...	...
1 VII 2019[1]	ESDF	1 280 743	...	...	651 710	...	...	629 033	...	...
Turkey - Turquie										
31 XII 2010[131]	ESDJ	73 722 988	52 340 830	71.0	37 043 182	26 348 394	71.1	36 679 806	25 992 436	70.9
3 X 2011[132]	CDJC	74 526 000	53 321 000	71.5	37 431 000	26 777 000	71.5	37 095 000	26 544 000	71.6
31 XII 2011[131]	ESDJ	74 724 269	53 630 845	71.8	37 532 954	26 947 983	71.8	37 191 315	26 682 862	71.7
31 XII 2012[131]	ESDJ	75 627 384	54 705 188	72.3	37 956 168	27 442 260	72.3	37 671 216	27 262 928	72.4
31 XII 2013[131]	ESDJ	76 667 864	66 488 105[133]	86.7	38 473 360	33 344 846[133]	86.7	38 194 504	33 143 259[133]	86.8
31 XII 2014[131]	ESDJ	77 695 904	67 720 318	87.2	38 984 302	33 954 681	87.1	38 711 602	33 765 637	87.2
31 XII 2015[131]	ESDJ	78 741 053	69 004 143	87.6	39 511 191	34 598 184	87.6	39 229 862	34 405 959	87.7
31 XII 2016[131]	ESDJ	79 814 871	70 165 359	87.9	40 043 650	35 162 317	87.8	39 771 221	35 003 042	88.0
31 XII 2017[131]	ESDJ	80 810 525	71 253 963	88.2	40 535 135	35 693 468	88.1	40 275 390	35 560 495	88.3
31 XII 2018[131]	ESDJ	82 003 882	72 073 198	87.9	41 139 980	36 085 213	87.7	40 863 902	35 987 985	88.1
United Arab Emirates - Émirats arabes unis[134]										
1 VII 2010	ESDF	8 264 070	...	...	6 161 820	...	...	2 102 250	...	...
31 XII 2011	ESDF	8 394 019	...	...	6 244 663	...	...	2 149 356	...	...
31 XII 2012	ESDF	8 526 425	...	...	6 328 827	...	...	2 197 598	...	...
31 XII 2013	ESDF	8 661 345	...	...	6 414 337	...	...	2 247 008	...	...
31 XII 2014	ESDF	8 798 841	...	...	6 501 224	...	...	2 297 617	...	...
31 XII 2015	ESDF	8 938 974	...	...	6 589 518	...	...	2 349 456	...	...
31 XII 2016	ESDF	9 121 167	...	...	6 298 296	...	...	2 822 871	...	...
31 XII 2017	ESDF	9 304 277	...	...	6 415 942	...	...	2 888 335	...	...
31 XII 2018	ESDF	9 366 829	...	...	6 297 663	...	...	3 069 166	...	...
Uzbekistan - Ouzbékistan[111]										
1 VII 2010	ESDJ	28 562 405	14 661 700	51.3	14 291 711	7 295 300	51.0	14 270 694	7 366 400	51.6
1 VII 2011	ESDJ	29 339 368	15 062 700	51.3	14 680 424	7 496 500	51.1	14 658 944	7 566 200	51.6

6. Total and urban population by sex: 2010 - 2019
Population totale et population urbaine selon le sexe : 2010 - 2019 (continued - suite)

Continent, country or area, and date Continent, pays ou zone et date	Code[a]	Both sexes - Les deux sexes Total	Urban - Urbaine Number Nombre	 Percent P.100	Male - Masculin Total	Urban - Urbaine Number Nombre	 Percent P.100	Female - Féminin Total	Urban - Urbaine Number Nombre	 Percent P.100
ASIA - ASIE										
Uzbekistan - Ouzbékistan[111]										
1 VII 2012	ESDJ	29 774 448	15 285 000	51.3	14 905 603	7 613 400	51.1	14 868 845	7 671 600	51.6
1 VII 2013	ESDJ	30 243 172	15 462 637	51.1	15 148 116	7 707 450	50.9	15 095 056	7 755 187	51.4
1 VII 2014	ESDJ	30 757 669	15 651 614	50.9	15 414 846	7 809 449	50.7	15 342 823	7 842 165	51.1
1 VII 2015	ESDJ	31 298 929	15 855 953	50.7	15 695 568	7 919 014	50.5	15 603 361	7 936 939	50.9
1 VII 2016	ESDJ	31 847 898	16 133 260	50.7	15 979 935	8 063 139	50.5	15 867 963	8 070 121	50.9
1 VII 2017	ESDJ	32 388 563	16 414 114	50.7	16 259 425	8 207 397	50.5	16 129 138	8 206 717	50.9
1 VII 2018	ESDJ	32 956 099	16 669 689	50.6	16 554 233	8 339 341	50.4	16 401 866	8 330 348	50.8
1 I 2019	ESDJ	33 255 538	16 806 721	50.5	16 710 577	8 410 413	50.3	16 544 961	8 396 308	50.7
Viet Nam										
1 VII 2010[135]	ESDJ	*86 947 439*	*26 515 900*	*30.5*	*42 993 487*	...	...	*43 953 952*	...	...
1 VII 2011[135]	ESDJ	*87 860 387*	*27 719 300*	*31.5*	*43 446 781*	...	...	*44 413 606*	...	...
1 VII 2012[135]	ESDJ	*88 809 279*	*28 269 200*	*31.8*	*43 908 201*	...	...	*44 901 078*	...	...
1 VII 2013[135]	ESDJ	*89 759 538*	*28 874 900*	*32.2*	*44 364 894*	...	...	*45 394 644*	...	...
1 VII 2014[135]	ESDJ	*90 728 941*	*30 035 405*	*33.1*	*44 758 132*	...	...	*45 970 809*	...	...
1 VII 2015[135]	ESDJ	*91 709 825*	*31 067 492*	*33.9*	*45 224 031*	...	...	*46 485 794*	...	...
1 VII 2016[135]	ESDJ	*92 695 121*	*31 985 992*	*34.5*	*45 705 601*	...	...	*46 989 520*	...	...
1 VII 2017*[135]	ESDJ	*93 677 594*	*32 823 139*	*35.0*	*46 266 288*	...	...	*47 411 306*	...	...
1 VII 2018*[135]	ESDJ	*94 665 973*	*33 829 988*	*35.7*	*46 785 200*	...	...	*47 880 773*	...	...
1 IV 2019	CDJC	96 208 984	33 122 548	34.4	47 881 061	16 268 095	34.0	48 327 923	16 854 453	34.9
1 VII 2019*[136]	ESDJ	*96 484 000*	*33 816 600*	*35.0*	*48 017 700*	...	...	*48 466 300*	...	...
Yemen - Yémen[1]										
1 VII 2010	ESDJ	*23 153 982*	*6 673 916*	*28.8*	*11 789 814*	...	...	*11 364 168*	...	...
1 VII 2011	ESDJ	*23 832 569*	*6 875 789*	*28.9*	*12 133 362*	...	...	*11 699 207*	...	...
1 VII 2012	ESDJ	*24 526 703*	*7 075 639*	*28.8*	*12 485 039*	...	...	*12 041 664*	...	...
1 VII 2013	ESDJ	*25 235 079*	*7 280 367*	*28.9*	*12 844 169*	...	...	*12 390 910*	...	...
1 VII 2014	ESDJ	*25 955 920*	*7 488 312*	*28.9*	*13 209 834*	...	...	*12 746 086*	...	...
1 VII 2015	ESDJ	*26 687 013*	*7 699 217*	*28.9*	*13 580 896*	...	...	*13 106 117*	...	...
1 VII 2016	ESDJ	*27 426 016*	*7 912 406*	*28.9*	*13 956 092*	...	...	*13 469 924*	...	...
1 VII 2017	ESDJ	*28 170 408*	*8 127 151*	*28.8*	*14 334 126*	...	...	*13 836 282*	...	...
EUROPE										
Åland Islands - Îles d'Åland[56]										
1 VII 2010	ESDJ	27 871	11 157	40.0	13 880	5 327	38.4	13 991	5 830	41.7
1 VII 2011	ESDJ	28 181	11 227	39.8	14 045	5 364	38.2	14 137	5 863	41.5
1 VII 2012	ESDJ	28 429	11 305	39.8	14 172	5 408	38.2	14 257	5 897	41.4
1 VII 2013	ESDJ	28 585	11 370	39.8	14 255	5 445	38.2	14 330	5 925	41.3
1 VII 2014	ESDJ	28 792	11 437	39.7	14 375	5 490	38.2	14 417	5 947	41.2
1 VII 2015	ESDJ	28 950	11 471	39.6	14 466	5 521	38.2	14 484	5 950	41.1
1 VII 2016	ESDJ	29 099	11 513	39.6	14 526	5 538	38.1	14 573	5 975	41.0
1 VII 2017	ESDJ	29 352	11 621	39.6	14 644	5 583	38.1	14 708	6 038	41.1
1 VII 2018	ESDJ	29 638	11 709	39.5	14 795	5 621	38.0	14 843	6 088	41.0
1 VII 2019	ESDJ	29 837	11 711	39.3	14 875	5 606	37.7	14 962	6 105	40.8
Albania - Albanie										
1 VII 2010	ESDF	2 913 021	1 541 310	52.9	1 457 661	763 780	52.4	1 455 360	777 530	53.4
1 VII 2011	ESDJ	2 904 780	1 564 139	53.8	1 455 074	775 313	53.3	1 449 706	788 826	54.4
1 X 2011	CDJC	2 800 138	1 498 508	53.5	1 403 059	742 671	52.9	1 397 079	755 837	54.1
1 VII 2012	ESDJ	2 900 401	...	...	1 459 681	...	...	1 440 720	...	...
1 VII 2013	ESDJ	2 895 092	...	...	1 461 076	...	...	1 434 016	...	...
1 VII 2014	ESDJ	2 889 104	...	...	1 461 389	...	...	1 427 715	...	...
1 VII 2015	ESDJ	2 880 703	...	...	1 459 831	...	...	1 420 872	...	...
1 VII 2016	ESDJ	2 876 101	...	...	1 456 000	...	...	1 420 101	...	...
1 VII 2017	ESDJ	2 873 457	...	...	1 446 071	...	...	1 427 386	...	...
1 VII 2018	ESDJ	2 866 376	...	...	1 434 102	...	...	1 432 274	...	...
1 I 2019	ESDJ	2 862 427	...	...	1 429 594	...	...	1 432 833	...	...
Andorra - Andorre[56]										
1 I 2010[137]	ESDJ	70 290	...	...	35 592	...	...	34 698	...	...
1 I 2011	ESDJ	69 772	...	...	35 204	...	...	34 568	...	...
31 XII 2011	CDJC	69 758	...	...	35 147	...	...	34 611	...	...
1 I 2012	ESDJ	69 758	...	...	35 147	...	...	34 611	...	...
1 VII 2013	ESDJ	69 929	...	...	35 206	...	...	34 723	...	...

6. Total and urban population by sex: 2010 - 2019
Population totale et population urbaine selon le sexe : 2010 - 2019 (continued - suite)

Continent, country or area, and date Continent, pays ou zone et date	Code[a]	Both sexes - Les deux sexes Total	Urban - Urbaine Number Nombre	 Percent P.100	Male - Masculin Total	Urban - Urbaine Number Nombre	 Percent P.100	Female - Féminin Total	Urban - Urbaine Number Nombre	 Percent P.100
EUROPE										
Andorra - Andorre[56]										
1 VII 2014	ESDJ	70 155	...	...	35 364	...	...	34 791	...	...
1 VII 2015	ESDJ	70 901	...	...	35 741	...	...	35 160	...	...
1 VII 2016	ESDJ	72 358	...	...	36 590	...	...	35 768	...	...
1 I 2017	ESDJ	73 105	...	...	37 047	...	...	36 058	...	...
1 I 2018	ESDJ	74 794	...	...	38 031	...	...	36 763	...	...
1 I 2019	ESDJ	76 177	...	...	38 789	...	...	37 388	...	...
Austria - Autriche										
1 VII 2010	ESDJ	8 361 069	...	...	4 071 773	...	...	4 289 296	...	...
1 VII 2011	ESDJ	8 388 534	...	...	4 087 188	...	...	4 301 346	...	...
31 X 2011	CDJC	8 401 940	5 643 239	67.2	4 093 938	2 713 930	66.3	4 308 002	2 929 309	68.0
1 VII 2012	ESDJ	8 426 311	...	...	4 109 431	...	...	4 316 880	...	...
1 VII 2013	ESDJ	8 477 230	...	...	4 138 693	...	...	4 338 537	...	...
1 VII 2014	ESDJ	8 543 975	...	...	4 176 554	...	...	4 367 421	...	...
1 VII 2015	ESDJ	8 629 496	...	...	4 229 064	...	...	4 400 432	...	...
1 VII 2016	ESDJ	8 739 806	...	...	4 295 164	...	...	4 444 642	...	...
1 VII 2017	ESDJ	8 795 073	...	...	4 324 737	...	...	4 470 336	...	...
1 VII 2018	ESDJ	8 837 707	...	...	4 346 748	...	...	4 490 959	...	...
1 I 2019	ESDJ	8 858 775	...	...	4 357 033	...	...	4 501 742	...	...
Belarus - Bélarus										
1 VII 2010	ESDJ	9 490 583	7 100 147	74.8	4 413 225	3 285 104	74.4	5 077 358	3 815 043	75.1
1 VII 2011	ESDJ	9 473 172	7 148 636	75.5	4 403 227	3 303 932	75.0	5 069 945	3 844 704	75.8
1 VII 2012	ESDJ	9 464 495	7 198 575	76.1	4 397 910	3 324 299	75.6	5 066 585	3 874 276	76.5
1 VII 2013	ESDJ	9 465 997	7 247 854	76.6	4 399 369	3 345 878	76.1	5 066 628	3 901 976	77.0
1 VII 2014	ESDJ	9 474 511	7 299 878	77.0	4 405 204	3 369 054	76.5	5 069 307	3 930 824	77.5
1 VII 2015	ESDJ	9 489 616	7 347 512	77.4	4 415 020	3 390 465	76.8	5 074 596	3 957 047	78.0
1 VII 2016[26]	ESDJ	9 501 534	7 385 438	77.7	4 423 680	3 407 394	77.0	5 077 854	3 978 044	78.3
1 VII 2017[26]	ESDJ	9 498 264	7 406 475	78.0	4 424 027	3 415 947	77.2	5 074 237	3 990 528	78.6
1 VII 2018[26]	ESDJ	9 483 499	7 420 666	78.2	4 418 640	3 421 748	77.4	5 064 859	3 998 918	79.0
1 I 2019	ESDJ	9 475 174	...	...	4 415 745	...	...	5 059 429	...	...
Belgium - Belgique										
1 VII 2010	ESDJ	10 895 638	10 739 291	98.6	5 341 252	5 262 796	98.5	5 554 386	5 476 495	98.6
1 I 2011	CDJC	11 000 638	10 842 520	98.6	5 401 718	5 322 172	98.5	5 598 920	5 520 348	98.6
1 VII 2011	ESDJ	11 043 788	10 884 939	98.6	5 425 814	5 345 964	98.5	5 617 974	5 538 975	98.6
1 VII 2012	ESDJ	11 128 246	...	...	5 469 608	...	...	5 658 638	...	...
1 VII 2013	ESDJ	11 182 817	...	...	5 497 753	...	...	5 685 065	...	...
1 VII 2014	ESDJ	11 231 213	...	...	5 522 163	...	...	5 709 051	...	...
1 VII 2015[26]	ESDJ	11 284 776	...	...	5 552 760	...	...	5 732 016	...	...
1 VII 2016[26]	ESDJ	11 331 422	...	...	5 579 268	...	...	5 752 154	...	...
1 VII 2017[26]	ESDJ	11 375 158	...	...	5 601 745	...	...	5 773 413	...	...
1 VII 2018[26]	ESDJ	11 427 054	...	...	5 629 522	...	...	5 797 532	...	...
1 I 2019	ESDJ	11 455 519	...	...	5 644 826	...	...	5 810 693	...	...
Bosnia and Herzegovina - Bosnie-Herzégovine										
1 VII 2010	ESDF	3 843 126	...	...	1 877 587	...	...	1 965 539	...	...
1 VII 2011	ESDF	3 841 224	...	...	1 876 546	...	...	1 964 678	...	...
1 VII 2012	ESDF	3 837 455	...	...	1 874 608	...	...	1 962 848	...	...
30 IX 2013	CDJC	3 531 159	...	...	1 732 270	...	...	1 798 889	...	...
Bulgaria - Bulgarie										
1 VII 2010	ESDJ	7 534 289	5 388 142	71.5	3 644 560	2 587 844	71.0	3 889 729	2 800 298	72.0
1 II 2011	CDJC	7 364 570	5 338 261	72.5	3 586 571	2 580 734	72.0	3 777 999	2 757 527	73.0
1 VII 2011	ESDJ	7 348 328	5 336 366	72.6	3 577 847	2 579 205	72.1	3 770 481	2 757 161	73.1
1 VII 2012	ESDJ	7 305 888	5 316 384	72.8	3 555 920	2 568 535	72.2	3 749 968	2 747 849	73.3
1 VII 2013	ESDJ	7 263 859	...	...	3 534 276	...	...	3 729 584	...	...
1 VII 2014	ESDJ	7 223 937	5 279 577	73.1	3 513 480	2 548 437	72.5	3 710 457	2 731 140	73.6
1 VII 2015	ESDJ	7 177 991	5 247 331	73.1	3 489 596	2 530 439	72.5	3 688 395	2 716 892	73.7
1 VII 2016[26]	ESDJ	7 127 822	5 215 784	73.2	3 463 578	2 512 987	72.6	3 664 244	2 702 797	73.8
1 VII 2017[26]	ESDJ	7 075 947	5 193 070	73.4	3 436 194	2 500 348	72.8	3 639 753	2 692 722	74.0
1 VII 2018[26]	ESDJ	7 025 037	5 170 442	73.6	3 409 055	2 487 598	73.0	3 615 982	2 682 844	74.2
1 I 2019	ESDJ	7 000 039	5 159 129	73.7	3 395 701	2 481 128	73.1	3 604 338	2 678 001	74.3
Croatia - Croatie										
1 VII 2010	ESDJ	4 295 427	...	...	2 071 195	...	...	2 224 232	...	...
1 IV 2011	CDJC	4 284 889	2 368 506	55.3	2 066 335	1 121 328	54.3	2 218 554	1 247 178	56.2
1 VII 2011	ESDJ	4 280 622	...	...	2 064 314	...	...	2 216 308	...	...
1 VII 2012	ESDJ	4 267 558	...	...	2 058 701	...	...	2 208 857	...	...

6. Total and urban population by sex: 2010 - 2019
Population totale et population urbaine selon le sexe : 2010 - 2019 (continued - suite)

Continent, country or area, and date / Continent, pays ou zone et date	Code[a]	Both sexes - Les deux sexes: Total	Both sexes - Urban - Urbaine: Number Nombre	Both sexes - Urban - Urbaine: Percent P.100	Male - Masculin: Total	Male - Urban - Urbaine: Number Nombre	Male - Urban - Urbaine: Percent P.100	Female - Féminin: Total	Female - Urban - Urbaine: Number Nombre	Female - Urban - Urbaine: Percent P.100
EUROPE										
Croatia - Croatie										
1 VII 2013	ESDJ	4 255 689	...	...	2 053 788	...	...	2 201 901	...	...
1 VII 2014	ESDJ	4 238 389	...	...	2 045 801	...	...	2 192 588	...	...
1 VII 2015	ESDJ	4 203 604	...	...	2 028 640	...	...	2 174 964	...	...
1 VII 2016	ESDJ	4 174 349	...	...	2 014 837	...	...	2 159 512	...	...
1 VII 2017	ESDJ	4 124 531	...	...	1 990 341	...	...	2 134 190	...	...
1 VII 2018	ESDJ	4 087 843	...	...	1 975 052	...	...	2 112 791	...	...
1 I 2019	ESDJ	4 076 246	...	...	1 972 572	...	...	2 103 674	...	...
Czechia - Tchéquie										
1 VII 2010	ESDJ	10 474 410	...	...	5 141 699	...	...	5 332 711	...	...
25 III 2011	CDJC	10 436 560	7 650 450	73.3	5 109 766	3 712 348	72.7	5 326 794	3 938 102	73.9
1 VII 2011	ESDJ	10 496 088	...	...	5 152 721	...	...	5 343 368	...	...
1 VII 2012	ESDJ	10 510 786	...	...	5 161 280	...	...	5 349 506	...	...
1 VII 2013	ESDJ	10 510 719	7 683 793	73.1	5 161 617	3 740 790	72.5	5 349 102	3 943 003	73.7
1 VII 2014	ESDJ	10 524 783	7 693 352	73.1	5 169 146	3 744 873	72.4	5 355 637	3 948 479	73.7
1 VII 2015	ESDJ	10 542 942	7 702 624	73.1	5 180 242	3 749 901	72.4	5 362 700	3 952 723	73.7
1 VII 2016	ESDJ	10 565 284	7 725 090	73.1	5 193 012	3 761 862	72.4	5 372 272	3 963 228	73.8
1 VII 2017	ESDJ	10 589 526	7 742 524	73.1	5 207 575	3 772 123	72.4	5 381 951	3 970 401	73.8
1 VII 2018	ESDJ	10 626 430	7 766 457	73.1	5 230 373	3 787 722	72.4	5 396 057	3 978 735	73.7
1 I 2019	ESDJ	10 649 800	7 777 376	73.0	5 244 194	3 795 042	72.4	5 405 606	3 982 334	73.7
Denmark - Danemark[138]										
1 VII 2010	ESDJ	5 545 039	...	...	2 748 439	...	...	2 796 600	...	...
1 I 2011	CDJC	5 560 628	...	...	2 756 582	...	...	2 804 046	...	...
1 VII 2011	ESDJ	5 566 856	...	...	2 760 140	...	...	2 806 716	...	...
1 VII 2012	ESDJ	5 587 085	...	...	2 771 208	...	...	2 815 877	...	...
1 VII 2013	ESDJ	5 608 784	...	...	2 782 661	...	...	2 826 123	...	...
1 VII 2014	ESDJ	5 639 719	...	...	2 799 895	...	...	2 839 824	...	...
1 VII 2015	ESDJ	5 678 348	...	...	2 822 535	...	...	2 855 813	...	...
1 VII 2016	ESDJ	5 724 456	...	...	2 848 030	...	...	2 876 426	...	...
1 VII 2017	ESDJ	5 760 694	...	...	2 866 952	...	...	2 893 742	...	...
1 VII 2018	ESDJ	5 789 957	...	...	2 881 620	...	...	2 908 337	...	...
1 VII 2019	ESDJ	5 814 461	...	...	2 893 956	...	...	2 920 505	...	...
Estonia - Estonie										
1 VII 2010	ESDJ	1 331 475	904 365	67.9	620 250	408 720	65.9	711 225	495 645	69.7
1 VII 2011	ESDJ	1 327 439	903 066	68.0	618 919	408 988	66.1	708 520	494 078	69.7
31 XII 2011	CDJC	1 294 455	879 157	67.9	600 526	396 719	66.1	693 929	482 438	69.5
1 VII 2012	ESDJ	1 322 696	902 743	68.3	617 153	409 784	66.4	705 543	492 959	69.9
1 VII 2013	ESDJ	1 317 997	900 071	68.3	615 543	408 564	66.4	702 454	491 507	70.0
1 VII 2014	ESDJ	1 314 545	897 901	68.3	614 654	407 677	66.3	699 891	490 224	70.0
1 VII 2015	ESDJ	1 314 608	899 288[105]	68.4	615 549	406 894[105]	66.1	699 059	492 395[105]	70.4
1 VII 2016[26]	ESDJ	1 315 790	900 266[105]	68.4	617 123	406 142[105]	65.8	698 667	494 124[105]	70.7
1 VII 2017	ESDJ	1 317 384	912 157[105]	69.2	619 311	414 881[105]	67.0	698 073	497 277[105]	71.2
1 VII 2018[26]	ESDJ	1 321 977	917 240[105]	69.4	623 360	418 778[105]	67.2	698 617	498 462[105]	71.3
1 I 2019	ESDJ	1 324 820	919 630[105]	69.4	625 635	420 569[105]	67.2	699 185	499 061[105]	71.4
Faroe Islands - Îles Féroé										
1 VII 2010	ESDJ	48 669	18 131	37.3	25 276	9 195	36.4	23 393	8 936	38.2
1 VII 2011	ESDJ	48 563	18 110	37.3	25 179	9 120	36.2	23 384	8 990	38.4
11 XI 2011	CDJC	48 346	...	...	25 125	...	...	23 221	...	...
1 VII 2012	ESDJ	48 319	18 033	37.3	25 074	9 072	36.2	23 245	8 961	38.6
1 VII 2013	ESDJ	48 286	18 220	37.7	25 014	9 147	36.6	23 272	9 073	39.0
1 VII 2014	ESDJ	48 462	18 373	37.9	25 048	9 207	36.8	23 414	9 166	39.1
1 VII 2015	ESDJ	48 929	18 663	38.1	25 312	9 381	37.1	23 617	9 282	39.3
1 VII 2016	ESDJ	49 496	18 963	38.3	25 545	9 513	37.2	23 951	9 450	39.5
1 VII 2017	ESDJ	50 203	19 240	38.3	25 880	9 666	37.3	24 323	9 574	39.4
1 VII 2018	ESDJ	51 025	19 601	38.4	26 340	9 875	37.5	24 685	9 726	39.4
1 VII 2019	ESDJ	51 842	19 903	38.4	26 815	10 040	37.4	25 027	9 863	39.4
Finland - Finlande										
1 VII 2010[139]	ESDJ	5 335 481	3 643 170	68.3	2 617 862	1 767 855	67.5	2 717 620	1 875 315	69.0
31 XII 2010	CDJC	5 375 276	3 662 915	68.1	2 638 416	1 777 697	67.4	2 736 860	1 885 218	68.9
1 VII 2011[139]	ESDJ	5 360 091	3 671 777	68.5	2 631 431	1 783 058	67.8	2 728 660	1 888 719	69.2
1 VII 2012[139]	ESDJ	5 385 543	3 701 923	68.7	2 645 408	1 799 025	68.0	2 740 136	1 902 898	69.4
1 VII 2013[139]	ESDJ	5 410 389	3 732 928	69.0	2 659 239	1 815 818	68.3	2 751 150	1 917 110	69.7
1 VII 2014[139]	ESDJ	5 432 721	3 762 906	69.3	2 671 740	1 831 826	68.6	2 760 981	1 931 080	69.9
1 VII 2015[139]	ESDJ	5 450 581	3 849 116	70.6	2 682 211	1 875 949	69.9	2 768 370	1 973 167	71.3

6. Total and urban population by sex: 2010 - 2019
Population totale et population urbaine selon le sexe : 2010 - 2019 (continued - suite)

Continent, country or area, and date / Continent, pays ou zone et date	Code[a]	Both sexes - Les deux sexes: Total	Both sexes - Urban - Urbaine: Number Nombre	Both sexes - Urban - Urbaine: Percent P.100	Male - Masculin: Total	Male - Urban - Urbaine: Number Nombre	Male - Urban - Urbaine: Percent P.100	Female - Féminin: Total	Female - Urban - Urbaine: Number Nombre	Female - Urban - Urbaine: Percent P.100
EUROPE										
Finland - Finlande										
1 VII 2016[139]	ESDJ	5 466 204	3 880 555	71.0	2 692 383	1 893 551	70.3	2 773 822	1 987 004	71.6
1 VII 2017[139]	ESDJ	5 478 862	3 904 835	71.3	2 701 086	1 907 533	70.6	2 777 777	1 997 303	71.9
1 VII 2018[139]	ESDJ	5 485 886	3 926 164	71.6	2 706 416	1 919 593	70.9	2 779 470	2 006 571	72.2
1 I 2019[56]	ESDJ	5 517 919	...	...	2 723 290	...	...	2 794 629	...	...
France										
1 I 2010[140]	CDJS	62 765 235	48 387 303	77.1	30 393 079	23 208 841	76.4	32 372 156	25 178 462	77.8
1 VII 2010[140]	ESDJ	62 917 790	...	...	30 475 789	...	...	32 442 001	...	...
1 VII 2011[140]	ESDJ	63 223 158	...	...	30 626 399	...	...	32 596 759	...	...
1 VII 2012[140]	ESDJ	63 536 918	...	...	30 782 589	...	...	32 754 329	...	...
1 VII 2013[140]	ESDJ	63 862 912	...	...	30 945 467	...	...	32 917 445	...	...
1 VII 2014[140]	ESDJ	64 164 390	...	...	31 086 155	...	...	33 078 235	...	...
1 I 2015	CDJC	64 300 821	49 781 175	77.4	31 138 550	23 891 441	76.7	33 162 271	25 889 734	78.1
1 VII 2015[140]	ESDJ	64 384 807	...	...	31 181 794	...	...	33 203 013	...	...
1 VII 2016*[140]	ESDJ	64 543 604	...	...	31 248 627	...	...	33 294 977	...	...
1 VII 2017*[140]	ESDJ	64 671 734	...	...	31 303 616	...	...	33 368 118	...	...
1 VII 2018*[140]	ESDJ	64 768 552	...	...	31 343 809	...	...	33 424 743	...	...
1 I 2019[140]	ESDJ	64 821 954	...	...	31 353 853	...	...	33 468 101	...	...
Germany - Allemagne										
1 VII 2010	ESDJ	81 757 471	...	...	40 099 871	...	...	41 657 600	...	...
9 V 2011	CDJC	80 219 695	64 444 232	80.3	39 145 941	31 227 832	79.8	41 073 754	33 216 400	80.9
1 VII 2011[5]	ESDJ	80 274 983	...	...	39 177 274	...	...	41 097 709	...	...
1 VII 2012[5]	ESDJ	80 425 823	...	...	39 305 462	...	...	41 120 362	...	...
1 VII 2013[5]	ESDJ	80 645 605	...	...	39 468 950	...	...	41 176 655	...	...
1 VII 2014[5]	ESDJ	80 982 500	...	...	39 696 190	...	...	41 286 310	...	...
1 VII 2015[5]	ESDJ	81 686 663	...	...	40 174 816	...	...	41 511 847	...	...
1 VII 2016[141]	ESDJ	82 348 669	...	...	40 605 621	...	...	41 743 048	...	...
1 VII 2017[141]	ESDJ	82 657 002	...	...	40 770 342	...	...	41 886 661	...	...
1 VII 2018[141]	ESDJ	82 905 782	...	...	40 905 128	...	...	42 000 654	...	...
1 I 2019[5]	ESDJ	83 019 213	...	...	40 966 691	...	...	42 052 522	...	...
Gibraltar[142]										
31 XII 2010	ESDF	31 465	...	...	15 666	...	...	15 799	...	...
31 XII 2011	ESDF	32 003	...	...	15 977	...	...	16 026	...	...
12 XI 2012	CDJC	32 194	...	...	16 061	...	...	16 133	...	...
31 XII 2012	ESDF	32 577	...	...	16 311	...	...	16 266	...	...
31 XII 2013	ESDF	32 734	...	...	16 460	...	...	16 274	...	...
31 XII 2014	ESDF	33 140	...	...	16 694	...	...	16 446	...	...
31 XII 2015	ESDF	33 573	...	...	16 938	...	...	16 635	...	...
31 XII 2016	ESDF	34 003	...	...	17 093	...	...	16 910	...	...
Greece - Grèce										
1 VII 2010	ESDF	11 121 383	...	...	5 457 186	...	...	5 664 197	...	...
9 V 2011	CDFC	10 816 286	8 285 259	76.6	5 303 223	4 022 889	75.9	5 513 063	4 262 370	77.3
1 VII 2011	ESDF	11 104 995	...	...	5 438 712	...	...	5 666 283	...	...
1 VII 2012	ESDF	11 045 040	...	...	5 395 104	...	...	5 649 936	...	...
1 VII 2013	ESDF	10 965 241	...	...	5 339 750	...	...	5 625 491	...	...
1 VII 2014	ESDF	10 892 369	...	...	5 290 797	...	...	5 601 572	...	...
1 VII 2015	ESDF	10 820 964	...	...	5 246 345	...	...	5 574 619	...	...
1 VII 2016	ESDF	10 775 989	...	...	5 222 749	...	...	5 553 240	...	...
1 VII 2017	ESDF	10 761 447	...	...	5 218 481	...	...	5 542 966	...	...
1 VII 2018	ESDF	10 732 898	...	...	5 209 178	...	...	5 523 720	...	...
1 I 2019	ESDF	10 724 599	...	...	5 208 293	...	...	5 516 306	...	...
Guernsey - Guernesey										
31 III 2010	ESDJ	62 431	...	...	30 695	...	...	31 736	...	...
31 III 2011	ESDJ	62 915	...	...	31 025	...	...	31 890	...	...
31 III 2012	ESDJ	63 085	...	...	31 147	...	...	31 938	...	...
31 III 2013	ESDJ	62 732	...	...	31 081	...	...	31 651	...	...
31 III 2014	ESDJ	62 341	...	...	30 804	...	...	31 537	...	...
31 III 2015	CDJC	62 234	...	...	30 819	...	...	31 415	...	...
31 III 2015	ESDJ	62 234	...	...	30 819	...	...	31 415	...	...
31 III 2016	ESDJ	62 208	...	...	30 824	...	...	31 384	...	...
31 III 2017	ESDJ	62 106	...	...	30 755	...	...	31 351	...	...
31 III 2018	ESDJ	62 333	...	...	30 874	...	...	31 459	...	...
31 III 2019	ESDJ	62 792	...	...	31 080	...	...	31 712	...	...

6. Total and urban population by sex: 2010 - 2019
Population totale et population urbaine selon le sexe : 2010 - 2019 (continued - suite)

Continent, country or area, and date / Continent, pays ou zone et date	Code[a]	Both sexes - Les deux sexes			Male - Masculin			Female - Féminin		
		Total	Urban - Urbaine		Total	Urban - Urbaine		Total	Urban - Urbaine	
			Number Nombre	Percent P.100		Number Nombre	Percent P.100		Number Nombre	Percent P.100
EUROPE										
Hungary - Hongrie										
1 VII 2010	ESDJ	10 000 023	6 953 071	69.5	4 750 401	3 260 344	68.6	5 249 623	3 692 727	70.3
1 VII 2011	ESDJ	9 971 727	6 945 873	69.7	4 737 813	3 256 796	68.7	5 233 914	3 689 077	70.5
1 X 2011	CDFC	9 937 628	6 903 858	69.5	4 718 479	3 241 911	68.7	5 219 149	3 661 947	70.2
1 VII 2012	ESDJ	9 920 362	6 877 231	69.3	4 720 310	3 234 447	68.5	5 200 052	3 642 785	70.1
1 VII 2013	ESDJ	9 893 082	6 864 757	69.4	4 709 672	3 229 480	68.6	5 183 410	3 635 277	70.1
1 VII 2014[8]	ESDJ	9 866 468	6 950 391	70.4	4 699 585	3 272 050	69.6	5 166 883	3 678 342	71.2
1 VII 2015[8]	ESDJ	9 843 028	6 937 836	70.5	4 692 149	3 267 756	69.6	5 150 879	3 670 081	71.3
1 VII 2016[8]	ESDJ	9 814 023	6 916 274	70.5	4 681 905	3 259 506	69.6	5 132 118	3 656 768	71.3
1 VII 2017[8]	ESDJ	9 787 966	6 896 039	70.5	4 673 447	3 252 609	69.6	5 114 520	3 643 431	71.2
1 VII 2018[8]	ESDJ	9 775 564	6 888 955	70.5	4 673 712	3 253 732	69.6	5 101 852	3 635 224	71.3
1 I 2019[8]	ESDJ	9 772 756	...	...	4 675 821	...	...	5 096 935	...	...
Iceland - Islande[126]										
1 VII 2010	ESDJ	318 006	297 432	93.5	159 838	148 901	93.2	158 168	148 531	93.9
1 VII 2011	ESDJ	319 014	300 395	94.2	160 185	...	...	158 829	...	...
31 XII 2011	CDJC	315 556	295 874	93.8	158 151	147 681	93.4	157 405	148 193	94.1
1 VII 2012	ESDJ	320 716	300 237	93.6	160 901	150 074	93.3	159 815	150 163	94.0
1 VII 2013	ESDJ	323 764	303 136	93.6	162 378	151 471	93.3	161 386	151 665	94.0
1 VII 2014	ESDJ	327 386	306 633	93.7	164 252	153 265	93.3	163 134	153 368	94.0
1 VII 2015	ESDJ	330 815	309 868	93.7	166 228	155 146	93.3	164 587	154 723	94.0
1 VII 2016	ESDJ	335 439	314 123	93.6	169 152	157 819	93.3	166 288	156 304	94.0
1 VII 2017	ESDJ	343 400	321 288	93.6	174 317	162 440	93.2	169 083	158 848	93.9
1 VII 2018	ESDJ	352 721	329 828	93.5	180 219	167 879	93.2	172 502	161 949	93.9
1 I 2019	ESDJ	356 991	...	...	182 837	...	...	174 154	...	...
Ireland - Irlande										
1 VII 2010	ESDF	4 560 155	...	...	2 265 200	...	...	2 294 955	...	...
10 IV 2011	CDFC	4 588 252	2 846 882	62.0	2 272 699	1 389 160	61.1	2 315 553	1 457 722	63.0
1 VII 2011	ESDF	4 580 084	...	...	2 271 713	...	...	2 308 372	...	...
1 VII 2012	ESDF	4 599 533	...	...	2 278 731	...	...	2 320 803	...	...
1 VII 2013	ESDF	4 623 816	...	...	2 289 656	...	...	2 334 160	...	...
1 VII 2014	ESDF	4 657 740	...	...	2 304 596	...	...	2 353 144	...	...
1 VII 2015	ESDF	4 701 957	...	...	2 326 242	...	...	2 375 715	...	...
24 IV 2016	CDJC	4 761 865	...	...	2 354 428	...	...	2 407 437	...	...
1 VII 2016[8]	ESDJ	4 755 335	...	...	2 353 530	...	...	2 401 805	...	...
1 VII 2017[8]	ESDJ	4 807 388	...	...	2 380 071	...	...	2 427 317	...	...
1 VII 2018[8]	ESDJ	4 867 316	...	...	2 410 552	...	...	2 456 764	...	...
1 I 2019[8]	ESDJ	4 904 240	...	...	2 428 881	...	...	2 475 359	...	...
Isle of Man - Île de Man										
30 IV 2010	ESDJ	82 691	...	...	41 053	...	...	41 638	...	...
27 III 2011	CDJC	84 497	...	...	41 971	...	...	42 526	...	...
30 IV 2012	ESDJ	85 047	...	...	42 273	...	...	42 775	...	...
30 IV 2013	ESDJ	85 682	...	...	42 622	...	...	43 060	...	...
30 IV 2014	ESDJ	86 322	...	...	42 971	...	...	43 352	...	...
30 IV 2015	ESDJ	86 963	...	...	43 319	...	...	43 644	...	...
24 IV 2016	CDJC	83 314	...	...	41 269	...	...	42 045	...	...
30 IV 2016	ESDJ	83 314	...	...	41 269	...	...	42 045	...	...
Italy - Italie										
1 VII 2010	ESDJ	59 277 417	...	...	28 682 321	...	...	30 595 096	...	...
1 VII 2011	ESDJ	59 379 449	...	...	28 720 928	...	...	30 658 521	...	...
9 X 2011	CDJC	59 433 744	...	...	28 745 507	...	...	30 688 237	...	...
1 VII 2012	ESDJ	59 539 717	...	...	28 808 098	...	...	30 731 619	...	...
1 VII 2013	ESDJ	60 233 948	...	...	29 187 081	...	...	31 046 867	...	...
1 VII 2014	ESDJ	60 789 140	...	...	29 493 077	...	...	31 296 063	...	...
1 VII 2015	ESDJ	60 730 582	...	...	29 478 956	...	...	31 251 626	...	...
1 VII 2016	ESDJ	60 627 498	...	...	29 451 031	...	...	31 176 467	...	...
1 VII 2017	ESDJ	60 536 709	...	...	29 436 674	...	...	31 100 035	...	...
1 VII 2018	ESDJ	60 421 760	...	...	29 406 187	...	...	31 015 573	...	...
Jersey										
1 I 2011	ESDJ	97 108	...	...	47 822	...	...	49 286	...	...
27 III 2011	CDJC	97 857	...	...	48 296	...	...	49 561	...	...
1 I 2012	ESDJ	98 105	...	...	48 360	...	...	49 745	...	...
1 I 2013	ESDJ	98 999	...	...	48 837	...	...	50 162	...	...
1 I 2014	ESDJ	100 208	...	...	49 478	...	...	50 730	...	...
1 I 2015	ESDJ	101 007	...	...	49 900	...	...	51 107	...	...
1 I 2016	ESDJ	102 704	...	...	50 768	...	...	51 936	...	...

6. Total and urban population by sex: 2010 - 2019
Population totale et population urbaine selon le sexe : 2010 - 2019 (continued - suite)

Continent, country or area, and date / Continent, pays ou zone et date	Code[a]	Both sexes - Les deux sexes			Male - Masculin			Female - Féminin		
		Total	Urban - Urbaine		Total	Urban - Urbaine		Total	Urban - Urbaine	
			Number Nombre	Percent P.100		Number Nombre	Percent P.100		Number Nombre	Percent P.100
EUROPE										
Jersey										
1 I 2017	ESDJ	104 190	...	...	51 636	...	...	52 554	...	...
1 I 2018	ESDJ	105 598	...	...	52 406	...	...	53 192	...	...
1 I 2019	ESDJ	106 800	...	...	53 061	...	...	53 739	...	...
Latvia - Lettonie										
1 VII 2010	ESDJ	2 097 555	1 422 675	67.8	959 435	634 393	66.1	1 138 120	788 282	69.3
1 III 2011	CDJC	2 070 371	1 404 251	67.8	946 102	625 150	66.1	1 124 269	779 101	69.3
1 VII 2011	ESDJ	2 059 709	1 394 429	67.7	941 375	620 484	65.9	1 118 334	773 945	69.2
1 VII 2012	ESDJ	2 034 319	1 374 215	67.6	930 696	611 604	65.7	1 103 623	762 611	69.1
1 VII 2013	ESDJ	2 012 647	1 362 004	67.7	921 813	606 624	65.8	1 090 834	755 380	69.2
1 VII 2014	ESDJ	1 993 782	1 353 269	67.9	914 126	603 112	66.0	1 079 656	750 157	69.5
1 VII 2015	ESDJ	1 977 527	1 344 291	68.0	907 753	599 629	66.1	1 069 774	744 662	69.6
1 VII 2016	ESDJ	1 959 537	1 336 137	68.2	899 991	596 307	66.3	1 059 546	739 830	69.8
1 VII 2017	ESDJ	1 942 248	...	...	892 662	...	...	1 049 586	...	...
1 VII 2018	ESDJ	1 927 174	1 319 941	68.5	887 275	590 284	66.5	1 039 899	729 657	70.2
1 I 2019	ESDJ	1 919 968	1 315 177	68.5	884 909	588 614	66.5	1 035 059	726 563	70.2
Liechtenstein										
1 VII 2010	ESDJ	36 010	...	...	17 817	...	...	18 193	...	...
31 XII 2010	CDJC	36 149	...	...	17 886	...	...	18 263	...	...
1 VII 2011	ESDJ	36 281	...	...	17 950	...	...	18 331	...	...
1 VII 2012	ESDJ	36 636	...	...	18 123	...	...	18 513	...	...
1 VII 2013	ESDJ	36 942	...	...	18 314	...	...	18 628	...	...
1 VII 2014	ESDJ	37 215	...	...	18 458	...	...	18 757	...	...
1 VII 2015	ESDJ	37 468	...	...	18 580	...	...	18 888	...	...
31 XII 2015	CDJC	37 622	...	...	18 660	...	...	18 962	...	...
1 VII 2016	ESDJ	37 686	...	...	18 673	...	...	19 013	...	...
1 VII 2017	ESDJ	37 877	...	...	18 768	...	...	19 109	...	...
1 VII 2018	ESDJ	38 201	...	...	18 949	...	...	19 252	...	...
1 VII 2019	ESDJ	38 557	...	...	19 119	...	...	19 438	...	...
Lithuania - Lituanie										
1 VII 2010	ESDJ	3 097 282	2 068 095	66.8	1 428 711	931 128	65.2	1 668 571	1 136 967	68.1
1 III 2011	CDJC	3 043 429	2 031 211	66.7	1 402 604	912 943	65.1	1 640 825	1 118 268	68.2
1 VII 2011	ESDJ	3 028 115	2 021 365	66.8	1 395 367	907 995	65.1	1 632 748	1 113 370	68.2
1 VII 2012	ESDJ	2 987 773	1 997 436	66.9	1 376 201	896 102	65.1	1 611 572	1 101 334	68.3
1 VII 2013	ESDJ	2 957 689	1 981 924	67.0	1 362 443	888 578	65.2	1 595 246	1 093 346	68.5
1 VII 2014[8]	ESDJ	2 932 367	1 968 596	67.1	1 351 126	881 978	65.3	1 581 241	1 086 618	68.7
1 VII 2015[8]	ESDJ	2 904 910	1 952 920	67.2	1 337 932	873 571	65.3	1 566 978	1 079 349	68.9
1 VII 2016[8]	ESDJ	2 868 231	1 927 148	67.2	1 320 897	860 905	65.2	1 547 334	1 066 243	68.9
1 VII 2017[8]	ESDJ	2 828 403	1 897 895	67.1	1 304 740	848 512	65.0	1 523 663	1 049 383	68.9
1 VII 2018[8]	ESDJ	2 801 543	1 880 046	67.1	1 296 442	842 614	65.0	1 505 101	1 037 432	68.9
1 I 2019[8]	ESDJ	2 794 184	...	...	1 295 591	...	...	1 498 593	...	...
Luxembourg										
1 VII 2010	ESDJ	506 953	...	...	252 013	...	...	254 941	...	...
1 II 2011	CDJC	512 353	...	...	254 967	...	...	257 386	...	...
1 VII 2011	ESDJ	518 347	...	...	258 220	...	...	260 127	...	...
1 VII 2012	ESDJ	530 946	...	...	265 116	...	...	265 830	...	...
1 VII 2013	ESDJ	543 360	...	...	271 765	...	...	271 595	...	...
1 VII 2014	ESDJ	556 319	...	...	278 544	...	...	277 775	...	...
1 VII 2015	ESDJ	569 604	...	...	285 583	...	...	284 021	...	...
1 VII 2016	ESDJ	583 458	...	...	292 917	...	...	290 541	...	...
1 VII 2017	ESDJ	596 336	...	...	299 611	...	...	296 726	...	...
1 VII 2018	ESDJ	607 950	...	...	305 650	...	...	302 300	...	...
1 I 2019	ESDJ	613 894	...	...	308 720	...	...	305 174	...	...
Malta - Malte										
1 VII 2010[143]	ESDJ	414 562	...	...	206 333	...	...	208 229	...	...
1 VII 2011[143]	ESDJ	416 318	...	...	207 072	...	...	209 246	...	...
20 XI 2011	CDFC	417 432	400 557	96.0	207 625	199 151	95.9	209 807	201 406	96.0
1 VII 2012[143]	ESDJ	420 082	...	...	209 066	...	...	211 016	...	...
1 VII 2013[143]	ESDJ	426 019	...	...	212 482	...	...	213 537	...	...
1 VII 2014[143]	ESDJ	434 606	...	...	217 537	...	...	217 069	...	...
1 VII 2015[143]	ESDJ	445 105	...	...	223 467	...	...	221 638	...	...
1 VII 2016[143]	ESDJ	455 410	...	...	229 058	...	...	226 352	...	...
1 VII 2017[143]	ESDJ	468 056	...	...	236 159	...	...	231 897	...	...
1 VII 2018[143]	ESDJ	484 682	...	...	246 244	...	...	238 438	...	...
1 I 2019[143]	ESDJ	493 559	...	...	251 836	...	...	241 723	...	...

6. Total and urban population by sex: 2010 - 2019
Population totale et population urbaine selon le sexe : 2010 - 2019 (continued - suite)

Continent, country or area, and date Continent, pays ou zone et date	Code[a]	Both sexes - Les deux sexes			Male - Masculin			Female - Féminin		
		Total	Urban - Urbaine		Total	Urban - Urbaine		Total	Urban - Urbaine	
			Number Nombre	Percent P.100		Number Nombre	Percent P.100		Number Nombre	Percent P.100
EUROPE										
Monaco[144]										
7 VI 2016	CDJC	37 308	...	...	18 240	...	...	19 068	...	...
Montenegro - Monténégro										
1 VII 2010	ESDJ	619 426	...	...	305 674	...	...	313 752	...	...
1 IV 2011	CDJC	620 029	399 264	64.4	306 236	193 691	63.2	313 793	205 573	65.5
1 VII 2011	ESDJ	620 079	...	...	306 242	...	...	313 837	...	...
1 VII 2012	ESDJ	620 601	...	...	306 580	...	...	314 021	...	...
1 VII 2013	ESDJ	621 207	...	...	306 978	...	...	314 229	...	...
1 VII 2014[8]	ESDJ	621 810	...	...	307 339	...	...	314 471	...	...
1 VII 2015[8]	ESDJ	622 159	...	...	307 628	...	...	314 531	...	...
1 VII 2016[8]	ESDJ	622 303	...	...	307 743	...	...	314 560	...	...
1 I 2017[8]	ESDJ	622 387	...	...	307 752	...	...	314 635	...	...
1 VII 2018[8]	ESDJ	622 271	...	...	307 727	...	...	314 544	...	...
1 I 2019[8]	ESDJ	622 182	...	...	307 712	...	...	314 470	...	...
Netherlands - Pays-Bas										
1 VII 2010	ESDJ	16 615 394	11 096 288	66.8	8 223 479	5 464 083	66.4	8 391 915	5 632 205	67.1
1 I 2011	CDJC	16 655 799	11 124 721	66.8	8 243 482	5 478 213	66.5	8 412 317	5 646 508	67.1
1 VII 2011	ESDJ	16 693 074	...	...	8 263 177	...	...	8 429 897	...	...
1 VII 2012	ESDJ	16 754 962	...	...	8 295 105	...	...	8 459 857	...	...
1 VII 2013	ESDJ	16 804 432	...	...	8 320 862	...	...	8 483 570	...	...
1 VII 2014	ESDJ	16 865 007	...	...	8 353 621	...	...	8 511 386	...	...
1 VII 2015	ESDJ	16 939 923	...	...	8 394 997	...	...	8 544 926	...	...
1 VII 2016	ESDJ	17 030 314	...	...	8 445 119	...	...	8 585 195	...	...
1 I 2017	ESDJ	17 081 507	...	...	8 475 102	...	...	8 606 405	...	...
1 VII 2018	ESDJ	17 231 624	...	...	8 554 064	...	...	8 677 560	...	...
1 I 2019	ESDJ	17 282 163	...	...	8 581 086	...	...	8 701 077	...	...
North Macedonia - Macédoine du Nord										
1 VII 2010	ESDJ	2 055 004	...	...	1 029 848	...	...	1 025 156	...	...
1 VII 2011	ESDJ	2 058 539	...	...	1 031 403	...	...	1 027 136	...	...
1 VII 2012	ESDJ	2 061 044	...	...	1 032 532	...	...	1 028 512	...	...
1 VII 2013	ESDJ	2 064 032	...	...	1 033 990	...	...	1 030 042	...	...
1 VII 2014	ESDJ	2 067 471	...	...	1 035 680	...	...	1 031 791	...	...
1 VII 2015	ESDJ	2 070 225	...	...	1 037 060	...	...	1 033 166	...	...
1 VII 2016	ESDJ	2 072 490	...	...	1 038 107	...	...	1 034 383	...	...
1 VII 2017	ESDJ	2 074 502	...	...	1 038 948	...	...	1 035 554	...	...
1 VII 2018	ESDJ	2 076 217	...	...	1 039 742	...	...	1 036 475	...	...
1 I 2019	ESDJ	2 077 132	...	...	1 040 200	...	...	1 036 932	...	...
Norway - Norvège										
1 VII 2010[8]	ESDJ	4 889 252	...	...	2 443 801	...	...	2 445 452	...	...
1 VII 2011[8]	ESDJ	4 953 088	...	...	2 479 860	...	...	2 473 228	...	...
19 XI 2011[145]	CDJC	4 979 955	3 951 427[105]	79.3	2 495 777	1 959 424[105]	78.5	2 484 178	1 992 003[105]	80.2
1 VII 2012[8]	ESDJ	5 018 573	...	...	2 517 390	...	...	2 501 183	...	...
1 VII 2013[8]	ESDJ	5 079 623	...	...	2 551 458	...	...	2 528 165	...	...
1 VII 2014[8]	ESDJ	5 137 232	...	...	2 583 105	...	...	2 554 127	...	...
1 VII 2015[8]	ESDJ	5 188 607	...	...	2 611 414	...	...	2 577 194	...	...
1 VII 2016[146]	ESDJ	5 234 519	...	...	2 636 378	...	...	2 598 142	...	...
1 VII 2017[146]	ESDJ	5 276 968	...	...	2 658 751	...	...	2 618 218	...	...
1 I 2018[8]	ESDJ	5 295 619	...	...	2 668 371	...	...	2 627 248	...	...
1 I 2019[8]	ESDJ	5 328 212	...	...	2 685 073	...	...	2 643 139	...	...
Poland - Pologne										
1 VII 2010[8]	ESDJ	38 042 403	23 156 309	60.9	18 422 344	11 000 170	59.7	19 620 059	12 156 139	62.0
31 III 2011	CDJC	38 044 565	23 116 673	60.8	18 420 389	10 977 424	59.6	19 624 176	12 139 249	61.9
1 VII 2011[8]	ESDJ	38 051 032	23 111 377	60.7	18 422 837	10 973 937	59.6	19 628 195	12 137 440	61.8
1 VII 2012[8]	ESDJ	38 059 134	23 066 408	60.6	18 424 160	10 948 639	59.4	19 634 974	12 117 769	61.7
1 VII 2013[8]	ESDJ	38 031 632	23 000 324	60.5	18 411 126	10 915 023	59.3	19 620 506	12 085 301	61.6
1 VII 2014[8]	ESDJ	38 006 154	22 951 357	60.4	18 397 470	10 888 729	59.2	19 608 684	12 062 628	61.5
1 VII 2015[8]	ESDJ	37 981 588	22 916 634	60.3	18 384 771	10 869 587	59.1	19 596 817	12 047 047	61.5
1 VII 2016[8]	ESDJ	37 956 779	22 872 493	60.3	18 370 677	10 846 647	59.0	19 586 102	12 025 846	61.4
1 VII 2017[8]	ESDJ	37 962 318	22 859 045	60.2	18 373 411	10 839 076	59.0	19 588 907	12 019 969	61.4
1 VII 2018[8]	ESDJ	37 956 268	22 833 502	60.2	18 370 760	10 825 597	58.9	19 585 508	12 007 905	61.3
1 I 2019[8]	ESDJ	37 972 812	...	...	18 380 376	...	...	19 592 436	...	...

6. Total and urban population by sex: 2010 - 2019
Population totale et population urbaine selon le sexe : 2010 - 2019 (continued - suite)

Continent, country or area, and date Continent, pays ou zone et date	Code[a]	Both sexes - Les deux sexes Total	Urban - Urbaine Number Nombre	Urban - Urbaine Percent P.100	Male - Masculin Total	Urban - Urbaine Number Nombre	Urban - Urbaine Percent P.100	Female - Féminin Total	Urban - Urbaine Number Nombre	Urban - Urbaine Percent P.100
EUROPE										
Portugal										
1 VII 2010	ESDJ	10 573 100	...	...	5 058 644	...	...	5 514 456	...	...
21 III 2011	CDFC	10 282 306	6 286 712	61.1	4 868 755	2 949 862	60.6	5 413 551	3 336 850	61.6
1 VII 2011	ESDJ	10 557 560	...	...	5 041 990	...	...	5 515 570	...	...
1 VII 2012	ESDJ	10 514 844	...	...	5 013 067	...	...	5 501 777	...	...
1 VII 2013	ESDJ	10 457 295	...	...	4 976 859	...	...	5 480 437	...	...
1 VII 2014	ESDJ	10 401 062	...	...	4 940 843	...	...	5 460 219	...	...
1 VII 2015	ESDJ	10 358 076	...	...	4 912 588	...	...	5 445 489	...	...
1 VII 2016	ESDJ	10 325 452	...	...	4 891 983	...	...	5 433 469	...	...
1 VII 2017	ESDJ	10 300 300	...	...	4 875 074	...	...	5 425 226	...	...
1 VII 2018	ESDJ	10 283 822	...	...	4 860 029	...	...	5 423 793	...	...
1 I 2019	ESDJ	10 276 617	...	...	4 852 366	...	...	5 424 251	...	...
Republic of Moldova - République de Moldova										
1 VII 2010[147]	ESDJ	3 562 045	1 479 196	41.5	1 712 783	695 603	40.6	1 849 262	783 593	42.4
1 VII 2011[147]	ESDJ	3 559 986	1 483 731	41.7	1 711 916	697 492	40.7	1 848 070	786 239	42.5
1 VII 2012[147]	ESDJ	3 559 520	1 488 966	41.8	1 712 036	699 880	40.9	1 847 484	789 086	42.7
12 V 2014[148]	CDFC	2 805 194	951 226	33.9	1 352 353	446 554	33.0	1 452 841	504 672	34.7
1 VII 2014[149]	ESDJ	2 856 950	...	...	1 371 528	...	...	1 485 422	...	...
1 VII 2015[149]	ESDJ	2 834 530	...	...	1 363 262	...	...	1 471 269	...	...
1 VII 2016[149]	ESDJ	2 802 170	...	...	1 346 567	...	...	1 455 603	...	...
1 VII 2017[149]	ESDJ	2 755 158	...	...	1 319 613	...	...	1 435 546	...	...
1 VII 2018[149]	ESDJ	2 706 049	...	...	1 291 242	...	...	1 414 807	...	...
Romania - Roumanie[8]										
1 VII 2010	ESDJ	20 246 798	10 922 169	53.9	9 856 669	5 223 471	53.0	10 390 129	5 698 698	54.8
1 VII 2011	ESDJ	20 147 657	10 878 099	54.0	9 805 108	5 198 460	53.0	10 342 549	5 679 639	54.9
20 X 2011	CDFC	20 121 641	10 858 790	54.0	9 788 577	5 185 636	53.0	10 333 064	5 673 154	54.9
1 VII 2012	ESDJ	20 060 182	10 823 218	54.0	9 770 353	5 170 875	52.9	10 289 829	5 652 343	54.9
1 VII 2013	ESDJ	19 988 694	10 772 678	53.9	9 756 310	5 153 631	52.8	10 232 384	5 619 047	54.9
1 VII 2014	ESDF	19 916 451	10 728 929	53.9	9 730 258	5 134 314	52.8	10 186 193	5 594 615	54.9
1 VII 2015	ESDF	19 822 250	10 671 868	53.8	9 681 656	5 099 405	52.7	10 140 594	5 572 463	55.0
1 VII 2016	ESDF	19 706 424	10 586 210	53.7	9 627 987	5 053 806	52.5	10 078 437	5 532 404	54.9
1 VII 2017	ESDF	19 591 668	10 519 506	53.7	9 579 992	5 021 154	52.4	10 011 676	5 498 352	54.9
1 VII 2018	ESDF	19 476 713	10 481 512	53.8	9 528 936	4 999 811	52.5	9 947 777	5 481 701	55.1
1 I 2019	ESDF	19 414 458	10 455 362	53.9	9 500 450	4 984 069	52.5	9 914 008	5 471 293	55.2
Russian Federation - Fédération de Russie										
1 VII 2010	ESDJ	142 849 468	105 241 319	73.7	66 033 070	48 081 267	72.8	76 816 398	57 160 052	74.4
14 X 2010	CDFC	143 436 145	...	...	66 457 074	...	...	76 979 071	...	...
1 VII 2011	ESDJ	142 960 908	105 581 615	73.9	66 113 269	48 243 019	73.0	76 847 639	57 338 596	74.6
1 VII 2012	ESDJ	143 201 730	105 930 122	74.0	66 264 910	48 419 208	73.1	76 936 820	57 510 914	74.8
San Marino - Saint-Marin										
1 VII 2010[56]	ESDF	33 270	...	...	16 171	...	...	17 099	...	...
7 XI 2010*	CDFC	30 652	...	...	14 791[74]	...	...	15 818[74]	...	...
1 VII 2011[56]	ESDF	33 389	...	...	16 221	...	...	17 169	...	...
1 VII 2012[56]	ESDF	33 518	...	...	16 296	...	...	17 222	...	...
1 VII 2013[56]	ESDF	33 469	...	...	16 280	...	...	17 189	...	...
1 VII 2014[56]	ESDF	33 648	...	...	16 396	...	...	17 252	...	...
1 I 2015[56]	ESDF	33 738	...	...	16 425	...	...	17 313	...	...
1 I 2016[56]	ESDF	34 006	...	...	16 560	...	...	17 446	...	...
1 I 2017[56]	ESDF	34 267	...	...	16 677	...	...	17 590	...	...
1 VII 2018[56]	ESDJ	34 536	34 536	100.0	16 835	16 835	100.0	17 701	17 701	100.0
Serbia - Serbie[150]										
1 VII 2010	ESDJ	7 291 436	4 283 985	58.8	3 546 374	2 041 975	57.6	3 745 062	2 242 010	59.9
1 VII 2011[5]	ESDJ	7 236 519	4 275 178	59.1	3 523 911	2 041 228	57.9	3 712 608	2 233 950	60.2
1 X 2011	CDJC	7 186 862	4 271 872	59.4	3 499 176	2 039 105	58.3	3 687 686	2 232 767	60.5
1 VII 2012[5]	ESDJ	7 201 497	4 273 861	59.3	3 506 947	2 039 649	58.2	3 694 550	2 234 212	60.5
1 VII 2013[5]	ESDJ	7 166 552	4 272 061	59.6	3 489 683	2 037 554	58.4	3 676 869	2 234 507	60.8
1 VII 2014[5]	ESDJ	7 131 787	4 270 367	59.9	3 472 746	2 035 772	58.6	3 659 041	2 234 595	61.1
1 VII 2015[5]	ESDJ	7 095 383	4 267 079	60.1	3 455 335	2 033 446	58.8	3 640 048	2 233 633	61.4
1 VII 2016[5]	ESDJ	7 058 322	4 262 256	60.4	3 437 630	2 030 532	59.1	3 620 692	2 231 724	61.6
1 VII 2017[5]	ESDJ	7 020 858	4 256 129	60.6	3 419 815	2 027 177	59.3	3 601 043	2 228 952	61.9
1 VII 2018[5]	ESDJ	6 982 604	4 248 451	60.8	3 401 706	2 023 097	59.5	3 580 898	2 225 354	62.1
1 I 2019[5]	ESDJ	6 963 764	...	...	3 392 811	...	...	3 570 953	...	...

6. Total and urban population by sex: 2010 - 2019
Population totale et population urbaine selon le sexe : 2010 - 2019 (continued - suite)

Continent, country or area, and date / Continent, pays ou zone et date	Code[a]	Both sexes - Les deux sexes			Male - Masculin			Female - Féminin		
		Total	Urban - Urbaine		Total	Urban - Urbaine		Total	Urban - Urbaine	
			Number Nombre	Percent P.100		Number Nombre	Percent P.100		Number Nombre	Percent P.100
EUROPE										
Slovakia - Slovaquie										
1 VII 2010	ESDJ	5 431 024	2 975 976	54.8	2 639 896	1 429 637	54.2	2 791 128	1 546 339	55.4
21 V 2011	CDJC	5 397 036	2 937 735	54.4	2 627 772	1 412 818	53.8	2 769 264	1 524 917	55.1
1 VII 2011	ESDJ	5 398 384	2 938 053	54.4	2 628 463	1 412 966	53.8	2 769 922	1 525 087	55.1
1 VII 2012	ESDJ	5 407 579	2 935 710	54.3	2 633 866	1 411 738	53.6	2 773 714	1 523 972	54.9
1 VII 2013	ESDJ	5 413 393	2 931 444	54.2	2 637 520	1 409 503	53.4	2 775 873	1 521 941	54.8
1 VII 2014	ESDJ	5 418 649	2 925 291	54.0	2 640 694	1 406 300	53.3	2 777 955	1 518 991	54.7
1 VII 2015	ESDJ	5 423 801	2 919 718	53.8	2 644 205	1 403 692	53.1	2 779 596	1 516 027	54.5
1 VII 2016	ESDJ	5 430 798	2 925 475	53.9	2 648 883	1 406 787	53.1	2 781 915	1 518 688	54.6
1 VII 2017	ESDJ	5 439 232	2 921 207	53.7	2 654 099	1 404 749	52.9	2 785 133	1 516 458	54.4
1 VII 2018	ESDJ	5 446 771	2 915 506	53.5	2 658 796	1 401 961	52.7	2 787 975	1 513 545	54.3
1 I 2019	ESDJ	5 450 421	...	...	2 661 077	...	...	2 789 344	...	...
Slovenia - Slovénie										
1 VII 2010	ESDJ	2 049 261	1 024 812	50.0	1 014 716	500 063	49.3	1 034 545	524 749	50.7
1 I 2011	CDFC	2 058 051	1 030 172	50.1	1 019 826	503 083	49.3	1 038 225	527 089	50.8
1 VII 2011	ESDJ	2 052 496	1 023 650	49.9	1 015 430	498 490	49.1	1 037 066	525 160	50.6
1 VII 2012	ESDJ	2 056 262	1 023 236	49.8	1 017 414	498 297	49.0	1 038 848	524 939	50.5
1 VII 2013	ESDJ	2 059 114	1 047 560	50.9	1 019 658	513 084	50.3	1 039 456	534 476	51.4
1 VII 2014	ESDJ	2 061 623	1 051 087	51.0	1 021 419	514 828	50.4	1 040 204	536 259	51.6
1 I 2015	CDJC	2 062 874	1 107 064	53.7	1 022 229	542 636	53.1	1 040 645	564 428	54.2
1 VII 2015	ESDJ	2 063 077	1 106 955	53.7	1 022 554	542 847	53.1	1 040 523	564 108	54.2
1 VII 2016	ESDJ	2 064 241	1 107 409	53.6	1 023 872	543 571	53.1	1 040 369	563 838	54.2
1 VII 2017	ESDJ	2 066 161	1 141 453	55.2	1 025 973	561 337	54.7	1 040 188	580 116	55.8
1 VII 2018	ESDJ	2 070 050	1 144 936	55.3	1 030 234	564 385	54.8	1 039 816	580 551	55.8
1 I 2019	ESDJ	2 080 908	...	...	1 038 656	...	...	1 042 252	...	...
Spain - Espagne										
1 VII 2010	ESDJ	46 562 486	...	...	23 008 587	...	...	23 553 899	...	...
1 VII 2011	ESDJ	46 736 255	...	...	23 073 274	...	...	23 662 981	...	...
1 XI 2011	CDJC	46 815 915	...	...	23 104 350	...	...	23 711 560	...	...
1 VII 2012	ESDJ	46 766 399	...	...	23 055 715	...	...	23 710 684	...	...
1 VII 2013	ESDJ	46 593 236	...	...	22 933 751	...	...	23 659 485	...	...
1 VII 2014[126]	ESDJ	46 480 882	...	...	22 852 004	...	...	23 628 879	...	...
1 VII 2015[126]	ESDJ	46 447 697	...	...	22 817 983	...	...	23 629 714	...	...
1 VII 2016[126]	ESDJ	46 450 439	...	...	22 805 443	...	...	23 644 996	...	...
1 VII 2017[126]	ESDJ	46 532 869	...	...	22 829 748	...	...	23 703 121	...	...
1 VII 2018[126]	ESDJ	46 728 814	...	...	22 911 649	...	...	23 817 165	...	...
1 I 2019[126]	ESDJ	46 937 060	...	...	23 009 259	...	...	23 927 801	...	...
Sweden - Suède[56]										
1 VII 2010	ESDJ	9 378 126	...	...	4 669 629	...	...	4 708 497	...	...
1 VII 2011	ESDJ	9 449 213	...	...	4 708 539	...	...	4 740 674	...	...
31 XII 2011	CDJC	9 482 855	...	...	4 726 834	...	...	4 756 021	...	...
1 VII 2012	ESDJ	9 519 375	...	...	4 746 370	...	...	4 773 005	...	...
1 VII 2013[126]	ESDJ	9 600 379	...	...	4 790 131	...	...	4 810 248	...	...
1 VII 2014[126]	ESDJ	9 696 110	...	...	4 843 299	...	...	4 852 811	...	...
1 VII 2015[126]	ESDJ	9 799 186	...	...	4 901 603	...	...	4 897 583	...	...
1 VII 2016[151]	ESDJ	9 923 085	...	...	4 972 157	...	...	4 950 929	...	...
1 VII 2017[151]	ESDJ	10 057 698	...	...	5 048 005	...	...	5 009 693	...	...
1 I 2018[126]	ESDJ	10 120 242	...	...	5 082 662	...	...	5 037 580	...	...
1 I 2019[126]	ESDJ	10 230 185	...	...	5 142 438	...	...	5 087 747	...	...
Switzerland - Suisse										
1 VII 2010	ESDJ	7 824 909	...	...	3 851 028	...	...	3 973 882	...	...
1 VII 2011	ESDJ	7 912 398	5 823 816	73.6	3 899 840	2 853 440	73.2	4 012 559	2 970 376	74.0
31 XII 2011	CDFC	8 035 391	5 920 706	73.7	3 973 280	2 909 793	73.2	4 062 111	3 010 913	74.1
1 VII 2012	ESDJ	7 996 861	5 887 939	73.6	3 945 389	2 887 886	73.2	4 051 473	3 000 053	74.0
1 VII 2013	ESDJ	8 089 346	5 958 174	73.7	3 995 308	2 925 500	73.2	4 094 038	3 032 674	74.1
1 VII 2014[152]	ESDJ	8 188 649	6 033 396[153]	73.7	4 047 986	2 964 948[153]	73.2	4 140 663	3 068 448[153]	74.1
1 VII 2015[152]	ESDJ	8 282 396	6 997 929	84.5	4 097 676	3 451 374	84.2	4 184 721	3 546 555	84.8
1 VII 2016[152]	ESDJ	8 373 338	7 078 247	84.5	4 147 454	3 494 909	84.3	4 225 884	3 583 339	84.8
1 VII 2017[154]	ESDJ	8 451 840	...	...	4 189 936	...	...	4 261 905	...	...
1 VII 2018[152]	ESDJ	8 507 202	7 213 978	84.8	4 218 732	3 566 243	84.5	4 288 470	3 647 735	85.1
Ukraine										
1 VII 2010	ESDF	45 870 741	31 483 222	68.6	21 175 816	14 436 554	68.2	24 694 925	17 046 668	69.0
1 VII 2011	ESDF	45 706 086	31 411 262	68.7	21 110 638	14 401 999	68.2	24 595 448	17 009 263	69.2
1 VII 2012	ESDF	45 593 342	31 379 757	68.8	21 075 702	14 392 490	68.3	24 517 640	16 987 267	69.3
1 I 2013	ESDF	45 553 047	31 378 639	68.9	21 068 718	14 397 904	68.3	24 484 329	16 980 735	69.4

6. Total and urban population by sex: 2010 - 2019
Population totale et population urbaine selon le sexe : 2010 - 2019 (continued - suite)

Continent, country or area, and date / Continent, pays ou zone et date	Code[a]	Both sexes - Les deux sexes: Total	Both sexes - Urban - Urbaine: Number Nombre	Both sexes - Urban - Urbaine: Percent P.100	Male - Masculin: Total	Male - Urban - Urbaine: Number Nombre	Male - Urban - Urbaine: Percent P.100	Female - Féminin: Total	Female - Urban - Urbaine: Number Nombre	Female - Urban - Urbaine: Percent P.100
EUROPE										
Ukraine										
1 I 2014	ESDF	45 426 249	31 336 623	69.0	21 024 262	14 382 728	68.4	24 401 987	16 953 895	69.5
1 VII 2015[155]	ESDF	42 844 907	29 629 033	69.2	19 851 984	13 612 229	68.6	22 992 924	16 016 804	69.7
1 VII 2016[155]	ESDF	42 672 529	29 533 633	69.2	19 780 361	13 569 991	68.6	22 892 169	15 963 642	69.7
1 VII 2017[155]	ESDF	42 485 473	29 426 654	69.3	19 700 510	13 520 068	68.6	22 784 963	15 906 587	69.8
1 I 2018[156]	ESDF	42 386 403	29 370 995	69.3	19 657 310	13 492 648	68.6	22 729 093	15 878 347	69.9
United Kingdom of Great Britain and Northern Ireland - Royaume-Uni de Grande-Bretagne et d'Irlande du Nord[157]										
1 VII 2010	ESDJ	62 759 456	...	...	30 805 490	...	...	31 953 966	...	...
27 III 2011	CDFC	63 379 787	51 399 714	81.1	31 126 054	25 214 631	81.0	32 253 733	26 185 083	81.2
1 VII 2011	ESDJ	63 285 145	...	...	31 097 259	...	...	32 187 886	...	...
1 VII 2012	ESDJ	63 705 030	...	...	31 315 222	...	...	32 389 808	...	...
1 VII 2013[8]	ESDJ	64 105 654	...	...	31 533 021	...	...	32 572 633	...	...
1 VII 2014[8]	ESDJ	64 596 752	...	...	31 793 752	...	...	32 803 000	...	...
1 VII 2015[8]	ESDJ	65 110 034	...	...	32 074 445	...	...	33 035 589	...	...
1 VII 2016[8]	ESDJ	65 648 054	...	...	32 377 674	...	...	33 270 380	...	...
1 VII 2017[146]	ESDJ	66 041 075	...	...	32 588 011	...	...	33 453 064	...	...
1 I 2018[8]	ESDJ	66 435 550	...	...	32 790 202	...	...	33 645 348	...	...
OCEANIA - OCÉANIE										
American Samoa - Samoas américaines[65]										
1 IV 2010	CDJC	55 519	...	...	28 164	...	...	27 355	...	...
1 VII 2016	ESDJ	60 200	...	...	29 597	...	...	30 603	...	...
Australia - Australie										
1 VII 2010[42]	ESDJ	22 031 750	18 886 173	85.7	10 967 831	9 354 529	85.3	11 063 919	9 531 644	86.2
1 VII 2011[42]	ESDJ	22 340 024	19 172 952	85.8	11 118 234	9 494 673	85.4	11 221 790	9 678 279	86.2
9 VIII 2011[158]	CDFC	21 727 158[159]	19 312 642	88.9	10 737 148[159]	9 471 918	88.2	10 990 010[159]	9 840 724	89.5
1 VII 2012[42]	ESDJ	22 733 465	19 536 489	85.9	11 312 979	9 675 582	85.5	11 420 486	9 860 907	86.3
1 VII 2013[42]	ESDJ	23 128 129	19 903 669	86.1	11 506 165	9 856 019	85.7	11 621 964	10 047 650	86.5
1 VII 2014[42]	ESDJ	23 475 686	20 235 122	86.2	11 667 886	10 012 749	85.8	11 807 800	10 222 373	86.6
1 VII 2015[42]	ESDJ	23 815 995	20 565 241	86.4	11 827 652	10 170 404	86.0	11 988 343	10 394 837	86.7
1 VII 2016[42]	ESDJ	24 190 907	20 924 730	86.5	12 003 039	10 341 382	86.2	12 187 868	10 583 348	86.8
9 VIII 2016[158]	CDFC	23 717 421[159]	21 806 740	91.9	11 686 665[159]	10 676 368	91.4	12 030 751[159]	11 130 367	92.5
1 VII 2017[42]	ESDJ	24 601 860	21 318 113	86.7	12 203 770	10 533 628	86.3	12 398 090	10 784 485	87.0
1 VII 2018*[42]	ESDJ	24 992 860	21 688 081	86.8	12 397 401	10 717 350	86.4	12 595 459	10 970 731	87.1
1 VII 2019*[42]	ESDJ	25 365 571	...	...	12 581 355	...	...	12 784 216	...	...
Cook Islands - Îles Cook										
1 XII 2011	CDFC	17 794	...	...	8 815	...	...	8 979	...	...
1 XII 2016	CDFC	17 434	...	...	8 520	...	...	8 914	...	...
Fiji - Fidji										
17 IX 2010	ESDF	849 380	...	...	432 782	...	...	416 598	...	...
17 IX 2011	ESDF	854 120	...	...	434 877	...	...	419 242	...	...
17 IX 2012	ESDF	858 404	...	...	436 760	...	...	421 644	...	...
17 IX 2013	ESDF	862 233	...	...	438 429	...	...	423 804	...	...
17 IX 2014	ESDF	865 611	...	...	439 886	...	...	425 724	...	...
17 IX 2015	ESDF	868 532	...	...	441 129	...	...	427 402	...	...
17 IX 2016	ESDF	870 984	...	...	442 151	...	...	428 833	...	...
17 IX 2017	CDFC	884 887	494 252	55.9	448 595	245 928	54.8	436 292	248 324	56.9
17 IX 2018	ESDF	887 104	...	...	449 759	...	...	437 344	...	...
17 IX 2019	ESDF	889 327	...	...	450 927	...	...	438 400	...	...
French Polynesia - Polynésie française										
1 VII 2010[33]	ESDJ	264 916	...	...	135 528	...	...	129 388	...	...
1 VII 2011[33]	ESDJ	266 639	...	...	136 324	...	...	130 315	...	...
1 VII 2012[33]	ESDJ	268 154	...	...	136 993	...	...	131 161	...	...
22 VIII 2012	CDFC	268 207	...	...	136 996	...	...	131 211	...	...
1 VII 2013[33]	ESDJ	269 716	...	...	137 688	...	...	132 028	...	...
1 VII 2014[33]	ESDJ	271 442	...	...	138 460	...	...	132 982	...	...

6. Total and urban population by sex: 2010 - 2019
Population totale et population urbaine selon le sexe : 2010 - 2019 (continued - suite)

Continent, country or area, and date / Continent, pays ou zone et date	Code[a]	Both sexes - Les deux sexes			Male - Masculin			Female - Féminin		
		Total	Urban - Urbaine		Total	Urban - Urbaine		Total	Urban - Urbaine	
			Number Nombre	Percent P.100		Number Nombre	Percent P.100		Number Nombre	Percent P.100
OCEANIA - OCÉANIE										
French Polynesia - Polynésie française										
1 VII 2015[33]	ESDJ	273 044	...	...	139 140	...	...	133 904	...	...
1 VII 2016[33]	ESDJ	274 570	...	...	139 788	...	...	134 782	...	...
1 VII 2017[33]	ESDJ	275 822	...	...	140 262	...	...	135 559	...	...
1 VII 2018[3]	ESDJ	276 867	...	...	140 622	...	...	136 245	...	...
Guam										
1 IV 2010	CDJC	159 358	149 918	94.1	81 552	...	...	77 806	...	...
1 VII 2011[65]	ESDJ	159 600	...	...	81 053	...	...	78 547	...	...
1 VII 2012[65]	ESDJ	159 914	...	...	81 165	...	...	78 749	...	...
1 VII 2013[65]	ESDJ	160 378	...	...	81 354	...	...	79 024	...	...
1 VII 2014[65]	ESDJ	161 001	...	...	81 625	...	...	79 376	...	...
1 VII 2015[65]	ESDJ	161 785	...	...	81 978	...	...	79 807	...	...
1 VII 2016[65]	ESDJ	162 742	...	...	82 420	...	...	80 322	...	...
1 VII 2017[65]	ESDJ	163 875	...	...	82 951	...	...	80 924	...	...
1 VII 2018[65]	ESDJ	167 772	...	...	86 329	...	...	81 443	...	...
1 VII 2019[65]	ESDJ	168 147	...	...	86 541	...	...	81 606	...	...
Kiribati										
10 X 2010	CDFC	103 058	...	...	50 796	...	...	52 262	...	...
7 XI 2015	CDFC	110 136	56 388	51.2	54 096	27 159	50.2	56 040	29 229	52.2
Marshall Islands - Îles Marshall										
1 VII 2010[160]	ESDF	*54 305*	...	...	*27 843*	...	...	*26 462*	...	...
3 IV 2011	CDFC	53 158	39 205	73.8	27 243	19 927	73.1	25 915	19 278	74.4
Micronesia (Federated States of) - Micronésie (États fédérés de)										
1 IV 2010	CDJC	102 843	22 924	22.3	52 193	...	...	50 650	...	...
1 VII 2010[1]	ESDJ	*107 839*	...	...	*54 158*	...	...	*53 681*	...	...
1 VII 2011[161]	ESDJ	*103 022*	...	...	*52 284*	...	...	*50 738*	...	...
1 VII 2012[161]	ESDJ	*103 202*	...	...	*52 375*	...	...	*50 827*	...	...
1 VII 2013[161]	ESDJ	*103 382*	...	...	*52 467*	...	...	*50 915*	...	...
1 VII 2014[161]	ESDJ	*103 562*	...	...	*52 558*	...	...	*51 004*	...	...
1 VII 2015[161]	ESDJ	*103 743*	...	...	*52 650*	...	...	*51 093*	...	...
1 VII 2016[161]	ESDJ	*103 923*	...	...	*52 741*	...	...	*51 182*	...	...
1 VII 2017[161]	ESDJ	*104 104*	...	...	*52 833*	...	...	*51 271*	...	...
1 VII 2018[161]	ESDJ	*104 286*	...	...	*52 925*	...	...	*51 361*	...	...
1 VII 2019[161]	ESDJ	*104 468*	...	...	*53 017*	...	...	*51 450*	...	...
Nauru										
31 X 2011	CDFC	10 084	...	...	5 105	...	...	4 979	...	...
1 VII 2012[1]	ESDF	*10 376*	...	...	*5 126*	...	...	*5 250*	...	...
1 VII 2015[1]	ESDF	*11 288*	...	...	*5 701*	...	...	*5 587*	...	...
1 VII 2016[1]	ESDF	*11 014*	...	...	*5 467*	...	...	*5 547*	...	...
New Caledonia - Nouvelle-Calédonie										
26 VIII 2014	CDFC	268 767	...	...	135 542	...	...	133 225	...	...
1 I 2016	ESDF	274 579	...	...	138 197	...	...	136 382	...	...
1 I 2017	ESDF	*278 495*	...	...	*140 000*	...	...	*138 495*	...	...
New Zealand - Nouvelle-Zélande										
1 VII 2010[91]	ESDJ	4 350 700	3 743 300[162]	86.0	2 127 700	1 816 700[162]	85.4	2 222 900	1 926 600[162]	86.7
1 VII 2011[91]	ESDJ	4 384 000	3 765 400[162]	85.9	2 143 600	1 826 900[162]	85.2	2 240 400	1 938 500[162]	86.5
1 VII 2012[91]	ESDJ	4 408 100	3 784 600[162]	85.9	2 155 000	1 836 200[162]	85.2	2 253 100	1 948 500[162]	86.5
5 III 2013[163]	CDFC	4 353 198	3 732 537	85.7	2 119 464	1 801 341	85.0	2 233 734	1 931 199	86.5
1 VII 2013[91]	ESDJ	4 442 100	3 818 300[162]	86.0	2 172 200	1 853 100[162]	85.3	2 269 900	1 965 200[162]	86.6
1 VII 2014[91]	ESDJ	4 509 700	3 884 000[162]	86.1	2 209 600	1 889 100[162]	85.5	2 300 200	1 995 000[162]	86.7
1 VII 2015[91]	ESDJ	4 595 700	3 959 200[162]	86.2	2 257 200	1 931 800[162]	85.6	2 338 500	2 027 400[162]	86.7
1 VII 2016[91]	ESDJ	4 693 200	4 056 200[162]	86.4	2 309 100	1 983 600[162]	85.9	2 384 100	2 072 600[162]	86.9
1 VII 2017[91]	ESDJ	4 793 900	4 144 300[162]	86.4	2 361 100	2 029 700[162]	86.0	2 432 800	2 114 600[162]	86.9
1 VII 2018[91]	ESDJ	4 841 000	4 054 900[162]	83.8	2 380 000	1 978 200[162]	83.1	2 461 000	2 076 800[162]	84.4
1 VII 2019[91]	ESDJ	4 917 000	4 117 100[162]	83.7	2 419 700	2 012 100[162]	83.2	2 497 300	2 105 000[162]	84.3
Niue - Nioué										
1 VII 2010	ESDJ	1 496	...	...	754	...	...	740	...	...
1 VII 2011	ESDJ	1 460	...	...	738	...	...	722	...	...

6. Total and urban population by sex: 2010 - 2019
Population totale et population urbaine selon le sexe : 2010 - 2019 (continued - suite)

Continent, country or area, and date / Continent, pays ou zone et date	Code[a]	Both sexes - Les deux sexes: Total	Both sexes: Urban - Urbaine: Number Nombre	Both sexes: Urban - Urbaine: Percent P.100	Male - Masculin: Total	Male: Urban - Urbaine: Number Nombre	Male: Urban - Urbaine: Percent P.100	Female - Féminin: Total	Female: Urban - Urbaine: Number Nombre	Female: Urban - Urbaine: Percent P.100
OCEANIA - OCÉANIE										
Niue - Nioué										
11 IX 2011	CDFC	1 611	...	...	802	...	...	809	...	...
1 VII 2012[164]	ESDJ	1 482	...	...	752	...	...	730	...	...
1 VII 2013[164]	ESDJ	1 503	...	...	767	...	...	736	...	...
1 VII 2014[164]	ESDJ	1 515	...	...	781	...	...	737	...	...
1 VII 2015[164]	ESDJ	1 541	...	...	797	...	...	744	...	...
1 VII 2016[164]	ESDJ	1 567	...	...	812	...	...	755	...	...
9 III 2017	CDFC	1 719	...	...	831	...	...	888	...	...
Norfolk Island - Île Norfolk										
9 VIII 2011	CDFC	2 302	...	...	1 082	...	...	1 220	...	...
Northern Mariana Islands - Îles Mariannes septentrionales										
1 IV 2010	CDFC	53 883	...	...	27 746	...	...	26 137	...	...
1 VII 2010	ESDF	*48 317*	...	...	*23 231*	...	...	*25 086*	...	...
1 VII 2011	ESDF	*46 050*	...	...	*22 153*	...	...	*23 897*	...	...
Palau - Palaos										
1 XII 2012	CDJC	17 501	14 202	81.1	9 217	7 506	81.4	8 284	6 696	80.8
13 IV 2015	CDJC	17 661	14 209	80.5	9 433	7 620	80.8	8 228	6 589	80.1
Papua New Guinea - Papouasie-Nouvelle-Guinée										
10 VII 2011	CDFC	7 275 324	...	...	3 772 864	...	...	3 502 460	...	...
1 VII 2016[165]	ESDF	*8 151 300*	...	...	*4 205 000*	...	...	*3 946 300*	...	...
Pitcairn										
10 VIII 2012	CDJC	48	...	...	22	...	...	26	...	...
31 XII 2013	CDJC	49	...	...	23	...	...	26	...	...
Samoa										
1 VII 2010	ESDF	*186 404*	*36 930*	*19.8*	*96 327*	*18 612*	*19.3*	*90 077*	*18 318*	*20.3*
7 XI 2011	CDFC	187 820	36 735	19.6	96 990	18 485	19.1	90 830	18 250	20.1
1 VII 2012	ESDF	*189 236*	*36 866*	*19.5*	*97 653*	*18 540*	*19.0*	*91 583*	*18 326*	*20.0*
1 VII 2013	ESDF	*190 652*	*36 997*	*19.4*	*98 315*	*18 595*	*18.9*	*92 336*	*18 402*	*19.9*
1 VII 2014	ESDF	*192 067*	*37 129*	*19.3*	*98 978*	*18 650*	*18.8*	*93 090*	*18 479*	*19.9*
1 VII 2015	ESDF	*193 483*	*37 260*	*19.3*	*99 640*	*18 705*	*18.8*	*93 843*	*18 555*	*19.8*
7 XI 2016	CDFC	195 979	37 391	19.1	100 892	18 760	18.6	95 087	18 631	19.6
1 VII 2017	ESDF	*197 611*	*37 522*	*19.0*	*101 672*	*18 815*	*18.5*	*95 938*	*18 707*	*19.5*
1 VII 2018	ESDF	*199 243*	*37 653*	*18.9*	*102 453*	*18 870*	*18.4*	*96 790*	*18 783*	*19.4*
1 VII 2019	ESDF	*200 874*	*37 785*	*18.8*	*103 233*	*18 925*	*18.3*	*97 641*	*18 860*	*19.3*
Solomon Islands - Îles Salomon[166]										
1 VII 2010	ESDF	*555 447*	...	...	*285 040*	...	...	*270 408*	...	...
1 VII 2011	ESDF	*569 600*	...	...	*292 105*	...	...	*277 495*	...	...
1 VII 2012	ESDF	*583 672*	...	...	*299 131*	...	...	*284 541*	...	...
1 VII 2013	ESDF	*597 653*	...	...	*306 112*	...	...	*291 541*	...	...
1 VII 2014	ESDF	*611 538*	...	...	*313 044*	...	...	*298 494*	...	...
1 VII 2015	ESDF	*625 374*	...	...	*319 954*	...	...	*305 420*	...	...
1 VII 2016	ESDF	*639 157*	...	...	*326 837*	...	...	*312 321*	...	...
1 VII 2017	ESDF	*652 886*	...	...	*333 693*	...	...	*319 193*	...	...
1 VII 2018	ESDF	*666 557*	...	...	*340 521*	...	...	*326 036*	...	...
Tokelau - Tokélaou										
18 X 2011	CDFC	1 205	...	...	600	...	...	605	...	...
1 XII 2013	ESDF	*1 383*	...	...	*683*	...	...	*700*	...	...
18 X 2016	CDFC	1 285	...	...	652	...	...	633	...	...
12 XII 2019[167]	ESDF	1 647	...	...	813	...	...	834	...	...
Tonga										
30 XI 2011	CDJC	103 252	24 229	23.5	51 979	12 156	23.4	51 273	12 073	23.5
30 XI 2016	CDFC	100 651	23 221	23.1	50 255	11 529	22.9	50 396	11 692	23.2
Tuvalu										
1 VII 2011	ESDF	*11 206*	...	...	*5 582*	...	...	*5 625*	...	...
1 VII 2013	ESDF	*10 730*	...	...	*5 600*	...	...	*5 400*	...	...
1 VII 2016	ESDF	*11 153*	...	...	*5 100*[165]	...	...	*5 000*[165]	...	...
Vanuatu										
1 VII 2010[168]	ESDF	*239 115*	*59 163*	*24.7*	*121 599*	...	...	*117 517*	...	...
1 VII 2011[168]	ESDF	*244 319*	*61 199*	*25.0*	*124 161*	...	...	*122 862*	...	...

6. Total and urban population by sex: 2010 - 2019
Population totale et population urbaine selon le sexe : 2010 - 2019 (continued - suite)

Continent, country or area, and date / Continent, pays ou zone et date	Code[a]	Both sexes - Les deux sexes			Male - Masculin			Female - Féminin		
		Total	Urban - Urbaine		Total	Urban - Urbaine		Total	Urban - Urbaine	
			Number Nombre	Percent P.100		Number Nombre	Percent P.100		Number Nombre	Percent P.100
OCEANIA - OCÉANIE										
Vanuatu										
1 VII 2012[168]	ESDF	*249 635*	*63 305*	*25.4*	*126 776*	...	...	*122 862*	...	...
1 VII 2013[168]	ESDF	*255 067*	*65 483*	*25.7*	*129 446*	...	...	*125 625*	...	...
1 VII 2014[168]	ESDF	*260 618*	*67 737*	*26.0*	*132 172*	...	...	*128 450*	...	...
1 VII 2015[168]	ESDF	*266 289*	*70 068*	*26.3*	*134 956*	...	...	*131 339*	...	...
7 XI 2016[169]	CDFC	272 459	67 749	24.9	138 265	34 506	25.0	134 194	32 933	24.5
1 VII 2017[170]	ESDF	*278 040*	*69 296*	*24.9*	*141 045*	*35 216*	*25.0*	*136 995*	*33 722*	*24.6*
1 VII 2018[170]	ESDF	*283 735*	*70 879*	*25.0*	*143 880*	*35 941*	*25.0*	*139 855*	*34 529*	*24.7*
1 VII 2019[170]	ESDF	*289 546*	*72 497*	*25.0*	*146 773*	*36 680*	*25.0*	*142 774*	*35 356*	*24.8*
Wallis and Futuna Islands - Îles Wallis et Futuna										
22 VII 2013	CDFC	12 197	...	...	5 927	...	...	6 270	...	...
1 VII 2016[165]	ESDF	*11 800*	...	...	*5 700*	...	...	*6 100*	...	...

FOOTNOTES - NOTES

Italics: estimates which are less reliable. - Italiques : estimations moins sûres.

* Provisional. - Données provisoires.

[a] 'Code' indicates the source of data, as follows:
CDFC - Census, de facto, complete tabulation
CDFS - Census, de facto, sample tabulation
CDJC - Census, de jure, complete tabulation
CDJS - Census, de jure, sample tabulation
SSDF - Sample survey, de facto
SSDJ - Sample survey, de jure
ESDF - Estimates, de facto
ESDJ - Estimates, de jure

Le 'Code' indique la source des données, comme suit :
CDFC - Recensement, population de fait, tabulation complète
CDFS - Recensement, population de fait, tabulation par sondage
CDJC - Recensement, population de droit, tabulation complète
CDJS - Recensement, population de droit, tabulation par sondage
SSDF - Enquête par sondage, population de fait
SSDJ - Enquête par sondage, population de droit
ESDF - Estimations, population de fait
ESDJ - Estimations, population de droit

1 Data refer to national projections. - Les données se réfèrent aux projections nationales.

2 Unrevised data that do not take into account the results of the 2014 population census. - Ces données n'ont pas été revisées et elles ne prennent pas en compte les résultats du recensement de la population de 2014.

3 Postcensal estimates. - Estimations post censitaires.

4 Projections based on the 2013 Population Census. - Projections fondées sur le recensement de la population de 2013.

5 Based on the results of the 2011 Population Census. - Basé sur les résultats du recencement de la population de 2011.

6 Source: Population projections and estimates of priority targets for the various health programs and interventions, National Institute of Statistics (2016). - Source : Projections démographiques et estimations des cibles prioritaires des différents programmes et interventions de sante, Institut National de la Statistique (2016).

7 Based on the results of the 2014 Population Census. - D'après les résultats du recensement de la population de 2014.

8 Data refer to usual resident population. - Les données se réfèrent à la population résidente habituelle.

9 Estimates or projections based on the 2015 population census. - Estimations ou projections fondées sur les résultats du recensement de la population de 2015.

10 Estimates based on the 2000 quick population count results and 1995, 2002 and 2010 Eritrea Demographic and Health Surveys. - Des estimations fondées sur le dénombrement rapide de la population de 2000 et sur les enquêtes érythréennes de la démographie et de la santé de 1995, 2002 et 2010.

11 Data refer to national projections based on 2007 census. - Les données sont des projections nationales d'après les résultats du recensement de la population de 2007.

12 Estimates considering also the results of the 2007 Population Census. - Estimations en prennant en considération les résultats du recensement de la population de 2007.

13 Source: Integrated Household Survey (IHS) 2015/2016. - Source: Enquête intégrée auprès des ménages (IHS) 2015/2016.

14 Data based on the 2010 Population Census. - Les données sont fondées sur le recensement de la population de 2010.

15 Intercensal estimates. Population in households only. - Estimations inter-censitaires. Population dans les ménages seulement.

16 Population in households only. Postcensal estimates. - Population dans les ménages seulement. Estimations post censitaires.

17 Post-censal estimates based on the 2009 Population Census. - Les estimations post-censitaire fondées sur le recensement de la population de 2009.

18 The figure for both sexes excludes a total of 1524 intersex persons (841 in Rural and 683 in urban). - Le chiffre pour les deux sexes exclut un total de 1 524 personnes intersexes (841 pour le milieu rural et 683 pour le milieu urbain).

19 Data are projections based on the 2006 Population Census. - Projections fondées sur le recensement de la population de 2006.

20 Data refer to Libyan nationals only. - Les données se raportent aux nationaux libyens seulement.

21 Data refer to projections based on the 1993 Population Census. - Les données se réfèrent aux projections basées sur le recensement de la population de 1993.

22 Projections considering also the results of the 2009 Population Census. - Projections en prennant en considération les résultats du recensement de la population de 2009.

23 Including nomadic population. - Y compris la population nomade.

24 Excludes the islands of St. Brandon and Agalega. - Non compris les îles St. Brandon et Agalega.

25 Based on the results of the 2000 Population Census. - Basé sur les résultats du recencement de la population de 2000.

26 Data refer to annual average population. - Les données correspondent à la population annuelle moyenne.

27 Data from the main operation. - Données de l'opération principale.

28 Based on the results of the 2004 Population Census. - D'après des résultats du recensement de la population de 2004.

29 Projections based on the results of national survey on population and health conducted between 2010 and 2011, and especially population and housing census 2014. - Des projections de la population fondées sur les résultats de l'enquête nationale de la population et de la santé réalisée entre 2010 et 2011 et, surtout, du recensement général de la population et de l'habitat de 2014.

[30] Projections based on the 2012 Population Census. - Projections fondées sur le recensement de la population de 2012.
[31] Data are projections based on the 2008 Population and Housing Census. - Projection basée sur le recensement 2008 de la population et des logements.
[32] Data refer to total resident population, Saint Helenian and other nationalities. - Les données concernent la population résidente totale, originaire de Sainte-Hélène ou possédant une autre nationalité.
[33] Intercensal estimates. - Estimations inter-censitaires.
[34] Data are de facto Census counts that have been adjusted for age and sex errors. - Les données correspondent aux valeurs du recensement de facto corrigées pour tenir compte des erreurs d'âge et de sexe.
[35] Unrevised data. - Les données n'ont pas été révisées.
[36] The urban area is reconfigured by extending the urban agglomeration of Lomé to include all the prefecture of Golfe and the new prefecture of Agoènyvé. - L'espace urbaine a été reconstitué par l'extension de l'agglomération de Lomé à toute la préfecture du Golfe et à la nouvelle préfecture d'Agoènyvé.
[37] Data for urban and rural do not add up to the total; reason for discrepancy not ascertained. - La somme des données pour la résidence urbaine et rurale n'est pas égale au total; on ne sait pas comment s'explique la divergence.
[38] Projections based on the 2002 Population Census. - Projections fondées sur le recensement de la population de 2002.
[39] Data have not been adjusted for underenumeration, estimated at 7 per cent. - Les données n'ont pas été ajustées pour compenser les lacunes du dénombrement, estimées à 7 p. 100.
[40] Data refers to resident population adjusted for the undercount of 18 per cent and including the institutional population. - Les données concernent la population résidente, y compris la population des institutions, et ont été ajustées pour tenir compte du sous-dénombrement estimé à 18 p. 100.
[41] Bermuda is 100 per cent urban. - 100 pour cent de la population des Bermudes est urbaine.
[42] Based on the results of the 2016 Population Census. - Basé sur les résultats du recencement de la population de 2016.
[43] Adjusted for census net undercoverage (including adjustment for incompletely enumerated Indian reserves). Final intercensal estimates. - Ajusté pour la sous-estimation du recensement (y compris les réservations en Inde incomplètement énumérées). Estimations inter-censitaires definitives.
[44] To ensure confidentiality, the values, including totals are randomly rounded either up or down to a multiple of '5' or '10.' As a result, when these data are summed or grouped, the total value may not match the individual values since totals and sub-totals are independently rounded. Similarly, percentages, which are calculated on rounded data, may not necessarily add up to 100%. - À des fins de confidentialité, les chiffres, y compris les totaux, sont aléatoirement arrondis au multiple de 5 ou de 10 inférieur ou supérieur. Par conséquent, lorsque ces chiffres sont additionnés, le total peut ne pas correspondre à la somme des valeurs individuelles, dans la mesure où les totaux et les totaux partiels sont arrondis indépendamment. De même, la somme des pourcentages, qui sont calculés à partir des données arrondies, peut ne pas correspondre à 100 %.
[45] Final postcensal estimates. Adjusted for census net undercoverage (including adjustment for incompletely enumerated Indian reserves). - Estimations postcensitaires definitives. Ajusté pour la sous-estimation du recensement (y compris les réservations en Inde incomplètement énumérées).
[46] Adjusted for census net undercoverage (including adjustment for incompletely enumerated Indian reserves). Updated postcensal estimates. - Ajusté pour la sous-estimation du recensement (y compris les réservations en Inde incomplètement énumérées). Estimations post censitaires mises à jour.
[47] Adjusted for census net undercoverage (including adjustment for incompletely enumerated Indian reserves). Postcensal estimates. - Ajusté pour la sous-estimation du recensement (y compris les réservations en Inde incomplètement énumérées). Estimations post censitaires.
[48] Excluding the institutional population. - Non compris la population dans les institutions.
[49] Based on the national household surveys 2010-2014 and the 2011 population census. - D'après les données de l'enquête nationale des ménages 2010-2014 et les résultats du recensement de la population de 2011.
[50] Definition of urban and rural distribution changed from the year 2010. - La définition des régions urbaines et rurales a changée depuis 2010.
[51] Based on the national household survey of 2015. - Basée sur l' enquête nationale auprès des ménages de 2015.
[52] Based on the national household survey of 2016. - D'après l'enquête nationale auprès des ménages de 2016.
[53] Based on the national household survey of 2017. - D'après l'enquête nationale auprès des ménages de 2017.
[54] Based on the national household survey of 2018. - D'après l'enquête nationale auprès des ménages de 2018.
[55] Based on the national household survey of 2019. - D'après l'enquête nationale auprès des ménages de 2019.
[56] Population statistics are compiled from registers. - Les statistiques de la population sont compilées à partir des registres.
[57] Excluding data for Saint Barthélémy and Saint Martin. - Non compris les données pour Saint Barthélémy et Saint Martin.
[58] Projections produced by l'Institut Haïtien de Statistique et d'Informatique (IHSI) and the Latin American and Caribbean Demographic Centre (CELADE) - Population Division of ECLAC. - Les données sont projections produits par l'Institut Haïtien de Statistique et d'Informatique (IHSI) et le centre démographique de l'Amérique latine et les Caraïbes - Division de la population de la CEPALC.
[59] Data refer to projections based on the 2001 Population Census. - Les données se réfèrent aux projections basées sur le recensement de la population de 2001.
[60] The figures represent the census counts adjusted for under-coverage. Adjustments are done by applying weights calculated (to 4 decimal places) for each sex and age group to the enumerated population when the tabulations are produced. Minor discrepancies between totals and the sum of the component parts of a table and minor discrepancies between the totals across tables are due to rounding after weights are applied. - Les chiffres représentent le dénombrement résultant du recensement ajusté pour tenir compte du sous-dénombrement. Les ajustements sont effectués en appliquant un coefficient de pondération calculé (à la quatrième décimale) pour chaque sexe et groupe d'âges de la population dénombrée lors de l'établissement des tableaux. Les écarts mineurs entre les totaux et la somme des éléments constitutifs d'un tableau ainsi qu'entre les totaux figurant dans différents tableaux sont dus au fait que les chiffres sont arrondis après la pondération.
[61] Including an estimation of 1 334 585 persons corresponding to 448 195 housing units without information of the occupants. - Y compris une estimation de 1 334 585 personnes correspondant aux 448 195 unités d'habitation sans information sur les occupants.
[62] Data revised by CONAPO (National Population Council). - Données révisées par CONAPO (Conseil national de la population).
[63] The population projections of CONAPO (National Population Council). - Les projections démographiques de la CONAPO (Conseil national de la population).
[64] Data refer to the intercensal population count. - Les données se réfèrent au dénombrement intercensitaire de la population.
[65] Including armed forces stationed in the area. - Y compris les militaires en garnison sur le territoire.
[66] Based on the results of the 2010 Population Census. - D'après le résultats du recensement de la population de 2010.
[67] Postcensal estimates. Excluding U.S. Armed Forces overseas and civilian U.S. citizens whose usual place of residence is outside the United States. - Estimations post censitaires. Non compris les militaires américains à l'étranger et les civils américains dont le lieu de résidence habituel est en dehors des États-Unis.
[68] Data include persons in remote areas, military personnel outside the country, merchant seamen at sea, civilian seasonal workers outside the country, and other civilians outside the country, and exclude nomads, foreign military, civilian aliens temporarily in the country, transients on ships and Indian jungle population. Data refer to national projections. - Y compris les personnes vivant dans des régions éloignées, le personel militaire en dehors du pays, les marins marchands, les ouvriers saisonniers en dehors du pays, et autres civils en dehors du pays, et non compris les nomades, les militaires étrangers, les étrangers civils temporairement dans le pays, les transiteurs sur des bateaux et les Indiens de la jungle. Les données se réfèrent aux projections nationales.
[69] Estimates or projections based on the 2017 Population Census. - Estimations ou projections fondées sur le recensement de la population de 2017.
[70] Data are revised projections taking into consideration also the results of the 2018 census. - Les données sont des projections révisées tenant compte également des résultats du recensement de 2018.
[71] Excludes nomadic Indian tribes. Data based on the 2010 Population Census. - Non compris les tribus d'Indiens nomades. Les données sont fondées sur le recensement de la population de 2010.
[72] A dispute exists between the governments of Argentina and the United Kingdom of Great Britain and Northern Ireland concerning sovereignty over the Falkland Islands (Malvinas). - La souveraineté sur les îles Falkland (Malvinas) fait l'objet d'un différend entre le Gouvernement argentin et le Gouvernement du Royaume-Uni de Grande-Bretagne et d'Irlande du Nord.
[73] Excluding military personnel and their families, visitors and transients. - Non compris les militaires et leur familles, ni les visiteurs et transients.
[74] Figures for male and female may not add up to the total, since they do not include the category "Unknown". - La somme des chiffres indiqués pour les sexes masculin et féminin peut n'être pas égale au total parce qu'elle n'inclut pas la catégorie " inconnue ".
[75] Estimates based on low variant projections. - Des estimations fondées sur des projections de variante basse.

[76] Estimates or projections considering also the results of the 2012 Population Census. - Estimations ou projections en prennant en considération les résultats du recensement de la population de 2012.
[77] Source: INEI – National population estimates and projections from bulletin No. 24 published in July 2019. - Source : INEI - Estimations et projections nationales de la population, publiées dans le bulletin numéro 24 , juillet 2019.
[78] Data have not been adjusted for underenumeration and exclude an estimated population of 1,855,501 at the national level. - Les données n'ont pas été ajustées pour compenser les lacunes du dénombrement. Les données excluent un nombre de personnes estimé à 1,855,501 à l'échelle nationale.
[79] Figures for male and female population do not add up to the figure for total population, because they exclude 108 homeless people of unknown sex. - Les chiffres relatifs à la population masculine et féminine ne correspondent pas au chiffre de la population totale, parce que l'on en a exclu 108 personnes sans toit dont le sexe n'est pas connu.
[80] For operational purposes, population centers with 2,500 and more inhabitants are considered as urban area and less than 2,500 are considered as rural area. - À des fins opérationnelles, les centres de population comptant 2 500 habitants ou plus sont considérés comme zones urbaines, ceux qui en comptent moins de 2 500 comme zones rurales.
[81] Data refer to the settled population based on the 1979 Population Census and the latest household prelisting. The refugees of Afghanistan in Iran, Pakistan, and an estimated 1.5 million nomads, are not included. - Les données se rapportent à la population stationnaire sur la base du recensement de 1979 et du recensement préliminaire des logements le plus récent. Sont exclus les réfugiés d'Afghanistan en Iran et au Pakistan et les nomades estimés à 1,5 million.
[82] Data have been adjusted for underenumeration. - Les données ont été ajustées pour compenser les lacunes du dénombrement.
[83] Data refer to projected figures based on the Population and Housing Census 2005 (district projection). - Les données se réfèrent aux projections basées sur le recensement de la population et de l'habitat de 2005 (projections locales).
[84] Excluding 8408 tourists and foreigners. - À l'exclusion de 8 408 touristes et étrangers.
[85] Source: 2016 Population and Housing Census Update. - Source : Révision des chiffres du recensement de la population et des logements de 2016.
[86] Excluding foreign diplomatic personnel and their dependants. Data based on the 2008 Population Census. - Non compris le personnel diplomatique étranger et les membres de leur famille les accompagnant. Données fondées sur le recensement de population de 2008.
[87] Based on the results of the Cambodia Intercensal Population Survey. Data exclude foreign diplomatic personnel and their dependants. - Sur la base de l'enquête intercensitaire de la population de Cambodge. Non compris le personnel diplomatique étranger et les membres de leur famille les accompagnant.
[88] Excluding migrants working abroad. - Non compris les migrants qui travaillent à l'étranger.
[89] For statistical purposes, the data for China do not include those for the Hong Kong Special Administrative Region (Hong Kong SAR), Macao Special Administrative Region (Macao SAR) and Taiwan province of China. - Pour la présentation des statistiques, les données pour la Chine ne comprennent pas la Région Administrative Spéciale de Hong Kong (Hong Kong RAS), la Région Administrative Spéciale de Macao (Macao RAS) et Taïwan province de Chine.
[90] Data have been estimated on the basis of the annual National Sample Survey on Population Changes. - Les données ont été estimées sur la base de l'enquête annuelle "National Sample Survey on Population Changes".
[91] Because of rounding, totals are not in all cases the sum of the respective components. - Les chiffres étant arrondis, les totaux ne correspondent pas toujours rigoureusement à la somme des composants respectifs.
[92] Because of rounding, totals are not in all cases the sum of the respective components. The military personnel are classified as urban population. - Les chiffres étant arrondis, les totaux ne correspondent pas toujours rigoureusement à la somme des composants respectifs. Le personnel militaire est classé dans la population urbaine.
[93] Data are from Communique of the National Bureau of Statistics of the People's Republic of China on Major Figures of the 2010 Population Census (No.1). - Données issues du communiqué du Bureau national de la statistique de la République populaire de Chine sur les chiffres importants du recensement de 2010 (n° 1).
[94] Data have been adjusted on the basis of the Population Census of 2010. - Les données ont été ajustées à partir des résultats du recensement de la population de 2010.
[95] The military personnel are classified as urban population. - Le personnel militaire est classé dans la population urbaine.
[96] Data refer to Hong Kong resident population at the census moment, which covers usual residents and mobile residents. Usual residents refer to two categories of people: (1) Hong Kong permanent residents who had stayed in Hong Kong for at least three months during the six months before or for at least three months during the six months after the census moment, regardless of whether they were in Hong Kong or not at the census moment; and (2) Hong Kong non-permanent residents who were in Hong Kong at the census moment. Mobile Residents, they are Hong Kong permanent residents who had stayed in Hong Kong for at least one month but less than three months during the six months before or for at least one month but less than three months during the six months after the census moment, regardless of whether they were in Hong Kong or not at the census moment. - Les données se rapportent à la population résidente à Hong Kong au moment du recensement. Cette population est composée des résidants habituels et des résidants mobiles. La population résidente est partagée en deux catégories: (1) les résidents permanents qui ont habité à Hong Kong au moins trois mois pendant les six mois précédents ou les six mois suivants le recensement; (2) les habitants non-permanents de Hong Kong qui étaient à Hong Kong au moment du recensement. La population mobile se rapporte aux résidents permanents de Hong Kong qui ont habité à Hong Kong pendant les six mois après le recensement pour une période comprise entre un mois et trois mois, indépendamment du fait qu'ils étaient à Hong Kong au moment du recensement au pays.
[97] Data refer to Hong Kong resident population at the census moment, which covers usual residents and mobile residents. Usual residents refer to two categories of people: (1) Hong Kong permanent residents who had stayed in Hong Kong for at least three months during the six months before or for at least three months during the six months after the census moment, regardless of whether they were in Hong Kong or not at the census moment; and (2) Hong Kong non-permanent residents who were in Hong Kong at the census moment. Mobile Residents, they are Hong Kong permanent residents who had stayed in Hong Kong for at least one month but less than three months during the six months before or for at least one month but less than three months during the six months after the census moment, regardless of whether they were in Hong Kong or not at the census moment. Data are estimates from sample enquiry. - Les données se rapportent à la population résidente à Hong Kong au moment du recensement. Cette population est composée des résidants habituels et des résidants mobiles. La population résidente est partagée en deux catégories: (1) les résidents permanents qui ont habité à Hong Kong au moins trois mois pendant les six mois précédents ou les six mois suivants le recensement; (2) les habitants non-permanents de Hong Kong qui étaient à Hong Kong au moment du recensement. La population mobile se rapporte aux résidents permanents de Hong Kong qui ont habité à Hong Kong pendant les six mois après le recensement pour une période comprise entre un mois et trois mois, indépendamment du fait qu'ils étaient à Hong Kong au moment du recensement au pays. Les données sont des chiffres estimatifs dérivés d'une enquête par sondage.
[98] Population by-census is conducted between two population censuses, adopting a sampling method to select 29,421 housing units in Macao for enumeration, with the unit of observation being the individuals residing in the selected housing units. - Aux fins du recensement partiel de la population, conduit entre deux recensements, la méthode d'échantillonnage adoptée a permis de sélectionner 29 421 unités d'habitation à Macao, l'unité d'observation étant les personnes qui y résident.
[99] Data refer to government controlled areas. - Les données se rapportent aux zones contrôlées par le Gouvernement.
[100] Data refer to annual average population. Based on the results of the 2014 Population Census. - Les données correspondent à la population annuelle moyenne. D'après les résultats du recensement de la population de 2014.
[101] Includes data for the Indian-held part of Jammu and Kashmir, the final status of which has not yet been determined. - Y compris les données pour la partie du Jammu et du Cachemire occupée par l'Inde dont le statut définitif n'a pas encore été déterminé.
[102] Data are based on the publication: "Indonesia Population Projection 2010-2035" - Les données sont basées sur la publication : << Indonesia Population Projection 2010-2035 >>
[103] Data are based on the publication: "Indonesia Population Projection 2015-2045" - Les données sont basées sur la publication : << Indonesia Population Projection 2015-2045 >>
[104] Data refer to the Iranian Year which begins on 21 March and ends on 20 March of the following year. - Les données concernent l'année iranienne, qui commence le 21 mars et se termine le 20 mars de l'année suivante.
[105] The total number may include 'Unknown residence', but the categories urban and rural do not. - Le nombre total peut inclure les personnes dont la résidence n'est pas connue, à l'inverse des catégories de population urbaine et rurale.
[106] Differences between the total country figures and sum of urban and rural areas are due to the inclusion of unsettled population. - Les différences entre les chiffres pour l'ensemble du pays et la somme des zones urbaines et rurales s'expliquent par l'inclusion de la population non sédentaire.
[107] Includes data for East Jerusalem and Israeli residents in certain other territories under occupation by Israeli military forces since June 1967. Data refer to Israeli citizens and permanent residents who are listed in the Population

Register. - Y compris les données pour Jérusalem-Est et les résidents israéliens dans certains autres territoires occupés depuis 1967 par les forces armées israéliennes. Les données se rapportent aux citoyens israéliens et aux résidents permanents qui sont répertoriés dans le registre de la population.

108 Excluding diplomatic personnel outside the country and foreign military and civilian personnel and their dependants stationed in the area. - Non compris le personnel diplomatique hors du pays ni les militaires et agents civils étrangers en poste sur le territoire et les membres de leur famille les accompagnant.

109 Because of rounding, totals are not in all cases the sum of the respective components. Estimates or projections based on the 2015 population census. - Les chiffres étant arrondis, les totaux ne correspondent pas toujours rigoureusement à la somme des composants respectifs. Estimations ou projections fondées sur les résultats du recensement de la population de 2015.

110 Excluding data for Jordanian territory under occupation since June 1967 by Israeli military forces. - Non compris les données pour le territoire jordanien occupé depuis juin 1967 par les forces armées israéliennes.

111 Data refer to resident population. - Les données concernent la population résidente.

112 Recalculated population estimates taking into account late registration of births and deaths until May 2017. - Réestimation du nombre d'habitants compte tenu de l'enregistrement tardif des naissances et des décès jusqu'en mai 2017.

113 Source: Living conditions of household survey, October 2011 to September 2012. - Source: Enquête sur les conditions de vie des ménages, octobre 2011 à septembre 2012.

114 Estimates based on the adjusted results of the Population and Housing Census of 2010. - Les estimations sont fondée sur les résultats ajustées du recensement de la population et de l'habitat de 2010.

115 Based on the results of the 2014 Population Census. Data refer to resident population which includes resident Maldivians and resident foreigners. - D'après les résultats du recensement de la population de 2014. Les données concernent la population résidente, qui comprend les Maldiviens et les étrangers.

116 Data refer to resident population which includes resident Maldivians and resident foreigners. - Les données concernent la population résidente, qui comprend les Maldiviens et les étrangers.

117 Urban refers to 170 out of 254 towns and Rural refers to 62 out of 158 townships. - « Urbain » se rapporte à 170 des 254 villes, « rural » à 62 des 158 cantons.

118 Data refer to enumerated population. The total for the whole country excludes 1,206,353 persons estimated not to have been counted in parts of States of Rakhine, Kachin and Kayin. - Les données se rapportent à la population dénombrée. L' effectif de la population pour le pays ne comprend pas les personnes qui ne sont pas dénombrées dans certaines régions des États de Rakhine, Kachin et Kayin estimées à un chiffre de 1 206 353 personnes.

119 Data refer to registered population data from Royal Oman Police. - Les données portent sur la population enregistrée par la police royale de l'Oman.

120 Data for the urban and rural population are based on the percentage distribution according to the 2010 census. - Les données de la population urbaine et rurale sont fondées sur la répartition des pourcentages d'après le recensement de 2010.

121 Data for the urban and rural population are based on percentage distribution according to the 2016 survey. - Les données de la population urbaine et rurale sont fondées sur la répartition des pourcentages d'après l'enquête de 2016.

122 Excluding data for the Pakistan-held part of Jammu and Kashmir, the final status of which has not yet been determined. - Non compris les données concernant la partie du Jammu et Cachemire occupée par le Pakistan dont le statut définitif n'a pas été déterminé.

123 Excluding 2739 Filipinos in Philippine Embassies, Consulates and Missions Abroad. - Excepté 2739 Philippins travaillant dans les ambassades, les consulats et les missions des Philippines à l'étranger.

124 Excluding 2134 Filipinos in Philippine Embassies, Consulates and Missions Abroad. - Excepté 2134 Philippins travaillant dans les ambassades, les consulats et les missions des Philippines à l'étranger.

125 Excluding usual residents not in the country at the time of census. - À l'exclusion des résidents habituels qui ne sont pas dans le pays au moment du recensement.

126 Data refer to registered resident population. - Les données concernent la population enregistrée résidente.

127 Data are based on the latest register-based population estimates for 2010. Data refer to resident population which comprises Singapore citizens and permanent residents. - Données basées sur les estimations démographiques les plus récentes fondées sur les registres de 2010. Les données se rapportent à la population résidente composé des citoyens de Singapour et des résidents permanents.

128 Data refer to total population, which comprises Singapore residents and non-residents. Data exclude residents who have been away from Singapore for a continuous period of 12 months or longer as at the reference date. - Les données se rapportent à la population totale composé des résidents de Singapour et les non résidents. Non compris les résidents hors de Singapour pour une période ininterrompue de 12 mois ou plus avant de la date de référence.

129 Data for urban include population in refugee camps. - Les données pour la population urbaine comprennent la population dans les camps réfugiés.

130 Including Palestinian refugees. - Y compris les réfugiés de Palestine.

131 Data based on Address Based Population Registration System. - Les données sont basées sur le registre national de la population basé sur l'adresse.

132 Based on a sample taken at the time of census. Because of rounding, totals are not in all cases the sum of the respective components. - D'après un échantillon obtenu au moment du recensement. Les chiffres étant arrondis, les totaux ne correspondent pas toujours rigoureusement à la somme des composants respectifs.

133 The reason for the differences in the urban-rural population from the previous years is the changes in administrative attachment, legal entity and borders, regulated by related laws. - La raison des différences dans la population urbaine-rurale par rapport aux années précédentes est la modification de l'attachement administratif, de l'entité juridique et des frontières, réglementée par des lois connexes.

134 Data include non-national population. - Les données comprennent les non-nationaux.

135 Data are adjusted according to the results of the 2009 census and 2014 intercensus. - Les données ont été ajustées à partir des résultats du recensement de la population de 2009 et des données intercensitaires de 2014.

136 Average population adjusted according to Population and Housing Census on 1 April 2019. - Population moyenne ajustée selon le recensement de la population et de l'habitat du 1er avril 2019.

137 Decrease in population due to revision in administrative registers. - Diminution de la population due à la révision des registres administratifs.

138 Excluding Faeroe Islands and Greenland shown separately, if available. Population statistics are compiled from registers. - Non compris les Iles Féroé et le Groenland, qui font l'objet de rubriques distinctes, si disponible. Les statistiques de la population sont compilées à partir des registres.

139 Population statistics are compiled from registers. Excluding Åland Islands. - Les statistiques de la population sont compilées à partir des registres. Non compris les Îles d'Åland.

140 Excluding diplomatic personnel outside the country and including members of alien armed forces not living in military camps and foreign diplomatic personnel not living in embassies or consulates. - Non compris le personnel diplomatique hors du pays et y compris les militaires étrangers ne vivant pas dans des camps militaires et le personnel diplomatique étranger ne vivant pas dans les ambassades ou les consulats.

141 Based on the results of the 2011 Population Census. Data refer to annual average population. - Basé sur les résultats du recencement de la population de 2011. Les données correspondent à la population annuelle moyenne.

142 Excluding military personnel, visitors and transients. - Non compris les militaires, ni les visiteurs et transients.

143 Including civilian nationals temporarily outside the country. - Y compris les civils nationaux temporairement hors du pays.

144 Data refer to resident population only. - Pour la population résidante seulement.

145 Including residents temporarily outside the country. Population statistics are compiled from registers. - Y compris les résidents se trouvant temporairement hors du pays. Les statistiques de la population sont compilées à partir des registres.

146 Data refer to annual average population. Data refer to usual resident population. - Les données correspondent à la population annuelle moyenne. Les données se réfèrent à la population résidente habituelle.

147 Excluding Transnistria and the municipality of Bender. - Les données ne tiennent pas compte de l'information sur la Transnistria et la municipalité de Bender.

148 Tiraspol, Bender, Slobozia, Ribnita, Camenca Yrigoricpol/Grigoriopol are districts from Transnistria where the census was not conducted. - Tiraspol, Bender, Slobozia, Ribnita, Camenca, Yrigoricpol/Grigoriopol sont des districts de la Transnistrie où le recensement n'a pas eu lieu.

149 Data refer to usual resident population based on the 2014 Census. Tiraspol, Bender, Slobozia, Ribnita, Camenca Yrigoricpol/Grigoriopol are districts from Transnistria where the 2014 census was not conducted. Excluding Transnistria and the municipality of Bender. - Les données se rapportent à la population habituellement résidente et sont fondées sur le recensement de 2014. Tiraspol, Bender, Slobozia, Ribnita, Camenca, Yrigoricpol/Grigoriopol sont des districts de la Transnistrie où le recensement n'a pas eu lieu. Les données ne tiennent pas compte de l'information sur la Transnistria et la municipalité de Bender.

150 Excludes data for Kosovo and Metohia. - Sans les données pour le Kosovo et Metohie.

[151] Data refer to annual average population. Data refer to registered resident population. - Les données correspondent à la population annuelle moyenne. Les données concernent la population enregistrée résidente.
[152] Data refer to legal resident population. - Les données concernent la population légalement résidente.
[153] From 2014, urban refers to urban centers and areas under the influence of urban centers. - A partir de 2014, le territoire urbain inclut l'espace des centres urbains ainsi que l'espace sous influence des centres urbains.
[154] Data refer to legal resident population. Data refer to annual average population. - Les données concernent la population légalement résidente. Les données correspondent à la population annuelle moyenne.
[155] Data refer to annual average population. The Government of Ukraine has informed the United Nations that it is not in a position to provide statistical data concerning the Autonomous Republic of Crimea and the city of Sevastopol. - Les données correspondent à la population annuelle moyenne. Le gouvernement Ukrainien a informé l'ONU qu'il n'est pas en mesure de fournir des données statistiques concernant la République autonome de Crimée et la ville de Sébastopol.
[156] The Government of Ukraine has informed the United Nations that it is not in a position to provide statistical data concerning the Autonomous Republic of Crimea and the city of Sevastopol. - Le gouvernement Ukrainien a informé l'ONU qu'il n'est pas en mesure de fournir des données statistiques concernant la République autonome de Crimée et la ville de Sébastopol.
[157] Excluding Channel Islands (Guernsey and Jersey) and Isle of Man, shown separately, if available. - Non compris les îles Anglo-Normandes (Guernesey et Jersey) et l'île de Man, qui font l'objet de rubriques distinctes, si disponible.
[158] These data have been randomly rounded to protect confidentiality. Individual figures may not add up to totals, and values for the same data may vary in different tables. - Ces données ont été arrondies de façon aléatoire afin d'en préserver la confidentialité. La somme de certains chiffres peut ne pas correspondre aux totaux indiqués et les valeurs des mêmes données peuvent varier d'un tableau à un autre.
[159] Including population in off-shore, migratory and shipping. - Y compris les populations extraterritoriales, les populations nomades et les populations maritimes.
[160] Projections are prepared by the Secretariat of the Pacific Community based on the 1999 census of population and housing. - Les projections sont preparées par le Secrétariat de la Communauté du Pacifique à partir des résultats du recensement de la population et de l'habitat de 1999.
[161] Based on the 2010 Population and Housing Census and 2013/2014 Household Income and Expenditure Survey. - Données fondées sur les résultat du recensement de la population et de l'habitat de 2010, et ceux de l'enquête auprès des ménages sur des revenus et des dépenses de 2013/2014.
[162] Population estimates by urban/rural residence exclude inland waters and oceanic areas. - Les estimations de la population par lieu de résidence urbaine ou rurale excluent les eaux intérieures et les zones océaniques.
[163] These data have been randomly rounded to protect confidentiality. Individual figures may not add up to totals, and values for the same data may vary in different tables. Data include overseas visitors in New Zealand on census night. - Ces données ont été arrondies de façon aléatoire afin d'en préserver la confidentialité. La somme de certains chiffres peut ne pas correspondre aux totaux indiqués et les valeurs des mêmes données peuvent varier d'un tableau à un autre. Y compris les visiteurs étrangers qui se trouvaient en Nouvelle-Zélande le soir du recensement.
[164] Intercensal estimates. Data refer to usual resident population. - Estimations inter-censitaires. Les données se réfèrent à la population résidente habituelle.
[165] Estimates are prepared by the Secretariat of the Pacific Community based on the last population and housing census. - Les estimations sont preparées par le Secrétariat de la Communauté du Pacifique à partir des résultats du dernier recensement de la population et de l'habitat.
[166] Projections based on adjusted 2009 census counts. - Projections fondées à partir des comptes rajustés du recensement de 2009.
[167] Data refers to 2019 Tokelau population count. - Les données se rapportent au dénombrement de la population tokélaouane de 2019.
[168] Estimates based on the results of 1999 and in 2009 censuses. - Estimations fondées sur les résultats des recensement de la population de 1999 and 2009.
[169] Data is based on mini-census taken in 2016. - Selon le mini-recensement de 2016.
[170] Estimates based on the results of 2009 census and 2016 mini-census. - Estimaions fondées sur les résultats du recensement de 2009 et du mini-recensement de 2016.

Table 7 - *Demographic Yearbook 2019*

Table 7 presents population by age, sex and urban/rural residence for the latest available year between 2010 and 2019.

Description of variables: Data in this table are either population census figures or estimates, some of which are based on sample surveys. The source of data is indicated by the 'code' explained at the end of the table.

The reference date of the census or estimate appears in the left-most column of the table. In general, the estimates refer to mid-year, i.e. 1 July.

Age is defined as age at last birthday, that is, the difference between the date of birth and the reference date of the age distribution expressed in completed solar years. The age classification used in this table is the following: under 1 year, 1-4 years, 5-year groups through 95-99 years, and 100 years or over.

Statistics are presented for one year, the most recent available. However, if more complete disaggregation is available for an earlier year, both are displayed.

The urban/rural classification of population is that provided by each country or area; it is presumed to be based on the national census definitions of urban population that have been set forth at the end of the technical notes to table 6.

Reliability of data: Estimates which are believed to be less reliable are set in *italics* rather than in roman type.

Limitations: Statistics on population by age and sex are subject to the same qualifications as have been set forth for population statistics in general and age distributions in particular, as discussed in sections 3 and 3.1.3, respectively, of the Technical Notes.

Comparability of population data classified by age and sex is limited by variations in the definition of total population, discussed in detail in section 3 of the Technical Notes, and by the accuracy of the original enumeration. Both factors are more important in relation to certain age groups than to others. For example, under-enumeration is known to be more prevalent among infants and young children than among older persons. Similarly, the exclusion from the total population of certain groups that tend to be of selected ages (such as the armed forces) can markedly affect the age structure and its comparability with that for other countries or areas. Consideration should be given to the implications of these basic limitations in using the data.

In addition to these general qualifications are the special problems of comparability that arise in relation to age statistics in particular. Age distributions of population are known to suffer from certain deficiencies that have their origin in irregularities in age reporting. Although some of the irregularities tend to be obscured or eliminated when data are tabulated in five-year age groups rather than by single years, precision still continues to be affected, though the degree of distortion is not always readily seen.

Another factor limiting comparability is the age classification employed by the various countries or areas. Age may be based on the year of birth rather than the age at last birthday, in other words, calculated using the day, month and year of birth. Distributions based only on the year of birth are footnoted when known.

The absence of data in the unknown age group does not necessarily indicate completely accurate reporting and tabulation of the age item. The unknowns may have been eliminated by assigning ages to them before tabulation, or by proportionately distributing the unknown category across the age groups after tabulation.

As noted in connection with table 5, intercensal estimates of total population are usually revised to accord with the results of a census of population if inexplicable discontinuities appear to exist. Intercensal age-sex distributions, however, are less likely to be revised in this way. When it is known that a total population estimate for a given year has been revised and the corresponding age distribution has not been revised, a note is provided. Distributions of this type should be used with caution when studying trends over a period of years, though their utility for studying age structure for the specified year is probably unimpaired.

The comparability of data by urban/rural residence is affected by the national definitions of urban and rural used in tabulating these data. When known, the definitions of urban used in national population censuses are presented at the end of the technical notes for table 6. As discussed in detail in the technical notes for table 6, these definitions vary considerably from one country or area to another.

Earlier data: Population by age, sex and urban/rural residence has been shown in previous issues of the *Demographic Yearbook*. For more information on specific topics, and years for which data are reported, readers should consult the Historical Index. In addition, population data by single years of age, sex and urban/rural residence, for censuses conducted since 1995, are shown in the *Demographic Yearbook* webpage https://unstats.un.org/unsd/demographic-social/products/dyb/index.cshtml#censusdatasets.

Tableau 7 – *Annuaire démographique 2019*

Le tableau 7 présente les données les plus récentes disponibles pour la période 2010-2019 sur la population selon l'âge, le sexe et le lieu de résidence (zone urbaine ou rurale).

Description des variables : les données de ce tableau proviennent de recensements de la population ou correspondent à des estimations, fondées dans certains cas, sur des enquêtes par sondage. Le 'code' indique comment les données ont été obtenues. Les codes utilisés sont expliqués à la fin du tableau.

La date du recensement ou de l'estimation figure dans la colonne de gauche du tableau. En général, les estimations se rapportent au milieu de l'année (1er juillet).

L'âge désigne l'âge au dernier anniversaire, c'est-à-dire la différence entre la date de naissance et la date de référence de la répartition par âge exprimée en années solaires révolues. La classification par âge utilisée dans ce tableau est la suivante : moins d'un an, 1 à 4 ans, groupes quinquennaux jusqu'à 95-99 ans et 100 ans ou plus.

Les statistiques portent sur une année, qui correspond à celle pour laquelle on dispose des statistiques les plus récentes. Toutefois, si l'on dispose de répartitions plus complètes pour des années antérieures, les statistiques sont alors présentées pour les deux années.

La classification par zones urbaines et rurales de la population est celle qui est communiquée par chaque pays ou zone ; on part du principe qu'elle repose sur les définitions de la population urbaine utilisées pour les recensements de la population nationaux telles qu'elles sont reproduites à la fin des notes techniques du tableau 6.

Fiabilité des données : les estimations considérées comme moins sûres sont indiquées en italique plutôt qu'en caractères romains.

Insuffisance des données : les statistiques de la population selon l'âge et le sexe appellent les mêmes réserves que celles qui ont été formulées aux sections 3 et 3.1.3 des Notes techniques à propos des statistiques de la population en général et des répartitions par âge en particulier.

La comparabilité des statistiques de la population selon l'âge et le sexe pâtit du manque d'uniformité dans la définition de la population totale (voir la section 3 des Notes techniques) et des lacunes des dénombrements. L'influence de ces deux facteurs varie selon les groupes d'âge. Ainsi, le dénombrement des enfants de moins d'un an et des jeunes enfants comporte souvent plus de lacunes que celui des personnes plus âgées. De même, le fait que certains groupes de personnes appartenant souvent à des groupes d'âge déterminés, par exemple les militaires, ne soient pas pris en compte dans la population totale peut influer sensiblement sur la structure par âge et sur la comparabilité des données avec celles d'autres pays ou zones. Il conviendra de tenir compte de ces facteurs fondamentaux lorsque l'on utilisera les données du tableau.

Outre ces difficultés d'ordre général, la comparabilité pose des problèmes particuliers lorsqu'il s'agit des données par âge. On sait que les répartitions de la population selon l'âge présentent certaines imperfections dues à l'inexactitude des déclarations d'âge. Certaines de ces anomalies ont tendance à s'estomper ou à disparaître lorsque l'on classe les données par groupes d'âge quinquennaux et non par années d'âge, mais une certaine imprécision subsiste, même s'il n'est pas toujours facile de voir à quel point il y a distorsion.

Le degré de comparabilité dépend également de la classification par âge employée dans les divers pays ou zones. L'âge retenu peut être défini par date exacte (jour, mois et année) de naissance ou par celle du dernier anniversaire. Lorsqu'elles étaient connues, les répartitions établies seulement d'après l'année de la naissance ont été signalées en note à la fin du tableau.

Si aucun nombre ne figure dans la rangée réservée aux âges inconnus, cela ne signifie pas nécessairement que les déclarations d'âge et l'exploitation des données par âge aient été tout à fait exactes. C'est souvent une indication que l'on a attribué un âge aux personnes d'âge inconnu avant l'exploitation des données ou qu'elles ont été réparties proportionnellement entre les différents groupes après cette opération.

Comme on l'a indiqué à propos du tableau 5, les estimations intercensitaires de la population totale sont d'ordinaire rectifiées d'après les résultats des recensements de population si l'on constate des discontinuités inexplicables. Les données intercensitaires concernant la répartition de la population par âge et par sexe ont toutefois moins de chance d'être rectifiées de cette manière. Lorsque l'on savait qu'une estimation de la population totale pour une année donnée avait été rectifiée sans qu'il en soit de même pour la répartition par âge correspondante, cela a été indiquée dans une note. Les répartitions de ce type doivent être utilisées avec prudence lorsque l'on étudie les tendances sur un certain nombre d'années, quoique leur utilité pour l'étude de la structure par âge de la population pour l'année visée reste probablement entière.

La comparabilité des données selon le lieu de résidence (zone urbaine ou rurale) peut être limitée par les définitions nationales des termes « urbain » et « rural » utilisées pour la mise en tableaux de ces données. Les définitions du terme « urbain » utilisées pour les recensements nationaux de population ont été présentées à la fin des notes techniques du tableau 6 lorsqu'elles étaient connues. Comme on l'a précisé dans les notes techniques relatives au tableau 6, ces définitions varient considérablement d'un pays ou d'une zone à l'autre.

Données publiées antérieurement : des statistiques concernant la population selon l'âge, le sexe et le lieu de résidence (zone urbaine ou rurale) ont été présentées dans des éditions antérieures de l'*Annuaire démographique*. Pour plus de précisions concernant les années et les sujets pour lesquels des données ont été publiées, se reporter à l'index historique. En plus, des statistiques disponibles concernant la « Population selon chaque année d'âge, le sexe et la résidence urbaine/rurale », pour les recensements depuis 1995, ont été présentées dans la page internet suivante de l'*Annuaire démographique* https://unstats.un.org/unsd/demographic-social/products/dyb/index.cshtml#censusdatasets.

7. Population by age, sex and urban/rural residence: latest available year, 2010 - 2019
Population selon l'âge, le sexe et la résidence, urbaine/rurale : dernière année disponible, 2010 - 2019

Continent, country or area, date, code[a] and age (in years) / Continent, pays ou zone, date, code[a] et âge (en années)	Total			Urban - Urbaine			Rural - Rurale		
	Both sexes / Les deux sexes	Male / Masculin	Female / Féminin	Both sexes / Les deux sexes	Male / Masculin	Female / Féminin	Both sexes / Les deux sexes	Male / Masculin	Female / Féminin
AFRICA - AFRIQUE									
Algeria - Algérie[1]									
1 VII 2019 (ESDJ)									
Total	*43 413 000*	*21 993 000*	*21 420 000*	...	...	...	...	...	...
0 - 4	*5 063 000*	*2 602 000*	*2 461 000*	...	...	...	...	...	...
5 - 9	*4 515 000*	*2 320 000*	*2 195 000*	...	...	...	...	...	...
10 - 14	*3 609 000*	*1 858 000*	*1 751 000*	...	...	...	...	...	...
15 - 19	*2 964 000*	*1 517 000*	*1 447 000*	...	...	...	...	...	...
20 - 24	*3 200 000*	*1 632 000*	*1 568 000*	...	...	...	...	...	...
25 - 29	*3 607 000*	*1 833 000*	*1 774 000*	...	...	...	...	...	...
30 - 34	*3 796 000*	*1 911 000*	*1 885 000*	...	...	...	...	...	...
35 - 39	*3 540 000*	*1 786 000*	*1 754 000*	...	...	...	...	...	...
40 - 44	*2 863 000*	*1 441 000*	*1 422 000*	...	...	...	...	...	...
45 - 49	*2 395 000*	*1 193 000*	*1 202 000*	...	...	...	...	...	...
50 - 54	*2 058 000*	*1 023 000*	*1 035 000*	...	...	...	...	...	...
55 - 59	*1 657 000*	*825 000*	*832 000*	...	...	...	...	...	...
60 - 64	*1 331 000*	*666 000*	*665 000*	...	...	...	...	...	...
65 - 69	*1 033 000*	*523 000*	*510 000*	...	...	...	...	...	...
70 - 74	*661 000*	*324 000*	*337 000*	...	...	...	...	...	...
75 - 79	*500 000*	*241 000*	*259 000*	...	...	...	...	...	...
80 - 84	*346 000*	*163 000*	*183 000*	...	...	...	...	...	...
85 +	*275 000*	*135 000*	*140 000*	...	...	...	...	...	...
Angola[2]									
1 VII 2019 (ESDF)									
Total	*30 175 553*	*14 691 938*	*15 483 615*	*19 087 816*	*9 336 450*	*9 751 366*	*11 087 737*	*5 355 488*	*5 732 249*
0	*1 060 585*	*531 059*	*529 526*	*677 857*	*340 036*	*337 821*	*382 728*	*191 023*	*191 705*
1 - 4	*3 765 554*	*1 880 414*	*1 885 140*	*2 416 870*	*1 212 564*	*1 204 306*	*1 348 684*	*667 850*	*680 834*
5 - 9	*5 064 472*	*2 511 075*	*2 553 397*	*2 982 560*	*1 481 551*	*1 501 009*	*2 081 912*	*1 029 524*	*1 052 388*
10 - 14	*4 059 758*	*2 010 400*	*2 049 358*	*2 486 026*	*1 219 402*	*1 266 624*	*1 573 732*	*790 998*	*782 734*
15 - 19	*3 202 373*	*1 570 566*	*1 631 807*	*2 046 523*	*994 446*	*1 052 077*	*1 155 850*	*576 120*	*579 730*
20 - 24	*2 611 936*	*1 271 739*	*1 340 197*	*1 725 464*	*835 285*	*890 179*	*886 472*	*436 454*	*450 018*
25 - 29	*2 160 838*	*1 038 142*	*1 122 696*	*1 467 348*	*706 372*	*760 976*	*693 490*	*331 770*	*361 720*
30 - 34	*1 809 922*	*861 627*	*948 295*	*1 239 988*	*595 325*	*644 663*	*569 934*	*266 302*	*303 632*
35 - 39	*1 521 392*	*719 259*	*802 133*	*1 033 674*	*497 989*	*535 685*	*487 718*	*221 270*	*266 448*
40 - 44	*1 265 355*	*597 672*	*667 683*	*847 224*	*410 676*	*436 548*	*418 131*	*186 996*	*231 135*
45 - 49	*1 019 730*	*485 132*	*534 598*	*659 599*	*324 219*	*335 380*	*360 131*	*160 913*	*199 218*
50 - 54	*814 869*	*386 718*	*428 151*	*510 277*	*251 498*	*258 779*	*304 592*	*135 220*	*169 372*
55 - 59	*619 970*	*291 330*	*328 640*	*369 027*	*180 867*	*188 160*	*250 943*	*110 463*	*140 480*
60 - 64	*461 277*	*213 726*	*247 551*	*262 269*	*126 776*	*135 493*	*199 008*	*86 950*	*112 058*
65 - 69	*313 312*	*141 535*	*171 777*	*167 439*	*78 191*	*89 248*	*145 873*	*63 344*	*82 529*
70 - 74	*205 882*	*90 751*	*115 131*	*102 718*	*45 948*	*56 770*	*103 164*	*44 803*	*58 361*
75 - 79	*120 014*	*51 377*	*68 637*	*53 655*	*22 041*	*31 614*	*66 359*	*29 336*	*37 023*
80 +	*98 314*	*39 416*	*58 898*	*39 298*	*13 264*	*26 034*	*59 016*	*26 152*	*32 864*
Benin - Bénin									
1 VII 2011 (ESDF)[1]									
Total	*9 067 076*	*4 446 877*	*4 620 199*	*4 072 574*	*2 003 366*	*2 069 208*	*4 994 502*	*2 443 511*	*2 550 991*
0 - 4	*1 629 512*	*828 064*	*801 448*	*633 629*	*321 667*	*311 962*	*995 883*	*506 397*	*489 486*
0	*350 292*	*178 565*	*171 727*	...	...	...	...	...	...
1 - 4	*1 279 220*	*649 499*	*629 721*	...	...	...	...	...	...
5 - 9	*1 335 166*	*675 912*	*659 254*	*511 822*	*251 283*	*260 539*	*823 344*	*424 629*	*398 715*
10 - 14	*1 137 068*	*572 756*	*564 312*	*517 373*	*244 437*	*272 936*	*619 695*	*328 319*	*291 376*
15 - 19	*1 081 199*	*553 241*	*527 958*	*550 694*	*279 420*	*271 274*	*530 505*	*273 821*	*256 684*
20 - 24	*767 946*	*398 920*	*369 026*	*406 496*	*224 092*	*182 404*	*361 450*	*174 828*	*186 622*
25 - 29	*609 489*	*291 598*	*317 891*	*303 896*	*153 731*	*150 165*	*305 593*	*137 867*	*167 726*
30 - 34	*537 893*	*227 400*	*310 493*	*264 521*	*117 596*	*146 925*	*273 372*	*109 804*	*163 568*
35 - 39	*494 619*	*213 385*	*281 234*	*236 804*	*106 800*	*130 004*	*257 815*	*106 585*	*151 230*
40 - 44	*378 111*	*175 956*	*202 155*	*178 115*	*86 225*	*91 890*	*199 996*	*89 731*	*110 265*
45 - 49	*308 866*	*142 056*	*166 810*	*145 334*	*68 351*	*76 983*	*163 532*	*73 705*	*89 827*
50 - 54	*232 650*	*110 074*	*122 576*	*101 866*	*48 831*	*53 035*	*130 784*	*61 243*	*69 541*
55 - 59	*171 970*	*82 190*	*89 780*	*77 819*	*37 319*	*40 500*	*94 151*	*44 871*	*49 280*
60 - 64	*135 768*	*64 968*	*70 800*	*52 261*	*24 642*	*27 619*	*83 507*	*40 326*	*43 181*
65 - 69	*75 534*	*35 915*	*39 619*	*31 238*	*14 546*	*16 692*	*44 296*	*21 369*	*22 927*
70 - 74	*82 740*	*36 511*	*46 229*	*30 032*	*12 558*	*17 474*	*52 708*	*23 953*	*28 755*
75 - 79	*36 453*	*15 591*	*20 862*	*14 064*	*5 573*	*8 491*	*22 389*	*10 018*	*12 371*
80 +	*52 092*	*22 340*	*29 752*	*16 610*	*6 295*	*10 315*	*35 482*	*16 045*	*19 437*

7. Population by age, sex and urban/rural residence: latest available year, 2010 - 2019
Population selon l'âge, le sexe et la résidence, urbaine/rurale : dernière année disponible, 2010 - 2019 (continued - suite)

Continent, country or area, date, code[a] and age (in years) / Continent, pays ou zone, date, code[a] et âge (en annèes)	Total			Urban - Urbaine			Rural - Rurale		
	Both sexes Les deux sexes	Male Masculin	Female Féminin	Both sexes Les deux sexes	Male Masculin	Female Féminin	Both sexes Les deux sexes	Male Masculin	Female Féminin
AFRICA - AFRIQUE									
Benin - Bénin									
1 VII 2018 (ESDF)[3]									
Total	11 496 140	5 647 059	5 849 081	...	...	...	...	...	...
0 - 4	1 771 128	903 445	867 683	...	...	...	...	...	...
5 - 9	1 660 861	838 292	822 569	...	...	...	...	...	...
10 - 14	1 654 258	838 200	816 058	...	...	...	...	...	...
15 - 19	1 289 410	663 989	625 421	...	...	...	...	...	...
20 - 24	1 007 377	510 094	497 283	...	...	...	...	...	...
25 - 29	850 692	383 835	466 857	...	...	...	...	...	...
30 - 34	761 689	325 539	436 150	...	...	...	...	...	...
35 - 39	639 136	291 441	347 695	...	...	...	...	...	...
40 - 44	503 488	236 956	266 532	...	...	...	...	...	...
45 - 49	399 400	197 278	202 122	...	...	...	...	...	...
50 - 54	263 321	130 076	133 245	...	...	...	...	...	...
55 - 59	247 442	119 534	127 908	...	...	...	...	...	...
60 - 64	121 624	60 776	60 848	...	...	...	...	...	...
65 - 69	143 917	67 214	76 703	...	...	...	...	...	...
70 - 74	61 754	28 963	32 791	...	...	...	...	...	...
75 - 79	62 810	27 607	35 203	...	...	...	...	...	...
80 +	57 833	23 820	34 013	...	...	...	...	...	...
Botswana[4]									
1 VII 2017 (ESDJ)									
Total	2 266 990	1 107 191	1 159 799	1 452 383	693 532	758 851	814 607	413 658	400 948
0 - 4	61 940	31 397	30 544	37 124	18 879	18 245	24 816	12 518	12 298
5 - 9	203 745	102 949	100 797	116 405	58 772	57 632	87 341	44 176	43 164
10 - 14	240 886	121 521	119 365	141 315	70 695	70 619	99 571	50 826	48 745
15 - 19	232 077	116 903	115 174	140 422	69 995	70 428	91 655	46 908	44 746
20 - 24	235 942	117 349	118 592	161 551	77 071	84 479	74 391	40 278	34 113
25 - 29	224 303	108 876	115 427	158 279	74 123	84 156	66 023	34 752	31 271
30 - 34	232 702	113 292	119 409	165 346	77 884	87 462	67 356	35 408	31 948
35 - 39	190 931	94 619	96 312	136 536	65 716	70 821	54 395	28 904	25 491
40 - 44	151 385	76 617	74 768	105 606	51 881	53 725	45 779	24 735	21 043
45 - 49	111 168	54 597	56 571	75 396	36 406	38 991	35 772	18 192	17 580
50 - 54	92 096	42 410	49 686	59 159	27 007	32 152	32 936	15 403	17 533
55 - 59	74 296	33 298	40 998	45 078	20 249	24 828	29 218	13 048	16 170
60 - 64	60 511	27 281	33 229	34 113	15 217	18 896	26 398	12 064	14 334
65 - 69	42 077	19 418	22 660	21 535	9 303	12 231	20 543	10 114	10 429
70 - 74	31 064	13 707	17 358	15 223	6 191	9 031	15 842	7 516	8 326
75 - 79	24 922	10 595	14 327	11 975	4 485	7 490	12 948	6 111	6 837
80 - 84	20 031	7 801	12 230	9 604	3 262	6 341	10 428	4 539	5 889
85 - 89	14 799	5 458	9 342	6 843	2 171	4 672	7 957	3 287	4 670
90 - 94	9 233	3 163	6 070	4 418	1 362	3 055	4 815	1 800	3 015
95 - 99	4 390	1 542	2 848	2 062	669	1 393	2 328	872	1 455
100 +	8 492	4 400	4 092	4 394	2 192	2 202	4 098	2 208	1 890
1 VII 2018 (ESDJ)									
Total	2 302 878	1 134 505	1 168 373	...	...	...	...	...	...
0 - 4	237 605	119 929	117 676	...	...	...	...	...	...
5 - 9	251 537	127 110	124 427	...	...	...	...	...	...
10 - 14	221 177	111 626	109 551	...	...	...	...	...	...
15 - 19	208 951	105 421	103 530	...	...	...	...	...	...
20 - 24	209 631	105 164	104 467	...	...	...	...	...	...
25 - 29	202 809	99 747	103 062	...	...	...	...	...	...
30 - 34	206 384	100 719	105 665	...	...	...	...	...	...
35 - 39	186 229	91 970	94 259	...	...	...	...	...	...
40 - 44	146 981	74 104	72 877	...	...	...	...	...	...
45 - 49	109 824	54 949	54 875	...	...	...	...	...	...
50 - 54	85 463	40 199	45 264	...	...	...	...	...	...
55 - 59	69 954	31 270	38 684	...	...	...	...	...	...
60 - 64	56 342	24 977	31 365	...	...	...	...	...	...
65 - 69	40 341	18 166	22 175	...	...	...	...	...	...
70 - 74	27 031	11 915	15 116	...	...	...	...	...	...
75 - 79	19 989	8 335	11 654	...	...	...	...	...	...
80 +	22 630	8 904	13 726	...	...	...	...	...	...

7. Population by age, sex and urban/rural residence: latest available year, 2010 - 2019
Population selon l'âge, le sexe et la résidence, urbaine/rurale : dernière année disponible, 2010 - 2019 (continued - suite)

Continent, country or area, date, code[a] and age (in years) / Continent, pays ou zone, date, code[a] et âge (en années)	Total			Urban - Urbaine			Rural - Rurale		
	Both sexes Les deux sexes	Male Masculin	Female Féminin	Both sexes Les deux sexes	Male Masculin	Female Féminin	Both sexes Les deux sexes	Male Masculin	Female Féminin
AFRICA - AFRIQUE									
Burkina Faso[1]									
1 VII 2019 (ESDJ)									
Total	*20 870 060*	*10 082 776*	*10 787 284*	...	...	...	...	...	...
0	*792 142*	*404 627*	*387 515*	...	...	...	...	...	...
1 - 4	*2 881 696*	*1 473 039*	*1 408 657*	...	...	...	...	...	...
5 - 9	*3 224 716*	*1 649 838*	*1 574 878*	...	...	...	...	...	...
10 - 14	*2 807 446*	*1 448 391*	*1 359 055*	...	...	...	...	...	...
15 - 19	*2 365 616*	*1 203 281*	*1 162 335*	...	...	...	...	...	...
20 - 24	*1 868 663*	*903 240*	*965 423*	...	...	...	...	...	...
25 - 29	*1 442 137*	*657 527*	*784 610*	...	...	...	...	...	...
30 - 34	*1 203 630*	*489 694*	*713 936*	...	...	...	...	...	...
35 - 39	*973 080*	*399 670*	*573 410*	...	...	...	...	...	...
40 - 44	*820 252*	*349 769*	*470 483*	...	...	...	...	...	...
45 - 49	*630 247*	*276 648*	*353 599*	...	...	...	...	...	...
50 - 54	*539 819*	*234 450*	*305 369*	...	...	...	...	...	...
55 - 59	*403 024*	*178 208*	*224 816*	...	...	...	...	...	...
60 - 64	*326 610*	*142 827*	*183 783*	...	...	...	...	...	...
65 - 69	*220 765*	*102 563*	*118 202*	...	...	...	...	...	...
70 - 74	*178 806*	*80 564*	*98 242*	...	...	...	...	...	...
75 - 79	*96 783*	*45 726*	*51 057*	...	...	...	...	...	...
80 +	*94 628*	*42 714*	*51 914*	...	...	...	...	...	...
Burundi									
1 VII 2015 (ESDF)[5]									
Total	*9 823 828*	*4 822 838*	*5 000 990*	*1 473 574*	*723 426*	*750 148*	*8 350 254*	*4 099 412*	*4 250 842*
0 - 4	*1 712 483*	*856 714*	*855 769*	*220 830*	*99 976*	*120 854*	*1 491 653*	*756 738*	*734 915*
5 - 9	*1 379 000*	*679 740*	*699 260*	*172 229*	*76 843*	*95 386*	*1 206 771*	*602 897*	*603 874*
10 - 14	*1 234 086*	*604 457*	*629 629*	*154 449*	*67 431*	*87 018*	*1 079 637*	*537 026*	*542 611*
15 - 19	*1 021 915*	*496 353*	*525 562*	*161 685*	*74 964*	*86 721*	*860 230*	*421 389*	*438 841*
20 - 24	*974 645*	*467 123*	*507 522*	*176 946*	*89 742*	*87 204*	*797 699*	*377 381*	*420 318*
25 - 29	*843 366*	*397 323*	*446 043*	*174 840*	*90 183*	*84 657*	*668 526*	*307 140*	*361 386*
30 - 34	*659 106*	*321 348*	*337 758*	*140 254*	*76 414*	*63 840*	*518 852*	*244 934*	*273 918*
35 - 39	*466 561*	*236 115*	*230 446*	*82 657*	*46 719*	*35 938*	*383 904*	*189 396*	*194 508*
40 - 44	*366 466*	*182 701*	*183 765*	*57 283*	*33 163*	*24 120*	*309 183*	*149 538*	*159 645*
45 - 49	*310 594*	*153 796*	*156 798*	*40 803*	*22 094*	*18 709*	*269 791*	*131 702*	*138 089*
50 - 54	*265 180*	*134 933*	*130 247*	*30 364*	*16 749*	*13 615*	*234 816*	*118 184*	*116 632*
55 - 59	*225 278*	*113 470*	*111 808*	*25 692*	*13 147*	*12 545*	*199 586*	*100 323*	*99 263*
60 - 64	*145 211*	*74 556*	*70 655*	*14 954*	*7 579*	*7 375*	*130 257*	*66 977*	*63 280*
65 - 69	*90 785*	*44 744*	*46 041*	*9 023*	*4 024*	*4 999*	*81 762*	*40 720*	*41 042*
70 - 74	*54 548*	*25 722*	*28 826*	*4 874*	*2 027*	*2 847*	*49 674*	*23 695*	*25 979*
75 - 79	*36 220*	*16 056*	*20 164*	*3 504*	*1 175*	*2 329*	*32 716*	*14 881*	*17 835*
80 +	*38 384*	*17 687*	*20 697*	*3 187*	*1 196*	*1 991*	*35 197*	*16 491*	*18 706*
1 VII 2019 (ESDF)									
Total	*12 044 164*	*5 949 575*	*6 094 589*	...	...	...	...	...	...
0	*359 039*	*181 294*	*177 745*	...	...	...	...	...	...
1 - 4	*1 386 638*	*696 491*	*690 147*	...	...	...	...	...	...
5 - 9	*1 749 738*	*876 679*	*873 059*	...	...	...	...	...	...
10 - 14	*1 565 190*	*780 597*	*784 594*	...	...	...	...	...	...
15 - 19	*1 235 302*	*610 996*	*624 306*	...	...	...	...	...	...
20 - 24	*1 076 995*	*527 926*	*549 069*	...	...	...	...	...	...
25 - 29	*1 013 718*	*490 407*	*523 311*	...	...	...	...	...	...
30 - 34	*898 228*	*431 491*	*466 737*	...	...	...	...	...	...
35 - 39	*701 326*	*344 185*	*357 141*	...	...	...	...	...	...
40 - 44	*503 374*	*251 998*	*251 376*	...	...	...	...	...	...
45 - 49	*374 076*	*183 680*	*190 396*	...	...	...	...	...	...
50 - 54	*329 484*	*161 316*	*168 168*	...	...	...	...	...	...
55 - 59	*279 323*	*138 630*	*140 693*	...	...	...	...	...	...
60 - 64	*233 046*	*114 754*	*118 292*	...	...	...	...	...	...
65 - 69	*157 099*	*76 739*	*80 360*	...	...	...	...	...	...
70 - 74	*86 233*	*40 680*	*45 553*	...	...	...	...	...	...
75 - 79	*53 631*	*24 112*	*29 519*	...	...	...	...	...	...
80 +	*41 725*	*17 601*	*24 124*	...	...	...	...	...	...
Cabo Verde									
16 VI 2010 (CDJC)									
Total	491 683	243 403	248 280	303 673	151 219	152 454	188 010	92 184	95 826
0 - 4	50 200	25 131	25 069	30 842	15 542	15 300	19 358	9 589	9 769

7. Population by age, sex and urban/rural residence: latest available year, 2010 - 2019
Population selon l'âge, le sexe et la résidence, urbaine/rurale : dernière année disponible, 2010 - 2019 (continued - suite)

Continent, country or area, date, code[a] and age (in years) Continent, pays ou zone, date, code[a] et âge (en annèes)	Total			Urban - Urbaine			Rural - Rurale		
	Both sexes Les deux sexes	Male Masculin	Female Féminin	Both sexes Les deux sexes	Male Masculin	Female Féminin	Both sexes Les deux sexes	Male Masculin	Female Féminin
AFRICA - AFRIQUE									
Cabo Verde									
16 VI 2010 (CDJC)									
5 - 9	50 208	25 168	25 040	29 705	14 799	14 906	20 503	10 369	10 134
10 - 14	55 225	27 864	27 361	30 408	15 260	15 148	24 817	12 604	12 213
15 - 19	59 060	29 655	29 405	33 772	16 678	17 094	25 288	12 977	12 311
20 - 24	52 905	27 327	25 578	34 402	17 504	16 898	18 503	9 823	8 680
25 - 29	44 341	23 336	21 005	30 990	16 055	14 935	13 351	7 281	6 070
30 - 34	34 504	18 165	16 339	24 684	13 012	11 672	9 820	5 153	4 667
35 - 39	27 236	14 106	13 130	18 641	9 726	8 915	8 595	4 380	4 215
40 - 44	26 291	12 988	13 303	17 086	8 680	8 406	9 205	4 308	4 897
45 - 49	23 512	11 347	12 165	15 227	7 625	7 602	8 285	3 722	4 563
50 - 54	18 161	8 162	9 999	11 243	5 392	5 851	6 918	2 770	4 148
55 - 59	12 143	4 947	7 196	7 183	3 229	3 954	4 960	1 718	3 242
60 - 64	6 193	2 613	3 580	3 656	1 663	1 993	2 537	950	1 587
65 - 69	6 215	2 499	3 716	3 420	1 411	2 009	2 795	1 088	1 707
70 - 74	8 666	3 437	5 229	4 237	1 656	2 581	4 429	1 781	2 648
75 - 79	7 433	2 980	4 453	3 602	1 377	2 225	3 831	1 603	2 228
80 - 84	5 277	2 092	3 185	2 485	891	1 594	2 792	1 201	1 591
85 - 89	2 185	827	1 358	1 058	331	727	1 127	496	631
90 - 94	1 073	377	696	520	171	349	553	206	347
95 +	497	172	325	248	65	183	249	107	142
Unknown - Inconnu	358	210	148	264	152	112	94	58	36
1 VII 2019 (ESDJ)[1]									
Total	550 483	277 720	272 764	...	...	...	...	...	...
0 - 4	52 376	26 795	25 583	...	...	...	...	...	...
5 - 9	50 566	25 745	24 823	...	...	...	...	...	...
10 - 14	51 146	25 507	25 638	...	...	...	...	...	...
15 - 19	47 442	23 931	23 511	...	...	...	...	...	...
20 - 24	48 411	24 857	23 554	...	...	...	...	...	...
25 - 29	54 533	28 384	26 149	...	...	...	...	...	...
30 - 34	52 125	27 773	24 352	...	...	...	...	...	...
35 - 39	42 372	23 047	19 325	...	...	...	...	...	...
40 - 44	33 125	17 807	15 319	...	...	...	...	...	...
45 - 49	26 212	13 537	12 676	...	...	...	...	...	...
50 - 54	24 979	12 185	12 794	...	...	...	...	...	...
55 - 59	21 461	10 125	11 336	...	...	...	...	...	...
60 - 64	14 917	6 258	8 660	...	...	...	...	...	...
65 - 69	9 439	3 706	5 733	...	...	...	...	...	...
70 - 74	4 900	1 995	2 905	...	...	...	...	...	...
75 - 79	4 735	1 797	2 938	...	...	...	...	...	...
80 - 84	5 511	2 056	3 455	...	...	...	...	...	...
85 - 89	3 874	1 463	2 411	...	...	...	...	...	...
90 - 94	1 697	605	1 091	...	...	...	...	...	...
95 +	659	147	512	...	...	...	...	...	...
Cameroon - Cameroun[6]									
1 VII 2019 (ESDJ)									
Total	25 492 354	12 609 256	12 883 098	...	...	...	...	...	...
0	850 672	417 102	433 570	...	...	...	...	...	...
1 - 4	3 029 041	1 486 955	1 542 086	...	...	...	...	...	...
5 - 9	3 478 312	1 720 605	1 757 707	...	...	...	...	...	...
10 - 14	3 098 803	1 574 388	1 524 415	...	...	...	...	...	...
15 - 19	2 733 108	1 386 436	1 346 672	...	...	...	...	...	...
20 - 24	2 385 459	1 213 959	1 171 500	...	...	...	...	...	...
25 - 29	2 020 938	1 035 624	985 314	...	...	...	...	...	...
30 - 34	1 855 951	888 422	967 529	...	...	...	...	...	...
35 - 39	1 471 188	684 460	786 728	...	...	...	...	...	...
40 - 44	1 235 586	584 695	650 891	...	...	...	...	...	...
45 - 49	885 267	438 096	447 171	...	...	...	...	...	...
50 - 54	745 791	352 927	392 864	...	...	...	...	...	...
55 - 59	557 586	275 690	281 896	...	...	...	...	...	...
60 - 64	463 341	220 891	242 450	...	...	...	...	...	...
65 - 69	285 064	143 542	141 522	...	...	...	...	...	...
70 - 74	212 422	101 474	110 948	...	...	...	...	...	...
75 - 79	104 705	49 486	55 219	...	...	...	...	...	...
80 +	79 120	34 504	44 616	...	...	...	...	...	...

7. Population by age, sex and urban/rural residence: latest available year, 2010 - 2019
Population selon l'âge, le sexe et la résidence, urbaine/rurale : dernière année disponible, 2010 - 2019 (continued - suite)

Continent, country or area, date, code[a] and age (in years) / Continent, pays ou zone, date, code[a] et âge (en années)	Total			Urban - Urbaine			Rural - Rurale		
	Both sexes Les deux sexes	Male Masculin	Female Féminin	Both sexes Les deux sexes	Male Masculin	Female Féminin	Both sexes Les deux sexes	Male Masculin	Female Féminin
AFRICA - AFRIQUE									
Chad - Tchad									
1 VII 2019 (ESDJ)									
Total	15 692 969	7 820 817	7 872 152	3 855 240	1 921 314	1 933 926	11 837 729	5 899 503	5 938 226
0	580 322	295 467	284 855	134 977	66 115	68 862	444 576	228 791	215 786
1 - 4	2 591 279	1 324 932	1 266 347	550 526	271 132	279 394	2 030 139	1 049 068	981 071
5 - 9	2 843 286	1 452 262	1 391 024	606 767	295 755	311 012	2 225 510	1 151 197	1 074 313
10 - 14	1 920 775	1 004 084	916 691	472 779	234 225	238 554	1 449 375	768 768	680 606
15 - 19	1 506 805	721 338	785 466	423 846	202 830	221 016	1 090 368	520 724	569 644
20 - 24	1 228 288	548 106	680 182	367 320	178 595	188 725	868 780	373 318	495 461
25 - 29	1 070 030	459 091	610 939	292 075	139 355	152 720	780 740	322 037	458 704
30 - 34	870 339	397 784	472 556	239 285	119 693	119 592	633 603	279 993	353 610
35 - 39	714 121	347 077	367 045	187 463	97 264	90 199	527 699	250 850	276 849
40 - 44	611 428	309 663	301 764	160 801	87 373	73 428	451 471	223 267	228 204
45 - 49	431 511	235 168	196 343	112 438	63 728	48 710	319 674	171 955	147 720
50 - 54	399 306	211 892	187 414	97 317	52 993	44 324	301 749	158 978	142 771
55 - 59	210 337	121 832	88 505	53 674	31 803	21 870	156 848	90 190	66 658
60 - 64	252 753	132 961	119 793	57 862	30 165	27 697	194 351	102 577	91 774
65 - 69	121 618	68 928	52 690	27 531	14 903	12 629	93 851	53 848	40 003
70 - 74	149 854	80 410	69 445	31 307	15 165	16 142	117 978	64 846	53 132
75 - 79	59 111	34 637	24 474	12 278	6 658	5 620	46 599	27 818	18 781
80 - 84	66 055	35 783	30 272	12 865	5 935	6 930	52 847	29 600	23 247
85 - 89	21 251	13 033	8 218	4 124	2 252	1 872	17 017	10 698	6 319
90 - 94	17 528	9 828	7 699	3 425	1 664	1 760	14 014	8 099	5 915
95 - 99	12 419	7 334	5 084	2 541	1 295	1 246	9 829	5 994	3 835
100 +	3 589	1 898	1 691	751	318	433	2 833	1 568	1 264
Unknown - Inconnu	10 959	7 304	3 654	3 290	2 097	1 192	7 877	5 318	2 559
Côte d'Ivoire[7]									
1 VII 2017 (ESDF)									
Total	24 571 044	12 648 124	11 922 920	12 678 659	6 526 432	6 152 227	11 892 385	6 121 692	5 770 693
0	830 679	422 830	407 849	371 171	190 700	180 471	459 508	232 130	227 378
1 - 4	3 054 526	1 566 438	1 488 088	1 364 848	706 478	658 370	1 689 678	859 959	829 697
5 - 9	3 502 451	1 804 903	1 697 548	1 583 344	809 635	773 709	1 919 107	995 268	923 839
10 - 14	2 942 549	1 535 496	1 407 053	1 556 643	785 508	771 135	1 385 906	749 988	635 918
15 - 19	2 380 938	1 250 881	1 130 057	1 427 256	740 842	686 414	953 682	510 039	443 643
20 - 24	2 052 959	1 020 756	1 032 203	1 177 474	590 233	587 241	875 484	430 523	444 961
25 - 29	2 083 203	1 005 785	1 077 418	1 154 531	555 762	598 769	928 671	450 022	478 649
30 - 34	1 938 494	959 503	978 991	1 061 166	528 354	532 812	877 327	431 148	446 179
35 - 39	1 584 277	835 508	748 769	872 829	468 853	403 976	711 448	366 655	344 793
40 - 44	1 174 597	650 422	524 175	624 850	353 876	270 974	549 748	296 547	253 201
45 - 49	868 173	475 047	393 126	441 488	243 974	197 514	426 684	231 072	195 612
50 - 54	689 484	362 925	326 559	348 864	185 197	163 667	340 620	177 728	162 892
55 - 59	524 814	274 600	250 214	267 036	142 470	124 566	257 778	132 130	125 648
60 - 64	354 683	189 578	165 105	173 791	96 277	77 514	180 893	93 301	87 592
65 - 69	250 087	130 570	119 517	114 005	61 409	52 596	136 082	69 161	66 921
70 - 74	156 528	76 914	79 614	66 327	32 729	33 598	90 201	44 185	46 016
75 - 79	93 253	44 218	49 035	38 231	18 011	20 220	55 022	26 207	28 815
80 +	89 350	41 751	47 599	34 807	16 123	18 684	54 543	25 628	28 915
Egypt - Égypte									
1 VII 2018 (ESDF)									
Total	97 147 368	50 070 213	47 077 155	41 398 653	21 293 773	20 104 880	55 748 715	28 776 440	26 972 275
0	2 658 783	1 368 026	1 290 757	957 984	485 509	472 475	1 700 799	882 517	818 282
1 - 4	10 564 944	5 386 205	5 178 739	3 966 493	2 009 164	1 957 329	6 598 451	3 377 041	3 221 410
5 - 9	10 776 815	5 596 177	5 180 638	4 144 629	2 156 134	1 988 495	6 632 186	3 440 043	3 192 143
10 - 14	9 255 844	4 821 179	4 434 665	3 675 362	1 911 282	1 764 080	5 580 482	2 909 897	2 670 585
15 - 19	9 231 529	4 791 188	4 440 341	3 824 678	1 978 063	1 846 615	5 406 851	2 813 125	2 593 726
20 - 24	8 437 449	4 338 842	4 098 607	3 693 287	1 890 684	1 802 603	4 744 162	2 448 158	2 296 004
25 - 29	8 370 330	4 132 410	4 237 920	3 620 282	1 787 135	1 833 147	4 750 048	2 345 275	2 404 773
30 - 34	7 524 727	3 855 156	3 669 571	3 336 873	1 693 221	1 643 652	4 187 854	2 161 935	2 025 919
35 - 39	6 645 161	3 417 387	3 227 774	2 969 056	1 527 673	1 441 383	3 676 105	1 889 714	1 786 391
40 - 44	5 278 799	2 721 411	2 557 388	2 451 967	1 240 623	1 211 344	2 826 832	1 480 788	1 346 044
45 - 49	4 500 010	2 339 623	2 160 387	2 092 000	1 086 246	1 005 754	2 408 010	1 253 377	1 154 633
50 - 54	4 095 879	2 099 684	1 996 195	1 944 691	997 897	946 794	2 151 188	1 101 787	1 049 401
55 - 59	3 340 192	1 755 327	1 584 865	1 610 878	842 829	768 049	1 729 314	912 498	816 816
60 - 64	2 714 395	1 450 387	1 264 008	1 355 106	729 497	625 609	1 359 289	720 890	638 399
65 - 69	1 762 281	965 085	797 196	860 788	480 177	380 611	901 493	484 908	416 585

7. Population by age, sex and urban/rural residence: latest available year, 2010 - 2019
Population selon l'âge, le sexe et la résidence, urbaine/rurale : dernière année disponible, 2010 - 2019 (continued - suite)

Continent, country or area, date, code[a] and age (in years) / Continent, pays ou zone, date, code[a] et âge (en annèes)	Total			Urban - Urbaine			Rural - Rurale		
	Both sexes Les deux sexes	Male Masculin	Female Féminin	Both sexes Les deux sexes	Male Masculin	Female Féminin	Both sexes Les deux sexes	Male Masculin	Female Féminin
AFRICA - AFRIQUE									
Egypt - Égypte									
1 VII 2018 (ESDF)									
70 - 74	*1 040 945*	*543 787*	*497 158*	*489 176*	*261 890*	*227 286*	*551 769*	*281 897*	*269 872*
75 +	*949 285*	*488 339*	*460 946*	*405 403*	*215 749*	*189 654*	*543 882*	*272 590*	*271 292*
Equatorial Guinea - Guinée équatoriale[8]									
1 VII 2019 (ESDF)									
Total	*1 405 704*	...	...	...	...	...	...	...	...
0 - 4	*193 848*	...	...	...	...	...	...	...	...
5 - 9	*176 516*	...	...	...	...	...	...	...	...
10 - 14	*142 682*	...	...	...	...	...	...	...	...
15 - 19	*116 262*	...	...	...	...	...	...	...	...
20 - 24	*107 580*	...	...	...	...	...	...	...	...
25 - 29	*122 412*	...	...	...	...	...	...	...	...
30 - 34	*104 289*	...	...	...	...	...	...	...	...
35 - 39	*85 123*	...	...	...	...	...	...	...	...
40 - 44	*77 696*	...	...	...	...	...	...	...	...
45 - 49	*63 890*	...	...	...	...	...	...	...	...
50 - 54	*61 453*	...	...	...	...	...	...	...	...
55 - 59	*40 760*	...	...	...	...	...	...	...	...
60 - 64	*35 777*	...	...	...	...	...	...	...	...
65 - 69	*23 193*	...	...	...	...	...	...	...	...
70 - 74	*20 097*	...	...	...	...	...	...	...	...
75 - 79	*15 564*	...	...	...	...	...	...	...	...
80 - 84	*9 668*	...	...	...	...	...	...	...	...
85 +	*8 894*	...	...	...	...	...	...	...	...
Eritrea - Érythrée[9]									
1 VII 2019 (ESDF)									
Total	*3 379 039*	*1 662 675*	*1 716 364*	*1 190 612*	*566 445*	*624 168*	*2 188 427*	*1 096 230*	*1 092 196*
0	*108 034*	*53 908*	*54 126*	*29 743*	*14 142*	*15 600*	*78 291*	*39 765*	*38 526*
1 - 4	*401 515*	*199 712*	*201 803*	*115 362*	*54 771*	*60 592*	*286 152*	*144 941*	*141 211*
5 - 9	*442 744*	*219 688*	*223 056*	*135 880*	*64 472*	*71 408*	*306 863*	*155 216*	*151 648*
10 - 14	*367 797*	*182 175*	*185 622*	*120 322*	*57 142*	*63 180*	*247 475*	*125 033*	*122 442*
15 - 19	*292 840*	*145 905*	*146 935*	*99 619*	*47 471*	*52 148*	*193 222*	*98 435*	*94 787*
20 - 24	*297 236*	*152 830*	*144 406*	*97 169*	*49 306*	*47 863*	*200 066*	*103 524*	*96 542*
25 - 29	*322 609*	*164 663*	*157 946*	*107 740*	*54 867*	*52 873*	*214 869*	*109 796*	*105 073*
30 - 34	*268 136*	*132 784*	*135 352*	*102 266*	*48 059*	*54 206*	*165 871*	*84 725*	*81 146*
35 - 39	*190 830*	*94 471*	*96 360*	*86 953*	*40 863*	*46 090*	*103 877*	*53 608*	*50 269*
40 - 44	*135 260*	*59 659*	*75 602*	*64 433*	*28 550*	*35 883*	*70 827*	*31 108*	*39 719*
45 - 49	*134 396*	*59 087*	*75 309*	*61 935*	*27 865*	*34 069*	*72 461*	*31 222*	*41 239*
50 - 54	*99 331*	*45 913*	*53 418*	*41 743*	*19 785*	*21 958*	*57 588*	*26 128*	*31 460*
55 - 59	*87 281*	*38 984*	*48 298*	*34 471*	*15 573*	*18 898*	*52 810*	*23 411*	*29 400*
60 - 64	*67 942*	*34 287*	*33 655*	*26 595*	*13 641*	*12 954*	*41 347*	*20 646*	*20 702*
65 - 69	*55 899*	*27 888*	*28 012*	*22 753*	*10 883*	*11 870*	*33 146*	*17 004*	*16 142*
70 - 74	*46 904*	*22 450*	*24 454*	*19 594*	*8 412*	*11 181*	*27 311*	*14 038*	*13 273*
75 - 79	*32 547*	*14 324*	*18 223*	*12 671*	*5 233*	*7 438*	*19 876*	*9 091*	*10 784*
80 - 84	*18 314*	*8 783*	*9 531*	*7 193*	*3 346*	*3 847*	*11 121*	*5 437*	*5 683*
85 +	*9 423*	*5 165*	*4 258*	*4 170*	*2 063*	*2 107*	*5 254*	*3 103*	*2 151*
Eswatini									
29 IV 2017 (CDJC)									
Total	1 093 238	531 111	562 127	259 766	128 701	131 065	833 472	402 410	431 062
0	25 472	12 768	12 704	5 799	2 927	2 872	19 673	9 841	9 832
1 - 4	104 736	52 450	52 286	20 107	10 046	10 061	84 629	42 404	42 225
5 - 9	129 828	65 109	64 719	22 573	11 144	11 429	107 255	53 965	53 290
10 - 14	127 437	63 783	63 654	20 609	10 096	10 513	106 828	53 687	53 141
15 - 19	120 168	60 955	59 213	21 489	10 194	11 295	98 679	50 761	47 918
20 - 24	106 516	52 280	54 236	27 870	12 845	15 025	78 646	39 435	39 211
25 - 29	96 739	46 551	50 188	31 988	15 419	16 569	64 751	31 132	33 619
30 - 34	86 370	42 148	44 222	30 431	15 171	15 260	55 939	26 977	28 962
35 - 39	66 981	33 443	33 538	23 886	12 609	11 277	43 095	20 834	22 261
40 - 44	49 696	24 428	25 268	16 683	9 002	7 681	33 013	15 426	17 587
45 - 49	41 278	19 194	22 084	12 138	6 535	5 603	29 140	12 659	16 481
50 - 54	32 818	14 094	18 724	8 435	4 320	4 115	24 383	9 774	14 609
55 - 59	27 816	12 062	15 754	6 033	3 137	2 896	21 783	8 925	12 858
60 - 64	22 869	10 059	12 810	3 852	1 751	2 101	19 017	8 308	10 709

7. Population by age, sex and urban/rural residence: latest available year, 2010 - 2019
Population selon l'âge, le sexe et la résidence, urbaine/rurale : dernière année disponible, 2010 - 2019 (continued - suite)

Continent, country or area, date, code[a] and age (in years) / Continent, pays ou zone, date, code[a] et âge (en années)	Total			Urban - Urbaine			Rural - Rurale		
	Both sexes Les deux sexes	Male Masculin	Female Féminin	Both sexes Les deux sexes	Male Masculin	Female Féminin	Both sexes Les deux sexes	Male Masculin	Female Féminin
AFRICA - AFRIQUE									
Eswatini									
29 IV 2017 (CDJC)									
65 - 69	17 359	7 322	10 037	2 484	1 103	1 381	14 875	6 219	8 656
70 - 74	13 254	4 998	8 256	1 515	602	913	11 739	4 396	7 343
75 - 79	9 148	3 484	5 664	984	401	583	8 164	3 083	5 081
80 +	9 039	2 846	6 193	817	273	544	8 222	2 573	5 649
Unknown - Inconnu	5 714	3 137	2 577	2 073	1 126	947	3 641	2 011	1 630
1 VII 2018 (ESDJ)[10]									
Total	1 159 250	551 317	607 933	...	...	...	...	...	...
0 - 4	152 990	77 918	75 072	...	...	...	...	...	...
5 - 9	140 917	72 116	68 801	...	...	...	...	...	...
10 - 14	126 497	64 384	62 113	...	...	...	...	...	...
15 - 19	127 464	63 576	63 888	...	...	...	...	...	...
20 - 24	122 436	59 855	62 581	...	...	...	...	...	...
25 - 29	108 144	51 178	56 966	...	...	...	...	...	...
30 - 34	89 880	39 779	50 101	...	...	...	...	...	...
35 - 39	72 969	30 248	42 721	...	...	...	...	...	...
40 - 44	55 572	22 171	33 401	...	...	...	...	...	...
45 - 49	43 681	17 388	26 293	...	...	...	...	...	...
50 - 54	33 613	13 795	19 818	...	...	...	...	...	...
55 - 59	25 996	11 059	14 937	...	...	...	...	...	...
60 - 64	19 794	8 693	11 101	...	...	...	...	...	...
65 - 69	14 831	6 851	7 980	...	...	...	...	...	...
70 - 74	10 683	5 183	5 500	...	...	...	...	...	...
75 - 79	6 917	3 555	3 362	...	...	...	...	...	...
80 +	6 866	3 568	3 298	...	...	...	...	...	...
Ethiopia - Éthiopie[11]									
1 VII 2019 (ESDF)									
Total	98 536 550	49 430 939	49 105 606	20 776 812	10 326 225	10 450 593	77 759 737	39 104 714	38 655 021
0	2 802 631	1 429 256	1 373 374	357 045	180 470	176 553	2 445 587	1 248 786	1 196 822
1 - 4	10 777 046	5 475 645	5 301 401	1 395 298	702 700	692 616	9 381 748	4 772 945	4 608 785
5 - 9	12 797 130	6 480 644	6 316 488	2 077 695	1 031 830	1 045 865	10 719 437	5 448 813	5 270 621
10 - 14	11 588 644	5 861 227	5 727 417	2 300 637	1 134 159	1 166 477	9 288 008	4 727 066	4 560 940
15 - 19	10 895 730	5 522 716	5 373 013	2 417 385	1 198 939	1 218 445	8 478 343	4 323 776	4 154 569
20 - 24	9 740 051	4 941 957	4 798 096	2 399 952	1 205 358	1 194 597	7 340 099	3 736 601	3 603 501
25 - 29	8 550 892	4 292 221	4 258 670	2 276 432	1 127 537	1 148 899	6 274 460	3 164 686	3 109 773
30 - 34	7 188 461	3 544 637	3 643 825	1 943 815	969 020	974 797	5 244 644	2 575 616	2 669 028
35 - 39	5 929 121	2 893 350	3 035 775	1 586 855	801 453	785 407	4 342 264	2 091 896	2 250 369
40 - 44	4 684 764	2 278 243	2 406 517	1 142 581	582 110	560 468	3 542 183	1 696 135	1 846 051
45 - 49	3 670 821	1 778 307	1 892 516	835 184	424 485	410 699	2 835 635	1 353 822	1 481 817
50 - 54	2 892 221	1 418 440	1 473 777	619 483	308 845	310 637	2 272 736	1 109 597	1 163 138
55 - 59	2 252 146	1 117 870	1 134 276	460 280	224 966	235 316	1 791 866	892 905	898 961
60 - 64	1 706 766	848 660	858 106	350 382	161 938	188 441	1 356 385	686 720	669 665
65 - 69	1 236 690	619 289	617 401	246 111	111 612	134 502	990 579	507 676	482 900
70 - 74	856 823	431 668	425 154	170 946	76 091	94 852	685 880	355 575	330 302
75 - 79	532 988	269 478	263 508	109 874	48 388	61 485	423 114	221 090	202 024
80 +	433 629	227 332	206 296	86 858	36 321	50 535	346 772	191 012	155 760
Gambia - Gambie[12]									
31 XII 2015 (SSDF)									
Total	1 922 950	915 357	1 007 593	1 057 467	503 304	554 163	865 483	412 053	453 430
0 - 4	311 156	155 654	155 502	156 283	76 198	80 085	154 874	79 456	75 418
5 - 9	298 089	150 122	147 966	145 387	71 306	74 081	152 702	78 816	73 886
10 - 14	228 988	115 261	113 727	114 825	58 394	56 431	114 164	56 868	57 296
15 - 19	198 367	87 274	111 093	114 445	47 786	66 660	83 922	39 489	44 433
20 - 24	180 479	76 050	104 429	115 445	47 655	67 790	65 034	28 395	36 639
25 - 29	151 669	62 431	89 237	96 080	40 579	55 501	55 589	21 852	33 737
30 - 34	127 754	57 532	70 222	78 401	38 439	39 962	49 352	19 093	30 259
35 - 39	109 161	49 913	59 248	66 199	32 130	34 069	42 961	17 783	25 178
40 - 44	81 698	39 032	42 666	47 312	23 918	23 394	34 386	15 114	19 272
45 - 49	61 757	32 235	29 522	34 649	19 389	15 260	27 107	12 846	14 262
50 - 54	52 727	27 286	25 441	28 742	16 285	12 457	23 985	11 001	12 984
55 - 59	35 759	18 075	17 685	20 122	9 561	10 562	15 637	8 514	7 123
60 - 64	30 155	16 034	14 121	14 511	8 600	5 911	15 644	7 434	8 210
65 +	55 191	28 457	26 734	25 063	13 063	12 000	30 128	15 393	14 734

7. Population by age, sex and urban/rural residence: latest available year, 2010 - 2019
Population selon l'âge, le sexe et la résidence, urbaine/rurale : dernière année disponible, 2010 - 2019 (continued - suite)

Continent, country or area, date, code[a] and age (in years) / Continent, pays ou zone, date, code[a] et âge (en années)	Total			Urban - Urbaine			Rural - Rurale		
	Both sexes Les deux sexes	Male Masculin	Female Féminin	Both sexes Les deux sexes	Male Masculin	Female Féminin	Both sexes Les deux sexes	Male Masculin	Female Féminin
AFRICA - AFRIQUE									
Ghana[13]									
1 VII 2015 (ESDF)									
Total	27 670 174	13 562 093	14 108 081	13 817 894	6 903 107	6 914 787	13 852 280	6 658 986	7 193 294
0	841 301	425 611	415 690	403 605	195 150	208 455	437 696	230 461	207 235
1 - 4	3 158 109	1 595 165	1 562 944	1 513 925	731 409	782 516	1 644 184	863 756	780 428
5 - 9	3 312 878	1 688 452	1 624 426	1 579 799	755 911	823 888	1 733 079	932 541	800 538
10 - 14	3 097 352	1 567 043	1 530 309	1 538 503	749 266	789 237	1 558 849	817 777	741 072
15 - 19	2 825 578	1 414 987	1 410 591	1 458 024	735 981	722 043	1 367 554	679 006	688 548
20 - 24	2 537 799	1 251 759	1 286 040	1 377 177	736 425	640 752	1 160 622	515 334	645 288
25 - 29	2 252 493	1 083 877	1 168 616	1 211 633	636 338	575 295	1 040 860	447 539	593 321
30 - 34	1 967 166	935 947	1 031 219	1 014 879	537 402	477 477	952 287	398 545	553 742
35 - 39	1 665 237	785 200	880 037	840 000	437 656	402 344	825 237	347 544	477 693
40 - 44	1 404 309	661 789	742 520	703 098	362 522	340 576	701 211	299 267	401 944
45 - 49	1 145 932	546 030	599 902	560 013	275 131	284 882	585 919	270 899	315 020
50 - 54	933 268	445 531	487 737	477 984	238 760	239 224	455 284	206 771	248 513
55 - 59	728 002	348 118	379 884	337 828	159 376	178 452	390 174	188 742	201 432
60 - 64	570 616	270 642	299 974	271 174	129 651	141 523	299 442	140 991	158 451
65 - 69	419 501	196 219	223 282	178 422	73 727	104 695	241 079	122 492	118 587
70 - 74	313 256	142 378	170 878	149 542	68 333	81 209	163 714	74 045	89 669
75 - 79	223 087	96 514	126 573	90 638	36 406	54 232	132 449	60 108	72 341
80 +	274 290	106 831	167 459	111 650	43 663	67 987	162 640	63 168	99 472
Guinea - Guinée[14]									
1 VII 2019 (ESDJ)									
Total	12 218 359	5 921 547	6 296 809	4 414 266	2 139 345	2 274 921	7 804 090	3 782 203	4 021 888
0	430 943	217 341	213 602	131 108	63 203	67 905	340 658	174 105	166 553
1 - 4	1 605 364	808 121	797 241	434 772	209 912	224 860	1 129 768	578 243	551 525
5 - 9	1 851 505	942 301	909 203	598 195	287 084	311 111	1 253 310	655 218	598 092
10 - 14	1 571 695	791 646	780 049	601 776	283 968	317 808	969 919	507 678	462 241
15 - 19	1 273 254	629 697	643 557	538 399	257 750	280 649	734 854	371 947	362 908
20 - 24	1 063 118	507 459	555 659	494 620	249 745	244 876	568 497	257 714	310 783
25 - 29	903 679	400 621	503 057	415 899	201 845	214 053	487 780	198 776	289 004
30 - 34	756 411	327 322	429 089	297 275	140 546	156 729	459 136	186 776	272 360
35 - 39	608 695	265 802	342 893	222 127	106 104	116 023	386 568	159 698	226 870
40 - 44	501 112	222 348	278 764	176 646	85 360	91 286	324 466	136 988	187 478
45 - 49	407 456	188 150	219 306	138 206	68 661	69 546	269 249	119 489	149 760
50 - 54	332 518	158 668	173 849	109 523	54 505	55 018	222 994	104 163	118 831
55 - 59	264 085	132 617	131 468	83 409	43 232	40 176	180 677	89 385	91 292
60 - 64	210 434	108 077	102 358	62 077	33 238	28 839	148 358	74 839	73 519
65 - 69	163 165	84 149	79 016	45 289	24 142	21 147	117 876	60 007	57 869
70 - 74	118 581	60 899	57 682	30 334	15 629	14 705	88 247	45 270	42 977
75 - 79	77 528	38 992	38 536	17 364	7 831	9 533	60 164	31 161	29 003
80 +	78 816	37 336	41 479	17 247	6 590	10 657	61 568	30 746	30 822
Guinea-Bissau - Guinée-Bissau[1]									
1 VII 2019 (ESDF)									
Total	1 604 561	790 873	813 688	703 994	346 992	357 002	900 567	443 881	456 686
0 - 4	268 611	137 507	131 104	98 051	48 670	49 381	170 560	88 837	81 723
5 - 9	244 171	125 195	118 976	92 850	44 730	48 120	151 321	80 465	70 856
10 - 14	182 370	91 543	90 827	80 745	37 606	43 139	101 625	53 937	47 688
15 - 19	169 884	85 443	84 441	84 820	41 747	43 073	85 064	43 696	41 368
20 - 24	142 667	72 130	70 537	75 801	39 710	36 091	66 866	32 420	34 446
25 - 29	136 681	67 422	69 259	68 733	35 885	32 848	67 948	31 537	36 411
30 - 34	115 417	54 779	60 638	57 654	28 953	28 701	57 763	25 826	31 937
35 - 39	102 024	46 871	55 153	46 596	22 627	23 969	55 428	24 244	31 184
40 - 44	64 959	30 186	34 773	30 251	14 964	15 287	34 708	15 222	19 486
45 - 49	55 633	25 238	30 395	24 439	11 763	12 676	31 194	13 475	17 719
50 - 54	37 338	17 056	20 282	15 716	7 775	7 941	21 622	9 281	12 341
55 - 59	33 402	15 067	18 335	12 903	5 994	6 909	20 499	9 073	11 426
60 - 64	20 646	9 076	11 570	6 861	3 092	3 769	13 785	5 984	7 801
65 - 69	13 381	6 482	6 899	4 131	1 928	2 203	9 250	4 554	4 696
70 - 74	8 837	3 823	5 014	2 460	989	1 471	6 377	2 834	3 543
75 - 79	4 687	1 806	2 881	1 161	366	795	3 526	1 440	2 086
80 +	3 853	1 249	2 604	822	193	629	3 031	1 056	1 975

7. Population by age, sex and urban/rural residence: latest available year, 2010 - 2019
Population selon l'âge, le sexe et la résidence, urbaine/rurale : dernière année disponible, 2010 - 2019 (continued - suite)

Continent, country or area, date, code[a] and age (in years) / Continent, pays ou zone, date, code[a] et âge (en annèes)	Total			Urban - Urbaine			Rural - Rurale		
	Both sexes Les deux sexes	Male Masculin	Female Féminin	Both sexes Les deux sexes	Male Masculin	Female Féminin	Both sexes Les deux sexes	Male Masculin	Female Féminin
AFRICA - AFRIQUE									
Kenya[15]									
1 VII 2017 (ESDF)									
Total	*46 595 199*	*23 117 881*	*23 477 319*	...	...	...	...	...	...
0	*1 479 846*	*749 229*	*730 617*	...	...	...	...	...	...
1 - 4	*5 649 697*	*2 848 841*	*2 800 856*	...	...	...	...	...	...
5 - 9	*6 409 780*	*3 233 878*	*3 175 902*	...	...	...	...	...	...
10 - 14	*5 668 486*	*2 867 168*	*2 801 317*	...	...	...	...	...	...
15 - 19	*4 948 884*	*2 510 323*	*2 438 561*	...	...	...	...	...	...
20 - 24	*4 335 111*	*2 139 798*	*2 195 314*	...	...	...	...	...	...
25 - 29	*3 909 855*	*1 871 462*	*2 038 393*	...	...	...	...	...	...
30 - 34	*3 366 938*	*1 587 480*	*1 779 458*	...	...	...	...	...	...
35 - 39	*2 696 724*	*1 306 876*	*1 389 848*	...	...	...	...	...	...
40 - 44	*2 057 867*	*1 032 134*	*1 025 733*	...	...	...	...	...	...
45 - 49	*1 631 976*	*818 166*	*813 809*	...	...	...	...	...	...
50 - 54	*1 240 344*	*618 971*	*621 373*	...	...	...	...	...	...
55 - 59	*949 533*	*472 914*	*476 619*	...	...	...	...	...	...
60 - 64	*728 997*	*358 931*	*370 066*	...	...	...	...	...	...
65 - 69	*521 927*	*251 108*	*270 819*	...	...	...	...	...	...
70 - 74	*391 353*	*184 500*	*206 853*	...	...	...	...	...	...
75 - 79	*254 042*	*116 739*	*137 303*	...	...	...	...	...	...
80 +	*353 840*	*149 363*	*204 477*	...	...	...	...	...	...
Lesotho									
10 IV 2016 (CDJC)									
Total	2 007 201	982 133	1 025 068	...	...	...	...	...	...
0 - 4	200 155	100 793	99 362	...	...	...	...	...	...
5 - 9	221 476	109 953	111 523	...	...	...	...	...	...
10 - 14	215 813	107 879	107 934	...	...	...	...	...	...
15 - 19	209 866	106 214	103 652	...	...	...	...	...	...
20 - 24	199 267	98 827	100 440	...	...	...	...	...	...
25 - 29	188 943	95 802	93 141	...	...	...	...	...	...
30 - 34	168 145	86 956	81 189	...	...	...	...	...	...
35 - 39	130 381	68 246	62 135	...	...	...	...	...	...
40 - 44	96 295	48 665	47 630	...	...	...	...	...	...
45 - 49	74 887	36 425	38 462	...	...	...	...	...	...
50 - 54	70 359	31 785	38 574	...	...	...	...	...	...
55 - 59	59 817	25 759	34 058	...	...	...	...	...	...
60 - 64	49 221	20 770	28 451	...	...	...	...	...	...
65 - 69	37 358	15 311	22 047	...	...	...	...	...	...
70 - 74	30 808	12 017	18 791	...	...	...	...	...	...
75 - 79	24 174	8 467	15 707	...	...	...	...	...	...
80 - 84	18 621	5 424	13 197	...	...	...	...	...	...
85 - 89	7 074	1 873	5 201	...	...	...	...	...	...
90 - 94	2 789	662	2 127	...	...	...	...	...	...
95 +	1 752	305	1 447	...	...	...	...	...	...
Libya - Libye[16]									
1 VII 2015 (ESDF)									
Total	*6 162 247*	*3 129 026*	*3 033 221*	...	...	...	...	...	...
0 - 4	*615 556*	*316 497*	*299 059*	...	...	...	...	...	...
5 - 9	*577 905*	*297 303*	*280 602*	...	...	...	...	...	...
10 - 14	*555 149*	*284 318*	*270 831*	...	...	...	...	...	...
15 - 19	*525 115*	*268 106*	*257 009*	...	...	...	...	...	...
20 - 24	*546 408*	*278 875*	*267 533*	...	...	...	...	...	...
25 - 29	*571 230*	*289 113*	*282 117*	...	...	...	...	...	...
30 - 34	*568 834*	*287 480*	*281 354*	...	...	...	...	...	...
35 - 39	*551 606*	*279 699*	*271 907*	...	...	...	...	...	...
40 - 44	*466 373*	*235 088*	*231 285*	...	...	...	...	...	...
45 - 49	*360 825*	*180 029*	*180 796*	...	...	...	...	...	...
50 - 54	*253 647*	*126 799*	*126 848*	...	...	...	...	...	...
55 - 59	*173 760*	*87 135*	*86 625*	...	...	...	...	...	...
60 - 64	*116 033*	*56 199*	*59 834*	...	...	...	...	...	...
65 - 69	*102 645*	*51 782*	*50 863*	...	...	...	...	...	...
70 - 74	*72 486*	*38 750*	*33 736*	...	...	...	...	...	...
75 - 79	*52 558*	*26 942*	*25 616*	...	...	...	...	...	...
80 - 84	*30 271*	*15 038*	*15 233*	...	...	...	...	...	...
85 +	*21 846*	*9 873*	*11 973*	...	...	...	...	...	...

7. Population by age, sex and urban/rural residence: latest available year, 2010 - 2019
Population selon l'âge, le sexe et la résidence, urbaine/rurale : dernière année disponible, 2010 - 2019 (continued - suite)

Continent, country or area, date, code[a] and age (in years) Continent, pays ou zone, date, code[a] et âge (en années)	Total			Urban - Urbaine			Rural - Rurale		
	Both sexes Les deux sexes	Male Masculin	Female Féminin	Both sexes Les deux sexes	Male Masculin	Female Féminin	Both sexes Les deux sexes	Male Masculin	Female Féminin
AFRICA - AFRIQUE									
Madagascar[17]									
1 VII 2019 (ESDF)									
Total	*25 588 517*	*12 668 593*	*12 919 924*	...	...	...	...	...	...
0 - 4	*4 349 320*	*2 140 990*	*2 208 330*	...	...	...	...	...	...
5 - 9	*4 101 267*	*2 046 090*	*2 055 178*	...	...	...	...	...	...
10 - 14	*3 502 776*	*1 787 232*	*1 715 544*	...	...	...	...	...	...
15 - 19	*2 749 436*	*1 395 251*	*1 354 185*	...	...	...	...	...	...
20 - 24	*1 930 504*	*894 670*	*1 035 834*	...	...	...	...	...	...
25 - 29	*1 662 969*	*791 824*	*871 146*	...	...	...	...	...	...
30 - 34	*1 492 914*	*723 266*	*769 648*	...	...	...	...	...	...
35 - 39	*1 358 897*	*657 405*	*701 492*	...	...	...	...	...	...
40 - 44	*1 106 753*	*529 353*	*577 400*	...	...	...	...	...	...
45 - 49	*1 020 081*	*499 305*	*520 776*	...	...	...	...	...	...
50 - 54	*825 746*	*446 371*	*379 375*	...	...	...	...	...	...
55 - 59	*539 601*	*292 937*	*246 664*	...	...	...	...	...	...
60 - 64	*341 806*	*163 388*	*178 418*	...	...	...	...	...	...
65 - 69	*219 993*	*111 931*	*108 062*	...	...	...	...	...	...
70 - 74	*181 811*	*91 962*	*89 849*	...	...	...	...	...	...
75 - 79	*109 474*	*53 430*	*56 044*	...	...	...	...	...	...
80 - 84	*62 977*	*29 565*	*33 412*	...	...	...	...	...	...
85 +	*32 193*	*13 625*	*18 568*	...	...	...	...	...	...
Malawi									
3 IX 2018 (CDJC)									
Total	17 563 749	8 521 460	9 042 289	2 816 492	1 401 373	1 415 119	14 747 257	7 120 087	7 627 170
0 - 4	2 552 406	1 265 971	1 286 435	363 248	180 649	182 599	2 189 158	1 085 322	1 103 836
5 - 9	2 632 878	1 298 962	1 333 916	356 343	175 089	181 254	2 276 535	1 123 873	1 152 662
10 - 14	2 533 303	1 247 212	1 286 091	357 385	170 863	186 522	2 175 918	1 076 349	1 099 569
15 - 19	2 035 945	1 004 780	1 031 165	326 916	158 140	168 776	1 709 029	846 640	862 389
20 - 24	1 651 576	777 577	873 999	325 879	154 120	171 759	1 325 697	623 457	702 240
25 - 29	1 229 411	582 866	646 545	262 278	127 606	134 672	967 133	455 260	511 873
30 - 34	1 107 226	516 505	590 721	235 218	115 871	119 347	872 008	400 634	471 374
35 - 39	968 998	468 188	500 810	198 212	103 760	94 452	770 786	364 428	406 358
40 - 44	729 600	367 171	362 429	136 555	76 737	59 818	593 045	290 434	302 611
45 - 49	535 868	273 749	262 119	84 480	48 491	35 989	451 388	225 258	226 130
50 - 54	387 812	188 400	199 412	56 344	30 748	25 596	331 468	157 652	173 816
55 - 59	306 921	144 046	162 875	38 354	20 244	18 110	268 567	123 802	144 765
60 - 64	234 918	107 820	127 098	27 551	14 907	12 644	207 367	92 913	114 454
65 - 69	240 551	107 911	132 640	20 628	10 951	9 677	219 923	96 960	122 963
70 - 74	144 788	63 805	80 983	11 580	6 113	5 467	133 208	57 692	75 516
75 - 79	124 718	51 598	73 120	7 750	3 808	3 942	116 968	47 790	69 178
80 - 84	63 675	24 130	39 545	3 732	1 649	2 083	59 943	22 481	37 462
85 - 89	54 754	20 751	34 003	2 642	1 104	1 538	52 112	19 647	32 465
90 - 94	15 130	5 245	9 885	785	290	495	14 345	4 955	9 390
95 +	13 271	4 773	8 498	612	233	379	12 659	4 540	8 119
Mali[18]									
1 VII 2018 (ESDF)									
Total	*19 418 097*	*9 631 376*	*9 786 721*	...	...	...	...	...	...
0 - 4	*3 678 867*	*1 824 718*	*1 854 149*	...	...	...	...	...	...
5 - 9	*2 987 117*	*1 481 610*	*1 505 507*	...	...	...	...	...	...
10 - 14	*2 491 512*	*1 235 790*	*1 255 722*	...	...	...	...	...	...
15 - 19	*2 072 065*	*1 027 744*	*1 044 321*	...	...	...	...	...	...
20 - 24	*1 758 810*	*872 370*	*886 440*	...	...	...	...	...	...
25 - 29	*1 493 750*	*740 900*	*752 850*	...	...	...	...	...	...
30 - 34	*1 226 430*	*608 309*	*618 121*	...	...	...	...	...	...
35 - 39	*970 444*	*481 340*	*489 104*	...	...	...	...	...	...
40 - 44	*733 463*	*363 798*	*369 665*	...	...	...	...	...	...
45 - 49	*545 909*	*270 771*	*275 138*	...	...	...	...	...	...
50 - 54	*427 156*	*211 869*	*215 287*	...	...	...	...	...	...
55 - 59	*347 731*	*172 475*	*175 257*	...	...	...	...	...	...
60 - 64	*257 835*	*127 886*	*129 949*	...	...	...	...	...	...
65 - 69	*208 033*	*103 184*	*104 848*	...	...	...	...	...	...
70 - 74	*122 637*	*60 828*	*61 809*	...	...	...	...	...	...
75 - 79	*64 443*	*31 964*	*32 479*	...	...	...	...	...	...
80 - 84	*31 895*	*15 820*	*16 075*	...	...	...	...	...	...

7. Population by age, sex and urban/rural residence: latest available year, 2010 - 2019
Population selon l'âge, le sexe et la résidence, urbaine/rurale : dernière année disponible, 2010 - 2019 (continued - suite)

Continent, country or area, date, code[a] and age (in years) / Continent, pays ou zone, date, code[a] et âge (en années)	Total			Urban - Urbaine			Rural - Rurale		
	Both sexes Les deux sexes	Male Masculin	Female Féminin	Both sexes Les deux sexes	Male Masculin	Female Féminin	Both sexes Les deux sexes	Male Masculin	Female Féminin
AFRICA - AFRIQUE									
Mauritania - Mauritanie[1]									
1 VII 2016 (ESDF)									
Total	*3 782 701*	...	...	...	...	...	...	...	...
0 - 4	*579 832*	...	...	...	...	...	...	...	...
5 - 9	*567 643*	...	...	...	...	...	...	...	...
10 - 14	*478 293*	...	...	...	...	...	...	...	...
15 - 19	*396 650*	...	...	...	...	...	...	...	...
20 - 24	*333 473*	...	...	...	...	...	...	...	...
25 - 29	*280 531*	...	...	...	...	...	...	...	...
30 - 34	*236 864*	...	...	...	...	...	...	...	...
35 - 39	*196 168*	...	...	...	...	...	...	...	...
40 - 44	*164 707*	...	...	...	...	...	...	...	...
45 - 49	*137 439*	...	...	...	...	...	...	...	...
50 - 54	*111 936*	...	...	...	...	...	...	...	...
55 - 59	*90 008*	...	...	...	...	...	...	...	...
60 - 64	*68 836*	...	...	...	...	...	...	...	...
65 - 69	*50 266*	...	...	...	...	...	...	...	...
70 - 74	*36 188*	...	...	...	...	...	...	...	...
75 - 79	*24 540*	...	...	...	...	...	...	...	...
80 +	*29 328*	...	...	...	...	...	...	...	...
Mauritius - Maurice[19]									
4 VII 2011 (CDJC)									
Total	1 236 817	610 848	625 969	499 349	244 688	254 661	737 468	366 160	371 308
0 - 4	73 078	36 702	36 376	26 297	13 220	13 077	46 781	23 482	23 299
5 - 9	89 015	44 947	44 068	32 036	16 177	15 859	56 979	28 770	28 209
10 - 14	93 639	47 302	46 337	35 028	17 523	17 505	58 611	29 779	28 832
15 - 19	101 008	50 715	50 293	39 403	19 725	19 678	61 605	30 990	30 615
20 - 24	92 671	46 871	45 800	37 224	18 836	18 388	55 447	28 035	27 412
25 - 29	90 937	45 589	45 348	35 908	17 899	18 009	55 029	27 690	27 339
30 - 34	103 429	52 182	51 247	39 099	19 805	19 294	64 330	32 377	31 953
35 - 39	87 797	44 241	43 556	32 781	16 142	16 639	55 016	28 099	26 917
40 - 44	89 386	45 150	44 236	34 449	17 010	17 439	54 937	28 140	26 797
45 - 49	99 341	49 800	49 541	41 705	20 637	21 068	57 636	29 163	28 473
50 - 54	86 337	42 996	43 341	37 429	18 627	18 802	48 908	24 369	24 539
55 - 59	73 054	35 713	37 341	32 421	15 983	16 438	40 633	19 730	20 903
60 - 64	57 342	27 143	30 199	25 449	12 058	13 391	31 893	15 085	16 808
65 - 69	35 439	15 846	19 593	16 700	7 527	9 173	18 739	8 319	10 420
70 - 74	25 375	10 986	14 389	12 872	5 661	7 211	12 503	5 325	7 178
75 - 79	18 044	7 349	10 695	9 320	3 851	5 469	8 724	3 498	5 226
80 - 84	11 369	4 176	7 193	6 028	2 253	3 775	5 341	1 923	3 418
85 - 89	6 368	2 135	4 233	3 427	1 179	2 248	2 941	956	1 985
90 - 94	1 982	512	1 470	1 046	275	771	936	237	699
95 - 99	491	107	384	297	60	237	194	47	147
100 +	96	13	83	55	7	48	41	6	35
Unknown - Inconnu	619	373	246	375	233	142	244	140	104
1 VII 2019 (ESDJ)[4]									
Total	1 265 711	626 167	639 544	...	...	...	...	...	...
0	12 970	6 605	6 365	...	...	...	...	...	...
1 - 4	51 519	26 359	25 160	...	...	...	...	...	...
5 - 9	71 236	36 111	35 125	...	...	...	...	...	...
10 - 14	85 423	43 349	42 074	...	...	...	...	...	...
15 - 19	97 244	49 436	47 808	...	...	...	...	...	...
20 - 24	96 121	48 601	47 520	...	...	...	...	...	...
25 - 29	97 457	49 294	48 163	...	...	...	...	...	...
30 - 34	84 286	42 673	41 613	...	...	...	...	...	...
35 - 39	95 111	48 123	46 988	...	...	...	...	...	...
40 - 44	93 085	47 368	45 717	...	...	...	...	...	...
45 - 49	81 919	41 368	40 551	...	...	...	...	...	...
50 - 54	90 187	44 965	45 222	...	...	...	...	...	...
55 - 59	88 703	43 536	45 167	...	...	...	...	...	...
60 - 64	74 494	35 777	38 717	...	...	...	...	...	...
65 - 69	60 996	28 304	32 692	...	...	...	...	...	...
70 - 74	37 723	16 466	21 257	...	...	...	...	...	...
75 - 79	22 371	9 106	13 265	...	...	...	...	...	...

7. Population by age, sex and urban/rural residence: latest available year, 2010 - 2019
Population selon l'âge, le sexe et la résidence, urbaine/rurale : dernière année disponible, 2010 - 2019 (continued - suite)

Continent, country or area, date, code[a] and age (in years) / Continent, pays ou zone, date, code[a] et âge (en années)	Total: Both sexes / Les deux sexes	Total: Male / Masculin	Total: Female / Féminin	Urban - Urbaine: Both sexes / Les deux sexes	Urban - Urbaine: Male / Masculin	Urban - Urbaine: Female / Féminin	Rural - Rurale: Both sexes / Les deux sexes	Rural - Rurale: Male / Masculin	Rural - Rurale: Female / Féminin
AFRICA - AFRIQUE									
Mauritius - Maurice[19]									
1 VII 2019 (ESDJ)[4]									
80 - 84	14 228	5 341	8 887	...	...	...	...	...	...
85 +	10 638	3 385	7 253	...	...	...	...	...	...
Mayotte									
5 IX 2017 (CDJC)[20]									
Total	256 518	122 261	134 257	242 091	115 314	126 777	14 427	6 947	7 480
0	8 169	4 165	4 004	7 731	3 944	3 786	439	221	218
1 - 4	32 135	16 194	15 942	30 351	15 265	15 086	1 784	928	856
5 - 9	37 649	18 523	19 126	35 694	17 529	18 165	1 955	994	962
10 - 14	34 302	16 910	17 392	32 578	16 061	16 517	1 724	848	876
15 - 19	25 625	12 391	13 234	24 271	11 728	12 543	1 354	663	691
20 - 24	16 542	6 959	9 583	15 636	6 598	9 038	906	361	545
25 - 29	17 093	6 882	10 211	16 132	6 489	9 643	961	393	568
30 - 34	17 559	7 252	10 307	16 578	6 840	9 738	981	412	569
35 - 39	17 030	7 561	9 469	16 021	7 099	8 921	1 010	462	548
40 - 44	14 297	6 723	7 574	13 468	6 329	7 139	829	394	435
45 - 49	11 507	6 064	5 443	10 817	5 690	5 127	690	374	316
50 - 54	7 476	3 823	3 653	6 983	3 592	3 390	494	231	263
55 - 59	6 063	3 142	2 921	5 652	2 936	2 716	411	206	205
60 - 64	4 212	2 231	1 981	3 894	2 062	1 832	318	169	149
65 - 69	2 884	1 540	1 344	2 678	1 426	1 252	206	114	92
70 - 74	1 630	788	842	1 484	722	762	146	66	80
75 - 79	1 146	546	600	1 030	489	541	116	57	59
80 - 84	633	315	318	577	290	287	56	25	31
85 - 89	322	143	179	290	124	166	32	19	13
90 - 94	121	58	63	115	55	60	6	3	3
95 - 99	67	30	37	60	24	36	7	6	1
100 +	53	21	32	51	20	31	2	1	1
1 I 2019 (ESDJ)									
Total	269 471	128 431	141 040	...	...	...	...	...	...
0	8 582	4 376	4 206	...	...	...	...	...	...
1 - 4	33 757	17 009	16 748	...	...	...	...	...	...
5 - 9	39 554	19 461	20 093	...	...	...	...	...	...
10 - 14	36 033	17 763	18 270	...	...	...	...	...	...
15 - 19	26 919	13 017	13 902	...	...	...	...	...	...
20 - 24	17 377	7 310	10 067	...	...	...	...	...	...
25 - 29	17 956	7 229	10 727	...	...	...	...	...	...
30 - 34	18 445	7 618	10 827	...	...	...	...	...	...
35 - 39	17 892	7 944	9 948	...	...	...	...	...	...
40 - 44	15 022	7 064	7 958	...	...	...	...	...	...
45 - 49	12 087	6 368	5 719	...	...	...	...	...	...
50 - 54	7 857	4 018	3 839	...	...	...	...	...	...
55 - 59	6 369	3 300	3 069	...	...	...	...	...	...
60 - 64	4 427	2 345	2 082	...	...	...	...	...	...
65 - 69	3 032	1 619	1 413	...	...	...	...	...	...
70 - 74	1 712	828	884	...	...	...	...	...	...
75 - 79	1 209	577	632	...	...	...	...	...	...
80 - 84	668	330	338	...	...	...	...	...	...
85 - 89	340	148	192	...	...	...	...	...	...
90 - 94	118	57	61	...	...	...	...	...	...
95 - 99	82	41	41	...	...	...	...	...	...
100 +	33	9	24	...	...	...	...	...	...
Morocco - Maroc[21]									
1 VII 2019 (ESDJ)									
Total	*35 586 616*	*17 725 947*	*17 860 669*	*22 376 115*	*11 019 826*	*11 356 289*	*13 210 501*	*6 706 121*	*6 504 380*
0	*588 227*	*300 673*	*287 554*	*355 957*	*181 927*	*174 030*	*232 270*	*118 746*	*113 524*
1 - 4	*2 338 380*	*1 194 244*	*1 144 136*	*1 392 585*	*710 761*	*681 824*	*945 795*	*483 483*	*462 312*
5 - 9	*3 399 533*	*1 738 294*	*1 661 239*	*1 940 110*	*991 504*	*948 606*	*1 459 423*	*746 790*	*712 633*
10 - 14	*3 024 157*	*1 541 759*	*1 482 398*	*1 722 401*	*877 501*	*844 900*	*1 301 756*	*664 258*	*637 498*
15 - 19	*3 029 035*	*1 546 568*	*1 482 467*	*1 742 543*	*883 799*	*858 744*	*1 286 492*	*662 769*	*623 723*
20 - 24	*2 954 723*	*1 481 963*	*1 472 760*	*1 819 589*	*896 783*	*922 806*	*1 135 134*	*585 180*	*549 954*
25 - 29	*3 003 714*	*1 486 188*	*1 517 526*	*1 980 114*	*951 826*	*1 028 288*	*1 023 600*	*534 362*	*489 238*
30 - 34	*2 760 451*	*1 354 635*	*1 405 816*	*1 835 911*	*882 004*	*953 907*	*924 540*	*472 631*	*451 909*
35 - 39	*2 597 081*	*1 269 651*	*1 327 430*	*1 725 663*	*830 825*	*894 838*	*871 418*	*438 826*	*432 592*

7. Population by age, sex and urban/rural residence: latest available year, 2010 - 2019
Population selon l'âge, le sexe et la résidence, urbaine/rurale : dernière année disponible, 2010 - 2019 (continued - suite)

Continent, country or area, date, code[a] and age (in years) / Continent, pays ou zone, date, code[a] et âge (en années)	Total			Urban - Urbaine			Rural - Rurale		
	Both sexes Les deux sexes	Male Masculin	Female Féminin	Both sexes Les deux sexes	Male Masculin	Female Féminin	Both sexes Les deux sexes	Male Masculin	Female Féminin
AFRICA - AFRIQUE									
Morocco - Maroc[21]									
1 VII 2019 (ESDJ)									
40 - 44	2 330 492	1 129 328	1 201 164	1 542 638	730 326	812 312	787 854	399 002	388 852
45 - 49	2 130 905	1 040 250	1 090 655	1 430 254	686 184	744 070	700 651	354 066	346 585
50 - 54	1 804 539	876 672	927 867	1 227 793	587 700	640 093	576 746	288 972	287 774
55 - 59	1 760 275	864 414	895 861	1 184 231	581 866	602 365	576 044	282 548	293 496
60 - 64	1 331 152	681 860	649 292	893 408	458 868	434 540	437 744	222 992	214 752
65 - 69	1 071 463	542 532	528 931	688 820	354 845	333 975	382 643	187 687	194 956
70 - 74	577 820	280 942	296 878	360 396	175 037	185 359	217 424	105 905	111 519
75 - 79	475 329	213 018	262 311	286 446	128 472	157 974	188 883	84 546	104 337
80 +	409 340	182 956	226 384	247 256	109 598	137 658	162 084	73 358	88 726
Mozambique[10]									
1 VII 2017 (ESDF)									
Total	27 128 530	13 106 447	14 022 083	8 766 777	4 281 319	4 485 458	18 361 753	8 825 128	9 536 625
0 - 4	4 557 840	2 277 526	2 280 314	1 163 788	580 924	582 864	3 394 052	1 696 602	1 697 450
5 - 9	3 997 583	1 992 967	2 004 616	1 108 187	552 191	555 996	2 889 396	1 440 776	1 448 620
10 - 14	3 519 245	1 749 479	1 769 766	1 092 175	539 751	552 424	2 427 070	1 209 728	1 217 342
15 - 19	2 946 806	1 473 812	1 472 994	1 044 149	515 419	528 730	1 902 657	958 393	944 264
20 - 24	2 470 502	1 179 270	1 291 232	965 641	476 936	488 705	1 504 861	702 334	802 527
25 - 29	2 035 518	914 196	1 121 322	807 851	387 340	420 511	1 227 667	526 856	700 811
30 - 34	1 692 760	752 742	940 018	640 494	297 453	343 041	1 052 266	455 289	596 977
35 - 39	1 362 667	634 117	728 550	502 245	237 161	265 084	860 422	396 956	463 466
40 - 44	1 123 344	528 397	594 947	396 939	191 051	205 888	726 405	337 346	389 059
45 - 49	918 912	430 645	488 267	314 503	152 578	161 925	604 409	278 067	326 342
50 - 54	696 087	342 800	353 287	222 907	112 234	110 673	473 180	230 566	242 614
55 - 59	550 481	264 269	286 212	170 928	84 738	86 190	379 553	179 531	200 022
60 - 64	428 657	194 900	233 757	123 516	59 143	64 373	305 141	135 757	169 384
65 - 69	319 540	145 236	174 304	88 321	41 584	46 737	231 219	103 652	127 567
70 - 74	225 428	102 256	123 172	57 447	25 630	31 817	167 981	76 626	91 355
75 - 79	146 194	65 188	81 006	35 638	15 096	20 542	110 556	50 092	60 464
80 +	136 966	58 647	78 319	32 048	12 090	19 958	104 918	46 557	58 361
Namibia - Namibie[4]									
1 VII 2019 (ESDF)									
Total	2 458 936	1 195 708	1 263 228	1 249 372	608 851	640 521	1 209 564	586 857	622 707
0	67 951	34 400	33 551	35 364	17 900	17 464	32 587	16 500	16 087
1 - 4	263 101	132 978	130 123	131 344	66 373	64 971	131 757	66 605	65 152
5 - 9	307 798	155 268	152 530	133 687	67 398	66 289	174 111	87 870	86 241
10 - 14	261 210	131 509	129 701	93 293	46 269	47 024	167 917	85 240	82 677
15 - 19	236 829	118 263	118 566	94 101	44 704	49 397	142 728	73 559	69 169
20 - 24	239 370	117 776	121 594	112 063	51 569	60 494	127 307	66 207	61 100
25 - 29	222 284	108 644	113 640	138 313	65 515	72 798	83 971	43 129	40 842
30 - 34	188 154	91 675	96 479	139 823	68 702	71 121	48 331	22 973	25 358
35 - 39	150 803	72 617	78 186	104 981	51 978	53 003	45 822	20 639	25 183
40 - 44	125 923	60 317	65 606	79 024	39 135	39 889	46 899	21 182	25 717
45 - 49	101 553	47 554	53 999	59 209	29 160	30 049	42 344	18 394	23 950
50 - 54	79 879	36 330	43 549	43 435	21 601	21 834	36 444	14 729	21 715
55 - 59	63 577	27 597	35 980	32 033	15 757	16 276	31 544	11 840	19 704
60 - 64	46 620	19 374	27 246	21 178	9 828	11 350	25 442	9 546	15 896
65 - 69	36 060	15 316	20 744	13 025	5 781	7 244	23 035	9 535	13 500
70 - 74	27 584	11 475	16 109	8 016	3 291	4 725	19 568	8 184	11 384
75 - 79	17 673	6 846	10 827	4 901	1 910	2 991	12 772	4 936	7 836
80 +	22 567	7 769	14 798	5 582	1 980	3 602	16 985	5 789	11 196
Niger[22]									
1 VII 2016 (ESDJ)									
Total	19 865 067	9 898 628	9 966 439	3 242 161	1 617 882	1 624 278	16 622 906	8 280 747	8 342 160
0 - 4	3 966 109	2 009 845	1 956 264	560 061	281 015	279 046	3 406 048	1 728 830	1 677 218
5 - 9	3 533 085	1 810 213	1 722 872	514 367	259 802	254 565	3 018 718	1 550 412	1 468 306
10 - 14	2 790 727	1 418 659	1 372 068	450 479	223 341	227 137	2 340 248	1 195 317	1 144 931
15 - 19	2 021 025	1 010 216	1 010 809	344 569	173 980	170 589	1 676 456	836 236	840 220
20 - 24	1 619 917	777 760	842 157	316 826	159 697	157 130	1 303 090	618 063	685 027
25 - 29	1 236 640	592 643	643 996	220 452	107 039	113 413	1 016 188	485 605	530 583
30 - 34	1 013 696	493 232	520 464	186 768	91 960	94 808	826 927	401 271	425 656
35 - 39	845 916	404 801	441 115	153 624	74 733	78 891	692 293	330 068	362 225
40 - 44	679 710	326 886	352 824	123 978	61 940	62 037	555 732	264 946	290 786
45 - 49	544 473	267 053	277 420	98 818	50 233	48 585	445 656	216 820	228 836

7. Population by age, sex and urban/rural residence: latest available year, 2010 - 2019
Population selon l'âge, le sexe et la résidence, urbaine/rurale : dernière année disponible, 2010 - 2019 (continued - suite)

Continent, country or area, date, code[a] and age (in years) / Continent, pays ou zone, date, code[a] et âge (en annèes)	Total			Urban - Urbaine			Rural - Rurale		
	Both sexes Les deux sexes	Male Masculin	Female Féminin	Both sexes Les deux sexes	Male Masculin	Female Féminin	Both sexes Les deux sexes	Male Masculin	Female Féminin
AFRICA - AFRIQUE									
Niger[22]									
1 VII 2016 (ESDJ)									
50 - 54	*460 236*	*223 786*	*236 450*	*81 307*	*40 036*	*41 271*	*378 929*	*183 750*	*195 179*
55 - 59	*351 487*	*174 412*	*177 075*	*62 257*	*30 864*	*31 393*	*289 230*	*143 548*	*145 681*
60 - 64	*264 109*	*129 848*	*134 261*	*45 097*	*22 523*	*22 574*	*219 012*	*107 324*	*111 687*
65 - 69	*192 038*	*94 284*	*97 754*	*31 661*	*15 974*	*15 688*	*160 376*	*78 310*	*82 066*
70 - 74	*145 168*	*69 830*	*75 338*	*22 937*	*11 136*	*11 801*	*122 231*	*58 694*	*63 537*
75 - 79	*99 975*	*48 349*	*51 626*	*15 105*	*7 379*	*7 725*	*84 870*	*40 970*	*43 900*
80 +	*100 757*	*46 811*	*53 946*	*13 855*	*6 229*	*7 626*	*86 902*	*40 582*	*46 320*
1 VII 2017 (ESDJ)									
Total	*20 651 074*	*10 296 315*	*10 354 759*	...	...	...	...	...	...
0 - 4	*4 111 966*	*2 079 319*	*2 032 648*	...	...	...	...	...	...
5 - 9	*3 600 471*	*1 845 949*	*1 754 522*	...	...	...	...	...	...
10 - 14	*2 953 806*	*1 503 877*	*1 449 930*	...	...	...	...	...	...
15 - 19	*2 133 819*	*1 073 645*	*1 060 174*	...	...	...	...	...	...
20 - 24	*1 698 985*	*820 282*	*878 703*	...	...	...	...	...	...
25 - 29	*1 295 439*	*619 222*	*676 218*	...	...	...	...	...	...
30 - 34	*1 048 771*	*510 322*	*538 449*	...	...	...	...	...	...
35 - 39	*876 209*	*420 240*	*455 969*	...	...	...	...	...	...
40 - 44	*708 952*	*339 682*	*369 270*	...	...	...	...	...	...
45 - 49	*561 219*	*274 985*	*286 234*	...	...	...	...	...	...
50 - 54	*475 582*	*230 659*	*244 922*	...	...	...	...	...	...
55 - 59	*366 130*	*181 127*	*185 004*	...	...	...	...	...	...
60 - 64	*274 970*	*134 934*	*140 036*	...	...	...	...	...	...
65 - 69	*196 914*	*96 579*	*100 335*	...	...	...	...	...	...
70 - 74	*146 638*	*70 314*	*76 325*	...	...	...	...	...	...
75 - 79	*100 134*	*48 176*	*51 958*	...	...	...	...	...	...
80 +	*101 065*	*47 003*	*54 062*	...	...	...	...	...	...
Nigeria - Nigéria[23]									
1 VII 2016 (ESDF)									
Total	*193 392 517*	...	...	...	...	...	...	...	...
0 - 4	*31 116 156*	...	...	...	...	...	...	...	...
5 - 9	*27 549 964*	...	...	...	...	...	...	...	...
10 - 14	*22 221 265*	...	...	...	...	...	...	...	...
15 - 19	*20 518 404*	...	...	...	...	...	...	...	...
20 - 24	*18 501 820*	...	...	...	...	...	...	...	...
25 - 29	*16 816 694*	...	...	...	...	...	...	...	...
30 - 34	*13 038 009*	...	...	...	...	...	...	...	...
35 - 39	*10 096 763*	...	...	...	...	...	...	...	...
40 - 44	*8 891 384*	...	...	...	...	...	...	...	...
45 - 49	*6 322 797*	...	...	...	...	...	...	...	...
50 - 54	*5 851 717*	...	...	...	...	...	...	...	...
55 - 59	*2 845 486*	...	...	...	...	...	...	...	...
60 - 64	*3 374 357*	...	...	...	...	...	...	...	...
65 - 69	*1 585 140*	...	...	...	...	...	...	...	...
70 - 74	*1 832 402*	...	...	...	...	...	...	...	...
75 - 79	*798 511*	...	...	...	...	...	...	...	...
80 - 84	*1 046 690*	...	...	...	...	...	...	...	...
85 +	*984 956*	...	...	...	...	...	...	...	...
Republic of South Sudan - République de Soudan du Sud[24]									
1 VII 2018 (ESDF)									
Total	12 323 420	6 311 618	6 011 801	...	...	...	...	...	...
0 - 4	2 583 635	1 301 082	1 282 553	...	...	...	...	...	...
5 - 9	2 063 286	1 036 396	1 026 890	...	...	...	...	...	...
10 - 14	1 283 328	674 769	608 559	...	...	...	...	...	...
15 - 19	1 272 679	674 552	598 127	...	...	...	...	...	...
20 - 24	1 026 431	552 586	473 845	...	...	...	...	...	...
25 - 29	851 834	442 942	408 891	...	...	...	...	...	...
30 - 34	703 523	343 313	360 210	...	...	...	...	...	...
35 - 39	661 345	317 791	343 554	...	...	...	...	...	...
40 - 44	504 869	243 196	261 673	...	...	...	...	...	...
45 - 49	440 328	221 473	218 855	...	...	...	...	...	...
50 - 54	307 725	157 507	150 218	...	...	...	...	...	...

Continent, country or area, date, code[a] and age (in years) / Continent, pays ou zone, date, code[a] et âge (en annès)	Total			Urban - Urbaine			Rural - Rurale		
	Both sexes Les deux sexes	Male Masculin	Female Féminin	Both sexes Les deux sexes	Male Masculin	Female Féminin	Both sexes Les deux sexes	Male Masculin	Female Féminin
AFRICA - AFRIQUE									
Republic of South Sudan - République de Soudan du Sud[24]									
1 VII 2018 (ESDF)									
55 - 59	240 125	130 983	109 143	...	...	...	...	...	...
60 - 64	161 580	86 498	75 082	...	...	...	...	...	...
65 - 69	89 691	50 690	39 001	...	...	...	...	...	...
70 - 74	73 472	41 750	31 722	...	...	...	...	...	...
75 - 79	34 683	20 477	14 206	...	...	...	...	...	...
80 - 84	18 816	11 648	7 168	...	...	...	...	...	...
85 - 89	4 503	2 942	1 561	...	...	...	...	...	...
90 - 94	1 483	965	518	...	...	...	...	...	...
95 +	83	57	26	...	...	...	...	...	...
Reunion - Réunion									
1 I 2015 (CDJC)									
Total	850 727	411 435	439 292	838 228	405 123	433 105	12 499	6 312	6 187
0 - 4	62 021	31 643	30 377	61 139	31 203	29 936	882	440	442
5 - 9	68 814	35 386	33 428	67 849	34 856	32 992	965	530	435
10 - 14	71 429	36 713	34 716	70 409	36 202	34 208	1 020	512	508
15 - 19	67 979	34 756	33 223	67 007	34 252	32 754	972	504	469
20 - 24	54 703	27 392	27 312	53 896	26 970	26 926	807	422	385
25 - 29	52 295	24 326	27 969	51 522	23 977	27 545	774	350	424
30 - 34	52 379	23 815	28 564	51 620	23 434	28 186	759	381	378
35 - 39	56 023	25 787	30 236	55 270	25 412	29 858	753	375	378
40 - 44	60 610	28 755	31 855	59 755	28 323	31 432	856	432	423
45 - 49	65 416	31 471	33 945	64 340	30 897	33 442	1 077	574	503
50 - 54	60 858	29 842	31 017	59 902	29 329	30 573	956	513	444
55 - 59	50 551	24 330	26 221	49 807	23 950	25 857	744	380	364
60 - 64	40 918	19 874	21 043	40 336	19 584	20 752	582	290	291
65 - 69	29 519	14 070	15 448	29 146	13 878	15 268	373	192	181
70 - 74	21 688	9 895	11 794	21 287	9 717	11 570	402	178	224
75 - 79	16 390	6 870	9 521	16 112	6 750	9 363	278	120	158
80 - 84	10 203	3 920	6 283	10 030	3 846	6 183	173	73	100
85 - 89	5 681	1 762	3 919	5 594	1 727	3 867	87	35	52
90 - 94	2 505	662	1 843	2 473	651	1 822	32	11	21
95 - 99	560	120	441	555	120	436	5	-	5
100 +	183	47	137	179	46	134	4	1	3
1 I 2019 (ESDJ)									
Total	857 961	408 736	449 225	...	...	...	...	...	...
0	11 485	5 737	5 748	...	...	...	...	...	...
1 - 4	47 811	24 158	23 653	...	...	...	...	...	...
5 - 9	64 243	32 457	31 786	...	...	...	...	...	...
10 - 14	69 495	35 698	33 797	...	...	...	...	...	...
15 - 19	66 176	33 377	32 799	...	...	...	...	...	...
20 - 24	49 953	24 827	25 126	...	...	...	...	...	...
25 - 29	50 001	23 120	26 881	...	...	...	...	...	...
30 - 34	51 420	22 698	28 722	...	...	...	...	...	...
35 - 39	54 015	23 852	30 163	...	...	...	...	...	...
40 - 44	55 490	25 197	30 293	...	...	...	...	...	...
45 - 49	59 984	28 341	31 643	...	...	...	...	...	...
50 - 54	65 396	31 537	33 859	...	...	...	...	...	...
55 - 59	58 322	28 542	29 780	...	...	...	...	...	...
60 - 64	48 062	22 785	25 277	...	...	...	...	...	...
65 - 69	37 940	18 157	19 783	...	...	...	...	...	...
70 - 74	25 372	11 725	13 647	...	...	...	...	...	...
75 - 79	18 747	8 150	10 597	...	...	...	...	...	...
80 - 84	13 062	4 883	8 179	...	...	...	...	...	...
85 - 89	6 817	2 346	4 471	...	...	...	...	...	...
90 - 94	3 080	909	2 171	...	...	...	...	...	...
95 - 99	911	176	735	...	...	...	...	...	...
100 +	179	64	115	...	...	...	...	...	...
Rwanda[22]									
1 VII 2019 (ESDF)									
Total	*12 374 397*	*6 008 384*	*6 366 013*	*2 626 466*	*1 275 280*	*1 351 186*	*9 747 931*	*4 733 105*	*5 014 827*
0 - 4	*1 672 663*	*844 359*	*828 304*	*318 688*	*151 077*	*167 611*	*1 353 975*	*693 282*	*660 693*

7. Population by age, sex and urban/rural residence: latest available year, 2010 - 2019
Population selon l'âge, le sexe et la résidence, urbaine/rurale : dernière année disponible, 2010 - 2019 (continued - suite)

Continent, country or area, date, code[a] and age (in years) / Continent, pays ou zone, date, code[a] et âge (en annèes)	Total			Urban - Urbaine			Rural - Rurale		
	Both sexes Les deux sexes	Male Masculin	Female Féminin	Both sexes Les deux sexes	Male Masculin	Female Féminin	Both sexes Les deux sexes	Male Masculin	Female Féminin
AFRICA - AFRIQUE									
Rwanda[22]									
1 VII 2019 (ESDF)									
5 - 9	*1 527 168*	*764 098*	*763 070*	*262 668*	*123 421*	*139 247*	*1 264 500*	*640 677*	*623 823*
10 - 14	*1 521 756*	*757 029*	*764 727*	*276 524*	*127 475*	*149 049*	*1 245 232*	*629 554*	*615 678*
15 - 19	*1 354 611*	*669 226*	*685 385*	*298 766*	*130 980*	*167 785*	*1 055 845*	*538 245*	*517 599*
20 - 24	*1 139 615*	*559 045*	*580 570*	*315 833*	*153 489*	*162 344*	*823 783*	*405 556*	*418 226*
25 - 29	*1 036 560*	*502 947*	*533 613*	*294 839*	*149 787*	*145 051*	*741 722*	*353 160*	*388 562*
30 - 34	*951 301*	*464 011*	*487 289*	*251 770*	*132 182*	*119 588*	*699 531*	*331 830*	*367 701*
35 - 39	*820 018*	*399 641*	*420 377*	*203 602*	*108 598*	*95 004*	*616 416*	*291 043*	*325 372*
40 - 44	*584 417*	*272 423*	*311 994*	*128 645*	*67 207*	*61 438*	*455 773*	*205 216*	*250 557*
45 - 49	*426 542*	*193 490*	*233 052*	*80 984*	*41 404*	*39 580*	*345 558*	*152 087*	*193 471*
50 - 54	*346 872*	*158 153*	*188 719*	*55 177*	*28 062*	*27 115*	*291 696*	*130 091*	*161 604*
55 - 59	*321 557*	*143 753*	*177 803*	*46 719*	*22 860*	*23 859*	*274 838*	*120 893*	*153 945*
60 - 64	*259 101*	*113 795*	*145 306*	*35 996*	*16 914*	*19 082*	*223 106*	*96 881*	*126 224*
65 - 69	*174 630*	*75 204*	*99 427*	*24 417*	*10 641*	*13 776*	*150 214*	*64 563*	*85 651*
70 - 74	*101 965*	*41 032*	*60 933*	*13 417*	*5 260*	*8 157*	*88 547*	*35 772*	*52 776*
75 - 79	*65 519*	*24 110*	*41 408*	*8 927*	*3 037*	*5 890*	*56 591*	*21 073*	*35 518*
80 +	*70 102*	*26 067*	*44 035*	*9 495*	*2 885*	*6 610*	*60 607*	*23 182*	*37 425*
Saint Helena ex. dep. - Sainte-Hélène sans dép.[25]									
7 II 2016 (CDJC)									
Total	4 534	2 396	2 138	...	...	...	...	...	...
0	50	24	26	...	...	...	...	...	...
1 - 4	163	83	80	...	...	...	...	...	...
5 - 9	209	116	93	...	...	...	...	...	...
10 - 14	191	98	93	...	...	...	...	...	...
15 - 19	236	123	113	...	...	...	...	...	...
20 - 24	203	122	81	...	...	...	...	...	...
25 - 29	235	128	107	...	...	...	...	...	...
30 - 34	288	141	147	...	...	...	...	...	...
35 - 39	249	130	119	...	...	...	...	...	...
40 - 44	334	184	150	...	...	...	...	...	...
45 - 49	403	222	181	...	...	...	...	...	...
50 - 54	357	182	175	...	...	...	...	...	...
55 - 59	365	188	177	...	...	...	...	...	...
60 - 64	314	176	138	...	...	...	...	...	...
65 - 69	343	178	165	...	...	...	...	...	...
70 - 74	269	159	110	...	...	...	...	...	...
75 - 79	152	74	78	...	...	...	...	...	...
80 - 84	102	52	50	...	...	...	...	...	...
85 - 89	44	12	32	...	...	...	...	...	...
90 - 94	23	4	19	...	...	...	...	...	...
95 - 99	3	-	3	...	...	...	...	...	...
100 +	1	-	1	...	...	...	...	...	...
Unknown - Inconnu	-	-	-	...	...	...	...	...	...
Sao Tome and Principe - Sao Tomé-et-Principe[22]									
1 VII 2017 (ESDJ)									
Total	*197 700*	*97 988*	*99 712*	*133 748*	*66 291*	*67 457*	*63 952*	*31 697*	*32 255*
0 - 4	*24 133*	*12 031*	*12 102*	*16 249*	*8 217*	*8 032*	*7 883*	*3 814*	*4 070*
5 - 9	*27 500*	*13 833*	*13 667*	*18 273*	*9 375*	*8 898*	*9 227*	*4 458*	*4 769*
10 - 14	*25 390*	*12 677*	*12 714*	*17 054*	*8 509*	*8 546*	*8 336*	*4 168*	*4 168*
15 - 19	*21 345*	*10 673*	*10 672*	*14 430*	*7 149*	*7 281*	*6 915*	*3 524*	*3 391*
20 - 24	*18 341*	*9 278*	*9 062*	*12 555*	*6 298*	*6 257*	*5 786*	*2 981*	*2 805*
25 - 29	*15 841*	*7 895*	*7 946*	*11 026*	*5 460*	*5 566*	*4 815*	*2 435*	*2 380*
30 - 34	*14 665*	*7 276*	*7 389*	*10 078*	*4 984*	*5 094*	*4 587*	*2 292*	*2 295*
35 - 39	*12 358*	*6 105*	*6 252*	*8 237*	*4 046*	*4 191*	*4 120*	*2 059*	*2 061*
40 - 44	*9 546*	*4 762*	*4 784*	*6 404*	*3 155*	*3 249*	*3 142*	*1 607*	*1 535*
45 - 49	*7 654*	*3 831*	*3 822*	*5 256*	*2 618*	*2 638*	*2 398*	*1 214*	*1 184*
50 - 54	*6 033*	*2 880*	*3 153*	*4 200*	*2 000*	*2 200*	*1 833*	*881*	*953*
55 - 59	*5 004*	*2 384*	*2 620*	*3 518*	*1 690*	*1 827*	*1 486*	*694*	*792*
60 - 64	*3 431*	*1 573*	*1 858*	*2 326*	*1 054*	*1 272*	*1 105*	*519*	*586*
65 - 69	*2 249*	*1 076*	*1 173*	*1 477*	*689*	*787*	*772*	*386*	*385*
70 - 74	*1 500*	*665*	*835*	*932*	*400*	*532*	*568*	*265*	*303*

7. Population by age, sex and urban/rural residence: latest available year, 2010 - 2019
Population selon l'âge, le sexe et la résidence, urbaine/rurale : dernière année disponible, 2010 - 2019 (continued - suite)

Continent, country or area, date, code[a] and age (in years) Continent, pays ou zone, date, code[a] et âge (en annèes)	Total			Urban - Urbaine			Rural - Rurale		
	Both sexes Les deux sexes	Male Masculin	Female Féminin	Both sexes Les deux sexes	Male Masculin	Female Féminin	Both sexes Les deux sexes	Male Masculin	Female Féminin
AFRICA - AFRIQUE									
Sao Tome and Principe - Sao Tomé-et-Principe[22]									
1 VII 2017 (ESDJ)									
75 - 79	*1 313*	*535*	*777*	*796*	*320*	*477*	*516*	*216*	*301*
80 +	*1 400*	*514*	*886*	*938*	*329*	*609*	*463*	*185*	*277*
Senegal - Sénégal[1]									
1 VII 2018 (ESDJ)									
Total	*15 726 037*	*7 829 997*	*7 896 040*	...	...	...	...	...	...
0	*551 259*	*278 116*	*273 143*	...	...	...	...	...	...
1 - 4	*2 038 804*	*1 029 758*	*1 009 046*	...	...	...	...	...	...
5 - 9	*2 092 692*	*1 076 178*	*1 016 514*	...	...	...	...	...	...
10 - 14	*1 878 331*	*965 827*	*912 504*	...	...	...	...	...	...
15 - 19	*1 642 809*	*841 976*	*800 833*	...	...	...	...	...	...
20 - 24	*1 434 420*	*722 007*	*712 413*	...	...	...	...	...	...
25 - 29	*1 235 457*	*596 590*	*638 867*	...	...	...	...	...	...
30 - 34	*1 046 205*	*499 273*	*546 932*	...	...	...	...	...	...
35 - 39	*853 457*	*411 077*	*442 380*	...	...	...	...	...	...
40 - 44	*702 228*	*336 729*	*365 499*	...	...	...	...	...	...
45 - 49	*550 874*	*258 930*	*291 944*	...	...	...	...	...	...
50 - 54	*451 727*	*212 380*	*239 347*	...	...	...	...	...	...
55 - 59	*381 550*	*183 461*	*198 089*	...	...	...	...	...	...
60 - 64	*301 316*	*146 061*	*155 255*	...	...	...	...	...	...
65 - 69	*214 026*	*104 396*	*109 630*	...	...	...	...	...	...
70 - 74	*150 018*	*73 037*	*76 981*	...	...	...	...	...	...
75 - 79	*96 838*	*46 595*	*50 243*	...	...	...	...	...	...
80 +	*104 026*	*47 606*	*56 420*	...	...	...	...	...	...
Seychelles									
1 VII 2019 (ESDF)									
Total	97 625	49 665	47 960	...	...	...	...	...	...
0	1 627	832	795	...	...	...	...	...	...
1 - 4	6 322	3 273	3 049	...	...	...	...	...	...
5 - 9	7 101	3 697	3 404	...	...	...	...	...	...
10 - 14	5 478	2 790	2 688	...	...	...	...	...	...
15 - 19	4 770	2 209	2 561	...	...	...	...	...	...
20 - 24	2 882	1 740	1 142	...	...	...	...	...	...
25 - 29	5 264	2 979	2 285	...	...	...	...	...	...
30 - 34	7 384	4 236	3 148	...	...	...	...	...	...
35 - 39	9 543	5 116	4 427	...	...	...	...	...	...
40 - 44	6 851	3 504	3 347	...	...	...	...	...	...
45 - 49	8 521	4 627	3 894	...	...	...	...	...	...
50 - 54	6 379	2 772	3 607	...	...	...	...	...	...
55 - 59	9 057	4 283	4 774	...	...	...	...	...	...
60 - 64	6 030	3 031	2 999	...	...	...	...	...	...
65 - 69	4 526	2 187	2 339	...	...	...	...	...	...
70 - 74	2 594	1 263	1 331	...	...	...	...	...	...
75 - 79	1 538	681	857	...	...	...	...	...	...
80 - 84	937	300	637	...	...	...	...	...	...
85 - 89	597	128	469	...	...	...	...	...	...
90 +	224	17	207	...	...	...	...	...	...
Sierra Leone[8]									
1 VII 2019 (ESDF)									
Total	*7 901 454*	*3 889 366*	*4 012 088*	*3 238 372*[26]	*1 603 675*[26]	*1 634 697*[26]	*4 663 082*[26]	*2 285 691*[26]	*2 377 391*[26]
0 - 4	*1 228 137*	*604 531*	*623 606*	*414 229*[26]	*205 130*[26]	*209 099*[26]	*854 877*[26]	*419 034*[26]	*435 843*[26]
5 - 9	*1 084 874*	*534 011*	*550 863*	*368 984*[26]	*182 725*[26]	*186 259*[26]	*638 255*[26]	*312 852*[26]	*325 403*[26]
10 - 14	*977 355*	*481 086*	*496 269*	*389 488*[26]	*192 879*[26]	*196 609*[26]	*560 615*[26]	*274 795*[26]	*285 820*[26]
15 - 19	*831 890*	*409 485*	*422 405*	*375 601*[26]	*186 001*[26]	*189 600*[26]	*483 417*[26]	*236 956*[26]	*246 461*[26]
20 - 24	*743 100*	*365 780*	*377 320*	*351 206*[26]	*173 921*[26]	*177 285*[26]	*405 227*[26]	*198 629*[26]	*206 598*[26]
25 - 29	*643 678*	*316 840*	*326 838*	*308 098*[26]	*152 574*[26]	*155 524*[26]	*344 312*[26]	*168 770*[26]	*175 542*[26]
30 - 34	*537 577*	*264 614*	*272 963*	*255 768*[26]	*126 660*[26]	*129 108*[26]	*296 204*[26]	*145 190*[26]	*151 014*[26]
35 - 39	*445 943*	*219 508*	*226 435*	*204 571*[26]	*101 305*[26]	*103 266*[26]	*245 624*[26]	*120 397*[26]	*125 227*[26]
40 - 44	*356 555*	*175 509*	*181 046*	*158 129*[26]	*78 308*[26]	*79 821*[26]	*207 121*[26]	*101 525*[26]	*105 596*[26]
45 - 49	*282 827*	*139 217*	*143 610*	*120 060*[26]	*59 456*[26]	*60 604*[26]	*164 441*[26]	*80 603*[26]	*83 838*[26]
50 - 54	*215 495*	*106 075*	*109 420*	*92 462*[26]	*45 788*[26]	*46 674*[26]	*129 353*[26]	*63 405*[26]	*65 948*[26]
55 - 59	*164 643*	*81 043*	*83 600*	*66 940*[26]	*33 149*[26]	*33 791*[26]	*97 293*[26]	*47 690*[26]	*49 603*[26]

7. Population by age, sex and urban/rural residence: latest available year, 2010 - 2019
Population selon l'âge, le sexe et la résidence, urbaine/rurale : dernière année disponible, 2010 - 2019 (continued - suite)

Continent, country or area, date, code[a] and age (in years) / Continent, pays ou zone, date, code[a] et âge (en annèes)	Total			Urban - Urbaine			Rural - Rurale		
	Both sexes Les deux sexes	Male Masculin	Female Féminin	Both sexes Les deux sexes	Male Masculin	Female Féminin	Both sexes Les deux sexes	Male Masculin	Female Féminin
AFRICA - AFRIQUE									
Sierra Leone[8]									
1 VII 2019 (ESDF)									
60 - 64	*126 369*	*62 204*	*64 165*	*49 078*[26]	*24 303*[26]	*24 775*[26]	*74 925*[26]	*36 727*[26]	*38 198*[26]
65 - 69	*93 408*	*45 979*	*47 429*	*34 021*[26]	*16 848*[26]	*17 173*[26]	*55 912*[26]	*27 406*[26]	*28 506*[26]
70 - 74	*66 773*	*32 867*	*33 906*	*22 313*[26]	*11 050*[26]	*11 263*[26]	*41 200*[26]	*20 195*[26]	*21 005*[26]
75 - 79	*45 031*	*22 166*	*22 865*	*12 759*[26]	*6 319*[26]	*6 440*[26]	*28 581*[26]	*14 010*[26]	*14 571*[26]
80 +	*57 799*	*28 451*	*29 348*	*14 665*[26]	*7 259*[26]	*7 406*[26]	*35 725*[26]	*17 507*[26]	*18 218*[26]
South Africa - Afrique du Sud[2]									
1 VII 2019 (ESDF)									
Total	*58 775 022*	*28 672 747*	*30 102 275*	...	...	...	...	...	...
0 - 4	*5 733 946*	*2 903 457*	*2 830 489*	...	...	...	...	...	...
5 - 9	*5 737 439*	*2 908 734*	*2 828 705*	...	...	...	...	...	...
10 - 14	*5 427 902*	*2 738 556*	*2 689 347*	...	...	...	...	...	...
15 - 19	*4 660 002*	*2 343 975*	*2 316 027*	...	...	...	...	...	...
20 - 24	*4 914 186*	*2 475 396*	*2 438 790*	...	...	...	...	...	...
25 - 29	*5 528 571*	*2 805 676*	*2 722 896*	...	...	...	...	...	...
30 - 34	*5 537 963*	*2 826 623*	*2 711 340*	...	...	...	...	...	...
35 - 39	*4 571 175*	*2 320 608*	*2 250 567*	...	...	...	...	...	...
40 - 44	*3 585 408*	*1 764 787*	*1 820 620*	...	...	...	...	...	...
45 - 49	*3 045 617*	*1 455 283*	*1 590 334*	...	...	...	...	...	...
50 - 54	*2 535 048*	*1 129 900*	*1 405 148*	...	...	...	...	...	...
55 - 59	*2 192 512*	*945 388*	*1 247 124*	...	...	...	...	...	...
60 - 64	*1 784 476*	*745 071*	*1 039 405*	...	...	...	...	...	...
65 - 69	*1 370 121*	*553 578*	*816 542*	...	...	...	...	...	...
70 - 74	*949 812*	*361 408*	*588 404*	...	...	...	...	...	...
75 - 79	*597 874*	*214 946*	*382 928*	...	...	...	...	...	...
80 +	*602 969*	*179 361*	*423 608*	...	...	...	...	...	...
Sudan - Soudan[5]									
1 VII 2016 (ESDF)									
Total	39 647 621	20 105 842	19 541 779	14 269 540	7 236 276	7 033 264	25 378 082	12 869 567	12 508 515
0	1 495 606	762 197	733 409	454 208	223 675	230 524	1 041 398	538 523	502 885
1 - 4	5 388 576	2 744 131	2 644 444	1 636 483	805 294	831 198	3 752 093	1 938 838	1 813 247
5 - 9	5 479 254	2 801 266	2 677 988	1 758 182	874 065	884 117	3 721 072	1 927 201	1 793 872
10 - 14	4 522 096	2 325 624	2 196 472	1 542 867	777 406	765 461	2 979 229	1 548 218	1 431 011
15 - 19	4 025 611	2 073 006	1 952 605	1 447 819	739 848	707 970	2 577 793	1 333 158	1 244 635
20 - 24	3 537 491	1 816 041	1 721 450	1 363 235	711 648	651 587	2 174 256	1 104 393	1 069 863
25 - 29	3 067 006	1 547 613	1 519 393	1 222 270	635 394	586 876	1 844 735	912 219	932 517
30 - 34	2 625 594	1 295 965	1 329 629	1 066 750	549 164	517 585	1 558 844	746 801	812 043
35 - 39	2 221 636	1 085 101	1 136 535	908 234	463 534	444 700	1 313 401	621 567	691 835
40 - 44	1 840 327	891 195	949 131	741 484	371 028	370 456	1 098 843	520 167	578 675
45 - 49	1 494 962	732 711	762 251	600 105	301 816	298 289	894 857	430 895	463 963
50 - 54	1 175 703	589 400	586 304	472 806	241 174	231 632	702 897	348 225	354 672
55 - 59	899 359	458 118	441 240	358 957	184 543	174 414	540 402	273 575	266 827
60 - 64	654 915	340 396	314 518	256 819	133 591	123 228	398 096	206 805	191 290
65 - 69	474 001	248 570	225 431	181 190	93 976	87 214	292 812	154 595	138 217
70 - 74	322 506	170 069	152 437	118 162	60 482	57 680	204 344	109 588	94 757
75 - 79	206 936	109 224	97 712	70 332	34 777	35 555	136 604	74 447	62 157
80 +	216 042	115 214	100 828	69 638	34 862	34 776	146 405	80 353	66 052
Togo[2]									
1 VII 2019 (ESDJ)									
Total	*7 617 279*	*3 716 473*	*3 900 807*	*3 179 803*[27]	*1 534 372*[27]	*1 645 431*[27]	*4 437 477*	*2 182 101*	*2 255 376*
0	*227 393*	*115 148*	*112 245*	*86 589*[27]	*43 799*[27]	*42 790*[27]	*140 805*	*71 349*	*69 456*
1 - 4	*862 299*	*433 250*	*429 050*	*327 574*[27]	*163 996*[27]	*163 578*[27]	*534 726*	*269 254*	*265 472*
5 - 9	*957 696*	*478 769*	*478 927*	*356 249*[27]	*176 868*[27]	*179 381*[27]	*601 447*	*301 901*	*299 546*
10 - 14	*911 958*	*457 452*	*454 506*	*306 291*[27]	*148 679*[27]	*157 612*[27]	*605 667*	*308 773*	*296 894*
15 - 19	*886 895*	*451 851*	*435 044*	*319 995*[27]	*147 626*[27]	*172 369*[27]	*566 901*	*304 225*	*262 676*
20 - 24	*683 838*	*355 945*	*327 894*	*316 577*[27]	*147 020*[27]	*169 557*[27]	*367 261*	*208 925*	*158 337*
25 - 29	*577 980*	*285 927*	*292 054*	*312 382*[27]	*150 953*[27]	*161 429*[27]	*265 599*	*134 974*	*130 625*
30 - 34	*521 965*	*231 954*	*290 012*	*279 235*[27]	*132 629*[27]	*146 606*[27]	*242 731*	*99 325*	*143 406*
35 - 39	*468 693*	*205 492*	*263 201*	*228 571*[27]	*106 822*[27]	*121 749*[27]	*240 122*	*98 670*	*141 452*
40 - 44	*379 441*	*179 276*	*200 166*	*174 294*[27]	*86 108*[27]	*88 187*[27]	*205 147*	*93 168*	*111 979*
45 - 49	*307 790*	*144 297*	*163 494*	*137 955*[27]	*67 914*[27]	*70 041*[27]	*169 836*	*76 383*	*93 453*
50 - 54	*241 456*	*115 461*	*125 995*	*106 339*[27]	*52 272*[27]	*54 067*[27]	*135 117*	*63 189*	*71 928*

Continent, country or area, date, code[a] and age (in years) / Continent, pays ou zone, date, code[a] et âge (en années)	Total			Urban - Urbaine			Rural - Rurale		
	Both sexes Les deux sexes	Male Masculin	Female Féminin	Both sexes Les deux sexes	Male Masculin	Female Féminin	Both sexes Les deux sexes	Male Masculin	Female Féminin
AFRICA - AFRIQUE									
Togo[2]									
1 VII 2019 (ESDJ)									
55 - 59	*182 037*	*86 379*	*95 659*	*78 752*[27]	*37 368*[27]	*41 384*[27]	*103 285*	*49 011*	*54 275*
60 - 64	*124 347*	*56 303*	*68 044*	*55 960*[27]	*27 284*[27]	*28 676*[27]	*68 387*	*29 019*	*39 368*
65 - 69	*104 614*	*46 959*	*57 655*	*44 049*[27]	*24 945*[27]	*19 104*[27]	*60 565*	*22 014*	*38 551*
70 - 74	*75 374*	*31 722*	*43 652*	*25 453*[27]	*12 972*[27]	*12 481*[27]	*49 922*	*18 751*	*31 171*
75 - 79	*50 036*	*19 891*	*30 145*	*11 700*[27]	*3 764*[27]	*7 936*[27]	*38 336*	*16 127*	*22 209*
80 +	*53 469*	*20 401*	*33 068*	*11 842*[27]	*3 355*[27]	*8 487*[27]	*41 628*	*17 047*	*24 581*
Tunisia - Tunisie									
1 VII 2017 (ESDF)									
Total	*11 435 100*	*5 679 700*	*5 755 400*	...	...	...	...	...	...
0 - 4	*1 089 000*	*562 500*	*526 500*	...	...	...	...	...	...
5 - 9	*916 700*	*479 100*	*437 600*	...	...	...	...	...	...
10 - 14	*817 300*	*425 400*	*391 900*	...	...	...	...	...	...
15 - 19	*792 900*	*408 100*	*384 800*	...	...	...	...	...	...
20 - 24	*861 100*	*430 900*	*430 200*	...	...	...	...	...	...
25 - 29	*916 100*	*438 700*	*477 400*	...	...	...	...	...	...
30 - 34	*946 400*	*447 100*	*499 300*	...	...	...	...	...	...
35 - 39	*921 100*	*444 000*	*477 100*	...	...	...	...	...	...
40 - 44	*764 300*	*372 600*	*391 700*	...	...	...	...	...	...
45 - 49	*701 200*	*342 100*	*359 100*	...	...	...	...	...	...
50 - 54	*667 800*	*326 300*	*341 500*	...	...	...	...	...	...
55 - 59	*600 700*	*300 200*	*300 500*	...	...	...	...	...	...
60 - 64	*480 700*	*240 300*	*240 400*	...	...	...	...	...	...
65 - 69	*342 200*	*168 800*	*173 400*	...	...	...	...	...	...
70 - 74	*219 300*	*104 800*	*114 500*	...	...	...	...	...	...
75 - 79	*176 100*	*84 000*	*92 100*	...	...	...	...	...	...
80 +	*222 200*	*104 800*	*117 400*	...	...	...	...	...	...
Uganda - Ouganda									
27 VIII 2014 (CDFC)									
Total	34 634 650	16 897 849	17 736 801	8 438 009	4 042 324	4 395 685	26 196 641	12 855 525	13 341 116
0 - 4	6 131 028	3 173 950	2 957 078	1 342 058	699 470	642 588	4 788 970	2 474 480	2 314 490
5 - 9	5 551 678	2 834 456	2 717 222	1 135 262	575 893	559 369	4 416 416	2 258 563	2 157 853
10 - 14	4 920 443	2 462 789	2 457 654	1 017 614	487 602	530 012	3 902 829	1 975 187	1 927 642
15 - 19	3 956 633	1 917 797	2 038 836	1 015 017	449 250	565 767	2 941 616	1 468 547	1 473 069
20 - 24	3 188 611	1 444 438	1 744 173	1 024 995	444 919	580 076	2 163 616	999 519	1 164 097
25 - 29	2 486 176	1 143 467	1 342 709	825 746	377 888	447 858	1 660 430	765 579	894 851
30 - 34	1 951 739	908 447	1 043 292	584 396	280 869	303 527	1 367 343	627 578	739 765
35 - 39	1 535 837	726 355	809 482	434 901	214 481	220 420	1 100 936	511 874	589 062
40 - 44	1 272 417	617 034	655 383	316 293	162 345	153 948	956 124	454 689	501 435
45 - 49	921 124	452 081	469 043	217 719	112 768	104 951	703 405	339 313	364 092
50 - 54	808 103	371 126	436 977	172 367	81 867	90 500	635 736	289 259	346 477
55 - 59	480 284	224 765	255 519	97 541	46 042	51 499	382 743	178 723	204 020
60 - 64	440 053	195 283	244 770	81 233	36 927	44 306	358 820	158 356	200 464
65 - 69	301 150	136 107	165 043	50 965	22 770	28 195	250 185	113 337	136 848
70 - 74	277 236	115 862	161 374	46 835	19 032	27 803	230 401	96 830	133 571
75 - 79	150 473	69 095	81 378	25 771	11 009	14 762	124 702	58 086	66 616
80 - 84	131 269	51 871	79 398	23 763	9 044	14 719	107 506	42 827	64 679
85 - 89	51 776	21 572	30 204	9 925	3 912	6 013	41 851	17 660	24 191
90 - 94	37 171	15 125	22 046	8 116	3 484	4 632	29 055	11 641	17 414
95 +	41 449	16 229	25 220	7 492	2 752	4 740	33 957	13 477	20 480
1 VII 2019 (ESDF)[7]									
Total	*40 308 000*	*19 780 500*	*20 527 500*	...	...	...	...	...	...
0	*1 481 200*	*750 100*	*731 100*	...	...	...	...	...	...
1 - 4	*5 507 100*	*2 788 700*	*2 718 400*	...	...	...	...	...	...
5 - 9	*5 950 400*	*3 079 800*	*2 870 600*	...	...	...	...	...	...
10 - 14	*5 457 600*	*2 785 700*	*2 671 900*	...	...	...	...	...	...
15 - 19	*4 839 100*	*2 420 500*	*2 418 600*	...	...	...	...	...	...
20 - 24	*3 875 300*	*1 874 300*	*2 001 000*	...	...	...	...	...	...
25 - 29	*3 110 900*	*1 405 800*	*1 705 100*	...	...	...	...	...	...
30 - 34	*2 414 900*	*1 108 000*	*1 306 900*	...	...	...	...	...	...
35 - 39	*1 885 500*	*874 500*	*1 011 000*	...	...	...	...	...	...
40 - 44	*1 473 200*	*693 400*	*779 800*	...	...	...	...	...	...
45 - 49	*1 213 000*	*584 900*	*628 100*	...	...	...	...	...	...
50 - 54	*869 000*	*423 200*	*445 800*	...	...	...	...	...	...

7. Population by age, sex and urban/rural residence: latest available year, 2010 - 2019
Population selon l'âge, le sexe et la résidence, urbaine/rurale : dernière année disponible, 2010 - 2019 (continued - suite)

Continent, country or area, date, code[a] and age (in years) / Continent, pays ou zone, date, code[a] et âge (en années)	Total			Urban - Urbaine			Rural - Rurale		
	Both sexes Les deux sexes	Male Masculin	Female Féminin	Both sexes Les deux sexes	Male Masculin	Female Féminin	Both sexes Les deux sexes	Male Masculin	Female Féminin
AFRICA - AFRIQUE									
Uganda - Ouganda									
1 VII 2019 (ESDF)[7]									
55 - 59	*754 000*	*343 000*	*411 000*	...	...	...	...	...	...
60 - 64	*439 600*	*203 400*	*236 200*	...	...	...	...	...	...
65 - 69	*387 200*	*169 400*	*217 800*	...	...	...	...	...	...
70 - 74	*247 600*	*110 200*	*137 400*	...	...	...	...	...	...
75 - 79	*203 600*	*83 400*	*120 200*	...	...	...	...	...	...
80 +	*198 800*	*82 200*	*116 600*	...	...	...	...	...	...
United Republic of Tanzania - République Unie de Tanzanie									
1 VII 2013 (ESDF)[28]									
Total	*47 132 580*	*23 267 957*	*23 864 623*	*12 909 536*	*6 386 303*	*6 523 233*	*34 223 044*	*16 881 654*	*17 341 390*
0	*1 776 107*	*895 971*	*880 136*	*403 952*	*203 710*	*200 242*	*1 372 155*	*692 261*	*679 894*
1 - 4	*6 536 000*	*3 295 033*	*3 240 967*	*1 521 372*	*766 466*	*754 906*	*5 014 628*	*2 528 567*	*2 486 061*
5 - 9	*7 160 846*	*3 608 891*	*3 551 955*	*1 723 220*	*857 109*	*866 111*	*5 437 626*	*2 751 782*	*2 685 844*
10 - 14	*5 464 181*	*2 735 494*	*2 728 687*	*1 364 854*	*661 195*	*703 659*	*4 099 327*	*2 074 299*	*2 025 028*
15 - 19	*4 985 943*	*2 494 983*	*2 490 960*	*1 427 786*	*682 734*	*745 052*	*3 558 157*	*1 812 249*	*1 745 908*
20 - 24	*4 340 143*	*2 179 173*	*2 160 970*	*1 333 476*	*672 789*	*660 687*	*3 006 667*	*1 506 384*	*1 500 283*
25 - 29	*3 484 607*	*1 730 600*	*1 754 007*	*1 134 814*	*563 796*	*571 018*	*2 349 793*	*1 166 804*	*1 182 989*
30 - 34	*2 852 197*	*1 289 114*	*1 563 083*	*974 580*	*450 823*	*523 757*	*1 877 617*	*838 291*	*1 039 326*
35 - 39	*2 601 610*	*1 207 182*	*1 394 428*	*867 422*	*418 436*	*448 986*	*1 734 188*	*788 746*	*945 442*
40 - 44	*2 121 302*	*1 032 605*	*1 088 697*	*672 984*	*346 836*	*326 148*	*1 448 318*	*685 769*	*762 549*
45 - 49	*1 568 017*	*770 149*	*797 868*	*469 417*	*248 681*	*220 736*	*1 098 600*	*521 468*	*577 132*
50 - 54	*1 234 201*	*604 621*	*629 580*	*339 138*	*180 385*	*158 753*	*895 063*	*424 236*	*470 827*
55 - 59	*881 484*	*422 141*	*459 343*	*223 562*	*117 172*	*106 390*	*657 922*	*304 969*	*352 953*
60 - 64	*734 938*	*347 604*	*387 334*	*172 297*	*88 004*	*84 293*	*562 641*	*259 600*	*303 041*
65 - 69	*466 882*	*223 365*	*243 517*	*100 337*	*50 363*	*49 974*	*366 545*	*173 002*	*193 543*
70 - 74	*387 755*	*179 960*	*207 795*	*78 544*	*35 541*	*43 003*	*309 211*	*144 419*	*164 792*
75 - 79	*245 872*	*115 076*	*130 796*	*46 843*	*20 380*	*26 463*	*199 029*	*94 696*	*104 333*
80 +	*290 495*	*135 995*	*154 500*	*54 938*	*21 883*	*33 055*	*235 557*	*114 112*	*121 445*
1 VII 2019 (ESDF)[22]									
Total	*55 890 747*	*27 356 189*	*28 534 558*	...	...	...	...	...	...
0	*2 061 343*	*1 042 032*	*1 019 311*	...	...	...	...	...	...
1 - 4	*7 567 502*	*3 818 061*	*3 749 441*	...	...	...	...	...	...
5 - 9	*7 632 205*	*3 831 301*	*3 800 904*	...	...	...	...	...	...
10 - 14	*7 093 434*	*3 559 067*	*3 534 367*	...	...	...	...	...	...
15 - 19	*6 110 532*	*3 043 631*	*3 066 901*	...	...	...	...	...	...
20 - 24	*4 771 878*	*2 363 081*	*2 408 797*	...	...	...	...	...	...
25 - 29	*4 417 067*	*2 030 400*	*2 386 667*	...	...	...	...	...	...
30 - 34	*3 300 712*	*1 506 575*	*1 794 137*	...	...	...	...	...	...
35 - 39	*3 321 031*	*1 532 666*	*1 788 365*	...	...	...	...	...	...
40 - 44	*2 293 654*	*1 113 669*	*1 179 985*	...	...	...	...	...	...
45 - 49	*2 192 273*	*1 064 475*	*1 127 798*	...	...	...	...	...	...
50 - 54	*1 315 291*	*653 814*	*661 477*	...	...	...	...	...	...
55 - 59	*1 371 622*	*635 873*	*735 749*	...	...	...	...	...	...
60 - 64	*708 152*	*355 380*	*352 772*	...	...	...	...	...	...
65 - 69	*705 914*	*333 756*	*372 158*	...	...	...	...	...	...
70 - 74	*378 680*	*184 048*	*194 632*	...	...	...	...	...	...
75 - 79	*341 949*	*149 626*	*192 323*	...	...	...	...	...	...
80 +	*307 508*	*138 734*	*168 774*	...	...	...	...	...	...
Zambia - Zambie[13]									
1 VII 2019 (ESDJ)									
Total	*17 381 168*	*8 602 112*	*8 779 056*	*7 483 937*	*3 700 550*	*3 783 387*	*9 897 231*	*4 901 562*	*4 995 669*
0 - 4	*3 069 839*	*1 547 434*	*1 522 405*	*1 228 591*	*621 543*	*607 048*	*1 841 248*	*925 891*	*915 357*
0	*665 873*	*336 628*	*329 245*	...	...	...	...	...	...
1 - 4	*2 403 966*	*1 210 806*	*1 193 160*	...	...	...	...	...	...
5 - 9	*2 641 809*	*1 327 193*	*1 314 616*	*988 403*	*498 963*	*489 440*	*1 653 406*	*828 230*	*825 176*
10 - 14	*2 231 890*	*1 119 107*	*1 112 783*	*856 527*	*428 870*	*427 657*	*1 375 363*	*690 237*	*685 126*
15 - 19	*1 865 551*	*933 078*	*932 473*	*799 993*	*391 211*	*408 782*	*1 065 558*	*541 867*	*523 691*
20 - 24	*1 649 920*	*814 881*	*835 039*	*759 288*	*357 779*	*401 509*	*890 632*	*457 102*	*433 530*
25 - 29	*1 363 260*	*659 879*	*703 381*	*702 378*	*335 105*	*367 273*	*660 882*	*324 774*	*336 108*
30 - 34	*1 045 773*	*480 107*	*565 666*	*555 992*	*260 654*	*295 338*	*489 781*	*219 453*	*270 328*
35 - 39	*901 565*	*426 302*	*475 263*	*465 430*	*225 988*	*239 442*	*436 135*	*200 314*	*235 821*
40 - 44	*701 612*	*354 680*	*346 932*	*349 967*	*183 372*	*166 595*	*351 645*	*171 308*	*180 337*

7. Population by age, sex and urban/rural residence: latest available year, 2010 - 2019
Population selon l'âge, le sexe et la résidence, urbaine/rurale : dernière année disponible, 2010 - 2019 (continued - suite)

Continent, country or area, date, code[a] and age (in years) / Continent, pays ou zone, date, code[a] et âge (en annèes)	Total			Urban - Urbaine			Rural - Rurale		
	Both sexes Les deux sexes	Male Masculin	Female Féminin	Both sexes Les deux sexes	Male Masculin	Female Féminin	Both sexes Les deux sexes	Male Masculin	Female Féminin
AFRICA - AFRIQUE									
Zambia - Zambie[13]									
1 VII 2019 (ESDJ)									
45 - 49	*554 324*	*285 789*	*268 535*	*256 496*	*138 484*	*118 012*	*297 828*	*147 305*	*150 523*
50 - 54	*380 936*	*195 603*	*185 333*	*163 133*	*86 703*	*76 430*	*217 803*	*108 900*	*108 903*
55 - 59	*304 344*	*147 309*	*157 035*	*123 874*	*60 980*	*62 894*	*180 470*	*86 329*	*94 141*
60 - 64	*219 903*	*103 844*	*116 059*	*88 429*	*42 533*	*45 896*	*131 474*	*61 311*	*70 163*
65 - 69	*147 329*	*70 311*	*77 018*	*57 518*	*28 457*	*29 061*	*89 811*	*41 854*	*47 957*
70 - 74	*119 926*	*53 039*	*66 887*	*39 198*	*18 621*	*20 577*	*80 728*	*34 418*	*46 310*
75 - 79	*77 301*	*34 227*	*43 074*	*22 751*	*10 310*	*12 441*	*54 550*	*23 917*	*30 633*
80 +	*105 886*	*49 329*	*56 557*	*25 969*	*10 977*	*14 992*	*79 917*	*38 352*	*41 565*
Zimbabwe[29]									
1 VII 2018 (ESDF)									
Total	*14 848 905*	*7 138 445*	*7 710 459*	*4 993 375*	*2 385 567*	*2 607 811*	*9 962 261*	*4 807 069*	*5 155 192*
0 - 4	*1 963 868*	*966 005*	*997 863*	*687 394*	*340 453*	*346 941*	*1 364 514*	*669 253*	*695 261*
5 - 9	*1 934 432*	*956 182*	*978 249*	*627 296*	*310 872*	*316 423*	*1 338 620*	*661 051*	*677 569*
10 - 14	*1 727 760*	*856 473*	*871 287*	*473 070*	*231 798*	*241 272*	*1 252 155*	*623 360*	*628 795*
15 - 19	*1 691 926*	*844 770*	*847 155*	*428 885*	*205 227*	*223 658*	*1 261 502*	*638 707*	*622 795*
20 - 24	*1 451 054*	*721 161*	*729 892*	*453 105*	*195 769*	*257 335*	*996 840*	*524 726*	*472 114*
25 - 29	*1 200 413*	*550 136*	*650 277*	*479 725*	*206 106*	*273 619*	*720 207*	*343 862*	*376 345*
30 - 34	*1 126 462*	*510 135*	*616 328*	*486 672*	*220 697*	*265 976*	*639 550*	*289 519*	*350 031*
35 - 39	*941 990*	*446 973*	*495 017*	*401 633*	*195 373*	*206 261*	*540 120*	*251 694*	*288 426*
40 - 44	*752 871*	*366 411*	*386 461*	*303 749*	*155 521*	*148 228*	*448 816*	*210 926*	*237 890*
45 - 49	*547 802*	*277 546*	*270 256*	*218 810*	*117 838*	*100 973*	*328 758*	*159 743*	*169 015*
50 - 54	*352 521*	*167 479*	*185 042*	*134 948*	*68 547*	*66 401*	*217 375*	*98 919*	*118 456*
55 - 59	*329 014*	*129 708*	*199 307*	*102 558*	*47 226*	*55 332*	*225 611*	*82 368*	*143 243*
60 - 64	*272 265*	*112 185*	*160 079*	*78 721*	*37 759*	*40 963*	*193 065*	*74 235*	*118 830*
65 - 69	*207 322*	*86 591*	*120 731*	*50 387*	*23 853*	*26 535*	*156 132*	*62 394*	*93 738*
70 - 74	*142 023*	*59 727*	*82 296*	*30 127*	*13 485*	*16 641*	*110 916*	*45 802*	*65 114*
75 - 79	*101 041*	*43 579*	*57 462*	*18 997*	*8 111*	*10 886*	*80 950*	*34 911*	*46 039*
80 +	*106 141*	*43 384*	*62 757*	*17 298*	*6 932*	*10 367*	*87 130*	*35 599*	*51 531*
AMERICA, NORTH - AMÉRIQUE DU NORD									
Anguilla									
11 V 2011 (CDFC)									
Total	13 572	6 707	6 865	...	...	...	...	...	...
0	245	130	115	...	...	...	...	...	...
1 - 4	813	416	397	...	...	...	...	...	...
5 - 9	1 056	529	527	...	...	...	...	...	...
10 - 14	1 069	530	539	...	...	...	...	...	...
15 - 19	916	466	450	...	...	...	...	...	...
20 - 24	917	466	451	...	...	...	...	...	...
25 - 29	1 120	533	587	...	...	...	...	...	...
30 - 34	1 016	480	536	...	...	...	...	...	...
35 - 39	1 145	569	576	...	...	...	...	...	...
40 - 44	1 138	567	571	...	...	...	...	...	...
45 - 49	1 089	538	551	...	...	...	...	...	...
50 - 54	878	425	453	...	...	...	...	...	...
55 - 59	694	347	347	...	...	...	...	...	...
60 - 64	453	228	225	...	...	...	...	...	...
65 - 69	323	161	162	...	...	...	...	...	...
70 - 74	250	118	132	...	...	...	...	...	...
75 +	450	204	246	...	...	...	...	...	...
Antigua and Barbuda - Antigua-et-Barbuda[4]									
1 VII 2019 (ESDJ)									
Total	96 453	46 180	50 273	...	...	...	...	...	...
0 - 4	6 870	3 468	3 402	...	...	...	...	...	...
5 - 9	6 837	3 446	3 391	...	...	...	...	...	...
10 - 14	7 013	3 572	3 441	...	...	...	...	...	...
15 - 19	7 109	3 589	3 520	...	...	...	...	...	...
20 - 24	7 841	3 934	3 907	...	...	...	...	...	...
25 - 29	7 465	3 680	3 785	...	...	...	...	...	...

7. Population by age, sex and urban/rural residence: latest available year, 2010 - 2019
Population selon l'âge, le sexe et la résidence, urbaine/rurale : dernière année disponible, 2010 - 2019 (continued - suite)

Continent, country or area, date, code[a] and age (in years) / Continent, pays ou zone, date, code[a] et âge (en annèes)	Total			Urban - Urbaine			Rural - Rurale		
	Both sexes Les deux sexes	Male Masculin	Female Féminin	Both sexes Les deux sexes	Male Masculin	Female Féminin	Both sexes Les deux sexes	Male Masculin	Female Féminin
AMERICA, NORTH - AMÉRIQUE DU NORD									
Antigua and Barbuda - Antigua-et-Barbuda[4]									
1 VII 2019 (ESDJ)									
30 - 34	7 096	3 364	3 732	...	...	...	...	...	...
35 - 39	7 020	3 284	3 736	...	...	...	...	...	...
40 - 44	6 966	3 209	3 757	...	...	...	...	...	...
45 - 49	6 956	3 164	3 792	...	...	...	...	...	...
50 - 54	6 636	3 074	3 562	...	...	...	...	...	...
55 - 59	5 774	2 659	3 115	...	...	...	...	...	...
60 - 64	4 325	2 009	2 316	...	...	...	...	...	...
65 - 69	3 079	1 409	1 670	...	...	...	...	...	...
70 - 74	2 293	1 022	1 271	...	...	...	...	...	...
75 - 79	1 450	634	816	...	...	...	...	...	...
80 - 84	739	307	432	...	...	...	...	...	...
85 - 89	635	243	392	...	...	...	...	...	...
90 - 94	243	82	161	...	...	...	...	...	...
95 +	106	31	75	...	...	...	...	...	...
Aruba									
1 VII 2019 (ESDJ)									
Total	112 019	52 998	59 022	...	...	...	...	...	...
0	1 037	523	514	...	...	...	...	...	...
1 - 4	5 078	2 639	2 439	...	...	...	...	...	...
5 - 9	6 743	3 402	3 341	...	...	...	...	...	...
10 - 14	7 106	3 645	3 461	...	...	...	...	...	...
15 - 19	7 075	3 597	3 478	...	...	...	...	...	...
20 - 24	6 280	3 213	3 066	...	...	...	...	...	...
25 - 29	6 864	3 398	3 465	...	...	...	...	...	...
30 - 34	6 915	3 318	3 597	...	...	...	...	...	...
35 - 39	7 261	3 320	3 941	...	...	...	...	...	...
40 - 44	7 535	3 437	4 098	...	...	...	...	...	...
45 - 49	8 466	3 910	4 556	...	...	...	...	...	...
50 - 54	8 702	3 980	4 722	...	...	...	...	...	...
55 - 59	9 215	4 265	4 950	...	...	...	...	...	...
60 - 64	7 717	3 503	4 214	...	...	...	...	...	...
65 - 69	5 979	2 765	3 214	...	...	...	...	...	...
70 - 74	4 174	1 783	2 391	...	...	...	...	...	...
75 - 79	2 735	1 174	1 562	...	...	...	...	...	...
80 - 84	1 802	675	1 127	...	...	...	...	...	...
85 - 89	912	331	581	...	...	...	...	...	...
90 - 94	330	98	232	...	...	...	...	...	...
95 - 99	82	19	63	...	...	...	...	...	...
100 +	12	4	8	...	...	...	...	...	...
Bahamas[13]									
1 VII 2019 (ESDJ)									
Total	385 340	186 480	198 860	...	...	...	...	...	...
0 - 4	29 060	14 910	14 150	...	...	...	...	...	...
5 - 9	28 360	14 290	14 070	...	...	...	...	...	...
10 - 14	31 900	15 800	16 100	...	...	...	...	...	...
15 - 19	32 090	15 860	16 230	...	...	...	...	...	...
20 - 24	31 650	15 760	15 890	...	...	...	...	...	...
25 - 29	30 020	15 040	14 980	...	...	...	...	...	...
30 - 34	26 490	12 960	13 530	...	...	...	...	...	...
35 - 39	27 390	12 980	14 410	...	...	...	...	...	...
40 - 44	28 160	13 490	14 670	...	...	...	...	...	...
45 - 49	28 650	13 630	15 020	...	...	...	...	...	...
50 - 54	25 140	11 970	13 170	...	...	...	...	...	...
55 - 59	22 670	10 670	12 000	...	...	...	...	...	...
60 - 64	16 270	7 370	8 900	...	...	...	...	...	...
65 - 69	10 820	4 870	5 950	...	...	...	...	...	...
70 - 74	7 290	3 200	4 090	...	...	...	...	...	...
75 - 79	4 910	2 020	2 890	...	...	...	...	...	...
80 +	4 470	1 660	2 810	...	...	...	...	...	...

7. Population by age, sex and urban/rural residence: latest available year, 2010 - 2019
Population selon l'âge, le sexe et la résidence, urbaine/rurale : dernière année disponible, 2010 - 2019 (continued - suite)

Continent, country or area, date, code[a] and age (in years) Continent, pays ou zone, date, code[a] et âge (en annèes)	Total			Urban - Urbaine			Rural - Rurale		
	Both sexes Les deux sexes	Male Masculin	Female Féminin	Both sexes Les deux sexes	Male Masculin	Female Féminin	Both sexes Les deux sexes	Male Masculin	Female Féminin
AMERICA, NORTH - AMÉRIQUE DU NORD									
Barbados - Barbade[30]									
1 V 2010 (CDJC)									
Total	277 821	133 018	144 803	...	...	...	...	...	...
0 - 4	17 352	8 873	8 479	...	...	...	...	...	...
5 - 9	18 838	9 683	9 155	...	...	...	...	...	...
10 - 14	18 567	9 445	9 122	...	...	...	...	...	...
15 - 19	18 870	9 452	9 418	...	...	...	...	...	...
20 - 24	18 169	9 061	9 108	...	...	...	...	...	...
25 - 29	19 088	9 313	9 775	...	...	...	...	...	...
30 - 34	18 785	9 150	9 635	...	...	...	...	...	...
35 - 39	20 516	9 884	10 632	...	...	...	...	...	...
40 - 44	20 113	9 663	10 450	...	...	...	...	...	...
45 - 49	21 365	10 062	11 303	...	...	...	...	...	...
50 - 54	20 050	9 411	10 639	...	...	...	...	...	...
55 - 59	16 653	7 871	8 782	...	...	...	...	...	...
60 - 64	13 486	6 326	7 160	...	...	...	...	...	...
65 - 69	10 151	4 511	5 640	...	...	...	...	...	...
70 - 74	8 680	3 804	4 876	...	...	...	...	...	...
75 - 79	6 937	2 863	4 074	...	...	...	...	...	...
80 - 84	5 153	1 986	3 167	...	...	...	...	...	...
85 +	5 048	1 660	3 388	...	...	...	...	...	...
Belize									
1 VII 2019 (ESDJ)									
Total	*408 487*	*204 247*	*204 240*	...	...	...	...	...	...
0	*9 387*	*4 781*	*4 606*	...	...	...	...	...	...
1 - 4	*38 536*	*19 666*	*18 870*	...	...	...	...	...	...
5 - 9	*49 701*	*25 033*	*24 668*	...	...	...	...	...	...
10 - 14	*47 762*	*23 899*	*23 863*	...	...	...	...	...	...
15 - 19	*43 895*	*21 958*	*21 937*	...	...	...	...	...	...
20 - 24	*38 692*	*19 004*	*19 688*	...	...	...	...	...	...
25 - 29	*33 581*	*16 248*	*17 333*	...	...	...	...	...	...
30 - 34	*28 931*	*14 042*	*14 889*	...	...	...	...	...	...
35 - 39	*26 197*	*12 790*	*13 407*	...	...	...	...	...	...
40 - 44	*21 971*	*10 917*	*11 054*	...	...	...	...	...	...
45 - 49	*18 943*	*9 675*	*9 268*	...	...	...	...	...	...
50 - 54	*14 852*	*7 533*	*7 319*	...	...	...	...	...	...
55 - 59	*10 943*	*5 703*	*5 240*	...	...	...	...	...	...
60 - 64	*7 883*	*4 168*	*3 715*	...	...	...	...	...	...
65 - 69	*5 570*	*2 964*	*2 606*	...	...	...	...	...	...
70 - 74	*4 427*	*2 348*	*2 079*	...	...	...	...	...	...
75 - 79	*3 246*	*1 647*	*1 599*	...	...	...	...	...	...
80 +	*3 970*	*1 871*	*2 099*	...	...	...	...	...	...
Bermuda - Bermudes[31]									
20 V 2016 (CDJC)									
Total	63 779	30 690	33 089	63 779	30 690	33 089	-	-	-
0	587	308	279	587	308	279	-	-	-
1 - 4	2 406	1 174	1 232	2 406	1 174	1 232	-	-	-
5 - 9	3 353	1 705	1 648	3 353	1 705	1 648	-	-	-
10 - 14	3 173	1 650	1 523	3 173	1 650	1 523	-	-	-
15 - 19	3 150	1 521	1 629	3 150	1 521	1 629	-	-	-
20 - 24	2 965	1 451	1 514	2 965	1 451	1 514	-	-	-
25 - 29	3 468	1 659	1 809	3 468	1 659	1 809	-	-	-
30 - 34	4 442	2 160	2 282	4 442	2 160	2 282	-	-	-
35 - 39	4 581	2 253	2 328	4 581	2 253	2 328	-	-	-
40 - 44	4 758	2 437	2 321	4 758	2 437	2 321	-	-	-
45 - 49	5 005	2 533	2 472	5 005	2 533	2 472	-	-	-
50 - 54	5 453	2 712	2 741	5 453	2 712	2 741	-	-	-
55 - 59	5 351	2 505	2 846	5 351	2 505	2 846	-	-	-
60 - 64	4 383	2 045	2 338	4 383	2 045	2 338	-	-	-
65 - 69	3 449	1 584	1 865	3 449	1 584	1 865	-	-	-
70 - 74	2 685	1 208	1 477	2 685	1 208	1 477	-	-	-
75 - 79	1 899	789	1 110	1 899	789	1 110	-	-	-
80 - 84	1 477	631	846	1 477	631	846	-	-	-
85 - 89	769	268	501	769	268	501	-	-	-

Continent, country or area, date, code[a] and age (in years) / Continent, pays ou zone, date, code[a] et âge (en années)	Total			Urban - Urbaine			Rural - Rurale		
	Both sexes Les deux sexes	Male Masculin	Female Féminin	Both sexes Les deux sexes	Male Masculin	Female Féminin	Both sexes Les deux sexes	Male Masculin	Female Féminin
AMERICA, NORTH - AMÉRIQUE DU NORD									
Bermuda - Bermudes[31]									
20 V 2016 (CDJC)									
90 - 94	346	88	258	346	88	258	-	-	-
95 - 99	72	9	63	72	9	63	-	-	-
100 +	7	-	7	7	-	7	-	-	-
1 VII 2019 (ESDJ)[32]									
Total	64 027	30 786	33 241	...	...	...	...	...	...
0	557	280	277	...	...	...	...	...	...
1 - 4	2 319	1 178	1 141	...	...	...	...	...	...
5 - 9	3 132	1 549	1 583	...	...	...	...	...	...
10 - 14	3 303	1 694	1 609	...	...	...	...	...	...
15 - 19	3 193	1 600	1 593	...	...	...	...	...	...
20 - 24	3 045	1 500	1 545	...	...	...	...	...	...
25 - 29	3 041	1 475	1 566	...	...	...	...	...	...
30 - 34	3 813	1 837	1 976	...	...	...	...	...	...
35 - 39	4 610	2 190	2 420	...	...	...	...	...	...
40 - 44	4 571	2 307	2 264	...	...	...	...	...	...
45 - 49	4 946	2 539	2 407	...	...	...	...	...	...
50 - 54	4 969	2 486	2 483	...	...	...	...	...	...
55 - 59	5 545	2 698	2 847	...	...	...	...	...	...
60 - 64	4 882	2 217	2 665	...	...	...	...	...	...
65 - 69	3 875	1 823	2 052	...	...	...	...	...	...
70 - 74	3 067	1 363	1 704	...	...	...	...	...	...
75 - 79	2 140	928	1 212	...	...	...	...	...	...
80 - 84	1 556	626	930	...	...	...	...	...	...
85 +	1 463	496	967	...	...	...	...	...	...
British Virgin Islands - Îles Vierges britanniques									
12 VII 2010 (CDFC)									
Total	28 054	13 820	14 234	...	...	...	...	...	...
0 - 4	2 134	1 126	1 008	...	...	...	...	...	...
5 - 9	2 090	1 065	1 025	...	...	...	...	...	...
10 - 14	2 044	1 032	1 012	...	...	...	...	...	...
15 - 19	1 767	867	900	...	...	...	...	...	...
20 - 24	1 720	789	931	...	...	...	...	...	...
25 - 29	2 316	1 126	1 190	...	...	...	...	...	...
30 - 34	2 537	1 165	1 372	...	...	...	...	...	...
35 - 39	2 599	1 226	1 373	...	...	...	...	...	...
40 - 44	2 559	1 236	1 323	...	...	...	...	...	...
45 - 49	2 338	1 193	1 145	...	...	...	...	...	...
50 - 54	1 842	962	880	...	...	...	...	...	...
55 - 59	1 387	680	707	...	...	...	...	...	...
60 - 64	1 028	541	487	...	...	...	...	...	...
65 - 69	670	350	320	...	...	...	...	...	...
70 - 74	415	204	211	...	...	...	...	...	...
75 - 79	230	98	132	...	...	...	...	...	...
80 - 84	216	91	125	...	...	...	...	...	...
85 - 89	84	39	45	...	...	...	...	...	...
90 +	78	30	48	...	...	...	...	...	...
Canada									
10 V 2016 (CDJC)[33]									
Total	35 151 730	17 264 200	17 887 530	28 575 665	13 912 050	14 663 615	6 576 065	3 352 150	3 223 910
0	369 735	189 085	180 645	303 795	155 030	148 765	65 935	34 055	31 880
1 - 4	1 529 060	783 945	745 115	1 248 230	639 935	608 295	280 830	144 010	136 820
5 - 9	2 018 130	1 034 685	983 445	1 633 720	836 950	796 770	384 410	197 740	186 670
10 - 14	1 922 645	985 200	937 445	1 546 225	791 500	754 730	376 420	193 700	182 720
15 - 19	2 026 160	1 039 215	986 940	1 641 330	839 980	801 345	384 830	199 235	185 595
20 - 24	2 242 695	1 144 495	1 098 200	1 907 165	967 775	939 390	335 525	176 715	158 805
25 - 29	2 285 990	1 144 475	1 141 515	1 976 755	986 505	990 255	309 235	157 970	151 265
30 - 34	2 329 400	1 148 290	1 181 105	1 989 865	978 690	1 011 170	339 535	169 605	169 935
35 - 39	2 288 365	1 118 635	1 169 730	1 924 280	935 630	988 645	364 085	183 000	181 085
40 - 44	2 255 135	1 104 445	1 150 690	1 871 860	910 205	961 655	383 280	194 240	189 035
45 - 49	2 359 965	1 157 755	1 202 205	1 925 635	939 350	986 290	434 325	218 410	215 915
50 - 54	2 678 070	1 318 755	1 359 320	2 120 605	1 038 360	1 082 250	557 465	280 395	277 070

7. Population by age, sex and urban/rural residence: latest available year, 2010 - 2019
Population selon l'âge, le sexe et la résidence, urbaine/rurale : dernière année disponible, 2010 - 2019 (continued - suite)

Continent, country or area, date, code[a] and age (in years) / Continent, pays ou zone, date, code[a] et âge (en années)	Total			Urban - Urbaine			Rural - Rurale		
	Both sexes Les deux sexes	Male Masculin	Female Féminin	Both sexes Les deux sexes	Male Masculin	Female Féminin	Both sexes Les deux sexes	Male Masculin	Female Féminin
AMERICA, NORTH - AMÉRIQUE DU NORD									
Canada									
10 V 2016 (CDJC)[33]									
55 - 59	2 620 240	1 285 190	1 335 050	2 029 030	986 135	1 042 895	591 210	299 055	292 155
60 - 64	2 290 510	1 114 880	1 175 630	1 745 665	835 295	910 375	544 850	279 585	265 260
65 - 69	1 972 475	953 070	1 019 405	1 506 495	710 615	795 875	465 985	242 455	223 535
70 - 74	1 420 875	677 975	742 900	1 097 395	507 680	589 710	323 480	170 290	153 190
75 - 79	1 021 850	469 550	552 305	817 520	363 230	454 285	204 335	106 315	98 020
80 - 84	749 645	325 760	423 885	622 775	262 700	360 075	126 875	63 065	63 810
85 - 89	482 525	185 535	296 985	413 945	155 020	258 925	68 575	30 510	38 065
90 - 94	223 505	68 675	154 835	196 075	58 750	137 325	27 435	9 920	17 510
95 - 99	56 525	13 245	43 280	49 945	11 535	38 410	6 585	1 705	4 870
100 +	8 230	1 340	6 895	7 355	1 175	6 180	875	160	710
1 VII 2019* (ESDJ)[34]									
Total	37 589 262	18 678 085	18 911 177	...	...	...	...	...	...
0	381 716	195 851	185 865	...	...	...	...	...	...
1 - 4	1 561 459	800 318	761 141	...	...	...	...	...	...
5 - 9	2 039 352	1 042 006	997 346	...	...	...	...	...	...
10 - 14	2 031 762	1 034 679	997 083	...	...	...	...	...	...
15 - 19	2 114 635	1 083 305	1 031 330	...	...	...	...	...	...
20 - 24	2 476 698	1 293 447	1 183 251	...	...	...	...	...	...
25 - 29	2 625 474	1 353 719	1 271 755	...	...	...	...	...	...
30 - 34	2 603 938	1 318 922	1 285 016	...	...	...	...	...	...
35 - 39	2 580 021	1 288 484	1 291 537	...	...	...	...	...	...
40 - 44	2 421 009	1 198 446	1 222 563	...	...	...	...	...	...
45 - 49	2 396 406	1 190 042	1 206 364	...	...	...	...	...	...
50 - 54	2 502 667	1 245 715	1 256 952	...	...	...	...	...	...
55 - 59	2 749 626	1 367 374	1 382 252	...	...	...	...	...	...
60 - 64	2 511 888	1 235 919	1 275 969	...	...	...	...	...	...
65 - 69	2 096 607	1 016 865	1 079 742	...	...	...	...	...	...
70 - 74	1 706 760	817 541	889 219	...	...	...	...	...	...
75 - 79	1 164 277	543 007	621 270	...	...	...	...	...	...
80 - 84	786 704	347 388	439 316	...	...	...	...	...	...
85 - 89	510 828	204 463	306 365	...	...	...	...	...	...
90 - 94	242 554	80 100	162 454	...	...	...	...	...	...
95 - 99	74 086	18 556	55 530	...	...	...	...	...	...
100 +	10 795	1 938	8 857	...	...	...	...	...	...
Cayman Islands - Îles Caïmanes									
31 XII 2019 (ESDJ)									
Total	69 914	34 539	35 375	...	...	...	...	...	...
0 - 14	10 652	5 172	5 480	...	...	...	...	...	...
15 - 24	6 250	3 156	3 094	...	...	...	...	...	...
25 - 34	11 877	5 774	6 103	...	...	...	...	...	...
35 - 44	13 921	6 880	7 041	...	...	...	...	...	...
45 - 54	12 782	6 266	6 515	...	...	...	...	...	...
55 - 64	8 269	4 336	3 933	...	...	...	...	...	...
65 +	5 552	2 769	2 783	...	...	...	...	...	...
Unknown - Inconnu	610	185	425	...	...	...	...	...	...
Costa Rica[35]									
1 VII 2019 (ESDJ)									
Total	5 059 730	2 452 241	2 607 489	3 670 174	1 758 286	1 911 888	1 389 556	693 955	695 601
0 - 4	293 210	149 816	143 394	199 213	102 708	96 505	93 997	47 108	46 889
5 - 9	357 296	178 724	178 572	247 898	122 585	125 313	109 398	56 139	53 259
10 - 14	376 661	195 268	181 393	250 856	129 986	120 870	125 805	65 282	60 523
15 - 19	417 720	215 941	201 779	294 424	152 857	141 567	123 296	63 084	60 212
20 - 24	408 621	216 055	192 566	304 406	160 586	143 820	104 215	55 469	48 746
25 - 29	380 496	185 610	194 886	283 871	139 829	144 042	96 625	45 781	50 844
30 - 34	390 532	186 124	204 408	289 856	142 109	147 747	100 676	44 015	56 661
35 - 39	364 710	170 203	194 507	266 515	123 673	142 842	98 195	46 530	51 665
40 - 44	329 400	156 093	173 307	244 208	114 703	129 505	85 192	41 390	43 802
45 - 49	292 935	133 375	159 560	210 168	96 840	113 328	82 767	36 535	46 232
50 - 54	315 591	146 131	169 460	228 275	102 614	125 661	87 316	43 517	43 799
55 - 59	304 287	140 983	163 304	224 964	101 395	123 569	79 323	39 588	39 735
60 - 64	257 241	120 881	136 360	194 727	86 027	108 700	62 514	34 854	27 660

7. Population by age, sex and urban/rural residence: latest available year, 2010 - 2019
Population selon l'âge, le sexe et la résidence, urbaine/rurale : dernière année disponible, 2010 - 2019 (continued - suite)

Continent, country or area, date, code[a] and age (in years) / Continent, pays ou zone, date, code[a] et âge (en annèes)	Total			Urban - Urbaine			Rural - Rurale		
	Both sexes Les deux sexes	Male Masculin	Female Féminin	Both sexes Les deux sexes	Male Masculin	Female Féminin	Both sexes Les deux sexes	Male Masculin	Female Féminin
AMERICA, NORTH - AMÉRIQUE DU NORD									
Costa Rica[35]									
1 VII 2019 (ESDJ)									
65 - 69	204 119	92 066	112 053	154 214	67 811	86 403	49 905	24 255	25 650
70 - 74	142 602	65 262	77 340	105 286	43 983	61 303	37 316	21 279	16 037
75 - 79	99 081	45 980	53 101	74 716	32 584	42 132	24 365	13 396	10 969
80 - 84	65 973	29 855	36 118	50 368	20 532	29 836	15 605	9 323	6 282
85 - 89	35 276	15 340	19 936	25 592	10 708	14 884	9 684	4 632	5 052
90 - 94	17 395	6 280	11 115	14 736	4 734	10 002	2 659	1 546	1 113
95 +	6 584	2 254	4 330	5 881	2 022	3 859	703	232	471
Cuba									
1 VII 2019 (ESDJ)									
Total	11 201 549	5 570 081	5 631 469	8 633 350	4 194 838	4 438 512	2 568 200	1 375 243	1 192 957
0	112 465	58 098	54 367	91 238	47 079	44 160	21 227	11 019	10 208
1 - 4	473 544	245 792	227 752	386 782	200 784	185 998	86 762	45 008	41 754
5 - 9	622 947	320 678	302 269	474 867	244 460	230 407	148 080	76 219	71 862
10 - 14	571 975	294 634	277 341	428 055	219 987	208 068	143 920	74 647	69 273
15 - 19	675 413	347 343	328 071	513 865	262 936	250 930	161 548	84 407	77 141
20 - 24	691 431	356 333	335 098	529 920	270 714	259 206	161 512	85 619	75 893
25 - 29	772 097	398 298	373 799	592 060	300 305	291 755	180 038	97 993	82 045
30 - 34	766 924	393 336	373 589	591 335	296 909	294 426	175 590	96 427	79 163
35 - 39	636 475	323 680	312 795	483 940	240 734	243 207	152 535	82 947	69 588
40 - 44	729 203	365 869	363 334	544 252	266 354	277 898	184 951	99 516	85 436
45 - 49	981 441	487 757	493 684	739 057	356 837	382 220	242 385	130 921	111 464
50 - 54	1 003 983	491 188	512 795	773 112	366 687	406 425	230 871	124 501	106 370
55 - 59	856 008	415 221	440 788	675 044	318 033	357 011	180 965	97 188	83 777
60 - 64	592 764	282 713	310 052	463 377	213 588	249 789	129 387	69 125	60 263
65 - 69	541 095	257 861	283 234	428 162	196 630	231 533	112 933	61 232	51 701
70 - 74	442 208	205 703	236 505	350 058	156 737	193 321	92 150	48 966	43 184
75 - 79	333 558	153 466	180 092	262 630	114 886	147 744	70 928	38 580	32 349
80 - 84	207 631	92 562	115 070	161 902	67 308	94 594	45 729	25 254	20 476
85 +	190 391	79 553	110 839	143 698	53 875	89 824	46 693	25 678	21 015
Curaçao[2]									
1 I 2019 (ESDJ)									
Total	158 659	72 538	86 121	...	...	...	...	...	...
0	1 680	895	785	...	...	...	...	...	...
1 - 4	7 123	3 631	3 492	...	...	...	...	...	...
5 - 9	9 797	5 069	4 728	...	...	...	...	...	...
10 - 14	9 487	4 825	4 662	...	...	...	...	...	...
15 - 19	9 895	5 072	4 823	...	...	...	...	...	...
20 - 24	8 684	4 384	4 300	...	...	...	...	...	...
25 - 29	9 058	4 270	4 788	...	...	...	...	...	...
30 - 34	9 267	4 200	5 067	...	...	...	...	...	...
35 - 39	9 274	4 004	5 270	...	...	...	...	...	...
40 - 44	9 531	4 105	5 426	...	...	...	...	...	...
45 - 49	11 544	5 188	6 356	...	...	...	...	...	...
50 - 54	12 239	5 420	6 819	...	...	...	...	...	...
55 - 59	12 725	5 484	7 241	...	...	...	...	...	...
60 - 64	10 865	4 711	6 154	...	...	...	...	...	...
65 - 69	9 368	4 086	5 282	...	...	...	...	...	...
70 - 74	7 286	3 105	4 181	...	...	...	...	...	...
75 - 79	4 857	1 955	2 902	...	...	...	...	...	...
80 - 84	3 285	1 256	2 029	...	...	...	...	...	...
85 - 89	1 732	603	1 129	...	...	...	...	...	...
90 - 94	674	199	475	...	...	...	...	...	...
95 - 99	239	63	176	...	...	...	...	...	...
100 +	49	13	36	...	...	...	...	...	...
Dominica - Dominique									
14 V 2011 (CDFC)									
Total	68 913	34 973	33 940	...	...	...	...	...	...
0 - 4	6 380	3 240	3 140	...	...	...	...	...	...
5 - 9	5 096	2 601	2 495	...	...	...	...	...	...
10 - 14	5 822	2 946	2 876	...	...	...	...	...	...
15 - 19	6 297	3 237	3 060	...	...	...	...	...	...
20 - 24	5 258	2 691	2 567	...	...	...	...	...	...

Continent, country or area, date, code[a] and age (in years) / Continent, pays ou zone, date, code[a] et âge (en années)	Total			Urban - Urbaine			Rural - Rurale		
	Both sexes Les deux sexes	Male Masculin	Female Féminin	Both sexes Les deux sexes	Male Masculin	Female Féminin	Both sexes Les deux sexes	Male Masculin	Female Féminin
AMERICA, NORTH - AMÉRIQUE DU NORD									
Dominica - Dominique									
14 V 2011 (CDFC)									
25 - 29	4 861	2 389	2 472	...	...	...	...	...	...
30 - 34	4 029	2 118	1 911	...	...	...	...	...	...
35 - 39	4 507	2 271	2 236	...	...	...	...	...	...
40 - 44	4 953	2 544	2 409	...	...	...	...	...	...
45 - 49	4 472	2 337	2 135	...	...	...	...	...	...
50 - 54	3 946	2 162	1 784	...	...	...	...	...	...
55 - 59	3 093	1 682	1 411	...	...	...	...	...	...
60 - 64	2 493	1 281	1 212	...	...	...	...	...	...
65 - 69	2 159	1 054	1 105	...	...	...	...	...	...
70 - 74	1 867	884	983	...	...	...	...	...	...
75 - 79	1 587	724	863	...	...	...	...	...	...
80 - 84	1 102	467	635	...	...	...	...	...	...
85 - 89	599	212	387	...	...	...	...	...	...
90 - 94	274	101	173	...	...	...	...	...	...
95 +	118	32	86	...	...	...	...	...	...
Dominican Republic - République dominicaine									
1 VII 2019 (ESDJ)									
Total	*10 358 320*	*5 174 343*	*5 183 977*	*8 457 450*	*4 155 896*	*4 301 554*	*1 900 870*	*1 018 447*	*882 423*
0	*190 745*	*97 488*	*93 257*	*156 185*	*79 361*	*76 824*	*34 560*	*18 127*	*16 433*
1 - 4	*766 628*	*391 198*	*375 430*	*622 823*	*316 521*	*306 302*	*143 805*	*74 677*	*69 128*
5 - 9	*966 756*	*492 668*	*474 088*	*781 656*	*395 787*	*385 869*	*185 100*	*96 881*	*88 219*
10 - 14	*957 529*	*486 135*	*471 394*	*774 208*	*389 084*	*385 124*	*183 321*	*97 051*	*86 270*
15 - 19	*953 622*	*481 306*	*472 316*	*777 224*	*386 560*	*390 664*	*176 398*	*94 746*	*81 652*
20 - 24	*909 207*	*455 599*	*453 608*	*748 696*	*368 727*	*379 969*	*160 511*	*86 872*	*73 639*
25 - 29	*858 147*	*428 375*	*429 772*	*711 338*	*349 046*	*362 292*	*146 809*	*79 329*	*67 480*
30 - 34	*782 714*	*388 336*	*394 378*	*648 749*	*316 747*	*332 002*	*133 965*	*71 589*	*62 376*
35 - 39	*707 756*	*350 506*	*357 250*	*585 004*	*284 972*	*300 032*	*122 752*	*65 534*	*57 218*
40 - 44	*638 298*	*315 536*	*322 762*	*526 354*	*255 607*	*270 747*	*111 944*	*59 929*	*52 015*
45 - 49	*575 040*	*283 505*	*291 535*	*472 983*	*228 423*	*244 560*	*102 057*	*55 082*	*46 975*
50 - 54	*512 801*	*253 168*	*259 633*	*420 432*	*202 935*	*217 497*	*92 369*	*50 233*	*42 136*
55 - 59	*442 576*	*218 520*	*224 056*	*359 703*	*173 127*	*186 576*	*82 873*	*45 393*	*37 480*
60 - 64	*354 804*	*174 613*	*180 191*	*285 600*	*136 640*	*148 960*	*69 204*	*37 973*	*31 231*
65 - 69	*270 007*	*131 426*	*138 581*	*214 766*	*101 226*	*113 540*	*55 241*	*30 200*	*25 041*
70 - 74	*191 825*	*93 344*	*98 481*	*151 620*	*71 195*	*80 425*	*40 205*	*22 149*	*18 056*
75 - 79	*130 032*	*62 579*	*67 453*	*102 240*	*47 233*	*55 007*	*27 792*	*15 346*	*12 446*
80 +	*149 833*	*70 041*	*79 792*	*117 869*	*52 705*	*65 164*	*31 964*	*17 336*	*14 628*
El Salvador[10]									
1 VII 2017 (ESDJ)									
Total	6 581 940	3 098 633	3 483 307	...	...	...	...	...	...
0	111 299	56 941	54 358	...	...	...	...	...	...
1 - 4	446 740	228 345	218 395	...	...	...	...	...	...
5 - 9	567 307	289 964	277 343	...	...	...	...	...	...
10 - 14	614 163	314 135	300 028	...	...	...	...	...	...
15 - 19	682 932	347 360	335 572	...	...	...	...	...	...
20 - 24	703 384	351 669	351 715	...	...	...	...	...	...
25 - 29	597 142	284 515	312 627	...	...	...	...	...	...
30 - 34	474 137	210 535	263 602	...	...	...	...	...	...
35 - 39	406 945	173 276	233 669	...	...	...	...	...	...
40 - 44	376 093	159 892	216 201	...	...	...	...	...	...
45 - 49	340 258	145 527	194 731	...	...	...	...	...	...
50 - 54	291 141	124 103	167 038	...	...	...	...	...	...
55 - 59	242 500	103 228	139 272	...	...	...	...	...	...
60 - 64	203 360	87 005	116 355	...	...	...	...	...	...
65 - 69	167 862	71 983	95 879	...	...	...	...	...	...
70 - 74	132 816	56 878	75 938	...	...	...	...	...	...
75 - 79	100 621	42 776	57 845	...	...	...	...	...	...
80 - 84	67 398	28 096	39 302	...	...	...	...	...	...
85 +	55 842	22 405	33 437	...	...	...	...	...	...

7. Population by age, sex and urban/rural residence: latest available year, 2010 - 2019
Population selon l'âge, le sexe et la résidence, urbaine/rurale : dernière année disponible, 2010 - 2019 (continued - suite)

Continent, country or area, date, code[a] and age (in years) Continent, pays ou zone, date, code[a] et âge (en annèes)	Total			Urban - Urbaine			Rural - Rurale		
	Both sexes Les deux sexes	Male Masculin	Female Féminin	Both sexes Les deux sexes	Male Masculin	Female Féminin	Both sexes Les deux sexes	Male Masculin	Female Féminin
AMERICA, NORTH - AMÉRIQUE DU NORD									
Greenland - Groenland[36]									
1 VII 2019 (ESDJ)									
Total	56 225	29 654	26 571	48 928	25 648	23 280	7 297	4 006	3 291
0	831	436	395	726	377	349	105	59	46
1 - 4	3 235	1 659	1 576	2 799	1 427	1 372	436	232	204
5 - 9	3 883	2 030	1 853	3 363	1 756	1 607	520	274	246
10 - 14	3 809	1 942	1 867	3 276	1 671	1 605	533	271	262
15 - 19	3 599	1 840	1 759	3 078	1 571	1 507	521	269	252
20 - 24	4 171	2 114	2 057	3 609	1 839	1 770	562	275	287
25 - 29	4 696	2 398	2 298	4 122	2 103	2 019	574	295	279
30 - 34	4 383	2 234	2 149	3 925	1 985	1 940	458	249	209
35 - 39	3 820	2 001	1 819	3 389	1 752	1 637	431	249	182
40 - 44	3 012	1 645	1 367	2 658	1 446	1 212	354	199	155
45 - 49	3 158	1 740	1 418	2 743	1 500	1 243	415	240	175
50 - 54	4 922	2 677	2 245	4 263	2 311	1 952	659	366	293
55 - 59	4 534	2 454	2 080	3 928	2 099	1 829	606	355	251
60 - 64	3 327	1 874	1 453	2 848	1 581	1 267	479	293	186
65 - 69	2 079	1 162	917	1 782	983	799	297	179	118
70 - 74	1 311	765	546	1 142	658	484	169	107	62
75 - 79	889	449	440	787	393	394	102	56	46
80 - 84	363	159	204	306	131	175	57	28	29
85 - 89	162	60	102	145	52	93	17	8	9
90 - 94	36	11	25	35	10	25	1	1	-
95 +	5	4	1	4	3	1	1	1	-
Grenada - Grenade									
1 VII 2017 (ESDF)									
Total	111 467	56 222	55 245	...	...	...	...	...	...
0	1 375	735	640	...	...	...	...	...	...
1 - 4	6 779	3 547	3 232	...	...	...	...	...	...
5 - 9	7 427	3 793	3 634	...	...	...	...	...	...
10 - 14	8 668	4 392	4 276	...	...	...	...	...	...
15 - 19	9 687	4 869	4 818	...	...	...	...	...	...
20 - 24	9 824	5 027	4 797	...	...	...	...	...	...
25 - 29	9 480	4 758	4 722	...	...	...	...	...	...
30 - 34	7 110	3 596	3 514	...	...	...	...	...	...
35 - 39	6 554	3 424	3 130	...	...	...	...	...	...
40 - 44	6 024	3 120	2 904	...	...	...	...	...	...
45 - 49	6 614	3 416	3 198	...	...	...	...	...	...
50 - 54	6 374	3 179	3 195	...	...	...	...	...	...
55 - 59	4 686	2 455	2 231	...	...	...	...	...	...
60 - 64	3 571	1 806	1 765	...	...	...	...	...	...
65 - 69	2 758	1 261	1 497	...	...	...	...	...	...
70 - 74	2 393	1 106	1 287	...	...	...	...	...	...
75 - 79	1 731	732	999	...	...	...	...	...	...
80 - 84	1 112	417	695	...	...	...	...	...	...
85 - 89	527	168	359	...	...	...	...	...	...
90 +	275	78	197	...	...	...	...	...	...
Guadeloupe[37]									
1 I 2015 (CDJC)									
Total	397 990	183 479	214 511	391 984	180 438	211 546	6 006	3 041	2 965
0	4 009	2 045	1 965	3 965	2 025	1 941	44	20	24
1 - 4	18 400	9 247	9 153	18 216	9 148	9 068	184	99	85
5 - 9	26 769	13 707	13 062	26 476	13 552	12 923	294	155	139
10 - 14	29 794	15 004	14 790	29 418	14 801	14 617	376	203	173
15 - 19	29 000	14 731	14 269	28 658	14 539	14 120	342	193	149
20 - 24	19 884	10 153	9 731	19 628	9 997	9 631	256	156	100
25 - 29	18 266	8 227	10 039	18 021	8 104	9 918	245	123	122
30 - 34	19 526	7 926	11 600	19 305	7 808	11 497	222	119	103
35 - 39	22 312	9 201	13 111	22 041	9 074	12 967	271	127	144
40 - 44	29 148	12 518	16 630	28 680	12 286	16 394	468	232	236
45 - 49	31 360	13 926	17 434	30 817	13 646	17 171	544	281	263
50 - 54	31 975	14 748	17 227	31 442	14 477	16 965	533	271	262
55 - 59	27 674	12 884	14 790	27 179	12 626	14 554	495	258	237
60 - 64	24 635	11 204	13 431	24 202	10 992	13 210	433	213	221

7. Population by age, sex and urban/rural residence: latest available year, 2010 - 2019
Population selon l'âge, le sexe et la résidence, urbaine/rurale : dernière année disponible, 2010 - 2019 (continued - suite)

Continent, country or area, date, code[a] and age (in years) / Continent, pays ou zone, date, code[a] et âge (en annèes)	Total			Urban - Urbaine			Rural - Rurale		
	Both sexes Les deux sexes	Male Masculin	Female Féminin	Both sexes Les deux sexes	Male Masculin	Female Féminin	Both sexes Les deux sexes	Male Masculin	Female Féminin
AMERICA, NORTH - AMÉRIQUE DU NORD									
Guadeloupe[37]									
1 I 2015 (CDJC)									
65 - 69	20 327	9 336	10 991	19 938	9 146	10 792	389	190	199
70 - 74	15 353	6 850	8 503	15 013	6 692	8 322	340	158	182
75 - 79	11 957	5 315	6 642	11 696	5 193	6 503	261	122	139
80 - 84	8 552	3 359	5 193	8 381	3 287	5 093	172	72	100
85 - 89	5 364	1 891	3 472	5 275	1 858	3 417	88	33	55
90 - 94	2 625	882	1 742	2 588	867	1 720	37	15	22
95 - 99	817	268	549	807	266	541	10	2	8
100 +	240	56	184	236	55	181	4	1	3
1 I 2018 (ESDJ)									
Total	422 290	194 321	227 969	...	...	...	...	...	...
0 - 4	22 562	11 424	11 138	...	...	...	...	...	...
5 - 9	26 544	13 520	13 024	...	...	...	...	...	...
10 - 14	30 261	15 223	15 038	...	...	...	...	...	...
15 - 19	28 783	14 731	14 052	...	...	...	...	...	...
20 - 24	20 013	10 025	9 988	...	...	...	...	...	...
25 - 29	20 104	9 293	10 811	...	...	...	...	...	...
30 - 34	20 025	8 365	11 660	...	...	...	...	...	...
35 - 39	22 090	9 060	13 030	...	...	...	...	...	...
40 - 44	27 554	11 619	15 935	...	...	...	...	...	...
45 - 49	31 981	14 069	17 912	...	...	...	...	...	...
50 - 54	33 590	15 213	18 377	...	...	...	...	...	...
55 - 59	32 162	15 100	17 062	...	...	...	...	...	...
60 - 64	28 369	13 094	15 275	...	...	...	...	...	...
65 - 69	24 777	11 371	13 406	...	...	...	...	...	...
70 - 74	19 125	8 700	10 425	...	...	...	...	...	...
75 - 79	13 415	5 828	7 587	...	...	...	...	...	...
80 - 84	10 306	4 048	6 258	...	...	...	...	...	...
85 - 89	6 245	2 244	4 001	...	...	...	...	...	...
90 - 94	3 198	1 026	2 172	...	...	...	...	...	...
95 - 99	1 057	338	719	...	...	...	...	...	...
100 +	129	30	99	...	...	...	...	...	...
Guatemala[28]									
1 VII 2018 (ESDJ)									
Total	17 311 086	8 469 989	8 841 097	...	...	...	...	...	...
0 - 4	2 304 007	1 174 848	1 129 159	...	...	...	...	...	...
5 - 9	2 209 740	1 125 844	1 083 896	...	...	...	...	...	...
10 - 14	2 085 169	1 059 860	1 025 310	...	...	...	...	...	...
15 - 19	1 889 494	954 428	935 065	...	...	...	...	...	...
20 - 24	1 686 608	843 100	843 508	...	...	...	...	...	...
25 - 29	1 413 323	693 436	719 886	...	...	...	...	...	...
30 - 34	1 202 126	574 360	627 766	...	...	...	...	...	...
35 - 39	999 618	461 515	538 103	...	...	...	...	...	...
40 - 44	801 107	356 135	444 972	...	...	...	...	...	...
45 - 49	633 751	277 730	356 020	...	...	...	...	...	...
50 - 54	510 636	225 694	284 941	...	...	...	...	...	...
55 - 59	408 107	183 916	224 191	...	...	...	...	...	...
60 - 64	348 127	160 872	187 255	...	...	...	...	...	...
65 +	819 274	378 250	441 024	...	...	...	...	...	...
Haiti - Haïti[38]									
1 VII 2010 (ESDJ)									
Total	*10 085 214*	*4 993 731*	*5 091 483*	*4 817 666*	*2 321 608*	*2 496 059*	*5 267 548*	*2 672 123*	*2 595 424*
0 - 4	*1 263 322*	*644 550*	*618 772*	*532 352*	*274 597*	*257 755*	*730 970*	*369 953*	*361 017*
5 - 9	*1 195 479*	*608 495*	*586 984*	*493 368*	*249 982*	*243 386*	*702 111*	*358 513*	*343 598*
10 - 14	*1 158 478*	*588 618*	*569 860*	*532 573*	*255 002*	*277 571*	*625 905*	*333 616*	*292 289*
15 - 19	*1 092 364*	*551 467*	*540 897*	*583 183*	*276 258*	*306 925*	*509 181*	*275 209*	*233 972*
20 - 24	*1 019 589*	*509 042*	*510 547*	*600 175*	*296 233*	*303 943*	*419 414*	*212 809*	*206 604*
25 - 29	*919 636*	*454 123*	*465 513*	*537 063*	*267 198*	*269 865*	*382 573*	*186 925*	*195 648*
30 - 34	*702 596*	*340 518*	*362 078*	*390 054*	*189 432*	*200 622*	*312 542*	*151 086*	*161 456*
35 - 39	*548 004*	*261 157*	*286 847*	*272 855*	*128 575*	*144 280*	*275 149*	*132 582*	*142 567*
40 - 44	*488 482*	*235 182*	*253 300*	*225 057*	*106 072*	*118 985*	*263 425*	*129 110*	*134 315*
45 - 49	*423 377*	*204 077*	*219 300*	*179 712*	*81 240*	*98 472*	*243 665*	*122 837*	*120 828*
50 - 54	*342 913*	*166 418*	*176 495*	*138 580*	*61 854*	*76 726*	*204 333*	*104 564*	*99 769*

7. Population by age, sex and urban/rural residence: latest available year, 2010 - 2019
Population selon l'âge, le sexe et la résidence, urbaine/rurale : dernière année disponible, 2010 - 2019 (continued - suite)

Continent, country or area, date, code[a] and age (in years) / Continent, pays ou zone, date, code[a] et âge (en annèes)	Total			Urban - Urbaine			Rural - Rurale		
	Both sexes Les deux sexes	Male Masculin	Female Féminin	Both sexes Les deux sexes	Male Masculin	Female Féminin	Both sexes Les deux sexes	Male Masculin	Female Féminin
AMERICA, NORTH - AMÉRIQUE DU NORD									
Haiti - Haïti[38]									
1 VII 2010 (ESDJ)									
55 - 59	*284 731*	*136 034*	*148 697*	*107 391*	*46 062*	*61 329*	*177 340*	*89 972*	*87 368*
60 - 64	*206 835*	*95 939*	*110 896*	*73 562*	*29 974*	*43 588*	*133 273*	*65 965*	*67 308*
65 - 69	*175 898*	*81 854*	*94 044*	*61 671*	*24 975*	*36 696*	*114 227*	*56 879*	*57 348*
70 - 74	*129 436*	*58 181*	*71 255*	*44 448*	*17 100*	*27 347*	*84 988*	*41 081*	*43 908*
75 - 79	*80 898*	*35 538*	*45 360*	*27 630*	*10 473*	*17 158*	*53 268*	*25 065*	*28 202*
80 +	*53 176*	*22 538*	*30 638*	*17 992*	*6 581*	*11 412*	*35 184*	*15 957*	*19 226*
1 VII 2018 (ESDJ)									
Total	*11 411 527*	*5 659 140*	*5 752 387*	...	...	...	...	...	...
0 - 4	*1 295 906*	*661 535*	*634 371*	...	...	...	...	...	...
5 - 9	*1 247 619*	*635 927*	*611 692*	...	...	...	...	...	...
10 - 14	*1 197 091*	*608 695*	*588 396*	...	...	...	...	...	...
15 - 19	*1 146 787*	*580 801*	*565 986*	...	...	...	...	...	...
20 - 24	*1 089 914*	*547 618*	*542 296*	...	...	...	...	...	...
25 - 29	*1 013 281*	*504 926*	*508 355*	...	...	...	...	...	...
30 - 34	*936 810*	*463 541*	*473 269*	...	...	...	...	...	...
35 - 39	*793 197*	*387 698*	*405 499*	...	...	...	...	...	...
40 - 44	*594 836*	*285 013*	*309 823*	...	...	...	...	...	...
45 - 49	*485 166*	*230 537*	*254 629*	...	...	...	...	...	...
50 - 54	*431 114*	*206 255*	*224 859*	...	...	...	...	...	...
55 - 59	*357 489*	*170 991*	*186 498*	...	...	...	...	...	...
60 - 64	*282 415*	*134 300*	*148 115*	...	...	...	...	...	...
65 - 69	*211 207*	*97 454*	*113 753*	...	...	...	...	...	...
70 - 74	*147 063*	*66 084*	*80 979*	...	...	...	...	...	...
75 - 79	*104 921*	*46 188*	*58 733*	...	...	...	...	...	...
80 +	*76 710*	*31 576*	*45 134*	...	...	...	...	...	...
Honduras[3]									
1 VII 2019 (ESDJ)									
Total	*9 158 345*	*4 459 196*	*4 699 149*	*5 017 687*	*2 333 620*	*2 684 067*	*4 140 658*	*2 125 576*	*2 015 082*
0	*196 852*	*100 307*	*96 545*	*104 662*	*53 361*	*51 301*	*92 190*	*46 946*	*45 244*
1 - 4	*772 229*	*393 120*	*379 109*	*403 124*	*205 379*	*197 745*	*369 105*	*187 741*	*181 364*
5 - 9	*966 323*	*491 718*	*474 605*	*500 114*	*252 347*	*247 767*	*466 209*	*239 371*	*226 838*
10 - 14	*984 539*	*496 707*	*487 832*	*534 756*	*267 830*	*266 926*	*449 783*	*228 877*	*220 906*
15 - 19	*954 480*	*470 870*	*483 610*	*525 607*	*252 081*	*273 526*	*428 873*	*218 789*	*210 084*
20 - 24	*887 466*	*430 102*	*457 364*	*486 449*	*221 231*	*265 218*	*401 017*	*208 871*	*192 146*
25 - 29	*816 847*	*391 843*	*425 004*	*455 831*	*204 493*	*251 338*	*361 016*	*187 350*	*173 666*
30 - 34	*724 114*	*345 012*	*379 102*	*406 987*	*180 720*	*226 267*	*317 127*	*164 292*	*152 835*
35 - 39	*594 269*	*281 228*	*313 041*	*335 201*	*148 119*	*187 082*	*259 068*	*133 109*	*125 959*
40 - 44	*494 119*	*232 859*	*261 260*	*279 539*	*123 191*	*156 348*	*214 580*	*109 668*	*104 912*
45 - 49	*407 282*	*191 676*	*215 606*	*229 330*	*100 741*	*128 589*	*177 952*	*90 935*	*87 017*
50 - 54	*337 566*	*158 690*	*178 876*	*189 312*	*82 827*	*106 485*	*148 254*	*75 863*	*72 391*
55 - 59	*277 808*	*130 791*	*147 017*	*155 415*	*67 912*	*87 503*	*122 393*	*62 879*	*59 514*
60 - 64	*225 392*	*105 824*	*119 568*	*125 487*	*54 500*	*70 987*	*99 905*	*51 324*	*48 581*
65 - 69	*178 520*	*83 065*	*95 455*	*99 153*	*42 246*	*56 907*	*79 367*	*40 819*	*38 548*
70 - 74	*132 089*	*61 005*	*71 084*	*71 552*	*29 939*	*41 613*	*60 537*	*31 066*	*29 471*
75 - 79	*95 526*	*43 874*	*51 652*	*51 047*	*21 122*	*29 925*	*44 479*	*22 752*	*21 727*
80 - 84	*56 988*	*25 795*	*31 193*	*31 528*	*12 811*	*18 717*	*25 460*	*12 984*	*12 476*
85 - 89	*33 829*	*15 202*	*18 627*	*19 076*	*7 654*	*11 422*	*14 753*	*7 548*	*7 205*
90 - 94	*16 029*	*7 032*	*8 997*	*9 710*	*3 755*	*5 955*	*6 319*	*3 277*	*3 042*
95 +	*6 078*	*2 476*	*3 602*	*3 807*	*1 361*	*2 446*	*2 271*	*1 115*	*1 156*
Jamaica - Jamaïque									
4 IV 2011 (CDJC)									
Total	2 697 983	1 334 533	1 363 450	1 454 151	700 957	753 194	1 243 832	633 576	610 256
0 - 4	209 871	106 107	103 764	109 121	55 157	53 965	100 750	50 950	49 799
5 - 9	226 378	114 792	111 586	114 520	57 817	56 703	111 858	56 975	54 883
10 - 14	266 586	136 183	130 403	138 596	70 428	68 168	127 990	65 755	62 235
15 - 19	274 658	139 777	134 881	143 644	72 173	71 471	131 014	67 604	63 410
20 - 24	250 711	125 243	125 468	140 770	68 692	72 078	109 941	56 551	53 390
25 - 29	226 120	109 919	116 201	129 961	61 980	67 981	96 159	47 939	48 220
30 - 34	185 495	87 810	97 685	106 228	49 452	56 776	79 267	38 358	40 909
35 - 39	183 756	86 647	97 109	103 560	47 408	56 152	80 196	39 239	40 957
40 - 44	173 924	85 656	88 268	97 069	46 377	50 693	76 855	39 279	37 575
45 - 49	155 389	79 201	76 188	88 044	41 385	46 658	67 345	37 816	29 530

Continent, country or area, date, code[a] and age (in years) Continent, pays ou zone, date, code[a] et âge (en annèes)	Total			Urban - Urbaine			Rural - Rurale		
	Both sexes Les deux sexes	Male Masculin	Female Féminin	Both sexes Les deux sexes	Male Masculin	Female Féminin	Both sexes Les deux sexes	Male Masculin	Female Féminin
AMERICA, NORTH - AMÉRIQUE DU NORD									
Jamaica - Jamaïque									
4 IV 2011 (CDJC)									
50 - 54	137 895	67 297	70 598	74 271	34 341	39 930	63 624	32 956	30 668
55 - 59	100 798	50 717	50 081	54 090	26 020	28 070	46 708	24 697	22 011
60 - 64	88 057	44 407	43 650	46 868	22 549	24 319	41 189	21 858	19 331
65 - 69	65 164	32 543	32 621	33 182	15 691	17 491	31 982	16 852	15 130
70 - 74	51 276	24 627	26 649	25 354	11 785	13 569	25 922	12 842	13 080
75 - 79	42 762	19 847	22 915	20 542	9 085	11 458	22 220	10 762	11 457
80 - 84	30 738	13 258	17 480	14 941	6 132	8 809	15 797	7 126	8 671
85 - 89	18 457	7 267	11 190	8 789	3 151	5 638	9 668	4 116	5 552
90 - 94	6 921	2 303	4 618	3 238	957	2 281	3 683	1 346	2 337
95 - 99	2 503	808	1 695	1 119	326	793	1 384	482	902
100 +	524	124	400	243	53	190	281	71	210
1 VII 2019 (ESDJ)									
Total	2 732 539	1 351 515	1 381 024	...	...	...	...	...	...
0 - 4	174 059	88 769	85 290	...	...	...	...	...	...
5 - 9	191 247	97 299	93 948	...	...	...	...	...	...
10 - 14	211 432	106 720	104 712	...	...	...	...	...	...
15 - 19	232 783	118 895	113 888	...	...	...	...	...	...
20 - 24	257 798	130 614	127 184	...	...	...	...	...	...
25 - 29	249 862	126 322	123 540	...	...	...	...	...	...
30 - 34	221 968	109 010	112 958	...	...	...	...	...	...
35 - 39	199 078	95 108	103 970	...	...	...	...	...	...
40 - 44	166 175	77 021	89 154	...	...	...	...	...	...
45 - 49	166 086	78 742	87 344	...	...	...	...	...	...
50 - 54	152 863	75 767	77 096	...	...	...	...	...	...
55 - 59	136 228	69 089	67 139	...	...	...	...	...	...
60 - 64	111 210	54 822	56 388	...	...	...	...	...	...
65 - 69	82 766	41 595	41 171	...	...	...	...	...	...
70 - 74	65 474	32 319	33 155	...	...	...	...	...	...
75 - 79	45 070	21 380	23 690	...	...	...	...	...	...
80 +	68 440	28 043	40 397	...	...	...	...	...	...
Martinique									
1 I 2015 (CDJC)									
Total	380 877	176 328	204 549	367 749	169 911	197 838	13 128	6 417	6 711
0 - 4	19 514	9 968	9 545	18 927	9 661	9 267	586	308	279
5 - 9	23 179	11 841	11 338	22 465	11 480	10 985	713	361	353
10 - 14	24 846	12 616	12 229	24 010	12 176	11 834	835	440	395
15 - 19	25 065	12 913	12 152	24 241	12 506	11 736	824	408	416
20 - 24	18 914	9 758	9 157	18 354	9 455	8 899	561	303	258
25 - 29	17 978	8 092	9 886	17 471	7 846	9 625	507	246	261
30 - 34	17 884	7 651	10 233	17 393	7 444	9 948	491	207	284
35 - 39	19 983	8 508	11 474	19 389	8 247	11 142	594	262	332
40 - 44	26 375	11 391	14 984	25 498	10 985	14 512	877	405	472
45 - 49	31 052	13 979	17 073	30 020	13 471	16 549	1 032	508	524
50 - 54	32 777	14 886	17 891	31 588	14 274	17 314	1 188	611	577
55 - 59	28 564	13 462	15 101	27 524	12 915	14 609	1 040	547	492
60 - 64	24 838	11 229	13 609	23 903	10 764	13 139	935	465	470
65 - 69	20 492	9 408	11 084	19 679	9 002	10 677	814	406	407
70 - 74	15 786	7 148	8 638	15 119	6 850	8 269	667	298	369
75 - 79	13 601	6 019	7 582	13 027	5 737	7 291	573	282	291
80 - 84	9 800	4 090	5 710	9 346	3 897	5 449	454	193	261
85 - 89	6 010	2 174	3 836	5 747	2 066	3 681	263	108	154
90 - 94	2 962	895	2 067	2 840	851	1 989	123	44	78
95 - 99	971	241	731	932	228	704	39	12	27
100 +	287	59	228	275	57	218	12	2	10
1 I 2018 (ESDJ)									
Total	368 640	169 594	199 046	...	...	...	...	...	...
0 - 4	17 297	8 702	8 595	...	...	...	...	...	...
5 - 9	20 661	10 461	10 200	...	...	...	...	...	...
10 - 14	23 134	11 676	11 458	...	...	...	...	...	...
15 - 19	23 451	12 065	11 386	...	...	...	...	...	...
20 - 24	16 735	8 585	8 150	...	...	...	...	...	...
25 - 29	17 058	7 869	9 189	...	...	...	...	...	...

7. Population by age, sex and urban/rural residence: latest available year, 2010 - 2019
Population selon l'âge, le sexe et la résidence, urbaine/rurale : dernière année disponible, 2010 - 2019 (continued - suite)

Continent, country or area, date, code[a] and age (in years) / Continent, pays ou zone, date, code[a] et âge (en années)	Total			Urban - Urbaine			Rural - Rurale		
	Both sexes Les deux sexes	Male Masculin	Female Féminin	Both sexes Les deux sexes	Male Masculin	Female Féminin	Both sexes Les deux sexes	Male Masculin	Female Féminin
AMERICA, NORTH - AMÉRIQUE DU NORD									
Martinique									
1 I 2018 (ESDJ)									
30 - 34	17 334	7 425	9 909	...	...	...	...	...	...
35 - 39	17 626	7 403	10 223	...	...	...	...	...	...
40 - 44	21 232	9 096	12 136	...	...	...	...	...	...
45 - 49	28 277	12 468	15 809	...	...	...	...	...	...
50 - 54	32 717	14 630	18 087	...	...	...	...	...	...
55 - 59	30 850	14 331	16 519	...	...	...	...	...	...
60 - 64	26 539	12 242	14 297	...	...	...	...	...	...
65 - 69	22 531	10 284	12 247	...	...	...	...	...	...
70 - 74	17 511	8 026	9 485	...	...	...	...	...	...
75 - 79	13 821	6 070	7 751	...	...	...	...	...	...
80 - 84	10 755	4 548	6 207	...	...	...	...	...	...
85 - 89	6 341	2 418	3 923	...	...	...	...	...	...
90 - 94	3 141	938	2 203	...	...	...	...	...	...
95 - 99	1 199	286	913	...	...	...	...	...	...
100 +	430	71	359	...	...	...	...	...	...
Mexico - Mexique									
12 VI 2010 (CDFC)[39]									
Total	112 336 538	54 855 231	57 481 307	86 287 410	41 946 540	44 340 870	26 049 128	12 908 691	13 140 437
0 - 4	10 528 322	5 346 943	5 181 379	7 766 149	3 945 636	3 820 513	2 762 173	1 401 307	1 360 866
5 - 9	11 047 537	5 604 175	5 443 362	8 124 337	4 124 524	3 999 813	2 923 200	1 479 651	1 443 549
10 - 14	10 939 937	5 547 613	5 392 324	7 974 649	4 041 649	3 933 000	2 965 288	1 505 964	1 459 324
15 - 19	11 026 112	5 520 121	5 505 991	8 191 229	4 097 876	4 093 353	2 834 883	1 422 245	1 412 638
20 - 24	9 892 271	4 813 204	5 079 067	7 725 598	3 775 245	3 950 353	2 166 673	1 037 959	1 128 714
25 - 29	8 788 177	4 205 975	4 582 202	6 985 279	3 354 569	3 630 710	1 802 898	851 406	951 492
30 - 34	8 470 798	4 026 031	4 444 767	6 719 047	3 188 789	3 530 258	1 751 751	837 242	914 509
35 - 39	8 292 987	3 964 738	4 328 249	6 642 253	3 160 713	3 481 540	1 650 734	804 025	846 709
40 - 44	7 009 226	3 350 322	3 658 904	5 633 205	2 676 230	2 956 975	1 376 021	674 092	701 929
45 - 49	5 928 730	2 824 364	3 104 366	4 739 911	2 241 753	2 498 158	1 188 819	582 611	606 208
50 - 54	5 064 291	2 402 451	2 661 840	4 051 487	1 904 317	2 147 170	1 012 804	498 134	514 670
55 - 59	3 895 365	1 869 537	2 025 828	3 043 924	1 443 868	1 600 056	851 441	425 669	425 772
60 - 64	3 116 466	1 476 667	1 639 799	2 403 645	1 119 077	1 284 568	712 821	357 590	355 231
65 - 69	2 317 265	1 095 273	1 221 992	1 719 078	794 137	924 941	598 187	301 136	297 051
70 - 74	1 873 934	873 893	1 000 041	1 338 906	603 945	734 961	535 028	269 948	265 080
75 - 79	1 245 483	579 689	665 794	892 237	399 026	493 211	353 246	180 663	172 583
80 - 84	798 936	355 277	443 659	576 855	244 082	332 773	222 081	111 195	110 886
85 - 89	454 164	197 461	256 703	322 844	132 826	190 018	131 320	64 635	66 685
90 - 94	164 924	68 130	96 794	116 950	45 123	71 827	47 974	23 007	24 967
95 - 99	65 732	25 920	39 812	44 084	16 122	27 962	21 648	9 798	11 850
100 +	18 475	7 228	11 247	10 451	3 753	6 698	8 024	3 475	4 549
Unknown - Inconnu	1 397 406	700 219	697 187	1 265 292	633 280	632 012	132 114	66 939	65 175
1 VII 2019 (ESDJ)[40]									
Total	126 577 691	61 977 632	64 600 059	...	...	...	...	...	...
0	2 152 703	1 096 055	1 056 648	...	...	...	...	...	...
1 - 4	8 739 233	4 447 737	4 291 496	...	...	...	...	...	...
5 - 9	11 063 085	5 630 791	5 432 294	...	...	...	...	...	...
10 - 14	11 143 813	5 671 487	5 472 326	...	...	...	...	...	...
15 - 19	11 060 233	5 610 235	5 449 998	...	...	...	...	...	...
20 - 24	10 860 364	5 474 227	5 386 137	...	...	...	...	...	...
25 - 29	10 579 511	5 270 602	5 308 909	...	...	...	...	...	...
30 - 34	9 753 419	4 733 498	5 019 921	...	...	...	...	...	...
35 - 39	8 862 603	4 186 478	4 676 125	...	...	...	...	...	...
40 - 44	8 295 137	3 891 159	4 403 978	...	...	...	...	...	...
45 - 49	7 734 457	3 672 817	4 061 640	...	...	...	...	...	...
50 - 54	6 721 901	3 207 504	3 514 397	...	...	...	...	...	...
55 - 59	5 675 731	2 700 637	2 975 094	...	...	...	...	...	...
60 - 64	4 523 043	2 135 451	2 387 592	...	...	...	...	...	...
65 - 69	3 355 193	1 563 434	1 791 759	...	...	...	...	...	...
70 - 74	2 416 176	1 106 225	1 309 951	...	...	...	...	...	...
75 - 79	1 666 269	744 542	921 727	...	...	...	...	...	...
80 - 84	1 053 840	456 014	597 826	...	...	...	...	...	...
85 - 89	583 444	243 908	339 536	...	...	...	...	...	...
90 - 94	251 054	101 271	149 783	...	...	...	...	...	...

7. Population by age, sex and urban/rural residence: latest available year, 2010 - 2019
Population selon l'âge, le sexe et la résidence, urbaine/rurale : dernière année disponible, 2010 - 2019 (continued - suite)

Continent, country or area, date, code[a] and age (in years) Continent, pays ou zone, date, code[a] et âge (en annèes)	Total			Urban - Urbaine			Rural - Rurale		
	Both sexes Les deux sexes	Male Masculin	Female Féminin	Both sexes Les deux sexes	Male Masculin	Female Féminin	Both sexes Les deux sexes	Male Masculin	Female Féminin
AMERICA, NORTH - AMÉRIQUE DU NORD									
Mexico - Mexique									
1 VII 2019 (ESDJ)[40]									
95 - 99	73 787	28 733	45 054	...	...	...	...	...	...
100 +	12 695	4 827	7 868	...	...	...	...	...	...
Montserrat[41]									
22 IX 2018 (ESDJ)									
Total	4 649	2 306	2 343	...	...	...	...	...	...
0 - 4	235	113	122	...	...	...	...	...	...
5 - 9	302	144	158	...	...	...	...	...	...
10 - 14	316	156	160	...	...	...	...	...	...
15 - 19	267	130	137	...	...	...	...	...	...
20 - 24	249	142	107	...	...	...	...	...	...
25 - 29	283	140	143	...	...	...	...	...	...
30 - 34	333	152	181	...	...	...	...	...	...
35 - 39	290	127	163	...	...	...	...	...	...
40 - 44	321	148	173	...	...	...	...	...	...
45 - 49	339	156	183	...	...	...	...	...	...
50 - 54	362	183	179	...	...	...	...	...	...
55 - 59	321	163	158	...	...	...	...	...	...
60 - 64	291	166	125	...	...	...	...	...	...
65 - 69	237	145	92	...	...	...	...	...	...
70 - 74	212	108	104	...	...	...	...	...	...
75 - 79	118	63	55	...	...	...	...	...	...
80 - 84	84	40	44	...	...	...	...	...	...
85 +	89	30	59	...	...	...	...	...	...
Nicaragua									
1 VII 2019 (ESDJ)									
Total	*6 527 691*	*3 220 940*	*3 306 751*	*3 817 763*	*1 839 908*	*1 977 855*	*2 709 928*	*1 381 032*	*1 328 896*
0 - 4	*667 913*	*341 298*	*326 615*	*328 370*	*170 693*	*157 677*	*339 543*	*170 605*	*168 938*
5 - 9	*677 247*	*345 824*	*331 423*	*353 839*	*181 640*	*172 199*	*323 408*	*164 184*	*159 224*
10 - 14	*656 735*	*334 723*	*322 012*	*358 451*	*182 185*	*176 266*	*298 284*	*152 538*	*145 746*
15 - 19	*616 738*	*313 589*	*303 149*	*340 141*	*170 580*	*169 561*	*276 597*	*143 009*	*133 588*
20 - 24	*613 537*	*309 280*	*304 257*	*353 785*	*172 922*	*180 863*	*259 752*	*136 358*	*123 394*
25 - 29	*590 804*	*292 347*	*298 457*	*351 657*	*168 682*	*182 975*	*239 147*	*123 665*	*115 482*
30 - 34	*514 972*	*251 175*	*263 797*	*314 911*	*148 513*	*166 398*	*200 061*	*102 662*	*97 399*
35 - 39	*467 743*	*224 949*	*242 794*	*296 452*	*136 233*	*160 219*	*171 291*	*88 716*	*82 575*
40 - 44	*383 432*	*180 105*	*203 327*	*249 876*	*115 946*	*133 930*	*133 556*	*64 159*	*69 397*
45 - 49	*311 958*	*147 517*	*164 441*	*204 316*	*95 743*	*108 573*	*107 642*	*51 774*	*55 868*
50 - 54	*257 225*	*122 759*	*134 466*	*167 033*	*77 227*	*89 806*	*90 192*	*45 532*	*44 660*
55 - 59	*223 055*	*105 610*	*117 445*	*145 126*	*65 647*	*79 479*	*77 929*	*39 963*	*37 966*
60 - 64	*190 381*	*88 973*	*101 408*	*122 634*	*54 950*	*67 684*	*67 747*	*34 023*	*33 724*
65 - 69	*136 846*	*64 122*	*72 724*	*87 522*	*38 879*	*48 643*	*49 324*	*25 243*	*24 081*
70 - 74	*78 020*	*36 422*	*41 598*	*50 195*	*22 038*	*28 157*	*27 825*	*14 384*	*13 441*
75 - 79	*67 929*	*31 248*	*36 681*	*44 858*	*19 369*	*25 489*	*23 071*	*11 879*	*11 192*
80 +	*73 156*	*30 999*	*42 157*	*48 597*	*18 661*	*29 936*	*24 559*	*12 338*	*12 221*
Panama[13]									
1 VII 2019 (ESDF)									
Total	4 218 808	2 115 458	2 103 350	2 965 759	1 459 649	1 506 110	1 253 049	655 809	597 240
0	74 183	37 915	36 268	46 561	23 824	22 737	27 622	14 091	13 531
1 - 4	295 813	151 131	144 682	184 907	94 589	90 318	110 906	56 542	54 364
5 - 9	367 710	187 796	179 914	231 430	118 262	113 168	136 280	69 534	66 746
10 - 14	363 266	185 416	177 850	228 349	116 094	112 255	134 917	69 322	65 595
15 - 19	359 157	183 074	176 083	231 879	116 708	115 171	127 278	66 366	60 912
20 - 24	342 939	174 159	168 780	237 207	118 717	118 490	105 732	55 442	50 290
25 - 29	321 839	162 533	159 306	223 359	110 803	112 556	98 480	51 730	46 750
30 - 34	310 632	156 412	154 220	225 254	111 291	113 963	85 378	45 121	40 257
35 - 39	297 232	149 725	147 507	225 327	111 972	113 355	71 905	37 753	34 152
40 - 44	284 199	142 835	141 364	224 196	111 219	112 977	60 003	31 616	28 387
45 - 49	265 049	132 530	132 519	209 506	102 556	106 950	55 543	29 974	25 569
50 - 54	230 756	114 708	116 048	182 685	88 859	93 826	48 071	25 849	22 222
55 - 59	195 779	96 489	99 290	151 729	72 934	78 795	44 050	23 555	20 495
60 - 64	155 052	75 497	79 555	116 170	54 265	61 905	38 882	21 232	17 650
65 - 69	118 700	56 953	61 747	84 145	38 339	45 806	34 555	18 614	15 941
70 - 74	88 880	41 974	46 906	60 586	26 737	33 849	28 294	15 237	13 057

7. Population by age, sex and urban/rural residence: latest available year, 2010 - 2019
Population selon l'âge, le sexe et la résidence, urbaine/rurale : dernière année disponible, 2010 - 2019 (continued - suite)

Continent, country or area, date, code[a] and age (in years) / Continent, pays ou zone, date, code[a] et âge (en années)	Total			Urban - Urbaine			Rural - Rurale		
	Both sexes Les deux sexes	Male Masculin	Female Féminin	Both sexes Les deux sexes	Male Masculin	Female Féminin	Both sexes Les deux sexes	Male Masculin	Female Féminin
AMERICA, NORTH - AMÉRIQUE DU NORD									
Panama[13]									
1 VII 2019 (ESDF)									
75 - 79	64 065	29 630	34 435	42 925	18 544	24 381	21 140	11 086	10 054
80 - 84	42 357	19 074	23 283	29 422	12 075	17 347	12 935	6 999	5 936
85 +	41 200	17 607	23 593	30 122	11 861	18 261	11 078	5 746	5 332
85 - 89	24 542	10 692	13 850	...	...	...	...	...	...
90 - 94	11 699	4 914	6 785	...	...	...	...	...	...
95 - 99	4 143	1 678	2 465	...	...	...	...	...	...
100 +	816	323	493	...	...	...	...	...	...
Puerto Rico - Porto Rico[42]									
1 VII 2018 (ESDJ)									
Total	3 195 153	1 518 043	1 677 110	...	...	...	...	...	...
0	22 637	11 649	10 988	...	...	...	...	...	...
1 - 4	103 984	53 070	50 914	...	...	...	...	...	...
5 - 9	163 105	82 505	80 600	...	...	...	...	...	...
10 - 14	184 834	94 142	90 692	...	...	...	...	...	...
15 - 19	205 289	105 006	100 283	...	...	...	...	...	...
20 - 24	218 348	110 620	107 728	...	...	...	...	...	...
25 - 29	215 642	107 461	108 181	...	...	...	...	...	...
30 - 34	179 107	85 917	93 190	...	...	...	...	...	...
35 - 39	193 463	91 276	102 187	...	...	...	...	...	...
40 - 44	199 040	94 230	104 810	...	...	...	...	...	...
45 - 49	205 928	98 017	107 911	...	...	...	...	...	...
50 - 54	216 303	100 503	115 800	...	...	...	...	...	...
55 - 59	218 120	100 331	117 789	...	...	...	...	...	...
60 - 64	208 138	95 438	112 700	...	...	...	...	...	...
65 - 69	188 840	85 428	103 412	...	...	...	...	...	...
70 - 74	172 973	77 819	95 154	...	...	...	...	...	...
75 - 79	126 496	55 804	70 692	...	...	...	...	...	...
80 - 84	86 807	36 884	49 923	...	...	...	...	...	...
85 +	86 099	31 943	54 156	...	...	...	...	...	...
Saint Barthélemy - Saint-Barthélemy									
1 I 2015 (CDJC)									
Total	9 625	5 117	4 508	...	...	...	...	...	...
0	91	46	44	...	...	...	...	...	...
1 - 4	409	215	195	...	...	...	...	...	...
5 - 9	500	270	230	...	...	...	...	...	...
10 - 14	462	241	221	...	...	...	...	...	...
15 - 19	346	177	169	...	...	...	...	...	...
20 - 24	624	309	316	...	...	...	...	...	...
25 - 29	929	505	424	...	...	...	...	...	...
30 - 34	866	467	399	...	...	...	...	...	...
35 - 39	830	430	400	...	...	...	...	...	...
40 - 44	803	425	378	...	...	...	...	...	...
45 - 49	949	563	386	...	...	...	...	...	...
50 - 54	814	459	356	...	...	...	...	...	...
55 - 59	684	384	300	...	...	...	...	...	...
60 - 64	419	219	201	...	...	...	...	...	...
65 - 69	299	152	147	...	...	...	...	...	...
70 - 74	242	116	125	...	...	...	...	...	...
75 - 79	160	67	93	...	...	...	...	...	...
80 - 84	118	43	75	...	...	...	...	...	...
85 - 89	48	18	30	...	...	...	...	...	...
90 - 94	26	11	15	...	...	...	...	...	...
95 - 99	5	-	5	...	...	...	...	...	...
100 +	-	-	-	...	...	...	...	...	...
Saint Kitts and Nevis - Saint-Kitts-et-Nevis									
15 V 2011 (CDFC)									
Total	47 195	23 012	24 183	...	...	...	...	...	...
0 - 4	3 108	1 512	1 596	...	...	...	...	...	...
5 - 9	3 472	1 698	1 774	...	...	...	...	...	...
10 - 14	4 111	2 048	2 063	...	...	...	...	...	...

Continent, country or area, date, code[a] and age (in years) / Continent, pays ou zone, date, code[a] et âge (en annèes)	Total			Urban - Urbaine			Rural - Rurale		
	Both sexes Les deux sexes	Male Masculin	Female Féminin	Both sexes Les deux sexes	Male Masculin	Female Féminin	Both sexes Les deux sexes	Male Masculin	Female Féminin
AMERICA, NORTH - AMÉRIQUE DU NORD									
Saint Kitts and Nevis - Saint-Kitts-et-Nevis									
15 V 2011 (CDFC)									
15 - 19	3 827	1 883	1 944	...	...	...	...	...	...
20 - 24	4 086	2 042	2 044	...	...	...	...	...	...
25 - 29	4 014	1 880	2 134	...	...	...	...	...	...
30 - 34	3 649	1 745	1 904	...	...	...	...	...	...
35 - 39	3 580	1 788	1 792	...	...	...	...	...	...
40 - 44	3 268	1 657	1 611	...	...	...	...	...	...
45 - 49	3 378	1 693	1 685	...	...	...	...	...	...
50 - 54	3 330	1 593	1 737	...	...	...	...	...	...
55 - 59	2 365	1 211	1 154	...	...	...	...	...	...
60 - 64	1 346	690	656	...	...	...	...	...	...
65 - 69	1 061	496	565	...	...	...	...	...	...
70 +	2 600	1 076	1 524	...	...	...	...	...	...
Saint Lucia - Sainte-Lucie									
1 VII 2018 (ESDF)									
Total	178 696	88 693	90 002	...	...	...	...	...	...
0 - 4	10 539	5 340	5 199	...	...	...	...	...	...
5 - 9	10 728	5 492	5 236	...	...	...	...	...	...
10 - 14	11 854	6 058	5 796	...	...	...	...	...	...
15 - 19	13 206	6 674	6 531	...	...	...	...	...	...
20 - 24	15 092	7 654	7 438	...	...	...	...	...	...
25 - 29	15 357	7 748	7 609	...	...	...	...	...	...
30 - 34	14 776	7 300	7 477	...	...	...	...	...	...
35 - 39	13 842	6 956	6 885	...	...	...	...	...	...
40 - 44	12 946	6 555	6 391	...	...	...	...	...	...
45 - 49	12 754	6 368	6 385	...	...	...	...	...	...
50 - 54	12 166	6 051	6 114	...	...	...	...	...	...
55 - 59	10 638	5 319	5 319	...	...	...	...	...	...
60 - 64	8 054	3 927	4 127	...	...	...	...	...	...
65 - 69	5 834	2 784	3 050	...	...	...	...	...	...
70 - 74	4 358	1 977	2 381	...	...	...	...	...	...
75 - 79	3 090	1 319	1 771	...	...	...	...	...	...
80 +	3 461	1 170	2 291	...	...	...	...	...	...
Saint Pierre and Miquelon - Saint Pierre-et-Miquelon									
1 I 2015 (CDJC)									
Total	6 021	2 940	3 081	...	...	...	...	...	...
0 - 4	315	142	172	...	...	...	...	...	...
5 - 9	392	200	191	...	...	...	...	...	...
10 - 14	392	197	194	...	...	...	...	...	...
15 - 19	335	174	160	...	...	...	...	...	...
20 - 24	205	117	88	...	...	...	...	...	...
25 - 29	271	140	131	...	...	...	...	...	...
30 - 34	378	172	205	...	...	...	...	...	...
35 - 39	390	188	201	...	...	...	...	...	...
40 - 44	452	219	233	...	...	...	...	...	...
45 - 49	567	281	286	...	...	...	...	...	...
50 - 54	531	273	258	...	...	...	...	...	...
55 - 59	450	233	217	...	...	...	...	...	...
60 - 64	377	198	179	...	...	...	...	...	...
65 - 69	301	138	163	...	...	...	...	...	...
70 - 74	214	101	112	...	...	...	...	...	...
75 - 79	195	92	102	...	...	...	...	...	...
80 - 84	134	38	96	...	...	...	...	...	...
85 - 89	78	24	54	...	...	...	...	...	...
90 - 94	32	8	25	...	...	...	...	...	...
95 - 99	11	3	8	...	...	...	...	...	...
100 +	1	-	1	...	...	...	...	...	...

7. Population by age, sex and urban/rural residence: latest available year, 2010 - 2019
Population selon l'âge, le sexe et la résidence, urbaine/rurale : dernière année disponible, 2010 - 2019 (continued - suite)

Continent, country or area, date, code[a] and age (in years) / Continent, pays ou zone, date, code[a] et âge (en années)	Total			Urban - Urbaine			Rural - Rurale		
	Both sexes Les deux sexes	Male Masculin	Female Féminin	Both sexes Les deux sexes	Male Masculin	Female Féminin	Both sexes Les deux sexes	Male Masculin	Female Féminin
AMERICA, NORTH - AMÉRIQUE DU NORD									
Saint Vincent and the Grenadines - Saint-Vincent-et-les Grenadines									
1 VII 2019 (ESDJ)									
Total	110 608	56 735	53 872	...	...	...	...	...	...
0	1 585	800	785	...	...	...	...	...	...
1 - 4	7 171	3 606	3 565	...	...	...	...	...	...
5 - 9	8 630	4 400	4 230	...	...	...	...	...	...
10 - 14	9 888	5 149	4 739	...	...	...	...	...	...
15 - 19	10 041	5 161	4 880	...	...	...	...	...	...
20 - 24	8 718	4 447	4 272	...	...	...	...	...	...
25 - 29	8 425	4 318	4 107	...	...	...	...	...	...
30 - 34	7 963	3 970	3 993	...	...	...	...	...	...
35 - 39	7 651	3 921	3 730	...	...	...	...	...	...
40 - 44	7 250	3 852	3 398	...	...	...	...	...	...
45 - 49	7 564	3 943	3 621	...	...	...	...	...	...
50 - 54	6 635	3 509	3 126	...	...	...	...	...	...
55 - 59	5 098	2 698	2 399	...	...	...	...	...	...
60 - 64	3 871	2 012	1 859	...	...	...	...	...	...
65 - 69	2 878	1 488	1 390	...	...	...	...	...	...
70 - 74	2 569	1 309	1 260	...	...	...	...	...	...
75 - 79	2 003	984	1 019	...	...	...	...	...	...
80 - 84	1 461	677	783	...	...	...	...	...	...
85 +	1 205	490	715	...	...	...	...	...	...
Saint-Martin (French part) - Saint-Martin (partie française)									
1 VII 2018 (ESDJ)									
Total	35 457	17 151	18 306	...	...	...	...	...	...
0	377	193	184	...	...	...	...	...	...
1 - 4	1 600	816	784	...	...	...	...	...	...
5 - 9	2 178	1 114	1 064	...	...	...	...	...	...
10 - 14	2 200	1 125	1 075	...	...	...	...	...	...
15 - 19	2 184	1 119	1 065	...	...	...	...	...	...
20 - 24	1 979	1 000	979	...	...	...	...	...	...
25 - 29	2 029	1 003	1 026	...	...	...	...	...	...
30 - 34	2 144	1 045	1 099	...	...	...	...	...	...
35 - 39	2 240	1 095	1 145	...	...	...	...	...	...
40 - 44	2 203	1 087	1 116	...	...	...	...	...	...
45 - 49	2 415	1 194	1 221	...	...	...	...	...	...
50 - 54	2 384	1 170	1 214	...	...	...	...	...	...
55 - 59	2 294	1 112	1 182	...	...	...	...	...	...
60 - 64	2 166	1 033	1 133	...	...	...	...	...	...
65 - 69	2 093	988	1 105	...	...	...	...	...	...
70 - 74	1 677	778	899	...	...	...	...	...	...
75 - 79	1 151	510	641	...	...	...	...	...	...
80 - 84	991	401	590	...	...	...	...	...	...
85 - 89	710	248	462	...	...	...	...	...	...
90 - 94	338	97	241	...	...	...	...	...	...
95 +	104	23	81	...	...	...	...	...	...
Sint Maarten (Dutch part) - Saint-Martin (partie néerlandaise)									
1 I 2018 (ESDF)									
Total	40 614	19 759	20 855	...	...	...	...	...	...
0 - 4	2 614	1 349	1 265	...	...	...	...	...	...
5 - 9	2 773	1 437	1 336	...	...	...	...	...	...
10 - 14	2 741	1 387	1 354	...	...	...	...	...	...
15 - 19	2 721	1 360	1 361	...	...	...	...	...	...
20 - 24	2 165	1 139	1 025	...	...	...	...	...	...
25 - 29	2 466	1 142	1 324	...	...	...	...	...	...
30 - 34	3 083	1 432	1 651	...	...	...	...	...	...
35 - 39	3 342	1 510	1 832	...	...	...	...	...	...

7. Population by age, sex and urban/rural residence: latest available year, 2010 - 2019
Population selon l'âge, le sexe et la résidence, urbaine/rurale : dernière année disponible, 2010 - 2019 (continued - suite)

Continent, country or area, date, code[a] and age (in years) / Continent, pays ou zone, date, code[a] et âge (en années)	Total			Urban - Urbaine			Rural - Rurale		
	Both sexes Les deux sexes	Male Masculin	Female Féminin	Both sexes Les deux sexes	Male Masculin	Female Féminin	Both sexes Les deux sexes	Male Masculin	Female Féminin
AMERICA, NORTH - AMÉRIQUE DU NORD									
Sint Maarten (Dutch part) - Saint-Martin (partie néerlandaise)									
1 I 2018 (ESDF)									
40 - 44	3 546	1 651	1 895	...	...	...	...	...	...
45 - 49	3 471	1 665	1 806	...	...	...	...	...	...
50 - 54	3 446	1 727	1 719	...	...	...	...	...	...
55 - 59	2 795	1 348	1 447	...	...	...	...	...	...
60 - 64	2 223	1 091	1 132	...	...	...	...	...	...
65 - 69	1 573	759	813	...	...	...	...	...	...
70 - 74	881	431	450	...	...	...	...	...	...
75 - 79	430	207	223	...	...	...	...	...	...
80 - 84	217	93	125	...	...	...	...	...	...
85 - 89	79	18	61	...	...	...	...	...	...
90 +	47	11	36	...	...	...	...	...	...
Trinidad and Tobago - Trinité-et-Tobago[4]									
1 VII 2019 (ESDJ)									
Total	1 363 985	684 350	679 635	...	...	...	...	...	...
0	17 223	8 868	8 355	...	...	...	...	...	...
1 - 4	79 447	40 275	39 172	...	...	...	...	...	...
5 - 9	93 804	47 635	46 169	...	...	...	...	...	...
10 - 14	90 345	46 170	44 175	...	...	...	...	...	...
15 - 19	101 043	51 055	49 988	...	...	...	...	...	...
20 - 24	117 334	58 962	58 372	...	...	...	...	...	...
25 - 29	126 863	63 954	62 909	...	...	...	...	...	...
30 - 34	108 439	55 357	53 083	...	...	...	...	...	...
35 - 39	95 045	48 131	46 914	...	...	...	...	...	...
40 - 44	88 497	44 669	43 828	...	...	...	...	...	...
45 - 49	98 717	50 004	48 713	...	...	...	...	...	...
50 - 54	89 545	45 172	44 373	...	...	...	...	...	...
55 - 59	75 198	37 713	37 484	...	...	...	...	...	...
60 - 64	60 235	30 448	29 787	...	...	...	...	...	...
65 - 69	45 847	22 168	23 679	...	...	...	...	...	...
70 - 74	31 108	14 594	16 514	...	...	...	...	...	...
75 - 79	21 311	9 537	11 773	...	...	...	...	...	...
80 +	23 982	9 638	14 344	...	...	...	...	...	...
Turks and Caicos Islands - Îles Turques et Caïques									
1 VII 2017 (ESDJ)									
Total	*39 792*	*20 296*	*19 496*	...	...	...	...	...	...
0 - 4	*2 824*	*1 426*	*1 398*	...	...	...	...	...	...
5 - 9	*2 499*	*1 270*	*1 229*	...	...	...	...	...	...
10 - 14	*2 303*	*1 146*	*1 157*	...	...	...	...	...	...
15 - 19	*2 266*	*1 111*	*1 155*	...	...	...	...	...	...
20 - 24	*2 671*	*1 306*	*1 365*	...	...	...	...	...	...
25 - 29	*3 232*	*1 582*	*1 650*	...	...	...	...	...	...
30 - 34	*3 774*	*1 889*	*1 885*	...	...	...	...	...	...
35 - 39	*4 388*	*2 248*	*2 140*	...	...	...	...	...	...
40 - 44	*4 172*	*2 162*	*2 010*	...	...	...	...	...	...
45 - 49	*3 718*	*1 948*	*1 770*	...	...	...	...	...	...
50 - 54	*2 949*	*1 553*	*1 396*	...	...	...	...	...	...
55 - 59	*1 983*	*1 050*	*933*	...	...	...	...	...	...
60 - 64	*1 366*	*730*	*636*	...	...	...	...	...	...
65 - 69	*820*	*445*	*375*	...	...	...	...	...	...
70 - 74	*471*	*258*	*213*	...	...	...	...	...	...
75 - 79	*206*	*112*	*94*	...	...	...	...	...	...
80 +	*150*	*60*	*90*	...	...	...	...	...	...
United States of America - États-Unis d'Amérique									
1 IV 2010 (CDJC)									
Total	308 745 538	151 781 326	156 964 212	249 253 271	121 698 595	127 554 676	59 492 267	30 082 731	29 409 536
0 - 4	20 201 362	10 319 427	9 881 935	16 838 001	8 597 234	8 240 767	3 363 361	1 722 193	1 641 168
5 - 9	20 348 657	10 389 638	9 959 019	16 597 127	8 464 939	8 132 188	3 751 530	1 924 699	1 826 831

7. Population by age, sex and urban/rural residence: latest available year, 2010 - 2019
Population selon l'âge, le sexe et la résidence, urbaine/rurale : dernière année disponible, 2010 - 2019 (continued - suite)

Continent, country or area, date, code[a] and age (in years) / Continent, pays ou zone, date, code[a] et âge (en annèes)	Total			Urban - Urbaine			Rural - Rurale		
	Both sexes Les deux sexes	Male Masculin	Female Féminin	Both sexes Les deux sexes	Male Masculin	Female Féminin	Both sexes Les deux sexes	Male Masculin	Female Féminin
AMERICA, NORTH - AMÉRIQUE DU NORD									
United States of America - États-Unis d'Amérique									
1 IV 2010 (CDJC)									
10 - 14	20 677 194	10 579 862	10 097 332	16 576 171	8 466 809	8 109 362	4 101 023	2 113 053	1 987 970
15 - 19	22 040 343	11 303 666	10 736 677	17 946 265	9 149 187	8 797 078	4 094 078	2 154 479	1 939 599
20 - 24	21 585 999	11 014 176	10 571 823	18 653 468	9 450 066	9 203 402	2 932 531	1 564 110	1 368 421
25 - 29	21 101 849	10 635 591	10 466 258	18 163 244	9 110 029	9 053 215	2 938 605	1 525 562	1 413 043
30 - 34	19 962 099	9 996 500	9 965 599	16 857 801	8 409 694	8 448 107	3 104 298	1 586 806	1 517 492
35 - 39	20 179 642	10 042 022	10 137 620	16 629 937	8 249 301	8 380 636	3 549 705	1 792 721	1 756 984
40 - 44	20 890 964	10 393 977	10 496 987	16 837 761	8 347 894	8 489 867	4 053 203	2 046 083	2 007 120
45 - 49	22 708 591	11 209 085	11 499 506	17 847 074	8 760 812	9 086 262	4 861 517	2 448 273	2 413 244
50 - 54	22 298 125	10 933 274	11 364 851	17 279 058	8 401 091	8 877 967	5 019 067	2 532 183	2 486 884
55 - 59	19 664 805	9 523 648	10 141 157	15 060 179	7 204 444	7 855 735	4 604 626	2 319 204	2 285 422
60 - 64	16 817 924	8 077 500	8 740 424	12 750 365	6 020 393	6 729 972	4 067 559	2 057 107	2 010 452
65 - 69	12 435 263	5 852 547	6 582 716	9 299 030	4 275 616	5 023 414	3 136 233	1 576 931	1 559 302
70 - 74	9 278 166	4 243 972	5 034 194	7 011 129	3 115 814	3 895 315	2 267 037	1 128 158	1 138 879
75 - 79	7 317 795	3 182 388	4 135 407	5 693 807	2 409 946	3 283 861	1 623 988	772 442	851 546
80 - 84	5 743 327	2 294 374	3 448 953	4 629 581	1 800 531	2 829 050	1 113 746	493 843	619 903
85 - 89	3 620 459	1 273 867	2 346 592	3 005 285	1 036 583	1 968 702	615 174	237 284	377 890
90 - 94	1 448 366	424 387	1 023 979	1 216 647	351 491	865 156	231 719	72 896	158 823
95 - 99	371 244	82 263	288 981	315 589	69 008	246 581	55 655	13 255	42 400
100 +	53 364	9 162	44 202	45 752	7 713	38 039	7 612	1 449	6 163
1 VII 2018 (ESDJ)[43]									
Total	327 167 434	161 128 679	166 038 755	...	...	...	...	...	...
0	3 848 208	1 968 505	1 879 703	...	...	...	...	...	...
1 - 4	15 962 067	8 163 697	7 798 370	...	...	...	...	...	...
5 - 9	20 195 642	10 315 990	9 879 652	...	...	...	...	...	...
10 - 14	20 879 527	10 658 840	10 220 687	...	...	...	...	...	...
15 - 19	21 097 221	10 774 908	10 322 313	...	...	...	...	...	...
20 - 24	21 873 579	11 201 547	10 672 032	...	...	...	...	...	...
25 - 29	23 561 756	12 018 838	11 542 918	...	...	...	...	...	...
30 - 34	22 136 018	11 191 871	10 944 147	...	...	...	...	...	...
35 - 39	21 563 587	10 790 190	10 773 397	...	...	...	...	...	...
40 - 44	19 714 301	9 797 410	9 916 891	...	...	...	...	...	...
45 - 49	20 747 135	10 263 995	10 483 140	...	...	...	...	...	...
50 - 54	20 884 564	10 277 207	10 607 357	...	...	...	...	...	...
55 - 59	21 940 985	10 669 327	11 271 658	...	...	...	...	...	...
60 - 64	20 331 651	9 729 536	10 602 115	...	...	...	...	...	...
65 - 69	17 086 893	8 034 813	9 052 080	...	...	...	...	...	...
70 - 74	13 405 423	6 211 272	7 194 151	...	...	...	...	...	...
75 - 79	9 267 066	4 144 674	5 122 392	...	...	...	...	...	...
80 - 84	6 127 308	2 590 366	3 536 942	...	...	...	...	...	...
85 - 89	3 898 995	1 496 255	2 402 740	...	...	...	...	...	...
90 - 94	1 958 772	646 642	1 312 130	...	...	...	...	...	...
95 - 99	592 809	162 814	429 995	...	...	...	...	...	...
100 +	93 927	19 982	73 945	...	...	...	...	...	...
United States Virgin Islands - Îles Vierges américaines[44]									
1 IV 2010 (CDJC)									
Total	106 405	50 854	55 551	...	...	...	...	...	...
0 - 4	7 500	3 736	3 764	...	...	...	...	...	...
5 - 9	7 150	3 694	3 456	...	...	...	...	...	...
10 - 14	7 484	3 849	3 635	...	...	...	...	...	...
15 - 19	7 560	3 765	3 795	...	...	...	...	...	...
20 - 24	5 894	2 707	3 187	...	...	...	...	...	...
25 - 29	5 969	2 695	3 274	...	...	...	...	...	...
30 - 34	6 137	2 825	3 312	...	...	...	...	...	...
35 - 39	6 675	3 133	3 542	...	...	...	...	...	...
40 - 44	7 450	3 506	3 944	...	...	...	...	...	...
45 - 49	7 743	3 680	4 063	...	...	...	...	...	...
50 - 54	7 900	3 800	4 100	...	...	...	...	...	...
55 - 59	7 192	3 341	3 851	...	...	...	...	...	...
60 - 64	7 367	3 510	3 857	...	...	...	...	...	...
65 - 69	5 853	2 883	2 970	...	...	...	...	...	...

Continent, country or area, date, code[a] and age (in years) / Continent, pays ou zone, date, code[a] et âge (en annèes)	Total			Urban - Urbaine			Rural - Rurale		
	Both sexes Les deux sexes	Male Masculin	Female Féminin	Both sexes Les deux sexes	Male Masculin	Female Féminin	Both sexes Les deux sexes	Male Masculin	Female Féminin
AMERICA, NORTH - AMÉRIQUE DU NORD									
United States Virgin Islands - Îles Vierges américaines[44]									
1 IV 2010 (CDJC)									
70 - 74	3 717	1 739	1 978	...	...	...	...	...	...
75 - 79	2 328	1 043	1 285	...	...	...	...	...	...
80 - 84	1 332	568	764	...	...	...	...	...	...
85 +	1 154	380	774	...	...	...	...	...	...
AMERICA, SOUTH - AMÉRIQUE DU SUD									
Argentina - Argentine[13]									
1 VII 2019 (ESDF)									
Total	44 938 712	22 050 332	22 888 380	41 317 551	20 125 215	21 192 336	3 621 161	1 925 117	1 696 044
0 - 4	3 726 162	1 917 283	1 808 879	3 353 779	1 724 639	1 629 140	372 383	192 644	179 739
0	740 709	381 186	359 523	...	...	...	...	...	...
1 - 4	2 985 453	1 536 097	1 449 356	...	...	...	...	...	...
5 - 9	3 743 931	1 926 816	1 817 115	3 369 490	1 730 604	1 638 886	374 441	196 212	178 229
10 - 14	3 542 513	1 821 015	1 721 498	3 218 541	1 650 364	1 568 177	323 972	170 651	153 321
15 - 19	3 508 965	1 791 833	1 717 132	3 200 146	1 628 790	1 571 356	308 819	163 043	145 776
20 - 24	3 548 389	1 797 945	1 750 444	3 208 449	1 615 163	1 593 286	339 940	182 782	157 158
25 - 29	3 522 333	1 768 349	1 753 984	3 229 000	1 607 556	1 621 444	293 333	160 793	132 540
30 - 34	3 287 553	1 636 833	1 650 720	3 056 715	1 513 163	1 543 552	230 838	123 670	107 168
35 - 39	3 141 871	1 556 369	1 585 502	2 926 659	1 446 581	1 480 078	215 212	109 788	105 424
40 - 44	3 027 334	1 491 146	1 536 188	2 827 240	1 387 782	1 439 458	200 094	103 364	96 730
45 - 49	2 579 461	1 261 819	1 317 642	2 403 765	1 167 221	1 236 544	175 696	94 598	81 098
50 - 54	2 241 959	1 087 301	1 154 658	2 085 431	999 721	1 085 710	156 528	87 580	68 948
55 - 59	2 084 864	998 296	1 086 568	1 939 569	916 797	1 022 772	145 295	81 499	63 796
60 - 64	1 879 409	883 685	995 724	1 746 432	809 633	936 799	132 977	74 052	58 925
65 - 69	1 631 170	745 973	885 197	1 515 761	682 076	833 685	115 409	63 897	51 512
70 - 74	1 311 495	574 148	737 347	1 219 092	523 347	695 745	92 403	50 801	41 602
75 - 79	945 129	385 901	559 228	878 565	350 588	527 977	66 564	35 313	31 251
80 - 84	627 708	230 624	397 084	585 013	209 704	375 309	42 695	20 920	21 775
85 - 89	364 728	117 216	247 512	341 954	107 567	234 387	22 774	9 649	13 125
90 - 94	166 561	44 963	121 598	157 441	41 826	115 615	9 120	3 137	5 983
95 - 99	48 440	11 155	37 285	46 226	10 540	35 686	2 214	615	1 599
100 +	8 737	1 662	7 075	8 283	1 553	6 730	454	109	345
Bolivia (Plurinational State of) - Bolivie (État plurinational de)[2]									
1 VII 2019 (ESDF)									
Total	*11 469 896*	*5 775 959*	*5 693 937*	*7 998 346*	*3 961 231*	*4 037 115*	*3 471 550*	*1 814 728*	*1 656 822*
0	*242 876*	*123 406*	*119 470*	*163 290*	*82 960*	*80 330*	*79 586*	*40 446*	*39 140*
1 - 4	*969 587*	*492 078*	*477 509*	*653 559*	*331 643*	*321 916*	*316 028*	*160 435*	*155 593*
5 - 9	*1 217 448*	*619 866*	*597 582*	*821 785*	*417 100*	*404 685*	*395 663*	*202 766*	*192 897*
10 - 14	*1 199 514*	*611 530*	*587 984*	*809 214*	*409 604*	*399 610*	*390 300*	*201 926*	*188 374*
15 - 19	*1 129 120*	*575 047*	*554 073*	*777 870*	*391 545*	*386 325*	*351 250*	*183 502*	*167 748*
20 - 24	*1 023 725*	*520 500*	*503 225*	*730 768*	*364 675*	*366 093*	*292 957*	*155 825*	*137 132*
25 - 29	*930 775*	*471 755*	*459 020*	*681 934*	*336 376*	*345 558*	*248 841*	*135 379*	*113 462*
30 - 34	*862 148*	*436 172*	*425 976*	*635 426*	*312 892*	*322 534*	*226 722*	*123 280*	*103 442*
35 - 39	*775 315*	*391 649*	*383 666*	*573 070*	*282 053*	*291 017*	*202 245*	*109 596*	*92 649*
40 - 44	*661 584*	*333 931*	*327 653*	*482 812*	*236 641*	*246 171*	*178 772*	*97 290*	*81 482*
45 - 49	*551 719*	*277 410*	*274 309*	*395 016*	*192 717*	*202 299*	*156 703*	*84 693*	*72 010*
50 - 54	*459 253*	*229 873*	*229 380*	*324 200*	*158 092*	*166 108*	*135 053*	*71 781*	*63 272*
55 - 59	*382 411*	*190 319*	*192 092*	*263 279*	*127 987*	*135 292*	*119 132*	*62 332*	*56 800*
60 - 64	*316 186*	*155 912*	*160 274*	*208 731*	*100 219*	*108 512*	*107 455*	*55 693*	*51 762*
65 - 69	*250 977*	*122 143*	*128 834*	*163 097*	*77 358*	*85 739*	*87 880*	*44 785*	*43 095*
70 - 74	*192 530*	*92 217*	*100 313*	*125 205*	*58 276*	*66 929*	*67 325*	*33 941*	*33 384*
75 - 79	*134 644*	*62 436*	*72 208*	*86 850*	*39 284*	*47 566*	*47 794*	*23 152*	*24 642*
80 - 84	*87 251*	*37 932*	*49 319*	*54 389*	*23 268*	*31 121*	*32 862*	*14 664*	*18 198*
85 - 89	*52 364*	*21 112*	*31 252*	*30 812*	*12 374*	*18 438*	*21 552*	*8 738*	*12 814*
90 - 94	*23 594*	*8 669*	*14 925*	*13 384*	*4 999*	*8 385*	*10 210*	*3 670*	*6 540*
95 +	*6 875*	*2 002*	*4 873*	*3 655*	*1 168*	*2 487*	*3 220*	*834*	*2 386*

7. Population by age, sex and urban/rural residence: latest available year, 2010 - 2019
Population selon l'âge, le sexe et la résidence, urbaine/rurale : dernière année disponible, 2010 - 2019 (continued - suite)

Continent, country or area, date, code[a] and age (in years) / Continent, pays ou zone, date, code[a] et âge (en annèes)	Total			Urban - Urbaine			Rural - Rurale		
	Both sexes Les deux sexes	Male Masculin	Female Féminin	Both sexes Les deux sexes	Male Masculin	Female Féminin	Both sexes Les deux sexes	Male Masculin	Female Féminin
AMERICA, SOUTH - AMÉRIQUE DU SUD									
Brazil - Brésil									
31 VII 2010 (CDJC)									
Total	190 755 799	93 406 990	97 348 809	160 925 804	77 710 179	83 215 625	29 829 995	15 696 811	14 133 184
0	2 713 244	1 378 532	1 334 712	2 246 034	1 141 784	1 104 250	467 210	236 748	230 462
1 - 4	11 082 914	5 638 455	5 444 459	9 055 114	4 603 340	4 451 774	2 027 800	1 035 115	992 685
5 - 9	14 969 375	7 624 144	7 345 231	12 135 285	6 169 531	5 965 754	2 834 090	1 454 613	1 379 477
10 - 14	17 166 761	8 725 413	8 441 348	13 956 987	7 062 057	6 894 930	3 209 774	1 663 356	1 546 418
15 - 19	16 990 872	8 558 868	8 432 004	14 039 001	6 998 102	7 040 899	2 951 871	1 560 766	1 391 105
20 - 24	17 245 192	8 630 229	8 614 963	14 706 068	7 276 963	7 429 105	2 539 124	1 353 266	1 185 858
25 - 29	17 104 414	8 460 995	8 643 419	14 772 957	7 225 732	7 547 225	2 331 457	1 235 263	1 096 194
30 - 34	15 744 512	7 717 658	8 026 854	13 611 921	6 586 877	7 025 044	2 132 591	1 130 781	1 001 810
35 - 39	13 888 579	6 766 664	7 121 915	11 975 407	5 750 498	6 224 909	1 913 172	1 016 166	897 006
40 - 44	13 009 364	6 320 568	6 688 796	11 187 429	5 344 982	5 842 447	1 821 935	975 586	846 349
45 - 49	11 833 352	5 692 014	6 141 338	10 181 394	4 806 322	5 375 072	1 651 958	885 692	766 266
50 - 54	10 140 402	4 834 995	5 305 407	8 708 339	4 074 679	4 633 660	1 432 063	760 316	671 747
55 - 59	8 276 221	3 902 344	4 373 877	7 025 474	3 238 531	3 786 943	1 250 747	663 813	586 934
60 - 64	6 509 120	3 041 035	3 468 085	5 474 944	2 479 882	2 995 062	1 034 176	561 153	473 023
65 - 69	4 840 810	2 224 065	2 616 745	4 040 016	1 792 798	2 247 218	800 794	431 267	369 527
70 - 74	3 741 636	1 667 372	2 074 264	3 142 173	1 349 329	1 792 844	599 463	318 043	281 420
75 - 79	2 563 447	1 090 517	1 472 930	2 174 038	889 908	1 284 130	389 409	200 609	188 800
80 - 84	1 666 972	668 623	998 349	1 423 603	546 865	876 738	243 369	121 758	121 611
85 - 89	819 483	310 759	508 724	695 385	251 112	444 273	124 098	59 647	64 451
90 - 94	326 558	114 964	211 594	273 348	90 960	182 388	53 210	24 004	29 206
95 - 99	98 335	31 529	66 806	81 121	24 365	56 756	17 214	7 164	10 050
100 +	24 236	7 247	16 989	19 766	5 562	14 204	4 470	1 685	2 785
1 VII 2018 (ESDJ)[45]									
Total	*208 494 900*	*101 971 173*	*106 523 727*	...	...	...	...	...	...
0 - 4	*14 787 557*	*7 565 301*	*7 222 256*	...	...	...	...	...	...
5 - 9	*14 537 829*	*7 432 381*	*7 105 448*	...	...	...	...	...	...
10 - 14	*15 182 024*	*7 751 948*	*7 430 076*	...	...	...	...	...	...
15 - 19	*16 439 846*	*8 364 062*	*8 075 784*	...	...	...	...	...	...
20 - 24	*17 294 780*	*8 716 490*	*8 578 290*	...	...	...	...	...	...
25 - 29	*17 068 593*	*8 512 314*	*8 556 279*	...	...	...	...	...	...
30 - 34	*17 296 659*	*8 555 280*	*8 741 379*	...	...	...	...	...	...
35 - 39	*16 661 965*	*8 148 183*	*8 513 782*	...	...	...	...	...	...
40 - 44	*14 879 035*	*7 213 769*	*7 665 266*	...	...	...	...	...	...
45 - 49	*13 281 287*	*6 401 687*	*6 879 600*	...	...	...	...	...	...
50 - 54	*12 293 932*	*5 877 917*	*6 416 015*	...	...	...	...	...	...
55 - 59	*10 746 091*	*5 059 761*	*5 686 330*	...	...	...	...	...	...
60 - 64	*8 797 470*	*4 076 794*	*4 720 676*	...	...	...	...	...	...
65 - 69	*6 823 731*	*3 103 440*	*3 720 291*	...	...	...	...	...	...
70 - 74	*4 938 529*	*2 194 687*	*2 743 842*	...	...	...	...	...	...
75 - 79	*3 376 250*	*1 439 622*	*1 936 628*	...	...	...	...	...	...
80 - 84	*2 191 860*	*881 564*	*1 310 296*	...	...	...	...	...	...
85 - 89	*1 165 517*	*435 871*	*729 646*	...	...	...	...	...	...
90 +	*731 945*	*240 102*	*491 843*	...	...	...	...	...	...
Chile - Chili[46]									
1 VII 2019 (ESDF)									
Total	19 107 216	9 424 139	9 683 077	16 883 696	8 254 179	8 629 517	2 223 520	1 169 960	1 053 560
0	229 927	117 153	112 774	207 125	105 731	101 394	22 802	11 422	11 380
1 - 4	972 249	495 460	476 789	869 868	443 097	426 771	102 381	52 363	50 018
5 - 9	1 275 472	649 322	626 150	1 133 183	576 548	556 635	142 289	72 774	69 515
10 - 14	1 236 524	629 243	607 281	1 089 809	553 479	536 330	146 715	75 764	70 951
15 - 19	1 272 967	647 322	625 645	1 137 472	575 978	561 494	135 495	71 344	64 151
20 - 24	1 446 985	735 379	711 606	1 315 712	666 493	649 219	131 273	68 886	62 387
25 - 29	1 627 783	827 193	800 590	1 483 248	751 862	731 386	144 535	75 331	69 204
30 - 34	1 515 386	769 391	745 995	1 370 573	693 805	676 768	144 813	75 586	69 227
35 - 39	1 396 728	705 386	691 342	1 247 538	626 617	620 921	149 190	78 769	70 421
40 - 44	1 328 559	665 145	663 414	1 170 432	580 376	590 056	158 127	84 769	73 358
45 - 49	1 243 929	616 547	627 382	1 080 292	528 196	552 096	163 637	88 351	75 286
50 - 54	1 218 076	597 164	620 912	1 054 261	507 832	546 429	163 815	89 332	74 483
55 - 59	1 118 091	540 699	577 392	965 892	457 237	508 655	152 199	83 462	68 737
60 - 64	964 318	458 457	505 861	830 884	386 253	444 631	133 434	72 204	61 230
65 - 69	777 714	361 643	416 071	665 433	301 868	363 565	112 281	59 775	52 506

7. Population by age, sex and urban/rural residence: latest available year, 2010 - 2019
Population selon l'âge, le sexe et la résidence, urbaine/rurale : dernière année disponible, 2010 - 2019 (continued - suite)

Continent, country or area, date, code[a] and age (in years) / Continent, pays ou zone, date, code[a] et âge (en années)	Total			Urban - Urbaine			Rural - Rurale		
	Both sexes Les deux sexes	Male Masculin	Female Féminin	Both sexes Les deux sexes	Male Masculin	Female Féminin	Both sexes Les deux sexes	Male Masculin	Female Féminin
AMERICA, SOUTH - AMÉRIQUE DU SUD									
Chile - Chili[46]									
1 VII 2019 (ESDF)									
70 - 74	557 691	251 433	306 258	474 121	207 197	266 924	83 570	44 236	39 334
75 - 79	398 309	168 861	229 448	337 343	137 933	199 410	60 966	30 928	30 038
80 - 84	265 424	103 122	162 302	225 677	83 958	141 719	39 747	19 164	20 583
85 - 89	162 733	56 558	106 175	140 165	46 434	93 731	22 568	10 124	12 444
90 - 94	74 779	22 932	51 847	64 426	18 712	45 714	10 353	4 220	6 133
95 - 99	19 491	4 950	14 541	16 493	3 880	12 613	2 998	1 070	1 928
100 +	4 081	779	3 302	3 749	693	3 056	332	86	246
Colombia - Colombie[47]									
1 VII 2019 (ESDJ)									
Total	*49 395 678*	*24 123 683*	*25 271 995*	*37 425 856*	*17 914 385*	*19 511 471*	*11 969 822*	*6 209 298*	*5 760 524*
0 - 4	*3 881 677*	*1 984 466*	*1 897 211*	*2 719 619*	*1 389 103*	*1 330 516*	*1 162 058*	*595 363*	*566 695*
0	*772 577*	*395 076*	*377 501*	...	...	...	...	...	...
1 - 4	*3 109 100*	*1 589 390*	*1 519 710*	...	...	...	...	...	...
5 - 9	*3 892 552*	*1 989 695*	*1 902 857*	*2 760 055*	*1 406 783*	*1 353 272*	*1 132 497*	*582 912*	*549 585*
10 - 14	*3 963 857*	*2 023 764*	*1 940 093*	*2 860 392*	*1 451 563*	*1 408 829*	*1 103 465*	*572 201*	*531 264*
15 - 19	*4 147 613*	*2 108 467*	*2 039 146*	*3 075 259*	*1 547 994*	*1 527 265*	*1 072 354*	*560 473*	*511 881*
20 - 24	*4 288 225*	*2 158 358*	*2 129 867*	*3 314 817*	*1 649 123*	*1 665 694*	*973 408*	*509 235*	*464 173*
25 - 29	*4 110 539*	*2 043 134*	*2 067 405*	*3 237 445*	*1 592 211*	*1 645 234*	*873 094*	*450 923*	*422 171*
30 - 34	*3 756 775*	*1 845 814*	*1 910 961*	*2 950 833*	*1 434 219*	*1 516 614*	*805 942*	*411 595*	*394 347*
35 - 39	*3 518 923*	*1 707 057*	*1 811 866*	*2 754 743*	*1 315 927*	*1 438 816*	*764 180*	*391 130*	*373 050*
40 - 44	*3 111 716*	*1 486 917*	*1 624 799*	*2 404 717*	*1 122 360*	*1 282 357*	*706 999*	*364 557*	*342 442*
45 - 49	*2 878 746*	*1 355 973*	*1 522 773*	*2 217 012*	*1 012 147*	*1 204 865*	*661 734*	*343 826*	*317 908*
50 - 54	*2 807 802*	*1 309 144*	*1 498 658*	*2 190 505*	*985 927*	*1 204 578*	*617 297*	*323 217*	*294 080*
55 - 59	*2 527 741*	*1 168 829*	*1 358 912*	*1 976 104*	*878 892*	*1 097 212*	*551 637*	*289 937*	*261 700*
60 - 64	*2 058 677*	*945 515*	*1 113 162*	*1 602 585*	*703 737*	*898 848*	*456 092*	*241 778*	*214 314*
65 - 69	*1 574 621*	*719 109*	*855 512*	*1 208 729*	*524 389*	*684 340*	*365 892*	*194 720*	*171 172*
70 - 74	*1 141 402*	*516 047*	*625 355*	*866 661*	*370 530*	*496 131*	*274 741*	*145 517*	*129 224*
75 - 79	*762 819*	*340 699*	*422 120*	*572 828*	*241 056*	*331 772*	*189 991*	*99 643*	*90 348*
80 - 84	*471 859*	*207 990*	*263 869*	*348 987*	*144 268*	*204 719*	*122 872*	*63 722*	*59 150*
85 - 89	*273 226*	*118 417*	*154 809*	*198 809*	*80 282*	*118 527*	*74 417*	*38 135*	*36 282*
90 - 94	*142 815*	*60 704*	*82 111*	*102 783*	*40 433*	*62 350*	*40 032*	*20 271*	*19 761*
95 - 99	*61 480*	*25 278*	*36 202*	*44 450*	*16 893*	*27 557*	*17 030*	*8 385*	*8 645*
100 +	*22 613*	*8 306*	*14 307*	*18 523*	*6 548*	*11 975*	*4 090*	*1 758*	*2 332*
Ecuador - Équateur[48]									
1 VII 2019 (ESDF)									
Total	*17 267 986*	*8 547 067*	*8 720 919*	*11 030 216*	*5 403 496*	*5 626 720*	*6 237 770*	*3 143 571*	*3 094 199*
0	*331 773*	*169 631*	*162 142*	*199 165*	*102 365*	*96 800*	*132 608*	*67 266*	*65 342*
1 - 4	*1 330 131*	*679 889*	*650 242*	*799 923*	*409 792*	*390 131*	*530 208*	*270 097*	*260 111*
5 - 9	*1 681 685*	*859 434*	*822 251*	*1 010 553*	*516 637*	*493 916*	*671 132*	*342 797*	*328 335*
10 - 14	*1 676 222*	*857 229*	*818 993*	*1 019 874*	*520 185*	*499 689*	*656 348*	*337 044*	*319 304*
15 - 19	*1 604 530*	*818 604*	*785 926*	*1 011 190*	*512 462*	*498 728*	*593 340*	*306 142*	*287 198*
20 - 24	*1 496 206*	*757 312*	*738 894*	*978 443*	*490 898*	*487 545*	*517 763*	*266 414*	*251 349*
25 - 29	*1 375 773*	*688 330*	*687 443*	*917 028*	*455 009*	*462 019*	*458 745*	*233 321*	*225 424*
30 - 34	*1 268 169*	*625 888*	*642 281*	*847 303*	*414 513*	*432 790*	*420 866*	*211 375*	*209 491*
35 - 39	*1 169 326*	*567 546*	*601 780*	*781 449*	*374 907*	*406 542*	*387 877*	*192 639*	*195 238*
40 - 44	*1 053 221*	*504 112*	*549 109*	*708 708*	*334 219*	*374 489*	*344 513*	*169 893*	*174 620*
45 - 49	*928 541*	*442 852*	*485 689*	*627 891*	*294 898*	*332 993*	*300 650*	*147 954*	*152 696*
50 - 54	*814 014*	*388 466*	*425 548*	*546 424*	*257 010*	*289 414*	*267 590*	*131 456*	*136 134*
55 - 59	*699 650*	*333 449*	*366 201*	*460 174*	*215 691*	*244 483*	*239 476*	*117 758*	*121 718*
60 - 64	*574 322*	*272 733*	*301 589*	*365 361*	*169 798*	*195 563*	*208 961*	*102 935*	*106 026*
65 - 69	*448 661*	*211 158*	*237 503*	*274 397*	*125 451*	*148 946*	*174 264*	*85 707*	*88 557*
70 - 74	*334 530*	*154 741*	*179 789*	*198 488*	*88 309*	*110 179*	*136 042*	*66 432*	*69 610*
75 - 79	*232 203*	*104 940*	*127 263*	*135 785*	*58 598*	*77 187*	*96 418*	*46 342*	*50 076*
80 - 84	*141 928*	*63 128*	*78 800*	*83 223*	*35 306*	*47 917*	*58 705*	*27 822*	*30 883*
85 - 89	*71 457*	*31 752*	*39 705*	*42 700*	*18 099*	*24 601*	*28 757*	*13 653*	*15 104*
90 - 94	*27 807*	*12 418*	*15 389*	*17 141*	*7 264*	*9 877*	*10 666*	*5 154*	*5 512*
95 - 99	*7 540*	*3 322*	*4 218*	*4 804*	*2 002*	*2 802*	*2 736*	*1 320*	*1 416*
100 +	*297*	*133*	*164*	*192*	*83*	*109*	*105*	*50*	*55*

7. Population by age, sex and urban/rural residence: latest available year, 2010 - 2019
Population selon l'âge, le sexe et la résidence, urbaine/rurale : dernière année disponible, 2010 - 2019 (continued - suite)

Continent, country or area, date, code[a] and age (in years) / Continent, pays ou zone, date, code[a] et âge (en annèes)	Total			Urban - Urbaine			Rural - Rurale		
	Both sexes Les deux sexes	Male Masculin	Female Féminin	Both sexes Les deux sexes	Male Masculin	Female Féminin	Both sexes Les deux sexes	Male Masculin	Female Féminin
AMERICA, SOUTH - AMÉRIQUE DU SUD									
Falkland Islands (Malvinas) - Îles Falkland (Malvinas)[49]									
9 X 2016 (CDJC)									
Total	3 200	1 687[50]	1 511[50]	...	...	...	...	...	...
0 - 4	197	105	92	...	...	...	...	...	...
5 - 9	185	96	89	...	...	...	...	...	...
10 - 14	182	96	86	...	...	...	...	...	...
15 - 19	142	61	81	...	...	...	...	...	...
20 - 24	158	71	87	...	...	...	...	...	...
25 - 29	222	101	121	...	...	...	...	...	...
30 - 34	242	126	116	...	...	...	...	...	...
35 - 39	276	148	128	...	...	...	...	...	...
40 - 44	303	159	144	...	...	...	...	...	...
45 - 49	282	165	117	...	...	...	...	...	...
50 - 54	252	145	107	...	...	...	...	...	...
55 - 59	235	123	112	...	...	...	...	...	...
60 - 64	161	99	62	...	...	...	...	...	...
65 - 69	121	65	56	...	...	...	...	...	...
70 - 74	91	50	41	...	...	...	...	...	...
75 - 79	65	37	28	...	...	...	...	...	...
80 - 84	37	18	19	...	...	...	...	...	...
85 +	36	14	22	...	...	...	...	...	...
Unknown - Inconnu	13	8[50]	3[50]	...	...	...	...	...	...
French Guiana - Guyane française									
1 I 2015 (CDJC)									
Total	259 865	128 973	130 892	224 631	110 366	114 265	35 234	18 606	16 628
0	5 715	2 805	2 910	4 912	2 407	2 505	803	398	405
1 - 4	23 246	11 995	11 251	19 865	10 303	9 562	3 380	1 692	1 688
5 - 9	29 563	15 050	14 512	24 945	12 721	12 224	4 618	2 330	2 288
10 - 14	28 237	14 151	14 085	23 887	11 964	11 923	4 350	2 187	2 163
15 - 19	23 941	12 158	11 784	20 668	10 423	10 245	3 273	1 734	1 539
20 - 24	18 529	8 960	9 569	15 668	7 490	8 177	2 861	1 470	1 392
25 - 29	18 563	8 674	9 890	15 921	7 291	8 630	2 642	1 382	1 259
30 - 34	19 077	9 230	9 846	16 297	7 658	8 639	2 780	1 572	1 207
35 - 39	18 394	9 068	9 326	15 956	7 716	8 240	2 438	1 352	1 086
40 - 44	17 650	8 701	8 949	15 506	7 498	8 009	2 144	1 203	941
45 - 49	14 715	7 357	7 359	13 056	6 400	6 656	1 659	956	703
50 - 54	12 133	6 042	6 091	10 795	5 289	5 507	1 338	754	585
55 - 59	9 951	5 010	4 941	8 961	4 447	4 514	990	562	427
60 - 64	7 749	3 959	3 790	7 048	3 579	3 470	701	381	320
65 - 69	5 038	2 574	2 464	4 512	2 283	2 229	526	291	235
70 - 74	3 066	1 496	1 570	2 747	1 343	1 404	319	153	166
75 - 79	1 859	860	999	1 648	751	897	211	109	102
80 - 84	1 237	479	758	1 107	431	676	129	47	82
85 - 89	723	257	466	677	236	442	46	21	25
90 - 94	356	102	254	335	94	241	20	8	12
95 - 99	100	32	68	95	30	65	5	2	3
100 +	24	13	10	23	12	10	1	1	-
1 I 2018 (ESDJ)									
Total	281 612	139 842	141 770	...	...	...	...	...	...
0 - 4	32 001	16 398	15 603	...	...	...	...	...	...
5 - 9	30 143	15 492	14 651	...	...	...	...	...	...
10 - 14	30 060	15 186	14 874	...	...	...	...	...	...
15 - 19	26 783	13 385	13 398	...	...	...	...	...	...
20 - 24	19 255	9 396	9 859	...	...	...	...	...	...
25 - 29	19 051	9 075	9 976	...	...	...	...	...	...
30 - 34	19 820	9 244	10 576	...	...	...	...	...	...
35 - 39	20 500	9 917	10 583	...	...	...	...	...	...
40 - 44	18 306	9 071	9 235	...	...	...	...	...	...
45 - 49	17 379	8 724	8 655	...	...	...	...	...	...
50 - 54	13 323	6 766	6 557	...	...	...	...	...	...
55 - 59	11 002	5 443	5 559	...	...	...	...	...	...
60 - 64	9 012	4 672	4 340	...	...	...	...	...	...

7. Population by age, sex and urban/rural residence: latest available year, 2010 - 2019
Population selon l'âge, le sexe et la résidence, urbaine/rurale : dernière année disponible, 2010 - 2019 (continued - suite)

Continent, country or area, date, code[a] and age (in years) / Continent, pays ou zone, date, code[a] et âge (en années)	Total			Urban - Urbaine			Rural - Rurale		
	Both sexes Les deux sexes	Male Masculin	Female Féminin	Both sexes Les deux sexes	Male Masculin	Female Féminin	Both sexes Les deux sexes	Male Masculin	Female Féminin
AMERICA, SOUTH - AMÉRIQUE DU SUD									
French Guiana - Guyane française									
1 I 2018 (ESDJ)									
65 - 69	6 208	3 123	3 085	...	...	...	...	...	...
70 - 74	4 019	2 055	1 964	...	...	...	...	...	...
75 - 79	2 046	910	1 136	...	...	...	...	...	...
80 - 84	1 330	544	786	...	...	...	...	...	...
85 - 89	789	283	506	...	...	...	...	...	...
90 - 94	378	95	283	...	...	...	...	...	...
95 +	207	63	144	...	...	...	...	...	...
Guyana									
15 IX 2012 (CDFC)									
Total	746 955	371 805	375 150	...	...	...	...	...	...
0 - 4	70 440	35 876	34 564	...	...	...	...	...	...
5 - 9	71 268	35 954	35 314	...	...	...	...	...	...
10 - 14	83 139	42 302	40 837	...	...	...	...	...	...
15 - 19	84 798	42 749	42 049	...	...	...	...	...	...
20 - 24	63 282	31 350	31 932	...	...	...	...	...	...
25 - 29	52 061	25 487	26 574	...	...	...	...	...	...
30 - 34	53 099	26 103	26 996	...	...	...	...	...	...
35 - 39	51 479	25 457	26 022	...	...	...	...	...	...
40 - 44	47 955	24 212	23 743	...	...	...	...	...	...
45 - 49	43 115	21 573	21 542	...	...	...	...	...	...
50 - 54	37 444	18 878	18 566	...	...	...	...	...	...
55 - 59	29 043	14 045	14 998	...	...	...	...	...	...
60 - 64	21 513	10 479	11 034	...	...	...	...	...	...
65 - 69	13 835	6 638	7 197	...	...	...	...	...	...
70 - 74	10 339	4 817	5 522	...	...	...	...	...	...
75 - 79	6 908	3 037	3 871	...	...	...	...	...	...
80 - 84	4 079	1 714	2 365	...	...	...	...	...	...
85 +	3 158	1 134	2 024	...	...	...	...	...	...
Paraguay[51]									
1 VII 2019 (ESDF)									
Total	*7 152 703*	*3 604 135*	*3 548 568*	*4 444 274*	*2 172 518*	*2 271 757*	*2 708 428*	*1 431 617*	*1 276 811*
0 - 4	*705 443*	*359 910*	*345 533*	*408 580*	*208 677*	*199 903*	*296 863*	*151 233*	*145 630*
5 - 9	*697 710*	*355 582*	*342 128*	*402 075*	*202 279*	*199 796*	*295 634*	*153 303*	*142 331*
10 - 14	*688 660*	*350 586*	*338 074*	*401 610*	*199 747*	*201 864*	*287 049*	*150 840*	*136 210*
15 - 19	*673 810*	*343 008*	*330 802*	*414 200*	*205 051*	*209 149*	*259 610*	*137 957*	*121 653*
20 - 24	*653 159*	*332 667*	*320 491*	*424 749*	*210 218*	*214 530*	*228 410*	*122 449*	*105 961*
25 - 29	*618 331*	*313 892*	*304 439*	*413 951*	*204 124*	*209 827*	*204 380*	*109 768*	*94 612*
30 - 34	*573 132*	*289 843*	*283 290*	*379 843*	*186 337*	*193 506*	*193 289*	*103 506*	*89 784*
35 - 39	*495 579*	*248 483*	*247 095*	*321 629*	*156 045*	*165 585*	*173 950*	*92 439*	*81 511*
40 - 44	*404 880*	*201 219*	*203 661*	*259 440*	*124 379*	*135 061*	*145 441*	*76 840*	*68 601*
45 - 49	*360 060*	*179 344*	*180 716*	*228 252*	*109 379*	*118 873*	*131 809*	*69 965*	*61 843*
50 - 54	*316 826*	*158 119*	*158 707*	*198 985*	*95 246*	*103 739*	*117 841*	*62 872*	*54 969*
55 - 59	*270 811*	*135 739*	*135 072*	*168 197*	*80 434*	*87 763*	*102 614*	*55 305*	*47 309*
60 - 64	*227 286*	*114 889*	*112 397*	*139 583*	*66 882*	*72 702*	*87 702*	*48 007*	*39 695*
65 - 69	*173 649*	*86 873*	*86 776*	*105 581*	*49 595*	*55 986*	*68 068*	*37 278*	*30 790*
70 - 74	*118 435*	*57 895*	*60 540*	*71 605*	*32 508*	*39 098*	*46 830*	*25 387*	*21 443*
75 - 79	*81 021*	*37 988*	*43 033*	*48 885*	*20 971*	*27 913*	*32 137*	*17 017*	*15 120*
80 +	*93 911*	*38 098*	*55 813*	*57 109*	*20 646*	*36 463*	*36 802*	*17 452*	*19 350*
Peru - Pérou									
30 VI 2018 (ESDF)									
Total	*32 162 184*	*16 105 008*	*16 057 176*	*25 156 589*	*12 427 084*	*12 729 505*	*7 005 595*	*3 677 924*	*3 327 671*
0 - 4	*2 817 164*	*1 438 133*	*1 379 031*	*2 019 234*	*1 034 545*	*984 689*	*797 930*	*403 588*	*394 342*
0	*561 564*	*286 966*	*274 598*	...	...	...	...	...	...
1 - 4	*2 255 600*	*1 151 167*	*1 104 433*	...	...	...	...	...	...
5 - 9	*2 871 130*	*1 463 817*	*1 407 313*	*2 084 165*	*1 061 211*	*1 022 954*	*786 965*	*402 606*	*384 359*
10 - 14	*2 913 831*	*1 484 041*	*1 429 790*	*2 145 319*	*1 086 105*	*1 059 214*	*768 512*	*397 936*	*370 576*
15 - 19	*2 886 398*	*1 466 914*	*1 419 484*	*2 203 356*	*1 106 376*	*1 096 980*	*683 042*	*360 538*	*322 504*
20 - 24	*2 839 502*	*1 438 445*	*1 401 057*	*2 275 786*	*1 135 369*	*1 140 417*	*563 716*	*303 076*	*260 640*
25 - 29	*2 738 402*	*1 383 393*	*1 355 009*	*2 207 175*	*1 095 905*	*1 111 270*	*531 227*	*287 488*	*243 739*
30 - 34	*2 528 404*	*1 273 217*	*1 255 187*	*2 010 384*	*991 862*	*1 018 522*	*518 020*	*281 355*	*236 665*
35 - 39	*2 317 407*	*1 164 344*	*1 153 063*	*1 874 116*	*919 732*	*954 384*	*443 291*	*244 612*	*198 679*

Continent, country or area, date, code[a] and age (in years) / Continent, pays ou zone, date, code[a] et âge (en années)	Total			Urban - Urbaine			Rural - Rurale		
	Both sexes Les deux sexes	Male Masculin	Female Féminin	Both sexes Les deux sexes	Male Masculin	Female Féminin	Both sexes Les deux sexes	Male Masculin	Female Féminin
AMERICA, SOUTH - AMÉRIQUE DU SUD									
Peru - Pérou									
30 VI 2018 (ESDF)									
40 - 44	*2 122 547*	*1 063 630*	*1 058 917*	*1 729 525*	*844 325*	*885 200*	*393 022*	*219 305*	*173 717*
45 - 49	*1 843 174*	*919 522*	*923 652*	*1 504 937*	*733 833*	*771 104*	*338 237*	*185 689*	*152 548*
50 - 54	*1 598 842*	*792 702*	*806 140*	*1 325 780*	*647 643*	*678 137*	*273 062*	*145 059*	*128 003*
55 - 59	*1 339 831*	*657 818*	*682 013*	*1 107 375*	*537 269*	*570 106*	*232 456*	*120 549*	*111 907*
60 - 64	*1 067 857*	*517 390*	*550 467*	*859 788*	*412 712*	*447 076*	*208 069*	*104 678*	*103 391*
65 - 69	*827 092*	*394 420*	*432 672*	*657 507*	*311 240*	*346 267*	*169 585*	*83 180*	*86 405*
70 - 74	*603 971*	*281 419*	*322 552*	*475 123*	*219 768*	*255 355*	*128 848*	*61 651*	*67 197*
75 - 79	*426 984*	*191 745*	*235 239*	*335 663*	*148 497*	*187 166*	*91 321*	*43 248*	*48 073*
80 +	*419 648*	*174 058*	*245 590*	*341 356*	*140 692*	*200 664*	*78 292*	*33 366*	*44 926*
30 VI 2019 (ESDF)[52]									
Total	*32 131 400*	*15 938 284*	*16 193 116*	...	...	...	...	...	...
0	*568 862*	*292 202*	*276 660*	...	...	...	...	...	...
1 - 4	*2 211 089*	*1 129 941*	*1 081 148*	...	...	...	...	...	...
5 - 9	*2 635 661*	*1 329 036*	*1 306 625*	...	...	...	...	...	...
10 - 14	*2 751 604*	*1 387 605*	*1 363 999*	...	...	...	...	...	...
15 - 19	*2 479 473*	*1 223 570*	*1 255 903*	...	...	...	...	...	...
20 - 24	*2 702 781*	*1 288 329*	*1 414 452*	...	...	...	...	...	...
25 - 29	*2 667 352*	*1 318 992*	*1 348 360*	...	...	...	...	...	...
30 - 34	*2 522 714*	*1 283 439*	*1 239 275*	...	...	...	...	...	...
35 - 39	*2 385 223*	*1 198 200*	*1 187 023*	...	...	...	...	...	...
40 - 44	*2 183 954*	*1 103 532*	*1 080 422*	...	...	...	...	...	...
45 - 49	*1 884 501*	*923 339*	*961 162*	...	...	...	...	...	...
50 - 54	*1 708 688*	*844 928*	*863 760*	...	...	...	...	...	...
55 - 59	*1 461 243*	*727 864*	*733 379*	...	...	...	...	...	...
60 - 64	*1 167 639*	*563 043*	*604 596*	...	...	...	...	...	...
65 - 69	*966 494*	*466 527*	*499 967*	...	...	...	...	...	...
70 - 74	*711 461*	*350 474*	*360 987*	...	...	...	...	...	...
75 - 79	*509 380*	*239 672*	*269 708*	...	...	...	...	...	...
80 +	*613 281*	*267 591*	*345 690*	...	...	...	...	...	...
Suriname									
1 VII 2018 (ESDJ)									
Total	590 100	294 200	295 900	391 200	193 100	198 100	198 900	101 100	97 800
0	9 809	5 024	4 785	6 335	3 209	3 126	3 474	1 815	1 659
1 - 4	44 191	22 376	21 815	26 565	13 591	12 974	17 626	8 785	8 841
5 - 9	50 700	26 100	24 600	30 200	15 600	14 600	20 500	10 500	10 000
10 - 14	49 400	25 500	23 900	30 300	15 600	14 700	19 100	9 900	9 200
15 - 19	48 600	24 800	23 800	30 900	15 700	15 200	17 700	9 100	8 600
20 - 24	47 100	23 900	23 200	30 800	15 500	15 300	16 300	8 400	7 900
25 - 29	45 700	23 000	22 700	31 100	15 500	15 600	14 600	7 500	7 100
30 - 34	43 800	21 900	21 900	30 300	15 000	15 300	13 500	6 900	6 600
35 - 39	41 400	20 600	20 800	28 800	14 200	14 600	12 600	6 400	6 200
40 - 44	38 900	19 400	19 500	27 000	13 300	13 700	11 900	6 100	5 800
45 - 49	37 300	18 600	18 700	25 700	12 600	13 100	11 600	6 000	5 600
50 - 54	33 600	16 700	16 900	23 200	11 300	11 900	10 400	5 400	5 000
55 - 59	28 800	14 100	14 700	20 000	9 600	10 400	8 800	4 500	4 300
60 - 64	23 700	11 400	12 300	16 500	7 700	8 800	7 200	3 700	3 500
65 - 69	17 500	8 100	9 400	12 300	5 600	6 700	5 200	2 500	2 700
70 - 74	12 800	5 700	7 100	9 100	4 000	5 100	3 700	1 700	2 000
75 - 79	8 400	3 600	4 800	6 000	2 600	3 400	2 400	1 000	1 400
80 +	8 400	3 400	5 000	6 100	2 500	3 600	2 300	900	1 400
Uruguay[1]									
1 VII 2019 (ESDJ)									
Total	3 518 552	1 704 782	1 813 771	3 354 867	1 614 457	1 740 410	163 686	90 324	73 361
0	45 235	23 153	22 082	43 504	22 265	21 239	1 731	888	843
1 - 4	182 337	93 318	89 020	175 086	89 579	85 506	7 252	3 738	3 513
5 - 9	231 826	118 513	113 313	222 047	113 455	108 592	9 779	5 058	4 721
10 - 14	239 597	122 513	117 084	228 748	116 840	111 908	10 849	5 673	5 176
15 - 19	256 939	131 227	125 711	246 145	125 447	120 698	10 794	5 780	5 014
20 - 24	271 389	137 888	133 500	261 079	132 213	128 866	10 310	5 675	4 634
25 - 29	257 617	129 941	127 675	247 093	124 026	123 067	10 523	5 916	4 608
30 - 34	245 772	123 361	122 410	235 169	117 375	117 794	10 603	5 986	4 617
35 - 39	237 063	117 597	119 466	225 895	111 355	114 540	11 168	6 241	4 926

7. Population by age, sex and urban/rural residence: latest available year, 2010 - 2019
Population selon l'âge, le sexe et la résidence, urbaine/rurale : dernière année disponible, 2010 - 2019 (continued - suite)

Continent, country or area, date, code[a] and age (in years) Continent, pays ou zone, date, code[a] et âge (en annèes)	Total			Urban - Urbaine			Rural - Rurale		
	Both sexes Les deux sexes	Male Masculin	Female Féminin	Both sexes Les deux sexes	Male Masculin	Female Féminin	Both sexes Les deux sexes	Male Masculin	Female Féminin
AMERICA, SOUTH - AMÉRIQUE DU SUD									
Uruguay[1]									
1 VII 2019 (ESDJ)									
40 - 44	241 209	118 783	122 426	229 407	112 147	117 260	11 802	6 636	5 166
45 - 49	219 035	106 948	112 087	207 721	100 542	107 179	11 314	6 405	4 909
50 - 54	201 498	96 859	104 639	190 777	90 793	99 984	10 721	6 067	4 654
55 - 59	200 537	95 445	105 092	189 885	89 318	100 567	10 652	6 127	4 525
60 - 64	181 229	84 630	96 599	171 346	79 008	92 338	9 883	5 622	4 262
65 - 69	149 254	67 439	81 815	140 637	62 481	78 156	8 617	4 958	3 659
70 - 74	123 034	52 937	70 097	116 104	48 954	67 150	6 930	3 983	2 947
75 - 79	95 905	38 482	57 423	90 974	35 709	55 265	4 931	2 773	2 158
80 - 84	69 197	24 872	44 325	66 007	23 244	42 763	3 190	1 627	1 562
85 - 89	44 594	14 085	30 509	42 839	13 284	29 555	1 755	801	954
90 +	25 287	6 790	18 498	24 405	6 421	17 984	882	369	513
Venezuela (Bolivarian Republic of) - Venezuela (République bolivarienne du)									
1 IX 2011 (CDJC)									
Total	27 227 930	13 549 752	13 678 178	24 180 964[53]	11 900 242[53]	12 280 722[53]	3 046 966[53]	1 649 510[53]	1 397 456[53]
0 - 4	2 437 631	1 254 208	1 183 423	2 130 561[53]	1 095 625[53]	1 034 936[53]	307 070[53]	158 583[53]	148 487[53]
5 - 9	2 402 364	1 236 217	1 166 147	2 083 248[53]	1 071 223[53]	1 012 025[53]	319 116[53]	164 994[53]	154 122[53]
10 - 14	2 516 779	1 298 191	1 218 588	2 179 907[53]	1 121 671[53]	1 058 236[53]	336 872[53]	176 520[53]	160 352[53]
15 - 19	2 641 320	1 336 159	1 305 161	2 317 888[53]	1 164 992[53]	1 152 896[53]	323 432[53]	171 167[53]	152 265[53]
20 - 24	2 560 649	1 280 125	1 280 524	2 289 728[53]	1 134 290[53]	1 155 438[53]	270 921[53]	145 835[53]	125 086[53]
25 - 29	2 344 332	1 159 400	1 184 932	2 104 335[53]	1 030 636[53]	1 073 699[53]	239 997[53]	128 764[53]	111 233[53]
30 - 34	2 219 741	1 105 617	1 114 124	1 994 628[53]	982 139[53]	1 012 489[53]	225 113[53]	123 478[53]	101 635[53]
35 - 39	1 905 253	942 311	962 942	1 708 084[53]	833 596[53]	874 488[53]	197 169[53]	108 715[53]	88 454[53]
40 - 44	1 755 490	873 509	881 981	1 578 118[53]	772 872[53]	805 246[53]	177 372[53]	100 637[53]	76 735[53]
45 - 49	1 528 781	747 704	781 077	1 377 721[53]	662 225[53]	715 496[53]	151 060[53]	85 479[53]	65 581[53]
50 - 54	1 337 934	651 255	686 679	1 208 133[53]	576 212[53]	631 921[53]	129 801[53]	75 043[53]	54 758[53]
55 - 59	1 108 799	530 935	577 864	1 002 491[53]	469 613[53]	532 878[53]	106 308[53]	61 322[53]	44 986[53]
60 - 64	848 358	407 656	440 702	763 622[53]	358 620[53]	405 002[53]	84 736[53]	49 036[53]	35 700[53]
65 - 69	568 688	267 691	300 997	507 772[53]	232 506[53]	275 266[53]	60 916[53]	35 185[53]	25 731[53]
70 - 74	410 455	189 285	221 170	364 425[53]	163 019[53]	201 406[53]	46 030[53]	26 266[53]	19 764[53]
75 - 79	292 992	130 126	162 866	259 357[53]	111 084[53]	148 273[53]	33 635[53]	19 042[53]	14 593[53]
80 - 84	188 895	78 996	109 899	168 413[53]	68 078[53]	100 335[53]	20 482[53]	10 918[53]	9 564[53]
85 - 89	104 141	40 560	63 581	93 151[53]	34 885[53]	58 266[53]	10 990[53]	5 675[53]	5 315[53]
90 - 94	40 370	14 875	25 495	36 160[53]	12 804[53]	23 356[53]	4 210[53]	2 071[53]	2 139[53]
95 +	14 958	4 932	10 026	13 222[53]	4 152[53]	9 070[53]	1 736[53]	780[53]	956[53]
1 VII 2019 (ESDF)									
Total	32 064 741	16 085 704	15 979 037	...	...	...	...	...	...
0	552 619	276 629	275 990	...	...	...	...	...	...
1 - 4	2 157 691	1 116 331	1 041 360	...	...	...	...	...	...
5 - 9	2 748 508	1 420 995	1 327 513	...	...	...	...	...	...
10 - 14	2 791 506	1 442 288	1 349 218	...	...	...	...	...	...
15 - 19	2 770 223	1 427 367	1 342 856	...	...	...	...	...	...
20 - 24	2 678 628	1 372 148	1 306 480	...	...	...	...	...	...
25 - 29	2 604 562	1 322 783	1 281 779	...	...	...	...	...	...
30 - 34	2 569 261	1 294 114	1 275 147	...	...	...	...	...	...
35 - 39	2 357 364	1 180 244	1 177 120	...	...	...	...	...	...
40 - 44	2 093 543	1 042 646	1 050 897	...	...	...	...	...	...
45 - 49	1 910 427	946 494	963 933	...	...	...	...	...	...
50 - 54	1 781 279	877 401	903 878	...	...	...	...	...	...
55 - 59	1 529 356	747 504	781 852	...	...	...	...	...	...
60 - 64	1 187 457	574 077	613 380	...	...	...	...	...	...
65 - 69	859 994	409 138	450 856	...	...	...	...	...	...
70 - 74	608 292	282 267	326 025	...	...	...	...	...	...
75 - 79	400 939	179 631	221 308	...	...	...	...	...	...
80 - 84	241 693	101 653	140 040	...	...	...	...	...	...
85 - 89	129 442	48 109	81 333	...	...	...	...	...	...
90 - 94	61 304	17 947	43 357	...	...	...	...	...	...
95 - 99	24 517	4 924	19 593	...	...	...	...	...	...
100 +	6 136	1 014	5 122	...	...	...	...	...	...

Continent, country or area, date, code[a] and age (in years) / Continent, pays ou zone, date, code[a] et âge (en années)	Total			Urban - Urbaine			Rural - Rurale		
	Both sexes Les deux sexes	Male Masculin	Female Féminin	Both sexes Les deux sexes	Male Masculin	Female Féminin	Both sexes Les deux sexes	Male Masculin	Female Féminin
ASIA - ASIE									
Afghanistan[54]									
1 VII 2019 (ESDF)									
Total	*30 725 560*	*15 643 288*	*15 082 272*	*7 761 765*	*3 921 208*	*3 840 557*	*22 963 795*	*11 722 080*	*11 241 715*
0	*1 033 481*	*514 870*	*518 611*	*231 050*	*116 237*	*114 813*	*802 430*	*398 632*	*403 798*
1 - 4	*4 231 844*	*2 149 063*	*2 082 781*	*899 888*	*461 395*	*438 493*	*3 331 957*	*1 687 669*	*1 644 288*
5 - 9	*5 036 120*	*2 620 321*	*2 415 799*	*1 110 870*	*578 633*	*532 238*	*3 925 250*	*2 041 689*	*1 883 561*
10 - 14	*4 278 993*	*2 250 077*	*2 028 915*	*1 086 947*	*563 858*	*523 089*	*3 192 045*	*1 686 219*	*1 505 826*
15 - 19	*3 368 354*	*1 723 661*	*1 644 693*	*956 717*	*487 233*	*469 485*	*2 411 636*	*1 236 428*	*1 175 208*
20 - 24	*2 677 215*	*1 299 423*	*1 377 792*	*786 709*	*373 359*	*413 350*	*1 890 506*	*926 064*	*964 442*
25 - 29	*2 304 537*	*1 098 240*	*1 206 297*	*604 015*	*278 770*	*325 245*	*1 700 523*	*819 470*	*881 052*
30 - 34	*1 514 924*	*768 960*	*745 964*	*386 715*	*193 077*	*193 639*	*1 128 208*	*575 883*	*552 325*
35 - 39	*1 404 551*	*701 846*	*702 705*	*388 580*	*199 471*	*189 109*	*1 015 972*	*502 376*	*513 596*
40 - 44	*1 125 673*	*552 384*	*573 290*	*300 828*	*150 064*	*150 764*	*824 845*	*402 320*	*422 526*
45 - 49	*1 008 318*	*482 881*	*525 437*	*257 326*	*121 775*	*135 551*	*750 991*	*361 106*	*389 886*
50 - 54	*795 209*	*387 913*	*407 296*	*217 233*	*106 034*	*111 199*	*577 976*	*281 879*	*296 097*
55 - 59	*581 361*	*298 882*	*282 478*	*157 717*	*75 966*	*81 750*	*423 644*	*222 916*	*200 728*
60 - 64	*531 040*	*283 791*	*247 250*	*140 506*	*75 938*	*64 568*	*390 535*	*207 852*	*182 682*
65 - 69	*350 466*	*214 664*	*135 802*	*94 644*	*54 974*	*39 670*	*255 822*	*159 690*	*96 132*
70 - 74	*242 498*	*146 338*	*96 161*	*60 128*	*34 104*	*26 024*	*182 370*	*112 233*	*70 137*
75 - 79	*112 183*	*69 699*	*42 484*	*32 673*	*20 179*	*12 494*	*79 510*	*49 520*	*29 990*
80 - 84	*79 210*	*47 963*	*31 248*	*30 216*	*18 350*	*11 866*	*48 994*	*29 613*	*19 381*
85 +	*49 583*	*32 312*	*17 271*	*19 002*	*11 791*	*7 211*	*30 582*	*20 522*	*10 060*
Armenia - Arménie									
1 VII 2018 (ESDJ)									
Total	2 969 001	1 404 965	1 564 036	1 895 362	878 143	1 017 219	1 073 639	526 822	546 817
0	36 891	19 353	17 538	24 286	12 675	11 611	12 605	6 678	5 927
1 - 4	163 883	86 662	77 221	106 441	55 891	50 550	57 442	30 771	26 671
5 - 9	210 379	111 969	98 410	130 525	68 859	61 666	79 854	43 110	36 744
10 - 14	188 723	100 968	87 755	116 858	61 908	54 950	71 865	39 060	32 805
15 - 19	165 184	87 644	77 540	99 796	52 595	47 201	65 388	35 049	30 339
20 - 24	189 870	95 261	94 609	110 521	55 399	55 122	79 349	39 862	39 487
25 - 29	258 280	122 919	135 361	155 423	72 116	83 307	102 857	50 803	52 054
30 - 34	263 053	124 623	138 430	165 515	75 596	89 919	97 538	49 027	48 511
35 - 39	226 507	107 564	118 943	150 740	70 282	80 458	75 767	37 282	38 485
40 - 44	183 307	85 090	98 217	123 011	57 120	65 891	60 296	27 970	32 326
45 - 49	164 816	74 568	90 248	105 906	47 223	58 683	58 910	27 345	31 565
50 - 54	177 007	78 338	98 669	106 446	44 679	61 767	70 561	33 659	36 902
55 - 59	214 851	95 373	119 478	135 084	56 790	78 294	79 767	38 583	41 184
60 - 64	177 391	77 194	100 197	120 608	50 350	70 258	56 783	26 844	29 939
65 - 69	125 079	52 400	72 679	91 097	37 583	53 514	33 982	14 817	19 165
70 - 74	66 516	26 217	40 299	49 815	19 676	30 139	16 701	6 541	10 160
75 - 79	71 755	27 428	44 327	49 040	19 143	29 897	22 715	8 285	14 430
80 - 84	55 546	20 267	35 279	36 002	13 193	22 809	19 544	7 074	12 470
85 +	29 963	11 127	18 836	18 248	7 065	11 183	11 715	4 062	7 653
1 I 2019 (ESDJ)									
Total	2 965 269	1 401 731	1 563 538	...	...	...	...	...	...
0	36 352	19 130	17 222	...	...	...	...	...	...
1 - 4	161 876	85 471	76 405	...	...	...	...	...	...
5 - 9	210 817	112 123	98 694	...	...	...	...	...	...
10 - 14	191 050	102 174	88 876	...	...	...	...	...	...
15 - 19	165 130	87 702	77 428	...	...	...	...	...	...
20 - 24	183 856	92 725	91 131	...	...	...	...	...	...
25 - 29	251 883	119 697	132 186	...	...	...	...	...	...
30 - 34	263 365	124 511	138 854	...	...	...	...	...	...
35 - 39	230 638	109 487	121 151	...	...	...	...	...	...
40 - 44	185 247	86 024	99 223	...	...	...	...	...	...
45 - 49	164 327	74 227	90 100	...	...	...	...	...	...
50 - 54	172 088	75 802	96 286	...	...	...	...	...	...
55 - 59	212 437	94 058	118 379	...	...	...	...	...	...
60 - 64	183 078	79 586	103 492	...	...	...	...	...	...
65 - 69	128 101	53 737	74 364	...	...	...	...	...	...
70 - 74	71 274	27 914	43 360	...	...	...	...	...	...
75 - 79	66 023	25 241	40 782	...	...	...	...	...	...
80 - 84	57 135	20 640	36 495	...	...	...	...	...	...
85 +	30 592	11 482	19 110	...	...	...	...	...	...

Continent, country or area, date, code[a] and age (in years) / Continent, pays ou zone, date, code[a] et âge (en années)	Total			Urban - Urbaine			Rural - Rurale		
	Both sexes Les deux sexes	Male Masculin	Female Féminin	Both sexes Les deux sexes	Male Masculin	Female Féminin	Both sexes Les deux sexes	Male Masculin	Female Féminin
ASIA - ASIE									
Azerbaijan - Azerbaïdjan									
1 I 2019 (ESDJ)									
Total	9 939 771	4 960 216	4 979 555	5 255 848	2 600 834	2 655 014	4 683 923	2 359 382	2 324 541
0	141 511	75 404	66 107	68 420	36 240	32 180	73 091	39 164	33 927
1 - 4	646 929	344 812	302 117	312 070	165 145	146 925	334 859	179 667	155 192
5 - 9	819 428	440 473	378 955	404 360	216 351	188 009	415 068	224 122	190 946
10 - 14	628 737	335 573	293 164	320 649	170 615	150 034	308 088	164 958	143 130
15 - 19	649 828	345 201	304 627	323 469	172 701	150 768	326 359	172 500	153 859
20 - 24	780 312	406 751	373 561	387 042	202 983	184 059	393 270	203 768	189 502
25 - 29	925 538	466 727	458 811	478 961	240 210	238 751	446 577	226 517	220 060
30 - 34	907 532	447 586	459 946	496 351	241 871	254 480	411 181	205 715	205 466
35 - 39	775 744	384 909	390 835	434 700	214 174	220 526	341 044	170 735	170 309
40 - 44	640 170	314 244	325 926	348 881	169 350	179 531	291 289	144 894	146 395
45 - 49	631 083	302 214	328 869	336 397	157 348	179 049	294 686	144 866	149 820
50 - 54	648 912	306 465	342 447	345 586	159 324	186 262	303 326	147 141	156 185
55 - 59	638 040	302 542	335 498	359 032	169 677	189 355	279 008	132 865	146 143
60 - 64	442 741	206 173	236 568	257 777	120 101	137 676	184 964	86 072	98 892
65 - 69	269 857	121 268	148 589	164 888	74 664	90 224	104 969	46 604	58 365
70 - 74	129 926	55 178	74 748	80 784	34 611	46 173	49 142	20 567	28 575
75 - 79	119 583	48 175	71 408	66 523	27 027	39 496	53 060	21 148	31 912
80 - 84	93 338	36 649	56 689	46 288	18 355	27 933	47 050	18 294	28 756
85 - 89	36 884	14 865	22 019	17 599	7 460	10 139	19 285	7 405	11 880
90 - 94	9 428	3 610	5 818	4 292	1 878	2 414	5 136	1 732	3 404
95 - 99	3 435	1 177	2 258	1 462	648	814	1 973	529	1 444
100 +	815	220	595	317	101	216	498	119	379
Bahrain - Bahreïn									
1 VII 2019 (ESDJ)									
Total	1 483 756	920 564	563 192	...	...	...	...	...	...
0	20 925	10 624	10 301	...	...	...	...	...	...
1 - 4	83 893	42 672	41 221	...	...	...	...	...	...
5 - 9	102 832	52 554	50 278	...	...	...	...	...	...
10 - 14	91 499	46 620	44 879	...	...	...	...	...	...
15 - 19	79 261	40 928	38 333	...	...	...	...	...	...
20 - 24	102 785	60 781	42 004	...	...	...	...	...	...
25 - 29	167 353	107 495	59 858	...	...	...	...	...	...
30 - 34	207 726	146 970	60 756	...	...	...	...	...	...
35 - 39	179 014	126 964	52 050	...	...	...	...	...	...
40 - 44	133 615	90 011	43 604	...	...	...	...	...	...
45 - 49	99 790	67 219	32 571	...	...	...	...	...	...
50 - 54	77 284	48 655	28 629	...	...	...	...	...	...
55 - 59	56 803	34 201	22 602	...	...	...	...	...	...
60 - 64	36 768	21 313	15 455	...	...	...	...	...	...
65 - 69	20 463	11 766	8 697	...	...	...	...	...	...
70 - 74	10 346	5 485	4 861	...	...	...	...	...	...
75 - 79	6 461	3 138	3 323	...	...	...	...	...	...
80 - 84	3 749	1 715	2 034	...	...	...	...	...	...
85 - 89	1 907	874	1 033	...	...	...	...	...	...
90 - 94	789	378	411	...	...	...	...	...	...
95 - 99	372	152	220	...	...	...	...	...	...
100 +	121	49	72	...	...	...	...	...	...
Bangladesh									
1 VII 2019 (ESDF)									
Total	166 500 000	83 330 000	83 170 000	50 366 250	25 207 325	25 158 925	116 133 750	58 122 675	58 011 075
0	2 638 688	1 355 632	1 283 056	697 021	357 484	339 537	1 941 667	998 148	943 519
1 - 4	11 557 190	5 915 416	5 641 774	3 279 506	1 682 187	1 597 319	8 277 684	4 233 229	4 044 455
5 - 9	15 703 735	7 941 017	7 762 718	4 530 203	2 333 356	2 196 847	11 173 532	5 607 660	5 565 871
10 - 14	18 069 747	9 072 580	8 997 167	5 024 978	2 502 208	2 522 770	13 044 769	6 570 372	6 474 397
15 - 19	16 528 998	9 113 484	7 415 514	4 753 578	2 550 858	2 202 719	11 775 420	6 562 626	5 212 795
20 - 24	14 611 077	7 047 446	7 563 631	4 659 351	2 111 756	2 547 595	9 951 726	4 935 690	5 016 036
25 - 29	13 646 660	6 193 731	7 452 929	4 488 792	1 993 961	2 494 832	9 157 868	4 199 771	4 958 097
30 - 34	13 442 405	6 218 586	7 223 819	4 447 364	2 081 282	2 366 082	8 995 041	4 137 304	4 857 737
35 - 39	12 251 327	5 869 826	6 381 500	4 041 647	1 969 368	2 072 279	8 209 680	3 900 458	4 309 222
40 - 44	10 595 963	5 276 648	5 319 315	3 446 094	1 761 044	1 685 050	7 149 869	3 515 604	3 634 265
45 - 49	8 933 635	4 652 659	4 280 976	2 866 173	1 533 117	1 333 056	6 067 462	3 119 542	2 947 920
50 - 54	8 084 269	4 033 789	4 050 480	2 533 701	1 307 507	1 226 195	5 550 567	2 726 283	2 824 285

Continent, country or area, date, code[a] and age (in years) Continent, pays ou zone, date, code[a] et âge (en annèes)	Total			Urban - Urbaine			Rural - Rurale		
	Both sexes Les deux sexes	Male Masculin	Female Féminin	Both sexes Les deux sexes	Male Masculin	Female Féminin	Both sexes Les deux sexes	Male Masculin	Female Féminin
ASIA - ASIE									
Bangladesh									
1 VII 2019 (ESDF)									
55 - 59	*6 404 618*	*3 232 711*	*3 171 907*	*1 879 368*	*997 426*	*881 942*	*4 525 250*	*2 235 285*	*2 289 965*
60 - 64	*4 927 804*	*2 644 825*	*2 282 978*	*1 421 919*	*797 032*	*624 887*	*3 505 885*	*1 847 794*	*1 658 091*
65 - 69	*3 776 128*	*1 993 666*	*1 782 462*	*1 006 321*	*556 274*	*450 047*	*2 769 808*	*1 437 393*	*1 332 415*
70 - 74	*2 450 720*	*1 309 539*	*1 141 181*	*632 140*	*346 168*	*285 973*	*1 818 580*	*963 371*	*855 209*
75 - 79	*1 411 462*	*763 241*	*648 221*	*331 328*	*171 703*	*159 625*	*1 080 134*	*591 538*	*488 596*
80 +	*1 465 575*	*695 203*	*770 371*	*326 766*	*154 595*	*172 171*	*1 138 809*	*540 609*	*598 200*
80 - 84	*749 774*	*373 636*	*376 139*	...	...	...	...	...	...
85 - 89	*378 090*	*176 892*	*201 197*	...	...	...	...	...	...
90 - 94	*183 566*	*81 339*	*102 228*	...	...	...	...	...	...
95 +	*154 144*	*63 337*	*90 808*	...	...	...	...	...	...
Bhutan - Bhoutan									
30 V 2017 (CDFC)[55]									
Total	727 145	380 453	346 692	274 316	143 313	131 003	452 829	237 140	215 689
0 - 4	57 474	29 176	28 298	21 453	11 059	10 394	36 021	18 117	17 904
5 - 9	62 991	32 035	30 956	22 567	11 429	11 138	40 424	20 606	19 818
10 - 14	68 952	34 656	34 296	24 285	12 129	12 156	44 667	22 527	22 140
15 - 19	68 286	34 679	33 607	30 378	15 058	15 320	37 908	19 621	18 287
20 - 24	75 415	41 075	34 340	35 689	18 941	16 748	39 726	22 134	17 592
25 - 29	79 280	42 802	36 478	35 586	18 698	16 888	43 694	24 104	19 590
30 - 34	65 180	35 059	30 121	27 753	14 698	13 055	37 427	20 361	17 066
35 - 39	55 549	29 689	25 860	22 460	12 039	10 421	33 089	17 650	15 439
40 - 44	41 495	22 274	19 221	14 868	8 387	6 481	26 627	13 887	12 740
45 - 49	35 533	18 865	16 668	11 938	6 810	5 128	23 595	12 055	11 540
50 - 54	29 317	15 456	13 861	8 334	4 706	3 628	20 983	10 750	10 233
55 - 59	23 898	12 379	11 519	5 494	2 895	2 599	18 404	9 484	8 920
60 - 64	20 711	10 498	10 213	4 321	2 150	2 171	16 390	8 348	8 042
65 - 69	14 654	7 585	7 069	2 998	1 481	1 517	11 656	6 104	5 552
70 - 74	11 468	5 876	5 592	2 401	1 069	1 332	9 067	4 807	4 260
75 - 79	7 871	3 965	3 906	1 715	802	913	6 156	3 163	2 993
80 - 84	5 397	2 651	2 746	1 172	542	630	4 225	2 109	2 116
85 +	3 674	1 733	1 941	904	420	484	2 770	1 313	1 457
30 V 2019 (ESDF)[46]									
Total	*741 672*	*387 402*	*354 270*	...	...	...	...	...	...
0	*12 125*	*6 158*	*5 967*	...	...	...	...	...	...
1 - 4	*45 273*	*22 883*	*22 390*	...	...	...	...	...	...
5 - 9	*60 767*	*31 021*	*29 746*	...	...	...	...	...	...
10 - 14	*67 031*	*33 825*	*33 206*	...	...	...	...	...	...
15 - 19	*68 119*	*34 151*	*33 968*	...	...	...	...	...	...
20 - 24	*71 800*	*38 209*	*33 591*	...	...	...	...	...	...
25 - 29	*79 238*	*43 071*	*36 167*	...	...	...	...	...	...
30 - 34	*71 058*	*38 217*	*32 841*	...	...	...	...	...	...
35 - 39	*58 968*	*31 527*	*27 441*	...	...	...	...	...	...
40 - 44	*46 294*	*24 779*	*21 515*	...	...	...	...	...	...
45 - 49	*37 000*	*19 718*	*17 282*	...	...	...	...	...	...
50 - 54	*31 350*	*16 553*	*14 797*	...	...	...	...	...	...
55 - 59	*25 267*	*13 212*	*12 055*	...	...	...	...	...	...
60 - 64	*21 560*	*10 959*	*10 601*	...	...	...	...	...	...
65 - 69	*16 409*	*8 389*	*8 020*	...	...	...	...	...	...
70 - 74	*11 788*	*6 068*	*5 720*	...	...	...	...	...	...
75 - 79	*8 423*	*4 238*	*4 185*	...	...	...	...	...	...
80 - 84	*5 331*	*2 595*	*2 736*	...	...	...	...	...	...
85 +	*3 871*	*1 829*	*2 042*	...	...	...	...	...	...
Brunei Darussalam - Brunéi Darussalam									
1 VII 2016 (ESDJ)[56]									
Total	*417 256*	*214 104*	*203 152*	*312 448*	*160 061*	*152 387*	*104 808*	*54 043*	*50 765*
0	*3 878*	*2 075*	*1 803*	*2 945*	*1 582*	*1 363*	*933*	*493*	*440*
1 - 4	*24 549*	*12 789*	*11 760*	*18 534*	*9 661*	*8 873*	*6 015*	*3 128*	*2 887*
5 - 9	*30 426*	*15 673*	*14 753*	*23 168*	*11 918*	*11 250*	*7 258*	*3 755*	*3 503*
10 - 14	*34 306*	*17 663*	*16 643*	*25 904*	*13 378*	*12 526*	*8 402*	*4 285*	*4 117*
15 - 19	*36 417*	*18 949*	*17 468*	*27 115*	*14 167*	*12 948*	*9 302*	*4 782*	*4 520*
20 - 24	*39 027*	*20 544*	*18 483*	*28 741*	*15 067*	*13 674*	*10 286*	*5 477*	*4 809*
25 - 29	*39 812*	*21 416*	*18 396*	*29 722*	*15 861*	*13 861*	*10 090*	*5 555*	*4 535*

Continent, country or area, date, code[a] and age (in years) / Continent, pays ou zone, date, code[a] et âge (en années)	Total			Urban - Urbaine			Rural - Rurale		
	Both sexes Les deux sexes	Male Masculin	Female Féminin	Both sexes Les deux sexes	Male Masculin	Female Féminin	Both sexes Les deux sexes	Male Masculin	Female Féminin
ASIA - ASIE									
Brunei Darussalam - Brunéi Darussalam									
1 VII 2016 (ESDJ)[56]									
30 - 34	*36 895*	*19 313*	*17 582*	*27 970*	*14 506*	*13 464*	*8 925*	*4 807*	*4 118*
35 - 39	*34 492*	*17 815*	*16 677*	*26 642*	*13 749*	*12 893*	*7 850*	*4 066*	*3 784*
40 - 44	*31 164*	*15 743*	*15 421*	*23 783*	*11 945*	*11 838*	*7 381*	*3 798*	*3 583*
45 - 49	*27 701*	*13 682*	*14 019*	*20 748*	*10 264*	*10 484*	*6 953*	*3 418*	*3 535*
50 - 54	*23 160*	*11 651*	*11 509*	*17 466*	*8 819*	*8 647*	*5 694*	*2 832*	*2 862*
55 - 59	*19 239*	*9 462*	*9 777*	*14 213*	*7 049*	*7 164*	*5 026*	*2 413*	*2 613*
60 - 64	*14 591*	*7 068*	*7 523*	*10 457*	*5 061*	*5 396*	*4 134*	*2 007*	*2 127*
65 - 69	*8 958*	*4 257*	*4 701*	*6 337*	*3 053*	*3 284*	*2 621*	*1 204*	*1 417*
70 - 74	*5 095*	*2 537*	*2 558*	*3 564*	*1 735*	*1 829*	*1 531*	*802*	*729*
75 - 79	*3 780*	*1 737*	*2 043*	*2 625*	*1 142*	*1 483*	*1 155*	*595*	*560*
80 - 84	*2 206*	*974*	*1 232*	*1 491*	*637*	*854*	*715*	*337*	*378*
85 - 89	*1 015*	*498*	*517*	*679*	*314*	*365*	*336*	*184*	*152*
90 - 94	*396*	*184*	*212*	*254*	*105*	*149*	*142*	*79*	*63*
95 - 99	*124*	*64*	*60*	*75*	*40*	*35*	*49*	*24*	*25*
100 +	*25*	*10*	*15*	*15*	*8*	*7*	*10*	*2*	*8*
1 VII 2019 (ESDJ)									
Total	*459 500*	*244 500*	*215 000*	...	...	...	...	...	...
0	*5 700*	*3 000*	*2 700*	...	...	...	...	...	...
1 - 4	*25 000*	*12 600*	*12 400*	...	...	...	...	...	...
5 - 9	*32 400*	*16 600*	*15 800*	...	...	...	...	...	...
10 - 14	*31 500*	*16 500*	*15 000*	...	...	...	...	...	...
15 - 19	*37 300*	*19 000*	*18 300*	...	...	...	...	...	...
20 - 24	*43 200*	*23 700*	*19 500*	...	...	...	...	...	...
25 - 29	*45 300*	*25 800*	*19 500*	...	...	...	...	...	...
30 - 34	*43 600*	*24 700*	*18 900*	...	...	...	...	...	...
35 - 39	*40 300*	*22 300*	*18 000*	...	...	...	...	...	...
40 - 44	*36 500*	*19 600*	*16 900*	...	...	...	...	...	...
45 - 49	*32 200*	*16 900*	*15 300*	...	...	...	...	...	...
50 - 54	*26 200*	*13 400*	*12 800*	...	...	...	...	...	...
55 - 59	*21 800*	*10 900*	*10 900*	...	...	...	...	...	...
60 - 64	*16 300*	*8 400*	*7 900*	...	...	...	...	...	...
65 - 69	*10 400*	*5 600*	*4 800*	...	...	...	...	...	...
70 - 74	*5 300*	*2 500*	*2 800*	...	...	...	...	...	...
75 - 79	*3 500*	*1 700*	*1 800*	...	...	...	...	...	...
80 - 84	*1 900*	*800*	*1 100*	...	...	...	...	...	...
85 +	*1 100*	*500*	*600*	...	...	...	...	...	...
Cambodia - Cambodge[57]									
1 VII 2015 (ESDF)									
Total	*15 405 157*	*7 551 944*	*7 853 213*	*3 540 575*	*1 705 018*	*1 835 557*	*11 864 582*	*5 846 926*	*6 017 656*
0	*343 968*	*175 388*	*168 580*	*86 946*	*44 740*	*42 206*	*257 022*	*130 648*	*126 374*
1 - 4	*1 256 559*	*639 680*	*616 879*	*287 909*	*146 676*	*141 233*	*968 650*	*493 004*	*475 646*
5 - 9	*1 478 056*	*751 537*	*726 519*	*266 331*	*135 468*	*130 863*	*1 211 725*	*616 069*	*595 656*
10 - 14	*1 424 533*	*727 116*	*697 417*	*222 335*	*114 171*	*108 164*	*1 202 198*	*612 945*	*589 253*
15 - 19	*1 637 111*	*838 821*	*798 290*	*273 601*	*136 051*	*137 550*	*1 363 510*	*702 770*	*660 740*
20 - 24	*1 698 824*	*877 158*	*821 666*	*407 469*	*188 296*	*219 173*	*1 291 355*	*688 862*	*602 493*
25 - 29	*1 478 710*	*737 077*	*741 633*	*484 549*	*223 014*	*261 535*	*994 161*	*514 063*	*480 098*
30 - 34	*1 333 262*	*649 670*	*683 592*	*427 395*	*205 047*	*222 348*	*905 867*	*444 623*	*461 244*
35 - 39	*879 004*	*427 791*	*451 213*	*237 471*	*117 764*	*119 707*	*641 533*	*310 027*	*331 506*
40 - 44	*761 990*	*367 586*	*394 404*	*177 884*	*89 396*	*88 488*	*584 106*	*278 190*	*305 916*
45 - 49	*793 754*	*374 975*	*418 779*	*175 105*	*87 482*	*87 623*	*618 649*	*287 493*	*331 156*
50 - 54	*677 057*	*312 718*	*364 339*	*144 559*	*70 342*	*74 217*	*532 498*	*242 376*	*290 122*
55 - 59	*533 368*	*224 272*	*309 096*	*119 460*	*52 954*	*66 506*	*413 908*	*171 318*	*242 590*
60 - 64	*398 784*	*159 105*	*239 679*	*89 373*	*37 736*	*51 637*	*309 411*	*121 369*	*188 042*
65 - 69	*282 114*	*117 449*	*164 665*	*58 973*	*24 909*	*34 064*	*223 141*	*92 540*	*130 601*
70 - 74	*191 298*	*79 144*	*112 154*	*36 584*	*14 784*	*21 800*	*154 714*	*64 360*	*90 354*
75 - 79	*126 227*	*50 567*	*75 660*	*23 103*	*8 844*	*14 259*	*103 124*	*41 723*	*61 401*
80 +	*110 538*	*41 890*	*68 648*	*21 528*	*7 344*	*14 184*	*89 010*	*34 546*	*54 464*
China - Chine[58]									
1 XI 2010 (CDJC)[59]									
Total	1332810869	682 329 104	650 481 765	670 005 546	343 040 783	326 964 763	662 805 323	339 288 321	323 517 002
0 - 4	75 532 610	41 062 566	34 470 044	30 936 470	16 749 729	14 186 741	44 596 140	24 312 837	20 283 303
5 - 9	70 881 549	38 464 665	32 416 884	30 565 659	16 580 910	13 984 749	40 315 890	21 883 755	18 432 135

7. Population by age, sex and urban/rural residence: latest available year, 2010 - 2019

Population selon l'âge, le sexe et la résidence, urbaine/rurale : dernière année disponible, 2010 - 2019 (continued - suite)

Continent, country or area, date, code[a] and age (in years) / Continent, pays ou zone, date, code[a] et âge (en annèes)	Total			Urban - Urbaine			Rural - Rurale		
	Both sexes Les deux sexes	Male Masculin	Female Féminin	Both sexes Les deux sexes	Male Masculin	Female Féminin	Both sexes Les deux sexes	Male Masculin	Female Féminin
ASIA - ASIE									
China - Chine[58]									
1 XI 2010 (CDJC)[59]									
10 - 14	74 908 462	40 267 277	34 641 185	32 807 526	17 664 790	15 142 736	42 100 936	22 602 487	19 498 449
15 - 19	99 889 114	51 904 830	47 984 284	53 589 992	27 603 777	25 986 215	46 299 122	24 301 053	21 998 069
20 - 24	127 412 518	64 008 573	63 403 945	71 058 518	36 041 784	35 016 734	56 354 000	27 966 789	28 387 211
25 - 29	101 013 852	50 837 038	50 176 814	57 679 956	28 973 516	28 706 440	43 333 896	21 863 522	21 470 374
30 - 34	97 138 203	49 521 822	47 616 381	56 010 957	28 432 073	27 578 884	41 127 246	21 089 749	20 037 497
35 - 39	118 025 959	60 391 104	57 634 855	65 025 365	33 349 280	31 676 085	53 000 594	27 041 824	25 958 770
40 - 44	124 753 964	63 608 678	61 145 286	63 786 496	32 845 769	30 940 727	60 967 468	30 762 909	30 204 559
45 - 49	105 594 553	53 776 418	51 818 135	53 629 541	27 723 132	25 906 409	51 965 012	26 053 286	25 911 726
50 - 54	78 753 171	40 363 234	38 389 937	39 186 388	20 130 395	19 055 993	39 566 783	20 232 839	19 333 944
55 - 59	81 312 474	41 082 938	40 229 536	37 437 535	18 762 887	18 674 648	43 874 939	22 320 051	21 554 888
60 - 64	58 667 282	29 834 426	28 832 856	26 036 917	13 067 045	12 969 872	32 630 365	16 767 381	15 862 984
65 - 69	41 113 282	20 748 471	20 364 811	17 910 329	8 866 594	9 043 735	23 202 953	11 881 877	11 321 076
70 - 74	32 972 397	16 403 453	16 568 944	14 777 260	7 241 891	7 535 369	18 195 137	9 161 562	9 033 575
75 - 79	23 852 133	11 278 859	12 573 274	10 531 503	5 048 471	5 483 032	13 320 630	6 230 388	7 090 242
80 - 84	13 373 198	5 917 502	7 455 696	5 762 828	2 665 218	3 097 610	7 610 370	3 252 284	4 358 086
85 - 89	5 631 928	2 199 810	3 432 118	2 392 190	982 284	1 409 906	3 239 738	1 217 526	2 022 212
90 - 94	1 578 307	530 872	1 047 435	687 763	246 031	441 732	890 544	284 841	605 703
95 - 99	369 979	117 716	252 263	176 542	60 991	115 551	193 437	56 725	136 712
100 +	35 934	8 852	27 082	15 811	4 216	11 595	20 123	4 636	15 487
31 XII 2011 (ESDF)[60]									
Total	*1347304706*	*690 634 118*	*656 670 588*	...	...	...	...	...	...
0 - 4	*76 270 588*	*41 467 059*	*34 803 529*	...	...	...	...	...	...
5 - 9	*72 092 941*	*39 108 235*	*32 984 706*	...	...	...	...	...	...
10 - 14	*73 507 059*	*39 657 647*	*33 849 412*	...	...	...	...	...	...
15 - 19	*94 574 118*	*49 489 412*	*45 084 706*	...	...	...	...	...	...
20 - 24	*127 725 882*	*64 991 765*	*62 732 941*	...	...	...	...	...	...
25 - 29	*105 010 588*	*52 912 941*	*52 096 471*	...	...	...	...	...	...
30 - 34	*96 644 706*	*49 303 529*	*47 341 176*	...	...	...	...	...	...
35 - 39	*113 994 118*	*58 317 647*	*55 676 471*	...	...	...	...	...	...
40 - 44	*126 342 353*	*64 477 647*	*61 864 706*	...	...	...	...	...	...
45 - 49	*118 650 588*	*60 510 588*	*58 140 000*	...	...	...	...	...	...
50 - 54	*73 181 176*	*37 436 471*	*35 744 706*	...	...	...	...	...	...
55 - 59	*84 314 118*	*42 603 529*	*41 709 412*	...	...	...	...	...	...
60 - 64	*62 009 412*	*31 397 647*	*30 611 765*	...	...	...	...	...	...
65 - 69	*42 416 471*	*21 251 765*	*21 164 706*	...	...	...	...	...	...
70 - 74	*33 912 941*	*16 934 118*	*16 978 824*	...	...	...	...	...	...
75 - 79	*24 910 588*	*11 716 471*	*13 195 294*	...	...	...	...	...	...
80 - 84	*14 075 294*	*6 263 529*	*7 811 765*	...	...	...	...	...	...
85 - 89	*5 642 353*	*2 182 353*	*3 460 000*	...	...	...	...	...	...
90 - 94	*1 690 588*	*524 706*	*1 165 882*	...	...	...	...	...	...
95 +	*341 176*	*85 882*	*254 118*	...	...	...	...	...	...
China, Hong Kong SAR - Chine, Hong Kong RAS									
1 VII 2019 (ESDJ)									
Total	7 507 400	3 423 000	4 084 400	...	...	...	...	...	...
0	48 600	25 100	23 500	...	...	...	...	...	...
1 - 4	229 000	119 000	110 000	...	...	...	...	...	...
5 - 9	307 600	158 700	148 900	...	...	...	...	...	...
10 - 14	289 700	147 900	141 800	...	...	...	...	...	...
15 - 19	285 600	146 400	139 200	...	...	...	...	...	...
20 - 24	413 500	204 200	209 300	...	...	...	...	...	...
25 - 29	491 700	226 300	265 400	...	...	...	...	...	...
30 - 34	557 100	227 700	329 400	...	...	...	...	...	...
35 - 39	611 200	238 200	373 000	...	...	...	...	...	...
40 - 44	566 600	227 000	339 600	...	...	...	...	...	...
45 - 49	582 200	242 200	340 000	...	...	...	...	...	...
50 - 54	579 900	254 800	325 100	...	...	...	...	...	...
55 - 59	647 900	306 300	341 600	...	...	...	...	...	...
60 - 64	574 800	283 100	291 700	...	...	...	...	...	...
65 - 69	444 000	217 600	226 400	...	...	...	...	...	...
70 - 74	307 600	151 300	156 300	...	...	...	...	...	...
75 - 79	190 700	95 400	95 300	...	...	...	...	...	...

7. Population by age, sex and urban/rural residence: latest available year, 2010 - 2019
Population selon l'âge, le sexe et la résidence, urbaine/rurale : dernière année disponible, 2010 - 2019 (continued - suite)

Continent, country or area, date, code[a] and age (in years) / Continent, pays ou zone, date, code[a] et âge (en annèes)	Total			Urban - Urbaine			Rural - Rurale		
	Both sexes Les deux sexes	Male Masculin	Female Féminin	Both sexes Les deux sexes	Male Masculin	Female Féminin	Both sexes Les deux sexes	Male Masculin	Female Féminin
ASIA - ASIE									
China, Hong Kong SAR - Chine, Hong Kong RAS									
1 VII 2019 (ESDJ)									
80 - 84	173 400	78 400	95 000	...	...	...	...	...	...
85 +	206 300	73 400	132 900	...	...	...	...	...	...
China, Macao SAR - Chine, Macao RAS									
1 VII 2019 (ESDJ)									
Total	672 000	314 500	357 500	...	...	...	...	...	...
0	5 900	3 100	2 800	...	...	...	...	...	...
1 - 4	28 200	14 700	13 500	...	...	...	...	...	...
5 - 9	31 800	16 800	15 000	...	...	...	...	...	...
10 - 14	23 400	12 300	11 100	...	...	...	...	...	...
15 - 19	26 300	13 300	13 000	...	...	...	...	...	...
20 - 24	45 700	22 200	23 500	...	...	...	...	...	...
25 - 29	53 300	25 800	27 500	...	...	...	...	...	...
30 - 34	73 600	33 100	40 500	...	...	...	...	...	...
35 - 39	60 900	27 800	33 100	...	...	...	...	...	...
40 - 44	48 600	21 700	26 900	...	...	...	...	...	...
45 - 49	50 800	21 200	29 600	...	...	...	...	...	...
50 - 54	48 200	19 600	28 600	...	...	...	...	...	...
55 - 59	53 100	24 000	29 100	...	...	...	...	...	...
60 - 64	45 800	22 500	23 300	...	...	...	...	...	...
65 - 69	30 800	15 000	15 800	...	...	...	...	...	...
70 - 74	19 700	10 200	9 500	...	...	...	...	...	...
75 - 79	9 700	5 000	4 700	...	...	...	...	...	...
80 - 84	7 800	3 400	4 400	...	...	...	...	...	...
85 +	8 400	2 800	5 600	...	...	...	...	...	...
Cyprus - Chypre[61]									
1 X 2011 (CDJC)									
Total	840 407	408 780	431 627	566 191	273 065	293 126	274 216	135 715	138 501
0 - 4	45 015	23 061	21 954	29 726	15 202	14 524	15 289	7 859	7 430
5 - 9	42 635	21 921	20 714	28 050	14 386	13 664	14 585	7 535	7 050
10 - 14	47 298	24 179	23 119	30 926	15 730	15 196	16 372	8 449	7 923
15 - 19	55 818	28 683	27 135	36 345	18 593	17 752	19 473	10 090	9 383
20 - 24	66 073	33 891	32 182	44 948	22 847	22 101	21 125	11 044	10 081
25 - 29	74 114	36 992	37 122	51 855	25 842	26 013	22 259	11 150	11 109
30 - 34	69 834	33 149	36 685	48 938	23 133	25 805	20 896	10 016	10 880
35 - 39	61 862	27 754	34 108	43 232	19 204	24 028	18 630	8 550	10 080
40 - 44	59 728	27 031	32 697	41 295	18 416	22 879	18 433	8 615	9 818
45 - 49	57 240	27 059	30 181	39 233	18 225	21 008	18 007	8 834	9 173
50 - 54	56 128	27 517	28 611	38 287	18 499	19 788	17 841	9 018	8 823
55 - 59	47 762	23 771	23 991	31 716	15 541	16 175	16 046	8 230	7 816
60 - 64	45 034	22 057	22 977	29 704	14 438	15 266	15 330	7 619	7 711
65 - 69	36 328	17 656	18 672	23 459	11 295	12 164	12 869	6 361	6 508
70 - 74	29 433	14 044	15 389	18 991	9 048	9 943	10 442	4 996	5 446
75 - 79	21 058	9 647	11 411	13 545	6 239	7 306	7 513	3 408	4 105
80 +	24 948	10 342	14 606	15 853	6 408	9 445	9 095	3 934	5 161
Unknown - Inconnu	99	26	73	88	19	69	11	7	4
1 I 2019 (ESDJ)									
Total	*875 899*	*427 831*	*448 068*	...	...	...	...	...	...
0	*9 289*	*4 757*	*4 532*	...	...	...	...	...	...
1 - 4	*37 341*	*19 259*	*18 082*	...	...	...	...	...	...
5 - 9	*49 104*	*24 966*	*24 138*	...	...	...	...	...	...
10 - 14	*45 470*	*23 200*	*22 270*	...	...	...	...	...	...
15 - 19	*48 856*	*24 429*	*24 427*	...	...	...	...	...	...
20 - 24	*63 295*	*30 018*	*33 277*	...	...	...	...	...	...
25 - 29	*74 578*	*36 530*	*38 048*	...	...	...	...	...	...
30 - 34	*73 209*	*35 955*	*37 254*	...	...	...	...	...	...
35 - 39	*66 650*	*32 678*	*33 972*	...	...	...	...	...	...
40 - 44	*56 158*	*27 240*	*28 918*	...	...	...	...	...	...
45 - 49	*54 054*	*26 325*	*27 729*	...	...	...	...	...	...
50 - 54	*53 871*	*26 614*	*27 257*	...	...	...	...	...	...
55 - 59	*54 546*	*26 958*	*27 588*	...	...	...	...	...	...
60 - 64	*48 366*	*23 846*	*24 520*	...	...	...	...	...	...

7. Population by age, sex and urban/rural residence: latest available year, 2010 - 2019
Population selon l'âge, le sexe et la résidence, urbaine/rurale : dernière année disponible, 2010 - 2019 (continued - suite)

Continent, country or area, date, code[a] and age (in years) / Continent, pays ou zone, date, code[a] et âge (en années)	Total			Urban - Urbaine			Rural - Rurale		
	Both sexes Les deux sexes	Male Masculin	Female Féminin	Both sexes Les deux sexes	Male Masculin	Female Féminin	Both sexes Les deux sexes	Male Masculin	Female Féminin
ASIA - ASIE									
Cyprus - Chypre[61]									
1 I 2019 (ESDJ)									
65 - 69	*45 193*	*21 966*	*23 227*	...	...	...	...	...	...
70 - 74	*36 574*	*17 152*	*19 422*	...	...	...	...	...	...
75 - 79	*27 332*	*12 590*	*14 742*	...	...	...	...	...	...
80 - 84	*18 411*	*7 999*	*10 412*	...	...	...	...	...	...
85 - 89	*9 828*	*3 932*	*5 896*	...	...	...	...	...	...
90 - 94	*2 930*	*1 109*	*1 821*	...	...	...	...	...	...
95 - 99	*716*	*263*	*453*	...	...	...	...	...	...
100 +	*128*	*45*	*83*	...	...	...	...	...	...
Georgia - Géorgie									
5 XI 2014 (CDJC)									
Total	3 713 804	1 772 864	1 940 940	2 122 623	980 985	1 141 638	1 591 181	791 879	799 302
0 - 4	255 089	132 700	122 389	152 766	78 799	73 967	102 323	53 901	48 422
5 - 9	230 024	121 245	108 779	139 301	72 526	66 775	90 723	48 719	42 004
10 - 14	206 216	109 481	96 735	119 287	62 645	56 642	86 929	46 836	40 093
15 - 19	226 022	118 877	107 145	130 446	66 924	63 522	95 576	51 953	43 623
20 - 24	266 125	135 305	130 820	162 336	79 100	83 236	103 789	56 205	47 584
25 - 29	278 662	139 945	138 717	168 601	80 608	87 993	110 061	59 337	50 724
30 - 34	262 060	129 921	132 139	160 622	76 264	84 358	101 438	53 657	47 781
35 - 39	248 549	121 943	126 606	150 707	71 177	79 530	97 842	50 766	47 076
40 - 44	243 281	118 318	124 963	143 846	67 326	76 520	99 435	50 992	48 443
45 - 49	239 407	114 036	125 371	133 670	60 443	73 227	105 737	53 593	52 144
50 - 54	271 386	126 710	144 676	150 014	66 843	83 171	121 372	59 867	61 505
55 - 59	245 391	111 641	133 750	133 348	57 828	75 520	112 043	53 813	58 230
60 - 64	211 385	92 412	118 973	114 908	47 738	67 170	96 477	44 674	51 803
65 - 69	155 702	64 889	90 813	84 433	33 489	50 944	71 269	31 400	39 869
70 - 74	123 605	48 483	75 122	61 257	22 399	38 858	62 348	26 084	36 264
75 - 79	135 764	49 895	85 869	64 993	21 828	43 165	70 771	28 067	42 704
80 - 84	71 675	25 100	46 575	32 119	10 106	22 013	39 556	14 994	24 562
85 - 89	34 508	10 166	24 342	15 957	4 154	11 803	18 551	6 012	12 539
90 - 94	7 495	1 620	5 875	3 473	712	2 761	4 022	908	3 114
95 - 99	1 171	163	1 008	456	69	387	715	94	621
100 +	287	14	273	83	7	76	204	7	197
1 I 2019 (ESDJ)[7]									
Total	3 723 464	1 790 899	1 932 565	...	...	...	...	...	...
0	50 991	26 450	24 541	...	...	...	...	...	...
1 - 4	228 645	118 180	110 465	...	...	...	...	...	...
5 - 9	256 101	133 324	122 777	...	...	...	...	...	...
10 - 14	218 763	115 653	103 110	...	...	...	...	...	...
15 - 19	205 771	109 149	96 622	...	...	...	...	...	...
20 - 24	220 569	115 686	104 883	...	...	...	...	...	...
25 - 29	262 452	132 675	129 777	...	...	...	...	...	...
30 - 34	271 863	136 404	135 459	...	...	...	...	...	...
35 - 39	252 347	125 265	127 082	...	...	...	...	...	...
40 - 44	241 238	119 450	121 788	...	...	...	...	...	...
45 - 49	234 369	114 750	119 619	...	...	...	...	...	...
50 - 54	236 258	113 033	123 225	...	...	...	...	...	...
55 - 59	262 403	121 364	141 039	...	...	...	...	...	...
60 - 64	229 009	101 154	127 855	...	...	...	...	...	...
65 - 69	191 733	79 925	111 808	...	...	...	...	...	...
70 - 74	123 632	48 307	75 325	...	...	...	...	...	...
75 - 79	108 187	38 731	69 456	...	...	...	...	...	...
80 - 84	85 385	28 418	56 967	...	...	...	...	...	...
85 - 89	33 436	10 551	22 885	...	...	...	...	...	...
90 - 94	9 340	2 266	7 074	...	...	...	...	...	...
95 - 99	965	157	808	...	...	...	...	...	...
100 +	7	7	-	...	...	...	...	...	...
India - Inde[62]									
9 II 2011 (CDFC)									
Total	1210854977	623 270 258	587 584 719	377 106 125	195 489 200	181 616 925	833 748 852	427 781 058	405 967 794
0 - 4	112 806 778	58 632 074	54 174 704	29 820 118	15 595 697	14 224 421	82 986 660	43 036 377	39 950 283
5 - 9	126 928 126	66 300 466	60 627 660	33 120 514	17 475 207	15 645 307	93 807 612	48 825 259	44 982 353
10 - 14	132 709 212	69 418 835	63 290 377	35 904 718	18 930 677	16 974 041	96 804 494	50 488 158	46 316 336
15 - 19	120 526 449	63 982 396	56 544 053	36 623 977	19 411 839	17 212 138	83 902 472	44 570 557	39 331 915

7. Population by age, sex and urban/rural residence: latest available year, 2010 - 2019
Population selon l'âge, le sexe et la résidence, urbaine/rurale : dernière année disponible, 2010 - 2019 (continued - suite)

Continent, country or area, date, code[a] and age (in years) / Continent, pays ou zone, date, code[a] et âge (en années)	Total			Urban - Urbaine			Rural - Rurale		
	Both sexes Les deux sexes	Male Masculin	Female Féminin	Both sexes Les deux sexes	Male Masculin	Female Féminin	Both sexes Les deux sexes	Male Masculin	Female Féminin
ASIA - ASIE									
India - Inde[62]									
9 II 2011 (CDFC)									
20 - 24	111 424 222	57 584 693	53 839 529	37 589 176	19 446 031	18 143 145	73 835 046	38 138 662	35 696 384
25 - 29	101 413 965	51 344 208	50 069 757	35 345 695	17 968 219	17 377 476	66 068 270	33 375 989	32 692 281
30 - 34	88 594 951	44 660 674	43 934 277	30 683 172	15 726 482	14 956 690	57 911 779	28 934 192	28 977 587
35 - 39	85 140 684	42 919 381	42 221 303	29 077 977	14 793 820	14 284 157	56 062 707	28 125 561	27 937 146
40 - 44	72 438 112	37 545 386	34 892 726	24 857 104	12 980 151	11 876 953	47 581 008	24 565 235	23 015 773
45 - 49	62 318 327	32 138 114	30 180 213	21 630 099	11 273 844	10 356 255	40 688 228	20 864 270	19 823 958
50 - 54	49 069 254	25 843 266	23 225 988	17 037 466	9 053 719	7 983 747	32 031 788	16 789 547	15 242 241
55 - 59	39 146 055	19 456 012	19 690 043	13 284 541	6 919 483	6 365 058	25 861 514	12 536 529	13 324 985
60 - 64	37 663 707	18 701 749	18 961 958	11 372 462	5 770 157	5 602 305	26 291 245	12 931 592	13 359 653
65 - 69	26 454 983	12 944 326	13 510 657	7 538 713	3 736 015	3 802 698	18 916 270	9 208 311	9 707 959
70 - 74	19 208 842	9 651 499	9 557 343	5 401 242	2 673 320	2 727 922	13 807 600	6 978 179	6 829 421
75 - 79	9 232 503	4 490 603	4 741 900	2 848 786	1 377 179	1 471 607	6 383 717	3 113 424	3 270 293
80 - 84	6 220 229	2 927 040	3 293 189	1 800 347	807 610	992 737	4 419 882	2 119 430	2 300 452
85 - 89	2 383 167	1 120 106	1 263 061	785 179	349 809	435 370	1 597 988	770 297	827 691
90 - 94	1 446 534	652 465	794 069	422 547	180 500	242 047	1 023 987	471 965	552 022
95 - 99	633 297	294 759	338 538	187 628	84 120	103 508	445 669	210 639	235 030
100 +	605 778	289 325	316 453	198 314	95 860	102 454	407 464	193 465	213 999
Unknown - Inconnu	4 489 802	2 372 881	2 116 921	1 576 350	839 461	736 889	2 913 452	1 533 420	1 380 032
Indonesia - Indonésie[63]									
1 VII 2019 (ESDJ)									
Total	*266 911 905*	*134 025 583*	*132 886 322*	*148 771 903*	*74 658 523*	*74 113 380*	*118 140 002*	*59 367 060*	*58 772 942*
0 - 4	*21 974 348*	*11 133 238*	*10 841 110*	*12 030 688*	*6 093 254*	*5 937 434*	*9 943 660*	*5 039 984*	*4 903 676*
0	*4 388 841*	*2 220 839*	*2 168 002*	...	...	...	...	...	...
1 - 4	*17 585 507*	*8 912 399*	*8 673 108*	...	...	...	...	...	...
5 - 9	*21 998 827*	*11 230 399*	*10 768 428*	*11 914 239*	*6 081 608*	*5 832 631*	*10 084 588*	*5 148 791*	*4 935 797*
10 - 14	*22 200 085*	*11 290 180*	*10 909 905*	*11 930 004*	*6 057 856*	*5 872 148*	*10 270 081*	*5 232 324*	*5 037 757*
15 - 19	*22 134 812*	*11 180 509*	*10 954 303*	*12 461 809*	*6 231 916*	*6 229 893*	*9 673 003*	*4 948 593*	*4 724 410*
20 - 24	*21 964 077*	*11 073 218*	*10 890 859*	*12 962 513*	*6 522 330*	*6 440 183*	*9 001 564*	*4 550 888*	*4 450 676*
25 - 29	*21 678 638*	*10 962 006*	*10 716 632*	*12 546 496*	*6 348 109*	*6 198 387*	*9 132 142*	*4 613 897*	*4 518 245*
30 - 34	*21 257 657*	*10 753 197*	*10 504 460*	*12 191 464*	*6 169 694*	*6 021 770*	*9 066 193*	*4 583 503*	*4 482 690*
35 - 39	*20 631 081*	*10 395 623*	*10 235 458*	*11 728 827*	*5 907 442*	*5 821 385*	*8 902 254*	*4 488 181*	*4 414 073*
40 - 44	*19 319 486*	*9 728 863*	*9 590 623*	*10 921 140*	*5 501 905*	*5 419 235*	*8 398 346*	*4 226 958*	*4 171 388*
45 - 49	*17 860 921*	*8 994 248*	*8 866 673*	*9 965 934*	*5 021 440*	*4 944 494*	*7 894 987*	*3 972 808*	*3 922 179*
50 - 54	*15 502 403*	*7 760 021*	*7 742 382*	*8 578 775*	*4 302 876*	*4 275 899*	*6 923 628*	*3 457 145*	*3 466 483*
55 - 59	*12 891 142*	*6 431 737*	*6 459 405*	*7 064 681*	*3 529 482*	*3 535 199*	*5 826 461*	*2 902 255*	*2 924 206*
60 - 64	*10 123 515*	*5 043 307*	*5 080 208*	*5 400 554*	*2 693 442*	*2 707 112*	*4 722 961*	*2 349 865*	*2 373 096*
65 - 69	*7 347 682*	*3 596 629*	*3 751 053*	*3 886 054*	*1 902 977*	*1 983 077*	*3 461 628*	*1 693 652*	*1 767 976*
70 - 74	*4 976 714*	*2 337 702*	*2 639 012*	*2 597 152*	*1 219 094*	*1 378 058*	*2 379 562*	*1 118 608*	*1 260 954*
75 +	*5 050 517*	*2 114 706*	*2 935 811*	*2 591 573*	*1 075 098*	*1 516 475*	*2 458 944*	*1 039 608*	*1 419 336*
Iran (Islamic Republic of) - Iran (République islamique d')[64]									
1 VII 2019 (ESDJ)									
Total	*83 075 062*	*42 017 710*	*41 057 352*	*62 367 382*	*31 539 435*	*30 827 947*	*20 707 680*	*10 478 275*	*10 229 405*
0 - 4	*7 339 376*	*3 757 592*	*3 581 784*	*5 256 319*	*2 696 519*	*2 559 800*	*2 083 057*	*1 061 073*	*1 021 984*
5 - 9	*6 976 861*	*3 581 310*	*3 395 551*	*5 021 036*	*2 584 662*	*2 436 374*	*1 955 825*	*996 648*	*959 177*
10 - 14	*6 084 252*	*3 115 873*	*2 968 379*	*4 401 814*	*2 260 237*	*2 141 577*	*1 682 438*	*855 636*	*826 802*
15 - 19	*5 488 287*	*2 806 096*	*2 682 191*	*4 032 624*	*2 053 556*	*1 979 068*	*1 455 663*	*752 540*	*703 123*
20 - 24	*5 668 880*	*2 881 992*	*2 786 888*	*4 130 139*	*2 058 782*	*2 071 357*	*1 538 741*	*823 210*	*715 531*
25 - 29	*7 112 245*	*3 594 700*	*3 517 545*	*5 345 979*	*2 661 190*	*2 684 789*	*1 766 266*	*933 510*	*832 756*
30 - 34	*8 586 457*	*4 332 743*	*4 253 714*	*6 677 971*	*3 351 692*	*3 326 279*	*1 908 486*	*981 051*	*927 435*
35 - 39	*8 097 926*	*4 091 703*	*4 006 223*	*6 289 428*	*3 174 669*	*3 114 759*	*1 808 498*	*917 034*	*891 464*
40 - 44	*6 318 239*	*3 213 162*	*3 105 077*	*4 863 810*	*2 480 532*	*2 383 278*	*1 454 429*	*732 630*	*721 799*
45 - 49	*5 151 778*	*2 622 292*	*2 529 486*	*4 019 111*	*2 060 303*	*1 958 808*	*1 132 667*	*561 989*	*570 678*
50 - 54	*4 420 625*	*2 232 401*	*2 188 224*	*3 473 396*	*1 771 128*	*1 702 268*	*947 229*	*461 273*	*485 956*
55 - 59	*3 600 060*	*1 795 384*	*1 804 676*	*2 785 471*	*1 406 697*	*1 378 774*	*814 589*	*388 687*	*425 902*
60 - 64	*2 947 641*	*1 452 188*	*1 495 453*	*2 242 256*	*1 128 340*	*1 113 916*	*705 385*	*323 848*	*381 537*
65 - 69	*2 066 218*	*990 450*	*1 075 768*	*1 536 075*	*753 411*	*782 664*	*530 143*	*237 039*	*293 104*
70 - 74	*1 320 883*	*613 412*	*707 471*	*965 899*	*454 773*	*511 126*	*354 984*	*158 639*	*196 345*
75 - 79	*855 813*	*412 530*	*443 283*	*610 392*	*293 101*	*317 291*	*245 421*	*119 429*	*125 992*
80 +	*1 039 521*	*523 882*	*515 639*	*715 662*	*349 843*	*365 819*	*323 859*	*174 039*	*149 820*

7. Population by age, sex and urban/rural residence: latest available year, 2010 - 2019
Population selon l'âge, le sexe et la résidence, urbaine/rurale : dernière année disponible, 2010 - 2019 (continued - suite)

Continent, country or area, date, code[a] and age (in years) Continent, pays ou zone, date, code[a] et âge (en annèes)	Total			Urban - Urbaine			Rural - Rurale		
	Both sexes Les deux sexes	Male Masculin	Female Féminin	Both sexes Les deux sexes	Male Masculin	Female Féminin	Both sexes Les deux sexes	Male Masculin	Female Féminin
ASIA - ASIE									
Iraq									
1 VII 2019 (ESDF)									
Total	*38 836 326*	*19 621 019*	*19 215 306*	*27 134 294*	*13 693 935*	*13 440 360*	*11 702 031*	*5 927 084*	*5 774 947*
0	*1 040 652*	*530 167*	*510 486*	*705 147*	*357 990*	*347 157*	*335 505*	*172 176*	*163 329*
1 - 4	*4 657 538*	*2 395 086*	*2 262 452*	*3 102 208*	*1 598 441*	*1 503 767*	*1 555 329*	*796 645*	*758 684*
5 - 9	*5 299 958*	*2 730 014*	*2 569 943*	*3 513 998*	*1 800 610*	*1 713 388*	*1 785 960*	*929 405*	*856 555*
10 - 14	*4 717 524*	*2 439 838*	*2 277 686*	*3 120 214*	*1 612 388*	*1 507 826*	*1 597 310*	*827 450*	*769 860*
15 - 19	*4 163 349*	*2 140 720*	*2 022 629*	*2 840 863*	*1 453 036*	*1 387 827*	*1 322 485*	*687 683*	*634 802*
20 - 24	*3 595 693*	*1 869 943*	*1 725 750*	*2 576 083*	*1 331 383*	*1 244 700*	*1 019 610*	*538 561*	*481 050*
25 - 29	*2 892 670*	*1 466 644*	*1 426 026*	*2 090 060*	*1 066 201*	*1 023 859*	*802 610*	*400 444*	*402 167*
30 - 34	*2 605 847*	*1 284 258*	*1 321 588*	*1 869 774*	*930 003*	*939 771*	*736 073*	*354 255*	*381 818*
35 - 39	*2 248 738*	*1 094 648*	*1 154 090*	*1 620 836*	*792 569*	*828 267*	*627 902*	*302 079*	*325 823*
40 - 44	*2 078 265*	*1 032 239*	*1 046 026*	*1 500 940*	*742 604*	*758 336*	*577 326*	*289 636*	*287 690*
45 - 49	*1 548 367*	*762 860*	*785 507*	*1 155 740*	*571 568*	*584 172*	*392 626*	*191 292*	*201 334*
50 - 54	*1 009 920*	*449 795*	*560 125*	*788 261*	*357 911*	*430 350*	*221 659*	*91 884*	*129 775*
55 - 59	*1 046 450*	*511 343*	*535 107*	*792 511*	*389 261*	*403 251*	*253 939*	*122 082*	*131 856*
60 - 64	*737 044*	*352 151*	*384 892*	*552 523*	*263 680*	*288 843*	*184 521*	*88 471*	*96 050*
65 - 69	*473 298*	*231 805*	*241 493*	*365 542*	*179 234*	*186 307*	*107 756*	*52 570*	*55 186*
70 - 74	*303 423*	*151 236*	*152 187*	*235 545*	*117 497*	*118 048*	*67 878*	*33 739*	*34 140*
75 - 79	*175 641*	*79 658*	*95 983*	*134 106*	*61 368*	*72 738*	*41 535*	*18 290*	*23 245*
80 +	*241 950*	*98 614*	*143 336*	*169 944*	*68 191*	*101 753*	*72 005*	*30 423*	*41 583*
Israel - Israël[65]									
1 VII 2018 (ESDJ)									
Total	8 882 764	4 407 285	4 475 480	8 114 294[66]	4 016 793[66]	4 097 502[66]	768 470[66]	390 492[66]	377 978[66]
0	183 378	94 072	89 306	167 689[66]	86 076[66]	81 613[66]	15 689[66]	7 996[66]	7 693[66]
1 - 4	721 408	371 058	350 350	654 651[66]	336 740[66]	317 910[66]	66 757[66]	34 317[66]	32 440[66]
5 - 9	845 379	432 985	412 395	760 940[66]	389 492[66]	371 448[66]	84 439[66]	43 493[66]	40 947[66]
10 - 14	757 176	388 148	369 029	681 781[66]	348 918[66]	332 863[66]	75 395[66]	39 230[66]	36 166[66]
15 - 19	699 314	357 804	341 509	630 316[66]	321 286[66]	309 029[66]	68 998[66]	36 518[66]	32 480[66]
20 - 24	637 002	324 631	312 371	584 023[66]	296 611[66]	287 412[66]	52 980[66]	28 020[66]	24 959[66]
25 - 29	610 241	308 477	301 763	565 329[66]	285 411[66]	279 918[66]	44 912[66]	23 066[66]	21 846[66]
30 - 34	594 125	297 376	296 749	548 426[66]	274 747[66]	273 679[66]	45 699[66]	22 629[66]	23 070[66]
35 - 39	571 383	283 949	287 433	522 293[66]	260 082[66]	262 211[66]	49 090[66]	23 867[66]	25 222[66]
40 - 44	553 210	274 349	278 861	501 550[66]	249 013[66]	252 537[66]	51 660[66]	25 336[66]	26 324[66]
45 - 49	491 958	242 982	248 976	447 197[66]	220 495[66]	226 703[66]	44 761[66]	22 487[66]	22 274[66]
50 - 54	416 989	205 145	211 845	381 844[66]	187 070[66]	194 774[66]	35 145[66]	18 075[66]	17 070[66]
55 - 59	392 683	189 053	203 630	361 781[66]	173 416[66]	188 366[66]	30 901[66]	15 637[66]	15 264[66]
60 - 64	371 431	176 316	195 115	342 585[66]	161 652[66]	180 934[66]	28 846[66]	14 664[66]	14 181[66]
65 - 69	347 020	162 804	184 216	321 196[66]	149 498[66]	171 698[66]	25 825[66]	13 306[66]	12 519[66]
70 - 74	263 081	121 400	141 680	244 520[66]	112 210[66]	132 310[66]	18 561[66]	9 191[66]	9 370[66]
75 - 79	165 221	72 662	92 559	154 109[66]	67 297[66]	86 812[66]	11 112[66]	5 365[66]	5 747[66]
80 - 84	134 921	56 400	78 522	126 140[66]	52 488[66]	73 653[66]	8 781[66]	3 912[66]	4 869[66]
85 - 89	78 113	30 356	47 757	72 733[66]	28 212[66]	44 521[66]	5 379[66]	2 144[66]	3 236[66]
90 - 94	36 208	12 609	23 599	33 597[66]	11 673[66]	21 924[66]	2 611[66]	936[66]	1 675[66]
95 - 99	9 432	3 338	6 094	8 720[66]	3 103[66]	5 617[66]	712[66]	235[66]	477[66]
100 +	3 092	1 372	1 720	2 874[66]	1 303[66]	1 571[66]	218[66]	68[66]	149[66]
Japan - Japon[67]									
1 X 2015 (CDJC)									
Total	127 094 745	61 841 738	65 253 007	116 137 232	56 532 149	59 605 083	10 957 513	5 309 589	5 647 924
0 - 4	4 987 706	2 550 921	2 436 785	4 585 047	2 344 645	2 240 402	402 659	206 276	196 383
5 - 9	5 299 787	2 714 591	2 585 196	4 842 315	2 480 103	2 362 212	457 472	234 488	222 984
10 - 14	5 599 317	2 868 024	2 731 293	5 098 044	2 611 161	2 486 883	501 273	256 863	244 410
15 - 19	6 008 388	3 085 416	2 922 972	5 512 237	2 829 307	2 682 930	496 151	256 109	240 042
20 - 24	5 968 127	3 046 392	2 921 735	5 557 062	2 834 296	2 722 766	411 065	212 096	198 969
25 - 29	6 409 612	3 255 717	3 153 895	5 947 621	3 016 085	2 931 536	461 991	239 632	222 359
30 - 34	7 290 878	3 684 747	3 606 131	6 748 938	3 407 192	3 341 746	541 940	277 555	264 385
35 - 39	8 316 157	4 204 202	4 111 955	7 682 014	3 879 376	3 802 638	634 143	324 826	309 317
40 - 44	9 732 218	4 914 018	4 818 200	9 002 172	4 540 962	4 461 210	730 046	373 056	356 990
45 - 49	8 662 804	4 354 877	4 307 927	8 008 263	4 026 225	3 982 038	654 541	328 652	325 889
50 - 54	7 930 296	3 968 311	3 961 985	7 266 826	3 636 156	3 630 670	663 470	332 155	331 315
55 - 59	7 515 246	3 729 523	3 785 723	6 791 248	3 368 519	3 422 729	723 998	361 004	362 994
60 - 64	8 455 010	4 151 119	4 303 891	7 593 671	3 722 143	3 871 528	861 339	428 976	432 363
65 - 69	9 643 867	4 659 662	4 984 205	8 719 913	4 203 013	4 516 900	923 954	456 649	467 305
70 - 74	7 695 811	3 582 440	4 113 371	6 983 090	3 247 479	3 735 611	712 721	334 961	377 760

Continent, country or area, date, code[a] and age (in years) / Continent, pays ou zone, date, code[a] et âge (en années)	Total			Urban - Urbaine			Rural - Rurale		
	Both sexes Les deux sexes	Male Masculin	Female Féminin	Both sexes Les deux sexes	Male Masculin	Female Féminin	Both sexes Les deux sexes	Male Masculin	Female Féminin
ASIA - ASIE									
Japan - Japon[67]									
1 X 2015 (CDJC)									
75 - 79	6 276 856	2 787 417	3 489 439	5 654 811	2 511 652	3 143 159	622 045	275 765	346 280
80 - 84	4 961 420	1 994 326	2 967 094	4 425 840	1 779 702	2 646 138	535 580	214 624	320 956
85 - 89	3 117 257	1 056 641	2 060 616	2 749 324	932 310	1 817 014	367 933	124 331	243 602
90 - 94	1 349 120	333 335	1 015 785	1 183 214	292 810	890 404	165 906	40 525	125 381
95 - 99	359 347	63 265	296 082	314 841	55 450	259 391	44 506	7 815	36 691
100 +	61 763	8 383	53 380	54 031	7 351	46 680	7 732	1 032	6 700
Unknown - Inconnu	1 453 758	828 411	625 347	1 416 710	806 212	610 498	37 048	22 199	14 849
1 VII 2019 (ESDJ)[68]									
Total	126 265 000	61 441 000	64 823 000	...	...	...	...	...	...
0 - 4	4 790 000	2 454 000	2 336 000	...	...	...	...	...	...
5 - 9	5 126 000	2 625 000	2 501 000	...	...	...	...	...	...
10 - 14	5 369 000	2 749 000	2 620 000	...	...	...	...	...	...
15 - 19	5 863 000	3 006 000	2 857 000	...	...	...	...	...	...
20 - 24	6 394 000	3 299 000	3 094 000	...	...	...	...	...	...
25 - 29	6 223 000	3 203 000	3 020 000	...	...	...	...	...	...
30 - 34	6 814 000	3 475 000	3 339 000	...	...	...	...	...	...
35 - 39	7 582 000	3 842 000	3 740 000	...	...	...	...	...	...
40 - 44	8 820 000	4 466 000	4 353 000	...	...	...	...	...	...
45 - 49	9 745 000	4 923 000	4 821 000	...	...	...	...	...	...
50 - 54	8 523 000	4 283 000	4 239 000	...	...	...	...	...	...
55 - 59	7 661 000	3 826 000	3 835 000	...	...	...	...	...	...
60 - 64	7 555 000	3 728 000	3 827 000	...	...	...	...	...	...
65 - 69	8 863 000	4 290 000	4 573 000	...	...	...	...	...	...
70 - 74	8 540 000	4 024 000	4 516 000	...	...	...	...	...	...
75 - 79	7 195 000	3 218 000	3 977 000	...	...	...	...	...	...
80 - 84	5 320 000	2 192 000	3 128 000	...	...	...	...	...	...
85 - 89	3 589 000	1 263 000	2 326 000	...	...	...	...	...	...
90 - 94	1 749 000	478 000	1 271 000	...	...	...	...	...	...
95 - 99	473 000	85 000	388 000	...	...	...	...	...	...
100 +	71 000	9 000	62 000	...	...	...	...	...	...
Jordan - Jordanie[69]									
30 XI 2015 (CDFC)									
Total	9 531 712	5 046 824	4 484 888	8 611 323	4 561 944	4 049 379	920 389	484 880	435 509
0	208 691	107 002	101 689	186 255	95 466	90 789	22 436	11 536	10 900
1 - 4	885 507	454 278	431 229	792 037	406 308	385 729	93 470	47 970	45 500
5 - 9	1 169 491	597 975	571 516	1 050 857	537 071	513 786	118 634	60 904	57 730
10 - 14	1 010 398	519 876	490 522	910 848	468 508	442 340	99 550	51 368	48 182
15 - 19	947 821	498 519	449 302	854 544	449 845	404 699	93 277	48 674	44 603
20 - 24	945 975	519 140	426 835	856 226	470 218	386 008	89 749	48 922	40 827
25 - 29	830 606	459 841	370 765	750 184	414 978	335 206	80 422	44 863	35 559
30 - 34	734 400	395 939	338 461	663 266	357 518	305 748	71 134	38 421	32 713
35 - 39	651 190	352 691	298 499	589 773	319 919	269 854	61 417	32 772	28 645
40 - 44	560 931	304 330	256 601	508 054	276 252	231 802	52 877	28 078	24 799
45 - 49	473 409	258 567	214 842	431 427	236 137	195 290	41 982	22 430	19 552
50 - 54	349 837	187 189	162 648	320 505	171 594	148 911	29 332	15 595	13 737
55 - 59	244 699	127 359	117 340	225 052	117 524	107 528	19 647	9 835	9 812
60 - 64	167 078	86 254	80 824	152 320	78 409	73 911	14 758	7 845	6 913
65 - 69	135 653	67 492	68 161	124 292	62 013	62 279	11 361	5 479	5 882
70 - 74	99 792	52 668	47 124	91 281	48 326	42 955	8 511	4 342	4 169
75 - 79	64 187	32 428	31 759	58 154	29 476	28 678	6 033	2 952	3 081
80 +	52 047	25 276	26 771	46 248	22 382	23 866	5 799	2 894	2 905
80 - 84	30 957	15 324	15 633	...	...	...	...	...	...
85 - 89	13 738	6 387	7 351	...	...	...	...	...	...
90 - 94	4 035	1 797	2 238	...	...	...	...	...	...
95 +	3 317	1 768	1 549	...	...	...	...	...	...
31 XII 2018 (ESDF)[66]									
Total	*10 309 000*	*5 458 000*	*4 851 000*	...	...	...	...	...	...
0	*225 710*	*115 720*	*109 990*	...	...	...	...	...	...
1 - 4	*957 720*	*491 290*	*466 430*	...	...	...	...	...	...
5 - 9	*1 264 870*	*646 690*	*618 180*	...	...	...	...	...	...
10 - 14	*1 092 790*	*562 230*	*530 560*	...	...	...	...	...	...
15 - 19	*1 025 110*	*539 130*	*485 980*	...	...	...	...	...	...
20 - 24	*1 023 120*	*561 440*	*461 680*	...	...	...	...	...	...

7. Population by age, sex and urban/rural residence: latest available year, 2010 - 2019
Population selon l'âge, le sexe et la résidence, urbaine/rurale : dernière année disponible, 2010 - 2019 (continued - suite)

Continent, country or area, date, code[a] and age (in years) / Continent, pays ou zone, date, code[a] et âge (en annèes)	Total			Urban - Urbaine			Rural - Rurale		
	Both sexes Les deux sexes	Male Masculin	Female Féminin	Both sexes Les deux sexes	Male Masculin	Female Féminin	Both sexes Les deux sexes	Male Masculin	Female Féminin
ASIA - ASIE									
Jordan - Jordanie[69]									
31 XII 2018 (ESDF)[66]									
25 - 29	*898 340*	*497 310*	*401 030*	...	...	...	...	...	...
30 - 34	*794 290*	*428 200*	*366 090*	...	...	...	...	...	...
35 - 39	*704 290*	*381 430*	*322 860*	...	...	...	...	...	...
40 - 44	*606 670*	*329 120*	*277 550*	...	...	...	...	...	...
45 - 49	*512 010*	*279 630*	*232 380*	...	...	...	...	...	...
50 - 54	*378 370*	*202 440*	*175 930*	...	...	...	...	...	...
55 - 59	*264 650*	*137 740*	*126 910*	...	...	...	...	...	...
60 - 64	*180 700*	*93 280*	*87 420*	...	...	...	...	...	...
65 - 69	*146 720*	*72 990*	*73 730*	...	...	...	...	...	...
70 - 74	*107 930*	*56 960*	*50 970*	...	...	...	...	...	...
75 - 79	*69 420*	*35 070*	*34 350*	...	...	...	...	...	...
80 - 84	*33 480*	*16 570*	*16 910*	...	...	...	...	...	...
85 - 89	*14 860*	*6 910*	*7 950*	...	...	...	...	...	...
90 - 94	*4 360*	*1 940*	*2 420*	...	...	...	...	...	...
95 +	*3 590*	*1 910*	*1 680*	...	...	...	...	...	...
Kazakhstan[70]									
1 VII 2019 (ESDF)									
Total	18 513 673	8 973 665	9 540 008	10 818 430	5 103 920	5 714 510	7 695 243	3 869 745	3 825 498
0	396 642	204 682	191 960	233 302	120 515	112 787	163 340	84 167	79 173
1 - 4	1 567 654	808 394	759 260	903 428	466 069	437 359	664 226	342 325	321 901
5 - 9	1 842 162	946 846	895 316	1 034 558	532 589	501 969	807 604	414 257	393 347
10 - 14	1 504 874	773 365	731 509	790 140	406 580	383 560	714 734	366 785	347 949
15 - 19	1 156 795	592 250	564 545	604 900	310 162	294 738	551 895	282 088	269 807
20 - 24	1 190 170	606 930	583 240	674 529	333 294	341 235	515 641	273 636	242 005
25 - 29	1 510 468	757 225	753 243	950 675	455 357	495 318	559 793	301 868	257 925
30 - 34	1 583 900	781 255	802 645	1 001 397	478 299	523 098	582 503	302 956	279 547
35 - 39	1 314 073	648 344	665 729	800 315	385 494	414 821	513 758	262 850	250 908
40 - 44	1 170 140	567 575	602 565	692 966	325 093	367 873	477 174	242 482	234 692
45 - 49	1 086 461	519 008	567 453	637 994	292 297	345 697	448 467	226 711	221 756
50 - 54	998 757	468 693	530 064	579 848	260 240	319 608	418 909	208 453	210 456
55 - 59	1 004 388	458 413	545 975	588 398	257 130	331 268	415 990	201 283	214 707
60 - 64	780 515	336 650	443 865	464 635	189 932	274 703	315 880	146 718	169 162
65 - 69	569 896	226 561	343 335	346 560	130 594	215 966	223 336	95 967	127 369
70 - 74	329 896	121 549	208 347	205 644	71 506	134 138	124 252	50 043	74 209
75 - 79	235 057	76 651	158 406	140 917	43 103	97 814	94 140	33 548	60 592
80 - 84	187 646	55 951	131 695	116 354	32 164	84 190	71 292	23 787	47 505
85 - 89	58 436	15 731	42 705	36 977	9 534	27 443	21 459	6 197	15 262
90 - 94	20 528	5 423	15 105	12 301	2 933	9 368	8 227	2 490	5 737
95 - 99	4 067	1 545	2 522	2 066	747	1 319	2 001	798	1 203
100 +	1 148	624	524	526	288	238	622	336	286
Kuwait - Koweït									
1 I 2019 (ESDF)									
Total	*4 420 110*	*2 736 531*	*1 683 579*	...	...	...	...	...	...
0	*55 410*	*28 775*	*26 635*	...	...	...	...	...	...
1 - 4	*246 265*	*131 645*	*114 620*	...	...	...	...	...	...
5 - 9	*335 374*	*187 399*	*147 975*	...	...	...	...	...	...
10 - 14	*286 571*	*159 269*	*127 302*	...	...	...	...	...	...
15 - 19	*240 149*	*132 220*	*107 929*	...	...	...	...	...	...
20 - 24	*225 745*	*125 138*	*100 607*	...	...	...	...	...	...
25 - 29	*217 633*	*118 763*	*98 870*	...	...	...	...	...	...
30 - 34	*408 208*	*238 759*	*169 449*	...	...	...	...	...	...
35 - 39	*548 398*	*360 536*	*187 862*	...	...	...	...	...	...
40 - 44	*550 547*	*371 081*	*179 466*	...	...	...	...	...	...
45 - 49	*473 177*	*321 182*	*151 995*	...	...	...	...	...	...
50 - 54	*324 954*	*220 768*	*104 186*	...	...	...	...	...	...
55 - 59	*218 589*	*148 785*	*69 804*	...	...	...	...	...	...
60 - 64	*138 498*	*96 414*	*42 084*	...	...	...	...	...	...
65 - 69	*77 121*	*52 069*	*25 052*	...	...	...	...	...	...
70 - 74	*37 793*	*23 219*	*14 574*	...	...	...	...	...	...
75 - 79	*18 914*	*10 894*	*8 020*	...	...	...	...	...	...
80 +	*16 764*	*9 615*	*7 149*	...	...	...	...	...	...

7. Population by age, sex and urban/rural residence: latest available year, 2010 - 2019
Population selon l'âge, le sexe et la résidence, urbaine/rurale : dernière année disponible, 2010 - 2019 (continued - suite)

Continent, country or area, date, code[a] and age (in years) / Continent, pays ou zone, date, code[a] et âge (en années)	Total			Urban - Urbaine			Rural - Rurale		
	Both sexes Les deux sexes	Male Masculin	Female Féminin	Both sexes Les deux sexes	Male Masculin	Female Féminin	Both sexes Les deux sexes	Male Masculin	Female Féminin
ASIA - ASIE									
Kyrgyzstan - Kirghizstan									
1 VII 2017 (ESDJ)[71]									
Total	6 198 465	3 072 164	3 126 301	2 097 487	996 210	1 101 277	4 100 978	2 075 954	2 025 024
0	153 674	78 878	74 796	50 790	26 021	24 769	102 884	52 857	50 027
1 - 4	624 235	321 049	303 186	207 427	106 993	100 434	416 808	214 056	202 752
5 - 9	673 907	344 573	329 334	217 396	111 126	106 270	456 511	233 447	223 064
10 - 14	543 470	276 917	266 553	157 585	79 774	77 811	385 885	197 143	188 742
15 - 19	497 079	253 073	244 006	139 125	70 665	68 460	357 954	182 408	175 546
20 - 24	556 096	283 536	272 560	162 667	80 353	82 314	393 429	203 183	190 246
25 - 29	580 904	292 693	288 211	227 567	105 940	121 627	353 337	186 753	166 584
30 - 34	502 049	251 984	250 065	186 909	87 950	98 959	315 140	164 034	151 106
35 - 39	391 950	196 453	195 497	143 343	67 797	75 546	248 607	128 656	119 951
40 - 44	340 627	167 218	173 409	121 854	55 533	66 321	218 773	111 685	107 088
45 - 49	319 033	154 326	164 707	117 362	52 751	64 611	201 671	101 575	100 096
50 - 54	291 181	138 139	153 042	103 823	46 607	57 216	187 358	91 532	95 826
55 - 59	264 854	123 125	141 729	94 203	41 445	52 758	170 651	81 680	88 971
60 - 64	178 026	79 396	98 630	63 155	26 243	36 912	114 871	53 153	61 718
65 - 69	117 727	49 495	68 232	44 195	17 150	27 045	73 532	32 345	41 187
70 - 74	49 872	20 066	29 806	19 795	7 161	12 634	30 077	12 905	17 172
75 - 79	55 296	20 911	34 385	20 717	6 905	13 812	34 579	14 006	20 573
80 - 84	32 500	11 258	21 242	11 394	3 408	7 986	21 106	7 850	13 256
85 - 89	17 356	5 815	11 541	5 597	1 574	4 023	11 759	4 241	7 518
90 - 94	6 687	2 619	4 068	2 027	649	1 378	4 660	1 970	2 690
95 - 99	1 596	505	1 091	434	129	305	1 162	376	786
100 +	346	135	211	122	36	86	224	99	125
1 I 2019 (ESDJ)									
Total	6 389 500	3 169 634	3 219 866	...	...	...	...	...	...
0	168 801	86 596	82 205	...	...	...	...	...	...
1 - 4	624 309	321 190	303 119	...	...	...	...	...	...
5 - 9	723 843	370 656	353 187	...	...	...	...	...	...
10 - 14	568 463	289 522	278 941	...	...	...	...	...	...
15 - 19	494 774	252 063	242 711	...	...	...	...	...	...
20 - 24	538 492	274 817	263 675	...	...	...	...	...	...
25 - 29	574 286	291 314	282 972	...	...	...	...	...	...
30 - 34	540 150	270 172	269 978	...	...	...	...	...	...
35 - 39	413 746	208 010	205 736	...	...	...	...	...	...
40 - 44	350 144	172 791	177 353	...	...	...	...	...	...
45 - 49	321 615	155 658	165 957	...	...	...	...	...	...
50 - 54	294 538	140 195	154 343	...	...	...	...	...	...
55 - 59	275 726	128 484	147 242	...	...	...	...	...	...
60 - 64	199 170	89 279	109 891	...	...	...	...	...	...
65 - 69	129 226	54 414	74 812	...	...	...	...	...	...
70 - 74	64 770	25 744	39 026	...	...	...	...	...	...
75 - 79	44 508	16 840	27 668	...	...	...	...	...	...
80 - 84	36 552	12 629	23 923	...	...	...	...	...	...
85 +	26 387	9 260	17 127	...	...	...	...	...	...
Lao People's Democratic Republic - République démocratique populaire lao									
1 III 2015 (CDJC)									
Total	6 492 228	3 254 770	3 237 458	2 137 831	1 076 928	1 060 903	4 354 397	2 177 842	2 176 555
0	118 387	60 356	58 031	33 508	17 278	16 230	84 879	43 078	41 801
1 - 4	563 596	286 106	277 490	155 156	79 243	75 913	408 440	206 863	201 577
5 - 9	679 209	345 380	333 829	175 575	89 631	85 944	503 634	255 749	247 885
10 - 14	718 606	363 026	355 580	189 707	96 093	93 614	528 899	266 933	261 966
15 - 19	699 010	354 360	344 650	222 599	112 931	109 668	476 411	241 429	234 982
20 - 24	654 037	325 601	328 436	247 125	126 005	121 120	406 912	199 596	207 316
25 - 29	615 988	308 988	307 000	231 466	117 561	113 905	384 522	191 427	193 095
30 - 34	496 234	250 383	245 851	184 851	92 976	91 875	311 383	157 407	153 976
35 - 39	420 083	212 523	207 560	150 894	75 793	75 101	269 189	136 730	132 459
40 - 44	343 870	170 808	173 062	125 290	61 840	63 450	218 580	108 968	109 612
45 - 49	295 907	149 656	146 251	109 574	55 072	54 502	186 333	94 584	91 749
50 - 54	267 418	127 272	140 146	95 530	46 444	49 086	171 888	80 828	91 060
55 - 59	197 607	98 615	98 992	70 696	35 929	34 767	126 911	62 686	64 225
60 - 64	147 179	74 106	73 073	49 885	25 446	24 439	97 294	48 660	48 634

7. Population by age, sex and urban/rural residence: latest available year, 2010 - 2019
Population selon l'âge, le sexe et la résidence, urbaine/rurale : dernière année disponible, 2010 - 2019 (continued - suite)

Continent, country or area, date, code[a] and age (in years) / Continent, pays ou zone, date, code[a] et âge (en annèes)	Total			Urban - Urbaine			Rural - Rurale		
	Both sexes Les deux sexes	Male Masculin	Female Féminin	Both sexes Les deux sexes	Male Masculin	Female Féminin	Both sexes Les deux sexes	Male Masculin	Female Féminin
ASIA - ASIE									
Lao People's Democratic Republic - République démocratique populaire lao									
1 III 2015 (CDJC)									
65 - 69	98 901	47 563	51 338	33 849	16 540	17 309	65 052	31 023	34 029
70 - 74	71 427	32 930	38 497	24 393	11 302	13 091	47 034	21 628	25 406
75 - 79	47 078	21 871	25 207	17 089	7 933	9 156	29 989	13 938	16 051
80 - 84	30 190	13 519	16 671	10 804	4 767	6 037	19 386	8 752	10 634
85 - 89	15 267	6 744	8 523	5 721	2 456	3 265	9 546	4 288	5 258
90 - 94	7 036	3 041	3 995	2 422	1 084	1 338	4 614	1 957	2 657
95 +	5 198	1 922	3 276	1 697	604	1 093	3 501	1 318	2 183
1 VII 2019 (ESDJ)[68]									
Total	*7 123 205*	*3 569 021*	*3 554 184*	...	...	...	...	...	...
0	*154 934*	*79 170*	*75 764*	...	...	...	...	...	...
1 - 4	*623 871*	*317 723*	*306 147*	...	...	...	...	...	...
5 - 9	*779 884*	*393 909*	*385 975*	...	...	...	...	...	...
10 - 14	*726 369*	*367 622*	*358 747*	...	...	...	...	...	...
15 - 19	*699 547*	*354 023*	*345 524*	...	...	...	...	...	...
20 - 24	*685 629*	*344 658*	*340 971*	...	...	...	...	...	...
25 - 29	*643 427*	*322 701*	*320 725*	...	...	...	...	...	...
30 - 34	*571 579*	*286 356*	*285 223*	...	...	...	...	...	...
35 - 39	*489 655*	*246 491*	*243 164*	...	...	...	...	...	...
40 - 44	*400 333*	*200 994*	*199 340*	...	...	...	...	...	...
45 - 49	*336 582*	*168 300*	*168 283*	...	...	...	...	...	...
50 - 54	*284 935*	*139 645*	*145 290*	...	...	...	...	...	...
55 - 59	*233 752*	*114 283*	*119 469*	...	...	...	...	...	...
60 - 64	*180 197*	*87 244*	*92 953*	...	...	...	...	...	...
65 - 69	*123 961*	*60 372*	*63 589*	...	...	...	...	...	...
70 - 74	*82 764*	*39 050*	*43 713*	...	...	...	...	...	...
75 - 79	*52 328*	*23 623*	*28 705*	...	...	...	...	...	...
80 +	*53 460*	*22 857*	*30 602*	...	...	...	...	...	...
Malaysia - Malaisie[72]									
1 VII 2019 (ESDJ)									
Total	32 581 387	16 830 551	15 750 836	24 817 031	12 780 768	12 036 263	7 764 356	4 049 783	3 714 573
0	502 584	259 578	243 006	374 328	193 583	180 745	128 256	65 995	62 261
1 - 4	2 055 928	1 060 382	995 546	1 533 097	792 213	740 884	522 831	268 169	254 662
5 - 9	2 521 718	1 305 998	1 215 720	1 880 142	977 004	903 138	641 576	328 994	312 582
10 - 14	2 519 573	1 295 811	1 223 762	1 890 895	971 481	919 414	628 678	324 330	304 348
15 - 19	2 866 058	1 486 109	1 379 949	2 092 464	1 083 486	1 008 978	773 594	402 623	370 971
20 - 24	3 220 332	1 702 463	1 517 869	2 369 625	1 253 232	1 116 393	850 707	449 231	401 476
25 - 29	3 317 469	1 779 761	1 537 708	2 491 370	1 323 210	1 168 160	826 099	456 551	369 548
30 - 34	2 894 806	1 522 413	1 372 393	2 296 491	1 185 906	1 110 585	598 315	336 507	261 808
35 - 39	2 525 041	1 314 281	1 210 760	2 025 752	1 039 499	986 253	499 289	274 782	224 507
40 - 44	1 973 717	1 026 455	947 262	1 589 291	820 584	768 707	384 426	205 871	178 555
45 - 49	1 770 962	896 205	874 757	1 406 014	709 628	696 386	364 948	186 577	178 371
50 - 54	1 621 052	808 024	813 028	1 270 655	632 991	637 664	350 397	175 033	175 364
55 - 59	1 438 722	733 781	704 941	1 114 486	573 750	540 736	324 236	160 031	164 205
60 - 64	1 167 361	583 099	584 262	887 267	447 761	439 506	280 094	135 338	144 756
65 - 69	868 095	427 483	440 612	648 959	322 169	326 790	219 136	105 314	113 822
70 - 74	611 811	294 225	317 586	449 092	216 727	232 365	162 719	77 498	85 221
75 - 79	346 409	162 903	183 506	247 289	117 580	129 709	99 120	45 323	53 797
80 - 84	209 653	96 660	112 993	149 025	69 195	79 830	60 628	27 465	33 163
85 +	150 096	74 920	75 176	100 789	50 769	50 020	49 307	24 151	25 156
Maldives[73]									
1 VII 2019 (ESDF)									
Total	533 941	337 167	196 774	221 678	137 614	84 064	312 264	199 554	112 710
0 - 4	39 281	20 540	18 740	15 697	8 174	7 523	23 584	12 366	11 217
0	7 920	4 140	3 779	...	...	...	...	...	...
1 - 4	31 367	16 405	14 962	...	...	...	...	...	...
5 - 9	36 258	19 088	17 171	12 996	6 810	6 187	23 262	12 278	10 984
10 - 14	32 049	16 489	15 560	11 152	5 730	5 422	20 897	10 759	10 138
15 - 19	30 262	17 187	13 075	10 247	5 769	4 478	20 015	11 418	8 597
20 - 24	62 434	45 325	17 109	27 807	19 658	8 149	34 627	25 667	8 960
25 - 29	83 190	61 625	21 565	37 907	27 063	10 844	45 283	34 562	10 721
30 - 34	70 757	48 501	22 256	30 323	19 973	10 351	40 434	28 529	11 905

7. Population by age, sex and urban/rural residence: latest available year, 2010 - 2019
Population selon l'âge, le sexe et la résidence, urbaine/rurale : dernière année disponible, 2010 - 2019 (continued - suite)

Continent, country or area, date, code[a] and age (in years) / Continent, pays ou zone, date, code[a] et âge (en années)	Total			Urban - Urbaine			Rural - Rurale		
	Both sexes / Les deux sexes	Male / Masculin	Female / Féminin	Both sexes / Les deux sexes	Male / Masculin	Female / Féminin	Both sexes / Les deux sexes	Male / Masculin	Female / Féminin
ASIA - ASIE									
Maldives[73]									
1 VII 2019 (ESDF)									
35 - 39	51 485	33 870	17 614	22 686	14 264	8 422	28 799	19 606	9 193
40 - 44	35 541	22 994	12 547	15 772	9 823	5 949	19 769	13 171	6 598
45 - 49	26 892	16 220	10 672	11 730	7 012	4 718	15 162	9 208	5 954
50 - 54	20 614	11 616	8 997	8 673	4 810	3 863	11 941	6 807	5 134
55 - 59	15 752	8 367	7 385	6 368	3 339	3 029	9 384	5 028	4 357
60 - 64	11 509	6 005	5 504	4 286	2 161	2 125	7 223	3 844	3 379
65 - 69	5 838	3 106	2 732	2 244	1 195	1 049	3 594	1 911	1 683
70 - 74	4 247	2 111	2 136	1 601	764	837	2 646	1 347	1 299
75 - 79	3 820	1 904	1 916	1 155	550	605	2 665	1 354	1 311
80 +	4 013	2 219	1 794	1 034	521	514	2 978	1 699	1 280
Mongolia - Mongolie									
11 XI 2010 (CDJC)									
Total	2 647 545	1 313 968	1 333 577	1 798 147	872 989	925 158	849 398	440 979	408 419
0 - 4	288 497	146 516	141 981	188 882	95 671	93 211	99 615	50 845	48 770
5 - 9	216 214	110 117	106 097	133 740	68 119	65 621	82 474	41 998	40 476
10 - 14	236 865	120 064	116 801	143 846	72 244	71 602	93 019	47 820	45 199
15 - 19	257 645	130 560	127 085	188 334	92 124	96 210	69 311	38 436	30 875
20 - 24	292 183	147 472	144 711	221 784	107 751	114 033	70 399	39 721	30 678
25 - 29	247 983	124 490	123 493	171 685	83 922	87 763	76 298	40 568	35 730
30 - 34	222 522	111 976	110 546	149 461	73 525	75 936	73 061	38 451	34 610
35 - 39	202 383	100 819	101 564	136 034	66 149	69 885	66 349	34 670	31 679
40 - 44	179 267	88 273	90 994	120 105	57 388	62 717	59 162	30 885	28 277
45 - 49	158 756	77 475	81 281	108 736	51 528	57 208	50 020	25 947	24 073
50 - 54	122 082	58 009	64 073	83 084	38 547	44 537	38 998	19 462	19 536
55 - 59	71 989	33 384	38 605	49 342	22 373	26 969	22 647	11 011	11 636
60 - 64	49 453	22 106	27 347	34 724	15 234	19 490	14 729	6 872	7 857
65 - 69	38 232	17 262	20 970	26 004	11 578	14 426	12 228	5 684	6 544
70 - 74	29 332	13 081	16 251	19 556	8 594	10 962	9 776	4 487	5 289
75 - 79	18 617	7 252	11 365	12 384	4 742	7 642	6 233	2 510	3 723
80 - 84	9 166	3 258	5 908	6 234	2 225	4 009	2 932	1 033	1 899
85 - 89	4 415	1 378	3 037	2 948	945	2 003	1 467	433	1 034
90 - 94	1 459	383	1 076	962	274	688	497	109	388
95 - 99	402	80	322	251	47	204	151	33	118
100 +	83	13	70	51	9	42	32	4	28
1 VII 2019 (ESDF)									
Total	3 267 673	1 605 711	1 661 962	...	...	...	...	...	...
0	76 152	39 047	37 105	...	...	...	...	...	...
1 - 4	312 250	160 311	151 939	...	...	...	...	...	...
5 - 9	365 694	186 955	178 739	...	...	...	...	...	...
10 - 14	265 922	135 684	130 238	...	...	...	...	...	...
15 - 19	225 739	114 855	110 884	...	...	...	...	...	...
20 - 24	242 286	122 454	119 832	...	...	...	...	...	...
25 - 29	285 970	143 512	142 458	...	...	...	...	...	...
30 - 34	299 912	149 318	150 594	...	...	...	...	...	...
35 - 39	247 954	122 266	125 688	...	...	...	...	...	...
40 - 44	223 052	108 241	114 811	...	...	...	...	...	...
45 - 49	194 950	92 978	101 972	...	...	...	...	...	...
50 - 54	164 931	76 382	88 549	...	...	...	...	...	...
55 - 59	138 972	62 563	76 409	...	...	...	...	...	...
60 - 64	92 112	39 568	52 544	...	...	...	...	...	...
65 - 69	52 795	21 616	31 179	...	...	...	...	...	...
70 - 74	32 468	12 782	19 686	...	...	...	...	...	...
75 - 79	24 671	9 860	14 811	...	...	...	...	...	...
80 - 84	12 963	4 767	8 196	...	...	...	...	...	...
85 - 89	6 548	1 957	4 591	...	...	...	...	...	...
90 - 94	1 786	490	1 296	...	...	...	...	...	...
95 - 99	485	95	390	...	...	...	...	...	...
100 +	61	10	51	...	...	...	...	...	...
Myanmar[7]									
1 X 2019 (ESDF)									
Total	*54 339 766*	*26 049 847*	*28 289 919*	*16 183 650*[74]	*7 669 067*[74]	*8 514 583*[74]	*38 156 116*[74]	*18 380 780*[74]	*19 775 336*[74]
0 - 4	*5 002 761*	*2 533 457*	*2 469 304*	*1 263 195*[74]	*640 815*[74]	*622 380*[74]	*3 739 566*[74]	*1 892 642*[74]	*1 846 924*[74]
0	*1 020 220*	*517 925*	*502 295*	...	...	...	...	...	...

7. Population by age, sex and urban/rural residence: latest available year, 2010 - 2019
Population selon l'âge, le sexe et la résidence, urbaine/rurale : dernière année disponible, 2010 - 2019 (continued - suite)

Continent, country or area, date, code[a] and age (in years) / Continent, pays ou zone, date, code[a] et âge (en années)	Total			Urban - Urbaine			Rural - Rurale		
	Both sexes Les deux sexes	Male Masculin	Female Féminin	Both sexes Les deux sexes	Male Masculin	Female Féminin	Both sexes Les deux sexes	Male Masculin	Female Féminin
ASIA - ASIE									
Myanmar[7]									
1 X 2019 (ESDF)									
1 - 4	3 982 541	2 015 532	1 967 009	...	...	...	...	...	...
5 - 9	4 784 854	2 416 554	2 368 300	1 171 455[74]	593 394[74]	578 061[74]	3 613 399[74]	1 823 160[74]	1 790 239[74]
10 - 14	5 037 372	2 556 565	2 480 807	1 213 435[74]	621 137[74]	592 298[74]	3 823 937[74]	1 935 428[74]	1 888 509[74]
15 - 19	5 037 089	2 550 720	2 486 369	1 458 207[74]	747 245[74]	710 962[74]	3 578 882[74]	1 803 475[74]	1 775 407[74]
20 - 24	4 608 265	2 269 657	2 338 608	1 634 559[74]	815 990[74]	818 569[74]	2 973 706[74]	1 453 667[74]	1 520 039[74]
25 - 29	4 261 834	2 033 348	2 228 486	1 533 345[74]	739 840[74]	793 505[74]	2 728 489[74]	1 293 508[74]	1 434 981[74]
30 - 34	4 090 452	1 939 847	2 150 605	1 329 068[74]	634 460[74]	694 608[74]	2 761 384[74]	1 305 387[74]	1 455 997[74]
35 - 39	3 865 579	1 838 755	2 026 824	1 212 158[74]	575 998[74]	636 160[74]	2 653 421[74]	1 262 757[74]	1 390 664[74]
40 - 44	3 538 788	1 668 004	1 870 784	1 073 221[74]	497 512[74]	575 709[74]	2 465 567[74]	1 170 492[74]	1 295 075[74]
45 - 49	3 255 409	1 509 563	1 745 846	997 858[74]	448 737[74]	549 121[74]	2 257 551[74]	1 060 826[74]	1 196 725[74]
50 - 54	2 912 336	1 332 423	1 579 913	895 460[74]	391 003[74]	504 457[74]	2 016 876[74]	941 420[74]	1 075 456[74]
55 - 59	2 508 549	1 130 258	1 378 291	752 991[74]	318 612[74]	434 379[74]	1 755 558[74]	811 646[74]	943 912[74]
60 - 64	1 967 508	865 980	1 101 528	592 819[74]	242 934[74]	349 885[74]	1 374 689[74]	623 046[74]	751 643[74]
65 - 69	1 445 174	618 539	826 635	430 313[74]	171 723[74]	258 590[74]	1 014 861[74]	446 816[74]	568 045[74]
70 - 74	915 216	373 459	541 757	285 112[74]	108 765[74]	176 347[74]	630 104[74]	264 694[74]	365 410[74]
75 - 79	536 675	206 594	330 081	163 141[74]	60 173[74]	102 968[74]	373 534[74]	146 421[74]	227 113[74]
80 - 84	342 435	127 457	214 978	104 789[74]	37 072[74]	67 717[74]	237 646[74]	90 385[74]	147 261[74]
85 - 89	167 681	59 023	108 658	51 792[74]	17 427[74]	34 365[74]	115 889[74]	41 596[74]	74 293[74]
90 +	61 789	19 644	42 145	20 732[74]	6 230[74]	14 502[74]	41 057[74]	13 414[74]	27 643[74]
Nepal - Népal									
22 VI 2011 (CDJC)									
Total	26 494 504	12 849 041	13 645 463	4 523 820	2 306 049	2 217 771	21 970 684	10 542 992	11 427 692
0 - 4	2 567 963	1 314 957	1 253 006	327 100	172 598	154 502	2 240 863	1 142 359	1 098 504
5 - 9	3 204 859	1 635 176	1 569 683	431 121	227 618	203 503	2 773 738	1 407 558	1 366 180
10 - 14	3 475 424	1 764 630	1 710 794	507 618	266 722	240 896	2 967 806	1 497 908	1 469 898
15 - 19	2 931 980	1 443 191	1 488 789	520 714	273 601	247 113	2 411 266	1 169 590	1 241 676
20 - 24	2 358 071	1 043 981	1 314 090	520 546	260 529	260 017	1 837 525	783 452	1 054 073
25 - 29	2 079 354	917 243	1 162 111	452 256	220 230	232 026	1 627 098	697 013	930 085
30 - 34	1 735 305	770 577	964 728	372 219	181 542	190 677	1 363 086	589 035	774 051
35 - 39	1 604 319	740 200	864 119	324 965	161 347	163 618	1 279 354	578 853	700 501
40 - 44	1 386 121	660 290	725 831	263 008	136 600	126 408	1 123 113	523 690	599 423
45 - 49	1 172 959	575 101	597 858	205 833	106 627	99 206	967 126	468 474	498 652
50 - 54	1 005 476	505 864	499 612	165 685	86 471	79 214	839 791	419 393	420 398
55 - 59	818 263	412 892	405 371	123 667	63 841	59 826	694 596	349 051	345 545
60 - 64	756 827	368 451	388 376	105 862	52 258	53 604	650 965	316 193	334 772
65 - 69	554 449	277 782	276 667	76 074	37 256	38 818	478 375	240 526	237 849
70 - 74	395 153	199 610	195 543	55 001	26 400	28 601	340 152	173 210	166 942
75 - 79	235 135	117 358	117 777	35 764	16 538	19 226	199 371	100 820	98 551
80 - 84	128 777	62 787	65 990	21 053	9 435	11 618	107 724	53 352	54 372
85 - 89	52 526	25 810	26 716	9 857	4 350	5 507	42 669	21 460	21 209
90 - 94	20 335	8 940	11 395	3 788	1 474	2 314	16 547	7 466	9 081
95 - 99	7 642	3 020	4 622	1 234	477	757	6 408	2 543	3 865
100 +	3 566	1 181	2 385	455	135	320	3 111	1 046	2 065
1 VII 2016 (ESDJ)[4]									
Total	28 431 494	13 784 009	14 647 486	...	...	...	...	...	...
0 - 4	2 950 167	1 525 630	1 424 537	...	...	...	...	...	...
5 - 9	2 674 278	1 368 495	1 305 783	...	...	...	...	...	...
10 - 14	3 062 865	1 564 080	1 498 784	...	...	...	...	...	...
15 - 19	3 317 315	1 680 525	1 636 790	...	...	...	...	...	...
20 - 24	3 021 919	1 476 611	1 545 309	...	...	...	...	...	...
25 - 29	2 340 931	1 033 222	1 307 709	...	...	...	...	...	...
30 - 34	1 998 816	860 512	1 138 303	...	...	...	...	...	...
35 - 39	1 740 784	771 970	968 815	...	...	...	...	...	...
40 - 44	1 521 989	691 192	830 797	...	...	...	...	...	...
45 - 49	1 334 086	632 128	701 958	...	...	...	...	...	...
50 - 54	1 140 179	552 834	587 346	...	...	...	...	...	...
55 - 59	930 950	462 675	468 275	...	...	...	...	...	...
60 - 64	770 098	382 738	387 360	...	...	...	...	...	...
65 - 69	627 821	303 255	324 567	...	...	...	...	...	...
70 - 74	482 949	231 131	251 818	...	...	...	...	...	...
75 - 79	339 914	162 123	177 791	...	...	...	...	...	...
80 +	176 432	84 889	91 543	...	...	...	...	...	...

7. Population by age, sex and urban/rural residence: latest available year, 2010 - 2019
Population selon l'âge, le sexe et la résidence, urbaine/rurale : dernière année disponible, 2010 - 2019 (continued - suite)

Continent, country or area, date, code[a] and age (in years) / Continent, pays ou zone, date, code[a] et âge (en annèes)	Total			Urban - Urbaine			Rural - Rurale		
	Both sexes Les deux sexes	Male Masculin	Female Féminin	Both sexes Les deux sexes	Male Masculin	Female Féminin	Both sexes Les deux sexes	Male Masculin	Female Féminin
ASIA - ASIE									
Oman[75]									
1 VII 2019 (ESDF)									
Total	*4 617 927*	*2 945 254*	*1 672 673*	...	...	...	...	...	...
0	*81 296*	*41 482*	*39 814*	...	...	...	...	...	...
1 - 4	*356 776*	*181 697*	*175 079*	...	...	...	...	...	...
5 - 9	*375 024*	*190 920*	*184 104*	...	...	...	...	...	...
10 - 14	*282 412*	*144 036*	*138 376*	...	...	...	...	...	...
15 - 19	*238 855*	*121 791*	*117 064*	...	...	...	...	...	...
20 - 24	*353 849*	*215 888*	*137 961*	...	...	...	...	...	...
25 - 29	*635 572*	*455 284*	*180 288*	...	...	...	...	...	...
30 - 34	*685 777*	*498 393*	*187 384*	...	...	...	...	...	...
35 - 39	*531 718*	*380 769*	*150 949*	...	...	...	...	...	...
40 - 44	*363 105*	*251 491*	*111 614*	...	...	...	...	...	...
45 - 49	*243 153*	*172 928*	*70 225*	...	...	...	...	...	...
50 - 54	*160 770*	*111 679*	*49 091*	...	...	...	...	...	...
55 - 59	*114 266*	*73 898*	*40 368*	...	...	...	...	...	...
60 - 64	*74 748*	*45 354*	*29 394*	...	...	...	...	...	...
65 - 69	*43 685*	*22 256*	*21 429*	...	...	...	...	...	...
70 - 74	*27 985*	*13 721*	*14 264*	...	...	...	...	...	...
75 - 79	*22 544*	*10 792*	*11 752*	...	...	...	...	...	...
80 - 84	*12 556*	*6 477*	*6 079*	...	...	...	...	...	...
85 - 89	*7 797*	*3 665*	*4 132*	...	...	...	...	...	...
90 - 94	*3 198*	*1 472*	*1 726*	...	...	...	...	...	...
95 - 99	*1 871*	*800*	*1 071*	...	...	...	...	...	...
100 +	*970*	*461*	*509*	...	...	...	...	...	...
Philippines									
1 VIII 2015 (CDJC)[76]									
Total	100 979 303	51 069 962	49 909 341	51 728 697	25 884 921	25 843 776	49 250 606	25 185 041	24 065 565
0	2 076 015	1 073 402	1 002 613	1 034 367	534 903	499 464	1 041 648	538 499	503 149
1 - 4	8 742 916	4 517 083	4 225 833	4 223 884	2 185 173	2 038 711	4 519 032	2 331 910	2 187 122
5 - 9	10 842 920	5 596 837	5 246 083	5 192 082	2 680 013	2 512 069	5 650 838	2 916 824	2 734 014
10 - 14	10 493 942	5 405 418	5 088 524	5 038 321	2 588 533	2 449 788	5 455 621	2 816 885	2 638 736
15 - 19	10 191 185	5 202 239	4 988 946	5 215 933	2 612 060	2 603 873	4 975 252	2 590 179	2 385 073
20 - 24	9 467 494	4 795 772	4 671 722	5 129 397	2 555 317	2 574 080	4 338 097	2 240 455	2 097 642
25 - 29	8 360 447	4 252 817	4 107 630	4 602 240	2 310 548	2 291 692	3 758 207	1 942 269	1 815 938
30 - 34	7 341 894	3 755 963	3 585 931	4 032 971	2 038 876	1 994 095	3 308 923	1 717 087	1 591 836
35 - 39	6 742 687	3 447 349	3 295 338	3 664 250	1 848 714	1 815 536	3 078 437	1 598 635	1 479 802
40 - 44	5 849 328	2 995 391	2 853 937	3 117 283	1 575 802	1 541 481	2 732 045	1 419 589	1 312 456
45 - 49	5 284 325	2 680 464	2 603 861	2 767 792	1 381 650	1 386 142	2 516 533	1 298 814	1 217 719
50 - 54	4 430 547	2 227 579	2 202 968	2 293 852	1 129 580	1 164 272	2 136 695	1 097 999	1 038 696
55 - 59	3 606 834	1 785 436	1 821 398	1 843 549	893 459	950 090	1 763 285	891 977	871 308
60 - 64	2 761 183	1 325 815	1 435 368	1 397 075	657 593	739 482	1 364 108	668 222	695 886
65 - 69	1 916 125	878 327	1 037 798	926 892	417 491	509 401	989 233	460 836	528 397
70 - 74	1 220 080	523 237	696 843	542 499	226 767	315 732	677 581	296 470	381 111
75 - 79	859 098	338 520	520 578	372 881	141 733	231 148	486 217	196 787	289 430
80 - 84	475 140	169 388	305 752	200 286	67 663	132 623	274 854	101 725	173 129
85 - 89	218 226	69 930	148 296	92 449	28 055	64 394	125 777	41 875	83 902
90 - 94	74 955	21 868	53 087	31 013	8 294	22 719	43 942	13 574	30 368
95 - 99	19 966	5 956	14 010	8 031	2 244	5 787	11 935	3 712	8 223
100 +	3 996	1 171	2 825	1 650	453	1 197	2 346	718	1 628
1 VII 2019 (ESDJ)[8]									
Total	*107 288 150*	*54 201 305*	*53 086 845*	...	...	...	...	...	...
0 - 4	*11 030 150*	*5 688 655*	*5 341 495*	...	...	...	...	...	...
5 - 9	*11 054 539*	*5 695 661*	*5 358 878*	...	...	...	...	...	...
10 - 14	*10 750 841*	*5 530 663*	*5 220 178*	...	...	...	...	...	...
15 - 19	*10 325 741*	*5 270 955*	*5 054 786*	...	...	...	...	...	...
20 - 24	*9 716 386*	*4 960 167*	*4 756 219*	...	...	...	...	...	...
25 - 29	*8 947 484*	*4 577 286*	*4 370 198*	...	...	...	...	...	...
30 - 34	*8 113 142*	*4 142 232*	*3 970 910*	...	...	...	...	...	...
35 - 39	*7 255 199*	*3 693 552*	*3 561 647*	...	...	...	...	...	...
40 - 44	*6 324 116*	*3 212 507*	*3 111 609*	...	...	...	...	...	...
45 - 49	*5 715 050*	*2 890 842*	*2 824 208*	...	...	...	...	...	...
50 - 54	*4 872 683*	*2 445 928*	*2 426 755*	...	...	...	...	...	...
55 - 59	*4 107 748*	*2 033 921*	*2 073 827*	...	...	...	...	...	...
60 - 64	*3 232 095*	*1 559 678*	*1 672 417*	...	...	...	...	...	...

Continent, country or area, date, code[a] and age (in years) / Continent, pays ou zone, date, code[a] et âge (en années)	Total			Urban - Urbaine			Rural - Rurale		
	Both sexes Les deux sexes	Male Masculin	Female Féminin	Both sexes Les deux sexes	Male Masculin	Female Féminin	Both sexes Les deux sexes	Male Masculin	Female Féminin
ASIA - ASIE									
Philippines									
1 VII 2019 (ESDJ)[8]									
65 - 69	*2 352 791*	*1 091 407*	*1 261 384*	...	...	...	...	...	...
70 - 74	*1 545 560*	*676 996*	*868 564*	...	...	...	...	...	...
75 - 79	*1 025 373*	*412 566*	*612 807*	...	...	...	...	...	...
80 +	*919 252*	*318 289*	*600 963*	...	...	...	...	...	...
Qatar									
1 VII 2019 (ESDF)									
Total	2 799 202	2 064 276	734 926	2 799 202	2 064 276	734 926	...	...	...
0	27 595	14 186	13 409	27 595	14 186	13 409	...	...	...
1 - 4	119 031	60 716	58 315	119 031	60 716	58 315	...	...	...
5 - 9	140 881	71 614	69 267	140 881	71 614	69 267	...	...	...
10 - 14	110 928	56 637	54 291	110 928	56 637	54 291	...	...	...
15 - 19	86 210	47 897	38 313	86 210	47 897	38 313	...	...	...
20 - 24	250 244	205 862	44 382	250 244	205 862	44 382	...	...	...
25 - 29	445 131	352 616	92 515	445 131	352 616	92 515	...	...	...
30 - 34	503 079	393 644	109 435	503 079	393 644	109 435	...	...	...
35 - 39	408 747	319 713	89 034	408 747	319 713	89 034	...	...	...
40 - 44	273 862	211 372	62 490	273 862	211 372	62 490	...	...	...
45 - 49	184 793	145 216	39 577	184 793	145 216	39 577	...	...	...
50 - 54	111 713	86 415	25 298	111 713	86 415	25 298	...	...	...
55 - 59	67 836	51 306	16 530	67 836	51 306	16 530	...	...	...
60 - 64	36 777	26 902	9 875	36 777	26 902	9 875	...	...	...
65 - 69	16 109	10 744	5 365	16 109	10 744	5 365	...	...	...
70 - 74	8 059	4 905	3 154	8 059	4 905	3 154	...	...	...
75 - 79	4 734	2 703	2 031	4 734	2 703	2 031	...	...	...
80 +	3 473	1 828	1 645	3 473	1 828	1 645	...	...	...
Republic of Korea - République de Corée									
1 XI 2015 (CDJC)									
Total	51 069 375	25 608 502	25 460 873	41 677 695	20 791 896	20 885 799	9 391 680	4 816 606	4 575 074
0	422 337	216 797	205 540	353 330	181 250	172 080	69 007	35 547	33 460
1 - 4	1 836 333	942 214	894 119	1 529 774	784 742	745 032	306 559	157 472	149 087
5 - 9	2 267 851	1 169 770	1 098 081	1 893 768	976 334	917 434	374 083	193 436	180 647
10 - 14	2 427 792	1 262 770	1 165 022	2 042 651	1 060 734	981 917	385 141	202 036	183 105
15 - 19	3 194 079	1 668 683	1 525 396	2 679 885	1 395 027	1 284 858	514 194	273 656	240 538
20 - 24	3 531 108	1 887 776	1 643 332	2 980 057	1 568 333	1 411 724	551 051	319 443	231 608
25 - 29	3 265 288	1 728 888	1 536 400	2 757 203	1 428 161	1 329 042	508 085	300 727	207 358
30 - 34	3 811 610	1 986 796	1 824 814	3 221 411	1 651 851	1 569 560	590 199	334 945	255 254
35 - 39	3 926 862	2 022 466	1 904 396	3 306 159	1 678 522	1 627 637	620 703	343 944	276 759
40 - 44	4 338 827	2 218 442	2 120 385	3 656 010	1 837 640	1 818 370	682 817	380 802	302 015
45 - 49	4 388 157	2 217 013	2 171 144	3 677 944	1 829 471	1 848 473	710 213	387 542	322 671
50 - 54	4 263 447	2 153 186	2 110 261	3 506 520	1 751 909	1 754 611	756 927	401 277	355 650
55 - 59	3 956 849	1 969 232	1 987 617	3 182 242	1 572 740	1 609 502	774 607	396 492	378 115
60 - 64	2 821 457	1 379 694	1 441 763	2 210 398	1 077 319	1 133 079	611 059	302 375	308 684
65 - 69	2 144 023	1 028 129	1 115 894	1 629 723	778 383	851 340	514 300	249 746	264 554
70 - 74	1 770 741	793 855	976 886	1 273 733	578 485	695 248	497 008	215 370	281 638
75 - 79	1 362 669	553 178	809 491	913 754	375 959	537 795	448 915	177 219	271 696
80 - 84	814 222	276 627	537 595	523 437	179 372	344 065	290 785	97 255	193 530
85 - 89	372 987	98 855	274 132	240 935	63 626	177 309	132 052	35 229	96 823
90 - 94	124 723	28 759	95 964	80 613	18 467	62 146	44 110	10 292	33 818
95 - 99	24 796	4 923	19 873	16 059	3 271	12 788	8 737	1 652	7 085
100 +	3 217	449	2 768	2 089	300	1 789	1 128	149	979
1 VII 2018 (ESDJ)									
Total	51 606 633	25 863 502	25 743 131	...	...	...	...	...	...
0	345 555	177 432	168 123	...	...	...	...	...	...
1 - 4	1 686 457	864 114	822 343	...	...	...	...	...	...
5 - 9	2 289 635	1 177 422	1 112 213	...	...	...	...	...	...
10 - 14	2 267 741	1 172 820	1 094 921	...	...	...	...	...	...
15 - 19	2 817 245	1 469 053	1 348 192	...	...	...	...	...	...
20 - 24	3 496 564	1 856 658	1 639 906	...	...	...	...	...	...
25 - 29	3 497 380	1 868 308	1 629 072	...	...	...	...	...	...
30 - 34	3 366 501	1 766 587	1 599 914	...	...	...	...	...	...
35 - 39	4 100 582	2 116 733	1 983 849	...	...	...	...	...	...
40 - 44	3 955 767	2 023 646	1 932 121	...	...	...	...	...	...

7. Population by age, sex and urban/rural residence: latest available year, 2010 - 2019
Population selon l'âge, le sexe et la résidence, urbaine/rurale : dernière année disponible, 2010 - 2019 (continued - suite)

Continent, country or area, date, code[a] and age (in years) / Continent, pays ou zone, date, code[a] et âge (en années)	Total			Urban - Urbaine			Rural - Rurale		
	Both sexes Les deux sexes	Male Masculin	Female Féminin	Both sexes Les deux sexes	Male Masculin	Female Féminin	Both sexes Les deux sexes	Male Masculin	Female Féminin
ASIA - ASIE									
Republic of Korea - République de Corée									
1 VII 2018 (ESDJ)									
45 - 49	4 556 757	2 311 564	2 245 193	...	...	...	...	...	...
50 - 54	4 123 542	2 076 615	2 046 927	...	...	...	...	...	...
55 - 59	4 339 919	2 163 953	2 175 966	...	...	...	...	...	...
60 - 64	3 390 828	1 669 024	1 721 804	...	...	...	...	...	...
65 - 69	2 358 389	1 133 201	1 225 188	...	...	...	...	...	...
70 - 74	1 796 287	826 425	969 862	...	...	...	...	...	...
75 - 79	1 580 370	664 618	915 752	...	...	...	...	...	...
80 - 84	988 370	355 962	632 408	...	...	...	...	...	...
85 - 89	459 474	128 560	330 914	...	...	...	...	...	...
90 - 94	148 457	32 990	115 467	...	...	...	...	...	...
95 - 99	36 841	7 260	29 581	...	...	...	...	...	...
100 +	3 972	557	3 415	...	...	...	...	...	...
Saudi Arabia - Arabie saoudite									
1 VII 2019 (ESDF)									
Total	34 218 169	19 739 056	14 479 113	...	...	...	...	...	...
0 - 4	2 844 501	1 449 705	1 394 796	...	...	...	...	...	...
5 - 9	2 956 437	1 506 148	1 450 289	...	...	...	...	...	...
10 - 14	2 589 025	1 317 077	1 271 948	...	...	...	...	...	...
15 - 19	2 359 981	1 205 027	1 154 954	...	...	...	...	...	...
20 - 24	2 627 694	1 401 128	1 226 566	...	...	...	...	...	...
25 - 29	3 266 711	1 806 124	1 460 587	...	...	...	...	...	...
30 - 34	3 313 375	1 950 461	1 362 914	...	...	...	...	...	...
35 - 39	3 707 231	2 326 154	1 381 077	...	...	...	...	...	...
40 - 44	3 316 507	2 118 142	1 198 365	...	...	...	...	...	...
45 - 49	2 460 559	1 628 848	831 711	...	...	...	...	...	...
50 - 54	1 714 639	1 175 456	539 183	...	...	...	...	...	...
55 - 59	1 183 229	786 126	397 103	...	...	...	...	...	...
60 - 64	779 129	487 714	291 415	...	...	...	...	...	...
65 - 69	433 752	236 215	197 537	...	...	...	...	...	...
70 - 74	288 076	150 559	137 517	...	...	...	...	...	...
75 - 79	172 838	91 832	81 006	...	...	...	...	...	...
80 +	204 485	102 340	102 145	...	...	...	...	...	...
Singapore - Singapour[77]									
30 VI 2019 (ESDJ)									
Total	4 026 209	1 969 382	2 056 827	...	...	...	...	...	...
0 - 4	185 355	94 666	90 689	...	...	...	...	...	...
5 - 9	197 775	101 051	96 724	...	...	...	...	...	...
10 - 14	207 926	105 661	102 265	...	...	...	...	...	...
15 - 19	222 222	113 555	108 667	...	...	...	...	...	...
20 - 24	249 079	126 764	122 315	...	...	...	...	...	...
25 - 29	288 194	142 465	145 729	...	...	...	...	...	...
30 - 34	293 446	140 208	153 238	...	...	...	...	...	...
35 - 39	300 818	142 118	158 700	...	...	...	...	...	...
40 - 44	300 763	143 869	156 894	...	...	...	...	...	...
45 - 49	311 682	151 637	160 045	...	...	...	...	...	...
50 - 54	301 682	149 121	152 561	...	...	...	...	...	...
55 - 59	306 759	153 477	153 282	...	...	...	...	...	...
60 - 64	278 828	138 324	140 504	...	...	...	...	...	...
65 - 69	221 296	108 655	112 641	...	...	...	...	...	...
70 - 74	150 127	71 234	78 893	...	...	...	...	...	...
75 - 79	94 600	42 201	52 399	...	...	...	...	...	...
80 - 84	62 293	26 077	36 216	...	...	...	...	...	...
85 - 89	33 935	12 484	21 451	...	...	...	...	...	...
90 +	19 429	5 815	13 614	...	...	...	...	...	...
Sri Lanka									
20 III 2012 (CDJC)									
Total	20 359 439	9 856 634	10 502 805	3 704 470	1 800 327	1 904 143	16 654 969	8 056 307	8 598 662
0 - 4	1 743 862	879 223	864 639	281 707	142 039	139 668	1 462 155	737 184	724 971
5 - 9	1 747 752	882 108	865 644	292 480	147 539	144 941	1 455 272	734 569	720 703
10 - 14	1 640 052	829 069	810 983	286 653	145 640	141 013	1 353 399	683 429	669 970
15 - 19	1 644 249	819 927	824 322	306 654	155 546	151 108	1 337 595	664 381	673 214

7. Population by age, sex and urban/rural residence: latest available year, 2010 - 2019
Population selon l'âge, le sexe et la résidence, urbaine/rurale : dernière année disponible, 2010 - 2019 (continued - suite)

Continent, country or area, date, code[a] and age (in years) / Continent, pays ou zone, date, code[a] et âge (en annèes)	Total			Urban - Urbaine			Rural - Rurale		
	Both sexes Les deux sexes	Male Masculin	Female Féminin	Both sexes Les deux sexes	Male Masculin	Female Féminin	Both sexes Les deux sexes	Male Masculin	Female Féminin
ASIA - ASIE									
Sri Lanka									
20 III 2012 (CDJC)									
20 - 24	1 532 883	742 316	790 567	308 605	151 666	156 939	1 224 278	590 650	633 628
25 - 29	1 552 848	743 510	809 338	290 825	142 387	148 438	1 262 023	601 123	660 900
30 - 34	1 639 415	796 866	842 549	294 944	145 860	149 084	1 344 471	651 006	693 465
35 - 39	1 409 077	686 037	723 040	260 479	127 396	133 083	1 148 598	558 641	589 957
40 - 44	1 359 209	661 623	697 586	253 831	124 363	129 468	1 105 378	537 260	568 118
45 - 49	1 285 830	618 140	667 690	237 646	113 675	123 971	1 048 184	504 465	543 719
50 - 54	1 219 460	581 293	638 167	223 940	106 249	117 691	995 520	475 044	520 476
55 - 59	1 064 229	500 871	563 358	192 715	90 444	102 271	871 514	410 427	461 087
60 - 64	917 910	425 428	492 482	169 167	78 370	90 797	748 743	347 058	401 685
65 - 69	633 289	283 764	349 525	121 751	54 401	67 350	511 538	229 363	282 175
70 - 74	412 414	181 846	230 568	77 909	33 807	44 102	334 505	148 039	186 466
75 - 79	283 186	116 389	166 797	52 087	21 036	31 051	231 099	95 353	135 746
80 - 84	159 379	64 250	95 129	30 707	11 775	18 932	128 672	52 475	76 197
85 - 89	73 441	28 293	45 148	14 121	5 097	9 024	59 320	23 196	36 124
90 - 94	24 258	9 293	14 965	4 932	1 790	3 142	19 326	7 503	11 823
95 +	16 696	6 388	10 308	3 317	1 247	2 070	13 379	5 141	8 238
1 VII 2019* (ESDJ)									
Total	*21 803 000*	*10 556 000*	*11 247 000*	...	...	...	...	...	...
0 - 4	*1 871 000*	*943 000*	*928 000*	...	...	...	...	...	...
5 - 9	*1 874 000*	*946 000*	*928 000*	...	...	...	...	...	...
10 - 14	*1 759 000*	*889 000*	*870 000*	...	...	...	...	...	...
15 - 19	*1 763 000*	*879 000*	*884 000*	...	...	...	...	...	...
20 - 24	*1 642 000*	*795 000*	*847 000*	...	...	...	...	...	...
25 - 29	*1 663 000*	*796 000*	*867 000*	...	...	...	...	...	...
30 - 34	*1 756 000*	*854 000*	*902 000*	...	...	...	...	...	...
35 - 39	*1 508 000*	*734 000*	*774 000*	...	...	...	...	...	...
40 - 44	*1 455 000*	*708 000*	*747 000*	...	...	...	...	...	...
45 - 49	*1 377 000*	*662 000*	*715 000*	...	...	...	...	...	...
50 - 54	*1 305 000*	*622 000*	*683 000*	...	...	...	...	...	...
55 - 59	*1 139 000*	*536 000*	*603 000*	...	...	...	...	...	...
60 - 64	*981 000*	*455 000*	*526 000*	...	...	...	...	...	...
65 - 69	*676 000*	*303 000*	*373 000*	...	...	...	...	...	...
70 - 74	*440 000*	*194 000*	*246 000*	...	...	...	...	...	...
75 - 79	*302 000*	*124 000*	*178 000*	...	...	...	...	...	...
80 +	*292 000*	*116 000*	*176 000*	...	...	...	...	...	...
State of Palestine - État de Palestine									
1 XII 2017 (CDFC)									
Total	4 705 855	2 394 359	2 311 496	4 018 942[78]	2 043 943[78]	1 974 999[78]	686 913	350 416	336 497
0	136 053	69 787	66 266	115 746[78]	59 361[78]	56 385[78]	20 307	10 426	9 881
1 - 4	517 004	265 487	251 517	444 934[78]	228 263[78]	216 671[78]	72 070	37 224	34 846
5 - 9	618 175	316 437	301 738	534 014[78]	273 318[78]	260 696[78]	84 161	43 119	41 042
10 - 14	545 086	278 732	266 354	467 636[78]	239 174[78]	228 462[78]	77 450	39 558	37 892
15 - 19	488 260	249 363	238 897	415 405[78]	212 194[78]	203 211[78]	72 855	37 169	35 686
20 - 24	479 002	244 964	234 038	408 830[78]	208 570[78]	200 260[78]	70 172	36 394	33 778
25 - 29	405 024	206 870	198 154	346 561[78]	176 567[78]	169 994[78]	58 463	30 303	28 160
30 - 34	304 841	153 069	151 772	260 571[78]	130 349[78]	130 222[78]	44 270	22 720	21 550
35 - 39	257 607	128 602	129 005	219 771[78]	109 480[78]	110 291[78]	37 836	19 122	18 714
40 - 44	225 066	113 829	111 237	190 779[78]	96 280[78]	94 499[78]	34 287	17 549	16 738
45 - 49	184 473	94 445	90 028	155 763[78]	79 749[78]	76 014[78]	28 710	14 696	14 014
50 - 54	162 121	83 982	78 139	138 210[78]	71 789[78]	66 421[78]	23 911	12 193	11 718
55 - 59	117 936	60 713	57 223	99 850[78]	51 597[78]	48 253[78]	18 086	9 116	8 970
60 - 64	81 856	40 599	41 257	69 264[78]	34 541[78]	34 723[78]	12 592	6 058	6 534
65 - 69	59 156	29 630	29 526	50 760[78]	25 437[78]	25 323[78]	8 396	4 193	4 203
70 - 74	39 556	18 249	21 307	33 716[78]	15 689[78]	18 027[78]	5 840	2 560	3 280
75 - 79	23 709	9 661	14 048	19 882[78]	8 188[78]	11 694[78]	3 827	1 473	2 354
80 - 84	16 257	6 662	9 595	13 503[78]	5 586[78]	7 917[78]	2 754	1 076	1 678
85 - 89	8 427	3 147	5 280	6 881[78]	2 570[78]	4 311[78]	1 546	577	969
90 - 94	2 970	1 127	1 843	2 393[78]	898[78]	1 495[78]	577	229	348
95 - 98	1 338	471	867	1 065[78]	374[78]	691[78]	273	97	176
Unknown - Inconnu	31 938	18 533	13 405	23 408[78]	13 969[78]	9 439[78]	8 530	4 564	3 966

7. Population by age, sex and urban/rural residence: latest available year, 2010 - 2019
Population selon l'âge, le sexe et la résidence, urbaine/rurale : dernière année disponible, 2010 - 2019 (continued - suite)

Continent, country or area, date, code[a] and age (in years) / Continent, pays ou zone, date, code[a] et âge (en années)	Total			Urban - Urbaine			Rural - Rurale		
	Both sexes Les deux sexes	Male Masculin	Female Féminin	Both sexes Les deux sexes	Male Masculin	Female Féminin	Both sexes Les deux sexes	Male Masculin	Female Féminin
ASIA - ASIE									
State of Palestine - État de Palestine									
1 VII 2019 (ESDF)									
Total	*4 976 684*	*2 530 966*	*2 445 718*	...	...	...	...	...	...
0	*146 915*	*74 829*	*72 086*	...	...	...	...	...	...
1 - 4	*538 421*	*275 965*	*262 456*	...	...	...	...	...	...
5 - 9	*644 597*	*330 420*	*314 177*	...	...	...	...	...	...
10 - 14	*582 683*	*297 958*	*284 725*	...	...	...	...	...	...
15 - 19	*508 984*	*260 072*	*248 912*	...	...	...	...	...	...
20 - 24	*483 355*	*247 429*	*235 926*	...	...	...	...	...	...
25 - 29	*446 586*	*228 507*	*218 079*	...	...	...	...	...	...
30 - 34	*349 277*	*176 501*	*172 776*	...	...	...	...	...	...
35 - 39	*272 632*	*136 165*	*136 467*	...	...	...	...	...	...
40 - 44	*238 472*	*120 260*	*118 212*	...	...	...	...	...	...
45 - 49	*201 026*	*102 321*	*98 705*	...	...	...	...	...	...
50 - 54	*170 179*	*87 648*	*82 531*	...	...	...	...	...	...
55 - 59	*136 406*	*70 421*	*65 985*	...	...	...	...	...	...
60 - 64	*94 101*	*47 618*	*46 483*	...	...	...	...	...	...
65 - 69	*64 953*	*32 014*	*32 939*	...	...	...	...	...	...
70 - 74	*43 244*	*20 529*	*22 715*	...	...	...	...	...	...
75 - 79	*26 542*	*11 450*	*15 092*	...	...	...	...	...	...
80 +	*28 311*	*10 859*	*17 452*	...	...	...	...	...	...
Syrian Arab Republic - République arabe syrienne[79]									
1 VII 2011 (ESDF)									
Total	*21 124 000*	*10 794 000*	*10 330 000*	*11 297 000*	*5 795 000*	*5 502 000*	*9 827 000*	*4 999 000*	*4 828 000*
0 - 4	*2 775 000*	*1 428 000*	*1 347 000*	*1 384 000*	*713 000*	*671 000*	*1 391 000*	*715 000*	*676 000*
5 - 9	*2 654 000*	*1 384 000*	*1 270 000*	*1 357 000*	*719 000*	*638 000*	*1 297 000*	*665 000*	*632 000*
10 - 14	*2 430 000*	*1 232 000*	*1 198 000*	*1 270 000*	*637 000*	*633 000*	*1 160 000*	*595 000*	*565 000*
15 - 19	*2 279 000*	*1 191 000*	*1 088 000*	*1 193 000*	*626 000*	*567 000*	*1 086 000*	*565 000*	*521 000*
20 - 24	*1 979 000*	*1 035 000*	*944 000*	*1 045 000*	*545 000*	*500 000*	*934 000*	*490 000*	*444 000*
25 - 29	*1 737 000*	*864 000*	*873 000*	*937 000*	*475 000*	*462 000*	*800 000*	*389 000*	*411 000*
30 - 34	*1 371 000*	*674 000*	*697 000*	*733 000*	*359 000*	*374 000*	*638 000*	*315 000*	*323 000*
35 - 39	*1 229 000*	*601 000*	*628 000*	*694 000*	*336 000*	*358 000*	*535 000*	*265 000*	*270 000*
40 - 44	*1 096 000*	*545 000*	*551 000*	*644 000*	*325 000*	*319 000*	*452 000*	*220 000*	*232 000*
45 - 49	*870 000*	*437 000*	*433 000*	*536 000*	*272 000*	*264 000*	*334 000*	*165 000*	*169 000*
50 - 54	*792 000*	*387 000*	*405 000*	*458 000*	*232 000*	*226 000*	*334 000*	*155 000*	*179 000*
55 - 59	*573 000*	*293 000*	*280 000*	*322 000*	*168 000*	*154 000*	*251 000*	*125 000*	*126 000*
60 - 64	*481 000*	*254 000*	*227 000*	*260 000*	*139 000*	*121 000*	*221 000*	*115 000*	*106 000*
65 +	*858 000*	*469 000*	*389 000*	*464 000*	*249 000*	*215 000*	*394 000*	*220 000*	*174 000*
Tajikistan - Tadjikistan									
1 VII 2019 (ESDF)									
Total	*9 126 560*	*4 627 300*	*4 499 260*	*2 384 777*	*1 216 680*	*1 168 097*	*6 741 675*	*3 410 557*	*3 331 118*
0	*228 995*	*120 494*	*108 501*	*51 821*	*27 616*	*24 205*	*177 174*	*92 878*	*84 296*
1 - 4	*908 155*	*479 437*	*428 718*	*204 459*	*108 606*	*95 853*	*703 696*	*370 831*	*332 865*
5 - 9	*1 090 964*	*564 566*	*526 398*	*259 754*	*134 126*	*125 628*	*831 210*	*430 440*	*400 770*
10 - 14	*901 745*	*463 608*	*438 137*	*220 674*	*113 531*	*107 143*	*681 071*	*350 077*	*330 994*
15 - 19	*845 326*	*433 006*	*412 320*	*224 307*	*117 752*	*106 555*	*621 019*	*315 254*	*305 765*
20 - 24	*860 694*	*437 754*	*422 940*	*233 081*	*124 131*	*108 950*	*627 613*	*313 623*	*313 990*
25 - 29	*838 413*	*422 000*	*416 413*	*242 738*	*132 801*	*109 937*	*595 675*	*289 199*	*306 476*
30 - 34	*772 329*	*386 691*	*385 638*	*196 371*	*100 173*	*96 198*	*575 958*	*286 518*	*289 440*
35 - 39	*574 914*	*291 069*	*283 845*	*149 049*	*73 704*	*75 345*	*425 865*	*217 365*	*208 500*
40 - 44	*461 773*	*230 148*	*231 625*	*128 903*	*60 967*	*67 936*	*332 870*	*169 181*	*163 689*
45 - 49	*413 577*	*203 542*	*210 035*	*123 325*	*58 177*	*65 148*	*290 252*	*145 365*	*144 887*
50 - 54	*372 252*	*181 436*	*190 816*	*109 926*	*52 588*	*57 338*	*262 326*	*128 848*	*133 478*
55 - 59	*329 037*	*161 141*	*167 896*	*95 174*	*45 546*	*49 628*	*233 863*	*115 595*	*118 268*
60 - 64	*218 629*	*105 866*	*112 763*	*62 347*	*29 525*	*32 822*	*156 282*	*76 341*	*79 941*
65 - 69	*134 669*	*64 143*	*70 526*	*38 524*	*17 807*	*20 717*	*96 145*	*46 336*	*49 809*
70 - 74	*65 804*	*32 100*	*33 704*	*18 770*	*8 595*	*10 175*	*47 034*	*23 505*	*23 529*
75 - 79	*53 241*	*25 998*	*27 243*	*14 051*	*6 431*	*7 620*	*39 190*	*19 567*	*19 623*
80 - 84	*33 742*	*14 767*	*18 975*	*7 574*	*3 060*	*4 514*	*26 168*	*11 707*	*14 461*
85 - 89	*15 097*	*6 416*	*8 681*	*2 797*	*1 104*	*1 693*	*12 300*	*5 312*	*6 988*
90 - 94	*6 065*	*2 664*	*3 401*	*958*	*363*	*595*	*5 107*	*2 301*	*2 806*
95 - 99	*1 031*	*391*	*640*	*174*	*77*	*97*	*857*	*314*	*543*
100 +	*108*	*63*	*45*	...	...	...	...	...	...

7. Population by age, sex and urban/rural residence: latest available year, 2010 - 2019
Population selon l'âge, le sexe et la résidence, urbaine/rurale : dernière année disponible, 2010 - 2019 (continued - suite)

Continent, country or area, date, code[a] and age (in years) / Continent, pays ou zone, date, code[a] et âge (en annèes)	Total			Urban - Urbaine			Rural - Rurale		
	Both sexes Les deux sexes	Male Masculin	Female Féminin	Both sexes Les deux sexes	Male Masculin	Female Féminin	Both sexes Les deux sexes	Male Masculin	Female Féminin
ASIA - ASIE									
Thailand - Thaïlande									
1 VII 2017 (ESDJ)									
Total	65 521 660	31 807 391	33 714 269	32 257 097	15 626 525	16 630 572	33 264 563	16 180 866	17 083 697
0 - 4	3 661 555	1 872 247	1 789 308	1 792 273	916 261	876 012	1 869 282	955 986	913 295
0	721 683	369 306	352 378	...	...	...	...	...	...
1 - 4	2 939 871	1 502 941	1 436 930	...	...	...	...	...	...
5 - 9	3 760 113	1 923 678	1 836 435	1 757 747	899 422	858 325	2 002 366	1 024 256	978 110
10 - 14	4 071 457	2 079 375	1 992 082	1 842 247	943 055	899 193	2 229 210	1 136 320	1 092 890
15 - 19	4 416 067	2 244 537	2 171 529	2 022 351	1 027 332	995 019	2 393 716	1 217 206	1 176 510
20 - 24	4 584 174	2 311 801	2 272 373	2 195 601	1 107 445	1 088 156	2 388 573	1 204 355	1 184 218
25 - 29	4 395 408	2 198 898	2 196 511	2 355 102	1 165 928	1 189 174	2 040 307	1 032 970	1 007 337
30 - 34	4 383 056	2 168 363	2 214 693	2 375 033	1 159 442	1 215 590	2 008 023	1 008 920	999 103
35 - 39	4 861 798	2 371 586	2 490 211	2 607 031	1 268 687	1 338 344	2 254 767	1 102 900	1 151 867
40 - 44	5 148 705	2 486 553	2 662 152	2 640 455	1 278 511	1 361 944	2 508 250	1 208 042	1 300 208
45 - 49	5 352 661	2 561 963	2 790 698	2 688 918	1 290 530	1 398 388	2 663 743	1 271 433	1 392 310
50 - 54	5 173 034	2 456 951	2 716 083	2 526 279	1 200 024	1 326 254	2 646 756	1 256 927	1 389 829
55 - 59	4 487 810	2 115 271	2 372 538	2 180 384	1 026 584	1 153 800	2 307 426	1 088 687	1 218 739
60 - 64	3 704 169	1 728 447	1 975 722	1 765 250	819 775	945 474	1 938 920	908 672	1 030 248
65 - 69	2 726 809	1 254 515	1 472 293	1 286 193	588 071	698 122	1 440 616	666 444	774 172
70 - 74	1 914 155	858 054	1 056 101	886 843	394 210	492 633	1 027 312	463 844	563 468
75 - 79	1 346 901	579 113	767 789	625 254	266 341	358 914	721 647	312 772	408 875
80 - 84	897 021	361 369	535 653	413 590	166 331	247 258	483 432	195 037	288 394
85 - 89	458 484	173 302	285 182	212 460	79 776	132 685	246 024	93 526	152 498
90 - 94	144 430	50 880	93 551	68 041	23 872	44 169	76 389	27 007	49 382
95 +	33 852	10 489	23 363	16 046	4 927	11 118	17 806	5 561	12 245
95 - 99	29 621	9 336	20 285	...	...	...	...	...	...
100 +	4 231	1 153	3 078	...	...	...	...	...	...
Timor-Leste									
11 VII 2015 (CDFC)									
Total	1 183 643	601 112	582 531	349 208	179 565	169 643	834 435	421 547	412 888
0 - 4	150 306	77 896	72 410	42 573	22 175	20 398	107 733	55 721	52 012
5 - 9	156 082	80 377	75 705	39 146	20 223	18 923	116 936	60 154	56 782
10 - 14	156 269	80 721	75 548	40 216	20 641	19 575	116 053	60 080	55 973
15 - 19	136 872	69 839	67 033	45 935	22 768	23 167	90 937	47 071	43 866
20 - 24	107 003	52 759	54 244	44 782	22 580	22 202	62 221	30 179	32 042
25 - 29	92 950	45 486	47 464	36 500	18 251	18 249	56 450	27 235	29 215
30 - 34	72 395	35 934	36 461	26 538	13 671	12 867	45 857	22 263	23 594
35 - 39	48 890	24 245	24 645	16 651	8 768	7 883	32 239	15 477	16 762
40 - 44	55 876	29 097	26 779	16 492	9 183	7 309	39 384	19 914	19 470
45 - 49	47 318	25 044	22 274	11 964	6 691	5 273	35 354	18 353	17 001
50 - 54	35 437	18 661	16 776	8 576	4 784	3 792	26 861	13 877	12 984
55 - 59	27 303	14 436	12 867	5 998	3 328	2 670	21 305	11 108	10 197
60 - 64	28 380	13 864	14 516	5 248	2 560	2 688	23 132	11 304	11 828
65 - 69	31 038	14 611	16 427	3 630	1 685	1 945	27 408	12 926	14 482
70 - 74	18 153	8 949	9 204	2 277	1 067	1 210	15 876	7 882	7 994
75 - 79	9 961	4 862	5 099	1 298	598	700	8 663	4 264	4 399
80 - 84	5 197	2 399	2 798	699	301	398	4 498	2 098	2 400
85 +	4 213	1 932	2 281	685	291	394	3 528	1 641	1 887
1 VII 2018 (ESDF)[1]									
Total	1 261 407	642 639	618 768	...	...	...	...	...	...
0	32 989	17 058	15 931	...	...	...	...	...	...
1 - 4	131 734	68 984	62 750	...	...	...	...	...	...
5 - 9	161 209	84 950	76 259	...	...	...	...	...	...
10 - 14	157 103	82 088	75 015	...	...	...	...	...	...
15 - 19	147 544	75 602	71 942	...	...	...	...	...	...
20 - 24	121 216	60 513	60 703	...	...	...	...	...	...
25 - 29	97 016	46 777	50 239	...	...	...	...	...	...
30 - 34	83 062	40 344	42 718	...	...	...	...	...	...
35 - 39	58 922	28 909	30 013	...	...	...	...	...	...
40 - 44	48 193	24 228	23 965	...	...	...	...	...	...
45 - 49	52 864	27 718	25 146	...	...	...	...	...	...
50 - 54	40 945	21 620	19 325	...	...	...	...	...	...
55 - 59	32 093	16 674	15 419	...	...	...	...	...	...
60 - 64	29 295	14 583	14 712	...	...	...	...	...	...
65 - 69	24 205	11 764	12 441	...	...	...	...	...	...

7. Population by age, sex and urban/rural residence: latest available year, 2010 - 2019
Population selon l'âge, le sexe et la résidence, urbaine/rurale : dernière année disponible, 2010 - 2019 (continued - suite)

Continent, country or area, date, code[a] and age (in years) Continent, pays ou zone, date, code[a] et âge (en années)	Total			Urban - Urbaine			Rural - Rurale		
	Both sexes Les deux sexes	Male Masculin	Female Féminin	Both sexes Les deux sexes	Male Masculin	Female Féminin	Both sexes Les deux sexes	Male Masculin	Female Féminin
ASIA - ASIE									
Timor-Leste									
1 VII 2018 (ESDF)[1]									
70 - 74	*18 575*	*9 187*	*9 388*	...	...	...	...	...	...
75 - 79	*13 241*	*6 452*	*6 789*	...	...	...	...	...	...
80 +	*11 201*	*5 188*	*6 013*	...	...	...	...	...	...
Turkey - Turquie[80]									
31 XII 2018 (ESDJ)									
Total	*82 003 882*	*41 139 980*	*40 863 902*	*72 073 198*	*36 085 213*	*35 987 985*	*9 930 684*	*5 054 767*	*4 875 917*
0	*1 215 156*	*623 658*	*591 498*	*1 092 517*	*560 465*	*532 052*	*122 639*	*63 193*	*59 446*
1 - 4	*5 269 830*	*2 704 122*	*2 565 708*	*4 736 982*	*2 430 508*	*2 306 474*	*532 848*	*273 614*	*259 234*
5 - 9	*6 358 920*	*3 264 508*	*3 094 412*	*5 691 655*	*2 922 571*	*2 769 084*	*667 265*	*341 937*	*325 328*
10 - 14	*6 340 423*	*3 254 277*	*3 086 146*	*5 616 114*	*2 883 138*	*2 732 976*	*724 309*	*371 139*	*353 170*
15 - 19	*6 424 267*	*3 299 449*	*3 124 818*	*5 635 188*	*2 889 197*	*2 745 991*	*789 079*	*410 252*	*378 827*
20 - 24	*6 547 129*	*3 347 297*	*3 199 832*	*5 784 643*	*2 921 896*	*2 862 747*	*762 486*	*425 401*	*337 085*
25 - 29	*6 276 469*	*3 190 023*	*3 086 446*	*5 632 691*	*2 834 109*	*2 798 582*	*643 778*	*355 914*	*287 864*
30 - 34	*6 333 153*	*3 205 205*	*3 127 948*	*5 749 790*	*2 889 034*	*2 860 756*	*583 363*	*316 171*	*267 192*
35 - 39	*6 576 072*	*3 316 603*	*3 259 469*	*5 966 248*	*2 995 022*	*2 971 226*	*609 824*	*321 581*	*288 243*
40 - 44	*5 846 026*	*2 953 329*	*2 892 697*	*5 267 542*	*2 653 770*	*2 613 772*	*578 484*	*299 559*	*278 925*
45 - 49	*5 310 707*	*2 670 183*	*2 640 524*	*4 709 802*	*2 365 723*	*2 344 079*	*600 905*	*304 460*	*296 445*
50 - 54	*4 701 324*	*2 372 182*	*2 329 142*	*4 087 383*	*2 060 579*	*2 026 804*	*613 941*	*311 603*	*302 338*
55 - 59	*4 172 341*	*2 076 882*	*2 095 459*	*3 546 414*	*1 764 535*	*1 781 879*	*625 927*	*312 347*	*313 580*
60 - 64	*3 445 861*	*1 692 130*	*1 753 731*	*2 860 813*	*1 405 322*	*1 455 491*	*585 048*	*286 808*	*298 240*
65 - 69	*2 612 207*	*1 245 979*	*1 366 228*	*2 119 631*	*1 012 006*	*1 107 625*	*492 576*	*233 973*	*258 603*
70 - 74	*1 856 922*	*835 353*	*1 021 569*	*1 475 049*	*664 383*	*810 666*	*381 873*	*170 970*	*210 903*
75 - 79	*1 262 550*	*539 825*	*722 725*	*980 942*	*418 418*	*562 524*	*281 608*	*121 407*	*160 201*
80 - 84	*793 736*	*318 882*	*474 854*	*613 948*	*243 068*	*370 880*	*179 788*	*75 814*	*103 974*
85 - 89	*485 914*	*182 957*	*302 957*	*369 053*	*135 344*	*233 709*	*116 861*	*47 613*	*69 248*
90 - 94	*146 272*	*41 296*	*104 976*	*114 050*	*31 488*	*82 562*	*32 222*	*9 808*	*22 414*
95 - 99	*23 401*	*5 142*	*18 259*	*18 742*	*4 095*	*14 647*	*4 659*	*1 047*	*3 612*
100 +	*5 202*	*698*	*4 504*	*4 001*	*542*	*3 459*	*1 201*	*156*	*1 045*
Uzbekistan - Ouzbékistan[70]									
1 I 2019 (ESDJ)									
Total	33 255 538	16 710 577	16 544 961	16 806 721	8 410 413	8 396 308	16 448 817	8 300 164	8 148 653
0	738 069	387 468	350 601	341 226	179 805	161 421	396 843	207 663	189 180
1 - 4	2 813 658	1 462 931	1 350 727	1 286 193	668 721	617 472	1 527 465	794 210	733 255
5 - 9	3 202 432	1 657 059	1 545 373	1 474 313	763 941	710 372	1 728 119	893 118	835 001
10 - 14	2 845 758	1 461 724	1 384 034	1 334 264	682 442	651 822	1 511 494	779 282	732 212
15 - 19	2 557 146	1 310 596	1 246 550	1 262 087	645 459	616 628	1 295 059	665 137	629 922
20 - 24	2 985 366	1 527 065	1 458 301	1 485 385	760 379	725 006	1 499 981	766 686	733 295
25 - 29	3 203 107	1 628 677	1 574 430	1 572 017	805 460	766 557	1 631 090	823 217	807 873
30 - 34	2 987 338	1 504 774	1 482 564	1 531 249	775 041	756 208	1 456 089	729 733	726 356
35 - 39	2 395 355	1 198 673	1 196 682	1 248 295	624 660	623 635	1 147 060	574 013	573 047
40 - 44	2 034 563	1 012 680	1 021 883	1 082 353	534 695	547 658	952 210	477 985	474 225
45 - 49	1 820 234	900 165	920 069	1 017 619	508 603	509 016	802 615	391 562	411 053
50 - 54	1 593 966	765 080	828 886	866 251	418 242	448 009	727 715	346 838	380 877
55 - 59	1 486 620	712 680	773 940	810 181	384 790	425 391	676 439	327 890	348 549
60 - 64	1 067 433	507 345	560 088	598 800	279 856	318 944	468 633	227 489	241 144
65 - 69	670 718	310 519	360 199	392 153	177 305	214 848	278 565	133 214	145 351
70 - 74	310 630	140 822	169 808	185 427	80 610	104 817	125 203	60 212	64 991
75 - 79	249 254	110 961	138 293	143 997	59 688	84 309	105 257	51 273	53 984
80 - 84	156 913	63 813	93 100	90 963	33 317	57 646	65 950	30 496	35 454
85 +	136 978	47 545	89 433	83 948	27 399	56 549	53 030	20 146	32 884
Viet Nam									
1 IV 2019 (CDJC)									
Total	96 208 984	47 881 061	48 327 923	33 122 548	16 268 095	16 854 453	63 086 436	31 612 966	31 473 470
0 - 4	7 819 326	4 100 479	3 718 847	2 436 970	1 279 623	1 157 347	5 382 356	2 820 856	2 561 500
5 - 9	8 332 719	4 354 887	3 977 832	2 638 637	1 384 755	1 253 882	5 694 082	2 970 132	2 723 950
10 - 14	7 219 837	3 737 030	3 482 807	2 301 523	1 193 320	1 108 203	4 918 314	2 543 710	2 374 604
15 - 19	6 506 217	3 352 386	3 153 831	2 271 322	1 144 545	1 126 777	4 234 895	2 207 841	2 027 054
20 - 24	6 675 703	3 417 149	3 258 554	2 535 087	1 235 901	1 299 186	4 140 616	2 181 248	1 959 368
25 - 29	8 447 977	4 301 210	4 146 767	3 064 686	1 486 402	1 578 284	5 383 291	2 814 808	2 568 483
30 - 34	8 393 810	4 276 404	4 117 406	3 064 953	1 501 326	1 563 627	5 328 857	2 775 078	2 553 779
35 - 39	7 692 386	3 891 950	3 800 436	2 860 531	1 418 373	1 442 158	4 831 855	2 473 577	2 358 278
40 - 44	6 684 119	3 366 147	3 317 972	2 378 278	1 185 366	1 192 912	4 305 841	2 180 781	2 125 060
45 - 49	6 257 471	3 132 172	3 125 299	2 180 612	1 086 509	1 094 103	4 076 859	2 045 663	2 031 196

7. Population by age, sex and urban/rural residence: latest available year, 2010 - 2019
Population selon l'âge, le sexe et la résidence, urbaine/rurale : dernière année disponible, 2010 - 2019 (continued - suite)

Continent, country or area, date, code[a] and age (in years) / Continent, pays ou zone, date, code[a] et âge (en années)	Total			Urban - Urbaine			Rural - Rurale		
	Both sexes Les deux sexes	Male Masculin	Female Féminin	Both sexes Les deux sexes	Male Masculin	Female Féminin	Both sexes Les deux sexes	Male Masculin	Female Féminin
ASIA - ASIE									
Viet Nam									
1 IV 2019 (CDJC)									
50 - 54	5 662 010	2 772 157	2 889 853	1 888 768	920 327	968 441	3 773 242	1 851 830	1 921 412
55 - 59	5 108 724	2 402 096	2 706 628	1 754 005	831 261	922 744	3 354 719	1 570 835	1 783 884
60 - 64	3 992 034	1 810 497	2 181 537	1 405 242	645 948	759 294	2 586 792	1 164 549	1 422 243
65 - 69	2 685 271	1 167 214	1 518 057	893 601	384 987	508 614	1 791 670	782 227	1 009 443
70 - 74	1 640 850	687 339	953 511	542 687	225 971	316 716	1 098 163	461 368	636 795
75 - 79	1 171 811	453 972	717 839	374 648	150 984	223 664	797 163	302 988	494 175
80 - 84	907 732	327 330	580 402	266 768	99 825	166 943	640 964	227 505	413 459
85 +	1 010 987	330 642	680 345	264 230	92 672	171 558	746 757	237 970	508 787
Yemen - Yémen[1]									
1 VII 2017 (ESDJ)									
Total	*28 170 408*	*14 334 126*	*13 836 282*	...	...	...	...	...	...
0 - 4	*4 331 851*	*2 213 674*	*2 118 177*	...	...	...	...	...	...
5 - 9	*3 893 155*	*1 992 122*	*1 901 034*	...	...	...	...	...	...
10 - 14	*3 213 221*	*1 639 285*	*1 573 936*	...	...	...	...	...	...
15 - 19	*2 981 060*	*1 529 732*	*1 451 328*	...	...	...	...	...	...
20 - 24	*2 907 826*	*1 509 363*	*1 398 464*	...	...	...	...	...	...
25 - 29	*2 627 986*	*1 367 680*	*1 260 306*	...	...	...	...	...	...
30 - 34	*2 074 340*	*1 063 494*	*1 010 846*	...	...	...	...	...	...
35 - 39	*1 589 008*	*799 595*	*789 413*	...	...	...	...	...	...
40 - 44	*1 165 508*	*577 738*	*587 770*	...	...	...	...	...	...
45 - 49	*854 059*	*415 599*	*438 461*	...	...	...	...	...	...
50 - 54	*714 875*	*343 155*	*371 721*	...	...	...	...	...	...
55 - 59	*586 832*	*279 808*	*307 024*	...	...	...	...	...	...
60 - 64	*425 188*	*206 651*	*218 537*	...	...	...	...	...	...
65 - 69	*299 382*	*148 672*	*150 710*	...	...	...	...	...	...
70 - 74	*213 416*	*105 257*	*108 159*	...	...	...	...	...	...
75 - 79	*141 596*	*69 010*	*72 586*	...	...	...	...	...	...
80 +	*151 104*	*73 292*	*77 812*	...	...	...	...	...	...
EUROPE									
Åland Islands - Îles d'Åland[36]									
1 VII 2019 (ESDJ)									
Total	29 837	14 875	14 962	11 711	5 606	6 105	18 126	9 269	8 857
0	278	145	134	85	40	45	194	105	89
1 - 4	1 264	650	614	442	221	221	822	429	394
5 - 9	1 704	864	840	579	298	281	1 125	566	559
10 - 14	1 703	886	817	572	280	292	1 131	606	525
15 - 19	1 557	822	735	605	306	300	952	517	436
20 - 24	1 297	710	587	648	354	294	649	356	293
25 - 29	1 730	903	827	783	425	359	947	479	468
30 - 34	1 831	939	892	779	406	373	1 053	533	520
35 - 39	1 896	975	922	728	374	354	1 169	601	568
40 - 44	1 849	935	914	702	331	371	1 147	604	543
45 - 49	1 953	974	979	737	359	378	1 216	615	602
50 - 54	2 190	1 080	1 111	811	383	428	1 380	697	683
55 - 59	1 980	961	1 019	725	311	414	1 256	650	606
60 - 64	1 905	892	1 014	741	321	420	1 165	571	594
65 - 69	1 953	926	1 027	777	337	440	1 176	589	587
70 - 74	1 877	933	945	776	357	419	1 101	576	526
75 - 79	1 241	636	606	528	246	282	714	390	324
80 - 84	806	344	462	355	140	215	452	205	247
85 - 89	508	208	300	214	86	129	294	123	172
90 - 94	253	78	175	103	26	77	151	52	99
95 - 99	61	18	43	25	8	17	36	11	26
100 +	5	1	4	3	1	3	2	1	2
Albania - Albanie									
1 VII 2013 (ESDJ)[5]									
Total	2 897 364	1 458 648	1 438 716	1 633 617	798 615	835 002	1 263 747	660 033	603 714
0 - 4	173 349	90 068	83 281	75 341	39 381	35 960	98 008	50 687	47 321
0	35 445	18 414	17 031	...	...	...	...	...	...
1 - 4	137 903	71 653	66 250	...	...	...	...	...	...

Continent, country or area, date, code[a] and age (in years) / Continent, pays ou zone, date, code[a] et âge (en annèes)	Total			Urban - Urbaine			Rural - Rurale		
	Both sexes / Les deux sexes	Male / Masculin	Female / Féminin	Both sexes / Les deux sexes	Male / Masculin	Female / Féminin	Both sexes / Les deux sexes	Male / Masculin	Female / Féminin
EUROPE									
Albania - Albanie									
1 VII 2013 (ESDJ)[5]									
5 - 9	171 833	90 701	81 132	100 478	52 421	48 057	71 355	38 280	33 075
10 - 14	220 582	114 164	106 418	117 500	60 576	56 924	103 082	53 587	49 494
15 - 19	261 669	132 810	128 859	134 718	67 303	67 414	126 952	65 507	61 445
20 - 24	235 615	126 936	108 680	153 986	75 706	78 280	81 630	51 230	30 400
25 - 29	209 075	112 236	96 839	136 959	65 999	70 960	72 116	46 237	25 879
30 - 34	187 077	92 149	94 928	95 098	44 074	51 024	91 979	48 075	43 904
35 - 39	173 587	82 445	91 142	89 169	40 432	48 737	84 418	42 013	42 405
40 - 44	189 099	89 772	99 327	106 471	50 381	56 091	82 627	39 391	43 236
45 - 49	197 020	95 657	101 363	113 719	55 342	58 377	83 301	40 315	42 986
50 - 54	209 575	104 084	105 490	121 293	60 655	60 638	88 282	43 430	44 852
55 - 59	184 593	92 037	92 556	105 093	51 906	53 188	79 500	40 131	39 369
60 - 64	141 532	71 276	70 256	83 065	40 768	42 296	58 467	30 508	27 960
65 - 69	106 945	54 278	52 666	60 973	29 333	31 640	45 971	24 945	21 026
70 - 74	102 875	49 827	53 048	55 109	26 020	29 089	47 766	23 807	23 959
75 - 79	71 589	35 241	36 348	41 911	19 956	21 955	29 678	15 285	14 393
80 - 84	38 203	16 977	21 226	25 030	11 374	13 656	13 174	5 603	7 570
85 +	23 147	7 992	15 155	17 705	6 988	10 717	5 443	1 004	4 438
1 I 2019 (ESDJ)									
Total	2 862 427	1 429 594	1 432 833	...	...	...	...	...	...
0	28 934	15 025	13 909	...	...	...	...	...	...
1 - 4	126 688	64 763	61 925	...	...	...	...	...	...
5 - 9	163 452	83 414	80 038	...	...	...	...	...	...
10 - 14	174 350	89 801	84 549	...	...	...	...	...	...
15 - 19	207 192	104 737	102 455	...	...	...	...	...	...
20 - 24	236 982	118 522	118 460	...	...	...	...	...	...
25 - 29	237 378	120 969	116 409	...	...	...	...	...	...
30 - 34	197 702	104 446	93 256	...	...	...	...	...	...
35 - 39	169 105	85 824	83 281	...	...	...	...	...	...
40 - 44	162 381	79 173	83 208	...	...	...	...	...	...
45 - 49	177 316	85 217	92 099	...	...	...	...	...	...
50 - 54	191 618	93 241	98 377	...	...	...	...	...	...
55 - 59	206 653	101 895	104 758	...	...	...	...	...	...
60 - 64	179 460	87 894	91 566	...	...	...	...	...	...
65 - 69	136 050	66 443	69 607	...	...	...	...	...	...
70 - 74	102 840	50 338	52 502	...	...	...	...	...	...
75 - 79	87 913	41 965	45 948	...	...	...	...	...	...
80 - 84	52 224	24 909	27 315	...	...	...	...	...	...
85 +	24 189	11 018	13 171	...	...	...	...	...	...
Andorra - Andorre[36]									
1 I 2019 (ESDJ)									
Total	76 177	38 789	37 388	...	...	...	...	...	...
0	308	165	143	...	...	...	...	...	...
1 - 4	2 411	1 226	1 185	...	...	...	...	...	...
5 - 9	3 823	1 912	1 911	...	...	...	...	...	...
10 - 14	4 027	2 124	1 903	...	...	...	...	...	...
15 - 19	4 077	2 096	1 981	...	...	...	...	...	...
20 - 24	4 005	2 164	1 841	...	...	...	...	...	...
25 - 29	4 570	2 356	2 214	...	...	...	...	...	...
30 - 34	5 062	2 563	2 499	...	...	...	...	...	...
35 - 39	6 269	3 125	3 144	...	...	...	...	...	...
40 - 44	7 035	3 511	3 524	...	...	...	...	...	...
45 - 49	7 083	3 628	3 455	...	...	...	...	...	...
50 - 54	6 792	3 524	3 268	...	...	...	...	...	...
55 - 59	5 926	3 062	2 864	...	...	...	...	...	...
60 - 64	4 443	2 322	2 121	...	...	...	...	...	...
65 - 69	3 333	1 719	1 614	...	...	...	...	...	...
70 - 74	2 668	1 416	1 252	...	...	...	...	...	...
75 - 79	1 785	832	953	...	...	...	...	...	...
80 - 84	1 190	524	666	...	...	...	...	...	...
85 - 89	852	340	512	...	...	...	...	...	...
90 - 94	393	137	256	...	...	...	...	...	...
95 - 99	108	38	70	...	...	...	...	...	...
100 - 104	14	5	9	...	...	...	...	...	...

7. Population by age, sex and urban/rural residence: latest available year, 2010 - 2019
Population selon l'âge, le sexe et la résidence, urbaine/rurale : dernière année disponible, 2010 - 2019 (continued - suite)

Continent, country or area, date, code[a] and age (in years) / Continent, pays ou zone, date, code[a] et âge (en annèes)	Total			Urban - Urbaine			Rural - Rurale		
	Both sexes Les deux sexes	Male Masculin	Female Féminin	Both sexes Les deux sexes	Male Masculin	Female Féminin	Both sexes Les deux sexes	Male Masculin	Female Féminin
EUROPE									
Andorra - Andorre[36]									
1 I 2019 (ESDJ)									
105 - 109	2	-	2	...	...	...	...	...	...
110 +	1	-	1	...	...	...	...	...	...
Austria - Autriche									
31 X 2011 (CDJC)									
Total	8 401 940	4 093 938	4 308 002	5 643 239	2 713 930	2 929 309	2 758 701	1 380 008	1 378 693
0 - 4	394 706	202 637	192 069	267 743	137 645	130 098	126 963	64 992	61 971
5 - 9	406 027	207 779	198 248	268 770	137 636	131 134	137 257	70 143	67 114
10 - 14	426 957	218 499	208 458	276 347	141 429	134 918	150 610	77 070	73 540
15 - 19	488 818	251 251	237 567	313 792	160 620	153 172	175 026	90 631	84 395
20 - 24	527 675	267 651	260 024	364 267	181 574	182 693	163 408	86 077	77 331
25 - 29	552 783	277 236	275 547	390 454	193 719	196 735	162 329	83 517	78 812
30 - 34	538 307	270 267	268 040	375 886	187 248	188 638	162 421	83 019	79 402
35 - 39	564 817	280 207	284 610	383 183	187 902	195 281	181 634	92 305	89 329
40 - 44	675 242	338 455	336 787	453 188	224 449	228 739	222 054	114 006	108 048
45 - 49	710 388	358 163	352 225	470 749	234 757	235 992	239 639	123 406	116 233
50 - 54	626 162	312 890	313 272	409 191	200 993	208 198	216 971	111 897	105 074
55 - 59	517 280	253 019	264 261	339 245	161 747	177 498	178 035	91 272	86 763
60 - 64	480 665	231 598	249 067	322 367	151 726	170 641	158 298	79 872	78 426
65 - 69	402 829	189 221	213 608	283 946	130 760	153 186	118 883	58 461	60 422
70 - 74	410 314	187 956	222 358	273 352	123 395	149 957	136 962	64 561	72 401
75 - 79	262 203	110 870	151 333	165 864	68 812	97 052	96 339	42 058	54 281
80 - 84	218 133	83 066	135 067	142 903	52 895	90 008	75 230	30 171	45 059
85 - 89	141 772	40 153	101 619	99 777	27 332	72 445	41 995	12 821	29 174
90 - 94	46 362	10 997	35 365	34 057	7 767	26 290	12 305	3 230	9 075
95 - 99	9 388	1 836	7 552	7 274	1 377	5 897	2 114	459	1 655
100 +	1 112	187	925	884	147	737	228	40	188
1 I 2019 (ESDJ)									
Total	8 858 775	4 357 033	4 501 742	...	...	...	...	...	...
0	84 177	43 139	41 038	...	...	...	...	...	...
1 - 4	350 956	180 933	170 023	...	...	...	...	...	...
5 - 9	420 286	216 360	203 926	...	...	...	...	...	...
10 - 14	423 273	217 140	206 133	...	...	...	...	...	...
15 - 19	439 004	226 869	212 135	...	...	...	...	...	...
20 - 24	530 763	273 309	257 454	...	...	...	...	...	...
25 - 29	603 708	308 820	294 888	...	...	...	...	...	...
30 - 34	603 166	306 621	296 545	...	...	...	...	...	...
35 - 39	599 958	302 548	297 410	...	...	...	...	...	...
40 - 44	566 656	283 265	283 391	...	...	...	...	...	...
45 - 49	642 560	319 069	323 491	...	...	...	...	...	...
50 - 54	715 583	359 620	355 963	...	...	...	...	...	...
55 - 59	666 885	332 571	334 314	...	...	...	...	...	...
60 - 64	543 241	263 940	279 301	...	...	...	...	...	...
65 - 69	446 045	211 022	235 023	...	...	...	...	...	...
70 - 74	387 425	177 376	210 049	...	...	...	...	...	...
75 - 79	392 572	172 699	219 873	...	...	...	...	...	...
80 - 84	216 579	88 550	128 029	...	...	...	...	...	...
85 - 89	144 327	51 531	92 796	...	...	...	...	...	...
90 - 94	64 959	18 401	46 558	...	...	...	...	...	...
95 - 99	15 646	3 119	12 527	...	...	...	...	...	...
100 - 104	945	123	822	...	...	...	...	...	...
105 - 109	59	8	51	...	...	...	...	...	...
110 +	2	-	2	...	...	...	...	...	...
Belarus - Bélarus									
1 I 2018 (ESDJ)									
Total	9 491 823	4 421 534	5 070 289	7 412 118	3 417 894	3 994 224	2 079 705	1 003 640	1 076 065
0	102 883	52 863	50 020	79 600	40 788	38 812	23 283	12 075	11 208
1 - 4	477 666	246 238	231 428	375 550	193 466	182 084	102 116	52 772	49 344
5 - 9	552 896	284 645	268 251	437 233	224 841	212 392	115 663	59 804	55 859
10 - 14	461 491	236 838	224 653	359 711	184 737	174 974	101 780	52 101	49 679
15 - 19	453 268	232 987	220 281	374 921	190 668	184 253	78 347	42 319	36 028
20 - 24	512 640	263 427	249 213	431 424	216 013	215 411	81 216	47 414	33 802
25 - 29	713 641	365 053	348 588	624 954	311 400	313 554	88 687	53 653	35 034
30 - 34	781 838	397 622	384 216	657 903	328 385	329 518	123 935	69 237	54 698

7. Population by age, sex and urban/rural residence: latest available year, 2010 - 2019
Population selon l'âge, le sexe et la résidence, urbaine/rurale : dernière année disponible, 2010 - 2019 (continued - suite)

Continent, country or area, date, code[a] and age (in years) / Continent, pays ou zone, date, code[a] et âge (en années)	Total			Urban - Urbaine			Rural - Rurale		
	Both sexes Les deux sexes	Male Masculin	Female Féminin	Both sexes Les deux sexes	Male Masculin	Female Féminin	Both sexes Les deux sexes	Male Masculin	Female Féminin
EUROPE									
Belarus - Bélarus									
1 I 2018 (ESDJ)									
35 - 39	700 453	349 879	350 574	580 271	285 878	294 393	120 182	64 001	56 181
40 - 44	654 091	318 786	335 305	516 299	248 187	268 112	137 792	70 599	67 193
45 - 49	637 421	303 200	334 221	480 034	222 219	257 815	157 387	80 981	76 406
50 - 54	661 130	308 180	352 950	491 194	220 265	270 929	169 936	87 915	82 021
55 - 59	741 293	335 591	405 702	555 536	239 626	315 910	185 757	95 965	89 792
60 - 64	621 451	263 836	357 615	469 599	190 785	278 814	151 852	73 051	78 801
65 - 69	499 210	195 226	303 984	376 541	142 596	233 945	122 669	52 630	70 039
70 - 74	273 350	97 352	175 998	195 799	69 753	126 046	77 551	27 599	49 952
75 - 79	287 101	84 804	202 297	188 093	56 476	131 617	99 008	28 328	70 680
80 - 84	204 091	52 459	151 632	121 652	32 077	89 575	82 439	20 382	62 057
85 - 89	112 479	24 493	87 986	64 118	13 953	50 165	48 361	10 540	37 821
90 - 94	36 538	6 917	29 621	25 323	4 794	20 529	11 215	2 123	9 092
95 - 99	5 783	985	4 798	5 288	839	4 449	495	146	349
100 +	1 109	153	956	1 075	148	927	34	5	29
1 I 2019 (ESDJ)									
Total	9 475 174	4 415 745	5 059 429	...	...	...	...	...	...
0	94 481	48 452	46 029	...	...	...	...	...	...
1 - 4	462 667	238 404	224 263	...	...	...	...	...	...
5 - 9	565 224	290 939	274 285	...	...	...	...	...	...
10 - 14	481 112	247 015	234 097	...	...	...	...	...	...
15 - 19	450 185	231 179	219 006	...	...	...	...	...	...
20 - 24	489 913	252 352	237 561	...	...	...	...	...	...
25 - 29	674 854	344 810	330 044	...	...	...	...	...	...
30 - 34	779 225	397 455	381 770	...	...	...	...	...	...
35 - 39	721 490	361 942	359 548	...	...	...	...	...	...
40 - 44	658 931	322 193	336 738	...	...	...	...	...	...
45 - 49	637 023	303 554	333 469	...	...	...	...	...	...
50 - 54	640 174	297 925	342 249	...	...	...	...	...	...
55 - 59	728 162	331 122	397 040	...	...	...	...	...	...
60 - 64	650 795	277 593	373 202	...	...	...	...	...	...
65 - 69	507 430	197 957	309 473	...	...	...	...	...	...
70 - 74	310 446	110 941	199 505	...	...	...	...	...	...
75 - 79	252 094	74 716	177 378	...	...	...	...	...	...
80 - 84	216 707	55 226	161 481	...	...	...	...	...	...
85 - 89	106 560	22 928	83 632	...	...	...	...	...	...
90 - 94	39 384	7 687	31 697	...	...	...	...	...	...
95 - 99	6 875	1 176	5 699	...	...	...	...	...	...
100 +	1 442	179	1 263	...	...	...	...	...	...
Belgium - Belgique									
1 I 2011 (CDJC)									
Total	11 000 638	5 401 718	5 598 920	10 842 520	5 322 172	5 520 348	158 118	79 546	78 572
0 - 4	645 512	330 184	315 328	636 217	325 336	310 881	9 295	4 848	4 447
5 - 9	607 325	310 560	296 765	597 723	305 654	292 069	9 602	4 906	4 696
10 - 14	614 460	313 738	300 722	604 574	308 723	295 851	9 886	5 015	4 871
15 - 19	649 018	331 790	317 228	638 725	326 452	312 273	10 293	5 338	4 955
20 - 24	684 093	344 647	339 446	674 173	339 520	334 653	9 920	5 127	4 793
25 - 29	700 373	351 045	349 328	691 593	346 539	345 054	8 780	4 506	4 274
30 - 34	722 936	364 728	358 208	713 667	360 044	353 623	9 269	4 684	4 585
35 - 39	741 204	375 815	365 389	730 809	370 490	360 319	10 395	5 325	5 070
40 - 44	789 895	401 530	388 365	778 159	395 446	382 713	11 736	6 084	5 652
45 - 49	828 167	418 827	409 340	816 018	412 531	403 487	12 149	6 296	5 853
50 - 54	781 240	391 809	389 431	770 016	385 999	384 017	11 224	5 810	5 414
55 - 59	702 331	349 489	352 842	692 496	344 347	348 149	9 835	5 142	4 693
60 - 64	650 904	320 714	330 190	641 771	316 010	325 761	9 133	4 704	4 429
65 - 69	480 199	230 217	249 982	473 668	226 987	246 681	6 531	3 230	3 301
70 - 74	448 374	205 382	242 992	441 884	202 344	239 540	6 490	3 038	3 452
75 - 79	401 594	171 538	230 056	395 900	168 962	226 938	5 694	2 576	3 118
80 - 84	304 788	115 591	189 197	300 342	113 821	186 521	4 446	1 770	2 676
85 - 89	180 495	57 963	122 532	177 932	57 048	120 884	2 563	915	1 648
90 - 94	52 708	13 541	39 167	52 007	13 341	38 666	701	200	501
95 - 99	13 392	2 412	10 980	13 233	2 381	10 852	159	31	128
100 +	1 630	198	1 432	1 613	197	1 416	17	1	16

7. Population by age, sex and urban/rural residence: latest available year, 2010 - 2019
Population selon l'âge, le sexe et la résidence, urbaine/rurale : dernière année disponible, 2010 - 2019 (continued - suite)

Continent, country or area, date, code[a] and age (in years) Continent, pays ou zone, date, code[a] et âge (en années)	Total			Urban - Urbaine			Rural - Rurale		
	Both sexes Les deux sexes	Male Masculin	Female Féminin	Both sexes Les deux sexes	Male Masculin	Female Féminin	Both sexes Les deux sexes	Male Masculin	Female Féminin
EUROPE									
Belgium - Belgique									
1 I 2019 (ESDJ)									
Total	11 455 519	5 644 826	5 810 693	...	...	...	...	...	...
0	118 269	60 344	57 925	...	...	...	...	...	...
1 - 4	497 907	254 833	243 074	...	...	...	...	...	...
5 - 9	666 585	340 923	325 662	...	...	...	...	...	...
10 - 14	656 805	336 284	320 521	...	...	...	...	...	...
15 - 19	631 502	323 790	307 712	...	...	...	...	...	...
20 - 24	670 320	341 598	328 722	...	...	...	...	...	...
25 - 29	746 547	374 924	371 623	...	...	...	...	...	...
30 - 34	736 780	368 166	368 614	...	...	...	...	...	...
35 - 39	751 784	377 157	374 627	...	...	...	...	...	...
40 - 44	731 374	368 567	362 807	...	...	...	...	...	...
45 - 49	777 528	393 483	384 045	...	...	...	...	...	...
50 - 54	802 929	406 309	396 620	...	...	...	...	...	...
55 - 59	791 327	395 854	395 473	...	...	...	...	...	...
60 - 64	710 403	349 994	360 409	...	...	...	...	...	...
65 - 69	615 632	298 587	317 045	...	...	...	...	...	...
70 - 74	531 538	249 942	281 596	...	...	...	...	...	...
75 - 79	371 320	165 281	206 039	...	...	...	...	...	...
80 - 84	319 385	131 154	188 231	...	...	...	...	...	...
85 - 89	215 262	76 742	138 520	...	...	...	...	...	...
90 - 94	89 787	26 044	63 743	...	...	...	...	...	...
95 - 99	21 050	4 640	16 410	...	...	...	...	...	...
100 - 104	1 389	201	1 188	...	...	...	...	...	...
105 - 109	93	9	84	...	...	...	...	...	...
110 +	3	-	3	...	...	...	...	...	...
Bosnia and Herzegovina - Bosnie-Herzégovine									
30 IX 2013 (CDJC)									
Total	3 531 159	1 732 270	1 798 889	...	...	...	...	...	...
0 - 4	174 064	89 442	84 622	...	...	...	...	...	...
5 - 9	176 980	90 881	86 099	...	...	...	...	...	...
10 - 14	192 675	98 653	94 022	...	...	...	...	...	...
15 - 19	242 742	124 900	117 842	...	...	...	...	...	...
20 - 24	228 056	116 883	111 173	...	...	...	...	...	...
25 - 29	252 318	129 248	123 070	...	...	...	...	...	...
30 - 34	252 633	128 593	124 040	...	...	...	...	...	...
35 - 39	249 266	126 145	123 121	...	...	...	...	...	...
40 - 44	241 138	121 595	119 543	...	...	...	...	...	...
45 - 49	260 928	130 087	130 841	...	...	...	...	...	...
50 - 54	276 575	136 153	140 422	...	...	...	...	...	...
55 - 59	258 537	125 576	132 961	...	...	...	...	...	...
60 - 64	223 251	104 970	118 281	...	...	...	...	...	...
65 - 69	153 569	69 066	84 503	...	...	...	...	...	...
70 - 74	140 455	59 854	80 601	...	...	...	...	...	...
75 - 79	117 267	47 403	69 864	...	...	...	...	...	...
80 - 84	62 636	23 769	38 867	...	...	...	...	...	...
85 +	28 069	9 052	19 017	...	...	...	...	...	...
Bulgaria - Bulgarie									
1 I 2019 (ESDJ)									
Total	7 000 039	3 395 701	3 604 338	5 159 129	2 481 128	2 678 001	1 840 910	914 573	926 337
0	62 039	32 063	29 976	46 843	24 193	22 650	15 196	7 870	7 326
1 - 4	263 686	135 484	128 202	200 420	102 862	97 558	63 266	32 622	30 644
5 - 9	344 667	176 901	167 766	262 014	134 544	127 470	82 653	42 357	40 296
10 - 14	334 453	172 140	162 313	247 599	127 187	120 412	86 854	44 953	41 901
15 - 19	315 547	162 291	153 256	230 637	118 421	112 216	84 910	43 870	41 040
20 - 24	307 744	158 591	149 153	231 943	118 481	113 462	75 801	40 110	35 691
25 - 29	419 624	215 814	203 810	322 373	163 283	159 090	97 251	52 531	44 720
30 - 34	479 506	247 397	232 109	375 746	190 630	185 116	103 760	56 767	46 993
35 - 39	489 908	254 064	235 844	381 251	194 730	186 521	108 657	59 334	49 323
40 - 44	544 398	279 842	264 556	425 300	215 707	209 593	119 098	64 135	54 963
45 - 49	518 322	265 640	252 682	393 882	198 375	195 507	124 440	67 265	57 175
50 - 54	469 131	236 143	232 988	346 726	170 841	175 885	122 405	65 302	57 103
55 - 59	477 398	234 382	243 016	349 763	167 284	182 479	127 635	67 098	60 537

7. Population by age, sex and urban/rural residence: latest available year, 2010 - 2019
Population selon l'âge, le sexe et la résidence, urbaine/rurale : dernière année disponible, 2010 - 2019 (continued - suite)

Continent, country or area, date, code[a] and age (in years) / Continent, pays ou zone, date, code[a] et âge (en années)	Total			Urban - Urbaine			Rural - Rurale		
	Both sexes Les deux sexes	Male Masculin	Female Féminin	Both sexes Les deux sexes	Male Masculin	Female Féminin	Both sexes Les deux sexes	Male Masculin	Female Féminin
EUROPE									
Bulgaria - Bulgarie									
1 I 2019 (ESDJ)									
60 - 64	480 497	224 905	255 592	347 659	158 736	188 923	132 838	66 169	66 669
65 - 69	473 587	209 008	264 579	333 956	145 166	188 790	139 631	63 842	75 789
70 - 74	401 524	165 752	235 772	269 547	110 070	159 477	131 977	55 682	76 295
75 - 79	279 398	107 489	171 909	177 499	67 524	109 975	101 899	39 965	61 934
80 - 84	197 996	70 638	127 358	124 835	43 268	81 567	73 161	27 370	45 791
85 - 89	105 034	36 025	69 009	67 415	22 398	45 017	37 619	13 627	23 992
90 - 94	30 838	9 737	21 101	20 575	6 488	14 087	10 263	3 249	7 014
95 - 99	4 539	1 337	3 202	3 011	897	2 114	1 528	440	1 088
100 +	203	58	145	135	43	92	68	15	53
100 - 104	196	55	141	...	...	...	...	...	...
105 - 109	7	3	4	...	...	...	...	...	...
110 +	-	-	-	...	...	...	...	...	...
Croatia - Croatie									
1 IV 2011 (CDJC)									
Total	4 284 889	2 066 335	2 218 554	2 368 506	1 121 328	1 247 178	1 916 383	945 007	971 376
0 - 4	212 709	109 251	103 458	116 367	59 768	56 599	96 342	49 483	46 859
5 - 9	204 317	104 841	99 476	108 481	55 715	52 766	95 836	49 126	46 710
10 - 14	235 402	120 633	114 769	124 241	63 763	60 478	111 161	56 870	54 291
15 - 19	244 177	124 918	119 259	130 369	66 506	63 863	113 808	58 412	55 396
20 - 24	261 658	133 455	128 203	142 681	72 037	70 644	118 977	61 418	57 559
25 - 29	289 066	147 416	141 650	164 754	82 466	82 288	124 312	64 950	59 362
30 - 34	294 619	149 998	144 621	173 166	86 363	86 803	121 453	63 635	57 818
35 - 39	284 754	143 984	140 770	165 450	81 745	83 705	119 304	62 239	57 065
40 - 44	286 933	143 603	143 330	161 295	78 845	82 450	125 638	64 758	60 880
45 - 49	307 561	152 446	155 115	167 593	80 182	87 411	139 968	72 264	67 704
50 - 54	320 502	157 981	162 521	174 963	81 945	93 018	145 539	76 036	69 503
55 - 59	311 818	153 750	158 068	174 376	81 746	92 630	137 442	72 004	65 438
60 - 64	272 740	127 851	144 889	154 706	69 577	85 129	118 034	58 274	59 760
65 - 69	202 002	89 364	112 638	114 109	49 018	65 091	87 893	40 346	47 547
70 - 74	212 401	88 912	123 489	113 737	47 978	65 759	98 664	40 934	57 730
75 - 79	175 526	66 456	109 070	91 966	35 801	56 165	83 560	30 655	52 905
80 - 84	108 104	35 999	72 105	56 658	19 022	37 636	51 446	16 977	34 469
85 - 89	47 641	12 415	35 226	26 213	7 045	19 168	21 428	5 370	16 058
90 - 94	10 758	2 580	8 178	6 081	1 517	4 564	4 677	1 063	3 614
95 - 99	2 003	446	1 557	1 181	270	911	822	176	646
100 +	198	36	162	119	19	100	79	17	62
1 I 2019 (ESDJ)									
Total	4 076 246	1 972 572	2 103 674	...	...	...	...	...	...
0	36 819	18 993	17 826	...	...	...	...	...	...
1 - 4	148 308	76 169	72 139	...	...	...	...	...	...
5 - 9	202 194	104 128	98 066	...	...	...	...	...	...
10 - 14	200 465	103 125	97 340	...	...	...	...	...	...
15 - 19	204 449	104 954	99 495	...	...	...	...	...	...
20 - 24	240 575	123 799	116 776	...	...	...	...	...	...
25 - 29	239 413	123 105	116 308	...	...	...	...	...	...
30 - 34	262 027	133 589	128 438	...	...	...	...	...	...
35 - 39	282 031	143 693	138 338	...	...	...	...	...	...
40 - 44	275 383	139 620	135 763	...	...	...	...	...	...
45 - 49	266 771	134 088	132 683	...	...	...	...	...	...
50 - 54	285 324	140 758	144 566	...	...	...	...	...	...
55 - 59	296 230	143 565	152 665	...	...	...	...	...	...
60 - 64	297 658	142 724	154 934	...	...	...	...	...	...
65 - 69	262 779	121 354	141 425	...	...	...	...	...	...
70 - 74	190 347	81 201	109 146	...	...	...	...	...	...
75 - 79	167 840	66 295	101 545	...	...	...	...	...	...
80 - 84	128 375	45 618	82 757	...	...	...	...	...	...
85 - 89	66 864	20 354	46 510	...	...	...	...	...	...
90 - 94	19 107	4 809	14 298	...	...	...	...	...	...
95 - 99	3 156	609	2 547	...	...	...	...	...	...
100 - 104	123	18	105	...	...	...	...	...	...
105 - 109	8	4	4	...	...	...	...	...	...
110 +	-	-	-	...	...	...	...	...	...

7. Population by age, sex and urban/rural residence: latest available year, 2010 - 2019
Population selon l'âge, le sexe et la résidence, urbaine/rurale : dernière année disponible, 2010 - 2019 (continued - suite)

Continent, country or area, date, code[a] and age (in years) Continent, pays ou zone, date, code[a] et âge (en annèes)	Total			Urban - Urbaine			Rural - Rurale		
	Both sexes Les deux sexes	Male Masculin	Female Féminin	Both sexes Les deux sexes	Male Masculin	Female Féminin	Both sexes Les deux sexes	Male Masculin	Female Féminin
EUROPE									
Czechia - Tchéquie									
1 I 2019 (ESDJ)									
Total	10 649 800	5 244 194	5 405 606	7 777 376	3 795 042	3 982 334	2 872 424	1 449 152	1 423 272
0	113 866	58 167	55 699	82 835	42 516	40 319	31 031	15 651	15 380
1 - 4	453 306	232 528	220 778	328 629	168 571	160 058	124 677	63 957	60 720
5 - 9	571 974	292 895	279 079	412 200	210 910	201 290	159 774	81 985	77 789
10 - 14	553 914	284 120	269 794	395 316	202 751	192 565	158 598	81 369	77 229
15 - 19	467 391	240 218	227 173	332 016	170 251	161 765	135 375	69 967	65 408
20 - 24	498 017	255 372	242 645	356 897	182 134	174 763	141 120	73 238	67 882
25 - 29	668 977	343 440	325 537	492 448	251 593	240 855	176 529	91 847	84 682
30 - 34	725 191	373 769	351 422	542 867	280 029	262 838	182 324	93 740	88 584
35 - 39	786 975	406 261	380 714	577 543	297 215	280 328	209 432	109 046	100 386
40 - 44	937 403	481 362	456 041	678 358	345 463	332 895	259 045	135 899	123 146
45 - 49	787 035	404 233	382 802	568 638	288 406	280 232	218 397	115 827	102 570
50 - 54	691 967	352 218	339 749	505 199	253 329	251 870	186 768	98 889	87 879
55 - 59	628 207	314 566	313 641	457 701	226 036	231 665	170 506	88 530	81 976
60 - 64	678 960	328 182	350 778	492 108	233 709	258 399	186 852	94 473	92 379
65 - 69	679 942	315 501	364 441	495 600	225 606	269 994	184 342	89 895	94 447
70 - 74	589 873	258 907	330 966	438 761	188 403	250 358	151 112	70 504	80 608
75 - 79	383 895	156 913	226 982	291 237	117 538	173 699	92 658	39 375	53 283
80 - 84	229 168	83 949	145 219	173 355	63 331	110 024	55 813	20 618	35 195
85 - 89	142 232	45 812	96 420	108 277	34 983	73 294	33 955	10 829	23 126
90 - 94	51 252	13 596	37 656	39 446	10 569	28 877	11 806	3 027	8 779
95 - 99	9 632	2 020	7 612	7 485	1 577	5 908	2 147	443	1 704
100 +	623	165	458	460	122	338	163	43	120
100 - 104	556	149	407	...	...	...	...	...	...
105 - 109	67	16	51	...	...	...	...	...	...
110 +	-	-	-	...	...	...	...	...	...
Denmark - Danemark[81]									
1 VII 2019 (ESDJ)									
Total	5 814 461	2 893 956	2 920 505	...	...	...	...	...	...
0	60 919	31 471	29 448	...	...	...	...	...	...
1 - 4	245 330	126 041	119 289	...	...	...	...	...	...
5 - 9	309 364	158 542	150 822	...	...	...	...	...	...
10 - 14	338 994	173 920	165 074	...	...	...	...	...	...
15 - 19	342 289	175 161	167 128	...	...	...	...	...	...
20 - 24	385 104	196 767	188 337	...	...	...	...	...	...
25 - 29	398 407	203 166	195 241	...	...	...	...	...	...
30 - 34	353 743	180 785	172 958	...	...	...	...	...	...
35 - 39	330 505	167 049	163 456	...	...	...	...	...	...
40 - 44	368 941	184 893	184 048	...	...	...	...	...	...
45 - 49	390 895	196 029	194 866	...	...	...	...	...	...
50 - 54	417 018	210 355	206 663	...	...	...	...	...	...
55 - 59	382 640	191 709	190 931	...	...	...	...	...	...
60 - 64	343 324	170 076	173 248	...	...	...	...	...	...
65 - 69	319 425	155 926	163 499	...	...	...	...	...	...
70 - 74	327 384	157 918	169 466	...	...	...	...	...	...
75 - 79	231 971	107 963	124 008	...	...	...	...	...	...
80 - 84	145 199	63 168	82 031	...	...	...	...	...	...
85 - 89	78 054	30 156	47 898	...	...	...	...	...	...
90 - 94	34 751	10 732	24 019	...	...	...	...	...	...
95 - 99	9 126	1 967	7 159	...	...	...	...	...	...
100 +	1 078	162	916	...	...	...	...	...	...
Estonia - Estonie									
1 I 2019 (ESDJ)									
Total	1 324 820	625 635	699 185	919 630[82]	420 569[82]	499 061[82]	403 771[82]	204 386[82]	199 385[82]
0	14 395	7 356	7 039	10 267[82]	5 279[82]	4 988[82]	4 126[82]	2 076[82]	2 050[82]
1 - 4	56 340	29 150	27 190	40 988[82]	21 119[82]	19 869[82]	15 346[82]	8 027[82]	7 319[82]
5 - 9	74 176	37 955	36 221	53 024[82]	27 024[82]	26 000[82]	21 150[82]	10 931[82]	10 219[82]
10 - 14	72 512	37 358	35 154	51 036[82]	26 182[82]	24 854[82]	21 474[82]	11 176[82]	10 298[82]
15 - 19	61 227	31 344	29 883	41 410[82]	21 032[82]	20 378[82]	19 807[82]	10 306[82]	9 501[82]
20 - 24	64 692	33 049	31 643	45 000[82]	22 222[82]	22 778[82]	19 650[82]	10 806[82]	8 844[82]
25 - 29	88 133	46 208	41 925	62 378[82]	31 407[82]	30 971[82]	25 707[82]	14 773[82]	10 934[82]
30 - 34	99 574	52 137	47 437	73 160[82]	36 799[82]	36 361[82]	26 318[82]	15 265[82]	11 053[82]
35 - 39	92 945	48 129	44 816	68 161[82]	33 948[82]	34 213[82]	24 679[82]	14 104[82]	10 575[82]

Continent, country or area, date, code[a] and age (in years) / Continent, pays ou zone, date, code[a] et âge (en années)	Total			Urban - Urbaine			Rural - Rurale		
	Both sexes Les deux sexes	Male Masculin	Female Féminin	Both sexes Les deux sexes	Male Masculin	Female Féminin	Both sexes Les deux sexes	Male Masculin	Female Féminin
EUROPE									
Estonia - Estonie									
1 I 2019 (ESDJ)									
40 - 44	90 701	46 483	44 218	64 417[82]	31 669[82]	32 748[82]	26 164[82]	14 732[82]	11 432[82]
45 - 49	91 347	46 055	45 292	61 959[82]	29 855[82]	32 104[82]	29 247[82]	16 120[82]	13 127[82]
50 - 54	83 105	40 588	42 517	54 536[82]	25 544[82]	28 992[82]	28 445[82]	14 974[82]	13 471[82]
55 - 59	88 719	41 833	46 886	58 367[82]	25 998[82]	32 369[82]	30 221[82]	15 776[82]	14 445[82]
60 - 64	85 106	37 809	47 297	57 130[82]	23 908[82]	33 222[82]	27 856[82]	13 852[82]	14 004[82]
65 - 69	77 344	31 841	45 503	52 800[82]	20 499[82]	32 301[82]	24 401[82]	11 287[82]	13 114[82]
70 - 74	58 104	21 967	36 137	39 040[82]	13 990[82]	25 050[82]	18 940[82]	7 942[82]	10 998[82]
75 - 79	51 683	17 256	34 427	34 712[82]	11 129[82]	23 583[82]	16 884[82]	6 110[82]	10 774[82]
80 - 84	40 544	11 517	29 027	27 959[82]	7 804[82]	20 155[82]	12 529[82]	3 699[82]	8 830[82]
85 - 89	23 198	5 624	17 574	15 746[82]	3 793[82]	11 953[82]	7 414[82]	1 825[82]	5 589[82]
90 - 94	9 170	1 738	7 432	6 355[82]	1 218[82]	5 137[82]	2 793[82]	517[82]	2 276[82]
95 - 99	1 672	222	1 450	1 094[82]	139[82]	955[82]	578[82]	83[82]	495[82]
100 +	133	16	117	91[82]	11[82]	80[82]	42[82]	5[82]	37[82]
100 - 104	127	16	111	...	...	...	...	...	...
105 - 109	6	-	6	...	...	...	...	...	...
110 +	-	-	-	...	...	...	...	...	...
Faroe Islands - Îles Féroé									
1 VII 2019 (ESDJ)									
Total	51 842	26 815	25 027	19 903	10 040	9 863	31 939	16 775	15 164
0	703	354	349	286	145	141	417	209	208
1 - 4	2 915	1 420	1 495	1 130	549	581	1 785	871	914
5 - 9	3 506	1 828	1 678	1 344	674	670	2 162	1 154	1 008
10 - 14	3 731	1 904	1 827	1 437	722	715	2 294	1 182	1 112
15 - 19	3 602	1 860	1 742	1 395	713	682	2 207	1 147	1 060
20 - 24	3 032	1 692	1 340	1 148	611	537	1 884	1 081	803
25 - 29	3 020	1 624	1 396	1 204	650	554	1 816	974	842
30 - 34	3 121	1 660	1 461	1 192	608	584	1 929	1 052	877
35 - 39	3 021	1 575	1 446	1 187	601	586	1 834	974	860
40 - 44	3 217	1 716	1 501	1 236	659	577	1 981	1 057	924
45 - 49	3 274	1 757	1 517	1 260	667	593	2 014	1 090	924
50 - 54	3 516	1 873	1 643	1 519	757	762	1 997	1 116	881
55 - 59	3 204	1 656	1 548	1 251	665	586	1 953	991	962
60 - 64	2 940	1 497	1 443	1 097	531	566	1 843	966	877
65 - 69	2 709	1 378	1 331	1 018	503	515	1 691	875	816
70 - 74	2 290	1 222	1 068	816	406	410	1 474	816	658
75 - 79	1 805	900	905	625	299	326	1 180	601	579
80 - 84	1 070	484	586	365	153	212	705	331	374
85 - 89	757	301	456	243	93	150	514	208	306
90 - 94	338	101	237	121	31	90	217	70	147
95 - 99	62	11	51	26	3	23	36	8	28
100 +	9	2	7	3	-	3	6	2	4
Finland - Finlande[36]									
1 VII 2018 (ESDJ)[83]									
Total	5 485 886	2 706 416	2 779 470	3 926 164	1 919 593	2 006 571	1 573 829	793 439	780 390
0	48 837	25 087	23 747	36 446	18 732	17 715	12 391	6 355	6 032
1 - 4	222 699	113 860	108 824	161 987	82 932	79 055	64 734	33 014	31 704
5 - 9	307 874	157 321	150 543	217 736	111 248	106 488	91 079	46 632	44 437
10 - 14	302 008	154 329	147 663	209 681	107 182	102 500	92 317	47 067	45 233
15 - 19	294 545	151 333	143 194	208 268	105 352	102 916	87 850	46 764	41 067
20 - 24	322 739	165 539	157 177	266 102	133 248	132 854	59 447	33 639	25 785
25 - 29	352 807	181 459	171 332	288 853	147 621	141 236	64 761	34 173	30 573
30 - 34	349 560	180 345	169 196	274 389	141 581	132 808	77 845	40 105	37 721
35 - 39	351 248	181 059	170 170	266 174	137 280	128 894	84 927	43 713	41 195
40 - 44	335 727	172 376	163 339	248 220	127 325	120 895	86 552	44 540	42 000
45 - 49	319 766	162 464	157 294	229 697	116 297	113 400	94 457	48 501	45 948
50 - 54	364 959	183 519	181 427	255 852	127 167	128 685	111 698	57 730	53 955
55 - 59	364 547	181 222	183 321	247 687	120 926	126 762	117 946	60 778	57 164
60 - 64	362 942	177 196	185 724	239 954	113 885	126 069	125 139	64 635	60 481
65 - 69	364 159	175 256	188 901	238 735	110 806	127 929	127 165	65 250	61 912
70 - 74	317 283	148 101	169 180	211 577	95 572	116 005	96 319	47 676	48 641
75 - 79	206 985	90 592	116 372	136 180	57 965	78 215	72 344	33 153	39 171
80 - 84	151 032	60 327	90 688	96 535	37 290	59 245	53 123	22 269	30 837

7. Population by age, sex and urban/rural residence: latest available year, 2010 - 2019
Population selon l'âge, le sexe et la résidence, urbaine/rurale : dernière année disponible, 2010 - 2019 (continued - suite)

Continent, country or area, date, code[a] and age (in years) Continent, pays ou zone, date, code[a] et âge (en années)	Total			Urban - Urbaine			Rural - Rurale		
	Both sexes Les deux sexes	Male Masculin	Female Féminin	Both sexes Les deux sexes	Male Masculin	Female Féminin	Both sexes Les deux sexes	Male Masculin	Female Féminin
EUROPE									
Finland - Finlande[36]									
1 VII 2018 (ESDJ)[83]									
85 - 89	95 919	32 354	63 542	60 726	19 733	40 994	35 548	12 538	22 987
90 - 94	40 561	10 752	29 790	25 370	6 418	18 956	14 737	4 062	10 657
95 - 99	8 689	1 593	7 091	5 428	1 042	4 460	3 044	590	2 451
100 +	866	132	734	584	83	510	273	55	218
1 I 2019 (ESDJ)									
Total	5 517 919	2 723 290	2 794 629	...	...	...	...	...	...
0	47 663	24 663	23 000	...	...	...	...	...	...
1 - 4	220 023	112 394	107 629	...	...	...	...	...	...
5 - 9	309 010	158 005	151 005	...	...	...	...	...	...
10 - 14	305 538	156 182	149 356	...	...	...	...	...	...
15 - 19	296 167	152 126	144 041	...	...	...	...	...	...
20 - 24	320 376	164 499	155 877	...	...	...	...	...	...
25 - 29	354 872	182 635	172 237	...	...	...	...	...	...
30 - 34	350 396	180 832	169 564	...	...	...	...	...	...
35 - 39	355 751	183 327	172 424	...	...	...	...	...	...
40 - 44	342 365	175 769	166 596	...	...	...	...	...	...
45 - 49	315 578	160 573	155 005	...	...	...	...	...	...
50 - 54	364 549	183 302	181 247	...	...	...	...	...	...
55 - 59	368 233	183 156	185 077	...	...	...	...	...	...
60 - 64	362 561	177 055	185 506	...	...	...	...	...	...
65 - 69	362 208	174 278	187 930	...	...	...	...	...	...
70 - 74	330 660	154 506	176 154	...	...	...	...	...	...
75 - 79	209 259	91 933	117 326	...	...	...	...	...	...
80 - 84	155 089	62 247	92 842	...	...	...	...	...	...
85 - 89	96 049	32 747	63 302	...	...	...	...	...	...
90 - 94	41 649	11 243	30 406	...	...	...	...	...	...
95 - 99	9 034	1 683	7 351	...	...	...	...	...	...
100 - 104	851	132	719	...	...	...	...	...	...
105 - 109	38	3	35	...	...	...	...	...	...
110 +	-	-	-	...	...	...	...	...	...
France									
1 I 2015 (CDJC)									
Total	64 300 821	31 138 550	33 162 271	49 781 175	23 891 441	25 889 734	14 519 646	7 247 109	7 272 537
0 - 4	3 779 312	1 932 140	1 847 172	2 943 961	1 505 149	1 438 812	835 351	426 991	408 360
5 - 9	3 974 070	2 031 848	1 942 222	3 018 642	1 542 952	1 475 690	955 429	488 896	466 533
10 - 14	3 958 786	2 024 518	1 934 267	2 993 243	1 530 322	1 462 921	965 543	494 196	471 346
15 - 19	3 889 075	1 996 718	1 892 357	3 107 020	1 586 257	1 520 763	782 055	410 461	371 594
20 - 24	3 716 644	1 877 169	1 839 475	3 186 247	1 592 313	1 593 934	530 397	284 856	245 541
25 - 29	3 816 224	1 882 618	1 933 606	3 154 967	1 554 787	1 600 180	661 257	327 831	333 426
30 - 34	3 991 417	1 960 633	2 030 784	3 154 039	1 548 166	1 605 872	837 378	412 467	424 911
35 - 39	3 988 088	1 973 599	2 014 489	3 082 418	1 523 069	1 559 349	905 670	450 530	455 140
40 - 44	4 341 471	2 155 883	2 185 588	3 298 789	1 626 585	1 672 204	1 042 682	529 298	513 384
45 - 49	4 361 803	2 155 308	2 206 495	3 307 842	1 613 857	1 693 985	1 053 962	541 451	512 510
50 - 54	4 307 213	2 111 783	2 195 431	3 264 358	1 577 384	1 686 973	1 042 856	534 398	508 457
55 - 59	4 113 250	1 992 506	2 120 744	3 093 196	1 474 501	1 618 695	1 020 054	518 005	502 049
60 - 64	3 990 376	1 912 839	2 077 537	2 969 500	1 393 394	1 576 105	1 020 877	519 445	501 432
65 - 69	3 605 489	1 713 389	1 892 099	2 700 040	1 255 492	1 444 548	905 449	457 897	447 551
70 - 74	2 458 426	1 138 687	1 319 739	1 879 526	854 092	1 025 434	578 900	284 595	294 305
75 - 79	2 167 384	938 443	1 228 941	1 657 310	703 262	954 049	510 074	235 181	274 893
80 - 84	1 865 044	731 105	1 133 939	1 432 760	549 227	883 533	432 284	181 878	250 406
85 - 89	1 249 877	420 854	829 023	963 811	315 642	648 168	286 066	105 212	180 855
90 - 94	589 014	161 109	427 905	462 115	123 242	338 872	126 899	37 866	89 033
95 - 99	114 657	23 412	91 245	92 480	18 509	73 971	22 177	4 903	17 274
100 +	23 202	3 989	19 212	18 913	3 237	15 676	4 289	752	3 536
1 I 2019 (ESDJ)[84]									
Total	64 821 954	31 353 853	33 468 101	...	...	...	...	...	...
0	678 543	346 895	331 648	...	...	...	...	...	...
1 - 4	2 893 525	1 476 024	1 417 501	...	...	...	...	...	...
5 - 9	3 944 258	2 017 255	1 927 003	...	...	...	...	...	...
10 - 14	3 996 692	2 043 994	1 952 698	...	...	...	...	...	...
15 - 19	3 965 611	2 038 061	1 927 550	...	...	...	...	...	...
20 - 24	3 612 818	1 828 640	1 784 178	...	...	...	...	...	...
25 - 29	3 667 054	1 815 393	1 851 661	...	...	...	...	...	...

7. Population by age, sex and urban/rural residence: latest available year, 2010 - 2019
Population selon l'âge, le sexe et la résidence, urbaine/rurale : dernière année disponible, 2010 - 2019 (continued - suite)

Continent, country or area, date, code[a] and age (in years) Continent, pays ou zone, date, code[a] et âge (en annèes)	Total			Urban - Urbaine			Rural - Rurale		
	Both sexes Les deux sexes	Male Masculin	Female Féminin	Both sexes Les deux sexes	Male Masculin	Female Féminin	Both sexes Les deux sexes	Male Masculin	Female Féminin
EUROPE									
France									
1 I 2019 (ESDJ)[84]									
30 - 34	3 935 915	1 917 425	2 018 490	...	...	...	...	...	...
35 - 39	4 105 434	2 008 334	2 097 100	...	...	...	...	...	...
40 - 44	3 975 678	1 966 705	2 008 973	...	...	...	...	...	...
45 - 49	4 410 048	2 187 169	2 222 879	...	...	...	...	...	...
50 - 54	4 308 847	2 118 506	2 190 341	...	...	...	...	...	...
55 - 59	4 186 166	2 034 336	2 151 830	...	...	...	...	...	...
60 - 64	3 962 481	1 888 253	2 074 228	...	...	...	...	...	...
65 - 69	3 821 201	1 802 846	2 018 355	...	...	...	...	...	...
70 - 74	3 195 884	1 481 970	1 713 914	...	...	...	...	...	...
75 - 79	2 129 395	944 980	1 184 415	...	...	...	...	...	...
80 - 84	1 836 937	744 505	1 092 432	...	...	...	...	...	...
85 - 89	1 330 941	465 998	864 943	...	...	...	...	...	...
90 - 94	652 577	182 981	469 596	...	...	...	...	...	...
95 - 99	193 047	40 485	152 562	...	...	...	...	...	...
100 - 104	16 435	2 602	13 833	...	...	...	...	...	...
105 - 109	2 171	496	1 675	...	...	...	...	...	...
110 +	296	-	296	...	...	...	...	...	...
Germany - Allemagne									
9 V 2011 (CDJC)									
Total	80 219 695	39 145 941	41 073 754	64 444 232	31 227 832	33 216 400	15 775 463	7 918 109	7 857 354
0 - 4	3 338 895	1 714 872	1 624 023	2 712 601	1 393 763	1 318 838	626 294	321 109	305 185
5 - 9	3 525 830	1 809 024	1 716 806	2 798 622	1 435 745	1 362 877	727 208	373 279	353 929
10 - 14	3 940 566	2 021 305	1 919 261	3 074 610	1 575 684	1 498 926	865 956	445 621	420 335
15 - 19	4 013 880	2 057 155	1 956 725	3 144 832	1 606 068	1 538 764	869 048	451 087	417 961
20 - 24	4 835 639	2 463 932	2 371 707	3 993 247	2 003 582	1 989 665	842 392	460 350	382 042
25 - 29	4 872 533	2 455 885	2 416 648	4 113 697	2 057 507	2 056 190	758 836	398 378	360 458
30 - 34	4 751 911	2 385 305	2 366 606	3 942 747	1 977 628	1 965 119	809 164	407 677	401 487
35 - 39	4 742 893	2 378 055	2 364 838	3 833 417	1 920 448	1 912 969	909 476	457 607	451 869
40 - 44	6 351 189	3 209 481	3 141 708	5 029 918	2 540 433	2 489 485	1 321 271	669 048	652 223
45 - 49	6 999 679	3 547 254	3 452 425	5 488 622	2 771 239	2 717 383	1 511 057	776 015	735 042
50 - 54	6 206 294	3 113 463	3 092 831	4 845 747	2 413 038	2 432 709	1 360 547	700 425	660 122
55 - 59	5 419 450	2 668 976	2 750 474	4 252 008	2 066 178	2 185 830	1 167 442	602 798	564 644
60 - 64	4 702 815	2 298 903	2 403 912	3 753 504	1 808 314	1 945 190	949 311	490 589	458 722
65 - 69	4 173 351	1 999 287	2 174 064	3 423 376	1 624 839	1 798 537	749 975	374 448	375 527
70 - 74	4 861 239	2 247 196	2 614 043	3 931 373	1 801 914	2 129 459	929 866	445 282	484 584
75 - 79	3 270 283	1 413 881	1 856 402	2 633 648	1 128 379	1 505 269	636 635	285 502	351 133
80 - 84	2 328 083	878 797	1 449 286	1 890 025	704 565	1 185 460	438 058	174 232	263 826
85 - 89	1 335 076	369 029	966 047	1 108 944	302 059	806 885	226 132	66 970	159 162
90 - 94	430 600	95 074	335 526	368 116	79 884	288 232	62 484	15 190	47 294
95 - 99	106 044	17 388	88 656	93 152	15 094	78 058	12 892	2 294	10 598
100 +	13 445	1 679	11 766	12 026	1 471	10 555	1 419	208	1 211
1 I 2019 (ESDJ)[4]									
Total	83 019 213	40 966 691	42 052 522	...	...	...	...	...	...
0	783 978	402 082	381 896	...	...	...	...	...	...
1 - 4	3 142 419	1 612 015	1 530 404	...	...	...	...	...	...
5 - 9	3 662 238	1 882 175	1 780 063	...	...	...	...	...	...
10 - 14	3 702 180	1 904 430	1 797 750	...	...	...	...	...	...
15 - 19	4 003 477	2 082 699	1 920 778	...	...	...	...	...	...
20 - 24	4 607 272	2 415 012	2 192 260	...	...	...	...	...	...
25 - 29	5 193 335	2 695 936	2 497 399	...	...	...	...	...	...
30 - 34	5 409 029	2 784 081	2 624 948	...	...	...	...	...	...
35 - 39	5 237 416	2 653 317	2 584 099	...	...	...	...	...	...
40 - 44	4 841 738	2 438 958	2 402 780	...	...	...	...	...	...
45 - 49	5 584 519	2 812 217	2 772 302	...	...	...	...	...	...
50 - 54	6 875 948	3 470 222	3 405 726	...	...	...	...	...	...
55 - 59	6 598 218	3 297 674	3 300 544	...	...	...	...	...	...
60 - 64	5 493 914	2 695 725	2 798 189	...	...	...	...	...	...
65 - 69	4 808 497	2 291 634	2 516 863	...	...	...	...	...	...
70 - 74	3 596 545	1 679 886	1 916 659	...	...	...	...	...	...
75 - 79	4 089 384	1 823 611	2 265 773	...	...	...	...	...	...
80 - 84	3 111 597	1 287 124	1 824 473	...	...	...	...	...	...
85 - 89	1 482 566	530 300	952 266	...	...	...	...	...	...
90 - 94	636 791	177 534	459 257	...	...	...	...	...	...

Continent, country or area, date, code[a] and age (in years) / Continent, pays ou zone, date, code[a] et âge (en annèes)	Total			Urban - Urbaine			Rural - Rurale		
	Both sexes Les deux sexes	Male Masculin	Female Féminin	Both sexes Les deux sexes	Male Masculin	Female Féminin	Both sexes Les deux sexes	Male Masculin	Female Féminin
EUROPE									
Germany - Allemagne									
1 I 2019 (ESDJ)[4]									
95 - 99	144 183	27 529	116 654	...	...	...	...	...	...
100 - 104	11 298	1 937	9 361	...	...	...	...	...	...
105 - 109	2 286	456	1 830	...	...	...	...	...	...
110 +	385	137	248	...	...	...	...	...	...
Gibraltar[85]									
12 XI 2012 (CDJC)									
Total	32 194	16 061	16 133	...	...	...	...	...	...
0 - 4	1 952	982	970	...	...	...	...	...	...
5 - 9	1 894	967	927	...	...	...	...	...	...
10 - 14	1 987	1 050	937	...	...	...	...	...	...
15 - 19	1 997	1 038	959	...	...	...	...	...	...
20 - 24	2 028	1 042	986	...	...	...	...	...	...
25 - 29	1 985	999	986	...	...	...	...	...	...
30 - 34	2 154	1 107	1 047	...	...	...	...	...	...
35 - 39	2 217	1 080	1 137	...	...	...	...	...	...
40 - 44	2 198	1 076	1 122	...	...	...	...	...	...
45 - 49	2 384	1 203	1 181	...	...	...	...	...	...
50 - 54	2 158	1 072	1 086	...	...	...	...	...	...
55 - 59	2 041	1 054	987	...	...	...	...	...	...
60 - 64	1 954	1 034	920	...	...	...	...	...	...
65 - 69	1 655	853	802	...	...	...	...	...	...
70 - 74	1 176	563	613	...	...	...	...	...	...
75 - 79	1 021	456	565	...	...	...	...	...	...
80 - 84	732	297	435	...	...	...	...	...	...
85 - 89	437	141	296	...	...	...	...	...	...
90 - 94	180	37	143	...	...	...	...	...	...
95 - 99	39	10	29	...	...	...	...	...	...
100 +	5	-	5	...	...	...	...	...	...
Greece - Grèce									
9 V 2011 (CDFC)									
Total	10 816 286	5 303 223	5 513 063	8 285 259	4 022 889	4 262 370	2 531 027	1 280 334	1 250 693
0 - 4	537 243	274 788	262 455	431 611	220 917	210 694	105 632	53 871	51 761
5 - 9	512 596	262 432	250 164	405 436	207 479	197 957	107 160	54 953	52 207
10 - 14	519 429	265 787	253 642	406 962	208 070	198 892	112 467	57 717	54 750
15 - 19	553 276	286 386	266 890	440 869	226 682	214 187	112 407	59 704	52 703
20 - 24	627 097	325 127	301 970	510 067	259 795	250 272	117 030	65 332	51 698
25 - 29	723 771	371 617	352 154	583 506	295 880	287 626	140 265	75 737	64 528
30 - 34	822 475	417 861	404 614	666 145	334 794	331 351	156 330	83 067	73 263
35 - 39	812 829	409 681	403 148	651 826	323 821	328 005	161 003	85 860	75 143
40 - 44	832 666	414 026	418 640	663 331	323 632	339 699	169 335	90 394	78 941
45 - 49	748 429	367 086	381 343	590 034	283 391	306 643	158 395	83 695	74 700
50 - 54	731 486	355 552	375 934	565 986	268 882	297 104	165 500	86 670	78 830
55 - 59	660 368	321 466	338 902	501 507	240 725	260 782	158 861	80 741	78 120
60 - 64	625 769	301 589	324 180	459 249	219 165	240 084	166 520	82 424	84 096
65 - 69	508 276	241 832	266 444	356 701	167 557	189 144	151 575	74 275	77 300
70 - 74	542 165	246 264	295 901	363 133	162 560	200 573	179 032	83 704	95 328
75 - 79	475 077	209 983	265 094	309 622	134 691	174 931	165 455	75 292	90 163
80 - 84	352 373	146 455	205 918	229 214	91 916	137 298	123 159	54 539	68 620
85 - 89	159 841	60 933	98 908	104 058	37 922	66 136	55 783	23 011	32 772
90 - 94	53 445	18 760	34 685	34 608	11 513	23 095	18 837	7 247	11 590
95 - 99	15 187	4 948	10 239	9 822	3 081	6 741	5 365	1 867	3 498
100 +	2 488	650	1 838	1 572	416	1 156	916	234	682
1 I 2019 (ESDF)									
Total	10 724 599	5 208 293	5 516 306	...	...	...	...	...	...
0	87 557	45 078	42 479	...	...	...	...	...	...
1 - 4	379 119	194 654	184 465	...	...	...	...	...	...
5 - 9	528 033	271 053	256 980	...	...	...	...	...	...
10 - 14	542 366	278 937	263 429	...	...	...	...	...	...
15 - 19	546 137	283 450	262 687	...	...	...	...	...	...
20 - 24	552 322	286 472	265 850	...	...	...	...	...	...
25 - 29	568 972	289 329	279 643	...	...	...	...	...	...
30 - 34	609 715	304 326	305 389	...	...	...	...	...	...
35 - 39	766 170	383 663	382 507	...	...	...	...	...	...

7. Population by age, sex and urban/rural residence: latest available year, 2010 - 2019
Population selon l'âge, le sexe et la résidence, urbaine/rurale : dernière année disponible, 2010 - 2019 (continued - suite)

Continent, country or area, date, code[a] and age (in years) Continent, pays ou zone, date, code[a] et âge (en années)	Total			Urban - Urbaine			Rural - Rurale		
	Both sexes Les deux sexes	Male Masculin	Female Féminin	Both sexes Les deux sexes	Male Masculin	Female Féminin	Both sexes Les deux sexes	Male Masculin	Female Féminin
EUROPE									
Greece - Grèce									
1 I 2019 (ESDF)									
40 - 44	802 186	397 530	404 656	...	...	...	...	...	...
45 - 49	806 053	393 951	412 102	...	...	...	...	...	...
50 - 54	782 207	376 235	405 972	...	...	...	...	...	...
55 - 59	718 583	338 020	380 563	...	...	...	...	...	...
60 - 64	671 906	316 380	355 526	...	...	...	...	...	...
65 - 69	606 852	285 694	321 158	...	...	...	...	...	...
70 - 74	557 393	255 713	301 680	...	...	...	...	...	...
75 - 79	438 594	195 153	243 441	...	...	...	...	...	...
80 - 84	394 625	163 766	230 859	...	...	...	...	...	...
85 - 89	240 780	98 676	142 104	...	...	...	...	...	...
90 - 94	92 672	36 371	56 301	...	...	...	...	...	...
95 - 99	23 025	10 028	12 997	...	...	...	...	...	...
100 +	9 332	3 814	5 518	...	...	...	...	...	...
Guernsey - Guernesey									
31 III 2019 (ESDJ)									
Total	62 792	31 080	31 712	...	...	...	...	...	...
0	500	251	249	...	...	...	...	...	...
1 - 4	2 352	1 197	1 155	...	...	...	...	...	...
5 - 9	3 346	1 733	1 613	...	...	...	...	...	...
10 - 14	3 154	1 662	1 492	...	...	...	...	...	...
15 - 19	3 335	1 705	1 630	...	...	...	...	...	...
20 - 24	3 577	1 824	1 753	...	...	...	...	...	...
25 - 29	3 990	2 065	1 925	...	...	...	...	...	...
30 - 34	3 912	2 011	1 901	...	...	...	...	...	...
35 - 39	3 902	1 988	1 914	...	...	...	...	...	...
40 - 44	3 825	1 884	1 941	...	...	...	...	...	...
45 - 49	4 665	2 283	2 382	...	...	...	...	...	...
50 - 54	4 919	2 373	2 546	...	...	...	...	...	...
55 - 59	4 757	2 334	2 423	...	...	...	...	...	...
60 - 64	4 007	2 040	1 967	...	...	...	...	...	...
65 - 69	3 532	1 717	1 815	...	...	...	...	...	...
70 - 74	3 368	1 610	1 758	...	...	...	...	...	...
75 - 79	2 143	996	1 147	...	...	...	...	...	...
80 - 84	1 795	806	989	...	...	...	...	...	...
85 - 89	1 071	413	658	...	...	...	...	...	...
90 - 94	498	149	349	...	...	...	...	...	...
95 - 99	128	37	91	...	...	...	...	...	...
100 +	16	2	14	...	...	...	...	...	...
Hungary - Hongrie									
1 VII 2018 (ESDJ)									
Total	9 775 564	4 673 712	5 101 852	6 888 955	3 253 732	3 635 224	2 886 609	1 419 980	1 466 629
0	93 429	47 957	45 472	64 320	33 026	31 294	29 109	14 931	14 178
1 - 4	373 552	191 766	181 787	262 599	134 950	127 649	110 954	56 816	54 138
5 - 9	463 826	238 161	225 665	326 595	167 657	158 938	137 231	70 504	66 727
10 - 14	491 022	252 090	238 932	334 093	171 487	162 606	156 929	80 603	76 327
15 - 19	488 197	251 029	237 168	334 356	170 773	163 583	153 842	80 256	73 586
20 - 24	570 243	293 629	276 614	392 331	200 138	192 193	177 912	93 491	84 421
25 - 29	627 446	324 321	303 125	441 065	225 239	215 826	186 381	99 082	87 299
30 - 34	609 264	312 804	296 461	436 753	221 538	215 215	172 512	91 266	81 246
35 - 39	699 256	354 197	345 059	506 352	252 984	253 368	192 904	101 213	91 691
40 - 44	849 146	430 056	419 090	612 009	306 219	305 790	237 137	123 837	113 300
45 - 49	718 070	361 296	356 774	504 874	250 895	253 979	213 197	110 402	102 795
50 - 54	624 554	308 155	316 400	429 454	208 166	221 288	195 100	99 989	95 112
55 - 59	588 213	278 789	309 424	398 455	184 302	214 154	189 758	94 488	95 270
60 - 64	708 387	320 984	387 403	493 744	217 334	276 410	214 643	103 650	110 994
65 - 69	609 958	261 617	348 341	434 652	182 338	252 314	175 306	79 279	96 028
70 - 74	469 128	189 326	279 803	343 515	137 399	206 116	125 614	51 927	73 687
75 - 79	361 395	131 032	230 363	261 282	95 646	165 637	100 113	35 387	64 726
80 - 84	235 066	73 676	161 390	168 797	54 107	114 690	66 269	19 570	46 700
85 - 89	133 385	37 925	95 460	97 599	28 433	69 167	35 786	9 493	26 293
90 - 94	48 239	11 626	36 613	35 985	8 726	27 259	12 254	2 900	9 354
95 - 99	12 033	2 711	9 322	8 871	1 967	6 904	3 163	745	2 418
100 +	1 761	569	1 192	1 260	412	848	501	157	344

7. Population by age, sex and urban/rural residence: latest available year, 2010 - 2019
Population selon l'âge, le sexe et la résidence, urbaine/rurale : dernière année disponible, 2010 - 2019 (continued - suite)

Continent, country or area, date, code[a] and age (in years) / Continent, pays ou zone, date, code[a] et âge (en annèes)	Total			Urban - Urbaine			Rural - Rurale		
	Both sexes Les deux sexes	Male Masculin	Female Féminin	Both sexes Les deux sexes	Male Masculin	Female Féminin	Both sexes Les deux sexes	Male Masculin	Female Féminin
EUROPE									
Hungary - Hongrie									
1 VII 2019 (ESDJ)[86]									
Total	9 772 756	4 675 821	5 096 935	...	...	...	...	...	...
0	92 771	47 642	45 129	...	...	...	...	...	...
1 - 4	375 834	192 895	182 939	...	...	...	...	...	...
5 - 9	459 179	235 885	223 294	...	...	...	...	...	...
10 - 14	493 955	253 532	240 423	...	...	...	...	...	...
15 - 19	487 054	250 546	236 508	...	...	...	...	...	...
20 - 24	561 803	289 541	272 262	...	...	...	...	...	...
25 - 29	629 354	325 446	303 908	...	...	...	...	...	...
30 - 34	611 717	315 030	296 687	...	...	...	...	...	...
35 - 39	681 817	345 806	336 011	...	...	...	...	...	...
40 - 44	856 450	433 920	422 530	...	...	...	...	...	...
45 - 49	719 721	362 642	357 079	...	...	...	...	...	...
50 - 54	637 730	315 080	322 650	...	...	...	...	...	...
55 - 59	580 541	275 799	304 742	...	...	...	...	...	...
60 - 64	694 871	314 966	379 905	...	...	...	...	...	...
65 - 69	617 337	265 009	352 328	...	...	...	...	...	...
70 - 74	475 183	191 850	283 333	...	...	...	...	...	...
75 - 79	364 406	132 807	231 599	...	...	...	...	...	...
80 - 84	235 835	73 952	161 883	...	...	...	...	...	...
85 - 89	134 068	38 279	95 789	...	...	...	...	...	...
90 - 94	48 623	11 748	36 875	...	...	...	...	...	...
95 - 99	12 661	2 853	9 808	...	...	...	...	...	...
100 - 104	1 400	415	985	...	...	...	...	...	...
105 - 109	410	157	253	...	...	...	...	...	...
110 +	36	21	15	...	...	...	...	...	...
Iceland - Islande[87]									
1 VII 2018 (ESDJ)									
Total	352 721	180 219	172 502	329 828	167 879	161 949	22 893	12 340	10 553
0	4 162	2 181	1 982	3 938	2 051	1 887	225	130	95
1 - 4	17 088	8 706	8 382	16 190	8 251	7 940	898	456	443
5 - 9	23 728	12 151	11 577	22 555	11 544	11 011	1 173	607	567
10 - 14	22 635	11 603	11 032	21 383	10 957	10 426	1 252	647	606
15 - 19	21 935	11 063	10 873	20 553	10 365	10 189	1 382	698	684
20 - 24	25 817	13 386	12 432	24 062	12 521	11 542	1 755	865	890
25 - 29	28 751	15 343	13 408	26 719	14 216	12 504	2 032	1 128	905
30 - 34	25 275	13 495	11 780	23 804	12 634	11 170	1 471	861	610
35 - 39	25 128	13 290	11 838	23 817	12 557	11 261	1 311	734	578
40 - 44	22 833	11 900	10 933	21 608	11 224	10 384	1 225	676	549
45 - 49	22 078	11 403	10 675	20 696	10 657	10 039	1 383	747	636
50 - 54	22 156	11 109	11 047	20 504	10 233	10 271	1 652	876	777
55 - 59	21 685	10 933	10 752	19 932	9 961	9 971	1 753	972	782
60 - 64	19 592	9 873	9 719	17 993	8 981	9 012	1 599	892	707
65 - 69	16 286	8 231	8 056	15 002	7 541	7 461	1 285	690	595
70 - 74	12 690	6 328	6 363	11 694	5 755	5 939	997	573	424
75 - 79	8 456	4 015	4 441	7 827	3 675	4 152	629	340	290
80 - 84	6 084	2 767	3 318	5 651	2 540	3 112	433	227	206
85 - 89	4 178	1 734	2 444	3 879	1 576	2 304	299	159	141
90 - 94	1 745	596	1 149	1 641	546	1 095	104	50	54
95 - 99	376	106	270	342	88	254	34	18	16
100 +	47	12	35	44	11	33	4	1	3
1 VII 2019 (ESDJ)									
Total	356 991	182 837	174 154	...	...	...	...	...	...
0	4 231	2 240	1 991	...	...	...	...	...	...
1 - 4	16 997	8 714	8 283	...	...	...	...	...	...
5 - 9	23 620	12 051	11 569	...	...	...	...	...	...
10 - 14	22 969	11 802	11 167	...	...	...	...	...	...
15 - 19	21 945	11 036	10 909	...	...	...	...	...	...
20 - 24	25 913	13 440	12 473	...	...	...	...	...	...
25 - 29	29 571	15 802	13 769	...	...	...	...	...	...
30 - 34	25 989	13 983	12 006	...	...	...	...	...	...
35 - 39	25 661	13 650	12 011	...	...	...	...	...	...
40 - 44	23 043	12 052	10 991	...	...	...	...	...	...
45 - 49	22 554	11 687	10 867	...	...	...	...	...	...

7. Population by age, sex and urban/rural residence: latest available year, 2010 - 2019
Population selon l'âge, le sexe et la résidence, urbaine/rurale : dernière année disponible, 2010 - 2019 (continued - suite)

Continent, country or area, date, code[a] and age (in years) Continent, pays ou zone, date, code[a] et âge (en années)	Total			Urban - Urbaine			Rural - Rurale		
	Both sexes Les deux sexes	Male Masculin	Female Féminin	Both sexes Les deux sexes	Male Masculin	Female Féminin	Both sexes Les deux sexes	Male Masculin	Female Féminin
EUROPE									
Iceland - Islande[87]									
1 VII 2019 (ESDJ)									
50 - 54	22 090	11 141	10 949	...	...	...	...	...	...
55 - 59	21 837	11 013	10 824	...	...	...	...	...	...
60 - 64	19 832	9 976	9 856	...	...	...	...	...	...
65 - 69	16 545	8 380	8 165	...	...	...	...	...	...
70 - 74	13 014	6 485	6 529	...	...	...	...	...	...
75 - 79	8 702	4 115	4 587	...	...	...	...	...	...
80 - 84	6 082	2 793	3 289	...	...	...	...	...	...
85 - 89	4 168	1 742	2 426	...	...	...	...	...	...
90 - 94	1 796	621	1 175	...	...	...	...	...	...
95 - 99	383	103	280	...	...	...	...	...	...
100 - 104	46	11	35	...	...	...	...	...	...
105 - 109	3	-	3	...	...	...	...	...	...
110 +	-	-	-	...	...	...	...	...	...
Ireland - Irlande									
10 IV 2011 (CDFC)									
Total	4 588 252	2 272 699	2 315 553	2 846 882	1 389 160	1 457 722	1 741 370	883 539	857 831
0 - 4	356 329	182 076	174 253	224 004	114 284	109 720	132 325	67 792	64 533
5 - 9	320 770	164 037	156 733	188 818	96 160	92 658	131 952	67 877	64 075
10 - 14	302 491	155 076	147 415	172 930	88 433	84 497	129 561	66 643	62 918
15 - 19	283 019	144 262	138 757	170 523	86 129	84 394	112 496	58 133	54 363
20 - 24	297 231	146 636	150 595	208 146	100 226	107 920	89 085	46 410	42 675
25 - 29	361 122	173 714	187 408	266 457	126 362	140 095	94 665	47 352	47 313
30 - 34	393 945	194 774	199 171	278 935	137 689	141 246	115 010	57 085	57 925
35 - 39	364 261	182 237	182 024	233 417	116 912	116 505	130 844	65 325	65 519
40 - 44	330 812	166 330	164 482	198 432	99 162	99 270	132 380	67 168	65 212
45 - 49	305 185	151 516	153 669	178 630	87 087	91 543	126 555	64 429	62 126
50 - 54	274 386	136 737	137 649	158 031	77 106	80 925	116 355	59 631	56 724
55 - 59	244 522	122 121	122 401	137 973	66 919	71 054	106 549	55 202	51 347
60 - 64	218 786	109 869	108 917	122 606	59 521	63 085	96 180	50 348	45 832
65 - 69	173 638	86 298	87 340	97 999	46 741	51 258	75 639	39 557	36 082
70 - 74	131 190	63 476	67 714	76 683	35 378	41 305	54 507	28 098	26 409
75 - 79	102 036	46 631	55 405	59 519	25 708	33 811	42 517	20 923	21 594
80 - 84	70 113	28 423	41 690	40 585	15 449	25 136	29 528	12 974	16 554
85 - 89	39 887	13 591	26 296	22 742	7 303	15 439	17 145	6 288	10 857
90 - 94	14 877	4 155	10 722	8 363	2 200	6 163	6 514	1 955	4 559
95 - 99	3 263	682	2 581	1 884	360	1 524	1 379	322	1 057
100 +	389	58	331	205	31	174	184	27	157
1 I 2019 (ESDJ)[86]									
Total	4 904 240	2 428 881	2 475 359	...	...	...	...	...	...
0	61 184	30 753	30 431	...	...	...	...	...	...
1 - 4	254 243	130 211	124 032	...	...	...	...	...	...
5 - 9	353 403	180 638	172 765	...	...	...	...	...	...
10 - 14	338 928	173 776	165 152	...	...	...	...	...	...
15 - 19	319 337	162 916	156 421	...	...	...	...	...	...
20 - 24	296 182	151 356	144 826	...	...	...	...	...	...
25 - 29	289 721	145 083	144 638	...	...	...	...	...	...
30 - 34	332 274	159 864	172 410	...	...	...	...	...	...
35 - 39	397 483	191 965	205 518	...	...	...	...	...	...
40 - 44	377 630	186 232	191 398	...	...	...	...	...	...
45 - 49	347 976	173 137	174 839	...	...	...	...	...	...
50 - 54	308 997	153 407	155 590	...	...	...	...	...	...
55 - 59	284 155	140 325	143 830	...	...	...	...	...	...
60 - 64	251 288	124 668	126 620	...	...	...	...	...	...
65 - 69	218 380	108 056	110 324	...	...	...	...	...	...
70 - 74	183 170	90 052	93 118	...	...	...	...	...	...
75 - 79	126 065	59 849	66 216	...	...	...	...	...	...
80 - 84	87 093	38 567	48 526	...	...	...	...	...	...
85 - 89	48 856	19 415	29 441	...	...	...	...	...	...
90 - 94	20 244	6 604	13 640	...	...	...	...	...	...
95 - 99	6 453	1 722	4 731	...	...	...	...	...	...
100 - 104	1 077	270	807	...	...	...	...	...	...
105 - 109	98	15	83	...	...	...	...	...	...
110 +	3	-	3	...	...	...	...	...	...

7. Population by age, sex and urban/rural residence: latest available year, 2010 - 2019
Population selon l'âge, le sexe et la résidence, urbaine/rurale : dernière année disponible, 2010 - 2019 (continued - suite)

Continent, country or area, date, code[a] and age (in years) / Continent, pays ou zone, date, code[a] et âge (en années)	Total			Urban - Urbaine			Rural - Rurale		
	Both sexes Les deux sexes	Male Masculin	Female Féminin	Both sexes Les deux sexes	Male Masculin	Female Féminin	Both sexes Les deux sexes	Male Masculin	Female Féminin
EUROPE									
Isle of Man - Île de Man									
24 IV 2016 (CDJC)									
Total	83 314	41 269	42 045	...	...	...	...	...	...
0 - 4	4 144	2 186	1 958	...	...	...	...	...	...
5 - 9	4 733	2 436	2 297	...	...	...	...	...	...
10 - 14	4 469	2 346	2 123	...	...	...	...	...	...
15 - 19	4 789	2 506	2 283	...	...	...	...	...	...
20 - 24	4 422	2 252	2 170	...	...	...	...	...	...
25 - 29	4 326	2 131	2 195	...	...	...	...	...	...
30 - 34	4 506	2 148	2 358	...	...	...	...	...	...
35 - 39	4 873	2 371	2 502	...	...	...	...	...	...
40 - 44	5 612	2 715	2 897	...	...	...	...	...	...
45 - 49	6 497	3 255	3 242	...	...	...	...	...	...
50 - 54	6 681	3 359	3 322	...	...	...	...	...	...
55 - 59	5 887	2 889	2 998	...	...	...	...	...	...
60 - 64	5 170	2 612	2 558	...	...	...	...	...	...
65 - 69	5 441	2 715	2 726	...	...	...	...	...	...
70 - 74	4 212	2 074	2 138	...	...	...	...	...	...
75 - 79	3 155	1 529	1 626	...	...	...	...	...	...
80 - 84	2 129	958	1 171	...	...	...	...	...	...
85 - 89	1 380	522	858	...	...	...	...	...	...
90 - 94	675	202	473	...	...	...	...	...	...
95 - 99	188	53	135	...	...	...	...	...	...
100 +	25	10	15	...	...	...	...	...	...
Italy - Italie									
1 VII 2018 (ESDJ)									
Total	60 421 760	29 406 187	31 015 573	...	...	...	...	...	...
0	447 240	230 084	217 156	...	...	...	...	...	...
1 - 4	1 952 433	1 003 176	949 257	...	...	...	...	...	...
5 - 9	2 753 250	1 416 328	1 336 923	...	...	...	...	...	...
10 - 14	2 868 273	1 477 108	1 391 166	...	...	...	...	...	...
15 - 19	2 897 610	1 503 402	1 394 208	...	...	...	...	...	...
20 - 24	2 988 383	1 562 130	1 426 253	...	...	...	...	...	...
25 - 29	3 229 975	1 653 297	1 576 678	...	...	...	...	...	...
30 - 34	3 382 024	1 706 640	1 675 384	...	...	...	...	...	...
35 - 39	3 759 128	1 884 741	1 874 387	...	...	...	...	...	...
40 - 44	4 489 044	2 237 850	2 251 194	...	...	...	...	...	...
45 - 49	4 845 913	2 400 580	2 445 333	...	...	...	...	...	...
50 - 54	4 923 890	2 424 592	2 499 298	...	...	...	...	...	...
55 - 59	4 358 599	2 118 108	2 240 491	...	...	...	...	...	...
60 - 64	3 812 030	1 832 793	1 979 238	...	...	...	...	...	...
65 - 69	3 524 057	1 678 304	1 845 753	...	...	...	...	...	...
70 - 74	3 166 781	1 478 367	1 688 415	...	...	...	...	...	...
75 - 79	2 754 597	1 225 496	1 529 101	...	...	...	...	...	...
80 - 84	2 142 709	882 385	1 260 324	...	...	...	...	...	...
85 - 89	1 365 619	486 735	878 884	...	...	...	...	...	...
90 - 94	597 406	169 331	428 075	...	...	...	...	...	...
95 - 99	147 753	32 304	115 449	...	...	...	...	...	...
100 +	15 052	2 441	12 611	...	...	...	...	...	...
Jersey									
1 I 2019 (ESDJ)									
Total	106 800	53 061	53 739	...	...	...	...	...	...
0 - 4	5 405	2 712	2 693	...	...	...	...	...	...
5 - 9	5 861	2 946	2 915	...	...	...	...	...	...
10 - 14	5 742	2 861	2 881	...	...	...	...	...	...
15 - 19	5 717	2 923	2 794	...	...	...	...	...	...
20 - 24	6 133	3 144	2 989	...	...	...	...	...	...
25 - 29	6 942	3 464	3 478	...	...	...	...	...	...
30 - 34	7 267	3 741	3 526	...	...	...	...	...	...
35 - 39	7 749	3 929	3 820	...	...	...	...	...	...
40 - 44	7 523	3 849	3 674	...	...	...	...	...	...
45 - 49	7 915	3 995	3 920	...	...	...	...	...	...
50 - 54	8 586	4 317	4 269	...	...	...	...	...	...
55 - 59	7 559	3 766	3 793	...	...	...	...	...	...
60 - 64	6 340	3 093	3 247	...	...	...	...	...	...

7. Population by age, sex and urban/rural residence: latest available year, 2010 - 2019
Population selon l'âge, le sexe et la résidence, urbaine/rurale : dernière année disponible, 2010 - 2019 (continued - suite)

Continent, country or area, date, code[a] and age (in years) / Continent, pays ou zone, date, code[a] et âge (en années)	Total			Urban - Urbaine			Rural - Rurale		
	Both sexes Les deux sexes	Male Masculin	Female Féminin	Both sexes Les deux sexes	Male Masculin	Female Féminin	Both sexes Les deux sexes	Male Masculin	Female Féminin
EUROPE									
Jersey									
1 I 2019 (ESDJ)									
65 - 69	5 363	2 619	2 744	...	...	...	...	...	...
70 - 74	4 623	2 222	2 401	...	...	...	...	...	...
75 - 79	3 161	1 465	1 696	...	...	...	...	...	...
80 - 84	2 537	1 147	1 390	...	...	...	...	...	...
85 - 89	1 491	585	906	...	...	...	...	...	...
90 +	886	283	603	...	...	...	...	...	...
Latvia - Lettonie									
1 I 2019 (ESDJ)									
Total	1 919 968	884 909	1 035 059	1 315 177	588 614	726 563	604 791	296 295	308 496
0	19 127	9 912	9 215	13 173	6 840	6 333	5 964	3 072	2 882
1 - 4	87 041	45 276	41 765	60 616	31 587	29 029	26 425	13 689	12 736
5 - 9	98 221	50 564	47 657	67 225	34 576	32 649	30 996	15 988	15 008
10 - 14	100 691	51 525	49 166	67 637	34 512	33 125	33 054	17 013	16 041
15 - 19	88 927	45 541	43 386	58 378	29 597	28 781	30 549	15 944	14 605
20 - 24	87 077	45 226	41 851	56 847	29 065	27 782	30 230	16 161	14 069
25 - 29	123 792	63 845	59 947	83 372	41 689	41 683	40 420	22 156	18 264
30 - 34	139 017	71 430	67 587	98 288	48 876	49 412	40 729	22 554	18 175
35 - 39	127 927	64 949	62 978	90 709	44 996	45 713	37 218	19 953	17 265
40 - 44	126 352	62 361	63 991	87 534	42 045	45 489	38 818	20 316	18 502
45 - 49	132 411	64 157	68 254	89 317	41 908	47 409	43 094	22 249	20 845
50 - 54	129 259	61 191	68 068	85 528	38 890	46 638	43 731	22 301	21 430
55 - 59	141 408	64 246	77 162	94 240	40 645	53 595	47 168	23 601	23 567
60 - 64	129 739	56 322	73 417	89 137	36 522	52 615	40 602	19 800	20 802
65 - 69	110 469	43 780	66 689	78 003	29 091	48 912	32 466	14 689	17 777
70 - 74	86 232	31 002	55 230	60 963	20 984	39 979	25 269	10 018	15 251
75 - 79	84 765	26 728	58 037	58 204	17 830	40 374	26 561	8 898	17 663
80 - 84	60 749	16 700	44 049	42 824	11 636	31 188	17 925	5 064	12 861
85 - 89	32 404	7 605	24 799	22 781	5 407	17 374	9 623	2 198	7 425
90 - 94	12 202	2 243	9 959	8 841	1 682	7 159	3 361	561	2 800
95 - 99	2 011	281	1 730	1 452	217	1 235	559	64	495
100 +	147	25	122	108	19	89	39	6	33
Liechtenstein									
1 I 2019 (ESDJ)									
Total	38 378	19 025	19 353	...	...	...	...	...	...
0	381	192	189	...	...	...	...	...	...
1 - 4	1 450	780	670	...	...	...	...	...	...
5 - 9	1 906	1 015	891	...	...	...	...	...	...
10 - 14	1 918	991	927	...	...	...	...	...	...
15 - 19	1 973	996	977	...	...	...	...	...	...
20 - 24	2 222	1 133	1 089	...	...	...	...	...	...
25 - 29	2 317	1 171	1 146	...	...	...	...	...	...
30 - 34	2 405	1 185	1 220	...	...	...	...	...	...
35 - 39	2 483	1 253	1 230	...	...	...	...	...	...
40 - 44	2 548	1 269	1 279	...	...	...	...	...	...
45 - 49	3 023	1 514	1 509	...	...	...	...	...	...
50 - 54	3 260	1 581	1 679	...	...	...	...	...	...
55 - 59	3 079	1 520	1 559	...	...	...	...	...	...
60 - 64	2 552	1 256	1 296	...	...	...	...	...	...
65 - 69	2 142	1 060	1 082	...	...	...	...	...	...
70 - 74	1 879	922	957	...	...	...	...	...	...
75 - 79	1 384	641	743	...	...	...	...	...	...
80 - 84	788	326	462	...	...	...	...	...	...
85 - 89	438	159	279	...	...	...	...	...	...
90 - 94	187	50	137	...	...	...	...	...	...
95 - 99	42	10	32	...	...	...	...	...	...
100 +	1	1	-	...	...	...	...	...	...
Lithuania - Lituanie[86]									
1 VII 2018 (ESDJ)									
Total	2 801 543	1 296 442	1 505 101	1 880 046	842 614	1 037 432	921 497	453 828	467 669
0	28 463	14 586	13 877	19 792	10 132	9 660	8 671	4 454	4 217
1 - 4	119 787	61 573	58 214	83 284	42 977	40 307	36 503	18 596	17 907
5 - 9	144 466	74 063	70 403	99 932	51 138	48 794	44 534	22 925	21 609
10 - 14	128 931	65 878	63 053	83 858	42 986	40 872	45 073	22 892	22 181

7. Population by age, sex and urban/rural residence: latest available year, 2010 - 2019
Population selon l'âge, le sexe et la résidence, urbaine/rurale : dernière année disponible, 2010 - 2019 (continued - suite)

Continent, country or area, date, code[a] and age (in years) / Continent, pays ou zone, date, code[a] et âge (en annèes)	Total			Urban - Urbaine			Rural - Rurale		
	Both sexes Les deux sexes	Male Masculin	Female Féminin	Both sexes Les deux sexes	Male Masculin	Female Féminin	Both sexes Les deux sexes	Male Masculin	Female Féminin
EUROPE									
Lithuania - Lituanie[86]									
1 VII 2018 (ESDJ)									
15 - 19	140 260	72 171	68 089	86 272	44 021	42 251	53 988	28 150	25 838
20 - 24	161 703	83 286	78 417	100 462	51 089	49 373	61 241	32 197	29 044
25 - 29	188 228	97 886	90 342	128 632	63 390	65 242	59 596	34 496	25 100
30 - 34	183 118	94 487	88 631	137 301	67 490	69 811	45 817	26 997	18 820
35 - 39	165 422	84 162	81 260	119 386	59 170	60 216	46 036	24 992	21 044
40 - 44	177 891	87 514	90 377	120 973	57 974	62 999	56 918	29 540	27 378
45 - 49	199 817	96 589	103 228	129 704	60 626	69 078	70 113	35 963	34 150
50 - 54	204 890	96 903	107 987	130 671	58 534	72 137	74 219	38 369	35 850
55 - 59	223 271	101 970	121 301	147 139	63 217	83 922	76 132	38 753	37 379
60 - 64	183 211	79 287	103 924	123 228	50 207	73 021	59 983	29 080	30 903
65 - 69	155 244	61 795	93 449	105 065	39 114	65 951	50 179	22 681	27 498
70 - 74	119 623	43 113	76 510	80 480	27 515	52 965	39 143	15 598	23 545
75 - 79	117 187	38 305	78 882	77 849	24 825	53 024	39 338	13 480	25 858
80 - 84	88 913	25 699	63 214	58 332	16 623	41 709	30 581	9 076	21 505
85 - 89	50 626	13 031	37 595	33 116	8 691	24 425	17 510	4 340	13 170
90 - 94	17 378	3 612	13 766	12 047	2 506	9 541	5 331	1 106	4 225
95 - 99	2 868	480	2 388	2 305	347	1 958	563	133	430
100 +	246	52	194	218	42	176	28	10	18
1 I 2019 (ESDJ)									
Total	2 794 184	1 295 591	1 498 593	...	...	...	...	...	...
0	28 166	14 364	13 802	...	...	...	...	...	...
1 - 4	119 535	61 531	58 004	...	...	...	...	...	...
5 - 9	144 688	74 096	70 592	...	...	...	...	...	...
10 - 14	129 468	66 121	63 347	...	...	...	...	...	...
15 - 19	136 819	70 331	66 488	...	...	...	...	...	...
20 - 24	157 609	81 359	76 250	...	...	...	...	...	...
25 - 29	187 713	97 849	89 864	...	...	...	...	...	...
30 - 34	183 846	95 412	88 434	...	...	...	...	...	...
35 - 39	166 624	85 415	81 209	...	...	...	...	...	...
40 - 44	176 104	87 125	88 979	...	...	...	...	...	...
45 - 49	198 150	96 254	101 896	...	...	...	...	...	...
50 - 54	203 195	96 263	106 932	...	...	...	...	...	...
55 - 59	221 849	101 577	120 272	...	...	...	...	...	...
60 - 64	188 045	81 572	106 473	...	...	...	...	...	...
65 - 69	155 351	62 020	93 331	...	...	...	...	...	...
70 - 74	119 763	43 246	76 517	...	...	...	...	...	...
75 - 79	115 720	37 689	78 031	...	...	...	...	...	...
80 - 84	89 469	25 937	63 532	...	...	...	...	...	...
85 - 89	50 862	13 099	37 763	...	...	...	...	...	...
90 - 94	17 938	3 780	14 158	...	...	...	...	...	...
95 - 99	3 042	510	2 532	...	...	...	...	...	...
100 - 104	179	28	151	...	...	...	...	...	...
105 - 109	36	7	29	...	...	...	...	...	...
110 +	13	6	7	...	...	...	...	...	...
Luxembourg									
1 I 2019 (ESDJ)									
Total	613 894	308 720	305 174	...	...	...	...	...	...
0	6 328	3 235	3 093	...	...	...	...	...	...
1 - 4	26 264	13 426	12 838	...	...	...	...	...	...
5 - 9	33 355	17 075	16 280	...	...	...	...	...	...
10 - 14	32 660	16 801	15 859	...	...	...	...	...	...
15 - 19	33 206	17 097	16 109	...	...	...	...	...	...
20 - 24	38 038	19 462	18 576	...	...	...	...	...	...
25 - 29	46 125	23 710	22 415	...	...	...	...	...	...
30 - 34	47 863	24 051	23 812	...	...	...	...	...	...
35 - 39	48 111	24 240	23 871	...	...	...	...	...	...
40 - 44	46 177	23 352	22 825	...	...	...	...	...	...
45 - 49	46 183	23 741	22 442	...	...	...	...	...	...
50 - 54	46 695	24 458	22 237	...	...	...	...	...	...
55 - 59	41 130	21 271	19 859	...	...	...	...	...	...
60 - 64	33 431	16 923	16 508	...	...	...	...	...	...
65 - 69	26 712	13 274	13 438	...	...	...	...	...	...
70 - 74	21 074	10 273	10 801	...	...	...	...	...	...

7. Population by age, sex and urban/rural residence: latest available year, 2010 - 2019
Population selon l'âge, le sexe et la résidence, urbaine/rurale : dernière année disponible, 2010 - 2019 (continued - suite)

Continent, country or area, date, code[a] and age (in years) Continent, pays ou zone, date, code[a] et âge (en annèes)	Total			Urban - Urbaine			Rural - Rurale		
	Both sexes Les deux sexes	Male Masculin	Female Féminin	Both sexes Les deux sexes	Male Masculin	Female Féminin	Both sexes Les deux sexes	Male Masculin	Female Féminin
EUROPE									
Luxembourg									
1 I 2019 (ESDJ)									
75 - 79	16 260	7 310	8 950	...	...	...	...	...	...
80 - 84	12 270	5 031	7 239	...	...	...	...	...	...
85 - 89	8 069	2 951	5 118	...	...	...	...	...	...
90 - 94	3 177	902	2 275	...	...	...	...	...	...
95 - 99	697	122	575	...	...	...	...	...	...
100 - 104	61	14	47	...	...	...	...	...	...
105 - 109	6	-	6	...	...	...	...	...	...
110 +	2	1	1	...	...	...	...	...	...
Unknown - Inconnu	-	-	-	...	...	...	...	...	...
Malta - Malte									
20 XI 2011 (CDFC)									
Total	417 432	207 625	209 807	400 557	199 151	201 406	16 875	8 474	8 401
0 - 4	20 061	10 347	9 714	19 247	9 926	9 321	814	421	393
5 - 9	19 419	9 971	9 448	18 602	9 562	9 040	817	409	408
10 - 14	22 248	11 355	10 893	21 218	10 854	10 364	1 030	501	529
15 - 19	26 182	13 509	12 673	25 026	12 907	12 119	1 156	602	554
20 - 24	29 450	15 062	14 388	28 269	14 475	13 794	1 181	587	594
25 - 29	30 320	15 722	14 598	29 154	15 110	14 044	1 166	612	554
30 - 34	30 194	15 641	14 553	29 141	15 074	14 067	1 053	567	486
35 - 39	28 799	14 757	14 042	27 712	14 202	13 510	1 087	555	532
40 - 44	25 236	12 840	12 396	24 151	12 293	11 858	1 085	547	538
45 - 49	26 895	13 574	13 321	25 716	12 972	12 744	1 179	602	577
50 - 54	30 596	15 292	15 304	29 293	14 628	14 665	1 303	664	639
55 - 59	29 246	14 655	14 591	28 127	14 052	14 075	1 119	603	516
60 - 64	30 595	15 130	15 465	29 452	14 551	14 901	1 143	579	564
65 - 69	23 728	11 429	12 299	22 791	10 986	11 805	937	443	494
70 - 74	16 205	7 389	8 816	15 572	7 106	8 466	633	283	350
75 - 79	13 287	5 579	7 708	12 749	5 332	7 417	538	247	291
80 - 84	8 494	3 181	5 313	8 121	3 036	5 085	373	145	228
85 - 89	4 567	1 622	2 945	4 371	1 546	2 825	196	76	120
90 - 94	1 583	480	1 103	1 532	455	1 077	51	25	26
95 - 99	296	82	214	284	77	207	12	5	7
100 +	31	8	23	29	7	22	2	1	1
1 I 2019 (ESDJ)									
Total	493 559	251 836	241 723	...	...	...	...	...	...
0	4 520	2 307	2 213	...	...	...	...	...	...
1 - 4	18 987	9 870	9 117	...	...	...	...	...	...
5 - 9	22 800	11 710	11 090	...	...	...	...	...	...
10 - 14	21 197	10 997	10 200	...	...	...	...	...	...
15 - 19	22 320	11 357	10 963	...	...	...	...	...	...
20 - 24	32 057	17 265	14 792	...	...	...	...	...	...
25 - 29	43 511	23 017	20 494	...	...	...	...	...	...
30 - 34	42 093	22 647	19 446	...	...	...	...	...	...
35 - 39	39 110	20 839	18 271	...	...	...	...	...	...
40 - 44	35 262	18 656	16 606	...	...	...	...	...	...
45 - 49	29 905	15 668	14 237	...	...	...	...	...	...
50 - 54	27 957	14 389	13 568	...	...	...	...	...	...
55 - 59	31 005	15 721	15 284	...	...	...	...	...	...
60 - 64	30 655	15 413	15 242	...	...	...	...	...	...
65 - 69	28 649	14 113	14 536	...	...	...	...	...	...
70 - 74	28 144	13 447	14 697	...	...	...	...	...	...
75 - 79	14 541	6 508	8 033	...	...	...	...	...	...
80 - 84	11 660	4 858	6 802	...	...	...	...	...	...
85 - 89	6 297	2 175	4 122	...	...	...	...	...	...
90 - 94	2 322	744	1 578	...	...	...	...	...	...
95 - 99	494	115	379	...	...	...	...	...	...
100 - 104	61	14	47	...	...	...	...	...	...
105 - 109	11	5	6	...	...	...	...	...	...
110 +	1	1	-	...	...	...	...	...	...
Monaco									
7 VI 2016 (CDJC)									
Total	37 308	18 240	19 068	...	...	...	...	...	...
0 - 4	1 571	785	786	...	...	...	...	...	...

7. Population by age, sex and urban/rural residence: latest available year, 2010 - 2019
Population selon l'âge, le sexe et la résidence, urbaine/rurale : dernière année disponible, 2010 - 2019 (continued - suite)

Continent, country or area, date, code[a] and age (in years) / Continent, pays ou zone, date, code[a] et âge (en années)	Total			Urban - Urbaine			Rural - Rurale		
	Both sexes Les deux sexes	Male Masculin	Female Féminin	Both sexes Les deux sexes	Male Masculin	Female Féminin	Both sexes Les deux sexes	Male Masculin	Female Féminin
EUROPE									
Monaco									
7 VI 2016 (CDJC)									
5 - 9	1 381	699	682	...	...	...	...	...	...
10 - 14	1 406	719	687	...	...	...	...	...	...
15 - 19	1 615	834	781	...	...	...	...	...	...
20 - 24	1 486	768	718	...	...	...	...	...	...
25 - 29	1 465	761	704	...	...	...	...	...	...
30 - 34	1 526	771	756	...	...	...	...	...	...
35 - 39	1 635	752	883	...	...	...	...	...	...
40 - 44	1 730	811	918	...	...	...	...	...	...
45 - 49	2 125	1 030	1 095	...	...	...	...	...	...
50 - 54	2 513	1 245	1 268	...	...	...	...	...	...
55 - 59	2 775	1 383	1 392	...	...	...	...	...	...
60 - 64	2 423	1 247	1 176	...	...	...	...	...	...
65 - 69	2 445	1 241	1 203	...	...	...	...	...	...
70 - 74	2 284	1 126	1 158	...	...	...	...	...	...
75 - 79	2 230	1 119	1 111	...	...	...	...	...	...
80 - 84	2 043	957	1 086	...	...	...	...	...	...
85 - 89	1 668	760	909	...	...	...	...	...	...
90 - 94	1 264	551	713	...	...	...	...	...	...
95 - 99	891	368	523	...	...	...	...	...	...
100 +	832	314	518	...	...	...	...	...	...
Montenegro - Monténégro									
1 IV 2011 (CDJC)									
Total	620 029	306 236	313 793	399 264	193 691	205 573	220 765	112 545	108 220
0 - 4	38 950	20 361	18 589	25 277	13 247	12 030	13 673	7 114	6 559
5 - 9	38 430	20 016	18 414	24 781	12 973	11 808	13 649	7 043	6 606
10 - 14	41 371	21 389	19 982	26 526	13 698	12 828	14 845	7 691	7 154
15 - 19	44 093	22 815	21 278	28 376	14 654	13 722	15 717	8 161	7 556
20 - 24	42 816	22 084	20 732	28 218	14 347	13 871	14 598	7 737	6 861
25 - 29	45 793	23 299	22 494	31 083	15 290	15 793	14 710	8 009	6 701
30 - 34	44 495	22 188	22 307	30 133	14 495	15 638	14 362	7 693	6 669
35 - 39	41 879	20 523	21 356	27 869	13 311	14 558	14 010	7 212	6 798
40 - 44	40 496	20 136	20 360	26 265	12 539	13 726	14 231	7 597	6 634
45 - 49	43 089	21 401	21 688	28 332	13 444	14 888	14 757	7 957	6 800
50 - 54	43 613	21 817	21 796	28 705	13 851	14 854	14 908	7 966	6 942
55 - 59	41 223	20 509	20 714	27 021	13 143	13 878	14 202	7 366	6 836
60 - 64	34 196	15 941	18 255	21 738	9 981	11 757	12 458	5 960	6 498
65 - 69	22 121	9 774	12 347	12 692	5 522	7 170	9 429	4 252	5 177
70 - 74	25 141	10 909	14 232	14 441	6 116	8 325	10 700	4 793	5 907
75 - 79	17 184	7 251	9 933	9 665	4 041	5 624	7 519	3 210	4 309
80 - 84	10 021	4 050	5 971	5 375	2 112	3 263	4 646	1 938	2 708
85 - 89	3 739	1 324	2 415	2 038	699	1 339	1 701	625	1 076
90 - 94	885	283	602	453	130	323	432	153	279
95 - 99	202	61	141	103	30	73	99	31	68
100 +	44	13	31	23	7	16	21	6	15
Unknown - Inconnu	248	92	156	150	61	89	98	31	67
1 I 2019 (ESDJ)									
Total	622 182	307 712	314 470	...	...	...	...	...	...
0	7 343	3 810	3 533	...	...	...	...	...	...
1 - 4	29 716	15 425	14 291	...	...	...	...	...	...
5 - 9	37 405	19 471	17 934	...	...	...	...	...	...
10 - 14	37 289	19 475	17 814	...	...	...	...	...	...
15 - 19	40 324	20 899	19 425	...	...	...	...	...	...
20 - 24	40 258	20 751	19 507	...	...	...	...	...	...
25 - 29	39 240	20 313	18 927	...	...	...	...	...	...
30 - 34	45 313	23 297	22 016	...	...	...	...	...	...
35 - 39	45 206	22 677	22 529	...	...	...	...	...	...
40 - 44	42 414	20 908	21 506	...	...	...	...	...	...
45 - 49	40 380	19 719	20 661	...	...	...	...	...	...
50 - 54	40 395	19 987	20 408	...	...	...	...	...	...
55 - 59	41 896	20 427	21 469	...	...	...	...	...	...
60 - 64	40 689	19 897	20 792	...	...	...	...	...	...
65 - 69	35 283	16 370	18 913	...	...	...	...	...	...
70 - 74	21 437	9 136	12 301	...	...	...	...	...	...

7. Population by age, sex and urban/rural residence: latest available year, 2010 - 2019
Population selon l'âge, le sexe et la résidence, urbaine/rurale : dernière année disponible, 2010 - 2019 (continued - suite)

Continent, country or area, date, code[a] and age (in years) / Continent, pays ou zone, date, code[a] et âge (en annèes)	Total			Urban - Urbaine			Rural - Rurale		
	Both sexes Les deux sexes	Male Masculin	Female Féminin	Both sexes Les deux sexes	Male Masculin	Female Féminin	Both sexes Les deux sexes	Male Masculin	Female Féminin
EUROPE									
Montenegro - Monténégro									
1 I 2019 (ESDJ)									
75 - 79	17 341	7 074	10 267	...	...	...	...	...	...
80 - 84	12 508	5 067	7 441	...	...	...	...	...	...
85 - 89	5 489	2 083	3 406	...	...	...	...	...	...
90 - 94	1 815	764	1 051	...	...	...	...	...	...
95 - 99	427	159	268	...	...	...	...	...	...
100 - 104	11	1	10	...	...	...	...	...	...
105 - 109	3	2	1	...	...	...	...	...	...
110 +	-	-	-	...	...	...	...	...	...
Netherlands - Pays-Bas									
1 I 2011 (CDJC)									
Total	16 655 799	8 243 482	8 412 317	11 124 721	5 478 213	5 646 508	5 531 078	2 765 269	2 765 809
0 - 4	923 106	472 308	450 798	633 381	323 854	309 527	289 725	148 454	141 271
0	184 007	93 892	90 115	...	...	...	...	...	...
1 - 4	739 099	378 416	360 683	...	...	...	...	...	...
5 - 9	985 229	503 882	481 347	640 541	327 757	312 784	344 688	176 125	168 563
10 - 14	998 740	510 974	487 766	633 115	323 581	309 534	365 625	187 393	178 232
15 - 19	1 006 744	514 830	491 914	658 458	333 676	324 782	348 286	181 154	167 132
20 - 24	1 034 729	522 667	512 062	757 280	373 366	383 914	277 449	149 301	128 148
25 - 29	1 001 538	504 117	497 421	749 880	373 340	376 540	251 658	130 777	120 881
30 - 34	1 004 764	503 323	501 441	736 350	368 630	367 720	268 414	134 693	133 721
35 - 39	1 121 568	560 289	561 279	779 994	391 390	388 604	341 574	168 899	172 675
40 - 44	1 295 925	653 664	642 261	861 292	436 235	425 057	434 633	217 429	217 204
45 - 49	1 298 292	655 302	642 990	850 566	428 796	421 770	447 726	226 506	221 220
50 - 54	1 196 319	601 040	595 279	776 285	388 221	388 064	420 034	212 819	207 215
55 - 59	1 090 247	546 952	543 295	700 036	348 502	351 534	390 211	198 450	191 761
60 - 64	1 103 652	553 446	550 206	700 926	349 188	351 738	402 726	204 258	198 468
65 - 69	790 560	390 725	399 835	488 433	238 792	249 641	302 127	151 933	150 194
70 - 74	637 518	302 542	334 976	401 165	187 850	213 315	236 353	114 692	121 661
75 - 79	499 321	219 108	280 213	316 949	136 949	180 000	182 372	82 159	100 213
80 - 84	360 828	139 348	221 480	234 884	89 412	145 472	125 944	49 936	76 008
85 - 89	212 056	66 949	145 107	141 532	44 184	97 348	70 524	22 765	47 759
90 - 94	76 191	18 812	57 379	51 102	12 438	38 664	25 089	6 374	18 715
95 +	18 472	3 204	15 268	12 552	2 052	10 500	5 920	1 152	4 768
1 I 2019 (ESDJ)									
Total	17 282 163	8 581 086	8 701 077	...	...	...	...	...	...
0	168 443	86 173	82 270	...	...	...	...	...	...
1 - 4	697 619	357 485	340 134	...	...	...	...	...	...
5 - 9	917 442	470 233	447 209	...	...	...	...	...	...
10 - 14	956 315	489 531	466 784	...	...	...	...	...	...
15 - 19	1 052 019	538 304	513 715	...	...	...	...	...	...
20 - 24	1 079 925	548 282	531 643	...	...	...	...	...	...
25 - 29	1 121 863	569 071	552 792	...	...	...	...	...	...
30 - 34	1 076 906	543 375	533 531	...	...	...	...	...	...
35 - 39	1 031 293	516 735	514 558	...	...	...	...	...	...
40 - 44	1 025 388	510 460	514 928	...	...	...	...	...	...
45 - 49	1 235 719	616 540	619 179	...	...	...	...	...	...
50 - 54	1 276 856	641 987	634 869	...	...	...	...	...	...
55 - 59	1 231 532	616 601	614 931	...	...	...	...	...	...
60 - 64	1 096 839	545 999	550 840	...	...	...	...	...	...
65 - 69	993 074	492 006	501 068	...	...	...	...	...	...
70 - 74	913 384	445 416	467 968	...	...	...	...	...	...
75 - 79	608 726	284 920	323 806	...	...	...	...	...	...
80 - 84	422 114	181 154	240 960	...	...	...	...	...	...
85 - 89	250 068	91 558	158 510	...	...	...	...	...	...
90 - 94	100 963	29 673	71 290	...	...	...	...	...	...
95 - 99	23 486	5 244	18 242	...	...	...	...	...	...
100 - 104	2 093	331	1 762	...	...	...	...	...	...
105 - 109	94	8	86	...	...	...	...	...	...
110 +	2	-	2	...	...	...	...	...	...

7. Population by age, sex and urban/rural residence: latest available year, 2010 - 2019
Population selon l'âge, le sexe et la résidence, urbaine/rurale : dernière année disponible, 2010 - 2019 (continued - suite)

Continent, country or area, date, code[a] and age (in years) / Continent, pays ou zone, date, code[a] et âge (en années)	Total			Urban - Urbaine			Rural - Rurale		
	Both sexes / Les deux sexes	Male / Masculin	Female / Féminin	Both sexes / Les deux sexes	Male / Masculin	Female / Féminin	Both sexes / Les deux sexes	Male / Masculin	Female / Féminin
EUROPE									
North Macedonia - Macédoine du Nord									
1 I 2019 (ESDJ)									
Total	2 077 132	1 040 200	1 036 932	...	...	...	...	...	...
0	21 226	11 114	10 112	...	...	...	...	...	...
1 - 4	90 460	46 641	43 819	...	...	...	...	...	...
5 - 9	116 038	60 265	55 773	...	...	...	...	...	...
10 - 14	112 231	57 825	54 406	...	...	...	...	...	...
15 - 19	119 670	61 733	57 937	...	...	...	...	...	...
20 - 24	137 043	70 585	66 458	...	...	...	...	...	...
25 - 29	155 266	79 680	75 586	...	...	...	...	...	...
30 - 34	163 906	83 762	80 144	...	...	...	...	...	...
35 - 39	161 837	83 099	78 738	...	...	...	...	...	...
40 - 44	152 703	77 785	74 918	...	...	...	...	...	...
45 - 49	144 811	73 030	71 781	...	...	...	...	...	...
50 - 54	144 760	72 716	72 044	...	...	...	...	...	...
55 - 59	137 168	68 475	68 693	...	...	...	...	...	...
60 - 64	127 913	63 208	64 705	...	...	...	...	...	...
65 - 69	108 010	50 790	57 220	...	...	...	...	...	...
70 - 74	76 843	34 514	42 329	...	...	...	...	...	...
75 - 79	54 862	23 930	30 932	...	...	...	...	...	...
80 - 84	34 428	14 381	20 047	...	...	...	...	...	...
85 - 89	13 868	5 322	8 546	...	...	...	...	...	...
90 - 94	2 777	995	1 782	...	...	...	...	...	...
95 +	1 133	317	816	...	...	...	...	...	...
Unknown - Inconnu	179	33	146	...	...	...	...	...	...
Norway - Norvège									
19 XI 2011 (CDJC)[88]									
Total	4 979 955	2 495 777	2 484 178	3 951 427[82]	1 959 424[82]	1 992 003[82]	1 011 071[82]	524 519[82]	486 552[82]
0 - 4	310 523	159 582	150 941	252 348[82]	129 655[82]	122 693[82]	57 552[82]	29 590[82]	27 962[82]
5 - 9	300 625	153 598	147 027	239 702[82]	122 174[82]	117 528[82]	60 262[82]	31 070[82]	29 192[82]
10 - 14	312 618	160 122	152 496	245 562[82]	125 764[82]	119 798[82]	66 422[82]	34 008[82]	32 414[82]
15 - 19	324 682	167 701	156 981	254 774[82]	131 385[82]	123 389[82]	69 376[82]	36 049[82]	33 327[82]
20 - 24	329 537	167 828	161 709	268 150[82]	135 424[82]	132 726[82]	60 351[82]	31 776[82]	28 575[82]
25 - 29	321 171	163 754	157 417	268 356[82]	135 940[82]	132 416[82]	51 166[82]	26 654[82]	24 512[82]
30 - 34	325 241	166 578	158 663	269 924[82]	137 478[82]	132 446[82]	53 565[82]	27 843[82]	25 722[82]
35 - 39	352 008	180 904	171 104	286 185[82]	146 143[82]	140 042[82]	64 091[82]	33 501[82]	30 590[82]
40 - 44	373 191	191 483	181 708	297 629[82]	151 231[82]	146 398[82]	73 666[82]	38 863[82]	34 803[82]
45 - 49	350 537	180 834	169 703	275 817[82]	140 624[82]	135 193[82]	73 001[82]	38 909[82]	34 092[82]
50 - 54	322 729	165 233	157 496	250 381[82]	126 209[82]	124 172[82]	70 881[82]	37 897[82]	32 984[82]
55 - 59	304 335	154 029	150 306	233 724[82]	116 035[82]	117 689[82]	69 504[82]	37 194[82]	32 310[82]
60 - 64	286 319	144 699	141 620	218 480[82]	108 289[82]	110 191[82]	67 016[82]	35 823[82]	31 193[82]
65 - 69	247 451	122 740	124 711	188 932[82]	91 896[82]	97 036[82]	57 895[82]	30 414[82]	27 481[82]
70 - 74	166 680	78 850	87 830	126 640[82]	58 122[82]	68 518[82]	39 687[82]	20 517[82]	19 170[82]
75 - 79	130 209	58 013	72 196	99 673[82]	42 842[82]	56 831[82]	30 271[82]	15 028[82]	15 243[82]
80 - 84	108 243	44 024	64 219	84 440[82]	32 980[82]	51 460[82]	23 582[82]	10 955[82]	12 627[82]
85 - 89	74 057	25 608	48 449	58 579[82]	19 436[82]	39 143[82]	15 272[82]	6 085[82]	9 187[82]
90 - 94	32 243	8 769	23 474	25 938[82]	6 706[82]	19 232[82]	6 185[82]	2 017[82]	4 168[82]
95 - 99	6 825	1 310	5 515	5 593[82]	1 001[82]	4 592[82]	1 199[82]	300[82]	899[82]
100 +	731	118	613	600[82]	90[82]	510[82]	127[82]	26[82]	101[82]
1 I 2019 (ESDJ)[86]									
Total	5 328 212	2 685 073	2 643 139	...	...	...	...	...	...
0	55 391	28 556	26 835	...	...	...	...	...	...
1 - 4	239 472	123 296	116 176	...	...	...	...	...	...
5 - 9	320 053	164 083	155 970	...	...	...	...	...	...
10 - 14	320 042	164 061	155 981	...	...	...	...	...	...
15 - 19	320 499	165 165	155 334	...	...	...	...	...	...
20 - 24	341 231	176 336	164 895	...	...	...	...	...	...
25 - 29	371 188	189 610	181 578	...	...	...	...	...	...
30 - 34	364 972	186 264	178 708	...	...	...	...	...	...
35 - 39	352 397	181 466	170 931	...	...	...	...	...	...
40 - 44	350 211	179 750	170 461	...	...	...	...	...	...
45 - 49	378 428	194 074	184 354	...	...	...	...	...	...
50 - 54	366 044	187 947	178 097	...	...	...	...	...	...

7. Population by age, sex and urban/rural residence: latest available year, 2010 - 2019
Population selon l'âge, le sexe et la résidence, urbaine/rurale : dernière année disponible, 2010 - 2019 (continued - suite)

Continent, country or area, date, code[a] and age (in years) / Continent, pays ou zone, date, code[a] et âge (en années)	Total			Urban - Urbaine			Rural - Rurale		
	Both sexes Les deux sexes	Male Masculin	Female Féminin	Both sexes Les deux sexes	Male Masculin	Female Féminin	Both sexes Les deux sexes	Male Masculin	Female Féminin
EUROPE									
Norway - Norvège									
1 I 2019 (ESDJ)[86]									
55 - 59	325 700	166 140	159 560	...	...	...	...	...	...
60 - 64	303 743	152 590	151 153	...	...	...	...	...	...
65 - 69	273 004	136 125	136 879	...	...	...	...	...	...
70 - 74	255 791	125 400	130 391	...	...	...	...	...	...
75 - 79	164 047	76 728	87 319	...	...	...	...	...	...
80 - 84	109 210	47 100	62 110	...	...	...	...	...	...
85 - 89	71 821	27 209	44 612	...	...	...	...	...	...
90 - 94	34 548	10 859	23 689	...	...	...	...	...	...
95 - 99	9 341	2 135	7 206	...	...	...	...	...	...
100 +	1 079	179	900	...	...	...	...	...	...
Poland - Pologne[86]									
1 VII 2018 (ESDJ)									
Total	37 956 268	18 370 760	19 585 508	22 833 502	10 825 597	12 007 905	15 122 766	7 545 163	7 577 603
0	386 873	199 098	187 775	227 930	117 468	110 462	158 943	81 630	77 313
1 - 4	1 521 947	781 443	740 504	892 887	458 314	434 573	629 060	323 129	305 931
5 - 9	2 019 326	1 036 957	982 369	1 152 237	592 093	560 144	867 089	444 864	422 225
10 - 14	1 881 194	964 622	916 572	1 037 030	531 689	505 341	844 164	432 933	411 231
15 - 19	1 825 354	935 313	890 041	978 154	499 689	478 465	847 200	435 624	411 576
20 - 24	2 146 223	1 094 654	1 051 569	1 132 747	575 458	557 289	1 013 476	519 196	494 280
25 - 29	2 618 938	1 335 435	1 283 503	1 489 395	747 245	742 150	1 129 543	588 190	541 353
30 - 34	3 012 945	1 535 095	1 477 850	1 858 460	933 551	924 909	1 154 485	601 544	552 941
35 - 39	3 087 766	1 567 318	1 520 448	1 924 849	966 041	958 808	1 162 917	601 277	561 640
40 - 44	2 877 390	1 454 222	1 423 168	1 753 331	874 743	878 588	1 124 059	579 479	544 580
45 - 49	2 426 971	1 218 658	1 208 313	1 425 198	703 964	721 234	1 001 773	514 694	487 079
50 - 54	2 253 070	1 117 369	1 135 701	1 311 980	630 892	681 088	941 090	486 477	454 613
55 - 59	2 528 048	1 224 095	1 303 953	1 528 406	708 379	820 027	999 642	515 716	483 926
60 - 64	2 760 541	1 292 647	1 467 894	1 783 749	798 881	984 868	976 792	493 766	483 026
65 - 69	2 370 996	1 058 171	1 312 825	1 576 998	678 643	898 355	793 998	379 528	414 470
70 - 74	1 524 539	640 969	883 570	1 020 924	420 616	600 308	503 615	220 353	283 262
75 - 79	1 063 618	403 164	660 454	693 460	259 986	433 474	370 158	143 178	226 980
80 - 84	873 586	295 115	578 471	559 902	189 120	370 782	313 684	105 995	207 689
85 - 89	535 448	158 666	376 782	335 124	101 871	233 253	200 324	56 795	143 529
90 - 94	196 956	48 047	148 909	122 367	30 727	91 640	74 589	17 320	57 269
95 - 99	39 265	8 571	30 694	24 725	5 428	19 297	14 540	3 143	11 397
100 +	5 274	1 131	4 143	3 649	799	2 850	1 625	332	1 293
1 I 2019 (ESDJ)									
Total	37 972 812	18 380 376	19 592 436	...	...	...	...	...	...
0	379 769	195 435	184 334	...	...	...	...	...	...
1 - 4	1 539 249	790 430	748 819	...	...	...	...	...	...
5 - 9	1 992 180	1 023 244	968 936	...	...	...	...	...	...
10 - 14	1 922 593	985 833	936 760	...	...	...	...	...	...
15 - 19	1 809 745	927 377	882 368	...	...	...	...	...	...
20 - 24	2 102 657	1 072 518	1 030 139	...	...	...	...	...	...
25 - 29	2 589 169	1 320 546	1 268 623	...	...	...	...	...	...
30 - 34	2 964 750	1 510 709	1 454 041	...	...	...	...	...	...
35 - 39	3 117 151	1 582 900	1 534 251	...	...	...	...	...	...
40 - 44	2 908 354	1 470 338	1 438 016	...	...	...	...	...	...
45 - 49	2 467 264	1 238 904	1 228 360	...	...	...	...	...	...
50 - 54	2 246 116	1 114 988	1 131 128	...	...	...	...	...	...
55 - 59	2 474 876	1 199 272	1 275 604	...	...	...	...	...	...
60 - 64	2 752 895	1 290 543	1 462 352	...	...	...	...	...	...
65 - 69	2 400 297	1 071 706	1 328 591	...	...	...	...	...	...
70 - 74	1 590 647	669 719	920 928	...	...	...	...	...	...
75 - 79	1 054 724	401 097	653 627	...	...	...	...	...	...
80 - 84	874 011	295 038	578 973	...	...	...	...	...	...
85 - 89	536 611	159 477	377 134	...	...	...	...	...	...
90 - 94	202 643	49 977	152 666	...	...	...	...	...	...
95 - 99	41 667	9 143	32 524	...	...	...	...	...	...
100 +	5 444	1 182	4 262	...	...	...	...	...	...
Portugal									
21 III 2011 (CDJC)									
Total	10 562 178	5 046 600	5 515 578	6 438 593	3 047 968	3 390 625	4 123 585	1 998 632	2 124 953
0 - 4	482 647	246 396	236 251	316 068	161 365	154 703	166 579	85 031	81 548

7. Population by age, sex and urban/rural residence: latest available year, 2010 - 2019
Population selon l'âge, le sexe et la résidence, urbaine/rurale : dernière année disponible, 2010 - 2019 (continued - suite)

Continent, country or area, date, code[a] and age (in years) / Continent, pays ou zone, date, code[a] et âge (en années)	Total			Urban - Urbaine			Rural - Rurale		
	Both sexes Les deux sexes	Male Masculin	Female Féminin	Both sexes Les deux sexes	Male Masculin	Female Féminin	Both sexes Les deux sexes	Male Masculin	Female Féminin
EUROPE									
Portugal									
21 III 2011 (CDJC)									
5 - 9	525 087	268 965	256 122	329 692	168 925	160 767	195 395	100 040	95 355
10 - 14	564 595	288 638	275 957	344 809	176 287	168 522	219 786	112 351	107 435
15 - 19	565 250	288 525	276 725	342 328	174 252	168 076	222 922	114 273	108 649
20 - 24	582 065	293 023	289 042	358 412	178 982	179 430	223 653	114 041	109 612
25 - 29	656 076	324 848	331 228	425 629	208 104	217 525	230 447	116 744	113 703
30 - 34	773 567	378 734	394 833	508 225	247 125	261 100	265 342	131 609	133 733
35 - 39	824 683	402 307	422 376	529 287	255 858	273 429	295 396	146 449	148 947
40 - 44	773 098	374 962	398 136	478 840	228 255	250 585	294 258	146 707	147 551
45 - 49	770 294	370 989	399 305	466 564	219 783	246 781	303 730	151 206	152 524
50 - 54	722 360	346 248	376 112	435 982	203 867	232 115	286 378	142 381	143 997
55 - 59	677 651	322 095	355 556	410 020	190 860	219 160	267 631	131 235	136 396
60 - 64	634 741	298 546	336 195	382 547	177 485	205 062	252 194	121 061	131 133
65 - 69	551 701	253 004	298 697	319 398	146 189	173 209	232 303	106 815	125 488
70 - 74	496 438	220 461	275 977	273 513	119 844	153 669	222 925	100 617	122 308
75 - 79	429 706	180 131	249 575	231 208	94 394	136 814	198 498	85 737	112 761
80 - 84	297 888	113 325	184 563	159 578	57 948	101 630	138 310	55 377	82 933
85 - 89	164 356	55 635	108 721	88 444	28 423	60 021	75 912	27 212	48 700
90 - 94	53 847	15 679	38 168	29 038	7 847	21 191	24 809	7 832	16 977
95 - 99	14 602	3 816	10 786	8 158	2 029	6 129	6 444	1 787	4 657
100 +	1 526	273	1 253	853	146	707	673	127	546
1 I 2019 (ESDJ)									
Total	10 276 617	4 852 366	5 424 251	...	...	...	...	...	...
0	86 965	44 222	42 743	...	...	...	...	...	...
1 - 4	343 496	175 790	167 706	...	...	...	...	...	...
5 - 9	466 754	238 215	228 539	...	...	...	...	...	...
10 - 14	510 351	260 712	249 639	...	...	...	...	...	...
15 - 19	552 744	282 330	270 414	...	...	...	...	...	...
20 - 24	538 705	272 727	265 978	...	...	...	...	...	...
25 - 29	547 330	272 620	274 710	...	...	...	...	...	...
30 - 34	576 115	282 370	293 745	...	...	...	...	...	...
35 - 39	685 764	328 594	357 170	...	...	...	...	...	...
40 - 44	801 116	381 711	419 405	...	...	...	...	...	...
45 - 49	775 377	368 384	406 993	...	...	...	...	...	...
50 - 54	749 983	354 097	395 886	...	...	...	...	...	...
55 - 59	728 938	342 424	386 514	...	...	...	...	...	...
60 - 64	668 754	311 098	357 656	...	...	...	...	...	...
65 - 69	618 173	284 295	333 878	...	...	...	...	...	...
70 - 74	538 440	236 729	301 711	...	...	...	...	...	...
75 - 79	426 156	179 163	246 993	...	...	...	...	...	...
80 - 84	351 182	136 786	214 396	...	...	...	...	...	...
85 - 89	215 054	74 197	140 857	...	...	...	...	...	...
90 - 94	77 359	21 106	56 253	...	...	...	...	...	...
95 - 99	13 749	3 072	10 677	...	...	...	...	...	...
100 +	4 112	1 724	2 388	...	...	...	...	...	...
Republic of Moldova - République de Moldova									
12 V 2014 (CDFC)[89]									
Total	2 804 801	1 352 099	1 452 702	950 994	446 386	504 608	1 853 807	905 713	948 094
0	34 742	17 769	16 973	11 564	5 908	5 656	23 178	11 861	11 317
1 - 4	137 250	70 542	66 708	45 992	23 671	22 321	91 258	46 871	44 387
5 - 9	160 684	82 455	78 229	51 998	26 779	25 219	108 686	55 676	53 010
10 - 14	150 027	77 275	72 752	42 183	21 853	20 330	107 844	55 422	52 422
15 - 19	183 692	93 727	89 965	57 768	29 495	28 273	125 924	64 232	61 692
20 - 24	231 153	118 376	112 777	77 320	37 799	39 521	153 833	80 577	73 256
25 - 29	251 465	129 771	121 694	90 050	44 660	45 390	161 415	85 111	76 304
30 - 34	214 870	109 201	105 669	80 739	40 112	40 627	134 131	69 089	65 042
35 - 39	190 795	95 575	95 220	68 490	33 899	34 591	122 305	61 676	60 629
40 - 44	176 906	87 451	89 455	60 280	28 942	31 338	116 626	58 509	58 117
45 - 49	173 564	84 288	89 276	56 962	25 991	30 971	116 602	58 297	58 305
50 - 54	208 674	98 512	110 162	70 891	31 525	39 366	137 783	66 987	70 796
55 - 59	203 825	93 612	110 213	71 363	30 767	40 596	132 462	62 845	69 617
60 - 64	181 690	79 681	102 009	66 059	27 851	38 208	115 631	51 830	63 801
65 - 69	95 407	39 652	55 755	35 591	14 688	20 903	59 816	24 964	34 852

Continent, country or area, date, code[a] and age (in years) / Continent, pays ou zone, date, code[a] et âge (en années)	Total			Urban - Urbaine			Rural - Rurale		
	Both sexes Les deux sexes	Male Masculin	Female Féminin	Both sexes Les deux sexes	Male Masculin	Female Féminin	Both sexes Les deux sexes	Male Masculin	Female Féminin
EUROPE									
Republic of Moldova - République de Moldova									
12 V 2014 (CDFC)[89]									
70 - 74	85 270	32 645	52 625	26 949	10 612	16 337	58 321	22 033	36 288
75 - 79	65 096	22 757	42 339	20 154	6 884	13 270	44 942	15 873	29 069
80 - 84	37 980	12 543	25 437	10 243	3 261	6 982	27 737	9 282	18 455
85 - 89	16 502	4 801	11 701	4 893	1 334	3 559	11 609	3 467	8 142
90 - 94	4 277	1 148	3 129	1 228	270	958	3 049	878	2 171
95 - 99	574	158	416	170	38	132	404	120	284
100 +	358	160	198	107	47	60	251	113	138
1 VII 2018 (ESDJ)[90]									
Total	2 706 049	1 291 242	1 414 807	...	...	...	...	...	...
0	35 104	18 091	17 013	...	...	...	...	...	...
1 - 4	148 338	76 301	72 037	...	...	...	...	...	...
5 - 9	170 506	87 343	83 163	...	...	...	...	...	...
10 - 14	154 419	79 238	75 180	...	...	...	...	...	...
15 - 19	142 072	73 085	68 988	...	...	...	...	...	...
20 - 24	165 584	82 963	82 620	...	...	...	...	...	...
25 - 29	204 018	101 138	102 880	...	...	...	...	...	...
30 - 34	223 407	111 552	111 855	...	...	...	...	...	...
35 - 39	192 657	95 083	97 574	...	...	...	...	...	...
40 - 44	174 885	86 132	88 751	...	...	...	...	...	...
45 - 49	166 413	81 548	84 867	...	...	...	...	...	...
50 - 54	171 141	82 284	88 857	...	...	...	...	...	...
55 - 59	205 566	95 568	110 000	...	...	...	...	...	...
60 - 64	187 145	82 578	104 567	...	...	...	...	...	...
65 - 69	164 029	67 974	96 056	...	...	...	...	...	...
70 - 74	71 370	27 336	44 034	...	...	...	...	...	...
75 - 79	66 261	23 321	42 940	...	...	...	...	...	...
80 - 84	40 645	13 001	27 644	...	...	...	...	...	...
85 +	22 487	6 706	15 781	...	...	...	...	...	...
Romania - Roumanie[86]									
1 VII 2018 (ESDF)									
Total	19 476 713	9 528 936	9 947 777	10 481 512	4 999 811	5 481 701	8 995 201	4 529 125	4 466 076
0	200 226	102 560	97 666	111 055	56 893	54 162	89 171	45 667	43 504
1 - 4	795 607	408 081	387 526	437 087	224 570	212 517	358 520	183 511	175 009
5 - 9	997 245	512 976	484 269	518 932	267 379	251 553	478 313	245 597	232 716
10 - 14	1 054 908	541 979	512 929	513 868	263 691	250 177	541 040	278 288	262 752
15 - 19	1 044 955	536 576	508 379	470 223	239 281	230 942	574 732	297 295	277 437
20 - 24	1 021 609	522 695	498 914	489 668	242 065	247 603	531 941	280 630	251 311
25 - 29	1 167 968	611 775	556 193	683 259	337 296	345 963	484 709	274 479	210 230
30 - 34	1 334 991	694 435	640 556	801 229	404 541	396 688	533 762	289 894	243 868
35 - 39	1 402 483	718 988	683 495	817 103	410 691	406 412	585 380	308 297	277 083
40 - 44	1 547 184	792 168	755 016	854 427	425 363	429 064	692 757	366 805	325 952
45 - 49	1 559 060	801 466	757 594	841 240	411 196	430 044	717 820	390 270	327 550
50 - 54	1 280 748	652 534	628 214	729 654	348 067	381 587	551 094	304 467	246 627
55 - 59	1 149 137	563 275	585 862	667 786	307 854	359 932	481 351	255 421	225 930
60 - 64	1 345 810	625 659	720 151	797 241	359 594	437 647	548 569	266 065	282 504
65 - 69	1 197 558	529 824	667 734	657 560	289 564	367 996	539 998	240 260	299 738
70 - 74	810 283	341 493	468 790	395 670	165 060	230 610	414 613	176 433	238 180
75 - 79	670 831	258 736	412 095	306 042	116 152	189 890	364 789	142 584	222 205
80 - 84	514 831	184 667	330 164	224 528	78 229	146 299	290 303	106 438	183 865
85 - 89	267 712	91 833	175 879	114 947	37 189	77 758	152 765	54 644	98 121
90 - 94	89 984	29 714	60 270	39 433	12 151	27 282	50 551	17 563	32 988
95 - 99	21 065	6 737	14 328	9 299	2 696	6 603	11 766	4 041	7 725
100 +	2 518	765	1 753	1 261	289	972	1 257	476	781
1 I 2019 (ESDF)									
Total	19 414 458	9 500 450	9 914 008	...	...	...	...	...	...
0	200 726	102 647	98 079	...	...	...	...	...	...
1 - 4	799 157	409 279	389 878	...	...	...	...	...	...
5 - 9	986 266	507 343	478 923	...	...	...	...	...	...
10 - 14	1 056 093	542 599	513 494	...	...	...	...	...	...
15 - 19	1 036 435	532 460	503 975	...	...	...	...	...	...
20 - 24	1 016 105	520 921	495 184	...	...	...	...	...	...
25 - 29	1 127 138	590 060	537 078	...	...	...	...	...	...

7. Population by age, sex and urban/rural residence: latest available year, 2010 - 2019
Population selon l'âge, le sexe et la résidence, urbaine/rurale : dernière année disponible, 2010 - 2019 (continued - suite)

Continent, country or area, date, code[a] and age (in years) / Continent, pays ou zone, date, code[a] et âge (en annèes)	Total			Urban - Urbaine			Rural - Rurale		
	Both sexes Les deux sexes	Male Masculin	Female Féminin	Both sexes Les deux sexes	Male Masculin	Female Féminin	Both sexes Les deux sexes	Male Masculin	Female Féminin
EUROPE									
Romania - Roumanie[86]									
1 I 2019 (ESDF)									
30 - 34	1 354 283	704 620	649 663	...	...	...	...	...	...
35 - 39	1 363 973	700 375	663 598	...	...	...	...	...	...
40 - 44	1 555 321	795 877	759 444	...	...	...	...	...	...
45 - 49	1 506 342	775 480	730 862	...	...	...	...	...	...
50 - 54	1 359 924	693 564	666 360	...	...	...	...	...	...
55 - 59	1 116 040	548 697	567 343	...	...	...	...	...	...
60 - 64	1 340 298	623 820	716 478	...	...	...	...	...	...
65 - 69	1 206 962	533 849	673 113	...	...	...	...	...	...
70 - 74	829 726	349 894	479 832	...	...	...	...	...	...
75 - 79	653 271	252 437	400 834	...	...	...	...	...	...
80 - 84	519 126	185 512	333 614	...	...	...	...	...	...
85 - 89	268 850	92 156	176 694	...	...	...	...	...	...
90 - 94	93 047	30 752	62 295	...	...	...	...	...	...
95 - 99	22 387	7 223	15 164	...	...	...	...	...	...
100 +	2 988	885	2 103	...	...	...	...	...	...
Russian Federation - Fédération de Russie									
1 VII 2012 (ESDJ)									
Total	143 201 730	66 264 910	76 936 820	105 930 122	48 419 208	57 510 914	37 271 608	17 845 702	19 425 906
0	1 837 406	944 299	893 107	1 299 253	668 312	630 941	538 153	275 987	262 166
1 - 4	6 695 802	3 433 227	3 262 575	4 714 200	2 419 141	2 295 059	1 981 602	1 014 086	967 516
5 - 9	7 350 838	3 762 806	3 588 032	5 189 787	2 657 166	2 532 621	2 161 051	1 105 640	1 055 411
10 - 14	6 628 125	3 396 364	3 231 761	4 584 611	2 348 219	2 236 392	2 043 514	1 048 145	995 369
15 - 19	7 391 866	3 776 026	3 615 840	5 367 803	2 718 897	2 648 906	2 024 063	1 057 129	966 934
20 - 24	11 223 730	5 708 187	5 515 543	8 636 085	4 330 536	4 305 549	2 587 645	1 377 651	1 209 994
25 - 29	12 442 007	6 262 379	6 179 628	9 541 009	4 744 648	4 796 361	2 900 998	1 517 731	1 383 267
30 - 34	11 231 149	5 583 513	5 647 636	8 675 785	4 272 864	4 402 921	2 555 364	1 310 649	1 244 715
35 - 39	10 419 383	5 087 565	5 331 818	7 966 185	3 854 320	4 111 865	2 453 198	1 233 245	1 219 953
40 - 44	9 451 487	4 589 504	4 861 983	7 068 002	3 394 309	3 673 693	2 383 485	1 195 195	1 188 290
45 - 49	9 784 092	4 632 279	5 151 813	7 108 256	3 298 718	3 809 538	2 675 836	1 333 561	1 342 275
50 - 54	11 498 441	5 279 364	6 219 077	8 339 186	3 721 713	4 617 473	3 159 255	1 557 651	1 601 604
55 - 59	10 298 414	4 480 855	5 817 559	7 573 444	3 197 844	4 375 600	2 724 970	1 283 011	1 441 959
60 - 64	8 534 857	3 523 990	5 010 867	6 428 296	2 585 856	3 842 440	2 106 561	938 134	1 168 427
65 - 69	4 174 510	1 602 839	2 571 671	3 204 644	1 214 486	1 990 158	969 866	388 353	581 513
70 - 74	5 965 072	1 989 724	3 975 348	4 331 090	1 428 165	2 902 925	1 633 982	561 559	1 072 423
75 - 79	3 888 860	1 179 476	2 709 384	2 762 682	822 673	1 940 009	1 126 178	356 803	769 375
80 - 84	2 795 954	722 151	2 073 803	1 965 242	501 515	1 463 727	830 712	220 636	610 076
85 - 89	1 261 655	253 028	1 008 627	927 939	193 530	734 409	333 716	59 498	274 218
90 - 94	266 163	46 736	219 427	200 155	37 401	162 754	66 008	9 335	56 673
95 - 99	52 622	8 634	43 988	39 307	7 154	32 153	13 315	1 480	11 835
100 +	9 297	1 964	7 333	7 161	1 741	5 420	2 136	223	1 913
San Marino - Saint-Marin[36]									
1 VII 2018 (ESDJ)									
Total	34 536	16 835	17 701	...	...	...	...	...	...
0	245	128	117	...	...	...	...	...	...
1 - 4	1 161	605	556	...	...	...	...	...	...
5 - 9	1 728	887	841	...	...	...	...	...	...
10 - 14	1 689	872	817	...	...	...	...	...	...
15 - 19	1 744	930	814	...	...	...	...	...	...
20 - 24	1 660	856	804	...	...	...	...	...	...
25 - 29	1 638	828	810	...	...	...	...	...	...
30 - 34	1 820	885	935	...	...	...	...	...	...
35 - 39	2 215	1 055	1 160	...	...	...	...	...	...
40 - 44	2 848	1 362	1 486	...	...	...	...	...	...
45 - 49	3 121	1 526	1 595	...	...	...	...	...	...
50 - 54	3 165	1 505	1 660	...	...	...	...	...	...
55 - 59	2 701	1 335	1 366	...	...	...	...	...	...
60 - 64	2 101	998	1 103	...	...	...	...	...	...
65 - 69	1 843	905	938	...	...	...	...	...	...
70 - 74	1 625	782	843	...	...	...	...	...	...
75 - 79	1 252	579	673	...	...	...	...	...	...
80 - 84	959	426	533	...	...	...	...	...	...
85 - 89	653	258	395	...	...	...	...	...	...

7. Population by age, sex and urban/rural residence: latest available year, 2010 - 2019
Population selon l'âge, le sexe et la résidence, urbaine/rurale : dernière année disponible, 2010 - 2019 (continued - suite)

Continent, country or area, date, code[a] and age (in years) / Continent, pays ou zone, date, code[a] et âge (en annèes)	Total			Urban - Urbaine			Rural - Rurale		
	Both sexes Les deux sexes	Male Masculin	Female Féminin	Both sexes Les deux sexes	Male Masculin	Female Féminin	Both sexes Les deux sexes	Male Masculin	Female Féminin
EUROPE									
San Marino - Saint-Marin[36]									
1 VII 2018 (ESDJ)									
90 - 94	279	92	187	...	...	...	...	...	...
95 - 99	76	20	56	...	...	...	...	...	...
100 +	13	1	12	...	...	...	...	...	...
Serbia - Serbie[91]									
1 VII 2018 (ESDJ)									
Total	6 982 604	3 401 706	3 580 898	4 248 451	2 023 097	2 225 354	2 734 153	1 378 609	1 355 544
0	64 117	33 089	31 028	42 924	22 164	20 760	21 193	10 925	10 268
1 - 4	260 473	134 416	126 057	179 125	92 458	86 667	81 348	41 958	39 390
5 - 9	331 121	170 607	160 514	217 474	112 065	105 409	113 647	58 542	55 105
10 - 14	344 885	177 307	167 578	207 834	106 667	101 167	137 051	70 640	66 411
15 - 19	351 160	180 585	170 575	207 829	106 763	101 066	143 331	73 822	69 509
20 - 24	387 671	199 567	188 104	229 462	116 652	112 810	158 209	82 915	75 294
25 - 29	427 573	218 691	208 882	264 614	131 374	133 240	162 959	87 317	75 642
30 - 34	472 406	241 029	231 377	305 382	150 484	154 898	167 024	90 545	76 479
35 - 39	490 823	249 342	241 481	324 308	160 201	164 107	166 515	89 141	77 374
40 - 44	499 185	251 790	247 395	320 141	157 182	162 959	179 044	94 608	84 436
45 - 49	469 669	233 808	235 861	288 763	139 911	148 852	180 906	93 897	87 009
50 - 54	463 118	226 708	236 410	275 623	130 177	145 446	187 495	96 531	90 964
55 - 59	488 497	235 035	253 462	288 259	132 556	155 703	200 238	102 479	97 759
60 - 64	523 570	247 332	276 238	305 748	138 063	167 685	217 822	109 269	108 553
65 - 69	504 656	230 907	273 749	294 384	128 632	165 752	210 272	102 275	107 997
70 - 74	326 873	143 016	183 857	186 957	78 885	108 072	139 916	64 131	75 785
75 - 79	260 032	107 678	152 354	141 395	56 496	84 899	118 637	51 182	67 455
80 - 84	190 609	74 658	115 951	103 237	39 742	63 495	87 372	34 916	52 456
85 - 89	92 009	34 127	57 882	47 002	16 624	30 378	45 007	17 503	27 504
90 - 94	27 028	9 604	17 424	14 205	4 782	9 423	12 823	4 822	8 001
95 - 99	6 433	2 151	4 282	3 431	1 103	2 328	3 002	1 048	1 954
100 +	696	259	437	354	116	238	342	143	199
1 I 2019 (ESDJ)									
Total	6 963 764	3 392 811	3 570 953	...	...	...	...	...	...
0	63 664	33 040	30 624	...	...	...	...	...	...
1 - 4	260 188	134 246	125 942	...	...	...	...	...	...
5 - 9	330 293	170 059	160 234	...	...	...	...	...	...
10 - 14	342 059	175 951	166 108	...	...	...	...	...	...
15 - 19	352 273	181 200	171 073	...	...	...	...	...	...
20 - 24	381 264	196 179	185 085	...	...	...	...	...	...
25 - 29	423 074	216 403	206 671	...	...	...	...	...	...
30 - 34	468 537	239 214	229 323	...	...	...	...	...	...
35 - 39	490 025	248 949	241 076	...	...	...	...	...	...
40 - 44	499 738	252 358	247 380	...	...	...	...	...	...
45 - 49	471 735	235 231	236 504	...	...	...	...	...	...
50 - 54	460 570	225 445	235 125	...	...	...	...	...	...
55 - 59	484 075	232 800	251 275	...	...	...	...	...	...
60 - 64	514 185	242 787	271 398	...	...	...	...	...	...
65 - 69	507 794	232 525	275 269	...	...	...	...	...	...
70 - 74	340 197	148 873	191 324	...	...	...	...	...	...
75 - 79	255 049	105 798	149 251	...	...	...	...	...	...
80 - 84	189 834	74 292	115 542	...	...	...	...	...	...
85 - 89	93 277	34 626	58 651	...	...	...	...	...	...
90 - 94	28 070	10 164	17 906	...	...	...	...	...	...
95 - 99	7 043	2 361	4 682	...	...	...	...	...	...
100 +	820	310	510	...	...	...	...	...	...
Slovakia - Slovaquie									
1 VII 2018 (ESDJ)									
Total	5 446 771	2 658 796	2 787 975	2 915 506	1 401 961	1 513 545	2 531 265	1 256 835	1 274 430
0	58 590	30 107	28 483	30 120	15 501	14 619	28 470	14 606	13 864
1 - 4	231 149	118 431	112 719	117 771	60 264	57 507	113 379	58 167	55 212
5 - 9	293 110	150 173	142 937	146 503	74 861	71 643	146 607	75 313	71 295
10 - 14	271 023	139 260	131 763	131 471	67 573	63 898	139 552	71 687	67 866
15 - 19	267 380	137 081	130 299	126 084	64 651	61 434	141 296	72 431	68 866
20 - 24	310 010	158 815	151 195	149 263	76 403	72 860	160 747	82 413	78 335
25 - 29	384 630	196 327	188 303	202 705	102 679	100 026	181 926	93 649	88 277
30 - 34	423 264	216 384	206 880	235 937	119 993	115 944	187 327	96 391	90 936

7. Population by age, sex and urban/rural residence: latest available year, 2010 - 2019
Population selon l'âge, le sexe et la résidence, urbaine/rurale : dernière année disponible, 2010 - 2019 (continued - suite)

Continent, country or area, date, code[a] and age (in years) / Continent, pays ou zone, date, code[a] et âge (en années)	Total			Urban - Urbaine			Rural - Rurale		
	Both sexes Les deux sexes	Male Masculin	Female Féminin	Both sexes Les deux sexes	Male Masculin	Female Féminin	Both sexes Les deux sexes	Male Masculin	Female Féminin
EUROPE									
Slovakia - Slovaquie									
1 VII 2018 (ESDJ)									
35 - 39	445 527	229 503	216 024	247 183	126 971	120 212	198 344	102 532	95 812
40 - 44	449 137	230 676	218 461	244 056	123 814	120 242	205 081	106 862	98 219
45 - 49	373 845	189 216	184 629	198 298	97 726	100 572	175 547	91 490	84 057
50 - 54	355 842	177 023	178 819	191 651	91 326	100 325	164 191	85 698	78 494
55 - 59	357 510	174 666	182 844	200 382	93 813	106 569	157 128	80 853	76 275
60 - 64	366 171	172 227	193 944	212 291	96 497	115 794	153 880	75 730	78 150
65 - 69	314 971	140 781	174 190	182 553	79 707	102 847	132 418	61 074	71 344
70 - 74	213 845	87 698	126 148	121 755	49 446	72 309	92 091	38 252	53 839
75 - 79	152 911	56 230	96 681	83 153	30 875	52 278	69 758	25 355	44 403
80 - 84	97 725	31 727	65 998	52 050	17 427	34 623	45 675	14 300	31 375
85 - 89	55 519	16 074	39 446	29 200	8 852	20 348	26 320	7 222	19 098
90 - 94	19 150	4 806	14 344	10 107	2 657	7 450	9 043	2 149	6 894
95 - 99	4 386	1 190	3 196	2 289	679	1 611	2 097	512	1 586
100 +	1 082	404	678	690	251	439	392	154	239
1 I 2019 (ESDJ)									
Total	5 450 421	2 661 077	2 789 344	...	...	...	...	...	...
0	58 445	30 077	28 368	...	...	...	...	...	...
1 - 4	233 087	119 456	113 631	...	...	...	...	...	...
5 - 9	292 822	149 972	142 850	...	...	...	...	...	...
10 - 14	273 688	140 628	133 060	...	...	...	...	...	...
15 - 19	264 777	135 752	129 025	...	...	...	...	...	...
20 - 24	302 237	154 833	147 404	...	...	...	...	...	...
25 - 29	380 385	194 291	186 094	...	...	...	...	...	...
30 - 34	420 036	214 575	205 461	...	...	...	...	...	...
35 - 39	442 733	228 112	214 621	...	...	...	...	...	...
40 - 44	452 499	232 624	219 875	...	...	...	...	...	...
45 - 49	381 710	193 358	188 352	...	...	...	...	...	...
50 - 54	352 022	175 160	176 862	...	...	...	...	...	...
55 - 59	356 275	174 262	182 013	...	...	...	...	...	...
60 - 64	365 386	172 047	193 339	...	...	...	...	...	...
65 - 69	319 800	143 218	176 582	...	...	...	...	...	...
70 - 74	220 261	90 809	129 452	...	...	...	...	...	...
75 - 79	154 745	57 184	97 561	...	...	...	...	...	...
80 - 84	98 306	31 861	66 445	...	...	...	...	...	...
85 - 89	55 964	16 266	39 698	...	...	...	...	...	...
90 - 94	19 408	4 890	14 518	...	...	...	...	...	...
95 - 99	4 686	1 274	3 412	...	...	...	...	...	...
100 +	1 149	428	721	...	...	...	...	...	...
Slovenia - Slovénie									
1 VII 2018 (ESDJ)									
Total	2 070 050	1 030 234	1 039 816	1 144 936	564 385	580 551	925 114	465 849	459 265
0	19 905	10 267	9 638	11 021	5 706	5 315	8 884	4 561	4 323
1 - 4	83 118	42 669	40 449	45 730	23 359	22 371	37 388	19 310	18 078
5 - 9	111 021	57 228	53 793	60 944	31 392	29 552	50 077	25 836	24 241
10 - 14	97 787	50 109	47 678	53 043	27 293	25 750	44 744	22 816	21 928
15 - 19	92 599	47 982	44 617	49 712	25 834	23 878	42 887	22 148	20 739
20 - 24	100 852	52 467	48 385	60 108	30 373	29 735	40 744	22 094	18 650
25 - 29	115 511	60 298	55 213	63 807	32 979	30 828	51 704	27 319	24 385
30 - 34	137 408	72 138	65 270	77 267	40 489	36 778	60 141	31 649	28 492
35 - 39	154 470	81 402	73 068	86 984	45 691	41 293	67 486	35 711	31 775
40 - 44	154 636	81 130	73 506	86 274	45 142	41 132	68 362	35 988	32 374
45 - 49	145 749	75 583	70 166	79 194	40 698	38 496	66 555	34 885	31 670
50 - 54	154 333	78 260	76 073	83 396	41 914	41 482	70 937	36 346	34 591
55 - 59	149 384	75 354	74 030	80 398	39 889	40 509	68 986	35 465	33 521
60 - 64	145 944	72 635	73 309	79 267	38 519	40 748	66 677	34 116	32 561
65 - 69	128 962	62 728	66 234	71 179	33 642	37 537	57 783	29 086	28 697
70 - 74	89 608	40 840	48 768	50 420	22 428	27 992	39 188	18 412	20 776
75 - 79	79 372	33 536	45 836	44 428	18 522	25 906	34 944	15 014	19 930
80 - 84	58 051	21 611	36 440	32 545	12 383	20 162	25 506	9 228	16 278
85 - 89	35 221	10 473	24 748	19 827	6 013	13 814	15 394	4 460	10 934
90 - 94	13 351	3 014	10 337	7 731	1 820	5 911	5 620	1 194	4 426
95 - 99	2 594	479	2 115	1 559	278	1 281	1 035	201	834
100 +	174	31	143	102	21	81	72	10	62

7. Population by age, sex and urban/rural residence: latest available year, 2010 - 2019
Population selon l'âge, le sexe et la résidence, urbaine/rurale : dernière année disponible, 2010 - 2019 (continued - suite)

Continent, country or area, date, code[a] and age (in years) / Continent, pays ou zone, date, code[a] et âge (en années)	Total			Urban - Urbaine			Rural - Rurale		
	Both sexes / Les deux sexes	Male / Masculin	Female / Féminin	Both sexes / Les deux sexes	Male / Masculin	Female / Féminin	Both sexes / Les deux sexes	Male / Masculin	Female / Féminin
EUROPE									
Slovenia - Slovénie									
1 I 2019 (ESDJ)									
Total	2 080 908	1 038 656	1 042 252	...	...	...	...	...	...
0	19 571	10 143	9 428	...	...	...	...	...	...
1 - 4	82 735	42 540	40 195	...	...	...	...	...	...
5 - 9	110 717	57 090	53 627	...	...	...	...	...	...
10 - 14	100 683	51 616	49 067	...	...	...	...	...	...
15 - 19	92 855	48 080	44 775	...	...	...	...	...	...
20 - 24	101 940	53 597	48 343	...	...	...	...	...	...
25 - 29	114 680	60 359	54 321	...	...	...	...	...	...
30 - 34	137 712	72 603	65 109	...	...	...	...	...	...
35 - 39	154 185	81 642	72 543	...	...	...	...	...	...
40 - 44	156 582	82 483	74 099	...	...	...	...	...	...
45 - 49	147 104	76 523	70 581	...	...	...	...	...	...
50 - 54	154 102	78 330	75 772	...	...	...	...	...	...
55 - 59	149 547	75 417	74 130	...	...	...	...	...	...
60 - 64	145 441	72 401	73 040	...	...	...	...	...	...
65 - 69	131 040	63 965	67 075	...	...	...	...	...	...
70 - 74	90 902	41 529	49 373	...	...	...	...	...	...
75 - 79	80 079	33 916	46 163	...	...	...	...	...	...
80 - 84	58 757	22 096	36 661	...	...	...	...	...	...
85 - 89	35 549	10 642	24 907	...	...	...	...	...	...
90 - 94	13 744	3 144	10 600	...	...	...	...	...	...
95 - 99	2 794	512	2 282	...	...	...	...	...	...
100 +	189	28	161	...	...	...	...	...	...
Spain - Espagne[87]									
1 I 2019 (ESDJ)									
Total	46 937 060	23 009 259	23 927 801	...	...	...	...	...	...
0	371 989	191 164	180 825	...	...	...	...	...	...
1 - 4	1 695 514	873 065	822 449	...	...	...	...	...	...
5 - 9	2 356 886	1 215 470	1 141 416	...	...	...	...	...	...
10 - 14	2 505 728	1 292 421	1 213 307	...	...	...	...	...	...
15 - 19	2 332 161	1 202 753	1 129 408	...	...	...	...	...	...
20 - 24	2 288 322	1 169 404	1 118 918	...	...	...	...	...	...
25 - 29	2 525 120	1 273 836	1 251 284	...	...	...	...	...	...
30 - 34	2 801 658	1 395 386	1 406 272	...	...	...	...	...	...
35 - 39	3 436 405	1 716 735	1 719 670	...	...	...	...	...	...
40 - 44	3 984 581	2 014 584	1 969 997	...	...	...	...	...	...
45 - 49	3 812 140	1 924 615	1 887 525	...	...	...	...	...	...
50 - 54	3 640 087	1 815 339	1 824 748	...	...	...	...	...	...
55 - 59	3 273 516	1 611 961	1 661 555	...	...	...	...	...	...
60 - 64	2 807 378	1 361 786	1 445 592	...	...	...	...	...	...
65 - 69	2 406 253	1 147 954	1 258 299	...	...	...	...	...	...
70 - 74	2 187 986	1 011 942	1 176 044	...	...	...	...	...	...
75 - 79	1 630 452	722 339	908 113	...	...	...	...	...	...
80 - 84	1 363 069	553 031	810 038	...	...	...	...	...	...
85 - 89	980 625	357 472	623 153	...	...	...	...	...	...
90 - 94	419 180	128 712	290 468	...	...	...	...	...	...
95 - 99	106 329	27 181	79 148	...	...	...	...	...	...
100 +	11 681	2 109	9 572	...	...	...	...	...	...
Sweden - Suède[92]									
1 I 2019 (ESDJ)									
Total	10 230 185	5 142 438	5 087 747	...	...	...	...	...	...
0	116 839	60 032	56 807	...	...	...	...	...	...
1 - 4	487 659	251 004	236 655	...	...	...	...	...	...
5 - 9	619 473	318 534	300 939	...	...	...	...	...	...
10 - 14	595 758	306 645	289 113	...	...	...	...	...	...
15 - 19	559 513	293 802	265 711	...	...	...	...	...	...
20 - 24	597 593	311 168	286 425	...	...	...	...	...	...
25 - 29	741 322	380 948	360 374	...	...	...	...	...	...
30 - 34	690 141	354 455	335 686	...	...	...	...	...	...
35 - 39	640 119	328 012	312 107	...	...	...	...	...	...
40 - 44	635 836	323 915	311 921	...	...	...	...	...	...
45 - 49	658 339	333 690	324 649	...	...	...	...	...	...
50 - 54	687 849	349 187	338 662	...	...	...	...	...	...

7. Population by age, sex and urban/rural residence: latest available year, 2010 - 2019
Population selon l'âge, le sexe et la résidence, urbaine/rurale : dernière année disponible, 2010 - 2019 (continued - suite)

Continent, country or area, date, code[a] and age (in years) / Continent, pays ou zone, date, code[a] et âge (en annèes)	Total			Urban - Urbaine			Rural - Rurale		
	Both sexes Les deux sexes	Male Masculin	Female Féminin	Both sexes Les deux sexes	Male Masculin	Female Féminin	Both sexes Les deux sexes	Male Masculin	Female Féminin
EUROPE									
Sweden - Suède[92]									
1 I 2019 (ESDJ)									
55 - 59	598 967	302 734	296 233	...	...	...	...	...	...
60 - 64	565 066	282 697	282 369	...	...	...	...	...	...
65 - 69	549 311	271 523	277 788	...	...	...	...	...	...
70 - 74	563 648	275 471	288 177	...	...	...	...	...	...
75 - 79	400 619	190 937	209 682	...	...	...	...	...	...
80 - 84	261 527	115 206	146 321	...	...	...	...	...	...
85 - 89	162 303	62 775	99 528	...	...	...	...	...	...
90 - 94	76 247	24 347	51 900	...	...	...	...	...	...
95 - 99	19 989	4 994	14 995	...	...	...	...	...	...
100 +	2 067	362	1 705	...	...	...	...	...	...
Switzerland - Suisse[93]									
31 XII 2018 (ESDJ)									
Total	8 544 527	4 237 121	4 307 406	7 241 546	3 579 833	3 661 713	1 302 981	657 288	645 693
0	86 168	44 120	42 048	73 635	37 698	35 937	12 533	6 422	6 111
1 - 4	351 712	180 632	171 080	299 076	153 447	145 629	52 636	27 185	25 451
5 - 9	430 304	221 007	209 297	363 203	186 494	176 709	67 101	34 513	32 588
10 - 14	415 562	213 495	202 067	349 466	179 658	169 808	66 096	33 837	32 259
15 - 19	425 712	219 776	205 936	356 753	184 055	172 698	68 959	35 721	33 238
20 - 24	483 445	249 100	234 345	408 085	209 377	198 708	75 360	39 723	35 637
25 - 29	569 288	288 954	280 334	491 405	248 392	243 013	77 883	40 562	37 321
30 - 34	606 490	306 152	300 338	526 437	265 039	261 398	80 053	41 113	38 940
35 - 39	608 706	307 401	301 305	526 092	265 561	260 531	82 614	41 840	40 774
40 - 44	583 783	293 717	290 066	502 192	252 103	250 089	81 591	41 614	39 977
45 - 49	620 649	311 949	308 700	526 675	264 435	262 240	93 974	47 514	46 460
50 - 54	671 146	338 894	332 252	565 572	284 789	280 783	105 574	54 105	51 469
55 - 59	610 732	307 700	303 032	509 835	256 347	253 488	100 897	51 353	49 544
60 - 64	503 529	251 173	252 356	418 014	207 322	210 692	85 515	43 851	41 664
65 - 69	427 996	206 561	221 435	355 301	169 436	185 865	72 695	37 125	35 570
70 - 74	398 116	188 848	209 268	333 894	156 827	177 067	64 222	32 021	32 201
75 - 79	307 537	139 426	168 111	260 082	117 007	143 075	47 455	22 419	25 036
80 - 84	220 832	92 810	128 022	186 981	78 201	108 780	33 851	14 609	19 242
85 - 89	142 816	52 618	90 198	120 864	44 349	76 515	21 952	8 269	13 683
90 - 94	62 959	18 823	44 136	53 359	15 886	37 473	9 600	2 937	6 663
95 - 99	15 473	3 708	11 765	13 281	3 189	10 092	2 192	519	1 673
100 +	1 572	257	1 315	1 344	221	1 123	228	36	192
Ukraine[94]									
1 I 2018 (ESDJ)									
Total	42 216 766	19 558 180	22 658 586	29 132 191	13 363 808	15 768 383	13 084 575	6 194 372	6 890 203
0	361 789	186 249	175 540	235 742	121 339	114 403	126 047	64 910	61 137
1 - 4	1 736 184	895 177	841 007	1 134 412	585 051	549 361	601 772	310 126	291 646
5 - 9	2 379 971	1 226 979	1 152 992	1 582 271	816 423	765 848	797 700	410 556	387 144
10 - 14	2 052 546	1 054 198	998 348	1 375 263	706 849	668 414	677 283	347 349	329 934
15 - 19	1 840 643	945 967	894 676	1 196 422	612 234	584 188	644 221	333 733	310 488
20 - 24	2 313 510	1 189 370	1 124 140	1 528 992	785 843	743 149	784 518	403 527	380 991
25 - 29	3 055 950	1 562 602	1 493 348	2 060 712	1 042 147	1 018 565	995 238	520 455	474 783
30 - 34	3 635 922	1 842 797	1 793 125	2 660 663	1 326 740	1 333 923	975 259	516 057	459 202
35 - 39	3 249 517	1 623 318	1 626 199	2 400 600	1 189 693	1 210 907	848 917	433 625	415 292
40 - 44	3 047 046	1 485 621	1 561 425	2 169 142	1 046 073	1 123 069	877 904	439 548	438 356
45 - 49	2 887 430	1 381 886	1 505 544	1 995 610	936 247	1 059 363	891 820	445 639	446 181
50 - 54	2 823 735	1 302 639	1 521 096	1 941 376	868 106	1 073 270	882 359	434 533	447 826
55 - 59	3 152 778	1 395 204	1 757 574	2 218 879	951 370	1 267 509	933 899	443 834	490 065
60 - 64	2 712 475	1 128 895	1 583 580	1 938 417	783 597	1 154 820	774 058	345 298	428 760
65 - 69	2 364 521	918 219	1 446 302	1 701 783	648 712	1 053 071	662 738	269 507	393 231
70 - 74	1 336 574	465 668	870 906	922 790	322 843	599 947	413 784	142 825	270 959
75 - 79	1 588 273	489 788	1 098 485	1 036 925	324 706	712 219	551 348	165 082	386 266
80 - 84	963 116	281 666	681 450	608 719	181 779	426 940	354 397	99 887	254 510
85 - 89	491 782	126 308	365 474	292 362	78 778	213 584	199 420	47 530	151 890
90 - 94	180 512	42 855	137 657	104 410	26 558	77 852	76 102	16 297	59 805
95 - 99	33 969	10 040	23 929	20 104	6 646	13 458	13 865	3 394	10 471
100 +	8 523	2 734	5 789	6 597	2 074	4 523	1 926	660	1 266

7. Population by age, sex and urban/rural residence: latest available year, 2010 - 2019
Population selon l'âge, le sexe et la résidence, urbaine/rurale : dernière année disponible, 2010 - 2019 (continued - suite)

Continent, country or area, date, code[a] and age (in years) / Continent, pays ou zone, date, code[a] et âge (en années)	Total			Urban - Urbaine			Rural - Rurale		
	Both sexes Les deux sexes	Male Masculin	Female Féminin	Both sexes Les deux sexes	Male Masculin	Female Féminin	Both sexes Les deux sexes	Male Masculin	Female Féminin
EUROPE									
United Kingdom of Great Britain and Northern Ireland - Royaume-Uni de Grande-Bretagne et d'Irlande du Nord[95]									
27 III 2011 (CDJC)									
Total	63 182 178	31 028 143	32 154 035	51 217 521	25 124 237	26 093 284	11 964 657	5 903 906	6 060 751
0 - 4	3 913 953	2 002 494	1 911 459	3 302 119	1 689 719	1 612 400	611 834	312 775	299 059
5 - 9	3 516 615	1 799 999	1 716 616	2 878 114	1 472 489	1 405 625	638 501	327 510	310 991
10 - 14	3 669 326	1 878 838	1 790 488	2 951 079	1 509 796	1 441 283	718 247	369 042	349 205
15 - 19	3 996 452	2 040 725	1 955 727	3 277 414	1 667 480	1 609 934	719 038	373 245	345 793
20 - 24	4 297 198	2 164 141	2 133 057	3 737 543	1 863 922	1 873 621	559 655	300 219	259 436
25 - 29	4 306 340	2 145 054	2 161 286	3 781 906	1 876 471	1 905 435	524 434	268 583	255 851
30 - 34	4 125 449	2 059 312	2 066 137	3 573 410	1 789 511	1 783 899	552 039	269 801	282 238
35 - 39	4 194 477	2 082 310	2 112 167	3 495 390	1 745 563	1 749 827	699 087	336 747	362 340
40 - 44	4 625 635	2 283 902	2 341 733	3 734 709	1 851 446	1 883 263	890 926	432 456	458 470
45 - 49	4 643 100	2 293 572	2 349 528	3 683 527	1 821 257	1 862 270	959 573	472 315	487 258
50 - 54	4 094 454	2 028 748	2 065 706	3 216 769	1 593 822	1 622 947	877 685	434 926	442 759
55 - 59	3 614 078	1 785 598	1 828 480	2 790 096	1 378 906	1 411 190	823 982	406 692	417 290
60 - 64	3 807 974	1 868 912	1 939 062	2 869 025	1 404 882	1 464 143	938 949	464 030	474 919
65 - 69	3 017 480	1 463 355	1 554 125	2 248 845	1 082 105	1 166 740	768 635	381 250	387 385
70 - 74	2 462 745	1 162 621	1 300 124	1 874 997	873 593	1 001 404	587 748	289 028	298 720
75 - 79	2 006 019	903 433	1 102 586	1 549 014	686 269	862 745	457 005	217 164	239 841
80 - 84	1 498 896	615 163	883 733	1 166 619	470 552	696 067	332 277	144 611	187 666
85 - 89	918 343	324 063	594 280	717 808	249 645	468 163	200 535	74 418	126 117
90 - 94	368 425	104 072	264 353	287 454	80 165	207 289	80 971	23 907	57 064
95 - 99	92 951	19 756	73 195	72 117	15 038	57 079	20 834	4 718	16 116
100 +	12 268	2 075	10 193	9 566	1 606	7 960	2 702	469	2 233
1 I 2018 (ESDJ)[86]									
Total	66 273 576	32 709 956	33 563 620	...	...	...	...	...	...
0	768 431	393 790	374 641	...	...	...	...	...	...
1 - 4	3 180 323	1 630 588	1 549 735	...	...	...	...	...	...
5 - 9	4 127 134	2 112 519	2 014 615	...	...	...	...	...	...
10 - 14	3 795 661	1 944 627	1 851 034	...	...	...	...	...	...
15 - 19	3 678 852	1 888 733	1 790 119	...	...	...	...	...	...
20 - 24	4 194 671	2 153 737	2 040 934	...	...	...	...	...	...
25 - 29	4 544 698	2 301 315	2 243 383	...	...	...	...	...	...
30 - 34	4 448 043	2 219 685	2 228 358	...	...	...	...	...	...
35 - 39	4 328 081	2 148 457	2 179 624	...	...	...	...	...	...
40 - 44	4 025 390	1 996 585	2 028 805	...	...	...	...	...	...
45 - 49	4 541 513	2 239 582	2 301 931	...	...	...	...	...	...
50 - 54	4 671 514	2 299 522	2 371 992	...	...	...	...	...	...
55 - 59	4 240 050	2 090 524	2 149 526	...	...	...	...	...	...
60 - 64	3 637 148	1 782 067	1 855 081	...	...	...	...	...	...
65 - 69	3 438 188	1 665 214	1 772 974	...	...	...	...	...	...
70 - 74	3 182 572	1 522 470	1 660 102	...	...	...	...	...	...
75 - 79	2 210 116	1 018 015	1 192 101	...	...	...	...	...	...
80 - 84	1 657 805	723 134	934 671	...	...	...	...	...	...
85 - 89	1 021 503	398 605	622 898	...	...	...	...	...	...
90 - 94	446 840	148 066	298 774	...	...	...	...	...	...
95 - 99	120 574	30 218	90 356	...	...	...	...	...	...
100 +	14 469	2 503	11 966	...	...	...	...	...	...
OCEANIA - OCÉANIE									
American Samoa - Samoas américaines[44]									
1 IV 2010 (CDJC)									
Total	55 519	28 164	27 355	...	...	...	...	...	...
0 - 4	6 611	3 417	3 194	...	...	...	...	...	...
5 - 9	6 535	3 470	3 065	...	...	...	...	...	...
10 - 14	6 279	3 214	3 065	...	...	...	...	...	...
15 - 19	6 296	3 218	3 078	...	...	...	...	...	...
20 - 24	3 891	1 944	1 947	...	...	...	...	...	...

Continent, country or area, date, code[a] and age (in years) / Continent, pays ou zone, date, code[a] et âge (en années)	Total			Urban - Urbaine			Rural - Rurale		
	Both sexes Les deux sexes	Male Masculin	Female Féminin	Both sexes Les deux sexes	Male Masculin	Female Féminin	Both sexes Les deux sexes	Male Masculin	Female Féminin
OCEANIA - OCÉANIE									
American Samoa - Samoas américaines[44]									
1 IV 2010 (CDJC)									
25 - 29	3 324	1 670	1 654	...	...	...	...	...	...
30 - 34	3 510	1 726	1 784	...	...	...	...	...	...
35 - 39	3 609	1 845	1 764	...	...	...	...	...	...
40 - 44	3 600	1 793	1 807	...	...	...	...	...	...
45 - 49	3 389	1 673	1 716	...	...	...	...	...	...
50 - 54	2 679	1 335	1 344	...	...	...	...	...	...
55 - 59	2 049	1 011	1 038	...	...	...	...	...	...
60 - 64	1 480	755	725	...	...	...	...	...	...
65 - 69	960	500	460	...	...	...	...	...	...
70 - 74	654	321	333	...	...	...	...	...	...
75 - 79	337	155	182	...	...	...	...	...	...
80 - 84	206	76	130	...	...	...	...	...	...
85 +	110	41	69	...	...	...	...	...	...
Australia - Australie[32]									
1 VII 2018* (ESDJ)									
Total	24 992 860	12 397 401	12 595 459	21 688 081	10 717 350	10 970 731	3 304 779	1 680 051	1 624 728
0	313 544	161 154	152 390	277 186	142 578	134 608	36 358	18 576	17 782
1 - 4	1 268 687	651 711	616 976	1 115 061	572 527	542 534	153 626	79 184	74 442
5 - 9	1 604 449	823 406	781 043	1 390 647	713 630	677 017	213 802	109 776	104 026
10 - 14	1 515 720	779 174	736 546	1 297 794	667 199	630 595	217 926	111 975	105 951
15 - 19	1 491 008	765 106	725 902	1 295 652	664 234	631 418	195 356	100 872	94 484
20 - 24	1 739 976	890 600	849 376	1 584 558	807 558	777 000	155 418	83 042	72 376
25 - 29	1 877 334	940 782	936 552	1 709 957	855 401	854 556	167 377	85 381	81 996
30 - 34	1 862 558	921 260	941 298	1 685 359	832 979	852 380	177 199	88 281	88 918
35 - 39	1 722 345	857 577	864 768	1 542 397	767 963	774 434	179 948	89 614	90 334
40 - 44	1 593 899	793 312	800 587	1 402 644	697 430	705 214	191 255	95 882	95 373
45 - 49	1 670 884	818 996	851 888	1 446 394	707 306	739 088	224 490	111 690	112 800
50 - 54	1 528 997	749 470	779 527	1 302 157	635 497	666 660	226 840	113 973	112 867
55 - 59	1 529 383	749 984	779 399	1 274 642	621 774	652 868	254 741	128 210	126 531
60 - 64	1 359 403	661 441	697 962	1 118 290	538 009	580 281	241 113	123 432	117 681
65 - 69	1 207 000	589 971	617 029	983 765	473 462	510 303	223 235	116 509	106 726
70 - 74	1 017 943	500 024	517 919	833 610	402 666	430 944	184 333	97 358	86 975
75 - 79	700 394	333 699	366 695	580 307	271 936	308 371	120 087	61 763	58 324
80 - 84	485 668	218 466	267 202	411 664	182 018	229 646	74 004	36 448	37 556
85 - 89	309 056	126 240	182 816	265 912	107 060	158 852	43 144	19 180	23 964
90 - 94	149 761	52 338	97 423	130 810	45 038	85 772	18 951	7 300	11 651
95 - 99	40 350	11 537	28 813	35 508	10 125	25 383	4 842	1 412	3 430
100 +	4 501	1 153	3 348	3 767	960	2 807	734	193	541
Cook Islands - Îles Cook									
1 XII 2016 (CDFC)									
Total	17 434	8 520	8 914	...	...	...	...	...	...
0 - 4	1 354	710	644	...	...	...	...	...	...
5 - 9	1 501	768	733	...	...	...	...	...	...
10 - 14	1 441	745	696	...	...	...	...	...	...
15 - 19	1 375	664	711	...	...	...	...	...	...
20 - 24	1 225	569	656	...	...	...	...	...	...
25 - 29	1 153	541	612	...	...	...	...	...	...
30 - 34	1 077	482	595	...	...	...	...	...	...
35 - 39	1 016	483	533	...	...	...	...	...	...
40 - 44	1 121	520	601	...	...	...	...	...	...
45 - 49	1 224	599	625	...	...	...	...	...	...
50 - 54	1 265	642	623	...	...	...	...	...	...
55 - 59	1 043	521	522	...	...	...	...	...	...
60 - 64	834	405	429	...	...	...	...	...	...
65 - 69	696	363	333	...	...	...	...	...	...
70 - 74	482	234	248	...	...	...	...	...	...
75 - 79	353	159	194	...	...	...	...	...	...
80 +	274	115	159	...	...	...	...	...	...
Fiji - Fidji									
17 IX 2017 (CDFC)									
Total	884 887	448 595	436 292	494 252	245 928	248 324	390 635	202 667	187 968
0 - 4	91 897	47 195	44 702	47 904	24 614	23 290	43 993	22 581	21 412

7. Population by age, sex and urban/rural residence: latest available year, 2010 - 2019
Population selon l'âge, le sexe et la résidence, urbaine/rurale : dernière année disponible, 2010 - 2019 (continued - suite)

Continent, country or area, date, code[a] and age (in years) / Continent, pays ou zone, date, code[a] et âge (en années)	Total			Urban - Urbaine			Rural - Rurale		
	Both sexes Les deux sexes	Male Masculin	Female Féminin	Both sexes Les deux sexes	Male Masculin	Female Féminin	Both sexes Les deux sexes	Male Masculin	Female Féminin
OCEANIA - OCÉANIE									
Fiji - Fidji									
17 IX 2017 (CDFC)									
5 - 9	88 295	45 243	43 052	45 436	23 231	22 205	42 859	22 012	20 847
10 - 14	79 596	40 715	38 881	40 784	20 676	20 108	38 812	20 039	18 773
15 - 19	74 088	38 032	36 056	42 045	20 713	21 332	32 043	17 319	14 724
20 - 24	73 616	37 464	36 152	46 942	23 397	23 545	26 674	14 067	12 607
25 - 29	69 308	35 253	34 055	41 756	21 030	20 726	27 552	14 223	13 329
30 - 34	68 818	35 266	33 552	40 741	20 609	20 132	28 077	14 657	13 420
35 - 39	65 150	33 382	31 768	37 684	18 904	18 780	27 466	14 478	12 988
40 - 44	53 514	27 697	25 817	30 590	15 476	15 114	22 924	12 221	10 703
45 - 49	49 504	25 314	24 190	27 872	13 998	13 874	21 632	11 316	10 316
50 - 54	48 610	24 649	23 961	26 585	13 241	13 344	22 025	11 408	10 617
55 - 59	42 008	21 263	20 745	23 113	11 249	11 864	18 895	10 014	8 881
60 - 64	30 615	14 891	15 724	16 744	7 805	8 939	13 871	7 086	6 785
65 - 69	21 328	10 076	11 252	11 469	5 138	6 331	9 859	4 938	4 921
70 - 74	14 148	6 367	7 781	7 342	3 131	4 211	6 806	3 236	3 570
75 +	14 392	5 788	8 604	7 245	2 716	4 529	7 147	3 072	4 075
17 IX 2019 (ESDF)									
Total	889 327	450 927	438 400	...	...	...	...	...	...
0	18 709	9 570	9 139	...	...	...	...	...	...
1 - 4	70 910	36 220	34 691	...	...	...	...	...	...
5 - 9	89 496	45 819	43 677	...	...	...	...	...	...
10 - 14	82 590	42 300	40 290	...	...	...	...	...	...
15 - 19	75 143	38 557	36 586	...	...	...	...	...	...
20 - 24	73 311	37 388	35 923	...	...	...	...	...	...
25 - 29	69 334	35 136	34 198	...	...	...	...	...	...
30 - 34	65 954	33 644	32 310	...	...	...	...	...	...
35 - 39	64 487	32 952	31 535	...	...	...	...	...	...
40 - 44	55 196	28 440	26 756	...	...	...	...	...	...
45 - 49	47 470	24 363	23 108	...	...	...	...	...	...
50 - 54	46 334	23 586	22 748	...	...	...	...	...	...
55 - 59	42 527	21 650	20 877	...	...	...	...	...	...
60 - 64	32 776	16 281	16 495	...	...	...	...	...	...
65 - 69	22 918	10 967	11 952	...	...	...	...	...	...
70 - 74	15 093	6 923	8 170	...	...	...	...	...	...
75 +	17 077	7 134	9 944	...	...	...	...	...	...
French Polynesia - Polynésie française[2]									
1 VII 2018 (ESDJ)									
Total	276 867	140 622	136 245	...	...	...	...	...	...
0	1 870	965	905	...	...	...	...	...	...
1 - 4	15 312	7 849	7 463	...	...	...	...	...	...
5 - 9	21 537	11 202	10 335	...	...	...	...	...	...
10 - 14	21 904	11 188	10 715	...	...	...	...	...	...
15 - 19	22 776	11 668	11 108	...	...	...	...	...	...
20 - 24	19 507	10 011	9 496	...	...	...	...	...	...
25 - 29	21 507	10 741	10 767	...	...	...	...	...	...
30 - 34	22 687	11 210	11 478	...	...	...	...	...	...
35 - 39	20 752	10 388	10 364	...	...	...	...	...	...
40 - 44	19 664	9 941	9 723	...	...	...	...	...	...
45 - 49	19 751	10 116	9 634	...	...	...	...	...	...
50 - 54	18 769	9 675	9 094	...	...	...	...	...	...
55 - 59	15 283	7 933	7 350	...	...	...	...	...	...
60 - 64	12 225	6 367	5 859	...	...	...	...	...	...
65 - 69	8 632	4 403	4 229	...	...	...	...	...	...
70 - 74	6 269	3 154	3 115	...	...	...	...	...	...
75 - 79	4 279	2 082	2 197	...	...	...	...	...	...
80 - 84	2 451	1 072	1 380	...	...	...	...	...	...
85 - 89	1 205	492	713	...	...	...	...	...	...
90 - 94	406	148	259	...	...	...	...	...	...
95 - 99	72	17	55	...	...	...	...	...	...
100 +	8	2	6	...	...	...	...	...	...

7. Population by age, sex and urban/rural residence: latest available year, 2010 - 2019
Population selon l'âge, le sexe et la résidence, urbaine/rurale : dernière année disponible, 2010 - 2019 (continued - suite)

Continent, country or area, date, code[a] and age (in years) / Continent, pays ou zone, date, code[a] et âge (en annèes)	Total			Urban - Urbaine			Rural - Rurale		
	Both sexes Les deux sexes	Male Masculin	Female Féminin	Both sexes Les deux sexes	Male Masculin	Female Féminin	Both sexes Les deux sexes	Male Masculin	Female Féminin
OCEANIA - OCÉANIE									
Guam[44]									
1 VII 2019 (ESDJ)									
Total	168 147	86 541	81 606	...	...	...	...	...	...
0	3 181	1 643	1 538	...	...	...	...	...	...
1 - 4	12 740	6 581	6 159	...	...	...	...	...	...
5 - 9	15 466	8 000	7 466	...	...	...	...	...	...
10 - 14	14 590	7 592	6 998	...	...	...	...	...	...
15 - 19	14 117	7 482	6 635	...	...	...	...	...	...
20 - 24	13 220	7 139	6 081	...	...	...	...	...	...
25 - 29	12 552	6 657	5 895	...	...	...	...	...	...
30 - 34	10 724	5 537	5 187	...	...	...	...	...	...
35 - 39	9 218	4 645	4 573	...	...	...	...	...	...
40 - 44	9 095	4 646	4 449	...	...	...	...	...	...
45 - 49	10 270	5 176	5 094	...	...	...	...	...	...
50 - 54	10 169	5 348	4 821	...	...	...	...	...	...
55 - 59	9 774	5 087	4 687	...	...	...	...	...	...
60 - 64	7 549	3 807	3 742	...	...	...	...	...	...
65 - 69	6 178	3 028	3 150	...	...	...	...	...	...
70 - 74	4 271	2 042	2 229	...	...	...	...	...	...
75 - 79	2 435	1 125	1 310	...	...	...	...	...	...
80 - 84	1 645	664	981	...	...	...	...	...	...
85 - 89	741	266	475	...	...	...	...	...	...
90 - 94	179	65	114	...	...	...	...	...	...
95 - 99	29	9	20	...	...	...	...	...	...
100 +	4	2	2	...	...	...	...	...	...
Kiribati									
7 XI 2015 (CDFC)									
Total	110 136	54 096	56 040	56 388	27 159	29 229	53 748	26 937	26 811
0 - 4	14 393	7 546	6 847	7 140	3 724	3 416	7 253	3 822	3 431
5 - 9	13 600	6 903	6 697	6 470	3 313	3 157	7 130	3 590	3 540
10 - 14	10 445	5 309	5 136	4 700	2 327	2 373	5 745	2 982	2 763
15 - 19	11 676	5 851	5 825	6 290	2 988	3 302	5 386	2 863	2 523
20 - 24	10 319	5 199	5 120	6 137	3 015	3 122	4 182	2 184	1 998
25 - 29	9 672	4 682	4 990	5 468	2 603	2 865	4 204	2 079	2 125
30 - 34	8 012	3 838	4 174	4 356	2 052	2 304	3 656	1 786	1 870
35 - 39	6 584	3 161	3 423	3 422	1 661	1 761	3 162	1 500	1 662
40 - 44	5 091	2 433	2 658	2 555	1 198	1 357	2 536	1 235	1 301
45 - 49	5 707	2 676	3 031	2 724	1 227	1 497	2 983	1 449	1 534
50 - 54	4 905	2 372	2 533	2 483	1 182	1 301	2 422	1 190	1 232
55 - 59	3 321	1 548	1 773	1 694	743	951	1 627	805	822
60 - 64	2 406	1 051	1 355	1 174	494	680	1 232	557	675
65 - 69	1 748	731	1 017	815	322	493	933	409	524
70 - 74	1 238	460	778	551	183	368	687	277	410
75 - 79	608	217	391	241	86	155	367	131	236
80 - 84	267	80	187	109	30	79	158	50	108
85 - 89	109	30	79	42	6	36	67	24	43
90 - 94	24	7	17	10	3	7	14	4	10
95 - 99	11	2	9	7	2	5	4	-	4
100 +	-	-	-	-	-	-	-	-	-
Marshall Islands - Îles Marshall									
3 IV 2011 (CDFC)									
Total	53 158	27 243	25 915	39 205	19 927	19 278	13 953	7 316	6 637
0 - 4	7 743	4 031	3 712	5 617	2 901	2 716	2 126	1 130	996
5 - 9	7 017	3 622	3 395	4 794	2 459	2 335	2 223	1 163	1 060
10 - 14	6 493	3 385	3 108	4 400	2 293	2 107	2 093	1 092	1 001
15 - 19	4 731	2 417	2 314	3 793	1 917	1 876	938	500	438
20 - 24	5 094	2 614	2 480	3 955	2 015	1 940	1 139	599	540
25 - 29	4 404	2 159	2 245	3 288	1 585	1 703	1 116	574	542
30 - 34	3 789	1 876	1 913	2 819	1 387	1 432	970	489	481
35 - 39	3 136	1 587	1 549	2 369	1 197	1 172	767	390	377
40 - 44	2 785	1 419	1 366	2 151	1 083	1 068	634	336	298
45 - 49	2 344	1 189	1 155	1 766	876	890	578	313	265
50 - 54	1 930	1 016	914	1 503	782	721	427	234	193
55 - 59	1 576	815	761	1 167	595	572	409	220	189

7. Population by age, sex and urban/rural residence: latest available year, 2010 - 2019
Population selon l'âge, le sexe et la résidence, urbaine/rurale : dernière année disponible, 2010 - 2019 (continued - suite)

Continent, country or area, date, code[a] and age (in years) / Continent, pays ou zone, date, code[a] et âge (en années)	Total			Urban - Urbaine			Rural - Rurale		
	Both sexes Les deux sexes	Male Masculin	Female Féminin	Both sexes Les deux sexes	Male Masculin	Female Féminin	Both sexes Les deux sexes	Male Masculin	Female Féminin
OCEANIA - OCÉANIE									
Marshall Islands - Îles Marshall									
3 IV 2011 (CDFC)									
60 - 64	1 052	583	469	803	444	359	249	139	110
65 - 69	522	284	238	399	219	180	123	65	58
70 - 74	250	131	119	182	95	87	68	36	32
75 - 79	152	62	90	103	44	59	49	18	31
80 - 84	92	31	61	61	19	42	31	12	19
85 - 89	36	21	15	26	16	10	10	5	5
90 - 94	12	1	11	9	-	9	3	1	2
95 +	-	-	-	-	-	-	-	-	-
Micronesia (Federated States of) - Micronésie (États fédérés de)[96]									
1 VII 2019 (ESDJ)									
Total	*104 468*	*53 017*	*51 450*	...	...	...	...	...	...
0	*2 551*	*1 320*	*1 231*	...	...	...	...	...	...
1 - 4	*9 713*	*4 920*	*4 794*	...	...	...	...	...	...
5 - 9	*12 128*	*6 235*	*5 893*	...	...	...	...	...	...
10 - 14	*12 885*	*6 620*	*6 265*	...	...	...	...	...	...
15 - 19	*12 177*	*6 337*	*5 841*	...	...	...	...	...	...
20 - 24	*9 509*	*4 983*	*4 525*	...	...	...	...	...	...
25 - 29	*7 769*	*3 904*	*3 865*	...	...	...	...	...	...
30 - 34	*6 695*	*3 451*	*3 244*	...	...	...	...	...	...
35 - 39	*6 041*	*2 974*	*3 067*	...	...	...	...	...	...
40 - 44	*5 671*	*2 762*	*2 909*	...	...	...	...	...	...
45 - 49	*5 273*	*2 684*	*2 589*	...	...	...	...	...	...
50 - 54	*4 697*	*2 338*	*2 359*	...	...	...	...	...	...
55 - 59	*3 669*	*1 905*	*1 764*	...	...	...	...	...	...
60 - 64	*2 328*	*1 187*	*1 141*	...	...	...	...	...	...
65 +	*3 361*	*1 399*	*1 963*	...	...	...	...	...	...
Nauru									
1 VII 2016 (ESDF)									
Total	*11 014*	*5 547*	*5 467*	...	...	...	...	...	...
0	*321*	*164*	*157*	...	...	...	...	...	...
1 - 4	*1 324*	*675*	*649*	...	...	...	...	...	...
5 - 9	*1 579*	*854*	*725*	...	...	...	...	...	...
10 - 14	*1 142*	*562*	*579*	...	...	...	...	...	...
15 - 19	*1 012*	*525*	*488*	...	...	...	...	...	...
20 - 24	*836*	*434*	*402*	...	...	...	...	...	...
25 - 29	*930*	*461*	*468*	...	...	...	...	...	...
30 - 34	*900*	*444*	*457*	...	...	...	...	...	...
35 - 39	*723*	*377*	*346*	...	...	...	...	...	...
40 - 44	*562*	*277*	*285*	...	...	...	...	...	...
45 - 49	*443*	*220*	*223*	...	...	...	...	...	...
50 - 54	*452*	*212*	*240*	...	...	...	...	...	...
55 - 59	*343*	*152*	*190*	...	...	...	...	...	...
60 - 64	*242*	*110*	*131*	...	...	...	...	...	...
65 - 69	*127*	*50*	*77*	...	...	...	...	...	...
70 - 74	*40*	*15*	*25*	...	...	...	...	...	...
75 +	*39*	*15*	*24*	...	...	...	...	...	...
New Caledonia - Nouvelle-Calédonie									
1 I 2017 (ESDF)									
Total	*278 495*	*140 000*	*138 495*	...	...	...	...	...	...
0 - 4	*20 587*	*10 481*	*10 106*	...	...	...	...	...	...
5 - 9	*21 295*	*11 009*	*10 286*	...	...	...	...	...	...
10 - 14	*21 505*	*10 922*	*10 583*	...	...	...	...	...	...
15 - 19	*22 963*	*11 621*	*11 342*	...	...	...	...	...	...
20 - 24	*19 937*	*10 329*	*9 608*	...	...	...	...	...	...
25 - 29	*20 738*	*10 338*	*10 400*	...	...	...	...	...	...
30 - 34	*21 487*	*10 760*	*10 727*	...	...	...	...	...	...
35 - 39	*20 717*	*10 255*	*10 462*	...	...	...	...	...	...
40 - 44	*21 555*	*10 853*	*10 702*	...	...	...	...	...	...
45 - 49	*19 744*	*9 795*	*9 949*	...	...	...	...	...	...

7. Population by age, sex and urban/rural residence: latest available year, 2010 - 2019
Population selon l'âge, le sexe et la résidence, urbaine/rurale : dernière année disponible, 2010 - 2019 (continued - suite)

Continent, country or area, date, code[a] and age (in years) Continent, pays ou zone, date, code[a] et âge (en années)	Total			Urban - Urbaine			Rural - Rurale		
	Both sexes Les deux sexes	Male Masculin	Female Féminin	Both sexes Les deux sexes	Male Masculin	Female Féminin	Both sexes Les deux sexes	Male Masculin	Female Féminin
OCEANIA - OCÉANIE									
New Caledonia - Nouvelle-Calédonie									
1 I 2017 (ESDF)									
50 - 54	*17 719*	*8 939*	*8 780*	...	...	...	...	...	...
55 - 59	*13 955*	*7 010*	*6 945*	...	...	...	...	...	...
60 - 64	*11 230*	*5 722*	*5 508*	...	...	...	...	...	...
65 - 69	*8 877*	*4 516*	*4 361*	...	...	...	...	...	...
70 - 74	*6 650*	*3 339*	*3 311*	...	...	...	...	...	...
75 - 79	*4 642*	*2 157*	*2 485*	...	...	...	...	...	...
80 - 84	*2 793*	*1 198*	*1 595*	...	...	...	...	...	...
85 - 89	*1 538*	*607*	*931*	...	...	...	...	...	...
90 - 94	*436*	*119*	*317*	...	...	...	...	...	...
95 +	*127*	*30*	*97*	...	...	...	...	...	...
New Zealand - Nouvelle-Zélande[66]									
1 VII 2018 (ESDJ)									
Total	4 885 570	2 408 890	2 476 680	4 223 710	2 071 350	2 152 360	661 860	337 540	324 320
0	60 220	30 870	29 350	52 500	26 880	25 620	7 730	3 990	3 730
1 - 4	246 290	126 530	119 760	214 390	110 130	104 270	31 890	16 400	15 490
5 - 9	327 240	167 910	159 330	281 220	144 250	136 970	46 020	23 660	22 360
10 - 14	310 950	159 200	151 740	263 170	134 750	128 420	47 780	24 460	23 320
15 - 19	314 160	161 060	153 090	273 550	139 520	134 020	40 610	21 540	19 070
20 - 24	358 260	186 440	171 820	323 780	167 460	156 320	34 480	18 980	15 500
25 - 29	380 050	193 850	186 200	345 970	176 010	169 960	34 080	17 850	16 240
30 - 34	330 720	161 920	168 800	298 490	145 850	152 630	32 230	16 060	16 170
35 - 39	297 660	144 100	153 560	264 360	127 800	136 560	33 300	16 310	16 990
40 - 44	291 120	140 050	151 060	252 110	120 880	131 230	39 010	19 170	19 840
45 - 49	324 420	155 190	169 230	275 290	131 160	144 130	49 130	24 020	25 110
50 - 54	312 930	150 970	161 960	261 360	125 580	135 780	51 570	25 390	26 190
55 - 59	312 600	150 880	161 710	257 510	123 400	134 110	55 090	27 480	27 610
60 - 64	272 010	131 400	140 610	222 290	106 130	116 170	49 720	25 280	24 440
65 - 69	237 180	115 320	121 850	194 770	93 350	101 420	42 410	21 970	20 430
70 - 74	195 330	94 430	100 890	163 380	77 580	85 800	31 940	16 850	15 090
75 - 79	138 330	65 030	73 310	119 400	55 030	64 370	18 930	9 990	8 940
80 - 84	89 370	40 270	49 100	79 910	35 330	44 580	9 460	4 940	4 520
85 - 89	55 710	22 970	32 750	51 150	20 610	30 540	4 570	2 360	2 210
90 +	31 020	10 500	20 520	29 110	9 660	19 450	1 910	840	1 070
Niue - Nioué[86]									
9 III 2017 (CDJC)									
Total	1 591	762	829	...	...	...	...	...	...
0 - 4	135	68	67	...	...	...	...	...	...
5 - 14	312	149	163	...	...	...	...	...	...
15 - 24	160	77	83	...	...	...	...	...	...
25 - 34	220	101	119	...	...	...	...	...	...
35 - 44	182	87	95	...	...	...	...	...	...
45 - 54	192	101	91	...	...	...	...	...	...
55 - 64	178	88	90	...	...	...	...	...	...
65 - 74	114	55	59	...	...	...	...	...	...
75 +	98	36	62	...	...	...	...	...	...
Norfolk Island - Île Norfolk									
9 VIII 2011 (CDFC)									
Total	2 302	1 082	1 220	...	...	...	...	...	...
0 - 4	106	53	53	...	...	...	...	...	...
5 - 9	123	63	60	...	...	...	...	...	...
10 - 14	132	69	63	...	...	...	...	...	...
15 - 19	73	35	38	...	...	...	...	...	...
20 - 24	41	20	21	...	...	...	...	...	...
25 - 29	60	19	41	...	...	...	...	...	...
30 - 34	100	48	52	...	...	...	...	...	...
35 - 39	127	56	71	...	...	...	...	...	...
40 - 44	146	64	82	...	...	...	...	...	...
45 - 49	167	81	86	...	...	...	...	...	...
50 - 54	180	86	94	...	...	...	...	...	...
55 - 59	232	103	129	...	...	...	...	...	...
60 - 64	262	120	142	...	...	...	...	...	...

7. Population by age, sex and urban/rural residence: latest available year, 2010 - 2019
Population selon l'âge, le sexe et la résidence, urbaine/rurale : dernière année disponible, 2010 - 2019 (continued - suite)

Continent, country or area, date, code[a] and age (in years) / Continent, pays ou zone, date, code[a] et âge (en annèes)	Total			Urban - Urbaine			Rural - Rurale		
	Both sexes Les deux sexes	Male Masculin	Female Féminin	Both sexes Les deux sexes	Male Masculin	Female Féminin	Both sexes Les deux sexes	Male Masculin	Female Féminin
OCEANIA - OCÉANIE									
Norfolk Island - Île Norfolk									
9 VIII 2011 (CDFC)									
65 - 69	205	99	106	...	...	...	...	...	...
70 - 74	142	70	72	...	...	...	...	...	...
75 - 79	96	49	47	...	...	...	...	...	...
80 - 84	58	24	34	...	...	...	...	...	...
85 +	52	23	29	...	...	...	...	...	...
Northern Mariana Islands - Îles Mariannes septentrionales									
1 VII 2011 (ESDF)									
Total	*46 050*	*22 153*	*23 897*	...	...	...	...	...	...
0 - 4	*4 852*	*2 495*	*2 357*	...	...	...	...	...	...
5 - 9	*3 622*	*1 883*	*1 739*	...	...	...	...	...	...
10 - 14	*3 500*	*1 971*	*1 529*	...	...	...	...	...	...
15 - 19	*3 802*	*2 121*	*1 681*	...	...	...	...	...	...
20 - 24	*3 398*	*1 607*	*1 791*	...	...	...	...	...	...
25 - 29	*3 831*	*1 050*	*2 781*	...	...	...	...	...	...
30 - 34	*3 696*	*1 008*	*2 688*	...	...	...	...	...	...
35 - 39	*3 211*	*1 550*	*1 661*	...	...	...	...	...	...
40 - 44	*3 584*	*1 858*	*1 726*	...	...	...	...	...	...
45 - 49	*3 738*	*1 967*	*1 771*	...	...	...	...	...	...
50 - 54	*3 441*	*1 824*	*1 617*	...	...	...	...	...	...
55 - 59	*2 270*	*1 260*	*1 010*	...	...	...	...	...	...
60 - 64	*1 440*	*769*	*671*	...	...	...	...	...	...
65 - 69	*794*	*366*	*428*	...	...	...	...	...	...
70 - 74	*416*	*248*	*168*	...	...	...	...	...	...
75 - 79	*239*	*101*	*138*	...	...	...	...	...	...
80 - 84	*147*	*54*	*93*	...	...	...	...	...	...
85 - 89	*53*	*17*	*36*	...	...	...	...	...	...
90 - 94	*14*	*3*	*11*	...	...	...	...	...	...
95 - 99	*1*	*1*	-	...	...	...	...	...	...
100 +	*1*	-	*1*	...	...	...	...	...	...
Palau - Palaos									
13 IV 2015 (CDJC)									
Total	17 661	9 433	8 228	14 209	7 620	6 589	3 452	1 813	1 639
0 - 4	1 200	653	547	962	528	434	238	125	113
5 - 9	1 219	614	605	932	483	449	287	131	156
10 - 14	1 209	636	573	916	489	427	293	147	146
15 - 19	1 201	624	577	975	495	480	226	129	97
20 - 24	1 195	687	508	1 018	587	431	177	100	77
25 - 29	1 217	694	523	1 041	581	460	176	113	63
30 - 34	1 338	759	579	1 163	661	502	175	98	77
35 - 39	1 420	813	607	1 215	701	514	205	112	93
40 - 44	1 501	861	640	1 235	715	520	266	146	120
45 - 49	1 538	820	718	1 248	657	591	290	163	127
50 - 54	1 363	708	655	1 067	549	518	296	159	137
55 - 59	1 126	605	521	856	459	397	270	146	124
60 - 64	851	432	419	641	318	323	210	114	96
65 - 69	554	271	283	414	202	212	140	69	71
70 - 74	314	137	177	233	106	127	81	31	50
75 +	415	119	296	293	89	204	122	30	92
Papua New Guinea - Papouasie-Nouvelle-Guinée[97]									
1 VII 2016 (ESDF)									
Total	*8 151 300*	...	...	...	...	...	...	...	...
0 - 14	*2 970 800*	...	...	...	...	...	...	...	...
15 - 24	*1 641 400*	...	...	...	...	...	...	...	...
25 - 59	*3 177 700*	...	...	...	...	...	...	...	...
60 +	*361 400*	...	...	...	...	...	...	...	...
Pitcairn									
31 XII 2013 (CDJC)									
Total	49	23	26	...	...	...	...	...	...
0 - 17	8	3	5	...	...	...	...	...	...

7. Population by age, sex and urban/rural residence: latest available year, 2010 - 2019
Population selon l'âge, le sexe et la résidence, urbaine/rurale : dernière année disponible, 2010 - 2019 (continued - suite)

Continent, country or area, date, code[a] and age (in years) / Continent, pays ou zone, date, code[a] et âge (en années)	Total			Urban - Urbaine			Rural - Rurale		
	Both sexes Les deux sexes	Male Masculin	Female Féminin	Both sexes Les deux sexes	Male Masculin	Female Féminin	Both sexes Les deux sexes	Male Masculin	Female Féminin
OCEANIA - OCÉANIE									
Pitcairn									
31 XII 2013 (CDJC)									
18 - 40	7	4	3	...	...	...	...	...	...
41 - 64	24	13	11	...	...	...	...	...	...
65 +	10	3	7	...	...	...	...	...	...
Samoa									
7 XI 2016 (CDFC)									
Total	195 979	100 892	95 087	37 391	18 760	18 631	158 588	82 132	76 456
0	5 554	2 870	2 684	964	484	480	4 590	2 386	2 204
1 - 4	22 605	11 731	10 874	3 866	1 985	1 881	18 739	9 746	8 993
5 - 9	25 019	13 151	11 868	4 444	2 312	2 132	20 575	10 839	9 736
10 - 14	21 438	11 056	10 382	3 813	1 942	1 871	17 625	9 114	8 511
15 - 19	18 952	9 968	8 984	3 771	1 870	1 901	15 181	8 098	7 083
20 - 24	15 919	8 184	7 735	3 391	1 699	1 692	12 528	6 485	6 043
25 - 29	13 332	6 700	6 632	2 780	1 363	1 417	10 552	5 337	5 215
30 - 34	11 916	6 051	5 865	2 482	1 230	1 252	9 434	4 821	4 613
35 - 39	10 799	5 564	5 235	2 150	1 115	1 035	8 649	4 449	4 200
40 - 44	10 252	5 333	4 919	1 959	950	1 009	8 293	4 383	3 910
45 - 49	9 774	5 240	4 534	1 843	960	883	7 931	4 280	3 651
50 - 54	8 448	4 336	4 112	1 682	845	837	6 766	3 491	3 275
55 - 59	7 010	3 658	3 352	1 356	683	673	5 654	2 975	2 679
60 - 64	5 225	2 667	2 558	1 039	508	531	4 186	2 159	2 027
65 - 69	3 475	1 702	1 773	689	333	356	2 786	1 369	1 417
70 - 74	2 688	1 267	1 421	513	246	267	2 175	1 021	1 154
75 - 79	1 750	746	1 004	334	136	198	1 416	610	806
80 - 84	1 011	365	646	184	63	121	827	302	525
85 - 89	476	163	313	90	24	66	386	139	247
90 - 94	159	48	111	21	1	20	138	47	91
95 - 99	27	6	21	4	-	4	23	6	17
100 +	6	2	4	1	-	1	5	2	3
Unknown - Inconnu	144	84	60	15	11	4	129	73	56
Solomon Islands - Îles Salomon[98]									
1 VII 2018 (ESDF)									
Total	*666 557*	*340 521*	*326 036*	...	...	...	...	...	...
0 - 4	*82 563*	*42 655*	*39 908*	...	...	...	...	...	...
5 - 9	*81 965*	*42 134*	*39 831*	...	...	...	...	...	...
10 - 14	*79 847*	*41 077*	*38 769*	...	...	...	...	...	...
15 - 19	*71 605*	*36 936*	*34 670*	...	...	...	...	...	...
20 - 24	*58 974*	*30 516*	*28 458*	...	...	...	...	...	...
25 - 29	*51 579*	*26 664*	*24 915*	...	...	...	...	...	...
30 - 34	*48 491*	*24 988*	*23 503*	...	...	...	...	...	...
35 - 39	*42 314*	*21 397*	*20 917*	...	...	...	...	...	...
40 - 44	*37 106*	*18 302*	*18 804*	...	...	...	...	...	...
45 - 49	*31 329*	*15 550*	*15 779*	...	...	...	...	...	...
50 - 54	*22 890*	*11 486*	*11 404*	...	...	...	...	...	...
55 - 59	*18 288*	*9 187*	*9 100*	...	...	...	...	...	...
60 - 64	*13 009*	*6 587*	*6 422*	...	...	...	...	...	...
65 - 69	*10 367*	*5 110*	*5 257*	...	...	...	...	...	...
70 - 74	*7 227*	*3 483*	*3 744*	...	...	...	...	...	...
75 - 79	*4 886*	*2 430*	*2 455*	...	...	...	...	...	...
80 +	*4 117*	*2 020*	*2 098*	...	...	...	...	...	...
Tokelau - Tokélaou[99]									
12 XII 2019 (ESDF)									
Total	1 647	813	834	...	...	...	...	...	...
0 - 4	161	80	81	...	...	...	...	...	...
5 - 9	173	86	87	...	...	...	...	...	...
10 - 14	187	106	81	...	...	...	...	...	...
15 - 19	140	68	72	...	...	...	...	...	...
20 - 24	139	74	65	...	...	...	...	...	...
25 - 29	118	58	60	...	...	...	...	...	...
30 - 34	102	42	60	...	...	...	...	...	...
35 - 39	107	53	54	...	...	...	...	...	...
40 - 44	88	41	47	...	...	...	...	...	...
45 - 49	91	53	38	...	...	...	...	...	...

7. Population by age, sex and urban/rural residence: latest available year, 2010 - 2019
Population selon l'âge, le sexe et la résidence, urbaine/rurale : dernière année disponible, 2010 - 2019 (continued - suite)

Continent, country or area, date, code[a] and age (in years) / Continent, pays ou zone, date, code[a] et âge (en années)	Total			Urban - Urbaine			Rural - Rurale		
	Both sexes Les deux sexes	Male Masculin	Female Féminin	Both sexes Les deux sexes	Male Masculin	Female Féminin	Both sexes Les deux sexes	Male Masculin	Female Féminin
OCEANIA - OCÉANIE									
Tokelau - Tokélaou[99]									
12 XII 2019 (ESDF)									
50 - 54	98	42	56	...	...	...	...	...	...
55 - 59	73	28	45	...	...	...	...	...	...
60 - 64	60	32	28	...	...	...	...	...	...
65 - 69	44	25	19	...	...	...	...	...	...
70 - 74	25	11	14	...	...	...	...	...	...
75 - 79	21	10	11	...	...	...	...	...	...
80 - 84	13	2	11	...	...	...	...	...	...
85 - 89	6	2	4	...	...	...	...	...	...
90 +	1	-	1	...	...	...	...	...	...
Tonga									
30 XI 2016 (CDFC)									
Total	100 651	50 255	50 396	23 221	11 529	11 692	77 430	38 726	38 704
0 - 4	12 499	6 440	6 059	2 648	1 357	1 291	9 851	5 083	4 768
5 - 9	12 153	6 417	5 736	2 557	1 351	1 206	9 596	5 066	4 530
10 - 14	11 882	6 139	5 743	2 518	1 244	1 274	9 364	4 895	4 469
15 - 19	10 502	5 449	5 053	2 374	1 246	1 128	8 128	4 203	3 925
20 - 24	8 234	4 106	4 128	2 070	1 029	1 041	6 164	3 077	3 087
25 - 29	6 629	3 162	3 467	1 762	888	874	4 867	2 274	2 593
30 - 34	6 521	2 994	3 527	1 641	790	851	4 880	2 204	2 676
35 - 39	5 645	2 704	2 941	1 368	641	727	4 277	2 063	2 214
40 - 44	5 189	2 473	2 716	1 209	577	632	3 980	1 896	2 084
45 - 49	5 181	2 600	2 581	1 220	605	615	3 961	1 995	1 966
50 - 54	4 150	2 129	2 021	1 012	519	493	3 138	1 610	1 528
55 - 59	3 254	1 571	1 683	803	369	434	2 451	1 202	1 249
60 - 64	2 696	1 297	1 399	628	301	327	2 068	996	1 072
65 - 69	2 030	968	1 062	474	215	259	1 556	753	803
70 - 74	1 601	735	866	345	154	191	1 256	581	675
75 - 79	1 250	575	675	269	121	148	981	454	527
80 - 84	725	315	410	175	70	105	550	245	305
85 - 89	358	127	231	78	23	55	280	104	176
90 - 94	99	25	74	27	5	22	72	20	52
95 - 99	10	5	5	2	1	1	8	4	4
100 +	2	1	1	-	-	-	2	1	1
Unknown - Inconnu	41	23	18	41	23	18	-	-	-
Tuvalu									
1 VII 2016 (ESDF)									
Total	*11 153*	...	...	...	...	...	...	...	...
0 - 4	*1 345*	...	...	...	...	...	...	...	...
5 - 9	*1 102*	...	...	...	...	...	...	...	...
10 - 14	*1 041*	...	...	...	...	...	...	...	...
15 - 19	*1 177*	...	...	...	...	...	...	...	...
20 - 24	*1 068*	...	...	...	...	...	...	...	...
25 - 29	*960*	...	...	...	...	...	...	...	...
30 - 34	*670*	...	...	...	...	...	...	...	...
35 - 39	*430*	...	...	...	...	...	...	...	...
40 - 44	*485*	...	...	...	...	...	...	...	...
45 - 49	*638*	...	...	...	...	...	...	...	...
50 - 54	*693*	...	...	...	...	...	...	...	...
55 - 59	*605*	...	...	...	...	...	...	...	...
60 - 64	*387*	...	...	...	...	...	...	...	...
65 - 69	*187*	...	...	...	...	...	...	...	...
70 - 74	*172*	...	...	...	...	...	...	...	...
75 - 79	*114*	...	...	...	...	...	...	...	...
80 +	*79*	...	...	...	...	...	...	...	...
Vanuatu[100]									
7 XI 2016 (CDFC)									
Total	272 459	138 265	134 194	67 749	34 506	33 243	204 710	103 759	100 951
0	6 699	3 367	3 332	1 491	708	783	5 208	2 659	2 549
1 - 4	32 237	16 805	15 432	6 793	3 546	3 247	25 444	13 259	12 185
5 - 9	37 148	19 276	17 872	7 344	3 752	3 592	29 804	15 524	14 280
10 - 14	29 846	15 560	14 286	5 972	3 069	2 903	23 874	12 491	11 383
15 - 19	25 902	13 207	12 695	6 844	3 372	3 472	19 058	9 835	9 223
20 - 24	24 862	11 738	13 124	7 983	3 921	4 062	16 879	7 817	9 062

7. Population by age, sex and urban/rural residence: latest available year, 2010 - 2019
Population selon l'âge, le sexe et la résidence, urbaine/rurale : dernière année disponible, 2010 - 2019 (continued - suite)

Continent, country or area, date, code[a] and age (in years) / Continent, pays ou zone, date, code[a] et âge (en annèes)	Total			Urban - Urbaine			Rural - Rurale		
	Both sexes Les deux sexes	Male Masculin	Female Féminin	Both sexes Les deux sexes	Male Masculin	Female Féminin	Both sexes Les deux sexes	Male Masculin	Female Féminin
OCEANIA - OCÉANIE									
Vanuatu[100]									
7 XI 2016 (CDFC)									
25 - 29	23 031	10 986	12 045	6 908	3 406	3 502	16 123	7 580	8 543
30 - 34	18 067	8 909	9 158	5 261	2 658	2 603	12 806	6 251	6 555
35 - 39	16 233	8 148	8 085	4 505	2 307	2 198	11 728	5 841	5 887
40 - 44	13 251	6 726	6 525	3 793	1 976	1 817	9 458	4 750	4 708
45 - 49	11 833	6 125	5 708	3 387	1 751	1 636	8 446	4 374	4 072
50 - 54	9 329	4 756	4 573	2 582	1 354	1 228	6 747	3 402	3 345
55 - 59	7 227	3 792	3 435	1 915	1 049	866	5 312	2 743	2 569
60 - 64	5 357	2 832	2 525	1 202	665	537	4 155	2 167	1 988
65 - 69	4 010	2 089	1 921	743	407	336	3 267	1 682	1 585
70 - 74	2 787	1 521	1 266	440	231	209	2 347	1 290	1 057
75 - 79	1 909	1 069	840	229	152	77	1 680	917	763
80 - 84	1 049	516	533	116	59	57	933	457	476
85 - 89	813	407	406	83	39	44	730	368	362
90 - 94	249	120	129	24	10	14	225	110	115
95 - 99	194	90	104	14	8	6	180	82	98
100 +	426	226	200	120	66	54	306	160	146
Unknown - Inconnu	202	111	91	...	...	...	...	...	...
Wallis and Futuna Islands - Îles Wallis et Futuna									
22 VII 2013 (CDFC)									
Total	12 197	5 927	6 270	...	...	...	...	...	...
0 - 4	997	507	490	...	...	...	...	...	...
5 - 9	1 136	560	576	...	...	...	...	...	...
10 - 14	1 297	687	610	...	...	...	...	...	...
15 - 19	1 168	615	553	...	...	...	...	...	...
20 - 24	583	257	326	...	...	...	...	...	...
25 - 29	600	266	334	...	...	...	...	...	...
30 - 34	719	315	404	...	...	...	...	...	...
35 - 39	864	398	466	...	...	...	...	...	...
40 - 44	922	434	488	...	...	...	...	...	...
45 - 49	762	354	408	...	...	...	...	...	...
50 - 54	761	344	417	...	...	...	...	...	...
55 - 59	669	352	317	...	...	...	...	...	...
60 - 64	571	310	261	...	...	...	...	...	...
65 - 69	462	238	224	...	...	...	...	...	...
70 - 74	309	153	156	...	...	...	...	...	...
75 - 79	201	82	119	...	...	...	...	...	...
80 - 84	111	35	76	...	...	...	...	...	...
85 - 89	50	17	33	...	...	...	...	...	...
90 - 94	15	3	12	...	...	...	...	...	...
95 +	-	-	-	...	...	...	...	...	...

FOOTNOTES - NOTES

Italics: estimates which are less reliable. - Italiques : estimations moins sûres.

* Provisional. - Données provisoires.

[a] 'Code' indicates the source of data, as follows:
CDFC - Census, de facto, complete tabulation
CDFS - Census, de facto, sample tabulation
CDJC - Census, de jure, complete tabulation
CDJS - Census, de jure, sample tabulation
SSDF - Sample survey, de facto
SSDJ - Sample survey, de jure
ESDF - Estimates, de facto
ESDJ - Estimates, de jure

Le 'Code' indique la source des données, comme suit :
CDFC - Recensement, population de fait, tabulation complète
CDFS - Recensement, population de fait, tabulation par sondage
CDJC - Recensement, population de droit, tabulation complète
CDJS - Recensement, population de droit, tabulation par sondage
SSDF - Enquête par sondage, population de fait
SSDJ - Enquête par sondage, population de droit
ESDF - Estimations, population de fait
ESDJ - Estimations, population de droit

[1] Data refer to national projections. - Les données se réfèrent aux projections nationales.
[2] Postcensal estimates. - Estimations post censitaires.
[3] Projections based on the 2013 Population Census. - Projections fondées sur le recensement de la population de 2013.
[4] Based on the results of the 2011 Population Census. - Basé sur les résultats du recencement de la population de 2011.
[5] Unrevised data. - Les données n'ont pas été révisées.
[6] Source: Population projections and estimates of priority targets for the various health programs and interventions, National Institute of Statistics (2016). - Source : Projections démographiques et estimations des cibles prioritaires des différents programmes et interventions de sante, Institut National de la Statistique (2016).

[7] Based on the results of the 2014 Population Census. - D'après les résultats du recensement de la population de 2014.
[8] Estimates or projections based on the 2015 population census. - Estimations ou projections fondées sur les résultats du recensement de la population de 2015.
[9] Estimates based on the 2000 quick population count results and 1995, 2002 and 2010 Eritrea Demographic and Health Surveys. - Des estimations fondées sur le dénombrement rapide de la population de 2000 et sur les enquêtes érythréennes de la démographie et de la santé de 1995, 2002 et 2010.
[10] Data refer to national projections based on 2007 census. - Les données sont des projections nationales d'après les résultats du recensement de la population de 2007.
[11] Estimates considering also the results of the 2007 Population Census. - Estimations en prennant en considération les résultats du recensement de la population de 2007.
[12] Source: Integrated Household Survey (IHS) 2015/2016. - Source: Enquête intégrée auprès des ménages (IHS) 2015/2016.
[13] Data based on the 2010 Population Census. - Les données sont fondées sur le recensement de la population de 2010.
[14] Population in households only. Postcensal estimates. - Population dans les ménages seulement. Estimations post censitaires.
[15] Post-censal estimates based on the 2009 Population Census. - Les estimations post-censitaire fondées sur le recensement de la population de 2009.
[16] Data refer to Libyan nationals only. - Les données se raportent aux nationaux libyens seulement.
[17] Unrevised data. Data refer to projections based on the 1993 Population Census. - Les données n'ont pas été révisées. Les données se réfèrent aux projections basées sur le recensement de la population de 1993.
[18] Projections considering also the results of the 2009 Population Census. - Projections en prennant en considération les résultats du recensement de la population de 2009.
[19] Excludes the islands of St. Brandon and Agalega. - Non compris les îles St. Brandon et Agalega.
[20] Data from the main operation. - Données de l'opération principale.
[21] Projections based on the results of national survey on population and health conducted between 2010 and 2011, and especially population and housing census 2014. - Des projections de la population fondées sur les résultats de l'enquête nationale de la population et de la santé réalisée entre 2010 et 2011 et, surtout, du recensement général de la population et de l'habitat de 2014.
[22] Projections based on the 2012 Population Census. - Projections fondées sur le recensement de la population de 2012.
[23] Data are projections based on the 2006 Population Census. - Projections fondées sur le recensement de la population de 2006.
[24] Data are projections based on the 2008 Population and Housing Census. - Projection basée sur le recensement 2008 de la population et des logements.
[25] Data refer to total resident population, Saint Helenian and other nationalities. - Les données concernent la population résidente totale, originaire de Sainte-Hélène ou possédant une autre nationalité.
[26] Data for urban and rural do not add up to the total; reason for discrepancy not ascertained. - La somme des données pour la résidence urbaine et rurale n'est pas égale au total; on ne sait pas comment s'explique la divergence.
[27] The urban area is reconfigured by extending the urban agglomeration of Lomé to include all the prefecture of Golfe and the new prefecture of Agoènyvé. - L'espace urbaine a été reconstitué par l'extension de l'agglomération de Lomé à toute la préfecture du Golfe et à la nouvelle préfecture d'Agoènyvé.
[28] Projections based on the 2002 Population Census. - Projections fondées sur le recensement de la population de 2002.
[29] Data for urban and rural do not add up to the total; reason for discrepancy not ascertained. Projections based on the 2012 Population Census. - La somme des données pour la résidence urbaine et rurale n'est pas égale au total; on ne sait pas comment s'explique la divergence. Projections fondées sur le recensement de la population de 2012.
[30] Data refers to resident population adjusted for the undercount of 18 per cent and including the institutional population. - Les données concernent la population résidente, y compris la population des institutions, et ont été ajustées pour tenir compte du sous-dénombrement estimé à 18 p. 100.
[31] Bermuda is 100 per cent urban. - 100 pour cent de la population des Bermudes est urbaine.
[32] Based on the results of the 2016 Population Census. - Basé sur les résultats du recencement de la population de 2016.
[33] To ensure confidentiality, the values, including totals are randomly rounded either up or down to a multiple of '5' or '10.' As a result, when these data are summed or grouped, the total value may not match the individual values since totals and sub-totals are independently rounded. Similarly, percentages, which are calculated on rounded data, may not necessarily add up to 100%. - À des fins de confidentialité, les chiffres, y compris les totaux, sont aléatoirement arrondis au multiple de 5 ou de 10 inférieur ou supérieur. Par conséquent, lorsque ces chiffres sont additionnés, le total peut ne pas correspondre à la somme des valeurs individuelles, dans la mesure où les totaux et les totaux partiels sont arrondis indépendamment. De même, la somme des pourcentages, qui sont calculés à partir des données arrondies, peut ne pas correspondre à 100 %.
[34] Adjusted for census net undercoverage (including adjustment for incompletely enumerated Indian reserves). Postcensal estimates. - Ajusté pour la sous-estimation du recensement (y compris les réservations en Inde incomplètement énumérées). Estimations post censitaires.
[35] Based on the national household survey of 2019. - D'après l'enquête nationale auprès des ménages de 2019.
[36] Population statistics are compiled from registers. - Les statistiques de la population sont compilées à partir des registres.
[37] Excluding data for Saint Barthélémy and Saint Martin. - Non compris les données pour Saint Barthélémy et Saint Martin.
[38] Projections produced by l'Institut Haïtien de Statistique et d'Informatique (IHSI) and the Latin American and Caribbean Demographic Centre (CELADE) - Population Division of ECLAC. - Les données sont projections produits par l'Institut Haïtien de Statistique et d'Informatique (IHSI) et le centre démographique de l'Amérique latine et les Caraïbes - Division de la population de la CEPALC.
[39] Including an estimation of 1 334 585 persons corresponding to 448 195 housing units without information of the occupants. - Y compris une estimation de 1 334 585 personnes correspondant aux 448 195 unités d'habitation sans information sur les occupants.
[40] The population projections of CONAPO (National Population Council). - Les projections démographiques de la CONAPO (Conseil national de la population).
[41] Data refer to the intercensal population count. - Les données se réfèrent au dénombrement intercensitaire de la population.
[42] Including armed forces stationed in the area. Postcensal estimates. - Y compris les militaires en garnison sur le territoire. Estimations post censitaires.
[43] Excluding U.S. Armed Forces overseas and civilian U.S. citizens whose usual place of residence is outside the United States. Postcensal estimates. - Non compris les militaires américains à l'étranger et les civils américains dont le lieu de résidence habituel est en dehors des États-Unis. Estimations post censitaires.
[44] Including armed forces stationed in the area. - Y compris les militaires en garnison sur le territoire.
[45] Data include persons in remote areas, military personnel outside the country, merchant seamen at sea, civilian seasonal workers outside the country, and other civilians outside the country, and exclude nomads, foreign military, civilian aliens temporarily in the country, transients on ships and Indian jungle population. Data refer to national projections. - Y compris les personnes vivant dans des régions éloignées, le personel militaire en dehors du pays, les marins marchands, les ouvriers saisonniers en dehors du pays, et autres civils en dehors du pays, et non compris les nomades, les militaires étrangers, les étrangers civils temporairement dans le pays, les transiteurs sur des bateaux et les Indiens de la jungle. Les données se réfèrent aux projections nationales.
[46] Estimates or projections based on the 2017 Population Census. - Estimations ou projections fondées sur le recensement de la population de 2017.
[47] Data are revised projections taking into consideration also the results of the 2018 census. - Les données sont des projections révisées tenant compte également des résultats du recensement de 2018.
[48] Excludes nomadic Indian tribes. Data based on the 2010 Population Census. - Non compris les tribus d'Indiens nomades. Les données sont fondées sur le recensement de la population de 2010.
[49] A dispute exists between the governments of Argentina and the United Kingdom of Great Britain and Northern Ireland concerning sovereignty over the Falkland Islands (Malvinas). - La souveraineté sur les îles Falkland (Malvinas) fait l'objet d'un différend entre le Gouvernement argentin et le Gouvernement du Royaume-Uni de Grande-Bretagne et d'Irlande du Nord.
[50] Figures for male and female may not add up to the total, since they do not include the category "Unknown". - La somme des chiffres indiqués pour les sexes masculin et féminin peut n'être pas égale au total parce qu'elle n'inclut pas la catégorie " inconnue ".
[51] Estimates or projections considering also the results of the 2012 Population Census. - Estimations ou projections en prennant en considération les résultats du recensement de la population de 2012.
[52] Source: INEI – National population estimates and projections from bulletin No. 24 published in July 2019. - Source : INEI - Estimations et projections nationales de la population, publiées dans le bulletin numéro 24 , juillet 2019.
[53] For operational purposes, population centers with 2,500 and more inhabitants are considered as urban area and less than 2,500 are considered as rural area. - À des fins opérationnelles, les centres de population comptant 2 500 habitants ou plus sont considérés comme zones urbaines, ceux qui en comptent moins de 2 500 comme zones rurales.

[54] Data refer to the settled population based on the 1979 Population Census and the latest household prelisting. The refugees of Afghanistan in Iran, Pakistan, and an estimated 1.5 million nomads, are not included. - Les données se rapportent à la population stationnaire sur la base du recensement de 1979 et du recensement préliminaire des logements le plus récent. Sont exclus les réfugiés d'Afghanistan en Iran et au Pakistan et les nomades estimés à 1,5 million.

[55] Excluding 8408 tourists and foreigners. - À l'exclusion de 8 408 touristes et étrangers.

[56] Source: 2016 Population and Housing Census Update. - Source : Révision des chiffres du recensement de la population et des logements de 2016.

[57] Excluding foreign diplomatic personnel and their dependants. Data based on the 2008 Population Census. - Non compris le personnel diplomatique étranger et les membres de leur famille les accompagnant. Données fondées sur le recensement de population de 2008.

[58] For statistical purposes, the data for China do not include those for the Hong Kong Special Administrative Region (Hong Kong SAR), Macao Special Administrative Region (Macao SAR) and Taiwan province of China. - Pour la présentation des statistiques, les données pour la Chine ne comprennent pas la Région Administrative Spéciale de Hong Kong (Hong Kong RAS), la Région Administrative Spéciale de Macao (Macao RAS) et Taïwan province de Chine.

[59] Data exclude 2.3 million servicemen, 4.65 million persons with permanent resident status difficult to define, and 0.12 per cent undercount based on the post enumeration survey. - Les données ne comprennent pas 2,3 millions de militaires, 4,65 millions de personnes ayant le statut de résident permanent mais difficiles à définir, et des lacunes estimées à 0,12 pour cent sur la base de l'enquête de vérification du recensement.

[60] Because of rounding, totals are not in all cases the sum of the respective components. Data have been adjusted on the basis of the Population Census of 2010. - Les chiffres étant arrondis, les totaux ne correspondent pas toujours rigoureusement à la somme des composants respectifs. Les données ont été ajustées à partir des résultats du recensement de la population de 2010.

[61] Data refer to government controlled areas. - Les données se rapportent aux zones contrôlées par le Gouvernement.

[62] Includes data for the Indian-held part of Jammu and Kashmir, the final status of which has not yet been determined. - Y compris les données pour la partie du Jammu et du Cachemire occupée par l'Inde dont le statut définitif n'a pas encore été déterminé.

[63] Data are based on the publication: "Indonesia Population Projection 2015-2045" - Les données sont basées sur la publication : << Indonesia Population Projection 2015-2045 >>

[64] Data refer to the Iranian Year which begins on 21 March and ends on 20 March of the following year. - Les données concernent l'année iranienne, qui commence le 21 mars et se termine le 20 mars de l'année suivante.

[65] Includes data for East Jerusalem and Israeli residents in certain other territories under occupation by Israeli military forces since June 1967. Data refer to Israeli citizens and permanent residents who are listed in the Population Register. - Y compris les données pour Jérusalem-Est et les résidents israéliens dans certains autres territoires occupés depuis 1967 par les forces armées israéliennes. Les données se rapportent aux citoyens israéliens et aux résidents permanents qui sont répertoriés dans le registre de la population.

[66] Because of rounding, totals are not in all cases the sum of the respective components. - Les chiffres étant arrondis, les totaux ne correspondent pas toujours rigoureusement à la somme des composants respectifs.

[67] Excluding diplomatic personnel outside the country and foreign military and civilian personnel and their dependants stationed in the area. - Non compris le personnel diplomatique hors du pays ni les militaires et agents civils étrangers en poste sur le territoire et les membres de leur famille les accompagnant.

[68] Because of rounding, totals are not in all cases the sum of the respective components. Estimates or projections based on the 2015 population census. - Les chiffres étant arrondis, les totaux ne correspondent pas toujours rigoureusement à la somme des composants respectifs. Estimations ou projections fondées sur les résultats du recensement de la population de 2015.

[69] Excluding data for Jordanian territory under occupation since June 1967 by Israeli military forces. - Non compris les données pour le territoire jordanien occupé depuis juin 1967 par les forces armées israéliennes.

[70] Data refer to resident population. - Les données concernent la population résidente.

[71] Data refer to annual average population. - Les données correspondent à la population annuelle moyenne.

[72] Estimates based on the adjusted results of the Population and Housing Census of 2010. - Les estimations sont fondée sur les résultats ajustées du recensement de la population et de l'habitat de 2010.

[73] Based on the results of the 2014 Population Census. Data refer to resident population which includes resident Maldivians and resident foreigners. - D'après les résultats du recensement de la population de 2014. Les données concernent la population résidente, qui comprend les Maldiviens et les étrangers.

[74] Urban refers to 170 out of 254 towns and Rural refers to 62 out of 158 townships. - « Urbain » se rapporte à 170 des 254 villes, « rural » à 62 des 158 cantons.

[75] Data refer to registered population data from Royal Oman Police. - Les données portent sur la population enregistrée par la police royale de l'Oman.

[76] Excluding 2134 Filipinos in Philippine Embassies, Consulates and Missions Abroad. - Excepté 2134 Philippins travaillant dans les ambassades, les consulats et les missions des Philippines à l'étranger.

[77] Data refer to resident population which comprises Singapore citizens and permanent residents. Data exclude residents who have been away from Singapore for a continuous period of 12 months or longer as at the reference date. - Les données se rapportent à la population résidente composé des citoyens de Singapour et des résidents permanents. Non compris les résidents hors de Singapour pour une période ininterrompue de 12 mois ou plus avant de la date de référence.

[78] Data for urban include population in refugee camps. - Les données pour la population urbaine comprennent la population dans les camps réfugiés.

[79] Including Palestinian refugees. - Y compris les réfugiés de Palestine.

[80] Data based on Address Based Population Registration System. - Les données sont basées sur le registre national de la population basé sur l'adresse.

[81] Excluding Faeroe Islands and Greenland shown separately, if available. Population statistics are compiled from registers. - Non compris les Iles Féroé et le Groenland, qui font l'objet de rubriques distinctes, si disponible. Les statistiques de la population sont compilées à partir des registres.

[82] The total number may include 'Unknown residence', but the categories urban and rural do not. - Le nombre total peut inclure les personnes dont la résidence n'est pas connue, à l'inverse des catégories de population urbaine et rurale.

[83] Excluding Åland Islands. - Non compris les Îles d'Åland.

[84] Excluding diplomatic personnel outside the country and including members of alien armed forces not living in military camps and foreign diplomatic personnel not living in embassies or consulates. - Non compris le personnel diplomatique hors du pays et y compris les militaires étrangers ne vivant pas dans des camps militaires et le personnel diplomatique étranger ne vivant pas dans les ambassades ou les consulats.

[85] Excluding military personnel, visitors and transients. - Non compris les militaires, ni les visiteurs et transients.

[86] Data refer to usual resident population. - Les données se réfèrent à la population résidente habituelle.

[87] Data refer to registered resident population. - Les données concernent la population enregistrée résidente.

[88] Including residents temporarily outside the country. Population statistics are compiled from registers. - Y compris les résidents se trouvant temporairement hors du pays. Les statistiques de la population sont compilées à partir des registres.

[89] Excludes non-residents present in country at time of census (visitors, foreigners temporarily residing in country, etc.). Tiraspol, Bender, Slobozia, Ribnita, Camenca Yrigoricpol/Grigoriopol are districts from Transnistria where the census was not conducted. - Exclue les non-résidents présents dans le pays au moment du recensement (visiteurs, étrangers résidant temporairement dans le pays, etc.). Tiraspol, Bender, Slobozia, Ribnita, Camenca, Yrigoricpol/Grigoriopol sont des districts de la Transnistrie où le recensement n'a pas eu lieu.

[90] Excluding Transnistria and the municipality of Bender. Data refer to usual resident population based on the 2014 Census. Tiraspol, Bender, Slobozia, Ribnita, Camenca Yrigoricpol/Grigoriopol are districts from Transnistria where the 2014 census was not conducted. - Les données ne tiennent pas compte de l'information sur la Transnistria et la municipalité de Bender. Les données se rapportent à la population habituellement résidente et sont fondées sur le recensement de 2014. Tiraspol, Bender, Slobozia, Ribnita, Camenca, Yrigoricpol/Grigoriopol sont des districts de la Transnistrie où le recensement n'a pas eu lieu.

[91] Excludes data for Kosovo and Metohia. Based on the results of the 2011 Population Census. - Sans les données pour le Kosovo et Metohie. Basé sur les résultats du recencement de la population de 2011.

[92] Population statistics are compiled from registers. Data refer to registered resident population. - Les statistiques de la population sont compilées à partir des registres. Les données concernent la population enregistrée résidente.

[93] Data refer to legal resident population. - Les données concernent la population légalement résidente.

[94] The Government of Ukraine has informed the United Nations that it is not in a position to provide statistical data concerning the Autonomous Republic of Crimea and the city of Sevastopol. - Le gouvernement Ukrainien a informé l'ONU qu'il n'est pas en mesure de fournir des données statistiques concernant la République autonome de Crimée et la ville de Sébastopol.

[95] Excluding Channel Islands (Guernsey and Jersey) and Isle of Man, shown separately, if available. - Non compris les îles Anglo-Normandes (Guernesey et Jersey) et l'île de Man, qui font l'objet de rubriques distinctes, si disponible.

[96] Based on the 2010 Population and Housing Census and 2013/2014 Household Income and Expenditure Survey. - Données fondées sur les résultat du recensement de la population et de l'habitat de 2010, et ceux de l'enquête auprès des ménages sur des revenus et des dépenses de 2013/2014.

[97] Estimates are prepared by the Secretariat of the Pacific Community based on the last population and housing census. - Les estimations sont preparées par le Secrétariat de la Communauté du Pacifique à partir des résultats du dernier recensement de la population et de l'habitat.

[98] Projections based on adjusted 2009 census counts. - Projections fondées à partir des comptes rajustés du recensement de 2009.

[99] Data refers to 2019 Tokelau population count. - Les données se rapportent au dénombrement de la population tokélaouane de 2019.

[100] Data is based on mini-census taken in 2016. - Selon le mini-recensement de 2016.

Table 8 - *Demographic Yearbook 2019*

Table 8 presents population of capital cities and cities of 100 000 or more inhabitants for the latest available year between 2000 and 2019.

Description of variables: Since the way in which cities are delimited differs from one country or area to another, the table not only presents data for the so-called city proper, but also for the urban agglomeration, if available.

City proper is defined as a locality with legally fixed boundaries and an administratively recognized urban status, usually characterized by some form of local government.

Urban agglomeration has been defined as comprising the city or town proper and also the suburban fringe or densely settled territory lying outside of, but adjacent to, the city boundaries.

For some countries or areas, however, the data relate to entire administrative divisions known, for example, as shi or municipalities (municipios) which are composed of a populated centre and adjoining territory, some of which may contain other, often separate urban localities or may be distinctively rural in character. For this group of countries or areas the type of civil division is given in a footnote.

The surface area of the city or urban agglomeration is presented, when available.

City names are presented in the original language of the country or area in which the cities are located. In cases where the original names are not in the Roman alphabet, they have been romanized. Cities are listed in English alphabetical order.

Capital cities are shown in the table regardless of their population size. The names of the capital cities are printed in capital letters. The designation of any specific city as a capital city is as reported by the country or area.

The table also covers cities whose urban agglomeration's population exceeds 100 000; that is, while the urban agglomeration should have a population of 100 000 or more to be included in the table, the city proper may be of a smaller population size.

The reference date of each population figure appears in the left-most column of the table. Estimates based on results of sample surveys and city censuses or from other sources are explained by the 'code' also appearing in the left-most column of the table. The codes are explained at the end of the table.

Reliability of data: Specific information is generally not available on the reliability of the estimates of the population of cities or urban agglomerations presented in this table.

In the absence of such quality assessment, data from population censuses, sample surveys and city censuses are considered reliable and, therefore, set in Roman type. Other estimates are considered reliable if they are based on a complete census (or a sample survey), and have been adjusted by a continuous population register or adjusted on the basis of the calculated balance of births, deaths, and migration.

Limitations: Statistics on the population of capital cities and cities of 100 000 or more inhabitants are subject to the same qualifications as have been set forth for population statistics in general as discussed in section 3 of the Technical Notes.

International comparability of data on city population is limited by variations in national concepts and definitions. Although an effort is made to reduce the sources of non-comparability somewhat by presenting the data for both city proper and urban agglomeration, many serious problems of comparability remain.

Data presented in the "city proper" column for some countries represent an urban administrative area legally distinguished from surrounding rural territory, while for other countries these data represent a commune or an equally small administrative unit. In still other countries, the administrative units may be relatively extensive and thereby include considerable territories beyond the urban centre itself.

City data are also especially affected by whether the data refer to *de facto* or *de jure* population, as well as variations among countries in how each of these concepts is applied. With reference to the total population, the difference between the *de facto* and *de jure* population is discussed at length in section 3.1.1 of the Technical Notes.

Data on city populations based on intercensal estimates present additional problems: comparability is impaired by the different methods used in making the estimates, and by the loss of precision in applying to selected segments of the population methods best suited for the whole population. For example, it is far more difficult to apply the component method of estimating population growth to cities than it is to the entire country.

Births and deaths occurring in the cities do not all originate in the population present in or resident of that area. Therefore, the use of natural increase to estimate the probable size of the city population is a potential source of error. Internal migration is another component of population change that cannot be measured with accuracy in many areas. Because of these factors, estimates in this table may be less valuable in general and in particular limited for purposes of international comparison.

City data, even when set in Roman type, are often not as reliable as estimates for the total population of the country or area. Furthermore, because the sources of these data include censuses (national or city), surveys and estimates, the years to which they refer vary widely. In addition, because city boundaries may alter over time, comparisons covering different years should be carried out with caution.

Earlier data: Population of capital cities and cities with a population of 100 000 or more have been shown in previous issues of the *Demographic Yearbook*. For more information on specific topics and years for which data are reported, readers should consult the Historical Index.

Tableau 8 – *Annuaire démographique 2019*

Le tableau 8 présente les données les plus récentes disponibles pour la période 2000 – 2019 sur la population des capitales et des villes de 100 000 habitants ou plus.

Description des variables : étant donné que les villes ne sont pas délimitées de la même manière dans tous les pays ou zones, on s'est efforcé de donner, dans ce tableau, des chiffres correspondant non seulement aux villes proprement dites, mais aussi, le cas échéant, aux agglomérations urbaines.

On entend par villes proprement dites les localités qui ont des limites juridiquement définies et sont administrativement considérées comme villes, ce qui se caractérise généralement par l'existence d'une autorité locale.

L'agglomération urbaine comprend, par définition, la ville proprement dite ainsi que la proche banlieue, c'est-à-dire la zone fortement peuplée qui est extérieure, mais contiguë aux limites de la ville.

En outre, dans certains pays ou zones, les données se rapportent à des divisions administratives entières, connues par exemple sous le nom de shi ou de municipios, qui comportent une agglomération et le territoire avoisinant, lequel peut englober d'autres agglomérations urbaines tout à fait distinctes ou être à caractère essentiellement rural. Pour ce groupe de pays ou zones, le type de division administrative est indiqué en note.

On trouvera en plus la superficie des villes ou des agglomérations urbaines chaque fois que possible.

Les noms des villes sont indiqués dans la langue du pays ou zone où ces villes sont situées. Les noms de villes qui ne sont pas à l'origine libellés en caractères latins ont été romanisés. Les villes sont énumérées dans l'ordre alphabétique anglais.

Les capitales figurent dans le tableau quel que soit le chiffre de leur population et leur nom a été imprimé en lettres majuscules. Ne sont indiquées comme capitales que les villes ainsi désignées par le pays ou zone intéressé.

En ce qui concerne les autres villes, le tableau indique celles dont la population est égale ou supérieure à 100 000 habitants. Ce chiffre limite s'applique à l'agglomération urbaine et non à la ville proprement dite, dont la population peut être moindre.

La date à laquelle se réfère le chiffre correspondant, figure dans la colonne de gauche du tableau. Le 'code' aussi figurant dans la colonne de gauche du tableau, permet de savoir si les estimations sont fondées sur les résultats d'enquêtes par sondage ou de recensements municipaux ou sont tirées d'autres sources. Les codes utilisés sont expliqués à la fin du tableau.

Fiabilité des données : on ne possède généralement pas de renseignements précis sur la fiabilité des estimations de la population des villes ou agglomérations urbaines présentées dans ce tableau.

Les données provenant de recensements de la population, d'enquêtes par sondage ou de recensements municipaux sont jugées sûres et figurent par conséquent en caractères romains. D'autres estimations sont considérées comme sûres si elles sont fondées sur un recensement complet (ou une enquête par sondage) et ont été ajustées en fonction des données provenant d'un registre permanent de population ou en fonction de la balance, établie par le calcul des naissances, des décès et des migrations.

Insuffisance des données : les statistiques portant sur la population des capitales et des villes de 100 000 habitants ou plus appellent toutes les réserves qui ont été formulées à la section 3 des Notes techniques à propos des statistiques de la population en général.

La comparabilité internationale des données portant sur la population des villes est compromise par la diversité des définitions nationales. Bien que l'on se soit efforcé de réduire les facteurs de non-comparabilité en présentant à la fois dans le tableau les données relatives aux villes proprement dites et celles concernant les agglomérations urbaines, de graves problèmes de comparabilité n'en subsistent pas moins.

Pour certains pays, les données figurant dans la colonne intitulée « Ville proprement dite » correspondent à une zone administrative urbaine juridiquement distincte du territoire rural environnant, tandis que pour d'autres pays ces données correspondent à une commune ou petite unité administrative analogue. Pour d'autres encore, les unités administratives en cause peuvent être relativement étendues et englober par conséquent un vaste territoire au-delà du centre urbain lui-même.

L'emploi de données se rapportant tantôt à la population de fait, tantôt à la population de droit, ainsi que les différences de traitement de ces deux notions d'un pays à l'autre influent particulièrement sur les statistiques urbaines. En ce qui concerne la population totale, la différence entre population de fait et population de droit est expliquée en détail à la section 3.1.1 des Notes techniques.

Les statistiques relatives à la population urbaine qui sont fondées sur des estimations intercensitaires posent encore plus de problèmes que les données issues de recensement. Leur comparabilité est compromise par la diversité des méthodes employées pour établir les estimations, et par l'imprécision qui résulte de l'application de certaines méthodes qui sont conçues pour être appliquées à l'ensemble de la population. La méthode des composantes, par exemple, est beaucoup plus difficile à appliquer en vue de l'estimation de l'accroissement de la population lorsqu'il s'agit de villes que lorsqu'il s'agit d'un pays tout entier.

Les naissances et décès qui surviennent dans les villes ne correspondent pas tous à la population présente ou résidente. En conséquence, des erreurs peuvent se produire si l'on établit pour les villes des estimations fondées sur l'accroissement naturel de la population. Les migrations intérieures constituent un second élément d'estimation que, dans bien des régions, on ne peut pas toujours mesurer avec exactitude. Pour ces raisons, les estimations présentées dans ce tableau risquent dans l'ensemble d'être peu fiables et leur valeur est particulièrement limitée du point de vue des comparaisons internationales.

Même lorsqu'elles figurent en caractères romains, il arrive souvent que les statistiques urbaines ne soient pas aussi fiables que les estimations concernant la population totale de la zone ou du pays considéré. De surcroît, comme ces statistiques proviennent aussi bien de recensements (nationaux ou municipaux) que d'enquêtes ou d'estimations, les années auxquelles elles se rapportent sont extrêmement variables. Enfin, comme les limites urbaines varient parfois d'une époque à une autre, il y a lieu d'être prudent lorsque l'on compare des données se rapportant à des années différentes.

Données publiées antérieurement : des statistiques concernant la population des capitales et des villes de 100 000 habitants ou plus ont été présentées dans des éditions antérieures de l'*Annuaire démographique*. Pour plus de précisions concernant les années et les sujets pour lesquels des données ont été publiées, se reporter à l'index historique.

8. Population of capital cities and cities of 100 000 or more inhabitants: latest available year, 2000 - 2019
Population des capitales et des villes de 100 000 habitants ou plus : dernière année disponible, 2000 - 2019

Continent, country or area, date, code[a] and city Continent, pays ou zone, date, code[a] et ville	City proper - Ville proprement dite				Urban agglomeration - Agglomération urbaine			
	Population			Surface area - Superficie (km²)	Population			Surface area - Superficie (km²)
	Both sexes - Les deux sexes	Male - Masculin	Female - Féminin		Both sexes - Les deux sexes	Male - Masculin	Female - Féminin	
AFRICA - AFRIQUE								
Algeria - Algérie								
16 IV 2008 (CDJC)								
Adrar	200 834	...	...	...	...	...	...	...
Ain Defla	450 280	...	...	...	...	...	...	...
Ain Temouchent	299 341	...	...	...	...	...	...	...
ALGIERS (EL DJAZAIR)	2 712 944	...	...	...	...	...	...	...
Annaba	442 230	...	...	...	...	...	...	...
Batna	768 444	...	...	...	...	...	...	...
Béchar	236 213	...	...	...	...	...	...	...
Bejaïa	559 981	...	...	...	...	...	...	...
Beskra (Biskra)	563 245	...	...	...	...	...	...	...
Bordj Bou Arreridj	422 986	...	...	...	...	...	...	...
Bouira	372 196	...	...	...	...	...	...	...
Boumerdes	459 250	...	...	...	...	...	...	...
Chlef	521 070	...	...	...	...	...	...	...
El Bayadh	192 958	...	...	...	...	...	...	...
El Boulaïda (Blida)	719 515	...	...	...	...	...	...	...
El Djelfa	825 411	...	...	...	...	...	...	...
El Oued	495 573	...	...	...	...	...	...	...
El Tarf	230 157	...	...	...	...	...	...	...
Ghardaïa	355 701	...	...	...	...	...	...	...
Ghilizane (Relizane)	432 386	...	...	...	...	...	...	...
Guelma	363 716	...	...	...	...	...	...	...
Jijel	391 096	...	...	...	...	...	...	...
Khenchela	288 849	...	...	...	...	...	...	...
Laghouat	371 204	...	...	...	...	...	...	...
Lemdiyya (Médéa)	519 383	...	...	...	...	...	...	...
Mestghanem (Mostaganem)	338 143	...	...	...	...	...	...	...
Mila	440 735	...	...	...	...	...	...	...
Mouaskar (Mascara)	513 432	...	...	...	...	...	...	...
M'Sila	666 848	...	...	...	...	...	...	...
Naama	160 381	...	...	...	...	...	...	...
Oum El Bouaghi	467 997	...	...	...	...	...	...	...
Qacentina (Constantine)	717 646	...	...	...	...	...	...	...
Saïda	248 939	...	...	...	...	...	...	...
Sidi-bel-Abbès	517 836	...	...	...	...	...	...	...
Skikda	543 402	...	...	...	...	...	...	...
Souq Ahras	308 319	...	...	...	...	...	...	...
Stif (Sétif)	856 457	...	...	...	...	...	...	...
Tamanrasset	136 822	...	...	...	...	...	...	...
Tbessa (Tébessa)	515 786	...	...	...	...	...	...	...
Tihert (Tiaret)	637 991	...	...	...	...	...	...	...
Tilimsen (Tlemcen)	672 490	...	...	...	...	...	...	...
Tipaza	343 838	...	...	...	...	...	...	...
Tissemsilt	193 011	...	...	...	...	...	...	...
Tizi Ouzou	585 775	...	...	...	...	...	...	...
Wahran (Oran)	1 165 687	...	...	...	...	...	...	...
Wargla (Ouargla)	473 543	...	...	...	...	...	...	...
Angola[1]								
1 VII 2019 (ESDF)								
Benguela	...	...	...	...	*640 372*[2]	*306 777*[2]	*333 595*[2]	2136.8
Cabinda	...	...	...	...	*718 915*[2]	*356 407*[2]	*362 507*[2]	2260.1
Cazengo	...	...	...	...	*197 516*[2]	*96 209*[2]	*101 307*[2]	2045.8
Cuanhama	...	...	...	...	*437 819*[2]	*205 661*[2]	*232 158*[2]	23575.5
Cuito	...	...	...	...	*529 564*[2]	*255 102*[2]	*274 461*[2]	4691.6
Dande	...	...	...	...	*278 092*[2]	*139 404*[2]	*138 688*[2]	6075
Huambo	...	...	...	...	*843 737*[2]	*407 741*[2]	*435 996*[2]	2812.9
LUANDA[3]	...	...	...	...	*1 632 647*[2]	*801 459*[2]	*831 188*[2]	78
Lubango	...	...	...	...	*903 564*[2]	*437 859*[2]	*465 705*[2]	2785.6
Lucapa	...	...	...	...	*179 020*[2]	*95 614*[2]	*83 405*[2]	18744.8
Luena	...	...	...	...	*292 011*[2]	*143 139*[2]	*148 872*[2]	41763.5
Malanje	...	...	...	...	*586 542*[2]	*285 353*[2]	*301 189*[2]	2837.6
M'banza-Kongo	...	...	...	...	*232 508*[2]	*116 383*[2]	*116 125*[2]	7090.6
Menongue	...	...	...	...	*513 374*[2]	*249 789*[2]	*263 584*[2]	23322.8

8. Population of capital cities and cities of 100 000 or more inhabitants: latest available year, 2000 - 2019
Population des capitales et des villes de 100 000 habitants ou plus : dernière année disponible, 2000 - 2019 (continued - suite)

Continent, country or area, date, code[a] and city / Continent, pays ou zone, date, code[a] et ville	City proper - Ville proprement dite: Population: Both sexes - Les deux sexes	Male - Masculin	Female - Féminin	Surface area - Superficie (km²)	Urban agglomeration - Agglomération urbaine: Population: Both sexes - Les deux sexes	Male - Masculin	Female - Féminin	Surface area - Superficie (km²)
AFRICA - AFRIQUE								
Angola[1]								
1 VII 2019 (ESDF)								
Namibe	...	...	...	...	*335 892*[2]	*164 812*[2]	*171 079*[2]	9110.3
Saurimo	...	...	...	...	*876 339*[2]	*424 076*[2]	*452 263*[2]	16977.2
Sumbe	...	...	...	...	*323 142*[2]	*154 882*[2]	*168 260*[2]	4058.1
Uíge	...	...	...	...	*598 906*[2]	*295 290*[2]	*303 616*[2]	1105.4
Benin - Bénin								
11 V 2013 (CDFC)								
Cotonou	679 012	325 872	353 140	...	...	...	...	...
Parakou	255 478	127 328	128 150	...	...	...	...	...
PORTO-NOVO	264 320	126 016	138 304	...	...	...	...	...
Botswana								
1 VII 2017 (ESDJ)								
Francistown	*110 077*[4]	...	...	199	...	...	...	...
GABORONE	*264 311*[4]	...	...	198	...	...	...	...
Burkina Faso								
9 XII 2006 (CDFC)								
Banfora	75 917	38 399	37 518	...	109 824	54 581	55 243	...
Bobo Dioulasso	489 967	244 136	245 831	...	554 042	275 703	278 339	...
Dori	21 078	10 431	10 647	...	106 808	52 992	53 816	...
Fada N'gourma	41 785	21 220	20 565	...	124 577	62 193	62 384	...
Gorom-Gorom	8 882	4 509	4 373	...	106 346	53 129	53 217	...
Kaya	54 365	26 989	27 376	...	117 122	56 209	60 913	...
Koudougou	88 184	42 803	45 381	...	138 209	64 362	73 847	...
OUAGADOUGOU	1 475 223	745 289	729 934	...	1 475 223	745 289	729 934	...
Ouahigouya	73 153	36 370	36 783	...	125 030	61 002	64 028	...
Solenzo	16 850	8 557	8 293	...	121 819	59 892	61 927	...
Tenkodogo	44 491	21 476	23 015	...	124 985	58 003	66 982	...
Burundi								
16 VIII 2008 (CDJC)								
BUJUMBURA	497 169	274 979	222 190	...	...	...	...	...
Cabo Verde[5]								
1 VII 2011 (ESDF)								
PRAIA	...	...	...	...	*133 863*	*65 412*	*68 451*	...
Cameroon - Cameroun[6]								
1 VII 2019 (ESDJ)								
Douala	*3 226 714*	*1 626 901*	*1 599 813*	...	...	...	...	...
YAOUNDE	*3 158 891*	*1 592 236*	*1 566 655*	...	...	...	...	...
Chad - Tchad[7]								
1 VII 2019 (ESDJ)								
Abéché	*152 107*	*53 709*	*98 398*	...	...	...	...	...
Moundou	*200 963*	*69 468*	*131 495*	...	...	...	...	...
N'DJAMENA	*1 521 882*	*506 218*	*1 015 664*	...	...	...	...	...
Sarh	*151 727*	*48 478*	*103 249*	...	...	...	...	...
Côte d'Ivoire								
15 V 2014 (CDJC)								
Abengourou	100 910	51 153	49 757	...	...	...	...	...
Abidjan	4 395 243	2 180 526	2 214 717	...	...	...	...	...
Anyama	103 297	52 169	51 128	...	...	...	...	...
Bouake	536 719	273 502	263 217	...	...	...	...	...
Daloa	245 360	128 922	116 438	...	...	...	...	...
Divo	105 397	54 614	50 783	...	...	...	...	...
Gagnoa	160 465	82 615	77 850	...	...	...	...	...
Korhogo	243 048	126 493	116 555	...	...	...	...	...
Man	148 945	77 005	71 940	...	...	...	...	...
San Pédro	164 944	85 168	79 776	...	...	...	...	...
Soubre	101 196	53 799	47 397	...	...	...	...	...
YAMOUSSOUKRO	212 670	107 871	104 799	...	...	...	...	...
Djibouti								
29 V 2009 (CDFC)								
DJIBOUTI	475 322	...	...	...	...	...	...	...
Egypt - Égypte[8]								
18 IV 2017 (CDJC)								
Alexandria	...	...	...	...	5 163 750	2 654 824	2 508 926	...
CAIRO	...	...	...	...	9 539 673	4 960 625	4 579 048	...

8. Population of capital cities and cities of 100 000 or more inhabitants: latest available year, 2000 - 2019
Population des capitales et des villes de 100 000 habitants ou plus : dernière année disponible, 2000 - 2019 (continued - suite)

Continent, country or area, date, code[a] and city Continent, pays ou zone, date, code[a] et ville	City proper - Ville proprement dite				Urban agglomeration - Agglomération urbaine			
	Population				Population			
	Both sexes - Les deux sexes	Male - Masculin	Female - Féminin	Surface area - Superficie (km²)	Both sexes - Les deux sexes	Male - Masculin	Female - Féminin	Surface area - Superficie (km²)
AFRICA - AFRIQUE								
Egypt - Égypte[8]								
18 IV 2017 (CDJC)								
Port Said	...	...	...	...	749 371	385 129	364 242	...
Suez	...	...	...	...	728 180	374 399	353 781	...
Equatorial Guinea - Guinée équatoriale								
1 VII 2001 (ESDF)								
MALABO	...	...	...	...	*211 276*	*106 923*	*104 353*	...
Eritrea - Érythrée								
1 VII 2019 (ESDF)								
ASMARA	*512 438*	*235 238*	*277 201*	59	*586 618*	*269 755*	*316 862*	184
Eswatini								
29 IV 2017 (CDJC)								
MBABANE	60 691	...	...	...	...	...	...	...
Ethiopia - Éthiopie								
1 VII 2019 (ESDF)								
ADDIS ABABA	*3 603 568*	*1 703 247*	*1 900 322*	...	...	...	...	...
Bahir Dar	*300 858*	*149 914*	*150 944*	...	...	...	...	...
Debre Zeit	*178 808*	*84 766*	*94 042*	...	...	...	...	...
Gondar	*400 555*	*196 225*	*204 330*	...	...	...	...	...
Jimma	*216 341*	*107 727*	*108 614*	...	...	...	...	...
Mekele	*360 181*	*200 749*	*159 432*	...	...	...	...	...
Nazareth	*393 922*	*192 827*	*201 095*	...	...	...	...	...
Gabon								
22 V 2013 (CDFC)								
Franceville	...	...	...	...	110 568	63 518	47 050	...
LIBREVILLE	...	...	...	...	703 939	360 012	343 927	...
Port-Gentil	...	...	...	...	136 462	69 978	66 484	...
Ghana								
26 IX 2010 (CDFC)								
ACCRA	1 594 419	763 870	830 549	...	...	...	...	...
Ashiaman	190 972	93 727	97 245	...	...	...	...	...
Koforidua	122 300	59 056	63 244	...	...	...	...	...
Kumasi	1 730 249	826 479	903 770	...	...	...	...	...
Madina	111 926	54 271	57 655	...	...	...	...	...
Obuasi	168 641	81 015	87 626	...	...	...	...	...
Tamale	223 252	111 109	112 143	...	...	...	...	...
Tema	292 773	139 958	152 815	...	...	...	...	...
Guinea - Guinée[9]								
1 VII 2019 (ESDJ)								
Boke	*215 849*	*109 948*	*105 901*	...	...	...	...	...
CONAKRY	*1 930 838*	*972 697*	*958 141*	...	*2 365 850*	*1 186 090*	*1 179 761*	...
Coyah	*252 354*	*121 068*	*131 285*	...	...	...	...	...
Dubreka	*182 659*	*92 325*	*90 334*	...	...	...	...	...
Kankan	*221 868*	*112 802*	*109 067*	...	...	...	...	...
Kindia	*161 345*	*79 141*	*82 204*	...	...	...	...	...
Kissidougou	*116 250*	*57 082*	*59 169*	...	...	...	...	...
Labé	*107 785*	*51 578*	*56 207*	...	...	...	...	...
Nzérékoré	*226 876*	*113 640*	*113 236*	...	...	...	...	...
Siguiri	*148 312*	*76 574*	*71 739*	...	...	...	...	...
Guinea-Bissau - Guinée-Bissau								
15 III 2009 (CDFC)								
BISSAU	387 909	...	...	...	...	...	...	...
Kenya								
24 VIII 2019 (CDFC)								
NAIROBI	4 397 073[10]	2 192 452	2 204 376	...	...	...	...	...
Lesotho[11]								
10 IV 2016 (CDJC)								
MASERU	330 760	...	...	...	...	...	...	...
Liberia - Libéria[12]								
21 III 2008 (CDFC)								
MONROVIA	...	...	...	...	970 824	476 473	494 351	...
Madagascar								
18 V 2018* (CDJC)								
ANTANANARIVO	1 275 207	616 106	659 101	85	...	...	...	...
Antsirabe	245 592	118 912	126 680	133	...	...	...	...

8. Population of capital cities and cities of 100 000 or more inhabitants: latest available year, 2000 - 2019
Population des capitales et des villes de 100 000 habitants ou plus : dernière année disponible, 2000 - 2019 (continued - suite)

Continent, country or area, date, code[a] and city / Continent, pays ou zone, date, code[a] et ville	City proper - Ville proprement dite: Population: Both sexes - Les deux sexes	Male - Masculin	Female - Féminin	Surface area - Superficie (km²)	Urban agglomeration - Agglomération urbaine: Population: Both sexes - Les deux sexes	Male - Masculin	Female - Féminin	Surface area - Superficie (km²)
AFRICA - AFRIQUE								
Madagascar								
18 V 2018* (CDJC)								
Antsiranana	131 165	61 178	69 987	72	...	...	...	...
Fianarantsoa	189 879	90 848	99 031	86	...	...	...	...
Mahajanga	244 722	116 007	128 715	51	...	...	...	...
Toamasina	326 286	154 778	171 508	31	...	...	...	...
Toliara	169 760	80 358	89 402	32	...	...	...	...
Malawi								
3 IX 2018 (CDJC)								
Blantyre City	800 264	401 172	399 092	...	...	...	...	...
LILONGWE	989 318	497 201	492 117	...	...	...	...	...
Mzuzu City	221 272	108 848	112 424	...	...	...	...	...
Zomba City	105 013	51 619	53 394	...	...	...	...	...
Mali								
1 IV 2009 (CDFC)								
BAMAKO[13]	...	...	...	...	1 810 366	907 643	902 723	...
Kayes	...	...	...	...	149 129	76 470	72 659	...
Koutiala	...	...	...	...	141 444	70 905	70 539	...
Mopti	...	...	...	...	120 786	60 080	60 706	...
Ségou	...	...	...	...	133 501	66 819	66 682	...
Sikasso	...	...	...	...	226 618	114 171	112 447	...
Mauritania - Mauritanie[5]								
1 VII 2018 (ESDF)								
NOUAKCHOTT	*1 155 482*	...	...	...	...	...	...	...
Mauritius - Maurice[14]								
1 VII 2019 (ESDJ)								
Beau Bassin - Rose Hill	103 740	51 448	52 292	21	...	...	...	...
PORT LOUIS	146 737	73 332	73 405	61	...	...	...	...
Vacoas - Phoenix	105 933	51 163	54 770	106	...	...	...	...
Morocco - Maroc								
1 VII 2014 (ESDF)								
Agadir	*505 765*	...	...	...	*598 484*	...	...	...
Al Hoceima	*137 024*	...	...	...	*399 586*	...	...	...
Azilal	*100 327*	...	...	...	*553 121*	...	...	...
Béni-Mellal	*325 405*	...	...	...	*549 559*	...	...	...
Benslimane	*113 341*	...	...	...	*232 509*	...	...	...
Berkane	*182 203*	...	...	...	*288 807*	...	...	...
Berrechid	*272 356*	...	...	...	*482 119*	...	...	...
Casablanca (Dar-el-Beida)	*3 352 399*	...	...	...	*3 352 399*	...	...	...
Chtouka-Ait Baha	*111 522*	...	...	...	*369 706*	...	...	...
El Hajeb	*121 226*	...	...	...	*246 461*	...	...	...
El Kelâa des Sraghna	*152 900*	...	...	...	*536 191*	...	...	...
El-Jadida	*311 038*	...	...	...	*784 432*	...	...	...
Errachidia	*193 748*	...	...	...	*418 069*	...	...	...
Essaouira	*106 319*	...	...	...	*450 569*	...	...	...
Fès	*1 126 551*	...	...	...	*1 146 967*	...	...	...
Fquih Ben Salah	*204 732*	...	...	...	*502 021*	...	...	...
Guelmim	*138 788*	...	...	...	*187 428*	...	...	...
Inezgane ait Melloul	*511 209*	...	...	...	*538 786*	...	...	...
Kénitra	*604 206*	...	...	...	*1 058 359*	...	...	...
Khemisset	*279 890*	...	...	...	*541 868*	...	...	...
Khénifra	*228 509*	...	...	...	*370 952*	...	...	...
Khouribga	*376 829*	...	...	...	*541 365*	...	...	...
Laayoune	*234 870*	...	...	...	*237 384*	...	...	...
Larache	*264 802*	...	...	...	*496 264*	...	...	...
Marrakech	*978 045*	...	...	...	*1 325 571*	...	...	...
M'Diq-Fnideq	*196 586*	...	...	...	*208 337*	...	...	...
Médiouna	*119 054*	...	...	...	*171 684*	...	...	...
Meknès	*685 408*	...	...	...	*833 456*	...	...	...
Midelt	*124 684*	...	...	...	*288 757*	...	...	...
Mohammedia	*288 131*	...	...	...	*403 087*	...	...	...
Nador	*390 913*	...	...	...	*564 354*	...	...	...
Nouaceur	*271 052*	...	...	...	*331 651*	...	...	...
Ouarzazate	*113 230*	...	...	...	*297 018*	...	...	...
Oued Ed-Dahab	*105 193*	...	...	...	*125 747*	...	...	...

8. Population of capital cities and cities of 100 000 or more inhabitants: latest available year, 2000 - 2019
Population des capitales et des villes de 100 000 habitants ou plus : dernière année disponible, 2000 - 2019 (continued - suite)

Continent, country or area, date, code[a] and city / Continent, pays ou zone, date, code[a] et ville	City proper - Ville proprement dite: Population: Both sexes - Les deux sexes	Male - Masculin	Female - Féminin	Surface area - Superficie (km²)	Urban agglomeration - Agglomération urbaine: Population: Both sexes - Les deux sexes	Male - Masculin	Female - Féminin	Surface area - Superficie (km²)
AFRICA - AFRIQUE								
Morocco - Maroc								
1 VII 2014 (ESDF)								
Oujda	*504 480*	...	...	...	*550 406*	...	...	...
RABAT	*578 644*	...	...	...	*578 644*	...	...	...
Rehamna	*102 715*	...	...	...	*314 605*	...	...	...
Safi	*345 595*	...	...	...	*691 128*	...	...	...
Salé	*912 957*	...	...	...	*979 228*	...	...	...
Sefrou	*154 973*	...	...	...	*286 009*	...	...	...
Settat	*215 665*	...	...	...	*633 500*	...	...	...
Sidi Kacem	*168 302*	...	...	...	*521 694*	...	...	...
Sidi Slimane	*130 576*	...	...	...	*319 528*	...	...	...
Skhirate-Témara	*512 867*	...	...	...	*570 855*	...	...	...
Tanger	*998 972*	...	...	...	*1 059 562*	...	...	...
Taourirt	*149 604*	...	...	...	*232 712*	...	...	...
Taroudannt	*247 428*	...	...	...	*837 797*	...	...	...
Taza	*207 719*	...	...	...	*528 917*	...	...	...
Tétouan	*396 806*	...	...	...	*549 062*	...	...	...
Youssoufia	*100 617*	...	...	...	*251 692*	...	...	...
Mozambique								
1 VII 2019 (ESDF)								
MAPUTO	*1 122 607*	*544 766*	*577 841*	...	...	...	...	...
Namibia - Namibie								
28 VIII 2011 (CDFC)								
WINDHOEK	325 858	160 730	165 128	5133	...	...	...	...
Niger[15]								
1 VII 2017 (ESDJ)								
Maradi	*326 804*	*162 292*	*164 512*	...	...	...	...	...
NIAMEY	*1 203 766*	*598 489*	*605 277*	...	...	...	...	...
Tahoua	*178 910*	*89 177*	*89 733*	...	...	...	...	...
Zinder	*392 835*	*196 954*	*195 881*	...	...	...	...	...
Republic of South Sudan - République de Soudan du Sud								
21 IV 2008 (CDFC)								
JUBA	230 195	129 427	100 768	56	...	...	...	...
Malakal	114 528	60 440	54 088	25	...	...	...	...
Wau	118 331	63 777	54 554	75	...	...	...	...
Reunion - Réunion								
1 I 2015 (CDJC)								
SAINT-DENIS	146 985	68 447	78 538	...	179 925	84 554	95 371	...
Saint-Paul	105 967	52 163	53 804	...	173 967	85 212	88 755	...
Rwanda								
15 VIII 2012 (CDJC)								
KIGALI	859 332	451 673	407 659	...	...	...	...	...
Saint Helena ex. dep. - Sainte-Hélène sans dép.								
7 II 2016 (CDJC)								
JAMESTOWN	657[16]	341[16]	316[16]	6	...	...	...	...
Sao Tome and Principe - Sao Tomé-et-Principe								
25 VIII 2001 (CDJC)								
SAO TOME	...	...	...	...	49 957	24 003	25 954	...
Senegal - Sénégal[17]								
31 XII 2011 (ESDJ)								
DAKAR	1 056 009	526 299	529 710	...	...	...	...	...
Diourbel	279 667	136 961	142 706	...	...	...	...	...
Guediawaye	317 464	157 992	159 472	...	...	...	...	...
Kaolack	410 577	199 057	211 520	...	...	...	...	...
Mbour	605 346	307 461	297 885	...	...	...	...	...
Pikine	941 245	472 868	468 377	...	...	...	...	...
Rufisque	333 032	167 942	165 090	...	...	...	...	...
Saint Louis	277 245	136 957	140 289	...	...	...	...	...
Thiès	618 436	304 087	314 349	...	...	...	...	...
Ziguinchor	337 295	167 048	170 247	...	...	...	...	...
Seychelles[18]								
26 VIII 2010 (CDFC)								
VICTORIA	...	...	...	...	26 450	...	...	...

8. Population of capital cities and cities of 100 000 or more inhabitants: latest available year, 2000 - 2019
Population des capitales et des villes de 100 000 habitants ou plus : dernière année disponible, 2000 - 2019 (continued - suite)

Continent, country or area, date, code[a] and city Continent, pays ou zone, date, code[a] et ville	City proper - Ville proprement dite				Urban agglomeration - Agglomération urbaine			
	Population				Population			
	Both sexes - Les deux sexes	Male - Masculin	Female - Féminin	Surface area - Superficie (km²)	Both sexes - Les deux sexes	Male - Masculin	Female - Féminin	Surface area - Superficie (km²)
AFRICA - AFRIQUE								
Sierra Leone								
5 XII 2015 (CDFC)								
Bo	174 369	83 998	90 371	...	...	...	...	...
FREETOWN	1 055 964	528 207	527 757	...	...	...	...	...
Kenema	200 443	97 818	102 625	...	...	...	...	...
Makeni	124 634	61 494	63 140	...	...	...	...	...
Somalia - Somalie								
1 VII 2001 (ESDF)								
MOGADISHU	*1 212 000*	...	...	...	...	...	...	...
South Africa - Afrique du Sud								
10 X 2011 (CDFC)								
CAPE TOWN[19]	433 688	209 082	224 607	...	...	...	...	...
Durban	595 061	288 871	306 189	...	...	...	...	...
Johannesburg	957 441	484 293	473 148	...	...	...	...	...
PRETORIA[19]	741 651	359 139	382 512	...	...	...	...	...
Togo[5]								
1 VII 2015 (ESDF)								
Kara	*104 400*	...	...	...	...	...	...	...
LOME	...	...	...	...	*1 788 600*	...	...	...
Sokode	*101 900*	...	...	...	...	...	...	...
Tunisia - Tunisie[20]								
23 IV 2014 (CDFC)								
Monastir	...	...	...	...	548 828	274 215	274 613	...
TUNIS	...	...	...	...	1 056 247	528 145	528 102	...
Uganda - Ouganda[21]								
1 VII 2019 (ESDF)								
KAMPALA	*1 650 800*	*781 700*	*869 100*	...	...	...	...	...
Kasese	*112 800*	*54 500*	*58 300*	...	...	...	...	...
Kira	*434 200*	*203 400*	*230 800*	...	...	...	...	...
Lira	*113 500*	*53 500*	*60 000*	...	...	...	...	...
Lugazi	*126 100*	*62 600*	*63 500*	...	...	...	...	...
Makindye Ssabagabo	*387 900*	*181 300*	*206 600*	...	...	...	...	...
Masaka	*114 300*	*54 600*	*59 700*	...	...	...	...	...
Mbarara	*241 700*	*118 700*	*123 000*	...	...	...	...	...
Mukono	*186 500*	*85 300*	*101 200*	...	...	...	...	...
Nansana	*499 900*	*235 100*	*264 800*	...	...	...	...	...
United Republic of Tanzania - République Unie de Tanzanie								
1 VII 2018 (ESDF)								
Arusha[22]	*1 000 923*	*481 431*	*519 492*	...	...	...	...	...
Dar es Salaam	*5 147 070*	*2 512 614*	*2 634 456*	1393	...	...	...	...
DODOMA[22]	*506 943*	*247 621*	*259 322*	...	...	...	...	...
Mbeya[22]	*471 971*	*225 384*	*246 587*	...	...	...	...	...
Tanga[22]	*326 515*	*156 419*	*170 096*	...	...	...	...	...
Zambia - Zambie								
16 X 2010 (CDJC)								
Chingola	216 626	108 464	108 162	...	...	...	...	...
Chipata	455 783	224 934	230 849	...	...	...	...	...
Kabwe	202 360	98 781	103 579	...	...	...	...	...
Kasama	231 824	114 208	117 616	...	...	...	...	...
Kitwe	517 543	256 740	260 803	...	...	...	...	...
Livingstone	139 509	68 763	70 746	...	...	...	...	...
Luanshya	156 059	77 368	78 691	...	...	...	...	...
LUSAKA	1 747 152	860 424	886 728	...	...	...	...	...
Mufulira	162 889	81 355	81 534	...	...	...	...	...
Ndola	451 246	223 020	228 226	...	...	...	...	...
Zimbabwe								
17 VIII 2012 (CDFC)								
Bulawayo	653 337	303 346	349 991	...	...	...	...	...
Chitungwiza	356 840	168 600	188 240	...	...	...	...	...
HARARE	1 485 231	716 595	768 636	...	...	...	...	...
Mutare	262 124	125 850	136 274	...	...	...	...	...

8. Population of capital cities and cities of 100 000 or more inhabitants: latest available year, 2000 - 2019
Population des capitales et des villes de 100 000 habitants ou plus : dernière année disponible, 2000 - 2019 (continued - suite)

Continent, country or area, date, code[a] and city Continent, pays ou zone, date, code[a] et ville	City proper - Ville proprement dite				Urban agglomeration - Agglomération urbaine			
	Population				Population			
	Both sexes - Les deux sexes	Male - Masculin	Female - Féminin	Surface area - Superficie (km²)	Both sexes - Les deux sexes	Male - Masculin	Female - Féminin	Surface area - Superficie (km²)
AMERICA, NORTH - AMÉRIQUE DU NORD								
Anguilla								
11 V 2011 (CDFC)								
THE VALLEY	2 812	...	...	...	...	...	...	...
Aruba								
29 IX 2010 (CDJC)								
ORANJESTAD	28 295	13 139	15 156	...	...	...	...	...
Bahamas								
1 VII 2016* (ESDF)								
NASSAU	266 100	128 100	138 000	...	...	...	...	...
Belize								
1 VII 2019 (ESDJ)								
BELMOPAN	*24 294*	*11 954*	*12 340*	...	...	...	...	...
Bermuda - Bermudes[23]								
20 V 2016 (CDJC)								
HAMILTON	854	480	374	...	...	...	...	...
Canada[24]								
1 VII 2019* (ESDJ)								
Abbotsford	158 457	79 931	78 526	...	...	...	...	...
Abbotsford-Mission	...	...	...	...	201 953	102 643	99 310	...
Ajax	129 490	63 339	66 151	...	...	...	...	...
Barrie	149 302	73 399	75 903	...	213 660	106 511	107 149	...
Belleville	54 633	26 505	28 128	...	111 311	55 185	56 126	...
Brampton	696 975	349 862	347 113	...	...	...	...	...
Brantford	104 902	51 679	53 223	...	149 018	74 103	74 915	...
Burlington	190 194	92 073	98 121	...	...	...	...	...
Burnaby	253 007	124 836	128 171	...	...	...	...	...
Calgary	1 335 145	668 451	666 694	...	1 514 723	758 966	755 757	...
Cambridge	139 996	69 898	70 098	...	...	...	...	...
Cape Breton	96 423	46 406	50 017	...	101 265	48 758	52 507	...
Chatham-Kent	105 666	52 350	53 316	...	106 091	52 581	53 510	...
Chilliwack	94 534	47 239	47 295	...	114 938	58 027	56 911	...
Coquitlam	149 894	74 005	75 889	...	...	...	...	...
Delta	109 490	54 043	55 447	...	...	...	...	...
Edmonton	1 025 096	514 045	511 051	...	1 447 143	725 988	721 155	...
Gatineau	287 868	141 565	146 303	...	...	...	...	...
Greater Sudbury / Grand Sudbury	168 813	83 537	85 276	...	172 216	85 368	86 848	...
Guelph	143 169	70 342	72 827	...	165 236	81 680	83 556	...
Halifax	440 051	215 477	224 574	...	440 348	215 620	224 728	...
Hamilton	574 263	284 191	290 072	...	794 716	391 238	403 478	...
Kamloops	100 046	49 904	50 142	...	115 957	58 028	57 929	...
Kelowna	142 146	69 906	72 240	...	217 229	107 324	109 905	...
Kingston	135 204	65 935	69 269	...	175 708	86 703	89 005	...
Kitchener	263 790	132 044	131 746	...	...	...	...	...
Kitchener-Cambridge-Waterloo	...	...	...	...	584 259	293 461	290 798	...
Langley	130 924	64 335	66 589	...	...	...	...	...
Laval	438 973	216 485	222 488	...	...	...	...	...
Lethbridge	100 323	49 427	50 896	...	127 232	63 437	63 795	...
Lévis V	147 673	73 251	74 422	...	...	...	...	...
London	426 139	209 070	217 069	...	545 441	268 613	276 828	...
Longueuil	249 997	123 656	126 341	...	...	...	...	...
Markham	343 698	168 885	174 813	...	...	...	...	...
Milton	129 334	64 520	64 814	...	...	...	...	...
Mississauga	769 050	381 046	388 004	...	...	...	...	...
Moncton	77 623	37 860	39 763	...	155 825	76 870	78 955	...
Montréal	1 806 022	897 291	908 731	...	4 318 505	2 140 785	2 177 720	...
Nanaimo	99 856	48 786	51 070	...	115 743	56 938	58 805	...
Oakville	212 551	103 596	108 955	...	...	...	...	...
Oshawa	175 220	86 517	88 703	...	413 936	204 552	209 384	...
OTTAWA	1 028 514	505 137	523 377	...	...	...	...	...
Ottawa - Gatineau	...	...	...	...	1 441 118	710 026	731 092	...
Peterborough	86 469	41 274	45 195	...	131 416	63 764	67 652	...
Québec	546 424	269 319	277 105	...	824 411	409 400	415 011	...
Red Deer	106 024	52 612	53 412	...	...	...	...	...
Regina	237 011	118 508	118 503	...	261 684	131 524	130 160	...
Richmond	212 276	102 240	110 036	...	...	...	...	...

8. Population of capital cities and cities of 100 000 or more inhabitants: latest available year, 2000 - 2019
Population des capitales et des villes de 100 000 habitants ou plus : dernière année disponible, 2000 - 2019 (continued - suite)

Continent, country or area, date, code[a] and city Continent, pays ou zone, date, code[a] et ville	City proper - Ville proprement dite				Urban agglomeration - Agglomération urbaine			
	Population			Surface area - Superficie (km²)	Population			Surface area - Superficie (km²)
	Both sexes - Les deux sexes	Male - Masculin	Female - Féminin		Both sexes - Les deux sexes	Male - Masculin	Female - Féminin	
AMERICA, NORTH - AMÉRIQUE DU NORD								
Canada[24]								
1 VII 2019* (ESDJ)								
Richmond Hill	203 996	99 876	104 120	...	...	...	...	...
Saanich	122 173	59 854	62 319	...	...	...	...	...
Saguenay	146 797	73 838	72 959	...	162 416	82 146	80 270	...
Saint John	70 817	34 235	36 582	...	131 025	64 052	66 973	...
Saskatoon	275 242	136 607	138 635	...	330 674	165 474	165 200	...
Sherbrooke	168 518	83 383	85 135	...	221 043	109 656	111 387	...
St. Catharines	141 294	68 603	72 691	...	...	...	...	...
St. Catharines-Niagara	...	...	...	...	434 927	213 960	220 967	...
St. John's	111 038	54 240	56 798	...	212 433	104 543	107 890	...
Surrey	584 526	291 432	293 094	...	...	...	...	...
Terrebonne	117 615	58 727	58 888	...	...	...	...	...
Thunder Bay	112 740	55 834	56 906	...	...	...	...	...
Toronto	2 965 713	1 443 833	1 521 880	...	6 471 850	3 179 904	3 291 946	...
Trois-Rivières	138 200	67 763	70 437	...	160 685	79 228	81 457	...
Vancouver	685 885	338 226	347 659	...	2 691 351	1 324 284	1 367 067	...
Vaughan	325 678	159 756	165 922	...	...	...	...	...
Victoria	94 005	45 119	48 886	...	402 271	196 330	205 941	...
Waterloo	119 869	61 069	58 800	...	...	...	...	...
Whitby	136 594	67 227	69 367	...	...	...	...	...
Windsor	234 048	116 910	117 138	...	354 917	177 080	177 837	...
Winnipeg	763 922	377 675	386 247	...	844 566	419 572	424 994	...
Cayman Islands - Îles Caïmanes[25]								
10 X 2010 (CDJC)								
GEORGE TOWN	28 089	14 253	13 836	...	...	...	...	...
Costa Rica[26]								
1 VII 2019 (ESDJ)								
Alajuela	310 248	157 338	152 910	...	...	...	...	...
Cartago	162 944	81 804	81 140	...	...	...	...	...
Desamparados	242 983	121 198	121 785	...	...	...	...	...
Goicoechea	137 328	67 785	69 543	...	...	...	...	...
Heredia	141 683	69 761	71 922	...	...	...	...	...
La Unión	111 369	55 904	55 465	...	...	...	...	...
Pérez Zeledón	142 997	71 282	71 715	...	...	...	...	...
Pococí	148 593	77 055	71 538	...	...	...	...	...
Puntarenas	138 222	70 740	67 482	...	...	...	...	...
San Carlos	197 218	101 058	96 160	...	...	...	...	...
SAN JOSÉ	344 851	170 813	174 038	...	...	...	...	...
Cuba								
1 VII 2019 (ESDJ)								
Bayamo	160 024	...	...	27	...	...	...	...
Camagüey	309 542	...	...	82	...	...	...	...
Ciego de Ávila	120 948	...	...	21	...	...	...	...
Cienfuegos	152 040	...	...	46	...	...	...	...
Guantánamo	215 545	...	...	34	...	...	...	...
Holguín	298 466	...	...	58	...	...	...	...
LA HABANA	2 131 937	...	...	721	...	...	...	...
Las Tunas	173 979	...	...	31	...	...	...	...
Matanzas	143 924	...	...	44	...	...	...	...
Pinar del Río	145 412	...	...	32	...	...	...	...
Sancti Spíritus	108 836	...	...	23	...	...	...	...
Santa Clara	217 205	...	...	44	...	...	...	...
Santiago de Cuba	433 494	...	...	70	...	...	...	...
Dominican Republic - République dominicaine								
1 VII 2019 (ESDJ)								
Bajos de Haina	*137 543*	*67 723*	*69 820*	12.7	...	...	...	...
Baní	*167 519*	*82 937*	*84 582*	363.3	...	...	...	...
Boca Chica	*170 814*	*84 503*	*86 311*	106.5	...	...	...	...
Bonao	*131 631*	*66 118*	*65 513*	678.1	...	...	...	...
Higüey	*318 036*	*163 813*	*154 223*	907.7	...	...	...	...
La Romana	*153 751*	*74 405*	*79 346*	272.2	...	...	...	...
La Vega	*258 024*	*130 147*	*127 877*	642.1	...	...	...	...
Los Alcarrizos	*328 077*	*163 230*	*164 847*	31.8	...	...	...	...
Moca	*185 115*	*93 639*	*91 476*	340.5	...	...	...	...

8. Population of capital cities and cities of 100 000 or more inhabitants: latest available year, 2000 - 2019
Population des capitales et des villes de 100 000 habitants ou plus : dernière année disponible, 2000 - 2019 (continued - suite)

Continent, country or area, date, code[a] and city Continent, pays ou zone, date, code[a] et ville	City proper - Ville proprement dite				Urban agglomeration - Agglomération urbaine			
	Population				Population			
	Both sexes - Les deux sexes	Male - Masculin	Female - Féminin	Surface area - Superficie (km²)	Both sexes - Les deux sexes	Male - Masculin	Female - Féminin	Surface area - Superficie (km²)
AMERICA, NORTH - AMÉRIQUE DU NORD								
Dominican Republic - République dominicaine								
1 VII 2019 (ESDJ)								
Puerto Plata	164 101	81 808	82 293	210.7	...	...	...	...
San Cristóbal	257 791	127 434	130 357	153.6	...	...	...	...
San Francisco de Macoris	193 742	96 630	97 112	284.5	...	...	...	...
San Juan de la Maguana	126 861	66 908	59 953	248.6	...	...	...	...
San Pedro de Macorís	204 282	98 768	105 514	146.7	...	...	...	...
Santiago de los Caballeros	744 890	362 850	382 040	165	...	...	...	...
SANTO DOMINGO	1 036 494	492 885	543 609	91.6	1 036 494	492 885	543 609	...
Santo Domingo East - Santo Domingo Este	1 141 371	549 321	592 050	123.3	...	...	...	...
Santo Domingo North - Santo Domingo Norte	636 727	315 880	320 847	172.1	...	...	...	...
Santo Domingo West - Santo Domingo Oeste	437 012	211 729	225 283	54	...	...	...	...
El Salvador								
1 VII 2017 (ESDJ)								
Ahuachapán	129 750	61 829	67 921	244.8	...	...	...	...
Apopa	185 073	84 297	100 776	51.8	...	...	...	...
Ciudad Delgado	128 012	59 141	68 871	33.4	...	...	...	...
Ilopango	135 703	61 394	74 309	34.6	...	...	...	...
Mejicanos	144 872	65 747	79 125	22.1	...	...	...	...
San Martin	103 245	47 568	55 677	55.8	...	...	...	...
San Miguel	265 921	123 506	142 415	594	...	...	...	...
SAN SALVADOR	238 244	108 919	129 325	72.3	...	...	...	...
Santa Ana	272 554	129 805	142 749	400.1	...	...	...	...
Santa Tecla	138 695	62 884	75 811	112.2	...	...	...	...
Soyapango	283 223	128 956	154 267	29.7	...	...	...	...
Greenland - Groenland								
1 VII 2019 (ESDJ)								
NUUK (GODTHAB)	18 128	9 554	8 574	...	...	...	...	...
Grenada - Grenade								
12 V 2011 (CDFC)								
ST. GEORGE'S	...	...	...	...	38 251	19 124	19 127	...
Guatemala								
24 XI 2002 (CDJC)								
CUIDAD DE GUATEMALA	942 348	444 429	497 919	...	...	...	...	...
Honduras								
10 VIII 2013 (CDJC)								
Choloma	163 818	77 659	86 159	...	...	...	...	...
El Progreso	114 934	53 849	61 086	...	...	...	...	...
La Ceiba	176 212	82 813	93 399	...	...	...	...	...
San Pedro Sula	598 519	284 362	314 157	...	...	...	...	...
TEGUCIGALPA	996 658	465 474	531 184	...	...	...	...	...
Jamaica - Jamaïque								
4 IV 2011 (CDJC)								
KINGSTON[27]	...	...	...	...	592 291	285 509	306 782	149
Montego Bay	...	...	...	...	111 037	53 601	57 436	76.7
Portmore	...	...	...	...	182 800	85 380	97 420	182.1
Spanish Town	...	...	...	...	149 479	72 885	76 594	64.6
Martinique								
1 I 2015 (CDJC)								
FORT-DE-FRANCE	82 502	36 647	45 855	...	123 369	55 149	68 220	...
Mexico - Mexique[5]								
1 VII 2018 (ESDJ)								
Acapulco	...	...	...	...	935 273	450 674	484 599	...
Acayucan	...	...	...	...	122 233	58 831	63 402	...
Aguascalientes	...	...	...	...	1 056 561	513 692	542 869	...
Apatzingán de la Constitución	...	...	...	...	102 668	...	...	...
Campeche	...	...	...	...	298 741	144 761	153 980	...
Cancún	...	...	...	...	869 665	438 425	431 240	...
Cárdenas	...	...	...	...	106 341	...	...	...
Celaya	...	...	...	...	748 825	357 790	391 035	...
Chetumal	...	...	...	...	258 539	128 157	130 381	...
Chihuahua	...	...	...	...	979 563	474 852	504 710	...
Chilpacingo de los Bravo	...	...	...	...	321 081	153 276	167 805	...
Ciudad Acuña	...	...	...	...	147 888	...	...	...
Ciudad Del Carmen	...	...	...	...	194 484	...	...	...

8. Population of capital cities and cities of 100 000 or more inhabitants: latest available year, 2000 - 2019
Population des capitales et des villes de 100 000 habitants ou plus : dernière année disponible, 2000 - 2019 (continued - suite)

Continent, country or area, date, code[a] and city / Continent, pays ou zone, date, code[a] et ville	City proper - Ville proprement dite				Urban agglomeration - Agglomération urbaine			
	Population				Population			
	Both sexes - Les deux sexes	Male - Masculin	Female - Féminin	Surface area - Superficie (km²)	Both sexes - Les deux sexes	Male - Masculin	Female - Féminin	Surface area - Superficie (km²)
AMERICA, NORTH - AMÉRIQUE DU NORD								
Mexico - Mexique[5]								
1 VII 2018 (ESDJ)								
Ciudad Guzmán	...	...	...	...	105 539	...	...	...
Ciudad Lázaro Cárdenas	...	...	...	...	145 394	...	...	...
Ciudad Obregón	...	...	...	...	347 857	...	...	...
Ciudad Valles	...	...	...	...	135 938	...	...	...
Ciudad Victoria	...	...	...	...	365 089	177 720	187 369	...
Coatzacoalcos	...	...	...	...	379 805	184 135	195 670	...
Colima-Villa de Álvarez	...	...	...	...	388 618	188 810	199 808	...
Comitán de Domínguez	...	...	...	...	114 136	...	...	...
Córdoba	...	...	...	...	341 041	161 527	179 514	...
Cuauhtemoc	...	...	...	...	134 525	...	...	...
Cuautla	...	...	...	...	491 750	237 210	254 540	...
Cuernavaca	...	...	...	...	1 032 278	495 869	536 409	...
Culiacán Rosales	...	...	...	...	966 609	471 964	494 645	...
Delicias	...	...	...	...	206 090	101 034	105 056	...
Ensenada	...	...	...	...	542 896	272 046	270 850	...
Fresnillo	...	...	...	...	136 448	...	...	...
Guadalajara	...	...	...	...	5 060 750	2 474 500	2 586 251	...
Guanajuato	...	...	...	...	187 490	89 790	97 700	...
Guaymas	...	...	...	...	231 206	115 076	116 130	...
Hermosillo	...	...	...	...	907 233	451 792	455 442	...
Heroica Nogales	...	...	...	...	256 387	128 644	127 743	...
Hidalgo del Parral	...	...	...	...	124 395	59 970	64 425	...
Iguala de la Independencia	...	...	...	...	122 790	...	...	...
Irapuato	...	...	...	...	420 702	...	...	...
Juárez	...	...	...	...	1 462 133	721 450	740 683	...
La Laguna	...	...	...	...	1 417 538	694 648	722 890	...
La Paz	...	...	...	...	313 204	156 237	156 967	...
La Piedad-Pénjamo	...	...	...	...	266 495	126 345	140 150	...
Lagos de Moreno	...	...	...	...	109 186	...	...	...
León	...	...	...	...	1 757 811	851 520	906 292	...
Los Mochis	...	...	...	...	294 684	...	...	...
Manzanillo	...	...	...	...	165 809	...	...	...
Matamoros	...	...	...	...	542 609	268 068	274 541	...
Mazatlán	...	...	...	...	492 420	241 214	251 206	...
Mérida	...	...	...	...	1 196 520	583 179	613 341	...
Mexicali	...	...	...	...	1 065 882	535 044	530 839	...
MEXICO, CIUDAD DE	...	...	...	...	21 800 320	10 550 177	11 250 142	...
Minatitlán	...	...	...	...	387 131	186 999	200 132	...
Monclova-Frontera	...	...	...	...	374 058	185 520	188 538	...
Monterrey	...	...	...	...	4 834 971	2 401 433	2 433 538	...
Morelia	...	...	...	...	908 203	433 134	475 069	...
Moroleón Uriangato - Moroleón-Uriangato	...	...	...	...	115 793	54 866	60 927	...
Navojoa	...	...	...	...	130 446	...	...	...
Nuevo Laredo	...	...	...	...	428 927	211 931	216 995	...
Oaxaca	...	...	...	...	683 128	321 071	362 057	...
Ocotlán	...	...	...	...	179 113	87 702	91 411	...
Orizaba	...	...	...	...	463 767	220 275	243 492	...
Pachuca	...	...	...	...	594 972	284 036	310 936	...
Piedras Negras	...	...	...	...	197 488	98 913	98 575	...
Playa del Carmen	...	...	...	...	214 734	...	...	...
Poza Rica	...	...	...	...	548 859	264 819	284 040	...
Puebla-Tlaxcala	...	...	...	...	3 046 766	1 459 887	1 586 878	...
Puerto Vallarta	...	...	...	...	469 204	234 997	234 207	...
Querétaro	...	...	...	...	1 337 686	648 702	688 984	...
Reynosa-Río Bravo	...	...	...	...	843 968	418 611	425 356	...
Rioverde-Ciudad Fernández	...	...	...	...	146 908	71 669	75 240	...
Salamanca	...	...	...	...	173 831	...	...	...
Saltillo	...	...	...	...	935 663	463 629	472 034	...
San Cristóbal de las Casas	...	...	...	...	179 648	...	...	...
San Francisco del Rincón	...	...	...	...	200 318	97 502	102 816	...
San José del Cabo	...	...	...	...	105 369	...	...	...
San Juan Bautista Tuxtepec	...	...	...	...	114 259	...	...	...
San Juan del Río	...	...	...	...	157 552	...	...	...

8. Population of capital cities and cities of 100 000 or more inhabitants: latest available year, 2000 - 2019
Population des capitales et des villes de 100 000 habitants ou plus : dernière année disponible, 2000 - 2019 (continued - suite)

Continent, country or area, date, code[a] and city / Continent, pays ou zone, date, code[a] et ville	City proper - Ville proprement dite: Population: Both sexes - Les deux sexes	Male - Masculin	Female - Féminin	Surface area - Superficie (km²)	Urban agglomeration - Agglomération urbaine: Population: Both sexes - Les deux sexes	Male - Masculin	Female - Féminin	Surface area - Superficie (km²)
AMERICA, NORTH - AMÉRIQUE DU NORD								
Mexico - Mexique[5]								
1 VII 2018 (ESDJ)								
San Luis Potosí-Soledad de Graciano Sánchez	...	...	...	...	1 188 221	572 625	615 596	...
San Luis Rio Colorado	...	...	...	...	182 121	...	...	...
Tampico	...	...	...	...	955 119	463 507	491 612	...
Tapachula de Cordova y Ordoñez	...	...	...	...	369 198	177 585	191 613	...
Tecomán	...	...	...	...	164 541	82 301	82 240	...
Tehuacán	...	...	...	...	329 094	155 552	173 543	...
Tehuantepec	...	...	...	...	180 296	86 835	93 461	...
Tepatitlán De Morelos	...	...	...	...	103 284	...	...	...
Tepic	...	...	...	...	512 386	248 821	263 565	...
Teziutlán	...	...	...	...	135 074	64 140	70 934	...
Tianguistenco	...	...	...	...	188 474	91 657	96 817	...
Tijuana	...	...	...	...	2 024 994	1 012 792	1 012 202	...
Tlaxcala	...	...	...	...	568 140	273 042	295 098	...
Toluca	...	...	...	...	2 386 157	1 165 288	1 220 869	...
Tula	...	...	...	...	227 415	110 541	116 873	...
Tulancingo	...	...	...	...	272 228	129 071	143 157	...
Túxpan de Rodríguez Cano	...	...	...	...	118 894	...	...	...
Tuxtla Gutiérrez	...	...	...	...	853 518	410 616	442 902	...
Uruapan	...	...	...	...	301 766	...	...	...
Veracruz	...	...	...	...	906 976	431 333	475 643	...
Victoria de Durango	...	...	...	...	660 663	319 622	341 041	...
Villahermosa	...	...	...	...	851 925	415 126	436 800	...
Xalapa	...	...	...	...	787 443	373 471	413 972	...
Zacatecas-Guadalupe	...	...	...	...	377 668	181 167	196 500	...
Zamora-Jacona	...	...	...	...	266 904	128 356	138 548	...
Nicaragua								
1 VII 2009 (ESDJ)								
Chinandega	...	...	...	...	*106 635*	...	...	...
León	...	...	...	...	*156 049*	...	...	...
MANAGUA	...	...	...	...	*985 143*	...	...	...
Masaya	...	...	...	...	*110 491*	...	...	...
Tipitapa	...	...	...	...	*105 773*	...	...	...
Panama								
1 VII 2019 (ESDF)								
CIUDAD DE PANAMÁ	434 458[28]	205 421[28]	229 037[28]	98	1 126 757[28]	556 499[28]	570 258[28]	288
San Miguelito	380 899[28]	186 193[28]	194 706[28]	50	...	...	...	...
Puerto Rico - Porto Rico								
1 VII 2018 (ESDJ)								
Bayamón	170 480[29]	80 211[29]	90 269[29]	71	...	...	...	...
Caguas	124 434[29]	57 761[29]	66 673[29]	94	...	...	...	...
Carolina	147 661[29]	67 442[29]	80 219[29]	73	...	...	...	...
Ponce	133 191[29]	63 943[29]	69 248[29]	184	...	...	...	...
SAN JUAN	320 967[29]	146 687[29]	174 280[29]	77	...	...	...	...
Saint Lucia - Sainte-Lucie[9]								
10 V 2010 (CDJC)								
CASTRIES	4 173	2 044	2 129	...	...	...	...	...
Saint Pierre and Miquelon - Saint Pierre-et-Miquelon								
1 I 2015 (CDJC)								
SAINT-PIERRE	5 415	2 639	2 776	...	...	...	...	...
Trinidad and Tobago - Trinité-et-Tobago								
9 I 2011 (CDJC)								
PORT-OF-SPAIN	37 074	18 008	19 066	12	...	...	...	...
Turks and Caicos Islands - Îles Turques et Caïques								
25 I 2012 (CDJC)								
GRAND TURK	4 831	2 325	2 506	...	...	...	...	...
United States of America - États-Unis d'Amérique[30]								
1 VII 2016 (ESDJ)								
Abilene (TX)	122 225[31]	...	...	276.3[32]	...	...	...	...
Akron (OH)	197 633[31]	...	...	160.7[32]	...	...	...	...
Albuquerque (NM)	559 277[31]	...	...	487.4[32]	...	...	...	...
Alexandria (VA)	155 810[31]	...	...	39[32]	...	...	...	...

8. Population of capital cities and cities of 100 000 or more inhabitants: latest available year, 2000 - 2019
Population des capitales et des villes de 100 000 habitants ou plus : dernière année disponible, 2000 - 2019 (continued - suite)

Continent, country or area, date, code[a] and city - Continent, pays ou zone, date, code[a] et ville	City proper - Ville proprement dite				Urban agglomeration - Agglomération urbaine			
	Population				Population			
	Both sexes - Les deux sexes	Male - Masculin	Female - Féminin	Surface area - Superficie (km²)	Both sexes - Les deux sexes	Male - Masculin	Female - Féminin	Surface area - Superficie (km²)
AMERICA, NORTH - AMÉRIQUE DU NORD								
United States of America - États-Unis d'Amérique[30]								
1 VII 2016 (ESDJ)								
Allentown (PA)	120 443[31]	...	...	45.4[32]	...	...	...	...
Amarillo (TX)	199 582[31]	...	...	262.5[32]	...	...	...	...
Anaheim (CA)	351 043[31]	...	...	129.4[32]	...	...	...	...
Anchorage (AK)	298 192[31]	...	...	4420.1[32]	...	...	...	...
Ann Arbor (MI)	120 782[31]	...	...	72.7[32]	...	...	...	...
Antioch (CA)	110 898[31]	...	...	76.2[32]	...	...	...	...
Arlington (TX)	392 772[31]	...	...	248.2[32]	...	...	...	...
Arvada (CO)	117 453[31]	...	...	100[32]	...	...	...	...
Athens (GA)	123 371[31]	...	...	301.4[32]	...	...	...	...
Atlanta (GA)	472 522[31]	...	...	345.7[32]	...	...	...	...
Augusta (GA)	197 081[31]	...	...	783.4[32]	...	...	...	...
Aurora (CO)	361 710[31]	...	...	397.6[32]	...	...	...	...
Aurora (IL)	201 110[31]	...	...	116.3[32]	...	...	...	...
Austin (TX)	947 890[31]	...	...	810[32]	...	...	...	...
Bakersfield (CA)	376 380[31]	...	...	385.4[32]	...	...	...	...
Baltimore (MD)	614 664[31]	...	...	209.6[32]	...	...	...	...
Baton Rouge (LA)	227 715[31]	...	...	222.5[32]	...	...	...	...
Beaumont (TX)	118 299[31]	...	...	212.8[32]	...	...	...	...
Bellevue (WA)	141 400[31]	...	...	86.7[32]	...	...	...	...
Berkeley (CA)	121 240[31]	...	...	27.1[32]	...	...	...	...
Billings (MT)	110 323[31]	...	...	113.2[32]	...	...	...	...
Birmingham (AL)	212 157[31]	...	...	378.4[32]	...	...	...	...
Boise City (ID)	223 154[31]	...	...	212.6[32]	...	...	...	...
Boston (MA)	673 184[31]	...	...	125.2[32]	...	...	...	...
Boulder (CO)	108 090[31]	...	...	64.3[32]	...	...	...	...
Bridgeport (CT)	145 936[31]	...	...	41.6[32]	...	...	...	...
Broken Arrow (OK)	107 403[31]	...	...	159.9[32]	...	...	...	...
Brownsville (TX)	183 823[31]	...	...	343.1[32]	...	...	...	...
Buffalo (NY)	256 902[31]	...	...	104.6[32]	...	...	...	...
Burbank (CA)	104 447[31]	...	...	44.9[32]	...	...	...	...
Cambridge (MA)	110 651[31]	...	...	16.6[32]	...	...	...	...
Cape Coral (FL)	179 804[31]	...	...	273.5[32]	...	...	...	...
Carlsbad (CA)	113 952[31]	...	...	97.7[32]	...	...	...	...
Carrollton (TX)	133 351[31]	...	...	94[32]	...	...	...	...
Cary (NC)	162 320[31]	...	...	146.3[32]	...	...	...	...
Cedar Rapids (IA)	131 127[31]	...	...	183.3[32]	...	...	...	...
Centennial (CO)	109 932[31]	...	...	76.5[32]	...	...	...	...
Chandler (AZ)	247 477[31]	...	...	168.2[32]	...	...	...	...
Charleston (SC)	134 385[31]	...	...	282.4[32]	...	...	...	...
Charlotte (NC)	842 051[31]	...	...	790.9[32]	...	...	...	...
Chattanooga (TN)	177 571[31]	...	...	370.6[32]	...	...	...	...
Chesapeake (VA)	237 940[31]	...	...	876.7[32]	...	...	...	...
Chicago (IL)	2 704 958[31]	...	...	588.8[32]	...	...	...	...
Chula Vista (CA)	267 172[31]	...	...	128.5[32]	...	...	...	...
Cincinnati (OH)	298 800[31]	...	...	200.4[32]	...	...	...	...
Clarksville (TN)	150 287[31]	...	...	254.5[32]	...	...	...	...
Clearwater (FL)	114 361[31]	...	...	67[32]	...	...	...	...
Cleveland (OH)	385 809[31]	...	...	201.3[32]	...	...	...	...
Clovis (CA)	106 583[31]	...	...	62.7[32]	...	...	...	...
College Station (TX)	112 141[31]	...	...	132.1[32]	...	...	...	...
Colorado Springs (CO)	465 101[31]	...	...	506.7[32]	...	...	...	...
Columbia (MO)	120 612[31]	...	...	168.3[32]	...	...	...	...
Columbia (SC)	134 309[31]	...	...	345.8[32]	...	...	...	...
Columbus (GA)	197 485[31]	...	...	560.5[32]	...	...	...	...
Columbus (OH)	860 090[31]	...	...	565.8[32]	...	...	...	...
Concord (CA)	128 726[31]	...	...	79.1[32]	...	...	...	...
Coral Springs (FL)	130 059[31]	...	...	61.6[32]	...	...	...	...
Corona (CA)	166 785[31]	...	...	102.2[32]	...	...	...	...
Corpus Christi (TX)	325 733[31]	...	...	452.1[32]	...	...	...	...

8. Population of capital cities and cities of 100 000 or more inhabitants: latest available year, 2000 - 2019
Population des capitales et des villes de 100 000 habitants ou plus : dernière année disponible, 2000 - 2019 (continued - suite)

Continent, country or area, date, code[a] and city Continent, pays ou zone, date, code[a] et ville	City proper - Ville proprement dite: Population: Both sexes - Les deux sexes	Male - Masculin	Female - Féminin	Surface area - Superficie (km²)	Urban agglomeration - Agglomération urbaine: Population: Both sexes - Les deux sexes	Male - Masculin	Female - Féminin	Surface area - Superficie (km²)
AMERICA, NORTH - AMÉRIQUE DU NORD								
United States of America - États-Unis d'Amérique[30]								
1 VII 2016 (ESDJ)								
Costa Mesa (CA)	112 822[31]	...	...	40.7[32]	...	...	...	...
Dallas (TX)	1 317 929[31]	...	...	882.9[32]	...	...	...	...
Daly City (CA)	106 472[31]	...	...	19.8[32]	...	...	...	...
Davenport (IA)	102 612[31]	...	...	162.9[32]	...	...	...	...
Davie (FL)	101 871[31]	...	...	90.4[32]	...	...	...	...
Dayton (OH)	140 489[31]	...	...	144.2[32]	...	...	...	...
Denton (TX)	133 808[31]	...	...	241.9[32]	...	...	...	...
Denver (CO)	693 060[31]	...	...	397.1[32]	...	...	...	...
Des Moines (IA)	215 472[31]	...	...	230.3[32]	...	...	...	...
Detroit (MI)	672 795[31]	...	...	359.4[32]	...	...	...	...
Downey (CA)	113 267[31]	...	...	32.1[32]	...	...	...	...
Durham (NC)	263 016[31]	...	...	284.3[32]	...	...	...	...
El Cajon (CA)	103 768[31]	...	...	37.5[32]	...	...	...	...
El Monte (CA)	115 807[31]	...	...	24.8[32]	...	...	...	...
El Paso (TX)	683 080[31]	...	...	665[32]	...	...	...	...
Elgin (IL)	112 123[31]	...	...	97[32]	...	...	...	...
Elizabeth (NJ)	128 640[31]	...	...	31.9[32]	...	...	...	...
Elk Grove (CA)	169 743[31]	...	...	109.3[32]	...	...	...	...
Escondido (CA)	151 613[31]	...	...	96[32]	...	...	...	...
Eugene (OR)	166 575[31]	...	...	114.3[32]	...	...	...	...
Evansville (IN)	119 477[31]	...	...	122.6[32]	...	...	...	...
Everett (WA)	109 043[31]	...	...	86.1[32]	...	...	...	...
Fairfield (CA)	114 756[31]	...	...	106[32]	...	...	...	...
Fargo (ND)	120 762[31]	...	...	127.7[32]	...	...	...	...
Fayetteville (NC)	204 759[31]	...	...	382.7[32]	...	...	...	...
Fontana (CA)	209 665[31]	...	...	111.4[32]	...	...	...	...
Fort Collins (CO)	164 207[31]	...	...	144.6[32]	...	...	...	...
Fort Lauderdale (FL)	178 752[31]	...	...	89.7[32]	...	...	...	...
Fort Wayne (IN)	264 488[31]	...	...	286.5[32]	...	...	...	...
Fort Worth (TX)	854 113[31]	...	...	888.1[32]	...	...	...	...
Fremont (CA)	233 136[31]	...	...	200.6[32]	...	...	...	...
Fresno (CA)	522 053[31]	...	...	296.3[32]	...	...	...	...
Frisco (TX)	163 656[31]	...	...	175.3[32]	...	...	...	...
Fullerton (CA)	140 721[31]	...	...	58.1[32]	...	...	...	...
Gainesville (FL)	131 591[31]	...	...	161.4[32]	...	...	...	...
Garden Grove (CA)	174 858[31]	...	...	46.5[32]	...	...	...	...
Garland (TX)	234 943[31]	...	...	147.7[32]	...	...	...	...
Gilbert (AZ)	237 133[31]	...	...	176.1[32]	...	...	...	...
Glendale (AZ)	245 895[31]	...	...	153[32]	...	...	...	...
Glendale (CA)	200 831[31]	...	...	78.8[32]	...	...	...	...
Grand Prairie (TX)	190 682[31]	...	...	187.2[32]	...	...	...	...
Grand Rapids (MI)	196 445[31]	...	...	115.1[32]	...	...	...	...
Greeley (CO)	103 990[31]	...	...	123.9[32]	...	...	...	...
Green Bay (WI)	105 139[31]	...	...	117.7[32]	...	...	...	...
Greensboro (NC)	287 027[31]	...	...	332.3[32]	...	...	...	...
Gresham (OR)	111 523[31]	...	...	60.3[32]	...	...	...	...
Hampton (VA)	135 410[31]	...	...	133.3[32]	...	...	...	...
Hartford (CT)	123 243[31]	...	...	45[32]	...	...	...	...
Hayward (CA)	158 937[31]	...	...	117.9[32]	...	...	...	...
Henderson (NV)	292 969[31]	...	...	271.2[32]	...	...	...	...
Hialeah (FL)	236 387[31]	...	...	55.6[32]	...	...	...	...
High Point City (NC)	111 223[31]	...	...	143[32]	...	...	...	...
Hillsboro (OR)	105 164[31]	...	...	64.7[32]	...	...	...	...
Hollywood (FL)	151 998[31]	...	...	70.6[32]	...	...	...	...
Houston (TX)	2 303 482[31]	...	...	1651.2[32]	...	...	...	...
Huntington Beach (CA)	200 652[31]	...	...	69.8[32]	...	...	...	...
Huntsville (AL)	193 079[31]	...	...	552.6[32]	...	...	...	...
Independence (MO)	117 030[31]	...	...	201.6[32]	...	...	...	...
Indianapolis (IN)	855 164[31]	...	...	936.3[32]	...	...	...	...

8. Population of capital cities and cities of 100 000 or more inhabitants: latest available year, 2000 - 2019
Population des capitales et des villes de 100 000 habitants ou plus : dernière année disponible, 2000 - 2019 (continued - suite)

Continent, country or area, date, code[a] and city / Continent, pays ou zone, date, code[a] et ville	City proper - Ville proprement dite: Population: Both sexes - Les deux sexes	City proper: Population: Male - Masculin	City proper: Population: Female - Féminin	City proper: Surface area - Superficie (km²)	Urban agglomeration - Agglomération urbaine: Population: Both sexes - Les deux sexes	Urban agglomeration: Population: Male - Masculin	Urban agglomeration: Population: Female - Féminin	Urban agglomeration: Surface area - Superficie (km²)
AMERICA, NORTH - AMÉRIQUE DU NORD								
United States of America - États-Unis d'Amérique[30]								
1 VII 2016 (ESDJ)								
Inglewood (CA)	110 654[31]	...	...	23.5[32]	...	...	...	...
Irvine (CA)	266 122[31]	...	...	169.9[32]	...	...	...	...
Irving (TX)	238 289[31]	...	...	173.6[32]	...	...	...	...
Jackson (MS)	169 148[31]	...	...	287.6[32]	...	...	...	...
Jacksonville (FL)	880 619[31]	...	...	1935.9[32]	...	...	...	...
Jersey City (NJ)	264 152[31]	...	...	38.3[32]	...	...	...	...
Joliet (IL)	148 262[31]	...	...	166.9[32]	...	...	...	...
Jurupa Valley (CA)	103 541[31]	...	...	111.2[32]	...	...	...	...
Kansas City (KS)	151 709[31]	...	...	323.3[32]	...	...	...	...
Kansas City (MO)	481 420[31]	...	...	815.8[32]	...	...	...	...
Kent (WA)	127 514[31]	...	...	87.4[32]	...	...	...	...
Killeen (TX)	143 400[31]	...	...	138.7[32]	...	...	...	...
Knoxville (TN)	186 239[31]	...	...	255.2[32]	...	...	...	...
Lafayette (LA)	127 626[31]	...	...	139.4[32]	...	...	...	...
Lakeland (FL)	106 420[31]	...	...	170.7[32]	...	...	...	...
Lakewood (CO)	154 393[31]	...	...	111[32]	...	...	...	...
Lancaster (CA)	160 106[31]	...	...	244.2[32]	...	...	...	...
Lansing (MI)	116 020[31]	...	...	101.3[32]	...	...	...	...
Laredo (TX)	257 156[31]	...	...	261.9[32]	...	...	...	...
Las Cruces (NM)	101 759[31]	...	...	199.3[32]	...	...	...	...
Las Vegas (NV)	632 912[31]	...	...	348[32]	...	...	...	...
League City (TX)	102 010[31]	...	...	132.6[32]	...	...	...	...
Lewisville (TX)	104 659[31]	...	...	95[32]	...	...	...	...
Lexington-Fayette (KY)	318 449[31]	...	...	734.6[32]	...	...	...	...
Lincoln (NE)	280 364[31]	...	...	238.6[32]	...	...	...	...
Little Rock (AR)	198 541[31]	...	...	307.4[32]	...	...	...	...
Long Beach (CA)	470 130[31]	...	...	130.3[32]	...	...	...	...
Los Angeles (CA)	3 976 322[31]	...	...	1214[32]	...	...	...	...
Louisville (KY)	616 261[31]	...	...	841.7[32]	...	...	...	...
Lowell (MA)	110 558[31]	...	...	35.2[32]	...	...	...	...
Lubbock (TX)	252 506[31]	...	...	322.8[32]	...	...	...	...
Macon-Bibb (GA)	152 555[31]	...	...	645.6[32]	...	...	...	...
Madison (WI)	252 551[31]	...	...	199.3[32]	...	...	...	...
Manchester (NH)	110 506[31]	...	...	85.6[32]	...	...	...	...
McAllen (TX)	142 212[31]	...	...	151.1[32]	...	...	...	...
McKinney City (TX)	172 298[31]	...	...	163.1[32]	...	...	...	...
Memphis (TN)	652 717[31]	...	...	822[32]	...	...	...	...
Mesa (AZ)	484 587[31]	...	...	357.1[32]	...	...	...	...
Mesquite (TX)	143 736[31]	...	...	122.3[32]	...	...	...	...
Miami (FL)	453 579[31]	...	...	93.2[32]	...	...	...	...
Miami Gardens (FL)	113 058[31]	...	...	47.2[32]	...	...	...	...
Midland City (TX)	134 610[31]	...	...	192.6[32]	...	...	...	...
Milwaukee (WI)	595 047[31]	...	...	249.1[32]	...	...	...	...
Minneapolis (MN)	413 651[31]	...	...	139.9[32]	...	...	...	...
Miramar (FL)	138 449[31]	...	...	76.1[32]	...	...	...	...
Mobile (AL)	192 904[31]	...	...	361[32]	...	...	...	...
Modesto (CA)	212 175[31]	...	...	111.3[32]	...	...	...	...
Montgomery (AL)	200 022[31]	...	...	414[32]	...	...	...	...
Moreno Valley (CA)	205 499[31]	...	...	132.8[32]	...	...	...	...
Murfreesboro (TN)	131 947[31]	...	...	144.7[32]	...	...	...	...
Murrieta (CA)	111 674[31]	...	...	87[32]	...	...	...	...
Naperville (IL)	147 122[31]	...	...	100.2[32]	...	...	...	...
Nashville-Davidson (TN)	660 388[31]	...	...	1232.7[32]	...	...	...	...
New Haven (CT)	129 934[31]	...	...	48.4[32]	...	...	...	...
New Orleans (LA)	391 495[31]	...	...	438.8[32]	...	...	...	...
New York (NY)	8 537 673[31]	...	...	780.8[32]	...	...	...	...
Newark (NJ)	281 764[31]	...	...	62.5[32]	...	...	...	...
Newport News (VA)	181 825[31]	...	...	178.9[32]	...	...	...	...
Norfolk (VA)	245 115[31]	...	...	138[32]	...	...	...	...

8. Population of capital cities and cities of 100 000 or more inhabitants: latest available year, 2000 - 2019
Population des capitales et des villes de 100 000 habitants ou plus : dernière année disponible, 2000 - 2019 (continued - suite)

Continent, country or area, date, code[a] and city / Continent, pays ou zone, date, code[a] et ville	City proper - Ville proprement dite				Urban agglomeration - Agglomération urbaine			
	Population				Population			
	Both sexes - Les deux sexes	Male - Masculin	Female - Féminin	Surface area - Superficie (km²)	Both sexes - Les deux sexes	Male - Masculin	Female - Féminin	Surface area - Superficie (km²)
AMERICA, NORTH - AMÉRIQUE DU NORD								
United States of America - États-Unis d'Amérique[30]								
1 VII 2016 (ESDJ)								
Norman (OK)	122 180[31]	...	...	463[32]	...	...	...	...
North Charleston (SC)	109 298[31]	...	...	190.8[32]	...	...	...	...
North Las Vegas (NV)	238 702[31]	...	...	253.9[32]	...	...	...	...
Norwalk (CA)	106 178[31]	...	...	25.1[32]	...	...	...	...
Oakland (CA)	420 005[31]	...	...	144.8[32]	...	...	...	...
Oceanside (CA)	175 464[31]	...	...	106.8[32]	...	...	...	...
Odessa (TX)	117 871[31]	...	...	117[32]	...	...	...	...
Oklahoma City (OK)	638 367[31]	...	...	1570.3[32]	...	...	...	...
Olathe (KS)	135 473[31]	...	...	157.6[32]	...	...	...	...
Omaha (NE)	446 970[31]	...	...	345[32]	...	...	...	...
Ontario (CA)	173 212[31]	...	...	129.3[32]	...	...	...	...
Orange (CA)	140 504[31]	...	...	65.7[32]	...	...	...	...
Orlando (FL)	277 173[31]	...	...	272.5[32]	...	...	...	...
Overland Park (KS)	188 966[31]	...	...	194.6[32]	...	...	...	...
Oxnard (CA)	207 906[31]	...	...	69.7[32]	...	...	...	...
Palm Bay City (FL)	110 104[31]	...	...	170.2[32]	...	...	...	...
Palmdale (CA)	157 356[31]	...	...	274.5[32]	...	...	...	...
Pasadena (CA)	142 059[31]	...	...	59.5[32]	...	...	...	...
Pasadena (TX)	153 351[31]	...	...	112.6[32]	...	...	...	...
Paterson (NJ)	147 000[31]	...	...	21.8[32]	...	...	...	...
Pearland (TX)	113 570[31]	...	...	120[32]	...	...	...	...
Pembroke Pines (FL)	168 587[31]	...	...	85.5[32]	...	...	...	...
Peoria (AZ)	164 173[31]	...	...	455[32]	...	...	...	...
Peoria (IL)	114 265[31]	...	...	124.9[32]	...	...	...	...
Philadelphia (PA)	1 567 872[31]	...	...	347.5[32]	...	...	...	...
Phoenix (AZ)	1 615 017[31]	...	...	1340.7[32]	...	...	...	...
Pittsburgh (PA)	303 625[31]	...	...	143.4[32]	...	...	...	...
Plano (TX)	286 057[31]	...	...	185.6[32]	...	...	...	...
Pomona (CA)	152 494[31]	...	...	59.4[32]	...	...	...	...
Pompano Beach (FL)	109 393[31]	...	...	62.3[32]	...	...	...	...
Port St. Lucie (FL)	185 132[31]	...	...	307.9[32]	...	...	...	...
Portland (OR)	639 863[31]	...	...	345.7[32]	...	...	...	...
Providence (RI)	179 219[31]	...	...	47.7[32]	...	...	...	...
Provo (UT)	116 868[31]	...	...	107.9[32]	...	...	...	...
Pueblo (CO)	110 291[31]	...	...	138.8[32]	...	...	...	...
Raleigh (NC)	458 880[31]	...	...	375.7[32]	...	...	...	...
Rancho Cucamonga (CA)	176 534[31]	...	...	103.6[32]	...	...	...	...
Reno (NV)	245 255[31]	...	...	277.9[32]	...	...	...	...
Renton (WA)	100 953[31]	...	...	60.7[32]	...	...	...	...
Rialto (CA)	103 314[31]	...	...	57.8[32]	...	...	...	...
Richardson (TX)	113 347[31]	...	...	74[32]	...	...	...	...
Richmond (CA)	109 813[31]	...	...	77.8[32]	...	...	...	...
Richmond (VA)	223 170[31]	...	...	154.9[32]	...	...	...	...
Riverside (CA)	324 722[31]	...	...	210.4[32]	...	...	...	...
Rochester (MN)	114 011[31]	...	...	141.3[32]	...	...	...	...
Rochester (NY)	208 880[31]	...	...	92.7[32]	...	...	...	...
Rockford (IL)	147 651[31]	...	...	164.4[32]	...	...	...	...
Roseville (CA)	132 671[31]	...	...	111.3[32]	...	...	...	...
Round Rock (TX)	120 892[31]	...	...	92.1[32]	...	...	...	...
Sacramento (CA)	495 234[31]	...	...	253.6[32]	...	...	...	...
Salem (OR)	167 419[31]	...	...	125.8[32]	...	...	...	...
Salinas (CA)	157 218[31]	...	...	61.2[32]	...	...	...	...
Salt Lake City (UT)	193 744[31]	...	...	288[32]	...	...	...	...
San Angelo (TX)	100 702[31]	...	...	155.3[32]	...	...	...	...
San Antonio (TX)	1 492 510[31]	...	...	1194[32]	...	...	...	...
San Bernardino (CA)	216 239[31]	...	...	159.3[32]	...	...	...	...
San Buenaventura (CA)	109 592[31]	...	...	56.5[32]	...	...	...	...
San Diego (CA)	1 406 630[31]	...	...	842.3[32]	...	...	...	...
San Francisco (CA)	870 887[31]	...	...	121.5[32]	...	...	...	...

8. Population of capital cities and cities of 100 000 or more inhabitants: latest available year, 2000 - 2019
Population des capitales et des villes de 100 000 habitants ou plus : dernière année disponible, 2000 - 2019 (continued - suite)

Continent, country or area, date, code[a] and city Continent, pays ou zone, date, code[a] et ville	City proper - Ville proprement dite				Urban agglomeration - Agglomération urbaine			
	Population				Population			
	Both sexes - Les deux sexes	Male - Masculin	Female - Féminin	Surface area - Superficie (km²)	Both sexes - Les deux sexes	Male - Masculin	Female - Féminin	Surface area - Superficie (km²)
AMERICA, NORTH - AMÉRIQUE DU NORD								
United States of America - États-Unis d'Amérique[30]								
1 VII 2016 (ESDJ)								
San Jose (CA)	1 025 350[31]	...	...	459.7[32]	...	...	...	...
San Mateo (CA)	103 959[31]	...	...	31.4[32]	...	...	...	...
Sandy Springs (GA)	105 703[31]	...	...	97.5[32]	...	...	...	...
Santa Ana (CA)	334 217[31]	...	...	70.3[32]	...	...	...	...
Santa Clara (CA)	125 948[31]	...	...	47.7[32]	...	...	...	...
Santa Clarita (CA)	181 972[31]	...	...	136.6[32]	...	...	...	...
Santa Maria (CA)	106 290[31]	...	...	59[32]	...	...	...	...
Santa Rosa (CA)	175 155[31]	...	...	106.9[32]	...	...	...	...
Savannah (GA)	146 763[31]	...	...	268.3[32]	...	...	...	...
Scottsdale (AZ)	246 645[31]	...	...	476.4[32]	...	...	...	...
Seattle (WA)	704 352[31]	...	...	217.1[32]	...	...	...	...
Shreveport (LA)	194 920[31]	...	...	277.5[32]	...	...	...	...
Simi Valley (CA)	126 327[31]	...	...	107.4[32]	...	...	...	...
Sioux Falls (SD)	174 360[31]	...	...	195.3[32]	...	...	...	...
South Bend (IN)	101 735[31]	...	...	107.2[32]	...	...	...	...
Spokane (WA)	215 973[31]	...	...	178[32]	...	...	...	...
Springfield (IL)	115 715[31]	...	...	155.6[32]	...	...	...	...
Springfield (MA)	154 074[31]	...	...	82.5[32]	...	...	...	...
Springfield (MO)	167 319[31]	...	...	213.2[32]	...	...	...	...
St. Louis (MO)	311 404[31]	...	...	160.5[32]	...	...	...	...
St. Paul (MN)	302 398[31]	...	...	134.6[32]	...	...	...	...
St. Petersburg (FL)	260 999[31]	...	...	159.9[32]	...	...	...	...
Stamford (CT)	129 113[31]	...	...	97.4[32]	...	...	...	...
Sterling Heights (MI)	132 427[31]	...	...	94.6[32]	...	...	...	...
Stockton (CA)	307 072[31]	...	...	159.7[32]	...	...	...	...
Sunnyvale (CA)	152 771[31]	...	...	56.9[32]	...	...	...	...
Surprise (AZ)	132 677[31]	...	...	279.3[32]	...	...	...	...
Syracuse (NY)	143 378[31]	...	...	64.9[32]	...	...	...	...
Tacoma (WA)	211 277[31]	...	...	128.8[32]	...	...	...	...
Tallahassee (FL)	190 894[31]	...	...	260.1[32]	...	...	...	...
Tampa (FL)	377 165[31]	...	...	293.7[32]	...	...	...	...
Temecula (CA)	113 054[31]	...	...	96.5[32]	...	...	...	...
Tempe (AZ)	182 498[31]	...	...	103.5[32]	...	...	...	...
Thornton (CO)	136 703[31]	...	...	92.5[32]	...	...	...	...
Thousand Oaks (CA)	128 888[31]	...	...	142.9[32]	...	...	...	...
Toledo (OH)	278 508[31]	...	...	209.1[32]	...	...	...	...
Topeka (KS)	126 808[31]	...	...	159.2[32]	...	...	...	...
Torrance (CA)	147 195[31]	...	...	53[32]	...	...	...	...
Tucson (AZ)	530 706[31]	...	...	597.8[32]	...	...	...	...
Tulsa (OK)	403 090[31]	...	...	509.8[32]	...	...	...	...
Tyler (TX)	104 798[31]	...	...	146.7[32]	...	...	...	...
Urban Honolulu (HI)	351 792[31]	...	...	156.8[32]	...	...	...	...
Vallejo (CA)	121 299[31]	...	...	79.4[32]	...	...	...	...
Vancouver (WA)	174 826[31]	...	...	121.6[32]	...	...	...	...
Victorville City (CA)	122 265[31]	...	...	189.9[32]	...	...	...	...
Virginia Beach (VA)	452 602[31]	...	...	633.8[32]	...	...	...	...
Visalia (CA)	131 074[31]	...	...	97.1[32]	...	...	...	...
Vista (CA)	101 659[31]	...	...	48.4[32]	...	...	...	...
Waco (TX)	134 432[31]	...	...	230.6[32]	...	...	...	...
Warren (MI)	135 125[31]	...	...	89.1[32]	...	...	...	...
WASHINGTON (DC)	681 170[31]	...	...	158.4[32]	...	...	...	...
Waterbury (CT)	108 272[31]	...	...	73.9[32]	...	...	...	...
West Covina (CA)	107 847[31]	...	...	41.5[32]	...	...	...	...
West Jordan (UT)	113 699[31]	...	...	83.7[32]	...	...	...	...
West Palm Beach (FL)	108 161[31]	...	...	142.8[32]	...	...	...	...
West Valley City (UT)	136 574[31]	...	...	91.9[32]	...	...	...	...
Westminster (CO)	113 875[31]	...	...	82.2[32]	...	...	...	...
Wichita (KS)	389 902[31]	...	...	415.4[32]	...	...	...	...
Wichita Falls (TX)	104 724[31]	...	...	187[32]	...	...	...	...

8. Population of capital cities and cities of 100 000 or more inhabitants: latest available year, 2000 - 2019
Population des capitales et des villes de 100 000 habitants ou plus : dernière année disponible, 2000 - 2019 (continued - suite)

Continent, country or area, date, code[a] and city Continent, pays ou zone, date, code[a] et ville	City proper - Ville proprement dite				Urban agglomeration - Agglomération urbaine			
	Population				Population			
	Both sexes - Les deux sexes	Male - Masculin	Female - Féminin	Surface area - Superficie (km²)	Both sexes - Les deux sexes	Male - Masculin	Female - Féminin	Surface area - Superficie (km²)
AMERICA, NORTH - AMÉRIQUE DU NORD								
United States of America - États-Unis d'Amérique[30]								
1 VII 2016 (ESDJ)								
Wilmington (NC)	117 525[31]	...	...	133.7[32]	...	...	...	...
Winston-Salem (NC)	242 203[31]	...	...	343.2[32]	...	...	...	...
Worcester (MA)	184 508[31]	...	...	96.8[32]	...	...	...	...
Yonkers (NY)	200 807[31]	...	...	46.7[32]	...	...	...	...
United States Virgin Islands - Îles Vierges américaines[33]								
1 IV 2010 (CDJC)								
CHARLOTTE AMALIE	10 354	...	...	...	...	...	...	...
AMERICA, SOUTH - AMÉRIQUE DU SUD								
Argentina - Argentine[28]								
1 VII 2019 (ESDF)								
Bahía Blanca-Cerri	...	...	...	...	312 806	150 631	162 176	...
BUENOS AIRES	...	...	...	...	15 263 441	7 439 127	7 824 314	...
Catamarca	...	...	...	...	220 519	107 151	113 369	...
Comodoro Rivadavia-Rada Tilly	...	...	...	...	231 781	118 684	113 097	...
Concordia	...	...	...	...	159 773	77 784	81 989	...
Córdoba	...	...	...	...	1 554 060	746 319	807 741	...
Corrientes	...	...	...	...	376 981	180 302	196 679	...
Formosa	...	...	...	...	250 125	120 114	130 011	...
La Plata	...	...	...	...	885 066	430 827	454 239	...
La Rioja	...	...	...	...	218 459	107 511	110 948	...
Mar del Plata-Batán	...	...	...	...	639 028	307 341	331 687	...
Mendoza	...	...	...	...	1 017 327	492 806	524 521	...
Neuquén-Plottier	...	...	...	...	303 766	149 248	154 518	...
Paraná	...	...	...	...	278 963	133 376	145 587	...
Posadas	...	...	...	...	367 368	176 379	190 989	...
Rawson-Trelew-Playa Unión	...	...	...	...	144 087	70 249	73 838	...
Resistencia	...	...	...	...	411 510	197 743	213 767	...
Río Cuarto	...	...	...	...	176 183	84 533	91 651	...
Rio Gallegos	...	...	...	...	120 017	60 829	59 187	...
Rosario	...	...	...	...	1 313 576	633 618	679 958	...
Salta	...	...	...	...	628 798	302 866	325 932	...
San Juan	...	...	...	...	531 124	256 821	274 303	...
San Luis - El Chorrillo	...	...	...	...	232 420	113 912	118 508	...
San Nicolás-Villa Constitución	...	...	...	...	193 186	94 337	98 848	...
San Salvador de Jujuy-Palpalá	...	...	...	...	343 607	165 546	178 061	...
Santa Fé	...	...	...	...	529 939	254 458	275 480	...
Santa Rosa-Toay	...	...	...	...	126 447	61 087	65 360	...
Santiago del Estero-La Banda	...	...	...	...	398 836	191 873	206 963	...
Tucumán-Tafí Viejo	...	...	...	...	894 753	431 201	463 552	...
Ushuaia-Río Grande	...	...	...	...	161 214	83 559	77 655	...
Bolivia (Plurinational State of) - Bolivie (État plurinational de)								
1 VII 2010 (ESDF)								
Cochabamba	*618 376*	*294 711*	*323 666*	...	...	...	...	...
El Alto	*953 253*	*463 069*	*490 184*	...	...	...	...	...
LA PAZ	*835 361*	*397 608*	*437 753*	...	...	...	...	...
Oruro	*216 724*	*104 294*	*112 430*	...	...	...	...	...
Potosí	*154 693*	*74 591*	*80 103*	...	...	...	...	...
Sacaba	*155 668*	*75 113*	*80 555*	...	...	...	...	...
Santa Cruz	*1 616 063*	*785 941*	*830 122*	...	...	...	...	...
SUCRE	*284 032*	*137 943*	*146 090*	...	...	...	...	...
Tarija	*194 313*	*94 231*	*100 082*	...	...	...	...	...
Yacuiba	*112 096*	*55 346*	*56 750*	...	...	...	...	...
Brazil - Brésil[34]								
1 VII 2016 (ESDJ)								
Abaetetuba	*151 934*	...	...	...	...	...	...	...
Açailândia	*110 543*	...	...	...	...	...	...	...
Aguas Lindas de Goiás	*191 499*	...	...	...	...	...	...	...
Alagoinhas	*155 362*	...	...	...	...	...	...	...

8. Population of capital cities and cities of 100 000 or more inhabitants: latest available year, 2000 - 2019
Population des capitales et des villes de 100 000 habitants ou plus : dernière année disponible, 2000 - 2019 (continued - suite)

Continent, country or area, date, code[a] and city Continent, pays ou zone, date, code[a] et ville	City proper - Ville proprement dite				Urban agglomeration - Agglomération urbaine			
	Population				Population			
	Both sexes - Les deux sexes	Male - Masculin	Female - Féminin	Surface area - Superficie (km²)	Both sexes - Les deux sexes	Male - Masculin	Female - Féminin	Surface area - Superficie (km²)
AMERICA, SOUTH - AMÉRIQUE DU SUD								
Brazil - Brésil[34]								
1 VII 2016 (ESDJ)								
Almirante Tamandaré	*114 129*	...	...	...	...	...	...	...
Altamira	*109 938*	...	...	...	...	...	...	...
Alvorada	*207 392*	...	...	...	...	...	...	...
Americana	*231 621*	...	...	...	...	...	...	...
Ananindeua	*510 834*	...	...	...	...	...	...	...
Anápolis	*370 875*	...	...	...	...	...	...	...
Angra dos Reis	*191 504*	...	...	...	...	...	...	...
Aparecida de Goiania	*532 135*	...	...	...	...	...	...	...
Apucarana	*131 571*	...	...	...	...	...	...	...
Aracaju	*641 523*	...	...	...	...	...	...	...
Araçatuba	*193 828*	...	...	...	...	...	...	...
Araguaina	*173 112*	...	...	...	...	...	...	...
Araguario	*116 871*	...	...	...	...	...	...	...
Arapiraca	*232 671*	...	...	...	...	...	...	...
Arapongas	*116 960*	...	...	...	...	...	...	...
Araraquara	*228 664*	...	...	...	...	...	...	...
Araras	*130 102*	...	...	...	...	...	...	...
Araruama	*124 940*	...	...	...	...	...	...	...
Araucária	*135 459*	...	...	...	...	...	...	...
Araxá	*103 287*	...	...	...	...	...	...	...
Ariquemes	*105 896*	...	...	...	...	...	...	...
Assis	*102 268*	...	...	...	...	...	...	...
Atibaia	*138 449*	...	...	...	...	...	...	...
Bacabal	*103 020*	...	...	...	...	...	...	...
Bagé	*121 986*	...	...	...	...	...	...	...
Balneário Camboriú	*131 727*	...	...	...	...	...	...	...
Barbacena	*135 829*	...	...	...	...	...	...	...
Barcarena	*118 537*	...	...	...	...	...	...	...
Barra Mansa	*180 126*	...	...	...	...	...	...	...
Barreiras	*155 519*	...	...	...	...	...	...	...
Barretos	*119 948*	...	...	...	...	...	...	...
Barueri	*264 935*	...	...	...	...	...	...	...
Bauru	*369 368*	...	...	...	...	...	...	...
Belém	*1 446 042*	...	...	...	...	...	...	...
Belford Roxo	*494 141*	...	...	...	...	...	...	...
Belo Horizonte	*2 513 451*	...	...	...	...	...	...	...
Bento Gonçalves	*114 203*	...	...	...	...	...	...	...
Betim	*422 354*	...	...	...	...	...	...	...
Birigui	*119 536*	...	...	...	...	...	...	...
Blumenou	*343 715*	...	...	...	...	...	...	...
Boa Vista	*326 419*	...	...	...	...	...	...	...
Botucatu	*141 032*	...	...	...	...	...	...	...
Bragança	*122 881*	...	...	...	...	...	...	...
Bragança Paulista	*162 435*	...	...	...	...	...	...	...
BRASILIA	*2 977 216*	...	...	...	...	...	...	...
Brusque	*125 810*	...	...	...	...	...	...	...
Cabo de Santo Agostinho	*202 636*	...	...	...	...	...	...	...
Cabo Frio	*212 289*	...	...	...	...	...	...	...
Cachoeirinha	*126 666*	...	...	...	...	...	...	...
Cachoeiro de Itapemirim	*210 325*	...	...	...	...	...	...	...
Camacari	*292 074*	...	...	...	...	...	...	...
Camaragibe	*155 228*	...	...	...	...	...	...	...
Cambé	*104 592*	...	...	...	...	...	...	...
Cametá	*132 515*	...	...	...	...	...	...	...
Campina Grande	*407 754*	...	...	...	...	...	...	...
Campinas	*1 173 370*	...	...	...	...	...	...	...
Campo Grande	*863 982*	...	...	...	...	...	...	...
Campo Largo	*125 719*	...	...	...	...	...	...	...
Campos dos Goytacazes	*487 186*	...	...	...	...	...	...	...
Canoas	*342 634*	...	...	...	...	...	...	...
Caraguatatuba	*115 071*	...	...	...	...	...	...	...
Carapicuíba	*394 465*	...	...	...	...	...	...	...
Cariacica	*384 621*	...	...	...	...	...	...	...

8. Population of capital cities and cities of 100 000 or more inhabitants: latest available year, 2000 - 2019
Population des capitales et des villes de 100 000 habitants ou plus : dernière année disponible, 2000 - 2019 (continued - suite)

Continent, country or area, date, code[a] and city Continent, pays ou zone, date, code[a] et ville	City proper - Ville proprement dite				Urban agglomeration - Agglomération urbaine			
	Population				Population			
	Both sexes - Les deux sexes	Male - Masculin	Female - Féminin	Surface area - Superficie (km²)	Both sexes - Les deux sexes	Male - Masculin	Female - Féminin	Surface area - Superficie (km²)
AMERICA, SOUTH - AMÉRIQUE DU SUD								
Brazil - Brésil[34]								
1 VII 2016 (ESDJ)								
Caruaru	*351 686*	...	...	...	...	...	...	...
Cascavel	*316 226*	...	...	...	...	...	...	...
Castanhal	*192 571*	...	...	...	...	...	...	...
Catalão	*100 590*	...	...	...	...	...	...	...
Catanduva	*120 092*	...	...	...	...	...	...	...
Caucaia	*358 164*	...	...	...	...	...	...	...
Caxias	*161 926*	...	...	...	...	...	...	...
Caxias do Sul	*479 236*	...	...	...	...	...	...	...
Chapecó	*209 553*	...	...	...	...	...	...	...
Codo	*120 548*	...	...	...	...	...	...	...
Colatina	*123 598*	...	...	...	...	...	...	...
Colombo	*234 941*	...	...	...	...	...	...	...
Conselheiro Lafaiete	*126 420*	...	...	...	...	...	...	...
Contagem	*653 800*	...	...	...	...	...	...	...
Coronel Fabriciano	*109 857*	...	...	...	...	...	...	...
Corumbá	*109 294*	...	...	...	...	...	...	...
Cotia	*233 696*	...	...	...	...	...	...	...
Crato	*129 662*	...	...	...	...	...	...	...
Criciúma	*209 153*	...	...	...	...	...	...	...
Cubatao	*127 887*	...	...	...	...	...	...	...
Cuiabá	*585 367*	...	...	...	...	...	...	...
Curitiba	*1 893 997*	...	...	...	...	...	...	...
Diadema	*415 180*	...	...	...	...	...	...	...
Divinópolis	*232 945*	...	...	...	...	...	...	...
Dourados	*215 486*	...	...	...	...	...	...	...
Duque de Caxias	*886 917*	...	...	...	...	...	...	...
Embu	*264 448*	...	...	...	...	...	...	...
Erechim	*102 906*	...	...	...	...	...	...	...
Eunápolis	*114 275*	...	...	...	...	...	...	...
Feira de Santana	*622 639*	...	...	...	...	...	...	...
Ferraz de Vasconcelos	*186 808*	...	...	...	...	...	...	...
Florianópolis	*477 798*	...	...	...	...	...	...	...
Formosa	*114 036*	...	...	...	...	...	...	...
Fortaleza	*2 609 716*	...	...	...	...	...	...	...
Foz do Iguaçu	*263 915*	...	...	...	...	...	...	...
Franca	*344 704*	...	...	...	...	...	...	...
Francisco Morato	*169 942*	...	...	...	...	...	...	...
Franco da Rocha	*147 650*	...	...	...	...	...	...	...
Garanhuns	*137 810*	...	...	...	...	...	...	...
Goiânia	*1 448 639*	...	...	...	...	...	...	...
Governador Valadares	*279 665*	...	...	...	...	...	...	...
Gravatai	*273 742*	...	...	...	...	...	...	...
Guarapari	*121 506*	...	...	...	...	...	...	...
Guarapuava	*179 256*	...	...	...	...	...	...	...
Guaratinguetá	*119 753*	...	...	...	...	...	...	...
Guarujá	*313 421*	...	...	...	...	...	...	...
Guarulhos	*1 337 087*	...	...	...	...	...	...	...
Hortolandia	*219 039*	...	...	...	...	...	...	...
Ibirité	*175 721*	...	...	...	...	...	...	...
Igarassu	*113 956*	...	...	...	...	...	...	...
Iguatu	*102 013*	...	...	...	...	...	...	...
Ilhéus	*178 210*	...	...	...	...	...	...	...
Imperatriz	*253 873*	...	...	...	...	...	...	...
Indaiatuba	*235 367*	...	...	...	...	...	...	...
Ipatinga	*259 324*	...	...	...	...	...	...	...
Itabiraí	*118 481*	...	...	...	...	...	...	...
Itaboraí	*230 786*	...	...	...	...	...	...	...
Itabuna	*220 386*	...	...	...	...	...	...	...
Itaguaí	*120 855*	...	...	...	...	...	...	...
Itajaí	*208 958*	...	...	...	...	...	...	...
Itapecerica da Serra	*169 103*	...	...	...	...	...	...	...
Itapetininga	*158 561*	...	...	...	...	...	...	...
Itapevi	*226 488*	...	...	...	...	...	...	...

8. Population of capital cities and cities of 100 000 or more inhabitants: latest available year, 2000 - 2019
Population des capitales et des villes de 100 000 habitants ou plus : dernière année disponible, 2000 - 2019 (continued - suite)

Continent, country or area, date, code[a] and city / Continent, pays ou zone, date, code[a] et ville	City proper - Ville proprement dite: Population: Both sexes - Les deux sexes	City proper: Population: Male - Masculin	City proper: Population: Female - Féminin	City proper: Surface area - Superficie (km²)	Urban agglomeration - Agglomération urbaine: Population: Both sexes - Les deux sexes	Urban agglomeration: Population: Male - Masculin	Urban agglomeration: Population: Female - Féminin	Urban agglomeration: Surface area - Superficie (km²)
AMERICA, SOUTH - AMÉRIQUE DU SUD								
Brazil - Brésil[34]								
1 VII 2016 (ESDJ)								
Itapipoca	*126 234*	...	...	...	...	...	...	...
Itaquaquecetuba	*356 774*	...	...	...	...	...	...	...
Itatiba	*114 912*	...	...	...	...	...	...	...
Itu	*168 643*	...	...	...	...	...	...	...
Ituiutaba	*103 945*	...	...	...	...	...	...	...
Itumbiara	*101 544*	...	...	...	...	...	...	...
Jaboatao dos Guarapes	*691 125*	...	...	...	...	...	...	...
Jacareí	*228 214*	...	...	...	...	...	...	...
Jandira	*120 177*	...	...	...	...	...	...	...
Japeri	*100 562*	...	...	...	...	...	...	...
Jaraguá do Sul	*167 300*	...	...	...	...	...	...	...
Jaú	*144 828*	...	...	...	...	...	...	...
Jequié	*161 880*	...	...	...	...	...	...	...
Ji-Paraná	*131 560*	...	...	...	...	...	...	...
Joao Pessoa	*801 718*	...	...	...	...	...	...	...
Joinville	*569 645*	...	...	...	...	...	...	...
Juazeiro	*220 253*	...	...	...	...	...	...	...
Juàzeiro do Norte	*268 248*	...	...	...	...	...	...	...
Juiz de Fora	*559 636*	...	...	...	...	...	...	...
Jundiaí	*405 740*	...	...	...	...	...	...	...
Lagarto	*103 188*	...	...	...	...	...	...	...
Lages	*158 620*	...	...	...	...	...	...	...
Lauro de Freitas	*194 641*	...	...	...	...	...	...	...
Lavras	*101 208*	...	...	...	...	...	...	...
Leme	*100 296*	...	...	...	...	...	...	...
Limeira	*298 701*	...	...	...	...	...	...	...
Linhares	*166 491*	...	...	...	...	...	...	...
Londrina	*553 393*	...	...	...	...	...	...	...
Luziânia	*196 864*	...	...	...	...	...	...	...
Macae	*239 471*	...	...	...	...	...	...	...
Macapá	*465 495*	...	...	...	...	...	...	...
Maceió	*1 021 709*	...	...	...	...	...	...	...
Magé	*236 319*	...	...	...	...	...	...	...
Manaus	*2 094 391*	...	...	...	...	...	...	...
Maraba	*266 932*	...	...	...	...	...	...	...
Maracanau	*223 188*	...	...	...	...	...	...	...
Maranguape	*125 058*	...	...	...	...	...	...	...
Maricá	*149 876*	...	...	...	...	...	...	...
Marília	*233 639*	...	...	...	...	...	...	...
Maringá	*403 063*	...	...	...	...	...	...	...
Marituba	*125 435*	...	...	...	...	...	...	...
Mauá	*457 696*	...	...	...	...	...	...	...
Mesquita	*171 020*	...	...	...	...	...	...	...
Moji das Cruzes	*429 321*	...	...	...	...	...	...	...
Moji-Guaçu	*148 327*	...	...	...	...	...	...	...
Montes Claros	*398 288*	...	...	...	...	...	...	...
Mossoró	*291 937*	...	...	...	...	...	...	...
Muriaé	*107 916*	...	...	...	...	...	...	...
Natal	*877 662*	...	...	...	...	...	...	...
Nilópolis	*158 319*	...	...	...	...	...	...	...
Niterói	*497 883*	...	...	...	...	...	...	...
Nossa Senhora do Socorro	*179 661*	...	...	...	...	...	...	...
Nova Friburgo	*185 102*	...	...	...	...	...	...	...
Nova Iguaçu	*797 435*	...	...	...	...	...	...	...
Novo Gama	*108 410*	...	...	...	...	...	...	...
Nôvo Hamburgo	*249 113*	...	...	...	...	...	...	...
Olinda	*390 144*	...	...	...	...	...	...	...
Osasco	*696 382*	...	...	...	...	...	...	...
Ourinhos	*111 056*	...	...	...	...	...	...	...
Paço do Lumiar	*119 915*	...	...	...	...	...	...	...
Palhoça	*161 395*	...	...	...	...	...	...	...
Palmas	*279 856*	...	...	...	...	...	...	...
Paragominas	*108 547*	...	...	...	...	...	...	...

8. Population of capital cities and cities of 100 000 or more inhabitants: latest available year, 2000 - 2019
Population des capitales et des villes de 100 000 habitants ou plus : dernière année disponible, 2000 - 2019 (continued - suite)

Continent, country or area, date, code[a] and city / Continent, pays ou zone, date, code[a] et ville	City proper - Ville proprement dite: Population: Both sexes - Les deux sexes	City proper: Population: Male - Masculin	City proper: Population: Female - Féminin	City proper: Surface area - Superficie (km²)	Urban agglomeration - Agglomération urbaine: Population: Both sexes - Les deux sexes	Urban agglomeration: Population: Male - Masculin	Urban agglomeration: Population: Female - Féminin	Urban agglomeration: Surface area - Superficie (km²)
AMERICA, SOUTH - AMÉRIQUE DU SUD								
Brazil - Brésil[34]								
1 VII 2016 (ESDJ)								
Paranaguá	*151 829*	...	...	...	...	...	...	...
Parauapebas	*196 259*	...	...	...	...	...	...	...
Parintins	*112 716*	...	...	...	...	...	...	...
Parnaíba	*150 201*	...	...	...	...	...	...	...
Parnamirim	*248 623*	...	...	...	...	...	...	...
Passo Fundo	*197 798*	...	...	...	...	...	...	...
Passos	*113 807*	...	...	...	...	...	...	...
Patos	*107 067*	...	...	...	...	...	...	...
Patos de Minas	*149 856*	...	...	...	...	...	...	...
Paulínia	*100 128*	...	...	...	...	...	...	...
Paulista	*325 590*	...	...	...	...	...	...	...
Paulo Afonso	*119 930*	...	...	...	...	...	...	...
Pelotas	*343 651*	...	...	...	...	...	...	...
Petrolina	*337 683*	...	...	...	...	...	...	...
Petrópolis	*298 158*	...	...	...	...	...	...	...
Pindamonhangaba	*162 327*	...	...	...	...	...	...	...
Pinhais	*128 256*	...	...	...	...	...	...	...
Piracicaba	*394 419*	...	...	...	...	...	...	...
Piraquara	*106 132*	...	...	...	...	...	...	...
Poà	*114 650*	...	...	...	...	...	...	...
Poços de Caldas	*164 912*	...	...	...	...	...	...	...
Ponta Grossa	*341 130*	...	...	...	...	...	...	...
Porto Alegre	*1 481 019*	...	...	...	...	...	...	...
Porto Seguro	*147 444*	...	...	...	...	...	...	...
Porto Velho	*511 219*	...	...	...	...	...	...	...
Pouso Alegre	*145 535*	...	...	...	...	...	...	...
Praia Grande	*304 705*	...	...	...	...	...	...	...
Presidente Prudente	*223 749*	...	...	...	...	...	...	...
Queimados	*144 525*	...	...	...	...	...	...	...
Recife	*1 625 583*	...	...	...	...	...	...	...
Resende	*126 084*	...	...	...	...	...	...	...
Ribeirao das Neves	*325 846*	...	...	...	...	...	...	...
Ribeirao Pires	*121 130*	...	...	...	...	...	...	...
Ribeirao Prêto	*674 405*	...	...	...	...	...	...	...
Rio Branco	*377 057*	...	...	...	...	...	...	...
Rio Claro	*201 473*	...	...	...	...	...	...	...
Rio das Ostras	*136 626*	...	...	...	...	...	...	...
Rio de Janeiro	*6 498 837*	...	...	...	...	...	...	...
Rio Grande	*208 641*	...	...	...	...	...	...	...
Rio Verde	*212 237*	...	...	...	...	...	...	...
Rondonópolis	*218 899*	...	...	...	...	...	...	...
Sabára	*135 196*	...	...	...	...	...	...	...
Salto	*115 193*	...	...	...	...	...	...	...
Salvador	*2 938 092*	...	...	...	...	...	...	...
Santa Bárbara D'Oeste	*191 024*	...	...	...	...	...	...	...
Santa Cruz do Capibaribe	*103 660*	...	...	...	...	...	...	...
Santa Cruz do Sul	*126 775*	...	...	...	...	...	...	...
Santa Luzia (Minas Gerais)	*217 610*	...	...	...	...	...	...	...
Santa Maria	*277 309*	...	...	...	...	...	...	...
Santa Rita	*135 915*	...	...	...	...	...	...	...
Santana	*113 854*	...	...	...	...	...	...	...
Santana de Parnaíba	*129 261*	...	...	...	...	...	...	...
Santarém	*294 447*	...	...	...	...	...	...	...
Santo André	*712 749*	...	...	...	...	...	...	...
Santo Antônio de Jesus	*102 469*	...	...	...	...	...	...	...
Santos	*434 359*	...	...	...	...	...	...	...
Sao Bernardo do Campo	*822 242*	...	...	...	...	...	...	...
Sao Caetano do Sul	*158 825*	...	...	...	...	...	...	...
Sao Carlo	*243 765*	...	...	...	...	...	...	...
São Félix do Xingu	*120 580*	...	...	...	...	...	...	...
Sao Gonçalo	*1 044 058*	...	...	...	...	...	...	...
Sao Joao de Meriti	*460 541*	...	...	...	...	...	...	...
Sao José	*236 029*	...	...	...	...	...	...	...

8. Population of capital cities and cities of 100 000 or more inhabitants: latest available year, 2000 - 2019
Population des capitales et des villes de 100 000 habitants ou plus : dernière année disponible, 2000 - 2019 (continued - suite)

Continent, country or area, date, code[a] and city - Continent, pays ou zone, date, code[a] et ville	City proper - Ville proprement dite				Urban agglomeration - Agglomération urbaine			
	Population				Population			
	Both sexes - Les deux sexes	Male - Masculin	Female - Féminin	Surface area - Superficie (km²)	Both sexes - Les deux sexes	Male - Masculin	Female - Féminin	Surface area - Superficie (km²)
AMERICA, SOUTH - AMÉRIQUE DU SUD								
Brazil - Brésil[34]								
1 VII 2016 (ESDJ)								
Sao José de Ribamar	*176 008*	...	...	...	...	...	...	...
Sao José do Rio Prêto	*446 649*	...	...	...	...	...	...	...
Sao José dos Campos	*695 992*	...	...	...	...	...	...	...
Sao José dos Pinhais	*302 759*	...	...	...	...	...	...	...
Sao Leopoldo	*229 678*	...	...	...	...	...	...	...
São Lourenço da Mata	*111 197*	...	...	...	...	...	...	...
Sao Luís	*1 082 935*	...	...	...	...	...	...	...
São Mateus	*126 437*	...	...	...	...	...	...	...
Sao Paulo	*12 038 175*	...	...	...	...	...	...	...
Sao Vicente	*357 989*	...	...	...	...	...	...	...
Sapucaia do Sul	*138 933*	...	...	...	...	...	...	...
Senador Canedo	*102 947*	...	...	...	...	...	...	...
Serra	*494 109*	...	...	...	...	...	...	...
Sertaozinho	*121 412*	...	...	...	...	...	...	...
Sete Lagoas	*234 221*	...	...	...	...	...	...	...
Simoes Filho	*134 674*	...	...	...	...	...	...	...
Sinop	*132 934*	...	...	...	...	...	...	...
Sobral	*203 682*	...	...	...	...	...	...	...
Sorocaba	*652 481*	...	...	...	...	...	...	...
Sumaré	*269 522*	...	...	...	...	...	...	...
Susano	*288 056*	...	...	...	...	...	...	...
Taboao da Serra	*275 948*	...	...	...	...	...	...	...
Tailândia	*100 300*	...	...	...	...	...	...	...
Tatuí	*117 823*	...	...	...	...	...	...	...
Taubaté	*305 174*	...	...	...	...	...	...	...
Teixeira de Freitas	*159 813*	...	...	...	...	...	...	...
Teófilo Otoni	*141 502*	...	...	...	...	...	...	...
Teresina	*847 430*	...	...	...	...	...	...	...
Teresópolis	*174 587*	...	...	...	...	...	...	...
Timon	*166 295*	...	...	...	...	...	...	...
Toledo	*133 824*	...	...	...	...	...	...	...
Três Lagoas	*115 561*	...	...	...	...	...	...	...
Trindade	*119 385*	...	...	...	...	...	...	...
Tubarão	*103 674*	...	...	...	...	...	...	...
Tucuruí	*108 885*	...	...	...	...	...	...	...
Ubá	*112 186*	...	...	...	...	...	...	...
Uberaba	*325 279*	...	...	...	...	...	...	...
Uberlândia	*669 672*	...	...	...	...	...	...	...
Umuarama	*109 132*	...	...	...	...	...	...	...
Uruguaiana	*129 720*	...	...	...	...	...	...	...
Valinhos	*122 163*	...	...	...	...	...	...	...
Valparaíso de Goiás	*156 419*	...	...	...	...	...	...	...
Varginha	*133 384*	...	...	...	...	...	...	...
Varzea Grande	*271 339*	...	...	...	...	...	...	...
Varzea Paulista	*117 772*	...	...	...	...	...	...	...
Vespasiano	*120 510*	...	...	...	...	...	...	...
Viamao	*252 872*	...	...	...	...	...	...	...
Vila Velha	*479 664*	...	...	...	...	...	...	...
Vitória	*359 555*	...	...	...	...	...	...	...
Vitória da Conquista	*346 069*	...	...	...	...	...	...	...
Vitória de Santo Antao	*136 706*	...	...	...	...	...	...	...
Volta Redonda	*263 659*	...	...	...	...	...	...	...
Votorantim	*118 858*	...	...	...	...	...	...	...
Chile - Chili								
1 VII 2017 (ESDF)								
Alto Hospicio	124 877	63 281	61 596	17[32]	...	...	...	...
Antofagasta	388 545	205 983	182 562	44[32]	...	...	...	...
Arica	229 689	114 441	115 248	42[32]	...	...	...	...
Calama	180 283	91 633	88 650	18[32]	...	...	...	...
Chiguallante	101 244	48 160	53 084	34[32]	...	...	...	...
Chillán	159 476	75 030	84 446	33[32]	...	...	...	...
Concepción	220 746	104 151	116 595	56[32]	...	...	...	...
Copiapó	175 162	88 912	86 250	48[32]	...	...	...	...

8. Population of capital cities and cities of 100 000 or more inhabitants: latest available year, 2000 - 2019
Population des capitales et des villes de 100 000 habitants ou plus : dernière année disponible, 2000 - 2019 (continued - suite)

Continent, country or area, date, code[a] and city Continent, pays ou zone, date, code[a] et ville	City proper - Ville proprement dite				Urban agglomeration - Agglomération urbaine			
	Population				Population			
	Both sexes - Les deux sexes	Male - Masculin	Female - Féminin	Surface area - Superficie (km²)	Both sexes - Les deux sexes	Male - Masculin	Female - Féminin	Surface area - Superficie (km²)
AMERICA, SOUTH - AMÉRIQUE DU SUD								
Chile - Chili								
1 VII 2017 (ESDF)								
Coquimbo	216 623	105 602	111 021	42[32]	...	...	...	...
Coronel	109 709	51 462	58 247	25[32]	...	...	...	...
Curicó	102 710	49 371	53 339	21[32]	...	...	...	...
Hualpén	108 803	50 733	58 070	11.9[32]	...	...	...	...
Iquique	196 562	98 599	97 963	22[32]	...	...	...	...
La Serena	205 635	100 151	105 484	66[32]	...	...	...	...
Los Ángeles	128 933	61 836	67 097	27[32]	...	...	...	...
Osorno	139 550	66 890	72 660	32[32]	...	...	...	...
Puente Alto	625 551	308 490	317 061	64[32]	...	...	...	...
Puerto Montt	213 119	106 266	106 853	40[32]	...	...	...	...
Punta Arenas	124 169	61 603	62 566	39[32]	...	...	...	...
Quilpué	172 049	83 317	88 732	38[32]	...	...	...	...
Rancagua	225 563	112 119	113 444	50[32]	...	...	...	...
San Bernardo	296 583	147 549	149 034	52[32]	...	...	...	...
San Pedro de la Paz	139 174	64 934	74 240	49[32]	...	...	...	...
SANTIAGO	5 613 962[35]	2 723 688[35]	2 890 274[35]	843[32]	...	...	...	...
Talca	203 873	97 557	106 316	46[32]	...	...	...	...
Temuco	221 375	105 706	115 669	46[32]	...	...	...	...
Valdivia	143 207	69 519	73 688	42[32]	...	...	...	...
Valparaíso	295 113	147 418	147 695	47[32]	...	...	...	...
Villa Alemana	144 417	70 578	73 839	31[32]	...	...	...	...
Viña del Mar	326 759	157 481	169 278	87[32]	...	...	...	...
Colombia - Colombie[36]								
1 VII 2019 (ESDJ)								
Apartadó	*200 931*	*101 466*	*99 465*	...	...	...	...	...
Armenia (Quindio)	*302 723*	*146 216*	*156 507*	...	...	...	...	...
Barrancabermeja	*191 340*	*94 571*	*96 769*	...	...	...	...	...
Barranquilla	*1 236 202*	*600 305*	*635 897*	...	...	...	...	...
Bello	*491 182*	*237 207*	*253 975*	...	...	...	...	...
BOGOTÁ, D.C.	*8 281 030*	*4 014 441*	*4 266 589*	...	...	...	...	...
Bucaramanga	*528 610*	*254 893*	*273 717*	...	...	...	...	...
Buenaventura	*432 501*	*210 328*	*222 173*	...	...	...	...	...
Cali	*2 470 852*	*1 181 058*	*1 289 794*	...	...	...	...	...
Cartagena	*1 047 005*	*506 895*	*540 110*	...	...	...	...	...
Cartago	*134 972*	*65 006*	*69 966*	...	...	...	...	...
Caucasia	*123 304*	*59 778*	*63 526*	...	...	...	...	...
Chía	*138 822*	*66 821*	*72 001*	...	...	...	...	...
Ciénaga (Magdalena)	*105 510*	*52 797*	*52 713*	...	...	...	...	...
Cúcuta	*674 831*	*326 351*	*348 480*	...	...	...	...	...
Dosquebradas	*206 692*	*101 249*	*105 443*	...	...	...	...	...
Duitama	*114 413*	*52 189*	*62 224*	...	...	...	...	...
Envigado	*243 609*	*117 080*	*126 529*	...	...	...	...	...
Facatativá	*141 762*	*70 866*	*70 896*	...	...	...	...	...
Florencia	*184 510*	*90 736*	*93 774*	...	...	...	...	...
Floridablanca	*267 538*	*127 664*	*139 874*	...	...	...	...	...
Fusagasugá	*145 039*	*71 880*	*73 159*	...	...	...	...	...
Girardot	*107 324*	*50 624*	*56 700*	...	...	...	...	...
Girón	*200 733*	*100 369*	*100 364*	...	...	...	...	...
Gudalajara de Buga	*114 316*	*56 014*	*58 302*	...	...	...	...	...
Ibagué	*574 568*	*278 876*	*295 692*	...	...	...	...	...
Ipiales	*151 533*	*74 834*	*76 699*	...	...	...	...	...
Itagüí	*279 871*	*136 532*	*143 339*	...	...	...	...	...
Jamundí	*129 877*	*63 033*	*66 844*	...	...	...	...	...
Lorica	*121 214*	*60 494*	*60 720*	...	...	...	...	...
Magangué	*123 982*	*62 758*	*61 224*	...	...	...	...	...
Maicao	*166 603*	*81 934*	*84 669*	...	...	...	...	...
Malambo	*129 148*	*65 914*	*63 234*	...	...	...	...	...
Manaure	*120 417*	*59 289*	*61 128*	...	...	...	...	...
Manizales	*401 398*	*191 476*	*209 922*	...	...	...	...	...
Medellín	*2 549 537*	*1 197 836*	*1 351 701*	...	...	...	...	...
Montería	*465 999*	*226 076*	*239 923*	...	...	...	...	...
Neiva	*348 964*	*166 896*	*182 068*	...	...	...	...	...

8. Population of capital cities and cities of 100 000 or more inhabitants: latest available year, 2000 - 2019
Population des capitales et des villes de 100 000 habitants ou plus : dernière année disponible, 2000 - 2019 (continued - suite)

Continent, country or area, date, code[a] and city / Continent, pays ou zone, date, code[a] et ville	City proper - Ville proprement dite: Population: Both sexes - Les deux sexes	Male - Masculin	Female - Féminin	Surface area - Superficie (km²)	Urban agglomeration - Agglomération urbaine: Population: Both sexes - Les deux sexes	Male - Masculin	Female - Féminin	Surface area - Superficie (km²)
AMERICA, SOUTH - AMÉRIQUE DU SUD								
Colombia - Colombie[36]								
1 VII 2019 (ESDJ)								
Ocaña	*101 158*	*49 988*	*51 170*	...	...	...	...	...
Palmira	*312 507*	*150 665*	*161 842*	...	...	...	...	...
Pasto	*460 454*	*222 932*	*237 522*	...	...	...	...	...
Pereira	*478 892*	*226 220*	*252 672*	...	...	...	...	...
Piedecuesta	*163 362*	*79 318*	*84 044*	...	...	...	...	...
Pitalito	*135 711*	*67 348*	*68 363*	...	...	...	...	...
Popayán	*286 724*	*139 246*	*147 478*	...	...	...	...	...
Quibdo	*116 256*	*58 548*	*57 708*	...	...	...	...	...
Riohacha	*295 984*	*145 944*	*150 040*	...	...	...	...	...
Rionegro (Antioquia)	*128 153*	*63 448*	*64 705*	...	...	...	...	...
Sabanalarga	*102 334*	*52 146*	*50 188*	...	...	...	...	...
San Andrés de Tumaco	*217 079*	*108 081*	*108 998*	...	...	...	...	...
Santa Marta	*515 717*	*252 573*	*263 144*	...	...	...	...	...
Sincelejo	*290 667*	*143 168*	*147 499*	...	...	...	...	...
Soacha	*556 268*	*274 728*	*281 540*	...	...	...	...	...
Sogamoso	*111 336*	*52 762*	*58 574*	...	...	...	...	...
Soledad	*683 580*	*338 478*	*345 102*	...	...	...	...	...
Tierralta	*109 770*	*55 606*	*54 164*	...	...	...	...	...
Tuluá	*221 701*	*106 459*	*115 242*	...	...	...	...	...
Tunja	*202 996*	*97 506*	*105 490*	...	...	...	...	...
Turbo	*176 813*	*88 933*	*87 880*	...	...	...	...	...
Uribia	*198 890*	*97 447*	*101 443*	...	...	...	...	...
Valledupar	*493 367*	*241 203*	*252 164*	...	...	...	...	...
Villavicencio	*527 673*	*256 303*	*271 370*	...	...	...	...	...
Yopal	*152 655*	*76 355*	*76 300*	...	...	...	...	...
Yumbo	*128 616*	*64 566*	*64 050*	...	...	...	...	...
Zipaquirá	*130 432*	*64 266*	*66 166*	...	...	...	...	...
Ecuador - Équateur[28]								
1 VII 2019 (ESDF)								
Ambato	*178 772*	...	...	...	...	...	...	...
Babahoyo	*103 564*	...	...	...	...	...	...	...
Cuenca	*403 745*	...	...	...	...	...	...	...
Daule	*110 394*	...	...	...	...	...	...	...
Durán	*302 227*	...	...	...	...	...	...	...
Esmeraldas	*200 327*	...	...	...	...	...	...	...
Guayaquil	*2 606 168*	...	...	...	...	...	...	...
Ibarra	*162 501*	...	...	...	...	...	...	...
La Libertad	*115 952*	...	...	...	...	...	...	...
Loja	*233 097*	...	...	...	...	...	...	...
Machala	*269 198*	...	...	...	...	...	...	...
Manta	*253 259*	...	...	...	...	...	...	...
Milagro	*156 041*	...	...	...	...	...	...	...
Portoviejo	*240 602*	...	...	...	...	...	...	...
Quevedo	*184 542*	...	...	...	...	...	...	...
QUITO	*1 817 229*	...	...	...	...	...	...	...
Riobamba	*170 449*	...	...	...	...	...	...	...
Santo Domingo de los Colorados	*342 057*	...	...	...	...	...	...	...
Falkland Islands (Malvinas) - Îles Falkland (Malvinas)[37]								
9 X 2016 (CDJC)								
STANLEY	2 460	1 261[38]	1 197[38]	...	...	...	...	...
French Guiana - Guyane française								
1 I 2015 (CDJC)								
CAYENNE	57 614	26 666	30 948	...	114 017	54 462	59 555	...
Guyana								
15 IX 2012 (CDFC)								
GEORGETOWN	24 849	...	...	...	118 368	...	...	...
Paraguay								
1 VII 2014 (ESDF)								
ASUNCIÓN[39]	*512 919*	*236 790*	*276 129*	117	*2 887 087*	*1 402 891*	*1 484 196*	2582
Capiatá	*257 116*	*127 676*	*129 440*	87.7	...	...	...	...
Ciudad del Este	*317 525*	*159 726*	*157 799*	149	...	...	...	...
Fernando de la Mora	*200 112*	*95 174*	*104 937*	21	...	...	...	...

8. Population of capital cities and cities of 100 000 or more inhabitants: latest available year, 2000 - 2019
Population des capitales et des villes de 100 000 habitants ou plus : dernière année disponible, 2000 - 2019 (continued - suite)

Continent, country or area, date, code[a] and city / Continent, pays ou zone, date, code[a] et ville	City proper - Ville proprement dite: Population: Both sexes - Les deux sexes	Male - Masculin	Female - Féminin	Surface area - Superficie (km²)	Urban agglomeration - Agglomération urbaine: Population: Both sexes - Les deux sexes	Male - Masculin	Female - Féminin	Surface area - Superficie (km²)
AMERICA, SOUTH - AMÉRIQUE DU SUD								
Paraguay								
1 VII 2014 (ESDF)								
Lambaré	*210 725*	*101 019*	*109 706*	26.8	...	...	...	...
Luque	*358 265*	*175 663*	*182 602*	152.5	...	...	...	...
San Lorenzo	*354 283*	*171 242*	*183 042*	54.2	...	...	...	...
Peru - Pérou								
30 VI 2018 (ESDF)								
Arequipa	*893 491*	*429 534*	*463 957*	...	...	...	...	...
Ayacucho	*190 861*	*94 254*	*96 607*	...	...	...	...	...
Cajamarca	*248 222*	*122 101*	*126 121*	...	...	...	...	...
Chiclayo	*617 089*	*293 991*	*323 098*	...	...	...	...	...
Chimbote	*380 011*	*191 689*	*188 322*	...	...	...	...	...
Chincha Alta	*185 054*	*92 784*	*92 270*	...	...	...	...	...
Cuzco	*448 124*	*217 973*	*230 151*	...	...	...	...	...
Huancayo	*375 857*	*178 123*	*197 734*	...	...	...	...	...
Huánuco	*181 318*	*86 297*	*95 021*	...	...	...	...	...
Huaral	*102 811*	*50 641*	*52 170*	...	...	...	...	...
Huaraz	*136 628*	*67 152*	*69 476*	...	...	...	...	...
Ica	*251 573*	*124 069*	*127 504*	...	...	...	...	...
Iquitos	*450 799*	*227 401*	*223 398*	...	...	...	...	...
Jaen	*100 551*	*49 999*	*50 552*	...	...	...	...	...
Juliaca	*294 921*	*143 315*	*151 606*	...	...	...	...	...
LIMA[40]	*10 350 721*	*5 026 529*	*5 324 192*	...	...	...	...	...
Paita	*104 367*	*51 908*	*52 459*	...	...	...	...	...
Pisco	*105 394*	*53 747*	*51 647*	...	...	...	...	...
Piura	*458 262*	*222 570*	*235 692*	...	...	...	...	...
Pucallpa	*211 708*	*110 628*	*101 080*	...	...	...	...	...
Puno	*147 385*	*71 407*	*75 978*	...	...	...	...	...
Sullana	*206 213*	*100 741*	*105 472*	...	...	...	...	...
Tacna	*306 021*	*155 738*	*150 283*	...	...	...	...	...
Tarapoto	*153 613*	*79 932*	*73 681*	...	...	...	...	...
Trujillo	*833 379*	*404 885*	*428 494*	...	...	...	...	...
Tumbes	*115 141*	*62 636*	*52 505*	...	...	...	...	...
Suriname								
13 VIII 2012 (CDJC)								
PARAMARIBO	240 924	119 439	121 485	182	...	...	...	...
Wanica	118 222	57 776	60 446	443	...	...	...	...
Uruguay[41]								
1 VII 2019 (ESDJ)								
MONTEVIDEO	1 382 579	651 365	731 214	...	...	...	...	...
Venezuela (Bolivarian Republic of) - Venezuela (République bolivarienne du)								
1 VII 2015 (ESDF)								
Anaco(F) (Capital)	140 496	...	...	...	...	...	...	...
Barinas	389 578	...	...	...	...	...	...	...
Barquisimeto	881 127	...	...	...	...	...	...	...
Baruta	358 221	...	...	...	...	...	...	...
Cabimas	293 365	...	...	...	...	...	...	...
Cagua	118 290	...	...	...	...	...	...	...
CARACAS	2 082 130	...	...	...	...	...	...	...
Carora	111 963	...	...	...	...	...	...	...
Carúpano	156 380	...	...	...	...	...	...	...
Ciudad Bolívar	407 452	...	...	...	...	...	...	...
Ciudad Guayana	877 547	...	...	...	...	...	...	...
Ciudad Ojeda	216 489	...	...	...	...	...	...	...
Cua	143 164	...	...	...	...	...	...	...
Cumaná	358 138	...	...	...	...	...	...	...
El Tigre	203 403	...	...	...	...	...	...	...
Guacara	192 536	...	...	...	...	...	...	...
Guanare	160 234	...	...	...	...	...	...	...
Guarenas	247 131	...	...	...	...	...	...	...
Guatire	177 794	...	...	...	...	...	...	...
Los Guayos	173 878	...	...	...	...	...	...	...
Los Teques	216 358	...	...	...	...	...	...	...
Maracaibo	1 653 215	...	...	...	...	...	...	...

8. Population of capital cities and cities of 100 000 or more inhabitants: latest available year, 2000 - 2019
Population des capitales et des villes de 100 000 habitants ou plus : dernière année disponible, 2000 - 2019 (continued - suite)

Continent, country or area, date, code[a] and city Continent, pays ou zone, date, code[a] et ville	City proper - Ville proprement dite				Urban agglomeration - Agglomération urbaine			
	Population				Population			
	Both sexes - Les deux sexes	Male - Masculin	Female - Féminin	Surface area - Superficie (km²)	Both sexes - Les deux sexes	Male - Masculin	Female - Féminin	Surface area - Superficie (km²)
AMERICA, SOUTH - AMÉRIQUE DU SUD								
Venezuela (Bolivarian Republic of) - Venezuela (République bolivarienne du)								
1 VII 2015 (ESDF)								
Maracay	419 052	...	...	...	...	...	...	...
Maturín	571 276	...	...	...	...	...	...	...
Mérida	248 410	...	...	...	...	...	...	...
Naguanagua	161 658	...	...	...	...	...	...	...
Ocumare Del Tuy	197 952	...	...	...	...	...	...	...
Petare	434 320	...	...	...	...	...	...	...
Pozuelos (F) (Capital)	144 045	...	...	...	...	...	...	...
Puerto Cabello	193 025	...	...	...	...	...	...	...
Punto Fijo	272 239	...	...	...	...	...	...	...
San Cristóbal	282 830	...	...	...	...	...	...	...
San Fernando de Apure	217 590	...	...	...	...	...	...	...
San Francisco	106 763	...	...	...	...	...	...	...
Santa Lucía	133 543	...	...	...	...	...	...	...
Táriba	132 657	...	...	...	...	...	...	...
Tocuyito	186 755	...	...	...	...	...	...	...
Turmero	238 570	...	...	...	...	...	...	...
Valencia	888 109	...	...	...	...	...	...	...
Valera	161 771	...	...	...	...	...	...	...
ASIA - ASIE								
Afghanistan								
1 VII 2019 (ESDF)								
Baghalan Center (Puli Khumry)	*237 888*	*120 992*	*116 896*	695.8	...	...	...	...
Balkh Center (Mazar- Sharif)	*469 247*	*236 335*	*232 912*	70.8	...	...	...	...
Herat Center	*556 205*	*277 346*	*278 859*	240.3	...	...	...	...
KABUL CENTER	*4 273 156*	*2 171 396*	*2 101 760*	384.2	...	...	...	...
Kandhar Center (Kndhar)	*614 254*	*311 385*	*302 869*	765.1	...	...	...	...
Kunduz Center	*356 536*	*180 418*	*176 118*	613.6	...	...	...	...
Ngarhar Center (Jlal Abad)	*263 312*	*133 088*	*130 224*	17.7	...	...	...	...
Armenia - Arménie								
1 VII 2018 (ESDJ)								
Gyumri (Leninakan)	113 977	52 087	61 890	44	...	...	...	...
YEREVAN	1 079 732	498 625	581 107	223	...	...	...	...
Azerbaijan - Azerbaïdjan								
1 I 2019 (ESDJ)								
BAKU	2 270 030	1 128 792	1 141 238	2140	...	...	...	...
Ganja	333 324	162 689	170 635	110	...	...	...	...
Sumgayit	342 166	168 878	173 288	90	...	...	...	...
Bahrain - Bahreïn								
1 VII 2006 (ESDF)								
MANAMA	*176 909*	*113 503*	*63 406*	30	...	...	...	...
Bangladesh								
15 III 2011 (CDFC)								
Barisal	339 308	174 980	164 328	...	...	...	...	...
Chittagong	2 591 681	1 367 282	1 224 399	...	...	...	...	...
Comilla	296 010	153 523	142 487	...	...	...	...	...
DHAKA	8 906 035	4 931 802	3 974 233	...	...	...	...	...
Khulna	664 728	346 069	318 659	...	...	...	...	...
Mymensingh	389 918	200 053	189 865	...	...	...	...	...
Narayanganj	286 330	148 214	138 116	...	...	...	...	...
Rajshahi	449 756	232 974	216 782	...	...	...	...	...
Saidpur	133 433	68 884	64 549	...	...	...	...	...
Bhutan - Bhoutan								
30 V 2017 (CDFC)								
THIMPHU	114 551	58 996	55 555	26.1	...	...	...	...
Brunei Darussalam - Brunéi Darussalam								
21 VIII 2001 (CDFC)								
BANDAR SERI BEGAWAN	27 285	13 639	13 646	100.4	...	...	...	...

8. Population of capital cities and cities of 100 000 or more inhabitants: latest available year, 2000 - 2019
Population des capitales et des villes de 100 000 habitants ou plus : dernière année disponible, 2000 - 2019 (continued - suite)

Continent, country or area, date, code[a] and city / Continent, pays ou zone, date, code[a] et ville	City proper - Ville proprement dite: Population: Both sexes - Les deux sexes	Male - Masculin	Female - Féminin	Surface area - Superficie (km²)	Urban agglomeration - Agglomération urbaine: Population: Both sexes - Les deux sexes	Male - Masculin	Female - Féminin	Surface area - Superficie (km²)
ASIA - ASIE								
Cambodia - Cambodge[42]								
1 VII 2011 (ESDF)								
Bat Dambang	*1 126 345*	*558 945*	*567 400*	...	...	...	...	...
PHNOM PENH	*1 570 791*	*738 159*	*832 631*	...	...	...	...	...
Seam Reab	*999 703*	*493 184*	*506 519*	...	...	...	...	...
China - Chine[43]								
1 VII 2016 (ESDF)								
BEIJING (PEKING)	...	...	...	...	*18 796 000*	...	...	...
China, Hong Kong SAR - Chine, Hong Kong RAS								
1 VII 2019 (ESDJ)								
HONG KONG SAR	7 507 400	3 423 000	4 084 400	...	...	...	...	...
China, Macao SAR - Chine, Macao RAS								
1 VII 2019 (ESDJ)								
MACAO	672 000	314 500	357 500	33[44]	...	...	...	...
Cyprus - Chypre								
1 I 2017 (ESDJ)								
LEFKOSIA[45]	...	...	...	...	*244 200*	...	...	...
Lemesos[46]	...	...	...	...	*182 600*	...	...	...
Democratic People's Republic of Korea - République populaire démocratique de Corée								
1 X 2008 (CDJC)								
Anju	167 646	79 187	88 459	...	...	...	...	...
Chongjin	614 892	292 741	322 151	...	...	...	...	...
Haeju	241 599	116 594	125 005	...	...	...	...	...
Hamhung	614 198	292 058	322 140	...	...	...	...	...
Huichon	136 093	64 547	71 546	...	...	...	...	...
Hyesan	174 015	82 604	91 411	...	...	...	...	...
Jongju	102 659	48 423	54 236	...	...	...	...	...
Kaechon	262 389	124 222	138 167	...	...	...	...	...
Kaesong	192 578	90 653	101 925	...	...	...	...	...
Kanggye	251 971	120 305	131 666	...	...	...	...	...
Kim Chaek	155 284	73 133	82 151	...	...	...	...	...
Kusong	155 181	73 677	81 504	...	...	...	...	...
Nampho	310 864	150 091	160 773	...	...	...	...	...
Phyongsong	236 583	115 817	120 766	...	...	...	...	...
PYONGYANG	2 581 076	1 233 765	1 347 311	...	...	...	...	...
Rason	158 337	74 777	83 560	...	...	...	...	...
Sariwon	271 434	130 181	141 253	...	...	...	...	...
Sinpho	130 951	63 207	67 744	...	...	...	...	...
Sinuiju	334 031	158 139	175 892	...	...	...	...	...
Sunchon	250 738	119 727	131 011	...	...	...	...	...
Tanchon	240 873	113 221	127 652	...	...	...	...	...
Tokchon	210 571	99 655	110 916	...	...	...	...	...
Wonsan	328 467	155 903	172 564	...	...	...	...	...
Georgia - Géorgie								
1 VII 2016 (ESDJ)								
Batumi	155 000	...	...	...	...	...	...	...
Kutaisi	147 500	...	...	...	...	...	...	...
Rustavi	126 200	...	...	...	...	...	...	...
TBILISI	1 113 800	...	...	...	...	...	...	...
India - Inde								
9 II 2011 (CDFC)								
Abohar	...	...	...	...	145 302	76 984	68 318	...
Achalpur	...	...	...	...	112 311	58 108	54 203	...
Adilabad	...	...	...	...	117 167	59 448	57 719	...
Adityapur	...	...	...	...	174 355	91 664	82 691	...
Adoni	...	...	...	...	184 625	91 736	92 889	...
Agartala	...	...	...	...	400 004	200 132	199 872	...
Agra	...	...	...	...	1 585 704	845 902	739 802	...
Ahmadabad	...	...	...	...	5 633 927	2 968 460	2 665 467	...
Ahmadnagar	...	...	...	...	350 859	178 899	171 960	...
Aizawl	...	...	...	...	293 416	144 913	148 503	...
Ajmer	...	...	...	...	542 321	278 545	263 776	...
Akbarpur	...	...	...	...	111 447	57 330	54 117	...
Akola	...	...	...	...	425 817	217 393	208 424	...

Continent, country or area, date, code[a] and city Continent, pays ou zone, date, code[a] et ville	City proper - Ville proprement dite				Urban agglomeration - Agglomération urbaine			
	Population				Population			
	Both sexes - Les deux sexes	Male - Masculin	Female - Féminin	Surface area - Superficie (km²)	Both sexes - Les deux sexes	Male - Masculin	Female - Féminin	Surface area - Superficie (km²)
ASIA - ASIE								
India - Inde								
9 II 2011 (CDFC)								
Alandur	...	...	...	...	164 430	82 332	82 098	...
Alappuzha	...	...	...	...	240 991	116 439	124 552	...
Aligarh	...	...	...	...	874 408	461 772	412 636	...
Allahabad	...	...	...	...	1 168 385	630 577	537 808	...
Alwar	...	...	...	...	322 568	170 530	152 038	...
Ambala	...	...	...	...	195 153	102 607	92 546	...
Ambala Sadar	...	...	...	...	104 974	54 680	50 294	...
Ambarnath	...	...	...	...	253 475	132 582	120 893	...
Ambattur	...	...	...	...	466 205	234 923	231 282	...
Ambikapur	...	...	...	...	121 071	62 776	58 295	...
Ambur	...	...	...	...	114 608	56 382	58 226	...
Amravati	...	...	...	...	647 057	329 992	317 065	...
Amreli	...	...	...	...	117 967	59 902	58 065	...
Amritsar	...	...	...	...	1 159 227	615 417	543 810	...
Amroha	...	...	...	...	198 471	103 097	95 374	...
Anand	...	...	...	...	209 410	108 403	101 007	...
Anantapur	...	...	...	...	267 161	133 919	133 242	...
Anantnag	...	...	...	...	150 592	77 712	72 880	...
Arrah	...	...	...	...	261 430	138 804	122 626	...
Asansol	...	...	...	...	563 917	292 387	271 530	...
Ashoknagar Kalyangarh	...	...	...	...	121 592	61 236	60 356	...
Aurangabad (Bihar)	...	...	...	...	102 244	53 542	48 702	...
Aurangabad (Maharashtra)	...	...	...	...	1 175 116	609 206	565 910	...
Avadi	...	...	...	...	345 996	175 658	170 338	...
Azamgarh	...	...	...	...	110 983	57 878	53 105	...
Badlapur	...	...	...	...	174 226	90 365	83 861	...
Bagaha	...	...	...	...	112 634	59 614	53 020	...
Bagalkot	...	...	...	...	111 933	56 378	55 555	...
Bahadurgarh	...	...	...	...	170 767	91 721	79 046	...
Baharampur	...	...	...	...	195 223	100 247	94 976	...
Bahraich	...	...	...	...	186 223	97 653	88 570	...
Baidyabati	...	...	...	...	121 110	62 485	58 625	...
Baleshwar Town	...	...	...	...	144 373	73 721	70 652	...
Ballia	...	...	...	...	104 424	55 459	48 965	...
Bally (Census Town)	...	...	...	...	113 377	58 530	54 847	...
Bally (Municipality)	...	...	...	...	293 373	156 911	136 462	...
Balurghat	...	...	...	...	153 279	76 730	76 549	...
Banda	...	...	...	...	160 473	85 370	75 103	...
Bankura	...	...	...	...	137 386	69 843	67 543	...
Bansberia	...	...	...	...	103 920	53 760	50 160	...
Banswara	...	...	...	...	101 017	51 585	49 432	...
Baran	...	...	...	...	117 992	61 071	56 921	...
Baranagar	...	...	...	...	245 213	126 187	119 026	...
Barasat	...	...	...	...	278 435	140 822	137 613	...
Baraut	...	...	...	...	103 764	55 013	48 751	...
Barddhaman	...	...	...	...	314 265	159 936	154 329	...
Bareilly	...	...	...	...	904 797	477 515	427 282	...
Baripada Town	...	...	...	...	116 849	60 489	56 360	...
Barnala	...	...	...	...	116 449	62 554	53 895	...
Barrackpur	...	...	...	...	152 783	78 349	74 434	...
Barshi	...	...	...	...	118 722	60 801	57 921	...
Basirhat	...	...	...	...	125 254	63 223	62 031	...
Basti	...	...	...	...	114 657	60 095	54 562	...
Batala	...	...	...	...	158 621	83 655	74 966	...
Bathinda	...	...	...	...	285 788	151 524	134 264	...
Beawar	...	...	...	...	151 152	77 616	73 536	...
Begusarai	...	...	...	...	252 008	133 722	118 286	...
Belgaum	...	...	...	...	490 045	246 537	243 508	...
Bellary	...	...	...	...	410 445	206 149	204 296	...
Bettiah	...	...	...	...	132 209	69 529	62 680	...
Betul	...	...	...	...	103 330	52 823	50 507	...
Bhadrak	...	...	...	...	121 338	62 335	59 003	...
Bhadravati	...	...	...	...	151 102	75 009	76 093	...

Continent, country or area, date, code[a] and city / Continent, pays ou zone, date, code[a] et ville	City proper - Ville proprement dite: Population: Both sexes - Les deux sexes	Male - Masculin	Female - Féminin	Surface area - Superficie (km²)	Urban agglomeration - Agglomération urbaine: Population: Both sexes - Les deux sexes	Male - Masculin	Female - Féminin	Surface area - Superficie (km²)
ASIA - ASIE								
India - Inde								
9 II 2011 (CDFC)								
Bhadreswar	...	...	...	...	101 477	53 330	48 147	...
Bhagalpur	...	...	...	...	400 146	212 813	187 333	...
Bhalswa Jahangir Pur	...	...	...	...	197 148	106 388	90 760	...
Bharatpur	...	...	...	...	252 838	134 040	118 798	...
Bharuch	...	...	...	...	169 007	86 810	82 197	...
Bhatpara	...	...	...	...	386 019	204 539	181 480	...
Bhavnagar	...	...	...	...	605 882	315 429	290 453	...
Bhilai Nagar	...	...	...	...	627 734	323 479	304 255	...
Bhilwara	...	...	...	...	359 483	187 081	172 402	...
Bhimavaram	...	...	...	...	146 961	72 441	74 520	...
Bhind	...	...	...	...	197 585	105 352	92 233	...
Bhiwadi	...	...	...	...	104 921	59 712	45 209	...
Bhiwandi	...	...	...	...	709 665	415 339	294 326	...
Bhiwani	...	...	...	...	196 057	104 026	92 031	...
Bhopal	...	...	...	...	1 798 218	936 168	862 050	...
Bhubaneswar Town	...	...	...	...	885 363	468 043	417 320	...
Bhuj	...	...	...	...	148 834	78 813	70 021	...
Bhusawal	...	...	...	...	187 421	96 147	91 274	...
Bid	...	...	...	...	146 709	75 566	71 143	...
Bidar	...	...	...	...	216 020	111 470	104 550	...
Bidhan Nagar	...	...	...	...	215 514	109 014	106 500	...
Biharsharif	...	...	...	...	297 268	155 216	142 052	...
Bijapur	...	...	...	...	327 427	165 177	162 250	...
Bikaner	...	...	...	...	644 406	338 442	305 964	...
Bilaspur	...	...	...	...	365 579	188 342	177 237	...
Bokaro Steel City	...	...	...	...	414 820	219 646	195 174	...
Bongaon	...	...	...	...	108 864	55 382	53 482	...
Botad	...	...	...	...	130 327	67 675	62 652	...
Brahmapur	...	...	...	...	356 598	185 754	170 844	...
Bruhat Bengaluru Mahanagara Palike (BBMP)	...	...	...	...	8 495 492	4 420 006	4 075 486	...
Budaun	...	...	...	...	159 285	83 176	76 109	...
Bulandshahar	...	...	...	...	230 024	120 275	109 749	...
Bundi	...	...	...	...	104 919	54 485	50 434	...
Burari	...	...	...	...	146 190	78 103	68 087	...
Burhanpur	...	...	...	...	210 886	108 187	102 699	...
Buxar	...	...	...	...	102 861	54 277	48 584	...
Champdani	...	...	...	...	111 251	59 350	51 901	...
Chandannagar	...	...	...	...	166 867	84 009	82 858	...
Chandausi	...	...	...	...	114 383	60 256	54 127	...
Chandigarh	...	...	...	...	970 602	531 051	439 551	...
Chandrapur	...	...	...	...	320 379	164 085	156 294	...
Chapra	...	...	...	...	202 352	106 501	95 851	...
Chas	...	...	...	...	141 640	74 727	66 913	...
Chennai	...	...	...	...	4 646 732	2 335 844	2 310 888	...
Chhatarpur	...	...	...	...	142 128	75 070	67 058	...
Chhindwara	...	...	...	...	175 052	89 396	85 656	...
Chikmagalur	...	...	...	...	118 401	58 702	59 699	...
Chilakaluripet	...	...	...	...	101 398	50 207	51 191	...
Chitradurga	...	...	...	...	145 853	73 020	72 833	...
Chittaurgarh	...	...	...	...	116 406	60 068	56 338	...
Chittoor	...	...	...	...	160 722	80 060	80 662	...
Churu	...	...	...	...	120 157	61 774	58 383	...
Coimbatore	...	...	...	...	1 050 721	526 163	524 558	...
Cuddalore	...	...	...	...	173 636	85 700	87 936	...
Cuttack	...	...	...	...	610 189	316 242	293 947	...
Dabgram	...	...	...	...	119 040	61 078	57 962	...
Dallo Pura	...	...	...	...	154 791	81 262	73 529	...
Damoh	...	...	...	...	139 561	72 869	66 692	...
Darbhanga	...	...	...	...	296 039	155 637	140 402	...
Darjiling	...	...	...	...	118 805	59 187	59 618	...
Datia	...	...	...	...	100 284	52 772	47 512	...
Davanagere	...	...	...	...	434 971	219 776	215 195	...
Deesa	...	...	...	...	111 160	58 657	52 503	...

8. Population of capital cities and cities of 100 000 or more inhabitants: latest available year, 2000 - 2019
Population des capitales et des villes de 100 000 habitants ou plus : dernière année disponible, 2000 - 2019 (continued - suite)

Continent, country or area, date, code[a] and city / Continent, pays ou zone, date, code[a] et ville	City proper - Ville proprement dite				Urban agglomeration - Agglomération urbaine			
	Population				Population			
	Both sexes - Les deux sexes	Male - Masculin	Female - Féminin	Surface area - Superficie (km²)	Both sexes - Les deux sexes	Male - Masculin	Female - Féminin	Surface area - Superficie (km²)
ASIA - ASIE								
India - Inde								
9 II 2011 (CDFC)								
Dehradun	...	...	...	...	574 840	301 207	273 633	...
Dehri	...	...	...	...	137 231	72 372	64 859	...
Delhi Cantonment	...	...	...	...	110 351	63 757	46 594	...
Delhi Municipal Corporation (DMC)	...	...	...	...	11 034 555	5 882 117	5 152 438	...
Deoghar	...	...	...	...	203 123	107 997	95 126	...
Deoli	...	...	...	...	169 122	90 914	78 208	...
Deoria	...	...	...	...	129 479	67 462	62 017	...
Dewas	...	...	...	...	289 550	150 081	139 469	...
Dhamtari	...	...	...	...	101 677	50 807	50 870	...
Dhanbad	...	...	...	...	1 162 472	614 722	547 750	...
Dharmavaram	...	...	...	...	121 874	62 250	59 624	...
Dhaulpur	...	...	...	...	133 075	71 298	61 777	...
Dhule	...	...	...	...	375 559	193 446	182 113	...
Dibrugarh	...	...	...	...	145 488	75 318	70 170	...
Dimapur	...	...	...	...	122 834	64 300	58 534	...
Dinapur Nizamat	...	...	...	...	182 429	96 875	85 554	...
Dindigul	...	...	...	...	207 327	103 027	104 300	...
Dohad	...	...	...	...	118 846	60 515	58 331	...
Dum Dum	...	...	...	...	114 786	58 566	56 220	...
Durg	...	...	...	...	268 806	136 641	132 165	...
Durgapur	...	...	...	...	566 517	294 255	272 262	...
Eluru	...	...	...	...	218 020	107 511	110 509	...
English Bazar	...	...	...	...	205 521	106 824	98 697	...
Erode	...	...	...	...	157 101	78 222	78 879	...
Etah	...	...	...	...	118 517	62 590	55 927	...
Etawah	...	...	...	...	256 838	135 439	121 399	...
Faizabad	...	...	...	...	165 228	85 620	79 608	...
Faridabad	...	...	...	...	1 414 050	754 542	659 508	...
Farrukhabad-cum-Fatehgarh	...	...	...	...	276 581	145 641	130 940	...
Fatehpur	...	...	...	...	193 193	101 263	91 930	...
Firozabad	...	...	...	...	604 214	319 415	284 799	...
Firozpur	...	...	...	...	110 313	58 451	51 862	...
Gadag-Betigeri	...	...	...	...	172 612	85 920	86 692	...
Gandhidham	...	...	...	...	247 992	131 484	116 508	...
Gandhinagar	...	...	...	...	292 797	153 443	139 354	...
Ganganagar	...	...	...	...	237 780	127 840	109 940	...
Gangapur City	...	...	...	...	119 090	62 829	56 261	...
Gangawati	...	...	...	...	114 642	57 230	57 412	...
Gangtok	...	...	...	...	100 286	52 459	47 827	...
Gaya	...	...	...	...	474 093	250 037	224 056	...
Ghaziabad	...	...	...	...	1 648 643	874 607	774 036	...
Ghazipur	...	...	...	...	121 020	63 513	57 507	...
Giridih	...	...	...	...	114 533	59 966	54 567	...
Godhra	...	...	...	...	143 644	74 230	69 414	...
Gokal Pur	...	...	...	...	121 870	64 857	57 013	...
Gonda	...	...	...	...	114 046	59 948	54 098	...
Gondal	...	...	...	...	112 197	58 300	53 897	...
Gondiya	...	...	...	...	132 813	66 500	66 313	...
Gorakhpur	...	...	...	...	673 446	353 907	319 539	...
Greater Hyderabad Municipal Corporation (GHMC)	...	...	...	...	6 993 262	3 576 640	3 416 622	...
Greater Mumbai	...	...	...	...	12 442 373	6 715 931	5 726 442	...
Greater Noida	...	...	...	...	102 054	55 540	46 514	...
Greater Visakhapatnam Municipal Corporation (GVMC)	...	...	...	...	1 728 128	873 599	854 529	...
Gudivada	...	...	...	...	118 167	59 062	59 105	...
Gulbarga	...	...	...	...	543 147	276 552	266 595	...
Guna	...	...	...	...	180 935	94 464	86 471	...
Guntakal	...	...	...	...	126 270	62 851	63 419	...
Guntur	...	...	...	...	670 073	331 435	338 638	...
Gurgaon	...	...	...	...	886 519	480 042	406 477	...
Guwahati	...	...	...	...	962 334	498 450	463 884	...
Gwalior	...	...	...	...	1 054 420	561 165	493 255	...

8. Population of capital cities and cities of 100 000 or more inhabitants: latest available year, 2000 - 2019
Population des capitales et des villes de 100 000 habitants ou plus : dernière année disponible, 2000 - 2019 (continued - suite)

Continent, country or area, date, code[a] and city / Continent, pays ou zone, date, code[a] et ville	City proper - Ville proprement dite: Population: Both sexes - Les deux sexes	Male - Masculin	Female - Féminin	Surface area - Superficie (km²)	Urban agglomeration - Agglomération urbaine: Population: Both sexes - Les deux sexes	Male - Masculin	Female - Féminin	Surface area - Superficie (km²)
ASIA - ASIE								
India - Inde								
9 II 2011 (CDFC)								
Habra	...	...	...	...	147 221	74 592	72 629	...
Hajipur	...	...	...	...	147 688	78 047	69 641	...
Haldia	...	...	...	...	200 827	104 841	95 986	...
Haldwani-cum-Kathgodam	...	...	...	...	201 461	105 580	95 881	...
Halisahar	...	...	...	...	124 939	65 467	59 472	...
Hanumangarh	...	...	...	...	150 958	79 709	71 249	...
Haora	...	...	...	...	1 077 075	561 220	515 855	...
Hapur	...	...	...	...	262 983	139 525	123 458	...
Hardoi	...	...	...	...	197 029	103 619	93 410	...
Hardwar	...	...	...	...	231 338	123 455	107 883	...
Hassan	...	...	...	...	155 006	77 051	77 955	...
Hastsal	...	...	...	...	176 877	94 833	82 044	...
Hathras	...	...	...	...	143 020	76 054	66 966	...
Hazaribag	...	...	...	...	142 489	74 132	68 357	...
Hindaun	...	...	...	...	105 452	55 834	49 618	...
Hindupur	...	...	...	...	151 677	76 370	75 307	...
Hinganghat	...	...	...	...	101 805	52 577	49 228	...
Hisar	...	...	...	...	307 024	166 494	140 530	...
Hoshangabad	...	...	...	...	117 988	61 716	56 272	...
Hoshiarpur	...	...	...	...	168 653	88 304	80 349	...
Hospet	...	...	...	...	206 167	102 668	103 499	...
Hosur	...	...	...	...	116 821	59 351	57 470	...
Hubli-Dharwad	...	...	...	...	943 788	474 518	469 270	...
Hugli-Chinsurah	...	...	...	...	179 931	90 217	89 714	...
Ichalkaranji	...	...	...	...	287 353	149 164	138 189	...
Imphal	...	...	...	...	277 196	135 059	142 137	...
Indore	...	...	...	...	1 994 397	1 035 912	958 485	...
Jabalpur	...	...	...	...	1 081 677	559 361	522 316	...
Jagadhri	...	...	...	...	124 894	67 685	57 209	...
Jagdalpur	...	...	...	...	125 463	63 989	61 474	...
Jagtial	...	...	...	...	103 930	51 828	52 102	...
Jaipur	...	...	...	...	3 046 163	1 603 125	1 443 038	...
Jalandhar	...	...	...	...	868 929	460 811	408 118	...
Jalgaon	...	...	...	...	460 228	240 590	219 638	...
Jalna	...	...	...	...	285 577	147 092	138 485	...
Jalpaiguri	...	...	...	...	107 341	53 708	53 633	...
Jamalpur	...	...	...	...	105 434	56 072	49 362	...
Jammu	...	...	...	...	576 198	303 689	272 509	...
Jamnagar	...	...	...	...	600 943	313 214	287 729	...
Jamshedpur	...	...	...	...	677 350	353 212	324 138	...
Jamuria	...	...	...	...	149 220	77 379	71 841	...
Jaunpur	...	...	...	...	180 362	93 718	86 644	...
Jehanabad	...	...	...	...	103 202	54 710	48 492	...
Jetpur Navagadh	...	...	...	...	118 302	62 174	56 128	...
Jhansi	...	...	...	...	505 693	265 449	240 244	...
Jhunjhunun	...	...	...	...	118 473	61 548	56 925	...
Jind	...	...	...	...	167 592	89 253	78 339	...
Jodhpur	...	...	...	...	1 056 191	555 371	500 820	...
Jorhat	...	...	...	...	126 736	65 489	61 247	...
Junagadh	...	...	...	...	319 462	163 413	156 049	...
Kadapa	...	...	...	...	344 893	173 314	171 579	...
Kaithal	...	...	...	...	144 915	76 794	68 121	...
Kakinada	...	...	...	...	384 182	188 308	195 874	...
Kalol	...	...	...	...	134 426	70 995	63 431	...
Kalyan Dombivali	...	...	...	...	1 247 327	649 626	597 701	...
Kalyani	...	...	...	...	100 575	50 727	49 848	...
Kamarhati	...	...	...	...	330 211	170 293	159 918	...
Kancheepuram	...	...	...	...	164 384	81 992	82 392	...
Kanchrapara	...	...	...	...	129 576	65 436	64 140	...
Kanhangad	...	...	...	...	125 564	58 564	67 000	...
Kanpur	...	...	...	...	2 768 057	1 490 547	1 277 510	...
Kanpur (Cantonment Board)	...	...	...	...	108 534	58 550	49 984	...
Karaikkudi	...	...	...	...	106 714	53 348	53 366	...

8. Population of capital cities and cities of 100 000 or more inhabitants: latest available year, 2000 - 2019
Population des capitales et des villes de 100 000 habitants ou plus : dernière année disponible, 2000 - 2019 (continued - suite)

Continent, country or area, date, code[a] and city / Continent, pays ou zone, date, code[a] et ville	City proper - Ville proprement dite: Population: Both sexes - Les deux sexes	Male - Masculin	Female - Féminin	Surface area - Superficie (km²)	Urban agglomeration - Agglomération urbaine: Population: Both sexes - Les deux sexes	Male - Masculin	Female - Féminin	Surface area - Superficie (km²)
ASIA - ASIE								
India - Inde								
9 II 2011 (CDFC)								
Karawal Nagar	...	...	...	...	224 281	119 951	104 330	...
Karimnagar	...	...	...	...	289 821	146 145	143 676	...
Karnal	...	...	...	...	302 140	159 653	142 487	...
Kasganj	...	...	...	...	101 277	53 552	47 725	...
Kashipur	...	...	...	...	121 623	63 609	58 014	...
Katihar	...	...	...	...	240 838	127 240	113 598	...
Khammam	...	...	...	...	196 283	96 898	99 385	...
Khandwa	...	...	...	...	200 738	102 901	97 837	...
Khanna	...	...	...	...	128 137	67 801	60 336	...
Kharagpur	...	...	...	...	207 604	106 559	101 045	...
Khardaha	...	...	...	...	108 496	54 879	53 617	...
Khargone	...	...	...	...	116 150	59 752	56 398	...
Khora	...	...	...	...	190 005	102 574	87 431	...
Khurja	...	...	...	...	121 207	63 825	57 382	...
Kirari Suleman Nagar	...	...	...	...	283 211	152 348	130 863	...
Kishanganj	...	...	...	...	105 782	55 143	50 639	...
Kishangarh	...	...	...	...	154 886	80 024	74 862	...
Kochi	...	...	...	...	633 553	312 358	321 195	...
Kolar	...	...	...	...	138 462	69 910	68 552	...
Kolhapur	...	...	...	...	549 236	280 366	268 870	...
Kolkata (Calcutta)	...	...	...	...	4 496 694	2 356 766	2 139 928	...
Kollam	...	...	...	...	367 107	177 072	190 035	...
Korba	...	...	...	...	365 253	189 772	175 481	...
Kota	...	...	...	...	1 001 694	528 601	473 093	...
Kozhikode	...	...	...	...	550 440	262 939	287 501	...
Krishnanagar	...	...	...	...	153 062	77 146	75 916	...
Kulti	...	...	...	...	313 809	163 193	150 616	...
Kumbakonam	...	...	...	...	140 156	69 340	70 816	...
Kurichi	...	...	...	...	123 667	61 815	61 852	...
Kurnool	...	...	...	...	457 633	228 148	229 485	...
Lakhimpur	...	...	...	...	151 993	80 523	71 470	...
Lalitpur	...	...	...	...	133 305	69 529	63 776	...
Latur	...	...	...	...	382 940	197 737	185 203	...
Loni	...	...	...	...	516 082	275 025	241 057	...
Lucknow	...	...	...	...	2 817 105	1 460 970	1 356 135	...
Ludhiana	...	...	...	...	1 618 879	874 908	743 971	...
Machilipatnam	...	...	...	...	169 892	83 594	86 298	...
Madanapalle	...	...	...	...	180 180	90 700	89 480	...
Madavaram	...	...	...	...	119 105	59 887	59 218	...
Madhyamgram	...	...	...	...	196 127	98 864	97 263	...
Madurai	...	...	...	...	1 017 865	509 302	508 563	...
Mahbubnagar	...	...	...	...	190 400	96 142	94 258	...
Mahesana	...	...	...	...	190 753	100 558	90 195	...
Maheshtala	...	...	...	...	448 317	229 693	218 624	...
Mainpuri	...	...	...	...	136 557	71 274	65 283	...
Malappuram	...	...	...	...	101 386	48 957	52 429	...
Malegaon	...	...	...	...	481 228	244 080	237 148	...
Malerkotla	...	...	...	...	135 424	71 376	64 048	...
Mandoli	...	...	...	...	120 417	64 159	56 258	...
Mandsaur	...	...	...	...	141 667	72 488	69 179	...
Mandya	...	...	...	...	137 358	68 662	68 696	...
Mangalagiri	...	...	...	...	107 197	53 301	53 896	...
Mangalore	...	...	...	...	499 487	247 903	251 584	...
Mango	...	...	...	...	223 805	115 970	107 835	...
Mathura	...	...	...	...	349 909	185 983	163 926	...
Maunath Bhanjan	...	...	...	...	278 745	142 967	135 778	...
Medinipur	...	...	...	...	169 264	84 977	84 287	...
Meerut	...	...	...	...	1 305 429	688 118	617 311	...
Mira Bhayandar	...	...	...	...	809 378	429 260	380 118	...
Miryalaguda	...	...	...	...	104 918	52 565	52 353	...
Mirzapur-cum-Vindhyachal	...	...	...	...	234 871	125 601	109 270	...
Modinagar	...	...	...	...	130 325	69 268	61 057	...
Moga	...	...	...	...	163 397	86 604	76 793	...

8. Population of capital cities and cities of 100 000 or more inhabitants: latest available year, 2000 - 2019
Population des capitales et des villes de 100 000 habitants ou plus : dernière année disponible, 2000 - 2019 (continued - suite)

Continent, country or area, date, code[a] and city / Continent, pays ou zone, date, code[a] et ville	City proper - Ville proprement dite				Urban agglomeration - Agglomération urbaine			
	Population				Population			
	Both sexes - Les deux sexes	Male - Masculin	Female - Féminin	Surface area - Superficie (km²)	Both sexes - Les deux sexes	Male - Masculin	Female - Féminin	Surface area - Superficie (km²)
ASIA - ASIE								
India - Inde								
9 II 2011 (CDFC)								
Moradabad	...	...	...	...	887 871	464 580	423 291	...
Morena	...	...	...	...	200 482	108 390	92 092	...
Morvi	...	...	...	...	210 451	109 451	101 000	...
Motihari	...	...	...	...	126 158	67 861	58 297	...
Mughalsarai	...	...	...	...	109 650	57 682	51 968	...
Muktsar	...	...	...	...	116 747	61 725	55 022	...
Munger	...	...	...	...	213 303	113 291	100 012	...
Murwara (Katni)	...	...	...	...	221 883	115 348	106 535	...
Mustafabad	...	...	...	...	127 167	66 889	60 278	...
Muzaffarnagar	...	...	...	...	392 768	206 782	185 986	...
Muzaffarpur	...	...	...	...	354 462	187 564	166 898	...
Mysore	...	...	...	...	920 550	461 042	459 508	...
Nabadwip	...	...	...	...	125 543	65 415	60 128	...
Nadiad	...	...	...	...	225 071	115 903	109 168	...
Nagaon	...	...	...	...	121 628	61 642	59 986	...
Nagapattinam	...	...	...	...	102 905	50 793	52 112	...
Nagaur	...	...	...	...	105 218	54 126	51 092	...
Nagda	...	...	...	...	100 039	51 373	48 666	...
Nagercoil	...	...	...	...	224 849	109 938	114 911	...
Nagpur	...	...	...	...	2 405 665	1 225 405	1 180 260	...
Naihati	...	...	...	...	217 900	109 849	108 051	...
Nalgonda	...	...	...	...	154 326	77 320	77 006	...
Nanded Waghala	...	...	...	...	550 439	285 433	265 006	...
Nandurbar	...	...	...	...	111 037	57 412	53 625	...
Nandyal	...	...	...	...	211 424	105 826	105 598	...
Nangloi Jat	...	...	...	...	205 596	110 056	95 540	...
Narasaraopet	...	...	...	...	117 489	59 424	58 065	...
Nashik	...	...	...	...	1 486 053	782 517	703 536	...
Navi Mumbai (New Bombay)	...	...	...	...	1 120 547	610 060	510 487	...
Navi Mumbai Panvel Raigad	...	...	...	...	195 373	107 342	88 031	...
Navsari	...	...	...	...	171 109	88 486	82 623	...
Neemuch	...	...	...	...	128 561	67 890	60 671	...
Nellore	...	...	...	...	547 621	278 787	268 834	...
New Delhi Municipal Council (NDMC)	...	...	...	...	257 803	140 234	117 569	...
Neyveli	...	...	...	...	105 731	53 409	52 322	...
Nizamabad	...	...	...	...	311 152	154 929	156 223	...
Noida	...	...	...	...	637 272	349 397	287 875	...
North Barrackpur	...	...	...	...	132 806	66 924	65 882	...
North Dum Dum	...	...	...	...	249 142	126 279	122 863	...
Ongole	...	...	...	...	208 344	104 646	103 698	...
Orai	...	...	...	...	190 575	101 306	89 269	...
Osmanabad	...	...	...	...	111 825	57 824	54 001	...
Ozhukarai	...	...	...	...	300 104	148 464	151 640	...
Palakkad	...	...	...	...	130 955	63 833	67 122	...
Palanpur	...	...	...	...	141 592	74 088	67 504	...
Pali	...	...	...	...	230 075	119 924	110 151	...
Pallavaram	...	...	...	...	233 984	117 405	116 579	...
Palwal	...	...	...	...	131 926	69 997	61 929	...
Panchkula	...	...	...	...	211 355	111 731	99 624	...
Panihati	...	...	...	...	377 347	189 446	187 901	...
Panipat	...	...	...	...	295 970	158 063	137 907	...
Panvel	...	...	...	...	180 020	92 484	87 536	...
Parbhani	...	...	...	...	307 170	156 520	150 650	...
Patan	...	...	...	...	133 737	69 898	63 839	...
Pathankot	...	...	...	...	156 306	82 045	74 261	...
Patiala	...	...	...	...	446 246	236 198	210 048	...
Patna	...	...	...	...	1 684 297	893 445	790 852	...
Pilibhit	...	...	...	...	127 988	67 614	60 374	...
Pimpri Chinchwad	...	...	...	...	1 727 692	942 533	785 159	...
Pithampur	...	...	...	...	126 200	70 250	55 950	...
Porbandar	...	...	...	...	152 760	78 604	74 156	...
Port Blair	...	...	...	...	108 058	57 761	50 297	...
Proddatur	...	...	...	...	163 970	81 874	82 096	...

8. Population of capital cities and cities of 100 000 or more inhabitants: latest available year, 2000 - 2019
Population des capitales et des villes de 100 000 habitants ou plus : dernière année disponible, 2000 - 2019 (continued - suite)

Continent, country or area, date, code[a] and city / Continent, pays ou zone, date, code[a] et ville	City proper - Ville proprement dite: Population: Both sexes - Les deux sexes	Male - Masculin	Female - Féminin	Surface area - Superficie (km²)	Urban agglomeration - Agglomération urbaine: Population: Both sexes - Les deux sexes	Male - Masculin	Female - Féminin	Surface area - Superficie (km²)
ASIA - ASIE								
India - Inde								
9 II 2011 (CDFC)								
Puducherry	...	...	...	...	244 377	119 430	124 947	...
Pudukkottai	...	...	...	...	117 630	58 737	58 893	...
Pune	...	...	...	...	3 124 458	1 603 675	1 520 783	...
Puri	...	...	...	...	200 564	104 086	96 478	...
Purnia	...	...	...	...	282 248	148 077	134 171	...
Puruliya	...	...	...	...	121 067	62 351	58 716	...
Rae Bareli	...	...	...	...	191 316	99 903	91 413	...
Raichur	...	...	...	...	234 073	117 657	116 416	...
Raiganj	...	...	...	...	183 612	96 388	87 224	...
Raigarh	...	...	...	...	150 019	76 865	73 154	...
Raipur	...	...	...	...	1 027 264	527 365	499 899	...
Rajahmundry	...	...	...	...	376 333	185 970	190 363	...
Rajapalayam	...	...	...	...	130 442	64 765	65 677	...
Rajarhat Gopalpur	...	...	...	...	402 844	203 911	198 933	...
Rajkot	...	...	...	...	1 323 363	693 473	629 890	...
Rajnandgaon	...	...	...	...	163 114	81 929	81 185	...
Rajpur Sonarpur	...	...	...	...	424 368	215 405	208 963	...
Ramagundam	...	...	...	...	242 979	123 430	119 549	...
Rampur	...	...	...	...	325 313	169 681	155 632	...
Ranchi	...	...	...	...	1 073 427	558 872	514 555	...
Ranibennur	...	...	...	...	106 406	54 040	52 366	...
Raniganj	...	...	...	...	129 441	67 578	61 863	...
Ratlam	...	...	...	...	264 914	134 915	129 999	...
Raurkela Industrial Township	...	...	...	...	216 410	112 897	103 513	...
Raurkela Town	...	...	...	...	320 040	169 095	150 945	...
Rewa	...	...	...	...	235 654	124 012	111 642	...
Rewari	...	...	...	...	143 021	75 764	67 257	...
Rishra	...	...	...	...	124 577	66 606	57 971	...
Robertson Pet	...	...	...	...	162 230	80 375	81 855	...
Rohtak	...	...	...	...	374 292	198 237	176 055	...
Roorkee	...	...	...	...	118 200	63 434	54 766	...
Rudrapur	...	...	...	...	154 554	81 340	73 214	...
S.A.S. Nagar	...	...	...	...	166 864	87 380	79 484	...
Sagar	...	...	...	...	274 556	143 425	131 131	...
Saharanpur	...	...	...	...	705 478	371 740	333 738	...
Saharsa	...	...	...	...	156 540	83 291	73 249	...
Salem	...	...	...	...	829 267	417 317	411 950	...
Sambalpur	...	...	...	...	189 366	97 460	91 906	...
Sambhal	...	...	...	...	220 813	115 767	105 046	...
Sangli-Miraj Kupwad	...	...	...	...	502 793	253 640	249 153	...
Santipur	...	...	...	...	151 777	77 011	74 766	...
Sasaram	...	...	...	...	147 408	77 599	69 809	...
Satara	...	...	...	...	120 195	61 129	59 066	...
Satna	...	...	...	...	282 977	149 415	133 562	...
Sawai Madhopur	...	...	...	...	121 106	63 014	58 092	...
Secunderabad	...	...	...	...	217 910	113 577	104 333	...
Sehore	...	...	...	...	109 118	56 335	52 783	...
Seoni	...	...	...	...	102 343	52 352	49 991	...
Serampore	...	...	...	...	181 842	93 694	88 148	...
Shahjahanpur	...	...	...	...	329 736	173 006	156 730	...
Shamli	...	...	...	...	107 266	57 187	50 079	...
Shikohabad	...	...	...	...	107 404	56 794	50 610	...
Shillong	...	...	...	...	143 229	70 135	73 094	...
Shimla	...	...	...	...	169 578	93 152	76 426	...
Shimoga	...	...	...	...	322 650	162 018	160 632	...
Shivpuri	...	...	...	...	179 977	95 132	84 845	...
Sikar	...	...	...	...	244 497	126 837	117 660	...
Silchar	...	...	...	...	178 865	89 961	88 904	...
Siliguri	...	...	...	...	513 264	263 702	249 562	...
Singrauli	...	...	...	...	220 257	116 867	103 390	...
Sirsa	...	...	...	...	182 534	96 175	86 359	...
Sitapur	...	...	...	...	177 234	92 696	84 538	...
Siwan	...	...	...	...	135 066	70 756	64 310	...

8. Population of capital cities and cities of 100 000 or more inhabitants: latest available year, 2000 - 2019
Population des capitales et des villes de 100 000 habitants ou plus : dernière année disponible, 2000 - 2019 (continued - suite)

Continent, country or area, date, code[a] and city / Continent, pays ou zone, date, code[a] et ville	City proper - Ville proprement dite: Population: Both sexes - Les deux sexes	Male - Masculin	Female - Féminin	Surface area - Superficie (km²)	Urban agglomeration - Agglomération urbaine: Population: Both sexes - Les deux sexes	Male - Masculin	Female - Féminin	Surface area - Superficie (km²)
ASIA - ASIE								
India - Inde								
9 II 2011 (CDFC)								
Solapur	...	...	...	...	951 558	481 064	470 494	...
Sonipat	...	...	...	...	289 333	154 407	134 926	...
South Dum Dum	...	...	...	...	403 316	202 214	201 102	...
Srikakulam	...	...	...	...	137 944	68 457	69 487	...
Srinagar	...	...	...	...	1 206 419	631 830	574 589	...
Sujangarh	...	...	...	...	101 523	51 906	49 617	...
Sultan Pur Majra	...	...	...	...	181 554	95 687	85 867	...
Sultanpur	...	...	...	...	107 640	56 420	51 220	...
Surat	...	...	...	...	4 501 610	2 565 803	1 935 807	...
Surendranagar Dudhrej	...	...	...	...	177 851	92 675	85 176	...
Suryapet	...	...	...	...	106 805	52 773	54 032	...
Tadepalligudem	...	...	...	...	104 032	51 438	52 594	...
Tadpatri	...	...	...	...	108 171	54 015	54 156	...
Tambaram	...	...	...	...	174 787	89 060	85 727	...
Tenali	...	...	...	...	164 937	81 427	83 510	...
Thane	...	...	...	...	1 841 488	975 399	866 089	...
Thanesar	...	...	...	...	155 152	83 994	71 158	...
Thanjavur	...	...	...	...	222 943	109 199	113 744	...
Thiruvananthapuram	...	...	...	...	788 271	384 004	404 267	...
Thoothukkudi	...	...	...	...	237 830	118 298	119 532	...
Thrissur	...	...	...	...	315 957	152 296	163 661	...
Tinsukia	...	...	...	...	116 322	62 303	54 019	...
Tiruchirappalli	...	...	...	...	847 387	418 400	428 987	...
Tirunelveli	...	...	...	...	473 637	233 659	239 978	...
Tirupati	...	...	...	...	295 323	150 125	145 198	...
Tiruppur	...	...	...	...	444 352	227 311	217 041	...
Tiruvannamalai	...	...	...	...	145 278	72 406	72 872	...
Tiruvottiyur	...	...	...	...	249 446	125 300	124 146	...
Titagarh	...	...	...	...	116 541	62 735	53 806	...
Tonk	...	...	...	...	165 294	84 806	80 488	...
Tumkur	...	...	...	...	302 143	152 925	149 218	...
Udaipur	...	...	...	...	451 100	233 959	217 141	...
Udgir	...	...	...	...	103 550	54 013	49 537	...
Udupi	...	...	...	...	144 960	71 614	73 346	...
Ujjain	...	...	...	...	515 215	264 871	250 344	...
Ulhasnagar	...	...	...	...	506 098	269 048	237 050	...
Uluberia	...	...	...	...	235 345	120 741	114 604	...
Unnao	...	...	...	...	177 658	93 021	84 637	...
Uttarpara Kotrung	...	...	...	...	159 147	81 410	77 737	...
Vadodara	...	...	...	...	1 752 371	912 721	839 650	...
Valsad	...	...	...	...	139 764	71 400	68 364	...
Vapi	...	...	...	...	163 630	94 105	69 525	...
Varanasi	...	...	...	...	1 198 491	635 140	563 351	...
Vasai-Virar City	...	...	...	...	1 222 390	648 172	574 218	...
Vellore	...	...	...	...	185 803	91 342	94 461	...
Veraval	...	...	...	...	171 121	87 009	84 112	...
Vidisha	...	...	...	...	155 951	81 488	74 463	...
Vijayawada	...	...	...	...	1 143 232	574 794	568 438	...
Vizianagaram	...	...	...	...	228 720	112 290	116 430	...
Warangal	...	...	...	...	704 570	353 309	351 261	...
Wardha	...	...	...	...	106 444	53 697	52 747	...
Yamunanagar	...	...	...	...	217 071	115 663	101 408	...
Yavatmal	...	...	...	...	116 551	58 549	58 002	...
Indonesia - Indonésie								
1 VII 2018 (ESDJ)								
Ambon	*431 092*	*215 223*	*215 869*	359.5	...	...	...	...
Balikpapan	*624 033*	*318 535*	*305 498*	512	...	...	...	...
Banda Aceh	*264 054*	*136 169*	*127 885*	61	...	...	...	...
Bandar Lampung	*1 033 601*	*518 960*	*514 641*	296	...	...	...	...
Bandjarmasin	*692 288*	*344 564*	*347 724*	73	...	...	...	...
Bandung	*2 525 220*	*1 275 030*	*1 250 190*	168	...	...	...	...
Batam	*1 347 762*	*688 198*	*659 564*	960	...	...	...	...
Bengkulu	*354 079*	*177 231*	*176 848*	145	...	...	...	...

8. Population of capital cities and cities of 100 000 or more inhabitants: latest available year, 2000 - 2019
Population des capitales et des villes de 100 000 habitants ou plus : dernière année disponible, 2000 - 2019 (continued - suite)

Continent, country or area, date, code[a] and city Continent, pays ou zone, date, code[a] et ville	City proper - Ville proprement dite				Urban agglomeration - Agglomération urbaine			
	Population				Population			
	Both sexes - Les deux sexes	Male - Masculin	Female - Féminin	Surface area - Superficie (km²)	Both sexes - Les deux sexes	Male - Masculin	Female - Féminin	Surface area - Superficie (km²)
ASIA - ASIE								
Indonesia - Indonésie								
1 VII 2018 (ESDJ)								
Binjai	*274 063*	*136 793*	*137 270*	59	...	...	...	...
Bitung	*193 883*	*98 202*	*95 681*	304	...	...	...	...
Blitar	*503 718*	*253 076*	*250 642*	33	...	...	...	...
Bogor	*5 162 044*	*2 644 661*	*2 517 383*	112	...	...	...	...
Cirebon (Tjirebon)	*1 891 957*	*967 609*	*924 348*	40	...	...	...	...
Denpasar	*938 188*	*478 816*	*459 372*	128	...	...	...	...
Gorontalo	*138 590*	*67 236*	*71 354*	66	...	...	...	...
JAKARTA[47]	*10 428 001*	*5 212 569*	*5 215 432*	662	...	...	...	...
Jambi	*585 392*	*292 509*	*292 883*	205	...	...	...	...
Kediri	*800 716*	*403 055*	*397 661*	63	...	...	...	...
Madiun	*237 668*	*117 818*	*119 850*	34	...	...	...	...
Magelang	*413 946*	*207 123*	*206 823*	18	...	...	...	...
Makasar (Ujung Pandang)	*1 502 459*	*744 057*	*758 402*	176	...	...	...	...
Malang	*1 382 786*	*695 308*	*687 478*	145	...	...	...	...
Manado	*427 409*	*213 250*	*214 159*	158	...	...	...	...
Mataram	*483 908*	*240 914*	*242 994*	61	...	...	...	...
Medan	*2 269 588*	*1 121 730*	*1 147 858*	265	...	...	...	...
Mojokerto	*598 783*	*300 406*	*298 377*	16	...	...	...	...
Padang	*941 136*	*470 051*	*471 085*	695	...	...	...	...
Pakalongan	*498 568*	*248 731*	*249 837*	45	...	...	...	...
Pakanbaru	*1 090 735*	*556 689*	*534 046*	632	...	...	...	...
Palangkaraya	*265 154*	*134 411*	*130 743*	2400	...	...	...	...
Palembang	*1 649 298*	*823 359*	*825 939*	364	...	...	...	...
Pangkal Pinang	*201 207*	*102 142*	*99 065*	119	...	...	...	...
Pare Pare	*142 391*	*69 925*	*72 466*	99	...	...	...	...
Pasuruan	*799 137*	*399 425*	*399 712*	35	...	...	...	...
Pematang Siantar	*254 010*	*123 897*	*130 113*	56	...	...	...	...
Probolinggo	*458 338*	*225 066*	*233 272*	57	...	...	...	...
Salatiga	*190 872*	*93 423*	*97 449*	53	...	...	...	...
Samarinda	*831 608*	*424 424*	*407 184*	717	...	...	...	...
Semarang	*459 358*	*222 781*	*236 577*	374	...	...	...	...
Sukabumi	*1 301 873*	*658 536*	*643 337*	49	...	...	...	...
Surabaya	*2 885 245*	*1 425 085*	*1 460 160*	351	...	...	...	...
Surakarta	*515 865*	*251 014*	*264 851*	44	...	...	...	...
Tangerang	*3 050 758*	*1 563 442*	*1 487 316*	154	...	...	...	...
Tanjung Balai	*174 049*	*87 794*	*86 255*	108	...	...	...	...
Tebing Tinggi	*163 292*	*80 763*	*82 529*	31	...	...	...	...
Tegal	*895 902*	*445 229*	*450 673*	34	...	...	...	...
Yogyakarta	*427 801*	*208 222*	*219 579*	33	...	...	...	...
Iran (Islamic Republic of) - Iran (République islamique d')								
24 IX 2016 (CDJC)								
Abadan	231 476	115 745	115 731	...	...	...	...	...
Ahar	100 641	50 386	50 255	...	...	...	...	...
Ahwaz	1 184 788	596 774	588 014	...	...	...	...	...
Amol	237 528	118 706	118 822	...	...	...	...	...
Andimeshk	135 116	68 218	66 898	...	...	...	...	...
Andisheh	116 062	58 717	57 345	...	...	...	...	...
Arak	520 944	263 143	257 801	...	...	...	...	...
Ardabil	529 374	269 387	259 987	...	...	...	...	...
Babol	250 217	124 863	125 354	...	...	...	...	...
Bam	127 396	65 128	62 268	...	...	...	...	...
Bandar-e-Abbas	526 648	269 033	257 615	...	...	...	...	...
Bandar-e-Anzali	118 564	58 802	59 762	...	...	...	...	...
Bandar-e-Mahshahr	162 797	81 717	81 080	...	...	...	...	...
Baneh	110 218	55 609	54 609	...	...	...	...	...
Behbahan	122 604	62 124	60 480	...	...	...	...	...
Birjand	203 636	102 399	101 237	...	...	...	...	...
Bojnurd	228 931	114 441	114 490	...	...	...	...	...
Borazjan	110 567	55 675	54 892	...	...	...	...	...
Borujerd	234 997	117 255	117 742	...	...	...	...	...
Bukand	193 501	97 659	95 842	...	...	...	...	...
Bushehr	223 504	115 260	108 244	...	...	...	...	...

8. Population of capital cities and cities of 100 000 or more inhabitants: latest available year, 2000 - 2019
Population des capitales et des villes de 100 000 habitants ou plus : dernière année disponible, 2000 - 2019 (continued - suite)

Continent, country or area, date, code[a] and city / Continent, pays ou zone, date, code[a] et ville	City proper - Ville proprement dite: Population: Both sexes - Les deux sexes	Male - Masculin	Female - Féminin	Surface area - Superficie (km²)	Urban agglomeration - Agglomération urbaine: Population: Both sexes - Les deux sexes	Male - Masculin	Female - Féminin	Surface area - Superficie (km²)
ASIA - ASIE								
Iran (Islamic Republic of) - Iran (République islamique d')								
24 IX 2016 (CDJC)								
Chabahar	106 739	54 657	52 082	...	...	...	...	...
Dezful	264 709	135 925	128 784	...	...	...	...	...
Dorud	121 638	61 395	60 243	...	...	...	...	...
Esfahan	1 961 260	989 168	972 092	...	...	...	...	...
Fardis	181 174	90 573	90 601	...	...	...	...	...
Fasa	110 825	55 650	55 175	...	...	...	...	...
Golestan (Soltanabad)	239 556	123 923	115 633	...	...	...	...	...
Gonbad-e-Kavus	151 910	75 899	76 011	...	...	...	...	...
Gorgan	350 676	174 797	175 879	...	...	...	...	...
Hamadan	554 406	276 455	277 951	...	...	...	...	...
Ilam	194 030	98 276	95 754	...	...	...	...	...
Iranshahr	113 750	58 143	55 607	...	...	...	...	...
Islam Shahr (Qasemabad)	448 129	227 808	220 321	...	...	...	...	...
Izeh	119 399	59 665	59 734	...	...	...	...	...
Jahrom	141 634	73 641	67 993	...	...	...	...	...
Jiroft	130 429	66 874	63 555	...	...	...	...	...
Kamal Shahr	141 669	72 661	69 008	...	...	...	...	...
Karaj	1 592 492	802 398	790 094	...	...	...	...	...
Kashan	304 487	154 100	150 387	...	...	...	...	...
Kashmar	102 282	51 616	50 666	...	...	...	...	...
Kerman	537 718	272 715	265 003	...	...	...	...	...
Kermanshah	946 651	474 073	472 578	...	...	...	...	...
Khomeini shahr	247 128	127 450	119 678	...	...	...	...	...
Khoramabad	373 416	186 481	186 935	...	...	...	...	...
Khoramshahr	133 097	66 113	66 984	...	...	...	...	...
Khoy	198 845	99 712	99 133	...	...	...	...	...
Lahijan	101 073	50 123	50 950	...	...	...	...	...
Mahabad	168 393	84 271	84 122	...	...	...	...	...
Malard	281 027	143 278	137 749	...	...	...	...	...
Malayer	170 237	85 487	84 750	...	...	...	...	...
Marand	130 825	66 671	64 154	...	...	...	...	...
Maraqeh	175 255	87 868	87 387	...	...	...	...	...
Marivan	136 654	69 679	66 975	...	...	...	...	...
Marvadsht	148 858	76 363	72 495	...	...	...	...	...
Mashhad	3 001 184	1 503 824	1 497 360	...	...	...	...	...
Masjed Soleyman	100 497	51 019	49 478	...	...	...	...	...
Miandoab	134 425	68 679	65 746	...	...	...	...	...
Mohammad Shahr	119 418	60 988	58 430	...	...	...	...	...
Najafabad	235 281	118 710	116 571	...	...	...	...	...
Nasim Shahr	200 393	103 371	97 022	...	...	...	...	...
Nazar Abad	119 512	61 074	58 438	...	...	...	...	...
Neyshabur	264 375	132 273	132 102	...	...	...	...	...
Orumiyeh	736 224	369 043	367 181	...	...	...	...	...
Pakdasht	236 319	120 459	115 860	...	...	...	...	...
Qaem shahr	204 953	101 999	102 954	...	...	...	...	...
Qarchak	231 075	118 260	112 815	...	...	...	...	...
Qazvin	402 748	203 702	199 046	...	...	...	...	...
Qods	309 605	158 567	151 038	...	...	...	...	...
Qom	1 201 158	609 541	591 617	...	...	...	...	...
Quchan	101 604	51 501	50 103	...	...	...	...	...
Rafsanjan	161 909	83 607	78 302	...	...	...	...	...
Rasht	679 995	336 313	343 682	...	...	...	...	...
Robatkarim	105 393	53 647	51 746	...	...	...	...	...
Sabzewar	243 700	121 667	122 033	...	...	...	...	...
Sanandaj	412 767	208 059	204 708	...	...	...	...	...
Saqez	165 258	82 984	82 274	...	...	...	...	...
Sari	309 820	153 823	155 997	...	...	...	...	...
Saveh	220 762	112 742	108 020	...	...	...	...	...
Semnan	185 129	94 411	90 718	...	...	...	...	...
Shahinshahr	173 329	86 008	87 321	...	...	...	...	...
Shahr-e-Kord	190 441	94 789	95 652	...	...	...	...	...
Shahreza	134 952	68 191	66 761	...	...	...	...	...

Continent, country or area, date, code[a] and city - Continent, pays ou zone, date, code[a] et ville	City proper - Ville proprement dite: Population: Both sexes - Les deux sexes	Male - Masculin	Female - Féminin	Surface area - Superficie (km²)	Urban agglomeration - Agglomération urbaine: Population: Both sexes - Les deux sexes	Male - Masculin	Female - Féminin	Surface area - Superficie (km²)
ASIA - ASIE								
Iran (Islamic Republic of) - Iran (République islamique d')								
24 IX 2016 (CDJC)								
Shahriar	309 607	156 085	153 522	...	...	...	...	...
Shahrud	150 129	75 656	74 473	...	...	...	...	...
Shiraz	1 565 572	785 450	780 122	...	...	...	...	...
Shoshtar	101 878	51 762	50 116	...	...	...	...	...
Sirjan	199 704	102 656	97 048	...	...	...	...	...
Tabriz	1 558 693	786 661	772 032	...	...	...	...	...
TEHRAN	8 693 706	4 324 155	4 369 551	...	...	...	...	...
Torbat-e-heydariyeh	140 019	71 603	68 416	...	...	...	...	...
Torbatejam	100 449	50 772	49 677	...	...	...	...	...
Varamin	225 628	114 215	111 413	...	...	...	...	...
Yasooj	134 532	68 427	66 105	...	...	...	...	...
Yazd	529 673	269 732	259 941	...	...	...	...	...
Zabol	134 950	67 691	67 259	...	...	...	...	...
Zahedan	587 730	299 550	288 180	...	...	...	...	...
Zanjan	430 871	217 406	213 465	...	...	...	...	...
Iraq								
1 VII 2015 (ESDF)								
Abi Gharaq Nahia	*108 630*	*55 009*	*53 621*	191	...	...	...	...
Abna'a Al-Rafidain Nahia	*153 712*	*77 827*	*75 885*	...	...	...	...	...
Abu Al-Khaseeb Qadha Center	*215 247*	*108 228*	*107 019*	1152	...	...	...	...
Abu-Gharib Qadha Center	*149 858*	*76 274*	*73 584*	431	...	...	...	...
Al-Adhamia Qadha Center	*286 036*	*144 825*	*141 211*	29	...	...	...	...
Al-Amara Qadha Center	*541 034*	*270 426*	*270 608*	2862	...	...	...	...
Al-Amirya Nahia	*101 119*	*51 899*	*49 220*	2532	...	...	...	...
Al-Basrah Qadha Center	*1 225 793*	*616 525*	*609 268*	1085	...	...	...	...
Al-Dair Nahia	*101 882*	*50 969*	*50 913*	825	...	...	...	...
Al-Dijail Qadha Center	*105 345*	*53 240*	*52 105*	1286	...	...	...	...
Al-Diwaniya Qadha Center	*421 571*	*212 293*	*209 278*	319	...	...	...	...
Al-Fahama Nahia	*619 474*	*313 651*	*305 823*	90	...	...	...	...
Al-Falluja Qadha Center	*321 106*	*165 111*	*155 995*	478	...	...	...	...
Al-Forat Nahia	*379 668*	*192 233*	*187 435*	...	...	...	...	...
Al-Garma Nahia	*129 783*	*66 577*	*63 206*	1038	...	...	...	...
Al-Gharraf Nahia	*118 081*	*59 318*	*58 763*	623	...	...	...	...
Al-Habbaniya Nahia	*133 202*	*68 366*	*64 836*	714	...	...	...	...
Al-Hamza Qadha Center	*128 472*	*64 739*	*63 733*	600	...	...	...	...
Al-Hartha Nahia	*156 391*	*78 509*	*77 882*	...	...	...	...	...
Al-Hassainya Nahia	*147 103*	*74 383*	*72 720*	334	...	...	...	...
Al-Hawiga Qadha Center	*115 910*	*58 508*	*57 402*	1903	...	...	...	...
Al-Hilla Qadha Center	*559 834*	*282 142*	*277 692*	161	...	...	...	...
Al-Hindiya Qadha Center	*113 021*	*57 001*	*56 020*	134	...	...	...	...
Al-Hur Nahia	*231 635*	*116 740*	*114 895*	...	...	...	...	...
Al-Iskandaria Nahia	*159 516*	*80 514*	*79 002*	283	...	...	...	...
Al-Jisr Nahia	*159 306*	*81 464*	*77 842*	153	...	...	...	...
Al-Kadimiya Qadha Center	*420 968*	*213 144*	*207 824*	32	...	...	...	...
Al-Kaim Qadha Center	*104 989*	*53 971*	*51 018*	6460	...	...	...	...
Al-Karkh Qadha Center	*113 397*	*57 415*	*55 982*	...	...	...	...	...
Al-Karrada Al-Sharqia Nahia	*318 615*	*161 321*	*157 294*	49	...	...	...	...
Al-Khalis Qadha Center	*139 713*	*70 624*	*69 089*	1109	...	...	...	...
Al-Kifl Nahia	*140 182*	*71 029*	*69 153*	526	...	...	...	...
Al-Kufa Qadha Center	*232 670*	*116 667*	*116 003*	129	...	...	...	...
Al-Kut Qadha Center	*436 673*	*220 490*	*216 183*	2540	...	...	...	...
Al-Madhatiya Nahia	*135 941*	*68 724*	*67 217*	498	...	...	...	...
Al-Mahawil Qadha Center	*116 899*	*59 181*	*57 718*	608	...	...	...	...
Al-Mamoon Nahia	*985 798*	*499 128*	*486 670*	82	...	...	...	...
Al-Mansour Nahia	*434 839*	*220 167*	*214 672*	119	...	...	...	...
Al-Mashroo Nahia	*127 344*	*64 449*	*62 895*	834	...	...	...	...
Al-Mejar Al-Kabir Qadha Center	*108 979*	*54 373*	*54 606*	506	...	...	...	...
Al-Mosal Qadha Center	*1 384 260*	*708 546*	*675 714*	1783	...	...	...	...
Al-Mounawara Nahia	*287 799*	*145 718*	*142 081*	...	...	...	...	...
Al-Muqdadya Qadha Center	*157 593*	*79 612*	*77 981*	768	...	...	...	...
Al-Najaf Qadha Center	*746 180*	*372 423*	*373 757*	1133	...	...	...	...
Al-Nasir & Al-Salam Nahia	*160 606*	*82 184*	*78 422*	262	...	...	...	...

8. Population of capital cities and cities of 100 000 or more inhabitants: latest available year, 2000 - 2019
Population des capitales et des villes de 100 000 habitants ou plus : dernière année disponible, 2000 - 2019 (continued - suite)

Continent, country or area, date, code[a] and city / Continent, pays ou zone, date, code[a] et ville	City proper - Ville proprement dite: Population: Both sexes - Les deux sexes	Male - Masculin	Female - Féminin	Surface area - Superficie (km²)	Urban agglomeration - Agglomération urbaine: Population: Both sexes - Les deux sexes	Male - Masculin	Female - Féminin	Surface area - Superficie (km²)
ASIA - ASIE								
Iraq								
1 VII 2015 (ESDF)								
Al-Nasiriya Qadha Center	*537 544*	*269 480*	*268 064*	1277	...	...	...	...
Al-Noamaniya Qadha Center	*111 647*	*56 363*	*55 284*	946	...	...	...	...
Al-Qasim Nahia	*159 420*	*80 545*	*78 875*	528	...	...	...	...
Al-Qayarra Nahia	*129 811*	*66 129*	*63 682*	686	...	...	...	...
Al-Qurna Qadha Center	*136 677*	*68 704*	*67 973*	1248	...	...	...	...
Al-Ramadi Qadha Center	*419 053*	*215 292*	*203 761*	7829	...	...	...	...
Al-Rifaai Qadha Center	*155 478*	*78 087*	*77 391*	1345	...	...	...	...
Al-Rumaitha Qadha Center	*118 011*	*59 581*	*58 430*	106	...	...	...	...
Al-Rusafa Qadha Center	*118 018*	*59 755*	*58 263*	...	...	...	...	...
Al-Samawa Qadha Center	*288 948*	*145 984*	*142 964*	941	...	...	...	...
Al-Shamal Nahia	*158 475*	*81 035*	*77 440*	...	...	...	...	...
Al-Shattra Qadha Center	*239 680*	*120 266*	*119 414*	384	...	...	...	...
Al-Shirqat Qadha Center	*208 586*	*105 453*	*103 133*	1515	...	...	...	...
Al-Sideeq Al-Akbar Nahia	*172 057*	*87 116*	*84 941*	...	...	...	...	...
Al-Suwaira Qadha Center	*142 924*	*72 148*	*70 776*	1345	...	...	...	...
Al-Taji Nahia	*164 894*	*84 470*	*80 424*	388	...	...	...	...
Al-Wihda Nahia	*204 585*	*104 438*	*100 147*	890	...	...	...	...
Al-Yousifya Nahia	*131 507*	*67 600*	*63 907*	486	...	...	...	...
Al-Zohour Nahia	*209 918*	*106 332*	*103 586*	...	...	...	...	...
Al-Zubair Qadha Center	*378 758*	*190 200*	*188 558*	1134	...	...	...	...
Arbil Qadha Center	*787 997*	*398 450*	*389 547*	2790	...	...	...	...
BAGHDAD	*1 211 934*[48]	*613 625*[48]	*598 309*[48]	111	...	...	...	...
Bakrago Nahia	*101 892*	*51 077*	*50 815*	...	...	...	...	...
Baquba Qadha Center	*276 029*	*138 681*	*137 348*	580	...	...	...	...
Bashiqa Nahia	*140 258*	*71 487*	*68 771*	497	...	...	...	...
Beni Saad Nahia	*127 268*	*64 496*	*62 772*	497	...	...	...	...
Beygee Qadha Center	*175 395*	*88 596*	*86 799*	1188	...	...	...	...
Duhouk Qadha Center	*328 113*	*164 245*	*163 868*	577	...	...	...	...
Kalar Qadha Center	*144 235*	*72 047*	*72 188*	2201	...	...	...	...
Kerbela Qadha Center	*514 356*	*259 193*	*255 163*	2397	...	...	...	...
Kirkuk Qadha Center	*938 336*	*471 419*	*466 917*	1956	...	...	...	...
Mahmudiya Qadha Center	*154 741*	*78 846*	*75 895*	68	...	...	...	...
Qalat Siker Nahia	*100 315*	*50 373*	*49 942*	614	...	...	...	...
Saddat Al-Hindin Nahia	*116 247*	*58 839*	*57 408*	388	...	...	...	...
Sader /1 Qadha Center	*130 153*	*65 899*	*64 254*	...	...	...	...	...
Samarra Qadha Center	*203 011*	*102 444*	*100 567*	4504	...	...	...	...
Shat Al-Arab Qadha Center	*136 043*	*68 413*	*67 630*	1516	...	...	...	...
Sulaimania Qadha Center	*651 173*	*325 147*	*326 026*	3404	...	...	...	...
Suq AL-Shoyolh Qadha Center	*126 652*	*63 493*	*63 159*	285	...	...	...	...
Telafar Qadha Center	*206 835*	*105 780*	*101 055*	3206	...	...	...	...
That Al Salasil Nahia	*277 494*	*140 647*	*136 847*	147	...	...	...	...
Tikrit Qadha Center	*182 464*	*92 119*	*90 345*	991	...	...	...	...
Tooz-Khormato Qadha Center	*117 458*	*59 233*	*58 225*	1253	...	...	...	...
Zummar Nahia	*128 017*	*65 210*	*62 807*	1247	...	...	...	...
Israel - Israël								
1 VII 2018 (ESDJ)								
Ashdod	223 755	109 160	114 595	46	...	...	...	...
Ashqelon	139 456	67 975	71 481	45	...	...	...	...
Bat Yam	128 714	61 287	67 427	8	...	...	...	...
Be'er Sheva	208 277	101 703	106 574	117	...	...	...	...
Bene Beraq	196 319	100 375	95 943	7	...	...	...	...
Bet Shemesh	116 523	58 229	58 294	38	...	...	...	...
Haifa	282 364	135 991	146 373	65	...	...	...	...
Holon	193 448	93 441	100 007	19	...	...	...	...
JERUSALEM[49]	910 370	453 833	456 537	126	...	...	...	...
Kefar Sava	100 401	48 329	52 072	14	...	...	...	...
Netanya	215 672	105 020	110 652	31	...	...	...	...
Petah Tiqwa	242 316	118 778	123 538	36	...	...	...	...
Ramat Gan	157 719	75 488	82 230	16	...	...	...	...
Rehovot	139 979	68 385	71 594	24	...	...	...	...
Rishon Leziyyon	250 789	122 904	127 885	59	...	...	...	...
Tel Aviv-Yafo	447 730	221 932	225 798	52	...	...	...	...

8. Population of capital cities and cities of 100 000 or more inhabitants: latest available year, 2000 - 2019
Population des capitales et des villes de 100 000 habitants ou plus : dernière année disponible, 2000 - 2019 (continued - suite)

Continent, country or area, date, code[a] and city / Continent, pays ou zone, date, code[a] et ville	City proper - Ville proprement dite				Urban agglomeration - Agglomération urbaine			
	Population				Population			
	Both sexes - Les deux sexes	Male - Masculin	Female - Féminin	Surface area - Superficie (km²)	Both sexes - Les deux sexes	Male - Masculin	Female - Féminin	Surface area - Superficie (km²)
ASIA - ASIE								
Japan - Japon								
1 X 2015 (CDJC)								
Abiko	131 606[50]	64 614[50]	66 992[50]	43.2[51]	...	...	...	...
Ageo	225 196[50]	112 157[50]	113 039[50]	45.5[51]	...	...	...	...
Aizuwakamatsu	124 062[50]	59 200[50]	64 862[50]	383[51]	...	...	...	...
Akashi	293 409[50]	141 801[50]	151 608[50]	49.4[51]	...	...	...	...
Akishima	111 539[50]	55 394[50]	56 145[50]	17.3[51]	...	...	...	...
Akita	315 814[50]	148 851[50]	166 963[50]	906.1[51]	...	...	...	...
Amagasaki	452 563[50]	219 059[50]	233 504[50]	50.7[51]	...	...	...	...
Anjo	184 140[50]	94 073[50]	90 067[50]	86.1[51]	...	...	...	...
Aomori	287 648[50]	133 560[50]	154 088[50]	824.6[51]	...	...	...	...
Asahikawa	339 605[50]	156 402[50]	183 203[50]	747.7[51]	...	...	...	...
Asaka	136 299[50]	69 971[50]	66 328[50]	18.3[51]	...	...	...	...
Ashikaga	149 452[50]	73 161[50]	76 291[50]	177.8[51]	...	...	...	...
Atsugi	225 714[50]	116 658[50]	109 056[50]	93.8[51]	...	...	...	...
Beppu	122 138[50]	55 482[50]	66 656[50]	125.3[51]	...	...	...	...
Chiba	971 882[50]	482 840[50]	489 042[50]	271.8[51]	...	...	...	...
Chigasaki	239 348[50]	116 894[50]	122 454[50]	35.7[51]	...	...	...	...
Chikusei	104 573[50]	51 663[50]	52 910[50]	205.3[51]	...	...	...	...
Chikushino	101 081[50]	47 995[50]	53 086[50]	87.7[51]	...	...	...	...
Chofu	229 061[50]	111 921[50]	117 140[50]	21.6[51]	...	...	...	...
Daito	123 217[50]	60 302[50]	62 915[50]	18.3[51]	...	...	...	...
Ebetsu	120 636[50]	57 391[50]	63 245[50]	187.4[51]	...	...	...	...
Ebina	130 190[50]	65 620[50]	64 570[50]	26.6[51]	...	...	...	...
Fuchu	260 274[50]	132 172[50]	128 102[50]	29.4[51]	...	...	...	...
Fuji	248 399[50]	121 901[50]	126 498[50]	245[51]	...	...	...	...
Fujieda	143 605[50]	70 049[50]	73 556[50]	194.1[51]	...	...	...	...
Fujimi	108 102[50]	53 312[50]	54 790[50]	19.8[51]	...	...	...	...
Fujimino	110 970[50]	54 910[50]	56 060[50]	14.6[51]	...	...	...	...
Fujinomiya	130 770[50]	64 281[50]	66 489[50]	389.1[51]	...	...	...	...
Fujisawa	423 894[50]	210 032[50]	213 862[50]	69.6[51]	...	...	...	...
Fukaya	143 811[50]	71 594[50]	72 217[50]	138.4[51]	...	...	...	...
Fukui	265 904[50]	128 892[50]	137 012[50]	536.4[51]	...	...	...	...
Fukuoka	1 538 681[50]	726 666[50]	812 015[50]	343.4[51]	...	...	...	...
Fukushima	294 247[50]	144 690[50]	149 557[50]	767.7[51]	...	...	...	...
Fukuyama	464 811[50]	225 414[50]	239 397[50]	518.1[51]	...	...	...	...
Funabashi	622 890[50]	311 358[50]	311 532[50]	85.6[51]	...	...	...	...
Gifu	406 735[50]	193 760[50]	212 975[50]	203.6[51]	...	...	...	...
Habikino	112 683[50]	53 243[50]	59 440[50]	26.5[51]	...	...	...	...
Hachinohe	231 257[50]	110 493[50]	120 764[50]	305.5[51]	...	...	...	...
Hachioji	577 513[50]	291 238[50]	286 275[50]	186.4[51]	...	...	...	...
Hadano	167 378[50]	85 552[50]	81 826[50]	103.8[51]	...	...	...	...
Hakodate	265 979[50]	120 376[50]	145 603[50]	677.9[51]	...	...	...	...
Hakusan	109 287[50]	53 085[50]	56 202[50]	754.9[51]	...	...	...	...
Hamamatsu	797 980[50]	395 509[50]	402 471[50]	1558.1[51]	...	...	...	...
Handa	116 908[50]	58 444[50]	58 464[50]	47.4[51]	...	...	...	...
Hatsukaichi	114 906[50]	54 654[50]	60 252[50]	489.5[51]	...	...	...	...
Higashihiroshima	192 907[50]	97 962[50]	94 945[50]	635.2[51]	...	...	...	...
Higashikurume	116 632[50]	56 738[50]	59 894[50]	12.9[51]	...	...	...	...
Higashimurayama	149 956[50]	73 314[50]	76 642[50]	17.1[51]	...	...	...	...
Higashiomi	114 180[50]	56 601[50]	57 579[50]	388.4[51]	...	...	...	...
Higashiosaka	502 784[50]	246 053[50]	256 731[50]	61.8[51]	...	...	...	...
Hikone	113 679[50]	56 090[50]	57 589[50]	196.9[51]	...	...	...	...
Himeji	535 664[50]	258 724[50]	276 940[50]	534.5[51]	...	...	...	...
Hino	186 283[50]	93 349[50]	92 934[50]	27.6[51]	...	...	...	...
Hirakata	404 152[50]	192 816[50]	211 336[50]	65.1[51]	...	...	...	...
Hiratsuka	258 227[50]	129 456[50]	128 771[50]	67.8[51]	...	...	...	...
Hirosaki	177 411[50]	81 367[50]	96 044[50]	524.2[51]	...	...	...	...
Hiroshima	1 194 034[50]	576 850[50]	617 184[50]	906.5[51]	...	...	...	...
Hitachi	185 054[50]	92 595[50]	92 459[50]	225.7[51]	...	...	...	...
Hitachinaka	155 689[50]	78 270[50]	77 419[50]	99.9[51]	...	...	...	...

8. Population of capital cities and cities of 100 000 or more inhabitants: latest available year, 2000 - 2019
Population des capitales et des villes de 100 000 habitants ou plus : dernière année disponible, 2000 - 2019 (continued - suite)

Continent, country or area, date, code[a] and city / Continent, pays ou zone, date, code[a] et ville	City proper - Ville proprement dite				Urban agglomeration - Agglomération urbaine			
	Population				Population			
	Both sexes - Les deux sexes	Male - Masculin	Female - Féminin	Surface area - Superficie (km²)	Both sexes - Les deux sexes	Male - Masculin	Female - Féminin	Surface area - Superficie (km²)
ASIA - ASIE								
Japan - Japon								
1 X 2015 (CDJC)								
Hofu	115 942[50]	55 910[50]	60 032[50]	189.4[51]	...	...	...	...
Ibaraki	280 033[50]	135 705[50]	144 328[50]	76.5[51]	...	...	...	...
Ichihara	274 656[50]	141 134[50]	133 522[50]	368.2[51]	...	...	...	...
Ichikawa	481 732[50]	242 652[50]	239 080[50]	57.5[51]	...	...	...	...
Ichinomiya	380 868[50]	185 869[50]	194 999[50]	113.8[51]	...	...	...	...
Ichinoseki	121 583[50]	58 804[50]	62 779[50]	1256.4[51]	...	...	...	...
Iida	101 581[50]	48 443[50]	53 138[50]	658.7[51]	...	...	...	...
Iizuka	129 146[50]	61 249[50]	67 897[50]	214.1[51]	...	...	...	...
Ikeda	103 069[50]	49 372[50]	53 697[50]	22.1[51]	...	...	...	...
Ikoma	118 233[50]	55 972[50]	62 261[50]	53.2[51]	...	...	...	...
Imabari	158 114[50]	74 336[50]	83 778[50]	419.1[51]	...	...	...	...
Inazawa	136 867[50]	67 500[50]	69 367[50]	79.4[51]	...	...	...	...
Iruma	148 390[50]	73 408[50]	74 982[50]	44.7[51]	...	...	...	...
Isahaya	138 078[50]	65 029[50]	73 049[50]	341.8[51]	...	...	...	...
Ise	127 817[50]	60 467[50]	67 350[50]	208.4[51]	...	...	...	...
Isehara	101 514[50]	51 429[50]	50 085[50]	55.6[51]	...	...	...	...
Isesaki	208 814[50]	104 234[50]	104 580[50]	139.4[51]	...	...	...	...
Ishinomaki	147 214[50]	71 826[50]	75 388[50]	554.6[51]	...	...	...	...
Itami	196 883[50]	95 641[50]	101 242[50]	25[51]	...	...	...	...
Iwaki	350 237[50]	172 829[50]	177 408[50]	1232[51]	...	...	...	...
Iwakuni	136 757[50]	64 455[50]	72 302[50]	873.7[51]	...	...	...	...
Iwata	167 210[50]	84 130[50]	83 080[50]	163.5[51]	...	...	...	...
Izumi (Osaka)	186 109[50]	89 868[50]	96 241[50]	85[51]	...	...	...	...
Izumisano	100 966[50]	48 506[50]	52 460[50]	56.5[51]	...	...	...	...
Izumo	171 938[50]	82 707[50]	89 231[50]	624.4[51]	...	...	...	...
Joetsu	196 987[50]	95 990[50]	100 997[50]	973.8[51]	...	...	...	...
Kadoma	123 576[50]	60 620[50]	62 956[50]	12.3[51]	...	...	...	...
Kagoshima	599 814[50]	279 108[50]	320 706[50]	547.6[51]	...	...	...	...
Kakamigahara	144 690[50]	71 167[50]	73 523[50]	87.8[51]	...	...	...	...
Kakegawa	114 602[50]	57 126[50]	57 476[50]	265.7[51]	...	...	...	...
Kakogawa	267 435[50]	131 170[50]	136 265[50]	138.5[51]	...	...	...	...
Kamagaya	108 917[50]	53 490[50]	55 427[50]	21.1[51]	...	...	...	...
Kamakura	173 019[50]	81 664[50]	91 355[50]	39.7[51]	...	...	...	...
Kanazawa	465 699[50]	226 007[50]	239 692[50]	468.6[51]	...	...	...	...
Kanoya	103 608[50]	49 555[50]	54 053[50]	448.2[51]	...	...	...	...
Karatsu	122 785[50]	57 547[50]	65 238[50]	487.6[51]	...	...	...	...
Kariya	149 765[50]	78 456[50]	71 309[50]	50.4[51]	...	...	...	...
Kashihara	124 111[50]	58 888[50]	65 223[50]	39.6[51]	...	...	...	...
Kashiwa	413 954[50]	205 971[50]	207 983[50]	114.7[51]	...	...	...	...
Kasuga	110 743[50]	53 284[50]	57 459[50]	14.2[51]	...	...	...	...
Kasugai	306 508[50]	151 955[50]	154 553[50]	92.8[51]	...	...	...	...
Kasukabe	232 709[50]	114 813[50]	117 896[50]	66[51]	...	...	...	...
Kawachinagano	106 987[50]	50 182[50]	56 805[50]	109.6[51]	...	...	...	...
Kawagoe	350 745[50]	175 559[50]	175 186[50]	109.1[51]	...	...	...	...
Kawaguchi	578 112[50]	292 067[50]	286 045[50]	62[51]	...	...	...	...
Kawanishi	156 375[50]	73 882[50]	82 493[50]	53.4[51]	...	...	...	...
Kawasaki	1 475 213[50]	749 038[50]	726 175[50]	143[51]	...	...	...	...
Kazo	112 229[50]	55 828[50]	56 401[50]	133.3[51]	...	...	...	...
Kirishima	125 857[50]	59 966[50]	65 891[50]	603.2[51]	...	...	...	...
Kiryu	114 714[50]	55 327[50]	59 387[50]	274.5[51]	...	...	...	...
Kisarazu	134 141[50]	67 450[50]	66 691[50]	139[51]	...	...	...	...
Kishiwada	194 911[50]	93 160[50]	101 751[50]	72.7[51]	...	...	...	...
Kitakyushu	961 286[50]	452 682[50]	508 604[50]	492[51]	...	...	...	...
Kitami	121 226[50]	58 020[50]	63 206[50]	1427.4[51]	...	...	...	...
Kobe	1 537 272[50]	726 700[50]	810 572[50]	557[51]	...	...	...	...
Kochi	337 190[50]	157 002[50]	180 188[50]	309[51]	...	...	...	...
Kodaira	190 005[50]	93 777[50]	96 228[50]	20.5[51]	...	...	...	...
Kofu	193 125[50]	94 448[50]	98 677[50]	212.5[51]	...	...	...	...
Koga	140 946[50]	70 354[50]	70 592[50]	123.6[51]	...	...	...	...

8. Population of capital cities and cities of 100 000 or more inhabitants: latest available year, 2000 - 2019
Population des capitales et des villes de 100 000 habitants ou plus : dernière année disponible, 2000 - 2019 (continued - suite)

Continent, country or area, date, code[a] and city / Continent, pays ou zone, date, code[a] et ville	City proper - Ville proprement dite				Urban agglomeration - Agglomération urbaine			
	Population				Population			
	Both sexes - Les deux sexes	Male - Masculin	Female - Féminin	Surface area - Superficie (km²)	Both sexes - Les deux sexes	Male - Masculin	Female - Féminin	Surface area - Superficie (km²)
ASIA - ASIE								
Japan - Japon								
1 X 2015 (CDJC)								
Koganei	121 396[50]	60 168[50]	61 228[50]	11.3[51]	...	...	...	...
Kokubunji	122 742[50]	60 274[50]	62 468[50]	11.5[51]	...	...	...	...
Komaki	149 462[50]	75 430[50]	74 032[50]	62.8[51]	...	...	...	...
Komatsu	106 919[50]	51 844[50]	55 075[50]	371.1[51]	...	...	...	...
Konosu	118 072[50]	58 346[50]	59 726[50]	67.4[51]	...	...	...	...
Koriyama	335 444[50]	167 096[50]	168 348[50]	757.2[51]	...	...	...	...
Koshigaya	337 498[50]	167 023[50]	170 475[50]	60.2[51]	...	...	...	...
Kuki	152 311[50]	75 993[50]	76 318[50]	82.4[51]	...	...	...	...
Kumagaya	198 742[50]	99 169[50]	99 573[50]	159.8[51]	...	...	...	...
Kumamoto	740 822[50]	348 470[50]	392 352[50]	390.3[51]	...	...	...	...
Kurashiki	477 118[50]	230 081[50]	247 037[50]	355.6[51]	...	...	...	...
Kure	228 552[50]	110 173[50]	118 379[50]	352.8[51]	...	...	...	...
Kurume	304 552[50]	144 971[50]	159 581[50]	230[51]	...	...	...	...
Kusatsu	137 247[50]	70 129[50]	67 118[50]	67.8[51]	...	...	...	...
Kushiro	174 742[50]	82 185[50]	92 557[50]	1362.9[51]	...	...	...	...
Kuwana	140 303[50]	68 740[50]	71 563[50]	136.7[51]	...	...	...	...
Kyoto	1 475 183[50]	699 748[50]	775 435[50]	827.8[51]	...	...	...	...
Machida	432 348[50]	212 312[50]	220 036[50]	71.8[51]	...	...	...	...
Maebashi	336 154[50]	164 136[50]	172 018[50]	311.6[51]	...	...	...	...
Marugame	110 010[50]	53 183[50]	56 827[50]	111.8[51]	...	...	...	...
Matsubara	120 750[50]	58 096[50]	62 654[50]	16.7[51]	...	...	...	...
Matsudo	483 480[50]	240 928[50]	242 552[50]	61.4[51]	...	...	...	...
Matsue	206 230[50]	99 565[50]	106 665[50]	573[51]	...	...	...	...
Matsumoto	243 293[50]	119 479[50]	123 814[50]	978.5[51]	...	...	...	...
Matsusaka	163 863[50]	78 548[50]	85 315[50]	623.7[51]	...	...	...	...
Matsuyama	514 865[50]	241 656[50]	273 209[50]	429.4[51]	...	...	...	...
Minoh	133 411[50]	63 938[50]	69 473[50]	47.9[51]	...	...	...	...
Misato	136 521[50]	68 950[50]	67 571[50]	30.1[51]	...	...	...	...
Mishima	110 046[50]	53 836[50]	56 210[50]	62[51]	...	...	...	...
Mitaka	186 936[50]	90 641[50]	96 295[50]	16.4[51]	...	...	...	...
Mito	270 783[50]	132 799[50]	137 984[50]	217.3[51]	...	...	...	...
Miyakonojo	165 029[50]	77 521[50]	87 508[50]	653.4[51]	...	...	...	...
Miyazaki	401 138[50]	188 177[50]	212 961[50]	643.7[51]	...	...	...	...
Moriguchi	143 042[50]	68 987[50]	74 055[50]	12.7[51]	...	...	...	...
Morioka	297 631[50]	141 089[50]	156 542[50]	886.5[51]	...	...	...	...
Musashino	144 730[50]	69 475[50]	75 255[50]	11[51]	...	...	...	...
Nagahama	118 193[50]	57 703[50]	60 490[50]	681[51]	...	...	...	...
Nagano	377 598[50]	182 843[50]	194 755[50]	834.8[51]	...	...	...	...
Nagaoka	275 133[50]	134 198[50]	140 935[50]	891.1[51]	...	...	...	...
Nagareyama	174 373[50]	86 249[50]	88 124[50]	35.3[51]	...	...	...	...
Nagasaki	429 508[50]	198 716[50]	230 792[50]	405.9[51]	...	...	...	...
Nagoya	2 295 638[50]	1 133 640[50]	1 161 998[50]	326.5[51]	...	...	...	...
Naha	319 435[50]	154 685[50]	164 750[50]	39.6[51]	...	...	...	...
Nara	360 310[50]	167 899[50]	192 411[50]	276.9[51]	...	...	...	...
Narashino	167 909[50]	84 323[50]	83 586[50]	21[51]	...	...	...	...
Narita	131 190[50]	65 928[50]	65 262[50]	213.8[51]	...	...	...	...
Nasushiobara	117 146[50]	58 148[50]	58 998[50]	592.7[51]	...	...	...	...
Neyagawa	237 518[50]	115 131[50]	122 387[50]	24.7[51]	...	...	...	...
Niigata	810 157[50]	389 512[50]	420 645[50]	726.5[51]	...	...	...	...
Niihama	119 903[50]	57 551[50]	62 352[50]	234.5[51]	...	...	...	...
Niiza	162 122[50]	80 627[50]	81 495[50]	22.8[51]	...	...	...	...
Nishinomiya	487 850[50]	228 354[50]	259 496[50]	100[51]	...	...	...	...
Nishio	167 990[50]	84 669[50]	83 321[50]	161.2[51]	...	...	...	...
Nishitokyo	200 012[50]	97 830[50]	102 182[50]	15.8[51]	...	...	...	...
Nobeoka	125 159[50]	58 993[50]	66 166[50]	868[51]	...	...	...	...
Noda	153 583[50]	76 541[50]	77 042[50]	103.6[51]	...	...	...	...
Numazu	195 633[50]	95 980[50]	99 653[50]	187[51]	...	...	...	...
Obihiro	169 327[50]	80 994[50]	88 333[50]	619.3[51]	...	...	...	...
Odawara	194 086[50]	94 697[50]	99 389[50]	113.8[51]	...	...	...	...

8. Population of capital cities and cities of 100 000 or more inhabitants: latest available year, 2000 - 2019
Population des capitales et des villes de 100 000 habitants ou plus : dernière année disponible, 2000 - 2019 (continued - suite)

Continent, country or area, date, code[a] and city / Continent, pays ou zone, date, code[a] et ville	City proper - Ville proprement dite				Urban agglomeration - Agglomération urbaine			
	Population				Population			
	Both sexes - Les deux sexes	Male - Masculin	Female - Féminin	Surface area - Superficie (km²)	Both sexes - Les deux sexes	Male - Masculin	Female - Féminin	Surface area - Superficie (km²)
ASIA - ASIE								
Japan - Japon								
1 X 2015 (CDJC)								
Ogaki	159 879[50]	77 430[50]	82 449[50]	206.6[51]	...	...	...	...
Oita	478 146[50]	229 844[50]	248 302[50]	502.4[51]	...	...	...	...
Okayama	719 474[50]	345 913[50]	373 561[50]	790[51]	...	...	...	...
Okazaki	381 051[50]	192 771[50]	188 280[50]	387.2[51]	...	...	...	...
Okinawa	139 279[50]	67 522[50]	71 757[50]	49.7[51]	...	...	...	...
Ome	137 381[50]	68 677[50]	68 704[50]	103.3[51]	...	...	...	...
Omuta	117 360[50]	53 859[50]	63 501[50]	81.5[51]	...	...	...	...
Onomichi	138 626[50]	66 292[50]	72 334[50]	285.1[51]	...	...	...	...
Osaka	2 691 185[50]	1 302 562[50]	1 388 623[50]	225.2[51]	...	...	...	...
Osaki	133 391[50]	65 120[50]	68 271[50]	796.8[51]	...	...	...	...
Oshu	119 422[50]	57 377[50]	62 045[50]	993.3[51]	...	...	...	...
Ota	219 807[50]	111 610[50]	108 197[50]	175.5[51]	...	...	...	...
Otaru	121 924[50]	54 985[50]	66 939[50]	243.8[51]	...	...	...	...
Otsu	340 973[50]	164 799[50]	176 174[50]	464.5[51]	...	...	...	...
Oyama	166 760[50]	84 100[50]	82 660[50]	171.8[51]	...	...	...	...
Saga	236 372[50]	111 453[50]	124 919[50]	431.8[51]	...	...	...	...
Sagamihara	720 780[50]	361 060[50]	359 720[50]	328.7[51]	...	...	...	...
Saijo	108 174[50]	51 807[50]	56 367[50]	510[51]	...	...	...	...
Saitama	1 263 979[50]	627 238[50]	636 741[50]	217.4[51]	...	...	...	...
Sakado	101 679[50]	51 307[50]	50 372[50]	41[51]	...	...	...	...
Sakai (Osaka)	839 310[50]	402 379[50]	436 931[50]	209.7[51]	...	...	...	...
Sakata	106 244[50]	50 293[50]	55 951[50]	603[51]	...	...	...	...
Sakura	172 739[50]	84 434[50]	88 305[50]	103.7[51]	...	...	...	...
Sanda	112 691[50]	54 184[50]	58 507[50]	210.3[51]	...	...	...	...
Sano	118 919[50]	58 507[50]	60 412[50]	356[51]	...	...	...	...
Sapporo	1 952 356[50]	910 614[50]	1 041 742[50]	1121.3[51]	...	...	...	...
Sasebo	255 439[50]	120 198[50]	135 241[50]	426.1[51]	...	...	...	...
Sayama	152 405[50]	76 580[50]	75 825[50]	49[51]	...	...	...	...
Sendai	1 082 159[50]	527 170[50]	554 989[50]	786.3[51]	...	...	...	...
Seto	129 046[50]	63 189[50]	65 857[50]	111.4[51]	...	...	...	...
Shimonoseki	268 517[50]	124 722[50]	143 795[50]	715.9[51]	...	...	...	...
Shizuoka	704 989[50]	343 338[50]	361 651[50]	1411.9[51]	...	...	...	...
Shunan	144 842[50]	69 819[50]	75 023[50]	656.3[51]	...	...	...	...
Soka	247 034[50]	125 225[50]	121 809[50]	27.5[51]	...	...	...	...
Suita	374 468[50]	180 669[50]	193 799[50]	36.1[51]	...	...	...	...
Suzuka	196 403[50]	97 500[50]	98 903[50]	194.5[51]	...	...	...	...
Tachikawa	176 295[50]	86 978[50]	89 317[50]	24.4[51]	...	...	...	...
Tajimi	110 441[50]	53 378[50]	57 063[50]	91.3[51]	...	...	...	...
Takamatsu	420 748[50]	205 049[50]	215 699[50]	375.4[51]	...	...	...	...
Takaoka	172 125[50]	82 802[50]	89 323[50]	209.6[51]	...	...	...	...
Takarazuka	224 903[50]	104 215[50]	120 688[50]	101.8[51]	...	...	...	...
Takasaki	370 884[50]	181 601[50]	189 283[50]	459.2[51]	...	...	...	...
Takatsuki	351 829[50]	168 057[50]	183 772[50]	105.3[51]	...	...	...	...
Tama	146 631[50]	71 762[50]	74 869[50]	21[51]	...	...	...	...
Tochigi	159 211[50]	78 209[50]	81 002[50]	331.5[51]	...	...	...	...
Toda	136 150[50]	69 674[50]	66 476[50]	18.2[51]	...	...	...	...
Tokai	111 944[50]	58 170[50]	53 774[50]	43.4[51]	...	...	...	...
Tokorozawa	340 386[50]	168 205[50]	172 181[50]	72.1[51]	...	...	...	...
Tokushima	258 554[50]	123 014[50]	135 540[50]	191.3[51]	...	...	...	...
TOKYO	9 272 740[52]	4 567 247[52]	4 705 493[52]	626.7[51]	...	...	...	...
Tomakomai	172 737[50]	84 605[50]	88 132[50]	561.6[51]	...	...	...	...
Tondabayashi	113 984[50]	53 693[50]	60 291[50]	39.7[51]	...	...	...	...
Toride	106 570[50]	52 489[50]	54 081[50]	69.9[51]	...	...	...	...
Tottori	193 717[50]	94 151[50]	99 566[50]	765.3[51]	...	...	...	...
Toyama	418 686[50]	203 427[50]	215 259[50]	1241.8[51]	...	...	...	...
Toyohashi	374 765[50]	187 801[50]	186 964[50]	261.9[51]	...	...	...	...
Toyokawa	182 436[50]	90 869[50]	91 567[50]	161.1[51]	...	...	...	...
Toyonaka	395 479[50]	187 319[50]	208 160[50]	36.4[51]	...	...	...	...
Toyota	422 542[50]	222 169[50]	200 373[50]	918.3[51]	...	...	...	...

Continent, country or area, date, code[a] and city Continent, pays ou zone, date, code[a] et ville	City proper - Ville proprement dite				Urban agglomeration - Agglomération urbaine			
	Population				Population			
	Both sexes - Les deux sexes	Male - Masculin	Female - Féminin	Surface area - Superficie (km²)	Both sexes - Les deux sexes	Male - Masculin	Female - Féminin	Surface area - Superficie (km²)
ASIA - ASIE								
Japan - Japon								
1 X 2015 (CDJC)								
Tsu	279 886[50]	135 718[50]	144 168[50]	711.1[51]	...	...	...	...
Tsuchiura	140 804[50]	70 101[50]	70 703[50]	122.9[51]	...	...	...	...
Tsukuba	226 963[50]	114 774[50]	112 189[50]	283.7[51]	...	...	...	...
Tsuruoka	129 652[50]	61 761[50]	67 891[50]	1311.5[51]	...	...	...	...
Tsuyama	103 746[50]	49 561[50]	54 185[50]	506.3[51]	...	...	...	...
Ube	169 429[50]	81 133[50]	88 296[50]	286.7[51]	...	...	...	...
Ueda	156 827[50]	76 776[50]	80 051[50]	552[51]	...	...	...	...
Uji	184 678[50]	89 014[50]	95 664[50]	67.5[51]	...	...	...	...
Urasoe	114 232[50]	55 471[50]	58 761[50]	19.5[51]	...	...	...	...
Urayasu	164 024[50]	81 057[50]	82 967[50]	17.3[51]	...	...	...	...
Uruma	118 898[50]	59 409[50]	59 489[50]	87[51]	...	...	...	...
Utsunomiya	518 594[50]	258 960[50]	259 634[50]	416.9[51]	...	...	...	...
Wakayama	364 154[50]	171 215[50]	192 939[50]	208.8[51]	...	...	...	...
Yachiyo	193 152[50]	95 224[50]	97 928[50]	51.4[51]	...	...	...	...
Yaizu	139 462[50]	68 168[50]	71 294[50]	70.3[51]	...	...	...	...
Yamagata	253 832[50]	121 575[50]	132 257[50]	381.3[51]	...	...	...	...
Yamaguchi	197 422[50]	94 245[50]	103 177[50]	1023.2[51]	...	...	...	...
Yamato	232 922[50]	116 714[50]	116 208[50]	27.1[51]	...	...	...	...
Yao	268 800[50]	128 284[50]	140 516[50]	41.7[51]	...	...	...	...
Yatsushiro	127 472[50]	59 221[50]	68 251[50]	681.4[51]	...	...	...	...
Yokkaichi	311 031[50]	154 674[50]	156 357[50]	206.4[51]	...	...	...	...
Yokohama	3 724 844[50]	1 855 985[50]	1 868 859[50]	437.5[51]	...	...	...	...
Yokosuka	406 586[50]	202 775[50]	203 811[50]	100.8[51]	...	...	...	...
Yonago	149 313[50]	70 628[50]	78 685[50]	132.4[51]	...	...	...	...
Zama	128 737[50]	64 478[50]	64 259[50]	17.6[51]	...	...	...	...
Jordan - Jordanie								
31 XII 2018 (ESDF)								
AMMAN	*3 728 346*	*1 989 375*	*1 738 971*	...	...	...	...	...
Aqaba	*160 265*	*92 006*	*68 259*	...	...	...	...	...
Irbid	*542 884*	*283 401*	*259 483*	...	...	...	...	...
Madaba	*113 771*	*60 689*	*53 082*	...	...	...	...	...
Mafraq	*114 490*	*59 900*	*54 590*	...	...	...	...	...
Mukhayyam Al-Za'tary	*122 152*	*60 816*	*61 336*	...	...	...	...	...
Ramtha	*168 134*	*87 719*	*80 415*	...	...	...	...	...
Russiefa	*510 391*	*272 134*	*238 257*	...	...	...	...	...
Salt	*107 874*	*56 263*	*51 611*	...	...	...	...	...
Zarqa	*685 941*	*358 769*	*327 172*	...	...	...	...	...
Kazakhstan[53]								
1 VII 2019 (ESDF)								
Aktau	185 944	89 227	96 717	...	...	...	...	...
Aktobe	494 376	233 786	260 590	...	...	...	...	...
Almaty	1 885 739	863 474	1 022 265	...	...	...	...	...
ASTANA	1 107 270	531 380	575 890	...	...	...	...	...
Atirau	280 210	134 548	145 662	...	...	...	...	...
Ekibastuz	133 783	63 808	69 975	...	...	...	...	...
Karaganda	497 745	229 031	268 714	...	...	...	...	...
Koktshetau	145 633	67 426	78 207	...	...	...	...	...
Kustanai	245 650	110 548	135 102	...	...	...	...	...
Kyzylorda	240 766	117 382	123 384	...	...	...	...	...
Pavlodar	333 734	151 101	182 633	...	...	...	...	...
Petropavlovsk (Severo- Kazakhstanskaya oblast)	219 094	98 760	120 334	...	...	...	...	...
Rudni	115 131	53 975	61 156	...	...	...	...	...
Semipalatinsk	323 591	151 043	172 548	...	...	...	...	...
Shimkent	1 023 619	492 506	531 113	...	...	...	...	...
Taldykorgan	145 547	67 631	77 916	...	...	...	...	...
Taraz	357 793	168 492	189 301	...	...	...	...	...
Temirtau	179 224	83 744	95 480	...	...	...	...	...
Turkestan	168 340	84 578	83 762	...	...	...	...	...
Uralsk	234 170	107 174	126 996	...	...	...	...	...
Ust-Kamenogorsk	332 364	150 276	182 088	...	...	...	...	...

8. Population of capital cities and cities of 100 000 or more inhabitants: latest available year, 2000 - 2019
Population des capitales et des villes de 100 000 habitants ou plus : dernière année disponible, 2000 - 2019 (continued - suite)

Continent, country or area, date, code[a] and city / Continent, pays ou zone, date, code[a] et ville	City proper - Ville proprement dite: Population: Both sexes - Les deux sexes	Male - Masculin	Female - Féminin	Surface area - Superficie (km²)	Urban agglomeration - Agglomération urbaine: Population: Both sexes - Les deux sexes	Male - Masculin	Female - Féminin	Surface area - Superficie (km²)
ASIA - ASIE								
Kuwait - Koweït								
1 VII 2010 (ESDF)								
Farwanyiah	*101 867*	*68 326*	*33 541*	...	...	...	...	...
Hawalli	*127 982*	*84 506*	*43 477*	...	...	...	...	...
Jaleeb Al-Shuykh	*219 629*	*180 786*	*38 843*	...	...	...	...	...
Salmiya	*177 009*	*103 119*	*73 890*	...	...	...	...	...
South Kheetan	*113 426*	*104 655*	*8 770*	...	...	...	...	...
Kyrgyzstan - Kirghizstan[54]								
1 VII 2017 (ESDJ)								
BISHKEK	976 734	456 400	520 334	...	991 257	463 566	527 691	...
Osh	256 763	123 228	133 535	...	285 372	137 889	147 483	...
Lao People's Democratic Republic - République démocratique populaire lao								
1 VII 2019 (ESDJ)								
VIENTIANE	...	...	...	...	*927 390*[55]	*459 215*[55]	*468 175*[55]	3920
Lebanon - Liban[56]								
1 X 2011 (SSDF)								
BEIRUT	...	...	...	...	363 033	179 737	183 296	...
Malaysia - Malaisie[57]								
1 VII 2019 (ESDJ)								
Alor Setar	136 423	...	...	...	...	...	...	...
Bintulu Townland	140 756	...	...	...	...	...	...	...
Georgetown	226 281	...	...	...	...	...	...	...
Kajang dan Sungai Chua	114 849	...	...	...	...	...	...	...
Klang	296 642	...	...	...	...	...	...	...
Kota Kinabalu	252 979	...	...	...	...	...	...	...
KUALA LUMPUR	1 839 451	...	...	...	...	...	...	...
Kuala Terengganu	246 266	...	...	...	...	...	...	...
Kuantan	418 219	...	...	...	...	...	...	...
Kuching "Bandaraya Kuching Utara dan Selatan"	157 668	...	...	...	...	...	...	...
Majlis Perbandaran Ipoh	488 172	...	...	...	...	...	...	...
MB Johor Bahru (Johor Bahru)	518 627	...	...	...	...	...	...	...
Miri Townland	155 746	...	...	...	...	...	...	...
MP Kota Bharu	332 288	...	...	...	...	...	...	...
Petaling Jaya	218 506	...	...	...	...	...	...	...
Sandakan	202 705	...	...	...	...	...	...	...
Selayang Baru	186 847	...	...	...	...	...	...	...
Seremban	385 935	...	...	...	...	...	...	...
Shah Alam	195 049	...	...	...	...	...	...	...
Sibu "Majlis Perbandaran Sibu"	192 707	...	...	...	...	...	...	...
Subang Jaya	211 602	...	...	...	...	...	...	...
Sungai Petani	201 745	...	...	...	...	...	...	...
Taiping	244 104	...	...	...	...	...	...	...
Tawau	147 090	...	...	...	...	...	...	...
Maldives								
1 VII 2019 (ESDF)								
MALÉ	221 678[58]	137 614[58]	84 064[58]	2	...	...	...	...
Mongolia - Mongolie								
1 VII 2019 (ESDF)								
Bayan-Olgii	106 810	53 374	53 436	46	...	...	...	...
Darkhan-Uul	106 470	52 339	54 131	3	...	...	...	...
Hovsgol	134 530	66 773	67 757	101	...	...	...	...
Orkhon	106 810	52 406	54 404	1	...	...	...	...
Ovorhangay	116 922	58 238	58 684	63	...	...	...	...
Selenge	110 757	56 122	54 635	41	...	...	...	...
ULAANBAATAR	1 515 593	729 428	786 165	5	...	...	...	...
Myanmar								
29 III 2014 (CDFC)								
Bago	...	...	...	...	491 434	235 529	255 905	...
Dawei	...	...	...	...	125 605	60 044	65 561	...
Hpa-an	...	...	...	...	421 575	203 910	217 665	...
Loikaw	...	...	...	...	128 401	63 109	65 292	...
Magway	...	...	...	...	289 247	135 103	154 144	...
Mandalay	...	...	...	...	1 225 546	598 429	627 117	...

Continent, country or area, date, code[a] and city / Continent, pays ou zone, date, code[a] et ville	City proper - Ville proprement dite				Urban agglomeration - Agglomération urbaine			
	Population			Surface area - Superficie (km²)	Population			Surface area - Superficie (km²)
	Both sexes - Les deux sexes	Male - Masculin	Female - Féminin		Both sexes - Les deux sexes	Male - Masculin	Female - Féminin	
ASIA - ASIE								
Myanmar								
29 III 2014 (CDFC)								
Mawlamyine	...	...	...	...	289 388	139 026	150 362	...
Monywa	...	...	...	...	372 095	171 951	200 144	...
Myitkyina	...	...	...	...	306 949	148 485	158 464	...
NAY PYI TAW[59]	...	...	...	...	1 160 242	565 155	595 087	...
Pathein	...	...	...	...	287 071	137 663	149 408	...
Sittway	...	...	...	...	147 899	70 470	77 429	...
Taunggyi	...	...	...	...	381 639	185 954	195 685	...
Yangon	...	...	...	...	5 211 431	2 466 918	2 744 513	...
Nepal - Népal								
22 VI 2011 (CDJC)								
Bharatpur	143 836	71 175	72 661	162.2	...	...	...	...
Bhimdutta	104 599	51 087	53 512	171.2	...	...	...	...
Biratnagar	201 125	101 949	99 176	58.5	...	...	...	...
Birgunj	135 904	72 580	63 324	21.2	...	...	...	...
Butwal	118 462	58 808	59 654	69.3	...	...	...	...
Dhangadhi	101 970	51 439	50 531	103.7	...	...	...	...
Dharan	116 181	54 599	61 582	103.4	...	...	...	...
KATHMANDU	975 453	511 841	463 612	49.5	...	...	...	...
Lalitpur	220 802	113 781	107 021	15.2	...	...	...	...
Pokhara	255 465	126 238	129 227	55.2	...	...	...	...
Oman								
1 VII 2019 (ESDF)								
Al Buraymi	*107 411*[60]	*71 386*[60]	*36 025*[60]	1222.9	...	...	...	...
Al Mudaybi	*119 731*[60]	*73 471*[60]	*46 260*[60]	12108.2	...	...	...	...
Al Rustaq	*124 858*[60]	*70 298*[60]	*54 560*[60]	2262.4	...	...	...	...
As Seeb	*463 960*[60]	*287 862*[60]	*176 098*[60]	488.8	...	...	...	...
As Suwayq	*184 482*[60]	*110 925*[60]	*73 557*[60]	1007.2	...	...	...	...
Barka	*157 273*[60]	*99 627*[60]	*57 646*[60]	698.1	...	...	...	...
Bawshar	*457 361*[60]	*359 794*[60]	*97 567*[60]	340	...	...	...	...
Ibri	*173 337*[60]	*104 171*[60]	*69 166*[60]	32697	...	...	...	...
Jaalan Bani Bu Ali	*104 829*[60]	*40 386*[60]	*64 443*[60]	2977.3	...	...	...	...
MUSCAT	*76 344*[60]	*39 717*[60]	*36 627*[60]	273.9	...	...	...	...
Mutrah	*269 507*[60]	*204 054*[60]	*65 453*[60]	90.3	...	...	...	...
Nizwa	*131 108*[60]	*78 318*[60]	*52 790*[60]	4489	...	...	...	...
Saham	*151 979*[60]	*90 222*[60]	*61 757*[60]	1459	...	...	...	...
Salalah	*363 427*[60]	*256 893*[60]	*106 534*[60]	4943	...	...	...	...
Sohar	*239 765*[60]	*159 224*[60]	*80 541*[60]	2025	...	...	...	...
Sur	*120 876*[60]	*46 651*[60]	*74 225*[60]	1908	...	...	...	...
Pakistan								
15 III 2017* (CDFC)								
Faisalabad (Lyallpur)	3 203 846	...	...	...	...	...	...	...
Gujranwala	2 027 001	...	...	...	...	...	...	...
Hyderabad	1 732 693	...	...	...	...	...	...	...
ISLAMABAD	1 014 825	...	...	...	...	...	...	...
Karachi	14 910 352	...	...	...	...	...	...	...
Lahore	11 126 285	...	...	...	...	...	...	...
Multan	1 871 843	...	...	...	...	...	...	...
Peshawar	1 970 042	...	...	...	...	...	...	...
Quetta	1 001 205	...	...	...	...	...	...	...
Rawalpindi	2 098 231	...	...	...	...	...	...	...
Philippines								
1 VIII 2015 (CDJC)								
Angeles	411 634	...	...	...	...	...	...	...
Bacolod	561 875	...	...	...	...	...	...	...
Baguio	345 366	...	...	...	...	...	...	...
Butuan	337 063	...	...	...	...	...	...	...
Cagayan de Oro	675 950	...	...	...	...	...	...	...
Caloocan	1 583 978	...	...	...	...	...	...	...
Cebu	922 611	...	...	...	...	...	...	...
Cotabato	299 438	...	...	...	...	...	...	...
Davao	1 632 991	...	...	...	...	...	...	...
General Santos	594 446	...	...	...	...	...	...	...

8. Population of capital cities and cities of 100 000 or more inhabitants: latest available year, 2000 - 2019
Population des capitales et des villes de 100 000 habitants ou plus : dernière année disponible, 2000 - 2019 (continued - suite)

Continent, country or area, date, code[a] and city Continent, pays ou zone, date, code[a] et ville	City proper - Ville proprement dite				Urban agglomeration - Agglomération urbaine			
	Population			Surface area - Superficie (km²)	Population			Surface area - Superficie (km²)
	Both sexes - Les deux sexes	Male - Masculin	Female - Féminin		Both sexes - Les deux sexes	Male - Masculin	Female - Féminin	
ASIA - ASIE								
Philippines								
1 VIII 2015 (CDJC)								
Iligan	342 618	...	...	...	...	...	...	...
Iloilo	447 992	...	...	...	...	...	...	...
Isabela	112 788	...	...	...	...	...	...	...
Lapu-Lapu	408 112	...	...	...	...	...	...	...
Las Piñas	588 894	...	...	...	...	...	...	...
Lucena City	266 248	...	...	...	...	...	...	...
Makati	582 602	...	...	...	...	...	...	...
Malabon	365 525	...	...	...	...	...	...	...
Mandaluyong	386 276	...	...	...	...	...	...	...
Mandaue	362 654	...	...	...	...	...	...	...
MANILA	1 780 148	...	...	...	...	...	...	...
Marikina	450 741	...	...	...	...	...	...	...
Muntinlupa	504 509	...	...	...	...	...	...	...
Navotas	249 463	...	...	...	...	...	...	...
Olongapo	233 040	...	...	...	...	...	...	...
Paranaque	665 822	...	...	...	...	...	...	...
Pasay	416 522	...	...	...	...	...	...	...
Pasig	755 300	...	...	...	...	...	...	...
Puerto Princesa	255 116	...	...	...	...	...	...	...
Quezon City	2 936 116	...	...	...	...	...	...	...
San Juan	122 180	...	...	...	...	...	...	...
Tacloban	242 089	...	...	...	...	...	...	...
Taguig	804 915	...	...	...	...	...	...	...
Valenzuela	620 422	...	...	...	...	...	...	...
Zamboanga	861 799	...	...	...	...	...	...	...
Qatar								
20 IV 2015 (CDFC)								
Al-Khoor	202 031	181 000	21 031	...	...	...	...	...
Al-Rayyan	605 712	406 783	198 929	...	...	...	...	...
Al-Wakrah	299 037	248 103	50 934	...	...	...	...	...
DOHA	956 457	706 430	250 027	...	...	...	...	...
Republic of Korea - République de Corée								
1 VII 2018 (ESDJ)								
Busan (Pusan)	3 400 027	1 671 846	1 728 181	770[61]	...	...	...	...
Daegu (Taegu)	2 449 789	1 215 762	1 234 027	884[61]	...	...	...	...
Daejeon (Taejon)	1 517 902	761 618	756 284	540[61]	...	...	...	...
Gwangju (Kwangchu)	1 493 417	743 700	749 717	501[61]	...	...	...	...
Incheon	2 938 875	1 478 502	1 460 373	1063[61]	...	...	...	...
Jeju (Cheju)	652 693	329 625	323 068	1850[61]	...	...	...	...
Sejong	303 582	152 729	150 853	465[61]	...	...	...	...
SEOUL	9 704 546	4 731 252	4 973 294	605[61]	...	...	...	...
Ulsan	1 154 482	598 784	555 698	1062[61]	...	...	...	...
Saudi Arabia - Arabie saoudite								
27 IV 2010 (CDFC)								
Abha	236 157	136 118	100 039	...	...	...	...	...
Ad-Dammam	903 312	546 924	356 388	...	...	...	...	...
Al-Hawiyah	148 151	78 735	69 416	...	...	...	...	...
Al-Hufuf	660 788	361 672	299 116	...	...	...	...	...
Al-Jubayl	337 778	237 912	99 866	...	...	...	...	...
Al-Khubar	219 679	131 646	88 033	...	...	...	...	...
Al-Madinah	1 100 093	608 720	491 373	...	...	...	...	...
Al-Qatif	118 327	66 504	51 823	...	...	...	...	...
Al-Qurrayyat	116 162	63 412	52 750	...	...	...	...	...
Al-Seeh	234 607	131 391	103 216	...	...	...	...	...
Ar'ar	167 057	90 771	76 286	...	...	...	...	...
Ath-Thuqbah	238 066	149 691	88 375	...	...	...	...	...
At-Ta'if	579 970	306 682	273 288	...	...	...	...	...
Buraydah	467 410	268 604	198 806	...	...	...	...	...
Dhahran	120 521	68 746	51 775	...	...	...	...	...
Hafar al-Batin	271 642	148 396	123 246	...	...	...	...	...
Ha'il	310 897	170 882	140 015	...	...	...	...	...
Jiddah	3 430 697	1 996 716	1 433 981	...	...	...	...	...
Jizan	127 743	76 987	50 756	...	...	...	...	...

8. Population of capital cities and cities of 100 000 or more inhabitants: latest available year, 2000 - 2019
Population des capitales et des villes de 100 000 habitants ou plus : dernière année disponible, 2000 - 2019 (continued - suite)

Continent, country or area, date, code[a] and city Continent, pays ou zone, date, code[a] et ville	City proper - Ville proprement dite: Population: Both sexes - Les deux sexes	Male - Masculin	Female - Féminin	Surface area - Superficie (km²)	Urban agglomeration - Agglomération urbaine: Population: Both sexes - Les deux sexes	Male - Masculin	Female - Féminin	Surface area - Superficie (km²)
ASIA - ASIE								
Saudi Arabia - Arabie saoudite								
27 IV 2010 (CDFC)								
Khamis Mushayt	430 828	245 756	185 072	...	...	...	...	...
Makkah	1 534 731	861 737	672 994	...	...	...	...	...
Najran (Aba as-Suud)	298 288	166 143	132 145	...	...	...	...	...
RIYADH	5 188 286	3 059 287	2 128 999	...	...	...	...	...
Sekaka	150 257	84 881	65 376	...	...	...	...	...
Tabuk	512 629	281 672	230 957	...	...	...	...	...
Unayzah	152 895	86 385	66 510	...	...	...	...	...
Yanbu al-Bahr	233 236	140 897	92 339	...	...	...	...	...
Singapore - Singapour								
30 VI 2019 (ESDJ)								
SINGAPORE	5 703 569[62]	...	...	725[63]	...	...	...	...
Sri Lanka[64]								
17 VII 2001 (CDFC)								
COLOMBO	647 100	346 366	300 734	...	...	...	...	...
Dehiwala-Mount Lavinia	210 546	105 522	105 024	...	...	...	...	...
Kandy	109 343	54 288	55 055	...	...	...	...	...
Moratuwa	177 563	87 313	90 250	...	...	...	...	...
Negombo	121 701	60 947	60 754	...	...	...	...	...
Sri Jayawardanapura Kotte	116 366	59 993	56 373	...	...	...	...	...
State of Palestine - État de Palestine								
1 VII 2019 (ESDF)								
EAST JERUSALEM - JÉRUSALEM-EST[65]	*291 378*	...	...	...	...	...	...	...
Gaza	*614 071*	...	...	...	...	...	...	...
Hebron	*210 081*	...	...	...	...	...	...	...
Jabalya	*182 658*	...	...	...	...	...	...	...
Khan Yunis	*251 621*	...	...	...	...	...	...	...
Nablus	*161 630*	...	...	...	...	...	...	...
Rafah	*180 354*	...	...	...	...	...	...	...
Syrian Arab Republic - République arabe syrienne								
1 VII 2008 (ESDF)								
Aleppo	*4 450 000*	*2 292 000*	*2 158 000*	...	...	...	...	...
Al-Hasakeh	*1 392 000*	*701 000*	*691 000*	...	...	...	...	...
Al-Raqqah	*865 000*	*456 000*	*409 000*	...	...	...	...	...
Al-Sweida	*349 000*	*171 000*	*178 000*	...	...	...	...	...
DAMASCUS	*1 680 000*	*857 000*	*823 000*	...	...	...	...	...
Damasus rural	*2 529 000*	*1 302 000*	*1 227 000*	...	...	...	...	...
Deir El-Zor	*1 111 000*	*563 000*	*548 000*	...	...	...	...	...
Dra'a	*930 000*	*472 000*	*458 000*	...	...	...	...	...
Hama	*1 508 000*	*768 000*	*740 000*	...	...	...	...	...
Homs	*1 667 000*	*852 000*	*815 000*	...	...	...	...	...
Idleb	*1 376 000*	*704 000*	*672 000*	...	...	...	...	...
Lattakia	*951 000*	*480 000*	*471 000*	...	...	...	...	...
Tartous	*756 000*	*383 000*	*373 000*	...	...	...	...	...
Tajikistan - Tadjikistan								
1 VII 2017 (ESDF)								
DUSHANBE	*823 787*	*430 622*	*393 165*	...	...	...	...	...
Khujand	*176 710*	...	...	...	...	...	...	...
Thailand - Thaïlande								
1 IX 2010 (CDJC)								
Ang Thong	...	...	...	...	109 207	51 540	57 667	...
BANGKOK	...	...	...	...	8 305 218	4 032 586	4 272 632	1569
Buri Ram	...	...	...	...	375 999	181 546	194 453	...
Chachoengsao	...	...	...	...	206 250	101 475	104 775	...
Chai Nat	...	...	...	...	205 456	97 373	108 083	...
Chaiyaphum	...	...	...	...	205 112	99 280	105 832	...
Chanthaburi	...	...	...	...	243 126	118 221	124 905	...
Chiang Mai	...	...	...	...	967 020	466 145	500 875	...
Chiang Rai	...	...	...	...	455 732	220 391	235 341	...
Chon Buri	...	...	...	...	1 158 989	575 208	583 781	...
Chumphon	...	...	...	...	147 912	75 339	72 573	...
Kalasin	...	...	...	...	428 940	208 863	220 077	...
Kamphaeng Phet	...	...	...	...	211 774	101 456	110 318	...
Kanchanaburi	...	...	...	...	292 521	143 986	148 535	...

8. Population of capital cities and cities of 100 000 or more inhabitants: latest available year, 2000 - 2019
Population des capitales et des villes de 100 000 habitants ou plus : dernière année disponible, 2000 - 2019 (continued - suite)

Continent, country or area, date, code[a] and city / Continent, pays ou zone, date, code[a] et ville	City proper - Ville proprement dite: Population: Both sexes - Les deux sexes	City proper: Population: Male - Masculin	City proper: Population: Female - Féminin	City proper: Surface area - Superficie (km²)	Urban agglomeration - Agglomération urbaine: Population: Both sexes - Les deux sexes	Urban agglomeration: Population: Male - Masculin	Urban agglomeration: Population: Female - Féminin	Urban agglomeration: Surface area - Superficie (km²)
ASIA - ASIE								
Thailand - Thaïlande								
1 IX 2010 (CDJC)								
Khon Kaen	...	...	...	...	703 123	339 011	364 112	...
Lampang	...	...	...	...	372 463	180 360	192 103	...
Lamphun	...	...	...	...	262 832	126 662	136 170	...
Loei	...	...	...	...	164 180	81 302	82 878	...
Lop Buri	...	...	...	...	235 827	118 964	116 863	...
Maha Sarakham	...	...	...	...	153 740	72 143	81 597	...
Mukdahan	...	...	...	...	180 600	89 190	91 410	...
Nakhon Pathom	...	...	...	...	339 736	166 150	173 586	...
Nakhon Phanom	...	...	...	...	123 720	59 683	64 037	...
Nakhon Ratchasima	...	...	...	...	653 075	316 329	336 746	...
Nakhon Sawan	...	...	...	...	225 903	107 298	118 605	...
Nakhon Si Thammarat	...	...	...	...	265 606	127 460	138 146	...
Narathiwat	...	...	...	...	133 718	64 616	69 102	...
Nong Bua Lam Phu	...	...	...	...	203 142	98 164	104 978	...
Nong Khai	...	...	...	...	232 798	113 989	118 809	...
Nonthaburi	...	...	...	...	797 739	383 826	413 913	...
Pathum Thani	...	...	...	...	757 175	358 679	398 496	...
Pattani	...	...	...	...	104 617	51 305	53 312	...
Phatthalung	...	...	...	...	244 783	117 039	127 744	...
Phayao	...	...	...	...	221 062	106 657	114 405	...
Phetchabun	...	...	...	...	172 275	82 257	90 018	...
Phetchaburi	...	...	...	...	175 675	83 735	91 940	...
Phichit	...	...	...	...	131 283	62 446	68 837	...
Phitsanulok	...	...	...	...	201 466	93 098	108 368	...
Phra Nakhon Si Ayutthaya	...	...	...	...	365 736	173 280	192 456	...
Phrae	...	...	...	...	156 099	75 175	80 924	...
Phuket	...	...	...	...	358 159	175 144	183 015	...
Prachuap Khiri Khan	...	...	...	...	177 011	87 525	89 486	...
Ranong	...	...	...	...	123 596	62 090	61 506	...
Ratchaburi	...	...	...	...	317 886	149 460	168 426	...
Rayong	...	...	...	...	445 939	224 068	221 871	...
Roi Et	...	...	...	...	365 113	176 648	188 465	...
Sa Kaeo	...	...	...	...	135 536	66 447	69 089	...
Sakon Nakhon	...	...	...	...	315 788	153 785	162 003	...
Samut Prakan	...	...	...	...	1 082 993	527 487	555 506	...
Samut Sakhon	...	...	...	...	479 186	237 778	241 408	...
Saraburi	...	...	...	...	239 281	114 885	124 396	...
Si Sa Ket	...	...	...	...	160 508	77 363	83 145	...
Songkhla	...	...	...	...	800 970	382 828	418 142	...
Sukhothai	...	...	...	...	166 782	79 139	87 643	...
Suphan Buri	...	...	...	...	228 496	108 666	119 830	...
Surat Thani	...	...	...	...	410 984	198 909	212 075	...
Surin	...	...	...	...	153 159	73 082	80 077	...
Tak	...	...	...	...	146 769	70 754	76 015	...
Trat	...	...	...	...	110 398	52 309	58 089	...
Ubon Ratchathani	...	...	...	...	411 954	198 655	213 299	...
Udon Thani	...	...	...	...	483 057	232 326	250 731	...
Uttaradit	...	...	...	...	151 047	72 244	78 803	...
Yala	...	...	...	...	119 744	58 041	61 703	...
Yasothon	...	...	...	...	127 173	63 885	63 288	...
Timor-Leste[66]								
11 VII 2015 (CDFC)								
DILI	222 323	114 792	107 531	...	...	...	...	...
Turkey - Turquie[67]								
31 XII 2018 (ESDJ)								
Adana	...	...	...	...	*2 220 125*	*1 106 811*	*1 113 314*	...
Adıyaman	*254 695*	*127 555*	*127 140*	...	...	...	...	...
Afyonkarahisar	*231 983*	*114 392*	*117 591*	...	...	...	...	...
Ağrı	*115 285*	*58 860*	*56 425*	...	...	...	...	...
Aksaray	*223 166*	*110 412*	*112 754*	...	...	...	...	...
Amasya	*113 932*	*58 871*	*55 061*	...	...	...	...	...
ANKARA	...	...	...	...	*5 503 985*	*2 728 900*	*2 775 085*	...
Antalya	...	...	...	...	*2 426 356*	*1 222 086*	*1 204 270*	...

8. Population of capital cities and cities of 100 000 or more inhabitants: latest available year, 2000 - 2019
Population des capitales et des villes de 100 000 habitants ou plus : dernière année disponible, 2000 - 2019 (continued - suite)

Continent, country or area, date, code[a] and city / Continent, pays ou zone, date, code[a] et ville	City proper - Ville proprement dite				Urban agglomeration - Agglomération urbaine			
	Population				Population			
	Both sexes - Les deux sexes	Male - Masculin	Female - Féminin	Surface area - Superficie (km²)	Both sexes - Les deux sexes	Male - Masculin	Female - Féminin	Surface area - Superficie (km²)
ASIA - ASIE								
Turkey - Turquie[67]								
31 XII 2018 (ESDJ)								
Aydın	...	...	...	...	1 097 746	546 092	551 654	...
Balıkesir	...	...	...	...	1 226 575	612 738	613 837	...
Batman	419 517	210 817	208 700	...	...	...	...	...
Bingöl	117 556	59 182	58 374	...	...	...	...	...
Bolu	171 180	85 591	85 589	...	...	...	...	...
Bursa	...	...	...	...	2 994 521	1 498 219	1 496 302	...
Çanakkale	136 002	67 456	68 546	...	...	...	...	...
Cizre	121 073	61 678	59 395	...	...	...	...	...
Çorum	263 895	130 300	133 595	...	...	...	...	...
Denizli	...	...	...	...	1 027 782	512 109	515 673	...
Diyarbakir	...	...	...	...	1 732 396	875 468	856 928	...
Düzce	173 838	85 896	87 942	...	...	...	...	...
Edirne	167 443	83 743	83 700	...	...	...	...	...
Elazığ	353 629	175 081	178 548	...	...	...	...	...
Ereğli	117 456	57 987	59 469	...	...	...	...	...
Erzincan	141 018	70 935	70 083	...	...	...	...	...
Erzurum	...	...	...	...	767 848	383 435	384 413	...
Eskişehir	...	...	...	...	871 187	434 112	437 075	...
Gaziantep	...	...	...	...	2 028 563	1 023 716	1 004 847	...
Giresun	113 761	55 434	58 327	...	...	...	...	...
Hatay	...	...	...	...	1 609 856	809 484	800 372	...
Isparta	236 749	117 458	119 291	...	...	...	...	...
İstanbul	...	...	...	...	15 067 724	7 542 231	7 525 493	...
İzmir	...	...	...	...	4 320 519	2 152 585	2 167 934	...
Kahramanmaraş	...	...	...	...	1 144 851	580 410	564 441	...
Karabük	118 776	57 459	61 317	...	...	...	...	...
Karaman	161 946	80 310	81 636	...	...	...	...	...
Kastamonu	118 282	58 308	59 974	...	...	...	...	...
Kayseri	...	...	...	...	1 389 680	696 658	693 022	...
Kilis	100 675	49 955	50 720	...	...	...	...	...
Kırıkkale	188 709	93 073	95 636	...	...	...	...	...
Kırşehir	139 134	68 998	70 136	...	...	...	...	...
Kocaeli	...	...	...	...	1 906 391	963 326	943 065	...
Konya	...	...	...	...	2 205 609	1 094 441	1 111 168	...
Kütahya	246 315	121 046	125 269	...	...	...	...	...
Lüleburgaz	117 739	59 426	58 313	...	...	...	...	...
Malatya	...	...	...	...	797 036	396 877	400 159	...
Manisa	...	...	...	...	1 429 643	720 337	709 306	...
Mardin	...	...	...	...	829 195	417 000	412 195	...
Mersin	...	...	...	...	1 814 468	905 520	908 948	...
Muğla	...	...	...	...	967 487	493 140	474 347	...
Muş	107 470	54 440	53 030	...	...	...	...	...
Nevşehir	110 098	53 542	56 556	...	...	...	...	...
Niğde	150 178	75 040	75 138	...	...	...	...	...
Ordu	...	...	...	...	771 932	386 547	385 385	...
Osmaniye	231 739	115 848	115 891	...	...	...	...	...
Rize	103 145	49 517	53 628	...	...	...	...	...
Sakarya	...	...	...	...	1 010 700	505 645	505 055	...
Samsun	...	...	...	...	1 335 716	662 086	673 630	...
Şanlıurfa	...	...	...	...	2 035 809	1 026 719	1 009 090	...
Siirt	153 647	80 328	73 319	...	...	...	...	...
Sivas	348 683	172 845	175 838	...	...	...	...	...
Tekirdağ	...	...	...	...	1 029 927	527 975	501 952	...
Tokat	154 495	77 360	77 135	...	...	...	...	...
Trabzon	...	...	...	...	807 903	399 377	408 526	...
Uşak	223 246	112 363	110 883	...	...	...	...	...
Van	...	...	...	...	1 123 784	574 461	549 323	...
Yalova	124 956	61 777	63 179	...	...	...	...	...
Zonguldak	105 529	51 283	54 246	...	...	...	...	...
United Arab Emirates - Émirats arabes unis								
1 VII 2002 (ESDF)								
ABU DHABI	527 000	359 000	168 000	...	...	...	...	...
Ajman	205 000	122 000	83 000	...	...	...	...	...

8. Population of capital cities and cities of 100 000 or more inhabitants: latest available year, 2000 - 2019
Population des capitales et des villes de 100 000 habitants ou plus : dernière année disponible, 2000 - 2019 (continued - suite)

Continent, country or area, date, code[a] and city / Continent, pays ou zone, date, code[a] et ville	City proper - Ville proprement dite: Population: Both sexes - Les deux sexes	City proper: Population: Male - Masculin	City proper: Population: Female - Féminin	City proper: Surface area - Superficie (km²)	Urban agglomeration - Agglomération urbaine: Population: Both sexes - Les deux sexes	Urban agglomeration: Population: Male - Masculin	Urban agglomeration: Population: Female - Féminin	Urban agglomeration: Surface area - Superficie (km²)
ASIA - ASIE								
United Arab Emirates - Émirats arabes unis								
1 VII 2002 (ESDF)								
Al-Ayn	*328 000*	*215 000*	*113 000*	...	...	...	...	...
Al-Sharjah	*488 000*	*317 000*	*171 000*	...	...	...	...	...
Dubai	*1 089 000*	*759 000*	*330 000*	...	...	...	...	...
Uzbekistan - Ouzbékistan[53]								
1 I 2019 (ESDJ)								
Almalyk	...	...	...	...	129 111	62 503	66 608	...
Andizhan	433 901	218 243	215 658	...	...	...	...	...
Angren	...	...	...	...	185 905	92 529	93 376	...
Bukhara	277 839	137 930	139 909	...	...	...	...	...
Chirchik	...	...	...	...	155 822	76 568	79 254	...
Fergana	283 791	140 343	143 448	...	...	...	...	...
Jizzax	174 400	87 223	87 177	...	...	...	...	...
Karshi	270 736	135 378	135 358	...	...	...	...	...
Kokand	...	...	...	...	248 740	121 618	127 122	...
Margilan	...	...	...	...	231 051	115 973	115 078	...
Namangan	612 208	314 718	297 490	...	...	...	...	...
Navoi	136 374	69 053	67 321	...	...	...	...	...
Nukus	314 928	155 222	159 706	...	...	...	...	...
Samarkand	538 211	260 365	277 846	...	...	...	...	...
Shahrisabz	...	...	...	...	137 076	69 452	67 624	...
TASHKENT	2 509 969	1 225 235	1 284 734	...	...	...	...	...
Termez	145 065	71 273	73 792	...	...	...	...	...
Urgentch	141 685	71 265	70 420	...	...	...	...	...
Yemen - Yémen								
1 VII 2009* (ESDF)								
Adan	*684 322*	...	...	...	*684 322*	...	...	...
SANA'A	*1 976 286*	...	...	...	*2 022 867*	...	...	...
EUROPE								
Åland Islands - Îles d'Åland								
1 VII 2019 (ESDJ)								
MARIEHAMN	11 711[68]	5 606[68]	6 105[68]	11.8	...	...	...	...
Albania - Albanie								
1 X 2011 (CDJC)								
Durrës	113 249	56 511	56 738	...	...	...	...	...
TIRANA	418 495	203 239	215 256	...	...	...	...	...
Andorra - Andorre[68]								
1 VII 2011 (ESDJ)								
ANDORRA LA VELLA	...	...	...	...	22 205	11 056	11 149	...
Austria - Autriche								
1 I 2019 (ESDJ)								
Graz	288 806	142 472	146 334	...	...	...	...	...
Innsbruck	132 110	64 622	67 488	...	...	...	...	...
Klagenfurt	100 817	47 764	53 053	...	...	...	...	...
Linz	205 726	99 917	105 809	...	...	...	...	...
Salzburg	154 211	74 006	80 205	...	...	...	...	...
WIEN	1 897 491	925 003	972 488	...	...	...	...	...
Belarus - Bélarus								
1 I 2018 (ESDJ)								
Baranovichi	179 166	81 256	97 910	85	...	...	...	...
Bobruisk	217 546	101 477	116 069	96	...	...	...	...
Borisov	143 051	67 061	75 990	46	...	...	...	...
Brest	347 576	160 790	186 786	146	...	...	...	...
Gomel	...	...	...	...	535 693	244 234	291 459	140
Grodno	370 919	168 336	202 583	142	...	...	...	...
Lida	101 616	47 496	54 120	...	...	...	...	...
MINSK	1 982 444	902 211	1 080 233	348	...	...	...	...
Mogilev	381 353	175 151	206 202	119	...	...	...	...
Mozir	111 733	52 974	58 759	44	...	...	...	...
Novopolotsk	...	...	...	...	107 479	51 228	56 251	48
Orsha	115 052	52 982	62 070	...	...	...	...	...

8. Population of capital cities and cities of 100 000 or more inhabitants: latest available year, 2000 - 2019
Population des capitales et des villes de 100 000 habitants ou plus : dernière année disponible, 2000 - 2019 (continued - suite)

Continent, country or area, date, code[a] and city / Continent, pays ou zone, date, code[a] et ville	City proper - Ville proprement dite				Urban agglomeration - Agglomération urbaine			
	Population				Population			
	Both sexes - Les deux sexes	Male - Masculin	Female - Féminin	Surface area - Superficie (km²)	Both sexes - Les deux sexes	Male - Masculin	Female - Féminin	Surface area - Superficie (km²)
EUROPE								
Belarus - Bélarus								
1 I 2018 (ESDJ)								
Pinsk	137 961	63 424	74 537	47	...	...	...	...
Soligorsk	106 627	49 882	56 745	15	...	...	...	...
Vitebsk	...	...	...	...	377 932	167 506	210 426	145
Belgium - Belgique								
1 I 2011 (CDJC)								
Anderlecht	108 940	53 707	55 233	18	...	...	...	...
Antwerpen (Anvers)	498 473	247 192	251 281	205	718 730	354 576	364 154	394
Brugge	117 260	56 952	60 308	138	117 260	56 952	60 308	138
BRUXELLES (BRUSSEL)	174 383	90 317	84 066	33	1 550 299[69]	754 208[69]	796 091[69]	573[69]
Charleroi	204 150	99 221	104 929	102	291 806	141 106	150 700	199
Gent (Gand)	248 358	122 457	125 901	156	280 151	137 980	142 171	207
Liège (Luik)	195 965	96 509	99 456	69	491 767	238 134	253 633	367
Namur	110 175	53 019	57 156	176	110 175	53 019	57 156	176
Schaerbeek	127 525	63 020	64 505	8	...	...	...	...
Bulgaria - Bulgarie								
1 I 2019 (ESDJ)								
Burgas	202 434	96 201	106 233	...	...	...	...	...
Plovdiv	346 893	164 739	182 154	...	...	...	...	...
Ruse	142 902	69 335	73 567	...	...	...	...	...
SOFIA	1 241 675	594 245	647 430	...	...	...	...	...
Stara Zagora	135 715	64 966	70 749	...	...	...	...	...
Varna	336 505	162 584	173 921	...	...	...	...	...
Croatia - Croatie								
1 IV 2011 (CDJC)								
Osijek	108 048	50 357	57 691	174	...	...	...	...
Rijeka	128 624	60 951	67 673	43	...	...	...	...
Split	178 102	84 477	93 625	79	...	...	...	...
ZAGREB	790 017	369 339	420 678	641	...	...	...	...
Czechia - Tchéquie								
1 I 2019 (ESDJ)								
Brno	380 681	184 048	196 633	225.7[32]	...	...	...	...
Liberec	104 445	50 623	53 822	105.1[32]	...	...	...	...
Olomouc	100 523	47 632	52 891	100.9[32]	...	...	...	...
Ostrava	289 128	140 369	148 759	204.8[32]	...	...	...	...
Plzen	172 441	83 871	88 570	133.3[32]	...	...	...	...
PRAHA	1 308 632	638 009	670 623	485.2[32]	...	...	...	...
Denmark - Danemark[70]								
1 VII 2019 (ESDJ)								
Ålborg	215 510[68]	108 653[68]	106 857[68]	1137.4	...	...	...	...
Århus	345 635[68]	170 020[68]	175 615[68]	467.9	...	...	...	...
Esbjerg	115 675[68]	57 981[68]	57 694[68]	795.2	...	...	...	...
Frederiksberg	103 725[68]	49 253[68]	54 472[68]	8.7	...	...	...	...
KOBENHAVN	626 508[68]	309 426[68]	317 082[68]	86.7	...	...	...	...
Odense	204 120[68]	101 079[68]	103 041[68]	305.6	...	...	...	...
Vejle	115 316[68]	57 719[68]	57 597[68]	1058.5	...	...	...	...
Estonia - Estonie								
1 I 2019 (ESDJ)								
TALLINN	434 562	196 700	237 862	...	...	...	...	...
Faroe Islands - Îles Féroé								
1 VII 2019 (ESDJ)								
TÓRSHAVN	13 408	6 718	6 690	6[71]	19 903[72]	10 040[72]	9 863[72]	15[73]
Finland - Finlande[74]								
1 VII 2018 (ESDJ)								
Espoo	281 338[68]	139 785[68]	141 554[68]	312.3	...	...	...	...
HELSINKI	645 657[68]	306 435[68]	339 222[68]	214.3	...	...	...	...
Jyvaskyla	140 747[68]	69 262[68]	71 485[68]	1171	...	...	...	...
Kuopio	118 437[68]	57 702[68]	60 735[68]	3241	...	...	...	...
Lahti	119 762[68]	57 833[68]	61 930[68]	459.5	...	...	...	...
Oulu	202 689[68]	101 238[68]	101 451[68]	2972	...	...	...	...
Tampere	233 546[68]	113 313[68]	120 234[68]	525	...	...	...	...
Turku	190 500[68]	91 022[68]	99 478[68]	245.7	...	...	...	...
Vantaa	225 597[68]	112 029[68]	113 568[68]	238.4	...	...	...	...

Continent, country or area, date, code[a] and city / Continent, pays ou zone, date, code[a] et ville	City proper - Ville proprement dite				Urban agglomeration - Agglomération urbaine			
	Population				Population			
	Both sexes - Les deux sexes	Male - Masculin	Female - Féminin	Surface area - Superficie (km²)	Both sexes - Les deux sexes	Male - Masculin	Female - Féminin	Surface area - Superficie (km²)
EUROPE								
France								
1 I 2015 (CDJC)								
Aix-en-Provence[75]	142 668	67 070	75 598	...	...	...	...	...
Amiens	132 874[75]	63 049[75]	69 825[75]	...	162 637	77 405	85 232	...
Angers	151 520[75]	70 013[75]	81 507[75]	...	225 978	105 860	120 118	...
Argenteuil[75]	110 388	54 149	56 239	...	...	...	...	...
Besançon	116 676[75]	54 726[75]	61 950[75]	...	135 448	63 794	71 654	...
Bordeaux	249 712[75]	117 403[75]	132 309[75]	...	904 359	431 444	472 915	...
Boulogne-Billancourt[75]	117 931	55 415	62 516	...	...	...	...	...
Brest	139 163[75]	68 320[75]	70 843[75]	...	200 530	98 235	102 295	...
Caen	106 260[75]	50 047[75]	56 213[75]	...	198 639	94 037	104 602	...
Clermont-Ferrand	141 398[75]	67 196[75]	74 202[75]	...	265 892	125 811	140 081	...
Dijon	155 114[75]	72 985[75]	82 129[75]	...	243 244	114 786	128 458	...
Grenoble	160 649[75]	77 519[75]	83 130[75]	...	512 591	249 141	263 450	...
Le Havre	172 366[75]	81 082[75]	91 284[75]	...	237 578	112 535	125 043	...
Le Mans	143 325[75]	66 870[75]	76 455[75]	...	210 018	99 384	110 634	...
Lille	232 741[75]	112 619[75]	120 122[75]	...	1 039 397	498 466	540 931	...
Limoges	133 627[75]	62 060[75]	71 567[75]	...	183 347	85 799	97 548	...
Lyon	513 275[75]	240 623[75]	272 652[75]	...	1 639 558	785 665	853 893	...
Marseille	861 635[75]	408 487[75]	453 148[75]	...	1 585 498[76]	756 867[76]	828 631[76]	...
Metz	117 492[75]	57 390[75]	60 102[75]	...	285 268	138 242	147 026	...
Montpellier	277 639[75]	130 109[75]	147 530[75]	...	428 909	203 366	225 543	...
Montreuil[75]	106 691	52 788	53 903	...	...	...	...	...
Mulhouse	110 370[75]	54 011[75]	56 359[75]	...	246 511	119 610	126 901	...
Nancy	105 162[75]	50 411[75]	54 751[75]	...	285 659	136 682	148 977	...
Nantes	303 382[75]	144 654[75]	158 728[75]	...	633 690	303 454	330 236	...
Nice	342 522[75]	160 123[75]	182 399[75]	...	943 354	445 620	497 734	...
Nîmes	150 672[75]	71 659[75]	79 013[75]	...	184 750	87 991	96 759	...
Orléans	114 644[75]	54 387[75]	60 257[75]	...	278 131	134 130	144 001	...
PARIS	2 206 488[75]	1 038 493[75]	1 167 995[75]	...	10 706 072[77]	5 158 244[77]	5 547 828[77]	...
Perpignan	121 934[75]	57 150[75]	64 784[75]	...	200 971	94 613	106 358	...
Reims	184 076[75]	86 890[75]	97 186[75]	...	212 949	100 629	112 320	...
Rennes	215 366[75]	101 905[75]	113 461[75]	...	330 871	158 754	172 117	...
Rouen	110 169[75]	52 690[75]	57 479[75]	...	467 133	221 315	245 818	...
Saint-Denis[75]	111 103	56 501	54 602	...	...	...	...	...
Saint-Étienne	171 057[75]	81 077[75]	89 980[75]	...	373 130	177 568	195 562	...
Strasbourg	277 270[75]	131 692[75]	145 578[75]	...	461 101	219 722	241 379	...
Toulon	167 479[75]	79 436[75]	88 043[75]	...	569 793	271 171	298 622	...
Toulouse	471 941[75]	228 540[75]	243 401[75]	...	948 433	461 054	487 379	...
Tours	136 252[75]	62 843[75]	73 409[75]	...	353 042	166 391	186 651	...
Villeurbanne[75]	148 665	72 291	76 374	...	...	...	...	...
Germany - Allemagne								
1 I 2019 (ESDJ)								
Aachen	247 380[4]	128 754[4]	118 626[4]	161	...	...	...	...
Augsburg	295 135[4]	145 158[4]	149 977[4]	147	...	...	...	...
Bergisch Gladbach	111 966[4]	53 737[4]	58 229[4]	83	...	...	...	...
BERLIN	3 644 826[4]	1 792 801[4]	1 852 025[4]	891	...	...	...	...
Bielefeld	333 786[4]	161 078[4]	172 708[4]	259	...	...	...	...
Bochum	364 628[4]	177 699[4]	186 929[4]	146	...	...	...	...
Bonn	327 258[4]	156 328[4]	170 930[4]	141	...	...	...	...
Bottrop	117 383[4]	57 101[4]	60 282[4]	101	...	...	...	...
Braunschweig	248 292[4]	122 985[4]	125 307[4]	193	...	...	...	...
Bremen	569 352[4]	281 336[4]	288 016[4]	318	...	...	...	...
Bremerhaven	113 634[4]	56 699[4]	56 935[4]	102	...	...	...	...
Chemnitz	247 237[4]	122 248[4]	124 989[4]	221	...	...	...	...
Cottbus	100 219[4]	49 201[4]	51 018[4]	166	...	...	...	...
Darmstadt	159 207[4]	81 217[4]	77 990[4]	122	...	...	...	...
Dortmund	587 010[4]	288 386[4]	298 624[4]	281	...	...	...	...
Dresden	554 649[4]	276 729[4]	277 920[4]	328	...	...	...	...
Duisburg	498 590[4]	246 588[4]	252 002[4]	233	...	...	...	...
Düsseldorf	619 294[4]	299 315[4]	319 979[4]	217	...	...	...	...
Erfurt	213 699[4]	103 920[4]	109 779[4]	270	...	...	...	...

8. Population of capital cities and cities of 100 000 or more inhabitants: latest available year, 2000 - 2019
Population des capitales et des villes de 100 000 habitants ou plus : dernière année disponible, 2000 - 2019 (continued - suite)

Continent, country or area, date, code[a] and city Continent, pays ou zone, date, code[a] et ville	City proper - Ville proprement dite				Urban agglomeration - Agglomération urbaine			
	Population				Population			
	Both sexes - Les deux sexes	Male - Masculin	Female - Féminin	Surface area - Superficie (km²)	Both sexes - Les deux sexes	Male - Masculin	Female - Féminin	Surface area - Superficie (km²)
EUROPE								
Germany - Allemagne								
1 I 2019 (ESDJ)								
Erlangen	111 962[4]	55 864[4]	56 098[4]	77	...	...	...	...
Essen	583 109[4]	283 005[4]	300 104[4]	210	...	...	...	...
Frankfurt am Main	753 056[4]	371 671[4]	381 385[4]	248	...	...	...	...
Freiburg im Breisgau	230 241[4]	109 829[4]	120 412[4]	153	...	...	...	...
Fürth	127 748[4]	62 603[4]	65 145[4]	63	...	...	...	...
Gelsenkirchen	260 654[4]	129 778[4]	130 876[4]	105	...	...	...	...
Göttingen	119 801[4]	58 326[4]	61 475[4]	117	...	...	...	...
Gütersloh	100 194[4]	49 807[4]	50 387[4]	112	...	...	...	...
Hagen	188 814[4]	92 168[4]	96 646[4]	160	...	...	...	...
Halle (Saale)	239 257[4]	115 713[4]	123 544[4]	135	...	...	...	...
Hamburg	1 841 179[4]	902 048[4]	939 131[4]	755	...	...	...	...
Hamm	179 111[4]	88 024[4]	91 087[4]	226	...	...	...	...
Hannover	538 068[4]	263 335[4]	274 733[4]	204	...	...	...	...
Heidelberg	160 355[4]	77 112[4]	83 243[4]	109	...	...	...	...
Heilbronn	125 960[4]	63 527[4]	62 433[4]	100	...	...	...	...
Herne	156 374[4]	76 649[4]	79 725[4]	51	...	...	...	...
Hildesheim	101 990[4]	48 558[4]	53 432[4]	92	...	...	...	...
Ingolstadt	136 981[4]	69 252[4]	67 729[4]	133	...	...	...	...
Jena	111 407[4]	55 665[4]	55 742[4]	115	...	...	...	...
Karlsruhe	313 092[4]	160 429[4]	152 663[4]	173	...	...	...	...
Kassel	201 585[4]	99 007[4]	102 578[4]	107	...	...	...	...
Kiel	247 548[4]	120 566[4]	126 982[4]	119	...	...	...	...
Koblenz	114 024[4]	55 628[4]	58 396[4]	105	...	...	...	...
Köln	1 085 664[4]	529 368[4]	556 296[4]	405	...	...	...	...
Krefeld	227 020[4]	110 745[4]	116 275[4]	138	...	...	...	...
Leipzig	587 857[4]	288 553[4]	299 304[4]	298	...	...	...	...
Leverkusen	163 838[4]	79 787[4]	84 051[4]	79	...	...	...	...
Lübeck	217 198[4]	104 371[4]	112 827[4]	214	...	...	...	...
Ludwigshafen am Rhein	171 061[4]	85 820[4]	85 241[4]	77	...	...	...	...
Magdeburg	238 697[4]	117 828[4]	120 869[4]	201	...	...	...	...
Mainz	217 118[4]	105 599[4]	111 519[4]	98	...	...	...	...
Mannheim	309 370[4]	154 273[4]	155 097[4]	145	...	...	...	...
Moers	103 725[4]	50 368[4]	53 357[4]	68	...	...	...	...
Mönchengladbach	261 454[4]	128 655[4]	132 799[4]	170	...	...	...	...
Mülheim an der Ruhr	170 880[4]	82 387[4]	88 493[4]	91	...	...	...	...
München	1 471 508[4]	717 308[4]	754 200[4]	311	...	...	...	...
Münster (Westf.)	314 319[4]	150 836[4]	163 483[4]	303	...	...	...	...
Neuss	153 796[4]	74 534[4]	79 262[4]	100	...	...	...	...
Nürnberg	518 365[4]	252 807[4]	265 558[4]	186	...	...	...	...
Oberhausen	210 829[4]	103 612[4]	107 217[4]	77	...	...	...	...
Offenbach am Main	128 744[4]	63 699[4]	65 045[4]	45	...	...	...	...
Oldenburg (Oldenburg)	168 210[4]	80 501[4]	87 709[4]	103	...	...	...	...
Osnabrück	164 748[4]	79 756[4]	84 992[4]	120	...	...	...	...
Paderborn	150 580[4]	74 978[4]	75 602[4]	180	...	...	...	...
Pforzheim	125 542[4]	61 699[4]	63 843[4]	98	...	...	...	...
Potsdam	178 089[4]	86 179[4]	91 910[4]	188	...	...	...	...
Recklinghausen	112 267[4]	54 592[4]	57 675[4]	67	...	...	...	...
Regensburg	152 610[4]	74 225[4]	78 385[4]	81	...	...	...	...
Remscheid	110 994[4]	54 664[4]	56 330[4]	75	...	...	...	...
Reutlingen	115 966[4]	57 332[4]	58 634[4]	87	...	...	...	...
Rostock	208 886[4]	102 911[4]	105 975[4]	181	...	...	...	...
Saarbrücken	180 741[4]	89 665[4]	91 076[4]	168	...	...	...	...
Salzgitter	104 948[4]	52 202[4]	52 746[4]	224	...	...	...	...
Siegen	102 836[4]	50 470[4]	52 366[4]	115	...	...	...	...
Solingen	159 360[4]	77 471[4]	81 889[4]	90	...	...	...	...
Stuttgart	634 830[4]	317 139[4]	317 691[4]	207	...	...	...	...
Trier	110 636[4]	54 444[4]	56 192[4]	117	...	...	...	...
Ulm	126 329[4]	62 660[4]	63 669[4]	119	...	...	...	...
Wiesbaden	278 342[4]	132 943[4]	145 399[4]	204	...	...	...	...

8. Population of capital cities and cities of 100 000 or more inhabitants: latest available year, 2000 - 2019
Population des capitales et des villes de 100 000 habitants ou plus : dernière année disponible, 2000 - 2019 (continued - suite)

Continent, country or area, date, code[a] and city / Continent, pays ou zone, date, code[a] et ville	City proper - Ville proprement dite				Urban agglomeration - Agglomération urbaine			
	Population				Population			
	Both sexes - Les deux sexes	Male - Masculin	Female - Féminin	Surface area - Superficie (km²)	Both sexes - Les deux sexes	Male - Masculin	Female - Féminin	Surface area - Superficie (km²)
EUROPE								
Germany - Allemagne								
1 I 2019 (ESDJ)								
Wolfsburg	124 151[4]	61 820[4]	62 331[4]	205	...	...	...	...
Wuppertal	354 382[4]	173 687[4]	180 695[4]	168	...	...	...	...
Würzburg	127 880[4]	61 151[4]	66 729[4]	88	...	...	...	...
Gibraltar								
31 XII 2016 (ESDF)								
GIBRALTAR	34 003[78]	17 093[78]	16 910[78]	6	...	...	...	...
Greece - Grèce								
9 V 2011 (CDFC)								
ATHINAI	664 046	315 210	348 836	...	...	...	...	...
Calithèa	100 641	46 782	53 859	...	...	...	...	...
Iraclion	140 730	68 024	72 706	...	...	...	...	...
Larissa	144 651	70 797	73 854	...	...	...	...	...
Patrai	167 446	81 114	86 332	...	...	...	...	...
Péesterion	139 981	68 563	71 418	...	...	...	...	...
Pireas	163 688	78 200	85 488	...	...	...	...	...
Thessaloniki	315 196	143 813	171 383	...	...	...	...	...
Guernsey - Guernesey								
31 III 2019 (ESDJ)								
ST. PETER PORT	18 958	...	...	6.4	...	...	...	...
Holy See - Saint-Siège[79]								
21 VI 2012 (ESDF)								
VATICAN CITY	451	...	...	...	...	...	...	...
Hungary - Hongrie								
1 VII 2018 (ESDJ)								
BUDAPEST	1 751 010	816 438	934 572	525.1	2 608 485	1 230 155	1 378 330	2538.4
Debrecen	201 823	94 393	107 430	461.7	265 647	125 983	139 664	1081.8
Györ	131 066	62 348	68 718	174.6	237 341	115 444	121 897	1607
Kecskemét	110 663	51 982	58 681	322.6	132 679	62 926	69 753	666.1
Miskolc	155 086	71 962	83 124	236.7	244 513	115 322	129 191	982.3
Nyiregyhaza	116 960	54 492	62 469	274.5	147 019	69 247	77 772	554.2
Pécs	143 531	65 835	77 696	162.8	179 070	83 319	95 751	671.3
Szeged	160 944	74 163	86 781	281	204 197	95 614	108 583	804.5
Iceland - Islande								
1 VII 2018 (ESDJ)								
REYKJAVIK	127 417[80]	64 607[80]	62 811[80]	274	225 358[80]	114 035[80]	111 323[80]	1044
Ireland - Irlande								
1 IV 2016 (ESDJ)								
Cork	124 391	61 255	63 136	...	...	...	...	...
DUBLIN	544 107	267 319	276 788	...	...	...	...	...
Isle of Man - Île de Man								
23 IV 2006 (CDJC)								
DOUGLAS	26 218	13 000	13 218	...	...	...	...	...
Italy - Italie								
1 VII 2018 (ESDJ)								
Ancona	100 984	48 452	52 532	...	...	...	...	...
Bari	322 116	154 794	167 322	...	...	...	...	...
Bergamo	121 281	57 344	63 937	...	...	...	...	...
Bologna	389 949	184 229	205 720	...	...	...	...	...
Bolzano	107 528	51 630	55 899	...	...	...	...	...
Brescia	197 641	93 659	103 982	...	...	...	...	...
Cagliari	154 187	72 053	82 134	...	...	...	...	...
Catania	311 602	150 114	161 488	...	...	...	...	...
Ferrara	132 165	62 316	69 850	...	...	...	...	...
Firenze	379 894	178 437	201 457	...	...	...	...	...
Foggia	151 288	73 391	77 897	...	...	...	...	...
Forli	117 831	56 797	61 034	...	...	...	...	...
Genova	579 049	273 664	305 385	...	...	...	...	...
Giugliano in Campania	123 926	61 426	62 500	...	...	...	...	...
Latina	126 608	61 604	65 004	...	...	...	...	...
Livorno	158 077	75 855	82 223	...	...	...	...	...
Messina	233 424	111 900	121 524	...	...	...	...	...
Milano	1 372 435	658 762	713 673	...	...	...	...	...
Modena	185 790	89 136	96 654	...	...	...	...	...

8. Population of capital cities and cities of 100 000 or more inhabitants: latest available year, 2000 - 2019
Population des capitales et des villes de 100 000 habitants ou plus : dernière année disponible, 2000 - 2019 (continued - suite)

Continent, country or area, date, code[a] and city / Continent, pays ou zone, date, code[a] et ville	City proper - Ville proprement dite				Urban agglomeration - Agglomération urbaine			
	Population				Population			
	Both sexes - Les deux sexes	Male - Masculin	Female - Féminin	Surface area - Superficie (km²)	Both sexes - Les deux sexes	Male - Masculin	Female - Féminin	Surface area - Superficie (km²)
EUROPE								
Italy - Italie								
1 VII 2018 (ESDJ)								
Monza	123 498	59 268	64 230	...	...	...	...	...
Napoli	962 666	460 237	502 429	...	...	...	...	...
Novara	104 231	50 331	53 901	...	...	...	...	...
Padova	210 676	99 404	111 273	...	...	...	...	...
Palermo	665 903	318 064	347 840	...	...	...	...	...
Parma	196 103	94 066	102 037	...	...	...	...	...
Perugia	165 820	79 336	86 484	...	...	...	...	...
Pescara	119 257	55 865	63 393	...	...	...	...	...
Piacenza	103 512	49 482	54 031	...	...	...	...	...
Prato	193 958	94 086	99 872	...	...	...	...	...
Ravenna	158 389	76 819	81 570	...	...	...	...	...
Reggio di Calabria	180 908	86 686	94 222	...	...	...	...	...
Reggio nell'Emilia	171 972	83 872	88 100	...	...	...	...	...
Rimini	149 990	71 922	78 068	...	...	...	...	...
ROMA	2 864 467	1 357 404	1 507 063	...	...	...	...	...
Salerno	133 667	62 477	71 190	...	...	...	...	...
Sassari	126 820	61 105	65 715	...	...	...	...	...
Siracusa	121 388	59 445	61 943	...	...	...	...	...
Taranto	197 493	94 287	103 206	...	...	...	...	...
Terni	110 969	52 323	58 646	...	...	...	...	...
Torino	879 111	419 299	459 812	...	...	...	...	...
Trento	118 143	56 861	61 282	...	...	...	...	...
Trieste	204 303	97 801	106 502	...	...	...	...	...
Venezia	260 921	124 099	136 822	...	...	...	...	...
Verona	257 634	121 976	135 658	...	...	...	...	...
Vicenza	111 205	52 681	58 525	...	...	...	...	...
Jersey								
11 III 2001 (CDJC)								
ST. HELIER	28 310	13 669	14 641	8.6	...	...	...	...
Latvia - Lettonie								
1 I 2019 (ESDJ)								
RIGA	632 614	281 558	351 056	304	...	...	...	...
Liechtenstein								
1 VII 2019 (ESDJ)								
VADUZ	5 668	2 778	2 890	17	...	...	...	...
Lithuania - Lituanie								
1 VII 2018 (ESDJ)								
Kaunas	287 559[81]	126 197[81]	161 362[81]	157	...	...	...	...
Klaipeda	148 400[81]	66 822[81]	81 578[81]	98	...	...	...	...
Shauliai	100 353[81]	45 732[81]	54 621[81]	81	...	...	...	...
VILNIUS	549 808[81]	247 940[81]	301 868[81]	401	...	...	...	...
Luxembourg								
1 I 2019 (ESDJ)								
LUXEMBOURG-VILLE	119 215	61 216	57 999	51	...	...	...	...
Malta - Malte[82]								
1 VII 2018 (ESDJ)								
VALLETTA	5 827	2 918	2 909	...	...	...	...	...
Monaco								
9 VI 2008 (CDJC)								
MONACO	31 109	15 076[83]	15 914[83]	...	...	...	...	...
Montenegro - Monténégro								
1 IV 2011 (CDJC)								
PODGORICA	185 937	90 614	95 323	1441	...	...	...	...
Netherlands - Pays-Bas								
1 I 2015 (ESDJ)								
Alkmaar	107 106	52 973	54 133	...	...	...	...	...
Almere	196 932	97 666	99 266	...	...	...	...	...
Alphen aan den	107 396	53 321	54 075	...	...	...	...	...
Amersfoort	152 481	74 967	77 514	...	...	...	...	...
AMSTERDAM	821 752	404 881	416 871	...	...	...	...	...
Apeldoorn	158 099	78 163	79 936	...	...	...	...	...
Arnhem	152 293	75 872	76 421	...	...	...	...	...
Breda	180 937	88 620	92 317	...	...	...	...	...

8. Population of capital cities and cities of 100 000 or more inhabitants: latest available year, 2000 - 2019
Population des capitales et des villes de 100 000 habitants ou plus : dernière année disponible, 2000 - 2019 (continued - suite)

Continent, country or area, date, code[a] and city Continent, pays ou zone, date, code[a] et ville	City proper - Ville proprement dite: Population: Both sexes - Les deux sexes	City proper: Population: Male - Masculin	City proper: Population: Female - Féminin	City proper: Surface area - Superficie (km²)	Urban agglomeration - Agglomération urbaine: Population: Both sexes - Les deux sexes	Urban agglomeration: Population: Male - Masculin	Urban agglomeration: Population: Female - Féminin	Urban agglomeration: Surface area - Superficie (km²)
EUROPE								
Netherlands - Pays-Bas								
1 I 2015 (ESDJ)								
Delft	101 030	54 035	46 995	...	...	...	...	...
Dordrecht	118 899	58 646	60 253	...	...	...	...	...
Ede	111 575	54 790	56 785	...	...	...	...	...
Eindhoven	223 209	114 034	109 175	...	...	...	...	...
Emmen	107 775	53 399	54 376	...	...	...	...	...
Enschede	158 553	80 411	78 142	...	...	...	...	...
Groningen	200 336	99 657	100 679	...	...	...	...	...
Haarlem	156 645	76 481	80 164	...	...	...	...	...
Haarlemmermeer	144 152	71 642	72 510	...	...	...	...	...
Leeuwarden	107 691	53 264	54 427	...	...	...	...	...
Leiden	121 562	59 084	62 478	...	...	...	...	...
Maastricht	122 397	58 799	63 598	...	...	...	...	...
Nijmegen	170 681	81 934	88 747	...	...	...	...	...
Rotterdam	623 652	307 001	316 651	...	...	...	...	...
s-Gravenhage	514 861	254 187	260 674	...	...	...	...	...
s-Hertogenbosch	150 889	74 424	76 465	...	...	...	...	...
Tilburg	211 648	105 179	106 469	...	...	...	...	...
Utrecht	334 176	162 556	171 620	...	...	...	...	...
Venlo	100 536	49 978	50 558	...	...	...	...	...
Westland	104 302	51 937	52 365	...	...	...	...	...
Zaanstad	151 418	74 778	76 640	...	...	...	...	...
Zoetermeer	124 025	60 554	63 471	...	...	...	...	...
Zwolle	123 861	60 759	63 102	...	...	...	...	...
North Macedonia - Macédoine du Nord								
1 VII 2016 (ESDJ)								
SKOPJE	546 824	267 738	279 086	...	...	...	...	...
Norway - Norvège								
1 I 2019 (ESDJ)								
OSLO	681 067	339 597	341 470	...	...	...	...	...
Poland - Pologne[84]								
1 VII 2018 (ESDJ)								
Bialystok	294 683[81]	138 357[81]	156 326[81]	102[85]	...	...	...	...
Bielsko-Biala	169 373[81]	80 059[81]	89 314[81]	125[85]	...	...	...	...
Bydgoszcz	351 273[81]	165 446[81]	185 827[81]	176[85]	...	...	...	...
Bytom	166 135[81]	79 284[81]	86 851[81]	69[85]	...	...	...	...
Chorzów	107 780[81]	51 200[81]	56 580[81]	33[85]	...	...	...	...
Czestochowa	221 508[81]	103 837[81]	117 671[81]	160[85]	...	...	...	...
Dabrowa Górnicza	119 816[81]	57 331[81]	62 485[81]	189[85]	...	...	...	...
Elblag	118 397[81]	56 502[81]	61 895[81]	80[85]	...	...	...	...
Gdansk	464 834[81]	220 748[81]	244 086[81]	262[85]	...	...	...	...
Gdynia	243 496[81]	114 899[81]	128 597[81]	135[85]	...	...	...	...
Gliwice	179 218[81]	86 400[81]	92 818[81]	134[85]	...	...	...	...
Gorzów Wielkopolski	122 455[81]	58 116[81]	64 339[81]	86[85]	...	...	...	...
Kalisz	100 223[81]	46 571[81]	53 652[81]	69[85]	...	...	...	...
Katowice	299 674[81]	143 308[81]	156 366[81]	165[85]	...	...	...	...
Kielce	194 632[81]	91 502[81]	103 130[81]	110[85]	...	...	...	...
Koszalin	106 118[81]	49 897[81]	56 221[81]	98[85]	...	...	...	...
Kraków	762 776[81]	356 584[81]	406 192[81]	327[85]	...	...	...	...
Lódz	686 874[81]	313 191[81]	373 683[81]	293[85]	...	...	...	...
Lublin	341 493[81]	157 363[81]	184 130[81]	147[85]	...	...	...	...
Olsztyn	174 023[81]	81 124[81]	92 899[81]	88[85]	...	...	...	...
Opole	127 434[81]	60 268[81]	67 166[81]	149[85]	...	...	...	...
Plock	119 175[81]	56 211[81]	62 964[81]	88[85]	...	...	...	...
Poznan	536 692[81]	250 673[81]	286 019[81]	262[85]	...	...	...	...
Radom	211 909[81]	100 554[81]	111 355[81]	112[85]	...	...	...	...
Ruda Slaska	137 093[81]	66 263[81]	70 830[81]	78[85]	...	...	...	...
Rybnik	137 316[81]	67 021[81]	70 295[81]	148[85]	...	...	...	...
Rzeszów	188 232[81]	89 244[81]	98 988[81]	120[85]	...	...	...	...
Sosnowiec	201 228[81]	95 091[81]	106 137[81]	91[85]	...	...	...	...
Szczecin	400 947[81]	190 816[81]	210 131[81]	301[85]	...	...	...	...
Tarnów	106 408[81]	50 187[81]	56 221[81]	72[85]	...	...	...	...

8. Population of capital cities and cities of 100 000 or more inhabitants: latest available year, 2000 - 2019
Population des capitales et des villes de 100 000 habitants ou plus : dernière année disponible, 2000 - 2019 (continued - suite)

Continent, country or area, date, code[a] and city Continent, pays ou zone, date, code[a] et ville	City proper - Ville proprement dite				Urban agglomeration - Agglomération urbaine			
	Population				Population			
	Both sexes - Les deux sexes	Male - Masculin	Female - Féminin	Surface area - Superficie (km²)	Both sexes - Les deux sexes	Male - Masculin	Female - Féminin	Surface area - Superficie (km²)
EUROPE								
Poland - Pologne[84]								
1 VII 2018 (ESDJ)								
Torun	199 531[81]	92 656[81]	106 875[81]	116[85]	...	...	...	...
Tychy	126 581[81]	60 962[81]	65 619[81]	82[85]	...	...	...	...
Walbrzych	111 803[81]	52 686[81]	59 117[81]	85[85]	...	...	...	...
WARSZAWA	1 766 212[81]	813 008[81]	953 204[81]	517[85]	...	...	...	...
Wloclawek	109 751[81]	51 589[81]	58 162[81]	84[85]	...	...	...	...
Wroclaw	636 722[81]	298 228[81]	338 494[81]	293[85]	...	...	...	...
Zabrze	171 756[81]	82 802[81]	88 954[81]	80[85]	...	...	...	...
Zielona Góra	140 219[81]	66 795[81]	73 424[81]	277[85]	...	...	...	...
Portugal								
1 VII 2018 (ESDJ)								
Amadora	180 833	84 025	96 809	...	...	...	...	...
LISBOA	506 654	232 019	274 636	...	...	...	...	...
Porto	214 936	96 613	118 323	...	...	...	...	...
Republic of Moldova - République de Moldova[86]								
12 V 2014 (CDFC)								
CHIŞINĂU (KISHINEV)	339 079	157 341	181 738	...	...	...	...	...
Romania - Roumanie								
1 I 2019 (ESDF)								
BUCURESTI	1 829 897	850 413	979 484	...	...	...	...	...
Russian Federation - Fédération de Russie								
1 VII 2012 (ESDJ)								
Abakan	168 655	77 052	91 603	...	...	...	...	...
Achinsk	107 943	48 069	59 874	...	109 229	...	...	...
Almetievsk	148 384	69 433	78 951	...	...	...	...	...
Anapa	...	...	...	...	156 928	...	...	...
Angarsk	231 944	105 405	126 539	...	...	...	...	...
Arkhangelsk	350 258	156 523	193 735	...	357 264	...	...	...
Armavir	190 831	87 524	103 307	...	209 742	...	...	...
Artem (Primorskiy Krai)	102 605	49 147	53 458	...	112 102	...	...	...
Arzamas	105 506	47 208	58 298	...	...	...	...	...
Astrakhan	526 363	241 489	284 874	...	...	...	...	...
Balakovo	196 918	88 075	108 843	...	...	...	...	...
Balashikha	228 567	112 191	116 376	...	238 284	...	...	...
Barnaul	625 679	279 300	346 379	...	686 306	...	...	...
Bataisk	115 016	54 477	60 539	...	...	...	...	...
Belgorod	369 815	167 120	202 695	...	...	...	...	...
Belovo	...	...	...	...	132 144	...	...	...
Berezniki	153 806	68 365	85 441	...	...	...	...	...
Biisk	206 327	91 943	114 384	...	215 780	...	...	...
Blagoveshchensk (Amurskaya oblast)	216 691	97 135	119 556	...	222 065	...	...	...
Bor	...	...	...	...	122 201	...	...	...
Bratsk	242 604	109 596	133 008	...	...	...	...	...
Bryansk	411 798	183 540	228 258	...	430 987	...	...	...
Cheboksary	462 669	206 721	255 948	...	473 189	...	...	...
Chelyabinsk	1 149 829	514 456	635 373	...	...	...	...	...
Cherepovets	315 186	142 977	172 209	...	...	...	...	...
Cherkessk	126 884	55 588	71 296	...	...	...	...	...
Chita	329 391	152 092	177 299	...	329 868	...	...	...
Derbent	119 647	57 527	62 120	...	...	...	...	...
Dimitrovgrad	120 750	55 838	64 912	...	...	...	...	...
Domodedovo	...	...	...	...	142 743	...	...	...
Dzerzhinsk (Nizhegorodskaya oblast)	238 327	105 346	132 981	...	248 649	...	...	...
Ekaterinburg	1 386 909	621 499	765 410	...	1 420 285	...	...	...
Elektrostal	156 136	71 093	85 043	...	...	...	...	...
Elets	107 347	48 757	58 590	...	...	...	...	...
Elista	104 177	47 317	56 860	...	108 753	...	...	...
Engels	210 190	95 953	114 237	...	211 825	...	...	...
Esentuky	101 851	45 327	56 524	...	...	...	...	...
Groznyi	276 524	136 615	139 909	...	...	...	...	...
Hasaviurt	133 188	63 867	69 321	...	...	...	...	...
Irkutsk	601 993	269 003	332 990	...	...	...	...	...
Ivanovo	408 952	180 083	228 869	...	...	...	...	...
Izhevsk	631 182	281 708	349 474	...	...	...	...	...

Continent, country or area, date, code[a] and city Continent, pays ou zone, date, code[a] et ville	City proper - Ville proprement dite				Urban agglomeration - Agglomération urbaine			
	Population				Population			
	Both sexes - Les deux sexes	Male - Masculin	Female - Féminin	Surface area - Superficie (km²)	Both sexes - Les deux sexes	Male - Masculin	Female - Féminin	Surface area - Superficie (km²)
EUROPE								
Russian Federation - Fédération de Russie								
1 VII 2012 (ESDJ)								
Kaliningrad (Kaliningradskaya oblast)	437 456	200 849	236 607	...	...	...	...	...
Kaluga	328 871	146 008	182 863	...	344 766	...	...	...
Kamensk-Uralsky	172 639	77 327	95 312	...	174 493	...	...	...
Kamyshin	117 352	53 822	63 530	...	...	...	...	...
Kaspiysk	102 421	49 393	53 028	...	...	...	...	...
Kazan	1 168 745	520 694	648 051	...	...	...	...	...
Kemerovo	538 188	240 431	297 757	...	...	...	...	...
Khabarovsk	589 596	273 949	315 647	...	...	...	...	...
Khimki	218 275	99 122	119 153	...	...	...	...	...
Kirov	480 594	211 205	269 389	...	505 346	...	...	...
Kiselevsk	...	...	...	...	101 180	...	...	...
Kislovodsk	129 313	58 854	70 459	...	136 142	...	...	...
Kolomna	144 838	66 469	78 369	...	...	...	...	...
Komsomolsk-na-Amure	259 081	120 197	138 884	...	...	...	...	...
Kopeysk	139 161	66 142	73 019	...	141 291	...	...	...
Korolev (Moskovskaya oblast)	186 460	84 232	102 228	...	...	...	...	...
Kostroma	270 366	120 622	149 744	...	...	...	...	...
Kovrov	...	...	...	...	346 922	154 144	192 778	...
Krasnodar	773 970	350 519	423 451	...	861 181	...	...	...
Krasnogorsk	125 198	56 432	68 766	...	125 787	...	...	...
Krasnoyarsk	1 006 856	456 171	550 685	...	1 007 654	...	...	...
Kurgan	326 729	146 140	180 589	...	...	...	...	...
Kursk	425 950	189 025	236 925	...	...	...	...	...
Kyzyl	112 659	52 137	60 522	...	...	...	...	...
Leninsk-Kuznetsky	100 073	45 651	54 422	...	102 285	...	...	...
Lipetsk	508 585	230 178	278 407	...	...	...	...	...
Lyubertsy	178 884	80 564	98 320	...	...	...	...	...
Magadan	95 263	45 084	50 179	...	101 933	...	...	...
Magnitogorsk	410 733	186 534	224 199	...	...	...	...	...
Maikop	144 579	64 512	80 067	...	167 281	...	...	...
Makhachkala	575 243	271 687	303 556	...	701 753	...	...	...
Mezhdurechensk	100 278	46 498	53 780	...	102 465	...	...	...
Miass	150 806	67 824	82 982	...	166 205	...	...	...
MOSKVA	11 918 057	5 495 477	6 422 580	...	...	...	...	...
Murmansk	303 754	139 944	163 810	...	...	...	...	...
Murom	113 330	50 293	63 037	...	122 545	...	...	...
Mytishchi	176 825	80 425	96 400	...	185 204	...	...	...
Naberezhnye Tchelny	517 831	237 620	280 211	...	...	...	...	...
Nakhodka	158 649	75 081	83 568	...	159 633	...	...	...
Naltchik	239 230	106 648	132 582	...	265 051	...	...	...
Nazran	100 574	44 126	56 448	...	...	...	...	...
Neftekamsk	123 202	57 271	65 931	...	135 013	...	...	...
Nefteyugansk	125 528	61 635	63 893	...	...	...	...	...
Nevinnomyssk	117 949	53 611	64 338	...	...	...	...	...
Nizhnekamsk	235 179	111 262	123 917	...	235 279	...	...	...
Nizhnevartovsk	261 011	125 937	135 074	...	...	...	...	...
Nizhny Novgorod	1 257 260	552 285	704 975	...	1 266 231	...	...	...
Nizhny Tagil	358 651	162 731	195 920	...	362 185	...	...	...
Noginsk	101 779	45 741	56 038	...	103 843	...	...	...
Norilsk	177 506	89 198	88 308	...	178 363	...	...	...
Novocheboksarsk	...	...	...	...	124 288	...	...	...
Novocherkassk	171 081	81 921	89 160	...	...	...	...	...
Novokuybishevsk	107 244	48 418	58 826	...	109 521	...	...	...
Novokuznetsk	549 383	247 386	301 997	...	...	...	...	...
Novomoskovsk (Tulskaya oblast)	129 555	57 961	71 594	...	141 893	...	...	...
Novorossiysk	248 857	117 707	131 150	...	305 421	...	...	...
Novoshakhtinsk	110 243	50 410	59 833	...	...	...	...	...
Novosibirsk	1 511 369	694 959	816 410	...	...	...	...	...
Novotroitsk	...	...	...	...	103 061	...	...	...
Novy Urengoy	114 332	59 841	54 491	...	...	...	...	...
Noyabrsk	108 662	53 237	55 425	...	...	...	...	...
Obninsk	105 722	48 323	57 399	...	...	...	...	...
Odintsovo	137 706	63 405	74 301	...	143 848	...	...	...

8. Population of capital cities and cities of 100 000 or more inhabitants: latest available year, 2000 - 2019
Population des capitales et des villes de 100 000 habitants ou plus : dernière année disponible, 2000 - 2019 (continued - suite)

Continent, country or area, date, code[a] and city / Continent, pays ou zone, date, code[a] et ville	City proper - Ville proprement dite				Urban agglomeration - Agglomération urbaine			
	Population				Population			
	Both sexes - Les deux sexes	Male - Masculin	Female - Féminin	Surface area - Superficie (km²)	Both sexes - Les deux sexes	Male - Masculin	Female - Féminin	Surface area - Superficie (km²)
EUROPE								
Russian Federation - Fédération de Russie								
1 VII 2012 (ESDJ)								
Oktyabrsky	111 109	51 956	59 153	...	...	...	...	...
Omsk	1 158 627	526 757	631 870	...	...	...	...	...
Orekhovo-Zuevo	121 341	53 443	67 898	...	...	...	...	...
Orel	318 642	139 662	178 980	...	...	...	...	...
Orenburg	555 420	252 906	302 514	...	571 041	...	...	...
Orsk	237 194	106 127	131 067	...	241 327	...	...	...
Penza	519 948	234 270	285 678	...	...	...	...	...
Perm	1 007 272	444 386	562 886	...	1 007 285	...	...	...
Pervouralsk	125 421	56 144	69 277	...	149 796	...	...	...
Petropavlovsk-Kamchatsky	180 702	88 743	91 959	...	...	...	...	...
Petrozavodsk	267 102	118 638	148 464	...	...	...	...	...
Podolsk	200 059	89 931	110 128	...	...	...	...	...
Prokopyevsk	206 023	91 944	114 079	...	...	...	...	...
Pskov	205 062	92 439	112 623	...	...	...	...	...
Pushkino	104 020	46 649	57 371	...	...	...	...	...
Pyatigorsk	144 603	64 578	80 025	...	212 968	...	...	...
Rostov-na-Donu	1 100 091	501 068	599 023	...	...	...	...	...
Rubtsovsk	146 075	69 084	76 991	...	...	...	...	...
Ryazan	526 919	237 791	289 128	...	...	...	...	...
Rybinsk	197 359	87 921	109 438	...	...	...	...	...
Salavat	155 174	72 449	82 725	...	...	...	...	...
Samara (Samarskaya oblast)	1 170 381	522 660	647 721	...	1 170 485	...	...	...
Saransk	298 103	132 543	165 560	...	326 473	...	...	...
Sarapyul	100 362	44 678	55 684	...	...	...	...	...
Saratov	838 321	373 676	464 645	...	...	...	...	...
Sergiev Posad	109 076	48 786	60 290	...	115 858	...	...	...
Serov	...	...	...	...	107 904	...	...	...
Serpukhov	126 729	57 494	69 235	...	...	...	...	...
Severodvinsk	189 313	87 781	101 532	...	190 513	...	...	...
Seversk	109 630	50 705	58 925	...	116 340	...	...	...
Shakhty	238 031	107 544	130 487	...	...	...	...	...
Shchelkovo	111 406	50 812	60 594	...	113 726	...	...	...
Smolensk	330 451	147 446	183 005	...	...	...	...	...
Sochi	364 171	164 632	199 539	...	441 407	...	...	...
St. Petersburg	4 990 602	2 247 375	2 743 227	...	...	...	...	...
Stary Oskol	220 719	100 902	119 817	...	256 790	...	...	...
Stavropol	408 361	187 593	220 768	...	408 560	...	...	...
Sterlitamak	275 087	125 443	149 644	...	...	...	...	...
Surgut	321 062	153 832	167 230	...	...	...	...	...
Syktivkar	239 341	107 945	131 396	...	255 283	...	...	...
Syzran	177 404	79 804	97 600	...	178 205	...	...	...
Taganrog	255 671	114 508	141 163	...	...	...	...	...
Tambov	281 348	126 427	154 921	...	...	...	...	...
Tobolsk	...	...	...	...	101 955	...	...	...
Tolyatti	719 363	331 248	388 115	...	...	...	...	...
Tomsk	543 596	252 173	291 423	...	565 000	...	...	...
Tula	496 656	220 675	275 981	...	...	...	...	...
Tver	407 896	180 459	227 437	...	...	...	...	...
Tyumen	621 918	288 291	333 627	...	644 799	...	...	...
Ufa	1 075 007	484 893	590 114	...	1 084 420	...	...	...
Uhta	99 680	47 563	52 117	...	121 479	...	...	...
Ulan-Ude	413 850	191 732	222 118	...	...	...	...	...
Ulyanovsk	614 878	278 103	336 775	...	637 637	...	...	...
Ussuriisk	163 465	79 562	83 903	...	189 502	...	...	...
Velikiy Novgorod	219 941	95 446	124 495	...	...	...	...	...
Vladikavkaz (Osetinskaya ASSR)	309 173	139 818	169 355	...	327 448	...	...	...
Vladimir	346 922	154 144	192 778	...	349 525	...	...	...
Vladivostok	598 927	282 260	316 667	...	624 281	...	...	...
Volgodonsk	170 189	78 251	91 938	...	...	...	...	...
Volgograd	1 018 762	460 095	558 667	...	...	...	...	...
Vologda	305 397	135 292	170 105	...	313 679	...	...	...
Volzhsky	320 761	148 339	172 422	...	327 460	...	...	...
Voronezh	997 447	447 484	549 963	...	...	...	...	...

8. Population of capital cities and cities of 100 000 or more inhabitants: latest available year, 2000 - 2019
Population des capitales et des villes de 100 000 habitants ou plus : dernière année disponible, 2000 - 2019 (continued - suite)

Continent, country or area, date, code[a] and city Continent, pays ou zone, date, code[a] et ville	City proper - Ville proprement dite: Population: Both sexes - Les deux sexes	Male - Masculin	Female - Féminin	Surface area - Superficie (km²)	Urban agglomeration - Agglomération urbaine: Population: Both sexes - Les deux sexes	Male - Masculin	Female - Féminin	Surface area - Superficie (km²)
EUROPE								
Russian Federation - Fédération de Russie								
1 VII 2012 (ESDJ)								
Yakutsk	282 419	132 612	149 807	...	298 926	...	...	...
Yaroslavl	597 161	262 042	335 119	...	...	...	...	...
Yoshkar-Ola	254 987	114 331	140 656	...	265 626	...	...	...
Yuzhno-Sakhalinsk	188 242	89 200	99 042	...	195 104	...	...	...
Zheleznodorozhny	138 814	62 719	76 095	...	...	...	...	...
Zhukovsky	106 555	49 027	57 528	...	...	...	...	...
Zlatoust	172 972	78 071	94 901	...	175 178	...	...	...
San Marino - Saint-Marin								
1 VII 2018 (ESDJ)								
SAN MARINO	4 127	2 008	2 119	...	...	...	...	...
Serbia - Serbie[87]								
1 VII 2018 (ESDJ)								
BEOGRAD (BELGRADE)	1 382 547	644 270	738 277	716	1 690 193[20]	798 019[20]	892 174[20]	3232[20]
Čačak	71 558	34 052	37 506	35	110 279[20]	53 518[20]	56 761[20]	636[20]
Kragujevac	150 192	72 233	77 959	83	177 383[20]	86 006[20]	91 377[20]	834[20]
Kraljevo	66 105	31 879	34 226	42	118 363[20]	58 155[20]	60 208[20]	1529[20]
Kruševac	56 799	26 954	29 845	11	121 293[20]	59 292[20]	62 001[20]	853[20]
Leskovac	63 247	30 610	32 637	64	135 591[20]	67 474[20]	68 117[20]	1024[20]
Niš	185 770	88 683	97 087	49	256 381[20]	124 307[20]	132 074[20]	596[20]
Novi Pazar	73 196	36 172	37 024	15	106 261[20]	52 940[20]	53 321[20]	742[20]
Novi Sad	294 082	137 740	156 342	164	358 572[20]	169 854[20]	188 718[20]	699[20]
Pancevo	88 852	42 672	46 180	263	119 960[20]	58 404[20]	61 556[20]	755[20]
Šabac	52 623	24 655	27 968	31	110 918[20]	54 193[20]	56 725[20]	797[20]
Smederevo	62 127	30 033	32 094	42	103 180[20]	50 909[20]	52 271[20]	484[20]
Subotica	103 407	49 228	54 179	205	137 173[20]	65 964[20]	71 209[20]	1007[20]
Zrenjanin	73 449	34 961	38 488	193	116 784[20]	56 847[20]	59 937[20]	1325[20]
Slovakia - Slovaquie								
1 VII 2018 (ESDJ)								
BRATISLAVA	431 214	202 794	228 420	368[61]	...	...	...	...
Kosice	238 927	114 534	124 393	244[61]	...	...	...	...
Slovenia - Slovénie								
1 VII 2018 (ESDJ)								
LJUBLJANA	281 226	135 857	145 369	164	283 055	136 755	146 300	171
Maribor	94 244	46 195	48 049	41	107 877	52 973	54 904	99
Spain - Espagne[88]								
1 VII 2018 (ESDJ)								
A Coruña	245 280	113 756	131 524	...	...	...	...	...
Albacete	173 189	84 650	88 539	...	...	...	...	...
Alcalá de Henares	194 700	94 796	99 904	...	...	...	...	...
Alcobendas	116 538	55 783	60 755	...	...	...	...	...
Alcorcón	170 008	81 944	88 064	...	...	...	...	...
Algeciras	121 685	59 986	61 699	...	...	...	...	...
Alicante/Alacant	333 232	161 393	171 839	...	...	...	...	...
Almería	197 692	96 474	101 218	...	...	...	...	...
Badajoz	150 616	73 033	77 583	...	...	...	...	...
Badalona	219 090	107 800	111 290	...	...	...	...	...
Barakaldo	100 658	48 615	52 043	...	...	...	...	...
Barcelona	1 628 552	770 790	857 762	...	...	...	...	...
Bilbao	346 332	163 247	183 085	...	...	...	...	...
Burgos	175 871	83 721	92 150	...	...	...	...	...
Cádiz	116 503	55 146	61 357	...	...	...	...	...
Cartagena	214 372	106 826	107 546	...	...	...	...	...
Castellón de la Plana/Castelló de la Plana	171 308	82 883	88 425	...	...	...	...	...
Córdoba	325 704	156 386	169 318	...	...	...	...	...
Donostia/San Sebastián	187 040	88 035	99 005	...	...	...	...	...
Dos Hermanas	133 568	65 684	67 884	...	...	...	...	...
Elche/Elx	231 571	114 741	116 830	...	...	...	...	...
Fuenlabrada	193 643	95 421	98 222	...	...	...	...	...
Getafe	182 060	89 082	92 978	...	...	...	...	...
Gijón	271 811	128 168	143 643	...	...	...	...	...
Girona	101 059	48 480	52 579	...	...	...	...	...
Granada	232 335	107 484	124 851	...	...	...	...	...

8. Population of capital cities and cities of 100 000 or more inhabitants: latest available year, 2000 - 2019
Population des capitales et des villes de 100 000 habitants ou plus : dernière année disponible, 2000 - 2019 (continued - suite)

Continent, country or area, date, code[a] and city Continent, pays ou zone, date, code[a] et ville	City proper - Ville proprement dite				Urban agglomeration - Agglomération urbaine			
	Population				Population			
	Both sexes - Les deux sexes	Male - Masculin	Female - Féminin	Surface area - Superficie (km²)	Both sexes - Les deux sexes	Male - Masculin	Female - Féminin	Surface area - Superficie (km²)
EUROPE								
Spain - Espagne[88]								
1 VII 2018 (ESDJ)								
Huelva	143 960	69 169	74 791	...	...	...	...	...
Jaén	113 228	54 476	58 752	...	...	...	...	...
Jerez de la Frontera	212 814	103 991	108 823	...	...	...	...	...
Las Palmas de Gran Canaria	379 221	183 225	195 996	...	...	...	...	...
Leganés	189 143	91 731	97 412	...	...	...	...	...
León	124 537	56 421	68 116	...	...	...	...	...
L'Hospitalet de Llobregat	262 995	127 023	135 972	...	...	...	...	...
Lleida	138 406	68 363	70 043	...	...	...	...	...
Logroño	151 124	71 789	79 335	...	...	...	...	...
MADRID	3 244 730	1 510 172	1 734 558	...	...	...	...	...
Málaga	572 840	275 187	297 653	...	...	...	...	...
Marbella	142 424	68 508	73 916	...	...	...	...	...
Mataró	127 626	63 291	64 335	...	...	...	...	...
Móstoles	208 139	101 417	106 722	...	...	...	...	...
Murcia	450 220	220 027	230 193	...	...	...	...	...
Ourense	105 369	47 828	57 541	...	...	...	...	...
Oviedo	219 853	101 819	118 034	...	...	...	...	...
Palma de Mallorca	412 863	201 423	211 440	...	...	...	...	...
Pamplona/Iruña	200 359	94 720	105 639	...	...	...	...	...
Parla	129 190	64 320	64 870	...	...	...	...	...
Reus	103 925	50 222	53 703	...	...	...	...	...
Sabadell	212 689	103 387	109 302	...	...	...	...	...
Salamanca	144 103	65 319	78 784	...	...	...	...	...
San Cristóbal de La Laguna	156 526	75 786	80 740	...	...	...	...	...
Santa Coloma de Gramenet	119 018	58 872	60 146	...	...	...	...	...
Santa Cruz de Tenerife	206 084	98 416	107 668	...	...	...	...	...
Santander	172 291	79 463	92 828	...	...	...	...	...
Sevilla	688 651	326 784	361 867	...	...	...	...	...
Tarragona	133 407	64 893	68 514	...	...	...	...	...
Telde	102 535	50 428	52 107	...	...	...	...	...
Terrassa	219 545	108 004	111 541	...	...	...	...	...
Torrejón de Ardoz	130 552	64 329	66 223	...	...	...	...	...
Valencia	792 850	377 126	415 724	...	...	...	...	...
Valladolid	298 639	140 220	158 419	...	...	...	...	...
Vigo	294 503	139 339	155 164	...	...	...	...	...
Vitoria-Gasteiz	250 475	122 034	128 441	...	...	...	...	...
Zaragoza	670 938	320 901	350 037	...	...	...	...	...
Sweden - Suède								
1 VII 2007 (ESDJ)								
Göteborg	491 630	242 916	248 714	449	...	...	...	...
Helsingborg	124 188	60 672	63 516	346	...	...	...	...
Jönköping	122 952	60 462	62 490	1485	...	...	...	...
Linköping	139 474	70 239	69 235	1431	...	...	...	...
Malmö	278 523	135 997	142 526	154	...	...	...	...
Norrköping	126 072	62 323	63 749	1491	...	...	...	...
Orebro	129 703	63 123	66 581	1371	...	...	...	...
STOCKHOLM	789 024	384 243	404 781	187	...	...	...	...
Umeå	111 503	55 549	55 955	2316	...	...	...	...
Uppsala	186 364	91 149	95 215	2465	...	...	...	...
Västerås	133 324	66 056	67 269	956	...	...	...	...
Switzerland - Suisse								
31 XII 2018 (ESDJ)								
Baden-Brugg	30 521	15 352	15 169	...	111 438[89]	55 593[89]	55 845[89]	...
Bâle	172 258	83 724	88 534	...	550 152[89]	269 043[89]	281 109[89]	...
BERNE	133 883	64 659	69 224	...	419 983[89]	204 459[89]	215 524[89]	...
Biel/Bienne	55 159	26 983	28 176	...	106 864[89]	52 305[89]	54 559[89]	...
Fribourg	38 365	19 117	19 248	...	109 106[89]	54 378[89]	54 728[89]	...
Genève	201 818	96 947	104 871	...	597 269[89]	289 909[89]	307 360[89]	...
Lausanne	139 111	67 301	71 810	...	424 622[89]	208 538[89]	216 084[89]	...
Lugano	63 185	30 489	32 696	...	151 122[89]	73 367[89]	77 755[89]	...
Luzern	81 691	39 341	42 350	...	231 246[89]	113 818[89]	117 428[89]	...
Olten-Zofingen	30 019	14 817	15 202	...	101 685[89]	50 791[89]	50 894[89]	...

8. Population of capital cities and cities of 100 000 or more inhabitants: latest available year, 2000 - 2019
Population des capitales et des villes de 100 000 habitants ou plus : dernière année disponible, 2000 - 2019 (continued - suite)

Continent, country or area, date, code[a] and city / Continent, pays ou zone, date, code[a] et ville	City proper - Ville proprement dite: Population: Both sexes - Les deux sexes	Male - Masculin	Female - Féminin	Surface area - Superficie (km²)	Urban agglomeration - Agglomération urbaine: Population: Both sexes - Les deux sexes	Male - Masculin	Female - Féminin	Surface area - Superficie (km²)
EUROPE								
Switzerland - Suisse								
31 XII 2018 (ESDJ)								
St. Gallen	75 833	37 259	38 574	...	167 214[89]	82 806[89]	84 408[89]	...
Winterthur	111 851	55 019	56 832	...	143 428[89]	70 789[89]	72 639[89]	...
Zug	30 542	15 491	15 051	...	132 206[89]	66 919[89]	65 287[89]	...
Zürich	415 367	207 415	207 952	...	1 384 728[89]	690 728[89]	694 000[89]	...
Ukraine								
1 I 2018 (ESDJ)								
Alchevsk	107 542	49 388	58 154	...	...	...	...	...
Berdyansk	111 955	49 467	62 488	...	114 999	50 916	64 083	...
Bila Tserkva	205 247	94 552	110 695	...	...	...	...	...
Cherkasy	275 469	125 816	149 653	...	276 363	126 286	150 077	...
Chernihiv	283 579	130 070	153 509	...	...	...	...	...
Chernivtsi	261 924	120 154	141 770	...	...	...	...	...
Dnepropetrovsk	990 381	448 624	541 757	...	992 812	449 811	543 001	...
Dniprodzerzhynsk	234 516	105 482	129 034	...	241 432	108 600	132 832	...
Donets'k	910 252	402 964	507 288	...	926 086	410 162	515 924	...
Enakievo (Yenakievo)	78 867	34 982	43 885	...	106 873	47 580	59 293	...
Gorlivka	243 536	109 276	134 260	...	260 223	116 767	143 456	...
Ivano-Frankivsk	232 502	108 571	123 931	...	254 696	118 538	136 158	...
Kharkiv	1 430 515	661 485	769 030	...	...	...	...	...
Kherson	287 826	129 252	158 574	...	324 888	146 606	178 282	...
Khmelnitsky (Hmilnyk)	265 583	122 358	143 225	...	...	...	...	...
Kirovograd	225 489	102 466	123 023	...	233 509	106 112	127 397	...
Kramatorsk	155 155	69 162	85 993	...	188 096	84 508	103 588	...
Krasny Lutch	80 602	37 365	43 237	...	120 539	56 080	64 459	...
Krementchug	220 271	99 788	120 483	...	...	...	...	...
Krivoy Rog	628 181	282 312	345 869	...	630 941	283 708	347 233	...
KYIV	2 893 215	1 338 208	1 555 007	...	...	...	...	...
Lugansk	403 254	179 899	223 355	...	429 077	192 140	236 937	...
Luts'k	213 422	96 046	117 376	...	...	...	...	...
Lviv	720 105	336 316	383 789	...	750 044	350 357	399 687	...
Lysychansk	97 935	44 135	53 800	...	112 489	50 742	61 747	...
Makijivka	343 102	154 621	188 481	...	380 789	172 086	208 703	...
Mariupol	441 098	200 308	240 790	...	462 319	210 216	252 103	...
Melitopol	153 839	69 496	84 343	...	...	...	...	...
Nikolaev	481 760	218 915	262 845	...	...	...	...	...
Nikopol	114 156	50 748	63 408	...	...	...	...	...
Odessa	993 831	465 195	528 636	...	...	...	...	...
Pavlograd	107 127	48 998	58 129	...	...	...	...	...
Poltava	282 523	130 579	151 944	...	...	...	...	...
Rivne	243 152	111 490	131 662	...	...	...	...	...
Sievierodonetsk	104 828	46 578	58 250	...	115 013	51 434	63 579	...
Slovyansk	109 374	47 524	61 850	...	112 479	48 958	63 521	...
Sumy	263 681	118 921	144 760	...	266 550	120 314	146 236	...
Ternopil	217 171	100 200	116 971	...	...	...	...	...
Uzhhorod	112 436	52 377	60 059	...	...	...	...	...
Vinnitsa	370 017	169 260	200 757	...	...	...	...	...
Zaporozhye	741 496	334 920	406 576	...	...	...	...	...
Zhytomyr	265 679	122 455	143 224	...	...	...	...	...
United Kingdom of Great Britain and Northern Ireland - Royaume-Uni de Grande-Bretagne et d'Irlande du Nord[90]								
27 III 2011 (CDJC)								
Aberdeen	207 932	102 858	105 078	...	...	...	...	...
Belfast	280 211	134 693	145 518	...	...	...	...	...
Birmingham	1 085 810	534 038	551 772	...	...	...	...	...
Bolton	194 189	95 924	98 265	...	...	...	...	...
Bournemouth	187 503	93 390	94 113	...	...	...	...	...
Bradford	349 561	173 024	176 537	...	...	...	...	...
Brighton and Hove	229 700	115 245	114 455	...	...	...	...	...
Bristol	535 907	265 968	269 939	...	...	...	...	...
Cardiff	335 145	164 427	170 718	...	...	...	...	...
Coventry	325 949	162 069	163 880	...	...	...	...	...
Derby	255 394	126 402	128 992	...	...	...	...	...

8. Population of capital cities and cities of 100 000 or more inhabitants: latest available year, 2000 - 2019
Population des capitales et des villes de 100 000 habitants ou plus : dernière année disponible, 2000 - 2019 (continued - suite)

Continent, country or area, date, code[a] and city Continent, pays ou zone, date, code[a] et ville	City proper - Ville proprement dite				Urban agglomeration - Agglomération urbaine			
	Population				Population			
	Both sexes - Les deux sexes	Male - Masculin	Female - Féminin	Surface area - Superficie (km²)	Both sexes - Les deux sexes	Male - Masculin	Female - Féminin	Surface area - Superficie (km²)
EUROPE								
United Kingdom of Great Britain and Northern Ireland - Royaume-Uni de Grande-Bretagne et d'Irlande du Nord[90]								
27 III 2011 (CDJC)								
Edinburgh	482 005	234 608	247 397	...	...	...	...	...
Glasgow[91]	1 209 143	580 857	628 286	...	...	...	...	...
Kingston-upon-Hull	284 321	141 905	142 416	...	...	...	...	...
Leeds	474 632	233 488	241 144	...	...	...	...	...
Leicester	443 760	218 722	225 038	...	...	...	...	...
Liverpool	552 267	271 342	280 925	...	...	...	...	...
LONDON[92]	8 135 667	4 015 297	4 120 370	...	...	...	...	...
Luton	211 228	105 905	105 323	...	...	...	...	...
Manchester	510 746	256 984	253 762	...	...	...	...	...
Newcastle-upon-Tyne	268 064	134 375	133 689	...	...	...	...	...
Northampton	215 173	105 617	109 556	...	...	...	...	...
Nottingham	289 301	145 855	143 446	...	...	...	...	...
Plymouth	234 982	116 444	118 538	...	...	...	...	...
Portsmouth	238 137	119 369	118 768	...	...	...	...	...
Reading	218 705	109 236	109 469	...	...	...	...	...
Sheffield	518 090	255 755	262 335	...	...	...	...	...
Southampton	253 651	127 630	126 021	...	...	...	...	...
Stoke-on-Trent	270 726	134 642	136 084	...	...	...	...	...
Wolverhampton	210 319	104 047	106 272	...	...	...	...	...
OCEANIA - OCÉANIE								
American Samoa - Samoas américaines[33]								
1 IV 2010 (CDJC)								
PAGO PAGO	3 656	...	...	...	...	...	...	...
Australia - Australie[93]								
1 VII 2018* (ESDJ)								
Adelaide	24 794	12 648	12 146	15.6	1 326 958	651 997	674 961	2246.2
Ballarat	107 325	52 032	55 293	739	...	...	...	...
Brisbane	1 231 605	608 693	622 912	1342.7	2 379 724	1 175 360	1 204 364	5326.7
Cairns	165 525	81 741	83 784	1689.3	...	...	...	...
CANBERRA	420 960	208 320	212 640	2358.2	420 960	208 320	212 640	2358.2
Canberra-Queanbeyan	480 919	238 491	242 428	7677.1	...	...	...	...
Central Coast	342 047	167 140	174 907	1681.1	...	...	...	...
Darwin	84 613	43 359	41 254	111.3	134 544	70 478	64 066	374.4
Geelong	252 217	123 628	128 589	1248	268 277	131 587	136 690	1329
Gold Coast	606 774	295 788	310 986	1333.7	622 048	303 299	318 749	1857.9
Gold Coast-Tweed Heads	702 882	342 315	360 567	2641.4	...	...	...	...
Greater Adelaide	...	...	...	...	1 345 777	661 528	684 249	3259.8
Greater Brisbane	...	...	...	...	2 462 637	1 217 722	1 244 915	15842
Greater Darwin	...	...	...	...	148 564	78 130	70 434	3163.9
Greater Hobart	...	...	...	...	232 606	115 767	116 839	1695.4
Greater Melbourne	...	...	...	...	4 963 349	2 455 249	2 508 100	9992.5
Greater Perth	...	...	...	...	2 059 484	1 024 207	1 035 277	6416.2
Greater Sydney	...	...	...	...	5 230 330	2 600 157	2 630 173	12368.2
Hobart	53 684	26 786	26 898	77.9	213 502	106 118	107 384	1149.3
Melbourne	169 961	83 605	86 356	37.4	4 784 608	2 366 735	2 417 873	6189.1
Newcastle	164 104	81 550	82 554	186.8	173 251	86 077	87 174	224.9
Newcastle-Maitland	247 307	122 290	125 017	578.3	486 704	240 185	246 519	1179.1
Perth	27 762	14 515	13 247	13.7	2 020 138	1 003 250	1 016 888	3531.9
Sunshine Coast	319 922	154 674	165 248	2253.9	...	...	...	...
Sydney	240 229	124 590	115 639	26.7	4 835 206	2 406 373	2 428 833	4196.3
Toowoomba	167 657	81 698	85 959	12957.2	...	...	...	...
Townsville	194 072	97 203	96 869	3730.8	...	...	...	...
Wollongong	216 071	107 200	108 871	684	...	...	...	...
Cook Islands - Îles Cook								
1 XII 2016 (CDFC)								
RAROTONGA	13 007	6 289	6 718	...	...	...	...	...

8. Population of capital cities and cities of 100 000 or more inhabitants: latest available year, 2000 - 2019
Population des capitales et des villes de 100 000 habitants ou plus : dernière année disponible, 2000 - 2019 (continued - suite)

Continent, country or area, date, code[a] and city / Continent, pays ou zone, date, code[a] et ville	City proper - Ville proprement dite				Urban agglomeration - Agglomération urbaine			
	Population				Population			
	Both sexes - Les deux sexes	Male - Masculin	Female - Féminin	Surface area - Superficie (km²)	Both sexes - Les deux sexes	Male - Masculin	Female - Féminin	Surface area - Superficie (km²)
OCEANIA - OCÉANIE								
Fiji - Fidji								
16 IX 2007 (CDFC)								
SUVA	74 481	37 032	37 449	...	...	...	...	...
French Polynesia - Polynésie française								
22 VIII 2012 (CDFC)								
PAPEETE	25 763	12 971	12 792	...	...	...	...	...
Guam								
1 VII 2010 (ESDJ)								
AGANA	1 051	625	426	3	...	...	...	...
Kiribati								
7 XI 2015 (CDFC)								
TARAWA	...	...	...	...	63 017	30 416	32 601	...
Marshall Islands - Îles Marshall								
3 IV 2011 (CDFC)								
MAJURO	27 797	...	...	...	...	...	...	...
Micronesia (Federated States of) - Micronésie (États fédérés de)								
1 IV 2000 (CDJC)								
PALIKIR	6 227	...	...	...	...	...	...	...
New Caledonia - Nouvelle-Calédonie								
26 VIII 2014 (CDFC)								
NOUMEA	99 926	49 218	50 708	...	...	...	...	...
New Zealand - Nouvelle-Zélande[94]								
1 VII 2018 (ESDJ)								
Auckland	1 695 900	837 600	858 300	...	...	...	...	...
Christchurch	388 500	195 000	193 500	...	404 600	203 100	201 500	...
Dunedin	130 700	63 300	67 400	...	...	...	...	...
Hamilton	169 300	82 200	87 100	...	241 200	117 400	123 900	...
Lower Hutt	105 900	51 900	54 000	...	...	...	...	...
Napier-Hastings	...	...	...	...	134 500	64 500	70 000	...
Tauranga	135 000	64 700	70 300	...	141 600	67 900	73 700	...
WELLINGTON	216 300	106 400	109 900	...	418 500	205 400	213 100	...
Niue - Nioué								
11 IX 2011 (CDFC)								
ALOFI	639	311	328	...	...	...	...	...
Northern Mariana Islands - Îles Mariannes septentrionales								
1 IV 2010 (CDFC)								
GARAPAN	3 983	1 953	2 030	...	...	...	...	...
Palau - Palaos								
13 IV 2015 (CDJC)								
KOROR	...	...	...	...	11 754	...	...	...
Papua New Guinea - Papouasie-Nouvelle-Guinée								
10 VII 2011 (CDFC)								
PORT MORESBY	364 125	194 834	169 291	...	...	...	...	...
Pitcairn								
31 XII 2013 (CDJC)								
ADAMSTOWN	49	23	26	...	...	...	...	...
Samoa								
7 XI 2016 (CDFC)								
APIA	37 391	18 760	18 631	...	...	...	...	...
Solomon Islands - Îles Salomon								
22 XI 2009 (CDFC)								
HONIARA	64 609	...	...	...	80 082	...	...	...
Tonga								
30 XI 2016 (CDFC)								
NUKU'ALOFA	...	...	...	...	35 184	17 490	17 694	...
Tuvalu								
4 XI 2012 (CDFC)								
FUNAFUTI	6 152	...	...	...	...	...	...	...
Vanuatu[95]								
7 XI 2016 (CDFC)								
PORT VILA	50 944	25 861	25 083	...	...	...	...	...

8. Population of capital cities and cities of 100 000 or more inhabitants: latest available year, 2000 - 2019
Population des capitales et des villes de 100 000 habitants ou plus : dernière année disponible, 2000 - 2019 (continued - suite)

Continent, country or area, date, code[a] and city Continent, pays ou zone, date, code[a] et ville	City proper - Ville proprement dite				Urban agglomeration - Agglomération urbaine			
	Population				Population			
	Both sexes - Les deux sexes	Male - Masculin	Female - Féminin	Surface area - Superficie (km²)	Both sexes - Les deux sexes	Male - Masculin	Female - Féminin	Surface area - Superficie (km²)
OCEANIA - OCÉANIE								
Wallis and Futuna Islands - Îles Wallis et Futuna								
21 VII 2008 (CDFC)								
META-UTU	1 126	...	...	...	...	...	...	...

FOOTNOTES - NOTES

The capital city of each country is shown in capital letters. Figures in italics are estimates of questionnable reliability. For definition of city proper and urban agglomeration, method of evaluation and limitations of data see Technical Notes for this table. - Le nom de la capitale de chaque pays est imprimé en majuscules. Les chiffres en italique sont des estimations dont la fiabilité n'est pas assurée. Pour la définition de la ville proprement dite et de l'agglomération urbaine, et pour les méthodes d'évaluation et les insuffisances de données, voir les notes techniques pour ce tableau.

Italics: estimates which are less reliable. - Italiques : estimations moins sûres.

* Provisional. - Données provisoires.

[a] 'Code' indicates the source of data, as follows:
CDFC - Census, de facto, complete tabulation
CDFS - Census, de facto, sample tabulation
CDJC - Census, de jure, complete tabulation
CDJS - Census, de jure, sample tabulation
SSDF - Sample survey, de facto
SSDJ - Sample survey, de jure
ESDF - Estimates, de facto
ESDJ - Estimates, de jure

Le 'Code' indique la source des données, comme suit :
CDFC - Recensement, population de fait, tabulation complète
CDFS - Recensement, population de fait, tabulation par sondage
CDJC - Recensement, population de droit, tabulation complète
CDJS - Recensement, population de droit, tabulation par sondage
SSDF - Enquête par sondage, population de fait
SSDJ - Enquête par sondage, population de droit
ESDF - Estimations, population de fait
ESDJ - Estimations, population de droit

[1] Data refer to provincial capitals. - Les données se rapportent aux capitales des provinces.
[2] Postcensal estimates. - Estimations post censitaires.
[3] There is a reduction of the surface area and population of Luanda (capital of the province of Luanda) compared to the previous year, due to a redistribution of the territory of the province of Luanda. - Il y a une réduction apparente de la superficie et de la population de Luanda (capitale de la province du même nom) par rapport à l'année précédente, due à la redistribution du territoire de la province de Luanda.
[4] Based on the results of the 2011 Population Census. - Basé sur les résultats du recencement de la population de 2011.
[5] Data refer to national projections. - Les données se réfèrent aux projections nationales.
[6] Source: Population projections and estimates of priority targets for the various health programs and interventions, National Institute of Statistics (2016). - Source : Projections démographiques et estimations des cibles prioritaires des différents programmes et interventions de sante, Institut National de la Statistique (2016).
[7] Data refer to departmental seat of government and not to urban or rural agglomeration. - Ville correspond au chef-lieu de departement, pas de milieu rural ou agglomeration.
[8] Data refer to usual resident population. Data refer to Total Urban Governorates. - Les données se réfèrent à la population résidente habituelle. Les données concernent les gouvernorats entièrement urbaines.
[9] Population in households only. - Population dans les ménages seulement.
[10] The figure for both sexes includes a total of 245 intersex persons. - Le chiffre pour les deux sexes comprend un total de 245 personnes intersexes.
[11] Data refer to Maseru Urban Centre. - Les données concernent le centre urbain de Maseru.
[12] Data refer to Greater Monrovia. - Les données concernent la région métropolitaine de Monrovia.
[13] Data refer to District de Bamako. - Les données concernent le district de Bamako.
[14] Excludes the islands of St. Brandon and Agalega. - Non compris les îles St. Brandon et Agalega.
[15] Projections based on the 2012 Population Census. - Projections fondées sur le recensement de la population de 2012.
[16] Data refer to total resident population, Saint Helenian and other nationalities. - Les données concernent la population résidente totale, originaire de Sainte-Hélène ou possédant une autre nationalité.
[17] Projections based on the 2002 Population Census. - Projections fondées sur le recensement de la population de 2002.
[18] Data refer to Greater Victoria. - Les données concernent la région métropolitaine de Victoria.
[19] Bloemfontein is the judicial capital, Cape Town is the legislative capital and Pretoria is the administrative capital. - Bloemfontein est la capitale judiciaire, Le Cap est la capitale législative et Pretoria est la capitale administrative.
[20] Data for urban agglomeration refer to communes which are administrative divisions. - Les données pour l'agglomération urbaine se rapportent aux communes qui sont des divisions administrative.
[21] Based on the results of the 2014 Population Census. - D'après les résultats du recensement de la population de 2014.
[22] Data refer to the City Council. - Les données se rapportent au conseil municipal.
[23] Bermuda is 100 per cent urban. - 100 pour cent de la population des Bermudes est urbaine.
[24] Adjusted for census net undercoverage (including adjustment for incompletely enumerated Indian reserves). Postcensal estimates. The "City proper" uses the geographic definition of Census Subdivision (CSD): Census subdivision (CSD) is the general term for municipalities (as determined by provincial/territorial legislation) or areas treated as municipal equivalents for statistical purposes. The "Urban Agglomeration" uses the geographic definition of Census Metropolitan Area\Census Agglomeration (CMA\CA). - Ajusté pour la sous-estimation du recensement (y compris les réservations en Inde incomplètement énumérées). Estimations post censitaires. La ville est délimitée selon la définition géographique de la subdivision pour le recensement, qui est le terme générique utilisé pour désigner les municipalités (telles que définies par la législation provinciale ou territoriale) et les zones considérées comme telles à des fins statistiques. L'agglomération urbaine correspond à la définition géographique de la région métropolitaine ou de l'agglomération pour le recensement.
[25] Excluding the institutional population. - Non compris la population dans les institutions.
[26] Data refers to "cantons" rather than to cities. Data are based on population estimates and projections. - Les données concernent les « cantons », et non les villes. Les données sont fondées sur des estimations et des projections démographiques.
[27] Data refer to Kingston Metropolitan Area. - Données pour la zone métropolitaine de Kingston.
[28] Data based on the 2010 Population Census. - Les données sont fondées sur le recensement de la population de 2010.
[29] Including armed forces stationed in the area. Postcensal estimates. - Y compris les militaires en garnison sur le territoire. Estimations post censitaires.
[30] City refers to a type of incorporated place in 49 states and the District of Columbia, that has an elected government and provides a range of government functions and services. Also included among the cities on this list is Urban

Honolulu, Hawaii Census Designated Place (CDP), for which the Census Bureau reports data under agreement with the State of Hawaii (instead of the combined city and county of Honolulu). - Par ville, on entend un lieu doté de la personnalité morale dans 49 États et dans le district de Columbia, qui a un gouvernement élu et fournit tout un ensemble de fonctions et de services publics. Sont également inclus Honolulu, lieu chargé du recensement pour Hawaii, pour lequel le Census Bureau établit les données en accord avec l'État de Hawaii (au lieu de la ville et du comté d'Honolulu).

[31] Excluding U.S. Armed Forces overseas and civilian U.S. citizens whose usual place of residence is outside the United States. - Non compris les militaires américains à l'étranger et les civils américains dont le lieu de résidence habituel est en dehors des États-Unis.

[32] Excluding inland water. - Exception faite des eaux intérieures.

[33] Including armed forces stationed in the area. - Y compris les militaires en garnison sur le territoire.

[34] Data refer to municipalities, which may contain an urban centre as well as rural areas. - Pour municipios qui peuvent comprendre un centre urbain et aussi une zone rurale.

[35] 'Metropolitan area' Grand Santiago. Data exclude the population of the cities of Puente Alto and San Bernardo. - 'Zone métropolitaine' Grand Santiago. Les données ne comprennent pas la population des villes de Puente Alto et de San Bernardo.

[36] Data are revised projections taking into consideration also the results of the 2005 census. - Les données sont des projections révisées tenant compte également des résultats du recensement de 2005.

[37] A dispute exists between the governments of Argentina and the United Kingdom of Great Britain and Northern Ireland concerning sovereignty over the Falkland Islands (Malvinas). - La souveraineté sur les îles Falkland (Malvinas) fait l'objet d'un différend entre le Gouvernement argentin et le Gouvernement du Royaume-Uni de Grande-Bretagne et d'Irlande du Nord.

[38] Figures for male and female may not add up to the total, since they do not include the category "Unknown". - La somme des chiffres indiqués pour les sexes masculin et féminin peut n'être pas égale au total parce qu'elle n'inclut pas la catégorie " inconnue ".

[39] The Metropolitan Area of Asunción is made up of Asunción and the 19 Central Department districts. - La zone métropolitaine d'Asunción est composée d'Asunción et de 19 districts du Département central.

[40] Data refer to the Province of Lima and the Constitutional Province of Callao. - Les données concernent la province de Lima et la province constitutionnelle de Callao.

[41] Data refer to national projections. Data refer to the department of Montevideo. - Les données se réfèrent aux projections nationales. Les données concernent le département de Montevideo.

[42] Excluding foreign diplomatic personnel and their dependants. Data based on the 2008 Population Census. - Non compris le personnel diplomatique étranger et les membres de leur famille les accompagnant. Données fondées sur le recensement de population de 2008.

[43] Data refer only to the population in urban areas of Beijing. - Les données ne concernent que la population des zones urbaines de Beijing.

[44] Inland waters include the reservoirs. - Les eaux intérieures comprennent les réservoirs.

[45] The urban agglomeration of Lefkosia is composed of Lefkosia municipality, Agios Dometios, Egkomi, Strovolos, Aglangia, Lakatameia, Anthoupoli, Latsia and Geri. - L'agglomération urbaine de Lefkosia est composée de la municipalité de Lefkosia et Agios Dometios, Egkomi, Strovolos, Aglangia, Lakatameia, Anthoupoli, Latsia et Geri.

[46] The urban agglomeration of Lemesos is composed of Lemesos municipality, Mesa Geitonia, Agios Athanasios, Germasogeia, Pano Polemidia, Ypsonas and Kato Polemidia. - L'agglomération de Lemesos comprend la municipalité du même nom, ainsi que Mesa Geitonia, Agios Athanasios, Germasogeia, Pano Polemidia, Ypsonas et Kato Polemidia.

[47] Including Kep. Seribu, North Jakarta, East Jakarta, South Jakarta, West Jakarta and Central Jakarta. - Y compris les îles Seribu, Jakarta-Nord, Jakarta-Est, Jakarta-Sud, Jakarta-Ouest et Jakarta-Centre.

[48] Data refer to "Baghdad Al-Jedeeda Nahia" - Les données concernent le district Al-Jadeeda de Bagdad (Baghdad Al-Jedeeda Nahiya).

[49] Designation and data provided by Israel. The position of the United Nations on the question of Jerusalem is contained in General Assembly resolution 181 (II) and subsequent resolutions of the General Assembly and the Security Council concerning this question. Including East Jerusalem. - Appelation de données fournies par Israel. La position des Nations Unies concernant la question de Jérusalem est décrite dans la resolution 181 (II) de l'Assemblée générale et résolutions ultérieures de l'Assemblée générale et du Conseil de sécurité sur cette question. Y compris Jérusalem-Est.

[50] Excluding diplomatic personnel outside the country and foreign military and civilian personnel and their dependants stationed in the area. - Non compris le personnel diplomatique hors du pays ni les militaires et agents civils étrangers en poste sur le territoire et les membres de leur famille les accompagnant.

[51] Land areas are based on the "Municipalities Area Statistics of Japan, 2015" published by the Geospatial Information Authority of Japan, Ministry of Land, Infrastructure, Transport and Tourism. - Les zones terrestres sont déterminées selon les statistiques relatives aux municipalités du Japon en 2015, publiées par l'Autorité japonaise d'information géospatiale du Ministère de l'aménagement foncier, des infrastructures, des transports et du tourisme.

[52] Excluding diplomatic personnel outside the country and foreign military and civilian personnel and their dependants stationed in the area. Data for Tokyo refer to 23 ku (wards) of Tokyo. - Non compris le personnel diplomatique hors du pays ni les militaires et agents civils étrangers en poste sur le territoire et les membres de leur famille les accompagnant. Données relatives à Tokyo concernant 23 ku (arrondissements de la ville).

[53] Data refer to resident population. - Les données concernent la population résidente.

[54] Data refer to annual average population. - Les données correspondent à la population annuelle moyenne.

[55] Estimates or projections based on the 2015 population census. - Estimations ou projections fondées sur les résultats du recensement de la population de 2015.

[56] Source: Living conditions of household survey, October 2011 to September 2012. - Source: Enquête sur les conditions de vie des ménages, octobre 2011 à septembre 2012.

[57] Estimates based on the adjusted results of the Population and Housing Census of 2010. - Les estimations sont fondée sur les résultats ajustées du recensement de la population et de l'habitat de 2010.

[58] Data refer to resident population which includes resident Maldivians and resident foreigners. - Les données concernent la population résidente, qui comprend les Maldiviens et les étrangers.

[59] Including population from all eight townships. - Y compris la population des huit municipalités.

[60] Data refer to registered population data from Royal Oman Police. - Les données portent sur la population enregistrée par la police royale de l'Oman.

[61] Land area includes inland water. - La zone terrestre comprend les eaux intérieures.

[62] Data refer to total population, which comprises Singapore residents and non-residents. Data exclude residents who have been away from Singapore for a continuous period of 12 months or longer as at the reference date. - Les données se rapportent à la population totale composé des résidents de Singapour et les non résidents. Non compris les résidents hors de Singapour pour une période ininterrompue de 12 mois ou plus avant de la date de référence.

[63] The land area of Singapore comprises the mainland and other islands. - La superficie terrestre de Singapour comprend l'île principale et les autres îles.

[64] The Population and Housing Census 2001 did not cover the whole area of the country due to the security problems; data refer to the 18 districts for which the census was completed only (in three districts it was not possible to conduct the census at all and in four districts it was partially conducted). - Le recensement de la population et du logement de 2001 n'a pas été réalisé sur la superficie totale du pays à cause de problèmes de sécurité; les données ne concernent que les 18 districts entièrement recensés (3 districts n'ont pas été recensés du tout, et 4 ont été recensés en partie).

[65] Designation and data provided by the State of Palestine. The position of the United Nations on the question of Jerusalem is contained in General Assembly resolution 181 (II) and subsequent resolutions of the General Assembly and the Security Council concerning this question. - Appellation de données fournies par l'État de Palestine. La position des Nations Unies concernant la question de Jérusalem est décrite dans la résolution 181 (II) de l'Assemblée générale et résolutions ultérieures de l'Assemblée générale et du Conseil de sécurité sur cette question.

[66] Data refer to urban area of municipality of Dili. - Les données se réfèrent à la zone urbaine de la municipalité de Dili.

[67] Data based on Address Based Population Registration System. - Les données sont basées sur le registre national de la population basé sur l'adresse.

[68] Population statistics are compiled from registers. - Les statistiques de la population sont compilées à partir des registres.

[69] Data include Anderlecht and Schaerbeek. - Les données comprennent Anderlecht et Schaerbeek.

[70] Excluding Faeroe Islands and Greenland shown separately, if available. - Non compris les Iles Féroé et le Groenland, qui font l'objet de rubriques distinctes, si disponible.

[71] Land area refers to built over area. - Partie du territoire désigne une zone bâtie.

[72] Urban Agglomeration refers to Tórshavn, Hoyvík, Argir and Hvítanes. - Agglomération urbaine fait référence à Tórshavn, Hoyvík, Argir et Hvitanes.
[73] Urban Agglomeration refers to Tórshavn, Hoyvík, Argir and Hvítanes. Land area refers to built over area. - Agglomération urbaine fait référence à Tórshavn, Hoyvík, Argir et Hvitanes. Partie du territoire désigne une zone bâtie.
[74] Excluding Åland Islands. - Non compris les Îles d'Åland.
[75] City proper refers to commune or municipality. - La ville proprement dite se rapporte à la commune ou à la municipalité.
[76] The city of Aix-en-Provence is part of the urban agglomeration of Marseille. - La ville d'Aix-en-Provence fait partie de l'agglomération urbaine de Marseille.
[77] The communes of Argenteuil, Boulogne-Billancourt and Montreuil are parts of the urban agglomeration of Paris. - Les communes de Argenteuil, Boulogne-Billancourt et Montreuil font partie de l'agglomération urbaine de Paris.
[78] Excluding military personnel, visitors and transients. - Non compris les militaires, ni les visiteurs et transients.
[79] Data refer to the Vatican City State. - Les données se rapportent à l'Etat de la Cité du Vatican.
[80] Data refer to registered resident population. - Les données concernent la population enregistrée résidente.
[81] Data refer to usual resident population. - Les données se réfèrent à la population résidente habituelle.
[82] Including civilian nationals temporarily outside the country. - Y compris les civils nationaux temporairement hors du pays.
[83] Figures for male and female population do not add up to the figure for total population, because they exclude 119 persons of unknown sex. - Les chiffres relatifs à la population masculine et féminine ne correspondent pas au chiffre de la population totale, parce que l'on en a exclu 119 personnes de sexe inconnu.
[84] City is defined as an administratively separated area entitled to civil (municipal) rights. - Une ville est définie comme une zone administrativement distincte dotée de droits municipaux.
[85] Surface area includes interior waters. - La superficie comprend les eaux intérieures.
[86] Excludes non-residents present in country at time of census (visitors, foreigners temporarily residing in country, etc.). - Exclue les non-résidents présents dans le pays au moment du recensement (visiteurs, étrangers résidant temporairement dans le pays, etc.).
[87] Excludes data for Kosovo and Metohia. - Sans les données pour le Kosovo et Metohie.
[88] Data refer to municipalities, which may contain an urban centre as well as rural areas. Data refer to registered resident population. - Pour municipios qui peuvent comprendre un centre urbain et aussi une zone rurale. Les données concernent la population enregistrée résidente.
[89] From 2014, urban refers to urban centers and areas under the influence of urban centers. - A partir de 2014, le territoire urbain inclut l'espace des centres urbains ainsi que l'espace sous influence des centres urbains.
[90] Excluding Channel Islands (Guernsey and Jersey) and Isle of Man, shown separately, if available. - Non compris les îles Anglo-Normandes (Guernesey et Jersey) et l'île de Man, qui font l'objet de rubriques distinctes, si disponible.
[91] Data refer to Greater Glasgow. - Les données concernent la région métropolitaine de Glasgow.
[92] Data refer to Greater London. - Les données concernent la région métropolitaine de London.
[93] Source: Regional Population by Age and Sex, Australia, 2018 released 29 August 2019 - Source : Statistiques australiennes relatives à la population régionale par âge et par sexe pour 2018, publiées le 29 août 2019.
[94] Because of rounding, totals are not in all cases the sum of the respective components. 1. Land area excludes inlet, inland water and oceanic areas. 2. A city is a territorial authority which is a distinct entity, is predominantly urban in character, has a minimum population of 50,000 and is a major centre of activity within its parent region. 3. Urban agglomerations refer to main urban areas that are centres with populations of 30,000 or more. Since 2011 Auckland includes Manukau city, North Shore city, and Waktakere city and Wellington urban area includes Lower Hutt. Napier-Hastings consist of two separate territorial authorities. Napier is a city, while Hastings is a district based on the New Zealand Standard Areas Classification. - Les chiffres étant arrondis, les totaux ne correspondent pas toujours rigoureusement à la somme des composants respectifs. 1. La superficie terrestre exclut les cours d'eau, les eaux intérieures et les zones océaniques. 2. Par « ville », on entend une autorité territoriale qui est une entité distincte, de caractère essentiellement urbain, dont la population s'élève à au moins 50 000 personnes et qui représente l'un des principaux centres d'activité de la région dans laquelle elle se trouve. 3. Par « agglomérations urbaines », on entend les grandes zones urbaines dont la population s'élève à au moins 30 000 personnes. Depuis 2011, Auckland comprend Manukau City, North Shore City et Waktakere city, tandis que la zone urbaine de Wellington comprend Lower Hutt. Napier-Hastings se compose de deux autorités territoriales distinctes. Ainsi, selon les règles de classification des territoires néo-zélandais, Napier est une ville et Hastings est un district.
[95] Data is based on mini-census taken in 2016. - Selon le mini-recensement de 2016.

Table 9 - *Demographic Yearbook 2019*

Table 9 presents live births and crude birth rates by urban/rural residence for as many years as possible between 2015 and 2019.

Description of variables: Live birth is defined as the complete expulsion or extraction from its mother of a product of conception, irrespective of the duration of pregnancy, which after such separation, breathes or shows any other evidence of life such as beating of the heart, pulsation of the umbilical cord, or definite movements of voluntary muscles, whether or not the umbilical cord has been cut or the placenta is attached; each product of such a birth is considered live-born[1].

Statistics on the number of live births are obtained from civil registers unless otherwise noted. For those countries or areas where civil registration statistics on live births are considered reliable the birth rates shown have been calculated on the basis of registered live births.

For certain countries, there is a discrepancy between the total number of live births shown in this table and those shown in subsequent tables for the same year. Usually this discrepancy arises because the total number of live births occurring in a given year is revised but not the remaining tabulations.

Rate computation: Crude birth rates are the annual number of live births per 1 000 mid-year population.

Rates by urban/rural residence are the annual number of live births, in the appropriate urban or rural category, per 1 000 corresponding mid-year population. Rates are calculated only for data considered complete, that is, coded with a "C" and for estimates and live births statistics for the 12 month period prior to the census date, coded with a "|". These rates are calculated by the Statistics Division of the United Nations based on the appropriate reference population (for example: total population, nationals only, etc.) if known and available. If the reference population is not known or unavailable, the total population is used to calculate the rates. Therefore, if the population that is used to calculate the rates is different from the correct reference population, the rates presented might under- or overstate the true situation in a country or area.

Rates presented in this table are limited to those countries or areas having a minimum number of 30 live births in a given year.

Reliability of data: Each country or area has been asked to indicate the estimated completeness of the live births recorded in its civil register. These national assessments are indicated by the quality codes "C" and "U" that appear in the first column of this table.

"C" indicates that the data are estimated to be virtually complete, that is, representing at least 90 per cent of the live births occurring each year, whereas "U" indicates that data are estimated to be incomplete, that is, representing less than 90 per cent of the live births occurring each year. A third code "..." indicates that no information was provided regarding completeness.

Data from civil registers that are reported as incomplete or of unknown completeness (coded "U" or "...") are considered unreliable. They appear in italics in this table and rates are not calculated for these data.

These quality codes apply only to data from civil registers. If data from other sources are presented, the symbol "|" is shown instead of the quality code. For more information about the quality of vital statistics data in general, and the information available on the basis of the completeness estimates in particular, see section 4.2 of the Technical Notes.

Limitations: Statistics on live births are subject to the same qualifications as have been set forth for vital statistics in general and birth statistics in particular as discussed in section 4 of the Technical Notes.

The reliability of data, an indication of which is described above, is an important factor in considering the limitations. In addition, some live births are tabulated by date of registration and not by date of occurrence; these have been indicated by a plus sign "+". Whenever the lag between the date of occurrence and date of registration is prolonged and, therefore, a large proportion of the live birth registrations are delayed, birth statistics for any given year may be seriously affected.

Another factor that limits international comparability is the practice of some countries or areas not to include in live birth statistics infants who were born alive but died before the registration of the birth or within the first 24 hours of life, thus underestimating the total number of life births. Statistics of this type are footnoted.

In addition, it should be noted that rates are affected also by the quality and limitations of the population estimates that are used in their computation. The problems of under-enumeration or over-enumeration and, to some extent, the differences in definition of total population have been discussed in section 3 of the Technical Notes dealing with population data in general, and specific information pertaining to individual countries or areas is given in the footnotes to table 3.

The rates estimated from the results of sample surveys are subject to possibilities of considerable error as a result of omissions in reporting of births, or as a result of erroneous reporting of births that occurred outside the reference period. However, rates estimated from sample surveys have the advantage of the availability of a built-in and strictly corresponding population base.

It should be emphasized that crude birth rates - like crude death, marriage and divorce rates - may be seriously affected by the age-sex structure of the populations to which they relate. Nevertheless, they do provide a simple measure of the level of and changes in fertility.

The urban/rural classification of birth may refer to the residence of mother or the place of delivery, according to the national practice and it is provided by each country or area. In addition, the comparability of data by urban/rural residence is affected by the national definition of urban and rural used in tabulating these data. It is assumed, in the absence of specific information to the contrary, that the definitions of urban and rural used in connection with the national population census were also used in the compilation of the vital statistics for each country or area. However, it cannot be ruled out that, for a given country or area, different definitions of urban and rural are used for the vital statistics data and the population census data respectively. When known, the definitions of urban used in national population census are presented at the end of the technical notes to table 6. As discussed in detail in the technical notes to table 6, these definitions vary considerably from one area or country to another. Urban/rural differentials in vital rates may also be affected by whether the vital events have been tabulated in terms of place of occurrence or place of usual residence. This problem is discussed in more detail in section 4.1.4.1 of the Technical notes.

Earlier data: Live births have been shown in each issue of the *Demographic Yearbook*. Information on the years and specific topics covered is presented in the Historical Index.

NOTES

[1] *Principles and Recommendations for a Vital Statistics System Revision 3,* Sales No. E.13.XVII.10, United Nations, New York, 2014.

Tableau 9 – *Annuaire démographique 2019*

Le tableau 9 présente des données sur les naissances vivantes et les taux bruts de natalité selon le lieu de résidence (zone urbaine ou rurale) pour le plus grand nombre d'années possible entre 2015 et 2019.

Description des variables : La naissance vivante est l'expulsion ou l'extraction complète du corps de la mère, indépendamment de la durée de gestation, d'un produit de la conception qui, après cette séparation, respire ou manifeste tout autre signe de vie, tel que battement de cœur, pulsation du cordon ombilical ou contraction effective d'un muscle soumis à l'action de la volonté, que le cordon ombilical ait été coupé ou non et que le placenta soit ou non demeuré attaché ; tout produit d'une telle naissance est considéré comme « enfant né vivant »[1].

Sauf indication contraire, les statistiques relatives au nombre de naissances vivantes sont établies sur la base des registres de l'état civil. Pour les pays ou zones où les statistiques obtenues auprès des services de l'état civil sont jugées sûres, les taux de natalité indiqués ont été calculés par la Division de statistique de l'ONU d'après les naissances vivantes enregistrées.

Pour quelques pays il y a une discordance entre le nombre total des naissances présenté dans ce tableau et ceux présentés après pour la même année. Habituellement ces différences apparaissent lorsque le nombre total des naissances pour une certaine année a été révisé alors que les autres tabulations ne l'ont pas été.

Calcul des taux : Les taux bruts de natalité représentent le nombre annuel de naissances vivantes pour 1 000 habitants au milieu de l'année.

Les taux selon le lieu de résidence (zone urbaine ou rurale) représentent le nombre annuel de naissances vivantes, classées selon la catégorie urbaine ou rurale appropriée pour 1 000 habitants au milieu de l'année. Les taux ont été calculés seulement pour les données considérées complètes, c'est-à-dire celles associées au code « C », ainsi que pour les estimations et les statistiques des naissances vivantes dans la periode des douze mois précédante la date de recensement associées au code « | ». Ces taux sont calculés par la division de statistique des Nations Unies sur la base de la population de référence adéquate (par exemple : population totale, nationaux seulement, etc.) si connue et disponible. Si la population de référence n'est pas connue ou n'est pas disponible, la population totale est utilisée pour calculer les taux. Par conséquent, si la population utilisée pour calculer les taux est différente de la population de référence adéquate, les taux présentés sont susceptibles de sous ou sur estimer la situation réelle d'un pays ou d'un territoire.

Les taux présentés dans ce tableau se rapportent seulement aux pays ou zones où l'on a enregistré un nombre minimal de 30 naissances vivantes au cours d'une année donnée.

Fiabilité des données : Il a été demandé à chaque pays ou zone d'indiquer le degré estimatif de complétude des données sur les naissances vivantes figurant dans ses registres d'état civil. Ces évaluations nationales sont signalées par les codes de qualité "C" et "U" qui apparaissent dans la deuxième colonne du tableau.

La lettre "C" indique que les données sont jugées à peu près complètes, c'est-à-dire qu'elles représentent au moins 90 p. 100 des naissances vivantes survenues chaque année ; la lettre "U" signifie que les données sont jugées incomplètes, c'est-à-dire qu'elles représentent moins de 90 p. 100 des naissances vivantes survenues chaque année. Un troisième code, "...", indique qu'aucun renseignement n'a été communiqué quant à la complétude des données.

Les données provenant des registres de l'état civil qui sont déclarées incomplètes ou dont le degré de complétude n'est pas connu (code "U" ou "...") sont jugées douteuses. Elles apparaissent en italique dans le tableau. Les taux pour ces données ne sont pas calculés.

Les codes de qualité ne s'appliquent qu'aux données provenant des registres de l'état civil. Si l'on présente des données autres que celles de l'état civil, le signe "|" est utilisé à la place du code de qualité. Pour plus de précisions sur la qualité des données reposant sur les statistiques de l'état civil en général et les estimations de complétude en particulier, voir la section 4.2 des Notes techniques.

Insuffisance des données : Les statistiques concernant les naissances vivantes appellent toutes les réserves qui ont été formulées à propos des statistiques de l'état civil en général et des statistiques des naissances en particulier (voir la section 4 des Notes techniques).

La fiabilité des données, au sujet de laquelle des indications ont été fournies plus haut, est un facteur important. Il faut également tenir compte du fait que, dans certains cas, les données relatives aux naissances vivantes sont exploitées selon la date de l'enregistrement et non selon la date de l'événement ; ces cas ont été signalés par le signe '+'. Chaque fois que le décalage entre l'événement et son enregistrement est grand et qu'une forte proportion des naissances vivantes fait l'objet d'un enregistrement tardif, les statistiques des naissances vivantes pour une année donnée peuvent être considérablement faussées.

Un autre facteur qui nuit à la comparabilité internationale est la pratique de certains pays ou zones qui consiste à ne pas inclure dans les statistiques des naissances vivantes les enfants nés vivants mais décédés avant l'enregistrement de leur naissance ou dans les 24 heures qui ont suivi la naissance, pratique qui conduit à sous-estimer le nombre total de naissances vivantes. Lorsque ce facteur a joué, cela a été signalé en note à la fin du tableau.

La qualité et les limitations des estimations concernant la population ont également une incidence sur le calcul des taux. Les problèmes liés au sur-dénombrement ou au sous-dénombrement et, dans une certaine mesure, aux différences dans la définition de la population totale ont été abordés à la section 3 des Notes techniques relative aux données sur la population en général et des précisions sur certains pays ou zones sont données dans les notes se rapportant au tableau 3.

Les taux estimatifs fondés sur les résultats d'enquêtes par sondage comportent des possibilités d'erreurs considérables dues soit à des omissions dans les déclarations, soit au fait que l'on a déclaré à tort des naissances survenues en réalité hors de la période considérée. Toutefois, les taux estimatifs fondés sur les résultats d'enquêtes par sondage présentent un gros avantage : le chiffre de population utilisé comme base est, par définition, rigoureusement correspondant.

Il faut souligner que les taux bruts de natalité, de même que les taux bruts de mortalité, de nuptialité et de divortialité, peuvent varier très sensiblement selon la structure par âge et par sexe de la population à laquelle ils se rapportent. Ils offrent néanmoins un moyen simple de mesurer le niveau et l'évolution de la natalité.

La classification des naissances selon le lieu de résidence (zone urbaine ou rurale) peut se rapporter au lieu de résidence de la mère ou au lieu d'occurrence et correspond à celle indiquée par chaque pays ou zone. En outre, la comparabilité des données selon le lieu de résidence (zone urbaine ou rurale) peut être limitée par les définitions nationales des termes « urbain » et « rural » utilisées pour la mise en tableaux de ces données. En l'absence d'indications contraires, on a supposé que les mêmes définitions avaient servi pour le recensement national de la population et pour l'établissement des statistiques de l'état civil pour chaque pays ou zone. Toutefois, il n'est pas exclu que, pour une zone ou un pays donné, des définitions différentes aient été retenues. Les définitions du terme « urbain » utilisées pour les recensements nationaux de population ont été présentées à la fin des notes techniques du tableau 6 lorsqu'elles étaient connues. Comme on l'a précisé dans les notes techniques relatives au tableau 6, ces définitions varient considérablement d'un pays ou d'une zone à l'autre. La différence entre ces taux pour les zones urbaines et rurales pourra aussi être faussée selon que les faits d'état civil auront été classés d'après le lieu de l'événement ou le lieu de résidence habituel. Ce problème est examiné plus en détail à la section 4.1.4.1 des Notes techniques.

Données publiées antérieurement : Les différentes éditions de l'*Annuaire démographique* contiennent des données sur les naissances vivantes. Pour plus de précisions concernant les années et les sujets pour lesquels des données ont été publiées, se reporter à l'index historique.

NOTES

[1] *Principes et recommandations pour un système de statistique de l'état civil, troisième révision,* numéro de vente : E.13.XVII.10, publication des Nations Unies, New York, 2014.

9. Live births and crude birth rates, by urban/rural residence: 2015 - 2019
Naissances vivantes et taux bruts de natalité selon la résidence, urbaine/rurale : 2015 - 2019

Continent, country or area, and urban/rural residence Continent, pays ou zone et résidence, urbaine/rurale	Code[a]	Number - Nombre					Rate - Taux				
		2015	2016	2017	2018	2019	2015	2016	2017	2018	2019
AFRICA - AFRIQUE											
Algeria - Algérie[1]											
Total	C	1 040 285	1 066 823	1 059 514	...	...	26.0	26.1	25.4	...	...
Botswana[2]											
Total	U	*46 765*	*49 984*	...	...	...	...	...	...	...	...
Total	C	...	...	43 290	54 023	...	...	...	19.1	23.5	...
Burundi[3]											
Total	+U	*266 820*	...	...	...	...	...	...	...	...	...
Cabo Verde[4]											
Total	+C	*9 740	*9 907	*9 831	*9 231	...	*18.6	*18.6	*18.3	*17.0	...
Côte d'Ivoire											
Total	+U	*626 783*	*659 247*	*619 181*	*635 924*	...	...	...	...	...	...
Egypt - Égypte											
Total	+C	2 685 276	2 600 173	2 557 440	...	...	30.2	28.6	26.9	...	...
Urban - Urbaine	+C	1 224 729	1 241 469	1 292 661	...	...	32.2	31.9	32.0	...	...
Rural - Rurale	+C	1 460 547	1 358 704	1 264 779	...	...	28.7	26.1	23.1	...	...
Eswatini[5]											
Total	U	...	*28 556*	*26 915*	*23 174*	...	...	...	...	...	...
Kenya											
Total	+U	*950 224*	*948 351*	*923 487*	*1 138 654*	*1 178 260*	...	...	...	...	...
Lesotho											
Total	+U	*10 800*[6]	*9 655*	*9 463*	*7 902*	*7 515*	...	...	...	...	...
Malawi[7]											
Total	I	...	...	...	576 525	...	...	...	...	32.8	...
Urban - Urbaine	I	...	...	...	84 639	...	...	...	...	30.1	...
Rural - Rurale	I	...	...	...	491 886	...	...	...	...	33.4	...
Mauritius - Maurice[8]											
Total	+C	12 640	12 948	13 385	12 980	12 846	10.0	10.2	10.6	10.3	10.1
Urban - Urbaine	+C	5 150	5 302	5 303	5 362	5 155	10.0	10.3	10.3	10.4	10.1
Rural - Rurale	+C	7 490	7 646	8 082	7 618	7 691	10.1	10.2	10.8	10.1	10.2
Mayotte											
Total	C	8 997	9 496	9 762	9 590	...	38.3	38.9	38.2	36.1	...
Mozambique[9]											
Total	U	...	...	...	*1 086 425*	*1 111 038*	...	...	...	...	...
Niger[10]											
Total	+U	*320 643*	*315 317*	...	...	...	...	...	...	...	...
Reunion - Réunion[11]											
Total	C	14 011	13 742	13 708	13 364	...	16.4	16.0	15.9	15.5	...
Urban - Urbaine	C	...	...	13 225	...	...	...	...	...	...	...
Rural - Rurale	C	...	...	483	...	...	...	...	...	...	...
Saint Helena ex. dep. - Sainte-Hélène sans dép.											
Total	C	40	35	36	26	31	8.9	7.5	7.9	...	6.9
Sao Tome and Principe - Sao Tomé-et-Principe											
Total	C	5 022	5 105	5 190	...	...	26.5	26.4	26.3	...	...
Seychelles											
Total	+C	1 592	1 645	1 651	1 650	1 605	17.0	17.4	17.2	17.1	16.4
Sierra Leone											
Total	+U	*353 187*	...	...	...	...	...	...	...	...	...
South Africa - Afrique du Sud											
Total	U	*966 162*	...	...	...	...	...	...	...	...	...
Total	C	...	906 375	913 499	...	...	...	16.1	16.0	...	...
Tunisia - Tunisie											
Total	C	222 534	219 441	208 000	...	...	19.9	19.4	18.2	...	...
Zambia - Zambie[12]											
Total	U	...	...	*104 816*	...	...	...	...	...	...	...
AMERICA, NORTH - AMÉRIQUE DU NORD											
Anguilla											
Total	+C	165	135	145	...	130	11.2	9.0	...	...	8.3
Antigua and Barbuda - Antigua-et-Barbuda											
Total	+C	1 159	1 063	1 108	1 015	...	12.8	11.5	11.8	10.7	...

9. Live births and crude birth rates, by urban/rural residence: 2015 - 2019
Naissances vivantes et taux bruts de natalité selon la résidence, urbaine/rurale : 2015 - 2019 (continued - suite)

Continent, country or area, and urban/rural residence / Continent, pays ou zone et résidence, urbaine/rurale	Code[a]	Number - Nombre 2015	2016	2017	2018	2019	Rate - Taux 2015	2016	2017	2018	2019
AMERICA, NORTH - AMÉRIQUE DU NORD											
Aruba											
Total	C	1 244	1 259	1 202	1 028	1 029	11.4	11.4	10.8	9.2	9.2
Bahamas											
Total	+U	*4 253	*4 093	*4 017	...	...	...	...	...	...	...
Belize											
Total	U	*7 459*	*7 226*	*7 252*	*7 775*	...	...	...	...	...	...
Urban - Urbaine[13]	U	*3 075*	*2 863*	...	...	...	...	...	...	...	...
Rural - Rurale[13]	U	*4 353*	*4 301*	...	...	...	...	...	...	...	...
Bermuda - Bermudes[14]											
Total	C	583	591	576	530	...	9.4	9.3	9.0	8.3	...
British Virgin Islands - Îles Vierges britanniques											
Total	C	266	269	248	...	...	9.1	...	...	...	...
Canada[15]											
Total	C	382 392	383 102	376 291	372 329	...	10.7	10.6	10.3	10.0	...
Cayman Islands - Îles Caïmanes											
Total	C	649	660	625	640	646	11.0	10.8	9.9	9.9	9.5
Costa Rica											
Total	C	71 819	70 004	68 816	68 479	*64 287	14.9	14.3	13.9	13.7	*12.7
Urban - Urbaine	C	49 744	48 392	47 273	46 647	*43 944	14.2	13.6	13.2	12.8	*12.0
Rural - Rurale	C	22 075	21 612	21 543	21 832	*20 343	16.7	16.2	15.9	15.9	*14.6
Cuba											
Total	C	125 064	116 872	114 971	116 333	...	11.1	10.4	10.2	10.4	...
Urban - Urbaine	C	99 434	93 565	93 370	94 825	...	11.5	10.8	10.8	11.0	...
Rural - Rurale	C	25 630	23 307	21 601	21 508	...	9.9	9.0	8.3	8.3	...
Curaçao											
Total	C	1 877	1 789	1 548	1 680	1 583	11.9	11.2	9.7	10.5	10.1
Dominica - Dominique											
Total	+C	861	796	647	...	...	12.1	11.2	9.6	...	...
Dominican Republic - République dominicaine											
Total	U	*167 178*	*158 252*	*165 550*	*171 249*	*167 686*	...	...	...	...	...
Urban - Urbaine[16]	U	*124 945*	...	...	...	...	...	...	...	...	...
Rural - Rurale[16]	U	*19 766*	...	...	...	...	...	...	...	...	...
El Salvador[17]											
Total	C	109 617	...	...	...	...	17.0	...	...	...	...
Greenland - Groenland											
Total	C	854	830	853	819	849	15.2	14.8	15.2	14.6	15.1
Urban - Urbaine	C	719	699	734	699	747	14.9	14.4	15.1	14.4	15.3
Rural - Rurale	C	135	131	119	120	102	17.2	16.9	15.6	16.1	14.0
Grenada - Grenade											
Total	+C	1 694	1 577	1 398	...	...	15.4	14.2	12.5	...	...
Guadeloupe[11]											
Total	C	5 368	5 276	4 626	4 249	...	13.5	13.4	11.8	10.1	...
Guatemala											
Total	C	391 425	390 382	381 664	383 263	...	24.2	23.6	22.5	22.1	...
Jamaica - Jamaïque											
Total	C	37 900	36 160	34 423	34 209	34 632	13.9	13.3	12.6	12.5	12.7
Martinique[11]											
Total	C	3 972	3 782	3 640	...	...	10.5	10.0	9.8	...	...
Urban - Urbaine	C	...	...	3 080	...	...	...	...	...	...	...
Rural - Rurale	C	...	...	560	...	...	...	...	...	...	...
Mexico - Mexique											
Total	C	2 096 274[18]	2 028 358[18]	2 000 591[18]	*2 162 535	...	17.3	16.5	16.1	*17.3	...
Urban - Urbaine[19]	C	1 540 464	1 476 247	1 468 199	...	...	17.6	16.6	16.4	...	...
Rural - Rurale[19]	C	442 539	440 219	438 619	...	...	13.3	13.1	12.9	...	...
Montserrat											
Total	C	48	46	55	45	47	9.6	9.1	...	9.7	...
Nicaragua											
Total	+U	...	*137 772*	*136 724*	*136 361*	...	...	...	...	...	...
Urban - Urbaine	+U	...	*71 668*	*70 080*	*70 061*	...	...	...	...	...	...
Rural - Rurale	+U	...	*66 104*	*66 644*	*66 300*	...	...	...	...	...	...
Panama											
Total	C	75 901	75 184	76 166	76 863	*72 256	19.1	18.6	18.6	18.5	*17.1
Urban - Urbaine	C	48 960	47 818	47 837	47 859	...	18.1	17.2	16.9	16.5	...
Rural - Rurale	C	26 941	27 366	28 329	29 004	...	21.3	21.6	22.5	23.1	...

9. Live births and crude birth rates, by urban/rural residence: 2015 - 2019
Naissances vivantes et taux bruts de natalité selon la résidence, urbaine/rurale : 2015 - 2019 (continued - suite)

Continent, country or area, and urban/rural residence Continent, pays ou zone et résidence, urbaine/rurale	Co-de[a]	Number - Nombre					Rate - Taux				
		2015	2016	2017	2018	2019	2015	2016	2017	2018	2019
AMERICA, NORTH - AMÉRIQUE DU NORD											
Puerto Rico - Porto Rico											
Total	C	31 241	28 344	24 395	21 492	20 409	9.0	8.3	7.3	6.7	6.4
Urban - Urbaine	C	18 995	18 210	16 368	13 946	13 354	...	...	...	...	...
Rural - Rurale	C	12 246	10 134	8 027	7 546	7 055	...	...	...	...	...
Saint Barthélemy - Saint-Barthélemy											
Total	C	...	...	72	...	...	...	...	...	...	...
Saint Kitts and Nevis - Saint-Kitts-et-Nevis											
Total	+C	632	676	648	593	594	...	...	...	...	...
Saint Pierre and Miquelon - Saint Pierre-et-Miquelon											
Total	C	...	...	30	...	...	...	...	4.8	...	...
Saint Vincent and the Grenadines - Saint-Vincent-et-les Grenadines											
Total	C	1 813	1 729	1 539	...	...	16.4	15.7	13.9	...	...
Saint-Martin (French part) - Saint-Martin (partie française)											
Total	C	...	...	500	...	...	...	...	14.0	...	...
Sint Maarten (Dutch part) - Saint-Martin (partie néerlandaise)											
Total	+C	500	458	363	...	...	13.1	11.6	9.0	...	...
Trinidad and Tobago - Trinité-et-Tobago											
Total	C	*18 062	*18 142[20]	*16 569[20]	*16 217[20]	*16 058[21]	*13.4	*13.4	*12.2	*11.9	*11.8
Turks and Caicos Islands - Îles Turques et Caïques											
Total	C	437	518	555	454	*487	11.9	13.7	13.9	11.0	*11.3
United States of America - États-Unis d'Amérique											
Total	C	3 978 497	3 945 875	3 855 500	3 791 712	...	12.4	12.2	11.9	11.6	...
United States Virgin Islands - Îles Vierges américaines[22]											
Total	C	1 325	1 187	...	*1 197	...	12.8	11.0	...	...	...
AMERICA, SOUTH - AMÉRIQUE DU SUD											
Argentina - Argentine											
Total	C	770 040	728 035	704 609	685 394	...	17.9	16.7	16.0	15.4	...
Bolivia (Plurinational State of) - Bolivie (État plurinational de)[23]											
Total	U	*209 154*	*199 574*	*197 348*	**178 710*	...	...	...	...	...	...
Brazil - Brésil											
Total	C	3 058 783	2 903 933	2 962 815	...	...	15.0	14.1	14.3	...	...
Chile - Chili											
Total	C	244 670	231 749	219 186	*221 724	...	13.6	12.8	11.9	*11.8	...
Urban - Urbaine	C	222 438	211 920	203 806	...	...	14.1	13.3	12.6	...	...
Rural - Rurale	C	22 232	19 829	15 380	...	...	10.2	9.1	7.0	...	...
Colombia - Colombie											
Total	U	*660 999*	*647 521*	*656 704*	*649 115*	**638 516*	...	...	...	...	...
Urban - Urbaine[16]	U	*526 365*	*514 829*	*515 706*	*504 539*	**493 196*	...	...	...	...	...
Rural - Rurale[16]	U	*134 215*	*132 183*	*139 651*	*140 485*	**133 739*	...	...	...	...	...
Ecuador - Équateur[24]											
Total	U	*283 313*	*272 090*	*291 397*	**293 139*	...	...	...	...	...	...
Urban - Urbaine	U	*222 575*	*212 673*	*225 165*	**226 685*	...	...	...	...	...	...
Rural - Rurale	U	*60 738*	*59 417*	*66 232*	**66 454*	...	...	...	...	...	...
French Guiana - Guyane française[11]											
Total	C	6 806	7 270	8 057	...	...	26.7	27.7	29.4	...	...
Guyana[25]											
Total	+U	*16 202*	*14 907*	*13 608*	...	...	...	...	...	...	...

9. Live births and crude birth rates, by urban/rural residence: 2015 - 2019
Naissances vivantes et taux bruts de natalité selon la résidence, urbaine/rurale : 2015 - 2019 (continued - suite)

Continent, country or area, and urban/rural residence Continent, pays ou zone et résidence, urbaine/rurale	Co-de[a]	Number - Nombre					Rate - Taux				
		2015	2016	2017	2018	2019	2015	2016	2017	2018	2019
AMERICA, SOUTH - AMÉRIQUE DU SUD											
Paraguay											
Total	+U	132 241	128 117	129 903	123 187	...	...	...	...	...	...
Peru - Pérou[26]											
Total	+U	529 029	522 269	511 867	511 960	*485 269[27]	...	...	...	...	...
Urban - Urbaine	+U	384 757	...	...	...	...	...	...	...	...	...
Rural - Rurale	+U	144 272	...	...	...	...	...	...	...	...	...
Suriname											
Total	C	10 148	9 910	9 785	9 809	...	17.9	17.2	16.8	16.6	...
Urban - Urbaine	C	6 683	6 561	6 471	6 335	...	...	...	16.7	16.2	...
Rural - Rurale	C	3 465	3 349	3 314	3 474	...	...	...	16.8	17.5	...
Uruguay											
Total	C	48 926	47 058	43 036	40 139	...	14.1	13.5	12.3	11.4	...
Venezuela (Bolivarian Republic of) - Venezuela (République bolivarienne du)											
Total	U	600 875	642 644	579 349	...	...	...	...	...	...	...
ASIA - ASIE											
Armenia - Arménie											
Total	C	41 763	40 592	37 700	36 574	36 041	13.9	13.6	12.7	12.3	12.2
Urban - Urbaine	C	27 124	26 474	24 611	24 259	...	14.2	13.9	13.0	12.8	...
Rural - Rurale	C	14 639	14 118	13 089	12 315	...	13.4	13.0	12.1	11.5	...
Azerbaijan - Azerbaïdjan[28]											
Total	+C	166 210	159 464	144 041	138 982	141 179	17.2	16.3	14.6	14.0	14.1
Urban - Urbaine	+C	81 149	76 954	69 479	67 362	...	15.8	14.9	13.3	12.8	...
Rural - Rurale	+C	85 061	82 510	74 562	71 620	...	18.8	18.0	16.1	15.3	...
Bahrain - Bahreïn[29]											
Total	C	20 983	20 714	20 581	19 740	20 245	15.3	14.5	13.7	13.1	13.6
Bangladesh											
Total	U	2 987 320	3 006 960	3 009 950	3 012 180	3 013 650	...	...	...	...	...
Urban - Urbaine	U	754 215	763 301	791 637	792 224	792 610	...	...	...	...	...
Rural - Rurale	U	2 233 105	2 243 659	2 218 313	2 219 956	2 221 040	...	...	...	...	...
Bhutan - Bhoutan[30]											
Total	|	...	...	11 239	...	...	...	...	15.5	...	...
Brunei Darussalam - Brunéi Darussalam											
Total	+C	6 699	6 437	6 452	6 199	...	16.2	15.4	15.0	14.0	...
China - Chine[31]											
Total	|	16 550 000	17 860 000	17 230 000	15 230 000	14 650 000	12.1	13.0	12.4	10.9	10.5
China, Hong Kong SAR - Chine, Hong Kong RAS											
Total	C	59 878	60 856	56 548	53 716	52 856	8.2	8.3	7.7	7.2	7.0
China, Macao SAR - Chine, Macao RAS											
Total	C	7 055	7 146	6 529	5 925	5 979	11.0	11.0	10.1	9.0	8.9
Cyprus - Chypre[32]											
Total	C	9 170	9 455	9 229	9 329	*9 625	10.8	11.1	10.7	10.7	*11.0
Georgia - Géorgie											
Total	C	59 249	56 569	53 293	51 138	48 296	15.9	15.2	14.3	13.7	13.0
Urban - Urbaine	C	33 898	32 227	...	...	...	15.9	15.1	...	...	...
Rural - Rurale	C	25 351	24 342	...	...	...	15.9	15.3	...	...	...
India - Inde[33]											
Total	|	...	...	...	...	...	20.8	20.4	20.2	20.0	...
Urban - Urbaine	|	...	...	...	...	...	17.3	17.0	16.8	16.7	...
Rural - Rurale	|	...	...	...	...	...	22.4	22.1	21.8	21.6	...
Iran (Islamic Republic of) - Iran (République islamique d')[34]											
Total	+C	1 570 219	1 528 053	1 487 913	1 366 519	...	19.9	19.1	18.4	16.6	...
Urban - Urbaine	+C	1 208 142	1 176 032	1 143 558	1 047 925	...	21.1	19.9	19.0	17.1	...
Rural - Rurale	+C	362 077	352 021	344 355	318 594	...	16.9	16.9	16.6	15.4	...
Iraq											
Total	U	...	777 823	803 010	...	...	...	...	...	...	...

9. Live births and crude birth rates, by urban/rural residence: 2015 - 2019
Naissances vivantes et taux bruts de natalité selon la résidence, urbaine/rurale : 2015 - 2019 (continued - suite)

Continent, country or area, and urban/rural residence — Continent, pays ou zone et résidence, urbaine/rurale	Code[a]	Number - Nombre					Rate - Taux				
		2015	2016	2017	2018	2019	2015	2016	2017	2018	2019
ASIA - ASIE											
Israel - Israël[35]											
Total	C	178 723	181 405	183 648	184 370	*181 709	21.3	21.2	21.1	20.8	*20.1
Urban - Urbaine	C	162 225	164 561	167 264	168 358	...	21.2	21.1	21.0	20.7	...
Rural - Rurale	C	16 498	16 844	16 384	16 012	...	22.4	22.5	21.5	20.8	...
Japan - Japon[36]											
Total	C	1 005 677[16]	976 978[16]	946 065[16]	918 400[16]	*865 234	7.9	7.7	7.5	7.3	*6.9
Urban - Urbaine[37]	C	928 962	902 855	875 127	850 041	...	...	...	...	...	...
Rural - Rurale[37]	C	76 662	74 058	70 887	68 320	...	...	...	...	...	...
Jordan - Jordanie[38]											
Total	C	198 018	197 789	211 441	...	...	20.7	20.2	21.0	...	...
Kazakhstan											
Total	C	398 458	400 694	390 262	397 799	402 310	22.7	22.5	21.6	21.8	21.7
Urban - Urbaine	C	225 808	229 731	226 847	235 014	239 496	22.7	22.6	21.9	22.2	22.1
Rural - Rurale	C	172 650	170 963	163 415	162 785	162 814	22.7	22.3	21.2	21.2	21.2
Kuwait - Koweït											
Total	C	59 271	58 797	59 172	56 121	...	14.9	14.4	14.7	13.6	...
Kyrgyzstan - Kirghizstan											
Total	C	163 452	158 160	153 620	171 149	...	27.4	26.0	24.8	27.1	...
Urban - Urbaine	C	52 477	51 610	52 829	62 046	...	26.1	25.2	25.2	28.9	...
Rural - Rurale	C	110 975	106 550	100 791	109 103	...	28.1	26.5	24.6	26.1	...
Lao People's Democratic Republic - République démocratique populaire lao[39]											
Total	I	125 614	...	...	...	...	18.8	...	...	...	...
Urban - Urbaine	I	35 443	...	...	...	...	...	...	...	...	...
Rural - Rurale	I	90 171	...	...	...	...	...	...	...	...	...
Malaysia - Malaisie											
Total	C	521 136	508 203	508 685	501 945	...	16.7	16.1	15.9	15.5	...
Urban - Urbaine	C	350 677	342 253	337 792	331 726	...	15.1	14.5	14.0	13.5	...
Rural - Rurale	C	170 459	165 950	170 893	170 219	...	21.3	20.9	21.5	21.6	...
Maldives[40]											
Total	C	6 986	6 756	6 723	...	...	20.3	19.3	18.8	...	...
Urban - Urbaine[16]	C	2 404	2 431	875	...	...	18.0	17.6	6.1	...	...
Rural - Rurale[16]	C	4 211	3 996	5 008	...	...	20.0	18.8	23.4	...	...
Mongolia - Mongolie											
Total	+C	82 130	79 920	75 321	78 444	79 580	27.1	25.9	23.9	24.5	24.4
Urban - Urbaine	+C	60 861	55 161	51 912	52 487	52 915	29.8	26.0	24.3	24.2	23.7
Rural - Rurale	+C	21 269	24 759	23 409	25 957	26 665	21.6	25.6	23.2	25.1	25.7
Myanmar[41]											
Total	+U	*739 152*	*765 844*	*787 172*	...	...	...	...	...	...	...
Urban - Urbaine	+U	*233 206*	*250 564*	*241 200*	...	...	...	...	...	...	...
Rural - Rurale	+U	*505 946*	*515 280*	*545 972*	...	...	...	...	...	...	...
Oman											
Total[42]	U	*86 286*	*88 346*	...	...	...	...	...	...	...	...
Total	C	...	...	90 371	89 071	86 819	...	...	19.8	19.4	18.8
Philippines											
Total	C	1 744 767	1 731 289	1 700 618	1 668 120	...	17.3	16.9	16.3	15.8	...
Qatar											
Total	C	26 622	26 816	27 906	28 069	28 412	10.9	10.2	10.2	10.2	10.2
Urban - Urbaine	C	26 622	26 816	27 906	28 069	28 412	10.9	10.2	10.2	10.2	10.2
Republic of Korea - République de Corée[43]											
Total	C	438 420	406 243	357 771	326 822	...	8.6	7.9	7.0	6.4	...
Urban - Urbaine	C	367 143	338 973	296 550	270 777	...	8.8	8.2	7.1	6.5	...
Rural - Rurale	C	71 277	67 270	61 221	56 045	...	7.5	7.1	6.4	5.8	...
Saudi Arabia - Arabie saoudite[44]											
Total	I	449 149[45]	447 040[45]	488 130	...	...	14.5	14.1	15.0	...	...
Singapore - Singapour											
Total	C	42 185	41 251	39 615	39 039	39 279	10.8	10.5	10.0	9.8	9.8
Sri Lanka											
Total	+C	336 097	*331 073	*326 052	*328 112	*319 010	16.0	*15.6	*15.2	*15.1	*14.6
Urban - Urbaine	+C	236 537	...	...	...	...	...	...	...	...	...
Rural - Rurale[46]	+C	99 560	...	...	...	...	...	...	...	...	...

9. Live births and crude birth rates, by urban/rural residence: 2015 - 2019
Naissances vivantes et taux bruts de natalité selon la résidence, urbaine/rurale : 2015 - 2019 (continued - suite)

Continent, country or area, and urban/rural residence Continent, pays ou zone et résidence, urbaine/rurale	Code[a]	Number - Nombre 2015	2016	2017	2018	2019	Rate - Taux 2015	2016	2017	2018	2019
ASIA - ASIE											
State of Palestine - État de Palestine[47]											
Total	U	*133 185*	*138 238*	*140 441*	*141 407*	...	...	...	...	...	...
Tajikistan - Tadjikistan[48]											
Total	U	*237 541*	*230 044*	*224 057*	*231 020*	...	...	...	...	...	...
Urban - Urbaine	U	*53 034*	*51 042*	*51 561*	*53 139*	...	...	...	...	...	...
Rural - Rurale	U	*184 507*	*179 002*	*172 496*	*177 881*	...	...	...	...	...	...
Thailand - Thaïlande											
Total	+U	*738 930*	*666 207*[49]	*656 570*[49]	*628 450*[49]	**596 736*	...	...	...	...	...
Timor-Leste[50]											
Total	I	36 202	...	...	...	...	30.2	...	...	...	...
Turkey - Turquie											
Total	C	1 335 564	1 313 615	1 295 784	1 248 847	*1 183 652	17.0	16.5	16.1	15.4	*14.4
United Arab Emirates - Émirats arabes unis											
Total[51]	...	*97 328*	*98 299*	...	...	...	...	...	...	...	...
Total	C	...	...	97 738	95 309	...	...	...	10.5	10.2	...
Uzbekistan - Ouzbékistan											
Total	+C	734 141	726 170	715 519	768 520	814 960	23.5	22.8	22.1	23.3	24.5
Urban - Urbaine	+C	325 660	332 035	325 152	353 257	...	20.5	20.6	19.8	21.2	...
Rural - Rurale	+C	408 481	394 135	390 367	415 263	...	26.5	25.1	24.4	25.5	...
Yemen - Yémen[52]											
Total	U	...	*575 556*	*645 833*	...	...	...	...	...	...	...
EUROPE											
Åland Islands - Îles d'Åland											
Total	C	275	293	279	280	*266	9.5	10.1	9.5	9.4	*8.9
Urban - Urbaine	C	97	112	109	80	*91	8.5	9.7	9.4	6.8	*7.8
Rural - Rurale	C	178	181	170	200	*175	10.2	10.3	9.6	11.2	*9.7
Albania - Albanie											
Total	C	32 715	31 733	30 869	28 934	28 561	11.4	11.0	10.7	10.1	10.0
Andorra - Andorre											
Total	C	659	634	588	543	539	9.3	8.8	8.0	7.3	7.1
Austria - Autriche											
Total	C	84 381[53]	87 675[53]	87 633[53]	85 535[53]	*84 952	9.8	10.0	10.0	9.7	*9.6
Belarus - Bélarus											
Total	C	119 028	117 779	102 556	94 042	*87 851	12.5	12.4	10.8	9.9	*9.3
Urban - Urbaine	C	91 870	91 005	78 852	72 238	...	12.5	12.3	10.6	9.7	...
Rural - Rurale	C	27 158	26 774	23 704	21 804	...	12.7	12.7	11.3	10.6	...
Belgium - Belgique[54]											
Total	C	122 274	121 896	119 690	118 319	*116 128	10.8	10.8	10.5	10.4	*10.1
Urban - Urbaine	C	120 591	...	...	...	...	...	...	...	...	...
Rural - Rurale	C	1 683	...	...	...	...	...	...	...	...	...
Bosnia and Herzegovina - Bosnie-Herzégovine											
Total	C	28 906	29 276	29 158	29 467	...	8.2	8.3	8.3	8.4	...
Bulgaria - Bulgarie											
Total	C	65 950	64 984	63 955	62 197	61 538	9.2	9.1	9.0	8.9	8.8
Urban - Urbaine	C	49 486	48 733	48 005	46 877	...	9.4	9.3	9.2	9.1	...
Rural - Rurale	C	16 464	16 251	15 950	15 320	...	8.5	8.5	8.5	8.3	...
Croatia - Croatie											
Total	C	37 503	37 537	36 556	36 945	*36 135	8.9	9.0	8.9	9.0	*8.9
Urban - Urbaine	C	21 802	21 645	21 156	21 148	...	...	...	...	...	...
Rural - Rurale	C	15 701	15 892	15 400	15 797	...	...	...	...	...	...
Czechia - Tchéquie											
Total	C	110 764	112 663	114 405	114 036	*112 231	10.5	10.7	10.8	10.7	*10.5
Urban - Urbaine	C	81 413	82 912	83 980	83 399	...	10.6	10.7	10.8	10.7	...
Rural - Rurale	C	29 351	29 751	30 425	30 637	...	10.3	10.5	10.7	10.7	...
Denmark - Danemark[55]											
Total	C	58 205	61 614	61 397	61 476	61 167	10.3	10.8	10.7	10.6	10.5
Estonia - Estonie											
Total	C	13 907	14 053	13 784	14 367	14 099	10.6	10.7	10.5	10.9	10.6
Urban - Urbaine	C	9 553[16]	9 566	10 049[16]	10 097[16]	...	10.6	10.6	11.0	11.0	...
Rural - Rurale	C	4 353[16]	4 487	3 731[16]	4 267[16]	...	10.5	10.8	9.2	10.6	...

9. Live births and crude birth rates, by urban/rural residence: 2015 - 2019
Naissances vivantes et taux bruts de natalité selon la résidence, urbaine/rurale : 2015 - 2019 (continued - suite)

Continent, country or area, and urban/rural residence — Continent, pays ou zone et résidence, urbaine/rurale	Code[a]	Number - Nombre 2015	2016	2017	2018	2019	Rate - Taux 2015	2016	2017	2018	2019
EUROPE											
Faroe Islands - Îles Féroé											
Total	C	605	674	656	684	683	12.4	13.6	13.1	13.4	13.2
Urban - Urbaine	C	227	274	247	268	270	12.2	14.4	12.8	13.7	13.6
Rural - Rurale	C	378	400	409	416	413	12.5	13.1	13.2	13.2	12.9
Finland - Finlande											
Total	C	55 197[56]	52 521[56]	50 042[56]	47 297[56]	*45 597	10.1	9.6	9.1	8.6	*8.3
Urban - Urbaine[56]	C	40 711	38 853	37 193	35 657	...	10.6	10.0	9.5	9.1	...
Rural - Rurale[56]	C	14 486	13 668	12 849	11 640	...	9.0	8.6	8.2	7.5	...
France											
Total	C	760 421	744 697	730 242	719 737	...	11.8	11.5	11.3	11.1	...
Urban - Urbaine[57]	C	611 062	601 770	591 457	...	...	...	...	...	...	...
Rural - Rurale[57]	C	147 304	140 951	136 626	...	...	...	...	...	...	...
Germany - Allemagne											
Total	C	737 575	792 131	784 884	787 523	*778 129	9.0	9.6	9.5	9.5	*9.4
Gibraltar[58]											
Total	+C	492	424	...	...	...	14.7	12.5	...	...	...
Greece - Grèce											
Total	C	91 847	92 898	88 553	86 440	*83 746	8.5	8.6	8.2	8.1	*7.8
Urban - Urbaine	C	63 283	64 223	61 004	59 541	...	...	...	...	...	...
Rural - Rurale	C	28 564	28 675	27 549	26 899	...	...	...	...	...	...
Guernsey - Guernesey[59]											
Total	C	580	595	571	542	497	9.3	9.6	9.2	8.7	7.9
Hungary - Hongrie[60]											
Total	C	92 135[61]	95 361[61]	94 646[61]	93 467[61]	93 100	9.4	9.7	9.7	9.6	9.5
Urban - Urbaine	C	63 961	65 866	64 894	63 720	...	9.2	9.5	9.4	9.2	...
Rural - Rurale	C	28 153	29 495	29 707	29 729	...	9.7	10.2	10.3	10.3	...
Iceland - Islande											
Total	C	4 129	4 034	4 071	4 228	...	12.5	12.0	11.9	12.0	...
Urban - Urbaine	C	3 924	3 617	3 860	4 000	...	12.7	11.5	12.0	12.1	...
Rural - Rurale	C	205	169	211	228	...	9.8	7.9	9.5	10.0	...
Ireland - Irlande											
Total	+C	65 537	63 836	61 824	61 022	59 796	13.9	13.4	12.9	12.5	12.2
Isle of Man - Île de Man											
Total	+C	785	758	753	717	710	9.0	9.1	9.0	...	...
Italy - Italie											
Total	C	485 780	473 438	458 151	439 747	*420 170	8.0	7.8	7.6	7.3	...
Jersey[18]											
Total	+C	1 021	1 020	954	942	...	10.1	9.9	9.2	8.9	...
Latvia - Lettonie											
Total	C	21 979	21 968	20 828	19 314	18 786	11.1	11.2	10.7	10.0	9.8
Urban - Urbaine	C	15 099	15 154	14 507	13 178	...	11.2	11.3	...	10.0	...
Rural - Rurale	C	6 880	6 814	6 321	6 136	...	10.9	10.9	...	10.1	...
Liechtenstein											
Total	C	325	378	338	378	...	8.7	10.0	8.9	9.9	...
Lithuania - Lituanie											
Total	C	31 475	30 623	28 696	28 149	27 393	10.8	10.7	10.1	10.0	9.8
Urban - Urbaine	C	21 589	21 256	19 851	19 446	...	11.1	11.0	10.5	10.3	...
Rural - Rurale	C	9 886	9 367	8 845	8 703	...	10.4	10.0	9.5	9.4	...
Luxembourg											
Total	C	6 115	6 050	6 174	6 274	6 230	10.7	10.4	10.4	10.3	10.1
Malta - Malte											
Total	C	4 325	4 476	4 319	4 444	4 350	9.7	9.8	9.2	9.2	8.8
Monaco[62]											
Total	C	1 067	938	958	983	...	28.4	24.6	25.5	25.7	...
Montenegro - Monténégro											
Total	C	7 386	7 569	7 432	7 264	7 223	11.9	12.2	11.9	11.7	11.6
Netherlands - Pays-Bas[63]											
Total	C	170 510	172 520	169 836	168 525	169 680	10.1	10.1	9.9	9.8	9.8
North Macedonia - Macédoine du Nord											
Total	C	23 075	23 002	21 754	21 333	*19 725	11.1	11.1	10.5	10.3	*9.5
Urban - Urbaine	C	13 357	13 536	12 841	12 598	...	...	...	...	...	...
Rural - Rurale	C	9 718	9 466	8 913	8 735	...	...	...	...	...	...
Norway - Norvège											
Total	C	58 815	58 890	56 633	55 120	*54 496	11.3	11.3	10.7	10.4	*10.2

9. Live births and crude birth rates, by urban/rural residence: 2015 - 2019
Naissances vivantes et taux bruts de natalité selon la résidence, urbaine/rurale : 2015 - 2019 (continued - suite)

Continent, country or area, and urban/rural residence Continent, pays ou zone et résidence, urbaine/rurale	Code[a]	Number - Nombre 2015	2016	2017	2018	2019	Rate - Taux 2015	2016	2017	2018	2019
EUROPE											
Poland - Pologne											
Total	C	369 308	382 257	401 982	388 178	374 954	9.7	10.1	10.6	10.2	9.8
Urban - Urbaine	C	217 391	226 296	236 143	228 714	...	9.5	9.9	10.3	10.0	...
Rural - Rurale	C	151 917	155 961	165 839	159 464	...	10.1	10.3	11.0	10.5	...
Portugal[18]											
Total	C	85 500	87 126	86 154	87 020	*87 019	8.3	8.4	8.4	8.5	*8.5
Republic of Moldova - République de Moldova[64]											
Total	C	38 610	37 394	34 060	32 606	*29 682	13.6	13.3	12.4	12.0	*11.1
Urban - Urbaine	C	13 555	13 359	12 392	11 998	...	...	...	...	...	...
Rural - Rurale	C	25 055	24 035	21 668	20 608	...	...	...	...	...	...
Romania - Roumanie											
Total	C	197 491	205 773	202 151	202 744	*185 733	10.0	10.4	10.3	10.4	*9.6
Urban - Urbaine	C	108 744	113 530	111 637	112 585	...	10.2	10.7	10.6	10.7	...
Rural - Rurale	C	88 747	92 243	90 514	90 159	...	9.7	10.1	10.0	10.0	...
San Marino - Saint-Marin											
Total	C	269	262	228	235	...	8.0	7.7	6.6	6.8	...
Serbia - Serbie[65]											
Total	+C	65 657	64 734	64 894	63 975	*63 723	9.3	9.2	9.2	9.2	*9.2
Urban - Urbaine	+C	45 640	44 794	43 783	42 601	...	10.7	10.5	10.3	10.0	...
Rural - Rurale	+C	20 017	19 940	21 111	21 374	...	7.1	7.1	7.6	7.8	...
Slovakia - Slovaquie											
Total	C	55 602	57 557	57 969	57 639	57 054	10.3	10.6	10.7	10.6	10.5
Urban - Urbaine	C	29 082	29 719	29 810	29 540	...	10.0	10.2	10.2	10.1	...
Rural - Rurale	C	26 520	27 838	28 159	28 099	...	10.6	11.1	11.2	11.1	...
Slovenia - Slovénie											
Total	C	20 641	20 345	20 241	19 585	*19 328	10.0	9.9	9.8	9.5	*9.3
Urban - Urbaine	C	10 871	10 765	11 023	10 826	...	9.8	9.7	9.7	9.5	...
Rural - Rurale	C	9 770	9 580	9 218	8 759	...	10.2	10.0	10.0	9.5	...
Spain - Espagne											
Total	C	418 432	408 734	391 265	370 827	*357 924	9.0	8.8	8.4	7.9	*7.6
Sweden - Suède											
Total	C	114 870	117 425	115 416	115 832	...	11.7	11.8	11.5	11.4	...
Switzerland - Suisse											
Total	C	86 559	87 883	87 381	87 851	*81 564	10.5	10.5	10.3	10.3	*9.6
Urban - Urbaine	C	74 039	75 327	74 978	75 215	...	10.6	10.6	...	10.4	...
Rural - Rurale	C	12 520	12 556	12 403	12 636	...	9.7	9.7	...	9.8	...
Ukraine[66]											
Total	+C	411 781	397 037	363 987	*335 874	*308 817	9.6	9.3	8.6	*7.9	*7.3
Urban - Urbaine	+C	266 082	258 688	237 874	...	...	9.0	8.8	8.1	...	...
Rural - Rurale	+C	145 699	138 349	126 113	...	...	11.0	10.5	9.7	...	...
United Kingdom of Great Britain and Northern Ireland - Royaume-Uni de Grande-Bretagne et d'Irlande du Nord[67]											
Total	C	776 746	774 386	754 754	730 918	*712 550	11.9	11.8	11.4	11.0	*10.7
OCEANIA - OCÉANIE											
American Samoa - Samoas américaines											
Total	C	1 096	1 013	1 001	...	...	18.0	16.8	16.6	...	...
Australia - Australie											
Total	C	305 377	311 104	309 142	315 147	...	12.8	12.9	12.6	12.6	...
Urban - Urbaine[68]	C	208 466	215 561	214 142	216 931	...	10.1	10.3	10.0	10.0	...
Rural - Rurale[68]	C	94 562	93 466	92 995	96 405	...	29.1	28.6	28.3	29.2	...
Cook Islands - Îles Cook											
Total	+C	205	242	222	*232	*225	11.1	12.5	11.4	*12.5	*11.1
Fiji - Fidji											
Total	+C	17 882	15 620	14 023	...	...	20.6	17.9	15.8	...	...
French Polynesia - Polynésie française											
Total	C	3 888	3 969	3 821	3 776	...	14.2	14.5	13.9	13.6	...
Guam[69]											
Total	C	3 367	3 433	3 292	3 175	*3 059	20.8	21.1	20.1	18.9	*18.2

9. Live births and crude birth rates, by urban/rural residence: 2015 - 2019
Naissances vivantes et taux bruts de natalité selon la résidence, urbaine/rurale : 2015 - 2019 (continued - suite)

Continent, country or area, and urban/rural residence Continent, pays ou zone et résidence, urbaine/rurale	Code[a]	Number - Nombre 2015	2016	2017	2018	2019	Rate - Taux 2015	2016	2017	2018	2019
OCEANIA - OCÉANIE											
Kiribati[70]											
Total	+U	*2 368*	...	...	...	...	...	...	...	...	...
Nauru											
Total	C	360	358	304	...	...	31.9	32.5	...	...	...
New Caledonia - Nouvelle-Calédonie											
Total	C	4 191	4 271	4 059	...	...	15.4	15.6	14.6	...	...
New Zealand - Nouvelle-Zélande[71]											
Total	+C	61 038	59 427[72]	59 610[72]	58 020[72]	59 637[72]	13.3	12.7	12.4	12.0	12.1
Urban - Urbaine[16]	+C	53 205	51 849[72]	51 876[72]	48 402[72]	49 659[72]	13.4	12.8	12.5	11.9	12.1
Rural - Rurale[16]	+C	7 827	7 572[72]	7 728[72]	9 603[72]	9 969[72]	12.3	11.9	11.9	12.2	12.5
Niue - Nioué											
Total	C	26	27	...	...	...	...	...	...	...	...
Palau - Palaos											
Total	C	242	213	221	256	...	13.7	12.0	12.4	14.0	...
Pitcairn											
Total	C	...	...	...	...	-	...	...	...	...	...
Samoa[73]											
Total	+U	*8 210*	*9 378*	*9 278*	*13 392*[74]	*9 604*	...	...	...	...	...
Tuvalu											
Total	+U	*208*	*210*	...	...	...	...	...	...	...	...

FOOTNOTES - NOTES

Italics: data from civil registers which are incomplete or of unknown completeness. - Italiques : données incomplètes ou dont le degré d'exactitude n'est pas connu, provenant des registres de l'état civil.

* Provisional. - Données provisoires.

[a] 'Code' indicates the source of data, as follows:
C - Civil registration, estimated over 90% complete
U - Civil registration, estimated less than 90% complete
| - Other source, estimated reliable
+ - Data tabulated by date of registration rather than occurence
... - Information not available

Le 'Code' indique la source des données, comme suit :
C - Registres de l'état civil considérés complets à 90 p. 100 au moins
U - Registres de l'état civil qui ne sont pas considérés complets à 90 p. 100 au moins
| - Autre source, considérée pas douteuses
+ - Données exploitées selon la date de l'enregistrement et non la date de l'événement
... - Information pas disponible

[1] Excluding live-born infants who died before their birth was registered. Data refer to Algerian population only. - Non compris les enfants nés vivants décédés avant l'enregistrement de leur naissance. Les données ne concernent que la population algérienne.
[2] Source: Vital Statistics Report. - Source: Vital Statistics Report.
[3] Data refer only to events recorded in hospitals and health centres. - Ces données ne concernent que les faits d'état civil enregistrés dans les hôpitaux et les centres de santé uniquement.
[4] Source: Vital Statistics Report, National Statistics Institute. Registered births only. - Source: Rapport sur les statistiques de l'état civil, Institut national de la statistique. Naissances enregistrées seulement.
[5] Data refers to births in health institution. Source: Reports of the Ministry of Health. - Les données se rapportent aux naissances dans les établissements de santé. Source : Rapports du Ministère de la Santé.
[6] The marked increase is due to the improvement in birth registration. - L'augmentation sensible s'explique par l'amélioration d'enregistrement des naissances.
[7] Data refer to the 12 months preceding the census in September. - Les données se rapportent aux 12 mois précédant le recensement de septembre.
[8] Excludes the islands of St. Brandon and Agalega. - Non compris les îles St. Brandon et Agalega.
[9] Source: Ministry of Health - Source : Ministère de la santé
[10] Source: Ministry of Public Health, Department of Statistics. - Source: Ministère de la Santé Publique, Direction des Statistiques.
[11] Excluding live-born infants who died before their birth was registered. - Non compris les enfants nés vivants décédés avant l'enregistrement de leur naissance.
[12] Completeness estimated at 15.3%. - Degré de complétude évalué à 15.3 pour cent.
[13] Unrevised data. - Les données n'ont pas été révisées.
[14] Excluding non-residents and foreign service personnel and their dependants. Bermuda is 100 per cent urban. - À l'exclusion des non-résidents et du personnel diplomatique et de leurs charges de famille. 100 pour cent de la population des Bermudes est urbaine.
[15] Including Canadian residents temporarily in the United States, but excluding United States residents temporarily in Canada. - Y compris les résidents canadiens se trouvant temporairement aux Etats-Unis, mais ne comprenant pas les résidents des Etats-Unis se trouvant temporairement au Canada.
[16] The total number may include 'Unknown residence', but the categories urban and rural do not. - Le nombre total peut inclure les personnes dont la résidence n'est pas connue, à l'inverse des catégories de population urbaine et rurale.
[17] Excluding children born in the country of non-resident mothers. - Exceptés les enfants nés dans le pays des mères non-résidentes.
[18] Data refer to births to resident mothers. - Ces données concernent les enfants nés de mères résidentes.
[19] Data refer to births to resident mothers. The total number may include 'Unknown residence', but the categories urban and rural do not. - Ces données concernent les enfants nés de mères résidentes. Le nombre total peut inclure les personnes dont la résidence n'est pas connue, à l'inverse des catégories de population urbaine et rurale.
[20] Source: Ministry of Legal Affairs. - Source : Ministère des affaires juridiques.
[21] Source: National Statistical Office. - Source : Service national de statistique.
[22] Source: U.S. National Center for Health Statistics, National Vital Statistics Reports (NVSR). - Source : US National Center for Health Statistics, National Vital Statistics Reports (NVSR).
[23] Data refer to the number of less than one year olds registered in the year. - Les données se rapportent au nombre d'enfants de moins d'un an enregistrés dans l'année.
[24] Excludes nomadic Indian tribes. - Non compris les tribus d'Indiens nomades.
[25] Source: General Registrar Office. Estimated completeness of registration is within 80-89 per cent. - Source : Bureau général de l'État civil. Degré de complétude de l'enregistrement est évalué à 80-89 pour cent.

[26] Source: Reports of the Ministry of Health. - Source : Rapports du Ministère de la Santé.
[27] Data extracted from online system representing only 85.6 per cent of estimated births. - Données extraites du système en ligne, qui ne représentent que 85.6 % du nombre total estimé de naissances.
[28] Excluding infants born alive of less than 28 weeks' gestation, of less than 1 000 g in weight and 35 cm in length, who die within seven days of birth. - Non compris les enfants nés vivants après moins de 28 semaines de gestations, pesant moins de 1 000 g, mesurant moins de 35 cm et décédés dans les sept jours qui ont suivi leur naissance.
[29] Sources: Births and Deaths National Registration System database, and medical records of government hospitals. Data refer to Bahraini and non-Bahraini births including some visitors, and Bahraini births abroad. - Les sources: Les bases de données des << Births and Deaths National Registration System >> et les dossiers médicaux des hôpitaux du gouvernement. Les données se rapportent aux naissances de Bahreïniens et de non-Bahreïniens, y compris d'enfants non résidents, ainsi que de Bahreïniens résidant à l'étranger.
[30] Data refer to the 12 months preceding the census in May. - Les données se rapportent aux 12 mois précédant le recensement de mai.
[31] Data have been estimated on the basis of the annual National Sample Survey on Population Changes. For statistical purposes, the data for China do not include those for the Hong Kong Special Administrative Region (Hong Kong SAR), Macao Special Administrative Region (Macao SAR) and Taiwan province of China. - Les données ont été estimées sur la base de l'enquête annuelle "National Sample Survey on Population Changes". Pour la présentation des statistiques, les données pour la Chine ne comprennent pas la Région Administrative Spéciale de Hong Kong (Hong Kong RAS), la Région Administrative Spéciale de Macao (Macao RAS) et Taïwan province de Chine.
[32] Data refer to government controlled areas. - Les données se rapportent aux zones contrôlées par le Gouvernement.
[33] Includes data for the Indian-held part of Jammu and Kashmir, the final status of which has not yet been determined. Rates were obtained by the Sample Registration System of India, which is a large demographic survey. - Y compris les données pour la partie du Jammu et du Cachemire occupée par l'Inde dont le statut définitif n'a pas encore été déterminé. Les taux ont été obtenus par le Système de l'enregistrement par échantillon de l'Inde qui est une large enquête démographique.
[34] Data refer to the Iranian Year which begins on 21 March and ends on 20 March of the following year. - Les données concernent l'année iranienne, qui commence le 21 mars et se termine le 20 mars de l'année suivante.
[35] Includes data for East Jerusalem and Israeli residents in certain other territories under occupation by Israeli military forces since June 1967. - Y compris les données pour Jérusalem-Est et les résidents israéliens dans certains autres territoires occupés depuis 1967 par les forces armées israéliennes.
[36] Data refer to Japanese nationals in Japan only. - Les données se raportent aux nationaux japonais au Japon seulement.
[37] The total number may include 'Unknown residence', but the categories urban and rural do not. Urban and rural distribution refers to the residence of the child. - Le nombre total peut inclure les personnes dont la résidence n'est pas connue, à l'inverse des catégories de population urbaine et rurale. La répartition urbain/rural se réfère au domicile de l'enfant.
[38] Excluding data for Jordanian territory under occupation since June 1967 by Israeli military forces. Excluding foreigners, including registered Palestinian refugees. - Non compris les données pour le territoire jordanien occupé depuis juin 1967 par les forces armées israéliennes. Non compris les étrangers, mais y compris les réfugiés de Palestine enregistrés.
[39] Data refer to the 12 months preceding the census in March. - Les données se rapportent aux 12 mois précédant le recensement de mars.
[40] Data do not include foreigners. - Les données sur les etrangers ne sont pas inclus.
[41] Data are from Vital Registration System (VRS). - Les données proviennent du système d'enregistrement des faits d'état civil.
[42] Data from Births and Deaths Notification System (Ministry of Health and all health care providers). - Les données proviennent du système de notification des naissances et des décès (Ministère de la santé et tous prestataires de soins de santé).
[43] Data refer to residence of child. Excluding alien armed forces, civilian aliens employed by armed forces, and foreign diplomatic personnel and their dependants. - Les données correspondent à la résidence de l'enfant. Non compris les militaires étrangers, les civils étrangers employés par les forces armées ni le personnel diplomatique étranger et les membres de leur famille les accompagnant.
[44] Survey based estimates. - Estimations basées sur des enquêtes.
[45] Data refer to Saudi Arabian nationals only. - Les données ne concernent que les ressortissants saoudiens.
[46] Data for rural areas include data of estate sectors consisting of all plantations which are 20 acres or more in extent and with ten or more resident labourers. - Les données pour les zones rurales comprennent celles pour les domaines, dont l'ensemble des plantations de plus de 10 hectares comptant au moins 10 travailleurs résidents.
[47] Data exclude Jerusalem ID holders. Source: Palestinian Central Bureau of Statistics, Population Register, updated version 2019. - Les données ne tiennent pas compte des détenteurs de carte d'identité de Jérusalem. Source: Bureau central de statistique palestinien, registre de la population, version actualisée jusqu'au 2019.
[48] Excluding infants born alive of less than 28 weeks' gestation, of less than 1 000 g in weight and 35 cm in length, who die within seven days of birth. Data have been adjusted for under-registration. - Non compris les enfants nés vivants après moins de 28 semaines de gestations, pesant moins de 1 000 g, mesurant moins de 35 cm et décédés dans les sept jours qui ont suivi leur naissance. Y compris un ajustement pour sous-enregistrement.
[49] Source: Strategy and Planning Division, Ministry of Public Health. - Source : Division de la stratégie et de la planification, Ministère de la Santé publique.
[50] Data refer to the 12 months preceding the census in July. - Les données se rapportent aux 12 mois précédant le recensement de juillet.
[51] The registration of births and deaths is conducted by the Ministry of Health. An estimate of completeness is not provided. - L'enregistrement des naissances et des décès est mené par le Ministère de la Santé. Le degré estimatif de complétude n'est pas fourni.
[52] Including Non-Yemeni births. - Y compris les naissances non-yéménites.
[53] Including births occurring abroad of mothers with residence in Austria. - Y compris les naissances survenues à l'étranger des mères avec résidence en Autriche.
[54] Including armed forces stationed outside the country, but excluding alien armed forces stationed in the area. - Y compris les militaires nationaux hors du pays, mais non compris les militaires étrangers en garnison sur le territoire.
[55] Excluding Faeroe Islands and Greenland shown separately, if available. - Non compris les Iles Féroé et le Groenland, qui font l'objet de rubriques distinctes, si disponible.
[56] Excluding Åland Islands. - Non compris les Îles d'Åland.
[57] Data for urban and rural exclude events corresponding to nationals residing outside the country, which may be included in the total. - Les données relatives à les categories urbaine et rurale n'englobent pas les faits d'état civil qui concernent les nationaux se trouvant à l'étranger, lesquels faits peuvent être inclus au total.
[58] Including live births by military personnel and their dependants. - Y compris les naissances vivantes parmi les membres du personnel militaire et leurs personnes à charge.
[59] For year ending 31 March. - Période annuelle se terminant le 31 mars.
[60] Data include the live births of women with Hungarian usual residence regardless of whether the live birth occurred in Hungary or in a foreign country, and do not include the live births of women with foreign country usual residence. - Les données concernent les enfants nés vivants de femmes dont la résidence habituelle est en Hongrie, que la naissance vivante ait eu lieu en Hongrie ou dans un pays étranger, et ne comprennent pas les enfants nés vivants de femmes dont la résidence habituelle est dans un pays étranger.
[61] Data include the live births of women with unknown residence and homeless. - Les données incluent les enfants nés vivants de femmes dont la résidence n'est pas connue et de femmes sans domicile fixe.
[62] Source: City Hall, Civil Status Registry Office, resident and non-resident births. - Source : La mairie, Bureau de l'État Civil, toutes les naissances.
[63] Including residents outside the country if listed in a Netherlands population register. - Englobe les résidents se trouvant à l'étranger à condition qu'ils soient inscrits sur le registre de population des Pays-Bas.
[64] Excluding Transnistria and the municipality of Bender. - Les données ne tiennent pas compte de l'information sur la Transnistria et la municipalité de Bender.
[65] Excludes data for Kosovo and Metohia. - Sans les données pour le Kosovo et Metohie.
[66] The Government of Ukraine has informed the United Nations that it is not in a position to provide statistical data concerning the Autonomous Republic of Crimea and the city of Sevastopol. Data refer to births with weight 500g and more (if weight is unknown - with length 25 centimeters and more, or with gestation during 22 weeks or more). - Le gouvernement Ukrainien a informé l'ONU qu'il n'est pas en mesure de fournir des données statistiques concernant la République autonome de Crimée et la ville de Sébastopol. Données concernant les nouveau-nés de 500 grammes ou plus (si le poids est inconnu – de 25 centimètres de long ou plus, ou après une grossesse de 22 semaines ou plus).
[67] Excluding Channel Islands (Guernsey and Jersey) and Isle of Man, shown separately, if available. Data tabulated by date of occurrence for England and Wales, and by date of registration for Northern Ireland and Scotland. - Non compris les îles Anglo-Normandes (Guernesey et Jersey) et l'île de Man, qui font l'objet de rubriques distinctes, si disponible. Données exploitées selon la date de

l'événement pour l'Angleterre et le pays de Galles, et selon la date de l'enregistrement pour l'Irlande du Nord et l'Ecosse.

[68] Urban refers to Greater Capital City Statistical Areas, and rural refers to other areas within the state or territory. Data for urban and rural figures do not add up to the total because they exclude the events occurred in Migratory, Special Purpose and Other Territories. - Urbain renvoie aux zones statistiques de la capitale métropolitaine, et rural aux autres zones de l'État ou territoire. La somme des chiffres des catégories « en zone urbaine » et « en zone rurale » ne correspond pas au total du fait qu'en sont exclus les événements qui ont eu lieu dans les territoires de migration, les territoires à destination spéciale et autres territoires.

[69] Including United States military personnel, their dependants and contract employees. - Y compris les militaires des Etats-Unis, les membres de leur famille les accompagnant et les agents contractuels des Etats-Unis.

[70] Data refer to registered events only within island councils and civil registration office. - Correspond aux événements enregistrés par les conseils des îles et par les services de l'état civil.

[71] Random rounding to base 3 is applied in this table as a confidentiality measure. - Les chiffres sont arrondis à la base 3 de manière aléatoire, pour des raisons de confidentialité.

[72] Data refers to births registered in the country to mothers resident in the country. - Les données se rapportent aux naissances enregistrées dans le pays pour lesquelles la mère réside dans le pays.

[73] Source: Births, Deaths, and Marriages Registration Division, Samoa Bureau of Statistics. - Source : Division de l'enregistrement des naissances, des décès et des mariages du Bureau de statistique du Samoa.

[74] The huge increase in 2018 is due to late registrations of all unregistered persons regardless of their age conducted mid-February to June. - La forte augmentation constatée en 2018 s'explique par l'organisation, de la mi-février au mois de juin, d'une campagne de déclaration tardive pour toutes les personnes qui n'étaient pas encore déclarées, quel que soit leur âge.

Table 10 presents live births by age of mother and sex of the child, general fertility rate, and age-specific fertility rates for the latest available year between 2010 and 2019.

Description of variables: Age is defined as age at last birthday, that is, the difference between the date of birth and the date of the occurrence of the event, expressed in completed solar years. The age classification used in this table is the following: under 15 years, 5-year age groups through 45-49 years, and 50 years and over. A different classification may appear as provided by the reporting country or area.

Rate computation: Age-specific fertility rates are the annual number of births to women in each age group per 1 000 female population in the same age group. These rates are calculated by the Statistics Division of the United Nations.

Since relatively few births occur to women below 15 or above 50 years of age, age-specific fertility rates for women under 20 years of age and for those 45 years of age or over are computed on the female population aged 15-19 and 45-49, respectively. Similarly, the rate for women of "All ages" is based on all live births irrespective of age of mother and is computed on the female population aged 15-49 years. This rate for "All ages" is known as the general fertility rate. The age-specific fertility rates for age groups of women below 15 or 50 and above years of age are not calculated.

Births to mothers of unknown age are distributed proportionately across the age groups, by the Statistics Division of the United Nations, in accordance with the distribution of births by age of mother prior to the calculation of the rates.

The population used in computing the rates is the estimated or enumerated distribution of females by age. First priority was given to the estimated population and second priority to the enumerated population, i.e. to census returns of the year to which the births referred.

Rates presented in this table are limited to those for countries or areas having at least a total of 100 live births in a given year.

Reliability of data: Data from civil registers of live births which are reported as incomplete (less than 90 per cent completeness) or of unknown completeness are considered unreliable and are set in *italics* rather than in roman type. Rates are not computed if the data on live births from civil registers are reported as incomplete (less than 90 per cent completeness) or of unknown completeness. Table 9 and the technical notes for that table provide more detailed information on the completeness of live-birth registration. For more information about the quality of vital statistics data in general, see section 4.2 of the Technical Notes.

Limitations: Statistics on live births by age of mother are subject to the same qualifications as have been set forth for vital statistics in general and birth statistics in particular as discussed in section 4 of the Technical Notes. These include differences in the completeness of registration, the method used to determine age of mother and the quality of the reported information relating to age of mother.

The reliability of the data described above, is an important factor in considering the limitations. In addition, some live births are tabulated by date of registration and not by date of occurrence; these are indicated in the table by a plus sign "+". Whenever the lag between the date of occurrence and date of registration is prolonged and, therefore, a large proportion of the live birth registrations are delayed, birth statistics for any given year may be seriously affected. For example, the age of the mother will almost always refer to the date of registration rather than to the date of birth of the child. Hence, in those countries or areas where registration of births is delayed, possibly for years, statistics on births by age of mother should be used with caution.

Another factor which limits international comparability is the practice of some countries or areas of not including in live birth statistics infants who were born alive but died before the registration of the birth or within the first 24 hours of life, thus underestimating the total number of live births. Statistics of this type are footnoted.

Because these statistics are classified according to age, they are subject to the limitations with respect to accuracy of age reporting similar to those already discussed in connection with section 3.1.3 of the Technical Notes. The factors influencing the accuracy of reporting may be somewhat dissimilar in vital statistics (because of the differences in the method of taking a census and registering a birth) but, in general, the same errors can be observed. The absence of frequencies in the unknown age group does not necessarily indicate completely accurate reporting and tabulation of the age item. It is often an indication that the unknowns have been eliminated by assigning ages to them before tabulation, or by proportionate distribution after tabulation.

On the other hand, large frequencies in the unknown age category may indicate that a large proportion of the births are born outside of wedlock, the records for which tend to be incomplete so far as characteristics of the parents are concerned.

Another limitation of age reporting may result from calculating age of mother at birth of child (or at time of registration) from year of birth rather than from day, month and year of birth. Information on this factor is given in footnotes when known.

In few countries, data by age refer to deliveries rather than to live births causing under-enumeration in the event of a multiple birth. This practice leads to lack of strict comparability, both among countries or areas relying on this practice and between data shown in this table and table 9.

Rates shown in this table are subject to the same limitations that affect the corresponding statistics on live births. In cases of rates based on births tabulated by date of registration and not by date of occurrence; the effect of including delayed registration on the distribution of births by age of mother may be noted in the age-specific fertility rates for women at older ages. In some cases, high age-specific rates for women aged 45 years and over may reflect age of mother at registration of birth and not fertility at these older ages.

Earlier data: Live births and live-birth rates by age of mother (i.e. age-specific fertility rates), have been shown for the latest available year in each issue of the Yearbook. Information on the years and specific topics covered is presented in the Historical Index.

Tableau 10 – *Annuaire démographique 2019*

Le tableau 10 présente les données les plus récentes disponibles pour la période 2010- 2019 sur les naissances vivantes selon l'âge de la mère et le sexe de l'enfant, le taux de fécondité et les taux de fécondité par âge.

Description des variables : l'âge désigne l'âge au dernier anniversaire, c'est-à-dire la différence entre la date de naissance et la date de l'événement exprimée en années solaires révolues. La classification par âge utilisée dans ce tableau comprend les catégories suivantes : moins de 15 ans, groupes quinquennaux jusqu'à 45-49 ans, 50 ans et plus, et âge inconnu. Des groupes d'âge différents sont parfois utilisés lorsque les pays ou territoires ont fourni les données dans une autre classification.

Les taux de fécondité par âge représentent le nombre annuel de naissances vivantes intervenues dans un groupe d'âge donné pour 1 000 femmes du groupe d'âge. Ces taux ont été calculés par la Division de statistique de l'ONU.

Étant donné que le nombre de naissances parmi les femmes de moins de 15 ans ou de plus de 50 ans est relativement peu élevé, les taux de fécondité par âge parmi les femmes âgées de moins de 20 ans et celles de 45 ans et plus ont été calculés sur la base des populations féminines âgées de 15 à 19 ans et de 45 à 49 ans, respectivement. De même, le taux pour les femmes de « tous âges » est fondé sur la totalité des naissances vivantes, indépendamment de l'âge de la mère et ce chiffre est rapporté à l'effectif de la population féminine âgée de 15 à 49 ans. Ce taux « tous âges » est le taux global de fécondité ou simplement taux de fécondité. Les taux de fécondité parmi les femmes âgées de moins de 15 ans ou celles de 50 ans et plus n'ont pas été calculés.

Les naissances pour lesquelles l'âge de la mère était inconnu ont été réparties par la Division de statistique de l'ONU, avant le calcul des taux, suivant les proportions observées pour celles où l'âge de la mère était connu.

Les chiffres de population utilisés pour le calcul des taux proviennent de dénombrements ou de répartitions estimatives de la population féminine selon l'âge. On a utilisé de préférence les estimations de la population; à défaut, on s'est contenté des données censitaires se rapportant à l'année des naissances.

Les taux présentés dans ce tableau ne concernent que les pays ou zones où l'on a enregistré un total d'au moins 100 naissances vivantes dans une année donnée.

Fiabilité des données : les données sur les naissances vivantes provenant des registres de l'état civil qui sont déclarées incomplètes (degré de complétude inférieur à 90 p. 100) ou dont le degré de complétude n'est pas connu, sont jugées douteuses et apparaissent en italique et non en caractères romains. On a choisi de ne pas faire figurer des taux calculés à partir de données sur les naissances vivantes issues de registres de l'état civil qui sont déclarées incomplètes (degré de complétude inférieur à 90 p. 100) ou dont le degré de complétude n'est pas connu. Le tableau 9 et les notes techniques qui s'y rapportent présentent des renseignements plus détaillés sur le degré de complétude de l'enregistrement des naissances vivantes. Pour plus de précisions sur la qualité des statistiques de l'état civil en général, voir la section 4.2 des Notes techniques.

Insuffisance des données : les statistiques relatives aux naissances vivantes selon l'âge de la mère appellent toutes les réserves qui ont été formulées à propos des statistiques de l'état civil en général et des statistiques de naissances en particulier (voir la section 4 des Notes techniques). Ceci inclut les différences de complétude d'enregistrement des faits d'état civil, de méthode pour déterminer l'âge de la mère et de qualité d'information concernant l'âge de la mère.

La fiabilité des données, au sujet de laquelle des indications ont été données plus haut, est un facteur important. Il faut également tenir compte du fait que, dans certains cas, les données relatives aux naissances vivantes sont exploitées selon la date de l'enregistrement et non la date de l'événement ; ces cas ont été signalés dans le tableau par le signe '+'. Chaque fois que le décalage entre l'événement et son enregistrement est grand et qu'une forte proportion des naissances vivantes fait l'objet d'un enregistrement tardif, les statistiques des naissances vivantes pour une année donnée peuvent être considérablement faussées. Par exemple, l'âge de la mère représente presque toujours son âge à la date de l'enregistrement et non à la date de la naissance de l'enfant. Ainsi, dans les pays ou zones où l'enregistrement des naissances est tardif, le retard atteignant parfois plusieurs années, il faut utiliser avec prudence les statistiques concernant les naissances selon l'âge de la mère.

Un autre facteur qui nuit à la comparabilité internationale est la pratique de certains pays ou zones qui consiste à ne pas inclure dans les statistiques des naissances vivantes les enfants nés vivants mais décédés avant l'enregistrement de leur naissance ou dans les 24 heures qui ont suivi la naissance, pratique qui conduit à sous-estimer le nombre total de naissances vivantes. Quand pareil facteur a joué, cela a été signalé en note à la fin du tableau.

Étant donné que les statistiques du tableau 10 sont classées selon l'âge, elles appellent les mêmes réserves concernant l'exactitude des déclarations d'âge que celles formulées à la section 3.1.3 des Notes techniques. Dans le cas des statistiques de l'état civil, les facteurs qui interviennent à cet égard sont parfois différents, étant donné que le recensement de la population et l'enregistrement des naissances se font par des méthodes différentes, mais, d'une manière générale, les erreurs observées seront les mêmes. Si aucun nombre ne figure dans la rangée réservée aux âges inconnus, cela ne signifie pas nécessairement que les déclarations d'âge et l'exploitation des données par âge ont été tout à fait exactes. C'est souvent une indication que l'on a attribué un âge aux personnes d'âge inconnu avant l'exploitation des données ou qu'elles ont été réparties proportionnellement entre les différents groupes après cette opération.

À l'inverse, lorsque le nombre des personnes d'âge inconnu est important, cela peut signifier que la proportion de naissances parmi les mères célibataires est élevée, étant donné qu'en pareil cas l'acte de naissance ne contient pas tous les renseignements concernant les parents.

Les déclarations par âge peuvent comporter des distorsions, du fait que l'âge de la mère au moment de la naissance d'un enfant (ou de la déclaration de naissance) est donné par année de naissance et non par date exacte (jour, mois et année).

Dans quelques pays, la classification par âges se réfère aux accouchements, et non aux naissances vivantes, ce qui conduit à un sous-dénombrement en cas de naissances gémellaires. Cette pratique nuit à la comparabilité des données, à la fois entre pays ou zones qui recourent à cette méthode et entre les données présentées dans le tableau 10 et celles du tableau 9.

Les taux présentés dans ce tableau sont sujets aux mêmes limitations qui affectent les statistiques correspondantes de naissances vivantes. Dans le cas des taux basés sur des naissances par date d'enregistrement et non par date d'occurrence, l'effet peut être visible sur les taux de fécondité par âge des femmes aux âges plus élevés. Dans certains cas, les taux de fécondité des femmes de plus de 45 ans peuvent refléter l'âge de la mère à l'enregistrement plus que la fécondité à ces âges.

Données publiées antérieurement : les différentes éditions de l'*Annuaire démographique* regroupent les dernières statistiques dont on disposait à l'époque sur les naissances vivantes selon l'âge de la mère et les taux des naissances vivantes selon l'âge de la mère (taux de fécondité par âge). Pour plus de précisions concernant les années pour lesquels des données ont été publiées, se reporter à l'index historique.

10. Live births by age of mother and sex of child, general and age-specific fertility rates: latest available year, 2010 - 2019
Naissances vivantes selon l'âge de la mère et le sexe de l'enfant, taux de fécondité et taux de fécondité par âge : dernière année disponible, 2010 - 2019

Continent, country or area, year, code[a] and age of mother (in years) — Continent, pays ou zone, année, code[a] et âge de la mère (en années)	Number - Nombre			Rate Taux
	Total	Male Masculin	Female Féminin	
AFRICA - AFRIQUE				
Botswana[1]				
2018 (C)				
Total	54 023	27 373	26 650	84.6
10 - 14	48	28	20	..
15 - 19	5 467	2 807	2 660	53.3
20 - 24	14 209	7 241	6 968	137.3
25 - 29	13 196	6 635	6 561	129.3
30 - 34	10 995	5 635	5 360	105.0
35 - 39	7 303	3 607	3 696	78.2
40 - 44	2 122	1 082	1 040	29.4
45 - 49	154	75	79	2.8
50 +	19	14	5	..
Unknown - Inconnu	510	249	261	..
Cabo Verde[2]				
2018* (+C)				
Total	9 231	4 596	4 635	64.2
10 - 14	26	14	12	..
15 - 19	1 396	676	720	58.8
20 - 24	2 455	1 203	1 252	100.2
25 - 29	2 323	1 192	1 131	88.7
30 - 34	1 765	873	892	75.2
35 - 39	977	488	489	53.2
40 - 44	266	135	131	18.3
45 - 49	16	12	4	♦1.3
50 +	-	-	-	..
Unknown - Inconnu	7	3	4	..
Congo				
2014 (+U)				
Total	*111 360*	*56 565*	*54 795*	...
0 - 14	*687*	*338*	*349*	..
15 - 19	*17 013*	*8 672*	*8 341*	...
20 - 24	*27 445*	*14 025*	*13 420*	...
25 - 29	*27 607*	*14 099*	*13 508*	...
30 - 34	*20 583*	*10 316*	*10 267*	...
35 - 39	*12 659*	*6 443*	*6 216*	...
40 - 44	*4 369*	*2 172*	*2 197*	...
45 - 49	*695*	*345*	*350*	...
50 +	*302*	*155*	*147*	..
Côte d'Ivoire[3]				
2014 (|)				
Total	841 081	426 128	414 953	154.0
0 - 14	3 653	1 875	1 778	..
15 - 19	77 375	39 411	37 964	74.5
20 - 24	192 965	97 499	95 466	178.1
25 - 29	221 215	112 113	109 102	210.1
30 - 34	183 792	92 806	90 986	213.2
35 - 39	105 637	53 532	52 105	171.7
40 - 44	40 638	20 721	19 917	91.0
45 +	15 806	8 171	7 635	43.7
Egypt - Égypte				
2012 (+C)				
Total	2 629 769	1 343 402	1 286 367	121.1
0 - 19	71 275	36 022	35 253	23.8
20 - 24	1 298 851	665 452	633 399	403.8
25 - 29	399 915	201 967	197 948	127.5
30 - 34	223 307	111 754	111 553	86.0
35 - 39	83 362	41 121	42 241	41.3
40 - 44	21 510	11 229	10 281	12.2
45 +	3 802	2 233	1 569	2.3
Unknown - Inconnu	527 747	273 624	254 123	..
Ghana[4]				
2010 (|)				
Total	623 700	306 159	317 541	98.1
0 - 14	917	381	536	..
15 - 19	40 307	19 067	21 240	31.0
AFRICA - AFRIQUE				
Ghana[4]				
2010 (|)				
20 - 24	126 417	61 277	65 140	103.4
25 - 29	167 306	82 741	84 565	151.1
30 - 34	130 724	64 600	66 124	147.1
35 - 39	92 751	46 285	46 466	124.6
40 - 44	41 898	20 783	21 115	68.3
45 - 49	14 742	7 071	7 671	30.4
50 +	8 638	3 954	4 684	..
Guinea - Guinée[5]				
2014 (|)				
Total	416 607	204 309	212 298	161.9
0 - 14	3 494	1 728	1 766	..
15 - 19	62 085	30 684	31 401	105.6
20 - 24	96 498	47 687	48 811	194.3
25 - 29	101 210	49 832	51 378	227.6
30 - 34	72 323	35 456	36 867	204.4
35 - 39	44 261	21 594	22 667	155.4
40 - 44	21 347	10 144	11 203	90.0
45 - 49	9 266	4 348	4 918	54.9
50 +	6 123	2 839	3 284	..
Kenya				
2018 (+U)				
Total	*1 138 654*	...	...	...
10 - 14	*4 214*	...	...	..
15 - 19	*134 184*	...	...	...
20 - 24	*330 605*	...	...	...
25 - 29	*300 873*	...	...	...
30 - 34	*210 822*	...	...	...
35 - 39	*100 949*	...	...	...
40 - 44	*27 403*	...	...	...
45 - 49	*4 354*	...	...	...
50 +	*747*	...	...	..
Unknown - Inconnu	*24 503*	...	...	..
Lesotho				
2019 (+U)				
Total	*7 515*	...	...	...
10 - 14	*6*	...	...	..
15 - 19	*575*	...	...	...
20 - 24	*1 637*	...	...	...
25 - 29	*2 061*	...	...	...
30 - 34	*1 842*	...	...	...
35 - 39	*1 109*	...	...	...
40 - 44	*266*	...	...	...
45 - 49	*19*	...	...	...
50 +	-	...	...	..
Malawi[4]				
2018 (|)				
Total	576 525	...	...	135.1
15 - 19	104 087	...	...	100.9
20 - 24	177 544	...	...	203.1
25 - 29	120 735	...	...	186.7
30 - 34	93 091	...	...	157.6
35 - 39	57 215	...	...	114.2
40 - 44	19 252	...	...	53.1
45 - 49	4 601	...	...	17.6
Mauritania - Mauritanie[6]				
2013 (|)				
Total	114 420	...	...	137.6
15 - 19	14 258	...	...	77.0
20 - 24	34 153	...	...	216.2
25 - 29	31 533	...	...	232.3
30 - 34	20 082	...	...	176.6
35 - 39	10 479	...	...	109.9

10. Live births by age of mother and sex of child, general and age-specific fertility rates: latest available year, 2010 - 2019
Naissances vivantes selon l'âge de la mère et le sexe de l'enfant, taux de fécondité et taux de fécondité par âge : dernière année disponible, 2010 - 2019 (continued - suite)

Continent, country or area, year, code[a] and age of mother (in years) / Continent, pays ou zone, année, code[a] et âge de la mère (en années)	Number - Nombre: Total	Number - Nombre: Male Masculin	Number - Nombre: Female Féminin	Rate Taux
AFRICA - AFRIQUE				
Mauritania - Mauritanie[6]				
2013 (|)				
40 - 44	3 421	...	...	43.2
45 - 49	493	...	...	7.6
Mauritius - Maurice[7]				
2019 (+C)				
Total	12 846	6 475	6 371	40.4
10 - 14	33	17	16	..
15 - 19	1 103	537	566	23.2
20 - 24	2 552	1 324	1 228	54.1
25 - 29	3 932	1 968	1 964	82.2
30 - 34	3 064	1 546	1 518	74.2
35 - 39	1 674	845	829	35.9
40 - 44	375	179	196	8.3
45 - 49	23	13	10	♦0.6
50 +	-	-	-	..
Unknown - Inconnu	90	46	44	..
Mayotte				
2017 (C)				
Total	9 762	4 993	4 769	148.9
0 - 14	56	...	...	..
10 - 14	56	29	27	..
15 - 19	1 047	531	516	79.4
20 - 24	2 342	1 188	1 154	245.3
25 - 29	2 468	1 279	1 189	242.7
30 - 34	2 097	1 092	1 005	204.3
35 - 39	1 304	639	665	138.3
40 - 44	418	216	202	55.4
45 - 49	30	19	11	♦5.5
50 +	-	-	-	..
2018 (C)				
Total	9 590	...	...	140.8
10 - 14	35	...	...	..
15 - 19	1 071	...	...	78.2
20 - 24	2 217	...	...	223.6
25 - 29	2 488	...	...	235.5
30 - 34	2 074	...	...	194.5
35 - 39	1 250	...	...	127.6
40 - 44	414	...	...	52.8
45 - 49	37	...	...	6.6
50 +	4	...	...	..
Namibia - Namibie[8]				
2011 (|)				
Total	61 523	30 560	30 963	110.8
0 - 14	873	443	430	..
15 - 19	7 593	3 723	3 870	62.5
20 - 24	16 655	8 235	8 420	152.3
25 - 29	14 296	7 109	7 187	157.7
30 - 34	11 017	5 632	5 385	145.3
35 - 39	7 237	3 531	3 706	113.0
40 - 44	2 982	1 451	1 531	58.4
45 +	870	436	434	20.2
Reunion - Réunion[9]				
2018 (C)				
Total	13 364	...	...	64.5
10 - 14	17	...	...	..
15 - 19	947	...	...	28.1
20 - 24	2 759	...	...	108.1
25 - 29	3 714	...	...	140.3
30 - 34	3 265	...	...	115.1
35 - 39	1 986	...	...	66.8
40 - 44	645	...	...	20.8
45 - 49	27	...	...	♦0.8
50 +	4	...	...	..
AFRICA - AFRIQUE				
Saint Helena ex. dep. - Sainte-Hélène sans dép.				
2018 (C)				
Total	26	11	15	...
10 - 14	-	-	-	..
15 - 19	1	1	-	...
20 - 24	5	2	3	...
25 - 29	4	1	3	...
30 - 34	8	3	5	...
35 - 39	4	2	2	...
40 - 44	2	-	2	...
45 +	-	-	-	...
Unknown - Inconnu	2	2	-	..
Seychelles				
2019 (+C)				
Total	1 605	813	792	77.1
10 - 14	9	4	5	..
15 - 19	228	121	107	89.0
20 - 24	373	166	207	326.6
25 - 29	388	193	195	169.8
30 - 34	329	176	153	104.5
35 - 39	205	112	93	46.3
40 - 44	69	40	29	20.6
45 +	4	1	3	♦1.0
South Africa - Afrique du Sud[10]				
2017 (C)				
Total	897 750	452 686	445 064	...
10 - 14	1 302	664	638	..
15 - 19	97 143	49 159	47 984	...
20 - 24	228 936	116 088	112 848	...
25 - 29	235 466	118 682	116 784	...
30 - 34	191 418	96 292	95 126	...
35 - 39	102 565	51 276	51 289	...
40 - 44	30 318	15 168	15 150	...
45 - 49	2 122	1 070	1 052	...
50 +	155	71	84	..
Unknown - Inconnu	8 325	4 216	4 109	..
Tunisia - Tunisie				
2017 (C)				
Total	208 000	...	...	68.9
15 - 19	2 632	...	...	7.3
20 - 24	25 312	...	...	62.9
25 - 29	58 644	...	...	131.2
30 - 34	62 186	...	...	133.1
35 - 39	35 767	...	...	80.1
40 - 44	9 392	...	...	25.6
45 +	757	...	...	2.3
Unknown - Inconnu	13 309	...	...	..
Zambia - Zambie[11]				
2010 (|)				
Total	442 998	224 756	218 242	141.4
12 - 14	921	470	451	..
15 - 19	58 999	29 701	29 298	75.4
20 - 24	128 270	65 048	63 222	200.0
25 - 29	114 701	58 366	56 335	205.1
30 - 34	74 066	37 666	36 400	178.4
35 - 39	45 452	23 072	22 380	139.5
40 - 44	16 150	8 181	7 969	72.5
45 - 49	4 439	2 252	2 187	23.7

Continent, country or area, year, code[a] and age of mother (in years) — Continent, pays ou zone, année, code[a] et âge de la mère (en années)	Number - Nombre Total	Male Masculin	Female Féminin	Rate Taux
AMERICA, NORTH - AMÉRIQUE DU NORD				
Antigua and Barbuda - Antigua-et-Barbuda				
2018 (+C)				
Total	1 015	...	...	38.9
10 - 14	1	...	...	..
15 - 19	100	...	...	27.6
20 - 24	272	...	...	70.8
25 - 29	252	...	...	67.7
30 - 34	223	...	...	60.1
35 - 39	138	...	...	37.4
40 - 44	28	...	...	♦7.4
45 +	1	...	...	♦0.3
Aruba				
2019 (C)				
Total	1 029	534	495	39.3
10 - 14	-	-	-	..
15 - 19	73	31	42	21.0
20 - 24	250	120	130	81.5
25 - 29	296	163	133	85.4
30 - 34	233	125	108	64.8
35 - 39	142	77	65	36.0
40 - 44	33	16	17	8.1
45 - 49	1	1	-	♦0.2
50 +	1	1	-	..
Bahamas				
2012 (+U)				
Total	*4 469*	*2 279*	*2 187*	...
0 - 14	*4*	*2*	*2*	..
15 - 19	*497*	*261*	*236*	...
20 - 24	*1 028*	*524*	*504*	...
25 - 29	*1 123*	*580*	*543*	...
30 - 34	*972*	*496*	*476*	...
35 - 39	*632*	*318*	*314*	...
40 - 44	*193*	*91*	*102*	...
45 - 49	*15*	*5*	*10*	...
50 +	*1*	*1*	-	..
Unknown - Inconnu	*1*	*1*	-	..
Belize				
2016 (U)[12]				
Total	*7 200*	*3 615*	*3 585*	...
0 - 14	*20*	*11*	*9*	..
15 - 19	*1 337*	*653*	*684*	...
20 - 24	*2 323*	*1 171*	*1 152*	...
25 - 29	*1 780*	*924*	*856*	...
30 - 34	*1 054*	*524*	*530*	...
35 - 39	*543*	*260*	*283*	...
40 - 44	*129*	*65*	*64*	...
45 - 49	*14*	*7*	*7*	...
50 +	-	-	-	..
2018 (U)				
Total	*7 775*	...	...	...
10 - 14	*13*	...	...	..
15 - 19	*1 395*	...	...	...
20 - 24	*2 446*	...	...	...
25 - 29	*1 938*	...	...	...
30 - 34	*1 170*	...	...	...
35 - 39	*627*	...	...	...
40 - 44	*172*	...	...	...
45 +	*14*	...	...	...
Bermuda - Bermudes[13]				
2018 (C)				
Total	530	256	274	38.0
10 - 14	-	-	-	..
15 - 19	7	1	6	♦4.3
20 - 24	56	32	24	37.6
AMERICA, NORTH - AMÉRIQUE DU NORD				
Bermuda - Bermudes[13]				
2018 (C)				
25 - 29	109	57	52	65.9
30 - 34	170	77	93	81.7
35 - 39	146	68	78	61.0
40 - 44	36	20	16	16.0
45 - 49	5	-	5	♦2.0
50 +	1	1	-	..
British Virgin Islands - Îles Vierges britanniques				
2017 (C)				
Total	248	...	...	...
13 - 19	16	...	...	...
20 - 24	35	...	...	...
25 - 29	51	...	...	...
30 - 34	86	...	...	...
35 - 39	32	...	...	...
40 +	20	...	...	...
Unknown - Inconnu	8	...	...	..
Canada[14]				
2018 (C)				
Total	372 329	190 879	181 450	44.4
10 - 14	55	27	28	..
15 - 19	6 736	3 510	3 226	6.6
20 - 24	39 409	20 400	19 009	33.8
25 - 29	104 284	53 425	50 859	83.5
30 - 34	134 240	68 798	65 442	106.3
35 - 39	72 096	36 777	35 319	57.0
40 - 44	14 493	7 429	7 064	12.0
45 - 49	944	476	468	0.8
50 +	72	37	35	..
Cayman Islands - Îles Caïmanes				
2019 (C)				
Total	646	...	...	...
10 - 14	1	...	...	..
15 - 19	12	...	...	...
20 - 24	78	...	...	...
25 - 29	154	...	...	...
30 - 34	207	...	...	...
35 - 39	148	...	...	...
40 - 44	46	...	...	...
Costa Rica				
2019* (C)				
Total	64 287	32 718	31 569	48.7
10 - 14	264	138	126	..
15 - 19	7 776	4 023	3 753	38.6
20 - 24	16 774	8 558	8 216	87.1
25 - 29	17 042	8 569	8 473	87.5
30 - 34	13 615	6 919	6 696	66.6
35 - 39	7 086	3 608	3 478	36.4
40 - 44	1 637	853	784	9.4
45 - 49	64	36	28	0.4
50 +	3	2	1	..
Unknown - Inconnu	26	12	14	..
Cuba				
2018 (C)				
Total	116 333	60 374	55 959	44.3
10 - 14	433	231	202	..
15 - 19	17 901	9 326	8 575	53.3
20 - 24	32 483	16 783	15 700	96.8
25 - 29	34 091	17 656	16 435	88.0
30 - 34	21 169	11 116	10 053	58.0
35 - 39	8 153	4 176	3 977	26.7
40 - 44	1 910	982	928	4.8

10. Live births by age of mother and sex of child, general and age-specific fertility rates: latest available year, 2010 - 2019
Naissances vivantes selon l'âge de la mère et le sexe de l'enfant, taux de fécondité et taux de fécondité par âge : dernière année disponible, 2010 - 2019 (continued - suite)

Continent, country or area, year, code[a] and age of mother (in years) / Continent, pays ou zone, année, code[a] et âge de la mère (en années)	Number - Nombre			
	Total	Male Masculin	Female Féminin	Rate Taux
AMERICA, NORTH - AMÉRIQUE DU NORD				
Cuba				
2018 (C)				
45 - 49	121	64	57	0.2
50 +	32	17	15	..
Unknown - Inconnu	40	23	17	..
Curaçao				
2016 (C)				
Total	1 789	901	888	47.8
0 - 14	4	2	2	..
15 - 19	113	64	49	22.9
20 - 24	417	202	215	91.6
25 - 29	465	233	232	98.2
30 - 34	421	211	210	82.8
35 - 39	255	136	119	49.9
40 - 44	65	33	32	11.2
45 - 49	6	2	4	♦0.9
50 +	-	-	-	..
Unknown - Inconnu	43	18	25	..
2018 (C)[12]				
Total	1 727	...	...	...
0 - 19	117	...	...	...
20 - 24	353	...	...	...
25 - 29	466	...	...	...
30 - 34	442	...	...	...
35 - 39	236	...	...	...
40 +	73	...	...	...
Unknown - Inconnu	40	...	...	..
Dominican Republic - République dominicaine				
2019 (U)				
Total	*167 686*	*85 419*	*82 267*	...
10 - 14	*746*	*380*	*366*	..
15 - 19	*25 178*	*12 819*	*12 359*	...
20 - 24	*47 961*	*24 434*	*23 527*	...
25 - 29	*45 896*	*23 395*	*22 501*	...
30 - 34	*29 086*	*14 781*	*14 305*	...
35 - 39	*13 130*	*6 658*	*6 472*	...
40 - 44	*2 897*	*1 488*	*1 409*	...
45 - 49	*155*	*82*	*73*	...
50 +	*14*	*7*	*7*	..
Unknown - Inconnu	*2 623*	*1 375*	*1 248*	..
El Salvador[15]				
2015 (C)				
Total	109 617	56 757	52 860	58.9
0 - 14	923	466	457	..
15 - 19	23 452	12 226	11 226	67.2
20 - 24	32 224	16 716	15 508	94.1
25 - 29	24 090	12 451	11 639	82.7
30 - 34	17 103	8 802	8 301	68.5
35 - 39	8 891	4 564	4 327	39.2
40 - 44	2 333	1 205	1 128	11.1
45 - 49	171	96	75	0.9
50 +	45	17	28	..
Unknown - Inconnu	385	214	171	..
Greenland - Groenland				
2019 (C)				
Total	849	420	429	66.0
10 - 14	-	-	-	..
15 - 19	65	35	30	37.0
20 - 24	224	112	112	108.9
25 - 29	245	123	122	106.6
30 - 34	213	106	107	99.1
35 - 39	88	36	52	48.4
40 - 44	13	7	6	♦9.5
45 +	1	1	-	♦0.7
AMERICA, NORTH - AMÉRIQUE DU NORD				
Grenada - Grenade				
2014 (+C)				
Total	1 750	900	850	62.8
10 - 14	4	1	3	..
15 - 19	169	91	78	35.9
20 - 24	481	252	229	101.2
25 - 29	500	257	243	103.1
30 - 34	351	179	172	88.9
35 - 39	166	85	81	52.3
40 - 44	50	24	26	16.8
45 - 49	5	2	3	♦1.6
Unknown - Inconnu	24	9	15	..
Guadeloupe[9]				
2018 (C)				
Total	4 249	...	...	45.5
0 - 19	133	...	...	9.5
20 - 24	652	...	...	65.3
25 - 29	1 013	...	...	93.7
30 - 34	1 195	...	...	102.5
35 - 39	903	...	...	69.3
40 +	353	...	...	10.4
Guatemala				
2011 (C)				
Total	373 692	189 724	183 968	102.4
0 - 14	2 841	1 426	1 415	..
15 - 19	75 175	38 415	36 760	92.4
20 - 24	108 949	55 558	53 391	157.0
25 - 29	85 914	43 599	42 315	142.0
30 - 34	58 050	29 264	28 786	113.4
35 - 39	30 892	15 540	15 352	73.8
40 - 44	10 220	5 136	5 084	30.5
45 - 49	1 176	573	603	4.4
50 +	290	127	163	..
Unknown - Inconnu	185	86	99	..
2018 (C)				
Total	383 263	...	...	85.8
10 - 14	2 004	...	...	..
15 - 19	72 615	...	...	77.7
20 - 24	117 125	...	...	138.9
25 - 29	89 425	...	...	124.3
30 - 34	59 125	...	...	94.2
35 - 39	32 409	...	...	60.3
40 - 44	9 744	...	...	21.9
45 - 49	633	...	...	1.8
50 +	44	...	...	..
Unknown - Inconnu	139	...	...	..
Honduras				
2012 (+U)				
Total	*196 119*	...	...	...
0 - 14	*1 571*	...	...	..
15 - 19	*41 882*	...	...	...
20 - 24	*56 501*	...	...	...
25 - 29	*43 429*	...	...	...
30 - 34	*28 675*	...	...	...
35 - 39	*14 730*	...	...	...
40 - 44	*4 791*	...	...	...
45 - 49	*575*	...	...	...
50 +	*471*	...	...	..
Unknown - Inconnu	*3 494*	...	...	..
Jamaica - Jamaïque[16]				
2011 (I)				
Total	49 676	23 949[17]	23 339[17]	66.0
15 - 19	6 167	3 034[17]	2 884[17]	50.5
20 - 24	13 977	6 852[17]	6 451[17]	129.9
25 - 29	12 348	5 923[17]	5 900[17]	108.7

10. Live births by age of mother and sex of child, general and age-specific fertility rates: latest available year, 2010 - 2019
Naissances vivantes selon l'âge de la mère et le sexe de l'enfant, taux de fécondité et taux de fécondité par âge : dernière année disponible, 2010 - 2019 (continued - suite)

Continent, country or area, year, code[a] and age of mother (in years) / Continent, pays ou zone, année, code[a] et âge de la mère (en années)	Number - Nombre Total	Male Masculin	Female Féminin	Rate Taux
AMERICA, NORTH - AMÉRIQUE DU NORD				
Jamaica - Jamaïque[16]				
2011 (I)				
30 - 34	8 746	4 182[17]	4 145[17]	73.9
35 - 39	6 001	2 816[17]	2 875[17]	48.9
40 - 44	2 109	1 014[17]	956[17]	21.2
45 - 49	328	128[17]	128[17]	4.8
Martinique[9]				
2017 (C)				
Total	3 640	...	...	46.5
10 - 14	3	...	...	..
15 - 19	213	...	...	18.6
20 - 24	666	...	...	79.5
25 - 29	926	...	...	98.9
30 - 34	987	...	...	99.0
35 - 39	630	...	...	61.3
40 - 44	199	...	...	15.7
45 - 49	16	...	...	♦1.0
50 +	-	...	...	..
Mexico - Mexique[18]				
2017 (C)				
Total	2 000 591	1 020 094[17]	980 490[17]	59.0
10 - 14	6 544	3 446[17]	3 098[17]	..
15 - 19	339 403	173 353[17]	166 047[17]	62.1
20 - 24	584 394	298 017[17]	286 375[17]	107.8
25 - 29	509 894	259 871[17]	250 022[17]	98.9
30 - 34	344 849	175 939[17]	168 909[17]	71.3
35 - 39	167 209	84 800[17]	82 409[17]	36.0
40 - 44	40 565	20 634[17]	19 931[17]	9.3
45 - 49	2 803	1 420[17]	1 383[17]	0.7
50 +	314	158[17]	156[17]	..
Unknown - Inconnu	4 616	2 456[17]	2 160[17]	..
Montserrat				
2016 (C)				
Total	46	23	23	...
0 - 14	-	-	-	..
15 - 19	2	-	2	...
20 - 24	10	5	5	...
25 - 29	11	7	4	...
30 - 34	11	6	5	...
35 - 39	8	4	4	...
40 - 44	4	1	3	...
45 +	-	-	-	...
Nicaragua				
2010 (+U)				
Total	*132 165*	*68 726*	*63 439*	...
0 - 14	*1 539*	*793*	*746*	..
15 - 19	*33 963*	*17 752*	*16 211*	...
20 - 24	*38 897*	*20 181*	*18 716*	...
25 - 29	*30 273*	*15 790*	*14 483*	...
30 - 34	*17 301*	*8 942*	*8 359*	...
35 - 39	*8 010*	*4 156*	*3 854*	...
40 - 44	*1 943*	*992*	*951*	...
45 - 49	*209*	*105*	*104*	...
50 +	*30*	*15*	*15*	..
Panama				
2018 (C)				
Total	76 863	39 620	37 243	72.0
10 - 14	522	276	246	..
15 - 19	12 840	6 626	6 214	73.5
20 - 24	21 903	11 312	10 591	131.7
25 - 29	18 602	9 496	9 106	117.9
30 - 34	13 506	7 011	6 495	88.4
35 - 39	7 368	3 813	3 555	50.5
40 - 44	1 965	1 011	954	14.0

Continent, country or area, year, code[a] and age of mother (in years) / Continent, pays ou zone, année, code[a] et âge de la mère (en années)	Number - Nombre Total	Male Masculin	Female Féminin	Rate Taux
AMERICA, NORTH - AMÉRIQUE DU NORD				
Panama				
2018 (C)				
45 - 49	137	66	71	1.1
50 +	9	4	5	..
Unknown - Inconnu	11	5	6	..
Puerto Rico - Porto Rico				
2019 (C)				
Total	20 409	10 465	9 944	...
10 - 14	15	6	9	..
15 - 19	1 890	958	932	...
20 - 24	6 241	3 222	3 019	...
25 - 29	5 680	2 908	2 772	...
30 - 34	3 977	2 023	1 954	...
35 - 39	2 064	1 080	984	...
40 - 44	515	255	260	...
45 - 49	27	13	14	...
50 +	-	-	-	..
Saint Barthélemy - Saint-Barthélemy				
2014 (C)				
Total	96	59	37	...
10 - 14	-	-	-	..
15 - 19	-	-	-	...
20 - 24	10	7	3	...
25 - 29	30	18	12	...
30 - 34	31	19	12	...
35 - 39	18	10	8	...
40 - 44	7	5	2	...
45 +	-	-	-	...
Saint Lucia - Sainte-Lucie				
2014 (+C)				
Total	2 026	...	...	42.3
10 - 14	6	...	...	..
15 - 19	295	...	...	40.3
20 - 24	536	...	...	70.7
25 - 29	481	...	...	66.7
30 - 34	391	...	...	57.0
35 - 39	245	...	...	38.7
40 - 44	64	...	...	10.1
45 +	8	...	...	♦1.3
Saint Pierre and Miquelon - Saint Pierre-et-Miquelon				
2014 (C)				
Total	61	30	31	...
10 - 14	5	3	2	..
15 - 19	25	12	13	...
20 - 24	17	11	6	...
25 - 29	11	3	8	...
30 - 34	2	1	1	...
35 - 39	1	-	1	...
40 +	-	-	-	...
Saint Vincent and the Grenadines - Saint-Vincent-et-les Grenadines				
2017 (C)				
Total	1 539	796	743	55.0
10 - 14	11	6	5	..
15 - 19	241	132	109	49.5
20 - 24	395	202	193	92.6
25 - 29	362	185	177	88.3
30 - 34	276	150	126	69.2
35 - 39	192	88	104	51.6
40 - 44	54	27	27	15.9

Continent, country or area, year, code[a] and age of mother (in years) / Continent, pays ou zone, année, code[a] et âge de la mère (en années)	Number - Nombre: Total	Male Masculin	Female Féminin	Rate Taux
AMERICA, NORTH - AMÉRIQUE DU NORD				
Saint Vincent and the Grenadines - Saint-Vincent-et-les Grenadines				
2017 (C)				
45 - 49	8	6	2	♦2.2
Unknown - Inconnu	-	-	-	..
Saint-Martin (French part) - Saint-Martin (partie française)				
2014 (C)				
Total	693	370	323	88.6
10 - 14	-	-	-	..
15 - 19	55	33	22	52.9
20 - 24	134	79	55	131.1
25 - 29	195	100	95	181.4
30 - 34	175	81	94	155.3
35 - 39	117	67	50	106.5
40 - 44	15	9	6	♦12.2
45 - 49	2	1	1	♦1.6
50 +	-	-	-	..
Turks and Caicos Islands - Îles Turques et Caïques				
2016 (C)				
Total	518	272	246	44.7
0 - 14	-	-	-	..
15 - 19	31	17	14	27.3
20 - 24	79	47	32	58.8
25 - 29	117	55	62	73.6
30 - 34	141	77	64	77.5
35 - 39	116	54	62	57.4
40 - 44	26	19	7	♦13.9
45 +	-	-	-	-
Unknown - Inconnu	8	3	5	..
2019* (C)				
Total	487	...	...	...
0 - 14	-	...	...	..
15 - 19	24	...	...	...
20 - 24	77	...	...	...
25 - 29	116	...	...	...
30 - 34	143	...	...	...
35 - 39	99	...	...	...
40 - 44	25	...	...	...
45 - 49	3	...	...	...
50 +	-	...	...	..
United States of America - États-Unis d'Amérique				
2015 (C)				
Total	3 978 497	2 036 161	1 942 336	53.7
0 - 14	2 500	1 265	1 235	..
15 - 19	229 715	118 021	111 694	22.3
20 - 24	850 509	435 461	415 048	76.8
25 - 29	1 152 311	589 719	562 592	104.3
30 - 34	1 094 693	560 429	534 264	101.5
35 - 39	527 996	269 784	258 212	51.8
40 - 44	111 848	56 922	54 926	11.0
45 - 49	8 171	4 172	3 999	0.8
50 +	754	388	366	..
2018 (C)				
Total	3 791 712	...	...	50.8
10 - 14	1 736	...	...	..
15 - 19	179 871	...	...	17.4
20 - 24	726 175	...	...	68.0
25 - 29	1 099 491	...	...	95.3
30 - 34	1 090 697	...	...	99.7

Continent, country or area, year, code[a] and age of mother (in years) / Continent, pays ou zone, année, code[a] et âge de la mère (en années)	Number - Nombre: Total	Male Masculin	Female Féminin	Rate Taux
AMERICA, NORTH - AMÉRIQUE DU NORD				
United States of America - États-Unis d'Amérique				
2018 (C)				
35 - 39	566 786	...	...	52.6
40 - 44	117 381	...	...	11.8
45 - 49	8 616	...	...	0.8
50 +	959	...	...	..
AMERICA, SOUTH - AMÉRIQUE DU SUD				
Argentina - Argentine				
2018 (C)				
Total	685 394	348 242[17]	330 910[17]	61.1
10 - 14	2 350	1 190[17]	1 142[17]	..
15 - 19	84 768	43 125[17]	41 055[17]	50.1
20 - 24	164 480	84 143[17]	78 910[17]	95.1
25 - 29	163 156	82 644[17]	79 230[17]	95.5
30 - 34	140 679	71 725[17]	67 925[17]	87.8
35 - 39	91 509	46 389[17]	44 418[17]	58.7
40 - 44	26 793	13 477[17]	13 091[17]	18.2
Unknown - Inconnu	11 659	5 549[17]	5 139[17]	..
Brazil - Brésil				
2017 (+C)				
Total	2 874 466	1 473 166[17]	1 400 998[17]	50.9
10 - 14	19 156	9 923[17]	9 227[17]	..
15 - 19	437 603	224 840[17]	212 705[17]	52.1
20 - 24	715 776	367 504[17]	348 205[17]	85.4
25 - 29	686 420	351 382[17]	334 982[17]	81.5
30 - 34	586 037	299 955[17]	286 027[17]	67.0
35 - 39	334 720	171 042[17]	163 640[17]	40.1
40 - 44	77 923	39 742[17]	38 177[17]	10.6
45 - 49	4 525	2 290[17]	2 235[17]	0.7
50 +	364	191[17]	173[17]	..
Unknown - Inconnu	11 942	6 297[17]	5 627[17]	..
Chile - Chili				
2017 (C)				
Total	219 186	111 660[17]	107 501[17]	46.9
10 - 14	472	236[17]	236[17]	..
15 - 19	16 897	8 576[17]	8 319[17]	27.0
20 - 24	45 057	22 950[17]	22 102[17]	65.1
25 - 29	59 455	30 150[17]	29 295[17]	79.0
30 - 34	53 929	27 573[17]	26 353[17]	75.9
35 - 39	33 523	17 144[17]	16 374[17]	52.7
40 - 44	9 095	4 656[17]	4 439[17]	14.6
45 - 49	537	264[17]	273[17]	0.9
50 +	19	10[17]	9[17]	..
Unknown - Inconnu	202	101[17]	101[17]	..
Colombia - Colombie				
2019* (U)				
Total	*638 516*	*327 875*[17]	*310 581*[17]	...
10 - 14	*4 758*	*2 451*[17]	*2 306*[17]	..
15 - 19	*117 633*	*60 467*[17]	*57 154*[17]	...
20 - 24	*184 243*	*95 054*[17]	*89 178*[17]	...
25 - 29	*155 920*	*79 973*[17]	*75 933*[17]	...
30 - 34	*104 699*	*53 593*[17]	*51 093*[17]	...
35 - 39	*56 245*	*28 754*[17]	*27 486*[17]	...
40 - 44	*13 934*	*7 056*[17]	*6 875*[17]	...
45 - 49	*949*	*449*[17]	*499*[17]	...
50 +	*124*	*73*[17]	*51*[17]	..
Unknown - Inconnu	*11*	*5*[17]	*6*[17]	..

10. Live births by age of mother and sex of child, general and age-specific fertility rates: latest available year, 2010 - 2019
Naissances vivantes selon l'âge de la mère et le sexe de l'enfant, taux de fécondité et taux de fécondité par âge : dernière année disponible, 2010 - 2019 (continued - suite)

Continent, country or area, year, code[a] and age of mother (in years) / Continent, pays ou zone, année, code[a] et âge de la mère (en années)	Number - Nombre			Rate Taux
	Total	Male Masculin	Female Féminin	
AMERICA, SOUTH - AMÉRIQUE DU SUD				
Ecuador - Équateur[19]				
2018* (U)				
Total	*293 139*	*149 198*	*143 941*	...
10 - 14	*2 089*	*1 040*	*1 049*	..
15 - 19	*53 940*	*27 423*	*26 517*	...
20 - 24	*77 445*	*39 479*	*37 966*	...
25 - 29	*69 170*	*35 155*	*34 015*	...
30 - 34	*50 321*	*25 683*	*24 638*	...
35 - 39	*27 443*	*13 984*	*13 459*	...
40 - 44	*7 158*	*3 661*	*3 497*	...
45 - 49	*473*	*222*	*251*	...
50 +	*35*	*14*	*21*	..
Unknown - Inconnu	*5 065*	*2 537*	*2 528*	..
French Guiana - Guyane française[9]				
2017 (C)				
Total	8 057	...	...	114.8
10 - 14	52	...	...	..
15 - 19	1 015	...	...	79.7
20 - 24	1 706	...	...	178.3
25 - 29	1 988	...	...	201.8
30 - 34	1 818	...	...	171.2
35 - 39	1 117	...	...	111.6
40 - 44	332	...	...	35.7
45 - 49	28	...	...	♦3.5
50 +	1	...	...	..
Guyana[4]				
2012 (I)				
Total	13 023	...	...	65.5
15 - 19	2 082	...	...	49.5
20 - 24	3 939	...	...	123.4
25 - 29	2 918	...	...	109.8
30 - 34	2 304	...	...	85.3
35 - 39	1 347	...	...	51.8
40 - 44	397	...	...	16.7
45 - 49	36	...	...	1.7
Paraguay[10]				
2016 (+U)				
Total	*122 336*	...	...	...
10 - 14	*215*	...	...	..
15 - 19	*15 391*	...	...	...
20 - 24	*32 373*	...	...	...
25 - 29	*30 646*	...	...	...
30 - 34	*22 502*	...	...	...
35 - 39	*11 900*	...	...	...
40 - 44	*3 863*	...	...	...
45 - 49	*776*	...	...	...
50 +	*253*	...	...	..
Unknown - Inconnu	*4 417*	...	...	..
Peru - Pérou[20]				
2019* (+U)				
Total	*485 269*	*248 672*	*236 597*	...
10 - 14	*1 294*	*644*	*650*	..
15 - 19	*52 005*	*26 861*	*25 144*	...
20 - 24	*110 654*	*57 049*	*53 605*	...
25 - 29	*119 585*	*61 169*	*58 416*	...
30 - 34	*104 635*	*53 402*	*51 233*	...
35 - 39	*69 264*	*35 476*	*33 788*	...
40 - 44	*25 528*	*12 938*	*12 590*	...
45 - 49	*2 193*	*1 086*	*1 107*	...
50 +	*102*	*43*	*59*	..
Unknown - Inconnu	*9*	*4*	*5*	..

Continent, country or area, year, code[a] and age of mother (in years) / Continent, pays ou zone, année, code[a] et âge de la mère (en années)	Number - Nombre			Rate Taux
	Total	Male Masculin	Female Féminin	
AMERICA, SOUTH - AMÉRIQUE DU SUD				
Suriname				
2018 (C)				
Total	9 809	5 024	4 785	65.1
10 - 14	54	...	...	..
15 - 19	1 283	...	...	53.9
20 - 24	2 451	...	...	105.6
25 - 29	2 568	...	...	113.1
30 - 34	2 055	...	...	93.8
35 - 39	1 064	...	...	51.2
40 - 44	318	...	...	16.3
45 - 49	16	...	...	♦0.9
50 +	-	...	...	..
Uruguay				
2018 (C)				
Total	40 139	20 683[17]	19 455[17]	46.6
10 - 14	71	36[17]	35[17]	..
15 - 19	4 554	2 328[17]	2 226[17]	35.8
20 - 24	9 623	4 986[17]	4 637[17]	71.9
25 - 29	9 330	4 794[17]	4 535[17]	73.8
30 - 34	9 204	4 689[17]	4 515[17]	76.0
35 - 39	5 716	3 009[17]	2 707[17]	47.4
40 - 44	1 537	786[17]	751[17]	12.7
45 - 49	98	52[17]	46[17]	0.9
50 +	5	3[17]	2[17]	..
Unknown - Inconnu	1	-[17]	1[17]	..
Venezuela (Bolivarian Republic of) - Venezuela (République bolivarienne du)				
2017 (U)				
Total	*579 349*	*298 705*	*280 644*	...
10 - 14	*4 275*	*2 213*	*2 062*	..
15 - 19	*107 018*	*55 351*	*51 667*	...
20 - 24	*166 164*	*85 845*	*80 319*	...
25 - 29	*140 277*	*72 002*	*68 275*	...
30 - 34	*94 664*	*48 667*	*45 997*	...
35 - 39	*48 719*	*25 195*	*23 524*	...
40 - 44	*12 698*	*6 442*	*6 256*	...
45 - 49	*1 248*	*669*	*579*	...
50 +	*293*	*154*	*139*	..
Unknown - Inconnu	*3 993*	*2 167*	*1 826*	..
ASIA - ASIE				
Armenia - Arménie				
2018 (C)				
Total	36 574	19 252	17 322	48.5
0 - 14	4	3	1	..
15 - 19	1 466	751	715	18.9
20 - 24	10 336	5 297	5 039	109.2
25 - 29	13 286	6 986	6 300	98.2
30 - 34	7 897	4 314	3 583	57.0
35 - 39	3 036	1 626	1 410	25.5
40 - 44	500	254	246	5.1
45 - 49	43	19	24	0.5
50 +	6	2	4	..
Azerbaijan - Azerbaïdjan[21]				
2018 (+C)				
Total	138 982	74 224	64 758	52.5
0 - 14	-	-	-	..
15 - 19	13 246	6 686	6 560	43.2
20 - 24	52 417	27 599	24 818	136.6
25 - 29	44 554	24 094	20 460	95.9
30 - 34	20 594	11 391	9 203	45.3
35 - 39	6 731	3 700	3 031	17.5

10. Live births by age of mother and sex of child, general and age-specific fertility rates: latest available year, 2010 - 2019
Naissances vivantes selon l'âge de la mère et le sexe de l'enfant, taux de fécondité et taux de fécondité par âge : dernière année disponible, 2010 - 2019 (continued - suite)

Continent, country or area, year, code[a] and age of mother (in years) / Continent, pays ou zone, année, code[a] et âge de la mère (en années)	Number - Nombre			Rate Taux
	Total	Male Masculin	Female Féminin	
ASIA - ASIE				
Azerbaijan - Azerbaïdjan[21]				
2018 (+C)				
40 - 44	1 301	676	625	4.1
45 - 49	117	66	51	0.4
50 +	22	12	10	..
Bahrain - Bahreïn[22]				
2018 (C)				
Total	19 740	10 206	9 534	60.2
10 - 14	-	-	-	..
15 - 19	464	250	214	12.4
20 - 24	3 614	1 892	1 722	81.6
25 - 29	6 233	3 219	3 014	101.5
30 - 34	5 493	2 808	2 685	90.4
35 - 39	3 000	1 532	1 468	59.0
40 - 44	861	467	394	20.8
45 - 49	61	31	30	1.9
50 +	12	5	7	..
Unknown - Inconnu	2	2	-	..
Bangladesh				
2010 (U)				
Total	*2 868 494*	*1 451 664*	*1 416 831*	...
15 - 19	*404 570*	*209 615*	*194 955*	...
20 - 24	*1 055 194*	*527 993*	*527 201*	...
25 - 29	*762 338*	*383 627*	*378 710*	...
30 - 34	*389 547*	*199 767*	*189 780*	...
35 - 39	*192 438*	*97 826*	*94 613*	...
40 - 44	*49 380*	*25 206*	*24 174*	...
45 +	*15 027*	*7 630*	*7 397*	...
Brunei Darussalam - Brunéi Darussalam				
2018 (+C)				
Total	6 199	3 239	2 960	50.0
10 - 14	6	4	2	..
15 - 19	165	86	79	9.0
20 - 24	771	402	369	40.2
25 - 29	1 913	1 005	908	101.2
30 - 34	1 968	1 030	938	105.3
35 - 39	1 086	557	529	62.1
40 - 44	270	141	129	16.6
45 - 49	19	14	5	♦1.3
50 +	-	-	-	..
Unknown - Inconnu	1	-	1	..
China, Hong Kong SAR - Chine, Hong Kong RAS				
2019 (C)				
Total	52 856	27 694[17]	25 161[17]	26.5
10 - 14	4	2	2	..
15 - 19	251	132	119	1.8
20 - 24	2 689	1 394	1 295	12.8
25 - 29	10 839	5 667	5 172	40.8
30 - 34	21 437	11 266[17]	10 170[17]	65.1
35 - 39	14 395	7 519	6 876	38.6
40 - 44	3 005	1 569	1 436	8.8
45 - 49	220	135	85	0.6
50 +	16	10	6	..
China, Macao SAR - Chine, Macao RAS				
2019 (C)				
Total	5 979	3 083	2 896	30.8
0 - 24	408	210	198	11.2
25 - 29	2 009	1 012	997	73.1
30 - 34	2 438	1 266	1 172	60.2
35 - 39	937	502	435	28.3
40 +	187	93	94	3.3

Continent, country or area, year, code[a] and age of mother (in years) / Continent, pays ou zone, année, code[a] et âge de la mère (en années)	Number - Nombre			Rate Taux
	Total	Male Masculin	Female Féminin	
ASIA - ASIE				
Cyprus - Chypre[23]				
2018 (C)				
Total	9 329	4 771	4 558	41.9
0 - 14	4	3	1	..
15 - 19	190	97	93	7.8
20 - 24	866	439	427	25.9
25 - 29	2 440	1 218	1 222	64.9
30 - 34	3 494	1 832	1 662	94.7
35 - 39	1 902	959	943	56.7
40 - 44	387	206	181	13.4
45 - 49	40	14	26	1.4
50 +	6	3	3	..
Georgia - Géorgie				
2018 (C)				
Total	51 138	26 538	24 600	60.8
0 - 14	5	3	2	..
15 - 19	3 112	1 627	1 485	32.0
20 - 24	12 786	6 592	6 194	120.4
25 - 29	16 548	8 620	7 928	124.7
30 - 34	11 564	6 099	5 465	85.2
35 - 39	5 627	2 838	2 789	44.3
40 - 44	1 344	681	663	11.0
45 - 49	126	65	61	1.0
50 +	26	13	13	..
Indonesia - Indonésie[24]				
2010 (I)				
Total	6 028 921	...	...	92.5
0 - 14	1 054	...	...	..
15 - 19	344 318	...	...	33.5
20 - 24	1 435 265	...	...	143.5
25 - 29	1 787 802	...	...	167.4
30 - 34	1 352 605	...	...	136.9
35 - 39	776 985	...	...	84.8
40 - 44	254 427	...	...	31.0
45 - 49	57 924	...	...	8.3
50 +	18 541	...	...	..
Iran (Islamic Republic of) - Iran (République islamique d')[25]				
2018 (+C)				
Total	1 334 962	688 453	646 509	58.5
10 - 14	1 502	741	761	..
15 - 19	82 440	42 125	40 315	31.2
20 - 24	255 656	132 040	123 616	89.2
25 - 29	385 790	198 812	186 978	104.5
30 - 34	362 336	186 626	175 710	84.8
35 - 39	190 824	98 816	92 008	50.1
40 - 44	44 068	22 763	21 305	15.0
45 - 49	3 416	1 763	1 653	1.4
50 +	345	158	187	..
Unknown - Inconnu	8 585	4 609	3 976	..
Israel - Israël[26]				
2018 (C)				
Total	184 370	94 510	89 860	89.2
10 - 14	-	-	-	..
15 - 19	2 801	1 490	1 311	8.2
20 - 24	31 908	16 344	15 564	102.3
25 - 29	53 360	27 473	25 887	177.1
30 - 34	54 653	28 064	26 589	184.4
35 - 39	31 692	16 112	15 580	110.4
40 - 44	8 767	4 427	4 340	31.5
45 - 49	810	406	404	3.3
50 +	110	46	64	..
Unknown - Inconnu	269	148	121	..

10. Live births by age of mother and sex of child, general and age-specific fertility rates: latest available year, 2010 - 2019
Naissances vivantes selon l'âge de la mère et le sexe de l'enfant, taux de fécondité et taux de fécondité par âge : dernière année disponible, 2010 - 2019 (continued - suite)

Continent, country or area, year, code[a] and age of mother (in years) / Continent, pays ou zone, année, code[a] et âge de la mère (en années)	Number - Nombre			Rate Taux
	Total	Male Masculin	Female Féminin	
ASIA - ASIE				
Japan - Japon[27]				
2018 (C)				
Total	918 400	470 851	447 549	36.0
10 - 14	37	19	18	..
15 - 19	8 741	4 591	4 150	3.0
20 - 24	77 023	39 468	37 555	25.2
25 - 29	233 754	120 033	113 721	76.8
30 - 34	334 906	171 800	163 106	97.7
35 - 39	211 021	108 170	102 851	55.3
40 - 44	51 258	25 959	25 299	11.3
45 - 49	1 591	773	818	0.3
50 +	68	37	31	..
Unknown - Inconnu	1	1	-	..
Kazakhstan				
2019 (C)				
Total	402 310	208 038	194 272	88.6
10 - 14	18	9	9	..
15 - 19	13 080	6 842	6 238	23.2
20 - 24	96 997	50 189	46 808	166.3
25 - 29	130 092	67 315	62 777	172.7
30 - 34	99 715	51 479	48 236	124.2
35 - 39	49 596	25 654	23 942	74.5
40 - 44	12 221	6 226	5 995	20.3
45 - 49	526	289	237	0.9
50 +	58	30	28	..
Unknown - Inconnu	7	5	2	..
Kuwait - Koweït				
2018 (C)				
Total	56 121	28 924	27 197	59.6
15 - 19	494	258	236	5.4
20 - 24	7 030	3 692	3 338	81.6
25 - 29	15 394	7 905	7 489	165.9
30 - 34	15 578	7 928	7 650	102.8
35 - 39	8 898	4 706	4 192	57.9
40 - 44	2 649	1 341	1 308	17.7
45 +	230	122	108	2.0
Unknown - Inconnu	5 848	2 972	2 876	..
Kyrgyzstan - Kirghizstan				
2018 (C)				
Total	171 149	87 927	83 222	106.8
10 - 14	2	-	2	..
15 - 19	8 722	4 493	4 229	35.9
20 - 24	55 327	28 387	26 940	207.9
25 - 29	53 020	27 182	25 838	186.0
30 - 34	34 346	17 697	16 649	130.4
35 - 39	15 701	8 117	7 584	77.5
40 - 44	3 733	1 888	1 845	21.3
45 - 49	220	123	97	1.3
50 +	8	5	3	..
Unknown - Inconnu	70	35	35	..
Lao People's Democratic Republic - République démocratique populaire lao[28]				
2015 (I)				
Total	125 614	59 336[17]	56 893[17]	71.3
15 - 19	16 718	7 489[17]	7 337[17]	48.5
20 - 24	37 732	17 659[17]	16 926[17]	115.0
25 - 29	35 905	17 153[17]	16 357[17]	121.7
30 - 34	20 533	9 843[17]	9 536[17]	80.6
35 - 39	10 105	4 997[17]	4 567[17]	48.2
40 - 44	3 495	1 661[17]	1 640[17]	19.8
45 +	1 126	534[17]	530[17]	7.3

Continent, country or area, year, code[a] and age of mother (in years) / Continent, pays ou zone, année, code[a] et âge de la mère (en années)	Number - Nombre			Rate Taux
	Total	Male Masculin	Female Féminin	
ASIA - ASIE				
Malaysia - Malaisie				
2018 (C)				
Total	501 945	259 582	242 363	57.2
0 - 14	181	98	83	..
15 - 19	11 757	6 108	5 649	8.5
20 - 24	66 818	34 536	32 282	43.8
25 - 29	157 636	81 740	75 896	103.5
30 - 34	159 166	82 261	76 905	116.9
35 - 39	84 067	43 266	40 801	72.3
40 - 44	20 354	10 509	9 845	21.7
45 - 49	1 378	737	641	1.6
50 +	53	31	22	..
Unknown - Inconnu	535	296	239	..
Maldives[29]				
2017 (C)				
Total	6 723	3 403	3 320	67.4
10 - 14	1	1	-	..
15 - 19	119	65	54	9.1
20 - 24	1 382	712	670	85.2
25 - 29	2 321	1 163	1 158	124.0
30 - 34	1 823	882	941	100.2
35 - 39	829	455	374	61.0
40 - 44	230	116	114	22.0
45 - 49	13	8	5	♦1.4
50 +	2	1	1	..
Unknown - Inconnu	3	-	3	..
Mongolia - Mongolie				
2019 (+C)				
Total	79 580	40 755	38 825	91.9
10 - 14	20	13	7	..
15 - 19	3 383	1 746	1 637	30.5
20 - 24	17 684	9 003	8 681	147.6
25 - 29	23 752	12 061	11 691	166.7
30 - 34	20 280	10 528	9 752	134.7
35 - 39	11 555	5 925	5 630	91.9
40 - 44	2 787	1 423	1 364	24.3
45 - 49	114	54	60	1.1
50 +	5	2	3	..
Myanmar[30]				
2017 (+U)				
Total	*787 172*	*404 997*	*382 175*	...
10 - 14	*123*	*62*	*61*	..
15 - 19	*47 710*	*24 437*	*23 273*	...
20 - 24	*190 660*	*97 934*	*92 726*	...
25 - 29	*212 292*	*109 454*	*102 838*	...
30 - 34	*171 990*	*88 634*	*83 356*	...
35 - 39	*100 281*	*51 658*	*48 623*	...
40 - 44	*29 502*	*15 178*	*14 324*	...
45 - 49	*3 008*	*1 532*	*1 476*	...
50 +	*45*	*23*	*22*	..
Unknown - Inconnu	*31 561*	*16 085*	*15 476*	..
Oman				
2019 (C)				
Total	86 819	44 361	42 458	90.9
10 - 14	4	3	1	..
15 - 19	968	498	470	8.3
20 - 24	11 316	5 736	5 580	82.0
25 - 29	25 875	13 228	12 647	143.5
30 - 34	26 361	13 461	12 900	140.7
35 - 39	16 509	8 442	8 067	109.4
40 - 44	5 317	2 758	2 559	47.6
45 - 49	434	213	221	6.2
50 +	35	22	13	..

10. Live births by age of mother and sex of child, general and age-specific fertility rates: latest available year, 2010 - 2019
Naissances vivantes selon l'âge de la mère et le sexe de l'enfant, taux de fécondité et taux de fécondité par âge : dernière année disponible, 2010 - 2019 (continued - suite)

Continent, country or area, year, code[a] and age of mother (in years) / Continent, pays ou zone, année, code[a] et âge de la mère (en années)	Number - Nombre			Rate Taux
	Total	Male Masculin	Female Féminin	
ASIA - ASIE				
Philippines				
2018 (C)				
Total	1 668 120	870 832	797 288	61.2
0 - 14	2 250	...	...	..
10 - 14	2 250	1 179	1 071	..
15 - 19	181 717	95 068	86 649	36.1
20 - 24	454 648	237 965	216 683	96.2
25 - 29	443 365	231 416	211 949	103.2
30 - 34	322 554	168 123	154 431	83.4
35 - 39	192 250	100 193	92 057	55.1
40 - 44	61 420	31 727	29 693	20.2
45 - 49	5 797	2 983	2 814	2.1
50 +	215	101	114	..
Unknown - Inconnu	3 904	2 077	1 827	..
Qatar				
2018 (C)				
Total	28 069	14 183	13 886	60.9
0 - 19	319	166	153	8.5
20 - 24	3 420	1 780	1 640	75.7
25 - 29	8 417	4 239	4 178	93.1
30 - 34	9 574	4 793	4 781	91.8
35 - 39	4 944	2 506	2 438	57.6
40 - 44	1 283	643	640	21.4
45 - 49	103	50	53	2.7
50 +	9	6	3	..
Republic of Korea - République de Corée[31]				
2018 (C)				
Total	326 822	167 686	159 136	26.4
10 - 14	8	7	1	..
15 - 19	1 292	676	616	1.0
20 - 24	13 313	6 768	6 545	8.1
25 - 29	65 029	33 349	31 680	39.9
30 - 34	143 067	73 513	69 554	89.5
35 - 39	91 101	46 809	44 292	45.9
40 - 44	12 417	6 359	6 058	6.4
45 - 49	389	183	206	0.2
50 +	18	6	12	..
Unknown - Inconnu	188	16	172	..
Saudi Arabia - Arabie saoudite[32]				
2017 (I)				
Total	488 130	254 511	233 619	59.3
15 - 19	10 679	5 299	5 380	9.6
20 - 24	80 426	39 573	40 853	68.0
25 - 29	155 776	82 107	73 669	111.6
30 - 34	126 583	61 190	65 393	97.2
35 - 39	84 258	49 267	34 991	64.1
40 - 44	20 430	11 607	8 823	17.9
45 - 49	9 069	5 454	3 615	11.4
50 +	909	14	895	..
Singapore - Singapour				
2019 (C)				
Total	39 279	19 918	19 361	39.1
10 - 14	3	1	2	..
15 - 19	277	135	142	2.5
20 - 24	1 645	827	818	13.4
25 - 29	9 459	4 865	4 594	64.9
30 - 34	16 571	8 331	8 240	108.1
35 - 39	9 453	4 796	4 657	59.6
40 - 44	1 787	924	863	11.4
45 - 49	79	35	44	0.5
50 +	5	4	1	..
ASIA - ASIE				
Sri Lanka				
2015 (+C)				
Total	336 097	172 049	164 048	60.9
10 - 14	38	24	14	..
15 - 19	13 568	6 998	6 570	16.0
20 - 24	64 173	32 928	31 245	78.8
25 - 29	101 615	52 054	49 561	121.8
30 - 34	98 371	50 326	48 045	113.3
35 - 39	46 912	23 947	22 965	63.0
40 - 44	10 336	5 230	5 106	14.4
45 - 49	1 042	520	522	1.5
50 +	42	22	20	..
Tajikistan - Tadjikistan[33]				
2017 (U)				
Total	*224 057*	...	...	...
10 - 14	-	...	...	..
15 - 19	*12 909*	...	...	...
20 - 24	*94 079*	...	...	...
25 - 29	*68 115*	...	...	...
30 - 34	*34 296*	...	...	...
35 - 39	*11 864*	...	...	...
40 - 44	*2 296*	...	...	...
45 - 49	*126*	...	...	...
50 +	*1*	...	...	..
Unknown - Inconnu	*371*	...	...	..
Thailand - Thaïlande[34]				
2018 (+U)				
Total	*628 450*	*323 809*	*304 641*	...
10 - 14	*2 385*	*1 226*	*1 159*	..
15 - 19	*70 181*	*36 176*	*34 005*	...
20 - 24	*143 958*	*74 431*	*69 527*	...
25 - 29	*164 831*	*85 225*	*79 606*	...
30 - 34	*141 958*	*72 854*	*69 104*	...
35 - 39	*84 225*	*43 175*	*41 050*	...
40 - 44	*19 380*	*9 924*	*9 456*	...
45 - 49	*1 065*	*540*	*525*	...
50 +	*50*	*29*	*21*	..
Unknown - Inconnu	*417*	*229*	*188*	..
Turkey - Turquie				
2018 (C)				
Total	1 248 847	641 056	607 791	58.5
0 - 14	167	100	67	..
15 - 19	59 997	31 046	28 951	19.4
20 - 24	284 121	146 095	138 026	89.6
25 - 29	391 236	200 940	190 296	127.9
30 - 34	304 138	156 098	148 040	98.1
35 - 39	161 706	82 412	79 294	50.1
40 - 44	33 813	17 412	16 401	11.8
45 - 49	2 382	1 147	1 235	0.9
50 +	289	152	137	..
Unknown - Inconnu	10 998	5 654	5 344	..
United Arab Emirates - Émirats arabes unis				
2018 (C)				
Total	95 309	48 730[17]	46 575[17]	...
10 - 14	-	-	-	..
15 - 19	697	371	326	...
20 - 24	9 708	4 949	4 759	...
25 - 29	25 721	13 113	12 608	...
30 - 34	32 575	16 622	15 953	...
35 - 39	20 463	10 545	9 918	...
40 - 44	5 654	2 871	2 783	...
45 - 49	451	239	212	...
50 +	36	20	16	..
Unknown - Inconnu	4	-[17]	-[17]	..

10. Live births by age of mother and sex of child, general and age-specific fertility rates: latest available year, 2010 - 2019
Naissances vivantes selon l'âge de la mère et le sexe de l'enfant, taux de fécondité et taux de fécondité par âge : dernière année disponible, 2010 - 2019 (continued - suite)

Continent, country or area, year, code[a] and age of mother (in years) / Continent, pays ou zone, année, code[a] et âge de la mère (en années)	Number - Nombre			Rate Taux
	Total	Male Masculin	Female Féminin	
ASIA - ASIE				
Uzbekistan - Ouzbékistan				
2018 (+C)				
Total	768 520	403 304	365 216	86.6
10 - 14	1	-	1	..
15 - 19	1 238	594	644	1.0
20 - 24	85 601	44 194	41 407	59.2
25 - 29	319 838	166 700	153 138	209.5
30 - 34	224 516	118 616	105 900	158.1
35 - 39	84 357	45 146	39 211	73.8
40 - 44	22 612	12 077	10 535	23.0
45 - 49	5 510	3 001	2 509	6.2
50 +	3 351	1 811	1 540	..
Unknown - Inconnu	21 497	11 165	10 332	..
EUROPE				
Åland Islands - Îles d'Åland				
2018 (C)				
Total	280	151	129	47.9
10 - 14	-	-	-	..
15 - 19	3	2	1	♦4.1
20 - 24	35	20	15	56.8
25 - 29	105	54	51	126.7
30 - 34	91	54	37	104.2
35 - 39	40	18	22	44.8
40 - 44	6	3	3	♦6.5
45 +	-	-	-	-
Albania - Albanie				
2018 (C)				
Total	28 934	15 025	13 909	41.9
0 - 14	22	6	16	..
15 - 19	1 486	748	738	14.3
20 - 24	7 299	3 755	3 544	60.6
25 - 29	10 314	5 357	4 957	90.1
30 - 34	6 812	3 594	3 218	73.9
35 - 39	2 482	1 295	1 187	30.1
40 - 44	444	230	214	5.3
45 - 49	41	23	18	0.4
50 +	4	2	2	..
Unknown - Inconnu	30	15	15	..
Andorra - Andorre				
2018 (C)				
Total	543	293	250	29.3
0 - 14	-	-	-	..
15 - 19	5	-	5	♦2.5
20 - 24	23	17	6	♦13.1
25 - 29	108	52	56	49.4
30 - 34	184	102	82	73.1
35 - 39	160	88	72	50.8
40 - 44	55	27	28	15.7
45 - 49	8	7	1	♦2.3
50 +	-	-	-	..
Austria - Autriche[35]				
2018 (C)				
Total	85 535	43 796	41 739	43.4
0 - 14	11	8	3	..
15 - 19	1 169	578	591	5.5
20 - 24	9 970	5 126	4 844	38.3
25 - 29	25 316	13 141	12 175	85.9
30 - 34	29 234	14 796	14 438	98.8
35 - 39	16 220	8 285	7 935	55.1
40 - 44	3 345	1 723	1 622	11.7
45 - 49	250	130	120	0.8
50 +	20	9	11	..

Continent, country or area, year, code[a] and age of mother (in years) / Continent, pays ou zone, année, code[a] et âge de la mère (en années)	Number - Nombre			Rate Taux
	Total	Male Masculin	Female Féminin	
EUROPE				
Belarus - Bélarus				
2018 (C)				
Total	94 042	...	...	42.5
0 - 14	6	...	...	..
15 - 19	2 558	...	...	11.6
20 - 24	17 961	...	...	73.8
25 - 29	31 530	...	...	92.9
30 - 34	27 421	...	...	71.6
35 - 39	12 197	...	...	34.4
40 - 44	2 247	...	...	6.7
45 - 49	90	...	...	0.3
50 +	9	...	...	..
Unknown - Inconnu	23	...	...	..
Belgium - Belgique[36]				
2018 (C)				
Total	118 319	60 398	57 921	47.4
0 - 14	21	9	12	..
15 - 19	1 689	889	800	5.5
20 - 24	11 694	5 935	5 759	35.7
25 - 29	38 333	19 696	18 637	104.0
30 - 34	42 136	21 390	20 746	115.9
35 - 39	19 032	9 751	9 281	51.2
40 - 44	4 213	2 133	2 080	11.7
45 - 49	307	156	151	0.8
50 +	24	14	10	..
Unknown - Inconnu	870	425	445	..
Bosnia and Herzegovina - Bosnie-Herzégovine				
2010 (C)				
Total	33 528	17 277	16 251	35.2
12 - 14	8	6	2	..
15 - 19	1 792	950	842	13.5
20 - 24	8 293	4 282	4 011	59.4
25 - 29	11 690	5 949	5 741	86.2
30 - 34	7 985	4 144	3 841	66.8
35 - 39	3 027	1 560	1 467	24.3
40 - 44	557	287	270	3.9
45 - 49	30	14	16	0.2
50 +	1	-	1	..
Unknown - Inconnu	145	85	60	..
2018 (C)				
Total	29 467	...	...	...
10 - 14	5	...	...	..
15 - 19	904	...	...	...
20 - 24	6 029	...	...	...
25 - 29	9 184	...	...	...
30 - 34	8 630	...	...	...
35 - 39	3 898	...	...	...
40 - 44	707	...	...	...
45 - 49	51	...	...	...
50 +	2	...	...	..
Unknown - Inconnu	57	...	...	..
Bulgaria - Bulgarie				
2018 (C)				
Total	62 197	32 144	30 053	41.3
0 - 14	252	132	120	..
15 - 19	5 939	3 094	2 845	38.9
20 - 24	10 625	5 546	5 079	69.3
25 - 29	18 644	9 625	9 019	88.8
30 - 34	16 770	8 645	8 125	72.3
35 - 39	7 825	3 998	3 827	32.9
40 - 44	1 917	993	924	7.2
45 - 49	192	95	97	0.8
50 +	30	14	16	..
Unknown - Inconnu	3	2	1	..

10. Live births by age of mother and sex of child, general and age-specific fertility rates: latest available year, 2010 - 2019
Naissances vivantes selon l'âge de la mère et le sexe de l'enfant, taux de fécondité et taux de fécondité par âge : dernière année disponible, 2010 - 2019 (continued - suite)

Continent, country or area, year, code[a] and age of mother (in years) / Continent, pays ou zone, année, code[a] et âge de la mère (en années)	Number - Nombre: Total	Number - Nombre: Male Masculin	Number - Nombre: Female Féminin	Rate Taux
EUROPE				
Croatia - Croatie				
2018 (C)				
Total	36 945	19 078	17 867	42.2
0 - 14	3	1	2	..
15 - 19	875	441	434	8.6
20 - 24	4 813	2 500	2 313	41.0
25 - 29	10 318	5 325	4 993	87.7
30 - 34	12 787	6 625	6 162	98.0
35 - 39	6 745	3 478	3 267	48.5
40 - 44	1 337	675	662	9.8
45 - 49	65	32	33	0.5
50 +	2	1	1	..
Czechia - Tchéquie				
2018 (C)				
Total	114 036	58 256	55 780	48.1
0 - 14	14	7	7	..
15 - 19	2 429	1 271	1 158	10.8
20 - 24	12 796	6 511	6 285	51.3
25 - 29	34 571	17 744	16 827	105.3
30 - 34	39 505	20 182	19 323	112.5
35 - 39	20 020	10 164	9 856	51.5
40 - 44	4 444	2 243	2 201	9.8
45 - 49	247	127	120	0.7
50 +	10	7	3	..
Denmark - Danemark[37]				
2018 (C)				
Total	61 476	31 611	29 865	48.6
0 - 14	-	-	-	..
15 - 19	409	208	201	2.4
20 - 24	6 022	3 160	2 862	31.9
25 - 29	20 895	10 719	10 176	109.0
30 - 34	21 541	10 978	10 563	128.4
35 - 39	10 107	5 248	4 859	60.9
40 - 44	2 345	1 222	1 123	12.5
45 - 49	141	70	71	0.7
50 +	16	6	10	..
Estonia - Estonie				
2018 (C)				
Total	14 367	7 345	7 022	50.3
0 - 14	2	-	2	..
15 - 19	283	152	131	9.6
20 - 24	1 499	764	735	46.8
25 - 29	4 411	2 267	2 144	102.0
30 - 34	4 872	2 517	2 355	103.5
35 - 39	2 554	1 276	1 278	57.5
40 - 44	705	351	354	15.9
45 - 49	38	16	22	0.8
50 +	3	2	1	..
Faroe Islands - Îles Féroé				
2019 (C)				
Total	683	343	340	65.7
10 - 14	-	-	-	..
15 - 19	15	8	7	♦8.7
20 - 24	105	52	53	79.4
25 - 29	220	117	103	159.7
30 - 34	213	109	104	147.7
35 - 39	98	42	56	68.7
40 - 44	23	9	14	♦15.5
45 +	-	-	-	-
Unknown - Inconnu	9	6	3	..
Finland - Finlande				
2018 (C)				
Total	47 577	24 630	22 947	42.0
0 - 14	-	-	-	..
15 - 19	622	327	295	4.3
EUROPE				
Finland - Finlande				
2018 (C)				
20 - 24	5 692	3 022	2 670	36.2
25 - 29	13 895	7 185	6 710	81.1
30 - 34	16 070	8 286	7 784	95.0
35 - 39	9 099	4 668	4 431	53.5
40 - 44	2 083	1 080	1 003	12.8
45 - 49	108	58	50	0.7
50 +	8	4	4	..
France				
2014 (C)				
Total	806 101	411 604	394 497	57.1
10 - 14	134	66	68	..
15 - 19	15 977	8 153	7 824	8.6
20 - 24	103 146	52 889	50 257	55.9
25 - 29	255 898	130 683	125 215	131.6
30 - 34	267 500	136 400	131 100	131.1
35 - 39	128 988	65 989	62 999	65.0
40 - 44	32 280	16 303	15 977	14.5
45 - 49	2 059	1 070	989	0.9
50 +	119	51	68	..
2018 (C)				
Total	719 737	...	...	51.6
0 - 19	8 869	...	...	4.6
20 - 24	71 872	...	...	40.2
25 - 29	200 722	...	...	107.0
30 - 34	254 936	...	...	126.9
35 - 39	143 921	...	...	68.8
40 - 44	36 493	...	...	18.0
45 - 49	2 752	...	...	1.2
50 +	172	...	...	..
Germany - Allemagne				
2018 (C)				
Total	787 523	404 052	383 471	46.2
0 - 14	109	54	55	..
15 - 19	14 351	7 474	6 877	7.4
20 - 24	78 339	40 379	37 960	35.8
25 - 29	212 596	108 965	103 631	84.3
30 - 34	285 291	146 180	139 111	109.8
35 - 39	162 555	83 457	79 098	63.3
40 - 44	32 170	16 451	15 719	13.5
45 - 49	1 846	957	889	0.6
50 +	167	85	82	..
Unknown - Inconnu	99	50	49	..
Gibraltar[38]				
2016 (+C)				
Total	424	201	223	...
0 - 19	6	3	3	...
20 - 24	53	23	30	...
25 - 29	120	57	63	...
30 - 34	128	61	67	...
35 - 39	92	45	47	...
40 +	25	12	13	...
Greece - Grèce				
2018 (C)				
Total	86 440	44 525	41 915	36.9
0 - 14	105	44	61	..
15 - 19	2 226	1 212	1 014	8.5
20 - 24	7 225	3 727	3 498	27.2
25 - 29	18 316	9 421	8 895	63.9
30 - 34	29 781	15 314	14 467	95.0
35 - 39	22 140	11 452	10 688	56.7
40 - 44	5 614	2 852	2 762	13.9
45 - 49	920	450	470	2.2
50 +	113	53	60	..

10. Live births by age of mother and sex of child, general and age-specific fertility rates: latest available year, 2010 - 2019
Naissances vivantes selon l'âge de la mère et le sexe de l'enfant, taux de fécondité et taux de fécondité par âge : dernière année disponible, 2010 - 2019 (continued - suite)

Continent, country or area, year, code[a] and age of mother (in years) Continent, pays ou zone, année, code[a] et âge de la mère (en années)	Number - Nombre Total	 Male Masculin	 Female Féminin	Rate Taux
EUROPE				
Hungary - Hongrie[39]				
2018 (C)				
Total	93 467	48 008	45 459	41.8
0 - 14	74	41	33	..
15 - 19	5 226	2 688	2 538	22.0
20 - 24	13 077	6 655	6 422	47.3
25 - 29	24 279	12 416	11 863	80.1
30 - 34	28 550	14 662	13 888	96.3
35 - 39	17 238	8 942	8 296	50.0
40 - 44	4 837	2 504	2 333	11.5
45 - 49	179	97	82	0.5
50 +	7	3	4	..
Unknown - Inconnu	-	-	-	..
Iceland - Islande				
2018 (C)				
Total	4 228	2 242	1 986	51.6
0 - 14	1	1	-	..
15 - 19	58	23	35	5.3
20 - 24	602	308	294	48.4
25 - 29	1 454	779	675	108.4
30 - 34	1 254	657	597	106.5
35 - 39	699	390	309	59.0
40 - 44	144	77	67	13.2
45 - 49	15	7	8	♦1.4
50 +	1	-	1	..
Ireland - Irlande				
2018 (+C)				
Total	61 022	31 306	29 716	52.0
0 - 14	1	1	-	..
15 - 19	955	505	450	6.2
20 - 24	5 070	2 594	2 476	36.2
25 - 29	10 486	5 325	5 161	72.0
30 - 34	20 881	10 670	10 211	118.6
35 - 39	19 010	9 843	9 167	93.4
40 - 44	4 301	2 203	2 098	23.2
45 - 49	299	157	142	1.8
50 +	19	8	11	..
Isle of Man - Île de Man[40]				
2016 (I)				
Total	731	...	...	41.4
10 - 14	1	...	...	..
15 - 19	23	...	...	♦10.1
20 - 24	111	...	...	51.2
25 - 29	178	...	...	81.1
30 - 34	238	...	...	100.9
35 - 39	146	...	...	58.4
40 - 44	33	...	...	11.4
45 - 49	1	...	...	♦0.3
50 +	-	...	...	..
Italy - Italie				
2018 (C)				
Total	439 747	226 217	213 530	34.8
0 - 14	8	5	3	..
15 - 19	5 731	2 946	2 785	4.1
20 - 24	35 626	18 477	17 149	25.0
25 - 29	97 738	50 393	47 345	62.0
30 - 34	149 464	76 900	72 564	89.2
35 - 39	111 897	57 502	54 395	59.7
40 - 44	35 405	18 034	17 371	15.7
45 - 49	3 483	1 754	1 729	1.4
50 +	395	206	189	..
Latvia - Lettonie				
2018 (C)				
Total	19 314	9 995	9 319	46.4
0 - 14	2	-	2	..
EUROPE				
Latvia - Lettonie				
2018 (C)				
15 - 19	520	259	261	12.2
20 - 24	2 429	1 229	1 200	54.0
25 - 29	6 110	3 212	2 898	95.7
30 - 34	6 173	3 182	2 991	90.4
35 - 39	3 199	1 663	1 536	51.5
40 - 44	825	418	407	12.6
45 - 49	52	30	22	0.8
50 +	2	1	1	..
Unknown - Inconnu	2	1	1	..
Liechtenstein				
2018 (C)				
Total	378	192	186	44.7
0 - 14	-	-	-	..
15 - 19	1	1	-	♦1.0
20 - 24	20	14	6	♦18.0
25 - 29	82	41	41	75.4
30 - 34	168	87	81	136.8
35 - 39	90	38	52	73.8
40 - 44	13	7	6	♦9.9
45 - 49	2	2	-	♦1.3
50 +	2	2	-	..
Lithuania - Lituanie				
2018 (C)				
Total	28 149	14 362	13 787	46.9
0 - 14	4	1	3	..
15 - 19	762	381	381	11.2
20 - 24	3 468	1 771	1 697	44.2
25 - 29	9 562	4 938	4 624	105.9
30 - 34	9 404	4 731	4 673	106.1
35 - 39	4 034	2 072	1 962	49.6
40 - 44	874	453	421	9.7
45 - 49	35	13	22	0.3
50 +	3	-	3	..
Unknown - Inconnu	3	2	1	..
Luxembourg				
2018 (C)				
Total	6 274	3 196	3 078	42.5
0 - 14	2	1	1	..
15 - 19	74	38	36	4.6
20 - 24	429	218	211	23.3
25 - 29	1 398	715	683	64.0
30 - 34	2 388	1 213	1 175	103.9
35 - 39	1 582	811	771	67.6
40 - 44	366	180	186	16.5
45 - 49	24	13	11	♦1.1
50 +	1	1	-	..
Unknown - Inconnu	10	6	4	..
Malta - Malte				
2018 (C)				
Total	4 444	2 278	2 166	39.5
0 - 14	1	-	1	..
15 - 19	133	63	70	12.1
20 - 24	440	233	207	29.9
25 - 29	1 199	607	592	60.4
30 - 34	1 647	850	797	87.8
35 - 39	862	441	421	48.4
40 - 44	155	81	74	9.5
45 - 49	7	3	4	♦0.5
50 +	-	-	-	..
Montenegro - Monténégro				
2018 (C)				
Total	7 264	3 771	3 493	50.0
0 - 14	-	-	-	..

Continent, country or area, year, code[a] and age of mother (in years) / Continent, pays ou zone, année, code[a] et âge de la mère (en années)	Number - Nombre: Total	Male Masculin	Female Féminin	Rate Taux
EUROPE				
Montenegro - Monténégro				
2018 (C)				
15 - 19	187	98	89	9.6
20 - 24	1 114	576	538	57.9
25 - 29	2 280	1 189	1 091	119.7
30 - 34	2 223	1 171	1 052	100.0
35 - 39	1 093	546	547	49.9
40 - 44	234	120	114	11.1
45 - 49	21	13	8	♦1.0
50 +	1	1	-	..
Unknown - Inconnu	111	57	54	..
Netherlands - Pays-Bas[41]				
2018 (C)				
Total	168 525	86 204	82 321	44.7
0 - 14	-	-	-	..
15 - 19	1 323	664	659	2.6
20 - 24	13 298	6 842	6 456	25.3
25 - 29	50 162	25 758	24 404	91.9
30 - 34	66 648	34 027	32 621	127.6
35 - 39	31 110	15 926	15 184	60.7
40 - 44	5 635	2 823	2 812	10.8
45 - 49	316	149	167	0.5
50 +	33	15	18	..
North Macedonia - Macédoine du Nord				
2018 (C)				
Total	21 333	11 173	10 160	42.1
0 - 14	19	8	11	..
10 - 14	19	...	...	..
15 - 19	909	479	430	15.5
20 - 24	3 991	2 052	1 939	59.1
25 - 29	7 281	3 850	3 431	95.3
30 - 34	6 055	3 148	2 907	75.6
35 - 39	2 603	1 390	1 213	33.2
40 - 44	447	231	216	6.0
45 - 49	26	14	12	♦0.4
50 +	2	1	1	..
Norway - Norvège				
2018 (C)				
Total	55 120	28 430	26 690	45.7
0 - 14	1	1	-	..
15 - 19	395	179	216	2.5
20 - 24	5 381	2 724	2 657	32.5
25 - 29	17 718	9 177	8 541	97.3
30 - 34	20 184	10 429	9 755	115.5
35 - 39	9 395	4 879	4 516	55.4
40 - 44	1 882	956	926	10.9
45 - 49	147	78	69	0.8
50 +	17	7	10	..
Poland - Pologne				
2018 (C)				
Total	388 178	199 820	188 358	43.8
0 - 14	39	23	16	..
15 - 19	9 185	4 796	4 389	10.3
20 - 24	51 745	26 605	25 140	49.2
25 - 29	127 208	65 494	61 714	99.1
30 - 34	128 762	66 354	62 408	87.1
35 - 39	59 546	30 498	29 048	39.2
40 - 44	11 210	5 807	5 403	7.9
45 - 49	470	236	234	0.4
50 +	13	7	6	..
Portugal[18]				
2018 (C)				
Total	87 020	44 309	42 711	37.9
0 - 14	35	21	14	..

Continent, country or area, year, code[a] and age of mother (in years) / Continent, pays ou zone, année, code[a] et âge de la mère (en années)	Number - Nombre: Total	Male Masculin	Female Féminin	Rate Taux
EUROPE				
Portugal[18]				
2018 (C)				
15 - 19	1 993	1 019	974	7.4
20 - 24	8 676	4 425	4 251	32.7
25 - 29	19 082	9 678	9 404	69.5
30 - 34	28 676	14 726	13 950	96.2
35 - 39	22 146	11 191	10 955	61.1
40 - 44	6 016	3 054	2 962	14.3
45 - 49	370	183	187	0.9
50 +	26	12	14	..
Republic of Moldova - République de Moldova[42]				
2018 (C)				
Total	32 606	16 864	15 742	51.1
10 - 14	6	4	2	..
15 - 19	2 190	1 129	1 061	31.7
20 - 24	8 219	4 231	3 988	99.5
25 - 29	10 316	5 417	4 899	100.3
30 - 34	8 000	4 097	3 903	71.5
35 - 39	3 246	1 667	1 579	33.3
40 - 44	601	306	295	6.8
45 - 49	27	13	14	♦0.3
50 +	1	-	1	..
Romania - Roumanie				
2018 (C)				
Total	202 744	104 005	98 739	46.1
0 - 14	725	388	337	..
15 - 19	18 485	9 416	9 069	36.4
20 - 24	37 040	18 946	18 094	74.2
25 - 29	60 219	31 035	29 184	108.3
30 - 34	55 040	28 137	26 903	85.9
35 - 39	25 055	12 895	12 160	36.7
40 - 44	5 851	3 008	2 843	7.7
45 - 49	303	167	136	0.4
50 +	26	13	13	..
Russian Federation - Fédération de Russie[21]				
2011 (C)				
Total	1 796 629	923 804	872 825	48.3
12 - 14	351	174	177	..
15 - 19	103 533	53 162	50 371	25.2
20 - 24	510 184	262 085	248 099	85.1
25 - 29	603 791	311 250	292 541	101.2
30 - 34	379 884	195 518	184 366	68.6
35 - 39	165 364	84 832	80 532	31.8
40 - 44	30 221	15 168	15 053	6.3
45 - 49	1 481	680	801	0.3
50 +	138	65	73	..
Unknown - Inconnu	1 682	870	812	..
San Marino - Saint-Marin				
2017 (C)				
Total	228	121	107	29.5
0 - 14	-	-	-	..
15 - 19	1	-	1	♦1.2
20 - 24	8	5	3	♦10.9
25 - 29	50	28	22	61.6
30 - 34	76	38	38	79.1
35 - 39	64	33	31	51.6
40 - 44	25	13	12	♦16.1
45 - 49	3	3	-	♦1.9
50 +	1	1	-	..
Serbia - Serbie[43]				
2018 (+C)				
Total	63 975	33 208	30 767	42.0
0 - 14	48	19	29	..

10. Live births by age of mother and sex of child, general and age-specific fertility rates: latest available year, 2010 - 2019
Naissances vivantes selon l'âge de la mère et le sexe de l'enfant, taux de fécondité et taux de fécondité par âge : dernière année disponible, 2010 - 2019 (continued - suite)

Continent, country or area, year, code[a] and age of mother (in years) / Continent, pays ou zone, année, code[a] et âge de la mère (en années)	Number - Nombre: Total	Male Masculin	Female Féminin	Rate Taux
EUROPE				
Serbia - Serbie[43]				
2018 (+C)				
15 - 19	2 383	1 206	1 177	14.0
20 - 24	10 526	5 518	5 008	56.1
25 - 29	18 977	9 898	9 079	91.0
30 - 34	19 598	10 187	9 411	84.9
35 - 39	9 964	5 129	4 835	41.3
40 - 44	2 179	1 101	1 078	8.8
45 - 49	151	75	76	0.6
50 +	25	11	14	..
Unknown - Inconnu	124	64	60	..
Slovakia - Slovaquie				
2018 (C)				
Total	57 639	29 674	27 965	44.5
0 - 14	38	18	20	..
15 - 19	3 431	1 759	1 672	26.3
20 - 24	8 649	4 420	4 229	57.2
25 - 29	17 011	8 736	8 275	90.3
30 - 34	18 100	9 377	8 723	87.5
35 - 39	8 693	4 462	4 231	40.2
40 - 44	1 656	863	793	7.6
45 - 49	60	38	22	0.3
50 +	1	1	-	..
Slovenia - Slovénie				
2018 (C)				
Total	19 585	10 157	9 428	45.5
0 - 14	1	1	-	..
15 - 19	172	103	69	3.9
20 - 24	2 074	1 099	975	42.9
25 - 29	6 062	3 154	2 908	109.8
30 - 34	7 056	3 580	3 476	108.1
35 - 39	3 502	1 847	1 655	47.9
40 - 44	674	344	330	9.2
45 - 49	39	26	13	0.6
50 +	5	3	2	..
Spain - Espagne				
2018 (C)				
Total	370 827	190 584	180 243	35.4
0 - 14	76	44	32	..
15 - 19	6 925	3 541	3 384	6.2
20 - 24	26 852	13 835	13 017	24.2
25 - 29	64 632	33 172	31 460	51.9
30 - 34	123 385	63 492	59 893	87.1
35 - 39	112 731	58 102	54 629	64.5
40 - 44	33 252	16 918	16 334	16.9
45 - 49	2 791	1 388	1 403	1.5
50 +	183	92	91	..
Sweden - Suède				
2018 (C)				
Total	115 832	59 534	56 298	53.1
0 - 14	7	6	1	..
15 - 19	1 105	570	535	4.3
20 - 24	11 789	6 069	5 720	39.6
25 - 29	37 393	19 236	18 157	104.9
30 - 34	40 199	20 649	19 550	124.9
35 - 39	20 519	10 545	9 974	66.9
40 - 44	4 483	2 282	2 201	14.2
45 - 49	308	164	144	1.0
50 +	28	12	16	..
Unknown - Inconnu	1	1	-	..
Switzerland - Suisse				
2018 (C)				
Total	87 851	45 013	42 838	45.7
0 - 14	2	1	1	..
15 - 19	481	232	249	2.3

Continent, country or area, year, code[a] and age of mother (in years) / Continent, pays ou zone, année, code[a] et âge de la mère (en années)	Number - Nombre: Total	Male Masculin	Female Féminin	Rate Taux
EUROPE				
Switzerland - Suisse				
2018 (C)				
20 - 24	5 783	2 951	2 832	24.7
25 - 29	21 634	11 086	10 548	77.2
30 - 34	34 008	17 463	16 545	113.2
35 - 39	21 145	10 830	10 315	70.2
40 - 44	4 451	2 281	2 170	15.3
45 - 49	320	155	165	1.0
50 +	27	14	13	..
Ukraine[44]				
2017 (+C)				
Total	363 987	...	...	36.2
0 - 14	157	...	...	..
15 - 19	18 616	...	...	20.6
20 - 24	85 744	...	...	74.2
25 - 29	119 038	...	...	77.8
30 - 34	91 477	...	...	51.2
35 - 39	39 072	...	...	24.3
40 - 44	8 360	...	...	5.3
45 - 49	683	...	...	0.5
50 +	179	...	...	..
Unknown - Inconnu	661	...	...	..
United Kingdom of Great Britain and Northern Ireland - Royaume-Uni de Grande-Bretagne et d'Irlande du Nord[45]				
2018 (C)				
Total	730 918	375 379	355 539	49.3
0 - 14	73	42	31	..
15 - 19	21 171	10 934	10 237	11.8
20 - 24	101 066	52 091	48 975	49.5
25 - 29	200 925	103 278	97 647	89.6
30 - 34	237 244	121 667	115 577	106.5
35 - 39	138 555	71 043	67 512	63.6
40 - 44	29 323	15 071	14 252	14.5
45 - 49	2 288	1 120	1 168	1.0
50 +	263	129	134	..
Unknown - Inconnu	10	4	6	..
OCEANIA - OCÉANIE				
American Samoa - Samoas américaines				
2017 (C)				
Total	1 001	471	530	...
10 - 14	-	...	...	..
15 - 19	95	...	...	...
20 - 24	292	...	...	...
25 - 29	272	...	...	...
30 - 34	173	...	...	...
35 - 39	121	...	...	...
40 - 44	45	...	...	...
45 - 49	3	...	...	...
50 +	-	...	...	..
Australia - Australie[46]				
2018 (C)				
Total	315 147	162 088	153 059	52.8
10 - 14	46	22	24	..
15 - 19	6 839	3 543	3 296	9.4
20 - 24	36 191	18 679	17 512	42.6
25 - 29	83 338	42 853	40 485	89.0
30 - 34	112 585	57 935	54 650	119.6
35 - 39	62 136	31 873	30 263	71.9

10. Live births by age of mother and sex of child, general and age-specific fertility rates: latest available year, 2010 - 2019
Naissances vivantes selon l'âge de la mère et le sexe de l'enfant, taux de fécondité et taux de fécondité par âge : dernière année disponible, 2010 - 2019 (continued - suite)

Continent, country or area, year, code[a] and age of mother (in years) / Continent, pays ou zone, année, code[a] et âge de la mère (en années)	Number - Nombre: Total	Number - Nombre: Male / Masculin	Number - Nombre: Female / Féminin	Rate / Taux
OCEANIA - OCÉANIE				
Australia - Australie[46]				
2018 (C)				
40 - 44	12 827	6 590	6 237	16.0
45 - 49	1 006	512	494	1.2
50 +	112	49	63	..
Unknown - Inconnu	67	32	35	..
Cook Islands - Îles Cook				
2019* (+C)				
Total	225	...	...	...
10 - 14	-	...	...	..
15 - 19	19	...	...	...
20 - 24	66	...	...	...
25 - 29	64	...	...	...
30 - 34	50	...	...	...
35 - 39	18	...	...	...
40 - 44	7	...	...	...
45 +	1	...	...	...
Fiji - Fidji				
2017 (+U)				
Total	*14 023*	*7 302*	*6 721*	...
10 - 14	*4*	*1*	*3*	..
15 - 19	*594*	*316*	*278*	...
20 - 24	*3 970*	*2 103*	*1 867*	...
25 - 29	*4 289*	*2 181*	*2 108*	...
30 - 34	*3 083*	*1 618*	*1 465*	...
35 - 39	*1 598*	*838*	*760*	...
40 - 44	*451*	*227*	*224*	...
45 - 49	*31*	*15*	*16*	...
50 +	*2*	*2*	-	..
Unknown - Inconnu	*1*	*1*	-	..
French Polynesia - Polynésie française				
2018 (C)				
Total	3 776	1 946	1 830	52.0
10 - 14	3	3	-	..
15 - 19	351	187	164	31.6
20 - 24	825	425	400	86.9
25 - 29	915	489	426	85.0
30 - 34	895	443	452	78.0
35 - 39	574	286	288	55.4
40 - 44	194	103	91	20.0
45 - 49	18	10	8	♦1.9
50 +	1	-	1	..
Guam[47]				
2018 (C)				
Total	3 175	1 655	1 520	83.3
10 - 14	3	2	1	..
15 - 19	234	143	91	35.1
20 - 24	833	441	392	135.7
25 - 29	927	479	448	158.2
30 - 34	692	346	346	137.0
35 - 39	388	200	188	84.1
40 - 44	90	42	48	19.6
45 - 49	7	2	5	♦1.4
50 +	-	-	-	..
Unknown - Inconnu	1	-	1	..
Nauru				
2011 (C)				
Total	370	190	180	...
15 - 19	40	22	18	...
20 - 24	126	69	57	...
25 - 29	111	57	54	...
30 - 34	55	22	33	...
35 - 39	33	17	16	...
OCEANIA - OCÉANIE				
Nauru				
2011 (C)				
40 - 44	5	3	2	...
45 - 49	-	-	-	...
New Caledonia - Nouvelle-Calédonie				
2015 (C)				
Total	4 191	...	...	...
0 - 19	197	...	...	...
20 - 24	888	...	...	...
25 - 29	1 148	...	...	...
30 - 34	1 046	...	...	...
35 - 39	671	...	...	...
40 - 44	233	...	...	...
45 - 49	6	...	...	...
50 +	2	...	...	..
New Zealand - Nouvelle-Zélande[48]				
2019 (+C)				
Total	59 640	30 567	29 070	...
10 - 14	18	9	9	..
15 - 19	1 974	1 023	951	...
20 - 24	8 511	4 407	4 107	...
25 - 29	16 428	8 433	7 995	...
30 - 34	19 740	10 086	9 651	...
35 - 39	10 548	5 415	5 133	...
40 - 44	2 265	1 122	1 146	...
45 - 49	144	72	75	...
50 +	6	-	6	..
Palau - Palaos				
2018 (C)				
Total	256	125	131	...
15 - 19	32	18	14	...
20 - 24	48	23	25	...
25 - 29	74	37	37	...
30 - 34	53	27	26	...
35 - 39	39	14	25	...
40 - 44	9	5	4	...
45 - 49	1	1	-	...
Samoa[49]				
2016 (I)				
Total	4 835	2 556	2 279	110.1
10 - 14	-	-	-	..
15 - 19	282	143	139	31.4
20 - 24	1 290	672	618	166.8
25 - 29	1 321	705	616	199.2
30 - 34	965	501	464	164.5
35 - 39	634	349	285	121.1
40 - 44	277	150	127	56.3
45 - 49	66	36	30	14.6
Tokelau - Tokélaou[50]				
2011 (I)				
Total	16	...	...	...
0 - 14	-	...	...	..
15 - 19	1	...	...	...
20 - 24	6	...	...	...
25 - 29	4	...	...	...
30 - 34	4	...	...	...
35 - 39	1	...	...	...
Tuvalu				
2016 (+U)				
Total	*210*	...	...	...
10 - 14	-	...	...	..
15 - 19	*14*	...	...	...
20 - 24	*67*	...	...	...

10. Live births by age of mother and sex of child, general and age-specific fertility rates: latest available year, 2010 - 2019
Naissances vivantes selon l'âge de la mère et le sexe de l'enfant, taux de fécondité et taux de fécondité par âge : dernière année disponible, 2010 - 2019 (continued - suite)

Continent, country or area, year, code[a] and age of mother (in years) / Continent, pays ou zone, année, code[a] et âge de la mère (en années)	Number - Nombre Total	Male Masculin	Female Féminin	Rate Taux
OCEANIA - OCÉANIE				
Tuvalu				
2016 (+U)				
25 - 29	*55*	...	...	...
30 - 34	*44*	...	...	...
35 - 39	*23*	...	...	...
40 - 44	*7*	...	...	...
45 - 49	-	...	...	...

FOOTNOTES - NOTES

♦ Rates based on 30 or fewer births. - Taux basés sur 30 naissances ou moins.

* Provisional. - Données provisoires.

[a] 'Code' indicates the source of data, as follows:
C - Civil registration, estimated over 90% complete
U - Civil registration, estimated less than 90% complete
| - Other source, estimated reliable
+ - Data tabulated by date of registration rather than occurrence
... Information not available

Le 'Code' indique la source des données, comme suit :
C - Registres de l'état civil considérés complets à 90 p. 100 au moins
U - Registres de l'état civil qui ne sont pas considérés complets à 90 p. 100 au moins
| - Autre source, considérée fiable
+ - Données exploitées selon la date de l'enregistrement et non la date de l'événement
... Information non disponible

1 Source: Vital Statistics Report. - Source: Vital Statistics Report.

2 Source: Vital Statistics Report, National Statistics Institute. Registered births only. - Source: Rapport sur les statistiques de l'état civil, Institut national de la statistique. Naissances enregistrées seulement.

3 Data refer to the 12 months preceding the census in May. - Les données se rapportent aux 12 mois précédant le recensement de mai.

4 Data refer to the 12 months preceding the census in September. - Les données se rapportent aux 12 mois précédant le recensement de septembre.

5 Unadjusted number of births in households referring to the 12 months preceding the census in March. - Le nombre non ajusté de naissances vivantes des ménages ordinaires se rapportent aux 12 mois précédant le recensement de mars.

6 Including nomadic population. Data refer to the 12 months preceding the census in March. - Y compris la population nomade. Les données se rapportent aux 12 mois précédant le recensement de mars.

7 Excludes the islands of St. Brandon and Agalega. - Non compris les îles St. Brandon et Agalega.

8 Data refer to the 12 months preceding the census in August. - Les données se rapportent aux 12 mois précédant le recensement d'août.

9 Excluding live-born infants who died before their birth was registered. - Non compris les enfants nés vivants décédés avant l'enregistrement de leur naissance.

10 Reason for discrepancy between these figures and corresponding figures shown elsewhere not ascertained. - On ne sait pas comment s'explique la divergence entre ces chiffres et les chiffres correspondants indiqués ailleurs.

11 Data refer to the 12 months preceding the census in October. - Les données se rapportent aux 12 mois précédant le recensement de octobre.

12 Unrevised data. - Les données n'ont pas été révisées.

13 Excluding non-residents and foreign service personnel and their dependants. - À l'exclusion des non-résidents et du personnel diplomatique et de leurs charges de famille.

14 Including Canadian residents temporarily in the United States, but excluding United States residents temporarily in Canada. - Y compris les résidents canadiens se trouvant temporairement aux Etats-Unis, mais ne comprenant pas les résidents des Etats-Unis se trouvant temporairement au Canada.

15 Excluding children born in the country of non-resident mothers. - Exceptés les enfants nés dans le pays des mères non-résidentes.

16 Data refer to population in private households. Data refer to period from 1 January 2010 to 3 April 2011. - Les données portent sur la population des ménages privés. Les données concernent la période du 1 janvier 2010 au 3 avril 2011.

17 Figures for male and female may not add up to the total, since they do not include the category "Unknown". - La somme des chiffres indiqués pour les sexes masculin et féminin peut n'être pas égale au total parce qu'elle n'inclut pas la catégorie " inconnue ".

18 Data refer to births to resident mothers. - Ces données concernent les enfants nés de mères résidentes.

19 Excludes nomadic Indian tribes. - Non compris les tribus d'Indiens nomades.

20 Source: Reports of the Ministry of Health. Data extracted from online system representing only 85.6 per cent of estimated births. - Source : Rapports du Ministère de la Santé. Données extraites du système en ligne, qui ne représentent que 85.6 % du nombre total estimé de naissances.

21 Excluding infants born alive of less than 28 weeks' gestation, of less than 1 000 g in weight and 35 cm in length, who die within seven days of birth. - Non compris les enfants nés vivants après moins de 28 semaines de gestations, pesant moins de 1 000 g, mesurant moins de 35 cm et décédés dans les sept jours qui ont suivi leur naissance.

22 Sources: Births and Deaths National Registration System database, and medical records of government hospitals. Data refer to Bahraini and non-Bahraini births including some visitors, and Bahraini births abroad. - Les sources: Les bases de données des << Births and Deaths National Registration System >> et les dossiers médicaux des hôpitaux du gouvernement. Les données se rapportent aux naissances de Bahreïniens et de non-Bahreïniens, y compris d'enfants non résidents, ainsi que de Bahreïniens résidant à l'étranger.

23 Data refer to government controlled areas. - Les données se rapportent aux zones contrôlées par le Gouvernement.

24 Data are from 1 January 2009 to 1 May 2010. - Les données vont du 1er janvier 2009 au 1er mai 2010.

25 Data refer to the Iranian Year which begins on 21 March and ends on 20 March of the following year. Data refer to current birth data; excluding delayed birth registrations. - Les données concernent l'année iranienne, qui commence le 21 mars et se termine le 20 mars de l'année suivante. Les données se rapportent aux naissances actuelles; les déclarations tardives des naissances ne sont pas compris.

26 Includes data for East Jerusalem and Israeli residents in certain other territories under occupation by Israeli military forces since June 1967. - Y compris les données pour Jérusalem-Est et les résidents israéliens dans certains autres territoires occupés depuis 1967 par les forces armées israéliennes.

27 Data refer to Japanese nationals in Japan only. - Les données se raportent aux nationaux japonais au Japon seulement.

28 Data refer to the 12 months preceding the census in March. - Les données se rapportent aux 12 mois précédant le recensement de mars.

29 Data do not include foreigners. - Les données sur les etrangers ne sont pas inclus.

30 Data are from Vital Registration System (VRS). - Les données proviennent du système d'enregistrement des faits d'état civil.

31 Excluding alien armed forces, civilian aliens employed by armed forces, and foreign diplomatic personnel and their dependants. - Non compris les militaires étrangers, les civils étrangers employés par les forces armées ni le personnel diplomatique étranger et les membres de leur famille les accompagnant.

32 Survey based estimates. - Estimations basées sur des enquêtes.

[33] Excluding infants born alive of less than 28 weeks' gestation, of less than 1 000 g in weight and 35 cm in length, who die within seven days of birth. Data have been adjusted for under-registration. - Non compris les enfants nés vivants après moins de 28 semaines de gestations, pesant moins de 1 000 g, mesurant moins de 35 cm et décédés dans les sept jours qui ont suivi leur naissance. Y compris un ajustement pour sous-enregistrement.
[34] Source: Strategy and Planning Division, Ministry of Public Health. - Source : Division de la stratégie et de la planification, Ministère de la Santé publique.
[35] Including births occurring abroad of mothers with residence in Austria. - Y compris les naissances survenues à l'étranger des mères avec résidence en Autriche.
[36] Including armed forces stationed outside the country, but excluding alien armed forces stationed in the area. - Y compris les militaires nationaux hors du pays, mais non compris les militaires étrangers en garnison sur le territoire.
[37] Excluding Faeroe Islands and Greenland shown separately, if available. - Non compris les Iles Féroé et le Groenland, qui font l'objet de rubriques distinctes, si disponible.
[38] Including live births by military personnel and their dependants. - Y compris les naissances vivantes parmi les membres du personnel militaire et leurs personnes à charge.
[39] Data include the live births of women with Hungarian usual residence regardless of whether the live birth occurred in Hungary or in a foreign country, and do not include the live births of women with foreign country usual residence. Data include the live births of women with unknown residence and homeless. - Les données concernent les enfants nés vivants de femmes dont la résidence habituelle est en Hongrie, que la naissance vivante ait eu lieu en Hongrie ou dans un pays étranger, et ne comprennent pas les enfants nés vivants de femmes dont la résidence habituelle est dans un pays étranger. Les données incluent les enfants nés vivants de femmes dont la résidence n'est pas connue et de femmes sans domicile fixe.
[40] Data refer to the 12 months preceding the census in April. - Les données se rapportent aux douze mois précédant le recensement d'avril.
[41] Including residents outside the country if listed in a Netherlands population register. - Englobe les résidents se trouvant à l'étranger à condition qu'ils soient inscrits sur le registre de population des Pays-Bas.
[42] Excluding Transnistria and the municipality of Bender. - Les données ne tiennent pas compte de l'information sur la Transnistria et la municipalité de Bender.
[43] Excludes data for Kosovo and Metohia. - Sans les données pour le Kosovo et Metohie.
[44] Data refer to births with weight 500g and more (if weight is unknown - with length 25 centimeters and more, or with gestation during 22 weeks or more). The Government of Ukraine has informed the United Nations that it is not in a position to provide statistical data concerning the Autonomous Republic of Crimea and the city of Sevastopol. - Données concernant les nouveau-nés de 500 grammes ou plus (si le poids est inconnu – de 25 centimètres de long ou plus, ou après une grossesse de 22 semaines ou plus). Le gouvernement Ukrainien a informé l'ONU qu'il n'est pas en mesure de fournir des données statistiques concernant la République autonome de Crimée et la ville de Sébastopol.
[45] Data tabulated by date of occurrence for England and Wales, and by date of registration for Northern Ireland and Scotland. Excluding Channel Islands (Guernsey and Jersey) and Isle of Man, shown separately, if available. - Données exploitées selon la date de l'événement pour l'Angleterre et le pays de Galles, et selon la date de l'enregistrement pour l'Irlande du Nord et l'Ecosse. Non compris les îles Anglo-Normandes (Guernesey et Jersey) et l'île de Man, qui font l'objet de rubriques distinctes, si disponible.
[46] Data of small values have been randomly adjusted to protect confidentiality. Some totals will not equal the sum of their components. Cells with 0 values have not been affected by confidentialisation. - Les valeurs peu élevées ont été arrondies de façon aléatoire pour des raisons de confidentialité. Certains totaux ne correspondront pas rigoureusement à la somme des composants. Les mesures de confidentialité ont été sans incidence sur les cellules présentant des valeurs nulles.
[47] Including United States military personnel, their dependants and contract employees. - Y compris les militaires des Etats-Unis, les membres de leur famille les accompagnant et les agents contractuels des Etats-Unis.
[48] Random rounding to base 3 is applied in this table as a confidentiality measure. Data refers to births registered in the country to mothers resident in the country. - Les chiffres sont arrondis à la base 3 de manière aléatoire, pour des raisons de confidentialité. Les données se rapportent aux naissances enregistrées dans le pays pour lesquelles la mère réside dans le pays.
[49] Data refer to the 12 months preceding the census in November. The question on live births was not asked to females fifty years of age or more. - Données se rapportant aux 12 mois précédant le recensement de novembre. La question sur les naissances vivantes n'était pas posée aux femmes âgées cinquante ans ou plus.
[50] Data refer to the 12 months preceding the census in October. Data refer to usually resident population present on census night. - Les données se rapportent aux 12 mois précédant le recensement de octobre. Les données concernent la population habituellement résidente présente la nuit du recensement.

Table 11 - *Demographic Yearbook 2019*

Table 11 presents live births by age of father and live birth rates by age of father for the latest available year between 2010 and 2019.

Description of variables: Age is defined as age at last birthday, that is, the difference between the date of birth and the date of the occurrence of the event, expressed in completed solar years. The age classification used in this table is the following: under 20 years, 5-year age groups through 60-64 years, 65 years and over, and age unknown. A different classification may appear as provided by reporting country or area.

Rate computation: Live-birth rates specific to age of father are the annual number of births to a man in each age group per 1 000 male population in the same age group. These rates are calculated by the Statistics Division of the United Nations.

Since relatively few births occur to men below 15 or above 59 years of age, birth rates for men under 20 years of age and for those 55 years of age or over are computed on the male population aged 15-19 and 55-59, respectively. Similarly, the rate for men of "All ages" is based on all live births irrespective of age of father, and it is computed on the male population aged 15-59 years.

Births to fathers of unknown age are distributed proportionately across the age groups, by the Statistics Division of the United Nations, in accordance with the distribution of births by age of father prior to the calculation of the rates.

The population used in computing the rates is the estimated or enumerated distribution of males by age. First priority is given to the estimated population and second priority to the enumerated population, i.e. to census returns of the year to which the births refer.

Rates presented in this table are limited to those for countries or areas having at least a total of 100 live births in a given year.

Reliability of data: Data from civil registers of live births which are reported as incomplete (less than 90 per cent completeness) or of unknown completeness are considered unreliable and are set in *italics* rather than in roman type. Rates are not computed if the data on live births from civil registers are reported as incomplete (less than 90 per cent completeness) or of unknown completeness. Table 9 and the technical notes for that table provide more detailed information on the completeness of birth registration. For more information about the quality of vital statistics data in general, see section 4.2 of the Technical Notes.

Limitations: Statistics on live births by age of father are subject to the same qualifications as have been set forth for vital statistics in general and birth statistics in particular as discussed in section 4 of the Technical Notes. These include differences in the completeness of registration, the method used to determine age of father and the quality of the reported information relating to age of father.

The reliability of the data described above, is an important factor in considering the limitations. In addition, some live births are tabulated by date of registration and not by date of occurrence; these are indicated in the table by a plus sign "+". Whenever the lag between the date of occurrence and date of registration is prolonged and, therefore, a large proportion of the live-birth registrations are delayed, birth statistics for any given year may be seriously affected. For example, the age of the father will almost always refer to the date of registration rather than to the date of birth of the child. Hence, in those countries or areas where registration of births is delayed, possibly for years, statistics on births by age of father should be used with caution.

Another factor which limits international comparability is the practice of some countries or areas of not including in live birth statistics infants who were born alive but died before the registration of the birth or within the first 24 hours of life, thus underestimating the total number of live births. Statistics of this type are footnoted.

Because these statistics are classified according to age, they are subject to the limitations with respect to accuracy of age reporting similar to those already discussed in connection with section 3.1.3 of the Technical Notes. The factors influencing the accuracy of reporting may be somewhat dissimilar in vital statistics (because of the differences in the method of taking a census and registering a birth) but, in general, the same errors can be observed. The absence of frequencies in the unknown age group does not necessarily indicate completely accurate reporting and tabulation of the age item. It is often an indication that the unknowns have been eliminated by assigning ages to them before tabulation, or by proportionate distribution after tabulation.

On the other hand, large frequencies in the unknown age category may indicate that a large proportion of the births are born outside of wedlock, the records for which tend to be incomplete so far as characteristics of the parents are concerned.

Another limitation of age reporting may result from calculating age of father at birth of child (or at time of registration) from year of birth rather than from day, month and year of birth. Information on this factor is given in footnotes when known.

In few countries, data by age refer to deliveries rather than to live births causing under-enumeration in the event of a multiple birth. This practice leads to lack of strict comparability, both among countries or areas relying on this practice and between data shown in this table and table 9.

Rates shown in this table are subject to the same limitations that affect the corresponding statistics on live births. In cases of rates based on births tabulated by date of registration and not by date of occurrence; the effect of including delayed registration on the distribution of births by age of father may be noted in the age-specific fertility rates for men at older ages. In some cases, high age-specific rates for men aged 55 years and over may reflect age of father at registration of birth and not fertility at these older ages.

Earlier data: Live births and live birth rates by age of father have been shown in previous issues of the *Demographic Yearbook*. Information on the specific years is presented in the Historical Index.

Tableau 11 – *Annuaire démographique 2019*

Le tableau 11 présente les données les plus récentes disponibles pour la période 2010 - 2019 sur les naissances vivantes selon l'âge du père et les taux des naissances vivantes selon l'âge du père.

Description des variables : l'âge désigne l'âge au dernier anniversaire, c'est-à-dire la différence entre la date de naissance et la date de l'événement exprimée en années solaires révolues. La classification par âge utilisée dans ce tableau comprend les catégories suivantes : moins de 20 ans, groupes quinquennaux jusqu'à 60-64 ans, 65 ans et plus, et âge inconnu. Des groupes d'âge différents sont parfois utilisés lorsque les pays ou territoires ont fourni les données dans une autre classification.

Les taux de natalité selon l'âge du père représentent le nombre annuel de naissances vivantes intervenues dans un groupe d'âge donné pour 1 000 hommes du groupe d'âge. Ces taux ont été calculés par la Division de statistique de l'ONU.

Étant donné que le nombre de naissances parmi les hommes de moins de 15 ans ou de plus de 59 ans est relativement peu élevé, les taux de natalité parmi les hommes âgées de moins de 20 ans et celles de 55 ans et plus ont été calculés sur la base des populations masculines âgées de 15 à 19 ans et de 55 à 59 ans, respectivement. De même, le taux pour les hommes de « tous âges » est fondé sur la totalité des naissances vivantes, indépendamment de l'âge du père et ce chiffre est rapporté à l'effectif de la population masculine âgée de 15 à 59 ans.

Les naissances pour lesquelles l'âge du père était inconnu ont été réparties par la Division de statistique de l'ONU, avant le calcul des taux, suivant les proportions observées pour celles où l'âge du père était connu.

Les chiffres de population utilisés pour le calcul des taux proviennent de dénombrements ou de répartitions estimatives de la population masculine selon l'âge. On a utilisé de préférence les estimations de la population; à défaut, on s'est contenté des données censitaires se rapportant à l'année des naissances.

Les taux présentés dans ce tableau ne concernent que les pays ou zones où l'on a enregistré un total d'au moins 100 naissances vivantes dans une année donnée.

Fiabilité des données : les données sur les naissances vivantes provenant des registres de l'état civil qui sont déclarées incomplètes (degré de complétude inférieur à 90 p. 100) ou dont le degré de complétude n'est pas connu sont jugées douteuses et apparaissent en italique et non en caractères romains. On a choisi de ne pas faire figurer dans le tableau 11 des taux calculés à partir de données sur les naissances vivantes issues de registres de l'état civil qui sont déclarées incomplètes (degré de complétude inférieur à 90 p. 100) ou dont le degré de complétude n'est pas connu. Le tableau 9 et les notes techniques qui s'y rapportent présentent des renseignements plus détaillés sur le degré de complétude de l'enregistrement des naissances vivantes. Pour plus de précisions sur la qualité des statistiques de l'état civil en général, voir la section 4.2 des Notes techniques.

Insuffisance des données : les statistiques relatives aux naissances vivantes selon l'âge du père appellent toutes les réserves qui ont été formulées à propos des statistiques de l'état civil en général et des statistiques de naissances en particulier (voir la section 4 des Notes techniques). Ceci inclut les différences de complétude d'enregistrement des faits d'état civil, de méthode pour déterminer l'âge du père et de qualité d'information concernant l'âge du père.

La fiabilité des données, au sujet de laquelle des indications ont été données plus haut, est un facteur important. Il faut également tenir compte du fait que, dans certains cas, les données relatives aux naissances vivantes sont exploitées selon la date de l'enregistrement et non la date de l'événement ; ces cas ont été signalés dans le tableau par le signe '+'. Chaque fois que le décalage entre l'événement et son enregistrement est grand et qu'une forte proportion des naissances vivantes fait l'objet d'un enregistrement tardif, les statistiques des naissances vivantes pour une année donnée peuvent être considérablement faussées. Par exemple, l'âge du père représente presque toujours son âge à la date de l'enregistrement et non à la date de la naissance de l'enfant. Ainsi, dans les pays ou zones où l'enregistrement des naissances est tardif, le retard atteignant parfois plusieurs années, il faut utiliser avec prudence les statistiques concernant les naissances selon l'âge du père.

Un autre facteur qui nuit à la comparabilité internationale est la pratique de certains pays ou zones qui consiste à ne pas inclure dans les statistiques des naissances vivantes les enfants nés vivants mais décédés avant l'enregistrement de leur naissance ou dans les 24 heures qui ont suivi la naissance, pratique qui conduit à sous-estimer le nombre total de naissances vivantes. Quand pareil facteur a joué, cela a été signalé en note à la fin du tableau.

Étant donné que les statistiques du tableau 11 sont classées selon l'âge, elles appellent les mêmes réserves concernant l'exactitude des déclarations d'âge que celles formulées à la section 3.1.3 des Notes techniques. Dans le cas des statistiques de l'état civil, les facteurs qui interviennent à cet égard sont parfois différents, étant donné que le recensement de la population et l'enregistrement des naissances se font par des méthodes différentes, mais, d'une manière générale, les erreurs observées seront les mêmes. Si aucun nombre ne figure dans la rangée réservée aux âges inconnus, cela ne signifie pas nécessairement que les déclarations d'âge et l'exploitation des données par âge ont été tout à fait exactes. C'est souvent une indication que l'on a attribué un âge aux personnes d'âge inconnu avant l'exploitation des données ou qu'elles ont été réparties proportionnellement entre les différents groupes après cette opération.

À l'inverse, lorsque le nombre des personnes d'âge inconnu est important, cela peut signifier que la proportion de naissances parmi les parents célibataires est élevée, étant donné qu'en pareil cas l'acte de naissance ne contient pas tous les renseignements concernant les parents.

Les déclarations par âge peuvent comporter des distorsions, du fait que l'âge du père au moment de la naissance d'un enfant (ou de la déclaration de naissance) est donné par année de naissance et non par date exacte (jour, mois et année).

Dans quelques pays, la classification par âges se réfère aux accouchements, et non aux naissances vivantes, ce qui conduit à un sous-dénombrement en cas de naissances gémellaires. Cette pratique nuit à la comparabilité des données, à la fois entre pays ou zones qui recourent à cette méthode et entre les données présentées dans le tableau 11 et celles du tableau 9.

Les taux présentés dans ce tableau, sont sujets aux mêmes limitations qui affectent les statistiques correspondantes de naissances vivantes. Dans le cas des taux basés sur des naissances par date d'enregistrement et non par date d'occurrence, l'effet peut être visible sur les taux de fécondité par âge des hommes aux âges plus élevés. Dans certains cas, les taux de fécondité des hommes de plus de 55 ans peuvent refléter l'âge du père à l'enregistrement plus que la fécondité à ces âges.

Données publiées antérieurement : Les données sur les naissances vivantes selon l'âge du père et les taux des naissances vivantes selon l'âge du père ont été publié antérieurement dans l'*Annuaire démographique*. Pour plus de précisions concernant les années pour lesquels des données ont été publiées, se reporter à l'index historique.

11. Live births and live birth rates by age of father: latest available year, 2010 - 2019
Naissances vivantes et taux de natalité selon l'âge du père : dernière année disponible, 2010 - 2019

Continent, country or area, year, code[a] and age of father (in years) / Continent, pays ou zone, année, code[a] et âge du père (en années)	Number - Nombre: Both sexes - Les deux sexes	Rate - Taux
AFRICA - AFRIQUE		
Egypt - Égypte		
2012 (+C)		
Total	2 629 769	101.6
0 - 19	4 700	1.2
20 - 24	119 826	28.3
25 - 29	1 489 063	364.7
30 - 34	502 329	150.1
35 - 39	288 404	111.4
40 - 44	134 381	59.4
45 - 49	60 206	29.0
50 - 54	19 391	10.6
55 - 59	6 333	4.2
60 +	5 136	..
Mauritius - Maurice[1]		
2019 (+C)		
Total	12 846	30.9
0 - 19	1 136	23.1
20 - 24	2 552	52.9
25 - 29	3 932	80.3
30 - 34	3 064	72.3
35 - 39	1 674	35.0
40 - 44	375	8.0
45 - 49	23	♦0.6
50 - 54	-	-
55 - 59	-	-
60 - 64	-	..
65 +	-	..
Unknown - Inconnu	90	..
Saint Helena ex. dep. - Sainte-Hélène sans dép.		
2018 (C)		
Total	26	...
0 - 19	-	...
20 - 24	3	...
25 - 29	8	...
30 - 34	3	...
35 - 39	6	...
40 - 44	2	...
45 - 49	1	...
50 - 54	-	...
55 - 59	-	...
60 - 64	-	..
65 +	-	..
Unknown - Inconnu	3	..
South Africa - Afrique du Sud[2]		
2016 (U)		
Total	*876 435*	...
0 - 19	*4 502*	...
20 - 24	*35 319*	...
25 - 29	*72 871*	...
30 - 34	*93 538*	...
35 - 39	*69 193*	...
40 - 44	*41 377*	...
45 - 49	*17 105*	...
50 - 54	*6 369*	...
55 - 59	*2 340*	...
60 - 64	*844*	..
Unknown - Inconnu	*532 977*	..
AMERICA, NORTH - AMÉRIQUE DU NORD		
Bahamas[3]		
2014* (+U)		
Total	*4 196*	...
0 - 19	*63*	...
20 - 24	*576*	...
25 - 29	*742*	...
AMERICA, NORTH - AMÉRIQUE DU NORD		
Bahamas[3]		
2014* (+U)		
30 - 34	*815*	...
35 - 39	*659*	...
40 - 44	*388*	...
45 - 49	*167*	...
50 - 54	*60*	...
55 - 59	*23*	...
60 - 64	*5*	..
65 +	*6*	..
Unknown - Inconnu	*692*	..
Canada[4]		
2018 (C)		
Total	372 329	33.1
0 - 19	2 423	2.4
20 - 24	20 174	16.7
25 - 29	70 023	55.5
30 - 34	121 080	98.6
35 - 39	89 105	74.7
40 - 44	35 350	31.5
45 - 49	11 631	10.2
50 - 54	3 419	2.8
55 - 59	1 050	0.8
60 - 64	303	..
65 +	121	..
Unknown - Inconnu	17 650	..
Costa Rica		
2019* (C)		
Total	64 287	41.5
0 - 19	812	6.0
20 - 24	5 123	37.6
25 - 29	8 323	71.1
30 - 34	9 117	77.7
35 - 39	6 375	59.4
40 - 44	2 993	30.4
45 - 49	1 233	14.7
50 - 54	515	5.6
55 - 59	204	2.3
60 - 64	61	..
65 +	5 781	..
Unknown - Inconnu	23 750	..
Cuba		
2018 (C)		
Total	116 333	32.4
0 - 19	2 972	9.7
20 - 24	17 020	55.0
25 - 29	28 098	78.7
30 - 34	23 504	70.9
35 - 39	12 585	46.2
40 - 44	8 490	24.7
45 - 49	4 965	11.6
50 - 54	2 060	4.8
55 - 59	604	1.8
60 - 64	132	..
65 +	102	..
Unknown - Inconnu	15 801	..
Dominican Republic - République dominicaine		
2019 (U)		
Total	*167 686*	...
0 - 19	*3 270*	...
20 - 24	*25 487*	...
25 - 29	*38 690*	...
30 - 34	*32 673*	...
35 - 39	*21 777*	...
40 - 44	*11 396*	...
45 - 49	*5 525*	...
50 +	*4 491*	...

Continent, country or area, year, code[a] and age of father (in years) / Continent, pays ou zone, année, code[a] et âge du père (en années)	Number - Nombre: Both sexes - Les deux sexes	Rate - Taux
AMERICA, NORTH - AMÉRIQUE DU NORD		
Dominican Republic - République dominicaine		
2019 (U)		
50 - 54	*2 641*	...
55 - 59	*1 148*	...
60 - 64	*505*	..
65 +	*197*	..
Unknown - Inconnu	*24 377*	..
El Salvador[5]		
2014 (C)		
Total	108 903	62.6
0 - 19	6 884	22.6
20 - 24	22 522	84.4
25 - 29	22 722	115.0
30 - 34	18 048	114.4
35 - 39	12 219	84.6
40 - 44	6 345	47.2
45 - 49	2 957	25.3
50 - 54	1 360	13.7
55 - 59	666	7.9
60 - 64	309	..
65 +	199	..
Unknown - Inconnu	14 672	..
Guatemala		
2018 (C)		
Total	383 263	83.9
0 - 19	17 551	21.4
20 - 24	85 266	117.8
25 - 29	85 779	144.1
30 - 34	62 506	126.8
35 - 39	41 309	104.3
40 - 44	21 622	70.7
45 - 49	8 777	36.8
50 +	6 217	17.7
Unknown - Inconnu	54 236	..
Mexico - Mexique[6]		
2017 (C)		
Total	2 000 591	53.7
0 - 19	125 895	24.6
20 - 24	436 745	89.3
25 - 29	478 241	108.0
30 - 34	379 969	95.0
35 - 39	229 717	60.9
40 - 44	108 051	30.4
45 - 49	40 938	12.7
50 - 54	15 282	5.6
55 - 59	6 219	2.8
60 - 64	2 414	..
65 +	1 466	..
Unknown - Inconnu	175 654	..
Panama		
2018 (C)		
Total	76 863	59.4
0 - 19	2 749	21.7
20 - 24	11 181	93.6
25 - 29	13 034	116.3
30 - 34	11 252	104.2
35 - 39	7 706	74.7
40 - 44	4 280	43.5
45 - 49	1 978	21.9
50 - 54	824	10.6
55 - 59	312	4.8
60 - 64	130	..
65 +	73	..
Unknown - Inconnu	23 344	..
AMERICA, NORTH - AMÉRIQUE DU NORD		
Puerto Rico - Porto Rico		
2019 (C)		
Total	20 409	...
0 - 19	678	...
20 - 24	4 381	...
25 - 29	5 138	...
30 - 34	4 220	...
35 - 39	2 792	...
40 - 44	1 258	...
45 - 49	503	...
50 - 54	157	...
55 - 59	69	...
60 - 64	44	..
65 +	15	..
Unknown - Inconnu	1 154	..
United States of America - États-Unis d'Amérique		
2015 (C)		
Total	3 978 497	41.1
0 - 19	78 966	8.3
20 - 24	477 664	46.6
25 - 29	866 460	86.4
30 - 34	1 031 310	107.7
35 - 39	648 051	72.5
40 - 44	263 377	29.9
45 - 49	89 921	9.9
50 - 54	29 105	3.0
55 +	12 911	1.4
Unknown - Inconnu	480 732	..
AMERICA, SOUTH - AMÉRIQUE DU SUD		
Chile - Chili		
2017 (C)		
Total	219 186	37.1
0 - 19	7 075	11.9
20 - 24	29 898	45.4
25 - 29	48 824	69.3
30 - 34	49 811	75.5
35 - 39	36 772	63.0
40 - 44	17 782	31.4
45 - 49	6 609	11.7
50 - 54	2 310	4.1
55 - 59	716	1.4
60 - 64	234	..
65 +	96	..
Unknown - Inconnu	19 059	..
Colombia - Colombie		
2019* (U)		
Total	*638 516*	...
0 - 19	*35 438*	...
20 - 24	*137 994*	...
25 - 29	*165 278*	...
30 - 34	*133 741*	...
35 - 39	*85 433*	...
40 - 44	*40 316*	...
45 - 49	*16 095*	...
50 - 54	*7 243*	...
55 - 59	*2 293*	...
60 - 64	*931*	..
65 +	*545*	..
Unknown - Inconnu	*13 209*	..
Ecuador - Équateur		
2011 (+U)		
Total	*229 780*	...
0 - 19	*4 219*	...
20 - 24	*16 514*	...

Continent, country or area, year, code[a] and age of father (in years) / Continent, pays ou zone, année, code[a] et âge du père (en années)	Number - Nombre: Both sexes - Les deux sexes	Rate - Taux
AMERICA, SOUTH - AMÉRIQUE DU SUD		
Ecuador - Équateur		
2011 (+U)		
25 - 29	*17 040*	...
30 - 34	*14 115*	...
35 - 39	*8 339*	...
40 - 44	*4 405*	...
45 - 49	*1 864*	...
50 - 54	*719*	...
55 - 59	*274*	...
60 - 64	*104*	..
65 +	*94*	..
Unknown - Inconnu	*162 093*	..
Uruguay		
2018 (C)		
Total	40 139	38.1
0 - 19	773	8.7
20 - 24	3 993	43.4
25 - 29	5 610	65.5
30 - 34	6 886	84.7
35 - 39	5 338	67.9
40 - 44	2 720	34.7
45 - 49	901	12.9
50 - 54	349	5.4
55 - 59	127	2.0
60 - 64	37	..
65 +	25	..
Unknown - Inconnu	13 380	..
Venezuela (Bolivarian Republic of) - Venezuela (République bolivarienne du)		
2017 (U)		
Total	*579 319*	...
0 - 19	*26 717*	...
20 - 24	*99 854*	...
25 - 29	*114 790*	...
30 - 34	*96 967*	...
35 - 39	*63 612*	...
40 - 44	*33 254*	...
45 - 49	*16 443*	...
50 - 54	*7 164*	...
55 - 59	*2 913*	...
60 - 64	*1 181*	..
65 +	*613*	..
Unknown - Inconnu	*115 811*	..
ASIA - ASIE		
Armenia - Arménie		
2018 (C)		
Total	36 574	42.0
17 - 19	28	0.6
20 - 24	2 253	25.4
25 - 29	10 781	94.1
30 - 34	11 417	98.3
35 - 39	6 393	63.8
40 - 44	2 208	27.8
45 - 49	638	9.2
50 - 54	143	2.0
55 - 59	54	0.6
60 - 64	20	..
65 +	144	..
Unknown - Inconnu	2 495	..
Azerbaijan - Azerbaïdjan[7]		
2018 (+C)		
Total	133 579	40.8
0 - 19	211	0.6
20 - 24	14 672	35.3
ASIA - ASIE		
Azerbaijan - Azerbaïdjan[7]		
2018 (+C)		
25 - 29	53 001	112.9
30 - 34	40 655	92.2
35 - 39	16 781	44.2
40 - 44	5 789	18.8
45 - 49	1 746	5.7
50 - 54	508	1.7
55 +	216	0.7
Bahrain - Bahreïn[8]		
2018 (C)		
Total	19 740	26.2
15 - 19	27	♦0.7
20 - 24	1 131	16.6
25 - 29	4 507	35.0
30 - 34	5 673	36.9
35 - 39	4 410	35.6
40 - 44	2 429	27.3
45 - 49	1 015	15.3
50 - 54	344	7.2
55 - 59	126	3.8
60 - 64	20	..
65 +	37	..
Unknown - Inconnu	21	..
Brunei Darussalam - Brunéi Darussalam		
2018 (+C)		
Total	6 199	36.8
0 - 19	13	♦0.7
20 - 24	366	17.7
25 - 29	1 343	60.4
30 - 34	1 880	87.4
35 - 39	1 289	65.6
40 - 44	572	32.7
45 - 49	198	12.9
50 - 54	68	5.5
55 +	41	4.3
Unknown - Inconnu	429	..
China, Hong Kong SAR - Chine, Hong Kong RAS		
2019 (C)		
Total	52 856	25.5
0 - 19	68	0.5
20 - 24	1 270	6.3
25 - 29	6 714	30.1
30 - 34	17 177	76.5
35 - 39	16 191	69.0
40 - 44	6 740	30.1
45 - 49	2 476	10.4
50 - 54	875	3.5
55 - 59	394	1.3
60 - 64	139	..
65 +	58	..
Unknown - Inconnu	754	..
China, Macao SAR - Chine, Macao RAS		
2019 (C)		
Total	5 979	28.6
0 - 24	172	4.9
25 - 29	1 352	53.1
30 - 34	2 383	72.9
35 - 39	1 171	42.6
40 - 44	493	23.0
45 +	335	5.2
Unknown - Inconnu	73	..
Cyprus - Chypre[9]		
2016 (C)		
Total	9 455	36.5
0 - 19	30	1.2
20 - 24	348	10.8

11. Live births and live birth rates by age of father: latest available year, 2010 - 2019
Naissances vivantes et taux de natalité selon l'âge du père : dernière année disponible, 2010 - 2019 (continued - suite)

Continent, country or area, year, code[a] and age of father (in years) / Continent, pays ou zone, année, code[a] et âge du père (en années)	Number - Nombre: Both sexes - Les deux sexes	Rate - Taux
ASIA - ASIE		
Cyprus - Chypre[9]		
2016 (C)		
25 - 29	1 731	49.6
30 - 34	3 400	106.2
35 - 39	2 472	86.6
40 - 44	889	35.4
45 - 49	308	12.2
50 +	139	2.7
Unknown - Inconnu	138	..
Georgia - Géorgie		
2016 (C)		
Total	56 569	51.1
0 - 19	569	5.1
20 - 24	8 640	72.2
25 - 29	16 650	121.9
30 - 34	14 105	107.3
35 - 39	8 738	72.8
40 - 44	4 421	38.0
45 - 49	1 529	13.7
50 - 54	394	3.3
55 +	154	1.3
Unknown - Inconnu	1 369	..
Israel - Israël[10]		
2018 (C)		
Total	184 370	74.2
0 - 19	394	1.1
20 - 24	15 395	48.8
25 - 29	41 469	138.4
30 - 34	55 408	191.9
35 - 39	40 370	146.4
40 - 44	18 842	70.7
45 - 49	5 271	22.3
50 - 54	1 248	6.3
55 - 59	427	2.3
60 - 64	150	..
65 +	83	..
Unknown - Inconnu	5 313	..
Japan - Japon[11]		
2018 (C)		
Total	897 359	26.0
0 - 19	3 103	1.0
20 - 24	49 549	15.3
25 - 29	179 057	55.9
30 - 34	300 636	84.7
35 - 39	223 833	57.1
40 - 44	103 008	22.1
45 - 49	29 804	6.1
50 - 54	6 271	1.5
55 - 59	1 509	0.4
60 - 64	399	..
65 +	186	..
Unknown - Inconnu	4	..
Kazakhstan		
2019 (C)		
Total	402 310	74.5
0 - 19	1 255	2.3
20 - 24	39 074	69.5
25 - 29	115 378	164.4
30 - 34	111 888	154.6
35 - 39	64 268	107.0
40 - 44	30 109	57.3
45 - 49	8 372	17.4
50 - 54	1 820	4.2
55 - 59	453	1.1
60 - 64	105	..
65 +	51	..
Unknown - Inconnu	29 537	..

Continent, country or area, year, code[a] and age of father (in years) / Continent, pays ou zone, année, code[a] et âge du père (en années)	Number - Nombre: Both sexes - Les deux sexes	Rate - Taux
ASIA - ASIE		
Kyrgyzstan - Kirghizstan		
2018 (C)		
Total	171 149	90.9
0 - 19	251	1.1
20 - 24	16 846	67.4
25 - 29	52 709	200.1
30 - 34	44 068	185.0
35 - 39	24 781	134.6
40 - 44	11 289	73.4
45 - 49	3 325	23.7
50 - 54	754	6.0
55 - 59	181	1.6
60 - 64	52	..
65 +	24	..
Unknown - Inconnu	16 869	..
Malaysia - Malaisie		
2018 (C)		
Total	501 945	44.9
0 - 19	2 061	1.4
20 - 24	29 145	17.8
25 - 29	119 404	70.8
30 - 34	157 298	108.8
35 - 39	103 278	84.4
40 - 44	45 971	47.3
45 - 49	16 637	19.5
50 - 54	5 500	7.0
55 - 59	1 939	2.8
60 - 64	615	..
65 +	226	..
Unknown - Inconnu	19 871	..
Maldives[12]		
2017 (C)		
Total	6 723	58.2
0 - 19	1	♦0.1
20 - 24	321	19.3
25 - 29	1 851	97.8
30 - 34	2 023	115.5
35 - 39	1 282	97.2
40 - 44	697	68.5
45 - 49	329	36.1
50 - 54	91	11.3
55 - 59	30	4.4
60 - 64	8	..
65 +	4	..
Unknown - Inconnu	86	..
Mongolia - Mongolie		
2019 (+C)		
Total	79 580	80.2
0 - 19	801	7.7
20 - 24	11 172	101.0
25 - 29	21 382	164.9
30 - 34	20 335	150.7
35 - 39	12 176	110.2
40 - 44	4 714	48.2
45 - 49	1 057	12.6
50 +	277	2.2
Unknown - Inconnu	7 666	..
Oman		
2019 (C)		
Total	86 819	38.0
0 - 19	38	0.3
20 - 24	3 590	17.4
25 - 29	19 699	45.3
30 - 34	25 495	53.5
35 - 39	18 516	50.9
40 - 44	9 504	39.5
45 - 49	3 658	22.1

11. Live births and live birth rates by age of father: latest available year, 2010 - 2019
Naissances vivantes et taux de natalité selon l'âge du père : dernière année disponible, 2010 - 2019 (continued - suite)

Continent, country or area, year, code[a] and age of father (in years) / Continent, pays ou zone, année, code[a] et âge du père (en années)	Number - Nombre: Both sexes Les deux sexes	Rate Taux
ASIA - ASIE		
Oman		
2019 (C)		
50 - 54	1 352	12.7
55 - 59	618	8.8
60 - 64	243	..
65 +	263	..
Unknown - Inconnu	3 843	..
Philippines		
2018 (C)		
Total	1 668 120	51.0
0 - 19	50 194	10.4
20 - 24	306 203	67.9
25 - 29	411 606	100.0
30 - 34	343 170	92.6
35 - 39	228 720	68.8
40 - 44	114 747	39.7
45 - 49	47 118	18.1
50 - 54	15 914	7.3
55 - 59	5 919	3.3
60 - 64	2 402	..
65 +	1 398	..
Unknown - Inconnu	140 729	..
Qatar		
2016 (C)		
Total	26 816	15.3
0 - 19	8	♦0.1
20 - 24	845	3.7
25 - 29	4 613	12.3
30 - 34	8 528	24.4
35 - 39	7 038	26.9
40 - 44	3 559	18.0
45 - 49	1 403	10.1
50 +	822	5.8
Republic of Korea - République de Corée[13]		
2018 (C)		
Total	326 822	18.5
0 - 19	254	0.2
20 - 24	4 350	2.4
25 - 29	31 212	16.9
30 - 34	116 784	66.8
35 - 39	123 549	59.0
40 - 44	36 679	18.3
45 - 49	8 671	3.8
50 - 54	1 489	0.7
55 - 59	352	0.2
60 - 64	80	..
65 +	19	..
Unknown - Inconnu	3 383	..
Singapore - Singapour		
2019 (C)		
Total	39 279	31.1
0 - 19	77	0.7
20 - 24	689	5.5
25 - 29	5 643	40.0
30 - 34	14 083	101.4
35 - 39	11 732	83.4
40 - 44	4 625	32.5
45 - 49	1 414	9.4
50 - 54	407	2.8
55 - 59	150	1.0
60 - 64	56	..
65 +	15	..
Unknown - Inconnu	388	..
Tajikistan - Tadjikistan[14]		
2017 (U)		
Total	*224 057*	...
0 - 19	*404*	...

Continent, country or area, year, code[a] and age of father (in years) / Continent, pays ou zone, année, code[a] et âge du père (en années)	Number - Nombre: Both sexes Les deux sexes	Rate Taux
ASIA - ASIE		
Tajikistan - Tadjikistan[14]		
2017 (U)		
20 - 24	*37 120*	...
25 - 29	*87 552*	...
30 - 34	*54 556*	...
35 - 39	*23 226*	...
40 - 44	*8 326*	...
45 - 49	*2 581*	...
50 - 54	*716*	...
55 - 59	*370*	...
60 - 64	*187*	..
65 +	*92*	..
Unknown - Inconnu	*8 927*	..
Turkey - Turquie		
2018 (C)		
Total	1 248 847	47.2
0 - 19	5 742	1.8
20 - 24	98 239	29.7
25 - 29	342 724	108.8
30 - 34	383 152	121.0
35 - 39	260 675	79.6
40 - 44	104 191	35.7
45 - 49	29 086	11.0
50 - 54	6 804	2.9
55 - 59	1 845	0.9
60 - 64	688	..
65 +	333	..
Unknown - Inconnu	15 368	..
Uzbekistan - Ouzbékistan[15]		
2018 (+C)		
Total	707 678	67.3
0 - 19	883	0.7
20 - 24	81 980	52.7
25 - 29	308 887	190.4
30 - 34	213 647	144.4
35 - 39	77 653	65.9
40 - 44	18 919	18.8
45 - 49	3 742	4.2
50 - 54	1 108	1.5
55 - 59	525	0.7
60 - 64	225	..
65 +	109	..
EUROPE		
Åland Islands - Îles d'Åland		
2018 (C)		
Total	280	33.7
0 - 19	1	♦1.2
20 - 24	7	♦10.1
25 - 29	56	59.3
30 - 34	102	115.5
35 - 39	63	65.5
40 - 44	39	42.2
45 - 49	7	♦7.2
50 - 54	1	♦0.9
55 - 59	-	-
60 - 64	-	..
65 +	-	..
Unknown - Inconnu	4	..
Albania - Albanie		
2018 (C)		
Total	28 934	32.2
0 - 19	62	0.6
20 - 24	1 148	9.6
25 - 29	6 767	56.9

11. Live births and live birth rates by age of father: latest available year, 2010 - 2019
Naissances vivantes et taux de natalité selon l'âge du père : dernière année disponible, 2010 - 2019 (continued - suite)

Continent, country or area, year, code[a] and age of father (in years) / Continent, pays ou zone, année, code[a] et âge du père (en années)	Number - Nombre: Both sexes - Les deux sexes	Rate - Taux
EUROPE		
Albania - Albanie		
2018 (C)		
30 - 34	10 463	102.6
35 - 39	6 322	76.2
40 - 44	2 621	33.6
45 - 49	775	9.2
50 - 54	201	2.2
55 - 59	47	0.5
60 - 64	15	..
65 +	4	..
Unknown - Inconnu	509	..
Andorra - Andorre		
2015 (C)		
Total	659	...
0 - 19	3	...
20 - 24	18	...
25 - 29	70	...
30 - 34	203	...
35 - 39	202	...
40 - 44	104	...
45 - 49	23	...
50 - 54	11	...
55 - 59	4	...
60 - 64	3	..
65 +	-	..
Unknown - Inconnu	18	..
Austria - Autriche[16]		
2018 (C)		
Total	50 271	18.5
0 - 19	33	0.1
20 - 24	1 856	6.7
25 - 29	9 448	30.6
30 - 34	17 012	55.7
35 - 39	13 522	45.1
40 - 44	5 616	19.8
45 - 49	1 921	5.9
50 - 54	621	1.7
55 - 59	164	0.5
60 - 64	53	..
65 +	25	..
Belarus - Bélarus[15]		
2018 (C)		
Total	81 836	28.6
0 - 19	446	1.9
20 - 24	8 256	32.0
25 - 29	25 392	71.5
30 - 34	26 812	67.4
35 - 39	14 093	39.6
40 - 44	4 941	15.4
45 - 49	1 406	4.6
50 - 54	329	1.1
55 +	161	0.5
Belgium - Belgique		
2014 (C)		
Total	125 014	37.3
0 - 19	532	1.7
20 - 24	6 420	18.9
25 - 29	27 224	79.5
30 - 34	41 459	116.9
35 - 39	25 524	72.7
40 - 44	11 502	30.7
45 - 49	4 559	11.7
50 - 54	1 602	4.1
55 - 59	502	1.4
60 - 64	153	..
65 +	64	..
Unknown - Inconnu	5 473	..
EUROPE		
Bosnia and Herzegovina - Bosnie-Herzégovine		
2010 (C)		
Total	33 528	28.0
0 - 19	99	0.7
20 - 24	3 174	23.3
25 - 29	9 300	75.0
30 - 34	10 238	90.1
35 - 39	5 624	49.2
40 - 44	2 203	16.5
45 - 49	672	4.8
50 - 54	150	1.2
55 - 59	29	0.3
60 - 64	9	..
65 +	4	..
Unknown - Inconnu	2 026	..
Bulgaria - Bulgarie		
2018 (C)		
Total	62 197	30.1
0 - 19	788	5.5
20 - 24	4 699	32.7
25 - 29	12 798	65.4
30 - 34	17 514	80.4
35 - 39	11 767	52.2
40 - 44	5 248	21.3
45 - 49	1 376	5.9
50 - 54	369	1.8
55 - 59	79	0.4
60 - 64	31	..
65 +	13	..
Unknown - Inconnu	7 515	..
Croatia - Croatie		
2018 (C)		
Total	36 945	31.0
0 - 19	238	2.3
20 - 24	2 192	18.0
25 - 29	7 194	59.0
30 - 34	12 256	92.4
35 - 39	9 431	66.6
40 - 44	3 666	26.8
45 - 49	1 025	7.8
50 - 54	286	2.1
55 - 59	82	0.6
60 - 64	18	..
65 +	4	..
Unknown - Inconnu	553	..
Czechia - Tchéquie		
2018 (C)		
Total	114 036	36.0
0 - 19	371	1.7
20 - 24	5 495	22.5
25 - 29	21 520	67.0
30 - 34	34 734	99.9
35 - 39	26 480	68.8
40 - 44	12 708	28.4
45 - 49	3 326	9.1
50 - 54	1 002	3.0
55 - 59	331	1.1
60 - 64	109	..
65 +	44	..
Unknown - Inconnu	7 916	..
Denmark - Danemark[17]		
2018 (C)		
Total	61 476	36.1
0 - 19	60	0.4
20 - 24	2 499	13.8
25 - 29	14 016	76.9
30 - 34	20 049	125.3

11. Live births and live birth rates by age of father: latest available year, 2010 - 2019
Naissances vivantes et taux de natalité selon l'âge du père : dernière année disponible, 2010 - 2019 (continued - suite)

Continent, country or area, year, code[a] and age of father (in years) / Continent, pays ou zone, année, code[a] et âge du père (en années)	Number - Nombre: Both sexes - Les deux sexes	Rate - Taux
EUROPE		
Denmark - Danemark[17]		
2018 (C)		
35 - 39	12 406	80.3
40 - 44	4 963	28.9
45 - 49	1 498	8.3
50 - 54	480	2.5
55 - 59	127	0.7
60 - 64	56	..
65 +	30	..
Unknown - Inconnu	5 292	..
Estonia - Estonie		
2018 (C)		
Total	14 367	37.3
0 - 19	59	2.0
20 - 24	699	21.5
25 - 29	3 122	67.9
30 - 34	4 643	93.3
35 - 39	3 162	68.9
40 - 44	1 480	33.0
45 - 49	519	11.8
50 - 54	146	3.7
55 - 59	50	1.2
60 - 64	14	..
65 +	3	..
Unknown - Inconnu	470	..
Faroe Islands - Îles Féroé		
2019 (C)		
Total	683	44.3
0 - 19	1	♦0.6
20 - 24	52	34.6
25 - 29	146	101.3
30 - 34	168	114.1
35 - 39	150	107.3
40 - 44	66	43.3
45 - 49	16	♦10.3
50 - 54	7	♦4.2
55 - 59	-	-
60 - 64	-	..
65 +	-	..
Unknown - Inconnu	77	..
Finland - Finlande[18]		
2018 (C)		
Total	47 297	30.3
0 - 19	247	1.7
20 - 24	3 184	19.7
25 - 29	10 180	57.5
30 - 34	14 980	85.2
35 - 39	11 017	62.4
40 - 44	4 485	26.7
45 - 49	1 393	8.8
50 - 54	440	2.5
55 - 59	145	0.8
60 - 64	39	..
65 +	20	..
Unknown - Inconnu	1 167	..
France		
2017 (C)		
Total	730 242	40.0
0 - 19	2 343	1.2
20 - 24	34 195	18.7
25 - 29	148 087	78.1
30 - 34	239 631	121.4
35 - 39	177 992	87.3
40 - 44	81 022	39.2
45 - 49	31 338	14.3
50 - 54	10 741	4.9
55 - 59	3 555	1.7

Continent, country or area, year, code[a] and age of father (in years) / Continent, pays ou zone, année, code[a] et âge du père (en années)	Number - Nombre: Both sexes - Les deux sexes	Rate - Taux
EUROPE		
France		
2017 (C)		
60 - 64	1 201	..
65 +	137	..
Germany - Allemagne		
2018 (C)		
Total	787 523	31.9
0 - 19	2 234	1.1
20 - 24	29 723	13.1
25 - 29	134 088	52.5
30 - 34	246 922	95.6
35 - 39	197 195	79.8
40 - 44	84 921	37.3
45 - 49	30 153	11.1
50 - 54	10 067	3.1
55 - 59	2 779	0.9
60 - 64	764	..
65 +	335	..
Unknown - Inconnu	48 342	..
Greece - Grèce		
2018 (C)		
Total	86 440	28.2
0 - 19	147	0.6
20 - 24	1 703	6.4
25 - 29	8 590	31.3
30 - 34	23 478	80.0
35 - 39	26 836	73.5
40 - 44	13 813	37.2
45 - 49	4 553	12.3
50 - 54	1 279	3.7
55 - 59	323	1.0
60 - 64	89	..
65 +	27	..
Unknown - Inconnu	5 602	..
Hungary - Hongrie[19]		
2018 (C)		
Total	93 467	32.1
0 - 19	989	4.6
20 - 24	5 746	22.8
25 - 29	14 219	51.0
30 - 34	23 025	85.7
35 - 39	20 696	68.0
40 - 44	11 324	30.7
45 - 49	3 139	10.1
50 - 54	799	3.0
55 - 59	226	0.9
60 - 64	94	..
65 +	32	..
Unknown - Inconnu	13 178	..
Iceland - Islande		
2018 (C)		
Total	4 228	37.8
0 - 19	18	♦1.6
20 - 24	349	26.1
25 - 29	1 159	75.5
30 - 34	1 255	93.0
35 - 39	832	62.6
40 - 44	349	29.3
45 - 49	106	9.3
50 - 54	44	4.0
55 - 59	9	♦0.8
60 - 64	2	..
65 +	105	..
Italy - Italie		
2018 (C)		
Total	439 747	25.1
0 - 19	1 302	0.9

11. Live births and live birth rates by age of father: latest available year, 2010 - 2019
Naissances vivantes et taux de natalité selon l'âge du père : dernière année disponible, 2010 - 2019 (continued - suite)

Continent, country or area, year, code[a] and age of father (in years) — Continent, pays ou zone, année, code[a] et âge du père (en années)	Number - Nombre: Both sexes - Les deux sexes	Rate - Taux
EUROPE		
Italy - Italie		
2018 (C)		
20 - 24	12 194	8.4
25 - 29	51 689	33.7
30 - 34	114 313	72.3
35 - 39	121 429	69.5
40 - 44	71 624	34.5
45 - 49	25 274	11.4
50 - 54	7 099	3.2
55 - 59	1 910	1.0
60 - 64	537	..
65 +	226	..
Unknown - Inconnu	32 150	..
Latvia - Lettonie		
2018 (C)		
Total	19 314	35.1
0 - 19	131	3.0
20 - 24	1 151	24.7
25 - 29	4 645	70.4
30 - 34	6 215	89.4
35 - 39	3 966	64.9
40 - 44	1 719	27.9
45 - 49	658	10.5
50 - 54	176	2.9
55 - 59	79	1.2
60 - 64	19	..
65 +	10	..
Unknown - Inconnu	545	..
Lithuania - Lituanie		
2018 (C)		
Total	28 149	34.5
0 - 19	116	1.7
20 - 24	1 646	20.4
25 - 29	6 978	73.7
30 - 34	10 078	110.2
35 - 39	5 479	67.3
40 - 44	2 060	24.3
45 - 49	642	6.9
50 - 54	169	1.8
55 - 59	48	0.5
60 - 64	12	..
65 +	7	..
Unknown - Inconnu	914	..
Luxembourg		
2018 (C)		
Total	6 274	31.8
0 - 19	19	♦1.1
20 - 24	199	10.5
25 - 29	880	39.6
30 - 34	2 032	89.8
35 - 39	1 759	76.3
40 - 44	790	35.3
45 - 49	300	13.0
50 - 54	92	3.9
55 - 59	25	♦1.3
60 - 64	9	..
65 +	3	..
Unknown - Inconnu	166	..
Malta - Malte		
2018 (C)		
Total	4 444	28.6
0 - 19	22	♦2.0
20 - 24	221	13.5
25 - 29	849	39.7
30 - 34	1 502	71.5
35 - 39	1 133	58.1
40 - 44	425	24.2

Continent, country or area, year, code[a] and age of father (in years) — Continent, pays ou zone, année, code[a] et âge du père (en années)	Number - Nombre: Both sexes - Les deux sexes	Rate - Taux
EUROPE		
Malta - Malte		
2018 (C)		
45 - 49	122	8.2
50 - 54	37	2.7
55 - 59	14	♦0.9
60 - 64	2	..
65 +	2	..
Unknown - Inconnu	115	..
Netherlands - Pays-Bas[20]		
2014 (C)		
Total	175 181	34.8
0 - 19	333	0.7
20 - 24	6 226	12.1
25 - 29	33 346	66.4
30 - 34	60 729	125.6
35 - 39	41 980	87.5
40 - 44	17 247	30.0
45 - 49	5 280	8.5
50 - 54	1 495	2.5
55 - 59	403	0.7
60 - 64	97	..
65 +	56	..
Unknown - Inconnu	7 989	..
North Macedonia - Macédoine du Nord		
2018 (C)		
Total	21 333	31.7
0 - 19	127	2.1
20 - 24	1 529	22.3
25 - 29	5 534	71.9
30 - 34	6 987	87.3
35 - 39	4 325	54.7
40 - 44	1 399	18.9
45 - 49	385	5.5
50 - 54	86	1.2
55 - 59	15	♦0.2
60 - 64	5	..
65 +	-	..
Unknown - Inconnu	941	..
Norway - Norvège		
2012 (C)		
Total	60 255	38.8
0 - 19	271	1.7
20 - 24	3 931	23.9
25 - 29	13 332	83.2
30 - 34	19 068	116.9
35 - 39	13 188	76.5
40 - 44	5 590	30.1
45 - 49	1 822	10.3
50 - 54	524	3.3
55 - 59	176	1.2
60 - 64	47	..
65 +	9	..
Unknown - Inconnu	2 297	..
Poland - Pologne		
2018 (C)		
Total	388 178	33.8
0 - 19	1 359	1.5
20 - 24	24 377	22.9
25 - 29	94 892	73.1
30 - 34	134 754	90.3
35 - 39	83 115	54.5
40 - 44	29 082	20.6
45 - 49	7 130	6.0
50 - 54	1 865	1.7
55 - 59	595	0.5
60 - 64	194	..

11. Live births and live birth rates by age of father: latest available year, 2010 - 2019
Naissances vivantes et taux de natalité selon l'âge du père : dernière année disponible, 2010 - 2019 (continued - suite)

Continent, country or area, year, code[a] and age of father (in years) / Continent, pays ou zone, année, code[a] et âge du père (en années)	Number - Nombre: Both sexes - Les deux sexes	Rate - Taux
EUROPE		
Poland - Pologne		
2018 (C)		
65 +	53	..
Unknown - Inconnu	10 762	..
Portugal[6]		
2018 (C)		
Total	87 020	30.0
0 - 19	760	2.7
20 - 24	5 139	19.2
25 - 29	14 200	52.7
30 - 34	25 186	89.5
35 - 39	24 032	73.4
40 - 44	11 571	30.6
45 - 49	3 340	9.2
50 - 54	909	2.6
55 - 59	329	1.0
60 - 64	102	..
65 +	32	..
Unknown - Inconnu	1 420	..
Republic of Moldova - République de Moldova[21]		
2018 (C)		
Total	32 606	40.3
0 - 19	170	2.5
20 - 24	3 634	47.5
25 - 29	9 526	102.0
30 - 34	9 303	90.3
35 - 39	4 887	55.7
40 - 44	1 853	23.3
45 - 49	527	7.0
50 +	198	1.2
Unknown - Inconnu	2 508	..
Romania - Roumanie		
2018 (C)		
Total	202 744	34.4
0 - 19	3 020	6.0
20 - 24	17 256	35.1
25 - 29	46 151	80.2
30 - 34	62 159	95.2
35 - 39	39 491	58.4
40 - 44	16 711	22.4
45 - 49	4 379	5.8
50 - 54	1 109	1.8
55 - 59	293	0.6
60 - 64	78	..
65 +	25	..
Unknown - Inconnu	12 072	..
Russian Federation - Fédération de Russie[22]		
2012 (C)		
Total	1 902 084	41.9
0 - 19	12 731	3.9
20 - 24	256 939	51.4
25 - 29	564 777	103.0
30 - 34	431 851	88.4
35 - 39	245 613	55.2
40 - 44	102 880	25.6
45 - 49	33 963	8.4
50 - 54	11 671	2.5
55 - 59	3 196	0.8
60 +	1 203	..
Unknown - Inconnu	237 260	..
San Marino - Saint-Marin		
2017 (C)		
Total	228	22.4
0 - 19	-	-
20 - 24	4	♦5.1
25 - 29	17	♦21.8
30 - 34	64	72.2
EUROPE		
San Marino - Saint-Marin		
2017 (C)		
35 - 39	73	67.7
40 - 44	44	32.2
45 - 49	16	♦10.9
50 - 54	2	♦1.4
55 - 59	1	♦0.8
60 - 64	-	..
65 +	-	..
Unknown - Inconnu	7	..
Serbia - Serbie[23]		
2018 (+C)		
Total	63 975	31.4
0 - 19	395	2.3
20 - 24	4 138	21.7
25 - 29	13 374	64.0
30 - 34	20 460	88.9
35 - 39	14 543	61.1
40 - 44	5 903	24.5
45 - 49	1 644	7.4
50 - 54	439	2.0
55 - 59	158	0.7
60 - 64	42	..
65 +	13	..
Unknown - Inconnu	2 866	..
Slovakia - Slovaquie		
2018 (C)		
Total	57 639	33.7
0 - 19	390	3.3
20 - 24	3 393	24.7
25 - 29	10 621	62.6
30 - 34	16 798	89.8
35 - 39	12 103	61.0
40 - 44	4 963	24.9
45 - 49	1 159	7.1
50 - 54	266	1.7
55 - 59	94	0.6
60 - 64	26	..
65 +	10	..
Unknown - Inconnu	7 816	..
Slovenia - Slovénie		
2018 (C)		
Total	19 585	31.4
0 - 19	47	1.0
20 - 24	865	16.8
25 - 29	4 107	69.3
30 - 34	6 845	96.5
35 - 39	4 842	60.5
40 - 44	1 888	23.7
45 - 49	486	6.5
50 - 54	142	1.8
55 - 59	31	0.4
60 - 64	5	..
65 +	3	..
Unknown - Inconnu	324	..
Spain - Espagne		
2018 (C)		
Total	370 827	26.3
0 - 19	1 971	1.7
20 - 24	12 223	10.8
25 - 29	39 694	32.2
30 - 34	97 198	71.1
35 - 39	121 767	71.3
40 - 44	63 125	32.2
45 - 49	18 553	10.0
50 - 54	4 625	2.6
55 - 59	1 175	0.8

11. Live births and live birth rates by age of father: latest available year, 2010 - 2019
Naissances vivantes et taux de natalité selon l'âge du père : dernière année disponible, 2010 - 2019 (continued - suite)

Continent, country or area, year, code[a] and age of father (in years) / Continent, pays ou zone, année, code[a] et âge du père (en années)	Number - Nombre: Both sexes - Les deux sexes	Rate - Taux
EUROPE		
Spain - Espagne		
2018 (C)		
60 - 64	360	..
65 +	138	..
Unknown - Inconnu	9 998	..
Sweden - Suède		
2012 (C)		
Total	113 177	40.2
0 - 19	443	1.5
20 - 24	7 043	21.2
25 - 29	23 661	77.8
30 - 34	36 139	122.1
35 - 39	26 932	86.6
40 - 44	11 433	35.6
45 - 49	4 023	12.0
50 - 54	1 169	4.0
55 - 59	404	1.4
60 - 64	116	..
65 +	52	..
Unknown - Inconnu	1 762	..
Switzerland - Suisse[15]		
2018 (C)		
Total	65 275	24.9
0 - 19	6	-
20 - 24	847	3.4
25 - 29	8 639	29.9
30 - 34	22 194	72.5
35 - 39	20 406	66.4
40 - 44	8 911	30.3
45 - 49	2 837	9.1
50 - 54	979	2.9
55 - 59	307	1.0
60 - 64	96	..
65 +	53	..
Unknown - Inconnu	-	..
Ukraine[24]		
2017 (+C)		
Total	363 987	28.4
0 - 19	2 271	2.7
20 - 24	39 307	36.4
25 - 29	100 369	71.0
30 - 34	96 216	59.3
35 - 39	51 522	36.4
40 - 44	21 653	16.5
45 - 49	6 819	5.6
50 - 54	1 977	1.7
55 - 59	950	0.8
Unknown - Inconnu	42 903	..
United Kingdom of Great Britain and Northern Ireland - Royaume-Uni de Grande-Bretagne et d'Irlande du Nord[25]		
2018 (C)		
Total	730 918	37.8
0 - 19	7 507	4.2
20 - 24	55 760	27.4
25 - 29	146 931	67.5
30 - 34	215 569	102.6
35 - 39	163 175	80.3
40 - 44	67 538	35.7
45 - 49	24 388	11.5
50 - 54	7 657	3.5
55 - 59	2 344	1.2
60 - 64	575	..
65 +	277	..
Unknown - Inconnu	39 197	..

Continent, country or area, year, code[a] and age of father (in years) / Continent, pays ou zone, année, code[a] et âge du père (en années)	Number - Nombre: Both sexes - Les deux sexes	Rate - Taux
OCEANIA - OCÉANIE		
Australia - Australie		
2018 (C)		
Total	315 147	42.1
0 - 19	2 645	3.6
20 - 24	20 455	23.9
25 - 29	58 517	64.8
30 - 34	102 328	115.7
35 - 39	75 517	91.7
40 - 44	29 362	38.5
45 - 49	9 432	12.0
50 - 54	2 837	3.9
55 - 59	974	1.4
60 - 64	346	..
65 +	167	..
Unknown - Inconnu[26]	12 567	..
French Polynesia - Polynésie française		
2018 (C)		
Total	3 776	41.2
0 - 19	135	12.1
20 - 24	569	59.3
25 - 29	821	79.8
30 - 34	819	76.2
35 - 39	626	62.9
40 - 44	357	37.5
45 - 49	181	18.7
50 - 54	75	8.1
55 - 59	27	♦3.6
60 - 64	6	..
65 +	3	..
Unknown - Inconnu	157	..
New Caledonia - Nouvelle-Calédonie		
2015 (C)		
Total	4 191	...
0 - 19	49	...
20 - 24	433	...
25 - 29	798	...
30 - 34	968	...
35 - 39	728	...
40 - 44	436	...
45 - 49	131	...
50 - 54	43	...
55 - 59	13	...
60 +	4	..
Unknown - Inconnu	588	..
New Zealand - Nouvelle-Zélande[27]		
2019 (+C)		
Total	59 637	...
0 - 19	1 011	...
20 - 24	5 694	...
25 - 29	12 282	...
30 - 34	18 039	...
35 - 39	12 252	...
40 - 44	4 800	...
45 - 49	1 707	...
50 - 54	504	...
55 - 59	150	...
60 - 64	54	..
65 +	27	..
Unknown - Inconnu	3 126	..

FOOTNOTES - NOTES

♦ Rates based on 30 or fewer births. - Taux basés sur 30 naissances ou moins.

* Provisional. - Données provisoires.

a 'Code' indicates the source of data, as follows:
C - Civil registration, estimated over 90% complete
U - Civil registration, estimated less than 90% complete
| - Other source, estimated reliable
+ - Data tabulated by date of registration rather than occurrence
... Information not available

Le 'Code' indique la source des données, comme suit :
C - Registres de l'état civil considérés complets à 90 p. 100 au moins
U - Registres de l'état civil qui ne sont pas considérés complets à 90 p. 100 au moins
| - Autre source, considérée fiable
+ - Données exploitées selon la date de l'enregistrement et non la date de l'événement
... Information non disponible

1 Excludes the islands of St. Brandon and Agalega. - Non compris les îles St. Brandon et Agalega.

2 Reason for discrepancy between these figures and corresponding figures shown elsewhere not ascertained. - On ne sait pas comment s'explique la divergence entre ces chiffres et les chiffres correspondants indiqués ailleurs.

3 Unrevised data. - Les données n'ont pas été révisées.

4 Including Canadian residents temporarily in the United States, but excluding United States residents temporarily in Canada. - Y compris les résidents canadiens se trouvant temporairement aux Etats-Unis, mais ne comprenant pas les résidents des Etats-Unis se trouvant temporairement au Canada.

5 Excluding children born in the country of non-resident mothers. - Exceptés les enfants nés dans le pays des mères non-résidentes.

6 Data refer to births to resident mothers. - Ces données concernent les enfants nés de mères résidentes.

7 Excluding infants born alive of less than 28 weeks' gestation, of less than 1 000 g in weight and 35 cm in length, who die within seven days of birth. Excluding newborns registered by application of mothers. - Non compris les enfants nés vivants après moins de 28 semaines de gestations, pesant moins de 1 000 g, mesurant moins de 35 cm et décédés dans les sept jours qui ont suivi leur naissance. Exception faite des nouveau-nés qui ont été enregistrés à la demande des mères.

8 Sources: Births and Deaths National Registration System database, and medical records of government hospitals. Data refer to Bahraini and non-Bahraini births including some visitors, and Bahraini births abroad. - Les sources: Les bases de données des << Births and Deaths National Registration System >> et les dossiers médicaux des hôpitaux du gouvernement. Les données se rapportent aux naissances de Bahreïniens et de non-Bahreïniens, y compris d'enfants non résidents, ainsi que de Bahreïniens résidant à l'étranger.

9 Data refer to government controlled areas. - Les données se rapportent aux zones contrôlées par le Gouvernement.

10 Includes data for East Jerusalem and Israeli residents in certain other territories under occupation by Israeli military forces since June 1967. - Y compris les données pour Jérusalem-Est et les résidents israéliens dans certains autres territoires occupés depuis 1967 par les forces armées israéliennes.

11 Data refer to Japanese nationals in Japan only. Data refer to live births in wedlock only. - Les données se raportent aux nationaux japonais au Japon seulement. Les données ne concernent que les naissances vivantes de parents mariés.

12 Data do not include foreigners. - Les données sur les etrangers ne sont pas inclus.

13 Excluding alien armed forces, civilian aliens employed by armed forces, and foreign diplomatic personnel and their dependants. - Non compris les militaires étrangers, les civils étrangers employés par les forces armées ni le personnel diplomatique étranger et les membres de leur famille les accompagnant.

14 Excluding infants born alive of less than 28 weeks' gestation, of less than 1 000 g in weight and 35 cm in length, who die within seven days of birth. Data have been adjusted for under-registration. - Non compris les enfants nés vivants après moins de 28 semaines de gestations, pesant moins de 1 000 g, mesurant moins de 35 cm et décédés dans les sept jours qui ont suivi leur naissance. Y compris un ajustement pour sous-enregistrement.

15 Data refer to live births in wedlock only. - Les données ne concernent que les naissances vivantes de parents mariés.

16 Data refer to live births in wedlock only. Including births occurring abroad of mothers with residence in Austria. - Les données ne concernent que les naissances vivantes de parents mariés. Y compris les naissances survenues à l'étranger des mères avec résidence en Autriche.

17 Excluding Faeroe Islands and Greenland shown separately, if available. - Non compris les Iles Féroé et le Groenland, qui font l'objet de rubriques distinctes, si disponible.

18 Excluding Åland Islands. - Non compris les Îles d'Åland.

19 Data include the live births of women with Hungarian usual residence regardless of whether the live birth occurred in Hungary or in a foreign country, and do not include the live births of women with foreign country usual residence. Data include the live births of women with unknown residence and homeless. - Les données concernent les enfants nés vivants de femmes dont la résidence habituelle est en Hongrie, que la naissance vivante ait eu lieu en Hongrie ou dans un pays étranger, et ne comprennent pas les enfants nés vivants de femmes dont la résidence habituelle est dans un pays étranger. Les données incluent les enfants nés vivants de femmes dont la résidence n'est pas connue et de femmes sans domicile fixe.

20 Including residents outside the country if listed in a Netherlands population register. - Englobe les résidents se trouvant à l'étranger à condition qu'ils soient inscrits sur le registre de population des Pays-Bas.

21 Excluding Transnistria and the municipality of Bender. - Les données ne tiennent pas compte de l'information sur la Transnistria et la municipalité de Bender.

22 Excluding infants born alive of less than 28 weeks' gestation, of less than 1 000 g in weight and 35 cm in length, who die within seven days of birth. - Non compris les enfants nés vivants après moins de 28 semaines de gestations, pesant moins de 1 000 g, mesurant moins de 35 cm et décédés dans les sept jours qui ont suivi leur naissance.

23 Excludes data for Kosovo and Metohia. - Sans les données pour le Kosovo et Metohie.

24 Data refer to births with weight 500g and more (if weight is unknown - with length 25 centimeters and more, or with gestation during 22 weeks or more). The Government of Ukraine has informed the United Nations that it is not in a position to provide statistical data concerning the Autonomous Republic of Crimea and the city of Sevastopol. - Données concernant les nouveau-nés de 500 grammes ou plus (si le poids est inconnu – de 25 centimètres de long ou plus, ou après une grossesse de 22 semaines ou plus). Le gouvernement Ukrainien a informé l'ONU qu'il n'est pas en mesure de fournir des données statistiques concernant la République autonome de Crimée et la ville de Sébastopol.

25 Data tabulated by date of occurrence for England and Wales, and by date of registration for Northern Ireland and Scotland. Excluding Channel Islands (Guernsey and Jersey) and Isle of Man, shown separately, if available. - Données exploitées selon la date de l'événement pour l'Angleterre et le pays de Galles, et selon la date de l'enregistrement pour l'Irlande du Nord et l'Ecosse. Non compris les îles Anglo-Normandes (Guernesey et Jersey) et l'île de Man, qui font l'objet de rubriques distinctes, si disponible.

26 Data includes births born in wedlock for which age of father is unknown and births born out of wedlock not acknowledged by the father for which therefore age of father is unknown. - Les données se rapportent aux enfants légitimes pour lesquels l'âge du père n'est pas connu et aux naissances hors mariage non reconnues par le père et pour lesquelles l'âge du père n'est par conséquent pas connu.

27 Random rounding to base 3 is applied in this table as a confidentiality measure. Data refers to births registered in the country to mothers resident in the country. - Les chiffres sont arrondis à la base 3 de manière aléatoire, pour des raisons de confidentialité. Les données se rapportent aux naissances enregistrées dans le pays pour lesquelles la mère réside dans le pays.

Table 12 - *Demographic Yearbook 2019*

Table 12 presents late foetal deaths and late foetal-death ratios by urban/rural residence for as many years as possible between 2015 and 2019.

Description of variables: Late foetal deaths are foetal deaths[1] of 28 or more completed weeks of gestation. Foetal deaths of unknown gestational age are included with those 28 or more weeks.

Statistics on the number of late foetal deaths are obtained from civil registers unless otherwise noted.

The urban/rural classification of late foetal deaths is as provided by each country or area; it is presumed to be based on the national census definitions of urban population that have been set forth at the end of the technical notes for table 6.

Ratio computation: Late foetal-death ratios are the annual number of late foetal deaths per 1 000 live births (as shown in table 9) in the same year. The live-birth base was adopted because it is assumed to be more comparable from one country or area to another than the sum of live births and foetal deaths.

Ratios by urban/rural residence are the annual number of late foetal deaths, in the appropriate urban or rural category, per 1 000 corresponding live births (as shown in table 9). These ratios are calculated by the United Nations Statistics Division.

Ratios presented in this table are limited to those for countries or areas and urban/rural areas having at least a total of 30 late foetal deaths in a given year.

Reliability of data: Each country or area is asked to indicate the estimated completeness of the late foetal deaths recorded in its civil register. These national assessments are indicated by the quality codes "C", "U" and "…" that appear in the first column of this table.

"C" indicates that the data are estimated to be virtually complete, that is, representing at least 90 per cent of the late foetal deaths occurring each year, while "U" indicates that data are estimated to be incomplete, that is, representing less than 90 per cent of the late foetal deaths occurring each year. The code "..." indicates that no information was provided regarding completeness.

Data from civil registers which are reported as incomplete or of unknown completeness (coded "U" or "...") are considered unreliable. They appear in italics in this table. Ratios are not computed for data so coded.

For more information about the quality of vital statistics data in general, see section 4.2 of the Technical Notes.

Limitations: Statistics on late foetal deaths are subject to the same qualifications as have been set forth for vital statistics in general and foetal-death statistics in particular as discussed in section 4 of the Technical Notes.

The reliability of the data is a very important factor. Of all vital statistics, the registration of foetal deaths is probably the most incomplete.

Variation in the definition of foetal deaths, and in particular late foetal deaths, also limits international comparability. The criterion of 28 or more completed weeks of gestation to distinguish late foetal deaths is not universally used; some countries or areas use different durations of gestation or other criteria such as size of the foetus. In addition, the difficulty of accurately determining gestational age further reduces comparability. However, to promote comparability, late foetal deaths shown in this table are restricted to those of at least 28 or more completed weeks of gestation. Wherever this is not possible, a footnote is provided.

Late foetal-death ratios are subject to the limitations of the data on live births with which they have been calculated. These have been set forth in the technical notes for table 9.

It must be pointed out that when late foetal deaths and live births are both under registered, the resulting ratios may be of reasonable magnitude. For the countries or areas where live-birth registration is poorest, the late foetal-death ratios may be the largest, effectively masking the completeness of the base data. For this reason, possible variations in birth-registration completeness as well as the reported completeness of late foetal deaths must always be borne in mind in evaluating late foetal-death ratios.

Finally, it may be noted that the counting of live-born infants as late foetal deaths, because they died before the registration of the birth or within the first 24 hours of life, has the effect of inflating the late foetal-death ratios unduly by decreasing the birth denominator and increasing the foetal-death numerator. This factor should not be overlooked in using data from this table.

The comparability of data by urban/rural residence is affected by the national definitions of urban and rural used in tabulating these data. It is assumed, in the absence of specific information to the contrary, that the definitions of urban and rural used in connection with the national population census were also used in the compilation of the vital statistics for each country or area. However, it cannot be excluded that, for a given country or area, different definitions of urban and rural are used for the vital statistics data and the population census data respectively. When known, the definitions of urban used in national population censuses are presented at the end of the technical notes for table 6. As discussed in detail in the technical notes for table 6, these definitions vary considerably from one country or area to another.

Urban/rural differentials in late foetal death ratios may also be affected by whether the late foetal deaths and live births have been tabulated in terms of place of occurrence or place of usual residence. This problem is discussed in more detail in section 4.1.4.1 of the Introduction.

Earlier data: Late foetal deaths and late foetal-death ratios have been shown in each issue of the Demographic Yearbook beginning with the 1951 issue. A special topic CD on natality published in 2001 presents the data for all available years from 1990 to 1998. For more information on specific topics, and years for which data are reported, readers should consult the Historical Index.

NOTES

[1] For definition, see section 4.1.1 of the Introduction.

Tableau 12 – *Annuaire démographique 2019*

Le tableau 12 présente des données sur les morts fœtales tardives et les rapports de mortinatalité selon le lieu de résidence (zone urbaine ou rurale) pour le plus grand nombre d'années possible entre 2015 et 2019.

Description des variables : Par mort fœtale tardive, on entend le décès d'un fœtus[1] survenu après 28 semaines complètes de gestation au moins. Les morts fœtales pour lesquelles la durée de la période de gestation n'est pas connue sont comprises dans cette catégorie.

Sauf indication contraire, les statistiques du nombre de morts fœtales tardives sont établies sur la base des registres de l'état civil.

La classification des morts fœtales tardives selon le lieu de résidence (zone urbaine ou rurale) est celle qui a été communiquée par chaque pays ou zone ; on part du principe qu'elle repose sur les définitions de la population urbaine utilisées pour les recensements nationaux, telles qu'elles sont reproduites à la fin des notes techniques du tableau 6.

Calcul des rapports : les rapports de mortinatalité représentent le nombre annuel de morts fœtales tardives pour 1 000 naissances vivantes (telles qu'elles sont présentées au tableau 9) survenues pendant la même année. On a pris pour base de calcul les naissances vivantes parce que l'on pense qu'elles sont plus facilement comparables d'un pays ou d'une zone à l'autre que la somme des naissances vivantes et des morts fœtales.

Les rapports selon le lieu de résidence (zone urbaine ou rurale) représentent le nombre annuel de morts fœtales tardives, classées selon la catégorie urbaine ou rurale appropriée pour 1 000 naissances vivantes (telles qu'elles sont présentées au tableau 9) survenues parmi la population correspondante. Ces rapports ont été calculés par la Division des statistiques de l'Organisation des Nations Unies.

Les rapports présentés dans le tableau 12 ne concernent que les pays ou zones où l'on a enregistré un total d'au moins 30 morts fœtales tardives pendant une année donnée.

Fiabilité des données : il a été demandé à chaque pays ou zone d'indiquer le degré estimatif de complétude des données sur les morts fœtales tardives figurant dans ses registres d'état civil. Ces évaluations nationales sont signalées par les codes de qualité “C”, “U” et “...” qui apparaissent dans la deuxième colonne du tableau.

La lettre “C” indique que les données sont jugées à peu près complètes, c'est-à-dire qu'elles représentent au moins 90 p. 100 des morts fœtales tardives survenues chaque année ; la lettre “U” signifie que les données sont jugées incomplètes, c'est-à-dire qu'elles représentent moins de 90 p.100 des morts fœtales tardives survenues chaque année. Le code “...” indique qu'aucun renseignement n'a été communiqué quant à la complétude des données.

Les données provenant des registres de l'état civil qui sont déclarées incomplètes ou dont le degré de complétude n'est pas connu (code “U” ou “...”) sont jugées douteuses. Elles apparaissent en italique dans le tableau ; les rapports, dans ces cas, n'ont pas été calculés.

Pour plus de précisions sur la qualité des données reposant sur les statistiques de l'état civil en général, voir la section 4.2 des Notes techniques.

Insuffisance des données : les statistiques des morts fœtales tardives appellent toutes les réserves qui ont été formulées à propos des statistiques de l'état civil en général et des statistiques concernant les morts fœtales en particulier (voir la section 4 des Notes techniques).

La fiabilité des données est un facteur très important. Les statistiques concernant les morts fœtales sont probablement les moins complètes de toutes les statistiques de l'état civil.

L'hétérogénéité des définitions de la mort fœtale et, en particulier, de la mort fœtale tardive nuit aussi à la comparabilité internationale des données. Le critère des 28 semaines complètes de gestation au moins n'est pas universellement utilisé ; certains pays ou zones retiennent des critères différents pour la durée de la période de gestation ou d'autres critères tels que la taille du fœtus. De surcroît, la comparabilité est rendue malaisée par le fait qu'il est difficile d'établir avec précision l'âge gestationnel. Pour faciliter les comparaisons, les morts fœtales tardives considérées ici sont exclusivement celles qui sont survenues au terme de 28 semaines de gestation au moins. Les exceptions sont signalées en note.

Les rapports de mortinatalité appellent en outre toutes les réserves qui ont été formulées à propos des statistiques des naissances vivantes qui ont servi à leur calcul (voir à ce sujet les notes techniques relatives au tableau 9).

En ce qui concerne le calcul des rapports, il convient de noter que, si l'enregistrement des morts fœtales tardives et celui des naissances vivantes sont loin d'être exhaustifs, les rapports de mortinatalité peuvent être raisonnables. C'est parfois pour les pays ou zones où l'enregistrement des naissances vivantes laisse le plus à désirer que les rapports de mortinatalité sont les plus élevés, ce qui masque le caractère incomplet des données de base. Aussi, pour porter un jugement sur la qualité des rapports de mortinatalité, il ne faut jamais oublier que la complétude de l'enregistrement des naissances comme celle de l'enregistrement des morts fœtales tardives peuvent varier sensiblement.

Enfin, on notera que l'inclusion parmi les morts fœtales tardives des décès d'enfants nés vivants qui sont décédés avant l'enregistrement de leur naissance ou dans les 24 heures qui ont suivi la naissance conduit à des rapports de mortinatalité exagérés parce que le dénominateur (nombre de naissances) se trouve alors diminué et le numérateur (morts fœtales) augmenté. Il importe de ne pas négliger ce facteur lorsque l'on utilise les données du tableau 12.

La comparabilité des données selon le lieu de résidence (zone urbaine ou rurale) peut être limitée par les définitions nationales des termes « urbain » et « rural » utilisées pour la mise en tableaux de ces données. En l'absence d'indications contraires, on a supposé que les mêmes définitions avaient servi pour le recensement national de la population et pour l'établissement des statistiques de l'état civil pour chaque pays ou zone. Toutefois, il n'est pas exclu que, pour une zone ou un pays donné, des définitions différentes aient été retenues. Les définitions du terme « urbain » utilisées pour les recensements nationaux de population ont été présentées à la fin des notes techniques du tableau 6 lorsqu'elles étaient connues. Comme on l'a précisé dans les notes techniques relatives au tableau 6, ces définitions varient considérablement d'un pays ou d'une zone à l'autre.

La différence entre les rapports de mortinatalité pour les zones urbaines et rurales pourra aussi être faussée selon que les morts fœtales tardives et les naissances vivantes auront été classées d'après le lieu de l'événement ou le lieu de résidence habituel. Ce problème est examiné plus en détail à la section 4.1.4.1 des Notes techniques.

Données publiées antérieurement : les éditions de l'*Annuaire démographique* parues à partir de 1951 contiennent des statistiques concernant les morts fœtales tardives et les rapports de mortinatalité. Un CD-ROM sur la natalité paru en 2001 présente les données pour toutes les années disponibles de 1990 à 1998. Pour plus de précisions concernant les années et les sujets pour lesquels des données ont été publiées, se reporter à l'index.

NOTE

[1] Pour la définition, voir la section 4.1.1 de l'Introduction.

12. Late foetal deaths and late foetal death ratios, by urban/rural residence: 2015 - 2019
Morts foetales tardives et rapports de mortinatalité, selon la résidence, urbaine/rurale : 2015 - 2019

Continent, country or area, and urban/rural residence Continent, pays ou zone et résidence, urbaine/rurale	Code[a]	Number - Nombre					Ratio - Rapport				
		2015	2016	2017	2018	2019	2015	2016	2017	2018	2019
AFRICA - AFRIQUE											
Algeria - Algérie											
Total	+U	*14 620*	*14 236*	*13 412*	*12 712*	*12 540*	...	...	...	...	...
Botswana											
Total	+U	...	*496*[1]	*371*[1]	*757*[2]	...	...	...	...	...	...
Cabo Verde[3]											
Total	C	104	121	112	...	...	10.7	12.2	11.4	...	...
Eswatini[4]											
Total	U	...	*217*	*240*	*210*	...	...	...	...	...	...
Kenya											
Total	+U	...	...	...	...	*7 596*	...	...	...	...	...
Mauritius - Maurice[5]											
Total	+C	125	127	135	130	139	9.9	9.8	10.1	10.0	10.8
Urban - Urbaine	+C	54	52	53	57	52	10.5	9.8	10.0	10.6	10.1
Rural - Rurale	+C	71	75	82	73	87	9.5	9.8	10.1	9.6	11.3
South Africa - Afrique du Sud											
Total	...	*14 341*	*11 961*	...	...	...	...	...	...	...	...
Tunisia - Tunisie											
Total	U	*2 268*	*2 475*	*2 463*	*2 335*	...	...	...	...	...	...
AMERICA, NORTH - AMÉRIQUE DU NORD											
Belize											
Total	U	*55*	*54*	...	...	...	...	...	...	...	...
Urban - Urbaine	U	*24*	*21*	...	...	...	...	...	...	...	...
Rural - Rurale	U	*31*	*33*	...	...	...	...	...	...	...	...
Bermuda - Bermudes[6]											
Total	C	2	4[7]	-[7]	4[7]	-[7]	...	...	...	...	...
British Virgin Islands - Îles Vierges britanniques											
Total	C	1	2	2	...	...	...	...	...	...	...
Canada[8]											
Total	C	1 078	1 068	1 073	1 040	...	2.8	2.8	2.9	2.8	...
Costa Rica											
Total	C	326	314	276	316	*233	4.5	4.5	4.0	4.6	*3.6
Urban - Urbaine	C	208	198	164	202	...	4.2	4.1	3.5	4.3	...
Rural - Rurale	C	118	116	112	114	...	5.3	5.4	5.2	5.2	...
Cuba[9]											
Total	C	1 190[2]	772	1 312[2]	1 350[2]	...	9.5	6.6	11.4	11.6	...
Dominican Republic - République dominicaine											
Total	U	*2 133*	*2 062*	*2 153*	*2 234*	...	...	...	...	...	...
Guatemala[2]											
Total	C	3 121	3 161	3 033	2 894	...	8.0	8.1	7.9	7.6	...
Mexico - Mexique[10]											
Total	+U	*9 685*	*9 068*	*8 968*	*8 255*	...	...	...	...	...	...
Urban - Urbaine[11]	+U	*7 005*	*6 623*	*6 257*	*5 006*	...	...	...	...	...	...
Rural - Rurale[11]	+U	*2 407*	*2 151*	*1 947*	*1 701*	...	...	...	...	...	...
Montserrat											
Total	C	1	-	...	...	...	...	...	...	...	...
Panama											
Total	U	*436*	*373*	*419*	*421*	...	...	...	...	...	...
Puerto Rico - Porto Rico[2]											
Total	C	358	311	257	241	205	11.5	11.0	10.5	11.2	10.0
Urban - Urbaine	C	205[11]	165	146	140	124	10.8	9.1	8.9	10.0	9.3
Rural - Rurale	C	130[11]	146	111	101	81	10.6	14.4	13.8	13.4	11.5
United States of America - États-Unis d'Amérique											
Total	C	11 354	...	...	...	...	2.9	...	...	...	...
AMERICA, SOUTH - AMÉRIQUE DU SUD											
Argentina - Argentine											
Total	C	3 785	3 782	3 604	3 633	...	4.9	5.2	5.1	5.3	...

12. Late foetal deaths and late foetal death ratios, by urban/rural residence: 2015 - 2019
Morts foetales tardives et rapports de mortinatalité, selon la résidence, urbaine/rurale : 2015 - 2019 (continued - suite)

Continent, country or area, and urban/rural residence Continent, pays ou zone et résidence, urbaine/rurale	Co-de[a]	Number - Nombre					Ratio - Rapport				
		2015	2016	2017	2018	2019	2015	2016	2017	2018	2019
AMERICA, SOUTH - AMÉRIQUE DU SUD											
Brazil - Brésil											
Total	U	*16 851*	*16 224*	*24 495*[2]	*25 018*[2]	...	...	...	...	...	...
Chile - Chili[12]											
Total	C	1 185	1 114	984	...	...	4.8	4.8	4.5	...	...
Urban - Urbaine	C	1 067	1 011	887	...	...	4.8	4.8	4.4	...	...
Rural - Rurale	C	118	103	97	...	...	5.3	5.2	6.3	...	...
Colombia - Colombie[13]											
Total	U	*5 935*	*5 728*	*5 939*	*6 305*	**6 167*	...	...	...	...	...
Urban - Urbaine[11]	U	*4 477*	*4 327*	*4 362*	*4 635*	**185*	...	...	...	...	...
Rural - Rurale[11]	U	*1 406*	*1 354*	*1 486*	*1 527*	**4 511*	...	...	...	...	...
Ecuador - Équateur[14]											
Total	...	*1 028*	*1 001*	*1 063*	*1 022*	...	...	...	...	...	...
Urban - Urbaine	...	*849*	*822*	*881*	*834*[15]	...	...	...	...	...	...
Rural - Rurale	...	*179*	*179*	*182*	*185*[15]	...	...	...	...	...	...
Uruguay											
Total	C	199	183	197	155	...	4.1	3.9	4.6	3.9	...
Venezuela (Bolivarian Republic of) - Venezuela (République bolivarienne du)											
Total	U	*2 483*	*3 028*	*2 202*	...	...	...	...	...	...	...
ASIA - ASIE											
Armenia - Arménie											
Total	C	796	699	634	623	...	19.1	17.2	16.8	17.0	...
Urban - Urbaine	C	509	431	408	410	...	18.8	16.3	16.6	16.9	...
Rural - Rurale	C	287	268	226	213	...	19.6	19.0	17.3	17.3	...
Azerbaijan - Azerbaïdjan											
Total	+C	904	920	1 158	907	...	5.4	5.8	8.0	6.5	...
Bahrain - Bahreïn[16]											
Total	...	*137*	*138*	*103*	...	...	...	...	...	...	...
China, Hong Kong SAR - Chine, Hong Kong RAS											
Total	...	*150*	*180*	*139*	*124*	*140*	...	...	...	...	...
China, Macao SAR - Chine, Macao RAS											
Total	C	6	11	12	7	7	...	...	...	...	...
Georgia - Géorgie											
Total	C	589	558	506	438	...	9.9	9.9	9.5	8.6	...
Urban - Urbaine	C	321	310	...	...	...	9.5	9.6	...	...	...
Rural - Rurale	C	268	248	...	...	...	10.6	10.2	...	...	...
Israel - Israël[17]											
Total	C	561	681	...	...	...	3.1	3.8	...	...	...
Urban - Urbaine[11]	C	511	596	...	...	...	3.1	3.6	...	...	...
Rural - Rurale[11]	C	42	76	...	...	...	2.5	4.5	...	...	...
Japan - Japon[18]											
Total	C	1 830	1 699	1 616	1 383	...	1.8	1.7	1.7	1.5	...
Urban - Urbaine[19]	C	1 695	1 584	1 499	1 265	...	1.8	1.8	1.7	1.5	...
Rural - Rurale[19]	C	134	114	117	118	...	1.7	1.5	1.7	1.7	...
Kazakhstan											
Total	C	2 344[20]	2 382[20]	2 361[21]	2 287[21]	2 225[21]	5.9	5.9	6.0	5.7	5.5
Urban - Urbaine	C	1 268[20]	1 251[20]	1 286[21]	1 217[21]	1 192[21]	5.6	5.4	5.7	5.2	5.0
Rural - Rurale	C	1 076[20]	1 131[20]	1 075[21]	1 070[21]	1 033[21]	6.2	6.6	6.6	6.6	6.3
Kuwait - Koweït											
Total	C	405	220	234	198	...	6.8	3.7	4.0	3.5	...
Kyrgyzstan - Kirghizstan											
Total	C	1 484	1 423	1 387	1 420	...	9.1	9.0	9.0	8.3	...
Urban - Urbaine[22]	C	1 080	1 006	1 039	1 072	...	20.6	19.5	19.7	17.3	...
Rural - Rurale[22]	C	404	417	348	348	...	3.6	3.9	3.5	3.2	...
Malaysia - Malaisie											
Total	C	2 325	2 648	2 769	2 755	...	4.5	5.2	5.4	5.5	...
Urban - Urbaine	C	1 507	...	...	...	...	4.3	...	...	...	...
Rural - Rurale	C	818	...	...	...	...	4.8	...	...	...	...

12. Late foetal deaths and late foetal death ratios, by urban/rural residence: 2015 - 2019
Morts foetales tardives et rapports de mortinatalité, selon la résidence, urbaine/rurale : 2015 - 2019 (continued - suite)

Continent, country or area, and urban/rural residence — Continent, pays ou zone et résidence, urbaine/rurale	Co-de[a]	Number - Nombre 2015	2016	2017	2018	2019	Ratio - Rapport 2015	2016	2017	2018	2019
ASIA - ASIE											
Maldives[2]											
Total	...	*47*	*41*	*34*	...	...	...	...	...	...	...
Urban - Urbaine	...	*12*	*16*	*2*[11]	...	...	...	...	...	...	...
Rural - Rurale	...	*35*	*25*	*31*[11]	...	...	...	...	...	...	...
Mongolia - Mongolie											
Total	+C	557	484	451	438	405	6.8	6.1	6.0	5.6	5.1
Myanmar[23]											
Total	+U	*5 382*	*5 328*	*4 722*	...	...	...	...	...	...	...
Urban - Urbaine	+U	*2 644*	*2 634*	*2 587*	...	...	...	...	...	...	...
Rural - Rurale	+U	*2 738*	*2 694*	*2 135*	...	...	...	...	...	...	...
Oman											
Total[24]	U	...	*403*	...	...	...	...	...	...	...	...
Total	C	...	...	404	434	412	...	...	4.5	4.9	4.7
Philippines											
Total	...	*4 151*	*4 468*	*4 360*	*4 756*	...	...	...	...	...	...
Republic of Korea - République de Corée[25]											
Total	C	836	709	606	559	...	1.9	1.7	1.7	1.7	...
Urban - Urbaine[11]	C	695	556	466	439	...	1.9	1.6	1.6	1.6	...
Rural - Rurale[11]	C	119	117	112	112	...	1.7	1.7	1.8	2.0	...
Singapore - Singapour											
Total	+C	90	89	99	89	73	2.1	2.2	2.5	2.3	1.9
Sri Lanka											
Total	+U	*715*	*959*	*1 039*	...	...	...	...	...	...	...
Tajikistan - Tadjikistan											
Total	U	*2 346*	*2 326*	*2 061*	...	...	...	...	...	...	...
Urban - Urbaine	U	*1 701*	*1 819*	*1 635*	...	...	...	...	...	...	...
Rural - Rurale	U	*645*	*507*	*426*	...	...	...	...	...	...	...
United Arab Emirates - Émirats arabes unis											
Total	...	*492*	*475*	*413*	*361*	...	...	...	...	...	...
Uzbekistan - Ouzbékistan											
Total	+C	6 636	6 471	6 488	6 466	...	9.0	8.9	9.1	8.4	...
Urban - Urbaine	+C	3 653	3 444	3 313	3 311	...	11.2	10.4	10.2	9.4	...
Rural - Rurale	+C	2 983	3 027	3 175	3 155	...	7.3	7.7	8.1	7.6	...
EUROPE											
Åland Islands - Îles d'Åland											
Total	C	-	1	-	-	...	...	...	...	...	...
Urban - Urbaine	C	-	...	-	-	...	...	...	...	...	...
Rural - Rurale	C	-	...	-	-	...	...	...	...	...	...
Albania - Albanie											
Total	C	132	113	118	93	...	4.0	3.6	3.8	3.2	...
Andorra - Andorre											
Total	C	1	...	...	2	...	...	...	...	...	...
Austria - Autriche											
Total	C	202	202	198	187	...	2.4	2.3	2.3	2.2	...
Belarus - Bélarus											
Total	C	271	282	202	204	...	2.3	2.4	2.0	2.2	...
Urban - Urbaine	C	192	207	151	134	...	2.1	2.3	1.9	1.9	...
Rural - Rurale	C	79	75	51	70	...	2.9	2.8	2.2	3.2	...
Belgium - Belgique											
Total	C	...	542	634	...	...	...	4.4	5.3	...	...
Bosnia and Herzegovina - Bosnie-Herzégovine											
Total	C	114	110	103	88	...	3.9	3.8	3.5	3.0	...
Bulgaria - Bulgarie[2]											
Total	C	420	462	404	379	...	6.4	7.1	6.3	6.1	...
Urban - Urbaine	C	284	333	290	277	...	5.7	6.8	6.0	5.9	...
Rural - Rurale	C	136	129	114	102	...	8.3	7.9	7.1	6.7	...
Croatia - Croatie[26]											
Total	C	163	169	149	164	...	4.3	4.5	4.1	4.4	...
Urban - Urbaine	C	91	97	84	89	...	4.2	4.5	4.0	4.2	...
Rural - Rurale	C	72	72	65	75	...	4.6	4.5	4.2	4.7	...

12. Late foetal deaths and late foetal death ratios, by urban/rural residence: 2015 - 2019
Morts foetales tardives et rapports de mortinatalité, selon la résidence, urbaine/rurale : 2015 - 2019 (continued - suite)

Continent, country or area, and urban/rural residence Continent, pays ou zone et résidence, urbaine/rurale	Code[a]	Number - Nombre					Ratio - Rapport				
		2015	2016	2017	2018	2019	2015	2016	2017	2018	2019
EUROPE											
Czechia - Tchéquie[27]											
Total	C	296	296	295	270	...	2.7	2.6	2.6	2.4	...
Urban - Urbaine	C	224	215	220	202	...	2.8	2.6	2.6	2.4	...
Rural - Rurale	C	72	81	75	68	...	2.5	2.7	2.5	2.2	...
Denmark - Danemark[28]											
Total	C	...	237	246	202	...	...	3.8	4.0	3.3	...
Estonia - Estonie											
Total	C	19	38	36	29	...	...	2.7	2.6	...	...
Urban - Urbaine	C	14	30	30	24	...	...	3.1	3.0	...	...
Rural - Rurale	C	5	8	6	5	...	...	...	...	...	...
Faroe Islands - Îles Féroé											
Total	C	3	2	1	1	2	...	...	...	...	...
Finland - Finlande[29]											
Total	C	115	116	96	99	...	2.1	2.2	1.9	2.1	...
Urban - Urbaine	C	77	86	79	74	...	1.9	2.2	2.1	2.1	...
Rural - Rurale	C	38	30	17	25	...	2.6	2.2	...	...	...
Germany - Allemagne											
Total	C	2 787	2 910	3 000	3 030	...	3.8	3.7	3.8	3.8	...
Greece - Grèce											
Total	C	272	283	316	279	...	3.0	3.0	3.6	3.2	...
Urban - Urbaine	C	196	203	234	205	...	3.1	3.2	3.8	3.4	...
Rural - Rurale	C	76	80	82	74	...	2.7	2.8	3.0	2.8	...
Hungary - Hongrie[30]											
Total	C	408	410	435	383	...	4.4	4.3	4.6	4.1	...
Urban - Urbaine[31]	C	265	250	272	203	...	4.1	3.8	4.2	3.2	...
Rural - Rurale[31]	C	138	156	161	180	...	4.9	5.3	5.4	6.1	...
Iceland - Islande											
Total	C	8	10	7	5	11	...	...	...	...	...
Urban - Urbaine	C	8	9	6	4	...	...	...	...	...	...
Rural - Rurale	C	-	1	1	1	...	...	...	...	...	...
Ireland - Irlande[32]											
Total	C	194	173	162	...	...	3.0	2.7	2.6	...	...
Italy - Italie											
Total	C	1 305	1 308	1 265	1 107	...	2.7	2.8	2.8	2.5	...
Latvia - Lettonie											
Total	C	72	88	70	72	...	3.3	4.0	3.4	3.7	...
Lithuania - Lituanie[26]											
Total	C	126	130	102	115	...	4.0	4.2	3.6	4.1	...
Urban - Urbaine	C	88	86	65	73	...	4.1	4.0	3.3	3.8	...
Rural - Rurale	C	38	44	37	42	...	3.8	4.7	4.2	4.8	...
Luxembourg											
Total	C	50	36	37	37	...	8.2	6.0	6.0	5.9	...
Netherlands - Pays-Bas[33]											
Total	C	500	493	482	506	...	2.9	2.9	2.8	3.0	...
North Macedonia - Macédoine du Nord											
Total	C	185	197	192	151	...	8.0	8.6	8.8	7.1	...
Urban - Urbaine	C	110	116	110	86	...	8.2	8.6	8.6	6.8	...
Rural - Rurale	C	75	81	82	65	...	7.7	8.6	9.2	7.4	...
Norway - Norvège											
Total	C	174	183	139	148	...	3.0	3.1	2.5	2.7	...
Poland - Pologne											
Total	C	...	...	...	924	...	...	...	...	2.4	...
Urban - Urbaine	C	...	...	...	523	...	...	...	...	2.3	...
Rural - Rurale	C	...	...	...	401	...	...	...	...	2.5	...
Portugal[34]											
Total	C	216	214	182	228	...	2.5	2.5	2.1	2.6	...
Romania - Roumanie[2]											
Total	C	735	732	697	682	...	3.7	3.6	3.4	3.4	...
Urban - Urbaine	C	340	...	347	330	...	3.1	...	3.1	2.9	...
Rural - Rurale	C	395	...	350	352	...	4.5	...	3.9	3.9	...
San Marino - Saint-Marin											
Total	C	-	2	-	-	...	...	...	...	...	...
Serbia - Serbie[35]											
Total	+C	388	377	349	345	...	5.9	5.8	5.4	5.4	...
Urban - Urbaine	+C	261	258	250	238	...	5.7	5.8	5.7	5.6	...
Rural - Rurale	+C	127	119	99	107	...	6.3	6.0	4.7	5.0	...

12. Late foetal deaths and late foetal death ratios, by urban/rural residence: 2015 - 2019
Morts foetales tardives et rapports de mortinatalité, selon la résidence, urbaine/rurale : 2015 - 2019 (continued - suite)

Continent, country or area, and urban/rural residence — Continent, pays ou zone et résidence, urbaine/rurale	Code[a]	Number - Nombre 2015	2016	2017	2018	2019	Ratio - Rapport 2015	2016	2017	2018	2019
EUROPE											
Slovakia - Slovaquie[36]											
Total	C	184	160	159	169	...	3.3	2.8	2.7	2.9	...
Urban - Urbaine	C	85	74	71	73	...	2.9	2.5	2.4	2.5	...
Rural - Rurale	C	99	86	88	96	...	3.7	3.1	3.1	3.4	...
Slovenia - Slovénie											
Total	C	55	67	55	36[37]	...	2.7	3.3	2.7	1.8	...
Spain - Espagne											
Total	C	1 287	1 295[2]	1 246[2]	1 148[2]	...	3.1	3.2	3.2	3.1	...
Sweden - Suède											
Total	C	429	414	399	442	...	3.7	3.5	3.5	3.8	...
Switzerland - Suisse[2]											
Total	C	357	371	362	381	...	4.1	4.2	4.1	4.3	...
Urban - Urbaine	C	314	317	305	329	...	4.2	4.2	4.1	4.4	...
Rural - Rurale	C	43	54	57	52	...	3.4	4.3	4.6	4.1	...
Ukraine[38]											
Total	+C	3 318	2 244	2 136	...	...	8.1	5.7	5.9	...	...
Urban - Urbaine	+C	2 035	1 387	1 326	...	...	7.6	5.4	5.6	...	...
Rural - Rurale	+C	1 283	857	810	...	...	8.8	6.2	6.4	...	...
United Kingdom of Great Britain and Northern Ireland - Royaume-Uni de Grande-Bretagne et d'Irlande du Nord[39]											
Total	C	3 434	3 377[40]	3 157	2 926	...	4.4	4.4	4.2	4.0	...
OCEANIA - OCÉANIE											
Australia - Australie[41]											
Total	C	364	364	365	353	...	1.2	1.2	1.2	1.1	...
Urban - Urbaine[42]	C	220	247	231	220	...	1.1	1.1	1.1	1.0	...
Rural - Rurale[42]	C	122	101	106	115	...	1.3	1.1	1.1	1.2	...
French Polynesia - Polynésie française											
Total	C	52	45	42	49	...	13.4	11.3	11.0	13.0	...
Guam[43]											
Total	C	45	44	43	51	...	13.4	12.8	13.1	16.1	...
New Zealand - Nouvelle-Zélande[44]											
Total	+C	117	144	141	126	129	1.9	2.4	2.4	2.2	2.2
Urban - Urbaine	+C	105	123	117	108	108	2.0	2.4	2.3	2.2	2.2
Rural - Rurale	+C	12	21	21	15	18	...	...	...	...	...
Palau - Palaos[45]											
Total	C	4	7	2	3	...	...	...	...	...	...

FOOTNOTES - NOTES

Italics: data from civil registers which are incomplete or of unknown completeness. - Italiques : données incomplètes ou dont le degré d'exactitude n'est pas connu, provenant des registres de l'état civil.

* Provisional. - Données provisoires.

a 'Code' indicates the source of data, as follows:
C - Civil registration, estimated over 90% complete
U - Civil registration, estimated less than 90% complete
| - Other source, estimated reliable
+ - Data tabulated by date of registration rather than occurence
... - Information not available

Le 'Code' indique la source des données, comme suit :
C - Registres de l'état civil considérés complets à 90 p. 100 au moins
U - Registres de l'état civil qui ne sont pas considérés complets à 90 p. 100 au moins
| - Autre source, considérée pas douteuses
+ - Données exploitées selon la date de l'enregistrement et non la date de l'événement
... - Information pas disponible

1 Source: Statistics Botswana. - Source: Statistics Botswana.
2 Data refer to total foetal deaths. - Y compris toutes les morts foetales.
3 Source: Statistical Report, Ministry of Health and Social Security. Data refer to foetal deaths of 22 weeks and over. - Source: Rapport statistique, ministère de la Santé et de la Sécurité sociale. Les données se réfèrent aux décès fœtaux de 22 semaines et plus.
4 Data refer to stillbirths. Source: Reports of the Ministry of Health. - Il s'agit ici du nombre d'enfants mort-nés, Source : Rapports du Ministère de la Santé.
5 Excludes the islands of St. Brandon and Agalega. - Non compris les îles St. Brandon et Agalega.
6 Bermuda is 100 per cent urban. - 100 pour cent de la population des Bermudes est urbaine.
7 Source: Bermuda Hospitals Board (BHB). - Source : Conseil des hôpitaux des Bermudes.
8 Including Canadian residents temporarily in the United States, but excluding United States residents temporarily in Canada. - Y compris les résidents canadiens se trouvant temporairement aux Etats-Unis, mais ne comprenant pas les résidents des Etats-Unis se trouvant temporairement au Canada.

[9] Late foetal death is indicated by the fact that the foetus is at least 500 g or more in weight. - Les décès foetaux tardifs sont caractérisés par le fait que le foetus pèse au moins 500 g.
[10] Data refer to resident population only. - Pour la population résidante seulement.
[11] The total number may include 'Unknown residence', but the categories urban and rural do not. - Le nombre total peut inclure les personnes dont la résidence n'est pas connue, à l'inverse des catégories de population urbaine et rurale.
[12] Late foetal death is indicated by the fact that the foetus is at least 22 completed weeks of gestational age. - Les décès intra-utérins tardifs sont définis comme survenant après 22 semaines au moins de gestation.
[13] Data refer to all foetal deaths with gestational age equal or greater than 22 weeks. - Les données concernent tous les décès intra-utérins de fœtus de 22 semaines ou plus.
[14] Excludes nomadic Indian tribes. - Non compris les tribus d'Indiens nomades.
[15] Data exclude late foetal deaths of unknown gestation period. - Les données relatives à la mortalité fœtale tardive pour lesquelles la durée de gestation était inconnue ont été exclues.
[16] Source: Health records from hospitals (Government and Private). - Source : Dossiers médicaux des hôpitaux (publics et privés).
[17] Includes data for East Jerusalem and Israeli residents in certain other territories under occupation by Israeli military forces since June 1967. - Y compris les données pour Jérusalem-Est et les résidents israéliens dans certains autres territoires occupés depuis 1967 par les forces armées israéliennes.
[18] Data refer to Japanese nationals in Japan only. The total number may include 'Unknown residence', but the categories urban and rural do not. Data exclude unknown duration of pregnancy. - Les données se raportent aux nationaux japonais au Japon seulement. Le nombre total peut inclure les personnes dont la résidence n'est pas connue, à l'inverse des catégories de population urbaine et rurale. Exception faite des grossesses dont la durée n'est pas connue.
[19] Urban and rural categories are tabulated only as the total number. - Pour les catégories urbaine et rurale, les données comprennent les personnes des deux sexes.
[20] Data refer to foetal deaths with a birth weight of 1000 grams or more. - Les données se rapportent aux décès intra-utérins de fœtus d'un poids à la naissance supérieur ou égal à 1 000 grammes.
[21] Data refer to foetal deaths of 28 and more completed weeks of gestation. - Les données se rapportent aux décès intra-utérins de fœtus de 28 semaines ou plus de gestation révolues.
[22] Urban and rural figures refer to the late foetal deaths collected based on the location of the medical facilities, regardless of the mothers' permanent residence location. - Les chiffres urbains et ruraux concernent les décès tardifs du fœtus recueillis sur la base de l'emplacement des établissements médicaux, indépendamment du lieu de résidence permanente des mères.
[23] Data are from Vital Registration System (VRS). - Les données proviennent du système d'enregistrement des faits d'état civil.
[24] Data from Births and Deaths Notification System (Ministry of Health and all health care providers). - Les données proviennent du système de notification des naissances et des décès (Ministère de la santé et tous prestataires de soins de santé).
[25] Excluding alien armed forces, civilian aliens employed by armed forces, and foreign diplomatic personnel and their dependants. - Non compris les militaires étrangers, les civils étrangers employés par les forces armées ni le personnel diplomatique étranger et les membres de leur famille les accompagnant.
[26] Late foetal death is defined as an infant born without any signs of life, weighing at least 500 g, after duration of pregnancy of at least 22 weeks. - On dit qu'il y a mort intra-utérine tardive lorsqu'un enfant pesant au minimum 500 g naît sans donner aucun signe de vie au terme d'une grossesse qui a duré au moins 22 semaines.
[27] Since 1 April 2012, a stillborn child is defined in guidelines for filling in a death certificate as a child fully expelled or removed out of the mother's body, not showing any sign of life and whose birth weight is 500 g or more. If the weight is not possible to determine then duration of pregnancy must be 22 weeks or more. If the duration of pregnancy is not possible to determine, the foetus length must be 25 cm or more. - Depuis le 1er avril 2012, un enfant mort-né est défini dans les directives relatives à l'établissement du certificat de décès comme un enfant complètement expulsé par la mère ou retiré de son corps, ne montrant aucun signe de vie et ayant atteint un poids de 500 g. S'il est impossible d'en déterminer le poids, la durée de gestation doit être au moins de 22 semaines. S'il est impossible de déterminer la durée de gestation, la longueur du fœtus doit être au moins de 25 cm.
[28] Excluding Faeroe Islands and Greenland shown separately, if available. - Non compris les Iles Féroé et le Groenland, qui font l'objet de rubriques distinctes, si disponible.
[29] Excluding Åland Islands. - Non compris les Îles d'Åland.
[30] Late foetal death is indicated by the fact that the foetus is at least 24 completed weeks of gestation (it was 28 weeks until 1996) and does not show any sign of life after the separation from its mother; the foetus has to be 30 cm or more in length or 500 g or more in weight if its gestational age cannot be determined. - Pour qu'il y ait mort foetale tardive, il faut que le décès d'un foetus survienne après 24 semaines complètes de gestation au moins (28 semaines jusqu'en 1996), que le foetus n'ait pas donné signe de vie après avoir été séparé de la mère, qu'il mesure 30 cm au moins ou pèse 500 g si la durée de la période de gestation n'est pas connue.
[31] The urban and rural categories do not include the data of foreigners, persons of unknown residence and the homeless, whereas the total category includes them. - Les chiffres portant sur la population urbaine et rurale n' incluent pas les données relatives aux étrangers, aux personnes dont la résidence n'est pas connue et aux personnes sans domicile fixe, à l'inverse, le total les inclut.
[32] Data refer to events registered within one year of occurrence. - Les données portent sur des événements enregistrés dans l'année pendant laquelle ils sont survenus.
[33] Including residents outside the country if listed in a Netherlands population register. - Englobe les résidents se trouvant à l'étranger à condition qu'ils soient inscrits sur le registre de population des Pays-Bas.
[34] Data refer to usual resident population. - Les données se réfèrent à la population résidente habituelle.
[35] Excludes data for Kosovo and Metohia. Data refer to total foetal deaths. - Sans les données pour le Kosovo et Metohie. Y compris toutes les morts foetales.
[36] Including foetal deaths of at least 1 000 g in weight or 28 weeks of gestation. - Y compris les morts de fœtus pesant au moins 1 000 g ou après 28 semaines de gestation.
[37] Source: National Institute of Public Health. - Source: Institut national de la santé publique.
[38] The Government of Ukraine has informed the United Nations that it is not in a position to provide statistical data concerning the Autonomous Republic of Crimea and the city of Sevastopol. - Le gouvernement Ukrainien a informé l'ONU qu'il n'est pas en mesure de fournir des données statistiques concernant la République autonome de Crimée et la ville de Sébastopol.
[39] Excluding Channel Islands (Guernsey and Jersey) and Isle of Man, shown separately, if available. - Non compris les îles Anglo-Normandes (Guernesey et Jersey) et l'île de Man, qui font l'objet de rubriques distinctes, si disponible.
[40] From 2016 onwards late foetal deaths to non-UK residents are excluded. Late foetal deaths that occurred in one of the constituent countries of UK to a resident of another constituent country of UK are also excluded. - À partir de 2016, les données ne tiennent plus compte des cas de mortalité fœtale tardive qui concernent des personnes ne résidant pas au Royaume-Uni. Sont également exclus les cas de mortalité fœtale tardive survenus dans l'un des pays constitutifs du Royaume-Uni et qui concernent un résident d'un autre de ces pays.
[41] Data exclude foetal deaths for which the period of gestation and birthweight was not stated on the Medical Certificate of Cause of Perinatal Death. - Les données ne tiennent pas compte des décès intra-utérins pour lesquels la période de gestation et le poids à la naissance n'étaient pas indiqués sur le certificat médical faisant état de la cause du décès périnatal.
[42] Data for urban and rural figures do not add up to the total because they exclude the events occurred in Migratory, Special Purpose and Other Territories. Urban refers to Greater Capital City Statistical Areas, and rural refers to other areas within the state or territory. - La somme des chiffres des catégories « en zone urbaine » et « en zone rurale » ne correspond pas au total du fait qu'en sont exclus les événements qui ont eu lieu dans les territoires de migration, les territoires à destination spéciale et autres territoires. Urbain renvoie aux zones statistiques de la capitale métropolitaine, et rural aux autres zones de l'État ou territoire.
[43] Data refer to total foetal deaths. Including United States military personnel, their dependants and contract employees. - Y compris toutes les morts foetales. Y compris les militaires des Etats-Unis, les membres de leur famille les accompagnant et les agents contractuels des Etats-Unis.
[44] The total number may include 'Unknown residence', but the categories urban and rural do not. Data refer to deaths of residents only. Random rounding to base 3 is applied in this table as a confidentiality measure. - Le nombre total peut inclure les personnes dont la résidence n'est pas connue, à l'inverse des catégories de population urbaine et rurale. Les données renvoient aux décès de résidents uniquement. Les chiffres sont arrondis à la base 3 de manière aléatoire, pour des raisons de confidentialité.
[45] Data includes abortions. - Les données comprennnent les avortement.

Table 13 - *Demographic Yearbook 2019*

Table 13 presents legally induced abortions for as many years as available between 2010 and 2019.

Description of variables: There are two major categories of abortion: spontaneous and induced. Induced abortions are those initiated by deliberate action undertaken with the intention of terminating pregnancy; all other abortions are considered spontaneous.

The induction of abortion is subject to governmental regulation in most, if not all, countries or areas. This regulation varies from complete prohibition in some countries or areas to abortion on request, with services provided by governmental health authorities, in others. More generally, governments have attempted to define the conditions under which a pregnancy may lawfully be terminated and have established procedures for authorizing abortion in individual cases.

Information on abortion policies is collected by the United Nations Population Division and published in the *Abortion Policies and Reproductive Health around the World*[1].

Reliability of data: Unlike data on live births and foetal deaths, which are generally collected through systems of vital registration, data on abortion are collected from a variety of sources. Because of this, the quality specification on the completeness of civil registers, which is presented for other tables, does not appear here.

Limitations: With regard to the collection of information on abortions, a variety of sources are used, but hospital records are the most common source of information. This implies that most cases that have no contact with hospitals are missed. Data from other sources are probably also incomplete. The data in the present table are limited to legally induced abortions, which, by their nature, might be assumed to be more complete than data on all induced abortions.

Earlier data: Legally induced abortions have been shown previously in all issues of the *Demographic Yearbook* since the twenty-third issue. For more information on specific topics and years for which data are reported, readers should consult the Historical Index.

NOTES

[1] United Nations, Department of Economic and Social Affairs, Population Division (2014). *Abortion Policies and Reproductive Health around the World* (United Nations publication, Sales No. E.14.XIII.11).

Tableau 13 – *Annuaire démographique 2019*

Le tableau 13 présente les données disponibles, relatives aux avortements provoqués légalement, entre 2010 et 2019.

Description des variables : l'avortement peut être spontané ou provoqué. L'avortement provoqué est celui qui résulte de manœuvres délibérées, entreprises afin d'interrompre la grossesse ; tous les autres avortements sont considérés comme spontanés.

L'interruption délibérée de la grossesse fait l'objet d'une réglementation officielle dans la plupart des pays ou zones, sinon dans tous. Cette réglementation va de l'interdiction totale à l'autorisation de l'avortement sur demande, pratiqué par des services de santé publique. Le plus souvent, les gouvernements se sont efforcés de définir les circonstances dans lesquelles la grossesse peut être interrompue licitement et de fixer une procédure d'autorisation.

La Division de la population des Nations Unies collecte des informations sur les politiques en matière d'avortement et les publient dans *Abortion Policies and Reproductive Health around the World*[1].

Fiabilité des données : à la différence des données sur les naissances vivantes et les morts fœtales, qui proviennent généralement des registres d'état civil, les données sur l'avortement sont tirées de sources diverses. Aussi ne trouve-t-on pas ici une évaluation de la qualité des données semblable à celle qui indique, pour les autres tableaux, le degré d'exhaustivité des données de l'état civil.

Insuffisance des données : en ce qui concerne les renseignements sur l'avortement, un grand nombre de sources sont utilisées, les relevés hospitaliers restant cependant la source la plus commune. Il s'ensuit que la plupart des cas qui ne passent pas par les hôpitaux sont ignorés. Il faut aussi tenir compte du fait que les données provenant d'autres sources sont probablement incomplètes. Les données du tableau 13 se limitent aux avortements provoqués pour raisons légales dont on peut supposer, en raison de leur nature même, que les statistiques sont plus complètes que les données concernant l'ensemble des avortements provoqués.

Données publiées antérieurement : des statistiques concernant les avortements provoqués pour raisons légales sont publiées dans *l'Annuaire démographique* depuis la vingt-troisième édition. Pour plus de précisions concernant les années et les sujets pour lesquels des données ont été publiées, se reporter à l'index historique.

NOTES

[1] United Nations, Department of Economic and Social Affairs, Population Division (2014). *Abortion Policies and Reproductive Health around the World* (United Nations publication, Sales No. E.14.XIII.11).

13. Legally induced abortions: 2010 - 2019
Avortements provoqués légalement : 2010 - 2019

Continent and country or area Continent et pays ou zone	Number - Nombre									
	2010	2011	2012	2013	2014	2015	2016	2017	2018	2019
AFRICA - AFRIQUE										
Burundi[1]	6 272	3 547	3 630	3 152	...	...	...	...	...	...
Cabo Verde[2]	0	1	0	0	0	0	0	0	...	...
Reunion - Réunion	4 349	4 508	4 280	...	...	...	...	...	...	...
Seychelles	556	579	533	515	549	478	509	521	473	431
AMERICA, NORTH - AMÉRIQUE DU NORD										
Bermuda - Bermudes[3]	275	268	271	270	239	227	226	231	183	234
Costa Rica[4]	7 697	7 882	7 405	7 283	*7 137	...	...	...	...	...
Cuba	71 398	83 943	83 682	84 373	85 782	91 500	85 445	83 904	85 045	...
Dominican Republic - République dominicaine	20 946	24 210	26 303	24 605	26 699	21 600	21 266	19 413	14 835	...
Greenland - Groenland	858	743	784	875	864	864	855	883	931	...
Mexico - Mexique[5]	*986[6]	1 041[6]	294[6]	271[6]	301[6]	411[6]	394[6]	489[7]	611[7]	...
AMERICA, SOUTH - AMÉRIQUE DU SUD										
Colombia - Colombie	*82*	*120*	*212*	*633*	*876*	*3 002*	*1 588*[8]	*577*[8]	*689*[8]	*1 347*[8]
Ecuador - Équateur[9]	*42 541*	*42 574*	*41 712*	*40 256*	*35 719*	*31 302*	*30 410*	*30 331*	*28 096*	...
Paraguay	...	...	*4 353*	...	...	...	...	...	...	...
ASIA - ASIE										
Armenia - Arménie	...	...	...	...	11 892	11 104	10 448	10 006	10 404	...
Azerbaijan - Azerbaïdjan	26 799[10]	27 787[10]	31 037	27 892	27 220	27 452	34 569	37 599	36 141	...
Bahrain - Bahreïn[11]	2 525	2 452	2 463	...	...	...	...	...	...	...
China, Hong Kong SAR - Chine, Hong Kong RAS	11 231	11 864	11 298	10 653	10 359	9 890	9 481	8 780	8 518	8 272
Georgia - Géorgie	25 585	30 590	39 225	37 018	33 469	33 377	29 641	24 937	22 733	...
Israel - Israël[12]	19 575	18 974	18 822	18 263	18 646	18 510	18 032	17 924	17 869	...
Japan - Japon	212 694[13]	202 106	196 639	186 253	181 905	176 388	168 015	164 621	161 741	...
Kazakhstan	106 074	95 288	95 654	84 265	83 709	81 440	78 857	80 328	78 545	*77 178
Kyrgyzstan - Kirghizstan[14]	21 675	23 728	23 547	21 673	24 456	22 084	20 783	19 486	19 176	...
Mongolia - Mongolie	12 492	17 504	18 473	15 628	18 145	18 168	18 316	17 530	15 822	15 166
Singapore - Singapour	12 079	11 940	10 624	9 216	8 514	7 946	7 237	6 834	6 413	6 066[15]
Tajikistan - Tadjikistan	19 510	17 503	16 618	15 984	17 347	16 864	14 957	13 963	...	...
Uzbekistan - Ouzbékistan	40 651	38 809	37 634	38 546	41 352	40 201	42 417	42 433	...	...
EUROPE										
Åland Islands - Îles d'Åland	70	73	60	70	66	69	76	74	75	...
Albania - Albanie	3 234	3 032	2 699	2 177	1 679	1 433	1 206	1 193	1 147	...
Belarus - Bélarus	33 262	32 031	28 628	31 206	29 797	29 217	27 467	25 249	23 305	...
Belgium - Belgique	19 095	19 578	...	...	...	...	...	...	...	...
Bulgaria - Bulgarie	31 548	31 716	29 992	29 505	28 145	27 782	26 412	24 287	23 437	...
Croatia - Croatie	4 043	4 347	3 571	3 161	3 020	3 002	2 520	2 416	2 558	...
Czechia - Tchéquie	23 998	24 055	23 032	22 714	21 893	20 403	20 406	19 415	18 298	...
Denmark - Danemark[16]	16 596	16 085	16 220	15 986	15 440	15 325	...	...	...	...
Estonia - Estonie[17]	7 068	6 668	6 056	5 777	6 901	4 889	6 248	3 997	3 799	...
Faroe Islands - Îles Féroé	33	33	34	23	30	21	26	...	...	...
Finland - Finlande[18]	10 231	10 622	10 177	10 060	9 714	9 372	9 311	9 258	8 523	...
France[19]	211 248	206 888	205 300	214 649	210 703	204 139	200 330	...	...	...
Germany - Allemagne	110 431	108 867	106 815	102 802	99 715	99 237	98 721	101 209	100 986	...
Hungary - Hongrie	40 449	38 443	36 118	34 891	32 663	31 176	30 439	28 496	26 941	...
Iceland - Islande	977	970	980	963	951	921	1 021	...	1 049	...
Italy - Italie	112 463[20]	110 041[20]	103 191[21]	100 342[22]	95 400[23]	87 369[24]	84 874	80 497[25]	76 044[26]	...
Jersey	200	200	220	190	160	190	180	170	190	...
Latvia - Lettonie	7 443	7 089	6 197	5 557	5 318	4 802	4 366	3 917	3 636	...
Lithuania - Lituanie	6 989	6 205	6 033	5 353	5 231	4 735	4 502	4 294	3 590	...
Montenegro - Monténégro	...	...	...	...	943	980	763	637	...	...

13. Legally induced abortions: 2010 - 2019
Avortements provoqués légalement : 2010 - 2019 (continued - suite)

Continent and country or area / Continent et pays ou zone	Number - Nombre									
	2010	2011	2012	2013	2014	2015	2016	2017	2018	2019
EUROPE										
North Macedonia - Macédoine du Nord	5 078	5 324	5 387	4 983	4 738	4 587	4 251	4 236	3 992	...
Norway - Norvège	15 735	15 343	...	...	...	...	...	...	...	...
Poland - Pologne[27]	644	669	752	745	970	1 040	1 098	1 057	1 076	...
Portugal	20 137	20 480	19 156	18 281	16 762	16 652	*15 959	*15 492	*14 928	...
Republic of Moldova - République de Moldova	14 785	15 710	14 838	...	13 930	14 059	13 285	12 025	10 830	10 889
Romania - Roumanie	101 915	103 386	87 975	86 432	78 371	70 885	63 518	56 238	52 318	...
Russian Federation - Fédération de Russie	1 186 108	1 124 880	1 063 982	1 012 399	...	...	...	...	...	...
Serbia - Serbie[28]	17 466	15 963	15 301	13 650	12 923	12 242	11 093	10 378	9 982	...
Slovakia - Slovaquie	12 582	11 789	11 214	11 105	10 582	10 058	9 390	9 083	9 039	...
Slovenia - Slovénie	4 328	4 263	4 106	4 011	4 060	3 682	3 736	3 529	3 474[29]	...
Spain - Espagne	113 031	118 359	112 390	108 690	94 796	94 188	...	94 123	95 917	...
Sweden - Suède	37 693	37 750	37 366	...	36 629	38 071	38 177	36 616	35 782	36 151
Switzerland - Suisse[30]	10 650	10 715	10 531	10 177	10 016	10 088	10 102	9 885	10 263	...
Ukraine	176 774	169 131	153 147	147 736	116 104[31]	106 357[31]	101 121[31]	94 665[31]	...	...
United Kingdom of Great Britain and Northern Ireland - Royaume-Uni de Grande-Bretagne et d'Irlande du Nord[32]	209 048	208 636	203 419[33]	...	...	...	197 659	...	...	...
OCEANIA - OCÉANIE										
Guam[34]	269	295	275	213	209	263	289	239	102	...
New Zealand - Nouvelle-Zélande	16 630	15 863	14 745	14 073	13 137	13 155	12 823	13 285	13 282	...

FOOTNOTES - NOTES

Italics: estimates which are less reliable. - Italiques : estimations moins sûres.

* Provisional. - Données provisoires.

1 Data refer only to events recorded in hospitals and health centres. - Ces données ne concernent que les faits d'état civil enregistrés dans les hôpitaux et les centres de santé uniquement.

2 Source: Statistical Report, Ministry of Health and Social Security. - Source: Rapport statistique, ministère de la Santé et de la Sécurité sociale.

3 Source: Bermuda Hospitals Board (BHB). - Source : Conseil des hôpitaux des Bermudes.

4 Excluding abortions performed in private hospitals. - Non comprises les interruptions volontaires de grossesse effectuées dans des hôpitaux privés.

5 Data refer to 'Therapeutic Abortions'. According to Mexican law, only induced abortions, prescribed by medical reasons or induced because of pregnancy coming from sexual aggression, are considered as legal; data refer only to the former. Refers to residence of the mother. Excluding abortions in the country by women with usual residence outside of the country. - Les données se rapportent aux « interruptions volontaires de grossesse pour des motifs thérapeutiques ». D'après la loi mexicaine, seuls sont considérés légaux les avortements déclenchés pour des raisons médicales ou parce que la grossesse est le résultat d'une agression sexuelle; les données se réfèrent seulement à la première. Correspond à la résidence de la mère. Hors avortements dans le pays par des femmes avec résidence habituelle en dehors du pays.

6 To calculate the total number of abortions, only foetal deaths of less than 20 weeks of gestation were considered. - Seuls les morts fœtales survenues à moins de 20 semaines de gestation ont été prises en compte aux fins du calcul du nombre total d'avortements.

7 To calculate the total number of abortions, only foetal deaths of less than 22 weeks of gestation were considered. - Seuls les morts fœtales survenues à moins de 22 semaines de gestation ont été prises en compte aux fins du calcul du nombre total d'avortements.

8 Affected by underreporting since, by law, legally induced abortions are not reported directly to the civil registry. - Font l'objet d'une sous-déclaration, toutes les interruptions volontaires de grossesse pratiquées légalement n'étant pas déclarées dans la mesure où la loi n'impose pas de les inscrire directement au registre civil.

9 Data refer to abortions registered in hospitals due to pregnancy complications. - Les données renvoient aux avortements enregistrés dans les hôpitaux du fait des complications de la grossesse.

10 Data are from the Ministry of Health only before expansion to include data form other sources. - Les données proviennent du Ministère de la santé uniquement, avant inclusion de données provenant d'autres sources.

11 Data refer to spontaneous abortions and miscarriages. - Données se rapportant aux avortements spontanés et fausses couches.

12 Includes data for East Jerusalem and Israeli residents in certain other territories under occupation by Israeli military forces since June 1967. Data refer to applications to commissions for termination of pregnancy and not to authorizations. - Y compris les données pour Jérusalem-Est et les résidents israéliens dans certains autres territoires occupés depuis 1967 par les forces armées israéliennes. Les données relatives aux avortements provoqués légalement se rapportent aux demandes d'autorisation et non aux autorisations elles-mêmes.

13 Excluding data of cities and towns in the jurisdiction of Sousou Public Health and Welfare Office of Fukushima Prefecture due to the impact of the Great East Japan Earthquake. - Ne sont pas incluses les données relatives aux agglomérations relevant du bureau de la santé publique et des services sociaux de Sousou dans la préfecture de Fukushima, en raison des conséquences du grand séisme dans l'est du Japon.

14 Based on administrative reporting of the Ministry of Health. - Les données reposent sur les rapports administratifs du Ministère de la santé.

15 Provisional data. - Données provisoires.

16 Excluding Faeroe Islands and Greenland shown separately, if available. - Non compris les Iles Féroé et le Groenland, qui font l'objet de rubriques distinctes, si disponible.

17 Data refer to resident population only. - Pour la population résidante seulement.

18 Excluding Åland Islands. - Non compris les Îles d'Åland.

19 Data refer to women between 15 and 49 years of age. - Le total se rapporte uniquement aux femmes dont l'âge est compris entre 15 et 49 ans.

20 Data are incomplete for Umbria, Campania and Sicilia regions. - Les données sont incomplètes pour l'Ombrie, la Campanie et la Sicile.

21 Data are incomplete for Umbria, Abruzzo, Campania, Puglia and Sicilia regions. - Les données sont incomplètes pour les régions d'Ombrio, des Abruzzes, de Campanie, des Pouilles et de Sicile.

[22] Data are incomplete for Liguria, Campania, Puglia and Sardegna regions. - Les données sont incomplètes pour les régions suivantes : Ligurie, Campanie, Pouilles et Sardaigne.
[23] Data are incomplete for Lombardia, Marche, Campania, Basilicata, Sicilia and Sardegna regions. - Les données sont incomplètes pour les régions suivantes : Lombardie, Marches, Campanie, Basilicate, Sicile et Sardaigne.
[24] Data are incomplete for Sicilia and Sardegna regions. - Les données sont incomplètes pour les régions suivantes : Sicile et Sardaigne.
[25] Data are incomplete for Lombardia region. - Les données sont incomplètes pour la région de Lombardie.
[26] Data are incomplete for Lombardia, Campania, Calabria and Sardegna regions. - Les données sont incomplètes pour les régions suivantes : Lombardie, Campanie, Calabre et Sardaigne.
[27] Based on hospital and polyclinic records. - D'après les registres des hôpitaux et des polycliniques.
[28] Excludes data for Kosovo and Metohia. - Sans les données pour le Kosovo et Metohie.
[29] Source: National Institute of Public Health. - Source: Institut national de la santé publique.
[30] Data refer to termination of pregnancy for women who are Switzerland residents. - Les données portent sur les interruptions de grossesse pratiquées sur des femmes qui résident en Suisse.
[31] The Government of Ukraine has informed the United Nations that it is not in a position to provide statistical data concerning the Autonomous Republic of Crimea and the city of Sevastopol. - Le gouvernement Ukrainien a informé l'ONU qu'il n'est pas en mesure de fournir des données statistiques concernant la République autonome de Crimée et la ville de Sébastopol.
[32] Excluding Northern Ireland. Excluding Channel Islands (Guernsey and Jersey) and Isle of Man, shown separately, if available. - Non compris l'Irlande du Nord. Non compris les îles Anglo-Normandes (Guernesey et Jersey) et l'île de Man, qui font l'objet de rubriques distinctes, si disponible.
[33] Including provisional data for Scotland. - Y compris les données provisoires pour l'Écosse.
[34] Including United States military personnel, their dependants and contract employees. - Y compris les militaires des Etats-Unis, les membres de leur famille les accompagnant et les agents contractuels des Etats-Unis.

Table 14 - *Demographic Yearbook 2019*

Table 14 presents legally induced abortions by age and number of previous live births of women for the latest available year between 2010 and 2019.

Description of variables: Age is defined as age at last birthday, that is, the difference between the date of birth and the date of the occurrence of the event, expressed in complete solar years. The age classification used in this table is the following: under 15 years, 5-year age groups through 45-49 years and 50 years and over.

Except where otherwise indicated, eight categories are used in classifying the number of previous live births: 0 through 5, 6 or more live births, and, if required, number of live births unknown.

Information on abortion policies is collected by the United Nations Population Division and published in the *Abortion Policies and Reproductive Health around the World*[1].

Reliability of data: Unlike data on live births and foetal deaths, which are generally collected through systems of vital registration, data on abortion are collected from a variety of sources. Because of this, the quality specification on the completeness of civil registers, which is presented for other tables, does not appear here.

Limitations: With regard to the collection of information on abortions, a variety of sources are used, but hospital records are the most common source of information. This implies that most cases that have no contact with hospitals are missed. Data from other sources are probably also incomplete. The data in the present table are limited to legally induced abortions, which, by their nature, might be assumed to be more complete than data on all induced abortions.

In addition, deficiencies in the reporting of age and number of previous live births of the woman, differences in the method used for obtaining the age of the woman, and the proportion of abortions for which age or previous live births of the woman are unknown must all be taken into account in using these data.

Earlier data: Legally induced abortions by age and previous live births of women have been shown previously in most issues of the *Demographic Yearbook* since the twenty-third issue. For more information on specific topics and years for which data are reported, readers should consult the Historical Index.

NOTES

[1] United Nations, Department of Economic and Social Affairs, Population Division (2014). *Abortion Policies and Reproductive Health around the World* (United Nations publication, Sales No. E.14.XIII.11).

Tableau 14 – *Annuaire démographique 2019*

Le tableau 14 présente les données les plus récentes disponibles entre 2010 et 2019 sur les avortements provoqués pour des raisons légales, selon l'âge de la mère et le nombre de naissances vivantes précédentes.

Description des variables : L'âge considéré est l'âge au dernier anniversaire, c'est-à-dire la différence entre la date de naissance et la date de l'avortement, exprimée en années solaires révolues. La classification par âge utilisée dans le tableau 14 est la suivante : moins de 15 ans, groupes quinquennaux jusqu'à 45-49 ans, 50 ans et plus, et âge inconnu.

Sauf indication contraire, les naissances vivantes antérieures sont classées dans les huit catégories suivantes: 0 à 5 naissances vivantes, 6 naissances vivantes ou plus et, le cas échéant, nombre de naissances vivantes inconnu.

La Division de la population des Nations Unies collecte des informations sur les politiques en matière d'avortement et les publient dans *Abortion Policies and Reproductive Health around the World*[1].

Fiabilité des données : à la différence des données sur les naissances vivantes et les morts fœtales, qui proviennent généralement des registres d'état civil, les données sur l'avortement sont tirées de sources diverses. Aussi ne trouve-t-on pas ici une évaluation de la qualité des données semblable à celle qui indique, pour les autres tableaux, le degré d'exhaustivité des données de l'état civil.

Insuffisance des données : en ce qui concerne les renseignements sur l'avortement, un grand nombre de sources sont utilisées, les relevés hospitaliers restant cependant la source la plus commune. Il s'ensuit que la plupart des cas qui ne passent pas par les hôpitaux sont ignorés. Il faut aussi tenir compte du fait que les données provenant d'autres sources sont probablement incomplètes. Les données du tableau 14 se limitent aux avortements provoqués pour raisons légales dont on peut supposer, en raison de leur nature même, que les statistiques sont plus complètes que les données concernant l'ensemble des avortements provoqués.

En outre, on doit tenir compte, lorsque l'on utilise ces données, des erreurs de déclaration de l'âge de la mère et du nombre des naissances vivantes précédentes, de l'hétérogénéité des méthodes de calcul de l'âge de la mère et de la proportion d'avortements pour lesquels l'âge de la mère ou le nombre des naissances vivantes ne sont pas connus.

Données publiées antérieurement : Depuis la vingt-troisième édition, la plupart des éditions de l'*Annuaire démographique* contiennent des statistiques concernant les avortements provoqués pour raisons légales, selon l'âge de la mère et le nombre de naissances vivantes antérieures. Pour plus de précisions concernant les années et les sujets pour lesquels des données ont été publiées, se reporter à l'index historique.

NOTES

[1] United Nations, Department of Economic and Social Affairs, Population Division (2014). *Abortion Policies and Reproductive Health around the World* (United Nations publication, Sales No. E.14.XIII.11).

14. Legally induced abortions by age and number of previous live births of women: latest available year, 2010 - 2019
Avortments provoqués légalement selon l'âge de la femme et selon le nombre des naissances vivantes précédentes : dernière année disponible, 2010 - 2019

Continent, country or area, year and age Continent, pays ou zone, année et âge	Number of previous live births - Nombre des naissances vivantes précédentes								
	Total	0	1	2	3	4	5	6+	Unknown - Inconnu
AFRICA - AFRIQUE									
Seychelles									
2018									
Total	473	...	...	...	...	...	...	...	...
10 - 14	6	...	...	...	...	...	...	...	...
15 - 19	73	...	...	...	...	...	...	...	...
20 - 24	77	...	...	...	...	...	...	...	...
25 - 29	100	...	...	...	...	...	...	...	...
30 - 34	107	...	...	...	...	...	...	...	...
35 - 39	70	...	...	...	...	...	...	...	...
40 - 44	34	...	...	...	...	...	...	...	...
45 - 49	6	...	...	...	...	...	...	...	...
AMERICA, NORTH - AMÉRIQUE DU NORD									
Bermuda - Bermudes[1]									
2019									
Total	234	...	...	...	...	...	...	...	234
0 - 14	-	...	...	...	...	...	...	...	-
15 - 19	13	...	...	...	...	...	...	...	13
20 - 24	47	...	...	...	...	...	...	...	47
25 - 29	70	...	...	...	...	...	...	...	70
30 - 34	56	...	...	...	...	...	...	...	56
35 - 39	38	...	...	...	...	...	...	...	38
40 - 44	10	...	...	...	...	...	...	...	10
45 - 49	-	...	...	...	...	...	...	...	-
50 +	-	...	...	...	...	...	...	...	-
Unknown - Inconnu	-	...	...	...	...	...	...	...	-
Cuba									
2018									
Total	85 045	...	...	...	...	...	...	...	...
12 - 14	1 403	...	...	...	...	...	...	...	...
15 - 19	19 746	...	...	...	...	...	...	...	...
20 - 34	55 570	...	...	...	...	...	...	...	...
35 - 49	8 326	...	...	...	...	...	...	...	...
Mexico - Mexique[2]									
2018									
Total	611	-	178	101	46	13	2	2	269
0 - 14	3	-	-	-	-	-	-	-	3
15 - 19	79	-	8	1	-	-	-	-	70
20 - 24	143	-	52	13	5	-	-	-	73
25 - 29	139	-	48	29	10	2	-	-	50
30 - 34	119	-	33	27	19	4	-	-	36
35 - 39	83	-	27	20	9	4	1	2	20
40 - 44	24	-	7	6	2	1	-	-	8
45 - 49	3	-	-	1	-	2	-	-	-
50 +	-	-	-	-	-	-	-	-	-
Unknown - Inconnu	18	-	3	4	1	-	1	-	9
AMERICA, SOUTH - AMÉRIQUE DU SUD									
Colombia - Colombie[3]									
2019									
Total	*1 347*	*485*	*475*	*241*	*86*	*32*	*14*	*9*	*5*
0 - 14	*37*	*36*	*1*	-	-	-	-	-	-
15 - 19	*221*	*157*	*52*	*10*	*2*	-	-	-	-
20 - 24	*410*	*164*	*168*	*63*	*10*	*4*	-	*1*	-
25 - 29	*279*	*67*	*112*	*68*	*22*	*8*	*2*	-	-
30 - 34	*208*	*41*	*74*	*49*	*31*	*5*	*8*	-	-
35 - 39	*118*	*15*	*45*	*29*	*14*	*9*	*2*	*4*	-
40 - 44	*67*	*5*	*22*	*21*	*7*	*6*	*2*	*4*	-
45 - 49	*2*	-	*1*	*1*	-	-	-	-	-
50 +	-	-	-	-	-	-	-	-	-
Unknown - Inconnu	*5*	-	-	-	-	-	-	-	*5*

14. Legally induced abortions by age and number of previous live births of women: latest available year, 2010 - 2019
Avortments provoqués légalement selon l'âge de la femme et selon le nombre des naissances vivantes précédentes : dernière année disponible, 2010 - 2019 (continued - suite)

Continent, country or area, year and age Continent, pays ou zone, année et âge	Number of previous live births Nombre des naissances vivantes précédentes								
	Total	0	1	2	3	4	5	6+	Unknown - Inconnu
AMERICA, SOUTH - AMÉRIQUE DU SUD									
Ecuador - Équateur[4]									
2018									
Total	*28 096*	...	...	...	...	...	...	...	...
0 - 14	*258*	...	...	...	...	...	...	...	...
15 - 19	*3 960*	...	...	...	...	...	...	...	...
20 - 24	*6 324*	...	...	...	...	...	...	...	...
25 - 29	*6 398*	...	...	...	...	...	...	...	...
30 - 34	*5 185*	...	...	...	...	...	...	...	...
35 - 39	*3 960*	...	...	...	...	...	...	...	...
40 - 44	*1 747*	...	...	...	...	...	...	...	...
45 - 49	*241*	...	...	...	...	...	...	...	...
50 +	*23*	...	...	...	...	...	...	...	...
Unknown - Inconnu	-	...	...	...	...	...	...	...	...
ASIA - ASIE									
Armenia - Arménie									
2018									
Total	10 404	...	...	...	...	...	...	...	...
0 - 14	-	...	...	...	...	...	...	...	...
15 - 29	436	...	...	...	...	...	...	...	...
30 - 44	7 558	...	...	...	...	...	...	...	...
45 +	2 410	...	...	...	...	...	...	...	...
Azerbaijan - Azerbaïdjan									
2018									
Total	36 141	...	...	...	...	...	...	...	...
0 - 14	-	...	...	...	...	...	...	...	...
15 - 19	1 238	...	...	...	...	...	...	...	...
20 - 24	7 545	...	...	...	...	...	...	...	...
25 - 29	11 578	...	...	...	...	...	...	...	...
30 - 34	10 293	...	...	...	...	...	...	...	...
35 - 49	5 435	...	...	...	...	...	...	...	...
50 +	52	...	...	...	...	...	...	...	...
Unknown - Inconnu	-	...	...	...	...	...	...	...	...
China, Hong Kong SAR - Chine, Hong Kong RAS									
2019									
Total	8 272	4 283	1 585	1 927	387	70	13	7	-
0 - 14	8	8	-	-	-	-	-	-	-
15 - 19	393	374	17	2	-	-	-	-	-
20 - 24	1 392	1 211	128	46	7	-	-	-	-
25 - 29	1 747	1 249	281	171	33	11	2	-	-
30 - 34	1 804	787	411	493	90	20	2	1	-
35 - 39	1 849	463	444	787	129	20	2	4	-
40 - 44	947	170	266	377	110	16	6	2	-
45 - 49	130	20	38	51	18	2	1	-	-
50 +	2	1	-	-	-	1	-	-	-
Unknown - Inconnu	-	-	-	-	-	-	-	-	-
Georgia - Géorgie									
2018									
Total	22 733	...	...	...	...	...	...	...	...
0 - 14	-	...	...	...	...	...	...	...	...
15 - 19	510	...	...	...	...	...	...	...	...
20 - 24	3 534	...	...	...	...	...	...	...	...
25 - 29	6 199	...	...	...	...	...	...	...	...
30 - 34	6 114	...	...	...	...	...	...	...	...
35 - 39	4 304	...	...	...	...	...	...	...	...
40 - 44	1 889	...	...	...	...	...	...	...	...
45 - 49	169	...	...	...	...	...	...	...	...
50 +	14	...	...	...	...	...	...	...	...
Unknown - Inconnu	-	...	...	...	...	...	...	...	...
Israel - Israël[5]									
2018									
Total	17 869	7 202	2 447	3 654	2 818	1 090	373	285	...
0 - 14	24	24	-	-	-	-	-	-	...
15 - 19	1 477	1 421	45	10	1	-	-	-	...
20 - 24	3 238	2 596	370	216	48	7	1	-	...

14. Legally induced abortions by age and number of previous live births of women: latest available year, 2010 - 2019
Avortments provoqués légalement selon l'âge de la femme et selon le nombre des naissances vivantes précédentes : dernière année disponible, 2010 - 2019 (continued - suite)

Continent, country or area, year and age Continent, pays ou zone, année et âge	Number of previous live births - Nombre des naissances vivantes précédentes								
	Total	0	1	2	3	4	5	6+	Unknown - Inconnu
ASIA - ASIE									
Israel - Israël[5]									
2018									
25 - 29	3 881	1 915	741	724	346	114	35	6	...
30 - 34	3 789	822	716	1 121	692	286	105	47	...
35 - 39	3 361	312	387	1 048	1 010	365	127	112	...
40 - 44	1 864	102	172	479	645	279	91	96	...
45 - 49	227	9	15	55	75	38	14	21	...
50 +	8	1	1	1	1	1	-	3	...
Japan - Japon									
2018									
Total	161 741	...	...	...	...	...	...	...	...
0 - 14	190	...	...	...	...	...	...	...	...
15 - 19	13 398	...	...	...	...	...	...	...	...
20 - 24	40 408	...	...	...	...	...	...	...	...
25 - 29	31 437	...	...	...	...	...	...	...	...
30 - 34	31 481	...	...	...	...	...	...	...	...
35 - 39	28 887	...	...	...	...	...	...	...	...
40 - 44	14 508	...	...	...	...	...	...	...	...
45 - 49	1 388	...	...	...	...	...	...	...	...
50 +	13	...	...	...	...	...	...	...	...
Unknown - Inconnu	31	...	...	...	...	...	...	...	...
Kyrgyzstan - Kirghizstan[6]									
2018									
Total	19 176	...	...	...	...	...	...	...	...
0 - 19	1 476	...	...	...	...	...	...	...	...
20 - 24	4 463	...	...	...	...	...	...	...	...
25 - 29	5 301	...	...	...	...	...	...	...	...
30 - 34	4 137	...	...	...	...	...	...	...	...
35 +	3 799	...	...	...	...	...	...	...	...
Mongolia - Mongolie									
2019									
Total	15 166	...	...	...	...	...	...	...	...
0 - 19	765	...	...	...	...	...	...	...	...
20 - 24	2 521	...	...	...	...	...	...	...	...
25 - 29	3 851	...	...	...	...	...	...	...	...
30 - 34	4 047	...	...	...	...	...	...	...	...
35 - 39	2 687	...	...	...	...	...	...	...	...
40 - 44	1 166	...	...	...	...	...	...	...	...
45 - 49	129	...	...	...	...	...	...	...	...
50 +	-	...	...	...	...	...	...	...	...
Tajikistan - Tadjikistan									
2017									
Total	13 963	...	...	...	...	...	...	...	...
0 - 14	-	...	...	...	...	...	...	...	...
15 - 17	8	...	...	...	...	...	...	...	...
18 - 19	1 068	...	...	...	...	...	...	...	...
20 - 34	10 085	...	...	...	...	...	...	...	...
35 +	2 802	...	...	...	...	...	...	...	...
Uzbekistan - Ouzbékistan									
2017									
Total	42 433	5 992	9 657	12 809	7 906	4 543	1 367	159	...
0 - 14	2	2	-	-	-	-	-	-	...
15 - 19	1 928	832	640	211	67	106	65	7	...
20 - 24	11 269	2 648	2 763	3 688	1 693	407	68	2	...
25 - 29	15 623	1 978	3 510	4 987	2 571	1 943	602	32	...
30 - 34	8 339	397	1 936	2 596	2 074	1 088	219	29	...
35 - 39	4 231	104	726	1 084	1 253	723	271	70	...
40 - 44	918	26	74	177	235	262	139	5	...
45 +	123	5	8	66	13	14	3	14	...
EUROPE									
Åland Islands - Îles d'Åland									
2012									
Total	60	31	12	10	5	-	2	-	...
0 - 14	-	-	-	-	-	-	-	-	...
15 - 19	9	9	-	-	-	-	-	-	...

14. Legally induced abortions by age and number of previous live births of women: latest available year, 2010 - 2019
Avortments provoqués légalement selon l'âge de la femme et selon le nombre des naissances vivantes précédentes : dernière année disponible, 2010 - 2019 (continued - suite)

Continent, country or area, year and age Continent, pays ou zone, année et âge	Number of previous live births Nombre des naissances vivantes précédentes								
	Total	0	1	2	3	4	5	6+	Unknown - Inconnu
EUROPE									
Åland Islands - Îles d'Åland									
2012									
20 - 24	15	11	3	1	-	-	-	-	...
25 - 29	17	6	4	4	1	-	2	-	...
30 - 34	7	2	1	3	1	-	-	-	...
35 - 39	7	1	3	1	2	-	-	-	...
40 - 44	5	2	1	1	1	-	-	-	...
45 - 49	-	-	-	-	-	-	-	-	...
50 +	-	-	-	-	-	-	-	-	...
2018									
Total	75	...	...	...	...	...	...	...	...
0 - 14	-	...	...	...	...	...	...	...	...
15 - 19	5	...	...	...	...	...	...	...	...
20 - 24	12	...	...	...	...	...	...	...	...
25 - 29	23	...	...	...	...	...	...	...	...
30 - 34	21	...	...	...	...	...	...	...	...
35 - 39	11	...	...	...	...	...	...	...	...
40 - 44	2	...	...	...	...	...	...	...	...
45 - 49	1	...	...	...	...	...	...	...	...
50 +	-	...	...	...	...	...	...	...	...
Albania - Albanie									
2018									
Total	1 147	249	192	345	147	29	5	2	178
0 - 14	-	-	-	-	-	-	-	-	-
15 - 19	28	23	4	1	-	-	-	-	-
20 - 24	147	93	33	18	3	-	-	-	-
25 - 29	222	65	58	77	19	3	-	-	-
30 - 34	230	34	51	96	42	5	-	1	1
35 - 39	191	17	24	83	47	16	3	-	1
40 - 44	112	7	15	50	32	5	2	1	-
45 - 49	12	-	2	7	3	-	-	-	-
50 +	1	-	-	1	-	-	-	-	-
Unknown - Inconnu	204	10	5	12	1	-	-	-	176
Belarus - Bélarus									
2018									
Total	23 305	...	...	...	...	...	...	...	...
0 - 14	9	...	...	...	...	...	...	...	...
15 - 19	782	...	...	...	...	...	...	...	...
20 - 24	3 182	...	...	...	...	...	...	...	...
25 - 29	5 833	...	...	...	...	...	...	...	...
30 - 34	6 956	...	...	...	...	...	...	...	...
35 - 39	4 567	...	...	...	...	...	...	...	...
40 - 44	1 819	...	...	...	...	...	...	...	...
45 +	157	...	...	...	...	...	...	...	...
Belgium - Belgique									
2011									
Total	19 578	9 145	4 266	3 698	1 636	581	174	78	...
0 - 14	87	86	1	-	-	-	-	-	...
15 - 19	2 575	2 339	207	28	1	-	-	-	...
20 - 24	5 027	3 430	1 070	425	87	12	3	-	...
25 - 29	4 688	1 992	1 249	983	332	104	20	8	...
30 - 34	3 745	863	997	1 131	512	176	46	20	...
35 - 39	2 454	349	538	796	483	184	70	34	...
40 - 44	923	78	188	308	207	99	30	13	...
45 - 49	78	7	16	27	14	6	5	3	...
50 +	1	1	-	-	-	-	-	-	...
Bulgaria - Bulgarie									
2018									
Total	23 437	...	...	...	...	...	...	...	...
0 - 14	117	...	...	...	...	...	...	...	...
15 - 19	2 003	...	...	...	...	...	...	...	...
20 - 24	4 069	...	...	...	...	...	...	...	...
25 - 29	5 710	...	...	...	...	...	...	...	...
30 - 34	5 632	...	...	...	...	...	...	...	...
35 - 39	4 173	...	...	...	...	...	...	...	...
40 - 44	1 550	...	...	...	...	...	...	...	...
45 - 49	176	...	...	...	...	...	...	...	...
50 +	7	...	...	...	...	...	...	...	...

14. Legally induced abortions by age and number of previous live births of women: latest available year, 2010 - 2019
Avortments provoqués légalement selon l'âge de la femme et selon le nombre des naissances vivantes précédentes : dernière année disponible, 2010 - 2019 (continued - suite)

Continent, country or area, year and age Continent, pays ou zone, année et âge	Number of previous live births Nombre des naissances vivantes précédentes								
	Total	0	1	2	3	4	5	6+	Unknown - Inconnu
EUROPE									
Croatia - Croatie									
2018									
Total	2 558	812	528	716	284	91	21	36	70
0 - 14	4	4	-	-	-	-	-	-	-
15 - 19	160	146	9	1	-	-	-	-	4
20 - 24	434	284	88	35	10	4	-	-	13
25 - 29	503	184	127	110	41	13	4	8	16
30 - 34	603	108	131	216	88	27	8	9	16
35 - 39	589	63	127	237	99	32	8	10	13
40 - 44	249	22	45	108	43	15	1	8	7
45 - 49	15	1	1	8	3	-	-	1	1
50 +	1	-	-	1	-	-	-	-	-
Czechia - Tchéquie									
2018									
Total	18 298	5 279	4 760	5 768	1 725	473	192	101	...
0 - 14	34	34	-	-	-	-	-	-	...
15 - 19	1 091	906	160	25	-	-	-	-	...
20 - 24	3 013	1 651	835	408	99	16	3	1	...
25 - 29	3 995	1 362	1 257	949	286	87	41	13	...
30 - 34	4 135	785	1 162	1 526	431	139	61	31	...
35 - 39	3 794	404	900	1 759	521	115	57	38	...
40 - 44	2 038	126	415	1 006	346	102	27	16	...
45 - 49	191	9	30	93	41	13	3	2	...
50 +	7	2	1	2	1	1	-	-	...
Denmark - Danemark[7]									
2014									
Total	15 097	...	...	...	...	...	...	...	...
0 - 19	2 051	...	...	...	...	...	...	...	...
20 - 24	4 023	...	...	...	...	...	...	...	...
25 - 29	3 324	...	...	...	...	...	...	...	...
30 - 34	2 609	...	...	...	...	...	...	...	...
35 - 39	2 045	...	...	...	...	...	...	...	...
40 - 44	967	...	...	...	...	...	...	...	...
45 +	78	...	...	...	...	...	...	...	...
Estonia - Estonie[8]									
2017									
Total	3 997	1 150	1 153	1 141	408	99	27	15	4
0 - 14	7	7	-	-	-	-	-	-	-
15 - 19	306	259	40	7	-	-	-	-	-
20 - 24	745	426	214	89	10	5	-	-	1
25 - 29	947	281	376	223	52	11	3	1	-
30 - 34	902	116	275	346	117	34	8	5	1
35 - 39	752	40	174	345	150	28	8	5	2
40 - 44	305	19	70	119	68	19	6	4	-
45 - 49	33	2	4	12	11	2	2	-	-
50 +	-	-	-	-	-	-	-	-	-
Faroe Islands - Îles Féroé									
2016									
Total	26	...	...	...	...	...	...	...	...
0 - 14	-	...	...	...	...	...	...	...	...
15 - 19	3	...	...	...	...	...	...	...	...
20 - 24	6	...	...	...	...	...	...	...	...
25 - 29	7	...	...	...	...	...	...	...	...
30 - 34	3	...	...	...	...	...	...	...	...
35 - 39	6	...	...	...	...	...	...	...	...
40 - 44	-	...	...	...	...	...	...	...	...
45 - 49	1	...	...	...	...	...	...	...	...
50 +	-	...	...	...	...	...	...	...	...
Finland - Finlande									
2018									
Total	8 598	3 663	1 610	1 666	743	247	81	53	535
0 - 14	15	14	-	-	-	-	-	-	1
15 - 19	903	774	43	2	-	-	-	-	84
20 - 24	2 128	1 369	408	133	17	1	-	-	200
25 - 29	2 094	857	505	404	142	37	8	1	140
30 - 34	1 732	402	340	541	268	81	22	6	72
35 - 39	1 227	183	239	412	213	87	35	27	31
40 - 44	468	62	72	160	97	36	16	19	6

14. Legally induced abortions by age and number of previous live births of women: latest available year, 2010 - 2019
Avortments provoqués légalement selon l'âge de la femme et selon le nombre des naissances vivantes précédentes : dernière année disponible, 2010 - 2019 (continued - suite)

Continent, country or area, year and age Continent, pays ou zone, année et âge	Number of previous live births Nombre des naissances vivantes précédentes								
	Total	0	1	2	3	4	5	6+	Unknown - Inconnu
EUROPE									
Finland - Finlande									
2018									
45 - 49	29	2	3	14	5	4	-	-	1
50 +	2	-	-	-	1	1	-	-	-
Germany - Allemagne									
2017									
Total	101 209	39 627	24 036	24 069	8 995	2 906	^1 576	...	...
0 - 14	280	280	-	-	-	-	^-	...	...
15 - 19	7 633	6 795	708	125	5	-	^-	...	...
20 - 24	19 942	12 802	4 431	2 054	519	96	^40	...	...
25 - 29	24 859	10 202	6 785	5 388	1 815	473	^196	...	...
30 - 34	23 127	5 729	6 080	7 193	2 714	954	^457	...	...
35 - 39	17 643	2 809	4 322	6 379	2 646	916	^571	...	...
40 - 44	7 018	936	1 557	2 657	1 175	422	^271	...	...
45 - 49	691	73	151	266	119	44	^38	...	...
50 +	16	1	2	7	2	1	^3	...	...
2018									
Total	100 986	40 417	23 051	24 005	9 023	2 955	1 010	525	...
0 - 14	240	...	...	...	...	...	...	...	...
15 - 19	7 458	...	...	...	...	...	...	...	...
20 - 24	19 832	...	...	...	...	...	...	...	...
25 - 29	24 361	...	...	...	...	...	...	...	...
30 - 34	23 773	...	...	...	...	...	...	...	...
35 - 39	17 652	...	...	...	...	...	...	...	...
40 - 44	7 025	...	...	...	...	...	...	...	...
45 - 49	631	...	...	...	...	...	...	...	...
50 +	14	...	...	...	...	...	...	...	...
Hungary - Hongrie									
2013									
Total	34 891	9 707	8 781	8 536	4 632	1 821	808	606	-
0 - 14	168	165	3	-	-	-	-	-	-
15 - 19	4 423	3 395	869	132	25	2	-	-	-
20 - 24	7 335	3 135	2 182	1 309	542	134	28	5	-
25 - 29	6 935	1 622	1 902	1 692	1 007	450	173	89	-
30 - 34	6 839	837	1 737	2 032	1 229	520	277	207	-
35 - 39	6 624	451	1 528	2 331	1 325	521	240	228	-
40 - 44	2 406	94	526	976	470	184	86	70	-
45 - 49	160	8	34	63	34	10	4	7	-
50 +	1	-	-	1	-	-	-	-	-
Unknown - Inconnu	-	-	-	-	-	-	-	-	-
2014									
Total	32 663	...	...	...	...	...	...	...	...
0 - 14	161	...	...	...	...	...	...	...	...
15 - 19	4 245	...	...	...	...	...	...	...	...
20 - 24	7 109	...	...	...	...	...	...	...	...
25 - 29	6 562	...	...	...	...	...	...	...	...
30 - 34	6 035	...	...	...	...	...	...	...	...
35 - 39	6 066	...	...	...	...	...	...	...	...
40 - 44	2 325	...	...	...	...	...	...	...	...
45 - 49	157	...	...	...	...	...	...	...	...
50 +	3	...	...	...	...	...	...	...	...
Unknown - Inconnu	-	...	...	...	...	...	...	...	...
Iceland - Islande									
2011									
Total	969	415	249	186	83	29	5	2	-
0 - 14	2	2	-	-	-	-	-	-	-
15 - 19	174	155	16	3	-	-	-	-	-
20 - 24	289	182	84	21	2	-	-	-	-
25 - 29	187	46	73	52	10	6	-	-	-
30 - 34	169	25	40	56	36	11	1	-	-
35 - 39	109	5	29	45	20	9	1	-	-
40 - 44	35	-	7	8	12	3	3	2	-
45 - 49	4	-	-	1	3	-	-	-	-
50 +	-	-	-	-	-	-	-	-	-
Unknown - Inconnu	-	-	-	-	-	-	-	-	-
Italy - Italie[9]									
2018									
Total	76 044	30 139	17 312	19 542	6 382	1 439	320	152	758
0 - 14	143	143	-	-	-	-	-	-	-

14. Legally induced abortions by age and number of previous live births of women: latest available year, 2010 - 2019
Avortments provoqués légalement selon l'âge de la femme et selon le nombre des naissances vivantes précédentes : dernière année disponible, 2010 - 2019 (continued - suite)

Continent, country or area, year and age Continent, pays ou zone, année et âge	Number of previous live births / Nombre des naissances vivantes précédentes								
	Total	0	1	2	3	4	5	6+	Unknown - Inconnu
EUROPE									
Italy - Italie[9]									
2018									
15 - 19	5 493	4 918	403	56	9	1	1	-	105
20 - 24	13 336	9 203	2 665	1 024	224	37	2	2	179
25 - 29	15 553	7 033	3 875	3 316	929	193	42	14	151
30 - 34	16 722	4 578	4 293	5 456	1 752	386	78	47	132
35 - 39	15 394	2 795	3 886	5 849	2 077	510	107	52	118
40 - 44	8 480	1 316	1 964	3 492	1 246	281	83	33	65
45 - 49	852	127	209	331	139	30	7	4	5
50 +	23	5	4	9	4	1	-	-	-
Unknown - Inconnu	48	21	13	9	2	-	-	-	3
Latvia - Lettonie									
2017									
Total	3 917	...	...	...	...	...	...	...	...
0 - 14	8	...	...	...	...	...	...	...	...
15 - 19	183	...	...	...	...	...	...	...	...
20 - 24	617	...	...	...	...	...	...	...	...
25 - 29	982	...	...	...	...	...	...	...	...
30 - 34	938	...	...	...	...	...	...	...	...
35 - 39	744	...	...	...	...	...	...	...	...
40 - 44	416	...	...	...	...	...	...	...	...
45 - 49	29	...	...	...	...	...	...	...	...
50 +	-	...	...	...	...	...	...	...	...
Unknown - Inconnu	-	...	...	...	...	...	...	...	...
Lithuania - Lituanie									
2017									
Total	4 294	-	-	-	-	-	-	-	4 294
0 - 14	1	-	-	-	-	-	-	-	1
15 - 19	226	-	-	-	-	-	-	-	226
20 - 24	736	-	-	-	-	-	-	-	736
25 - 29	992	-	-	-	-	-	-	-	992
30 - 34	987	-	-	-	-	-	-	-	987
35 - 39	889	-	-	-	-	-	-	-	889
40 - 44	401	-	-	-	-	-	-	-	401
45 - 49	62	-	-	-	-	-	-	-	62
50 +	...	-	-	-	-	-	-	-	...
Unknown - Inconnu	-	-	-	-	-	-	-	-	-
2018									
Total	3 590	...	...	...	...	...	...	...	...
0 - 14	3	...	...	...	...	...	...	...	...
15 - 19	180	...	...	...	...	...	...	...	...
20 - 24	614	...	...	...	...	...	...	...	...
25 - 29	747	...	...	...	...	...	...	...	...
30 - 34	816	...	...	...	...	...	...	...	...
35 - 39	806	...	...	...	...	...	...	...	...
40 - 44	374	...	...	...	...	...	...	...	...
45 - 49	50	...	...	...	...	...	...	...	...
50 +	-	...	...	...	...	...	...	...	...
Unknown - Inconnu	-	...	...	...	...	...	...	...	...
Poland - Pologne[10]									
2018									
Total	1 076	...	...	...	...	...	...	...	...
0 - 19	-	...	...	...	...	...	...	...	...
20 - 24	105	...	...	...	...	...	...	...	...
25 - 29	104	...	...	...	...	...	...	...	...
30 - 34	175	...	...	...	...	...	...	...	...
35 - 39	283	...	...	...	...	...	...	...	...
40 - 44	409	...	...	...	...	...	...	...	...
Portugal									
2018*									
Total	14 928	6 469	4 275	3 012	837	237	72	26	-
0 - 14	51	46	1	2	1	1	-	-	-
15 - 19	1 318	1 245	65	7	1	-	-	-	-
20 - 24	3 352	2 339	816	175	17	3	1	1	-
25 - 29	3 380	1 526	1 106	564	145	30	8	1	-
30 - 34	2 914	751	980	829	254	79	17	4	-
35 - 39	2 519	413	847	897	237	87	27	11	-
40 - 44	1 241	119	414	477	171	35	17	8	-
45 - 49	131	16	44	55	11	2	2	1	-

14. Legally induced abortions by age and number of previous live births of women: latest available year, 2010 - 2019
Avortments provoqués légalement selon l'âge de la femme et selon le nombre des naissances vivantes précédentes : dernière année disponible, 2010 - 2019 (continued - suite)

Continent, country or area, year and age / Continent, pays ou zone, année et âge	Number of previous live births / Nombre des naissances vivantes précédentes								
	Total	0	1	2	3	4	5	6+	Unknown - Inconnu
EUROPE									
Portugal									
2018*									
50 +	-	-	-	-	-	-	-	-	-
Unknown - Inconnu	22	14	2	6	-	-	-	-	-
Republic of Moldova - République de Moldova									
2019									
Total	10 889	...	...	...	...	...	...	...	...
0 - 14	7	...	...	...	...	...	...	...	...
15 - 19	610	...	...	...	...	...	...	...	...
20 - 34	7 414	...	...	...	...	...	...	...	...
35 +	2 858	...	...	...	...	...	...	...	...
Romania - Roumanie									
2018									
Total	52 318	...	...	...	...	...	...	...	...
0 - 14	289	...	...	...	...	...	...	...	...
15 - 19	4 883	...	...	...	...	...	...	...	...
20 - 24	9 602	...	...	...	...	...	...	...	...
25 - 29	11 942	...	...	...	...	...	...	...	...
30 - 34	11 839	...	...	...	...	...	...	...	...
35 - 39	9 195	...	...	...	...	...	...	...	...
40 - 44	4 154	...	...	...	...	...	...	...	...
45 - 49	403	...	...	...	...	...	...	...	...
50 +	11	...	...	...	...	...	...	...	...
Unknown - Inconnu	-	...	...	...	...	...	...	...	...
Russian Federation - Fédération de Russie									
2013									
Total	1 012 399	...	...	...	...	...	...	...	...
0 - 14	474	...	...	...	...	...	...	...	...
15 - 19	47 732	...	...	...	...	...	...	...	...
20 - 24	203 802	...	...	...	...	...	...	...	...
25 - 29	285 859	...	...	...	...	...	...	...	...
30 - 34	242 437	...	...	...	...	...	...	...	...
35 - 39	165 856	...	...	...	...	...	...	...	...
40 - 44	61 059	...	...	...	...	...	...	...	...
45 - 49	5 029	...	...	...	...	...	...	...	...
50 +	151	...	...	...	...	...	...	...	...
Serbia - Serbie[11]									
2018									
Total	9 982	2 839	2 022	3 382	1 207	357	101	74	-
0 - 14	4	4	-	-	-	-	-	-	-
15 - 19	345	297	33	14	1	-	-	-	-
20 - 24	1 337	802	250	182	65	26	7	5	-
25 - 29	1 925	679	421	526	193	65	27	14	-
30 - 34	2 624	539	595	972	345	119	34	20	-
35 - 39	2 412	344	485	1 063	375	99	25	21	-
40 - 44	1 210	160	218	558	208	44	8	14	-
45 - 49	120	11	20	65	20	4	-	-	-
50 +	5	3	-	2	-	-	-	-	-
Unknown - Inconnu	-	-	-	-	-	-	-	-	-
Slovakia - Slovaquie									
2018									
Total	9 039	2 858	2 510	2 329	788	277	130	147	-
0 - 14	17	17	-	-	-	-	-	-	-
15 - 19	576	440	103	26	6	1	-	-	-
20 - 24	1 382	715	387	205	44	23	5	3	-
25 - 29	2 067	794	590	426	150	61	26	20	-
30 - 34	2 103	535	636	610	185	55	34	48	-
35 - 39	1 924	257	571	685	253	76	39	43	-
40 - 44	907	93	213	350	134	59	25	33	-
45 - 49	62	6	10	27	16	2	1	-	-
50 +	1	1	-	-	-	-	-	-	-
Unknown - Inconnu	-	-	-	-	-	-	-	-	-
Slovenia - Slovénie[12]									
2018									
Total	3 474	1 192	771	1 090	307	77	19	17	1
0 - 14	4	4	-	-	-	-	-	-	-
15 - 19	209	196	9	3	1	-	-	-	-
20 - 24	504	392	77	25	8	2	-	-	-

14. Legally induced abortions by age and number of previous live births of women: latest available year, 2010 - 2019
Avortments provoqués légalement selon l'âge de la femme et selon le nombre des naissances vivantes précédentes : dernière année disponible, 2010 - 2019 (continued - suite)

Continent, country or area, year and age Continent, pays ou zone, année et âge	Number of previous live births - Nombre des naissances vivantes précédentes: Total	0	1	2	3	4	5	6+	Unknown - Inconnu
EUROPE									
Slovenia - Slovénie[12]									
2018									
25 - 29	706	302	179	154	53	12	3	3	-
30 - 34	879	183	225	365	76	20	7	3	-
35 - 39	804	89	202	369	103	26	6	8	1
40 - 44	339	25	71	161	59	17	3	3	-
45 - 49	29	1	8	13	7	-	-	-	-
50 +	-	-	-	-	-	-	-	-	-
Unknown - Inconnu	-	-	-	-	-	-	-	-	-
Spain - Espagne									
2018									
Total	95 917	44 199	24 644	19 263	5 640	1 568	^603	...	...
0 - 14	310	306	4	-	-	-	^-	...	...
15 - 19	9 518	8 583	822	100	10	1	^2	...	...
20 - 24	20 595	14 271	4 656	1 390	228	40	^10	...	...
25 - 29	20 876	10 056	5 859	3 735	953	210	^63	...	...
30 - 34	19 856	6 209	5 959	5 398	1 690	450	^150	...	...
35 - 39	16 953	3 519	5 090	5 705	1 849	564	^226	...	...
40 - 44	7 201	1 152	2 091	2 716	821	282	^139	...	...
45 +	608	103	163	219	89	21	^13	...	...
Sweden - Suède[13]									
2019									
Total	36 151	19 334	9 396	^7 163	...	...	...	...	258
0 - 19	2 583	2 180	308	^78	...	...	...	...	17
20 - 24	6 886	4 306	1 705	^836	...	...	...	...	39
25 - 29	9 823	5 023	2 693	^2 060	...	...	...	...	47
30 - 34	8 406	3 879	2 284	^2 178	...	...	...	...	65
35 - 39	5 728	2 624	1 621	^1 433	...	...	...	...	50
40 +	2 714	1 321	784	^578	...	...	...	...	31
Unknown - Inconnu	11	1	1	^-	...	...	...	...	9
Switzerland - Suisse[14]									
2018									
Total	10 263	2 544	991	1 094	400	^124	...	...	5 110
0 - 14	9	4	1	-	-	^-	...	...	4
15 - 19	684	341	8	4	-	^-	...	...	331
20 - 24	1 871	787	136	48	5	^2	...	...	893
25 - 29	2 416	705	269	195	57	^12	...	...	1 178
30 - 34	2 418	439	279	314	131	^31	...	...	1 224
35 - 39	1 892	190	206	320	141	^55	...	...	980
40 - 44	868	73	84	184	57	^16	...	...	454
45 - 49	96	3	5	27	9	^7	...	...	45
50 +	1	-	-	-	-	^-	...	...	1
Unknown - Inconnu	8	2	3	2	-	^1	...	...	-
Ukraine[15]									
2017									
Total	94 665	...	...	...	...	...	...	...	...
0 - 14	39	...	...	...	...	...	...	...	...
15 - 19	4 221	...	...	...	...	...	...	...	...
20 - 34	68 707	...	...	...	...	...	...	...	...
35 +	21 698	...	...	...	...	...	...	...	...
United Kingdom of Great Britain and Northern Ireland - Royaume-Uni de Grande-Bretagne et d'Irlande du Nord[16]									
2016									
Total	197 659	...	...	...	...	...	...	...	...
0 - 14	492	...	...	...	...	...	...	...	...
15 - 19	25 761	...	...	...	...	...	...	...	...
20 - 24	53 834	...	...	...	...	...	...	...	...
25 - 29	49 248	...	...	...	...	...	...	...	...
30 - 34	36 146	...	...	...	...	...	...	...	...
35 - 39	23 219	...	...	...	...	...	...	...	...
40 - 44	8 181	...	...	...	...	...	...	...	...
45 - 49	749	...	...	...	...	...	...	...	...
50 +	29	...	...	...	...	...	...	...	...
Unknown - Inconnu	-	...	...	...	...	...	...	...	...

14. Legally induced abortions by age and number of previous live births of women: latest available year, 2010 - 2019
Avortments provoqués légalement selon l'âge de la femme et selon le nombre des naissances vivantes précédentes : dernière année disponible, 2010 - 2019 (continued - suite)

Continent, country or area, year and age Continent, pays ou zone, année et âge	Number of previous live births Nombre des naissances vivantes précédentes Total	0	1	2	3	4	5	6+	Unknown - Inconnu
OCEANIA - OCÉANIE									
Guam[17]									
2015									
Total	263	...	...	...	...	...	...	...	...
0 - 14	-	...	...	...	...	...	...	...	...
15 - 19	20	...	...	...	...	...	...	...	...
20 - 24	89	...	...	...	...	...	...	...	...
25 - 29	60	...	...	...	...	...	...	...	...
30 - 34	52	...	...	...	...	...	...	...	...
35 - 39	27	...	...	...	...	...	...	...	...
40 - 44	12	...	...	...	...	...	...	...	...
45 - 49	2	...	...	...	...	...	...	...	...
50 +	-	...	...	...	...	...	...	...	...
Unknown - Inconnu	1	...	...	...	...	...	...	...	...
New Zealand - Nouvelle-Zélande									
2018									
Total	13 282	5 543	2 666	2 976	1 330	482	184	101	...
0 - 14	22	22	-	-	-	-	-	-	...
15 - 19	1 289	1 143	129	15	2	-	-	-	...
20 - 24	3 334	2 101	692	408	113	20	-	-	...
25 - 29	3 598	1 415	818	777	395	129	47	17	...
30 - 34	2 650	577	549	842	425	168	58	31	...
35 - 39	1 679	209	350	651	261	116	55	37	...
40 - 44	660	69	116	266	126	46	22	15	...
45 +	50	7	12	17	8	3	2	1	...

FOOTNOTES - NOTES

Italics: estimates which are less reliable. - Italiques : estimations moins sûres.

* Provisional. - Données provisoires.

^ Indicates an open-ended group, for example 4+. - indique un groupe d'âge ouvert, par exemple 4 ou plus.

1 Source: Bermuda Hospitals Board (BHB). - Source : Conseil des hôpitaux des Bermudes.

2 To calculate the total number of abortions, only foetal deaths of less than 22 weeks of gestation were considered. Excluding abortions in the country by women with usual residence outside of the country. Data refer to 'Therapeutic Abortions'. According to Mexican law, only induced abortions, prescribed by medical reasons or induced because of pregnancy coming from sexual aggression, are considered as legal; data refer only to the former. Refers to residence of the mother. - Seuls les morts fœtales survenues à moins de 22 semaines de gestation ont été prises en compte aux fins du calcul du nombre total d'avortements. Hors avortements dans le pays par des femmes avec résidence habituelle en dehors du pays. Les données se rapportent aux « interruptions volontaires de grossesse pour des motifs thérapeutiques ». D'après la loi mexicaine, seuls sont considérés légaux les avortements déclenchés pour des raisons médicales ou parce que la grossesse est le résultat d'une agression sexuelle; les données se réfèrent seulement à la première. Correspond à la résidence de la mère.

3 Affected by underreporting since, by law, legally induced abortions are not reported directly to the civil registry. - Font l'objet d'une sous-déclaration, toutes les interruptions volontaires de grossesse pratiquées légalement n'étant pas déclarées dans la mesure où la loi n'impose pas de les inscrire directement au registre civil.

4 Data refer to abortions registered in hospitals due to pregnancy complications. - Les données renvoient aux avortements enregistrés dans les hôpitaux du fait des complications de la grossesse.

5 Data refer to applications to commissions for termination of pregnancy and not to authorizations. Includes data for East Jerusalem and Israeli residents in certain other territories under occupation by Israeli military forces since June 1967. - Les données relatives aux avortements provoqués légalement se rapportent aux demandes d'autorisation et non aux autorisations elles-mêmes. Y compris les données pour Jérusalem-Est et les résidents israéliens dans certains autres territoires occupés depuis 1967 par les forces armées israéliennes.

6 Based on administrative reporting of the Ministry of Health. - Les données reposent sur les rapports administratifs du Ministère de la santé.

7 Unrevised data. Excluding Faeroe Islands and Greenland shown separately, if available. - Les données n'ont pas été révisées. Non compris les Iles Féroé et le Groenland, qui font l'objet de rubriques distinctes, si disponible.

8 Data refer to resident population only. - Pour la population résidante seulement.

9 Data are incomplete for Lombardia, Campania, Calabria and Sardegna regions. - Les données sont incomplètes pour les régions suivantes : Lombardie, Campanie, Calabre et Sardaigne.

10 Based on hospital and polyclinic records. - D'après les registres des hôpitaux et des polycliniques.

11 Excludes data for Kosovo and Metohia. - Sans les données pour le Kosovo et Metohie.

12 Source: National Institute of Public Health. - Source: Institut national de la santé publique.

13 Data refer to abortions by previous deliveries of mother rather than previous live births of mother. - Avortements selon les accouchements précédents de la mère plutôt que selon les naissances vivantes de la mère.

14 Data refer to termination of pregnancy for women who are Switzerland residents. - Les données portent sur les interruptions de grossesse pratiquées sur des femmes qui résident en Suisse.

15 The Government of Ukraine has informed the United Nations that it is not in a position to provide statistical data concerning the Autonomous Republic of Crimea and the city of Sevastopol. - Le gouvernement Ukrainien a informé l'ONU qu'il n'est pas en mesure de fournir des données statistiques concernant la République autonome de Crimée et la ville de Sébastopol.

16 Excluding Channel Islands (Guernsey and Jersey) and Isle of Man, shown separately, if available. Excluding Northern Ireland. - Non compris les îles Anglo-Normandes (Guernesey et Jersey) et l'île de Man, qui font l'objet de rubriques distinctes, si disponible. Non compris l'Irlande du Nord.

17 Including United States military personnel, their dependants and contract employees. - Y compris les militaires des Etats-Unis, les membres de leur famille les accompagnant et les agents contractuels des Etats-Unis.

Table 15 - *Demographic Yearbook 2019*

Table 15 presents infant deaths and infant mortality rates by urban/rural residence for as many years as possible between 2015 and 2019.

Description of variables: Infant deaths are deaths of live-born infants under one year of age.

Statistics on the number of infant deaths are obtained from civil registers unless otherwise noted. Infant mortality rates are, in most instances, calculated from data on registered infant deaths and registered live births for a country or area where civil registration is considered reliable (that is, with an estimated completeness of 90 per cent or more).

The urban/rural classification of infant deaths is that provided by each reporting country or area; it is presumed to be based on the national census definitions of urban population that have been set forth at the end of the technical notes of table 6.

Rate computation: Infant mortality rates are the annual number of deaths of infants under one year of age per 1 000 live births (as shown in table 9) in the same year.

Rates by urban/rural residence are the annual number of infant deaths, in the appropriate urban or rural category, per 1 000 corresponding live births (as shown in table 9). These rates have been calculated by the United Nations Statistics Division.

Rates presented in this table have been limited to those countries or areas having at least a total of 30 infant deaths in a given year and for which the quality code is represented by a "C" or a symbol "|".

Reliability of data: Each country or area has been asked to indicate the estimated completeness of the infant deaths recorded in its civil register. These national assessments are indicated by the quality codes "C", "U" and "|" that appear in the first column of this table.

"C" indicates that the data are estimated to be virtually complete, that is, representing at least 90 per cent of the infant deaths occurring each year, while "U" indicates that data are estimated to be incomplete that is, representing less than 90 per cent of the infant deaths occurring each year. The code "|" indicates that the source of data is not civil registration, but it is still considered reliable. The code "..." indicates that no information was provided regarding completeness.

Data from civil registers that are reported as incomplete or of unknown completeness (coded "U" or "...") are considered unreliable. They appear in italics in this table; rates are not computed for data so coded.

Limitations: Statistics on infant deaths are subject to the same qualifications as have been set forth for vital statistics and particularly for death statistics discussed in section 4 of the Technical Notes.

The reliability of the data, an indication of which is described above, is an important factor in considering the limitations. In addition, some infant deaths are tabulated by date of registration and not by date of occurrence; these have been indicated by a plus sign "+". Whenever the lag between the date of occurrence and date of registration is prolonged and, therefore, a large proportion of the infant-death registrations are delayed, infant-death statistics for any given year may be seriously affected.

Another factor that limits international comparability is the practice of some countries or areas not to include in infant-death statistics infants who were born alive but died before the registration of the birth or within the first 24 hours of life, thus underestimating the total number of infant deaths. Statistics of this type are footnoted.

The method of reckoning age at death for infants may also introduce non-comparability. If year alone, rather than completed minutes, hours, days and months elapsed since birth, is used to calculate age at time of death, many of the infants who died during the eleventh month of life and some of those who died at younger ages will be classified as having completed one year of age and thus be excluded. The effect would be to underestimate the number of infant deaths. Information on this factor is given in footnotes when known. Reckoning of infant age is further discussed in the technical notes for table 16.

In addition, infant mortality rates are subject to the limitations of the data on live births that have been used as denominators for these rates. These have been set forth in the technical notes for table 9.

Because the two components of the infant mortality rate, infant deaths in the numerator and live births in the denominator, are both obtained from systems of civil registration, the limitations which affect live birth statistics are very similar to those which have been mentioned above in connection with the infant death statistics. It is important to consider the reliability of the data (the completeness of registration) and the method of tabulation (by date of occurrence or by date of registration) of live birth statistics as well as infant death statistics, both of which are used to calculate infant mortality rates. The quality code and use of italics to indicate unreliable data presented in this table refer only to infant deaths. Similarly, the indication of the basis of tabulation (the use of the symbol "+" to indicate data tabulated by date of registration) presented in this table also refers only to infant deaths. Table 9 provides the corresponding information for live births.

If the registration of infant deaths is more complete than the registration of live births, then infant mortality rates would be biased upwards. If, however, the registration of live births is more complete than registration of infant deaths, infant mortality rates would be biased downwards.

Infant mortality rates may be seriously affected by the practice of some countries or areas of not considering infants that were born alive but died before the registration of the birth or within the first 24 hours of life as live birth and subsequently infant death. Although this practice results in both the number of infant deaths in the numerator and the number of live births in the denominator being underestimated, its impact is greater on the numerator of the infant mortality rate. As a result, this practice causes infant mortality rates to be biased downwards.

Infant mortality rates will also be underestimated if the method of reckoning age at death results in an underestimation of the number of infant deaths. This point has been discussed above.

Because of all these factors care should be taken in comparing infant mortality rates.

With respect to the method of calculating infant mortality rates used in this table, it should be noted that no adjustment was made to take account of the fact that a proportion of the infant deaths that occur during a given year are deaths of infants that were born during the preceding year and hence are not taken from the universe of births used to compute the rates. However, unless the number of live births or infant deaths is changing rapidly, the error involved is insignificant.

The comparability of data by urban/rural residence is affected by the national definitions of urban and rural used in tabulating these data. It is assumed, in the absence of specific information to the contrary, that the definitions of urban and rural used in connection with the national population census were also used in the compilation of the vital statistics for each country or area. However, it cannot be denied that, for some countries or areas, different definitions of urban and rural may be used for the vital statistics data and the population census data respectively. When known, the definitions of urban used in national population censuses are presented at the end of the technical notes for table 6. As discussed in detail in the technical notes for table 6, these definitions vary considerably from one country or area to another.

Urban/rural differentials in infant mortality rates may also be affected by whether the infant deaths and live births have been tabulated in terms of place of occurrence or place of usual residence. This problem is discussed in more detail in section 4.1.4.1 of the Technical Notes.

Earlier data: Infant deaths and infant mortality rates have been shown in previous issues of the *Demographic Yearbook*. For more information on specific topics and years for which data are reported, readers should consult the Historical Index.

Tableau 15 – *Annuaire démographique 2019*

Le tableau 15 présente des données sur les décès d'enfants de moins d'un an et les taux de mortalité infantile selon le lieu de résidence (zone urbaine ou rurale) pour le plus grand nombre d'années possible entre 2015 et 2019.

Description des variables : les chiffres se rapportent aux décès d'enfants de moins d'un an.

Sauf indication contraire, les statistiques concernant le nombre de décès d'enfants de moins d'un an sont établies à partir des registres de l'état civil. Dans la plupart des cas, les taux de mortalité infantile sont calculés à partir des données relatives aux décès enregistrés d'enfants de moins d'un an et aux naissances vivantes enregistrées dans un pays ou une zone lorsque les registres de l'état civil sont jugés fiables (exhaustivité estimée à 90 p. 100 ou plus).

La classification des décès d'enfants de moins d'un an selon le lieu de résidence (zone urbaine ou rurale) est celle qui a été communiquée par chaque pays ou zone ; on part du principe qu'elle repose sur les définitions de la population urbaine utilisées pour les recensements nationaux, telles qu'elles sont reproduites à la fin des notes techniques du tableau 6.

Calcul des taux : Les taux de mortalité infantile représentent le nombre annuel de décès d'enfants de moins d'un an pour 1 000 naissances vivantes (présentées dans le tableau 9) survenues pendant la même année.

Les taux selon le lieu de résidence (zone urbaine ou rurale) représentent le nombre annuel de décès d'enfants de moins d'un an, classés selon la catégorie urbaine ou rurale appropriée pour 1 000 naissances vivantes survenues parmi la population correspondante (présentées dans le tableau 9). Ces taux ont été calculés par la Division des statistiques de l'Organisation des Nations Unies.

Les taux présentés dans ce tableau se rapportent seulement aux pays ou zones où l'on a enregistré au moins un total de 30 décès d'enfants de moins d'un an au cours d'une année donnée et pour lesquels le code de qualité est soit "C" ou "|".

Fiabilité des données : il a été demandé à chaque pays ou zone d'indiquer le degré estimatif de complétude des données sur les décès d'enfants de moins d'un an figurant dans ses registres d'état civil. Ces évaluations nationales sont signalées par les codes de qualité "C", "U" et "|" qui apparaissent dans la deuxième colonne du tableau.

La lettre "C" indique que les données sont jugées à peu près complètes, c'est-à-dire qu'elles représentent au moins 90 p. 100 des décès d'enfants de moins d'un an survenus chaque année ; la lettre "U" signifie que les données sont jugées incomplètes, c'est-à-dire qu'elles représentent moins de 90 p.100 des décès d'enfants de moins d'un an survenus chaque année. Le symbole 'I' indique que la source des données n'est pas un registre de l'état civil, mais est quand même considérée fiable. Le code "..." dénote qu'aucun renseignement n'a été communiqué quant à la complétude des données.

Les données provenant des registres de l'état civil qui sont déclarées incomplètes ou dont le degré de complétude n'est pas connu (code "U" ou "...") sont jugées douteuses. Elles apparaissent en italique dans le tableau ; les taux, dans ces cas là, n'ont pas été calculés.

Insuffisance des données : les statistiques des décès d'enfants de moins d'un an appellent toutes les réserves qui ont été formulées à propos des statistiques de l'état civil en général et des statistiques concernant les décès en particulier (voir la section 4 des notes techniques).

La fiabilité des données, au sujet de laquelle des indications ont été fournies plus haut, est un facteur important. Il faut également tenir compte du fait que, dans certains cas, les données relatives aux décès d'enfants de moins d'un an sont exploitées selon la date de l'enregistrement et non la date de l'événement ; ces cas ont été signalés par le signe "+". Chaque fois que le décalage entre l'événement et son enregistrement est grand et qu'une forte proportion des décès d'enfants de moins d'un an fait l'objet d'un enregistrement tardif, les statistiques des décès d'enfants de moins d'un an pour une année donnée peuvent être considérablement faussées.

Un autre facteur qui nuit à la comparabilité internationale est la pratique de certains pays ou zones qui consiste à ne pas inclure dans les statistiques des décès d'enfants de moins d'un an les enfants nés vivants mais décédés avant l'enregistrement de leur naissance ou dans les 24 heures qui ont suivi la naissance, pratique qui conduit à sous-estimer le nombre total de décès d'enfants de moins d'un an. Quand pareil facteur a joué, cela a été signalé en note.

Les méthodes appliquées pour calculer l'âge au moment du décès peuvent également nuire à la comparabilité des données. Si l'on utilise à cet effet l'année seulement, et non pas les minutes, heures, jours et mois qui se sont écoulés depuis la naissance, de nombreux enfants décédés au cours du onzième mois qui a suivi leur naissance et certains enfants décédés encore plus jeunes seront classés comme décédés à un an révolu et donc exclus des données. Cette pratique conduit à sous-estimer le nombre de décès d'enfants de moins d'un an. Les renseignements dont on dispose sur ce facteur apparaissent en note à la fin du tableau. La question du calcul de l'âge au moment du décès est examinée plus en détail dans les notes techniques se rapportant au tableau 16.

Les taux de mortalité infantile appellent en outre toutes les réserves qui ont été formulées à propos des statistiques des naissances vivantes qui ont servi à leur calcul (voir à ce sujet les notes techniques relatives au tableau 9).

Les deux composantes du taux de mortalité infantile - décès d'enfants de moins d'un an au numérateur et naissances vivantes au dénominateur - étant obtenues à partir des registres de l'état civil, les statistiques des naissances vivantes appellent des réserves presque identiques à celles qui ont été formulées plus haut à propos des statistiques des décès d'enfants de moins d'un an. Il importe de prendre en considération la fiabilité des données (complétude de l'enregistrement) et le mode d'exploitation (selon la date de l'événement ou selon la date de l'enregistrement) dans le cas des statistiques des naissances vivantes tout comme dans le cas de celles des décès d'enfants de moins d'un an, puisque les unes et les autres servent au calcul des taux de mortalité infantile. Dans le tableau 15, le code de qualité et l'emploi de caractères italiques pour signaler les données moins sûres ne concernent que les décès d'enfants de moins d'un an. L'indication du mode d'exploitation des données (emploi du signe "+" pour signaler les données exploitées selon la date de l'enregistrement) ne porte là aussi que sur les décès d'enfants de moins d'un an. Le tableau 9 contient les renseignements correspondants pour les naissances vivantes.

Si l'enregistrement des décès d'enfants de moins d'un an est plus complet que l'enregistrement des naissances vivantes, les taux de mortalité infantile seront entachés d'une erreur par excès. En revanche, si l'enregistrement des naissances vivantes est plus complet que l'enregistrement des décès d'enfants de moins d'un an, les taux de mortalité infantile seront entachés d'une erreur par défaut.

Les taux de mortalité infantile peuvent être gravement faussés par la pratique de certains pays ou zones qui consiste à ne pas classer dans les naissances vivantes et ensuite dans les décès d'enfants de moins d'un an les enfants nés vivants mais décédés soit avant l'enregistrement de leur naissance, soit dans les 24 heures qui ont suivi la naissance. Cette pratique conduit à sous-estimer aussi bien le nombre des décès d'enfants de moins d'un an, qui constitue le numérateur, que le nombre des naissances vivantes, qui constitue le dénominateur, mais c'est pour le numérateur du taux de mortalité infantile que la distorsion est la plus marquée. Ce système a pour effet d'introduire une erreur par défaut dans les taux de mortalité infantile.

Les taux de mortalité infantile seront également sous-estimés si la méthode utilisée pour calculer l'âge au moment du décès conduit à sous-estimer le nombre de décès d'enfants de moins d'un an. Cette question a été examinée plus haut.

Tous ces facteurs sont importants et il faut donc en tenir compte lorsque l'on compare les taux de mortalité infantile.

En ce qui concerne la méthode de calcul des taux de mortalité infantile utilisée dans le tableau, il convient de noter qu'il n'a pas été tenu compte du fait qu'une partie des décès survenus pendant une année donnée sont des décès d'enfants nés l'année précédente et ne correspondent donc pas à l'ensemble des naissances utilisé pour le calcul des taux. Toutefois, l'erreur n'est pas grave, à moins que le nombre des naissances vivantes ou des décès d'enfants de moins d'un an ne varie rapidement.

La comparabilité des données selon le lieu de résidence (zone urbaine ou rurale) peut être limitée par les définitions nationales des termes « urbain » et « rural » utilisées pour la mise en tableaux de ces données. En l'absence d'indications contraires, on a supposé que les mêmes définitions avaient servi pour le recensement national de la population et pour l'établissement des statistiques de l'état civil pour chaque pays ou zone. Toutefois, il n'est pas exclu que, pour une zone ou un pays donné, des définitions différentes aient été retenues. Les définitions du terme « urbain » utilisées pour les recensements nationaux de population ont été présentées à la fin des notes techniques du tableau 6 lorsqu'elles étaient connues. Comme on l'a précisé dans les notes techniques relatives au tableau 6, ces définitions varient considérablement d'un pays ou d'une zone à l'autre.

La différence entre les taux de mortalité infantile pour les zones urbaines et rurales pourra aussi être faussée selon que les décès d'enfants de moins d'un an et les naissances vivantes auront été classés d'après le lieu de l'événement ou le lieu de résidence habituel. Ce problème est examiné plus en détail à la section 4.1.4.1 des Notes techniques.

Données publiées antérieurement : des statistiques concernant les décès d'enfants de moins d'un an et les taux de mortalité infantile ont déjà été présentées dans des éditions antérieures de l'*Annuaire démographique*. Pour plus de précisions concernant les années et les sujets pour lesquels des données ont été publiées, se reporter à l'index historique.

15. Infant deaths and infant mortality rates, by urban/rural residence: 2015 - 2019
Décès d'enfants de moins d'un an et taux de mortalité infantile, selon la résidence, urbaine/rurale : 2015 - 2019

Continent, country or area, and urban/rural residence Continent, pays ou zone et résidence, urbaine/rurale	Code[a]	Number - Nombre					Rate - Taux				
		2015	2016	2017	2018	2019	2015	2016	2017	2018	2019
AFRICA - AFRIQUE											
Algeria - Algérie[1]											
Total	U	*23 150*	*22 271*	*21 416*	*21 846*	*21 030*	...	...	...	...	...
Botswana[2]											
Total	U	*1 012*	*1 041*	*985*	*891*	...	...	...	...	...	...
Cabo Verde[3]											
Total	C	163	164	167	...	...	16.7	16.6	17.0	...	...
Egypt - Égypte											
Total	C	42 050	39 301	38 685	...	...	15.7	15.1	15.1	...	...
Urban - Urbaine	C	25 528	24 370	24 674	...	...	20.8	19.6	19.1	...	...
Rural - Rurale	C	16 522	14 931	14 011	...	...	11.3	11.0	11.1	...	...
Eswatini[4]											
Total	+U	...	*162*	*123*	*156*	...	...	...	...	...	...
Kenya											
Total	+U	*23 123*	*21 475*	*19 895*	*20 350*	...	...	...	...	...	...
Lesotho											
Total	+U	*218*	*17*	*158*	*150*	*180*	...	...	...	...	...
Mauritius - Maurice[5]											
Total	+C	173	154	164	181	187	13.7	11.9	12.3	13.9	14.6
Urban - Urbaine	+C	81	57	57	74	73	15.7	10.8	10.7	13.8	14.2
Rural - Rurale	+C	92	97	107	107	114	12.3	12.7	13.2	14.0	14.8
Mayotte											
Total	C	71	96	86	94	...	7.9	10.1	8.8	9.8	...
Reunion - Réunion											
Total	C	93	98	87	82	...	6.6	7.1	6.3	6.1	...
Urban - Urbaine	C	...	...	80	...	...	...	...	6.0	...	...
Rural - Rurale	C	...	...	7	...	...	...	...	...	...	...
Saint Helena ex. dep. - Sainte-Hélène sans dép.											
Total	C	1	1	-	-	...	...	...	...	...	...
Seychelles											
Total	+C	17	22	18	31	27	...	...	...	18.8	...
South Africa - Afrique du Sud											
Total	U	*24 994*	*20 649*	...	...	...	...	...	...	...	...
AMERICA, NORTH - AMÉRIQUE DU NORD											
Antigua and Barbuda - Antigua-et-Barbuda											
Total	+C	10	13	...	...	...	...	...	...	...	...
Aruba											
Total	+C	6	5	6	9	5	...	...	...	...	...
Bahamas											
Total	+C	*82	*70	*72	...	...	*19.3	*17.1	*17.9	...	...
Belize											
Total	U	*129*	*100*	*104*	*98*	...	...	...	...	...	...
Urban - Urbaine[6]	U	*58*	*44*	...	...	...	...	...	...	...	...
Rural - Rurale[6]	U	*69*	*59*	...	...	...	...	...	...	...	...
Bermuda - Bermudes[7]											
Total	C	2	2	-	1	...	...	...	...	...	...
British Virgin Islands - Îles Vierges britanniques											
Total	C	4	4	7	...	...	...	...	...	...	...
Canada[8]											
Total	C	1 737	1 741	1 699	1 750	...	4.5	4.5	4.5	4.7	...
Costa Rica											
Total	C	557	555	548	573	*533	7.8	7.9	8.0	8.4	*8.3
Urban - Urbaine	C	404	422	381	401	*363	8.1	8.7	8.1	8.6	*8.3
Rural - Rurale	C	153	133	167	172	*170	6.9	6.2	7.8	7.9	*8.4
Cuba											
Total	C	535	497	465	461	...	4.3	4.3	4.0	4.0	...
Urban - Urbaine	C	429	419	399	364	...	4.3	4.5	4.3	3.8	...
Rural - Rurale	C	106	78	66	97	...	4.1	3.3	3.1	4.5	...
Curaçao											
Total	C	20	20	16	14	9	...	...	...	...	...

15. Infant deaths and infant mortality rates, by urban/rural residence: 2015 - 2019
Décès d'enfants de moins d'un an et taux de mortalité infantile, selon la résidence, urbaine/rurale : 2015 - 2019 (continued - suite)

Continent, country or area, and urban/rural residence Continent, pays ou zone et résidence, urbaine/rurale	Code[a]	Number - Nombre 2015	2016	2017	2018	2019	Rate - Taux 2015	2016	2017	2018	2019
AMERICA, NORTH - AMÉRIQUE DU NORD											
Dominican Republic - République dominicaine											
Total	U	*937*	*811*	*685*	*247*	*748*	...	...	...	...	...
Urban - Urbaine[9]	U	*775*	*705*	...	...	...	...	...	...	...	...
Rural - Rurale[9]	U	*35*	*52*	...	...	...	...	...	...	...	...
Greenland - Groenland											
Total	C	9	6	6	6	10	...	...	...	...	...
Urban - Urbaine	C	9	6	6	...	7	...	...	...	...	...
Rural - Rurale	C	-	-	-	...	3	...	...	...	...	...
Grenada - Grenade											
Total	+C	28	31	34	...	...	...	19.7	24.3	...	...
Guadeloupe[10]											
Total	C	43	41	40	32	...	8.0	7.8	8.6	7.5	...
Guatemala											
Total	C	8 202	8 366	7 626	7 564	...	21.0	21.4	20.0	19.7	...
Martinique											
Total	C	...	...	40	...	...	...	...	11.0	...	...
Urban - Urbaine	C	...	...	36	...	...	...	...	11.7	...	...
Rural - Rurale	C	...	...	4	...	...	...	...	...	...	...
Mexico - Mexique[11]											
Total	+C	26 045	24 722	25 180	23 142	...	12.4	12.2	12.6	10.7	...
Urban - Urbaine[9]	+C	19 753	18 766	19 114	17 955	...	12.8	12.7	13.0	...	...
Rural - Rurale[9]	+C	5 832	5 593	5 766	4 447	...	13.2	12.7	13.1	...	...
Montserrat											
Total	C	3	-	...	...	...	...	...	...	...	...
Panama											
Total	C	935	1 046	1 063	1 092	*1 005	12.3	13.9	14.0	14.2	*13.9
Urban - Urbaine	C	543	556	589	676	*554	11.1	11.6	12.3	14.1	...
Rural - Rurale	C	392	490	474	416	*451	14.6	17.9	16.7	14.3	...
Puerto Rico - Porto Rico											
Total	C	222	222	172	142	135	7.1	7.8	7.1	6.6	6.6
Urban - Urbaine	C	124	122	100	83	91	6.5	6.7	6.1	6.0	6.8
Rural - Rurale	C	98	100	72	59	44	8.0	9.9	9.0	7.8	6.2
Saint Barthélemy - Saint-Barthélemy											
Total	C	...	...	-	...	...	...	...	...	...	...
Saint Pierre and Miquelon - Saint Pierre-et-Miquelon											
Total	C	...	...	-	...	...	...	...	...	...	...
Saint Vincent and the Grenadines - Saint-Vincent-et-les Grenadines											
Total	C	26	25	17	...	...	...	...	...	...	...
Saint-Martin (French part) - Saint-Martin (partie française)											
Total	C	...	...	5	...	...	...	...	...	...	...
Trinidad and Tobago - Trinité-et-Tobago											
Total	C	*182	*223	*190	*172	...	*10.1	*12.3	*11.5	*10.6	...
Turks and Caicos Islands - Îles Turques et Caïques											
Total	C	1	...	3	*-	...	...	...	...	...	...
United States of America - États-Unis d'Amérique											
Total	C	23 455	23 161	22 341	21 498	...	5.9	5.9	5.8	5.7	...
United States Virgin Islands - Îles Vierges américaines[12]											
Total	C	4	3	10	...	...	...	...	...	...	...
AMERICA, SOUTH - AMÉRIQUE DU SUD											
Argentina - Argentine											
Total	C	7 445	7 093	6 579	6 048	...	9.7	9.7	9.3	8.8	...

15. Infant deaths and infant mortality rates, by urban/rural residence: 2015 - 2019
Décès d'enfants de moins d'un an et taux de mortalité infantile, selon la résidence, urbaine/rurale : 2015 - 2019 (continued - suite)

Continent, country or area, and urban/rural residence / Continent, pays ou zone et résidence, urbaine/rurale	Code[a]	Number - Nombre					Rate - Taux				
		2015	2016	2017	2018	2019	2015	2016	2017	2018	2019
AMERICA, SOUTH - AMÉRIQUE DU SUD											
Brazil - Brésil[13]											
Total	+C	31 238	30 541	30 636	...	...	10.2	10.5	10.3	...	...
Chile - Chili											
Total	C	1 683	1 629	1 557	*1 235	...	6.9	7.0	7.1	*5.6	...
Urban - Urbaine	C	1 506	1 471	1 402	...	...	6.8	6.9	6.9	...	...
Rural - Rurale	C	177	158	155	...	...	8.0	8.0	10.1	...	...
Colombia - Colombie											
Total	U	7 244	7 220	7 044	7 329	*7 166	...	...	...	...	...
Urban - Urbaine[9]	U	5 384	5 365	5 246	5 342	*5 157	...	...	...	...	...
Rural - Rurale[9]	U	1 799	1 800	1 713	1 854	*1 801	...	...	...	...	...
Ecuador - Équateur[14]											
Total	U	3 011	3 078	3 298	*3 350	...	...	...	...	...	...
Urban - Urbaine	U	2 503	2 505	2 697	*2 737	...	...	...	...	...	...
Rural - Rurale	U	508	573	601	*613	...	...	...	...	...	...
Paraguay											
Total	+U	...	485	...	490	...	...	...	...	...	...
Peru - Pérou[15]											
Total	+U	3 852	3 756	5 224	5 739	*4 758	...	...	...	...	...
Suriname											
Total	C	149	170	199	190	...	14.7	17.2	20.3	19.4	...
Urban - Urbaine	C	101	131	146	141	...	15.1	20.0	22.6	22.3	...
Rural - Rurale	C	48	39	53	49	...	13.9	11.6	16.0	14.1	...
Uruguay											
Total	C	367	376	280	273	...	7.5	8.0	6.5	6.8	...
Venezuela (Bolivarian Republic of) - Venezuela (République bolivarienne du)											
Total	C	9 276	11 783	11 671	...	...	15.4	18.3	20.1	...	...
ASIA - ASIE											
Armenia - Arménie[16]											
Total	C	370	352	311	261	...	8.9	8.7	8.2	7.1	...
Urban - Urbaine	C	233	201	178	162	...	8.6	7.6	7.2	6.7	...
Rural - Rurale	C	137	151	133	99	...	9.4	10.7	10.2	8.0	...
Azerbaijan - Azerbaïdjan[16]											
Total	+C	2 033	1 666	1 700	1 547	...	12.2	10.4	11.8	11.1	...
Urban - Urbaine	+C	1 602	1 380	1 363	1 101	...	19.7	17.9	19.6	16.3	...
Rural - Rurale	+C	431	286	337	446	...	5.1	3.5	4.5	6.2	...
Bahrain - Bahreïn[17]											
Total	C	156	109	133	129	...	7.4	5.3	6.5	6.5	...
Bangladesh											
Total	U	86 632	84 195	72 239	66 268	63 287	...	...	...	...	...
Urban - Urbaine	U	21 118	21 373	17 416	15 976	15 258	...	...	...	...	...
Rural - Rurale	U	65 514	62 822	54 823	50 292	48 029	...	...	...	...	...
Brunei Darussalam - Brunéi Darussalam											
Total	+C	58	52	60	56	...	8.7	8.1	9.3	9.0	...
China, Hong Kong SAR - Chine, Hong Kong RAS											
Total	C	85	109	97	80	78	1.4	1.8	1.7	1.5	1.5
China, Macao SAR - Chine, Macao RAS											
Total	C	11	12	15	20	9	...	...	...	...	...
Cyprus - Chypre[18]											
Total	C	25	25	...	22	...	...	...	...	...	...
Georgia - Géorgie[16]											
Total	C	507	507	512	416	...	8.6	9.0	9.6	8.1	...
Urban - Urbaine	C	259	253	...	...	...	7.6	7.9	...	...	...
Rural - Rurale	C	248	254	...	...	...	9.8	10.4	...	...	...
India - Inde[19]											
Total	I	...	...	...	...	...	37.0	34.0	33.0	32.0	...
Urban - Urbaine	I	...	...	...	...	...	25.0	23.0	23.0	23.0	...
Rural - Rurale	I	...	...	...	...	...	41.0	38.0	37.0	36.0	...

15. Infant deaths and infant mortality rates, by urban/rural residence: 2015 - 2019
Décès d'enfants de moins d'un an et taux de mortalité infantile, selon la résidence, urbaine/rurale : 2015 - 2019 (continued - suite)

Continent, country or area, and urban/rural residence Continent, pays ou zone et résidence, urbaine/rurale	Code[a]	Number - Nombre					Rate - Taux				
		2015	2016	2017	2018	2019	2015	2016	2017	2018	2019
ASIA - ASIE											
Iran (Islamic Republic of) - Iran (République islamique d')[20]											
Total	+C	...	8 261	8 304	7 530	...	...	5.4	5.6	5.5	...
Urban - Urbaine	+C	...	6 115	6 296	5 612	...	...	5.2	5.5	5.4	...
Rural - Rurale	+C	...	2 146	2 008	1 918	...	...	6.1	5.8	6.0	...
Iraq											
Total	U	...	...	*18 611*	...	...	...	...	...	...	...
Israel - Israël[21]											
Total	C	563	570	564	550	534	3.2	3.1	3.1	3.0	2.9
Urban - Urbaine[9]	C	496	491	509	484	465	3.1	3.0	3.0	2.9	...
Rural - Rurale[9]	C	63	78	55	66	60	3.8	4.6	3.4	4.1	...
Japan - Japon[22]											
Total	C	1 916	1 928	1 761	1 748	...	1.9	2.0	1.9	1.9	...
Urban - Urbaine	C	1 754	1 768	1 636	1 628	...	1.9	2.0	1.9	1.9	...
Rural - Rurale	C	161	158	122	115	...	2.1	2.1	1.7	1.7	...
Kazakhstan											
Total	C	3 751	3 438	3 109	3 184	3 360	9.4	8.6	8.0	8.0	8.4
Urban - Urbaine	C	2 177	1 936	1 700	1 846	2 057	9.6	8.4	7.5	7.9	8.6
Rural - Rurale	C	1 574	1 502	1 409	1 338	1 303	9.1	8.8	8.6	8.2	8.0
Kuwait - Koweït											
Total	C	456	448	413	417	...	7.7	7.6	7.0	7.4	...
Kyrgyzstan - Kirghizstan											
Total	C	2 945	2 621	2 401	2 535	...	18.0	16.6	15.6	14.8	...
Urban - Urbaine	C	1 853	1 586	1 586	1 752	...	35.3	30.7	30.0	28.2	...
Rural - Rurale	C	1 092	1 035	815	783	...	9.8	9.7	8.1	7.2	...
Lao People's Democratic Republic - République démocratique populaire lao[23]											
Total	I	3 164	...	...	...	...	25.2	...	...	...	...
Urban - Urbaine	I	559	...	...	...	...	15.8	...	...	...	...
Rural - Rurale	I	2 605	...	...	...	...	28.9	...	...	...	...
Malaysia - Malaisie											
Total	C	3 582	3 390	3 496	3 622	...	6.9	6.7	6.9	7.2	...
Urban - Urbaine	C	2 301	2 186	2 288	2 316	...	6.6	6.4	6.8	7.0	...
Rural - Rurale	C	1 281	1 204	1 208	1 306	...	7.5	7.3	7.1	7.7	...
Maldives[24]											
Total	C	63	53	64	...	...	9.0	7.8	9.5	...	...
Urban - Urbaine[9]	C	8	35	6	...	...	...	14.4	...	...	...
Rural - Rurale[9]	C	17	14	55	...	...	...	...	11.0	...	...
Mongolia - Mongolie											
Total	+C	1 234	1 315	1 009	1 037	1 041	15.0	16.5	13.4	13.2	13.1
Urban - Urbaine	+C	...	...	...	809	805	...	...	...	15.4	15.2
Rural - Rurale	+C	...	...	...	228	236	...	...	...	8.8	8.9
Myanmar[25]											
Total	+U	*9 849*	*9 476*	*9 761*	...	...	...	...	...	...	...
Urban - Urbaine	+U	*6 256*	*4 819*	*3 718*	...	...	...	...	...	...	...
Rural - Rurale	+U	*3 593*	*4 657*	*6 043*	...	...	...	...	...	...	...
Oman											
Total[26]	U	*818*	*816*	...	...	...	...	...	...	...	...
Total	C	...	...	850	762	686	...	...	9.4	8.6	7.9
Philippines											
Total	C	20 750	21 874	20 311	21 019	...	11.9	12.6	11.9	12.6	...
Qatar											
Total	C	197	161	151	172	...	7.4	6.0	5.4	6.1	...
Urban - Urbaine	C	197	161	151	172	...	7.4	6.0	5.4	6.1	...
Republic of Korea - République de Corée[27]											
Total	C	1 190	1 154	1 000	931	...	2.7	2.8	2.8	2.8	...
Urban - Urbaine	C	1 010	945	821	764	...	2.8	2.8	2.8	2.8	...
Rural - Rurale	C	180	209	179	167	...	2.5	3.1	2.9	3.0	...
Saudi Arabia - Arabie saoudite[28]											
Total	I	...	5 084[29]	6 608	...	...	...	11.4	13.5	...	...
Singapore - Singapour											
Total	+C	84	101	94	88	75	2.0	2.4	2.4	2.3	1.9

15. Infant deaths and infant mortality rates, by urban/rural residence: 2015 - 2019
Décès d'enfants de moins d'un an et taux de mortalité infantile, selon la résidence, urbaine/rurale : 2015 - 2019 (continued - suite)

Continent, country or area, and urban/rural residence Continent, pays ou zone et résidence, urbaine/rurale	Co-de[a]	Number - Nombre					Rate - Taux				
		2015	2016	2017	2018	2019	2015	2016	2017	2018	2019
ASIA - ASIE											
Sri Lanka											
Total	+C	*2 845	...	...	...	...	*8.5	...	...	...	...
State of Palestine - État de Palestine[30]											
Total	U	*871*	*880*	*821*	*897*	...	...	...	...	...	...
Tajikistan - Tadjikistan[16]											
Total	U	*3 082*	*2 725*	*2 405*	...	...	...	...	...	...	...
Urban - Urbaine	U	*1 617*	*1 479*	*1 362*	...	...	...	...	...	...	...
Rural - Rurale	U	*1 465*	*1 246*	*1 043*	...	...	...	...	...	...	...
Thailand - Thaïlande[31]											
Total	+U	*4 221*	*4 233*	*3 861*	*3 800*	...	...	...	...	...	...
Turkey - Turquie[32]											
Total	C	13 677	12 915	12 118	11 629	...	10.2	9.8	9.4	9.3	...
United Arab Emirates - Émirats arabes unis											
Total[33]	...	*640*	*597*	...	...	...	...	...	...	...	...
Total	C	...	...	607	500	...	...	...	6.2	5.2	...
Uzbekistan - Ouzbékistan[16]											
Total	+C	8 320	7 764	8 235	7 557	...	11.3	10.7	11.5	9.8	...
Urban - Urbaine	+C	4 494	4 235	4 473	4 117	...	13.8	12.8	13.8	11.7	...
Rural - Rurale	+C	3 826	3 529	3 762	3 440	...	9.4	9.0	9.6	8.3	...
EUROPE											
Åland Islands - Îles d'Åland											
Total	C	-	1	-	-	...	...	...	...	...	...
Urban - Urbaine	C	-	-	-	-	...	...	...	...	...	...
Rural - Rurale	C	-	1	-	-	...	...	...	...	...	...
Albania - Albanie											
Total	C	233	277	248	257	...	7.1	8.7	8.0	8.9	...
Andorra - Andorre											
Total	C	-	...	...	1	...	...	...	...	...	...
Austria - Autriche											
Total	C	259	269	256	231	...	3.1	3.1	2.9	2.7	...
Belarus - Bélarus											
Total	C	352	373	332	238	...	3.0	3.2	3.2	2.5	...
Urban - Urbaine	C	254	288	225	169	...	2.8	3.2	2.9	2.3	...
Rural - Rurale	C	98	85	107	69	...	3.6	3.2	4.5	3.2	...
Belgium - Belgique[34]											
Total	C	400	387	429	444	...	3.3	3.2	3.6	3.8	...
Urban - Urbaine	C	396	...	...	...	...	3.3	...	...	...	...
Rural - Rurale	C	4	...	...	...	...	...	...	...	...	...
Bosnia and Herzegovina - Bosnie-Herzégovine											
Total	C	174	152	183	183	...	6.0	5.2	6.3	6.2	...
Bulgaria - Bulgarie											
Total	C	434	423	408	358	...	6.6	6.5	6.4	5.8	...
Urban - Urbaine	C	255	285	257	234	...	5.2	5.8	5.4	5.0	...
Rural - Rurale	C	179	138	151	124	...	10.9	8.5	9.5	8.1	...
Croatia - Croatie											
Total	C	154	161	148	157	...	4.1	4.3	4.0	4.2	...
Urban - Urbaine	C	91	82	99	101	...	4.2	3.8	4.7	4.8	...
Rural - Rurale	C	63	79	49	56	...	4.0	5.0	3.2	3.5	...
Czechia - Tchéquie											
Total	C	272	317	304	292	...	2.5	2.8	2.7	2.6	...
Urban - Urbaine	C	193	231	225	229	...	2.4	2.8	2.7	2.7	...
Rural - Rurale	C	79	86	79	63	...	2.7	2.9	2.6	2.1	...
Denmark - Danemark[35]											
Total	C	216	194	231	226	...	3.7	3.1	3.8	3.7	...
Estonia - Estonie											
Total	C	35	33	32	23	...	2.5	2.3	2.3	...	...
Urban - Urbaine	C	24	24	23	16	...	...	...	...	...	...
Rural - Rurale	C	11	9	9	7	...	...	...	...	...	...

15. Infant deaths and infant mortality rates, by urban/rural residence: 2015 - 2019
Décès d'enfants de moins d'un an et taux de mortalité infantile, selon la résidence, urbaine/rurale : 2015 - 2019 (continued - suite)

Continent, country or area, and urban/rural residence Continent, pays ou zone et résidence, urbaine/rurale	Code[a]	Number - Nombre					Rate - Taux				
		2015	2016	2017	2018	2019	2015	2016	2017	2018	2019
EUROPE											
Faroe Islands - Îles Féroé											
Total	C	-	3	6	-	3	...	...	...	...	...
Urban - Urbaine	C	-	1	2	-	1	...	...	...	...	...
Rural - Rurale	C	-	2	4	-	2	...	...	...	...	...
Finland - Finlande[36]											
Total	C	97	99	102	101	...	1.8	1.9	2.0	2.1	...
Urban - Urbaine	C	66	72	73	71	...	1.6	1.9	2.0	2.0	...
Rural - Rurale	C	31	27	29	30	...	2.1	...	...	2.6	...
France											
Total	C	2 655	2 577	2 639	2 600	...	3.5	3.5	3.6	3.6	...
Urban - Urbaine[37]	C	2 219	2 165	2 211	...	...	3.6	3.6	3.7	...	...
Rural - Rurale[37]	C	408	386	406	...	...	2.8	2.7	3.0	...	...
Germany - Allemagne											
Total	C	2 405	2 698	2 566	2 505	...	3.3	3.4	3.3	3.2	...
Greece - Grèce											
Total	C	364	387	306	300	...	4.0	4.2	3.5	3.5	...
Urban - Urbaine	C	335	351	286	278	...	5.3	5.5	4.7	4.7	...
Rural - Rurale	C	29	36	20	22	...	...	1.3	...	...	...
Hungary - Hongrie[38]											
Total	C	383	368	328	304	...	4.2	3.9	3.5	3.3	...
Urban - Urbaine[39]	C	242	231	182	190	...	3.8	3.5	2.8	3.0	...
Rural - Rurale[39]	C	140	136	145	114	...	5.0	4.6	4.9	3.8	...
Iceland - Islande											
Total	C	9	3	11	7	...	...	...	...	...	...
Urban - Urbaine	C	8	3	11	6	...	...	...	...	...	...
Rural - Rurale	C	1	-	-	1	...	...	...	...	...	...
Ireland - Irlande											
Total	+C	225	208	174	174	...	3.4	3.3	2.8	2.9	...
Isle of Man - Île de Man[40]											
Total	|	...	2	...	...	...	...	...	...	...	...
Italy - Italie											
Total	C	1 398	1 427	1 347	1 228	...	2.9	3.0	2.9	2.8	...
Latvia - Lettonie											
Total	C	90	81	86	61	...	4.1	3.7	4.1	3.2	...
Urban - Urbaine	C	59	53	64	44	...	3.9	3.5	4.4	3.3	...
Rural - Rurale	C	31	28	22	17	...	4.5	...	...	...	...
Liechtenstein											
Total	C	2	1	-	-	...	...	...	...	...	...
Lithuania - Lituanie											
Total	C	132	139	85	96	...	4.2	4.5	3.0	3.4	...
Urban - Urbaine	C	92	96	59	72	...	4.3	4.5	3.0	3.7	...
Rural - Rurale	C	40	43	26	24	...	4.0	4.6	...	...	...
Luxembourg											
Total	C	17	23	20	27	...	...	...	...	...	...
Malta - Malte											
Total	C	25	33	30	25	...	...	7.4	6.9	...	...
Montenegro - Monténégro											
Total	C	16	26	10	12	17	...	...	...	...	...
Netherlands - Pays-Bas[41]											
Total	C	561	597	607	582	...	3.3	3.5	3.6	3.5	...
North Macedonia - Macédoine du Nord											
Total	C	198	273	201	122	...	8.6	11.9	9.2	5.7	...
Urban - Urbaine	C	116	153	102	...	...	8.7	11.3	7.9	...	...
Rural - Rurale	C	82	120	99	...	...	8.4	12.7	11.1	...	...
Norway - Norvège[42]											
Total	C	133	128	130	129	...	2.3	2.2	2.3	2.3	...
Poland - Pologne											
Total	C	1 476	1 522	1 604	1 494	...	4.0	4.0	4.0	3.8	...
Urban - Urbaine	C	859	876	931	823	...	4.0	3.9	3.9	3.6	...
Rural - Rurale	C	617	646	673	671	...	4.1	4.1	4.1	4.2	...
Portugal[43]											
Total	C	250	282	229	287	...	2.9	3.2	2.7	3.3	...

15. Infant deaths and infant mortality rates, by urban/rural residence: 2015 - 2019
Décès d'enfants de moins d'un an et taux de mortalité infantile, selon la résidence, urbaine/rurale : 2015 - 2019 (continued - suite)

Continent, country or area, and urban/rural residence Continent, pays ou zone et résidence, urbaine/rurale	Code[a]	Number - Nombre					Rate - Taux				
		2015	2016	2017	2018	2019	2015	2016	2017	2018	2019
EUROPE											
Republic of Moldova - République de Moldova[44]											
Total	C	375	353	330	326	...	9.7	9.4	9.7	10.0	...
Urban - Urbaine	C	141	131	107	120	...	10.4	9.8	8.6	10.0	...
Rural - Rurale	C	234	222	223	206	...	9.3	9.2	10.3	10.0	...
Romania - Roumanie											
Total	C	1 500	1 399	1 364	1 226	...	7.6	6.8	6.7	6.0	...
Urban - Urbaine	C	648	615	587	550	...	6.0	5.4	5.3	4.9	...
Rural - Rurale	C	852	784	777	676	...	9.6	8.5	8.6	7.5	...
San Marino - Saint-Marin											
Total	C	-	1	-	1	...	...	...	...	...	...
Serbia - Serbie[45]											
Total	+C	346	348	305	311	...	5.3	5.4	4.7	4.9	...
Urban - Urbaine	+C	258	265	212	209	...	5.7	5.9	4.8	4.9	...
Rural - Rurale	+C	88	83	93	102	...	4.4	4.2	4.4	4.8	...
Slovakia - Slovaquie											
Total	C	285	311	263	288	...	5.1	5.4	4.5	5.0	...
Urban - Urbaine	C	117	133	107	125	...	4.0	4.5	3.6	4.2	...
Rural - Rurale	C	168	178	156	163	...	6.3	6.4	5.5	5.8	...
Slovenia - Slovénie											
Total	C	33	41	42	33	...	1.6	2.0	2.1	1.7	...
Urban - Urbaine	C	17	15	26	20	...	...	...	...	...	...
Rural - Rurale	C	16	26	16	13	...	...	...	...	...	...
Spain - Espagne											
Total	C	1 117	1 097	1 064	998	...	2.7	2.7	2.7	2.7	...
Sweden - Suède											
Total	C	282	292	278	235	...	2.5	2.5	2.4	2.0	...
Switzerland - Suisse											
Total	C	340	316	310	287	...	3.9	3.6	3.5	3.3	...
Urban - Urbaine	C	282	279	268	246	...	3.8	3.7	3.6	3.3	...
Rural - Rurale	C	58	37	42	41	...	4.6	2.9	3.4	3.2	...
Ukraine[46]											
Total	+C	3 318	2 955	2 786	2 397	...	8.1	7.4	7.7	7.1	...
Urban - Urbaine	+C	2 035	1 788	1 666	...	...	7.6	6.9	7.0	...	...
Rural - Rurale	+C	1 283	1 167	1 120	...	...	8.8	8.4	8.9	...	...
United Kingdom of Great Britain and Northern Ireland - Royaume-Uni de Grande-Bretagne et d'Irlande du Nord[47]											
Total	+C	3 004	2 976	2 947	2 818	...	3.9	3.8	3.9	3.9	...
OCEANIA - OCÉANIE											
American Samoa - Samoas américaines											
Total	C	11	14	14	...	...	...	...	...	...	...
Australia - Australie											
Total	C	991	970	1 019	988	...	3.2	3.1	3.3	3.1	...
Urban - Urbaine[48]	C	606	630	655	658	...	2.9	2.9	3.1	3.0	...
Rural - Rurale[48]	C	361	326	355	326	...	3.8	3.5	3.8	3.4	...
Cook Islands - Îles Cook											
Total	+C	-	-	1	*4	*2	...	...	...	...	...
Fiji - Fidji[49]											
Total	+C	226	216	300	...	...	12.6	13.8	21.4	...	...
French Polynesia - Polynésie française											
Total	C	27	25	29	38	...	...	...	...	10.1	...
Guam[50]											
Total	C	47	37	28	37	...	14.0	10.8	...	11.7	...
New Caledonia - Nouvelle-Calédonie											
Total	C	25	16	20	...	...	...	...	...	...	...

15. Infant deaths and infant mortality rates, by urban/rural residence: 2015 - 2019
Décès d'enfants de moins d'un an et taux de mortalité infantile, selon la résidence, urbaine/rurale : 2015 - 2019 (continued - suite)

Continent, country or area, and urban/rural residence Continent, pays ou zone et résidence, urbaine/rurale	Code[a]	Number - Nombre					Rate - Taux				
		2015	2016	2017	2018	2019	2015	2016	2017	2018	2019
OCEANIA - OCÉANIE											
New Zealand - Nouvelle-Zélande[51]											
Total	+C	249	213	228	219	267	4.1	3.6	3.8	3.8	4.5
Urban - Urbaine[9]	+C	216	189	198	186	243	4.1	3.6	3.8	3.8	4.9
Rural - Rurale[9]	+C	30	18	27	33	27	3.8	...	...	3.4	...
Palau - Palaos											
Total	C	4	-	5	3	...	...	...	...	...	...
Samoa[52]											
Total	+U	*5*	*10*	*10*	*2*	*7*	...	...	...	...	...

FOOTNOTES - NOTES

Italics: data from civil registers which are incomplete or of unknown completeness. - Italiques : données incomplètes ou dont le degré d'exactitude n'est pas connu, provenant des registres de l'état civil.

* Provisional. - Données provisoires.

[a] 'Code' indicates the source of data, as follows:
C - Civil registration, estimated over 90% complete
U - Civil registration, estimated less than 90% complete
| - Other source, estimated reliable
\+ - Data tabulated by date of registration rather than occurence
... - Information not available

Le 'Code' indique la source des données, comme suit :
C - Registres de l'état civil considérés complets à 90 p. 100 au moins
U - Registres de l'état civil qui ne sont pas considérés complets à 90 p. 100 au moins
| - Autre source, considérée pas douteuses
\+ - Données exploitées selon la date de l'enregistrement et non la date de l'événement
... - Information pas disponible

[1] Excluding live-born infants who died before their birth was registered. Data refer to Algerian population only. - Non compris les enfants nés vivants décédés avant l'enregistrement de leur naissance. Les données ne concernent que la population algérienne.
[2] Source: Vital Statistics Report. - Source: Vital Statistics Report.
[3] Source: Statistical Report, Ministry of Health and Social Security. - Source: Rapport statistique, ministère de la Santé et de la Sécurité sociale.
[4] Source: Ministry of Home Affairs. - Source : Ministère de l'intérieur.
[5] Excludes the islands of St. Brandon and Agalega. - Non compris les îles St. Brandon et Agalega.
[6] Unrevised data. - Les données n'ont pas été révisées.
[7] Bermuda is 100 per cent urban. - 100 pour cent de la population des Bermudes est urbaine.
[8] Including Canadian residents temporarily in the United States, but excluding United States residents temporarily in Canada. - Y compris les résidents canadiens se trouvant temporairement aux Etats-Unis, mais ne comprenant pas les résidents des Etats-Unis se trouvant temporairement au Canada.
[9] The total number may include 'Unknown residence', but the categories urban and rural do not. - Le nombre total peut inclure les personnes dont la résidence n'est pas connue, à l'inverse des catégories de population urbaine et rurale.
[10] Excluding live-born infants who died before their birth was registered. - Non compris les enfants nés vivants décédés avant l'enregistrement de leur naissance.
[11] Data refer to resident population only. - Pour la population résidante seulement.
[12] Source: U.S. National Center for Health Statistics, National Vital Statistics Reports (NVSR). - Source : US National Center for Health Statistics, National Vital Statistics Reports (NVSR).
[13] Including deaths abroad and deaths of unknown residence of mother. - Y compris décès à l'étranger et décès de nourrissons nés de mères dont le lieu de résidence n'est pas connu.
[14] Excludes nomadic Indian tribes. - Non compris les tribus d'Indiens nomades.
[15] Source: Reports of the Ministry of Health. - Source : Rapports du Ministère de la Santé.
[16] Excluding infants born alive of less than 28 weeks' gestation, of less than 1 000 g in weight and 35 cm in length, who die within seven days of birth. - Non compris les enfants nés vivants après moins de 28 semaines de gestations, pesant moins de 1 000 g, mesurant moins de 35 cm et décédés dans les sept jours qui ont suivi leur naissance.
[17] Sources: Births and Deaths National Registration System database, and medical records of government hospitals. Data refer to Bahraini and non-Bahraini deaths including some visitors, and Bahraini deaths abroad. - Les sources: Les bases de données des << Births and Deaths National Registration System >> et les dossiers médicaux des hôpitaux du gouvernement. Les données se rapportent aux décès de Bahreïniens et de non-Bahreïniens, y compris de non-résidents, ainsi que de Bahreïniens résidant à l'étranger.
[18] Data refer to government controlled areas. - Les données se rapportent aux zones contrôlées par le Gouvernement.
[19] Rates were obtained by the Sample Registration System of India, which is a large demographic survey. Includes data for the Indian-held part of Jammu and Kashmir, the final status of which has not yet been determined. - Les taux ont été obtenus par le Système de l'enregistrement par échantillon de l'Inde qui est une large enquête démographique. Y compris les données pour la partie du Jammu et du Cachemire occupée par l'Inde dont le statut définitif n'a pas encore été déterminé.
[20] Data refer to the Iranian Year which begins on 21 March and ends on 20 March of the following year. - Les données concernent l'année iranienne, qui commence le 21 mars et se termine le 20 mars de l'année suivante.
[21] Including deaths abroad of Israeli residents who were out of the country for less than a year. Includes data for East Jerusalem and Israeli residents in certain other territories under occupation by Israeli military forces since June 1967. - Y compris les décès à l'étranger de résidents israéliens qui ont quitté le pays depuis moins d'un an. Y compris les données pour Jérusalem-Est et les résidents israéliens dans certains autres territoires occupés depuis 1967 par les forces armées israéliennes.
[22] Data refer to Japanese nationals in Japan only. The total number may include 'Unknown residence', but the categories urban and rural do not. - Les données se raportent aux nationaux japonais au Japon seulement. Le nombre total peut inclure les personnes dont la résidence n'est pas connue, à l'inverse des catégories de population urbaine et rurale.
[23] Data refer to the 12 months preceding the census in March. - Les données se rapportent aux 12 mois précédant le recensement de mars.
[24] Data do not include foreigners. - Les données sur les etrangers ne sont pas inclus.
[25] Data are from Vital Registration System (VRS). - Les données proviennent du système d'enregistrement des faits d'état civil.
[26] Data from Births and Deaths Notification System (Ministry of Health and all health care providers). - Les données proviennent du système de notification des naissances et des décès (Ministère de la santé et tous prestataires de soins de santé).
[27] Excluding alien armed forces, civilian aliens employed by armed forces, and foreign diplomatic personnel and their dependants. - Non compris les militaires étrangers, les civils étrangers employés par les forces armées ni le personnel diplomatique étranger et les membres de leur famille les accompagnant.
[28] Survey based estimates. - Estimations basées sur des enquêtes.
[29] Data refer to Saudi Arabian nationals only. - Les données ne concernent que les ressortissants saoudiens.

30 Source: Palestinian Central Bureau of Statistics, Population Register, updated version 2019. Data exclude Jerusalem ID holders. - Source: Bureau central de statistique palestinien, registre de la population, version actualisée jusqu'au 2019. Les données ne tiennent pas compte des détenteurs de carte d'identité de Jérusalem.
31 Source: Strategy and Planning Division, Ministry of Public Health. - Source : Division de la stratégie et de la planification, Ministère de la Santé publique.
32 Data from MERNIS (Central Population Administrative System). - Données de MERNIS (Système central de données démographiques).
33 The registration of births and deaths is conducted by the Ministry of Health. An estimate of completeness is not provided. - L'enregistrement des naissances et des décès est mené par le Ministère de la Santé. Le degré estimatif de complétude n'est pas fourni.
34 Including armed forces stationed outside the country, but excluding alien armed forces stationed in the area. - Y compris les militaires nationaux hors du pays, mais non compris les militaires étrangers en garnison sur le territoire.
35 Excluding Faeroe Islands and Greenland shown separately, if available. - Non compris les Iles Féroé et le Groenland, qui font l'objet de rubriques distinctes, si disponible.
36 Excluding Åland Islands. - Non compris les Îles d'Åland.
37 Data for urban and rural exclude events corresponding to nationals residing outside the country, which may be included in the total. - Les données relatives à les categories urbaine et rurale n'englobent pas les faits d'état civil qui concernent les nationaux se trouvant à l'étranger, lesquels faits peuvent être inclus au total.
38 Data include the deceased infants with Hungarian usual residence regardless of whether the death occurred in Hungary or in a foreign country, and do not include the deceased infants with foreign country usual residence. - Les données comprennent les nourrissons décédés alors que leur résidence habituelle était en Hongrie, que le décès ait eu lieu en Hongrie ou dans un pays étranger, et ne comprennent pas les nourrissons décédés dont la residence habituelle était dans un pays étranger.
39 The urban and rural categories do not include the data of foreigners, persons of unknown residence and the homeless, whereas the total category includes them. - Les chiffres portant sur la population urbaine et rurale n' incluent pas les données relatives aux étrangers, aux personnes dont la résidence n'est pas connue et aux personnes sans domicile fixe, à l'inverse, le total les inclut.
40 Data refer to the 12 months preceding the census in April. - Les données se rapportent aux douze mois précédant le recensement d'avril.
41 Including residents outside the country if listed in a Netherlands population register. - Englobe les résidents se trouvant à l'étranger à condition qu'ils soient inscrits sur le registre de population des Pays-Bas.
42 Including residents temporarily outside the country. - Y compris les résidents se trouvant temporairement hors du pays.
43 Data refer to usual resident population. - Les données se réfèrent à la population résidente habituelle.
44 Excluding Transnistria and the municipality of Bender. - Les données ne tiennent pas compte de l'information sur la Transnistria et la municipalité de Bender.
45 Excludes data for Kosovo and Metohia. - Sans les données pour le Kosovo et Metohie.
46 Data includes deaths resulting from births with weight 500 g and more (if weight is unknown - with length 25 cm and more, or with gestation during 22 weeks or more). The Government of Ukraine has informed the United Nations that it is not in a position to provide statistical data concerning the Autonomous Republic of Crimea and the city of Sevastopol. - Y compris les décès de nouveau-nés de 500 g ou plus (si le poids est inconnu – de 25 cm de long ou plus, ou après une grossesse de 22 semaines ou plus). Le gouvernement Ukrainien a informé l'ONU qu'il n'est pas en mesure de fournir des données statistiques concernant la République autonome de Crimée et la ville de Sébastopol.
47 Excluding Channel Islands (Guernsey and Jersey) and Isle of Man, shown separately, if available. - Non compris les îles Anglo-Normandes (Guernesey et Jersey) et l'île de Man, qui font l'objet de rubriques distinctes, si disponible.
48 Urban refers to Greater Capital City Statistical Areas, and rural refers to other areas within the state or territory. Data for urban and rural figures do not add up to the total because they exclude the events occurred in Migratory, Special Purpose and Other Territories. - Urbain renvoie aux zones statistiques de la capitale métropolitaine, et rural aux autres zones de l'État ou territoire. La somme des chiffres des catégories « en zone urbaine » et « en zone rurale » ne correspond pas au total du fait qu'en sont exclus les événements qui ont eu lieu dans les territoires de migration, les territoires à destination spéciale et autres territoires.
49 Data recorded by Ministry of Health and Medical Services (MoHMS). - Données enregistrées par le Ministère de la santé et des services médicaux (MoHMS).
50 Including United States military personnel, their dependants and contract employees. - Y compris les militaires des Etats-Unis, les membres de leur famille les accompagnant et les agents contractuels des Etats-Unis.
51 Random rounding to base 3 is applied in this table as a confidentiality measure. Data refer to deaths of residents only. - Les chiffres sont arrondis à la base 3 de manière aléatoire, pour des raisons de confidentialité. Les données renvoient aux décès de résidents uniquement.
52 Source: Births, Deaths, and Marriages Registration Division, Samoa Bureau of Statistics. - Source : Division de l'enregistrement des naissances, des décès et des mariages du Bureau de statistique du Samoa.

Table 16 - *Demographic Yearbook 2019*

Table 16 presents infant deaths and infant mortality rates by age and sex for latest available year between 2010 and 2019.

Description of variables: Age is defined as hours, days and months of life completed, based on the difference between the hour, day, month and year of birth and the hour, day, month and year of death. The age classification used in this table is as follows: Main categories are "under 1 day", "1-6 days", "7-27 days" and "28 days – 11 months". Additional subcategories are shown within "7-27 days" and "28 days to 11 months" wherever available.

Rate computation: Infant mortality rates by age and sex are the annual number of infant deaths that occurred in a specific age-sex group per 1 000 live births of the corresponding sex. These rates have been calculated by the United Nations Statistics Division. The denominator for all these rates, regardless of age of infant at death, is the total number of live births by sex.

Infant deaths of unknown age are included only in the rate for under one year of age. Infant deaths of unknown sex are included in the rate for the total and, hence, these rates, should agree with the infant mortality rates shown in table 15. Discrepancies are explained in footnotes.

Rates presented in this table have been limited to those countries or areas having at least a total of 100 deaths in a given year. Moreover, rates specific for individual sub-categories based on 30 or fewer infant deaths are identified by the symbol "♦".

Reliability of data: Data from civil registers of infant deaths which are reported as incomplete (less than 90 percent completeness) or of unknown completeness are considered unreliable and are set in italics rather than in roman type. Rates on these data are not computed. Table 15 and its technical notes provide more detailed information on the completeness of infant death registration. For more information about the quality of vital statistics, and the information available on their completeness, see section 4.2 of the Technical Notes.

Limitations: Statistics on infant deaths by age and sex are subject to the same qualifications as have been set forth for vital statistics and particularly for death statistics discussed in section 4 of the Technical Notes.

The reliability of the data, an indication of which is described above, is an important factor in considering the limitations. In addition, some infant deaths are tabulated by date of registration and not by date of occurrence; these have been indicated by a plus sign "+". Whenever the lag between the date of occurrence and date of registration is prolonged and, therefore, a large proportion of the infant-death registrations are delayed, infant-death statistics for any given year may be seriously affected.

Another factor that limits international comparability is the practice of some countries or areas of not including in infant-death statistics infants who were born alive but died before the registration of the birth or within the first 24 hours of life, thus underestimating the total number of infant deaths. Statistics of this type are footnoted. In this table, this practice may contribute to the lack of comparability among deaths under one year, under 28 days, under one week and under one day.

Variation in the method of reckoning age at the time of death may also introduce non-comparability. Although it is to some degree a limiting factor throughout the age span, it is an especially important consideration with respect to deaths at ages under one day, under one week (early neonatal deaths) and under 28 days (neonatal deaths). As noted above, the recommended method of reckoning infant age at death is to calculate duration of life in minutes, hours and days, as appropriate. This gives age in completed units of time. In some countries or areas, however, infant age is calculated to the nearest day only, that is, age at death for an infant is the difference between the day, month and year of birth and the day, month and year of death. The result of this procedure is to classify as deaths at age one day, many deaths of infants that occurred before the infants had completed 24 hours of life. The under-one-day class is thus understated while the frequency in the 1-6-day age group is inflated.

A special limitation on comparability of neonatal (under 28 days) deaths is the variation in the classification of infant age used. Some countries or areas continue to report infant age in calendar, rather than lunar month (4-week or 28-day) periods. This failure to tabulate infant deaths under 4 weeks of age in terms of completed days introduces another source of variation between countries or areas. Deaths classified as occurring under one month usually connote deaths within any one calendar month; these frequencies are not strictly comparable with those referring to deaths within 4 weeks or 27 completed days.

In addition, infant mortality rates by age and sex are subject to the limitations of the data on live births with which they have been calculated. These have been set forth in the technical notes for table 9. These limitations have also been discussed in the technical notes for table 15.

In addition, it should be noted that infant mortality rates by age are affected by the problems related to the practice of excluding infants who were born alive but died before the registration of the birth or within the first 24 hours of life from both infant-death and live-birth statistics and the problems related to the reckoning of infant age at death. These factors, which have been described above, may affect certain age groups more than others. In so far as the numbers of infant deaths for the various age groups are underestimated or overestimated, the corresponding rates for the various age groups will also be underestimated or overestimated. The youngest age groups are more likely to be underestimated than other age groups; the youngest age group (under one day) is likely to be the most seriously affected.

Earlier data: Infant deaths and infant mortality rates by age and sex have been shown in previous issues of the *Demographic Yearbook*. For information on specific years covered, readers should consult the Historical Index.

Tableau 16 – *Annuaire démographique 2019*

Le tableau 16 présente les données les plus récentes disponible, entre 2010 et 2019, sur les décès d'enfants de moins d'un an et les taux de mortalité infantile selon l'âge et le sexe.

Description des variables : l'âge est exprimé en heures, jours et mois révolus et est calculé en retranchant la date de la naissance (heure, jour, mois et année) de celle du décès (heure, jour, mois et année). Les tranches d'âge utilisées dans ce tableau se présentent comme suit : les catégories principales sont « moins d'un jour », « 1-6 jours », « 7-27 jours » et « 28 jours à 11 mois ». Des sous-catégories additionnelles pour « 7-27 jours » et « 28 jours à 11 mois » sont présentées lorsque disponibles.

Calcul des taux : les taux de mortalité infantile selon l'âge et le sexe représentent le nombre annuel de décès d'enfants de moins d'un an intervenu dans un groupe d'âge donné parmi la population de sexe masculin ou féminin pour 1 000 naissances vivantes survenues parmi la population du même sexe. Ces taux ont été calculés par la Division de statistique du Département des affaires économiques et sociales de l'Organisation des Nations Unies. Le dénominateur de tous ces taux, quel que soit l'âge de l'enfant au moment du décès, est le nombre total de naissances vivantes selon le sexe.

Il n'est tenu compte des décès d'enfants d'âge « inconnu » que pour le calcul du taux relatif à l'ensemble des décès de moins d'un an. Étant donné que les décès d'enfants de sexe inconnu sont compris dans le numérateur des taux concernant le total, les chiffres obtenus devraient concorder avec les taux de mortalité infantile du tableau 15. Les divergences sont expliquées en note.

Les taux présentés dans le tableau 16 ne concernent que les pays ou zones où l'on a enregistré un total d'au moins 100 décès au cours d'une année donnée. Les taux relatifs à des sous-catégories qui sont fondées sur un nombre égal ou inférieur à 30 décès d'enfants âgés de moins d'un an sont signalés par le signe "♦".

Fiabilité des données : les données relatives aux décès d'enfants de moins d'un an provenant de registres de l'état civil qui sont déclarées incomplètes (degré de complétude inférieur à 90 p.100) ou dont le degré de complétude n'est pas connu sont jugées douteuses et apparaissent en italique et non en caractères romains. Les taux à partir de ces données n'ont pas été calculés. Le tableau 15 et les notes techniques se rapportant à ce tableau comportent des renseignements plus détaillés sur le degré de complétude de l'enregistrement des décès d'enfants de moins d'un an. Pour plus de précisions sur la qualité des données reposant sur les statistiques de l'état civil en général et les estimations de complétude en particulier, voir la section 4.2 des Notes techniques.

Insuffisance des données : les statistiques des décès d'enfants de moins d'un an selon l'âge et le sexe appellent toutes les réserves qui ont été formulées à propos des statistiques de l'état civil en général et des statistiques concernant les décès en particulier (voir la section 4 des Notes techniques).

La fiabilité des données, au sujet de laquelle des indications ont été fournies plus haut, est un facteur important. Il faut également tenir compte du fait que, dans certains cas, les données relatives aux décès d'enfants de moins d'un an sont exploitées selon la date de l'enregistrement et non la date de l'événement ; ces cas ont été signalés par le signe "+". Chaque fois que le décalage entre l'événement et son enregistrement est grand et qu'une forte proportion des décès d'enfants de moins d'un an fait l'objet d'un enregistrement tardif, les statistiques des décès d'enfants de moins d'un an pour une année donnée peuvent être considérablement faussées.

Un autre facteur qui nuit à la comparabilité internationale est la pratique de certains pays ou zones qui consiste à ne pas inclure dans les statistiques des décès d'enfants de moins d'un an les enfants nés vivants mais décédés soit avant l'enregistrement de leur naissance, soit dans les 24 heures qui ont suivi la naissance, pratique qui conduit à sous-estimer le nombre total de décès d'enfants de moins d'un an. Quand pareil facteur a joué, cela a été signalé en note. Dans le tableau 16 en particulier, ce système peut limiter la comparabilité des données concernant les décès d'enfants de moins d'un an, de moins de 28 jours, de moins d'une semaine et de moins d'un jour.

Le manque d'uniformité des méthodes suivies pour calculer l'âge au moment du décès nuit également à la comparabilité des données. Ce facteur influe dans une certaine mesure sur les données relatives à la mortalité à tous les âges, mais il a des répercussions particulièrement marquées sur les statistiques des décès de moins d'un jour et de moins d'une semaine (mortalité néo-natale précoce) et de moins de 28 jours (mortalité néo-natale). Comme on l'a dit, l'âge d'un enfant de moins d'un an à son décès est calculé, selon la méthode recommandée, en évaluant la durée de vie en minutes, heures et jours, selon le cas. L'âge est ainsi exprimé en unités de temps révolues. Toutefois, dans certains pays ou zones, l'âge de ces enfants est ramené au jour le plus proche en retranchant la date de la naissance (jour, mois et année) de celle du décès (jour, mois et année). Il s'ensuit que de nombreux décès survenus dans les vingt-quatre heures qui suivent la naissance sont classés comme décès d'un jour. Dans ces conditions, les données concernant les décès de moins d'un jour sont entachées d'une erreur par défaut et celles qui se rapportent aux décès de 1 à 6 jours d'une erreur par excès.

La comparabilité des données relatives à la mortalité néo-natale (moins de 28 jours) est influencée par un facteur spécial : l'hétérogénéité de la classification par âge utilisée pour les enfants de moins d'un an. Dans un certain nombre de pays ou zones, on continue d'utiliser le mois civil au lieu du mois lunaire (4 semaines ou 28 jours).

Lorsque les données relatives aux décès de moins de 4 semaines ne sont pas exploitées sur la base de l'âge en jours révolus, il existe une nouvelle cause de non-comparabilité internationale. Les décès de moins d'un mois sont généralement ceux qui se produisent au cours d'un mois civil ; les taux calculés sur la base de ces données ne sont pas strictement comparables à ceux qui sont établis à partir des données concernant les décès survenus dans les 4 semaines ou 27 jours révolus qui suivent la naissance.

Les taux de mortalité infantile selon l'âge et le sexe appellent en outre toutes les réserves qui ont été formulées à propos des statistiques des naissances vivantes qui ont servi à leur calcul (voir à ce sujet les notes techniques relatives au tableau 9). Ces insuffisances ont également été examinées dans les notes techniques relatives au tableau 15.

Il convient de signaler aussi que les taux de mortalité infantile selon l'âge peuvent être gravement faussés par la pratique qui consiste à ne pas classer dans les naissances vivantes et ensuite dans les décès d'enfants de moins d'un an les enfants nés vivants mais décédés soit avant l'enregistrement de leur naissance, soit dans les 24 heures qui ont suivi la naissance, et par les problèmes que pose le calcul de l'âge de l'enfant au moment du décès. Ces facteurs, qui ont été décrits plus haut, peuvent fausser les statistiques concernant certains groupes d'âge plus que d'autres. Si le nombre des décès d'enfants de moins d'un an pour chaque groupe d'âge est sous-estimé ou surestimé, les taux correspondants pour chacun de ces groupes d'âge seront eux aussi sous-estimés ou surestimés. Les risques de sous-estimation sont plus grands pour les groupes les plus jeunes ; c'est pour le groupe d'âge le plus jeune de tous (moins d'un jour) que les données risquent de comporter les plus grosses erreurs.

Données publiées antérieurement : des statistiques des décès d'enfants de moins d'un an et des taux de mortalité infantile selon l'âge et le sexe ont déjà été présentées dans des éditions antérieures de l'*Annuaire démographique*. Pour plus de précisions concernant les années pour lesquelles ces données ont été publiées, se reporter à l'index historique.

16. Infant deaths and infant mortality rates by age and sex: latest available year, 2010 - 2019
Décès d'enfants de moins d'un an et taux de mortalité infantile selon l'âge et le sexe : dernière année disponible, 2010 - 2019

Continent, country or area, year, code[a] and age Continent, pays ou zone, année, code[a] et âge	Number - Nombre			Rate - Taux		
	Both sexes Les deux sexes	Male Masculin	Female Féminin	Both sexes Les deux sexes	Male Masculin	Female Féminin
AFRICA - AFRIQUE						
Botswana[1]						
2017 (U)						
Total	*985*	*539*	*446*	...	...	...
Less than 1 day - Moins de 1 jour	*102*	*59*	*43*	...	...	...
1 - 6 days - 1 - 6 jours	*324*	*180*	*144*	...	...	...
7 - 27 days - 7 - 27 jours	*193*	*103*	*90*	...	...	...
7 - 13 days - 7 - 13 jours	*99*	*51*	*48*	...	...	...
14 - 20 days - 14 - 20 jours	*57*	*29*	*28*	...	...	...
21 - 27 days - 21 - 27 jours	*37*	*23*	*14*	...	...	...
28 days - 11 months - 28 jours - 11 mois	*366*	*197*	*169*	...	...	...
28 days - less than 2 months - 28 jours - moins de 2 mois	*83*	*53*	*30*	...	...	...
2 months - 2 mois	*50*	*27*	*23*	...	...	...
3 months - 3 mois	*36*	*17*	*19*	...	...	...
4 months - 4 mois	*30*	*13*	*17*	...	...	...
5 months - 5 mois	*29*	*18*	*11*	...	...	...
6 months - 6 mois	*26*	*11*	*15*	...	...	...
7 months - 7 mois	*19*	*9*	*10*	...	...	...
8 months - 8 mois	*23*	*12*	*11*	...	...	...
9 months - 9 mois	*24*	*12*	*12*	...	...	...
10 months - 10 mois	*22*	*12*	*10*	...	...	...
11 months - 11 mois	*24*	*13*	*11*	...	...	...
Cabo Verde[2]						
2017 (C)						
Total	167	100	67	17.0	19.9	14.0
Less than 7 days - Moins de 7 jours	88	53	35	9.0	10.5	7.3
7 - 27 days - 7 - 27 jours	28	19	9	♦2.8	♦3.8	♦1.9
28 days - 11 months - 28 jours - 11 mois	51	28	23	5.2	♦5.6	♦4.8
Egypt - Égypte						
2017 (C)						
Total	38 685	...	...	15.1	...	...
1 - 6 days - 1 - 6 jours	7 454	...	...	2.9	...	...
7 - 27 days - 7 - 27 jours	10 325	...	...	4.0	...	...
7 - 13 days - 7 - 13 jours	5 165	...	...	2.0	...	...
14 - 20 days - 14 - 20 jours	3 222	...	...	1.3	...	...
21 - 27 days - 21 - 27 jours	1 938	...	...	0.8	...	...
28 days - 11 months - 28 jours - 11 mois	20 906	...	...	8.2	...	...
28 days - less than 2 months - 28 jours - moins de 2 mois	5 334	...	...	2.1	...	...
2 months - 2 mois	3 644	...	...	1.4	...	...
3 months - 3 mois	2 580	...	...	1.0	...	...
4 months - 4 mois	2 153	...	...	0.8	...	...
5 months - 5 mois	1 698	...	...	0.7	...	...
6 months - 6 mois	1 424	...	...	0.6	...	...
7 months - 7 mois	1 138	...	...	0.4	...	...
8 months - 8 mois	965	...	...	0.4	...	...
9 months - 9 mois	767	...	...	0.3	...	...
10 months - 10 mois	671	...	...	0.3	...	...
11 months - 11 mois	532	...	...	0.2	...	...
Mauritius - Maurice[3]						
2019 (+C)						
Total	187	103	84	14.6	15.9	13.2
Less than 1 day - Moins de 1 jour	10	6	4	♦0.8	♦0.9	♦0.6
1 - 6 days - 1 - 6 jours	82	44	38	6.4	6.8	6.0
7 - 27 days - 7 - 27 jours	41	21	20	3.2	♦3.2	♦3.1
7 - 13 days - 7 - 13 jours	15	7	8	♦1.2	♦1.1	♦1.3
14 - 20 days - 14 - 20 jours	16	10	6	♦1.2	♦1.5	♦0.9
21 - 27 days - 21 - 27 jours	10	4	6	♦0.8	♦0.6	♦0.9
28 days - 11 months - 28 jours - 11 mois	54	32	22	4.2	4.9	♦3.5
28 days - less than 2 months - 28 jours - moins de 2 mois	22	13	9	♦1.7	♦2.0	♦1.4
2 months - 2 mois	6	4	2	♦0.5	♦0.6	♦0.3
3 months - 3 mois	12	8	4	♦0.9	♦1.2	♦0.6
4 months - 4 mois	3	1	2	♦0.2	♦0.2	♦0.3
5 months - 5 mois	1	1	-	♦0.1	♦0.2	-
6 months - 6 mois	2	2	-	♦0.2	♦0.3	-
7 months - 7 mois	2	1	1	♦0.2	♦0.2	♦0.2
8 months - 8 mois	2	-	2	♦0.2	-	♦0.3
9 months - 9 mois	1	-	1	♦0.1	-	♦0.2
10 months - 10 mois	2	1	1	♦0.2	♦0.2	♦0.2
11 months - 11 mois	1	1	-	♦0.1	♦0.2	-

16. Infant deaths and infant mortality rates by age and sex: latest available year, 2010 - 2019
Décès d'enfants de moins d'un an et taux de mortalité infantile selon l'âge et le sexe : dernière année disponible, 2010 - 2019 (continued - suite)

Continent, country or area, year, code[a] and age Continent, pays ou zone, année, code[a] et âge	Number - Nombre			Rate - Taux		
	Both sexes Les deux sexes	Male Masculin	Female Féminin	Both sexes Les deux sexes	Male Masculin	Female Féminin
AFRICA - AFRIQUE						
Mayotte						
2018 (C)						
Total	94	...	...	...	...	...
Less than 1 day - Moins de 1 jour	13	...	...	...	...	...
1 - 6 days - 1 - 6 jours	13	...	...	...	...	...
7 - 27 days - 7 - 27 jours	20	...	...	...	...	...
28 days - 11 months - 28 jours - 11 mois	48	...	...	...	...	...
Reunion - Réunion						
2018 (C)						
Total	82	...	...	...	...	...
Less than 1 day - Moins de 1 jour	31	...	...	...	...	...
1 - 6 days - 1 - 6 jours	13	...	...	...	...	...
7 - 27 days - 7 - 27 jours	18	...	...	...	...	...
28 days - 11 months - 28 jours - 11 mois	20	...	...	...	...	...
Saint Helena ex. dep. - Sainte-Hélène sans dép.						
2018 (C)						
Total	-	-	-	...	...	...
Less than 1 day - Moins de 1 jour	-	-	-	...	...	...
1 - 6 days - 1 - 6 jours	-	-	-	...	...	...
7 - 27 days - 7 - 27 jours	-	-	-	...	...	...
7 - 13 days - 7 - 13 jours	-	-	-	...	...	...
14 - 20 days - 14 - 20 jours	-	-	-	...	...	...
21 - 27 days - 21 - 27 jours	-	-	-	...	...	...
28 days - 11 months - 28 jours - 11 mois	-	-	-	...	...	...
28 days - less than 2 months - 28 jours - moins de 2 mois	-	-	-	...	...	...
2 months - 2 mois	-	-	-	...	...	...
3 months - 3 mois	-	-	-	...	...	...
4 months - 4 mois	-	-	-	...	...	...
5 months - 5 mois	-	-	-	...	...	...
6 months - 6 mois	-	-	-	...	...	...
7 months - 7 mois	-	-	-	...	...	...
8 months - 8 mois	-	-	-	...	...	...
9 months - 9 mois	-	-	-	...	...	...
10 months - 10 mois	-	-	-	...	...	...
11 months - 11 mois	-	-	-	...	...	...
South Africa - Afrique du Sud						
2016 (U)						
Total	*20 649*	*10 963*[4]	*9 284*[4]	...	...	...
Less than 1 day - Moins de 1 jour	*2 363*	*1 265*[4]	*978*[4]	...	...	...
1 - 6 days - 1 - 6 jours	*4 109*	*2 266*[4]	*1 735*[4]	...	...	...
7 - 27 days - 7 - 27 jours	*2 709*	*1 401*[4]	*1 249*[4]	...	...	...
7 - 13 days - 7 - 13 jours	*1 315*	*666*[4]	*624*[4]	...	...	...
14 - 20 days - 14 - 20 jours	*769*	*406*[4]	*342*[4]	...	...	...
21 - 27 days - 21 - 27 jours	*625*	*329*[4]	*283*[4]	...	...	...
28 days - 11 months - 28 jours - 11 mois	*11 468*	*6 031*[4]	*5 322*[4]	...	...	...
28 days - less than 2 months - 28 jours - moins de 2 mois	*2 403*	*1 269*[4]	*1 104*[4]	...	...	...
2 months - 2 mois	*1 701*	*887*[4]	*792*[4]	...	...	...
3 months - 3 mois	*1 512*	*746*[4]	*754*[4]	...	...	...
4 months - 4 mois	*1 107*	*594*[4]	*501*[4]	...	...	...
5 months - 5 mois	*875*	*476*[4]	*393*[4]	...	...	...
6 months - 6 mois	*821*	*438*[4]	*376*[4]	...	...	...
7 months - 7 mois	*732*	*398*[4]	*328*[4]	...	...	...
8 months - 8 mois	*650*	*343*[4]	*303*[4]	...	...	...
9 months - 9 mois	*615*	*323*[4]	*288*[4]	...	...	...
10 months - 10 mois	*546*	*279*[4]	*258*[4]	...	...	...
11 months - 11 mois	*506*	*278*[4]	*225*[4]	...	...	...
AMERICA, NORTH - AMÉRIQUE DU NORD						
Aruba						
2019 (+C)						
Total	5	1	4	...	...	...
Less than 1 day - Moins de 1 jour	3	-	3	...	...	...
1 - 6 days - 1 - 6 jours	-	-	-	...	...	...

16. Infant deaths and infant mortality rates by age and sex: latest available year, 2010 - 2019
Décès d'enfants de moins d'un an et taux de mortalité infantile selon l'âge et le sexe : dernière année disponible, 2010 - 2019 (continued - suite)

Continent, country or area, year, code[a] and age Continent, pays ou zone, année, code[a] et âge	Number - Nombre			Rate - Taux		
	Both sexes Les deux sexes	Male Masculin	Female Féminin	Both sexes Les deux sexes	Male Masculin	Female Féminin
AMERICA, NORTH - AMÉRIQUE DU NORD						
Aruba						
2019 (+C)						
7 - 27 days - 7 - 27 jours	-	-	-	...	...	...
7 - 13 days - 7 - 13 jours	-	-	-	...	...	...
14 - 20 days - 14 - 20 jours	-	-	-	...	...	...
21 - 27 days - 21 - 27 jours	-	-	-	...	...	...
28 days - 11 months - 28 jours - 11 mois	2	1	1	...	...	...
28 days - less than 2 months - 28 jours - moins de 2 mois	-	-	-	...	...	...
2 months - 2 mois	2	1	1	...	...	...
3 months - 3 mois	-	-	-	...	...	...
4 months - 4 mois	-	-	-	...	...	...
5 months - 5 mois	-	-	-	...	...	...
6 months - 6 mois	-	-	-	...	...	...
7 months - 7 mois	-	-	-	...	...	...
8 months - 8 mois	-	-	-	...	...	...
9 months - 9 mois	-	-	-	...	...	...
10 months - 10 mois	-	-	-	...	...	...
11 months - 11 mois	-	-	-	...	...	...
Bahamas						
2012 (+C)						
Total	57	26	31	...	...	...
Less than 1 day - Moins de 1 jour	-	-	-	...	...	...
1 - 6 days - 1 - 6 jours	18	10	8	...	...	...
7 - 27 days - 7 - 27 jours	19	8	11	...	...	...
7 - 13 days - 7 - 13 jours	16	6	10	...	...	...
14 - 20 days - 14 - 20 jours	2	1	1	...	...	...
21 - 27 days - 21 - 27 jours	1	1	-	...	...	...
28 days - 11 months - 28 jours - 11 mois	20	8	12	...	...	...
28 days - less than 2 months - 28 jours - moins de 2 mois	9	5	4	...	...	...
2 months - 2 mois	3	1	2	...	...	...
3 months - 3 mois	2	1	1	...	...	...
4 months - 4 mois	3	-	3	...	...	...
5 months - 5 mois	-	-	-	...	...	...
6 months - 6 mois	-	-	-	...	...	...
7 months - 7 mois	1	-	1	...	...	...
8 months - 8 mois	1	1	-	...	...	...
9 months - 9 mois	1	-	1	...	...	...
10 months - 10 mois	-	-	-	...	...	...
11 months - 11 mois	-	-	-	...	...	...
Belize[5]						
2016 (U)						
Total	*103*	*61*	*42*	...	...	...
Less than 1 day - Moins de 1 jour	*29*	*14*	*15*	...	...	...
1 - 6 days - 1 - 6 jours	*36*	*26*	*10*	...	...	...
7 - 27 days - 7 - 27 jours	*15*	*8*	*7*	...	...	...
7 - 13 days - 7 - 13 jours	*2*	*1*	*1*	...	...	...
14 - 20 days - 14 - 20 jours	*5*	*2*	*3*	...	...	...
21 - 27 days - 21 - 27 jours	*8*	*5*	*3*	...	...	...
28 days - 11 months - 28 jours - 11 mois	*23*	*13*	*10*	...	...	...
28 days - less than 2 months - 28 jours - moins de 2 mois	*1*	-	*1*	...	...	...
2 months - 2 mois	*4*	*2*	*2*	...	...	...
3 months - 3 mois	*7*	*4*	*3*	...	...	...
4 months - 4 mois	*3*	*3*	-	...	...	...
5 months - 5 mois	*2*	*1*	*1*	...	...	...
6 months - 6 mois	*2*	*1*	*1*	...	...	...
7 months - 7 mois	*1*	*1*	-	...	...	...
8 months - 8 mois	-	-	-	...	...	...
9 months - 9 mois	*3*	*1*	*2*	...	...	...
10 months - 10 mois	-	-	-	...	...	...
11 months - 11 mois	-	-	-	...	...	...
Bermuda - Bermudes						
2018 (C)						
Total	1	1	-	...	...	...
Less than 1 day - Moins de 1 jour	-	-	-	...	...	...
1 - 6 days - 1 - 6 jours	-	-	-	...	...	...
7 - 27 days - 7 - 27 jours	-	-	-	...	...	...
7 - 13 days - 7 - 13 jours	-	-	-	...	...	...
14 - 20 days - 14 - 20 jours	-	-	-	...	...	...

16. Infant deaths and infant mortality rates by age and sex: latest available year, 2010 - 2019
Décès d'enfants de moins d'un an et taux de mortalité infantile selon l'âge et le sexe : dernière année disponible, 2010 - 2019 (continued - suite)

Continent, country or area, year, code[a] and age Continent, pays ou zone, année, code[a] et âge	Number - Nombre			Rate - Taux		
	Both sexes Les deux sexes	Male Masculin	Female Féminin	Both sexes Les deux sexes	Male Masculin	Female Féminin
AMERICA, NORTH - AMÉRIQUE DU NORD						
Bermuda - Bermudes						
2018 (C)						
21 - 27 days - 21 - 27 jours	-	-	-	...	...	...
28 days - 11 months - 28 jours - 11 mois	1	1	-	...	...	...
28 days - less than 2 months - 28 jours - moins de 2 mois	-	-	-	...	...	...
2 - 11 months - 2 - 11 mois	1	1	-	...	...	...
Canada[6]						
2018 (C)						
Total	1 750	953	797	4.7	5.0	4.4
Less than 1 day - Moins de 1 jour	886	501	385	2.4	2.6	2.1
1 - 6 days - 1 - 6 jours	230	121	109	0.6	0.6	0.6
7 - 27 days - 7 - 27 jours	194	99	95	0.5	0.5	0.5
7 - 13 days - 7 - 13 jours	80	40	40	0.2	0.2	0.2
14 - 20 days - 14 - 20 jours	64	32	32	0.2	0.2	0.2
21 - 27 days - 21 - 27 jours	50	27	23	0.1	♦0.1	♦0.1
28 days - 11 months - 28 jours - 11 mois	440	232	208	1.2	1.2	1.1
28 days - less than 2 months - 28 jours - moins de 2 mois	144	70	74	0.4	0.4	0.4
2 months - 2 mois	76	42	34	0.2	0.2	0.2
3 months - 3 mois	46	33	13	0.1	0.2	♦0.1
4 months - 4 mois	47	24	23	0.1	♦0.1	♦0.1
5 months - 5 mois	34	17	17	0.1	♦0.1	♦0.1
6 months - 6 mois	21	7	14	♦0.1	-	♦0.1
7 months - 7 mois	23	15	8	♦0.1	♦0.1	-
8 months - 8 mois	15	7	8	-	-	-
9 months - 9 mois	16	6	10	-	-	♦0.1
10 months - 10 mois	8	6	2	-	-	-
11 months - 11 mois	10	5	5	-	-	-
Costa Rica						
2019* (C)						
Total	533	262	271	8.3	8.0	8.6
Less than 1 day - Moins de 1 jour	177	88	89	2.8	2.7	2.8
1 - 6 days - 1 - 6 jours	132	67	65	2.1	2.0	2.1
7 - 27 days - 7 - 27 jours	94	47	47	1.5	1.4	1.5
7 - 13 days - 7 - 13 jours	47	25	22	0.7	♦0.8	♦0.7
14 - 20 days - 14 - 20 jours	33	18	15	0.5	♦0.6	♦0.5
21 - 27 days - 21 - 27 jours	14	4	10	♦0.2	♦0.1	♦0.3
28 days - 11 months - 28 jours - 11 mois	130	60	70	2.0	1.8	2.2
28 days - less than 2 months - 28 jours - moins de 2 mois	46	20	26	0.7	♦0.6	♦0.8
2 months - 2 mois	15	10	5	♦0.2	♦0.3	♦0.2
3 months - 3 mois	17	8	9	♦0.3	♦0.2	♦0.3
4 months - 4 mois	8	3	5	♦0.1	♦0.1	♦0.2
5 months - 5 mois	6	3	3	♦0.1	♦0.1	♦0.1
6 months - 6 mois	12	5	7	♦0.2	♦0.2	♦0.2
7 months - 7 mois	4	1	3	♦0.1	-	♦0.1
8 months - 8 mois	5	2	3	♦0.1	♦0.1	♦0.1
9 months - 9 mois	6	4	2	♦0.1	♦0.1	♦0.1
10 months - 10 mois	5	2	3	♦0.1	♦0.1	♦0.1
11 months - 11 mois	6	2	4	♦0.1	♦0.1	♦0.1
Cuba						
2018 (C)						
Total	461	264	197	4.0	4.4	3.5
Less than 1 day - Moins de 1 jour	52	29	23	0.4	♦0.5	♦0.4
1 - 6 days - 1 - 6 jours	119	74	45	1.0	1.2	0.8
7 - 27 days - 7 - 27 jours	92	51	41	0.8	0.8	0.7
7 - 13 days - 7 - 13 jours	44	25	19	0.4	♦0.4	♦0.3
14 - 20 days - 14 - 20 jours	28	12	16	♦0.2	♦0.2	♦0.3
21 - 27 days - 21 - 27 jours	20	14	6	♦0.2	♦0.2	♦0.1
28 days - 11 months - 28 jours - 11 mois	198	110	88	1.7	1.8	1.6
28 days - less than 2 months - 28 jours - moins de 2 mois	51	26	25	0.4	♦0.4	♦0.4
2 months - 2 mois	44	28	16	0.4	♦0.5	♦0.3
3 months - 3 mois	27	15	12	♦0.2	♦0.2	♦0.2
4 months - 4 mois	23	13	10	♦0.2	♦0.2	♦0.2
5 months - 5 mois	13	9	4	♦0.1	♦0.1	♦0.1
6 months - 6 mois	8	3	5	♦0.1	-	♦0.1
7 months - 7 mois	8	4	4	♦0.1	♦0.1	♦0.1
8 months - 8 mois	6	5	1	♦0.1	♦0.1	-
9 months - 9 mois	3	1	2	-	-	-

16. Infant deaths and infant mortality rates by age and sex: latest available year, 2010 - 2019
Décès d'enfants de moins d'un an et taux de mortalité infantile selon l'âge et le sexe : dernière année disponible, 2010 - 2019 (continued - suite)

Continent, country or area, year, code[a] and age Continent, pays ou zone, année, code[a] et âge	Number - Nombre			Rate - Taux		
	Both sexes Les deux sexes	Male Masculin	Female Féminin	Both sexes Les deux sexes	Male Masculin	Female Féminin
AMERICA, NORTH - AMÉRIQUE DU NORD						
Cuba						
2018 (C)						
10 months - 10 mois	7	3	4	♦0.1	-	♦0.1
11 months - 11 mois	8	3	5	♦0.1	-	♦0.1
Curaçao						
2016 (C)						
Total	20	11	9	...	...	...
Less than 1 day - Moins de 1 jour	7	3	4	...	...	...
1 - 6 days - 1 - 6 jours	3	1	2	...	...	...
7 - 27 days - 7 - 27 jours	7	5	2	...	...	...
7 - 13 days - 7 - 13 jours	6	4	2	...	...	...
14 - 20 days - 14 - 20 jours	1	1	-	...	...	...
21 - 27 days - 21 - 27 jours	-	-	-	...	...	...
28 days - 11 months - 28 jours - 11 mois	39	20	19	...	...	...
28 days - less than 2 months - 28 jours - moins de 2 mois	1	-	1	...	...	...
2 months - 2 mois	18	9	9	...	...	...
3 months - 3 mois	20	11	9	...	...	...
4 months - 4 mois	-	-	-	...	...	...
5 months - 5 mois	-	-	-	...	...	...
6 months - 6 mois	-	-	-	...	...	...
7 months - 7 mois	-	-	-	...	...	...
8 months - 8 mois	-	-	-	...	...	...
9 months - 9 mois	-	-	-	...	...	...
10 months - 10 mois	-	-	-	...	...	...
11 months - 11 mois	-	-	-	...	...	...
Dominican Republic - République dominicaine						
2019 (U)						
Total	*747*	*426*	*321*	...	...	...
Less than 1 day - Moins de 1 jour	*87*	*50*	*37*	...	...	...
1 - 6 days - 1 - 6 jours	*295*	*168*	*127*	...	...	...
7 - 27 days - 7 - 27 jours	*139*	*87*	*52*	...	...	...
7 - 13 days - 7 - 13 jours	*81*	*54*	*27*	...	...	...
14 - 20 days - 14 - 20 jours	*44*	*25*	*19*	...	...	...
21 - 27 days - 21 - 27 jours	*14*	*8*	*6*	...	...	...
28 days - 11 months - 28 jours - 11 mois	*226*	*121*	*105*	...	...	...
28 days - less than 2 months - 28 jours - moins de 2 mois	*56*	*31*	*25*	...	...	...
2 months - 2 mois	*40*	*20*	*20*	...	...	...
3 months - 3 mois	*27*	*16*	*11*	...	...	...
4 months - 4 mois	*16*	*8*	*8*	...	...	...
5 months - 5 mois	*16*	*10*	*6*	...	...	...
6 months - 6 mois	*11*	*5*	*6*	...	...	...
7 months - 7 mois	*17*	*8*	*9*	...	...	...
8 months - 8 mois	*15*	*8*	*7*	...	...	...
9 months - 9 mois	*11*	*6*	*5*	...	...	...
10 months - 10 mois	*9*	*3*	*6*	...	...	...
11 months - 11 mois	*8*	*6*	*2*	...	...	...
El Salvador[7]						
2014 (C)						
Total	876	491	385	8.0	8.8	7.3
Less than 1 day - Moins de 1 jour	158	90	68	1.5	1.6	1.3
1 - 6 days - 1 - 6 jours	163	91	72	1.5	1.6	1.4
7 - 27 days - 7 - 27 jours	141	78	63	1.3	1.4	1.2
7 - 13 days - 7 - 13 jours	65	32	33	0.6	0.6	0.6
14 - 20 days - 14 - 20 jours	42	24	18	0.4	♦0.4	♦0.3
21 - 27 days - 21 - 27 jours	34	22	12	0.3	♦0.4	♦0.2
28 days - 11 months - 28 jours - 11 mois	414	232	182	3.8	4.1	3.4
28 days - less than 2 months - 28 jours - moins de 2 mois	97	49	48	0.9	0.9	0.9
2 months - 2 mois	56	33	23	0.5	0.6	♦0.4
3 months - 3 mois	44	28	16	0.4	♦0.5	♦0.3
4 months - 4 mois	35	23	12	0.3	♦0.4	♦0.2
5 months - 5 mois	26	16	10	♦0.2	♦0.3	♦0.2
6 months - 6 mois	38	27	11	0.3	♦0.5	♦0.2
7 months - 7 mois	28	13	15	♦0.3	♦0.2	♦0.3
8 months - 8 mois	20	10	10	♦0.2	♦0.2	♦0.2
9 months - 9 mois	21	9	12	♦0.2	♦0.2	♦0.2
10 months - 10 mois	21	9	12	♦0.2	♦0.2	♦0.2
11 months - 11 mois	28	15	13	♦0.3	♦0.3	♦0.2

16. Infant deaths and infant mortality rates by age and sex: latest available year, 2010 - 2019
Décès d'enfants de moins d'un an et taux de mortalité infantile selon l'âge et le sexe : dernière année disponible, 2010 - 2019 (continued - suite)

Continent, country or area, year, code[a] and age Continent, pays ou zone, année, code[a] et âge	Number - Nombre			Rate - Taux		
	Both sexes Les deux sexes	Male Masculin	Female Féminin	Both sexes Les deux sexes	Male Masculin	Female Féminin
AMERICA, NORTH - AMÉRIQUE DU NORD						
Grenada - Grenade						
2014 (+C)						
Total	33	21	12	...	...	...
Less than 1 day - Moins de 1 jour	18	11	7	...	...	...
1 - 6 days - 1 - 6 jours	6	4	2	...	...	...
7 - 27 days - 7 - 27 jours	3	1	2	...	...	...
28 days - 11 months - 28 jours - 11 mois	6	5	1	...	...	...
28 days - 3 months - 28 jours - 3 mois	2	1	1	...	...	...
4 - 6 months - 4 - 6 mois	1	1	-	...	...	...
7 - 11 months - 7 - 11 mois	3	3	-	...	...	...
Guadeloupe[8]						
2018 (C)						
Total	32	...	...	...	...	...
Less than 1 day - Moins de 1 jour	3	...	...	...	...	...
1 - 6 days - 1 - 6 jours	16	...	...	...	...	...
7 - 27 days - 7 - 27 jours	7	...	...	...	...	...
28 days - less than 2 months - 28 jours - moins de 2 mois	6	...	...	...	...	...
Guatemala						
2018 (C)						
Total	7 564	4 285	3 279	19.7	22.0	17.4
Less than 1 day - Moins de 1 jour	634	343	291	1.7	1.8	1.5
1 - 6 days - 1 - 6 jours	1 841	1 050	791	4.8	5.4	4.2
7 - 27 days - 7 - 27 jours	1 474	850	624	3.8	4.4	3.3
7 - 13 days - 7 - 13 jours	727	434	293	1.9	2.2	1.6
14 - 27 days - 14 - 27 jours	747	416	331	1.9	2.1	1.8
28 days - 11 months - 28 jours - 11 mois	3 615	2 042	1 573	9.4	10.5	8.4
28 days - less than 2 months - 28 jours - moins de 2 mois	1 527	903	624	4.0	4.6	3.3
2 - 11 months - 2 - 11 mois	2 088	1 139	949	5.4	5.8	5.0
Mexico - Mexique[9]						
2018 (+C)						
Total	23 142	12 854[4]	10 208[4]	10.7	...	...
Less than 1 day - Moins de 1 jour	4 272	2 263[4]	1 951[4]	2.0	...	...
1 - 6 days - 1 - 6 jours	5 969	3 448[4]	2 505[4]	2.8	...	...
7 - 27 days - 7 - 27 jours	4 556	2 548[4]	2 003[4]	2.1	...	...
7 - 13 days - 7 - 13 jours	2 446	1 369[4]	1 075[4]	1.1	...	...
14 - 20 days - 14 - 20 jours	1 264	692[4]	571[4]	0.6	...	...
21 - 27 days - 21 - 27 jours	846	487[4]	357[4]	0.4	...	...
28 days - 11 months - 28 jours - 11 mois	8 344	4 594[4]	3 749[4]	3.9	...	...
28 days - less than 2 months - 28 jours - moins de 2 mois	2 476	1 409[4]	1 067[4]	1.1	...	...
2 months - 2 mois	1 458	813[4]	645[4]	0.7	...	...
3 months - 3 mois	967	519[4]	447[4]	0.4	...	...
4 months - 4 mois	759	414[4]	345[4]	0.4	...	...
5 months - 5 mois	597	326[4]	271[4]	0.3	...	...
6 months - 6 mois	486	266[4]	220[4]	0.2	...	...
7 months - 7 mois	399	222[4]	177[4]	0.2	...	...
8 months - 8 mois	364	177[4]	187[4]	0.2	...	...
9 months - 9 mois	299	148[4]	151[4]	0.1	...	...
10 months - 10 mois	279	155[4]	124[4]	0.1	...	...
11 months - 11 mois	260	145[4]	115[4]	0.1	...	...
Unknown - Inconnu	1	1[4]	-[4]	-	...	...
Montserrat						
2016 (C)						
Total	-	-	-	...	...	...
Less than 1 day - Moins de 1 jour	-	-	-	...	...	...
1 - 6 days - 1 - 6 jours	-	-	-	...	...	...
7 - 27 days - 7 - 27 jours	-	-	-	...	...	...
28 days - 11 months - 28 jours - 11 mois	-	-	-	...	...	...
Panama						
2018 (C)						
Total	1 092	591	501	14.2	14.9	13.5
Less than 1 day - Moins de 1 jour	150	83	67	2.0	2.1	1.8
1 - 6 days - 1 - 6 jours	283	152	131	3.7	3.8	3.5
7 - 27 days - 7 - 27 jours	228	129	99	3.0	3.3	2.7
7 - 13 days - 7 - 13 jours	107	63	44	1.4	1.6	1.2
14 - 20 days - 14 - 20 jours	52	28	24	0.7	♦0.7	♦0.6
21 - 27 days - 21 - 27 jours	69	38	31	0.9	1.0	0.8

16. Infant deaths and infant mortality rates by age and sex: latest available year, 2010 - 2019
Décès d'enfants de moins d'un an et taux de mortalité infantile selon l'âge et le sexe : dernière année disponible, 2010 - 2019 (continued - suite)

Continent, country or area, year, code[a] and age Continent, pays ou zone, année, code[a] et âge	Number - Nombre			Rate - Taux		
	Both sexes Les deux sexes	Male Masculin	Female Féminin	Both sexes Les deux sexes	Male Masculin	Female Féminin
AMERICA, NORTH - AMÉRIQUE DU NORD						
Panama						
2018 (C)						
28 days - 11 months - 28 jours - 11 mois	431	227	204	5.6	5.7	5.5
28 days - less than 2 months - 28 jours - moins de 2 mois	156	84	72	2.0	2.1	1.9
2 months - 2 mois	49	30	19	0.6	0.8	♦0.5
3 months - 3 mois	48	22	26	0.6	♦0.6	♦0.7
4 months - 4 mois	43	24	19	0.6	♦0.6	♦0.5
5 months - 5 mois	14	8	6	♦0.2	♦0.2	♦0.2
6 months - 6 mois	23	8	15	♦0.3	♦0.2	♦0.4
7 months - 7 mois	20	14	6	♦0.3	♦0.4	♦0.2
8 months - 8 mois	19	8	11	♦0.2	♦0.2	♦0.3
9 months - 9 mois	11	7	4	♦0.1	♦0.2	♦0.1
10 months - 10 mois	22	10	12	♦0.3	♦0.3	♦0.3
11 months - 11 mois	26	12	14	♦0.3	♦0.3	♦0.4
Puerto Rico - Porto Rico						
2019 (C)						
Total	135	72	63	6.6	6.9	6.3
Less than 1 day - Moins de 1 jour	20	8	12	♦1.0	♦0.8	♦1.2
1 - 6 days - 1 - 6 jours	39	18	21	1.9	♦1.7	♦2.1
7 - 27 days - 7 - 27 jours	20	11	9	♦1.0	♦1.1	♦0.9
7 - 13 days - 7 - 13 jours	8	3	5	♦0.4	♦0.3	♦0.5
14 - 20 days - 14 - 20 jours	9	6	3	♦0.4	♦0.6	♦0.3
21 - 27 days - 21 - 27 jours	3	2	1	♦0.1	♦0.2	♦0.1
28 days - 11 months - 28 jours - 11 mois	56	35	21	2.7	3.3	♦2.1
28 days - less than 2 months - 28 jours - moins de 2 mois	11	6	5	♦0.5	♦0.6	♦0.5
2 months - 2 mois	11	8	3	♦0.5	♦0.8	♦0.3
3 months - 3 mois	11	9	2	♦0.5	♦0.9	♦0.2
4 months - 4 mois	3	-	3	♦0.1	-	♦0.3
5 months - 5 mois	5	2	3	♦0.2	♦0.2	♦0.3
6 months - 6 mois	6	6	-	♦0.3	♦0.6	-
7 months - 7 mois	3	1	2	♦0.1	♦0.1	♦0.2
8 months - 8 mois	1	-	1	-	-	♦0.1
9 months - 9 mois	2	1	1	♦0.1	♦0.1	♦0.1
10 months - 10 mois	1	-	1	-	-	♦0.1
11 months - 11 mois	2	2	-	♦0.1	♦0.2	-
Saint Vincent and the Grenadines - Saint-Vincent-et-les Grenadines						
2017 (C)						
Total	17	8	9	...	...	...
Less than 1 day - Moins de 1 jour	3	2	1	...	...	...
1 - 6 days - 1 - 6 jours	5	2	3	...	...	...
7 - 27 days - 7 - 27 jours	3	1	2	...	...	...
28 days - 11 months - 28 jours - 11 mois	6	3	3	...	...	...
28 days - 6 months - 28 jours - 6 mois	3	2	1	...	...	...
7 - 11 months - 7 - 11 mois	3	1	2	...	...	...
Trinidad and Tobago - Trinité-et-Tobago						
2018* (C)						
Total	172	94[10]	75[10]	10.6	11.3	9.5
Less than 1 day - Moins de 1 jour	26	11	15	♦1.6	♦1.3	♦1.9
1 - 6 days - 1 - 6 jours	36	24	12	2.2	♦2.9	♦1.5
7 - 27 days - 7 - 27 jours	43	25[10]	16[10]	2.7	♦3.0	♦2.0
7 - 13 days - 7 - 13 jours	18	12	6	♦1.1	♦1.4	♦0.8
14 - 20 days - 14 - 20 jours	17	8[10]	8[10]	♦1.0	♦1.0	♦1.0
21 - 27 days - 21 - 27 jours	8	5[10]	2[10]	♦0.5	♦0.6	♦0.3
28 days - 11 months - 28 jours - 11 mois	67	34[10]	32[10]	4.1	4.1	4.0
28 days - less than 2 months - 28 jours - moins de 2 mois	38	19[10]	18[10]	2.3	♦2.3	♦2.3
2 months - 2 mois	12	8	4	♦0.7	♦1.0	♦0.5
3 - 5 months - 3 - 5 mois	6	2	4	♦0.4	♦0.2	♦0.5
6 - 8 months - 6 - 8 mois	8	3	5	♦0.5	♦0.4	♦0.6
9 - 11 months - 9 - 11 mois	3	2	1	♦0.2	♦0.2	♦0.1
United States of America - États-Unis d'Amérique						
2017 (C)						
Total	22 341	...	...	5.8	...	...
Less than 7 days - Moins de 7 jours	11 971	...	...	3.1	...	...
7 - 27 days - 7 - 27 jours	2 873	...	...	0.7	...	...
28 days - 11 months - 28 jours - 11 mois	7 497	...	...	1.9	...	...

16. Infant deaths and infant mortality rates by age and sex: latest available year, 2010 - 2019
Décès d'enfants de moins d'un an et taux de mortalité infantile selon l'âge et le sexe : dernière année disponible, 2010 - 2019 (continued - suite)

Continent, country or area, year, code[a] and age Continent, pays ou zone, année, code[a] et âge	Number - Nombre			Rate - Taux		
	Both sexes Les deux sexes	Male Masculin	Female Féminin	Both sexes Les deux sexes	Male Masculin	Female Féminin
AMERICA, SOUTH - AMÉRIQUE DU SUD						
Argentina - Argentine						
2018 (C)						
Total	6 048	3 471[10]	2 564[10]	8.8	10.0	7.7
Less than 1 day - Moins de 1 jour	1 309	735[10]	566[10]	1.9	2.1	1.7
1 - 6 days - 1 - 6 jours	1 631	962[10]	665[10]	2.4	2.8	2.0
7 - 27 days - 7 - 27 jours	1 181	694[10]	486[10]	1.7	2.0	1.5
7 - 13 days - 7 - 13 jours	638	387	251	0.9	1.1	0.8
14 - 20 days - 14 - 20 jours	315	186	129	0.5	0.5	0.4
21 - 27 days - 21 - 27 jours	228	121[10]	106[10]	0.3	0.3	0.3
28 days - 11 months - 28 jours - 11 mois	1 927	1 080	847	2.8	3.1	2.6
28 days - less than 2 months - 28 jours - moins de 2 mois	612	343	269	0.9	1.0	0.8
2 months - 2 mois	346	222	124	0.5	0.6	0.4
3 months - 3 mois	237	129	108	0.3	0.4	0.3
4 months - 4 mois	157	83	74	0.2	0.2	0.2
5 months - 5 mois	122	72	50	0.2	0.2	0.2
6 months - 6 mois	100	52	48	0.1	0.1	0.1
7 months - 7 mois	85	45	40	0.1	0.1	0.1
8 months - 8 mois	86	41	45	0.1	0.1	0.1
9 months - 9 mois	59	29	30	0.1	♦0.1	0.1
10 months - 10 mois	66	32	34	0.1	0.1	0.1
11 months - 11 mois	57	32	25	0.1	0.1	♦0.1
Brazil - Brésil						
2017 (+C)						
Total	30 636[11]	16 597[4]	13 682[4]	10.3	10.9	9.5
Less than 1 day - Moins de 1 jour	6 678[11]	3 609[4]	2 948[4]	2.3	2.4	2.0
1 - 6 days - 1 - 6 jours	9 168[11]	5 105[4]	3 982[4]	3.1	3.4	2.8
7 - 27 days - 7 - 27 jours	5 359[11]	2 875[4]	2 453[4]	1.8	1.9	1.7
7 - 13 days - 7 - 13 jours	2 847[11]	1 499[4]	1 332[4]	1.0	1.0	0.9
14 - 20 days - 14 - 20 jours	1 518[11]	826[4]	684[4]	0.5	0.5	0.5
21 - 27 days - 21 - 27 jours	994[11]	550[4]	437[4]	0.3	0.4	0.3
28 days - 11 months - 28 jours - 11 mois	9 431[11]	5 008[4]	4 299[4]	3.2	3.3	3.0
28 days - less than 2 months - 28 jours - moins de 2 mois	3 045[11]	1 648[4]	1 372[4]	1.0	1.1	1.0
2 months - 2 mois	1 520[11]	852[4]	655[4]	0.5	0.6	0.5
3 months - 3 mois	1 053[11]	542[4]	498[4]	0.4	0.4	0.3
4 months - 4 mois	799[11]	422[4]	363[4]	0.3	0.3	0.3
5 months - 5 mois	661[11]	342[4]	305[4]	0.2	0.2	0.2
6 months - 6 mois	548[11]	271[4]	268[4]	0.2	0.2	0.2
7 months - 7 mois	451[11]	243[4]	202[4]	0.2	0.2	0.1
8 months - 8 mois	388[11]	208[4]	174[4]	0.1	0.1	0.1
9 months - 9 mois	388[11]	189[4]	191[4]	0.1	0.1	0.1
10 months - 10 mois	316[11]	161[4]	143[4]	0.1	0.1	0.1
11 months - 11 mois	262[11]	130[4]	128[4]	0.1	0.1	0.1
Chile - Chili						
2017 (C)						
Total	1 557	830[10]	705[10]	7.1	7.4	6.6
Less than 1 day - Moins de 1 jour	641	328[10]	295[10]	2.9	2.9	2.7
1 - 6 days - 1 - 6 jours	315	170[10]	142[10]	1.4	1.5	1.3
7 - 27 days - 7 - 27 jours	246	142[10]	103[10]	1.1	1.3	1.0
7 - 13 days - 7 - 13 jours	128	71[10]	56[10]	0.6	0.6	0.5
14 - 20 days - 14 - 20 jours	74	45[10]	29[10]	0.3	0.4	♦0.3
21 - 27 days - 21 - 27 jours	44	26[10]	18[10]	0.2	♦0.2	♦0.2
28 days - 11 months - 28 jours - 11 mois	355	190[10]	165[10]	1.6	1.7	1.5
28 days - less than 2 months - 28 jours - moins de 2 mois	113	59[10]	54[10]	0.5	0.5	0.5
2 months - 2 mois	55	29[10]	26[10]	0.3	♦0.3	♦0.2
3 months - 3 mois	43	29[10]	14[10]	0.2	♦0.3	♦0.1
4 months - 4 mois	35	20[10]	15[10]	0.2	♦0.2	♦0.1
5 months - 5 mois	21	11[10]	10[10]	♦0.1	♦0.1	♦0.1
6 months - 6 mois	15	8[10]	7[10]	♦0.1	♦0.1	♦0.1
7 months - 7 mois	18	8[10]	10[10]	♦0.1	♦0.1	♦0.1
8 months - 8 mois	16	7[10]	9[10]	♦0.1	♦0.1	♦0.1
9 months - 9 mois	17	8[10]	9[10]	♦0.1	♦0.1	♦0.1
10 months - 10 mois	17	9[10]	8[10]	♦0.1	♦0.1	♦0.1
11 months - 11 mois	5	2[10]	3[10]	-	-	-

16. Infant deaths and infant mortality rates by age and sex: latest available year, 2010 - 2019
Décès d'enfants de moins d'un an et taux de mortalité infantile selon l'âge et le sexe : dernière année disponible, 2010 - 2019 (continued - suite)

Continent, country or area, year, code[a] and age Continent, pays ou zone, année, code[a] et âge	Number - Nombre			Rate - Taux		
	Both sexes Les deux sexes	Male Masculin	Female Féminin	Both sexes Les deux sexes	Male Masculin	Female Féminin
AMERICA, SOUTH - AMÉRIQUE DU SUD						
Colombia - Colombie						
2019* (U)						
Total	7 166	4 080[10]	3 084[10]	...	...	...
Less than 1 day - Moins de 1 jour	1 249	719[10]	530[10]	...	...	...
1 - 6 days - 1 - 6 jours	1 720	1 024[10]	696[10]	...	...	...
7 - 27 days - 7 - 27 jours	1 401	770[10]	630[10]	...	...	...
7 - 13 days - 7 - 13 jours	755	419[10]	336[10]	...	...	...
14 - 20 days - 14 - 20 jours	379	209[10]	169[10]	...	...	...
21 - 27 days - 21 - 27 jours	267	142[10]	125[10]	...	...	...
28 days - 11 months - 28 jours - 11 mois	2 796	1 567[10]	1 228[10]	...	...	...
28 days - less than 2 months - 28 jours - moins de 2 mois	658	355[10]	303[10]	...	...	...
2 months - 2 mois	447	264[10]	183[10]	...	...	...
3 months - 3 mois	309	178[10]	130[10]	...	...	...
4 months - 4 mois	267	156[10]	111[10]	...	...	...
5 months - 5 mois	198	112[10]	86[10]	...	...	...
6 months - 6 mois	201	113[10]	88[10]	...	...	...
7 months - 7 mois	158	87[10]	71[10]	...	...	...
8 months - 8 mois	171	80[10]	91[10]	...	...	...
9 months - 9 mois	150	86[10]	64[10]	...	...	...
10 months - 10 mois	118	70[10]	48[10]	...	...	...
11 months - 11 mois	119	66[10]	53[10]	...	...	...
Ecuador - Équateur[12]						
2018* (U)						
Total	3 350	1 852	1 498	...	...	...
Less than 1 day - Moins de 1 jour	402	234	168	...	...	...
1 - 6 days - 1 - 6 jours	917	548	369	...	...	...
7 - 27 days - 7 - 27 jours	671	347	324	...	...	...
7 - 13 days - 7 - 13 jours	357	173	184	...	...	...
14 - 20 days - 14 - 20 jours	193	106	87	...	...	...
21 - 27 days - 21 - 27 jours	121	68	53	...	...	...
28 days - 11 months - 28 jours - 11 mois	1 360	723	637	...	...	...
28 days - less than 2 months - 28 jours - moins de 2 mois	513	272	241	...	...	...
2 months - 2 mois	226	122	104	...	...	...
3 months - 3 mois	130	61	69	...	...	...
4 months - 4 mois	106	58	48	...	...	...
5 months - 5 mois	94	50	44	...	...	...
6 months - 6 mois	62	37	25	...	...	...
7 months - 7 mois	61	34	27	...	...	...
8 months - 8 mois	45	23	22	...	...	...
9 months - 9 mois	60	35	25	...	...	...
10 months - 10 mois	32	20	12	...	...	...
11 months - 11 mois	31	11	20	...	...	...
Peru - Pérou[13]						
2019* (+U)						
Total	4 758	2 604	2 154	...	...	...
Less than 1 day - Moins de 1 jour	948	530	418	...	...	...
1 - 6 days - 1 - 6 jours	1 058	591	467	...	...	...
7 - 27 days - 7 - 27 jours	860	473	387	...	...	...
7 - 13 days - 7 - 13 jours	432	229	203	...	...	...
14 - 20 days - 14 - 20 jours	225	124	101	...	...	...
21 - 27 days - 21 - 27 jours	203	120	83	...	...	...
28 days - 11 months - 28 jours - 11 mois	1 878	1 002	876	...	...	...
28 days - less than 2 months - 28 jours - moins de 2 mois	604	322	282	...	...	...
2 months - 2 mois	350	200	150	...	...	...
3 months - 3 mois	192	82	110	...	...	...
4 months - 4 mois	176	91	85	...	...	...
5 months - 5 mois	121	75	46	...	...	...
6 months - 6 mois	94	49	45	...	...	...
7 months - 7 mois	88	38	50	...	...	...
8 months - 8 mois	81	47	34	...	...	...
9 months - 9 mois	58	30	28	...	...	...
10 months - 10 mois	62	39	23	...	...	...
11 months - 11 mois	52	29	23	...	...	...
Unknown - Inconnu	14	8	6	...	...	...

16. Infant deaths and infant mortality rates by age and sex: latest available year, 2010 - 2019
Décès d'enfants de moins d'un an et taux de mortalité infantile selon l'âge et le sexe : dernière année disponible, 2010 - 2019 (continued - suite)

Continent, country or area, year, code[a] and age Continent, pays ou zone, année, code[a] et âge	Number - Nombre			Rate - Taux		
	Both sexes Les deux sexes	Male Masculin	Female Féminin	Both sexes Les deux sexes	Male Masculin	Female Féminin
AMERICA, SOUTH - AMÉRIQUE DU SUD						
Uruguay						
2018 (C)						
Total	273	156[4]	116[4]	6.8	7.5	6.0
Less than 1 day - Moins de 1 jour	46	32[4]	14[4]	1.1	1.5	♦0.7
1 - 6 days - 1 - 6 jours	86	51[4]	34[4]	2.1	2.5	1.7
7 - 27 days - 7 - 27 jours	54	30[4]	24[4]	1.3	1.5	♦1.2
7 - 13 days - 7 - 13 jours	33	21[4]	12[4]	0.8	♦1.0	♦0.6
14 - 20 days - 14 - 20 jours	14	6[4]	8[4]	♦0.3	♦0.3	♦0.4
21 - 27 days - 21 - 27 jours	7	3[4]	4[4]	♦0.2	♦0.1	♦0.2
28 days - 11 months - 28 jours - 11 mois	87	43[4]	44[4]	2.2	2.1	2.3
28 days - less than 2 months - 28 jours - moins de 2 mois	25	14[4]	11[4]	♦0.6	♦0.7	♦0.6
2 months - 2 mois	15	5[4]	10[4]	♦0.4	♦0.2	♦0.5
3 months - 3 mois	5	4[4]	1[4]	♦0.1	♦0.2	♦0.1
4 months - 4 mois	9	2[4]	7[4]	♦0.2	♦0.1	♦0.4
5 months - 5 mois	9	3[4]	6[4]	♦0.2	♦0.1	♦0.3
6 months - 6 mois	5	5[4]	-[4]	♦0.1	♦0.2	-
7 months - 7 mois	4	2[4]	2[4]	♦0.1	♦0.1	♦0.1
8 months - 8 mois	4	2[4]	2[4]	♦0.1	♦0.1	♦0.1
9 months - 9 mois	4	4[4]	-[4]	♦0.1	♦0.2	-
10 months - 10 mois	4	1[4]	3[4]	♦0.1	-	♦0.2
11 months - 11 mois	3	1[4]	2[4]	♦0.1	-	♦0.1
Venezuela (Bolivarian Republic of) - Venezuela (République bolivarienne du)						
2017 (C)						
Total	11 671	6 626	5 045	...	...	...
ASIA - ASIE						
Armenia - Arménie[14]						
2018 (C)						
Total	261	143	118	7.1	7.4	6.8
Less than 1 day - Moins de 1 jour	35	21	14	1.0	♦1.1	♦0.8
1 - 6 days - 1 - 6 jours	88	53	35	2.4	2.8	2.0
7 - 27 days - 7 - 27 jours	59	27	32	1.6	♦1.4	1.8
7 - 13 days - 7 - 13 jours	37	19	18	1.0	♦1.0	♦1.0
14 - 20 days - 14 - 20 jours	12	4	8	♦0.3	♦0.2	♦0.5
21 - 27 days - 21 - 27 jours	10	4	6	♦0.3	♦0.2	♦0.3
28 days - 11 months - 28 jours - 11 mois	79	42	37	2.2	2.2	2.1
28 days - less than 2 months - 28 jours - moins de 2 mois	24	14	10	♦0.7	♦0.7	♦0.6
2 months - 2 mois	10	4	6	♦0.3	♦0.2	♦0.3
3 months - 3 mois	6	5	1	♦0.2	♦0.3	♦0.1
4 months - 4 mois	11	5	6	♦0.3	♦0.3	♦0.3
5 months - 5 mois	10	4	6	♦0.3	♦0.2	♦0.3
6 months - 6 mois	3	3	-	♦0.1	♦0.2	-
7 months - 7 mois	3	2	1	♦0.1	♦0.1	♦0.1
8 months - 8 mois	4	3	1	♦0.1	♦0.2	♦0.1
9 months - 9 mois	3	-	3	♦0.1	-	♦0.2
10 months - 10 mois	2	1	1	♦0.1	♦0.1	♦0.1
11 months - 11 mois	3	1	2	♦0.1	♦0.1	♦0.1
Azerbaijan - Azerbaïdjan[14]						
2018 (+C)						
Total	1 547	892	655	11.1	12.0	10.1
Less than 1 day - Moins de 1 jour	222	132	90	1.6	1.8	1.4
1 - 6 days - 1 - 6 jours	506	286	220	3.6	3.9	3.4
7 - 27 days - 7 - 27 jours	169	88	81	1.2	1.2	1.3
7 - 13 days - 7 - 13 jours	102	51	51	0.7	0.7	0.8
14 - 20 days - 14 - 20 jours	37	19	18	0.3	♦0.3	♦0.3
21 - 27 days - 21 - 27 jours	30	18	12	0.2	♦0.2	♦0.2
28 days - 11 months - 28 jours - 11 mois	650	386	264	4.7	5.2	4.1
28 days - less than 2 months - 28 jours - moins de 2 mois	110	76	34	0.8	1.0	0.5
2 months - 2 mois	78	37	41	0.6	0.5	0.6
3 months - 3 mois	68	44	24	0.5	0.6	♦0.4
4 months - 4 mois	61	37	24	0.4	0.5	♦0.4
5 months - 5 mois	54	37	17	0.4	0.5	♦0.3
6 months - 6 mois	75	41	34	0.5	0.6	0.5

16. Infant deaths and infant mortality rates by age and sex: latest available year, 2010 - 2019
Décès d'enfants de moins d'un an et taux de mortalité infantile selon l'âge et le sexe : dernière année disponible, 2010 - 2019 (continued - suite)

Continent, country or area, year, code[a] and age Continent, pays ou zone, année, code[a] et âge	Number - Nombre			Rate - Taux		
	Both sexes Les deux sexes	Male Masculin	Female Féminin	Both sexes Les deux sexes	Male Masculin	Female Féminin
ASIA - ASIE						
Azerbaijan - Azerbaïdjan[14]						
2018 (+C)						
7 months - 7 mois	58	39	19	0.4	0.5	♦0.3
8 months - 8 mois	43	19	24	0.3	♦0.3	♦0.4
9 months - 9 mois	37	7	30	0.3	♦0.1	0.5
10 months - 10 mois	49	34	15	0.4	0.5	♦0.2
11 months - 11 mois	17	15	2	♦0.1	♦0.2	-
Bahrain - Bahreïn[15]						
2018 (C)						
Total	129	67	62	6.5	6.6	6.5
Less than 1 day - Moins de 1 jour	8	5	3	♦0.4	♦0.5	♦0.3
1 - 6 days - 1 - 6 jours	31	17	14	1.6	♦1.7	♦1.5
7 - 27 days - 7 - 27 jours	36	18	18	1.8	♦1.8	♦1.9
7 - 13 days - 7 - 13 jours	20	7	13	♦1.0	♦0.7	♦1.4
14 - 20 days - 14 - 20 jours	9	5	4	♦0.5	♦0.5	♦0.4
21 - 27 days - 21 - 27 jours	7	6	1	♦0.4	♦0.6	♦0.1
28 days - 11 months - 28 jours - 11 mois	54	27	27	2.7	♦2.6	♦2.8
28 days - less than 2 months - 28 jours - moins de 2 mois	18	12	6	♦0.9	♦1.2	♦0.6
2 months - 2 mois	10	2	8	♦0.5	♦0.2	♦0.8
3 months - 3 mois	5	1	4	♦0.3	♦0.1	♦0.4
4 months - 4 mois	5	3	2	♦0.3	♦0.3	♦0.2
5 months - 5 mois	5	4	1	♦0.3	♦0.4	♦0.1
6 months - 6 mois	2	1	1	♦0.1	♦0.1	♦0.1
7 months - 7 mois	1	-	1	♦0.1	-	♦0.1
8 months - 8 mois	3	-	3	♦0.2	-	♦0.3
9 months - 9 mois	1	1	-	♦0.1	♦0.1	-
10 months - 10 mois	1	1	-	♦0.1	♦0.1	-
11 months - 11 mois	3	2	1	♦0.2	♦0.2	♦0.1
Bangladesh						
2010 (U)						
Total	*104 591*	*55 178*	*49 413*	...	...	...
1 - 6 days - 1 - 6 jours	*56 108*	*30 276*	*25 832*	...	...	...
7 - 27 days - 7 - 27 jours	*17 576*	*9 234*	*8 342*	...	...	...
7 - 13 days - 7 - 13 jours	*8 488*	*4 491*	*3 997*	...	...	...
14 - 20 days - 14 - 20 jours	*4 845*	*2 546*	*2 299*	...	...	...
21 - 27 days - 21 - 27 jours	*4 243*	*2 197*	*2 046*	...	...	...
28 days - 11 months - 28 jours - 11 mois	*30 907*	*15 668*	*15 239*	...	...	...
28 days - less than 2 months - 28 jours - moins de 2 mois	*7 377*	*3 906*	*3 471*	...	...	...
2 months - 2 mois	*5 234*	*2 674*	*2 560*	...	...	...
3 months - 3 mois	*4 381*	*2 248*	*2 133*	...	...	...
4 months - 4 mois	*2 628*	*1 333*	*1 295*	...	...	...
5 months - 5 mois	*1 188*	*606*	*582*	...	...	...
6 months - 6 mois	*2 123*	*1 050*	*1 073*	...	...	...
7 months - 7 mois	*1 361*	*669*	*692*	...	...	...
8 months - 8 mois	*1 905*	*918*	*987*	...	...	...
9 months - 9 mois	*1 420*	*696*	*724*	...	...	...
10 months - 10 mois	*1 188*	*566*	*622*	...	...	...
11 months - 11 mois	*2 102*	*1 002*	*1 100*	...	...	...
China, Hong Kong SAR - Chine, Hong Kong RAS						
2019 (C)						
Total	78	44[4]	33[4]	...	...	...
Less than 1 day - Moins de 1 jour	7	2	5	...	...	...
1 - 6 days - 1 - 6 jours	27	15	12	...	...	...
7 - 27 days - 7 - 27 jours	14	9	5	...	...	...
7 - 13 days - 7 - 13 jours	5	3	2	...	...	...
14 - 20 days - 14 - 20 jours	6	3	3	...	...	...
21 - 27 days - 21 - 27 jours	3	3	-	...	...	...
28 days - 11 months - 28 jours - 11 mois	27	16	11	...	...	...
28 days - less than 2 months - 28 jours - moins de 2 mois	6	4	2	...	...	...
2 months - 2 mois	1	1	-	...	...	...
3 months - 3 mois	3	2	1	...	...	...
4 months - 4 mois	2	-	2	...	...	...
5 months - 5 mois	3	1	2	...	...	...
6 months - 6 mois	3	2	1	...	...	...
7 months - 7 mois	3	3	-	...	...	...
8 months - 8 mois	4	2	2	...	...	...
9 months - 9 mois	-	-	-	...	...	...
10 months - 10 mois	1	1	-	...	...	...

16. Infant deaths and infant mortality rates by age and sex: latest available year, 2010 - 2019
Décès d'enfants de moins d'un an et taux de mortalité infantile selon l'âge et le sexe : dernière année disponible, 2010 - 2019 (continued - suite)

Continent, country or area, year, code[a] and age Continent, pays ou zone, année, code[a] et âge	Number - Nombre			Rate - Taux		
	Both sexes Les deux sexes	Male Masculin	Female Féminin	Both sexes Les deux sexes	Male Masculin	Female Féminin
ASIA - ASIE						
China, Hong Kong SAR - Chine, Hong Kong RAS						
2019 (C)						
11 months - 11 mois	1	-	1	...	...	...
Unknown - Inconnu	3	2[4]	-[4]	...	...	...
China, Macao SAR - Chine, Macao RAS						
2010 (C)						
Total	15	7	8	...	...	...
Less than 1 day - Moins de 1 jour	7	3	4	...	...	...
1 - 6 days - 1 - 6 jours	4	2	2	...	...	...
7 - 27 days - 7 - 27 jours	2	1	1	...	...	...
7 - 13 days - 7 - 13 jours	-	-	-	...	...	...
14 - 20 days - 14 - 20 jours	1	-	1	...	...	...
21 - 27 days - 21 - 27 jours	1	1	-	...	...	...
28 days - 11 months - 28 jours - 11 mois	2	1	1	...	...	...
28 days - less than 2 months - 28 jours - moins de 2 mois	1	-	1	...	...	...
2 months - 2 mois	-	-	-	...	...	...
3 months - 3 mois	-	-	-	...	...	...
4 months - 4 mois	1	1	-	...	...	...
5 months - 5 mois	-	-	-	...	...	...
6 months - 6 mois	-	-	-	...	...	...
7 months - 7 mois	-	-	-	...	...	...
8 months - 8 mois	-	-	-	...	...	...
9 months - 9 mois	-	-	-	...	...	...
10 months - 10 mois	-	-	-	...	...	...
11 months - 11 mois	-	-	-	...	...	...
Cyprus - Chypre[16]						
2011 (C)						
Total	30	18	12	...	...	...
Less than 1 day - Moins de 1 jour	10	6	4	...	...	...
1 - 6 days - 1 - 6 jours	8	4	4	...	...	...
7 - 27 days - 7 - 27 jours	3	2	1	...	...	...
28 days - 11 months - 28 jours - 11 mois	9	6	3	...	...	...
Georgia - Géorgie[14]						
2018 (C)						
Total	416	246	170	8.1	9.3	6.9
Less than 1 day - Moins de 1 jour	65	40	25	1.3	1.5	♦1.0
1 - 6 days - 1 - 6 jours	101	63	38	2.0	2.4	1.5
7 - 27 days - 7 - 27 jours	88	49	39	1.7	1.8	1.6
28 days - 11 months - 28 jours - 11 mois	162	94	68	3.2	3.5	2.8
Israel - Israël[17]						
2019 (C)						
Total	534	316[4]	216[4]	2.9	...	...
Less than 1 day - Moins de 1 jour	113	60[4]	52[4]	0.6	...	...
1 - 6 days - 1 - 6 jours	141	96[4]	44[4]	0.8	...	...
7 - 27 days - 7 - 27 jours	101	61[4]	40[4]	0.6	...	...
7 - 13 days - 7 - 13 jours	50	32[4]	18[4]	0.3	...	...
14 - 20 days - 14 - 20 jours	31	18[4]	13[4]	0.2	...	...
21 - 27 days - 21 - 27 jours	20	11[4]	9[4]	♦0.1	...	...
28 days - 11 months - 28 jours - 11 mois	179	99[4]	80[4]	1.0	...	...
28 days - less than 2 months - 28 jours - moins de 2 mois	49	29[4]	20[4]	0.3	...	...
2 months - 2 mois	26	9[4]	17[4]	♦0.1	...	...
3 months - 3 mois	23	12[4]	11[4]	♦0.1	...	...
4 months - 4 mois	18	10[4]	8[4]	♦0.1	...	...
5 months - 5 mois	16	12[4]	4[4]	♦0.1	...	...
6 months - 6 mois	7	4[4]	3[4]	-	...	...
7 months - 7 mois	5	3[4]	2[4]	-	...	...
8 months - 8 mois	7	4[4]	3[4]	-	...	...
9 months - 9 mois	11	8[4]	3[4]	♦0.1	...	...
10 months - 10 mois	13	5[4]	8[4]	♦0.1	...	...
11 months - 11 mois	4	3[4]	1[4]	-	...	...
Japan - Japon[18]						
2018 (C)						
Total	1 748	932	816	1.9	2.0	1.8
Less than 1 day - Moins de 1 jour	424	221	203	0.5	0.5	0.5
1 - 6 days - 1 - 6 jours	190	103	87	0.2	0.2	0.2

16. Infant deaths and infant mortality rates by age and sex: latest available year, 2010 - 2019
Décès d'enfants de moins d'un an et taux de mortalité infantile selon l'âge et le sexe : dernière année disponible, 2010 - 2019 (continued - suite)

Continent, country or area, year, code[a] and age Continent, pays ou zone, année, code[a] et âge	Number - Nombre			Rate - Taux		
	Both sexes Les deux sexes	Male Masculin	Female Féminin	Both sexes Les deux sexes	Male Masculin	Female Féminin
ASIA - ASIE						
Japan - Japon[18]						
2018 (C)						
7 - 27 days - 7 - 27 jours	187	103	84	0.2	0.2	0.2
7 - 13 days - 7 - 13 jours	63	34	29	0.1	0.1	♦0.1
14 - 20 days - 14 - 20 jours	62	31	31	0.1	0.1	0.1
21 - 27 days - 21 - 27 jours	62	38	24	0.1	0.1	♦0.1
28 days - 11 months - 28 jours - 11 mois	947	505	442	1.0	1.1	1.0
28 days - less than 2 months - 28 jours - moins de 2 mois	198	105	93	0.2	0.2	0.2
2 months - 2 mois	161	79	82	0.2	0.2	0.2
3 months - 3 mois	102	53	49	0.1	0.1	0.1
4 months - 4 mois	112	68	44	0.1	0.1	0.1
5 months - 5 mois	79	49	30	0.1	0.1	0.1
6 months - 6 mois	75	43	32	0.1	0.1	0.1
7 months - 7 mois	62	29	33	0.1	♦0.1	0.1
8 months - 8 mois	48	20	28	0.1	-	♦0.1
9 months - 9 mois	42	22	20	-	-	-
10 months - 10 mois	36	20	16	-	-	-
11 months - 11 mois	32	17	15	-	-	-
Kazakhstan						
2019 (C)						
Total	3 360	1 944	1 416	8.4	9.3	7.3
Less than 1 day - Moins de 1 jour	193	112	81	0.5	0.5	0.4
1 - 6 days - 1 - 6 jours	978	590	388	2.4	2.8	2.0
7 - 27 days - 7 - 27 jours	763	449	314	1.9	2.2	1.6
7 - 13 days - 7 - 13 jours	378	234	144	0.9	1.1	0.7
14 - 20 days - 14 - 20 jours	228	127	101	0.6	0.6	0.5
21 - 27 days - 21 - 27 jours	157	88	69	0.4	0.4	0.4
28 days - 11 months - 28 jours - 11 mois	1 426	793	633	3.5	3.8	3.3
28 days - less than 2 months - 28 jours - moins de 2 mois	452	279	173	1.1	1.3	0.9
2 months - 2 mois	215	114	101	0.5	0.5	0.5
3 months - 3 mois	141	71	70	0.4	0.3	0.4
4 months - 4 mois	129	65	64	0.3	0.3	0.3
5 months - 5 mois	99	57	42	0.2	0.3	0.2
6 months - 6 mois	81	41	40	0.2	0.2	0.2
7 months - 7 mois	86	40	46	0.2	0.2	0.2
8 months - 8 mois	57	32	25	0.1	0.2	♦0.1
9 months - 9 mois	58	28	30	0.1	♦0.1	0.2
10 months - 10 mois	65	40	25	0.2	0.2	♦0.1
11 months - 11 mois	43	26	17	0.1	♦0.1	♦0.1
Kuwait - Koweït						
2018 (C)						
Total	417	229	188	7.4	7.9	6.9
Less than 1 day - Moins de 1 jour	99	54	45	1.8	1.9	1.7
1 - 6 days - 1 - 6 jours	91	55	36	1.6	1.9	1.3
7 - 27 days - 7 - 27 jours	92	45	47	1.6	1.6	1.7
7 - 13 days - 7 - 13 jours	48	18	30	0.9	♦0.6	1.1
14 - 20 days - 14 - 20 jours	24	12	12	♦0.4	♦0.4	♦0.4
21 - 27 days - 21 - 27 jours	20	15	5	♦0.4	♦0.5	♦0.2
28 days - 11 months - 28 jours - 11 mois	135	75	60	2.4	2.6	2.2
28 days - less than 2 months - 28 jours - moins de 2 mois	43	23	20	0.8	♦0.8	♦0.7
2 months - 2 mois	25	16	9	♦0.4	♦0.6	♦0.3
3 months - 3 mois	13	9	4	♦0.2	♦0.3	♦0.1
4 months - 4 mois	18	8	10	♦0.3	♦0.3	♦0.4
5 months - 5 mois	10	6	4	♦0.2	♦0.2	♦0.1
6 months - 6 mois	7	3	4	♦0.1	♦0.1	♦0.1
7 months - 7 mois	4	1	3	♦0.1	-	♦0.1
8 months - 8 mois	6	3	3	♦0.1	♦0.1	♦0.1
9 months - 9 mois	1	-	1	-	-	-
10 months - 10 mois	2	2	-	-	♦0.1	-
11 months - 11 mois	6	4	2	♦0.1	♦0.1	♦0.1
Kyrgyzstan - Kirghizstan						
2018 (C)						
Total	2 535	1 442	1 093	14.8	16.4	13.1
Less than 1 day - Moins de 1 jour	569	333	236	3.3	3.8	2.8
1 - 6 days - 1 - 6 jours	1 154	637	517	6.7	7.2	6.2
7 - 27 days - 7 - 27 jours	329	192	137	1.9	2.2	1.6
7 - 13 days - 7 - 13 jours	214	123	91	1.3	1.4	1.1
14 - 20 days - 14 - 20 jours	75	49	26	0.4	0.6	♦0.3

16. Infant deaths and infant mortality rates by age and sex: latest available year, 2010 - 2019
Décès d'enfants de moins d'un an et taux de mortalité infantile selon l'âge et le sexe : dernière année disponible, 2010 - 2019 (continued - suite)

Continent, country or area, year, code[a] and age / Continent, pays ou zone, année, code[a] et âge	Number - Nombre			Rate - Taux		
	Both sexes Les deux sexes	Male Masculin	Female Féminin	Both sexes Les deux sexes	Male Masculin	Female Féminin
ASIA - ASIE						
Kyrgyzstan - Kirghizstan						
2018 (C)						
21 - 27 days - 21 - 27 jours	40	20	20	0.2	♦0.2	♦0.2
28 days - 11 months - 28 jours - 11 mois	483	280	203	2.8	3.2	2.4
28 days - less than 2 months - 28 jours - moins de 2 mois	110	70	40	0.6	0.8	0.5
2 months - 2 mois	63	36	27	0.4	0.4	♦0.3
3 months - 3 mois	61	29	32	0.4	♦0.3	0.4
4 months - 4 mois	48	24	24	0.3	♦0.3	♦0.3
5 months - 5 mois	32	18	14	0.2	♦0.2	♦0.2
6 months - 6 mois	33	19	14	0.2	♦0.2	♦0.2
7 months - 7 mois	29	20	9	♦0.2	♦0.2	♦0.1
8 months - 8 mois	25	15	10	♦0.1	♦0.2	♦0.1
9 months - 9 mois	34	16	18	0.2	♦0.2	♦0.2
10 months - 10 mois	25	18	7	♦0.1	♦0.2	♦0.1
11 months - 11 mois	23	15	8	♦0.1	♦0.2	♦0.1
Maldives[19]						
2017 (C)						
Total	64	42	22	...	...	...
Less than 1 day - Moins de 1 jour	17	13	4	...	...	...
1 - 6 days - 1 - 6 jours	28	16	12	...	...	...
7 - 27 days - 7 - 27 jours	6	3	3	...	...	...
7 - 13 days - 7 - 13 jours	3	1	2	...	...	...
14 - 20 days - 14 - 20 jours	3	2	1	...	...	...
21 - 27 days - 21 - 27 jours	-	-	-	...	...	...
28 days - 11 months - 28 jours - 11 mois	13	10	3	...	...	...
28 days - less than 2 months - 28 jours - moins de 2 mois	5	4	1	...	...	...
2 months - 2 mois	3	2	1	...	...	...
3 months - 3 mois	2	1	1	...	...	...
4 months - 4 mois	1	1	-	...	...	...
5 months - 5 mois	-	-	-	...	...	...
6 months - 6 mois	2	2	-	...	...	...
7 months - 7 mois	-	-	-	...	...	...
8 months - 8 mois	-	-	-	...	...	...
9 months - 9 mois	-	-	-	...	...	...
10 months - 10 mois	-	-	-	...	...	...
11 months - 11 mois	-	-	-	...	...	...
Mongolia - Mongolie						
2019 (+C)						
Total	1 041	583	458	13.1	14.3	11.8
Less than 1 day - Moins de 1 jour	113	66	47	1.4	1.6	1.2
1 - 6 days - 1 - 6 jours	349	203	146	4.4	5.0	3.8
7 - 27 days - 7 - 27 jours	183	106	77	2.3	2.6	2.0
7 - 13 days - 7 - 13 jours	114	71	43	1.4	1.7	1.1
14 - 20 days - 14 - 20 jours	45	22	23	0.6	♦0.5	♦0.6
21 - 27 days - 21 - 27 jours	24	13	11	♦0.3	♦0.3	♦0.3
28 days - 11 months - 28 jours - 11 mois	396	208	188	5.0	5.1	4.8
28 days - less than 2 months - 28 jours - moins de 2 mois	94	53	41	1.2	1.3	1.1
2 months - 2 mois	71	41	30	0.9	1.0	0.8
3 months - 3 mois	46	22	24	0.6	♦0.5	♦0.6
4 months - 4 mois	40	24	16	0.5	♦0.6	♦0.4
5 months - 5 mois	37	16	21	0.5	♦0.4	♦0.5
6 months - 6 mois	22	10	12	♦0.3	♦0.2	♦0.3
7 months - 7 mois	23	12	11	♦0.3	♦0.3	♦0.3
8 months - 8 mois	24	11	13	♦0.3	♦0.3	♦0.3
9 months - 9 mois	11	4	7	♦0.1	♦0.1	♦0.2
10 months - 10 mois	12	5	7	♦0.2	♦0.1	♦0.2
11 months - 11 mois	16	10	6	♦0.2	♦0.2	♦0.2
Myanmar[20]						
2017 (+U)						
Total	*9 761*	*5 485*	*4 276*	...	...	...
Less than 1 day - Moins de 1 jour	*545*	*319*	*226*	...	...	...
1 - 6 days - 1 - 6 jours	*4 453*	*2 555*	*1 898*	...	...	...
7 - 27 days - 7 - 27 jours	*1 362*	*757*	*605*	...	...	...
7 - 13 days - 7 - 13 jours	*719*	*398*	*321*	...	...	...
14 - 20 days - 14 - 20 jours	*349*	*192*	*157*	...	...	...
21 - 27 days - 21 - 27 jours	*294*	*167*	*127*	...	...	...
28 days - 11 months - 28 jours - 11 mois	*2 960*	*1 604*	*1 356*	...	...	...
28 days - less than 2 months - 28 jours - moins de 2 mois	*742*	*436*	*306*	...	...	...

16. Infant deaths and infant mortality rates by age and sex: latest available year, 2010 - 2019
Décès d'enfants de moins d'un an et taux de mortalité infantile selon l'âge et le sexe : dernière année disponible, 2010 - 2019 (continued - suite)

Continent, country or area, year, code[a] and age Continent, pays ou zone, année, code[a] et âge	Number - Nombre			Rate - Taux		
	Both sexes Les deux sexes	Male Masculin	Female Féminin	Both sexes Les deux sexes	Male Masculin	Female Féminin
ASIA - ASIE						
Myanmar[20]						
2017 (+U)						
2 months - 2 mois	*457*	*262*	*195*	...	...	...
3 months - 3 mois	*334*	*167*	*167*	...	...	...
4 months - 4 mois	*284*	*158*	*126*	...	...	...
5 months - 5 mois	*212*	*117*	*95*	...	...	...
6 months - 6 mois	*236*	*112*	*124*	...	...	...
7 months - 7 mois	*211*	*104*	*107*	...	...	...
8 months - 8 mois	*165*	*86*	*79*	...	...	...
9 months - 9 mois	*121*	*63*	*58*	...	...	...
10 months - 10 mois	*109*	*57*	*52*	...	...	...
11 months - 11 mois	*89*	*42*	*47*	...	...	...
Unknown - Inconnu	*441*	*250*	*191*	...	...	...
Oman						
2019 (C)						
Total	686	367	319	7.9	8.3	7.5
Less than 1 day - Moins de 1 jour	122	79	43	1.4	1.8	1.0
1 - 6 days - 1 - 6 jours	191	102	89	2.2	2.3	2.1
7 - 27 days - 7 - 27 jours	129	62	67	1.5	1.4	1.6
7 - 13 days - 7 - 13 jours	57	26	31	0.7	♦0.6	0.7
14 - 20 days - 14 - 20 jours	42	21	21	0.5	♦0.5	♦0.5
21 - 27 days - 21 - 27 jours	30	15	15	0.3	♦0.3	♦0.4
28 days - 11 months - 28 jours - 11 mois	244	124	120	2.8	2.8	2.8
28 days - less than 2 months - 28 jours - moins de 2 mois	67	33	34	0.8	0.7	0.8
2 months - 2 mois	29	14	15	♦0.3	♦0.3	♦0.4
3 months - 3 mois	34	17	17	0.4	♦0.4	♦0.4
4 months - 4 mois	26	16	10	♦0.3	♦0.4	♦0.2
5 months - 5 mois	15	8	7	♦0.2	♦0.2	♦0.2
6 months - 6 mois	22	12	10	♦0.3	♦0.3	♦0.2
7 months - 7 mois	16	11	5	♦0.2	♦0.2	♦0.1
8 months - 8 mois	8	2	6	♦0.1	-	♦0.1
9 months - 9 mois	13	4	9	♦0.1	♦0.1	♦0.2
10 months - 10 mois	7	3	4	♦0.1	♦0.1	♦0.1
11 months - 11 mois	7	4	3	♦0.1	♦0.1	♦0.1
Philippines						
2018 (C)						
Total	21 019	12 174	8 845	12.6	14.0	11.1
Less than 1 day - Moins de 1 jour	3 063	1 703	1 360	1.8	2.0	1.7
1 - 6 days - 1 - 6 jours	5 992	3 594	2 398	3.6	4.1	3.0
7 - 27 days - 7 - 27 jours	2 893	1 706	1 187	1.7	2.0	1.5
7 - 13 days - 7 - 13 jours	1 474	900	574	0.9	1.0	0.7
14 - 20 days - 14 - 20 jours	770	439	331	0.5	0.5	0.4
21 - 27 days - 21 - 27 jours	649	367	282	0.4	0.4	0.4
28 days - 11 months - 28 jours - 11 mois	9 071	5 171	3 900	5.4	5.9	4.9
28 days - less than 2 months - 28 jours - moins de 2 mois	2 223	1 278	945	1.3	1.5	1.2
2 months - 2 mois	1 141	689	452	0.7	0.8	0.6
3 months - 3 mois	925	513	412	0.6	0.6	0.5
4 months - 4 mois	836	499	337	0.5	0.6	0.4
5 months - 5 mois	722	408	314	0.4	0.5	0.4
6 months - 6 mois	748	403	345	0.4	0.5	0.4
7 months - 7 mois	610	342	268	0.4	0.4	0.3
8 months - 8 mois	567	315	252	0.3	0.4	0.3
9 months - 9 mois	507	278	229	0.3	0.3	0.3
10 months - 10 mois	403	230	173	0.2	0.3	0.2
11 months - 11 mois	389	216	173	0.2	0.2	0.2
Qatar						
2018 (C)						
Total	172	83	89	6.1	5.9	6.4
Less than 1 day - Moins de 1 jour	-	-	-	-	-	-
1 - 6 days - 1 - 6 jours	79	39	40	2.8	2.7	2.9
7 - 27 days - 7 - 27 jours	28	15	13	♦1.0	♦1.1	♦0.9
7 - 13 days - 7 - 13 jours	13	6	7	♦0.5	♦0.4	♦0.5
14 - 20 days - 14 - 20 jours	11	7	4	♦0.4	♦0.5	♦0.3
21 - 27 days - 21 - 27 jours	4	2	2	♦0.1	♦0.1	♦0.1
28 days - 11 months - 28 jours - 11 mois	65	29	36	2.3	♦2.0	2.6
28 days - less than 2 months - 28 jours - moins de 2 mois	20	6	14	♦0.7	♦0.4	♦1.0
2 months - 2 mois	15	9	6	♦0.5	♦0.6	♦0.4
3 months - 3 mois	10	5	5	♦0.4	♦0.4	♦0.4

16. Infant deaths and infant mortality rates by age and sex: latest available year, 2010 - 2019
Décès d'enfants de moins d'un an et taux de mortalité infantile selon l'âge et le sexe : dernière année disponible, 2010 - 2019 (continued - suite)

Continent, country or area, year, code[a] and age Continent, pays ou zone, année, code[a] et âge	Number - Nombre			Rate - Taux		
	Both sexes Les deux sexes	Male Masculin	Female Féminin	Both sexes Les deux sexes	Male Masculin	Female Féminin
ASIA - ASIE						
Qatar						
2018 (C)						
4 months - 4 mois	4	2	2	♦0.1	♦0.1	♦0.1
5 months - 5 mois	5	3	2	♦0.2	♦0.2	♦0.1
6 months - 6 mois	5	1	4	♦0.2	♦0.1	♦0.3
7 months - 7 mois	2	1	1	♦0.1	♦0.1	♦0.1
8 months - 8 mois	2	1	1	♦0.1	♦0.1	♦0.1
9 months - 9 mois	1	-	1	-	-	♦0.1
10 months - 10 mois	1	1	-	-	♦0.1	-
11 months - 11 mois	-	-	-	-	-	-
Republic of Korea - République de Corée[21]						
2018 (C)						
Total	931	534	397	2.8	3.2	2.5
Less than 1 day - Moins de 1 jour	143	88	55	0.4	0.5	0.3
1 - 6 days - 1 - 6 jours	202	117	85	0.6	0.7	0.5
7 - 27 days - 7 - 27 jours	188	108	80	0.6	0.6	0.5
7 - 13 days - 7 - 13 jours	91	57	34	0.3	0.3	0.2
14 - 20 days - 14 - 20 jours	65	35	30	0.2	0.2	0.2
21 - 27 days - 21 - 27 jours	32	16	16	0.1	♦0.1	♦0.1
28 days - 11 months - 28 jours - 11 mois	398	221	177	1.2	1.3	1.1
28 days - less than 2 months - 28 jours - moins de 2 mois	102	59	43	0.3	0.4	0.3
2 months - 2 mois	65	26	39	0.2	♦0.2	0.2
3 months - 3 mois	51	25	26	0.2	♦0.1	♦0.2
4 months - 4 mois	43	23	20	0.1	♦0.1	♦0.1
5 months - 5 mois	34	24	10	0.1	♦0.1	♦0.1
6 months - 6 mois	27	14	13	♦0.1	♦0.1	♦0.1
7 months - 7 mois	20	12	8	♦0.1	♦0.1	♦0.1
8 months - 8 mois	19	11	8	♦0.1	♦0.1	♦0.1
9 months - 9 mois	16	11	5	-	♦0.1	-
10 months - 10 mois	8	6	2	-	-	-
11 months - 11 mois	13	10	3	-	♦0.1	-
Singapore - Singapour						
2019 (+C)						
Total	75	39	36	...	...	...
Less than 1 day - Moins de 1 jour	16	4	12	...	...	...
1 - 6 days - 1 - 6 jours	8	4	4	...	...	...
7 - 27 days - 7 - 27 jours	7	6	1	...	...	...
7 - 13 days - 7 - 13 jours	3	3	-	...	...	...
14 - 20 days - 14 - 20 jours	1	1	-	...	...	...
21 - 27 days - 21 - 27 jours	3	2	1	...	...	...
28 days - 11 months - 28 jours - 11 mois	44	25	19	...	...	...
28 days - less than 2 months - 28 jours - moins de 2 mois	14	8	6	...	...	...
2 months - 2 mois	2	2	-	...	...	...
3 months - 3 mois	4	2	2	...	...	...
4 months - 4 mois	6	3	3	...	...	...
5 months - 5 mois	3	1	2	...	...	...
6 months - 6 mois	6	4	2	...	...	...
7 months - 7 mois	2	1	1	...	...	...
8 months - 8 mois	1	1	-	...	...	...
9 months - 9 mois	2	1	1	...	...	...
10 months - 10 mois	1	1	-	...	...	...
11 months - 11 mois	3	1	2	...	...	...
Sri Lanka						
2014 (+C)						
Total	2 662	1 505	1 157	7.6	8.4	6.8
1 - 6 days - 1 - 6 jours	1 291	735	556	3.7	4.1	3.3
7 - 27 days - 7 - 27 jours	587	333	254	1.7	1.9	1.5
28 days - 11 months - 28 jours - 11 mois	784	437	347	2.2	2.4	2.0
28 days - 2 months - 28 jours - 2 mois	328	199	129	0.9	1.1	0.8
3 - 5 months - 3 - 5 mois	246	125	121	0.7	0.7	0.7
6 - 8 months - 6 - 8 mois	128	66	62	0.4	0.4	0.4
9 - 11 months - 9 - 11 mois	82	47	35	0.2	0.3	0.2
Tajikistan - Tadjikistan[14]						
2017 (U)						
Total	*2 405*	*1 384*	*1 021*	...	...	...
Less than 1 day - Moins de 1 jour	*539*	*313*	*226*	...	...	...
1 - 6 days - 1 - 6 jours	*875*	*536*	*339*	...	...	...

16. Infant deaths and infant mortality rates by age and sex: latest available year, 2010 - 2019
Décès d'enfants de moins d'un an et taux de mortalité infantile selon l'âge et le sexe : dernière année disponible, 2010 - 2019 (continued - suite)

Continent, country or area, year, code[a] and age Continent, pays ou zone, année, code[a] et âge	Number - Nombre			Rate - Taux		
	Both sexes Les deux sexes	Male Masculin	Female Féminin	Both sexes Les deux sexes	Male Masculin	Female Féminin
ASIA - ASIE						
Tajikistan - Tadjikistan[14]						
2017 (U)						
7 - 27 days - 7 - 27 jours	*212*	*108*	*104*	...	...	...
7 - 13 days - 7 - 13 jours	*136*	*66*	*70*	...	...	...
14 - 20 days - 14 - 20 jours	*48*	*27*	*21*	...	...	...
21 - 27 days - 21 - 27 jours	*28*	*15*	*13*	...	...	...
28 days - 11 months - 28 jours - 11 mois	*779*	*427*	*352*	...	...	...
28 days - less than 2 months - 28 jours - moins de 2 mois	*16*	*10*	*6*	...	...	...
2 - 11 months - 2 - 11 mois	*763*	*417*	*346*	...	...	...
Thailand - Thaïlande[22]						
2016 (+U)						
Total	*4 233*	*2 360*	*1 873*	...	...	...
Less than 1 day - Moins de 1 jour	*340*	*168*	*172*	...	...	...
1 - 6 days - 1 - 6 jours	*1 171*	*666*	*505*	...	...	...
7 - 27 days - 7 - 27 jours	*1 384*	*789*	*595*	...	...	...
7 - 13 days - 7 - 13 jours	*450*	*274*	*176*	...	...	...
14 - 20 days - 14 - 20 jours	*238*	*134*	*104*	...	...	...
21 - 27 days - 21 - 27 jours	*165*	*93*	*72*	...	...	...
28 days - 11 months - 28 jours - 11 mois	*1 869*	*1 035*	*844*	...	...	...
28 days - less than 2 months - 28 jours - moins de 2 mois	*531*	*288*	*243*	...	...	...
2 months - 2 mois	*303*	*172*	*131*	...	...	...
3 months - 3 mois	*239*	*126*	*113*	...	...	...
4 months - 4 mois	*179*	*96*	*83*	...	...	...
5 months - 5 mois	*126*	*75*	*51*	...	...	...
6 months - 6 mois	*98*	*53*	*45*	...	...	...
7 months - 7 mois	*87*	*59*	*38*	...	...	...
8 months - 8 mois	*90*	*50*	*40*	...	...	...
9 months - 9 mois	*78*	*42*	*36*	...	...	...
10 months - 10 mois	*74*	*34*	*40*	...	...	...
11 months - 11 mois	*64*	*40*	*24*	...	...	...
Turkey - Turquie[23]						
2018 (C)						
Total	11 629	6 311	5 318	9.3	9.8	8.7
Less than 1 day - Moins de 1 jour	1 475	781	694	1.2	1.2	1.1
1 - 6 days - 1 - 6 jours	3 661	2 103	1 558	2.9	3.3	2.6
7 - 27 days - 7 - 27 jours	2 355	1 282	1 073	1.9	2.0	1.8
7 - 13 days - 7 - 13 jours	1 228	656	572	1.0	1.0	0.9
14 - 20 days - 14 - 20 jours	667	378	289	0.5	0.6	0.5
21 - 27 days - 21 - 27 jours	460	248	212	0.4	0.4	0.3
28 days - 11 months - 28 jours - 11 mois	4 138	2 145	1 993	3.3	3.3	3.3
28 days - less than 2 months - 28 jours - moins de 2 mois	1 194	634	560	1.0	1.0	0.9
2 months - 2 mois	622	309	313	0.5	0.5	0.5
3 months - 3 mois	476	254	222	0.4	0.4	0.4
4 months - 4 mois	389	206	183	0.3	0.3	0.3
5 months - 5 mois	334	175	159	0.3	0.3	0.3
6 months - 6 mois	287	144	143	0.2	0.2	0.2
7 months - 7 mois	192	103	89	0.2	0.2	0.1
8 months - 8 mois	205	100	105	0.2	0.2	0.2
9 months - 9 mois	199	93	106	0.2	0.1	0.2
10 months - 10 mois	144	74	70	0.1	0.1	0.1
11 months - 11 mois	96	53	43	0.1	0.1	0.1
United Arab Emirates - Émirats arabes unis						
2018 (C)						
Total	500	276	224	5.2	5.7	4.8
Less than 1 day - Moins de 1 jour	126	71	55	1.3	1.5	1.2
1 - 6 days - 1 - 6 jours	149	88	61	1.6	1.8	1.3
7 - 27 days - 7 - 27 jours	86	45	41	0.9	0.9	0.9
7 - 13 days - 7 - 13 jours	42	22	20	0.4	♦0.5	♦0.4
14 - 20 days - 14 - 20 jours	25	14	11	♦0.3	♦0.3	♦0.2
21 - 27 days - 21 - 27 jours	19	9	10	♦0.2	♦0.2	♦0.2
28 days - 11 months - 28 jours - 11 mois	139	72	67	1.5	1.5	1.4
28 days - less than 2 months - 28 jours - moins de 2 mois	35	19	16	0.4	♦0.4	♦0.3
2 months - 2 mois	17	11	6	♦0.2	♦0.2	♦0.1
3 months - 3 mois	9	5	4	♦0.1	♦0.1	♦0.1
4 months - 4 mois	11	4	7	♦0.1	♦0.1	♦0.2
5 months - 5 mois	16	6	10	♦0.2	♦0.1	♦0.2
6 months - 6 mois	11	9	2	♦0.1	♦0.2	-
7 months - 7 mois	13	8	5	♦0.1	♦0.2	♦0.1

16. Infant deaths and infant mortality rates by age and sex: latest available year, 2010 - 2019
Décès d'enfants de moins d'un an et taux de mortalité infantile selon l'âge et le sexe : dernière année disponible, 2010 - 2019 (continued - suite)

Continent, country or area, year, code[a] and age Continent, pays ou zone, année, code[a] et âge	Number - Nombre			Rate - Taux		
	Both sexes Les deux sexes	Male Masculin	Female Féminin	Both sexes Les deux sexes	Male Masculin	Female Féminin
ASIA - ASIE						
United Arab Emirates - Émirats arabes unis						
2018 (C)						
8 months - 8 mois	7	4	3	♦0.1	♦0.1	♦0.1
9 months - 9 mois	8	3	5	♦0.1	♦0.1	♦0.1
10 months - 10 mois	3	-	3	-	-	♦0.1
11 months - 11 mois	9	3	6	♦0.1	♦0.1	♦0.1
Uzbekistan - Ouzbékistan[14]						
2018 (+C)						
Total	7 557	4 372	3 185	9.8	10.8	8.7
Less than 1 day - Moins de 1 jour	931	546	385	1.2	1.4	1.1
1 - 6 days - 1 - 6 jours	3 075	1 803	1 272	4.0	4.5	3.5
7 - 27 days - 7 - 27 jours	1 334	782	552	1.7	1.9	1.5
7 - 13 days - 7 - 13 jours	825	496	329	1.1	1.2	0.9
14 - 20 days - 14 - 20 jours	314	173	141	0.4	0.4	0.4
21 - 27 days - 21 - 27 jours	195	113	82	0.3	0.3	0.2
28 days - 11 months - 28 jours - 11 mois	2 217	1 241	976	2.9	3.1	2.7
28 days - less than 2 months - 28 jours - moins de 2 mois	494	290	204	0.6	0.7	0.6
2 months - 2 mois	282	178	104	0.4	0.4	0.3
3 months - 3 mois	284	153	131	0.4	0.4	0.4
4 months - 4 mois	224	136	88	0.3	0.3	0.2
5 months - 5 mois	208	118	90	0.3	0.3	0.2
6 months - 6 mois	186	98	88	0.2	0.2	0.2
7 months - 7 mois	135	64	71	0.2	0.2	0.2
8 months - 8 mois	147	69	78	0.2	0.2	0.2
9 months - 9 mois	107	47	60	0.1	0.1	0.2
10 months - 10 mois	79	51	28	0.1	0.1	♦0.1
11 months - 11 mois	71	37	34	0.1	0.1	0.1
EUROPE						
Åland Islands - Îles d'Åland						
2018 (C)						
Total	-	-	-	...	...	...
Less than 1 day - Moins de 1 jour	-	-	-	...	...	...
1 - 6 days - 1 - 6 jours	-	-	-	...	...	...
7 - 27 days - 7 - 27 jours	-	-	-	...	...	...
7 - 13 days - 7 - 13 jours	-	-	-	...	...	...
14 - 20 days - 14 - 20 jours	-	-	-	...	...	...
21 - 27 days - 21 - 27 jours	-	-	-	...	...	...
28 days - 11 months - 28 jours - 11 mois	-	-	-	...	...	...
28 days - less than 2 months - 28 jours - moins de 2 mois	-	-	-	...	...	...
2 - 11 months - 2 - 11 mois	-	-	-	...	...	...
Albania - Albanie						
2018 (C)						
Total	257	146	111	8.9	9.7	8.0
Less than 1 day - Moins de 1 jour	87	45	42	3.0	3.0	3.0
1 - 6 days - 1 - 6 jours	71	47	24	2.5	3.1	♦1.7
7 - 27 days - 7 - 27 jours	53	28	25	1.8	♦1.9	♦1.8
7 - 13 days - 7 - 13 jours	36	17	19	1.2	♦1.1	♦1.4
14 - 20 days - 14 - 20 jours	10	7	3	♦0.3	♦0.5	♦0.2
21 - 27 days - 21 - 27 jours	7	4	3	♦0.2	♦0.3	♦0.2
28 days - 11 months - 28 jours - 11 mois	46	26	20	1.6	♦1.7	♦1.4
28 days - less than 2 months - 28 jours - moins de 2 mois	16	11	5	♦0.6	♦0.7	♦0.4
2 months - 2 mois	6	2	4	♦0.2	♦0.1	♦0.3
3 months - 3 mois	5	3	2	♦0.2	♦0.2	♦0.1
4 months - 4 mois	1	-	1	-	-	♦0.1
5 months - 5 mois	2	1	1	♦0.1	♦0.1	♦0.1
6 months - 6 mois	4	2	2	♦0.1	♦0.1	♦0.1
7 months - 7 mois	3	1	2	♦0.1	♦0.1	♦0.1
8 months - 8 mois	6	4	2	♦0.2	♦0.3	♦0.1
9 months - 9 mois	1	1	-	-	♦0.1	-
10 months - 10 mois	1	1	-	-	♦0.1	-
11 months - 11 mois	1	-	1	-	-	♦0.1
Andorra - Andorre						
2018 (C)						
Total	1	-	1	...	...	...
Less than 1 day - Moins de 1 jour	-	-	-	...	...	...

16. Infant deaths and infant mortality rates by age and sex: latest available year, 2010 - 2019
Décès d'enfants de moins d'un an et taux de mortalité infantile selon l'âge et le sexe : dernière année disponible, 2010 - 2019 (continued - suite)

Continent, country or area, year, code[a] and age Continent, pays ou zone, année, code[a] et âge	Number - Nombre			Rate - Taux		
	Both sexes Les deux sexes	Male Masculin	Female Féminin	Both sexes Les deux sexes	Male Masculin	Female Féminin
EUROPE						
Andorra - Andorre						
2018 (C)						
1 - 6 days - 1 - 6 jours	1	-	1	...	...	...
7 - 27 days - 7 - 27 jours	-	-	-	...	...	...
28 days - 11 months - 28 jours - 11 mois	-	-	-	...	...	...
Austria - Autriche						
2018 (C)						
Total	231	132	99	2.7	3.0	2.4
Less than 1 day - Moins de 1 jour	98	56	42	1.1	1.3	1.0
1 - 6 days - 1 - 6 jours	38	18	20	0.4	♦0.4	♦0.5
7 - 27 days - 7 - 27 jours	38	20	18	0.4	♦0.5	♦0.4
7 - 13 days - 7 - 13 jours	16	9	7	♦0.2	♦0.2	♦0.2
14 - 20 days - 14 - 20 jours	16	8	8	♦0.2	♦0.2	♦0.2
21 - 27 days - 21 - 27 jours	6	3	3	♦0.1	♦0.1	♦0.1
28 days - 11 months - 28 jours - 11 mois	53	35	18	0.6	0.8	♦0.4
28 days - less than 2 months - 28 jours - moins de 2 mois	15	9	6	♦0.2	♦0.2	♦0.1
2 months - 2 mois	11	8	3	♦0.1	♦0.2	♦0.1
3 months - 3 mois	6	3	3	♦0.1	♦0.1	♦0.1
4 months - 4 mois	4	2	2	-	-	-
5 months - 5 mois	3	3	-	-	♦0.1	-
6 months - 6 mois	3	2	1	-	-	-
7 months - 7 mois	2	2	-	-	-	-
8 months - 8 mois	4	3	1	-	♦0.1	-
9 months - 9 mois	3	2	1	-	-	-
10 months - 10 mois	-	-	-	-	-	-
11 months - 11 mois	2	1	1	-	-	-
Unknown - Inconnu	4	3	1	-	♦0.1	-
Belarus - Bélarus						
2018 (C)						
Total	238	143	95	2.5	3.0	2.1
Less than 1 day - Moins de 1 jour	11	9	2	♦0.1	♦0.2	-
1 - 6 days - 1 - 6 jours	55	34	21	0.6	0.7	♦0.5
7 - 27 days - 7 - 27 jours	42	21	21	0.4	♦0.4	♦0.5
7 - 13 days - 7 - 13 jours	17	10	7	♦0.2	♦0.2	♦0.2
14 - 20 days - 14 - 20 jours	10	4	6	♦0.1	♦0.1	♦0.1
21 - 27 days - 21 - 27 jours	15	7	8	♦0.2	♦0.1	♦0.2
28 days - 11 months - 28 jours - 11 mois	130	79	51	1.4	1.6	1.1
28 days - less than 2 months - 28 jours - moins de 2 mois	46	29	17	0.5	♦0.6	♦0.4
2 months - 2 mois	15	8	7	♦0.2	♦0.2	♦0.2
3 months - 3 mois	14	10	4	♦0.1	♦0.2	♦0.1
4 months - 4 mois	12	5	7	♦0.1	♦0.1	♦0.2
5 months - 5 mois	7	6	1	♦0.1	♦0.1	-
6 months - 6 mois	8	5	3	♦0.1	♦0.1	♦0.1
7 months - 7 mois	5	3	2	♦0.1	♦0.1	-
8 months - 8 mois	6	3	3	♦0.1	♦0.1	♦0.1
9 months - 9 mois	2	1	1	-	-	-
10 months - 10 mois	9	6	3	♦0.1	♦0.1	♦0.1
11 months - 11 mois	6	3	3	♦0.1	♦0.1	♦0.1
Belgium - Belgique[24]						
2014 (C)						
Total	423	247	176	3.4	3.8	2.9
Less than 1 day - Moins de 1 jour	115	61	54	0.9	1.0	0.9
1 - 6 days - 1 - 6 jours	91	58	33	0.7	0.9	0.5
7 - 27 days - 7 - 27 jours	79	39	40	0.6	0.6	0.7
7 - 13 days - 7 - 13 jours	40	21	19	0.3	♦0.3	♦0.3
14 - 20 days - 14 - 20 jours	25	11	14	♦0.2	♦0.2	♦0.2
21 - 27 days - 21 - 27 jours	14	7	7	♦0.1	♦0.1	♦0.1
28 days - 11 months - 28 jours - 11 mois	138	89	49	1.1	1.4	0.8
28 days - less than 2 months - 28 jours - moins de 2 mois	42	25	17	0.3	♦0.4	♦0.3
2 months - 2 mois	23	17	6	♦0.2	♦0.3	♦0.1
3 months - 3 mois	13	9	4	♦0.1	♦0.1	♦0.1
4 months - 4 mois	15	12	3	♦0.1	♦0.2	-
5 months - 5 mois	11	7	4	♦0.1	♦0.1	♦0.1
6 months - 6 mois	8	3	5	♦0.1	-	♦0.1
7 months - 7 mois	9	8	1	♦0.1	♦0.1	-
8 months - 8 mois	7	4	3	♦0.1	♦0.1	-
9 months - 9 mois	2	2	-	-	-	-

16. Infant deaths and infant mortality rates by age and sex: latest available year, 2010 - 2019
Décès d'enfants de moins d'un an et taux de mortalité infantile selon l'âge et le sexe : dernière année disponible, 2010 - 2019 (continued - suite)

Continent, country or area, year, code[a] and age Continent, pays ou zone, année, code[a] et âge	Number - Nombre			Rate - Taux		
	Both sexes Les deux sexes	Male Masculin	Female Féminin	Both sexes Les deux sexes	Male Masculin	Female Féminin
EUROPE						
Belgium - Belgique[24]						
2014 (C)						
10 months - 10 mois	5	1	4	-	-	♦0.1
11 months - 11 mois	3	1	2	-	-	-
Bosnia and Herzegovina - Bosnie-Herzégovine						
2010 (C)						
Total	216	125	91	6.4	7.2	5.6
Less than 1 day - Moins de 1 jour	74	43	31	2.2	2.5	1.9
1 - 6 days - 1 - 6 jours	89	56	33	2.7	3.2	2.0
7 - 27 days - 7 - 27 jours	19	13	6	♦0.6	♦0.8	♦0.4
7 - 13 days - 7 - 13 jours	10	6	4	♦0.3	♦0.3	♦0.2
14 - 20 days - 14 - 20 jours	6	6	-	♦0.2	♦0.3	-
21 - 27 days - 21 - 27 jours	3	1	2	♦0.1	♦0.1	♦0.1
28 days - 11 months - 28 jours - 11 mois	34	13	21	1.0	♦0.8	♦1.3
28 days - less than 2 months - 28 jours - moins de 2 mois	5	2	3	♦0.1	♦0.1	♦0.2
2 months - 2 mois	10	6	4	♦0.3	♦0.3	♦0.2
3 months - 3 mois	1	-	1	-	-	♦0.1
4 months - 4 mois	5	2	3	♦0.1	♦0.1	♦0.2
5 months - 5 mois	3	1	2	♦0.1	♦0.1	♦0.1
6 months - 6 mois	3	1	2	♦0.1	♦0.1	♦0.1
7 months - 7 mois	-	-	-	-	-	-
8 months - 8 mois	1	-	1	-	-	♦0.1
9 months - 9 mois	4	-	4	♦0.1	-	♦0.2
10 months - 10 mois	1	1	-	-	♦0.1	-
11 months - 11 mois	1	-	1	-	-	♦0.1
Bulgaria - Bulgarie						
2018 (C)						
Total	358	200	158	5.8	6.2	5.3
Less than 1 day - Moins de 1 jour	67	42	25	1.1	1.3	♦0.8
1 - 6 days - 1 - 6 jours	88	40	48	1.4	1.2	1.6
7 - 27 days - 7 - 27 jours	72	45	27	1.2	1.4	♦0.9
7 - 13 days - 7 - 13 jours	34	23	11	0.5	♦0.7	♦0.4
14 - 20 days - 14 - 20 jours	22	12	10	♦0.4	♦0.4	♦0.3
21 - 27 days - 21 - 27 jours	16	10	6	♦0.3	♦0.3	♦0.2
28 days - 11 months - 28 jours - 11 mois	131	73	58	2.1	2.3	1.9
28 days - less than 2 months - 28 jours - moins de 2 mois	40	20	20	0.6	♦0.6	♦0.7
2 months - 2 mois	25	15	10	♦0.4	♦0.5	♦0.3
3 months - 3 mois	15	9	6	♦0.2	♦0.3	♦0.2
4 months - 4 mois	9	7	2	♦0.1	♦0.2	♦0.1
5 months - 5 mois	10	5	5	♦0.2	♦0.2	♦0.2
6 months - 6 mois	5	2	3	♦0.1	♦0.1	♦0.1
7 months - 7 mois	3	1	2	-	-	♦0.1
8 months - 8 mois	8	4	4	♦0.1	♦0.1	♦0.1
9 months - 9 mois	4	3	1	♦0.1	♦0.1	-
10 months - 10 mois	8	5	3	♦0.1	♦0.2	♦0.1
11 months - 11 mois	4	2	2	♦0.1	♦0.1	♦0.1
Croatia - Croatie						
2018 (C)						
Total	157	104	53	4.2	5.5	3.0
Less than 1 day - Moins de 1 jour	48	26	22	1.3	♦1.4	♦1.2
1 - 6 days - 1 - 6 jours	39	25	14	1.1	♦1.3	♦0.8
7 - 27 days - 7 - 27 jours	33	27	6	0.9	♦1.4	♦0.3
7 - 13 days - 7 - 13 jours	18	16	2	♦0.5	♦0.8	♦0.1
14 - 20 days - 14 - 20 jours	13	9	4	♦0.4	♦0.5	♦0.2
21 - 27 days - 21 - 27 jours	2	2	-	♦0.1	♦0.1	-
28 days - 11 months - 28 jours - 11 mois	37	26	11	1.0	♦1.4	♦0.6
28 days - less than 2 months - 28 jours - moins de 2 mois	11	7	4	♦0.3	♦0.4	♦0.2
2 months - 2 mois	8	7	1	♦0.2	♦0.4	♦0.1
3 months - 3 mois	2	1	1	♦0.1	♦0.1	♦0.1
4 months - 4 mois	4	2	2	♦0.1	♦0.1	♦0.1
5 months - 5 mois	2	2	-	♦0.1	♦0.1	-
6 months - 6 mois	1	-	1	-	-	♦0.1
7 months - 7 mois	1	1	-	-	♦0.1	-
8 months - 8 mois	2	1	1	♦0.1	♦0.1	♦0.1
9 months - 9 mois	3	3	-	♦0.1	♦0.2	-
10 months - 10 mois	1	-	1	-	-	♦0.1
11 months - 11 mois	2	2	-	♦0.1	♦0.1	-

Continent, country or area, year, code[a] and age Continent, pays ou zone, année, code[a] et âge	Number - Nombre			Rate - Taux		
	Both sexes Les deux sexes	Male Masculin	Female Féminin	Both sexes Les deux sexes	Male Masculin	Female Féminin
EUROPE						
Czechia - Tchéquie						
2018 (C)						
Total	292	159	133	2.6	2.7	2.4
Less than 1 day - Moins de 1 jour	58	27	31	0.5	♦0.5	0.6
1 - 6 days - 1 - 6 jours	65	35	30	0.6	0.6	0.5
7 - 27 days - 7 - 27 jours	64	36	28	0.6	0.6	♦0.5
7 - 13 days - 7 - 13 jours	34	22	12	0.3	♦0.4	♦0.2
14 - 20 days - 14 - 20 jours	18	11	7	♦0.2	♦0.2	♦0.1
21 - 27 days - 21 - 27 jours	12	3	9	♦0.1	♦0.1	♦0.2
28 days - 11 months - 28 jours - 11 mois	105	61	44	0.9	1.0	0.8
28 days - less than 2 months - 28 jours - moins de 2 mois	26	10	16	♦0.2	♦0.2	♦0.3
2 months - 2 mois	18	17	1	♦0.2	♦0.3	-
3 months - 3 mois	11	7	4	♦0.1	♦0.1	♦0.1
4 months - 4 mois	9	3	6	♦0.1	♦0.1	♦0.1
5 months - 5 mois	8	4	4	♦0.1	♦0.1	♦0.1
6 months - 6 mois	4	4	-	-	♦0.1	-
7 months - 7 mois	6	3	3	♦0.1	♦0.1	♦0.1
8 months - 8 mois	8	4	4	♦0.1	♦0.1	♦0.1
9 months - 9 mois	6	4	2	♦0.1	♦0.1	-
10 months - 10 mois	4	3	1	-	♦0.1	-
11 months - 11 mois	5	2	3	-	-	♦0.1
Denmark - Danemark[25]						
2018 (C)						
Total	226	130	96	3.7	4.1	3.2
Less than 1 day - Moins de 1 jour	109	66	43	1.8	2.1	1.4
1 - 6 days - 1 - 6 jours	47	30	17	0.8	0.9	♦0.6
7 - 27 days - 7 - 27 jours	18	8	10	♦0.3	♦0.3	♦0.3
7 - 13 days - 7 - 13 jours	9	4	5	♦0.1	♦0.1	♦0.2
14 - 20 days - 14 - 20 jours	7	3	4	♦0.1	♦0.1	♦0.1
21 - 27 days - 21 - 27 jours	2	1	1	-	-	-
28 days - 11 months - 28 jours - 11 mois	52	26	26	0.8	♦0.8	♦0.9
28 days - less than 2 months - 28 jours - moins de 2 mois	15	5	10	♦0.2	♦0.2	♦0.3
2 months - 2 mois	5	2	3	♦0.1	♦0.1	♦0.1
3 months - 3 mois	5	2	3	♦0.1	♦0.1	♦0.1
4 months - 4 mois	7	5	2	♦0.1	♦0.2	♦0.1
5 months - 5 mois	2	1	1	-	-	-
6 months - 6 mois	6	5	1	♦0.1	♦0.2	-
7 months - 7 mois	2	1	1	-	-	-
8 months - 8 mois	2	2	-	-	♦0.1	-
9 months - 9 mois	4	1	3	♦0.1	-	♦0.1
10 months - 10 mois	2	1	1	-	-	-
11 months - 11 mois	2	1	1	-	-	-
Estonia - Estonie						
2018 (C)						
Total	23	14	9	...	...	...
Less than 1 day - Moins de 1 jour	3	1	2	...	...	...
1 - 6 days - 1 - 6 jours	8	5	3	...	...	...
7 - 27 days - 7 - 27 jours	2	1	1	...	...	...
7 - 13 days - 7 - 13 jours	1	1	-	...	...	...
14 - 20 days - 14 - 20 jours	1	-	1	...	...	...
21 - 27 days - 21 - 27 jours	-	-	-	...	...	...
28 days - 11 months - 28 jours - 11 mois	10	7	3	...	...	...
28 days - less than 2 months - 28 jours - moins de 2 mois	3	1	2	...	...	...
2 months - 2 mois	3	3	-	...	...	...
3 months - 3 mois	-	-	-	...	...	...
4 months - 4 mois	1	1	-	...	...	...
5 months - 5 mois	1	1	-	...	...	...
6 months - 6 mois	-	-	-	...	...	...
7 months - 7 mois	-	-	-	...	...	...
8 months - 8 mois	1	1	-	...	...	...
9 months - 9 mois	1	-	1	...	...	...
10 months - 10 mois	-	-	-	...	...	...
11 months - 11 mois	-	-	-	...	...	...
Faroe Islands - Îles Féroé						
2019 (C)						
Total	3	2	1	...	...	...
Less than 1 day - Moins de 1 jour	-	-	-	...	...	...
1 - 6 days - 1 - 6 jours	2	1	1	...	...	...

16. Infant deaths and infant mortality rates by age and sex: latest available year, 2010 - 2019
Décès d'enfants de moins d'un an et taux de mortalité infantile selon l'âge et le sexe : dernière année disponible, 2010 - 2019 (continued - suite)

Continent, country or area, year, code[a] and age / Continent, pays ou zone, année, code[a] et âge	Number - Nombre			Rate - Taux		
	Both sexes Les deux sexes	Male Masculin	Female Féminin	Both sexes Les deux sexes	Male Masculin	Female Féminin
EUROPE						
Faroe Islands - Îles Féroé						
2019 (C)						
7 - 27 days - 7 - 27 jours	1	1	-	...	...	...
7 - 13 days - 7 - 13 jours	-	-	-	...	...	...
14 - 20 days - 14 - 20 jours	-	-	-	...	...	...
21 - 27 days - 21 - 27 jours	-	-	-	...	...	...
28 days - 11 months - 28 jours - 11 mois	-	-	-	...	...	...
28 days - less than 2 months - 28 jours - moins de 2 mois	-	-	-	...	...	...
2 months - 2 mois	-	-	-	...	...	...
3 months - 3 mois	-	-	-	...	...	...
4 months - 4 mois	-	-	-	...	...	...
5 months - 5 mois	-	-	-	...	...	...
6 months - 6 mois	-	-	-	...	...	...
7 months - 7 mois	-	-	-	...	...	...
8 months - 8 mois	-	-	-	...	...	...
9 months - 9 mois	-	-	-	...	...	...
10 months - 10 mois	-	-	-	...	...	...
11 months - 11 mois	-	-	-	...	...	...
Finland - Finlande[26]						
2018 (C)						
Total	101	52	49	2.1	2.1	2.1
Less than 1 day - Moins de 1 jour	34	17	17	0.7	♦0.7	♦0.7
1 - 6 days - 1 - 6 jours	26	17	9	♦0.5	♦0.7	♦0.4
7 - 27 days - 7 - 27 jours	16	8	8	♦0.3	♦0.3	♦0.4
7 - 13 days - 7 - 13 jours	2	2	-	-	♦0.1	-
14 - 20 days - 14 - 20 jours	10	4	6	♦0.2	♦0.2	♦0.3
21 - 27 days - 21 - 27 jours	4	2	2	♦0.1	♦0.1	♦0.1
28 days - 11 months - 28 jours - 11 mois	25	10	15	♦0.5	♦0.4	♦0.7
28 days - less than 2 months - 28 jours - moins de 2 mois	10	2	8	♦0.2	♦0.1	♦0.4
2 months - 2 mois	4	1	3	♦0.1	-	♦0.1
3 months - 3 mois	-	-	-	-	-	-
4 months - 4 mois	1	1	-	-	-	-
5 months - 5 mois	3	2	1	♦0.1	♦0.1	-
6 months - 6 mois	4	3	1	♦0.1	♦0.1	-
7 months - 7 mois	1	-	1	-	-	-
8 months - 8 mois	1	-	1	-	-	-
9 months - 9 mois	1	1	-	-	-	-
10 months - 10 mois	-	-	-	-	-	-
11 months - 11 mois	-	-	-	-	-	-
France						
2017 (C)						
Total	2 639	1 444	1 195	3.6	3.9	3.4
Less than 1 day - Moins de 1 jour	711	389	322	1.0	1.0	0.9
1 - 6 days - 1 - 6 jours	643	372	271	0.9	1.0	0.8
7 - 27 days - 7 - 27 jours	581	306	275	0.8	0.8	0.8
7 - 13 days - 7 - 13 jours	319	166	153	0.4	0.4	0.4
14 - 20 days - 14 - 20 jours	152	82	70	0.2	0.2	0.2
21 - 27 days - 21 - 27 jours	110	58	52	0.2	0.2	0.1
28 days - 11 months - 28 jours - 11 mois	704	377	327	1.0	1.0	0.9
28 days - less than 2 months - 28 jours - moins de 2 mois	240	129	111	0.3	0.3	0.3
2 months - 2 mois	103	56	47	0.1	0.1	0.1
3 months - 3 mois	84	43	41	0.1	0.1	0.1
4 months - 4 mois	63	35	28	0.1	0.1	♦0.1
5 months - 5 mois	48	31	17	0.1	0.1	-
6 months - 6 mois	39	21	18	0.1	♦0.1	♦0.1
7 months - 7 mois	35	20	15	-	♦0.1	-
8 months - 8 mois	28	16	12	-	-	-
9 months - 9 mois	24	11	13	-	-	-
10 months - 10 mois	24	9	15	-	-	-
11 months - 11 mois	16	6	10	-	-	-
Germany - Allemagne						
2018 (C)						
Total	2 505	1 399	1 106	3.2	3.5	2.9
Less than 1 day - Moins de 1 jour	915	481	434	1.2	1.2	1.1
1 - 6 days - 1 - 6 jours	494	303	191	0.6	0.7	0.5
7 - 27 days - 7 - 27 jours	378	210	168	0.5	0.5	0.4
7 - 13 days - 7 - 13 jours	199	109	90	0.3	0.3	0.2
14 - 20 days - 14 - 20 jours	110	67	43	0.1	0.2	0.1

16. Infant deaths and infant mortality rates by age and sex: latest available year, 2010 - 2019
Décès d'enfants de moins d'un an et taux de mortalité infantile selon l'âge et le sexe : dernière année disponible, 2010 - 2019 (continued - suite)

Continent, country or area, year, code[a] and age / Continent, pays ou zone, année, code[a] et âge	Number - Nombre			Rate - Taux		
	Both sexes Les deux sexes	Male Masculin	Female Féminin	Both sexes Les deux sexes	Male Masculin	Female Féminin
EUROPE						
Germany - Allemagne						
2018 (C)						
21 - 27 days - 21 - 27 jours	69	34	35	0.1	0.1	0.1
28 days - 11 months - 28 jours - 11 mois	717	405	312	0.9	1.0	0.8
28 days - less than 2 months - 28 jours - moins de 2 mois	201	110	91	0.3	0.3	0.2
2 months - 2 mois	103	60	43	0.1	0.1	0.1
3 months - 3 mois	77	50	27	0.1	0.1	♦0.1
4 months - 4 mois	77	44	33	0.1	0.1	0.1
5 months - 5 mois	53	31	22	0.1	0.1	♦0.1
6 months - 6 mois	49	27	22	0.1	♦0.1	♦0.1
7 months - 7 mois	41	23	18	0.1	♦0.1	-
8 months - 8 mois	32	17	15	-	-	-
9 months - 9 mois	35	17	18	-	-	-
10 months - 10 mois	26	11	15	-	-	-
11 months - 11 mois	23	15	8	-	-	-
Greece - Grèce						
2018 (C)						
Total	300	169	131	3.5	3.8	3.1
Less than 1 day - Moins de 1 jour	61	35	26	0.7	0.8	♦0.6
1 - 6 days - 1 - 6 jours	79	51	28	0.9	1.1	♦0.7
7 - 27 days - 7 - 27 jours	65	34	31	0.8	0.8	0.7
7 - 13 days - 7 - 13 jours	36	16	20	0.4	♦0.4	♦0.5
14 - 20 days - 14 - 20 jours	18	12	6	♦0.2	♦0.3	♦0.1
21 - 27 days - 21 - 27 jours	11	6	5	♦0.1	♦0.1	♦0.1
28 days - 11 months - 28 jours - 11 mois	94	48	46	1.1	1.1	1.1
28 days - less than 2 months - 28 jours - moins de 2 mois	27	16	11	♦0.3	♦0.4	♦0.3
2 months - 2 mois	21	10	11	♦0.2	♦0.2	♦0.3
3 months - 3 mois	6	4	2	♦0.1	♦0.1	-
4 months - 4 mois	4	1	3	-	-	♦0.1
5 months - 5 mois	6	3	3	♦0.1	♦0.1	♦0.1
6 months - 6 mois	5	2	3	♦0.1	-	♦0.1
7 months - 7 mois	5	1	4	♦0.1	-	♦0.1
8 months - 8 mois	4	2	2	-	-	-
9 months - 9 mois	9	5	4	♦0.1	♦0.1	♦0.1
Unknown - Inconnu	1	1	-	-	-	-
Hungary - Hongrie[27]						
2018 (C)						
Total	304	161	143	3.3	3.4	3.1
Less than 1 day - Moins de 1 jour	70	35	35	0.7	0.7	0.8
1 - 6 days - 1 - 6 jours	80	43	37	0.9	0.9	0.8
7 - 27 days - 7 - 27 jours	50	24	26	0.5	♦0.5	♦0.6
7 - 13 days - 7 - 13 jours	27	13	14	♦0.3	♦0.3	♦0.3
14 - 20 days - 14 - 20 jours	15	7	8	♦0.2	♦0.1	♦0.2
21 - 27 days - 21 - 27 jours	8	4	4	♦0.1	♦0.1	♦0.1
28 days - 11 months - 28 jours - 11 mois	104	59	45	1.1	1.2	1.0
28 days - less than 2 months - 28 jours - moins de 2 mois	35	22	13	0.4	♦0.5	♦0.3
2 months - 2 mois	11	4	7	♦0.1	♦0.1	♦0.2
3 months - 3 mois	11	8	3	♦0.1	♦0.2	♦0.1
4 months - 4 mois	8	4	4	♦0.1	♦0.1	♦0.1
5 months - 5 mois	14	7	7	♦0.1	♦0.1	♦0.2
6 months - 6 mois	5	3	2	♦0.1	♦0.1	-
7 months - 7 mois	5	2	3	♦0.1	-	♦0.1
8 months - 8 mois	2	2	-	-	-	-
9 months - 9 mois	5	2	3	♦0.1	-	♦0.1
10 months - 10 mois	2	1	1	-	-	-
11 months - 11 mois	6	4	2	♦0.1	♦0.1	-
Iceland - Islande						
2018 (C)						
Total	7	5	2	...	...	...
Less than 1 day - Moins de 1 jour	2	2	-	...	...	...
1 - 6 days - 1 - 6 jours	2	1	1	...	...	...
7 - 27 days - 7 - 27 jours	1	1	-	...	...	...
7 - 13 days - 7 - 13 jours	1	1	-	...	...	...
14 - 20 days - 14 - 20 jours	-	-	-	...	...	...
21 - 27 days - 21 - 27 jours	-	-	-	...	...	...
28 days - 11 months - 28 jours - 11 mois	2	1	1	...	...	...
28 days - less than 2 months - 28 jours - moins de 2 mois	-	-	-	...	...	...
2 months - 2 mois	-	-	-	...	...	...

16. Infant deaths and infant mortality rates by age and sex: latest available year, 2010 - 2019
Décès d'enfants de moins d'un an et taux de mortalité infantile selon l'âge et le sexe : dernière année disponible, 2010 - 2019 (continued - suite)

Continent, country or area, year, code[a] and age Continent, pays ou zone, année, code[a] et âge	Number - Nombre			Rate - Taux		
	Both sexes Les deux sexes	Male Masculin	Female Féminin	Both sexes Les deux sexes	Male Masculin	Female Féminin
EUROPE						
Iceland - Islande						
2018 (C)						
3 months - 3 mois	-	-	-	...	...	...
4 months - 4 mois	-	-	-	...	...	...
5 months - 5 mois	-	-	-	...	...	...
6 months - 6 mois	-	-	-	...	...	...
7 months - 7 mois	1	-	1	...	...	...
8 months - 8 mois	-	-	-	...	...	...
9 months - 9 mois	1	1	-	...	...	...
10 months - 10 mois	-	-	-	...	...	...
11 months - 11 mois	-	-	-	...	...	...
Ireland - Irlande						
2011 (+C)						
Total	262	150	112	3.5	4.0	3.1
Less than 1 day - Moins de 1 jour	88	43	45	1.2	1.1	1.2
1 - 6 days - 1 - 6 jours	59	38	21	0.8	1.0	♦0.6
7 - 27 days - 7 - 27 jours	41	30	11	0.6	0.8	♦0.3
7 - 13 days - 7 - 13 jours	18	13	5	♦0.2	♦0.3	♦0.1
14 - 20 days - 14 - 20 jours	17	13	4	♦0.2	♦0.3	♦0.1
21 - 27 days - 21 - 27 jours	6	4	2	♦0.1	♦0.1	♦0.1
28 days - 11 months - 28 jours - 11 mois	74	39	35	1.0	1.0	1.0
28 days - less than 2 months - 28 jours - moins de 2 mois	20	12	8	♦0.3	♦0.3	♦0.2
2 months - 2 mois	17	7	10	♦0.2	♦0.2	♦0.3
3 months - 3 mois	11	4	7	♦0.1	♦0.1	♦0.2
4 months - 4 mois	5	5	-	♦0.1	♦0.1	-
5 months - 5 mois	6	3	3	♦0.1	♦0.1	♦0.1
6 months - 6 mois	3	1	2	-	-	♦0.1
7 months - 7 mois	2	1	1	-	-	-
8 months - 8 mois	1	-	1	-	-	-
9 months - 9 mois	4	3	1	♦0.1	♦0.1	-
10 months - 10 mois	4	2	2	♦0.1	♦0.1	♦0.1
11 months - 11 mois	1	1	-	-	-	-
Italy - Italie						
2013 (C)						
Total	1 493	864	629	2.9	3.3	2.5
Less than 1 day - Moins de 1 jour	268	153	115	0.5	0.6	0.5
1 - 6 days - 1 - 6 jours	447	279	168	0.9	1.1	0.7
7 - 27 days - 7 - 27 jours	311	175	136	0.6	0.7	0.5
7 - 13 days - 7 - 13 jours	151	87	64	0.3	0.3	0.3
14 - 20 days - 14 - 20 jours	92	47	45	0.2	0.2	0.2
21 - 27 days - 21 - 27 jours	68	41	27	0.1	0.2	♦0.1
28 days - 11 months - 28 jours - 11 mois	467	257	210	0.9	1.0	0.8
28 days - less than 2 months - 28 jours - moins de 2 mois	149	90	59	0.3	0.3	0.2
2 months - 2 mois	69	31	38	0.1	0.1	0.2
3 months - 3 mois	50	20	30	0.1	♦0.1	0.1
4 months - 4 mois	44	26	18	0.1	♦0.1	♦0.1
5 months - 5 mois	35	21	14	0.1	♦0.1	♦0.1
6 months - 6 mois	33	21	12	0.1	♦0.1	-
7 months - 7 mois	27	10	17	♦0.1	-	♦0.1
8 months - 8 mois	20	16	4	-	♦0.1	-
9 months - 9 mois	18	11	7	-	-	-
10 months - 10 mois	13	6	7	-	-	-
11 months - 11 mois	9	5	4	-	-	-
Latvia - Lettonie						
2018 (C)						
Total	61	33	28	...	...	...
Less than 1 day - Moins de 1 jour	16	8	8	...	...	...
1 - 6 days - 1 - 6 jours	8	5	3	...	...	...
7 - 27 days - 7 - 27 jours	10	5	5	...	...	...
7 - 13 days - 7 - 13 jours	6	2	4	...	...	...
14 - 20 days - 14 - 20 jours	2	1	1	...	...	...
21 - 27 days - 21 - 27 jours	2	2	-	...	...	...
28 days - 11 months - 28 jours - 11 mois	27	15	12	...	...	...
28 days - less than 2 months - 28 jours - moins de 2 mois	3	2	1	...	...	...
2 months - 2 mois	7	5	2	...	...	...
3 months - 3 mois	5	2	3	...	...	...
4 months - 4 mois	3	-	3	...	...	...
5 months - 5 mois	-	-	-	...	...	...

16. Infant deaths and infant mortality rates by age and sex: latest available year, 2010 - 2019
Décès d'enfants de moins d'un an et taux de mortalité infantile selon l'âge et le sexe : dernière année disponible, 2010 - 2019 (continued - suite)

Continent, country or area, year, code[a] and age Continent, pays ou zone, année, code[a] et âge	Number - Nombre			Rate - Taux		
	Both sexes Les deux sexes	Male Masculin	Female Féminin	Both sexes Les deux sexes	Male Masculin	Female Féminin
EUROPE						
Latvia - Lettonie						
2018 (C)						
6 months - 6 mois	1	-	1	...	...	...
7 months - 7 mois	4	3	1	...	...	...
8 months - 8 mois	-	-	-	...	...	...
9 months - 9 mois	2	1	1	...	...	...
10 months - 10 mois	1	1	-	...	...	...
11 months - 11 mois	1	1	-	...	...	...
Liechtenstein						
2015 (C)						
Total	2	2	-	...	...	...
1 - 6 days - 1 - 6 jours	2	2	-	...	...	...
Lithuania - Lituanie						
2018 (C)						
Total	96	55	41	...	...	...
Less than 1 day - Moins de 1 jour	19	10	9	...	...	...
1 - 6 days - 1 - 6 jours	19	8	11	...	...	...
7 - 27 days - 7 - 27 jours	25	18	7	...	...	...
7 - 13 days - 7 - 13 jours	12	7	5	...	...	...
14 - 20 days - 14 - 20 jours	4	3	1	...	...	...
21 - 27 days - 21 - 27 jours	9	8	1	...	...	...
28 days - 11 months - 28 jours - 11 mois	33	19	14	...	...	...
28 days - less than 2 months - 28 jours - moins de 2 mois	13	7	6	...	...	...
2 months - 2 mois	5	4	1	...	...	...
3 months - 3 mois	6	4	2	...	...	...
4 months - 4 mois	1	1	-	...	...	...
5 months - 5 mois	4	2	2	...	...	...
6 months - 6 mois	2	1	1	...	...	...
7 months - 7 mois	1	-	1	...	...	...
8 months - 8 mois	-	-	-	...	...	...
9 months - 9 mois	1	-	1	...	...	...
10 months - 10 mois	-	-	-	...	...	...
11 months - 11 mois	-	-	-	...	...	...
Luxembourg						
2018 (C)						
Total	27	13	14	...	...	...
Less than 1 day - Moins de 1 jour	18	7	11	...	...	...
1 - 6 days - 1 - 6 jours	1	1	-	...	...	...
7 - 27 days - 7 - 27 jours	-	-	-	...	...	...
7 - 13 days - 7 - 13 jours	-	-	-	...	...	...
14 - 20 days - 14 - 20 jours	-	-	-	...	...	...
21 - 27 days - 21 - 27 jours	-	-	-	...	...	...
28 days - 11 months - 28 jours - 11 mois	8	5	3	...	...	...
28 days - less than 2 months - 28 jours - moins de 2 mois	3	2	1	...	...	...
2 months - 2 mois	-	-	-	...	...	...
3 months - 3 mois	2	1	1	...	...	...
4 months - 4 mois	-	-	-	...	...	...
5 months - 5 mois	2	2	-	...	...	...
6 months - 6 mois	-	-	-	...	...	...
7 months - 7 mois	-	-	-	...	...	...
8 months - 8 mois	1	-	1	...	...	...
9 months - 9 mois	-	-	-	...	...	...
10 months - 10 mois	-	-	-	...	...	...
11 months - 11 mois	-	-	-	...	...	...
Malta - Malte						
2018 (C)						
Total	25	16	9	...	...	...
Less than 1 day - Moins de 1 jour	7	3	4	...	...	...
1 - 6 days - 1 - 6 jours	7	5	2	...	...	...
7 - 27 days - 7 - 27 jours	6	5	1	...	...	...
7 - 13 days - 7 - 13 jours	3	2	1	...	...	...
14 - 20 days - 14 - 20 jours	3	3	-	...	...	...
21 - 27 days - 21 - 27 jours	-	-	-	...	...	...
28 days - 11 months - 28 jours - 11 mois	5	3	2	...	...	...
28 days - less than 2 months - 28 jours - moins de 2 mois	3	2	1	...	...	...
2 months - 2 mois	2	1	1	...	...	...
3 months - 3 mois	-	-	-	...	...	...
4 months - 4 mois	-	-	-	...	...	...

16. Infant deaths and infant mortality rates by age and sex: latest available year, 2010 - 2019
Décès d'enfants de moins d'un an et taux de mortalité infantile selon l'âge et le sexe : dernière année disponible, 2010 - 2019 (continued - suite)

Continent, country or area, year, code[a] and age / Continent, pays ou zone, année, code[a] et âge	Number - Nombre			Rate - Taux		
	Both sexes Les deux sexes	Male Masculin	Female Féminin	Both sexes Les deux sexes	Male Masculin	Female Féminin
EUROPE						
Malta - Malte						
2018 (C)						
5 months - 5 mois	-	-	-	...	...	...
6 months - 6 mois	-	-	-	...	...	...
7 months - 7 mois	-	-	-	...	...	...
8 months - 8 mois	-	-	-	...	...	...
9 months - 9 mois	-	-	-	...	...	...
10 months - 10 mois	-	-	-	...	...	...
11 months - 11 mois	-	-	-	...	...	...
Montenegro - Monténégro						
2018 (C)						
Total	12	8	4	...	...	...
Less than 1 day - Moins de 1 jour	-	-	-	...	...	...
1 - 6 days - 1 - 6 jours	2	2	-	...	...	...
7 - 27 days - 7 - 27 jours	3	2	1	...	...	...
28 days - 11 months - 28 jours - 11 mois	7	4	3	...	...	...
Netherlands - Pays-Bas[28]						
2018 (C)						
Total	582	332	250	3.5	3.9	3.0
Less than 1 day - Moins de 1 jour	173	101	72	1.0	1.2	0.9
1 - 6 days - 1 - 6 jours	154	87	67	0.9	1.0	0.8
7 - 27 days - 7 - 27 jours	102	55	47	0.6	0.6	0.6
28 days - 11 months - 28 jours - 11 mois	153	89	64	0.9	1.0	0.8
North Macedonia - Macédoine du Nord						
2018 (C)						
Total	122	71	51	5.7	6.4	5.0
Less than 1 day - Moins de 1 jour	23	12	11	♦1.1	♦1.1	♦1.1
1 - 6 days - 1 - 6 jours	50	29	21	2.3	♦2.6	♦2.1
7 - 27 days - 7 - 27 jours	14	8	6	♦0.7	♦0.7	♦0.6
7 - 13 days - 7 - 13 jours	6	5	1	♦0.3	♦0.4	♦0.1
14 - 20 days - 14 - 20 jours	5	2	3	♦0.2	♦0.2	♦0.3
21 - 27 days - 21 - 27 jours	3	1	2	♦0.1	♦0.1	♦0.2
28 days - 11 months - 28 jours - 11 mois	35	22	13	1.6	♦2.0	♦1.3
28 days - less than 2 months - 28 jours - moins de 2 mois	8	6	2	♦0.4	♦0.5	♦0.2
2 months - 2 mois	4	2	2	♦0.2	♦0.2	♦0.2
3 months - 3 mois	4	3	1	♦0.2	♦0.3	♦0.1
4 months - 4 mois	3	2	1	♦0.1	♦0.2	♦0.1
5 months - 5 mois	3	2	1	♦0.1	♦0.2	♦0.1
6 months - 6 mois	5	2	3	♦0.2	♦0.2	♦0.3
7 months - 7 mois	1	1	-	-	♦0.1	-
8 months - 8 mois	2	1	1	♦0.1	♦0.1	♦0.1
9 months - 9 mois	3	1	2	♦0.1	♦0.1	♦0.2
10 months - 10 mois	1	1	-	-	♦0.1	-
11 months - 11 mois	1	1	-	-	♦0.1	-
Norway - Norvège[29]						
2018 (C)						
Total	129	70	59	2.3	2.5	2.2
Less than 1 day - Moins de 1 jour	34	21	13	0.6	♦0.7	♦0.5
1 - 6 days - 1 - 6 jours	36	21	15	0.7	♦0.7	♦0.6
7 - 27 days - 7 - 27 jours	24	12	12	♦0.4	♦0.4	♦0.4
28 days - 11 months - 28 jours - 11 mois	35	16	19	0.6	♦0.6	♦0.7
Poland - Pologne						
2018 (C)						
Total	1 494	834	660	3.8	4.2	3.5
Less than 1 day - Moins de 1 jour	488	289	199	1.3	1.4	1.1
1 - 6 days - 1 - 6 jours	314	173	141	0.8	0.9	0.7
7 - 27 days - 7 - 27 jours	266	145	121	0.7	0.7	0.6
7 - 13 days - 7 - 13 jours	140	73	67	0.4	0.4	0.4
14 - 20 days - 14 - 20 jours	67	37	30	0.2	0.2	0.2
21 - 27 days - 21 - 27 jours	59	35	24	0.2	0.2	♦0.1
28 days - 11 months - 28 jours - 11 mois	426	227	199	1.1	1.1	1.1
28 days - less than 2 months - 28 jours - moins de 2 mois	127	65	62	0.3	0.3	0.3
2 months - 2 mois	68	35	33	0.2	0.2	0.2
3 months - 3 mois	48	29	19	0.1	♦0.1	♦0.1
4 months - 4 mois	42	20	22	0.1	♦0.1	♦0.1
5 months - 5 mois	30	16	14	0.1	♦0.1	♦0.1
6 months - 6 mois	35	20	15	0.1	♦0.1	♦0.1
7 months - 7 mois	23	9	14	♦0.1	-	♦0.1

16. Infant deaths and infant mortality rates by age and sex: latest available year, 2010 - 2019
Décès d'enfants de moins d'un an et taux de mortalité infantile selon l'âge et le sexe : dernière année disponible, 2010 - 2019 (continued - suite)

Continent, country or area, year, code[a] and age Continent, pays ou zone, année, code[a] et âge	Number - Nombre			Rate - Taux		
	Both sexes Les deux sexes	Male Masculin	Female Féminin	Both sexes Les deux sexes	Male Masculin	Female Féminin
EUROPE						
Poland - Pologne						
2018 (C)						
8 months - 8 mois	20	12	8	♦0.1	♦0.1	-
9 months - 9 mois	10	6	4	-	-	-
10 months - 10 mois	13	10	3	-	♦0.1	-
11 months - 11 mois	10	5	5	-	-	-
Portugal[30]						
2018 (C)						
Total	287	159	128	3.3	3.6	3.0
Less than 1 day - Moins de 1 jour	73	46	27	0.8	1.0	♦0.6
1 - 6 days - 1 - 6 jours	69	37	32	0.8	0.8	0.7
7 - 27 days - 7 - 27 jours	49	24	25	0.6	♦0.5	♦0.6
7 - 13 days - 7 - 13 jours	27	14	13	♦0.3	♦0.3	♦0.3
14 - 20 days - 14 - 20 jours	15	6	9	♦0.2	♦0.1	♦0.2
21 - 27 days - 21 - 27 jours	7	4	3	♦0.1	♦0.1	♦0.1
28 days - 11 months - 28 jours - 11 mois	96	...	...	1.1	...	...
28 days - less than 2 months - 28 jours - moins de 2 mois	33	19	14	0.4	♦0.4	♦0.3
2 months - 2 mois	11	7	4	♦0.1	♦0.2	♦0.1
3 months - 3 mois	7	3	4	♦0.1	♦0.1	♦0.1
4 months - 4 mois	10	6	4	♦0.1	♦0.1	♦0.1
5 months - 5 mois	10	3	7	♦0.1	♦0.1	♦0.2
6 months - 6 mois	4	2	2	-	-	-
7 months - 7 mois	8	6	2	♦0.1	♦0.1	-
8 months - 8 mois	2	...	2	-	...	-
9 months - 9 mois	4	...	3	-	...	♦0.1
10 months - 10 mois	4	...	...	-	...	...
11 months - 11 mois	3	...	...	-	...	...
Republic of Moldova - République de Moldova[31]						
2016 (C)						
Total	353	204	149	9.4	10.6	8.2
Less than 1 day - Moins de 1 jour	75	41	34	2.0	2.1	1.9
1 - 6 days - 1 - 6 jours	94	59	35	2.5	3.1	1.9
7 - 27 days - 7 - 27 jours	73	42	31	2.0	2.2	1.7
28 days - 11 months - 28 jours - 11 mois	111	62	49	3.0	3.2	2.7
Romania - Roumanie						
2018 (C)						
Total	1 226	691	535	6.0	6.6	5.4
Less than 1 day - Moins de 1 jour	160	88	72	0.8	0.8	0.7
1 - 6 days - 1 - 6 jours	304	168	136	1.5	1.6	1.4
7 - 27 days - 7 - 27 jours	237	139	98	1.2	1.3	1.0
7 - 13 days - 7 - 13 jours	108	63	45	0.5	0.6	0.5
14 - 20 days - 14 - 20 jours	73	40	33	0.4	0.4	0.3
21 - 27 days - 21 - 27 jours	56	36	20	0.3	0.3	♦0.2
28 days - 11 months - 28 jours - 11 mois	525	296	229	2.6	2.8	2.3
28 days - less than 2 months - 28 jours - moins de 2 mois	151	91	60	0.7	0.9	0.6
2 months - 2 mois	73	46	27	0.4	0.4	♦0.3
3 months - 3 mois	64	35	29	0.3	0.3	♦0.3
4 months - 4 mois	53	29	24	0.3	♦0.3	♦0.2
5 months - 5 mois	40	27	13	0.2	♦0.3	♦0.1
6 months - 6 mois	33	13	20	0.2	♦0.1	♦0.2
7 months - 7 mois	25	13	12	♦0.1	♦0.1	♦0.1
8 months - 8 mois	23	12	11	♦0.1	♦0.1	♦0.1
9 months - 9 mois	32	17	15	0.2	♦0.2	♦0.2
10 months - 10 mois	18	7	11	♦0.1	♦0.1	♦0.1
11 months - 11 mois	13	6	7	♦0.1	♦0.1	♦0.1
Russian Federation - Fédération de Russie[14]						
2012 (C)						
Total	16 306	9 219	7 087	8.6	9.4	7.7
Less than 1 day - Moins de 1 jour	1 897	1 009	888	1.0	1.0	1.0
1 - 6 days - 1 - 6 jours	5 072	2 961	2 111	2.7	3.0	2.3
7 - 27 days - 7 - 27 jours	3 438	1 958	1 480	1.8	2.0	1.6
7 - 13 days - 7 - 13 jours	1 798	1 020	778	0.9	1.0	0.8
14 - 20 days - 14 - 20 jours	952	560	392	0.5	0.6	0.4
21 - 27 days - 21 - 27 jours	688	378	310	0.4	0.4	0.3
28 days - 11 months - 28 jours - 11 mois	5 898	3 290	2 608	3.1	3.4	2.8
28 days - less than 2 months - 28 jours - moins de 2 mois	2 063	1 166	897	1.1	1.2	1.0
2 months - 2 mois	942	525	417	0.5	0.5	0.5
3 months - 3 mois	691	372	319	0.4	0.4	0.3

Continent, country or area, year, code[a] and age / Continent, pays ou zone, année, code[a] et âge	Number - Nombre			Rate - Taux		
	Both sexes Les deux sexes	Male Masculin	Female Féminin	Both sexes Les deux sexes	Male Masculin	Female Féminin
EUROPE						
Russian Federation - Fédération de Russie[14]						
2012 (C)						
4 months - 4 mois	562	333	229	0.3	0.3	0.2
5 months - 5 mois	417	221	196	0.2	0.2	0.2
6 months - 6 mois	334	184	150	0.2	0.2	0.2
7 months - 7 mois	252	139	113	0.1	0.1	0.1
8 months - 8 mois	219	127	92	0.1	0.1	0.1
9 months - 9 mois	172	86	86	0.1	0.1	0.1
10 months - 10 mois	134	74	60	0.1	0.1	0.1
11 months - 11 mois	112	63	49	0.1	0.1	0.1
Unknown - Inconnu	1	1	-	-	-	-
San Marino - Saint-Marin						
2014 (C)						
Total	1	1	-	...	...	...
Less than 1 day - Moins de 1 jour	-	-	-	...	...	...
1 - 6 days - 1 - 6 jours	-	-	-	...	...	...
7 - 27 days - 7 - 27 jours	-	-	-	...	...	...
28 days - 11 months - 28 jours - 11 mois	1	1	-	...	...	...
Serbia - Serbie[32]						
2018 (+C)						
Total	311	168	143	4.9	5.1	4.6
Less than 1 day - Moins de 1 jour	94	45	49	1.5	1.4	1.6
1 - 6 days - 1 - 6 jours	88	52	36	1.4	1.6	1.2
7 - 27 days - 7 - 27 jours	53	33	20	0.8	1.0	♦0.7
7 - 13 days - 7 - 13 jours	33	22	11	0.5	♦0.7	♦0.4
14 - 20 days - 14 - 20 jours	11	4	7	♦0.2	♦0.1	♦0.2
21 - 27 days - 21 - 27 jours	9	7	2	♦0.1	♦0.2	♦0.1
28 days - 11 months - 28 jours - 11 mois	76	38	38	1.2	1.1	1.2
28 days - less than 2 months - 28 jours - moins de 2 mois	16	11	5	♦0.3	♦0.3	♦0.2
2 months - 2 mois	14	5	9	♦0.2	♦0.2	♦0.3
3 months - 3 mois	10	4	6	♦0.2	♦0.1	♦0.2
4 months - 4 mois	8	4	4	♦0.1	♦0.1	♦0.1
5 months - 5 mois	8	4	4	♦0.1	♦0.1	♦0.1
6 months - 6 mois	4	3	1	♦0.1	♦0.1	-
7 months - 7 mois	2	-	2	-	-	♦0.1
8 months - 8 mois	3	2	1	-	♦0.1	-
9 months - 9 mois	6	2	4	♦0.1	♦0.1	♦0.1
10 months - 10 mois	1	1	-	-	-	-
11 months - 11 mois	4	2	2	♦0.1	♦0.1	♦0.1
Slovakia - Slovaquie						
2018 (C)						
Total	288	159	129	5.0	5.4	4.6
Less than 1 day - Moins de 1 jour	58	29	29	1.0	♦1.0	♦1.0
1 - 6 days - 1 - 6 jours	59	36	23	1.0	1.2	♦0.8
7 - 27 days - 7 - 27 jours	56	30	26	1.0	1.0	♦0.9
7 - 13 days - 7 - 13 jours	26	16	10	♦0.5	♦0.5	♦0.4
14 - 20 days - 14 - 20 jours	21	9	12	♦0.4	♦0.3	♦0.4
21 - 27 days - 21 - 27 jours	9	5	4	♦0.2	♦0.2	♦0.1
28 days - 11 months - 28 jours - 11 mois	115	64	51	2.0	2.2	1.8
28 days - less than 2 months - 28 jours - moins de 2 mois	41	25	16	0.7	♦0.8	♦0.6
2 months - 2 mois	15	7	8	♦0.3	♦0.2	♦0.3
3 months - 3 mois	10	7	3	♦0.2	♦0.2	♦0.1
4 months - 4 mois	11	6	5	♦0.2	♦0.2	♦0.2
5 months - 5 mois	13	7	6	♦0.2	♦0.2	♦0.2
6 months - 6 mois	5	3	2	♦0.1	♦0.1	♦0.1
7 months - 7 mois	6	1	5	♦0.1	-	♦0.2
8 months - 8 mois	5	2	3	♦0.1	♦0.1	♦0.1
9 months - 9 mois	3	3	-	♦0.1	♦0.1	-
10 months - 10 mois	3	1	2	♦0.1	-	♦0.1
11 months - 11 mois	3	2	1	♦0.1	♦0.1	-
Slovenia - Slovénie						
2018 (C)						
Total	33	22	11	...	...	...
Less than 1 day - Moins de 1 jour	10	5	5	...	...	...
1 - 6 days - 1 - 6 jours	8	7	1	...	...	...
7 - 27 days - 7 - 27 jours	10	7	3	...	...	...
7 - 13 days - 7 - 13 jours	5	5	-	...	...	...
14 - 20 days - 14 - 20 jours	4	1	3	...	...	...

Continent, country or area, year, code[a] and age Continent, pays ou zone, année, code[a] et âge	Number - Nombre			Rate - Taux		
	Both sexes Les deux sexes	Male Masculin	Female Féminin	Both sexes Les deux sexes	Male Masculin	Female Féminin
EUROPE						
Slovenia - Slovénie						
2018 (C)						
21 - 27 days - 21 - 27 jours	1	1	-	...	...	...
28 days - 11 months - 28 jours - 11 mois	5	3	2	...	...	...
28 days - less than 2 months - 28 jours - moins de 2 mois	-	-	-	...	...	...
2 months - 2 mois	2	1	1	...	...	...
3 months - 3 mois	-	-	-	...	...	...
4 months - 4 mois	-	-	-	...	...	...
5 months - 5 mois	2	2	-	...	...	...
6 months - 6 mois	1	-	1	...	...	...
7 months - 7 mois	-	-	-	...	...	...
8 months - 8 mois	-	-	-	...	...	...
9 months - 9 mois	-	-	-	...	...	...
10 months - 10 mois	-	-	-	...	...	...
11 months - 11 mois	-	-	-	...	...	...
Spain - Espagne						
2018 (C)						
Total	998	543	455	2.7	2.8	2.5
Less than 1 day - Moins de 1 jour	211	114	97	0.6	0.6	0.5
1 - 6 days - 1 - 6 jours	267	147	120	0.7	0.8	0.7
7 - 27 days - 7 - 27 jours	216	121	95	0.6	0.6	0.5
7 - 13 days - 7 - 13 jours	115	63	52	0.3	0.3	0.3
14 - 20 days - 14 - 20 jours	66	38	28	0.2	0.2	♦0.2
21 - 27 days - 21 - 27 jours	35	20	15	0.1	♦0.1	♦0.1
28 days - 11 months - 28 jours - 11 mois	304	161	143	0.8	0.8	0.8
28 days - less than 2 months - 28 jours - moins de 2 mois	81	45	36	0.2	0.2	0.2
2 months - 2 mois	50	30	20	0.1	0.2	♦0.1
3 months - 3 mois	30	16	14	0.1	♦0.1	♦0.1
4 months - 4 mois	33	18	15	0.1	♦0.1	♦0.1
5 months - 5 mois	26	9	17	♦0.1	-	♦0.1
6 months - 6 mois	17	10	7	-	♦0.1	-
7 months - 7 mois	21	12	9	♦0.1	♦0.1	-
8 months - 8 mois	13	5	8	-	-	-
9 months - 9 mois	14	6	8	-	-	-
10 months - 10 mois	11	6	5	-	-	-
11 months - 11 mois	8	4	4	-	-	-
Sweden - Suède						
2018 (C)						
Total	235	132	103	2.0	2.2	1.8
Less than 1 day - Moins de 1 jour	37	21	16	0.3	♦0.4	♦0.3
1 - 6 days - 1 - 6 jours	70	43	27	0.6	0.7	♦0.5
7 - 27 days - 7 - 27 jours	41	20	21	0.4	♦0.3	♦0.4
28 days - 11 months - 28 jours - 11 mois	87	48	39	0.8	0.8	0.7
Switzerland - Suisse						
2018 (C)						
Total	287	154	133	3.3	3.4	3.1
Less than 1 day - Moins de 1 jour	157	75	82	1.8	1.7	1.9
1 - 6 days - 1 - 6 jours	47	30	17	0.5	0.7	♦0.4
7 - 27 days - 7 - 27 jours	34	22	12	0.4	♦0.5	♦0.3
7 - 13 days - 7 - 13 jours	16	10	6	♦0.2	♦0.2	♦0.1
14 - 20 days - 14 - 20 jours	12	8	4	♦0.1	♦0.2	♦0.1
21 - 27 days - 21 - 27 jours	6	4	2	♦0.1	♦0.1	-
28 days - 11 months - 28 jours - 11 mois	49	27	22	0.6	♦0.6	♦0.5
28 days - less than 2 months - 28 jours - moins de 2 mois	15	6	9	♦0.2	♦0.1	♦0.2
2 months - 2 mois	7	4	3	♦0.1	♦0.1	♦0.1
3 months - 3 mois	4	4	-	-	♦0.1	-
4 months - 4 mois	6	4	2	♦0.1	♦0.1	-
5 months - 5 mois	2	1	1	-	-	-
6 months - 6 mois	-	-	-	-	-	-
7 months - 7 mois	3	1	2	-	-	-
8 months - 8 mois	3	1	2	-	-	-
9 months - 9 mois	5	3	2	♦0.1	♦0.1	-
10 months - 10 mois	2	1	1	-	-	-
11 months - 11 mois	2	2	-	-	-	-
Ukraine[33]						
2017 (+C)						
Total	2 786	1 608	1 178	7.7	8.6	6.7
Less than 1 day - Moins de 1 jour	455	247	208	1.3	1.3	1.2

Continent, country or area, year, code[a] and age Continent, pays ou zone, année, code[a] et âge	Number - Nombre			Rate - Taux		
	Both sexes Les deux sexes	Male Masculin	Female Féminin	Both sexes Les deux sexes	Male Masculin	Female Féminin
EUROPE						
Ukraine[33]						
2017 (+C)						
1 - 6 days - 1 - 6 jours	764	463	301	2.1	2.5	1.7
7 - 27 days - 7 - 27 jours	579	338	241	1.6	1.8	1.4
7 - 13 days - 7 - 13 jours	313	181	132	0.9	1.0	0.7
14 - 20 days - 14 - 20 jours	154	95	59	0.4	0.5	0.3
21 - 27 days - 21 - 27 jours	112	62	50	0.3	0.3	0.3
28 days - 11 months - 28 jours - 11 mois	988	560	428	2.7	3.0	2.4
28 days - less than 2 months - 28 jours - moins de 2 mois	296	161	135	0.8	0.9	0.8
2 months - 2 mois	152	90	62	0.4	0.5	0.4
3 months - 3 mois	117	66	51	0.3	0.4	0.3
4 months - 4 mois	105	65	40	0.3	0.3	0.2
5 months - 5 mois	66	34	32	0.2	0.2	0.2
6 months - 6 mois	64	32	32	0.2	0.2	0.2
7 months - 7 mois	52	28	24	0.1	♦0.1	♦0.1
8 months - 8 mois	32	20	12	0.1	♦0.1	♦0.1
9 months - 9 mois	34	20	14	0.1	♦0.1	♦0.1
10 months - 10 mois	33	20	13	0.1	♦0.1	♦0.1
11 months - 11 mois	37	24	13	0.1	♦0.1	♦0.1
United Kingdom of Great Britain and Northern Ireland - Royaume-Uni de Grande-Bretagne et d'Irlande du Nord[34]						
2018 (+C)						
Total	2 818	1 562	1 256	3.9	4.2	3.5
Less than 1 day - Moins de 1 jour	1 046	589	457	1.4	1.6	1.3
1 - 6 days - 1 - 6 jours	550	299	251	0.8	0.8	0.7
7 - 27 days - 7 - 27 jours	425	237	188	0.6	0.6	0.5
7 - 13 days - 7 - 13 jours	212	120	92	0.3	0.3	0.3
14 - 20 days - 14 - 20 jours	140	73	67	0.2	0.2	0.2
21 - 27 days - 21 - 27 jours	73	44	29	0.1	0.1	♦0.1
28 days - 11 months - 28 jours - 11 mois	799	437	362	1.1	1.2	1.0
28 days - less than 2 months - 28 jours - moins de 2 mois	277	154	123	0.4	0.4	0.3
2 months - 2 mois	126	70	56	0.2	0.2	0.2
3 months - 3 mois	83	49	34	0.1	0.1	0.1
4 months - 4 mois	78	47	31	0.1	0.1	0.1
5 months - 5 mois	61	38	23	0.1	0.1	♦0.1
6 months - 6 mois	44	26	18	0.1	♦0.1	♦0.1
7 months - 7 mois	41	10	31	0.1	-	0.1
8 months - 8 mois	22	12	10	-	-	-
9 months - 9 mois	29	10	19	-	-	♦0.1
10 months - 10 mois	23	12	11	-	-	-
11 months - 11 mois	15	9	6	-	-	-
OCEANIA - OCÉANIE						
Australia - Australie[35]						
2018 (C)						
Total	988	571	417	3.1	3.5	2.7
Less than 1 day - Moins de 1 jour	435	246	189	1.4	1.5	1.2
1 - 6 days - 1 - 6 jours	143	90	53	0.5	0.6	0.3
7 - 27 days - 7 - 27 jours	159	89	70	0.5	0.5	0.5
7 - 13 days - 7 - 13 jours	87	51	36	0.3	0.3	0.2
14 - 20 days - 14 - 20 jours	37	16	21	0.1	♦0.1	♦0.1
21 - 27 days - 21 - 27 jours	35	22	13	0.1	♦0.1	♦0.1
28 days - 11 months - 28 jours - 11 mois	251	146	101	0.8	0.9	0.7
28 days - less than 2 months - 28 jours - moins de 2 mois	78	39	39	0.2	0.2	0.3
2 months - 2 mois	38	21	17	0.1	♦0.1	♦0.1
3 months - 3 mois	30	19	11	0.1	♦0.1	♦0.1
4 months - 4 mois	29	19	10	♦0.1	♦0.1	♦0.1
5 months - 5 mois	18	13	5	♦0.1	♦0.1	-
6 months - 6 mois	22	16	6	♦0.1	♦0.1	-
7 months - 7 mois	9	5	3	-	-	-
8 months - 8 mois	6	2	4	-	-	-
9 months - 9 mois	10	6	2	-	-	-
10 months - 10 mois	5	3	1	-	-	-
11 months - 11 mois	6	3	3	-	-	-

16. Infant deaths and infant mortality rates by age and sex: latest available year, 2010 - 2019
Décès d'enfants de moins d'un an et taux de mortalité infantile selon l'âge et le sexe : dernière année disponible, 2010 - 2019 (continued - suite)

Continent, country or area, year, code[a] and age Continent, pays ou zone, année, code[a] et âge	Number - Nombre			Rate - Taux		
	Both sexes Les deux sexes	Male Masculin	Female Féminin	Both sexes Les deux sexes	Male Masculin	Female Féminin
OCEANIA - OCÉANIE						
French Polynesia - Polynésie française						
2018 (C)						
Total	38	24	14	...	...	...
Less than 1 day - Moins de 1 jour	21	14	7	...	...	...
1 - 6 days - 1 - 6 jours	5	4	1	...	...	...
7 - 27 days - 7 - 27 jours	4	1	3	...	...	...
7 - 13 days - 7 - 13 jours	4	1	3	...	...	...
14 - 20 days - 14 - 20 jours	-	-	-	...	...	...
21 - 27 days - 21 - 27 jours	-	-	-	...	...	...
28 days - 11 months - 28 jours - 11 mois	8	5	3	...	...	...
28 days - less than 2 months - 28 jours - moins de 2 mois	5	3	2	...	...	...
2 months - 2 mois	1	-	1	...	...	...
3 months - 3 mois	1	1	-	...	...	...
4 months - 4 mois	-	-	-	...	...	...
5 months - 5 mois	-	-	-	...	...	...
6 months - 6 mois	-	-	-	...	...	...
7 months - 7 mois	-	-	-	...	...	...
8 months - 8 mois	-	-	-	...	...	...
9 months - 9 mois	-	-	-	...	...	...
10 months - 10 mois	-	-	-	...	...	...
11 months - 11 mois	1	1	-	...	...	...
Guam[36]						
2015 (C)						
Total	47	23	24	...	...	...
Less than 1 day - Moins de 1 jour	10	4	6	...	...	...
1 - 6 days - 1 - 6 jours	16	9	7	...	...	...
7 - 27 days - 7 - 27 jours	7	1	6	...	...	...
7 - 13 days - 7 - 13 jours	2	-	2	...	...	...
14 - 20 days - 14 - 20 jours	4	1	3	...	...	...
21 - 27 days - 21 - 27 jours	1	-	1	...	...	...
28 days - 11 months - 28 jours - 11 mois	14	9	5	...	...	...
28 days - less than 2 months - 28 jours - moins de 2 mois	2	2	-	...	...	...
2 months - 2 mois	3	3	-	...	...	...
3 months - 3 mois	3	-	3	...	...	...
4 months - 4 mois	-	-	-	...	...	...
5 months - 5 mois	-	-	-	...	...	...
6 months - 6 mois	2	1	1	...	...	...
7 months - 7 mois	-	-	-	...	...	...
8 months - 8 mois	2	2	-	...	...	...
9 months - 9 mois	1	1	-	...	...	...
10 months - 10 mois	1	-	1	...	...	...
11 months - 11 mois	-	-	-	...	...	...
New Caledonia - Nouvelle-Calédonie						
2015 (C)						
Total	25	18	7	...	...	...
Less than 1 day - Moins de 1 jour	4	3	1	...	...	...
1 - 6 days - 1 - 6 jours	5	4	1	...	...	...
7 - 27 days - 7 - 27 jours	7	5	2	...	...	...
7 - 13 days - 7 - 13 jours	5	4	1	...	...	...
14 - 20 days - 14 - 20 jours	2	1	1	...	...	...
21 - 27 days - 21 - 27 jours	-	-	-	...	...	...
28 days - 11 months - 28 jours - 11 mois	9	6	3	...	...	...
28 days - less than 2 months - 28 jours - moins de 2 mois	3	1	2	...	...	...
2 - 11 months - 2 - 11 mois	6	5	1	...	...	...
New Zealand - Nouvelle-Zélande[37]						
2019 (+C)						
Total	270	144	126	4.5	4.7	4.3
Less than 1 day - Moins de 1 jour	96	39	54	1.6	1.3	1.9
1 - 6 days - 1 - 6 jours	45	27	18	0.8	♦0.9	♦0.6
7 - 27 days - 7 - 27 jours	33	21	12	0.6	♦0.7	♦0.4
7 - 13 days - 7 - 13 jours	15	9	6	♦0.3	♦0.3	♦0.2
14 - 20 days - 14 - 20 jours	9	6	3	♦0.2	♦0.2	♦0.1
21 - 27 days - 21 - 27 jours	9	6	3	♦0.2	♦0.2	♦0.1
28 days - 11 months - 28 jours - 11 mois	99	54	39	1.7	1.8	1.3
28 days - less than 2 months - 28 jours - moins de 2 mois	30	15	12	0.5	♦0.5	♦0.4
2 months - 2 mois	21	9	12	♦0.4	♦0.3	♦0.4
3 months - 3 mois	9	6	3	♦0.2	♦0.2	♦0.1
4 months - 4 mois	9	6	3	♦0.2	♦0.2	♦0.1

16. Infant deaths and infant mortality rates by age and sex: latest available year, 2010 - 2019
Décès d'enfants de moins d'un an et taux de mortalité infantile selon l'âge et le sexe : dernière année disponible, 2010 - 2019 (continued - suite)

Continent, country or area, year, code[a] and age Continent, pays ou zone, année, code[a] et âge	Number - Nombre			Rate - Taux		
	Both sexes Les deux sexes	Male Masculin	Female Féminin	Both sexes Les deux sexes	Male Masculin	Female Féminin
OCEANIA - OCÉANIE						
New Zealand - Nouvelle-Zélande[37]						
2019 (+C)						
5 months - 5 mois	6	3	3	♦0.1	♦0.1	♦0.1
6 months - 6 mois	6	6	-	♦0.1	♦0.2	-
7 months - 7 mois	3	-	3	♦0.1	-	♦0.1
8 months - 8 mois	6	3	-	♦0.1	♦0.1	-
9 months - 9 mois	3	3	-	♦0.1	♦0.1	-
10 months - 10 mois	3	3	3	♦0.1	♦0.1	♦0.1
11 months - 11 mois	3	-	-	♦0.1	-	-

FOOTNOTES - NOTES

Italics: data from civil registers which are incomplete or of unknown completeness. - Italiques : données incomplètes ou dont le degré d'exactitude n'est pas connu, provenant des registres de l'état civil.

♦ Rates based on 30 or fewer infant deaths. - Taux basés sur 30 dècès d'enfants ou moins.

* Provisional. - Données provisoires.

a 'Code' indicates the source of data, as follows:
C - Civil registration, estimated over 90% complete
U - Civil registration, estimated less than 90% complete
| - Other source, estimated reliable
+ - Data tabulated by date of registration rather than occurence
... - Information not available

Le 'Code' indique la source des données, comme suit :
C - Registres de l'état civil considérés complèts à 90 p. 100 au moins
U - Registres de l'état civil qui ne sont pas considérés complèts à 90 p. 100 au moins
| - Autre source, considérée pas douteuses
+ - Données exploitées selon la date de l'enregistrement et non la date de l'événement
... - Information pas disponible

1 Source: Statistics Botswana. - Source: Statistics Botswana.
2 Source: Statistical Report, Ministry of Health and Social Security. - Source: Rapport statistique, ministère de la Santé et de la Sécurité sociale.
3 Excludes the islands of St. Brandon and Agalega. - Non compris les Îles St. Brandon et Agalega.
4 Data for male and female categories may exclude infant deaths of unknown sex. - Les données pour les catégories hommes et femmes peuvent exclure décès d'enfant de sexe inconnu.
5 Unrevised data. - Les données n'ont pas été révisées.
6 Including Canadian residents temporarily in the United States, but excluding United States residents temporarily in Canada. - Y compris les résidents canadiens se trouvant temporairement aux Etats-Unis, mais ne comprenant pas les résidents des Etats-Unis se trouvant temporairement au Canada.
7 Excluding infant deaths to mothers living abroad. - Exception faite des décès d'enfants en bas âge survenus lorsque la mère résidait à l'étranger.
8 Excluding live-born infants who died before their birth was registered. - Non compris les enfants nés vivants décédés avant l'enregistrement de leur naissance.
9 Data refer to resident population only. - Pour la population résidante seulement.
10 Figures for male and female may not add up to the total, since they do not include the category "Unknown". - La somme des chiffres indiqués pour les sexes masculin et féminin peut n'être pas égale au total parce qu'elle n'inclut pas la catégorie " inconnue ".
11 Including deaths abroad and deaths of unknown residence of mother. - Y compris décès à l'étranger et décès de nourrissons nés de mères dont le lieu de résidence n'est pas connu.
12 Excludes nomadic Indian tribes. - Non compris les tribus d'Indiens nomades.
13 Source: Reports of the Ministry of Health. - Source : Rapports du Ministère de la Santé.
14 Excluding infants born alive of less than 28 weeks' gestation, of less than 1 000 g in weight and 35 cm in length, who die within seven days of birth. - Non compris les enfants nés vivants après moins de 28 semaines de gestations, pesant moins de 1 000 g, mesurant moins de 35 cm et décédés dans les sept jours qui ont suivi leur naissance.
15 Sources: Births and Deaths National Registration System database, and medical records of government hospitals. Data refer to Bahraini and non-Bahraini deaths including some visitors, and Bahraini deaths abroad. - Les sources: Les bases de données des << Births and Deaths National Registration System >> et les dossiers médicaux des hôpitaux du gouvernement. Les données se rapportent aux décès de Bahreïniens et de non-Bahreïniens, y compris de non-résidents, ainsi que de Bahreïniens résidant à l'étranger.
16 Data refer to government controlled areas. - Les données se rapportent aux zones contrôlées par le Gouvernement.
17 Includes data for East Jerusalem and Israeli residents in certain other territories under occupation by Israeli military forces since June 1967. Including deaths abroad of Israeli residents who were out of the country for less than a year. - Y compris les données pour Jérusalem-Est et les résidents israéliens dans certains autres territoires occupés depuis 1967 par les forces armées israéliennes. Y compris les décès à l'étranger de résidents israéliens qui ont quitté le pays depuis moins d'un an.
18 Data refer to Japanese nationals in Japan only. - Les données se raportent aux nationaux japonais au Japon seulement.
19 Data do not include foreigners. - Les données sur les etrangers ne sont pas inclus.
20 Data are from Vital Registration System (VRS). - Les données proviennent du système d'enregistrement des faits d'état civil.
21 Excluding alien armed forces, civilian aliens employed by armed forces, and foreign diplomatic personnel and their dependants. - Non compris les militaires étrangers, les civils étrangers employés par les forces armées ni le personnel diplomatique étranger et les membres de leur famille les accompagnant.
22 Source: Strategy and Planning Division, Ministry of Public Health. - Source : Division de la stratégie et de la planification, Ministère de la Santé publique.
23 Data from MERNIS (Central Population Administrative System). - Données de MERNIS (Système central de données démographiques).
24 Including armed forces stationed outside the country, but excluding alien armed forces stationed in the area. - Y compris les militaires nationaux hors du pays, mais non compris les militaires étrangers en garnison sur le territoire.
25 Excluding Faeroe Islands and Greenland shown separately, if available. - Non compris les Iles Féroé et le Groenland, qui font l'objet de rubriques distinctes, si disponible.
26 Excluding Åland Islands. - Non compris les Îles d'Åland.
27 Data include the deceased infants with Hungarian usual residence regardless of whether the death occurred in Hungary or in a foreign country, and do not include the deceased infants with foreign country usual residence. - Les données comprennent les nourrissons décédés alors que leur résidence habituelle était en Hongrie, que le décès ait eu lieu en Hongrie ou dans un pays étranger, et ne comprennent pas les nourrissons décédés dont la residence habituelle était dans un pays étranger.
28 Including residents outside the country if listed in a Netherlands population register. - Englobe les résidents se trouvant à l'étranger à condition qu'ils soient inscrits sur le registre de population des Pays-Bas.
29 Including residents temporarily outside the country. - Y compris les résidents se trouvant temporairement hors du pays.
30 Data refer to usual resident population. - Les données se réfèrent à la population résidente habituelle.

[31] Excluding Transnistria and the municipality of Bender. - Les données ne tiennent pas compte de l'information sur la Transnistria et la municipalité de Bender.
[32] Excludes data for Kosovo and Metohia. - Sans les données pour le Kosovo et Metohie.
[33] Data includes deaths resulting from births with weight 500 g and more (if weight is unknown - with length 25 cm and more, or with gestation during 22 weeks or more). The Government of Ukraine has informed the United Nations that it is not in a position to provide statistical data concerning the Autonomous Republic of Crimea and the city of Sevastopol. - Y compris les décès de nouveau-nés de 500 g ou plus (si le poids est inconnu – de 25 cm de long ou plus, ou après une grossesse de 22 semaines ou plus). Le gouvernement Ukrainien a informé l'ONU qu'il n'est pas en mesure de fournir des données statistiques concernant la République autonome de Crimée et la ville de Sébastopol.
[34] Excluding Channel Islands (Guernsey and Jersey) and Isle of Man, shown separately, if available. - Non compris les îles Anglo-Normandes (Guernesey et Jersey) et l'île de Man, qui font l'objet de rubriques distinctes, si disponible.
[35] Data of small values have been randomly adjusted to protect confidentiality. Some totals will not equal the sum of their components. Cells with 0 values have not been affected by confidentialisation. - Les valeurs peu élevées ont été arrondies de façon aléatoire pour des raisons de confidentialité. Certains totaux ne correspondront pas rigoureusement à la somme des composants. Les mesures de confidentialité ont été sans incidence sur les cellules présentant des valeurs nulles.
[36] Including United States military personnel, their dependants and contract employees. - Y compris les militaires des Etats-Unis, les membres de leur famille les accompagnant et les agents contractuels des Etats-Unis.
[37] Data refer to deaths of residents only. Random rounding to base 3 is applied in this table as a confidentiality measure. - Les données renvoient aux décès de résidents uniquement. Les chiffres sont arrondis à la base 3 de manière aléatoire, pour des raisons de confidentialité.

Table 17 - *Demographic Yearbook 2019*

Table 17 presents maternal deaths and maternal mortality ratios for as many years available between 2009 and 2018.

Description of variables: Maternal deaths are defined for the purposes of the *Demographic Yearbook* as those caused by deliveries and complications of pregnancy, childbirth and the puerperium, within 42 days of termination of pregnancy. They are usually defined as deaths coded "38-41" for ICD-9 Basic Tabulation List or as deaths coded "A34", "O00-O95", "O98-O99" for ICD-10, respectively. However, data for ICD-10 shown in this table include deaths due to "O96" and "O97" which refer to deaths from any obstetric cause occurring more than 42 days but less than one year after delivery and death from sequelae of direct obstetric causes occurring one year or more after delivery.

For further information on the definition of maternal mortality from the tenth revisions of the *International Statistical Classification of Diseases and Related Health Problems*[1], see also section 4.3 of the Technical Notes.

Statistics on maternal death presented in this table are provided by the World Health Organisation. They are limited to countries or areas that meet the criterion that cause-of-death statistics are either classified by or convertible to the ninth or tenth revisions mentioned above. Data that are classified by the tenth revision are set in bold in the table.

Ratios computation: Maternal mortality ratios are the annual number of maternal deaths per 100 000 live births (table 9) in the same year. These ratios have been calculated by the Statistics Division of the United Nations Department of Economic and Social Affairs. If maternal mortality data are considered incomplete, or if live birth data for the year are not available, no ratio has been calculated. Ratios based on 30 or fewer maternal deaths are identified by the symbol "♦".

Reliability of data: Countries and areas that have incomplete (less than 90 per cent completeness) or of unknown completeness of cause of deaths data coverage are considered to provide unreliable data, which are set in *italics* rather than in roman type. Ratios on these data are not computed. Information on completeness is normally provided by the World Health Organisation. When this is not the case, information on completeness is set to coincide with that of table 18. The reliability of data for the completeness of cause of death provided by the World Health Organisation[2] may differ from the reliability of data for the total number of reported deaths. Therefore, there are cases when the quality code in table 18 does not correspond with the typeface used in this table.

Territorial composition, as set in Section 2.2 of "Technical Notes on the Statistical Tables", including or excluding certain population of a country, refers only to the denominator.

Limitations: Statistics on maternal deaths are subject to the same qualifications that have been set forth for vital statistics in general and death statistics in particular as discussed in section 4 of the Technical Notes. The reliability of the data, an indication of which is described above, is an important factor in considering the limitations. In addition, maternal-death statistics are subject to all the qualifications relating to cause-of-death statistics. These have been set forth in section 4 of the Technical Notes.

Maternal mortality ratios are subject to the limitations of the data on live births with which they have been calculated. These have been set forth in the technical notes for table 9. Specific information pertaining to individual countries or areas is given in the footnotes to table 9.

The calculation of the maternal mortality ratios based on the total number of live births approximates the risk of dying from complications of pregnancy, childbirth or puerperium. Ideally this rate should be based on the number of women exposed to the risk of pregnancy, in other words, the number of women conceiving. Since it is impossible to know how many women have conceived, the total number of live births is used in calculating this rate.

Earlier data: Maternal deaths and maternal mortality ratios have been shown in previous issues of the *Demographic Yearbook*. For information on specific years covered, the reader should consult the Index.

It should however be noted that in issues prior to 1975, maternal mortality rates were calculated using the female population rather than live births for the denominators. Therefore, maternal mortality ratios published since 1975 are not comparable to the earlier maternal death rates.

---

[1] *International Statistical Classification of Diseases and Related Health Problems*, Tenth Revision, Volume 2, World Health Organization, Geneva, 1992. The publication is available online at: http://www.who.int/classifications/icd/en/

[2] For more information on specific method used for countries, see "Mathers CD, Bernard C, Iburg KM, Inoue M, Ma Fat D, Shibuya K et al. *Global burden of disease in 2002: data sources, methods and results*. Geneva, World Health Organization, 2003 (GPE Discussion Paper No. 54).

Tableau 17 – *Annuaire démographique 2019*

Le tableau 17 présente des statistiques et des taux de mortalité liée à la maternité pour les années disponibles entre 2009 et 2018.

Description des variables : aux fins de *l'Annuaire démographique*, les décès liés à la maternité sont ceux entraînés par l'accouchement ou les complications de la grossesse, de l'accouchement et des suites de couches dans un délai de 42 jours après la terminaison de la grossesse. Ils sont généralement associés aux codes 38 à 41 dans le cas de la liste de base pour la mise en tableaux de la CIM-9 et aux codes A34, O00 à O95 et O98 et O99 dans le cas de la CIM-10. Les statistiques associées à des codes correspondant à la CIM-10 englobent des décès de type O96 et O97, qui désignent les décès liés à des causes obstétriques se produisant après 42 jours mais moins d'un an après l'accouchement et les décès entraînés par les séquelles de complications obstétriques directes qui se produisent un an ou plus après l'accouchement.

Pour plus de précisions concernant les définitions de la mortalité liée à la maternité dans la dixième révision de la *Classification statistique internationale des maladies et des problèmes de santé connexes*[1], se reporter également à la section 4.3 des Notes techniques.

Les statistiques de mortalité liée à la maternité présentées dans le tableau 17 émanent de l'Organisation mondiale de la santé. Elles ne se rapportent qu'aux pays ou zones qui répondent aux critères selon lesquels les statistiques relatives à la cause des décès sont conformes à la liste de la neuvième ou de la dixième révision de la CIM ou peuvent être aisément comparées aux catégories de cette liste. Les données conformes à la dixième révision sont indiquées en gras dans le tableau.

Calcul des taux : les taux de mortalité maternelle représentent le nombre annuel de décès dus à la maternité pour 100 000 naissances vivantes (données du tableau 9) de la même année. Ces taux ont été calculés par la Division de statistique du Département des affaires économiques et sociales de l'Organisation des Nations Unies. Si les données des décès dus à la maternité sont incomplètes ou si les naissances vivantes pour l'année ne sont pas disponibles, les taux ne sont pas calculés. Les taux fondés sur 30 décès liés à la maternité ou moins sont signalés par le signe "♦".

Fiabilité des données : les statistiques relatives aux pays et aux zones pour lesquels la couverture des données concernant les causes de décès est incomplète (mois de 90 pour cent) ou dont le degré de complétude n'est pas connue sont jugés douteuses et apparaissent en *italique* et non en caractères romains. Les taux correspondant ne sont pas calculés. L'information sur la complétude est normalement fournie par l'Organisation Mondiale de la Santé. Si ce n'est pas le cas, l'information sur la complétude est reprise de tableau 18. La fiabilité des données relatives aux causes de décès fournie par l'Organisation Mondiale de la Santé[2] peut différer de la fiabilité des données relatives au nombre de décès enregistrés. En conséquence, il peut apparaitre de différences entre les codes de fiabilité du tableau 18 et du présent tableau.

La composition territoriale est définie dans la Section 2.2 des "Notes Techniques sur les tableaux statistiques". L'inclusion ou l'exclusion de certaines populations d'un pays ne concerne que le dénominateur.

Insuffisance des données : les statistiques de la mortalité liée à la maternité appellent toutes les réserves qui ont été formulées à propos des statistiques de l'état civil en général et des statistiques relatives à la mortalité en particulier (voir la section 4 des Notes techniques). La fiabilité des données, au sujet de laquelle des indications ont été fournies plus haut, est un facteur important. En outre, les statistiques de la mortalité liée à la maternité appellent les mêmes réserves que celles exposées à la section 4 des Notes techniques en ce qui concerne les statistiques des causes de décès.

Les taux de mortalité maternelle appellent également toutes les réserves formulées à propos des statistiques des naissances vivantes qui ont servi à leur calcul (voir à ce sujet les notes techniques relatives au tableau 9). Des précisions sur certains pays ou zones sont données dans les notes se rapportant au tableau 9.

En prenant le nombre total des naissances vivantes comme base pour le calcul des taux de mortalité maternelle, on obtient une mesure approximative de la probabilité de décès dus aux complications de la grossesse, de l'accouchement et des suites de couches. Idéalement, ces taux devraient être calculés sur la base du nombre de femmes exposées aux risques liés à la grossesse, c'est-à-dire sur la base du nombre de femmes qui conçoivent. Étant donné qu'il est impossible de connaître le nombre de femmes ayant conçu, c'est le nombre total de naissances vivantes que l'on utilise pour calculer ces taux.

Données publiées antérieurement : des statistiques concernant les décès liés à la maternité (nombre de décès et taux) ont déjà été présentées dans des éditions antérieures de *l'Annuaire démographique*. Pour plus de précisions concernant les années pour lesquelles ces données ont été publiées, se reporter à l'index.

Il faut souligner que, avant 1975, les taux de mortalité maternelle étaient calculés sur la base de la population féminine et non sur celle du nombre de naissances vivantes. Ils ne sont donc pas comparables à ceux qui figurent dans les éditions de l'*Annuaire démographique* parues après 1975.

---

[1] *Classification statistique internationale des maladies et des problèmes de santé connexes*, dixième révision, volume 2. Genève, Organisation mondiale de la santé, 1992.
[2] Pour plus d'information sur les méthodes spécifiques utilisées pour les pays, voir "Mathers CD, Bernard C, Iburg KM, Inoue M, Ma Fat D, Shibuya K et al. *Global burden of disease in 2002: data sources, methods and results.* Geneva, World Health Organization, 2003 (GPE Discussion Paper No. 54).

17. Maternal deaths and maternal mortality ratios: 2009 - 2018
Mortalité liée à la maternité, nombre de décès et taux : 2009 - 2018

Continent and country or area Continent et pays ou zone	Code[a]	2009	2010	2011	2012	2013	2014	2015	2016	2017	2018
AFRICA - AFRIQUE											
Cabo Verde											
Number - Nombre	C	...	...	5	1	...	...	...	...	...	...
Rate - Taux	C	...	...	♦46.0	♦9.9	...	...	...	...	...	...
Egypt - Égypte											
Number - Nombre	C	579	519	550	531	503	497	410	...	...	...
Rate - Taux	C	26.1	23.0	22.5	20.2	19.2	18.3	15.3	...	...	...
Mauritius - Maurice											
Number - Nombre	+C	10	4	5	9	9	7	4	6	10	5
Rate - Taux	+C	♦65.2	♦26.7	♦34.0	♦62.1	♦66.7	♦52.7	♦31.6	♦46.3	♦74.7	♦38.5
Mayotte											
Number - Nombre	...	...	...	-[1]	1[1]	1[1]	2[1]	2	2	...	...
Rate - Taux	...	...	...	...	...	...	♦27.4	...	...	...	...
Morocco - Maroc											
Number - Nombre	U	...	*65*	*98*	*93*	*62*	*77*	...	...	...	...
Reunion - Réunion											
Number - Nombre	...	*1*	*1*	*5*	*2*	*2*	*2*	*1*	*2*	...	...
Seychelles											
Number - Nombre	+C	1	2	-	-	-	-	3	...	...	...
Rate - Taux	+C	♦63.3	♦133.0	-	-	-	-	♦188.4	...	...	...
South Africa - Afrique du Sud											
Number - Nombre	C	1 880	1 658	1 260	1 050	946	1 027	942	...	...	...
Rate - Taux	C	178.2	161.3	121.6	101.5	92.8	100.7	97.5	...	...	...
Tunisia - Tunisie											
Number - Nombre	U	...	...	...	...	*28*	...	...	...	...	...
AMERICA, NORTH - AMÉRIQUE DU NORD											
Anguilla											
Number - Nombre	...	-	*1*	-	-	-	-	-	-	*1*	-
Antigua and Barbuda - Antigua-et-Barbuda											
Number - Nombre	+U	-	...	...	*1*	-	-	-	*1*	-	...
Aruba											
Number - Nombre	...	-	-	*2*	-	-	-	-	*2*	...	...
Bahamas											
Number - Nombre	...	7[2]	5[2]	-[2]	*3*[3]	*3*[3]	*3*[3]	...	...	...	...
Rate - Taux	...	♦130.9	♦99.0	-	...	...	...	...	...	...	...
Barbados - Barbade											
Number - Nombre	...	-[1]	-[1]	2[1]	*1*[4]	*1*[4]	...	...	...	...	...
Rate - Taux	...	-	-	♦60.9	...	...	...	...	...	...	...
Belize											
Number - Nombre	...	4[1]	4[1]	-[1]	*2*[4]	-[4]	-[4]	-[4]	*1*[4]	...	...
Rate - Taux	...	♦53.9	♦55.3	-	...	...	...	...	...	...	...
Bermuda - Bermudes											
Number - Nombre	...	-	-	-	-	-	-	-	-	-	...
British Virgin Islands - Îles Vierges britanniques											
Number - Nombre	...	-	-	...	...	...	...	...	...	...	...
Canada											
Number - Nombre	C	29	24	18	22	23	23	27	24	25	...
Rate - Taux	C	♦7.6	♦6.4	♦4.8	♦5.8	♦6.0	♦6.0	♦7.1	♦6.3	♦6.6	...
Cayman Islands - Îles Caïmanes											
Number - Nombre	...	-	-	...	...	-	...	...	...	...	...
Costa Rica											
Number - Nombre	...	10[2]	14[2]	17[2]	22[3]	*10*[3]	*21*[3]	*20*[3]	*20*[3]	*15*[3]	...
Rate - Taux	...	♦13.3	♦19.7	♦23.1	...	...	...	...	...	...	...
Cuba											
Number - Nombre	C	66	61	61	55	56	50	58	61	49	...
Rate - Taux	C	50.8	47.8	45.8	43.8	44.5	40.8	46.4	52.2	42.6	...
Dominica - Dominique											
Number - Nombre	+C	-	2	-	-	-	-	-	...	...	...
Rate - Taux	+C	-	♦214.4	-	-	-	-	-	...	...	...
Dominican Republic - République dominicaine											
Number - Nombre	U	*56*	*37*	*188*	*177*	*215*	...	...	...	...	...

17. Maternal deaths and maternal mortality ratios: 2009 - 2018
Mortalité liée à la maternité, nombre de décès et taux : 2009 - 2018 (continued - suite)

Continent and country or area Continent et pays ou zone	Code[a]	2009	2010	2011	2012	2013	2014	2015	2016	2017	2018
AMERICA, NORTH - AMÉRIQUE DU NORD											
El Salvador											
Number - Nombre	...	*14*[3]	*19*[3]	*16*[3]	17[2]	39[2]	52[2]	47[2]	...	...	...
Rate - Taux	...	...	...	...	♦15.3	35.6	47.7	42.9	...	...	...
Grenada - Grenade											
Number - Nombre	C	-	-	-	2	1	-	-	2	-	-
Rate - Taux	C	-	-	-	♦120.4	♦54.4	-	-	♦126.8	-	...
Guadeloupe											
Number - Nombre	...	*1*	*1*	-	*4*	*1*	-	-	*1*	...	...
Guatemala											
Number - Nombre	...	*346*[4]	355[1]	315[1]	356[1]	318[1]	291[1]	298[1]	301[1]	260[1]	...
Rate - Taux	...	...	98.1	84.3	91.6	82.1	75.4	76.1	77.1	68.1	...
Honduras											
Number - Nombre	+U	...	*28*	*47*	*31*	*37*	...	...	...	...	...
Jamaica - Jamaïque											
Number - Nombre	...	...	*28*	*28*	...	...	36[1]	...	...	...	...
Rate - Taux	...	...	...	...	...	...	97.3	...	...	...	...
Martinique											
Number - Nombre	...	*2*	-	*2*	*1*	*3*	-	*3*	*1*	...	...
Mexico - Mexique											
Number - Nombre	+C	1 230	1 030	1 027	1 036	969	995	905	929	902	...
Rate - Taux	+C	54.6	47.5	45.4	47.3	44.7	46.7	43.2	45.8	45.1	...
Montserrat											
Number - Nombre	...	-	-	-	-	-	-	-	-	-	-
Nicaragua											
Number - Nombre	+U	*78*	*80*	*71*	*72*	*71*	*53*	*59*	*52*	*47*	*47*
Panama											
Number - Nombre	+C	29	41	59	49	41	44	40	37	27	...
Rate - Taux	+C	♦42.4	60.3	80.5	64.9	55.6	58.5	52.7	49.2	♦35.4	...
Puerto Rico - Porto Rico											
Number - Nombre	...	*10*	*6*	*5*	*1*	*2*	*3*	*15*	*11*	*12*	...
Saint Kitts and Nevis - Saint-Kitts-et-Nevis											
Number - Nombre	+U	-	-	*1*	*1*	...	-	-	-	...	...
Saint Lucia - Sainte-Lucie											
Number - Nombre	...	...	*3*[4]	*1*[4]	1[1]	1[1]	2[1]	-[1]	...	...	...
Rate - Taux	...	...	...	...	♦49.9	♦46.0	♦98.7	...	...	...	...
Saint Pierre and Miquelon - Saint Pierre-et-Miquelon											
Number - Nombre	...	-	-	...	...	...	...	...	...	...	...
Saint Vincent and the Grenadines - Saint-Vincent-et-les Grenadines											
Number - Nombre	+C	-	2	1	-	2	1	-	-	2	...
Rate - Taux	+C	-	♦112.1	♦58.0	-	♦115.1	♦54.3	-	-	♦130.0	...
Turks and Caicos Islands - Îles Turques et Caïques											
Number - Nombre	...	*1*	...	...	...	-	-	-	...	...	...
United States of America - États-Unis d'Amérique											
Number - Nombre	C	962	825	931	990	1 138	1 123	1 140	1 231	1 208	...
Rate - Taux	C	23.3	20.6	23.5	25.0	28.9	28.2	28.7	31.2	31.3	...
United States Virgin Islands - Îles Vierges américaines											
Number - Nombre	...	-	-	-	-	...	...	-	-	-	...
AMERICA, SOUTH - AMÉRIQUE DU SUD											
Argentina - Argentine											
Number - Nombre	+C	422	331	318	280	274	307	333	284	246	...
Rate - Taux	+C	56.6	43.8	42.0	37.9	36.3	39.5	43.2	39.0	34.9	...
Brazil - Brésil											
Number - Nombre	C	1 884	1 728	1 680	1 647	1 788	1 889	1 896	1 814	1 874	...
Rate - Taux	C	68.4	62.6	59.5	58.2	63.1	64.8	62.0	62.5	63.3	...

Continent and country or area Continent et pays ou zone	Code[a]	2009	2010	2011	2012	2013	2014	2015	2016	2017	2018
AMERICA, SOUTH - AMÉRIQUE DU SUD											
Chile - Chili											
Number - Nombre	C	43	46	46	54	52	56	56	51	58	...
Rate - Taux	C	17.0	18.4	18.6	22.2	21.5	22.3	22.9	22.0	26.5	...
Colombia - Colombie											
Number - Nombre	...	496[1]	474[1]	459[1]	*452*[4]	*381*[4]	*491*[4]	*476*[4]	*476*[4]	*485*[4]	...
Rate - Taux	...	70.9	72.4	69.0	...	...	...	...	...	...	...
Ecuador - Équateur											
Number - Nombre	U	*208*	*202*	*239*	*202*	*158*	*169*	*183*	*154*	*211*	...
French Guiana - Guyane française											
Number - Nombre	...	*1*	*3*	-	*2*	*1*	*3*	*1*	*1*	...	...
Guyana											
Number - Nombre	...	*9*[4]	*20*[4]	*14*[4]	14[1]	9[1]	17[1]	...	...	...	...
Rate - Taux	...	...	...	...	♦93.0	♦61.9	♦112.4	...	...	...	...
Paraguay											
Number - Nombre	+U	*128*	*100*	*94*	*91*	*100*	*71*	*114*	*115*	*100*	...
Peru - Pérou											
Number - Nombre	+U	*163*	*137*	*148*	*126*	*97*	*112*	*110*	*72*	*315*	...
Suriname											
Number - Nombre	...	11[1]	6[1]	7[1]	*2*[4]	*11*[4]	*7*[4]	...	...	...	...
Rate - Taux	...	♦112.3	♦61.8	♦72.1	...	...	...	...	...	...	...
Uruguay											
Number - Nombre	C	11	2	...	5	9	9	11	9	8	...
Rate - Taux	C	♦23.3	♦4.2	...	♦10.4	♦18.5	♦18.6	♦22.5	♦19.1	♦18.6	...
Venezuela (Bolivarian Republic of) - Venezuela (République bolivarienne du)											
Number - Nombre	...	434[1]	412[1]	436[1]	*416*[4]	*410*[4]	*490*[4]	...	...	...	...
Rate - Taux	...	73.1	69.7	70.9	...	...	...	...	...	...	...
ASIA - ASIE											
Armenia - Arménie											
Number - Nombre	...	*12*[4]	*4*[4]	*6*[4]	5[1]	9[1]	8[1]	7[1]	14[1]	...	...
Rate - Taux	...	...	...	...	♦11.8	♦21.5	♦18.6	♦16.8	♦34.5	...	...
Bahrain - Bahreïn											
Number - Nombre	...	*3*[4]	*1*[4]	*2*[4]	2[1]	4[1]	2[1]	...	...	...	...
Rate - Taux	...	...	...	...	♦10.5	♦20.0	♦9.6	...	...	...	...
Brunei Darussalam - Brunéi Darussalam											
Number - Nombre	...	1[2]	*1*[3]	*-*[3]	3[2]	1[2]	-[2]	2[2]	-[2]	4[2]	-[2]
Rate - Taux	...	♦15.1	...	...	♦43.4	♦15.0	-	♦29.9	-	♦62.0	-
China, Hong Kong SAR - Chine, Hong Kong RAS											
Number - Nombre	...	*2*	*1*	*1*	*2*	-	*2*	*1*	-	*1*	...
Cyprus - Chypre											
Number - Nombre	U	-	*1*	-	-	*1*	*2*	-	-	...	...
Georgia - Géorgie											
Number - Nombre	C	32	13	21	12	16	18	19	12	12	20
Rate - Taux	C	50.5	♦20.8	♦36.2	♦21.0	♦27.6	♦29.7	♦32.1	♦21.2	♦22.5	♦39.1
Iran (Islamic Republic of) - Iran (République islamique d')											
Number - Nombre	...	...	...	...	...	*113*[4]	*104*[4]	*111*[4]	135[1]	...	...
Rate - Taux	...	...	...	...	...	...	...	...	8.8	...	...
Iraq											
Number - Nombre	U	...	...	...	...	...	...	*1*	*94*	...	...
Israel - Israël											
Number - Nombre	C	5	7	2	9	14	10	7	8	8	...
Rate - Taux	C	♦3.1	♦4.2	♦1.2	♦5.3	♦8.2	♦5.7	♦3.9	♦4.4	♦4.4	...
Japan - Japon											
Number - Nombre	C	61	49	43	50	41	33	44	36	36	...
Rate - Taux	C	5.7	4.6	4.1	4.8	4.0	3.3	4.4	3.7	3.8	...
Jordan - Jordanie											
Number - Nombre	U	*26*	*46*	*34*	*44*	...	...	*38*	...	...	...

17. Maternal deaths and maternal mortality ratios: 2009 - 2018
Mortalité liée à la maternité, nombre de décès et taux : 2009 - 2018 (continued - suite)

Continent and country or area / Continent et pays ou zone	Code[a]	2009	2010	2011	2012	2013	2014	2015	2016	2017	2018
ASIA - ASIE											
Kazakhstan											
Number - Nombre	...	94[1]	65[1]	48[1]	41[4]	41[4]	37[4]	35[4]	...	36[4]	...
Rate - Taux	...	26.4	17.7	12.9	...	...	...	...	...	...	...
Kuwait - Koweït											
Number - Nombre	...	7[1]	3[1]	6[1]	1[4]	4[4]	7[4]	5[4]	2[4]	3[4]	...
Rate - Taux	...	♦12.4	♦5.2	♦10.3	...	...	...	...	...	...	...
Kyrgyzstan - Kirghizstan											
Number - Nombre	C	86	75	81	76	56	81	63	48	...	...
Rate - Taux	C	63.5	51.3	54.1	49.1	36.0	50.1	38.5	30.3	...	...
Lebanon - Liban											
Number - Nombre	...	...	...	...	...	...	...	...	...	5	...
Malaysia - Malaisie											
Number - Nombre	U	...	...	...	122	108	119	...	...	...	...
Maldives											
Number - Nombre	...	...	7[3]	4[3]	...	...	2[2]	2[2]	2[2]	7[2]	...
Rate - Taux	...	...	...	...	...	...	♦27.6	♦28.6	♦29.6	♦104.1	...
Mongolia - Mongolie											
Number - Nombre	U	...	...	...	...	...	...	...	38	...	...
Oman											
Number - Nombre	U	3	6	...	...	...	-	...	3	3	...
Philippines											
Number - Nombre	U	...	1 718	1 465	...	...	1 570	...	...	...	...
Qatar											
Number - Nombre	...	4[1]	2[4]	1[4]	1[4]	-[4]	1[4]	3[4]	-[4]	-[4]	...
Rate - Taux	...	♦21.8	...	...	...	...	...	...	...	...	...
Republic of Korea - République de Corée											
Number - Nombre	C	48	75	85	56	51	48	42	37	32	...
Rate - Taux	C	10.8	16.0	18.0	11.6	11.7	11.0	9.6	9.1	8.9	...
Saudi Arabia - Arabie saoudite											
Number - Nombre	U	54	...	...	45	...	...	...	...	...	...
Singapore - Singapour											
Number - Nombre	+U	-	1	2	1	-	-	3	2	-	...
Syrian Arab Republic - République arabe syrienne											
Number - Nombre	+C	...	23	...	...	...	...	...	...	...	...
Rate - Taux	+C	...	♦2.6	...	...	...	...	...	...	...	...
Tajikistan - Tadjikistan											
Number - Nombre	U	...	...	...	...	...	...	...	18	...	...
Thailand - Thaïlande											
Number - Nombre	+U	...	78	71	141	166	166	167	177	143	...
Turkey - Turquie											
Number - Nombre	...	37[3]	46[3]	58[3]	55[3]	302[3]	273[3]	220[3]	251[2]	...	...
Rate - Taux	...	...	...	...	...	...	...	...	19.1	...	...
Turkmenistan - Turkménistan											
Number - Nombre	U	...	...	...	7	9	4	5	...	...	...
United Arab Emirates - Émirats arabes unis											
Number - Nombre	+U	2	4	...	...	...	...	...	...	...	...
Uzbekistan - Ouzbékistan											
Number - Nombre	C	...	...	...	103	120	131	134	128	...	...
Rate - Taux	C	...	...	...	16.5	17.7	18.2	18.3	17.6	...	...
EUROPE											
Andorra - Andorre											
Number - Nombre	C	...	...	...	-	-	-	-	...	...	...
Austria - Autriche											
Number - Nombre	C	2	1	2	1	1	7	4	5	2	...
Rate - Taux	C	♦2.6	♦1.3	♦2.6	♦1.3	♦1.3	♦8.6	♦4.7	♦5.7	♦2.3	...
Belarus - Bélarus											
Number - Nombre	C	1	1	1	...	-	1	...	...	...	3
Rate - Taux	C	♦0.9	♦0.9	♦0.9	...	-	♦0.8	...	...	...	♦3.2
Belgium - Belgique											
Number - Nombre	C	6	8	9	5	3	6	4	4	...	...
Rate - Taux	C	♦4.7	♦6.1	♦7.0	♦3.9	♦2.4	♦4.8	♦3.3	♦3.3	...	...

17. Maternal deaths and maternal mortality ratios: 2009 - 2018
Mortalité liée à la maternité, nombre de décès et taux : 2009 - 2018 (continued - suite)

Continent and country or area Continent et pays ou zone	Code[a]	2009	2010	2011	2012	2013	2014	2015	2016	2017	2018
EUROPE											
Bosnia and Herzegovina - Bosnie-Herzégovine											
Number - Nombre	...	...	...	2[4]	...	...	-[1]	...	1[1]	...	...
Rate - Taux	...	...	...	...	...	...	-	...	♦3.4	...	...
Bulgaria - Bulgarie											
Number - Nombre	C	4	6	2	3	8	5	4	...	...	...
Rate - Taux	C	♦4.9	♦7.9	♦2.8	♦4.3	♦12.0	♦7.4	♦6.1	...	...	...
Croatia - Croatie											
Number - Nombre	C	6	4	4	3	2	1	1	1	-	...
Rate - Taux	C	♦13.5	♦9.2	♦9.7	♦7.2	♦5.0	♦2.5	♦2.7	♦2.7	-	...
Czechia - Tchéquie											
Number - Nombre	C	3	3	2	6	1	4	2	1	2	...
Rate - Taux	C	♦2.5	♦2.6	♦1.8	♦5.5	♦0.9	♦3.6	♦1.8	♦0.9	♦1.7	...
Denmark - Danemark											
Number - Nombre	C	4	-	2	-	1	3	-	...	...	...
Rate - Taux	C	♦6.4	-	♦3.4	-	♦1.8	♦5.3	-	...	...	...
Estonia - Estonie											
Number - Nombre	C	-	1	1	1	1	-	-	2	-	-
Rate - Taux	C	-	♦6.3	♦6.8	♦7.1	♦7.4	-	-	♦14.2	-	-
Finland - Finlande											
Number - Nombre	C	1	3	-	2	1	3	2	...	...	...
Rate - Taux	C	♦1.7	♦4.9	-	♦3.4	♦1.7	♦5.3	♦3.6	...	...	...
France											
Number - Nombre	C	75	68	45	44	38	37	34	33	...	...
Rate - Taux	C	9.5	8.5	5.7	5.6	4.9	4.6	4.5	4.4	...	...
Germany - Allemagne											
Number - Nombre	C	35	37	32	31	29	29	24	23	22	...
Rate - Taux	C	5.3	5.5	4.8	4.6	♦4.3	♦4.1	♦3.3	♦2.9	♦2.8	...
Greece - Grèce											
Number - Nombre	C	4	6	4	1	-	4	5	6	...	...
Rate - Taux	C	♦3.4	♦5.2	♦3.8	♦1.0	-	♦4.3	♦5.4	♦6.5	...	...
Hungary - Hongrie											
Number - Nombre	C	18	14	9	9	13	6	5	11	14	...
Rate - Taux	C	♦18.7	♦15.5	♦10.2	♦10.0	♦14.5	♦6.4	♦5.4	♦11.5	♦14.8	...
Iceland - Islande											
Number - Nombre	C	-	...	...	-	-	-	-	-	-	-
Ireland - Irlande											
Number - Nombre	+C	3	3	2	2	3	1	1	...	...	...
Rate - Taux	+C	♦4.0	♦4.0	♦2.7	♦2.8	♦4.4	♦1.5	♦1.5	...	...	...
Italy - Italie											
Number - Nombre	C	19	16	14	11	14	6	16	13	...	...
Rate - Taux	C	♦3.3	♦2.8	♦2.6	♦2.1	♦2.7	♦1.2	♦3.3	♦2.7	...	...
Latvia - Lettonie											
Number - Nombre	+C	7	4	-	4	2	2	12	...	...	...
Rate - Taux	+C	♦31.8	♦20.2	-	♦20.1	♦9.7	♦9.2	♦54.6	...	...	...
Lithuania - Lituanie											
Number - Nombre	+C	-	2	2	3	2	1	3	2	2	4
Rate - Taux	+C	-	♦6.5	♦6.6	♦9.8	♦6.7	♦3.3	♦9.5	♦6.5	♦7.0	♦14.2
Luxembourg											
Number - Nombre	+C	-	1	-	1	1	-	-	-	...	...
Rate - Taux	+C	-	♦17.0	-	♦16.6	♦16.4	-	-	-	...	...
Malta - Malte											
Number - Nombre	+C	-	1	-	-	-	-	-	-	...	...
Rate - Taux	+C	-	♦25.7	-	-	-	-	-	-	...	...
Montenegro - Monténégro											
Number - Nombre	C	-	...	...	...	...	...	...	...	...	...
Netherlands - Pays-Bas											
Number - Nombre	+C	9	4	3	6	5	5	6	6	3	...
Rate - Taux	+C	♦4.9	♦2.2	♦1.7	♦3.4	♦2.9	♦2.9	♦3.5	♦3.5	♦1.8	...
North Macedonia - Macédoine du Nord[1]											
Number - Nombre	C	1	2	...	1	1	...	...	...	...	...
Rate - Taux	C	♦4.2	♦8.2	...	♦4.2	♦4.3	...	...	...	...	...
Norway - Norvège											
Number - Nombre	+C	1	3	3	-	2	2	-	-	...	...
Rate - Taux	+C	♦1.6	♦4.9	♦5.0	-	♦3.4	♦3.4	-	-	...	...
Poland - Pologne											
Number - Nombre	C	8	9	9	4	7	8	6	9	9	...
Rate - Taux	C	♦1.9	♦2.2	♦2.3	♦1.0	♦1.9	♦2.1	♦1.6	♦2.4	♦2.2	...

17. Maternal deaths and maternal mortality ratios: 2009 - 2018
Mortalité liée à la maternité, nombre de décès et taux : 2009 - 2018 (continued - suite)

Continent and country or area Continent et pays ou zone	Code[a]	2009	2010	2011	2012	2013	2014	2015	2016	2017	2018
EUROPE											
Portugal											
Number - Nombre	+C	7	8	5	4	5	6	6	7	9	...
Rate - Taux	+C	♦7.0	♦7.9	♦5.2	♦4.5	♦6.0	♦7.3	♦7.0	♦8.0	♦10.4	...
Republic of Moldova - République de Moldova											
Number - Nombre	...	7[2]	18[2]	6[2]	*12*[3]	*6*[3]	*7*[3]	*12*[3]	*7*[3]	*6*[3]	*5*[3]
Rate - Taux	...	♦17.2	♦44.5	♦15.3	...	...	...	...	...	...	...
Romania - Roumanie											
Number - Nombre	+C	47	51	50	23	27	24	27	17	24	...
Rate - Taux	+C	21.1	24.0	25.5	♦11.4	♦14.8	♦12.1	♦13.7	♦8.3	♦11.9	...
Russian Federation - Fédération de Russie											
Number - Nombre	+C	388	298	291	221	216	...	...	189	150	147
Rate - Taux	+C	22.0	16.7	16.2	11.6	11.4	...	...	...	...	...
San Marino - Saint-Marin											
Number - Nombre	+C	...	...	...	-	-	-	-	...	...	...
Serbia - Serbie											
Number - Nombre	...	*6*[3]	12[2]	7[2]	10[2]	9[2]	8[2]	8[2]	7[2]	7[2]	...
Rate - Taux	...	...	♦17.6	♦10.7	♦14.9	♦13.7	♦12.0	♦12.2	♦10.8	♦10.8	...
Slovakia - Slovaquie											
Number - Nombre	C	6	-	...	3	1	2	...	...	...	...
Rate - Taux	C	♦9.8	-	...	♦5.4	♦1.8	♦3.6	...	...	...	...
Slovenia - Slovénie											
Number - Nombre	C	1	-	...	1	1	2	1	1	-	...
Rate - Taux	C	♦4.6	-	...	♦4.6	♦4.7	♦9.4	♦4.8	♦4.9	-	...
Spain - Espagne											
Number - Nombre	C	17	20	14	10	18	9	15	15	13	...
Rate - Taux	C	♦3.4	♦4.1	♦3.0	♦2.2	♦4.2	♦2.1	♦3.6	♦3.7	♦3.3	...
Sweden - Suède											
Number - Nombre	C	6	3	1	5	7	4	1	3	4	...
Rate - Taux	C	♦5.4	♦2.6	♦0.9	♦4.4	♦6.2	♦3.5	♦0.9	♦2.6	♦3.5	...
Switzerland - Suisse											
Number - Nombre	C	3	3	3	7	2	5	6	3	...	...
Rate - Taux	C	♦3.8	♦3.7	♦3.7	♦8.5	♦2.4	♦5.9	♦6.9	♦3.4	...	...
Ukraine											
Number - Nombre	+C	129	116	85	66	...	69	60	...	30	...
Rate - Taux	+C	25.2	23.3	16.9	12.7	...	14.8	14.6	...	♦8.2	...
United Kingdom of Great Britain and Northern Ireland - Royaume-Uni de Grande-Bretagne et d'Irlande du Nord											
Number - Nombre	+C	74	40	53	51	50	52	35	51	...	...
Rate - Taux	+C	9.4	5.0	6.6	6.3	6.4	6.7	4.5	6.6	...	...
OCEANIA - OCÉANIE											
Australia - Australie											
Number - Nombre	C	9	12	12	16	6	12	8	12	5	...
Rate - Taux	C	♦3.0	♦4.0	♦4.0	♦5.2	♦1.9	♦4.0	♦2.6	♦3.9	♦1.6	...
Fiji - Fidji											
Number - Nombre	+C	5	...	4	8	...	...	...	...	...	...
Rate - Taux	+C	♦27.5	...	♦20.5	♦43.4	...	...	...	...	...	...
New Zealand - Nouvelle-Zélande											
Number - Nombre	+C	11	6	7	7	10	3	6	...	...	...
Rate - Taux	+C	♦17.6	♦9.4	♦11.4	♦11.4	♦17.0	♦5.2	♦9.8	...	...	...
Solomon Islands - Îles Salomon											
Number - Nombre	...	...	...	...	...	...	...	...	...	*3*	*2*

FOOTNOTES - NOTES

Data in bold refer to maternal deaths based on ICD-10 Classification, otherwise data refer to maternal deaths based on ICD-9 Classification. - Les données en typographie gras se rapportent aux décès maternelles basées sur la classification CIM-10, autrement les données se rapportent aux décès maternelles basées sur la classification CIM-9.

Italics: data from civil registers which are incomplete or of unknown completeness. - Italiques : données incomplètes ou dont le degré d'exactitude n'est pas connu, provenant des registres de l'état civil.

* Provisional. - Données provisoires.

♦ Rates based on 30 or fewer deaths. - Taux basés sur 30 décès ou moins.

[a] 'Code' indicates the source of data, as follows:
C - Civil registration, estimated over 90% complete
U - Civil registration, estimated less than 90% complete
| - Other source, estimated reliable
+ - Data tabulated by date of registration rather than occurence
... - Information not available

Le 'Code' indique la source des données, comme suit :
C - Registres de l'état civil considérés complèts à 90 p. 100 au moins
U - Registres de l'état civil qui ne sont pas considérés complèts à 90 p. 100 au moins
| - Autre source, considérée pas douteuses
+ - Données exploitées selon la date de l'enregistrement et non la date de l'événement
... - Information pas disponible

[1] The code is C. - Le code est C.
[2] The code is +C. - Le code est +C.
[3] The code is +U. - Le code est +U.
[4] The code is U. - Le code est U.

Table 18 - *Demographic Yearbook 2019*

Table 18 presents deaths and crude death rates by urban/rural residence for as many years as possible between 2015 and 2019.

Description of variables: Death is defined as the permanent disappearance of all evidence of life at any time after live birth has taken place (post-natal cessation of vital functions without capability of resuscitation).

Statistics on the number of deaths are obtained from civil registers unless otherwise noted. For those countries or areas where civil registration statistics on deaths are considered reliable (estimated completeness of 90 per cent or more), the death rates shown have been calculated on the basis of registered deaths.

The urban/rural classification of deaths is that provided by each country or area; it is presumed to be based on the national census definitions of urban population that have been set forth at the end of the technical notes for table 6.

For certain countries, there is a discrepancy between the total number of deaths shown in this table and those shown in subsequent tables for the same year. Usually this discrepancy arises because the total number of deaths occurring in a given year is revised although the remaining tabulations are not.

Rate computation: Crude death rates are the annual number of deaths per 1 000 mid-year population.

Rates by urban/rural residence are the annual number of deaths, in the appropriate urban or rural category, per 1 000 corresponding mid-year population. These rates are calculated by the Statistics Division of the United Nations based on the appropriate reference population (for example: total population, nationals only etc.) if known and available. If the reference population is not known or unavailable, the total population is used to calculate the rates. Therefore, if the population that is used to calculate the rates is different from the correct reference population, the rates presented might under- or overstate the true situation in a country or area.

Rates presented in this table are limited to those countries or areas with a minimum number of 30 deaths in a given year.

Reliability of data: Each country or area has been asked to indicate the estimated completeness of the deaths recorded in its civil register. These national assessments are indicated by the quality codes "C", "U" and "|" that appear in the first column of this table. "C" indicates that the data are estimated to be virtually complete, that is, representing at least 90 per cent of the deaths occurring each year, while "U" indicates that data are estimated to be incomplete that is, representing less than 90 per cent of the deaths occurring each year. The code "|" indicates that the source of data is different than civil registration and is explained by a footnote. The code "..." indicates that no information was provided regarding completeness or no assessment has been done in the country.

Data from civil registers that are reported as incomplete or of unknown completeness (code "U" or "...") are considered unreliable. They appear in italics in this table; rates based on these data are not computed.

Limitations: Statistics on deaths are subject to the same qualifications as have been set forth for vital statistics and particularly for death statistics discussed in section 4 of the Technical Notes.

The reliability of the data, an indication of which is described above, is an important factor in considering the limitations. In addition, some deaths are tabulated by date of registration and not by date of occurrence; these have been indicated with a plus sign "+". Whenever the lag between the date of occurrence and date of registration is prolonged and, therefore, a large proportion of the death registrations are delayed, death statistics for any given year may be seriously affected. However, delays in the registration of deaths are less common and shorter than in the registration of live births.

International comparability in mortality statistics may also be affected by the exclusion of deaths of infants who were born alive but died before the registration of the birth or within the first 24 hours of life. Statistics of this type are footnoted.

In addition, it should be noted that rates are affected also by the quality and limitations of the population estimates that are used in their computation. The problems of under-enumeration or over-enumeration and, to some extent, the differences in definition of total population have been discussed in section 3 of the Technical Notes dealing generally with population data. Specific information pertaining to individual countries or areas is given in the footnotes to table 3.

It should be emphasized that crude death rates -- like other crude rates, such as of birth, marriage and divorce -- may be seriously affected by the age-sex structure of the populations to which they relate. Nevertheless, they do provide a simple measure of the level and changes in mortality.

The comparability of data by urban/rural residence is affected by the national definitions of urban and rural used in tabulating these data. It is assumed, in the absence of specific information to the contrary, that the definitions of urban and rural used in connection with the national population census were also used in the compilation of the vital statistics for each country or area. However, it cannot be excluded that, for a given country or area, different definitions of urban and rural are used for the vital statistics data and the population census data respectively. When known, the definitions of urban used in national population censuses are presented at the end of the technical notes for table 6. As discussed in detail in the technical notes for table 6, these definitions vary considerably from one country or area to another.

Earlier data: Deaths and crude death rates have been presented in each issue of the *Demographic Yearbook*. For information on specific years covered, the reader should consult the Historical Index.

Tableau 18 – *Annuaire démographique 2019*

Le tableau 18 présente le nombre des décès et les taux bruts de mortalité selon le lieu de résidence (zone urbaine ou rurale) pour le plus grand nombre d'années possible entre 2015 et 2019.

Description des variables : Le décès est défini comme la disparition permanente de tout signe de vie à un moment quelconque postérieur à la naissance vivante (cessation des fonctions vitales après la naissance sans possibilité de réanimation).

Sauf indication contraire, les statistiques relatives au nombre de décès sont établies sur la base des registres d'état civil. Pour les pays ou zones où les données concernant l'enregistrement des décès par les services de l'état civil sont jugées sûres (complétude estimée à 90 p. 100 ou plus), les taux de mortalité ont été calculés d'après les décès enregistrés.

La répartition des décès entre zones urbaines et zones rurales est celle qui a été communiquée par chaque pays ou zone ; on part du principe qu'elle repose sur les définitions de la population urbaine utilisées pour les recensements nationaux, qui sont reproduites à la fin des notes techniques du tableau 6.

Pour quelques pays il y a une discordance entre le nombre total des décès présenté dans ce tableau et ceux présentés après pour la même année. Habituellement ces différences apparaissent lorsque le nombre total des décès pour une certaine année a été révisé alors que les autres tabulations ne l'ont pas été.

Calcul des taux : Les taux bruts de mortalité représentent le nombre annuel de décès pour 1 000 habitants en milieu d'année.

Les taux selon le lieu de résidence (zone urbaine ou rurale) représentent le nombre annuel de décès, classés selon la catégorie urbaine ou rurale appropriée, pour 1 000 habitants en milieu d'année. Ces taux sont calculés par la division de statistique des Nations Unies sur la base de la population de référence adéquate (par exemple : population totale, nationaux seulement, etc.) si connue et disponible. Si la population de référence n'est pas connue ou n'est pas disponible, la population totale est utilisée pour calculer les taux. Par conséquent, si la population utilisée pour calculer les taux est différente de la population de référence adéquate, les taux présentés sont susceptibles de sous ou sur estimer la situation réelle d'un pays ou d'un territoire.

Les taux présentés dans ce tableau se rapportent seulement aux pays ou zones où l'on a enregistré un nombre minimal de 30 décès au cours d'une année donnée.

Fiabilité des données : Il a été demandé à chaque pays ou zone d'indiquer le degré estimatif de complétude des données sur les décès d'enfants de moins d'un an figurant dans ses registres d'état civil. Ces évaluations nationales sont signalées par les codes de qualité "C", "U" et "|" qui apparaissent dans la deuxième colonne du tableau.

La lettre "C" indique que les données sont jugées à peu près complètes, c'est-à-dire qu'elles représentent au moins 90 p. 100 des décès survenus chaque année ; la lettre "U" signifie que les données sont jugées incomplètes, c'est-à-dire qu'elles représentent moins de 90 p.100 des décès survenus chaque année. Le symbole "|" indique que la source des données n'est pas un registre de l'état civil ; le symbole, dans ce cas, est accompagné par une note explicative. Le code "..." dénote qu'aucun renseignement n'a été communiqué quant à la complétude des données.

Les données provenant des registres de l'état civil qui sont déclarées incomplètes ou dont le degré de complétude n'est pas connu (code "U" ou "...") sont jugées douteuses. Elles apparaissent en italique dans le présent tableau et les taux correspondants n'ont pas été calculés.

Insuffisance des données : Les statistiques relatives à la mortalité appellent les mêmes réserves que celles qui ont été formulées à propos des statistiques de l'état civil en général et des statistiques relatives aux décès en particulier (voir la section 4 des Notes techniques).

La fiabilité des données, au sujet de laquelle des indications ont été fournies plus haut, est un facteur important. Il faut également tenir compte du fait que, dans certains cas, les décès sont classés par date d'enregistrement et non par date d'occurrence ; ces cas ont été signalés par le signe "+". Chaque fois que le décalage entre le décès et son enregistrement est grand et qu'une forte proportion des décès fait l'objet d'un enregistrement tardif, les statistiques relatives aux décès survenus pendant l'année peuvent être considérablement faussées.

En règle générale, toutefois, les décès sont enregistrés beaucoup plus rapidement que les naissances vivantes, et les retards prolongés sont rares.

Un autre facteur qui nuit à la comparabilité internationale est la pratique qui consiste à ne pas inclure dans les statistiques de la mortalité les enfants nés vivants mais décédés avant l'enregistrement de leur naissance ou dans les 24 heures qui ont suivi la naissance. Quand pareil facteur a joué, cela a été signalé en note à la fin du tableau.

Il convient de noter par ailleurs que l'exactitude des taux dépend également de la qualité et des limitations des estimations de la population qui sont utilisées pour leur calcul. Le problème des erreurs par excès ou par défaut commises lors du dénombrement et, dans une certaine mesure, le problème de l'hétérogénéité des définitions de la population totale ont été examinés à la section 3 des Notes techniques, relative à la population en général ; des indications concernant certains pays ou zones sont données en note à la fin du tableau 3.

Il faut souligner que les taux bruts de mortalité, de même que les taux bruts de natalité, de nuptialité et de divortialité, peuvent varier très sensiblement selon la composition par âge et par sexe de la population à laquelle ils se rapportent. Ils offrent néanmoins un moyen simple de mesurer le niveau et l'évolution de la mortalité.

La comparabilité des données selon le lieu de résidence (zone urbaine ou rurale) peut être limitée par les définitions nationales des termes « urbain » et « rural » utilisées pour le classement de ces données. En l'absence d'indications contraires, on a supposé que les mêmes définitions avaient servi pour le recensement national de la population et pour l'établissement des statistiques de l'état civil pour chaque pays ou zone. Toutefois, il n'est pas exclu que, pour une zone ou un pays donné, des définitions différentes aient été retenues. Les définitions du terme « urbain » utilisées pour les recensements nationaux de population ont été présentées à la fin du tableau 6 lorsqu'elles étaient connues. Comme on l'a précisé dans les notes techniques relatives au tableau 6, ces définitions varient considérablement d'un pays ou d'une zone à l'autre.

Données publiées antérieurement : les différentes éditions de l'*Annuaire démographique* contiennent des statistiques des décès et des taux bruts de mortalité. Pour plus de précisions concernant les années pour lesquelles ces données ont été publiées, se reporter à l'index historique.

18. Deaths and crude death rates, by urban/rural residence: 2015 - 2019
Décès et taux bruts de mortalité, selon la résidence, urbaine/rurale : 2015 - 2019

Continent, country or area, and urban/rural residence Continent, pays ou zone et résidence, urbaine/rurale	Co-de[a]	Number - Nombre 2015	2016	2017	2018	2019	Rate - Taux 2015	2016	2017	2018	2019
AFRICA - AFRIQUE											
Algeria - Algérie[1]											
Total	U	182 570	180 404	174 168	...	...	...	...	...	...	...
Botswana[2]											
Total	U	13 030	12 825	12 386	12 609	...	...	...	...	...	...
Cabo Verde[3]											
Total	C	2 744	2 580	2 497	...	...	5.2	4.9	4.6	...	...
Côte d'Ivoire[4]											
Total	+U	47 065	45 995	44 813	46 385	...	...	...	...	...	...
Urban - Urbaine	+U	...	37 487	37 965	40 520	...	...	...	...	...	...
Rural - Rurale	+U	...	8 508	6 848	5 865	...	...	...	...	...	...
Egypt - Égypte											
Total	C	573 879	556 148	547 208	...	...	6.5	6.1	5.7	...	...
Urban - Urbaine	C	324 422	319 409	319 980	...	...	8.5	8.2	7.9	...	...
Rural - Rurale	C	249 457	236 739	227 228	...	...	4.9	4.5	4.1	...	...
Eswatini[5]											
Total	+U	...	5 309	5 073	5 032	...	...	...	...	...	...
Kenya											
Total	+U	200 205	189 930	190 877	192 019	190 696	...	...	...	...	...
Lesotho											
Total	+U	17 929	13 768	13 671	13 406	13 494	...	...	...	...	...
Malawi[6]											
Total	I	...	...	...	110 776	...	...	...	...	6.3	...
Urban - Urbaine	I	...	...	...	13 724	...	...	...	...	4.9	...
Rural - Rurale	I	...	...	...	97 052	...	...	...	...	6.6	...
Mauritius - Maurice[7]											
Total	+C	9 747	10 174	10 140	10 787	11 174	7.7	8.1	8.0	8.5	8.8
Urban - Urbaine	+C	4 454	4 658	4 560	4 891	5 029	8.6	9.0	8.9	9.5	9.8
Rural - Rurale	+C	5 293	5 516	5 580	5 896	6 145	7.1	7.4	7.4	7.8	8.2
Mayotte											
Total	C	636	705	735	758	...	2.7	2.9	2.9	2.9	...
Reunion - Réunion											
Total	C	4 531	4 689	4 673	5 011	...	5.3	5.5	5.4	5.8	...
Urban - Urbaine	C	...	...	4 458	...	...	...	...	...	...	...
Rural - Rurale	C	...	...	215	...	...	...	...	...	...	...
Saint Helena ex. dep. - Sainte-Hélène sans dép.											
Total	C	55	45	58	52	38	12.3	9.7	12.7	11.3	8.5
Sao Tome and Principe - Sao Tomé-et-Principe											
Total	C	1 226	1 212	1 202	...	...	6.5	6.3	6.1	...	...
Seychelles											
Total	+C	703	747	748	818	795	7.5	7.9	7.8	8.5	8.1
South Africa - Afrique du Sud											
Total	U	473 266	456 612	...	...	...	...	...	...	...	...
Tunisia - Tunisie											
Total	U	65 743	62 601	68 846	...	...	...	...	...	...	...
Zambia - Zambie[8]											
Total	U	...	...	39 150	...	...	...	...	...	...	...
AMERICA, NORTH - AMÉRIQUE DU NORD											
Anguilla[9]											
Total	+C	61	*83	...	...	...	4.1	*5.5	...	...	...
Antigua and Barbuda - Antigua-et-Barbuda											
Total	+C	527	542	599	581	...	5.8	5.9	6.4	6.1	...
Aruba											
Total	C	679	781	707	717	665	6.2	7.1	6.4	6.4	5.9
Bahamas											
Total	+C	*2 243	*2 288	*2 372	...	...	*6.1	*6.1	*6.3	...	...
Belize											
Total	U	1 792	1 805	1 872	1 886	...	...	...	...	...	...
Urban - Urbaine[10]	U	910	958	...	...	...	...	...	...	...	...
Rural - Rurale[10]	U	862	838	...	...	...	...	...	...	...	...

18. Deaths and crude death rates, by urban/rural residence: 2015 - 2019
Décès et taux bruts de mortalité, selon la résidence, urbaine/rurale : 2015 - 2019 (continued - suite)

Continent, country or area, and urban/rural residence Continent, pays ou zone et résidence, urbaine/rurale	Code[a]	Number - Nombre 2015	2016	2017	2018	2019	Rate - Taux 2015	2016	2017	2018	2019
AMERICA, NORTH - AMÉRIQUE DU NORD											
Bermuda - Bermudes[11]											
Total	C	478	492	481	533	...	7.7	7.7	7.5	8.3	...
British Virgin Islands - Îles Vierges britanniques											
Total	C	136	120	155	...	...	4.7	...	...	...	...
Canada[12]											
Total	C	264 333	267 213	276 689	283 706	...	7.4	7.4	7.6	7.7	...
Cayman Islands - Îles Caïmanes[13]											
Total	C	170	193	216	214	250	2.9	3.1	3.4	3.3	3.7
Costa Rica											
Total	C	21 039	22 603	23 251	23 786	*24 237	4.4	4.6	4.7	4.8	*4.8
Urban - Urbaine	C	17 103	17 988	17 879	18 031	*18 409	4.9	5.1	5.0	5.0	*5.0
Rural - Rurale	C	3 936	4 615	5 372	5 755	*5 828	3.0	3.4	4.0	4.2	*4.2
Cuba											
Total	C	99 691	99 388	106 949	106 196	...	8.9	8.8	9.5	9.5	...
Urban - Urbaine	C	84 365	84 574	89 855	88 174	...	9.8	9.8	10.4	10.2	...
Rural - Rurale	C	15 326	14 814	17 094	18 022	...	5.9	5.7	6.6	7.0	...
Curaçao											
Total	C	1 398	1 482	1 420	1 399	1 387	8.8	9.3	8.9	8.8	8.8
Dominica - Dominique											
Total	+C	664	686	...	...	...	9.3	9.6	...	...	...
Dominican Republic - République dominicaine											
Total	U	*41 598*	*43 843*	*42 862*	*41 997*	*42 811*	...	...	...	...	...
Urban - Urbaine[14]	U	*33 228*	*35 004*	...	...	...	...	...	...	...	...
Rural - Rurale[14]	U	*7 107*	*6 953*	...	...	...	...	...	...	...	...
Greenland - Groenland											
Total	C	472	487	499	487	548	8.4	8.7	8.9	8.7	9.7
Urban - Urbaine	C	407	408	428	421	470	8.4	8.4	8.8	8.7	9.6
Rural - Rurale	C	65	79	71	66	78	8.3	10.2	9.3	8.9	10.7
Grenada - Grenade											
Total	+C	869	898	885	...	...	7.9	8.1	7.9	...	...
Guadeloupe[15]											
Total	C	3 052	3 383	3 273	3 258	...	7.7	8.6	8.3	7.7	...
Guatemala											
Total	C	80 876	82 565	81 726	83 071	...	5.0	5.0	4.8	4.8	...
Jamaica - Jamaïque											
Total	U	*19 249*	*19 761*	*19 661*	*19 762*	*18 233*	...	...	...	...	...
Martinique[15]											
Total	C	3 058	3 284	3 217	...	...	8.1	8.7	8.7	...	...
Urban - Urbaine	C	...	...	2 631	...	...	...	...	...	...	...
Rural - Rurale	C	...	...	586	...	...	...	...	...	...	...
Mexico - Mexique[16]											
Total	+C	654 593	684 437	693 848	704 803	...	5.4	5.6	5.6	5.6	...
Urban - Urbaine[14]	+C	496 737	520 912	535 703	552 024	...	5.7	5.9	6.0	6.0	...
Rural - Rurale[14]	+C	147 354	153 699	152 136	130 382	...	4.4	4.6	4.5	4.0	...
Montserrat											
Total	C	49	43	39	38	59	9.8	8.5	...	8.2	...
Nicaragua											
Total	+U	...	*23 205*	*23 826*	*23 818*	...	...	...	...	...	...
Urban - Urbaine	+U	...	*15 198*	*15 461*	*15 776*	...	...	...	...	...	...
Rural - Rurale	+U	...	*8 007*	*8 365*	*8 042*	...	...	...	...	...	...
Panama											
Total	C	18 182	18 882	19 482	19 720	*18 591	4.6	4.7	4.8	4.7	*4.4
Urban - Urbaine	C	12 265	12 617	12 974	13 488	...	4.5	4.6	4.6	4.6	...
Rural - Rurale	C	5 917	6 265	6 508	6 232	...	4.7	5.0	5.2	5.0	...
Puerto Rico - Porto Rico											
Total	C	28 409	29 649	31 140	29 284	29 638	8.2	8.7	9.4	9.2	9.3
Urban - Urbaine	C	14 824[14]	15 038[14]	16 236	15 475	15 361	...	...	...	...	...
Rural - Rurale	C	13 099[14]	14 019[14]	14 904	13 809	14 277	...	...	...	...	...
Saint Barthélemy - Saint-Barthélemy											
Total	C	...	...	40	...	...	...	...	...	...	...
Saint Pierre and Miquelon - Saint Pierre-et-Miquelon											
Total	C	...	...	65	...	...	...	...	10.4	...	...

18. Deaths and crude death rates, by urban/rural residence: 2015 - 2019
Décès et taux bruts de mortalité, selon la résidence, urbaine/rurale : 2015 - 2019 (continued - suite)

Continent, country or area, and urban/rural residence Continent, pays ou zone et résidence, urbaine/rurale	Co-de[a]	Number - Nombre					Rate - Taux				
		2015	2016	2017	2018	2019	2015	2016	2017	2018	2019
AMERICA, NORTH - AMÉRIQUE DU NORD											
Saint Vincent and the Grenadines - Saint-Vincent-et-les Grenadines[17]											
Total	C	885	934	917	...	...	8.0	8.5	8.3	...	...
Saint-Martin (French part) - Saint-Martin (partie française)											
Total	C	...	...	152	...	...	...	...	4.3	...	...
Sint Maarten (Dutch part) - Saint-Martin (partie néerlandaise)											
Total	+C	197	160	172	...	...	5.2	4.1	4.2	...	...
Trinidad and Tobago - Trinité-et-Tobago											
Total	C	*10 651	*11 460	*11 410	*11 564	*11 266[18]	*7.9	*8.5	*8.4	*8.5	*8.3
Turks and Caicos Islands - Îles Turques et Caïques[19]											
Total	C	97	89	122	102	*126	2.6	2.3	3.1	2.5	*2.9
United States of America - États-Unis d'Amérique											
Total	C	2 712 630	2 744 248	2 813 503	...	...	8.5	8.5	8.7	...	...
United States Virgin Islands - Îles Vierges américaines[20]											
Total	C	673	632	707	...	...	6.5	5.9	6.6	...	...
AMERICA, SOUTH - AMÉRIQUE DU SUD											
Argentina - Argentine											
Total	C	333 407	352 992	341 688	336 823	...	7.7	8.1	7.8	7.6	...
Brazil - Brésil[21]											
Total	+C	1 231 400	1 274 630	1 277 579	...	...	6.0	6.2	6.2	...	...
Chile - Chili											
Total	C	103 327	104 026	106 388	*106 786	...	5.7	5.7	5.8	*5.7	...
Urban - Urbaine	C	89 935	90 010	93 008	...	...	5.7	5.6	5.7	...	...
Rural - Rurale	C	13 392	14 016	13 380	...	...	6.2	6.4	6.1	...	...
Colombia - Colombie											
Total	U	219 472	223 078	227 624	236 932	*242 609	...	...	...	...	...
Urban - Urbaine[14]	U	177 609	179 379	183 065	190 557	*194 357	...	...	...	...	...
Rural - Rurale[14]	U	39 828	41 536	41 752	44 147	*44 730	...	...	...	...	...
Ecuador - Équateur[22]											
Total	U	65 391	68 304	70 144	*71 007	...	...	...	...	...	...
Urban - Urbaine	U	50 239	52 752	53 909	*54 577	...	...	...	...	...	...
Rural - Rurale	U	15 152	15 552	16 235	*16 430	...	...	...	...	...	...
French Guiana - Guyane française[15]											
Total	C	834	901	964	...	...	3.3	3.4	3.5	...	...
Guyana[23]											
Total	+C	4 922	5 109	...	...	...	6.6	6.9	...	...	...
Total[24]	+U	...	...	*5 637	*4 949	*5 766	...	...	...	...	...
Paraguay											
Total	+U	24 885	27 243	26 404	29 139	...	...	...	...	...	...
Peru - Pérou[25]											
Total	+U	96 240	97 241	121 024	126 291	*114 945	...	...	...	...	...
Suriname											
Total	C	3 663	3 591	3 508	3 763	...	6.5	6.2	6.0	6.4	...
Urban - Urbaine	C	2 536	2 489	2 404	676	...	...	...	6.2	1.7	...
Rural - Rurale	C	1 127	1 102	1 104	3 087	...	...	...	5.6	15.5	...
Uruguay											
Total	C	32 967	34 273	33 173	34 412	...	9.5	9.8	9.5	9.8	...
Venezuela (Bolivarian Republic of) - Venezuela (République bolivarienne du)											
Total	C	163 712	188 725	190 236	...	...	5.4	6.1	6.1	...	...

18. Deaths and crude death rates, by urban/rural residence: 2015 - 2019
Décès et taux bruts de mortalité, selon la résidence, urbaine/rurale : 2015 - 2019 (continued - suite)

Continent, country or area, and urban/rural residence Continent, pays ou zone et résidence, urbaine/rurale	Co-de[a]	Number - Nombre					Rate - Taux				
		2015	2016	2017	2018	2019	2015	2016	2017	2018	2019
ASIA - ASIE											
Armenia - Arménie[26]											
Total	C	27 878	28 226	27 157	25 751	26 286	9.3	9.4	9.1	8.7	8.9
Urban - Urbaine	C	17 743	18 257	17 418	16 687	...	9.3	9.6	9.2	8.8	...
Rural - Rurale	C	10 135	9 969	9 739	9 064	...	9.3	9.2	9.0	8.4	...
Azerbaijan - Azerbaïdjan[26]											
Total	+C	54 697	56 648	57 109	57 250	55 916	5.7	5.8	5.8	5.8	5.6
Urban - Urbaine	+C	29 628	31 385	31 222	31 469	...	5.8	6.1	6.0	6.0	...
Rural - Rurale	+C	25 069	25 263	25 887	25 781	...	5.5	5.5	5.6	5.5	...
Bahrain - Bahreïn[27]											
Total	C	2 787	2 858	2 902	3 052	3 016	2.0	2.0	1.9	2.0	2.0
Bangladesh											
Total	U	*810 390*	*820 080*	*829 770*	*823 000*	*815 850*	...	...	...	...	...
Urban - Urbaine	U	*210 266*	*199 122*	*206 514*	*204 829*	*203 050*	...	...	...	...	...
Rural - Rurale	U	*600 124*	*620 958*	*623 256*	*618 171*	*612 800*	...	...	...	...	...
Bhutan - Bhoutan[28]											
Total	|	...	...	4 894	...	...	...	...	6.7	...	...
Brunei Darussalam - Brunéi Darussalam											
Total	+C	1 547	1 632	1 696	1 612	...	3.8	3.9	3.9	3.6	...
China - Chine[29]											
Total	|	9 750 000	9 770 000	9 860 000	9 930 000	9 980 000	7.1	7.1	7.1	7.1	7.1
China, Hong Kong SAR - Chine, Hong Kong RAS											
Total	C	46 108	46 905	46 829	47 400	48 957	6.3	6.4	6.3	6.4	6.5
China, Macao SAR - Chine, Macao RAS											
Total	C	2 002	2 248	2 120	2 069	2 282	3.1	3.4	3.3	3.1	3.4
Cyprus - Chypre[30]											
Total	C	5 859	5 471	5 996	5 768	*6 020	6.9	6.4	7.0	6.6	*6.9
Georgia - Géorgie[26]											
Total	C	49 121	50 771	47 822	46 524	46 659	13.2	13.7	12.8	12.5	12.5
Urban - Urbaine	C	26 139	26 788	...	...	...	12.3	12.6	...	...	...
Rural - Rurale	C	22 982	23 983	...	...	...	14.4	15.1	...	...	...
India - Inde[31]											
Total	|	...	...	...	...	...	6.5	6.4	6.3	6.2	...
Urban - Urbaine	|	...	...	...	...	...	5.4	5.4	5.3	5.1	...
Rural - Rurale	|	...	...	...	...	...	7.1	6.9	6.9	6.7	...
Iran (Islamic Republic of) - Iran (République islamique d')[32]											
Total	+C	374 827	369 751	376 678	377 193	*395 392	4.8	4.6	4.6	4.6	*4.8
Urban - Urbaine	+C	280 765	274 870[14]	278 448	279 525	...	4.9	4.6	4.6	4.6	...
Rural - Rurale	+C	94 062	94 788[14]	98 230	97 668	...	4.4	4.6	4.7	4.7	...
Iraq											
Total	U	...	*140 111*	*142 766*	...	...	...	...	...	...	...
Israel - Israël[33]											
Total	C	44 507	44 244	44 923	44 802	45 961	5.3	5.2	5.2	5.0	5.1
Urban - Urbaine[14]	C	41 775	41 560	42 201	42 140	43 131	5.5	5.3	5.3	5.2	...
Rural - Rurale[14]	C	2 723	2 677	2 720	2 660	2 819	3.7	3.6	3.6	3.5	...
Japan - Japon[34]											
Total	C	1 290 444[14]	1 307 748[14]	1 340 397[14]	1 362 470[14]	*1 381 098	10.1	10.3	10.6	10.8	*10.9
Urban - Urbaine[14]	C	1 147 467	1 162 734	1 194 280	1 215 476	...	...	...	...	...	...
Rural - Rurale[14]	C	141 799	143 801	144 963	145 981	...	...	...	...	...	...
Jordan - Jordanie[35]											
Total	U	*26 640*	*27 608*	*27 516*	...	...	...	...	...	...	...
Kazakhstan											
Total	U	*130 811*	*131 231*	*129 009*	*130 448*	*133 128*	...	...	...	...	...
Urban - Urbaine	U	*77 319*	*78 001*	*76 522*	*79 172*	*81 572*	...	...	...	...	...
Rural - Rurale	U	*53 492*	*53 230*	*52 487*	*51 276*	*51 556*	...	...	...	...	...
Kuwait - Koweït											
Total	C	6 481	6 338	6 679	6 807	...	1.6	1.6	1.7	1.7	...
Kyrgyzstan - Kirghizstan											
Total	C	34 808	33 475	33 166	32 989	...	5.8	5.5	5.4	5.2	...
Urban - Urbaine	C	12 294	11 664	11 647	11 574	...	6.1	5.7	5.6	5.4	...
Rural - Rurale	C	22 514	21 811	21 519	21 415	...	5.7	5.4	5.2	5.1	...

18. Deaths and crude death rates, by urban/rural residence: 2015 - 2019
Décès et taux bruts de mortalité, selon la résidence, urbaine/rurale : 2015 - 2019 (continued - suite)

Continent, country or area, and urban/rural residence Continent, pays ou zone et résidence, urbaine/rurale	Code[a]	Number - Nombre 2015	2016	2017	2018	2019	Rate - Taux 2015	2016	2017	2018	2019
ASIA - ASIE											
Lao People's Democratic Republic - République démocratique populaire lao[36]											
Total	I	27 083	...	...	...	...	4.1	...	...	...	...
Urban - Urbaine	I	7 571	...	...	...	...	...	...	...	...	...
Rural - Rurale	I	19 512	...	...	...	...	...	...	...	...	...
Malaysia - Malaisie											
Total	C	155 786	162 201	168 168	172 031	...	5.0	5.1	5.3	5.3	...
Urban - Urbaine	C	101 309	104 817	108 772	111 913	...	4.4	4.4	4.5	4.6	...
Rural - Rurale	C	54 477	57 384	59 396	60 118	...	6.8	7.2	7.5	7.6	...
Maldives[37]											
Total	C	1 130	1 226	1 241	...	...	3.3	3.5	3.5	...	...
Urban - Urbaine[14]	C	260	263	207	...	...	1.9	1.9	1.4	...	...
Rural - Rurale[14]	C	744	846	1 015	...	...	3.5	4.0	4.7	...	...
Mongolia - Mongolie											
Total	+C	17 620	17 763	17 357	17 864	18 403	5.8	5.8	5.5	5.6	5.6
Urban - Urbaine	+C	11 753	11 182	11 425	11 575	11 924	5.8	5.3	5.3	5.3	5.4
Rural - Rurale	+C	5 867	6 581	5 932	6 289	6 479	6.0	6.8	5.9	6.1	6.2
Myanmar[38]											
Total	+U	*225 526*	*213 187*	*231 210*	...	...	...	...	...	...	...
Urban - Urbaine	+U	*102 923*	*88 606*	*89 779*	...	...	...	...	...	...	...
Rural - Rurale	+U	*122 603*	*124 581*	*141 431*	...	...	...	...	...	...	...
Oman											
Total	U	*8 167*[39]	*8 196*[39]	*8 861*	*8 979*	*8 581*	...	...	...	...	...
Philippines											
Total	C	560 605	582 183	579 237	590 709	...	5.6	5.7	5.6	5.6	...
Qatar											
Total	C	2 317	2 347	2 294	2 385	2 200	1.0	0.9	0.8	0.9	0.8
Urban - Urbaine	C	2 317	2 347	2 294	2 385	2 200	1.0	0.9	0.8	0.9	0.8
Republic of Korea - République de Corée[40]											
Total	C	275 895	280 827	285 534	298 820	...	5.4	5.5	5.6	5.8	...
Urban - Urbaine	C	189 851[14]	193 664[14]	196 654	206 800[14]	...	4.6	4.7	4.7	5.0	...
Rural - Rurale	C	86 038[14]	87 162[14]	88 880	92 017[14]	...	9.1	9.1	9.2	9.5	...
Saudi Arabia - Arabie saoudite[41]											
Total	I	69 206[42]	58 097[42]	58 915[43]	...	...	2.2	1.8	1.8	...	...
Singapore - Singapour											
Total	+C	19 862	20 017	20 905	21 282	21 446	5.1	5.1	5.3	5.3	5.3
Sri Lanka											
Total	+C	*131 614	*130 765	*139 822	*139 498	*146 053	*6.3	*6.2	*6.5	*6.4	*6.7
State of Palestine - État de Palestine[44]											
Total	U	*12 075*	*12 202*	*11 778*	*12 296*	...	...	...	...	...	...
Tajikistan - Tadjikistan[26]											
Total	U	*33 563*	*34 134*	*32 027*	*32 699*	...	...	...	...	...	...
Urban - Urbaine	U	*9 959*	*9 944*	*9 556*	*9 881*	...	...	...	...	...	...
Rural - Rurale	U	*23 604*	*24 190*	*22 471*	*22 818*	...	...	...	...	...	...
Thailand - Thaïlande											
Total	+U	*445 964*[45]	*469 085*[45]	*458 010*[45]	*461 818*[45]	**494 339*	...	...	...	...	...
Timor-Leste[46]											
Total	I	9 209	...	...	...	...	7.7	...	...	...	...
Turkey - Turquie[47]											
Total	C	405 528	422 827	426 504	426 106	*435 941	5.2	5.3	5.3	5.2	*5.3
United Arab Emirates - Émirats arabes unis											
Total[48]	...	*8 755*	*8 988*	...	...	...	...	...	...	...	...
Total	C	...	...	8 826	8 794	...	...	...	0.9	0.9	...
Uzbekistan - Ouzbékistan[26]											
Total	+C	152 035	154 791	160 723	154 913	154 570	4.9	4.9	5.0	4.7	4.6
Urban - Urbaine	+C	81 094	81 736	84 969	82 633	...	5.1	5.1	5.2	5.0	...
Rural - Rurale	+C	70 941	73 055	75 754	72 280	...	4.6	4.6	4.7	4.4	...
Viet Nam											
Total	C	...	...	...	569 338	556 015	...	...	...	6.0	5.8
Yemen - Yémen[49]											
Total	U	...	*25 927*	*31 999*	...	...	...	...	...	...	...

18. Deaths and crude death rates, by urban/rural residence: 2015 - 2019
Décès et taux bruts de mortalité, selon la résidence, urbaine/rurale : 2015 - 2019 (continued - suite)

Continent, country or area, and urban/rural residence Continent, pays ou zone et résidence, urbaine/rurale	Code[a]	Number - Nombre 2015	2016	2017	2018	2019	Rate - Taux 2015	2016	2017	2018	2019
EUROPE											
Åland Islands - Îles d'Åland											
Total	C	285	297	235	272	*265	9.8	10.2	8.0	9.2	*8.9
Urban - Urbaine	C	114	120	96	135	*111	9.9	10.4	8.3	11.5	*9.5
Rural - Rurale	C	171	177	139	137	*154	9.8	10.1	7.8	7.6	*8.5
Albania - Albanie											
Total	C	22 418	21 388	22 232	21 804	21 937	7.8	7.4	7.7	7.6	7.7
Andorra - Andorre											
Total	C	282	310	323	335	301	4.0	4.3	4.4	4.5	4.0
Austria - Autriche[50]											
Total	C	83 073	80 669	83 270	83 975	*83 386	9.6	9.2	9.5	9.5	*9.4
Belarus - Bélarus											
Total	C	120 026	119 379	119 311	120 053	*120 913	12.6	12.6	12.6	12.7	*12.8
Urban - Urbaine	C	73 563	73 599	73 972	75 529	...	10.0	10.0	10.0	10.2	...
Rural - Rurale	C	46 463	45 780	45 339	44 524	...	21.7	21.6	21.7	21.6	...
Belgium - Belgique[51]											
Total	C	110 541	108 097	109 666	110 693	*108 783	9.8	9.5	9.6	9.7	*9.5
Urban - Urbaine	C	108 942	...	...	...	...	...	...	...	...	...
Rural - Rurale	C	1 599	...	...	...	...	...	...	...	...	...
Bosnia and Herzegovina - Bosnie-Herzégovine											
Total	C	37 070	35 530	36 336	37 744	...	10.5	10.1	10.4	10.8	...
Bulgaria - Bulgarie											
Total	C	110 117	107 580	109 791	108 526	108 083	15.3	15.1	15.5	15.4	15.4
Urban - Urbaine	C	67 749	67 192	68 418	68 011	...	12.9	12.9	13.2	13.2	...
Rural - Rurale	C	42 368	40 388	41 373	40 515	...	21.9	21.1	22.0	21.8	...
Croatia - Croatie											
Total	C	54 205	51 542	53 477	52 706	*51 794	12.9	12.3	13.0	12.9	*12.7
Urban - Urbaine	C	28 365	27 000	28 311	28 216	...	...	...	...	...	...
Rural - Rurale	C	25 840	24 542	25 166	24 490	...	...	...	...	...	...
Czechia - Tchéquie											
Total	C	111 173	107 750	111 443	112 920	*112 362	10.5	10.2	10.5	10.6	*10.5
Urban - Urbaine	C	81 854	79 384	82 135	83 298	...	10.6	10.3	10.6	10.7	...
Rural - Rurale	C	29 319	28 366	29 308	29 622	...	10.3	10.0	10.3	10.4	...
Denmark - Danemark[52]											
Total	C	52 555	52 824	53 261	55 232	53 958	9.3	9.2	9.2	9.5	9.3
Estonia - Estonie											
Total	C	15 243	15 392	15 543	15 751	15 401	11.6	11.7	11.8	11.9	11.6
Urban - Urbaine[14]	C	10 491	10 539	10 030	10 119	...	11.7	11.7	11.0	11.0	...
Rural - Rurale[14]	C	4 744	4 836	5 503	5 606	...	11.4	11.7	13.6	13.9	...
Faroe Islands - Îles Féroé											
Total	C	377	379	447	394	411	7.7	7.7	8.9	7.7	7.9
Urban - Urbaine	C	102	122	159	144	147	5.5	6.4	8.3	7.3	7.4
Rural - Rurale	C	275	257	288	250	264	9.1	8.4	9.3	8.0	8.3
Finland - Finlande											
Total	C	52 207[53]	53 626[53]	53 487[53]	54 255[53]	*53 559	9.6	9.8	9.8	9.9	*9.7
Urban - Urbaine[53]	C	32 941	33 949	33 748	34 705	...	8.6	8.7	8.6	8.8	...
Rural - Rurale[53]	C	19 266	19 677	19 739	19 550	...	12.0	12.4	12.5	12.5	...
France											
Total	C	581 770	581 073	593 606	596 422	...	9.0	9.0	9.2	9.2	...
Urban - Urbaine[54]	C	441 398	441 334	451 637	...	...	...	...	...	...	...
Rural - Rurale[54]	C	138 220	137 674	139 881	...	...	...	...	...	...	...
Germany - Allemagne											
Total	C	925 200	910 899	932 263	954 874	*939 536	11.3	11.1	11.3	11.5	*11.3
Gibraltar[55]											
Total	+C	235	249	...	...	...	7.0	7.3	...	...	...
Greece - Grèce											
Total	C	121 183	118 788	124 495	120 296	*125 016	11.2	11.0	11.6	11.2	*11.7
Urban - Urbaine	C	67 843	67 121	70 276	68 911	...	...	...	...	...	...
Rural - Rurale	C	53 340	51 667	54 219	51 385	...	...	...	...	...	...
Guernsey - Guernesey[56]											
Total	C	557	536	586	574	539	9.0	8.6	9.4	9.2	8.6
Hungary - Hongrie[57]											
Total	C	131 575	127 098	131 877	131 247	129 892	13.4	13.0	13.5	13.4	13.3
Urban - Urbaine[58]	C	89 692	86 815	89 822	89 482	...	12.9	12.6	13.0	13.0	...
Rural - Rurale[58]	C	41 717	40 130	41 911	41 598	...	14.4	13.8	14.5	14.4	...

18. Deaths and crude death rates, by urban/rural residence: 2015 - 2019
Décès et taux bruts de mortalité, selon la résidence, urbaine/rurale : 2015 - 2019 (continued - suite)

Continent, country or area, and urban/rural residence / Continent, pays ou zone et résidence, urbaine/rurale	Code[a]	Number - Nombre 2015	2016	2017	2018	2019	Rate - Taux 2015	2016	2017	2018	2019
EUROPE											
Iceland - Islande											
Total	C	2 178	2 309	2 238	2 254	...	6.6	6.9	6.5	6.4	...
Urban - Urbaine	C	2 009	2 038	2 070	2 086	...	6.5	6.5	6.4	6.3	...
Rural - Rurale	C	169	183	168	168	...	8.1	8.6	7.6	7.3	...
Ireland - Irlande											
Total	+C	30 064	30 390	30 317	31 009	31 134	6.4	6.4	6.3	6.4	6.3
Isle of Man - Île de Man											
Total	+C	...	852	837	876	850	...	10.2	10.0	...	...
Italy - Italie											
Total	C	647 571	615 261	649 061	633 133	*634 432	10.7	10.1	10.7	10.5	...
Jersey											
Total	+C	762	831	803	820	...	7.5	8.1	7.7	7.8	...
Latvia - Lettonie											
Total	C	28 478	28 580	28 757	28 820	27 719	14.4	14.6	14.8	15.0	14.4
Urban - Urbaine	C	18 884	18 877	19 134	19 127	...	14.0	14.1	...	14.5	...
Rural - Rurale	C	9 594	9 701	9 623	9 693	...	15.2	15.6	...	16.0	...
Liechtenstein											
Total	C	252	271	249	274	...	6.7	7.2	6.6	7.2	...
Lithuania - Lituanie											
Total	C	41 776	41 106	40 142	39 574	38 281	14.4	14.3	14.2	14.1	13.7
Urban - Urbaine	C	25 850	25 817	24 941	24 933	...	13.2	13.4	13.1	13.3	...
Rural - Rurale	C	15 926	15 289	15 201	14 641	...	16.7	16.2	16.3	15.9	...
Luxembourg											
Total	C	3 983	3 967	4 263	4 318	4 283	7.0	6.8	7.1	7.1	7.0
Malta - Malte											
Total	C	3 442	3 342	3 571	3 688	3 688	7.7	7.3	7.6	7.6	7.5
Monaco[59]											
Total	C	595	503[60]	490	528	...	15.8	13.2	13.0	13.8	...
Montenegro - Monténégro											
Total	C	6 329	6 464	6 523	6 504	6 595	10.2	10.4	10.5	10.5	10.6
Netherlands - Pays-Bas[61]											
Total	C	147 134	148 997	150 214	153 363	151 885	8.7	8.7	8.8	8.9	8.8
North Macedonia - Macédoine du Nord											
Total	C	20 461	20 417	20 318	19 727	*20 412	9.9	9.9	9.8	9.5	*9.8
Urban - Urbaine	C	12 462	12 438	12 426	12 091	...	...	...	...	...	...
Rural - Rurale	C	7 999	7 983	7 892	7 636	...	...	...	...	...	...
Norway - Norvège[62]											
Total	C	40 676	40 726	40 774	40 840	*40 727	7.8	7.8	7.7	7.7	*7.6
Poland - Pologne											
Total	C	394 921	388 009	402 852	414 200	409 709	10.4	10.2	10.6	10.9	10.7
Urban - Urbaine	C	242 067	236 749	247 346	255 280	...	10.6	10.4	10.8	11.2	...
Rural - Rurale	C	152 854	151 260	155 506	158 920	...	10.1	10.0	10.3	10.5	...
Portugal[63]											
Total	C	108 539	110 573	109 758	113 051	*112 278	10.5	10.7	10.7	11.0	*10.9
Republic of Moldova - République de Moldova[64]											
Total	C	39 906	38 489	36 768	37 200	*36 794	14.1	13.7	13.3	13.7	*13.7
Urban - Urbaine	C	...	12 766	12 473	12 866	...	...	...	...	...	...
Rural - Rurale	C	...	25 723	24 295	24 334	...	...	...	...	...	...
Romania - Roumanie											
Total	C	261 294	258 404	261 402	263 911	*259 506	13.2	13.1	13.3	13.6	*13.4
Urban - Urbaine	C	121 616	121 610	123 079	124 957	...	11.4	11.5	11.7	11.9	...
Rural - Rurale	C	139 678	136 794	138 323	138 954	...	15.3	15.0	15.2	15.4	...
San Marino - Saint-Marin											
Total	C	235	253	278	244	...	6.9	7.4	8.1	7.1	...
Serbia - Serbie[65]											
Total	+C	103 678	100 834	103 722	101 655	*102 131	14.6	14.3	14.8	14.6	*14.7
Urban - Urbaine	+C	56 161	54 902	56 387	56 112	...	13.2	12.9	13.2	13.2	...
Rural - Rurale	+C	47 517	45 932	47 335	45 543	...	16.8	16.4	17.1	16.7	...
Slovakia - Slovaquie											
Total	C	53 826	52 351	53 914	54 293	53 234	9.9	9.6	9.9	10.0	9.8
Urban - Urbaine	C	27 254	27 070	27 666	28 205	...	9.3	9.3	9.5	9.7	...
Rural - Rurale	C	26 572	25 281	26 248	26 088	...	10.6	10.1	10.4	10.3	...

18. Deaths and crude death rates, by urban/rural residence: 2015 - 2019
Décès et taux bruts de mortalité, selon la résidence, urbaine/rurale : 2015 - 2019 (continued - suite)

Continent, country or area, and urban/rural residence Continent, pays ou zone et résidence, urbaine/rurale	Co-de[a]	Number - Nombre					Rate - Taux				
		2015	2016	2017	2018	2019	2015	2016	2017	2018	2019
EUROPE											
Slovenia - Slovénie											
Total	C	19 834	19 689	20 509	20 485	*20 588	9.6	9.5	9.9	9.9	*9.9
Urban - Urbaine	C	10 098	9 890	10 753	10 666	...	9.1	8.9	9.4	9.3	...
Rural - Rurale	C	9 736	9 799	9 756	9 819	...	10.2	10.2	10.6	10.6	...
Spain - Espagne											
Total	C	420 408	408 231	422 037	425 153	*415 070	9.1	8.8	9.1	9.1	*8.8
Sweden - Suède											
Total	C	90 907	90 982	91 972	92 185	...	9.3	9.2	9.1	9.1	...
Switzerland - Suisse											
Total	C	67 606	64 964	66 971	67 088	*66 315	8.2	7.8	7.9	7.9	*7.8
Urban - Urbaine	C	56 647	54 293	56 155	56 496	...	8.1	7.7	...	7.8	...
Rural - Rurale	C	10 959	10 671	10 816	10 592	...	8.5	8.2	...	8.2	...
Ukraine[66]											
Total	+C	594 796	583 631	574 123	*587 665	*581 114	13.9	13.7	13.5	*13.9	*13.8
Urban - Urbaine	+C	358 749	354 634	350 549	...	...	12.1	12.0	11.9	...	...
Rural - Rurale	+C	236 047	228 997	223 574	...	...	17.9	17.4	17.1	...	...
United Kingdom of Great Britain and Northern Ireland - Royaume-Uni de Grande-Bretagne et d'Irlande du Nord[67]											
Total	+C	601 272	595 655	605 748	614 313	*603 419	9.2	9.1	9.2	9.2	*9.0
OCEANIA - OCÉANIE											
American Samoa - Samoas américaines											
Total	C	314	280	310	...	...	5.2	4.7	5.1	...	...
Australia - Australie											
Total	C	159 052	158 504	160 909	158 493	...	6.7	6.6	6.5	6.3	...
Urban - Urbaine[68]	C	94 156	93 337	95 223	93 028	...	4.6	4.5	4.5	4.3	...
Rural - Rurale[68]	C	64 388	64 638	65 170	64 883	...	19.8	19.8	19.8	19.6	...
Cook Islands - Îles Cook											
Total	+C	102	87	93	*121	*105	5.5	4.5	4.8	*6.5	*5.2
Fiji - Fidji											
Total	+C	6 672	7 476[69]	6 992[69]	...	...	7.7	8.6	7.9	...	...
French Polynesia - Polynésie française											
Total	C	1 409	1 394	1 608	1 616	...	5.2	5.1	5.8	5.8	...
Guam[70]											
Total	C	1 009	1 022	1 008	1 056	*1 037	6.2	6.3	6.2	6.3	*6.2
Kiribati[71]											
Total	+U	*709*	...	...	...	...	...	...	...	...	...
Nauru											
Total	C	90	100	94	...	...	8.0	9.1	...	...	...
New Caledonia - Nouvelle-Calédonie											
Total	C	1 465	1 569	1 529	...	...	5.4	5.7	5.5	...	...
New Zealand - Nouvelle-Zélande[72]											
Total	+C	31 608	31 179[73]	33 339[73]	33 216[73]	34 242[73]	6.9	6.6	7.0	6.9	7.0
Urban - Urbaine[14]	+C	28 455	27 912[73]	29 913[73]	29 166[73]	30 249[73]	7.2	6.9	7.2	7.2	7.3
Rural - Rurale[14]	+C	3 132	3 246[73]	3 411[73]	4 050[73]	3 993[73]	4.9	5.1	5.3	5.2	5.0
Niue - Nioué											
Total	C	16	7	...	...	...	...	...	...	...	...
Norfolk Island - Île Norfolk[74]											
Total	+C	11	...	...	...	...	...	...	...	...	...
Palau - Palaos											
Total	C	136	175	183	143	...	7.7	9.9	10.3	7.8	...
Pitcairn											
Total	C	...	...	...	...	3	...	...	...	...	...
Samoa[75]											
Total	+U	*1 112*	*2 020*	*1 037*	*1 114*	...	...	...	...	...	...
Tuvalu											
Total	+U	*66*	*90*	...	...	...	...	...	...	...	...

FOOTNOTES - NOTES

Italics: data from civil registers which are incomplete or of unknown completeness. - Italiques : données incomplètes ou dont le degré d'exactitude n'est pas connu, provenant des registres de l'état civil.

* Provisional. - Données provisoires.

[a] 'Code' indicates the source of data, as follows:
C - Civil registration, estimated over 90% complete
U - Civil registration, estimated less than 90% complete
| - Other source, estimated reliable
+ - Data tabulated by date of registration rather than occurence
... - Information not available

Le 'Code' indique la source des données, comme suit :
C - Registres de l'état civil considérés complets à 90 p. 100 au moins
U - Registres de l'état civil qui ne sont pas considérés complets à 90 p. 100 au moins
| - Autre source, considérée pas douteuses
+ - Données exploitées selon la date de l'enregistrement et non la date de l'événement
... - Information pas disponible

[1] Excluding live-born infants who died before their birth was registered. Data refer to Algerian population only. - Non compris les enfants nés vivants décédés avant l'enregistrement de leur naissance. Les données ne concernent que la population algérienne.
[2] Source: Vital Statistics Report. - Source: Vital Statistics Report.
[3] Source: Statistical Report, Ministry of Health and Social Security. - Source: Rapport statistique, ministère de la Santé et de la Sécurité sociale.
[4] The rate of registration of deaths is less than 20 per cent at the national level. - Le taux d'enregistrement des décès est inférieur à 20 p. 100 au niveau national.
[5] Source: Ministry of Home Affairs. - Source : Ministère de l'intérieur.
[6] Data refer to the 12 months preceding the census in September. - Les données se rapportent aux 12 mois précédant le recensement de septembre.
[7] Excludes the islands of St. Brandon and Agalega. - Non compris les îles St. Brandon et Agalega.
[8] Completeness estimated at 19%. - Degré de complétude évalué à 19 pour cent.
[9] Excluding visitors. - Ne comprend pas les visiteurs.
[10] Unrevised data. - Les données n'ont pas été révisées.
[11] Excluding non-residents and foreign service personnel and their dependants. Bermuda is 100 per cent urban. - À l'exclusion des non-résidents et du personnel diplomatique et de leurs charges de famille. 100 pour cent de la population des Bermudes est urbaine.
[12] Including Canadian residents temporarily in the United States, but excluding United States residents temporarily in Canada. - Y compris les résidents canadiens se trouvant temporairement aux Etats-Unis, mais ne comprenant pas les résidents des Etats-Unis se trouvant temporairement au Canada.
[13] Including resident deaths outside of the islands but buried in the islands. - Y compris les décès de résidents hors des îles mais inhumés dans les îles.
[14] The total number may include 'Unknown residence', but the categories urban and rural do not. - Le nombre total peut inclure les personnes dont la résidence n'est pas connue, à l'inverse des catégories de population urbaine et rurale.
[15] Excluding live-born infants who died before their birth was registered. - Non compris les enfants nés vivants décédés avant l'enregistrement de leur naissance.
[16] Data refer to resident population only. - Pour la population résidante seulement.
[17] Data refer to resident and non resident deaths that occurred in Saint Vincent and the Grenadines. - Les données concernent les décès de résidents et de non-résidents survenus à St Vincent-et-les-Grenadines.
[18] Source: National Statistical Office. - Source : Service national de statistique.
[19] Excluding deaths of persons living abroad. - Exception faite des personnes décédées à l'étranger.
[20] Source: U.S. National Center for Health Statistics, National Vital Statistics Reports (NVSR). - Source : US National Center for Health Statistics, National Vital Statistics Reports (NVSR).
[21] Including deaths abroad and deaths of unknown place of residence. - Y compris décès à l'étranger et décès dont le lieu de résidence n'est pas connu.
[22] Excludes nomadic Indian tribes. - Non compris les tribus d'Indiens nomades.
[23] Source: General Registrar Office. - Source : Bureau général de l'État civil.
[24] Estimated completeness of registration is within 80-89 per cent. - Degré de complétude de l'enregistrement est évalué à 80-89 pour cent.
[25] Source: Reports of the Ministry of Health. - Source : Rapports du Ministère de la Santé.
[26] Excluding infants born alive of less than 28 weeks' gestation, of less than 1 000 g in weight and 35 cm in length, who die within seven days of birth. - Non compris les enfants nés vivants après moins de 28 semaines de gestations, pesant moins de 1 000 g, mesurant moins de 35 cm et décédés dans les sept jours qui ont suivi leur naissance.
[27] Sources: Births and Deaths National Registration System database, and medical records of government hospitals. Data refer to Bahraini and non-Bahraini deaths including some visitors, and Bahraini deaths abroad. - Les sources: Les bases de données des << Births and Deaths National Registration System >> et les dossiers médicaux des hôpitaux du gouvernement. Les données se rapportent aux décès de Bahreïniens et de non-Bahreïniens, y compris de non-résidents, ainsi que de Bahreïniens résidant à l'étranger.
[28] Data refer to the 12 months preceding the census in May. - Les données se rapportent aux 12 mois précédant le recensement de mai.
[29] Data have been estimated on the basis of the annual National Sample Survey on Population Changes. For statistical purposes, the data for China do not include those for the Hong Kong Special Administrative Region (Hong Kong SAR), Macao Special Administrative Region (Macao SAR) and Taiwan province of China. - Les données ont été estimées sur la base de l'enquête annuelle "National Sample Survey on Population Changes". Pour la présentation des statistiques, les données pour la Chine ne comprennent pas la Région Administrative Spéciale de Hong Kong (Hong Kong RAS), la Région Administrative Spéciale de Macao (Macao RAS) et Taïwan province de Chine.
[30] Data refer to government controlled areas. Data refer to deaths of residents only. - Les données se rapportent aux zones contrôlées par le Gouvernement. Les données renvoient aux décès de résidents uniquement.
[31] Includes data for the Indian-held part of Jammu and Kashmir, the final status of which has not yet been determined. Rates were obtained by the Sample Registration System of India, which is a large demographic survey. - Y compris les données pour la partie du Jammu et du Cachemire occupée par l'Inde dont le statut définitif n'a pas encore été déterminé. Les taux ont été obtenus par le Système de l'enregistrement par échantillon de l'Inde qui est une large enquête démographique.
[32] Data refer to the Iranian Year which begins on 21 March and ends on 20 March of the following year. - Les données concernent l'année iranienne, qui commence le 21 mars et se termine le 20 mars de l'année suivante.
[33] Including deaths abroad of Israeli residents who were out of the country for less than a year. Includes data for East Jerusalem and Israeli residents in certain other territories under occupation by Israeli military forces since June 1967. - Y compris les décès à l'étranger de résidents israéliens qui ont quitté le pays depuis moins d'un an. Y compris les données pour Jérusalem-Est et les résidents israéliens dans certains autres territoires occupés depuis 1967 par les forces armées israéliennes.
[34] Data refer to Japanese nationals in Japan only. - Les données se raportent aux nationaux japonais au Japon seulement.
[35] Excluding data for Jordanian territory under occupation since June 1967 by Israeli military forces. Excluding foreigners, including registered Palestinian refugees. - Non compris les données pour le territoire jordanien occupé depuis juin 1967 par les forces armées israéliennes. Non compris les étrangers, mais y compris les réfugiés de Palestine enregistrés.
[36] Data refer to the 12 months preceding the census in March. - Les données se rapportent aux 12 mois précédant le recensement de mars.
[37] Data do not include foreigners. - Les données sur les etrangers ne sont pas inclus.
[38] Data are from Vital Registration System (VRS). - Les données proviennent du système d'enregistrement des faits d'état civil.
[39] Data from Births and Deaths Notification System (Ministry of Health and all health care providers). - Les données proviennent du système de notification des naissances et des décès (Ministère de la santé et tous prestataires de soins de santé).
[40] Excluding alien armed forces, civilian aliens employed by armed forces, and foreign diplomatic personnel and their dependants. - Non compris les militaires étrangers, les civils étrangers employés par les forces armées ni le personnel diplomatique étranger et les membres de leur famille les accompagnant.
[41] Data refer to Saudi Arabian nationals only. - Les données ne concernent que les ressortissants saoudiens.
[42] Based on 2010 population census and 2016 demographic survey. - D'après le recensement de la population de 2010 et l'enquête démographique de 2016.
[43] Survey based estimates. - Estimations basées sur des enquêtes.
[44] Data exclude Jerusalem ID holders. Source: Palestinian Central Bureau of Statistics, Population Register, updated version 2019. - Les données ne tiennent pas compte des détenteurs de carte d'identité de Jérusalem. Source: Bureau

central de statistique palestinien, registre de la population, version actualisée jusqu'au 2019.

[45] Source: Strategy and Planning Division, Ministry of Public Health. - Source : Division de la stratégie et de la planification, Ministère de la Santé publique.

[46] Data refer to the 12 months preceding the census in July. - Les données se rapportent aux 12 mois précédant le recensement de juillet.

[47] Data from MERNIS (Central Population Administrative System). - Données de MERNIS (Système central de données démographiques).

[48] The registration of births and deaths is conducted by the Ministry of Health. An estimate of completeness is not provided. - L'enregistrement des naissances et des décès est mené par le Ministère de la Santé. Le degré estimatif de complétude n'est pas fourni.

[49] Including Non-Yemeni deaths. - Y compris les décès non-yéménites.

[50] Including deaths of nationals abroad. - Y compris les décès des nationaux survenus à l'étranger.

[51] Including armed forces stationed outside the country, but excluding alien armed forces stationed in the area. - Y compris les militaires nationaux hors du pays, mais non compris les militaires étrangers en garnison sur le territoire.

[52] Excluding Faeroe Islands and Greenland shown separately, if available. - Non compris les Iles Féroé et le Groenland, qui font l'objet de rubriques distinctes, si disponible.

[53] Excluding Åland Islands. - Non compris les Îles d'Åland.

[54] Data for urban and rural exclude events corresponding to nationals residing outside the country, which may be included in the total. - Les données relatives à les categories urbaine et rurale n'englobent pas les faits d'état civil qui concernent les nationaux se trouvant à l'étranger, lesquels faits peuvent être inclus au total.

[55] Excluding armed forces. - Non compris les militaires en garnison.

[56] For year ending 31 March. - Période annuelle se terminant le 31 mars.

[57] Data include the deceased persons with Hungarian usual residence regardless of whether the death occurred in Hungary or in a foreign country, and do not include the deceased persons with foreign country usual residence. - Les données comprennent tous les décès survenus alors que leur résidence habituelle était en Hongrie, que le décès ait eu lieu en Hongrie ou dans un pays étranger, et ne comprennent pas les décès des personnes dont la residence habituelle était dans un pays étranger.

[58] The urban and rural categories do not include the data of foreigners, persons of unknown residence and the homeless, whereas the total category includes them. - Les chiffres portant sur la population urbaine et rurale n' incluent pas les données relatives aux étrangers, aux personnes dont la résidence n'est pas connue et aux personnes sans domicile fixe, à l'inverse, le total les inclut.

[59] Source: City Hall, Civil Status Registry Office, resident and non-resident deaths. - Source : La mairie, Bureau de l'État Civil, toutes les décès.

[60] Including still births. - Les données comprennent les mortinaissances.

[61] Including residents outside the country if listed in a Netherlands population register. - Englobe les résidents se trouvant à l'étranger à condition qu'ils soient inscrits sur le registre de population des Pays-Bas.

[62] Including residents temporarily outside the country. - Y compris les résidents se trouvant temporairement hors du pays.

[63] Data refer to usual resident population. - Les données se réfèrent à la population résidente habituelle.

[64] Excluding Transnistria and the municipality of Bender. - Les données ne tiennent pas compte de l'information sur la Transnistria et la municipalité de Bender.

[65] Excludes data for Kosovo and Metohia. - Sans les données pour le Kosovo et Metohie.

[66] The Government of Ukraine has informed the United Nations that it is not in a position to provide statistical data concerning the Autonomous Republic of Crimea and the city of Sevastopol. Data includes deaths resulting from births with weight 500 g and more (if weight is unknown - with length 25 cm and more, or with gestation during 22 weeks or more). - Le gouvernement Ukrainien a informé l'ONU qu'il n'est pas en mesure de fournir des données statistiques concernant la République autonome de Crimée et la ville de Sébastopol. Y compris les décès de nouveau-nés de 500 g ou plus (si le poids est inconnu – de 25 cm de long ou plus, ou après une grossesse de 22 semaines ou plus).

[67] Excluding Channel Islands (Guernsey and Jersey) and Isle of Man, shown separately, if available. - Non compris les îles Anglo-Normandes (Guernesey et Jersey) et l'île de Man, qui font l'objet de rubriques distinctes, si disponible.

[68] Urban refers to Greater Capital City Statistical Areas, and rural refers to other areas within the state or territory. Data for urban and rural figures do not add up to the total because they exclude the events occurred in Migratory, Special Purpose and Other Territories. - Urbain renvoie aux zones statistiques de la capitale métropolitaine, et rural aux autres zones de l'État ou territoire. La somme des chiffres des catégories « en zone urbaine » et « en zone rurale » ne correspond pas au total du fait qu'en sont exclus les événements qui ont eu lieu dans les territoires de migration, les territoires à destination spéciale et autres territoires.

[69] Data recorded by Ministry of Health and Medical Services (MoHMS). - Données enregistrées par le Ministère de la santé et des services médicaux (MoHMS).

[70] Including United States military personnel, their dependants and contract employees. - Y compris les militaires des Etats-Unis, les membres de leur famille les accompagnant et les agents contractuels des Etats-Unis.

[71] Data refer to registered events only within island councils and civil registration office. - Correspond aux événements enregistrés par les conseils des îles et par les services de l'état civil.

[72] Random rounding to base 3 is applied in this table as a confidentiality measure. - Les chiffres sont arrondis à la base 3 de manière aléatoire, pour des raisons de confidentialité.

[73] Data refer to deaths of residents only. - Les données renvoient aux décès de résidents uniquement.

[74] Data cover the period from 1 July of the previous year to 30 June of the present year. - Pour la période allant du 1er juillet de l'année précédente au 30 juin de l'année en cours.

[75] Source: Births, Deaths, and Marriages Registration Division, Samoa Bureau of Statistics. - Source : Division de l'enregistrement des naissances, des décès et des mariages du Bureau de statistique du Samoa.

Table 19 - *Demographic Yearbook 2019*

Table 19 presents deaths by age and sex and age-specific death rates by sex for the latest available year between 2010 and 2019.

Description of variables: Age is defined as age at last birthday, that is, the difference between the date of birth and the date of the occurrence of the event, expressed in completed solar years. The age classification used in this table is the following: under 1 year, 1-4 years, 5-year age groups through 95-99 years, and 100 years or over.

Rate computation: Age-specific death rates by sex are the annual number of deaths in each age-sex group per 1 000 population in the same age-sex group. These rates are calculated by the United Nations Statistics Division.

Deaths at unknown age and the population of unknown age are excluded from age-specific rate calculations but are part of the death rate for all ages combined.

Death rates for infants under one year of age in this table differ from the infant mortality rates shown elsewhere, because the latter are computed per 1 000 live births rather than per 1 000 population.

The population used in computing the rates is the estimated or the enumerated population by age and sex reported to United Nations Statistics Division. First priority is given to an estimate and second priority to census returns of the year to which the deaths refer.

Rates presented in this table have been limited to those countries or areas having at least a total of 100 deaths in a given year. Moreover, rates specific for individual sub-categories that are based on 30 or fewer deaths are identified by the symbol "♦".

Reliability of data: Data from civil registers of deaths that are reported as incomplete (less than 90 per cent completeness) or of unknown completeness are considered unreliable and are set in italics rather than in roman type. Table 18 and the technical notes for that table provide more detailed information on the completeness of death registration. For more information about the quality of vital statistics data in general and the information available on the basis of the completeness estimates in particular, see section 4.2 of the Technical Notes.

Rates are not computed if data from civil registers of deaths are reported as incomplete (less than 90 per cent completeness) or of unknown completeness, and therefore deemed unreliable.

Limitations: Statistics on deaths by age and sex are subject to the same qualifications as are set forth for vital statistics and particularly for death statistics discussed in section 4 of the Technical Notes.

The reliability of the data is an important factor in considering the limitations. In addition, some deaths are tabulated by date of registration and not by date of occurrence; these have been indicated by a plus sign "+". Whenever the lag between the date of occurrence and date of registration is prolonged and, therefore, a large proportion of the death registrations are delayed, death statistics for any given year may be seriously affected. However, delays in the registration of deaths are less common and shorter than in the registration of live births.

International comparability in mortality statistics may also be affected by the exclusion of deaths of infants who were born alive but died before the registration of the birth or within the first 24 hours of life. Statistics of this type are footnoted.

Because these statistics are classified according to age, they are subject to the limitations with respect to accuracy of age reporting similar to those already discussed in connection with section 3.1.3 of the Technical Notes. The factors influencing the accuracy of reporting may be somewhat dissimilar in vital statistics (because of the differences in the method of taking a census and registering a death) but, in general, the same errors can be observed.

The absence of data in the unknown age group does not necessarily indicate completely accurate reporting and tabulation of the age item. It is often an indication that the unknowns have been eliminated by assigning ages to them before tabulation, or by proportionate distribution after tabulation.

International comparability of statistics on deaths by age is also affected by the use of different methods to determine age at death. If age is obtained from an item that simply requests age at death in completed years or is derived from information on year of birth and death rather than from information on complete date (day, month and year) of birth and death, the number of deaths classified in the under-one-year age group will tend to be reduced and the number of deaths in the next age group will tend to be somewhat increased. A similar bias may affect other age groups but its impact is usually negligible. Information on this factor is given in the footnotes when known.

Limitations of rates: Rates shown in this table are subject to the same limitations that affect the corresponding data and are set forth in the technical notes for table 18. These include differences in the completeness of registration, the treatment of infants who were born alive but died before the registration of their birth or within the first 24 hours of life, the method used to determine age at death and the quality of the reported information relating to age at death. In addition, some rates are based on deaths tabulated by date of registration and not by date of occurrence; these have been indicated with a plus sign "+".

The problem of obtaining precise correspondence between deaths (numerator) and population (denominator) as regards the inclusion or exclusion of armed forces, refugees, displaced persons and other special groups is particularly difficult where age-specific death rates are concerned. Even when deaths and population do correspond conceptually, comparability of the rates may be affected by abnormal conditions such as absence from the country or area of large numbers of young men in the military forces or working abroad as temporary workers. Death rates may appear high in the younger ages, simply because a large section of the able-bodied members of the age group, whose death rates under normal conditions might be less than the average for persons of their age, is not included. Therefore, care should be exercised in using these rates for comparative purposes.

Also, in a number of cases the rates shown here for all ages combined differ from crude death rates shown elsewhere, because in this table they are computed on the population for which an appropriate age-sex distribution was available, while the crude death rates shown elsewhere may utilize a different total population. The population by age and sex might refer to a census date within the year rather than to the mid-point, or it might be more or less inclusive as regards ethnic groups, armed forces and so forth. In a few instances, the difference is attributable to the fact that the rates in this table were computed on the mean population whereas the corresponding rates in other tables were computed on an estimate for 1 July.

Earlier data: Age-specific deaths and death rates by sex have been shown for the latest available year in each issue of the *Demographic Yearbook* since the 1955 issue. For information on specific years covered, the reader should consult the Historical Index.

Tableau 19 – *Annuaire démographique 2019*

Le tableau 19 présente les données disponibles les plus récentes, entre 2010 et 2019, sur les décès et les taux de mortalité selon l'âge et le sexe.

Description des variables : L'âge considéré est l'âge au dernier anniversaire, c'est-à-dire la différence entre la date de naissance et la date du décès, exprimée en années solaires révolues. La classification par âge est la suivante : moins d'un an, 1 à 4 ans, groupes quinquennaux jusqu'à 95-99 ans et 100 ans et plus.

Calcul des taux : les taux de mortalité selon l'âge et le sexe représentent le nombre annuel de décès survenus pour chaque sexe et chaque groupe d'âge pour 1 000 personnes du même groupe. Ces taux ont été calculés par la Division de statistique de l'ONU.

On n'a pas tenu compte des décès à un âge inconnu ni de la population d'âge inconnu, sauf dans les taux de mortalité pour tous les âges combinés.

Il convient de noter que, dans ce tableau, les taux de mortalité des groupes de moins d'un an sont différents des taux de mortalité infantile qui figurent dans d'autres tableaux, ces derniers ayant été établis pour 1 000 naissances vivantes et non pour 1 000 habitants.

Les chiffres de population utilisés pour le calcul des taux proviennent de dénombrements ou de répartitions estimatives de la population selon l'âge et le sexe. On a utilisé de préférence les estimations de la population; à défaut, on s'est contenté des données censitaires se rapportant à l'année des décès.

Les taux présentés dans ce tableau ne se rapportent qu'aux pays ou zones où l'on a enregistré un total d'au moins 100 décès pendant l'année. Les taux relatifs à des sous-catégories, qui sont fondés sur 30 décès ou moins, sont signalés par le signe "♦".

Fiabilité des données : Les données sur les décès issues des registres d'état civil qui sont déclarées incomplètes (degré d'exhaustivité inférieur à 90 p.100) ou dont le degré d'exhaustivité n'est pas connu sont jugées douteuses et apparaissent en italique et non en caractères romains. Le tableau 18 et les notes techniques s'y rapportant présentent des renseignements plus détaillés sur le degré d'exhaustivité de l'enregistrement des décès. Pour plus de précisions sur la qualité des statistiques de l'état civil en général et le degré de complétude en particulier, voir la section 4.2 de l'Introduction.

On a choisi de ne pas faire figurer dans le tableau 19 des taux calculés à partir de données sur les décès issues de registres d'état civil qui sont déclarées incomplètes (degré d'exhaustivité inférieur à 90 p. 100) ou dont le degré d'exhaustivité n'est pas connu.

Insuffisance des données : Les statistiques des décès selon l'âge et le sexe appellent les mêmes réserves que les statistiques de l'état civil en général et les statistiques relatives à la mortalité en particulier (voir la section 4 des Notes techniques).

La fiabilité des données est un facteur important. Il faut également tenir compte du fait que, dans certains cas, les données relatives aux décès sont classées par date d'enregistrement et non par date d'occurrence ; ces cas ont été signalés par le signe "+". Chaque fois que le décalage entre le décès et son enregistrement est grand et qu'une forte proportion des décès fait l'objet d'un enregistrement tardif, les statistiques des décès de l'année peuvent être considérablement faussées. En règle générale, toutefois, les décès sont enregistrés beaucoup plus rapidement que les naissances vivantes, et les retards prolongés sont rares.

Un autre facteur qui nuit à la comparabilité internationale est la pratique de certains pays ou zones qui consiste à ne pas inclure dans les statistiques des décès les enfants nés vivants mais décédés avant l'enregistrement de leur naissance ou dans les 24 heures qui ont suivi la naissance, pratique qui conduit à sous-évaluer le nombre de décès à moins d'un an. Quand pareil facteur a joué, cela a été signalé en note à la fin du tableau.

Étant donné que les statistiques relatives à la mortalité sont classées selon l'âge, elles appellent les mêmes réserves concernant l'exactitude des déclarations d'âge que celles qui ont été formulées à la section 3.1.3 des Notes techniques. Dans le cas des données d'état civil, les facteurs qui interviennent à cet égard sont parfois un peu différents, du fait que le recensement et l'enregistrement des décès se font par des méthodes différentes, mais, d'une manière générale, les erreurs observées sont les mêmes.

Si aucun nombre ne figure dans la rangée réservée aux âges inconnus, cela ne signifie pas nécessairement que les déclarations d'âge et le classement par âge sont tout à fait exacts. C'est souvent une indication que l'on a attribué un âge aux personnes d'âge inconnu avant l'exploitation des données ou qu'elles ont été réparties proportionnellement entre les différents groupes après cette opération.

Le manque d'uniformité des méthodes suivies pour obtenir l'âge au moment du décès nuit également à la comparabilité internationale des données. Si l'âge est connu, soit d'après la réponse à une simple question sur l'âge du décès en années révolues, soit d'après l'année de la naissance et l'année du décès, et non d'après des renseignements concernant la date exacte (jour, mois et année) de la naissance et du décès, le nombre de décès classés dans la catégorie « moins d'un an » sera entaché d'une erreur par défaut et le chiffre figurant dans la catégorie suivante d'une erreur par excès.

Les données pour les autres groupes d'âge pourront être entachées d'une distorsion analogue, mais les répercussions seront généralement négligeables. Les imperfections, lorsqu'elles étaient connues, ont été signalées en note à la fin du tableau.

Insuffisance des taux : les taux présentés dans le tableau 19 appellent les mêmes réserves que celles formulées à propos des fréquences correspondantes (voir à ce sujet les notes techniques se rapportant au tableau 18). Leurs imperfections tiennent notamment aux différences d'exhaustivité de l'enregistrement, au classement des enfants nés vivants mais décédés avant l'enregistrement de leur naissance ou dans les 24 heures qui ont suivi la naissance, à la méthode utilisée pour obtenir l'âge au moment du décès, et à la qualité des déclarations concernant l'âge au moment du décès. En outre, dans certains cas, les données relatives aux décès sont classées par date d'enregistrement et non par date de l'événement ; ces cas ont été signalés par le signe "+".

S'agissant des taux de mortalité par âge, il est particulièrement difficile d'établir une correspondance exacte entre les décès (numérateur) et la population (dénominateur) du fait de l'inclusion ou de l'exclusion des militaires, des réfugiés, des personnes déplacées et d'autres groupes spéciaux. Il convient d'ajouter que, même lorsque population et décès correspondent, la comparabilité des taux peut être compromise par des conditions anormales telles que l'absence du pays ou de la zone d'un grand nombre de jeunes gens qui sont sous les drapeaux ou qui travaillent à l'étranger comme travailleurs temporaires. Il arrive ainsi que les taux de mortalité paraissent élevés parmi les groupes les plus jeunes simplement parce que l'on en a exclu un grand nombre d'individus en bonne santé pour lesquels le taux de mortalité pourrait être, dans des conditions normales, inférieur à la moyenne observée pour les personnes du même âge. Par conséquent, il importe d'être prudent quand on les utilise ces taux de mortalité dans des comparaisons.

De même, les taux indiqués pour tous les âges combinés diffèrent dans plusieurs cas des taux bruts de mortalité qui figurent dans d'autres tableaux, parce qu'ils se rapportent à une population pour laquelle on disposait d'une répartition par âge et par sexe appropriée, tandis que les taux bruts de mortalité indiqués ailleurs peuvent avoir été calculés sur la base d'un chiffre de population totale différent. Ainsi, il est possible que les chiffres de population par âge et par sexe proviennent d'un recensement effectué dans le courant de l'année et non au milieu de l'année, et qu'ils se différencient des autres chiffres de population en excluant ou en incluant certains groupes ethniques, les militaires, etc. Quelquefois, la différence tient à ce que les taux du tableau 19 ont été calculés sur la base de la population moyenne, alors que les taux correspondants des autres tableaux reposent sur une estimation au 1er juillet.

Données publiées antérieurement : Les éditions de l'*Annuaire démographique* parues depuis 1955 présentent les statistiques les plus récentes dont on disposait à l'époque sur les décès selon l'âge et le sexe et sur les taux de mortalité selon l'âge et le sexe. Pour plus de précisions concernant les années pour lesquelles ces données ont été publiées, se reporter à l'index historique.

19. Deaths by age and sex and age-specific death rates by sex: latest available year, 2010 - 2019
Décès et taux de mortalité selon l'âge et le sexe : dernière année disponible, 2010 - 2019

Continent, country or area, date, code[a] and age (in years) / Continent, pays ou zone, date, code[a] et âge (en annèes)	Number - Nombre			Rate - Taux		
	Both sexes Les deux sexes	Male Masculin	Female Féminin	Both sexes Les deux sexes	Male Masculin	Female Féminin
AFRICA - AFRIQUE						
Algeria - Algérie[1]						
2016 (U)						
Total	*180 404*	*92 981*	*87 423*	...	...	...
0	*22 271*	*12 157*	*10 114*	...	...	...
1 - 4	*2 986*	*1 581*	*1 406*	...	...	...
5 - 9	*1 458*	*795*	*664*	...	...	...
10 - 14	*1 066*	*570*	*495*	...	...	...
15 - 19	*1 610*	*1 008*	*601*	...	...	...
20 - 24	*2 440*	*1 630*	*810*	...	...	...
25 - 29	*2 741*	*1 710*	*1 031*	...	...	...
30 - 34	*3 362*	*1 892*	*1 470*	...	...	...
35 - 39	*3 685*	*1 957*	*1 728*	...	...	...
40 - 44	*4 206*	*2 134*	*2 071*	...	...	...
45 - 49	*5 321*	*2 711*	*2 611*	...	...	...
50 - 54	*6 817*	*3 651*	*3 166*	...	...	...
55 - 59	*8 144*	*4 457*	*3 687*	...	...	...
60 - 64	*11 005*	*6 279*	*4 726*	...	...	...
65 - 69	*11 794*	*6 649*	*5 145*	...	...	...
70 - 74	*12 746*	*6 905*	*5 841*	...	...	...
75 - 79	*18 197*	*9 162*	*9 035*	...	...	...
80 - 84	*22 572*	*10 897*	*11 675*	...	...	...
85 +	*37 984*	*16 836*	*21 147*	...	...	...
Botswana[2]						
2018 (U)						
Total	*12 609*	*6 624*	*5 985*	...	...	...
0	*891*	*460*	*431*	...	...	...
1 - 4	*250*	*139*	*111*	...	...	...
5 - 9	*87*	*46*	*41*	...	...	...
10 - 14	*97*	*53*	*44*	...	...	...
15 - 19	*141*	*69*	*72*	...	...	...
20 - 24	*315*	*186*	*129*	...	...	...
25 - 29	*455*	*270*	*185*	...	...	...
30 - 34	*607*	*329*	*278*	...	...	...
35 - 39	*710*	*405*	*305*	...	...	...
40 - 44	*799*	*446*	*353*	...	...	...
45 - 49	*733*	*409*	*324*	...	...	...
50 - 54	*676*	*368*	*308*	...	...	...
55 - 59	*727*	*445*	*282*	...	...	...
60 - 64	*857*	*498*	*359*	...	...	...
65 - 69	*779*	*475*	*304*	...	...	...
70 - 74	*767*	*431*	*336*	...	...	...
75 - 79	*835*	*428*	*407*	...	...	...
80 - 84	*703*	*323*	*380*	...	...	...
85 - 89	*889*	*362*	*527*	...	...	...
90 - 94	*722*	*263*	*459*	...	...	...
95 - 99	*323*	*114*	*209*	...	...	...
100 +	*178*	*57*	*121*	...	...	...
Unknown - Inconnu	*68*	*48*	*20*	..	..	..
Cabo Verde[3]						
2017 (C)						
Total	2 497	1 371	1 126	4.6	5.1	4.2
0 - 4	180	105	75	3.4	3.9	2.9
5 - 9	7	2	5	♦0.1	♦0.1	♦0.2
10 - 14	13	6	7	♦0.3	♦0.2	♦0.3
15 - 49	402	290	112	1.3	1.9	0.8
50 - 64	442	303	139	7.8	11.8	4.5
65 +	1 453	665	788	49.1	58.6	43.2
Congo						
2014 (+U)						
Total	*13 413*	*7 106*	*6 307*	...	...	...
0	*2 240*	*1 241*	*999*	...	...	...
1 - 4	*1 072*	*542*	*530*	...	...	...
5 - 14	*582*	*325*	*257*	...	...	...
15 - 59	*5 352*	*2 873*	*2 479*	...	...	...
60 +	*4 165*	*2 123*	*2 042*	...	...	...

19. Deaths by age and sex and age-specific death rates by sex: latest available year, 2010 - 2019
Décès et taux de mortalité selon l'âge et le sexe : dernière année disponible, 2010 - 2019 (continued - suite)

Continent, country or area, date, code[a] and age (in years) Continent, pays ou zone, date, code[a] et âge (en années)	Number - Nombre			Rate - Taux		
	Both sexes Les deux sexes	Male Masculin	Female Féminin	Both sexes Les deux sexes	Male Masculin	Female Féminin
AFRICA - AFRIQUE						
Egypt - Égypte						
2017 (C)						
Total	547 208	300 898	246 310	5.7	6.1	5.3
0	38 685	20 964	17 721	14.9	15.6	14.0
1 - 4	11 184	6 046	5 138	1.1	1.1	1.0
5 - 9	4 599	2 720	1 879	0.4	0.5	0.4
10 - 14	3 788	2 448	1 340	0.4	0.5	0.3
15 - 19	6 292	4 305	1 987	0.7	0.9	0.5
20 - 24	6 565	4 637	1 928	0.8	1.1	0.5
25 - 29	7 201	4 862	2 339	0.9	1.2	0.6
30 - 34	8 695	5 646	3 049	1.2	1.5	0.8
35 - 39	10 005	6 393	3 612	1.5	1.9	1.1
40 - 44	12 343	7 758	4 585	2.4	2.9	1.8
45 - 49	17 557	11 229	6 328	4.0	4.9	3.0
50 - 54	32 080	20 586	11 494	8.0	10.0	5.9
55 - 59	45 493	28 810	16 683	13.9	16.7	10.7
60 - 64	59 405	36 007	23 398	22.3	25.3	18.9
65 - 69	67 018	37 985	29 033	38.8	40.1	37.2
70 - 74	61 623	32 111	29 512	60.4	60.2	60.6
75 +	154 675	68 391	86 284	166.2	142.8	191.1
75 - 79	56 925	27 754	29 171	...	...	...
80 - 84	47 982	21 385	26 597	...	...	...
85 +	49 768	19 252	30 516	...	...	...
Eswatini[4]						
2018 (+U)						
Total	*5 032*	*2 442*	*2 590*	...	...	...
0	*156*	*80*	*76*	...	...	...
1 - 4	*64*	*36*	*28*	...	...	...
5 - 9	*41*	*21*	*20*	...	...	...
10 - 14	*53*	*24*	*29*	...	...	...
15 - 19	*85*	*38*	*47*	...	...	...
20 - 24	*141*	*61*	*80*	...	...	...
25 - 44	*1 599*	*682*	*917*	...	...	...
45 - 49	*291*	*152*	*139*	...	...	...
50 - 54	*319*	*165*	*154*	...	...	...
55 - 59	*289*	*144*	*145*	...	...	...
60 - 64	*370*	*206*	*164*	...	...	...
65 - 69	*350*	*189*	*161*	...	...	...
70 - 74	*405*	*180*	*225*	...	...	...
75 - 79	*408*	*192*	*216*	...	...	...
80 +	*461*	*272*	*189*	...	...	...
Ghana[5]						
2010 (I)						
Total	163 534	84 214	79 320	6.6	7.0	6.3
0	28 068	15 807	12 261	38.4	42.7	34.0
1 - 4	17 868	9 424	8 444	6.7	6.9	6.4
5 - 9	6 275	3 437	2 838	2.0	2.2	1.8
10 - 14	3 641	1 587	2 054	1.2	1.1	1.4
15 - 19	4 399	1 752	2 647	1.7	1.3	2.0
20 - 24	5 467	2 117	3 350	2.4	1.9	2.7
25 - 29	6 325	2 516	3 809	3.1	2.7	3.4
30 - 34	8 218	3 397	4 821	4.9	4.3	5.4
35 - 39	8 215	3 579	4 636	5.8	5.3	6.2
40 - 44	8 855	4 141	4 714	7.5	7.2	7.7
45 - 49	7 573	3 715	3 858	8.1	8.2	8.0
50 - 54	8 577	4 376	4 201	10.3	11.1	9.6
55 - 59	5 656	3 564	2 092	10.8	13.8	7.9
60 - 64	7 159	4 418	2 741	15.0	19.5	11.0
65 - 69	5 670	3 360	2 310	19.3	24.7	14.7
70 - 74	8 443	5 096	3 347	24.0	34.1	16.6
75 - 79	6 197	3 599	2 598	30.1	40.4	22.2
80 - 84	6 543	3 346	3 197	41.1	53.7	33.1
85 - 89	4 436	2 166	2 270	53.4	65.8	45.3
90 - 94	3 650	1 797	1 853	71.5	94.6	57.8
95 +	2 299	1 020	1 279	99.3	116.6	88.9

19. Deaths by age and sex and age-specific death rates by sex: latest available year, 2010 - 2019
Décès et taux de mortalité selon l'âge et le sexe : dernière année disponible, 2010 - 2019 (continued - suite)

Continent, country or area, date, code[a] and age (in years) / Continent, pays ou zone, date, code[a] et âge (en annèes)	Number - Nombre			Rate - Taux		
	Both sexes / Les deux sexes	Male / Masculin	Female / Féminin	Both sexes / Les deux sexes	Male / Masculin	Female / Féminin
AFRICA - AFRIQUE						
Guinea - Guinée[6]						
2014 (|)						
Total	129 896	70 815	59 081	12.3	13.9	10.9
0	36 556	20 751	15 805	112.1	125.9	97.9
1 - 4	21 083	11 308	9 775	14.7	15.6	13.7
5 - 9	5 661	3 128	2 533	3.3	3.6	3.0
10 - 14	3 237	1 821	1 416	2.6	2.9	2.3
15 - 19	3 585	1 630	1 955	3.2	3.1	3.3
20 - 24	3 775	1 806	1 969	4.2	4.4	4.0
25 - 29	4 350	1 934	2 416	5.6	5.7	5.4
30 - 34	4 366	2 077	2 289	6.9	7.5	6.5
35 - 39	3 909	1 986	1 923	7.6	8.7	6.8
40 - 44	4 168	2 226	1 942	9.5	11.1	8.2
45 - 49	3 567	2 063	1 504	10.9	12.9	8.9
50 - 54	4 461	2 562	1 899	15.0	17.5	12.5
55 - 59	2 963	1 857	1 106	14.0	16.2	11.4
60 - 64	4 659	2 695	1 964	22.8	25.6	19.8
65 - 69	3 490	2 070	1 420	27.4	30.4	23.9
70 - 74	5 181	2 884	2 297	44.4	50.7	38.4
75 - 79	3 461	2 029	1 432	54.2	59.8	47.9
80 - 84	4 300	2 248	2 052	84.3	91.1	78.0
85 - 89	2 350	1 297	1 053	113.4	120.2	106.0
90 - 94	1 673	929	744	142.4	165.0	121.6
95 +	3 101	1 514	1 587	259.3	264.8	254.2
95 - 99	1 886	963	923	...	...	...
100 +	1 215	551	664	...	...	...
Kenya						
2018 (+U)						
Total	*192 019*	*106 318*	*85 701*	...	...	...
0	*20 350*	*10 598*	*9 752*	...	...	...
1 - 4	*8 238*	*4 558*	*3 680*	...	...	...
5 - 14	*7 303*	*3 958*	*3 345*	...	...	...
15 - 24	*12 333*	*7 017*	*5 316*	...	...	...
25 - 34	*20 409*	*11 383*	*9 026*	...	...	...
35 - 44	*23 249*	*13 671*	*9 578*	...	...	...
45 - 54	*21 306*	*12 518*	*8 788*	...	...	...
55 - 74	*39 505*	*23 020*	*16 485*	...	...	...
75 +	*39 326*	*19 595*	*19 731*	...	...	...
Lesotho						
2019 (+U)						
Total	*13 494*	*6 991*	*6 503*	...	...	...
0 - 4	*307*	*158*	*149*	...	...	...
5 - 9	*91*	*50*	*41*	...	...	...
10 - 14	*87*	*62*	*25*	...	...	...
15 - 19	*179*	*100*	*79*	...	...	...
20 - 24	*375*	*249*	*126*	...	...	...
25 - 29	*605*	*360*	*245*	...	...	...
30 - 34	*914*	*528*	*386*	...	...	...
35 - 39	*972*	*574*	*398*	...	...	...
40 - 44	*852*	*501*	*351*	...	...	...
45 - 49	*772*	*439*	*333*	...	...	...
50 - 54	*697*	*380*	*317*	...	...	...
55 - 59	*847*	*492*	*355*	...	...	...
60 - 64	*996*	*581*	*415*	...	...	...
65 - 69	*1 036*	*593*	*443*	...	...	...
70 - 74	*987*	*525*	*462*	...	...	...
75 +	*3 777*	*1 399*	*2 378*	...	...	...
Malawi[5]						
2018 (|)						
Total	110 776	61 881	48 895	6.3	7.3	5.4
0	12 586	6 787	5 799	24.1	26.2	22.0
1 - 4	11 362	6 037	5 325	5.6	6.0	5.2
5 - 9	4 902	2 594	2 308	1.9	2.0	1.7
10 - 14	3 249	1 745	1 504	1.3	1.4	1.2
15 - 19	3 596	1 930	1 666	1.8	1.9	1.6
20 - 24	4 614	2 608	2 006	2.8	3.4	2.3
25 - 29	5 267	3 124	2 143	4.3	5.4	3.3

19. Deaths by age and sex and age-specific death rates by sex: latest available year, 2010 - 2019
Décès et taux de mortalité selon l'âge et le sexe : dernière année disponible, 2010 - 2019 (continued - suite)

Continent, country or area, date, code[a] and age (in years) / Continent, pays ou zone, date, code[a] et âge (en années)	Number - Nombre			Rate - Taux		
	Both sexes / Les deux sexes	Male / Masculin	Female / Féminin	Both sexes / Les deux sexes	Male / Masculin	Female / Féminin
AFRICA - AFRIQUE						
Malawi[5]						
2018 (|)						
30 - 34	6 010	3 588	2 422	5.4	6.9	4.1
35 - 39	6 790	4 087	2 703	7.0	8.7	5.4
40 - 44	5 849	3 657	2 192	8.0	10.0	6.0
45 - 49	5 554	3 537	2 017	10.4	12.9	7.7
50 - 54	5 032	3 043	1 989	13.0	16.2	10.0
55 - 59	4 321	2 586	1 735	14.1	18.0	10.7
60 - 64	4 394	2 611	1 783	18.7	24.2	14.0
65 - 69	4 477	2 568	1 909	18.6	23.8	14.4
70 - 74	4 835	2 756	2 079	33.4	43.2	25.7
75 - 79	5 054	2 717	2 337	40.5	52.7	32.0
80 - 84	4 465	2 121	2 344	70.1	87.9	59.3
85 - 89	3 825	1 796	2 029	69.9	86.6	59.7
90 - 94	1 938	876	1 062	128.1	167.0	107.4
95 +	2 656	1 113	1 543	200.1	233.2	181.6
95 - 99	1 716	760	956	...	...	...
100 +	940	353	587	...	...	...
Mauritius - Maurice[7]						
2019 (+C)						
Total	11 174	6 124	5 050	8.8	9.8	7.9
0	187	103	84	14.4	15.6	13.2
1 - 4	19	9	10	♦0.4	♦0.3	♦0.4
5 - 9	17	12	5	♦0.2	♦0.3	♦0.1
10 - 14	21	14	7	♦0.2	♦0.3	♦0.2
15 - 19	54	36	18	0.6	0.7	♦0.4
20 - 24	105	83	22	1.1	1.7	♦0.5
25 - 29	118	83	35	1.2	1.7	0.7
30 - 34	161	118	43	1.9	2.8	1.0
35 - 39	245	180	65	2.6	3.7	1.4
40 - 44	325	212	113	3.5	4.5	2.5
45 - 49	436	295	141	5.3	7.1	3.5
50 - 54	648	417	231	7.2	9.3	5.1
55 - 59	912	569	343	10.3	13.1	7.6
60 - 64	1 205	811	394	16.2	22.7	10.2
65 - 69	1 390	831	559	22.8	29.4	17.1
70 - 74	1 239	654	585	32.8	39.7	27.5
75 - 79	1 218	611	607	54.4	67.1	45.8
80 - 84	1 152	536	616	81.0	100.4	69.3
85 +	1 722	550	1 172	161.9	162.5	161.6
85 - 89	853	309	544	...	...	...
90 - 94	599	178	421	...	...	...
95 - 99	215	49	166	...	...	...
100 +	55	14	41	...	...	...
Mayotte						
2018 (C)						
Total	758	404	354	2.9	3.2	2.5
0	94	53	41	11.1	12.3	9.9
1 - 4	23	12	11	♦0.7	♦0.7	♦0.7
5 - 9	9	4	5	♦0.2	♦0.2	♦0.3
10 - 14	10	5	5	♦0.3	♦0.3	♦0.3
15 - 19	14	9	5	♦0.5	♦0.7	♦0.4
20 - 24	13	10	3	♦0.8	♦1.4	♦0.3
25 - 29	13	6	7	♦0.7	♦0.8	♦0.7
30 - 34	24	12	12	♦1.3	♦1.6	♦1.1
35 - 39	34	17	17	1.9	♦2.2	♦1.7
40 - 44	23	12	11	♦1.6	♦1.7	♦1.4
45 - 49	47	22	25	3.9	♦3.5	♦4.4
50 - 54	43	24	19	5.6	♦6.1	♦5.0
55 - 59	51	28	23	8.1	♦8.6	♦7.6
60 - 64	40	27	13	9.2	♦11.7	♦6.3
65 - 69	70	42	28	23.4	26.3	♦20.1
70 - 74	54	19	35	32.0	♦23.4	40.1
75 - 79	66	37	29	55.2	64.8	♦46.4
80 - 84	54	24	30	82.7	♦74.3	♦90.9
85 - 89	48	27	21	150.9	♦192.9	♦118.0
90 - 94	16	10	6	♦163.3	♦200.0	♦125.0

19. Deaths by age and sex and age-specific death rates by sex: latest available year, 2010 - 2019
Décès et taux de mortalité selon l'âge et le sexe : dernière année disponible, 2010 - 2019 (continued - suite)

Continent, country or area, date, code[a] and age (in years) / Continent, pays ou zone, date, code[a] et âge (en années)	Number - Nombre			Rate - Taux		
	Both sexes / Les deux sexes	Male / Masculin	Female / Féminin	Both sexes / Les deux sexes	Male / Masculin	Female / Féminin
AFRICA - AFRIQUE						
Mayotte						
2018 (C)						
95 +	12	4	8	♦110.1	♦78.4	♦137.9
95 - 99	9	3	6	...	...	...
100 +	3	1	2	...	...	...
Namibia - Namibie[8]						
2011 (|)						
Total	22 668	12 491	10 177	10.7	12.2	9.3
0	2 685	1 411	1 274	41.9	44.1	39.6
1 - 4	1 346	719	627	6.1	6.5	5.7
5 - 9	447	255	192	1.9	2.1	1.6
10 - 14	384	212	172	1.6	1.7	1.4
15 - 19	577	298	279	2.4	2.5	2.3
20 - 24	918	537	381	4.3	5.1	3.5
25 - 29	1 233	645	588	7.0	7.4	6.5
30 - 34	1 591	890	701	10.7	12.1	9.2
35 - 39	1 487	873	614	11.9	14.3	9.6
40 - 44	1 323	807	516	13.5	17.2	10.1
45 - 49	1 140	698	442	14.2	18.6	10.3
50 - 54	917	535	382	14.9	19.5	11.2
55 - 59	891	562	329	18.6	26.1	12.5
60 - 64	994	584	410	24.4	31.7	18.3
65 - 69	766	424	342	24.6	32.3	19.0
70 - 74	739	424	315	30.7	41.3	22.8
75 - 79	682	382	300	39.5	54.5	29.3
80 - 84	792	402	390	55.3	76.2	43.1
85 - 89	638	282	356	68.6	90.2	57.6
90 - 94	549	234	315	80.6	98.4	71.1
95 +	1 003	403	600	178.7	228.6	155.8
Unknown - Inconnu	1 566	914	652	..	..	..
Niger						
2011 (+U)						
Total	*6 761*	...	...	...	...	...
0	*236*	...	...	...	...	...
1 - 4	*329*	...	...	...	...	...
5 - 9	*120*	...	...	...	...	...
10 - 14	*81*	...	...	...	...	...
15 - 19	*147*	...	...	...	...	...
20 - 24	*242*	...	...	...	...	...
25 - 29	*319*	...	...	...	...	...
30 - 34	*378*	...	...	...	...	...
35 - 39	*414*	...	...	...	...	...
40 - 44	*470*	...	...	...	...	...
45 - 49	*485*	...	...	...	...	...
50 - 54	*495*	...	...	...	...	...
55 - 59	*443*	...	...	...	...	...
60 - 64	*541*	...	...	...	...	...
65 - 69	*443*	...	...	...	...	...
70 - 74	*517*	...	...	...	...	...
75 - 79	*347*	...	...	...	...	...
80 - 84	*298*	...	...	...	...	...
85 - 89	*112*	...	...	...	...	...
90 - 94	*90*	...	...	...	...	...
95 - 99	*26*	...	...	...	...	...
100 +	*53*	...	...	...	...	...
Unknown - Inconnu	*175*	...	...	..	..	..
Reunion - Réunion						
2018 (C)						
Total	5 011	2 719	2 292	5.8	6.6	5.1
0	82	40	42	6.8	6.5	7.1
1 - 4	13	8	5	♦0.3	♦0.3	♦0.2
5 - 9	5	2	3	♦0.1	♦0.1	♦0.1
10 - 14	7	4	3	♦0.1	♦0.1	♦0.1
15 - 19	15	9	6	♦0.2	♦0.3	♦0.2
20 - 24	20	17	3	♦0.4	♦0.7	♦0.1
25 - 29	22	17	5	♦0.4	♦0.7	♦0.2
30 - 34	58	45	13	1.1	2.0	♦0.5

Continent, country or area, date, code[a] and age (in years) / Continent, pays ou zone, date, code[a] et âge (en années)	Number - Nombre			Rate - Taux		
	Both sexes / Les deux sexes	Male / Masculin	Female / Féminin	Both sexes / Les deux sexes	Male / Masculin	Female / Féminin
AFRICA - AFRIQUE						
Reunion - Réunion						
2018 (C)						
35 - 39	60	44	16	1.1	1.8	♦0.5
40 - 44	95	67	28	1.7	2.5	♦0.9
45 - 49	153	97	56	2.5	3.3	1.7
50 - 54	232	158	74	3.5	4.9	2.2
55 - 59	309	205	104	5.5	7.5	3.6
60 - 64	393	273	120	8.3	12.0	4.8
65 - 69	444	295	149	12.3	17.3	7.8
70 - 74	431	266	165	17.4	23.1	12.5
75 - 79	547	299	248	29.5	37.0	23.7
80 - 84	689	337	352	53.8	69.8	44.1
85 - 89	655	289	366	101.3	132.3	85.5
90 - 94	492	176	316	173.5	209.8	158.3
95 +	289	71	218	320.4	388.0	303.2
95 - 99	226	62	164	...	...	...
100 +	63	9	54	...	...	...
Saint Helena ex. dep. - Sainte-Hélène sans dép.						
2018 (C)						
Total	52	32	20	...	...	...
0	-	-	-	...	...	...
1 - 4	-	-	-	...	...	...
5 - 9	-	-	-	...	...	...
10 - 14	-	-	-	...	...	...
15 - 19	-	-	-	...	...	...
20 - 24	-	-	-	...	...	...
25 - 29	-	-	-	...	...	...
30 - 34	-	-	-	...	...	...
35 - 39	-	-	-	...	...	...
40 - 44	-	-	-	...	...	...
45 - 49	1	-	1	...	...	...
50 - 54	3	1	2	...	...	...
55 - 59	3	3	-	...	...	...
60 - 64	2	2	-	...	...	...
65 - 69	10	7	3	...	...	...
70 - 74	5	4	1	...	...	...
75 - 79	12	7	5	...	...	...
80 - 84	6	5	1	...	...	...
85 - 89	4	2	2	...	...	...
90 - 94	3	1	2	...	...	...
95 - 99	2	-	2	...	...	...
100 +	1	-	1	...	...	...
Sao Tome and Principe - Sao Tomé-et-Principe[9]						
2012 (|)						
Total	1 287	735	552	7.2	8.3	6.1
0	132	82	50	23.1	27.8	18.0
1 - 4	69	41	29	3.1	3.7	♦2.6
5 - 9	18	5	13	♦0.7	♦0.4	♦1.0
10 - 14	29	20	10	♦1.4	♦1.9	♦0.9
15 - 19	29	23	6	♦1.6	♦2.5	♦0.7
20 - 24	54	36	18	3.4	4.5	♦2.3
25 - 29	39	26	13	2.6	♦3.5	♦1.7
30 - 34	41	31	10	3.3	5.0	♦1.6
35 - 39	61	41	20	6.3	8.4	♦4.1
40 - 44	51	34	17	6.5	8.6	♦4.4
45 - 49	49	24	25	7.8	♦7.9	♦7.7
50 - 54	77	44	33	14.4	16.9	12.0
55 - 59	52	21	31	13.6	♦11.6	15.4
60 - 64	86	59	27	32.3	44.1	♦20.4
65 - 69	60	33	27	31.2	35.9	♦26.8
70 - 74	102	60	42	54.3	70.6	40.9
75 - 79	103	51	52	73.0	83.7	64.8
80 +	234	104	130	170.1	198.1	152.8
Seychelles						
2019 (+C)						
Total	795	438	357	8.1	8.8	7.4
0	27	14	13	♦16.6	♦16.8	♦16.4

19. Deaths by age and sex and age-specific death rates by sex: latest available year, 2010 - 2019
Décès et taux de mortalité selon l'âge et le sexe : dernière année disponible, 2010 - 2019 (continued - suite)

Continent, country or area, date, code[a] and age (in years) / Continent, pays ou zone, date, code[a] et âge (en années)	Number - Nombre			Rate - Taux		
	Both sexes / Les deux sexes	Male / Masculin	Female / Féminin	Both sexes / Les deux sexes	Male / Masculin	Female / Féminin
AFRICA - AFRIQUE						
Seychelles						
2019 (+C)						
1 - 4	1	1	-	♦0.2	♦0.3	-
5 - 9	-	-	-	-	-	-
10 - 14	2	-	2	♦0.4	-	♦0.7
15 - 19	8	8	-	♦1.7	♦3.6	-
20 - 24	5	5	-	♦1.7	♦2.9	-
25 - 29	14	11	3	♦2.7	♦3.7	♦1.3
30 - 34	16	12	4	♦2.2	♦2.8	♦1.3
35 - 39	16	11	5	♦1.7	♦2.2	♦1.1
40 - 44	32	20	12	4.7	♦5.7	♦3.6
45 - 49	31	24	7	3.6	♦5.2	♦1.8
50 - 54	57	39	18	8.9	14.1	♦5.0
55 - 59	65	42	23	7.2	9.8	♦4.8
60 - 64	61	36	25	10.1	11.9	♦8.3
65 - 69	64	40	24	14.1	18.3	♦10.3
70 - 74	74	45	29	28.5	35.6	♦21.8
75 - 79	82	44	38	53.3	64.6	44.3
80 - 84	76	33	43	81.1	110.0	67.5
85 - 89	76	33	43	127.3	257.8	91.7
90 +	88	20	68	392.9	♦1176.5	328.5
90 - 94	59	14	45	...	...	...
95 - 99	25	6	19	...	...	...
100 +	4	-	4	...	...	...
Sierra Leone[10]						
2013 (+U)						
Total	*19 403*	*9 982*	*9 421*	...	...	...
0	*2 276*	*1 151*	*1 125*	...	...	...
1 - 4	*2 413*	*1 168*	*1 245*	...	...	...
5 - 14	*2 904*	*1 447*	*1 457*	...	...	...
15 +	*11 810*	*6 216*	*5 594*	...	...	...
South Africa - Afrique du Sud						
2016 (U)						
Total	*456 612*	*240 001*[11]	*214 988*[11]	...	...	...
0	*20 649*	*10 963*[11]	*9 284*[11]	...	...	...
1 - 4	*7 008*	*3 686*[11]	*3 281*[11]	...	...	...
5 - 9	*2 965*	*1 672*[11]	*1 287*[11]	...	...	...
10 - 14	*3 083*	*1 781*[11]	*1 298*[11]	...	...	...
15 - 19	*6 821*	*4 019*[11]	*2 781*[11]	...	...	...
20 - 24	*13 708*	*8 272*[11]	*5 375*[11]	...	...	...
25 - 29	*22 209*	*12 851*[11]	*9 238*[11]	...	...	...
30 - 34	*28 519*	*16 597*[11]	*11 769*[11]	...	...	...
35 - 39	*28 244*	*16 535*[11]	*11 558*[11]	...	...	...
40 - 44	*29 290*	*17 270*[11]	*11 898*[11]	...	...	...
45 - 49	*28 635*	*16 890*[11]	*11 656*[11]	...	...	...
50 - 54	*31 618*	*18 470*[11]	*13 093*[11]	...	...	...
55 - 59	*33 917*	*19 796*[11]	*14 055*[11]	...	...	...
60 - 64	*36 372*	*20 689*[11]	*15 633*[11]	...	...	...
65 - 69	*35 684*	*19 486*[11]	*16 168*[11]	...	...	...
70 - 74	*31 418*	*15 753*[11]	*15 632*[11]	...	...	...
75 - 79	*32 210*	*14 361*[11]	*17 829*[11]	...	...	...
80 - 84	*25 323*	*9 280*[11]	*16 031*[11]	...	...	...
85 - 89	*21 280*	*6 736*[11]	*14 525*[11]	...	...	...
90 - 94	*10 508*	*2 975*[11]	*7 527*[11]	...	...	...
95 - 99	*5 114*	*1 211*[11]	*3 897*[11]	...	...	...
100 +	*1 325*	*304*[11]	*1 018*[11]	...	...	...
Unknown - Inconnu	*712*	*404*[11]	*155*[11]	..	..	..
Zambia - Zambie[12]						
2017 (U)						
Total	*39 150*	*16 610*[11]	*22 537*[11]	...	...	...
0	*4 654*	*2 249*	*2 405*	...	...	...
1 - 4	*2 213*	*988*	*1 225*	...	...	...
5 - 9	*724*	*325*	*399*	...	...	...
10 - 14	*606*	*286*	*320*	...	...	...
15 - 19	*982*	*423*	*559*	...	...	...
20 - 24	*1 748*	*776*	*972*	...	...	...

Continent, country or area, date, code[a] and age (in years) / Continent, pays ou zone, date, code[a] et âge (en années)	Number - Nombre: Both sexes / Les deux sexes	Male / Masculin	Female / Féminin	Rate - Taux: Both sexes / Les deux sexes	Male / Masculin	Female / Féminin
AFRICA - AFRIQUE						
Zambia - Zambie[12]						
2017 (U)						
25 - 29	*2 474*	*989*	*1 485*	...	...	...
30 - 34	*3 383*	*1 323*	*2 060*	...	...	...
35 - 39	*3 738*	*1 431*	*2 307*	...	...	...
40 - 44	*3 259*	*1 103*	*2 156*	...	...	...
45 - 49	*2 505*	*895*	*1 610*	...	...	...
50 - 54	*1 919*	*793*	*1 126*	...	...	...
55 - 59	*1 659*	*689*	*970*	...	...	...
60 - 64	*1 549*	*661*	*888*	...	...	...
65 - 69	*1 502*	*639*	*863*	...	...	...
70 - 74	*1 427*	*659*	*768*	...	...	...
75 - 79	*1 336*	*696*	*640*	...	...	...
80 - 84	*1 133*	*595*	*538*	...	...	...
85 +	*1 395*	*726*	*669*	...	...	...
Unknown - Inconnu	*944*	*364*[11]	*577*[11]	..	..	..
AMERICA, NORTH - AMÉRIQUE DU NORD						
Anguilla[13]						
2013 (+C)[14]						
Total	72	43	29	...	...	...
0	3	2	1	...	...	...
1 - 4	-	-	-	...	...	...
5 - 9	-	-	-	...	...	...
10 - 14	-	-	-	...	...	...
15 - 19	2	2	-	...	...	...
20 - 24	1	1	-	...	...	...
25 - 29	2	2	-	...	...	...
30 - 34	-	-	-	...	...	...
35 - 39	2	1	1	...	...	...
40 - 44	-	-	-	...	...	...
45 - 49	1	1	-	...	...	...
50 - 54	5	3	2	...	...	...
55 - 59	5	3	2	...	...	...
60 - 64	3	3	-	...	...	...
65 - 69	7	3	4	...	...	...
70 - 74	4	3	1	...	...	...
75 - 79	9	5	4	...	...	...
80 - 84	8	5	3	...	...	...
85 +	20	9	11	...	...	...
2015 (+C)						
Total	61	...	...	...	...	...
0 - 4	5	...	...	...	...	...
5 - 14	-	...	...	...	...	...
15 - 29	3	...	...	...	...	...
30 - 44	5	...	...	...	...	...
45 - 59	8	...	...	...	...	...
60 - 64	-	...	...	...	...	...
65 - 69	1	...	...	...	...	...
70 - 74	6	...	...	...	...	...
75 - 79	8	...	...	...	...	...
80 - 84	8	...	...	...	...	...
85 +	15	...	...	...	...	...
Antigua and Barbuda - Antigua-et-Barbuda						
2016 (+C)						
Total	542	...	...	5.9	...	...
0	13	...	...	...	...	...
1 - 4	2	...	...	...	...	...
5 - 9	1	...	...	♦0.1	...	...
10 - 14	2	...	...	♦0.3	...	...
15 - 19	4	...	...	♦0.5	...	...
20 - 24	7	...	...	♦0.9	...	...
25 - 29	9	...	...	♦1.3	...	...
30 - 34	6	...	...	♦0.9	...	...
35 - 39	14	...	...	♦2.1	...	...

19. Deaths by age and sex and age-specific death rates by sex: latest available year, 2010 - 2019
Décès et taux de mortalité selon l'âge et le sexe : dernière année disponible, 2010 - 2019 (continued - suite)

Continent, country or area, date, code[a] and age (in years) / Continent, pays ou zone, date, code[a] et âge (en années)	Number - Nombre			Rate - Taux		
	Both sexes / Les deux sexes	Male / Masculin	Female / Féminin	Both sexes / Les deux sexes	Male / Masculin	Female / Féminin
AMERICA, NORTH - AMÉRIQUE DU NORD						
Antigua and Barbuda - Antigua-et-Barbuda						
2016 (+C)						
40 - 44	14	...	...	♦2.0	...	...
45 - 49	14	...	...	♦2.1	...	...
50 - 54	30	...	...	♦4.8	...	...
55 - 59	43	...	...	8.5	...	...
60 - 64	39	...	...	10.9	...	...
65 - 69	48	...	...	17.2	...	...
70 - 74	59	...	...	29.3	...	...
75 - 79	46	...	...	37.2	...	...
80 - 84	67	...	...	84.3	...	...
85 +	124	...	...	131.8	...	...
Aruba						
2019 (C)						
Total	665	342	323	5.9	6.5	5.5
0	5	1	4	♦4.8	♦1.9	♦7.8
1 - 4	-	-	-	-	-	-
5 - 9	-	-	-	-	-	-
10 - 14	-	-	-	-	-	-
15 - 19	2	2	-	♦0.3	♦0.6	-
20 - 24	3	3	-	♦0.5	♦0.9	-
25 - 29	8	5	3	♦1.2	♦1.5	♦0.9
30 - 34	10	5	5	♦1.4	♦1.5	♦1.4
35 - 39	1	-	1	♦0.1	-	♦0.3
40 - 44	8	3	5	♦1.1	♦0.9	♦1.2
45 - 49	11	7	4	♦1.3	♦1.8	♦0.9
50 - 54	20	12	8	♦2.3	♦3.0	♦1.7
55 - 59	36	19	17	3.9	♦4.5	♦3.4
60 - 64	64	40	24	8.3	11.4	♦5.7
65 - 69	73	44	29	12.2	15.9	♦9.0
70 - 74	92	56	36	22.0	31.4	15.1
75 - 79	95	51	44	34.7	43.5	28.2
80 - 84	91	47	44	50.5	69.6	39.0
85 - 89	82	30	52	89.9	♦90.6	89.5
90 - 94	44	11	33	133.4	♦112.0	142.5
95 - 99	18	5	13	♦219.5	♦263.2	♦206.3
100 +	2	1	1	♦166.7	♦266.7	♦121.2
Bahamas						
2012 (+C)						
Total	1 995	1 094	901	5.5	6.2	4.9
0	57	26	31	8.6	♦7.6	9.7
1 - 4	18	10	8	♦0.7	♦0.8	♦0.7
5 - 9	9	5	4	♦0.3	♦0.3	♦0.3
10 - 14	8	6	2	♦0.3	♦0.4	♦0.1
15 - 19	27	17	10	♦0.9	♦1.1	♦0.6
20 - 24	57	42	15	1.9	2.9	♦1.0
25 - 29	49	42	7	1.8	3.2	♦0.5
30 - 34	72	52	20	2.8	4.1	♦1.5
35 - 39	84	47	37	3.1	3.5	2.6
40 - 44	100	58	42	3.6	4.4	2.9
45 - 49	130	72	58	4.9	5.6	4.2
50 - 54	159	84	75	6.8	7.5	6.2
55 - 59	147	94	53	8.5	11.4	5.9
60 - 64	149	83	66	12.2	14.5	10.2
65 - 69	147	87	60	16.1	21.0	12.1
70 - 74	183	96	87	27.6	32.9	23.5
75 - 79	176	93	83	43.0	54.4	34.9
80 - 84	170	81	89	98.0	154.6	74.0
85 - 89	116	61	55	143.7	279.8	91.5
90 +	137	38	99	259.0	351.9	222.0
90 - 94	90	30	60	...	...	...
95 - 99	36	6	30	...	...	...
100 +	11	2	9	...	...	...
Belize						
2018 (U)						
Total	*1 886*	*1 092*	*794*	...	...	...
0	*98*	*54*	*44*	...	...	...

19. Deaths by age and sex and age-specific death rates by sex: latest available year, 2010 - 2019
Décès et taux de mortalité selon l'âge et le sexe : dernière année disponible, 2010 - 2019 (continued - suite)

Continent, country or area, date, code[a] and age (in years) / Continent, pays ou zone, date, code[a] et âge (en années)	Number - Nombre			Rate - Taux		
	Both sexes / Les deux sexes	Male / Masculin	Female / Féminin	Both sexes / Les deux sexes	Male / Masculin	Female / Féminin
AMERICA, NORTH - AMÉRIQUE DU NORD						
Belize						
2018 (U)						
1 - 4	*17*	*10*	*7*	...	...	...
5 - 9	*9*	*5*	*4*	...	...	...
10 - 14	*20*	*12*	*8*	...	...	...
15 - 19	*28*	*18*	*10*	...	...	...
20 - 24	*58*	*45*	*13*	...	...	...
25 - 29	*78*	*58*	*20*	...	...	...
30 - 34	*63*	*40*	*23*	...	...	...
35 - 39	*87*	*54*	*33*	...	...	...
40 - 44	*78*	*47*	*31*	...	...	...
45 - 49	*102*	*60*	*42*	...	...	...
50 - 54	*97*	*51*	*46*	...	...	...
55 - 59	*126*	*73*	*53*	...	...	...
60 - 64	*163*	*88*	*75*	...	...	...
65 +	*862*	*477*	*385*	...	...	...
Bermuda - Bermudes[15]						
2018 (C)						
Total	533	265	268	8.3	8.6	8.1
0	1	1	-	♦1.8	♦3.5	-
1 - 4	-	-	-	-	-	-
5 - 9	-	-	-	-	-	-
10 - 14	1	-	1	♦0.3	-	♦0.6
15 - 19	1	-	1	♦0.3	-	♦0.6
20 - 24	1	1	-	♦0.3	♦0.7	-
25 - 29	3	2	1	♦0.9	♦1.3	♦0.6
30 - 34	5	5	-	♦1.2	♦2.6	-
35 - 39	2	1	1	♦0.4	♦0.5	♦0.4
40 - 44	3	2	1	♦0.7	♦0.9	♦0.4
45 - 49	15	8	7	♦3.0	♦3.2	♦2.9
50 - 54	18	14	4	♦3.5	♦5.4	♦1.6
55 - 59	25	15	10	♦4.5	♦5.7	♦3.5
60 - 64	38	20	18	8.0	♦9.2	♦7.1
65 - 69	37	22	15	10.0	♦12.8	♦7.5
70 - 74	61	34	27	20.7	26.1	♦16.5
75 - 79	46	24	22	22.3	♦26.8	♦18.8
80 - 84	85	37	48	55.7	57.7	54.3
85 +	191	79	112	139.4	179.5	120.4
85 - 89	84	42	42	...	...	...
90 - 94	62	26	36	...	...	...
95 - 99	36	9	27	...	...	...
100 +	9	2	7	...	...	...
British Virgin Islands - Îles Vierges britanniques						
2017 (C)						
Total	155	102	53	...	...	...
0 - 4	1	1	-	...	...	...
5 - 9	-	-	-	...	...	...
10 - 14	1	-	1	...	...	...
15 - 19	2	2	-	...	...	...
20 - 24	4	3	1	...	...	...
25 - 29	3	2	1	...	...	...
30 - 34	5	5	-	...	...	...
35 - 39	4	2	2	...	...	...
40 - 44	7	5	2	...	...	...
45 - 49	7	4	3	...	...	...
50 - 54	9	7	2	...	...	...
55 - 59	13	11	2	...	...	...
60 - 64	11	6	5	...	...	...
65 - 69	20	15	5	...	...	...
70 - 74	12	9	3	...	...	...
75 - 79	15	11	4	...	...	...
80 - 84	9	2	7	...	...	...
85 +	24	10	14	...	...	...
Unknown - Inconnu	1	1	-	..	..	..

19. Deaths by age and sex and age-specific death rates by sex: latest available year, 2010 - 2019
Décès et taux de mortalité selon l'âge et le sexe : dernière année disponible, 2010 - 2019 (continued - suite)

Continent, country or area, date, code[a] and age (in years) / Continent, pays ou zone, date, code[a] et âge (en années)	Number - Nombre			Rate - Taux		
	Both sexes / Les deux sexes	Male / Masculin	Female / Féminin	Both sexes / Les deux sexes	Male / Masculin	Female / Féminin
AMERICA, NORTH - AMÉRIQUE DU NORD						
Canada						
2018 (C)						
Total	283 706	144 483	139 223	7.7	7.9	7.5
0	1 750	953	797	4.6	4.9	4.3
1 - 4	256	131	125	0.2	0.2	0.2
5 - 9	164	90	74	0.1	0.1	0.1
10 - 14	212	117	95	0.1	0.1	0.1
15 - 19	710	478	232	0.3	0.4	0.2
20 - 24	1 423	994	429	0.6	0.8	0.4
25 - 29	1 850	1 285	565	0.7	1.0	0.5
30 - 34	2 048	1 383	665	0.8	1.1	0.5
35 - 39	2 407	1 563	844	1.0	1.2	0.7
40 - 44	2 941	1 867	1 074	1.2	1.6	0.9
45 - 49	4 346	2 696	1 650	1.8	2.3	1.4
50 - 54	7 542	4 660	2 882	2.9	3.6	2.2
55 - 59	12 417	7 506	4 911	4.6	5.5	3.6
60 - 64	17 665	10 764	6 901	7.2	8.9	5.5
65 - 69	22 566	13 490	9 076	11.1	13.6	8.7
70 - 74	28 003	16 193	11 810	17.2	20.8	14.0
75 - 79	32 140	18 032	14 108	29.0	35.0	23.8
80 - 84	38 741	20 293	18 448	50.6	60.3	43.0
85 - 89	46 123	21 737	24 386	91.6	109.0	80.2
90 - 94	38 522	14 547	23 975	162.5	190.0	149.4
95 - 99	18 048	4 977	13 071	259.6	291.9	249.0
100 +	3 832	727	3 105	387.3	413.5	381.6
Cayman Islands - Îles Caïmanes[16]						
2019 (C)						
Total	250	105	145	3.6	3.0	4.1
0 - 14	4	2	2	♦0.4	♦0.4	♦0.4
15 - 19	-	-	-	...	...	...
20 - 24	1	-	1	...	...	...
25 - 29	5	1	4	...	...	...
30 - 34	6	1	5	...	...	...
35 - 39	3	1	2	...	...	...
40 - 49	22	8	14	...	...	...
50 - 59	24	9	15	...	...	...
60 - 69	31	8	23	...	...	...
70 - 79	51	22	29	...	...	...
80 - 89	70	31	39	...	...	...
90 +	33	22	11	...	...	...
Costa Rica						
2019* (C)						
Total	24 237	13 558	10 679	4.8	5.5	4.1
0	533	262	271	...	...	...
1 - 4	103	59	44	...	...	...
5 - 9	55	31	24	0.2	0.2	♦0.1
10 - 14	73	43	30	0.2	0.2	♦0.2
15 - 19	211	160	51	0.5	0.7	0.3
20 - 24	410	315	95	1.0	1.5	0.5
25 - 29	439	342	97	1.2	1.8	0.5
30 - 34	474	345	129	1.2	1.9	0.6
35 - 39	534	367	167	1.5	2.2	0.9
40 - 44	635	430	205	1.9	2.8	1.2
45 - 49	735	472	263	2.5	3.5	1.6
50 - 54	1 040	658	382	3.3	4.5	2.3
55 - 59	1 442	889	553	4.7	6.3	3.4
60 - 64	1 794	1 083	711	7.0	9.0	5.2
65 - 69	2 101	1 232	869	10.3	13.4	7.8
70 - 74	2 218	1 327	891	15.6	20.3	11.5
75 - 79	2 498	1 377	1 121	25.2	29.9	21.1
80 - 84	2 926	1 501	1 425	44.4	50.3	39.5
85 - 89	2 745	1 273	1 472	77.8	83.0	73.8
90 - 94	2 077	923	1 154	119.4	147.0	103.8
95 +	1 180	458	722	179.2	203.2	166.7
95 - 99	936	376	560	...	...	...
100 +	244	82	162	...	...	...
Unknown - Inconnu	14	11	3	..	..	..

19. Deaths by age and sex and age-specific death rates by sex: latest available year, 2010 - 2019
Décès et taux de mortalité selon l'âge et le sexe : dernière année disponible, 2010 - 2019 (continued - suite)

Continent, country or area, date, code[a] and age (in years) / Continent, pays ou zone, date, code[a] et âge (en annèes)	Number - Nombre			Rate - Taux		
	Both sexes / Les deux sexes	Male / Masculin	Female / Féminin	Both sexes / Les deux sexes	Male / Masculin	Female / Féminin
AMERICA, NORTH - AMÉRIQUE DU NORD						
Cuba						
2018 (C)						
Total	106 196	57 931	48 265	9.5	10.4	8.6
0	461	264	197	4.0	4.4	3.6
1 - 4	150	75	75	0.3	0.3	0.3
5 - 9	123	74	49	0.2	0.2	0.2
10 - 14	116	78	38	0.2	0.3	0.1
15 - 19	262	180	82	0.4	0.5	0.2
20 - 24	381	260	121	0.5	0.7	0.4
25 - 29	505	345	160	0.6	0.8	0.4
30 - 34	628	412	216	0.8	1.1	0.6
35 - 39	820	535	285	1.3	1.7	0.9
40 - 44	1 425	928	497	1.8	2.3	1.3
45 - 49	2 750	1 772	978	2.8	3.6	1.9
50 - 54	4 725	2 979	1 746	4.6	6.0	3.4
55 - 59	6 305	3 923	2 382	8.0	10.3	5.9
60 - 64	7 581	4 574	3 007	12.8	16.2	9.7
65 - 69	10 108	5 973	4 135	19.0	23.5	14.9
70 - 74	12 715	7 297	5 418	29.2	36.0	23.3
75 - 79	14 773	8 178	6 595	45.6	54.6	37.8
80 - 84	14 509	7 516	6 993	72.3	83.6	63.1
85 +	27 808	12 526	15 282	149.1	160.4	141.0
85 - 89	13 277	6 327	6 950	...	...	...
90 - 94	9 257	4 106	5 151	...	...	...
95 - 99	4 094	1 671	2 423	...	...	...
100 +	1 180	422	758	...	...	...
Unknown - Inconnu	51	42	9	..	..	..
Curaçao						
2019 (C)						
Total	1 387	709	678	8.7	9.8	7.9
0	9	...	...	♦5.4	...	...
1 - 19	11	...	...	♦0.3	...	...
20 - 24	6	...	...	♦0.7	...	...
25 - 29	11	...	...	♦1.2	...	...
30 - 34	7	...	...	♦0.8	...	...
35 - 39	7	...	...	♦0.8	...	...
40 - 44	19	...	...	♦2.0	...	...
45 - 49	24	...	...	♦2.1	...	...
50 - 54	42	...	...	3.4	...	...
55 - 59	84	...	...	6.6	...	...
60 - 64	100	...	...	9.2	...	...
65 - 69	149	...	...	15.9	...	...
70 - 74	187	...	...	25.7	...	...
75 - 79	147	...	...	30.3	...	...
80 - 84	198	...	...	60.3	...	...
85 - 89	196	...	...	113.2	...	...
90 - 94	124	...	...	184.0	...	...
95 - 99	51	...	...	213.4	...	...
100 +	15	...	...	♦306.1	...	...
Dominican Republic - République dominicaine						
2019 (U)						
Total	*42 811*	*24 606*	*18 205*	...	...	...
0	*748*	*426*	*322*	...	...	...
1 - 4	*155*	*88*	*67*	...	...	...
5 - 9	*126*	*68*	*58*	...	...	...
10 - 14	*125*	*63*	*62*	...	...	...
15 - 19	*572*	*422*	*150*	...	...	...
20 - 24	*928*	*715*	*213*	...	...	...
25 - 29	*997*	*741*	*256*	...	...	...
30 - 34	*1 015*	*680*	*335*	...	...	...
35 - 39	*1 179*	*758*	*421*	...	...	...
40 - 44	*1 309*	*832*	*477*	...	...	...
45 - 49	*1 765*	*1 101*	*664*	...	...	...
50 - 54	*2 273*	*1 411*	*862*	...	...	...
55 - 59	*2 782*	*1 752*	*1 030*	...	...	...
60 - 64	*3 282*	*2 023*	*1 259*	...	...	...
65 - 69	*3 946*	*2 369*	*1 577*	...	...	...

Continent, country or area, date, code[a] and age (in years) / Continent, pays ou zone, date, code[a] et âge (en annèes)	Number - Nombre: Both sexes / Les deux sexes	Male / Masculin	Female / Féminin	Rate - Taux: Both sexes / Les deux sexes	Male / Masculin	Female / Féminin
AMERICA, NORTH - AMÉRIQUE DU NORD						
Dominican Republic - République dominicaine						
2019 (U)						
70 - 74	*4 039*	*2 381*	*1 658*	...	...	...
75 - 79	*4 455*	*2 534*	*1 921*	...	...	...
80 - 84	*4 628*	*2 409*	*2 219*	...	...	...
85 - 89	*4 109*	*1 926*	*2 183*	...	...	...
90 - 94	*2 506*	*1 135*	*1 371*	...	...	...
95 +	*1 485*	*565*	*920*	...	...	...
Unknown - Inconnu	*387*	*207*	*180*	..	..	..
El Salvador						
2014 (C)						
Total	37 461	21 326	16 135	5.9	7.2	4.8
0	876	491	385	7.0	7.7	6.3
1 - 4	240	131	109	0.5	0.5	0.5
5 - 9	125	66	59	0.2	0.2	0.2
10 - 14	250	160	90	0.4	0.5	0.3
15 - 19	983	813	170	1.4	2.3	0.5
20 - 24	1 139	926	213	1.8	3.0	0.6
25 - 29	1 047	869	178	2.1	3.8	0.6
30 - 34	1 249	1 015	234	2.9	5.6	1.0
35 - 39	1 348	1 061	287	3.5	6.4	1.3
40 - 44	1 313	942	371	3.6	6.1	1.8
45 - 49	1 492	985	507	4.7	7.3	2.8
50 - 54	1 669	1 022	647	6.3	8.9	4.2
55 - 59	1 991	1 129	862	8.9	11.6	6.8
60 - 64	2 302	1 275	1 027	12.1	15.4	9.6
65 - 69	2 678	1 398	1 280	17.1	20.4	14.6
70 - 74	3 107	1 644	1 463	24.7	29.7	20.8
75 - 79	3 687	1 826	1 861	38.6	44.0	34.4
80 +	11 965	5 573	6 392	109.6	120.9	101.3
80 - 84	4 057	1 977	2 080	...	...	...
85 - 89	3 853	1 851	2 002	...	...	...
90 - 94	2 642	1 186	1 456	...	...	...
95 +	1 413	559	854	...	...	...
Greenland - Groenland						
2019 (C)						
Total	548	321	227	9.7	10.8	8.5
0	10	4	6	♦12.0	♦9.2	♦15.2
1 - 4	2	2	-	♦0.6	♦1.2	-
5 - 9	-	-	-	-	-	-
10 - 14	1	1	-	♦0.3	♦0.5	-
15 - 19	14	7	7	♦3.9	♦3.8	♦4.0
20 - 24	14	10	4	♦3.4	♦4.7	♦1.9
25 - 29	11	8	3	♦2.3	♦3.3	♦1.3
30 - 34	12	9	3	♦2.7	♦4.0	♦1.4
35 - 39	6	3	3	♦1.6	♦1.5	♦1.6
40 - 44	5	4	1	♦1.7	♦2.4	♦0.7
45 - 49	12	10	2	♦3.8	♦5.7	♦1.4
50 - 54	32	20	12	6.5	♦7.5	♦5.3
55 - 59	41	22	19	9.0	♦9.0	♦9.1
60 - 64	58	32	26	17.4	17.1	♦17.9
65 - 69	70	47	23	33.7	40.4	♦25.1
70 - 74	64	39	25	48.8	51.0	♦45.8
75 - 79	91	54	37	102.4	120.3	84.1
80 - 84	50	29	21	137.7	♦182.4	♦102.9
85 - 89	40	15	25	246.9	♦250.0	♦245.1
90 - 94	15	5	10	♦416.7	♦454.5	♦400.0
95 +	-	-	-	-	-	-
Grenada - Grenade						
2014 (+C)						
Total	958	514	444	8.8	9.3	8.2
0 - 4	35	23	12	4.1	♦5.2	♦2.9
0	33	21	12	...	...	...
1 - 4	2	2	-	...	...	...
5 - 9	1	-	1	♦0.1	-	♦0.3
10 - 14	5	3	2	♦0.7	♦0.8	♦0.5
15 - 19	4	3	1	♦0.4	♦0.6	♦0.2

19. Deaths by age and sex and age-specific death rates by sex: latest available year, 2010 - 2019
Décès et taux de mortalité selon l'âge et le sexe : dernière année disponible, 2010 - 2019 (continued - suite)

Continent, country or area, date, code[a] and age (in years) / Continent, pays ou zone, date, code[a] et âge (en années)	Number - Nombre			Rate - Taux		
	Both sexes / Les deux sexes	Male / Masculin	Female / Féminin	Both sexes / Les deux sexes	Male / Masculin	Female / Féminin
AMERICA, NORTH - AMÉRIQUE DU NORD						
Grenada - Grenade						
2014 (+C)						
20 - 24	14	8	6	♦1.4	♦1.6	♦1.2
25 - 29	12	8	4	♦1.2	♦1.6	♦0.8
30 - 34	16	10	6	♦2.0	♦2.4	♦1.5
35 - 39	17	8	9	♦2.6	♦2.4	♦2.8
40 - 44	19	11	8	♦3.0	♦3.3	♦2.7
45 - 49	25	16	9	♦3.9	♦4.9	♦2.9
50 - 54	58	39	19	8.7	11.4	♦5.9
55 - 59	57	32	25	9.8	10.7	♦9.0
60 - 64	64	43	21	15.1	19.8	♦10.2
65 - 69	64	39	25	19.8	24.4	♦15.3
70 +	567	271	296	67.2	75.0	61.3
70 - 74	85	50	35	...	...	...
75 - 79	114	67	47	...	...	...
80 - 84	127	59	68	...	...	...
85 - 89	122	58	64	...	...	...
90 - 94	71	22	49	...	...	...
95 - 99	32	12	20	...	...	...
100 +	16	3	13	...	...	...
Guadeloupe[17]						
2018 (C)						
Total	3 258	1 778	1 480	7.7	9.1	6.5
0	30	20	10	♦7.4	♦9.7	♦5.1
1 - 4	5	3	2	♦0.3	♦0.3	♦0.2
5 - 9	-	-	-	-	-	-
10 - 14	1	1	-	-	♦0.1	-
15 - 19	12	9	3	♦0.4	♦0.6	♦0.2
20 - 24	15	14	1	♦0.7	♦1.4	♦0.1
25 - 29	24	16	8	♦1.2	♦1.7	♦0.7
30 - 34	29	21	8	♦1.4	♦2.5	♦0.7
35 - 39	34	23	11	1.5	♦2.5	♦0.8
40 - 44	41	28	13	1.5	♦2.4	♦0.8
45 - 49	83	48	35	2.6	3.4	2.0
50 - 54	127	78	49	3.8	5.1	2.7
55 - 59	182	128	54	5.7	8.5	3.2
60 - 64	212	146	66	7.5	11.2	4.3
65 - 69	249	159	90	10.0	14.0	6.7
70 - 74	277	180	97	14.5	20.7	9.3
75 - 79	340	196	144	25.3	33.6	19.0
80 - 84	441	230	211	42.8	56.8	33.7
85 - 89	429	191	238	68.7	85.1	59.5
90 - 94	392	164	228	122.6	159.8	105.0
95 - 99	224	88	136	211.9	260.4	189.2
100 +	111	35	76	860.5	1166.7	767.7
Guatemala						
2018 (C)						
Total	83 071	45 784	37 287	4.8	5.4	4.2
0	7 564	4 285	3 279	...	...	...
1 - 4	2 158	1 151	1 007	...	...	...
5 - 9	711	379	332	0.3	0.3	0.3
10 - 14	769	411	358	0.4	0.4	0.3
15 - 19	2 094	1 457	637	1.1	1.5	0.7
20 - 24	2 811	2 102	709	1.7	2.5	0.8
25 - 29	2 650	1 990	660	1.9	2.9	0.9
30 - 34	2 548	1 800	748	2.1	3.1	1.2
35 - 39	3 016	2 030	986	3.0	4.4	1.8
40 - 44	3 144	1 977	1 167	3.9	5.6	2.6
45 - 49	3 320	1 982	1 338	5.2	7.1	3.8
50 - 54	3 870	2 175	1 695	7.6	9.6	5.9
55 - 59	4 719	2 481	2 238	11.6	13.5	10.0
60 - 64	5 535	2 786	2 749	15.9	17.3	14.7
65 +	37 837	18 576	19 261	46.2	49.1	43.7
65 - 69	6 236	3 179	3 057	...	...	...
70 - 74	6 445	3 236	3 209	...	...	...
75 - 79	6 387	3 188	3 199	...	...	...
80 - 84	6 885	3 383	3 502	...	...	...

19. Deaths by age and sex and age-specific death rates by sex: latest available year, 2010 - 2019
Décès et taux de mortalité selon l'âge et le sexe : dernière année disponible, 2010 - 2019 (continued - suite)

Continent, country or area, date, code[a] and age (in years) - Continent, pays ou zone, date, code[a] et âge (en années)	Number - Nombre: Both sexes - Les deux sexes	Male - Masculin	Female - Féminin	Rate - Taux: Both sexes - Les deux sexes	Male - Masculin	Female - Féminin
AMERICA, NORTH - AMÉRIQUE DU NORD						
Guatemala						
2018 (C)						
85 - 89	6 356	3 068	3 288	...	...	...
90 - 94	3 997	1 863	2 134	...	...	...
95 +	1 531	659	872	...	...	...
Unknown - Inconnu	325	202	123	..	..	..
Jamaica - Jamaïque[18]						
2011 (I)						
Total	21 001	10 061[11]	8 618[11]	7.8	7.6	6.3
0 - 4	361	187[11]	163[11]	1.6	1.7	1.5
5 - 9	118	53[11]	61[11]	0.5	0.4	0.5
10 - 14	128	74[11]	54[11]	0.5	0.5	0.4
15 - 19	382	288[11]	90[11]	1.5	2.3	0.7
20 - 24	521	423[11]	92[11]	2.5	4.2	0.9
25 - 29	515	367[11]	136[11]	2.4	3.6	1.2
30 - 34	451	304[11]	134[11]	2.0	2.9	1.1
35 - 39	557	319[11]	224[11]	2.4	3.0	1.8
40 - 44	609	329[11]	268[11]	3.1	3.3	2.7
45 - 49	631	324[11]	299[11]	4.7	4.8	4.4
50 - 54	749	418[11]	320[11]	6.4	6.8	5.7
55 - 59	702	367[11]	319[11]	8.1	8.1	7.8
60 - 64	1 003	501[11]	482[11]	14.6	14.9	13.7
65 - 69	1 031	554[11]	448[11]	15.7	17.5	13.2
70 - 74	1 343	700[11]	610[11]	22.4	24.6	19.3
75 +	9 932	4 853[11]	4 918[11]	94.6	115.9	77.9
75 - 79	1 567	805[11]	722[11]	...	...	...
80 - 84	1 721	876[11]	806[11]	...	...	...
85 - 89	3 057	1 259[11]	1 798[11]	...	...	...
90 +	3 505	1 913[11]	1 592[11]	...	...	...
Unknown - Inconnu	1 968	-[11]	-[11]	..	..	..
Martinique[17]						
2017 (C)						
Total	3 217	1 660	1 557	8.7	9.7	7.8
0 - 4	41	24	17	2.3	♦2.7	♦1.9
0	40	23	17	12.2	♦13.9	♦10.5
5 - 9	4	4	-	♦0.2	♦0.4	-
10 - 14	4	2	2	♦0.2	♦0.2	♦0.2
15 - 19	15	10	5	♦0.6	♦0.8	♦0.4
20 - 24	10	7	3	♦0.6	♦0.8	♦0.4
25 - 29	14	9	5	♦0.8	♦1.1	♦0.5
30 - 34	19	14	5	♦1.1	♦1.9	♦0.5
35 - 39	12	6	6	♦0.7	♦0.8	♦0.6
40 - 44	39	20	19	1.8	♦2.1	♦1.5
45 - 49	62	37	25	2.2	2.9	♦1.6
50 - 54	100	61	39	3.0	4.1	2.1
55 - 59	146	99	47	4.8	7.0	2.9
60 - 64	184	126	58	7.0	10.4	4.1
65 - 69	233	147	86	10.5	14.6	7.1
70 - 74	282	168	114	16.3	21.2	12.2
75 - 79	321	186	135	23.4	30.8	17.6
80 - 84	490	245	245	46.4	55.3	40.0
85 - 89	510	241	269	80.4	100.1	68.4
90 - 94	428	173	255	138.5	186.2	118.0
95 +	303	81	222	193.2	231.4	182.3
95 - 99	221	65	156	...	...	...
100 +	82	16	66	...	...	...
Mexico - Mexique[19]						
2018 (+C)						
Total	704 803	394 131[11]	310 573[11]	5.6	6.4	4.9
0	23 142	12 854[11]	10 208[11]	10.7	11.6	9.6
1 - 4	4 536	2 448[11]	2 088[11]	0.5	0.5	0.5
5 - 9	2 415	1 295[11]	1 120[11]	0.2	0.2	0.2
10 - 14	3 095	1 790[11]	1 305[11]	0.3	0.3	0.2
15 - 19	8 983	6 574[11]	2 409[11]	0.8	1.2	0.4
20 - 24	14 409	11 305[11]	3 104[11]	1.3	2.1	0.6

19. Deaths by age and sex and age-specific death rates by sex: latest available year, 2010 - 2019
Décès et taux de mortalité selon l'âge et le sexe : dernière année disponible, 2010 - 2019 (continued - suite)

Continent, country or area, date, code[a] and age (in years) / Continent, pays ou zone, date, code[a] et âge (en années)	Number - Nombre			Rate - Taux		
	Both sexes / Les deux sexes	Male / Masculin	Female / Féminin	Both sexes / Les deux sexes	Male / Masculin	Female / Féminin
AMERICA, NORTH - AMÉRIQUE DU NORD						
Mexico - Mexique[19]						
2018 (+C)						
25 - 29	16 543	12 928[11]	3 615[11]	1.6	2.5	0.7
30 - 34	16 897	12 768[11]	4 128[11]	1.8	2.8	0.8
35 - 39	19 493	14 188[11]	5 304[11]	2.2	3.4	1.1
40 - 44	24 447	16 851[11]	7 596[11]	3.0	4.3	1.7
45 - 49	30 267	19 718[11]	10 547[11]	4.0	5.5	2.7
50 - 54	37 699	23 206[11]	14 493[11]	5.7	7.4	4.2
55 - 59	47 165	27 871[11]	19 294[11]	8.6	10.6	6.7
60 - 64	55 392	31 552[11]	23 839[11]	12.7	15.4	10.4
65 - 69	59 873	33 367[11]	26 505[11]	18.6	22.2	15.4
70 - 74	65 512	35 722[11]	29 790[11]	28.1	33.4	23.6
75 - 79	71 057	37 082[11]	33 974[11]	44.0	51.4	38.1
80 - 84	73 956	36 470[11]	37 484[11]	72.2	82.3	64.6
85 - 89	65 431	29 780[11]	35 650[11]	115.3	125.5	108.0
90 - 94	42 110	17 547[11]	24 563[11]	173.5	179.2	169.6
95 - 99	17 744	6 991[11]	10 753[11]	249.1	252.0	247.2
100 +	4 237	1 492[11]	2 744[11]	343.7	318.3	359.2
Unknown - Inconnu	400	332[11]	60[11]	..	..	..
Montserrat						
2016 (C)						
Total	43	26	17	...	...	...
0	-	-	-	...	...	...
1 - 4	-	-	-	...	...	...
5 - 9	-	-	-	...	...	...
10 - 14	-	-	-	...	...	...
15 - 19	-	-	-	...	...	...
20 - 24	1	-	1	...	...	...
25 - 29	1	1	-	...	...	...
30 - 34	-	-	-	...	...	...
35 - 39	-	-	-	...	...	...
40 - 44	-	-	-	...	...	...
45 - 49	-	-	-	...	...	...
50 - 54	1	-	1	...	...	...
55 - 59	-	-	-	...	...	...
60 - 64	3	2	1	...	...	...
65 - 69	7	4	3	...	...	...
70 - 74	7	7	-	...	...	...
75 - 79	1	1	-	...	...	...
80 - 84	8	3	5	...	...	...
85 - 89	5	4	1	...	...	...
90 +	9	4	5	...	...	...
Nicaragua						
2010 (+U)						
Total	*19 944*	*11 416*	*8 528*	...	...	...
0	*1 891*	*1 077*	*814*	...	...	...
1 - 4	*252*	*155*	*97*	...	...	...
5 - 9	*155*	*86*	*69*	...	...	...
10 - 14	*182*	*95*	*87*	...	...	...
15 - 19	*458*	*313*	*145*	...	...	...
20 - 24	*564*	*428*	*136*	...	...	...
25 - 29	*672*	*514*	*158*	...	...	...
30 - 34	*615*	*458*	*157*	...	...	...
35 - 39	*697*	*491*	*206*	...	...	...
40 - 44	*758*	*495*	*263*	...	...	...
45 - 49	*843*	*540*	*303*	...	...	...
50 - 54	*997*	*594*	*403*	...	...	...
55 - 59	*1 166*	*693*	*473*	...	...	...
60 - 64	*1 258*	*704*	*554*	...	...	...
65 - 69	*1 385*	*787*	*598*	...	...	...
70 - 74	*1 584*	*863*	*721*	...	...	...
75 - 79	*1 740*	*931*	*809*	...	...	...
80 +	*4 727*	*2 192*	*2 535*	...	...	...

19. Deaths by age and sex and age-specific death rates by sex: latest available year, 2010 - 2019
Décès et taux de mortalité selon l'âge et le sexe : dernière année disponible, 2010 - 2019 (continued - suite)

Continent, country or area, date, code[a] and age (in years) / Continent, pays ou zone, date, code[a] et âge (en années)	Number - Nombre			Rate - Taux		
	Both sexes Les deux sexes	Male Masculin	Female Féminin	Both sexes Les deux sexes	Male Masculin	Female Féminin
AMERICA, NORTH - AMÉRIQUE DU NORD						
Panama						
2018 (C)						
Total	19 720	11 358	8 362	4.7	5.4	4.0
0	1 092	591	501	14.7	15.6	13.8
1 - 4	269	166	103	0.9	1.1	0.7
5 - 9	86	47	39	0.2	0.3	0.2
10 - 14	99	61	38	0.3	0.3	0.2
15 - 19	236	171	65	0.7	0.9	0.4
20 - 24	378	292	86	1.1	1.7	0.5
25 - 29	422	317	105	1.3	2.0	0.7
30 - 34	378	275	103	1.2	1.8	0.7
35 - 39	435	284	151	1.5	1.9	1.0
40 - 44	500	300	200	1.8	2.1	1.4
45 - 49	634	390	244	2.4	3.0	1.9
50 - 54	745	463	282	3.3	4.2	2.5
55 - 59	1 039	666	373	5.5	7.1	3.9
60 - 64	1 250	775	475	8.4	10.7	6.2
65 - 69	1 487	918	569	13.1	16.8	9.6
70 - 74	1 785	1 083	702	20.8	26.7	15.5
75 - 79	1 996	1 178	818	32.4	41.3	24.7
80 - 84	2 078	1 128	950	51.2	61.6	42.6
85 - 89	2 105	1 064	1 041	89.8	104.0	78.7
90 - 94	1 554	713	841	139.8	152.6	130.5
95 - 99	837	346	491	214.6	219.0	211.5
100 +	276	103	173	365.6	345.6	378.6
Unknown - Inconnu	39	27	12	..	..	..
Puerto Rico - Porto Rico						
2019 (C)						
Total	29 638	16 150	13 488	...	...	...
0	135	73	62	...	...	...
1 - 4	20	10	10	...	...	...
5 - 9	15	9	6	...	...	...
10 - 14	19	15	4	...	...	...
15 - 19	75	59	16	...	...	...
20 - 24	260	216	44	...	...	...
25 - 29	307	264	43	...	...	...
30 - 34	322	252	70	...	...	...
35 - 39	425	300	125	...	...	...
40 - 44	530	389	141	...	...	...
45 - 49	644	436	208	...	...	...
50 - 54	1 010	682	328	...	...	...
55 - 59	1 405	897	508	...	...	...
60 - 64	1 881	1 210	671	...	...	...
65 - 69	2 437	1 513	924	...	...	...
70 - 74	3 123	1 881	1 242	...	...	...
75 - 79	3 727	2 056	1 671	...	...	...
80 - 84	4 169	2 125	2 044	...	...	...
85 - 89	4 161	1 889	2 272	...	...	...
90 - 94	3 088	1 226	1 862	...	...	...
95 - 99	1 481	514	967	...	...	...
100 +	372	109	263	...	...	...
Unknown - Inconnu	32	25	7	..	..	..
Saint Barthélemy - Saint-Barthélemy						
2014 (C)						
Total	53	30	23	...	...	...
0	-	-	-	...	...	...
1 - 4	-	-	-	...	...	...
5 - 9	-	-	-	...	...	...
10 - 14	-	-	-	...	...	...
15 - 19	-	-	-	...	...	...
20 - 24	1	1	-	...	...	...
25 - 29	-	-	-	...	...	...
30 - 34	-	-	-	...	...	...
35 - 39	1	1	-	...	...	...
40 - 44	1	-	1	...	...	...
45 - 49	1	1	-	...	...	...
50 - 54	5	2	3	...	...	...

19. Deaths by age and sex and age-specific death rates by sex: latest available year, 2010 - 2019
Décès et taux de mortalité selon l'âge et le sexe : dernière année disponible, 2010 - 2019 (continued - suite)

Continent, country or area, date, code[a] and age (in years) / Continent, pays ou zone, date, code[a] et âge (en années)	Number - Nombre			Rate - Taux		
	Both sexes / Les deux sexes	Male / Masculin	Female / Féminin	Both sexes / Les deux sexes	Male / Masculin	Female / Féminin
AMERICA, NORTH - AMÉRIQUE DU NORD						
Saint Barthélemy - Saint-Barthélemy						
2014 (C)						
55 - 59	4	3	1	...	...	...
60 - 64	3	2	1	...	...	...
65 - 69	6	4	2	...	...	...
70 - 74	4	2	2	...	...	...
75 - 79	9	6	3	...	...	...
80 - 84	5	2	3	...	...	...
85 - 89	4	2	2	...	...	...
90 - 94	6	2	4	...	...	...
95 - 99	3	2	1	...	...	...
100 +	-	-	-	...	...	...
Saint Pierre and Miquelon - Saint Pierre-et-Miquelon						
2014 (C)						
Total	50	21	29	...	...	...
0	-	-	-	...	...	...
1 - 4	-	-	-	...	...	...
5 - 9	-	-	-	...	...	...
10 - 14	-	-	-	...	...	...
15 - 19	-	-	-	...	...	...
20 - 24	-	-	-	...	...	...
25 - 29	-	-	-	...	...	...
30 - 34	-	-	-	...	...	...
35 - 39	-	-	-	...	...	...
40 - 44	2	1	1	...	...	...
45 - 49	-	-	-	...	...	...
50 - 54	-	-	-	...	...	...
55 - 59	3	2	1	...	...	...
60 - 64	5	4	1	...	...	...
65 - 69	7	4	3	...	...	...
70 - 74	4	3	1	...	...	...
75 - 79	3	1	2	...	...	...
80 - 84	7	3	4	...	...	...
85 - 89	3	1	2	...	...	...
90 - 94	9	2	7	...	...	...
95 - 99	5	-	5	...	...	...
100 +	2	-	2	...	...	...
Saint Vincent and the Grenadines - Saint-Vincent-et-les Grenadines[20]						
2017 (C)						
Total	917	504	413	8.3	8.9	7.7
0	17	8	9	♦10.7	♦10.0	♦11.5
1 - 4	7	4	3	♦1.0	♦1.1	♦0.8
5 - 9	3	-	3	♦0.3	-	♦0.7
10 - 14	4	2	2	♦0.4	♦0.4	♦0.4
15 - 19	11	9	2	♦1.1	♦1.7	♦0.4
20 - 24	11	6	5	♦1.3	♦1.4	♦1.2
25 - 29	16	8	8	♦1.9	♦1.9	♦2.0
30 - 34	20	14	6	♦2.5	♦3.5	♦1.5
35 - 39	15	9	6	♦2.0	♦2.3	♦1.6
40 - 44	41	26	15	5.7	♦6.8	♦4.4
45 - 49	45	25	20	6.0	♦6.3	♦5.5
50 - 54	57	39	18	8.6	11.1	♦5.8
55 - 59	66	42	24	13.0	15.6	♦10.0
60 - 64	71	40	31	18.4	19.9	16.7
65 - 69	69	44	25	24.0	29.6	♦18.0
70 - 74	82	44	38	32.0	33.7	30.2
75 - 79	101	55	46	50.5	56.0	45.2
80 - 84	100	55	45	68.6	81.4	57.5
85 +	180	74	106	149.6	151.2	148.5
Unknown - Inconnu	1	-	1	..	..	..
Saint-Martin (French part) - Saint-Martin (partie française)						
2014 (C)						
Total	161	97	64	4.5	5.7	3.5
0	5	3	2	...	...	...
1 - 4	-	-	-	...	...	...

19. Deaths by age and sex and age-specific death rates by sex: latest available year, 2010 - 2019
Décès et taux de mortalité selon l'âge et le sexe : dernière année disponible, 2010 - 2019 (continued - suite)

Continent, country or area, date, code[a] and age (in years) / Continent, pays ou zone, date, code[a] et âge (en années)	Number - Nombre: Both sexes / Les deux sexes	Male / Masculin	Female / Féminin	Rate - Taux: Both sexes / Les deux sexes	Male / Masculin	Female / Féminin
AMERICA, NORTH - AMÉRIQUE DU NORD						
Saint-Martin (French part) - Saint-Martin (partie française)						
2014 (C)						
5 - 9	2	2	-	♦0.9	♦1.8	-
10 - 14	1	1	-	♦0.5	♦0.9	-
15 - 19	4	4	-	♦1.9	♦3.7	-
20 - 24	3	2	1	♦1.5	♦1.9	♦1.0
25 - 29	1	1	-	♦0.5	♦1.0	-
30 - 34	4	1	3	♦1.8	♦0.9	♦2.7
35 - 39	4	4	-	♦1.8	♦3.7	-
40 - 44	6	6	-	♦2.5	♦4.9	-
45 - 49	11	6	5	♦4.6	♦5.0	♦4.1
50 - 54	13	7	6	♦5.5	♦6.0	♦4.9
55 - 59	13	8	5	♦5.8	♦7.3	♦4.3
60 - 64	15	10	5	♦6.8	♦9.5	♦4.4
65 - 69	12	9	3	♦6.2	♦9.8	♦3.0
70 - 74	6	4	2	♦4.6	♦6.7	♦2.9
75 - 79	19	10	9	♦15.9	♦19.5	♦13.3
80 - 84	14	5	9	♦13.9	♦12.7	♦14.6
85 - 89	14	9	5	♦21.2	♦40.7	♦11.4
90 - 94	11	4	7	♦35.5	♦47.6	♦31.0
95 - 99	2	1	1	♦39.2	♦90.9	♦25.0
100 +	1	-	1	♦90.9	-	♦100.0
Trinidad and Tobago - Trinité-et-Tobago						
2018* (C)						
Total	11 564	6 633[11]	4 925[11]	8.5	9.7	7.3
0	172	94[11]	75[11]	...	...	...
1 - 4	12	4	8	...	...	...
5 - 9	24	15	9	♦0.3	♦0.3	♦0.2
10 - 14	26	16	10	♦0.3	♦0.3	♦0.2
15 - 19	70	54	16	0.7	1.1	♦0.3
20 - 24	156	128	28	1.3	2.2	♦0.5
25 - 29	245	190	55	1.9	3.0	0.9
30 - 34	264	195	69	2.4	3.5	1.3
35 - 39	331	226	105	3.5	4.7	2.2
40 - 44	332	200	132	3.8	4.5	3.0
45 - 49	405	246	159	4.1	4.9	3.3
50 - 54	620	369[11]	250[11]	6.9	8.2	5.7
55 - 59	867	542	325	11.6	14.4	8.7
60 - 64	1 147	718	429	19.1	23.7	14.5
65 - 69	1 183	725	458	25.9	32.8	19.4
70 - 74	1 379	810	569	44.5	55.7	34.6
75 - 79	1 268	691	577	59.7	72.7	49.2
80 +	3 041	1 397	1 644	127.2	145.5	115.0
80 - 84	1 235	638	597	...	...	...
85 +	1 806	759	1 047	...	...	...
Unknown - Inconnu	22	13[11]	7[11]	..	..	..
Turks and Caicos Islands - Îles Turques et Caïques[21]						
2019* (C)						
Total	126	80	46	...	...	...
0	2	1	1	...	...	...
1 - 4	-	-	-	...	...	...
5 - 9	1	1	-	...	...	...
10 - 14	-	-	-	...	...	...
15 - 19	-	-	-	...	...	...
20 - 24	3	2	1	...	...	...
25 - 29	10	10	-	...	...	...
30 - 34	1	1	-	...	...	...
35 - 39	4	4	-	...	...	...
40 - 44	3	2	1	...	...	...
45 - 49	6	4	2	...	...	...
50 - 54	2	-	2	...	...	...
55 - 59	9	2	7	...	...	...
60 - 64	12	5	7	...	...	...
65 - 69	11	9	2	...	...	...
70 - 74	15	10	5	...	...	...
75 - 79	9	8	1	...	...	...

19. Deaths by age and sex and age-specific death rates by sex: latest available year, 2010 - 2019
Décès et taux de mortalité selon l'âge et le sexe : dernière année disponible, 2010 - 2019 (continued - suite)

Continent, country or area, date, code[a] and age (in years) / Continent, pays ou zone, date, code[a] et âge (en années)	Number - Nombre			Rate - Taux		
	Both sexes Les deux sexes	Male Masculin	Female Féminin	Both sexes Les deux sexes	Male Masculin	Female Féminin
AMERICA, NORTH - AMÉRIQUE DU NORD						
Turks and Caicos Islands - Îles Turques et Caïques[21]						
2019* (C)						
80 - 84	8	3	5	...	...	...
85 +	14	7	7	...	...	...
Unknown - Inconnu	16	11	5	..	..	..
United States of America - États-Unis d'Amérique						
2017 (C)						
Total	2 813 503	1 439 111	1 374 392	8.7	9.0	8.3
0	22 335	12 468	9 867	5.7	6.3	5.2
1 - 4	3 880	2 232	1 648	0.2	0.3	0.2
5 - 9	2 354	1 299	1 055	0.1	0.1	0.1
10 - 14	3 217	1 970	1 247	0.2	0.2	0.1
15 - 19	10 886	7 849	3 037	0.5	0.7	0.3
20 - 24	21 139	15 654	5 485	1.0	1.4	0.5
25 - 29	28 276	20 385	7 891	1.2	1.7	0.7
30 - 34	31 939	21 764	10 175	1.5	2.0	0.9
35 - 39	36 901	24 105	12 796	1.7	2.3	1.2
40 - 44	42 895	26 687	16 208	2.2	2.7	1.6
45 - 49	65 698	40 223	25 475	3.1	3.9	2.4
50 - 54	104 444	63 581	40 863	4.9	6.1	3.8
55 - 59	162 098	98 387	63 711	7.4	9.2	5.6
60 - 64	209 908	126 948	82 960	10.5	13.3	8.0
65 - 69	248 087	145 258	102 829	14.8	18.4	11.6
70 - 74	283 523	158 673	124 850	22.1	26.7	18.1
75 - 79	307 498	163 505	143 993	35.2	42.0	29.8
80 - 84	350 261	173 166	177 095	58.8	69.1	51.3
85 +	878 035	334 866	543 169	135.7	146.9	129.6
Unknown - Inconnu	129	91	38	..	..	..
AMERICA, SOUTH - AMÉRIQUE DU SUD						
Argentina - Argentine						
2018 (C)						
Total	336 823	173 950[11]	162 408[11]	7.6	8.0	7.2
0	6 048	3 471[11]	2 564[11]	8.1	9.1	7.1
1 - 4	1 214	655[11]	558[11]	0.4	0.4	0.4
5 - 9	593	318[11]	274[11]	0.2	0.2	0.2
10 - 14	725	401[11]	324[11]	0.2	0.2	0.2
15 - 19	2 458	1 734[11]	722[11]	0.7	1.0	0.4
20 - 24	3 528	2 559[11]	964[11]	1.0	1.4	0.5
25 - 29	3 404	2 393[11]	1 006[11]	1.0	1.4	0.6
30 - 34	3 624	2 362[11]	1 254[11]	1.1	1.5	0.8
35 - 39	4 728	2 947[11]	1 772[11]	1.5	1.9	1.1
40 - 44	5 920	3 557[11]	2 360[11]	2.0	2.4	1.6
45 - 49	7 705	4 631[11]	3 063[11]	3.1	3.8	2.4
50 - 54	10 907	6 743[11]	4 147[11]	4.9	6.3	3.6
55 - 59	15 949	9 986[11]	5 946[11]	7.7	10.1	5.5
60 - 64	23 553	14 716[11]	8 802[11]	12.7	16.9	8.9
65 - 69	31 531	19 577[11]	11 914[11]	19.7	26.7	13.7
70 - 74	37 732	22 158[11]	15 515[11]	29.7	39.8	21.7
75 - 79	41 123	22 528[11]	18 547[11]	44.8	60.3	34.1
80 - 84	45 054	21 291[11]	23 728[11]	73.1	94.3	60.8
85 +	89 123	30 875[11]	58 142[11]	155.7	181.9	144.4
Unknown - Inconnu	1 904	1 048[11]	806[11]	..	..	..
Bolivia (Plurinational State of) - Bolivie (État plurinational de)[22]						
2012 (I)						
Total	127 050	59 027	68 023	12.6	11.8	13.5
0	5 363	2 406	2 957	26.6	23.4	29.9
1 - 4	6 695	3 085	3 610	7.5	6.8	8.3
5 - 9	2 531	1 183	1 348	2.5	2.3	2.8
10 - 14	1 961	827	1 134	1.8	1.5	2.1
15 - 19	3 699	1 460	2 239	3.3	2.6	4.1
20 - 24	4 767	1 618	3 149	4.9	3.3	6.5
25 - 29	4 089	1 393	2 696	5.0	3.4	6.6

19. Deaths by age and sex and age-specific death rates by sex: latest available year, 2010 - 2019
Décès et taux de mortalité selon l'âge et le sexe : dernière année disponible, 2010 - 2019 (continued - suite)

Continent, country or area, date, code[a] and age (in years) / Continent, pays ou zone, date, code[a] et âge (en années)	Number - Nombre			Rate - Taux		
	Both sexes / Les deux sexes	Male / Masculin	Female / Féminin	Both sexes / Les deux sexes	Male / Masculin	Female / Féminin
AMERICA, SOUTH - AMÉRIQUE DU SUD						
Bolivia (Plurinational State of) - Bolivie (État plurinational de)[22]						
2012 (I)						
30 - 34	4 323	1 556	2 767	5.7	4.2	7.3
35 - 39	4 670	1 868	2 802	7.4	6.0	8.7
40 - 44	4 597	1 849	2 748	8.4	6.8	10.0
45 - 49	5 769	2 483	3 286	12.5	10.9	14.0
50 - 54	6 298	2 849	3 449	15.6	14.3	16.9
55 - 59	6 851	2 946	3 905	21.1	18.5	23.7
60 - 64	9 105	4 256	4 849	32.5	31.7	33.3
65 - 69	9 801	4 792	5 009	47.9	48.8	47.1
70 - 74	9 701	4 649	5 052	63.6	64.7	62.7
75 - 79	9 798	4 756	5 042	98.7	105.7	92.9
80 - 84	11 190	5 952	5 238	138.0	172.7	112.3
85 - 89	8 493	4 674	3 819	224.0	294.3	173.3
90 - 94	3 927	2 332	1 595	267.8	388.9	184.0
95 +	3 422	2 093	1 329	415.6	633.3	269.6
Brazil - Brésil						
2017 (+C)						
Total	1 277 579[23]	714 528[11]	562 577[11]	6.2	7.0	5.3
0	30 636[23]	16 753[11]	13 779[11]	10.9	11.7	10.1
1 - 4	5 516[23]	3 004[11]	2 508[11]	0.5	0.5	0.4
5 - 9	3 062[23]	1 795[11]	1 267[11]	0.2	0.2	0.2
10 - 14	4 388[23]	2 687[11]	1 701[11]	0.3	0.3	0.2
15 - 19	20 082[23]	16 529[11]	3 546[11]	1.2	1.9	0.4
20 - 24	27 498[23]	23 105[11]	4 386[11]	1.6	2.7	0.5
25 - 29	25 585[23]	20 397[11]	5 182[11]	1.5	2.4	0.6
30 - 34	28 339[23]	20 987[11]	7 346[11]	1.6	2.4	0.8
35 - 39	33 317[23]	23 039[11]	10 271[11]	2.0	2.8	1.2
40 - 44	38 192[23]	25 286[11]	12 903[11]	2.6	3.5	1.8
45 - 49	48 759[23]	31 139[11]	17 617[11]	3.7	4.9	2.6
50 - 54	66 216[23]	41 845[11]	24 366[11]	5.5	7.2	3.9
55 - 59	84 208[23]	52 132[11]	32 065[11]	8.1	10.4	5.9
60 - 64	103 303[23]	62 634[11]	40 657[11]	12.3	15.9	9.1
65 - 69	116 441[23]	68 697[11]	47 734[11]	18.2	23.5	13.8
70 - 74	125 124[23]	70 133[11]	54 979[11]	28.0	35.5	22.0
75 - 79	136 631[23]	71 852[11]	64 763[11]	44.3	55.5	36.2
80 - 84	137 690[23]	65 906[11]	71 767[11]	70.4	85.2	60.8
85 - 89	122 817[23]	52 132[11]	70 670[11]	117.1	134.2	107.0
90 +	116 311[23]	41 918[11]	74 363[11]	188.7	211.3	177.9
90 - 94	76 538[23]	29 058[11]	47 469[11]	...	...	...
95 - 99	30 338[23]	10 062[11]	20 266[11]	...	...	...
100 +	9 435[23]	2 798[11]	6 628[11]	...	...	...
Unknown - Inconnu	3 464[23]	2 558[11]	707[11]	..	..	..
Chile - Chili						
2017 (C)						
Total	106 388	55 773[11]	50 593[11]	5.8	6.1	5.5
0	1 557	830[11]	705[11]	6.3	6.6	5.8
1 - 4	223	119[11]	104[11]	0.2	0.2	0.2
5 - 9	143	72[11]	71[11]	0.1	0.1	0.1
10 - 14	176	92[11]	84[11]	0.1	0.2	0.1
15 - 19	542	384[11]	158[11]	0.4	0.6	0.3
20 - 24	875	656[11]	219[11]	0.6	0.9	0.3
25 - 29	1 052	800[11]	252[11]	0.7	1.0	0.3
30 - 34	1 154	823[11]	331[11]	0.8	1.1	0.5
35 - 39	1 347	939[11]	408[11]	1.1	1.5	0.6
40 - 44	1 933	1 291[11]	642[11]	1.6	2.1	1.0
45 - 49	2 754	1 758[11]	996[11]	2.2	2.8	1.6
50 - 54	4 233	2 678[11]	1 555[11]	3.4	4.4	2.5
55 - 59	5 829	3 703[11]	2 126[11]	5.2	6.7	3.7
60 - 64	7 251	4 453[11]	2 798[11]	8.1	10.3	6.1
65 - 69	8 861	5 277[11]	3 584[11]	12.8	16.2	9.8
70 - 74	11 217	6 489[11]	4 728[11]	21.2	27.1	16.4
75 - 79	12 848	7 083[11]	5 765[11]	34.8	44.9	27.3
80 +	44 392	18 325[11]	26 067[11]	106.5	124.4	96.7

Continent, country or area, date, code[a] and age (in years) / Continent, pays ou zone, date, code[a] et âge (en années)	Number - Nombre			Rate - Taux		
	Both sexes Les deux sexes	Male Masculin	Female Féminin	Both sexes Les deux sexes	Male Masculin	Female Féminin
AMERICA, SOUTH - AMÉRIQUE DU SUD						
Chile - Chili						
2017 (C)						
80 - 84	14 102	7 028[11]	7 074[11]	...	...	...
85 - 89	15 466	6 561[11]	8 905[11]	...	...	...
90 - 94	9 878	3 458[11]	6 420[11]	...	...	...
95 - 99	3 974	1 086[11]	2 888[11]	...	...	...
100 +	972	192[11]	780[11]	...	...	...
Unknown - Inconnu	1	1[11]	-[11]	..	..	..
Colombia - Colombie						
2019* (U)						
Total	*242 609*	*133 594*[11]	*108 883*[11]	...	...	...
0	*7 166*	*4 080*[11]	*3 084*[11]	...	...	...
1 - 4	*1 483*	*783*[11]	*699*[11]	...	...	...
5 - 9	*841*	*473*[11]	*367*[11]	...	...	...
10 - 14	*1 125*	*653*[11]	*472*[11]	...	...	...
15 - 19	*3 749*	*2 841*[11]	*904*[11]	...	...	...
20 - 24	*5 839*	*4 700*[11]	*1 139*[11]	...	...	...
25 - 29	*5 890*	*4 615*[11]	*1 275*[11]	...	...	...
30 - 34	*5 604*	*4 148*[11]	*1 442*[11]	...	...	...
35 - 39	*5 656*	*3 891*[11]	*1 762*[11]	...	...	...
40 - 44	*5 923*	*3 727*[11]	*2 191*[11]	...	...	...
45 - 49	*6 865*	*4 050*[11]	*2 812*[11]	...	...	...
50 - 54	*9 398*	*5 535*[11]	*3 853*[11]	...	...	...
55 - 59	*12 612*	*7 310*[11]	*5 300*[11]	...	...	...
60 - 64	*16 449*	*9 596*[11]	*6 843*[11]	...	...	...
65 - 69	*19 654*	*11 365*[11]	*8 288*[11]	...	...	...
70 - 74	*22 500*	*12 797*[11]	*9 692*[11]	...	...	...
75 - 79	*26 242*	*14 295*[11]	*11 944*[11]	...	...	...
80 - 84	*29 875*	*15 046*[11]	*14 818*[11]	...	...	...
85 - 89	*27 770*	*12 647*[11]	*15 122*[11]	...	...	...
90 - 94	*18 623*	*7 698*[11]	*10 922*[11]	...	...	...
95 - 99	*7 470*	*2 752*[11]	*4 713*[11]	...	...	...
100 +	*1 827*	*580*[11]	*1 238*[11]	...	...	...
Unknown - Inconnu	*48*	*12*[11]	*3*[11]	..	..	..
Ecuador - Équateur[24]						
2018* (U)						
Total	*71 007*	*39 040*	*31 967*	...	...	...
0	*3 350*	*1 852*	*1 498*	...	...	...
1 - 4	*709*	*383*	*326*	...	...	...
5 - 9	*422*	*235*	*187*	...	...	...
10 - 14	*516*	*296*	*220*	...	...	...
15 - 19	*1 108*	*767*	*341*	...	...	...
20 - 24	*1 539*	*1 180*	*359*	...	...	...
25 - 29	*1 603*	*1 215*	*388*	...	...	...
30 - 34	*1 600*	*1 131*	*469*	...	...	...
35 - 39	*1 796*	*1 193*	*603*	...	...	...
40 - 44	*1 862*	*1 184*	*678*	...	...	...
45 - 49	*2 249*	*1 368*	*881*	...	...	...
50 - 54	*2 849*	*1 674*	*1 175*	...	...	...
55 - 59	*3 707*	*2 206*	*1 501*	...	...	...
60 - 64	*4 496*	*2 576*	*1 920*	...	...	...
65 - 69	*5 167*	*2 883*	*2 284*	...	...	...
70 - 74	*5 929*	*3 279*	*2 650*	...	...	...
75 - 79	*6 805*	*3 724*	*3 081*	...	...	...
80 - 84	*7 718*	*4 072*	*3 646*	...	...	...
85 - 89	*8 001*	*3 863*	*4 138*	...	...	...
90 - 94	*5 867*	*2 529*	*3 338*	...	...	...
95 - 99	*2 870*	*1 130*	*1 740*	...	...	...
100 +	*831*	*287*	*544*	...	...	...
Unknown - Inconnu	*13*	*13*	-	..	..	..
French Guiana - Guyane française[17]						
2017 (C)						
Total	964	546	418	3.5	4.0	3.0
0	84	48	36	13.2	14.8	11.5
1 - 4	11	5	6	♦0.4	♦0.4	♦0.5

19. Deaths by age and sex and age-specific death rates by sex: latest available year, 2010 - 2019
Décès et taux de mortalité selon l'âge et le sexe : dernière année disponible, 2010 - 2019 (continued - suite)

Continent, country or area, date, code[a] and age (in years) / Continent, pays ou zone, date, code[a] et âge (en années)	Number - Nombre			Rate - Taux		
	Both sexes / Les deux sexes	Male / Masculin	Female / Féminin	Both sexes / Les deux sexes	Male / Masculin	Female / Féminin
AMERICA, SOUTH - AMÉRIQUE DU SUD						
French Guiana - Guyane française[17]						
2017 (C)						
5 - 9	-	-	-	-	-	-
10 - 14	7	2	5	♦0.2	♦0.1	♦0.3
15 - 19	15	8	7	♦0.6	♦0.6	♦0.5
20 - 24	10	7	3	♦0.5	♦0.8	♦0.3
25 - 29	21	13	8	♦1.1	♦1.5	♦0.8
30 - 34	13	9	4	♦0.7	♦1.0	♦0.4
35 - 39	34	20	14	1.7	♦2.1	♦1.4
40 - 44	41	25	16	2.2	♦2.8	♦1.7
45 - 49	48	27	21	2.9	♦3.2	♦2.6
50 - 54	48	36	12	3.7	5.5	♦1.8
55 - 59	64	44	20	6.0	8.3	♦3.8
60 - 64	78	42	36	9.0	9.4	8.5
65 - 69	84	49	35	14.5	16.8	12.1
70 - 74	85	54	31	23.1	28.9	17.1
75 - 79	78	52	26	40.3	58.6	♦24.8
80 - 84	75	37	38	57.2	71.0	48.1
85 - 89	81	39	42	101.8	130.4	84.5
90 - 94	57	22	35	158.8	♦258.8	127.7
95 - 99	24	5	19	♦164.4	♦151.5	♦168.1
100 +	5	2	3	♦108.7	♦90.9	♦125.0
Unknown - Inconnu	1	-	1	..	..	..
Paraguay						
2018 (+U)						
Total	*29 139*	*16 575*[11]	*12 513*[11]	...	...	...
0	*490*	*283*[11]	*205*[11]	...	...	...
1 - 4	*166*	*99*[11]	*67*[11]	...	...	...
5 - 9	*119*	*66*[11]	*53*[11]	...	...	...
10 - 14	*147*	*83*[11]	*63*[11]	...	...	...
15 - 19	*414*	*285*[11]	*128*[11]	...	...	...
20 - 24	*586*	*446*[11]	*138*[11]	...	...	...
25 - 29	*564*	*411*[11]	*153*[11]	...	...	...
30 - 34	*547*	*363*[11]	*183*[11]	...	...	...
35 - 39	*661*	*431*[11]	*228*[11]	...	...	...
40 - 44	*749*	*464*[11]	*285*[11]	...	...	...
45 - 49	*1 022*	*655*[11]	*366*[11]	...	...	...
50 - 54	*1 416*	*900*[11]	*514*[11]	...	...	...
55 - 59	*1 918*	*1 249*[11]	*668*[11]	...	...	...
60 - 64	*2 315*	*1 477*[11]	*834*[11]	...	...	...
65 - 69	*2 635*	*1 596*[11]	*1 037*[11]	...	...	...
70 - 74	*2 926*	*1 726*[11]	*1 195*[11]	...	...	...
75 - 79	*3 214*	*1 781*[11]	*1 426*[11]	...	...	...
80 - 84	*3 119*	*1 601*[11]	*1 509*[11]	...	...	...
85 +	*6 062*	*2 621*[11]	*3 434*[11]	...	...	...
Unknown - Inconnu	*69*	*38*[11]	*27*[11]	..	..	..
Peru - Pérou[25]						
2019* (+U)						
Total	*114 945*	*61 660*	*53 285*	...	...	...
0	*4 758*	*2 604*	*2 154*	...	...	...
1 - 4	*1 049*	*567*	*482*	...	...	...
5 - 9	*640*	*361*	*279*	...	...	...
10 - 14	*742*	*417*	*325*	...	...	...
15 - 19	*1 357*	*856*	*501*	...	...	...
20 - 24	*1 936*	*1 370*	*566*	...	...	...
25 - 29	*2 231*	*1 558*	*673*	...	...	...
30 - 34	*2 358*	*1 572*	*786*	...	...	...
35 - 39	*2 676*	*1 726*	*950*	...	...	...
40 - 44	*3 180*	*1 954*	*1 226*	...	...	...
45 - 49	*3 846*	*2 211*	*1 635*	...	...	...
50 - 54	*4 719*	*2 710*	*2 009*	...	...	...
55 - 59	*5 811*	*3 317*	*2 494*	...	...	...
60 - 64	*7 087*	*3 949*	*3 138*	...	...	...
65 - 69	*8 560*	*4 703*	*3 857*	...	...	...
70 - 74	*10 516*	*5 784*	*4 732*	...	...	...
75 - 79	*11 942*	*6 249*	*5 693*	...	...	...

19. Deaths by age and sex and age-specific death rates by sex: latest available year, 2010 - 2019
Décès et taux de mortalité selon l'âge et le sexe : dernière année disponible, 2010 - 2019 (continued - suite)

Continent, country or area, date, code[a] and age (in years) Continent, pays ou zone, date, code[a] et âge (en années)	Number - Nombre Both sexes Les deux sexes	Male Masculin	Female Féminin	Rate - Taux Both sexes Les deux sexes	Male Masculin	Female Féminin
AMERICA, SOUTH - AMÉRIQUE DU SUD						
Peru - Pérou[25]						
2019* (+U)						
80 - 84	*14 056*	*7 263*	*6 793*	...	...	...
85 - 89	*13 696*	*6 601*	*7 095*	...	...	...
90 - 94	*9 313*	*4 147*	*5 166*	...	...	...
95 - 99	*3 601*	*1 429*	*2 172*	...	...	...
100 +	*790*	*267*	*523*	...	...	...
Unknown - Inconnu	*81*	*45*	*36*	..	..	..
Suriname						
2018 (C)						
Total	3 763	2 120	1 643	6.4	7.2	5.6
0	190	105	85	19.4	20.9	17.8
1 - 4	33	21	12	0.7	♦0.9	♦0.6
5 - 9	19	12	7	♦0.4	♦0.5	♦0.3
10 - 14	21	9	12	♦0.4	♦0.4	♦0.5
15 - 19	40	22	18	0.8	♦0.9	♦0.8
20 - 24	59	41	18	1.3	1.7	♦0.8
25 - 29	60	34	26	1.3	1.5	♦1.1
30 - 34	77	47	30	1.8	2.1	♦1.4
35 - 39	125	69	56	3.0	3.3	2.7
40 - 44	116	82	34	3.0	4.2	1.7
45 - 49	157	102	55	4.2	5.5	2.9
50 - 54	253	164	89	7.5	9.8	5.3
55 - 59	324	210	114	11.3	14.9	7.8
60 - 64	330	199	131	13.9	17.5	10.7
65 - 69	368	208	160	21.0	25.7	17.0
70 - 74	352	199	153	27.5	34.9	21.5
75 - 79	378	206	172	45.0	57.2	35.8
80 +	861	390	471	102.5	114.7	94.2
80 - 84	373	195	178	...	...	...
85 - 89	286	128	158	...	...	...
90 - 94	149	47	102	...	...	...
95 - 99	46	17	29	...	...	...
100 +	7	3	4	...	...	...
Uruguay[26]						
2018 (C)						
Total	34 127	17 315	16 812	9.7	10.2	9.3
0	272	156	116	6.0	6.7	5.2
1 - 4	64	36	28	0.3	0.4	♦0.3
5 - 9	34	17	17	0.1	♦0.1	♦0.1
10 - 14	52	26	26	0.2	♦0.2	♦0.2
15 - 19	187	149	38	0.7	1.1	0.3
20 - 24	302	240	62	1.1	1.7	0.5
25 - 29	266	218	48	1.0	1.7	0.4
30 - 34	301	208	93	1.2	1.7	0.8
35 - 39	405	277	128	1.7	2.3	1.1
40 - 44	505	306	199	2.1	2.6	1.6
45 - 49	632	370	262	2.9	3.5	2.4
50 - 54	957	601	356	4.7	6.2	3.4
55 - 59	1 545	995	550	7.8	10.5	5.3
60 - 64	2 171	1 355	816	12.2	16.3	8.6
65 - 69	2 858	1 785	1 073	19.6	27.1	13.4
70 - 74	3 526	2 054	1 472	29.1	39.4	21.3
75 - 79	4 170	2 293	1 877	43.9	60.4	33.0
80 - 84	5 072	2 473	2 599	73.3	99.8	58.6
85 - 89	5 389	2 137	3 252	121.1	152.5	106.6
90 +	5 370	1 588	3 782	220.7	244.3	212.2
90 - 94	3 680	1 179	2 501	...	...	...
95 +	1 690	409	1 281	...	...	...
Unknown - Inconnu	49	31	18	..	..	..
Venezuela (Bolivarian Republic of) - Venezuela (République bolivarienne du)						
2017 (C)						
Total	190 236	113 648	76 588	6.1	7.2	4.9
0	13 873	7 875	5 998	25.7	28.3	23.0
1 - 4	1 957	1 040	917	0.9	0.9	0.9
5 - 9	909	518	391	0.3	0.4	0.3

19. Deaths by age and sex and age-specific death rates by sex: latest available year, 2010 - 2019
Décès et taux de mortalité selon l'âge et le sexe : dernière année disponible, 2010 - 2019 (continued - suite)

Continent, country or area, date, code[a] and age (in years) / Continent, pays ou zone, date, code[a] et âge (en annèes)	Number - Nombre			Rate - Taux		
	Both sexes / Les deux sexes	Male / Masculin	Female / Féminin	Both sexes / Les deux sexes	Male / Masculin	Female / Féminin
AMERICA, SOUTH - AMÉRIQUE DU SUD						
Venezuela (Bolivarian Republic of) - Venezuela (République bolivarienne du)						
2017 (C)						
10 - 14	1 170	742	428	0.4	0.5	0.3
15 - 19	4 612	3 769	843	1.7	2.7	0.6
20 - 24	7 957	6 879	1 078	3.0	5.1	0.8
25 - 29	7 168	5 924	1 244	2.8	4.5	1.0
30 - 34	6 068	4 669	1 399	2.4	3.7	1.1
35 - 39	5 832	4 090	1 742	2.6	3.6	1.5
40 - 44	5 716	3 726	1 990	2.8	3.7	2.0
45 - 49	6 790	4 178	2 612	3.6	4.5	2.8
50 - 54	8 859	5 538	3 321	5.2	6.6	3.8
55 - 59	11 711	7 163	4 548	8.2	10.3	6.3
60 - 64	14 295	8 709	5 586	13.2	16.6	10.0
65 - 69	16 026	9 719	6 307	20.4	26.1	15.3
70 - 74	16 026	9 503	6 523	28.8	36.7	21.9
75 - 79	16 755	9 318	7 437	45.4	56.2	36.6
80 - 84	16 708	8 552	8 156	75.0	90.9	63.3
85 - 89	14 648	6 815	7 833	121.5	152.4	103.3
90 - 94	9 023	3 534	5 489	157.2	209.9	135.3
95 - 99	3 287	1 123	2 164	145.1	236.6	120.8
100 +	846	264	582	152.3	260.9	128.1
ASIA - ASIE						
Armenia - Arménie[27]						
2018 (C)						
Total	25 751	13 021	12 730	8.7	9.3	8.1
0	261	143	118	7.1	7.4	6.7
1 - 4	56	33	23	0.3	0.4	♦0.3
5 - 9	26	17	9	♦0.1	♦0.2	♦0.1
10 - 14	26	13	13	♦0.1	♦0.1	♦0.1
15 - 19	50	39	11	0.3	0.4	♦0.1
20 - 24	100	78	22	0.5	0.8	♦0.2
25 - 29	139	108	31	0.5	0.9	0.2
30 - 34	200	146	54	0.8	1.2	0.4
35 - 39	248	168	80	1.1	1.6	0.7
40 - 44	331	227	104	1.8	2.7	1.1
45 - 49	511	348	163	3.1	4.7	1.8
50 - 54	893	653	240	5.0	8.3	2.4
55 - 59	1 731	1 166	565	8.1	12.2	4.7
60 - 64	2 223	1 434	789	12.5	18.6	7.9
65 - 69	2 594	1 540	1 054	20.7	29.4	14.5
70 - 74	2 148	1 223	925	32.3	46.6	23.0
75 - 79	3 407	1 606	1 801	47.5	58.6	40.6
80 - 84	4 840	2 032	2 808	87.1	100.3	79.6
85 +	5 967	2 047	3 920	199.1	184.0	208.1
85 - 89	3 785	1 404	2 381	...	...	...
90 - 94	1 854	570	1 284	...	...	...
95 - 99	273	58	215	...	...	...
100 +	55	15	40	...	...	...
Azerbaijan - Azerbaïdjan[27]						
2018 (+C)						
Total	57 250	30 643	26 607	5.8	6.2	5.4
0	1 547	892	655	10.7	11.6	9.7
1 - 4	278	173	105	0.4	0.5	0.3
5 - 9	213	128	85	0.3	0.3	0.2
10 - 14	213	140	73	0.3	0.4	0.3
15 - 19	304	209	95	0.5	0.6	0.3
20 - 24	441	299	142	0.6	0.7	0.4
25 - 29	582	380	202	0.6	0.8	0.4
30 - 34	699	475	224	0.8	1.1	0.5
35 - 39	777	529	248	1.0	1.4	0.6
40 - 44	1 199	860	339	1.9	2.8	1.1
45 - 49	1 927	1 346	581	3.0	4.4	1.7
50 - 54	3 304	2 210	1 094	5.1	7.2	3.2

19. Deaths by age and sex and age-specific death rates by sex: latest available year, 2010 - 2019
Décès et taux de mortalité selon l'âge et le sexe : dernière année disponible, 2010 - 2019 (continued - suite)

Continent, country or area, date, code[a] and age (in years) / Continent, pays ou zone, date, code[a] et âge (en années)	Number - Nombre			Rate - Taux		
	Both sexes Les deux sexes	Male Masculin	Female Féminin	Both sexes Les deux sexes	Male Masculin	Female Féminin
ASIA - ASIE						
Azerbaijan - Azerbaïdjan[27]						
2018 (+C)						
55 - 59	5 158	3 414	1 744	8.2	11.4	5.3
60 - 64	6 056	3 785	2 271	14.4	19.4	10.1
65 - 69	5 877	3 407	2 470	22.4	28.9	17.1
70 - 74	4 211	2 238	1 973	35.7	44.6	29.1
75 - 79	7 182	3 422	3 760	55.3	65.4	48.5
80 - 84	9 177	3 866	5 311	103.4	110.3	98.9
85 - 89	5 540	2 128	3 412	150.2	144.5	154.0
90 - 94	1 953	635	1 318	236.3	200.6	258.4
95 - 99	450	89	361	140.9	81.5	171.8
100 +	162	18	144	216.3	♦98.4	254.4
Bahrain - Bahreïn[28]						
2018 (C)						
Total	3 052	1 794	1 258	2.0	1.9	2.3
0	129	68	61	6.1	6.3	5.9
1 - 4	31	19	12	0.4	♦0.4	♦0.3
5 - 9	18	14	4	♦0.2	♦0.3	♦0.1
10 - 14	17	8	9	♦0.2	♦0.2	♦0.2
15 - 19	32	17	15	0.4	♦0.4	♦0.4
20 - 24	48	33	15	0.4	0.5	♦0.3
25 - 29	83	66	17	0.4	0.5	♦0.3
30 - 34	93	71	22	0.4	0.5	♦0.4
35 - 39	120	89	31	0.7	0.7	0.6
40 - 44	129	97	32	1.0	1.1	0.8
45 - 49	150	106	44	1.5	1.6	1.4
50 - 54	197	127	70	2.6	2.7	2.5
55 - 59	267	165	102	4.8	4.9	4.7
60 - 64	269	165	104	7.8	8.2	7.3
65 - 69	284	175	109	15.4	16.3	14.2
70 - 74	246	129	117	24.8	24.9	24.8
75 - 79	310	156	154	48.6	48.5	48.7
80 - 84	285	127	158	76.5	72.9	79.7
85 - 89	187	90	97	97.6	97.3	97.9
90 - 94	98	51	47	111.1	121.1	102.0
95 - 99	40	18	22	101.0	♦94.7	♦106.8
100 +	17	2	15	♦89.0	♦25.3	♦133.9
Unknown - Inconnu	2	1	1	..	..	..
Brunei Darussalam - Brunéi Darussalam						
2018 (+C)						
Total	1 612	878	734	3.6	3.8	3.5
0	56	34	22	...	...	...
1 - 4	11	5	6	...	...	...
5 - 9	5	3	2	♦0.2	♦0.2	♦0.1
10 - 14	7	3	4	♦0.2	♦0.2	♦0.3
15 - 19	13	10	3	♦0.3	♦0.5	♦0.2
20 - 24	12	6	6	♦0.3	♦0.3	♦0.3
25 - 29	27	21	6	♦0.6	♦0.9	♦0.3
30 - 34	38	27	11	0.9	♦1.2	♦0.6
35 - 39	62	38	24	1.6	1.8	♦1.4
40 - 44	72	43	29	2.1	2.3	♦1.8
45 - 49	111	68	43	3.5	4.1	2.9
50 - 54	119	71	48	4.7	5.4	3.9
55 - 59	127	69	58	6.0	6.8	5.4
60 - 64	162	95	67	10.7	12.0	9.2
65 - 69	146	80	66	15.2	15.4	15.0
70 - 74	146	79	67	31.1	34.3	27.9
75 - 79	174	85	89	51.2	60.7	44.5
80 - 84	146	59	87	91.3	73.8	108.8
85 +	178	82	96	197.8	205.0	192.0
85 - 89	110	52	58	...	...	...
90 - 94	51	27	24	...	...	...
95 - 99	15	3	12	...	...	...
100 +	2	-	2	...	...	...

19. Deaths by age and sex and age-specific death rates by sex: latest available year, 2010 - 2019
Décès et taux de mortalité selon l'âge et le sexe : dernière année disponible, 2010 - 2019 (continued - suite)

Continent, country or area, date, code[a] and age (in years) / Continent, pays ou zone, date, code[a] et âge (en années)	Number - Nombre			Rate - Taux		
	Both sexes / Les deux sexes	Male / Masculin	Female / Féminin	Both sexes / Les deux sexes	Male / Masculin	Female / Féminin
ASIA - ASIE						
China - Chine[29]						
2010 (|)						
Total	7 421 990	4 293 783	3 128 207	5.6	6.3	4.8
0	60 217	32 026	28 191	4.4	4.3	4.5
1 - 4	39 591	23 119	16 472	0.6	0.7	0.6
5 - 9	21 183	13 621	7 562	0.3	0.4	0.2
10 - 14	23 088	15 243	7 845	0.3	0.4	0.2
15 - 19	40 469	28 088	12 381	0.4	0.5	0.3
20 - 24	62 552	43 738	18 814	0.5	0.7	0.3
25 - 29	60 661	42 497	18 164	0.6	0.8	0.4
30 - 34	79 960	55 804	24 156	0.8	1.1	0.5
35 - 39	140 531	98 382	42 149	1.2	1.6	0.7
40 - 44	216 353	149 111	67 242	1.7	2.3	1.1
45 - 49	262 531	179 446	83 085	2.5	3.3	1.6
50 - 54	337 397	226 888	110 509	4.3	5.6	2.9
55 - 59	494 339	324 817	169 522	6.1	7.9	4.2
60 - 64	586 160	377 069	209 091	10.0	12.6	7.3
65 - 69	695 662	435 007	260 655	16.9	21.0	12.8
70 - 74	999 653	599 394	400 259	30.3	36.5	24.2
75 - 79	1 162 694	657 140	505 554	48.7	58.3	40.2
80 - 84	1 081 704	553 704	528 000	80.9	93.6	70.8
85 - 89	686 462	306 678	379 784	121.9	139.4	110.7
90 - 94	279 569	104 048	175 521	177.1	196.0	167.6
95 - 99	74 729	23 292	51 437	202.0	197.9	203.9
100 +	16 485	4 671	11 814	458.8	527.7	436.2
China, Hong Kong SAR - Chine, Hong Kong RAS						
2019 (C)						
Total	48 957	27 232[11]	21 721[11]	6.5	8.0	5.3
0	75	42	33	1.5	1.7	1.4
1 - 4	27	16	11	♦0.1	♦0.1	♦0.1
5 - 9	14	6	8	-	-	♦0.1
10 - 14	28	13	15	♦0.1	♦0.1	♦0.1
15 - 19	61	37	24	0.2	0.3	♦0.2
20 - 24	83	53	30	0.2	0.3	♦0.1
25 - 29	148	100	48	0.3	0.4	0.2
30 - 34	227	136	91	0.4	0.6	0.3
35 - 39	321	187	134	0.5	0.8	0.4
40 - 44	539	323	216	1.0	1.4	0.6
45 - 49	863	512	351	1.5	2.1	1.0
50 - 54	1 437	847	590	2.5	3.3	1.8
55 - 59	2 295	1 455	840	3.5	4.8	2.5
60 - 64	3 329	2 226	1 103	5.8	7.9	3.8
65 - 69	3 926	2 648	1 278	8.8	12.2	5.6
70 - 74	4 320	2 924	1 396	14.0	19.3	8.9
75 - 79	4 656	3 117	1 539	24.4	32.7	16.1
80 - 84	7 111	4 210	2 901	41.0	53.7	30.5
85 +	19 442	8 345	11 097	94.2	113.7	83.5
Unknown - Inconnu	55	35[11]	16[11]	..	..	..
China, Macao SAR - Chine, Macao RAS						
2019 (C)						
Total	2 282	1 320	962	3.4	4.2	2.7
0 - 19	15	8	7	♦0.1	♦0.1	♦0.1
20 - 24	11	8	3	♦0.2	♦0.4	♦0.1
25 - 29	9	6	3	♦0.2	♦0.2	♦0.1
30 - 34	19	11	8	♦0.3	♦0.3	♦0.2
35 - 39	24	15	9	♦0.4	♦0.5	♦0.3
40 - 44	38	23	15	0.8	♦1.1	♦0.6
45 - 49	61	45	16	1.2	2.1	♦0.5
50 - 54	59	35	24	1.2	1.8	♦0.8
55 - 59	132	79	53	2.5	3.3	1.8
60 - 64	248	168	80	5.4	7.5	3.4
65 - 69	226	157	69	7.3	10.5	4.4
70 - 74	234	181	53	11.9	17.7	5.6
75 - 79	186	127	59	19.2	25.4	12.6
80 - 84	275	164	111	35.3	48.2	25.2
85 +	745	293	452	88.7	104.6	80.7

Continent, country or area, date, code[a] and age (in years) / Continent, pays ou zone, date, code[a] et âge (en années)	Number - Nombre			Rate - Taux		
	Both sexes Les deux sexes	Male Masculin	Female Féminin	Both sexes Les deux sexes	Male Masculin	Female Féminin
ASIA - ASIE						
Cyprus - Chypre[30]						
2018 (C)						
Total	5 768	3 033	2 735	6.6	7.1	6.1
0	22	16	6	♦2.4	♦3.4	♦1.3
1 - 4	1	-	1	-	-	♦0.1
5 - 9	5	2	3	♦0.1	♦0.1	♦0.1
10 - 14	6	3	3	♦0.1	♦0.1	♦0.1
15 - 19	10	8	2	♦0.2	♦0.3	♦0.1
20 - 24	17	13	4	♦0.3	♦0.4	♦0.1
25 - 29	17	12	5	♦0.2	♦0.3	♦0.1
30 - 34	33	19	14	0.5	♦0.5	♦0.4
35 - 39	34	25	9	0.5	♦0.8	♦0.3
40 - 44	48	28	20	0.9	♦1.0	♦0.7
45 - 49	69	49	20	1.3	1.9	♦0.7
50 - 54	114	69	45	2.1	2.6	1.6
55 - 59	188	111	77	3.5	4.1	2.8
60 - 64	302	190	112	6.3	8.1	4.6
65 - 69	422	279	143	9.3	12.7	6.2
70 - 74	651	422	229	18.3	25.3	12.2
75 - 79	711	400	311	26.2	31.9	21.3
80 - 84	1 055	545	510	58.5	69.9	49.8
85 - 89	1 076	463	613	113.0	122.0	107.1
90 - 94	723	283	440	244.0	253.4	238.4
95 - 99	227	81	146	366.7	355.3	373.4
100 +	37	15	22	334.8	♦384.6	♦307.7
Georgia - Géorgie[27]						
2018 (C)						
Total	46 524	23 836	22 688	12.5	13.3	11.7
0	416	246	170	8.0	9.1	6.8
1 - 4	83	39	44	0.4	0.3	0.4
5 - 9	55	33	22	0.2	0.2	♦0.2
10 - 14	51	36	15	0.2	0.3	♦0.1
15 - 19	105	73	32	0.5	0.7	0.3
20 - 24	185	143	42	0.8	1.2	0.4
25 - 29	272	210	62	1.0	1.6	0.5
30 - 34	332	247	85	1.2	1.8	0.6
35 - 39	456	359	97	1.8	2.9	0.8
40 - 44	770	612	158	3.2	5.1	1.3
45 - 49	1 068	799	269	4.5	7.0	2.2
50 - 54	1 790	1 329	461	7.4	11.6	3.7
55 - 59	2 903	2 094	809	11.1	17.3	5.7
60 - 64	3 569	2 448	1 121	15.8	24.5	8.9
65 - 69	4 358	2 781	1 577	23.0	35.2	14.3
70 - 74	3 868	2 220	1 648	33.3	48.8	23.3
75 - 79	7 293	3 445	3 848	62.2	82.1	51.2
80 - 84	8 704	3 600	5 104	105.6	129.7	93.3
85 - 89	6 503	2 206	4 297	191.7	207.9	184.4
90 - 94	3 104	812	2 292	340.7	372.4	330.8
95 - 99	541	92	449	535.9	582.3	527.3
100 +	98	12	86	16333.3	♦2000.0	...
Indonesia - Indonésie[31]						
2010 (I)						
Total	1 236 154	687 976	548 178	5.2	5.8	4.6
0	106 846	61 546	45 300	24.3	27.2	21.2
1 - 4	37 689	20 958	16 731	2.1	2.2	1.9
5 - 9	19 409	10 807	8 602	0.8	0.9	0.8
10 - 14	15 382	9 029	6 353	0.7	0.8	0.6
15 - 19	23 642	14 948	8 694	1.1	1.4	0.8
20 - 24	27 089	16 020	11 069	1.4	1.6	1.1
25 - 29	31 020	17 855	13 165	1.5	1.7	1.2
30 - 34	31 290	17 168	14 122	1.6	1.7	1.4
35 - 39	38 257	20 382	17 875	2.1	2.2	1.9
40 - 44	49 757	26 901	22 856	3.0	3.2	2.8
45 - 49	65 139	36 351	28 788	4.6	5.2	4.1
50 - 54	89 078	51 820	37 258	7.7	8.8	6.5
55 - 59	86 308	53 355	32 953	10.2	12.1	8.1
60 - 64	105 991	62 663	43 328	17.5	21.4	13.8

19. Deaths by age and sex and age-specific death rates by sex: latest available year, 2010 - 2019
Décès et taux de mortalité selon l'âge et le sexe : dernière année disponible, 2010 - 2019 (continued - suite)

Continent, country or area, date, code[a] and age (in years) / Continent, pays ou zone, date, code[a] et âge (en annèes)	Number - Nombre			Rate - Taux		
	Both sexes / Les deux sexes	Male / Masculin	Female / Féminin	Both sexes / Les deux sexes	Male / Masculin	Female / Féminin
ASIA - ASIE						
Indonesia - Indonésie[31]						
2010 (|)						
65 - 69	107 730	62 508	45 222	23.0	28.1	18.3
70 - 74	138 235	76 159	62 076	40.0	49.7	32.2
75 - 79	92 062	49 343	42 719	46.5	58.6	37.6
80 - 84	86 057	42 547	43 510	75.3	88.4	65.8
85 +	85 173	37 616	47 557	119.4	133.2	110.3
Iran (Islamic Republic of) - Iran (République islamique d')[32]						
2018 (+U)						
Total	*357 687*	*203 195*	*154 492*	...	...	...
0	*7 530*	*4 060*	*3 470*	...	...	...
1 - 4	*3 385*	*1 825*	*1 560*	...	...	...
5 - 9	*2 431*	*1 324*	*1 107*	...	...	...
10 - 14	*2 132*	*1 227*	*905*	...	...	...
15 - 19	*4 408*	*3 128*	*1 280*	...	...	...
20 - 24	*5 517*	*4 093*	*1 424*	...	...	...
25 - 29	*6 954*	*5 040*	*1 914*	...	...	...
30 - 34	*8 553*	*5 764*	*2 789*	...	...	...
35 - 39	*9 063*	*6 149*	*2 914*	...	...	...
40 - 44	*9 111*	*6 090*	*3 021*	...	...	...
45 - 49	*11 445*	*7 691*	*3 754*	...	...	...
50 - 54	*14 278*	*9 340*	*4 938*	...	...	...
55 - 59	*20 220*	*13 054*	*7 166*	...	...	...
60 - 64	*25 694*	*16 006*	*9 688*	...	...	...
65 - 69	*28 838*	*16 382*	*12 456*	...	...	...
70 - 74	*31 458*	*16 870*	*14 588*	...	...	...
75 +	*163 272*	*83 306*	*79 966*	...	...	...
Unknown - Inconnu	*3 398*	*1 846*	*1 552*	..	..	..
Israel - Israël[33]						
2019 (C)						
Total	45 961	22 984	22 975	...	...	...
0	534	316	216	...	...	...
1 - 4	131	73	58	...	...	...
5 - 9	50	31	19	...	...	...
10 - 14	66	32	34	...	...	...
15 - 19	176	130	46	...	...	...
20 - 24	192	139	53	...	...	...
25 - 29	230	165	65	...	...	...
30 - 34	265	187	78	...	...	...
35 - 39	380	241	139	...	...	...
40 - 44	470	284	186	...	...	...
45 - 49	707	460	247	...	...	...
50 - 54	1 006	623	383	...	...	...
55 - 59	1 589	1 026	563	...	...	...
60 - 64	2 381	1 481	900	...	...	...
65 - 69	3 459	2 029	1 430	...	...	...
70 - 74	4 486	2 593	1 893	...	...	...
75 - 79	4 757	2 595	2 162	...	...	...
80 - 84	7 165	3 506	3 659	...	...	...
85 - 89	7 954	3 424	4 530	...	...	...
90 - 94	6 566	2 436	4 130	...	...	...
95 - 99	2 867	1 029	1 838	...	...	...
100 +	516	176	340	...	...	...
Japan - Japon[34]						
2018 (C)						
Total	1 362 470	699 138	663 332	10.8	11.4	10.2
0	1 748	932	816	...	...	...
1 - 4	645	334	311	...	...	...
5 - 9	363	206	157	0.1	0.1	0.1
10 - 14	463	266	197	0.1	0.1	0.1
15 - 19	1 143	747	396	0.2	0.2	0.1
20 - 24	2 006	1 406	600	0.3	0.4	0.2
25 - 29	2 216	1 518	698	0.4	0.5	0.2
30 - 34	3 114	2 065	1 049	0.4	0.6	0.3
35 - 39	4 610	2 955	1 655	0.6	0.8	0.4
40 - 44	8 338	5 243	3 095	0.9	1.1	0.7

19. Deaths by age and sex and age-specific death rates by sex: latest available year, 2010 - 2019
Décès et taux de mortalité selon l'âge et le sexe : dernière année disponible, 2010 - 2019 (continued - suite)

Continent, country or area, date, code[a] and age (in years) / Continent, pays ou zone, date, code[a] et âge (en annèes)	Number - Nombre: Both sexes - Les deux sexes	Number - Nombre: Male - Masculin	Number - Nombre: Female - Féminin	Rate - Taux: Both sexes - Les deux sexes	Rate - Taux: Male - Masculin	Rate - Taux: Female - Féminin
ASIA - ASIE						
Japan - Japon[34]						
2018 (C)						
45 - 49	14 001	8 757	5 244	1.5	1.8	1.1
50 - 54	19 491	12 582	6 909	2.4	3.0	1.7
55 - 59	27 382	18 310	9 072	3.6	4.8	2.4
60 - 64	43 347	30 002	13 345	5.7	8.0	3.5
65 - 69	86 373	59 936	26 437	9.1	13.1	5.4
70 - 74	114 528	77 805	36 723	14.1	20.3	8.5
75 - 79	158 276	101 156	57 120	23.2	33.2	15.1
80 - 84	225 139	129 610	95 529	42.1	59.1	30.2
85 - 89	276 699	133 396	143 303	79.1	109.6	62.8
90 - 94	234 656	83 799	150 857	142.0	188.7	124.9
95 - 99	109 209	23 781	85 428	251.1	312.9	238.0
100 +	28 324	4 026	24 298	404.6	447.3	398.3
Unknown - Inconnu	399	306	93	..	..	..
Kazakhstan						
2019 (U)						
Total	*133 128*	*72 222*	*60 906*	...	...	...
0	*3 360*	*1 944*	*1 416*	...	...	...
1 - 4	*940*	*559*	*381*	...	...	...
5 - 9	*510*	*319*	*191*	...	...	...
10 - 14	*433*	*278*	*155*	...	...	...
15 - 19	*683*	*445*	*238*	...	...	...
20 - 24	*1 081*	*778*	*303*	...	...	...
25 - 29	*1 632*	*1 204*	*428*	...	...	...
30 - 34	*2 674*	*1 966*	*708*	...	...	...
35 - 39	*3 529*	*2 559*	*970*	...	...	...
40 - 44	*4 671*	*3 363*	*1 308*	...	...	...
45 - 49	*5 950*	*4 172*	*1 778*	...	...	...
50 - 54	*7 285*	*5 109*	*2 176*	...	...	...
55 - 59	*10 960*	*7 473*	*3 487*	...	...	...
60 - 64	*13 506*	*8 806*	*4 700*	...	...	...
65 - 69	*14 819*	*8 955*	*5 864*	...	...	...
70 - 74	*12 459*	*6 749*	*5 710*	...	...	...
75 - 79	*14 182*	*6 362*	*7 820*	...	...	...
80 - 84	*18 320*	*6 954*	*11 366*	...	...	...
85 - 89	*9 097*	*2 678*	*6 419*	...	...	...
90 - 94	*5 630*	*1 257*	*4 373*	...	...	...
95 - 99	*1 179*	*232*	*947*	...	...	...
100 +	*198*	*35*	*163*	...	...	...
Unknown - Inconnu	*30*	*25*	*5*	..	..	..
Kuwait - Koweït						
2018 (C)						
Total	6 807	4 333	2 474	1.7	1.7	1.6
0	417	229	188	15.7	16.7	14.6
1 - 4	75	41	34	0.3	0.3	0.3
5 - 9	52	31	21	0.2	0.2	♦0.2
10 - 14	52	27	25	0.2	♦0.2	♦0.2
15 - 19	82	69	13	0.4	0.6	♦0.1
20 - 24	157	128	29	0.7	1.1	♦0.3
25 - 29	218	178	40	1.0	1.4	0.4
30 - 34	221	172	49	0.5	0.7	0.3
35 - 39	291	227	64	0.6	0.7	0.4
40 - 44	368	290	78	0.7	0.8	0.5
45 - 49	448	333	115	1.1	1.2	0.9
50 - 54	535	417	118	1.9	2.2	1.3
55 - 59	505	362	143	2.7	2.8	2.4
60 - 64	547	359	188	4.6	4.4	5.1
65 - 69	529	305	224	8.3	7.2	10.3
70 - 74	569	296	273	17.8	15.5	21.1
75 - 79	601	299	302	35.8	31.4	41.4
80 +	1 078	528	550	72.8	63.3	85.0
80 - 84	564	292	272	...	...	...
85 - 89	306	149	157	...	...	...
90 - 94	142	67	75	...	...	...
95 +	66	20	46	...	...	...
Unknown - Inconnu	62	42	20	..	..	..

Continent, country or area, date, code[a] and age (in years) / Continent, pays ou zone, date, code[a] et âge (en années)	Number - Nombre			Rate - Taux		
	Both sexes / Les deux sexes	Male / Masculin	Female / Féminin	Both sexes / Les deux sexes	Male / Masculin	Female / Féminin
ASIA - ASIE						
Kyrgyzstan - Kirghizstan						
2018 (C)						
Total	32 989	18 457	14 532	5.2	5.9	4.6
0	2 535	1 442	1 093	15.8	17.6	14.0
1 - 4	432	241	191	0.7	0.7	0.6
5 - 9	168	110	58	0.2	0.3	0.2
10 - 14	196	118	78	0.3	0.4	0.3
15 - 19	259	153	106	0.5	0.6	0.4
20 - 24	435	273	162	0.8	1.0	0.6
25 - 29	510	352	158	0.9	1.2	0.6
30 - 34	644	436	208	1.2	1.6	0.8
35 - 39	926	680	246	2.3	3.3	1.2
40 - 44	1 222	885	337	3.5	5.2	1.9
45 - 49	1 658	1 189	469	5.2	7.6	2.8
50 - 54	2 042	1 378	664	7.0	9.9	4.3
55 - 59	2 884	1 902	982	10.6	15.0	6.7
60 - 64	3 038	1 939	1 099	15.9	22.6	10.4
65 - 69	3 206	1 900	1 306	25.5	35.9	17.9
70 - 74	1 941	1 043	898	33.0	44.5	25.4
75 - 79	3 333	1 603	1 730	68.5	86.8	57.2
80 - 84	3 451	1 477	1 974	98.7	122.3	86.3
85 +	4 108	1 336	2 772	155.7	144.5	161.7
85 - 89	2 608	906	1 702	...	...	...
90 - 94	1 176	383	793	...	...	...
95 - 99	261	44	217	...	...	...
100 +	63	3	60	...	...	...
Unknown - Inconnu	1	-	1	..	..	..
Lao People's Democratic Republic - République démocratique populaire lao[35]						
2015 (|)						
Total	27 083	17 507	9 576	4.1	5.2	2.9
0	3 164	1 938	1 226	...	...	...
1 - 4	2 840	1 790	1 050	...	...	...
5 - 9	1 103	730	373	1.5	2.0	1.0
10 - 14	789	500	289	1.1	1.4	0.8
15 - 19	1 023	687	336	1.5	2.0	1.0
20 - 24	893	628	265	1.4	1.9	0.8
25 - 29	832	579	253	1.4	2.0	0.9
30 - 34	709	477	232	1.4	1.8	0.9
35 - 39	918	634	284	2.2	3.0	1.4
40 - 44	1 026	692	334	2.9	3.9	1.9
45 - 49	1 296	857	439	4.3	5.7	2.9
50 - 54	1 486	982	504	5.8	7.8	3.9
55 - 59	1 580	1 044	536	7.7	10.4	5.1
60 - 64	1 749	1 198	551	11.8	16.2	7.4
65 - 69	1 634	1 079	555	15.4	20.8	10.2
70 - 74	1 494	971	523	20.5	28.3	13.6
75 - 79	1 478	920	558	25.0	34.3	17.3
80 +	3 069	1 801	1 268	67.9	93.2	49.0
80 - 84	1 214	732	482	...	...	...
85 - 89	933	567	366	...	...	...
90 - 94	500	291	209	...	...	...
95 - 99	376	184	192	...	...	...
100 +	46	27	19	...	...	...
Malaysia - Malaisie						
2018 (C)						
Total	172 031	98 949	73 082	5.3	5.9	4.7
0	3 622	2 004	1 618	7.1	7.6	6.5
1 - 4	805	438	367	0.4	0.4	0.4
5 - 9	627	375	252	0.2	0.3	0.2
10 - 14	691	443	248	0.3	0.3	0.2
15 - 19	1 759	1 336	423	0.6	0.9	0.3
20 - 24	2 307	1 711	596	0.7	1.0	0.4
25 - 29	2 414	1 691	723	0.7	1.0	0.5
30 - 34	3 120	2 174	946	1.1	1.4	0.7
35 - 39	4 113	2 854	1 259	1.7	2.2	1.1
40 - 44	5 323	3 664	1 659	2.7	3.6	1.8

19. Deaths by age and sex and age-specific death rates by sex: latest available year, 2010 - 2019
Décès et taux de mortalité selon l'âge et le sexe : dernière année disponible, 2010 - 2019 (continued - suite)

Continent, country or area, date, code[a] and age (in years) / Continent, pays ou zone, date, code[a] et âge (en années)	Number - Nombre			Rate - Taux		
	Both sexes / Les deux sexes	Male / Masculin	Female / Féminin	Both sexes / Les deux sexes	Male / Masculin	Female / Féminin
ASIA - ASIE						
Malaysia - Malaisie						
2018 (C)						
45 - 49	7 382	4 963	2 419	4.2	5.6	2.8
50 - 54	10 883	7 095	3 788	6.7	8.7	4.7
55 - 59	14 544	9 347	5 197	10.3	12.9	7.5
60 - 64	17 480	10 856	6 624	15.4	19.2	11.7
65 - 69	19 048	11 563	7 485	22.6	27.8	17.5
70 - 74	19 494	11 389	8 105	34.0	41.2	27.3
75 - 79	20 010	10 745	9 265	59.2	67.5	51.8
80 - 84	19 183	9 122	10 061	97.1	99.8	94.8
85 +	19 226	7 179	12 047	131.0	100.4	160.0
85 - 89	11 612	4 616	6 996	...	...	...
90 - 94	5 440	1 909	3 531	...	...	...
95 +	2 174	654	1 520	...	...	...
Maldives[36]						
2017 (C)						
Total	1 241	750	491	3.5	4.1	2.8
0	64	42	22	8.2	10.3	♦5.8
1 - 4	8	5	3	♦0.3	♦0.3	♦0.2
5 - 9	8	2	6	♦0.2	♦0.1	♦0.4
10 - 14	5	2	3	♦0.2	♦0.1	♦0.2
15 - 19	13	9	4	♦0.5	♦0.7	♦0.3
20 - 24	16	10	6	♦0.5	♦0.6	♦0.4
25 - 29	29	18	11	♦0.8	♦0.9	♦0.6
30 - 34	25	18	7	♦0.7	♦1.0	♦0.4
35 - 39	20	16	4	♦0.7	♦1.2	♦0.3
40 - 44	18	10	8	♦0.9	♦1.0	♦0.8
45 - 49	31	24	7	1.7	♦2.6	♦0.7
50 - 54	36	21	15	2.2	♦2.6	♦1.9
55 - 59	76	47	29	5.6	6.8	♦4.4
60 - 64	79	51	28	8.7	10.8	♦6.4
65 - 69	72	48	24	14.5	18.6	♦10.1
70 - 74	148	82	66	33.4	37.3	29.6
75 - 79	246	130	116	60.8	63.4	58.1
80 +	347	215	132	101.2	111.6	87.9
80 - 84	186	118	68	...	...	...
85 - 89	98	57	41	...	...	...
90 - 94	43	28	15	...	...	...
95 - 99	13	8	5	...	...	...
100 +	7	4	3	...	...	...
Mongolia - Mongolie						
2019 (+C)						
Total	18 403	11 349	7 054	5.6	7.1	4.2
0	1 041	583	458	13.7	14.9	12.3
1 - 4	216	120	96	0.7	0.7	0.6
5 - 9	111	67	44	0.3	0.4	0.2
10 - 14	89	58	31	0.3	0.4	0.2
15 - 19	148	96	52	0.7	0.8	0.5
20 - 24	239	165	74	1.0	1.3	0.6
25 - 29	375	276	99	1.3	1.9	0.7
30 - 34	517	397	120	1.7	2.7	0.8
35 - 39	769	571	198	3.1	4.7	1.6
40 - 44	1 087	813	274	4.9	7.5	2.4
45 - 49	1 455	1 076	379	7.5	11.6	3.7
50 - 54	1 702	1 224	478	10.3	16.0	5.4
55 - 59	2 061	1 431	630	14.8	22.9	8.2
60 - 64	1 836	1 215	621	19.9	30.7	11.8
65 - 69	1 474	891	583	27.9	41.2	18.7
70 - 74	1 267	673	594	39.0	52.7	30.2
75 - 79	1 475	701	774	59.8	71.1	52.3
80 - 84	1 110	527	583	85.6	110.6	71.1
85 - 89	868	310	558	132.6	158.4	121.5
90 - 94	368	106	262	206.0	216.3	202.2
95 - 99	166	46	120	342.3	484.2	307.7
100 +	29	3	26	♦475.4	♦300.0	♦509.8

19. Deaths by age and sex and age-specific death rates by sex: latest available year, 2010 - 2019
Décès et taux de mortalité selon l'âge et le sexe : dernière année disponible, 2010 - 2019 (continued - suite)

Continent, country or area, date, code[a] and age (in years) Continent, pays ou zone, date, code[a] et âge (en années)	Number - Nombre			Rate - Taux		
	Both sexes Les deux sexes	Male Masculin	Female Féminin	Both sexes Les deux sexes	Male Masculin	Female Féminin
ASIA - ASIE						
Myanmar[37]						
2017 (+U)						
Total	*231 210*	*134 669*	*96 541*	...	...	...
0	*9 761*	*5 485*	*4 276*	...	...	...
1 - 4	*1 979*	*1 037*	*942*	...	...	...
5 - 9	*1 800*	*1 004*	*796*	...	...	...
10 - 14	*1 734*	*1 011*	*723*	...	...	...
15 - 19	*2 988*	*1 984*	*1 004*	...	...	...
20 - 24	*4 544*	*3 105*	*1 439*	...	...	...
25 - 29	*6 116*	*4 438*	*1 678*	...	...	...
30 - 34	*8 933*	*6 876*	*2 057*	...	...	...
35 - 39	*11 307*	*8 819*	*2 488*	...	...	...
40 - 44	*12 361*	*9 277*	*3 084*	...	...	...
45 - 49	*14 255*	*10 214*	*4 041*	...	...	...
50 - 54	*15 836*	*10 643*	*5 193*	...	...	...
55 - 59	*17 030*	*10 688*	*6 342*	...	...	...
60 - 64	*19 061*	*11 193*	*7 868*	...	...	...
65 - 69	*20 308*	*11 124*	*9 184*	...	...	...
70 - 74	*19 326*	*9 978*	*9 348*	...	...	...
75 - 79	*19 697*	*9 518*	*10 179*	...	...	...
80 - 84	*18 924*	*8 329*	*10 595*	...	...	...
85 +	*24 344*	*9 347*	*14 997*	...	...	...
Unknown - Inconnu	*906*	*599*	*307*	..	..	..
Nepal - Népal[38]						
2011 (I)						
Total	129 978	73 961[11]	54 621[11]	4.5	5.2	3.8
0	10 132	5 902[11]	4 127[11]	...	...	...
1 - 4	5 128	2 563[11]	2 396[11]	...	...	...
5 - 9	2 416	1 409[11]	982[11]	0.7	0.8	0.6
10 - 14	2 056	1 177[11]	866[11]	0.7	0.7	0.6
15 - 19	2 911	1 540[11]	1 351[11]	1.0	1.0	0.9
20 - 24	3 344	1 915[11]	1 407[11]	1.2	1.3	1.0
25 - 29	3 216	1 940[11]	1 256[11]	1.3	1.6	1.0
30 - 34	2 980	1 869[11]	1 097[11]	1.4	1.9	1.0
35 - 39	3 820	2 387[11]	1 402[11]	2.2	2.9	1.5
40 - 44	4 066	2 574[11]	1 463[11]	2.7	3.6	1.9
45 - 49	4 951	2 963[11]	1 951[11]	4.0	4.9	3.1
50 - 54	5 952	3 605[11]	2 289[11]	5.9	7.2	4.5
55 - 59	6 618	3 965[11]	2 587[11]	8.2	9.8	6.4
60 - 64	10 616	6 012[11]	4 514[11]	16.9	19.0	14.5
65 - 69	11 061	6 284[11]	4 691[11]	23.6	26.7	20.1
70 - 74	12 951	7 363[11]	5 472[11]	39.4	45.3	32.9
75 - 79	10 936	6 135[11]	4 694[11]	53.6	61.2	45.2
80 +	23 700	12 661[11]	10 808[11]	136.2	146.6	123.3
Unknown - Inconnu	3 124	1 697[11]	1 268[11]	..	..	..
Oman						
2019 (U)						
Total	*8 581*	*5 371*	*3 210*	...	...	...
0	*686*	*367*	*319*	...	...	...
1 - 4	*193*	*100*	*93*	...	...	...
5 - 9	*95*	*52*	*43*	...	...	...
10 - 14	*71*	*40*	*31*	...	...	...
15 - 19	*100*	*72*	*28*	...	...	...
20 - 24	*187*	*140*	*47*	...	...	...
25 - 29	*279*	*223*	*56*	...	...	...
30 - 34	*325*	*251*	*74*	...	...	...
35 - 39	*364*	*275*	*89*	...	...	...
40 - 44	*362*	*289*	*73*	...	...	...
45 - 49	*359*	*279*	*80*	...	...	...
50 - 54	*380*	*292*	*88*	...	...	...
55 - 59	*499*	*361*	*138*	...	...	...
60 - 64	*634*	*380*	*254*	...	...	...
65 +	*4 047*	*2 250*	*1 797*	...	...	...

Continent, country or area, date, code[a] and age (in years) / Continent, pays ou zone, date, code[a] et âge (en années)	Number - Nombre			Rate - Taux		
	Both sexes / Les deux sexes	Male / Masculin	Female / Féminin	Both sexes / Les deux sexes	Male / Masculin	Female / Féminin
ASIA - ASIE						
Philippines						
2018 (C)						
Total	590 709	337 789	252 920	5.6	6.3	4.8
0	21 019	12 174	8 845	...	...	...
1 - 4	7 805	4 215	3 590	...	...	...
5 - 9	5 212	2 830	2 382	0.5	0.5	0.4
10 - 14	4 670	2 718	1 952	0.4	0.5	0.4
15 - 19	7 788	5 172	2 616	0.8	1.0	0.5
20 - 24	11 171	7 715	3 456	1.2	1.6	0.7
25 - 29	13 180	9 088	4 092	1.5	2.0	1.0
30 - 34	14 526	9 828	4 698	1.8	2.4	1.2
35 - 39	18 831	12 547	6 284	2.6	3.5	1.8
40 - 44	23 109	15 243	7 866	3.7	4.8	2.6
45 - 49	31 150	20 368	10 782	5.6	7.2	3.9
50 - 54	39 148	25 383	13 765	8.2	10.6	5.8
55 - 59	47 841	31 055	16 786	12.0	15.8	8.4
60 - 64	55 893	35 710	20 183	18.0	23.8	12.5
65 - 69	60 201	37 129	23 072	26.9	35.8	19.2
70 - 74	57 696	33 346	24 350	39.5	52.3	29.5
75 - 79	57 158	29 640	27 518	58.1	75.3	46.7
80 +	114 166	43 513	70 653	128.7	142.4	121.5
80 - 84	51 526	22 615	28 911	...	...	...
85 - 89	36 544	13 333	23 211	...	...	...
90 - 94	18 388	5 495	12 893	...	...	...
95 +	7 708	2 070	5 638	...	...	...
Unknown - Inconnu	145	115	30	..	..	..
Qatar						
2018 (C)						
Total	2 385	1 725	660	0.9	0.8	0.9
0	172	83	89	6.1	5.8	6.5
1 - 4	41	27	14	0.4	♦0.5	♦0.2
5 - 9	7	4	3	♦0.1	♦0.1	-
10 - 14	20	8	12	♦0.2	♦0.1	♦0.2
15 - 19	52	45	7	0.6	0.9	♦0.2
20 - 24	91	80	11	0.3	0.4	♦0.2
25 - 29	129	115	14	0.3	0.3	♦0.2
30 - 34	163	146	17	0.3	0.4	♦0.2
35 - 39	145	127	18	0.4	0.4	♦0.2
40 - 44	165	146	19	0.6	0.7	♦0.3
45 - 49	162	139	23	0.9	1.0	♦0.6
50 - 54	166	128	38	1.5	1.5	1.6
55 - 59	179	140	39	2.7	2.7	2.5
60 - 64	164	117	47	4.7	4.6	5.0
65 - 69	161	98	63	10.7	9.8	12.6
70 - 74	137	82	55	17.7	17.5	18.0
75 - 79	149	80	69	32.7	31.1	34.7
80 +	280	158	122	66.7	69.0	63.9
80 - 84	132	72	60	...	...	...
85 - 89	88	52	36	...	...	...
90 - 94	40	26	14	...	...	...
95 +	20	8	12	...	...	...
Unknown - Inconnu	2	2	-	..	..	..
Republic of Korea - République de Corée[39]						
2018 (C)						
Total	298 820	161 187	137 633	5.8	6.2	5.3
0	931	534	397	2.7	3.0	2.4
1 - 4	220	111	109	0.1	0.1	0.1
5 - 9	177	102	75	0.1	0.1	0.1
10 - 14	221	118	103	0.1	0.1	0.1
15 - 19	620	386	234	0.2	0.3	0.2
20 - 24	1 144	728	416	0.3	0.4	0.3
25 - 29	1 384	926	458	0.4	0.5	0.3
30 - 34	1 861	1 175	686	0.6	0.7	0.4
35 - 39	3 204	2 057	1 147	0.8	1.0	0.6
40 - 44	4 513	3 006	1 507	1.1	1.5	0.8
45 - 49	8 071	5 653	2 418	1.8	2.4	1.1
50 - 54	11 207	8 127	3 080	2.7	3.9	1.5

19. Deaths by age and sex and age-specific death rates by sex: latest available year, 2010 - 2019
Décès et taux de mortalité selon l'âge et le sexe : dernière année disponible, 2010 - 2019 (continued - suite)

Continent, country or area, date, code[a] and age (in years) / Continent, pays ou zone, date, code[a] et âge (en annèes)	Number - Nombre			Rate - Taux		
	Both sexes / Les deux sexes	Male / Masculin	Female / Féminin	Both sexes / Les deux sexes	Male / Masculin	Female / Féminin
ASIA - ASIE						
Republic of Korea - République de Corée[39]						
2018 (C)						
55 - 59	16 667	12 347	4 320	3.8	5.7	2.0
60 - 64	18 793	13 872	4 921	5.5	8.3	2.9
65 - 69	20 397	14 568	5 829	8.6	12.9	4.8
70 - 74	25 964	17 340	8 624	14.5	21.0	8.9
75 - 79	45 173	26 917	18 256	28.6	40.5	19.9
80 - 84	53 905	26 823	27 082	54.5	75.4	42.8
85 - 89	46 046	16 805	29 241	100.2	130.7	88.4
90 - 94	26 788	7 154	19 634	180.4	216.9	170.0
95 - 99	9 810	2 152	7 658	266.3	296.4	258.9
100 +	1 681	261	1 420	423.2	468.6	415.8
Unknown - Inconnu	43	25	18	..	..	..
Saudi Arabia - Arabie saoudite[40]						
2016 (|)						
Total	58 097	35 497	22 600	1.8	1.9	1.7
0 - 4	5 084	2 273	2 811	1.9	1.7	2.1
5 - 9	1 033	577	456	0.4	0.4	0.3
10 - 14	2 125	1 206	919	0.9	1.0	0.8
15 - 19	1 487	1 368	119	0.7	1.2	0.1
20 - 24	4 859	3 146	1 713	2.0	2.4	1.5
25 - 29	3 926	2 673	1 253	1.3	1.6	0.9
30 - 34	2 106	1 582	524	0.7	0.9	0.4
35 - 39	3 232	2 207	1 025	1.0	1.0	0.8
40 - 44	2 714	2 027	687	0.9	1.0	0.6
45 - 49	2 629	1 233	1 396	1.2	0.8	1.8
50 - 54	3 031	2 571	460	1.9	2.4	0.9
55 - 59	3 901	2 404	1 497	3.6	3.3	4.0
60 - 64	2 895	1 844	1 051	4.0	4.1	3.8
65 - 69	2 547	1 181	1 366	6.3	5.4	7.4
70 - 74	4 186	2 922	1 264	15.5	20.7	9.8
75 - 79	1 846	709	1 137	11.5	8.3	14.9
80 +	10 496	5 574	4 922	54.6	58.1	51.1
80 - 84	4 678	1 900	2 778	...	...	...
85 +	5 818	3 674	2 144	...	...	...
Singapore - Singapour						
2019 (+C)						
Total	21 446	11 653	9 793	5.3	5.9	4.8
0	75	39	36	...	...	...
1 - 4	29	13	16	...	...	...
5 - 9	19	8	11	♦0.1	♦0.1	♦0.1
10 - 14	9	6	3	-	♦0.1	-
15 - 19	48	24	24	0.2	♦0.2	♦0.2
20 - 24	85	61	24	0.3	0.5	♦0.2
25 - 29	125	82	43	0.4	0.6	0.3
30 - 34	178	117	61	0.6	0.8	0.4
35 - 39	211	139	72	0.7	1.0	0.5
40 - 44	293	189	104	1.0	1.3	0.7
45 - 49	466	304	162	1.5	2.0	1.0
50 - 54	723	443	280	2.4	3.0	1.8
55 - 59	1 192	739	453	3.9	4.8	3.0
60 - 64	1 732	1 115	617	6.2	8.1	4.4
65 - 69	2 099	1 349	750	9.5	12.4	6.7
70 - 74	2 398	1 492	906	16.0	20.9	11.5
75 - 79	2 663	1 527	1 136	28.2	36.2	21.7
80 - 84	3 174	1 704	1 470	51.0	65.3	40.6
85 - 89	2 945	1 323	1 622	86.8	106.0	75.6
90 +	2 982	979	2 003	153.5	168.4	147.1
90 - 94	2 042	731	1 311	...	...	...
95 - 99	735	213	522	...	...	...
100 +	205	35	170	...	...	...
Sri Lanka						
2014 (+C)						
Total	128 185	72 634	55 551	6.2	7.2	5.2
0	2 662	1 505	1 157	...	...	...
1 - 4	533	302	231	...	...	...
5 - 9	384	219	165	0.2	0.2	0.2

19. Deaths by age and sex and age-specific death rates by sex: latest available year, 2010 - 2019
Décès et taux de mortalité selon l'âge et le sexe : dernière année disponible, 2010 - 2019 (continued - suite)

Continent, country or area, date, code[a] and age (in years) / Continent, pays ou zone, date, code[a] et âge (en années)	Number - Nombre: Both sexes / Les deux sexes	Number - Nombre: Male / Masculin	Number - Nombre: Female / Féminin	Rate - Taux: Both sexes / Les deux sexes	Rate - Taux: Male / Masculin	Rate - Taux: Female / Féminin
ASIA - ASIE						
Sri Lanka						
2014 (+C)						
10 - 14	406	231	175	0.2	0.3	0.2
15 - 19	903	611	292	0.5	0.7	0.3
20 - 24	1 185	837	348	0.8	1.1	0.4
25 - 29	1 232	869	363	0.8	1.1	0.4
30 - 34	1 617	1 118	499	1.0	1.4	0.6
35 - 39	1 943	1 321	622	1.4	1.9	0.8
40 - 44	2 604	1 805	799	1.9	2.7	1.1
45 - 49	4 271	2 996	1 275	3.3	4.7	1.9
50 - 54	6 617	4 481	2 136	5.3	7.6	3.3
55 - 59	8 599	5 800	2 799	7.9	11.4	4.9
60 - 64	11 743	7 616	4 127	12.5	17.5	8.2
65 - 69	14 024	8 651	5 373	21.7	29.8	15.1
70 - 74	15 975	9 097	6 878	37.9	48.9	29.3
75 - 79	15 993	8 382	7 611	55.3	70.4	44.8
80 +	37 443	16 760	20 683	134.2	152.4	122.4
80 - 84	16 638	7 790	8 848	...	...	...
85 +	20 805	8 970	11 835	...	...	...
Unknown - Inconnu	51	33	18	..	..	..
State of Palestine - État de Palestine[41]						
2018 (U)						
Total	*12 296*	*6 846*	*5 450*	...	...	...
0	*897*	*486*	*411*	...	...	...
1 - 4	*300*	*174*	*126*	...	...	...
5 - 9	*134*	*89*	*45*	...	...	...
10 - 14	*151*	*100*	*51*	...	...	...
15 - 19	*176*	*142*	*34*	...	...	...
20 - 24	*247*	*193*	*54*	...	...	...
25 - 29	*265*	*199*	*66*	...	...	...
30 - 34	*198*	*142*	*56*	...	...	...
35 - 39	*210*	*125*	*85*	...	...	...
40 - 44	*267*	*163*	*104*	...	...	...
45 - 49	*368*	*234*	*134*	...	...	...
50 - 54	*577*	*383*	*194*	...	...	...
55 - 59	*844*	*555*	*289*	...	...	...
60 - 64	*973*	*619*	*354*	...	...	...
65 - 69	*1 076*	*643*	*433*	...	...	...
70 - 74	*1 340*	*700*	*640*	...	...	...
75 - 79	*1 198*	*560*	*638*	...	...	...
80 - 84	*1 306*	*585*	*721*	...	...	...
85 - 89	*1 014*	*421*	*593*	...	...	...
90 - 94	*507*	*231*	*276*	...	...	...
95 - 99	*189*	*72*	*117*	...	...	...
100 +	*59*	*30*	*29*	...	...	...
Tajikistan - Tadjikistan[27]						
2017 (U)						
Total	*32 027*	*17 894*	*14 133*	...	...	...
0	*2 405*	*1 384*	*1 021*	...	...	...
1 - 4	*610*	*335*	*275*	...	...	...
5 - 9	*230*	*128*	*102*	...	...	...
10 - 14	*186*	*120*	*66*	...	...	...
15 - 19	*268*	*161*	*107*	...	...	...
20 - 24	*363*	*231*	*132*	...	...	...
25 - 29	*561*	*336*	*225*	...	...	...
30 - 34	*670*	*415*	*255*	...	...	...
35 - 39	*704*	*435*	*269*	...	...	...
40 - 44	*952*	*602*	*350*	...	...	...
45 - 49	*1 219*	*671*	*548*	...	...	...
50 - 54	*1 732*	*1 004*	*728*	...	...	...
55 - 59	*2 599*	*1 550*	*1 049*	...	...	...
60 - 64	*2 870*	*1 605*	*1 265*	...	...	...
65 - 69	*3 024*	*1 723*	*1 301*	...	...	...
70 - 74	*2 433*	*1 427*	*1 006*	...	...	...
75 - 79	*4 025*	*2 264*	*1 761*	...	...	...
80 - 84	*3 599*	*1 848*	*1 751*	...	...	...
85 - 89	*2 381*	*1 169*	*1 212*	...	...	...

19. Deaths by age and sex and age-specific death rates by sex: latest available year, 2010 - 2019
Décès et taux de mortalité selon l'âge et le sexe : dernière année disponible, 2010 - 2019 (continued - suite)

Continent, country or area, date, code[a] and age (in years) Continent, pays ou zone, date, code[a] et âge (en années)	Number - Nombre Both sexes Les deux sexes	 Male Masculin	 Female Féminin	Rate - Taux Both sexes Les deux sexes	 Male Masculin	 Female Féminin
ASIA - ASIE						
Tajikistan - Tadjikistan[27]						
2017 (U)						
90 - 94	882	395	487	...	...	...
95 - 99	247	74	173	...	...	...
100 +	10	4	6	...	...	...
Unknown - Inconnu	57	13	44	..	..	..
Thailand - Thaïlande[42]						
2018 (+U)						
Total	461 818	262 171	199 647	...	...	...
0	3 800	2 180	1 620	...	...	...
1 - 4	1 502	867	635	...	...	...
5 - 9	1 160	727	433	...	...	...
10 - 14	1 722	1 127	595	...	...	...
15 - 19	4 224	3 269	955	...	...	...
20 - 24	5 508	4 225	1 283	...	...	...
25 - 29	6 399	4 877	1 522	...	...	...
30 - 34	7 905	5 856	2 049	...	...	...
35 - 39	11 992	8 838	3 154	...	...	...
40 - 44	17 427	12 710	4 717	...	...	...
45 - 49	23 348	16 429	6 919	...	...	...
50 - 54	30 368	20 379	9 989	...	...	...
55 - 59	35 683	23 428	12 255	...	...	...
60 - 64	39 681	24 895	14 786	...	...	...
65 - 69	44 667	26 363	18 304	...	...	...
70 - 74	44 904	24 880	20 024	...	...	...
75 - 79	50 472	26 177	24 295	...	...	...
80 - 84	54 315	25 172	29 143	...	...	...
85 - 89	43 694	18 006	25 688	...	...	...
90 - 94	23 550	8 745	14 805	...	...	...
95 - 99	7 685	2 513	5 172	...	...	...
100 +	1 807	505	1 302	...	...	...
Unknown - Inconnu	5	3	2	..	..	..
Turkey - Turquie[43]						
2018 (C)						
Total	426 106	232 799	193 307	5.2	5.7	4.7
0	11 629	6 311	5 318	9.6	10.1	9.0
1 - 4	2 611	1 420	1 191	0.5	0.5	0.5
5 - 9	1 176	663	513	0.2	0.2	0.2
10 - 14	1 315	796	519	0.2	0.2	0.2
15 - 19	2 692	1 920	772	0.4	0.6	0.2
20 - 24	3 153	2 403	750	0.5	0.7	0.2
25 - 29	3 242	2 406	836	0.5	0.8	0.3
30 - 34	3 619	2 487	1 132	0.6	0.8	0.4
35 - 39	4 882	3 259	1 623	0.7	1.0	0.5
40 - 44	6 599	4 306	2 293	1.1	1.5	0.8
45 - 49	9 943	6 502	3 441	1.9	2.4	1.3
50 - 54	15 830	10 767	5 063	3.4	4.5	2.2
55 - 59	23 336	16 112	7 224	5.6	7.8	3.4
60 - 64	33 141	22 429	10 712	9.6	13.3	6.1
65 - 69	40 342	26 055	14 287	15.4	20.9	10.5
70 - 74	46 722	27 791	18 931	25.2	33.3	18.5
75 - 79	57 054	30 418	26 636	45.2	56.3	36.9
80 - 84	62 507	30 236	32 271	78.8	94.8	68.0
85 - 89	60 214	25 162	35 052	123.9	137.5	115.7
90 - 94	28 786	9 528	19 258	196.8	230.7	183.5
95 - 99	6 074	1 655	4 419	259.6	321.9	242.0
100 +	1 239	173	1 066	238.2	247.9	236.7
United Arab Emirates - Émirats arabes unis						
2018 (C)						
Total	8 794	6 197	2 597	...	...	...
0	500	276	224	...	...	...
1 - 4	159	81	78	...	...	...
5 - 9	54	25	29	...	...	...
10 - 14	53	32	21	...	...	...
15 - 19	103	73	30	...	...	...
20 - 24	299	260	39	...	...	...
25 - 29	392	329	63	...	...	...

19. Deaths by age and sex and age-specific death rates by sex: latest available year, 2010 - 2019
Décès et taux de mortalité selon l'âge et le sexe : dernière année disponible, 2010 - 2019 (continued - suite)

Continent, country or area, date, code[a] and age (in years) / Continent, pays ou zone, date, code[a] et âge (en années)	Number - Nombre			Rate - Taux		
	Both sexes / Les deux sexes	Male / Masculin	Female / Féminin	Both sexes / Les deux sexes	Male / Masculin	Female / Féminin
ASIA - ASIE						
United Arab Emirates - Émirats arabes unis						
2018 (C)						
30 - 34	536	452	84	...	...	...
35 - 39	606	500	106	...	...	...
40 - 44	594	478	116	...	...	...
45 - 49	636	536	100	...	...	...
50 - 54	628	518	110	...	...	...
55 - 59	649	520	129	...	...	...
60 - 64	662	491	171	...	...	...
65 - 69	607	389	218	...	...	...
70 - 74	579	344	235	...	...	...
75 - 79	552	312	240	...	...	...
80 - 84	480	244	236	...	...	...
85 +	703	337	366	...	...	...
Unknown - Inconnu	2	-	2	..	..	..
Uzbekistan - Ouzbékistan[27]						
2018 (+C)						
Total	154 913	84 592	70 321	4.7	5.1	4.3
0	7 569	4 382	3 187	10.6	11.8	9.4
1 - 4	2 272	1 330	942	0.8	0.9	0.7
5 - 9	987	592	395	0.3	0.4	0.3
10 - 14	991	574	417	0.4	0.4	0.3
15 - 19	1 609	930	679	0.6	0.7	0.5
20 - 24	2 241	1 311	930	0.7	0.8	0.6
25 - 29	2 518	1 535	983	0.8	0.9	0.6
30 - 34	3 190	1 969	1 221	1.1	1.3	0.8
35 - 39	3 876	2 416	1 460	1.6	2.1	1.2
40 - 44	4 849	3 093	1 756	2.4	3.1	1.7
45 - 49	6 474	4 005	2 469	3.6	4.5	2.7
50 - 54	9 062	5 621	3 441	5.7	7.4	4.2
55 - 59	14 047	8 829	5 218	9.6	12.5	6.8
60 - 64	16 207	9 675	6 532	15.8	19.9	12.2
65 - 69	16 637	9 289	7 348	25.8	31.2	21.2
70 - 74	11 807	6 220	5 587	40.3	46.6	35.1
75 - 79	17 684	8 896	8 788	67.6	77.0	60.2
80 - 84	16 275	7 475	8 800	106.8	121.1	97.0
85 +	16 618	6 450	10 168	122.0	135.2	114.9
EUROPE						
Åland Islands - Îles d'Åland						
2018 (C)						
Total	272	141	131	9.2	9.5	8.8
0	-	-	-	-	-	-
1 - 4	-	-	-	-	-	-
5 - 9	-	-	-	-	-	-
10 - 14	-	-	-	-	-	-
15 - 19	-	-	-	-	-	-
20 - 24	1	-	1	♦0.8	-	♦1.6
25 - 29	-	-	-	-	-	-
30 - 34	1	-	1	♦0.6	-	♦1.1
35 - 39	1	-	1	♦0.5	-	♦1.1
40 - 44	5	4	1	♦2.7	♦4.3	♦1.1
45 - 49	1	1	-	♦0.5	♦1.0	-
50 - 54	5	3	2	♦2.3	♦2.8	♦1.8
55 - 59	6	5	1	♦3.1	♦5.2	♦1.0
60 - 64	14	10	4	♦7.2	♦10.8	♦3.9
65 - 69	22	12	10	♦11.3	♦13.0	♦9.8
70 - 74	27	16	11	♦15.0	♦17.8	♦12.2
75 - 79	35	24	11	30.0	♦40.5	♦19.2
80 - 84	50	30	20	62.7	♦87.2	♦44.2
85 - 89	45	22	23	91.9	♦110.3	♦79.3
90 - 94	43	12	31	174.4	♦171.4	175.6
95 - 99	13	2	11	♦218.5	♦125.0	♦252.9
100 +	3	-	3	♦750.0	-	♦1000.0

19. Deaths by age and sex and age-specific death rates by sex: latest available year, 2010 - 2019
Décès et taux de mortalité selon l'âge et le sexe : dernière année disponible, 2010 - 2019 (continued - suite)

Continent, country or area, date, code[a] and age (in years) Continent, pays ou zone, date, code[a] et âge (en années)	Number - Nombre Both sexes Les deux sexes	Male Masculin	Female Féminin	Rate - Taux Both sexes Les deux sexes	Male Masculin	Female Féminin
EUROPE						
Albania - Albanie						
2018 (C)						
Total	21 804	11 667	10 137	7.6	8.1	7.1
0	257	146	111	8.6	9.3	7.8
1 - 4	34	20	14	0.3	♦0.3	♦0.2
5 - 9	32	13	19	0.2	♦0.2	♦0.2
10 - 14	43	23	20	0.2	♦0.3	♦0.2
15 - 19	71	38	33	0.3	0.4	0.3
20 - 24	105	76	29	0.4	0.6	♦0.2
25 - 29	106	77	29	0.4	0.6	♦0.3
30 - 34	116	86	30	0.6	0.8	♦0.3
35 - 39	155	102	53	0.9	1.2	0.6
40 - 44	201	123	78	1.2	1.5	0.9
45 - 49	338	218	120	1.9	2.5	1.3
50 - 54	572	391	181	3.0	4.1	1.8
55 - 59	995	651	344	4.8	6.4	3.3
60 - 64	1 386	908	478	7.9	10.5	5.3
65 - 69	1 683	1 093	590	12.6	16.7	8.7
70 - 74	2 098	1 282	816	20.8	25.9	15.9
75 - 79	3 717	2 013	1 704	42.4	48.3	37.1
80 - 84	4 400	2 260	2 140	86.6	93.2	80.5
85 +	5 495	2 147	3 348	232.8	203.3	256.8
85 - 89	3 232	1 457	1 775	...	...	...
90 - 94	1 532	499	1 033	...	...	...
95 - 99	575	170	405	...	...	...
100 +	156	21	135	...	...	...
Andorra - Andorre						
2018 (C)						
Total	335	178	157	4.5	4.7	4.3
0	1	-	1	...	...	...
1 - 4	-	-	-	...	...	...
5 - 9	-	-	-	-	-	-
10 - 14	-	-	-	-	-	-
15 - 19	2	1	1	♦0.5	♦0.5	♦0.5
20 - 24	1	1	-	♦0.3	♦0.5	-
25 - 29	1	-	1	♦0.2	-	♦0.5
30 - 34	3	2	1	♦0.6	♦0.8	♦0.4
35 - 39	2	1	1	♦0.3	♦0.3	♦0.3
40 - 44	4	3	1	♦0.6	♦0.8	♦0.3
45 - 49	15	9	6	♦2.2	♦2.5	♦1.8
50 - 54	3	2	1	♦0.5	♦0.6	♦0.3
55 - 59	28	16	12	♦5.0	♦5.5	♦4.4
60 - 64	22	12	10	♦5.2	♦5.4	♦5.0
65 - 69	25	20	5	♦7.7	♦11.8	♦3.2
70 - 74	26	21	5	♦10.2	♦15.7	♦4.1
75 - 79	38	23	15	23.3	♦30.4	♦17.2
80 - 84	50	30	20	41.7	♦56.1	♦30.1
85 +	114	37	77	83.9	73.3	90.2
85 - 89	50	18	32	...	...	...
90 - 94	40	16	24	...	...	...
95 - 99	22	3	19	...	...	...
100 +	2	-	2	...	...	...
Austria - Autriche[44]						
2018 (C)						
Total	83 975	40 851	43 124	9.5	9.4	9.6
0	231	132	99	2.7	3.0	2.4
1 - 4	43	24	19	0.1	♦0.1	♦0.1
5 - 9	31	18	13	0.1	♦0.1	♦0.1
10 - 14	33	21	12	0.1	♦0.1	♦0.1
15 - 19	120	85	35	0.3	0.4	0.2
20 - 24	189	154	35	0.4	0.6	0.1
25 - 29	241	167	74	0.4	0.5	0.3
30 - 34	304	199	105	0.5	0.7	0.4
35 - 39	403	247	156	0.7	0.8	0.5
40 - 44	636	384	252	1.1	1.4	0.9
45 - 49	1 109	712	397	1.7	2.2	1.2
50 - 54	1 994	1 261	733	2.8	3.5	2.1

Continent, country or area, date, code[a] and age (in years) / Continent, pays ou zone, date, code[a] et âge (en années)	Number - Nombre			Rate - Taux		
	Both sexes / Les deux sexes	Male / Masculin	Female / Féminin	Both sexes / Les deux sexes	Male / Masculin	Female / Féminin
EUROPE						
Austria - Autriche[44]						
2018 (C)						
55 - 59	3 249	2 132	1 117	5.0	6.5	3.4
60 - 64	4 069	2 654	1 415	7.6	10.3	5.2
65 - 69	5 608	3 551	2 057	12.5	16.8	8.7
70 - 74	7 555	4 606	2 949	19.7	26.2	14.2
75 - 79	11 597	6 666	4 931	29.9	39.0	22.7
80 - 84	11 784	5 886	5 898	55.2	67.8	46.5
85 - 89	15 789	6 623	9 166	109.3	129.2	98.4
90 - 94	13 471	4 103	9 368	207.5	228.8	199.4
95 - 99	5 032	1 149	3 883	333.9	383.5	321.6
100 +	487	77	410	481.0	554.0	469.4
Belarus - Bélarus						
2018 (C)						
Total	120 053	59 830	60 223	12.7	13.5	11.9
0	238	143	95	2.4	2.8	2.0
1 - 4	100	66	34	0.2	0.3	0.1
5 - 9	43	31	12	0.1	0.1	-
10 - 14	74	42	32	0.2	0.2	0.1
15 - 19	153	111	42	0.3	0.5	0.2
20 - 24	239	189	50	0.5	0.7	0.2
25 - 29	576	429	147	0.8	1.2	0.4
30 - 34	1 118	861	257	1.4	2.2	0.7
35 - 39	1 591	1 197	394	2.2	3.4	1.1
40 - 44	2 339	1 734	605	3.6	5.4	1.8
45 - 49	3 373	2 491	882	5.3	8.2	2.6
50 - 54	5 012	3 705	1 307	7.7	12.2	3.8
55 - 59	8 631	6 283	2 348	11.7	18.8	5.8
60 - 64	11 268	8 072	3 196	17.7	29.8	8.7
65 - 69	12 633	8 262	4 371	25.1	42.0	14.3
70 - 74	10 475	6 080	4 395	35.9	58.4	23.4
75 - 79	15 160	6 805	8 355	56.2	85.3	44.0
80 - 84	18 930	6 721	12 209	90.0	124.8	78.0
85 - 89	17 005	4 441	12 564	155.3	187.3	146.4
90 - 94	9 077	1 850	7 227	239.1	253.4	235.7
95 - 99	1 798	280	1 518	284.1	259.1	289.2
100 +	209	29	180	163.9	♦174.7	162.2
Unknown - Inconnu	11	8	3	..	..	..
Belgium - Belgique[45]						
2018 (C)						
Total	110 693	54 092	56 601	9.7	9.6	9.8
0	444	252	192	3.7	4.2	3.3
1 - 4	79	42	37	0.2	0.2	0.2
5 - 9	54	31	23	0.1	0.1	♦0.1
10 - 14	55	35	20	0.1	0.1	♦0.1
15 - 19	131	85	46	0.2	0.3	0.1
20 - 24	252	187	65	0.4	0.5	0.2
25 - 29	299	210	89	0.4	0.6	0.2
30 - 34	422	280	142	0.6	0.8	0.4
35 - 39	618	403	215	0.8	1.1	0.6
40 - 44	866	524	342	1.2	1.4	0.9
45 - 49	1 509	927	582	1.9	2.3	1.5
50 - 54	2 428	1 489	939	3.0	3.6	2.4
55 - 59	3 903	2 424	1 479	5.0	6.2	3.8
60 - 64	5 813	3 556	2 257	8.3	10.3	6.3
65 - 69	7 707	4 819	2 888	12.5	16.2	9.1
70 - 74	9 920	6 031	3 889	19.1	24.7	14.1
75 - 79	11 667	6 669	4 998	31.4	40.5	24.2
80 - 84	17 669	9 088	8 581	55.6	69.9	45.7
85 - 89	22 459	9 665	12 794	105.0	127.7	92.6
90 - 94	17 029	5 552	11 477	192.2	218.3	181.7
95 - 99	6 579	1 703	4 876	325.4	380.4	309.7
100 +	790	120	670	511.2	588.2	499.4
Bosnia and Herzegovina - Bosnie-Herzégovine						
2010 (C)						
Total	35 118	17 900	17 218	9.1	9.5	8.8
0 - 4	252	143	109	1.5	1.7	1.3

Continent, country or area, date, code[a] and age (in years) / Continent, pays ou zone, date, code[a] et âge (en annèes)	Number - Nombre			Rate - Taux		
	Both sexes / Les deux sexes	Male / Masculin	Female / Féminin	Both sexes / Les deux sexes	Male / Masculin	Female / Féminin
EUROPE						
Bosnia and Herzegovina - Bosnie-Herzégovine						
2010 (C)						
0	216	125	91	6.5	7.3	5.6
1 - 4	36	18	18	0.3	♦0.3	♦0.3
5 - 9	28	19	9	♦0.1	♦0.2	♦0.1
10 - 14	27	14	13	♦0.1	♦0.1	♦0.1
15 - 19	84	58	26	0.3	0.4	♦0.2
20 - 24	120	92	28	0.4	0.6	♦0.2
25 - 29	165	130	35	0.6	1.0	0.3
30 - 34	160	109	51	0.7	0.9	0.4
35 - 39	254	180	74	1.0	1.5	0.6
40 - 44	432	265	167	1.5	1.9	1.2
45 - 49	844	553	291	2.7	3.7	1.9
50 - 54	1 465	980	485	5.5	7.2	3.7
55 - 59	2 141	1 429	712	9.2	13.6	5.6
60 - 64	2 610	1 647	963	14.3	19.1	10.0
65 - 69	3 390	2 032	1 358	16.8	22.6	12.1
70 - 74	6 045	3 199	2 846	32.8	38.8	27.9
75 - 79	6 948	3 344	3 604	57.7	66.1	51.6
80 - 84	6 006	2 440	3 566	125.3	124.5	125.9
85 +	4 119	1 254	2 865	164.3	175.6	159.9
85 - 89	3 105	966	2 139	...	...	...
90 - 94	737	210	527	...	...	...
95 - 99	245	69	176	...	...	...
100 +	32	9	23	...	...	...
Unknown - Inconnu	28	12	16	..	..	..
Bulgaria - Bulgarie						
2018 (C)						
Total	108 526	56 367	52 159	15.4	16.5	14.4
0	358	200	158	5.7	6.2	5.2
1 - 4	93	46	47	0.4	0.3	0.4
5 - 9	61	35	26	0.2	0.2	♦0.2
10 - 14	70	50	20	0.2	0.3	♦0.1
15 - 19	145	97	48	0.5	0.6	0.3
20 - 24	176	118	58	0.6	0.7	0.4
25 - 29	304	219	85	0.7	1.0	0.4
30 - 34	488	356	132	1.0	1.4	0.6
35 - 39	757	518	239	1.5	2.0	1.0
40 - 44	1 331	885	446	2.4	3.2	1.7
45 - 49	2 203	1 521	682	4.2	5.7	2.7
50 - 54	3 285	2 293	992	7.0	9.8	4.3
55 - 59	5 474	3 820	1 654	11.4	16.2	6.8
60 - 64	8 001	5 406	2 595	16.5	23.9	10.1
65 - 69	11 132	7 187	3 945	23.4	34.2	14.8
70 - 74	13 510	7 975	5 535	34.2	48.9	23.9
75 - 79	15 069	7 656	7 413	54.3	71.6	43.4
80 - 84	18 976	8 179	10 797	94.9	114.1	84.1
85 - 89	16 748	6 445	10 303	161.9	181.0	151.8
90 - 94	8 466	2 785	5 681	279.0	290.9	273.4
95 - 99	1 751	540	1 211	400.0	418.0	392.5
100 +	128	36	92	622.9	620.7	623.7
Croatia - Croatie						
2018 (C)						
Total	52 706	25 964	26 742	12.9	13.1	12.7
0	157	104	53	4.3	5.5	3.0
1 - 4	29	19	10	♦0.2	♦0.2	♦0.1
5 - 9	19	13	6	♦0.1	♦0.1	♦0.1
10 - 14	21	12	9	♦0.1	♦0.1	♦0.1
15 - 19	61	41	20	0.3	0.4	♦0.2
20 - 24	100	80	20	0.4	0.6	♦0.2
25 - 29	109	79	30	0.5	0.6	♦0.3
30 - 34	158	122	36	0.6	0.9	0.3
35 - 39	249	171	78	0.9	1.2	0.6
40 - 44	411	294	117	1.5	2.1	0.9
45 - 49	659	477	182	2.5	3.6	1.4
50 - 54	1 320	896	424	4.6	6.3	2.9
55 - 59	2 248	1 557	691	7.5	10.7	4.5

19. Deaths by age and sex and age-specific death rates by sex: latest available year, 2010 - 2019
Décès et taux de mortalité selon l'âge et le sexe : dernière année disponible, 2010 - 2019 (continued - suite)

Continent, country or area, date, code[a] and age (in years) / Continent, pays ou zone, date, code[a] et âge (en années)	Number - Nombre			Rate - Taux		
	Both sexes / Les deux sexes	Male / Masculin	Female / Féminin	Both sexes / Les deux sexes	Male / Masculin	Female / Féminin
EUROPE						
Croatia - Croatie						
2018 (C)						
60 - 64	3 587	2 520	1 067	12.1	17.7	6.9
65 - 69	4 721	3 147	1 574	18.1	26.1	11.2
70 - 74	4 898	2 989	1 909	26.3	37.8	17.9
75 - 79	7 651	3 994	3 657	45.0	59.5	35.5
80 - 84	10 490	4 470	6 020	81.9	98.4	72.8
85 - 89	9 688	3 354	6 334	148.1	169.3	138.9
90 - 94	4 884	1 341	3 543	264.0	292.2	254.7
95 - 99	1 170	269	901	385.8	438.8	372.3
100 +	76	15	61	558.8	♦789.5	521.4
Czechia - Tchéquie						
2018 (C)						
Total	112 920	57 273	55 647	10.6	10.9	10.3
0	292	159	133	2.6	2.7	2.4
1 - 4	71	39	32	0.2	0.2	0.1
5 - 9	53	24	29	0.1	♦0.1	♦0.1
10 - 14	38	24	14	0.1	♦0.1	♦0.1
15 - 19	148	108	40	0.3	0.5	0.2
20 - 24	248	189	59	0.5	0.7	0.2
25 - 29	338	254	84	0.5	0.7	0.3
30 - 34	479	346	133	0.7	0.9	0.4
35 - 39	759	536	223	0.9	1.3	0.6
40 - 44	1 274	901	373	1.4	1.9	0.8
45 - 49	1 738	1 163	575	2.3	3.0	1.5
50 - 54	2 794	1 974	820	4.0	5.6	2.4
55 - 59	3 928	2 684	1 244	6.3	8.6	4.0
60 - 64	7 574	5 014	2 560	11.0	15.1	7.2
65 - 69	11 670	7 579	4 091	17.1	24.0	11.2
70 - 74	15 468	9 314	6 154	26.7	36.7	18.9
75 - 79	15 192	8 251	6 941	40.9	54.5	31.6
80 - 84	16 475	7 544	8 931	72.3	90.7	61.7
85 - 89	19 068	7 048	12 020	134.2	154.8	124.5
90 - 94	11 742	3 367	8 375	232.3	254.6	224.4
95 - 99	3 330	714	2 616	367.6	378.9	364.7
100 +	241	41	200	376.3	250.8	419.3
Denmark - Danemark[46]						
2018 (C)						
Total	55 232	27 992	27 240	9.5	9.7	9.4
0	226	130	96	3.6	4.1	3.2
1 - 4	28	17	11	♦0.1	♦0.1	♦0.1
5 - 9	21	12	9	♦0.1	♦0.1	♦0.1
10 - 14	19	13	6	♦0.1	♦0.1	-
15 - 19	77	57	20	0.2	0.3	♦0.1
20 - 24	79	60	19	0.2	0.3	♦0.1
25 - 29	130	96	34	0.3	0.5	0.2
30 - 34	175	114	61	0.5	0.7	0.4
35 - 39	228	136	92	0.7	0.8	0.6
40 - 44	397	242	155	1.1	1.3	0.8
45 - 49	649	405	244	1.7	2.1	1.3
50 - 54	1 272	790	482	3.0	3.7	2.3
55 - 59	1 998	1 219	779	5.4	6.6	4.2
60 - 64	2 921	1 795	1 126	8.5	10.6	6.5
65 - 69	4 374	2 609	1 765	13.6	16.6	10.7
70 - 74	6 719	3 941	2 778	20.5	24.9	16.4
75 - 79	7 552	4 203	3 349	34.8	41.7	28.8
80 - 84	8 763	4 581	4 182	62.9	75.8	53.0
85 - 89	8 922	4 125	4 797	117.0	142.0	101.7
90 - 94	7 082	2 541	4 541	206.0	247.7	188.2
95 - 99	3 053	819	2 234	341.7	414.7	320.9
100 +	547	87	460	505.5	595.9	491.5
Estonia - Estonie						
2018 (C)						
Total	15 751	7 401	8 350	11.9	11.9	12.0
0	23	14	9	♦1.6	♦1.9	♦1.3
1 - 4	14	10	4	♦0.2	♦0.3	♦0.1
5 - 9	5	4	1	♦0.1	♦0.1	-

19. Deaths by age and sex and age-specific death rates by sex: latest available year, 2010 - 2019
Décès et taux de mortalité selon l'âge et le sexe : dernière année disponible, 2010 - 2019 (continued - suite)

Continent, country or area, date, code[a] and age (in years) / Continent, pays ou zone, date, code[a] et âge (en années)	Number - Nombre			Rate - Taux		
	Both sexes / Les deux sexes	Male / Masculin	Female / Féminin	Both sexes / Les deux sexes	Male / Masculin	Female / Féminin
EUROPE						
Estonia - Estonie						
2018 (C)						
10 - 14	10	4	6	♦0.1	♦0.1	♦0.2
15 - 19	27	19	8	♦0.4	♦0.6	♦0.3
20 - 24	22	18	4	♦0.3	♦0.5	♦0.1
25 - 29	58	43	15	0.6	0.9	♦0.3
30 - 34	94	70	24	1.0	1.4	♦0.5
35 - 39	132	95	37	1.4	2.0	0.8
40 - 44	179	134	45	2.0	2.9	1.0
45 - 49	291	223	68	3.2	4.9	1.5
50 - 54	424	304	120	5.1	7.5	2.8
55 - 59	754	564	190	8.5	13.5	4.0
60 - 64	1 043	743	300	12.3	19.8	6.4
65 - 69	1 439	904	535	18.7	28.6	11.8
70 - 74	1 511	892	619	26.9	42.0	17.7
75 - 79	2 085	1 042	1 043	39.1	59.0	29.3
80 - 84	2 520	975	1 545	63.6	86.6	54.4
85 - 89	2 741	861	1 880	117.7	153.2	106.4
90 - 94	1 820	381	1 439	204.7	229.0	199.2
95 - 99	502	96	406	321.7	445.5	301.9
100 +	57	5	52	471.1	♦416.7	477.1
Faroe Islands - Îles Féroé						
2019 (C)						
Total	411	218	193	7.9	8.1	7.7
0	3	2	1	♦4.3	♦5.6	♦2.9
1 - 4	-	-	-	-	-	-
5 - 9	-	-	-	-	-	-
10 - 14	-	-	-	-	-	-
15 - 19	1	1	-	♦0.3	♦0.5	-
20 - 24	1	1	-	♦0.3	♦0.6	-
25 - 29	1	1	-	♦0.3	♦0.6	-
30 - 34	-	-	-	-	-	-
35 - 39	3	3	-	♦1.0	♦1.9	-
40 - 44	1	1	-	♦0.3	♦0.6	-
45 - 49	-	-	-	-	-	-
50 - 54	6	4	2	♦1.7	♦2.1	♦1.2
55 - 59	14	10	4	♦4.4	♦6.0	♦2.6
60 - 64	25	15	10	♦8.5	♦10.0	♦6.9
65 - 69	36	19	17	13.3	♦13.8	♦12.8
70 - 74	31	21	10	13.5	♦17.2	♦9.4
75 - 79	55	31	24	30.5	34.4	♦26.5
80 - 84	69	33	36	64.5	68.2	61.4
85 - 89	78	45	33	103.0	149.5	72.4
90 - 94	68	27	41	201.2	♦267.3	173.0
95 - 99	15	4	11	♦241.9	♦363.6	♦215.7
100 +	4	-	4	♦444.4	-	♦571.4
Finland - Finlande						
2018 (C)						
Total	54 527	27 184	27 343	9.9	10.0	9.8
0	101	52	49	2.1	2.1	2.1
1 - 4	31	17	14	0.1	♦0.1	♦0.1
5 - 9	14	8	6	-	♦0.1	-
10 - 14	23	13	10	♦0.1	♦0.1	♦0.1
15 - 19	109	80	29	0.4	0.5	♦0.2
20 - 24	165	119	46	0.5	0.7	0.3
25 - 29	198	139	59	0.6	0.8	0.3
30 - 34	233	176	57	0.7	1.0	0.3
35 - 39	299	204	95	0.9	1.1	0.6
40 - 44	394	273	121	1.2	1.6	0.7
45 - 49	622	417	205	1.9	2.6	1.3
50 - 54	1 122	752	370	3.1	4.1	2.0
55 - 59	1 795	1 190	605	4.9	6.6	3.3
60 - 64	2 899	1 927	972	8.0	10.9	5.2
65 - 69	4 318	2 801	1 517	11.9	16.0	8.0
70 - 74	5 767	3 634	2 133	18.2	24.5	12.6
75 - 79	6 348	3 667	2 681	30.7	40.5	23.0
80 - 84	8 424	4 340	4 084	55.8	71.9	45.0

Continent, country or area, date, code[a] and age (in years) / Continent, pays ou zone, date, code[a] et âge (en années)	Number - Nombre: Both sexes / Les deux sexes	Number - Nombre: Male / Masculin	Number - Nombre: Female / Féminin	Rate - Taux: Both sexes / Les deux sexes	Rate - Taux: Male / Masculin	Rate - Taux: Female / Féminin
EUROPE						
Finland - Finlande						
2018 (C)						
85 - 89	10 253	4 226	6 027	106.9	130.6	94.9
90 - 94	7 997	2 473	5 524	197.2	230.0	185.4
95 - 99	2 965	601	2 364	341.2	377.3	333.4
100 +	450	75	375	519.6	568.2	510.9
France						
2018 (C)						
Total	596 422	296 524	299 898	9.2	9.5	9.0
0	2 600	1 456	1 144	...	...	...
1 - 4	468	260	208	0.2	0.2	0.1
5 - 9	278	144	134	0.1	0.1	0.1
10 - 14	342	212	130	0.1	0.1	0.1
15 - 19	913	640	273	0.2	0.3	0.1
20 - 24	1 446	1 096	350	0.4	0.6	0.2
25 - 29	1 723	1 227	496	0.5	0.7	0.3
30 - 34	2 286	1 601	685	0.6	0.8	0.3
35 - 39	3 561	2 454	1 107	0.9	1.2	0.5
40 - 44	5 334	3 419	1 915	1.3	1.7	0.9
45 - 49	9 431	6 113	3 318	2.1	2.8	1.5
50 - 54	14 799	9 595	5 204	3.4	4.5	2.4
55 - 59	22 283	14 507	7 776	5.3	7.1	3.6
60 - 64	31 472	20 968	10 504	7.9	11.1	5.1
65 - 69	42 320	27 830	14 490	11.0	15.3	7.1
70 - 74	47 782	30 413	17 369	15.5	21.2	10.5
75 - 79	52 490	31 228	21 262	24.8	33.3	18.1
80 - 84	81 371	42 920	38 451	44.5	58.1	35.3
85 - 89	114 067	50 737	63 330	86.9	110.6	74.1
90 - 94	103 897	36 020	67 877	166.2	203.6	151.4
95 +	57 559	13 684	43 875	307.5	345.2	297.3
95 - 99	49 924	12 598	37 326	...	...	...
100 +	7 635	1 086	6 549	...	...	...
Germany - Allemagne						
2018 (C)						
Total	954 874	470 032	484 842	11.5	11.5	11.5
0	2 505	1 399	1 106	3.2	3.5	2.9
1 - 4	494	260	234	0.2	0.2	0.2
5 - 9	290	171	119	0.1	0.1	0.1
10 - 14	324	187	137	0.1	0.1	0.1
15 - 19	943	639	304	0.2	0.3	0.2
20 - 24	1 423	1 054	369	0.3	0.4	0.2
25 - 29	1 836	1 281	555	0.4	0.5	0.2
30 - 34	2 637	1 724	913	0.5	0.6	0.4
35 - 39	3 833	2 477	1 356	0.7	0.9	0.5
40 - 44	5 547	3 587	1 960	1.2	1.5	0.8
45 - 49	11 060	7 029	4 031	1.9	2.4	1.4
50 - 54	22 654	14 672	7 982	3.3	4.2	2.3
55 - 59	36 452	23 716	12 736	5.6	7.3	3.9
60 - 64	49 584	31 978	17 606	9.1	12.0	6.3
65 - 69	65 660	41 388	24 272	13.8	18.2	9.8
70 - 74	75 437	45 755	29 682	20.9	27.2	15.4
75 - 79	137 300	78 513	58 787	33.0	42.3	25.5
80 - 84	176 688	90 025	86 663	58.9	72.8	49.2
85 - 89	174 068	72 977	101 091	116.9	138.0	105.3
90 - 94	131 971	40 294	91 677	210.5	236.9	200.6
95 - 99	48 715	10 159	38 556	344.6	378.5	336.7
100 +	5 453	747	4 706	387.2	302.6	405.2
Greece - Grèce						
2018 (C)						
Total	120 296	61 386	58 910	11.2	11.8	10.7
0	300	169	131	3.4	3.7	3.0
1 - 4	51	28	23	0.1	♦0.1	♦0.1
5 - 9	42	20	22	0.1	♦0.1	♦0.1
10 - 14	58	41	17	0.1	0.1	♦0.1
15 - 19	125	92	33	0.2	0.3	0.1
20 - 24	219	167	52	0.4	0.6	0.2
25 - 29	216	157	59	0.4	0.5	0.2

19. Deaths by age and sex and age-specific death rates by sex: latest available year, 2010 - 2019
Décès et taux de mortalité selon l'âge et le sexe : dernière année disponible, 2010 - 2019 (continued - suite)

Continent, country or area, date, code[a] and age (in years) / Continent, pays ou zone, date, code[a] et âge (en annèes)	Number - Nombre: Both sexes / Les deux sexes	Male / Masculin	Female / Féminin	Rate - Taux: Both sexes / Les deux sexes	Male / Masculin	Female / Féminin
EUROPE						
Greece - Grèce						
2018 (C)						
30 - 34	355	254	101	0.6	0.8	0.3
35 - 39	626	452	174	0.8	1.2	0.4
40 - 44	899	618	281	1.1	1.6	0.7
45 - 49	1 508	973	535	1.9	2.5	1.3
50 - 54	2 531	1 697	834	3.3	4.6	2.1
55 - 59	3 811	2 633	1 178	5.3	7.8	3.1
60 - 64	5 327	3 638	1 689	8.0	11.6	4.8
65 - 69	6 954	4 627	2 327	11.4	16.2	7.2
70 - 74	10 166	6 434	3 732	18.7	25.7	12.7
75 - 79	13 090	7 542	5 548	29.2	38.0	22.2
80 - 84	22 688	11 315	11 373	57.9	69.4	49.7
85 - 89	26 867	11 619	15 248	114.4	120.8	110.0
90 - 94	18 323	7 003	11 320	206.5	202.5	209.1
95 - 99	5 121	1 656	3 465	222.4	169.8	261.0
100 +	1 019	251	768	115.8	72.7	143.5
Unknown - Inconnu	19	18	1	..	..	..
Hungary - Hongrie[47]						
2018 (C)						
Total	131 247	64 139	67 108	13.4	13.7	13.2
0	304	161	143	3.3	3.4	3.1
1 - 4	73	46	27	0.2	0.2	♦0.1
5 - 9	27	14	13	♦0.1	♦0.1	♦0.1
10 - 14	38	25	13	0.1	♦0.1	♦0.1
15 - 19	133	90	43	0.3	0.4	0.2
20 - 24	243	157	86	0.4	0.5	0.3
25 - 29	312	226	86	0.5	0.7	0.3
30 - 34	453	320	133	0.7	1.0	0.4
35 - 39	753	503	250	1.1	1.4	0.7
40 - 44	1 548	1 062	486	1.8	2.5	1.2
45 - 49	2 448	1 648	800	3.4	4.6	2.2
50 - 54	4 080	2 830	1 250	6.5	9.2	4.0
55 - 59	6 735	4 562	2 173	11.4	16.4	7.0
60 - 64	12 480	8 218	4 262	17.6	25.6	11.0
65 - 69	14 495	9 035	5 460	23.8	34.5	15.7
70 - 74	15 211	8 785	6 426	32.4	46.4	23.0
75 - 79	17 824	8 663	9 161	49.3	66.1	39.8
80 - 84	20 130	7 849	12 281	85.6	106.5	76.1
85 - 89	19 401	6 302	13 099	145.5	166.2	137.2
90 - 94	10 953	2 838	8 115	227.1	244.1	221.6
95 - 99	3 299	737	2 562	274.2	271.9	274.8
100 +	307	68	239	174.4	119.5	200.6
Iceland - Islande						
2018 (C)						
Total	2 254	1 139	1 115	6.4	6.3	6.5
0	7	5	2	♦1.7	♦2.3	♦1.0
1 - 4	3	1	2	♦0.2	♦0.1	♦0.2
5 - 9	-	-	-	-	-	-
10 - 14	-	-	-	-	-	-
15 - 19	9	8	1	♦0.4	♦0.7	♦0.1
20 - 24	9	7	2	♦0.3	♦0.5	♦0.2
25 - 29	14	14	-	♦0.5	♦0.9	-
30 - 34	22	17	5	♦0.9	♦1.3	♦0.4
35 - 39	25	13	12	♦1.0	♦1.0	♦1.0
40 - 44	22	16	6	♦1.0	♦1.3	♦0.5
45 - 49	29	16	13	♦1.3	♦1.4	♦1.2
50 - 54	44	24	20	2.0	♦2.2	♦1.8
55 - 59	87	54	33	4.0	4.9	3.1
60 - 64	113	71	42	5.8	7.2	4.3
65 - 69	138	89	49	8.5	10.8	6.1
70 - 74	197	117	80	15.5	18.5	12.6
75 - 79	261	131	130	30.9	32.6	29.3
80 - 84	354	168	186	58.2	60.7	56.1
85 - 89	470	224	246	112.5	129.2	100.7
90 - 94	299	116	183	171.3	194.6	159.3

19. Deaths by age and sex and age-specific death rates by sex: latest available year, 2010 - 2019
Décès et taux de mortalité selon l'âge et le sexe : dernière année disponible, 2010 - 2019 (continued - suite)

Continent, country or area, date, code[a] and age (in years) / Continent, pays ou zone, date, code[a] et âge (en années)	Number - Nombre			Rate - Taux		
	Both sexes / Les deux sexes	Male / Masculin	Female / Féminin	Both sexes / Les deux sexes	Male / Masculin	Female / Féminin
EUROPE						
Iceland - Islande						
2018 (C)						
95 - 99	128	39	89	340.9	367.9	330.2
100 +	23	9	14	♦489.4	♦750.0	♦400.0
Ireland - Irlande						
2018 (+C)						
Total	31 009	15 962	15 047	6.4	6.7	6.2
0	174	99	75	2.8	3.1	2.5
1 - 4	24	8	16	♦0.1	♦0.1	♦0.1
5 - 9	12	9	3	-	-	-
10 - 14	35	21	14	0.1	♦0.1	♦0.1
15 - 19	61	41	20	0.2	0.3	♦0.1
20 - 24	91	62	29	0.3	0.4	♦0.2
25 - 29	115	74	41	0.4	0.5	0.3
30 - 34	183	109	74	0.5	0.7	0.4
35 - 39	247	145	102	0.6	0.8	0.5
40 - 44	386	242	144	1.1	1.3	0.8
45 - 49	576	346	230	1.7	2.0	1.4
50 - 54	790	464	326	2.6	3.1	2.1
55 - 59	1 192	726	466	4.3	5.3	3.3
60 - 64	1 626	1 009	617	6.6	8.3	5.0
65 - 69	2 421	1 454	967	11.3	13.7	8.9
70 - 74	3 252	1 935	1 317	18.5	22.4	14.8
75 - 79	3 990	2 308	1 682	33.1	40.5	26.5
80 - 84	5 016	2 615	2 401	59.1	70.0	50.5
85 - 89	5 307	2 514	2 793	111.1	135.4	95.6
90 - 94	3 908	1 414	2 494	206.7	239.3	191.9
95 - 99	1 398	343	1 055	250.9	241.5	254.1
100 +	205	24	181	246.4	♦129.7	279.8
Isle of Man - Île de Man[48]						
2016 (|)						
Total	870	437	433	10.4	10.6	10.3
0	2	-	2	♦2.5	-	♦5.3
1 - 4	1	1	-	♦0.3	♦0.6	-
5 - 9	-	-	-	-	-	-
10 - 14	3	2	1	♦0.7	♦0.9	♦0.5
15 - 19	1	1	-	♦0.2	♦0.4	-
20 - 24	3	2	1	♦0.7	♦0.9	♦0.5
25 - 29	3	3	-	♦0.7	♦1.4	-
30 - 34	5	3	2	♦1.1	♦1.4	♦0.8
35 - 39	5	4	1	♦1.0	♦1.7	♦0.4
40 - 44	8	6	2	♦1.4	♦2.2	♦0.7
45 - 49	11	7	4	♦1.7	♦2.2	♦1.2
50 - 54	22	15	7	♦3.3	♦4.5	♦2.1
55 - 59	28	16	12	♦4.8	♦5.5	♦4.0
60 - 64	36	23	13	7.0	♦8.8	♦5.1
65 - 69	60	38	22	11.0	14.0	♦8.1
70 - 74	85	50	35	20.2	24.1	16.4
75 - 79	126	78	48	39.9	51.0	29.5
80 - 84	128	64	64	60.1	66.8	54.7
85 +	343	124	219	151.2	157.6	147.9
85 - 89	153	67	86	...	...	...
90 - 94	118	38	80	174.8	188.1	169.1
95 - 99	58	15	43	...	...	...
100 +	14	4	10	...	...	...
Italy - Italie						
2018 (C)						
Total	633 133	302 495	330 638	10.5	10.3	10.7
0	1 228	689	539	2.7	3.0	2.5
1 - 4	259	153	106	0.1	0.2	0.1
5 - 9	198	122	76	0.1	0.1	0.1
10 - 14	247	134	113	0.1	0.1	0.1
15 - 19	596	422	174	0.2	0.3	0.1
20 - 24	840	648	192	0.3	0.4	0.1
25 - 29	1 062	785	277	0.3	0.5	0.2
30 - 34	1 342	892	450	0.4	0.5	0.3
35 - 39	2 121	1 337	784	0.6	0.7	0.4

19. Deaths by age and sex and age-specific death rates by sex: latest available year, 2010 - 2019
Décès et taux de mortalité selon l'âge et le sexe : dernière année disponible, 2010 - 2019 (continued - suite)

Continent, country or area, date, code[a] and age (in years) Continent, pays ou zone, date, code[a] et âge (en années)	Number - Nombre Both sexes Les deux sexes	 Male Masculin	 Female Féminin	Rate - Taux Both sexes Les deux sexes	 Male Masculin	 Female Féminin
EUROPE						
Italy - Italie						
2018 (C)						
40 - 44	3 952	2 440	1 512	0.9	1.1	0.7
45 - 49	6 911	4 239	2 672	1.4	1.8	1.1
50 - 54	11 598	7 017	4 581	2.4	2.9	1.8
55 - 59	16 435	10 263	6 172	3.8	4.8	2.8
60 - 64	23 140	14 535	8 605	6.1	7.9	4.3
65 - 69	34 076	21 312	12 764	9.7	12.7	6.9
70 - 74	49 587	30 522	19 065	15.7	20.6	11.3
75 - 79	75 479	43 604	31 875	27.4	35.6	20.8
80 - 84	108 840	55 983	52 857	50.8	63.4	41.9
85 - 89	135 177	58 609	76 568	99.0	120.4	87.1
90 - 94	109 421	36 679	72 742	183.2	216.6	169.9
95 - 99	43 757	10 916	32 841	296.2	337.9	284.5
100 +	6 867	1 194	5 673	456.2	489.2	449.8
Latvia - Lettonie						
2018 (C)						
Total	28 820	13 546	15 274	14.9	15.2	14.6
0 - 4	75	41	34	0.7	0.7	0.7
0	61	33	28	3.0	3.1	♦2.8
1 - 4	14	8	6	♦0.2	♦0.2	♦0.1
5 - 9	15	10	5	♦0.2	♦0.2	♦0.1
10 - 14	16	11	5	♦0.2	♦0.2	♦0.1
15 - 19	45	35	10	0.5	0.8	♦0.2
20 - 24	68	44	24	0.7	0.9	♦0.5
25 - 29	120	101	19	0.9	1.5	♦0.3
30 - 34	245	192	53	1.8	2.7	0.8
35 - 39	285	215	70	2.3	3.4	1.1
40 - 44	491	359	132	3.8	5.7	2.0
45 - 49	663	479	184	5.0	7.4	2.7
50 - 54	1 040	741	299	7.9	11.9	4.3
55 - 59	1 605	1 141	464	11.2	17.4	5.9
60 - 64	2 050	1 372	678	16.3	25.3	9.5
65 - 69	2 636	1 636	1 000	23.6	37.2	14.8
70 - 74	2 751	1 540	1 211	32.5	51.0	22.2
75 - 79	4 105	1 977	2 128	46.5	71.0	35.2
80 - 84	4 668	1 737	2 931	80.3	109.2	69.4
85 - 89	4 446	1 265	3 181	135.9	165.3	126.9
90 - 94	2 759	538	2 221	238.9	270.2	232.4
95 - 99	664	97	567	375.4	386.5	373.5
100 +	73	15	58	532.8	♦681.8	504.3
Liechtenstein						
2018 (C)						
Total	274	143	131	7.2	7.5	6.8
0	-	-	-	-	-	-
1 - 4	-	-	-	-	-	-
5 - 9	-	-	-	-	-	-
10 - 14	1	-	1	♦0.5	-	♦1.1
15 - 19	-	-	-	-	-	-
20 - 24	2	2	-	♦0.9	♦1.7	-
25 - 29	1	1	-	♦0.4	♦0.9	-
30 - 34	1	1	-	♦0.4	♦0.9	-
35 - 39	2	2	-	♦0.8	♦1.6	-
40 - 44	3	2	1	♦1.2	♦1.5	♦0.8
45 - 49	5	4	1	♦1.6	♦2.6	♦0.7
50 - 54	7	6	1	♦2.2	♦3.8	♦0.6
55 - 59	7	5	2	♦2.3	♦3.3	♦1.3
60 - 64	8	3	5	♦3.2	♦2.4	♦3.9
65 - 69	19	11	8	♦8.8	♦10.4	♦7.2
70 - 74	34	23	11	18.4	♦25.1	♦11.8
75 - 79	41	30	11	31.1	♦50.0	♦15.3
80 - 84	45	23	22	57.3	♦71.0	♦47.6
85 - 89	41	16	25	97.2	♦101.9	♦94.3
90 - 94	40	11	29	224.7	♦261.9	♦213.2
95 - 99	13	1	12	♦309.5	♦100.0	♦375.0
100 +	4	2	2	♦2000.0	♦1000.0	...

19. Deaths by age and sex and age-specific death rates by sex: latest available year, 2010 - 2019
Décès et taux de mortalité selon l'âge et le sexe : dernière année disponible, 2010 - 2019 (continued - suite)

Continent, country or area, date, code[a] and age (in years) / Continent, pays ou zone, date, code[a] et âge (en années)	Number - Nombre			Rate - Taux		
	Both sexes Les deux sexes	Male Masculin	Female Féminin	Both sexes Les deux sexes	Male Masculin	Female Féminin
EUROPE						
Lithuania - Lituanie						
2018 (C)						
Total	39 574	19 024	20 550	14.1	14.7	13.7
0	96	55	41	3.4	3.8	3.0
1 - 4	22	14	8	♦0.2	♦0.2	♦0.1
5 - 9	14	8	6	♦0.1	♦0.1	♦0.1
10 - 14	24	12	12	♦0.2	♦0.2	♦0.2
15 - 19	68	47	21	0.5	0.7	♦0.3
20 - 24	113	83	30	0.7	1.0	♦0.4
25 - 29	192	157	35	1.0	1.6	0.4
30 - 34	294	230	64	1.6	2.4	0.7
35 - 39	412	322	90	2.5	3.8	1.1
40 - 44	588	426	162	3.3	4.9	1.8
45 - 49	917	685	232	4.6	7.1	2.2
50 - 54	1 400	996	404	6.8	10.3	3.7
55 - 59	2 129	1 499	630	9.5	14.7	5.2
60 - 64	2 699	1 853	846	14.7	23.4	8.1
65 - 69	3 312	2 168	1 144	21.3	35.1	12.2
70 - 74	3 568	2 147	1 421	29.8	49.8	18.6
75 - 79	5 259	2 563	2 696	44.9	66.9	34.2
80 - 84	6 409	2 513	3 896	72.1	97.8	61.6
85 - 89	6 719	2 034	4 685	132.7	156.1	124.6
90 - 94	4 160	984	3 176	239.4	272.4	230.7
95 - 99	1 039	193	846	362.3	402.1	354.3
100 +	140	35	105	569.1	673.1	541.2
Luxembourg						
2018 (C)						
Total	4 318	2 195	2 123	7.2	7.3	7.1
0	27	13	14	♦4.4	♦4.1	♦4.7
1 - 4	3	2	1	♦0.1	♦0.2	♦0.1
5 - 9	1	1	-	-	♦0.1	-
10 - 14	3	3	-	♦0.1	♦0.2	-
15 - 19	4	2	2	♦0.1	♦0.1	♦0.1
20 - 24	11	7	4	♦0.3	♦0.4	♦0.2
25 - 29	14	7	7	♦0.3	♦0.3	♦0.3
30 - 34	26	16	10	♦0.6	♦0.7	♦0.4
35 - 39	20	15	5	♦0.4	♦0.6	♦0.2
40 - 44	44	31	13	1.0	1.3	♦0.6
45 - 49	63	41	22	1.4	1.7	♦1.0
50 - 54	135	88	47	2.9	3.7	2.1
55 - 59	175	107	68	4.4	5.2	3.5
60 - 64	244	165	79	7.5	10.1	4.9
65 - 69	301	188	113	11.5	14.4	8.6
70 - 74	391	247	144	19.3	25.1	13.9
75 - 79	500	276	224	31.1	38.8	25.0
80 - 84	696	379	317	58.0	76.3	45.1
85 - 89	830	362	468	103.5	123.8	91.9
90 - 94	620	197	423	203.2	250.0	186.9
95 - 99	183	46	137	300.0	383.3	279.6
100 +	27	2	25	♦355.3	♦181.8	♦384.6
Malta - Malte						
2018 (C)						
Total	3 688	1 876	1 812	7.6	7.6	7.6
0	25	16	9	♦5.6	♦7.0	♦4.1
1 - 4	4	3	1	♦0.2	♦0.3	♦0.1
5 - 9	2	-	2	♦0.1	-	♦0.2
10 - 14	-	-	-	-	-	-
15 - 19	2	2	-	♦0.1	♦0.2	-
20 - 24	8	6	2	♦0.3	♦0.4	♦0.1
25 - 29	16	13	3	♦0.4	♦0.6	♦0.2
30 - 34	19	10	9	♦0.5	♦0.5	♦0.5
35 - 39	28	17	11	♦0.7	♦0.8	♦0.6
40 - 44	32	16	16	0.9	♦0.9	♦1.0
45 - 49	37	22	15	1.3	♦1.4	♦1.1
50 - 54	81	53	28	2.9	3.7	♦2.1
55 - 59	130	80	50	4.2	5.1	3.2
60 - 64	210	129	81	6.9	8.5	5.4

19. Deaths by age and sex and age-specific death rates by sex: latest available year, 2010 - 2019
Décès et taux de mortalité selon l'âge et le sexe : dernière année disponible, 2010 - 2019 (continued - suite)

Continent, country or area, date, code[a] and age (in years) / Continent, pays ou zone, date, code[a] et âge (en années)	Number - Nombre			Rate - Taux		
	Both sexes / Les deux sexes	Male / Masculin	Female / Féminin	Both sexes / Les deux sexes	Male / Masculin	Female / Féminin
EUROPE						
Malta - Malte						
2018 (C)						
65 - 69	299	192	107	10.3	13.5	7.3
70 - 74	465	293	172	17.1	22.6	12.1
75 - 79	422	238	184	29.6	37.4	23.3
80 - 84	656	323	333	57.3	68.1	49.6
85 - 89	643	263	380	105.3	125.0	95.0
90 - 94	441	160	281	192.8	221.0	179.8
95 - 99	149	38	111	306.6	330.4	299.2
100 +	19	2	17	♦260.3	♦100.0	♦320.8
Montenegro - Monténégro						
2018 (C)						
Total	6 504	3 353	3 151	10.5	10.9	10.0
0	12	8	4	♦1.6	♦2.0	♦1.1
1 - 4	9	4	5	♦0.3	♦0.3	♦0.3
5 - 9	1	1	-	-	♦0.1	-
10 - 14	7	5	2	♦0.2	♦0.3	♦0.1
15 - 19	8	8	-	♦0.2	♦0.4	-
20 - 24	19	13	6	♦0.5	♦0.6	♦0.3
25 - 29	17	11	6	♦0.4	♦0.5	♦0.3
30 - 34	31	21	10	0.7	♦0.9	♦0.4
35 - 39	38	27	11	0.9	♦1.2	♦0.5
40 - 44	79	52	27	1.9	2.5	♦1.3
45 - 49	136	85	51	3.4	4.3	2.5
50 - 54	187	118	69	4.5	5.8	3.3
55 - 59	376	247	129	8.9	12.0	6.0
60 - 64	522	340	182	12.9	17.2	8.8
65 - 69	718	459	259	21.2	29.5	14.1
70 - 74	656	380	276	33.0	44.6	24.3
75 - 79	1 042	505	537	56.0	66.0	49.0
80 - 84	1 223	514	709	100.6	106.4	96.8
85 - 89	948	405	543	174.3	185.3	167.0
90 - 94	371	122	249	238.3	199.3	263.5
95 - 99	93	25	68	213.8	♦172.4	234.5
100 +	11	3	8	♦846.2	♦750.0	♦888.9
Netherlands - Pays-Bas[49]						
2018 (C)						
Total	153 363	74 522	78 841	8.9	8.7	9.1
0	582	332	250	3.4	3.8	3.0
1 - 4	94	51	43	0.1	0.1	0.1
5 - 9	67	33	34	0.1	0.1	0.1
10 - 14	70	47	23	0.1	0.1	-
15 - 19	211	138	73	0.2	0.3	0.1
20 - 24	290	204	86	0.3	0.4	0.2
25 - 29	382	253	129	0.3	0.5	0.2
30 - 34	461	288	173	0.4	0.5	0.3
35 - 39	621	390	231	0.6	0.8	0.5
40 - 44	971	557	414	0.9	1.1	0.8
45 - 49	1 906	1 107	799	1.5	1.7	1.3
50 - 54	3 349	1 893	1 456	2.6	2.9	2.3
55 - 59	5 469	3 089	2 380	4.5	5.1	3.9
60 - 64	8 058	4 629	3 429	7.5	8.6	6.3
65 - 69	11 454	6 821	4 633	11.5	13.8	9.2
70 - 74	16 706	9 810	6 896	19.2	23.1	15.4
75 - 79	19 066	10 740	8 326	32.4	39.2	26.4
80 - 84	24 381	12 574	11 807	59.7	72.8	50.2
85 - 89	28 824	12 427	16 397	116.9	140.0	104.0
90 - 94	21 284	7 075	14 209	214.1	245.9	201.2
95 - 99	7 939	1 876	6 063	351.6	392.8	340.5
100 +	1 178	188	990	540.4	582.0	533.1
North Macedonia - Macédoine du Nord						
2018 (C)						
Total	19 727	10 339	9 388	9.5	9.9	9.1
0	122	71	51	5.7	6.4	4.9
1 - 4	14	11	3	♦0.2	♦0.2	♦0.1
5 - 9	13	6	7	♦0.1	♦0.1	♦0.1
10 - 14	22	15	7	♦0.2	♦0.3	♦0.1

Continent, country or area, date, code[a] and age (in years) / Continent, pays ou zone, date, code[a] et âge (en années)	Number - Nombre: Both sexes / Les deux sexes	Number - Nombre: Male / Masculin	Number - Nombre: Female / Féminin	Rate - Taux: Both sexes / Les deux sexes	Rate - Taux: Male / Masculin	Rate - Taux: Female / Féminin
EUROPE						
North Macedonia - Macédoine du Nord						
2018 (C)						
15 - 24	70	54	16	0.3	0.4	♦0.1
15 - 19	31	22	9	0.3	♦0.4	♦0.2
20 - 24	39	32	7	0.3	0.4	♦0.1
25 - 34	166	114	52	0.5	0.7	0.3
25 - 29	71	52	19	0.5	0.6	♦0.2
30 - 34	95	62	33	0.6	0.7	0.4
35 - 44	372	244	128	1.2	1.5	0.8
35 - 39	149	100	49	0.9	1.2	0.6
40 - 44	223	144	79	1.5	1.9	1.1
45 - 54	1 000	656	344	3.5	4.5	2.4
45 - 49	355	224	131	2.5	3.1	1.8
50 - 54	645	432	213	4.5	5.9	3.0
55 - 64	2 716	1 736	980	10.3	13.2	7.4
55 - 59	1 097	710	387	8.0	10.4	5.7
60 - 64	1 619	1 026	593	12.7	16.3	9.2
65 - 74	4 610	2 656	1 954	25.4	31.8	20.0
65 - 69	2 205	1 331	874	20.6	26.5	15.3
70 - 74	2 405	1 325	1 080	32.4	39.7	26.4
75 - 84	6 877	3 243	3 634	77.4	85.0	71.7
75 - 79	3 193	1 582	1 611	58.8	66.7	52.6
80 - 84	3 684	1 661	2 023	106.7	114.9	100.7
85 - 89	2 592	1 073	1 519	194.0	209.7	184.3
90 - 94	940	395	545	342.6	402.7	309.1
95 +	213	65	148	190.0	209.7	182.5
95 - 99	199	61	138	...	...	...
100 +	14	4	10	...	...	...
Norway - Norvège[50]						
2018 (C)						
Total	40 840	19 870	20 970	7.7	7.4	8.0
0	129	70	59	2.3	2.4	2.1
1 - 4	13	7	6	♦0.1	♦0.1	♦0.1
5 - 9	18	11	7	♦0.1	♦0.1	-
10 - 14	31	16	15	0.1	♦0.1	♦0.1
15 - 19	67	43	24	0.2	0.3	♦0.2
20 - 24	125	103	22	0.4	0.6	♦0.1
25 - 29	163	119	44	0.4	0.6	0.2
30 - 34	180	133	47	0.5	0.7	0.3
35 - 39	242	168	74	0.7	0.9	0.4
40 - 44	314	197	117	0.9	1.1	0.7
45 - 49	509	304	205	1.3	1.6	1.1
50 - 54	792	480	312	2.2	2.6	1.8
55 - 59	1 243	751	492	3.9	4.6	3.1
60 - 64	1 862	1 117	745	6.2	7.4	5.0
65 - 69	2 765	1 641	1 124	10.2	12.1	8.3
70 - 74	4 149	2 444	1 705	16.9	20.3	13.6
75 - 79	4 768	2 680	2 088	30.7	37.2	25.0
80 - 84	5 896	3 058	2 838	55.8	67.6	46.9
85 - 89	7 451	3 383	4 068	103.0	125.0	89.9
90 - 94	6 576	2 305	4 271	191.1	217.6	179.3
95 - 99	3 045	748	2 297	329.3	370.5	317.7
100 +	502	92	410	488.8	528.7	480.7
Poland - Pologne						
2018 (C)						
Total	414 200	213 647	200 553	10.9	11.6	10.2
0	1 494	834	660	3.9	4.2	3.5
1 - 4	239	132	107	0.2	0.2	0.1
5 - 9	182	105	77	0.1	0.1	0.1
10 - 14	265	145	120	0.1	0.2	0.1
15 - 19	673	464	209	0.4	0.5	0.2
20 - 24	1 244	982	262	0.6	0.9	0.2
25 - 29	1 806	1 454	352	0.7	1.1	0.3
30 - 34	2 842	2 222	620	0.9	1.4	0.4
35 - 39	4 172	3 215	957	1.4	2.1	0.6
40 - 44	6 180	4 696	1 484	2.1	3.2	1.0
45 - 49	8 345	6 155	2 190	3.4	5.1	1.8

19. Deaths by age and sex and age-specific death rates by sex: latest available year, 2010 - 2019
Décès et taux de mortalité selon l'âge et le sexe : dernière année disponible, 2010 - 2019 (continued - suite)

Continent, country or area, date, code[a] and age (in years) / Continent, pays ou zone, date, code[a] et âge (en années)	Number - Nombre: Both sexes Les deux sexes	Male Masculin	Female Féminin	Rate - Taux: Both sexes Les deux sexes	Male Masculin	Female Féminin
EUROPE						
Poland - Pologne						
2018 (C)						
50 - 54	12 450	9 027	3 423	5.5	8.1	3.0
55 - 59	22 893	15 990	6 903	9.1	13.1	5.3
60 - 64	37 661	25 329	12 332	13.6	19.6	8.4
65 - 69	47 195	30 624	16 571	19.9	28.9	12.6
70 - 74	41 901	24 914	16 987	27.5	38.9	19.2
75 - 79	45 045	23 752	21 293	42.4	58.9	32.2
80 - 84	60 412	26 666	33 746	69.2	90.4	58.3
85 - 89	65 473	23 104	42 369	122.3	145.6	112.4
90 - 94	40 541	11 028	29 513	205.8	229.5	198.2
95 - 99	11 853	2 583	9 270	301.9	301.4	302.0
100 +	1 334	226	1 108	252.9	199.8	267.4
Portugal[51]						
2018 (C)						
Total	113 051	56 729	56 322	11.0	11.7	10.4
0	287	159	128	3.3	3.6	3.0
1 - 4	63	31	32	0.2	0.2	0.2
5 - 9	38	17	21	0.1	♦0.1	♦0.1
10 - 14	49	23	26	0.1	♦0.1	♦0.1
15 - 19	121	81	40	0.2	0.3	0.1
20 - 24	165	119	46	0.3	0.4	0.2
25 - 29	230	149	81	0.4	0.5	0.3
30 - 34	331	215	116	0.6	0.8	0.4
35 - 39	484	321	163	0.7	1.0	0.4
40 - 44	1 053	675	378	1.3	1.8	0.9
45 - 49	1 766	1 206	560	2.3	3.3	1.4
50 - 54	2 667	1 860	807	3.5	5.2	2.0
55 - 59	3 901	2 734	1 167	5.4	8.0	3.0
60 - 64	5 253	3 674	1 579	7.9	11.9	4.4
65 - 69	6 878	4 594	2 284	11.1	16.1	6.8
70 - 74	9 448	5 929	3 519	17.8	25.5	11.8
75 - 79	13 252	7 468	5 784	31.1	41.7	23.4
80 - 84	20 008	10 013	9 995	57.1	73.7	46.6
85 - 89	23 117	9 870	13 247	109.7	136.2	95.8
90 - 94	16 771	5 749	11 022	223.8	281.5	202.2
95 - 99	6 091	1 639	4 452	433.5	497.9	413.8
100 +	1 078	203	875	257.3	119.7	350.8
Republic of Moldova - République de Moldova[52]						
2018 (C)						
Total	37 200	19 720	17 480	13.7	15.3	12.4
0	326	195	131	9.3	10.8	7.7
1 - 4	59	31	28	0.4	0.4	♦0.4
5 - 9	44	28	16	0.3	♦0.3	♦0.2
10 - 14	44	25	19	0.3	♦0.3	♦0.3
15 - 19	95	68	27	0.7	0.9	♦0.4
20 - 24	130	102	28	0.8	1.2	♦0.3
25 - 29	227	177	50	1.1	1.8	0.5
30 - 34	410	318	92	1.8	2.9	0.8
35 - 39	584	445	139	3.0	4.7	1.4
40 - 44	876	639	237	5.0	7.4	2.7
45 - 49	1 173	858	315	7.0	10.5	3.7
50 - 54	1 718	1 231	487	10.0	15.0	5.5
55 - 59	3 011	2 048	963	14.6	21.4	8.8
60 - 64	4 256	2 883	1 373	22.7	34.9	13.1
65 - 69	5 299	3 124	2 175	32.3	46.0	22.6
70 - 74	3 223	1 658	1 565	45.2	60.7	35.5
75 - 79	5 121	2 277	2 844	77.3	97.6	66.2
80 - 84	5 049	1 916	3 133	124.2	147.4	113.3
85 +	5 536	1 682	3 854	246.2	250.8	244.2
85 - 89	3 628	1 151	2 477	...	...	...
90 - 94	1 537	424	1 113	...	...	...
95 - 99	348	98	250	...	...	...
100 +	23	9	14	...	...	...
Unknown - Inconnu	19	15	4	..	..	..

19. Deaths by age and sex and age-specific death rates by sex: latest available year, 2010 - 2019
Décès et taux de mortalité selon l'âge et le sexe : dernière année disponible, 2010 - 2019 (continued - suite)

Continent, country or area, date, code[a] and age (in years) / Continent, pays ou zone, date, code[a] et âge (en années)	Number - Nombre			Rate - Taux		
	Both sexes Les deux sexes	Male Masculin	Female Féminin	Both sexes Les deux sexes	Male Masculin	Female Féminin
EUROPE						
Romania - Roumanie						
2018 (C)						
Total	263 911	138 224	125 687	13.6	14.5	12.6
0	1 226	691	535	6.1	6.7	5.5
1 - 4	294	164	130	0.4	0.4	0.3
5 - 9	151	85	66	0.2	0.2	0.1
10 - 14	213	126	87	0.2	0.2	0.2
15 - 19	416	285	131	0.4	0.5	0.3
20 - 24	493	368	125	0.5	0.7	0.3
25 - 29	815	581	234	0.7	0.9	0.4
30 - 34	1 158	824	334	0.9	1.2	0.5
35 - 39	2 019	1 441	578	1.4	2.0	0.8
40 - 44	3 837	2 792	1 045	2.5	3.5	1.4
45 - 49	6 789	4 888	1 901	4.4	6.1	2.5
50 - 54	9 170	6 648	2 522	7.2	10.2	4.0
55 - 59	13 285	9 555	3 730	11.6	17.0	6.4
60 - 64	22 412	15 507	6 905	16.7	24.8	9.6
65 - 69	27 727	17 933	9 794	23.2	33.8	14.7
70 - 74	26 677	15 552	11 125	32.9	45.5	23.7
75 - 79	35 819	18 027	17 792	53.4	69.7	43.2
80 - 84	46 640	19 922	26 718	90.6	107.9	80.9
85 - 89	39 887	14 768	25 119	149.0	160.8	142.8
90 - 94	20 008	6 632	13 376	222.4	223.2	221.9
95 - 99	4 563	1 357	3 206	216.6	201.4	223.8
100 +	312	78	234	123.9	102.0	133.5
Russian Federation - Fédération de Russie[27]						
2011 (C)						
Total	1 925 720	997 494	928 226	13.5	15.1	12.1
0 - 4	16 465	9 472	6 993	2.1	2.3	1.8
0	13 168	7 572	5 596	8.0	9.0	7.0
1 - 4	3 297	1 900	1 397	0.5	0.6	0.5
5 - 9	1 972	1 160	812	0.3	0.3	0.2
10 - 14	2 006	1 249	757	0.3	0.4	0.2
15 - 19	6 656	4 634	2 022	0.8	1.1	0.5
20 - 24	18 666	14 374	4 292	1.5	2.3	0.7
25 - 29	32 160	24 684	7 476	2.7	4.1	1.3
30 - 34	45 451	34 852	10 599	4.1	6.4	1.9
35 - 39	50 630	38 270	12 360	5.0	7.7	2.4
40 - 44	55 007	40 708	14 299	6.0	9.1	3.0
45 - 49	81 813	60 225	21 588	7.7	12.0	3.8
50 - 54	124 961	89 971	34 990	10.9	17.1	5.6
55 - 59	156 587	108 205	48 382	15.6	24.9	8.5
60 - 64	177 990	118 728	59 262	22.7	36.6	12.9
65 - 69	111 156	66 246	44 910	27.8	44.4	17.9
70 - 74	263 633	136 875	126 758	40.8	62.8	29.6
75 - 79	232 616	99 250	133 366	65.5	92.9	53.7
80 - 84	290 314	94 614	195 700	101.1	129.8	91.4
85 - 89	172 178	35 533	136 645	166.8	187.8	162.0
90 - 94	56 714	9 585	47 129	244.6	241.3	245.3
95 - 99	18 647	2 652	15 995	320.7	294.4	325.5
100 +	2 562	320	2 242	352.6	232.1	380.8
Unknown - Inconnu	7 536	5 887	1 649	..	..	..
San Marino - Saint-Marin						
2017 (C)						
Total	278	125	153	8.1	7.5	8.7
0	-	-	-	-	-	-
1 - 4	1	-	1	♦0.8	-	♦1.7
5 - 9	-	-	-	-	-	-
10 - 14	-	-	-	-	-	-
15 - 19	-	-	-	-	-	-
20 - 24	-	-	-	-	-	-
25 - 29	-	-	-	-	-	-
30 - 34	-	-	-	-	-	-
35 - 39	1	1	-	♦0.4	♦0.9	-
40 - 44	1	-	1	♦0.3	-	♦0.6
45 - 49	7	4	3	♦2.2	♦2.6	♦1.9
50 - 54	5	4	1	♦1.6	♦2.7	♦0.6

19. Deaths by age and sex and age-specific death rates by sex: latest available year, 2010 - 2019
Décès et taux de mortalité selon l'âge et le sexe : dernière année disponible, 2010 - 2019 (continued - suite)

Continent, country or area, date, code[a] and age (in years) Continent, pays ou zone, date, code[a] et âge (en annèes)	Number - Nombre			Rate - Taux		
	Both sexes Les deux sexes	Male Masculin	Female Féminin	Both sexes Les deux sexes	Male Masculin	Female Féminin
EUROPE						
San Marino - Saint-Marin						
2017 (C)						
55 - 59	12	5	7	♦4.8	♦4.1	♦5.6
60 - 64	6	5	1	♦2.9	♦5.1	♦0.9
65 - 69	15	10	5	♦8.2	♦11.4	♦5.3
70 - 74	18	12	6	♦11.8	♦16.3	♦7.6
75 - 79	32	19	13	26.0	♦32.5	♦20.2
80 - 84	46	23	23	50.1	♦56.8	♦44.8
85 - 89	56	19	37	86.7	♦82.6	88.9
90 - 94	53	18	35	202.3	♦222.2	193.4
95 - 99	22	5	17	♦293.3	♦294.1	♦293.1
100 +	3	-	3	♦375.0	...	♦375.0
Serbia - Serbie[53]						
2018 (+C)						
Total	101 655	50 990	50 665	14.6	15.0	14.1
0	311	168	143	4.9	5.1	4.6
1 - 4	68	34	34	0.3	0.3	0.3
5 - 9	44	26	18	0.1	♦0.2	♦0.1
10 - 14	42	21	21	0.1	♦0.1	♦0.1
15 - 19	104	76	28	0.3	0.4	♦0.2
20 - 24	179	132	47	0.5	0.7	0.2
25 - 29	208	155	53	0.5	0.7	0.3
30 - 34	330	227	103	0.7	0.9	0.4
35 - 39	556	372	184	1.1	1.5	0.8
40 - 44	894	592	302	1.8	2.4	1.2
45 - 49	1 494	941	553	3.2	4.0	2.3
50 - 54	2 607	1 708	899	5.6	7.5	3.8
55 - 59	4 694	3 048	1 646	9.6	13.0	6.5
60 - 64	7 839	5 057	2 782	15.0	20.4	10.1
65 - 69	11 507	7 098	4 409	22.8	30.7	16.1
70 - 74	11 179	6 257	4 922	34.2	43.8	26.8
75 - 79	15 339	7 514	7 825	59.0	69.8	51.4
80 - 84	20 329	8 747	11 582	106.7	117.2	99.9
85 - 89	16 275	6 289	9 986	176.9	184.3	172.5
90 - 94	6 406	2 143	4 263	237.0	223.1	244.7
95 - 99	1 184	368	816	184.1	171.1	190.6
100 +	66	17	49	94.8	♦65.6	112.1
Slovakia - Slovaquie						
2018 (C)						
Total	54 293	27 777	26 516	10.0	10.4	9.5
0	288	159	129	4.9	5.3	4.5
1 - 4	57	36	21	0.2	0.3	♦0.2
5 - 9	39	17	22	0.1	♦0.1	♦0.2
10 - 14	41	22	19	0.2	♦0.2	♦0.1
15 - 19	96	64	32	0.4	0.5	0.2
20 - 24	164	119	45	0.5	0.7	0.3
25 - 29	215	155	60	0.6	0.8	0.3
30 - 34	324	247	77	0.8	1.1	0.4
35 - 39	500	385	115	1.1	1.7	0.5
40 - 44	823	578	245	1.8	2.5	1.1
45 - 49	1 158	815	343	3.1	4.3	1.9
50 - 54	1 993	1 402	591	5.6	7.9	3.3
55 - 59	3 076	2 166	910	8.6	12.4	5.0
60 - 64	4 846	3 294	1 552	13.2	19.1	8.0
65 - 69	6 175	4 021	2 154	19.6	28.6	12.4
70 - 74	6 005	3 473	2 532	28.1	39.6	20.1
75 - 79	7 060	3 504	3 556	46.2	62.3	36.8
80 - 84	7 978	3 237	4 741	81.6	102.0	71.8
85 - 89	7 994	2 676	5 318	144.0	166.5	134.8
90 - 94	4 296	1 145	3 151	224.3	238.2	219.7
95 - 99	1 084	251	833	247.2	210.9	260.6
100 +	81	11	70	74.9	♦27.2	103.3
Slovenia - Slovénie						
2018 (C)						
Total	20 485	10 113	10 372	9.9	9.8	10.0
0	33	22	11	1.7	♦2.1	♦1.1
1 - 4	13	5	8	♦0.2	♦0.1	♦0.2

19. Deaths by age and sex and age-specific death rates by sex: latest available year, 2010 - 2019
Décès et taux de mortalité selon l'âge et le sexe : dernière année disponible, 2010 - 2019 (continued - suite)

Continent, country or area, date, code[a] and age (in years) / Continent, pays ou zone, date, code[a] et âge (en années)	Number - Nombre			Rate - Taux		
	Both sexes / Les deux sexes	Male / Masculin	Female / Féminin	Both sexes / Les deux sexes	Male / Masculin	Female / Féminin
EUROPE						
Slovenia - Slovénie						
2018 (C)						
5 - 9	8	3	5	♦0.1	♦0.1	♦0.1
10 - 14	8	6	2	♦0.1	♦0.1	-
15 - 19	28	21	7	♦0.3	♦0.4	♦0.2
20 - 24	33	29	4	0.3	♦0.6	♦0.1
25 - 29	45	32	13	0.4	0.5	♦0.2
30 - 34	59	42	17	0.4	0.6	♦0.3
35 - 39	122	88	34	0.8	1.1	0.5
40 - 44	179	127	52	1.2	1.6	0.7
45 - 49	231	159	72	1.6	2.1	1.0
50 - 54	512	333	179	3.3	4.3	2.4
55 - 59	791	536	255	5.3	7.1	3.4
60 - 64	1 323	891	432	9.1	12.3	5.9
65 - 69	1 751	1 161	590	13.6	18.5	8.9
70 - 74	1 778	1 140	638	19.8	27.9	13.1
75 - 79	2 649	1 501	1 148	33.4	44.8	25.0
80 - 84	3 434	1 637	1 797	59.2	75.7	49.3
85 - 89	4 017	1 507	2 510	114.1	143.9	101.4
90 - 94	2 637	707	1 930	197.5	234.6	186.7
95 - 99	757	156	601	291.8	325.7	284.2
100 +	77	10	67	442.5	♦322.6	468.5
Spain - Espagne						
2018 (C)						
Total	425 153	214 671	210 482	9.1	9.4	8.8
0	998	543	455	2.6	2.8	2.5
1 - 4	221	136	85	0.1	0.2	0.1
5 - 9	172	101	71	0.1	0.1	0.1
10 - 14	192	102	90	0.1	0.1	0.1
15 - 19	386	250	136	0.2	0.2	0.1
20 - 24	562	393	169	0.2	0.3	0.2
25 - 29	774	560	214	0.3	0.4	0.2
30 - 34	1 105	741	364	0.4	0.5	0.3
35 - 39	1 893	1 224	669	0.5	0.7	0.4
40 - 44	3 397	2 170	1 227	0.9	1.1	0.6
45 - 49	5 758	3 716	2 042	1.5	1.9	1.1
50 - 54	9 872	6 560	3 312	2.7	3.6	1.8
55 - 59	14 451	9 768	4 683	4.5	6.1	2.8
60 - 64	18 864	12 890	5 974	6.8	9.6	4.2
65 - 69	24 094	16 462	7 632	10.0	14.4	6.1
70 - 74	33 275	22 067	11 208	15.4	22.1	9.7
75 - 79	41 046	24 830	16 216	25.9	35.5	18.4
80 - 84	69 771	36 952	32 819	50.2	65.7	39.7
85 - 89	92 115	40 809	51 306	95.6	116.6	83.6
90 - 94	72 292	25 642	46 650	177.1	205.2	164.7
95 - 99	28 557	7 780	20 777	277.2	296.8	270.5
100 +	5 358	975	4 383	470.6	490.3	466.4
Sweden - Suède						
2018 (C)						
Total	92 185	45 416	46 769	9.1	8.9	9.3
0	235	132	103	2.0	2.2	1.8
1 - 4	70	37	33	0.1	0.1	0.1
5 - 9	31	12	19	0.1	-	♦0.1
10 - 14	63	36	27	0.1	0.1	♦0.1
15 - 19	140	89	51	0.3	0.3	0.2
20 - 24	289	202	87	0.5	0.6	0.3
25 - 29	366	268	98	0.5	0.7	0.3
30 - 34	373	247	126	0.6	0.7	0.4
35 - 39	393	268	125	0.6	0.8	0.4
40 - 44	553	354	199	0.9	1.1	0.6
45 - 49	841	503	338	1.3	1.5	1.0
50 - 54	1 498	938	560	2.2	2.7	1.7
55 - 59	2 154	1 293	861	3.7	4.4	3.0
60 - 64	3 596	2 162	1 434	6.4	7.7	5.1
65 - 69	5 944	3 542	2 402	10.6	12.8	8.5
70 - 74	9 702	5 575	4 127	17.4	20.5	14.5
75 - 79	11 470	6 522	4 948	30.5	36.5	25.0

19. Deaths by age and sex and age-specific death rates by sex: latest available year, 2010 - 2019
Décès et taux de mortalité selon l'âge et le sexe : dernière année disponible, 2010 - 2019 (continued - suite)

Continent, country or area, date, code[a] and age (in years) / Continent, pays ou zone, date, code[a] et âge (en années)	Number - Nombre			Rate - Taux		
	Both sexes / Les deux sexes	Male / Masculin	Female / Féminin	Both sexes / Les deux sexes	Male / Masculin	Female / Féminin
EUROPE						
Sweden - Suède						
2018 (C)						
80 - 84	14 316	7 564	6 752	56.8	68.6	47.6
85 - 89	17 484	8 034	9 450	107.2	128.7	93.8
90 - 94	15 076	5 616	9 460	199.1	234.7	182.7
95 - 99	6 525	1 811	4 714	333.2	378.1	318.7
100 +	1 066	211	855	511.5	599.4	493.6
Switzerland - Suisse						
2018 (C)						
Total	67 088	32 396	34 692	7.9	7.6	8.1
0	287	154	133	3.3	3.5	3.2
1 - 4	55	25	30	0.2	♦0.1	♦0.2
5 - 9	33	20	13	0.1	♦0.1	♦0.1
10 - 14	36	18	18	0.1	♦0.1	♦0.1
15 - 19	109	74	35	0.3	0.3	0.2
20 - 24	149	108	41	0.3	0.4	0.2
25 - 29	178	123	55	0.3	0.4	0.2
30 - 34	206	129	77	0.3	0.4	0.3
35 - 39	309	215	94	0.5	0.7	0.3
40 - 44	476	296	180	0.8	1.0	0.6
45 - 49	829	518	311	1.3	1.7	1.0
50 - 54	1 469	901	568	2.2	2.7	1.7
55 - 59	2 087	1 278	809	3.4	4.2	2.7
60 - 64	2 904	1 807	1 097	5.8	7.2	4.3
65 - 69	4 008	2 475	1 533	9.4	12.0	6.9
70 - 74	5 848	3 536	2 312	14.7	18.7	11.0
75 - 79	7 365	4 157	3 208	23.9	29.8	19.1
80 - 84	10 540	5 407	5 133	47.7	58.3	40.1
85 - 89	13 424	5 760	7 664	94.0	109.5	85.0
90 - 94	11 488	4 020	7 468	182.5	213.6	169.2
95 - 99	4 558	1 226	3 332	294.6	330.6	283.2
100 +	730	149	581	464.4	579.8	441.8
Ukraine[54]						
2017 (+C)						
Total	574 123	281 784	292 339	13.6	14.4	12.9
0	2 786	1 608	1 178	7.4	8.2	6.4
1 - 4	598	357	241	0.3	0.4	0.3
5 - 9	391	214	177	0.2	0.2	0.2
10 - 14	402	254	148	0.2	0.2	0.2
15 - 19	890	633	257	0.5	0.7	0.3
20 - 24	1 908	1 492	416	0.8	1.2	0.4
25 - 29	4 071	3 091	980	1.3	1.9	0.6
30 - 34	7 460	5 679	1 781	2.1	3.1	1.0
35 - 39	10 358	7 706	2 652	3.2	4.8	1.6
40 - 44	13 614	10 018	3 596	4.5	6.7	2.3
45 - 49	17 043	12 408	4 635	6.0	9.1	3.1
50 - 54	23 962	17 277	6 685	8.3	13.1	4.3
55 - 59	36 678	25 946	10 732	11.6	18.6	6.1
60 - 64	46 399	31 156	15 243	17.2	27.8	9.7
65 - 69	58 382	35 464	22 918	25.2	39.4	16.2
70 - 74	49 917	26 199	23 718	37.9	57.4	27.5
75 - 79	99 211	43 174	56 037	59.4	83.4	48.6
80 - 84	82 511	29 856	52 655	91.7	113.2	82.8
85 - 89	73 757	20 398	53 359	147.4	159.0	143.3
90 - 94	36 507	7 556	28 951	211.5	188.0	218.7
95 - 99	6 549	1 127	5 422	203.3	119.4	238.1
100 +	729	171	558	94.9	71.2	105.7
United Kingdom of Great Britain and Northern Ireland - Royaume-Uni de Grande-Bretagne et d'Irlande du Nord[55]						
2018 (+C)						
Total	614 313	303 338	310 975	9.3	9.3	9.3
0	2 817	1 562	1 255	3.7	4.0	3.3
1 - 4	411	232	179	0.1	0.1	0.1
5 - 9	301	154	147	0.1	0.1	0.1
10 - 14	347	213	134	0.1	0.1	0.1
15 - 19	966	649	317	0.3	0.3	0.2

19. Deaths by age and sex and age-specific death rates by sex: latest available year, 2010 - 2019
Décès et taux de mortalité selon l'âge et le sexe : dernière année disponible, 2010 - 2019 (continued - suite)

Continent, country or area, date, code[a] and age (in years) / Continent, pays ou zone, date, code[a] et âge (en années)	Number - Nombre			Rate - Taux		
	Both sexes Les deux sexes	Male Masculin	Female Féminin	Both sexes Les deux sexes	Male Masculin	Female Féminin
EUROPE						
United Kingdom of Great Britain and Northern Ireland - Royaume-Uni de Grande-Bretagne et d'Irlande du Nord[55]						
2018 (+C)						
20 - 24	1 571	1 134	437	0.4	0.5	0.2
25 - 29	2 148	1 482	666	0.5	0.6	0.3
30 - 34	2 939	1 931	1 008	0.7	0.9	0.5
35 - 39	4 244	2 655	1 589	1.0	1.2	0.7
40 - 44	5 858	3 712	2 146	1.5	1.9	1.1
45 - 49	10 064	6 089	3 975	2.2	2.7	1.7
50 - 54	14 998	9 030	5 968	3.2	3.9	2.5
55 - 59	21 043	12 435	8 608	5.0	5.9	4.0
60 - 64	28 112	16 554	11 558	7.7	9.3	6.2
65 - 69	41 218	24 340	16 878	12.0	14.6	9.5
70 - 74	61 885	35 566	26 319	19.4	23.4	15.9
75 - 79	74 876	41 126	33 750	33.9	40.4	28.3
80 - 84	98 768	50 715	48 053	59.6	70.1	51.4
85 - 89	111 927	50 485	61 442	109.6	126.7	98.6
90 - 94	85 994	31 816	54 178	192.4	214.9	181.3
95 - 99	37 619	10 383	27 236	312.0	343.6	301.4
100 +	6 207	1 075	5 132	429.0	429.5	428.9
OCEANIA - OCÉANIE						
American Samoa - Samoas américaines						
2017 (C)						
Total	310	176	134	...	...	...
0	14	5	9	...	...	...
1 - 4	1	1	-	...	...	...
5 - 9	2	1	1	...	...	...
10 - 14	1	1	-	...	...	...
15 - 19	3	3	-	...	...	...
20 - 24	6	6	-	...	...	...
25 - 29	4	3	1	...	...	...
30 - 34	5	4	1	...	...	...
35 - 39	7	3	4	...	...	...
40 - 44	7	3	4	...	...	...
45 - 49	19	14	5	...	...	...
50 - 54	25	12	13	...	...	...
55 - 59	22	17	5	...	...	...
60 - 64	31	20	11	...	...	...
65 - 69	34	18	16	...	...	...
70 - 74	36	21	15	...	...	...
75 - 79	37	22	15	...	...	...
80 - 84	23	12	11	...	...	...
85 +	33	10	23	...	...	...
Australia - Australie[56]						
2018 (C)						
Total	158 493	82 320	76 173	6.3	6.6	6.0
0	988	571	417	3.2	3.5	2.7
1 - 4	158	89	69	0.1	0.1	0.1
5 - 9	102	51	51	0.1	0.1	0.1
10 - 14	136	80	56	0.1	0.1	0.1
15 - 19	457	304	153	0.3	0.4	0.2
20 - 24	677	510	167	0.4	0.6	0.2
25 - 29	797	580	217	0.4	0.6	0.2
30 - 34	1 043	724	319	0.6	0.8	0.3
35 - 39	1 459	966	493	0.8	1.1	0.6
40 - 44	1 822	1 125	697	1.1	1.4	0.9
45 - 49	2 864	1 763	1 101	1.7	2.2	1.3
50 - 54	3 979	2 391	1 588	2.6	3.2	2.0
55 - 59	6 021	3 689	2 332	3.9	4.9	3.0
60 - 64	8 075	4 955	3 120	5.9	7.5	4.5
65 - 69	10 774	6 612	4 162	8.9	11.2	6.7
70 - 74	14 837	9 009	5 828	14.6	18.0	11.3
75 - 79	17 754	10 262	7 492	25.3	30.8	20.4

19. Deaths by age and sex and age-specific death rates by sex: latest available year, 2010 - 2019
Décès et taux de mortalité selon l'âge et le sexe : dernière année disponible, 2010 - 2019 (continued - suite)

Continent, country or area, date, code[a] and age (in years) / Continent, pays ou zone, date, code[a] et âge (en années)	Number - Nombre			Rate - Taux		
	Both sexes / Les deux sexes	Male / Masculin	Female / Féminin	Both sexes / Les deux sexes	Male / Masculin	Female / Féminin
OCEANIA - OCÉANIE						
Australia - Australie[56]						
2018 (C)						
80 - 84	22 688	12 330	10 358	46.7	56.4	38.8
85 - 89	27 860	13 457	14 403	90.1	106.6	78.8
90 - 94	24 265	9 532	14 733	162.0	182.1	151.2
95 - 99	9 939	2 947	6 992	246.3	255.4	242.7
100 +	1 797	372	1 425	399.2	322.6	425.6
Unknown - Inconnu	3	3	-	..	..	..
Fiji - Fidji[57]						
2017 (+C)						
Total	6 992	3 766	3 226	7.9	8.4	7.4
0	300	170	130	...	...	...
1 - 4	134	74	60	...	...	...
5 - 9	49	25	24	0.6	♦0.6	♦0.6
10 - 14	46	18	28	0.6	♦0.4	♦0.7
15 - 19	50	22	28	0.7	♦0.6	♦0.8
20 - 24	92	53	39	1.2	1.4	1.1
25 - 29	108	63	45	1.6	1.8	1.3
30 - 34	140	71	69	2.0	2.0	2.1
35 - 39	191	109	82	2.9	3.3	2.6
40 - 44	264	143	121	4.9	5.2	4.7
45 - 49	352	197	155	7.1	7.8	6.4
50 - 54	592	345	247	12.2	14.0	10.3
55 - 59	756	450	306	18.0	21.2	14.8
60 - 64	830	481	349	27.1	32.3	22.2
65 - 69	752	394	358	35.3	39.1	31.8
70 - 74	736	393	343	52.0	61.7	44.1
75 +	1 600	758	842	111.2	131.0	97.9
75 - 79	687	358	329	...	...	...
80 - 84	490	231	259	...	...	...
85 +	423	169	254	...	...	...
French Polynesia - Polynésie française						
2018 (C)						
Total	1 616	938	678	5.8	6.7	5.0
0	36	23	13	19.3	♦23.8	♦14.4
1 - 4	6	3	3	♦0.4	♦0.4	♦0.4
5 - 9	-	-	-	-	-	-
10 - 14	9	6	3	♦0.4	♦0.5	♦0.3
15 - 19	13	8	5	♦0.6	♦0.7	♦0.5
20 - 24	11	9	2	♦0.6	♦0.9	♦0.2
25 - 29	25	20	5	♦1.2	♦1.9	♦0.5
30 - 34	27	21	6	♦1.2	♦1.9	♦0.5
35 - 39	28	19	9	♦1.3	♦1.8	♦0.9
40 - 44	44	30	14	2.2	♦3.0	♦1.4
45 - 49	50	38	12	2.5	3.8	♦1.2
50 - 54	100	62	38	5.3	6.4	4.2
55 - 59	124	78	46	8.1	9.8	6.3
60 - 64	152	83	69	12.4	13.0	11.8
65 - 69	160	104	56	18.5	23.6	13.2
70 - 74	204	131	73	32.5	41.5	23.4
75 - 79	182	105	77	42.5	50.4	35.1
80 - 84	203	101	102	82.8	94.3	73.9
85 - 89	146	64	82	121.1	130.0	115.0
90 - 94	74	31	43	182.0	209.9	166.2
95 - 99	18	2	16	♦249.4	♦118.7	♦289.3
100 +	4	-	4	♦521.2	-	♦649.1
Guam[58]						
2018 (C)						
Total	1 056	638	418	6.3	7.4	5.1
0	37	16	21	11.5	♦9.6	♦13.5
1 - 4	6	4	2	♦0.5	♦0.6	♦0.3
5 - 9	2	2	-	♦0.1	♦0.2	-
10 - 14	2	1	1	♦0.1	♦0.1	♦0.1
15 - 19	10	9	1	♦0.7	♦1.2	♦0.1
20 - 24	23	20	3	♦1.7	♦2.8	♦0.5
25 - 29	25	16	9	♦2.0	♦2.4	♦1.5
30 - 34	19	16	3	♦1.8	♦2.9	♦0.6

19. Deaths by age and sex and age-specific death rates by sex: latest available year, 2010 - 2019
Décès et taux de mortalité selon l'âge et le sexe : dernière année disponible, 2010 - 2019 (continued - suite)

Continent, country or area, date, code[a] and age (in years) / Continent, pays ou zone, date, code[a] et âge (en années)	Number - Nombre			Rate - Taux		
	Both sexes / Les deux sexes	Male / Masculin	Female / Féminin	Both sexes / Les deux sexes	Male / Masculin	Female / Féminin
OCEANIA - OCÉANIE						
Guam[58]						
2018 (C)						
35 - 39	40	31	9	4.3	6.7	♦1.9
40 - 44	36	28	8	3.9	♦5.9	♦1.7
45 - 49	50	30	20	4.7	♦5.6	♦3.9
50 - 54	81	56	25	7.8	10.3	♦5.1
55 - 59	101	63	38	10.7	12.8	8.4
60 - 64	106	68	38	14.3	18.4	10.3
65 - 69	107	61	46	17.7	20.4	15.0
70 - 74	105	65	40	26.7	34.7	19.5
75 - 79	84	48	36	34.1	42.7	26.9
80 - 84	92	41	51	57.7	64.4	53.3
85 - 89	55	30	25	79.9	♦118.1	♦57.6
90 - 94	59	25	34	345.0	♦403.2	311.9
95 - 99	15	7	8	♦555.6	♦777.8	♦444.4
100 +	1	1	-	♦333.3	♦1000.0	-
Kiribati[59]						
2011 (U)						
Total	*481*	*279*	*202*	...	...	...
0 - 4	*132*	*75*	*57*	...	...	...
5 - 19	*14*	*10*	*4*	...	...	...
20 - 29	*34*	*24*	*10*	...	...	...
30 - 39	*28*	*15*	*13*	...	...	...
40 - 49	*60*	*37*	*23*	...	...	...
50 - 59	*74*	*42*	*32*	...	...	...
60 - 69	*54*	*34*	*20*	...	...	...
70 +	*85*	*42*	*43*	...	...	...
Nauru						
2011 (C)						
Total	75	41	34	...	...	...
0	10	5	5	...	...	...
1 - 4	1	1	-	...	...	...
5 - 9	-	-	-	...	...	...
10 - 14	1	1	-	...	...	...
15 - 19	-	-	-	...	...	...
20 - 24	2	2	-	...	...	...
25 - 29	5	1	4	...	...	...
30 - 34	4	1	3	...	...	...
35 - 39	2	1	1	...	...	...
40 - 44	2	2	-	...	...	...
45 - 49	6	3	3	...	...	...
50 - 54	15	7	8	...	...	...
55 - 59	9	7	2	...	...	...
60 - 64	6	2	4	...	...	...
65 - 69	4	2	2	...	...	...
70 +	8	6	2	...	...	...
New Caledonia - Nouvelle-Calédonie						
2015 (C)						
Total	1 465	853	612	...	...	...
0	25	18	7	...	...	...
1 - 4	7	4	3	...	...	...
5 - 9	2	-	2	...	...	...
10 - 14	6	4	2	...	...	...
15 - 19	19	13	6	...	...	...
20 - 24	26	22	4	...	...	...
25 - 29	19	17	2	...	...	...
30 - 34	32	23	9	...	...	...
35 - 39	24	21	3	...	...	...
40 - 44	58	45	13	...	...	...
45 - 49	58	41	17	...	...	...
50 - 54	77	48	29	...	...	...
55 - 59	83	46	37	...	...	...
60 - 64	120	76	44	...	...	...
65 - 69	144	95	49	...	...	...
70 - 74	154	91	63	...	...	...
75 - 79	177	94	83	...	...	...
80 - 84	167	83	84	...	...	...

19. Deaths by age and sex and age-specific death rates by sex: latest available year, 2010 - 2019
Décès et taux de mortalité selon l'âge et le sexe : dernière année disponible, 2010 - 2019 (continued - suite)

Continent, country or area, date, code[a] and age (in years) / Continent, pays ou zone, date, code[a] et âge (en années)	Number - Nombre			Rate - Taux		
	Both sexes / Les deux sexes	Male / Masculin	Female / Féminin	Both sexes / Les deux sexes	Male / Masculin	Female / Féminin
OCEANIA - OCÉANIE						
New Caledonia - Nouvelle-Calédonie						
2015 (C)						
85 - 89	144	66	78	...	...	...
90 - 94	76	29	47	...	...	...
95 +	47	17	30	...	...	...
New Zealand - Nouvelle-Zélande[60]						
2019 (+C)						
Total	34 260	17 580	16 677	...	...	...
0	270	141	126	...	...	...
1 - 4	57	30	27	...	...	...
5 - 9	27	15	15	...	...	...
10 - 14	54	30	24	...	...	...
15 - 19	132	87	45	...	...	...
20 - 24	201	150	51	...	...	...
25 - 29	213	153	60	...	...	...
30 - 34	261	174	84	...	...	...
35 - 39	264	180	84	...	...	...
40 - 44	366	207	159	...	...	...
45 - 49	648	366	282	...	...	...
50 - 54	990	588	402	...	...	...
55 - 59	1 428	867	564	...	...	...
60 - 64	1 818	1 062	753	...	...	...
65 - 69	2 466	1 449	1 014	...	...	...
70 - 74	3 372	1 977	1 398	...	...	...
75 - 79	4 113	2 337	1 773	...	...	...
80 - 84	4 881	2 568	2 316	...	...	...
85 - 89	5 889	2 805	3 084	...	...	...
90 - 94	4 599	1 785	2 814	...	...	...
95 - 99	1 890	552	1 338	...	...	...
100 +	324	54	267	...	...	...
Palau - Palaos						
2018 (C)						
Total	143	79	64	...	...	...
0	3	1	2	...	...	...
1 - 14	-	-	-	...	...	...
15 - 24	3	2	1	...	...	...
25 - 44	11	7	4	...	...	...
45 - 64	43	33	10	...	...	...
65 +	83	36	47	...	...	...
Samoa[22]						
2016 (|)						
Total	853	446	407	4.4	4.4	4.3
0	69	32	37	12.4	11.1	13.8
1 - 4	26	14	12	♦1.2	♦1.2	♦1.1
5 - 9	9	4	5	♦0.4	♦0.3	♦0.4
10 - 14	4	2	2	♦0.2	♦0.2	♦0.2
15 - 19	16	8	7	♦0.8	♦0.8	♦0.8
20 - 24	17	9	8	♦1.1	♦1.1	♦1.0
25 - 29	10	4	6	♦0.8	♦0.6	♦0.9
30 - 34	25	16	10	♦2.1	♦2.6	♦1.7
35 - 39	16	7	10	♦1.5	♦1.3	♦1.9
40 - 44	27	14	13	♦2.6	♦2.6	♦2.6
45 - 49	37	16	21	3.8	♦3.1	♦4.6
50 - 54	67	40	28	7.9	9.2	♦6.8
55 - 59	80	52	27	11.4	14.2	♦8.1
60 - 64	78	50	27	14.9	18.7	♦10.6
65 - 69	67	37	30	19.3	21.7	♦16.9
70 - 74	60	29	32	22.3	♦22.9	22.5
75 - 79	79	40	39	45.1	53.6	38.8
80 - 84	58	29	29	57.4	♦79.5	♦44.9
85 - 89	43	17	26	90.3	♦104.3	♦83.1
90 - 94	32	9	23	201.3	♦187.5	♦207.2
95 - 99	8	2	6	♦296.3	♦333.3	♦285.7
100 +	2	2	-	♦333.3	♦1000.0	-
Unknown - Inconnu	22	14	8	..	..	..

19. Deaths by age and sex and age-specific death rates by sex: latest available year, 2010 - 2019
Décès et taux de mortalité selon l'âge et le sexe : dernière année disponible, 2010 - 2019 (continued - suite)

Continent, country or area, date, code[a] and age (in years) / Continent, pays ou zone, date, code[a] et âge (en annèes)	Number - Nombre			Rate - Taux		
	Both sexes Les deux sexes	Male Masculin	Female Féminin	Both sexes Les deux sexes	Male Masculin	Female Féminin
OCEANIA - OCÉANIE						
Tuvalu						
2016 (+U)						
Total	*90*	*45*	*45*	...	...	...
0 - 4	*9*	*4*	*5*	...	...	...
5 - 9	-	-	-	...	...	...
10 - 14	-	-	-	...	...	...
15 - 19	-	-	-	...	...	...
20 - 24	-	-	-	...	...	...
25 - 29	*4*	*3*	*1*	...	...	...
30 - 34	*1*	-	*1*	...	...	...
35 - 39	-	-	-	...	...	...
40 - 44	*4*	-	*4*	...	...	...
45 - 49	*2*	*1*	*1*	...	...	...
50 - 54	*5*	*4*	*1*	...	...	...
55 - 59	*12*	*8*	*4*	...	...	...
60 - 64	*9*	*6*	*3*	...	...	...
65 - 69	*9*	*3*	*6*	...	...	...
70 - 74	*8*	*3*	*5*	...	...	...
75 - 79	*17*	*8*	*9*	...	...	...
80 +	*10*	*5*	*5*	...	...	...
Vanuatu						
2014 (+U)						
Total	*614*	*370*[11]	*234*[11]	...	...	...
0 - 4	*133*	*56*[11]	*68*[11]	...	...	...
5 - 9	*3*	*1*	*2*	...	...	...
10 - 14	*4*	*2*	*2*	...	...	...
15 - 19	*9*	*6*	*3*	...	...	...
20 - 24	*11*	*7*	*4*	...	...	...
25 - 29	*9*	*7*	*2*	...	...	...
30 - 34	*15*	*11*	*4*	...	...	...
35 - 39	*17*	*10*	*7*	...	...	...
40 - 44	*37*	*25*	*12*	...	...	...
45 - 49	*51*	*34*	*17*	...	...	...
50 - 54	*53*	*37*	*16*	...	...	...
55 - 59	*38*	*26*	*12*	...	...	...
60 - 64	*62*	*39*	*23*	...	...	...
65 - 69	*25*	*16*	*9*	...	...	...
70 - 74	*41*	*25*	*16*	...	...	...
75 - 79	*26*	*22*	*4*	...	...	...
80 +	*42*	*26*[11]	*15*[11]	...	...	...
Unknown - Inconnu	*38*	*20*	*18*	..	..	..

FOOTNOTES - NOTES

♦ Rates based on 30 or fewer deaths. - Taux basés sur 30 décès ou moins.

Italics: estimates which are less reliable. - Italiques : estimations moins sûres.

* Provisional. - Données provisoires.

[a] 'Code' indicates the source of data, as follows:
C - Civil registration, estimated over 90% complete
U - Civil registration, estimated less than 90% complete
| - Other source, estimated reliable
+ - Data tabulated by date of registration rather than occurence
... - Information not available

Le 'Code' indique la source des données, comme suit :
C - Registres de l'état civil considérés complets à 90 p. 100 au moins
U - Registres de l'état civil qui ne sont pas considérés complets à 90 p. 100 au moins
| - Autre source, considérée pas douteuses
+ - Données exploitées selon la date de l'enregistrement et non la date de l'événement
... - Information pas disponible

[1] Excluding live-born infants who died before their birth was registered. Data refer to Algerian population only. - Non compris les enfants nés vivants décédés avant l'enregistrement de leur naissance. Les données ne concernent que la population algérienne.

[2] Source: Vital Statistics Report. - Source: Vital Statistics Report.

[3] Source: Statistical Report, Ministry of Health and Social Security. - Source: Rapport statistique, ministère de la Santé et de la Sécurité sociale.

[4] Source: Ministry of Home Affairs. - Source : Ministère de l'intérieur.

[5] Data refer to the 12 months preceding the census in September. - Les données se rapportent aux 12 mois précédant le recensement de septembre.

[6] Unadjusted number of deaths in households referring to the 12 months preceding the census in March. - Le nombre non ajusté de décès des ménages ordinaires se rapportent aux 12 mois précédant le recensement de mars.

[7] Excludes the islands of St. Brandon and Agalega. - Non compris les îles St. Brandon et Agalega.

[8] Data refer to the 12 months preceding the census in August. - Les données se rapportent aux 12 mois précédant le recensement d'août.

[9] Data refer to the 12 months preceding the census in May. - Les données se rapportent aux 12 mois précédant le recensement de mai.

[10] Source: National Office of Births and Deaths. - Source : Le bureau national des naissances et des décès.

[11] Figures for male and female may not add up to the total, since they do not include the category "Unknown". - La somme des chiffres indiqués pour les

sexes masculin et féminin peut n'être pas égale au total parce qu'elle n'inclut pas la catégorie " inconnue ".

[12] Completeness estimated at 19%. - Degré de complétude évalué à 19 pour cent.

[13] Excluding visitors. - Ne comprend pas les visiteurs.

[14] Unrevised data. - Les données n'ont pas été révisées.

[15] Excluding non-residents and foreign service personnel and their dependants. - À l'exclusion des non-résidents et du personnel diplomatique et de leurs charges de famille.

[16] Including resident deaths outside of the islands but buried in the islands. - Y compris les décès de résidents hors des îles mais inhumés dans les îles.

[17] Excluding live-born infants who died before their birth was registered. - Non compris les enfants nés vivants décédés avant l'enregistrement de leur naissance.

[18] Data refer to population in private households. Data refer to period from 1 January 2010 to 3 April 2011. - Les données portent sur la population des ménages privés. Les données concernent la période du 1 janvier 2010 au 3 avril 2011.

[19] Data refer to resident population only. - Pour la population résidante seulement.

[20] Data refer to resident and non resident deaths that occurred in Saint Vincent and the Grenadines. - Les données concernent les décès de résidents et de non-résidents survenus à St Vincent-et-les-Grenadines.

[21] Excluding deaths of persons living abroad. - Exception faite des personnes décédées à l'étranger.

[22] Data refer to the 12 months preceding the census in November. - Données se rapportant aux 12 mois précédant le recensement de novembre.

[23] Including deaths abroad and deaths of unknown place of residence. - Y compris décès à l'étranger et décès dont le lieu de résidence n'est pas connu.

[24] Excludes nomadic Indian tribes. - Non compris les tribus d'Indiens nomades.

[25] Source: Reports of the Ministry of Health. - Source : Rapports du Ministère de la Santé.

[26] Excluding deaths of unknown sex. - Non compris les décès dont on ignore le sexe.

[27] Excluding infants born alive of less than 28 weeks' gestation, of less than 1 000 g in weight and 35 cm in length, who die within seven days of birth. - Non compris les enfants nés vivants après moins de 28 semaines de gestations, pesant moins de 1 000 g, mesurant moins de 35 cm et décédés dans les sept jours qui ont suivi leur naissance.

[28] Sources: Births and Deaths National Registration System database, and medical records of government hospitals. Data refer to Bahraini and non-Bahraini deaths including some visitors, and Bahraini deaths abroad. - Les sources: Les bases de données des << Births and Deaths National Registration System >> et les dossiers médicaux des hôpitaux du gouvernement. Les données se rapportent aux décès de Bahreïniens et de non-Bahreïniens, y compris de non-résidents, ainsi que de Bahreïniens résidant à l'étranger.

[29] For statistical purposes, the data for China do not include those for the Hong Kong Special Administrative Region (Hong Kong SAR), Macao Special Administrative Region (Macao SAR) and Taiwan province of China. Data refer to the 12 months preceding the census in November. - Pour la présentation des statistiques, les données pour la Chine ne comprennent pas la Région Administrative Spéciale de Hong Kong (Hong Kong RAS), la Région Administrative Spéciale de Macao (Macao RAS) et Taïwan province de Chine. Données se rapportant aux 12 mois précédant le recensement de novembre.

[30] Data refer to government controlled areas. Data refer to deaths of residents only. - Les données se rapportent aux zones contrôlées par le Gouvernement. Les données renvoient aux décès de résidents uniquement.

[31] Data are from 1 January 2009 to 1 May 2010. - Les données vont du 1er janvier 2009 au 1er mai 2010.

[32] Data refer to the Iranian Year which begins on 21 March and ends on 20 March of the following year. Data refer to current deaths; excluding delayed registrations. - Les données concernent l'année iranienne, qui commence le 21 mars et se termine le 20 mars de l'année suivante. Les données se rapportent aux décès actuels; les déclarations tardives des décès ne sont pas compris.

[33] Includes data for East Jerusalem and Israeli residents in certain other territories under occupation by Israeli military forces since June 1967. Including deaths abroad of Israeli residents who were out of the country for less than a year. - Y compris les données pour Jérusalem-Est et les résidents israéliens dans certains autres territoires occupés depuis 1967 par les forces armées israéliennes. Y compris les décès à l'étranger de résidents israéliens qui ont quitté le pays depuis moins d'un an.

[34] Data refer to Japanese nationals in Japan only. - Les données se raportent aux nationaux japonais au Japon seulement.

[35] Data refer to the 12 months preceding the census in March. - Les données se rapportent aux 12 mois précédant le recensement de mars.

[36] Data do not include foreigners. - Les données sur les etrangers ne sont pas inclus.

[37] Data are from Vital Registration System (VRS). - Les données proviennent du système d'enregistrement des faits d'état civil.

[38] Data refer to the 12 months preceding the census in June. - Les données se rapportent aux 12 mois précédant le recensement de juin.

[39] Excluding alien armed forces, civilian aliens employed by armed forces, and foreign diplomatic personnel and their dependants. - Non compris les militaires étrangers, les civils étrangers employés par les forces armées ni le personnel diplomatique étranger et les membres de leur famille les accompagnant.

[40] Data refer to Saudi Arabian nationals only. Based on 2010 population census and 2016 demographic survey. - Les données ne concernent que les ressortissants saoudiens. D'après le recensement de la population de 2010 et l'enquête démographique de 2016.

[41] Source: Palestinian Central Bureau of Statistics, Population Register, updated version 2019. Data exclude Jerusalem ID holders. - Source: Bureau central de statistique palestinien, registre de la population, version actualisée jusqu'au 2019. Les données ne tiennent pas compte des détenteurs de carte d'identité de Jérusalem.

[42] Source: Strategy and Planning Division, Ministry of Public Health. - Source : Division de la stratégie et de la planification, Ministère de la Santé publique.

[43] Data from MERNIS (Central Population Administrative System). - Données de MERNIS (Système central de données démographiques).

[44] Including deaths of nationals abroad. - Y compris les décès des nationaux survenus à l'étranger.

[45] Including armed forces stationed outside the country, but excluding alien armed forces stationed in the area. - Y compris les militaires nationaux hors du pays, mais non compris les militaires étrangers en garnison sur le territoire.

[46] Excluding Faeroe Islands and Greenland shown separately, if available. - Non compris les Iles Féroé et le Groenland, qui font l'objet de rubriques distinctes, si disponible.

[47] Data include the deceased persons with Hungarian usual residence regardless of whether the death occurred in Hungary or in a foreign country, and do not include the deceased persons with foreign country usual residence. - Les données comprennent tous les décès survenus alors que leur résidence habituelle était en Hongrie, que le décès ait eu lieu en Hongrie ou dans un pays étranger, et ne comprennent pas les décès des personnes dont la residence habituelle était dans un pays étranger.

[48] Data refer to the 12 months preceding the census in April. - Les données se rapportent aux douze mois précédant le recensement d'avril.

[49] Including residents outside the country if listed in a Netherlands population register. - Englobe les résidents se trouvant à l'étranger à condition qu'ils soient inscrits sur le registre de population des Pays-Bas.

[50] Including residents temporarily outside the country. - Y compris les résidents se trouvant temporairement hors du pays.

[51] Data refer to usual resident population. - Les données se réfèrent à la population résidente habituelle.

[52] Excluding Transnistria and the municipality of Bender. - Les données ne tiennent pas compte de l'information sur la Transnistria et la municipalité de Bender.

[53] Excludes data for Kosovo and Metohia. - Sans les données pour le Kosovo et Metohie.

[54] Data includes deaths resulting from births with weight 500 g and more (if weight is unknown - with length 25 cm and more, or with gestation during 22 weeks or more). The Government of Ukraine has informed the United Nations that it is not in a position to provide statistical data concerning the Autonomous Republic of Crimea and the city of Sevastopol. - Y compris les décès de nouveau-nés de 500 g ou plus (si le poids est inconnu – de 25 cm de long ou plus, ou après une grossesse de 22 semaines ou plus). Le gouvernement Ukrainien a informé l'ONU qu'il n'est pas en mesure de fournir des données statistiques concernant la République autonome de Crimée et la ville de Sébastopol.

[55] Excluding Channel Islands (Guernsey and Jersey) and Isle of Man, shown separately, if available. - Non compris les îles Anglo-Normandes (Guernesey et Jersey) et l'île de Man, qui font l'objet de rubriques distinctes, si disponible.

[56] Data of small values have been randomly adjusted to protect confidentiality. Some totals will not equal the sum of their components. Cells with 0 values have not been affected by confidentialisation. - Les valeurs peu élevées ont été arrondies de façon aléatoire pour des raisons de confidentialité. Certains totaux ne correspondront pas rigoureusement à la somme des composants. Les mesures de confidentialité ont été sans incidence sur les cellules présentant des valeurs nulles.

[57] Data recorded by Ministry of Health and Medical Services (MoHMS). - Données enregistrées par le Ministère de la santé et des services médicaux (MoHMS).

[58] Including United States military personnel, their dependants and contract employees. - Y compris les militaires des Etats-Unis, les membres de leur famille les accompagnant et les agents contractuels des Etats-Unis.

[59] Excluding deaths of unknown age or sex. - Les données ne comprennent pas les décès d'âge ou de sexe inconnus.

[60] Data refer to deaths of residents only. Random rounding to base 3 is applied in this table as a confidentiality measure. - Les données renvoient aux décès de résidents uniquement. Les chiffres sont arrondis à la base 3 de manière aléatoire, pour des raisons de confidentialité.

Table 20 – *Demographic Yearbook 2019*

Table 20 presents deaths and death rates by cause and sex for the two latest available years between 2014 and 2018.

Description of variables: Causes of death are all those diseases, morbid conditions or injuries which either resulted in or contributed to death and the circumstances of the accident or violence which produced any such injuries.[1]

The underlying cause of death, rather than direct or intermediate antecedent cause, is the one recommended as the main cause for tabulation of mortality statistics. It is defined as (a) the disease or injury which initiated the train of events leading directly to death, or (b) the circumstances of the accident or violence which produced the fatal injury.[1]

Statistics on deaths by cause presented in this table are provided by the World Health Organisation. They are limited to countries or areas that meet the criterion that cause-of-death statistics are classified to the ninth or tenth revisions of the International Classification of Diseases (ICD-9 or ICD-10). Data that are classified by the tenth revision are set in bold in the table.

Rate computation: Rates are the annual number of deaths in each cause group by sex reported for the year per 100 000 corresponding mid-year population. For certain causes, the population that more nearly approximates the population at risk is used as denominator, as specified below:

- rates for malignant neoplasm of female breast and malignant neoplasm of cervix uteri are computed per 100 000 female population 15 years and over;
- rates for hyperplasia of prostate are computed per 100 000 male population 50 years and over; and
- rates for direct and indirect obstetric causes, and rates for conditions originating in the perinatal period are computed per 100 000 total live births in the same year.

Rates presented in this table have been limited to those countries or areas having a total of at least 1 000 deaths from all causes in a given year. In certain cases, death rates by cause have not been calculated because the population data needed for the denominator are not available (no data on population at risk are available). Moreover, rates based on 30 or fewer deaths shown in this table are identified by the symbol (♦).

Reliability of data: Countries and areas that have incomplete (less than 90 per cent completeness) or of unknown completeness of cause of deaths data coverage are considered unreliable and are set in *italics* rather than in roman type. Rates on these data are not computed. Information on completeness is normally provided by the World Health Organisation, when this is not the case, information on completeness is set to coincide with that of Table 18. Similarly, the reliability of data for the completeness of cause of death is provided by the World Health Organisation and it may differ from the reliability of data for the total number of reported deaths. Therefore, there are cases when the quality code in table 18 does not correspond with the typeface used in this table.

Territorial composition as set in Section 2.2 of "Technical Notes on the Statistical Tables", including or excluding certain population of a country refers only to the denominator.

Limitations: Statistics on deaths by cause are subject to the same qualifications as have been set forth for vital statistics in general and death statistics in particular as discussed in section 4 of the Technical Notes.

In considering cause-of-death statistics it is important to take account of the differences among countries or areas in the quality, availability, and efficiency of medical services, certification procedures, and coding practices. When a death is registered and reported for statistical purposes, the cause of death if available will be stated in the death registration form. This statement of cause may have several sources: (1) If the death has been followed by an autopsy, presumably the "true" cause will have been discovered; (2) If an autopsy is not performed but the decedent was treated prior to death by a medical attendant, the reported cause of death will reflect the opinion of that physician based on observation of the patient while he or she was alive; and (3) If, on the other hand, the decedent has died without medical attendance, the body

---

NOTES

[1] *International Statistical Classification of Diseases and Related Health Problems*, Tenth Revision, Volume 2, World Health Organization, Geneva, 1992

may be examined (without autopsy) by a physician who, aided by the questioning of persons who saw the patient before death, may come to a decision as to the probable cause of death. These three possible sources of information on cause of death constitute in general three degrees of decreasing accuracy in reporting.

Serious difficulties of comparability may stem also from differences in the form of death certificate being used, an increasing tendency to enter more than one cause of death on the certificate and diversity in the principles by which the primary or underlying cause is selected for statistical use when more than one is entered.

Differences in terminology used to identify the same disease also result in lack of comparability in statistics. These differences may arise in the same language in various parts of one country or area, but they are particularly troublesome between different languages.

Coding problems, and problems in interpretation of rules, arise constantly in using the various revisions of the International Statistical Classification of Diseases and Related Health Problems. Lack of uniformity between countries or areas in these interpretations and in adapting rules to national needs, results in a lack of comparability that can be observed in the statistics. It is particularly evident in causes that are coded differently according to the age of the decedent, such as pneumonia, diarrhoeal diseases and others. Changing interpretations and new rules can also introduce disparities into the time series for one country or area. Hence, large increases or decreases in deaths reported from specified diseases should be examined carefully for possible explanations in terms of coding practice, before they are accepted as changes in mortality.

Further limitations of statistics by cause of death result from the periodic revision of the International Classification of Diseases. Data might not be comparable among countries or areas if different revisions of the Classification were used. Similarly, comparison over time for one country or area is not appropriate if different revisions were applied in the country. For a correspondence between ICD-10 and ICD-9, please see table 20-1 below.

In addition to the qualifications explained in footnotes, particular care must be taken in using distributions with relatively large numbers of deaths attributed to ill-defined causes. Large frequencies in this category may indicate that cause of death among whole segments of the population has been undiagnosed, and the distribution of known causes in such cases is likely to be quite unrepresentative of the situation as a whole.

The possibility of error being introduced by the exclusion of deaths of infants who were born alive but died before the registration of the birth or within the first 24 hours of life should not be overlooked. These infant deaths are incorrectly classified as late foetal deaths. In several countries or areas, tabulation procedures have been devised to separate these pseudo-late-foetal deaths from true late foetal deaths and to incorporate them into the total deaths, but even in these cases there is no way of knowing the cause of death.

In addition, it should be noted that rates are affected also by the quality and limitations of the population at risk that are used in their computation. The problems of under-enumeration or over-enumeration and, to some extent, the differences in definition of population and live births have been discussed in section 3 of the Technical Notes dealing with population data in general and section 4 with vital statistics, respectively, Specific information pertaining to individual countries or areas is given in the footnotes to table 3 on total population and to table 9 on live births.

Earlier data: Deaths and death rates by cause have been shown annually since the 1951 issue of the *Demographic Yearbook* and every other year since the 2000 issue. For information on specific years covered, readers should consult the Historical Index.

Table 20-1. Tabulation list for ICD-9 and ICD-10 data for presentation in the Demographic Yearbook

Disease	ICD-10	ICD-9 Basic Tabulation List
All causes	**A00-Y89**	**01-56**
Certain infectious and parasitic diseases	**A00-A33, A35-B99**	**01-07, 184**
Intestinal infectious diseases	A00-A09	01
Tuberculosis	A15-A19	02
Tetanus[1]	A33, A35	037
Diphtheria	A36	033
Whooping cough	A37	034
Meningococcal infection	A39	036
Septicaemia	A40-A41	038
Acute poliomyelitis	A80	040
Measles	B05	042
Viral hepatitis	B15-B19	046
Human immunodeficiency virus [HIV] disease	B20-B24	184
Malaria	B50-B54	052
Neoplasms	**C00-D48**	**08-17**
Malignant neoplasms	**C00-C97**	**08-14**
Malignant neoplasm of lip, oral cavity and pharynx	C00-C14	08
Malignant neoplasm of oesophagus	C15	090
Malignant neoplasm of stomach	C16	091
Malignant neoplasm of colon, rectosigmoid junction, rectum, anus and anal canal	C18-C21	093-094
Malignant neoplasm of liver and intrahepatic bile ducts	C22	095
Malignant neoplasm of pancreas	C25	096
Malignant neoplasm of trachea, bronchus and lung	C33-C34	101
Malignant neoplasm of **female** breast	C50	113
Malignant neoplasm of cervix uteri	C53	120
Malignant neoplasm of prostate	C61	124
Malignant neoplasm of lymphoid, haematopoietic and related tissue	C81-C96	14
Disorders of the blood and blood-forming organs and certain disorders involving the immune mechanism	**D50-D89**	**20**
Anaemias	D50-D64	200
Endocrine, nutritional and metabolic diseases	**E00-E88**	**18-19, minus 184**
Diabetes mellitus	E10-E14	181
Malnutrition	E40-E46	190-192
Mental and behavioural disorders	**F01-F99**	**21**
Diseases of the nervous system	**G00-G98**	**22**
Diseases of the circulatory system	**I00-I99**	**25-30**
Acute rheumatic fever and chronic rheumatic heart diseases	I01-I09	25
Hypertensive diseases	I10-I13	26
Ischaemic heart diseases	I20-I25	27
Cerebrovascular diseases	I60-I69	29
Diseases of arteries, arterioles and capillaries	I70-I79	300-302
Diseases of the respiratory system	**J00-J98**	**31-32**
Influenza	J10-J11	322

Table 20-1. Tabulation list for ICD-9 and ICD-10 data for presentation in the Demographic Yearbook

Disease	ICD-10	ICD-9 Basic Tabulation List
Pneumonia	J12-J18	321
Chronic lower respiratory diseases	J40-J47	323-325
Diseases of the digestive system	**K00-K92**	**33-34**
Gastric and duodenal ulcer	K25-K27	341
Diseases of the liver	K70-K76	347
Diseases of the musculoskeletal system and connective tissue	**M00-M99**	**43**
Diseases of the genitourinary system	**N00-N98**	**35-37**
Disorders of kidney and ureter	N00-N28	350-351
Hyperplasia of prostate	N40	360
Pregnancy, childbirth and the puerperium	**O00-O99, A34**	**38-41**
Pregnancy with abortive outcome	O00-O07	38
Other direct obstetric causes[1]	O10-092, O95, A34	39
Indirect obstetric causes	O98-O99	40
Certain conditions originating in the perinatal period	**P00-P96**	**45**
Congenital malformations, deformations and chromosomal abnormalities	**Q00-Q99**	**44**
Symptoms, signs and abnormal clinical and laboratory findings, not elsewhere classified	**R00-R99**	**46**
All other diseases	**H00-H95, L00-L98**	**23-24, 42**
External causes	**V01-Y89**	**E47-E56**
Accidents	**V01-X59**	**E47-E53**
Transport accidents	V01-V99	E47
Falls	W00-W19	E50
Accidental drowning and submersion	W65-W74	E521
Exposure to smoke, fire and flames	X00-X09	E51
Accidental poisoning by and exposure to noxious substances	X40-X49	E48
Intentional self-harm	**X60-X84**	**E54**
Assault	**X85-Y09**	**E55**
All other external causes	Y10-Y89	E56

[1] In ICD-10 obstetrical tetanus is classified to A34 but in this table it is included with "Other direct obstetric causes", except for Belarus, Russian Federation, Seychelles, Turkmenistan and Ukraine, where obstetrical tetanus is included in "Tetanus" and "Other direct obstetric causes" excludes A34 and O95.

Tableau 20 - *Annuaire démographique 2019*

Le tableau 20 présente la statistique des décès par cause et sexe pour les deux dernières années entre 2014 et 2018.

Description des variables : les causes des décès sont toutes les maladies, états morbides ou traumatismes qui ont abouti ou contribué au décès et les circonstances de l'accident ou de la violence qui ont entraîné ces traumatismes[1].

La cause initiale de décès, plutôt que la cause directe du décès, est recommandée pour les statistiques de la mortalité. La cause initiale de décès est définie comme : a) la maladie ou le traumatisme qui a déclenché l'évolution morbide conduisant directement au décès ; b) les circonstances de l'accident ou de la violence qui ont entraîné le traumatisme mortel[1].

Les statistiques sur les décès classés en fonction de la cause qui les a provoqués émanent de l'Organisation mondiale de la santé. Elles ne portent que sur les pays ou les zones dans lesquels les statistiques relatives à la cause des décès sont conformes à la liste de la neuvième ou de la dixième révision de la *Classification statistique internationale des maladies* (CIM-9 ou CIM-10). Les données conformes à la liste de la dixième révision sont indiquées en caractères gras dans le tableau.

Calcul des taux : les taux représentent le nombre annuel de décès signalés dans chaque groupe, pour l'année, dans une population de 100 000 habitants en milieu d'année.

Les taux relatifs à certaines catégories de causes correspondent aux populations les plus semblables à la population exposée comme spécifié ci-dessous :

- les taux correspondant aux catégories « tumeur maligne du sein chez la femme » et « tumeur maligne du col de l'utérus » sont calculés sur une population de 100 000 femmes de 15 ans ou plus.
- les taux correspondant à la catégorie « tumeur maligne de la prostate » sont calculés sur une population de 100 000 personnes de sexe masculin âgées de 50 ans ou plus, et
- les taux pour les catégories « décès maternels directs », « décès maternels indirects » et « affections dont l'origine se situe dans la période périnatale » sont calculés sur 100 000 naissances vivantes dans la même année.

Les taux figurant dans ce tableau ne concernent que les pays ou zones où l'on a relevé au moins 1 000 décès, toutes causes confondues, dans l'année. Dans certains cas, on n'a pas calculé les taux de mortalité selon la cause car l'on ne disposait pas des informations sur la population qui étaient nécessaires pour déterminer le dénominateur (pas d'informations sur la population exposée au risque). De plus, les taux calculés sur la base de 30 décès ou moins, qui sont indiqués dans le tableau, sont signalés par le signe '♦'.

Fiabilité des données : les statistiques relatives aux pays et aux zones pour lesquels la couverture des données concernant les causes de décès est incomplète (mois de 90 pour cent) ou dont le degré de complétude n'est pas connue sont jugés douteuses et apparaissent en *italique* et non en caractères romains. Les taux correspondant ne sont pas calculés. L'information sur la complétude est normalement fournie par l'Organisation Mondiale de la Santé. Si ce n'est pas le cas, l'information sur la complétude est reprise de tableau 18. De même, la fiabilité des données relatives aux causes de décès est fournie par l'Organisation Mondiale de la Santé et peut différer de la fiabilité des données relatives au nombre de décès enregistrés. En conséquence, il peut apparaitre de différences entre les codes de fiabilité du tableau 18 et du présent tableau.

La composition territoriale est définie dans la Section 2.2 des "Notes Techniques sur les tableaux statistiques". L'inclusion ou l'exclusion de certaines populations d'un pays ne concerne que le dénominateur.

Insuffisance des données : les statistiques des décès selon la cause appellent les mêmes réserves que celles qui ont été formulées à propos des statistiques de l'état civil en général et des statistiques relatives aux décès en particulier (voir la section 4 des Notes techniques).

Lorsque l'on étudie les statistiques des causes des décès, il importe de prendre en considération les disparités existant entre pays ou zones du point de vue de la qualité, de la disponibilité et de l'efficacité des services médicaux, ainsi que des méthodes d'établissement des certificats de décès et des procédés de codage. Lorsqu'un décès est enregistré et déclaré aux fins de statistiques, le bulletin établi doit mentionner la cause du décès si elle est connue. Or la déclaration de la cause peut émaner de plusieurs sources : 1) si le décès a été suivi d'une autopsie, il est probable qu'on en aura décelé la cause « véritable » ; 2) s'il n'y a pas eu d'autopsie mais que le défunt a reçu, avant sa mort, les soins d'un médecin, la déclaration de la cause du décès reflétera l'opinion de ce médecin fondée sur l'observation du malade alors qu'il vivait encore ; 3) si, au contraire, le défunt est mort sans avoir reçu de soins médicaux, il se peut qu'un médecin examine le corps (sans qu'il soit fait d'autopsie), auquel cas il pourra, en questionnant les personnes qui ont vu le défunt avant sa mort, se former une opinion sur la cause probable du décès. À ces trois sources de renseignements possibles correspondent généralement trois degrés décroissants d'exactitude des données.

La comparabilité est aussi parfois très difficile à assurer par suite des différences existant dans la forme des certificats de décès utilisés, de la tendance croissante à indiquer plus d'une cause de décès sur le certificat et de la diversité des principes régissant le choix de la cause principale ou initiale à retenir dans les statistiques quand le certificat indique plus d'une cause.

Les différences entre les termes utilisés pour désigner une même maladie compromettent aussi la comparabilité des statistiques. On en rencontre parfois d'une région à l'autre dans un même pays ou une même zone où toute la population parle la même langue, mais elles sont particulièrement gênantes lorsque plusieurs langues interviennent.

En outre, des problèmes de codage et d'interprétation des règles se posent constamment lorsque l'on utilise les diverses révisions de la *Classification statistique internationale des maladies et des problèmes de santé connexes*. Les pays ou zones n'interprètent pas ces règles de manière uniforme et ne les adaptent pas de la même façon à leurs besoins ; la comparabilité s'en ressent comme le montrent les statistiques. Cela est particulièrement vrai pour les causes comme la pneumonie et les maladies diarrhéiques et autres, qui sont codées différemment selon l'âge du défunt. Les changements d'interprétation et l'adoption de nouvelles règles peuvent aussi introduire des divergences dans les séries chronologiques d'un même pays ou d'une même zone. En conséquence, il convient d'examiner attentivement les cas où le nombre de décès attribués à des maladies déterminées s'accroît ou diminue fortement, pour s'assurer, avant de conclure à une évolution de la mortalité, que le changement n'est pas dû à la méthode de codage.

D'autres irrégularités statistiques résultent des révisions périodiques de la *Classification statistique internationale des maladies*. Il est possible que les données ne soient pas comparables d'un pays ou d'une zone à un autre si différentes révisions de la classification ont été utilisées. De même, il n'est pas possible de comparer les données dans le temps pour un même pays ou zone lorsque différentes révisions y ont été utilisées. Pour une correspondance entre CIM-10 et CIM-9, veuillez voir le tableau 20-2 ci-dessous.

Outre les réserves expliquées dans les notes, il faut interpréter avec circonspection les répartitions comportant un nombre relativement élevé de décès attribués à des causes mal définies. Si les chiffres donnés pour cette catégorie sont importants, c'est peut-être parce que les décès survenus parmi des pans entiers de la population n'ont fait l'objet d'aucun diagnostic ; en pareil cas, il est probable que la répartition des causes connues est loin de donner une vue exacte de la situation d'ensemble.

Il ne faut pas négliger non plus le risque d'erreur que peut présenter l'exclusion des enfants nés vivants mais décédés avant l'enregistrement de leur naissance ou dans les 24 heures qui ont suivi la naissance. Ces décès sont classés à tort dans les morts foetales tardives. Dans plusieurs pays ou zones, les méthodes d'exploitation permettent de différencier ces pseudo-morts fœtales tardives des morts fœtales tardives véritables et de les ajouter au nombre total des décès, mais, là encore, il est impossible de connaître la cause du décès.

De plus, il convient de noter que les taux sont également fonction de la qualité de l'évaluation de la population à risque et des caractéristiques de celle-ci dont il est tenu compte dans leur calcul. Les problèmes du sous-enregistrement et du sur-enregistrement et, à un certain degré, les différences entre les définitions de la population et des naissances vivantes ont été examinés, respectivement, à la section 3 des Notes techniques, qui traite des données démographiques en général, et à la section 4, qui traite des statistiques de l'état civil. Des informations sur certains pays ou certaines zones sont données dans les notes du tableau 3, relatif à la population totale, et dans celles du tableau 9, relatif aux naissances vivantes.

Données antérieures : Le nombre des décès et les taux de mortalité par cause ont été publiés chaque année dans les éditions de l'*Annuaire démographique* 1951 à 2000, et tous les deux ans depuis. Pour obtenir ces informations pour une année donnée, les lecteurs doivent se reporter à l'index historique.

Tableau 20-2. Liste de tabulation pour les données CIM-9 et CIM-10 pour la présentation dans l'annuaire démographique

Maladie	CIM-10	CIM-9 (Liste de base pour la mise en tableaux)
Toutes causes	**A00-Y89**	**01-56**
Certaines maladies infectieuses et parasitaires	**A00-A33, A35-B99**	**01-07, 184**
Maladies infectieuses intestinales	A00-A09	01
Tuberculose	A15-A19	02
Tétanos[2]	A33, A35	037
Diphtérie	A36	033
Coqueluche	A37	034
Infection à méningocoques	A39	036
Septicémie	A40-A41	038
Poliomyélite aiguë	A80	040
Rougeole	B05	042
Hépatite virale	B15-B19	046
Maladies dues au virus de l'immunodéficience humaine (VIH)	B20-B24	184
Malaria	B50-B54	052
Tumeurs	**C00-D48**	**08-17**
Tumeurs malignes	**C00-C97**	**08-14**
Tumeur maligne de la lèvre, de la cavité buccale et du pharynx	C00-C14	08
Tumeur maligne de l'oesophage	C15	090
Tumeur maligne de l'estomac	C16	091
sigmoïdienne, du rectum, de l'anus et du canal anal	C18-C21	093-094
Tumeur maligne du foie et des voies bilaires intrahépatiques	C22	095
Tumeur maligne du pancréas	C25	096
Tumeur maligne de la trachée, des bronches et du poumon	C33-C34	101
Tumeur maligne du sein chez la femme	C50	113
Tumeur maligne du col de l'utérus	C53	120
Tumeur maligne de la prostate	C61	124
Tumeurs malignes primitives ou présumées primitives des tissus lymphoïde, hématopoïétique et apparentés	C81-C96	14
Maladies du sang et des organes hématopoïétiques et certains troubles du système immunitaire	**D50-D89**	**20**
Anémies	D50-D64	200
Maladies endocriniennes, nutritionnelles et métaboliques	**E00-E88**	**18-19, minus 184**
Diabète sucré	E10-E14	181
Malnutrition	E40-E46	190-192
Troubles mentaux et du comportement	**F01-F99**	**21**
Maladies du système nerveux	**G00-G98**	**22**
Maladies de l'appareil circulatoire	**I00-I99**	**25-30**
Rhumatisme articularie aigu et cardiopathies rhumatismales chroniques	I01-I09	25
Maladies hypertensives	I10-I13	26
Cardiopathies ischémiques	I20-I25	27
Maladies cérébrovasculaires	I60-I69	29
Maladies des artères, artérioles et capillaires	I70-I79	300-302
Maladies de l'appareil respiratoire	**J00-J98**	**31-32**

Tableau 20-2. Liste de tabulation pour les données CIM-9 et CIM-10 pour la présentation dans l'annuaire démographique

Maladie		CIM-10	CIM-9 (Liste de base pour la mise en tableaux)
	Grippe	J10-J11	322
	Pneumopathies	J12-J18	321
	Maladies chroniques des voies respiratoires inférieures	J40-J47	323-325
Maladies de l'appareil digestif		**K00-K92**	**33-34**
	Ulcère de l'estomac et du duodénum	K25-K27	341
	Maladies du foie	K70-K76	347
Maladies du système ostéo-articularie, des muscles et du tissu conjonctif		**M00-M99**	**43**
Maladies de l'appareil génito-urinaire		**N00-N98**	**35-37**
	Affections du rein et de l'uretère	N00-N28	350-351
	Hyperplasie de la prostate	N40	360
Grossesse, accouchement et puerpéralité		**O00-O99, A34**	**38-41**
	Grossesse se terminant par un avortement	O00-O07	38
	Autres décès maternels directs[2]	O10-O92, O95, A34	39
	Décès maternels indirects	O98-O99	40
Certaines affections dont l'origine se situe dans la période périnatale		**P00-P96**	**45**
Malformations congénitales et anomalies chromosomiques		**Q00-Q99**	**44**
Symptômes, signes et résultats anormaux d'examens cliniques et de laboratoire, non classés ailleurs		**R00-R99**	**46**
Toutes autres maladies		**H00-H95, L00-L98**	**23-24, 42**
Causes externes		**V01-Y89**	**E47-E56**
Accidents		**V01-X59**	**E47-E53**
	Accidents de transport	V01-V99	E47
	Chutes	W00-W19	E50
	Noyade et submersion accidentelles	W65-W74	E521
	Exposition à la fumée, au feu et aux flammes	X00-X09	E51
	Intoxication accidentelle par des substances nocives et exposition à ces substances	X40-X49	E48
Lésions auto-infligées		**X60-X84**	**E54**
Agresssions		**X85-Y09**	**E55**
Toutes autres causes externes		Y10-Y89	E56

NOTES

[1] *Classification statistique internationale des maladies et des problèmes de santé connexes*, dixième révision, volume 2. Genève, Organisation mondiale de la santé, 1992.

[2] Dans la Classification internationale des maladies (CIM-10), le tétanos obstétrique est classé à la rubrique A34 mais, dans ce tableau, il est inclus dans les « Autres causes obstétriques directes », sauf pour Bélarus, Fédération de Russie, Seychelles, Turkménistan et Ukraine où le tétanos obstétrique est inclus dans « Tétanos » et « Autres causes obstétriques directes » exclut A34 et O95.

20. Death and death rates by cause and sex: 2014 - 2018
Décès et taux de mortalité par cause et sexe : 2014 - 2018

Egypt - Égypte

Cause of death — Cause de décès	2014 (C)				2015 (C)			
	Male — Masculin		Female — Féminin		Male — Masculin		Female — Féminin	
	Number Nombre	Rate Taux	Number Nombre	Rate Taux	Number Nombre	Rate Taux	Number Nombre	Rate Taux
TOTAL	**293 313**	**662.1**	**238 551**	**561.2**	**313 392**	**690.6**	**260 487**	**597.7**
Certain infectious and parasitic diseases — Certaines maladies infectieuses et parasitaires								
Total	10 536	23.8	7 829	18.4	11 172	24.6	8 779	20.1
Intestinal infectious diseases — Maladies infectieuses intestinales	1 940	4.4	2 079	4.9	2 020	4.5	2 282	5.2
Tuberculosis — Tuberculose	171	0.4	62	0.1	231	0.5	89	0.2
Tetanus — Tétanos	51	0.1	8	♦0.0	55	0.1	20	♦0.0
Diphtheria — Diphtérie	-	-	-	-	-	-	-	-
Whooping cough — Coqueluche	-	-	-	-	-	-	1	♦0.0
Meningococcal infection — Infection à méningocoques	18	♦0.0	8	♦0.0	11	♦0.0	11	♦0.0
Septicaemia — Septicémie	2 201	5.0	1 938	4.6	2 558	5.6	2 412	5.5
Acute poliomyelitis — Poliomyélite aiguë	7	♦0.0	6	♦0.0	7	♦0.0	3	♦0.0
Measles — Rougeole	9	♦0.0	7	♦0.0	5	♦0.0	8	♦0.0
Viral hepatitis — Hépatite virale	4 619	10.4	2 651	6.2	5 116	11.3	3 139	7.2
Human immunodeficiency virus [HIV] disease — Maladies dues au virus de l'immunodéficience humaine (VIH)	9	♦0.0	8	♦0.0	8	♦0.0	6	♦0.0
Malaria — Paludisme	3	♦0.0	1	♦0.0	-	-	2	♦0.0
Neoplasms — Tumeurs	19 589	44.2	15 746	37.0	18 894	41.6	15 839	36.3
Malignant neoplasms — Tumeurs malignes								
Total	18 547	41.9	14 317	33.7	17 855	39.3	14 531	33.3
Malignant neoplasm of lip, oral cavity and pharynx — Tumeur maligne de la lèvre, de la cavité buccale et du pharynx	235	0.5	156	0.4	222	0.5	164	0.4
Malignant neoplasm of oesophagus — Tumeur maligne de l'oesophage	215	0.5	112	0.3	199	0.4	104	0.2
Malignant neoplasm of stomach — Tumeur maligne de l'estomac	919	2.1	802	1.9	883	1.9	802	1.8
Malignant neoplasm of colon, rectosigmoid junction, rectum, anus and anal canal — Tumeur maligne du côlon, de la jonction recto-sigmoïdienne, du rectum, de l'anus et du canal anal	928	2.1	791	1.9	894	2.0	788	1.8
Malignant neoplasm of liver and intrahepatic bile ducts — Tumeur maligne du foie et des voies bilaires intrahépatiques	4 952	11.2	2 284	5.4	4 599	10.1	2 186	5.0
Malignant neoplasm of pancreas — Tumeur maligne du pancréas	765	1.7	423	1.0	724	1.6	433	1.0
Malignant neoplasm of trachea, bronchus and lung — Tumeur maligne de la trachée, des bronches et du poumon	2 347	5.3	1 115	2.6	2 437	5.4	1 148	2.6
Malignant neoplasm of female breast — Tumeur maligne du sein chez la femme	..	..	2 503	8.5	..	..	2 646	8.7
Malignant neoplasm of cervix uteri — Tumeur maligne du col de l'utérus	..	..	156	0.5	..	..	166	0.5
Malignant neoplasm of prostate — Tumeur maligne de la prostate	750	11.7	..	..	793	11.4	..	..
Malignant neoplasm of lymphoid, haematopoietic and related tissue — Tumeurs malignes primitives ou présumées primitives des tissus lymphoïde, hématopoïétique et apparentés	1 927	4.3	1 556	3.7	1 794	4.0	1 530	3.5
Disorders of the blood and blood-forming organs and certain disorders involving the immune mechanism — Maladies du sang et des organes hématopoïétiques et certains troubles du système immunitaire								
Total	2 858	6.5	2 711	6.4	3 257	7.2	2 961	6.8
Anaemias — Anémies	439	1.0	515	1.2	492	1.1	537	1.2
Endocrine, nutritional and metabolic diseases — Maladies endocriniennes, nutritionnelles et métaboliques								
Total	11 551	26.1	13 311	31.3	6 285	13.9	7 147	16.4
Diabetes mellitus — Diabète sucré	9 240	20.9	10 598	24.9	3 898	8.6	4 544	10.4
Malnutrition — Malnutrition	119	0.3	109	0.3	98	0.2	82	0.2
Mental and behavioural disorders — Troubles mentaux et du comportement	532	1.2	362	0.9	316	0.7	272	0.6
Diseases of the nervous system — Maladies du système nerveux	3 166	7.1	2 978	7.0	3 179	7.0	3 095	7.1
Diseases of the circulatory system — Maladies de l'appareil circulatoire								
Total	134 419	303.4	119 592	281.3	143 366	315.9	126 163	289.5
Acute rheumatic fever and chronic rheumatic heart diseases — Rhumatisme articularie aigu et cardiopathies rhumatismales chroniques	1 199	2.7	1 215	2.9	914	2.0	914	2.1
Hypertensive diseases — Maladies hypertensives	16 008	36.1	16 064	37.8	21 922	48.3	22 007	50.5
Ischaemic heart disease — Cardiopathie ischémique	12 866	29.0	9 651	22.7	17 640	38.9	13 474	30.9
Cerebrovascular disease — Maladie cérébrovasculaire	21 652	48.9	19 575	46.0	20 020	44.1	17 185	39.4

20. Death and death rates by cause and sex: 2014 - 2018
Décès et taux de mortalité par cause et sexe : 2014 - 2018

Egypt - Égypte

Cause of death — Cause de décès	2014 (C)				2015 (C)			
	Male — Masculin		Female — Féminin		Male — Masculin		Female — Féminin	
	Number Nombre	Rate Taux	Number Nombre	Rate Taux	Number Nombre	Rate Taux	Number Nombre	Rate Taux
Diseases of arteries, arterioles and capillaries — Maladies des artères, artérioles et capillaires	13 862	31.3	12 763	30.0	12 762	28.1	12 024	27.6
Diseases of the respiratory system — Maladies de l'appareil respiratoire								
Total	21 965	49.6	18 704	44.0	22 710	50.0	19 410	44.5
Influenza — Grippe	16	♦0.0	10	♦0.0	7	♦0.0	6	♦0.0
Pneumonia — Pneumopathies	8 319	18.8	7 487	17.6	8 653	19.1	7 835	18.0
Chronic lower respiratory diseases — Maladies chroniques des voies respiratoires inférieures	2 582	5.8	1 920	4.5	2 606	5.7	1 884	4.3
Diseases of the digestive system — Maladies de l'appareil digestif								
Total	36 094	81.5	22 396	52.7	34 943	77.0	22 664	52.0
Gastric and duodenal ulcer — Ulcère de l'estomac et du duodénum	178	0.4	132	0.3	216	0.5	166	0.4
Diseases of the liver — Maladies du foie	34 202	77.2	21 022	49.5	32 991	72.7	21 317	48.9
Diseases of the musculoskeletal system and connective tissue — Maladies du système ostéo-articularie, des muscles et du tissu conjonctif	117	0.3	197	0.5	99	0.2	149	0.3
Diseases of the genitourinary system — Maladies de l'appareil génito-urinaire								
Total	11 464	25.9	9 221	21.7	12 338	27.2	9 901	22.7
Disorders of kidney and ureter — Affections du rein et de l'uretère	11 316	25.5	9 138	21.5	12 137	26.7	9 793	22.5
Hyperplasia of prostate — Hyperplasie de la prostate	77	1.2	..	..	116	1.7	..	..
Pregnancy, childbirth and the puerperium — Grossesse, accouchement et puerpéralité								
Total	..	..	497	18.3	..	..	410	15.3
Pregnancy with abortive outcome — Grossesse se terminant par un avortement	..	..	14	♦0.5	..	..	13	♦0.5
Other direct obstetric causes — Autres décès maternels directs	..	..	464	17.1	..	..	385	14.3
Indirect obstetric causes — Décès maternels indirects	..	..	6	♦0.2	..	..	3	♦0.1
Certain conditions originating in the perinatal period — Certaines affections dont l'origine se situe dans la période périnatale	2 796	201.1	2 035	153.0	2 375	173.0	1 852	141.1
Congenital malformations, deformations and chromosomal abnormalities — Malformations congénitales et anomalies chromosomiques	4 628	332.8	4 026	302.7	4 209	306.7	3 690	281.1
Symptoms, signs and abnormal clinical and laboratory findings, not elsewhere classified — Symptômes, signes et résultats anormaux d'examens cliniques et de laboratoire, non classés ailleurs	16 465	37.2	14 252	33.5	33 817	74.5	32 844	75.4
All other diseases — Toutes autres maladies	175	0.4	277	0.7	204	0.4	348	0.8
External causes — Causes externes								
Total	16 958	38.3	4 417	10.4	16 228	35.8	4 963	11.4
Accidents								
Total	14 569	32.9	3 504	8.2	10 659	23.5	2 779	6.4
Transport accidents — Accidents de transport	9 024	20.4	1 976	4.6	6 648	14.7	1 563	3.6
Falls — Chutes	1 418	3.2	463	1.1	986	2.2	325	0.7
Accidental drowning and submersion — Noyade et submersion accidentelles	1 648	3.7	292	0.7	1 360	3.0	255	0.6
Exposure to smoke, fire and flames — Exposition à la fumée, au feu et aux flammes	320	0.7	278	0.7	175	0.4	144	0.3
Accidental poisoning by and exposure to noxious substances — Intoxication accidentelle par des substances nocives et exposition à ces substances	70	0.2	58	0.1	62	0.1	49	0.1
Intentional self-harm — Lésions auto-infligées	71	0.2	17	♦0.0	35	0.1	14	♦0.0
Assault — Agresssions	195	0.4	34	0.1	121	0.3	25	♦0.1
All other external causes — Toutes autres causes externes	2 123	4.8	862	2.0	5 413	11.9	2 145	4.9

20. Death and death rates by cause and sex: 2014 - 2018
Décès et taux de mortalité par cause et sexe : 2014 - 2018 (continued - suite)

Mauritius - Maurice

Cause of death — Cause de décès	2017 (+C)				2018 (+C)			
	Male — Masculin		Female — Féminin		Male — Masculin		Female — Féminin	
	Number Nombre	Rate Taux	Number Nombre	Rate Taux	Number Nombre	Rate Taux	Number Nombre	Rate Taux
TOTAL	**5 446**	**870.3**	**4 468**	**699.3**	**5 939**	**948.7**	**4 848**	**758.4**
Certain infectious and parasitic diseases — Certaines maladies infectieuses et parasitaires								
Total	158	25.3	77	12.1	174	27.8	75	11.7
Intestinal infectious diseases — Maladies infectieuses intestinales	8	♦1.3	7	♦1.1	9	♦1.4	10	♦1.6
Tuberculosis — Tuberculose	13	♦2.1	4	♦0.6	9	♦1.4	6	♦0.9
Tetanus — Tétanos	-	-	-	-	-	-	-	-
Diphtheria — Diphtérie	-	-	-	-	-	-	-	-
Whooping cough — Coqueluche	-	-	-	-	-	-	-	-
Meningococcal infection — Infection à méningocoques	-	-	-	-	-	-	1	♦0.2
Septicaemia — Septicémie	26	♦4.2	36	5.6	39	6.2	29	♦4.5
Acute poliomyelitis — Poliomyélite aiguë	-	-	-	-	-	-	-	-
Measles — Rougeole	-	-	-	-	-	-	2	♦0.3
Viral hepatitis — Hépatite virale	10	♦1.6	3	♦0.5	9	♦1.4	2	♦0.3
Human immunodeficiency virus [HIV] disease — Maladies dues au virus de l'immunodéficience humaine (VIH)	97	15.5	26	♦4.1	102	16.3	21	♦3.3
Malaria — Paludisme	-	-	-	-	-	-	-	-
Neoplasms — Tumeurs	**657**	**105.0**	**718**	**112.4**	**676**	**108.0**	**704**	**110.1**
Malignant neoplasms — Tumeurs malignes								
Total	633	101.2	684	107.1	648	103.5	670	104.8
Malignant neoplasm of lip, oral cavity and pharynx — Tumeur maligne de la lèvre, de la cavité buccale et du pharynx	55	8.8	18	♦2.8	47	7.5	16	♦2.5
Malignant neoplasm of oesophagus — Tumeur maligne de l'oesophage	17	♦2.7	9	♦1.4	17	♦2.7	11	♦1.7
Malignant neoplasm of stomach — Tumeur maligne de l'estomac	49	7.8	26	♦4.1	61	9.7	19	♦3.0
Malignant neoplasm of colon, rectosigmoid junction, rectum, anus and anal canal — Tumeur maligne du côlon, de la jonction recto-sigmoïdienne, du rectum, de l'anus et du canal anal	85	13.6	68	10.6	83	13.3	59	9.2
Malignant neoplasm of liver and intrahepatic bile ducts — Tumeur maligne du foie et des voies bilaires intrahépatiques	25	♦4.0	16	♦2.5	29	♦4.6	25	♦3.9
Malignant neoplasm of pancreas — Tumeur maligne du pancréas	39	6.2	43	6.7	27	♦4.3	24	♦3.8
Malignant neoplasm of trachea, bronchus and lung — Tumeur maligne de la trachée, des bronches et du poumon	102	16.3	43	6.7	93	14.9	54	8.4
Malignant neoplasm of female breast — Tumeur maligne du sein chez la femme	..	..	189	36.1	..	..	173	32.8
Malignant neoplasm of cervix uteri — Tumeur maligne du col de l'utérus	..	..	43	8.2	..	..	42	8.0
Malignant neoplasm of prostate — Tumeur maligne de la prostate	73	40.7	..	..	99	53.9	..	..
Malignant neoplasm of lymphoid, haematopoietic and related tissue — Tumeurs malignes primitives ou présumées primitives des tissus lymphoïde, hématopoïétique et apparentés	59	9.4	43	6.7	43	6.9	42	6.6
Disorders of the blood and blood-forming organs and certain disorders involving the immune mechanism — Maladies du sang et des organes hématopoïétiques et certains troubles du système immunitaire								
Total	30	♦4.8	41	6.4	37	5.9	50	7.8
Anaemias — Anémies	22	♦3.5	35	5.5	24	♦3.8	34	5.3
Endocrine, nutritional and metabolic diseases — Maladies endocriniennes, nutritionnelles et métaboliques								
Total	1 216	194.3	1 150	180.0	1 198	191.4	1 089	170.3
Diabetes mellitus — Diabète sucré	1 191	190.3	1 113	174.2	1 164	185.9	1 045	163.5
Malnutrition — Malnutrition	7	♦1.1	10	♦1.6	7	♦1.1	5	♦0.8
Mental and behavioural disorders — Troubles mentaux et du comportement	88	14.1	7	♦1.1	76	12.1	6	♦0.9
Diseases of the nervous system — Maladies du système nerveux	82	13.1	55	8.6	102	16.3	53	8.3
Diseases of the circulatory system — Maladies de l'appareil circulatoire								
Total	1 714	273.9	1 492	233.5	2 047	327.0	1 756	274.7
Acute rheumatic fever and chronic rheumatic heart diseases — Rhumatisme articularie aigu et cardiopathies rhumatismales chroniques	2	♦0.3	3	♦0.5	3	♦0.5	1	♦0.2
Hypertensive diseases — Maladies hypertensives	215	34.4	290	45.4	305	48.7	353	55.2
Ischaemic heart disease — Cardiopathie ischémique	660	105.5	456	71.4	776	124.0	555	86.8
Cerebrovascular disease — Maladie cérébrovasculaire	430	68.7	379	59.3	493	78.8	471	73.7

20. Death and death rates by cause and sex: 2014 - 2018
Décès et taux de mortalité par cause et sexe : 2014 - 2018 (continued - suite)

Mauritius - Maurice

Cause of death — Cause de décès	2017 (+C)				2018 (+C)			
	Male — Masculin		Female — Féminin		Male — Masculin		Female — Féminin	
	Number Nombre	Rate Taux	Number Nombre	Rate Taux	Number Nombre	Rate Taux	Number Nombre	Rate Taux
Diseases of arteries, arterioles and capillaries — Maladies des artères, artérioles et capillaires	13	♦2.1	6	♦0.9	14	♦2.2	3	♦0.5
Diseases of the respiratory system — Maladies de l'appareil respiratoire								
Total	602	96.2	430	67.3	691	110.4	560	87.6
Influenza — Grippe	3	♦0.5	4	♦0.6	4	♦0.6	3	♦0.5
Pneumonia — Pneumopathies	137	21.9	105	16.4	155	24.8	154	24.1
Chronic lower respiratory diseases — Maladies chroniques des voies respiratoires inférieures	127	20.3	67	10.5	121	19.3	76	11.9
Diseases of the digestive system — Maladies de l'appareil digestif								
Total	232	37.1	118	18.5	248	39.6	113	17.7
Gastric and duodenal ulcer — Ulcère de l'estomac et du duodénum	12	♦1.9	8	♦1.3	8	♦1.3	2	♦0.3
Diseases of the liver — Maladies du foie	132	21.1	28	♦4.4	131	20.9	26	♦4.1
Diseases of the musculoskeletal system and connective tissue — Maladies du système ostéo-articularie, des muscles et du tissu conjonctif	5	♦0.8	18	♦2.8	2	♦0.3	14	♦2.2
Diseases of the genitourinary system — Maladies de l'appareil génito-urinaire								
Total	90	14.4	68	10.6	99	15.8	93	14.5
Disorders of kidney and ureter — Affections du rein et de l'uretère	50	8.0	36	5.6	53	8.5	47	7.4
Hyperplasia of prostate — Hyperplasie de la prostate	2	♦1.1	..	..	3	♦1.6	..	..
Pregnancy, childbirth and the puerperium — Grossesse, accouchement et puerpéralité								
Total	..	..	10	♦74.7	..	..	5	♦38.5
Pregnancy with abortive outcome — Grossesse se terminant par un avortement	..	..	1	♦7.5	..	..	-	-
Other direct obstetric causes — Autres décès maternels directs	..	..	6	♦44.8	..	..	4	♦30.8
Indirect obstetric causes — Décès maternels indirects	..	..	3	♦22.4	..	..	1	♦7.7
Certain conditions originating in the perinatal period — Certaines affections dont l'origine se situe dans la période périnatale	57	837.1	36	547.4	62	923.9	55	877.3
Congenital malformations, deformations and chromosomal abnormalities — Malformations congénitales et anomalies chromosomiques	27	♦396.5	17	♦258.5	26	♦387.4	15	♦239.3
Symptoms, signs and abnormal clinical and laboratory findings, not elsewhere classified — Symptômes, signes et résultats anormaux d'examens cliniques et de laboratoire, non classés ailleurs	64	10.2	64	10.0	55	8.8	100	15.6
All other diseases — Toutes autres maladies	29	♦4.6	31	4.9	28	♦4.5	32	5.0
External causes — Causes externes								
Total	395	63.1	136	21.3	418	66.8	128	20.0
Accidents								
Total	263	42.0	63	9.9	277	44.2	66	10.3
Transport accidents — Accidents de transport	139	22.2	29	♦4.5	138	22.0	31	4.8
Falls — Chutes	39	6.2	19	♦3.0	64	10.2	7	♦1.1
Accidental drowning and submersion — Noyade et submersion accidentelles	36	5.8	8	♦1.3	36	5.8	6	♦0.9
Exposure to smoke, fire and flames — Exposition à la fumée, au feu et aux flammes	11	♦1.8	3	♦0.5	6	♦1.0	7	♦1.1
Accidental poisoning by and exposure to noxious substances — Intoxication accidentelle par des substances nocives et exposition à ces substances	13	♦2.1	1	♦0.2	10	♦1.6	2	♦0.3
Intentional self-harm — Lésions auto-infligées	81	12.9	25	♦3.9	80	12.8	27	♦4.2
Assault — Agressions	26	♦4.2	16	♦2.5	26	♦4.2	14	♦2.2
All other external causes — Toutes autres causes externes	25	♦4.0	32	5.0	35	5.6	21	♦3.3

20. Death and death rates by cause and sex: 2014 - 2018
Décès et taux de mortalité par cause et sexe : 2014 - 2018 (continued - suite)

Cause of death — Cause de décès	Mayotte				Morocco - Maroc		Reunion - Réunion	
	2015 (...)		2016 (...)		2014 (U)		2015 (...)	
	Male — Masculin	Female — Féminin	Male — Masculin	Female — Féminin	Male — Masculin	Female — Féminin	Male — Masculin	Female — Féminin
	Number Nombre	Number Nombre	Number Nombre	Number Nombre	Number Nombre	Number Nombre	Number Nombre	Number Nombre
TOTAL	*339*	*296*	*399*	*318*	*29 382*	*23 062*	*2 459*	*2 072*
Certain infectious and parasitic diseases — Certaines maladies infectieuses et parasitaires								
Total	*7*	*12*	*16*	*11*	*1 147*	*764*	*40*	*48*
Intestinal infectious diseases — Maladies infectieuses intestinales	-	*4*	*5*	*3*	*52*	*64*	*5*	*6*
Tuberculosis — Tuberculose	*1*	*1*	*2*	*2*	*406*	*157*	*2*	*1*
Tetanus — Tétanos	-	-	-	-	*14*	*3*	-	-
Diphtheria — Diphtérie	-	-	-	-	-	-	-	-
Whooping cough — Coqueluche	-	-	-	-	-	*1*	-	-
Meningococcal infection — Infection à méningocoques	-	-	-	-	*2*	*1*	-	-
Septicaemia — Septicémie	*4*	*2*	*2*	*1*	*466*	*370*	*18*	*21*
Acute poliomyelitis — Poliomyélite aiguë	-	-	-	-	-	-	-	-
Measles — Rougeole	-	-	-	-	-	-	-	-
Viral hepatitis — Hépatite virale	-	*2*	*3*	*1*	*94*	*109*	*4*	*5*
Human immunodeficiency virus [HIV] disease — Maladies dues au virus de l'immunodéficience humaine (VIH)	-	-	*2*	*1*	*27*	*13*	*2*	-
Malaria — Paludisme	-	-	-	-	*1*	*1*	*1*	-
Neoplasms — Tumeurs	*49*	*56*	*62*	*44*	*3 599*	*2 534*	*683*	*467*
Malignant neoplasms — Tumeurs malignes								
Total	*44*	*48*	*59*	*41*	*3 410*	*2 363*	*660*	*449*
Malignant neoplasm of lip, oral cavity and pharynx — Tumeur maligne de la lèvre, de la cavité buccale et du pharynx	*1*	*2*	-	*1*	*78*	*41*	*27*	*9*
Malignant neoplasm of oesophagus — Tumeur maligne de l'oesophage	*1*	-	-	*1*	*30*	*19*	*24*	*1*
Malignant neoplasm of stomach — Tumeur maligne de l'estomac	*5*	*1*	*2*	*1*	*209*	*126*	*40*	*16*
Malignant neoplasm of colon, rectosigmoid junction, rectum, anus and anal canal — Tumeur maligne du côlon, de la jonction recto-sigmoïdienne, du rectum, de l'anus et du canal anal	-	*4*	*2*	*1*	*146*	*146*	*82*	*63*
Malignant neoplasm of liver and intrahepatic bile ducts — Tumeur maligne du foie et des voies bilaires intrahépatiques	*6*	-	*7*	*2*	*163*	*137*	*43*	*25*
Malignant neoplasm of pancreas — Tumeur maligne du pancréas	-	*1*	*2*	*3*	*139*	*91*	*33*	*26*
Malignant neoplasm of trachea, bronchus and lung — Tumeur maligne de la trachée, des bronches et du poumon	*5*	*3*	*7*	*1*	*832*	*145*	*155*	*50*
Malignant neoplasm of female breast — Tumeur maligne du sein chez la femme	..	*10*	..	*13*	..	*385*	..	*63*
Malignant neoplasm of cervix uteri — Tumeur maligne du col de l'utérus	..	*7*	..	*2*	..	*102*	..	*17*
Malignant neoplasm of prostate — Tumeur maligne de la prostate	*9*	..	*15*	..	*336*	..	*57*	..
Malignant neoplasm of lymphoid, haematopoietic and related tissue — Tumeurs malignes primitives ou présumées primitives des tissus lymphoïde, hématopoïétique et apparentés	*4*	*4*	*10*	*5*	*274*	*181*	*51*	*47*
Disorders of the blood and blood-forming organs and certain disorders involving the immune mechanism — Maladies du sang et des organes hématopoïétiques et certains troubles du système immunitaire								
Total	*3*	*2*	*5*	*2*	*160*	*151*	*9*	*8*
Anaemias — Anémies	*3*	*1*	*4*	-	*116*	*100*	*5*	*5*
Endocrine, nutritional and metabolic diseases — Maladies endocriniennes, nutritionnelles et métaboliques								
Total	*24*	*16*	*26*	*25*	*1 479*	*1 538*	*131*	*206*
Diabetes mellitus — Diabète sucré	*16*	*12*	*19*	*21*	*1 325*	*1 395*	*102*	*172*
Malnutrition — Malnutrition	*2*	-	*1*	*1*	*6*	-	*5*	*11*
Mental and behavioural disorders — Troubles mentaux et du comportement	*4*	-	*6*	*5*	*84*	*54*	*117*	*51*
Diseases of the nervous system — Maladies du système nerveux	*14*	*6*	*21*	*10*	*485*	*440*	*80*	*103*
Diseases of the circulatory system — Maladies de l'appareil circulatoire								
Total	*79*	*81*	*76*	*84*	*6 288*	*5 274*	*540*	*538*
Acute rheumatic fever and chronic rheumatic heart diseases — Rhumatisme articularie aigu et cardiopathies rhumatismales chroniques	-	*1*	*1*	*1*	*45*	*31*	*5*	*6*
Hypertensive diseases — Maladies hypertensives	*8*	*14*	*12*	*9*	*342*	*487*	*27*	*56*
Ischaemic heart disease — Cardiopathie ischémique	*9*	*9*	*9*	*5*	*538*	*269*	*186*	*118*

20. Death and death rates by cause and sex: 2014 - 2018
Décès et taux de mortalité par cause et sexe : 2014 - 2018 (continued - suite)

Cause of death — Cause de décès	Mayotte				Morocco - Maroc		Reunion - Réunion	
	2015 (...)		2016 (...)		2014 (U)		2015 (...)	
	Male — Masculin	Female — Féminin	Male — Masculin	Female — Féminin	Male — Masculin	Female — Féminin	Male — Masculin	Female — Féminin
	Number Nombre	Number Nombre	Number Nombre	Number Nombre	Number Nombre	Number Nombre	Number Nombre	Number Nombre
Cerebrovascular disease — Maladie cérébrovasculaire	*32*	*27*	*27*	*38*	*1 223*	*1 191*	*143*	*149*
Diseases of arteries, arterioles and capillaries — Maladies des artères, artérioles et capillaires	*7*	*1*	*2*	*1*	*65*	*32*	*42*	*17*
Diseases of the respiratory system — Maladies de l'appareil respiratoire								
Total	*11*	*12*	*22*	*22*	*1 652*	*905*	*168*	*133*
Influenza — Grippe	-	-	-	*1*	*7*	*6*	*1*	*8*
Pneumonia — Pneumopathies	*2*	*4*	*5*	*5*	*579*	*265*	*37*	*45*
Chronic lower respiratory diseases — Maladies chroniques des voies respiratoires inférieures	*2*	*6*	*9*	*6*	*382*	*184*	*79*	*36*
Diseases of the digestive system — Maladies de l'appareil digestif								
Total	*14*	*3*	*9*	*2*	*757*	*586*	*133*	*96*
Gastric and duodenal ulcer — Ulcère de l'estomac et du duodénum	*2*	-	*1*	-	*29*	*17*	*6*	*1*
Diseases of the liver — Maladies du foie	*5*	-	*5*	*2*	*303*	*255*	*61*	*27*
Diseases of the musculoskeletal system and connective tissue — Maladies du système ostéo-articularie, des muscles et du tissu conjonctif	*1*	*1*	-	*2*	*36*	*48*	*14*	*18*
Diseases of the genitourinary system — Maladies de l'appareil génito-urinaire								
Total	*5*	*1*	*8*	*4*	*810*	*529*	*30*	*53*
Disorders of kidney and ureter — Affections du rein et de l'uretère	*3*	*1*	*4*	*4*	*646*	*497*	*21*	*45*
Hyperplasia of prostate — Hyperplasie de la prostate	*1*	..	*1*	..	*29*	..	-	..
Pregnancy, childbirth and the puerperium — Grossesse, accouchement et puerpéralité								
Total	..	*2*	..	*2*	..	*77*	..	*1*
Pregnancy with abortive outcome — Grossesse se terminant par un avortement	..	-	..	-	..	*1*	..	-
Other direct obstetric causes — Autres décès maternels directs	..	*2*	..	*2*	..	*75*	..	-
Indirect obstetric causes — Décès maternels indirects	..	-	..	-	..	*1*	..	*1*
Certain conditions originating in the perinatal period — Certaines affections dont l'origine se situe dans la période périnatale	*13*	*14*	*18*	*11*	*2 307*	*1 713*	*28*	*25*
Congenital malformations, deformations and chromosomal abnormalities — Malformations congénitales et anomalies chromosomiques	*14*	*14*	*16*	*13*	*376*	*273*	*23*	*13*
Symptoms, signs and abnormal clinical and laboratory findings, not elsewhere classified — Symptômes, signes et résultats anormaux d'examens cliniques et de laboratoire, non classés ailleurs	*69*	*62*	*76*	*67*	*7 572*	*7 402*	*207*	*196*
All other diseases — Toutes autres maladies	*1*	*1*	*1*	-	*24*	*20*	*5*	*9*
External causes — Causes externes								
Total	*31*	*13*	*37*	*14*	*2 606*	*754*	*251*	*107*
Accidents								
Total	*25*	*11*	*30*	*13*	*2 414*	*684*	*149*	*76*
Transport accidents — Accidents de transport	*5*	-	*3*	*1*	*720*	*167*	*42*	*9*
Falls — Chutes	*2*	*1*	*3*	*1*	*106*	*38*	*31*	*15*
Accidental drowning and submersion — Noyade et submersion accidentelles	*9*	*2*	*9*	*2*	*255*	*55*	*11*	*5*
Exposure to smoke, fire and flames — Exposition à la fumée, au feu et aux flammes	*1*	*3*	*2*	*3*	*27*	*17*	*4*	-
Accidental poisoning by and exposure to noxious substances — Intoxication accidentelle par des substances nocives et exposition à ces substances	*1*	-	*2*	-	*52*	*51*	*13*	*8*
Intentional self-harm — Lésions auto-infligées	*2*	-	*3*	*1*	*82*	*36*	*79*	*20*
Assault — Agresssions	*2*	-	*4*	-	*98*	*24*	*9*	*3*
All other external causes — Toutes autres causes externes	*2*	*2*	-	-	*12*	*10*	*14*	*8*

20. Death and death rates by cause and sex: 2014 - 2018
Décès et taux de mortalité par cause et sexe : 2014 - 2018 (continued - suite)

Cause of death — Cause de décès	Reunion - Réunion		Seychelles			
	2016 (...)		2014 (+C)		2015 (+C)	
	Male — Masculin	Female — Féminin	Male — Masculin	Female — Féminin	Male — Masculin	Female — Féminin
	Number Nombre	Number Nombre	Number Nombre	Number Nombre	Number Nombre	Number Nombre
TOTAL	*2 579*	*2 135*	425	300	401	302
Certain infectious and parasitic diseases — Certaines maladies infectieuses et parasitaires						
Total	*51*	*44*	50	32	28	19
Intestinal infectious diseases — Maladies infectieuses intestinales	*10*	*6*	1	2	1	2
Tuberculosis — Tuberculose	*3*	-	-	-	1	-
Tetanus — Tétanos	-	-	-	-	-	-
Diphtheria — Diphtérie	-	-	-	-	-	-
Whooping cough — Coqueluche	-	*1*	-	-	-	-
Meningococcal infection — Infection à méningocoques	-	-	-	-	-	-
Septicaemia — Septicémie	*18*	*25*	26	23	18	14
Acute poliomyelitis — Poliomyélite aiguë	-	-	-	-	-	-
Measles — Rougeole	-	-	-	-	-	-
Viral hepatitis — Hépatite virale	*6*	-	1	-	2	-
Human immunodeficiency virus [HIV] disease — Maladies dues au virus de l'immunodéficience humaine (VIH)	*2*	-	9	6	3	2
Malaria — Paludisme	-	-	-	-	-	-
Neoplasms — Tumeurs	*721*	*507*	69	56	88	63
Malignant neoplasms — Tumeurs malignes						
Total	*695*	*480*	69	56	87	62
Malignant neoplasm of lip, oral cavity and pharynx — Tumeur maligne de la lèvre, de la cavité buccale et du pharynx	*37*	*7*	11	1	12	2
Malignant neoplasm of oesophagus — Tumeur maligne de l'oesophage	*34*	*4*	2	-	3	2
Malignant neoplasm of stomach — Tumeur maligne de l'estomac	*34*	*29*	2	4	2	2
Malignant neoplasm of colon, rectosigmoid junction, rectum, anus and anal canal — Tumeur maligne du côlon, de la jonction recto-sigmoïdienne, du rectum, de l'anus et du canal anal	*79*	*63*	11	13	8	11
Malignant neoplasm of liver and intrahepatic bile ducts — Tumeur maligne du foie et des voies bilaires intrahépatiques	*42*	*31*	6	2	4	2
Malignant neoplasm of pancreas — Tumeur maligne du pancréas	*44*	*29*	3	1	2	2
Malignant neoplasm of trachea, bronchus and lung — Tumeur maligne de la trachée, des bronches et du poumon	*143*	*44*	7	3	8	3
Malignant neoplasm of female breast — Tumeur maligne du sein chez la femme	..	*87*	..	10	..	9
Malignant neoplasm of cervix uteri — Tumeur maligne du col de l'utérus	..	*16*	..	7	..	6
Malignant neoplasm of prostate — Tumeur maligne de la prostate	*70*	..	15	..	22	..
Malignant neoplasm of lymphoid, haematopoietic and related tissue — Tumeurs malignes primitives ou présumées primitives des tissus lymphoïde, hématopoïétique et apparentés	*53*	*43*	...	...	...	...
Disorders of the blood and blood-forming organs and certain disorders involving the immune mechanism — Maladies du sang et des organes hématopoïétiques et certains troubles du système immunitaire						
Total	*11*	*7*	6	9	1	3
Anaemias — Anémies	*4*	*3*	5	8	1	3
Endocrine, nutritional and metabolic diseases — Maladies endocriniennes, nutritionnelles et métaboliques						
Total	*144*	*165*	9	9	8	7
Diabetes mellitus — Diabète sucré	*103*	*136*	8	9	5	5
Malnutrition — Malnutrition	*7*	*10*	-	-	2	1
Mental and behavioural disorders — Troubles mentaux et du comportement	*116*	*75*	1	1	4	1
Diseases of the nervous system — Maladies du système nerveux	*112*	*126*	3	3	3	7
Diseases of the circulatory system — Maladies de l'appareil circulatoire						
Total	*587*	*587*	108	94	118	98
Acute rheumatic fever and chronic rheumatic heart diseases — Rhumatisme articularie aigu et cardiopathies rhumatismales chroniques	*3*	*8*	2	1	1	-
Hypertensive diseases — Maladies hypertensives	*44*	*61*	20	38	20	26
Ischaemic heart disease — Cardiopathie ischémique	*177*	*132*	24	12	16	15
Cerebrovascular disease — Maladie cérébrovasculaire	*183*	*170*	24	8	32	26
Diseases of arteries, arterioles and capillaries — Maladies des artères, artérioles et capillaires	*35*	*27*	...	...	...	...

20. Death and death rates by cause and sex: 2014 - 2018
Décès et taux de mortalité par cause et sexe : 2014 - 2018 (continued - suite)

Cause of death — Cause de décès	Reunion - Réunion		Seychelles			
	2016 (...)		2014 (+C)		2015 (+C)	
	Male — Masculin	Female — Féminin	Male — Masculin	Female — Féminin	Male — Masculin	Female — Féminin
	Number Nombre	Number Nombre	Number Nombre	Number Nombre	Number Nombre	Number Nombre
Diseases of the respiratory system — Maladies de l'appareil respiratoire						
Total	223	161	54	41	44	40
Influenza — Grippe	7	17	-	-	-	-
Pneumonia — Pneumopathies	62	47	36	29	33	34
Chronic lower respiratory diseases — Maladies chroniques des voies respiratoires inférieures	82	36	12	4	7	3
Diseases of the digestive system — Maladies de l'appareil digestif						
Total	134	111	37	17	19	23
Gastric and duodenal ulcer — Ulcère de l'estomac et du duodénum	4	5	4	1	3	-
Diseases of the liver — Maladies du foie	65	39	16	8	11	11
Diseases of the musculoskeletal system and connective tissue — Maladies du système ostéo-articularie, des muscles et du tissu conjonctif	14	18	-	-	-	-
Diseases of the genitourinary system — Maladies de l'appareil génito-urinaire						
Total	34	38	30	17	20	18
Disorders of kidney and ureter — Affections du rein et de l'uretère	24	29	...	...	...	...
Hyperplasia of prostate — Hyperplasie de la prostate	2	..	...	..	...	..
Pregnancy, childbirth and the puerperium — Grossesse, accouchement et puerpéralité						
Total	..	2	..	-	..	3
Pregnancy with abortive outcome — Grossesse se terminant par un avortement	..	-	..	-	..	-
Other direct obstetric causes — Autres décès maternels directs	..	2	..	-	..	-
Indirect obstetric causes — Décès maternels indirects	..	-	..	-	..	3
Certain conditions originating in the perinatal period — Certaines affections dont l'origine se situe dans la période périnatale	23	30	8	3	3	5
Congenital malformations, deformations and chromosomal abnormalities — Malformations congénitales et anomalies chromosomiques	11	20	6	-	2	3
Symptoms, signs and abnormal clinical and laboratory findings, not elsewhere classified — Symptômes, signes et résultats anormaux d'examens cliniques et de laboratoire, non classés ailleurs	138	134	9	4	9	8
All other diseases — Toutes autres maladies	10	6	1	2	3	3
External causes — Causes externes						
Total	250	104	34	12	51	1
Accidents						
Total	170	69	...	...	...	...
Transport accidents — Accidents de transport	45	6	8	4	13	-
Falls — Chutes	28	19	2	-	6	-
Accidental drowning and submersion — Noyade et submersion accidentelles	11	-	8	4	19	-
Exposure to smoke, fire and flames — Exposition à la fumée, au feu et aux flammes	7	2	3	-	-	-
Accidental poisoning by and exposure to noxious substances — Intoxication accidentelle par des substances nocives et exposition à ces substances	16	7	-	-	-	-
Intentional self-harm — Lésions auto-infligées	68	17	2	2	6	1
Assault — Agresssions	5	7	6	2	1	-
All other external causes — Toutes autres causes externes	7	11	...	...	...	...

20. Death and death rates by cause and sex: 2014 - 2018
Décès et taux de mortalité par cause et sexe : 2014 - 2018 (continued - suite)

South Africa - Afrique du Sud

Cause of death — Cause de décès	2014 (C)				2015 (C)			
	Male — Masculin		Female — Féminin		Male — Masculin		Female — Féminin	
	Number Nombre	Rate Taux	Number Nombre	Rate Taux	Number Nombre	Rate Taux	Number Nombre	Rate Taux
TOTAL	**236 613**	**891.6**	**214 826**	**766.2**	**241 156**	**894.4**	**217 087**	**763.2**
Certain infectious and parasitic diseases — Certaines maladies infectieuses et parasitaires								
Total	**52 412**	**197.5**	**45 980**	**164.0**	**48 081**	**178.3**	**41 274**	**145.1**
Intestinal infectious diseases — Maladies infectieuses intestinales	**6 795**	**25.6**	**7 607**	**27.1**	**4 615**	**17.1**	**5 292**	**18.6**
Tuberculosis — Tuberculose	**22 545**	**85.0**	**15 174**	**54.1**	**20 111**	**74.6**	**12 811**	**45.0**
Tetanus — Tétanos	**7**	**♦0.0**	**4**	**♦0.0**	**8**	**♦0.0**	**4**	**♦0.0**
Diphtheria — Diphtérie	**-**	**-**	**-**	**-**	**2**	**♦0.0**	**-**	**-**
Whooping cough — Coqueluche	**2**	**♦0.0**	**-**	**-**	**4**	**♦0.0**	**4**	**♦0.0**
Meningococcal infection — Infection à méningocoques	**23**	**♦0.1**	**34**	**0.1**	**9**	**♦0.0**	**15**	**♦0.1**
Septicaemia — Septicémie	**2 452**	**9.2**	**3 066**	**10.9**	**2 324**	**8.6**	**2 722**	**9.6**
Acute poliomyelitis — Poliomyélite aiguë	**-**	**-**	**-**	**-**	**2**	**♦0.0**	**-**	**-**
Measles — Rougeole	**1**	**♦0.0**	**3**	**♦0.0**	**2**	**♦0.0**	**4**	**♦0.0**
Viral hepatitis — Hépatite virale	**166**	**0.6**	**113**	**0.4**	**187**	**0.7**	**129**	**0.5**
Human immunodeficiency virus [HIV] disease — Maladies dues au virus de l'immunodéficience humaine (VIH)	**11 160**	**42.1**	**10 685**	**38.1**	**11 275**	**41.8**	**10 545**	**37.1**
Malaria — Paludisme	**227**	**0.9**	**156**	**0.6**	**211**	**0.8**	**119**	**0.4**
Neoplasms — Tumeurs	**19 319**	**72.8**	**19 776**	**70.5**	**20 710**	**76.8**	**21 032**	**73.9**
Malignant neoplasms — Tumeurs malignes								
Total	**18 668**	**70.3**	**19 098**	**68.1**	**20 065**	**74.4**	**20 339**	**71.5**
Malignant neoplasm of lip, oral cavity and pharynx — Tumeur maligne de la lèvre, de la cavité buccale et du pharynx	**737**	**2.8**	**297**	**1.1**	**700**	**2.6**	**336**	**1.2**
Malignant neoplasm of oesophagus — Tumeur maligne de l'oesophage	**1 683**	**6.3**	**1 089**	**3.9**	**1 696**	**6.3**	**1 112**	**3.9**
Malignant neoplasm of stomach — Tumeur maligne de l'estomac	**631**	**2.4**	**471**	**1.7**	**749**	**2.8**	**512**	**1.8**
Malignant neoplasm of colon, rectosigmoid junction, rectum, anus and anal canal — Tumeur maligne du côlon, de la jonction recto-sigmoïdienne, du rectum, de l'anus et du canal anal	**1 239**	**4.7**	**1 142**	**4.1**	**1 338**	**5.0**	**1 244**	**4.4**
Malignant neoplasm of liver and intrahepatic bile ducts — Tumeur maligne du foie et des voies bilaires intrahépatiques	**983**	**3.7**	**581**	**2.1**	**1 114**	**4.1**	**721**	**2.5**
Malignant neoplasm of pancreas — Tumeur maligne du pancréas	**671**	**2.5**	**659**	**2.4**	**750**	**2.8**	**725**	**2.5**
Malignant neoplasm of trachea, bronchus and lung — Tumeur maligne de la trachée, des bronches et du poumon	**3 522**	**13.3**	**1 720**	**6.1**	**3 746**	**13.9**	**1 852**	**6.5**
Malignant neoplasm of female breast — Tumeur maligne du sein chez la femme	..	..	**3 122**	**15.9**	..	..	**3 297**	...
Malignant neoplasm of cervix uteri — Tumeur maligne du col de l'utérus	..	..	**3 444**	**17.6**	..	..	**3 619**	...
Malignant neoplasm of prostate — Tumeur maligne de la prostate	**2 729**	**70.5**	..	..	**3 033**	...	..	..
Malignant neoplasm of lymphoid, haematopoietic and related tissue — Tumeurs malignes primitives ou présumées primitives des tissus lymphoïde, hématopoïétique et apparentés	**1 532**	**5.8**	**1 316**	**4.7**	**1 724**	**6.4**	**1 316**	**4.6**
Disorders of the blood and blood-forming organs and certain disorders involving the immune mechanism — Maladies du sang et des organes hématopoïétiques et certains troubles du système immunitaire								
Total	**4 466**	**16.8**	**5 100**	**18.2**	**6 143**	**22.8**	**6 749**	**23.7**
Anaemias — Anémies	**868**	**3.3**	**1 258**	**4.5**	**815**	**3.0**	**1 203**	**4.2**
Endocrine, nutritional and metabolic diseases — Maladies endocriniennes, nutritionnelles et métaboliques								
Total	**12 137**	**45.7**	**17 465**	**62.3**	**12 722**	**47.2**	**18 848**	**66.3**
Diabetes mellitus — Diabète sucré	**8 914**	**33.6**	**13 819**	**49.3**	**9 657**	**35.8**	**15 396**	**54.1**
Malnutrition — Malnutrition	**1 006**	**3.8**	**858**	**3.1**	**961**	**3.6**	**799**	**2.8**
Mental and behavioural disorders — Troubles mentaux et du comportement	**900**	**3.4**	**1 091**	**3.9**	**940**	**3.5**	**956**	**3.4**
Diseases of the nervous system — Maladies du système nerveux	**5 722**	**21.6**	**4 520**	**16.1**	**6 030**	**22.4**	**4 672**	**16.4**
Diseases of the circulatory system — Maladies de l'appareil circulatoire								
Total	**35 140**	**132.4**	**42 985**	**153.3**	**36 653**	**135.9**	**44 988**	**158.2**
Acute rheumatic fever and chronic rheumatic heart diseases — Rhumatisme articularie aigu et cardiopathies rhumatismales chroniques	**122**	**0.5**	**203**	**0.7**	**111**	**0.4**	**203**	**0.7**
Hypertensive diseases — Maladies hypertensives	**6 670**	**25.1**	**11 081**	**39.5**	**7 342**	**27.2**	**12 078**	**42.5**
Ischaemic heart disease — Cardiopathie ischémique	**6 200**	**23.4**	**4 696**	**16.7**	**6 944**	**25.8**	**5 280**	**18.6**
Cerebrovascular disease — Maladie cérébrovasculaire	**9 908**	**37.3**	**13 149**	**46.9**	**9 696**	**36.0**	**13 146**	**46.2**

20. Death and death rates by cause and sex: 2014 - 2018
Décès et taux de mortalité par cause et sexe : 2014 - 2018 (continued - suite)

South Africa - Afrique du Sud

Cause of death — Cause de décès	2014 (C)				2015 (C)			
	Male — Masculin		Female — Féminin		Male — Masculin		Female — Féminin	
	Number Nombre	Rate Taux	Number Nombre	Rate Taux	Number Nombre	Rate Taux	Number Nombre	Rate Taux
Diseases of arteries, arterioles and capillaries — Maladies des artères, artérioles et capillaires	**840**	**3.2**	**606**	**2.2**	**831**	**3.1**	**591**	**2.1**
Diseases of the respiratory system — Maladies de l'appareil respiratoire								
Total	**24 576**	**92.6**	**20 649**	**73.6**	**24 267**	**90.0**	**19 891**	**69.9**
Influenza — Grippe	**192**	**0.7**	**280**	**1.0**	**215**	**0.8**	**226**	**0.8**
Pneumonia — Pneumopathies	**11 011**	**41.5**	**10 459**	**37.3**	**10 290**	**38.2**	**9 736**	**34.2**
Chronic lower respiratory diseases — Maladies chroniques des voies respiratoires inférieures	**7 300**	**27.5**	**4 785**	**17.1**	**7 691**	**28.5**	**4 948**	**17.4**
Diseases of the digestive system — Maladies de l'appareil digestif								
Total	**6 358**	**24.0**	**5 537**	**19.7**	**6 513**	**24.2**	**5 599**	**19.7**
Gastric and duodenal ulcer — Ulcère de l'estomac et du duodénum	**766**	**2.9**	**720**	**2.6**	**792**	**2.9**	**736**	**2.6**
Diseases of the liver — Maladies du foie	**2 390**	**9.0**	**1 770**	**6.3**	**2 466**	**9.1**	**1 695**	**6.0**
Diseases of the musculoskeletal system and connective tissue — Maladies du système ostéo-articularie, des muscles et du tissu conjonctif	**597**	**2.2**	**1 020**	**3.6**	**623**	**2.3**	**1 040**	**3.7**
Diseases of the genitourinary system — Maladies de l'appareil génito-urinaire								
Total	**4 534**	**17.1**	**4 220**	**15.1**	**4 666**	**17.3**	**4 341**	**15.3**
Disorders of kidney and ureter — Affections du rein et de l'uretère	**4 101**	**15.5**	**3 776**	**13.5**	**4 163**	**15.4**	**3 891**	**13.7**
Hyperplasia of prostate — Hyperplasie de la prostate	**156**	**4.0**	..	..	**174**	...	..	..
Pregnancy, childbirth and the puerperium — Grossesse, accouchement et puerpéralité								
Total	..	..	**1 027**	**100.7**	..	..	**942**	**97.5**
Pregnancy with abortive outcome — Grossesse se terminant par un avortement	..	..	**103**	**10.1**	..	..	**110**	**11.4**
Other direct obstetric causes — Autres décès maternels directs	..	..	**612**	**60.0**	..	..	**586**	**60.7**
Indirect obstetric causes — Décès maternels indirects	..	..	**312**	**30.6**	..	..	**246**	**25.5**
Certain conditions originating in the perinatal period — Certaines affections dont l'origine se situe dans la période périnatale	**5 041**	**980.1**	**4 035**	**798.8**	**5 081**	**1 043.6**	**4 108**	**857.1**
Congenital malformations, deformations and chromosomal abnormalities — Malformations congénitales et anomalies chromosomiques	**1 127**	**219.1**	**967**	**191.4**	**1 131**	**232.3**	**1 063**	**221.8**
Symptoms, signs and abnormal clinical and laboratory findings, not elsewhere classified — Symptômes, signes et résultats anormaux d'examens cliniques et de laboratoire, non classés ailleurs	**27 614**	**104.1**	**28 937**	**103.2**	**27 726**	**102.8**	**29 232**	**102.8**
All other diseases — Toutes autres maladies	**363**	**1.4**	**500**	**1.8**	**568**	**2.1**	**837**	**2.9**
External causes — Causes externes								
Total	**36 307**	**136.8**	**11 017**	**39.3**	**39 302**	**145.8**	**11 515**	**40.5**
Accidents								
Total	**23 998**	**90.4**	**7 736**	**27.6**	**29 141**	**108.1**	**8 834**	**31.1**
Transport accidents — Accidents de transport	**4 393**	**16.6**	**1 504**	**5.4**	**4 680**	**17.4**	**1 588**	**5.6**
Falls — Chutes	**129**	**0.5**	**54**	**0.2**	**139**	**0.5**	**72**	**0.3**
Accidental drowning and submersion — Noyade et submersion accidentelles	**1 225**	**4.6**	**343**	**1.2**	**1 125**	**4.2**	**278**	**1.0**
Exposure to smoke, fire and flames — Exposition à la fumée, au feu et aux flammes	**1 416**	**5.3**	**854**	**3.0**	**1 441**	**5.3**	**894**	**3.1**
Accidental poisoning by and exposure to noxious substances — Intoxication accidentelle par des substances nocives et exposition à ces substances	**477**	**1.8**	**382**	**1.4**	**548**	**2.0**	**384**	**1.3**
Intentional self-harm — Lésions auto-infligées	**461**	**1.7**	**121**	**0.4**	**377**	**1.4**	**105**	**0.4**
Assault — Agresssions	**4 670**	**17.6**	**601**	**2.1**	**6 353**	**23.6**	**801**	**2.8**
All other external causes — Toutes autres causes externes	**7 178**	**27.0**	**2 559**	**9.1**	**3 431**	**12.7**	**1 775**	**6.2**

20. Death and death rates by cause and sex: 2014 - 2018
Décès et taux de mortalité par cause et sexe : 2014 - 2018 (continued - suite)

Cause of death — Cause de décès	Anguilla				Antigua and Barbuda - Antigua-et-Barbuda			
	2017 (...)		2018 (...)		2016 (+U)		2017 (+U)	
	Male — Masculin	Female — Féminin	Male — Masculin	Female — Féminin	Male — Masculin	Female — Féminin	Male — Masculin	Female — Féminin
	Number Nombre	Number Nombre	Number Nombre	Number Nombre	Number Nombre	Number Nombre	Number Nombre	Number Nombre
TOTAL	*59*	*27*	*64*	*36*	*288*	*254*	*304*	*259*
Certain infectious and parasitic diseases — Certaines maladies infectieuses et parasitaires								
Total	*1*	-	*2*	*1*	*15*	*7*	*15*	*8*
Intestinal infectious diseases — Maladies infectieuses intestinales	-	-	-	-	-	-	*1*	-
Tuberculosis — Tuberculose	-	-	-	-	-	-	-	-
Tetanus — Tétanos	-	-	-	-	-	-	-	-
Diphtheria — Diphtérie	-	-	-	-	-	-	-	-
Whooping cough — Coqueluche	-	-	-	-	-	-	-	-
Meningococcal infection — Infection à méningocoques	-	-	-	-	-	-	-	-
Septicaemia — Septicémie	-	-	-	-	*10*	*2*	*5*	*6*
Acute poliomyelitis — Poliomyélite aiguë	-	-	-	-	-	-	-	-
Measles — Rougeole	-	-	-	-	-	-	-	-
Viral hepatitis — Hépatite virale	-	-	-	-	-	-	-	-
Human immunodeficiency virus [HIV] disease — Maladies dues au virus de l'immunodéficience humaine (VIH)	*1*	-	*2*	*1*	*2*	*4*	*7*	*1*
Malaria — Paludisme	-	-	-	-	-	-	-	-
Neoplasms — Tumeurs	*14*	*5*	*15*	*7*	*50*	*59*	*53*	*59*
Malignant neoplasms — Tumeurs malignes								
Total	*14*	*5*	*15*	*6*	*49*	*59*	*52*	*56*
Malignant neoplasm of lip, oral cavity and pharynx — Tumeur maligne de la lèvre, de la cavité buccale et du pharynx	*1*	-	*1*	-	*2*	*2*	-	-
Malignant neoplasm of oesophagus — Tumeur maligne de l'oesophage	*1*	-	-	-	-	-	-	-
Malignant neoplasm of stomach — Tumeur maligne de l'estomac	-	-	-	*1*	*4*	*2*	*1*	*2*
Malignant neoplasm of colon, rectosigmoid junction, rectum, anus and anal canal — Tumeur maligne du côlon, de la jonction recto-sigmoïdienne, du rectum, de l'anus et du canal anal	*1*	-	*1*	*1*	*3*	*9*	*5*	*4*
Malignant neoplasm of liver and intrahepatic bile ducts — Tumeur maligne du foie et des voies bilaires intrahépatiques	-	-	-	-	*2*	*1*	*1*	-
Malignant neoplasm of pancreas — Tumeur maligne du pancréas	-	-	-	-	*3*	*2*	*1*	*2*
Malignant neoplasm of trachea, bronchus and lung — Tumeur maligne de la trachée, des bronches et du poumon	*1*	-	-	-	*8*	*1*	*4*	*1*
Malignant neoplasm of female breast — Tumeur maligne du sein chez la femme	..	*3*	..	*2*	..	*21*	..	*20*
Malignant neoplasm of cervix uteri — Tumeur maligne du col de l'utérus	..	-	..	-	..	*6*	..	*3*
Malignant neoplasm of prostate — Tumeur maligne de la prostate	*9*	..	*9*	..	*16*	..	*22*	..
Malignant neoplasm of lymphoid, haematopoietic and related tissue — Tumeurs malignes primitives ou présumées primitives des tissus lymphoïde, hématopoïétique et apparentés	-	-	*1*	-	*3*	*3*	*7*	*5*
Disorders of the blood and blood-forming organs and certain disorders involving the immune mechanism — Maladies du sang et des organes hématopoïétiques et certains troubles du système immunitaire								
Total	-	-	-	*1*	*4*	*4*	*8*	*7*
Anaemias — Anémies	-	-	-	*1*	*3*	*3*	*6*	*3*
Endocrine, nutritional and metabolic diseases — Maladies endocriniennes, nutritionnelles et métaboliques								
Total	*7*	*7*	*6*	*8*	*33*	*42*	*28*	*38*
Diabetes mellitus — Diabète sucré	*6*	*7*	*5*	*6*	*28*	*33*	*20*	*33*
Malnutrition — Malnutrition	-	-	-	-	*1*	*1*	-	-
Mental and behavioural disorders — Troubles mentaux et du comportement	*2*	*1*	*2*	-	*3*	-	*4*	*3*
Diseases of the nervous system — Maladies du système nerveux	*1*	*1*	*3*	*2*	*12*	*5*	*7*	*8*
Diseases of the circulatory system — Maladies do l'appareil circulatoire								
Total	*18*	*7*	*15*	*13*	*94*	*88*	*102*	*99*
Acute rheumatic fever and chronic rheumatic heart diseases — Rhumatisme articularie aigu et cardiopathies rhumatismales chroniques	-	-	-	-	-	-	-	*2*
Hypertensive diseases — Maladies hypertensives	*4*	*4*	*1*	*5*	*21*	*27*	*25*	*30*
Ischaemic heart disease — Cardiopathie ischémique	*3*	-	*6*	*4*	*22*	*17*	*24*	*26*

20. Death and death rates by cause and sex: 2014 - 2018
Décès et taux de mortalité par cause et sexe : 2014 - 2018 (continued - suite)

Cause of death — Cause de décès	Anguilla				Antigua and Barbuda - Antigua-et-Barbuda			
	2017 (...)		2018 (...)		2016 (+U)		2017 (+U)	
	Male — Masculin	Female — Féminin	Male — Masculin	Female — Féminin	Male — Masculin	Female — Féminin	Male — Masculin	Female — Féminin
	Number Nombre	Number Nombre	Number Nombre	Number Nombre	Number Nombre	Number Nombre	Number Nombre	Number Nombre
Cerebrovascular disease — Maladie cérébrovasculaire	*3*	*2*	*4*	*3*	*24*	*25*	*21*	*18*
Diseases of arteries, arterioles and capillaries — Maladies des artères, artérioles et capillaires	*1*	-	-	*1*	*4*	*2*	*7*	*5*
Diseases of the respiratory system — Maladies de l'appareil respiratoire								
Total	*1*	*3*	*1*	-	*22*	*15*	*15*	*16*
Influenza — Grippe	-	-	-	-	-	-	-	-
Pneumonia — Pneumopathies	*1*	*1*	-	-	*2*	*4*	-	*5*
Chronic lower respiratory diseases — Maladies chroniques des voies respiratoires inférieures	-	*2*	-	-	*4*	*1*	*7*	*2*
Diseases of the digestive system — Maladies de l'appareil digestif								
Total	*3*	-	*2*	-	*10*	*5*	*11*	*1*
Gastric and duodenal ulcer — Ulcère de l'estomac et du duodénum	*1*	-	-	-	*2*	-	-	-
Diseases of the liver — Maladies du foie	*2*	-	-	-	*2*	*2*	*6*	-
Diseases of the musculoskeletal system and connective tissue — Maladies du système ostéo-articularie, des muscles et du tissu conjonctif	-	-	-	-	-	*1*	-	*1*
Diseases of the genitourinary system — Maladies de l'appareil génito-urinaire								
Total	*3*	-	*1*	-	*10*	*6*	*14*	*3*
Disorders of kidney and ureter — Affections du rein et de l'uretère	*1*	-	-	-	*4*	*3*	*10*	*3*
Hyperplasia of prostate — Hyperplasie de la prostate	*1*	..	-	..	*5*	..	*1*	..
Pregnancy, childbirth and the puerperium — Grossesse, accouchement et puerpéralité								
Total	..	*1*	..	-	..	*1*	..	-
Pregnancy with abortive outcome — Grossesse se terminant par un avortement	..	*1*	..	-	..	-	..	-
Other direct obstetric causes — Autres décès maternels directs	..	-	..	-	..	*1*	..	-
Indirect obstetric causes — Décès maternels indirects	..	-	..	-	..	-	..	-
Certain conditions originating in the perinatal period — Certaines affections dont l'origine se situe dans la période périnatale	*2*	*1*	-	*1*	*2*	*4*	*5*	-
Congenital malformations, deformations and chromosomal abnormalities — Malformations congénitales et anomalies chromosomiques	-	-	*1*	-	*2*	*3*	*1*	*2*
Symptoms, signs and abnormal clinical and laboratory findings, not elsewhere classified — Symptômes, signes et résultats anormaux d'examens cliniques et de laboratoire, non classés ailleurs	-	-	-	*1*	*1*	*2*	*1*	*8*
All other diseases — Toutes autres maladies	-	-	*2*	-	*7*	*4*	*3*	-
External causes — Causes externes								
Total	*7*	*1*	*14*	*2*	*23*	*8*	*37*	*6*
Accidents								
Total	*5*	-	*8*	*1*	*22*	*8*	*37*	*6*
Transport accidents — Accidents de transport	*3*	-	*2*	-	-	-	-	-
Falls — Chutes	-	-	*4*	-	-	-	-	-
Accidental drowning and submersion — Noyade et submersion accidentelles	*1*	-	*1*	*1*	*3*	*2*	*2*	-
Exposure to smoke, fire and flames — Exposition à la fumée, au feu et aux flammes	-	-	-	-	-	-	*1*	-
Accidental poisoning by and exposure to noxious substances — Intoxication accidentelle par des substances nocives et exposition à ces substances	-	-	-	-	*1*	-	*2*	-
Intentional self-harm — Lésions auto-infligées	-	-	-	-	-	-	-	-
Assault — Agresssions	*2*	*1*	*5*	-	-	-	-	-
All other external causes — Toutes autres causes externes	-	-	*1*	*1*	*1*	-	-	-

20. Death and death rates by cause and sex: 2014 - 2018
Décès et taux de mortalité par cause et sexe : 2014 - 2018 (continued - suite)

Cause of death — Cause de décès	Aruba				Bahamas		Belize	
	2015 (...)		2016 (...)		2014 (+U)		2015 (U)	
	Male — Masculin	Female — Féminin	Male — Masculin	Female — Féminin	Male — Masculin	Female — Féminin	Male — Masculin	Female — Féminin
	Number Nombre	Number Nombre	Number Nombre	Number Nombre	Number Nombre	Number Nombre	Number Nombre	Number Nombre
TOTAL	*382*	*311*	*394*	*370*	*1 193*	*966*	*1 095*	*677*
Certain infectious and parasitic diseases — Certaines maladies infectieuses et parasitaires								
Total	*15*	*8*	*11*	*7*	*98*	*75*	*103*	*52*
Intestinal infectious diseases — Maladies infectieuses intestinales	-	*1*	*1*	-	*5*	*2*	*5*	*3*
Tuberculosis — Tuberculose	*2*	-	-	-	*1*	*1*	*6*	*2*
Tetanus — Tétanos	-	-	-	-	-	-	-	-
Diphtheria — Diphtérie	-	-	-	-	-	-	-	-
Whooping cough — Coqueluche	-	-	-	-	-	-	-	-
Meningococcal infection — Infection à méningocoques	-	-	-	-	*1*	-	-	-
Septicaemia — Septicémie	*7*	*3*	*6*	*5*	*31*	*28*	*14*	*8*
Acute poliomyelitis — Poliomyélite aiguë	-	-	-	-	-	-	-	-
Measles — Rougeole	-	-	-	-	-	-	-	-
Viral hepatitis — Hépatite virale	*1*	-	*1*	-	-	-	-	*1*
Human immunodeficiency virus [HIV] disease — Maladies dues au virus de l'immunodéficience humaine (VIH)	*4*	-	*2*	-	*57*	*43*	*77*	*37*
Malaria — Paludisme	-	-	-	-	*1*	-	-	-
Neoplasms — Tumeurs	*85*	*77*	*89*	*124*	*194*	*191*	*121*	*99*
Malignant neoplasms — Tumeurs malignes								
Total	*81*	*75*	*86*	*121*	*187*	*185*	*115*	*91*
Malignant neoplasm of lip, oral cavity and pharynx — Tumeur maligne de la lèvre, de la cavité buccale et du pharynx	*4*	-	*4*	*1*	*9*	*4*	*4*	-
Malignant neoplasm of oesophagus — Tumeur maligne de l'oesophage	*2*	-	*5*	-	*5*	*1*	*3*	-
Malignant neoplasm of stomach — Tumeur maligne de l'estomac	*1*	*1*	*5*	*5*	*11*	*9*	*9*	*7*
Malignant neoplasm of colon, rectosigmoid junction, rectum, anus and anal canal — Tumeur maligne du côlon, de la jonction recto-sigmoïdienne, du rectum, de l'anus et du canal anal	*11*	*9*	*12*	*16*	*20*	*14*	*10*	*8*
Malignant neoplasm of liver and intrahepatic bile ducts — Tumeur maligne du foie et des voies bilaires intrahépatiques	*1*	*3*	*4*	*5*	*7*	*4*	*16*	*5*
Malignant neoplasm of pancreas — Tumeur maligne du pancréas	*3*	*4*	*7*	*4*	*3*	*3*	-	*3*
Malignant neoplasm of trachea, bronchus and lung — Tumeur maligne de la trachée, des bronches et du poumon	*14*	*6*	*16*	*9*	*15*	*7*	*17*	*9*
Malignant neoplasm of female breast — Tumeur maligne du sein chez la femme	..	*21*	..	*34*	..	*57*	..	*17*
Malignant neoplasm of cervix uteri — Tumeur maligne du col de l'utérus	..	*2*	..	*6*	..	*16*	..	*13*
Malignant neoplasm of prostate — Tumeur maligne de la prostate	*13*	..	*11*	..	*46*	..	*30*	..
Malignant neoplasm of lymphoid, haematopoietic and related tissue — Tumeurs malignes primitives ou présumées primitives des tissus lymphoïde, hématopoïétique et apparentés	*14*	*7*	*8*	*12*	*20*	*14*	*8*	*4*
Disorders of the blood and blood-forming organs and certain disorders involving the immune mechanism — Maladies du sang et des organes hématopoïétiques et certains troubles du système immunitaire								
Total	*4*	-	*3*	*3*	*9*	*9*	*7*	*4*
Anaemias — Anémies	*1*	-	*3*	*2*	*5*	*8*	*7*	*4*
Endocrine, nutritional and metabolic diseases — Maladies endocriniennes, nutritionnelles et métaboliques								
Total	*18*	*31*	*27*	*30*	*82*	*86*	*92*	*107*
Diabetes mellitus — Diabète sucré	*16*	*26*	*19*	*26*	*54*	*54*	*80*	*98*
Malnutrition — Malnutrition	*1*	*1*	-	*1*	*4*	*9*	*2*	*3*
Mental and behavioural disorders — Troubles mentaux et du comportement	*5*	*1*	*8*	*1*	*9*	*2*	*5*	*1*
Diseases of the nervous system — Maladies du système nerveux	*13*	*22*	*25*	*20*	*32*	*39*	*22*	*16*
Diseases of the circulatory system — Maladies de l'appareil circulatoire								
Total	*126*	*99*	*116*	*98*	*347*	*339*	*213*	*184*
Acute rheumatic fever and chronic rheumatic heart diseases — Rhumatisme articularie aigu et cardiopathies rhumatismales chroniques	*1*	-	-	-	-	*1*	-	-
Hypertensive diseases — Maladies hypertensives	*10*	*5*	*12*	*14*	*89*	*96*	*28*	*38*
Ischaemic heart disease — Cardiopathie ischémique	*34*	*27*	*35*	*17*	*105*	*78*	*76*	*52*

20. Death and death rates by cause and sex: 2014 - 2018
Décès et taux de mortalité par cause et sexe : 2014 - 2018 (continued - suite)

Cause of death — Cause de décès	Aruba				Bahamas		Belize	
	2015 (...)		2016 (...)		2014 (+U)		2015 (U)	
	Male — Masculin	Female — Féminin	Male — Masculin	Female — Féminin	Male — Masculin	Female — Féminin	Male — Masculin	Female — Féminin
	Number Nombre	Number Nombre	Number Nombre	Number Nombre	Number Nombre	Number Nombre	Number Nombre	Number Nombre
Cerebrovascular disease — Maladie cérébrovasculaire	37	31	25	24	62	80	61	38
Diseases of arteries, arterioles and capillaries — Maladies des artères, artérioles et capillaires	5	1	3	3	9	2	5	2
Diseases of the respiratory system — Maladies de l'appareil respiratoire								
Total	25	16	29	21	61	50	119	66
Influenza — Grippe	1	1	1	2	-	-	-	1
Pneumonia — Pneumopathies	12	11	14	12	31	27	50	42
Chronic lower respiratory diseases — Maladies chroniques des voies respiratoires inférieures	7	3	7	3	8	7	36	8
Diseases of the digestive system — Maladies de l'appareil digestif								
Total	21	18	20	17	65	43	66	33
Gastric and duodenal ulcer — Ulcère de l'estomac et du duodénum	1	1	1	-	7	1	1	-
Diseases of the liver — Maladies du foie	11	6	9	5	32	12	44	16
Diseases of the musculoskeletal system and connective tissue — Maladies du système ostéo-articularie, des muscles et du tissu conjonctif	1	6	2	4	5	17	1	4
Diseases of the genitourinary system — Maladies de l'appareil génito-urinaire								
Total	13	4	15	12	34	28	22	16
Disorders of kidney and ureter — Affections du rein et de l'uretère	10	2	13	6	17	17	20	8
Hyperplasia of prostate — Hyperplasie de la prostate	-	..	-	..	7	..	1	..
Pregnancy, childbirth and the puerperium — Grossesse, accouchement et puerpéralité								
Total	..	-	..	2	..	3	..	-
Pregnancy with abortive outcome — Grossesse se terminant par un avortement	..	-	..	1	..	1	..	-
Other direct obstetric causes — Autres décès maternels directs	..	-	..	1	..	2	..	-
Indirect obstetric causes — Décès maternels indirects	..	-	..	-	..	-	..	-
Certain conditions originating in the perinatal period — Certaines affections dont l'origine se situe dans la période périnatale	1	-	1	-	20	10	40	35
Congenital malformations, deformations and chromosomal abnormalities — Malformations congénitales et anomalies chromosomiques	5	1	1	1	5	12	19	15
Symptoms, signs and abnormal clinical and laboratory findings, not elsewhere classified — Symptômes, signes et résultats anormaux d'examens cliniques et de laboratoire, non classés ailleurs	18	17	9	13	14	15	15	4
All other diseases — Toutes autres maladies	1	4	2	6	4	15	1	2
External causes — Causes externes								
Total	31	7	36	11	214	32	249	39
Accidents								
Total	19	5	23	7	87	20	124	24
Transport accidents — Accidents de transport	9	4	8	3	55	5	74	14
Falls — Chutes	-	-	3	-	5	-	10	3
Accidental drowning and submersion — Noyade et submersion accidentelles	2	1	6	1	14	4	20	2
Exposure to smoke, fire and flames — Exposition à la fumée, au feu et aux flammes	-	-	-	-	3	-	1	1
Accidental poisoning by and exposure to noxious substances — Intoxication accidentelle par des substances nocives et exposition à ces substances	1	-	1	-	-	-	2	3
Intentional self-harm — Lésions auto-infligées	7	2	4	2	3	-	22	4
Assault — Agresssions	2	-	5	1	116	10	103	10
All other external causes — Toutes autres causes externes	3	-	4	1	8	2	-	1

20. Death and death rates by cause and sex: 2014 - 2018
Décès et taux de mortalité par cause et sexe : 2014 - 2018 (continued - suite)

Cause of death — Cause de décès	Belize		Bermuda - Bermudes			
	2016 (U)		2016 (...)		2017 (...)	
	Male — Masculin	Female — Féminin	Male — Masculin	Female — Féminin	Male — Masculin	Female — Féminin
	Number Nombre	Number Nombre	Number Nombre	Number Nombre	Number Nombre	Number Nombre
TOTAL	*1 126*	*676*	*265*	*235*	*250*	*242*
Certain infectious and parasitic diseases — Certaines maladies infectieuses et parasitaires						
Total	*99*	*63*	*4*	*2*	*10*	-
Intestinal infectious diseases — Maladies infectieuses intestinales	*4*	*2*	-	*1*	-	-
Tuberculosis — Tuberculose	*6*	*1*	-	-	-	-
Tetanus — Tétanos	-	-	-	-	-	-
Diphtheria — Diphtérie	-	-	-	-	-	-
Whooping cough — Coqueluche	-	-	-	-	-	-
Meningococcal infection — Infection à méningocoques	-	-	-	-	-	-
Septicaemia — Septicémie	*16*	*10*	*3*	*1*	*5*	-
Acute poliomyelitis — Poliomyélite aiguë	-	-	-	-	-	-
Measles — Rougeole	-	-	-	-	-	-
Viral hepatitis — Hépatite virale	-	-	-	-	-	-
Human immunodeficiency virus [HIV] disease — Maladies dues au virus de l'immunodéficience humaine (VIH)	*71*	*50*	*1*	-	*3*	-
Malaria — Paludisme	-	-	-	-	-	-
Neoplasms — Tumeurs	*115*	*86*	*76*	*65*	*68*	*59*
Malignant neoplasms — Tumeurs malignes						
Total	*109*	*82*	*76*	*65*	*68*	*56*
Malignant neoplasm of lip, oral cavity and pharynx — Tumeur maligne de la lèvre, de la cavité buccale et du pharynx	-	-	*2*	-	*7*	*2*
Malignant neoplasm of oesophagus — Tumeur maligne de l'oesophage	*1*	-	*1*	*1*	*2*	-
Malignant neoplasm of stomach — Tumeur maligne de l'estomac	*9*	*2*	*1*	*3*	*4*	*1*
Malignant neoplasm of colon, rectosigmoid junction, rectum, anus and anal canal — Tumeur maligne du côlon, de la jonction recto-sigmoïdienne, du rectum, de l'anus et du canal anal	*15*	*6*	*7*	*5*	*7*	*10*
Malignant neoplasm of liver and intrahepatic bile ducts — Tumeur maligne du foie et des voies biliaires intrahépatiques	*7*	*10*	*3*	*1*	*3*	*1*
Malignant neoplasm of pancreas — Tumeur maligne du pancréas	*4*	*6*	*4*	*7*	*1*	*2*
Malignant neoplasm of trachea, bronchus and lung — Tumeur maligne de la trachée, des bronches et du poumon	*16*	*3*	*18*	*8*	*14*	*6*
Malignant neoplasm of female breast — Tumeur maligne du sein chez la femme	..	*12*	..	*12*	..	*7*
Malignant neoplasm of cervix uteri — Tumeur maligne du col de l'utérus	..	*15*	..	*2*	..	*2*
Malignant neoplasm of prostate — Tumeur maligne de la prostate	*23*	..	*14*	..	*11*	..
Malignant neoplasm of lymphoid, haematopoietic and related tissue — Tumeurs malignes primitives ou présumées primitives des tissus lymphoïde, hématopoïétique et apparentés	*10*	*6*	*3*	*5*	*6*	*7*
Disorders of the blood and blood-forming organs and certain disorders involving the immune mechanism — Maladies du sang et des organes hématopoïétiques et certains troubles du système immunitaire						
Total	*8*	*7*	*2*	*3*	*3*	*2*
Anaemias — Anémies	*7*	*5*	*1*	*2*	*3*	*1*
Endocrine, nutritional and metabolic diseases — Maladies endocriniennes, nutritionnelles et métaboliques						
Total	*102*	*118*	*11*	*18*	*14*	*17*
Diabetes mellitus — Diabète sucré	*84*	*109*	*9*	*14*	*9*	*16*
Malnutrition — Malnutrition	*7*	*2*	-	-	-	-
Mental and behavioural disorders — Troubles mentaux et du comportement	*6*	*1*	*1*	*2*	*2*	-
Diseases of the nervous system — Maladies du système nerveux	*17*	*16*	*23*	*34*	*25*	*34*
Diseases of the circulatory system — Maladies de l'appareil circulatoire						
Total	*226*	*175*	*100*	*67*	*80*	*78*
Acute rheumatic fever and chronic rheumatic heart diseases — Rhumatisme articularie aigu et cardiopathies rhumatismales chroniques	*1*	*1*	*2*	*1*	*1*	-
Hypertensive diseases — Maladies hypertensives	*39*	*31*	*10*	*11*	*5*	*10*
Ischaemic heart disease — Cardiopathie ischémique	*73*	*46*	*45*	*23*	*36*	*19*
Cerebrovascular disease — Maladie cérébrovasculaire	*65*	*55*	*18*	*9*	*13*	*21*
Diseases of arteries, arterioles and capillaries — Maladies des artères, artérioles et capillaires	*6*	*1*	*7*	*7*	*2*	*4*

20. Death and death rates by cause and sex: 2014 - 2018
Décès et taux de mortalité par cause et sexe : 2014 - 2018 (continued - suite)

Cause of death — Cause de décès	Belize		Bermuda - Bermudes			
	2016 (U)		2016 (...)		2017 (...)	
	Male — Masculin	Female — Féminin	Male — Masculin	Female — Féminin	Male — Masculin	Female — Féminin
	Number Nombre	Number Nombre	Number Nombre	Number Nombre	Number Nombre	Number Nombre
Diseases of the respiratory system — Maladies de l'appareil respiratoire						
Total	*101*	*58*	*12*	*15*	*6*	*17*
Influenza — Grippe	-	-	-	-	-	*1*
Pneumonia — Pneumopathies	*32*	*29*	*1*	*4*	*2*	*4*
Chronic lower respiratory diseases — Maladies chroniques des voies respiratoires inférieures	*38*	*10*	*7*	*6*	*2*	*5*
Diseases of the digestive system — Maladies de l'appareil digestif						
Total	*82*	*34*	*6*	*6*	*8*	*13*
Gastric and duodenal ulcer — Ulcère de l'estomac et du duodénum	*3*	*1*	-	-	-	-
Diseases of the liver — Maladies du foie	*61*	*23*	*4*	*1*	*4*	*3*
Diseases of the musculoskeletal system and connective tissue — Maladies du système ostéo-articularie, des muscles et du tissu conjonctif	*2*	*6*	-	*2*	*2*	*1*
Diseases of the genitourinary system — Maladies de l'appareil génito-urinaire						
Total	*32*	*11*	*5*	*8*	*4*	*12*
Disorders of kidney and ureter — Affections du rein et de l'uretère	*28*	*8*	*4*	*7*	*3*	*9*
Hyperplasia of prostate — Hyperplasie de la prostate	*2*	..	-	..	*1*	..
Pregnancy, childbirth and the puerperium — Grossesse, accouchement et puerpéralité						
Total	..	*1*	..	-	..	-
Pregnancy with abortive outcome — Grossesse se terminant par un avortement	..	-	..	-	..	-
Other direct obstetric causes — Autres décès maternels directs	..	*1*	..	-	..	-
Indirect obstetric causes — Décès maternels indirects	..	-	..	-	..	-
Certain conditions originating in the perinatal period — Certaines affections dont l'origine se situe dans la période périnatale	*39*	*25*	*2*	-	-	-
Congenital malformations, deformations and chromosomal abnormalities — Malformations congénitales et anomalies chromosomiques	*13*	*12*	*1*	*2*	-	-
Symptoms, signs and abnormal clinical and laboratory findings, not elsewhere classified — Symptômes, signes et résultats anormaux d'examens cliniques et de laboratoire, non classés ailleurs	*8*	*10*	*1*	*3*	*1*	*2*
All other diseases — Toutes autres maladies	-	*4*	-	*3*	-	-
External causes — Causes externes						
Total	*276*	*49*	*21*	*5*	*27*	*7*
Accidents						
Total	*133*	*28*	*15*	*2*	*18*	*6*
Transport accidents — Accidents de transport	*88*	*16*	*9*	*2*	*11*	*4*
Falls — Chutes	*6*	*4*	*1*	-	*1*	*2*
Accidental drowning and submersion — Noyade et submersion accidentelles	*23*	*6*	*3*	-	*4*	-
Exposure to smoke, fire and flames — Exposition à la fumée, au feu et aux flammes	-	*1*	*1*	-	-	-
Accidental poisoning by and exposure to noxious substances — Intoxication accidentelle par des substances nocives et exposition à ces substances	*2*	-	*1*	-	-	-
Intentional self-harm — Lésions auto-infligées	*13*	*8*	*1*	-	*1*	-
Assault — Agresssions	*129*	*13*	*3*	-	*5*	-
All other external causes — Toutes autres causes externes	*1*	-	*2*	*3*	*3*	*1*

20. Death and death rates by cause and sex: 2014 - 2018
Décès et taux de mortalité par cause et sexe : 2014 - 2018 (continued - suite)

Canada

Cause of death — Cause de décès	2016 (C)				2017 (C)			
	Male — Masculin		Female — Féminin		Male — Masculin		Female — Féminin	
	Number Nombre	Rate Taux	Number Nombre	Rate Taux	Number Nombre	Rate Taux	Number Nombre	Rate Taux
TOTAL	**135 772**	**757.8**	**131 441**	**722.5**	**141 099**	**778.0**	**135 590**	**736.6**
Certain infectious and parasitic diseases — Certaines maladies infectieuses et parasitaires								
Total	2 092	11.7	2 076	11.4	2 117	11.7	2 155	11.7
Intestinal infectious diseases — Maladies infectieuses intestinales	387	2.2	569	3.1	377	2.1	537	2.9
Tuberculosis — Tuberculose	57	0.3	31	0.2	65	0.4	27	♦0.1
Tetanus — Tétanos	-	-	-	-	-	-	-	-
Diphtheria — Diphtérie	-	-	-	-	-	-	-	-
Whooping cough — Coqueluche	-	-	-	-	1	♦0.0	-	-
Meningococcal infection — Infection à méningocoques	4	♦0.0	5	♦0.0	2	♦0.0	2	♦0.0
Septicaemia — Septicémie	912	5.1	997	5.5	963	5.3	1 078	5.9
Acute poliomyelitis — Poliomyélite aiguë	-	-	-	-	-	-	-	-
Measles — Rougeole	-	-	-	-	-	-	-	-
Viral hepatitis — Hépatite virale	295	1.6	151	0.8	232	1.3	136	0.7
Human immunodeficiency virus [HIV] disease — Maladies dues au virus de l'immunodéficience humaine (VIH)	134	0.7	41	0.2	116	0.6	23	♦0.1
Malaria — Paludisme	-	-	-	-	-	-	-	-
Neoplasms — Tumeurs	42 290	236.0	38 423	211.2	43 033	237.3	38 432	208.8
Malignant neoplasms — Tumeurs malignes								
Total	41 447	231.3	37 637	206.9	42 167	232.5	37 677	204.7
Malignant neoplasm of lip, oral cavity and pharynx — Tumeur maligne de la lèvre, de la cavité buccale et du pharynx	1 030	5.7	496	2.7	1 027	5.7	436	2.4
Malignant neoplasm of oesophagus — Tumeur maligne de l'oesophage	1 531	8.5	456	2.5	1 615	8.9	473	2.6
Malignant neoplasm of stomach — Tumeur maligne de l'estomac	1 265	7.1	761	4.2	1 209	6.7	729	4.0
Malignant neoplasm of colon, rectosigmoid junction, rectum, anus and anal canal — Tumeur maligne du côlon, de la jonction recto-sigmoïdienne, du rectum, de l'anus et du canal anal	4 676	26.1	4 082	22.4	4 656	25.7	3 951	21.5
Malignant neoplasm of liver and intrahepatic bile ducts — Tumeur maligne du foie et des voies bilaires intrahépatiques	1 929	10.8	1 062	5.8	2 005	11.1	1 139	6.2
Malignant neoplasm of pancreas — Tumeur maligne du pancréas	2 551	14.2	2 349	12.9	2 572	14.2	2 424	13.2
Malignant neoplasm of trachea, bronchus and lung — Tumeur maligne de la trachée, des bronches et du poumon	10 481	58.5	9 590	52.7	10 637	58.7	9 551	51.9
Malignant neoplasm of female breast — Tumeur maligne du sein chez la femme	..	..	5 298	34.6	..	..	5 318	34.3
Malignant neoplasm of cervix uteri — Tumeur maligne du col de l'utérus	..	..	410	2.7	..	..	410	2.6
Malignant neoplasm of prostate — Tumeur maligne de la prostate	4 242	65.0	..	..	4 314	64.9	..	..
Malignant neoplasm of lymphoid, haematopoietic and related tissue — Tumeurs malignes primitives ou présumées primitives des tissus lymphoïde, hématopoïétique et apparentés	4 094	22.9	3 192	17.5	4 367	24.1	3 216	17.5
Disorders of the blood and blood-forming organs and certain disorders involving the immune mechanism — Maladies du sang et des organes hématopoïétiques et certains troubles du système immunitaire								
Total	408	2.3	467	2.6	446	2.5	519	2.8
Anaemias — Anémies	210	1.2	264	1.5	225	1.2	311	1.7
Endocrine, nutritional and metabolic diseases — Maladies endocriniennes, nutritionnelles et métaboliques								
Total	4 928	27.5	4 568	25.1	5 186	28.6	4 371	23.7
Diabetes mellitus — Diabète sucré	3 686	20.6	3 152	17.3	3 883	21.4	2 999	16.3
Malnutrition — Malnutrition	61	0.3	106	0.6	88	0.5	112	0.6
Mental and behavioural disorders — Troubles mentaux et du comportement	7 868	43.9	12 520	68.8	8 687	47.9	14 137	76.8
Diseases of the nervous system — Maladies du système nerveux	6 290	35.1	7 810	42.9	6 770	37.3	8 187	44.5
Diseases of the circulatory system — Maladies de l'appareil circulatoire								
Total	35 605	198.7	34 340	188.8	37 085	204.5	34 912	189.7
Acute rheumatic fever and chronic rheumatic heart diseases — Rhumatisme articularie aigu et cardiopathies rhumatismales chroniques	216	1.2	450	2.5	209	1.2	402	2.2
Hypertensive diseases — Maladies hypertensives	1 497	8.4	2 015	11.1	1 516	8.4	2 046	11.1
Ischaemic heart disease — Cardiopathie ischémique	19 103	106.6	13 751	75.6	19 540	107.7	13 831	75.1
Cerebrovascular disease — Maladie cérébrovasculaire	5 678	31.7	7 873	43.3	6 018	33.2	7 875	42.8

20. Death and death rates by cause and sex: 2014 - 2018
Décès et taux de mortalité par cause et sexe : 2014 - 2018 (continued - suite)

Canada

Cause of death — Cause de décès	2016 (C)				2017 (C)			
	Male — Masculin		Female — Féminin		Male — Masculin		Female — Féminin	
	Number Nombre	Rate Taux	Number Nombre	Rate Taux	Number Nombre	Rate Taux	Number Nombre	Rate Taux
Diseases of arteries, arterioles and capillaries — Maladies des artères, artérioles et capillaires	1 631	9.1	1 486	8.2	1 744	9.6	1 552	8.4
Diseases of the respiratory system — Maladies de l'appareil respiratoire								
Total	12 062	67.3	11 665	64.1	12 695	70.0	13 072	71.0
Influenza — Grippe	318	1.8	349	1.9	509	2.8	764	4.2
Pneumonia — Pneumopathies	2 637	14.7	2 931	16.1	2 800	15.4	3 323	18.1
Chronic lower respiratory diseases — Maladies chroniques des voies respiratoires inférieures	6 170	34.4	6 123	33.7	6 293	34.7	6 554	35.6
Diseases of the digestive system — Maladies de l'appareil digestif								
Total	5 800	32.4	5 627	30.9	5 871	32.4	5 682	30.9
Gastric and duodenal ulcer — Ulcère de l'estomac et du duodénum	205	1.1	197	1.1	223	1.2	213	1.2
Diseases of the liver — Maladies du foie	2 607	14.6	1 666	9.2	2 613	14.4	1 710	9.3
Diseases of the musculoskeletal system and connective tissue — Maladies du système ostéo-articularie, des muscles et du tissu conjonctif	643	3.6	1 220	6.7	700	3.9	1 270	6.9
Diseases of the genitourinary system — Maladies de l'appareil génito-urinaire								
Total	2 413	13.5	2 678	14.7	2 632	14.5	2 848	15.5
Disorders of kidney and ureter — Affections du rein et de l'uretère	1 664	9.3	1 750	9.6	1 835	10.1	1 851	10.1
Hyperplasia of prostate — Hyperplasie de la prostate	134	2.1	..	..	132	2.0	..	..
Pregnancy, childbirth and the puerperium — Grossesse, accouchement et puerpéralité								
Total	..	..	24	♦6.3	..	..	25	♦6.6
Pregnancy with abortive outcome — Grossesse se terminant par un avortement	..	..	3	♦0.8	..	..	1	♦0.3
Other direct obstetric causes — Autres décès maternels directs	..	..	15	♦3.9	..	..	17	♦4.5
Indirect obstetric causes — Décès maternels indirects	..	..	3	♦0.8	..	..	4	♦1.1
Certain conditions originating in the perinatal period — Certaines affections dont l'origine se situe dans la période périnatale	543	276.5	488	261.3	584	302.3	457	249.6
Congenital malformations, deformations and chromosomal abnormalities — Malformations congénitales et anomalies chromosomiques	549	279.6	495	265.1	517	267.6	473	258.3
Symptoms, signs and abnormal clinical and laboratory findings, not elsewhere classified — Symptômes, signes et résultats anormaux d'examens cliniques et de laboratoire, non classés ailleurs	3 090	17.2	2 193	12.1	2 281	12.6	1 862	10.1
All other diseases — Toutes autres maladies	277	1.5	400	2.2	310	1.7	409	2.2
External causes — Causes externes								
Total	10 914	60.9	6 447	35.4	12 185	67.2	6 779	36.8
Accidents								
Total	7 231	40.4	5 067	27.9	8 346	46.0	5 355	29.1
Transport accidents — Accidents de transport	1 463	8.2	612	3.4	1 367	7.5	548	3.0
Falls — Chutes	2 214	12.4	2 467	13.6	2 342	12.9	2 562	13.9
Accidental drowning and submersion — Noyade et submersion accidentelles	189	1.1	64	0.4	222	1.2	68	0.4
Exposure to smoke, fire and flames — Exposition à la fumée, au feu et aux flammes	131	0.7	65	0.4	96	0.5	66	0.4
Accidental poisoning by and exposure to noxious substances — Intoxication accidentelle par des substances nocives et exposition à ces substances	2 224	12.4	893	4.9	3 291	18.1	1 101	6.0
Intentional self-harm — Lésions auto-infligées	2 935	16.4	1 039	5.7	3 110	17.1	1 042	5.7
Assault — Agresssions	300	1.7	90	0.5	329	1.8	126	0.7
All other external causes — Toutes autres causes externes	448	2.5	251	1.4	400	2.2	256	1.4

20. Death and death rates by cause and sex: 2014 - 2018
Décès et taux de mortalité par cause et sexe : 2014 - 2018 (continued - suite)

Cause of death — Cause de décès	Costa Rica				Cuba			
	2016 (+U)		2017 (+U)		2016 (C)			
	Male — Masculin	Female — Féminin	Male — Masculin	Female — Féminin	Male — Masculin		Female — Féminin	
	Number Nombre	Number Nombre	Number Nombre	Number Nombre	Number Nombre	Rate Taux	Number Nombre	Rate Taux
TOTAL	*12 663*	*9 681*	*12 926*	*10 033*	54 284	969.5	45 104	799.7
Certain infectious and parasitic diseases — Certaines maladies infectieuses et parasitaires								
Total	*280*	*172*	*281*	*159*	713	12.7	375	6.6
Intestinal infectious diseases — Maladies infectieuses intestinales	*62*	*72*	*59*	*76*	92	1.6	98	1.7
Tuberculosis — Tuberculose	*15*	*13*	*22*	*9*	31	0.6	7	♦0.1
Tetanus — Tétanos	-	-	-	-	-	-	-	-
Diphtheria — Diphtérie	-	-	-	-	-	-	-	-
Whooping cough — Coqueluche	*1*	*1*	-	-	-	-	-	-
Meningococcal infection — Infection à méningocoques	*1*	-	-	-	1	♦0.0	2	♦0.0
Septicaemia — Septicémie	*16*	*25*	*17*	*28*	51	0.9	44	0.8
Acute poliomyelitis — Poliomyélite aiguë	-	-	-	-	-	-	-	-
Measles — Rougeole	-	-	-	-	-	-	-	-
Viral hepatitis — Hépatite virale	*6*	*2*	*5*	*4*	74	1.3	99	1.8
Human immunodeficiency virus [HIV] disease — Maladies dues au virus de l'immunodéficience humaine (VIH)	*136*	*32*	*125*	*19*	397	7.1	80	1.4
Malaria — Paludisme	-	-	-	-	1	♦0.0	-	-
Neoplasms — Tumeurs	*2 649*	*2 340*	*2 637*	*2 441*	14 446	258.0	10 715	190.0
Malignant neoplasms — Tumeurs malignes								
Total	*2 560*	*2 240*	*2 545*	*2 354*	14 018	250.4	10 327	183.1
Malignant neoplasm of lip, oral cavity and pharynx — Tumeur maligne de la lèvre, de la cavité buccale et du pharynx	*47*	*22*	*67*	*21*	595	10.6	165	2.9
Malignant neoplasm of oesophagus — Tumeur maligne de l'oesophage	*36*	*16*	*50*	*7*	621	11.1	147	2.6
Malignant neoplasm of stomach — Tumeur maligne de l'estomac	*382*	*268*	*399*	*252*	526	9.4	369	6.5
Malignant neoplasm of colon, rectosigmoid junction, rectum, anus and anal canal — Tumeur maligne du côlon, de la jonction recto-sigmoïdienne, du rectum, de l'anus et du canal anal	*290*	*273*	*271*	*275*	1 146	20.5	1 495	26.5
Malignant neoplasm of liver and intrahepatic bile ducts — Tumeur maligne du foie et des voies bilaires intrahépatiques	*192*	*114*	*185*	*142*	421	7.5	361	6.4
Malignant neoplasm of pancreas — Tumeur maligne du pancréas	*132*	*136*	*127*	*147*	433	7.7	416	7.4
Malignant neoplasm of trachea, bronchus and lung — Tumeur maligne de la trachée, des bronches et du poumon	*186*	*117*	*193*	*107*	3 496	62.4	2 048	36.3
Malignant neoplasm of female breast — Tumeur maligne du sein chez la femme	..	*327*	..	*366*	..	..	1 527	32.2
Malignant neoplasm of cervix uteri — Tumeur maligne du col de l'utérus	..	*143*	..	*142*	..	..	506	10.7
Malignant neoplasm of prostate — Tumeur maligne de la prostate	*406*	..	*357*	..	3 041	165.3	..	..
Malignant neoplasm of lymphoid, haematopoietic and related tissue — Tumeurs malignes primitives ou présumées primitives des tissus lymphoïde, hématopoïétique et apparentés	*293*	*228*	*259*	*252*	890	15.9	696	12.3
Disorders of the blood and blood-forming organs and certain disorders involving the immune mechanism — Maladies du sang et des organes hématopoïétiques et certains troubles du système immunitaire								
Total	*61*	*34*	*54*	*47*	104	1.9	108	1.9
Anaemias — Anémies	*43*	*21*	*37*	*29*	81	1.4	88	1.6
Endocrine, nutritional and metabolic diseases — Maladies endocriniennes, nutritionnelles et métaboliques								
Total	*605*	*661*	*677*	*720*	1 121	20.0	1 525	27.0
Diabetes mellitus — Diabète sucré	*543*	*586*	*623*	*659*	988	17.6	1 361	24.1
Malnutrition — Malnutrition	*9*	*12*	*7*	*7*	42	0.8	18	♦0.3
Mental and behavioural disorders — Troubles mentaux et du comportement	*129*	*169*	*184*	*237*	2 444	43.6	2 687	47.6
Diseases of the nervous system — Maladies du système nerveux	*337*	*316*	*341*	*318*	942	16.8	748	13.3
Diseases of the circulatory system — Maladies de l'appareil circulatoire								
Total	*3 174*	*2 639*	*3 274*	*2 662*	19 478	347.9	17 454	309.5
Acute rheumatic fever and chronic rheumatic heart diseases — Rhumatisme articularie aigu et cardiopathies rhumatismales chroniques	*15*	*23*	*17*	*15*	68	1.2	80	1.4
Hypertensive diseases — Maladies hypertensives	*332*	*333*	*328*	*362*	1 887	33.7	1 835	32.5
Ischaemic heart disease — Cardiopathie ischémique	*1 664*	*1 112*	*1 609*	*1 092*	8 855	158.1	7 495	132.9

20. Death and death rates by cause and sex: 2014 - 2018
Décès et taux de mortalité par cause et sexe : 2014 - 2018 (continued - suite)

Cause of death — Cause de décès	Costa Rica				Cuba			
	2016 (+U)		2017 (+U)		2016 (C)			
	Male — Masculin	Female — Féminin	Male — Masculin	Female — Féminin	Male — Masculin		Female — Féminin	
	Number Nombre	Number Nombre	Number Nombre	Number Nombre	Number Nombre	Rate Taux	Number Nombre	Rate Taux
Cerebrovascular disease — Maladie cérébrovasculaire	*598*	*634*	*753*	*654*	4 802	85.8	4 654	82.5
Diseases of arteries, arterioles and capillaries — Maladies des artères, artérioles et capillaires	*106*	*55*	*115*	*56*	1 429	25.5	1 225	21.7
Diseases of the respiratory system — Maladies de l'appareil respiratoire								
Total	*1 202*	*1 045*	*1 136*	*1 052*	5 924	105.8	5 080	90.1
Influenza — Grippe	*13*	*7*	*4*	*1*	-	-	1	♦0.0
Pneumonia — Pneumopathies	*433*	*317*	*432*	*375*	3 437	61.4	3 043	54.0
Chronic lower respiratory diseases — Maladies chroniques des voies respiratoires inférieures	*484*	*468*	*476*	*433*	2 312	41.3	1 858	32.9
Diseases of the digestive system — Maladies de l'appareil digestif								
Total	*950*	*739*	*937*	*760*	2 496	44.6	1 567	27.8
Gastric and duodenal ulcer — Ulcère de l'estomac et du duodénum	*44*	*26*	*47*	*36*	241	4.3	143	2.5
Diseases of the liver — Maladies du foie	*509*	*313*	*510*	*334*	1 297	23.2	381	6.8
Diseases of the musculoskeletal system and connective tissue — Maladies du système ostéo-articularie, des muscles et du tissu conjonctif	*80*	*145*	*74*	*156*	242	4.3	464	8.2
Diseases of the genitourinary system — Maladies de l'appareil génito-urinaire								
Total	*432*	*368*	*501*	*384*	699	12.5	524	9.3
Disorders of kidney and ureter — Affections du rein et de l'uretère	*320*	*221*	*364*	*241*	518	9.3	408	7.2
Hyperplasia of prostate — Hyperplasie de la prostate	*8*	..	*7*	..	80	4.3	..	..
Pregnancy, childbirth and the puerperium — Grossesse, accouchement et puerpéralité								
Total	..	*20*	..	*15*	..	..	61	52.2
Pregnancy with abortive outcome — Grossesse se terminant par un avortement	..	*1*	..	*1*	..	..	7	♦6.0
Other direct obstetric causes — Autres décès maternels directs	..	*9*	..	*9*	..	..	25	♦21.4
Indirect obstetric causes — Décès maternels indirects	..	*10*	..	*5*	..	..	17	♦14.5
Certain conditions originating in the perinatal period — Certaines affections dont l'origine se situe dans la période périnatale	*159*	*109*	*150*	*117*	136	223.3	110	196.6
Congenital malformations, deformations and chromosomal abnormalities — Malformations congénitales et anomalies chromosomiques	*120*	*125*	*120*	*126*	201	330.0	175	312.8
Symptoms, signs and abnormal clinical and laboratory findings, not elsewhere classified — Symptômes, signes et résultats anormaux d'examens cliniques et de laboratoire, non classés ailleurs	*275*	*172*	*540*	*236*	410	7.3	269	4.8
All other diseases — Toutes autres maladies	*38*	*52*	*44*	*50*	132	2.4	171	3.0
External causes — Causes externes								
Total	*2 172*	*575*	*1 976*	*553*	4 796	85.7	3 071	54.5
Accidents								
Total	*1 272*	*394*	*1 145*	*359*	2 673	47.7	1 686	29.9
Transport accidents — Accidents de transport	*755*	*140*	*690*	*123*	852	15.2	199	3.5
Falls — Chutes	*102*	*25*	*93*	*23*	1 165	20.8	1 326	23.5
Accidental drowning and submersion — Noyade et submersion accidentelles	*89*	*15*	*116*	*10*	231	4.1	29	♦0.5
Exposure to smoke, fire and flames — Exposition à la fumée, au feu et aux flammes	*6*	*5*	*10*	*3*	31	0.6	13	♦0.2
Accidental poisoning by and exposure to noxious substances — Intoxication accidentelle par des substances nocives et exposition à ces substances	*59*	*15*	*26*	*4*	81	1.4	11	♦0.2
Intentional self-harm — Lésions auto-infligées	*284*	*52*	*226*	*55*	1 145	20.4	290	5.1
Assault — Agresssions	*466*	*56*	*492*	*58*	452	8.1	120	2.1
All other external causes — Toutes autres causes externes	*150*	*73*	*113*	*81*	526	9.4	975	17.3

20. Death and death rates by cause and sex: 2014 - 2018
Décès et taux de mortalité par cause et sexe : 2014 - 2018 (continued - suite)

Cause of death — Cause de décès	Cuba				Dominica - Dominique			
	2017 (C)				2014 (+C)		2015 (+C)	
	Male — Masculin		Female — Féminin		Male — Masculin	Female — Féminin	Male — Masculin	Female — Féminin
	Number Nombre	Rate Taux	Number Nombre	Rate Taux	Number Nombre	Number Nombre	Number Nombre	Number Nombre
TOTAL	**58 283**	**1 042.3**	**48 666**	**863.1**	**318**	**296**	**381**	**280**
Certain infectious and parasitic diseases — Certaines maladies infectieuses et parasitaires								
Total	687	12.3	379	6.7	12	17	10	11
Intestinal infectious diseases — Maladies infectieuses intestinales	81	1.4	117	2.1	3	1	2	2
Tuberculosis — Tuberculose	26	♦0.5	8	♦0.1	-	-	-	-
Tetanus — Tétanos	2	♦0.0	-	-	-	-	-	-
Diphtheria — Diphtérie	-	-	-	-	-	-	-	-
Whooping cough — Coqueluche	-	-	-	-	-	-	-	-
Meningococcal infection — Infection à méningocoques	1	♦0.0	1	♦0.0	-	-	-	-
Septicaemia — Septicémie	55	1.0	54	1.0	3	13	5	6
Acute poliomyelitis — Poliomyélite aiguë	-	-	-	-	-	-	-	-
Measles — Rougeole	-	-	-	-	-	-	-	-
Viral hepatitis — Hépatite virale	65	1.2	93	1.6	-	-	-	-
Human immunodeficiency virus [HIV] disease — Maladies dues au virus de l'immunodéficience humaine (VIH)	388	6.9	69	1.2	2	-	1	1
Malaria — Paludisme	-	-	1	♦0.0	-	-	-	-
Neoplasms — Tumeurs	**14 993**	**268.1**	**10 978**	**194.7**	**61**	**46**	**91**	**45**
Malignant neoplasms — Tumeurs malignes								
Total	14 599	261.1	10 633	188.6	60	42	82	43
Malignant neoplasm of lip, oral cavity and pharynx — Tumeur maligne de la lèvre, de la cavité buccale et du pharynx	675	12.1	157	2.8	1	-	3	-
Malignant neoplasm of oesophagus — Tumeur maligne de l'oesophage	680	12.2	151	2.7	1	-	2	-
Malignant neoplasm of stomach — Tumeur maligne de l'estomac	560	10.0	335	5.9	2	5	3	3
Malignant neoplasm of colon, rectosigmoid junction, rectum, anus and anal canal — Tumeur maligne du côlon, de la jonction recto-sigmoïdienne, du rectum, de l'anus et du canal anal	1 164	20.8	1 629	28.9	3	8	5	4
Malignant neoplasm of liver and intrahepatic bile ducts — Tumeur maligne du foie et des voies bilaires intrahépatiques	395	7.1	372	6.6	2	4	2	4
Malignant neoplasm of pancreas — Tumeur maligne du pancréas	446	8.0	391	6.9	1	2	5	3
Malignant neoplasm of trachea, bronchus and lung — Tumeur maligne de la trachée, des bronches et du poumon	3 619	64.7	2 102	37.3	6	2	6	3
Malignant neoplasm of female breast — Tumeur maligne du sein chez la femme	..	..	1 519	31.9	..	6	..	8
Malignant neoplasm of cervix uteri — Tumeur maligne du col de l'utérus	..	..	530	11.1	..	2	..	1
Malignant neoplasm of prostate — Tumeur maligne de la prostate	3 132	165.8	..	..	25	..	39	..
Malignant neoplasm of lymphoid, haematopoietic and related tissue — Tumeurs malignes primitives ou présumées primitives des tissus lymphoïde, hématopoïétique et apparentés	885	15.8	702	12.4	10	3	7	6
Disorders of the blood and blood-forming organs and certain disorders involving the immune mechanism — Maladies du sang et des organes hématopoïétiques et certains troubles du système immunitaire								
Total	118	2.1	115	2.0	9	3	12	5
Anaemias — Anémies	81	1.4	80	1.4	5	3	8	3
Endocrine, nutritional and metabolic diseases — Maladies endocriniennes, nutritionnelles et métaboliques								
Total	1 177	21.0	1 598	28.3	12	20	20	32
Diabetes mellitus — Diabète sucré	1 012	18.1	1 428	25.3	10	18	16	28
Malnutrition — Malnutrition	36	0.6	21	♦0.4	1	1	4	1
Mental and behavioural disorders — Troubles mentaux et du comportement	**2 686**	**48.0**	**2 749**	**48.8**	**-**	**-**	**3**	**3**
Diseases of the nervous system — Maladies du système nerveux	**1 047**	**18.7**	**813**	**14.4**	**8**	**3**	**8**	**7**
Diseases of the circulatory system — Maladies de l'appareil circulatoire								
Total	21 213	379.4	19 349	343.2	129	136	117	103
Acute rheumatic fever and chronic rheumatic heart diseases — Rhumatisme articularie aigu et cardiopathies rhumatismales chroniques	57	1.0	100	1.8	-	1	1	2
Hypertensive diseases — Maladies hypertensives	2 261	40.4	2 287	40.6	24	28	26	24
Ischaemic heart disease — Cardiopathie ischémique	9 448	169.0	8 274	146.7	11	18	21	16

20. Death and death rates by cause and sex: 2014 - 2018
Décès et taux de mortalité par cause et sexe : 2014 - 2018 (continued - suite)

Cause of death — Cause de décès	Cuba				Dominica - Dominique			
	2017 (C)				2014 (+C)		2015 (+C)	
	Male — Masculin		Female — Féminin		Male — Masculin	Female — Féminin	Male — Masculin	Female — Féminin
	Number Nombre	Rate Taux	Number Nombre	Rate Taux	Number Nombre	Number Nombre	Number Nombre	Number Nombre
Cerebrovascular disease — Maladie cérébrovasculaire	**5 031**	**90.0**	**4 912**	**87.1**	**36**	**33**	**23**	**27**
Diseases of arteries, arterioles and capillaries — Maladies des artères, artérioles et capillaires	**1 575**	**28.2**	**1 374**	**24.4**	**3**	**3**	**3**	**3**
Diseases of the respiratory system — Maladies de l'appareil respiratoire								
Total	**6 814**	**121.9**	**6 053**	**107.3**	**20**	**14**	**28**	**14**
Influenza — Grippe	**-**	**-**	**2**	**♦0.0**	**-**	**-**	**-**	**-**
Pneumonia — Pneumopathies	**4 144**	**74.1**	**3 805**	**67.5**	**11**	**4**	**15**	**7**
Chronic lower respiratory diseases — Maladies chroniques des voies respiratoires inférieures	**2 416**	**43.2**	**2 041**	**36.2**	**2**	**2**	**6**	**5**
Diseases of the digestive system — Maladies de l'appareil digestif								
Total	**2 773**	**49.6**	**1 594**	**28.3**	**5**	**9**	**8**	**12**
Gastric and duodenal ulcer — Ulcère de l'estomac et du duodénum	**256**	**4.6**	**159**	**2.8**	**-**	**-**	**2**	**-**
Diseases of the liver — Maladies du foie	**1 477**	**26.4**	**355**	**6.3**	**2**	**5**	**2**	**3**
Diseases of the musculoskeletal system and connective tissue — Maladies du système ostéo-articularie, des muscles et du tissu conjonctif	**234**	**4.2**	**474**	**8.4**	**2**	**-**	**1**	**2**
Diseases of the genitourinary system — Maladies de l'appareil génito-urinaire								
Total	**725**	**13.0**	**593**	**10.5**	**1**	**2**	**9**	**1**
Disorders of kidney and ureter — Affections du rein et de l'uretère	**541**	**9.7**	**463**	**8.2**	**1**	**1**	**4**	**1**
Hyperplasia of prostate — Hyperplasie de la prostate	**65**	**3.4**	..	..	**-**	..	**2**	..
Pregnancy, childbirth and the puerperium — Grossesse, accouchement et puerpéralité								
Total	..	..	**49**	**42.6**	..	**-**	..	**-**
Pregnancy with abortive outcome — Grossesse se terminant par un avortement	..	..	**5**	**♦4.3**	..	**-**	..	**-**
Other direct obstetric causes — Autres décès maternels directs	..	..	**21**	**♦18.3**	..	**-**	..	**-**
Indirect obstetric causes — Décès maternels indirects	..	..	**19**	**♦16.5**	..	**-**	..	**-**
Certain conditions originating in the perinatal period — Certaines affections dont l'origine se situe dans la période périnatale	**127**	**212.7**	**85**	**153.8**	**16**	**18**	**13**	**7**
Congenital malformations, deformations and chromosomal abnormalities — Malformations congénitales et anomalies chromosomiques	**159**	**266.3**	**157**	**284.0**	**3**	**1**	**3**	**6**
Symptoms, signs and abnormal clinical and laboratory findings, not elsewhere classified — Symptômes, signes et résultats anormaux d'examens cliniques et de laboratoire, non classés ailleurs	**531**	**9.5**	**375**	**6.7**	**11**	**8**	**19**	**16**
All other diseases — Toutes autres maladies	**119**	**2.1**	**160**	**2.8**	**3**	**11**	**1**	**3**
External causes — Causes externes								
Total	**4 880**	**87.3**	**3 145**	**55.8**	**26**	**8**	**38**	**13**
Accidents								
Total	**2 668**	**47.7**	**1 680**	**29.8**	**16**	**5**	**23**	**10**
Transport accidents — Accidents de transport	**822**	**14.7**	**184**	**3.3**	**4**	**2**	**7**	**2**
Falls — Chutes	**1 218**	**21.8**	**1 341**	**23.8**	**1**	**-**	**1**	**-**
Accidental drowning and submersion — Noyade et submersion accidentelles	**191**	**3.4**	**21**	**♦0.4**	**1**	**-**	**2**	**-**
Exposure to smoke, fire and flames — Exposition à la fumée, au feu et aux flammes	**27**	**♦0.5**	**19**	**♦0.3**	**-**	**-**	**-**	**1**
Accidental poisoning by and exposure to noxious substances — Intoxication accidentelle par des substances nocives et exposition à ces substances	**71**	**1.3**	**14**	**♦0.2**	**-**	**-**	**-**	**1**
Intentional self-harm — Lésions auto-infligées	**1 229**	**22.0**	**340**	**6.0**	**3**	**-**	**4**	**1**
Assault — Agresssions	**386**	**6.9**	**130**	**2.3**	**6**	**2**	**9**	**2**
All other external causes — Toutes autres causes externes	**597**	**10.7**	**995**	**17.6**	**1**	**1**	**2**	**-**

20. Death and death rates by cause and sex: 2014 - 2018
Décès et taux de mortalité par cause et sexe : 2014 - 2018 (continued - suite)

El Salvador

Cause of death — Cause de décès	2014 (+C)				2015 (+C)			
	Male — Masculin		Female — Féminin		Male — Masculin		Female — Féminin	
	Number Nombre	Rate Taux	Number Nombre	Rate Taux	Number Nombre	Rate Taux	Number Nombre	Rate Taux
TOTAL	**21 335**	**719.0**	**16 139**	**480.2**	**23 839**	**783.7**	**17 030**	**498.2**
Certain infectious and parasitic diseases — Certaines maladies infectieuses et parasitaires								
Total	999	33.7	821	24.4	1 031	33.9	1 011	29.6
Intestinal infectious diseases — Maladies infectieuses intestinales	64	2.2	52	1.5	48	1.6	55	1.6
Tuberculosis — Tuberculose	49	1.7	15	♦0.4	31	1.0	18	♦0.5
Tetanus — Tétanos	1	♦0.0	-	-	2	♦0.1	1	♦0.0
Diphtheria — Diphtérie	-	-	1	♦0.0	-	-	-	-
Whooping cough — Coqueluche	-	-	-	-	-	-	-	-
Meningococcal infection — Infection à méningocoques	1	♦0.0	-	-	-	-	-	-
Septicaemia — Septicémie	622	21.0	644	19.2	740	24.3	802	23.5
Acute poliomyelitis — Poliomyélite aiguë	-	-	-	-	-	-	-	-
Measles — Rougeole	-	-	-	-	-	-	-	-
Viral hepatitis — Hépatite virale	3	♦0.1	-	-	2	♦0.1	1	♦0.0
Human immunodeficiency virus [HIV] disease — Maladies dues au virus de l'immunodéficience humaine (VIH)	206	6.9	76	2.3	128	4.2	64	1.9
Malaria — Paludisme	-	-	1	♦0.0	-	-	-	-
Neoplasms — Tumeurs	**1 660**	**55.9**	**2 087**	**62.1**	**1 468**	**48.3**	**1 865**	**54.6**
Malignant neoplasms — Tumeurs malignes								
Total	1 648	55.5	2 071	61.6	1 330	43.7	1 666	48.7
Malignant neoplasm of lip, oral cavity and pharynx — Tumeur maligne de la lèvre, de la cavité buccale et du pharynx	43	1.4	28	♦0.8	23	♦0.8	22	♦0.6
Malignant neoplasm of oesophagus — Tumeur maligne de l'oesophage	31	1.0	20	♦0.6	25	♦0.8	19	♦0.6
Malignant neoplasm of stomach — Tumeur maligne de l'estomac	258	8.7	229	6.8	221	7.3	179	5.2
Malignant neoplasm of colon, rectosigmoid junction, rectum, anus and anal canal — Tumeur maligne du côlon, de la jonction recto-sigmoïdienne, du rectum, de l'anus et du canal anal	95	3.2	131	3.9	88	2.9	84	2.5
Malignant neoplasm of liver and intrahepatic bile ducts — Tumeur maligne du foie et des voies bilaires intrahépatiques	115	3.9	145	4.3	102	3.4	152	4.4
Malignant neoplasm of pancreas — Tumeur maligne du pancréas	73	2.5	70	2.1	48	1.6	57	1.7
Malignant neoplasm of trachea, bronchus and lung — Tumeur maligne de la trachée, des bronches et du poumon	123	4.1	122	3.6	95	3.1	87	2.5
Malignant neoplasm of female breast — Tumeur maligne du sein chez la femme	..	..	196	7.9	..	..	149	5.9
Malignant neoplasm of cervix uteri — Tumeur maligne du col de l'utérus	..	..	198	8.0	..	..	181	7.1
Malignant neoplasm of prostate — Tumeur maligne de la prostate	241	47.7	..	..	155	30.1	..	..
Malignant neoplasm of lymphoid, haematopoietic and related tissue — Tumeurs malignes primitives ou présumées primitives des tissus lymphoïde, hématopoïétique et apparentés	190	6.4	170	5.1	162	5.3	152	4.4
Disorders of the blood and blood-forming organs and certain disorders involving the immune mechanism — Maladies du sang et des organes hématopoïétiques et certains troubles du système immunitaire								
Total	86	2.9	95	2.8	107	3.5	96	2.8
Anaemias — Anémies	64	2.2	70	2.1	77	2.5	60	1.8
Endocrine, nutritional and metabolic diseases — Maladies endocriniennes, nutritionnelles et métaboliques								
Total	876	29.5	1 311	39.0	714	23.5	1 079	31.6
Diabetes mellitus — Diabète sucré	779	26.3	1 181	35.1	577	19.0	915	26.8
Malnutrition — Malnutrition	62	2.1	79	2.4	57	1.9	80	2.3
Mental and behavioural disorders — Troubles mentaux et du comportement	518	17.5	34	1.0	481	15.8	31	0.9
Diseases of the nervous system — Maladies du système nerveux	363	12.2	327	9.7	352	11.6	349	10.2
Diseases of the circulatory system — Maladies de l'appareil circulatoire								
Total	2 853	96.1	2 956	88.0	4 248	139.6	4 566	133.6
Acute rheumatic fever and chronic rheumatic heart diseases — Rhumatisme articularie aigu et cardiopathies rhumatismales chroniques	1	♦0.0	3	♦0.1	3	♦0.1	5	♦0.1
Hypertensive diseases — Maladies hypertensives	338	11.4	397	11.8	321	10.6	391	11.4
Ischaemic heart disease — Cardiopathie ischémique	1 217	41.0	1 043	31.0	1 335	43.9	1 212	35.5
Cerebrovascular disease — Maladie cérébrovasculaire	495	16.7	566	16.8	486	16.0	578	16.9

20. Death and death rates by cause and sex: 2014 - 2018
Décès et taux de mortalité par cause et sexe : 2014 - 2018 (continued - suite)

El Salvador

Cause of death — Cause de décès	2014 (+C)				2015 (+C)			
	Male — Masculin		Female — Féminin		Male — Masculin		Female — Féminin	
	Number Nombre	Rate Taux	Number Nombre	Rate Taux	Number Nombre	Rate Taux	Number Nombre	Rate Taux
Diseases of arteries, arterioles and capillaries — Maladies des artères, artérioles et capillaires	**20**	**♦0.7**	**24**	**♦0.7**	**19**	**♦0.6**	**35**	**1.0**
Diseases of the respiratory system — Maladies de l'appareil respiratoire								
Total	**1 639**	**55.2**	**1 473**	**43.8**	**1 635**	**53.7**	**1 534**	**44.9**
Influenza — Grippe	**-**	**-**	**1**	**♦0.0**	**1**	**♦0.0**	**1**	**♦0.0**
Pneumonia — Pneumopathies	**941**	**31.7**	**796**	**23.7**	**915**	**30.1**	**831**	**24.3**
Chronic lower respiratory diseases — Maladies chroniques des voies respiratoires inférieures	**274**	**9.2**	**287**	**8.5**	**205**	**6.7**	**250**	**7.3**
Diseases of the digestive system — Maladies de l'appareil digestif								
Total	**1 048**	**35.3**	**757**	**22.5**	**1 118**	**36.8**	**796**	**23.3**
Gastric and duodenal ulcer — Ulcère de l'estomac et du duodénum	**59**	**2.0**	**71**	**2.1**	**53**	**1.7**	**52**	**1.5**
Diseases of the liver — Maladies du foie	**677**	**22.8**	**391**	**11.6**	**657**	**21.6**	**394**	**11.5**
Diseases of the musculoskeletal system and connective tissue — Maladies du système ostéo-articularie, des muscles et du tissu conjonctif	**24**	**♦0.8**	**69**	**2.1**	**35**	**1.2**	**66**	**1.9**
Diseases of the genitourinary system — Maladies de l'appareil génito-urinaire								
Total	**2 230**	**75.2**	**994**	**29.6**	**2 030**	**66.7**	**1 020**	**29.8**
Disorders of kidney and ureter — Affections du rein et de l'uretère	**2 114**	**71.2**	**922**	**27.4**	**1 903**	**62.6**	**932**	**27.3**
Hyperplasia of prostate — Hyperplasie de la prostate	**44**	**8.7**	..	..	**32**	**6.2**	..	..
Pregnancy, childbirth and the puerperium — Grossesse, accouchement et puerpéralité								
Total	..	..	**52**	**47.7**	..	..	**47**	**42.9**
Pregnancy with abortive outcome — Grossesse se terminant par un avortement	..	..	**2**	**♦1.8**	..	..	**3**	**♦2.7**
Other direct obstetric causes — Autres décès maternels directs	..	..	**34**	**31.2**	..	..	**40**	**36.5**
Indirect obstetric causes — Décès maternels indirects	..	..	**16**	**♦14.7**	..	..	**4**	**♦3.6**
Certain conditions originating in the perinatal period — Certaines affections dont l'origine se situe dans la période périnatale	**199**	**355.8**	**163**	**307.7**	**219**	**385.9**	**170**	**321.6**
Congenital malformations, deformations and chromosomal abnormalities — Malformations congénitales et anomalies chromosomiques	**125**	**223.5**	**117**	**220.9**	**116**	**204.4**	**88**	**166.5**
Symptoms, signs and abnormal clinical and laboratory findings, not elsewhere classified — Symptômes, signes et résultats anormaux d'examens cliniques et de laboratoire, non classés ailleurs	**3 875**	**130.6**	**4 062**	**120.9**	**3 339**	**109.8**	**3 254**	**95.2**
All other diseases — Toutes autres maladies	**33**	**1.1**	**41**	**1.2**	**44**	**1.4**	**78**	**2.3**
External causes — Causes externes								
Total	**4 807**	**162.0**	**780**	**23.2**	**6 902**	**226.9**	**980**	**28.7**
Accidents								
Total	**1 377**	**46.4**	**351**	**10.4**	**1 411**	**46.4**	**340**	**9.9**
Transport accidents — Accidents de transport	**809**	**27.3**	**208**	**6.2**	**747**	**24.6**	**187**	**5.5**
Falls — Chutes	**174**	**5.9**	**86**	**2.6**	**162**	**5.3**	**77**	**2.3**
Accidental drowning and submersion — Noyade et submersion accidentelles	**150**	**5.1**	**17**	**♦0.5**	**101**	**3.3**	**15**	**♦0.4**
Exposure to smoke, fire and flames — Exposition à la fumée, au feu et aux flammes	**13**	**♦0.4**	**4**	**♦0.1**	**9**	**♦0.3**	**7**	**♦0.2**
Accidental poisoning by and exposure to noxious substances — Intoxication accidentelle par des substances nocives et exposition à ces substances	**136**	**4.6**	**10**	**♦0.3**	**171**	**5.6**	**14**	**♦0.4**
Intentional self-harm — Lésions auto-infligées	**278**	**9.4**	**108**	**3.2**	**257**	**8.4**	**89**	**2.6**
Assault — Agresssions	**3 051**	**102.8**	**293**	**8.7**	**4 965**	**163.2**	**496**	**14.5**
All other external causes — Toutes autres causes externes	**101**	**3.4**	**28**	**♦0.8**	**269**	**8.8**	**55**	**1.6**

20. Death and death rates by cause and sex: 2014 - 2018
Décès et taux de mortalité par cause et sexe : 2014 - 2018 (continued - suite)

Cause of death — Cause de décès	Grenada - Grenade				Guadeloupe			
	2017 (C)		2018 (C)		2015 (...)		2016 (...)	
	Male — Masculin	Female — Féminin	Male — Masculin	Female — Féminin	Male — Masculin	Female — Féminin	Male — Masculin	Female — Féminin
	Number Nombre	Number Nombre	Number Nombre	Number Nombre	Number Nombre	Number Nombre	Number Nombre	Number Nombre
TOTAL	488	392	522	440	1 554	1 352	1 706	1 521
Certain infectious and parasitic diseases — Certaines maladies infectieuses et parasitaires								
Total	13	15	11	12	36	43	40	37
Intestinal infectious diseases — Maladies infectieuses intestinales	-	2	1	-	3	9	4	3
Tuberculosis — Tuberculose	-	-	-	-	-	-	-	1
Tetanus — Tétanos	-	-	-	-	-	-	-	-
Diphtheria — Diphtérie	-	-	-	-	-	-	-	-
Whooping cough — Coqueluche	-	-	-	-	-	-	-	-
Meningococcal infection — Infection à méningocoques	-	-	-	-	-	-	-	-
Septicaemia — Septicémie	10	13	8	11	18	14	11	14
Acute poliomyelitis — Poliomyélite aiguë	-	-	-	-	-	-	-	-
Measles — Rougeole	-	-	-	-	-	-	-	-
Viral hepatitis — Hépatite virale	-	-	-	-	2	3	4	1
Human immunodeficiency virus [HIV] disease — Maladies dues au virus de l'immunodéficience humaine (VIH)	2	-	1	1	4	7	6	3
Malaria — Paludisme	-	-	-	-	-	-	-	-
Neoplasms — Tumeurs	108	80	94	84	394	317	418	349
Malignant neoplasms — Tumeurs malignes								
Total	104	79	92	79	380	307	403	340
Malignant neoplasm of lip, oral cavity and pharynx — Tumeur maligne de la lèvre, de la cavité buccale et du pharynx	3	1	4	-	10	2	20	4
Malignant neoplasm of oesophagus — Tumeur maligne de l'oesophage	3	-	4	-	21	-	17	4
Malignant neoplasm of stomach — Tumeur maligne de l'estomac	3	3	4	1	39	22	32	19
Malignant neoplasm of colon, rectosigmoid junction, rectum, anus and anal canal — Tumeur maligne du côlon, de la jonction recto-sigmoïdienne, du rectum, de l'anus et du canal anal	12	9	5	6	34	34	28	36
Malignant neoplasm of liver and intrahepatic bile ducts — Tumeur maligne du foie et des voies bilaires intrahépatiques	7	3	2	1	14	15	22	9
Malignant neoplasm of pancreas — Tumeur maligne du pancréas	6	3	8	6	24	27	30	25
Malignant neoplasm of trachea, bronchus and lung — Tumeur maligne de la trachée, des bronches et du poumon	8	3	7	5	41	24	44	26
Malignant neoplasm of female breast — Tumeur maligne du sein chez la femme	..	21	..	17	..	42	..	78
Malignant neoplasm of cervix uteri — Tumeur maligne du col de l'utérus	..	9	..	7	..	5	..	9
Malignant neoplasm of prostate — Tumeur maligne de la prostate	47	..	35	..	79	..	94	..
Malignant neoplasm of lymphoid, haematopoietic and related tissue — Tumeurs malignes primitives ou présumées primitives des tissus lymphoïde, hématopoïétique et apparentés	3	1	6	7	34	28	32	33
Disorders of the blood and blood-forming organs and certain disorders involving the immune mechanism — Maladies du sang et des organes hématopoïétiques et certains troubles du système immunitaire								
Total	7	7	7	8	15	4	6	10
Anaemias — Anémies	5	6	3	5	6	3	4	9
Endocrine, nutritional and metabolic diseases — Maladies endocriniennes, nutritionnelles et métaboliques								
Total	49	53	61	69	80	110	103	109
Diabetes mellitus — Diabète sucré	44	43	56	61	53	81	70	76
Malnutrition — Malnutrition	1	-	2	-	9	12	11	17
Mental and behavioural disorders — Troubles mentaux et du comportement	8	4	10	1	51	28	51	47
Diseases of the nervous system — Maladies du système nerveux	3	7	13	12	77	72	94	83
Diseases of the circulatory system — Maladies de l'appareil circulatoire								
Total	147	140	177	141	309	327	365	396
Acute rheumatic fever and chronic rheumatic heart diseases — Rhumatisme articularie aigu et cardiopathies rhumatismales chroniques	2	-	-	1	-	2	6	2
Hypertensive diseases — Maladies hypertensives	24	18	24	20	45	57	52	69
Ischaemic heart disease — Cardiopathie ischémique	52	44	72	53	51	40	49	36

20. Death and death rates by cause and sex: 2014 - 2018
Décès et taux de mortalité par cause et sexe : 2014 - 2018 (continued - suite)

Cause of death — Cause de décès	Grenada - Grenade				Guadeloupe			
	2017 (C)		2018 (C)		2015 (...)		2016 (...)	
	Male — Masculin	Female — Féminin	Male — Masculin	Female — Féminin	Male — Masculin	Female — Féminin	Male — Masculin	Female — Féminin
	Number Nombre	Number Nombre	Number Nombre	Number Nombre	Number Nombre	Number Nombre	Number Nombre	Number Nombre
Cerebrovascular disease — Maladie cérébrovasculaire	39	52	47	43	94	95	101	128
Diseases of arteries, arterioles and capillaries — Maladies des artères, artérioles et capillaires	8	6	6	6	14	21	21	20
Diseases of the respiratory system — Maladies de l'appareil respiratoire								
Total	32	33	39	41	69	63	87	84
Influenza — Grippe	-	-	-	1	6	3	-	5
Pneumonia — Pneumopathies	17	21	20	29	21	21	31	36
Chronic lower respiratory diseases — Maladies chroniques des voies respiratoires inférieures	5	5	8	5	13	10	24	11
Diseases of the digestive system — Maladies de l'appareil digestif								
Total	29	13	26	16	91	43	77	64
Gastric and duodenal ulcer — Ulcère de l'estomac et du duodénum	2	-	5	2	3	-	4	-
Diseases of the liver — Maladies du foie	13	-	8	3	34	9	36	11
Diseases of the musculoskeletal system and connective tissue — Maladies du système ostéo-articularie, des muscles et du tissu conjonctif	1	4	1	1	6	19	2	8
Diseases of the genitourinary system — Maladies de l'appareil génito-urinaire								
Total	21	7	20	6	31	33	28	24
Disorders of kidney and ureter — Affections du rein et de l'uretère	13	4	12	4	21	29	18	22
Hyperplasia of prostate — Hyperplasie de la prostate	6	..	2	..	1	..	-	..
Pregnancy, childbirth and the puerperium — Grossesse, accouchement et puerpéralité								
Total	..	-	..	-	..	-	..	1
Pregnancy with abortive outcome — Grossesse se terminant par un avortement	..	-	..	-	..	-	..	-
Other direct obstetric causes — Autres décès maternels directs	..	-	..	-	..	-	..	1
Indirect obstetric causes — Décès maternels indirects	..	-	..	-	..	-	..	-
Certain conditions originating in the perinatal period — Certaines affections dont l'origine se situe dans la période périnatale	13	3	7	8	2	-	-	1
Congenital malformations, deformations and chromosomal abnormalities — Malformations congénitales et anomalies chromosomiques	4	3	2	3	2	1	7	6
Symptoms, signs and abnormal clinical and laboratory findings, not elsewhere classified — Symptômes, signes et résultats anormaux d'examens cliniques et de laboratoire, non classés ailleurs	5	5	5	6	245	238	250	229
All other diseases — Toutes autres maladies	5	6	7	15	4	4	6	12
External causes — Causes externes								
Total	43	12	42	17	142	50	172	61
Accidents								
Total	36	9	36	16	95	37	134	53
Transport accidents — Accidents de transport	8	-	4	1	28	8	42	4
Falls — Chutes	-	1	5	3	8	11	19	12
Accidental drowning and submersion — Noyade et submersion accidentelles	2	2	4	-	3	2	17	3
Exposure to smoke, fire and flames — Exposition à la fumée, au feu et aux flammes	1	1	4	2	4	2	1	-
Accidental poisoning by and exposure to noxious substances — Intoxication accidentelle par des substances nocives et exposition à ces substances	-	-	-	-	8	6	6	5
Intentional self-harm — Lésions auto-infligées	-	1	-	-	16	7	18	4
Assault — Agresssions	6	2	6	-	6	2	4	1
All other external causes — Toutes autres causes externes	1	-	-	1	25	4	16	3

20. Death and death rates by cause and sex: 2014 - 2018
Décès et taux de mortalité par cause et sexe : 2014 - 2018 (continued - suite)

Guatemala

Cause of death — Cause de décès	2016 (C)				2017 (C)			
	Male — Masculin		Female — Féminin		Male — Masculin		Female — Féminin	
	Number Nombre	Rate Taux	Number Nombre	Rate Taux	Number Nombre	Rate Taux	Number Nombre	Rate Taux
TOTAL	**45 162**	**558.1**	**35 424**	**418.6**	**44 464**	**536.9**	**35 032**	**404.9**
Certain infectious and parasitic diseases — Certaines maladies infectieuses et parasitaires								
Total	2 301	28.4	1 892	22.4	2 142	25.9	1 711	19.8
Intestinal infectious diseases — Maladies infectieuses intestinales	1 245	15.4	1 108	13.1	999	12.1	914	10.6
Tuberculosis — Tuberculose	200	2.5	103	1.2	194	2.3	100	1.2
Tetanus — Tétanos	4	♦0.0	-	-	8	♦0.1	1	♦0.0
Diphtheria — Diphtérie	-	-	-	-	-	-	-	-
Whooping cough — Coqueluche	11	♦0.1	11	♦0.1	10	♦0.1	7	♦0.1
Meningococcal infection — Infection à méningocoques	-	-	2	♦0.0	-	-	1	♦0.0
Septicaemia — Septicémie	430	5.3	435	5.1	551	6.7	482	5.6
Acute poliomyelitis — Poliomyélite aiguë	-	-	-	-	-	-	-	-
Measles — Rougeole	-	-	-	-	-	-	-	-
Viral hepatitis — Hépatite virale	25	♦0.3	25	♦0.3	29	♦0.4	17	♦0.2
Human immunodeficiency virus [HIV] disease — Maladies dues au virus de l'immunodéficience humaine (VIH)	248	3.1	100	1.2	231	2.8	86	1.0
Malaria — Paludisme	1	♦0.0	5	♦0.1	1	♦0.0	3	♦0.0
Neoplasms — Tumeurs	**3 650**	**45.1**	**4 298**	**50.8**	**3 672**	**44.3**	**4 441**	**51.3**
Malignant neoplasms — Tumeurs malignes								
Total	3 414	42.2	4 051	47.9	3 411	41.2	4 150	48.0
Malignant neoplasm of lip, oral cavity and pharynx — Tumeur maligne de la lèvre, de la cavité buccale et du pharynx	60	0.7	51	0.6	55	0.7	52	0.6
Malignant neoplasm of oesophagus — Tumeur maligne de l'oesophage	66	0.8	42	0.5	64	0.8	37	0.4
Malignant neoplasm of stomach — Tumeur maligne de l'estomac	568	7.0	662	7.8	563	6.8	634	7.3
Malignant neoplasm of colon, rectosigmoid junction, rectum, anus and anal canal — Tumeur maligne du côlon, de la jonction recto-sigmoïdienne, du rectum, de l'anus et du canal anal	134	1.7	166	2.0	148	1.8	173	2.0
Malignant neoplasm of liver and intrahepatic bile ducts — Tumeur maligne du foie et des voies bilaires intrahépatiques	674	8.3	690	8.2	656	7.9	739	8.5
Malignant neoplasm of pancreas — Tumeur maligne du pancréas	114	1.4	106	1.3	113	1.4	116	1.3
Malignant neoplasm of trachea, bronchus and lung — Tumeur maligne de la trachée, des bronches et du poumon	214	2.6	188	2.2	197	2.4	180	2.1
Malignant neoplasm of female breast — Tumeur maligne du sein chez la femme	..	..	321	6.1	..	..	353	6.5
Malignant neoplasm of cervix uteri — Tumeur maligne du col de l'utérus	..	..	400	7.6	..	..	389	7.1
Malignant neoplasm of prostate — Tumeur maligne de la prostate	552	61.2	..	..	564	61.0	..	..
Malignant neoplasm of lymphoid, haematopoietic and related tissue — Tumeurs malignes primitives ou présumées primitives des tissus lymphoïde, hématopoïétique et apparentés	355	4.4	309	3.7	384	4.6	345	4.0
Disorders of the blood and blood-forming organs and certain disorders involving the immune mechanism — Maladies du sang et des organes hématopoïétiques et certains troubles du système immunitaire								
Total	385	4.8	378	4.5	373	4.5	342	4.0
Anaemias — Anémies	238	2.9	254	3.0	214	2.6	212	2.5
Endocrine, nutritional and metabolic diseases — Maladies endocriniennes, nutritionnelles et métaboliques								
Total	3 349	41.4	4 424	52.3	3 280	39.6	4 484	51.8
Diabetes mellitus — Diabète sucré	2 390	29.5	3 460	40.9	2 433	29.4	3 556	41.1
Malnutrition — Malnutrition	488	6.0	510	6.0	420	5.1	458	5.3
Mental and behavioural disorders — Troubles mentaux et du comportement	**451**	**5.6**	**93**	**1.1**	**471**	**5.7**	**109**	**1.3**
Diseases of the nervous system — Maladies du système nerveux	**868**	**10.7**	**726**	**8.6**	**836**	**10.1**	**734**	**8.5**
Diseases of the circulatory system — Maladies de l'appareil circulatoire								
Total	6 425	79.4	6 233	73.7	6 405	77.3	6 332	73.2
Acute rheumatic fever and chronic rheumatic heart diseases — Rhumatisme articularie aigu et cardiopathies rhumatismales chroniques	11	♦0.1	14	♦0.2	8	♦0.1	9	♦0.1
Hypertensive diseases — Maladies hypertensives	579	7.2	671	7.9	545	6.6	683	7.9
Ischaemic heart disease — Cardiopathie ischémique	3 009	37.2	2 561	30.3	3 011	36.4	2 554	29.5
Cerebrovascular disease — Maladie cérébrovasculaire	1 510	18.7	1 573	18.6	1 517	18.3	1 615	18.7

20. Death and death rates by cause and sex: 2014 - 2018
Décès et taux de mortalité par cause et sexe : 2014 - 2018 (continued - suite)

Guatemala

Cause of death — Cause de décès	2016 (C)				2017 (C)			
	Male — Masculin		Female — Féminin		Male — Masculin		Female — Féminin	
	Number Nombre	Rate Taux	Number Nombre	Rate Taux	Number Nombre	Rate Taux	Number Nombre	Rate Taux
Diseases of arteries, arterioles and capillaries — Maladies des artères, artérioles et capillaires	**47**	**0.6**	**44**	**0.5**	**56**	**0.7**	**64**	**0.7**
Diseases of the respiratory system — Maladies de l'appareil respiratoire								
Total	**5 014**	**62.0**	**4 478**	**52.9**	**4 999**	**60.4**	**4 401**	**50.9**
Influenza — Grippe	**8**	**♦0.1**	**7**	**♦0.1**	**11**	**♦0.1**	**8**	**♦0.1**
Pneumonia — Pneumopathies	**3 614**	**44.7**	**3 191**	**37.7**	**3 591**	**43.4**	**3 163**	**36.6**
Chronic lower respiratory diseases — Maladies chroniques des voies respiratoires inférieures	**642**	**7.9**	**650**	**7.7**	**619**	**7.5**	**591**	**6.8**
Diseases of the digestive system — Maladies de l'appareil digestif								
Total	**3 981**	**49.2**	**2 505**	**29.6**	**3 668**	**44.3**	**2 245**	**25.9**
Gastric and duodenal ulcer — Ulcère de l'estomac et du duodénum	**278**	**3.4**	**252**	**3.0**	**243**	**2.9**	**262**	**3.0**
Diseases of the liver — Maladies du foie	**2 545**	**31.4**	**1 249**	**14.8**	**2 347**	**28.3**	**1 097**	**12.7**
Diseases of the musculoskeletal system and connective tissue — Maladies du système ostéo-articularie, des muscles et du tissu conjonctif	**116**	**1.4**	**214**	**2.5**	**118**	**1.4**	**229**	**2.6**
Diseases of the genitourinary system — Maladies de l'appareil génito-urinaire								
Total	**1 736**	**21.5**	**1 551**	**18.3**	**1 776**	**21.4**	**1 550**	**17.9**
Disorders of kidney and ureter — Affections du rein et de l'uretère	**1 505**	**18.6**	**1 404**	**16.6**	**1 545**	**18.7**	**1 393**	**16.1**
Hyperplasia of prostate — Hyperplasie de la prostate	**97**	**10.8**	..	..	**90**	**9.7**	..	..
Pregnancy, childbirth and the puerperium — Grossesse, accouchement et puerpéralité								
Total	..	..	**301**	**77.1**	..	..	**260**	**68.1**
Pregnancy with abortive outcome — Grossesse se terminant par un avortement	..	..	**20**	**♦5.1**	..	..	**9**	**♦2.4**
Other direct obstetric causes — Autres décès maternels directs	..	..	**252**	**64.6**	..	..	**242**	**63.4**
Indirect obstetric causes — Décès maternels indirects	..	..	**29**	**♦7.4**	..	..	**9**	**♦2.4**
Certain conditions originating in the perinatal period — Certaines affections dont l'origine se situe dans la période périnatale	**1 807**	**910.3**	**1 308**	**681.7**	**1 804**	**927.5**	**1 187**	**634.2**
Congenital malformations, deformations and chromosomal abnormalities — Malformations congénitales et anomalies chromosomiques	**750**	**377.8**	**643**	**335.1**	**683**	**351.1**	**584**	**312.0**
Symptoms, signs and abnormal clinical and laboratory findings, not elsewhere classified — Symptômes, signes et résultats anormaux d'examens cliniques et de laboratoire, non classés ailleurs	**4 400**	**54.4**	**4 255**	**50.3**	**4 706**	**56.8**	**4 342**	**50.2**
All other diseases — Toutes autres maladies	**110**	**1.4**	**123**	**1.5**	**87**	**1.1**	**91**	**1.1**
External causes — Causes externes								
Total	**9 819**	**121.3**	**2 002**	**23.7**	**9 444**	**114.0**	**1 990**	**23.0**
Accidents								
Total	**6 058**	**74.9**	**1 297**	**15.3**	**5 907**	**71.3**	**1 334**	**15.4**
Transport accidents — Accidents de transport	**1 292**	**16.0**	**248**	**2.9**	**1 248**	**15.1**	**230**	**2.7**
Falls — Chutes	**5**	**♦0.1**	**-**	**-**	**3**	**♦0.0**	**2**	**♦0.0**
Accidental drowning and submersion — Noyade et submersion accidentelles	**247**	**3.1**	**33**	**0.4**	**277**	**3.3**	**37**	**0.4**
Exposure to smoke, fire and flames — Exposition à la fumée, au feu et aux flammes	**74**	**0.9**	**39**	**0.5**	**81**	**1.0**	**76**	**0.9**
Accidental poisoning by and exposure to noxious substances — Intoxication accidentelle par des substances nocives et exposition à ces substances	**808**	**10.0**	**147**	**1.7**	**829**	**10.0**	**184**	**2.1**
Intentional self-harm — Lésions auto-infligées	**398**	**4.9**	**148**	**1.7**	**389**	**4.7**	**128**	**1.5**
Assault — Agresssions	**3 335**	**41.2**	**531**	**6.3**	**3 135**	**37.9**	**520**	**6.0**
All other external causes — Toutes autres causes externes	**28**	**♦0.3**	**26**	**♦0.3**	**13**	**♦0.2**	**8**	**♦0.1**

20. Death and death rates by cause and sex: 2014 - 2018
Décès et taux de mortalité par cause et sexe : 2014 - 2018 (continued - suite)

Cause of death — Cause de décès	Jamaica - Jamaïque				Martinique			
	2014 (C)				2015 (...)		2016 (...)	
	Male — Masculin		Female — Féminin		Male — Masculin	Female — Féminin	Male — Masculin	Female — Féminin
	Number Nombre	Rate Taux	Number Nombre	Rate Taux	Number Nombre	Number Nombre	Number Nombre	Number Nombre
TOTAL	**9 514**	**706.5**	**8 806**	**641.0**	***1 515***	***1 540***	***1 640***	***1 645***
Certain infectious and parasitic diseases — Certaines maladies infectieuses et parasitaires								
Total	613	45.5	435	31.7	*42*	*36*	*52*	*42*
Intestinal infectious diseases — Maladies infectieuses intestinales	39	2.9	30	♦2.2	*4*	*8*	*7*	*9*
Tuberculosis — Tuberculose	6	♦0.4	1	♦0.1	*1*	-	-	-
Tetanus — Tétanos	2	♦0.1	-	-	*1*	-	-	-
Diphtheria — Diphtérie	-	-	-	-	-	-	-	-
Whooping cough — Coqueluche	-	-	-	-	-	-	-	-
Meningococcal infection — Infection à méningocoques	-	-	-	-	-	-	-	-
Septicaemia — Septicémie	111	8.2	94	6.8	*24*	*11*	*25*	*18*
Acute poliomyelitis — Poliomyélite aiguë	-	-	-	-	-	-	-	-
Measles — Rougeole	-	-	-	-	-	-	-	-
Viral hepatitis — Hépatite virale	7	♦0.5	10	♦0.7	*1*	*1*	*3*	*2*
Human immunodeficiency virus [HIV] disease — Maladies dues au virus de l'immunodéficience humaine (VIH)	349	25.9	246	17.9	*5*	*3*	*3*	*3*
Malaria — Paludisme	-	-	-	-	-	-	-	-
Neoplasms — Tumeurs	**2 051**	**152.3**	**1 634**	**118.9**	***406***	***400***	***454***	***391***
Malignant neoplasms — Tumeurs malignes								
Total	1 979	147.0	1 557	113.3	*393*	*381*	*432*	*368*
Malignant neoplasm of lip, oral cavity and pharynx — Tumeur maligne de la lèvre, de la cavité buccale et du pharynx	30	♦2.2	10	♦0.7	*16*	*1*	*15*	*1*
Malignant neoplasm of oesophagus — Tumeur maligne de l'oesophage	37	2.7	20	♦1.5	*11*	*4*	*4*	*3*
Malignant neoplasm of stomach — Tumeur maligne de l'estomac	117	8.7	49	3.6	*48*	*30*	*40*	*26*
Malignant neoplasm of colon, rectosigmoid junction, rectum, anus and anal canal — Tumeur maligne du côlon, de la jonction recto-sigmoïdienne, du rectum, de l'anus et du canal anal	179	13.3	166	12.1	*37*	*59*	*51*	*44*
Malignant neoplasm of liver and intrahepatic bile ducts — Tumeur maligne du foie et des voies bilaires intrahépatiques	43	3.2	46	3.3	*16*	*13*	*14*	*9*
Malignant neoplasm of pancreas — Tumeur maligne du pancréas	72	5.3	36	2.6	*23*	*25*	*29*	*35*
Malignant neoplasm of trachea, bronchus and lung — Tumeur maligne de la trachée, des bronches et du poumon	294	21.8	105	7.6	*44*	*23*	*44*	*24*
Malignant neoplasm of female breast — Tumeur maligne du sein chez la femme	..	..	393	37.5	..	*54*	..	*72*
Malignant neoplasm of cervix uteri — Tumeur maligne du col de l'utérus	..	..	167	15.9	..	*9*	..	*10*
Malignant neoplasm of prostate — Tumeur maligne de la prostate	676	239.6	..	..	*96*	..	*106*	..
Malignant neoplasm of lymphoid, haematopoietic and related tissue — Tumeurs malignes primitives ou présumées primitives des tissus lymphoïde, hématopoïétique et apparentés	181	13.4	145	10.6	*30*	*45*	*40*	*41*
Disorders of the blood and blood-forming organs and certain disorders involving the immune mechanism — Maladies du sang et des organes hématopoïétiques et certains troubles du système immunitaire								
Total	107	7.9	90	6.6	*7*	*15*	*1*	*9*
Anaemias — Anémies	84	6.2	65	4.7	*7*	*10*	*1*	*6*
Endocrine, nutritional and metabolic diseases — Maladies endocriniennes, nutritionnelles et métaboliques								
Total	968	71.9	1 538	111.9	*95*	*115*	*90*	*112*
Diabetes mellitus — Diabète sucré	811	60.2	1 330	96.8	*58*	*77*	*58*	*65*
Malnutrition — Malnutrition	23	♦1.7	22	♦1.6	*12*	*17*	*14*	*16*
Mental and behavioural disorders — Troubles mentaux et du comportement	**12**	**♦0.9**	**4**	**♦0.3**	***37***	***31***	***53***	***35***
Diseases of the nervous system — Maladies du système nerveux	**221**	**16.4**	**235**	**17.1**	***99***	***124***	***93***	***123***
Diseases of the circulatory system — Maladies de l'appareil circulatoire								
Total	3 227	239.6	3 277	238.5	*351*	*398*	*381*	*436*
Acute rheumatic fever and chronic rheumatic heart diseases — Rhumatisme articularie aigu et cardiopathies rhumatismales chroniques	8	♦0.6	18	♦1.3	*1*	*3*	*2*	*4*
Hypertensive diseases — Maladies hypertensives	696	51.7	694	50.5	*38*	*43*	*34*	*54*
Ischaemic heart disease — Cardiopathie ischémique	822	61.0	747	54.4	*63*	*44*	*75*	*47*

20. Death and death rates by cause and sex: 2014 - 2018
Décès et taux de mortalité par cause et sexe : 2014 - 2018 (continued - suite)

Cause of death — Cause de décès	Jamaica - Jamaïque				Martinique			
	2014 (C)				2015 (...)		2016 (...)	
	Male — Masculin		Female — Féminin		Male — Masculin	Female — Féminin	Male — Masculin	Female — Féminin
	Number Nombre	Rate Taux	Number Nombre	Rate Taux	Number Nombre	Number Nombre	Number Nombre	Number Nombre
Cerebrovascular disease — Maladie cérébrovasculaire	1 248	92.7	1 389	101.1	103	138	130	147
Diseases of arteries, arterioles and capillaries — Maladies des artères, artérioles et capillaires	88	6.5	62	4.5	21	19	23	20
Diseases of the respiratory system — Maladies de l'appareil respiratoire								
Total	703	52.2	431	31.4	84	86	84	97
Influenza — Grippe	5	♦0.4	-	-	4	1	4	5
Pneumonia — Pneumopathies	187	13.9	171	12.4	29	33	41	45
Chronic lower respiratory diseases — Maladies chroniques des voies respiratoires inférieures	363	27.0	97	7.1	13	8	11	3
Diseases of the digestive system — Maladies de l'appareil digestif								
Total	306	22.7	206	15.0	69	62	63	65
Gastric and duodenal ulcer — Ulcère de l'estomac et du duodénum	60	4.5	26	♦1.9	2	3	-	3
Diseases of the liver — Maladies du foie	56	4.2	34	2.5	24	10	23	7
Diseases of the musculoskeletal system and connective tissue — Maladies du système ostéo-articularie, des muscles et du tissu conjonctif	34	2.5	78	5.7	8	8	11	9
Diseases of the genitourinary system — Maladies de l'appareil génito-urinaire								
Total	323	24.0	118	8.6	36	33	38	29
Disorders of kidney and ureter — Affections du rein et de l'uretère	111	8.2	57	4.1	21	23	21	21
Hyperplasia of prostate — Hyperplasie de la prostate	114	40.4	..	..	1	..	1	..
Pregnancy, childbirth and the puerperium — Grossesse, accouchement et puerpéralité								
Total	..	..	36	97.3	..	3	..	1
Pregnancy with abortive outcome — Grossesse se terminant par un avortement	..	..	4	♦10.8	..	-	..	-
Other direct obstetric causes — Autres décès maternels directs	..	..	31	83.8	..	3	..	1
Indirect obstetric causes — Décès maternels indirects	..	..	1	♦2.7	..	-	..	-
Certain conditions originating in the perinatal period — Certaines affections dont l'origine se situe dans la période périnatale	296	...	245	...	7	7	15	11
Congenital malformations, deformations and chromosomal abnormalities — Malformations congénitales et anomalies chromosomiques	85	...	80	...	3	7	7	1
Symptoms, signs and abnormal clinical and laboratory findings, not elsewhere classified — Symptômes, signes et résultats anormaux d'examens cliniques et de laboratoire, non classés ailleurs	20	♦1.5	30	♦2.2	137	155	160	209
All other diseases — Toutes autres maladies	101	7.5	167	12.2	7	11	9	12
External causes — Causes externes								
Total	447	33.2	202	14.7	127	49	129	63
Accidents								
Total	142	10.5	102	7.4	91	42	87	50
Transport accidents — Accidents de transport	70	5.2	27	♦2.0	22	3	20	5
Falls — Chutes	15	♦1.1	8	♦0.6	10	11	22	12
Accidental drowning and submersion — Noyade et submersion accidentelles	13	♦1.0	1	♦0.1	7	1	2	2
Exposure to smoke, fire and flames — Exposition à la fumée, au feu et aux flammes	3	♦0.2	7	♦0.5	-	1	1	1
Accidental poisoning by and exposure to noxious substances — Intoxication accidentelle par des substances nocives et exposition à ces substances	3	♦0.2	1	♦0.1	8	7	5	5
Intentional self-harm — Lésions auto-infligées	6	♦0.4	-	-	18	2	20	6
Assault — Agresssions	22	♦1.6	8	♦0.6	6	1	8	-
All other external causes — Toutes autres causes externes	277	20.6	92	6.7	12	4	14	7

20. Death and death rates by cause and sex: 2014 - 2018
Décès et taux de mortalité par cause et sexe : 2014 - 2018 (continued - suite)

Mexico - Mexique

Cause of death — Cause de décès	2016 (+C)				2017 (+C)			
	Male — Masculin		Female — Féminin		Male — Masculin		Female — Féminin	
	Number Nombre	Rate Taux	Number Nombre	Rate Taux	Number Nombre	Rate Taux	Number Nombre	Rate Taux
TOTAL	**374 600**	**623.4**	**296 594**	**473.6**	**386 125**	**635.7**	**301 979**	**477.1**
Certain infectious and parasitic diseases — Certaines maladies infectieuses et parasitaires								
Total	9 841	16.4	5 951	9.5	9 797	16.1	5 907	9.3
Intestinal infectious diseases — Maladies infectieuses intestinales	1 826	3.0	2 016	3.2	1 676	2.8	1 880	3.0
Tuberculosis — Tuberculose	1 443	2.4	605	1.0	1 388	2.3	595	0.9
Tetanus — Tétanos	12	♦0.0	-	-	9	♦0.0	2	♦0.0
Diphtheria — Diphtérie	-	-	-	-	-	-	-	-
Whooping cough — Coqueluche	16	♦0.0	4	♦0.0	5	♦0.0	16	♦0.0
Meningococcal infection — Infection à méningocoques	1	♦0.0	3	♦0.0	4	♦0.0	2	♦0.0
Septicaemia — Septicémie	1 387	2.3	1 291	2.1	1 489	2.5	1 303	2.1
Acute poliomyelitis — Poliomyélite aiguë	-	-	-	-	-	-	-	-
Measles — Rougeole	-	-	-	-	-	-	-	-
Viral hepatitis — Hépatite virale	547	0.9	638	1.0	348	0.6	375	0.6
Human immunodeficiency virus [HIV] disease — Maladies dues au virus de l'immunodéficience humaine (VIH)	3 792	6.3	813	1.3	3 857	6.3	818	1.3
Malaria — Paludisme	1	♦0.0	-	-	-	-	-	-
Neoplasms — Tumeurs	42 596	70.9	44 277	70.7	43 469	71.6	45 353	71.6
Malignant neoplasms — Tumeurs malignes								
Total	39 649	66.0	41 304	66.0	40 276	66.3	42 215	66.7
Malignant neoplasm of lip, oral cavity and pharynx — Tumeur maligne de la lèvre, de la cavité buccale et du pharynx	780	1.3	411	0.7	745	1.2	464	0.7
Malignant neoplasm of oesophagus — Tumeur maligne de l'oesophage	829	1.4	304	0.5	824	1.4	265	0.4
Malignant neoplasm of stomach — Tumeur maligne de l'estomac	3 307	5.5	2 872	4.6	3 302	5.4	2 880	4.5
Malignant neoplasm of colon, rectosigmoid junction, rectum, anus and anal canal — Tumeur maligne du côlon, de la jonction recto-sigmoïdienne, du rectum, de l'anus et du canal anal	3 177	5.3	2 778	4.4	3 425	5.6	2 961	4.7
Malignant neoplasm of liver and intrahepatic bile ducts — Tumeur maligne du foie et des voies bilaires intrahépatiques	3 135	5.2	3 253	5.2	3 118	5.1	3 331	5.3
Malignant neoplasm of pancreas — Tumeur maligne du pancréas	1 944	3.2	2 157	3.4	2 145	3.5	2 270	3.6
Malignant neoplasm of trachea, bronchus and lung — Tumeur maligne de la trachée, des bronches et du poumon	4 253	7.1	2 629	4.2	4 247	7.0	2 654	4.2
Malignant neoplasm of female breast — Tumeur maligne du sein chez la femme	..	..	6 548	14.1	..	..	6 756	14.4
Malignant neoplasm of cervix uteri — Tumeur maligne du col de l'utérus	..	..	3 974	8.6	..	..	3 951	8.4
Malignant neoplasm of prostate — Tumeur maligne de la prostate	6 762	61.1	..	..	6 521	57.1	..	..
Malignant neoplasm of lymphoid, haematopoietic and related tissue — Tumeurs malignes primitives ou présumées primitives des tissus lymphoïde, hématopoïétique et apparentés	4 811	8.0	4 053	6.5	5 016	8.3	4 143	6.5
Disorders of the blood and blood-forming organs and certain disorders involving the immune mechanism — Maladies du sang et des organes hématopoïétiques et certains troubles du système immunitaire								
Total	2 307	3.8	2 323	3.7	2 259	3.7	2 281	3.6
Anaemias — Anémies	1 687	2.8	1 736	2.8	1 624	2.7	1 708	2.7
Endocrine, nutritional and metabolic diseases — Maladies endocriniennes, nutritionnelles et métaboliques								
Total	58 793	97.8	60 928	97.3	59 288	97.6	61 243	96.7
Diabetes mellitus — Diabète sucré	50 734	84.4	52 759	84.2	51 252	84.4	53 046	83.8
Malnutrition — Malnutrition	3 522	5.9	3 583	5.7	3 375	5.6	3 510	5.5
Mental and behavioural disorders — Troubles mentaux et du comportement	3 202	5.3	1 131	1.8	3 138	5.2	991	1.6
Diseases of the nervous system — Maladies du système nerveux	6 265	10.4	5 276	8.4	6 396	10.5	5 379	8.5
Diseases of the circulatory system — Maladies de l'appareil circulatoire								
Total	89 143	148.3	82 022	131.0	92 400	152.1	84 092	132.8
Acute rheumatic fever and chronic rheumatic heart diseases — Rhumatisme articularie aigu et cardiopathies rhumatismales chroniques	275	0.5	599	1.0	278	0.5	480	0.8
Hypertensive diseases — Maladies hypertensives	9 790	16.3	12 288	19.6	10 323	17.0	12 337	19.5
Ischaemic heart disease — Cardiopathie ischémique	53 416	88.9	42 152	67.3	55 484	91.3	44 054	69.6
Cerebrovascular disease — Maladie cérébrovasculaire	16 521	27.5	17 505	28.0	16 986	28.0	17 496	27.6

20. Death and death rates by cause and sex: 2014 - 2018
Décès et taux de mortalité par cause et sexe : 2014 - 2018 (continued - suite)

Mexico - Mexique

Cause of death — Cause de décès	2016 (+C)				2017 (+C)			
	Male — Masculin		Female — Féminin		Male — Masculin		Female — Féminin	
	Number Nombre	Rate Taux	Number Nombre	Rate Taux	Number Nombre	Rate Taux	Number Nombre	Rate Taux
Diseases of arteries, arterioles and capillaries — Maladies des artères, artérioles et capillaires	1 147	1.9	1 052	1.7	1 096	1.8	949	1.5
Diseases of the respiratory system — Maladies de l'appareil respiratoire								
Total	31 540	52.5	26 783	42.8	30 810	50.7	27 122	42.8
Influenza — Grippe	147	0.2	106	0.2	124	0.2	111	0.2
Pneumonia — Pneumopathies	11 502	19.1	9 021	14.4	11 524	19.0	9 446	14.9
Chronic lower respiratory diseases — Maladies chroniques des voies respiratoires inférieures	14 739	24.5	13 226	21.1	14 129	23.3	13 148	20.8
Diseases of the digestive system — Maladies de l'appareil digestif								
Total	41 704	69.4	24 177	38.6	41 926	69.0	24 321	38.4
Gastric and duodenal ulcer — Ulcère de l'estomac et du duodénum	1 459	2.4	1 189	1.9	1 426	2.3	1 225	1.9
Diseases of the liver — Maladies du foie	27 636	46.0	10 350	16.5	27 851	45.9	10 223	16.1
Diseases of the musculoskeletal system and connective tissue — Maladies du système ostéo-articularie, des muscles et du tissu conjonctif	1 488	2.5	3 166	5.1	1 524	2.5	3 226	5.1
Diseases of the genitourinary system — Maladies de l'appareil génito-urinaire								
Total	12 062	20.1	10 688	17.1	12 338	20.3	10 966	17.3
Disorders of kidney and ureter — Affections du rein et de l'uretère	8 600	14.3	7 152	11.4	8 751	14.4	7 277	11.5
Hyperplasia of prostate — Hyperplasie de la prostate	794	7.2	..	..	835	7.3	..	..
Pregnancy, childbirth and the puerperium — Grossesse, accouchement et puerpéralité								
Total	..	..	929	45.8	..	..	902	45.1
Pregnancy with abortive outcome — Grossesse se terminant par un avortement	..	..	70	3.5	..	..	74	3.7
Other direct obstetric causes — Autres décès maternels directs	..	..	502	24.7	..	..	477	23.8
Indirect obstetric causes — Décès maternels indirects	..	..	241	11.9	..	..	209	10.4
Certain conditions originating in the perinatal period — Certaines affections dont l'origine se situe dans la période périnatale	7 234	700.9	5 281	530.1	7 428	728.2	5 551	566.1
Congenital malformations, deformations and chromosomal abnormalities — Malformations congénitales et anomalies chromosomiques	4 858	470.7	4 174	419.0	4 807	471.2	4 337	442.3
Symptoms, signs and abnormal clinical and laboratory findings, not elsewhere classified — Symptômes, signes et résultats anormaux d'examens cliniques et de laboratoire, non classés ailleurs	4 664	7.8	4 612	7.4	4 839	8.0	4 619	7.3
All other diseases — Toutes autres maladies	1 233	2.1	1 639	2.6	1 326	2.2	1 613	2.5
External causes — Causes externes								
Total	57 669	96.0	13 237	21.1	64 380	106.0	14 076	22.2
Accidents								
Total	27 405	45.6	8 200	13.1	26 350	43.4	8 154	12.9
Transport accidents — Accidents de transport	13 195	22.0	3 290	5.3	13 006	21.4	3 182	5.0
Falls — Chutes	2 183	3.6	502	0.8	1 965	3.2	459	0.7
Accidental drowning and submersion — Noyade et submersion accidentelles	1 644	2.7	281	0.4	1 602	2.6	252	0.4
Exposure to smoke, fire and flames — Exposition à la fumée, au feu et aux flammes	398	0.7	142	0.2	466	0.8	183	0.3
Accidental poisoning by and exposure to noxious substances — Intoxication accidentelle par des substances nocives et exposition à ces substances	866	1.4	208	0.3	729	1.2	227	0.4
Intentional self-harm — Lésions auto-infligées	5 116	8.5	1 173	1.9	5 279	8.7	1 213	1.9
Assault — Agresssions	21 225	35.3	2 746	4.4	27 905	45.9	3 357	5.3
All other external causes — Toutes autres causes externes	3 923	6.5	1 118	1.8	4 846	8.0	1 352	2.1

20. Death and death rates by cause and sex: 2014 - 2018
Décès et taux de mortalité par cause et sexe : 2014 - 2018 (continued - suite)

Cause of death — Cause de décès	Montserrat				Nicaragua			
	2017 (...)		2018 (...)		2017 (+U)		2018 (+U)	
	Male — Masculin	Female — Féminin	Male — Masculin	Female — Féminin	Male — Masculin	Female — Féminin	Male — Masculin	Female — Féminin
	Number Nombre	Number Nombre	Number Nombre	Number Nombre	Number Nombre	Number Nombre	Number Nombre	Number Nombre
TOTAL	*22*	*17*	*20*	*17*	*13 257*	*10 559*	*13 283*	*10 242*
Certain infectious and parasitic diseases — Certaines maladies infectieuses et parasitaires								
Total	*1*	*1*	-	*1*	*403*	*249*	*364*	*225*
Intestinal infectious diseases — Maladies infectieuses intestinales	*1*	-	-	-	*46*	*47*	*49*	*44*
Tuberculosis — Tuberculose	-	-	-	-	*83*	*39*	*63*	*38*
Tetanus — Tétanos	-	-	-	-	-	-	-	-
Diphtheria — Diphtérie	-	-	-	-	-	-	-	-
Whooping cough — Coqueluche	-	-	-	-	-	-	-	-
Meningococcal infection — Infection à méningocoques	-	-	-	-	-	-	-	-
Septicaemia — Septicémie	-	*1*	-	*1*	*63*	*70*	*53*	*52*
Acute poliomyelitis — Poliomyélite aiguë	-	-	-	-	-	-	-	-
Measles — Rougeole	-	-	-	-	-	-	-	-
Viral hepatitis — Hépatite virale	-	-	-	-	*6*	*6*	*1*	*4*
Human immunodeficiency virus [HIV] disease — Maladies dues au virus de l'immunodéficience humaine (VIH)	-	-	-	-	*173*	*68*	*170*	*62*
Malaria — Paludisme	-	-	-	-	-	*1*	*1*	*2*
Neoplasms — Tumeurs	*1*	*2*	*3*	*1*	*1 407*	*1 558*	*1 374*	*1 627*
Malignant neoplasms — Tumeurs malignes								
Total	*1*	*2*	*3*	*1*	*1 339*	*1 486*	*1 311*	*1 520*
Malignant neoplasm of lip, oral cavity and pharynx — Tumeur maligne de la lèvre, de la cavité buccale et du pharynx	-	-	*1*	-	*27*	*14*	*26*	*13*
Malignant neoplasm of oesophagus — Tumeur maligne de l'oesophage	-	-	-	-	*23*	*4*	*16*	*7*
Malignant neoplasm of stomach — Tumeur maligne de l'estomac	-	-	-	-	*188*	*119*	*182*	*129*
Malignant neoplasm of colon, rectosigmoid junction, rectum, anus and anal canal — Tumeur maligne du côlon, de la jonction recto-sigmoïdienne, du rectum, de l'anus et du canal anal	-	-	-	-	*103*	*98*	*81*	*112*
Malignant neoplasm of liver and intrahepatic bile ducts — Tumeur maligne du foie et des voies bilaires intrahépatiques	-	-	-	-	*188*	*172*	*175*	*176*
Malignant neoplasm of pancreas — Tumeur maligne du pancréas	-	-	-	-	*58*	*72*	*53*	*59*
Malignant neoplasm of trachea, bronchus and lung — Tumeur maligne de la trachée, des bronches et du poumon	-	-	*1*	-	*100*	*78*	*102*	*73*
Malignant neoplasm of female breast — Tumeur maligne du sein chez la femme	..	*2*	..	-	..	*202*	..	*216*
Malignant neoplasm of cervix uteri — Tumeur maligne du col de l'utérus	..	-	..	*1*	..	*272*	..	*259*
Malignant neoplasm of prostate — Tumeur maligne de la prostate	*1*	..	*1*	..	*207*	..	*185*	..
Malignant neoplasm of lymphoid, haematopoietic and related tissue — Tumeurs malignes primitives ou présumées primitives des tissus lymphoïde, hématopoïétique et apparentés	-	-	-	-	*163*	*123*	*175*	*133*
Disorders of the blood and blood-forming organs and certain disorders involving the immune mechanism — Maladies du sang et des organes hématopoïétiques et certains troubles du système immunitaire								
Total	-	-	-	-	*46*	*54*	*57*	*59*
Anaemias — Anémies	-	-	-	-	*22*	*37*	*36*	*41*
Endocrine, nutritional and metabolic diseases — Maladies endocriniennes, nutritionnelles et métaboliques								
Total	*3*	*3*	*2*	*3*	*1 094*	*1 402*	*1 122*	*1 390*
Diabetes mellitus — Diabète sucré	*3*	*3*	*2*	*3*	*999*	*1 314*	*1 039*	*1 302*
Malnutrition — Malnutrition	-	-	-	-	*72*	*50*	*62*	*57*
Mental and behavioural disorders — Troubles mentaux et du comportement	*1*	-	-	-	*261*	*27*	*230*	*25*
Diseases of the nervous system — Maladies du système nerveux	*1*	-	*1*	-	*202*	*172*	*198*	*183*
Diseases of the circulatory system — Maladies de l'appareil circulatoire								
Total	*10*	*8*	*14*	*12*	*3 179*	*3 224*	*3 303*	*3 200*
Acute rheumatic fever and chronic rheumatic heart diseases — Rhumatisme articularie aigu et cardiopathies rhumatismales chroniques	-	-	-	-	*8*	*8*	*8*	*17*
Hypertensive diseases — Maladies hypertensives	*2*	*2*	*2*	*2*	*472*	*461*	*514*	*380*
Ischaemic heart disease — Cardiopathie ischémique	*1*	*1*	*3*	*3*	*1 728*	*1 634*	*1 752*	*1 659*

20. Death and death rates by cause and sex: 2014 - 2018
Décès et taux de mortalité par cause et sexe : 2014 - 2018 (continued - suite)

Cause of death — Cause de décès	Montserrat				Nicaragua			
	2017 (...)		2018 (...)		2017 (+U)		2018 (+U)	
	Male — Masculin	Female — Féminin	Male — Masculin	Female — Féminin	Male — Masculin	Female — Féminin	Male — Masculin	Female — Féminin
	Number Nombre	Number Nombre	Number Nombre	Number Nombre	Number Nombre	Number Nombre	Number Nombre	Number Nombre
Cerebrovascular disease — Maladie cérébrovasculaire	*4*	*2*	*6*	*4*	*634*	*731*	*683*	*759*
Diseases of arteries, arterioles and capillaries — Maladies des artères, artérioles et capillaires	-	*1*	-	-	*35*	*26*	*19*	*28*
Diseases of the respiratory system — Maladies de l'appareil respiratoire								
Total	*2*	*2*	-	-	*1 113*	*1 042*	*847*	*846*
Influenza — Grippe	-	*1*	-	-	-	-	*1*	*1*
Pneumonia — Pneumopathies	-	-	-	-	*414*	*367*	*312*	*267*
Chronic lower respiratory diseases — Maladies chroniques des voies respiratoires inférieures	-	-	-	-	*511*	*515*	*385*	*428*
Diseases of the digestive system — Maladies de l'appareil digestif								
Total	*1*	-	-	-	*1 259*	*670*	*1 330*	*678*
Gastric and duodenal ulcer — Ulcère de l'estomac et du duodénum	-	-	-	-	*24*	*29*	*32*	*22*
Diseases of the liver — Maladies du foie	-	-	-	-	*942*	*371*	*994*	*372*
Diseases of the musculoskeletal system and connective tissue — Maladies du système ostéo-articularie, des muscles et du tissu conjonctif	-	*1*	-	-	*31*	*96*	*37*	*104*
Diseases of the genitourinary system — Maladies de l'appareil génito-urinaire								
Total	*2*	-	-	-	*1 334*	*549*	*1 332*	*548*
Disorders of kidney and ureter — Affections du rein et de l'uretère	*2*	-	-	-	*1 281*	*489*	*1 282*	*480*
Hyperplasia of prostate — Hyperplasie de la prostate	-	..	-	..	*12*	..	*12*	..
Pregnancy, childbirth and the puerperium — Grossesse, accouchement et puerpéralité								
Total	..	-	..	-	..	*47*	..	*47*
Pregnancy with abortive outcome — Grossesse se terminant par un avortement	..	-	..	-	..	*3*	..	*5*
Other direct obstetric causes — Autres décès maternels directs	..	-	..	-	..	*35*	..	*39*
Indirect obstetric causes — Décès maternels indirects	..	-	..	-	..	*9*	..	*3*
Certain conditions originating in the perinatal period — Certaines affections dont l'origine se situe dans la période périnatale	-	-	-	-	*607*	*413*	*494*	*354*
Congenital malformations, deformations and chromosomal abnormalities — Malformations congénitales et anomalies chromosomiques	-	-	-	-	*260*	*259*	*254*	*217*
Symptoms, signs and abnormal clinical and laboratory findings, not elsewhere classified — Symptômes, signes et résultats anormaux d'examens cliniques et de laboratoire, non classés ailleurs	-	-	-	-	*318*	*277*	*310*	*252*
All other diseases — Toutes autres maladies	-	-	-	-	*44*	*67*	*41*	*72*
External causes — Causes externes								
Total	-	-	-	-	*1 699*	*453*	*1 990*	*415*
Accidents								
Total	-	-	-	-	*1 113*	*312*	*1 132*	*264*
Transport accidents — Accidents de transport	-	-	-	-	*605*	*110*	*598*	*81*
Falls — Chutes	-	-	-	-	*86*	*100*	*130*	*92*
Accidental drowning and submersion — Noyade et submersion accidentelles	-	-	-	-	*162*	*29*	*139*	*7*
Exposure to smoke, fire and flames — Exposition à la fumée, au feu et aux flammes	-	-	-	-	*9*	*3*	*9*	*1*
Accidental poisoning by and exposure to noxious substances — Intoxication accidentelle par des substances nocives et exposition à ces substances	-	-	-	-	*38*	*5*	*37*	*9*
Intentional self-harm — Lésions auto-infligées	-	-	-	-	*261*	*76*	*273*	*75*
Assault — Agresssions	-	-	-	-	*280*	*36*	*512*	*48*
All other external causes — Toutes autres causes externes	-	-	-	-	*45*	*29*	*73*	*28*

20. Death and death rates by cause and sex: 2014 - 2018
Décès et taux de mortalité par cause et sexe : 2014 - 2018 (continued - suite)

Panama

Cause of death — Cause de décès	2016 (+C)				2017 (+C)			
	Male — Masculin		Female — Féminin		Male — Masculin		Female — Féminin	
	Number Nombre	Rate Taux	Number Nombre	Rate Taux	Number Nombre	Rate Taux	Number Nombre	Rate Taux
TOTAL	**10 859**	**536.0**	**8 023**	**399.0**	**11 096**	**539.7**	**8 386**	**410.7**
Certain infectious and parasitic diseases — Certaines maladies infectieuses et parasitaires								
Total	776	38.3	378	18.8	786	38.2	440	21.5
Intestinal infectious diseases — Maladies infectieuses intestinales	94	4.6	98	4.9	120	5.8	100	4.9
Tuberculosis — Tuberculose	123	6.1	53	2.6	126	6.1	69	3.4
Tetanus — Tétanos	-	-	-	-	-	-	1	♦0.0
Diphtheria — Diphtérie	-	-	-	-	-	-	-	-
Whooping cough — Coqueluche	-	-	-	-	1	♦0.0	-	-
Meningococcal infection — Infection à méningocoques	-	-	-	-	-	-	-	-
Septicaemia — Septicémie	106	5.2	69	3.4	82	4.0	89	4.4
Acute poliomyelitis — Poliomyélite aiguë	-	-	-	-	-	-	-	-
Measles — Rougeole	-	-	-	-	-	-	-	-
Viral hepatitis — Hépatite virale	5	♦0.2	2	♦0.1	8	♦0.4	4	♦0.2
Human immunodeficiency virus [HIV] disease — Maladies dues au virus de l'immunodéficience humaine (VIH)	419	20.7	134	6.7	400	19.5	151	7.4
Malaria — Paludisme	-	-	-	-	-	-	-	-
Neoplasms — Tumeurs	1 700	83.9	1 521	75.6	1 740	84.6	1 603	78.5
Malignant neoplasms — Tumeurs malignes								
Total	1 568	77.4	1 412	70.2	1 586	77.1	1 475	72.2
Malignant neoplasm of lip, oral cavity and pharynx — Tumeur maligne de la lèvre, de la cavité buccale et du pharynx	47	2.3	14	♦0.7	55	2.7	15	♦0.7
Malignant neoplasm of oesophagus — Tumeur maligne de l'oesophage	28	♦1.4	9	♦0.4	33	1.6	8	♦0.4
Malignant neoplasm of stomach — Tumeur maligne de l'estomac	223	11.0	122	6.1	184	8.9	123	6.0
Malignant neoplasm of colon, rectosigmoid junction, rectum, anus and anal canal — Tumeur maligne du côlon, de la jonction recto-sigmoïdienne, du rectum, de l'anus et du canal anal	146	7.2	130	6.5	175	8.5	143	7.0
Malignant neoplasm of liver and intrahepatic bile ducts — Tumeur maligne du foie et des voies bilaires intrahépatiques	70	3.5	63	3.1	68	3.3	94	4.6
Malignant neoplasm of pancreas — Tumeur maligne du pancréas	63	3.1	60	3.0	73	3.6	58	2.8
Malignant neoplasm of trachea, bronchus and lung — Tumeur maligne de la trachée, des bronches et du poumon	162	8.0	96	4.8	157	7.6	82	4.0
Malignant neoplasm of female breast — Tumeur maligne du sein chez la femme	..	..	228	15.5	..	..	241	16.0
Malignant neoplasm of cervix uteri — Tumeur maligne du col de l'utérus	..	..	137	9.3	..	..	144	9.6
Malignant neoplasm of prostate — Tumeur maligne de la prostate	297	73.3	..	..	338	80.4	..	..
Malignant neoplasm of lymphoid, haematopoietic and related tissue — Tumeurs malignes primitives ou présumées primitives des tissus lymphoïde, hématopoïétique et apparentés	180	8.9	182	9.1	183	8.9	144	7.1
Disorders of the blood and blood-forming organs and certain disorders involving the immune mechanism — Maladies du sang et des organes hématopoïétiques et certains troubles du système immunitaire								
Total	91	4.5	69	3.4	76	3.7	65	3.2
Anaemias — Anémies	73	3.6	52	2.6	55	2.7	44	2.2
Endocrine, nutritional and metabolic diseases — Maladies endocriniennes, nutritionnelles et métaboliques								
Total	747	36.9	798	39.7	733	35.7	830	40.6
Diabetes mellitus — Diabète sucré	580	28.6	637	31.7	584	28.4	671	32.9
Malnutrition — Malnutrition	62	3.1	62	3.1	49	2.4	44	2.2
Mental and behavioural disorders — Troubles mentaux et du comportement	78	3.8	69	3.4	69	3.4	51	2.5
Diseases of the nervous system — Maladies du système nerveux	319	15.7	277	13.8	307	14.9	282	13.8
Diseases of the circulatory system — Maladies de l'appareil circulatoire								
Total	3 027	149.4	2 481	123.4	3 137	152.6	2 503	122.6
Acute rheumatic fever and chronic rheumatic heart diseases — Rhumatismo articularie aigu et cardiopathies rhumatismales chroniques	5	♦0.2	16	♦0.8	14	♦0.7	12	♦0.6
Hypertensive diseases — Maladies hypertensives	512	25.3	443	22.0	345	16.8	330	16.2
Ischaemic heart disease — Cardiopathie ischémique	849	41.9	600	29.8	953	46.4	670	32.8
Cerebrovascular disease — Maladie cérébrovasculaire	857	42.3	751	37.3	909	44.2	758	37.1

20. Death and death rates by cause and sex: 2014 - 2018
Décès et taux de mortalité par cause et sexe : 2014 - 2018 (continued - suite)

Panama

Cause of death — Cause de décès	2016 (+C)				2017 (+C)			
	Male — Masculin		Female — Féminin		Male — Masculin		Female — Féminin	
	Number Nombre	Rate Taux	Number Nombre	Rate Taux	Number Nombre	Rate Taux	Number Nombre	Rate Taux
Diseases of arteries, arterioles and capillaries — Maladies des artères, artérioles et capillaires	132	6.5	82	4.1	114	5.5	78	3.8
Diseases of the respiratory system — Maladies de l'appareil respiratoire								
Total	920	45.4	765	38.0	912	44.4	761	37.3
Influenza — Grippe	2	♦0.1	-	-	3	♦0.1	-	-
Pneumonia — Pneumopathies	285	14.1	190	9.4	247	12.0	197	9.6
Chronic lower respiratory diseases — Maladies chroniques des voies respiratoires inférieures	256	12.6	288	14.3	306	14.9	252	12.3
Diseases of the digestive system — Maladies de l'appareil digestif								
Total	488	24.1	346	17.2	495	24.1	393	19.2
Gastric and duodenal ulcer — Ulcère de l'estomac et du duodénum	22	♦1.1	4	♦0.2	26	♦1.3	6	♦0.3
Diseases of the liver — Maladies du foie	232	11.5	163	8.1	213	10.4	155	7.6
Diseases of the musculoskeletal system and connective tissue — Maladies du système ostéo-articularie, des muscles et du tissu conjonctif	40	2.0	67	3.3	32	1.6	74	3.6
Diseases of the genitourinary system — Maladies de l'appareil génito-urinaire								
Total	476	23.5	277	13.8	584	28.4	346	16.9
Disorders of kidney and ureter — Affections du rein et de l'uretère	393	19.4	230	11.4	498	24.2	291	14.3
Hyperplasia of prostate — Hyperplasie de la prostate	21	♦5.2	..	..	32	7.6	..	..
Pregnancy, childbirth and the puerperium — Grossesse, accouchement et puerpéralité								
Total	..	..	37	49.2	..	..	27	♦35.4
Pregnancy with abortive outcome — Grossesse se terminant par un avortement	..	..	4	♦5.3	..	..	7	♦9.2
Other direct obstetric causes — Autres décès maternels directs	..	..	27	♦35.9	..	..	19	♦24.9
Indirect obstetric causes — Décès maternels indirects	..	..	6	♦8.0	..	..	1	♦1.3
Certain conditions originating in the perinatal period — Certaines affections dont l'origine se situe dans la période périnatale	230	589.8	188	519.5	254	644.5	199	541.5
Congenital malformations, deformations and chromosomal abnormalities — Malformations congénitales et anomalies chromosomiques	207	530.8	177	489.1	191	484.6	169	459.8
Symptoms, signs and abnormal clinical and laboratory findings, not elsewhere classified — Symptômes, signes et résultats anormaux d'examens cliniques et de laboratoire, non classés ailleurs	405	20.0	288	14.3	483	23.5	352	17.2
All other diseases — Toutes autres maladies	70	3.5	58	2.9	61	3.0	69	3.4
External causes — Causes externes								
Total	1 285	63.4	227	11.3	1 236	60.1	222	10.9
Accidents								
Total	661	32.6	130	6.5	625	30.4	132	6.5
Transport accidents — Accidents de transport	394	19.4	81	4.0	386	18.8	80	3.9
Falls — Chutes	51	2.5	11	♦0.5	53	2.6	16	♦0.8
Accidental drowning and submersion — Noyade et submersion accidentelles	115	5.7	10	♦0.5	81	3.9	21	♦1.0
Exposure to smoke, fire and flames — Exposition à la fumée, au feu et aux flammes	11	♦0.5	3	♦0.1	5	♦0.2	1	♦0.0
Accidental poisoning by and exposure to noxious substances — Intoxication accidentelle par des substances nocives et exposition à ces substances	8	♦0.4	4	♦0.2	7	♦0.3	2	♦0.1
Intentional self-harm — Lésions auto-infligées	107	5.3	16	♦0.8	109	5.3	15	♦0.7
Assault — Agressions	365	18.0	49	2.4	382	18.6	47	2.3
All other external causes — Toutes autres causes externes	152	7.5	32	1.6	120	5.8	28	♦1.4

20. Death and death rates by cause and sex: 2014 - 2018
Décès et taux de mortalité par cause et sexe : 2014 - 2018 (continued - suite)

Cause of death — Cause de décès	Puerto Rico - Porto Rico				Saint Kitts and Nevis - Saint-Kitts-et-Nevis			
	2016 (...)		2017 (...)		2015 (+U)		2016 (+U)	
	Male — Masculin	Female — Féminin	Male — Masculin	Female — Féminin	Male — Masculin	Female — Féminin	Male — Masculin	Female — Féminin
	Number Nombre	Number Nombre	Number Nombre	Number Nombre	Number Nombre	Number Nombre	Number Nombre	Number Nombre
TOTAL	***15 868***	***13 470***	***16 715***	***14 062***	***209***	***162***	***243***	***158***
Certain infectious and parasitic diseases — Certaines maladies infectieuses et parasitaires								
Total	*674*	*473*	*708*	*553*	*2*	*-*	*6*	*2*
Intestinal infectious diseases — Maladies infectieuses intestinales	*17*	*20*	*20*	*28*	*-*	*-*	*-*	*-*
Tuberculosis — Tuberculose	*7*	*6*	*4*	*1*	*-*	*-*	*-*	*-*
Tetanus — Tétanos	*-*	*1*	*1*	*-*	*-*	*-*	*-*	*-*
Diphtheria — Diphtérie	*-*	*-*	*-*	*-*	*-*	*-*	*-*	*-*
Whooping cough — Coqueluche	*-*	*-*	*-*	*-*	*-*	*-*	*-*	*-*
Meningococcal infection — Infection à méningocoques	*-*	*-*	*-*	*-*	*-*	*-*	*-*	*-*
Septicaemia — Septicémie	*364*	*343*	*422*	*408*	*-*	*-*	*-*	*-*
Acute poliomyelitis — Poliomyélite aiguë	*-*	*-*	*-*	*-*	*-*	*-*	*-*	*-*
Measles — Rougeole	*-*	*-*	*-*	*-*	*-*	*-*	*-*	*-*
Viral hepatitis — Hépatite virale	*66*	*14*	*54*	*17*	*-*	*-*	*-*	*-*
Human immunodeficiency virus [HIV] disease — Maladies dues au virus de l'immunodéficience humaine (VIH)	*151*	*50*	*127*	*54*	*1*	*-*	*5*	*2*
Malaria — Paludisme	*-*	*-*	*-*	*-*	*-*	*-*	*-*	*-*
Neoplasms — Tumeurs	*2 928*	*2 384*	*3 007*	*2 359*	*47*	*40*	*47*	*29*
Malignant neoplasms — Tumeurs malignes								
Total	*2 816*	*2 308*	*2 927*	*2 283*	*47*	*39*	*47*	*28*
Malignant neoplasm of lip, oral cavity and pharynx — Tumeur maligne de la lèvre, de la cavité buccale et du pharynx	*100*	*17*	*101*	*26*	*2*	*1*	*-*	*-*
Malignant neoplasm of oesophagus — Tumeur maligne de l'oesophage	*88*	*17*	*89*	*18*	*-*	*-*	*-*	*-*
Malignant neoplasm of stomach — Tumeur maligne de l'estomac	*94*	*78*	*102*	*65*	*1*	*-*	*-*	*2*
Malignant neoplasm of colon, rectosigmoid junction, rectum, anus and anal canal — Tumeur maligne du côlon, de la jonction recto-sigmoïdienne, du rectum, de l'anus et du canal anal	*381*	*317*	*386*	*289*	*6*	*6*	*3*	*2*
Malignant neoplasm of liver and intrahepatic bile ducts — Tumeur maligne du foie et des voies bilaires intrahépatiques	*215*	*119*	*218*	*93*	*5*	*-*	*3*	*-*
Malignant neoplasm of pancreas — Tumeur maligne du pancréas	*152*	*126*	*182*	*153*	*4*	*4*	*-*	*-*
Malignant neoplasm of trachea, bronchus and lung — Tumeur maligne de la trachée, des bronches et du poumon	*323*	*204*	*358*	*201*	*2*	*5*	*7*	*1*
Malignant neoplasm of female breast — Tumeur maligne du sein chez la femme	..	*436*	..	*445*	..	*10*	..	*9*
Malignant neoplasm of cervix uteri — Tumeur maligne du col de l'utérus	..	*50*	..	*46*	..	*-*	..	*4*
Malignant neoplasm of prostate — Tumeur maligne de la prostate	*483*	..	*472*	..	*13*	..	*23*	..
Malignant neoplasm of lymphoid, haematopoietic and related tissue — Tumeurs malignes primitives ou présumées primitives des tissus lymphoïde, hématopoïétique et apparentés	*284*	*232*	*270*	*225*	*1*	*3*	*1*	*1*
Disorders of the blood and blood-forming organs and certain disorders involving the immune mechanism — Maladies du sang et des organes hématopoïétiques et certains troubles du système immunitaire								
Total	*175*	*168*	*153*	*167*	*-*	*-*	*1*	*2*
Anaemias — Anémies	*115*	*106*	*107*	*113*	*-*	*-*	*1*	*2*
Endocrine, nutritional and metabolic diseases — Maladies endocriniennes, nutritionnelles et métaboliques								
Total	*1 934*	*1 896*	*2 059*	*1 980*	*17*	*19*	*29*	*30*
Diabetes mellitus — Diabète sucré	*1 572*	*1 549*	*1 658*	*1 580*	*15*	*18*	*27*	*24*
Malnutrition — Malnutrition	*29*	*38*	*54*	*35*	*-*	*1*	*1*	*2*
Mental and behavioural disorders — Troubles mentaux et du comportement	*267*	*195*	*276*	*221*	*3*	*-*	*6*	*-*
Diseases of the nervous system — Maladies du système nerveux	*1 055*	*1 633*	*1 067*	*1 802*	*4*	*5*	*5*	*7*
Diseases of the circulatory system — Maladies de l'appareil circulatoire								
Total	*3 789*	*3 433*	*3 972*	*3 592*	*64*	*70*	*70*	*63*
Acute rheumatic fever and chronic rheumatic heart diseases — Rhumatisme articularie aigu et cardiopathies rhumatismales chroniques	*10*	*8*	*10*	*17*	*-*	*-*	*-*	*-*
Hypertensive diseases — Maladies hypertensives	*602*	*649*	*604*	*687*	*17*	*11*	*17*	*16*
Ischaemic heart disease — Cardiopathie ischémique	*1 861*	*1 503*	*2 018*	*1 566*	*17*	*13*	*13*	*14*

20. Death and death rates by cause and sex: 2014 - 2018
Décès et taux de mortalité par cause et sexe : 2014 - 2018 (continued - suite)

Cause of death — Cause de décès	Puerto Rico - Porto Rico				Saint Kitts and Nevis - Saint-Kitts-et-Nevis			
	2016 (...)		2017 (...)		2015 (+U)		2016 (+U)	
	Male — Masculin	Female — Féminin	Male — Masculin	Female — Féminin	Male — Masculin	Female — Féminin	Male — Masculin	Female — Féminin
	Number Nombre	Number Nombre	Number Nombre	Number Nombre	Number Nombre	Number Nombre	Number Nombre	Number Nombre
Cerebrovascular disease — Maladie cérébrovasculaire	*556*	*606*	*589*	*627*	*19*	*29*	*17*	*18*
Diseases of arteries, arterioles and capillaries — Maladies des artères, artérioles et capillaires	*100*	*76*	*101*	*76*	*4*	*2*	*5*	*1*
Diseases of the respiratory system — Maladies de l'appareil respiratoire								
Total	*1 346*	*1 296*	*1 323*	*1 325*	*7*	*5*	*6*	*7*
Influenza — Grippe	*36*	*52*	*17*	*25*	-	-	-	*1*
Pneumonia — Pneumopathies	*380*	*348*	*387*	*389*	-	-	-	*3*
Chronic lower respiratory diseases — Maladies chroniques des voies respiratoires inférieures	*588*	*554*	*592*	*584*	*1*	*1*	*2*	*2*
Diseases of the digestive system — Maladies de l'appareil digestif								
Total	*855*	*491*	*797*	*500*	*8*	*1*	*11*	*9*
Gastric and duodenal ulcer — Ulcère de l'estomac et du duodénum	*15*	*9*	*12*	*11*	*1*	-	-	-
Diseases of the liver — Maladies du foie	*529*	*222*	*518*	*209*	*6*	-	*5*	*2*
Diseases of the musculoskeletal system and connective tissue — Maladies du système ostéo-articularie, des muscles et du tissu conjonctif	*60*	*94*	*91*	*121*	-	*2*	-	*1*
Diseases of the genitourinary system — Maladies de l'appareil génito-urinaire								
Total	*687*	*582*	*730*	*633*	*6*	*3*	*12*	-
Disorders of kidney and ureter — Affections du rein et de l'uretère	*597*	*459*	*609*	*498*	*4*	*3*	*4*	-
Hyperplasia of prostate — Hyperplasie de la prostate	*5*	..	*8*	..	-	..	*1*	..
Pregnancy, childbirth and the puerperium — Grossesse, accouchement et puerpéralité								
Total	..	*11*	..	*12*	..	-	..	-
Pregnancy with abortive outcome — Grossesse se terminant par un avortement	..	-	..	-	..	-	..	-
Other direct obstetric causes — Autres décès maternels directs	..	*8*	..	*7*	..	-	..	-
Indirect obstetric causes — Décès maternels indirects	..	-	..	*1*	..	-	..	-
Certain conditions originating in the perinatal period — Certaines affections dont l'origine se situe dans la période périnatale	*61*	*46*	*50*	*42*	*5*	*7*	*8*	*3*
Congenital malformations, deformations and chromosomal abnormalities — Malformations congénitales et anomalies chromosomiques	*51*	*37*	*55*	*37*	*2*	*3*	*2*	-
Symptoms, signs and abnormal clinical and laboratory findings, not elsewhere classified — Symptômes, signes et résultats anormaux d'examens cliniques et de laboratoire, non classés ailleurs	*423*	*181*	*678*	*176*	*1*	-	-	*1*
All other diseases — Toutes autres maladies	*97*	*131*	*109*	*151*	-	*1*	*2*	-
External causes — Causes externes								
Total	*1 466*	*419*	*1 640*	*391*	*43*	*6*	*38*	*4*
Accidents								
Total	*577*	*253*	*704*	*247*	*14*	*4*	*8*	-
Transport accidents — Accidents de transport	*259*	*69*	*281*	*70*	*6*	*1*	*3*	-
Falls — Chutes	*152*	*99*	*208*	*85*	-	*2*	*1*	-
Accidental drowning and submersion — Noyade et submersion accidentelles	*18*	*3*	*18*	*9*	-	-	*1*	-
Exposure to smoke, fire and flames — Exposition à la fumée, au feu et aux flammes	*10*	*1*	*7*	*2*	-	-	-	-
Accidental poisoning by and exposure to noxious substances — Intoxication accidentelle par des substances nocives et exposition à ces substances	*33*	*11*	*62*	*9*	*1*	*1*	-	-
Intentional self-harm — Lésions auto-infligées	*168*	*19*	*212*	*35*	-	-	-	-
Assault — Agresssions	*618*	*57*	*647*	*36*	*23*	-	*28*	*2*
All other external causes — Toutes autres causes externes	*103*	*90*	*77*	*73*	*6*	*2*	*2*	*2*

20. Death and death rates by cause and sex: 2014 - 2018
Décès et taux de mortalité par cause et sexe : 2014 - 2018 (continued - suite)

Saint Lucia - Sainte-Lucie

Cause of death — Cause de décès	2014 (+C)				2015 (+C)			
	Male — Masculin		Female — Féminin		Male — Masculin		Female — Féminin	
	Number Nombre	Rate Taux	Number Nombre	Rate Taux	Number Nombre	Rate Taux	Number Nombre	Rate Taux
TOTAL	**727**	**848.9**	**572**	**657.6**	**628**	**726.2**	**469**	**534.3**
Certain infectious and parasitic diseases — Certaines maladies infectieuses et parasitaires								
Total	28	♦32.7	24	♦27.6	18	♦20.8	17	♦19.4
Intestinal infectious diseases — Maladies infectieuses intestinales	1	♦1.2	-	-	1	♦1.2	1	♦1.1
Tuberculosis — Tuberculose	3	♦3.5	-	-	1	♦1.2	1	♦1.1
Tetanus — Tétanos	-	-	-	-	-	-	-	-
Diphtheria — Diphtérie	-	-	-	-	-	-	-	-
Whooping cough — Coqueluche	-	-	-	-	-	-	-	-
Meningococcal infection — Infection à méningocoques	-	-	-	-	-	-	-	-
Septicaemia — Septicémie	13	♦15.2	11	♦12.6	8	♦9.3	11	♦12.5
Acute poliomyelitis — Poliomyélite aiguë	-	-	-	-	-	-	-	-
Measles — Rougeole	-	-	-	-	-	-	-	-
Viral hepatitis — Hépatite virale	-	-	-	-	-	-	-	-
Human immunodeficiency virus [HIV] disease — Maladies dues au virus de l'immunodéficience humaine (VIH)	1	♦1.2	1	♦1.1	1	♦1.2	-	-
Malaria — Paludisme	-	-	-	-	-	-	-	-
Neoplasms — Tumeurs	147	171.7	102	117.3	129	149.2	96	109.4
Malignant neoplasms — Tumeurs malignes								
Total	143	167.0	97	111.5	123	142.2	91	103.7
Malignant neoplasm of lip, oral cavity and pharynx — Tumeur maligne de la lèvre, de la cavité buccale et du pharynx	8	♦9.3	1	♦1.1	5	♦5.8	1	♦1.1
Malignant neoplasm of oesophagus — Tumeur maligne de l'oesophage	5	♦5.8	1	♦1.1	5	♦5.8	-	-
Malignant neoplasm of stomach — Tumeur maligne de l'estomac	12	♦14.0	7	♦8.0	7	♦8.1	3	♦3.4
Malignant neoplasm of colon, rectosigmoid junction, rectum, anus and anal canal — Tumeur maligne du côlon, de la jonction recto-sigmoïdienne, du rectum, de l'anus et du canal anal	11	♦12.8	13	♦14.9	9	♦10.4	6	♦6.8
Malignant neoplasm of liver and intrahepatic bile ducts — Tumeur maligne du foie et des voies bilaires intrahépatiques	4	♦4.7	4	♦4.6	4	♦4.6	2	♦2.3
Malignant neoplasm of pancreas — Tumeur maligne du pancréas	7	♦8.2	4	♦4.6	4	♦4.6	4	♦4.6
Malignant neoplasm of trachea, bronchus and lung — Tumeur maligne de la trachée, des bronches et du poumon	12	♦14.0	2	♦2.3	16	♦18.5	6	♦6.8
Malignant neoplasm of female breast — Tumeur maligne du sein chez la femme	..	..	14	♦20.1	..	..	22	♦31.1
Malignant neoplasm of cervix uteri — Tumeur maligne du col de l'utérus	..	..	10	♦14.3	..	..	7	♦9.9
Malignant neoplasm of prostate — Tumeur maligne de la prostate	42	212.9	..	..	42	205.5	..	..
Malignant neoplasm of lymphoid, haematopoietic and related tissue — Tumeurs malignes primitives ou présumées primitives des tissus lymphoïde, hématopoïétique et apparentés	11	♦12.8	6	♦6.9	9	♦10.4	6	♦6.8
Disorders of the blood and blood-forming organs and certain disorders involving the immune mechanism — Maladies du sang et des organes hématopoïétiques et certains troubles du système immunitaire								
Total	9	♦10.5	7	♦8.0	8	♦9.3	5	♦5.7
Anaemias — Anémies	6	♦7.0	5	♦5.7	4	♦4.6	3	♦3.4
Endocrine, nutritional and metabolic diseases — Maladies endocriniennes, nutritionnelles et métaboliques								
Total	50	58.4	93	106.9	50	57.8	73	83.2
Diabetes mellitus — Diabète sucré	44	51.4	78	89.7	37	42.8	59	67.2
Malnutrition — Malnutrition	1	♦1.2	2	♦2.3	2	♦2.3	-	-
Mental and behavioural disorders — Troubles mentaux et du comportement	3	♦3.5	1	♦1.1	4	♦4.6	2	♦2.3
Diseases of the nervous system — Maladies du système nerveux	10	♦11.7	11	♦12.6	12	♦13.9	10	♦11.4
Diseases of the circulatory system — Maladies de l'appareil circulatoire								
Total	214	249.9	196	225.3	197	227.8	150	170.9
Acute rheumatic fever and chronic rheumatic heart diseases — Rhumatisme articularie aigu et cardiopathies rhumatismales chroniques	-	-	2	♦2.3	1	♦1.2	1	♦1.1
Hypertensive diseases — Maladies hypertensives	37	43.2	49	56.3	34	39.3	37	42.1
Ischaemic heart disease — Cardiopathie ischémique	50	58.4	32	36.8	35	40.5	14	♦15.9
Cerebrovascular disease — Maladie cérébrovasculaire	61	71.2	62	71.3	69	79.8	61	69.5

20. Death and death rates by cause and sex: 2014 - 2018
Décès et taux de mortalité par cause et sexe : 2014 - 2018 (continued - suite)

Saint Lucia - Sainte-Lucie

Cause of death — Cause de décès	2014 (+C)				2015 (+C)			
	Male — Masculin		Female — Féminin		Male — Masculin		Female — Féminin	
	Number Nombre	Rate Taux	Number Nombre	Rate Taux	Number Nombre	Rate Taux	Number Nombre	Rate Taux
Diseases of arteries, arterioles and capillaries — Maladies des artères, artérioles et capillaires	7	♦8.2	6	♦6.9	10	♦11.6	7	♦8.0
Diseases of the respiratory system — Maladies de l'appareil respiratoire								
Total	68	79.4	33	37.9	50	57.8	29	♦33.0
Influenza — Grippe	-	-	-	-	-	-	-	-
Pneumonia — Pneumopathies	16	♦18.7	10	♦11.5	13	♦15.0	9	♦10.3
Chronic lower respiratory diseases — Maladies chroniques des voies respiratoires inférieures	36	42.0	10	♦11.5	25	♦28.9	10	♦11.4
Diseases of the digestive system — Maladies de l'appareil digestif								
Total	39	45.5	27	♦31.0	31	35.8	19	♦21.6
Gastric and duodenal ulcer — Ulcère de l'estomac et du duodénum	4	♦4.7	2	♦2.3	6	♦6.9	3	♦3.4
Diseases of the liver — Maladies du foie	21	♦24.5	10	♦11.5	18	♦20.8	7	♦8.0
Diseases of the musculoskeletal system and connective tissue — Maladies du système ostéo-articularie, des muscles et du tissu conjonctif	3	♦3.5	5	♦5.7	3	♦3.5	2	♦2.3
Diseases of the genitourinary system — Maladies de l'appareil génito-urinaire								
Total	21	♦24.5	11	♦12.6	15	♦17.3	5	♦5.7
Disorders of kidney and ureter — Affections du rein et de l'uretère	11	♦12.8	6	♦6.9	6	♦6.9	3	♦3.4
Hyperplasia of prostate — Hyperplasie de la prostate	3	♦15.2	..	..	4	♦19.6	..	..
Pregnancy, childbirth and the puerperium — Grossesse, accouchement et puerpéralité								
Total	..	..	2	♦98.7	..	..	-	...
Pregnancy with abortive outcome — Grossesse se terminant par un avortement	..	..	-	-	..	..	-	...
Other direct obstetric causes — Autres décès maternels directs	..	..	2	♦98.7	..	..	-	...
Indirect obstetric causes — Décès maternels indirects	..	..	-	-	..	..	-	...
Certain conditions originating in the perinatal period — Certaines affections dont l'origine se situe dans la période périnatale	16	♦1 564.0	9	♦897.3	19	...	19	...
Congenital malformations, deformations and chromosomal abnormalities — Malformations congénitales et anomalies chromosomiques	7	♦684.3	1	♦99.7	9	...	8	...
Symptoms, signs and abnormal clinical and laboratory findings, not elsewhere classified — Symptômes, signes et résultats anormaux d'examens cliniques et de laboratoire, non classés ailleurs	10	♦11.7	18	♦20.7	12	♦13.9	8	♦9.1
All other diseases — Toutes autres maladies	6	♦7.0	14	♦16.1	5	♦5.8	9	♦10.3
External causes — Causes externes								
Total	96	112.1	18	♦20.7	66	76.3	17	♦19.4
Accidents								
Total	48	56.0	8	♦9.2	39	45.1	10	♦11.4
Transport accidents — Accidents de transport	21	♦24.5	1	♦1.1	5	♦5.8	2	♦2.3
Falls — Chutes	-	-	-	-	-	-	-	-
Accidental drowning and submersion — Noyade et submersion accidentelles	13	♦15.2	-	-	10	♦11.6	-	-
Exposure to smoke, fire and flames — Exposition à la fumée, au feu et aux flammes	-	-	-	-	1	♦1.2	-	-
Accidental poisoning by and exposure to noxious substances — Intoxication accidentelle par des substances nocives et exposition à ces substances	4	♦4.7	-	-	4	♦4.6	2	♦2.3
Intentional self-harm — Lésions auto-infligées	11	♦12.8	3	♦3.4	8	♦9.3	-	-
Assault — Agresssions	34	39.7	-	-	14	♦16.2	2	♦2.3
All other external causes — Toutes autres causes externes	3	♦3.5	7	♦8.0	5	♦5.8	5	♦5.7

20. Death and death rates by cause and sex: 2014 - 2018
Décès et taux de mortalité par cause et sexe : 2014 - 2018 (continued - suite)

Cause of death — Cause de décès	Saint Vincent and the Grenadines - Saint-Vincent-et-les Grenadines				Turks and Caicos Islands - Îles Turques et Caïques			
	2016 (+C)		2017 (+C)		2014 (...)		2015 (...)	
	Male — Masculin	Female — Féminin	Male — Masculin	Female — Féminin	Male — Masculin	Female — Féminin	Male — Masculin	Female — Féminin
	Number Nombre	Number Nombre	Number Nombre	Number Nombre	Number Nombre	Number Nombre	Number Nombre	Number Nombre
TOTAL	502	421	485	400	*52*	*25*	*58*	*37*
Certain infectious and parasitic diseases — Certaines maladies infectieuses et parasitaires								
Total	38	32	25	20	*1*	-	*1*	*2*
Intestinal infectious diseases — Maladies infectieuses intestinales	1	-	-	1	-	-	-	-
Tuberculosis — Tuberculose	-	-	1	-	-	-	-	*1*
Tetanus — Tétanos	-	-	-	-	-	-	-	-
Diphtheria — Diphtérie	-	-	-	-	-	-	-	-
Whooping cough — Coqueluche	-	-	-	-	-	-	-	-
Meningococcal infection — Infection à méningocoques	-	-	-	-	-	-	-	-
Septicaemia — Septicémie	21	27	12	11	-	-	-	-
Acute poliomyelitis — Poliomyélite aiguë	-	-	-	-	-	-	-	-
Measles — Rougeole	-	-	-	-	-	-	-	-
Viral hepatitis — Hépatite virale	-	-	-	-	-	-	-	-
Human immunodeficiency virus [HIV] disease — Maladies dues au virus de l'immunodéficience humaine (VIH)	12	5	8	7	*1*	-	*1*	*1*
Malaria — Paludisme	-	-	-	-	-	-	-	-
Neoplasms — Tumeurs	76	72	95	79	*7*	*3*	*9*	*4*
Malignant neoplasms — Tumeurs malignes								
Total	76	70	95	79	*7*	*3*	*9*	*4*
Malignant neoplasm of lip, oral cavity and pharynx — Tumeur maligne de la lèvre, de la cavité buccale et du pharynx	7	1	4	1	-	-	-	-
Malignant neoplasm of oesophagus — Tumeur maligne de l'oesophage	1	1	3	1	-	-	-	-
Malignant neoplasm of stomach — Tumeur maligne de l'estomac	4	2	4	-	*1*	-	*2*	-
Malignant neoplasm of colon, rectosigmoid junction, rectum, anus and anal canal — Tumeur maligne du côlon, de la jonction recto-sigmoïdienne, du rectum, de l'anus et du canal anal	4	3	5	6	-	-	*1*	*1*
Malignant neoplasm of liver and intrahepatic bile ducts — Tumeur maligne du foie et des voies bilaires intrahépatiques	6	2	3	3	-	-	-	-
Malignant neoplasm of pancreas — Tumeur maligne du pancréas	4	1	9	5	*1*	-	-	-
Malignant neoplasm of trachea, bronchus and lung — Tumeur maligne de la trachée, des bronches et du poumon	3	2	5	5	*2*	*1*	*3*	-
Malignant neoplasm of female breast — Tumeur maligne du sein chez la femme	..	15	..	18	..	-	..	*2*
Malignant neoplasm of cervix uteri — Tumeur maligne du col de l'utérus	..	7	..	3	..	*1*	..	-
Malignant neoplasm of prostate — Tumeur maligne de la prostate	20	..	26	..	*1*	..	*1*	..
Malignant neoplasm of lymphoid, haematopoietic and related tissue — Tumeurs malignes primitives ou présumées primitives des tissus lymphoïde, hématopoïétique et apparentés	6	3	8	8	-	*1*	-	-
Disorders of the blood and blood-forming organs and certain disorders involving the immune mechanism — Maladies du sang et des organes hématopoïétiques et certains troubles du système immunitaire								
Total	5	3	9	5	-	*1*	*2*	*1*
Anaemias — Anémies	2	3	8	3	-	-	-	*1*
Endocrine, nutritional and metabolic diseases — Maladies endocriniennes, nutritionnelles et métaboliques								
Total	30	46	24	41	*2*	*4*	*6*	*4*
Diabetes mellitus — Diabète sucré	25	40	20	40	*2*	*3*	*4*	*3*
Malnutrition — Malnutrition	3	1	1	-	-	-	-	-
Mental and behavioural disorders — Troubles mentaux et du comportement	-	1	2	-	-	-	*1*	-
Diseases of the nervous system — Maladies du système nerveux	8	3	4	3	*2*	*2*	-	-
Diseases of the circulatory system — Maladies de l'appareil circulatoire								
Total	159	161	159	159	*18*	*11*	*21*	*18*
Acute rheumatic fever and chronic rheumatic heart diseases — Rhumatisme articularie aigu et cardiopathies rhumatismales chroniques	2	2	-	2	-	-	-	-
Hypertensive diseases — Maladies hypertensives	12	29	39	33	*2*	*1*	*6*	*5*
Ischaemic heart disease — Cardiopathie ischémique	47	46	35	42	*11*	*5*	*11*	*7*

20. Death and death rates by cause and sex: 2014 - 2018
Décès et taux de mortalité par cause et sexe : 2014 - 2018 (continued - suite)

Cause of death — Cause de décès	Saint Vincent and the Grenadines - Saint-Vincent-et-les Grenadines				Turks and Caicos Islands - Îles Turques et Caïques			
	2016 (+C)		2017 (+C)		2014 (...)		2015 (...)	
	Male — Masculin	Female — Féminin	Male — Masculin	Female — Féminin	Male — Masculin	Female — Féminin	Male — Masculin	Female — Féminin
	Number Nombre	Number Nombre	Number Nombre	Number Nombre	Number Nombre	Number Nombre	Number Nombre	Number Nombre
Cerebrovascular disease — Maladie cérébrovasculaire	33	42	50	46	*1*	*3*	*2*	*1*
Diseases of arteries, arterioles and capillaries — Maladies des artères, artérioles et capillaires	2	4	3	-	*1*	*2*	*1*	-
Diseases of the respiratory system — Maladies de l'appareil respiratoire								
Total	41	37	41	29	*5*	*1*	*4*	*3*
Influenza — Grippe	-	-	-	-	-	-	-	-
Pneumonia — Pneumopathies	17	15	20	16	*4*	*1*	*3*	*2*
Chronic lower respiratory diseases — Maladies chroniques des voies respiratoires inférieures	3	3	3	4	-	-	-	-
Diseases of the digestive system — Maladies de l'appareil digestif								
Total	22	13	20	7	*2*	*1*	-	*1*
Gastric and duodenal ulcer — Ulcère de l'estomac et du duodénum	6	-	6	1	-	-	-	-
Diseases of the liver — Maladies du foie	7	1	6	3	*1*	-	-	-
Diseases of the musculoskeletal system and connective tissue — Maladies du système ostéo-articularie, des muscles et du tissu conjonctif	-	2	-	2	-	-	-	-
Diseases of the genitourinary system — Maladies de l'appareil génito-urinaire								
Total	14	8	17	8	*1*	-	-	-
Disorders of kidney and ureter — Affections du rein et de l'uretère	11	6	8	6	*1*	-	-	-
Hyperplasia of prostate — Hyperplasie de la prostate	-	..	3	..	-	..	-	..
Pregnancy, childbirth and the puerperium — Grossesse, accouchement et puerpéralité								
Total	..	-	..	2	..	-	..	-
Pregnancy with abortive outcome — Grossesse se terminant par un avortement	..	-	..	-	..	-	..	-
Other direct obstetric causes — Autres décès maternels directs	..	-	..	2	..	-	..	-
Indirect obstetric causes — Décès maternels indirects	..	-	..	-	..	-	..	-
Certain conditions originating in the perinatal period — Certaines affections dont l'origine se situe dans la période périnatale	7	8	3	4	-	-	*1*	-
Congenital malformations, deformations and chromosomal abnormalities — Malformations congénitales et anomalies chromosomiques	2	4	3	5	-	-	-	-
Symptoms, signs and abnormal clinical and laboratory findings, not elsewhere classified — Symptômes, signes et résultats anormaux d'examens cliniques et de laboratoire, non classés ailleurs	30	15	11	13	*5*	*1*	-	-
All other diseases — Toutes autres maladies	3	2	7	12	-	-	-	-
External causes — Causes externes								
Total	67	14	65	11	*9*	*1*	*13*	*4*
Accidents								
Total	31	9	30	7	*4*	*1*	*1*	*1*
Transport accidents — Accidents de transport	6	2	5	1	*3*	-	-	-
Falls — Chutes	6	-	6	1	-	-	-	-
Accidental drowning and submersion — Noyade et submersion accidentelles	6	2	5	-	*1*	*1*	*1*	*1*
Exposure to smoke, fire and flames — Exposition à la fumée, au feu et aux flammes	-	4	2	1	-	-	-	-
Accidental poisoning by and exposure to noxious substances — Intoxication accidentelle par des substances nocives et exposition à ces substances	-	-	-	-	-	-	-	-
Intentional self-harm — Lésions auto-infligées	-	-	-	-	*1*	-	*1*	*1*
Assault — Agresssions	32	4	31	4	*2*	-	*5*	*1*
All other external causes — Toutes autres causes externes	4	1	4	-	*2*	-	*6*	*1*

20. Death and death rates by cause and sex: 2014 - 2018
Décès et taux de mortalité par cause et sexe : 2014 - 2018 (continued - suite)

United States of America - États-Unis d'Amérique

Cause of death — Cause de décès	2016 (C)				2017 (C)			
	Male — Masculin		Female — Féminin		Male — Masculin		Female — Féminin	
	Number Nombre	Rate Taux	Number Nombre	Rate Taux	Number Nombre	Rate Taux	Number Nombre	Rate Taux
TOTAL	**1 400 232**	**880.2**	**1 344 016**	**819.3**	**1 439 111**	**898.7**	**1 374 392**	**832.9**
Certain infectious and parasitic diseases — Certaines maladies infectieuses et parasitaires								
Total	**36 187**	**22.7**	**33 865**	**20.6**	**35 481**	**22.2**	**33 904**	**20.5**
Intestinal infectious diseases — Maladies infectieuses intestinales	**3 766**	**2.4**	**5 611**	**3.4**	**3 592**	**2.2**	**5 269**	**3.2**
Tuberculosis — Tuberculose	**333**	**0.2**	**195**	**0.1**	**321**	**0.2**	**194**	**0.1**
Tetanus — Tétanos	**1**	**♦0.0**	**1**	**♦0.0**	**1**	**♦0.0**	**-**	**-**
Diphtheria — Diphtérie	**-**	**-**	**-**	**-**	**-**	**-**	**-**	**-**
Whooping cough — Coqueluche	**5**	**♦0.0**	**6**	**♦0.0**	**6**	**♦0.0**	**3**	**♦0.0**
Meningococcal infection — Infection à méningocoques	**22**	**♦0.0**	**14**	**♦0.0**	**16**	**♦0.0**	**15**	**♦0.0**
Septicaemia — Septicémie	**19 678**	**12.4**	**20 935**	**12.8**	**19 603**	**12.2**	**21 319**	**12.9**
Acute poliomyelitis — Poliomyélite aiguë	**-**	**-**	**-**	**-**	**-**	**-**	**-**	**-**
Measles — Rougeole	**-**	**-**	**-**	**-**	**-**	**-**	**-**	**-**
Viral hepatitis — Hépatite virale	**4 185**	**2.6**	**2 236**	**1.4**	**3 685**	**2.3**	**1 926**	**1.2**
Human immunodeficiency virus [HIV] disease — Maladies dues au virus de l'immunodéficience humaine (VIH)	**4 554**	**2.9**	**1 606**	**1.0**	**4 207**	**2.6**	**1 491**	**0.9**
Malaria — Paludisme	**3**	**♦0.0**	**2**	**♦0.0**	**6**	**♦0.0**	**1**	**♦0.0**
Neoplasms — Tumeurs	**322 978**	**203.0**	**290 917**	**177.3**	**323 675**	**202.1**	**291 313**	**176.5**
Malignant neoplasms — Tumeurs malignes								
Total	**314 586**	**197.8**	**283 485**	**172.8**	**315 162**	**196.8**	**283 974**	**172.1**
Malignant neoplasm of lip, oral cavity and pharynx — Tumeur maligne de la lèvre, de la cavité buccale et du pharynx	**7 150**	**4.5**	**3 020**	**1.8**	**7 235**	**4.5**	**2 891**	**1.8**
Malignant neoplasm of oesophagus — Tumeur maligne de l'oesophage	**12 317**	**7.7**	**3 142**	**1.9**	**12 314**	**7.7**	**3 007**	**1.8**
Malignant neoplasm of stomach — Tumeur maligne de l'estomac	**6 845**	**4.3**	**4 588**	**2.8**	**6 680**	**4.2**	**4 478**	**2.7**
Malignant neoplasm of colon, rectosigmoid junction, rectum, anus and anal canal — Tumeur maligne du côlon, de la jonction recto-sigmoïdienne, du rectum, de l'anus et du canal anal	**27 934**	**17.6**	**25 211**	**15.4**	**28 093**	**17.5**	**25 354**	**15.4**
Malignant neoplasm of liver and intrahepatic bile ducts — Tumeur maligne du foie et des voies bilaires intrahépatiques	**17 843**	**11.2**	**8 726**	**5.3**	**18 246**	**11.4**	**8 860**	**5.4**
Malignant neoplasm of pancreas — Tumeur maligne du pancréas	**21 899**	**13.8**	**20 858**	**12.7**	**22 919**	**14.3**	**21 093**	**12.8**
Malignant neoplasm of trachea, bronchus and lung — Tumeur maligne de la trachée, des bronches et du poumon	**80 815**	**50.8**	**68 130**	**41.5**	**78 743**	**49.2**	**67 189**	**40.7**
Malignant neoplasm of female breast — Tumeur maligne du sein chez la femme	..	..	**41 488**	**30.9**	..	..	**42 000**	**31.1**
Malignant neoplasm of cervix uteri — Tumeur maligne du col de l'utérus	..	..	**4 188**	**3.1**	..	..	**4 208**	**3.1**
Malignant neoplasm of prostate — Tumeur maligne de la prostate	**30 370**	**57.8**	..	..	**30 488**	**57.3**	..	..
Malignant neoplasm of lymphoid, haematopoietic and related tissue — Tumeurs malignes primitives ou présumées primitives des tissus lymphoïde, hématopoïétique et apparentés	**32 244**	**20.3**	**25 023**	**15.3**	**32 951**	**20.6**	**24 814**	**15.0**
Disorders of the blood and blood-forming organs and certain disorders involving the immune mechanism — Maladies du sang et des organes hématopoïétiques et certains troubles du système immunitaire								
Total	**4 970**	**3.1**	**5 894**	**3.6**	**4 978**	**3.1**	**5 756**	**3.5**
Anaemias — Anémies	**2 293**	**1.4**	**3 056**	**1.9**	**2 395**	**1.5**	**2 987**	**1.8**
Endocrine, nutritional and metabolic diseases — Maladies endocriniennes, nutritionnelles et métaboliques								
Total	**63 415**	**39.9**	**57 843**	**35.3**	**67 375**	**42.1**	**60 572**	**36.7**
Diabetes mellitus — Diabète sucré	**43 763**	**27.5**	**36 295**	**22.1**	**46 302**	**28.9**	**37 262**	**22.6**
Malnutrition — Malnutrition	**2 341**	**1.5**	**3 786**	**2.3**	**2 776**	**1.7**	**4 816**	**2.9**
Mental and behavioural disorders — Troubles mentaux et du comportement	**49 520**	**31.1**	**83 084**	**50.6**	**51 001**	**31.9**	**84 771**	**51.4**
Diseases of the nervous system — Maladies du système nerveux	**80 351**	**50.5**	**122 001**	**74.4**	**86 359**	**53.9**	**129 994**	**78.8**
Diseases of the circulatory system — Maladies de l'appareil circulatoire								
Total	**428 424**	**269.3**	**412 232**	**251.3**	**440 448**	**275.1**	**418 650**	**253.7**
Acute rheumatic fever and chronic rheumatic heart diseases — Rhumatisme articularie aigu et cardiopathies rhumatismales chroniques	**1 208**	**0.8**	**2 345**	**1.4**	**1 103**	**0.7**	**2 217**	**1.3**
Hypertensive diseases — Maladies hypertensives	**39 571**	**24.9**	**43 147**	**26.3**	**43 121**	**26.9**	**46 960**	**28.5**
Ischaemic heart disease — Cardiopathie ischémique	**210 156**	**132.1**	**153 296**	**93.4**	**213 295**	**133.2**	**152 619**	**92.5**
Cerebrovascular disease — Maladie cérébrovasculaire	**59 355**	**37.3**	**82 787**	**50.5**	**61 645**	**38.5**	**84 738**	**51.3**

20. Death and death rates by cause and sex: 2014 - 2018
Décès et taux de mortalité par cause et sexe : 2014 - 2018 (continued - suite)

United States of America - États-Unis d'Amérique

Cause of death — Cause de décès	2016 (C)				2017 (C)			
	Male — Masculin		Female — Féminin		Male — Masculin		Female — Féminin	
	Number Nombre	Rate Taux	Number Nombre	Rate Taux	Number Nombre	Rate Taux	Number Nombre	Rate Taux
Diseases of arteries, arterioles and capillaries — Maladies des artères, artérioles et capillaires	12 845	8.1	12 454	7.6	12 768	8.0	12 466	7.6
Diseases of the respiratory system — Maladies de l'appareil respiratoire								
Total	129 707	81.5	136 330	83.1	134 855	84.2	143 818	87.2
Influenza — Grippe	1 280	0.8	1 372	0.8	2 816	1.8	3 664	2.2
Pneumonia — Pneumopathies	23 583	14.8	25 049	15.3	23 725	14.8	25 432	15.4
Chronic lower respiratory diseases — Maladies chroniques des voies respiratoires inférieures	73 045	45.9	81 551	49.7	75 005	46.8	85 196	51.6
Diseases of the digestive system — Maladies de l'appareil digestif								
Total	56 191	35.3	49 747	30.3	57 137	35.7	50 543	30.6
Gastric and duodenal ulcer — Ulcère de l'estomac et du duodénum	1 628	1.0	1 544	0.9	1 690	1.1	1 606	1.0
Diseases of the liver — Maladies du foie	32 390	20.4	20 723	12.6	33 005	20.6	21 390	13.0
Diseases of the musculoskeletal system and connective tissue — Maladies du système ostéo-articularie, des muscles et du tissu conjonctif	5 046	3.2	8 753	5.3	5 287	3.3	8 553	5.2
Diseases of the genitourinary system — Maladies de l'appareil génito-urinaire								
Total	33 815	21.3	36 501	22.3	34 687	21.7	36 766	22.3
Disorders of kidney and ureter — Affections du rein et de l'uretère	28 259	17.8	27 762	16.9	29 004	18.1	28 326	17.2
Hyperplasia of prostate — Hyperplasie de la prostate	642	1.2	..	..	619	1.2	..	..
Pregnancy, childbirth and the puerperium — Grossesse, accouchement et puerpéralité								
Total	..	..	1 231	31.2	..	..	1 208	31.3
Pregnancy with abortive outcome — Grossesse se terminant par un avortement	..	..	22	♦0.6	..	..	19	♦0.5
Other direct obstetric causes — Autres décès maternels directs	..	..	579	14.7	..	..	589	15.3
Indirect obstetric causes — Décès maternels indirects	..	..	261	6.6	..	..	224	5.8
Certain conditions originating in the perinatal period — Certaines affections dont l'origine se situe dans la période périnatale	6 415	...	5 078	...	6 303	319.5	4 805	255.2
Congenital malformations, deformations and chromosomal abnormalities — Malformations congénitales et anomalies chromosomiques	5 250	...	4 881	...	5 198	263.5	4 704	249.9
Symptoms, signs and abnormal clinical and laboratory findings, not elsewhere classified — Symptômes, signes et résultats anormaux d'examens cliniques et de laboratoire, non classés ailleurs	15 833	10.0	17 540	10.7	15 391	9.6	17 359	10.5
All other diseases — Toutes autres maladies	2 231	1.4	2 824	1.7	2 249	1.4	2 865	1.7
External causes — Causes externes								
Total	159 899	100.5	75 295	45.9	168 687	105.3	78 811	47.8
Accidents								
Total	102 453	64.4	56 887	34.7	108 327	67.7	59 556	36.1
Transport accidents — Accidents de transport	30 215	19.0	12 020	7.3	30 193	18.9	11 966	7.3
Falls — Chutes	17 370	10.9	17 303	10.5	18 392	11.5	17 946	10.9
Accidental drowning and submersion — Noyade et submersion accidentelles	2 931	1.8	855	0.5	2 802	1.7	907	0.5
Exposure to smoke, fire and flames — Exposition à la fumée, au feu et aux flammes	1 602	1.0	1 128	0.7	1 666	1.0	1 146	0.7
Accidental poisoning by and exposure to noxious substances — Intoxication accidentelle par des substances nocives et exposition à ces substances	39 810	25.0	18 525	11.3	44 545	27.8	20 250	12.3
Intentional self-harm — Lésions auto-infligées	34 656	21.8	10 220	6.2	36 726	22.9	10 381	6.3
Assault — Agresssions	15 253	9.6	3 850	2.3	15 317	9.6	3 952	2.4
All other external causes — Toutes autres causes externes	7 537	4.7	4 338	2.6	8 317	5.2	4 922	3.0

20. Death and death rates by cause and sex: 2014 - 2018
Décès et taux de mortalité par cause et sexe : 2014 - 2018 (continued - suite)

Cause of death — Cause de décès	United States Virgin Islands - Îles Vierges américaines				Argentina - Argentine			
	2016 (...)		2017 (...)		2016 (+C)			
	Male — Masculin	Female — Féminin	Male — Masculin	Female — Féminin	Male — Masculin		Female — Féminin	
	Number Nombre	Number Nombre	Number Nombre	Number Nombre	Number Nombre	Rate Taux	Number Nombre	Rate Taux
TOTAL	*376*	*256*	*429*	*278*	179 673	841.0	170 203	765.8
Certain infectious and parasitic diseases — Certaines maladies infectieuses et parasitaires								
Total	*8*	*7*	*11*	*4*	6 914	32.4	6 876	30.9
Intestinal infectious diseases — Maladies infectieuses intestinales	-	-	-	-	191	0.9	308	1.4
Tuberculosis — Tuberculose	-	-	-	-	403	1.9	219	1.0
Tetanus — Tétanos	-	-	-	-	2	♦0.0	3	♦0.0
Diphtheria — Diphtérie	-	-	-	-	-	-	-	-
Whooping cough — Coqueluche	-	-	-	-	11	♦0.1	12	♦0.1
Meningococcal infection — Infection à méningocoques	-	-	-	-	11	♦0.1	5	♦0.0
Septicaemia — Septicémie	*3*	*4*	*9*	*3*	4 701	22.0	5 305	23.9
Acute poliomyelitis — Poliomyélite aiguë	-	-	-	-	-	-	-	-
Measles — Rougeole	-	-	-	-	-	-	-	-
Viral hepatitis — Hépatite virale	*1*	*1*	-	-	103	0.5	87	0.4
Human immunodeficiency virus [HIV] disease — Maladies dues au virus de l'immunodéficience humaine (VIH)	*4*	*1*	*1*	-	1 005	4.7	469	2.1
Malaria — Paludisme	-	-	-	-	-	-	-	-
Neoplasms — Tumeurs	*86*	*48*	*77*	*44*	33 979	159.0	31 329	141.0
Malignant neoplasms — Tumeurs malignes								
Total	*85*	*46*	*73*	*42*	32 312	151.2	29 926	134.6
Malignant neoplasm of lip, oral cavity and pharynx — Tumeur maligne de la lèvre, de la cavité buccale et du pharynx	*2*	*2*	-	-	602	2.8	289	1.3
Malignant neoplasm of oesophagus — Tumeur maligne de l'oesophage	*3*	*1*	-	*1*	1 193	5.6	554	2.5
Malignant neoplasm of stomach — Tumeur maligne de l'estomac	*5*	*1*	*2*	*1*	1 874	8.8	1 053	4.7
Malignant neoplasm of colon, rectosigmoid junction, rectum, anus and anal canal — Tumeur maligne du côlon, de la jonction recto-sigmoïdienne, du rectum, de l'anus et du canal anal	*9*	*5*	*13*	*4*	4 098	19.2	3 492	15.7
Malignant neoplasm of liver and intrahepatic bile ducts — Tumeur maligne du foie et des voies bilaires intrahépatiques	*2*	*1*	*2*	*1*	1 083	5.1	787	3.5
Malignant neoplasm of pancreas — Tumeur maligne du pancréas	*12*	*3*	*6*	*1*	1 967	9.2	2 219	10.0
Malignant neoplasm of trachea, bronchus and lung — Tumeur maligne de la trachée, des bronches et du poumon	*9*	*6*	*4*	*4*	6 343	29.7	3 137	14.1
Malignant neoplasm of female breast — Tumeur maligne du sein chez la femme	..	*13*	..	*15*	..	..	5 851	34.6
Malignant neoplasm of cervix uteri — Tumeur maligne du col de l'utérus	..	*1*	..	*3*	..	..	1 197	7.1
Malignant neoplasm of prostate — Tumeur maligne de la prostate	*15*	..	*21*	..	3 832	79.4	..	..
Malignant neoplasm of lymphoid, haematopoietic and related tissue — Tumeurs malignes primitives ou présumées primitives des tissus lymphoïde, hématopoïétique et apparentés	*9*	*1*	*2*	*3*	2 369	11.1	1 871	8.4
Disorders of the blood and blood-forming organs and certain disorders involving the immune mechanism — Maladies du sang et des organes hématopoïétiques et certains troubles du système immunitaire								
Total	*4*	*1*	*1*	-	607	2.8	833	3.7
Anaemias — Anémies	*2*	*1*	*1*	-	387	1.8	579	2.6
Endocrine, nutritional and metabolic diseases — Maladies endocriniennes, nutritionnelles et métaboliques								
Total	*12*	*23*	*26*	*20*	6 552	30.7	6 686	30.1
Diabetes mellitus — Diabète sucré	*7*	*19*	*23*	*15*	5 045	23.6	4 477	20.1
Malnutrition — Malnutrition	*1*	*1*	-	*1*	392	1.8	449	2.0
Mental and behavioural disorders — Troubles mentaux et du comportement	*13*	*7*	*11*	*17*	1 238	5.8	1 610	7.2
Diseases of the nervous system — Maladies du système nerveux	*18*	*22*	*24*	*30*	2 638	12.3	3 078	13.8
Diseases of the circulatory system — Maladies de l'appareil circulatoire								
Total	*121*	*77*	*123*	*107*	50 166	234.8	50 928	229.1
Acute rheumatic fever and chronic rheumatic heart diseases — Rhumatisme articularie aigu et cardiopathies rhumatismales chroniques	-	-	-	*1*	55	0.3	97	0.4
Hypertensive diseases — Maladies hypertensives	*19*	*11*	*33*	*35*	3 683	17.2	5 037	22.7
Ischaemic heart disease — Cardiopathie ischémique	*61*	*35*	*45*	*20*	13 475	63.1	9 650	43.4

20. Death and death rates by cause and sex: 2014 - 2018
Décès et taux de mortalité par cause et sexe : 2014 - 2018 (continued - suite)

Cause of death — Cause de décès	United States Virgin Islands - Îles Vierges américaines				Argentina - Argentine			
	2016 (...)		2017 (...)		2016 (+C)			
	Male — Masculin	Female — Féminin	Male — Masculin	Female — Féminin	Male — Masculin		Female — Féminin	
	Number Nombre	Number Nombre	Number Nombre	Number Nombre	Number Nombre	Rate Taux	Number Nombre	Rate Taux
Cerebrovascular disease — Maladie cérébrovasculaire	*20*	*15*	*24*	*23*	10 598	49.6	10 769	48.5
Diseases of arteries, arterioles and capillaries — Maladies des artères, artérioles et capillaires	*3*	*2*	-	*1*	1 489	7.0	974	4.4
Diseases of the respiratory system — Maladies de l'appareil respiratoire								
Total	*16*	*18*	*13*	*8*	31 166	145.9	33 575	151.1
Influenza — Grippe	-	-	-	-	25	♦0.1	23	♦0.1
Pneumonia — Pneumopathies	*5*	*6*	*4*	*2*	15 713	73.5	17 555	79.0
Chronic lower respiratory diseases — Maladies chroniques des voies respiratoires inférieures	*5*	*8*	*6*	*4*	4 315	20.2	2 990	13.5
Diseases of the digestive system — Maladies de l'appareil digestif								
Total	*16*	*6*	*14*	*10*	10 104	47.3	6 758	30.4
Gastric and duodenal ulcer — Ulcère de l'estomac et du duodénum	*1*	-	*1*	-	280	1.3	176	0.8
Diseases of the liver — Maladies du foie	*10*	*2*	*9*	*5*	4 751	22.2	1 494	6.7
Diseases of the musculoskeletal system and connective tissue — Maladies du système ostéo-articularie, des muscles et du tissu conjonctif	*4*	*1*	*1*	*3*	366	1.7	791	3.6
Diseases of the genitourinary system — Maladies de l'appareil génito-urinaire								
Total	*14*	*12*	*15*	*13*	6 265	29.3	6 985	31.4
Disorders of kidney and ureter — Affections du rein et de l'uretère	*13*	*10*	*10*	*11*	4 512	21.1	4 320	19.4
Hyperplasia of prostate — Hyperplasie de la prostate	-	..	-	..	34	0.7	..	..
Pregnancy, childbirth and the puerperium — Grossesse, accouchement et puerpéralité								
Total	..	-	..	-	..	..	284	39.0
Pregnancy with abortive outcome — Grossesse se terminant par un avortement	..	-	..	-	..	..	43	5.9
Other direct obstetric causes — Autres décès maternels directs	..	-	..	-	..	..	134	18.4
Indirect obstetric causes — Décès maternels indirects	..	-	..	-	..	..	66	9.1
Certain conditions originating in the perinatal period — Certaines affections dont l'origine se situe dans la période périnatale	-	*2*	*5*	*3*	2 005	534.8	1 424	403.5
Congenital malformations, deformations and chromosomal abnormalities — Malformations congénitales et anomalies chromosomiques	*1*	-	-	-	1 298	346.2	1 140	323.1
Symptoms, signs and abnormal clinical and laboratory findings, not elsewhere classified — Symptômes, signes et résultats anormaux d'examens cliniques et de laboratoire, non classés ailleurs	*7*	*17*	*16*	*7*	11 248	52.6	11 201	50.4
All other diseases — Toutes autres maladies	-	*3*	*1*	*2*	1 077	5.0	1 767	8.0
External causes — Causes externes								
Total	*56*	*12*	*91*	*10*	14 050	65.8	4 938	22.2
Accidents								
Total	*18*	*7*	*29*	*7*	6 388	29.9	2 749	12.4
Transport accidents — Accidents de transport	*6*	*4*	*13*	*3*	3 324	15.6	997	4.5
Falls — Chutes	*2*	-	*3*	*1*	280	1.3	136	0.6
Accidental drowning and submersion — Noyade et submersion accidentelles	*6*	*2*	*8*	*1*	368	1.7	61	0.3
Exposure to smoke, fire and flames — Exposition à la fumée, au feu et aux flammes	-	-	-	-	164	0.8	74	0.3
Accidental poisoning by and exposure to noxious substances — Intoxication accidentelle par des substances nocives et exposition à ces substances	*1*	-	-	-	134	0.6	63	0.3
Intentional self-harm — Lésions auto-infligées	*2*	-	*9*	*1*	2 477	11.6	569	2.6
Assault — Agresssions	*36*	*5*	*52*	*2*	1 769	8.3	304	1.4
All other external causes — Toutes autres causes externes	-	-	*1*	-	3 416	16.0	1 316	5.9

20. Death and death rates by cause and sex: 2014 - 2018
Décès et taux de mortalité par cause et sexe : 2014 - 2018 (continued - suite)

Cause of death — Cause de décès	Argentina - Argentine				Brazil - Brésil			
	2017 (+C)				2016 (C)			
	Male — Masculin		Female — Féminin		Male — Masculin		Female — Féminin	
	Number Nombre	Rate Taux	Number Nombre	Rate Taux	Number Nombre	Rate Taux	Number Nombre	Rate Taux
TOTAL	**174 222**	**806.7**	**166 730**	**742.7**	**736 842**	**724.3**	**572 359**	**548.5**
Certain infectious and parasitic diseases — Certaines maladies infectieuses et parasitaires								
Total	7 115	32.9	7 047	31.4	32 164	31.6	25 007	24.0
Intestinal infectious diseases — Maladies infectieuses intestinales	282	1.3	365	1.6	2 108	2.1	2 683	2.6
Tuberculosis — Tuberculose	366	1.7	217	1.0	3 340	3.3	1 142	1.1
Tetanus — Tétanos	1	♦0.0	1	♦0.0	69	0.1	12	♦0.0
Diphtheria — Diphtérie	-	-	-	-	2	♦0.0	3	♦0.0
Whooping cough — Coqueluche	-	-	5	♦0.0	4	♦0.0	5	♦0.0
Meningococcal infection — Infection à méningocoques	8	♦0.0	9	♦0.0	103	0.1	88	0.1
Septicaemia — Septicémie	4 815	22.3	5 470	24.4	9 769	9.6	10 091	9.7
Acute poliomyelitis — Poliomyélite aiguë	-	-	-	-	-	-	-	-
Measles — Rougeole	-	-	-	-	-	-	1	♦0.0
Viral hepatitis — Hépatite virale	93	0.4	85	0.4	1 772	1.7	1 065	1.0
Human immunodeficiency virus [HIV] disease — Maladies dues au virus de l'immunodéficience humaine (VIH)	984	4.6	468	2.1	8 254	8.1	4 282	4.1
Malaria — Paludisme	-	-	-	-	17	♦0.0	18	♦0.0
Neoplasms — Tumeurs	33 857	156.8	31 532	140.5	114 257	112.3	100 964	96.8
Malignant neoplasms — Tumeurs malignes								
Total	32 395	150.0	30 241	134.7	112 277	110.4	99 065	94.9
Malignant neoplasm of lip, oral cavity and pharynx — Tumeur maligne de la lèvre, de la cavité buccale et du pharynx	644	3.0	300	1.3	6 360	6.3	1 606	1.5
Malignant neoplasm of oesophagus — Tumeur maligne de l'oesophage	1 173	5.4	547	2.4	6 499	6.4	1 839	1.8
Malignant neoplasm of stomach — Tumeur maligne de l'estomac	1 907	8.8	1 095	4.9	9 424	9.3	5 226	5.0
Malignant neoplasm of colon, rectosigmoid junction, rectum, anus and anal canal — Tumeur maligne du côlon, de la jonction recto-sigmoïdienne, du rectum, de l'anus et du canal anal	4 087	18.9	3 412	15.2	8 829	8.7	8 869	8.5
Malignant neoplasm of liver and intrahepatic bile ducts — Tumeur maligne du foie et des voies bilaires intrahépatiques	1 158	5.4	827	3.7	5 681	5.6	4 105	3.9
Malignant neoplasm of pancreas — Tumeur maligne du pancréas	2 062	9.5	2 240	10.0	5 004	4.9	4 907	4.7
Malignant neoplasm of trachea, bronchus and lung — Tumeur maligne de la trachée, des bronches et du poumon	6 309	29.2	3 176	14.1	15 968	15.7	11 297	10.8
Malignant neoplasm of female breast — Tumeur maligne du sein chez la femme	..	..	6 049	35.3	..	..	16 069	19.7
Malignant neoplasm of cervix uteri — Tumeur maligne du col de l'utérus	..	..	1 216	7.1	..	..	5 847	7.2
Malignant neoplasm of prostate — Tumeur maligne de la prostate	3 771	76.8	..	..	14 926	69.0	..	..
Malignant neoplasm of lymphoid, haematopoietic and related tissue — Tumeurs malignes primitives ou présumées primitives des tissus lymphoïde, hématopoïétique et apparentés	2 363	10.9	1 875	8.4	8 309	8.2	6 988	6.7
Disorders of the blood and blood-forming organs and certain disorders involving the immune mechanism — Maladies du sang et des organes hématopoïétiques et certains troubles du système immunitaire								
Total	636	2.9	784	3.5	3 382	3.3	3 476	3.3
Anaemias — Anémies	403	1.9	553	2.5	2 240	2.2	2 333	2.2
Endocrine, nutritional and metabolic diseases — Maladies endocriniennes, nutritionnelles et métaboliques								
Total	6 082	28.2	6 304	28.1	35 690	35.1	42 379	40.6
Diabetes mellitus — Diabète sucré	4 655	21.6	4 214	18.8	27 740	27.3	33 653	32.2
Malnutrition — Malnutrition	360	1.7	408	1.8	3 193	3.1	2 914	2.8
Mental and behavioural disorders — Troubles mentaux et du comportement	991	4.6	1 285	5.7	8 819	8.7	3 729	3.6
Diseases of the nervous system — Maladies du système nerveux	2 392	11.1	2 741	12.2	16 848	16.6	20 020	19.2
Diseases of the circulatory system — Maladies de l'appareil circulatoire								
Total	48 321	223.8	48 690	216.9	190 219	187.0	171 802	164.6
Acute rheumatic fever and chronic rheumatic heart diseases — Rhumatisme articularie aigu et cardiopathies rhumatismales chroniques	41	0.2	82	0.4	778	0.8	1 289	1.2
Hypertensive diseases — Maladies hypertensives	3 629	16.8	4 766	21.2	23 529	23.1	26 106	25.0
Ischaemic heart disease — Cardiopathie ischémique	12 985	60.1	9 348	41.6	68 018	66.9	48 104	46.1
Cerebrovascular disease — Maladie cérébrovasculaire	9 941	46.0	9 936	44.3	51 753	50.9	51 198	49.1

20. Death and death rates by cause and sex: 2014 - 2018
Décès et taux de mortalité par cause et sexe : 2014 - 2018 (continued - suite)

Cause of death — Cause de décès	Argentina - Argentine				Brazil - Brésil			
	2017 (+C)				2016 (C)			
	Male — Masculin		Female — Féminin		Male — Masculin		Female — Féminin	
	Number Nombre	Rate Taux	Number Nombre	Rate Taux	Number Nombre	Rate Taux	Number Nombre	Rate Taux
Diseases of arteries, arterioles and capillaries — Maladies des artères, artérioles et capillaires	1 420	6.6	943	4.2	7 368	7.2	6 084	5.8
Diseases of the respiratory system — Maladies de l'appareil respiratoire								
Total	30 480	141.1	34 253	152.6	81 437	80.1	76 583	73.4
Influenza — Grippe	15	♦0.1	18	♦0.1	400	0.4	358	0.3
Pneumonia — Pneumopathies	15 304	70.9	18 074	80.5	40 779	40.1	41 550	39.8
Chronic lower respiratory diseases — Maladies chroniques des voies respiratoires inférieures	4 237	19.6	3 032	13.5	25 551	25.1	20 770	19.9
Diseases of the digestive system — Maladies de l'appareil digestif								
Total	9 140	42.3	6 523	29.1	40 850	40.2	25 207	24.2
Gastric and duodenal ulcer — Ulcère de l'estomac et du duodénum	229	1.1	184	0.8	2 205	2.2	1 349	1.3
Diseases of the liver — Maladies du foie	4 082	18.9	1 457	6.5	20 584	20.2	6 290	6.0
Diseases of the musculoskeletal system and connective tissue — Maladies du système ostéo-articularie, des muscles et du tissu conjonctif	360	1.7	753	3.4	2 184	2.1	3 603	3.5
Diseases of the genitourinary system — Maladies de l'appareil génito-urinaire								
Total	6 202	28.7	6 884	30.7	19 012	18.7	20 348	19.5
Disorders of kidney and ureter — Affections du rein et de l'uretère	4 368	20.2	4 188	18.7	10 589	10.4	9 088	8.7
Hyperplasia of prostate — Hyperplasie de la prostate	44	0.9	..	..	838	3.9	..	..
Pregnancy, childbirth and the puerperium — Grossesse, accouchement et puerpéralité								
Total	..	..	246	34.9	..	..	1 814	62.5
Pregnancy with abortive outcome — Grossesse se terminant par un avortement	..	..	30	♦4.3	..	..	127	4.4
Other direct obstetric causes — Autres décès maternels directs	..	..	118	16.7	..	..	1 075	37.0
Indirect obstetric causes — Décès maternels indirects	..	..	54	7.7	..	..	448	15.4
Certain conditions originating in the perinatal period — Certaines affections dont l'origine se situe dans la période périnatale	1 927	539.1	1 457	425.2	11 922	801.5	9 071	640.5
Congenital malformations, deformations and chromosomal abnormalities — Malformations congénitales et anomalies chromosomiques	1 217	340.5	1 138	332.1	5 603	376.7	5 148	363.5
Symptoms, signs and abnormal clinical and laboratory findings, not elsewhere classified — Symptômes, signes et résultats anormaux d'examens cliniques et de laboratoire, non classés ailleurs	10 269	47.6	10 222	45.5	43 448	42.7	32 335	31.0
All other diseases — Toutes autres maladies	1 061	4.9	1 684	7.5	2 747	2.7	3 317	3.2
External causes — Causes externes								
Total	14 172	65.6	5 187	23.1	128 260	126.1	27 556	26.4
Accidents								
Total	6 533	30.3	2 844	12.7	52 673	51.8	16 903	16.2
Transport accidents — Accidents de transport	3 606	16.7	1 062	4.7	31 565	31.0	6 685	6.4
Falls — Chutes	256	1.2	136	0.6	8 618	8.5	6 212	6.0
Accidental drowning and submersion — Noyade et submersion accidentelles	309	1.4	64	0.3	4 443	4.4	625	0.6
Exposure to smoke, fire and flames — Exposition à la fumée, au feu et aux flammes	150	0.7	74	0.3	640	0.6	318	0.3
Accidental poisoning by and exposure to noxious substances — Intoxication accidentelle par des substances nocives et exposition à ces substances	141	0.7	82	0.4	808	0.8	256	0.2
Intentional self-harm — Lésions auto-infligées	2 580	11.9	636	2.8	9 052	8.9	2 377	2.3
Assault — Agresssions	1 424	6.6	294	1.3	56 409	55.5	4 635	4.4
All other external causes — Toutes autres causes externes	3 635	16.8	1 413	6.3	10 126	10.0	3 641	3.5

20. Death and death rates by cause and sex: 2014 - 2018
Décès et taux de mortalité par cause et sexe : 2014 - 2018 (continued - suite)

Cause of death — Cause de décès	Brazil - Brésil				Chile - Chili			
	2017 (C)				2016 (C)			
	Male — Masculin		Female — Féminin		Male — Masculin		Female — Féminin	
	Number Nombre	Rate Taux	Number Nombre	Rate Taux	Number Nombre	Rate Taux	Number Nombre	Rate Taux
TOTAL	**734 470**	**716.8**	**577 573**	**549.1**	**54 761**	**612.3**	**49 239**	**533.8**
Certain infectious and parasitic diseases — Certaines maladies infectieuses et parasitaires								
Total	30 787	30.0	24 080	22.9	1 328	14.8	955	10.4
Intestinal infectious diseases — Maladies infectieuses intestinales	2 031	2.0	2 764	2.6	131	1.5	196	2.1
Tuberculosis — Tuberculose	3 443	3.4	1 170	1.1	149	1.7	70	0.8
Tetanus — Tétanos	62	0.1	18	♦0.0	1	♦0.0	1	♦0.0
Diphtheria — Diphtérie	5	♦0.0	5	♦0.0	-	-	-	-
Whooping cough — Coqueluche	8	♦0.0	9	♦0.0	3	♦0.0	3	♦0.0
Meningococcal infection — Infection à méningocoques	110	0.1	108	0.1	11	♦0.1	17	♦0.2
Septicaemia — Septicémie	9 175	9.0	9 670	9.2	250	2.8	307	3.3
Acute poliomyelitis — Poliomyélite aiguë	-	-	-	-	-	-	-	-
Measles — Rougeole	2	♦0.0	-	-	-	-	-	-
Viral hepatitis — Hépatite virale	1 517	1.5	942	0.9	33	0.4	22	♦0.2
Human immunodeficiency virus [HIV] disease — Maladies dues au virus de l'immunodéficience humaine (VIH)	7 781	7.6	3 952	3.8	484	5.4	81	0.9
Malaria — Paludisme	26	♦0.0	8	♦0.0	-	-	-	-
Neoplasms — Tumeurs	116 628	113.8	105 207	100.0	14 269	159.5	12 914	140.0
Malignant neoplasms — Tumeurs malignes								
Total	114 570	111.8	103 124	98.0	13 656	152.7	12 371	134.1
Malignant neoplasm of lip, oral cavity and pharynx — Tumeur maligne de la lèvre, de la cavité buccale et du pharynx	6 453	6.3	1 672	1.6	187	2.1	101	1.1
Malignant neoplasm of oesophagus — Tumeur maligne de l'oesophage	6 647	6.5	1 907	1.8	431	4.8	219	2.4
Malignant neoplasm of stomach — Tumeur maligne de l'estomac	9 206	9.0	5 107	4.9	2 153	24.1	1 097	11.9
Malignant neoplasm of colon, rectosigmoid junction, rectum, anus and anal canal — Tumeur maligne du côlon, de la jonction recto-sigmoïdienne, du rectum, de l'anus et du canal anal	9 207	9.0	9 660	9.2	1 268	14.2	1 326	14.4
Malignant neoplasm of liver and intrahepatic bile ducts — Tumeur maligne du foie et des voies bilaires intrahépatiques	5 908	5.8	4 292	4.1	692	7.7	600	6.5
Malignant neoplasm of pancreas — Tumeur maligne du pancréas	5 316	5.2	5 438	5.2	662	7.4	816	8.8
Malignant neoplasm of trachea, bronchus and lung — Tumeur maligne de la trachée, des bronches et du poumon	16 137	15.7	11 792	11.2	1 875	21.0	1 292	14.0
Malignant neoplasm of female breast — Tumeur maligne du sein chez la femme	..	..	16 724	20.2	..	..	1 490	20.2
Malignant neoplasm of cervix uteri — Tumeur maligne du col de l'utérus	..	..	6 385	7.7	..	..	624	8.4
Malignant neoplasm of prostate — Tumeur maligne de la prostate	15 391	68.9	..	..	2 108	88.1	..	..
Malignant neoplasm of lymphoid, haematopoietic and related tissue — Tumeurs malignes primitives ou présumées primitives des tissus lymphoïde, hématopoïétique et apparentés	8 194	8.0	7 002	6.7	1 108	12.4	917	9.9
Disorders of the blood and blood-forming organs and certain disorders involving the immune mechanism — Maladies du sang et des organes hématopoïétiques et certains troubles du système immunitaire								
Total	3 207	3.1	3 394	3.2	217	2.4	309	3.4
Anaemias — Anémies	2 125	2.1	2 184	2.1	153	1.7	255	2.8
Endocrine, nutritional and metabolic diseases — Maladies endocriniennes, nutritionnelles et métaboliques								
Total	36 914	36.0	42 741	40.6	2 773	31.0	3 292	35.7
Diabetes mellitus — Diabète sucré	29 115	28.4	34 367	32.7	2 247	25.1	2 582	28.0
Malnutrition — Malnutrition	2 922	2.9	2 729	2.6	212	2.4	236	2.6
Mental and behavioural disorders — Troubles mentaux et du comportement	8 926	8.7	3 809	3.6	718	8.0	1 076	11.7
Diseases of the nervous system — Maladies du système nerveux	17 465	17.0	21 314	20.3	1 641	18.3	2 066	22.4
Diseases of the circulatory system — Maladies de l'appareil circulatoire								
Total	187 934	183.4	170 880	162.4	14 287	159.7	13 861	150.3
Acute rheumatic fever and chronic rheumatic heart diseases — Rhumatisme articularie aigu et cardiopathies rhumatismales chroniques	741	0.7	1 293	1.2	45	0.5	75	0.8
Hypertensive diseases — Maladies hypertensives	24 719	24.1	27 832	26.5	2 457	27.5	3 447	37.4
Ischaemic heart disease — Cardiopathie ischémique	67 210	65.6	47 840	45.5	4 962	55.5	3 193	34.6
Cerebrovascular disease — Maladie cérébrovasculaire	50 919	49.7	50 269	47.8	4 148	46.4	4 289	46.5

20. Death and death rates by cause and sex: 2014 - 2018
Décès et taux de mortalité par cause et sexe : 2014 - 2018 (continued - suite)

Cause of death — Cause de décès	Brazil - Brésil				Chile - Chili			
	2017 (C)				2016 (C)			
	Male — Masculin		Female — Féminin		Male — Masculin		Female — Féminin	
	Number Nombre	Rate Taux	Number Nombre	Rate Taux	Number Nombre	Rate Taux	Number Nombre	Rate Taux
Diseases of arteries, arterioles and capillaries — Maladies des artères, artérioles et capillaires	7 458	7.3	6 053	5.8	476	5.3	385	4.2
Diseases of the respiratory system — Maladies de l'appareil respiratoire								
Total	78 785	76.9	76 812	73.0	4 854	54.3	4 993	54.1
Influenza — Grippe	247	0.2	284	0.3	42	0.5	35	0.4
Pneumonia — Pneumopathies	38 531	37.6	40 822	38.8	1 540	17.2	1 626	17.6
Chronic lower respiratory diseases — Maladies chroniques des voies respiratoires inférieures	26 298	25.7	22 518	21.4	1 633	18.3	1 704	18.5
Diseases of the digestive system — Maladies de l'appareil digestif								
Total	40 575	39.6	25 504	24.2	4 649	52.0	3 048	33.0
Gastric and duodenal ulcer — Ulcère de l'estomac et du duodénum	2 300	2.2	1 491	1.4	115	1.3	75	0.8
Diseases of the liver — Maladies du foie	20 069	19.6	6 135	5.8	3 132	35.0	1 326	14.4
Diseases of the musculoskeletal system and connective tissue — Maladies du système ostéo-articularie, des muscles et du tissu conjonctif	2 174	2.1	3 736	3.6	183	2.0	532	5.8
Diseases of the genitourinary system — Maladies de l'appareil génito-urinaire								
Total	19 261	18.8	21 206	20.2	1 562	17.5	1 777	19.3
Disorders of kidney and ureter — Affections du rein et de l'uretère	10 756	10.5	9 400	8.9	1 054	11.8	1 135	12.3
Hyperplasia of prostate — Hyperplasie de la prostate	882	3.9	..	..	62	2.6	..	..
Pregnancy, childbirth and the puerperium — Grossesse, accouchement et puerpéralité								
Total	..	..	1 874	63.3	..	..	51	22.0
Pregnancy with abortive outcome — Grossesse se terminant par un avortement	..	..	138	4.7	..	..	1	♦0.4
Other direct obstetric causes — Autres décès maternels directs	..	..	1 124	37.9	..	..	16	♦6.9
Indirect obstetric causes — Décès maternels indirects	..	..	437	14.7	..	..	4	♦1.7
Certain conditions originating in the perinatal period — Certaines affections dont l'origine se situe dans la période périnatale	11 904	784.0	9 484	656.8	404	343.0	302	265.1
Congenital malformations, deformations and chromosomal abnormalities — Malformations congénitales et anomalies chromosomiques	5 693	374.9	5 161	357.4	480	407.5	463	406.4
Symptoms, signs and abnormal clinical and laboratory findings, not elsewhere classified — Symptômes, signes et résultats anormaux d'examens cliniques et de laboratoire, non classés ailleurs	41 534	40.5	30 170	28.7	1 349	15.1	1 417	15.4
All other diseases — Toutes autres maladies	2 695	2.6	3 602	3.4	184	2.1	273	3.0
External causes — Causes externes								
Total	129 988	126.9	28 599	27.2	5 863	65.6	1 910	20.7
Accidents								
Total	51 210	50.0	17 397	16.5	3 603	40.3	1 452	15.7
Transport accidents — Accidents de transport	29 935	29.2	6 466	6.1	1 677	18.8	475	5.1
Falls — Chutes	8 788	8.6	6 877	6.5	414	4.6	518	5.6
Accidental drowning and submersion — Noyade et submersion accidentelles	4 370	4.3	644	0.6	280	3.1	43	0.5
Exposure to smoke, fire and flames — Exposition à la fumée, au feu et aux flammes	604	0.6	295	0.3	197	2.2	93	1.0
Accidental poisoning by and exposure to noxious substances — Intoxication accidentelle par des substances nocives et exposition à ces substances	767	0.7	251	0.2	160	1.8	51	0.6
Intentional self-harm — Lésions auto-infligées	9 826	9.6	2 664	2.5	1 541	17.2	317	3.4
Assault — Agresssions	58 713	57.3	4 928	4.7	616	6.9	85	0.9
All other external causes — Toutes autres causes externes	10 239	10.0	3 610	3.4	103	1.2	56	0.6

20. Death and death rates by cause and sex: 2014 - 2018
Décès et taux de mortalité par cause et sexe : 2014 - 2018 (continued - suite)

Cause of death — Cause de décès	Chile - Chili				Colombia - Colombie			
	2017 (C)				2016 (U)		2017 (U)	
	Male — Masculin		Female — Féminin		Male — Masculin	Female — Féminin	Male — Masculin	Female — Féminin
	Number Nombre	Rate Taux	Number Nombre	Rate Taux	Number Nombre	Number Nombre	Number Nombre	Number Nombre
TOTAL	**55 773**	**614.6**	**50 593**	**541.4**	***123 806***	***99 242***	***125 450***	***102 119***
Certain infectious and parasitic diseases — Certaines maladies infectieuses et parasitaires								
Total	1 280	14.1	1 020	10.9	*4 314*	*2 320*	*4 105*	*2 038*
Intestinal infectious diseases — Maladies infectieuses intestinales	102	1.1	217	2.3	*360*	*408*	*321*	*372*
Tuberculosis — Tuberculose	152	1.7	58	0.6	*706*	*291*	*699*	*251*
Tetanus — Tétanos	1	♦0.0	-	-	*13*	*6*	*8*	*2*
Diphtheria — Diphtérie	-	-	-	-	*1*	-	-	-
Whooping cough — Coqueluche	3	♦0.0	6	♦0.1	*6*	*6*	*5*	*3*
Meningococcal infection — Infection à méningocoques	11	♦0.1	18	♦0.2	*10*	*13*	*7*	*10*
Septicaemia — Septicémie	293	3.2	348	3.7	*513*	*530*	*506*	*466*
Acute poliomyelitis — Poliomyélite aiguë	-	-	-	-	-	-	-	-
Measles — Rougeole	-	-	-	-	-	*1*	-	-
Viral hepatitis — Hépatite virale	28	♦0.3	25	♦0.3	*60*	*57*	*63*	*59*
Human immunodeficiency virus [HIV] disease — Maladies dues au virus de l'immunodéficience humaine (VIH)	401	4.4	80	0.9	*2 024*	*594*	*1 972*	*543*
Malaria — Paludisme	-	-	-	-	*25*	*20*	*11*	*9*
Neoplasms — Tumeurs	**14 343**	**158.1**	**13 161**	**140.8**	***21 604***	***22 497***	***22 593***	***23 392***
Malignant neoplasms — Tumeurs malignes								
Total	13 669	150.6	12 560	134.4	*19 999*	*20 860*	*20 918*	*21 692*
Malignant neoplasm of lip, oral cavity and pharynx — Tumeur maligne de la lèvre, de la cavité buccale et du pharynx	148	1.6	98	1.0	*394*	*280*	*393*	*291*
Malignant neoplasm of oesophagus — Tumeur maligne de l'oesophage	400	4.4	225	2.4	*468*	*235*	*468*	*223*
Malignant neoplasm of stomach — Tumeur maligne de l'estomac	2 191	24.1	1 107	11.8	*3 112*	*1 974*	*3 202*	*1 999*
Malignant neoplasm of colon, rectosigmoid junction, rectum, anus and anal canal — Tumeur maligne du côlon, de la jonction recto-sigmoïdienne, du rectum, de l'anus et du canal anal	1 302	14.3	1 356	14.5	*1 820*	*1 867*	*1 785*	*2 107*
Malignant neoplasm of liver and intrahepatic bile ducts — Tumeur maligne du foie et des voies bilaires intrahépatiques	649	7.2	580	6.2	*889*	*994*	*897*	*934*
Malignant neoplasm of pancreas — Tumeur maligne du pancréas	649	7.2	815	8.7	*863*	*975*	*939*	*948*
Malignant neoplasm of trachea, bronchus and lung — Tumeur maligne de la trachée, des bronches et du poumon	1 897	20.9	1 379	14.8	*2 712*	*1 945*	*2 788*	*2 009*
Malignant neoplasm of female breast — Tumeur maligne du sein chez la femme	..	..	1 504	20.1	..	*3 157*	..	*3 300*
Malignant neoplasm of cervix uteri — Tumeur maligne du col de l'utérus	..	..	601	8.0	..	*1 732*	..	*1 715*
Malignant neoplasm of prostate — Tumeur maligne de la prostate	2 185	88.5	..	..	*2 955*	..	*3 065*	..
Malignant neoplasm of lymphoid, haematopoietic and related tissue — Tumeurs malignes primitives ou présumées primitives des tissus lymphoïde, hématopoïétique et apparentés	1 120	12.3	937	10.0	*2 202*	*1 846*	*2 349*	*1 888*
Disorders of the blood and blood-forming organs and certain disorders involving the immune mechanism — Maladies du sang et des organes hématopoïétiques et certains troubles du système immunitaire								
Total	240	2.6	307	3.3	*409*	*391*	*381*	*403*
Anaemias — Anémies	170	1.9	226	2.4	*200*	*193*	*194*	*217*
Endocrine, nutritional and metabolic diseases — Maladies endocriniennes, nutritionnelles et métaboliques								
Total	2 811	31.0	3 105	33.2	*4 460*	*5 270*	*4 531*	*5 264*
Diabetes mellitus — Diabète sucré	2 330	25.7	2 464	26.4	*3 289*	*3 964*	*3 383*	*4 117*
Malnutrition — Malnutrition	199	2.2	193	2.1	*839*	*907*	*832*	*732*
Mental and behavioural disorders — Troubles mentaux et du comportement	803	8.8	1 126	12.0	*279*	*439*	*261*	*376*
Diseases of the nervous system — Maladies du système nerveux	1 770	19.5	2 208	23.6	*2 159*	*1 950*	*1 977*	*1 868*
Diseases of the circulatory system — Maladies de l'appareil circulatoire								
Total	14 433	159.1	14 156	151.5	*36 843*	*33 778*	*37 434*	*35 040*
Acute rheumatic fever and chronic rheumatic heart diseases — Rhumatisme articularie aigu et cardiopathies rhumatismales chroniques	29	♦0.3	57	0.6	*9*	*24*	*14*	*19*
Hypertensive diseases — Maladies hypertensives	2 576	28.4	3 702	39.6	*4 115*	*4 315*	*4 250*	*4 591*
Ischaemic heart disease — Cardiopathie ischémique	4 976	54.8	3 327	35.6	*20 625*	*16 827*	*21 012*	*17 606*

20. Death and death rates by cause and sex: 2014 - 2018
Décès et taux de mortalité par cause et sexe : 2014 - 2018 (continued - suite)

Cause of death — Cause de décès	Chile - Chili				Colombia - Colombie			
	2017 (C)				2016 (U)		2017 (U)	
	Male — Masculin		Female — Féminin		Male — Masculin	Female — Féminin	Male — Masculin	Female — Féminin
	Number Nombre	Rate Taux	Number Nombre	Rate Taux	Number Nombre	Number Nombre	Number Nombre	Number Nombre
Cerebrovascular disease — Maladie cérébrovasculaire	4 063	44.8	4 229	45.3	6 988	8 006	7 134	8 126
Diseases of arteries, arterioles and capillaries — Maladies des artères, artérioles et capillaires	549	6.1	347	3.7	1 139	741	1 124	780
Diseases of the respiratory system — Maladies de l'appareil respiratoire								
Total	5 355	59.0	5 506	58.9	13 887	12 943	13 949	13 939
Influenza — Grippe	25	♦0.3	32	0.3	20	15	9	7
Pneumonia — Pneumopathies	1 650	18.2	1 738	18.6	4 721	4 419	4 586	4 686
Chronic lower respiratory diseases — Maladies chroniques des voies respiratoires inférieures	1 751	19.3	1 889	20.2	6 936	6 594	7 163	7 304
Diseases of the digestive system — Maladies de l'appareil digestif								
Total	4 697	51.8	3 127	33.5	5 792	5 080	5 676	5 204
Gastric and duodenal ulcer — Ulcère de l'estomac et du duodénum	127	1.4	73	0.8	397	303	376	300
Diseases of the liver — Maladies du foie	3 081	34.0	1 257	13.5	1 861	1 232	1 814	1 218
Diseases of the musculoskeletal system and connective tissue — Maladies du système ostéo-articularie, des muscles et du tissu conjonctif	190	2.1	467	5.0	657	1 536	635	1 513
Diseases of the genitourinary system — Maladies de l'appareil génito-urinaire								
Total	1 687	18.6	2 028	21.7	3 738	3 312	3 808	3 198
Disorders of kidney and ureter — Affections du rein et de l'uretère	1 155	12.7	1 255	13.4	2 421	1 889	2 488	1 850
Hyperplasia of prostate — Hyperplasie de la prostate	61	2.5	..	..	325	..	300	..
Pregnancy, childbirth and the puerperium — Grossesse, accouchement et puerpéralité								
Total	..	..	58	26.5	..	476	..	485
Pregnancy with abortive outcome — Grossesse se terminant par un avortement	..	..	3	♦1.4	..	28	..	23
Other direct obstetric causes — Autres décès maternels directs	..	..	24	♦10.9	..	198	..	188
Indirect obstetric causes — Décès maternels indirects	..	..	11	♦5.0	..	106	..	124
Certain conditions originating in the perinatal period — Certaines affections dont l'origine se situe dans la période périnatale	394	352.9	332	308.8	2 123	1 612	2 163	1 603
Congenital malformations, deformations and chromosomal abnormalities — Malformations congénitales et anomalies chromosomiques	432	386.9	407	378.6	1 326	1 114	1 345	1 037
Symptoms, signs and abnormal clinical and laboratory findings, not elsewhere classified — Symptômes, signes et résultats anormaux d'examens cliniques et de laboratoire, non classés ailleurs	1 342	14.8	1 336	14.3	2 196	1 653	2 024	1 574
All other diseases — Toutes autres maladies	247	2.7	420	4.5	461	600	478	634
External causes — Causes externes								
Total	5 749	63.4	1 829	19.6	23 558	4 271	24 090	4 551
Accidents								
Total	3 577	39.4	1 377	14.7	9 187	2 248	9 129	2 370
Transport accidents — Accidents de transport	1 467	16.2	363	3.9	6 126	1 369	5 880	1 338
Falls — Chutes	400	4.4	463	5.0	989	370	887	368
Accidental drowning and submersion — Noyade et submersion accidentelles	256	2.8	44	0.5	618	137	701	108
Exposure to smoke, fire and flames — Exposition à la fumée, au feu et aux flammes	202	2.2	99	1.1	88	30	82	42
Accidental poisoning by and exposure to noxious substances — Intoxication accidentelle par des substances nocives et exposition à ces substances	117	1.3	55	0.6	122	43	174	35
Intentional self-harm — Lésions auto-infligées	1 570	17.3	309	3.3	2 033	447	2 203	506
Assault — Agresssions	499	5.5	76	0.8	10 987	1 006	11 018	1 066
All other external causes — Toutes autres causes externes	103	1.1	67	0.7	1 351	570	1 740	609

20. Death and death rates by cause and sex: 2014 - 2018
Décès et taux de mortalité par cause et sexe : 2014 - 2018 (continued - suite)

Cause of death — Cause de décès	Ecuador - Équateur				French Guiana - Guyane française			
	2016 (U)		2017 (U)		2015 (...)		2016 (...)	
	Male — Masculin	Female — Féminin	Male — Masculin	Female — Féminin	Male — Masculin	Female — Féminin	Male — Masculin	Female — Féminin
	Number Nombre	Number Nombre	Number Nombre	Number Nombre	Number Nombre	Number Nombre	Number Nombre	Number Nombre
TOTAL	*36 905*	*30 601*	*37 996*	*31 251*	*471*	*361*	*508*	*393*
Certain infectious and parasitic diseases — Certaines maladies infectieuses et parasitaires								
Total	*1 254*	*686*	*1 381*	*724*	*13*	*16*	*18*	*16*
Intestinal infectious diseases — Maladies infectieuses intestinales	*75*	*72*	*60*	*78*	*1*	-	*2*	*3*
Tuberculosis — Tuberculose	*281*	*112*	*327*	*114*	*1*	-	*2*	*1*
Tetanus — Tétanos	*6*	*1*	*3*	*3*	-	-	-	-
Diphtheria — Diphtérie	-	-	-	-	-	-	-	-
Whooping cough — Coqueluche	-	*1*	*2*	*2*	-	-	-	-
Meningococcal infection — Infection à méningocoques	*1*	-	-	*1*	-	-	-	-
Septicaemia — Septicémie	*186*	*211*	*227*	*231*	*4*	*3*	*3*	*4*
Acute poliomyelitis — Poliomyélite aiguë	-	-	*1*	-	-	-	-	-
Measles — Rougeole	-	-	-	-	-	-	-	-
Viral hepatitis — Hépatite virale	*18*	*12*	*9*	*13*	-	*2*	*1*	*1*
Human immunodeficiency virus [HIV] disease — Maladies dues au virus de l'immunodéficience humaine (VIH)	*582*	*195*	*634*	*208*	*4*	*8*	*8*	*3*
Malaria — Paludisme	-	-	-	-	-	-	-	-
Neoplasms — Tumeurs	*5 437*	*5 735*	*5 648*	*5 844*	*93*	*70*	*104*	*88*
Malignant neoplasms — Tumeurs malignes								
Total	*5 173*	*5 464*	*5 340*	*5 554*	*89*	*65*	*101*	*83*
Malignant neoplasm of lip, oral cavity and pharynx — Tumeur maligne de la lèvre, de la cavité buccale et du pharynx	*76*	*70*	*74*	*64*	*3*	*1*	*9*	*2*
Malignant neoplasm of oesophagus — Tumeur maligne de l'oesophage	*88*	*28*	*112*	*23*	*3*	*1*	*3*	*2*
Malignant neoplasm of stomach — Tumeur maligne de l'estomac	*984*	*655*	*957*	*660*	*5*	*2*	*11*	*5*
Malignant neoplasm of colon, rectosigmoid junction, rectum, anus and anal canal — Tumeur maligne du côlon, de la jonction recto-sigmoïdienne, du rectum, de l'anus et du canal anal	*366*	*445*	*396*	*437*	*6*	*3*	*6*	*3*
Malignant neoplasm of liver and intrahepatic bile ducts — Tumeur maligne du foie et des voies bilaires intrahépatiques	*301*	*394*	*328*	*353*	*9*	*4*	*4*	*1*
Malignant neoplasm of pancreas — Tumeur maligne du pancréas	*192*	*219*	*222*	*257*	*7*	*3*	*9*	*5*
Malignant neoplasm of trachea, bronchus and lung — Tumeur maligne de la trachée, des bronches et du poumon	*380*	*348*	*435*	*388*	*21*	*9*	*14*	*4*
Malignant neoplasm of female breast — Tumeur maligne du sein chez la femme	..	*638*	..	*667*	..	*13*	..	*16*
Malignant neoplasm of cervix uteri — Tumeur maligne du col de l'utérus	..	*414*	..	*421*	..	*2*	..	*7*
Malignant neoplasm of prostate — Tumeur maligne de la prostate	*967*	..	*916*	..	*13*	..	*16*	..
Malignant neoplasm of lymphoid, haematopoietic and related tissue — Tumeurs malignes primitives ou présumées primitives des tissus lymphoïde, hématopoïétique et apparentés	*647*	*570*	*705*	*574*	*6*	*7*	*9*	*12*
Disorders of the blood and blood-forming organs and certain disorders involving the immune mechanism — Maladies du sang et des organes hématopoïétiques et certains troubles du système immunitaire								
Total	*274*	*306*	*234*	*260*	*4*	*4*	*1*	*2*
Anaemias — Anémies	*204*	*241*	*163*	*181*	*4*	*1*	*1*	*1*
Endocrine, nutritional and metabolic diseases — Maladies endocriniennes, nutritionnelles et métaboliques								
Total	*2 735*	*3 129*	*2 761*	*3 105*	*19*	*24*	*16*	*22*
Diabetes mellitus — Diabète sucré	*2 278*	*2 628*	*2 289*	*2 606*	*14*	*19*	*11*	*14*
Malnutrition — Malnutrition	*259*	*272*	*237*	*232*	*1*	-	*1*	*1*
Mental and behavioural disorders — Troubles mentaux et du comportement	*95*	*56*	*78*	*61*	*11*	*3*	*4*	*11*
Diseases of the nervous system — Maladies du système nerveux	*827*	*753*	*825*	*763*	*10*	*7*	*24*	*11*
Diseases of the circulatory system — Maladies de l'appareil circulatoire								
Total	*8 615*	*8 008*	*9 262*	*8 402*	*90*	*83*	*107*	*87*
Acute rheumatic fever and chronic rheumatic heart diseases — Rhumatisme articularie aigu et cardiopathies rhumatismales chroniques	*36*	*60*	*37*	*55*	*1*	*1*	*1*	*3*
Hypertensive diseases — Maladies hypertensives	*1 600*	*1 875*	*1 635*	*1 762*	*9*	*11*	*9*	*12*
Ischaemic heart disease — Cardiopathie ischémique	*3 750*	*2 767*	*4 230*	*3 174*	*19*	*10*	*19*	*7*

20. Death and death rates by cause and sex: 2014 - 2018
Décès et taux de mortalité par cause et sexe : 2014 - 2018 (continued - suite)

Cause of death — Cause de décès	Ecuador - Équateur				French Guiana - Guyane française			
	2016 (U)		2017 (U)		2015 (...)		2016 (...)	
	Male — Masculin	Female — Féminin	Male — Masculin	Female — Féminin	Male — Masculin	Female — Féminin	Male — Masculin	Female — Féminin
	Number Nombre	Number Nombre	Number Nombre	Number Nombre	Number Nombre	Number Nombre	Number Nombre	Number Nombre
Cerebrovascular disease — Maladie cérébrovasculaire	*2 144*	*2 148*	*2 151*	*2 149*	*38*	*26*	*29*	*32*
Diseases of arteries, arterioles and capillaries — Maladies des artères, artérioles et capillaires	*144*	*109*	*139*	*105*	*5*	*5*	*4*	*4*
Diseases of the respiratory system — Maladies de l'appareil respiratoire								
Total	*3 569*	*2 943*	*3 841*	*3 359*	*22*	*18*	*17*	*24*
Influenza — Grippe	*18*	*26*	*11*	*17*	-	*1*	*1*	*1*
Pneumonia — Pneumopathies	*1 773*	*1 593*	*1 952*	*1 820*	*6*	*9*	*8*	*7*
Chronic lower respiratory diseases — Maladies chroniques des voies respiratoires inférieures	*1 020*	*795*	*1 027*	*797*	*8*	*2*	*1*	*6*
Diseases of the digestive system — Maladies de l'appareil digestif								
Total	*2 416*	*1 870*	*2 554*	*1 889*	*25*	*11*	*15*	*12*
Gastric and duodenal ulcer — Ulcère de l'estomac et du duodénum	*100*	*95*	*109*	*84*	-	-	-	-
Diseases of the liver — Maladies du foie	*1 397*	*926*	*1 427*	*915*	*17*	*5*	*10*	*5*
Diseases of the musculoskeletal system and connective tissue — Maladies du système ostéo-articularie, des muscles et du tissu conjonctif	*109*	*275*	*117*	*300*	*1*	*3*	-	*2*
Diseases of the genitourinary system — Maladies de l'appareil génito-urinaire								
Total	*1 078*	*883*	*1 096*	*877*	*9*	*13*	*9*	*8*
Disorders of kidney and ureter — Affections du rein et de l'uretère	*908*	*722*	*898*	*684*	*7*	*12*	*8*	*8*
Hyperplasia of prostate — Hyperplasie de la prostate	*85*	..	*86*	..	-	..	-	..
Pregnancy, childbirth and the puerperium — Grossesse, accouchement et puerpéralité								
Total	..	*154*	..	*211*	..	*1*	..	*1*
Pregnancy with abortive outcome — Grossesse se terminant par un avortement	..	*13*	..	*12*	..	-	..	-
Other direct obstetric causes — Autres décès maternels directs	..	*86*	..	*86*	..	*1*	..	*1*
Indirect obstetric causes — Décès maternels indirects	..	*34*	..	*45*	..	-	..	-
Certain conditions originating in the perinatal period — Certaines affections dont l'origine se situe dans la période périnatale	*905*	*657*	*939*	*690*	*16*	*12*	*14*	*19*
Congenital malformations, deformations and chromosomal abnormalities — Malformations congénitales et anomalies chromosomiques	*516*	*482*	*586*	*519*	*7*	*7*	*7*	*13*
Symptoms, signs and abnormal clinical and laboratory findings, not elsewhere classified — Symptômes, signes et résultats anormaux d'examens cliniques et de laboratoire, non classés ailleurs	*2 451*	*2 441*	*2 464*	*2 388*	*65*	*53*	*72*	*46*
All other diseases — Toutes autres maladies	*62*	*96*	*97*	*141*	*1*	*2*	-	-
External causes — Causes externes								
Total	*6 562*	*2 127*	*6 113*	*1 718*	*85*	*34*	*100*	*31*
Accidents								
Total	*4 708*	*1 629*	*4 131*	*1 210*	*55*	*22*	*64*	*22*
Transport accidents — Accidents de transport	*2 378*	*563*	*2 434*	*598*	*20*	*5*	*20*	*8*
Falls — Chutes	*445*	*131*	*285*	*85*	*2*	*2*	*5*	*5*
Accidental drowning and submersion — Noyade et submersion accidentelles	*303*	*70*	*231*	*48*	*11*	*3*	*10*	*3*
Exposure to smoke, fire and flames — Exposition à la fumée, au feu et aux flammes	*63*	*29*	*52*	*27*	*1*	*1*	*1*	-
Accidental poisoning by and exposure to noxious substances — Intoxication accidentelle par des substances nocives et exposition à ces substances	*195*	*24*	*144*	*16*	*4*	*2*	*6*	-
Intentional self-harm — Lésions auto-infligées	*953*	*266*	*943*	*241*	*12*	*7*	*15*	*5*
Assault — Agresssions	*745*	*174*	*760*	*175*	*7*	-	*9*	*2*
All other external causes — Toutes autres causes externes	*156*	*58*	*279*	*92*	*11*	*5*	*12*	*2*

20. Death and death rates by cause and sex: 2014 - 2018
Décès et taux de mortalité par cause et sexe : 2014 - 2018 (continued - suite)

Cause of death — Cause de décès	Guyana				Paraguay			
	2014 (C)				2016 (+U)		2017 (+U)	
	Male — Masculin		Female — Féminin		Male — Masculin	Female — Féminin	Male — Masculin	Female — Féminin
	Number Nombre	Rate Taux	Number Nombre	Rate Taux	Number Nombre	Number Nombre	Number Nombre	Number Nombre
TOTAL	**3 164**	**851.6**	**2 383**	**636.6**	***17 792***	***13 517***	***16 389***	***12 620***
Certain infectious and parasitic diseases — Certaines maladies infectieuses et parasitaires								
Total	246	66.2	173	46.2	*654*	*414*	*508*	*307*
Intestinal infectious diseases — Maladies infectieuses intestinales	12	♦3.2	14	♦3.7	*43*	*54*	*44*	*49*
Tuberculosis — Tuberculose	55	14.8	21	♦5.6	*150*	*48*	*117*	*42*
Tetanus — Tétanos	-	-	-	-	*1*	-	*3*	-
Diphtheria — Diphtérie	-	-	-	-	-	-	-	-
Whooping cough — Coqueluche	-	-	-	-	-	-	-	-
Meningococcal infection — Infection à méningocoques	-	-	-	-	-	*2*	*3*	*1*
Septicaemia — Septicémie	52	14.0	50	13.4	*91*	*88*	*87*	*81*
Acute poliomyelitis — Poliomyélite aiguë	-	-	-	-	-	-	-	-
Measles — Rougeole	-	-	-	-	-	-	-	-
Viral hepatitis — Hépatite virale	2	♦0.5	-	-	*3*	*3*	*11*	*5*
Human immunodeficiency virus [HIV] disease — Maladies dues au virus de l'immunodéficience humaine (VIH)	106	28.5	81	21.6	*174*	*82*	*162*	*82*
Malaria — Paludisme	6	♦1.6	-	-	-	*1*	-	-
Neoplasms — Tumeurs	236	63.5	282	75.3	*2 399*	*2 165*	*2 521*	*2 215*
Malignant neoplasms — Tumeurs malignes								
Total	226	60.8	262	70.0	*2 212*	*1 987*	*2 289*	*2 040*
Malignant neoplasm of lip, oral cavity and pharynx — Tumeur maligne de la lèvre, de la cavité buccale et du pharynx	10	♦2.7	1	♦0.3	*82*	*17*	*82*	*11*
Malignant neoplasm of oesophagus — Tumeur maligne de l'oesophage	4	♦1.1	1	♦0.3	*88*	*17*	*102*	*14*
Malignant neoplasm of stomach — Tumeur maligne de l'estomac	6	♦1.6	10	♦2.7	*169*	*85*	*154*	*87*
Malignant neoplasm of colon, rectosigmoid junction, rectum, anus and anal canal — Tumeur maligne du côlon, de la jonction recto-sigmoïdienne, du rectum, de l'anus et du canal anal	21	♦5.7	18	♦4.8	*218*	*171*	*227*	*201*
Malignant neoplasm of liver and intrahepatic bile ducts — Tumeur maligne du foie et des voies bilaires intrahépatiques	12	♦3.2	12	♦3.2	*74*	*50*	*63*	*59*
Malignant neoplasm of pancreas — Tumeur maligne du pancréas	3	♦0.8	6	♦1.6	*99*	*107*	*103*	*87*
Malignant neoplasm of trachea, bronchus and lung — Tumeur maligne de la trachée, des bronches et du poumon	16	♦4.3	10	♦2.7	*411*	*135*	*451*	*114*
Malignant neoplasm of female breast — Tumeur maligne du sein chez la femme	..	..	60	...	..	*370*	..	*391*
Malignant neoplasm of cervix uteri — Tumeur maligne du col de l'utérus	..	..	36	...	..	*290*	..	*365*
Malignant neoplasm of prostate — Tumeur maligne de la prostate	74	...	..	..	*376*	..	*390*	..
Malignant neoplasm of lymphoid, haematopoietic and related tissue — Tumeurs malignes primitives ou présumées primitives des tissus lymphoïde, hématopoïétique et apparentés	19	♦5.1	21	♦5.6	*219*	*169*	*223*	*160*
Disorders of the blood and blood-forming organs and certain disorders involving the immune mechanism — Maladies du sang et des organes hématopoïétiques et certains troubles du système immunitaire								
Total	33	8.9	37	9.9	*92*	*99*	*81*	*57*
Anaemias — Anémies	31	8.3	32	8.5	*61*	*68*	*59*	*39*
Endocrine, nutritional and metabolic diseases — Maladies endocriniennes, nutritionnelles et métaboliques								
Total	277	74.6	316	84.4	*1 440*	*1 780*	*1 202*	*1 565*
Diabetes mellitus — Diabète sucré	207	55.7	252	67.3	*1 112*	*1 426*	*931*	*1 246*
Malnutrition — Malnutrition	21	♦5.7	10	♦2.7	*158*	*151*	*112*	*128*
Mental and behavioural disorders — Troubles mentaux et du comportement	5	♦1.3	1	♦0.3	*345*	*38*	*261*	*41*
Diseases of the nervous system — Maladies du système nerveux	34	9.2	21	♦5.6	*285*	*251*	*244*	*217*
Diseases of the circulatory system — Maladies de l'appareil circulatoire								
Total	1 036	278.9	953	254.6	*4 473*	*3 751*	*4 231*	*3 641*
Acute rheumatic fever and chronic rheumatic heart diseases — Rhumatisme articularie aigu et cardiopathies rhumatismales chroniques	5	♦1.3	5	♦1.3	*16*	*18*	*22*	*17*
Hypertensive diseases — Maladies hypertensives	195	52.5	233	62.2	*707*	*686*	*605*	*632*
Ischaemic heart disease — Cardiopathie ischémique	334	89.9	231	61.7	*1 783*	*1 209*	*1 634*	*1 159*

20. Death and death rates by cause and sex: 2014 - 2018
Décès et taux de mortalité par cause et sexe : 2014 - 2018 (continued - suite)

Cause of death — Cause de décès	Guyana				Paraguay			
	2014 (C)				2016 (+U)		2017 (+U)	
	Male — Masculin		Female — Féminin		Male — Masculin	Female — Féminin	Male — Masculin	Female — Féminin
	Number Nombre	Rate Taux	Number Nombre	Rate Taux	Number Nombre	Number Nombre	Number Nombre	Number Nombre
Cerebrovascular disease — Maladie cérébrovasculaire	253	68.1	286	76.4	1 171	1 129	1 224	1 144
Diseases of arteries, arterioles and capillaries — Maladies des artères, artérioles et capillaires	30	♦8.1	32	8.5	100	70	111	65
Diseases of the respiratory system — Maladies de l'appareil respiratoire								
Total	199	53.6	153	40.9	1 678	1 228	1 462	1 082
Influenza — Grippe	-	-	1	♦0.3	57	55	22	29
Pneumonia — Pneumopathies	118	31.8	99	26.4	676	627	622	572
Chronic lower respiratory diseases — Maladies chroniques des voies respiratoires inférieures	52	14.0	21	♦5.6	632	261	575	270
Diseases of the digestive system — Maladies de l'appareil digestif								
Total	229	61.6	117	31.3	942	540	832	511
Gastric and duodenal ulcer — Ulcère de l'estomac et du duodénum	35	9.4	19	♦5.1	35	29	26	23
Diseases of the liver — Maladies du foie	140	37.7	53	14.2	440	87	392	79
Diseases of the musculoskeletal system and connective tissue — Maladies du système ostéo-articularie, des muscles et du tissu conjonctif	1	♦0.3	5	♦1.3	72	148	80	139
Diseases of the genitourinary system — Maladies de l'appareil génito-urinaire								
Total	49	13.2	44	11.8	551	445	533	424
Disorders of kidney and ureter — Affections du rein et de l'uretère	39	10.5	31	8.3	409	305	397	294
Hyperplasia of prostate — Hyperplasie de la prostate	4	...	..	..	47	..	44	..
Pregnancy, childbirth and the puerperium — Grossesse, accouchement et puerpéralité								
Total	..	..	17	♦112.4	..	115	..	100
Pregnancy with abortive outcome — Grossesse se terminant par un avortement	..	..	4	♦26.4	..	24	..	10
Other direct obstetric causes — Autres décès maternels directs	..	..	13	♦85.9	..	36	..	40
Indirect obstetric causes — Décès maternels indirects	..	..	-	-	..	36	..	28
Certain conditions originating in the perinatal period — Certaines affections dont l'origine se situe dans la période périnatale	99	...	65	...	441	338	443	308
Congenital malformations, deformations and chromosomal abnormalities — Malformations congénitales et anomalies chromosomiques	37	...	23	...	275	242	292	257
Symptoms, signs and abnormal clinical and laboratory findings, not elsewhere classified — Symptômes, signes et résultats anormaux d'examens cliniques et de laboratoire, non classés ailleurs	28	♦7.5	11	♦2.9	1 453	1 152	1 220	997
All other diseases — Toutes autres maladies	-	-	3	♦0.8	66	76	41	68
External causes — Causes externes								
Total	655	176.3	162	43.3	2 626	735	2 438	691
Accidents								
Total	268	72.1	64	17.1	1 650	500	1 603	443
Transport accidents — Accidents de transport	116	31.2	21	♦5.6	1 000	208	1 002	199
Falls — Chutes	2	♦0.5	-	-	67	18	55	17
Accidental drowning and submersion — Noyade et submersion accidentelles	75	20.2	8	♦2.1	142	16	133	18
Exposure to smoke, fire and flames — Exposition à la fumée, au feu et aux flammes	4	♦1.1	3	♦0.8	39	21	32	14
Accidental poisoning by and exposure to noxious substances — Intoxication accidentelle par des substances nocives et exposition à ces substances	2	♦0.5	4	♦1.1	22	11	15	9
Intentional self-harm — Lésions auto-infligées	164	44.1	40	10.7	271	85	265	94
Assault — Agresssions	105	28.3	33	8.8	561	63	449	64
All other external causes — Toutes autres causes externes	118	31.8	25	♦6.7	144	87	121	90

20. Death and death rates by cause and sex: 2014 - 2018
Décès et taux de mortalité par cause et sexe : 2014 - 2018 (continued - suite)

Cause of death — Cause de décès	Peru - Pérou				Suriname	
	2016 (+U)		2017 (+U)		2014 (U)	
	Male — Masculin	Female — Féminin	Male — Masculin	Female — Féminin	Male — Masculin	Female — Féminin
	Number Nombre	Number Nombre	Number Nombre	Number Nombre	Number Nombre	Number Nombre
TOTAL	*51 894*	*45 334*	*63 938*	*57 204*	*1 792*	*1 356*
Certain infectious and parasitic diseases — Certaines maladies infectieuses et parasitaires						
Total	*3 874*	*2 758*	*5 377*	*4 464*	*127*	*98*
Intestinal infectious diseases — Maladies infectieuses intestinales	*156*	*144*	*149*	*144*	*3*	*5*
Tuberculosis — Tuberculose	*999*	*477*	*928*	*420*	*9*	*1*
Tetanus — Tétanos	*4*	-	*4*	*4*	-	-
Diphtheria — Diphtérie	-	-	-	-	-	-
Whooping cough — Coqueluche	-	*3*	*9*	*10*	-	*3*
Meningococcal infection — Infection à méningocoques	-	*1*	-	*3*	-	*1*
Septicaemia — Septicémie	*1 769*	*1 739*	*3 260*	*3 461*	*29*	*36*
Acute poliomyelitis — Poliomyélite aiguë	*1*	-	-	-	-	-
Measles — Rougeole	-	-	-	-	-	-
Viral hepatitis — Hépatite virale	*42*	*37*	*49*	*40*	*4*	*5*
Human immunodeficiency virus [HIV] disease — Maladies dues au virus de l'immunodéficience humaine (VIH)	*662*	*164*	*682*	*162*	*61*	*35*
Malaria — Paludisme	*3*	*1*	*2*	-	-	-
Neoplasms — Tumeurs	*8 741*	*10 001*	*9 790*	*11 209*	*240*	*195*
Malignant neoplasms — Tumeurs malignes						
Total	*8 190*	*9 411*	*9 165*	*10 573*	*239*	*193*
Malignant neoplasm of lip, oral cavity and pharynx — Tumeur maligne de la lèvre, de la cavité buccale et du pharynx	*117*	*110*	*136*	*108*	*12*	*4*
Malignant neoplasm of oesophagus — Tumeur maligne de l'oesophage	*129*	*54*	*134*	*44*	*4*	*1*
Malignant neoplasm of stomach — Tumeur maligne de l'estomac	*1 401*	*1 229*	*1 542*	*1 354*	*12*	*5*
Malignant neoplasm of colon, rectosigmoid junction, rectum, anus and anal canal — Tumeur maligne du côlon, de la jonction recto-sigmoïdienne, du rectum, de l'anus et du canal anal	*542*	*621*	*610*	*728*	*21*	*17*
Malignant neoplasm of liver and intrahepatic bile ducts — Tumeur maligne du foie et des voies bilaires intrahépatiques	*514*	*551*	*575*	*699*	*21*	*8*
Malignant neoplasm of pancreas — Tumeur maligne du pancréas	*328*	*396*	*389*	*527*	*6*	*7*
Malignant neoplasm of trachea, bronchus and lung — Tumeur maligne de la trachée, des bronches et du poumon	*773*	*730*	*878*	*827*	*46*	*18*
Malignant neoplasm of female breast — Tumeur maligne du sein chez la femme	..	*923*	..	*1 030*	..	*37*
Malignant neoplasm of cervix uteri — Tumeur maligne du col de l'utérus	..	*926*	..	*996*	..	*34*
Malignant neoplasm of prostate — Tumeur maligne de la prostate	*1 373*	..	*1 468*	..	*46*	..
Malignant neoplasm of lymphoid, haematopoietic and related tissue — Tumeurs malignes primitives ou présumées primitives des tissus lymphoïde, hématopoïétique et apparentés	*1 105*	*946*	*1 147*	*897*	*20*	*18*
Disorders of the blood and blood-forming organs and certain disorders involving the immune mechanism — Maladies du sang et des organes hématopoïétiques et certains troubles du système immunitaire						
Total	*517*	*453*	*434*	*445*	*2*	*8*
Anaemias — Anémies	*397*	*375*	*289*	*332*	*2*	*6*
Endocrine, nutritional and metabolic diseases — Maladies endocriniennes, nutritionnelles et métaboliques						
Total	*2 556*	*2 757*	*2 549*	*2 848*	*93*	*117*
Diabetes mellitus — Diabète sucré	*1 746*	*1 782*	*1 670*	*1 804*	*83*	*109*
Malnutrition — Malnutrition	*524*	*606*	*518*	*616*	*1*	*1*
Mental and behavioural disorders — Troubles mentaux et du comportement	*181*	*123*	*204*	*158*	*8*	*2*
Diseases of the nervous system — Maladies du système nerveux	*1 528*	*1 068*	*1 918*	*1 391*	*32*	*15*
Diseases of the circulatory system — Maladies de l'appareil circulatoire						
Total	*8 450*	*7 752*	*10 425*	*9 774*	*528*	*398*
Acute rheumatic fever and chronic rheumatic heart diseases — Rhumatisme articularie aigu et cardiopathies rhumatismales chroniques	*41*	*60*	*45*	*71*	-	*1*
Hypertensive diseases — Maladies hypertensives	*992*	*1 086*	*1 003*	*1 205*	*47*	*43*
Ischaemic heart disease — Cardiopathie ischémique	*3 296*	*2 487*	*3 729*	*2 840*	*159*	*89*
Cerebrovascular disease — Maladie cérébrovasculaire	*2 462*	*2 412*	*2 985*	*3 113*	*189*	*161*
Diseases of arteries, arterioles and capillaries — Maladies des artères, artérioles et capillaires	*171*	*165*	*160*	*133*	*20*	*3*

20. Death and death rates by cause and sex: 2014 - 2018
Décès et taux de mortalité par cause et sexe : 2014 - 2018 (continued - suite)

Cause of death — Cause de décès	Peru - Pérou				Suriname	
	2016 (+U)		2017 (+U)		2014 (U)	
	Male — Masculin	Female — Féminin	Male — Masculin	Female — Féminin	Male — Masculin	Female — Féminin
	Number Nombre	Number Nombre	Number Nombre	Number Nombre	Number Nombre	Number Nombre
Diseases of the respiratory system — Maladies de l'appareil respiratoire						
Total	*10 680*	*10 045*	*14 040*	*13 085*	*126*	*76*
Influenza — Grippe	*14*	*10*	*5*	*2*	-	-
Pneumonia — Pneumopathies	*6 025*	*5 706*	*7 113*	*6 912*	*79*	*48*
Chronic lower respiratory diseases — Maladies chroniques des voies respiratoires inférieures	*825*	*831*	*844*	*826*	*25*	*12*
Diseases of the digestive system — Maladies de l'appareil digestif						
Total	*3 952*	*2 870*	*4 590*	*3 410*	*94*	*49*
Gastric and duodenal ulcer — Ulcère de l'estomac et du duodénum	*146*	*97*	*127*	*112*	*10*	*3*
Diseases of the liver — Maladies du foie	*2 323*	*1 336*	*2 688*	*1 690*	*34*	*12*
Diseases of the musculoskeletal system and connective tissue — Maladies du système ostéo-articularie, des muscles et du tissu conjonctif	*226*	*447*	*246*	*490*	*5*	*11*
Diseases of the genitourinary system — Maladies de l'appareil génito-urinaire						
Total	*2 070*	*2 009*	*2 112*	*2 123*	*59*	*49*
Disorders of kidney and ureter — Affections du rein et de l'uretère	*1 449*	*1 393*	*1 508*	*1 501*	*39*	*29*
Hyperplasia of prostate — Hyperplasie de la prostate	*185*	..	*197*	..	-	..
Pregnancy, childbirth and the puerperium — Grossesse, accouchement et puerpéralité						
Total	..	*72*	..	*315*	..	*7*
Pregnancy with abortive outcome — Grossesse se terminant par un avortement	..	*14*	..	*31*	..	*1*
Other direct obstetric causes — Autres décès maternels directs	..	*57*	..	*228*	..	*4*
Indirect obstetric causes — Décès maternels indirects	..	-	..	*1*	..	*2*
Certain conditions originating in the perinatal period — Certaines affections dont l'origine se situe dans la période périnatale	*948*	*671*	*1 410*	*1 098*	*55*	*48*
Congenital malformations, deformations and chromosomal abnormalities — Malformations congénitales et anomalies chromosomiques	*522*	*505*	*781*	*718*	*17*	*12*
Symptoms, signs and abnormal clinical and laboratory findings, not elsewhere classified — Symptômes, signes et résultats anormaux d'examens cliniques et de laboratoire, non classés ailleurs	*1 424*	*1 300*	*3 304*	*2 669*	*149*	*157*
All other diseases — Toutes autres maladies	*240*	*359*	*304*	*419*	*12*	*24*
External causes — Causes externes						
Total	*5 985*	*2 144*	*6 454*	*2 588*	*245*	*90*
Accidents						
Total	*5 088*	*1 858*	*5 160*	*2 148*	*114*	*35*
Transport accidents — Accidents de transport	*1 317*	*447*	*1 005*	*413*	*54*	*17*
Falls — Chutes	*97*	*54*	*100*	*48*	*9*	*3*
Accidental drowning and submersion — Noyade et submersion accidentelles	*345*	*91*	*379*	*93*	*22*	*2*
Exposure to smoke, fire and flames — Exposition à la fumée, au feu et aux flammes	*63*	*33*	*58*	*38*	*3*	*4*
Accidental poisoning by and exposure to noxious substances — Intoxication accidentelle par des substances nocives et exposition à ces substances	*154*	*73*	*110*	*51*	*2*	*1*
Intentional self-harm — Lésions auto-infligées	*288*	*130*	*273*	*111*	*94*	*36*
Assault — Agresssions	*484*	*89*	*323*	*73*	*23*	*12*
All other external causes — Toutes autres causes externes	*125*	*67*	*698*	*256*	*14*	*7*

20. Death and death rates by cause and sex: 2014 - 2018
Décès et taux de mortalité par cause et sexe : 2014 - 2018 (continued - suite)

Uruguay

Cause of death — Cause de décès	2016 (C)				2017 (C)			
	Male — Masculin		Female — Féminin		Male — Masculin		Female — Féminin	
	Number Nombre	Rate Taux	Number Nombre	Rate Taux	Number Nombre	Rate Taux	Number Nombre	Rate Taux
TOTAL	**17 214**	**1 022.1**	**17 049**	**949.2**	**16 674**	**986.0**	**16 497**	**915.4**
Certain infectious and parasitic diseases — Certaines maladies infectieuses et parasitaires								
Total	**324**	**19.2**	**263**	**14.6**	**411**	**24.3**	**362**	**20.1**
Intestinal infectious diseases — Maladies infectieuses intestinales	**44**	**2.6**	**59**	**3.3**	**37**	**2.2**	**63**	**3.5**
Tuberculosis — Tuberculose	**42**	**2.5**	**16**	**♦0.9**	**37**	**2.2**	**18**	**♦1.0**
Tetanus — Tétanos	**1**	**♦0.1**	**-**	**-**	**-**	**-**	**-**	**-**
Diphtheria — Diphtérie	**-**	**-**	**-**	**-**	**-**	**-**	**-**	**-**
Whooping cough — Coqueluche	**1**	**♦0.1**	**1**	**♦0.1**	**-**	**-**	**-**	**-**
Meningococcal infection — Infection à méningocoques	**1**	**♦0.1**	**-**	**-**	**1**	**♦0.1**	**1**	**♦0.1**
Septicaemia — Septicémie	**84**	**5.0**	**98**	**5.5**	**187**	**11.1**	**190**	**10.5**
Acute poliomyelitis — Poliomyélite aiguë	**-**	**-**	**-**	**-**	**-**	**-**	**-**	**-**
Measles — Rougeole	**-**	**-**	**-**	**-**	**-**	**-**	**-**	**-**
Viral hepatitis — Hépatite virale	**2**	**♦0.1**	**1**	**♦0.1**	**11**	**♦0.7**	**3**	**♦0.2**
Human immunodeficiency virus [HIV] disease — Maladies dues au virus de l'immunodéficience humaine (VIH)	**119**	**7.1**	**53**	**3.0**	**104**	**6.1**	**53**	**2.9**
Malaria — Paludisme	**1**	**♦0.1**	**-**	**-**	**-**	**-**	**-**	**-**
Neoplasms — Tumeurs	**4 523**	**268.6**	**3 829**	**213.2**	**4 446**	**262.9**	**3 703**	**205.5**
Malignant neoplasms — Tumeurs malignes								
Total	**4 367**	**259.3**	**3 662**	**203.9**	**4 114**	**243.3**	**3 425**	**190.1**
Malignant neoplasm of lip, oral cavity and pharynx — Tumeur maligne de la lèvre, de la cavité buccale et du pharynx	**106**	**6.3**	**40**	**2.2**	**81**	**4.8**	**29**	**♦1.6**
Malignant neoplasm of oesophagus — Tumeur maligne de l'oesophage	**166**	**9.9**	**85**	**4.7**	**123**	**7.3**	**69**	**3.8**
Malignant neoplasm of stomach — Tumeur maligne de l'estomac	**257**	**15.3**	**139**	**7.7**	**204**	**12.1**	**141**	**7.8**
Malignant neoplasm of colon, rectosigmoid junction, rectum, anus and anal canal — Tumeur maligne du côlon, de la jonction recto-sigmoïdienne, du rectum, de l'anus et du canal anal	**469**	**27.8**	**482**	**26.8**	**504**	**29.8**	**466**	**25.9**
Malignant neoplasm of liver and intrahepatic bile ducts — Tumeur maligne du foie et des voies bilaires intrahépatiques	**91**	**5.4**	**44**	**2.4**	**96**	**5.7**	**31**	**1.7**
Malignant neoplasm of pancreas — Tumeur maligne du pancréas	**289**	**17.2**	**310**	**17.3**	**244**	**14.4**	**311**	**17.3**
Malignant neoplasm of trachea, bronchus and lung — Tumeur maligne de la trachée, des bronches et du poumon	**945**	**56.1**	**370**	**20.6**	**947**	**56.0**	**326**	**18.1**
Malignant neoplasm of female breast — Tumeur maligne du sein chez la femme	..	..	**688**	**47.6**	..	..	**611**	**42.0**
Malignant neoplasm of cervix uteri — Tumeur maligne du col de l'utérus	..	..	**79**	**5.5**	..	..	**91**	**6.3**
Malignant neoplasm of prostate — Tumeur maligne de la prostate	**574**	**123.0**	..	..	**541**	**114.8**	..	..
Malignant neoplasm of lymphoid, haematopoietic and related tissue — Tumeurs malignes primitives ou présumées primitives des tissus lymphoïde, hématopoïétique et apparentés	**311**	**18.5**	**300**	**16.7**	**288**	**17.0**	**260**	**14.4**
Disorders of the blood and blood-forming organs and certain disorders involving the immune mechanism — Maladies du sang et des organes hématopoïétiques et certains troubles du système immunitaire								
Total	**86**	**5.1**	**133**	**7.4**	**97**	**5.7**	**107**	**5.9**
Anaemias — Anémies	**54**	**3.2**	**86**	**4.8**	**56**	**3.3**	**62**	**3.4**
Endocrine, nutritional and metabolic diseases — Maladies endocriniennes, nutritionnelles et métaboliques								
Total	**615**	**36.5**	**697**	**38.8**	**542**	**32.1**	**642**	**35.6**
Diabetes mellitus — Diabète sucré	**438**	**26.0**	**476**	**26.5**	**390**	**23.1**	**427**	**23.7**
Malnutrition — Malnutrition	**38**	**2.3**	**33**	**1.8**	**23**	**♦1.4**	**16**	**♦0.9**
Mental and behavioural disorders — Troubles mentaux et du comportement	**360**	**21.4**	**672**	**37.4**	**558**	**33.0**	**1 011**	**56.1**
Diseases of the nervous system — Maladies du système nerveux	**507**	**30.1**	**701**	**39.0**	**571**	**33.8**	**677**	**37.6**
Diseases of the circulatory system — Maladies de l'appareil circulatoire								
Total	**4 403**	**261.4**	**4 965**	**276.4**	**4 072**	**240.8**	**4 645**	**257.8**
Acute rheumatic fever and chronic rheumatic heart diseases — Rhumatisme articularie aigu et cardiopathies rhumatismales chroniques	**23**	**♦1.4**	**25**	**♦1.4**	**10**	**♦0.6**	**14**	**♦0.8**
Hypertensive diseases — Maladies hypertensives	**358**	**21.3**	**560**	**31.2**	**379**	**22.4**	**538**	**29.9**
Ischaemic heart disease — Cardiopathie ischémique	**1 384**	**82.2**	**1 035**	**57.6**	**1 231**	**72.8**	**961**	**53.3**
Cerebrovascular disease — Maladie cérébrovasculaire	**1 080**	**64.1**	**1 528**	**85.1**	**910**	**53.8**	**1 321**	**73.3**

20. Death and death rates by cause and sex: 2014 - 2018
Décès et taux de mortalité par cause et sexe : 2014 - 2018 (continued - suite)

Uruguay

Cause of death — Cause de décès	2016 (C)				2017 (C)			
	Male — Masculin		Female — Féminin		Male — Masculin		Female — Féminin	
	Number Nombre	Rate Taux	Number Nombre	Rate Taux	Number Nombre	Rate Taux	Number Nombre	Rate Taux
Diseases of arteries, arterioles and capillaries — Maladies des artères, artérioles et capillaires	241	14.3	170	9.5	236	14.0	185	10.3
Diseases of the respiratory system — Maladies de l'appareil respiratoire								
Total	1 921	114.1	1 894	105.5	1 621	95.9	1 681	93.3
Influenza — Grippe	2	♦0.1	5	♦0.3	2	♦0.1	3	♦0.2
Pneumonia — Pneumopathies	551	32.7	769	42.8	444	26.3	631	35.0
Chronic lower respiratory diseases — Maladies chroniques des voies respiratoires inférieures	861	51.1	472	26.3	703	41.6	390	21.6
Diseases of the digestive system — Maladies de l'appareil digestif								
Total	695	41.3	647	36.0	620	36.7	600	33.3
Gastric and duodenal ulcer — Ulcère de l'estomac et du duodénum	29	♦1.7	22	♦1.2	19	♦1.1	28	♦1.6
Diseases of the liver — Maladies du foie	230	13.7	85	4.7	207	12.2	64	3.6
Diseases of the musculoskeletal system and connective tissue — Maladies du système ostéo-articularie, des muscles et du tissu conjonctif	93	5.5	165	9.2	117	6.9	170	9.4
Diseases of the genitourinary system — Maladies de l'appareil génito-urinaire								
Total	498	29.6	644	35.9	490	29.0	589	32.7
Disorders of kidney and ureter — Affections du rein et de l'uretère	340	20.2	366	20.4	323	19.1	324	18.0
Hyperplasia of prostate — Hyperplasie de la prostate	8	♦1.7	..	..	7	♦1.5	..	..
Pregnancy, childbirth and the puerperium — Grossesse, accouchement et puerpéralité								
Total	..	..	9	♦19.1	..	..	8	♦18.6
Pregnancy with abortive outcome — Grossesse se terminant par un avortement	..	..	2	♦4.3	..	..	2	♦4.6
Other direct obstetric causes — Autres décès maternels directs	..	..	4	♦8.5	..	..	4	♦9.3
Indirect obstetric causes — Décès maternels indirects	..	..	3	♦6.4	..	..	2	♦4.6
Certain conditions originating in the perinatal period — Certaines affections dont l'origine se situe dans la période périnatale	106	437.2	56	245.5	65	293.6	54	258.5
Congenital malformations, deformations and chromosomal abnormalities — Malformations congénitales et anomalies chromosomiques	88	362.9	83	363.9	77	347.8	69	330.3
Symptoms, signs and abnormal clinical and laboratory findings, not elsewhere classified — Symptômes, signes et résultats anormaux d'examens cliniques et de laboratoire, non classés ailleurs	1 347	80.0	1 480	82.4	1 323	78.2	1 377	76.4
All other diseases — Toutes autres maladies	34	2.0	75	4.2	41	2.4	74	4.1
External causes — Causes externes								
Total	1 614	95.8	736	41.0	1 623	96.0	728	40.4
Accidents								
Total	756	44.9	447	24.9	752	44.5	448	24.9
Transport accidents — Accidents de transport	321	19.1	100	5.6	331	19.6	102	5.7
Falls — Chutes	24	♦1.4	22	♦1.2	33	2.0	27	♦1.5
Accidental drowning and submersion — Noyade et submersion accidentelles	56	3.3	11	♦0.6	52	3.1	12	♦0.7
Exposure to smoke, fire and flames — Exposition à la fumée, au feu et aux flammes	33	2.0	35	1.9	27	♦1.6	21	♦1.2
Accidental poisoning by and exposure to noxious substances — Intoxication accidentelle par des substances nocives et exposition à ces substances	26	♦1.5	10	♦0.6	11	♦0.7	10	♦0.6
Intentional self-harm — Lésions auto-infligées	551	32.7	163	9.1	554	32.8	134	7.4
Assault — Agresssions	218	12.9	34	1.9	243	14.4	53	2.9
All other external causes — Toutes autres causes externes	89	5.3	92	5.1	74	4.4	93	5.2

20. Death and death rates by cause and sex: 2014 - 2018
Décès et taux de mortalité par cause et sexe : 2014 - 2018 (continued - suite)

Cause of death — Cause de décès	Venezuela (Bolivarian Republic of) - Venezuela (République bolivarienne du)		Armenia - Arménie			
	2014 (U)		2015 (C)			
	Male — Masculin	Female — Féminin	Male — Masculin		Female — Féminin	
	Number Nombre	Number Nombre	Number Nombre	Rate Taux	Number Nombre	Rate Taux
TOTAL	*97 701*	*64 424*	14 302	993.8	13 576	863.9
Certain infectious and parasitic diseases — Certaines maladies infectieuses et parasitaires						
Total	*4 288*	*2 650*	223	15.5	85	5.4
Intestinal infectious diseases — Maladies infectieuses intestinales	*705*	*685*	6	♦0.4	3	♦0.2
Tuberculosis — Tuberculose	*486*	*210*	57	4.0	7	♦0.4
Tetanus — Tétanos	*4*	-	-	-	-	-
Diphtheria — Diphtérie	-	-	-	-	-	-
Whooping cough — Coqueluche	*3*	*6*	-	-	-	-
Meningococcal infection — Infection à méningocoques	*9*	*6*	-	-	2	♦0.1
Septicaemia — Septicémie	*575*	*581*	19	♦1.3	16	♦1.0
Acute poliomyelitis — Poliomyélite aiguë	-	-	-	-	-	-
Measles — Rougeole	-	-	-	-	-	-
Viral hepatitis — Hépatite virale	*32*	*27*	87	6.0	16	♦1.0
Human immunodeficiency virus [HIV] disease — Maladies dues au virus de l'immunodéficience humaine (VIH)	*1 644*	*574*	25	♦1.7	8	♦0.5
Malaria — Paludisme	*21*	*23*	-	-	-	-
Neoplasms — Tumeurs	*13 379*	*13 098*	3 371	234.2	2 732	173.9
Malignant neoplasms — Tumeurs malignes						
Total	*12 189*	*12 010*	3 360	233.5	2 709	172.4
Malignant neoplasm of lip, oral cavity and pharynx — Tumeur maligne de la lèvre, de la cavité buccale et du pharynx	*358*	*155*	45	3.1	9	♦0.6
Malignant neoplasm of oesophagus — Tumeur maligne de l'oesophage	*230*	*69*	36	2.5	13	♦0.8
Malignant neoplasm of stomach — Tumeur maligne de l'estomac	*1 113*	*726*	305	21.2	203	12.9
Malignant neoplasm of colon, rectosigmoid junction, rectum, anus and anal canal — Tumeur maligne du côlon, de la jonction recto-sigmoïdienne, du rectum, de l'anus et du canal anal	*917*	*934*	221	15.4	286	18.2
Malignant neoplasm of liver and intrahepatic bile ducts — Tumeur maligne du foie et des voies bilaires intrahépatiques	*506*	*423*	246	17.1	178	11.3
Malignant neoplasm of pancreas — Tumeur maligne du pancréas	*488*	*529*	174	12.1	170	10.8
Malignant neoplasm of trachea, bronchus and lung — Tumeur maligne de la trachée, des bronches et du poumon	*2 151*	*1 457*	1 020	70.9	222	14.1
Malignant neoplasm of female breast — Tumeur maligne du sein chez la femme	..	*2 204*	..	..	568	43.7
Malignant neoplasm of cervix uteri — Tumeur maligne du col de l'utérus	..	*1 563*	..	..	73	5.6
Malignant neoplasm of prostate — Tumeur maligne de la prostate	*2 585*	..	304	77.9	..	..
Malignant neoplasm of lymphoid, haematopoietic and related tissue — Tumeurs malignes primitives ou présumées primitives des tissus lymphoïde, hématopoïétique et apparentés	*1 077*	*913*	153	10.6	116	7.4
Disorders of the blood and blood-forming organs and certain disorders involving the immune mechanism — Maladies du sang et des organes hématopoïétiques et certains troubles du système immunitaire						
Total	*247*	*240*	10	♦0.7	5	♦0.3
Anaemias — Anémies	*160*	*165*	4	♦0.3	5	♦0.3
Endocrine, nutritional and metabolic diseases — Maladies endocriniennes, nutritionnelles et métaboliques						
Total	*7 303*	*7 170*	496	34.5	827	52.6
Diabetes mellitus — Diabète sucré	*6 749*	*6 673*	475	33.0	801	51.0
Malnutrition — Malnutrition	*290*	*238*	1	♦0.1	1	♦0.1
Mental and behavioural disorders — Troubles mentaux et du comportement	*45*	*4*	6	♦0.4	8	♦0.5
Diseases of the nervous system — Maladies du système nerveux	*1 506*	*1 203*	67	4.7	51	3.2
Diseases of the circulatory system — Maladies de l'appareil circulatoire						
Total	*28 166*	*22 355*	6 164	428.3	6 653	423.4
Acute rheumatic fever and chronic rheumatic heart diseases — Rhumatisme articularie aigu et cardiopathies rhumatismales chroniques	*31*	*43*	38	2.6	117	7.4
Hypertensive diseases — Maladies hypertensives	*3 594*	*3 605*	273	19.0	425	27.0
Ischaemic heart disease — Cardiopathie ischémique	*16 073*	*10 816*	4 181	290.5	3 937	250.5
Cerebrovascular disease — Maladie cérébrovasculaire	*6 147*	*5 779*	1 000	69.5	1 428	90.9
Diseases of arteries, arterioles and capillaries — Maladies des artères, artérioles et capillaires	*387*	*336*	389	27.0	422	26.9

20. Death and death rates by cause and sex: 2014 - 2018
Décès et taux de mortalité par cause et sexe : 2014 - 2018 (continued - suite)

Cause of death — Cause de décès	Venezuela (Bolivarian Republic of) - Venezuela (République bolivarienne du)		Armenia - Arménie			
	2014 (U)		2015 (C)			
	Male — Masculin	Female — Féminin	Male — Masculin		Female — Féminin	
	Number Nombre	Number Nombre	Number Nombre	Rate Taux	Number Nombre	Rate Taux
Diseases of the respiratory system — Maladies de l'appareil respiratoire						
Total	*6 456*	*5 652*	1 041	72.3	1 085	69.0
Influenza — Grippe	*4*	*4*	-	-	2	♦0.1
Pneumonia — Pneumopathies	*2 561*	*2 210*	311	21.6	351	22.3
Chronic lower respiratory diseases — Maladies chroniques des voies respiratoires inférieures	*2 637*	*2 264*	623	43.3	626	39.8
Diseases of the digestive system — Maladies de l'appareil digestif						
Total	*4 456*	*2 453*	870	60.5	782	49.8
Gastric and duodenal ulcer — Ulcère de l'estomac et du duodénum	*250*	*166*	134	9.3	116	7.4
Diseases of the liver — Maladies du foie	*2 704*	*752*	541	37.6	409	26.0
Diseases of the musculoskeletal system and connective tissue — Maladies du système ostéo-articularie, des muscles et du tissu conjonctif	*111*	*453*	25	♦1.7	39	2.5
Diseases of the genitourinary system — Maladies de l'appareil génito-urinaire						
Total	*1 754*	*1 349*	432	30.0	409	26.0
Disorders of kidney and ureter — Affections du rein et de l'uretère	*1 405*	*1 079*	344	23.9	402	25.6
Hyperplasia of prostate — Hyperplasie de la prostate	*156*	..	83	21.3	..	..
Pregnancy, childbirth and the puerperium — Grossesse, accouchement et puerpéralité						
Total	..	*490*	..	..	7	♦16.8
Pregnancy with abortive outcome — Grossesse se terminant par un avortement	..	*42*	..	..	1	♦2.4
Other direct obstetric causes — Autres décès maternels directs	..	*249*	..	..	3	♦7.2
Indirect obstetric causes — Décès maternels indirects	..	*197*	..	..	3	♦7.2
Certain conditions originating in the perinatal period — Certaines affections dont l'origine se situe dans la période périnatale	*3 284*	*2 321*	86	388.6	69	351.5
Congenital malformations, deformations and chromosomal abnormalities — Malformations congénitales et anomalies chromosomiques	*1 330*	*1 144*	250	1 129.5	151	769.2
Symptoms, signs and abnormal clinical and laboratory findings, not elsewhere classified — Symptômes, signes et résultats anormaux d'examens cliniques et de laboratoire, non classés ailleurs	*427*	*425*	259	18.0	300	19.1
All other diseases — Toutes autres maladies	*12*	*15*	13	♦0.9	7	♦0.4
External causes — Causes externes						
Total	*24 937*	*3 402*	989	68.7	366	23.3
Accidents						
Total	*7 311*	*1 898*	383	26.6	91	5.8
Transport accidents — Accidents de transport	*5 488*	*1 144*	256	17.8	63	4.0
Falls — Chutes	*431*	*254*	9	♦0.6	1	♦0.1
Accidental drowning and submersion — Noyade et submersion accidentelles	*334*	*55*	22	♦1.5	1	♦0.1
Exposure to smoke, fire and flames — Exposition à la fumée, au feu et aux flammes	*109*	*48*	3	♦0.2	2	♦0.1
Accidental poisoning by and exposure to noxious substances — Intoxication accidentelle par des substances nocives et exposition à ces substances	*44*	*27*	10	♦0.7	3	♦0.2
Intentional self-harm — Lésions auto-infligées	*472*	*97*	55	3.8	19	♦1.2
Assault — Agresssions	*8 725*	*524*	25	♦1.7	13	♦0.8
All other external causes — Toutes autres causes externes	*8 429*	*883*	526	36.5	243	15.5

Cause of death — Cause de décès	Armenia - Arménie				Bahrain - Bahreïn			
	2016 (C)				2014 (C)			
	Male — Masculin		Female — Féminin		Male — Masculin		Female — Féminin	
	Number Nombre	Rate Taux	Number Nombre	Rate Taux	Number Nombre	Rate Taux	Number Nombre	Rate Taux
TOTAL	**14 536**	**1 020.9**	**13 690**	**872.8**	**1 638**	**203.1**	**1 057**	**208.0**
Certain infectious and parasitic diseases — Certaines maladies infectieuses et parasitaires								
Total	175	12.3	66	4.2	40	5.0	21	♦4.1
Intestinal infectious diseases — Maladies infectieuses intestinales	3	♦0.2	4	♦0.3	2	♦0.2	1	♦0.2
Tuberculosis — Tuberculose	46	3.2	9	♦0.6	6	♦0.7	-	-
Tetanus — Tétanos	-	-	-	-	-	-	-	-
Diphtheria — Diphtérie	-	-	-	-	-	-	-	-
Whooping cough — Coqueluche	-	-	-	-	-	-	-	-
Meningococcal infection — Infection à méningocoques	-	-	-	-	-	-	-	-
Septicaemia — Septicémie	15	♦1.1	12	♦0.8	8	♦1.0	12	♦2.4
Acute poliomyelitis — Poliomyélite aiguë	-	-	-	-	-	-	-	-
Measles — Rougeole	-	-	-	-	-	-	-	-
Viral hepatitis — Hépatite virale	74	5.2	13	♦0.8	15	♦1.9	6	♦1.2
Human immunodeficiency virus [HIV] disease — Maladies dues au virus de l'immunodéficience humaine (VIH)	21	♦1.5	8	♦0.5	8	♦1.0	-	-
Malaria — Paludisme	-	-	-	-	-	-	-	-
Neoplasms — Tumeurs	**3 208**	**225.3**	**2 487**	**158.6**	**146**	**18.1**	**146**	**28.7**
Malignant neoplasms — Tumeurs malignes								
Total	3 197	224.5	2 465	157.2	140	17.4	139	27.4
Malignant neoplasm of lip, oral cavity and pharynx — Tumeur maligne de la lèvre, de la cavité buccale et du pharynx	38	2.7	12	♦0.8	3	♦0.4	2	♦0.4
Malignant neoplasm of oesophagus — Tumeur maligne de l'oesophage	34	2.4	20	♦1.3	2	♦0.2	-	-
Malignant neoplasm of stomach — Tumeur maligne de l'estomac	303	21.3	162	10.3	10	♦1.2	3	♦0.6
Malignant neoplasm of colon, rectosigmoid junction, rectum, anus and anal canal — Tumeur maligne du côlon, de la jonction recto-sigmoïdienne, du rectum, de l'anus et du canal anal	209	14.7	253	16.1	22	♦2.7	13	♦2.6
Malignant neoplasm of liver and intrahepatic bile ducts — Tumeur maligne du foie et des voies biliaires intrahépatiques	209	14.7	166	10.6	5	♦0.6	4	♦0.8
Malignant neoplasm of pancreas — Tumeur maligne du pancréas	190	13.3	171	10.9	9	♦1.1	8	♦1.6
Malignant neoplasm of trachea, bronchus and lung — Tumeur maligne de la trachée, des bronches et du poumon	975	68.5	195	12.4	23	♦2.9	5	♦1.0
Malignant neoplasm of female breast — Tumeur maligne du sein chez la femme	..	..	464	35.9	..	..	43	11.4
Malignant neoplasm of cervix uteri — Tumeur maligne du col de l'utérus	..	..	59	4.6	..	..	5	♦1.3
Malignant neoplasm of prostate — Tumeur maligne de la prostate	267	68.4	..	..	16	♦14.1	..	..
Malignant neoplasm of lymphoid, haematopoietic and related tissue — Tumeurs malignes primitives ou présumées primitives des tissus lymphoïde, hématopoïétique et apparentés	140	9.8	106	6.8	12	♦1.5	7	♦1.4
Disorders of the blood and blood-forming organs and certain disorders involving the immune mechanism — Maladies du sang et des organes hématopoïétiques et certains troubles du système immunitaire								
Total	14	♦1.0	13	♦0.8	23	♦2.9	23	♦4.5
Anaemias — Anémies	11	♦0.8	11	♦0.7	18	♦2.2	19	♦3.7
Endocrine, nutritional and metabolic diseases — Maladies endocriniennes, nutritionnelles et métaboliques								
Total	460	32.3	747	47.6	295	36.6	235	46.3
Diabetes mellitus — Diabète sucré	450	31.6	721	46.0	270	33.5	204	40.2
Malnutrition — Malnutrition	-	-	2	♦0.1	-	-	-	-
Mental and behavioural disorders — Troubles mentaux et du comportement	3	♦0.2	2	♦0.1	9	♦1.1	7	♦1.4
Diseases of the nervous system — Maladies du système nerveux	79	5.5	76	4.8	28	♦3.5	19	♦3.7
Diseases of the circulatory system — Maladies de l'appareil circulatoire								
Total	6 521	458.0	7 049	449.4	595	73.8	270	53.1
Acute rheumatic fever and chronic rheumatic heart diseases — Rhumatisme articularie aigu et cardiopathies rhumatismales chroniques	44	3.1	85	5.4	2	♦0.2	8	♦1.6
Hypertensive diseases — Maladies hypertensives	241	16.9	389	24.8	113	14.0	80	15.7
Ischaemic heart disease — Cardiopathie ischémique	4 405	309.4	4 200	267.8	62	7.7	24	♦4.7
Cerebrovascular disease — Maladie cérébrovasculaire	1 054	74.0	1 407	89.7	50	6.2	31	6.1

Cause of death — Cause de décès	Armenia - Arménie				Bahrain - Bahreïn			
	2016 (C)				2014 (C)			
	Male — Masculin		Female — Féminin		Male — Masculin		Female — Féminin	
	Number Nombre	Rate Taux	Number Nombre	Rate Taux	Number Nombre	Rate Taux	Number Nombre	Rate Taux
Diseases of arteries, arterioles and capillaries — Maladies des artères, artérioles et capillaires	372	26.1	486	31.0	3	♦0.4	4	♦0.8
Diseases of the respiratory system — Maladies de l'appareil respiratoire								
Total	1 079	75.8	1 069	68.2	46	5.7	37	7.3
Influenza — Grippe	4	♦0.3	4	♦0.3	-	-	-	-
Pneumonia — Pneumopathies	393	27.6	437	27.9	15	♦1.9	13	♦2.6
Chronic lower respiratory diseases — Maladies chroniques des voies respiratoires inférieures	582	40.9	539	34.4	17	♦2.1	13	♦2.6
Diseases of the digestive system — Maladies de l'appareil digestif								
Total	988	69.4	855	54.5	34	4.2	19	♦3.7
Gastric and duodenal ulcer — Ulcère de l'estomac et du duodénum	134	9.4	129	8.2	3	♦0.4	1	♦0.2
Diseases of the liver — Maladies du foie	667	46.8	505	32.2	19	♦2.4	7	♦1.4
Diseases of the musculoskeletal system and connective tissue — Maladies du système ostéo-articularie, des muscles et du tissu conjonctif	14	♦1.0	28	♦1.8	6	♦0.7	8	♦1.6
Diseases of the genitourinary system — Maladies de l'appareil génito-urinaire								
Total	448	31.5	422	26.9	33	4.1	23	♦4.5
Disorders of kidney and ureter — Affections du rein et de l'uretère	377	26.5	411	26.2	22	♦2.7	16	♦3.1
Hyperplasia of prostate — Hyperplasie de la prostate	65	16.7	..	..	2	♦1.8	..	..
Pregnancy, childbirth and the puerperium — Grossesse, accouchement et puerpéralité								
Total	..	..	14	♦34.5	..	..	2	♦9.6
Pregnancy with abortive outcome — Grossesse se terminant par un avortement	..	..	2	♦4.9	..	..	1	♦4.8
Other direct obstetric causes — Autres décès maternels directs	..	..	8	♦19.7	..	..	1	♦4.8
Indirect obstetric causes — Décès maternels indirects	..	..	4	♦9.9	..	..	-	-
Certain conditions originating in the perinatal period — Certaines affections dont l'origine se situe dans la période périnatale	96	447.7	56	292.5	43	398.7	34	335.1
Congenital malformations, deformations and chromosomal abnormalities — Malformations congénitales et anomalies chromosomiques	226	1 053.9	174	908.8	32	296.7	33	325.3
Symptoms, signs and abnormal clinical and laboratory findings, not elsewhere classified — Symptômes, signes et résultats anormaux d'examens cliniques et de laboratoire, non classés ailleurs	246	17.3	302	19.3	125	15.5	140	27.6
All other diseases — Toutes autres maladies	18	♦1.3	6	♦0.4	9	♦1.1	4	♦0.8
External causes — Causes externes								
Total	961	67.5	324	20.7	174	21.6	36	7.1
Accidents								
Total	290	20.4	83	5.3	129	16.0	27	♦5.3
Transport accidents — Accidents de transport	168	11.8	53	3.4	64	7.9	14	♦2.8
Falls — Chutes	10	♦0.7	5	♦0.3	12	♦1.5	2	♦0.4
Accidental drowning and submersion — Noyade et submersion accidentelles	12	♦0.8	1	♦0.1	7	♦0.9	-	-
Exposure to smoke, fire and flames — Exposition à la fumée, au feu et aux flammes	7	♦0.5	-	-	8	♦1.0	4	♦0.8
Accidental poisoning by and exposure to noxious substances — Intoxication accidentelle par des substances nocives et exposition à ces substances	6	♦0.4	3	♦0.2	-	-	-	-
Intentional self-harm — Lésions auto-infligées	53	3.7	14	♦0.9	8	♦1.0	1	♦0.2
Assault — Agresssions	26	♦1.8	8	♦0.5	7	♦0.9	-	-
All other external causes — Toutes autres causes externes	592	41.6	219	14.0	30	♦3.7	8	♦1.6

20. Death and death rates by cause and sex: 2014 - 2018
Décès et taux de mortalité par cause et sexe : 2014 - 2018 (continued - suite)

Brunei Darussalam - Brunéi Darussalam

Cause of death — Cause de décès	2017 (+C)				2018 (+C)			
	Male — Masculin		Female — Féminin		Male — Masculin		Female — Féminin	
	Number Nombre	Rate Taux	Number Nombre	Rate Taux	Number Nombre	Rate Taux	Number Nombre	Rate Taux
TOTAL	**911**	**407.8**	**785**	**380.9**	**878**	**376.2**	**734**	**351.2**
Certain infectious and parasitic diseases — Certaines maladies infectieuses et parasitaires								
Total	47	21.0	54	26.2	48	20.6	42	20.1
Intestinal infectious diseases — Maladies infectieuses intestinales	1	♦0.4	1	♦0.5	2	♦0.9	2	♦1.0
Tuberculosis — Tuberculose	8	♦3.6	6	♦2.9	4	♦1.7	4	♦1.9
Tetanus — Tétanos	-	-	-	-	-	-	-	-
Diphtheria — Diphtérie	-	-	-	-	-	-	-	-
Whooping cough — Coqueluche	-	-	-	-	-	-	-	-
Meningococcal infection — Infection à méningocoques	-	-	-	-	-	-	-	-
Septicaemia — Septicémie	28	♦12.5	38	18.4	26	♦11.1	26	♦12.4
Acute poliomyelitis — Poliomyélite aiguë	-	-	-	-	-	-	-	-
Measles — Rougeole	-	-	-	-	-	-	-	-
Viral hepatitis — Hépatite virale	2	♦0.9	1	♦0.5	6	♦2.6	4	♦1.9
Human immunodeficiency virus [HIV] disease — Maladies dues au virus de l'immunodéficience humaine (VIH)	2	♦0.9	-	-	-	-	-	-
Malaria — Paludisme	-	-	-	-	-	-	-	-
Neoplasms — Tumeurs	159	71.2	180	87.3	149	63.8	164	78.5
Malignant neoplasms — Tumeurs malignes								
Total	159	71.2	168	81.5	145	62.1	159	76.1
Malignant neoplasm of lip, oral cavity and pharynx — Tumeur maligne de la lèvre, de la cavité buccale et du pharynx	7	♦3.1	2	♦1.0	13	♦5.6	1	♦0.5
Malignant neoplasm of oesophagus — Tumeur maligne de l'oesophage	1	♦0.4	1	♦0.5	4	♦1.7	1	♦0.5
Malignant neoplasm of stomach — Tumeur maligne de l'estomac	16	♦7.2	6	♦2.9	11	♦4.7	9	♦4.3
Malignant neoplasm of colon, rectosigmoid junction, rectum, anus and anal canal — Tumeur maligne du côlon, de la jonction recto-sigmoïdienne, du rectum, de l'anus et du canal anal	36	16.1	24	♦11.6	28	♦12.0	19	♦9.1
Malignant neoplasm of liver and intrahepatic bile ducts — Tumeur maligne du foie et des voies bilaires intrahépatiques	11	♦4.9	7	♦3.4	17	♦7.3	8	♦3.8
Malignant neoplasm of pancreas — Tumeur maligne du pancréas	1	♦0.4	6	♦2.9	3	♦1.3	8	♦3.8
Malignant neoplasm of trachea, bronchus and lung — Tumeur maligne de la trachée, des bronches et du poumon	29	♦13.0	23	♦11.2	25	♦10.7	22	♦10.5
Malignant neoplasm of female breast — Tumeur maligne du sein chez la femme	..	..	30	♦18.5	..	..	27	♦16.4
Malignant neoplasm of cervix uteri — Tumeur maligne du col de l'utérus	..	..	11	♦6.8	..	..	11	♦6.7
Malignant neoplasm of prostate — Tumeur maligne de la prostate	12	♦30.9	..	..	12	♦29.0	..	..
Malignant neoplasm of lymphoid, haematopoietic and related tissue — Tumeurs malignes primitives ou présumées primitives des tissus lymphoïde, hématopoïétique et apparentés	16	♦7.2	11	♦5.3	18	♦7.7	20	♦9.6
Disorders of the blood and blood-forming organs and certain disorders involving the immune mechanism — Maladies du sang et des organes hématopoïétiques et certains troubles du système immunitaire								
Total	6	♦2.7	4	♦1.9	14	♦6.0	7	♦3.3
Anaemias — Anémies	1	♦0.4	1	♦0.5	1	♦0.4	2	♦1.0
Endocrine, nutritional and metabolic diseases — Maladies endocriniennes, nutritionnelles et métaboliques								
Total	98	43.9	104	50.5	105	45.0	97	46.4
Diabetes mellitus — Diabète sucré	79	35.4	92	44.6	83	35.6	77	36.8
Malnutrition — Malnutrition	-	-	-	-	1	♦0.4	-	-
Mental and behavioural disorders — Troubles mentaux et du comportement	17	♦7.6	17	♦8.2	14	♦6.0	20	♦9.6
Diseases of the nervous system — Maladies du système nerveux	28	♦12.5	24	♦11.6	24	♦10.3	17	♦8.1
Diseases of the circulatory system — Maladies de l'appareil circulatoire								
Total	299	133.8	192	93.2	283	121.3	179	85.6
Acute rheumatic fever and chronic rheumatic heart diseases — Rhumatisme articularie aigu et cardiopathies rhumatismales chroniques	3	♦1.3	-	-	1	♦0.4	1	♦0.5
Hypertensive diseases — Maladies hypertensives	51	22.8	34	16.5	26	♦11.1	26	♦12.4
Ischaemic heart disease — Cardiopathie ischémique	131	58.6	53	25.7	132	56.6	59	28.2
Cerebrovascular disease — Maladie cérébrovasculaire	78	34.9	65	31.5	78	33.4	69	33.0

20. Death and death rates by cause and sex: 2014 - 2018
Décès et taux de mortalité par cause et sexe : 2014 - 2018 (continued - suite)

Brunei Darussalam - Brunéi Darussalam

Cause of death — Cause de décès	2017 (+C)				2018 (+C)			
	Male — Masculin		Female — Féminin		Male — Masculin		Female — Féminin	
	Number Nombre	Rate Taux	Number Nombre	Rate Taux	Number Nombre	Rate Taux	Number Nombre	Rate Taux
Diseases of arteries, arterioles and capillaries — Maladies des artères, artérioles et capillaires	**4**	**♦1.8**	**4**	**♦1.9**	**10**	**♦4.3**	**4**	**♦1.9**
Diseases of the respiratory system — Maladies de l'appareil respiratoire								
Total	**62**	**27.8**	**68**	**33.0**	**62**	**26.6**	**61**	**29.2**
Influenza — Grippe	**-**	**-**	**-**	**-**	**-**	**-**	**-**	**-**
Pneumonia — Pneumopathies	**31**	**13.9**	**36**	**17.5**	**21**	**♦9.0**	**24**	**♦11.5**
Chronic lower respiratory diseases — Maladies chroniques des voies respiratoires inférieures	**22**	**♦9.8**	**23**	**♦11.2**	**31**	**13.3**	**26**	**♦12.4**
Diseases of the digestive system — Maladies de l'appareil digestif								
Total	**23**	**♦10.3**	**23**	**♦11.2**	**29**	**♦12.4**	**19**	**♦9.1**
Gastric and duodenal ulcer — Ulcère de l'estomac et du duodénum	**2**	**♦0.9**	**3**	**♦1.5**	**3**	**♦1.3**	**2**	**♦1.0**
Diseases of the liver — Maladies du foie	**6**	**♦2.7**	**5**	**♦2.4**	**7**	**♦3.0**	**2**	**♦1.0**
Diseases of the musculoskeletal system and connective tissue — Maladies du système ostéo-articularie, des muscles et du tissu conjonctif	**5**	**♦2.2**	**17**	**♦8.2**	**3**	**♦1.3**	**13**	**♦6.2**
Diseases of the genitourinary system — Maladies de l'appareil génito-urinaire								
Total	**27**	**♦12.1**	**24**	**♦11.6**	**19**	**♦8.1**	**22**	**♦10.5**
Disorders of kidney and ureter — Affections du rein et de l'uretère	**23**	**♦10.3**	**20**	**♦9.7**	**17**	**♦7.3**	**20**	**♦9.6**
Hyperplasia of prostate — Hyperplasie de la prostate	**3**	**♦7.7**	..	..	**1**	**♦2.4**	..	..
Pregnancy, childbirth and the puerperium — Grossesse, accouchement et puerpéralité								
Total	..	..	**4**	**♦62.0**	..	..	**-**	**-**
Pregnancy with abortive outcome — Grossesse se terminant par un avortement	..	..	**-**	**-**	..	..	**-**	**-**
Other direct obstetric causes — Autres décès maternels directs	..	..	**1**	**♦15.5**	..	..	**-**	**-**
Indirect obstetric causes — Décès maternels indirects	..	..	**3**	**♦46.5**	..	..	**-**	**-**
Certain conditions originating in the perinatal period — Certaines affections dont l'origine se situe dans la période périnatale	**19**	**♦562.8**	**15**	**♦487.6**	**22**	**♦679.2**	**14**	**♦473.0**
Congenital malformations, deformations and chromosomal abnormalities — Malformations congénitales et anomalies chromosomiques	**10**	**♦296.2**	**13**	**♦422.6**	**11**	**♦339.6**	**8**	**♦270.3**
Symptoms, signs and abnormal clinical and laboratory findings, not elsewhere classified — Symptômes, signes et résultats anormaux d'examens cliniques et de laboratoire, non classés ailleurs	**28**	**♦12.5**	**21**	**♦10.2**	**25**	**♦10.7**	**37**	**17.7**
All other diseases — Toutes autres maladies	**3**	**♦1.3**	**4**	**♦1.9**	**8**	**♦3.4**	**8**	**♦3.8**
External causes — Causes externes								
Total	**80**	**35.8**	**21**	**♦10.2**	**62**	**26.6**	**26**	**♦12.4**
Accidents								
Total	**61**	**27.3**	**16**	**♦7.8**	**44**	**18.9**	**17**	**♦8.1**
Transport accidents — Accidents de transport	**32**	**14.3**	**4**	**♦1.9**	**16**	**♦6.9**	**8**	**♦3.8**
Falls — Chutes	**9**	**♦4.0**	**3**	**♦1.5**	**10**	**♦4.3**	**5**	**♦2.4**
Accidental drowning and submersion — Noyade et submersion accidentelles	**9**	**♦4.0**	**-**	**-**	**7**	**♦3.0**	**1**	**♦0.5**
Exposure to smoke, fire and flames — Exposition à la fumée, au feu et aux flammes	**3**	**♦1.3**	**2**	**♦1.0**	**-**	**-**	**1**	**♦0.5**
Accidental poisoning by and exposure to noxious substances — Intoxication accidentelle par des substances nocives et exposition à ces substances	**-**	**-**	**-**	**-**	**1**	**♦0.4**	**-**	**-**
Intentional self-harm — Lésions auto-infligées	**11**	**♦4.9**	**-**	**-**	**10**	**♦4.3**	**3**	**♦1.4**
Assault — Agresssions	**2**	**♦0.9**	**2**	**♦1.0**	**1**	**♦0.4**	**-**	**-**
All other external causes — Toutes autres causes externes	**6**	**♦2.7**	**3**	**♦1.5**	**7**	**♦3.0**	**6**	**♦2.9**

20. Death and death rates by cause and sex: 2014 - 2018
Décès et taux de mortalité par cause et sexe : 2014 - 2018 (continued - suite)

Cause of death — Cause de décès	China, Hong Kong SAR - Chine, Hong Kong RAS				Cyprus - Chypre			
	2016 (...)		2017 (...)		2015 (U)		2016 (U)	
	Male — Masculin	Female — Féminin	Male — Masculin	Female — Féminin	Male — Masculin	Female — Féminin	Male — Masculin	Female — Féminin
	Number Nombre	Number Nombre	Number Nombre	Number Nombre	Number Nombre	Number Nombre	Number Nombre	Number Nombre
TOTAL	***26 002***	***20 659***	***25 408***	***20 471***	***3 138***	***2 850***	***3 012***	***2 575***
Certain infectious and parasitic diseases — Certaines maladies infectieuses et parasitaires								
Total	*738*	*610*	*779*	*602*	*72*	*74*	*62*	*70*
Intestinal infectious diseases — Maladies infectieuses intestinales	*25*	*29*	*22*	*36*	*21*	*17*	*12*	*26*
Tuberculosis — Tuberculose	*117*	*41*	*131*	*48*	*1*	-	*1*	-
Tetanus — Tétanos	-	-	-	-	-	-	-	-
Diphtheria — Diphtérie	-	-	-	-	-	-	-	-
Whooping cough — Coqueluche	-	-	-	-	-	-	-	-
Meningococcal infection — Infection à méningocoques	*1*	-	-	*1*	-	*1*	-	-
Septicaemia — Septicémie	*490*	*480*	*524*	*447*	*38*	*50*	*34*	*37*
Acute poliomyelitis — Poliomyélite aiguë	-	-	-	-	-	-	-	-
Measles — Rougeole	-	-	-	-	-	-	-	-
Viral hepatitis — Hépatite virale	*40*	*18*	*30*	*19*	*4*	*1*	*5*	*1*
Human immunodeficiency virus [HIV] disease — Maladies dues au virus de l'immunodéficience humaine (VIH)	*14*	*2*	*11*	*4*	*4*	-	*1*	-
Malaria — Paludisme	-	-	-	*1*	-	-	-	-
Neoplasms — Tumeurs	*8 628*	*5 922*	*8 623*	*6 036*	*791*	*592*	*778*	*546*
Malignant neoplasms — Tumeurs malignes								
Total	*8 447*	*5 762*	*8 487*	*5 867*	*769*	*566*	*758*	*522*
Malignant neoplasm of lip, oral cavity and pharynx — Tumeur maligne de la lèvre, de la cavité buccale et du pharynx	*403*	*147*	*368*	*142*	*12*	*5*	*14*	*6*
Malignant neoplasm of oesophagus — Tumeur maligne de l'oesophage	*273*	*62*	*241*	*56*	*6*	*1*	*7*	*1*
Malignant neoplasm of stomach — Tumeur maligne de l'estomac	*427*	*283*	*420*	*262*	*43*	*18*	*31*	*28*
Malignant neoplasm of colon, rectosigmoid junction, rectum, anus and anal canal — Tumeur maligne du côlon, de la jonction recto-sigmoïdienne, du rectum, de l'anus et du canal anal	*1 208*	*881*	*1 274*	*864*	*61*	*54*	*74*	*42*
Malignant neoplasm of liver and intrahepatic bile ducts — Tumeur maligne du foie et des voies bilaires intrahépatiques	*1 135*	*405*	*1 126*	*426*	*34*	*17*	*29*	*21*
Malignant neoplasm of pancreas — Tumeur maligne du pancréas	*368*	*310*	*387*	*303*	*50*	*35*	*46*	*36*
Malignant neoplasm of trachea, bronchus and lung — Tumeur maligne de la trachée, des bronches et du poumon	*2 529*	*1 251*	*2 596*	*1 294*	*183*	*53*	*197*	*62*
Malignant neoplasm of female breast — Tumeur maligne du sein chez la femme	..	*702*	..	*721*	..	*113*	..	*106*
Malignant neoplasm of cervix uteri — Tumeur maligne du col de l'utérus	..	*151*	..	*150*	..	*14*	..	*13*
Malignant neoplasm of prostate — Tumeur maligne de la prostate	*410*	..	*443*	..	*100*	..	*90*	..
Malignant neoplasm of lymphoid, haematopoietic and related tissue — Tumeurs malignes primitives ou présumées primitives des tissus lymphoïde, hématopoïétique et apparentés	*531*	*315*	*498*	*351*	*71*	*74*	*70*	*46*
Disorders of the blood and blood-forming organs and certain disorders involving the immune mechanism — Maladies du sang et des organes hématopoïétiques et certains troubles du système immunitaire								
Total	*53*	*50*	*35*	*54*	*17*	*16*	*22*	*25*
Anaemias — Anémies	*19*	*27*	*19*	*27*	*8*	*9*	*12*	*15*
Endocrine, nutritional and metabolic diseases — Maladies endocriniennes, nutritionnelles et métaboliques								
Total	*284*	*322*	*223*	*275*	*219*	*232*	*207*	*178*
Diabetes mellitus — Diabète sucré	*246*	*252*	*185*	*215*	*186*	*189*	*178*	*133*
Malnutrition — Malnutrition	*1*	*4*	*3*	*2*	*2*	*1*	*2*	*1*
Mental and behavioural disorders — Troubles mentaux et du comportement	*553*	*822*	*562*	*900*	*50*	*100*	*54*	*108*
Diseases of the nervous system — Maladies du système nerveux	*266*	*179*	*213*	*197*	*107*	*128*	*107*	*116*
Diseases of the circulatory system — Maladies de l'appareil circulatoire								
Total	*5 404*	*4 647*	*5 209*	*4 624*	*1 058*	*1 025*	*981*	*871*
Acute rheumatic fever and chronic rheumatic heart diseases — Rhumatisme articularie aigu et cardiopathies rhumatismales chroniques	*24*	*47*	*27*	*59*	*9*	*19*	*11*	*22*
Hypertensive diseases — Maladies hypertensives	*399*	*401*	*408*	*434*	*85*	*131*	*55*	*118*
Ischaemic heart disease — Cardiopathie ischémique	*2 398*	*1 634*	*2 274*	*1 593*	*426*	*243*	*443*	*203*

20. Death and death rates by cause and sex: 2014 - 2018
Décès et taux de mortalité par cause et sexe : 2014 - 2018 (continued - suite)

Cause of death — Cause de décès	China, Hong Kong SAR - Chine, Hong Kong RAS				Cyprus - Chypre			
	2016 (...)		2017 (...)		2015 (U)		2016 (U)	
	Male — Masculin	Female — Féminin	Male — Masculin	Female — Féminin	Male — Masculin	Female — Féminin	Male — Masculin	Female — Féminin
	Number Nombre	Number Nombre	Number Nombre	Number Nombre	Number Nombre	Number Nombre	Number Nombre	Number Nombre
Cerebrovascular disease — Maladie cérébrovasculaire	*1 666*	*1 558*	*1 546*	*1 578*	*170*	*206*	*163*	*200*
Diseases of arteries, arterioles and capillaries — Maladies des artères, artérioles et capillaires	*247*	*169*	*250*	*128*	*51*	*27*	*45*	*17*
Diseases of the respiratory system — Maladies de l'appareil respiratoire								
Total	*6 080*	*4 573*	*6 006*	*4 396*	*313*	*237*	*276*	*220*
Influenza — Grippe	*43*	*50*	*70*	*85*	*2*	-	*1*	*1*
Pneumonia — Pneumopathies	*4 393*	*3 899*	*4 360*	*3 672*	*31*	*39*	*34*	*30*
Chronic lower respiratory diseases — Maladies chroniques des voies respiratoires inférieures	*1 256*	*383*	*1 149*	*356*	*94*	*40*	*96*	*56*
Diseases of the digestive system — Maladies de l'appareil digestif								
Total	*854*	*708*	*840*	*725*	*100*	*94*	*112*	*82*
Gastric and duodenal ulcer — Ulcère de l'estomac et du duodénum	*56*	*23*	*60*	*39*	*2*	*4*	*9*	*3*
Diseases of the liver — Maladies du foie	*296*	*157*	*259*	*164*	*40*	*16*	*38*	*12*
Diseases of the musculoskeletal system and connective tissue — Maladies du système ostéo-articularie, des muscles et du tissu conjonctif	*88*	*101*	*84*	*95*	*10*	*18*	*8*	*18*
Diseases of the genitourinary system — Maladies de l'appareil génito-urinaire								
Total	*1 075*	*1 225*	*1 059*	*1 201*	*114*	*103*	*98*	*104*
Disorders of kidney and ureter — Affections du rein et de l'uretère	*871*	*905*	*857*	*878*	*68*	*58*	*57*	*49*
Hyperplasia of prostate — Hyperplasie de la prostate	*5*	..	*2*	..	*5*	..	*4*	..
Pregnancy, childbirth and the puerperium — Grossesse, accouchement et puerpéralité								
Total	..	-	..	*1*	..	-	..	-
Pregnancy with abortive outcome — Grossesse se terminant par un avortement	..	-	..	-	..	-	..	-
Other direct obstetric causes — Autres décès maternels directs	..	-	..	*1*	..	-	..	-
Indirect obstetric causes — Décès maternels indirects	..	-	..	-	..	-	..	-
Certain conditions originating in the perinatal period — Certaines affections dont l'origine se situe dans la période périnatale	*19*	*20*	*18*	*24*	*9*	*9*	*12*	*7*
Congenital malformations, deformations and chromosomal abnormalities — Malformations congénitales et anomalies chromosomiques	*32*	*28*	*33*	*37*	*7*	*8*	*11*	*8*
Symptoms, signs and abnormal clinical and laboratory findings, not elsewhere classified — Symptômes, signes et résultats anormaux d'examens cliniques et de laboratoire, non classés ailleurs	*663*	*722*	*560*	*609*	*79*	*100*	*69*	*98*
All other diseases — Toutes autres maladies	*89*	*93*	*82*	*80*	*8*	*13*	*11*	*25*
External causes — Causes externes								
Total	*1 176*	*637*	*1 082*	*615*	*184*	*101*	*204*	*99*
Accidents								
Total	*516*	*297*	*515*	*283*	*134*	*84*	*155*	*81*
Transport accidents — Accidents de transport	*67*	*48*	*95*	*47*	*49*	*26*	*47*	*16*
Falls — Chutes	*189*	*88*	*156*	*81*	*16*	*6*	*28*	*12*
Accidental drowning and submersion — Noyade et submersion accidentelles	*30*	*8*	*22*	*8*	*9*	*3*	*17*	*5*
Exposure to smoke, fire and flames — Exposition à la fumée, au feu et aux flammes	*2*	*1*	*8*	*5*	*1*	*4*	*1*	*1*
Accidental poisoning by and exposure to noxious substances — Intoxication accidentelle par des substances nocives et exposition à ces substances	*85*	*27*	*81*	*13*	*11*	*1*	*12*	*5*
Intentional self-harm — Lésions auto-infligées	*617*	*314*	*531*	*314*	*31*	*9*	*31*	*5*
Assault — Agresssions	*9*	*6*	*9*	*5*	*10*	*3*	*7*	*5*
All other external causes — Toutes autres causes externes	*34*	*20*	*27*	*13*	*9*	*5*	*11*	*8*

20. Death and death rates by cause and sex: 2014 - 2018
Décès et taux de mortalité par cause et sexe : 2014 - 2018 (continued - suite)

Georgia - Géorgie

Cause of death — Cause de décès	2017 (C)				2018 (C)			
	Male — Masculin		Female — Féminin		Male — Masculin		Female — Féminin	
	Number Nombre	Rate Taux	Number Nombre	Rate Taux	Number Nombre	Rate Taux	Number Nombre	Rate Taux
TOTAL	**24 423**	**1 367.1**	**23 399**	**1 207.8**	**23 836**	**1 330.7**	**22 688**	**1 172.3**
Certain infectious and parasitic diseases — Certaines maladies infectieuses et parasitaires								
Total	491	27.5	226	11.7	429	24.0	159	8.2
Intestinal infectious diseases — Maladies infectieuses intestinales	9	♦0.5	14	♦0.7	6	♦0.3	6	♦0.3
Tuberculosis — Tuberculose	57	3.2	19	♦1.0	69	3.9	23	♦1.2
Tetanus — Tétanos	2	♦0.1	2	♦0.1	3	♦0.2	1	♦0.1
Diphtheria — Diphtérie	-	-	-	-	-	-	-	-
Whooping cough — Coqueluche	-	-	-	-	-	-	-	-
Meningococcal infection — Infection à méningocoques	1	♦0.1	2	♦0.1	3	♦0.2	1	♦0.1
Septicaemia — Septicémie	88	4.9	101	5.2	21	♦1.2	38	2.0
Acute poliomyelitis — Poliomyélite aiguë	-	-	-	-	-	-	-	-
Measles — Rougeole	-	-	-	-	2	♦0.1	-	-
Viral hepatitis — Hépatite virale	266	14.9	53	2.7	230	12.8	55	2.8
Human immunodeficiency virus [HIV] disease — Maladies dues au virus de l'immunodéficience humaine (VIH)	28	♦1.6	8	♦0.4	44	2.5	11	♦0.6
Malaria — Paludisme	-	-	-	-	-	-	-	-
Neoplasms — Tumeurs	**3 978**	**222.7**	**3 116**	**160.8**	**3 984**	**222.4**	**3 345**	**172.8**
Malignant neoplasms — Tumeurs malignes								
Total	3 868	216.5	3 016	155.7	3 906	218.1	3 241	167.5
Malignant neoplasm of lip, oral cavity and pharynx — Tumeur maligne de la lèvre, de la cavité buccale et du pharynx	137	7.7	37	1.9	167	9.3	35	1.8
Malignant neoplasm of oesophagus — Tumeur maligne de l'oesophage	42	2.4	20	♦1.0	44	2.5	28	♦1.4
Malignant neoplasm of stomach — Tumeur maligne de l'estomac	306	17.1	194	10.0	316	17.6	199	10.3
Malignant neoplasm of colon, rectosigmoid junction, rectum, anus and anal canal — Tumeur maligne du côlon, de la jonction recto-sigmoïdienne, du rectum, de l'anus et du canal anal	285	16.0	219	11.3	297	16.6	276	14.3
Malignant neoplasm of liver and intrahepatic bile ducts — Tumeur maligne du foie et des voies bilaires intrahépatiques	231	12.9	84	4.3	242	13.5	127	6.6
Malignant neoplasm of pancreas — Tumeur maligne du pancréas	131	7.3	120	6.2	115	6.4	142	7.3
Malignant neoplasm of trachea, bronchus and lung — Tumeur maligne de la trachée, des bronches et du poumon	923	51.7	152	7.8	974	54.4	183	9.5
Malignant neoplasm of female breast — Tumeur maligne du sein chez la femme	..	..	708	44.6	..	..	737	46.7
Malignant neoplasm of cervix uteri — Tumeur maligne du col de l'utérus	..	..	157	9.9	..	..	166	10.5
Malignant neoplasm of prostate — Tumeur maligne de la prostate	365	67.7	..	..	380	70.0	..	..
Malignant neoplasm of lymphoid, haematopoietic and related tissue — Tumeurs malignes primitives ou présumées primitives des tissus lymphoïde, hématopoïétique et apparentés	224	12.5	216	11.1	240	13.4	206	10.6
Disorders of the blood and blood-forming organs and certain disorders involving the immune mechanism — Maladies du sang et des organes hématopoïétiques et certains troubles du système immunitaire								
Total	287	16.1	270	13.9	254	14.2	237	12.2
Anaemias — Anémies	219	12.3	220	11.4	161	9.0	181	9.4
Endocrine, nutritional and metabolic diseases — Maladies endocriniennes, nutritionnelles et métaboliques								
Total	446	25.0	544	28.1	308	17.2	367	19.0
Diabetes mellitus — Diabète sucré	399	22.3	492	25.4	289	16.1	350	18.1
Malnutrition — Malnutrition	4	♦0.2	4	♦0.2	-	-	1	♦0.1
Mental and behavioural disorders — Troubles mentaux et du comportement	**61**	**3.4**	**45**	**2.3**	**15**	**♦0.8**	**37**	**1.9**
Diseases of the nervous system — Maladies du système nerveux	**345**	**19.3**	**278**	**14.3**	**269**	**15.0**	**252**	**13.0**
Diseases of the circulatory system — Maladies de l'appareil circulatoire								
Total	9 364	524.1	10 493	541.6	10 269	573.3	11 279	582.8
Acute rheumatic fever and chronic rheumatic heart diseases — Rhumatisme articularie aigu et cardiopathies rhumatismales chroniques	65	3.6	81	4.2	18	♦1.0	17	♦0.9
Hypertensive diseases — Maladies hypertensives	857	48.0	1 338	69.1	898	50.1	1 331	68.8
Ischaemic heart disease — Cardiopathie ischémique	2 278	127.5	2 020	104.3	3 030	169.2	2 378	122.9
Cerebrovascular disease — Maladie cérébrovasculaire	2 893	161.9	3 578	184.7	4 106	229.2	5 239	270.7

20. Death and death rates by cause and sex: 2014 - 2018
Décès et taux de mortalité par cause et sexe : 2014 - 2018 (continued - suite)

Georgia - Géorgie

Cause of death — Cause de décès	2017 (C)				2018 (C)			
	Male — Masculin		Female — Féminin		Male — Masculin		Female — Féminin	
	Number Nombre	Rate Taux	Number Nombre	Rate Taux	Number Nombre	Rate Taux	Number Nombre	Rate Taux
Diseases of arteries, arterioles and capillaries — Maladies des artères, artérioles et capillaires	205	11.5	146	7.5	234	13.1	135	7.0
Diseases of the respiratory system — Maladies de l'appareil respiratoire								
Total	1 417	79.3	1 192	61.5	1 934	108.0	1 737	89.8
Influenza — Grippe	6	♦0.3	13	♦0.7	4	♦0.2	8	♦0.4
Pneumonia — Pneumopathies	415	23.2	417	21.5	721	40.3	722	37.3
Chronic lower respiratory diseases — Maladies chroniques des voies respiratoires inférieures	232	13.0	150	7.7	247	13.8	133	6.9
Diseases of the digestive system — Maladies de l'appareil digestif								
Total	836	46.8	551	28.4	965	53.9	623	32.2
Gastric and duodenal ulcer — Ulcère de l'estomac et du duodénum	85	4.8	78	4.0	126	7.0	125	6.5
Diseases of the liver — Maladies du foie	409	22.9	118	6.1	456	25.5	143	7.4
Diseases of the musculoskeletal system and connective tissue — Maladies du système ostéo-articularie, des muscles et du tissu conjonctif	21	♦1.2	43	2.2	10	♦0.6	20	♦1.0
Diseases of the genitourinary system — Maladies de l'appareil génito-urinaire								
Total	502	28.1	317	16.4	351	19.6	290	15.0
Disorders of kidney and ureter — Affections du rein et de l'uretère	408	22.8	252	13.0	281	15.7	216	11.2
Hyperplasia of prostate — Hyperplasie de la prostate	18	♦3.3	..	..	7	♦1.3	..	..
Pregnancy, childbirth and the puerperium — Grossesse, accouchement et puerpéralité								
Total	..	..	12	♦22.5	..	..	20	♦39.1
Pregnancy with abortive outcome — Grossesse se terminant par un avortement	..	..	1	♦1.9	..	..	1	♦2.0
Other direct obstetric causes — Autres décès maternels directs	..	..	6	♦11.3	..	..	12	♦23.5
Indirect obstetric causes — Décès maternels indirects	..	..	5	♦9.4	..	..	7	♦13.7
Certain conditions originating in the perinatal period — Certaines affections dont l'origine se situe dans la période périnatale	199	719.5	158	616.3	170	640.6	127	516.3
Congenital malformations, deformations and chromosomal abnormalities — Malformations congénitales et anomalies chromosomiques	75	271.2	71	277.0	62	233.6	43	174.8
Symptoms, signs and abnormal clinical and laboratory findings, not elsewhere classified — Symptômes, signes et résultats anormaux d'examens cliniques et de laboratoire, non classés ailleurs	4 952	277.2	5 618	290.0	3 320	185.3	3 620	187.0
All other diseases — Toutes autres maladies	34	1.9	33	1.7	7	♦0.4	13	♦0.7
External causes — Causes externes								
Total	1 415	79.2	432	22.3	1 489	83.1	519	26.8
Accidents								
Total	1 083	60.6	349	18.0	1 103	61.6	399	20.6
Transport accidents — Accidents de transport	390	21.8	95	4.9	385	21.5	129	6.7
Falls — Chutes	148	8.3	48	2.5	205	11.4	111	5.7
Accidental drowning and submersion — Noyade et submersion accidentelles	46	2.6	5	♦0.3	48	2.7	10	♦0.5
Exposure to smoke, fire and flames — Exposition à la fumée, au feu et aux flammes	79	4.4	43	2.2	60	3.3	41	2.1
Accidental poisoning by and exposure to noxious substances — Intoxication accidentelle par des substances nocives et exposition à ces substances	45	2.5	21	♦1.1	51	2.8	18	♦0.9
Intentional self-harm — Lésions auto-infligées	120	6.7	30	♦1.5	205	11.4	45	2.3
Assault — Agresssions	41	2.3	10	♦0.5	53	3.0	14	♦0.7
All other external causes — Toutes autres causes externes	171	9.6	43	2.2	128	7.1	61	3.2

20. Death and death rates by cause and sex: 2014 - 2018
Décès et taux de mortalité par cause et sexe : 2014 - 2018 (continued - suite)

Cause of death — Cause de décès	Iran (Islamic Republic of) - Iran (République islamique d')						Iraq	
	2015 (U)		2016 (C)				2015 (U)	
	Male — Masculin	Female — Féminin	Male — Masculin		Female — Féminin		Male — Masculin	Female — Féminin
	Number Nombre	Number Nombre	Number Nombre	Rate Taux	Number Nombre	Rate Taux	Number Nombre	Number Nombre
TOTAL	189 429	137 716	195 010	480.9	144 795	366.7	62 021	62 021
Certain infectious and parasitic diseases — Certaines maladies infectieuses et parasitaires								
Total	3 601	2 356	3 291	8.1	2 215	5.6	2 197	2 197
Intestinal infectious diseases — Maladies infectieuses intestinales	462	380	487	1.2	418	1.1	88	88
Tuberculosis — Tuberculose	478	314	422	1.0	313	0.8	208	208
Tetanus — Tétanos	3	1	3	♦0.0	2	♦0.0	4	4
Diphtheria — Diphtérie	-	-	2	♦0.0	-	-	4	4
Whooping cough — Coqueluche	1	1	1	♦0.0	1	♦0.0	-	-
Meningococcal infection — Infection à méningocoques	155	106	82	0.2	58	0.1	1	1
Septicaemia — Septicémie	604	490	503	1.2	454	1.1	1 510	1 510
Acute poliomyelitis — Poliomyélite aiguë	9	3	5	♦0.0	7	♦0.0	3	3
Measles — Rougeole	3	-	1	♦0.0	1	♦0.0	7	7
Viral hepatitis — Hépatite virale	644	197	655	1.6	233	0.6	53	53
Human immunodeficiency virus [HIV] disease — Maladies dues au virus de l'immunodéficience humaine (VIH)	263	71	251	0.6	57	0.1	3	3
Malaria — Paludisme	2	-	-	-	-	-	-	-
Neoplasms — Tumeurs	28 838	20 083	31 409	77.5	21 993	55.7	5 046	4 785
Malignant neoplasms — Tumeurs malignes								
Total	27 491	19 078	29 962	73.9	20 901	52.9	5 001	4 740
Malignant neoplasm of lip, oral cavity and pharynx — Tumeur maligne de la lèvre, de la cavité buccale et du pharynx	292	212	248	0.6	214	0.5	97	97
Malignant neoplasm of oesophagus — Tumeur maligne de l'oesophage	1 005	719	1 081	2.7	752	1.9	54	54
Malignant neoplasm of stomach — Tumeur maligne de l'estomac	4 841	2 451	5 004	12.3	2 565	6.5	248	248
Malignant neoplasm of colon, rectosigmoid junction, rectum, anus and anal canal — Tumeur maligne du côlon, de la jonction recto-sigmoïdienne, du rectum, de l'anus et du canal anal	1 923	1 418	2 194	5.4	1 650	4.2	257	257
Malignant neoplasm of liver and intrahepatic bile ducts — Tumeur maligne du foie et des voies bilaires intrahépatiques	1 619	1 182	1 787	4.4	1 355	3.4	323	323
Malignant neoplasm of pancreas — Tumeur maligne du pancréas	1 031	675	1 278	3.2	751	1.9	275	275
Malignant neoplasm of trachea, bronchus and lung — Tumeur maligne de la trachée, des bronches et du poumon	3 529	1 511	3 931	9.7	1 756	4.4	1 103	1 103
Malignant neoplasm of female breast — Tumeur maligne du sein chez la femme	..	2 793	..	..	3 188	10.5	..	28
Malignant neoplasm of cervix uteri — Tumeur maligne du col de l'utérus	..	184	..	..	199	0.7	..	-
Malignant neoplasm of prostate — Tumeur maligne de la prostate	2 586	..	2 911	41.2	..	..	244	..
Malignant neoplasm of lymphoid, haematopoietic and related tissue — Tumeurs malignes primitives ou présumées primitives des tissus lymphoïde, hématopoïétique et apparentés	3 270	2 065	3 508	8.7	2 173	5.5	603	603
Disorders of the blood and blood-forming organs and certain disorders involving the immune mechanism — Maladies du sang et des organes hématopoïétiques et certains troubles du système immunitaire								
Total	909	744	880	2.2	701	1.8	123	123
Anaemias — Anémies	394	362	399	1.0	326	0.8	102	102
Endocrine, nutritional and metabolic diseases — Maladies endocriniennes, nutritionnelles et métaboliques								
Total	8 604	9 816	9 268	22.9	11 078	28.1	2 034	2 034
Diabetes mellitus — Diabète sucré	7 361	8 710	8 344	20.6	10 234	25.9	1 901	1 901
Malnutrition — Malnutrition	67	75	84	0.2	108	0.3	28	28
Mental and behavioural disorders — Troubles mentaux et du comportement	1 154	624	1 182	2.9	556	1.4	14	14
Diseases of the nervous system — Maladies du système nerveux	3 994	3 389	4 128	10.2	3 639	9.2	1 176	1 176
Diseases of the circulatory system — Maladies de l'appareil circulatoire								
Total	74 071	61 690	76 660	189.0	65 033	164.7	20 864	20 864
Acute rheumatic fever and chronic rheumatic heart diseases — Rhumatisme articularie aigu et cardiopathies rhumatismales chroniques	684	655	462	1.1	568	1.4	85	85
Hypertensive diseases — Maladies hypertensives	10 069	10 359	11 329	27.9	11 643	29.5	2 983	2 983
Ischaemic heart disease — Cardiopathie ischémique	29 259	21 677	34 212	84.4	25 750	65.2	5 337	5 337

20. Death and death rates by cause and sex: 2014 - 2018
Décès et taux de mortalité par cause et sexe : 2014 - 2018 (continued - suite)

Cause of death — Cause de décès	Iran (Islamic Republic of) - Iran (République islamique d')						Iraq	
	2015 (U)		2016 (C)				2015 (U)	
	Male — Masculin	Female — Féminin	Male — Masculin		Female — Féminin		Male — Masculin	Female — Féminin
	Number Nombre	Number Nombre	Number Nombre	Rate Taux	Number Nombre	Rate Taux	Number Nombre	Number Nombre
Cerebrovascular disease — Maladie cérébrovasculaire	*14 265*	*13 137*	15 101	37.2	14 267	36.1	*5 785*	*5 785*
Diseases of arteries, arterioles and capillaries — Maladies des artères, artérioles et capillaires	*2 540*	*2 014*	1 768	4.4	1 292	3.3	*341*	*341*
Diseases of the respiratory system — Maladies de l'appareil respiratoire								
Total	*12 145*	*8 770*	13 137	32.4	9 795	24.8	*1 912*	*1 912*
Influenza — Grippe	*241*	*208*	78	0.2	85	0.2	*2*	*2*
Pneumonia — Pneumopathies	*3 275*	*2 560*	3 585	8.8	2 942	7.5	*786*	*786*
Chronic lower respiratory diseases — Maladies chroniques des voies respiratoires inférieures	*4 242*	*2 705*	4 732	11.7	3 260	8.3	*244*	*244*
Diseases of the digestive system — Maladies de l'appareil digestif								
Total	*4 553*	*3 339*	4 993	12.3	3 814	9.7	*832*	*832*
Gastric and duodenal ulcer — Ulcère de l'estomac et du duodénum	*375*	*213*	407	1.0	289	0.7	*53*	*53*
Diseases of the liver — Maladies du foie	*1 674*	*1 059*	1 889	4.7	1 202	3.0	*571*	*571*
Diseases of the musculoskeletal system and connective tissue — Maladies du système ostéo-articularie, des muscles et du tissu conjonctif	*826*	*851*	440	1.1	626	1.6	*30*	*30*
Diseases of the genitourinary system — Maladies de l'appareil génito-urinaire								
Total	*4 832*	*3 503*	4 837	11.9	3 883	9.8	*3 771*	*3 760*
Disorders of kidney and ureter — Affections du rein et de l'uretère	*4 411*	*3 201*	4 368	10.8	3 533	8.9	*3 756*	*3 756*
Hyperplasia of prostate — Hyperplasie de la prostate	*86*	..	70	1.0	..	..	*8*	..
Pregnancy, childbirth and the puerperium — Grossesse, accouchement et puerpéralité								
Total	..	*111*	..	..	135	8.8	..	*1*
Pregnancy with abortive outcome — Grossesse se terminant par un avortement	..	*25*	..	..	16	♦1.0	..	-
Other direct obstetric causes — Autres décès maternels directs	..	*65*	..	..	87	5.7	..	*1*
Indirect obstetric causes — Décès maternels indirects	..	*17*	..	..	23	♦1.5	..	-
Certain conditions originating in the perinatal period — Certaines affections dont l'origine se situe dans la période périnatale	*6 093*	*4 994*	6 194	787.9	5 077	684.3	*4 526*	*4 526*
Congenital malformations, deformations and chromosomal abnormalities — Malformations congénitales et anomalies chromosomiques	*2 667*	*2 179*	2 607	331.6	2 296	309.5	*1 690*	*1 686*
Symptoms, signs and abnormal clinical and laboratory findings, not elsewhere classified — Symptômes, signes et résultats anormaux d'examens cliniques et de laboratoire, non classés ailleurs	*10 808*	*6 842*	9 501	23.4	5 665	14.3	*4 880*	*5 155*
All other diseases — Toutes autres maladies	*577*	*643*	474	1.2	512	1.3	*28*	*28*
External causes — Causes externes								
Total	*25 754*	*7 781*	26 009	64.1	7 775	19.7	*12 898*	*12 898*
Accidents								
Total	*19 450*	*5 988*	20 103	49.6	5 972	15.1	*2 824*	*2 824*
Transport accidents — Accidents de transport	*11 595*	*3 359*	11 762	29.0	3 221	8.2	*1 041*	*1 041*
Falls — Chutes	*839*	*325*	863	2.1	408	1.0	*22*	*22*
Accidental drowning and submersion — Noyade et submersion accidentelles	*615*	*149*	632	1.6	131	0.3	*103*	*103*
Exposure to smoke, fire and flames — Exposition à la fumée, au feu et aux flammes	*468*	*364*	665	1.6	402	1.0	*23*	*23*
Accidental poisoning by and exposure to noxious substances — Intoxication accidentelle par des substances nocives et exposition à ces substances	*1 105*	*318*	1 180	2.9	302	0.8	*1*	*1*
Intentional self-harm — Lésions auto-infligées	*1 669*	*706*	2 073	5.1	851	2.2	*3*	*3*
Assault — Agresssions	*697*	*157*	3 297	8.1	643	1.6	*311*	*311*
All other external causes — Toutes autres causes externes	*3 938*	*930*	536	1.3	309	0.8	*9 760*	*9 760*

20. Death and death rates by cause and sex: 2014 - 2018
Décès et taux de mortalité par cause et sexe : 2014 - 2018 (continued - suite)

Cause of death — Cause de décès	Iraq		Israel - Israël			
	2016 (U)		2016 (C)			
	Male — Masculin	Female — Féminin	Male — Masculin		Female — Féminin	
	Number Nombre	Number Nombre	Number Nombre	Rate Taux	Number Nombre	Rate Taux
TOTAL	64 607	48 223	21 733	512.9	22 233	516.0
Certain infectious and parasitic diseases — Certaines maladies infectieuses et parasitaires						
Total	2 279	2 027	1 239	29.2	1 317	30.6
Intestinal infectious diseases — Maladies infectieuses intestinales	61	64	87	2.1	100	2.3
Tuberculosis — Tuberculose	160	109	6	♦0.1	7	♦0.2
Tetanus — Tétanos	6	4	-	-	-	-
Diphtheria — Diphtérie	7	4	-	-	-	-
Whooping cough — Coqueluche	2	2	-	-	1	♦0.0
Meningococcal infection — Infection à méningocoques	2	1	1	♦0.0	1	♦0.0
Septicaemia — Septicémie	1 520	1 386	1 026	24.2	1 114	25.9
Acute poliomyelitis — Poliomyélite aiguë	4	1	-	-	-	-
Measles — Rougeole	-	-	-	-	-	-
Viral hepatitis — Hépatite virale	65	47	30	♦0.7	24	♦0.6
Human immunodeficiency virus [HIV] disease — Maladies dues au virus de l'immunodéficience humaine (VIH)	32	32	20	♦0.5	8	♦0.2
Malaria — Paludisme	-	-	-	-	-	-
Neoplasms — Tumeurs	5 295	5 319	5 726	135.1	5 662	131.4
Malignant neoplasms — Tumeurs malignes						
Total	5 243	5 256	5 580	131.7	5 497	127.6
Malignant neoplasm of lip, oral cavity and pharynx — Tumeur maligne de la lèvre, de la cavité buccale et du pharynx	81	68	70	1.7	34	0.8
Malignant neoplasm of oesophagus — Tumeur maligne de l'oesophage	58	46	78	1.8	44	1.0
Malignant neoplasm of stomach — Tumeur maligne de l'estomac	248	235	272	6.4	191	4.4
Malignant neoplasm of colon, rectosigmoid junction, rectum, anus and anal canal — Tumeur maligne du côlon, de la jonction recto-sigmoïdienne, du rectum, de l'anus et du canal anal	285	244	648	15.3	655	15.2
Malignant neoplasm of liver and intrahepatic bile ducts — Tumeur maligne du foie et des voies bilaires intrahépatiques	344	294	207	4.9	133	3.1
Malignant neoplasm of pancreas — Tumeur maligne du pancréas	296	226	498	11.8	457	10.6
Malignant neoplasm of trachea, bronchus and lung — Tumeur maligne de la trachée, des bronches et du poumon	1 163	541	1 264	29.8	633	14.7
Malignant neoplasm of female breast — Tumeur maligne du sein chez la femme	..	1 156	..	..	1 038	33.1
Malignant neoplasm of cervix uteri — Tumeur maligne du col de l'utérus	..	67	..	..	82	2.6
Malignant neoplasm of prostate — Tumeur maligne de la prostate	265	..	410	41.7	..	..
Malignant neoplasm of lymphoid, haematopoietic and related tissue — Tumeurs malignes primitives ou présumées primitives des tissus lymphoïde, hématopoïétique et apparentés	662	547	656	15.5	614	14.2
Disorders of the blood and blood-forming organs and certain disorders involving the immune mechanism — Maladies du sang et des organes hématopoïétiques et certains troubles du système immunitaire						
Total	132	117	110	2.6	179	4.2
Anaemias — Anémies	107	89	65	1.5	122	2.8
Endocrine, nutritional and metabolic diseases — Maladies endocriniennes, nutritionnelles et métaboliques						
Total	1 937	2 194	1 437	33.9	1 733	40.2
Diabetes mellitus — Diabète sucré	1 826	2 074	1 089	25.7	1 202	27.9
Malnutrition — Malnutrition	25	17	12	♦0.3	17	♦0.4
Mental and behavioural disorders — Troubles mentaux et du comportement	16	14	672	15.9	1 109	25.7
Diseases of the nervous system — Maladies du système nerveux	1 067	992	796	18.8	945	21.9
Diseases of the circulatory system — Maladies de l'appareil circulatoire						
Total	22 777	21 425	4 957	117.0	5 353	124.2
Acute rheumatic fever and chronic rheumatic heart diseases — Rhumatisme articularie aigu et cardiopathies rhumatismales chroniques	65	71	60	1.4	97	2.3
Hypertensive diseases — Maladies hypertensives	3 362	3 778	393	9.3	649	15.1
Ischaemic heart disease — Cardiopathie ischémique	5 367	4 461	2 157	50.9	1 658	38.5
Cerebrovascular disease — Maladie cérébrovasculaire	6 592	6 024	1 026	24.2	1 246	28.9
Diseases of arteries, arterioles and capillaries — Maladies des artères, artérioles et capillaires	345	359	219	5.2	165	3.8

20. Death and death rates by cause and sex: 2014 - 2018
Décès et taux de mortalité par cause et sexe : 2014 - 2018 (continued - suite)

Cause of death — Cause de décès	Iraq		Israel - Israël			
	2016 (U)		2016 (C)			
	Male — Masculin	Female — Féminin	Male — Masculin		Female — Féminin	
	Number Nombre	Number Nombre	Number Nombre	Rate Taux	Number Nombre	Rate Taux
Diseases of the respiratory system — Maladies de l'appareil respiratoire						
Total	*1 887*	*1 622*	1 783	42.1	1 738	40.3
Influenza — Grippe	*4*	*9*	28	♦0.7	37	0.9
Pneumonia — Pneumopathies	*688*	*610*	563	13.3	596	13.8
Chronic lower respiratory diseases — Maladies chroniques des voies respiratoires inférieures	*246*	*194*	659	15.6	562	13.0
Diseases of the digestive system — Maladies de l'appareil digestif						
Total	*789*	*579*	694	16.4	754	17.5
Gastric and duodenal ulcer — Ulcère de l'estomac et du duodénum	*38*	*16*	11	♦0.3	13	♦0.3
Diseases of the liver — Maladies du foie	*550*	*414*	217	5.1	196	4.5
Diseases of the musculoskeletal system and connective tissue — Maladies du système ostéo-articularie, des muscles et du tissu conjonctif	*27*	*34*	133	3.1	171	4.0
Diseases of the genitourinary system — Maladies de l'appareil génito-urinaire						
Total	*3 908*	*3 250*	1 063	25.1	1 099	25.5
Disorders of kidney and ureter — Affections du rein et de l'uretère	*3 892*	*3 240*	838	19.8	814	18.9
Hyperplasia of prostate — Hyperplasie de la prostate	*11*	..	28	♦2.8	..	..
Pregnancy, childbirth and the puerperium — Grossesse, accouchement et puerpéralité						
Total	..	*94*	..	..	8	♦4.4
Pregnancy with abortive outcome — Grossesse se terminant par un avortement	..	*3*	..	..	-	-
Other direct obstetric causes — Autres décès maternels directs	..	*87*	..	..	1	♦0.6
Indirect obstetric causes — Décès maternels indirects	..	*3*	..	..	3	♦1.7
Certain conditions originating in the perinatal period — Certaines affections dont l'origine se situe dans la période périnatale	*4 625*	*3 180*	156	167.1	96	109.0
Congenital malformations, deformations and chromosomal abnormalities — Malformations congénitales et anomalies chromosomiques	*1 616*	*1 398*	135	144.6	120	136.3
Symptoms, signs and abnormal clinical and laboratory findings, not elsewhere classified — Symptômes, signes et résultats anormaux d'examens cliniques et de laboratoire, non classés ailleurs	*6 155*	*3 424*	1 430	33.7	1 142	26.5
All other diseases — Toutes autres maladies	*18*	*54*	185	4.4	208	4.8
External causes — Causes externes						
Total	*12 079*	*2 500*	1 217	28.7	599	13.9
Accidents						
Total	*2 734*	*690*	724	17.1	452	10.5
Transport accidents — Accidents de transport	*1 213*	*331*	295	7.0	97	2.3
Falls — Chutes	-	-	81	1.9	51	1.2
Accidental drowning and submersion — Noyade et submersion accidentelles	*136*	*37*	42	1.0	11	♦0.3
Exposure to smoke, fire and flames — Exposition à la fumée, au feu et aux flammes	*19*	*24*	14	♦0.3	7	♦0.2
Accidental poisoning by and exposure to noxious substances — Intoxication accidentelle par des substances nocives et exposition à ces substances	*1*	*1*	4	♦0.1	4	♦0.1
Intentional self-harm — Lésions auto-infligées	*4*	-	321	7.6	69	1.6
Assault — Agresssions	*266*	*78*	88	2.1	29	♦0.7
All other external causes — Toutes autres causes externes	*9 075*	*1 732*	84	2.0	49	1.1

20. Death and death rates by cause and sex: 2014 - 2018
Décès et taux de mortalité par cause et sexe : 2014 - 2018 (continued - suite)

Cause of death — Cause de décès	Israel - Israël				Japan - Japon			
	2017 (C)				2016 (C)			
	Male — Masculin		Female — Féminin		Male — Masculin		Female — Féminin	
	Number Nombre	Rate Taux	Number Nombre	Rate Taux	Number Nombre	Rate Taux	Number Nombre	Rate Taux
TOTAL	**22 648**	**524.0**	**21 948**	**499.8**	**674 733**	**1 092.1**	**633 015**	**970.7**
Certain infectious and parasitic diseases — Certaines maladies infectieuses et parasitaires								
Total	1 244	28.8	1 274	29.0	12 130	19.6	12 969	19.9
Intestinal infectious diseases — Maladies infectieuses intestinales	64	1.5	82	1.9	1 135	1.8	1 416	2.2
Tuberculosis — Tuberculose	5	♦0.1	4	♦0.1	1 133	1.8	759	1.2
Tetanus — Tétanos	-	-	-	-	7	♦0.0	1	♦0.0
Diphtheria — Diphtérie	-	-	-	-	-	-	-	-
Whooping cough — Coqueluche	-	-	-	-	1	♦0.0	-	-
Meningococcal infection — Infection à méningocoques	2	♦0.0	1	♦0.0	2	♦0.0	1	♦0.0
Septicaemia — Septicémie	1 000	23.1	1 065	24.3	5 597	9.1	5 913	9.1
Acute poliomyelitis — Poliomyélite aiguë	-	-	-	-	-	-	-	-
Measles — Rougeole	-	-	-	-	-	-	-	-
Viral hepatitis — Hépatite virale	30	♦0.7	18	♦0.4	1 677	2.7	2 171	3.3
Human immunodeficiency virus [HIV] disease — Maladies dues au virus de l'immunodéficience humaine (VIH)	19	♦0.4	6	♦0.1	60	0.1	6	♦0.0
Malaria — Paludisme	-	-	-	-	1	♦0.0	1	♦0.0
Neoplasms — Tumeurs	**5 892**	**136.3**	**5 772**	**131.4**	**225 800**	**365.5**	**158 692**	**243.3**
Malignant neoplasms — Tumeurs malignes								
Total	5 682	131.5	5 541	126.2	219 790	355.8	153 205	234.9
Malignant neoplasm of lip, oral cavity and pharynx — Tumeur maligne de la lèvre, de la cavité buccale et du pharynx	76	1.8	61	1.4	5 396	8.7	2 279	3.5
Malignant neoplasm of oesophagus — Tumeur maligne de l'oesophage	79	1.8	37	0.8	9 533	15.4	1 950	3.0
Malignant neoplasm of stomach — Tumeur maligne de l'estomac	275	6.4	197	4.5	29 854	48.3	15 677	24.0
Malignant neoplasm of colon, rectosigmoid junction, rectum, anus and anal canal — Tumeur maligne du côlon, de la jonction recto-sigmoïdienne, du rectum, de l'anus et du canal anal	635	14.7	632	14.4	27 222	44.1	23 295	35.7
Malignant neoplasm of liver and intrahepatic bile ducts — Tumeur maligne du foie et des voies bilaires intrahépatiques	174	4.0	117	2.7	18 510	30.0	10 018	15.4
Malignant neoplasm of pancreas — Tumeur maligne du pancréas	470	10.9	470	10.7	17 060	27.6	16 415	25.2
Malignant neoplasm of trachea, bronchus and lung — Tumeur maligne de la trachée, des bronches et du poumon	1 231	28.5	611	13.9	52 430	84.9	21 408	32.8
Malignant neoplasm of female breast — Tumeur maligne du sein chez la femme	..	..	1 078	33.8	..	..	14 015	24.4
Malignant neoplasm of cervix uteri — Tumeur maligne du col de l'utérus	..	..	81	2.5	..	..	2 710	4.7
Malignant neoplasm of prostate — Tumeur maligne de la prostate	479	47.6	..	..	11 803	44.2	..	..
Malignant neoplasm of lymphoid, haematopoietic and related tissue — Tumeurs malignes primitives ou présumées primitives des tissus lymphoïde, hématopoïétique et apparentés	725	16.8	620	14.1	14 526	23.5	11 052	16.9
Disorders of the blood and blood-forming organs and certain disorders involving the immune mechanism — Maladies du sang et des organes hématopoïétiques et certains troubles du système immunitaire								
Total	126	2.9	172	3.9	1 985	3.2	2 524	3.9
Anaemias — Anémies	75	1.7	100	2.3	842	1.4	1 275	2.0
Endocrine, nutritional and metabolic diseases — Maladies endocriniennes, nutritionnelles et métaboliques								
Total	1 539	35.6	1 777	40.5	10 734	17.4	10 597	16.2
Diabetes mellitus — Diabète sucré	1 121	25.9	1 220	27.8	7 243	11.7	6 237	9.6
Malnutrition — Malnutrition	24	♦0.6	22	♦0.5	776	1.3	860	1.3
Mental and behavioural disorders — Troubles mentaux et du comportement	**788**	**18.2**	**1 250**	**28.5**	**4 414**	**7.1**	**9 767**	**15.0**
Diseases of the nervous system — Maladies du système nerveux	**812**	**18.8**	**887**	**20.2**	**14 940**	**24.2**	**18 417**	**28.2**
Diseases of the circulatory system — Maladies de l'appareil circulatoire								
Total	5 197	120.3	4 990	113.6	161 565	261.5	178 257	273.3
Acute rheumatic fever and chronic rheumatic heart diseases — Rhumatisme articularie aigu et cardiopathies rhumatismales chroniques	37	0.9	88	2.0	748	1.2	1 532	2.3
Hypertensive diseases — Maladies hypertensives	380	8.8	619	14.1	2 720	4.4	4 121	6.3
Ischaemic heart disease — Cardiopathie ischémique	2 236	51.7	1 528	34.8	40 429	65.4	30 031	46.1
Cerebrovascular disease — Maladie cérébrovasculaire	1 019	23.6	1 069	24.3	52 706	85.3	56 614	86.8

20. Death and death rates by cause and sex: 2014 - 2018
Décès et taux de mortalité par cause et sexe : 2014 - 2018 (continued - suite)

Cause of death — Cause de décès	Israel - Israël				Japan - Japon			
	2017 (C)				2016 (C)			
	Male — Masculin		Female — Féminin		Male — Masculin		Female — Féminin	
	Number Nombre	Rate Taux	Number Nombre	Rate Taux	Number Nombre	Rate Taux	Number Nombre	Rate Taux
Diseases of arteries, arterioles and capillaries — Maladies des artères, artérioles et capillaires	205	4.7	130	3.0	10 914	17.7	10 934	16.8
Diseases of the respiratory system — Maladies de l'appareil respiratoire								
Total	1 955	45.2	1 800	41.0	120 238	194.6	88 365	135.5
Influenza — Grippe	32	0.7	38	0.9	748	1.2	715	1.1
Pneumonia — Pneumopathies	573	13.3	569	13.0	65 636	106.2	53 664	82.3
Chronic lower respiratory diseases — Maladies chroniques des voies respiratoires inférieures	735	17.0	587	13.4	13 624	22.1	4 801	7.4
Diseases of the digestive system — Maladies de l'appareil digestif								
Total	692	16.0	743	16.9	25 616	41.5	23 146	35.5
Gastric and duodenal ulcer — Ulcère de l'estomac et du duodénum	13	♦0.3	17	♦0.4	1 527	2.5	1 130	1.7
Diseases of the liver — Maladies du foie	221	5.1	161	3.7	10 112	16.4	5 661	8.7
Diseases of the musculoskeletal system and connective tissue — Maladies du système ostéo-articularie, des muscles et du tissu conjonctif	165	3.8	165	3.8	2 552	4.1	3 893	6.0
Diseases of the genitourinary system — Maladies de l'appareil génito-urinaire								
Total	1 002	23.2	993	22.6	17 438	28.2	21 159	32.4
Disorders of kidney and ureter — Affections du rein et de l'uretère	786	18.2	761	17.3	14 907	24.1	16 532	25.4
Hyperplasia of prostate — Hyperplasie de la prostate	16	♦1.6	..	..	125	0.5	..	..
Pregnancy, childbirth and the puerperium — Grossesse, accouchement et puerpéralité								
Total	..	..	8	♦4.4	..	..	36	3.7
Pregnancy with abortive outcome — Grossesse se terminant par un avortement	..	..	-	-	..	..	3	♦0.3
Other direct obstetric causes — Autres décès maternels directs	..	..	4	♦2.2	..	..	24	♦2.5
Indirect obstetric causes — Décès maternels indirects	..	..	1	♦0.5	..	..	7	♦0.7
Certain conditions originating in the perinatal period — Certaines affections dont l'origine se situe dans la période périnatale	130	137.8	106	118.7	258	51.4	268	56.4
Congenital malformations, deformations and chromosomal abnormalities — Malformations congénitales et anomalies chromosomiques	156	165.4	128	143.3	951	189.5	1 069	225.0
Symptoms, signs and abnormal clinical and laboratory findings, not elsewhere classified — Symptômes, signes et résultats anormaux d'examens cliniques et de laboratoire, non classés ailleurs	1 564	36.2	1 089	24.8	35 030	56.7	77 416	118.7
All other diseases — Toutes autres maladies	145	3.4	190	4.3	628	1.0	1 046	1.6
External causes — Causes externes								
Total	1 241	28.7	604	13.8	40 454	65.5	25 394	38.9
Accidents								
Total	731	16.9	436	9.9	22 066	35.7	16 240	24.9
Transport accidents — Accidents de transport	297	6.9	94	2.1	3 665	5.9	1 613	2.5
Falls — Chutes	60	1.4	49	1.1	4 488	7.3	3 542	5.4
Accidental drowning and submersion — Noyade et submersion accidentelles	23	♦0.5	4	♦0.1	4 002	6.5	3 703	5.7
Exposure to smoke, fire and flames — Exposition à la fumée, au feu et aux flammes	23	♦0.5	7	♦0.2	542	0.9	349	0.5
Accidental poisoning by and exposure to noxious substances — Intoxication accidentelle par des substances nocives et exposition à ces substances	17	♦0.4	10	♦0.2	358	0.6	207	0.3
Intentional self-harm — Lésions auto-infligées	305	7.1	97	2.2	14 639	23.7	6 378	9.8
Assault — Agresssions	106	2.5	26	♦0.6	148	0.2	142	0.2
All other external causes — Toutes autres causes externes	99	2.3	45	1.0	3 601	5.8	2 634	4.0

20. Death and death rates by cause and sex: 2014 - 2018
Décès et taux de mortalité par cause et sexe : 2014 - 2018 (continued - suite)

Cause of death — Cause de décès	Japan - Japon				Jordan - Jordanie		Kazakhstan	
	2017 (C)				2015 (U)		2015 (U)	
	Male — Masculin		Female — Féminin		Male — Masculin	Female — Féminin	Male — Masculin	Female — Féminin
	Number Nombre	Rate Taux	Number Nombre	Rate Taux	Number Nombre	Number Nombre	Number Nombre	Number Nombre
TOTAL	**690 683**	**1 119.8**	**649 714**	**997.9**	**10 888**	**8 302**	**71 389**	**59 640**
Certain infectious and parasitic diseases — Certaines maladies infectieuses et parasitaires								
Total	12 020	19.5	12 739	19.6	288	245	988	520
Intestinal infectious diseases — Maladies infectieuses intestinales	1 012	1.6	1 346	2.1	13	8	28	34
Tuberculosis — Tuberculose	1 423	2.3	883	1.4	3	3	514	170
Tetanus — Tétanos	4	♦0.0	4	♦0.0	-	-	-	-
Diphtheria — Diphtérie	-	-	-	-	-	-	-	1
Whooping cough — Coqueluche	1	♦0.0	-	-	-	-	-	-
Meningococcal infection — Infection à méningocoques	1	♦0.0	-	-	-	-	16	10
Septicaemia — Septicémie	4 854	7.9	5 359	8.2	230	209	128	137
Acute poliomyelitis — Poliomyélite aiguë	-	-	-	-	-	-	-	-
Measles — Rougeole	-	-	-	-	-	-	1	-
Viral hepatitis — Hépatite virale	1 718	2.8	2 025	3.1	33	22	26	25
Human immunodeficiency virus [HIV] disease — Maladies dues au virus de l'immunodéficience humaine (VIH)	37	0.1	1	♦0.0	4	-	154	63
Malaria — Paludisme	1	♦0.0	1	♦0.0	1	-	-	-
Neoplasms — Tumeurs	**227 353**	**368.6**	**159 001**	**244.2**	**1 690**	**1 480**	**8 745**	**7 708**
Malignant neoplasms — Tumeurs malignes								
Total	220 398	357.3	152 936	234.9	1 574	1 412	8 592	7 552
Malignant neoplasm of lip, oral cavity and pharynx — Tumeur maligne de la lèvre, de la cavité buccale et du pharynx	5 328	8.6	2 126	3.3	18	14	359	178
Malignant neoplasm of oesophagus — Tumeur maligne de l'oesophage	9 580	15.5	1 988	3.1	22	9	530	399
Malignant neoplasm of stomach — Tumeur maligne de l'estomac	29 745	48.2	15 481	23.8	62	49	1 267	674
Malignant neoplasm of colon, rectosigmoid junction, rectum, anus and anal canal — Tumeur maligne du côlon, de la jonction recto-sigmoïdienne, du rectum, de l'anus et du canal anal	27 548	44.7	23 574	36.2	180	144	783	812
Malignant neoplasm of liver and intrahepatic bile ducts — Tumeur maligne du foie et des voies biliaires intrahépatiques	17 822	28.9	9 292	14.3	73	44	436	296
Malignant neoplasm of pancreas — Tumeur maligne du pancréas	17 401	28.2	16 823	25.8	61	75	445	377
Malignant neoplasm of trachea, bronchus and lung — Tumeur maligne de la trachée, des bronches et du poumon	53 002	85.9	21 118	32.4	350	127	2 202	515
Malignant neoplasm of female breast — Tumeur maligne du sein chez la femme	..	..	14 285	24.9	..	362	..	1 290
Malignant neoplasm of cervix uteri — Tumeur maligne du col de l'utérus	..	..	2 795	4.9	..	12	..	630
Malignant neoplasm of prostate — Tumeur maligne de la prostate	12 013	44.6	..	..	105	..	370	..
Malignant neoplasm of lymphoid, haematopoietic and related tissue — Tumeurs malignes primitives ou présumées primitives des tissus lymphoïde, hématopoïétique et apparentés	14 604	23.7	10 993	16.9	274	173	444	382
Disorders of the blood and blood-forming organs and certain disorders involving the immune mechanism — Maladies du sang et des organes hématopoïétiques et certains troubles du système immunitaire								
Total	1 884	3.1	2 486	3.8	40	52	80	92
Anaemias — Anémies	832	1.3	1 321	2.0	18	25	41	59
Endocrine, nutritional and metabolic diseases — Maladies endocriniennes, nutritionnelles et métaboliques								
Total	11 502	18.6	10 882	16.7	810	740	1 410	2 519
Diabetes mellitus — Diabète sucré	7 730	12.5	6 239	9.6	735	655	1 323	2 349
Malnutrition — Malnutrition	1 044	1.7	1 074	1.6	-	-	25	39
Mental and behavioural disorders — Troubles mentaux et du comportement	**7 977**	**12.9**	**13 506**	**20.7**	**1**	**2**	**565**	**1 144**
Diseases of the nervous system — Maladies du système nerveux	**21 168**	**34.3**	**23 856**	**36.6**	**196**	**174**	**4 503**	**6 335**
Diseases of the circulatory system — Maladies de l'appareil circulatoire								
Total	166 545	270.0	184 421	283.3	4 255	3 267	18 145	15 844
Acute rheumatic fever and chronic rheumatic heart diseases — Rhumatisme articularie aigu et cardiopathies rhumatismales chroniques	779	1.3	1 532	2.4	-	3	115	165
Hypertensive diseases — Maladies hypertensives	3 915	6.3	5 651	8.7	1 005	1 014	645	610
Ischaemic heart disease — Cardiopathie ischémique	40 475	65.6	29 382	45.1	1 333	562	7 218	5 355

20. Death and death rates by cause and sex: 2014 - 2018
Décès et taux de mortalité par cause et sexe : 2014 - 2018 (continued - suite)

Cause of death — Cause de décès	Japan - Japon				Jordan - Jordanie		Kazakhstan	
	2017 (C)				2015 (U)		2015 (U)	
	Male — Masculin		Female — Féminin		Male — Masculin	Female — Féminin	Male — Masculin	Female — Féminin
	Number Nombre	Rate Taux	Number Nombre	Rate Taux	Number Nombre	Number Nombre	Number Nombre	Number Nombre
Cerebrovascular disease — Maladie cérébrovasculaire	53 188	86.2	56 692	87.1	1 084	1 006	5 804	6 787
Diseases of arteries, arterioles and capillaries — Maladies des artères, artérioles et capillaires	11 467	18.6	11 639	17.9	49	26	790	893
Diseases of the respiratory system — Maladies de l'appareil respiratoire								
Total	110 890	179.8	78 711	120.9	674	479	10 127	8 294
Influenza — Grippe	1 202	1.9	1 367	2.1	-	1	5	3
Pneumonia — Pneumopathies	53 134	86.1	43 707	67.1	318	258	2 367	1 733
Chronic lower respiratory diseases — Maladies chroniques des voies respiratoires inférieures	16 425	26.6	5 478	8.4	201	80	7 199	6 127
Diseases of the digestive system — Maladies de l'appareil digestif								
Total	26 861	43.5	24 408	37.5	389	274	7 421	5 602
Gastric and duodenal ulcer — Ulcère de l'estomac et du duodénum	1 403	2.3	1 110	1.7	23	12	449	253
Diseases of the liver — Maladies du foie	10 980	17.8	6 038	9.3	162	92	5 686	4 285
Diseases of the musculoskeletal system and connective tissue — Maladies du système ostéo-articularie, des muscles et du tissu conjonctif	3 284	5.3	5 053	7.8	14	31	491	1 362
Diseases of the genitourinary system — Maladies de l'appareil génito-urinaire								
Total	17 338	28.1	20 659	31.7	403	305	2 447	2 352
Disorders of kidney and ureter — Affections du rein et de l'uretère	14 950	24.2	16 389	25.2	375	280	1 657	2 321
Hyperplasia of prostate — Hyperplasie de la prostate	164	0.6	..	..	-	..	689	..
Pregnancy, childbirth and the puerperium — Grossesse, accouchement et puerpéralité								
Total	..	..	36	3.8	..	38	..	35
Pregnancy with abortive outcome — Grossesse se terminant par un avortement	..	..	1	♦0.1	..	-	..	-
Other direct obstetric causes — Autres décès maternels directs	..	..	19	♦2.0	..	36	..	19
Indirect obstetric causes — Décès maternels indirects	..	..	13	♦1.4	..	2	..	16
Certain conditions originating in the perinatal period — Certaines affections dont l'origine se situe dans la période périnatale	271	55.9	215	46.6	444	367	1 174	814
Congenital malformations, deformations and chromosomal abnormalities — Malformations congénitales et anomalies chromosomiques	1 006	207.7	1 122	243.1	400	295	611	537
Symptoms, signs and abnormal clinical and laboratory findings, not elsewhere classified — Symptômes, signes et résultats anormaux d'examens cliniques et de laboratoire, non classés ailleurs	39 653	64.3	84 506	129.8	118	119	3 312	3 246
All other diseases — Toutes autres maladies	927	1.5	1 540	2.4	11	29	62	76
External causes — Causes externes								
Total	42 004	68.1	26 573	40.8	1 155	405	11 308	3 160
Accidents								
Total	23 091	37.4	17 238	26.5	758	247	6 288	1 906
Transport accidents — Accidents de transport	3 392	5.5	1 612	2.5	513	162	1 970	674
Falls — Chutes	5 303	8.6	4 370	6.7	65	13	509	145
Accidental drowning and submersion — Noyade et submersion accidentelles	4 253	6.9	3 910	6.0	45	14	650	138
Exposure to smoke, fire and flames — Exposition à la fumée, au feu et aux flammes	591	1.0	372	0.6	60	33	235	87
Accidental poisoning by and exposure to noxious substances — Intoxication accidentelle par des substances nocives et exposition à ces substances	375	0.6	223	0.3	22	3	1 265	398
Intentional self-harm — Lésions auto-infligées	14 333	23.2	6 132	9.4	7	1	2 343	530
Assault — Agresssions	159	0.3	129	0.2	109	23	814	232
All other external causes — Toutes autres causes externes	4 421	7.2	3 074	4.7	281	134	1 863	492

20. Death and death rates by cause and sex: 2014 - 2018
Décès et taux de mortalité par cause et sexe : 2014 - 2018 (continued - suite)

Cause of death — Cause de décès	Kazakhstan		Kuwait - Koweït			
	2017 (U)		2016 (U)		2017 (U)	
	Male — Masculin	Female — Féminin	Male — Masculin	Female — Féminin	Male — Masculin	Female — Féminin
	Number Nombre	Number Nombre	Number Nombre	Number Nombre	Number Nombre	Number Nombre
TOTAL	*69 104*	*59 905*	*3 944*	*2 394*	*4 309*	*2 370*
Certain infectious and parasitic diseases — Certaines maladies infectieuses et parasitaires						
Total	*920*	*488*	*113*	*121*	*149*	*125*
Intestinal infectious diseases — Maladies infectieuses intestinales	*19*	*17*	*2*	*2*	-	*1*
Tuberculosis — Tuberculose	*399*	*141*	*9*	*8*	*10*	*8*
Tetanus — Tétanos	-	-	-	-	-	-
Diphtheria — Diphtérie	-	-	-	-	-	-
Whooping cough — Coqueluche	-	-	-	-	-	-
Meningococcal infection — Infection à méningocoques	*11*	-	*1*	-	-	-
Septicaemia — Septicémie	*164*	*145*	*76*	*97*	*119*	*102*
Acute poliomyelitis — Poliomyélite aiguë	*1*	-	-	-	-	-
Measles — Rougeole	-	-	-	-	-	-
Viral hepatitis — Hépatite virale	*25*	*25*	*16*	*10*	*15*	*8*
Human immunodeficiency virus [HIV] disease — Maladies dues au virus de l'immunodéficience humaine (VIH)	*193*	*73*	*1*	-	-	*2*
Malaria — Paludisme	*1*	-	-	-	-	-
Neoplasms — Tumeurs	*8 202*	*7 277*	*400*	*465*	*491*	*461*
Malignant neoplasms — Tumeurs malignes						
Total	*8 007*	*7 126*	*378*	*446*	*479*	*452*
Malignant neoplasm of lip, oral cavity and pharynx — Tumeur maligne de la lèvre, de la cavité buccale et du pharynx	*322*	*167*	*12*	*6*	*9*	*1*
Malignant neoplasm of oesophagus — Tumeur maligne de l'oesophage	*429*	*321*	*5*	*5*	*5*	*5*
Malignant neoplasm of stomach — Tumeur maligne de l'estomac	*1 095*	*621*	*18*	*12*	*19*	*10*
Malignant neoplasm of colon, rectosigmoid junction, rectum, anus and anal canal — Tumeur maligne du côlon, de la jonction recto-sigmoïdienne, du rectum, de l'anus et du canal anal	*757*	*749*	*60*	*49*	*64*	*47*
Malignant neoplasm of liver and intrahepatic bile ducts — Tumeur maligne du foie et des voies biliaires intrahépatiques	*375*	*303*	*28*	*16*	*36*	*21*
Malignant neoplasm of pancreas — Tumeur maligne du pancréas	*433*	*385*	*25*	*15*	*34*	*22*
Malignant neoplasm of trachea, bronchus and lung — Tumeur maligne de la trachée, des bronches et du poumon	*2 016*	*455*	*68*	*26*	*96*	*33*
Malignant neoplasm of female breast — Tumeur maligne du sein chez la femme	..	*1 214*	..	*124*	..	*109*
Malignant neoplasm of cervix uteri — Tumeur maligne du col de l'utérus	..	*610*	..	*5*	..	*15*
Malignant neoplasm of prostate — Tumeur maligne de la prostate	*412*	..	*25*	..	*34*	..
Malignant neoplasm of lymphoid, haematopoietic and related tissue — Tumeurs malignes primitives ou présumées primitives des tissus lymphoïde, hématopoïétique et apparentés	*443*	*435*	*45*	*55*	*55*	*42*
Disorders of the blood and blood-forming organs and certain disorders involving the immune mechanism — Maladies du sang et des organes hématopoïétiques et certains troubles du système immunitaire						
Total	*68*	*92*	*10*	*12*	*16*	*8*
Anaemias — Anémies	*39*	*54*	*3*	*4*	*8*	*4*
Endocrine, nutritional and metabolic diseases — Maladies endocriniennes, nutritionnelles et métaboliques						
Total	*1 606*	*2 931*	*208*	*238*	*187*	*207*
Diabetes mellitus — Diabète sucré	*1 450*	*2 694*	*187*	*217*	*172*	*193*
Malnutrition — Malnutrition	*58*	*93*	-	-	-	-
Mental and behavioural disorders — Troubles mentaux et du comportement	*809*	*1 710*	*34*	*2*	*76*	*6*
Diseases of the nervous system — Maladies du système nerveux	*6 123*	*9 171*	*57*	*37*	*56*	*26*
Diseases of the circulatory system — Maladies de l'appareil circulatoire						
Total	*17 529*	*14 006*	*1 789*	*834*	*1 924*	*837*
Acute rheumatic fever and chronic rheumatic heart diseases — Rhumatisme articularie aigu et cardiopathies rhumatismales chroniques	*115*	*145*	*3*	*3*	-	*1*
Hypertensive diseases — Maladies hypertensives	*439*	*404*	*66*	*95*	*67*	*84*
Ischaemic heart disease — Cardiopathie ischémique	*6 774*	*4 695*	*1 270*	*279*	*1 311*	*324*
Cerebrovascular disease — Maladie cérébrovasculaire	*5 877*	*5 987*	*275*	*170*	*261*	*165*
Diseases of arteries, arterioles and capillaries — Maladies des artères, artérioles et capillaires	*773*	*752*	*8*	*9*	*16*	*6*

20. Death and death rates by cause and sex: 2014 - 2018
Décès et taux de mortalité par cause et sexe : 2014 - 2018 (continued - suite)

Cause of death — Cause de décès	Kazakhstan		Kuwait - Koweït			
	2017 (U)		2016 (U)		2017 (U)	
	Male — Masculin	Female — Féminin	Male — Masculin	Female — Féminin	Male — Masculin	Female — Féminin
	Number Nombre	Number Nombre	Number Nombre	Number Nombre	Number Nombre	Number Nombre
Diseases of the respiratory system — Maladies de l'appareil respiratoire						
Total	*9 587*	*7 042*	*183*	*176*	*211*	*158*
Influenza — Grippe	*7*	*4*	*1*	*2*	*2*	*-*
Pneumonia — Pneumopathies	*2 136*	*1 471*	*135*	*142*	*170*	*119*
Chronic lower respiratory diseases — Maladies chroniques des voies respiratoires inférieures	*7 002*	*5 235*	*17*	*18*	*12*	*16*
Diseases of the digestive system — Maladies de l'appareil digestif						
Total	*6 328*	*5 245*	*106*	*69*	*119*	*99*
Gastric and duodenal ulcer — Ulcère de l'estomac et du duodénum	*409*	*277*	*2*	*7*	*3*	*1*
Diseases of the liver — Maladies du foie	*4 725*	*3 806*	*60*	*27*	*52*	*35*
Diseases of the musculoskeletal system and connective tissue — Maladies du système ostéo-articularie, des muscles et du tissu conjonctif	*483*	*1 135*	*5*	*10*	*6*	*8*
Diseases of the genitourinary system — Maladies de l'appareil génito-urinaire						
Total	*2 628*	*2 357*	*40*	*49*	*64*	*65*
Disorders of kidney and ureter — Affections du rein et de l'uretère	*1 906*	*2 327*	*28*	*40*	*51*	*46*
Hyperplasia of prostate — Hyperplasie de la prostate	*659*	..	*-*	..	*-*	..
Pregnancy, childbirth and the puerperium — Grossesse, accouchement et puerpéralité						
Total	..	*36*	..	*2*	..	*3*
Pregnancy with abortive outcome — Grossesse se terminant par un avortement	..	*-*	..	*2*	..	*1*
Other direct obstetric causes — Autres décès maternels directs	..	*22*	..	*-*	..	*2*
Indirect obstetric causes — Décès maternels indirects	..	*14*	..	*-*	..	*-*
Certain conditions originating in the perinatal period — Certaines affections dont l'origine se situe dans la période périnatale	*902*	*679*	*119*	*70*	*113*	*76*
Congenital malformations, deformations and chromosomal abnormalities — Malformations congénitales et anomalies chromosomiques	*589*	*474*	*121*	*116*	*119*	*84*
Symptoms, signs and abnormal clinical and laboratory findings, not elsewhere classified — Symptômes, signes et résultats anormaux d'examens cliniques et de laboratoire, non classés ailleurs	*3 529*	*4 348*	*56*	*23*	*85*	*37*
All other diseases — Toutes autres maladies	*77*	*100*	*1*	*1*	*1*	*4*
External causes — Causes externes						
Total	*9 724*	*2 814*	*702*	*169*	*692*	*166*
Accidents						
Total	*5 210*	*1 710*	*590*	*123*	*586*	*112*
Transport accidents — Accidents de transport	*1 689*	*664*	*397*	*66*	*396*	*67*
Falls — Chutes	*433*	*169*	*82*	*9*	*86*	*13*
Accidental drowning and submersion — Noyade et submersion accidentelles	*592*	*112*	*28*	*6*	*18*	*7*
Exposure to smoke, fire and flames — Exposition à la fumée, au feu et aux flammes	*218*	*84*	*26*	*29*	*20*	*12*
Accidental poisoning by and exposure to noxious substances — Intoxication accidentelle par des substances nocives et exposition à ces substances	*926*	*308*	*16*	*2*	*10*	*6*
Intentional self-harm — Lésions auto-infligées	*2 166*	*498*	*54*	*12*	*54*	*18*
Assault — Agresssions	*732*	*176*	*17*	*10*	*17*	*12*
All other external causes — Toutes autres causes externes	*1 616*	*430*	*41*	*24*	*35*	*24*

20. Death and death rates by cause and sex: 2014 - 2018
Décès et taux de mortalité par cause et sexe : 2014 - 2018 (continued - suite)

Kyrgyzstan - Kirghizstan

Cause of death — Cause de décès	2015 (C)				2016 (C)			
	Male — Masculin		Female — Féminin		Male — Masculin		Female — Féminin	
	Number Nombre	Rate Taux	Number Nombre	Rate Taux	Number Nombre	Rate Taux	Number Nombre	Rate Taux
TOTAL	**19 376**	**657.1**	**15 433**	**513.0**	**18 564**	**616.4**	**14 911**	**486.0**
Certain infectious and parasitic diseases — Certaines maladies infectieuses et parasitaires								
Total	591	20.0	295	9.8	520	17.3	268	8.7
Intestinal infectious diseases — Maladies infectieuses intestinales	60	2.0	54	1.8	47	1.6	33	1.1
Tuberculosis — Tuberculose	324	11.0	129	4.3	305	10.1	118	3.8
Tetanus — Tétanos	1	♦0.0	-	-	-	-	-	-
Diphtheria — Diphtérie	-	-	-	-	-	-	-	-
Whooping cough — Coqueluche	-	-	-	-	-	-	-	-
Meningococcal infection — Infection à méningocoques	7	♦0.2	11	♦0.4	4	♦0.1	5	♦0.2
Septicaemia — Septicémie	16	♦0.5	10	♦0.3	20	♦0.7	13	♦0.4
Acute poliomyelitis — Poliomyélite aiguë	-	-	-	-	-	-	-	-
Measles — Rougeole	1	♦0.0	2	♦0.1	-	-	-	-
Viral hepatitis — Hépatite virale	39	1.3	19	♦0.6	38	1.3	28	♦0.9
Human immunodeficiency virus [HIV] disease — Maladies dues au virus de l'immunodéficience humaine (VIH)	89	3.0	27	♦0.9	82	2.7	36	1.2
Malaria — Paludisme	-	-	-	-	-	-	-	-
Neoplasms — Tumeurs	**1 970**	**66.8**	**1 871**	**62.2**	**2 087**	**69.3**	**1 832**	**59.7**
Malignant neoplasms — Tumeurs malignes								
Total	1 938	65.7	1 839	61.1	2 065	68.6	1 803	58.8
Malignant neoplasm of lip, oral cavity and pharynx — Tumeur maligne de la lèvre, de la cavité buccale et du pharynx	76	2.6	45	1.5	85	2.8	43	1.4
Malignant neoplasm of oesophagus — Tumeur maligne de l'oesophage	80	2.7	47	1.6	104	3.5	56	1.8
Malignant neoplasm of stomach — Tumeur maligne de l'estomac	473	16.0	225	7.5	491	16.3	197	6.4
Malignant neoplasm of colon, rectosigmoid junction, rectum, anus and anal canal — Tumeur maligne du côlon, de la jonction recto-sigmoïdienne, du rectum, de l'anus et du canal anal	112	3.8	131	4.4	104	3.5	114	3.7
Malignant neoplasm of liver and intrahepatic bile ducts — Tumeur maligne du foie et des voies bilaires intrahépatiques	190	6.4	125	4.2	203	6.7	134	4.4
Malignant neoplasm of pancreas — Tumeur maligne du pancréas	88	3.0	77	2.6	104	3.5	104	3.4
Malignant neoplasm of trachea, bronchus and lung — Tumeur maligne de la trachée, des bronches et du poumon	341	11.6	112	3.7	368	12.2	138	4.5
Malignant neoplasm of female breast — Tumeur maligne du sein chez la femme	..	..	258	12.3	..	..	223	10.5
Malignant neoplasm of cervix uteri — Tumeur maligne du col de l'utérus	..	..	259	12.4	..	..	222	10.5
Malignant neoplasm of prostate — Tumeur maligne de la prostate	65	15.4	..	..	72	16.5	..	..
Malignant neoplasm of lymphoid, haematopoietic and related tissue — Tumeurs malignes primitives ou présumées primitives des tissus lymphoïde, hématopoïétique et apparentés	117	4.0	75	2.5	127	4.2	73	2.4
Disorders of the blood and blood-forming organs and certain disorders involving the immune mechanism — Maladies du sang et des organes hématopoïétiques et certains troubles du système immunitaire								
Total	27	♦0.9	17	♦0.6	17	♦0.6	19	♦0.6
Anaemias — Anémies	15	♦0.5	12	♦0.4	11	♦0.4	13	♦0.4
Endocrine, nutritional and metabolic diseases — Maladies endocriniennes, nutritionnelles et métaboliques								
Total	168	5.7	225	7.5	183	6.1	260	8.5
Diabetes mellitus — Diabète sucré	153	5.2	206	6.8	163	5.4	245	8.0
Malnutrition — Malnutrition	5	♦0.2	5	♦0.2	3	♦0.1	4	♦0.1
Mental and behavioural disorders — Troubles mentaux et du comportement	23	♦0.8	19	♦0.6	25	♦0.8	15	♦0.5
Diseases of the nervous system — Maladies du système nerveux	319	10.8	190	6.3	324	10.8	200	6.5
Diseases of the circulatory system — Maladies de l'appareil circulatoire								
Total	8 951	303.5	8 745	290.7	8 568	284.5	8 438	275.0
Acute rheumatic fever and chronic rheumatic heart diseases — Rhumatisme articularie aigu et cardiopathies rhumatismales chroniques	85	2.9	92	3.1	63	2.1	85	2.8
Hypertensive diseases — Maladies hypertensives	255	8.6	237	7.9	210	7.0	191	6.2
Ischaemic heart disease — Cardiopathie ischémique	5 589	189.5	5 826	193.7	5 330	177.0	5 786	188.6
Cerebrovascular disease — Maladie cérébrovasculaire	2 322	78.7	2 231	74.2	2 164	71.9	1 981	64.6

20. Death and death rates by cause and sex: 2014 - 2018
Décès et taux de mortalité par cause et sexe : 2014 - 2018 (continued - suite)

Kyrgyzstan - Kirghizstan

Cause of death — Cause de décès	2015 (C)				2016 (C)			
	Male — Masculin		Female — Féminin		Male — Masculin		Female — Féminin	
	Number Nombre	Rate Taux	Number Nombre	Rate Taux	Number Nombre	Rate Taux	Number Nombre	Rate Taux
Diseases of arteries, arterioles and capillaries — Maladies des artères, artérioles et capillaires	123	4.2	93	3.1	120	4.0	133	4.3
Diseases of the respiratory system — Maladies de l'appareil respiratoire								
Total	1 039	35.2	800	26.6	1 124	37.3	879	28.6
Influenza — Grippe	11	♦0.4	12	♦0.4	16	♦0.5	23	♦0.7
Pneumonia — Pneumopathies	293	9.9	215	7.1	354	11.8	263	8.6
Chronic lower respiratory diseases — Maladies chroniques des voies respiratoires inférieures	669	22.7	526	17.5	690	22.9	545	17.8
Diseases of the digestive system — Maladies de l'appareil digestif								
Total	1 462	49.6	832	27.7	1 386	46.0	742	24.2
Gastric and duodenal ulcer — Ulcère de l'estomac et du duodénum	54	1.8	29	♦1.0	64	2.1	33	1.1
Diseases of the liver — Maladies du foie	1 252	42.5	691	23.0	1 194	39.6	615	20.0
Diseases of the musculoskeletal system and connective tissue — Maladies du système ostéo-articularie, des muscles et du tissu conjonctif	26	♦0.9	58	1.9	27	♦0.9	47	1.5
Diseases of the genitourinary system — Maladies de l'appareil génito-urinaire								
Total	291	9.9	193	6.4	273	9.1	188	6.1
Disorders of kidney and ureter — Affections du rein et de l'uretère	285	9.7	189	6.3	266	8.8	186	6.1
Hyperplasia of prostate — Hyperplasie de la prostate	4	♦1.0	..	..	6	♦1.4	..	..
Pregnancy, childbirth and the puerperium — Grossesse, accouchement et puerpéralité								
Total	..	..	63	38.5	..	..	48	30.3
Pregnancy with abortive outcome — Grossesse se terminant par un avortement	..	..	3	♦1.8	..	..	2	♦1.3
Other direct obstetric causes — Autres décès maternels directs	..	..	49	30.0	..	..	28	♦17.7
Indirect obstetric causes — Décès maternels indirects	..	..	11	♦6.7	..	..	18	♦11.4
Certain conditions originating in the perinatal period — Certaines affections dont l'origine se situe dans la période périnatale	1 265	1 494.4	959	1 217.0	1 073	1 320.9	893	1 160.8
Congenital malformations, deformations and chromosomal abnormalities — Malformations congénitales et anomalies chromosomiques	181	213.8	164	208.1	167	205.6	174	226.2
Symptoms, signs and abnormal clinical and laboratory findings, not elsewhere classified — Symptômes, signes et résultats anormaux d'examens cliniques et de laboratoire, non classés ailleurs	700	23.7	241	8.0	648	21.5	262	8.5
All other diseases — Toutes autres maladies	10	♦0.3	6	♦0.2	6	♦0.2	5	♦0.2
External causes — Causes externes								
Total	2 353	79.8	755	25.1	2 136	70.9	641	20.9
Accidents								
Total	1 630	55.3	552	18.3	1 498	49.7	449	14.6
Transport accidents — Accidents de transport	681	23.1	249	8.3	599	19.9	213	6.9
Falls — Chutes	59	2.0	20	♦0.7	66	2.2	25	♦0.8
Accidental drowning and submersion — Noyade et submersion accidentelles	174	5.9	51	1.7	157	5.2	63	2.1
Exposure to smoke, fire and flames — Exposition à la fumée, au feu et aux flammes	16	♦0.5	11	♦0.4	35	1.2	1	♦0.0
Accidental poisoning by and exposure to noxious substances — Intoxication accidentelle par des substances nocives et exposition à ces substances	338	11.5	81	2.7	303	10.1	64	2.1
Intentional self-harm — Lésions auto-infligées	327	11.1	90	3.0	330	11.0	89	2.9
Assault — Agresssions	158	5.4	55	1.8	120	4.0	46	1.5
All other external causes — Toutes autres causes externes	238	8.1	58	1.9	188	6.2	57	1.9

20. Death and death rates by cause and sex: 2014 - 2018
Décès et taux de mortalité par cause et sexe : 2014 - 2018 (continued - suite)

Cause of death — Cause de décès	Lebanon - Liban		Malaysia - Malaisie		Maldives			
	2017 (...)		2014 (U)		2016 (+C)			
	Male — Masculin	Female — Féminin	Male — Masculin	Female — Féminin	Male — Masculin		Female — Féminin	
	Number Nombre	Number Nombre	Number Nombre	Number Nombre	Number Nombre	Rate Taux	Number Nombre	Rate Taux
TOTAL	*8 471*	*7 106*	*47 871*	*29 494*	676	380.0	584	339.1
Certain infectious and parasitic diseases — Certaines maladies infectieuses et parasitaires								
Total	*407*	*357*	*4 475*	*2 877*	31	17.4	41	23.8
Intestinal infectious diseases — Maladies infectieuses intestinales	*10*	*11*	*126*	*131*	1	♦0.6	1	♦0.6
Tuberculosis — Tuberculose	*1*	*2*	*536*	*189*	5	♦2.8	1	♦0.6
Tetanus — Tétanos	-	-	*3*	*1*	-	-	-	-
Diphtheria — Diphtérie	-	-	-	-	-	-	-	-
Whooping cough — Coqueluche	-	-	-	*1*	-	-	-	-
Meningococcal infection — Infection à méningocoques	-	-	*1*	*6*	-	-	-	-
Septicaemia — Septicémie	*324*	*286*	*2 627*	*2 071*	21	♦11.8	32	18.6
Acute poliomyelitis — Poliomyélite aiguë	-	-	-	-	-	-	-	-
Measles — Rougeole	-	-	-	*1*	-	-	-	-
Viral hepatitis — Hépatite virale	*4*	*4*	*124*	*45*	-	-	-	-
Human immunodeficiency virus [HIV] disease — Maladies dues au virus de l'immunodéficience humaine (VIH)	*9*	*3*	*380*	*56*	-	-	-	-
Malaria — Paludisme	*2*	-	*5*	*1*	-	-	-	-
Neoplasms — Tumeurs	*1 752*	*1 402*	*5 646*	*5 151*	44	24.7	33	19.2
Malignant neoplasms — Tumeurs malignes								
Total	*1 704*	*1 362*	*5 347*	*4 871*	40	22.5	28	♦16.3
Malignant neoplasm of lip, oral cavity and pharynx — Tumeur maligne de la lèvre, de la cavité buccale et du pharynx	*18*	*5*	*315*	*154*	-	-	2	♦1.2
Malignant neoplasm of oesophagus — Tumeur maligne de l'oesophage	*10*	*5*	*87*	*31*	-	-	-	-
Malignant neoplasm of stomach — Tumeur maligne de l'estomac	*73*	*62*	*208*	*142*	2	♦1.1	1	♦0.6
Malignant neoplasm of colon, rectosigmoid junction, rectum, anus and anal canal — Tumeur maligne du côlon, de la jonction recto-sigmoïdienne, du rectum, de l'anus et du canal anal	*142*	*118*	*515*	*407*	2	♦1.1	-	-
Malignant neoplasm of liver and intrahepatic bile ducts — Tumeur maligne du foie et des voies bilaires intrahépatiques	*105*	*42*	*665*	*244*	7	♦3.9	2	♦1.2
Malignant neoplasm of pancreas — Tumeur maligne du pancréas	*127*	*93*	*202*	*137*	1	♦0.6	-	-
Malignant neoplasm of trachea, bronchus and lung — Tumeur maligne de la trachée, des bronches et du poumon	*497*	*240*	*1 220*	*521*	3	♦1.7	3	♦1.7
Malignant neoplasm of female breast — Tumeur maligne du sein chez la femme	..	*287*	..	*1 060*	..	..	1	♦0.8
Malignant neoplasm of cervix uteri — Tumeur maligne du col de l'utérus	..	*13*	..	*253*	..	..	1	♦0.8
Malignant neoplasm of prostate — Tumeur maligne de la prostate	*115*	..	*252*	..	3	♦10.9	..	..
Malignant neoplasm of lymphoid, haematopoietic and related tissue — Tumeurs malignes primitives ou présumées primitives des tissus lymphoïde, hématopoïétique et apparentés	*206*	*159*	*677*	*466*	4	♦2.2	-	-
Disorders of the blood and blood-forming organs and certain disorders involving the immune mechanism — Maladies du sang et des organes hématopoïétiques et certains troubles du système immunitaire								
Total	*52*	*45*	*296*	*258*	4	♦2.2	5	♦2.9
Anaemias — Anémies	*17*	*25*	*82*	*91*	2	♦1.1	5	♦2.9
Endocrine, nutritional and metabolic diseases — Maladies endocriniennes, nutritionnelles et métaboliques								
Total	*193*	*167*	*574*	*620*	26	♦14.6	31	18.0
Diabetes mellitus — Diabète sucré	*128*	*91*	*198*	*269*	12	♦6.7	22	♦12.8
Malnutrition — Malnutrition	*2*	*2*	*3*	*2*	-	-	-	-
Mental and behavioural disorders — Troubles mentaux et du comportement	*18*	*20*	*15*	*2*	5	♦2.8	1	♦0.6
Diseases of the nervous system — Maladies du système nerveux	*149*	*114*	*701*	*433*	16	♦9.0	9	♦5.2
Diseases of the circulatory system — Maladies de l'appareil circulatoire								
Total	*2 847*	*2 432*	*13 537*	*7 451*	254	142.8	217	126.0
Acute rheumatic fever and chronic rheumatic heart diseases — Rhumatisme articularie aigu et cardiopathies rhumatismales chroniques	*5*	*10*	*45*	*39*	-	-	-	-
Hypertensive diseases — Maladies hypertensives	*66*	*83*	*433*	*299*	27	♦15.2	39	22.6
Ischaemic heart disease — Cardiopathie ischémique	*486*	*336*	*7 295*	*3 137*	76	42.7	46	26.7

20. Death and death rates by cause and sex: 2014 - 2018
Décès et taux de mortalité par cause et sexe : 2014 - 2018 (continued - suite)

Cause of death — Cause de décès	Lebanon - Liban		Malaysia - Malaisie		Maldives			
	2017 (...)		2014 (U)		2016 (+C)			
	Male — Masculin	Female — Féminin	Male — Masculin	Female — Féminin	Male — Masculin		Female — Féminin	
	Number Nombre	Number Nombre	Number Nombre	Number Nombre	Number Nombre	Rate Taux	Number Nombre	Rate Taux
Cerebrovascular disease — Maladie cérébrovasculaire	338	321	3 170	2 304	54	30.4	45	26.1
Diseases of arteries, arterioles and capillaries — Maladies des artères, artérioles et capillaires	56	32	309	142	2	♦1.1	1	♦0.6
Diseases of the respiratory system — Maladies de l'appareil respiratoire								
Total	791	641	8 062	5 695	96	54.0	96	55.7
Influenza — Grippe	5	3	-	-	1	♦0.6	-	-
Pneumonia — Pneumopathies	354	263	5 333	3 917	14	♦7.9	11	♦6.4
Chronic lower respiratory diseases — Maladies chroniques des voies respiratoires inférieures	159	142	834	385	34	19.1	48	27.9
Diseases of the digestive system — Maladies de l'appareil digestif								
Total	237	219	2 136	1 044	9	♦5.1	4	♦2.3
Gastric and duodenal ulcer — Ulcère de l'estomac et du duodénum	14	5	162	83	-	-	-	-
Diseases of the liver — Maladies du foie	87	55	1 028	367	5	♦2.8	-	-
Diseases of the musculoskeletal system and connective tissue — Maladies du système ostéo-articularie, des muscles et du tissu conjonctif	13	19	332	332	1	♦0.6	1	♦0.6
Diseases of the genitourinary system — Maladies de l'appareil génito-urinaire								
Total	436	429	1 623	1 648	29	♦16.3	19	♦11.0
Disorders of kidney and ureter — Affections du rein et de l'uretère	373	348	1 136	958	23	♦12.9	18	♦10.5
Hyperplasia of prostate — Hyperplasie de la prostate	7	..	1	..	1	♦3.6	..	..
Pregnancy, childbirth and the puerperium — Grossesse, accouchement et puerpéralité								
Total	..	5	..	119	..	..	2	♦29.6
Pregnancy with abortive outcome — Grossesse se terminant par un avortement	..	-	..	18	..	..	-	-
Other direct obstetric causes — Autres décès maternels directs	..	5	..	76	..	..	2	♦29.6
Indirect obstetric causes — Décès maternels indirects	..	-	..	25	..	..	-	-
Certain conditions originating in the perinatal period — Certaines affections dont l'origine se situe dans la période périnatale	195	135	713	506	14	♦413.0	23	♦683.3
Congenital malformations, deformations and chromosomal abnormalities — Malformations congénitales et anomalies chromosomiques	69	48	575	481	3	♦88.5	1	♦29.7
Symptoms, signs and abnormal clinical and laboratory findings, not elsewhere classified — Symptômes, signes et résultats anormaux d'examens cliniques et de laboratoire, non classés ailleurs	869	807	1 675	897	105	59.0	85	49.4
All other diseases — Toutes autres maladies	18	49	434	456	5	♦2.8	1	♦0.6
External causes — Causes externes								
Total	425	217	7 077	1 524	34	19.1	15	♦8.7
Accidents								
Total	351	150	4 453	886	13	♦7.3	8	♦4.6
Transport accidents — Accidents de transport	62	12	3 636	668	1	♦0.6	2	♦1.2
Falls — Chutes	15	9	89	22	2	♦1.1	3	♦1.7
Accidental drowning and submersion — Noyade et submersion accidentelles	7	1	347	63	6	♦3.4	3	♦1.7
Exposure to smoke, fire and flames — Exposition à la fumée, au feu et aux flammes	14	10	6	4	-	-	-	-
Accidental poisoning by and exposure to noxious substances — Intoxication accidentelle par des substances nocives et exposition à ces substances	9	7	35	9	-	-	-	-
Intentional self-harm — Lésions auto-infligées	7	7	19	2	3	♦1.7	2	♦1.2
Assault — Agresssions	9	4	116	16	2	♦1.1	1	♦0.6
All other external causes — Toutes autres causes externes	58	56	2 489	620	16	♦9.0	4	♦2.3

20. Death and death rates by cause and sex: 2014 - 2018
Décès et taux de mortalité par cause et sexe : 2014 - 2018 (continued - suite)

Cause of death — Cause de décès	Maldives				Mongolia - Mongolie		Oman	
	2017 (+C)				2016 (U)		2016 (U)	
	Male — Masculin		Female — Féminin		Male — Masculin	Female — Féminin	Male — Masculin	Female — Féminin
	Number Nombre	Rate Taux	Number Nombre	Rate Taux	Number Nombre	Number Nombre	Number Nombre	Number Nombre
TOTAL	**750**	**413.9**	**491**	**279.8**	***9 662***	***6 520***	***5 281***	***2 915***
Certain infectious and parasitic diseases — Certaines maladies infectieuses et parasitaires								
Total	35	19.3	27	♦15.4	*289*	*181*	*132*	*69*
Intestinal infectious diseases — Maladies infectieuses intestinales	-	-	3	♦1.7	-	-	*9*	*10*
Tuberculosis — Tuberculose	3	♦1.7	2	♦1.1	*174*	*100*	*3*	*3*
Tetanus — Tétanos	1	♦0.6	-	-	-	-	-	-
Diphtheria — Diphtérie	-	-	-	-	-	-	-	-
Whooping cough — Coqueluche	-	-	-	-	-	-	-	-
Meningococcal infection — Infection à méningocoques	-	-	-	-	*1*	*1*	*1*	-
Septicaemia — Septicémie	27	♦14.9	19	♦10.8	*7*	*9*	*66*	*35*
Acute poliomyelitis — Poliomyélite aiguë	-	-	-	-	-	-	-	-
Measles — Rougeole	-	-	-	-	*75*	*56*	-	-
Viral hepatitis — Hépatite virale	-	-	1	♦0.6	*4*	*1*	*16*	*7*
Human immunodeficiency virus [HIV] disease — Maladies dues au virus de l'immunodéficience humaine (VIH)	-	-	-	-	*6*	*1*	*5*	-
Malaria — Paludisme	-	-	-	-	*1*	-	-	*1*
Neoplasms — Tumeurs	**62**	**34.2**	**34**	**19.4**	***2 309***	***1 838***	***256***	***172***
Malignant neoplasms — Tumeurs malignes								
Total	58	32.0	33	18.8	*2 293*	*1 823*	*234*	*166*
Malignant neoplasm of lip, oral cavity and pharynx — Tumeur maligne de la lèvre, de la cavité buccale et du pharynx	4	♦2.2	-	-	*41*	*20*	*6*	*6*
Malignant neoplasm of oesophagus — Tumeur maligne de l'oesophage	1	♦0.6	-	-	*157*	*107*	*6*	-
Malignant neoplasm of stomach — Tumeur maligne de l'estomac	-	-	-	-	*458*	*250*	*15*	*12*
Malignant neoplasm of colon, rectosigmoid junction, rectum, anus and anal canal — Tumeur maligne du côlon, de la jonction recto-sigmoïdienne, du rectum, de l'anus et du canal anal	1	♦0.6	-	-	*53*	*60*	*16*	*15*
Malignant neoplasm of liver and intrahepatic bile ducts — Tumeur maligne du foie et des voies bilaires intrahépatiques	7	♦3.9	-	-	*942*	*799*	*29*	*10*
Malignant neoplasm of pancreas — Tumeur maligne du pancréas	1	♦0.6	1	♦0.6	*81*	*54*	*14*	*7*
Malignant neoplasm of trachea, bronchus and lung — Tumeur maligne de la trachée, des bronches et du poumon	4	♦2.2	1	♦0.6	*287*	*67*	*24*	*6*
Malignant neoplasm of female breast — Tumeur maligne du sein chez la femme	..	..	1	♦0.8	..	*48*	..	*17*
Malignant neoplasm of cervix uteri — Tumeur maligne du col de l'utérus	..	..	2	♦1.6	..	*130*	..	*4*
Malignant neoplasm of prostate — Tumeur maligne de la prostate	2	♦7.0	..	..	*27*	..	*9*	..
Malignant neoplasm of lymphoid, haematopoietic and related tissue — Tumeurs malignes primitives ou présumées primitives des tissus lymphoïde, hématopoïétique et apparentés	6	♦3.3	3	♦1.7	*52*	*54*	*27*	*15*
Disorders of the blood and blood-forming organs and certain disorders involving the immune mechanism — Maladies du sang et des organes hématopoïétiques et certains troubles du système immunitaire								
Total	6	♦3.3	6	♦3.4	*3*	*12*	*52*	*36*
Anaemias — Anémies	3	♦1.7	6	♦3.4	*2*	*8*	*25*	*17*
Endocrine, nutritional and metabolic diseases — Maladies endocriniennes, nutritionnelles et métaboliques								
Total	35	19.3	22	♦12.5	*104*	*100*	*190*	*137*
Diabetes mellitus — Diabète sucré	23	♦12.7	12	♦6.8	*84*	*83*	*129*	*80*
Malnutrition — Malnutrition	-	-	-	-	*2*	-	-	*1*
Mental and behavioural disorders — Troubles mentaux et du comportement	**7**	**♦3.9**	**5**	**♦2.8**	***9***	***9***	***8***	***5***
Diseases of the nervous system — Maladies du système nerveux	**11**	**♦6.1**	**5**	**♦2.8**	***180***	***130***	***57***	***47***
Diseases of the circulatory system — Maladies de l'appareil circulatoire								
Total	304	167.7	184	104.9	*3 120*	*2 274*	*1 382*	*840*
Acute rheumatic fever and chronic rheumatic heart diseases — Rhumatisme articularie aigu et cardiopathies rhumatismales chroniques	1	♦0.6	1	♦0.6	*26*	*25*	*3*	*6*
Hypertensive diseases — Maladies hypertensives	41	22.6	32	18.2	*77*	*94*	*201*	*186*
Ischaemic heart disease — Cardiopathie ischémique	84	46.4	48	27.4	*1 497*	*982*	*215*	*106*

20. Death and death rates by cause and sex: 2014 - 2018
Décès et taux de mortalité par cause et sexe : 2014 - 2018 (continued - suite)

Cause of death — Cause de décès	Maldives				Mongolia - Mongolie		Oman	
	2017 (+C)				2016 (U)		2016 (U)	
	Male — Masculin		Female — Féminin		Male — Masculin	Female — Féminin	Male — Masculin	Female — Féminin
	Number Nombre	Rate Taux	Number Nombre	Rate Taux	Number Nombre	Number Nombre	Number Nombre	Number Nombre
Cerebrovascular disease — Maladie cérébrovasculaire	63	34.8	28	♦16.0	1 128	891	183	94
Diseases of arteries, arterioles and capillaries — Maladies des artères, artérioles et capillaires	6	♦3.3	3	♦1.7	56	59	12	8
Diseases of the respiratory system — Maladies de l'appareil respiratoire								
Total	73	40.3	79	45.0	403	294	362	258
Influenza — Grippe	-	-	-	-	5	3	1	1
Pneumonia — Pneumopathies	11	♦6.1	11	♦6.3	248	182	134	90
Chronic lower respiratory diseases — Maladies chroniques des voies respiratoires inférieures	26	♦14.3	45	25.6	96	83	42	22
Diseases of the digestive system — Maladies de l'appareil digestif								
Total	10	♦5.5	9	♦5.1	643	557	121	67
Gastric and duodenal ulcer — Ulcère de l'estomac et du duodénum	-	-	-	-	56	31	7	3
Diseases of the liver — Maladies du foie	6	♦3.3	5	♦2.8	414	390	51	27
Diseases of the musculoskeletal system and connective tissue — Maladies du système ostéo-articularie, des muscles et du tissu conjonctif	1	♦0.6	-	-	16	36	14	7
Diseases of the genitourinary system — Maladies de l'appareil génito-urinaire								
Total	30	♦16.6	24	♦13.7	129	117	174	125
Disorders of kidney and ureter — Affections du rein et de l'uretère	24	♦13.2	17	♦9.7	118	108	116	90
Hyperplasia of prostate — Hyperplasie de la prostate	1	♦3.5	..	..	2	..	5	..
Pregnancy, childbirth and the puerperium — Grossesse, accouchement et puerpéralité								
Total	..	..	7	♦104.1	..	38	..	3
Pregnancy with abortive outcome — Grossesse se terminant par un avortement	..	..	-	-	..	3	..	-
Other direct obstetric causes — Autres décès maternels directs	..	..	6	♦89.2	..	21	..	3
Indirect obstetric causes — Décès maternels indirects	..	..	1	♦14.9	..	14	..	-
Certain conditions originating in the perinatal period — Certaines affections dont l'origine se situe dans la période périnatale	30	♦881.6	18	♦542.2	342	242	168	111
Congenital malformations, deformations and chromosomal abnormalities — Malformations congénitales et anomalies chromosomiques	5	♦146.9	4	♦120.5	118	101	92	86
Symptoms, signs and abnormal clinical and laboratory findings, not elsewhere classified — Symptômes, signes et résultats anormaux d'examens cliniques et de laboratoire, non classés ailleurs	103	56.8	58	33.1	52	83	1 506	784
All other diseases — Toutes autres maladies	3	♦1.7	-	-	14	10	48	41
External causes — Causes externes								
Total	35	19.3	9	♦5.1	1 931	498	719	127
Accidents								
Total	13	♦7.2	4	♦2.3	1 309	372	615	103
Transport accidents — Accidents de transport	3	♦1.7	-	-	365	119	513	83
Falls — Chutes	-	-	-	-	109	55	46	8
Accidental drowning and submersion — Noyade et submersion accidentelles	3	♦1.7	-	-	119	16	31	6
Exposure to smoke, fire and flames — Exposition à la fumée, au feu et aux flammes	-	-	-	-	27	12	5	3
Accidental poisoning by and exposure to noxious substances — Intoxication accidentelle par des substances nocives et exposition à ces substances	-	-	-	-	424	87	2	-
Intentional self-harm — Lésions auto-infligées	-	-	-	-	387	63	6	2
Assault — Agresssions	2	♦1.1	-	-	155	42	3	-
All other external causes — Toutes autres causes externes	20	♦11.0	5	♦2.8	80	21	95	22

20. Death and death rates by cause and sex: 2014 - 2018
Décès et taux de mortalité par cause et sexe : 2014 - 2018 (continued - suite)

Cause of death — Cause de décès	Oman		Philippines		Qatar			
	2017 (U)		2014 (U)		2016 (U)		2017 (U)	
	Male — Masculin	Female — Féminin	Male — Masculin	Female — Féminin	Male — Masculin	Female — Féminin	Male — Masculin	Female — Féminin
	Number Nombre	Number Nombre	Number Nombre	Number Nombre	Number Nombre	Number Nombre	Number Nombre	Number Nombre
TOTAL	*5 266*	*3 207*	*307 861*	*229 138*	*1 647*	*560*	*1 602*	*583*
Certain infectious and parasitic diseases — Certaines maladies infectieuses et parasitaires								
Total	*253*	*157*	*25 643*	*13 772*	*17*	*14*	*25*	*15*
Intestinal infectious diseases — Maladies infectieuses intestinales	*12*	*11*	*2 228*	*1 765*	*2*	*2*	*1*	*2*
Tuberculosis — Tuberculose	*4*	-	*16 678*	*7 069*	-	-	*3*	-
Tetanus — Tétanos	-	-	*410*	*111*	-	-	-	-
Diphtheria — Diphtérie	-	-	*13*	*11*	-	-	-	-
Whooping cough — Coqueluche	*1*	*1*	*1*	*2*	-	-	-	-
Meningococcal infection — Infection à méningocoques	*1*	*1*	*47*	*47*	-	*1*	*1*	-
Septicaemia — Septicémie	*195*	*129*	*3 466*	*3 144*	*5*	*2*	*7*	*8*
Acute poliomyelitis — Poliomyélite aiguë	-	*1*	*12*	*8*	-	-	-	-
Measles — Rougeole	-	-	*287*	*210*	-	-	-	-
Viral hepatitis — Hépatite virale	*11*	*7*	*541*	*225*	*4*	*4*	*4*	*1*
Human immunodeficiency virus [HIV] disease — Maladies dues au virus de l'immunodéficience humaine (VIH)	*3*	*1*	*187*	*11*	-	-	*2*	*1*
Malaria — Paludisme	-	-	*12*	*10*	-	*2*	-	-
Neoplasms — Tumeurs	*234*	*164*	*28 766*	*29 057*	*170*	*120*	*169*	*130*
Malignant neoplasms — Tumeurs malignes								
Total	*216*	*155*	*26 920*	*27 357*	*168*	*117*	*162*	*122*
Malignant neoplasm of lip, oral cavity and pharynx — Tumeur maligne de la lèvre, de la cavité buccale et du pharynx	*7*	*2*	*1 376*	*784*	*5*	*3*	*1*	-
Malignant neoplasm of oesophagus — Tumeur maligne de l'oesophage	*4*	*2*	*322*	*176*	*3*	-	*1*	*1*
Malignant neoplasm of stomach — Tumeur maligne de l'estomac	*21*	*10*	*749*	*591*	*6*	*4*	*9*	*3*
Malignant neoplasm of colon, rectosigmoid junction, rectum, anus and anal canal — Tumeur maligne du côlon, de la jonction recto-sigmoïdienne, du rectum, de l'anus et du canal anal	*15*	*9*	*3 252*	*2 606*	*29*	*7*	*15*	*15*
Malignant neoplasm of liver and intrahepatic bile ducts — Tumeur maligne du foie et des voies bilaires intrahépatiques	*23*	*10*	*4 355*	*1 907*	*23*	*10*	*22*	*8*
Malignant neoplasm of pancreas — Tumeur maligne du pancréas	*7*	*3*	*810*	*839*	*10*	*6*	*9*	*4*
Malignant neoplasm of trachea, bronchus and lung — Tumeur maligne de la trachée, des bronches et du poumon	*21*	*5*	*5 712*	*2 465*	*14*	*4*	*25*	*12*
Malignant neoplasm of female breast — Tumeur maligne du sein chez la femme	..	*34*	..	*7 145*	..	*39*	..	*33*
Malignant neoplasm of cervix uteri — Tumeur maligne du col de l'utérus	..	*2*	..	*1 731*	..	*2*	..	*4*
Malignant neoplasm of prostate — Tumeur maligne de la prostate	*14*	..	*2 697*	..	*5*	..	*12*	..
Malignant neoplasm of lymphoid, haematopoietic and related tissue — Tumeurs malignes primitives ou présumées primitives des tissus lymphoïde, hématopoïétique et apparentés	*38*	*16*	*2 313*	*2 064*	*32*	*8*	*28*	*5*
Disorders of the blood and blood-forming organs and certain disorders involving the immune mechanism — Maladies du sang et des organes hématopoïétiques et certains troubles du système immunitaire								
Total	*41*	*23*	*1 959*	*2 129*	*2*	*4*	*8*	*8*
Anaemias — Anémies	*22*	*13*	*1 466*	*1 605*	*1*	*1*	*3*	-
Endocrine, nutritional and metabolic diseases — Maladies endocriniennes, nutritionnelles et métaboliques								
Total	*166*	*96*	*18 905*	*20 464*	*73*	*36*	*99*	*49*
Diabetes mellitus — Diabète sucré	*108*	*58*	*15 176*	*15 486*	*62*	*28*	*85*	*41*
Malnutrition — Malnutrition	*1*	*2*	*1 034*	*1 360*	-	-	-	-
Mental and behavioural disorders — Troubles mentaux et du comportement	*12*	*3*	*535*	*252*	-	-	-	-
Diseases of the nervous system — Maladies du système nerveux	*72*	*36*	*4 196*	*3 262*	*21*	*11*	*19*	*8*
Diseases of the circulatory system — Maladies de l'appareil circulatoire								
Total	*1 255*	*799*	*105 273*	*82 478*	*579*	*143*	*562*	*150*
Acute rheumatic fever and chronic rheumatic heart diseases — Rhumatisme articularie aigu et cardiopathies rhumatismales chroniques	*5*	*5*	*767*	*1 049*	*2*	-	*3*	-
Hypertensive diseases — Maladies hypertensives	*202*	*152*	*18 655*	*15 285*	*42*	*24*	*39*	*23*
Ischaemic heart disease — Cardiopathie ischémique	*195*	*101*	*38 139*	*25 703*	*167*	*30*	*177*	*31*

20. Death and death rates by cause and sex: 2014 - 2018
Décès et taux de mortalité par cause et sexe : 2014 - 2018 (continued - suite)

Cause of death — Cause de décès	Oman		Philippines		Qatar			
	2017 (U)		2014 (U)		2016 (U)		2017 (U)	
	Male — Masculin	Female — Féminin	Male — Masculin	Female — Féminin	Male — Masculin	Female — Féminin	Male — Masculin	Female — Féminin
	Number Nombre	Number Nombre	Number Nombre	Number Nombre	Number Nombre	Number Nombre	Number Nombre	Number Nombre
Cerebrovascular disease — Maladie cérébrovasculaire	*151*	*89*	*28 850*	*22 463*	*78*	*25*	*35*	*23*
Diseases of arteries, arterioles and capillaries — Maladies des artères, artérioles et capillaires	*12*	*5*	*1 214*	*1 332*	*9*	*1*	*10*	*1*
Diseases of the respiratory system — Maladies de l'appareil respiratoire								
Total	*290*	*263*	*46 532*	*35 988*	*171*	*50*	*159*	*61*
Influenza — Grippe	*3*	*10*	*28*	*20*	*1*	-	*1*	-
Pneumonia — Pneumopathies	*112*	*86*	*26 464*	*25 968*	*46*	*14*	*52*	*23*
Chronic lower respiratory diseases — Maladies chroniques des voies respiratoires inférieures	*27*	*24*	*16 790*	*7 292*	*13*	*7*	*6*	*10*
Diseases of the digestive system — Maladies de l'appareil digestif								
Total	*83*	*58*	*14 807*	*6 368*	*39*	*16*	*39*	*18*
Gastric and duodenal ulcer — Ulcère de l'estomac et du duodénum	*3*	*3*	*3 603*	*1 880*	*1*	-	*1*	-
Diseases of the liver — Maladies du foie	*47*	*29*	*6 282*	*2 142*	*20*	*7*	*22*	*12*
Diseases of the musculoskeletal system and connective tissue — Maladies du système ostéo-articularie, des muscles et du tissu conjonctif	*10*	*7*	*734*	*1 008*	*1*	-	-	*2*
Diseases of the genitourinary system — Maladies de l'appareil génito-urinaire								
Total	*161*	*120*	*12 093*	*8 446*	*41*	*37*	*66*	*47*
Disorders of kidney and ureter — Affections du rein et de l'uretère	*111*	*94*	*10 949*	*7 590*	*39*	*33*	*58*	*44*
Hyperplasia of prostate — Hyperplasie de la prostate	*3*	..	*456*	..	-	..	*1*	..
Pregnancy, childbirth and the puerperium — Grossesse, accouchement et puerpéralité								
Total	..	*3*	..	*1 570*	..	-	..	-
Pregnancy with abortive outcome — Grossesse se terminant par un avortement	..	-	..	*167*	..	-	..	-
Other direct obstetric causes — Autres décès maternels directs	..	*2*	..	*1 344*	..	-	..	-
Indirect obstetric causes — Décès maternels indirects	..	*1*	..	*59*	..	-	..	-
Certain conditions originating in the perinatal period — Certaines affections dont l'origine se situe dans la période périnatale	*134*	*107*	*5 859*	*4 007*	*23*	*27*	*37*	*30*
Congenital malformations, deformations and chromosomal abnormalities — Malformations congénitales et anomalies chromosomiques	*81*	*82*	*2 354*	*1 943*	*33*	*34*	*42*	*30*
Symptoms, signs and abnormal clinical and laboratory findings, not elsewhere classified — Symptômes, signes et résultats anormaux d'examens cliniques et de laboratoire, non classés ailleurs	*1 861*	*1 127*	*10 387*	*10 531*	*97*	*31*	*22*	*9*
All other diseases — Toutes autres maladies	*36*	*33*	*958*	*1 276*	*3*	-	*1*	*2*
External causes — Causes externes								
Total	*577*	*129*	*28 860*	*6 587*	*377*	*37*	*354*	*24*
Accidents								
Total	*371*	*74*	*13 098*	*3 860*	*308*	*28*	*291*	*19*
Transport accidents — Accidents de transport	*308*	*57*	*6 955*	*1 711*	*186*	*10*	*186*	*9*
Falls — Chutes	*26*	*5*	*1 445*	*719*	*29*	-	*33*	*1*
Accidental drowning and submersion — Noyade et submersion accidentelles	*22*	*6*	*2 272*	*688*	*13*	*5*	*12*	*1*
Exposure to smoke, fire and flames — Exposition à la fumée, au feu et aux flammes	*3*	*3*	*204*	*159*	*19*	*3*	*4*	*1*
Accidental poisoning by and exposure to noxious substances — Intoxication accidentelle par des substances nocives et exposition à ces substances	-	*1*	*126*	*43*	*3*	*1*	*10*	*4*
Intentional self-harm — Lésions auto-infligées	*9*	*4*	*1 723*	*384*	*63*	*7*	*49*	*5*
Assault — Agresssions	*1*	*1*	*9 831*	*987*	*3*	*1*	*11*	-
All other external causes — Toutes autres causes externes	*196*	*50*	*4 208*	*1 356*	*3*	*1*	*3*	-

20. Death and death rates by cause and sex: 2014 - 2018
Décès et taux de mortalité par cause et sexe : 2014 - 2018 (continued - suite)

Republic of Korea - République de Corée

Cause of death — Cause de décès	2016 (C)				2017 (C)			
	Male — Masculin		Female — Féminin		Male — Masculin		Female — Féminin	
	Number Nombre	Rate Taux	Number Nombre	Rate Taux	Number Nombre	Rate Taux	Number Nombre	Rate Taux
TOTAL	**152 529**	**597.5**	**128 298**	**501.5**	**154 328**	**603.4**	**131 206**	**511.4**
Certain infectious and parasitic diseases — Certaines maladies infectieuses et parasitaires								
Total	**3 980**	**15.6**	**3 966**	**15.5**	**3 830**	**15.0**	**4 156**	**16.2**
Intestinal infectious diseases — Maladies infectieuses intestinales	**306**	**1.2**	**536**	**2.1**	**325**	**1.3**	**568**	**2.2**
Tuberculosis — Tuberculose	**1 349**	**5.3**	**837**	**3.3**	**1 107**	**4.3**	**709**	**2.8**
Tetanus — Tétanos	**2**	**♦0.0**	**1**	**♦0.0**	**3**	**♦0.0**	**2**	**♦0.0**
Diphtheria — Diphtérie	-	-	-	-	-	-	-	-
Whooping cough — Coqueluche	-	-	-	-	-	-	-	-
Meningococcal infection — Infection à méningocoques	-	-	**2**	**♦0.0**	-	-	**1**	**♦0.0**
Septicaemia — Septicémie	**1 523**	**6.0**	**2 073**	**8.1**	**1 626**	**6.4**	**2 368**	**9.2**
Acute poliomyelitis — Poliomyélite aiguë	-	-	-	-	-	-	-	-
Measles — Rougeole	-	-	-	-	-	-	-	-
Viral hepatitis — Hépatite virale	**364**	**1.4**	**264**	**1.0**	**317**	**1.2**	**231**	**0.9**
Human immunodeficiency virus [HIV] disease — Maladies dues au virus de l'immunodéficience humaine (VIH)	**82**	**0.3**	**6**	**♦0.0**	**83**	**0.3**	**8**	**♦0.0**
Malaria — Paludisme	**4**	**♦0.0**	-	-	**3**	**♦0.0**	-	-
Neoplasms — Tumeurs	**49 009**	**192.0**	**30 720**	**120.1**	**49 629**	**194.0**	**30 691**	**119.6**
Malignant neoplasms — Tumeurs malignes								
Total	**48 208**	**188.8**	**29 986**	**117.2**	**48 866**	**191.1**	**29 997**	**116.9**
Malignant neoplasm of lip, oral cavity and pharynx — Tumeur maligne de la lèvre, de la cavité buccale et du pharynx	**909**	**3.6**	**294**	**1.1**	**928**	**3.6**	**271**	**1.1**
Malignant neoplasm of oesophagus — Tumeur maligne de l'oesophage	**1 379**	**5.4**	**145**	**0.6**	**1 290**	**5.0**	**133**	**0.5**
Malignant neoplasm of stomach — Tumeur maligne de l'estomac	**5 318**	**20.8**	**2 946**	**11.5**	**5 166**	**20.2**	**2 868**	**11.2**
Malignant neoplasm of colon, rectosigmoid junction, rectum, anus and anal canal — Tumeur maligne du côlon, de la jonction recto-sigmoïdienne, du rectum, de l'anus et du canal anal	**4 686**	**18.4**	**3 746**	**14.6**	**5 009**	**19.6**	**3 757**	**14.6**
Malignant neoplasm of liver and intrahepatic bile ducts — Tumeur maligne du foie et des voies bilaires intrahépatiques	**8 044**	**31.5**	**2 957**	**11.6**	**7 982**	**31.2**	**2 739**	**10.7**
Malignant neoplasm of pancreas — Tumeur maligne du pancréas	**2 901**	**11.4**	**2 713**	**10.6**	**2 976**	**11.6**	**2 806**	**10.9**
Malignant neoplasm of trachea, bronchus and lung — Tumeur maligne de la trachée, des bronches et du poumon	**13 324**	**52.2**	**4 639**	**18.1**	**13 272**	**51.9**	**4 708**	**18.4**
Malignant neoplasm of female breast — Tumeur maligne du sein chez la femme	..	..	**2 456**	**11.1**	..	..	**2 497**	**11.2**
Malignant neoplasm of cervix uteri — Tumeur maligne du col de l'utérus	..	..	**897**	**4.0**	..	..	**868**	**3.9**
Malignant neoplasm of prostate — Tumeur maligne de la prostate	**1 745**	**20.6**	..	..	**1 821**	**20.8**	..	..
Malignant neoplasm of lymphoid, haematopoietic and related tissue — Tumeurs malignes primitives ou présumées primitives des tissus lymphoïde, hématopoïétique et apparentés	**2 669**	**10.5**	**2 079**	**8.1**	**2 698**	**10.5**	**2 103**	**8.2**
Disorders of the blood and blood-forming organs and certain disorders involving the immune mechanism — Maladies du sang et des organes hématopoïétiques et certains troubles du système immunitaire								
Total	**282**	**1.1**	**421**	**1.6**	**308**	**1.2**	**469**	**1.8**
Anaemias — Anémies	**172**	**0.7**	**293**	**1.1**	**175**	**0.7**	**324**	**1.3**
Endocrine, nutritional and metabolic diseases — Maladies endocriniennes, nutritionnelles et métaboliques								
Total	**5 551**	**21.7**	**5 512**	**21.5**	**5 168**	**20.2**	**5 364**	**20.9**
Diabetes mellitus — Diabète sucré	**4 891**	**19.2**	**4 916**	**19.2**	**4 514**	**17.6**	**4 670**	**18.2**
Malnutrition — Malnutrition	**40**	**0.2**	**44**	**0.2**	**48**	**0.2**	**61**	**0.2**
Mental and behavioural disorders — Troubles mentaux et du comportement	**2 270**	**8.9**	**3 029**	**11.8**	**2 286**	**8.9**	**3 088**	**12.0**
Diseases of the nervous system — Maladies du système nerveux	**4 434**	**17.4**	**6 407**	**25.0**	**4 531**	**17.7**	**6 666**	**26.0**
Diseases of the circulatory system — Maladies de l'appareil circulatoire								
Total	**28 433**	**111.4**	**31 955**	**124.9**	**28 674**	**112.1**	**32 592**	**127.0**
Acute rheumatic fever and chronic rheumatic heart diseases — Rhumatisme articularie aigu et cardiopathies rhumatismales chroniques	**57**	**0.2**	**108**	**0.4**	**74**	**0.3**	**131**	**0.5**
Hypertensive diseases — Maladies hypertensives	**1 671**	**6.5**	**3 745**	**14.6**	**1 777**	**6.9**	**3 998**	**15.6**
Ischaemic heart disease — Cardiopathie ischémique	**7 924**	**31.0**	**6 730**	**26.3**	**7 855**	**30.7**	**6 402**	**25.0**
Cerebrovascular disease — Maladie cérébrovasculaire	**11 284**	**44.2**	**12 131**	**47.4**	**10 921**	**42.7**	**11 824**	**46.1**

20. Death and death rates by cause and sex: 2014 - 2018
Décès et taux de mortalité par cause et sexe : 2014 - 2018 (continued - suite)

Republic of Korea - République de Corée

Cause of death — Cause de décès	2016 (C)				2017 (C)			
	Male — Masculin		Female — Féminin		Male — Masculin		Female — Féminin	
	Number Nombre	Rate Taux	Number Nombre	Rate Taux	Number Nombre	Rate Taux	Number Nombre	Rate Taux
Diseases of arteries, arterioles and capillaries — Maladies des artères, artérioles et capillaires	815	3.2	671	2.6	818	3.2	660	2.6
Diseases of the respiratory system — Maladies de l'appareil respiratoire								
Total	16 394	64.2	13 010	50.8	18 128	70.9	14 515	56.6
Influenza — Grippe	104	0.4	118	0.5	99	0.4	163	0.6
Pneumonia — Pneumopathies	8 586	33.6	7 890	30.8	10 067	39.4	9 311	36.3
Chronic lower respiratory diseases — Maladies chroniques des voies respiratoires inférieures	4 358	17.1	2 634	10.3	4 275	16.7	2 475	9.6
Diseases of the digestive system — Maladies de l'appareil digestif								
Total	7 594	29.7	4 355	17.0	7 551	29.5	4 581	17.9
Gastric and duodenal ulcer — Ulcère de l'estomac et du duodénum	264	1.0	233	0.9	256	1.0	214	0.8
Diseases of the liver — Maladies du foie	5 165	20.2	1 633	6.4	5 124	20.0	1 673	6.5
Diseases of the musculoskeletal system and connective tissue — Maladies du système ostéo-articularie, des muscles et du tissu conjonctif	531	2.1	965	3.8	504	2.0	1 017	4.0
Diseases of the genitourinary system — Maladies de l'appareil génito-urinaire								
Total	3 282	12.9	3 886	15.2	3 303	12.9	4 279	16.7
Disorders of kidney and ureter — Affections du rein et de l'uretère	2 867	11.2	2 970	11.6	2 821	11.0	3 197	12.5
Hyperplasia of prostate — Hyperplasie de la prostate	64	0.8	..	..	49	0.6	..	..
Pregnancy, childbirth and the puerperium — Grossesse, accouchement et puerpéralité								
Total	..	..	37	9.1	..	..	32	8.9
Pregnancy with abortive outcome — Grossesse se terminant par un avortement	..	..	2	♦0.5	..	..	-	-
Other direct obstetric causes — Autres décès maternels directs	..	..	26	♦6.4	..	..	22	♦6.1
Indirect obstetric causes — Décès maternels indirects	..	..	6	♦1.5	..	..	6	♦1.7
Certain conditions originating in the perinatal period — Certaines affections dont l'origine se situe dans la période périnatale	353	169.7	263	132.7	308	167.1	215	123.9
Congenital malformations, deformations and chromosomal abnormalities — Malformations congénitales et anomalies chromosomiques	216	103.8	210	106.0	196	106.3	175	100.9
Symptoms, signs and abnormal clinical and laboratory findings, not elsewhere classified — Symptômes, signes et résultats anormaux d'examens cliniques et de laboratoire, non classés ailleurs	10 760	42.2	14 261	55.7	11 005	43.0	14 492	56.5
All other diseases — Toutes autres maladies	175	0.7	348	1.4	214	0.8	412	1.6
External causes — Causes externes								
Total	19 265	75.5	8 953	35.0	18 692	73.1	8 462	33.0
Accidents								
Total	8 327	32.6	4 039	15.8	8 119	31.7	3 870	15.1
Transport accidents — Accidents de transport	3 762	14.7	1 388	5.4	3 729	14.6	1 299	5.1
Falls — Chutes	1 903	7.5	700	2.7	1 922	7.5	750	2.9
Accidental drowning and submersion — Noyade et submersion accidentelles	500	2.0	149	0.6	452	1.8	133	0.5
Exposure to smoke, fire and flames — Exposition à la fumée, au feu et aux flammes	196	0.8	87	0.3	200	0.8	122	0.5
Accidental poisoning by and exposure to noxious substances — Intoxication accidentelle par des substances nocives et exposition à ces substances	199	0.8	100	0.4	198	0.8	86	0.3
Intentional self-harm — Lésions auto-infligées	9 243	36.2	3 849	15.0	8 922	34.9	3 541	13.8
Assault — Agresssions	214	0.8	222	0.9	216	0.8	199	0.8
All other external causes — Toutes autres causes externes	1 481	5.8	843	3.3	1 435	5.6	852	3.3

20. Death and death rates by cause and sex: 2014 - 2018
Décès et taux de mortalité par cause et sexe : 2014 - 2018 (continued - suite)

Cause of death — Cause de décès	Singapore - Singapour				Tajikistan - Tadjikistan		Thailand - Thaïlande	
	2016 (+U)		2017 (+U)		2016 (U)		2016 (+U)	
	Male — Masculin	Female — Féminin	Male — Masculin	Female — Féminin	Male — Masculin	Female — Féminin	Male — Masculin	Female — Féminin
	Number Nombre	Number Nombre	Number Nombre	Number Nombre	Number Nombre	Number Nombre	Number Nombre	Number Nombre
TOTAL	*10 269*	*8 587*	*10 674*	*9 089*	*19 068*	*15 058*	*265 439*	*203 646*
Certain infectious and parasitic diseases — Certaines maladies infectieuses et parasitaires								
Total	*103*	*56*	*113*	*61*	*415*	*356*	*21 828*	*15 437*
Intestinal infectious diseases — Maladies infectieuses intestinales	*18*	*16*	*18*	*21*	*114*	*109*	*1 135*	*1 098*
Tuberculosis — Tuberculose	*32*	*7*	*25*	*4*	*227*	*187*	*4 475*	*1 632*
Tetanus — Tétanos	-	-	-	-	-	-	*22*	*14*
Diphtheria — Diphtérie	-	-	-	-	-	-	*4*	*1*
Whooping cough — Coqueluche	-	-	-	*1*	-	-	-	-
Meningococcal infection — Infection à méningocoques	-	-	-	-	*5*	*8*	*5*	-
Septicaemia — Septicémie	*12*	*16*	*24*	*17*	*12*	*9*	*11 191*	*9 909*
Acute poliomyelitis — Poliomyélite aiguë	-	-	-	-	-	-	-	-
Measles — Rougeole	-	-	-	-	-	-	*2*	-
Viral hepatitis — Hépatite virale	*1*	*1*	*1*	*1*	*40*	*27*	*683*	*308*
Human immunodeficiency virus [HIV] disease — Maladies dues au virus de l'immunodéficience humaine (VIH)	*23*	*1*	*28*	*2*	-	-	*3 203*	*1 751*
Malaria — Paludisme	-	-	-	-	-	-	*20*	*6*
Neoplasms — Tumeurs	*3 154*	*2 528*	*3 206*	*2 726*	*1 405*	*1 372*	*44 490*	*33 076*
Malignant neoplasms — Tumeurs malignes								
Total	*3 120*	*2 496*	*3 119*	*2 661*	*1 397*	*1 366*	*43 966*	*32 538*
Malignant neoplasm of lip, oral cavity and pharynx — Tumeur maligne de la lèvre, de la cavité buccale et du pharynx	*170*	*43*	*150*	*54*	*36*	*35*	*2 183*	*972*
Malignant neoplasm of oesophagus — Tumeur maligne de l'oesophage	*89*	*15*	*76*	*11*	*70*	*44*	*1 512*	*213*
Malignant neoplasm of stomach — Tumeur maligne de l'estomac	*190*	*139*	*175*	*130*	*421*	*296*	*1 136*	*935*
Malignant neoplasm of colon, rectosigmoid junction, rectum, anus and anal canal — Tumeur maligne du côlon, de la jonction recto-sigmoïdienne, du rectum, de l'anus et du canal anal	*457*	*389*	*467*	*399*	*83*	*41*	*2 540*	*2 018*
Malignant neoplasm of liver and intrahepatic bile ducts — Tumeur maligne du foie et des voies bilaires intrahépatiques	*430*	*177*	*399*	*194*	*101*	*97*	*12 086*	*4 984*
Malignant neoplasm of pancreas — Tumeur maligne du pancréas	*166*	*160*	*181*	*183*	*32*	*28*	*631*	*611*
Malignant neoplasm of trachea, bronchus and lung — Tumeur maligne de la trachée, des bronches et du poumon	*799*	*388*	*804*	*396*	*127*	*77*	*8 726*	*4 688*
Malignant neoplasm of female breast — Tumeur maligne du sein chez la femme	..	*445*	..	*458*	..	*194*	..	*4 099*
Malignant neoplasm of cervix uteri — Tumeur maligne du col de l'utérus	..	*79*	..	*72*	..	*98*	..	*2 193*
Malignant neoplasm of prostate — Tumeur maligne de la prostate	*187*	..	*177*	..	*30*	..	*1 404*	..
Malignant neoplasm of lymphoid, haematopoietic and related tissue — Tumeurs malignes primitives ou présumées primitives des tissus lymphoïde, hématopoïétique et apparentés	*203*	*133*	*217*	*176*	*93*	*68*	*2 248*	*1 908*
Disorders of the blood and blood-forming organs and certain disorders involving the immune mechanism — Maladies du sang et des organes hématopoïétiques et certains troubles du système immunitaire								
Total	*5*	*6*	*4*	*12*	*60*	*71*	*467*	*579*
Anaemias — Anémies	*1*	*4*	*1*	*6*	*36*	*50*	*289*	*326*
Endocrine, nutritional and metabolic diseases — Maladies endocriniennes, nutritionnelles et métaboliques								
Total	*162*	*190*	*147*	*190*	*713*	*694*	*6 709*	*9 177*
Diabetes mellitus — Diabète sucré	*153*	*181*	*137*	*181*	*711*	*694*	*6 006*	*8 481*
Malnutrition — Malnutrition	-	-	-	-	-	-	*140*	*136*
Mental and behavioural disorders — Troubles mentaux et du comportement	*1*	*1*	-	*1*	*48*	*22*	*1 201*	*194*
Diseases of the nervous system — Maladies du système nerveux	*118*	*97*	*101*	*70*	*512*	*308*	*4 935*	*7 007*
Diseases of the circulatory system — Maladies de l'appareil circulatoire								
Total	*3 261*	*2 470*	*3 460*	*2 665*	*8 972*	*7 173*	*39 358*	*30 339*
Acute rheumatic fever and chronic rheumatic heart diseases — Rhumatisme articularie aigu et cardiopathies rhumatismales chroniques	*4*	*16*	*6*	*14*	*11*	*14*	*92*	*200*
Hypertensive diseases — Maladies hypertensives	*415*	*343*	*351*	*304*	*2 034*	*1 924*	*3 830*	*4 100*
Ischaemic heart disease — Cardiopathie ischémique	*1 992*	*1 202*	*2 233*	*1 395*	*2 902*	*2 171*	*12 634*	*8 374*

20. Death and death rates by cause and sex: 2014 - 2018
Décès et taux de mortalité par cause et sexe : 2014 - 2018 (continued - suite)

Cause of death — Cause de décès	Singapore - Singapour				Tajikistan - Tadjikistan		Thailand - Thaïlande	
	2016 (+U)		2017 (+U)		2016 (U)		2016 (+U)	
	Male — Masculin	Female — Féminin	Male — Masculin	Female — Féminin	Male — Masculin	Female — Féminin	Male — Masculin	Female — Féminin
	Number Nombre	Number Nombre	Number Nombre	Number Nombre	Number Nombre	Number Nombre	Number Nombre	Number Nombre
Cerebrovascular disease — Maladie cérébrovasculaire	605	648	556	677	1 877	1 430	18 273	13 412
Diseases of arteries, arterioles and capillaries — Maladies des artères, artérioles et capillaires	100	97	132	106	868	810	916	614
Diseases of the respiratory system — Maladies de l'appareil respiratoire								
Total	2 251	2 054	2 446	2 158	1 010	801	25 891	16 197
Influenza — Grippe	-	1	1	3	6	12	35	37
Pneumonia — Pneumopathies	1 870	1 875	2 083	2 007	232	176	16 551	11 919
Chronic lower respiratory diseases — Maladies chroniques des voies respiratoires inférieures	311	132	305	102	318	252	7 300	2 670
Diseases of the digestive system — Maladies de l'appareil digestif								
Total	240	206	232	230	865	609	14 039	6 364
Gastric and duodenal ulcer — Ulcère de l'estomac et du duodénum	25	20	25	17	39	31	400	286
Diseases of the liver — Maladies du foie	118	61	92	75	731	498	8 564	3 203
Diseases of the musculoskeletal system and connective tissue — Maladies du système ostéo-articularie, des muscles et du tissu conjonctif	42	37	36	46	25	21	1 326	1 703
Diseases of the genitourinary system — Maladies de l'appareil génito-urinaire								
Total	346	542	342	551	447	382	11 421	12 732
Disorders of kidney and ureter — Affections du rein et de l'uretère	197	228	214	282	419	381	10 116	10 690
Hyperplasia of prostate — Hyperplasie de la prostate	1	..	1	..	21	..	141	..
Pregnancy, childbirth and the puerperium — Grossesse, accouchement et puerpéralité								
Total	..	2	..	-	..	18	..	177
Pregnancy with abortive outcome — Grossesse se terminant par un avortement	..	-	..	-	..	1	..	15
Other direct obstetric causes — Autres décès maternels directs	..	2	..	-	..	17	..	118
Indirect obstetric causes — Décès maternels indirects	..	-	..	-	..	-	..	44
Certain conditions originating in the perinatal period — Certaines affections dont l'origine se situe dans la période périnatale	14	17	13	21	792	553	1 271	922
Congenital malformations, deformations and chromosomal abnormalities — Malformations congénitales et anomalies chromosomiques	34	30	23	19	612	397	881	809
Symptoms, signs and abnormal clinical and laboratory findings, not elsewhere classified — Symptômes, signes et résultats anormaux d'examens cliniques et de laboratoire, non classés ailleurs	39	27	49	32	2 149	1 970	59 294	59 349
All other diseases — Toutes autres maladies	43	105	38	75	2	1	1 082	1 272
External causes — Causes externes								
Total	456	219	464	232	1 041	310	31 246	8 312
Accidents								
Total	216	78	204	92	696	176	19 055	5 180
Transport accidents — Accidents de transport	81	32	79	33	304	74	12 215	3 259
Falls — Chutes	93	36	86	45	75	16	1 341	435
Accidental drowning and submersion — Noyade et submersion accidentelles	11	2	10	1	175	51	2 850	650
Exposure to smoke, fire and flames — Exposition à la fumée, au feu et aux flammes	1	1	1	2	31	8	193	98
Accidental poisoning by and exposure to noxious substances — Intoxication accidentelle par des substances nocives et exposition à ces substances	16	4	12	4	-	-	38	20
Intentional self-harm — Lésions auto-infligées	212	124	198	109	154	82	3 283	848
Assault — Agresssions	9	6	8	6	60	17	1 494	279
All other external causes — Toutes autres causes externes	19	11	54	25	131	35	7 414	2 005

20. Death and death rates by cause and sex: 2014 - 2018
Décès et taux de mortalité par cause et sexe : 2014 - 2018 (continued - suite)

Cause of death — Cause de décès	Thailand - Thaïlande		Turkey - Turquie					
	2017 (+U)		2015 (+U)		2016 (+C)			
	Male — Masculin	Female — Féminin	Male — Masculin	Female — Féminin	Male — Masculin		Female — Féminin	
	Number Nombre	Number Nombre	Number Nombre	Number Nombre	Number Nombre	Rate Taux	Number Nombre	Rate Taux
TOTAL	*260 701*	*197 309*	*215 977*	*180 994*	228 954	571.8	191 170	480.7
Certain infectious and parasitic diseases — Certaines maladies infectieuses et parasitaires								
Total	*21 855*	*15 108*	*4 307*	*4 021*	4 494	11.2	4 130	10.4
Intestinal infectious diseases — Maladies infectieuses intestinales	*1 149*	*1 045*	*244*	*342*	223	0.6	290	0.7
Tuberculosis — Tuberculose	*4 418*	*1 652*	*273*	*139*	298	0.7	141	0.4
Tetanus — Tétanos	*22*	*19*	*6*	*5*	7	♦0.0	2	♦0.0
Diphtheria — Diphtérie	*2*	-	-	-	-	-	-	-
Whooping cough — Coqueluche	*1*	-	-	-	-	-	1	♦0.0
Meningococcal infection — Infection à méningocoques	*3*	*3*	*9*	*10*	14	♦0.0	16	♦0.0
Septicaemia — Septicémie	*11 161*	*9 654*	*2 876*	*2 827*	3 026	7.6	3 053	7.7
Acute poliomyelitis — Poliomyélite aiguë	-	-	*1*	*1*	-	-	-	-
Measles — Rougeole	*2*	*4*	*1*	*2*	1	♦0.0	1	♦0.0
Viral hepatitis — Hépatite virale	*751*	*297*	*383*	*324*	365	0.9	257	0.6
Human immunodeficiency virus [HIV] disease — Maladies dues au virus de l'immunodéficience humaine (VIH)	*3 026*	*1 579*	*71*	*20*	75	0.2	10	♦0.0
Malaria — Paludisme	*9*	*6*	*2*	*1*	6	♦0.0	2	♦0.0
Neoplasms — Tumeurs	*45 016*	*33 524*	*51 256*	*27 903*	52 910	132.1	28 737	72.3
Malignant neoplasms — Tumeurs malignes								
Total	*44 108*	*32 594*	*50 275*	*27 188*	51 980	129.8	27 990	70.4
Malignant neoplasm of lip, oral cavity and pharynx — Tumeur maligne de la lèvre, de la cavité buccale et du pharynx	*2 173*	*965*	*569*	*275*	633	1.6	294	0.7
Malignant neoplasm of oesophagus — Tumeur maligne de l'oesophage	*1 555*	*237*	*471*	*346*	495	1.2	362	0.9
Malignant neoplasm of stomach — Tumeur maligne de l'estomac	*1 077*	*903*	*4 394*	*2 305*	4 560	11.4	2 357	5.9
Malignant neoplasm of colon, rectosigmoid junction, rectum, anus and anal canal — Tumeur maligne du côlon, de la jonction recto-sigmoïdienne, du rectum, de l'anus et du canal anal	*2 679*	*2 102*	*4 060*	*2 907*	4 195	10.5	2 935	7.4
Malignant neoplasm of liver and intrahepatic bile ducts — Tumeur maligne du foie et des voies bilaires intrahépatiques	*11 578*	*4 804*	*1 913*	*1 125*	2 087	5.2	1 178	3.0
Malignant neoplasm of pancreas — Tumeur maligne du pancréas	*706*	*677*	*2 667*	*1 904*	2 804	7.0	1 984	5.0
Malignant neoplasm of trachea, bronchus and lung — Tumeur maligne de la trachée, des bronches et du poumon	*8 998*	*4 706*	*19 466*	*3 531*	20 063	50.1	3 684	9.3
Malignant neoplasm of female breast — Tumeur maligne du sein chez la femme	..	*4 177*	..	*3 876*	..	..	3 981	13.0
Malignant neoplasm of cervix uteri — Tumeur maligne du col de l'utérus	..	*2 251*	..	*473*	..	..	524	1.7
Malignant neoplasm of prostate — Tumeur maligne de la prostate	*1 372*	..	*3 515*	..	3 595	40.9	..	..
Malignant neoplasm of lymphoid, haematopoietic and related tissue — Tumeurs malignes primitives ou présumées primitives des tissus lymphoïde, hématopoïétique et apparentés	*2 384*	*1 881*	*3 769*	*2 599*	3 753	9.4	2 716	6.8
Disorders of the blood and blood-forming organs and certain disorders involving the immune mechanism — Maladies du sang et des organes hématopoïétiques et certains troubles du système immunitaire								
Total	*541*	*541*	*639*	*655*	594	1.5	616	1.5
Anaemias — Anémies	*301*	*345*	*311*	*329*	251	0.6	285	0.7
Endocrine, nutritional and metabolic diseases — Maladies endocriniennes, nutritionnelles et métaboliques								
Total	*6 573*	*9 027*	*8 386*	*11 417*	8 788	21.9	11 942	30.0
Diabetes mellitus — Diabète sucré	*6 018*	*8 304*	*6 810*	*9 158*	6 945	17.3	9 643	24.2
Malnutrition — Malnutrition	*104*	*156*	*228*	*407*	239	0.6	367	0.9
Mental and behavioural disorders — Troubles mentaux et du comportement	*1 128*	*177*	*288*	*283*	244	0.6	287	0.7
Diseases of the nervous system — Maladies du système nerveux	*4 675*	*6 807*	*8 591*	*10 514*	8 970	22.4	11 233	28.2
Diseases of the circulatory system — Maladies de l'appareil circulatoire								
Total	*38 336*	*29 245*	*79 216*	*79 975*	82 536	206.1	83 532	210.0
Acute rheumatic fever and chronic rheumatic heart diseases — Rhumatisme articularie aigu et cardiopathies rhumatismales chroniques	*103*	*123*	*162*	*301*	195	0.5	295	0.7
Hypertensive diseases — Maladies hypertensives	*4 003*	*4 522*	*5 664*	*9 334*	5 225	13.0	8 828	22.2
Ischaemic heart disease — Cardiopathie ischémique	*12 677*	*8 069*	*36 902*	*27 789*	38 129	95.2	29 283	73.6

20. Death and death rates by cause and sex: 2014 - 2018
Décès et taux de mortalité par cause et sexe : 2014 - 2018 (continued - suite)

Cause of death — Cause de décès	Thailand - Thaïlande				Turkey - Turquie			
	2017 (+U)		2015 (+U)		2016 (+C)			
	Male — Masculin	Female — Féminin	Male — Masculin	Female — Féminin	Male — Masculin		Female — Féminin	
	Number Nombre	Number Nombre	Number Nombre	Number Nombre	Number Nombre	Rate Taux	Number Nombre	Rate Taux
Cerebrovascular disease — Maladie cérébrovasculaire	*17 889*	*13 283*	*17 442*	*21 206*	17 609	44.0	21 349	53.7
Diseases of arteries, arterioles and capillaries — Maladies des artères, artérioles et capillaires	*975*	*593*	*1 796*	*965*	1 792	4.5	961	2.4
Diseases of the respiratory system — Maladies de l'appareil respiratoire								
Total	*25 679*	*16 049*	*25 593*	*18 227*	28 481	71.1	20 814	52.3
Influenza — Grippe	*51*	*50*	*102*	*103*	183	0.5	163	0.4
Pneumonia — Pneumopathies	*17 297*	*12 246*	*6 523*	*6 172*	8 591	21.5	8 230	20.7
Chronic lower respiratory diseases — Maladies chroniques des voies respiratoires inférieures	*6 668*	*2 418*	*16 521*	*9 755*	17 089	42.7	10 035	25.2
Diseases of the digestive system — Maladies de l'appareil digestif								
Total	*13 171*	*6 200*	*5 242*	*4 861*	5 350	13.4	4 917	12.4
Gastric and duodenal ulcer — Ulcère de l'estomac et du duodénum	*361*	*259*	*310*	*226*	334	0.8	258	0.6
Diseases of the liver — Maladies du foie	*7 621*	*2 917*	*2 132*	*1 549*	2 133	5.3	1 612	4.1
Diseases of the musculoskeletal system and connective tissue — Maladies du système ostéo-articularie, des muscles et du tissu conjonctif	*1 288*	*1 636*	*433*	*723*	424	1.1	740	1.9
Diseases of the genitourinary system — Maladies de l'appareil génito-urinaire								
Total	*10 863*	*12 105*	*6 755*	*6 684*	7 582	18.9	7 652	19.2
Disorders of kidney and ureter — Affections du rein et de l'uretère	*9 543*	*10 290*	*5 977*	*6 041*	6 798	17.0	6 974	17.5
Hyperplasia of prostate — Hyperplasie de la prostate	*170*	..	*247*	..	234	2.7	..	..
Pregnancy, childbirth and the puerperium — Grossesse, accouchement et puerpéralité								
Total	..	*143*	..	*220*	..	..	251	19.1
Pregnancy with abortive outcome — Grossesse se terminant par un avortement	..	*9*	..	*2*	..	..	2	♦0.2
Other direct obstetric causes — Autres décès maternels directs	..	*91*	..	*101*	..	..	144	11.0
Indirect obstetric causes — Décès maternels indirects	..	*43*	..	*115*	..	..	104	7.9
Certain conditions originating in the perinatal period — Certaines affections dont l'origine se situe dans la période périnatale	*1 134*	*892*	*4 565*	*3 518*	4 598	681.9	3 604	563.7
Congenital malformations, deformations and chromosomal abnormalities — Malformations congénitales et anomalies chromosomiques	*763*	*728*	*2 988*	*2 611*	2 939	435.9	2 626	410.7
Symptoms, signs and abnormal clinical and laboratory findings, not elsewhere classified — Symptômes, signes et résultats anormaux d'examens cliniques et de laboratoire, non classés ailleurs	*57 535*	*55 599*	*4 192*	*3 711*	5 129	12.8	4 297	10.8
All other diseases — Toutes autres maladies	*1 225*	*1 369*	*88*	*176*	87	0.2	149	0.4
External causes — Causes externes								
Total	*30 919*	*8 159*	*13 438*	*5 495*	15 828	39.5	5 643	14.2
Accidents								
Total	*19 823*	*5 367*	*10 907*	*4 695*	12 488	31.2	4 694	11.8
Transport accidents — Accidents de transport	*12 461*	*3 255*	*5 079*	*1 628*	5 447	13.6	1 518	3.8
Falls — Chutes	*1 507*	*511*	*2 163*	*1 959*	1 980	4.9	1 898	4.8
Accidental drowning and submersion — Noyade et submersion accidentelles	*3 123*	*756*	*577*	*172*	691	1.7	220	0.6
Exposure to smoke, fire and flames — Exposition à la fumée, au feu et aux flammes	*157*	*86*	*149*	*106*	207	0.5	149	0.4
Accidental poisoning by and exposure to noxious substances — Intoxication accidentelle par des substances nocives et exposition à ces substances	*179*	*43*	*600*	*217*	1 008	2.5	242	0.6
Intentional self-harm — Lésions auto-infligées	*3 481*	*848*	*1 135*	*397*	1 422	3.6	434	1.1
Assault — Agresssions	*1 248*	*242*	*869*	*213*	1 180	2.9	256	0.6
All other external causes — Toutes autres causes externes	*6 367*	*1 702*	*527*	*190*	738	1.8	259	0.7

20. Death and death rates by cause and sex: 2014 - 2018
Décès et taux de mortalité par cause et sexe : 2014 - 2018 (continued - suite)

Cause of death — Cause de décès	Turkmenistan - Turkménistan				Uzbekistan - Ouzbékistan			
	2014 (U)		2015 (U)		2015 (C)			
	Male — Masculin	Female — Féminin	Male — Masculin	Female — Féminin	Male — Masculin		Female — Féminin	
	Number Nombre	Number Nombre	Number Nombre	Number Nombre	Number Nombre	Rate Taux	Number Nombre	Rate Taux
TOTAL	*18 079*	*13 672*	*18 112*	*14 135*	83 051	529.1	68 984	442.1
Certain infectious and parasitic diseases — Certaines maladies infectieuses et parasitaires								
Total	*513*	*294*	*496*	*226*	1 975	12.6	1 131	7.2
Intestinal infectious diseases — Maladies infectieuses intestinales	*20*	*22*	*30*	*33*	42	0.3	43	0.3
Tuberculosis — Tuberculose	*322*	*151*	*324*	*104*	1 175	7.5	605	3.9
Tetanus — Tétanos	*9*	*3*	*2*	*1*	-	-	-	-
Diphtheria — Diphtérie	-	-	-	-	-	-	-	-
Whooping cough — Coqueluche	-	-	-	-	-	-	-	-
Meningococcal infection — Infection à méningocoques	*2*	*2*	*2*	*6*	15	♦0.1	24	♦0.2
Septicaemia — Septicémie	*80*	*65*	*64*	*46*	274	1.7	184	1.2
Acute poliomyelitis — Poliomyélite aiguë	-	-	-	-	-	-	-	-
Measles — Rougeole	-	-	-	-	-	-	-	-
Viral hepatitis — Hépatite virale	*44*	*16*	*46*	*21*	183	1.2	121	0.8
Human immunodeficiency virus [HIV] disease — Maladies dues au virus de l'immunodéficience humaine (VIH)	-	-	-	-	240	1.5	125	0.8
Malaria — Paludisme	-	-	-	-	-	-	-	-
Neoplasms — Tumeurs	*1 264*	*1 311*	*1 324*	*1 367*	6 501	41.4	6 867	44.0
Malignant neoplasms — Tumeurs malignes								
Total	*1 245*	*1 299*	*1 309*	*1 359*	6 452	41.1	6 810	43.6
Malignant neoplasm of lip, oral cavity and pharynx — Tumeur maligne de la lèvre, de la cavité buccale et du pharynx	*79*	*42*	*63*	*33*	366	2.3	217	1.4
Malignant neoplasm of oesophagus — Tumeur maligne de l'oesophage	*115*	*109*	*129*	*119*	384	2.4	385	2.5
Malignant neoplasm of stomach — Tumeur maligne de l'estomac	*160*	*80*	*187*	*102*	1 088	6.9	669	4.3
Malignant neoplasm of colon, rectosigmoid junction, rectum, anus and anal canal — Tumeur maligne du côlon, de la jonction recto-sigmoïdienne, du rectum, de l'anus et du canal anal	*55*	*47*	*52*	*62*	373	2.4	351	2.2
Malignant neoplasm of liver and intrahepatic bile ducts — Tumeur maligne du foie et des voies biliaires intrahépatiques	*104*	*62*	*107*	*72*	534	3.4	390	2.5
Malignant neoplasm of pancreas — Tumeur maligne du pancréas	*39*	*29*	*53*	*42*	245	1.6	185	1.2
Malignant neoplasm of trachea, bronchus and lung — Tumeur maligne de la trachée, des bronches et du poumon	*203*	*68*	*201*	*65*	986	6.3	339	2.2
Malignant neoplasm of female breast — Tumeur maligne du sein chez la femme	..	*270*	..	*243*	..	..	1 293	11.4
Malignant neoplasm of cervix uteri — Tumeur maligne du col de l'utérus	..	*166*	..	*133*	..	..	760	6.7
Malignant neoplasm of prostate — Tumeur maligne de la prostate	*38*	..	*32*	..	161	6.9	..	..
Malignant neoplasm of lymphoid, haematopoietic and related tissue — Tumeurs malignes primitives ou présumées primitives des tissus lymphoïde, hématopoïétique et apparentés	...	...	...	...	555	3.5	410	2.6
Disorders of the blood and blood-forming organs and certain disorders involving the immune mechanism — Maladies du sang et des organes hématopoïétiques et certains troubles du système immunitaire								
Total	*32*	*29*	*22*	*23*	108	0.7	120	0.8
Anaemias — Anémies	*12*	*11*	*6*	*11*	55	0.4	75	0.5
Endocrine, nutritional and metabolic diseases — Maladies endocriniennes, nutritionnelles et métaboliques								
Total	*252*	*371*	*294*	*387*	2 507	16.0	2 790	17.9
Diabetes mellitus — Diabète sucré	*241*	*363*	*291*	*375*	2 473	15.8	2 753	17.6
Malnutrition — Malnutrition	-	-	-	-	4	♦0.0	3	♦0.0
Mental and behavioural disorders — Troubles mentaux et du comportement	*14*	*9*	*16*	*7*	8	♦0.1	1	♦0.0
Diseases of the nervous system — Maladies du système nerveux	*186*	*149*	*208*	*165*	1 474	9.4	1 017	6.5
Diseases of the circulatory system — Maladies de l'appareil circulatoire								
Total	*7 720*	*6 614*	*7 654*	*6 710*	47 239	301.0	42 710	273.7
Acute rheumatic fever and chronic rheumatic heart diseases — Rhumatisme articularie aigu et cardiopathies rhumatismales chroniques	*26*	*53*	*32*	*44*	248	1.6	369	2.4
Hypertensive diseases — Maladies hypertensives	*1 198*	*1 102*	*1 140*	*964*	11 138	71.0	10 902	69.9
Ischaemic heart disease — Cardiopathie ischémique	*3 760*	*3 199*	*3 838*	*3 394*	21 868	139.3	19 037	122.0

20. Death and death rates by cause and sex: 2014 - 2018
Décès et taux de mortalité par cause et sexe : 2014 - 2018 (continued - suite)

Cause of death — Cause de décès	Turkmenistan - Turkménistan				Uzbekistan - Ouzbékistan			
	2014 (U)		2015 (U)		2015 (C)			
	Male — Masculin	Female — Féminin	Male — Masculin	Female — Féminin	Male — Masculin		Female — Féminin	
	Number Nombre	Number Nombre	Number Nombre	Number Nombre	Number Nombre	Rate Taux	Number Nombre	Rate Taux
Cerebrovascular disease — Maladie cérébrovasculaire	*2 127*	*1 827*	*2 183*	*1 910*	6 958	44.3	6 028	38.6
Diseases of arteries, arterioles and capillaries — Maladies des artères, artérioles et capillaires	...	...	...	...	1 785	11.4	2 303	14.8
Diseases of the respiratory system — Maladies de l'appareil respiratoire								
Total	*1 102*	*811*	*1 066*	*880*	4 357	27.8	3 369	21.6
Influenza — Grippe	-	*4*	*2*	*4*	92	0.6	97	0.6
Pneumonia — Pneumopathies	*452*	*335*	*482*	*387*	1 903	12.1	1 406	9.0
Chronic lower respiratory diseases — Maladies chroniques des voies respiratoires inférieures	*100*	*75*	*103*	*87*	845	5.4	709	4.5
Diseases of the digestive system — Maladies de l'appareil digestif								
Total	*1 523*	*805*	*1 581*	*868*	5 209	33.2	3 812	24.4
Gastric and duodenal ulcer — Ulcère de l'estomac et du duodénum	*84*	*25*	*83*	*31*	357	2.3	193	1.2
Diseases of the liver — Maladies du foie	*1 287*	*681*	*1 381*	*731*	4 347	27.7	3 241	20.8
Diseases of the musculoskeletal system and connective tissue — Maladies du système ostéo-articularie, des muscles et du tissu conjonctif	*16*	*36*	*11*	*24*	30	♦0.2	88	0.6
Diseases of the genitourinary system — Maladies de l'appareil génito-urinaire								
Total	*254*	*196*	*229*	*166*	1 460	9.3	1 137	7.3
Disorders of kidney and ureter — Affections du rein et de l'uretère	...	...	...	...	1 409	9.0	1 129	7.2
Hyperplasia of prostate — Hyperplasie de la prostate	...	..	...	..	29	♦1.2	..	..
Pregnancy, childbirth and the puerperium — Grossesse, accouchement et puerpéralité								
Total	..	*4*	..	*5*	..	..	134	18.3
Pregnancy with abortive outcome — Grossesse se terminant par un avortement	..	*1*	..	-	..	..	2	♦0.3
Other direct obstetric causes — Autres décès maternels directs	..	*3*	..	*5*	..	..	118	16.1
Indirect obstetric causes — Décès maternels indirects	..	-	..	-	..	..	13	♦1.8
Certain conditions originating in the perinatal period — Certaines affections dont l'origine se situe dans la période périnatale	*907*	*579*	*912*	*643*	2 986	780.3	1 985	564.8
Congenital malformations, deformations and chromosomal abnormalities — Malformations congénitales et anomalies chromosomiques	*460*	*331*	*444*	*351*	518	135.4	408	116.1
Symptoms, signs and abnormal clinical and laboratory findings, not elsewhere classified — Symptômes, signes et résultats anormaux d'examens cliniques et de laboratoire, non classés ailleurs	*2 925*	*1 865*	*2 943*	*1 970*	1 080	6.9	828	5.3
All other diseases — Toutes autres maladies	*3*	*2*	*4*	*2*	9	♦0.1	7	♦0.0
External causes — Causes externes								
Total	*908*	*266*	*908*	*341*	7 590	48.4	2 580	16.5
Accidents								
Total	...	...	...	...	5 056	32.2	1 494	9.6
Transport accidents — Accidents de transport	*115*	*29*	*98*	*33*	2 322	14.8	540	3.5
Falls — Chutes	*36*	*2*	*37*	*9*	185	1.2	38	0.2
Accidental drowning and submersion — Noyade et submersion accidentelles	*62*	*16*	*61*	*16*	780	5.0	291	1.9
Exposure to smoke, fire and flames — Exposition à la fumée, au feu et aux flammes	*43*	*26*	*20*	*20*	194	1.2	145	0.9
Accidental poisoning by and exposure to noxious substances — Intoxication accidentelle par des substances nocives et exposition à ces substances	*44*	*23*	*39*	*30*	243	1.5	92	0.6
Intentional self-harm — Lésions auto-infligées	*92*	*44*	*92*	*41*	1 598	10.2	794	5.1
Assault — Agresssions	*71*	*18*	*50*	*13*	379	2.4	120	0.8
All other external causes — Toutes autres causes externes	...	...	...	...	557	3.5	172	1.1

20. Death and death rates by cause and sex: 2014 - 2018
Décès et taux de mortalité par cause et sexe : 2014 - 2018 (continued - suite)

Cause of death — Cause de décès	Uzbekistan - Ouzbékistan				Andorra - Andorre			
	2016 (C)				2014 (C)		2015 (C)	
	Male — Masculin		Female — Féminin		Male — Masculin	Female — Féminin	Male — Masculin	Female — Féminin
	Number Nombre	Rate Taux	Number Nombre	Rate Taux	Number Nombre	Number Nombre	Number Nombre	Number Nombre
TOTAL	**84 394**	**528.1**	**70 397**	**443.6**	**168**	**108**	**150**	**132**
Certain infectious and parasitic diseases — Certaines maladies infectieuses et parasitaires								
Total	**1 841**	**11.5**	**1 039**	**6.5**	**-**	**2**	**5**	**4**
Intestinal infectious diseases — Maladies infectieuses intestinales	**62**	**0.4**	**49**	**0.3**	**-**	**-**	**-**	**-**
Tuberculosis — Tuberculose	**1 164**	**7.3**	**535**	**3.4**	**-**	**-**	**-**	**-**
Tetanus — Tétanos	**-**	**-**	**-**	**-**	**-**	**-**	**-**	**-**
Diphtheria — Diphtérie	**-**	**-**	**-**	**-**	**-**	**-**	**-**	**-**
Whooping cough — Coqueluche	**-**	**-**	**-**	**-**	**-**	**-**	**-**	**-**
Meningococcal infection — Infection à méningocoques	**14**	**♦0.1**	**8**	**♦0.1**	**-**	**-**	**-**	**-**
Septicaemia — Septicémie	**221**	**1.4**	**187**	**1.2**	**-**	**1**	**1**	**1**
Acute poliomyelitis — Poliomyélite aiguë	**2**	**♦0.0**	**-**	**-**	**-**	**-**	**-**	**-**
Measles — Rougeole	**1**	**♦0.0**	**-**	**-**	**-**	**-**	**-**	**-**
Viral hepatitis — Hépatite virale	**106**	**0.7**	**93**	**0.6**	**-**	**1**	**1**	**-**
Human immunodeficiency virus [HIV] disease — Maladies dues au virus de l'immunodéficience humaine (VIH)	**243**	**1.5**	**129**	**0.8**	**-**	**-**	**2**	**1**
Malaria — Paludisme	**-**	**-**	**-**	**-**	**-**	**-**	**-**	**-**
Neoplasms — Tumeurs	**7 014**	**43.9**	**7 244**	**45.7**	**76**	**36**	**54**	**34**
Malignant neoplasms — Tumeurs malignes								
Total	**6 979**	**43.7**	**7 198**	**45.4**	**75**	**36**	**52**	**34**
Malignant neoplasm of lip, oral cavity and pharynx — Tumeur maligne de la lèvre, de la cavité buccale et du pharynx	**386**	**2.4**	**252**	**1.6**	**1**	**1**	**1**	**-**
Malignant neoplasm of oesophagus — Tumeur maligne de l'oesophage	**461**	**2.9**	**382**	**2.4**	**3**	**-**	**4**	**-**
Malignant neoplasm of stomach — Tumeur maligne de l'estomac	**1 041**	**6.5**	**596**	**3.8**	**3**	**-**	**2**	**3**
Malignant neoplasm of colon, rectosigmoid junction, rectum, anus and anal canal — Tumeur maligne du côlon, de la jonction recto-sigmoïdienne, du rectum, de l'anus et du canal anal	**481**	**3.0**	**445**	**2.8**	**5**	**6**	**10**	**1**
Malignant neoplasm of liver and intrahepatic bile ducts — Tumeur maligne du foie et des voies bilaires intrahépatiques	**539**	**3.4**	**393**	**2.5**	**9**	**1**	**-**	**1**
Malignant neoplasm of pancreas — Tumeur maligne du pancréas	**237**	**1.5**	**174**	**1.1**	**3**	**2**	**2**	**1**
Malignant neoplasm of trachea, bronchus and lung — Tumeur maligne de la trachée, des bronches et du poumon	**988**	**6.2**	**415**	**2.6**	**23**	**1**	**13**	**8**
Malignant neoplasm of female breast — Tumeur maligne du sein chez la femme	**..**	**..**	**1 370**	**11.9**	**..**	**5**	**..**	**5**
Malignant neoplasm of cervix uteri — Tumeur maligne du col de l'utérus	**..**	**..**	**732**	**6.4**	**..**	**2**	**..**	**1**
Malignant neoplasm of prostate — Tumeur maligne de la prostate	**203**	**8.4**	**..**	**..**	**3**	**..**	**3**	**..**
Malignant neoplasm of lymphoid, haematopoietic and related tissue — Tumeurs malignes primitives ou présumées primitives des tissus lymphoïde, hématopoïétique et apparentés	**618**	**3.9**	**476**	**3.0**	**...**	**...**	**...**	**...**
Disorders of the blood and blood-forming organs and certain disorders involving the immune mechanism — Maladies du sang et des organes hématopoïétiques et certains troubles du système immunitaire								
Total	**98**	**0.6**	**112**	**0.7**	**2**	**-**	**-**	**-**
Anaemias — Anémies	**58**	**0.4**	**83**	**0.5**	**-**	**-**	**-**	**-**
Endocrine, nutritional and metabolic diseases — Maladies endocriniennes, nutritionnelles et métaboliques								
Total	**2 484**	**15.5**	**2 875**	**18.1**	**1**	**-**	**-**	**2**
Diabetes mellitus — Diabète sucré	**2 462**	**15.4**	**2 831**	**17.8**	**1**	**-**	**-**	**-**
Malnutrition — Malnutrition	**3**	**♦0.0**	**6**	**♦0.0**	**-**	**-**	**-**	**-**
Mental and behavioural disorders — Troubles mentaux et du comportement	**11**	**♦0.1**	**2**	**♦0.0**	**2**	**7**	**11**	**14**
Diseases of the nervous system — Maladies du système nerveux	**1 525**	**9.5**	**1 084**	**6.8**	**1**	**3**	**2**	**9**
Diseases of the circulatory system — Maladies de l'appareil circulatoire								
Total	**48 765**	**305.2**	**43 955**	**277.0**	**32**	**30**	**32**	**33**
Acute rheumatic fever and chronic rheumatic heart diseases — Rhumatisme articularie aigu et cardiopathies rhumatismales chroniques	**337**	**2.1**	**383**	**2.4**	**-**	**-**	**-**	**1**
Hypertensive diseases — Maladies hypertensives	**11 749**	**73.5**	**11 603**	**73.1**	**6**	**9**	**4**	**8**
Ischaemic heart disease — Cardiopathie ischémique	**21 564**	**134.9**	**18 472**	**116.4**	**9**	**8**	**12**	**5**

20. Death and death rates by cause and sex: 2014 - 2018
Décès et taux de mortalité par cause et sexe : 2014 - 2018 (continued - suite)

Cause of death — Cause de décès	Uzbekistan - Ouzbékistan				Andorra - Andorre			
	2016 (C)				2014 (C)		2015 (C)	
	Male — Masculin		Female — Féminin		Male — Masculin	Female — Féminin	Male — Masculin	Female — Féminin
	Number Nombre	Rate Taux	Number Nombre	Rate Taux	Number Nombre	Number Nombre	Number Nombre	Number Nombre
Cerebrovascular disease — Maladie cérébrovasculaire	7 446	46.6	6 219	39.2	5	4	8	6
Diseases of arteries, arterioles and capillaries — Maladies des artères, artérioles et capillaires	2 611	16.3	3 215	20.3	...	...	...	...
Diseases of the respiratory system — Maladies de l'appareil respiratoire								
Total	4 291	26.9	3 509	22.1	15	13	14	13
Influenza — Grippe	38	0.2	37	0.2	-	1	-	-
Pneumonia — Pneumopathies	1 730	10.8	1 452	9.2	4	2	1	5
Chronic lower respiratory diseases — Maladies chroniques des voies respiratoires inférieures	878	5.5	689	4.3	4	4	5	3
Diseases of the digestive system — Maladies de l'appareil digestif								
Total	5 225	32.7	3 776	23.8	5	3	9	4
Gastric and duodenal ulcer — Ulcère de l'estomac et du duodénum	354	2.2	165	1.0	-	-	-	-
Diseases of the liver — Maladies du foie	4 375	27.4	3 238	20.4	3	1	2	2
Diseases of the musculoskeletal system and connective tissue — Maladies du système ostéo-articularie, des muscles et du tissu conjonctif	40	0.3	108	0.7	-	-	-	1
Diseases of the genitourinary system — Maladies de l'appareil génito-urinaire								
Total	1 559	9.8	1 289	8.1	2	1	4	2
Disorders of kidney and ureter — Affections du rein et de l'uretère	1 517	9.5	1 278	8.1	...	...	...	...
Hyperplasia of prostate — Hyperplasie de la prostate	16	♦0.7	..	..	...	..	...	..
Pregnancy, childbirth and the puerperium — Grossesse, accouchement et puerpéralité								
Total	..	..	128	17.6	..	-	..	-
Pregnancy with abortive outcome — Grossesse se terminant par un avortement	..	..	1	♦0.1	..	-	..	-
Other direct obstetric causes — Autres décès maternels directs	..	..	115	15.8	..	-	..	-
Indirect obstetric causes — Décès maternels indirects	..	..	11	♦1.5	..	-	..	-
Certain conditions originating in the perinatal period — Certaines affections dont l'origine se situe dans la période périnatale	2 525	668.5	1 789	513.4	1	1	-	-
Congenital malformations, deformations and chromosomal abnormalities — Malformations congénitales et anomalies chromosomiques	595	157.5	432	124.0	1	-	-	1
Symptoms, signs and abnormal clinical and laboratory findings, not elsewhere classified — Symptômes, signes et résultats anormaux d'examens cliniques et de laboratoire, non classés ailleurs	727	4.5	442	2.8	22	6	9	5
All other diseases — Toutes autres maladies	9	♦0.1	5	♦0.0	-	-	-	-
External causes — Causes externes								
Total	7 685	48.1	2 608	16.4	8	6	10	10
Accidents								
Total	4 895	30.6	1 441	9.1	...	...	...	...
Transport accidents — Accidents de transport	2 096	13.1	517	3.3	2	2	1	1
Falls — Chutes	254	1.6	43	0.3	3	3	5	6
Accidental drowning and submersion — Noyade et submersion accidentelles	819	5.1	307	1.9	-	-	-	-
Exposure to smoke, fire and flames — Exposition à la fumée, au feu et aux flammes	147	0.9	110	0.7	-	-	-	-
Accidental poisoning by and exposure to noxious substances — Intoxication accidentelle par des substances nocives et exposition à ces substances	229	1.4	94	0.6	-	-	-	-
Intentional self-harm — Lésions auto-infligées	1 658	10.4	809	5.1	3	1	3	2
Assault — Agresssions	409	2.6	130	0.8	-	-	-	-
All other external causes — Toutes autres causes externes	723	4.5	228	1.4	...	...	...	...

20. Death and death rates by cause and sex: 2014 - 2018
Décès et taux de mortalité par cause et sexe : 2014 - 2018 (continued - suite)

Austria - Autriche

Cause of death — Cause de décès	2016 (C)				2017 (C)			
	Male — Masculin		Female — Féminin		Male — Masculin		Female — Féminin	
	Number Nombre	Rate Taux	Number Nombre	Rate Taux	Number Nombre	Rate Taux	Number Nombre	Rate Taux
TOTAL	**39 022**	**914.9**	**41 647**	**941.2**	**39 902**	**925.3**	**43 368**	**972.3**
Certain infectious and parasitic diseases — Certaines maladies infectieuses et parasitaires								
Total	398	9.3	469	10.6	404	9.4	490	11.0
Intestinal infectious diseases — Maladies infectieuses intestinales	52	1.2	87	2.0	81	1.9	108	2.4
Tuberculosis — Tuberculose	22	♦0.5	9	♦0.2	15	♦0.3	10	♦0.2
Tetanus — Tétanos	-	-	-	-	-	-	1	♦0.0
Diphtheria — Diphtérie	-	-	-	-	-	-	-	-
Whooping cough — Coqueluche	1	♦0.0	-	-	-	-	1	♦0.0
Meningococcal infection — Infection à méningocoques	1	♦0.0	2	♦0.0	2	♦0.0	1	♦0.0
Septicaemia — Septicémie	116	2.7	121	2.7	112	2.6	136	3.0
Acute poliomyelitis — Poliomyélite aiguë	1	♦0.0	-	-	1	♦0.0	1	♦0.0
Measles — Rougeole	-	-	-	-	1	♦0.0	-	-
Viral hepatitis — Hépatite virale	76	1.8	105	2.4	73	1.7	89	2.0
Human immunodeficiency virus [HIV] disease — Maladies dues au virus de l'immunodéficience humaine (VIH)	28	♦0.7	7	♦0.2	16	♦0.4	9	♦0.2
Malaria — Paludisme	-	-	-	-	1	♦0.0	1	♦0.0
Neoplasms — Tumeurs	**11 119**	**260.7**	**9 799**	**221.5**	**11 329**	**262.7**	**9 670**	**216.8**
Malignant neoplasms — Tumeurs malignes								
Total	10 763	252.3	9 419	212.9	10 989	254.8	9 272	207.9
Malignant neoplasm of lip, oral cavity and pharynx — Tumeur maligne de la lèvre, de la cavité buccale et du pharynx	447	10.5	135	3.1	392	9.1	134	3.0
Malignant neoplasm of oesophagus — Tumeur maligne de l'oesophage	277	6.5	97	2.2	316	7.3	76	1.7
Malignant neoplasm of stomach — Tumeur maligne de l'estomac	425	10.0	353	8.0	483	11.2	339	7.6
Malignant neoplasm of colon, rectosigmoid junction, rectum, anus and anal canal — Tumeur maligne du côlon, de la jonction recto-sigmoïdienne, du rectum, de l'anus et du canal anal	1 215	28.5	908	20.5	1 213	28.1	932	20.9
Malignant neoplasm of liver and intrahepatic bile ducts — Tumeur maligne du foie et des voies bilaires intrahépatiques	596	14.0	211	4.8	632	14.7	288	6.5
Malignant neoplasm of pancreas — Tumeur maligne du pancréas	787	18.5	891	20.1	836	19.4	898	20.1
Malignant neoplasm of trachea, bronchus and lung — Tumeur maligne de la trachée, des bronches et du poumon	2 415	56.6	1 534	34.7	2 402	55.7	1 472	33.0
Malignant neoplasm of female breast — Tumeur maligne du sein chez la femme	..	..	1 588	41.6	..	..	1 566	40.7
Malignant neoplasm of cervix uteri — Tumeur maligne du col de l'utérus	..	..	138	3.6	..	..	159	4.1
Malignant neoplasm of prostate — Tumeur maligne de la prostate	1 225	77.8	..	..	1 260	78.2	..	..
Malignant neoplasm of lymphoid, haematopoietic and related tissue — Tumeurs malignes primitives ou présumées primitives des tissus lymphoïde, hématopoïétique et apparentés	978	22.9	847	19.1	990	23.0	794	17.8
Disorders of the blood and blood-forming organs and certain disorders involving the immune mechanism — Maladies du sang et des organes hématopoïétiques et certains troubles du système immunitaire								
Total	84	2.0	115	2.6	78	1.8	138	3.1
Anaemias — Anémies	38	0.9	63	1.4	41	1.0	75	1.7
Endocrine, nutritional and metabolic diseases — Maladies endocriniennes, nutritionnelles et métaboliques								
Total	1 987	46.6	2 162	48.9	1 877	43.5	2 195	49.2
Diabetes mellitus — Diabète sucré	1 521	35.7	1 779	40.2	1 423	33.0	1 735	38.9
Malnutrition — Malnutrition	-	-	1	♦0.0	6	♦0.1	4	♦0.1
Mental and behavioural disorders — Troubles mentaux et du comportement	943	22.1	1 158	26.2	1 130	26.2	1 823	40.9
Diseases of the nervous system — Maladies du système nerveux	1 249	29.3	1 615	36.5	1 363	31.6	1 834	41.1
Diseases of the circulatory system — Maladies de l'appareil circulatoire								
Total	14 352	336.5	18 896	427.1	14 174	328.7	18 951	424.9
Acute rheumatic fever and chronic rheumatic heart diseases — Rhumatisme articularie aigu et cardiopathies rhumatismales chroniques	98	2.3	181	4.1	109	2.5	214	4.8
Hypertensive diseases — Maladies hypertensives	1 513	35.5	3 284	74.2	1 374	31.9	2 935	65.8
Ischaemic heart disease — Cardiopathie ischémique	7 062	165.6	7 002	158.2	7 052	163.5	6 931	155.4
Cerebrovascular disease — Maladie cérébrovasculaire	1 852	43.4	2 760	62.4	1 852	42.9	2 896	64.9

20. Death and death rates by cause and sex: 2014 - 2018
Décès et taux de mortalité par cause et sexe : 2014 - 2018 (continued - suite)

Austria - Autriche

Cause of death — Cause de décès	2016 (C)				2017 (C)			
	Male — Masculin		Female — Féminin		Male — Masculin		Female — Féminin	
	Number Nombre	Rate Taux	Number Nombre	Rate Taux	Number Nombre	Rate Taux	Number Nombre	Rate Taux
Diseases of arteries, arterioles and capillaries — Maladies des artères, artérioles et capillaires	558	13.1	671	15.2	549	12.7	650	14.6
Diseases of the respiratory system — Maladies de l'appareil respiratoire								
Total	2 319	54.4	2 016	45.6	2 702	62.7	2 605	58.4
Influenza — Grippe	22	♦0.5	16	♦0.4	50	1.2	65	1.5
Pneumonia — Pneumopathies	424	9.9	518	11.7	597	13.8	694	15.6
Chronic lower respiratory diseases — Maladies chroniques des voies respiratoires inférieures	1 584	37.1	1 248	28.2	1 708	39.6	1 515	34.0
Diseases of the digestive system — Maladies de l'appareil digestif								
Total	1 659	38.9	1 197	27.1	1 576	36.5	1 315	29.5
Gastric and duodenal ulcer — Ulcère de l'estomac et du duodénum	87	2.0	78	1.8	65	1.5	85	1.9
Diseases of the liver — Maladies du foie	1 076	25.2	436	9.9	1 007	23.4	456	10.2
Diseases of the musculoskeletal system and connective tissue — Maladies du système ostéo-articularie, des muscles et du tissu conjonctif	106	2.5	212	4.8	108	2.5	221	5.0
Diseases of the genitourinary system — Maladies de l'appareil génito-urinaire								
Total	696	16.3	1 043	23.6	730	16.9	1 113	25.0
Disorders of kidney and ureter — Affections du rein et de l'uretère	575	13.5	843	19.1	592	13.7	865	19.4
Hyperplasia of prostate — Hyperplasie de la prostate	11	♦0.7	..	..	16	♦1.0	..	..
Pregnancy, childbirth and the puerperium — Grossesse, accouchement et puerpéralité								
Total	..	..	5	♦5.7	..	..	2	♦2.3
Pregnancy with abortive outcome — Grossesse se terminant par un avortement	..	..	-	-	..	..	-	-
Other direct obstetric causes — Autres décès maternels directs	..	..	4	♦4.6	..	..	1	♦1.1
Indirect obstetric causes — Décès maternels indirects	..	..	1	♦1.1	..	..	-	-
Certain conditions originating in the perinatal period — Certaines affections dont l'origine se situe dans la période périnatale	73	162.0	62	145.5	74	163.5	58	136.9
Congenital malformations, deformations and chromosomal abnormalities — Malformations congénitales et anomalies chromosomiques	145	321.9	120	281.5	130	287.3	115	271.4
Symptoms, signs and abnormal clinical and laboratory findings, not elsewhere classified — Symptômes, signes et résultats anormaux d'examens cliniques et de laboratoire, non classés ailleurs	1 270	29.8	1 108	25.0	1 411	32.7	1 201	26.9
All other diseases — Toutes autres maladies	25	♦0.6	54	1.2	34	0.8	46	1.0
External causes — Causes externes								
Total	2 597	60.9	1 616	36.5	2 782	64.5	1 591	35.7
Accidents								
Total	1 326	31.1	1 063	24.0	1 390	32.2	1 085	24.3
Transport accidents — Accidents de transport	307	7.2	116	2.6	305	7.1	101	2.3
Falls — Chutes	442	10.4	408	9.2	468	10.9	388	8.7
Accidental drowning and submersion — Noyade et submersion accidentelles	32	0.8	8	♦0.2	27	♦0.6	6	♦0.1
Exposure to smoke, fire and flames — Exposition à la fumée, au feu et aux flammes	15	♦0.4	15	♦0.3	10	♦0.2	17	♦0.4
Accidental poisoning by and exposure to noxious substances — Intoxication accidentelle par des substances nocives et exposition à ces substances	14	♦0.3	10	♦0.2	19	♦0.4	12	♦0.3
Intentional self-harm — Lésions auto-infligées	904	21.2	294	6.6	964	22.4	260	5.8
Assault — Agresssions	17	♦0.4	26	♦0.6	19	♦0.4	27	♦0.6
All other external causes — Toutes autres causes externes	350	8.2	233	5.3	409	9.5	219	4.9

20. Death and death rates by cause and sex: 2014 - 2018
Décès et taux de mortalité par cause et sexe : 2014 - 2018 (continued - suite)

Belarus - Bélarus

Cause of death — Cause de décès	2014 (C)				2018 (C)			
	Male — Masculin		Female — Féminin		Male — Masculin		Female — Féminin	
	Number Nombre	Rate Taux	Number Nombre	Rate Taux	Number Nombre	Rate Taux	Number Nombre	Rate Taux
TOTAL	**61 274**	**1 390.9**	**60 268**	**1 188.9**	**59 830**	**1 354.0**	**60 223**	**1 189.0**
Certain infectious and parasitic diseases — Certaines maladies infectieuses et parasitaires								
Total	661	15.0	232	4.6	477	10.8	214	4.2
Intestinal infectious diseases — Maladies infectieuses intestinales	2	♦0.0	5	♦0.1	3	♦0.1	8	♦0.2
Tuberculosis — Tuberculose	383	8.7	62	1.2	199	4.5	42	0.8
Tetanus — Tétanos	-	-	-	-	-	-	-	-
Diphtheria — Diphtérie	-	-	-	-	-	-	-	-
Whooping cough — Coqueluche	-	-	-	-	-	-	-	-
Meningococcal infection — Infection à méningocoques	3	♦0.1	6	♦0.1	1	♦0.0	2	♦0.0
Septicaemia — Septicémie	31	0.7	23	♦0.5	35	0.8	31	0.6
Acute poliomyelitis — Poliomyélite aiguë	-	-	-	-	-	-	-	-
Measles — Rougeole	-	-	-	-	-	-	-	-
Viral hepatitis — Hépatite virale	23	♦0.5	8	♦0.2	25	♦0.6	15	♦0.3
Human immunodeficiency virus [HIV] disease — Maladies dues au virus de l'immunodéficience humaine (VIH)	179	4.1	96	1.9	183	4.1	83	1.6
Malaria — Paludisme	-	-	-	-	-	-	-	-
Neoplasms — Tumeurs	**10 156**	**230.5**	**7 171**	**141.5**	**11 221**	**253.9**	**7 626**	**150.6**
Malignant neoplasms — Tumeurs malignes								
Total	10 050	228.1	7 018	138.4	11 100	251.2	7 497	148.0
Malignant neoplasm of lip, oral cavity and pharynx — Tumeur maligne de la lèvre, de la cavité buccale et du pharynx	706	16.0	88	1.7	840	19.0	119	2.3
Malignant neoplasm of oesophagus — Tumeur maligne de l'oesophage	351	8.0	40	0.8	395	8.9	40	0.8
Malignant neoplasm of stomach — Tumeur maligne de l'estomac	1 124	25.5	719	14.2	1 064	24.1	679	13.4
Malignant neoplasm of colon, rectosigmoid junction, rectum, anus and anal canal — Tumeur maligne du côlon, de la jonction recto-sigmoïdienne, du rectum, de l'anus et du canal anal	1 089	24.7	1 107	21.8	1 213	27.5	1 207	23.8
Malignant neoplasm of liver and intrahepatic bile ducts — Tumeur maligne du foie et des voies bilaires intrahépatiques	213	4.8	114	2.2	308	7.0	142	2.8
Malignant neoplasm of pancreas — Tumeur maligne du pancréas	510	11.6	409	8.1	583	13.2	433	8.5
Malignant neoplasm of trachea, bronchus and lung — Tumeur maligne de la trachée, des bronches et du poumon	2 550	57.9	339	6.7	2 740	62.0	382	7.5
Malignant neoplasm of female breast — Tumeur maligne du sein chez la femme	..	..	1 106	25.5	..	..	1 138	26.5
Malignant neoplasm of cervix uteri — Tumeur maligne du col de l'utérus	..	..	318	7.3	..	..	306	7.1
Malignant neoplasm of prostate — Tumeur maligne de la prostate	799	60.0	..	..	907	66.0	..	..
Malignant neoplasm of lymphoid, haematopoietic and related tissue — Tumeurs malignes primitives ou présumées primitives des tissus lymphoïde, hématopoïétique et apparentés	...	...	...	...	640	14.5	612	12.1
Disorders of the blood and blood-forming organs and certain disorders involving the immune mechanism — Maladies du sang et des organes hématopoïétiques et certains troubles du système immunitaire								
Total	34	0.8	34	0.7	23	♦0.5	27	♦0.5
Anaemias — Anémies	7	♦0.2	19	♦0.4	8	♦0.2	13	♦0.3
Endocrine, nutritional and metabolic diseases — Maladies endocriniennes, nutritionnelles et métaboliques								
Total	131	3.0	154	3.0	178	4.0	212	4.2
Diabetes mellitus — Diabète sucré	84	1.9	110	2.2	121	2.7	143	2.8
Malnutrition — Malnutrition	2	♦0.0	2	♦0.0	1	♦0.0	1	♦0.0
Mental and behavioural disorders — Troubles mentaux et du comportement	**831**	**18.9**	**883**	**17.4**	**520**	**11.8**	**750**	**14.8**
Diseases of the nervous system — Maladies du système nerveux	**1 094**	**24.8**	**1 299**	**25.6**	**2 345**	**53.1**	**4 310**	**85.1**
Diseases of the circulatory system — Maladies de l'appareil circulatoire								
Total	32 671	741.6	34 802	686.5	32 237	729.6	35 858	708.0
Acute rheumatic fever and chronic rheumatic heart diseases — Rhumatisme articularie aigu et cardiopathies rhumatismales chroniques	107	2.4	158	3.1	65	1.5	123	2.4
Hypertensive diseases — Maladies hypertensives	92	2.1	59	1.2	78	1.8	66	1.3
Ischaemic heart disease — Cardiopathie ischémique	24 096	547.0	24 881	490.8	23 646	535.1	26 036	514.1
Cerebrovascular disease — Maladie cérébrovasculaire	5 810	131.9	7 904	155.9	5 678	128.5	7 584	149.7

20. Death and death rates by cause and sex: 2014 - 2018
Décès et taux de mortalité par cause et sexe : 2014 - 2018 (continued - suite)

Belarus - Bélarus

Cause of death — Cause de décès	2014 (C)				2018 (C)			
	Male — Masculin		Female — Féminin		Male — Masculin		Female — Féminin	
	Number Nombre	Rate Taux	Number Nombre	Rate Taux	Number Nombre	Rate Taux	Number Nombre	Rate Taux
Diseases of arteries, arterioles and capillaries — Maladies des artères, artérioles et capillaires	...	...	...	...	**1 637**	**37.0**	**1 529**	**30.2**
Diseases of the respiratory system — Maladies de l'appareil respiratoire								
Total	**1 508**	**34.2**	**357**	**7.0**	**1 755**	**39.7**	**469**	**9.3**
Influenza — Grippe	**-**	**-**	**4**	**♦0.1**	**2**	**♦0.0**	**1**	**♦0.0**
Pneumonia — Pneumopathies	**468**	**10.6**	**81**	**1.6**	**695**	**15.7**	**156**	**3.1**
Chronic lower respiratory diseases — Maladies chroniques des voies respiratoires inférieures	**868**	**19.7**	**222**	**4.4**	**890**	**20.1**	**255**	**5.0**
Diseases of the digestive system — Maladies de l'appareil digestif								
Total	**2 235**	**50.7**	**1 646**	**32.5**	**2 022**	**45.8**	**1 670**	**33.0**
Gastric and duodenal ulcer — Ulcère de l'estomac et du duodénum	**132**	**3.0**	**65**	**1.3**	**151**	**3.4**	**58**	**1.1**
Diseases of the liver — Maladies du foie	**1 302**	**29.6**	**815**	**16.1**	**1 041**	**23.6**	**740**	**14.6**
Diseases of the musculoskeletal system and connective tissue — Maladies du système ostéo-articularie, des muscles et du tissu conjonctif	**51**	**1.2**	**88**	**1.7**	**103**	**2.3**	**110**	**2.2**
Diseases of the genitourinary system — Maladies de l'appareil génito-urinaire								
Total	**340**	**7.7**	**324**	**6.4**	**410**	**9.3**	**342**	**6.8**
Disorders of kidney and ureter — Affections du rein et de l'uretère	...	...	...	...	**341**	**7.7**	**325**	**6.4**
Hyperplasia of prostate — Hyperplasie de la prostate	...	...	..	..	**57**	**4.1**	..	..
Pregnancy, childbirth and the puerperium — Grossesse, accouchement et puerpéralité								
Total	..	..	**1**	**♦0.8**	..	..	**3**	**♦3.2**
Pregnancy with abortive outcome — Grossesse se terminant par un avortement	..	..	**-**	**-**	..	..	**-**	**-**
Other direct obstetric causes — Autres décès maternels directs	..	..	**-**	**-**	..	..	**2**	**♦2.1**
Indirect obstetric causes — Décès maternels indirects	..	..	**-**	**-**	..	..	**1**	**♦1.1**
Certain conditions originating in the perinatal period — Certaines affections dont l'origine se situe dans la période périnatale	**107**	**174.6**	**72**	**125.7**	**67**	**138.9**	**42**	**91.7**
Congenital malformations, deformations and chromosomal abnormalities — Malformations congénitales et anomalies chromosomiques	**140**	**228.5**	**113**	**197.4**	**120**	**248.8**	**113**	**246.7**
Symptoms, signs and abnormal clinical and laboratory findings, not elsewhere classified — Symptômes, signes et résultats anormaux d'examens cliniques et de laboratoire, non classés ailleurs	**3 693**	**83.8**	**10 949**	**216.0**	**2 057**	**46.6**	**6 620**	**130.7**
All other diseases — Toutes autres maladies	**34**	**0.8**	**47**	**0.9**	**51**	**1.2**	**83**	**1.6**
External causes — Causes externes								
Total	**7 588**	**172.3**	**2 096**	**41.3**	**6 244**	**141.3**	**1 774**	**35.0**
Accidents								
Total	...	...	...	...	**4 441**	**100.5**	**1 285**	**25.4**
Transport accidents — Accidents de transport	**747**	**17.0**	**255**	**5.0**	**563**	**12.7**	**196**	**3.9**
Falls — Chutes	**531**	**12.1**	**173**	**3.4**	**874**	**19.8**	**312**	**6.2**
Accidental drowning and submersion — Noyade et submersion accidentelles	**535**	**12.1**	**94**	**1.9**	**381**	**8.6**	**68**	**1.3**
Exposure to smoke, fire and flames — Exposition à la fumée, au feu et aux flammes	**569**	**12.9**	**211**	**4.2**	**431**	**9.8**	**139**	**2.7**
Accidental poisoning by and exposure to noxious substances — Intoxication accidentelle par des substances nocives et exposition à ces substances	**1 388**	**31.5**	**367**	**7.2**	**1 426**	**32.3**	**339**	**6.7**
Intentional self-harm — Lésions auto-infligées	**1 466**	**33.3**	**276**	**5.4**	**1 459**	**33.0**	**347**	**6.9**
Assault — Agresssions	**238**	**5.4**	**118**	**2.3**	**212**	**4.8**	**93**	**1.8**
All other external causes — Toutes autres causes externes	...	...	...	...	**132**	**3.0**	**49**	**1.0**

20. Death and death rates by cause and sex: 2014 - 2018
Décès et taux de mortalité par cause et sexe : 2014 - 2018 (continued - suite)

Belgium - Belgique

Cause of death — Cause de décès	2015 (C)				2016 (C)			
	Male — Masculin		Female — Féminin		Male — Masculin		Female — Féminin	
	Number Nombre	Rate Taux	Number Nombre	Rate Taux	Number Nombre	Rate Taux	Number Nombre	Rate Taux
TOTAL	**53 631**	**965.8**	**56 910**	**992.8**	**53 326**	**955.8**	**54 771**	**952.2**
Certain infectious and parasitic diseases — Certaines maladies infectieuses et parasitaires								
Total	**1 006**	**18.1**	**1 319**	**23.0**	**940**	**16.8**	**1 158**	**20.1**
Intestinal infectious diseases — Maladies infectieuses intestinales	**162**	**2.9**	**298**	**5.2**	**143**	**2.6**	**238**	**4.1**
Tuberculosis — Tuberculose	**17**	**♦0.3**	**14**	**♦0.2**	**9**	**♦0.2**	**9**	**♦0.2**
Tetanus — Tétanos	-	-	-	-	-	-	-	-
Diphtheria — Diphtérie	-	-	-	-	-	-	**1**	**♦0.0**
Whooping cough — Coqueluche	**1**	**♦0.0**	**1**	**♦0.0**	-	-	-	-
Meningococcal infection — Infection à méningocoques	**3**	**♦0.1**	**3**	**♦0.1**	**3**	**♦0.1**	**3**	**♦0.1**
Septicaemia — Septicémie	**413**	**7.4**	**471**	**8.2**	**404**	**7.2**	**426**	**7.4**
Acute poliomyelitis — Poliomyélite aiguë	-	-	-	-	-	-	-	-
Measles — Rougeole	-	-	-	-	-	-	-	-
Viral hepatitis — Hépatite virale	**35**	**0.6**	**35**	**0.6**	**22**	**♦0.4**	**37**	**0.6**
Human immunodeficiency virus [HIV] disease — Maladies dues au virus de l'immunodéficience humaine (VIH)	**20**	**♦0.4**	**9**	**♦0.2**	**29**	**♦0.5**	**7**	**♦0.1**
Malaria — Paludisme	**1**	**♦0.0**	-	-	**2**	**♦0.0**	**1**	**♦0.0**
Neoplasms — Tumeurs	**15 864**	**285.7**	**12 743**	**222.3**	**15 922**	**285.4**	**12 650**	**219.9**
Malignant neoplasms — Tumeurs malignes								
Total	**15 112**	**272.2**	**12 043**	**210.1**	**15 182**	**272.1**	**11 937**	**207.5**
Malignant neoplasm of lip, oral cavity and pharynx — Tumeur maligne de la lèvre, de la cavité buccale et du pharynx	**424**	**7.6**	**162**	**2.8**	**414**	**7.4**	**150**	**2.6**
Malignant neoplasm of oesophagus — Tumeur maligne de l'oesophage	**554**	**10.0**	**201**	**3.5**	**583**	**10.4**	**207**	**3.6**
Malignant neoplasm of stomach — Tumeur maligne de l'estomac	**472**	**8.5**	**268**	**4.7**	**442**	**7.9**	**269**	**4.7**
Malignant neoplasm of colon, rectosigmoid junction, rectum, anus and anal canal — Tumeur maligne du côlon, de la jonction recto-sigmoïdienne, du rectum, de l'anus et du canal anal	**1 545**	**27.8**	**1 300**	**22.7**	**1 493**	**26.8**	**1 287**	**22.4**
Malignant neoplasm of liver and intrahepatic bile ducts — Tumeur maligne du foie et des voies bilaires intrahépatiques	**600**	**10.8**	**336**	**5.9**	**596**	**10.7**	**312**	**5.4**
Malignant neoplasm of pancreas — Tumeur maligne du pancréas	**815**	**14.7**	**895**	**15.6**	**854**	**15.3**	**852**	**14.8**
Malignant neoplasm of trachea, bronchus and lung — Tumeur maligne de la trachée, des bronches et du poumon	**4 338**	**78.1**	**1 936**	**33.8**	**4 363**	**78.2**	**1 936**	**33.7**
Malignant neoplasm of female breast — Tumeur maligne du sein chez la femme	..	..	**2 167**	**45.2**	..	..	**2 227**	**46.3**
Malignant neoplasm of cervix uteri — Tumeur maligne du col de l'utérus	..	..	**161**	**3.4**	..	..	**146**	**3.0**
Malignant neoplasm of prostate — Tumeur maligne de la prostate	**1 532**	**76.4**	..	..	**1 523**	**74.8**	..	..
Malignant neoplasm of lymphoid, haematopoietic and related tissue — Tumeurs malignes primitives ou présumées primitives des tissus lymphoïde, hématopoïétique et apparentés	**1 233**	**22.2**	**1 131**	**19.7**	**1 294**	**23.2**	**1 063**	**18.5**
Disorders of the blood and blood-forming organs and certain disorders involving the immune mechanism — Maladies du sang et des organes hématopoïétiques et certains troubles du système immunitaire								
Total	**162**	**2.9**	**211**	**3.7**	**162**	**2.9**	**217**	**3.8**
Anaemias — Anémies	**84**	**1.5**	**140**	**2.4**	**85**	**1.5**	**139**	**2.4**
Endocrine, nutritional and metabolic diseases — Maladies endocriniennes, nutritionnelles et métaboliques								
Total	**1 107**	**19.9**	**1 666**	**29.1**	**1 093**	**19.6**	**1 460**	**25.4**
Diabetes mellitus — Diabète sucré	**670**	**12.1**	**836**	**14.6**	**682**	**12.2**	**766**	**13.3**
Malnutrition — Malnutrition	**76**	**1.4**	**194**	**3.4**	**51**	**0.9**	**135**	**2.3**
Mental and behavioural disorders — Troubles mentaux et du comportement	**2 004**	**36.1**	**3 355**	**58.5**	**1 973**	**35.4**	**3 320**	**57.7**
Diseases of the nervous system — Maladies du système nerveux	**2 398**	**43.2**	**3 193**	**55.7**	**2 405**	**43.1**	**3 106**	**54.0**
Diseases of the circulatory system — Maladies de l'appareil circulatoire								
Total	**14 158**	**255.0**	**17 184**	**299.8**	**13 716**	**245.8**	**16 224**	**282.1**
Acute rheumatic fever and chronic rheumatic heart diseases — Rhumatisme articulaire aigu et cardiopathies rhumatismales chroniques	**96**	**1.7**	**184**	**3.2**	**92**	**1.6**	**173**	**3.0**
Hypertensive diseases — Maladies hypertensives	**326**	**5.9**	**708**	**12.4**	**326**	**5.8**	**702**	**12.2**
Ischaemic heart disease — Cardiopathie ischémique	**4 528**	**81.5**	**3 317**	**57.9**	**4 303**	**77.1**	**3 073**	**53.4**
Cerebrovascular disease — Maladie cérébrovasculaire	**2 732**	**49.2**	**4 140**	**72.2**	**2 772**	**49.7**	**4 001**	**69.6**

20. Death and death rates by cause and sex: 2014 - 2018
Décès et taux de mortalité par cause et sexe : 2014 - 2018 (continued - suite)

Belgium - Belgique

Cause of death — Cause de décès	2015 (C)				2016 (C)			
	Male — Masculin		Female — Féminin		Male — Masculin		Female — Féminin	
	Number Nombre	Rate Taux	Number Nombre	Rate Taux	Number Nombre	Rate Taux	Number Nombre	Rate Taux
Diseases of arteries, arterioles and capillaries — Maladies des artères, artérioles et capillaires	776	14.0	585	10.2	691	12.4	520	9.0
Diseases of the respiratory system — Maladies de l'appareil respiratoire								
Total	6 133	110.4	5 715	99.7	5 976	107.1	5 228	90.9
Influenza — Grippe	89	1.6	219	3.8	49	0.9	65	1.1
Pneumonia — Pneumopathies	1 955	35.2	2 165	37.8	1 906	34.2	2 050	35.6
Chronic lower respiratory diseases — Maladies chroniques des voies respiratoires inférieures	2 728	49.1	1 949	34.0	2 629	47.1	1 799	31.3
Diseases of the digestive system — Maladies de l'appareil digestif								
Total	2 377	42.8	2 387	41.6	2 396	42.9	2 430	42.2
Gastric and duodenal ulcer — Ulcère de l'estomac et du duodénum	90	1.6	101	1.8	96	1.7	109	1.9
Diseases of the liver — Maladies du foie	993	17.9	580	10.1	985	17.7	594	10.3
Diseases of the musculoskeletal system and connective tissue — Maladies du système ostéo-articularie, des muscles et du tissu conjonctif	225	4.1	402	7.0	225	4.0	377	6.6
Diseases of the genitourinary system — Maladies de l'appareil génito-urinaire								
Total	1 174	21.1	1 679	29.3	1 192	21.4	1 719	29.9
Disorders of kidney and ureter — Affections du rein et de l'uretère	897	16.2	1 231	21.5	908	16.3	1 217	21.2
Hyperplasia of prostate — Hyperplasie de la prostate	20	♦1.0	..	..	16	♦0.8	..	..
Pregnancy, childbirth and the puerperium — Grossesse, accouchement et puerpéralité								
Total	..	..	4	♦3.3	..	..	4	♦3.3
Pregnancy with abortive outcome — Grossesse se terminant par un avortement	..	..	-	-	..	..	-	-
Other direct obstetric causes — Autres décès maternels directs	..	..	4	♦3.3	..	..	4	♦3.3
Indirect obstetric causes — Décès maternels indirects	..	..	-	-	..	..	-	-
Certain conditions originating in the perinatal period — Certaines affections dont l'origine se situe dans la période périnatale	111	177.4	87	145.7	135	216.2	72	121.1
Congenital malformations, deformations and chromosomal abnormalities — Malformations congénitales et anomalies chromosomiques	107	171.0	107	179.2	136	217.9	112	188.3
Symptoms, signs and abnormal clinical and laboratory findings, not elsewhere classified — Symptômes, signes et résultats anormaux d'examens cliniques et de laboratoire, non classés ailleurs	2 793	50.3	3 684	64.3	3 014	54.0	3 704	64.4
All other diseases — Toutes autres maladies	87	1.6	210	3.7	118	2.1	214	3.7
External causes — Causes externes								
Total	3 925	70.7	2 964	51.7	3 922	70.3	2 776	48.3
Accidents								
Total	2 258	40.7	2 178	38.0	2 188	39.2	1 990	34.6
Transport accidents — Accidents de transport	502	9.0	191	3.3	483	8.7	154	2.7
Falls — Chutes	726	13.1	892	15.6	763	13.7	771	13.4
Accidental drowning and submersion — Noyade et submersion accidentelles	74	1.3	18	♦0.3	47	0.8	22	♦0.4
Exposure to smoke, fire and flames — Exposition à la fumée, au feu et aux flammes	38	0.7	36	0.6	35	0.6	31	0.5
Accidental poisoning by and exposure to noxious substances — Intoxication accidentelle par des substances nocives et exposition à ces substances	155	2.8	83	1.4	128	2.3	75	1.3
Intentional self-harm — Lésions auto-infligées	1 314	23.7	552	9.6	1 362	24.4	543	9.4
Assault — Agresssions	65	1.2	54	0.9	77	1.4	48	0.8
All other external causes — Toutes autres causes externes	288	5.2	180	3.1	295	5.3	195	3.4

20. Death and death rates by cause and sex: 2014 - 2018
Décès et taux de mortalité par cause et sexe : 2014 - 2018 (continued - suite)

Bosnia and Herzegovina - Bosnie-Herzégovine

Cause of death — Cause de décès	2014 (C)				2016 (C)			
	Male — Masculin		Female — Féminin		Male — Masculin		Female — Féminin	
	Number Nombre	Rate Taux	Number Nombre	Rate Taux	Number Nombre	Rate Taux	Number Nombre	Rate Taux
TOTAL	**18 360**	...	**17 620**	...	**18 542**	...	**18 029**	...
Certain infectious and parasitic diseases — Certaines maladies infectieuses et parasitaires								
Total	168	...	126	...	215	...	200	...
Intestinal infectious diseases — Maladies infectieuses intestinales	5	...	8	...	9	...	22	...
Tuberculosis — Tuberculose	74	...	35	...	62	...	39	...
Tetanus — Tétanos	-	...	-	...	-	...	1	...
Diphtheria — Diphtérie	-	...	-	...	-	...	-	...
Whooping cough — Coqueluche	-	...	-	...	-	...	-	...
Meningococcal infection — Infection à méningocoques	-	...	2	...	3	...	1	...
Septicaemia — Septicémie	48	...	58	...	105	...	120	...
Acute poliomyelitis — Poliomyélite aiguë	-	...	-	...	-	...	-	...
Measles — Rougeole	-	...	-	...	-	...	-	...
Viral hepatitis — Hépatite virale	23	...	15	...	17	...	6	...
Human immunodeficiency virus [HIV] disease — Maladies dues au virus de l'immunodéficience humaine (VIH)	1	...	1	...	1	...	-	...
Malaria — Paludisme	-	...	-	...	-	...	-	...
Neoplasms — Tumeurs	**4 569**	...	**3 252**	...	**4 464**	...	**3 297**	...
Malignant neoplasms — Tumeurs malignes								
Total	4 531	...	3 231	...	4 404	...	3 251	...
Malignant neoplasm of lip, oral cavity and pharynx — Tumeur maligne de la lèvre, de la cavité buccale et du pharynx	106	...	26	...	111	...	37	...
Malignant neoplasm of oesophagus — Tumeur maligne de l'oesophage	77	...	16	...	70	...	18	...
Malignant neoplasm of stomach — Tumeur maligne de l'estomac	315	...	196	...	310	...	183	...
Malignant neoplasm of colon, rectosigmoid junction, rectum, anus and anal canal — Tumeur maligne du côlon, de la jonction recto-sigmoïdienne, du rectum, de l'anus et du canal anal	527	...	382	...	561	...	401	...
Malignant neoplasm of liver and intrahepatic bile ducts — Tumeur maligne du foie et des voies bilaires intrahépatiques	212	...	181	...	240	...	183	...
Malignant neoplasm of pancreas — Tumeur maligne du pancréas	234	...	203	...	225	...	199	...
Malignant neoplasm of trachea, bronchus and lung — Tumeur maligne de la trachée, des bronches et du poumon	1 468	...	390	...	1 311	...	435	...
Malignant neoplasm of female breast — Tumeur maligne du sein chez la femme	..	..	520	...	..	..	498	...
Malignant neoplasm of cervix uteri — Tumeur maligne du col de l'utérus	..	..	107	...	..	..	145	...
Malignant neoplasm of prostate — Tumeur maligne de la prostate	383	...	..	..	322	...	..	..
Malignant neoplasm of lymphoid, haematopoietic and related tissue — Tumeurs malignes primitives ou présumées primitives des tissus lymphoïde, hématopoïétique et apparentés	189	...	161	...	212	...	164	...
Disorders of the blood and blood-forming organs and certain disorders involving the immune mechanism — Maladies du sang et des organes hématopoïétiques et certains troubles du système immunitaire								
Total	14	...	26	...	20	...	30	...
Anaemias — Anémies	8	...	20	...	14	...	17	...
Endocrine, nutritional and metabolic diseases — Maladies endocriniennes, nutritionnelles et métaboliques								
Total	925	...	1 342	...	789	...	1 171	...
Diabetes mellitus — Diabète sucré	907	...	1 324	...	769	...	1 147	...
Malnutrition — Malnutrition	1	...	-	...	1	...	1	...
Mental and behavioural disorders — Troubles mentaux et du comportement	130	...	65	...	132	...	72	...
Diseases of the nervous system — Maladies du système nerveux	198	...	185	...	206	...	171	...
Diseases of the circulatory system — Maladies de l'appareil circulatoire								
Total	8 320	...	9 586	...	8 772	...	10 155	...
Acute rheumatic fever and chronic rheumatic heart diseases — Rhumatisme articularie aigu et cardiopathies rhumatismales chroniques	11	...	5	...	8	...	7	...
Hypertensive diseases — Maladies hypertensives	529	...	801	...	553	...	894	...
Ischaemic heart disease — Cardiopathie ischémique	2 082	...	1 800	...	2 311	...	2 023	...
Cerebrovascular disease — Maladie cérébrovasculaire	1 893	...	2 293	...	2 051	...	2 536	...

20. Death and death rates by cause and sex: 2014 - 2018
Décès et taux de mortalité par cause et sexe : 2014 - 2018 (continued - suite)

Bosnia and Herzegovina - Bosnie-Herzégovine

Cause of death — Cause de décès	2014 (C)				2016 (C)			
	Male — Masculin		Female — Féminin		Male — Masculin		Female — Féminin	
	Number Nombre	Rate Taux	Number Nombre	Rate Taux	Number Nombre	Rate Taux	Number Nombre	Rate Taux
Diseases of arteries, arterioles and capillaries — Maladies des artères, artérioles et capillaires	317	...	379	...	293	...	339	...
Diseases of the respiratory system — Maladies de l'appareil respiratoire								
Total	822	...	549	...	874	...	603	...
Influenza — Grippe	1	...	2	...	9	...	7	...
Pneumonia — Pneumopathies	77	...	82	...	190	...	146	...
Chronic lower respiratory diseases — Maladies chroniques des voies respiratoires inférieures	532	...	291	...	422	...	244	...
Diseases of the digestive system — Maladies de l'appareil digestif								
Total	544	...	403	...	615	...	456	...
Gastric and duodenal ulcer — Ulcère de l'estomac et du duodénum	36	...	42	...	54	...	36	...
Diseases of the liver — Maladies du foie	305	...	101	...	264	...	108	...
Diseases of the musculoskeletal system and connective tissue — Maladies du système ostéo-articularie, des muscles et du tissu conjonctif	16	...	44	...	8	...	37	...
Diseases of the genitourinary system — Maladies de l'appareil génito-urinaire								
Total	259	...	273	...	343	...	351	...
Disorders of kidney and ureter — Affections du rein et de l'uretère	243	...	269	...	317	...	341	...
Hyperplasia of prostate — Hyperplasie de la prostate	7	...	..	..	11	...	..	..
Pregnancy, childbirth and the puerperium — Grossesse, accouchement et puerpéralité								
Total	..	..	-	-	..	..	1	♦3.4
Pregnancy with abortive outcome — Grossesse se terminant par un avortement	..	..	-	-	..	..	-	-
Other direct obstetric causes — Autres décès maternels directs	..	..	-	-	..	..	1	♦3.4
Indirect obstetric causes — Décès maternels indirects	..	..	-	-	..	..	-	-
Certain conditions originating in the perinatal period — Certaines affections dont l'origine se situe dans la période périnatale	42	277.6	44	311.6	74	487.5	43	305.0
Congenital malformations, deformations and chromosomal abnormalities — Malformations congénitales et anomalies chromosomiques	20	♦132.2	28	♦198.3	9	♦59.3	7	♦49.7
Symptoms, signs and abnormal clinical and laboratory findings, not elsewhere classified — Symptômes, signes et résultats anormaux d'examens cliniques et de laboratoire, non classés ailleurs	1 512	...	1 432	...	1 209	...	1 156	...
All other diseases — Toutes autres maladies	16	...	21	...	18	...	19	...
External causes — Causes externes								
Total	805	...	244	...	794	...	260	...
Accidents								
Total	448	...	138	...	11	...	3	...
Transport accidents — Accidents de transport	196	...	48	...	1	...	1	...
Falls — Chutes	26	...	6	...	-	...	-	...
Accidental drowning and submersion — Noyade et submersion accidentelles	45	...	17	...	-	...	2	...
Exposure to smoke, fire and flames — Exposition à la fumée, au feu et aux flammes	16	...	8	...	1	...	-	...
Accidental poisoning by and exposure to noxious substances — Intoxication accidentelle par des substances nocives et exposition à ces substances	7	...	5	...	-	...	-	...
Intentional self-harm — Lésions auto-infligées	243	...	70	...	-	...	-	...
Assault — Agresssions	34	...	12	...	-	...	-	...
All other external causes — Toutes autres causes externes	80	...	24	...	783	...	257	...

20. Death and death rates by cause and sex: 2014 - 2018
Décès et taux de mortalité par cause et sexe : 2014 - 2018 (continued - suite)

Bulgaria - Bulgarie

Cause of death — Cause de décès	2014 (C)				2015 (C)			
	Male — Masculin		Female — Féminin		Male — Masculin		Female — Féminin	
	Number Nombre	Rate Taux	Number Nombre	Rate Taux	Number Nombre	Rate Taux	Number Nombre	Rate Taux
TOTAL	**56 630**	**1 611.8**	**52 322**	**1 410.1**	**57 040**	**1 634.6**	**53 077**	**1 439.0**
Certain infectious and parasitic diseases — Certaines maladies infectieuses et parasitaires								
Total	**285**	**8.1**	**173**	**4.7**	**359**	**10.3**	**243**	**6.6**
Intestinal infectious diseases — Maladies infectieuses intestinales	**13**	**♦0.4**	**16**	**♦0.4**	**3**	**♦0.1**	**19**	**♦0.5**
Tuberculosis — Tuberculose	**95**	**2.7**	**28**	**♦0.8**	**84**	**2.4**	**30**	**♦0.8**
Tetanus — Tétanos	**-**	**-**	**-**	**-**	**-**	**-**	**-**	**-**
Diphtheria — Diphtérie	**-**	**-**	**-**	**-**	**-**	**-**	**-**	**-**
Whooping cough — Coqueluche	**-**	**-**	**1**	**♦0.0**	**-**	**-**	**-**	**-**
Meningococcal infection — Infection à méningocoques	**4**	**♦0.1**	**2**	**♦0.1**	**3**	**♦0.1**	**2**	**♦0.1**
Septicaemia — Septicémie	**101**	**2.9**	**79**	**2.1**	**202**	**5.8**	**161**	**4.4**
Acute poliomyelitis — Poliomyélite aiguë	**-**	**-**	**-**	**-**	**-**	**-**	**-**	**-**
Measles — Rougeole	**-**	**-**	**-**	**-**	**-**	**-**	**-**	**-**
Viral hepatitis — Hépatite virale	**21**	**♦0.6**	**14**	**♦0.4**	**17**	**♦0.5**	**5**	**♦0.1**
Human immunodeficiency virus [HIV] disease — Maladies dues au virus de l'immunodéficience humaine (VIH)	**12**	**♦0.3**	**4**	**♦0.1**	**14**	**♦0.4**	**3**	**♦0.1**
Malaria — Paludisme	**-**	**-**	**1**	**♦0.0**	**-**	**-**	**-**	**-**
Neoplasms — Tumeurs	**10 552**	**300.3**	**7 561**	**203.8**	**10 457**	**299.7**	**7 564**	**205.1**
Malignant neoplasms — Tumeurs malignes								
Total	**10 476**	**298.2**	**7 494**	**202.0**	**10 410**	**298.3**	**7 520**	**203.9**
Malignant neoplasm of lip, oral cavity and pharynx — Tumeur maligne de la lèvre, de la cavité buccale et du pharynx	**327**	**9.3**	**92**	**2.5**	**339**	**9.7**	**66**	**1.8**
Malignant neoplasm of oesophagus — Tumeur maligne de l'oesophage	**146**	**4.2**	**28**	**♦0.8**	**169**	**4.8**	**42**	**1.1**
Malignant neoplasm of stomach — Tumeur maligne de l'estomac	**718**	**20.4**	**441**	**11.9**	**719**	**20.6**	**453**	**12.3**
Malignant neoplasm of colon, rectosigmoid junction, rectum, anus and anal canal — Tumeur maligne du côlon, de la jonction recto-sigmoïdienne, du rectum, de l'anus et du canal anal	**1 508**	**42.9**	**1 052**	**28.4**	**1 437**	**41.2**	**1 070**	**29.0**
Malignant neoplasm of liver and intrahepatic bile ducts — Tumeur maligne du foie et des voies bilaires intrahépatiques	**424**	**12.1**	**255**	**6.9**	**422**	**12.1**	**254**	**6.9**
Malignant neoplasm of pancreas — Tumeur maligne du pancréas	**624**	**17.8**	**520**	**14.0**	**612**	**17.5**	**492**	**13.3**
Malignant neoplasm of trachea, bronchus and lung — Tumeur maligne de la trachée, des bronches et du poumon	**2 746**	**78.2**	**739**	**19.9**	**2 717**	**77.9**	**735**	**19.9**
Malignant neoplasm of female breast — Tumeur maligne du sein chez la femme	..	..	**1 343**	**41.6**	..	..	**1 312**	**41.0**
Malignant neoplasm of cervix uteri — Tumeur maligne du col de l'utérus	..	..	**349**	**10.8**	..	..	**381**	**11.9**
Malignant neoplasm of prostate — Tumeur maligne de la prostate	**949**	**72.5**	..	..	**967**	**74.1**	..	..
Malignant neoplasm of lymphoid, haematopoietic and related tissue — Tumeurs malignes primitives ou présumées primitives des tissus lymphoïde, hématopoïétique et apparentés	**510**	**14.5**	**380**	**10.2**	**527**	**15.1**	**392**	**10.6**
Disorders of the blood and blood-forming organs and certain disorders involving the immune mechanism — Maladies du sang et des organes hématopoïétiques et certains troubles du système immunitaire								
Total	**87**	**2.5**	**69**	**1.9**	**72**	**2.1**	**67**	**1.8**
Anaemias — Anémies	**61**	**1.7**	**49**	**1.3**	**54**	**1.5**	**51**	**1.4**
Endocrine, nutritional and metabolic diseases — Maladies endocriniennes, nutritionnelles et métaboliques								
Total	**659**	**18.8**	**883**	**23.8**	**822**	**23.6**	**996**	**27.0**
Diabetes mellitus — Diabète sucré	**644**	**18.3**	**853**	**23.0**	**807**	**23.1**	**975**	**26.4**
Malnutrition — Malnutrition	**2**	**♦0.1**	**-**	**-**	**-**	**-**	**-**	**-**
Mental and behavioural disorders — Troubles mentaux et du comportement	**47**	**1.3**	**29**	**♦0.8**	**51**	**1.5**	**43**	**1.2**
Diseases of the nervous system — Maladies du système nerveux	**562**	**16.0**	**494**	**13.3**	**613**	**17.6**	**517**	**14.0**
Diseases of the circulatory system — Maladies de l'appareil circulatoire								
Total	**34 727**	**988.4**	**37 032**	**998.0**	**34 706**	**994.6**	**37 321**	**1 011.8**
Acute rheumatic fever and chronic rheumatic heart diseases — Rhumatisme articulaire aigu et cardiopathies rhumatismales chroniques	**35**	**1.0**	**49**	**1.3**	**14**	**♦0.4**	**20**	**♦0.5**
Hypertensive diseases — Maladies hypertensives	**3 164**	**90.1**	**3 840**	**103.5**	**3 702**	**106.1**	**4 591**	**124.5**
Ischaemic heart disease — Cardiopathie ischémique	**6 831**	**194.4**	**5 821**	**156.9**	**7 093**	**203.3**	**5 953**	**161.4**
Cerebrovascular disease — Maladie cérébrovasculaire	**10 355**	**294.7**	**12 157**	**327.6**	**9 771**	**280.0**	**11 718**	**317.7**

20. Death and death rates by cause and sex: 2014 - 2018
Décès et taux de mortalité par cause et sexe : 2014 - 2018 (continued - suite)

Bulgaria - Bulgarie

Cause of death — Cause de décès	2014 (C)				2015 (C)			
	Male — Masculin		Female — Féminin		Male — Masculin		Female — Féminin	
	Number Nombre	Rate Taux	Number Nombre	Rate Taux	Number Nombre	Rate Taux	Number Nombre	Rate Taux
Diseases of arteries, arterioles and capillaries — Maladies des artères, artérioles et capillaires	1 154	32.8	1 454	39.2	1 362	39.0	1 587	43.0
Diseases of the respiratory system — Maladies de l'appareil respiratoire								
Total	2 420	68.9	1 515	40.8	2 475	70.9	1 570	42.6
Influenza — Grippe	14	♦0.4	7	♦0.2	-	-	3	♦0.1
Pneumonia — Pneumopathies	855	24.3	621	16.7	766	22.0	536	14.5
Chronic lower respiratory diseases — Maladies chroniques des voies respiratoires inférieures	909	25.9	442	11.9	971	27.8	476	12.9
Diseases of the digestive system — Maladies de l'appareil digestif								
Total	2 567	73.1	1 286	34.7	2 564	73.5	1 292	35.0
Gastric and duodenal ulcer — Ulcère de l'estomac et du duodénum	194	5.5	96	2.6	177	5.1	114	3.1
Diseases of the liver — Maladies du foie	1 476	42.0	430	11.6	1 531	43.9	407	11.0
Diseases of the musculoskeletal system and connective tissue — Maladies du système ostéo-articularie, des muscles et du tissu conjonctif	23	♦0.7	32	0.9	17	♦0.5	25	♦0.7
Diseases of the genitourinary system — Maladies de l'appareil génito-urinaire								
Total	741	21.1	609	16.4	752	21.5	674	18.3
Disorders of kidney and ureter — Affections du rein et de l'uretère	714	20.3	599	16.1	734	21.0	671	18.2
Hyperplasia of prostate — Hyperplasie de la prostate	17	♦1.3	..	..	8	♦0.6	..	..
Pregnancy, childbirth and the puerperium — Grossesse, accouchement et puerpéralité								
Total	..	..	5	♦7.4	..	..	4	♦6.1
Pregnancy with abortive outcome — Grossesse se terminant par un avortement	..	..	-	-	..	..	-	-
Other direct obstetric causes — Autres décès maternels directs	..	..	5	♦7.4	..	..	3	♦4.5
Indirect obstetric causes — Décès maternels indirects	..	..	-	-	..	..	-	-
Certain conditions originating in the perinatal period — Certaines affections dont l'origine se situe dans la période périnatale	149	429.0	113	344.0	99	290.6	89	279.2
Congenital malformations, deformations and chromosomal abnormalities — Malformations congénitales et anomalies chromosomiques	64	184.3	60	182.6	96	281.8	56	175.7
Symptoms, signs and abnormal clinical and laboratory findings, not elsewhere classified — Symptômes, signes et résultats anormaux d'examens cliniques et de laboratoire, non classés ailleurs	1 550	44.1	1 661	44.8	1 803	51.7	1 849	50.1
All other diseases — Toutes autres maladies	25	♦0.7	27	♦0.7	25	♦0.7	26	♦0.7
External causes — Causes externes								
Total	2 172	61.8	773	20.8	2 129	61.0	741	20.1
Accidents								
Total	1 352	38.5	489	13.2	1 355	38.8	496	13.4
Transport accidents — Accidents de transport	483	13.7	156	4.2	509	14.6	154	4.2
Falls — Chutes	277	7.9	141	3.8	253	7.3	133	3.6
Accidental drowning and submersion — Noyade et submersion accidentelles	117	3.3	39	1.1	121	3.5	25	♦0.7
Exposure to smoke, fire and flames — Exposition à la fumée, au feu et aux flammes	50	1.4	27	♦0.7	63	1.8	33	0.9
Accidental poisoning by and exposure to noxious substances — Intoxication accidentelle par des substances nocives et exposition à ces substances	65	1.9	20	♦0.5	60	1.7	29	♦0.8
Intentional self-harm — Lésions auto-infligées	551	15.7	171	4.6	518	14.8	159	4.3
Assault — Agresssions	64	1.8	32	0.9	77	2.2	23	♦0.6
All other external causes — Toutes autres causes externes	205	5.8	81	2.2	179	5.1	63	1.7

20. Death and death rates by cause and sex: 2014 - 2018
Décès et taux de mortalité par cause et sexe : 2014 - 2018 (continued - suite)

Croatia - Croatie

Cause of death — Cause de décès	2016 (C)				2017 (C)			
	Male — Masculin		Female — Féminin		Male — Masculin		Female — Féminin	
	Number Nombre	Rate Taux	Number Nombre	Rate Taux	Number Nombre	Rate Taux	Number Nombre	Rate Taux
TOTAL	**25 344**	**1 252.9**	**26 198**	**1 208.5**	**25 861**	**1 289.7**	**27 616**	**1 285.1**
Certain infectious and parasitic diseases — Certaines maladies infectieuses et parasitaires								
Total	241	11.9	216	10.0	310	15.5	305	14.2
Intestinal infectious diseases — Maladies infectieuses intestinales	23	♦1.1	40	1.8	37	1.8	41	1.9
Tuberculosis — Tuberculose	39	1.9	19	♦0.9	38	1.9	22	♦1.0
Tetanus — Tétanos	-	-	1	♦0.0	-	-	-	-
Diphtheria — Diphtérie	-	-	-	-	-	-	-	-
Whooping cough — Coqueluche	1	♦0.0	-	-	-	-	-	-
Meningococcal infection — Infection à méningocoques	2	♦0.1	1	♦0.0	2	♦0.1	-	-
Septicaemia — Septicémie	103	5.1	136	6.3	175	8.7	222	10.3
Acute poliomyelitis — Poliomyélite aiguë	-	-	-	-	-	-	-	-
Measles — Rougeole	-	-	-	-	-	-	-	-
Viral hepatitis — Hépatite virale	61	3.0	14	♦0.6	39	1.9	15	♦0.7
Human immunodeficiency virus [HIV] disease — Maladies dues au virus de l'immunodéficience humaine (VIH)	6	♦0.3	-	-	8	♦0.4	-	-
Malaria — Paludisme	-	-	-	-	-	-	-	-
Neoplasms — Tumeurs	8 236	407.2	6 124	282.5	7 952	396.6	6 012	279.8
Malignant neoplasms — Tumeurs malignes								
Total	8 099	400.4	5 966	275.2	7 817	389.8	5 899	274.5
Malignant neoplasm of lip, oral cavity and pharynx — Tumeur maligne de la lèvre, de la cavité buccale et du pharynx	272	13.4	64	3.0	272	13.6	53	2.5
Malignant neoplasm of oesophagus — Tumeur maligne de l'oesophage	163	8.1	34	1.6	153	7.6	24	♦1.1
Malignant neoplasm of stomach — Tumeur maligne de l'estomac	449	22.2	308	14.2	438	21.8	279	13.0
Malignant neoplasm of colon, rectosigmoid junction, rectum, anus and anal canal — Tumeur maligne du côlon, de la jonction recto-sigmoïdienne, du rectum, de l'anus et du canal anal	1 273	62.9	896	41.3	1 174	58.5	863	40.2
Malignant neoplasm of liver and intrahepatic bile ducts — Tumeur maligne du foie et des voies bilaires intrahépatiques	376	18.6	159	7.3	322	16.1	171	8.0
Malignant neoplasm of pancreas — Tumeur maligne du pancréas	377	18.6	380	17.5	397	19.8	372	17.3
Malignant neoplasm of trachea, bronchus and lung — Tumeur maligne de la trachée, des bronches et du poumon	2 122	104.9	744	34.3	2 142	106.8	852	39.6
Malignant neoplasm of female breast — Tumeur maligne du sein chez la femme	..	..	990	52.9	..	..	853	46.0
Malignant neoplasm of cervix uteri — Tumeur maligne du col de l'utérus	..	..	115	6.1	..	..	109	5.9
Malignant neoplasm of prostate — Tumeur maligne de la prostate	769	101.4	..	..	785	102.9	..	..
Malignant neoplasm of lymphoid, haematopoietic and related tissue — Tumeurs malignes primitives ou présumées primitives des tissus lymphoïde, hématopoïétique et apparentés	483	23.9	445	20.5	460	22.9	455	21.2
Disorders of the blood and blood-forming organs and certain disorders involving the immune mechanism — Maladies du sang et des organes hématopoïétiques et certains troubles du système immunitaire								
Total	18	♦0.9	27	♦1.2	17	♦0.8	39	1.8
Anaemias — Anémies	4	♦0.2	13	♦0.6	6	♦0.3	26	♦1.2
Endocrine, nutritional and metabolic diseases — Maladies endocriniennes, nutritionnelles et métaboliques								
Total	793	39.2	1 153	53.2	947	47.2	1 435	66.8
Diabetes mellitus — Diabète sucré	770	38.1	1 119	51.6	927	46.2	1 404	65.3
Malnutrition — Malnutrition	-	-	-	-	-	-	-	-
Mental and behavioural disorders — Troubles mentaux et du comportement	436	21.6	653	30.1	468	23.3	728	33.9
Diseases of the nervous system — Maladies du système nerveux	512	25.3	599	27.6	574	28.6	708	32.9
Diseases of the circulatory system — Maladies de l'appareil circulatoire								
Total	10 054	497.0	13 136	605.9	10 086	503.0	13 418	624.4
Acute rheumatic fever and chronic rheumatic heart diseases — Rhumatisme articularie aigu et cardiopathies rhumatismales chroniques	50	2.5	89	4.1	69	3.4	100	4.7
Hypertensive diseases — Maladies hypertensives	515	25.5	982	45.3	296	14.8	628	29.2
Ischaemic heart disease — Cardiopathie ischémique	4 835	239.0	5 561	256.5	4 963	247.5	6 106	284.1
Cerebrovascular disease — Maladie cérébrovasculaire	2 724	134.7	3 870	178.5	2 561	127.7	3 586	166.9

20. Death and death rates by cause and sex: 2014 - 2018
Décès et taux de mortalité par cause et sexe : 2014 - 2018 (continued - suite)

Croatia - Croatie

Cause of death — Cause de décès	2016 (C)				2017 (C)			
	Male — Masculin		Female — Féminin		Male — Masculin		Female — Féminin	
	Number Nombre	Rate Taux	Number Nombre	Rate Taux	Number Nombre	Rate Taux	Number Nombre	Rate Taux
Diseases of arteries, arterioles and capillaries — Maladies des artères, artérioles et capillaires	497	24.6	666	30.7	517	25.8	598	27.8
Diseases of the respiratory system — Maladies de l'appareil respiratoire								
Total	1 392	68.8	1 048	48.3	1 687	84.1	1 452	67.6
Influenza — Grippe	12	♦0.6	7	♦0.3	43	2.1	32	1.5
Pneumonia — Pneumopathies	309	15.3	269	12.4	473	23.6	519	24.2
Chronic lower respiratory diseases — Maladies chroniques des voies respiratoires inférieures	1 008	49.8	727	33.5	1 107	55.2	859	40.0
Diseases of the digestive system — Maladies de l'appareil digestif								
Total	1 228	60.7	845	39.0	1 287	64.2	968	45.0
Gastric and duodenal ulcer — Ulcère de l'estomac et du duodénum	97	4.8	83	3.8	114	5.7	132	6.1
Diseases of the liver — Maladies du foie	723	35.7	246	11.3	738	36.8	225	10.5
Diseases of the musculoskeletal system and connective tissue — Maladies du système ostéo-articularie, des muscles et du tissu conjonctif	17	♦0.8	120	5.5	21	♦1.0	95	4.4
Diseases of the genitourinary system — Maladies de l'appareil génito-urinaire								
Total	507	25.1	766	35.3	536	26.7	933	43.4
Disorders of kidney and ureter — Affections du rein et de l'uretère	351	17.4	510	23.5	378	18.9	599	27.9
Hyperplasia of prostate — Hyperplasie de la prostate	42	5.5	..	..	36	4.7	..	..
Pregnancy, childbirth and the puerperium — Grossesse, accouchement et puerpéralité								
Total	..	..	1	♦2.7	..	..	-	-
Pregnancy with abortive outcome — Grossesse se terminant par un avortement	..	..	-	-	..	..	-	-
Other direct obstetric causes — Autres décès maternels directs	..	..	1	♦2.7	..	..	-	-
Indirect obstetric causes — Décès maternels indirects	..	..	-	-	..	..	-	-
Certain conditions originating in the perinatal period — Certaines affections dont l'origine se situe dans la période périnatale	40	209.7	35	189.5	49	260.0	26	♦146.8
Congenital malformations, deformations and chromosomal abnormalities — Malformations congénitales et anomalies chromosomiques	55	288.4	48	260.0	52	275.9	43	242.8
Symptoms, signs and abnormal clinical and laboratory findings, not elsewhere classified — Symptômes, signes et résultats anormaux d'examens cliniques et de laboratoire, non classés ailleurs	150	7.4	250	11.5	242	12.1	382	17.8
All other diseases — Toutes autres maladies	3	♦0.1	5	♦0.2	4	♦0.2	7	♦0.3
External causes — Causes externes								
Total	1 662	82.2	1 172	54.1	1 629	81.2	1 065	49.6
Accidents								
Total	1 066	52.7	900	41.5	1 049	52.3	817	38.0
Transport accidents — Accidents de transport	314	15.5	76	3.5	319	15.9	85	4.0
Falls — Chutes	439	21.7	657	30.3	300	15.0	426	19.8
Accidental drowning and submersion — Noyade et submersion accidentelles	68	3.4	25	♦1.2	58	2.9	21	♦1.0
Exposure to smoke, fire and flames — Exposition à la fumée, au feu et aux flammes	17	♦0.8	7	♦0.3	31	1.5	13	♦0.6
Accidental poisoning by and exposure to noxious substances — Intoxication accidentelle par des substances nocives et exposition à ces substances	61	3.0	25	♦1.2	84	4.2	25	♦1.2
Intentional self-harm — Lésions auto-infligées	515	25.5	168	7.7	474	23.6	159	7.4
Assault — Agresssions	30	♦1.5	21	♦1.0	31	1.5	20	♦0.9
All other external causes — Toutes autres causes externes	51	2.5	83	3.8	75	3.7	69	3.2

20. Death and death rates by cause and sex: 2014 - 2018
Décès et taux de mortalité par cause et sexe : 2014 - 2018 (continued - suite)

Czechia - Tchéquie

Cause of death — Cause de décès	2016 (C)				2017 (C)			
	Male — Masculin		Female — Féminin		Male — Masculin		Female — Féminin	
	Number Nombre	Rate Taux	Number Nombre	Rate Taux	Number Nombre	Rate Taux	Number Nombre	Rate Taux
TOTAL	**54 880**	**1 058.2**	**52 870**	**985.0**	**56 442**	**1 085.3**	**55 001**	**1 022.7**
Certain infectious and parasitic diseases — Certaines maladies infectieuses et parasitaires								
Total	**980**	**18.9**	**1 054**	**19.6**	**947**	**18.2**	**1 121**	**20.8**
Intestinal infectious diseases — Maladies infectieuses intestinales	**105**	**2.0**	**158**	**2.9**	**92**	**1.8**	**147**	**2.7**
Tuberculosis — Tuberculose	**31**	**0.6**	**9**	**♦0.2**	**21**	**♦0.4**	**13**	**♦0.2**
Tetanus — Tétanos	**-**	**-**	**-**	**-**	**-**	**-**	**-**	**-**
Diphtheria — Diphtérie	**-**	**-**	**-**	**-**	**-**	**-**	**-**	**-**
Whooping cough — Coqueluche	**-**	**-**	**1**	**♦0.0**	**-**	**-**	**-**	**-**
Meningococcal infection — Infection à méningocoques	**5**	**♦0.1**	**5**	**♦0.1**	**2**	**♦0.0**	**1**	**♦0.0**
Septicaemia — Septicémie	**716**	**13.8**	**738**	**13.7**	**706**	**13.6**	**829**	**15.4**
Acute poliomyelitis — Poliomyélite aiguë	**1**	**♦0.0**	**1**	**♦0.0**	**-**	**-**	**-**	**-**
Measles — Rougeole	**-**	**-**	**-**	**-**	**-**	**-**	**-**	**-**
Viral hepatitis — Hépatite virale	**17**	**♦0.3**	**13**	**♦0.2**	**18**	**♦0.3**	**5**	**♦0.1**
Human immunodeficiency virus [HIV] disease — Maladies dues au virus de l'immunodéficience humaine (VIH)	**11**	**♦0.2**	**6**	**♦0.1**	**12**	**♦0.2**	**2**	**♦0.0**
Malaria — Paludisme	**3**	**♦0.1**	**-**	**-**	**-**	**-**	**-**	**-**
Neoplasms — Tumeurs	**15 385**	**296.6**	**12 421**	**231.4**	**15 485**	**297.7**	**12 367**	**229.9**
Malignant neoplasms — Tumeurs malignes								
Total	**15 095**	**291.1**	**12 166**	**226.7**	**15 239**	**293.0**	**12 081**	**224.6**
Malignant neoplasm of lip, oral cavity and pharynx — Tumeur maligne de la lèvre, de la cavité buccale et du pharynx	**542**	**10.5**	**214**	**4.0**	**533**	**10.2**	**197**	**3.7**
Malignant neoplasm of oesophagus — Tumeur maligne de l'oesophage	**416**	**8.0**	**100**	**1.9**	**446**	**8.6**	**107**	**2.0**
Malignant neoplasm of stomach — Tumeur maligne de l'estomac	**599**	**11.5**	**399**	**7.4**	**582**	**11.2**	**391**	**7.3**
Malignant neoplasm of colon, rectosigmoid junction, rectum, anus and anal canal — Tumeur maligne du côlon, de la jonction recto-sigmoïdienne, du rectum, de l'anus et du canal anal	**2 105**	**40.6**	**1 404**	**26.2**	**2 142**	**41.2**	**1 418**	**26.4**
Malignant neoplasm of liver and intrahepatic bile ducts — Tumeur maligne du foie et des voies bilaires intrahépatiques	**515**	**9.9**	**314**	**5.9**	**566**	**10.9**	**327**	**6.1**
Malignant neoplasm of pancreas — Tumeur maligne du pancréas	**1 058**	**20.4**	**1 020**	**19.0**	**1 078**	**20.7**	**1 006**	**18.7**
Malignant neoplasm of trachea, bronchus and lung — Tumeur maligne de la trachée, des bronches et du poumon	**3 618**	**69.8**	**1 715**	**32.0**	**3 639**	**70.0**	**1 824**	**33.9**
Malignant neoplasm of female breast — Tumeur maligne du sein chez la femme	..	..	**1 685**	**36.8**	..	..	**1 620**	**35.4**
Malignant neoplasm of cervix uteri — Tumeur maligne du col de l'utérus	..	..	**314**	**6.9**	..	..	**323**	**7.1**
Malignant neoplasm of prostate — Tumeur maligne de la prostate	**1 421**	**78.1**	..	..	**1 372**	**74.6**	..	..
Malignant neoplasm of lymphoid, haematopoietic and related tissue — Tumeurs malignes primitives ou présumées primitives des tissus lymphoïde, hématopoïétique et apparentés	**1 010**	**19.5**	**888**	**16.5**	**1 076**	**20.7**	**890**	**16.5**
Disorders of the blood and blood-forming organs and certain disorders involving the immune mechanism — Maladies du sang et des organes hématopoïétiques et certains troubles du système immunitaire								
Total	**93**	**1.8**	**135**	**2.5**	**100**	**1.9**	**119**	**2.2**
Anaemias — Anémies	**32**	**0.6**	**61**	**1.1**	**23**	**♦0.4**	**41**	**0.8**
Endocrine, nutritional and metabolic diseases — Maladies endocriniennes, nutritionnelles et métaboliques								
Total	**1 995**	**38.5**	**2 526**	**47.1**	**2 025**	**38.9**	**2 472**	**46.0**
Diabetes mellitus — Diabète sucré	**1 701**	**32.8**	**2 065**	**38.5**	**1 724**	**33.1**	**2 001**	**37.2**
Malnutrition — Malnutrition	**75**	**1.4**	**132**	**2.5**	**91**	**1.7**	**143**	**2.7**
Mental and behavioural disorders — Troubles mentaux et du comportement	**591**	**11.4**	**819**	**15.3**	**686**	**13.2**	**1 047**	**19.5**
Diseases of the nervous system — Maladies du système nerveux	**1 432**	**27.6**	**1 724**	**32.1**	**1 408**	**27.1**	**1 861**	**34.6**
Diseases of the circulatory system — Maladies de l'appareil circulatoire								
Total	**22 257**	**429.1**	**25 354**	**472.4**	**22 840**	**439.2**	**26 506**	**492.8**
Acute rheumatic fever and chronic rheumatic heart diseases — Rhumatisme articularie aigu et cardiopathies rhumatismales chroniques	**113**	**2.2**	**174**	**3.2**	**99**	**1.9**	**172**	**3.2**
Hypertensive diseases — Maladies hypertensives	**1 178**	**22.7**	**1 779**	**33.1**	**1 321**	**25.4**	**2 019**	**37.5**
Ischaemic heart disease — Cardiopathie ischémique	**11 787**	**227.3**	**11 961**	**222.8**	**11 882**	**228.5**	**12 505**	**232.5**
Cerebrovascular disease — Maladie cérébrovasculaire	**3 707**	**71.5**	**5 088**	**94.8**	**3 633**	**69.9**	**4 871**	**90.6**

20. Death and death rates by cause and sex: 2014 - 2018
Décès et taux de mortalité par cause et sexe : 2014 - 2018 (continued - suite)

Czechia - Tchéquie

Cause of death — Cause de décès	2016 (C)				2017 (C)			
	Male — Masculin		Female — Féminin		Male — Masculin		Female — Féminin	
	Number Nombre	Rate Taux	Number Nombre	Rate Taux	Number Nombre	Rate Taux	Number Nombre	Rate Taux
Diseases of arteries, arterioles and capillaries — Maladies des artères, artérioles et capillaires	1 086	20.9	1 226	22.8	1 075	20.7	1 183	22.0
Diseases of the respiratory system — Maladies de l'appareil respiratoire								
Total	3 984	76.8	3 144	58.6	4 392	84.5	3 675	68.3
Influenza — Grippe	64	1.2	47	0.9	80	1.5	73	1.4
Pneumonia — Pneumopathies	1 455	28.1	1 323	24.6	1 675	32.2	1 599	29.7
Chronic lower respiratory diseases — Maladies chroniques des voies respiratoires inférieures	1 956	37.7	1 358	25.3	2 132	41.0	1 482	27.6
Diseases of the digestive system — Maladies de l'appareil digestif								
Total	2 552	49.2	1 960	36.5	2 734	52.6	2 035	37.8
Gastric and duodenal ulcer — Ulcère de l'estomac et du duodénum	240	4.6	181	3.4	224	4.3	179	3.3
Diseases of the liver — Maladies du foie	1 392	26.8	719	13.4	1 559	30.0	763	14.2
Diseases of the musculoskeletal system and connective tissue — Maladies du système ostéo-articularie, des muscles et du tissu conjonctif	86	1.7	107	2.0	82	1.6	145	2.7
Diseases of the genitourinary system — Maladies de l'appareil génito-urinaire								
Total	684	13.2	852	15.9	750	14.4	855	15.9
Disorders of kidney and ureter — Affections du rein et de l'uretère	508	9.8	578	10.8	539	10.4	641	11.9
Hyperplasia of prostate — Hyperplasie de la prostate	21	♦1.2	..	..	21	♦1.1	..	..
Pregnancy, childbirth and the puerperium — Grossesse, accouchement et puerpéralité								
Total	..	..	1	♦0.9	..	..	2	♦1.7
Pregnancy with abortive outcome — Grossesse se terminant par un avortement	..	..	-	-	..	..	-	-
Other direct obstetric causes — Autres décès maternels directs	..	..	1	♦0.9	..	..	2	♦1.7
Indirect obstetric causes — Décès maternels indirects	..	..	-	-	..	..	-	-
Certain conditions originating in the perinatal period — Certaines affections dont l'origine se situe dans la période périnatale	118	204.0	76	138.6	103	175.6	74	132.8
Congenital malformations, deformations and chromosomal abnormalities — Malformations congénitales et anomalies chromosomiques	87	150.4	78	142.3	90	153.4	72	129.2
Symptoms, signs and abnormal clinical and laboratory findings, not elsewhere classified — Symptômes, signes et résultats anormaux d'examens cliniques et de laboratoire, non classés ailleurs	908	17.5	664	12.4	899	17.3	725	13.5
All other diseases — Toutes autres maladies	61	1.2	111	2.1	92	1.8	126	2.3
External causes — Causes externes								
Total	3 667	70.7	1 844	34.4	3 809	73.2	1 799	33.5
Accidents								
Total	2 260	43.6	1 371	25.5	2 358	45.3	1 305	24.3
Transport accidents — Accidents de transport	536	10.3	179	3.3	515	9.9	174	3.2
Falls — Chutes	359	6.9	203	3.8	406	7.8	196	3.6
Accidental drowning and submersion — Noyade et submersion accidentelles	114	2.2	29	♦0.5	106	2.0	34	0.6
Exposure to smoke, fire and flames — Exposition à la fumée, au feu et aux flammes	31	0.6	22	♦0.4	27	♦0.5	7	♦0.1
Accidental poisoning by and exposure to noxious substances — Intoxication accidentelle par des substances nocives et exposition à ces substances	324	6.2	140	2.6	347	6.7	117	2.2
Intentional self-harm — Lésions auto-infligées	1 059	20.4	257	4.8	1 106	21.3	289	5.4
Assault — Agresssions	27	♦0.5	26	♦0.5	35	0.7	30	♦0.6
All other external causes — Toutes autres causes externes	321	6.2	190	3.5	310	6.0	175	3.3

20. Death and death rates by cause and sex: 2014 - 2018
Décès et taux de mortalité par cause et sexe : 2014 - 2018 (continued - suite)

Denmark - Danemark

Cause of death — Cause de décès	2014 (C)				2015 (C)			
	Male — Masculin		Female — Féminin		Male — Masculin		Female — Féminin	
	Number Nombre	Rate Taux	Number Nombre	Rate Taux	Number Nombre	Rate Taux	Number Nombre	Rate Taux
TOTAL	**25 458**	**909.2**	**25 535**	**899.2**	**26 047**	**922.8**	**26 177**	**916.6**
Certain infectious and parasitic diseases — Certaines maladies infectieuses et parasitaires								
Total	381	13.6	501	17.6	408	14.5	528	18.5
Intestinal infectious diseases — Maladies infectieuses intestinales	72	2.6	131	4.6	53	1.9	112	3.9
Tuberculosis — Tuberculose	9	♦0.3	3	♦0.1	10	♦0.4	6	♦0.2
Tetanus — Tétanos	-	-	-	-	-	-	-	-
Diphtheria — Diphtérie	-	-	-	-	-	-	-	-
Whooping cough — Coqueluche	-	-	-	-	-	-	-	-
Meningococcal infection — Infection à méningocoques	1	♦0.0	2	♦0.1	-	-	1	♦0.0
Septicaemia — Septicémie	148	5.3	183	6.4	178	6.3	244	8.5
Acute poliomyelitis — Poliomyélite aiguë	2	♦0.1	1	♦0.0	-	-	-	-
Measles — Rougeole	-	-	-	-	2	♦0.1	-	-
Viral hepatitis — Hépatite virale	17	♦0.6	11	♦0.4	11	♦0.4	7	♦0.2
Human immunodeficiency virus [HIV] disease — Maladies dues au virus de l'immunodéficience humaine (VIH)	11	♦0.4	5	♦0.2	9	♦0.3	4	♦0.1
Malaria — Paludisme	-	-	-	-	-	-	1	♦0.0
Neoplasms — Tumeurs	8 205	293.0	7 405	260.8	8 284	293.5	7 430	260.2
Malignant neoplasms — Tumeurs malignes								
Total	8 050	287.5	7 254	255.4	8 125	287.9	7 275	254.7
Malignant neoplasm of lip, oral cavity and pharynx — Tumeur maligne de la lèvre, de la cavité buccale et du pharynx	252	9.0	96	3.4	241	8.5	99	3.5
Malignant neoplasm of oesophagus — Tumeur maligne de l'oesophage	292	10.4	105	3.7	299	10.6	97	3.4
Malignant neoplasm of stomach — Tumeur maligne de l'estomac	247	8.8	168	5.9	246	8.7	131	4.6
Malignant neoplasm of colon, rectosigmoid junction, rectum, anus and anal canal — Tumeur maligne du côlon, de la jonction recto-sigmoïdienne, du rectum, de l'anus et du canal anal	950	33.9	800	28.2	960	34.0	876	30.7
Malignant neoplasm of liver and intrahepatic bile ducts — Tumeur maligne du foie et des voies bilaires intrahépatiques	310	11.1	152	5.4	276	9.8	164	5.7
Malignant neoplasm of pancreas — Tumeur maligne du pancréas	455	16.3	512	18.0	481	17.0	480	16.8
Malignant neoplasm of trachea, bronchus and lung — Tumeur maligne de la trachée, des bronches et du poumon	1 970	70.4	1 746	61.5	1 894	67.1	1 788	62.6
Malignant neoplasm of female breast — Tumeur maligne du sein chez la femme	..	..	1 115	47.1	..	..	1 069	44.8
Malignant neoplasm of cervix uteri — Tumeur maligne du col de l'utérus	..	..	97	4.1	..	..	97	4.1
Malignant neoplasm of prostate — Tumeur maligne de la prostate	1 142	112.7	..	..	1 170	113.4	..	..
Malignant neoplasm of lymphoid, haematopoietic and related tissue — Tumeurs malignes primitives ou présumées primitives des tissus lymphoïde, hématopoïétique et apparentés	590	21.1	442	15.6	623	22.1	472	16.5
Disorders of the blood and blood-forming organs and certain disorders involving the immune mechanism — Maladies du sang et des organes hématopoïétiques et certains troubles du système immunitaire								
Total	109	3.9	109	3.8	109	3.9	142	5.0
Anaemias — Anémies	65	2.3	77	2.7	64	2.3	109	3.8
Endocrine, nutritional and metabolic diseases — Maladies endocriniennes, nutritionnelles et métaboliques								
Total	904	32.3	789	27.8	887	31.4	841	29.4
Diabetes mellitus — Diabète sucré	746	26.6	547	19.3	741	26.3	611	21.4
Malnutrition — Malnutrition	4	♦0.1	3	♦0.1	4	♦0.1	7	♦0.2
Mental and behavioural disorders — Troubles mentaux et du comportement	1 327	47.4	1 788	63.0	1 515	53.7	1 920	67.2
Diseases of the nervous system — Maladies du système nerveux	924	33.0	1 119	39.4	1 019	36.1	1 237	43.3
Diseases of the circulatory system — Maladies de l'appareil circulatoire								
Total	6 109	218.2	6 000	211.3	6 289	222.8	6 215	217.6
Acute rheumatic fever and chronic rheumatic heart diseases — Rhumatisme articularie aigu et cardiopathies rhumatismales chroniques	35	1.3	49	1.7	32	1.1	42	1.5
Hypertensive diseases — Maladies hypertensives	355	12.7	481	16.9	426	15.1	536	18.8
Ischaemic heart disease — Cardiopathie ischémique	2 201	78.6	1 632	57.5	2 174	77.0	1 605	56.2
Cerebrovascular disease — Maladie cérébrovasculaire	1 434	51.2	1 832	64.5	1 500	53.1	1 890	66.2

20. Death and death rates by cause and sex: 2014 - 2018
Décès et taux de mortalité par cause et sexe : 2014 - 2018 (continued - suite)

Denmark - Danemark

Cause of death — Cause de décès	2014 (C)				2015 (C)			
	Male — Masculin		Female — Féminin		Male — Masculin		Female — Féminin	
	Number Nombre	Rate Taux	Number Nombre	Rate Taux	Number Nombre	Rate Taux	Number Nombre	Rate Taux
Diseases of arteries, arterioles and capillaries — Maladies des artères, artérioles et capillaires	460	16.4	393	13.8	473	16.8	412	14.4
Diseases of the respiratory system — Maladies de l'appareil respiratoire								
Total	2 641	94.3	2 881	101.4	2 813	99.7	3 032	106.2
Influenza — Grippe	6	♦0.2	7	♦0.2	13	♦0.5	8	♦0.3
Pneumonia — Pneumopathies	748	26.7	808	28.5	830	29.4	915	32.0
Chronic lower respiratory diseases — Maladies chroniques des voies respiratoires inférieures	1 558	55.6	1 805	63.6	1 663	58.9	1 839	64.4
Diseases of the digestive system — Maladies de l'appareil digestif								
Total	1 107	39.5	1 062	37.4	1 098	38.9	976	34.2
Gastric and duodenal ulcer — Ulcère de l'estomac et du duodénum	82	2.9	135	4.8	111	3.9	122	4.3
Diseases of the liver — Maladies du foie	520	18.6	269	9.5	496	17.6	220	7.7
Diseases of the musculoskeletal system and connective tissue — Maladies du système ostéo-articularie, des muscles et du tissu conjonctif	120	4.3	241	8.5	124	4.4	239	8.4
Diseases of the genitourinary system — Maladies de l'appareil génito-urinaire								
Total	390	13.9	398	14.0	396	14.0	399	14.0
Disorders of kidney and ureter — Affections du rein et de l'uretère	244	8.7	219	7.7	243	8.6	225	7.9
Hyperplasia of prostate — Hyperplasie de la prostate	23	♦2.3	..	..	23	♦2.2	..	..
Pregnancy, childbirth and the puerperium — Grossesse, accouchement et puerpéralité								
Total	..	..	3	♦5.3	..	..	-	-
Pregnancy with abortive outcome — Grossesse se terminant par un avortement	..	..	1	♦1.8	..	..	-	-
Other direct obstetric causes — Autres décès maternels directs	..	..	2	♦3.5	..	..	-	-
Indirect obstetric causes — Décès maternels indirects	..	..	-	-	..	..	-	-
Certain conditions originating in the perinatal period — Certaines affections dont l'origine se situe dans la période périnatale	66	225.6	49	177.4	63	211.1	55	194.0
Congenital malformations, deformations and chromosomal abnormalities — Malformations congénitales et anomalies chromosomiques	85	290.6	67	242.6	67	224.5	63	222.2
Symptoms, signs and abnormal clinical and laboratory findings, not elsewhere classified — Symptômes, signes et résultats anormaux d'examens cliniques et de laboratoire, non classés ailleurs	1 809	64.6	2 312	81.4	1 789	63.4	2 305	80.7
All other diseases — Toutes autres maladies	22	♦0.8	31	1.1	27	♦1.0	34	1.2
External causes — Causes externes								
Total	1 259	45.0	780	27.5	1 159	41.1	761	26.6
Accidents								
Total	731	26.1	577	20.3	702	24.9	551	19.3
Transport accidents — Accidents de transport	163	5.8	47	1.7	152	5.4	56	2.0
Falls — Chutes	227	8.1	268	9.4	207	7.3	256	9.0
Accidental drowning and submersion — Noyade et submersion accidentelles	32	1.1	2	♦0.1	19	♦0.7	6	♦0.2
Exposure to smoke, fire and flames — Exposition à la fumée, au feu et aux flammes	39	1.4	18	♦0.6	43	1.5	15	♦0.5
Accidental poisoning by and exposure to noxious substances — Intoxication accidentelle par des substances nocives et exposition à ces substances	134	4.8	59	2.1	122	4.3	51	1.8
Intentional self-harm — Lésions auto-infligées	469	16.8	160	5.6	390	13.8	174	6.1
Assault — Agresssions	19	♦0.7	19	♦0.7	21	♦0.7	12	♦0.4
All other external causes — Toutes autres causes externes	40	1.4	24	♦0.8	46	1.6	24	♦0.8

20. Death and death rates by cause and sex: 2014 - 2018
Décès et taux de mortalité par cause et sexe : 2014 - 2018 (continued - suite)

Estonia - Estonie

Cause of death — Cause de décès	2017 (C)				2018 (C)			
	Male — Masculin		Female — Féminin		Male — Masculin		Female — Féminin	
	Number Nombre	Rate Taux	Number Nombre	Rate Taux	Number Nombre	Rate Taux	Number Nombre	Rate Taux
TOTAL	**7 295**	**1 181.3**	**8 147**	**1 167.0**	**7 352**	**1 183.7**	**8 254**	**1 182.4**
Certain infectious and parasitic diseases — Certaines maladies infectieuses et parasitaires								
Total	72	11.7	80	11.5	81	13.0	71	10.2
Intestinal infectious diseases — Maladies infectieuses intestinales	-	-	5	♦0.7	2	♦0.3	6	♦0.9
Tuberculosis — Tuberculose	12	♦1.9	5	♦0.7	5	♦0.8	-	-
Tetanus — Tétanos	-	-	-	-	-	-	-	-
Diphtheria — Diphtérie	-	-	-	-	-	-	-	-
Whooping cough — Coqueluche	-	-	-	-	-	-	-	-
Meningococcal infection — Infection à méningocoques	-	-	1	♦0.1	-	-	-	-
Septicaemia — Septicémie	11	♦1.8	29	♦4.2	13	♦2.1	19	♦2.7
Acute poliomyelitis — Poliomyélite aiguë	-	-	-	-	-	-	-	-
Measles — Rougeole	-	-	-	-	-	-	-	-
Viral hepatitis — Hépatite virale	4	♦0.6	5	♦0.7	5	♦0.8	7	♦1.0
Human immunodeficiency virus [HIV] disease — Maladies dues au virus de l'immunodéficience humaine (VIH)	27	♦4.4	15	♦2.1	35	5.6	13	♦1.9
Malaria — Paludisme	-	-	-	-	-	-	-	-
Neoplasms — Tumeurs	**2 067**	**334.7**	**1 841**	**263.7**	**2 141**	**344.7**	**1 872**	**268.2**
Malignant neoplasms — Tumeurs malignes								
Total	2 029	328.6	1 787	256.0	2 100	338.1	1 800	257.9
Malignant neoplasm of lip, oral cavity and pharynx — Tumeur maligne de la lèvre, de la cavité buccale et du pharynx	70	11.3	26	♦3.7	93	15.0	18	♦2.6
Malignant neoplasm of oesophagus — Tumeur maligne de l'oesophage	56	9.1	16	♦2.3	61	9.8	9	♦1.3
Malignant neoplasm of stomach — Tumeur maligne de l'estomac	141	22.8	126	18.0	140	22.5	153	21.9
Malignant neoplasm of colon, rectosigmoid junction, rectum, anus and anal canal — Tumeur maligne du côlon, de la jonction recto-sigmoïdienne, du rectum, de l'anus et du canal anal	257	41.6	247	35.4	224	36.1	273	39.1
Malignant neoplasm of liver and intrahepatic bile ducts — Tumeur maligne du foie et des voies bilaires intrahépatiques	71	11.5	50	7.2	74	11.9	50	7.2
Malignant neoplasm of pancreas — Tumeur maligne du pancréas	93	15.1	131	18.8	140	22.5	156	22.3
Malignant neoplasm of trachea, bronchus and lung — Tumeur maligne de la trachée, des bronches et du poumon	474	76.8	165	23.6	505	81.3	166	23.8
Malignant neoplasm of female breast — Tumeur maligne du sein chez la femme	..	..	263	44.3	..	..	260	43.8
Malignant neoplasm of cervix uteri — Tumeur maligne du col de l'utérus	..	..	70	11.8	..	..	54	9.1
Malignant neoplasm of prostate — Tumeur maligne de la prostate	277	134.7	..	..	289	139.2	..	..
Malignant neoplasm of lymphoid, haematopoietic and related tissue — Tumeurs malignes primitives ou présumées primitives des tissus lymphoïde, hématopoïétique et apparentés	157	25.4	164	23.5	159	25.6	132	18.9
Disorders of the blood and blood-forming organs and certain disorders involving the immune mechanism — Maladies du sang et des organes hématopoïétiques et certains troubles du système immunitaire								
Total	13	♦2.1	20	♦2.9	11	♦1.8	17	♦2.4
Anaemias — Anémies	6	♦1.0	7	♦1.0	3	♦0.5	9	♦1.3
Endocrine, nutritional and metabolic diseases — Maladies endocriniennes, nutritionnelles et métaboliques								
Total	102	16.5	123	17.6	96	15.5	148	21.2
Diabetes mellitus — Diabète sucré	88	14.3	112	16.0	91	14.7	139	19.9
Malnutrition — Malnutrition	1	♦0.2	1	♦0.1	2	♦0.3	1	♦0.1
Mental and behavioural disorders — Troubles mentaux et du comportement	82	13.3	68	9.7	80	12.9	62	8.9
Diseases of the nervous system — Maladies du système nerveux	166	26.9	164	23.5	178	28.7	192	27.5
Diseases of the circulatory system — Maladies de l'appareil circulatoire								
Total	3 198	517.9	4 805	688.3	3 150	507.2	4 803	688.1
Acute rheumatic fever and chronic rheumatic heart diseases — Rhumatisme articularie aigu et cardiopathies rhumatismales chroniques	5	♦0.8	26	♦3.7	4	♦0.6	14	♦2.0
Hypertensive diseases — Maladies hypertensives	896	145.1	1 902	272.5	884	142.3	1 928	276.2
Ischaemic heart disease — Cardiopathie ischémique	1 339	216.8	1 682	240.9	1 312	211.2	1 605	229.9
Cerebrovascular disease — Maladie cérébrovasculaire	373	60.4	522	74.8	354	57.0	531	76.1

20. Death and death rates by cause and sex: 2014 - 2018
Décès et taux de mortalité par cause et sexe : 2014 - 2018 (continued - suite)

Estonia - Estonie

Cause of death — Cause de décès	2017 (C)				2018 (C)			
	Male — Masculin		Female — Féminin		Male — Masculin		Female — Féminin	
	Number Nombre	Rate Taux	Number Nombre	Rate Taux	Number Nombre	Rate Taux	Number Nombre	Rate Taux
Diseases of arteries, arterioles and capillaries — Maladies des artères, artérioles et capillaires	88	14.3	96	13.8	96	15.5	92	13.2
Diseases of the respiratory system — Maladies de l'appareil respiratoire								
Total	327	53.0	231	33.1	370	59.6	282	40.4
Influenza — Grippe	22	♦3.6	29	♦4.2	43	6.9	61	8.7
Pneumonia — Pneumopathies	137	22.2	105	15.0	127	20.4	116	16.6
Chronic lower respiratory diseases — Maladies chroniques des voies respiratoires inférieures	146	23.6	80	11.5	163	26.2	82	11.7
Diseases of the digestive system — Maladies de l'appareil digestif								
Total	352	57.0	273	39.1	350	56.4	292	41.8
Gastric and duodenal ulcer — Ulcère de l'estomac et du duodénum	33	5.3	29	♦4.2	26	♦4.2	34	4.9
Diseases of the liver — Maladies du foie	205	33.2	87	12.5	222	35.7	113	16.2
Diseases of the musculoskeletal system and connective tissue — Maladies du système ostéo-articularie, des muscles et du tissu conjonctif	21	♦3.4	40	5.7	24	♦3.9	49	7.0
Diseases of the genitourinary system — Maladies de l'appareil génito-urinaire								
Total	67	10.8	79	11.3	64	10.3	86	12.3
Disorders of kidney and ureter — Affections du rein et de l'uretère	48	7.8	57	8.2	46	7.4	53	7.6
Hyperplasia of prostate — Hyperplasie de la prostate	8	♦3.9	..	..	5	♦2.4	..	..
Pregnancy, childbirth and the puerperium — Grossesse, accouchement et puerpéralité								
Total	..	..	-	-	..	..	-	-
Pregnancy with abortive outcome — Grossesse se terminant par un avortement	..	..	-	-	..	..	-	-
Other direct obstetric causes — Autres décès maternels directs	..	..	-	-	..	..	-	-
Indirect obstetric causes — Décès maternels indirects	..	..	-	-	..	..	-	-
Certain conditions originating in the perinatal period — Certaines affections dont l'origine se situe dans la période périnatale	11	♦153.0	7	♦106.2	10	♦136.1	6	♦85.4
Congenital malformations, deformations and chromosomal abnormalities — Malformations congénitales et anomalies chromosomiques	16	♦222.5	18	♦273.0	22	♦299.5	18	♦256.3
Symptoms, signs and abnormal clinical and laboratory findings, not elsewhere classified — Symptômes, signes et résultats anormaux d'examens cliniques et de laboratoire, non classés ailleurs	149	24.1	185	26.5	153	24.6	142	20.3
All other diseases — Toutes autres maladies	4	♦0.6	12	♦1.7	7	♦1.1	7	♦1.0
External causes — Causes externes								
Total	648	104.9	201	28.8	615	99.0	207	29.7
Accidents								
Total	429	69.5	135	19.3	404	65.0	145	20.8
Transport accidents — Accidents de transport	46	7.4	17	♦2.4	60	9.7	23	♦3.3
Falls — Chutes	76	12.3	35	5.0	76	12.2	23	♦3.3
Accidental drowning and submersion — Noyade et submersion accidentelles	32	5.2	7	♦1.0	29	♦4.7	10	♦1.4
Exposure to smoke, fire and flames — Exposition à la fumée, au feu et aux flammes	31	5.0	13	♦1.9	35	5.6	14	♦2.0
Accidental poisoning by and exposure to noxious substances — Intoxication accidentelle par des substances nocives et exposition à ces substances	184	29.8	48	6.9	132	21.3	42	6.0
Intentional self-harm — Lésions auto-infligées	172	27.9	54	7.7	150	24.2	46	6.6
Assault — Agresssions	21	♦3.4	8	♦1.1	23	♦3.7	5	♦0.7
All other external causes — Toutes autres causes externes	26	♦4.2	4	♦0.6	38	6.1	11	♦1.6

Finland - Finlande

Cause of death — Cause de décès	2014 (C)				2015 (C)			
	Male — Masculin		Female — Féminin		Male — Masculin		Female — Féminin	
	Number Nombre	Rate Taux	Number Nombre	Rate Taux	Number Nombre	Rate Taux	Number Nombre	Rate Taux
TOTAL	**25 864**	**964.9**	**26 545**	**958.0**	**25 884**	**961.6**	**26 418**	**950.3**
Certain infectious and parasitic diseases — Certaines maladies infectieuses et parasitaires								
Total	**139**	**5.2**	**171**	**6.2**	**132**	**4.9**	**126**	**4.5**
Intestinal infectious diseases — Maladies infectieuses intestinales	**6**	**♦0.2**	**11**	**♦0.4**	**12**	**♦0.4**	**11**	**♦0.4**
Tuberculosis — Tuberculose	**12**	**♦0.4**	**8**	**♦0.3**	**10**	**♦0.4**	**8**	**♦0.3**
Tetanus — Tétanos	-	-	-	-	-	-	-	-
Diphtheria — Diphtérie	-	-	-	-	-	-	-	-
Whooping cough — Coqueluche	**1**	**♦0.0**	-	-	-	-	-	-
Meningococcal infection — Infection à méningocoques	**1**	**♦0.0**	**1**	**♦0.0**	-	-	**4**	**♦0.1**
Septicaemia — Septicémie	**63**	**2.4**	**83**	**3.0**	**68**	**2.5**	**53**	**1.9**
Acute poliomyelitis — Poliomyélite aiguë	-	-	-	-	-	-	-	-
Measles — Rougeole	-	-	-	-	-	-	-	-
Viral hepatitis — Hépatite virale	**4**	**♦0.1**	**5**	**♦0.2**	**4**	**♦0.1**	**2**	**♦0.1**
Human immunodeficiency virus [HIV] disease — Maladies dues au virus de l'immunodéficience humaine (VIH)	-	-	**3**	**♦0.1**	-	-	-	-
Malaria — Paludisme	-	-	-	-	**1**	**♦0.0**	-	-
Neoplasms — Tumeurs	**6 476**	**241.6**	**5 794**	**209.1**	**6 623**	**246.0**	**5 858**	**210.7**
Malignant neoplasms — Tumeurs malignes								
Total	**6 318**	**235.7**	**5 602**	**202.2**	**6 481**	**240.8**	**5 687**	**204.6**
Malignant neoplasm of lip, oral cavity and pharynx — Tumeur maligne de la lèvre, de la cavité buccale et du pharynx	**143**	**5.3**	**74**	**2.7**	**134**	**5.0**	**98**	**3.5**
Malignant neoplasm of oesophagus — Tumeur maligne de l'oesophage	**185**	**6.9**	**89**	**3.2**	**168**	**6.2**	**65**	**2.3**
Malignant neoplasm of stomach — Tumeur maligne de l'estomac	**244**	**9.1**	**169**	**6.1**	**249**	**9.3**	**192**	**6.9**
Malignant neoplasm of colon, rectosigmoid junction, rectum, anus and anal canal — Tumeur maligne du côlon, de la jonction recto-sigmoïdienne, du rectum, de l'anus et du canal anal	**646**	**24.1**	**583**	**21.0**	**654**	**24.3**	**557**	**20.0**
Malignant neoplasm of liver and intrahepatic bile ducts — Tumeur maligne du foie et des voies bilaires intrahépatiques	**303**	**11.3**	**186**	**6.7**	**321**	**11.9**	**188**	**6.8**
Malignant neoplasm of pancreas — Tumeur maligne du pancréas	**535**	**20.0**	**545**	**19.7**	**540**	**20.1**	**597**	**21.5**
Malignant neoplasm of trachea, bronchus and lung — Tumeur maligne de la trachée, des bronches et du poumon	**1 381**	**51.5**	**771**	**27.8**	**1 458**	**54.2**	**776**	**27.9**
Malignant neoplasm of female breast — Tumeur maligne du sein chez la femme	..	..	**813**	**34.8**	..	..	**816**	**34.8**
Malignant neoplasm of cervix uteri — Tumeur maligne du col de l'utérus	..	..	**53**	**2.3**	..	..	**63**	**2.7**
Malignant neoplasm of prostate — Tumeur maligne de la prostate	**859**	**84.9**	..	..	**898**	**87.6**	..	..
Malignant neoplasm of lymphoid, haematopoietic and related tissue — Tumeurs malignes primitives ou présumées primitives des tissus lymphoïde, hématopoïétique et apparentés	**604**	**22.5**	**578**	**20.9**	**636**	**23.6**	**529**	**19.0**
Disorders of the blood and blood-forming organs and certain disorders involving the immune mechanism — Maladies du sang et des organes hématopoïétiques et certains troubles du système immunitaire								
Total	**35**	**1.3**	**29**	**♦1.0**	**34**	**1.3**	**52**	**1.9**
Anaemias — Anémies	**13**	**♦0.5**	**12**	**♦0.4**	**14**	**♦0.5**	**12**	**♦0.4**
Endocrine, nutritional and metabolic diseases — Maladies endocriniennes, nutritionnelles et métaboliques								
Total	**352**	**13.1**	**327**	**11.8**	**326**	**12.1**	**311**	**11.2**
Diabetes mellitus — Diabète sucré	**270**	**10.1**	**228**	**8.2**	**251**	**9.3**	**232**	**8.3**
Malnutrition — Malnutrition	**1**	**♦0.0**	-	-	**3**	**♦0.1**	**7**	**♦0.3**
Mental and behavioural disorders — Troubles mentaux et du comportement	**853**	**31.8**	**1 472**	**53.1**	**841**	**31.2**	**1 512**	**54.4**
Diseases of the nervous system — Maladies du système nerveux	**2 805**	**104.6**	**5 111**	**184.5**	**3 036**	**112.8**	**5 263**	**189.3**
Diseases of the circulatory system — Maladies de l'appareil circulatoire								
Total	**9 496**	**354.3**	**10 147**	**366.2**	**9 528**	**354.0**	**9 907**	**356.4**
Acute rheumatic fever and chronic rheumatic heart diseases — Rhumatisme articularie aigu et cardiopathies rhumatismales chroniques	**8**	**♦0.3**	**17**	**♦0.6**	**10**	**♦0.4**	**27**	**♦1.0**
Hypertensive diseases — Maladies hypertensives	**518**	**19.3**	**1 061**	**38.3**	**613**	**22.8**	**1 150**	**41.4**
Ischaemic heart disease — Cardiopathie ischémique	**5 532**	**206.4**	**4 805**	**173.4**	**5 549**	**206.1**	**4 660**	**167.6**
Cerebrovascular disease — Maladie cérébrovasculaire	**1 786**	**66.6**	**2 642**	**95.3**	**1 800**	**66.9**	**2 499**	**89.9**

20. Death and death rates by cause and sex: 2014 - 2018
Décès et taux de mortalité par cause et sexe : 2014 - 2018 (continued - suite)

Finland - Finlande

Cause of death — Cause de décès	2014 (C)				2015 (C)			
	Male — Masculin		Female — Féminin		Male — Masculin		Female — Féminin	
	Number Nombre	Rate Taux	Number Nombre	Rate Taux	Number Nombre	Rate Taux	Number Nombre	Rate Taux
Diseases of arteries, arterioles and capillaries — Maladies des artères, artérioles et capillaires	**550**	**20.5**	**472**	**17.0**	**494**	**18.4**	**495**	**17.8**
Diseases of the respiratory system — Maladies de l'appareil respiratoire								
Total	**1 149**	**42.9**	**688**	**24.8**	**1 158**	**43.0**	**782**	**28.1**
Influenza — Grippe	**9**	**♦0.3**	**17**	**♦0.6**	**52**	**1.9**	**66**	**2.4**
Pneumonia — Pneumopathies	**99**	**3.7**	**81**	**2.9**	**63**	**2.3**	**80**	**2.9**
Chronic lower respiratory diseases — Maladies chroniques des voies respiratoires inférieures	**813**	**30.3**	**443**	**16.0**	**819**	**30.4**	**490**	**17.6**
Diseases of the digestive system — Maladies de l'appareil digestif								
Total	**1 478**	**55.1**	**951**	**34.3**	**1 331**	**49.4**	**895**	**32.2**
Gastric and duodenal ulcer — Ulcère de l'estomac et du duodénum	**94**	**3.5**	**51**	**1.8**	**91**	**3.4**	**54**	**1.9**
Diseases of the liver — Maladies du foie	**904**	**33.7**	**335**	**12.1**	**787**	**29.2**	**331**	**11.9**
Diseases of the musculoskeletal system and connective tissue — Maladies du système ostéo-articularie, des muscles et du tissu conjonctif	**72**	**2.7**	**133**	**4.8**	**65**	**2.4**	**145**	**5.2**
Diseases of the genitourinary system — Maladies de l'appareil génito-urinaire								
Total	**141**	**5.3**	**174**	**6.3**	**132**	**4.9**	**150**	**5.4**
Disorders of kidney and ureter — Affections du rein et de l'uretère	**124**	**4.6**	**149**	**5.4**	**108**	**4.0**	**133**	**4.8**
Hyperplasia of prostate — Hyperplasie de la prostate	**9**	**♦0.9**	..	..	**9**	**♦0.9**	..	..
Pregnancy, childbirth and the puerperium — Grossesse, accouchement et puerpéralité								
Total	..	..	**3**	**♦5.3**	..	..	**2**	**♦3.6**
Pregnancy with abortive outcome — Grossesse se terminant par un avortement	..	..	**-**	**-**	..	..	**-**	**-**
Other direct obstetric causes — Autres décès maternels directs	..	..	**2**	**♦3.5**	..	..	**2**	**♦3.6**
Indirect obstetric causes — Décès maternels indirects	..	..	**1**	**♦1.8**	..	..	**-**	**-**
Certain conditions originating in the perinatal period — Certaines affections dont l'origine se situe dans la période périnatale	**20**	**♦68.7**	**26**	**♦93.4**	**24**	**♦84.7**	**29**	**♦107.9**
Congenital malformations, deformations and chromosomal abnormalities — Malformations congénitales et anomalies chromosomiques	**87**	**298.7**	**90**	**323.4**	**87**	**307.1**	**75**	**279.1**
Symptoms, signs and abnormal clinical and laboratory findings, not elsewhere classified — Symptômes, signes et résultats anormaux d'examens cliniques et de laboratoire, non classés ailleurs	**426**	**15.9**	**259**	**9.3**	**333**	**12.4**	**218**	**7.8**
All other diseases — Toutes autres maladies	**17**	**♦0.6**	**11**	**♦0.4**	**14**	**♦0.5**	**16**	**♦0.6**
External causes — Causes externes								
Total	**2 318**	**86.5**	**1 159**	**41.8**	**2 220**	**82.5**	**1 077**	**38.7**
Accidents								
Total	**1 525**	**56.9**	**874**	**31.5**	**1 484**	**55.1**	**845**	**30.4**
Transport accidents — Accidents de transport	**232**	**8.7**	**69**	**2.5**	**222**	**8.2**	**74**	**2.7**
Falls — Chutes	**587**	**21.9**	**554**	**20.0**	**605**	**22.5**	**538**	**19.4**
Accidental drowning and submersion — Noyade et submersion accidentelles	**87**	**3.2**	**28**	**♦1.0**	**92**	**3.4**	**19**	**♦0.7**
Exposure to smoke, fire and flames — Exposition à la fumée, au feu et aux flammes	**50**	**1.9**	**20**	**♦0.7**	**44**	**1.6**	**17**	**♦0.6**
Accidental poisoning by and exposure to noxious substances — Intoxication accidentelle par des substances nocives et exposition à ces substances	**383**	**14.3**	**110**	**4.0**	**361**	**13.4**	**120**	**4.3**
Intentional self-harm — Lésions auto-infligées	**595**	**22.2**	**188**	**6.8**	**556**	**20.7**	**173**	**6.2**
Assault — Agresssions	**48**	**1.8**	**27**	**♦1.0**	**52**	**1.9**	**16**	**♦0.6**
All other external causes — Toutes autres causes externes	**150**	**5.6**	**70**	**2.5**	**128**	**4.8**	**43**	**1.5**

France

Cause of death — Cause de décès	2015 (C)				2016 (C)			
	Male — Masculin		Female — Féminin		Male — Masculin		Female — Féminin	
	Number Nombre	Rate Taux	Number Nombre	Rate Taux	Number Nombre	Rate Taux	Number Nombre	Rate Taux
TOTAL	**289 378**	**928.0**	**290 513**	**875.0**	**289 065**	**923.2**	**290 423**	**872.3**
Certain infectious and parasitic diseases — Certaines maladies infectieuses et parasitaires								
Total	5 217	16.7	5 713	17.2	4 825	15.4	5 356	16.1
Intestinal infectious diseases — Maladies infectieuses intestinales	692	2.2	1 032	3.1	692	2.2	1 116	3.4
Tuberculosis — Tuberculose	133	0.4	90	0.3	121	0.4	97	0.3
Tetanus — Tétanos	1	♦0.0	1	♦0.0	-	-	2	♦0.0
Diphtheria — Diphtérie	-	-	-	-	-	-	-	-
Whooping cough — Coqueluche	2	♦0.0	2	♦0.0	-	-	2	♦0.0
Meningococcal infection — Infection à méningocoques	12	♦0.0	8	♦0.0	14	♦0.0	6	♦0.0
Septicaemia — Septicémie	2 765	8.9	2 936	8.8	2 343	7.5	2 416	7.3
Acute poliomyelitis — Poliomyélite aiguë	-	-	-	-	-	-	-	-
Measles — Rougeole	-	-	-	-	-	-	-	-
Viral hepatitis — Hépatite virale	312	1.0	268	0.8	296	0.9	269	0.8
Human immunodeficiency virus [HIV] disease — Maladies dues au virus de l'immunodéficience humaine (VIH)	278	0.9	81	0.2	238	0.8	67	0.2
Malaria — Paludisme	12	♦0.0	4	♦0.0	9	♦0.0	3	♦0.0
Neoplasms — Tumeurs	**94 968**	**304.6**	**71 278**	**214.7**	**95 354**	**304.5**	**72 764**	**218.6**
Malignant neoplasms — Tumeurs malignes								
Total	91 279	292.7	67 648	203.7	91 635	292.7	69 091	207.5
Malignant neoplasm of lip, oral cavity and pharynx — Tumeur maligne de la lèvre, de la cavité buccale et du pharynx	2 944	9.4	909	2.7	2 936	9.4	904	2.7
Malignant neoplasm of oesophagus — Tumeur maligne de l'oesophage	2 961	9.5	865	2.6	2 948	9.4	883	2.7
Malignant neoplasm of stomach — Tumeur maligne de l'estomac	2 816	9.0	1 536	4.6	2 880	9.2	1 526	4.6
Malignant neoplasm of colon, rectosigmoid junction, rectum, anus and anal canal — Tumeur maligne du côlon, de la jonction recto-sigmoïdienne, du rectum, de l'anus et du canal anal	9 267	29.7	8 074	24.3	9 354	29.9	8 366	25.1
Malignant neoplasm of liver and intrahepatic bile ducts — Tumeur maligne du foie et des voies bilaires intrahépatiques	6 083	19.5	2 288	6.9	6 170	19.7	2 469	7.4
Malignant neoplasm of pancreas — Tumeur maligne du pancréas	5 417	17.4	5 339	16.1	5 501	17.6	5 593	16.8
Malignant neoplasm of trachea, bronchus and lung — Tumeur maligne de la trachée, des bronches et du poumon	22 728	72.9	9 055	27.3	22 322	71.3	9 211	27.7
Malignant neoplasm of female breast — Tumeur maligne du sein chez la femme	..	..	12 233	44.5	..	..	12 434	45.2
Malignant neoplasm of cervix uteri — Tumeur maligne du col de l'utérus	..	..	723	2.6	..	..	757	2.7
Malignant neoplasm of prostate — Tumeur maligne de la prostate	8 665	76.9	..	..	8 724	77.2	..	..
Malignant neoplasm of lymphoid, haematopoietic and related tissue — Tumeurs malignes primitives ou présumées primitives des tissus lymphoïde, hématopoïétique et apparentés	7 575	24.3	6 334	19.1	7 665	24.5	6 380	19.2
Disorders of the blood and blood-forming organs and certain disorders involving the immune mechanism — Maladies du sang et des organes hématopoïétiques et certains troubles du système immunitaire								
Total	916	2.9	1 220	3.7	986	3.1	1 253	3.8
Anaemias — Anémies	495	1.6	784	2.4	497	1.6	738	2.2
Endocrine, nutritional and metabolic diseases — Maladies endocriniennes, nutritionnelles et métaboliques								
Total	9 288	29.8	11 526	34.7	9 192	29.4	11 264	33.8
Diabetes mellitus — Diabète sucré	5 788	18.6	5 883	17.7	5 575	17.8	5 710	17.2
Malnutrition — Malnutrition	1 160	3.7	2 216	6.7	1 225	3.9	2 237	6.7
Mental and behavioural disorders — Troubles mentaux et du comportement	**10 139**	**32.5**	**14 932**	**45.0**	**10 050**	**32.1**	**15 565**	**46.8**
Diseases of the nervous system — Maladies du système nerveux	**14 384**	**46.1**	**22 941**	**69.1**	**14 853**	**47.4**	**23 243**	**69.8**
Diseases of the circulatory system — Maladies de l'appareil circulatoire								
Total	65 721	210.8	76 293	229.8	65 005	207.6	75 475	226.7
Acute rheumatic fever and chronic rheumatic heart diseases — Rhumatisme articularie aigu et cardiopathies rhumatismales chroniques	422	1.4	774	2.3	446	1.4	698	2.1
Hypertensive diseases — Maladies hypertensives	3 643	11.7	6 695	20.2	3 557	11.4	6 792	20.4
Ischaemic heart disease — Cardiopathie ischémique	19 802	63.5	13 621	41.0	19 351	61.8	13 119	39.4
Cerebrovascular disease — Maladie cérébrovasculaire	12 852	41.2	18 487	55.7	12 946	41.3	18 302	55.0

20. Death and death rates by cause and sex: 2014 - 2018
Décès et taux de mortalité par cause et sexe : 2014 - 2018 (continued - suite)

France

Cause of death — Cause de décès	2015 (C)				2016 (C)			
	Male — Masculin		Female — Féminin		Male — Masculin		Female — Féminin	
	Number Nombre	Rate Taux	Number Nombre	Rate Taux	Number Nombre	Rate Taux	Number Nombre	Rate Taux
Diseases of arteries, arterioles and capillaries — Maladies des artères, artérioles et capillaires	**4 314**	**13.8**	**3 410**	**10.3**	**4 275**	**13.7**	**3 656**	**11.0**
Diseases of the respiratory system — Maladies de l'appareil respiratoire								
Total	**20 925**	**67.1**	**21 147**	**63.7**	**20 365**	**65.0**	**20 162**	**60.6**
Influenza — Grippe	**611**	**2.0**	**1 017**	**3.1**	**351**	**1.1**	**395**	**1.2**
Pneumonia — Pneumopathies	**6 001**	**19.2**	**7 166**	**21.6**	**6 003**	**19.2**	**7 022**	**21.1**
Chronic lower respiratory diseases — Maladies chroniques des voies respiratoires inférieures	**6 652**	**21.3**	**4 809**	**14.5**	**6 454**	**20.6**	**4 705**	**14.1**
Diseases of the digestive system — Maladies de l'appareil digestif								
Total	**12 491**	**40.1**	**10 962**	**33.0**	**12 681**	**40.5**	**10 956**	**32.9**
Gastric and duodenal ulcer — Ulcère de l'estomac et du duodénum	**430**	**1.4**	**405**	**1.2**	**421**	**1.3**	**426**	**1.3**
Diseases of the liver — Maladies du foie	**5 510**	**17.7**	**2 408**	**7.3**	**5 375**	**17.2**	**2 353**	**7.1**
Diseases of the musculoskeletal system and connective tissue — Maladies du système ostéo-articularie, des muscles et du tissu conjonctif	**1 612**	**5.2**	**2 516**	**7.6**	**1 651**	**5.3**	**2 437**	**7.3**
Diseases of the genitourinary system — Maladies de l'appareil génito-urinaire								
Total	**4 815**	**15.4**	**5 040**	**15.2**	**4 781**	**15.3**	**5 125**	**15.4**
Disorders of kidney and ureter — Affections du rein et de l'uretère	**3 504**	**11.2**	**3 950**	**11.9**	**3 421**	**10.9**	**3 995**	**12.0**
Hyperplasia of prostate — Hyperplasie de la prostate	**71**	**0.6**	..	..	**46**	**0.4**	..	..
Pregnancy, childbirth and the puerperium — Grossesse, accouchement et puerpéralité								
Total	..	..	**34**	**4.5**	..	..	**33**	**4.4**
Pregnancy with abortive outcome — Grossesse se terminant par un avortement	..	..	**1**	**♦0.1**	..	..	**-**	**-**
Other direct obstetric causes — Autres décès maternels directs	..	..	**32**	**4.2**	..	..	**30**	**♦4.0**
Indirect obstetric causes — Décès maternels indirects	..	..	**1**	**♦0.1**	..	..	**3**	**♦0.4**
Certain conditions originating in the perinatal period — Certaines affections dont l'origine se situe dans la période périnatale	**825**	**212.0**	**619**	**166.7**	**769**	**201.7**	**590**	**162.4**
Congenital malformations, deformations and chromosomal abnormalities — Malformations congénitales et anomalies chromosomiques	**843**	**216.6**	**760**	**204.7**	**814**	**213.5**	**760**	**209.1**
Symptoms, signs and abnormal clinical and laboratory findings, not elsewhere classified — Symptômes, signes et résultats anormaux d'examens cliniques et de laboratoire, non classés ailleurs	**24 266**	**77.8**	**28 969**	**87.2**	**24 934**	**79.6**	**29 190**	**87.7**
All other diseases — Toutes autres maladies	**514**	**1.6**	**908**	**2.7**	**564**	**1.8**	**962**	**2.9**
External causes — Causes externes								
Total	**22 454**	**72.0**	**15 655**	**47.1**	**22 241**	**71.0**	**15 288**	**45.9**
Accidents								
Total	**14 209**	**45.6**	**12 620**	**38.0**	**14 168**	**45.2**	**12 311**	**37.0**
Transport accidents — Accidents de transport	**2 257**	**7.2**	**758**	**2.3**	**2 237**	**7.1**	**762**	**2.3**
Falls — Chutes	**3 558**	**11.4**	**4 032**	**12.1**	**3 648**	**11.7**	**4 009**	**12.0**
Accidental drowning and submersion — Noyade et submersion accidentelles	**580**	**1.9**	**272**	**0.8**	**601**	**1.9**	**262**	**0.8**
Exposure to smoke, fire and flames — Exposition à la fumée, au feu et aux flammes	**237**	**0.8**	**166**	**0.5**	**262**	**0.8**	**135**	**0.4**
Accidental poisoning by and exposure to noxious substances — Intoxication accidentelle par des substances nocives et exposition à ces substances	**1 108**	**3.6**	**876**	**2.6**	**1 028**	**3.3**	**721**	**2.2**
Intentional self-harm — Lésions auto-infligées	**6 853**	**22.0**	**2 099**	**6.3**	**6 449**	**20.6**	**1 982**	**6.0**
Assault — Agresssions	**177**	**0.6**	**121**	**0.4**	**188**	**0.6**	**87**	**0.3**
All other external causes — Toutes autres causes externes	**1 215**	**3.9**	**815**	**2.5**	**1 436**	**4.6**	**908**	**2.7**

20. Death and death rates by cause and sex: 2014 - 2018
Décès et taux de mortalité par cause et sexe : 2014 - 2018 (continued - suite)

Germany - Allemagne

Cause of death — Cause de décès	2016 (C)				2017 (C)			
	Male — Masculin		Female — Féminin		Male — Masculin		Female — Féminin	
	Number Nombre	Rate Taux	Number Nombre	Rate Taux	Number Nombre	Rate Taux	Number Nombre	Rate Taux
TOTAL	**448 304**	**1 106.5**	**462 595**	**1 110.4**	**457 756**	**1 124.8**	**474 507**	**1 134.5**
Certain infectious and parasitic diseases — Certaines maladies infectieuses et parasitaires								
Total	8 005	19.8	8 994	21.6	8 194	20.1	9 092	21.7
Intestinal infectious diseases — Maladies infectieuses intestinales	1 824	4.5	2 931	7.0	1 749	4.3	2 763	6.6
Tuberculosis — Tuberculose	158	0.4	82	0.2	133	0.3	88	0.2
Tetanus — Tétanos	-	-	2	♦0.0	-	-	-	-
Diphtheria — Diphtérie	-	-	-	-	-	-	-	-
Whooping cough — Coqueluche	3	♦0.0	1	♦0.0	2	♦0.0	2	♦0.0
Meningococcal infection — Infection à méningocoques	11	♦0.0	12	♦0.0	13	♦0.0	14	♦0.0
Septicaemia — Septicémie	3 736	9.2	3 662	8.8	3 789	9.3	3 676	8.8
Acute poliomyelitis — Poliomyélite aiguë	4	♦0.0	2	♦0.0	6	♦0.0	5	♦0.0
Measles — Rougeole	1	♦0.0	1	♦0.0	-	-	2	♦0.0
Viral hepatitis — Hépatite virale	442	1.1	347	0.8	418	1.0	320	0.8
Human immunodeficiency virus [HIV] disease — Maladies dues au virus de l'immunodéficience humaine (VIH)	284	0.7	59	0.1	243	0.6	68	0.2
Malaria — Paludisme	4	♦0.0	1	♦0.0	2	♦0.0	2	♦0.0
Neoplasms — Tumeurs	**128 826**	**318.0**	**109 570**	**263.0**	**127 002**	**312.1**	**108 698**	**259.9**
Malignant neoplasms — Tumeurs malignes								
Total	125 128	308.9	105 597	253.5	123 130	302.6	104 479	249.8
Malignant neoplasm of lip, oral cavity and pharynx — Tumeur maligne de la lèvre, de la cavité buccale et du pharynx	4 070	10.0	1 387	3.3	3 963	9.7	1 402	3.4
Malignant neoplasm of oesophagus — Tumeur maligne de l'oesophage	4 434	10.9	1 245	3.0	4 266	10.5	1 233	2.9
Malignant neoplasm of stomach — Tumeur maligne de l'estomac	5 370	13.3	3 861	9.3	5 266	12.9	3 700	8.8
Malignant neoplasm of colon, rectosigmoid junction, rectum, anus and anal canal — Tumeur maligne du côlon, de la jonction recto-sigmoïdienne, du rectum, de l'anus et du canal anal	13 615	33.6	11 699	28.1	13 102	32.2	11 215	26.8
Malignant neoplasm of liver and intrahepatic bile ducts — Tumeur maligne du foie et des voies bilaires intrahépatiques	5 411	13.4	2 625	6.3	5 213	12.8	2 697	6.4
Malignant neoplasm of pancreas — Tumeur maligne du pancréas	9 008	22.2	9 044	21.7	8 947	22.0	9 058	21.7
Malignant neoplasm of trachea, bronchus and lung — Tumeur maligne de la trachée, des bronches et du poumon	29 324	72.4	16 481	39.6	28 692	70.5	16 382	39.2
Malignant neoplasm of female breast — Tumeur maligne du sein chez la femme	..	..	18 570	51.1	..	..	18 401	50.5
Malignant neoplasm of cervix uteri — Tumeur maligne du col de l'utérus	..	..	1 562	4.3	..	..	1 588	4.4
Malignant neoplasm of prostate — Tumeur maligne de la prostate	14 417	87.1	..	..	14 318	85.1	..	..
Malignant neoplasm of lymphoid, haematopoietic and related tissue — Tumeurs malignes primitives ou présumées primitives des tissus lymphoïde, hématopoïétique et apparentés	10 700	26.4	9 021	21.7	10 762	26.4	8 776	21.0
Disorders of the blood and blood-forming organs and certain disorders involving the immune mechanism — Maladies du sang et des organes hématopoïétiques et certains troubles du système immunitaire								
Total	1 367	3.4	1 851	4.4	1 631	4.0	2 054	4.9
Anaemias — Anémies	615	1.5	1 031	2.5	749	1.8	1 196	2.9
Endocrine, nutritional and metabolic diseases — Maladies endocriniennes, nutritionnelles et métaboliques								
Total	13 839	34.2	17 410	41.8	15 122	37.2	18 788	44.9
Diabetes mellitus — Diabète sucré	10 454	25.8	12 605	30.3	11 412	28.0	13 443	32.1
Malnutrition — Malnutrition	116	0.3	293	0.7	177	0.4	412	1.0
Mental and behavioural disorders — Troubles mentaux et du comportement	18 065	44.6	28 193	67.7	19 993	49.1	32 645	78.1
Diseases of the nervous system — Maladies du système nerveux	14 802	36.5	14 959	35.9	16 328	40.1	16 020	38.3
Diseases of the circulatory system — Maladies de l'appareil circulatoire								
Total	152 820	377.2	185 867	446.1	156 180	383.8	188 350	450.3
Acute rheumatic fever and chronic rheumatic heart diseases — Rhumatisme articularie aigu et cardiopathies rhumatismales chroniques	1 277	3.2	2 432	5.8	1 483	3.6	2 852	6.8
Hypertensive diseases — Maladies hypertensives	12 781	31.5	27 849	66.8	13 699	33.7	29 876	71.4
Ischaemic heart disease — Cardiopathie ischémique	66 789	164.9	55 485	133.2	68 794	169.0	56 820	135.9
Cerebrovascular disease — Maladie cérébrovasculaire	23 263	57.4	32 693	78.5	23 780	58.4	31 625	75.6

20. Death and death rates by cause and sex: 2014 - 2018
Décès et taux de mortalité par cause et sexe : 2014 - 2018 (continued - suite)

Germany - Allemagne

Cause of death — Cause de décès	2016 (C)				2017 (C)			
	Male — Masculin		Female — Féminin		Male — Masculin		Female — Féminin	
	Number Nombre	Rate Taux	Number Nombre	Rate Taux	Number Nombre	Rate Taux	Number Nombre	Rate Taux
Diseases of arteries, arterioles and capillaries — Maladies des artères, artérioles et capillaires	6 991	17.3	7 637	18.3	6 225	15.3	6 515	15.6
Diseases of the respiratory system — Maladies de l'appareil respiratoire								
Total	34 905	86.2	29 509	70.8	36 210	89.0	32 198	77.0
Influenza — Grippe	155	0.4	122	0.3	594	1.5	540	1.3
Pneumonia — Pneumopathies	9 539	23.5	9 166	22.0	9 716	23.9	9 862	23.6
Chronic lower respiratory diseases — Maladies chroniques des voies respiratoires inférieures	18 493	45.6	15 020	36.1	19 421	47.7	16 938	40.5
Diseases of the digestive system — Maladies de l'appareil digestif								
Total	21 422	52.9	19 251	46.2	21 747	53.4	19 294	46.1
Gastric and duodenal ulcer — Ulcère de l'estomac et du duodénum	1 122	2.8	1 263	3.0	1 124	2.8	1 161	2.8
Diseases of the liver — Maladies du foie	10 433	25.8	5 430	13.0	10 381	25.5	5 493	13.1
Diseases of the musculoskeletal system and connective tissue — Maladies du système ostéo-articularie, des muscles et du tissu conjonctif	1 503	3.7	2 508	6.0	1 753	4.3	3 059	7.3
Diseases of the genitourinary system — Maladies de l'appareil génito-urinaire								
Total	10 458	25.8	13 344	32.0	10 532	25.9	12 939	30.9
Disorders of kidney and ureter — Affections du rein et de l'uretère	7 959	19.6	10 094	24.2	7 842	19.3	9 774	23.4
Hyperplasia of prostate — Hyperplasie de la prostate	204	1.2	..	..	273	1.6	..	..
Pregnancy, childbirth and the puerperium — Grossesse, accouchement et puerpéralité								
Total	..	..	23	♦2.9	..	..	22	♦2.8
Pregnancy with abortive outcome — Grossesse se terminant par un avortement	..	..	2	♦0.3	..	..	1	♦0.1
Other direct obstetric causes — Autres décès maternels directs	..	..	20	♦2.5	..	..	19	♦2.4
Indirect obstetric causes — Décès maternels indirects	..	..	1	♦0.1	..	..	2	♦0.3
Certain conditions originating in the perinatal period — Certaines affections dont l'origine se situe dans la période périnatale	848	209.1	653	168.9	838	208.2	645	168.7
Congenital malformations, deformations and chromosomal abnormalities — Malformations congénitales et anomalies chromosomiques	1 039	256.2	962	248.9	1 077	267.6	995	260.2
Symptoms, signs and abnormal clinical and laboratory findings, not elsewhere classified — Symptômes, signes et résultats anormaux d'examens cliniques et de laboratoire, non classés ailleurs	17 148	42.3	12 743	30.6	16 975	41.7	12 397	29.6
All other diseases — Toutes autres maladies	614	1.5	1 018	2.4	624	1.5	989	2.4
External causes — Causes externes								
Total	22 643	55.9	15 740	37.8	23 550	57.9	16 322	39.0
Accidents								
Total	13 027	32.2	11 580	27.8	13 843	34.0	11 901	28.5
Transport accidents — Accidents de transport	2 621	6.5	926	2.2	2 516	6.2	897	2.1
Falls — Chutes	6 721	16.6	7 714	18.5	6 979	17.1	7 699	18.4
Accidental drowning and submersion — Noyade et submersion accidentelles	336	0.8	111	0.3	278	0.7	105	0.3
Exposure to smoke, fire and flames — Exposition à la fumée, au feu et aux flammes	194	0.5	131	0.3	212	0.5	123	0.3
Accidental poisoning by and exposure to noxious substances — Intoxication accidentelle par des substances nocives et exposition à ces substances	694	1.7	253	0.6	815	2.0	281	0.7
Intentional self-harm — Lésions auto-infligées	7 374	18.2	2 464	5.9	6 990	17.2	2 251	5.4
Assault — Agresssions	189	0.5	183	0.4	182	0.4	170	0.4
All other external causes — Toutes autres causes externes	2 053	5.1	1 513	3.6	2 535	6.2	2 000	4.8

20. Death and death rates by cause and sex: 2014 - 2018
Décès et taux de mortalité par cause et sexe : 2014 - 2018 (continued - suite)

Greece - Grèce

Cause of death — Cause de décès	2015 (C)				2016 (C)			
	Male — Masculin		Female — Féminin		Male — Masculin		Female — Féminin	
	Number Nombre	Rate Taux	Number Nombre	Rate Taux	Number Nombre	Rate Taux	Number Nombre	Rate Taux
TOTAL	**61 950**	**1 175.9**	**59 535**	**1 065.1**	**60 632**	**1 160.6**	**58 320**	**1 049.0**
Certain infectious and parasitic diseases — Certaines maladies infectieuses et parasitaires								
Total	**1 580**	**30.0**	**2 356**	**42.1**	**1 636**	**31.3**	**2 377**	**42.8**
Intestinal infectious diseases — Maladies infectieuses intestinales	**10**	**♦0.2**	**26**	**♦0.5**	**24**	**♦0.5**	**28**	**♦0.5**
Tuberculosis — Tuberculose	**25**	**♦0.5**	**17**	**♦0.3**	**32**	**0.6**	**13**	**♦0.2**
Tetanus — Tétanos	-	-	-	-	**1**	**♦0.0**	-	-
Diphtheria — Diphtérie	-	-	-	-	-	-	-	-
Whooping cough — Coqueluche	-	-	-	-	**1**	**♦0.0**	-	-
Meningococcal infection — Infection à méningocoques	-	-	**1**	**♦0.0**	**3**	**♦0.1**	-	-
Septicaemia — Septicémie	**1 392**	**26.4**	**2 218**	**39.7**	**1 402**	**26.8**	**2 230**	**40.1**
Acute poliomyelitis — Poliomyélite aiguë	-	-	-	-	-	-	-	-
Measles — Rougeole	-	-	-	-	-	-	-	-
Viral hepatitis — Hépatite virale	**53**	**1.0**	**25**	**♦0.4**	**47**	**0.9**	**29**	**♦0.5**
Human immunodeficiency virus [HIV] disease — Maladies dues au virus de l'immunodéficience humaine (VIH)	**34**	**0.6**	**5**	**♦0.1**	**44**	**0.8**	**7**	**♦0.1**
Malaria — Paludisme	-	-	-	-	**1**	**♦0.0**	-	-
Neoplasms — Tumeurs	**18 438**	**350.0**	**11 814**	**211.4**	**18 387**	**352.0**	**12 289**	**221.0**
Malignant neoplasms — Tumeurs malignes								
Total	**18 132**	**344.2**	**11 554**	**206.7**	**18 031**	**345.1**	**12 023**	**216.3**
Malignant neoplasm of lip, oral cavity and pharynx — Tumeur maligne de la lèvre, de la cavité buccale et du pharynx	**250**	**4.7**	**121**	**2.2**	**259**	**5.0**	**118**	**2.1**
Malignant neoplasm of oesophagus — Tumeur maligne de l'oesophage	**158**	**3.0**	**29**	**♦0.5**	**155**	**3.0**	**56**	**1.0**
Malignant neoplasm of stomach — Tumeur maligne de l'estomac	**842**	**16.0**	**515**	**9.2**	**832**	**15.9**	**512**	**9.2**
Malignant neoplasm of colon, rectosigmoid junction, rectum, anus and anal canal — Tumeur maligne du côlon, de la jonction recto-sigmoïdienne, du rectum, de l'anus et du canal anal	**1 583**	**30.0**	**1 222**	**21.9**	**1 643**	**31.4**	**1 248**	**22.4**
Malignant neoplasm of liver and intrahepatic bile ducts — Tumeur maligne du foie et des voies bilaires intrahépatiques	**1 036**	**19.7**	**522**	**9.3**	**1 018**	**19.5**	**554**	**10.0**
Malignant neoplasm of pancreas — Tumeur maligne du pancréas	**1 011**	**19.2**	**848**	**15.2**	**952**	**18.2**	**881**	**15.8**
Malignant neoplasm of trachea, bronchus and lung — Tumeur maligne de la trachée, des bronches et du poumon	**5 745**	**109.0**	**1 413**	**25.3**	**5 652**	**108.2**	**1 475**	**26.5**
Malignant neoplasm of female breast — Tumeur maligne du sein chez la femme	..	..	**2 117**	**43.9**	..	..	**2 163**	**45.1**
Malignant neoplasm of cervix uteri — Tumeur maligne du col de l'utérus	..	..	**139**	**2.9**	..	..	**174**	**3.6**
Malignant neoplasm of prostate — Tumeur maligne de la prostate	**1 763**	**88.2**	..	..	**1 646**	**81.7**	..	..
Malignant neoplasm of lymphoid, haematopoietic and related tissue — Tumeurs malignes primitives ou présumées primitives des tissus lymphoïde, hématopoïétique et apparentés	**1 232**	**23.4**	**1 023**	**18.3**	**1 312**	**25.1**	**1 002**	**18.0**
Disorders of the blood and blood-forming organs and certain disorders involving the immune mechanism — Maladies du sang et des organes hématopoïétiques et certains troubles du système immunitaire								
Total	**88**	**1.7**	**151**	**2.7**	**126**	**2.4**	**142**	**2.6**
Anaemias — Anémies	**44**	**0.8**	**75**	**1.3**	**65**	**1.2**	**71**	**1.3**
Endocrine, nutritional and metabolic diseases — Maladies endocriniennes, nutritionnelles et métaboliques								
Total	**1 029**	**19.5**	**1 007**	**18.0**	**1 016**	**19.4**	**990**	**17.8**
Diabetes mellitus — Diabète sucré	**914**	**17.3**	**866**	**15.5**	**894**	**17.1**	**859**	**15.5**
Malnutrition — Malnutrition	**1**	**♦0.0**	**1**	**♦0.0**	-	-	-	-
Mental and behavioural disorders — Troubles mentaux et du comportement	**460**	**8.7**	**699**	**12.5**	**505**	**9.7**	**896**	**16.1**
Diseases of the nervous system — Maladies du système nerveux	**1 455**	**27.6**	**1 508**	**27.0**	**1 576**	**30.2**	**1 659**	**29.8**
Diseases of the circulatory system — Maladies de l'appareil circulatoire								
Total	**22 140**	**420.2**	**24 272**	**434.2**	**21 068**	**403.3**	**23 100**	**415.5**
Acute rheumatic fever and chronic rheumatic heart diseases — Rhumatisme articularie aigu et cardiopathies rhumatismales chroniques	**33**	**0.6**	**65**	**1.2**	**21**	**♦0.4**	**72**	**1.3**
Hypertensive diseases — Maladies hypertensives	**1 735**	**32.9**	**2 087**	**37.3**	**1 831**	**35.0**	**2 172**	**39.1**
Ischaemic heart disease — Cardiopathie ischémique	**7 519**	**142.7**	**4 777**	**85.5**	**7 257**	**138.9**	**4 530**	**81.5**
Cerebrovascular disease — Maladie cérébrovasculaire	**6 088**	**115.6**	**8 357**	**149.5**	**5 774**	**110.5**	**8 005**	**144.0**

20. Death and death rates by cause and sex: 2014 - 2018
Décès et taux de mortalité par cause et sexe : 2014 - 2018 (continued - suite)

Greece - Grèce

Cause of death — Cause de décès	2015 (C)				2016 (C)			
	Male — Masculin		Female — Féminin		Male — Masculin		Female — Féminin	
	Number Nombre	Rate Taux	Number Nombre	Rate Taux	Number Nombre	Rate Taux	Number Nombre	Rate Taux
Diseases of arteries, arterioles and capillaries — Maladies des artères, artérioles et capillaires	822	15.6	444	7.9	903	17.3	408	7.3
Diseases of the respiratory system — Maladies de l'appareil respiratoire								
Total	7 238	137.4	7 597	135.9	6 767	129.5	7 042	126.7
Influenza — Grippe	21	♦0.4	22	♦0.4	72	1.4	63	1.1
Pneumonia — Pneumopathies	599	11.4	551	9.9	587	11.2	579	10.4
Chronic lower respiratory diseases — Maladies chroniques des voies respiratoires inférieures	2 043	38.8	1 443	25.8	1 761	33.7	1 215	21.9
Diseases of the digestive system — Maladies de l'appareil digestif								
Total	1 765	33.5	1 546	27.7	1 882	36.0	1 618	29.1
Gastric and duodenal ulcer — Ulcère de l'estomac et du duodénum	279	5.3	255	4.6	255	4.9	236	4.2
Diseases of the liver — Maladies du foie	656	12.5	290	5.2	697	13.3	280	5.0
Diseases of the musculoskeletal system and connective tissue — Maladies du système ostéo-articularie, des muscles et du tissu conjonctif	74	1.4	159	2.8	95	1.8	215	3.9
Diseases of the genitourinary system — Maladies de l'appareil génito-urinaire								
Total	1 633	31.0	2 030	36.3	1 464	28.0	1 812	32.6
Disorders of kidney and ureter — Affections du rein et de l'uretère	1 319	25.0	1 432	25.6	1 179	22.6	1 297	23.3
Hyperplasia of prostate — Hyperplasie de la prostate	-	-	..	..	-	-	..	..
Pregnancy, childbirth and the puerperium — Grossesse, accouchement et puerpéralité								
Total	..	..	5	♦5.4	..	..	6	♦6.5
Pregnancy with abortive outcome — Grossesse se terminant par un avortement	..	..	-	-	..	..	1	♦1.1
Other direct obstetric causes — Autres décès maternels directs	..	..	4	♦4.4	..	..	3	♦3.2
Indirect obstetric causes — Décès maternels indirects	..	..	1	♦1.1	..	..	2	♦2.2
Certain conditions originating in the perinatal period — Certaines affections dont l'origine se situe dans la période périnatale	102	215.7	93	208.7	147	307.0	72	159.9
Congenital malformations, deformations and chromosomal abnormalities — Malformations congénitales et anomalies chromosomiques	108	228.4	74	166.1	129	269.4	109	242.1
Symptoms, signs and abnormal clinical and laboratory findings, not elsewhere classified — Symptômes, signes et résultats anormaux d'examens cliniques et de laboratoire, non classés ailleurs	2 916	55.3	4 850	86.8	2 936	56.2	4 625	83.2
All other diseases — Toutes autres maladies	19	♦0.4	32	0.6	13	♦0.2	31	0.6
External causes — Causes externes								
Total	2 905	55.1	1 342	24.0	2 885	55.2	1 337	24.0
Accidents								
Total	2 156	40.9	996	17.8	2 139	40.9	1 038	18.7
Transport accidents — Accidents de transport	935	17.7	322	5.8	880	16.8	276	5.0
Falls — Chutes	312	5.9	272	4.9	330	6.3	328	5.9
Accidental drowning and submersion — Noyade et submersion accidentelles	239	4.5	111	2.0	290	5.6	127	2.3
Exposure to smoke, fire and flames — Exposition à la fumée, au feu et aux flammes	41	0.8	46	0.8	57	1.1	47	0.8
Accidental poisoning by and exposure to noxious substances — Intoxication accidentelle par des substances nocives et exposition à ces substances	236	4.5	48	0.9	189	3.6	49	0.9
Intentional self-harm — Lésions auto-infligées	422	8.0	107	1.9	404	7.7	81	1.5
Assault — Agresssions	68	1.3	31	0.6	64	1.2	23	♦0.4
All other external causes — Toutes autres causes externes	259	4.9	208	3.7	278	5.3	195	3.5

20. Death and death rates by cause and sex: 2014 - 2018
Décès et taux de mortalité par cause et sexe : 2014 - 2018 (continued - suite)

Hungary - Hongrie

Cause of death — Cause de décès	2016 (C)				2017 (C)			
	Male — Masculin		Female — Féminin		Male — Masculin		Female — Féminin	
	Number Nombre	Rate Taux	Number Nombre	Rate Taux	Number Nombre	Rate Taux	Number Nombre	Rate Taux
TOTAL	**62 658**	**1 338.3**	**64 395**	**1 254.7**	**64 025**	**1 370.0**	**67 649**	**1 322.7**
Certain infectious and parasitic diseases — Certaines maladies infectieuses et parasitaires								
Total	349	7.5	411	8.0	329	7.0	398	7.8
Intestinal infectious diseases — Maladies infectieuses intestinales	111	2.4	206	4.0	110	2.4	202	3.9
Tuberculosis — Tuberculose	36	0.8	12	♦0.2	25	♦0.5	11	♦0.2
Tetanus — Tétanos	1	♦0.0	4	♦0.1	-	-	-	-
Diphtheria — Diphtérie	-	-	-	-	-	-	-	-
Whooping cough — Coqueluche	-	-	-	-	-	-	-	-
Meningococcal infection — Infection à méningocoques	4	♦0.1	4	♦0.1	4	♦0.1	2	♦0.0
Septicaemia — Septicémie	38	0.8	36	0.7	35	0.7	38	0.7
Acute poliomyelitis — Poliomyélite aiguë	-	-	-	-	-	-	-	-
Measles — Rougeole	-	-	-	-	-	-	-	-
Viral hepatitis — Hépatite virale	88	1.9	88	1.7	76	1.6	75	1.5
Human immunodeficiency virus [HIV] disease — Maladies dues au virus de l'immunodéficience humaine (VIH)	8	♦0.2	1	♦0.0	3	♦0.1	5	♦0.1
Malaria — Paludisme	1	♦0.0	1	♦0.0	-	-	-	-
Neoplasms — Tumeurs	**18 335**	**391.6**	**15 283**	**297.8**	**18 050**	**386.2**	**15 498**	**303.0**
Malignant neoplasms — Tumeurs malignes								
Total	18 020	384.9	14 967	291.6	17 716	379.1	15 128	295.8
Malignant neoplasm of lip, oral cavity and pharynx — Tumeur maligne de la lèvre, de la cavité buccale et du pharynx	1 122	24.0	273	5.3	1 035	22.1	298	5.8
Malignant neoplasm of oesophagus — Tumeur maligne de l'oesophage	471	10.1	87	1.7	427	9.1	104	2.0
Malignant neoplasm of stomach — Tumeur maligne de l'estomac	930	19.9	649	12.6	845	18.1	627	12.3
Malignant neoplasm of colon, rectosigmoid junction, rectum, anus and anal canal — Tumeur maligne du côlon, de la jonction recto-sigmoïdienne, du rectum, de l'anus et du canal anal	2 845	60.8	2 214	43.1	2 816	60.3	2 169	42.4
Malignant neoplasm of liver and intrahepatic bile ducts — Tumeur maligne du foie et des voies bilaires intrahépatiques	581	12.4	269	5.2	590	12.6	305	6.0
Malignant neoplasm of pancreas — Tumeur maligne du pancréas	1 056	22.6	1 122	21.9	1 084	23.2	1 144	22.4
Malignant neoplasm of trachea, bronchus and lung — Tumeur maligne de la trachée, des bronches et du poumon	5 542	118.4	3 341	65.1	5 393	115.4	3 447	67.4
Malignant neoplasm of female breast — Tumeur maligne du sein chez la femme	..	..	2 223	50.1	..	..	2 123	48.0
Malignant neoplasm of cervix uteri — Tumeur maligne du col de l'utérus	..	..	396	8.9	..	..	377	8.5
Malignant neoplasm of prostate — Tumeur maligne de la prostate	1 301	81.4	..	..	1 389	86.5	..	..
Malignant neoplasm of lymphoid, haematopoietic and related tissue — Tumeurs malignes primitives ou présumées primitives des tissus lymphoïde, hématopoïétique et apparentés	914	19.5	873	17.0	940	20.1	912	17.8
Disorders of the blood and blood-forming organs and certain disorders involving the immune mechanism — Maladies du sang et des organes hématopoïétiques et certains troubles du système immunitaire								
Total	72	1.5	107	2.1	76	1.6	98	1.9
Anaemias — Anémies	35	0.7	62	1.2	44	0.9	61	1.2
Endocrine, nutritional and metabolic diseases — Maladies endocriniennes, nutritionnelles et métaboliques								
Total	1 420	30.3	1 725	33.6	1 521	32.5	1 966	38.4
Diabetes mellitus — Diabète sucré	1 265	27.0	1 521	29.6	1 368	29.3	1 729	33.8
Malnutrition — Malnutrition	7	♦0.1	5	♦0.1	7	♦0.1	7	♦0.1
Mental and behavioural disorders — Troubles mentaux et du comportement	**1 292**	**27.6**	**2 072**	**40.4**	**1 402**	**30.0**	**2 416**	**47.2**
Diseases of the nervous system — Maladies du système nerveux	**936**	**20.0**	**981**	**19.1**	**1 021**	**21.8**	**1 097**	**21.4**
Diseases of the circulatory system — Maladies de l'appareil circulatoire								
Total	27 919	596.3	34 927	680.6	28 883	618.0	36 715	717.9
Acute rheumatic fever and chronic rheumatic heart diseases — Rhumatisme articularie aigu et cardiopathies rhumatismales chroniques	66	1.4	196	3.8	94	2.0	159	3.1
Hypertensive diseases — Maladies hypertensives	3 370	72.0	5 902	115.0	3 613	77.3	6 352	124.2
Ischaemic heart disease — Cardiopathie ischémique	14 454	308.7	16 830	327.9	14 831	317.3	17 814	348.3
Cerebrovascular disease — Maladie cérébrovasculaire	4 713	100.7	5 988	116.7	4 960	106.1	6 424	125.6

20. Death and death rates by cause and sex: 2014 - 2018
Décès et taux de mortalité par cause et sexe : 2014 - 2018 (continued - suite)

Hungary - Hongrie

Cause of death — Cause de décès	2016 (C)				2017 (C)			
	Male — Masculin		Female — Féminin		Male — Masculin		Female — Féminin	
	Number Nombre	Rate Taux	Number Nombre	Rate Taux	Number Nombre	Rate Taux	Number Nombre	Rate Taux
Diseases of arteries, arterioles and capillaries — Maladies des artères, artérioles et capillaires	1 475	31.5	1 748	34.1	1 546	33.1	1 939	37.9
Diseases of the respiratory system — Maladies de l'appareil respiratoire								
Total	3 920	83.7	3 285	64.0	4 322	92.5	3 826	74.8
Influenza — Grippe	8	♦0.2	-	-	21	♦0.4	25	♦0.5
Pneumonia — Pneumopathies	499	10.7	499	9.7	548	11.7	577	11.3
Chronic lower respiratory diseases — Maladies chroniques des voies respiratoires inférieures	3 061	65.4	2 494	48.6	3 320	71.0	2 857	55.9
Diseases of the digestive system — Maladies de l'appareil digestif								
Total	3 646	77.9	2 556	49.8	3 649	78.1	2 615	51.1
Gastric and duodenal ulcer — Ulcère de l'estomac et du duodénum	361	7.7	347	6.8	324	6.9	322	6.3
Diseases of the liver — Maladies du foie	2 284	48.8	893	17.4	2 296	49.1	947	18.5
Diseases of the musculoskeletal system and connective tissue — Maladies du système ostéo-articularie, des muscles et du tissu conjonctif	113	2.4	283	5.5	137	2.9	258	5.0
Diseases of the genitourinary system — Maladies de l'appareil génito-urinaire								
Total	417	8.9	420	8.2	384	8.2	397	7.8
Disorders of kidney and ureter — Affections du rein et de l'uretère	193	4.1	280	5.5	170	3.6	262	5.1
Hyperplasia of prostate — Hyperplasie de la prostate	127	7.9	..	..	103	6.4	..	..
Pregnancy, childbirth and the puerperium — Grossesse, accouchement et puerpéralité								
Total	..	..	11	♦11.5	..	..	14	♦14.8
Pregnancy with abortive outcome — Grossesse se terminant par un avortement	..	..	-	-	..	..	-	-
Other direct obstetric causes — Autres décès maternels directs	..	..	9	♦9.4	..	..	9	♦9.5
Indirect obstetric causes — Décès maternels indirects	..	..	2	♦2.1	..	..	5	♦5.3
Certain conditions originating in the perinatal period — Certaines affections dont l'origine se situe dans la période périnatale	107	218.6	90	194.0	102	209.9	82	178.0
Congenital malformations, deformations and chromosomal abnormalities — Malformations congénitales et anomalies chromosomiques	169	345.2	124	267.2	168	345.7	130	282.3
Symptoms, signs and abnormal clinical and laboratory findings, not elsewhere classified — Symptômes, signes et résultats anormaux d'examens cliniques et de laboratoire, non classés ailleurs	106	2.3	127	2.5	121	2.6	127	2.5
All other diseases — Toutes autres maladies	59	1.3	92	1.8	48	1.0	77	1.5
External causes — Causes externes								
Total	3 798	81.1	1 901	37.0	3 812	81.6	1 935	37.8
Accidents								
Total	2 266	48.4	1 334	26.0	2 372	50.8	1 410	27.6
Transport accidents — Accidents de transport	666	14.2	195	3.8	640	13.7	213	4.2
Falls — Chutes	898	19.2	806	15.7	906	19.4	821	16.1
Accidental drowning and submersion — Noyade et submersion accidentelles	98	2.1	27	♦0.5	128	2.7	32	0.6
Exposure to smoke, fire and flames — Exposition à la fumée, au feu et aux flammes	58	1.2	43	0.8	79	1.7	50	1.0
Accidental poisoning by and exposure to noxious substances — Intoxication accidentelle par des substances nocives et exposition à ces substances	77	1.6	27	♦0.5	104	2.2	36	0.7
Intentional self-harm — Lésions auto-infligées	1 316	28.1	446	8.7	1 241	26.6	393	7.7
Assault — Agresssions	60	1.3	39	0.8	45	1.0	39	0.8
All other external causes — Toutes autres causes externes	156	3.3	82	1.6	154	3.3	93	1.8

Iceland - Islande

Cause of death — Cause de décès	2017 (C)				2018 (C)			
	Male — Masculin		Female — Féminin		Male — Masculin		Female — Féminin	
	Number Nombre	Rate Taux	Number Nombre	Rate Taux	Number Nombre	Rate Taux	Number Nombre	Rate Taux
TOTAL	**1 124**	**657.2**	**1 112**	**664.6**	**1 137**	**640.2**	**1 115**	**652.6**
Certain infectious and parasitic diseases — Certaines maladies infectieuses et parasitaires								
Total	10	♦5.8	12	♦7.2	10	♦5.6	11	♦6.4
Intestinal infectious diseases — Maladies infectieuses intestinales	3	♦1.8	5	♦3.0	1	♦0.6	1	♦0.6
Tuberculosis — Tuberculose	-	-	-	-	-	-	-	-
Tetanus — Tétanos	-	-	-	-	-	-	-	-
Diphtheria — Diphtérie	-	-	-	-	-	-	-	-
Whooping cough — Coqueluche	-	-	-	-	-	-	-	-
Meningococcal infection — Infection à méningocoques	-	-	-	-	-	-	-	-
Septicaemia — Septicémie	4	♦2.3	2	♦1.2	4	♦2.3	7	♦4.1
Acute poliomyelitis — Poliomyélite aiguë	-	-	-	-	-	-	-	-
Measles — Rougeole	-	-	-	-	-	-	-	-
Viral hepatitis — Hépatite virale	-	-	-	-	1	♦0.6	-	-
Human immunodeficiency virus [HIV] disease — Maladies dues au virus de l'immunodéficience humaine (VIH)	-	-	-	-	-	-	-	-
Malaria — Paludisme	-	-	-	-	-	-	-	-
Neoplasms — Tumeurs	309	180.7	289	172.7	304	171.2	288	168.6
Malignant neoplasms — Tumeurs malignes								
Total	308	180.1	286	170.9	299	168.4	285	166.8
Malignant neoplasm of lip, oral cavity and pharynx — Tumeur maligne de la lèvre, de la cavité buccale et du pharynx	7	♦4.1	4	♦2.4	5	♦2.8	4	♦2.3
Malignant neoplasm of oesophagus — Tumeur maligne de l'oesophage	12	♦7.0	3	♦1.8	24	♦13.5	4	♦2.3
Malignant neoplasm of stomach — Tumeur maligne de l'estomac	8	♦4.7	6	♦3.6	8	♦4.5	5	♦2.9
Malignant neoplasm of colon, rectosigmoid junction, rectum, anus and anal canal — Tumeur maligne du côlon, de la jonction recto-sigmoïdienne, du rectum, de l'anus et du canal anal	29	♦17.0	31	18.5	32	18.0	32	18.7
Malignant neoplasm of liver and intrahepatic bile ducts — Tumeur maligne du foie et des voies bilaires intrahépatiques	14	♦8.2	5	♦3.0	13	♦7.3	6	♦3.5
Malignant neoplasm of pancreas — Tumeur maligne du pancréas	22	♦12.9	20	♦12.0	16	♦9.0	15	♦8.8
Malignant neoplasm of trachea, bronchus and lung — Tumeur maligne de la trachée, des bronches et du poumon	64	37.4	60	35.9	63	35.5	67	39.2
Malignant neoplasm of female breast — Tumeur maligne du sein chez la femme	..	..	40	29.7	..	..	47	34.1
Malignant neoplasm of cervix uteri — Tumeur maligne du col de l'utérus	..	..	7	♦5.2	..	..	7	♦5.1
Malignant neoplasm of prostate — Tumeur maligne de la prostate	50	93.5	..	..	49	89.1	..	..
Malignant neoplasm of lymphoid, haematopoietic and related tissue — Tumeurs malignes primitives ou présumées primitives des tissus lymphoïde, hématopoïétique et apparentés	27	♦15.8	21	♦12.6	29	♦16.3	21	♦12.3
Disorders of the blood and blood-forming organs and certain disorders involving the immune mechanism — Maladies du sang et des organes hématopoïétiques et certains troubles du système immunitaire								
Total	6	♦3.5	3	♦1.8	-	-	4	♦2.3
Anaemias — Anémies	1	♦0.6	1	♦0.6	-	-	4	♦2.3
Endocrine, nutritional and metabolic diseases — Maladies endocriniennes, nutritionnelles et métaboliques								
Total	25	♦14.6	31	18.5	33	18.6	20	♦11.7
Diabetes mellitus — Diabète sucré	20	♦11.7	17	♦10.2	25	♦14.1	12	♦7.0
Malnutrition — Malnutrition	-	-	3	♦1.8	-	-	1	♦0.6
Mental and behavioural disorders — Troubles mentaux et du comportement	35	20.5	49	29.3	38	21.4	53	31.0
Diseases of the nervous system — Maladies du système nerveux	102	59.6	143	85.5	113	63.6	169	98.9
Diseases of the circulatory system — Maladies de l'appareil circulatoire								
Total	357	208.7	335	200.2	347	195.4	308	180.3
Acute rheumatic fever and chronic rheumatic heart diseases — Rhumatisme articularie aigu et cardiopathies rhumatismales chroniques	-	-	3	♦1.8	-	-	-	-
Hypertensive diseases — Maladies hypertensives	16	♦9.4	16	♦9.6	17	♦9.6	19	♦11.1
Ischaemic heart disease — Cardiopathie ischémique	189	110.5	123	73.5	178	100.2	121	70.8
Cerebrovascular disease — Maladie cérébrovasculaire	57	33.3	70	41.8	61	34.3	71	41.6

20. Death and death rates by cause and sex: 2014 - 2018
Décès et taux de mortalité par cause et sexe : 2014 - 2018 (continued - suite)

Iceland - Islande

Cause of death — Cause de décès	2017 (C)				2018 (C)			
	Male — Masculin		Female — Féminin		Male — Masculin		Female — Féminin	
	Number Nombre	Rate Taux	Number Nombre	Rate Taux	Number Nombre	Rate Taux	Number Nombre	Rate Taux
Diseases of arteries, arterioles and capillaries — Maladies des artères, artérioles et capillaires	7	♦4.1	11	♦6.6	14	♦7.9	15	♦8.8
Diseases of the respiratory system — Maladies de l'appareil respiratoire								
Total	106	62.0	134	80.1	104	58.6	126	73.7
Influenza — Grippe	4	♦2.3	5	♦3.0	8	♦4.5	1	♦0.6
Pneumonia — Pneumopathies	35	20.5	49	29.3	39	22.0	40	23.4
Chronic lower respiratory diseases — Maladies chroniques des voies respiratoires inférieures	53	31.0	69	41.2	42	23.6	76	44.5
Diseases of the digestive system — Maladies de l'appareil digestif								
Total	34	19.9	34	20.3	27	♦15.2	29	♦17.0
Gastric and duodenal ulcer — Ulcère de l'estomac et du duodénum	4	♦2.3	4	♦2.4	3	♦1.7	-	-
Diseases of the liver — Maladies du foie	12	♦7.0	3	♦1.8	6	♦3.4	5	♦2.9
Diseases of the musculoskeletal system and connective tissue — Maladies du système ostéo-articularie, des muscles et du tissu conjonctif	4	♦2.3	9	♦5.4	4	♦2.3	7	♦4.1
Diseases of the genitourinary system — Maladies de l'appareil génito-urinaire								
Total	12	♦7.0	9	♦5.4	18	♦10.1	20	♦11.7
Disorders of kidney and ureter — Affections du rein et de l'uretère	10	♦5.8	6	♦3.6	14	♦7.9	14	♦8.2
Hyperplasia of prostate — Hyperplasie de la prostate	-	-	..	..	2	♦3.6	..	..
Pregnancy, childbirth and the puerperium — Grossesse, accouchement et puerpéralité								
Total	..	..	-	-	..	..	-	-
Pregnancy with abortive outcome — Grossesse se terminant par un avortement	..	..	-	-	..	..	-	-
Other direct obstetric causes — Autres décès maternels directs	..	..	-	-	..	..	-	-
Indirect obstetric causes — Décès maternels indirects	..	..	-	-	..	..	-	-
Certain conditions originating in the perinatal period — Certaines affections dont l'origine se situe dans la période périnatale	5	♦236.7	3	♦153.1	2	♦89.2	1	♦50.4
Congenital malformations, deformations and chromosomal abnormalities — Malformations congénitales et anomalies chromosomiques	3	♦142.0	4	♦204.2	3	♦133.8	-	-
Symptoms, signs and abnormal clinical and laboratory findings, not elsewhere classified — Symptômes, signes et résultats anormaux d'examens cliniques et de laboratoire, non classés ailleurs	14	♦8.2	9	♦5.4	30	♦16.9	13	♦7.6
All other diseases — Toutes autres maladies	1	♦0.6	2	♦1.2	2	♦1.1	2	♦1.2
External causes — Causes externes								
Total	101	59.1	46	27.5	102	57.4	64	37.5
Accidents								
Total	66	38.6	39	23.3	69	38.9	53	31.0
Transport accidents — Accidents de transport	4	♦2.3	4	♦2.4	8	♦4.5	2	♦1.2
Falls — Chutes	15	♦8.8	10	♦6.0	10	♦5.6	11	♦6.4
Accidental drowning and submersion — Noyade et submersion accidentelles	2	♦1.2	2	♦1.2	-	-	-	-
Exposure to smoke, fire and flames — Exposition à la fumée, au feu et aux flammes	1	♦0.6	1	♦0.6	-	-	-	-
Accidental poisoning by and exposure to noxious substances — Intoxication accidentelle par des substances nocives et exposition à ces substances	28	♦16.4	8	♦4.8	35	19.7	18	♦10.5
Intentional self-harm — Lésions auto-infligées	32	18.7	2	♦1.2	29	♦16.3	5	♦2.9
Assault — Agresssions	1	♦0.6	2	♦1.2	1	♦0.6	-	-
All other external causes — Toutes autres causes externes	2	♦1.2	3	♦1.8	3	♦1.7	6	♦3.5

Ireland - Irlande

Cause of death — Cause de décès	2014 (+C)				2015 (+C)			
	Male — Masculin		Female — Féminin		Male — Masculin		Female — Féminin	
	Number Nombre	Rate Taux	Number Nombre	Rate Taux	Number Nombre	Rate Taux	Number Nombre	Rate Taux
TOTAL	**14 897**	**648.9**	**14 355**	**612.9**	**15 228**	**658.3**	**14 899**	**630.2**
Certain infectious and parasitic diseases — Certaines maladies infectieuses et parasitaires								
Total	131	5.7	165	7.0	176	7.6	191	8.1
Intestinal infectious diseases — Maladies infectieuses intestinales	15	♦0.7	38	1.6	17	♦0.7	35	1.5
Tuberculosis — Tuberculose	6	♦0.3	9	♦0.4	12	♦0.5	4	♦0.2
Tetanus — Tétanos	-	-	-	-	-	-	-	-
Diphtheria — Diphtérie	-	-	-	-	-	-	-	-
Whooping cough — Coqueluche	-	-	-	-	-	-	-	-
Meningococcal infection — Infection à méningocoques	-	-	2	♦0.1	1	♦0.0	2	♦0.1
Septicaemia — Septicémie	56	2.4	85	3.6	100	4.3	111	4.7
Acute poliomyelitis — Poliomyélite aiguë	-	-	-	-	-	-	-	-
Measles — Rougeole	-	-	-	-	-	-	-	-
Viral hepatitis — Hépatite virale	16	♦0.7	8	♦0.3	18	♦0.8	6	♦0.3
Human immunodeficiency virus [HIV] disease — Maladies dues au virus de l'immunodéficience humaine (VIH)	7	♦0.3	1	♦0.0	5	♦0.2	3	♦0.1
Malaria — Paludisme	1	♦0.0	-	-	-	-	-	-
Neoplasms — Tumeurs	**4 840**	**210.8**	**4 380**	**187.0**	**4 834**	**209.0**	**4 240**	**179.3**
Malignant neoplasms — Tumeurs malignes								
Total	4 724	205.8	4 298	183.5	4 742	205.0	4 135	174.9
Malignant neoplasm of lip, oral cavity and pharynx — Tumeur maligne de la lèvre, de la cavité buccale et du pharynx	116	5.1	51	2.2	140	6.1	46	1.9
Malignant neoplasm of oesophagus — Tumeur maligne de l'oesophage	270	11.8	114	4.9	274	11.8	132	5.6
Malignant neoplasm of stomach — Tumeur maligne de l'estomac	225	9.8	144	6.1	193	8.3	135	5.7
Malignant neoplasm of colon, rectosigmoid junction, rectum, anus and anal canal — Tumeur maligne du côlon, de la jonction recto-sigmoïdienne, du rectum, de l'anus et du canal anal	555	24.2	432	18.4	615	26.6	398	16.8
Malignant neoplasm of liver and intrahepatic bile ducts — Tumeur maligne du foie et des voies bilaires intrahépatiques	187	8.1	139	5.9	192	8.3	103	4.4
Malignant neoplasm of pancreas — Tumeur maligne du pancréas	274	11.9	240	10.2	297	12.8	250	10.6
Malignant neoplasm of trachea, bronchus and lung — Tumeur maligne de la trachée, des bronches et du poumon	1 062	46.3	872	37.2	1 043	45.1	785	33.2
Malignant neoplasm of female breast — Tumeur maligne du sein chez la femme	..	..	735	...	..	..	678	36.2
Malignant neoplasm of cervix uteri — Tumeur maligne du col de l'utérus	..	..	96	...	..	..	87	4.6
Malignant neoplasm of prostate — Tumeur maligne de la prostate	540	...	..	..	527	78.8	..	..
Malignant neoplasm of lymphoid, haematopoietic and related tissue — Tumeurs malignes primitives ou présumées primitives des tissus lymphoïde, hématopoïétique et apparentés	433	18.9	292	12.5	407	17.6	326	13.8
Disorders of the blood and blood-forming organs and certain disorders involving the immune mechanism — Maladies du sang et des organes hématopoïétiques et certains troubles du système immunitaire								
Total	38	1.7	51	2.2	45	1.9	43	1.8
Anaemias — Anémies	16	♦0.7	26	♦1.1	18	♦0.8	21	♦0.9
Endocrine, nutritional and metabolic diseases — Maladies endocriniennes, nutritionnelles et métaboliques								
Total	361	15.7	319	13.6	360	15.6	345	14.6
Diabetes mellitus — Diabète sucré	271	11.8	211	9.0	281	12.1	237	10.0
Malnutrition — Malnutrition	1	♦0.0	1	♦0.0	-	-	1	♦0.0
Mental and behavioural disorders — Troubles mentaux et du comportement	473	20.6	879	37.5	555	24.0	1 002	42.4
Diseases of the nervous system — Maladies du système nerveux	657	28.6	763	32.6	683	29.5	872	36.9
Diseases of the circulatory system — Maladies de l'appareil circulatoire								
Total	4 448	193.7	4 404	188.0	4 741	204.9	4 630	195.8
Acute rheumatic fever and chronic rheumatic heart diseases — Rhumatisme articularie aigu et cardiopathies rhumatismales chroniques	22	♦1.0	36	1.5	25	♦1.1	47	2.0
Hypertensive diseases — Maladies hypertensives	98	4.3	183	7.8	110	4.8	231	9.8
Ischaemic heart disease — Cardiopathie ischémique	2 498	108.8	1 785	76.2	2 625	113.5	1 867	79.0
Cerebrovascular disease — Maladie cérébrovasculaire	752	32.8	1 100	47.0	831	35.9	1 089	46.1

20. Death and death rates by cause and sex: 2014 - 2018
Décès et taux de mortalité par cause et sexe : 2014 - 2018 (continued - suite)

Ireland - Irlande

Cause of death — Cause de décès	2014 (+C)				2015 (+C)			
	Male — Masculin		Female — Féminin		Male — Masculin		Female — Féminin	
	Number Nombre	Rate Taux	Number Nombre	Rate Taux	Number Nombre	Rate Taux	Number Nombre	Rate Taux
Diseases of arteries, arterioles and capillaries — Maladies des artères, artérioles et capillaires	222	9.7	223	9.5	228	9.9	229	9.7
Diseases of the respiratory system — Maladies de l'appareil respiratoire								
Total	1 713	74.6	1 779	76.0	1 855	80.2	2 010	85.0
Influenza — Grippe	12	♦0.5	17	♦0.7	15	♦0.6	17	♦0.7
Pneumonia — Pneumopathies	439	19.1	564	24.1	486	21.0	679	28.7
Chronic lower respiratory diseases — Maladies chroniques des voies respiratoires inférieures	773	33.7	778	33.2	846	36.6	855	36.2
Diseases of the digestive system — Maladies de l'appareil digestif								
Total	549	23.9	490	20.9	503	21.7	462	19.5
Gastric and duodenal ulcer — Ulcère de l'estomac et du duodénum	35	1.5	39	1.7	39	1.7	20	♦0.8
Diseases of the liver — Maladies du foie	222	9.7	98	4.2	228	9.9	139	5.9
Diseases of the musculoskeletal system and connective tissue — Maladies du système ostéo-articularie, des muscles et du tissu conjonctif	70	3.0	164	7.0	59	2.6	137	5.8
Diseases of the genitourinary system — Maladies de l'appareil génito-urinaire								
Total	299	13.0	315	13.5	279	12.1	338	14.3
Disorders of kidney and ureter — Affections du rein et de l'uretère	221	9.6	197	8.4	212	9.2	227	9.6
Hyperplasia of prostate — Hyperplasie de la prostate	18	...	..	..	13	♦1.9	..	..
Pregnancy, childbirth and the puerperium — Grossesse, accouchement et puerpéralité								
Total	..	..	1	♦1.5	..	..	1	♦1.5
Pregnancy with abortive outcome — Grossesse se terminant par un avortement	..	..	-	-	..	..	1	♦1.5
Other direct obstetric causes — Autres décès maternels directs	..	..	1	♦1.5	..	..	-	-
Indirect obstetric causes — Décès maternels indirects	..	..	-	-	..	..	-	-
Certain conditions originating in the perinatal period — Certaines affections dont l'origine se situe dans la période périnatale	54	155.7	46	141.1	61	182.2	42	131.0
Congenital malformations, deformations and chromosomal abnormalities — Malformations congénitales et anomalies chromosomiques	100	288.4	75	230.0	89	265.8	82	255.8
Symptoms, signs and abnormal clinical and laboratory findings, not elsewhere classified — Symptômes, signes et résultats anormaux d'examens cliniques et de laboratoire, non classés ailleurs	44	1.9	53	2.3	59	2.6	53	2.2
All other diseases — Toutes autres maladies	23	♦1.0	38	1.6	26	♦1.1	38	1.6
External causes — Causes externes								
Total	1 097	47.8	433	18.5	903	39.0	413	17.5
Accidents								
Total	621	27.0	323	13.8	512	22.1	302	12.8
Transport accidents — Accidents de transport	121	5.3	48	2.0	94	4.1	30	♦1.3
Falls — Chutes	145	6.3	121	5.2	121	5.2	123	5.2
Accidental drowning and submersion — Noyade et submersion accidentelles	44	1.9	10	♦0.4	53	2.3	12	♦0.5
Exposure to smoke, fire and flames — Exposition à la fumée, au feu et aux flammes	18	♦0.8	15	♦0.6	12	♦0.5	13	♦0.5
Accidental poisoning by and exposure to noxious substances — Intoxication accidentelle par des substances nocives et exposition à ces substances	181	7.9	69	2.9	158	6.8	78	3.3
Intentional self-harm — Lésions auto-infligées	399	17.4	87	3.7	335	14.5	90	3.8
Assault — Agresssions	27	♦1.2	5	♦0.2	18	♦0.8	3	♦0.1
All other external causes — Toutes autres causes externes	50	2.2	18	♦0.8	38	1.6	18	♦0.8

20. Death and death rates by cause and sex: 2014 - 2018
Décès et taux de mortalité par cause et sexe : 2014 - 2018 (continued - suite)

Italy - Italie

Cause of death — Cause de décès	2015 (C)				2016 (C)			
	Male — Masculin		Female — Féminin		Male — Masculin		Female — Féminin	
	Number Nombre	Rate Taux	Number Nombre	Rate Taux	Number Nombre	Rate Taux	Number Nombre	Rate Taux
TOTAL	**307 392**	**1 042.0**	**338 656**	**1 082.2**	**297 665**	**1 010.5**	**320 418**	**1 026.7**
Certain infectious and parasitic diseases — Certaines maladies infectieuses et parasitaires								
Total	7 408	25.1	8 402	26.8	5 918	20.1	6 932	22.2
Intestinal infectious diseases — Maladies infectieuses intestinales	379	1.3	609	1.9	585	2.0	933	3.0
Tuberculosis — Tuberculose	161	0.5	112	0.4	146	0.5	96	0.3
Tetanus — Tétanos	5	♦0.0	14	♦0.0	8	♦0.0	8	♦0.0
Diphtheria — Diphtérie	-	-	-	-	-	-	-	-
Whooping cough — Coqueluche	-	-	2	♦0.0	-	-	-	-
Meningococcal infection — Infection à méningocoques	6	♦0.0	10	♦0.0	6	♦0.0	9	♦0.0
Septicaemia — Septicémie	4 385	14.9	5 344	17.1	2 947	10.0	3 692	11.8
Acute poliomyelitis — Poliomyélite aiguë	-	-	-	-	-	-	-	-
Measles — Rougeole	-	-	1	♦0.0	1	♦0.0	-	-
Viral hepatitis — Hépatite virale	1 354	4.6	1 531	4.9	1 302	4.4	1 443	4.6
Human immunodeficiency virus [HIV] disease — Maladies dues au virus de l'immunodéficience humaine (VIH)	536	1.8	168	0.5	348	1.2	112	0.4
Malaria — Paludisme	2	♦0.0	-	-	3	♦0.0	-	-
Neoplasms — Tumeurs	**99 437**	**337.1**	**79 443**	**253.9**	**100 003**	**339.5**	**79 499**	**254.7**
Malignant neoplasms — Tumeurs malignes								
Total	94 870	321.6	75 469	241.2	95 099	322.8	75 187	240.9
Malignant neoplasm of lip, oral cavity and pharynx — Tumeur maligne de la lèvre, de la cavité buccale et du pharynx	1 899	6.4	990	3.2	2 228	7.6	988	3.2
Malignant neoplasm of oesophagus — Tumeur maligne de l'oesophage	1 359	4.6	485	1.5	1 417	4.8	515	1.7
Malignant neoplasm of stomach — Tumeur maligne de l'estomac	5 491	18.6	3 933	12.6	5 458	18.5	3 823	12.2
Malignant neoplasm of colon, rectosigmoid junction, rectum, anus and anal canal — Tumeur maligne du côlon, de la jonction recto-sigmoïdienne, du rectum, de l'anus et du canal anal	10 110	34.3	8 869	28.3	10 652	36.2	8 923	28.6
Malignant neoplasm of liver and intrahepatic bile ducts — Tumeur maligne du foie et des voies bilaires intrahépatiques	6 369	21.6	3 333	10.7	6 428	21.8	3 274	10.5
Malignant neoplasm of pancreas — Tumeur maligne du pancréas	5 555	18.8	5 945	19.0	5 834	19.8	6 215	19.9
Malignant neoplasm of trachea, bronchus and lung — Tumeur maligne de la trachée, des bronches et du poumon	24 405	82.7	9 570	30.6	24 059	81.7	9 779	31.3
Malignant neoplasm of female breast — Tumeur maligne du sein chez la femme	..	..	12 312	...	..	..	12 616	46.4
Malignant neoplasm of cervix uteri — Tumeur maligne du col de l'utérus	..	..	442	...	..	..	509	1.9
Malignant neoplasm of prostate — Tumeur maligne de la prostate	7 214	...	..	..	7 540	63.6	..	..
Malignant neoplasm of lymphoid, haematopoietic and related tissue — Tumeurs malignes primitives ou présumées primitives des tissus lymphoïde, hématopoïétique et apparentés	8 091	27.4	6 721	21.5	8 217	27.9	6 852	22.0
Disorders of the blood and blood-forming organs and certain disorders involving the immune mechanism — Maladies du sang et des organes hématopoïétiques et certains troubles du système immunitaire								
Total	1 229	4.2	1 909	6.1	1 220	4.1	1 883	6.0
Anaemias — Anémies	808	2.7	1 377	4.4	815	2.8	1 394	4.5
Endocrine, nutritional and metabolic diseases — Maladies endocriniennes, nutritionnelles et métaboliques								
Total	12 646	42.9	16 612	53.1	12 218	41.5	15 429	49.4
Diabetes mellitus — Diabète sucré	9 882	33.5	12 364	39.5	9 616	32.6	11 738	37.6
Malnutrition — Malnutrition	205	0.7	376	1.2	235	0.8	387	1.2
Mental and behavioural disorders — Troubles mentaux et du comportement	**6 946**	**23.5**	**14 451**	**46.2**	**7 134**	**24.2**	**14 401**	**46.1**
Diseases of the nervous system — Maladies du système nerveux	**11 918**	**40.4**	**16 220**	**51.8**	**11 928**	**40.5**	**15 704**	**50.3**
Diseases of the circulatory system — Maladies de l'appareil circulatoire								
Total	103 247	350.0	136 267	435.4	96 728	328.4	125 186	401.1
Acute rheumatic fever and chronic rheumatic heart diseases — Rhumatisme articularie aigu et cardiopathies rhumatismales chroniques	696	2.4	1 547	4.9	702	2.4	1 526	4.9
Hypertensive diseases — Maladies hypertensives	11 838	40.1	22 929	73.3	11 503	39.1	21 789	69.8
Ischaemic heart disease — Cardiopathie ischémique	37 366	126.7	35 806	114.4	34 869	118.4	31 999	102.5
Cerebrovascular disease — Maladie cérébrovasculaire	24 342	82.5	37 442	119.6	22 442	76.2	34 516	110.6

20. Death and death rates by cause and sex: 2014 - 2018
Décès et taux de mortalité par cause et sexe : 2014 - 2018 (continued - suite)

Italy - Italie

Cause of death — Cause de décès	2015 (C)				2016 (C)			
	Male — Masculin		Female — Féminin		Male — Masculin		Female — Féminin	
	Number Nombre	Rate Taux	Number Nombre	Rate Taux	Number Nombre	Rate Taux	Number Nombre	Rate Taux
Diseases of arteries, arterioles and capillaries — Maladies des artères, artérioles et capillaires	**4 056**	**13.7**	**3 444**	**11.0**	**4 113**	**14.0**	**3 437**	**11.0**
Diseases of the respiratory system — Maladies de l'appareil respiratoire								
Total	**25 512**	**86.5**	**23 006**	**73.5**	**24 981**	**84.8**	**21 556**	**69.1**
Influenza — Grippe	**196**	**0.7**	**378**	**1.2**	**130**	**0.4**	**168**	**0.5**
Pneumonia — Pneumopathies	**5 491**	**18.6**	**6 141**	**19.6**	**5 286**	**17.9**	**5 551**	**17.8**
Chronic lower respiratory diseases — Maladies chroniques des voies respiratoires inférieures	**12 953**	**43.9**	**9 545**	**30.5**	**13 683**	**46.5**	**10 027**	**32.1**
Diseases of the digestive system — Maladies de l'appareil digestif								
Total	**11 419**	**38.7**	**11 867**	**37.9**	**11 120**	**37.8**	**11 523**	**36.9**
Gastric and duodenal ulcer — Ulcère de l'estomac et du duodénum	**356**	**1.2**	**326**	**1.0**	**311**	**1.1**	**315**	**1.0**
Diseases of the liver — Maladies du foie	**4 668**	**15.8**	**2 944**	**9.4**	**4 706**	**16.0**	**3 072**	**9.8**
Diseases of the musculoskeletal system and connective tissue — Maladies du système ostéo-articularie, des muscles et du tissu conjonctif	**980**	**3.3**	**2 492**	**8.0**	**968**	**3.3**	**2 242**	**7.2**
Diseases of the genitourinary system — Maladies de l'appareil génito-urinaire								
Total	**6 315**	**21.4**	**7 303**	**23.3**	**5 027**	**17.1**	**5 908**	**18.9**
Disorders of kidney and ureter — Affections du rein et de l'uretère	**5 125**	**17.4**	**5 963**	**19.1**	**3 847**	**13.1**	**4 576**	**14.7**
Hyperplasia of prostate — Hyperplasie de la prostate	**258**	...	..	..	**217**	**1.8**	..	..
Pregnancy, childbirth and the puerperium — Grossesse, accouchement et puerpéralité								
Total	..	..	**16**	**♦3.3**	..	..	**13**	**♦2.7**
Pregnancy with abortive outcome — Grossesse se terminant par un avortement	..	..	**1**	**♦0.2**	..	..	**2**	**♦0.4**
Other direct obstetric causes — Autres décès maternels directs	..	..	**15**	**♦3.1**	..	..	**11**	**♦2.3**
Indirect obstetric causes — Décès maternels indirects	..	..	**-**	**-**	..	..	**-**	**-**
Certain conditions originating in the perinatal period — Certaines affections dont l'origine se situe dans la période périnatale	**464**	**185.6**	**393**	**166.6**	**482**	**198.3**	**409**	**177.5**
Congenital malformations, deformations and chromosomal abnormalities — Malformations congénitales et anomalies chromosomiques	**753**	**301.3**	**641**	**271.8**	**654**	**269.0**	**578**	**250.9**
Symptoms, signs and abnormal clinical and laboratory findings, not elsewhere classified — Symptômes, signes et résultats anormaux d'examens cliniques et de laboratoire, non classés ailleurs	**4 964**	**16.8**	**8 512**	**27.2**	**4 863**	**16.5**	**7 943**	**25.5**
All other diseases — Toutes autres maladies	**439**	**1.5**	**909**	**2.9**	**393**	**1.3**	**888**	**2.8**
External causes — Causes externes								
Total	**13 715**	**46.5**	**10 213**	**32.6**	**14 028**	**47.6**	**10 324**	**33.1**
Accidents								
Total	**9 688**	**32.8**	**8 088**	**25.8**	**9 973**	**33.9**	**8 193**	**26.3**
Transport accidents — Accidents de transport	**2 970**	**10.1**	**783**	**2.5**	**2 847**	**9.7**	**788**	**2.5**
Falls — Chutes	**2 105**	**7.1**	**1 853**	**5.9**	**2 060**	**7.0**	**1 766**	**5.7**
Accidental drowning and submersion — Noyade et submersion accidentelles	**283**	**1.0**	**77**	**0.2**	**268**	**0.9**	**72**	**0.2**
Exposure to smoke, fire and flames — Exposition à la fumée, au feu et aux flammes	**136**	**0.5**	**95**	**0.3**	**134**	**0.5**	**101**	**0.3**
Accidental poisoning by and exposure to noxious substances — Intoxication accidentelle par des substances nocives et exposition à ces substances	**345**	**1.2**	**167**	**0.5**	**335**	**1.1**	**151**	**0.5**
Intentional self-harm — Lésions auto-infligées	**3 104**	**10.5**	**884**	**2.8**	**3 038**	**10.3**	**830**	**2.7**
Assault — Agresssions	**280**	**0.9**	**112**	**0.4**	**235**	**0.8**	**129**	**0.4**
All other external causes — Toutes autres causes externes	**643**	**2.2**	**1 129**	**3.6**	**782**	**2.7**	**1 172**	**3.8**

20. Death and death rates by cause and sex: 2014 - 2018
Décès et taux de mortalité par cause et sexe : 2014 - 2018 (continued - suite)

Latvia - Lettonie

Cause of death — Cause de décès	2014 (+C)				2015 (+C)			
	Male — Masculin		Female — Féminin		Male — Masculin		Female — Féminin	
	Number Nombre	Rate Taux	Number Nombre	Rate Taux	Number Nombre	Rate Taux	Number Nombre	Rate Taux
TOTAL	**13 557**	**1 483.1**	**14 644**	**1 356.4**	**13 164**	**1 444.7**	**15 021**	**1 397.4**
Certain infectious and parasitic diseases — Certaines maladies infectieuses et parasitaires								
Total	184	20.1	105	9.7	203	22.3	106	9.9
Intestinal infectious diseases — Maladies infectieuses intestinales	1	♦0.1	3	♦0.3	2	♦0.2	5	♦0.5
Tuberculosis — Tuberculose	37	4.0	10	♦0.9	73	8.0	14	♦1.3
Tetanus — Tétanos	-	-	-	-	-	-	-	-
Diphtheria — Diphtérie	-	-	1	♦0.1	1	♦0.1	-	-
Whooping cough — Coqueluche	-	-	-	-	-	-	-	-
Meningococcal infection — Infection à méningocoques	-	-	-	-	-	-	-	-
Septicaemia — Septicémie	15	♦1.6	18	♦1.7	10	♦1.1	20	♦1.9
Acute poliomyelitis — Poliomyélite aiguë	-	-	-	-	-	-	-	-
Measles — Rougeole	-	-	-	-	-	-	-	-
Viral hepatitis — Hépatite virale	28	♦3.1	18	♦1.7	36	4.0	18	♦1.7
Human immunodeficiency virus [HIV] disease — Maladies dues au virus de l'immunodéficience humaine (VIH)	70	7.7	32	3.0	59	6.5	27	♦2.5
Malaria — Paludisme	-	-	-	-	-	-	-	-
Neoplasms — Tumeurs	3 273	358.0	2 807	260.0	3 093	339.4	2 898	269.6
Malignant neoplasms — Tumeurs malignes								
Total	3 233	353.7	2 739	253.7	3 044	334.1	2 832	263.5
Malignant neoplasm of lip, oral cavity and pharynx — Tumeur maligne de la lèvre, de la cavité buccale et du pharynx	154	16.8	37	3.4	148	16.2	36	3.3
Malignant neoplasm of oesophagus — Tumeur maligne de l'oesophage	113	12.4	20	♦1.9	106	11.6	21	♦2.0
Malignant neoplasm of stomach — Tumeur maligne de l'estomac	252	27.6	202	18.7	278	30.5	194	18.0
Malignant neoplasm of colon, rectosigmoid junction, rectum, anus and anal canal — Tumeur maligne du côlon, de la jonction recto-sigmoïdienne, du rectum, de l'anus et du canal anal	336	36.8	353	32.7	311	34.1	392	36.5
Malignant neoplasm of liver and intrahepatic bile ducts — Tumeur maligne du foie et des voies bilaires intrahépatiques	85	9.3	65	6.0	80	8.8	54	5.0
Malignant neoplasm of pancreas — Tumeur maligne du pancréas	173	18.9	202	18.7	170	18.7	202	18.8
Malignant neoplasm of trachea, bronchus and lung — Tumeur maligne de la trachée, des bronches et du poumon	760	83.1	186	17.2	674	74.0	217	20.2
Malignant neoplasm of female breast — Tumeur maligne du sein chez la femme	..	..	439	46.9	..	..	445	47.9
Malignant neoplasm of cervix uteri — Tumeur maligne du col de l'utérus	..	..	111	11.9	..	..	117	12.6
Malignant neoplasm of prostate — Tumeur maligne de la prostate	409	132.7	..	..	392	126.9	..	..
Malignant neoplasm of lymphoid, haematopoietic and related tissue — Tumeurs malignes primitives ou présumées primitives des tissus lymphoïde, hématopoïétique et apparentés	195	21.3	238	22.0	171	18.8	206	19.2
Disorders of the blood and blood-forming organs and certain disorders involving the immune mechanism — Maladies du sang et des organes hématopoïétiques et certains troubles du système immunitaire								
Total	16	♦1.8	24	♦2.2	12	♦1.3	16	♦1.5
Anaemias — Anémies	10	♦1.1	15	♦1.4	6	♦0.7	11	♦1.0
Endocrine, nutritional and metabolic diseases — Maladies endocriniennes, nutritionnelles et métaboliques								
Total	187	20.5	342	31.7	191	21.0	315	29.3
Diabetes mellitus — Diabète sucré	178	19.5	326	30.2	182	20.0	290	27.0
Malnutrition — Malnutrition	1	♦0.1	1	♦0.1	-	-	-	-
Mental and behavioural disorders — Troubles mentaux et du comportement	145	15.9	161	14.9	200	21.9	209	19.4
Diseases of the nervous system — Maladies du système nerveux	150	16.4	156	14.4	171	18.8	203	18.9
Diseases of the circulatory system — Maladies de l'appareil circulatoire								
Total	6 699	732.8	9 372	868.1	6 573	721.4	9 562	889.6
Acute rheumatic fever and chronic rheumatic heart diseases — Rhumatisme articularie aigu et cardiopathies rhumatismales chroniques	9	♦1.0	40	3.7	13	♦1.4	25	♦2.3
Hypertensive diseases — Maladies hypertensives	374	40.9	703	65.1	334	36.7	740	68.8
Ischaemic heart disease — Cardiopathie ischémique	3 551	388.5	4 536	420.1	3 498	383.9	4 536	422.0
Cerebrovascular disease — Maladie cérébrovasculaire	1 717	187.8	3 157	292.4	1 730	189.9	3 379	314.4

20. Death and death rates by cause and sex: 2014 - 2018
Décès et taux de mortalité par cause et sexe : 2014 - 2018 (continued - suite)

Latvia - Lettonie

Cause of death — Cause de décès	2014 (+C)				2015 (+C)			
	Male — Masculin		Female — Féminin		Male — Masculin		Female — Féminin	
	Number Nombre	Rate Taux	Number Nombre	Rate Taux	Number Nombre	Rate Taux	Number Nombre	Rate Taux
Diseases of arteries, arterioles and capillaries — Maladies des artères, artérioles et capillaires	**202**	**22.1**	**228**	**21.1**	**179**	**19.6**	**233**	**21.7**
Diseases of the respiratory system — Maladies de l'appareil respiratoire								
Total	**476**	**52.1**	**220**	**20.4**	**475**	**52.1**	**237**	**22.0**
Influenza — Grippe	**-**	**-**	**2**	**♦0.2**	**10**	**♦1.1**	**10**	**♦0.9**
Pneumonia — Pneumopathies	**220**	**24.1**	**126**	**11.7**	**209**	**22.9**	**130**	**12.1**
Chronic lower respiratory diseases — Maladies chroniques des voies respiratoires inférieures	**218**	**23.8**	**64**	**5.9**	**208**	**22.8**	**82**	**7.6**
Diseases of the digestive system — Maladies de l'appareil digestif								
Total	**529**	**57.9**	**460**	**42.6**	**506**	**55.5**	**509**	**47.4**
Gastric and duodenal ulcer — Ulcère de l'estomac et du duodénum	**66**	**7.2**	**75**	**6.9**	**49**	**5.4**	**77**	**7.2**
Diseases of the liver — Maladies du foie	**249**	**27.2**	**164**	**15.2**	**267**	**29.3**	**155**	**14.4**
Diseases of the musculoskeletal system and connective tissue — Maladies du système ostéo-articularie, des muscles et du tissu conjonctif	**25**	**♦2.7**	**46**	**4.3**	**38**	**4.2**	**54**	**5.0**
Diseases of the genitourinary system — Maladies de l'appareil génito-urinaire								
Total	**186**	**20.3**	**188**	**17.4**	**165**	**18.1**	**224**	**20.8**
Disorders of kidney and ureter — Affections du rein et de l'uretère	**113**	**12.4**	**152**	**14.1**	**116**	**12.7**	**189**	**17.6**
Hyperplasia of prostate — Hyperplasie de la prostate	**46**	**14.9**	..	..	**32**	**10.4**	..	..
Pregnancy, childbirth and the puerperium — Grossesse, accouchement et puerpéralité								
Total	..	..	**2**	**♦9.2**	..	..	**12**	**♦54.6**
Pregnancy with abortive outcome — Grossesse se terminant par un avortement	..	..	**-**	**-**	..	..	**-**	**-**
Other direct obstetric causes — Autres décès maternels directs	..	..	**1**	**♦4.6**	..	..	**9**	**♦40.9**
Indirect obstetric causes — Décès maternels indirects	..	..	**1**	**♦4.6**	..	..	**3**	**♦13.6**
Certain conditions originating in the perinatal period — Certaines affections dont l'origine se situe dans la période périnatale	**26**	**♦231.5**	**16**	**♦152.1**	**26**	**♦227.2**	**17**	**♦161.3**
Congenital malformations, deformations and chromosomal abnormalities — Malformations congénitales et anomalies chromosomiques	**27**	**♦240.4**	**20**	**♦190.2**	**29**	**♦253.5**	**23**	**♦218.3**
Symptoms, signs and abnormal clinical and laboratory findings, not elsewhere classified — Symptômes, signes et résultats anormaux d'examens cliniques et de laboratoire, non classés ailleurs	**191**	**20.9**	**215**	**19.9**	**141**	**15.5**	**165**	**15.4**
All other diseases — Toutes autres maladies	**24**	**♦2.6**	**59**	**5.5**	**22**	**♦2.4**	**36**	**3.3**
External causes — Causes externes								
Total	**1 419**	**155.2**	**451**	**41.8**	**1 319**	**144.8**	**435**	**40.5**
Accidents								
Total	**863**	**94.4**	**283**	**26.2**	**787**	**86.4**	**266**	**24.7**
Transport accidents — Accidents de transport	**182**	**19.9**	**58**	**5.4**	**164**	**18.0**	**54**	**5.0**
Falls — Chutes	**115**	**12.6**	**62**	**5.7**	**132**	**14.5**	**74**	**6.9**
Accidental drowning and submersion — Noyade et submersion accidentelles	**152**	**16.6**	**30**	**♦2.8**	**94**	**10.3**	**25**	**♦2.3**
Exposure to smoke, fire and flames — Exposition à la fumée, au feu et aux flammes	**73**	**8.0**	**37**	**3.4**	**67**	**7.4**	**35**	**3.3**
Accidental poisoning by and exposure to noxious substances — Intoxication accidentelle par des substances nocives et exposition à ces substances	**121**	**13.2**	**29**	**♦2.7**	**125**	**13.7**	**26**	**♦2.4**
Intentional self-harm — Lésions auto-infligées	**311**	**34.0**	**71**	**6.6**	**305**	**33.5**	**81**	**7.5**
Assault — Agresssions	**97**	**10.6**	**40**	**3.7**	**69**	**7.6**	**30**	**♦2.8**
All other external causes — Toutes autres causes externes	**148**	**16.2**	**57**	**5.3**	**158**	**17.3**	**58**	**5.4**

20. Death and death rates by cause and sex: 2014 - 2018
Décès et taux de mortalité par cause et sexe : 2014 - 2018 (continued - suite)

Lithuania - Lituanie

Cause of death — Cause de décès	2017 (+C)				2018 (+C)			
	Male — Masculin		Female — Féminin		Male — Masculin		Female — Féminin	
	Number Nombre	Rate Taux	Number Nombre	Rate Taux	Number Nombre	Rate Taux	Number Nombre	Rate Taux
TOTAL	**19 286**	**1 469.8**	**20 856**	**1 358.1**	**19 024**	**1 466.4**	**20 550**	**1 359.5**
Certain infectious and parasitic diseases — Certaines maladies infectieuses et parasitaires								
Total	336	25.6	297	19.3	320	24.7	293	19.4
Intestinal infectious diseases — Maladies infectieuses intestinales	13	♦1.0	43	2.8	19	♦1.5	42	2.8
Tuberculosis — Tuberculose	123	9.4	28	♦1.8	85	6.6	23	♦1.5
Tetanus — Tétanos	-	-	1	♦0.1	-	-	1	♦0.1
Diphtheria — Diphtérie	-	-	-	-	-	-	-	-
Whooping cough — Coqueluche	-	-	-	-	-	-	-	-
Meningococcal infection — Infection à méningocoques	5	♦0.4	4	♦0.3	2	♦0.2	4	♦0.3
Septicaemia — Septicémie	115	8.8	182	11.9	142	10.9	179	11.8
Acute poliomyelitis — Poliomyélite aiguë	-	-	-	-	-	-	-	-
Measles — Rougeole	-	-	-	-	-	-	-	-
Viral hepatitis — Hépatite virale	16	♦1.2	10	♦0.7	17	♦1.3	11	♦0.7
Human immunodeficiency virus [HIV] disease — Maladies dues au virus de l'immunodéficience humaine (VIH)	29	♦2.2	2	♦0.1	19	♦1.5	5	♦0.3
Malaria — Paludisme	-	-	-	-	-	-	2	♦0.1
Neoplasms — Tumeurs	**4 473**	**340.9**	**3 711**	**241.6**	**4 505**	**347.3**	**3 700**	**244.8**
Malignant neoplasms — Tumeurs malignes								
Total	4 389	334.5	3 607	234.9	4 424	341.0	3 604	238.4
Malignant neoplasm of lip, oral cavity and pharynx — Tumeur maligne de la lèvre, de la cavité buccale et du pharynx	245	18.7	57	3.7	280	21.6	55	3.6
Malignant neoplasm of oesophagus — Tumeur maligne de l'oesophage	158	12.0	35	2.3	159	12.3	25	♦1.7
Malignant neoplasm of stomach — Tumeur maligne de l'estomac	391	29.8	256	16.7	345	26.6	247	16.3
Malignant neoplasm of colon, rectosigmoid junction, rectum, anus and anal canal — Tumeur maligne du côlon, de la jonction recto-sigmoïdienne, du rectum, de l'anus et du canal anal	453	34.5	458	29.8	456	35.2	431	28.5
Malignant neoplasm of liver and intrahepatic bile ducts — Tumeur maligne du foie et des voies bilaires intrahépatiques	132	10.1	84	5.5	133	10.3	83	5.5
Malignant neoplasm of pancreas — Tumeur maligne du pancréas	229	17.5	276	18.0	244	18.8	260	17.2
Malignant neoplasm of trachea, bronchus and lung — Tumeur maligne de la trachée, des bronches et du poumon	962	73.3	269	17.5	931	71.8	269	17.8
Malignant neoplasm of female breast — Tumeur maligne du sein chez la femme	..	..	489	36.8	..	..	521	39.9
Malignant neoplasm of cervix uteri — Tumeur maligne du col de l'utérus	..	..	199	15.0	..	..	189	14.5
Malignant neoplasm of prostate — Tumeur maligne de la prostate	525	113.9	..	..	524	113.2	..	..
Malignant neoplasm of lymphoid, haematopoietic and related tissue — Tumeurs malignes primitives ou présumées primitives des tissus lymphoïde, hématopoïétique et apparentés	257	19.6	283	18.4	272	21.0	290	19.2
Disorders of the blood and blood-forming organs and certain disorders involving the immune mechanism — Maladies du sang et des organes hématopoïétiques et certains troubles du système immunitaire								
Total	14	♦1.1	28	♦1.8	10	♦0.8	34	2.2
Anaemias — Anémies	3	♦0.2	12	♦0.8	5	♦0.4	25	♦1.7
Endocrine, nutritional and metabolic diseases — Maladies endocriniennes, nutritionnelles et métaboliques								
Total	202	15.4	256	16.7	220	17.0	343	22.7
Diabetes mellitus — Diabète sucré	186	14.2	234	15.2	206	15.9	322	21.3
Malnutrition — Malnutrition	6	♦0.5	2	♦0.1	1	♦0.1	2	♦0.1
Mental and behavioural disorders — Troubles mentaux et du comportement	86	6.6	192	12.5	76	5.9	191	12.6
Diseases of the nervous system — Maladies du système nerveux	318	24.2	395	25.7	352	27.1	420	27.8
Diseases of the circulatory system — Maladies de l'appareil circulatoire								
Total	9 286	707.7	13 225	861.2	8 994	693.3	12 928	855.2
Acute rheumatic fever and chronic rheumatic heart diseases — Rhumatisme articularie aigu et cardiopathies rhumatismales chroniques	16	♦1.2	30	♦2.0	12	♦0.9	33	2.2
Hypertensive diseases — Maladies hypertensives	361	27.5	552	35.9	399	30.8	648	42.9
Ischaemic heart disease — Cardiopathie ischémique	6 004	457.6	8 492	553.0	5 744	442.8	8 152	539.3
Cerebrovascular disease — Maladie cérébrovasculaire	1 950	148.6	3 418	222.6	1 962	151.2	3 390	224.3

20. Death and death rates by cause and sex: 2014 - 2018
Décès et taux de mortalité par cause et sexe : 2014 - 2018 (continued - suite)

Lithuania - Lituanie

Cause of death — Cause de décès	2017 (+C)				2018 (+C)			
	Male — Masculin		Female — Féminin		Male — Masculin		Female — Féminin	
	Number Nombre	Rate Taux	Number Nombre	Rate Taux	Number Nombre	Rate Taux	Number Nombre	Rate Taux
Diseases of arteries, arterioles and capillaries — Maladies des artères, artérioles et capillaires	248	18.9	189	12.3	205	15.8	162	10.7
Diseases of the respiratory system — Maladies de l'appareil respiratoire								
Total	867	66.1	477	31.1	910	70.1	479	31.7
Influenza — Grippe	6	♦0.5	8	♦0.5	10	♦0.8	14	♦0.9
Pneumonia — Pneumopathies	351	26.7	227	14.8	398	30.7	253	16.7
Chronic lower respiratory diseases — Maladies chroniques des voies respiratoires inférieures	466	35.5	219	14.3	431	33.2	175	11.6
Diseases of the digestive system — Maladies de l'appareil digestif								
Total	1 037	79.0	956	62.3	1 020	78.6	880	58.2
Gastric and duodenal ulcer — Ulcère de l'estomac et du duodénum	151	11.5	163	10.6	158	12.2	150	9.9
Diseases of the liver — Maladies du foie	499	38.0	274	17.8	467	36.0	256	16.9
Diseases of the musculoskeletal system and connective tissue — Maladies du système ostéo-articularie, des muscles et du tissu conjonctif	44	3.4	60	3.9	49	3.8	67	4.4
Diseases of the genitourinary system — Maladies de l'appareil génito-urinaire								
Total	139	10.6	204	13.3	135	10.4	173	11.4
Disorders of kidney and ureter — Affections du rein et de l'uretère	120	9.1	175	11.4	111	8.6	137	9.1
Hyperplasia of prostate — Hyperplasie de la prostate	5	♦1.1	..	..	8	♦1.7	..	..
Pregnancy, childbirth and the puerperium — Grossesse, accouchement et puerpéralité								
Total	..	..	2	♦7.0	..	..	4	♦14.2
Pregnancy with abortive outcome — Grossesse se terminant par un avortement	..	..	-	-	..	..	-	-
Other direct obstetric causes — Autres décès maternels directs	..	..	-	-	..	..	3	♦10.7
Indirect obstetric causes — Décès maternels indirects	..	..	2	♦7.0	..	..	1	♦3.6
Certain conditions originating in the perinatal period — Certaines affections dont l'origine se situe dans la période périnatale	14	♦94.8	15	♦107.8	23	♦160.1	19	♦137.8
Congenital malformations, deformations and chromosomal abnormalities — Malformations congénitales et anomalies chromosomiques	33	223.4	33	237.1	34	236.7	36	261.1
Symptoms, signs and abnormal clinical and laboratory findings, not elsewhere classified — Symptômes, signes et résultats anormaux d'examens cliniques et de laboratoire, non classés ailleurs	376	28.7	192	12.5	478	36.8	205	13.6
All other diseases — Toutes autres maladies	24	♦1.8	40	2.6	20	♦1.5	38	2.5
External causes — Causes externes								
Total	2 037	155.2	773	50.3	1 878	144.8	740	49.0
Accidents								
Total	1 153	87.9	504	32.8	1 033	79.6	505	33.4
Transport accidents — Accidents de transport	179	13.6	71	4.6	161	12.4	63	4.2
Falls — Chutes	227	17.3	197	12.8	237	18.3	214	14.2
Accidental drowning and submersion — Noyade et submersion accidentelles	107	8.2	35	2.3	117	9.0	38	2.5
Exposure to smoke, fire and flames — Exposition à la fumée, au feu et aux flammes	18	♦1.4	11	♦0.7	21	♦1.6	8	♦0.5
Accidental poisoning by and exposure to noxious substances — Intoxication accidentelle par des substances nocives et exposition à ces substances	305	23.2	92	6.0	246	19.0	71	4.7
Intentional self-harm — Lésions auto-infligées	595	45.3	153	10.0	543	41.9	140	9.3
Assault — Agresssions	56	4.3	22	♦1.4	60	4.6	12	♦0.8
All other external causes — Toutes autres causes externes	233	17.8	94	6.1	242	18.7	83	5.5

20. Death and death rates by cause and sex: 2014 - 2018
Décès et taux de mortalité par cause et sexe : 2014 - 2018 (continued - suite)

Luxembourg

Cause of death — Cause de décès	2015 (+C)				2016 (+C)			
	Male — Masculin		Female — Féminin		Male — Masculin		Female — Féminin	
	Number Nombre	Rate Taux	Number Nombre	Rate Taux	Number Nombre	Rate Taux	Number Nombre	Rate Taux
TOTAL	**1 869**	**662.8**	**1 970**	**701.1**	**1 945**	**672.6**	**1 913**	**666.4**
Certain infectious and parasitic diseases — Certaines maladies infectieuses et parasitaires								
Total	35	12.4	33	11.7	24	♦8.3	27	♦9.4
Intestinal infectious diseases — Maladies infectieuses intestinales	2	♦0.7	1	♦0.4	-	-	1	♦0.3
Tuberculosis — Tuberculose	1	♦0.4	-	-	-	-	1	♦0.3
Tetanus — Tétanos	-	-	-	-	-	-	-	-
Diphtheria — Diphtérie	-	-	-	-	-	-	-	-
Whooping cough — Coqueluche	-	-	-	-	-	-	-	-
Meningococcal infection — Infection à méningocoques	-	-	-	-	-	-	-	-
Septicaemia — Septicémie	22	♦7.8	27	♦9.6	14	♦4.8	14	♦4.9
Acute poliomyelitis — Poliomyélite aiguë	-	-	-	-	-	-	-	-
Measles — Rougeole	-	-	-	-	-	-	-	-
Viral hepatitis — Hépatite virale	3	♦1.1	-	-	1	♦0.3	1	♦0.3
Human immunodeficiency virus [HIV] disease — Maladies dues au virus de l'immunodéficience humaine (VIH)	4	♦1.4	-	-	1	♦0.3	1	♦0.3
Malaria — Paludisme	-	-	-	-	-	-	-	-
Neoplasms — Tumeurs	**561**	**199.0**	**519**	**184.7**	**616**	**213.0**	**470**	**163.7**
Malignant neoplasms — Tumeurs malignes								
Total	535	189.7	499	177.6	597	206.4	449	156.4
Malignant neoplasm of lip, oral cavity and pharynx — Tumeur maligne de la lèvre, de la cavité buccale et du pharynx	10	♦3.5	7	♦2.5	12	♦4.1	4	♦1.4
Malignant neoplasm of oesophagus — Tumeur maligne de l'oesophage	12	♦4.3	7	♦2.5	23	♦8.0	8	♦2.8
Malignant neoplasm of stomach — Tumeur maligne de l'estomac	15	♦5.3	16	♦5.7	32	11.1	15	♦5.2
Malignant neoplasm of colon, rectosigmoid junction, rectum, anus and anal canal — Tumeur maligne du côlon, de la jonction recto-sigmoïdienne, du rectum, de l'anus et du canal anal	56	19.9	58	20.6	60	20.7	43	15.0
Malignant neoplasm of liver and intrahepatic bile ducts — Tumeur maligne du foie et des voies bilaires intrahépatiques	31	11.0	12	♦4.3	31	10.7	17	♦5.9
Malignant neoplasm of pancreas — Tumeur maligne du pancréas	27	♦9.6	34	12.1	42	14.5	34	11.8
Malignant neoplasm of trachea, bronchus and lung — Tumeur maligne de la trachée, des bronches et du poumon	145	51.4	79	28.1	169	58.4	69	24.0
Malignant neoplasm of female breast — Tumeur maligne du sein chez la femme	..	..	93	39.0	..	..	89	36.9
Malignant neoplasm of cervix uteri — Tumeur maligne du col de l'utérus	..	..	10	♦4.2	..	..	4	♦1.7
Malignant neoplasm of prostate — Tumeur maligne de la prostate	55	60.0	..	..	50	53.6	..	..
Malignant neoplasm of lymphoid, haematopoietic and related tissue — Tumeurs malignes primitives ou présumées primitives des tissus lymphoïde, hématopoïétique et apparentés	56	19.9	44	15.7	44	15.2	43	15.0
Disorders of the blood and blood-forming organs and certain disorders involving the immune mechanism — Maladies du sang et des organes hématopoïétiques et certains troubles du système immunitaire								
Total	12	♦4.3	8	♦2.8	12	♦4.1	12	♦4.2
Anaemias — Anémies	6	♦2.1	5	♦1.8	5	♦1.7	5	♦1.7
Endocrine, nutritional and metabolic diseases — Maladies endocriniennes, nutritionnelles et métaboliques								
Total	52	18.4	69	24.6	49	16.9	56	19.5
Diabetes mellitus — Diabète sucré	41	14.5	42	14.9	31	10.7	30	♦10.5
Malnutrition — Malnutrition	4	♦1.4	7	♦2.5	9	♦3.1	10	♦3.5
Mental and behavioural disorders — Troubles mentaux et du comportement	**94**	**33.3**	**136**	**48.4**	**95**	**32.9**	**136**	**47.4**
Diseases of the nervous system — Maladies du système nerveux	**81**	**28.7**	**102**	**36.3**	**83**	**28.7**	**85**	**29.6**
Diseases of the circulatory system — Maladies de l'appareil circulatoire								
Total	536	190.1	626	222.8	572	197.8	658	229.2
Acute rheumatic fever and chronic rheumatic heart diseases — Rhumatisme articularie aigu et cardiopathies rhumatismales chroniques	7	♦2.5	9	♦3.2	8	♦2.8	13	♦4.5
Hypertensive diseases — Maladies hypertensives	18	♦6.4	52	18.5	19	♦6.6	46	16.0
Ischaemic heart disease — Cardiopathie ischémique	184	65.3	124	44.1	212	73.3	148	51.6
Cerebrovascular disease — Maladie cérébrovasculaire	104	36.9	127	45.2	93	32.2	121	42.2

20. Death and death rates by cause and sex: 2014 - 2018
Décès et taux de mortalité par cause et sexe : 2014 - 2018 (continued - suite)

Luxembourg

Cause of death — Cause de décès	2015 (+C)				2016 (+C)			
	Male — Masculin		Female — Féminin		Male — Masculin		Female — Féminin	
	Number Nombre	Rate Taux	Number Nombre	Rate Taux	Number Nombre	Rate Taux	Number Nombre	Rate Taux
Diseases of arteries, arterioles and capillaries — Maladies des artères, artérioles et capillaires	36	12.8	22	♦7.8	21	♦7.3	22	♦7.7
Diseases of the respiratory system — Maladies de l'appareil respiratoire								
Total	148	52.5	171	60.9	147	50.8	145	50.5
Influenza — Grippe	4	♦1.4	4	♦1.4	1	♦0.3	2	♦0.7
Pneumonia — Pneumopathies	38	13.5	47	16.7	40	13.8	45	15.7
Chronic lower respiratory diseases — Maladies chroniques des voies respiratoires inférieures	79	28.0	83	29.5	72	24.9	73	25.4
Diseases of the digestive system — Maladies de l'appareil digestif								
Total	78	27.7	88	31.3	105	36.3	100	34.8
Gastric and duodenal ulcer — Ulcère de l'estomac et du duodénum	1	♦0.4	8	♦2.8	3	♦1.0	1	♦0.3
Diseases of the liver — Maladies du foie	38	13.5	27	♦9.6	61	21.1	25	♦8.7
Diseases of the musculoskeletal system and connective tissue — Maladies du système ostéo-articularie, des muscles et du tissu conjonctif	8	♦2.8	18	♦6.4	3	♦1.0	14	♦4.9
Diseases of the genitourinary system — Maladies de l'appareil génito-urinaire								
Total	36	12.8	36	12.8	31	10.7	27	♦9.4
Disorders of kidney and ureter — Affections du rein et de l'uretère	31	11.0	26	♦9.3	26	♦9.0	23	♦8.0
Hyperplasia of prostate — Hyperplasie de la prostate	1	♦1.1	..	..	2	♦2.1	..	..
Pregnancy, childbirth and the puerperium — Grossesse, accouchement et puerpéralité								
Total	..	..	-	-	..	..	-	-
Pregnancy with abortive outcome — Grossesse se terminant par un avortement	..	..	-	-	..	..	-	-
Other direct obstetric causes — Autres décès maternels directs	..	..	-	-	..	..	-	-
Indirect obstetric causes — Décès maternels indirects	..	..	-	-	..	..	-	-
Certain conditions originating in the perinatal period — Certaines affections dont l'origine se situe dans la période périnatale	3	♦94.7	1	♦33.9	7	♦227.5	4	♦134.5
Congenital malformations, deformations and chromosomal abnormalities — Malformations congénitales et anomalies chromosomiques	6	♦189.4	2	♦67.9	4	♦130.0	7	♦235.5
Symptoms, signs and abnormal clinical and laboratory findings, not elsewhere classified — Symptômes, signes et résultats anormaux d'examens cliniques et de laboratoire, non classés ailleurs	52	18.4	65	23.1	54	18.7	66	23.0
All other diseases — Toutes autres maladies	1	♦0.4	3	♦1.1	-	-	3	♦1.0
External causes — Causes externes								
Total	166	58.9	93	33.1	143	49.4	103	35.9
Accidents								
Total	87	30.9	62	22.1	85	29.4	77	26.8
Transport accidents — Accidents de transport	20	♦7.1	5	♦1.8	23	♦8.0	10	♦3.5
Falls — Chutes	29	♦10.3	24	♦8.5	24	♦8.3	28	♦9.8
Accidental drowning and submersion — Noyade et submersion accidentelles	3	♦1.1	1	♦0.4	-	-	1	♦0.3
Exposure to smoke, fire and flames — Exposition à la fumée, au feu et aux flammes	-	-	2	♦0.7	-	-	1	♦0.3
Accidental poisoning by and exposure to noxious substances — Intoxication accidentelle par des substances nocives et exposition à ces substances	6	♦2.1	6	♦2.1	2	♦0.7	1	♦0.3
Intentional self-harm — Lésions auto-infligées	45	16.0	19	♦6.8	32	11.1	11	♦3.8
Assault — Agresssions	3	♦1.1	2	♦0.7	2	♦0.7	1	♦0.3
All other external causes — Toutes autres causes externes	31	11.0	10	♦3.6	24	♦8.3	14	♦4.9

20. Death and death rates by cause and sex: 2014 - 2018
Décès et taux de mortalité par cause et sexe : 2014 - 2018 (continued - suite)

Malta - Malte

Cause of death — Cause de décès	2015 (+C)				2016 (+C)			
	Male — Masculin		Female — Féminin		Male — Masculin		Female — Féminin	
	Number Nombre	Rate Taux	Number Nombre	Rate Taux	Number Nombre	Rate Taux	Number Nombre	Rate Taux
TOTAL	**1 734**	**776.0**	**1 709**	**771.1**	**1 645**	**718.2**	**1 698**	**750.2**
Certain infectious and parasitic diseases — Certaines maladies infectieuses et parasitaires								
Total	9	♦4.0	13	♦5.9	18	♦7.9	18	♦8.0
Intestinal infectious diseases — Maladies infectieuses intestinales	-	-	2	♦0.9	1	♦0.4	-	-
Tuberculosis — Tuberculose	1	♦0.4	-	-	-	-	-	-
Tetanus — Tétanos	-	-	-	-	-	-	-	-
Diphtheria — Diphtérie	-	-	-	-	-	-	-	-
Whooping cough — Coqueluche	-	-	-	-	-	-	-	-
Meningococcal infection — Infection à méningocoques	-	-	-	-	-	-	1	♦0.4
Septicaemia — Septicémie	5	♦2.2	8	♦3.6	7	♦3.1	14	♦6.2
Acute poliomyelitis — Poliomyélite aiguë	-	-	-	-	-	-	-	-
Measles — Rougeole	-	-	-	-	-	-	-	-
Viral hepatitis — Hépatite virale	-	-	-	-	2	♦0.9	-	-
Human immunodeficiency virus [HIV] disease — Maladies dues au virus de l'immunodéficience humaine (VIH)	2	♦0.9	1	♦0.5	6	♦2.6	1	♦0.4
Malaria — Paludisme	-	-	-	-	-	-	-	-
Neoplasms — Tumeurs	510	228.2	427	192.7	513	224.0	436	192.6
Malignant neoplasms — Tumeurs malignes								
Total	502	224.6	413	186.3	503	219.6	426	188.2
Malignant neoplasm of lip, oral cavity and pharynx — Tumeur maligne de la lèvre, de la cavité buccale et du pharynx	17	♦7.6	8	♦3.6	9	♦3.9	7	♦3.1
Malignant neoplasm of oesophagus — Tumeur maligne de l'oesophage	12	♦5.4	5	♦2.3	9	♦3.9	5	♦2.2
Malignant neoplasm of stomach — Tumeur maligne de l'estomac	17	♦7.6	17	♦7.7	29	♦12.7	17	♦7.5
Malignant neoplasm of colon, rectosigmoid junction, rectum, anus and anal canal — Tumeur maligne du côlon, de la jonction recto-sigmoïdienne, du rectum, de l'anus et du canal anal	67	30.0	55	24.8	60	26.2	60	26.5
Malignant neoplasm of liver and intrahepatic bile ducts — Tumeur maligne du foie et des voies bilaires intrahépatiques	15	♦6.7	9	♦4.1	31	13.5	8	♦3.5
Malignant neoplasm of pancreas — Tumeur maligne du pancréas	50	22.4	33	14.9	42	18.3	44	19.4
Malignant neoplasm of trachea, bronchus and lung — Tumeur maligne de la trachée, des bronches et du poumon	148	66.2	41	18.5	132	57.6	52	23.0
Malignant neoplasm of female breast — Tumeur maligne du sein chez la femme	..	..	81	43.6	..	..	73	37.4
Malignant neoplasm of cervix uteri — Tumeur maligne du col de l'utérus	..	..	5	♦2.7	..	..	1	♦0.5
Malignant neoplasm of prostate — Tumeur maligne de la prostate	39	48.6	..	..	49	59.1	..	..
Malignant neoplasm of lymphoid, haematopoietic and related tissue — Tumeurs malignes primitives ou présumées primitives des tissus lymphoïde, hématopoïétique et apparentés	38	17.0	33	14.9	33	14.4	33	14.6
Disorders of the blood and blood-forming organs and certain disorders involving the immune mechanism — Maladies du sang et des organes hématopoïétiques et certains troubles du système immunitaire								
Total	1	♦0.4	6	♦2.7	2	♦0.9	4	♦1.8
Anaemias — Anémies	1	♦0.4	3	♦1.4	-	-	4	♦1.8
Endocrine, nutritional and metabolic diseases — Maladies endocriniennes, nutritionnelles et métaboliques								
Total	101	45.2	83	37.4	77	33.6	106	46.8
Diabetes mellitus — Diabète sucré	95	42.5	78	35.2	72	31.4	100	44.2
Malnutrition — Malnutrition	-	-	1	♦0.5	-	-	-	-
Mental and behavioural disorders — Troubles mentaux et du comportement	41	18.3	98	44.2	56	24.4	100	44.2
Diseases of the nervous system — Maladies du système nerveux	49	21.9	50	22.6	47	20.5	47	20.8
Diseases of the circulatory system — Maladies de l'appareil circulatoire								
Total	643	287.7	691	311.8	550	240.1	656	289.8
Acute rheumatic fever and chronic rheumatic heart diseases — Rhumatisme articularie aigu et cardiopathies rhumatismales chroniques	-	-	2	♦0.9	-	-	1	♦0.4
Hypertensive diseases — Maladies hypertensives	14	♦6.3	33	14.9	11	♦4.8	25	♦11.0
Ischaemic heart disease — Cardiopathie ischémique	380	170.0	352	158.8	329	143.6	330	145.8
Cerebrovascular disease — Maladie cérébrovasculaire	126	56.4	153	69.0	108	47.1	151	66.7

20. Death and death rates by cause and sex: 2014 - 2018
Décès et taux de mortalité par cause et sexe : 2014 - 2018 (continued - suite)

Malta - Malte

Cause of death — Cause de décès	2015 (+C)				2016 (+C)			
	Male — Masculin		Female — Féminin		Male — Masculin		Female — Féminin	
	Number Nombre	Rate Taux	Number Nombre	Rate Taux	Number Nombre	Rate Taux	Number Nombre	Rate Taux
Diseases of arteries, arterioles and capillaries — Maladies des artères, artérioles et capillaires	19	♦8.5	19	♦8.6	28	♦12.2	19	♦8.4
Diseases of the respiratory system — Maladies de l'appareil respiratoire								
Total	190	85.0	158	71.3	177	77.3	157	69.4
Influenza — Grippe	-	-	-	-	4	♦1.7	2	♦0.9
Pneumonia — Pneumopathies	43	19.2	55	24.8	37	16.2	52	23.0
Chronic lower respiratory diseases — Maladies chroniques des voies respiratoires inférieures	77	34.5	22	♦9.9	64	27.9	26	♦11.5
Diseases of the digestive system — Maladies de l'appareil digestif								
Total	44	19.7	54	24.4	48	21.0	51	22.5
Gastric and duodenal ulcer — Ulcère de l'estomac et du duodénum	2	♦0.9	4	♦1.8	3	♦1.3	4	♦1.8
Diseases of the liver — Maladies du foie	14	♦6.3	4	♦1.8	20	♦8.7	6	♦2.7
Diseases of the musculoskeletal system and connective tissue — Maladies du système ostéo-articularie, des muscles et du tissu conjonctif	5	♦2.2	11	♦5.0	2	♦0.9	4	♦1.8
Diseases of the genitourinary system — Maladies de l'appareil génito-urinaire								
Total	35	15.7	49	22.1	35	15.3	39	17.2
Disorders of kidney and ureter — Affections du rein et de l'uretère	14	♦6.3	23	♦10.4	20	♦8.7	18	♦8.0
Hyperplasia of prostate — Hyperplasie de la prostate	3	♦3.7	..	..	2	♦2.4	..	..
Pregnancy, childbirth and the puerperium — Grossesse, accouchement et puerpéralité								
Total	..	..	-	-	..	..	-	-
Pregnancy with abortive outcome — Grossesse se terminant par un avortement	..	..	-	-	..	..	-	-
Other direct obstetric causes — Autres décès maternels directs	..	..	-	-	..	..	-	-
Indirect obstetric causes — Décès maternels indirects	..	..	-	-	..	..	-	-
Certain conditions originating in the perinatal period — Certaines affections dont l'origine se situe dans la période périnatale	9	♦407.6	3	♦141.7	13	♦549.7	10	♦473.7
Congenital malformations, deformations and chromosomal abnormalities — Malformations congénitales et anomalies chromosomiques	5	♦226.4	10	♦472.4	9	♦380.5	6	♦284.2
Symptoms, signs and abnormal clinical and laboratory findings, not elsewhere classified — Symptômes, signes et résultats anormaux d'examens cliniques et de laboratoire, non classés ailleurs	5	♦2.2	10	♦4.5	9	♦3.9	10	♦4.4
All other diseases — Toutes autres maladies	8	♦3.6	11	♦5.0	4	♦1.7	13	♦5.7
External causes — Causes externes								
Total	79	35.4	35	15.8	85	37.1	41	18.1
Accidents								
Total	49	21.9	26	♦11.7	63	27.5	33	14.6
Transport accidents — Accidents de transport	9	♦4.0	3	♦1.4	19	♦8.3	6	♦2.7
Falls — Chutes	19	♦8.5	16	♦7.2	26	♦11.4	26	♦11.5
Accidental drowning and submersion — Noyade et submersion accidentelles	2	♦0.9	1	♦0.5	2	♦0.9	-	-
Exposure to smoke, fire and flames — Exposition à la fumée, au feu et aux flammes	-	-	-	-	-	-	-	-
Accidental poisoning by and exposure to noxious substances — Intoxication accidentelle par des substances nocives et exposition à ces substances	7	♦3.1	1	♦0.5	5	♦2.2	-	-
Intentional self-harm — Lésions auto-infligées	27	♦12.1	7	♦3.2	19	♦8.3	5	♦2.2
Assault — Agresssions	2	♦0.9	1	♦0.5	2	♦0.9	2	♦0.9
All other external causes — Toutes autres causes externes	1	♦0.4	1	♦0.5	1	♦0.4	1	♦0.4

20. Death and death rates by cause and sex: 2014 - 2018
Décès et taux de mortalité par cause et sexe : 2014 - 2018 (continued - suite)

Netherlands - Pays-Bas

Cause of death — Cause de décès	2016 (+C)				2017 (+C)			
	Male — Masculin		Female — Féminin		Male — Masculin		Female — Féminin	
	Number Nombre	Rate Taux	Number Nombre	Rate Taux	Number Nombre	Rate Taux	Number Nombre	Rate Taux
TOTAL	**72 180**	**857.5**	**76 817**	**897.2**	**72 661**	**857.3**	**77 553**	**901.1**
Certain infectious and parasitic diseases — Certaines maladies infectieuses et parasitaires								
Total	1 444	17.2	1 610	18.8	1 430	16.9	1 702	19.8
Intestinal infectious diseases — Maladies infectieuses intestinales	207	2.5	307	3.6	170	2.0	345	4.0
Tuberculosis — Tuberculose	8	♦0.1	7	♦0.1	9	♦0.1	5	♦0.1
Tetanus — Tétanos	-	-	-	-	-	-	-	-
Diphtheria — Diphtérie	-	-	-	-	-	-	-	-
Whooping cough — Coqueluche	1	♦0.0	1	♦0.0	1	♦0.0	1	♦0.0
Meningococcal infection — Infection à méningocoques	2	♦0.0	4	♦0.0	4	♦0.0	4	♦0.0
Septicaemia — Septicémie	786	9.3	768	9.0	739	8.7	759	8.8
Acute poliomyelitis — Poliomyélite aiguë	-	-	-	-	-	-	-	-
Measles — Rougeole	-	-	-	-	-	-	-	-
Viral hepatitis — Hépatite virale	25	♦0.3	17	♦0.2	23	♦0.3	8	♦0.1
Human immunodeficiency virus [HIV] disease — Maladies dues au virus de l'immunodéficience humaine (VIH)	27	♦0.3	15	♦0.2	21	♦0.2	4	♦0.0
Malaria — Paludisme	2	♦0.0	1	♦0.0	2	♦0.0	-	-
Neoplasms — Tumeurs	**25 350**	**301.2**	**21 626**	**252.6**	**25 311**	**298.7**	**21 245**	**246.9**
Malignant neoplasms — Tumeurs malignes								
Total	24 542	291.6	20 737	242.2	24 547	289.6	20 361	236.6
Malignant neoplasm of lip, oral cavity and pharynx — Tumeur maligne de la lèvre, de la cavité buccale et du pharynx	435	5.2	242	2.8	406	4.8	258	3.0
Malignant neoplasm of oesophagus — Tumeur maligne de l'oesophage	1 392	16.5	477	5.6	1 374	16.2	510	5.9
Malignant neoplasm of stomach — Tumeur maligne de l'estomac	758	9.0	481	5.6	808	9.5	438	5.1
Malignant neoplasm of colon, rectosigmoid junction, rectum, anus and anal canal — Tumeur maligne du côlon, de la jonction recto-sigmoïdienne, du rectum, de l'anus et du canal anal	2 769	32.9	2 438	28.5	2 775	32.7	2 328	27.0
Malignant neoplasm of liver and intrahepatic bile ducts — Tumeur maligne du foie et des voies bilaires intrahépatiques	678	8.1	418	4.9	717	8.5	403	4.7
Malignant neoplasm of pancreas — Tumeur maligne du pancréas	1 417	16.8	1 413	16.5	1 436	16.9	1 429	16.6
Malignant neoplasm of trachea, bronchus and lung — Tumeur maligne de la trachée, des bronches et du poumon	6 300	74.8	4 391	51.3	6 139	72.4	4 257	49.5
Malignant neoplasm of female breast — Tumeur maligne du sein chez la femme	..	..	3 150	43.8	..	..	3 107	42.9
Malignant neoplasm of cervix uteri — Tumeur maligne du col de l'utérus	..	..	229	3.2	..	..	206	2.8
Malignant neoplasm of prostate — Tumeur maligne de la prostate	2 770	87.6	..	..	2 865	89.0	..	..
Malignant neoplasm of lymphoid, haematopoietic and related tissue — Tumeurs malignes primitives ou présumées primitives des tissus lymphoïde, hématopoïétique et apparentés	2 075	24.7	1 546	18.1	2 042	24.1	1 546	18.0
Disorders of the blood and blood-forming organs and certain disorders involving the immune mechanism — Maladies du sang et des organes hématopoïétiques et certains troubles du système immunitaire								
Total	243	2.9	268	3.1	230	2.7	280	3.3
Anaemias — Anémies	147	1.7	209	2.4	153	1.8	211	2.5
Endocrine, nutritional and metabolic diseases — Maladies endocriniennes, nutritionnelles et métaboliques								
Total	1 700	20.2	1 911	22.3	1 664	19.6	1 903	22.1
Diabetes mellitus — Diabète sucré	1 381	16.4	1 510	17.6	1 315	15.5	1 466	17.0
Malnutrition — Malnutrition	-	-	10	♦0.1	6	♦0.1	10	♦0.1
Mental and behavioural disorders — Troubles mentaux et du comportement	4 173	49.6	7 784	90.9	4 391	51.8	8 207	95.4
Diseases of the nervous system — Maladies du système nerveux	3 680	43.7	4 674	54.6	3 695	43.6	4 712	54.7
Diseases of the circulatory system — Maladies de l'appareil circulatoire								
Total	18 148	215.6	20 499	239.4	18 097	213.5	20 056	233.0
Acute rheumatic fever and chronic rheumatic heart diseases — Rhumatisme articularie aigu et cardiopathies rhumatismales chroniques	66	0.8	160	1.9	80	0.9	187	2.2
Hypertensive diseases — Maladies hypertensives	526	6.2	905	10.6	594	7.0	852	9.9
Ischaemic heart disease — Cardiopathie ischémique	5 065	60.2	3 575	41.8	4 985	58.8	3 352	38.9
Cerebrovascular disease — Maladie cérébrovasculaire	3 931	46.7	5 576	65.1	3 770	44.5	5 429	63.1

20. Death and death rates by cause and sex: 2014 - 2018
Décès et taux de mortalité par cause et sexe : 2014 - 2018 (continued - suite)

Netherlands - Pays-Bas

Cause of death — Cause de décès	2016 (+C)				2017 (+C)			
	Male — Masculin		Female — Féminin		Male — Masculin		Female — Féminin	
	Number Nombre	Rate Taux	Number Nombre	Rate Taux	Number Nombre	Rate Taux	Number Nombre	Rate Taux
Diseases of arteries, arterioles and capillaries — Maladies des artères, artérioles et capillaires	1 552	18.4	1 145	13.4	1 542	18.2	1 192	13.9
Diseases of the respiratory system — Maladies de l'appareil respiratoire								
Total	6 055	71.9	5 929	69.2	6 311	74.5	6 654	77.3
Influenza — Grippe	157	1.9	183	2.1	197	2.3	292	3.4
Pneumonia — Pneumopathies	1 489	17.7	1 641	19.2	1 598	18.9	1 942	22.6
Chronic lower respiratory diseases — Maladies chroniques des voies respiratoires inférieures	3 438	40.8	3 258	38.1	3 521	41.5	3 495	40.6
Diseases of the digestive system — Maladies de l'appareil digestif								
Total	2 207	26.2	2 442	28.5	2 090	24.7	2 385	27.7
Gastric and duodenal ulcer — Ulcère de l'estomac et du duodénum	60	0.7	76	0.9	50	0.6	58	0.7
Diseases of the liver — Maladies du foie	672	8.0	454	5.3	698	8.2	406	4.7
Diseases of the musculoskeletal system and connective tissue — Maladies du système ostéo-articularie, des muscles et du tissu conjonctif	376	4.5	773	9.0	366	4.3	807	9.4
Diseases of the genitourinary system — Maladies de l'appareil génito-urinaire								
Total	1 444	17.2	1 766	20.6	1 486	17.5	1 819	21.1
Disorders of kidney and ureter — Affections du rein et de l'uretère	922	11.0	1 052	12.3	922	10.9	1 095	12.7
Hyperplasia of prostate — Hyperplasie de la prostate	32	1.0	..	..	37	1.1	..	..
Pregnancy, childbirth and the puerperium — Grossesse, accouchement et puerpéralité								
Total	..	..	6	♦3.5	..	..	3	♦1.8
Pregnancy with abortive outcome — Grossesse se terminant par un avortement	..	..	-	-	..	..	-	-
Other direct obstetric causes — Autres décès maternels directs	..	..	6	♦3.5	..	..	3	♦1.8
Indirect obstetric causes — Décès maternels indirects	..	..	-	-	..	..	-	-
Certain conditions originating in the perinatal period — Certaines affections dont l'origine se situe dans la période périnatale	193	217.9	160	190.6	205	235.2	169	204.4
Congenital malformations, deformations and chromosomal abnormalities — Malformations congénitales et anomalies chromosomiques	220	248.3	221	263.3	263	301.7	208	251.6
Symptoms, signs and abnormal clinical and laboratory findings, not elsewhere classified — Symptômes, signes et résultats anormaux d'examens cliniques et de laboratoire, non classés ailleurs	2 779	33.0	3 309	38.6	2 852	33.7	3 379	39.3
All other diseases — Toutes autres maladies	92	1.1	184	2.1	111	1.3	212	2.5
External causes — Causes externes								
Total	4 068	48.3	3 646	42.6	4 159	49.1	3 812	44.3
Accidents								
Total	2 466	29.3	2 610	30.5	2 475	29.2	2 708	31.5
Transport accidents — Accidents de transport	474	5.6	182	2.1	460	5.4	164	1.9
Falls — Chutes	1 389	16.5	1 914	22.4	1 414	16.7	2 045	23.8
Accidental drowning and submersion — Noyade et submersion accidentelles	65	0.8	21	♦0.2	67	0.8	18	♦0.2
Exposure to smoke, fire and flames — Exposition à la fumée, au feu et aux flammes	27	♦0.3	15	♦0.2	25	♦0.3	15	♦0.2
Accidental poisoning by and exposure to noxious substances — Intoxication accidentelle par des substances nocives et exposition à ces substances	148	1.8	39	0.5	181	2.1	43	0.5
Intentional self-harm — Lésions auto-infligées	1 279	15.2	614	7.2	1 304	15.4	613	7.1
Assault — Agresssions	63	0.7	32	0.4	89	1.1	43	0.5
All other external causes — Toutes autres causes externes	260	3.1	390	4.6	291	3.4	448	5.2

20. Death and death rates by cause and sex: 2014 - 2018
Décès et taux de mortalité par cause et sexe : 2014 - 2018 (continued - suite)

Norway - Norvège

Cause of death — Cause de décès	2015 (+C)				2016 (+C)			
	Male — Masculin		Female — Féminin		Male — Masculin		Female — Féminin	
	Number Nombre	Rate Taux	Number Nombre	Rate Taux	Number Nombre	Rate Taux	Number Nombre	Rate Taux
TOTAL	**19 695**	**757.7**	**20 991**	**817.6**	**19 623**	**747.9**	**20 986**	**811.2**
Certain infectious and parasitic diseases — Certaines maladies infectieuses et parasitaires								
Total	424	16.3	520	20.3	378	14.4	477	18.4
Intestinal infectious diseases — Maladies infectieuses intestinales	60	2.3	78	3.0	30	♦1.1	61	2.4
Tuberculosis — Tuberculose	2	♦0.1	1	♦0.0	1	♦0.0	2	♦0.1
Tetanus — Tétanos	-	-	-	-	-	-	-	-
Diphtheria — Diphtérie	-	-	-	-	-	-	-	-
Whooping cough — Coqueluche	-	-	1	♦0.0	1	♦0.0	-	-
Meningococcal infection — Infection à méningocoques	1	♦0.0	1	♦0.0	2	♦0.1	1	♦0.0
Septicaemia — Septicémie	155	6.0	163	6.3	127	4.8	139	5.4
Acute poliomyelitis — Poliomyélite aiguë	-	-	-	-	-	-	-	-
Measles — Rougeole	-	-	-	-	-	-	-	-
Viral hepatitis — Hépatite virale	13	♦0.5	5	♦0.2	12	♦0.5	5	♦0.2
Human immunodeficiency virus [HIV] disease — Maladies dues au virus de l'immunodéficience humaine (VIH)	4	♦0.2	5	♦0.2	6	♦0.2	2	♦0.1
Malaria — Paludisme	-	-	-	-	1	♦0.0	-	-
Neoplasms — Tumeurs	**5 956**	**229.1**	**5 095**	**198.5**	**5 876**	**224.0**	**5 250**	**202.9**
Malignant neoplasms — Tumeurs malignes								
Total	5 821	224.0	4 941	192.5	5 728	218.3	5 086	196.6
Malignant neoplasm of lip, oral cavity and pharynx — Tumeur maligne de la lèvre, de la cavité buccale et du pharynx	112	4.3	54	2.1	120	4.6	64	2.5
Malignant neoplasm of oesophagus — Tumeur maligne de l'oesophage	160	6.2	56	2.2	167	6.4	58	2.2
Malignant neoplasm of stomach — Tumeur maligne de l'estomac	204	7.8	121	4.7	190	7.2	105	4.1
Malignant neoplasm of colon, rectosigmoid junction, rectum, anus and anal canal — Tumeur maligne du côlon, de la jonction recto-sigmoïdienne, du rectum, de l'anus et du canal anal	811	31.2	779	30.3	783	29.8	827	32.0
Malignant neoplasm of liver and intrahepatic bile ducts — Tumeur maligne du foie et des voies bilaires intrahépatiques	166	6.4	96	3.7	182	6.9	97	3.7
Malignant neoplasm of pancreas — Tumeur maligne du pancréas	376	14.5	385	15.0	364	13.9	346	13.4
Malignant neoplasm of trachea, bronchus and lung — Tumeur maligne de la trachée, des bronches et du poumon	1 191	45.8	984	38.3	1 191	45.4	1 043	40.3
Malignant neoplasm of female breast — Tumeur maligne du sein chez la femme	..	..	585	27.7	..	..	623	29.2
Malignant neoplasm of cervix uteri — Tumeur maligne du col de l'utérus	..	..	79	3.7	..	..	95	4.5
Malignant neoplasm of prostate — Tumeur maligne de la prostate	1 045	122.0	..	..	957	109.4	..	..
Malignant neoplasm of lymphoid, haematopoietic and related tissue — Tumeurs malignes primitives ou présumées primitives des tissus lymphoïde, hématopoïétique et apparentés	526	20.2	408	15.9	497	18.9	362	14.0
Disorders of the blood and blood-forming organs and certain disorders involving the immune mechanism — Maladies du sang et des organes hématopoïétiques et certains troubles du système immunitaire								
Total	46	1.8	87	3.4	66	2.5	73	2.8
Anaemias — Anémies	25	♦1.0	60	2.3	30	♦1.1	55	2.1
Endocrine, nutritional and metabolic diseases — Maladies endocriniennes, nutritionnelles et métaboliques								
Total	460	17.7	510	19.9	472	18.0	533	20.6
Diabetes mellitus — Diabète sucré	319	12.3	285	11.1	328	12.5	305	11.8
Malnutrition — Malnutrition	38	1.5	91	3.5	39	1.5	82	3.2
Mental and behavioural disorders — Troubles mentaux et du comportement	**827**	**31.8**	**1 803**	**70.2**	**955**	**36.4**	**1 827**	**70.6**
Diseases of the nervous system — Maladies du système nerveux	**823**	**31.7**	**1 082**	**42.1**	**928**	**35.4**	**1 119**	**43.3**
Diseases of the circulatory system — Maladies de l'appareil circulatoire								
Total	5 436	209.1	6 177	240.6	5 136	195.8	5 800	224.2
Acute rheumatic fever and chronic rheumatic heart diseases — Rhumatisme articularie aigu et cardiopathies rhumatismales chroniques	18	♦0.7	52	2.0	25	♦1.0	48	1.9
Hypertensive diseases — Maladies hypertensives	145	5.6	298	11.6	159	6.1	277	10.7
Ischaemic heart disease — Cardiopathie ischémique	2 301	88.5	1 913	74.5	2 164	82.5	1 671	64.6
Cerebrovascular disease — Maladie cérébrovasculaire	1 110	42.7	1 513	58.9	1 000	38.1	1 406	54.3

20. Death and death rates by cause and sex: 2014 - 2018
Décès et taux de mortalité par cause et sexe : 2014 - 2018 (continued - suite)

Norway - Norvège

Cause of death — Cause de décès	2015 (+C)				2016 (+C)			
	Male — Masculin		Female — Féminin		Male — Masculin		Female — Féminin	
	Number Nombre	Rate Taux	Number Nombre	Rate Taux	Number Nombre	Rate Taux	Number Nombre	Rate Taux
Diseases of arteries, arterioles and capillaries — Maladies des artères, artérioles et capillaires	372	14.3	317	12.3	337	12.8	300	11.6
Diseases of the respiratory system — Maladies de l'appareil respiratoire								
Total	2 069	79.6	2 155	83.9	2 073	79.0	2 269	87.7
Influenza — Grippe	58	2.2	66	2.6	24	♦0.9	43	1.7
Pneumonia — Pneumopathies	675	26.0	809	31.5	689	26.3	867	33.5
Chronic lower respiratory diseases — Maladies chroniques des voies respiratoires inférieures	1 097	42.2	1 104	43.0	1 086	41.4	1 161	44.9
Diseases of the digestive system — Maladies de l'appareil digestif								
Total	607	23.4	664	25.9	596	22.7	663	25.6
Gastric and duodenal ulcer — Ulcère de l'estomac et du duodénum	76	2.9	69	2.7	75	2.9	84	3.2
Diseases of the liver — Maladies du foie	160	6.2	103	4.0	165	6.3	102	3.9
Diseases of the musculoskeletal system and connective tissue — Maladies du système ostéo-articularie, des muscles et du tissu conjonctif	112	4.3	202	7.9	90	3.4	208	8.0
Diseases of the genitourinary system — Maladies de l'appareil génito-urinaire								
Total	385	14.8	412	16.0	380	14.5	416	16.1
Disorders of kidney and ureter — Affections du rein et de l'uretère	233	9.0	249	9.7	222	8.5	233	9.0
Hyperplasia of prostate — Hyperplasie de la prostate	22	♦2.6	..	..	29	♦3.3	..	..
Pregnancy, childbirth and the puerperium — Grossesse, accouchement et puerpéralité								
Total	..	..	-	-	..	..	-	-
Pregnancy with abortive outcome — Grossesse se terminant par un avortement	..	..	-	-	..	..	-	-
Other direct obstetric causes — Autres décès maternels directs	..	..	-	-	..	..	-	-
Indirect obstetric causes — Décès maternels indirects	..	..	-	-	..	..	-	-
Certain conditions originating in the perinatal period — Certaines affections dont l'origine se situe dans la période périnatale	41	135.6	26	♦91.0	39	128.3	24	♦84.2
Congenital malformations, deformations and chromosomal abnormalities — Malformations congénitales et anomalies chromosomiques	58	191.8	60	210.0	66	217.2	70	245.6
Symptoms, signs and abnormal clinical and laboratory findings, not elsewhere classified — Symptômes, signes et résultats anormaux d'examens cliniques et de laboratoire, non classés ailleurs	1 011	38.9	1 102	42.9	1 004	38.3	1 133	43.8
All other diseases — Toutes autres maladies	38	1.5	64	2.5	49	1.9	68	2.6
External causes — Causes externes								
Total	1 402	53.9	1 032	40.2	1 515	57.7	1 056	40.8
Accidents								
Total	974	37.5	806	31.4	1 062	40.5	830	32.1
Transport accidents — Accidents de transport	127	4.9	34	1.3	159	6.1	26	♦1.0
Falls — Chutes	377	14.5	438	17.1	422	16.1	463	17.9
Accidental drowning and submersion — Noyade et submersion accidentelles	38	1.5	9	♦0.4	52	2.0	3	♦0.1
Exposure to smoke, fire and flames — Exposition à la fumée, au feu et aux flammes	23	♦0.9	17	♦0.7	20	♦0.8	17	♦0.7
Accidental poisoning by and exposure to noxious substances — Intoxication accidentelle par des substances nocives et exposition à ces substances	225	8.7	95	3.7	235	9.0	107	4.1
Intentional self-harm — Lésions auto-infligées	399	15.4	190	7.4	418	15.9	195	7.5
Assault — Agresssions	9	♦0.3	12	♦0.5	18	♦0.7	13	♦0.5
All other external causes — Toutes autres causes externes	20	♦0.8	24	♦0.9	17	♦0.6	18	♦0.7

20. Death and death rates by cause and sex: 2014 - 2018
Décès et taux de mortalité par cause et sexe : 2014 - 2018 (continued - suite)

Poland - Pologne

Cause of death — Cause de décès	2016 (C)				2017 (C)			
	Male — Masculin		Female — Féminin		Male — Masculin		Female — Féminin	
	Number Nombre	Rate Taux	Number Nombre	Rate Taux	Number Nombre	Rate Taux	Number Nombre	Rate Taux
TOTAL	**202 150**	**1 100.0**	**185 859**	**948.7**	**207 671**	**1 130.0**	**195 181**	**996.1**
Certain infectious and parasitic diseases — Certaines maladies infectieuses et parasitaires								
Total	1 093	5.9	837	4.3	1 049	5.7	882	4.5
Intestinal infectious diseases — Maladies infectieuses intestinales	226	1.2	339	1.7	303	1.6	508	2.6
Tuberculosis — Tuberculose	418	2.3	125	0.6	383	2.1	107	0.5
Tetanus — Tétanos	2	♦0.0	-	-	-	-	-	-
Diphtheria — Diphtérie	-	-	-	-	-	-	-	-
Whooping cough — Coqueluche	-	-	-	-	-	-	-	-
Meningococcal infection — Infection à méningocoques	7	♦0.0	8	♦0.0	9	♦0.0	6	♦0.0
Septicaemia — Septicémie	81	0.4	88	0.4	33	0.2	32	0.2
Acute poliomyelitis — Poliomyélite aiguë	-	-	-	-	-	-	-	-
Measles — Rougeole	-	-	-	-	-	-	-	-
Viral hepatitis — Hépatite virale	144	0.8	143	0.7	128	0.7	90	0.5
Human immunodeficiency virus [HIV] disease — Maladies dues au virus de l'immunodéficience humaine (VIH)	87	0.5	15	♦0.1	69	0.4	20	♦0.1
Malaria — Paludisme	-	-	-	-	-	-	-	-
Neoplasms — Tumeurs	58 352	317.5	47 601	243.0	58 359	317.6	48 582	247.9
Malignant neoplasms — Tumeurs malignes								
Total	55 248	300.6	44 707	228.2	54 559	296.9	45 084	230.1
Malignant neoplasm of lip, oral cavity and pharynx — Tumeur maligne de la lèvre, de la cavité buccale et du pharynx	2 124	11.6	653	3.3	2 246	12.2	724	3.7
Malignant neoplasm of oesophagus — Tumeur maligne de l'oesophage	1 205	6.6	334	1.7	1 189	6.5	312	1.6
Malignant neoplasm of stomach — Tumeur maligne de l'estomac	3 353	18.2	1 867	9.5	3 156	17.2	1 777	9.1
Malignant neoplasm of colon, rectosigmoid junction, rectum, anus and anal canal — Tumeur maligne du côlon, de la jonction recto-sigmoïdienne, du rectum, de l'anus et du canal anal	6 837	37.2	5 336	27.2	6 900	37.5	5 370	27.4
Malignant neoplasm of liver and intrahepatic bile ducts — Tumeur maligne du foie et des voies bilaires intrahépatiques	1 143	6.2	879	4.5	1 212	6.6	927	4.7
Malignant neoplasm of pancreas — Tumeur maligne du pancréas	2 396	13.0	2 512	12.8	2 409	13.1	2 455	12.5
Malignant neoplasm of trachea, bronchus and lung — Tumeur maligne de la trachée, des bronches et du poumon	16 190	88.1	7 643	39.0	15 514	84.4	7 837	40.0
Malignant neoplasm of female breast — Tumeur maligne du sein chez la femme	..	..	6 493	38.6	..	..	6 670	39.7
Malignant neoplasm of cervix uteri — Tumeur maligne du col de l'utérus	..	..	1 570	9.3	..	..	1 609	9.6
Malignant neoplasm of prostate — Tumeur maligne de la prostate	5 220	84.8	..	..	5 365	86.6	..	..
Malignant neoplasm of lymphoid, haematopoietic and related tissue — Tumeurs malignes primitives ou présumées primitives des tissus lymphoïde, hématopoïétique et apparentés	3 306	18.0	3 025	15.4	3 346	18.2	3 009	15.4
Disorders of the blood and blood-forming organs and certain disorders involving the immune mechanism — Maladies du sang et des organes hématopoïétiques et certains troubles du système immunitaire								
Total	139	0.8	138	0.7	134	0.7	155	0.8
Anaemias — Anémies	55	0.3	55	0.3	27	♦0.1	62	0.3
Endocrine, nutritional and metabolic diseases — Maladies endocriniennes, nutritionnelles et métaboliques								
Total	3 957	21.5	4 958	25.3	4 196	22.8	5 255	26.8
Diabetes mellitus — Diabète sucré	3 655	19.9	4 640	23.7	3 900	21.2	4 881	24.9
Malnutrition — Malnutrition	115	0.6	99	0.5	113	0.6	151	0.8
Mental and behavioural disorders — Troubles mentaux et du comportement	2 489	13.5	715	3.6	2 851	15.5	872	4.5
Diseases of the nervous system — Maladies du système nerveux	2 607	14.2	3 150	16.1	2 901	15.8	3 563	18.2
Diseases of the circulatory system — Maladies de l'appareil circulatoire								
Total	77 293	420.6	90 680	462.9	75 861	412.8	91 214	465.5
Acute rheumatic fever and chronic rheumatic heart diseases — Rhumatisme articularie aigu et cardiopathies rhumatismales chroniques	250	1.4	405	2.1	191	1.0	414	2.1
Hypertensive diseases — Maladies hypertensives	2 146	11.7	3 087	15.8	3 076	16.7	4 202	21.4
Ischaemic heart disease — Cardiopathie ischémique	21 044	114.5	18 087	92.3	23 245	126.5	21 471	109.6
Cerebrovascular disease — Maladie cérébrovasculaire	12 862	70.0	16 206	82.7	13 651	74.3	16 979	86.6

20. Death and death rates by cause and sex: 2014 - 2018
Décès et taux de mortalité par cause et sexe : 2014 - 2018 (continued - suite)

Poland - Pologne

Cause of death — Cause de décès	2016 (C)				2017 (C)			
	Male — Masculin		Female — Féminin		Male — Masculin		Female — Féminin	
	Number Nombre	Rate Taux	Number Nombre	Rate Taux	Number Nombre	Rate Taux	Number Nombre	Rate Taux
Diseases of arteries, arterioles and capillaries — Maladies des artères, artérioles et capillaires	13 122	71.4	21 780	111.2	13 321	72.5	22 598	115.3
Diseases of the respiratory system — Maladies de l'appareil respiratoire								
Total	13 021	70.9	9 992	51.0	14 312	77.9	11 997	61.2
Influenza — Grippe	67	0.4	36	0.2	35	0.2	44	0.2
Pneumonia — Pneumopathies	7 213	39.3	6 110	31.2	8 162	44.4	7 812	39.9
Chronic lower respiratory diseases — Maladies chroniques des voies respiratoires inférieures	4 063	22.1	2 524	12.9	4 510	24.5	2 831	14.4
Diseases of the digestive system — Maladies de l'appareil digestif								
Total	9 366	51.0	6 684	34.1	9 618	52.3	7 105	36.3
Gastric and duodenal ulcer — Ulcère de l'estomac et du duodénum	1 286	7.0	1 106	5.6	1 541	8.4	1 428	7.3
Diseases of the liver — Maladies du foie	5 113	27.8	2 227	11.4	5 116	27.8	2 402	12.3
Diseases of the musculoskeletal system and connective tissue — Maladies du système ostéo-articularie, des muscles et du tissu conjonctif	153	0.8	426	2.2	158	0.9	413	2.1
Diseases of the genitourinary system — Maladies de l'appareil génito-urinaire								
Total	1 642	8.9	1 933	9.9	1 797	9.8	2 134	10.9
Disorders of kidney and ureter — Affections du rein et de l'uretère	1 236	6.7	1 313	6.7	1 236	6.7	1 311	6.7
Hyperplasia of prostate — Hyperplasie de la prostate	25	♦0.4	..	..	28	♦0.5	..	..
Pregnancy, childbirth and the puerperium — Grossesse, accouchement et puerpéralité								
Total	..	..	9	♦2.4	..	..	9	♦2.2
Pregnancy with abortive outcome — Grossesse se terminant par un avortement	..	..	-	-	..	..	-	-
Other direct obstetric causes — Autres décès maternels directs	..	..	8	♦2.1	..	..	9	♦2.2
Indirect obstetric causes — Décès maternels indirects	..	..	1	♦0.3	..	..	-	-
Certain conditions originating in the perinatal period — Certaines affections dont l'origine se situe dans la période périnatale	482	245.6	349	187.6	495	239.8	364	186.1
Congenital malformations, deformations and chromosomal abnormalities — Malformations congénitales et anomalies chromosomiques	454	231.4	368	197.8	465	225.3	424	216.8
Symptoms, signs and abnormal clinical and laboratory findings, not elsewhere classified — Symptômes, signes et résultats anormaux d'examens cliniques et de laboratoire, non classés ailleurs	16 659	90.7	12 965	66.2	21 041	114.5	17 015	86.8
All other diseases — Toutes autres maladies	127	0.7	165	0.8	154	0.8	227	1.2
External causes — Causes externes								
Total	14 316	77.9	4 889	25.0	14 280	77.7	4 970	25.4
Accidents								
Total	8 330	45.3	3 719	19.0	8 573	46.6	3 797	19.4
Transport accidents — Accidents de transport	2 784	15.1	871	4.4	2 630	14.3	847	4.3
Falls — Chutes	2 386	13.0	2 065	10.5	2 513	13.7	2 078	10.6
Accidental drowning and submersion — Noyade et submersion accidentelles	512	2.8	105	0.5	504	2.7	105	0.5
Exposure to smoke, fire and flames — Exposition à la fumée, au feu et aux flammes	326	1.8	106	0.5	343	1.9	124	0.6
Accidental poisoning by and exposure to noxious substances — Intoxication accidentelle par des substances nocives et exposition à ces substances	876	4.8	185	0.9	1 071	5.8	205	1.0
Intentional self-harm — Lésions auto-infligées	4 075	22.2	596	3.0	3 881	21.1	601	3.1
Assault — Agresssions	204	1.1	80	0.4	190	1.0	73	0.4
All other external causes — Toutes autres causes externes	1 707	9.3	494	2.5	1 636	8.9	499	2.5

20. Death and death rates by cause and sex: 2014 - 2018
Décès et taux de mortalité par cause et sexe : 2014 - 2018 (continued - suite)

Cause of death — Cause de décès	Romania - Roumanie				Russian Federation - Fédération de Russie			
	2017 (+C)				2017 (+C)		2018 (+C)	
	Male — Masculin		Female — Féminin		Male — Masculin	Female — Féminin	Male — Masculin	Female — Féminin
	Number Nombre	Rate Taux	Number Nombre	Rate Taux	Number Nombre	Number Nombre	Number Nombre	Number Nombre
TOTAL	**136 154**	**1 417.9**	**125 248**	**1 247.3**	**910 820**	**915 305**	**913 359**	**915 551**
Certain infectious and parasitic diseases — Certaines maladies infectieuses et parasitaires								
Total	1 975	20.6	1 339	13.3	23 966	11 079	23 495	11 131
Intestinal infectious diseases — Maladies infectieuses intestinales	100	1.0	124	1.2	134	194	143	140
Tuberculosis — Tuberculose	741	7.7	187	1.9	7 478	2 136	6 767	1 850
Tetanus — Tétanos	1	♦0.0	-	-	-	2	3	3
Diphtheria — Diphtérie	-	-	-	-	-	-	-	-
Whooping cough — Coqueluche	-	-	-	-	-	1	-	3
Meningococcal infection — Infection à méningocoques	3	♦0.0	3	♦0.0	98	72	102	88
Septicaemia — Septicémie	865	9.0	799	8.0	827	672	801	658
Acute poliomyelitis — Poliomyélite aiguë	-	-	-	-	-	1	-	-
Measles — Rougeole	6	♦0.1	8	♦0.1	-	-	1	-
Viral hepatitis — Hépatite virale	49	0.5	82	0.8	1 314	810	1 345	884
Human immunodeficiency virus [HIV] disease — Maladies dues au virus de l'immunodéficience humaine (VIH)	130	1.4	55	0.5	13 456	6 589	13 720	6 877
Malaria — Paludisme	-	-	-	-	1	3	-	1
Neoplasms — Tumeurs	**30 559**	**318.2**	**21 297**	**212.1**	**157 451**	**137 136**	**159 870**	**138 126**
Malignant neoplasms — Tumeurs malignes								
Total	30 391	316.5	21 171	210.8	155 752	134 908	157 941	135 762
Malignant neoplasm of lip, oral cavity and pharynx — Tumeur maligne de la lèvre, de la cavité buccale et du pharynx	1 920	20.0	285	2.8	7 796	1 961	7 983	2 057
Malignant neoplasm of oesophagus — Tumeur maligne de l'oesophage	549	5.7	123	1.2	5 504	1 399	5 467	1 495
Malignant neoplasm of stomach — Tumeur maligne de l'estomac	2 241	23.3	1 092	10.9	16 628	11 884	16 390	11 465
Malignant neoplasm of colon, rectosigmoid junction, rectum, anus and anal canal — Tumeur maligne du côlon, de la jonction recto-sigmoïdienne, du rectum, de l'anus et du canal anal	3 731	38.9	2 662	26.5	18 083	21 299	18 450	21 044
Malignant neoplasm of liver and intrahepatic bile ducts — Tumeur maligne du foie et des voies bilaires intrahépatiques	1 952	20.3	1 097	10.9	5 618	4 241	5 826	4 192
Malignant neoplasm of pancreas — Tumeur maligne du pancréas	1 592	16.6	1 337	13.3	9 035	8 985	9 148	9 221
Malignant neoplasm of trachea, bronchus and lung — Tumeur maligne de la trachée, des bronches et du poumon	7 840	81.6	2 410	24.0	40 616	9 570	40 912	9 862
Malignant neoplasm of female breast — Tumeur maligne du sein chez la femme	..	..	3 495	40.9	..	22 098	..	21 967
Malignant neoplasm of cervix uteri — Tumeur maligne du col de l'utérus	..	..	1 560	18.2	..	6 480	..	6 404
Malignant neoplasm of prostate — Tumeur maligne de la prostate	2 307	72.7	..	..	12 565	..	12 979	..
Malignant neoplasm of lymphoid, haematopoietic and related tissue — Tumeurs malignes primitives ou présumées primitives des tissus lymphoïde, hématopoïétique et apparentés	1 404	14.6	1 107	11.0	...	...	...	...
Disorders of the blood and blood-forming organs and certain disorders involving the immune mechanism — Maladies du sang et des organes hématopoïétiques et certains troubles du système immunitaire								
Total	64	0.7	81	0.8	622	955	718	991
Anaemias — Anémies	33	0.3	58	0.6	354	583	449	632
Endocrine, nutritional and metabolic diseases — Maladies endocriniennes, nutritionnelles et métaboliques								
Total	1 246	13.0	1 489	14.8	12 021	27 262	13 324	29 751
Diabetes mellitus — Diabète sucré	1 160	12.1	1 403	14.0	11 065	25 897	12 276	27 981
Malnutrition — Malnutrition	53	0.6	39	0.4	257	235	233	220
Mental and behavioural disorders — Troubles mentaux et du comportement	**154**	**1.6**	**70**	**0.7**	**8 102**	**10 641**	**8 880**	**11 739**
Diseases of the nervous system — Maladies du système nerveux	**1 764**	**18.4**	**2 428**	**24.2**	**37 654**	**64 896**	**40 034**	**70 085**
Diseases of the circulatory system — Maladies de l'appareil circulatoire								
Total	69 630	725.1	80 709	803.7	402 134	460 761	402 450	453 677
Acute rheumatic fever and chronic rheumatic heart diseases — Rhumatisme articularie aigu et cardiopathies rhumatismales chroniques	201	2.1	253	2.5	744	1 783	748	1 744
Hypertensive diseases — Maladies hypertensives	12 377	128.9	17 730	176.6	6 812	10 293	6 629	9 574
Ischaemic heart disease — Cardiopathie ischémique	24 726	257.5	25 116	250.1	221 584	240 202	219 623	233 683

20. Death and death rates by cause and sex: 2014 - 2018
Décès et taux de mortalité par cause et sexe : 2014 - 2018 (continued - suite)

Cause of death — Cause de décès	Romania - Roumanie				Russian Federation - Fédération de Russie			
	2017 (+C)				2017 (+C)		2018 (+C)	
	Male — Masculin		Female — Féminin		Male — Masculin	Female — Féminin	Male — Masculin	Female — Féminin
	Number Nombre	Rate Taux	Number Nombre	Rate Taux	Number Nombre	Number Nombre	Number Nombre	Number Nombre
Cerebrovascular disease — Maladie cérébrovasculaire	**18 915**	**197.0**	**23 816**	**237.2**	**106 994**	**157 474**	**107 374**	**156 199**
Diseases of arteries, arterioles and capillaries — Maladies des artères, artérioles et capillaires	**4 732**	**49.3**	**6 498**	**64.7**	...	...	...	...
Diseases of the respiratory system — Maladies de l'appareil respiratoire								
Total	**9 534**	**99.3**	**6 003**	**59.8**	**42 050**	**19 982**	**41 243**	**19 907**
Influenza — Grippe	**10**	**♦0.1**	**12**	**♦0.1**	**41**	**46**	**122**	**103**
Pneumonia — Pneumopathies	**4 288**	**44.7**	**2 964**	**29.5**	**17 411**	**8 672**	**16 727**	**8 915**
Chronic lower respiratory diseases — Maladies chroniques des voies respiratoires inférieures	**4 095**	**42.6**	**2 136**	**21.3**	**21 360**	**9 497**	**20 765**	**8 950**
Diseases of the digestive system — Maladies de l'appareil digestif								
Total	**9 084**	**94.6**	**5 927**	**59.0**	**50 538**	**42 451**	**51 551**	**43 879**
Gastric and duodenal ulcer — Ulcère de l'estomac et du duodénum	**328**	**3.4**	**175**	**1.7**	**6 115**	**4 569**	**6 095**	**4 635**
Diseases of the liver — Maladies du foie	**6 501**	**67.7**	**3 709**	**36.9**	**26 079**	**18 429**	**26 484**	**18 963**
Diseases of the musculoskeletal system and connective tissue — Maladies du système ostéo-articularie, des muscles et du tissu conjonctif	**38**	**0.4**	**23**	**♦0.2**	**1 479**	**3 319**	**1 682**	**3 861**
Diseases of the genitourinary system — Maladies de l'appareil génito-urinaire								
Total	**2 084**	**21.7**	**1 837**	**18.3**	**9 101**	**9 858**	**9 624**	**11 059**
Disorders of kidney and ureter — Affections du rein et de l'uretère	**1 922**	**20.0**	**1 785**	**17.8**	...	...	...	...
Hyperplasia of prostate — Hyperplasie de la prostate	**121**	**3.8**	..	..	...	..	...	..
Pregnancy, childbirth and the puerperium — Grossesse, accouchement et puerpéralité								
Total	..	..	**24**	**♦11.9**	..	**150**	..	**147**
Pregnancy with abortive outcome — Grossesse se terminant par un avortement	..	..	**2**	**♦1.0**	..	**23**	..	**16**
Other direct obstetric causes — Autres décès maternels directs	..	..	**10**	**♦4.9**	..	**86**	..	**92**
Indirect obstetric causes — Décès maternels indirects	..	..	**12**	**♦5.9**	..	**40**	..	**38**
Certain conditions originating in the perinatal period — Certaines affections dont l'origine se situe dans la période périnatale	**280**	**269.7**	**208**	**211.5**	**2 791**	**2 150**	**2 395**	**1 711**
Congenital malformations, deformations and chromosomal abnormalities — Malformations congénitales et anomalies chromosomiques	**204**	**196.5**	**178**	**181.0**	**2 194**	**1 833**	**2 068**	**1 819**
Symptoms, signs and abnormal clinical and laboratory findings, not elsewhere classified — Symptômes, signes et résultats anormaux d'examens cliniques et de laboratoire, non classés ailleurs	**1 848**	**19.2**	**1 305**	**13.0**	**42 563**	**84 470**	**44 012**	**81 263**
All other diseases — Toutes autres maladies	**40**	**0.4**	**59**	**0.6**	**1 598**	**2 177**	**1 606**	**2 200**
External causes — Causes externes								
Total	**7 650**	**79.7**	**2 271**	**22.6**	**116 556**	**36 185**	**110 407**	**34 205**
Accidents								
Total	**5 618**	**58.5**	**1 781**	**17.7**	...	...	...	...
Transport accidents — Accidents de transport	**1 784**	**18.6**	**606**	**6.0**	**14 581**	**5 329**	**13 938**	**4 924**
Falls — Chutes	**1 074**	**11.2**	**328**	**3.3**	**4 923**	**2 681**	**5 032**	**2 588**
Accidental drowning and submersion — Noyade et submersion accidentelles	**482**	**5.0**	**101**	**1.0**	**4 332**	**748**	**4 135**	**739**
Exposure to smoke, fire and flames — Exposition à la fumée, au feu et aux flammes	**262**	**2.7**	**156**	**1.6**	**2 675**	**1 284**	**2 619**	**1 228**
Accidental poisoning by and exposure to noxious substances — Intoxication accidentelle par des substances nocives et exposition à ces substances	**494**	**5.1**	**180**	**1.8**	**17 362**	**4 724**	**15 786**	**4 251**
Intentional self-harm — Lésions auto-infligées	**1 595**	**16.6**	**331**	**3.3**	**16 830**	**3 448**	**15 079**	**3 127**
Assault — Agresssions	**183**	**1.9**	**89**	**0.9**	**6 758**	**2 290**	**5 953**	**2 033**
All other external causes — Toutes autres causes externes	**254**	**2.6**	**70**	**0.7**	...	...	...	...

20. Death and death rates by cause and sex: 2014 - 2018
Décès et taux de mortalité par cause et sexe : 2014 - 2018 (continued - suite)

Cause of death — Cause de décès	San Marino - Saint-Marin				Serbia - Serbie			
	2014 (+C)		2015 (+C)		2016 (+C)			
	Male — Masculin	Female — Féminin	Male — Masculin	Female — Féminin	Male — Masculin		Female — Féminin	
	Number Nombre	Number Nombre	Number Nombre	Number Nombre	Number Nombre	Rate Taux	Number Nombre	Rate Taux
TOTAL	**100**	**98**	**97**	**84**	**50 708**	**1 475.1**	**50 126**	**1 384.4**
Certain infectious and parasitic diseases — Certaines maladies infectieuses et parasitaires								
Total	-	-	-	-	317	9.2	258	7.1
Intestinal infectious diseases — Maladies infectieuses intestinales	-	-	-	-	56	1.6	74	2.0
Tuberculosis — Tuberculose	-	-	-	-	44	1.3	29	♦0.8
Tetanus — Tétanos	-	-	-	-	-	-	1	♦0.0
Diphtheria — Diphtérie	-	-	-	-	-	-	-	-
Whooping cough — Coqueluche	-	-	-	-	-	-	-	-
Meningococcal infection — Infection à méningocoques	-	-	-	-	1	♦0.0	-	-
Septicaemia — Septicémie	-	-	-	-	139	4.0	110	3.0
Acute poliomyelitis — Poliomyélite aiguë	-	-	-	-	-	-	-	-
Measles — Rougeole	-	-	-	-	-	-	-	-
Viral hepatitis — Hépatite virale	-	-	-	-	23	♦0.7	16	♦0.4
Human immunodeficiency virus [HIV] disease — Maladies dues au virus de l'immunodéficience humaine (VIH)	-	-	-	-	9	♦0.3	2	♦0.1
Malaria — Paludisme	-	-	-	-	-	-	-	-
Neoplasms — Tumeurs	**37**	**25**	**33**	**24**	**12 497**	**363.5**	**9 507**	**262.6**
Malignant neoplasms — Tumeurs malignes								
Total	35	25	32	22	12 253	356.4	9 273	256.1
Malignant neoplasm of lip, oral cavity and pharynx — Tumeur maligne de la lèvre, de la cavité buccale et du pharynx	4	-	-	-	430	12.5	131	3.6
Malignant neoplasm of oesophagus — Tumeur maligne de l'oesophage	-	-	1	-	195	5.7	56	1.5
Malignant neoplasm of stomach — Tumeur maligne de l'estomac	4	4	1	2	632	18.4	320	8.8
Malignant neoplasm of colon, rectosigmoid junction, rectum, anus and anal canal — Tumeur maligne du côlon, de la jonction recto-sigmoïdienne, du rectum, de l'anus et du canal anal	7	2	3	5	1 627	47.3	1 004	27.7
Malignant neoplasm of liver and intrahepatic bile ducts — Tumeur maligne du foie et des voies bilaires intrahépatiques	-	-	2	-	445	12.9	303	8.4
Malignant neoplasm of pancreas — Tumeur maligne du pancréas	2	-	2	2	599	17.4	552	15.2
Malignant neoplasm of trachea, bronchus and lung — Tumeur maligne de la trachée, des bronches et du poumon	6	3	6	3	3 861	112.3	1 511	41.7
Malignant neoplasm of female breast — Tumeur maligne du sein chez la femme	..	5	..	3	..	..	1 713	54.8
Malignant neoplasm of cervix uteri — Tumeur maligne du col de l'utérus	..	-	..	-	..	..	453	14.5
Malignant neoplasm of prostate — Tumeur maligne de la prostate	3	..	2	..	981	74.5	..	..
Malignant neoplasm of lymphoid, haematopoietic and related tissue — Tumeurs malignes primitives ou présumées primitives des tissus lymphoïde, hématopoïétique et apparentés	...	...	...	...	653	19.0	527	14.6
Disorders of the blood and blood-forming organs and certain disorders involving the immune mechanism — Maladies du sang et des organes hématopoïétiques et certains troubles du système immunitaire								
Total	-	-	-	-	123	3.6	127	3.5
Anaemias — Anémies	-	-	-	-	73	2.1	87	2.4
Endocrine, nutritional and metabolic diseases — Maladies endocriniennes, nutritionnelles et métaboliques								
Total	4	3	6	5	1 397	40.6	1 890	52.2
Diabetes mellitus — Diabète sucré	4	3	5	5	1 352	39.3	1 807	49.9
Malnutrition — Malnutrition	-	-	-	-	6	♦0.2	5	♦0.1
Mental and behavioural disorders — Troubles mentaux et du comportement	2	2	2	3	663	19.3	782	21.6
Diseases of the nervous system — Maladies du système nerveux	6	8	5	9	1 007	29.3	1 327	36.7
Diseases of the circulatory system — Maladies de l'appareil circulatoire								
Total	33	41	29	22	23 788	692.0	28 314	782.0
Acute rheumatic fever and chronic rheumatic heart diseases — Rhumatisme articularie aigu et cardiopathies rhumatismales chroniques	-	-	-	-	49	1.4	45	1.2
Hypertensive diseases — Maladies hypertensives	-	8	1	1	2 747	79.9	3 888	107.4
Ischaemic heart disease — Cardiopathie ischémique	9	5	6	2	4 935	143.6	4 172	115.2

20. Death and death rates by cause and sex: 2014 - 2018
Décès et taux de mortalité par cause et sexe : 2014 - 2018 (continued - suite)

Cause of death — Cause de décès	San Marino - Saint-Marin				Serbia - Serbie			
	2014 (+C)		2015 (+C)		2016 (+C)			
	Male — Masculin	Female — Féminin	Male — Masculin	Female — Féminin	Male — Masculin		Female — Féminin	
	Number Nombre	Number Nombre	Number Nombre	Number Nombre	Number Nombre	Rate Taux	Number Nombre	Rate Taux
Cerebrovascular disease — Maladie cérébrovasculaire	4	7	4	8	5 014	145.9	6 334	174.9
Diseases of arteries, arterioles and capillaries — Maladies des artères, artérioles et capillaires	...	...	...	...	1 128	32.8	1 379	38.1
Diseases of the respiratory system — Maladies de l'appareil respiratoire								
Total	6	7	6	6	2 908	84.6	1 969	54.4
Influenza — Grippe	-	-	-	-	18	♦0.5	11	♦0.3
Pneumonia — Pneumopathies	1	1	-	1	726	21.1	464	12.8
Chronic lower respiratory diseases — Maladies chroniques des voies respiratoires inférieures	3	4	4	5	1 603	46.6	1 066	29.4
Diseases of the digestive system — Maladies de l'appareil digestif								
Total	3	3	2	6	1 803	52.4	1 427	39.4
Gastric and duodenal ulcer — Ulcère de l'estomac et du duodénum	1	-	-	-	259	7.5	214	5.9
Diseases of the liver — Maladies du foie	1	-	2	1	632	18.4	171	4.7
Diseases of the musculoskeletal system and connective tissue — Maladies du système ostéo-articularie, des muscles et du tissu conjonctif	-	-	-	-	45	1.3	107	3.0
Diseases of the genitourinary system — Maladies de l'appareil génito-urinaire								
Total	2	1	1	2	1 184	34.4	1 080	29.8
Disorders of kidney and ureter — Affections du rein et de l'uretère	...	...	...	...	1 112	32.3	1 044	28.8
Hyperplasia of prostate — Hyperplasie de la prostate	...	..	...	..	36	2.7	..	..
Pregnancy, childbirth and the puerperium — Grossesse, accouchement et puerpéralité								
Total	..	-	..	-	..	..	7	♦10.8
Pregnancy with abortive outcome — Grossesse se terminant par un avortement	..	-	..	-	..	..	1	♦1.5
Other direct obstetric causes — Autres décès maternels directs	..	-	..	-	..	..	2	♦3.1
Indirect obstetric causes — Décès maternels indirects	..	-	..	-	..	..	4	♦6.2
Certain conditions originating in the perinatal period — Certaines affections dont l'origine se situe dans la période périnatale	1	-	-	-	153	457.0	91	291.1
Congenital malformations, deformations and chromosomal abnormalities — Malformations congénitales et anomalies chromosomiques	-	-	-	-	57	170.3	55	176.0
Symptoms, signs and abnormal clinical and laboratory findings, not elsewhere classified — Symptômes, signes et résultats anormaux d'examens cliniques et de laboratoire, non classés ailleurs	1	2	1	3	2 647	77.0	2 338	64.6
All other diseases — Toutes autres maladies	-	-	-	-	53	1.5	55	1.5
External causes — Causes externes								
Total	5	6	12	4	2 066	60.1	792	21.9
Accidents								
Total	...	...	...	...	1 034	30.1	360	9.9
Transport accidents — Accidents de transport	1	-	3	-	418	12.2	97	2.7
Falls — Chutes	1	2	4	1	230	6.7	138	3.8
Accidental drowning and submersion — Noyade et submersion accidentelles	-	-	-	-	55	1.6	16	♦0.4
Exposure to smoke, fire and flames — Exposition à la fumée, au feu et aux flammes	-	-	-	-	42	1.2	20	♦0.6
Accidental poisoning by and exposure to noxious substances — Intoxication accidentelle par des substances nocives et exposition à ces substances	-	-	-	-	28	♦0.8	12	♦0.3
Intentional self-harm — Lésions auto-infligées	-	1	5	1	704	20.5	258	7.1
Assault — Agresssions	-	-	-	-	77	2.2	46	1.3
All other external causes — Toutes autres causes externes	...	...	...	...	251	7.3	128	3.5

20. Death and death rates by cause and sex: 2014 - 2018
Décès et taux de mortalité par cause et sexe : 2014 - 2018 (continued - suite)

Cause of death — Cause de décès	Serbia - Serbie				Slovakia - Slovaquie			
	2017 (+C)				2014 (C)			
	Male — Masculin		Female — Féminin		Male — Masculin		Female — Féminin	
	Number Nombre	Rate Taux	Number Nombre	Rate Taux	Number Nombre	Rate Taux	Number Nombre	Rate Taux
TOTAL	**51 756**	**1 509.3**	**51 966**	**1 439.0**	**26 498**	**1 004.1**	**24 847**	**894.8**
Certain infectious and parasitic diseases — Certaines maladies infectieuses et parasitaires								
Total	307	9.0	247	6.8	168	6.4	200	7.2
Intestinal infectious diseases — Maladies infectieuses intestinales	35	1.0	51	1.4	21	♦0.8	28	♦1.0
Tuberculosis — Tuberculose	45	1.3	19	♦0.5	21	♦0.8	11	♦0.4
Tetanus — Tétanos	-	-	1	♦0.0	-	-	-	-
Diphtheria — Diphtérie	-	-	-	-	-	-	-	-
Whooping cough — Coqueluche	-	-	-	-	1	♦0.0	-	-
Meningococcal infection — Infection à méningocoques	-	-	2	♦0.1	4	♦0.2	4	♦0.1
Septicaemia — Septicémie	163	4.8	141	3.9	92	3.5	121	4.4
Acute poliomyelitis — Poliomyélite aiguë	-	-	-	-	-	-	-	-
Measles — Rougeole	1	♦0.0	-	-	-	-	-	-
Viral hepatitis — Hépatite virale	17	♦0.5	10	♦0.3	11	♦0.4	10	♦0.4
Human immunodeficiency virus [HIV] disease — Maladies dues au virus de l'immunodéficience humaine (VIH)	12	♦0.3	2	♦0.1	1	♦0.0	-	-
Malaria — Paludisme	2	♦0.1	-	-	-	-	-	-
Neoplasms — Tumeurs	11 821	344.7	9 219	255.3	7 650	289.9	5 978	215.3
Malignant neoplasms — Tumeurs malignes								
Total	11 566	337.3	9 005	249.4	7 616	288.6	5 927	213.4
Malignant neoplasm of lip, oral cavity and pharynx — Tumeur maligne de la lèvre, de la cavité buccale et du pharynx	408	11.9	104	2.9	554	21.0	89	3.2
Malignant neoplasm of oesophagus — Tumeur maligne de l'oesophage	201	5.9	43	1.2	251	9.5	37	1.3
Malignant neoplasm of stomach — Tumeur maligne de l'estomac	591	17.2	336	9.3	371	14.1	285	10.3
Malignant neoplasm of colon, rectosigmoid junction, rectum, anus and anal canal — Tumeur maligne du côlon, de la jonction recto-sigmoïdienne, du rectum, de l'anus et du canal anal	1 613	47.0	1 070	29.6	1 133	42.9	856	30.8
Malignant neoplasm of liver and intrahepatic bile ducts — Tumeur maligne du foie et des voies bilaires intrahépatiques	423	12.3	327	9.1	278	10.5	149	5.4
Malignant neoplasm of pancreas — Tumeur maligne du pancréas	619	18.1	537	14.9	428	16.2	394	14.2
Malignant neoplasm of trachea, bronchus and lung — Tumeur maligne de la trachée, des bronches et du poumon	3 701	107.9	1 580	43.8	1 607	60.9	567	20.4
Malignant neoplasm of female breast — Tumeur maligne du sein chez la femme	..	..	1 766	56.6	..	..	898	...
Malignant neoplasm of cervix uteri — Tumeur maligne du col de l'utérus	..	..	487	15.6	..	..	228	...
Malignant neoplasm of prostate — Tumeur maligne de la prostate	1 006	76.5	..	..	738	...	..	..
Malignant neoplasm of lymphoid, haematopoietic and related tissue — Tumeurs malignes primitives ou présumées primitives des tissus lymphoïde, hématopoïétique et apparentés	653	19.0	545	15.1	507	19.2	513	18.5
Disorders of the blood and blood-forming organs and certain disorders involving the immune mechanism — Maladies du sang et des organes hématopoïétiques et certains troubles du système immunitaire								
Total	123	3.6	154	4.3	24	♦0.9	30	♦1.1
Anaemias — Anémies	71	2.1	101	2.8	7	♦0.3	12	♦0.4
Endocrine, nutritional and metabolic diseases — Maladies endocriniennes, nutritionnelles et métaboliques								
Total	1 618	47.2	2 008	55.6	451	17.1	583	21.0
Diabetes mellitus — Diabète sucré	1 563	45.6	1 928	53.4	392	14.9	503	18.1
Malnutrition — Malnutrition	3	♦0.1	4	♦0.1	14	♦0.5	18	♦0.6
Mental and behavioural disorders — Troubles mentaux et du comportement	699	20.4	819	22.7	405	15.3	542	19.5
Diseases of the nervous system — Maladies du système nerveux	1 197	34.9	1 533	42.5	527	20.0	620	22.3
Diseases of the circulatory system — Maladies de l'appareil circulatoire								
Total	24 045	701.2	28 973	802.3	10 540	399.4	12 349	444.7
Acute rheumatic fever and chronic rheumatic heart diseases — Rhumatisme articularie aigu et cardiopathies rhumatismales chroniques	19	♦0.6	32	0.9	30	♦1.1	54	1.9
Hypertensive diseases — Maladies hypertensives	2 860	83.4	4 143	114.7	534	20.2	778	28.0
Ischaemic heart disease — Cardiopathie ischémique	4 940	144.1	4 411	122.1	6 138	232.6	7 200	259.3
Cerebrovascular disease — Maladie cérébrovasculaire	4 954	144.5	6 257	173.3	2 358	89.3	2 829	101.9

20. Death and death rates by cause and sex: 2014 - 2018
Décès et taux de mortalité par cause et sexe : 2014 - 2018 (continued - suite)

Cause of death — Cause de décès	Serbia - Serbie				Slovakia - Slovaquie			
	2017 (+C)				2014 (C)			
	Male — Masculin		Female — Féminin		Male — Masculin		Female — Féminin	
	Number Nombre	Rate Taux	Number Nombre	Rate Taux	Number Nombre	Rate Taux	Number Nombre	Rate Taux
Diseases of arteries, arterioles and capillaries — Maladies des artères, artérioles et capillaires	1 178	34.4	1 429	39.6	246	9.3	239	8.6
Diseases of the respiratory system — Maladies de l'appareil respiratoire								
Total	3 046	88.8	2 319	64.2	1 578	59.8	1 150	41.4
Influenza — Grippe	23	♦0.7	11	♦0.3	1	♦0.0	-	-
Pneumonia — Pneumopathies	795	23.2	658	18.2	860	32.6	717	25.8
Chronic lower respiratory diseases — Maladies chroniques des voies respiratoires inférieures	1 731	50.5	1 188	32.9	574	21.8	310	11.2
Diseases of the digestive system — Maladies de l'appareil digestif								
Total	1 631	47.6	1 285	35.6	1 734	65.7	1 158	41.7
Gastric and duodenal ulcer — Ulcère de l'estomac et du duodénum	248	7.2	227	6.3	124	4.7	108	3.9
Diseases of the liver — Maladies du foie	637	18.6	205	5.7	1 113	42.2	409	14.7
Diseases of the musculoskeletal system and connective tissue — Maladies du système ostéo-articularie, des muscles et du tissu conjonctif	47	1.4	120	3.3	29	♦1.1	51	1.8
Diseases of the genitourinary system — Maladies de l'appareil génito-urinaire								
Total	1 259	36.7	1 061	29.4	367	13.9	441	15.9
Disorders of kidney and ureter — Affections du rein et de l'uretère	1 172	34.2	1 028	28.5	300	11.4	351	12.6
Hyperplasia of prostate — Hyperplasie de la prostate	47	3.6	..	..	7	...	..	..
Pregnancy, childbirth and the puerperium — Grossesse, accouchement et puerpéralité								
Total	..	..	7	♦10.8	..	..	2	♦3.6
Pregnancy with abortive outcome — Grossesse se terminant par un avortement	..	..	-	-	..	..	1	♦1.8
Other direct obstetric causes — Autres décès maternels directs	..	..	5	♦7.7	..	..	1	♦1.8
Indirect obstetric causes — Décès maternels indirects	..	..	2	♦3.1	..	..	-	-
Certain conditions originating in the perinatal period — Certaines affections dont l'origine se situe dans la période périnatale	112	336.1	90	285.1	78	277.6	63	233.9
Congenital malformations, deformations and chromosomal abnormalities — Malformations congénitales et anomalies chromosomiques	61	183.1	49	155.2	101	359.4	69	256.2
Symptoms, signs and abnormal clinical and laboratory findings, not elsewhere classified — Symptômes, signes et résultats anormaux d'examens cliniques et de laboratoire, non classés ailleurs	2 655	77.4	2 318	64.2	553	21.0	571	20.6
All other diseases — Toutes autres maladies	33	1.0	23	♦0.6	71	2.7	96	3.5
External causes — Causes externes								
Total	442	12.9	154	4.3	2 222	84.2	944	34.0
Accidents								
Total	436	12.7	144	4.0	1 228	46.5	543	19.6
Transport accidents — Accidents de transport	436	12.7	144	4.0	316	12.0	112	4.0
Falls — Chutes	-	-	-	-	426	16.1	305	11.0
Accidental drowning and submersion — Noyade et submersion accidentelles	-	-	-	-	103	3.9	26	♦0.9
Exposure to smoke, fire and flames — Exposition à la fumée, au feu et aux flammes	-	-	-	-	14	♦0.5	6	♦0.2
Accidental poisoning by and exposure to noxious substances — Intoxication accidentelle par des substances nocives et exposition à ces substances	-	-	-	-	118	4.5	31	1.1
Intentional self-harm — Lésions auto-infligées	-	-	-	-	471	17.8	82	3.0
Assault — Agresssions	-	-	-	-	29	♦1.1	18	♦0.6
All other external causes — Toutes autres causes externes	6	♦0.2	10	♦0.3	494	18.7	301	10.8

20. Death and death rates by cause and sex: 2014 - 2018
Décès et taux de mortalité par cause et sexe : 2014 - 2018 (continued - suite)

Slovenia - Slovénie

Cause of death — Cause de décès	2016 (C)				2017 (C)			
	Male — Masculin		Female — Féminin		Male — Masculin		Female — Féminin	
	Number Nombre	Rate Taux	Number Nombre	Rate Taux	Number Nombre	Rate Taux	Number Nombre	Rate Taux
TOTAL	9 673	944.7	10 016	962.7	10 136	987.9	10 373	997.2
Certain infectious and parasitic diseases — Certaines maladies infectieuses et parasitaires								
Total	46	4.5	84	8.1	41	4.0	72	6.9
Intestinal infectious diseases — Maladies infectieuses intestinales	2	♦0.2	7	♦0.7	-	-	1	♦0.1
Tuberculosis — Tuberculose	4	♦0.4	3	♦0.3	5	♦0.5	1	♦0.1
Tetanus — Tétanos	-	-	-	-	-	-	1	♦0.1
Diphtheria — Diphtérie	-	-	-	-	-	-	-	-
Whooping cough — Coqueluche	-	-	-	-	-	-	-	-
Meningococcal infection — Infection à méningocoques	1	♦0.1	-	-	1	♦0.1	-	-
Septicaemia — Septicémie	26	♦2.5	66	6.3	18	♦1.8	46	4.4
Acute poliomyelitis — Poliomyélite aiguë	-	-	-	-	-	-	-	-
Measles — Rougeole	-	-	-	-	-	-	-	-
Viral hepatitis — Hépatite virale	-	-	2	♦0.2	1	♦0.1	1	♦0.1
Human immunodeficiency virus [HIV] disease — Maladies dues au virus de l'immunodéficience humaine (VIH)	-	-	-	-	2	♦0.2	2	♦0.2
Malaria — Paludisme	-	-	-	-	-	-	-	-
Neoplasms — Tumeurs	3 499	341.7	2 734	262.8	3 537	344.7	2 823	271.4
Malignant neoplasms — Tumeurs malignes								
Total	3 486	340.5	2 708	260.3	3 518	342.9	2 788	268.0
Malignant neoplasm of lip, oral cavity and pharynx — Tumeur maligne de la lèvre, de la cavité buccale et du pharynx	135	13.2	33	3.2	119	11.6	24	♦2.3
Malignant neoplasm of oesophagus — Tumeur maligne de l'oesophage	73	7.1	21	♦2.0	72	7.0	21	♦2.0
Malignant neoplasm of stomach — Tumeur maligne de l'estomac	202	19.7	120	11.5	198	19.3	129	12.4
Malignant neoplasm of colon, rectosigmoid junction, rectum, anus and anal canal — Tumeur maligne du côlon, de la jonction recto-sigmoïdienne, du rectum, de l'anus et du canal anal	429	41.9	347	33.4	408	39.8	283	27.2
Malignant neoplasm of liver and intrahepatic bile ducts — Tumeur maligne du foie et des voies bilaires intrahépatiques	180	17.6	86	8.3	196	19.1	85	8.2
Malignant neoplasm of pancreas — Tumeur maligne du pancréas	182	17.8	197	18.9	185	18.0	194	18.7
Malignant neoplasm of trachea, bronchus and lung — Tumeur maligne de la trachée, des bronches et du poumon	812	79.3	393	37.8	779	75.9	457	43.9
Malignant neoplasm of female breast — Tumeur maligne du sein chez la femme	..	..	378	42.4	..	..	433	48.7
Malignant neoplasm of cervix uteri — Tumeur maligne du col de l'utérus	..	..	41	4.6	..	..	43	4.8
Malignant neoplasm of prostate — Tumeur maligne de la prostate	398	102.9	..	..	456	116.0	..	..
Malignant neoplasm of lymphoid, haematopoietic and related tissue — Tumeurs malignes primitives ou présumées primitives des tissus lymphoïde, hématopoïétique et apparentés	308	30.1	258	24.8	309	30.1	255	24.5
Disorders of the blood and blood-forming organs and certain disorders involving the immune mechanism — Maladies du sang et des organes hématopoïétiques et certains troubles du système immunitaire								
Total	8	♦0.8	22	♦2.1	7	♦0.7	10	♦1.0
Anaemias — Anémies	3	♦0.3	3	♦0.3	2	♦0.2	1	♦0.1
Endocrine, nutritional and metabolic diseases — Maladies endocriniennes, nutritionnelles et métaboliques								
Total	162	15.8	195	18.7	182	17.7	205	19.7
Diabetes mellitus — Diabète sucré	130	12.7	165	15.9	154	15.0	173	16.6
Malnutrition — Malnutrition	-	-	1	♦0.1	-	-	-	-
Mental and behavioural disorders — Troubles mentaux et du comportement	260	25.4	42	4.0	298	29.0	70	6.7
Diseases of the nervous system — Maladies du système nerveux	190	18.6	242	23.3	287	28.0	333	32.0
Diseases of the circulatory system — Maladies de l'appareil circulatoire								
Total	3 135	306.2	4 675	449.4	3 302	321.8	4 702	452.0
Acute rheumatic fever and chronic rheumatic heart diseases — Rhumatisme articularie aigu et cardiopathies rhumatismales chroniques	38	3.7	71	6.8	62	6.0	92	8.8
Hypertensive diseases — Maladies hypertensives	210	20.5	541	52.0	226	22.0	582	56.0
Ischaemic heart disease — Cardiopathie ischémique	1 096	107.0	791	76.0	1 148	111.9	814	78.3
Cerebrovascular disease — Maladie cérébrovasculaire	771	75.3	1 177	113.1	802	78.2	1 159	111.4

20. Death and death rates by cause and sex: 2014 - 2018
Décès et taux de mortalité par cause et sexe : 2014 - 2018 (continued - suite)

Slovenia - Slovénie

Cause of death — Cause de décès	2016 (C)				2017 (C)			
	Male — Masculin		Female — Féminin		Male — Masculin		Female — Féminin	
	Number Nombre	Rate Taux	Number Nombre	Rate Taux	Number Nombre	Rate Taux	Number Nombre	Rate Taux
Diseases of arteries, arterioles and capillaries — Maladies des artères, artérioles et capillaires	156	15.2	204	19.6	171	16.7	217	20.9
Diseases of the respiratory system — Maladies de l'appareil respiratoire								
Total	604	59.0	662	63.6	628	61.2	652	62.7
Influenza — Grippe	12	♦1.2	18	♦1.7	24	♦2.3	33	3.2
Pneumonia — Pneumopathies	257	25.1	363	34.9	232	22.6	328	31.5
Chronic lower respiratory diseases — Maladies chroniques des voies respiratoires inférieures	240	23.4	167	16.1	293	28.6	206	19.8
Diseases of the digestive system — Maladies de l'appareil digestif								
Total	478	46.7	418	40.2	508	49.5	404	38.8
Gastric and duodenal ulcer — Ulcère de l'estomac et du duodénum	23	♦2.2	33	3.2	17	♦1.7	37	3.6
Diseases of the liver — Maladies du foie	289	28.2	96	9.2	287	28.0	94	9.0
Diseases of the musculoskeletal system and connective tissue — Maladies du système ostéo-articularie, des muscles et du tissu conjonctif	21	♦2.1	32	3.1	20	♦1.9	59	5.7
Diseases of the genitourinary system — Maladies de l'appareil génito-urinaire								
Total	96	9.4	212	20.4	87	8.5	190	18.3
Disorders of kidney and ureter — Affections du rein et de l'uretère	64	6.3	109	10.5	53	5.2	89	8.6
Hyperplasia of prostate — Hyperplasie de la prostate	-	-	..	..	-	-	..	..
Pregnancy, childbirth and the puerperium — Grossesse, accouchement et puerpéralité								
Total	..	..	1	♦4.9	..	..	-	-
Pregnancy with abortive outcome — Grossesse se terminant par un avortement	..	..	1	♦4.9	..	..	-	-
Other direct obstetric causes — Autres décès maternels directs	..	..	-	-	..	..	-	-
Indirect obstetric causes — Décès maternels indirects	..	..	-	-	..	..	-	-
Certain conditions originating in the perinatal period — Certaines affections dont l'origine se situe dans la période périnatale	10	♦96.5	12	♦120.3	11	♦104.9	13	♦133.2
Congenital malformations, deformations and chromosomal abnormalities — Malformations congénitales et anomalies chromosomiques	20	♦192.9	20	♦200.4	19	♦181.2	19	♦194.7
Symptoms, signs and abnormal clinical and laboratory findings, not elsewhere classified — Symptômes, signes et résultats anormaux d'examens cliniques et de laboratoire, non classés ailleurs	248	24.2	162	15.6	286	27.9	199	19.1
All other diseases — Toutes autres maladies	7	♦0.7	7	♦0.7	5	♦0.5	5	♦0.5
External causes — Causes externes								
Total	889	86.8	496	47.7	918	89.5	617	59.3
Accidents								
Total	467	45.6	355	34.1	490	47.8	462	44.4
Transport accidents — Accidents de transport	113	11.0	29	♦2.8	87	8.5	29	♦2.8
Falls — Chutes	230	22.5	277	26.6	292	28.5	388	37.3
Accidental drowning and submersion — Noyade et submersion accidentelles	15	♦1.5	5	♦0.5	18	♦1.8	2	♦0.2
Exposure to smoke, fire and flames — Exposition à la fumée, au feu et aux flammes	1	♦0.1	2	♦0.2	8	♦0.8	2	♦0.2
Accidental poisoning by and exposure to noxious substances — Intoxication accidentelle par des substances nocives et exposition à ces substances	39	3.8	9	♦0.9	44	4.3	11	♦1.1
Intentional self-harm — Lésions auto-infligées	294	28.7	77	7.4	327	31.9	84	8.1
Assault — Agresssions	9	♦0.9	5	♦0.5	15	♦1.5	8	♦0.8
All other external causes — Toutes autres causes externes	119	11.6	59	5.7	86	8.4	63	6.1

20. Death and death rates by cause and sex: 2014 - 2018
Décès et taux de mortalité par cause et sexe : 2014 - 2018 (continued - suite)

Spain - Espagne

Cause of death — Cause de décès	2016 (C)				2017 (C)			
	Male — Masculin		Female — Féminin		Male — Masculin		Female — Féminin	
	Number Nombre	Rate Taux	Number Nombre	Rate Taux	Number Nombre	Rate Taux	Number Nombre	Rate Taux
TOTAL	**208 993**	**916.4**	**201 618**	**852.7**	**214 236**	**938.4**	**210 287**	**887.2**
Certain infectious and parasitic diseases — Certaines maladies infectieuses et parasitaires								
Total	**3 326**	**14.6**	**3 707**	**15.7**	**3 286**	**14.4**	**3 533**	**14.9**
Intestinal infectious diseases — Maladies infectieuses intestinales	**342**	**1.5**	**604**	**2.6**	**340**	**1.5**	**615**	**2.6**
Tuberculosis — Tuberculose	**109**	**0.5**	**80**	**0.3**	**128**	**0.6**	**58**	**0.2**
Tetanus — Tétanos	**1**	**♦0.0**	**1**	**♦0.0**	**2**	**♦0.0**	**-**	**-**
Diphtheria — Diphtérie	**-**	**-**	**-**	**-**	**-**	**-**	**-**	**-**
Whooping cough — Coqueluche	**1**	**♦0.0**	**3**	**♦0.0**	**1**	**♦0.0**	**1**	**♦0.0**
Meningococcal infection — Infection à méningocoques	**12**	**♦0.1**	**8**	**♦0.0**	**2**	**♦0.0**	**10**	**♦0.0**
Septicaemia — Septicémie	**1 704**	**7.5**	**2 183**	**9.2**	**1 708**	**7.5**	**2 092**	**8.8**
Acute poliomyelitis — Poliomyélite aiguë	**-**	**-**	**-**	**-**	**-**	**-**	**-**	**-**
Measles — Rougeole	**-**	**-**	**-**	**-**	**-**	**-**	**-**	**-**
Viral hepatitis — Hépatite virale	**393**	**1.7**	**383**	**1.6**	**338**	**1.5**	**291**	**1.2**
Human immunodeficiency virus [HIV] disease — Maladies dues au virus de l'immunodéficience humaine (VIH)	**385**	**1.7**	**113**	**0.5**	**342**	**1.5**	**100**	**0.4**
Malaria — Paludisme	**3**	**♦0.0**	**-**	**-**	**5**	**♦0.0**	**1**	**♦0.0**
Neoplasms — Tumeurs	**68 619**	**300.9**	**44 320**	**187.4**	**68 508**	**300.1**	**44 758**	**188.8**
Malignant neoplasms — Tumeurs malignes								
Total	**66 358**	**291.0**	**42 335**	**179.0**	**66 198**	**290.0**	**42 875**	**180.9**
Malignant neoplasm of lip, oral cavity and pharynx — Tumeur maligne de la lèvre, de la cavité buccale et du pharynx	**1 801**	**7.9**	**627**	**2.7**	**1 836**	**8.0**	**621**	**2.6**
Malignant neoplasm of oesophagus — Tumeur maligne de l'oesophage	**1 558**	**6.8**	**283**	**1.2**	**1 519**	**6.7**	**331**	**1.4**
Malignant neoplasm of stomach — Tumeur maligne de l'estomac	**3 311**	**14.5**	**2 107**	**8.9**	**3 213**	**14.1**	**1 941**	**8.2**
Malignant neoplasm of colon, rectosigmoid junction, rectum, anus and anal canal — Tumeur maligne du côlon, de la jonction recto-sigmoïdienne, du rectum, de l'anus et du canal anal	**9 430**	**41.3**	**6 363**	**26.9**	**9 103**	**39.9**	**6 307**	**26.6**
Malignant neoplasm of liver and intrahepatic bile ducts — Tumeur maligne du foie et des voies bilaires intrahépatiques	**3 410**	**15.0**	**1 579**	**6.7**	**3 584**	**15.7**	**1 608**	**6.8**
Malignant neoplasm of pancreas — Tumeur maligne du pancréas	**3 434**	**15.1**	**3 355**	**14.2**	**3 590**	**15.7**	**3 278**	**13.8**
Malignant neoplasm of trachea, bronchus and lung — Tumeur maligne de la trachée, des bronches et du poumon	**17 624**	**77.3**	**4 563**	**19.3**	**17 268**	**75.6**	**4 853**	**20.5**
Malignant neoplasm of female breast — Tumeur maligne du sein chez la femme	..	..	**6 385**	**31.6**	..	..	**6 489**	**31.9**
Malignant neoplasm of cervix uteri — Tumeur maligne du col de l'utérus	..	..	**620**	**3.1**	..	..	**680**	**3.3**
Malignant neoplasm of prostate — Tumeur maligne de la prostate	**5 752**	**69.8**	..	..	**5 938**	**70.0**	..	..
Malignant neoplasm of lymphoid, haematopoietic and related tissue — Tumeurs malignes primitives ou présumées primitives des tissus lymphoïde, hématopoïétique et apparentés	**4 576**	**20.1**	**3 753**	**15.9**	**4 571**	**20.0**	**3 931**	**16.6**
Disorders of the blood and blood-forming organs and certain disorders involving the immune mechanism — Maladies du sang et des organes hématopoïétiques et certains troubles du système immunitaire								
Total	**807**	**3.5**	**1 079**	**4.6**	**856**	**3.7**	**1 117**	**4.7**
Anaemias — Anémies	**462**	**2.0**	**734**	**3.1**	**481**	**2.1**	**774**	**3.3**
Endocrine, nutritional and metabolic diseases — Maladies endocriniennes, nutritionnelles et métaboliques								
Total	**5 515**	**24.2**	**7 185**	**30.4**	**5 667**	**24.8**	**7 629**	**32.2**
Diabetes mellitus — Diabète sucré	**4 090**	**17.9**	**5 220**	**22.1**	**4 293**	**18.8**	**5 480**	**23.1**
Malnutrition — Malnutrition	**112**	**0.5**	**140**	**0.6**	**135**	**0.6**	**158**	**0.7**
Mental and behavioural disorders — Troubles mentaux et du comportement	**7 152**	**31.4**	**13 828**	**58.5**	**7 408**	**32.4**	**14 314**	**60.4**
Diseases of the nervous system — Maladies du système nerveux	**9 762**	**42.8**	**15 446**	**65.3**	**10 124**	**44.3**	**16 178**	**68.3**
Diseases of the circulatory system — Maladies de l'appareil circulatoire								
Total	**55 307**	**242.5**	**64 471**	**272.7**	**56 179**	**246.1**	**66 286**	**279.7**
Acute rheumatic fever and chronic rheumatic heart diseases — Rhumatisme articularie aigu et cardiopathies rhumatismales chroniques	**490**	**2.1**	**1 166**	**4.9**	**472**	**2.1**	**1 106**	**4.7**
Hypertensive diseases — Maladies hypertensives	**3 908**	**17.1**	**8 245**	**34.9**	**3 986**	**17.5**	**8 574**	**36.2**
Ischaemic heart disease — Cardiopathie ischémique	**19 071**	**83.6**	**12 985**	**54.9**	**19 132**	**83.8**	**13 193**	**55.7**
Cerebrovascular disease — Maladie cérébrovasculaire	**11 556**	**50.7**	**15 566**	**65.8**	**11 555**	**50.6**	**15 382**	**64.9**

20. Death and death rates by cause and sex: 2014 - 2018
Décès et taux de mortalité par cause et sexe : 2014 - 2018 (continued - suite)

Spain - Espagne

Cause of death — Cause de décès	2016 (C)				2017 (C)			
	Male — Masculin		Female — Féminin		Male — Masculin		Female — Féminin	
	Number Nombre	Rate Taux	Number Nombre	Rate Taux	Number Nombre	Rate Taux	Number Nombre	Rate Taux
Diseases of arteries, arterioles and capillaries — Maladies des artères, artérioles et capillaires	3 008	13.2	2 044	8.6	3 084	13.5	1 992	8.4
Diseases of the respiratory system — Maladies de l'appareil respiratoire								
Total	26 197	114.9	20 615	87.2	28 277	123.9	23 338	98.5
Influenza — Grippe	335	1.5	312	1.3	498	2.2	677	2.9
Pneumonia — Pneumopathies	4 767	20.9	4 393	18.6	5 279	23.1	4 943	20.9
Chronic lower respiratory diseases — Maladies chroniques des voies respiratoires inférieures	11 011	48.3	4 060	17.2	11 233	49.2	4 253	17.9
Diseases of the digestive system — Maladies de l'appareil digestif								
Total	10 582	46.4	9 514	40.2	10 666	46.7	9 781	41.3
Gastric and duodenal ulcer — Ulcère de l'estomac et du duodénum	287	1.3	182	0.8	277	1.2	181	0.8
Diseases of the liver — Maladies du foie	3 805	16.7	1 519	6.4	3 947	17.3	1 548	6.5
Diseases of the musculoskeletal system and connective tissue — Maladies du système ostéo-articularie, des muscles et du tissu conjonctif	1 442	6.3	2 814	11.9	1 699	7.4	3 371	14.2
Diseases of the genitourinary system — Maladies de l'appareil génito-urinaire								
Total	5 357	23.5	6 816	28.8	5 782	25.3	7 406	31.2
Disorders of kidney and ureter — Affections du rein et de l'uretère	3 183	14.0	3 650	15.4	3 352	14.7	3 940	16.6
Hyperplasia of prostate — Hyperplasie de la prostate	192	2.3	..	..	190	2.2	..	..
Pregnancy, childbirth and the puerperium — Grossesse, accouchement et puerpéralité								
Total	..	..	15	♦3.7	..	..	13	♦3.3
Pregnancy with abortive outcome — Grossesse se terminant par un avortement	..	..	3	♦0.7	..	..	2	♦0.5
Other direct obstetric causes — Autres décès maternels directs	..	..	12	♦2.9	..	..	11	♦2.8
Indirect obstetric causes — Décès maternels indirects	..	..	-	-	..	..	-	-
Certain conditions originating in the perinatal period — Certaines affections dont l'origine se situe dans la période périnatale	375	178.5	262	131.9	356	176.7	273	143.8
Congenital malformations, deformations and chromosomal abnormalities — Malformations congénitales et anomalies chromosomiques	430	204.7	416	209.4	437	216.9	377	198.6
Symptoms, signs and abnormal clinical and laboratory findings, not elsewhere classified — Symptômes, signes et résultats anormaux d'examens cliniques et de laboratoire, non classés ailleurs	3 766	16.5	4 267	18.0	4 494	19.7	4 839	20.4
All other diseases — Toutes autres maladies	549	2.4	1 002	4.2	574	2.5	1 160	4.9
External causes — Causes externes								
Total	9 807	43.0	5 861	24.8	9 923	43.5	5 914	25.0
Accidents								
Total	6 774	29.7	4 705	19.9	6 758	29.6	4 665	19.7
Transport accidents — Accidents de transport	1 600	7.0	472	2.0	1 670	7.3	472	2.0
Falls — Chutes	1 599	7.0	1 420	6.0	1 603	7.0	1 454	6.1
Accidental drowning and submersion — Noyade et submersion accidentelles	344	1.5	95	0.4	387	1.7	88	0.4
Exposure to smoke, fire and flames — Exposition à la fumée, au feu et aux flammes	98	0.4	74	0.3	110	0.5	82	0.3
Accidental poisoning by and exposure to noxious substances — Intoxication accidentelle par des substances nocives et exposition à ces substances	676	3.0	293	1.2	618	2.7	311	1.3
Intentional self-harm — Lésions auto-infligées	2 662	11.7	907	3.8	2 718	11.9	961	4.1
Assault — Agresssions	178	0.8	104	0.4	207	0.9	118	0.5
All other external causes — Toutes autres causes externes	193	0.8	145	0.6	240	1.1	170	0.7

Sweden - Suède

Cause of death — Cause de décès	2016 (C)				2017 (C)			
	Male — Masculin		Female — Féminin		Male — Masculin		Female — Féminin	
	Number Nombre	Rate Taux	Number Nombre	Rate Taux	Number Nombre	Rate Taux	Number Nombre	Rate Taux
TOTAL	**44 485**	**894.7**	**46 586**	**941.0**	**44 933**	**890.1**	**47 142**	**941.0**
Certain infectious and parasitic diseases — Certaines maladies infectieuses et parasitaires								
Total	961	19.3	1 064	21.5	1 015	20.1	1 097	21.9
Intestinal infectious diseases — Maladies infectieuses intestinales	99	2.0	167	3.4	108	2.1	185	3.7
Tuberculosis — Tuberculose	12	♦0.2	4	♦0.1	8	♦0.2	6	♦0.1
Tetanus — Tétanos	-	-	-	-	-	-	1	♦0.0
Diphtheria — Diphtérie	-	-	1	♦0.0	-	-	-	-
Whooping cough — Coqueluche	-	-	-	-	-	-	-	-
Meningococcal infection — Infection à méningocoques	3	♦0.1	2	♦0.0	3	♦0.1	6	♦0.1
Septicaemia — Septicémie	409	8.2	366	7.4	430	8.5	371	7.4
Acute poliomyelitis — Poliomyélite aiguë	-	-	-	-	-	-	-	-
Measles — Rougeole	-	-	-	-	-	-	-	-
Viral hepatitis — Hépatite virale	38	0.8	18	♦0.4	31	0.6	13	♦0.3
Human immunodeficiency virus [HIV] disease — Maladies dues au virus de l'immunodéficience humaine (VIH)	10	♦0.2	3	♦0.1	7	♦0.1	6	♦0.1
Malaria — Paludisme	-	-	-	-	-	-	-	-
Neoplasms — Tumeurs	**12 335**	**248.1**	**11 176**	**225.7**	**12 368**	**245.0**	**11 514**	**229.8**
Malignant neoplasms — Tumeurs malignes								
Total	11 842	238.2	10 676	215.6	11 908	235.9	11 047	220.5
Malignant neoplasm of lip, oral cavity and pharynx — Tumeur maligne de la lèvre, de la cavité buccale et du pharynx	238	4.8	114	2.3	227	4.5	134	2.7
Malignant neoplasm of oesophagus — Tumeur maligne de l'oesophage	384	7.7	142	2.9	339	6.7	135	2.7
Malignant neoplasm of stomach — Tumeur maligne de l'estomac	329	6.6	248	5.0	327	6.5	215	4.3
Malignant neoplasm of colon, rectosigmoid junction, rectum, anus and anal canal — Tumeur maligne du côlon, de la jonction recto-sigmoïdienne, du rectum, de l'anus et du canal anal	1 421	28.6	1 354	27.3	1 399	27.7	1 363	27.2
Malignant neoplasm of liver and intrahepatic bile ducts — Tumeur maligne du foie et des voies bilaires intrahépatiques	487	9.8	245	4.9	498	9.9	267	5.3
Malignant neoplasm of pancreas — Tumeur maligne du pancréas	839	16.9	901	18.2	900	17.8	959	19.1
Malignant neoplasm of trachea, bronchus and lung — Tumeur maligne de la trachée, des bronches et du poumon	1 855	37.3	1 827	36.9	1 873	37.1	1 933	38.6
Malignant neoplasm of female breast — Tumeur maligne du sein chez la femme	..	..	1 391	33.9	..	..	1 413	34.1
Malignant neoplasm of cervix uteri — Tumeur maligne du col de l'utérus	..	..	135	3.3	..	..	149	3.6
Malignant neoplasm of prostate — Tumeur maligne de la prostate	2 347	129.7	..	..	2 345	127.4	..	..
Malignant neoplasm of lymphoid, haematopoietic and related tissue — Tumeurs malignes primitives ou présumées primitives des tissus lymphoïde, hématopoïétique et apparentés	1 123	22.6	866	17.5	1 109	22.0	857	17.1
Disorders of the blood and blood-forming organs and certain disorders involving the immune mechanism — Maladies du sang et des organes hématopoïétiques et certains troubles du système immunitaire								
Total	138	2.8	181	3.7	158	3.1	190	3.8
Anaemias — Anémies	66	1.3	118	2.4	81	1.6	139	2.8
Endocrine, nutritional and metabolic diseases — Maladies endocriniennes, nutritionnelles et métaboliques								
Total	1 359	27.3	1 254	25.3	1 451	28.7	1 393	27.8
Diabetes mellitus — Diabète sucré	1 116	22.4	930	18.8	1 186	23.5	1 050	21.0
Malnutrition — Malnutrition	37	0.7	60	1.2	33	0.7	62	1.2
Mental and behavioural disorders — Troubles mentaux et du comportement	**2 325**	**46.8**	**4 164**	**84.1**	**2 324**	**46.0**	**4 236**	**84.6**
Diseases of the nervous system — Maladies du système nerveux	**2 201**	**44.3**	**2 810**	**56.8**	**2 245**	**44.5**	**3 167**	**63.2**
Diseases of the circulatory system — Maladies de l'appareil circulatoire								
Total	15 231	306.3	16 385	330.9	15 159	300.3	15 867	316.7
Acute rheumatic fever and chronic rheumatic heart diseases — Rhumatisme articularie aigu et cardiopathies rhumatismales chroniques	38	0.8	76	1.5	28	♦0.6	65	1.3
Hypertensive diseases — Maladies hypertensives	878	17.7	1 626	32.8	1 048	20.8	1 700	33.9
Ischaemic heart disease — Cardiopathie ischémique	6 552	131.8	5 050	102.0	6 517	129.1	4 657	93.0
Cerebrovascular disease — Maladie cérébrovasculaire	2 705	54.4	3 403	68.7	2 550	50.5	3 185	63.6

20. Death and death rates by cause and sex: 2014 - 2018
Décès et taux de mortalité par cause et sexe : 2014 - 2018 (continued - suite)

Sweden - Suède

Cause of death — Cause de décès	2016 (C)				2017 (C)			
	Male — Masculin		Female — Féminin		Male — Masculin		Female — Féminin	
	Number Nombre	Rate Taux	Number Nombre	Rate Taux	Number Nombre	Rate Taux	Number Nombre	Rate Taux
Diseases of arteries, arterioles and capillaries — Maladies des artères, artérioles et capillaires	863	17.4	841	17.0	861	17.1	863	17.2
Diseases of the respiratory system — Maladies de l'appareil respiratoire								
Total	2 993	60.2	3 258	65.8	3 168	62.8	3 553	70.9
Influenza — Grippe	115	2.3	111	2.2	199	3.9	234	4.7
Pneumonia — Pneumopathies	929	18.7	885	17.9	901	17.8	944	18.8
Chronic lower respiratory diseases — Maladies chroniques des voies respiratoires inférieures	1 338	26.9	1 837	37.1	1 443	28.6	1 919	38.3
Diseases of the digestive system — Maladies de l'appareil digestif								
Total	1 493	30.0	1 424	28.8	1 476	29.2	1 351	27.0
Gastric and duodenal ulcer — Ulcère de l'estomac et du duodénum	138	2.8	126	2.5	133	2.6	126	2.5
Diseases of the liver — Maladies du foie	551	11.1	337	6.8	532	10.5	309	6.2
Diseases of the musculoskeletal system and connective tissue — Maladies du système ostéo-articularie, des muscles et du tissu conjonctif	159	3.2	339	6.8	173	3.4	322	6.4
Diseases of the genitourinary system — Maladies de l'appareil génito-urinaire								
Total	630	12.7	604	12.2	722	14.3	681	13.6
Disorders of kidney and ureter — Affections du rein et de l'uretère	443	8.9	438	8.8	496	9.8	522	10.4
Hyperplasia of prostate — Hyperplasie de la prostate	31	1.7	..	..	46	2.5	..	..
Pregnancy, childbirth and the puerperium — Grossesse, accouchement et puerpéralité								
Total	..	..	3	♦2.6	..	..	4	♦3.5
Pregnancy with abortive outcome — Grossesse se terminant par un avortement	..	..	-	-	..	..	-	-
Other direct obstetric causes — Autres décès maternels directs	..	..	2	♦1.7	..	..	4	♦3.5
Indirect obstetric causes — Décès maternels indirects	..	..	1	♦0.9	..	..	-	-
Certain conditions originating in the perinatal period — Certaines affections dont l'origine se situe dans la période périnatale	83	137.9	65	113.6	85	143.4	74	131.8
Congenital malformations, deformations and chromosomal abnormalities — Malformations congénitales et anomalies chromosomiques	138	229.2	140	244.6	162	273.4	132	235.0
Symptoms, signs and abnormal clinical and laboratory findings, not elsewhere classified — Symptômes, signes et résultats anormaux d'examens cliniques et de laboratoire, non classés ailleurs	1 320	26.5	1 782	36.0	1 195	23.7	1 589	31.7
All other diseases — Toutes autres maladies	74	1.5	115	2.3	89	1.8	131	2.6
External causes — Causes externes								
Total	3 045	61.2	1 822	36.8	3 143	62.3	1 841	36.7
Accidents								
Total	1 871	37.6	1 261	25.5	1 907	37.8	1 290	25.8
Transport accidents — Accidents de transport	226	4.5	65	1.3	220	4.4	64	1.3
Falls — Chutes	535	10.8	484	9.8	556	11.0	506	10.1
Accidental drowning and submersion — Noyade et submersion accidentelles	90	1.8	19	♦0.4	67	1.3	15	♦0.3
Exposure to smoke, fire and flames — Exposition à la fumée, au feu et aux flammes	31	0.6	21	♦0.4	44	0.9	28	♦0.6
Accidental poisoning by and exposure to noxious substances — Intoxication accidentelle par des substances nocives et exposition à ces substances	420	8.4	122	2.5	470	9.3	128	2.6
Intentional self-harm — Lésions auto-infligées	783	15.7	351	7.1	841	16.7	348	6.9
Assault — Agresssions	62	1.2	24	♦0.5	82	1.6	24	♦0.5
All other external causes — Toutes autres causes externes	329	6.6	186	3.8	313	6.2	179	3.6

20. Death and death rates by cause and sex: 2014 - 2018
Décès et taux de mortalité par cause et sexe : 2014 - 2018 (continued - suite)

Switzerland - Suisse

Cause of death — Cause de décès	2015 (C)				2016 (C)			
	Male — Masculin		Female — Féminin		Male — Masculin		Female — Féminin	
	Number Nombre	Rate Taux	Number Nombre	Rate Taux	Number Nombre	Rate Taux	Number Nombre	Rate Taux
TOTAL	**32 646**	**796.7**	**34 960**	**835.4**	**31 283**	**754.3**	**33 681**	**797.0**
Certain infectious and parasitic diseases — Certaines maladies infectieuses et parasitaires								
Total	397	9.7	431	10.3	359	8.7	394	9.3
Intestinal infectious diseases — Maladies infectieuses intestinales	54	1.3	110	2.6	52	1.3	100	2.4
Tuberculosis — Tuberculose	8	♦0.2	4	♦0.1	10	♦0.2	6	♦0.1
Tetanus — Tétanos	-	-	1	♦0.0	-	-	-	-
Diphtheria — Diphtérie	-	-	-	-	-	-	-	-
Whooping cough — Coqueluche	1	♦0.0	-	-	-	-	-	-
Meningococcal infection — Infection à méningocoques	3	♦0.1	5	♦0.1	3	♦0.1	-	-
Septicaemia — Septicémie	109	2.7	105	2.5	92	2.2	103	2.4
Acute poliomyelitis — Poliomyélite aiguë	-	-	-	-	-	-	-	-
Measles — Rougeole	-	-	-	-	-	-	-	-
Viral hepatitis — Hépatite virale	15	♦0.4	8	♦0.2	13	♦0.3	7	♦0.2
Human immunodeficiency virus [HIV] disease — Maladies dues au virus de l'immunodéficience humaine (VIH)	29	♦0.7	6	♦0.1	17	♦0.4	4	♦0.1
Malaria — Paludisme	-	-	-	-	-	-	-	-
Neoplasms — Tumeurs	**9 834**	**240.0**	**7 974**	**190.6**	**9 623**	**232.0**	**8 159**	**193.1**
Malignant neoplasms — Tumeurs malignes								
Total	9 571	233.6	7 690	183.8	9 372	226.0	7 829	185.3
Malignant neoplasm of lip, oral cavity and pharynx — Tumeur maligne de la lèvre, de la cavité buccale et du pharynx	293	7.2	121	2.9	356	8.6	131	3.1
Malignant neoplasm of oesophagus — Tumeur maligne de l'oesophage	343	8.4	112	2.7	356	8.6	98	2.3
Malignant neoplasm of stomach — Tumeur maligne de l'estomac	332	8.1	198	4.7	339	8.2	217	5.1
Malignant neoplasm of colon, rectosigmoid junction, rectum, anus and anal canal — Tumeur maligne du côlon, de la jonction recto-sigmoïdienne, du rectum, de l'anus et du canal anal	976	23.8	792	18.9	913	22.0	779	18.4
Malignant neoplasm of liver and intrahepatic bile ducts — Tumeur maligne du foie et des voies bilaires intrahépatiques	532	13.0	223	5.3	520	12.5	201	4.8
Malignant neoplasm of pancreas — Tumeur maligne du pancréas	605	14.8	668	16.0	718	17.3	713	16.9
Malignant neoplasm of trachea, bronchus and lung — Tumeur maligne de la trachée, des bronches et du poumon	2 056	50.2	1 186	28.3	1 949	47.0	1 300	30.8
Malignant neoplasm of female breast — Tumeur maligne du sein chez la femme	..	..	1 424	39.7	..	..	1 405	38.6
Malignant neoplasm of cervix uteri — Tumeur maligne du col de l'utérus	..	..	75	2.1	..	..	87	2.4
Malignant neoplasm of prostate — Tumeur maligne de la prostate	1 356	91.0	..	..	1 257	81.5	..	..
Malignant neoplasm of lymphoid, haematopoietic and related tissue — Tumeurs malignes primitives ou présumées primitives des tissus lymphoïde, hématopoïétique et apparentés	873	21.3	737	17.6	860	20.7	707	16.7
Disorders of the blood and blood-forming organs and certain disorders involving the immune mechanism — Maladies du sang et des organes hématopoïétiques et certains troubles du système immunitaire								
Total	100	2.4	96	2.3	94	2.3	124	2.9
Anaemias — Anémies	56	1.4	58	1.4	55	1.3	81	1.9
Endocrine, nutritional and metabolic diseases — Maladies endocriniennes, nutritionnelles et métaboliques								
Total	834	20.4	963	23.0	766	18.5	965	22.8
Diabetes mellitus — Diabète sucré	631	15.4	685	16.4	573	13.8	701	16.6
Malnutrition — Malnutrition	25	♦0.6	59	1.4	17	♦0.4	42	1.0
Mental and behavioural disorders — Troubles mentaux et du comportement	**1 820**	**44.4**	**3 661**	**87.5**	**1 722**	**41.5**	**3 343**	**79.1**
Diseases of the nervous system — Maladies du système nerveux	**1 640**	**40.0**	**2 024**	**48.4**	**1 444**	**34.8**	**1 886**	**44.6**
Diseases of the circulatory system — Maladies de l'appareil circulatoire								
Total	9 715	237.1	11 878	283.8	9 356	225.6	11 356	268.7
Acute rheumatic fever and chronic rheumatic heart diseases — Rhumatisme articularie aigu et cardiopathies rhumatismales chroniques	21	♦0.5	47	1.1	29	♦0.7	47	1.1
Hypertensive diseases — Maladies hypertensives	1 030	25.1	2 119	50.6	974	23.5	2 061	48.8
Ischaemic heart disease — Cardiopathie ischémique	4 001	97.6	3 372	80.6	3 854	92.9	3 136	74.2
Cerebrovascular disease — Maladie cérébrovasculaire	1 455	35.5	2 113	50.5	1 379	33.2	2 099	49.7

20. Death and death rates by cause and sex: 2014 - 2018
Décès et taux de mortalité par cause et sexe : 2014 - 2018 (continued - suite)

Switzerland - Suisse

Cause of death — Cause de décès	2015 (C)				2016 (C)			
	Male — Masculin		Female — Féminin		Male — Masculin		Female — Féminin	
	Number Nombre	Rate Taux	Number Nombre	Rate Taux	Number Nombre	Rate Taux	Number Nombre	Rate Taux
Diseases of arteries, arterioles and capillaries — Maladies des artères, artérioles et capillaires	502	12.3	455	10.9	498	12.0	488	11.5
Diseases of the respiratory system — Maladies de l'appareil respiratoire								
Total	2 315	56.5	2 299	54.9	2 183	52.6	1 925	45.6
Influenza — Grippe	74	1.8	145	3.5	37	0.9	45	1.1
Pneumonia — Pneumopathies	664	16.2	805	19.2	571	13.8	619	14.6
Chronic lower respiratory diseases — Maladies chroniques des voies respiratoires inférieures	1 145	27.9	979	23.4	1 084	26.1	918	21.7
Diseases of the digestive system — Maladies de l'appareil digestif								
Total	1 228	30.0	1 250	29.9	1 145	27.6	1 314	31.1
Gastric and duodenal ulcer — Ulcère de l'estomac et du duodénum	68	1.7	49	1.2	49	1.2	70	1.7
Diseases of the liver — Maladies du foie	474	11.6	261	6.2	448	10.8	249	5.9
Diseases of the musculoskeletal system and connective tissue — Maladies du système ostéo-articularie, des muscles et du tissu conjonctif	224	5.5	453	10.8	186	4.5	435	10.3
Diseases of the genitourinary system — Maladies de l'appareil génito-urinaire								
Total	557	13.6	623	14.9	509	12.3	562	13.3
Disorders of kidney and ureter — Affections du rein et de l'uretère	356	8.7	384	9.2	339	8.2	356	8.4
Hyperplasia of prostate — Hyperplasie de la prostate	26	♦1.7	..	..	29	♦1.9	..	..
Pregnancy, childbirth and the puerperium — Grossesse, accouchement et puerpéralité								
Total	..	..	6	♦6.9	..	..	3	♦3.4
Pregnancy with abortive outcome — Grossesse se terminant par un avortement	..	..	-	-	..	..	-	-
Other direct obstetric causes — Autres décès maternels directs	..	..	3	♦3.5	..	..	3	♦3.4
Indirect obstetric causes — Décès maternels indirects	..	..	3	♦3.5	..	..	-	-
Certain conditions originating in the perinatal period — Certaines affections dont l'origine se situe dans la période périnatale	96	215.0	80	190.9	85	189.2	79	183.9
Congenital malformations, deformations and chromosomal abnormalities — Malformations congénitales et anomalies chromosomiques	154	344.9	132	315.0	135	300.5	153	356.2
Symptoms, signs and abnormal clinical and laboratory findings, not elsewhere classified — Symptômes, signes et résultats anormaux d'examens cliniques et de laboratoire, non classés ailleurs	1 382	33.7	1 468	35.1	1 464	35.3	1 337	31.6
All other diseases — Toutes autres maladies	51	1.2	94	2.2	39	0.9	104	2.5
External causes — Causes externes								
Total	2 299	56.1	1 528	36.5	2 173	52.4	1 542	36.5
Accidents								
Total	1 419	34.6	1 179	28.2	1 329	32.0	1 223	28.9
Transport accidents — Accidents de transport	231	5.6	70	1.7	198	4.8	66	1.6
Falls — Chutes	805	19.6	930	22.2	809	19.5	974	23.0
Accidental drowning and submersion — Noyade et submersion accidentelles	48	1.2	12	♦0.3	44	1.1	8	♦0.2
Exposure to smoke, fire and flames — Exposition à la fumée, au feu et aux flammes	19	♦0.5	3	♦0.1	9	♦0.2	6	♦0.1
Accidental poisoning by and exposure to noxious substances — Intoxication accidentelle par des substances nocives et exposition à ces substances	113	2.8	48	1.1	86	2.1	45	1.1
Intentional self-harm — Lésions auto-infligées	792	19.3	279	6.7	759	18.3	257	6.1
Assault — Agresssions	26	♦0.6	21	♦0.5	13	♦0.3	19	♦0.4
All other external causes — Toutes autres causes externes	62	1.5	49	1.2	72	1.7	43	1.0

20. Death and death rates by cause and sex: 2014 - 2018
Décès et taux de mortalité par cause et sexe : 2014 - 2018 (continued - suite)

Ukraine

Cause of death — Cause de décès	2015 (+C)				2017 (+C)			
	Male — Masculin		Female — Féminin		Male — Masculin		Female — Féminin	
	Number Nombre	Rate Taux	Number Nombre	Rate Taux	Number Nombre	Rate Taux	Number Nombre	Rate Taux
TOTAL	291 561	1 466.1	303 235	1 316.0	281 784	1 427.2	292 339	1 279.9
Certain infectious and parasitic diseases — Certaines maladies infectieuses et parasitaires								
Total	7 218	36.3	2 682	11.6	6 198	31.4	2 516	11.0
Intestinal infectious diseases — Maladies infectieuses intestinales	17	♦0.1	11	♦0.0	19	♦0.1	5	♦0.0
Tuberculosis — Tuberculose	3 765	18.9	837	3.6	3 050	15.4	685	3.0
Tetanus — Tétanos	2	♦0.0	1	♦0.0	1	♦0.0	4	♦0.0
Diphtheria — Diphtérie	-	-	-	-	-	-	-	-
Whooping cough — Coqueluche	2	♦0.0	-	-	1	♦0.0	1	♦0.0
Meningococcal infection — Infection à méningocoques	36	0.2	24	♦0.1	32	0.2	17	♦0.1
Septicaemia — Septicémie	218	1.1	192	0.8	250	1.3	160	0.7
Acute poliomyelitis — Poliomyélite aiguë	-	-	-	-	-	-	-	-
Measles — Rougeole	-	-	-	-	-	-	3	♦0.0
Viral hepatitis — Hépatite virale	159	0.8	114	0.5	153	0.8	86	0.4
Human immunodeficiency virus [HIV] disease — Maladies dues au virus de l'immunodéficience humaine (VIH)	2 669	13.4	1 363	5.9	2 392	12.1	1 382	6.1
Malaria — Paludisme	4	♦0.0	-	-	2	♦0.0	1	♦0.0
Neoplasms — Tumeurs	44 518	223.9	35 012	151.9	43 720	221.4	34 604	151.5
Malignant neoplasms — Tumeurs malignes								
Total	44 148	222.0	34 602	150.2	43 375	219.7	34 205	149.8
Malignant neoplasm of lip, oral cavity and pharynx — Tumeur maligne de la lèvre, de la cavité buccale et du pharynx	3 111	15.6	428	1.9	3 028	15.3	440	1.9
Malignant neoplasm of oesophagus — Tumeur maligne de l'oesophage	1 390	7.0	173	0.8	1 353	6.9	172	0.8
Malignant neoplasm of stomach — Tumeur maligne de l'estomac	4 389	22.1	2 707	11.7	4 200	21.3	2 667	11.7
Malignant neoplasm of colon, rectosigmoid junction, rectum, anus and anal canal — Tumeur maligne du côlon, de la jonction recto-sigmoïdienne, du rectum, de l'anus et du canal anal	5 653	28.4	5 268	22.9	5 560	28.2	5 247	23.0
Malignant neoplasm of liver and intrahepatic bile ducts — Tumeur maligne du foie et des voies bilaires intrahépatiques	925	4.7	655	2.8	1 081	5.5	680	3.0
Malignant neoplasm of pancreas — Tumeur maligne du pancréas	2 356	11.8	1 920	8.3	2 401	12.2	2 049	9.0
Malignant neoplasm of trachea, bronchus and lung — Tumeur maligne de la trachée, des bronches et du poumon	10 264	51.6	2 109	9.2	9 847	49.9	2 182	9.6
Malignant neoplasm of female breast — Tumeur maligne du sein chez la femme	..	..	6 832	34.4	..	..	6 592	33.6
Malignant neoplasm of cervix uteri — Tumeur maligne du col de l'utérus	..	..	1 922	9.7	..	..	1 869	9.5
Malignant neoplasm of prostate — Tumeur maligne de la prostate	3 644	59.7	..	..	3 740	60.9	..	..
Malignant neoplasm of lymphoid, haematopoietic and related tissue — Tumeurs malignes primitives ou présumées primitives des tissus lymphoïde, hématopoïétique et apparentés	...	...	...	...	...	...	...	...
Disorders of the blood and blood-forming organs and certain disorders involving the immune mechanism — Maladies du sang et des organes hématopoïétiques et certains troubles du système immunitaire								
Total	129	0.6	115	0.5	114	0.6	115	0.5
Anaemias — Anémies	40	0.2	62	0.3	37	0.2	66	0.3
Endocrine, nutritional and metabolic diseases — Maladies endocriniennes, nutritionnelles et métaboliques								
Total	923	4.6	1 246	5.4	966	4.9	1 220	5.3
Diabetes mellitus — Diabète sucré	809	4.1	1 096	4.8	866	4.4	1 099	4.8
Malnutrition — Malnutrition	21	♦0.1	16	♦0.1	20	♦0.1	11	♦0.0
Mental and behavioural disorders — Troubles mentaux et du comportement	853	4.3	452	2.0	724	3.7	354	1.5
Diseases of the nervous system — Maladies du système nerveux	2 884	14.5	1 980	8.6	2 823	14.3	1 815	7.9
Diseases of the circulatory system — Maladies de l'appareil circulatoire								
Total	175 080	880.4	229 471	995.9	167 069	846.2	217 741	953.3
Acute rhoumatic fever and chronic rheumatic heart diseases — Rhumatisme articularie aigu et cardiopathies rhumatismales chroniques	287	1.4	453	2.0	256	1.3	343	1.5
Hypertensive diseases — Maladies hypertensives	336	1.7	184	0.8	265	1.3	134	0.6
Ischaemic heart disease — Cardiopathie ischémique	121 276	609.8	157 438	683.3	115 186	583.4	149 740	655.6
Cerebrovascular disease — Maladie cérébrovasculaire	32 961	165.7	46 814	203.2	31 420	159.1	44 313	194.0

20. Death and death rates by cause and sex: 2014 - 2018
Décès et taux de mortalité par cause et sexe : 2014 - 2018 (continued - suite)

Ukraine

Cause of death — Cause de décès	2015 (+C)				2017 (+C)			
	Male — Masculin		Female — Féminin		Male — Masculin		Female — Féminin	
	Number Nombre	Rate Taux	Number Nombre	Rate Taux	Number Nombre	Rate Taux	Number Nombre	Rate Taux
Diseases of arteries, arterioles and capillaries — Maladies des artères, artérioles et capillaires	...	...	...	...	...	...	...	...
Diseases of the respiratory system — Maladies de l'appareil respiratoire								
Total	9 970	50.1	3 981	17.3	8 816	44.7	3 350	14.7
Influenza — Grippe	12	♦0.1	9	♦0.0	2	♦0.0	8	♦0.0
Pneumonia — Pneumopathies	3 656	18.4	1 298	5.6	3 705	18.8	1 231	5.4
Chronic lower respiratory diseases — Maladies chroniques des voies respiratoires inférieures	5 347	26.9	2 328	10.1	4 222	21.4	1 771	7.8
Diseases of the digestive system — Maladies de l'appareil digestif								
Total	14 108	70.9	8 710	37.8	13 647	69.1	8 352	36.6
Gastric and duodenal ulcer — Ulcère de l'estomac et du duodénum	1 126	5.7	628	2.7	1 187	6.0	704	3.1
Diseases of the liver — Maladies du foie	9 529	47.9	5 174	22.5	8 952	45.3	4 737	20.7
Diseases of the musculoskeletal system and connective tissue — Maladies du système ostéo-articularie, des muscles et du tissu conjonctif	182	0.9	297	1.3	191	1.0	259	1.1
Diseases of the genitourinary system — Maladies de l'appareil génito-urinaire								
Total	1 327	6.7	1 242	5.4	1 318	6.7	1 259	5.5
Disorders of kidney and ureter — Affections du rein et de l'uretère	...	...	...	...	...	...	...	...
Hyperplasia of prostate — Hyperplasie de la prostate	...	...	..	..	...	...	..	..
Pregnancy, childbirth and the puerperium — Grossesse, accouchement et puerpéralité								
Total	..	..	60	14.6	..	..	30	♦8.2
Pregnancy with abortive outcome — Grossesse se terminant par un avortement	..	..	3	♦0.7	..	..	1	♦0.3
Other direct obstetric causes — Autres décès maternels directs	..	..	30	♦7.3	..	..	18	♦4.9
Indirect obstetric causes — Décès maternels indirects	..	..	27	♦6.6	..	..	11	♦3.0
Certain conditions originating in the perinatal period — Certaines affections dont l'origine se situe dans la période périnatale	978	459.5	752	378.0	900	479.9	650	368.4
Congenital malformations, deformations and chromosomal abnormalities — Malformations congénitales et anomalies chromosomiques	809	380.1	634	318.7	674	359.4	578	327.6
Symptoms, signs and abnormal clinical and laboratory findings, not elsewhere classified — Symptômes, signes et résultats anormaux d'examens cliniques et de laboratoire, non classés ailleurs	5 057	25.4	9 074	39.4	9 536	48.3	12 890	56.4
All other diseases — Toutes autres maladies	234	1.2	249	1.1	262	1.3	247	1.1
External causes — Causes externes								
Total	27 291	137.2	7 278	31.6	24 826	125.7	6 359	27.8
Accidents								
Total	...	...	...	...	...	...	...	...
Transport accidents — Accidents de transport	3 662	18.4	1 145	5.0	3 445	17.4	1 084	4.7
Falls — Chutes	1 551	7.8	470	2.0	1 464	7.4	444	1.9
Accidental drowning and submersion — Noyade et submersion accidentelles	1 669	8.4	296	1.3	1 444	7.3	255	1.1
Exposure to smoke, fire and flames — Exposition à la fumée, au feu et aux flammes	886	4.5	440	1.9	844	4.3	342	1.5
Accidental poisoning by and exposure to noxious substances — Intoxication accidentelle par des substances nocives et exposition à ces substances	3 552	17.9	797	3.5	3 591	18.2	812	3.6
Intentional self-harm — Lésions auto-infligées	6 149	30.9	1 426	6.2	5 327	27.0	1 161	5.1
Assault — Agresssions	1 510	7.6	601	2.6	1 160	5.9	493	2.2
All other external causes — Toutes autres causes externes	...	...	...	...	...	...	...	...

20. Death and death rates by cause and sex: 2014 - 2018
Décès et taux de mortalité par cause et sexe : 2014 - 2018 (continued - suite)

United Kingdom of Great Britain and Northern Ireland - Royaume-Uni de Grande-Bretagne et d'Irlande du Nord

Cause of death — Cause de décès	2015 (+C)				2016 (+C)			
	Male — Masculin		Female — Féminin		Male — Masculin		Female — Féminin	
	Number Nombre	Rate Taux	Number Nombre	Rate Taux	Number Nombre	Rate Taux	Number Nombre	Rate Taux
TOTAL	**292 707**	**916.2**	**310 074**	**941.7**	**292 999**	**909.2**	**304 205**	**917.4**
Certain infectious and parasitic diseases — Certaines maladies infectieuses et parasitaires								
Total	3 075	9.6	3 649	11.1	3 046	9.5	3 599	10.9
Intestinal infectious diseases — Maladies infectieuses intestinales	526	1.6	1 036	3.1	532	1.7	919	2.8
Tuberculosis — Tuberculose	179	0.6	116	0.4	136	0.4	81	0.2
Tetanus — Tétanos	-	-	-	-	-	-	-	-
Diphtheria — Diphtérie	-	-	-	-	-	-	-	-
Whooping cough — Coqueluche	4	♦0.0	2	♦0.0	-	-	3	♦0.0
Meningococcal infection — Infection à méningocoques	42	0.1	29	♦0.1	29	♦0.1	42	0.1
Septicaemia — Septicémie	1 406	4.4	1 838	5.6	1 423	4.4	1 891	5.7
Acute poliomyelitis — Poliomyélite aiguë	-	-	-	-	-	-	-	-
Measles — Rougeole	-	-	-	-	1	♦0.0	-	-
Viral hepatitis — Hépatite virale	236	0.7	101	0.3	178	0.6	77	0.2
Human immunodeficiency virus [HIV] disease — Maladies dues au virus de l'immunodéficience humaine (VIH)	125	0.4	56	0.2	141	0.4	39	0.1
Malaria — Paludisme	5	♦0.0	2	♦0.0	2	♦0.0	5	♦0.0
Neoplasms — Tumeurs	**89 669**	**280.7**	**78 939**	**239.7**	**90 410**	**280.6**	**79 930**	**241.1**
Malignant neoplasms — Tumeurs malignes								
Total	87 676	274.4	77 102	234.2	88 435	274.4	78 087	235.5
Malignant neoplasm of lip, oral cavity and pharynx — Tumeur maligne de la lèvre, de la cavité buccale et du pharynx	1 927	6.0	913	2.8	2 040	6.3	990	3.0
Malignant neoplasm of oesophagus — Tumeur maligne de l'oesophage	5 466	17.1	2 494	7.6	5 507	17.1	2 510	7.6
Malignant neoplasm of stomach — Tumeur maligne de l'estomac	2 817	8.8	1 581	4.8	2 867	8.9	1 603	4.8
Malignant neoplasm of colon, rectosigmoid junction, rectum, anus and anal canal — Tumeur maligne du côlon, de la jonction recto-sigmoïdienne, du rectum, de l'anus et du canal anal	8 873	27.8	7 589	23.0	9 038	28.0	7 772	23.4
Malignant neoplasm of liver and intrahepatic bile ducts — Tumeur maligne du foie et des voies bilaires intrahépatiques	3 091	9.7	2 088	6.3	3 290	10.2	2 159	6.5
Malignant neoplasm of pancreas — Tumeur maligne du pancréas	4 469	14.0	4 472	13.6	4 738	14.7	4 548	13.7
Malignant neoplasm of trachea, bronchus and lung — Tumeur maligne de la trachée, des bronches et du poumon	19 200	60.1	16 357	49.7	19 357	60.1	16 328	49.2
Malignant neoplasm of female breast — Tumeur maligne du sein chez la femme	..	..	11 470	42.0	..	..	11 512	41.9
Malignant neoplasm of cervix uteri — Tumeur maligne du col de l'utérus	..	..	855	3.1	..	..	854	3.1
Malignant neoplasm of prostate — Tumeur maligne de la prostate	11 827	106.9	..	..	11 645	103.2	..	..
Malignant neoplasm of lymphoid, haematopoietic and related tissue — Tumeurs malignes primitives ou présumées primitives des tissus lymphoïde, hématopoïétique et apparentés	7 403	23.2	5 721	17.4	7 446	23.1	5 776	17.4
Disorders of the blood and blood-forming organs and certain disorders involving the immune mechanism — Maladies du sang et des organes hématopoïétiques et certains troubles du système immunitaire								
Total	584	1.8	706	2.1	601	1.9	596	1.8
Anaemias — Anémies	208	0.7	335	1.0	225	0.7	282	0.9
Endocrine, nutritional and metabolic diseases — Maladies endocriniennes, nutritionnelles et métaboliques								
Total	4 367	13.7	4 622	14.0	4 655	14.4	4 706	14.2
Diabetes mellitus — Diabète sucré	3 238	10.1	3 321	10.1	3 438	10.7	3 330	10.0
Malnutrition — Malnutrition	37	0.1	66	0.2	48	0.1	52	0.2
Mental and behavioural disorders — Troubles mentaux et du comportement	18 483	57.9	35 590	108.1	18 682	58.0	34 990	105.5
Diseases of the nervous system — Maladies du système nerveux	14 070	44.0	18 462	56.1	14 890	46.2	19 845	59.8
Diseases of the circulatory system — Maladies de l'appareil circulatoire								
Total	80 108	250.8	78 053	237.0	78 324	243.1	74 155	223.6
Acute rheumatic fever and chronic rheumatic heart diseases — Rhumatisme articularie aigu et cardiopathies rhumatismales chroniques	310	1.0	624	1.9	318	1.0	637	1.9
Hypertensive diseases — Maladies hypertensives	2 979	9.3	4 146	12.6	3 079	9.6	4 311	13.0
Ischaemic heart disease — Cardiopathie ischémique	41 955	131.3	27 828	84.5	40 299	125.1	25 777	77.7
Cerebrovascular disease — Maladie cérébrovasculaire	16 560	51.8	23 612	71.7	16 025	49.7	21 750	65.6

20. Death and death rates by cause and sex: 2014 - 2018
Décès et taux de mortalité par cause et sexe : 2014 - 2018 (continued - suite)

United Kingdom of Great Britain and Northern Ireland - Royaume-Uni de Grande-Bretagne et d'Irlande du Nord

Cause of death — Cause de décès	2015 (+C)				2016 (+C)			
	Male — Masculin		Female — Féminin		Male — Masculin		Female — Féminin	
	Number Nombre	Rate Taux	Number Nombre	Rate Taux	Number Nombre	Rate Taux	Number Nombre	Rate Taux
Diseases of arteries, arterioles and capillaries — Maladies des artères, artérioles et capillaires	5 097	16.0	4 382	13.3	4 947	15.4	4 217	12.7
Diseases of the respiratory system — Maladies de l'appareil respiratoire								
Total	40 693	127.4	44 752	135.9	39 765	123.4	41 749	125.9
Influenza — Grippe	164	0.5	210	0.6	209	0.6	186	0.6
Pneumonia — Pneumopathies	14 315	44.8	18 018	54.7	13 417	41.6	16 198	48.9
Chronic lower respiratory diseases — Maladies chroniques des voies respiratoires inférieures	17 925	56.1	18 682	56.7	17 691	54.9	18 026	54.4
Diseases of the digestive system — Maladies de l'appareil digestif								
Total	14 008	43.8	14 801	44.9	14 380	44.6	14 642	44.2
Gastric and duodenal ulcer — Ulcère de l'estomac et du duodénum	1 129	3.5	966	2.9	1 098	3.4	925	2.8
Diseases of the liver — Maladies du foie	5 623	17.6	3 631	11.0	5 950	18.5	3 661	11.0
Diseases of the musculoskeletal system and connective tissue — Maladies du système ostéo-articularie, des muscles et du tissu conjonctif	1 539	4.8	3 021	9.2	1 562	4.8	2 818	8.5
Diseases of the genitourinary system — Maladies de l'appareil génito-urinaire								
Total	4 737	14.8	6 151	18.7	4 619	14.3	5 873	17.7
Disorders of kidney and ureter — Affections du rein et de l'uretère	2 121	6.6	2 561	7.8	2 091	6.5	2 448	7.4
Hyperplasia of prostate — Hyperplasie de la prostate	170	1.5	..	..	179	1.6	..	..
Pregnancy, childbirth and the puerperium — Grossesse, accouchement et puerpéralité								
Total	..	..	35	4.5	..	..	51	6.6
Pregnancy with abortive outcome — Grossesse se terminant par un avortement	..	..	1	♦0.1	..	..	2	♦0.3
Other direct obstetric causes — Autres décès maternels directs	..	..	22	♦2.8	..	..	33	4.3
Indirect obstetric causes — Décès maternels indirects	..	..	12	♦1.5	..	..	16	♦2.1
Certain conditions originating in the perinatal period — Certaines affections dont l'origine se situe dans la période périnatale	943	236.5	676	178.8	919	231.2	746	197.9
Congenital malformations, deformations and chromosomal abnormalities — Malformations congénitales et anomalies chromosomiques	1 128	282.9	907	240.0	1 129	284.0	965	256.0
Symptoms, signs and abnormal clinical and laboratory findings, not elsewhere classified — Symptômes, signes et résultats anormaux d'examens cliniques et de laboratoire, non classés ailleurs	3 450	10.8	9 145	27.8	3 606	11.2	9 013	27.2
All other diseases — Toutes autres maladies	741	2.3	1 411	4.3	789	2.4	1 424	4.3
External causes — Causes externes								
Total	15 112	47.3	9 154	27.8	15 622	48.5	9 103	27.5
Accidents								
Total	9 752	30.5	6 991	21.2	10 266	31.9	6 946	20.9
Transport accidents — Accidents de transport	1 407	4.4	446	1.4	1 384	4.3	438	1.3
Falls — Chutes	3 103	9.7	3 282	10.0	3 334	10.3	3 346	10.1
Accidental drowning and submersion — Noyade et submersion accidentelles	195	0.6	70	0.2	193	0.6	71	0.2
Exposure to smoke, fire and flames — Exposition à la fumée, au feu et aux flammes	155	0.5	101	0.3	191	0.6	106	0.3
Accidental poisoning by and exposure to noxious substances — Intoxication accidentelle par des substances nocives et exposition à ces substances	2 757	8.6	1 064	3.2	2 931	9.1	1 136	3.4
Intentional self-harm — Lésions auto-infligées	3 732	11.7	1 178	3.6	3 676	11.4	1 110	3.3
Assault — Agresssions	73	0.2	47	0.1	72	0.2	45	0.1
All other external causes — Toutes autres causes externes	1 555	4.9	938	2.8	1 608	5.0	1 002	3.0

20. Death and death rates by cause and sex: 2014 - 2018
Décès et taux de mortalité par cause et sexe : 2014 - 2018 (continued - suite)

Australia - Australie

Cause of death — Cause de décès	2016 (C)				2017 (C)			
	Male — Masculin		Female — Féminin		Male — Masculin		Female — Féminin	
	Number Nombre	Rate Taux	Number Nombre	Rate Taux	Number Nombre	Rate Taux	Number Nombre	Rate Taux
TOTAL	81 867	682.1	76 637	628.8	82 858	679.0	78 051	629.5
Certain infectious and parasitic diseases — Certaines maladies infectieuses et parasitaires								
Total	1 445	12.0	1 384	11.4	1 329	10.9	1 307	10.5
Intestinal infectious diseases — Maladies infectieuses intestinales	112	0.9	161	1.3	124	1.0	197	1.6
Tuberculosis — Tuberculose	21	♦0.2	25	♦0.2	21	♦0.2	25	♦0.2
Tetanus — Tétanos	1	♦0.0	-	-	-	-	1	♦0.0
Diphtheria — Diphtérie	-	-	-	-	-	-	-	-
Whooping cough — Coqueluche	-	-	1	♦0.0	-	-	1	♦0.0
Meningococcal infection — Infection à méningocoques	6	♦0.0	7	♦0.1	13	♦0.1	9	♦0.1
Septicaemia — Septicémie	816	6.8	873	7.2	702	5.8	780	6.3
Acute poliomyelitis — Poliomyélite aiguë	-	-	-	-	-	-	-	-
Measles — Rougeole	-	-	-	-	-	-	-	-
Viral hepatitis — Hépatite virale	187	1.6	76	0.6	142	1.2	64	0.5
Human immunodeficiency virus [HIV] disease — Maladies dues au virus de l'immunodéficience humaine (VIH)	52	0.4	6	♦0.0	55	0.5	1	♦0.0
Malaria — Paludisme	-	-	-	-	1	♦0.0	-	-
Neoplasms — Tumeurs	26 158	217.9	20 167	165.5	26 162	214.4	20 237	163.2
Malignant neoplasms — Tumeurs malignes								
Total	25 539	212.8	19 622	161.0	25 524	209.1	19 706	158.9
Malignant neoplasm of lip, oral cavity and pharynx — Tumeur maligne de la lèvre, de la cavité buccale et du pharynx	596	5.0	250	2.1	601	4.9	238	1.9
Malignant neoplasm of oesophagus — Tumeur maligne de l'oesophage	988	8.2	350	2.9	925	7.6	340	2.7
Malignant neoplasm of stomach — Tumeur maligne de l'estomac	707	5.9	381	3.1	719	5.9	442	3.6
Malignant neoplasm of colon, rectosigmoid junction, rectum, anus and anal canal — Tumeur maligne du côlon, de la jonction recto-sigmoïdienne, du rectum, de l'anus et du canal anal	2 451	20.4	1 966	16.1	2 371	19.4	1 927	15.5
Malignant neoplasm of liver and intrahepatic bile ducts — Tumeur maligne du foie et des voies bilaires intrahépatiques	1 232	10.3	634	5.2	1 241	10.2	673	5.4
Malignant neoplasm of pancreas — Tumeur maligne du pancréas	1 500	12.5	1 411	11.6	1 566	12.8	1 430	11.5
Malignant neoplasm of trachea, bronchus and lung — Tumeur maligne de la trachée, des bronches et du poumon	5 024	41.9	3 387	27.8	4 911	40.2	3 351	27.0
Malignant neoplasm of female breast — Tumeur maligne du sein chez la femme	..	..	2 978	29.9	..	..	2 898	28.6
Malignant neoplasm of cervix uteri — Tumeur maligne du col de l'utérus	..	..	259	2.6	..	..	230	2.3
Malignant neoplasm of prostate — Tumeur maligne de la prostate	3 250	84.6	..	..	3 275	83.6	..	..
Malignant neoplasm of lymphoid, haematopoietic and related tissue — Tumeurs malignes primitives ou présumées primitives des tissus lymphoïde, hématopoïétique et apparentés	2 562	21.3	1 811	14.9	2 660	21.8	1 839	14.8
Disorders of the blood and blood-forming organs and certain disorders involving the immune mechanism — Maladies du sang et des organes hématopoïétiques et certains troubles du système immunitaire								
Total	234	1.9	257	2.1	265	2.2	272	2.2
Anaemias — Anémies	111	0.9	128	1.1	121	1.0	162	1.3
Endocrine, nutritional and metabolic diseases — Maladies endocriniennes, nutritionnelles et métaboliques								
Total	3 527	29.4	3 240	26.6	3 493	28.6	3 327	26.8
Diabetes mellitus — Diabète sucré	2 584	21.5	2 197	18.0	2 583	21.2	2 256	18.2
Malnutrition — Malnutrition	57	0.5	57	0.5	45	0.4	59	0.5
Mental and behavioural disorders — Troubles mentaux et du comportement	3 795	31.6	6 140	50.4	3 807	31.2	6 350	51.2
Diseases of the nervous system — Maladies du système nerveux	4 129	34.4	4 676	38.4	4 269	35.0	4 936	39.8
Diseases of the circulatory system — Maladies de l'appareil circulatoire								
Total	21 843	182.0	22 314	183.1	21 391	175.3	22 086	178.1
Acute rheumatic fever and chronic rheumatic heart diseases — Rhumatisme articularie aigu et cardiopathies rhumatismales chroniques	144	1.2	248	2.0	147	1.2	234	1.9
Hypertensive diseases — Maladies hypertensives	879	7.3	1 357	11.1	850	7.0	1 467	11.8
Ischaemic heart disease — Cardiopathie ischémique	10 949	91.2	8 236	67.6	10 514	86.2	8 076	65.1
Cerebrovascular disease — Maladie cérébrovasculaire	4 244	35.4	6 225	51.1	4 302	35.3	5 884	47.5

20. Death and death rates by cause and sex: 2014 - 2018
Décès et taux de mortalité par cause et sexe : 2014 - 2018 (continued - suite)

Australia - Australie

Cause of death — Cause de décès	2016 (C)				2017 (C)			
	Male — Masculin		Female — Féminin		Male — Masculin		Female — Féminin	
	Number Nombre	Rate Taux	Number Nombre	Rate Taux	Number Nombre	Rate Taux	Number Nombre	Rate Taux
Diseases of arteries, arterioles and capillaries — Maladies des artères, artérioles et capillaires	1 006	8.4	883	7.2	973	8.0	850	6.9
Diseases of the respiratory system — Maladies de l'appareil respiratoire								
Total	7 482	62.3	7 340	60.2	8 190	67.1	8 013	64.6
Influenza — Grippe	184	1.5	271	2.2	508	4.2	740	6.0
Pneumonia — Pneumopathies	1 240	10.3	1 641	13.5	1 432	11.7	1 582	12.8
Chronic lower respiratory diseases — Maladies chroniques des voies respiratoires inférieures	4 169	34.7	3 896	32.0	4 268	35.0	4 089	33.0
Diseases of the digestive system — Maladies de l'appareil digestif								
Total	2 910	24.2	2 863	23.5	3 021	24.8	2 909	23.5
Gastric and duodenal ulcer — Ulcère de l'estomac et du duodénum	131	1.1	133	1.1	138	1.1	122	1.0
Diseases of the liver — Maladies du foie	1 179	9.8	610	5.0	1 295	10.6	621	5.0
Diseases of the musculoskeletal system and connective tissue — Maladies du système ostéo-articularie, des muscles et du tissu conjonctif	473	3.9	903	7.4	490	4.0	911	7.3
Diseases of the genitourinary system — Maladies de l'appareil génito-urinaire								
Total	1 569	13.1	1 894	15.5	1 702	13.9	1 996	16.1
Disorders of kidney and ureter — Affections du rein et de l'uretère	1 168	9.7	1 318	10.8	1 276	10.5	1 310	10.6
Hyperplasia of prostate — Hyperplasie de la prostate	67	1.7	..	..	65	1.7	..	..
Pregnancy, childbirth and the puerperium — Grossesse, accouchement et puerpéralité								
Total	..	..	12	♦3.9	..	..	5	♦1.6
Pregnancy with abortive outcome — Grossesse se terminant par un avortement	..	..	1	♦0.3	..	..	1	♦0.3
Other direct obstetric causes — Autres décès maternels directs	..	..	7	♦2.3	..	..	4	♦1.3
Indirect obstetric causes — Décès maternels indirects	..	..	4	♦1.3	..	..	-	-
Certain conditions originating in the perinatal period — Certaines affections dont l'origine se situe dans la période périnatale	316	198.1	237	156.4	339	212.9	243	162.1
Congenital malformations, deformations and chromosomal abnormalities — Malformations congénitales et anomalies chromosomiques	330	206.8	261	172.2	331	207.9	303	202.1
Symptoms, signs and abnormal clinical and laboratory findings, not elsewhere classified — Symptômes, signes et résultats anormaux d'examens cliniques et de laboratoire, non classés ailleurs	572	4.8	736	6.0	1 012	8.3	926	7.5
All other diseases — Toutes autres maladies	239	2.0	312	2.6	258	2.1	320	2.6
External causes — Causes externes								
Total	6 845	57.0	3 901	32.0	6 799	55.7	3 910	31.5
Accidents								
Total	4 239	35.3	2 912	23.9	4 041	33.1	2 903	23.4
Transport accidents — Accidents de transport	1 099	9.2	368	3.0	1 019	8.3	352	2.8
Falls — Chutes	1 311	10.9	1 408	11.6	1 313	10.8	1 469	11.8
Accidental drowning and submersion — Noyade et submersion accidentelles	153	1.3	48	0.4	117	1.0	43	0.3
Exposure to smoke, fire and flames — Exposition à la fumée, au feu et aux flammes	38	0.3	14	♦0.1	31	0.3	20	♦0.2
Accidental poisoning by and exposure to noxious substances — Intoxication accidentelle par des substances nocives et exposition à ces substances	994	8.3	432	3.5	920	7.5	385	3.1
Intentional self-harm — Lésions auto-infligées	2 171	18.1	736	6.0	2 346	19.2	778	6.3
Assault — Agresssions	172	1.4	82	0.7	124	1.0	56	0.5
All other external causes — Toutes autres causes externes	263	2.2	171	1.4	288	2.4	173	1.4

New Zealand - Nouvelle-Zélande

Cause of death — Cause de décès	2014 (+C)				2015 (+C)			
	Male — Masculin		Female — Féminin		Male — Masculin		Female — Féminin	
	Number Nombre	Rate Taux	Number Nombre	Rate Taux	Number Nombre	Rate Taux	Number Nombre	Rate Taux
TOTAL	**15 707**	**710.9**	**15 457**	**672.0**	**15 929**	**705.7**	**15 867**	**678.5**
Certain infectious and parasitic diseases — Certaines maladies infectieuses et parasitaires								
Total	181	8.2	180	7.8	161	7.1	154	6.6
Intestinal infectious diseases — Maladies infectieuses intestinales	45	2.0	51	2.2	27	♦1.2	42	1.8
Tuberculosis — Tuberculose	5	♦0.2	1	♦0.0	5	♦0.2	5	♦0.2
Tetanus — Tétanos	-	-	1	♦0.0	-	-	-	-
Diphtheria — Diphtérie	-	-	-	-	-	-	-	-
Whooping cough — Coqueluche	-	-	-	-	-	-	1	♦0.0
Meningococcal infection — Infection à méningocoques	1	♦0.0	4	♦0.2	1	♦0.0	3	♦0.1
Septicaemia — Septicémie	61	2.8	77	3.3	64	2.8	60	2.6
Acute poliomyelitis — Poliomyélite aiguë	-	-	-	-	-	-	-	-
Measles — Rougeole	-	-	-	-	-	-	-	-
Viral hepatitis — Hépatite virale	35	1.6	18	♦0.8	26	♦1.2	13	♦0.6
Human immunodeficiency virus [HIV] disease — Maladies dues au virus de l'immunodéficience humaine (VIH)	14	♦0.6	3	♦0.1	5	♦0.2	-	-
Malaria — Paludisme	-	-	-	-	-	-	1	♦0.0
Neoplasms — Tumeurs	**4 942**	**223.7**	**4 413**	**191.9**	**5 145**	**227.9**	**4 558**	**194.9**
Malignant neoplasms — Tumeurs malignes								
Total	4 822	218.2	4 306	187.2	5 036	223.1	4 444	190.0
Malignant neoplasm of lip, oral cavity and pharynx — Tumeur maligne de la lèvre, de la cavité buccale et du pharynx	91	4.1	52	2.3	101	4.5	44	1.9
Malignant neoplasm of oesophagus — Tumeur maligne de l'oesophage	185	8.4	78	3.4	174	7.7	73	3.1
Malignant neoplasm of stomach — Tumeur maligne de l'estomac	181	8.2	95	4.1	151	6.7	108	4.6
Malignant neoplasm of colon, rectosigmoid junction, rectum, anus and anal canal — Tumeur maligne du côlon, de la jonction recto-sigmoïdienne, du rectum, de l'anus et du canal anal	648	29.3	625	27.2	689	30.5	578	24.7
Malignant neoplasm of liver and intrahepatic bile ducts — Tumeur maligne du foie et des voies bilaires intrahépatiques	166	7.5	90	3.9	193	8.6	92	3.9
Malignant neoplasm of pancreas — Tumeur maligne du pancréas	248	11.2	235	10.2	238	10.5	267	11.4
Malignant neoplasm of trachea, bronchus and lung — Tumeur maligne de la trachée, des bronches et du poumon	889	40.2	790	34.3	953	42.2	852	36.4
Malignant neoplasm of female breast — Tumeur maligne du sein chez la femme	..	..	607	32.7	..	..	669	35.3
Malignant neoplasm of cervix uteri — Tumeur maligne du col de l'utérus	..	..	46	2.5	..	..	53	2.8
Malignant neoplasm of prostate — Tumeur maligne de la prostate	651	91.7	..	..	647	88.9	..	..
Malignant neoplasm of lymphoid, haematopoietic and related tissue — Tumeurs malignes primitives ou présumées primitives des tissus lymphoïde, hématopoïétique et apparentés	492	22.3	362	15.7	500	22.2	335	14.3
Disorders of the blood and blood-forming organs and certain disorders involving the immune mechanism — Maladies du sang et des organes hématopoïétiques et certains troubles du système immunitaire								
Total	31	1.4	37	1.6	35	1.6	27	♦1.2
Anaemias — Anémies	11	♦0.5	15	♦0.7	15	♦0.7	16	♦0.7
Endocrine, nutritional and metabolic diseases — Maladies endocriniennes, nutritionnelles et métaboliques								
Total	570	25.8	493	21.4	540	23.9	554	23.7
Diabetes mellitus — Diabète sucré	431	19.5	360	15.7	423	18.7	415	17.7
Malnutrition — Malnutrition	9	♦0.4	5	♦0.2	2	♦0.1	9	♦0.4
Mental and behavioural disorders — Troubles mentaux et du comportement	**586**	**26.5**	**974**	**42.3**	**677**	**30.0**	**1 145**	**49.0**
Diseases of the nervous system — Maladies du système nerveux	**630**	**28.5**	**695**	**30.2**	**670**	**29.7**	**729**	**31.2**
Diseases of the circulatory system — Maladies de l'appareil circulatoire								
Total	5 137	232.5	5 224	227.1	5 003	221.6	5 254	224.7
Acute rheumatic fever and chronic rheumatic heart diseases — Rhumatisme articularie aigu et cardiopathies rhumatismales chroniques	56	2.5	88	3.8	39	1.7	67	2.9
Hypertensive diseases — Maladies hypertensives	164	7.4	243	10.6	148	6.6	270	11.5
Ischaemic heart disease — Cardiopathie ischémique	2 836	128.3	2 263	98.4	2 802	124.1	2 216	94.8
Cerebrovascular disease — Maladie cérébrovasculaire	1 036	46.9	1 533	66.6	970	43.0	1 497	64.0

20. Death and death rates by cause and sex: 2014 - 2018
Décès et taux de mortalité par cause et sexe : 2014 - 2018 (continued - suite)

New Zealand - Nouvelle-Zélande

Cause of death — Cause de décès	2014 (+C)				2015 (+C)			
	Male — Masculin		Female — Féminin		Male — Masculin		Female — Féminin	
	Number Nombre	Rate Taux	Number Nombre	Rate Taux	Number Nombre	Rate Taux	Number Nombre	Rate Taux
Diseases of arteries, arterioles and capillaries — Maladies des artères, artérioles et capillaires	272	12.3	263	11.4	270	12.0	265	11.3
Diseases of the respiratory system — Maladies de l'appareil respiratoire								
Total	1 410	63.8	1 504	65.4	1 433	63.5	1 535	65.6
Influenza — Grippe	15	♦0.7	17	♦0.7	29	♦1.3	30	♦1.3
Pneumonia — Pneumopathies	283	12.8	375	16.3	283	12.5	423	18.1
Chronic lower respiratory diseases — Maladies chroniques des voies respiratoires inférieures	872	39.5	955	41.5	911	40.4	907	38.8
Diseases of the digestive system — Maladies de l'appareil digestif								
Total	461	20.9	508	22.1	458	20.3	494	21.1
Gastric and duodenal ulcer — Ulcère de l'estomac et du duodénum	27	♦1.2	35	1.5	34	1.5	28	♦1.2
Diseases of the liver — Maladies du foie	103	4.7	71	3.1	119	5.3	64	2.7
Diseases of the musculoskeletal system and connective tissue — Maladies du système ostéo-articularie, des muscles et du tissu conjonctif	69	3.1	164	7.1	72	3.2	152	6.5
Diseases of the genitourinary system — Maladies de l'appareil génito-urinaire								
Total	207	9.4	241	10.5	225	10.0	230	9.8
Disorders of kidney and ureter — Affections du rein et de l'uretère	136	6.2	139	6.0	138	6.1	139	5.9
Hyperplasia of prostate — Hyperplasie de la prostate	18	♦2.5	..	..	19	♦2.6	..	..
Pregnancy, childbirth and the puerperium — Grossesse, accouchement et puerpéralité								
Total	..	..	3	♦5.2	..	..	6	♦9.8
Pregnancy with abortive outcome — Grossesse se terminant par un avortement	..	..	-	-	..	..	-	-
Other direct obstetric causes — Autres décès maternels directs	..	..	2	♦3.5	..	..	3	♦4.9
Indirect obstetric causes — Décès maternels indirects	..	..	1	♦1.7	..	..	3	♦4.9
Certain conditions originating in the perinatal period — Certaines affections dont l'origine se situe dans la période périnatale	91	307.5	84	303.8	70	223.2	53	178.6
Congenital malformations, deformations and chromosomal abnormalities — Malformations congénitales et anomalies chromosomiques	109	368.3	68	245.9	93	296.6	90	303.2
Symptoms, signs and abnormal clinical and laboratory findings, not elsewhere classified — Symptômes, signes et résultats anormaux d'examens cliniques et de laboratoire, non classés ailleurs	75	3.4	103	4.5	86	3.8	114	4.9
All other diseases — Toutes autres maladies	37	1.7	70	3.0	50	2.2	61	2.6
External causes — Causes externes								
Total	1 171	53.0	696	30.3	1 211	53.7	711	30.4
Accidents								
Total	703	31.8	524	22.8	723	32.0	514	22.0
Transport accidents — Accidents de transport	247	11.2	114	5.0	289	12.8	110	4.7
Falls — Chutes	237	10.7	306	13.3	231	10.2	314	13.4
Accidental drowning and submersion — Noyade et submersion accidentelles	38	1.7	15	♦0.7	44	1.9	11	♦0.5
Exposure to smoke, fire and flames — Exposition à la fumée, au feu et aux flammes	10	♦0.5	5	♦0.2	10	♦0.4	6	♦0.3
Accidental poisoning by and exposure to noxious substances — Intoxication accidentelle par des substances nocives et exposition à ces substances	63	2.9	30	♦1.3	67	3.0	29	♦1.2
Intentional self-harm — Lésions auto-infligées	377	17.1	130	5.7	386	17.1	144	6.2
Assault — Agresssions	31	1.4	14	♦0.6	40	1.8	19	♦0.8
All other external causes — Toutes autres causes externes	60	2.7	28	♦1.2	62	2.7	34	1.5

20. Death and death rates by cause and sex: 2014 - 2018
Décès et taux de mortalité par cause et sexe : 2014 - 2018 (continued - suite)

Solomon Islands - Îles Salomon

Cause of death — Cause de décès	2017 (...)		2018 (...)	
	Male — Masculin	Female — Féminin	Male — Masculin	Female — Féminin
	Number Nombre	Number Nombre	Number Nombre	Number Nombre
TOTAL	*253*	*165*	*314*	*246*
Certain infectious and parasitic diseases — Certaines maladies infectieuses et parasitaires				
Total	*39*	*20*	*36*	*32*
Intestinal infectious diseases — Maladies infectieuses intestinales	*11*	*1*	*4*	*6*
Tuberculosis — Tuberculose	*5*	*1*	*2*	*7*
Tetanus — Tétanos	-	-	*1*	-
Diphtheria — Diphtérie	-	-	-	-
Whooping cough — Coqueluche	-	-	-	-
Meningococcal infection — Infection à méningocoques	-	-	-	-
Septicaemia — Septicémie	*8*	*9*	*13*	*12*
Acute poliomyelitis — Poliomyélite aiguë	-	-	-	-
Measles — Rougeole	-	-	-	-
Viral hepatitis — Hépatite virale	*7*	*4*	*8*	*2*
Human immunodeficiency virus [HIV] disease — Maladies dues au virus de l'immunodéficience humaine (VIH)	-	-	-	-
Malaria — Paludisme	-	*1*	*1*	*3*
Neoplasms — Tumeurs	*28*	*26*	*33*	*35*
Malignant neoplasms — Tumeurs malignes				
Total	*27*	*24*	*33*	*31*
Malignant neoplasm of lip, oral cavity and pharynx — Tumeur maligne de la lèvre, de la cavité buccale et du pharynx	-	*1*	*1*	-
Malignant neoplasm of oesophagus — Tumeur maligne de l'oesophage	-	*1*	*1*	*2*
Malignant neoplasm of stomach — Tumeur maligne de l'estomac	*1*	*1*	-	*1*
Malignant neoplasm of colon, rectosigmoid junction, rectum, anus and anal canal — Tumeur maligne du côlon, de la jonction recto-sigmoïdienne, du rectum, de l'anus et du canal anal	*1*	-	*2*	*4*
Malignant neoplasm of liver and intrahepatic bile ducts — Tumeur maligne du foie et des voies bilaires intrahépatiques	*3*	*1*	*1*	*1*
Malignant neoplasm of pancreas — Tumeur maligne du pancréas	-	-	*1*	-
Malignant neoplasm of trachea, bronchus and lung — Tumeur maligne de la trachée, des bronches et du poumon	*3*	*2*	*6*	*2*
Malignant neoplasm of female breast — Tumeur maligne du sein chez la femme	..	*2*	..	*3*
Malignant neoplasm of cervix uteri — Tumeur maligne du col de l'utérus	..	*4*	..	*5*
Malignant neoplasm of prostate — Tumeur maligne de la prostate	*3*	..	*3*	..
Malignant neoplasm of lymphoid, haematopoietic and related tissue — Tumeurs malignes primitives ou présumées primitives des tissus lymphoïde, hématopoïétique et apparentés	*8*	*4*	*6*	*6*
Disorders of the blood and blood-forming organs and certain disorders involving the immune mechanism — Maladies du sang et des organes hématopoïétiques et certains troubles du système immunitaire				
Total	*2*	*2*	*1*	*4*
Anaemias — Anémies	*2*	*2*	-	*2*
Endocrine, nutritional and metabolic diseases — Maladies endocriniennes, nutritionnelles et métaboliques				
Total	*28*	*20*	*35*	*26*
Diabetes mellitus — Diabète sucré	*23*	*17*	*29*	*20*
Malnutrition — Malnutrition	*3*	*1*	*2*	*2*
Mental and behavioural disorders — Troubles mentaux et du comportement	-	-	*2*	-
Diseases of the nervous system — Maladies du système nerveux	*7*	*9*	*8*	*9*
Diseases of the circulatory system — Maladies de l'appareil circulatoire				
Total	*67*	*33*	*85*	*46*
Acute rheumatic fever and chronic rheumatic heart diseases — Rhumatisme articularie aigu et cardiopathies rhumatismales chroniques	*2*	*6*	*6*	*8*
Hypertensive diseases — Maladies hypertensives	*8*	*2*	*5*	*2*
Ischaemic heart disease — Cardiopathie ischémique	*34*	*6*	*36*	*5*
Cerebrovascular disease — Maladie cérébrovasculaire	*16*	*14*	*28*	*20*
Diseases of arteries, arterioles and capillaries — Maladies des artères, artérioles et capillaires	-	*1*	-	-
Diseases of the respiratory system — Maladies de l'appareil respiratoire				
Total	*9*	*5*	*11*	*10*
Influenza — Grippe	-	-	-	-
Pneumonia — Pneumopathies	-	-	*3*	*1*
Chronic lower respiratory diseases — Maladies chroniques des voies respiratoires inférieures	*5*	*4*	*7*	*4*

20. Death and death rates by cause and sex: 2014 - 2018
Décès et taux de mortalité par cause et sexe : 2014 - 2018 (continued - suite)

Solomon Islands - Îles Salomon

Cause of death — Cause de décès	2017 (...)		2018 (...)	
	Male — Masculin	Female — Féminin	Male — Masculin	Female — Féminin
	Number Nombre	Number Nombre	Number Nombre	Number Nombre
Diseases of the digestive system — Maladies de l'appareil digestif				
Total	*13*	*7*	*24*	*7*
Gastric and duodenal ulcer — Ulcère de l'estomac et du duodénum	*1*	*-*	*7*	*1*
Diseases of the liver — Maladies du foie	*5*	*1*	*8*	*3*
Diseases of the musculoskeletal system and connective tissue — Maladies du système ostéo-articularie, des muscles et du tissu conjonctif	*-*	*2*	*2*	*6*
Diseases of the genitourinary system — Maladies de l'appareil génito-urinaire				
Total	*2*	*2*	*7*	*8*
Disorders of kidney and ureter — Affections du rein et de l'uretère	*2*	*1*	*3*	*6*
Hyperplasia of prostate — Hyperplasie de la prostate	*-*	..	*1*	..
Pregnancy, childbirth and the puerperium — Grossesse, accouchement et puerpéralité				
Total	..	*3*	..	*2*
Pregnancy with abortive outcome — Grossesse se terminant par un avortement	..	*-*	..	*1*
Other direct obstetric causes — Autres décès maternels directs	..	*3*	..	*1*
Indirect obstetric causes — Décès maternels indirects	..	*-*	..	*-*
Certain conditions originating in the perinatal period — Certaines affections dont l'origine se situe dans la période périnatale	*32*	*22*	*48*	*39*
Congenital malformations, deformations and chromosomal abnormalities — Malformations congénitales et anomalies chromosomiques	*4*	*5*	*8*	*12*
Symptoms, signs and abnormal clinical and laboratory findings, not elsewhere classified — Symptômes, signes et résultats anormaux d'examens cliniques et de laboratoire, non classés ailleurs	*10*	*3*	*1*	*4*
All other diseases — Toutes autres maladies	*-*	*1*	*3*	*2*
External causes — Causes externes				
Total	*12*	*5*	*10*	*4*
Accidents				
Total	*7*	*3*	*6*	*1*
Transport accidents — Accidents de transport	*4*	*-*	*1*	*-*
Falls — Chutes	*-*	*2*	*1*	*-*
Accidental drowning and submersion — Noyade et submersion accidentelles	*1*	*-*	*-*	*1*
Exposure to smoke, fire and flames — Exposition à la fumée, au feu et aux flammes	*-*	*-*	*-*	*-*
Accidental poisoning by and exposure to noxious substances — Intoxication accidentelle par des substances nocives et exposition à ces substances	*-*	*1*	*-*	*-*
Intentional self-harm — Lésions auto-infligées	*1*	*-*	*-*	*-*
Assault — Agresssions	*-*	*-*	*1*	*-*
All other external causes — Toutes autres causes externes	*4*	*2*	*3*	*3*

FOOTNOTES — NOTES

Data in bold refer to deaths based on ICD-10 Classification, otherwise data refer to deaths based on ICD-9 Classification. - Les données en typographie gras se rapportent aux décès basées sur la classification CIM-10, autrement les données se rapportent aux décès basées sur la classification CIM-9.

Italics: data from civil registers that are incomplete or of unknown completeness. — Italiques : données incomplètes ou dont le degré d'exactitude n'est pas connu provenant des registres de l'état civil.

* Provisional. - Données provisoires.

♦ Rates based on 30 or fewer deaths. - Taux basés sur 30 décès ou moins.

'Code' indicates the source of data, as follows:
C - Civil registration, estimated over 90% complete
U - Civil registration, estimated less than 90% complete
| - Other source, estimated reliable
+ - Data tabulated by date of registration rather than occurence
... - Information not available

Le 'Code' indique la source des données, comme suit :
C - Registres de l'état civil considérés complèts à 90 p. 100 au moins
U - Registres de l'état civil qui ne sont pas considérés complèts à 90 p. 100 au moins
| - Autre source, considérée pas douteuses
+ - Données exploitées selon la date de l'enregistrement et non la date de l'événement
... - Information pas disponible

Table 21 - *Demographic Yearbook 2019*

Table 21 presents the life tables' probabilities of dying in the five year interval following specified ages ($_5q_x$), for each sex, for the latest available year between 2005 and 2019. The probabilities are multiplied by a thousand, that is, the values presented in the table are 1000*$_5q_x$.

Male and female probabilities of dying are shown separately for selected ages beginning at birth and proceeding at every fifth age thereafter up to age 100.

The values presented in the table are derived by the United Nations Statistics Division from the official complete life tables reported by the countries or areas.

Data are shown with one decimal regardless of the number of digits provided in the original computation.

The life table is a statistical device for summarizing the mortality experience of a population, from which the probability of dying, survivorship and expectation of life can be calculated. It is based on the assumption that the theoretical cohort is subject, throughout its existence, to the age-specific mortality rates observed at a particular time. Thus, levels of mortality prevailing at the time a life table is constructed are assumed to remain unchanged into the future until all members of the cohort have died.

Reliability of data: The values shown in this table are derived from official complete life tables. It is assumed that, if necessary, the basic data (population and deaths classified by age and sex) have been adjusted for deficiencies before their use in constructing the complete life tables.

Limitations: The life tables' probabilities of dying are subject to the same qualifications as have been set forth for population statistics in general and death statistics in particular, as discussed in sections 3 and 4, respectively, of the Technical Notes. They must be interpreted strictly using the underlying assumption that surviving cohorts are subjected to the same age-specific mortality rates of the period to which the life table refers.

Earlier data: The life tables' probabilities of dying at specified ages, for each sex, have been shown in previous issues of the *Demographic Yearbook*. For information on specific years covered, the reader should consult the Historical Index.

Tableau 21 – *Annuaire démographique 2019*

Le tableau 21 donne les probabilités de décès dans l'intervalle de cinq ans que suit l'âge spécifié ($_5q_x$), pour chaque sexe, pour la dernière année disponible entre 2005 et 2019. Les probabilités sont multipliées par mille, c'est-à-dire que les valeurs indiquées dans le tableau sont égales à $1000{*}{_5q_x}$.

Les probabilités de décès sont indiquées séparément pour les hommes et les femmes pour différents âges, depuis la naissance puis tous les cinq ans jusqu'à 100 ans.

Les chiffres indiqués dans ce tableau ont été calculés par la Division de statistique de l'Organisation des Nations Unies à partir des tables de mortalité complètes communiquées par les pays ou zones.

Les données sont arrondies à la première décimale, indépendamment du nombre de décimales qui figurent dans le calcul initial.

La table de mortalité est un moyen statistique que s'utilise pour donner un aperçu complet de la mortalité d'une population incluant les probabilités de décès et l'espérance de vie à chaque âge. Les tables de mortalité reposent sur l'hypothèse que chaque cohorte théoriquement distinguée connaît, pendant toute son existence, les taux de mortalité par âge observé à un moment donné. Les taux de mortalité correspondant à l'époque à laquelle sont calculées les tables de mortalité sont ainsi censés demeurer inchangées dans l'avenir jusqu'au décès de tous les membres de la cohorte.

Fiabilité des donnés : Les chiffres indiqués dans ce tableau ont été calculés à partir des tables officielles de mortalité complètes. En ce qui concerne les chiffres extraits de tables officielles de mortalité, on part du principe que les données de base (effectif de la population et nombre de décès selon l'âge et le sexe) ont été ajustées, en tant que de besoin, avant de servir à l'établissement de la table de mortalité.

Insuffisance des données : Les probabilités de décès appellent les mêmes réserves que celles qui ont été formulées à propos des statistiques de la population en général et des statistiques de mortalité en particulier (voir les sections 3 et 4 des Notes techniques). Lorsque l'on interprète les données, il ne faut jamais perdre de vue que, par hypothèse, les cohortes de survivants sont soumises, pour chaque âge, aux conditions de mortalité de la période visée par la table de mortalité.

Données publiées antérieurement : Les probabilités de décès pour chaque sexe figuraient déjà dans des éditions antérieures de *l'Annuaire démographique*. Pour plus de précisions concernant les années pour lesquelles ces données ont été publiées, se reporter à l'index historique.

21. Probability of dying in the five year interval following specified age (5qx), by sex, latest available year: 2005 - 2019
Probabilité de décès dans l'intervalle de cinq ans qui suit un âge donné (5qx), par sexe, dernière année disponible : 2005 - 2019

Continent, country or area and date	Age (in years) - Age (en années)																				
Continent, pays ou zone et date	0	5	10	15	20	25	30	35	40	45	50	55	60	65	70	75	80	85	90	95	100
AFRICA - AFRIQUE																					
Republic of South Sudan - République de Soudan du Sud																					
2010																					
Male - Hommes	130.6	14.1	10.8	18.5	25.6	27.0	28.8	33.1	40.1	51.8	70.0	98.7	143.7	213.2	316.6	457.7	624.2	785.1	907.0	...	...
Female - Femmes	111.9	13.7	10.7	18.4	25.9	27.8	30.2	35.2	43.3	56.8	78.0	111.6	164.6	245.8	362.8	513.5	678.3	826.7	931.7	...	...
AMERICA, NORTH - AMÉRIQUE DU NORD																					
Canada																					
2016 - 2018																					
Male - Hommes	5.5	0.4	0.6	2.1	4.0	4.7	5.5	6.1	8.0	11.6	17.5	26.9	42.1	66.5	106.2	170.3	272.0	425.5	626.5	804.2	913.2
Female - Femmes	4.9	0.4	0.5	1.2	1.8	2.1	2.6	3.1	4.7	7.4	11.2	17.2	27.1	43.5	71.3	118.7	199.4	332.7	528.8	733.4	878.1
Costa Rica																					
2019																					
Male - Hommes	7.9	0.6	1.2	3.3	5.7	6.7	7.4	8.7	11.2	15.6	22.4	33.3	50.6	79.6	122.4	192.7	288.0	415.4	579.7	755.1	*1000
Female - Femmes	6.4	0.5	0.8	1.3	1.5	1.7	2.3	3.2	4.7	7.7	11.6	19.3	30.4	49.9	79.9	133.9	227.0	360.2	528.6	717.4	*1000
Cuba																					
2011 - 2013																					
Male - Hommes	6.0	1.0	1.3	2.4	3.5	4.5	5.7	7.3	10.5	17.5	29.3	44.9	67.2	100.5	148.8	223.2	334.7	477.3	602.9	645.4	*1000
Female - Femmes	5.6	0.9	0.9	1.4	1.9	2.4	3.0	4.1	6.5	11.0	18.7	29.3	44.6	67.0	104.8	168.7	270.2	421.1	577.7	655.4	*1000
Curaçao																					
2016																					
Male - Hommes	9.6	0.4	0.5	2.1	5.8	7.2	7.2	8.9	11.0	15.4	28.1	49.3	69.2	103.7	158.6	226.0	359.1	525.1	701.4	841.0	...
Female - Femmes	14.6	0.3	0.2	0.7	1.8	2.5	2.9	3.9	6.2	8.9	12.1	19.1	33.3	53.2	83.1	148.5	257.1	388.1	571.7	776.1	...
Dominican Republic - République dominicaine																					
2010 - 2015																					
Male - Hommes	33.8	1.5	2.2	6.6	12.0	13.8	15.2	17.5	21.3	28.4	42.9	61.1	86.0	127.0	178.3	282.0	*1000	...	...	...	...
Female - Femmes	25.6	1.4	1.5	2.8	4.8	6.6	8.4	10.7	14.3	19.4	30.9	45.6	64.3	98.8	145.1	253.9	*1000	...	...	...	...
Greenland - Groenland																					
2009 - 2013																					
Male - Hommes	15.4	0.5	2.8	15.7	22.9	16.2	14.3	13.6	18.4	25.9	35.9	72.3	87.1	167.8	303.9	470.3	648.6	758.8	...	...	...
Female - Femmes	7.0	0.5	2.7	10.3	8.0	2.5	6.9	10.8	9.1	20.1	26.0	50.6	83.8	147.4	209.0	326.2	565.3	731.9	970.6	...	...
Jamaica - Jamaïque																					
2006																					
Male - Hommes	31.7	2.8	2.5	4.5	6.5	6.5	7.0	9.4	14.5	23.2	37.5	60.5	96.9	153.2	236.8	353.8	502.7	667.6	817.2	921.8	*1000
Female - Femmes	18.0	1.3	1.1	1.7	2.6	3.4	4.3	5.9	8.7	13.9	22.8	38.0	63.2	104.5	169.8	268.2	405.3	574.1	747.0	883.6	*1000
Martinique																					
2007																					
Male - Hommes	11.6	1.0	1.1	4.2	8.8	7.5	8.8	8.5	10.4	13.5	26.7	28.9	42.2	87.6	122.7	202.9	325.3	532.7	663.7	834.4	*1000
Female - Femmes	7.8	0.4	0.7	0.6	2.1	2.9	4.6	4.1	4.8	5.3	11.3	14.8	28.6	45.6	76.8	135.3	216.7	362.2	508.4	810.4	*1000
Mexico - Mexique																					
2005																					
Male - Hommes	21.6	1.7	2.2	4.3	7.4	9.9	12.0	15.1	20.3	28.7	41.3	59.9	86.6	124.3	176.5	246.8	337.7	448.7	574.2	702.2	*1000
Female - Femmes	17.4	1.3	1.2	1.8	2.4	3.1	4.3	6.4	9.9	15.4	23.9	37.2	57.5	88.4	134.4	201.1	293.6	414.1	557.1	705.8	*1000
Panama[1]																					
2018																					
Male - Hommes	20.9	1.9	2.3	6.8	12.2	13.7	12.6	12.2	13.9	18.4	26.5	39.0	58.0	86.0	126.6	184.2	263.5	367.3	494.2	634.3	*1000
Female - Femmes	15.7	1.2	1.4	2.3	3.2	4.1	5.1	6.3	8.0	10.9	15.6	23.3	35.7	55.8	87.6	137.0	211.0	316.5	455.2	615.9	*1000
Puerto Rico - Porto Rico																					
2017 - 2019																					
Male - Hommes	8.2	0.4	0.5	3.3	10.3	12.1	15.2	16.6	20.2	22.9	33.1	46.3	62.0	89.4	116.3	174.1	256.4	*1000	...	...	...
Female - Femmes	6.6	0.4	0.5	1.0	2.0	1.9	3.8	5.2	6.7	9.9	14.6	20.7	29.4	45.5	68.5	112.4	190.9	*1000	...	...	...
United States of America - États-Unis d'Amérique																					
2017																					
Male - Hommes	7.4	0.6	0.9	3.6	6.9	8.5	9.8	11.3	13.6	19.1	29.7	45.0	64.5	88.3	127.2	195.7	306.4	472.7	675.2	840.1	*1000
Female - Femmes	6.1	0.5	0.6	1.5	2.5	3.4	4.7	6.0	8.2	11.9	18.6	27.8	39.1	56.6	88.3	142.7	237.3	386.5	590.2	782.2	*1000

21. Probability of dying in the five year interval following specified age (5qx), by sex, latest available year: 2005 - 2019
Probabilité de décès dans l'intervalle de cinq ans qui suit un âge donné (5qx), par sexe, dernière année disponible : 2005 - 2019 (continued - suite)

Continent, country or area and date / Continent, pays ou zone et date	Age (in years) - Age (en années)																				
	0	5	10	15	20	25	30	35	40	45	50	55	60	65	70	75	80	85	90	95	100
AMERICA, SOUTH - AMÉRIQUE DU SUD																					
Argentina - Argentine																					
2008 - 2010																					
Male - Hommes	15.8	1.3	1.8	5.3	7.5	7.9	8.1	10.0	14.5	22.1	37.3	59.5	89.5	133.8	194.0	289.6	431.2	568.1	692.6	804.3	*1000
Female - Femmes	13.0	1.0	1.2	2.2	2.6	3.1	4.0	5.7	8.4	13.2	20.4	31.0	45.5	68.2	105.9	175.1	309.8	460.7	614.6	762.3	*1000
Bolivia (Plurinational State of) - Bolivie (État plurinational de)[2]																					
2016 - 2017																					
Male - Hommes	44.2	5.3	4.1	8.9	13.6	14.2	16.1	18.9	24.3	30.8	41.6	57.2	83.1	117.2	167.4	233.2	329.5	416.5	609.4	*1000	...
Female - Femmes	34.5	3.5	2.4	4.7	5.3	5.9	7.4	9.9	14.4	20.0	27.8	39.3	57.6	84.3	119.8	165.8	236.7	317.6	487.2	*1000	...
Brazil - Brésil																					
2015																					
Male - Hommes	17.4	1.5	1.9	8.2	12.5	12.6	13.5	15.7	20.2	28.1	40.3	56.8	79.0	114.1	168.7	246.7	*1000	...	...	...	...
Female - Femmes	14.7	1.1	1.2	2.2	2.8	3.5	4.7	6.4	9.6	14.8	21.7	31.6	46.7	71.9	112.3	173.9	*1000	...	...	...	...
Chile - Chili[3]																					
2019 - 2020																					
Male - Hommes	8.1	0.6	0.9	2.9	4.5	5.2	6.2	7.9	10.9	15.5	23.2	34.3	52.6	82.6	126.4	195.3	303.5	437.3	584.9	741.3	*1000
Female - Femmes	6.8	0.5	0.7	1.3	1.5	1.7	2.3	3.4	5.3	8.3	12.4	18.9	29.9	48.8	77.6	127.1	216.7	348.1	498.7	654.4	*1000
Ecuador - Équateur[4]																					
2018																					
Male - Hommes	20.7	0.9	1.0	3.2	4.5	6.2	8.9	10.3	12.8	19.2	28.7	41.4	67.3	102.7	161.8	251.6	380.6	549.2	722.5	854.0	*1000
Female - Femmes	17.9	0.9	1.0	1.8	2.2	2.8	3.2	4.1	5.6	8.4	13.5	20.0	31.6	52.4	94.4	173.2	309.4	492.6	691.8	846.0	*1000
French Guiana - Guyane française																					
2007																					
Male - Hommes	16.3	1.5	2.1	4.9	7.7	8.1	10.0	14.0	17.2	29.4	16.0	32.3	52.4	79.5	135.5	261.3	306.7	474.0	733.7	...	...
Female - Femmes	15.1	1.9	1.3	1.4	1.2	3.0	4.6	4.2	11.9	11.0	10.4	11.6	26.7	85.4	77.4	203.8	253.1	321.1	434.3	...	...
Guyana[5]																					
2012																					
Male - Hommes	43.5	5.5	6.1	11.8	20.7	25.5	26.5	28.2	33.3	42.8	57.2	77.5	105.0	141.6	189.3	250.3	325.9	415.9	517.9	625.9	*1000
Female - Femmes	35.2	3.5	3.1	5.5	9.8	12.8	14.1	15.4	18.4	24.3	33.9	48.6	70.0	100.6	143.5	202.3	280.1	378.7	495.8	623.5	*1000
ASIA - ASIE																					
Armenia - Arménie																					
2017 - 2018																					
Male - Hommes	9.8	0.9	0.9	3.2	4.2	4.8	5.3	7.6	13.8	23.8	46.9	62.9	89.8	144.6	206.0	231.2	481.2	862.1	899.7	729.2	...
Female - Femmes	8.4	0.8	0.7	1.2	1.5	1.5	1.9	2.9	4.7	8.9	15.0	23.5	39.1	72.6	118.6	149.7	353.7	783.1	916.9	946.9	...
Azerbaijan - Azerbaïdjan																					
2018																					
Male - Hommes	13.8	1.5	2.1	3.0	3.7	4.1	5.3	6.9	13.7	21.9	35.4	55.0	89.6	132.3	186.3	295.1	422.3	517.9	567.9	302.8	...
Female - Femmes	11.3	1.1	1.2	1.6	1.9	2.2	2.4	3.2	5.2	8.8	15.8	25.8	48.1	81.2	126.9	226.0	388.6	555.4	681.7	553.3	...
China, Hong Kong SAR - Chine, Hong Kong RAS																					
2019																					
Male - Hommes	2.2	0.3	0.5	1.1	1.4	2.1	2.9	4.1	6.9	10.7	16.0	23.9	38.3	59.3	94.0	152.4	240.6	357.2	506.8	677.8	*1000
Female - Femmes	1.8	0.3	0.5	0.8	0.7	0.9	1.3	1.9	3.1	5.3	8.7	12.5	18.6	27.7	44.3	78.8	143.5	242.8	390.2	583.9	*1000
China, Macao SAR - Chine, Macao RAS																					
2002 - 2005																					
Male - Hommes	7.2	0.6	0.4	1.7	3.9	5.4	6.2	7.6	9.0	13.6	17.8	25.8	43.1	72.1	128.9	239.9	369.5	574.4	841.2	991.4	*1000
Female - Femmes	5.2	0.4	0.2	0.9	1.5	1.9	2.3	3.8	4.7	5.9	7.4	10.9	19.3	33.3	70.4	186.2	317.0	485.2	717.3	923.7	*1000
Israel - Israël[6]																					
2014 - 2018																					
Male - Hommes	4.1	0.5	0.7	1.6	2.6	2.7	2.8	3.7	5.9	10.1	16.8	26.5	40.9	64.9	106.5	176.3	284.7	434.0	605.7	764.0	*1000
Female - Femmes	3.6	0.4	0.4	0.6	0.9	1.1	1.5	2.2	3.6	5.8	9.3	14.5	22.7	37.7	67.1	123.0	222.3	377.5	574.5	763.7	*1000
Japan - Japon[7]																					
2015																					
Male - Hommes	2.9	0.5	0.5	1.3	2.5	2.7	3.2	4.1	6.2	10.0	16.2	25.7	41.2	65.8	100.6	160.7	278.5	450.1	652.9	810.7	...
Female - Femmes	2.5	0.4	0.4	0.7	1.0	1.3	1.7	2.4	3.7	5.8	8.9	12.3	18.0	27.3	43.9	77.2	150.4	286.0	501.4	728.1	...

21. Probability of dying in the five year interval following specified age (5qx), by sex, latest available year: 2005 - 2019
Probabilité de décès dans l'intervalle de cinq ans qui suit un âge donné (5qx), par sexe, dernière année disponible : 2005 - 2019 (continued - suite)

Continent, country or area and date / Continent, pays ou zone et date	Age (in years) - Age (en années) 0	5	10	15	20	25	30	35	40	45	50	55	60	65	70	75	80	85	90	95	100
ASIA - ASIE																					
Kazakhstan																					
2019																					
Male - Hommes	12.0	1.7	1.8	3.8	6.4	7.9	12.6	19.6	29.2	39.4	53.1	78.5	124.5	181.2	244.2	335.3	473.4	583.7	672.0	503.6	...
Female - Femmes	9.3	1.1	1.1	2.1	2.6	2.8	4.4	7.3	10.8	15.6	20.3	31.5	52.2	82.5	132.3	211.1	364.2	539.9	785.6	836.3	...
Kyrgyzstan - Kirghizstan																					
2017																					
Male - Hommes	20.1	2.0	2.3	3.6	5.2	6.8	11.3	16.6	25.6	35.8	52.6	75.4	115.9	160.2	362.2	542.6	691.1	780.5	844.8	907.0	*1000
Female - Femmes	16.4	1.0	1.3	2.0	2.5	3.1	4.6	7.1	10.6	14.9	21.0	33.1	56.4	90.6	161.1	328.1	426.5	551.9	668.3	773.7	*1000
Qatar																					
2006																					
Male - Hommes	10.2	0.8	1.8	9.4	8.9	6.5	5.6	6.6	7.1	9.0	16.1	22.1	42.2	88.0	167.5	248.6	376.7	*1000	...	...	...
Female - Femmes	9.0	1.3	0.9	2.2	1.4	2.4	1.2	1.8	3.8	6.7	9.8	22.1	76.0	120.2	253.6	354.1	348.3	*1000	...	...	...
Republic of Korea - République de Corée																					
2018																					
Male - Hommes	3.7	0.4	0.5	1.3	2.0	2.6	3.6	5.0	7.4	12.2	19.3	28.5	41.4	63.5	101.9	187.3	325.1	500.8	686.4	839.4	*1000
Female - Femmes	3.0	0.3	0.5	0.8	1.3	1.5	2.2	2.9	3.9	5.4	7.6	10.1	14.6	24.0	44.2	95.9	199.2	372.1	584.9	779.2	*1000
Singapore - Singapour[8]																					
2019																					
Male - Hommes	2.6	0.3	0.4	1.2	1.8	1.7	2.2	3.0	5.0	8.8	14.1	24.3	39.6	61.8	103.7	169.7	276.2	422.2	600.5	779.9	*1000
Female - Femmes	2.4	0.5	0.3	0.4	0.7	0.9	1.3	1.8	2.8	5.0	8.8	14.0	21.6	33.0	57.0	106.7	191.8	330.1	514.4	711.7	*1000
Turkey - Turquie																					
2016 - 2018																					
Male - Hommes	12.3	1.2	1.4	3.2	4.1	4.2	4.2	5.2	7.8	13.3	23.5	40.6	66.9	105.2	165.1	258.2	385.4	558.2	720.4	818.3	*1000
Female - Femmes	11.0	0.9	0.9	1.3	1.3	1.5	1.8	2.7	4.2	7.0	11.2	18.2	31.1	53.8	97.4	179.0	301.6	468.0	633.6	719.5	*1000
EUROPE																					
Austria - Autriche																					
2018																					
Male - Hommes	3.8	0.3	0.5	1.8	2.4	2.9	3.0	4.4	6.5	10.5	18.1	32.0	50.5	79.2	124.7	175.8	299.8	497.7	705.3	880.5	...
Female - Femmes	3.3	0.3	0.4	0.9	0.8	1.1	1.5	2.3	3.7	5.8	10.4	16.0	27.3	43.0	69.0	110.3	216.7	407.3	651.4	835.3	...
Belarus - Bélarus																					
2017																					
Male - Hommes	3.9	0.8	0.8	2.3	4.2	6.2	10.2	16.8	26.4	39.5	57.7	88.1	139.0	188.0	257.4	359.3	485.0	627.6	769.8	887.4	...
Female - Femmes	3.3	0.7	0.7	1.1	1.5	2.1	3.1	5.7	8.8	12.9	18.2	27.2	44.0	68.1	113.7	202.6	340.2	529.0	741.7	911.5	...
Belgium - Belgique[9]																					
2015																					
Male - Hommes	4.2	0.5	0.4	1.4	3.2	3.0	4.0	5.4	7.7	12.4	20.1	35.5	55.2	81.7	122.3	193.8	315.6	506.2	717.7	872.7	*1000
Female - Femmes	3.6	0.4	0.5	0.8	1.1	1.3	2.0	2.8	4.9	8.3	12.6	21.3	33.1	44.8	71.3	119.0	222.4	406.4	643.5	832.8	*1000
Bulgaria - Bulgarie																					
2016 - 2018																					
Male - Hommes	8.4	1.0	1.2	2.9	4.0	5.0	6.7	10.1	16.0	28.7	49.3	76.8	113.8	161.1	214.6	303.5	446.5	611.8	785.7	883.5	...
Female - Femmes	7.2	0.4	0.7	1.4	1.7	2.1	2.8	4.6	8.2	13.7	21.5	33.7	49.5	70.8	114.1	200.4	357.7	556.8	755.7	872.7	...
Czechia - Tchéquie																					
2018																					
Male - Hommes	3.4	0.4	0.4	2.2	3.6	3.8	4.5	6.5	9.3	15.0	27.0	43.1	72.2	113.3	169.8	244.2	371.0	548.0	729.7	869.6	...
Female - Femmes	2.9	0.5	0.4	0.8	1.2	1.3	1.8	2.8	4.2	7.6	11.8	20.3	34.9	54.7	90.9	149.6	270.1	475.7	696.4	865.4	...
Denmark - Danemark[10]																					
2017 - 2018																					
Male - Hommes	4.5	0.2	0.4	1.5	2.2	2.4	3.2	3.6	6.0	11.2	18.7	32.0	53.6	78.8	117.2	191.2	326.9	515.7	733.7	879.9	...
Female - Femmes	3.3	0.3	0.2	0.6	0.7	1.1	1.8	2.6	3.8	6.5	12.0	20.7	32.5	50.1	80.5	134.9	243.0	409.4	620.4	816.6	...
Estonia - Estonie																					
2018																					
Male - Hommes	3.3	0.5	0.6	3.1	2.6	4.6	6.8	10.0	14.4	24.1	36.9	65.4	94.6	134.1	191.9	257.0	359.4	551.2	718.4	941.9	*1000
Female - Femmes	1.7	0.1	0.9	1.3	0.6	1.7	2.6	4.2	5.1	7.5	14.0	19.9	31.3	57.1	85.0	135.4	244.5	425.3	654.5	819.1	*1000
Faroe Islands - Îles Féroé																					
2018 - 2019																					
Male - Hommes	0.0	0.0	0.0	2.9	3.2	2.7	0.0	5.7	0.0	6.3	10.4	28.3	49.9	85.7	110.4	124.9	355.2	492.4	738.3	962.5	...
Female - Femmes	0.0	0.0	0.0	0.0	0.0	0.0	0.0	0.0	3.5	3.2	3.1	6.2	31.0	57.2	54.3	130.8	232.1	300.2	582.5	847.2	...

21. Probability of dying in the five year interval following specified age (5qx), by sex, latest available year: 2005 - 2019
Probabilité de décès dans l'intervalle de cinq ans qui suit un âge donné (5qx), par sexe, dernière année disponible : 2005 - 2019 (continued - suite)

Continent, country or area and date / Continent, pays ou zone et date	0	5	10	15	20	25	30	35	40	45	50	55	60	65	70	75	80	85	90	95	100
	Age (in years) - Age (en années)																				
EUROPE																					
Finland - Finlande[11]																					
2018																					
Male - Hommes	2.7	0.3	0.4	2.6	3.6	3.8	4.9	5.6	7.8	12.6	20.2	32.3	52.7	76.4	117.7	183.8	307.9	488.3	714.8	855.6	...
Female - Femmes	2.7	0.2	0.3	1.0	1.4	1.7	1.6	2.8	3.7	6.4	10.1	16.3	25.7	39.0	62.2	108.7	204.7	383.4	623.5	831.3	...
France																					
2014 - 2016																					
Male - Hommes	4.5	0.4	0.5	1.7	2.9	3.6	4.4	5.9	9.0	14.9	23.5	38.2	55.4	74.0	104.2	159.5	268.8	447.6	660.4	832.5	...
Female - Femmes	3.8	0.3	0.4	0.8	1.1	1.3	1.7	2.8	4.6	7.8	12.1	17.8	24.8	34.2	52.4	88.6	169.0	326.2	553.1	771.3	...
Germany - Allemagne																					
2016 - 2018																					
Male - Hommes	4.2	0.4	0.5	1.5	2.2	2.4	3.3	4.8	7.3	12.1	21.0	36.4	58.4	87.1	126.1	191.0	317.3	512.7	719.6	874.3	...
Female - Femmes	3.6	0.4	0.4	0.8	0.9	1.1	1.7	2.5	4.1	7.1	11.7	19.6	30.9	47.3	73.1	117.6	226.8	414.7	648.9	829.6	...
Greece - Grèce																					
2018																					
Male - Hommes	4.4	0.4	0.7	1.8	2.8	2.8	4.2	5.7	7.9	12.7	22.6	38.2	57.1	79.6	119.0	179.4	305.2	453.4	601.4	759.8	...
Female - Femmes	3.7	0.4	0.5	0.8	1.0	1.2	1.9	2.8	4.4	6.8	10.2	15.7	23.0	37.7	66.9	136.1	263.2	423.6	577.7	742.5	...
Hungary - Hongrie																					
2018																					
Male - Hommes	4.3	0.3	0.5	1.6	2.8	3.6	5.0	7.0	11.7	22.7	45.4	78.5	118.0	159.4	206.6	292.3	413.0	618.1	861.8	987.5	...
Female - Femmes	3.9	0.3	0.3	1.0	1.5	1.4	2.2	3.3	5.8	11.1	19.7	34.1	52.8	74.0	109.7	188.2	318.0	549.8	835.8	985.8	...
Iceland - Islande																					
2017 - 2018																					
Male - Hommes	2.5	0.0	0.6	2.4	2.7	3.9	6.3	5.9	5.6	7.6	13.8	25.2	31.5	53.5	93.5	154.7	296.0	469.8	666.6	846.8	...
Female - Femmes	3.2	0.4	0.0	0.7	0.8	0.4	2.1	3.6	2.0	5.3	8.3	13.9	22.2	31.7	63.8	140.6	244.5	402.7	595.1	825.1	...
Ireland - Irlande																					
2005 - 2007																					
Male - Hommes	4.9	0.6	0.8	3.6	5.4	4.7	5.1	5.7	8.6	13.3	21.1	33.3	54.5	88.7	148.8	247.0	395.4	567.3	730.3	919.0	...
Female - Femmes	4.5	0.4	0.7	1.6	1.5	1.6	2.0	3.0	5.2	9.2	13.6	21.3	33.8	53.6	90.1	153.4	284.4	460.3	643.4	800.7	...
Italy - Italie																					
2018																					
Male - Hommes	3.7	0.4	0.5	1.4	2.0	2.3	2.7	3.7	5.8	9.1	14.5	24.1	39.1	63.1	98.8	167.1	276.2	465.6	680.6	821.5	...
Female - Femmes	3.2	0.3	0.4	0.6	0.8	0.9	1.3	2.2	3.5	5.7	9.1	13.8	21.6	34.6	55.3	100.6	193.1	364.4	593.5	767.0	...
Latvia - Lettonie																					
2006																					
Male - Hommes	10.5	1.4	1.6	3.0	6.2	11.3	18.6	28.3	40.6	56.3	76.6	104.3	143.2	199.8	282.1	397.7	547.0	712.6	...	...	...
Female - Femmes	12.7	1.3	1.2	1.5	2.2	3.2	4.8	7.3	11.2	17.3	26.7	41.0	63.0	96.1	145.1	215.5	312.2	436.5	...	...	...
Lithuania - Lituanie																					
2018																					
Male - Hommes	4.7	0.5	0.9	3.2	5.0	7.6	12.2	18.7	23.8	35.0	50.0	71.6	111.7	161.9	220.9	287.1	394.5	554.0	764.6	907.6	*1000
Female - Femmes	3.5	0.4	1.0	1.5	2.0	2.0	3.5	5.4	8.5	11.7	17.8	25.7	40.6	59.0	89.6	157.1	271.9	478.6	713.5	837.1	*1000
Luxembourg																					
2016 - 2018																					
Male - Hommes	3.2	0.2	0.0	1.1	1.9	1.8	3.0	3.1	5.8	9.9	16.9	27.3	46.5	79.2	117.9	176.4	300.6	470.5	730.8	*1000	...
Female - Femmes	2.4	0.0	0.2	0.2	1.0	1.3	1.2	1.9	3.8	6.0	9.8	14.4	23.9	42.8	74.1	111.0	206.2	383.2	598.6	*1000	...
Malta - Malte																					
2012																					
Male - Hommes	5.6	0.5	0.4	0.4	2.3	2.2	5.4	4.8	6.1	12.6	14.8	26.8	46.3	77.4	112.0	220.3	378.6	640.6	887.5	975.9	*1000
Female - Femmes	6.0	0.6	0.9	0.8	0.0	2.0	2.7	1.8	5.6	4.5	11.8	13.5	27.6	41.3	67.7	130.5	273.1	474.9	737.6	853.6	*1000
Netherlands - Pays-Bas																					
2009																					
Male - Hommes	4.8	0.5	0.6	1.4	2.3	2.4	3.0	4.1	6.6	10.7	18.7	30.3	49.9	79.1	132.1	225.2	363.5	539.8	738.0	...	...
Female - Femmes	4.1	0.4	0.5	0.8	1.0	1.3	1.7	2.9	5.0	8.9	15.0	21.5	32.5	47.8	76.4	136.1	249.6	428.5	644.7	...	...
North Macedonia - Macédoine du Nord																					
2017																					
Male - Hommes	10.1	0.7	1.1	1.8	2.5	3.1	3.5	5.6	10.2	15.6	29.8	52.5	83.4	127.0	189.0	298.9	470.2	688.5	885.8	...	...
Female - Femmes	9.7	0.4	0.7	1.0	0.7	1.5	1.9	3.2	5.3	9.4	15.6	27.3	45.9	77.2	131.2	248.4	426.7	638.8	801.9	...	...
Norway - Norvège																					
2018																					
Male - Hommes	2.6	0.3	0.5	1.3	2.9	3.1	3.6	4.6	5.4	7.8	12.9	22.5	36.4	58.7	95.7	167.7	288.9	478.9	677.5	858.5	...
Female - Femmes	2.4	0.2	0.5	0.8	0.7	1.2	1.3	2.2	3.4	5.5	8.8	15.4	24.5	40.5	65.0	117.1	210.6	373.1	608.6	814.9	...
Poland - Pologne																					
2018																					
Male - Hommes	4.9	0.5	0.7	2.4	4.4	5.3	7.0	10.0	15.8	24.6	38.8	61.9	93.8	134.3	180.7	254.8	369.1	501.3	642.5	778.5	...
Female - Femmes	4.1	0.4	0.6	1.1	1.3	1.4	1.9	3.1	5.1	8.9	14.7	25.6	40.8	61.4	94.0	147.1	260.3	417.2	588.6	758.0	...

21. Probability of dying in the five year interval following specified age (5qx), by sex, latest available year: 2005 - 2019
Probabilité de décès dans l'intervalle de cinq ans qui suit un âge donné (5qx), par sexe, dernière année disponible : 2005 - 2019 (continued - suite)

Continent, country or area and date / Continent, pays ou zone et date	Age (in years) - Age (en années) 0	5	10	15	20	25	30	35	40	45	50	55	60	65	70	75	80	85	90	95	100
EUROPE																					
Portugal																					
2016 - 2018																					
Male - Hommes	4.0	0.4	0.6	1.5	2.3	3.0	3.3	5.3	8.9	15.8	26.8	40.0	58.2	77.7	118.7	192.8	334.6	617.1	848.8	966.6	...
Female - Femmes	3.2	0.4	0.4	0.7	1.1	1.2	1.6	2.7	4.5	7.1	10.9	14.9	22.5	35.1	59.8	112.2	226.6	506.6	780.7	945.3	...
Republic of Moldova - République de Moldova																					
2012																					
Male - Hommes	12.2	1.4	2.0	4.4	5.6	7.1	11.3	19.8	30.9	50.0	71.2	102.2	157.9	176.7	292.1	388.4	503.1	558.6	*1000	...	...
Female - Femmes	12.1	1.1	1.2	1.6	1.8	2.4	3.6	8.1	10.6	16.1	26.8	44.1	78.0	103.1	191.4	289.0	418.9	550.8	*1000	...	...
Romania - Roumanie																					
2016 - 2018																					
Male - Hommes	8.8	0.8	1.2	2.8	3.4	3.9	4.8	7.7	14.1	26.1	45.7	73.7	107.6	147.3	202.4	295.1	422.1	567.6	708.6	827.7	...
Female - Femmes	7.1	0.6	0.8	1.3	1.2	1.6	2.1	3.4	6.0	10.0	17.2	28.0	44.1	69.6	113.4	195.9	339.7	521.6	700.9	845.7	...
Russian Federation - Fédération de Russie																					
2012																					
Male - Hommes	11.6	1.7	1.8	5.4	11.6	19.0	30.3	36.8	42.1	56.4	77.9	110.6	155.6	193.8	273.2	361.6	481.9	577.2	694.9	771.0	*1000
Female - Femmes	9.5	1.1	1.2	2.5	3.4	5.6	9.0	11.6	14.3	18.9	26.2	39.5	57.7	84.1	137.1	230.5	372.9	543.1	716.4	825.0	*1000
San Marino - Saint-Marin																					
2017																					
Male - Hommes	2.5	0.0	0.0	1.9	2.7	1.9	0.5	2.4	3.2	4.1	11.1	20.6	29.4	49.1	76.1	153.8	285.3	430.4	655.9	933.0	...
Female - Femmes	2.7	0.0	0.0	1.3	0.0	0.0	0.5	0.8	3.7	5.0	6.2	11.3	14.0	27.7	45.6	74.0	170.1	341.0	564.7	821.0	...
Serbia - Serbie[12]																					
2010 - 2012																					
Male - Hommes	8.1	0.5	0.9	2.4	3.7	4.7	6.4	8.2	13.3	25.5	44.0	69.0	101.6	145.8	216.4	334.2	492.1	676.0	856.4	973.0	...
Female - Femmes	6.5	0.6	0.9	1.1	1.5	2.0	2.6	4.3	7.4	12.8	21.1	33.3	50.4	82.2	147.2	265.6	432.9	632.3	840.3	975.2	...
Slovakia - Slovaquie																					
2018																					
Male - Hommes	6.4	0.6	0.8	2.3	3.7	4.0	5.7	8.3	12.5	21.7	38.6	60.3	91.5	134.1	181.9	271.8	408.4	591.6	788.7	934.6	...
Female - Femmes	5.3	0.7	0.8	1.3	1.4	1.6	1.9	2.8	5.5	9.3	16.4	24.7	39.0	60.2	96.9	170.8	307.4	524.1	782.7	957.8	...
Slovenia - Slovénie																					
2018																					
Male - Hommes	2.6	0.3	0.6	2.2	2.8	2.6	2.9	5.4	7.8	10.4	21.1	35.1	59.5	89.0	133.5	203.3	322.0	531.3	709.1	804.7	...
Female - Femmes	2.0	0.5	0.2	0.8	0.4	1.2	1.3	2.3	3.6	5.1	11.6	17.2	29.0	43.8	63.8	119.0	220.8	407.2	626.8	791.4	...
Spain - Espagne																					
2018																					
Male - Hommes	3.4	0.4	0.4	1.1	1.7	2.2	2.6	3.5	5.4	9.7	18.1	30.3	47.3	69.4	105.2	165.4	280.7	451.0	654.1	770.5	*1000
Female - Femmes	2.9	0.3	0.4	0.6	0.8	0.9	1.3	1.9	3.1	5.4	9.1	14.2	20.9	29.9	47.4	89.3	180.0	348.9	574.0	750.5	*1000
Sweden - Suède																					
2012																					
Male - Hommes	3.5	0.4	0.5	1.4	3.2	3.6	3.2	3.8	5.4	9.2	15.2	25.0	40.8	65.6	109.3	186.3	322.6	519.0	727.6	886.1	...
Female - Femmes	2.7	0.3	0.5	0.9	1.1	1.1	1.6	2.8	3.4	6.4	11.0	16.2	26.3	45.6	71.4	126.8	229.8	416.2	644.1	827.2	...
Switzerland - Suisse																					
2017																					
Male - Hommes	4.7	0.3	0.3	1.3	2.3	2.0	2.5	3.4	4.9	8.0	14.1	23.3	36.6	57.6	92.5	152.1	261.2	457.6	696.1	855.0	...
Female - Femmes	3.5	0.3	0.3	0.4	0.6	0.9	1.3	1.8	2.8	4.7	8.1	13.2	20.6	32.7	55.0	98.9	188.0	359.9	606.4	815.6	...
Ukraine[13]																					
2017																					
Male - Hommes	10.0	1.0	1.4	3.6	6.4	10.2	16.6	25.5	35.8	48.0	67.8	97.2	142.0	194.1	269.7	370.4	492.4	608.2	711.8	802.9	...
Female - Femmes	7.8	0.8	0.8	1.5	1.9	3.3	5.4	8.8	12.3	16.7	23.2	33.0	51.9	85.1	141.2	235.8	388.7	563.4	750.7	901.0	...
United Kingdom of Great Britain and Northern Ireland - Royaume-Uni de Grande-Bretagne et d'Irlande du Nord[14]																					
2016 - 2018																					
Male - Hommes	4.8	0.4	0.5	1.6	2.5	3.2	4.3	6.1	9.3	13.4	19.2	29.3	46.2	71.3	111.6	185.1	301.9	479.7	675.0	842.7	...
Female - Femmes	4.1	0.3	0.4	0.8	1.1	1.4	2.3	3.5	5.4	8.4	12.7	19.7	30.8	47.2	76.7	133.0	230.6	399.0	608.4	795.6	...

21. Probability of dying in the five year interval following specified age (5qx), by sex, latest available year: 2005 - 2019
Probabilité de décès dans l'intervalle de cinq ans qui suit un âge donné (5qx), par sexe, dernière année disponible : 2005 - 2019 (continued - suite)

Continent, country or area and date / Continent, pays ou zone et date	0	5	10	15	20	25	30	35	40	45	50	55	60	65	70	75	80	85	90	95	100
OCEANIA - OCÉANIE																					
Australia - Australie																					
2016 - 2018																					
Male - Hommes	4.2	0.4	0.6	1.9	3.0	3.4	4.2	5.8	7.9	11.6	16.9	25.8	38.9	58.4	93.5	155.0	264.9	438.8	641.2	776.9	...
Female - Femmes	3.6	0.3	0.4	1.0	1.2	1.4	2.0	3.0	4.7	7.0	10.6	15.6	23.0	35.4	59.3	103.3	189.5	346.4	563.3	760.7	...
French Polynesia - Polynésie française																					
2018																					
Male - Hommes	25.0	0.0	2.7	3.4	4.4	9.3	9.4	9.3	14.9	18.6	31.7	48.9	63.2	114.3	186.7	227.0	379.9	527.6	792.0	...	...
Female - Femmes	15.9	0.0	1.4	2.2	1.0	2.3	2.6	4.4	7.3	6.3	20.4	30.7	57.3	66.6	112.6	164.1	316.8	469.5	692.8	...	...
New Zealand - Nouvelle-Zélande																					
2012 - 2014																					
Male - Hommes	5.9	0.7	0.9	3.2	4.1	4.0	4.2	5.6	7.6	11.6	17.6	26.2	40.3	65.4	108.3	176.2	298.2	485.4	667.7	822.5	*1000
Female - Femmes	4.9	0.5	0.7	1.5	1.6	1.5	2.3	3.2	5.1	8.0	12.5	17.9	28.2	43.2	71.4	126.3	219.4	391.0	615.3	807.3	*1000

Age (in years) - Age (en années)

FOOTNOTES - NOTES

* Open-ended group (e.g. 80 years or over). - Groupe d'âge ouvert (par exemple, 80 ans ou plus).

1 Excluding Indian jungle population. - Non compris les Indiens de la jungle.

2 Data refer to the 12 months from 30 June 2016 to 30 June 2017. - Les données font référence aux douze mois de 30 juin 2016 à 30 juin 2017.

3 Estimates or projections based on the 2017 Population Census. - Estimations ou projections fondées sur le recensement de la population de 2017.

4 Data based on the 2010 Population Census. Excludes nomadic Indian tribes. - Les données sont fondées sur le recensement de la population de 2010. Non compris les tribus d'Indiens nomades.

5 Based on the results of the 2012 Population and Housing Census. - D'après les résultats du recensement de la population et des logements de 2012.

6 Includes data for East Jerusalem and Israeli residents in certain other territories under occupation by Israeli military forces since June 1967. - Y compris les données pour Jérusalem-Est et les résidents israéliens dans certains autres territoires occupés depuis 1967 par les forces armées israéliennes.

7 Data refer to Japanese nationals in Japan only. - Les données se raportent aux nationaux japonais au Japon seulement.

8 Provisional data. Data refer to resident population which comprises Singapore citizens and permanent residents. - Données provisoires. Les données se rapportent à la population résidente composé des citoyens de Singapour et des résidents permanents.

9 Provisional data. - Données provisoires.

10 Excluding Faeroe Islands and Greenland shown separately, if available. - Non compris les Iles Féroé et le Groenland, qui font l'objet de rubriques distinctes, si disponible.

11 Excluding Åland Islands. - Non compris les Îles d'Åland.

12 Excludes data for Kosovo and Metohia. - Sans les données pour le Kosovo et Metohie.

13 The Government of Ukraine has informed the United Nations that it is not in a position to provide statistical data concerning the Autonomous Republic of Crimea and the city of Sevastopol. - Le gouvernement Ukrainien a informé l'ONU qu'il n'est pas en mesure de fournir des données statistiques concernant la République autonome de Crimée et la ville de Sébastopol.

14 Excluding Channel Islands (Guernsey and Jersey) and Isle of Man, shown separately, if available. - Non compris les îles Anglo-Normandes (Guernesey et Jersey) et l'île de Man, qui font l'objet de rubriques distinctes, si disponible.

Table 22 presents life expectancy at specified ages for each sex, for the latest available year between 2000 and 2019.

Description of variables: Life expectancy at age x, e_x, is defined as the average number of years of life remaining to persons who have reached age *x* if they continue to be subject to the mortality conditions of the period indicated in the life table.

Male and female life expectancy values are shown separately at selected ages beginning at birth and proceeding at every fifth age thereafter up to age 100.

The table shows life expectancy derived from a complete or abridged life table as reported by the country or area.

Data are shown with one decimal regardless of the number of digits provided in the original computation.

The life table is a statistical device for summarizing the mortality experience of a population, from which the probability of dying, survivorship and life expectancy can be calculated. It is based on the assumption that the theoretical cohort is subject, throughout its existence, to the age-specific mortality rates observed at a particular time period. Thus, levels of mortality prevailing at the time a life table is constructed are assumed to remain unchanged into the future until all members of the cohort have died.

Reliability of data: The values shown in this table come from official life tables. It is assumed that, if necessary, the basic data (population and deaths classified by age and sex) have been adjusted for deficiencies before their use in constructing the life tables.

Limitations: Life expectancy values are subject to the same qualifications as have been set forth for population statistics in general and death statistics in particular, as discussed in sections 3 and 4, respectively, of the Technical Notes. They must be interpreted strictly using the underlying assumption that surviving cohorts are subjected to the same age-specific mortality rates of the period to which the life table refers.

Earlier data: Life expectancy values at specified ages for each sex have been shown in previous issues of the *Demographic Yearbook*. For information on specific years covered, the reader should consult the Historical Index.

Tableau 22 – *Annuaire démographique 2019*

Le tableau 22 présente les espérances de vie à des âges déterminés, pour chaque sexe, pour la dernière année disponible entre 2000 et 2019.

Description des variables : L'espérance de vie à l'âge x, e_x, se définit comme le nombre moyen d'années restant à vivre aux hommes et aux femmes qui ont atteint l'âge *x*, à supposer qu'ils continuent de connaître les mêmes conditions de mortalité observées pendant la période sur laquelle porte la table de mortalité.

Les chiffres sont présentés séparément pour chaque sexe à partir de la naissance et puis tous les cinq ans jusqu'à 100 ans.

Dans le tableau figurent les espérances de vie calculées selon les tables de mortalité complètes ou abrégées communiquées par les pays et les zones.

Les données sont arrondies à la première décimale, indépendamment du nombre de décimales qui figurent dans le calcul initial.

La table de mortalité est un moyen statistique que s'utilise pour donner un aperçu complet de la mortalité d'une population incluant les probabilités de décès et l'espérance de vie à chaque âge. Les tables de mortalité reposent sur l'hypothèse que chaque cohorte théoriquement distinguée connaît, pendant toute son existence, les taux de mortalité par âge observé à un moment donné. Les taux de mortalité correspondant à l'époque à laquelle sont calculées les tables de mortalité sont ainsi censés demeurer inchangées dans l'avenir jusqu'au décès de tous les membres de la cohorte.

Fiabilité des donnés : Les chiffres figurant dans ce tableau proviennent de tables officielles de mortalité. En ce qui concerne les chiffres extraits de tables officielles de mortalité, on part du principe que les données de base (effectif de la population et nombre de décès selon l'âge et le sexe) ont été ajustées, en tant que de besoin, avant de servir à l'établissement de la table de mortalité.

Insuffisance des données : les espérances de vie appellent les mêmes réserves que celles qui ont été formulées à propos des statistiques de la population en général et des statistiques de mortalité en particulier (voir les sections 3 et 4 des Notes techniques). Lorsque l'on interprète les données, il ne faut jamais perdre de vue que, par hypothèse, les cohortes de survivants sont soumises, pour chaque âge, aux conditions de mortalité de la période visée par la table de mortalité.

Données publiées antérieurement : les espérances de vie à des âges déterminés pour chaque sexe figuraient déjà dans des éditions antérieures de *l'Annuaire démographique*. Pour plus de précisions concernant les années pour lesquelles ces données ont été publiées, se reporter à l'index historique.

22. Life expectancy at specified ages for each sex: latest available year, 2000 - 2019
Espérance de vie à un âge donné pour chaque sexe : dernière année disponible, 2000 - 2019

Continent, country or area and date / Continent, pays ou zone et date	Age (in years) - Age (en années)																				
	0	5	10	15	20	25	30	35	40	45	50	55	60	65	70	75	80	85	90	95	100
AFRICA - AFRIQUE																					
Algeria - Algérie[1]																					
2019																					
Male - Hommes	77.2	74.2	69.3	64.5	59.7	54.9	50.2	45.4	40.6	35.9	31.4	26.9	22.7	18.7	15.0	11.6	8.7	6.4	...	...	...
Female - Femmes	78.6	75.4	70.5	65.6	60.7	55.8	51.0	46.2	41.4	36.7	32.1	27.5	23.1	18.9	14.9	11.2	7.9	5.2	...	...	...
Angola																					
2019																					
Male - Hommes	60.8	...	...	...	...	...	...	...	...	...	...	...	...	...	...	...	...	...	...	...	...
Female - Femmes	63.7	...	...	...	...	...	...	...	...	...	...	...	...	...	...	...	...	...	...	...	...
Benin - Bénin[2]																					
2002																					
Male - Hommes	57.2	63.4	59.1	54.7	50.2	45.9	41.8	37.8	33.8	30.0	26.2	22.7	19.4	16.2	13.2	10.6	8.1	5.5	3.8	...	...
Female - Femmes	61.3	65.4	61.2	56.7	52.3	48.1	43.9	39.9	36.0	32.1	28.3	24.6	21.2	18.0	14.2	10.8	7.7	4.8	2.9	...	...
Botswana[3]																					
2016																					
Male - Hommes	64.9	62.0	57.4	52.6	48.1	43.9	40.3	37.3	34.4	31.7	28.4	24.9	21.3	17.7	14.1	10.4	6.7	...	...	...	...
Female - Femmes	65.9	62.8	58.1	53.3	48.6	44.1	39.8	36.0	32.5	29.2	25.7	22.3	19.0	15.6	12.4	9.1	5.8	...	...	...	...
Burkina Faso[4]																					
2006																					
Male - Hommes	55.8	60.0	55.9	51.3	46.9	42.8	38.6	34.5	30.5	26.6	22.8	19.3	16.0	12.9	10.3	8.1	6.2	4.8	...	...	...
Female - Femmes	57.5	61.6	57.6	53.1	48.6	44.4	40.2	36.1	32.0	28.0	24.1	20.3	16.8	13.5	10.7	8.4	6.4	4.9	...	...	...
Burundi																					
2008																					
Male - Hommes	46.0	49.7	46.5	42.5	39.0	35.8	32.4	28.9	25.4	21.9	18.6	15.3	12.3	9.5	7.2	5.2	3.8	...	...	...	...
Female - Femmes	51.8	55.4	52.1	47.9	44.0	40.3	36.7	33.0	29.2	25.4	21.5	17.8	14.2	11.0	8.3	6.0	4.4	...	...	...	...
2017																					
Male - Hommes	56.9	...	...	...	...	...	...	...	...	...	...	...	...	...	...	...	...	...	...	...	...
Female - Femmes	61.3	...	...	...	...	...	...	...	...	...	...	...	...	...	...	...	...	...	...	...	...
Cabo Verde																					
2010[5]																					
Male - Hommes	69.7	66.3	61.4	56.6	51.9	47.3	42.8	38.5	34.4	30.6	26.8	23.3	20.1	17.0	14.2	11.6	9.4	...	...	...	...
Female - Femmes	79.2	75.4	70.5	65.6	60.7	55.9	51.1	46.3	41.7	37.1	32.6	28.3	24.2	20.3	16.6	13.4	10.8	...	...	...	...
2018[6]																					
Male - Hommes	72.6	...	...	...	...	...	...	...	...	...	...	...	...	...	...	...	...	...	...	...	...
Female - Femmes	80.4	...	...	...	...	...	...	...	...	...	...	...	...	...	...	...	...	...	...	...	...
Congo																					
2007																					
Male - Hommes	50.1	...	...	...	...	...	...	...	...	...	...	...	...	...	...	...	...	...	...	...	...
Female - Femmes	53.3	...	...	...	...	...	...	...	...	...	...	...	...	...	...	...	...	...	...	...	...
Côte d'Ivoire																					
2019																					
Male - Hommes	55.5	...	...	...	...	...	...	...	...	...	...	...	...	...	...	...	...	...	...	...	...
Female - Femmes	58.0	...	...	...	...	...	...	...	...	...	...	...	...	...	...	...	...	...	...	...	...
Djibouti[7]																					
2002																					
Male - Hommes	51.8	...	...	...	...	...	...	...	...	...	...	...	...	...	...	...	...	...	...	...	...
Female - Femmes	54.1	...	...	...	...	...	...	...	...	...	...	...	...	...	...	...	...	...	...	...	...
Egypt - Égypte																					
2016																					
Male - Hommes	70.5	67.0	62.1	57.2	52.4	47.5	42.7	37.9	33.1	28.5	24.1	20.1	16.3	12.8	9.5	6.6	3.6	...	...	...	...
Female - Femmes	73.3	69.6	64.7	59.7	54.8	49.9	44.9	40.0	35.1	30.3	25.6	21.1	16.9	12.9	9.3	6.0	2.4	...	...	...	...
2019																					
Male - Hommes	72.7	...	...	...	...	...	...	...	...	...	...	...	...	...	...	...	...	...	...	...	...
Female - Femmes	75.1	...	...	...	...	...	...	...	...	...	...	...	...	...	...	...	...	...	...	...	...
Equatorial Guinea - Guinée équatoriale																					
2001																					
Male - Hommes	58.4	...	...	...	...	...	...	...	...	...	...	...	...	...	...	...	...	...	...	...	...
Female - Femmes	59.6	...	...	...	...	...	...	...	...	...	...	...	...	...	...	...	...	...	...	...	...
Eritrea - Érythrée																					
2010																					
Male - Hommes	60.0	60.8	56.3	51.6	47.0	42.7	38.3	34.0	29.7	25.7	21.8	18.2	14.9	11.9	9.3	7.1	5.3	4.0	2.9	2.2	1.7
Female - Femmes	64.8	64.5	59.9	55.2	50.6	46.1	41.7	37.2	32.9	28.7	24.6	20.7	17.0	13.6	10.6	8.0	5.9	4.4	3.2	2.3	1.8
Eswatini																					
2007																					
Male - Hommes	42.2	44.9	40.5	36.0	31.5	27.5	24.9	23.3	22.1	20.9	19.1	17.4	15.4	13.6	10.9	8.9	...	...	...	...	...
Female - Femmes	43.1	48.2	43.9	39.3	35.0	32.3	30.9	30.3	29.5	27.6	25.1	22.7	19.5	16.8	13.5	10.5	...	...	...	...	...

22. Life expectancy at specified ages for each sex: latest available year, 2000 - 2019
Espérance de vie à un âge donné pour chaque sexe : dernière année disponible, 2000 - 2019 (continued - suite)

Continent, country or area and date Continent, pays ou zone et date	Age (in years) - Age (en années) 0	5	10	15	20	25	30	35	40	45	50	55	60	65	70	75	80	85	90	95	100
AFRICA - AFRIQUE																					
2018[8]																					
Male - Hommes	44.1	...	...	...	...	...	...	...	...	...	...	...	...	...	...	...	...	...	...	...	...
Female - Femmes	48.1	...	...	...	...	...	...	...	...	...	...	...	...	...	...	...	...	...	...	...	...
Ghana[9]																					
2010																					
Male - Hommes	59.4	60.9	57.0	52.5	48.3	44.2	40.2	36.1	32.0	27.9	24.0	20.2	16.6	13.3	10.4	7.9	5.9	...	...	...	...
Female - Femmes	64.4	64.9	60.7	56.1	51.7	47.3	43.0	38.7	34.4	30.2	26.1	22.1	18.2	14.6	11.4	8.7	6.5	...	...	...	...
Guinea - Guinée																					
2014[10]																					
Male - Hommes	57.4	62.5	58.3	53.9	49.5	45.3	41.2	37.2	33.3	29.6	25.9	22.3	18.7	15.1	11.8	8.4	5.0	...	...	...	...
Female - Femmes	60.4	65.5	61.1	56.6	52.3	48.0	43.9	39.9	35.8	31.8	27.8	23.9	19.8	16.1	12.3	8.8	5.0	...	...	...	...
2017																					
Male - Hommes	58.4	...	...	...	...	...	...	...	...	...	...	...	...	...	...	...	...	...	...	...	...
Female - Femmes	61.4	...	...	...	...	...	...	...	...	...	...	...	...	...	...	...	...	...	...	...	...
Guinea-Bissau - Guinée-Bissau																					
2008 - 2009																					
Male - Hommes	49.2	49.8	45.3	41.0	36.8	32.8	29.3	26.2	23.3	20.7	18.0	15.5	13.1	11.2	9.4	8.0	6.8	...	...	...	...
Female - Femmes	51.2	50.1	45.7	41.5	37.8	34.4	31.3	28.4	25.6	22.9	20.0	17.4	14.9	12.8	10.6	8.8	7.1	...	...	...	...
2014																					
Male - Hommes	51.2	...	...	...	...	...	...	...	...	...	...	...	...	...	...	...	...	...	...	...	...
Female - Femmes	53.6	...	...	...	...	...	...	...	...	...	...	...	...	...	...	...	...	...	...	...	...
Kenya[2]																					
2009																					
Male - Hommes	57.8	58.1	53.9	49.7	45.3	41.0	36.9	33.3	30.2	27.1	23.9	20.4	16.7	13.2	10.0	7.0	4.0	...	...	...	...
Female - Femmes	60.7	60.1	55.8	51.4	46.9	42.6	38.7	35.7	33.0	29.8	26.2	22.3	18.3	14.5	11.0	7.7	4.7	...	...	...	...
Lesotho[11]																					
2006																					
Male - Hommes	39.8	40.4	36.0	31.5	27.2	23.6	20.9	19.2	18.2	17.3	16.4	14.9	13.2	11.3	9.4	7.4	5.3	2.9	...	...	...
Female - Femmes	42.9	42.7	38.4	33.8	29.6	26.3	24.2	23.2	22.8	22.3	21.5	20.2	18.6	16.7	14.5	12.1	9.6	7.4	...	...	...
2016																					
Male - Hommes	51.7	...	...	...	...	...	...	...	...	...	...	...	...	...	...	...	...	...	...	...	...
Female - Femmes	59.6	...	...	...	...	...	...	...	...	...	...	...	...	...	...	...	...	...	...	...	...
Madagascar[12]																					
2018																					
Male - Hommes	63.3	...	...	...	...	...	...	...	...	...	...	...	...	...	...	...	...	...	...	...	...
Female - Femmes	65.2	...	...	...	...	...	...	...	...	...	...	...	...	...	...	...	...	...	...	...	...
Malawi																					
2008																					
Male - Hommes	47.4	...	...	...	...	...	...	...	...	...	...	...	...	...	...	...	...	...	...	...	...
Female - Femmes	50.6	...	...	...	...	...	...	...	...	...	...	...	...	...	...	...	...	...	...	...	...
Mali																					
2017																					
Male - Hommes	65.7	...	...	...	...	...	...	...	...	...	...	...	...	...	...	...	...	...	...	...	...
Female - Femmes	68.2	...	...	...	...	...	...	...	...	...	...	...	...	...	...	...	...	...	...	...	...
Mauritania - Mauritanie																					
2013																					
Male - Hommes	58.3	61.5	57.5	53.0	48.7	44.6	40.5	36.4	32.2	28.2	24.2	20.4	16.8	13.5	10.5	8.0	6.0	...	...	...	...
Female - Femmes	61.8	63.8	59.8	55.3	50.9	46.6	42.4	38.1	33.9	29.8	25.6	21.7	17.8	14.3	11.2	8.5	6.4	...	...	...	...
Mauritius - Maurice[13]																					
2017 - 2019																					
Male - Hommes	71.1	67.2	62.3	57.4	52.6	47.9	43.3	38.8	34.4	30.1	26.0	22.2	18.6	15.3	12.3	9.5	7.4	5.4	...	...	...
Female - Femmes	77.6	73.6	68.7	63.7	58.8	54.0	49.2	44.4	39.7	35.2	30.7	26.4	22.2	18.3	14.7	11.4	8.7	6.2	...	...	...
Mayotte[14]																					
2018																					
Male - Hommes	74.8	...	...	...	56.2	...	...	...	37.7	...	...	...	20.2	...	...	...	...	...	...	...	...
Female - Femmes	76.9	...	...	...	58.0	...	...	...	38.9	...	...	...	21.4	...	...	...	...	...	...	...	...
Morocco - Maroc																					
2013																					
Male - Hommes	72.4	...	...	...	...	...	...	...	...	...	...	...	...	...	...	...	...	...	...	...	...
Female - Femmes	75.1	...	...	...	...	...	...	...	...	...	...	...	...	...	...	...	...	...	...	...	...
Mozambique																					
2014																					
Male - Hommes	50.2	54.0	50.0	45.6	41.6	37.7	33.9	30.1	26.5	22.9	19.6	16.4	13.5	10.9	8.7	6.8	5.0	...	...	...	...
Female - Femmes	55.4	59.0	54.8	50.3	46.1	42.1	38.1	34.1	30.2	26.3	22.5	19.0	15.7	12.7	10.0	7.7	5.8	...	...	...	...

22. Life expectancy at specified ages for each sex: latest available year, 2000 - 2019
Espérance de vie à un âge donné pour chaque sexe : dernière année disponible, 2000 - 2019 (continued - suite)

Continent, country or area and date / Continent, pays ou zone et date	Age (in years) - Age (en années) 0	5	10	15	20	25	30	35	40	45	50	55	60	65	70	75	80	85	90	95	100
AFRICA - AFRIQUE																					
2019[3]																					
Male - Hommes	51.7	...	...	...	...	...	...	...	...	...	...	...	...	...	...	...	...	...	...	...	...
Female - Femmes	57.4	...	...	...	...	...	...	...	...	...	...	...	...	...	...	...	...	...	...	...	...
Namibia - Namibie																					
2011																					
Male - Hommes	53.3	52.4	48.0	43.4	39.0	35.1	31.5	28.6	25.8	23.2	20.6	17.7	15.1	12.6	9.8	7.4	5.6	...	...	...	...
Female - Femmes	60.5	59.6	55.1	50.5	46.1	42.0	38.4	35.2	32.0	28.7	25.2	21.6	17.9	14.5	11.3	8.6	6.5	...	...	...	...
Republic of South Sudan - République de Soudan du Sud																					
2010																					
Male - Hommes	54.4	57.4	53.2	48.8	44.6	40.7	36.8	32.8	28.9	25.0	21.2	17.6	14.2	11.2	8.5	6.3	4.5	3.2	2.2	1.5	...
Female - Femmes	54.5	56.2	51.9	47.5	43.3	39.4	35.4	31.5	27.5	23.7	19.9	16.4	13.1	10.2	7.7	5.6	4.1	2.9	2.0	1.4	...
Reunion - Réunion																					
2015																					
Male - Hommes	77.1	...	...	...	58.1	...	...	...	39.3	...	...	...	21.8	...	...	...	...	...	...	...	...
Female - Femmes	83.6	...	...	...	64.3	...	...	...	44.8	...	...	...	26.2	...	...	...	...	...	...	...	...
2017																					
Male - Hommes	78.1	...	...	...	...	...	...	...	...	...	...	...	...	...	...	...	...	...	...	...	...
Female - Femmes	84.5	...	...	...	...	...	...	...	...	...	...	...	...	...	...	...	...	...	...	...	...
Rwanda																					
2002																					
Male - Hommes	48.4	58.4	54.4	49.9	45.6	41.6	37.5	33.5	29.4	25.4	21.6	17.9	14.5	11.4	8.6	6.3	4.6	...	...	...	...
Female - Femmes	53.8	63.1	58.8	54.3	49.9	45.7	41.4	37.2	32.9	28.7	24.5	20.4	16.5	12.9	9.8	7.1	5.1	...	...	...	...
2017																					
Male - Hommes	64.6	...	...	...	...	...	...	...	...	...	...	...	...	...	...	...	...	...	...	...	...
Female - Femmes	68.4	...	...	...	...	...	...	...	...	...	...	...	...	...	...	...	...	...	...	...	...
Saint Helena ex. dep. - Sainte-Hélène sans dép.[15]																					
2003 - 2012																					
Male - Hommes	72.0	68.1	63.4	...	53.9	...	44.2	...	35.5	...	27.1	...	19.3	...	12.5	...	7.2	...	...	...	...
Female - Femmes	79.7	75.3	70.3	...	60.3	...	51.0	...	41.8	...	32.0	...	23.0	...	15.5	...	8.6	...	...	...	...
2009 - 2018																					
Male - Hommes	74.3	...	...	...	...	...	...	...	...	...	...	...	...	...	...	...	...	...	...	...	...
Female - Femmes	80.4	...	...	...	...	...	...	...	...	...	...	...	...	...	...	...	...	...	...	...	...
Sao Tome and Principe - Sao Tomé-et-Principe																					
2011 - 2012																					
Male - Hommes	62.1	59.5	54.6	50.1	45.8	41.6	37.5	33.4	29.6	25.8	22.1	18.4	15.2	12.0	9.8	7.4	5.0	...	...	...	...
Female - Femmes	68.7	65.9	61.2	56.5	51.8	47.1	42.5	38.0	33.5	29.3	25.3	21.7	18.2	14.9	11.8	9.0	6.6	...	...	...	...
2017																					
Male - Hommes	64.0	...	...	...	...	...	...	...	...	...	...	...	...	...	...	...	...	...	...	...	...
Female - Femmes	70.5	...	...	...	...	...	...	...	...	...	...	...	...	...	...	...	...	...	...	...	...
Senegal - Sénégal[3]																					
2019																					
Male - Hommes	66.2	...	...	...	...	...	...	...	...	...	...	...	...	...	...	...	...	...	...	...	...
Female - Femmes	68.5	...	...	...	...	...	...	...	...	...	...	...	...	...	...	...	...	...	...	...	...
Seychelles																					
2007																					
Male - Hommes	68.9	65.0	60.2	55.3	50.5	45.9	41.6	37.0	32.7	28.7	24.4	20.9	17.1	14.1	11.0	9.0	7.4	...	...	...	...
Female - Femmes	77.7	73.3	68.5	63.5	58.5	53.7	48.9	44.3	39.5	35.3	31.0	26.4	22.2	18.5	15.1	12.1	9.2	...	...	...	...
2019																					
Male - Hommes	69.7	...	...	...	...	...	...	...	...	...	...	...	...	...	...	...	...	...	...	...	...
Female - Femmes	78.4	...	...	...	...	...	...	...	...	...	...	...	...	...	...	...	...	...	...	...	...
Sierra Leone[16]																					
2015																					
Male - Hommes	48.3	50.2	46.4	42.4	38.5	34.8	31.5	28.3	25.4	22.5	19.8	17.0	14.7	12.3	10.4	8.5	7.1	5.7	4.8	3.6	1.7
Female - Femmes	50.8	52.2	48.3	44.2	40.4	36.9	33.8	30.8	27.7	25.1	22.3	19.9	16.9	14.9	12.1	10.3	8.0	6.7	5.2	3.8	1.6
South Africa - Afrique du Sud																					
2014																					
Male - Hommes	59.1	...	...	...	...	...	...	...	...	...	...	...	...	...	...	...	...	...	...	...	...
Female - Femmes	63.1	...	...	...	...	...	...	...	...	...	...	...	...	...	...	...	...	...	...	...	...

22. Life expectancy at specified ages for each sex: latest available year, 2000 - 2019
Espérance de vie à un âge donné pour chaque sexe : dernière année disponible, 2000 - 2019 (continued - suite)

Continent, country or area and date / Continent, pays ou zone et date	Age (in years) - Age (en années) 0	5	10	15	20	25	30	35	40	45	50	55	60	65	70	75	80	85	90	95	100
AFRICA - AFRIQUE																					
Sudan - Soudan																					
2008																					
Male - Hommes	58.1	...	...	...	...	...	...	...	...	...	...	...	...	...	...	...	...	...	...	...	...
Female - Femmes	61.4	...	...	...	...	...	...	...	...	...	...	...	...	...	...	...	...	...	...	...	...
Tunisia - Tunisie																					
2017																					
Male - Hommes	74.5	...	...	...	...	...	...	...	...	...	...	...	...	...	...	...	...	...	...	...	...
Female - Femmes	78.1	...	...	...	...	...	...	...	...	...	...	...	...	...	...	...	...	...	...	...	...
Uganda - Ouganda																					
2002[17]																					
Male - Hommes	48.8	53.0	49.2	44.8	40.5	36.6	33.6	31.0	28.4	25.8	23.2	20.4	17.2	14.4	11.6	9.2	6.7	4.1	...	...	...
Female - Femmes	52.0	56.0	52.1	47.6	43.3	39.6	36.7	34.2	31.5	28.6	25.6	22.3	18.9	15.7	12.6	9.9	7.0	4.2	...	...	...
2014[18]																					
Male - Hommes	62.2	...	...	...	...	...	...	...	...	...	...	...	...	...	...	...	...	...	...	...	...
Female - Femmes	64.2	...	...	...	...	...	...	...	...	...	...	...	...	...	...	...	...	...	...	...	...
Zimbabwe																					
2001 - 2002																					
Male - Hommes	45.8	44.2	40.0	35.4	30.9	26.8	23.8	22.1	21.8	21.3	20.4	19.2	17.7	15.7	13.7	11.4	9.5	7.5	6.2	5.2	...
Female - Femmes	50.3	48.6	44.2	39.7	35.3	32.1	30.4	30.1	30.2	29.0	27.6	25.3	22.9	20.2	17.6	14.8	12.2	9.9	8.1	7.3	...
2012																					
Male - Hommes	57.4	...	...	...	...	...	...	...	...	...	...	...	...	...	...	...	...	...	...	...	...
Female - Femmes	64.0	...	...	...	...	...	...	...	...	...	...	...	...	...	...	...	...	...	...	...	...
AMERICA, NORTH - AMÉRIQUE DU NORD																					
Anguilla																					
2000 - 2002																					
Male - Hommes	76.5	72.1	67.1	62.1	57.3	53.1	48.4	43.7	39.4	34.7	30.2	25.4	21.1	16.5	12.7	10.0	8.0	6.9	...	...	...
Female - Femmes	81.1	76.4	71.4	66.4	61.4	57.1	52.7	47.7	42.7	38.3	33.5	28.7	24.0	19.4	15.3	10.8	8.3	7.6	...	...	...
Antigua and Barbuda - Antigua-et-Barbuda																					
2017																					
Male - Hommes	74.4	...	...	...	...	...	...	...	...	...	...	...	...	...	...	...	...	...	...	...	...
Female - Femmes	80.5	...	...	...	...	...	...	...	...	...	...	...	...	...	...	...	...	...	...	...	...
Aruba																					
2010 - 2011																					
Male - Hommes	73.9	69.4	64.4	59.5	54.6	50.0	45.4	40.8	36.3	31.7	27.3	23.1	19.1	15.3	12.3	9.4	7.3	5.0	3.5	2.7	...
Female - Femmes	79.8	76.2	71.2	66.2	61.3	56.4	51.5	46.6	42.0	37.3	32.6	27.9	23.8	19.7	16.0	12.5	9.5	6.8	5.0	3.8	...
Bahamas																					
1999 - 2001																					
Male - Hommes	69.9	...	...	...	...	...	...	...	...	...	...	...	...	...	...	...	...	...	...	...	...
Female - Femmes	76.4	...	...	...	...	...	...	...	...	...	...	...	...	...	...	...	...	...	...	...	...
Belize																					
2010																					
Male - Hommes	71.0	...	...	...	...	...	...	...	...	...	...	...	...	...	...	...	...	...	...	...	...
Female - Femmes	76.6	...	...	...	...	...	...	...	...	...	...	...	...	...	...	...	...	...	...	...	...
Bermuda - Bermudes																					
2019																					
Male - Hommes	79.6	74.9	70.0	65.0	60.1	55.4	50.9	46.2	41.5	36.8	32.2	27.8	23.6	19.8	16.1	12.7	9.6	6.6	...	...	...
Female - Femmes	85.8	81.0	76.0	71.1	66.2	61.3	56.3	51.4	46.5	41.7	36.9	32.3	27.7	23.2	19.0	15.0	11.4	8.2	...	...	...
British Virgin Islands - Îles Vierges britanniques																					
2015																					
Male - Hommes	72.9	...	...	...	...	...	...	...	...	...	...	...	...	...	...	...	...	...	...	...	...
Female - Femmes	80.8	...	...	...	...	...	...	...	...	...	...	...	...	...	...	...	...	...	...	...	...
Canada																					
2016 - 2018																					
Male - Hommes	79.9	75.3	70.4	65.4	60.5	55.8	51.0	46.3	41.6	36.9	32.3	27.8	23.5	19.4	15.6	12.1	9.1	6.5	4.5	3.1	2.2
Female - Femmes	84.1	79.5	74.5	69.5	64.6	59.7	54.8	50.0	45.1	40.3	35.6	31.0	26.5	22.1	18.0	14.2	10.8	7.8	5.3	3.6	2.5

22. Life expectancy at specified ages for each sex: latest available year, 2000 - 2019
Espérance de vie à un âge donné pour chaque sexe : dernière année disponible, 2000 - 2019 (continued - suite)

Continent, country or area and date / Continent, pays ou zone et date	Age (in years) - Age (en années) 0	5	10	15	20	25	30	35	40	45	50	55	60	65	70	75	80	85	90	95	100
AMERICA, NORTH - AMÉRIQUE DU NORD																					
Cayman Islands - Îles Caïmanes[19]																					
2010																					
Male - Hommes	79.8	75.5	70.5	65.6	61.1	56.8	52.2	47.4	42.5	37.6	32.9	28.3	23.9	19.6	15.2	11.6	8.9	6.2	5.0	3.6	2.5
Female - Femmes	84.7	80.1	75.1	70.1	65.1	60.3	55.3	50.4	45.4	40.5	35.7	30.8	26.1	21.5	17.0	13.2	9.8	7.2	4.9	3.8	2.5
Costa Rica																					
2019																					
Male - Hommes	77.7	73.5	68.6	63.7	58.9	54.2	49.5	44.9	40.3	35.7	31.2	26.9	22.7	18.8	15.2	11.9	9.1	6.8	4.9	3.3	2.1
Female - Femmes	82.7	78.6	73.6	68.7	63.8	58.9	53.9	49.1	44.2	39.4	34.7	30.1	25.6	21.3	17.3	13.6	10.3	7.5	5.3	3.6	2.3
Cuba																					
2011 - 2013																					
Male - Hommes	76.5	72.0	67.0	62.1	57.3	52.5	47.7	42.9	38.2	33.6	29.2	25.0	21.0	17.3	14.0	11.0	8.4	6.3	4.9	3.8	2.0
Female - Femmes	80.4	75.9	71.0	66.0	61.1	56.2	51.4	46.5	41.7	36.9	32.3	27.9	23.6	19.6	15.8	12.4	9.4	6.9	5.1	3.8	2.1
Curaçao																					
2016																					
Male - Hommes	74.9	71.1	66.2	61.2	56.3	51.6	47.0	42.3	37.7	33.0	28.5	24.3	20.4	16.7	13.3	10.4	7.6	5.5	3.9	2.8	2.4
Female - Femmes	81.0	77.7	72.7	67.7	62.8	57.9	53.0	48.2	43.3	38.6	33.9	29.3	24.8	20.6	16.6	12.8	9.6	7.0	4.9	3.3	2.2
2015 - 2017																					
Male - Hommes	74.7	...	...	...	...	...	...	...	...	...	...	...	...	...	...	...	...	...	...	...	...
Female - Femmes	81.5	...	...	...	...	...	...	...	...	...	...	...	...	...	...	...	...	...	...	...	...
Dominica - Dominique																					
2008																					
Male - Hommes	73.8	...	...	...	...	...	...	...	...	...	...	...	...	...	...	...	...	...	...	...	...
Female - Femmes	78.2	...	...	...	...	...	...	...	...	...	...	...	...	...	...	...	...	...	...	...	...
Dominican Republic - République dominicaine																					
2010 - 2015																					
Male - Hommes	70.0	67.5	62.6	57.7	53.0	48.7	44.3	40.0	35.6	31.3	27.2	23.3	19.6	16.2	13.2	10.5	8.6	...	...	...	...
Female - Femmes	74.8	71.8	66.9	62.0	57.1	52.4	47.7	43.1	38.5	34.1	29.7	25.5	21.6	17.9	14.6	11.7	9.7	...	...	...	...
El Salvador[20]																					
2000 - 2005																					
Male - Hommes	65.4	62.6	57.8	52.9	48.7	45.0	41.5	37.8	34.1	30.4	26.8	23.3	20.0	16.7	13.8	11.1	9.0	...	...	...	...
Female - Femmes	74.9	72.0	67.1	62.3	57.5	52.9	48.2	43.6	39.0	34.6	30.3	26.1	22.1	18.4	15.0	12.0	9.6	...	...	...	...
Greenland - Groenland																					
2015 - 2019																					
Male - Hommes	68.3	64.2	59.4	54.5	50.6	46.5	42.1	37.6	33.0	28.5	24.0	19.8	15.7	12.2	9.3	6.6	5.1	3.5	3.1	1.9	...
Female - Femmes	73.0	68.6	63.7	58.7	54.3	49.8	45.1	40.3	35.6	30.9	26.2	21.8	17.5	13.8	10.6	7.7	5.6	4.0	2.6	1.5	...
Guadeloupe																					
2015																					
Male - Hommes	77.0	...	...	...	58.2	...	...	...	40.4	...	...	...	23.5	...	...	...	...	...	...	...	...
Female - Femmes	84.8	...	...	...	65.6	...	...	...	46.1	...	...	...	27.4	...	...	...	...	...	...	...	...
Guatemala																					
1995 - 2000																					
Male - Hommes	61.4	60.6	56.0	51.2	46.8	42.7	38.8	34.9	31.2	27.4	23.7	20.1	16.8	13.6	10.7	8.2	6.1	...	...	...	...
Female - Femmes	67.2	66.2	62.6	56.9	52.3	47.7	43.3	38.9	34.6	30.4	26.3	22.3	18.6	15.2	12.0	9.2	6.9	...	...	...	...
2010 - 2015																					
Male - Hommes	67.9	...	...	...	...	...	...	...	...	...	...	...	...	...	...	...	...	...	...	...	...
Female - Femmes	75.0	...	...	...	...	...	...	...	...	...	...	...	...	...	...	...	...	...	...	...	...
Jamaica - Jamaïque																					
2011																					
Male - Hommes	70.4	67.0	62.1	57.2	52.7	48.7	44.7	40.6	36.6	32.4	28.3	24.2	20.3	16.4	12.8	9.5	6.5	...	...	...	...
Female - Femmes	78.0	74.3	69.5	64.6	59.7	54.8	50.0	45.3	40.6	36.0	31.5	27.1	22.9	18.7	14.7	11.0	7.6	...	...	...	...
Martinique																					
2015																					
Male - Hommes	79.4	...	...	...	60.1	...	...	...	41.7	...	...	...	24.1	...	...	...	...	...	...	...	...
Female - Femmes	84.7	...	...	...	65.4	...	...	...	45.9	...	...	...	27.4	...	...	...	...	...	...	...	...
Mexico - Mexique																					
2008																					
Male - Hommes	72.8	69.2	64.3	59.4	54.7	50.0	45.5	40.9	36.5	32.1	27.9	23.9	20.2	16.8	13.7	11.0	8.7	6.6	4.9	3.5	2.6
Female - Femmes	77.5	73.8	68.9	63.9	59.0	54.2	49.3	44.5	39.7	35.1	30.6	26.2	22.1	18.3	14.8	11.7	9.0	6.8	4.9	3.5	2.6
2018																					
Male - Hommes	72.2	...	...	...	...	...	...	...	...	...	...	...	...	...	...	...	...	...	...	...	...
Female - Femmes	77.9	...	...	...	...	...	...	...	...	...	...	...	...	...	...	...	...	...	...	...	...

22. Life expectancy at specified ages for each sex: latest available year, 2000 - 2019
Espérance de vie à un âge donné pour chaque sexe : dernière année disponible, 2000 - 2019 (continued - suite)

Continent, country or area and date / Continent, pays ou zone et date	Age (in years) - Age (en années)																				
	0	5	10	15	20	25	30	35	40	45	50	55	60	65	70	75	80	85	90	95	100
AMERICA, NORTH - AMÉRIQUE DU NORD																					
Nicaragua																					
2005 - 2010																					
Male - Hommes	63.4	61.1	56.5	51.8	47.9	44.2	40.5	36.5	32.5	28.6	24.9	21.3	17.7	14.6	11.6	9.0	6.5	...	...	...	...
Female - Femmes	68.9	66.2	61.4	56.7	52.1	47.6	43.0	38.5	34.1	29.8	25.7	21.9	18.1	14.9	11.8	9.3	6.9	...	...	...	...
Panama[21]																					
2018																					
Male - Hommes	75.3	71.9	67.1	62.2	57.6	53.3	49.0	44.6	40.1	35.6	31.3	27.0	23.0	19.3	15.8	12.8	10.1	7.8	5.8	4.2	2.5
Female - Femmes	81.4	77.6	72.7	67.8	63.0	58.2	53.4	48.7	44.0	39.3	34.7	30.2	25.9	21.7	17.8	14.3	11.2	8.4	6.2	4.3	2.5
Puerto Rico - Porto Rico																					
2017 - 2019																					
Male - Hommes	76.3	72.0	67.0	62.0	57.2	52.8	48.4	44.1	39.8	35.6	31.4	27.3	23.5	19.9	16.6	13.5	10.8	8.6	...	...	...
Female - Femmes	84.8	80.4	75.4	70.4	65.5	60.6	55.7	50.9	46.2	41.5	36.9	32.4	28.0	23.8	19.8	16.0	12.7	10.1	...	...	...
Saint Lucia - Sainte-Lucie																					
2005																					
Male - Hommes	69.9	66.4	61.5	56.6	52.0	47.4	43.1	38.6	34.3	30.1	25.9	21.7	17.9	14.7	11.8	9.0	7.2	5.2	...	...	...
Female - Femmes	75.7	72.2	67.3	62.4	57.5	52.6	47.8	43.2	38.4	33.8	29.2	25.0	20.8	17.2	13.8	10.4	7.7	4.8	...	...	...
2012																					
Male - Hommes	75.3	...	...	...	...	...	...	...	...	...	...	...	...	...	...	...	...	...	...	...	...
Female - Femmes	82.5	...	...	...	...	...	...	...	...	...	...	...	...	...	...	...	...	...	...	...	...
Saint Vincent and the Grenadines - Saint-Vincent-et-les Grenadines																					
2017																					
Male - Hommes	71.1	67.1	62.1	57.2	52.7	48.1	43.5	39.2	34.6	30.7	26.6	23.0	19.6	16.4	13.7	10.7	8.3	6.2	4.4	4.1	...
Female - Femmes	75.1	71.2	66.5	61.6	56.7	52.0	47.5	42.9	38.2	34.0	29.9	25.7	21.9	18.5	14.9	12.0	9.3	6.6	4.6	2.4	...
Sint Maarten (Dutch part) - Saint-Martin (partie néerlandaise)																					
2015 - 2017																					
Male - Hommes	74.0	70.1	65.3	60.4	55.6	51.1	46.8	42.1	37.5	32.7	28.2	24.0	20.0	16.4	12.6	9.6	6.8	4.2	4.8	...	...
Female - Femmes	82.8	79.2	74.2	69.2	64.2	59.5	54.5	49.6	44.8	40.0	35.2	30.5	26.1	21.8	17.6	14.3	11.3	8.1	6.8	...	...
Trinidad and Tobago - Trinité-et-Tobago[2]																					
2011																					
Male - Hommes	71.4	67.6	62.7	57.8	53.2	49.0	44.7	40.4	36.0	31.7	27.5	23.5	19.6	16.2	12.9	10.2	7.9	6.0	...	...	...
Female - Femmes	77.8	74.1	69.2	64.2	59.4	54.6	49.9	45.3	40.6	36.2	31.7	27.5	23.3	19.4	15.9	12.6	9.7	7.6	...	...	...
Turks and Caicos Islands - Îles Turques et Caïques																					
2012																					
Male - Hommes	75.8	73.3	68.4	63.5	58.8	54.4	49.9	45.1	40.4	35.6	31.0	...	26.6	22.3	18.4	14.7	11.5	8.7	...	...	...
Female - Femmes	77.8	73.9	69.1	64.2	59.4	54.7	49.9	45.0	40.2	35.5	30.8	...	26.2	21.9	17.8	14.1	10.8	8.0	...	...	...
United States of America - États-Unis d'Amérique																					
2017																					
Male - Hommes	76.1	71.7	66.7	61.8	57.0	52.4	47.8	43.2	38.7	34.2	29.8	25.6	21.7	18.0	14.5	11.3	8.4	5.9	4.1	2.8	2.0
Female - Femmes	81.1	76.6	71.6	66.7	61.8	56.9	52.1	47.3	42.6	37.9	33.4	28.9	24.7	20.6	16.7	13.0	9.8	7.0	4.8	3.2	2.2
AMERICA, SOUTH - AMÉRIQUE DU SUD																					
Argentina - Argentine																					
2008 - 2010																					
Male - Hommes	72.1	68.2	63.3	58.4	53.7	49.1	44.5	39.8	35.2	30.7	26.3	22.2	18.5	15.0	11.9	9.2	6.9	5.2	4.0	3.1	2.6
Female - Femmes	78.8	74.8	69.9	65.0	60.1	55.3	50.5	45.6	40.9	36.2	31.7	27.3	23.1	19.0	15.2	11.7	8.6	6.3	4.7	3.5	2.9
2015[6]																					
Male - Hommes	73.7	...	...	...	...	...	...	...	...	...	...	...	...	...	...	...	...	...	...	...	...
Female - Femmes	80.3	...	...	...	...	...	...	...	...	...	...	...	...	...	...	...	...	...	...	...	...

22. Life expectancy at specified ages for each sex: latest available year, 2000 - 2019
Espérance de vie à un âge donné pour chaque sexe : dernière année disponible, 2000 - 2019 (continued - suite)

Continent, country or area and date / Continent, pays ou zone et date	0	5	10	15	20	25	30	35	40	45	50	55	60	65	70	75	80	85	90	95	100
	Age (in years) - Age (en années)																				
AMERICA, SOUTH - AMÉRIQUE DU SUD																					
Bolivia (Plurinational State of) - Bolivie (État plurinational de)																					
2016 - 2017[22]																					
Male - Hommes	69.1	67.3	62.6	57.9	53.4	49.1	44.7	40.4	36.2	32.0	27.9	24.0	20.3	16.9	13.8	11.1	8.7	6.8	4.9	3.7	...
Female - Femmes	75.9	73.6	68.9	64.0	59.3	54.6	50.0	45.3	40.7	36.3	32.0	27.8	23.8	20.1	16.8	13.7	10.9	8.5	6.3	4.8	...
2018 - 2019[23]																					
Male - Hommes	70.0	...	...	...	...	...	...	...	...	...	...	...	...	...	...	...	...	...	...	...	...
Female - Femmes	77.0	...	...	...	...	...	...	...	...	...	...	...	...	...	...	...	...	...	...	...	...
Brazil - Brésil																					
2015																					
Male - Hommes	71.9	68.2	63.3	58.4	53.9	49.5	45.1	40.7	36.3	32.0	27.9	23.9	20.2	16.7	13.5	10.7	8.4	...	...	...	...
Female - Femmes	79.1	75.3	70.4	65.4	60.6	55.7	50.9	46.2	41.4	36.8	32.3	28.0	23.8	19.8	16.2	12.9	10.1	...	...	...	...
Chile - Chili[24]																					
2019 - 2020																					
Male - Hommes	77.9	73.5	68.6	63.6	58.8	54.0	49.3	44.6	39.9	35.3	30.9	26.5	22.4	18.5	14.9	11.7	8.9	6.6	4.9	3.6	3.0
Female - Femmes	83.4	79.0	74.0	69.1	64.2	59.3	54.4	49.5	44.6	39.9	35.2	30.6	26.1	21.8	17.8	14.1	10.8	8.0	5.9	4.5	3.7
Colombia - Colombie																					
2010 - 2015																					
Male - Hommes	72.1	68.9	64.0	59.1	54.5	50.1	45.7	41.3	36.8	32.3	27.9	23.7	19.7	16.0	12.7	9.8	7.4	...	...	...	...
Female - Femmes	78.5	74.9	70.0	65.1	60.2	55.4	50.6	45.8	41.0	36.3	31.7	27.2	22.9	18.8	15.0	11.6	8.7	...	...	...	...
2015 - 2020																					
Male - Hommes	73.1	...	...	...	...	...	...	...	...	...	...	...	...	...	...	...	...	...	...	...	...
Female - Femmes	79.4	...	...	...	...	...	...	...	...	...	...	...	...	...	...	...	...	...	...	...	...
Ecuador - Équateur[25]																					
2018																					
Male - Hommes	74.1	70.7	65.7	60.8	56.0	51.2	46.5	41.9	37.3	32.8	28.4	24.1	20.0	16.3	12.9	9.8	7.3	5.2	3.6	2.4	0.5
Female - Femmes	79.7	76.2	71.3	66.3	61.4	56.6	51.7	46.9	42.1	37.3	32.6	28.0	23.5	19.2	15.1	11.4	8.2	5.7	3.8	2.5	0.5
Falkland Islands (Malvinas) - Îles Falkland (Malvinas)																					
2006 - 2012																					
Male - Hommes	75.6	72.4	67.4	62.4	57.9	53.5	48.5	44.0	40.2	35.2	30.4	27.1	22.5	19.2	15.3	11.2	7.7	5.4	2.2	...	...
Female - Femmes	79.6	74.6	69.6	64.6	60.1	55.1	50.1	45.1	40.4	35.7	31.0	26.5	22.3	18.6	14.1	10.3	6.9	4.6	2.2	...	...
French Guiana - Guyane française																					
2015																					
Male - Hommes	76.4	...	...	...	58.0	...	...	...	39.5	...	...	...	22.0	...	...	...	...	...	...	...	...
Female - Femmes	82.0	...	...	...	63.0	...	...	...	43.6	...	...	...	25.3	...	...	...	...	...	...	...	...
Guyana[26]																					
2012																					
Male - Hommes	65.5	63.4	58.8	54.1	49.7	45.7	41.9	37.9	34.0	30.0	26.3	22.7	19.4	16.4	13.6	11.2	9.1	7.3	5.9	4.6	3.7
Female - Femmes	72.6	70.3	65.5	60.7	56.0	51.5	47.2	42.8	38.4	34.1	29.9	25.9	22.0	18.5	15.3	12.4	9.9	7.8	6.0	4.6	3.5
Paraguay																					
2018																					
Male - Hommes	71.4	...	...	...	...	...	...	...	...	...	...	...	...	...	...	...	...	...	...	...	...
Female - Femmes	77.2	...	...	...	...	...	...	...	...	...	...	...	...	...	...	...	...	...	...	...	...
Peru - Pérou																					
2015 - 2020																					
Male - Hommes	73.7	70.0	65.2	60.4	55.7	51.1	46.7	42.2	37.7	33.2	28.9	24.7	20.7	16.9	13.4	10.4	7.7	5.7	4.2	3.2	2.5
Female - Femmes	79.2	75.4	70.5	65.6	60.7	55.9	51.2	46.5	41.8	37.2	32.6	28.2	23.8	19.7	15.8	12.3	9.3	6.8	4.9	3.6	2.7
Suriname																					
2016 - 2018																					
Male - Hommes	71.0	67.7	62.9	57.9	53.2	48.6	44.0	39.5	35.1	30.7	26.5	22.7	19.2	15.7	12.4	9.2	6.2	4.1	...	...	...
Female - Femmes	75.9	72.3	67.4	62.5	57.8	53.0	48.3	43.6	39.1	34.5	30.0	25.7	21.6	17.6	13.8	10.2	6.8	4.3	...	...	...
Uruguay																					
2010																					
Male - Hommes	72.8	68.5	63.6	58.7	54.0	49.4	44.8	40.2	35.6	31.0	26.6	22.4	18.6	15.1	12.0	9.3	7.0	5.2	4.0	...	...
Female - Femmes	80.0	75.6	70.7	65.8	60.9	56.1	51.2	46.4	41.6	36.9	32.3	27.9	23.6	19.5	15.6	12.0	8.9	6.4	4.5	...	...
2016																					
Male - Hommes	73.8	...	...	...	...	...	...	...	...	...	...	...	...	...	...	...	...	...	...	...	...
Female - Femmes	80.6	...	...	...	...	...	...	...	...	...	...	...	...	...	...	...	...	...	...	...	...

Continent, country or area and date / Continent, pays ou zone et date	Age (in years) - Age (en années) 0	5	10	15	20	25	30	35	40	45	50	55	60	65	70	75	80	85	90	95	100
AMERICA, SOUTH - AMÉRIQUE DU SUD																					
Venezuela (Bolivarian Republic of) - Venezuela (République bolivarienne du)																					
1995 - 2000																					
Male - Hommes	68.6	66.6	61.8	56.9	52.3	47.8	43.3	38.8	34.3	29.9	25.6	21.6	17.9	14.5	11.4	8.6	5.9	...	...	...	...
Female - Femmes	74.5	72.1	67.2	62.3	57.5	52.6	47.8	43.1	38.4	33.7	29.2	24.9	20.8	16.9	13.3	9.9	6.9	...	...	...	...
2018[27]																					
Male - Hommes	72.6	...	...	...	...	...	...	...	...	...	...	...	...	...	...	...	...	...	...	...	...
Female - Femmes	78.7	...	...	...	...	...	...	...	...	...	...	...	...	...	...	...	...	...	...	...	...
ASIA - ASIE																					
Afghanistan																					
2004																					
Male - Hommes	45.0	...	...	...	...	...	...	...	...	...	...	...	...	...	...	...	...	...	...	...	...
Female - Femmes	44.0	...	...	...	...	...	...	...	...	...	...	...	...	...	...	...	...	...	...	...	...
Armenia - Arménie																					
2017 - 2018																					
Male - Hommes	72.4	68.1	63.2	58.2	53.4	48.6	43.8	39.1	34.3	29.8	25.4	21.6	17.8	14.3	11.3	8.6	5.4	2.7	2.1	2.9	1.0
Female - Femmes	79.0	74.7	69.7	64.8	59.9	54.9	50.0	45.1	40.2	35.4	30.7	26.1	21.7	17.5	13.6	10.1	6.4	3.3	2.1	1.8	0.8
Azerbaijan - Azerbaïdjan																					
2018																					
Male - Hommes	73.3	69.4	64.5	59.6	54.8	49.9	45.1	40.4	35.6	31.1	26.7	22.6	18.8	15.4	12.3	9.6	7.5	6.2	5.3	4.8	1.0
Female - Femmes	78.2	74.1	69.1	64.2	59.3	54.4	49.6	44.7	39.8	35.0	30.3	25.7	21.3	17.3	13.6	10.2	7.3	5.4	4.1	3.7	0.9
Bahrain - Bahreïn																					
2001																					
Male - Hommes	73.2	69.3	64.4	59.5	54.7	49.9	45.2	40.4	35.6	30.9	26.4	22.0	17.8	14.1	11.3	9.5	...	...	...	...	...
Female - Femmes	76.2	72.0	67.1	62.1	57.2	52.3	47.4	42.5	37.7	32.9	28.2	23.7	19.6	15.9	12.9	10.9	...	...	...	...	...
2015 - 2020																					
Male - Hommes	76.3	...	...	...	...	...	...	...	...	...	...	...	...	...	...	...	...	...	...	...	...
Female - Femmes	78.2	...	...	...	...	...	...	...	...	...	...	...	...	...	...	...	...	...	...	...	...
Bangladesh																					
2017																					
Male - Hommes	70.6	71.7	68.3	63.5	58.7	54.2	49.4	44.7	39.9	35.2	30.6	26.2	22.3	18.5	15.2	11.9	9.5	7.1	...	...	...
Female - Femmes	73.5	74.6	71.1	66.3	61.4	56.8	52.0	47.1	42.4	37.7	33.1	28.8	24.6	20.4	16.7	13.1	10.2	6.9	...	...	...
2019																					
Male - Hommes	71.1	...	...	...	...	...	...	...	...	...	...	...	...	...	...	...	...	...	...	...	...
Female - Femmes	74.2	...	...	...	...	...	...	...	...	...	...	...	...	...	...	...	...	...	...	...	...
Bhutan - Bhoutan																					
2005																					
Male - Hommes	65.7	...	...	...	...	...	...	...	...	...	...	...	...	...	...	...	...	...	...	...	...
Female - Femmes	66.9	...	...	...	...	...	...	...	...	...	...	...	...	...	...	...	...	...	...	...	...
Brunei Darussalam - Brunéi Darussalam																					
2018																					
Male - Hommes	76.4	...	...	...	...	...	...	...	...	...	...	...	...	...	...	...	...	...	...	...	...
Female - Femmes	78.5	...	...	...	...	...	...	...	...	...	...	...	...	...	...	...	...	...	...	...	...
China - Chine[28]																					
2010																					
Male - Hommes	66.8	...	...	...	...	...	...	...	...	...	...	...	...	...	...	...	...	...	...	...	...
Female - Femmes	70.5	...	...	...	...	...	...	...	...	...	...	...	...	...	...	...	...	...	...	...	...
China, Hong Kong SAR - Chine, Hong Kong RAS																					
2019																					
Male - Hommes	82.2	77.4	72.4	67.5	62.5	57.6	52.7	47.9	43.1	38.3	33.7	29.2	24.9	20.8	16.9	13.4	10.3	7.8	5.7	4.0	2.8
Female - Femmes	88.1	83.3	78.3	73.4	68.4	63.5	58.5	53.6	48.7	43.8	39.0	34.4	29.8	25.3	20.9	16.8	13.0	9.7	7.0	4.8	3.2
China, Macao SAR - Chine, Macao RAS																					
2016 - 2019																					
Male - Hommes	80.8	76.0	71.0	66.1	61.1	56.4	51.5	46.7	42.0	37.4	33.0	28.6	24.3	20.4	16.6	13.3	10.3	8.1	...	...	...
Female - Femmes	86.7	81.9	77.0	72.0	67.1	62.2	57.3	52.3	47.5	42.7	37.9	33.2	28.6	24.2	19.9	15.8	12.1	9.1	...	...	...

22. Life expectancy at specified ages for each sex: latest available year, 2000 - 2019
Espérance de vie à un âge donné pour chaque sexe : dernière année disponible, 2000 - 2019 (continued - suite)

Continent, country or area and date / Continent, pays ou zone et date	0	5	10	15	20	25	30	35	40	45	50	55	60	65	70	75	80	85	90	95	100
	Age (in years) - Age (en années)																				
ASIA - ASIE																					
Cyprus - Chypre[29]																					
2013																					
Male - Hommes	80.0	75.1	70.2	65.3	60.4	55.5	50.7	45.8	41.0	36.3	31.6	27.0	22.6	18.5	14.7	11.2	8.2	5.9	...	...	...
Female - Femmes	84.8	79.8	74.9	69.9	64.9	60.0	55.0	50.1	45.2	40.3	35.4	30.6	25.9	21.4	17.2	13.1	9.5	6.6	...	...	...
2017																					
Male - Hommes	80.0	...	...	...	...	...	...	...	...	...	...	...	...	...	...	...	...	...	...	...	...
Female - Femmes	84.1	...	...	...	...	...	...	...	...	...	...	...	...	...	...	...	...	...	...	...	...
Democratic People's Republic of Korea - République populaire démocratique de Corée																					
2008																					
Male - Hommes	65.6	...	...	...	...	...	...	...	...	...	...	...	...	...	...	...	...	...	...	...	...
Female - Femmes	72.7	...	...	...	...	...	...	...	...	...	...	...	...	...	...	...	...	...	...	...	...
Georgia - Géorgie																					
2016																					
Male - Hommes	68.2	64.1	59.1	54.2	49.4	44.7	40.1	35.6	31.2	27.0	23.0	19.4	16.0	12.9	10.1	7.6	5.5	3.7	...	...	...
Female - Femmes	77.1	72.8	67.9	62.9	58.0	53.2	48.3	43.5	38.7	33.9	29.3	24.8	20.6	16.5	12.7	9.3	6.5	4.4	...	...	...
India - Inde[30]																					
2014 - 2018																					
Male - Hommes	68.2	66.1	61.3	56.5	51.7	47.0	42.4	37.8	33.4	29.1	24.9	21.0	17.4	14.1	11.1	8.5	6.2	...	...	...	...
Female - Femmes	70.7	69.0	64.2	59.4	54.6	49.9	45.2	40.5	35.8	31.3	26.9	22.8	18.9	15.3	12.1	9.2	6.6	...	...	...	...
Indonesia - Indonésie[31]																					
2019																					
Male - Hommes	71.3	...	...	...	...	...	...	...	...	...	...	...	...	...	...	...	...	...	...	...	...
Female - Femmes	75.1	...	...	...	...	...	...	...	...	...	...	...	...	...	...	...	...	...	...	...	...
Iran (Islamic Republic of) - Iran (République islamique d')[32]																					
2016																					
Male - Hommes	72.5	...	...	...	...	...	...	...	...	...	...	...	...	...	...	...	...	...	...	...	...
Female - Femmes	75.5	...	...	...	...	...	...	...	...	...	...	...	...	...	...	...	...	...	...	...	...
Iraq																					
2018																					
Male - Hommes	71.7	...	...	...	...	...	...	...	...	...	...	...	...	...	...	...	...	...	...	...	...
Female - Femmes	75.6	...	...	...	...	...	...	...	...	...	...	...	...	...	...	...	...	...	...	...	...
Israel - Israël[33]																					
2014 - 2018																					
Male - Hommes	80.6	75.9	70.9	66.0	61.1	56.2	51.4	46.5	41.7	36.9	32.3	27.8	23.4	19.3	15.5	12.0	9.0	6.6	4.7	3.4	2.5
Female - Femmes	84.4	79.7	74.7	69.7	64.8	59.8	54.9	50.0	45.1	40.2	35.4	30.8	26.2	21.7	17.5	13.5	10.0	7.1	4.9	3.4	2.3
Japan - Japon[34]																					
2018																					
Male - Hommes	81.3	76.5	71.5	66.5	61.6	56.7	51.9	47.0	42.2	37.4	32.7	28.2	23.8	19.7	15.8	12.3	9.1	6.4	4.3	2.9	1.8
Female - Femmes	87.3	82.5	77.6	72.6	67.6	62.7	57.8	52.9	48.0	43.1	38.4	33.7	29.0	24.5	20.1	15.9	11.9	8.4	5.7	3.6	2.3
Jordan - Jordanie[35]																					
2012																					
Male - Hommes	72.7	69.1	64.2	59.3	54.4	49.6	44.8	40.0	35.2	30.5	26.0	21.7	17.8	14.2	10.9	8.2	6.0	...	...	...	...
Female - Femmes	76.7	73.1	68.1	63.2	58.2	53.3	48.4	43.6	38.7	33.9	29.3	24.7	20.3	16.2	12.4	9.2	6.8	...	...	...	...
2017																					
Male - Hommes	72.4	...	...	...	...	...	...	...	...	...	...	...	...	...	...	...	...	...	...	...	...
Female - Femmes	74.6	...	...	...	...	...	...	...	...	...	...	...	...	...	...	...	...	...	...	...	...
Kazakhstan																					
2019																					
Male - Hommes	68.8	64.7	59.8	54.9	50.1	45.4	40.7	36.2	31.9	27.7	23.8	20.0	16.4	13.4	10.8	8.5	6.5	5.2	4.1	3.7	0.5
Female - Femmes	77.3	73.0	68.1	63.2	58.3	53.4	48.6	43.8	39.1	34.5	30.0	25.6	21.3	17.3	13.6	10.3	7.4	5.1	3.2	2.3	0.5
Kuwait - Koweït																					
2018																					
Male - Hommes	80.1	...	...	...	...	...	...	...	...	...	...	...	...	...	...	...	...	...	...	...	...
Female - Femmes	83.3	...	...	...	...	...	...	...	...	...	...	...	...	...	...	...	...	...	...	...	...
Kyrgyzstan - Kirghizstan																					
2018																					
Male - Hommes	67.4	63.8	58.9	54.0	49.1	44.4	39.6	34.9	30.5	26.2	22.1	18.1	14.3	10.7	7.4	5.2	4.1	3.1	2.5	2.1	1.8
Female - Femmes	75.6	71.8	66.9	62.0	57.1	52.3	47.4	42.6	37.8	33.2	28.6	24.2	19.9	15.9	12.1	8.6	6.3	4.7	3.5	2.6	1.9

22. Life expectancy at specified ages for each sex: latest available year, 2000 - 2019
Espérance de vie à un âge donné pour chaque sexe : dernière année disponible, 2000 - 2019 (continued - suite)

Continent, country or area and date / Continent, pays ou zone et date	Age (in years) - Age (en années) 0	5	10	15	20	25	30	35	40	45	50	55	60	65	70	75	80	85	90	95	100
ASIA - ASIE																					
Lao People's Democratic Republic - République démocratique populaire lao[36]																					
2018																					
Male - Hommes	64.0	...	...	...	...	...	...	...	...	...	...	...	...	...	...	...	...	...	...	...	...
Female - Femmes	68.0	...	...	...	...	...	...	...	...	...	...	...	...	...	...	...	...	...	...	...	...
Malaysia - Malaisie																					
2019																					
Male - Hommes	72.2	67.9	62.9	58.1	53.3	48.6	43.8	39.1	34.5	30.1	25.9	21.9	18.2	14.8	11.6	8.6	6.1	...	...	...	...
Female - Femmes	77.3	72.9	68.0	63.0	58.1	53.2	48.4	43.5	38.7	34.1	29.5	25.2	21.0	17.1	13.4	9.9	7.0	...	...	...	...
Maldives																					
2015																					
Male - Hommes	73.1	69.0	64.0	59.1	54.3	49.4	44.6	39.7	34.8	29.9	25.2	20.7	16.2	11.9	7.9	4.7	...	...	...	...	...
Female - Femmes	74.6	70.3	65.4	60.5	55.6	50.7	45.7	40.7	35.8	31.0	26.1	21.4	16.7	12.2	7.8	4.4	...	...	...	...	...
2016																					
Male - Hommes	73.0	...	...	...	...	...	...	...	...	...	...	...	...	...	...	...	...	...	...	...	...
Female - Femmes	74.7	...	...	...	...	...	...	...	...	...	...	...	...	...	...	...	...	...	...	...	...
Mongolia - Mongolie																					
2019																					
Male - Hommes	66.4	62.6	57.8	52.9	48.2	43.7	39.1	34.8	30.6	26.7	23.2	20.0	17.1	14.6	12.4	...	...	...	...	...	...
Female - Femmes	76.0	72.5	67.6	62.7	57.9	53.1	48.3	43.6	39.0	34.4	30.1	26.0	22.1	18.6	15.5	...	...	...	...	...	...
Myanmar[37]																					
2017																					
Male - Hommes	60.8	60.4	55.8	51.2	46.5	42.1	37.9	34.0	30.4	26.8	23.3	19.9	16.6	13.4	10.5	7.9	5.7	4.3	...	...	...
Female - Femmes	70.2	69.5	64.8	60.1	55.3	50.6	45.9	41.3	36.7	32.2	27.9	23.6	19.6	15.8	12.4	9.3	6.5	4.9	...	...	...
Nepal - Népal																					
2011																					
Male - Hommes	65.5	...	...	...	...	...	...	...	...	...	...	...	...	...	...	...	...	...	...	...	...
Female - Femmes	67.9	...	...	...	...	...	...	...	...	...	...	...	...	...	...	...	...	...	...	...	...
Oman																					
2013																					
Male - Hommes	74.8	70.9	66.0	61.1	56.4	51.8	47.1	42.4	37.6	33.0	28.5	24.3	20.4	16.9	13.6	10.4	...	...	...	...	...
Female - Femmes	78.5	74.3	69.4	64.4	59.5	54.6	49.7	44.8	39.9	35.1	30.5	25.9	21.6	17.5	13.8	10.2	...	...	...	...	...
2019[38]																					
Male - Hommes	75.2	...	...	...	...	...	...	...	...	...	...	...	...	...	...	...	...	...	...	...	...
Female - Femmes	79.2	...	...	...	...	...	...	...	...	...	...	...	...	...	...	...	...	...	...	...	...
Pakistan[39]																					
2007																					
Male - Hommes	63.6	65.3	60.7	55.9	51.3	46.7	42.2	37.7	33.3	29.0	25.0	21.3	18.1	15.2	12.7	10.8	9.2	7.3	...	...	...
Female - Femmes	67.6	68.6	64.1	59.5	54.9	50.3	45.7	41.1	36.5	32.1	27.7	23.5	19.6	16.2	13.4	10.9	8.6	6.1	...	...	...
Philippines[40]																					
2015 - 2020																					
Male - Hommes	69.9	...	...	...	...	...	...	...	...	...	...	...	...	...	...	...	...	...	...	...	...
Female - Femmes	75.9	...	...	...	...	...	...	...	...	...	...	...	...	...	...	...	...	...	...	...	...
Qatar																					
2018																					
Male - Hommes	79.1	74.6	69.6	64.8	60.2	55.6	50.9	46.2	41.4	36.6	32.0	27.8	23.8	20.2	16.7	13.0	9.6	...	...	...	...
Female - Femmes	82.4	77.7	72.8	67.8	62.9	57.9	53.0	48.0	43.1	38.2	33.4	28.8	24.6	20.8	17.5	14.1	11.8	...	...	...	...
Republic of Korea - République de Corée																					
2018																					
Male - Hommes	79.7	75.0	70.1	65.1	60.2	55.3	50.4	45.6	40.8	36.1	31.5	27.1	22.8	18.7	14.8	11.1	8.1	5.7	4.0	2.8	2.0
Female - Femmes	85.7	81.0	76.0	71.1	66.1	61.2	56.3	51.4	46.5	41.7	36.9	32.2	27.5	22.9	18.3	14.1	10.3	7.1	4.8	3.3	2.3
Saudi Arabia - Arabie saoudite[41]																					
2018																					
Male - Hommes	73.7	...	...	...	...	...	...	...	...	...	...	...	...	...	...	...	...	...	...	...	...
Female - Femmes	76.4	...	...	...	...	...	...	...	...	...	...	...	...	...	...	...	...	...	...	...	...
Singapore - Singapour[42]																					
2019																					
Male - Hommes	81.4	76.6	71.6	66.6	61.7	56.8	51.9	47.0	42.1	37.3	32.7	28.1	23.7	19.6	15.7	12.2	9.1	6.7	4.7	3.2	2.2
Female - Femmes	85.7	80.9	76.0	71.0	66.0	61.1	56.1	51.2	46.3	41.4	36.6	31.9	27.3	22.9	18.6	14.5	10.9	7.9	5.5	3.8	2.5

22. Life expectancy at specified ages for each sex: latest available year, 2000 - 2019
Espérance de vie à un âge donné pour chaque sexe : dernière année disponible, 2000 - 2019 (continued - suite)

Continent, country or area and date / Continent, pays ou zone et date	0	5	10	15	20	25	30	35	40	45	50	55	60	65	70	75	80	85	90	95	100
	Age (in years) - Age (en années)																				
ASIA - ASIE																					
Sri Lanka																					
2000 - 2002																					
Male - Hommes	68.8	65.0	60.2	55.3	50.6	46.2	41.9	37.6	33.2	29.0	24.9	21.1	17.6	14.5	11.6	9.2	7.2	5.5	4.2	...	...
Female - Femmes	77.2	73.3	68.4	63.5	58.6	53.9	49.1	44.3	39.5	34.8	30.2	25.7	21.5	17.5	13.9	10.7	8.0	5.8	4.1	...	...
State of Palestine - État de Palestine																					
2001																					
Male - Hommes	70.5	67.5	62.7	57.8	53.1	48.4	43.6	38.9	34.2	29.6	25.2	21.1	17.2	13.8	10.7	8.1	6.1	...	...	...	...
Female - Femmes	73.6	70.3	65.5	60.5	55.7	50.9	46.1	41.3	36.6	32.0	27.5	23.2	19.0	15.2	11.7	8.8	6.4	...	...	...	...
2018																					
Male - Hommes	72.9	...	...	...	...	...	...	...	...	...	...	...	...	...	...	...	...	...	...	...	...
Female - Femmes	75.2	...	...	...	...	...	...	...	...	...	...	...	...	...	...	...	...	...	...	...	...
Tajikistan - Tadjikistan																					
2008																					
Male - Hommes	69.7	67.9	63.0	58.1	53.3	48.5	43.7	39.1	34.6	30.1	25.7	21.6	17.9	14.7	12.2	10.4	9.2	...	...	...	...
Female - Femmes	74.8	72.5	67.6	62.7	57.8	52.9	48.1	43.4	38.6	33.9	29.4	25.0	21.0	17.5	14.7	12.5	11.1	...	...	...	...
2017																					
Male - Hommes	73.0	...	...	...	...	...	...	...	...	...	...	...	...	...	...	...	...	...	...	...	...
Female - Femmes	76.9	...	...	...	...	...	...	...	...	...	...	...	...	...	...	...	...	...	...	...	...
Thailand - Thaïlande																					
2019																					
Male - Hommes	73.0	...	...	...	...	...	...	...	...	...	...	...	...	...	...	...	...	...	...	...	...
Female - Femmes	80.1	...	...	...	...	...	...	...	...	...	...	...	...	...	...	...	...	...	...	...	...
Timor-Leste[3]																					
2018																					
Male - Hommes	66.3	...	...	...	...	...	...	...	...	...	...	...	...	...	...	...	...	...	...	...	...
Female - Femmes	68.8	...	...	...	...	...	...	...	...	...	...	...	...	...	...	...	...	...	...	...	...
Turkey - Turquie																					
2016 - 2018																					
Male - Hommes	75.6	71.5	66.6	61.7	56.9	52.1	47.3	42.5	37.7	33.0	28.4	24.0	19.9	16.2	12.8	9.8	7.3	5.2	3.8	3.1	3.7
Female - Femmes	81.0	76.9	72.0	67.1	62.1	57.2	52.3	47.4	42.5	37.7	32.9	28.3	23.7	19.4	15.4	11.7	8.7	6.3	4.7	4.0	4.2
United Arab Emirates - Émirats arabes unis																					
2006																					
Male - Hommes	76.7	72.5	67.6	62.7	57.9	53.1	48.3	43.5	38.7	33.9	29.3	24.8	20.7	16.9	13.8	11.3	10.2	...	...	...	...
Female - Femmes	78.8	74.5	69.5	64.6	59.7	54.8	49.8	44.9	40.0	35.2	30.4	25.8	21.6	18.0	15.4	14.0	14.5	...	...	...	...
2018																					
Male - Hommes	78.4	...	...	...	...	...	...	...	...	...	...	...	...	...	...	...	...	...	...	...	...
Female - Femmes	81.8	...	...	...	...	...	...	...	...	...	...	...	...	...	...	...	...	...	...	...	...
Uzbekistan - Ouzbékistan																					
2018																					
Male - Hommes	72.3	68.4	63.5	58.6	53.8	49.1	44.3	39.6	34.9	30.4	26.1	22.0	18.2	14.9	12.0	9.5	7.8	7.4	...	...	...
Female - Femmes	77.0	72.9	68.0	63.1	58.3	53.4	48.6	43.8	39.1	34.4	29.8	25.4	21.2	17.4	14.0	11.2	9.3	8.7	...	...	...
2019																					
Male - Hommes	72.8	...	...	...	...	...	...	...	...	...	...	...	...	...	...	...	...	...	...	...	...
Female - Femmes	77.4	...	...	...	...	...	...	...	...	...	...	...	...	...	...	...	...	...	...	...	...
Viet Nam																					
2018																					
Male - Hommes	70.9	67.9	63.1	58.2	53.5	48.7	44.0	39.3	34.6	30.1	25.9	21.9	18.3	15.1	12.3	10.1	8.3	...	...	...	...
Female - Femmes	76.2	72.3	67.4	62.5	57.6	52.7	47.8	43.0	38.3	33.6	29.1	24.8	20.7	16.9	13.7	11.0	8.9	...	...	...	...
2019[11]																					
Male - Hommes	71.0	...	...	...	...	...	...	...	...	...	...	...	...	...	...	...	...	...	...	...	...
Female - Femmes	76.3	...	...	...	...	...	...	...	...	...	...	...	...	...	...	...	...	...	...	...	...
Yemen - Yémen																					
2004																					
Male - Hommes	60.2	...	...	...	...	...	...	...	...	...	...	...	...	...	...	...	...	...	...	...	...
Female - Femmes	62.0	...	...	...	...	...	...	...	...	...	...	...	...	...	...	...	...	...	...	...	...
EUROPE																					
Åland Islands - Îles d'Åland																					
2018																					
Male - Hommes	80.9	75.9	70.9	65.9	60.9	55.9	50.9	45.9	40.9	36.8	31.9	27.4	23.0	19.1	15.1	11.3	8.4	6.7	5.0	3.7	1.0
Female - Femmes	85.0	80.0	75.0	70.0	65.0	60.5	55.5	50.8	46.0	41.3	36.3	31.6	26.7	22.2	18.2	14.2	10.4	7.3	4.7	3.3	1.0

22. Life expectancy at specified ages for each sex: latest available year, 2000 - 2019
Espérance de vie à un âge donné pour chaque sexe : dernière année disponible, 2000 - 2019 (continued - suite)

Continent, country or area and date / Continent, pays ou zone et date	Age (in years) - Age (en années) 0	5	10	15	20	25	30	35	40	45	50	55	60	65	70	75	80	85	90	95	100
EUROPE																					
Albania - Albanie																					
2018																					
Male - Hommes	77.4	73.2	68.2	63.3	58.4	53.6	48.8	44.0	39.2	34.5	29.9	25.5	21.2	17.2	13.5	10.0	7.1	4.9	...	...	...
Female - Femmes	80.5	76.2	71.3	66.4	61.5	56.6	51.6	46.7	41.9	37.0	32.3	27.5	22.9	18.5	14.2	10.2	6.8	3.9	...	...	...
Austria - Autriche																					
2018																					
Male - Hommes	79.3	74.6	69.6	64.6	59.7	54.9	50.0	45.2	40.4	35.6	31.0	26.5	22.3	18.3	14.7	11.4	8.2	5.7	3.8	2.5	1.7
Female - Femmes	83.9	79.2	74.2	69.2	64.3	59.3	54.4	49.5	44.6	39.7	34.9	30.3	25.7	21.4	17.2	13.3	9.6	6.5	4.2	2.8	1.9
Belarus - Bélarus																					
2018																					
Male - Hommes	69.3	64.5	59.6	54.6	49.7	44.9	40.2	35.6	31.1	26.9	22.9	19.2	15.9	13.0	10.5	8.3	6.3	4.9	...	...	...
Female - Femmes	79.5	74.7	69.7	64.8	59.8	54.9	50.0	45.2	40.4	35.7	31.2	26.7	22.4	18.3	14.5	11.0	8.0	5.7	...	...	...
Belgium - Belgique																					
2018																					
Male - Hommes	79.2	74.6	69.6	64.6	59.7	54.9	50.0	45.2	40.4	35.7	31.1	26.6	22.4	18.4	14.7	11.3	8.3	5.8	3.9	2.5	1.6
Female - Femmes	83.7	79.0	74.0	69.1	64.1	59.2	54.2	49.3	44.5	39.7	35.0	30.3	25.9	21.6	17.5	13.6	10.0	6.9	4.5	3.0	2.0
Bosnia and Herzegovina - Bosnie-Herzégovine																					
2003																					
Male - Hommes	71.3	...	...	...	...	...	...	...	...	...	...	...	...	...	...	...	...	...	...	...	...
Female - Femmes	76.7	...	...	...	...	...	...	...	...	...	...	...	...	...	...	...	...	...	...	...	...
Bulgaria - Bulgarie																					
2016 - 2018																					
Male - Hommes	71.4	67.0	62.0	57.1	52.3	47.5	42.7	37.9	33.3	28.8	24.6	20.7	17.2	14.1	11.3	8.7	6.4	4.6	3.1	2.2	0.5
Female - Femmes	78.4	74.0	69.0	64.0	59.1	54.2	49.3	44.5	39.6	35.0	30.4	26.0	21.8	17.8	14.0	10.4	7.4	5.1	3.4	2.3	0.5
Croatia - Croatie																					
2018																					
Male - Hommes	74.9	70.4	65.5	60.5	55.6	50.8	45.9	41.1	36.4	31.7	27.2	23.0	19.1	15.7	12.5	9.6	7.1	5.0	...	...	...
Female - Femmes	81.5	76.8	71.8	66.8	61.9	56.9	52.0	47.1	42.2	37.4	32.6	28.0	23.6	19.3	15.3	11.5	8.2	5.7	...	...	...
Czechia - Tchéquie																					
2018																					
Male - Hommes	76.1	71.3	66.4	61.4	56.5	51.7	46.9	42.1	37.4	32.7	28.2	23.9	19.8	16.1	12.9	10.0	7.4	5.2	3.6	2.5	1.9
Female - Femmes	81.9	77.1	72.2	67.2	62.2	57.3	52.4	47.5	42.6	37.8	33.0	28.4	23.9	19.7	15.7	12.0	8.6	5.9	3.9	2.6	1.8
Denmark - Danemark[43]																					
2017 - 2018																					
Male - Hommes	79.0	74.4	69.4	64.4	59.5	54.6	49.8	44.9	40.1	35.3	30.6	26.2	22.0	18.0	14.4	10.9	7.9	5.4	3.6	2.4	...
Female - Femmes	82.9	78.2	73.2	68.3	63.3	58.3	53.4	48.5	43.6	38.8	34.0	29.4	24.9	20.7	16.6	12.9	9.5	6.6	4.5	2.9	...
Estonia - Estonie																					
2018																					
Male - Hommes	73.9	69.1	64.1	59.2	54.3	49.5	44.7	40.0	35.4	30.8	26.5	22.5	18.8	15.5	12.5	9.9	7.5	5.2	3.7	2.3	1.0
Female - Femmes	82.4	77.6	72.6	67.6	62.7	57.8	52.9	48.0	43.2	38.4	33.7	29.1	24.6	20.3	16.4	12.7	9.3	6.4	4.3	3.0	2.1
Faroe Islands - Îles Féroé																					
2018 - 2019																					
Male - Hommes	80.4	75.4	70.4	65.4	60.5	55.7	50.9	45.9	41.1	36.1	31.3	26.6	22.3	18.4	14.8	11.4	7.6	5.4	3.6	1.7	2.0
Female - Femmes	85.3	80.3	75.3	70.3	65.3	60.3	55.3	50.3	45.3	40.5	35.6	30.7	25.9	21.6	17.8	13.7	10.3	7.6	4.8	3.0	1.9
Finland - Finlande[44]																					
2018																					
Male - Hommes	78.9	74.1	69.1	64.1	59.3	54.5	49.7	44.9	40.2	35.5	30.9	26.5	22.3	18.4	14.7	11.3	8.2	5.7	3.8	2.6	2.2
Female - Femmes	84.3	79.5	74.5	69.6	64.6	59.7	54.8	49.9	45.0	40.2	35.4	30.8	26.2	21.8	17.6	13.6	9.9	6.8	4.4	2.8	2.2
France																					
2014 - 2016																					
Male - Hommes	79.2	74.6	69.6	64.6	59.7	54.9	50.1	45.3	40.6	35.9	31.4	27.1	23.1	19.3	15.6	12.1	8.9	6.2	4.2	2.9	2.4
Female - Femmes	85.3	80.6	75.6	70.7	65.7	60.8	55.9	51.0	46.1	41.3	36.6	32.0	27.5	23.2	18.9	14.8	11.0	7.7	5.1	3.3	2.3
Germany - Allemagne																					
2016 - 2018																					
Male - Hommes	78.5	73.8	68.8	63.9	59.0	54.1	49.2	44.4	39.6	34.8	30.2	25.8	21.7	17.9	14.3	11.0	8.0	5.5	3.7	2.5	1.8
Female - Femmes	83.3	78.6	73.6	68.6	63.7	58.7	53.8	48.9	44.0	39.2	34.4	29.8	25.3	21.1	17.0	13.1	9.5	6.5	4.3	2.9	2.1
Gibraltar																					
2001																					
Male - Hommes	78.5	73.5	68.5	63.5	58.5	53.5	...	43.5	...	33.9	...	25.8	...	17.9	...	11.3	...	...	...	...	...
Female - Femmes	83.3	79.5	75.0	70.0	65.0	60.0	...	50.3	...	40.3	...	30.3	...	20.6	...	13.7	...	...	...	...	...

22. Life expectancy at specified ages for each sex: latest available year, 2000 - 2019
Espérance de vie à un âge donné pour chaque sexe : dernière année disponible, 2000 - 2019 (continued - suite)

Continent, country or area and date / Continent, pays ou zone et date	Age (in years) - Age (en années) 0	5	10	15	20	25	30	35	40	45	50	55	60	65	70	75	80	85	90	95	100
EUROPE																					
Greece - Grèce																					
2018																					
Male - Hommes	78.9	74.2	69.2	64.3	59.4	54.6	49.7	44.9	40.1	35.4	30.9	26.5	22.5	18.7	15.1	11.7	8.7	6.4	4.7	3.4	2.3
Female - Femmes	83.5	78.9	73.9	68.9	64.0	59.0	54.1	49.2	44.3	39.5	34.8	30.1	25.5	21.1	16.8	12.8	9.4	6.8	4.9	3.5	2.4
Guernsey - Guernesey[45]																					
2016 - 2018																					
Male - Hommes	80.2	...	...	...	...	...	...	...	...	...	...	...	...	...	...	...	...	...	...	...	...
Female - Femmes	84.4	...	...	...	...	...	...	...	...	...	...	...	...	...	...	...	...	...	...	...	...
Hungary - Hongrie																					
2018																					
Male - Hommes	72.6	67.9	62.9	57.9	53.0	48.2	43.3	38.5	33.8	29.2	24.8	20.8	17.4	14.3	11.6	8.9	6.6	4.4	2.7	1.5	0.6
Female - Femmes	79.2	74.5	69.5	64.5	59.6	54.7	49.8	44.9	40.0	35.2	30.6	26.2	22.0	18.1	14.3	10.7	7.6	4.9	2.9	1.5	0.6
Iceland - Islande																					
2017 - 2018																					
Male - Hommes	81.0	76.2	71.2	66.2	61.4	56.5	51.8	47.1	42.3	37.5	32.8	28.2	23.9	19.6	15.5	11.9	8.6	6.0	4.1	2.7	1.5
Female - Femmes	84.1	79.4	74.4	69.4	64.5	59.5	54.5	49.6	44.8	39.9	35.1	30.4	25.8	21.3	16.9	12.9	9.5	6.7	4.6	2.7	1.5
Ireland - Irlande																					
2018																					
Male - Hommes	80.5	75.8	70.8	65.8	60.9	56.0	51.1	46.3	41.5	36.7	32.1	27.5	23.2	19.1	15.2	11.7	8.7	6.3	...	...	...
Female - Femmes	84.1	79.4	74.4	69.4	64.5	59.5	54.6	49.7	44.8	40.0	35.2	30.6	26.1	21.6	17.5	13.6	10.2	7.3	...	...	...
Italy - Italie																					
2018																					
Male - Hommes	80.9	76.2	71.2	66.2	61.3	56.5	51.6	46.7	41.9	37.1	32.4	27.9	23.5	19.3	15.4	11.8	8.7	6.0	4.1	2.8	2.0
Female - Femmes	85.2	80.5	75.5	70.5	65.6	60.6	55.7	50.7	45.8	41.0	36.2	31.5	26.9	22.5	18.2	14.1	10.3	7.2	4.8	3.2	2.2
Latvia - Lettonie																					
2018																					
Male - Hommes	70.0	65.3	60.4	55.4	50.7	45.9	41.2	36.7	32.3	28.2	24.1	20.5	17.1	14.0	11.4	9.0	6.8	5.0	3.6	2.6	1.9
Female - Femmes	79.6	74.9	69.9	65.0	60.0	55.2	50.3	45.5	40.7	36.1	31.6	27.2	22.9	18.9	15.2	11.6	8.4	5.8	3.9	2.7	2.0
Lithuania - Lituanie																					
2018																					
Male - Hommes	70.9	66.2	61.3	56.3	51.5	46.8	42.1	37.6	33.2	29.0	24.9	21.1	17.5	14.4	11.7	9.3	7.1	5.0	3.4	2.3	1.5
Female - Femmes	80.6	75.9	70.9	66.0	61.1	56.2	51.3	46.5	41.7	37.0	32.4	28.0	23.6	19.5	15.6	11.9	8.6	5.8	3.8	2.7	1.8
Luxembourg																					
2016 - 2018																					
Male - Hommes	80.0	75.2	70.2	65.2	60.3	55.4	50.5	45.6	40.8	36.0	31.3	26.8	22.5	18.5	14.8	11.5	8.3	5.8	3.7	2.8	...
Female - Femmes	84.5	79.7	74.7	69.7	64.7	59.8	54.9	49.9	45.0	40.2	35.4	30.7	26.1	21.7	17.6	13.7	10.1	7.0	4.8	3.3	...
Malta - Malte																					
2018																					
Male - Hommes	80.4	76.1	71.1	66.1	61.1	56.2	51.4	46.5	41.7	36.9	32.1	27.7	23.3	19.2	15.3	11.9	8.8	6.4	...	...	...
Female - Femmes	84.6	80.0	75.0	70.0	65.0	60.1	55.1	50.3	45.4	40.6	35.8	31.2	26.6	22.3	18.0	14.0	10.4	7.6	...	...	...
Netherlands - Pays-Bas																					
2018																					
Male - Hommes	80.3	75.6	70.7	65.7	60.8	55.9	51.0	46.1	41.3	36.5	31.8	27.2	22.9	18.7	14.9	11.4	8.3	5.8	...	...	...
Female - Femmes	83.4	78.7	73.7	68.7	63.8	58.8	53.9	49.0	44.1	39.3	34.5	29.9	25.4	21.1	17.0	13.1	9.6	6.6	...	...	...
North Macedonia - Macédoine du Nord																					
2018																					
Male - Hommes	74.6	70.1	65.2	60.3	55.4	50.5	45.6	40.8	36.0	31.3	26.8	22.5	18.6	14.9	11.7	8.7	6.2	4.2	...	...	...
Female - Femmes	78.8	74.2	69.2	64.3	59.3	54.4	49.4	44.5	39.6	34.8	30.1	25.5	21.2	17.1	13.2	9.7	6.9	4.9	...	...	...
Norway - Norvège																					
2018																					
Male - Hommes	81.0	76.2	71.2	66.3	61.4	56.5	51.7	46.9	42.1	37.3	32.6	28.0	23.5	19.3	15.4	11.7	8.5	5.9	4.0	2.6	1.8
Female - Femmes	84.5	79.7	74.7	69.7	64.8	59.8	54.9	50.0	45.1	40.2	35.4	30.7	26.2	21.8	17.6	13.6	10.0	7.0	4.6	3.0	2.1
Poland - Pologne																					
2018																					
Male - Hommes	73.9	69.2	64.2	59.3	54.4	49.7	44.9	40.2	35.6	31.1	26.8	22.8	19.1	15.8	12.9	10.2	7.8	5.9	4.4	3.3	2.4
Female - Femmes	81.7	77.0	72.0	67.1	62.2	57.2	52.3	47.4	42.6	37.8	33.1	28.5	24.2	20.1	16.3	12.7	9.4	6.8	4.8	3.4	2.4
Portugal																					
2016 - 2018																					
Male - Hommes	77.8	73.1	68.1	63.2	58.2	53.4	48.5	43.7	38.9	34.2	29.7	25.5	21.4	17.6	13.8	10.3	7.2	4.5	2.7	1.7	1.1
Female - Femmes	83.4	78.7	73.7	68.8	63.8	58.9	53.9	49.0	44.1	39.3	34.6	29.9	25.4	20.9	16.5	12.4	8.6	5.4	3.2	2.0	1.2

22. Life expectancy at specified ages for each sex: latest available year, 2000 - 2019
Espérance de vie à un âge donné pour chaque sexe : dernière année disponible, 2000 - 2019 (continued - suite)

Continent, country or area and date - Continent, pays ou zone et date	Age (in years) - Age (en années) 0	5	10	15	20	25	30	35	40	45	50	55	60	65	70	75	80	85	90	95	100
EUROPE																					
Republic of Moldova - République de Moldova[46]																					
2012																					
Male - Hommes	67.2	63.1	58.1	53.3	48.5	43.7	39.0	34.5	30.1	26.0	22.2	18.7	15.5	13.0	10.2	8.4	7.1	6.9	7.8	...	...
Female - Femmes	75.0	70.9	66.0	61.0	56.1	51.2	46.4	41.5	36.8	32.2	27.7	23.4	19.3	15.7	12.2	9.5	7.4	5.9	5.3	...	...
2017																					
Male - Hommes	69.4	...	...	...	...	...	...	...	...	...	...	...	...	...	...	...	...	...	...	...	...
Female - Femmes	77.0	...	...	...	...	...	...	...	...	...	...	...	...	...	...	...	...	...	...	...	...
Romania - Roumanie																					
2016 - 2018																					
Male - Hommes	72.4	68.0	63.1	58.2	53.3	48.5	43.7	38.9	34.2	29.6	25.3	21.4	17.9	14.7	11.8	9.1	6.9	5.1	3.8	2.8	0.9
Female - Femmes	79.4	75.0	70.0	65.1	60.1	55.2	50.3	45.4	40.5	35.8	31.1	26.6	22.3	18.2	14.4	10.9	7.9	5.5	3.9	2.6	0.8
Russian Federation - Fédération de Russie																					
2012																					
Male - Hommes	64.6	60.3	55.4	50.5	45.8	41.3	37.0	33.1	29.3	25.4	21.8	18.4	15.4	12.8	10.2	8.1	6.4	5.1	4.0	3.0	1.4
Female - Femmes	75.9	71.6	66.7	61.7	56.9	52.1	47.3	42.8	38.2	33.7	29.3	25.1	21.0	17.1	13.4	10.2	7.4	5.3	3.8	2.8	1.8
San Marino - Saint-Marin																					
2017																					
Male - Hommes	82.7	77.9	72.9	67.9	63.0	58.2	53.3	48.3	43.4	38.5	33.7	29.0	24.6	20.2	16.1	12.2	8.9	6.4	4.2	2.2	...
Female - Femmes	86.8	82.0	77.0	72.0	67.1	62.1	57.1	52.2	47.2	42.4	37.6	32.8	28.1	23.5	19.1	14.8	10.8	7.4	4.8	2.7	...
Serbia - Serbie[47]																					
2018																					
Male - Hommes	73.2	68.7	63.7	58.8	53.9	49.0	44.2	39.4	34.7	30.1	25.6	21.5	17.8	14.4	11.4	8.6	6.2	4.3	...	...	...
Female - Femmes	78.1	73.5	68.6	63.6	58.7	53.7	48.8	43.9	39.1	34.3	29.6	25.2	20.9	16.9	13.1	9.6	6.7	4.5	...	...	...
Slovakia - Slovaquie																					
2018																					
Male - Hommes	73.7	69.2	64.2	59.3	54.4	49.6	44.8	40.0	35.3	30.8	26.4	22.3	18.6	15.2	12.1	9.3	6.8	4.7	3.2	2.0	1.3
Female - Femmes	80.4	75.8	70.8	65.9	61.0	56.0	51.1	46.2	41.3	36.5	31.9	27.4	23.0	18.8	14.8	11.1	7.9	5.2	3.2	1.9	1.1
Slovenia - Slovénie																					
2018																					
Male - Hommes	78.3	73.5	68.5	63.6	58.7	53.9	49.0	44.1	39.4	34.7	30.0	25.6	21.4	17.6	14.1	10.8	7.9	5.4	3.8	2.9	2.0
Female - Femmes	84.0	79.1	74.2	69.2	64.2	59.3	54.3	49.4	44.5	39.7	34.9	30.2	25.7	21.4	17.3	13.3	9.7	6.7	4.5	3.1	2.1
Spain - Espagne																					
2018																					
Male - Hommes	80.5	75.7	70.8	65.8	60.9	56.0	51.1	46.2	41.3	36.6	31.9	27.4	23.2	19.2	15.5	12.0	8.8	6.2	4.3	3.0	1.8
Female - Femmes	85.8	81.1	76.1	71.1	66.2	61.2	56.3	51.4	46.4	41.6	36.8	32.1	27.5	23.1	18.7	14.5	10.6	7.4	4.9	3.3	2.1
Sweden - Suède																					
2018																					
Male - Hommes	80.9	76.1	71.1	66.1	61.2	56.4	51.6	46.8	42.0	37.2	32.4	27.8	23.4	19.2	15.3	11.7	8.5	5.9	...	...	...
Female - Femmes	84.3	79.5	74.5	69.5	64.6	59.7	54.8	49.9	45.0	40.1	35.3	30.6	26.0	21.6	17.4	13.5	9.9	6.9	...	...	...
Switzerland - Suisse																					
2018																					
Male - Hommes	81.9	77.2	72.2	67.3	62.4	57.5	52.6	47.7	42.9	38.1	33.4	28.8	24.4	20.2	16.3	12.6	9.3	6.6	...	...	...
Female - Femmes	85.7	81.0	76.0	71.1	66.1	61.2	56.2	51.3	46.4	41.5	36.7	32.0	27.4	23.0	18.7	14.6	10.8	7.7	...	...	...
Ukraine[48]																					
2017																					
Male - Hommes	67.0	62.7	57.7	52.8	48.0	43.3	38.7	34.3	30.2	26.2	22.4	18.8	15.5	12.7	10.1	7.9	6.2	4.8	3.8	3.0	2.1
Female - Femmes	76.8	72.4	67.4	62.5	57.6	52.7	47.9	43.1	38.5	33.9	29.4	25.1	20.8	16.8	13.2	9.9	7.1	5.0	3.4	2.3	1.5
United Kingdom of Great Britain and Northern Ireland - Royaume-Uni de Grande-Bretagne et d'Irlande du Nord[49]																					
2016 - 2018																					
Male - Hommes	79.3	74.6	69.7	64.7	59.8	54.9	50.1	45.3	40.6	35.9	31.4	26.9	22.7	18.6	14.9	11.4	8.4	5.9	4.1	2.8	2.0
Female - Femmes	82.9	78.3	73.3	68.3	63.4	58.4	53.5	48.6	43.8	39.0	34.3	29.7	25.3	21.0	16.9	13.1	9.7	6.8	4.6	3.1	2.2

22. Life expectancy at specified ages for each sex: latest available year, 2000 - 2019
Espérance de vie à un âge donné pour chaque sexe : dernière année disponible, 2000 - 2019 (continued - suite)

Continent, country or area and date / Continent, pays ou zone et date	Age (in years) - Age (en années) 0	5	10	15	20	25	30	35	40	45	50	55	60	65	70	75	80	85	90	95	100
OCEANIA - OCÉANIE																					
American Samoa - Samoas américaines																					
2011																					
Male - Hommes	71.1	66.8	61.9	57.0	52.2	47.4	42.6	38.0	33.5	29.1	25.3	21.4	18.0	14.6	11.7	9.6	...	...	...	...	...
Female - Femmes	77.8	73.3	68.3	63.4	58.5	53.6	48.9	44.4	39.6	35.0	30.6	26.5	22.8	19.2	16.1	13.8	...	...	...	...	...
Australia - Australie																					
2016 - 2018																					
Male - Hommes	80.7	76.1	71.1	66.1	61.3	56.4	51.6	46.8	42.1	37.4	32.8	28.3	24.0	19.9	15.9	12.3	9.1	6.4	4.4	3.2	2.1
Female - Femmes	84.9	80.2	75.2	70.2	65.3	60.4	55.5	50.6	45.7	40.9	36.2	31.5	27.0	22.6	18.3	14.3	10.6	7.5	5.0	3.4	2.2
Cook Islands - Îles Cook																					
2006																					
Male - Hommes	69.5	66.0	61.3	56.5	52.0	47.4	42.8	38.1	33.6	29.1	24.8	20.9	17.5	14.3	11.4	9.0	7.3	...	...	...	...
Female - Femmes	76.2	72.4	67.4	62.4	57.4	52.7	48.0	43.2	38.4	33.6	29.1	24.7	20.4	16.4	12.6	9.5	6.9	...	...	...	...
Fiji - Fidji																					
2015 - 2017																					
Male - Hommes	65.4	62.1	57.3	52.4	47.6	42.9	38.3	33.7	29.2	24.8	20.8	17.1	13.8	10.7	7.7	4.6	...	...	...	...	...
Female - Femmes	68.5	64.8	60.0	55.1	50.3	45.6	40.8	36.2	31.6	27.2	22.9	19.0	15.3	11.8	8.3	4.7	...	...	...	...	...
French Polynesia - Polynésie française																					
2018																					
Male - Hommes	73.2	71.1	66.1	61.3	56.5	51.7	47.2	42.6	37.9	33.5	29.0	24.9	20.9	17.1	13.8	11.3	8.5	6.7	4.9	4.3	...
Female - Femmes	78.8	76.1	71.1	66.2	61.4	56.4	51.5	46.7	41.8	37.1	32.3	27.9	23.7	19.9	16.1	12.6	9.4	7.0	5.0	2.8	...
Guam																					
2017																					
Male - Hommes	73.6	...	...	...	...	...	...	...	...	...	...	...	...	...	...	...	...	...	...	...	...
Female - Femmes	78.6	...	...	...	...	...	...	...	...	...	...	...	...	...	...	...	...	...	...	...	...
Kiribati																					
2005																					
Male - Hommes	58.9	58.2	53.6	48.9	44.4	40.0	35.6	31.3	27.1	23.1	19.4	16.0	13.0	10.4	8.3	6.6	5.3	4.2	...	...	...
Female - Femmes	63.1	62.6	57.9	53.1	48.6	44.1	39.7	35.4	31.2	27.1	23.2	19.5	16.1	13.1	10.4	8.1	6.2	4.7	...	...	...
Marshall Islands - Îles Marshall																					
2004																					
Male - Hommes	67.0	...	...	...	...	...	...	...	...	...	...	...	...	...	...	...	...	...	...	...	...
Female - Femmes	70.6	...	...	...	...	...	...	...	...	...	...	...	...	...	...	...	...	...	...	...	...
Micronesia (Federated States of) - Micronésie (États fédérés de)																					
2000																					
Male - Hommes	66.5	...	...	...	...	...	...	...	...	...	...	...	...	...	...	...	...	...	...	...	...
Female - Femmes	67.5	...	...	...	...	...	...	...	...	...	...	...	...	...	...	...	...	...	...	...	...
Nauru[50]																					
2011																					
Male - Hommes	56.8	...	...	...	...	...	...	...	...	...	...	...	...	...	...	...	...	...	...	...	...
Female - Femmes	62.7	...	...	...	...	...	...	...	...	...	...	...	...	...	...	...	...	...	...	...	...
New Caledonia - Nouvelle-Calédonie																					
2017																					
Male - Hommes	75.1	70.1	65.2	60.2	55.2	50.3	45.5	40.6	35.8	31.1	26.5	...	21.9	...	13.4	...	6.2	...	...	...	...
Female - Femmes	80.1	75.1	70.2	65.2	60.3	55.3	50.4	45.5	40.6	35.7	30.9	...	26.2	...	17.0	...	8.6	...	...	...	...
New Zealand - Nouvelle-Zélande																					
2017 - 2019																					
Male - Hommes	80.0	75.4	70.4	65.5	60.7	55.9	51.1	46.4	41.6	36.9	32.3	27.9	23.6	19.5	15.6	12.0	8.8	6.3	...	...	...
Female - Femmes	83.5	78.9	74.0	69.0	64.1	59.2	54.3	49.5	44.6	39.8	35.1	30.5	26.0	21.7	17.5	13.6	10.0	7.0	...	...	...
Niue - Nioué																					
2007 - 2011																					
Male - Hommes	70.1	...	...	...	...	...	...	...	...	...	...	...	...	...	...	...	...	...	...	...	...
Female - Femmes	76.3	...	...	...	...	...	...	...	...	...	...	...	...	...	...	...	...	...	...	...	...
Northern Mariana Islands - Îles Mariannes septentrionales																					
2009																					
Male - Hommes	74.5	...	...	...	...	...	...	...	...	...	...	...	...	...	...	...	...	...	...	...	...
Female - Femmes	79.9	...	...	...	...	...	...	...	...	...	...	...	...	...	...	...	...	...	...	...	...

22. Life expectancy at specified ages for each sex: latest available year, 2000 - 2019
Espérance de vie à un âge donné pour chaque sexe : dernière année disponible, 2000 - 2019 (continued - suite)

Continent, country or area and date / Continent, pays ou zone et date	Age (in years) - Age (en années)																				
	0	5	10	15	20	25	30	35	40	45	50	55	60	65	70	75	80	85	90	95	100
OCEANIA - OCÉANIE																					
Palau - Palaos																					
2005																					
Male - Hommes	66.3	...	...	...	...	...	...	...	...	...	...	...	...	...	...	...	...	...	...	...	...
Female - Femmes	72.1	...	...	...	...	...	...	...	...	...	...	...	...	...	...	...	...	...	...	...	...
Papua New Guinea - Papouasie-Nouvelle-Guinée																					
2000																					
Male - Hommes	53.7	54.1	50.2	45.7	41.6	37.7	33.7	29.8	25.9	22.1	18.5	15.0	11.9	9.2	6.9	5.0	3.6	2.6	1.7	0.6	...
Female - Femmes	54.8	54.7	50.8	46.3	42.1	38.1	34.1	30.1	26.2	22.3	18.6	15.2	12.0	9.2	6.8	5.0	3.6	2.5	1.6	0.6	...
Samoa																					
2016																					
Male - Hommes	73.7	69.9	65.0	60.0	55.3	50.6	45.7	41.2	36.5	31.9	27.4	23.5	20.1	16.9	13.5	9.9	7.2	4.5	...	...	...
Female - Femmes	76.0	72.4	67.6	62.7	57.9	53.2	48.4	43.8	39.2	34.6	30.4	26.4	22.4	18.5	14.9	11.3	8.2	4.6	...	...	...
Solomon Islands - Îles Salomon																					
2009																					
Male - Hommes	66.2	...	...	...	...	...	...	...	...	...	...	...	...	...	...	...	...	...	...	...	...
Female - Femmes	73.1	...	...	...	...	...	...	...	...	...	...	...	...	...	...	...	...	...	...	...	...
Tonga																					
2006																					
Male - Hommes	67.3	64.1	59.3	54.5	49.9	45.4	40.7	36.2	31.6	27.2	23.4	19.4	15.9	13.0	9.4	6.3	4.0	...	...	...	...
Female - Femmes	73.0	69.3	64.6	59.8	55.0	50.1	45.2	40.4	35.7	31.3	27.1	23.0	19.0	15.3	11.6	8.6	6.1	...	...	...	...
2010																					
Male - Hommes	65.0	...	...	...	...	...	...	...	...	...	...	...	...	...	...	...	...	...	...	...	...
Female - Femmes	69.0	...	...	...	...	...	...	...	...	...	...	...	...	...	...	...	...	...	...	...	...
Tuvalu																					
1997 - 2002																					
Male - Hommes	61.7	59.5	54.8	50.0	45.2	40.6	35.9	32.1	28.0	24.1	20.0	17.1	13.7	10.8	9.0	6.9	5.4	...	...	...	...
Female - Femmes	65.1	62.6	57.7	53.7	50.0	45.3	40.9	36.6	32.2	28.1	23.8	20.3	16.9	13.2	10.6	7.9	6.4	...	...	...	...
Vanuatu[51]																					
2009																					
Male - Hommes	69.6	66.4	61.6	56.8	52.1	47.5	42.8	38.1	33.5	29.0	24.7	20.6	16.8	13.4	10.4	7.9	6.0	...	...	...	...
Female - Femmes	72.7	69.3	64.5	59.5	54.7	49.9	45.1	40.3	35.5	30.8	26.3	22.0	18.0	14.4	11.2	8.5	6.4	...	...	...	...
Wallis and Futuna Islands - Îles Wallis et Futuna																					
2003																					
Male - Hommes	73.1	...	...	...	...	...	...	...	...	...	...	...	...	...	...	...	...	...	...	...	...
Female - Femmes	75.5	...	...	...	...	...	...	...	...	...	...	...	...	...	...	...	...	...	...	...	...

FOOTNOTES - NOTES

[1] Data refer to Algerian population only. - Les données ne concernent que la population algérienne.

[2] Based on the results of the Population Census. - D'après les résultats du recensement de la population.

[3] Data refer to national projections. - Les données se réfèrent aux projections nationales.

[4] Based on the results of the 2006 Population and Housing Census. - Données fondées sur les résultats du recensement de la population et de l'habitat de 2006.

[5] Data refer to the 12 months preceding the census in June. - Les données se rapportent aux 12 mois précédant le recensement de juin.

[6] Data based on the 2010 Population Census. - Les données sont fondées sur le recensement de la population de 2010.

[7] Source: Department of Statistics and Demographic Studies (DISED); 2002 EDAM-IS2 and 2002 EDSF/PAPFAM surveys - Source : Direction de la Statistique et des Etudes Démographiques (DISED); 2002 Enquête Djiboutienne auprès des Ménages (EDAM-IS2) et 2002 Enquête Djiboutienne sur la Sante de la Famille (EDSF/PAPFAM - 2002)

[8] Data refer to projections based on the 2007 Population Census. - Les données se réfèrent aux projections basées sur le recensement de la population de 2007.

[9] Based on the results of the 2010 Population Census. - D'après le résultats du recensement de la population de 2010.

[10] Based on underlying data of the Population and Housing Census 2014. - Données fondées sur le recensement de la population de 2014.

[11] Data refer to the 12 months preceding the census in April. - Les données se rapportent aux douze mois précédant le recensement d'avril.

[12] Data refer to projections based on the 1993 Population Census. - Les données se réfèrent aux projections basées sur le recensement de la population de 1993.

[13] Excludes the islands of St. Brandon and Agalega. - Non compris les îles St. Brandon et Agalega.

[14] Provisional data. - Données provisoires.

[15] Data refer to Saint Helenian resident population. - Pour la population résidante de Sainte-Hélène.

[16] Data refer to the 12 months preceding the census in December. - Les données se rapportent aux 12 mois précédant le recensement de décembre.

[17] Based on underlying data of the 2002 Population Census. - Données fondées sur le recensement de la population de 2002.

[18] Based on the results of the 2014 Population Census. Provisional data. - D'après les résultats du recensement de la population de 2014. Données provisoires.

[19] Data are based on a small number of deaths. - Les données sont basées sur un nombre limité de décès.

[20] Data refer to projections based on the 1992 Population Census. - Les données se réfèrent aux projections basées sur le recensement de la population de 1992.

[21] Excluding Indian jungle population. - Non compris les Indiens de la jungle.

22 Data refer to the 12 months from 30 June 2016 to 30 June 2017. - Les données font référence aux douze mois de 30 juin 2016 à 30 juin 2017.
23 Data refer to the 12 months from 30 June 2018 to 30 June 2019. Data refer to national projections. - Les données font référence aux douze mois de 30 juin 2018 à 30 juin 2019. Les données se réfèrent aux projections nationales.
24 Estimates or projections based on the 2017 Population Census. - Estimations ou projections fondées sur le recensement de la population de 2017.
25 Excludes nomadic Indian tribes. Data based on the 2010 Population Census. - Non compris les tribus d'Indiens nomades. Les données sont fondées sur le recensement de la population de 2010.
26 Based on the results of the 2012 Population and Housing Census. - D'après les résultats du recensement de la population et des logements de 2012.
27 Based on the results of the 2011 Population Census. - Basé sur les résultats du recencement de la population de 2011.
28 For statistical purposes, the data for China do not include those for the Hong Kong Special Administrative Region (Hong Kong SAR), Macao Special Administrative Region (Macao SAR) and Taiwan province of China. - Pour la présentation des statistiques, les données pour la Chine ne comprennent pas la Région Administrative Spéciale de Hong Kong (Hong Kong RAS), la Région Administrative Spéciale de Macao (Macao RAS) et Taïwan province de Chine.
29 Data refer to government controlled areas. - Les données se rapportent aux zones contrôlées par le Gouvernement.
30 Includes data for the Indian-held part of Jammu and Kashmir, the final status of which has not yet been determined. Based on the Sample Registration System of India, which is a large demographic survey. - Y compris les données pour la partie du Jammu et du Cachemire occupée par l'Inde dont le statut définitif n'a pas encore été déterminé. Les données sont fondées sur le Système de l'enregistrement par échantillon de l'Inde qui est une large enquête démographique.
31 Data are based on the publication: "Indonesia Population Projection 2015-2045" - Les données sont basées sur la publication : << Indonesia Population Projection 2015-2045 >>
32 Data refer to the Iranian Year which begins on 21 March and ends on 20 March of the following year. - Les données concernent l'année iranienne, qui commence le 21 mars et se termine le 20 mars de l'année suivante.
33 Includes data for East Jerusalem and Israeli residents in certain other territories under occupation by Israeli military forces since June 1967. - Y compris les données pour Jérusalem-Est et les résidents israéliens dans certains autres territoires occupés depuis 1967 par les forces armées israéliennes.
34 Data refer to Japanese nationals in Japan only. - Les données se raportent aux nationaux japonais au Japon seulement.
35 Excluding data for Jordanian territory under occupation since June 1967 by Israeli military forces. Excluding foreigners, including registered Palestinian refugees. - Non compris les données pour le territoire jordanien occupé depuis juin 1967 par les forces armées israéliennes. Non compris les étrangers, mais y compris les réfugiés de Palestine enregistrés.
36 Based on underlying data of the 2015 census. - Données fondées sur celles extraites du recensement de 2015.
37 Based on Vital Registration System (VRS). - Système d'enregistrement des faits d'état civil.
38 Data refer to Omani citizen only. - Les données concernent les citoyens d'Oman uniquement.
39 Based on the results of the Pakistan Demographic Survey. Excluding data for the Pakistan-held part of Jammu and Kashmir, the final status of which has not yet been determined. - Données extraites de l'enquête démographique effectuée par le Pakistan. Non compris les données concernant la partie du Jammu et Cachemire occupée par le Pakistan dont le statut définitif n'a pas été déterminé.
40 Data taken from the 2010 Census-based population projection. - Données tirées de la projection démographique établie à partir du recensement de 2010.
41 Data refer to Saudi Arabian nationals only. - Les données ne concernent que les ressortissants saoudiens.
42 Data refer to resident population which comprises Singapore citizens and permanent residents. Provisional data. - Les données se rapportent à la population résidente composé des citoyens de Singapour et des résidents permanents. Données provisoires.
43 Excluding Faeroe Islands and Greenland shown separately, if available. - Non compris les Iles Féroé et le Groenland, qui font l'objet de rubriques distinctes, si disponible.
44 Excluding Åland Islands. - Non compris les Îles d'Åland.
45 Data is a three year average for the years 2016-2018. - Les données correspondent à une moyenne de trois ans couvrant les années 2016 à 2018.
46 Excluding Transnistria and the municipality of Bender. - Les données ne tiennent pas compte de l'information sur la Transnistria et la municipalité de Bender.
47 Excludes data for Kosovo and Metohia. - Sans les données pour le Kosovo et Metohie.
48 The Government of Ukraine has informed the United Nations that it is not in a position to provide statistical data concerning the Autonomous Republic of Crimea and the city of Sevastopol. - Le gouvernement Ukrainien a informé l'ONU qu'il n'est pas en mesure de fournir des données statistiques concernant la République autonome de Crimée et la ville de Sébastopol.
49 Excluding Channel Islands (Guernsey and Jersey) and Isle of Man, shown separately, if available. - Non compris les îles Anglo-Normandes (Guernesey et Jersey) et l'île de Man, qui font l'objet de rubriques distinctes, si disponible.
50 Data refer to the 12 months preceding the census in October. - Les données se rapportent aux 12 mois précédant le recensement de octobre.
51 Based on underlying data of the 2009 census. - Données fondées sur celles extraites du recensement de 2009.

Table 23 - *Demographic Yearbook 2019*

Table 23 presents the number of marriages and crude marriage rates by urban/rural residence for every year with available data between 2015 and 2019.

Description of variables: Marriage is defined as the act, ceremony or process by which the legal relationship of spouses is constituted. The legality of the union may be established by civil, religious or other means as recognized by the laws of each country[1].

Marriage statistics in this table, therefore, include both first marriages and remarriages after divorce, widowhood or annulment. They do not, unless otherwise noted, include resumption of marriage ties after legal separation. These statistics refer to the number of marriages performed, and not to the number of persons marrying.

Statistics shown are obtained from civil registers of marriage. Exceptions, such as data from church registers, are identified in footnotes.

The urban/rural classification of marriages is that provided by each country or area; it is presumed to be based on the national census definitions of urban population which have been set forth at the end of the notes for table 6.

For certain countries, there is a discrepancy between the total number of marriages shown in this table and those shown in subsequent tables for the same year. Usually this discrepancy arises because the total number of marriages occurring in a given year is revised although the remaining tabulations are not.

Rate computation: Crude marriage rates are the annual number of marriages per 1 000 mid-year population. Rates by urban/rural residence are the annual number of marriages, in the appropriate urban or rural category, per 1 000 corresponding mid-year population. Rates presented in this table have been limited to those for countries or areas having at least a total of 30 marriages in a given year. These rates are calculated by the Statistics Division of the United Nations based on the appropriate reference population (for example: total population, nationals only, etc.) if known and available. If the reference population is not known or unavailable the total population is used to calculate the rates. Therefore, if the population that is used to calculate the rates is different from the correct reference population, the rates presented might under- or overstate the true situation in a country or area.

Reliability of data: Each country or area has been asked to indicate the estimated completeness of the number of marriages recorded in its civil register. These national assessments are indicated by the quality codes "C" and "U" that appear in the first column of this table.

"C" indicates that the data are estimated to be virtually complete, that is, representing at least 90 per cent of the marriages occurring each year, while "U" indicates that data are estimated to be incomplete, that is representing less than 90 per cent of the marriages occurring each year. The code "..." indicates that no information was provided regarding completeness.

Data from civil registers which are reported as incomplete or of unknown completeness (coded "U" or "...") are considered unreliable. They appear in italics in this table; rates are not computed for these data.

These quality codes apply only to data from civil registers. For more information about the quality of vital statistics data in general, see section 4.2 of the Technical Notes.

Limitations: Statistics on marriages are subject to the same qualifications that have been set forth for vital statistics in general and marriage statistics in particular as discussed in section 4 of the Technical Notes.

The fact that marriage is a legal event, unlike birth and death that are biological events, has implications for international comparability of data. Marriage has been defined, for statistical purposes, in terms of the laws of individual countries or areas. These laws vary throughout the world. In addition, comparability is further limited because some countries or areas compile statistics only for civil marriages although religious marriages may also be legally recognized; in other countries or areas, the only available records are church registers and, therefore, the statistics may not reflect marriages that are civil marriages only.

Because in many countries or areas marriage is a civil legal contract which, to establish its legality, must be celebrated before a civil officer, it follows that for these countries or areas registration would tend to be almost automatic at the time of, or immediately following, the marriage ceremony. This factor should be kept in mind when considering the reliability of data, described above. For this reason the practice of tabulating data by date of registration does not generally pose serious problems of comparability as it does in the case of birth and death statistics.

As indicators of family formation, the statistics on the number of marriages presented in this table are bound to be deficient to the extent that they do not include either customary unions, which are not registered even though they are considered legal and binding under customary law, or consensual unions (also known as extra-legal or de facto unions). In general, lower marriage rates over a period of years are an indication of higher incidence of customary or consensual unions.

In addition, rates are affected also by the quality and limitations of the population estimates that are used in their computation. The problems of under-enumeration or over-enumeration and, to some extent, the differences in definition of total population have been discussed in section 3 of the Technical Notes dealing with population data in general, and specific information pertaining to individual countries or areas is given in the footnotes to table 3.

Strict correspondence between the numerator of the rate and the denominator is not always obtained; for example, marriages among civilian and military segments of the population may be related to civilian population. The effect of this may be to increase the rates, but, in most cases, this effect is negligible.

It should be emphasized that crude marriage rates like crude birth, death and divorce rates, may be seriously affected by the age-sex-marital structure of the population to which they relate. Crude marriage rates do, however, provide a simple measure of the level and changes in marriage.

The comparability of data by urban/rural residence is affected by the national definitions of urban and rural used in tabulating these data. It is assumed, in the absence of specific information to the contrary, that the definitions of urban and rural used in connection with the national population census were also used in the compilation of the vital statistics for each country or area. However, it cannot be excluded that, for a given country or area, different definitions of urban and rural are used for the vital statistics data and the population census data respectively. When known, the definitions of urban in national population censuses are presented at the end of the technical notes for table 6. As discussed in detail in the notes, these definitions vary considerably from one country or area to another.

In addition to problems of comparability, marriage rates classified by urban/rural residence are also subject to certain special types of bias. If, when calculating marriage rates, different definitions of urban are used in connection with the vital events and the population data, and if this results in a net difference between the numerator and denominator of the rate in the population at risk, then the marriage rates would be biased. Urban/rural differentials in marriage rates may also be affected by whether the vital events have been tabulated in terms of place of occurrence or place of usual residence. This problem is discussed in more detail in section 4.1.4.1 of the Technical Notes.

Earlier data: Marriages and crude marriage rates have been shown in each issue of the *Demographic Yearbook*. For more information on specific topics, and years for which data are reported, readers should consult the Historical Index.

NOTES

[1] *Principles and Recommendations for a Vital Statistics System Revision 3,* Sales No. E.13.XVII.10, United Nations, New York, 2014.

Tableau 23 – *Annuaire démographique 2019*

Le tableau 23 présente des données sur les mariages et les taux bruts de nuptialité selon le lieu de résidence (zone urbaine ou rurale) pour les années où l'information est disponible entre 2015 et 2019.

Description des variables : le mariage désigne l'acte, la cérémonie ou la procédure qui établit un rapport légal entre les époux. L'union peut être rendue légale par une procédure civile ou religieuse, ou par toute autre procédure, conformément à la législation du pays[1].

Les statistiques de la nuptialité présentées dans ce tableau comprennent donc les premiers mariages et les remariages faisant suite à un divorce, un veuvage ou une annulation. Toutefois, sauf indication contraire, elles ne comprennent pas les unions reconstituées après une séparation légale. Ces statistiques se rapportent au nombre de mariages célébrés, non au nombre de personnes qui se marient.

Les statistiques présentées reposent sur l'enregistrement des mariages par les services de l'état civil. Les exceptions (données provenant des registres des églises, par exemple) font l'objet d'une note à la fin du tableau.

La classification des mariages selon le lieu de résidence (zone urbaine ou rurale) est celle qui a été communiquée par chaque pays ou zone ; on part du principe qu'elle repose sur les définitions de la population urbaine utilisées pour les recensements nationaux telles qu'elles sont reproduites à la fin des notes se rapportant au tableau 6.

Pour quelques pays il y a une discordance entre le nombre total de mariages présenté dans ce tableau et ceux présentés après pour la même année. Habituellement ces différences apparaissent lorsque le nombre total des mariages pour une certaine année a été révisé alors que les autres tabulations ne l'ont pas été.

Calcul des taux : les taux bruts de nuptialité représentent le nombre annuel de mariages pour 1 000 habitants au milieu de l'année. Les taux selon le lieu de résidence (zone urbaine ou rurale) représentent le nombre annuel de mariages, classés selon la catégorie urbaine ou rurale appropriée, pour 1 000 habitants au milieu de l'année. Les taux de ce tableau ne se rapportent qu'aux pays ou zones où l'on a enregistré un total d'au moins 30 mariages pendant une année donnée. Ces taux sont calculés par la division de statistique des Nations Unies sur la base de la population de référence adéquate (par exemple : population totale, nationaux seulement, etc.) si connue et disponible. Si la population de référence n'est pas connue ou n'est pas disponible, la population totale est utilisée pour calculer les taux. Par conséquent, si la population utilisée pour calculer les taux est différente de la population de référence adéquate, les taux présentés sont susceptibles de sous ou sur estimer la situation réelle d'un pays ou d'un territoire.

Fiabilité des données : il a été demandé à chaque pays ou zone d'indiquer le degré estimatif de complétude des données sur les mariages figurant dans ses registres d'état civil. Ces évaluations nationales sont signalées par les codes de qualité "C" et "U" qui apparaissent dans la deuxième colonne du tableau.

La lettre "C" indique que les données sont jugées à peu près complètes, c'est-à-dire qu'elles représentent au moins 90 p. 100 des mariages survenus chaque année ; la lettre "U" signale que les données sont jugées incomplètes, c'est-à-dire qu'elles représentent moins de 90 p. 100 des mariages survenus chaque année. Le code "..." indique qu'aucun renseignement n'a été communiqué quant à la complétude des données.

Les données issues des registres de l'état civil qui sont déclarées incomplètes ou dont le degré de complétude n'est pas connu (code "U" ou "...") sont jugées douteuses. Elles apparaissent en italique dans le tableau et les taux correspondants n'ont pas été calculés.

Les codes de qualité ne s'appliquent qu'aux données provenant des registres de l'état civil. Pour plus de précisions sur la qualité des données reposant sur les statistiques de l'état civil en général, voir la section 4.2 des Notes techniques.

Insuffisance des données : les statistiques relatives aux mariages appellent les mêmes réserves que celles qui ont été formulées à propos des statistiques de l'état civil en général et des statistiques concernant la nuptialité en particulier (voir la section 4 des Notes techniques).

Le fait que le mariage soit un acte juridique, à la différence de la naissance et du décès, qui sont des faits biologiques, a des répercussions sur la comparabilité internationale des données. Aux fins de la statistique, le mariage est défini par la législation de chaque pays ou zone. Cette législation varie d'un pays à l'autre. La comparabilité est limitée en outre du fait que certains pays ou zones ne réunissent des statistiques que pour les mariages civils, bien que les mariages religieux y soient également reconnus par la loi ; dans d'autres, les seuls relevés disponibles sont les registres des églises et, en conséquence, les statistiques peuvent ne pas rendre compte des mariages exclusivement civils.

Étant donné que, dans de nombreux pays ou zones, le mariage est un contrat juridique civil qui, pour être légal, doit être conclu devant un officier d'état civil, il s'ensuit que dans ces pays ou zones l'enregistrement se fait à peu près systématiquement au moment de la cérémonie ou immédiatement après. Il faut tenir compte de cet élément lorsque l'on évalue la fiabilité des données, dont il est question plus haut. C'est pourquoi la pratique consistant à exploiter les données selon la date de l'enregistrement ne pose généralement pas les graves problèmes de comparabilité auxquels on se heurte dans le cas des statistiques concernant les naissances et les décès.

Les statistiques relatives au nombre des mariages présentées dans ce tableau donnent une idée forcément trompeuse de la formation des familles, dans la mesure où elles ne tiennent compte ni des mariages coutumiers, qui ne sont pas enregistrés bien qu'ils soient considérés comme légaux et créateurs d'obligations en vertu du droit coutumier, ni des unions consensuelles (appelées également unions non légalisées ou unions de fait). En général, une diminution du taux de nuptialité pendant un certain nombre d'années indique une augmentation des mariages coutumiers ou des unions consensuelles.

L'exactitude des taux dépend également de la qualité et des insuffisances des estimations de population qui sont utilisées pour leur calcul. Le problème des erreurs par excès ou par défaut commises lors du dénombrement et, dans une certaine mesure, le problème de l'hétérogénéité des définitions de la population totale ont été examinés à la section 3 des Notes techniques relative à la population en général ; des indications concernant les différents pays ou zones sont données en note à la fin du tableau 3.

Il n'a pas toujours été possible d'obtenir une correspondance rigoureuse entre le numérateur et le dénominateur pour le calcul des taux. Par exemple, les mariages parmi la population civile et les militaires sont parfois rapportés à la population civile. Cela peut avoir pour effet d'accroître les taux, mais, dans la plupart des cas, il est probable que la différence sera négligeable.

Il faut souligner que les taux bruts de nuptialité, de même que les taux bruts de natalité, de mortalité et de divortialité, peuvent varier sensiblement selon la structure par âge et par sexe de la population à laquelle ils se rapportent. Les taux bruts de nuptialité offrent néanmoins un moyen simple de mesurer la fréquence et l'évolution des mariages.

La comparabilité des données selon le lieu de résidence (zone urbaine ou rurale) peut être limitée par les définitions nationales des termes « urbain » et « rural » utilisées pour le classement de ces données. En l'absence d'indications contraires, on a supposé que les mêmes définitions avaient servi pour le recensement national de la population et pour l'établissement des statistiques de l'état civil pour chaque pays ou zone. Toutefois, il n'est pas exclu que, pour une zone ou un pays donné, des définitions différentes aient été retenues. Les définitions du terme « urbain » utilisées pour les recensements nationaux de population ont été présentées à la fin des notes techniques du tableau 6 lorsqu'elles étaient connues. Comme on l'a précisé dans les notes techniques relatives au tableau 6, ces définitions varient considérablement d'un pays ou d'une zone à l'autre.

Outre les problèmes de comparabilité, les taux de nuptialité classés selon le lieu de résidence (zone urbaine ou rurale) sont également sujets à des distorsions particulières. Si l'on utilise des définitions différentes du terme « urbain » pour classer les faits d'état civil et les données relatives à la population lors du calcul des taux et qu'il en résulte une différence nette entre le numérateur et le dénominateur pour le taux de la population exposée au risque, les taux de nuptialité s'en trouveront faussés. La différence entre ces taux pour les zones urbaines et rurales pourra aussi être faussée selon que les faits d'état civil auront été classés d'après le lieu où ils se sont produits ou d'après le lieu de résidence habituel. Ce problème est examiné plus en détail à la section 4.1.4.1 des Notes techniques.

Données publiées antérieurement : les différentes éditions de *l'Annuaire démographique* regroupent des données sur le nombre des mariages. Pour plus de précisions concernant les années et les sujets pour lesquels des données ont été publiées, se reporter à l'index historique.

NOTE

[1] *Principes et recommandations pour un système de statistique de l'état civil, troisième révision,* numéro de vente : E.13.XVII.10, publication des Nations Unies, New York, 2014.

23. Marriages and crude marriage rates, by urban/rural residence: 2015 - 2019
Mariages et taux bruts de nuptialité, selon la résidence, urbaine/rurale : 2015 - 2019

Continent, country or area, and urban/rural residence Continent, pays ou zone et résidence, urbaine/rurale	Co-de[a]	Number - Nombre					Rate - Taux				
		2015	2016	2017	2018	2019	2015	2016	2017	2018	2019
AFRICA - AFRIQUE											
Algeria - Algérie[1]											
Total	...	*369 074*	*356 600*	*339 691*	...	...	...	...	...	...	...
Botswana[2]											
Total	+U	*6 677*	*6 051*	*6 203*	*5 489*	...	...	...	...	...	...
Cabo Verde[3]											
Total	+C	*1 554	*1 840	*2 184	*2 337	...	*3.0	*3.5	*4.1	*4.3	...
Côte d'Ivoire											
Total	+U	*25 689*	*26 678*	*26 316*	*30 554*	...	...	...	...	...	...
Urban - Urbaine	+U	*23 750*	*25 189*	...	*28 221*	...	...	...	...	...	...
Rural - Rurale	+U	*1 939*	*1 489*	...	*2 333*	...	...	...	...	...	...
Egypt - Égypte											
Total	+C	969 399[4]	938 526[4]	912 606	...	...	10.9	10.3	9.6	...	...
Urban - Urbaine	+C	409 906[4]	370 411[4]	356 634	...	...	10.8	9.5	8.8	...	...
Rural - Rurale	+C	559 493[4]	568 115[4]	555 972	...	...	11.0	10.9	10.2	...	...
Guinea - Guinée[5]											
Total	+U	*11 475*	*12 614*	...	*32 714*	...	...	...	...	...	...
Lesotho											
Total	+U	*2 660*	*2 640*	...	...	...	...	...	...	...	...
Mauritius - Maurice[6]											
Total	+C	9 709	10 042	9 757	10 034	9 709	7.7	7.9	7.7	7.9	7.7
Urban - Urbaine	+C	3 194	3 224	3 186	3 326	3 196	6.2	6.2	6.2	6.5	6.2
Rural - Rurale	+C	6 515	6 818	6 571	6 708	6 513	8.7	9.1	8.8	8.9	8.6
Mayotte											
Total	C	346	346	378[7]	346[7]	...	1.5	1.4	1.5	1.3	...
Reunion - Réunion											
Total	C	2 827	2 882	2 866	2 955[7]	...	3.3	3.4	3.3	3.4	...
Urban - Urbaine	C	...	...	2 782	...	...	...	...	...	...	...
Rural - Rurale	C	...	...	84	...	...	...	...	...	...	...
Saint Helena ex. dep. - Sainte-Hélène sans dép.											
Total	C	9	9	18	10	...	...	...	...	...	...
Sao Tome and Principe - Sao Tomé-et-Principe											
Total	C	305	302	215	...	...	1.6	1.6	1.1	...	...
Seychelles[8]											
Total	+C	1 845	2 147	2 821	3 131	3 078	19.7	22.7	29.4	32.4	31.5
South Africa - Afrique du Sud											
Total	...	*138 627*	*139 512*	*135 458*	*131 240*	...	...	...	...	...	...
Sudan - Soudan											
Total	U	*158 051*	...	...	...	...	...	...	...	...	...
Tunisia - Tunisie											
Total	...	*108 453*	*98 125*	*95 336*	*92 800*	...	...	...	...	...	...
AMERICA, NORTH - AMÉRIQUE DU NORD											
Anguilla											
Total	C	40[9]	64[9]	64[9]	...	153	2.7	4.2	...	...	9.8
Aruba											
Total	C	696	639	537	...	...	6.4	5.8	4.8	...	...
Bahamas[10]											
Total	+C	*3 829	*3 950	*3 574	...	...	*10.4	*10.6	*9.5	...	...
Bermuda - Bermudes[11]											
Total	C	509	450	430	473[12]	...	8.2	7.1	6.7	7.4	...
British Virgin Islands - Îles Vierges britanniques											
Total	C	236	229	177	...	...	8.1	...	...	...	...
Cayman Islands - Îles Caïmanes[13]											
Total	+C	468	493	513	516	503	7.9	8.0	8.1	8.0	7.4
Costa Rica[14]											
Total	C	26 512	26 718	25 501	23 604	*22 680	5.5	5.5	5.2	4.7	*4.5
Urban - Urbaine	C	21 258	21 565	20 129	18 695	*17 822	6.1	6.1	5.6	5.1	*4.9
Rural - Rurale	C	5 254	5 153	5 372	4 909	*4 858	4.0	3.9	4.0	3.6	*3.5

23. Marriages and crude marriage rates, by urban/rural residence: 2015 - 2019
Mariages et taux bruts de nuptialité, selon la résidence, urbaine/rurale : 2015 - 2019 (continued - suite)

Continent, country or area, and urban/rural residence / Continent, pays ou zone et résidence, urbaine/rurale	Code[a]	Number - Nombre 2015	2016	2017	2018	2019	Rate - Taux 2015	2016	2017	2018	2019
AMERICA, NORTH - AMÉRIQUE DU NORD											
Cuba[15]											
Total	C	61 902	61 903	53 684	58 070	...	5.5	5.5	4.8	5.2	...
Urban - Urbaine	C	57 600	57 596	49 874	53 737	...	6.7	6.7	5.8	6.2	...
Rural - Rurale	C	4 302	4 307	3 810	4 333	...	1.7	1.7	1.5	1.7	...
Curaçao[16]											
Total	C	703	695	729	669	563	4.4	4.4	4.6	4.2	3.6
Dominica - Dominique											
Total	+C	238	314	282	...	...	3.3	4.4	4.2	...	...
Dominican Republic - République dominicaine											
Total	+C	50 158	52 898	49 625	50 067	51 938	5.0	5.3	4.9	4.9	5.0
Grenada - Grenade											
Total	+C	669	635	629	...	...	6.1	5.7	5.6	...	...
Guadeloupe											
Total	C	1 172	1 185	1 104	1 191[7]	...	3.0	3.0	2.8	2.8	...
Guatemala											
Total	C	79 177	69 613	71 597	74 777	...	4.9	4.2	4.2	4.3	...
Jamaica - Jamaïque											
Total	+C	18 373	17 609	17 411	16 719	...	6.7	6.5	6.4	6.1	...
Martinique											
Total	C	1 017	1 067	1 034	...	...	2.7	2.8	2.8	...	...
Urban - Urbaine	C	...	...	877	...	...	...	...	...	...	...
Rural - Rurale	C	...	...	157	...	...	...	...	...	...	...
Mexico - Mexique[7]											
Total	+C	558 022	543 749	528 678	501 298	...	4.6	4.4	4.3	4.0	...
Urban - Urbaine[17]	+C	416 507	411 481	405 427	382 824	...	4.7	4.6	4.5	4.1	...
Rural - Rurale[17]	+C	108 675	100 862	104 059	92 246	...	3.3	3.0	3.1	2.8	...
Montserrat											
Total	C	14	10	...	...	...	...	...	...	...	...
Nicaragua											
Total	+U	*26 628*	*22 097*	*30 628*	*29 130*	...	...	...	...	...	...
Panama[14]											
Total	C	14 341	14 233	13 360	11 112	*8 829	3.6	3.5	3.3	2.7	*2.1
Urban - Urbaine	C	11 824	11 730	10 863	8 995	*7 160	4.4	4.2	3.8	3.1	*2.4
Rural - Rurale	C	2 517	2 503	2 497	2 117	*1 669	2.0	2.0	2.0	1.7	*1.3
Puerto Rico - Porto Rico											
Total	C	17 002	15 907	12 793	14 091	12 511	4.9	4.7	3.8	4.4	3.9
Saint Barthélemy - Saint-Barthélemy											
Total	C	...	...	26	...	...	...	...	...	...	...
Saint Pierre and Miquelon - Saint Pierre-et-Miquelon											
Total	C	...	...	8	...	...	...	...	...	...	...
Saint Vincent and the Grenadines - Saint-Vincent-et-les Grenadines											
Total	C	574	583	536	...	...	5.2	5.3	4.9	...	...
Saint-Martin (French part) - Saint-Martin (partie française)											
Total	C	...	...	88	...	...	...	...	2.5	...	...
Sint Maarten (Dutch part) - Saint-Martin (partie néerlandaise)											
Total	+C	251	306	158	...	...	6.6	7.8	3.9	...	...
Trinidad and Tobago - Trinité-et-Tobago											
Total	C	*7 981	*8 324[18]	*7 869[18]	...	...	*5.9	*6.1	*5.8	...	...
Turks and Caicos Islands - Îles Turques et Caïques											
Total	C	474	621	295	464	...	12.9	16.4	7.4	11.2	...
United States of America - États-Unis d'Amérique											
Total	C	2 221 579	...	...	...	...	6.9	...	...	...	...

23. Marriages and crude marriage rates, by urban/rural residence: 2015 - 2019
Mariages et taux bruts de nuptialité, selon la résidence, urbaine/rurale : 2015 - 2019 (continued - suite)

Continent, country or area, and urban/rural residence Continent, pays ou zone et résidence, urbaine/rurale	Code[a]	Number - Nombre 2015	2016	2017	2018	2019	Rate - Taux 2015	2016	2017	2018	2019
AMERICA, SOUTH - AMÉRIQUE DU SUD											
Argentina - Argentine											
Total	C	118 809	119 334	127 378	124 218	...	2.8	2.7	2.9	2.8	...
Bolivia (Plurinational State of) - Bolivie (État plurinational de)											
Total	+U	42 408	55 635	36 962	*48 502	...	...	...	...	...	...
Brazil - Brésil											
Total	+U	1 137 348[7]	1 095 535[7]	1 064 489	...	...	...	...	...	...	...
Chile - Chili											
Total	+C	61 744	62 464	61 320	*63 187	...	3.4	3.4	3.3	*3.4	...
Urban - Urbaine[19]	+C	56 984	57 413	55 736	...	...	3.6	3.6	3.4	...	...
Rural - Rurale[19]	+C	4 760	5 051	5 584	...	...	2.2	2.3	2.5	...	...
Ecuador - Équateur[20]											
Total	U	60 636	57 738	60 353	60 849	...	...	...	...	...	...
Urban - Urbaine[19]	U	50 425	47 322	48 946	49 445	...	...	...	...	...	...
Rural - Rurale[19]	U	10 211	10 416	11 407	11 404	...	...	...	...	...	...
French Guiana - Guyane française											
Total	C	590	631	...	...	...	2.3	2.4	...	...	...
Guyana											
Total	+U	4 744	4 445	3 990	4 008	...	...	...	...	...	...
Paraguay											
Total	U	19 504	19 440	19 760	19 660	...	...	...	...	...	...
Peru - Pérou[21]											
Total	+C	86 191	94 094	90 806	92 440	*93 453	2.9	3.1	2.9	2.9	*2.9
Suriname											
Total	C	2 010	2 125	1 996	1 927	...	3.5	3.7	3.4	3.3	...
Uruguay											
Total	C	9 501	9 820	9 518	9 395	...	2.7	2.8	2.7	2.7	...
Venezuela (Bolivarian Republic of) - Venezuela (République bolivarienne du)											
Total	C	91 688	84 349	82 213	...	...	3.0	2.7	2.6	...	...
ASIA - ASIE											
Armenia - Arménie											
Total	+C	17 603	16 294	15 214	14 822	...	5.9	5.4	5.1	5.0	...
Urban - Urbaine	+C	11 836	11 113	10 469	10 310	...	6.2	5.8	5.5	5.4	...
Rural - Rurale	+C	5 767	5 181	4 745	4 512	...	5.3	4.8	4.4	4.2	...
Azerbaijan - Azerbaïdjan											
Total	+C	68 773	66 771	62 923	62 484	...	7.1	6.8	6.4	6.3	...
Urban - Urbaine	+C	36 623	36 739	33 047	32 760	...	7.1	7.1	6.3	6.2	...
Rural - Rurale	+C	32 150	30 032	29 876	29 724	...	7.1	6.6	6.4	6.3	...
Bahrain - Bahreïn											
Total	...	6 953	7 019	6 691	6 039	5 524	...	...	...	...	...
Bangladesh											
Total	...	2 020 095	2 263 889	2 327 608	2 419 620	2 480 850	...	...	...	...	...
Urban - Urbaine	...	...	...	...	731 935	750 457	...	...	...	...	...
Rural - Rurale	...	...	...	...	1 687 685	1 730 393	...	...	...	...	...
Brunei Darussalam - Brunéi Darussalam											
Total	+C	2 750	2 532	2 540	2 653	...	6.7	6.1	5.9	6.0	...
China, Hong Kong SAR - Chine, Hong Kong RAS											
Total	C	51 609	50 008	51 817	49 331	44 247	7.1	6.8	7.0	6.6	5.9
China, Macao SAR - Chine, Macao RAS											
Total	+C	3 719	3 891	3 883	3 842	3 724	5.8	6.0	6.0	5.8	5.5
Cyprus - Chypre[22]											
Total	C	6 092	6 375	5 882	6 777	...	7.2	7.5	6.8	7.8	...
Georgia - Géorgie											
Total	C	29 157	25 101	23 684	23 202	...	7.8	6.7	6.4	6.2	...
Urban - Urbaine[19]	C	17 127	14 961	...	...	...	8.1	7.0	...	...	...
Rural - Rurale[19]	C	12 030	10 140	...	...	...	7.6	6.4	...	...	...

Continent, country or area, and urban/rural residence — Continent, pays ou zone et résidence, urbaine/rurale	Code[a]	Number - Nombre					Rate - Taux				
		2015	2016	2017	2018	2019	2015	2016	2017	2018	2019
ASIA - ASIE											
Indonesia - Indonésie											
Total	U	*1 958 394*	...	...	...	...	...	...	...	...	...
Iran (Islamic Republic of) - Iran (République islamique d')[23]											
Total	+C	685 352	668 303	608 956	550 565	...	8.7	8.3	7.5	6.7	...
Urban - Urbaine	+C	562 671	588 460	539 421	486 661	...	9.8	9.9	8.9	7.9	...
Rural - Rurale	+C	122 681	79 843	69 535	63 904	...	5.7	3.8	3.3	3.1	...
Israel - Israël[24]											
Total	C	53 579	52 809	50 029	...	...	6.4	6.2	5.7	...	...
Urban - Urbaine[25]	C	48 236	47 651	45 372	...	...	6.3	6.1	5.7	...	...
Rural - Rurale[25]	C	3 936	3 828	3 523	...	...	5.3	5.1	4.6	...	...
Japan - Japon[26]											
Total	+C	635 156	620 531	606 866	586 481	...	5.0	4.9	4.8	4.6	...
Urban - Urbaine[19]	+C	590 947	578 265	566 338	547 934	...	...	...	...	...	...
Rural - Rurale[19]	+C	44 209	42 266	40 528	38 547	...	...	...	...	...	...
Jordan - Jordanie[27]											
Total	+C	81 373	81 343	77 700	70 734	...	8.5	8.3	7.7	6.9	...
Kazakhstan											
Total	+C	148 769	141 702	141 791	137 797	139 504	8.5	8.0	7.9	7.5	7.5
Urban - Urbaine	+C	98 927	94 672	96 865	95 964	98 230	10.0	9.3	9.4	9.0	9.1
Rural - Rurale	+C	49 842	47 030	44 926	41 833	41 274	6.6	6.1	5.8	5.5	5.4
Kuwait - Koweït											
Total	C	15 412	14 693	13 932	14 400	...	3.9	3.6	3.5	3.5	...
Kyrgyzstan - Kirghizstan											
Total	C	52 043	47 837	43 350	49 579	...	8.7	7.9	7.0	7.8	...
Urban - Urbaine	C	15 875	15 990	16 274	15 756	...	7.9	7.8	7.8	7.3	...
Rural - Rurale	C	36 168	31 847	27 076	33 823	...	9.2	7.9	6.6	8.1	...
Malaysia - Malaisie											
Total	+C	...	200 274	203 741	206 253	...	...	6.3	6.4	6.4	...
Maldives											
Total	...	*5 763*	*5 488*	*5 237*	*5 290*	*5 350*	...	...	...	...	...
Urban - Urbaine	...	*2 610*	*2 527*	...	...	...	...	...	...	...	...
Rural - Rurale	...	*3 153*	*2 961*	...	...	...	...	...	...	...	...
Mongolia - Mongolie											
Total	+C	17 586	16 778	20 470	21 020	20 043	5.8	5.4	6.5	6.6	6.1
Urban - Urbaine	+C	12 506	11 915	14 617	15 332	15 057	6.1	5.6	6.8	7.1	6.8
Rural - Rurale	+C	5 080	4 863	5 853	5 688	4 986	5.2	5.0	5.8	5.5	4.8
Oman											
Total	U	*25 659*	*24 014*	*22 284*	*20 005*	*18 243*	...	...	...	...	...
Philippines[28]											
Total	U	*439 424*	*419 628*	*434 932*	*449 169*	...	...	...	...	...	...
Qatar											
Total	C	3 724	3 830	3 718	3 758	...	1.5	1.5	1.4	1.4	...
Urban - Urbaine	C	3 724	3 830	3 718	3 758	...	1.5	1.5	1.4	1.4	...
Republic of Korea - République de Corée[29]											
Total	+C	302 828	281 635	264 455	257 622	239 159	5.9	5.5	5.2	5.0	4.7
Urban - Urbaine[25]	+C	247 486	229 747	214 584	208 646	193 438	6.0	5.5	5.2	5.0	4.6
Rural - Rurale[25]	+C	48 638	46 792	44 756	43 693	40 473	5.1	4.9	4.7	4.5	4.2
Singapore - Singapour[30]											
Total	+C	28 322	27 971	28 212	27 007	25 434	7.3	7.1	7.1	6.8	6.3
Sri Lanka											
Total	+C	*175 939	*173 990	*169 365	*170 027	*163 378	*8.4	*8.2	*7.9	*7.8	*7.5
State of Palestine - État de Palestine											
Total	C	50 438	49 930	47 218	43 515	...	11.1	10.8	10.0	9.0	...
Tajikistan - Tadjikistan											
Total	+C	76 956	72 499	78 638	82 647	...	9.1	8.4	8.9	9.3	...
Urban - Urbaine	+C	19 810	18 378	20 184	...	...	8.9	8.1	8.7	...	...
Rural - Rurale	+C	57 146	54 121	58 454	...	...	9.2	8.5	9.0	...	...
Thailand - Thaïlande[31]											
Total	U	*304 392*	*307 746*	*297 501*	*307 936*	*328 875*	...	...	...	...	...
Turkey - Turquie[32]											
Total	C	602 982	594 493	569 459	553 202	...	7.7	7.4	7.1	6.8	...

23. Marriages and crude marriage rates, by urban/rural residence: 2015 - 2019
Mariages et taux bruts de nuptialité, selon la résidence, urbaine/rurale : 2015 - 2019 (continued - suite)

Continent, country or area, and urban/rural residence Continent, pays ou zone et résidence, urbaine/rurale	Co-de[a]	Number - Nombre 2015	2016	2017	2018	2019	Rate - Taux 2015	2016	2017	2018	2019
ASIA - ASIE											
United Arab Emirates - Émirats arabes unis											
Total	...	*16 248*	*15 778*	*15 150*	*14 804*	*14 909*	...	...	...	...	...
Uzbekistan - Ouzbékistan											
Total	+C	287 582	275 048	306 197	311 379	310 899	9.2	8.6	9.5	9.4	9.3
Urban - Urbaine	+C	131 216	125 820	138 681	145 756	147 501	8.3	7.8	8.4	8.7	8.8
Rural - Rurale	+C	156 366	149 228	167 516	165 623	163 398	10.1	9.5	10.5	10.2	9.9
Viet Nam											
Total	C	...	...	...	735 292	699 265	...	...	...	7.8	7.2
EUROPE											
Åland Islands - Îles d'Åland											
Total	C	118	123	115	107	*135	4.1	4.2	3.9	3.6	*4.5
Urban - Urbaine	C	49	49	48	45	...	4.3	4.3	4.1	3.8	...
Rural - Rurale	C	69	74	67	62	...	3.9	4.2	3.8	3.5	...
Albania - Albanie											
Total	C	24 997	22 562	22 641	23 104	...	8.7	7.8	7.9	8.1	...
Andorra - Andorre											
Total	C	285	295	320	293	325	4.0	4.1	4.4	3.9	4.3
Austria - Autriche[33]											
Total	C	44 502	44 890	44 981	46 468	...	5.2	5.1	5.1	5.3	...
Belarus - Bélarus											
Total	C	82 030	64 536	66 215	60 714	...	8.6	6.8	7.0	6.4	...
Urban - Urbaine	C	68 305	53 819	55 372	51 137	...	9.3	7.3	7.5	6.9	...
Rural - Rurale	C	13 725	10 717	10 843	9 577	...	6.4	5.1	5.2	4.6	...
Belgium - Belgique[34]											
Total	C	40 049	44 725	44 329	45 059	...	3.5	3.9	3.9	3.9	...
Urban - Urbaine	C	39 500	...	...	...	...	...	...	...	...	...
Rural - Rurale	C	549	...	...	...	...	...	...	...	...	...
Bosnia and Herzegovina - Bosnie-Herzégovine											
Total	C	19 680	19 233	19 617	19 911	...	5.6	5.5	5.6	5.7	...
Bulgaria - Bulgarie[35]											
Total	C	27 720	26 803	28 593	28 961	...	3.9	3.8	4.0	4.1	...
Urban - Urbaine	C	20 795	19 977	21 536	21 463	...	4.0	3.8	4.1	4.2	...
Rural - Rurale	C	6 925	6 826	7 057	7 498	...	3.6	3.6	3.7	4.0	...
Croatia - Croatie[14]											
Total	C	19 834	20 467	20 310	19 921	...	4.7	4.9	4.9	4.9	...
Urban - Urbaine	C	10 937	11 287	11 231	10 957	...	...	...	...	...	...
Rural - Rurale	C	8 897	9 180	9 079	8 964	...	...	...	...	...	...
Czechia - Tchéquie[14]											
Total	C	48 191	50 768	52 567	54 470	...	4.6	4.8	5.0	5.1	...
Urban - Urbaine	C	35 192	37 207	38 240	39 320	...	4.6	4.8	4.9	5.1	...
Rural - Rurale	C	12 999	13 561	14 327	15 150	...	4.6	4.8	5.0	5.3	...
Denmark - Danemark[36]											
Total	C	28 853	30 767	31 777	32 525	30 635	5.1	5.4	5.5	5.6	5.3
Estonia - Estonie											
Total	C	6 815	6 360	6 447	6 573	...	5.2	4.8	4.9	5.0	...
Urban - Urbaine[37]	C	4 660	4 214	4 493	4 456	...	5.2	4.7	4.9	4.9	...
Rural - Rurale[37]	C	1 733	1 748	1 548	1 635	...	4.2	4.2	3.8	4.1	...
Faroe Islands - Îles Féroé											
Total	C	268	268	275	285	244	5.5	5.4	5.5	5.6	4.7
Finland - Finlande[38]											
Total	C	24 590	24 341	23 731	21 921	...	4.5	4.5	4.3	4.0	...
Urban - Urbaine	C	18 838	18 676	18 470	16 909	...	4.9	4.8	4.7	4.3	...
Rural - Rurale	C	5 752	5 665	5 261	5 012	...	3.6	3.6	3.3	3.2	...
France[7]											
Total	C	230 364	226 614	227 758	*229 000	...	3.6	3.5	3.5	*3.5	...
Urban - Urbaine[39]	C	179 606	177 747	...	...	...	...	...	...	...	...
Rural - Rurale[39]	C	48 118	46 219	...	...	...	...	...	...	...	...
Germany - Allemagne											
Total	C	400 115	410 426	407 466	449 466[7]	...	4.9	5.0	4.9	5.4	...
Gibraltar[13]											
Total	+C	195	199	...	...	...	5.8	5.9	...	...	...

23. Marriages and crude marriage rates, by urban/rural residence: 2015 - 2019
Mariages et taux bruts de nuptialité, selon la résidence, urbaine/rurale : 2015 - 2019 (continued - suite)

Continent, country or area, and urban/rural residence Continent, pays ou zone et résidence, urbaine/rurale	Code[a]	Number - Nombre 2015	2016	2017	2018	2019	Rate - Taux 2015	2016	2017	2018	2019
EUROPE											
Greece - Grèce											
Total	C	53 672	49 632	50 138	47 428	...	5.0	4.6	4.7	4.4	...
Urban - Urbaine	C	38 031	35 268	35 888	34 047	...	...	...	...	...	...
Rural - Rurale	C	15 641	14 364	14 250	13 381	...	...	...	...	...	...
Hungary - Hongrie[15]											
Total	C	46 137	51 805	50 572	50 828	...	4.7	5.3	5.2	5.2	...
Urban - Urbaine[40]	C	33 144	36 422	35 416	35 585	...	4.8	5.3	5.1	5.2	...
Rural - Rurale[40]	C	12 492	14 810	14 528	14 613	...	4.3	5.1	5.0	5.1	...
Ireland - Irlande[7]											
Total	+C	22 116	22 626	22 021	21 053	...	4.7	4.8	4.6	4.3	...
Isle of Man - Île de Man											
Total	+C	195	235	240	347	221	2.2	2.8	2.9	...	...
Italy - Italie											
Total	C	194 377	203 258	191 287	195 778	...	3.2	3.4	3.2	3.2	...
Latvia - Lettonie[14]											
Total	C	13 617	13 002	13 150	13 058	...	6.9	6.6	6.8	6.8	...
Urban - Urbaine	C	...	...	...	8 906	...	...	...	...	6.7	...
Rural - Rurale	C	...	...	...	4 152	...	...	...	...	6.8	...
Liechtenstein[14]											
Total	C	205	198	229	242	...	5.5	5.3	6.0	6.3	...
Lithuania - Lituanie											
Total	C	21 987	21 347	21 186	19 734	...	7.6	7.4	7.5	7.0	...
Urban - Urbaine	C	15 219	14 914	14 684	13 530	...	7.8	7.7	7.7	7.2	...
Rural - Rurale	C	6 768	6 433	6 502	6 204	...	7.1	6.8	7.0	6.7	...
Luxembourg[41]											
Total	C	2 052	1 884	1 908	1 898	...	3.6	3.2	3.2	3.1	...
Malta - Malte											
Total	C	3 002	3 034	2 934	2 831	...	6.7	6.7	6.3	5.8	...
Monaco											
Total	C	213	193	206	182	...	5.7	5.1	5.5	4.8	...
Montenegro - Monténégro											
Total	C	3 837	3 178	3 272	3 321	3 523	6.2	5.1	5.3	5.3	5.7
Netherlands - Pays-Bas[42]											
Total	C	64 308	65 249	64 402	64 315	...	3.8	3.8	3.8	3.7	...
North Macedonia - Macédoine du Nord											
Total	C	14 186	13 199	13 781	13 494[14]	...	6.9	6.4	6.6	6.5	...
Urban - Urbaine	C	8 168	7 328	8 868	8 794[14]	...	...	...	...	...	...
Rural - Rurale	C	6 018	5 871	4 913	4 700[14]	...	...	...	...	...	...
Norway - Norvège[7]											
Total	C	23 227	23 672	23 134	22 578	...	4.5	4.5	4.4	4.3	...
Poland - Pologne											
Total	C	188 832	193 455	192 576	192 443	...	5.0	5.1	5.1	5.1	...
Urban - Urbaine	C	111 246	114 612	114 338	114 841	...	4.9	5.0	5.0	5.0	...
Rural - Rurale	C	77 586	78 843	78 238	77 602	...	5.2	5.2	5.2	5.1	...
Portugal[43]											
Total	C	32 393	32 399	33 634	34 637	...	3.1	3.1	3.3	3.4	...
Republic of Moldova - République de Moldova											
Total	C	24 709	21 992	20 924	20 399	...	8.7	7.8	7.6	7.5	...
Urban - Urbaine	C	12 919	11 233	10 980	10 799	...	...	...	...	...	...
Rural - Rurale	C	11 790	10 759	9 944	9 600	...	...	...	...	...	...
Romania - Roumanie											
Total	C	125 454	133 183	142 613	143 292	...	6.3	6.8	7.3	7.4	...
Urban - Urbaine	C	80 975	84 226	91 212	91 960	...	7.6	8.0	8.7	8.8	...
Rural - Rurale	C	44 479	48 957	51 401	51 332	...	4.9	5.4	5.7	5.7	...
San Marino - Saint-Marin[44]											
Total	C	182	181	159[45]	151[45]	...	5.4	5.3	4.6	4.4	...
Serbia - Serbie[46]											
Total	+C	36 949	35 921	36 047	36 321	...	5.2	5.1	5.1	5.2	...
Urban - Urbaine	+C	24 521	23 554	23 757	24 068	...	5.7	5.5	5.6	5.7	...
Rural - Rurale	+C	12 428	12 367	12 290	12 253	...	4.4	4.4	4.4	4.5	...
Slovakia - Slovaquie[14]											
Total	C	28 775	29 897	31 309	31 177	...	5.3	5.5	5.8	5.7	...
Urban - Urbaine	C	16 443	16 793	17 588	17 196	...	5.6	5.7	6.0	5.9	...
Rural - Rurale	C	12 332	13 104	13 721	13 981	...	4.9	5.2	5.4	5.5	...

23. Marriages and crude marriage rates, by urban/rural residence: 2015 - 2019
Mariages et taux bruts de nuptialité, selon la résidence, urbaine/rurale : 2015 - 2019 (continued - suite)

Continent, country or area, and urban/rural residence Continent, pays ou zone et résidence, urbaine/rurale	Co-de[a]	Number - Nombre					Rate - Taux				
		2015	2016	2017	2018	2019	2015	2016	2017	2018	2019
EUROPE											
Slovenia - Slovénie											
Total	C	6 449[47]	6 667[47]	6 481[47]	7 256[48]	...	3.1	3.2	3.1	3.5	...
Urban - Urbaine	C	3 418[47]	3 665[47]	3 630[47]	3 989[48]	...	3.1	3.3	3.2	3.5	...
Rural - Rurale	C	3 031[47]	3 002[47]	2 851[47]	3 267[48]	...	3.2	3.1	3.1	3.5	...
Spain - Espagne											
Total	C	166 651	173 049	171 320	165 527	*165 578	3.6	3.7	3.7	3.5	*3.5
Sweden - Suède[7]											
Total	C	52 314	53 817	52 497	50 796	...	5.3	5.4	5.2	5.0	...
Switzerland - Suisse[49]											
Total	C	41 437	41 646	40 599	40 716	...	5.0	5.0	4.8	4.8	...
Urban - Urbaine	C	35 758	35 995	35 208	35 096	...	5.1	5.1	...	4.9	...
Rural - Rurale	C	5 679	5 651	5 391	5 620	...	4.4	4.4	...	4.3	...
Ukraine[50]											
Total	+C	299 038	229 453	249 522	...	...	7.0	5.4	5.9	...	...
Urban - Urbaine	+C	222 747	172 663	191 826	...	...	7.5	5.8	6.5	...	...
Rural - Rurale	+C	76 291	56 790	57 696	...	...	5.8	4.3	4.4	...	...
United Kingdom of Great Britain and Northern Ireland - Royaume-Uni de Grande-Bretagne et d'Irlande du Nord[51]											
Total	C	283 559	287 328	...	...	...	4.4	4.4	...	...	...
OCEANIA - OCÉANIE											
American Samoa - Samoas américaines											
Total	C	264	253	228	...	...	4.3	4.2	3.8	...	...
Australia - Australie											
Total	+C	113 595	118 401	112 954	119 188	...	4.8	4.9	4.6	4.8	...
Cook Islands - Îles Cook[10]											
Total	+C	720	707	725	*703	*570	39.1	36.6	37.2	*37.8	*28.2
French Polynesia - Polynésie française											
Total	C	1 367	1 487	1 293	1 381	...	5.0	5.4	4.7	5.0	...
Guam[52]											
Total	C	1 348	1 185	1 244	1 251	...	8.3	7.3	7.6	7.5	...
New Caledonia - Nouvelle-Calédonie[7]											
Total	C	983	894	904	...	...	3.6	3.3	3.2	...	...
New Zealand - Nouvelle-Zélande[53]											
Total	+C	19 947	20 235	20 685	20 949	19 071	4.3	4.3	4.3	4.3	3.9
Niue - Nioué[8]											
Total	C	...	15	14	17	11	...	...	...	...	...
Norfolk Island - Île Norfolk[54]											
Total	+C	24	...	...	...	...	...	...	...	...	...
Pitcairn											
Total	C	...	...	...	...	-	...	...	...	...	...
Samoa											
Total	U	*865*	...	...	*2 861*[55]	...	...	...	...	...	...

FOOTNOTES - NOTES

Italics: data from civil registers which are incomplete or of unknown completeness. - Italiques : données incomplètes ou dont le degré d'exactitude n'est pas connu, provenant des registres de l'état civil.

* Provisional. - Données provisoires.

[a] 'Code' indicates the source of data, as follows:
C - Civil registration, estimated over 90% complete
U - Civil registration, estimated less than 90% complete
| - Other source, estimated reliable

+ - Data tabulated by date of registration rather than occurence
... - Information not available

Le 'Code' indique la source des données, comme suit :
C - Registres de l'état civil considérés complèts à 90 p. 100 au moins
U - Registres de l'état civil qui ne sont pas considérés complèts à 90 p. 100 au moins
| - Autre source, considérée pas douteuses
+ - Données exploitées selon la date de l'enregistrement et non la date de l'événement
... - Information pas disponible

[1] Data refer to Algerian population only. - Les données ne concernent que la population algérienne.
[2] Source: Vital Statistics Report. - Source: Vital Statistics Report.
[3] Source: Vital Statistics Report, National Statistics Institute. - Source: Rapport sur les statistiques de l'état civil, Institut national de la statistique.
[4] Including marriages resumed after 'revocable divorce' (among Moslem population), which approximates legal separation. - Y compris les unions reconstituées après un 'divorce révocable' (parmi la population musulmane), qui est à peu près l'équivalent d'une séparation légale.
[5] Registered and centralized marriages. National Directorate of Civil Status. - Mariages enregistrés et centralisés. Direction nationale de l'Etat civil.
[6] Excludes the islands of St. Brandon and Agalega. - Non compris les îles St. Brandon et Agalega.
[7] Including same-sex marriages. - Y compris les mariages entre personnes du même sexe.
[8] Including visitors. - Y compris les visiteurs.
[9] Excluding visitors. - Ne comprend pas les visiteurs.
[10] Including non-residents. - Y compris les non-résidents.
[11] Bermuda is 100 per cent urban. - 100 pour cent de la population des Bermudes est urbaine.
[12] Data includes 6 same sex marriages. - Dont six mariages homosexuels.
[13] Data refer to marriages where one or both partners are residents. - Les données portent sur les mariages pour lesquels l'un des deux partenaires ou les deux sont résidents.
[14] Data refer to marriages registered by residence of groom. - Les données concernent les mariages enregistrés selon la résidence du marié.
[15] Data refer to marriages registered by residence of bride. - Les données concernent les mariages enregistrés selon le lieu de résidence de la mariée.
[16] Data refers to the number of marriages of which at least one of the partners is a resident of Curacao. - Les données concernent le nombre de mariages dont au moins l'un des partenaires est un résident de Curaçao.
[17] Urban and rural distribution refers to the usual residence of the bride. The total number may include 'Unknown residence', but the categories urban and rural do not. - La répartition entre résidence urbaine et résidence rurale fait référence au lieu de résidence habituel de la mariée. Le nombre total peut inclure les personnes dont la résidence n'est pas connue, à l'inverse des catégories de population urbaine et rurale.
[18] Source: Ministry of Legal Affairs. - Source : Ministère des affaires juridiques.
[19] Urban and rural residence refers to the place of usual residence of groom. - Le lieu de résidence (zone urbaine ou zone rurale) correspond au lieu de résidence habituel du marié.
[20] Excludes nomadic Indian tribes. - Non compris les tribus d'Indiens nomades.
[21] Data are compiled from the National Registers of Identification and Civil Status (RENIEC). - Les données sont rédigées à partir des Registres Nationaux d'Identification et d'État Civil (RENIEC).
[22] Data refer to marriages of residents only. Data refer to government controlled areas. - Les données ne portent que sur les mariages de résidents. Les données se rapportent aux zones contrôlées par le Gouvernement.
[23] Data refer to the Iranian Year which begins on 21 March and ends on 20 March of the following year. - Les données concernent l'année iranienne, qui commence le 21 mars et se termine le 20 mars de l'année suivante.
[24] Includes data for East Jerusalem and Israeli residents in certain other territories under occupation by Israeli military forces since June 1967. - Y compris les données pour Jérusalem-Est et les résidents israéliens dans certains autres territoires occupés depuis 1967 par les forces armées israéliennes.
[25] The total number may include 'Unknown residence', but the categories urban and rural do not. Urban and rural residence refers to the place of usual residence of groom. - Le nombre total peut inclure les personnes dont la résidence n'est pas connue, à l'inverse des catégories de population urbaine et rurale. Le lieu de résidence (zone urbaine ou zone rurale) correspond au lieu de résidence habituel du marié.
[26] Data refer to Japanese nationals in Japan only. - Les données se raportent aux nationaux japonais au Japon seulement.
[27] Excluding data for Jordanian territory under occupation since June 1967 by Israeli military forces. Excluding foreigners, including registered Palestinian refugees. - Non compris les données pour le territoire jordanien occupé depuis juin 1967 par les forces armées israéliennes. Non compris les étrangers, mais y compris les réfugiés de Palestine enregistrés.
[28] Residence refers to place of occurrence of marriage. - « Résidence » désigne le lieu du mariage.
[29] Excluding alien armed forces, civilian aliens employed by armed forces, and foreign diplomatic personnel and their dependants. - Non compris les militaires étrangers, les civils étrangers employés par les forces armées ni le personnel diplomatique étranger et les membres de leur famille les accompagnant.
[30] Excluding marriages previously officiated outside Singapore or under religious and customary rites. Data comprise civil marriages registered under the Women's Charter and Muslim marriages registered under the Administration of Muslim Law Act. - Ne comprend pas les mariages prononcés ailleurs qu'à Singapour ni les mariages religieux ou coutumiers. Les données comprennent les mariages civils enregistrés en vertu de la Charte des droits de la femme, ainsi que les mariages musulmans enregistrés en vertu de la loi sur l'administration du droit islamique.
[31] Source: Department of Local Administration, Ministry of Interior. - Source : Département de l'administration locale, Ministère de l'intérieur.
[32] Data from MERNIS (Central Population Administrative System). - Données de MERNIS (Système central de données démographiques).
[33] Excluding marriages of aliens temporarily in the area, but including marriages abroad of persons with residence in Austria. - Non compris les mariages d'étrangers temporairement dans la région, mais y compris des mariages à l'étranger de personnes ayant leur résidence en Autriche.
[34] Including armed forces stationed outside the country and alien armed forces in the area, if the marriage is performed by local authority. Including same-sex marriages. - Y compris les militaires nationaux hors du pays et les militaires étrangers en garnison sur le territoire, si le mariage a été célébré par l'autorité locale. Y compris les mariages entre personnes du même sexe.
[35] Including nationals outside the country, but excluding foreigners in the country. - Y compris les nationaux à l'étranger, mais non compris les étrangers sur le territoire.
[36] Excluding Faeroe Islands and Greenland shown separately, if available. - Non compris les Iles Féroé et le Groenland, qui font l'objet de rubriques distinctes, si disponible.
[37] The difference between 'Total' and the sum of urban and rural is due to the unknown place of residence of grooms and to grooms living outside the country. Urban and rural residence refers to the place of usual residence of groom. - La différence entre le « Total » et la somme des chiffres urbains et ruraux s'explique par le fait que la résidence du marié n'est pas toujours connue ou est située à l'étranger. Le lieu de résidence (zone urbaine ou zone rurale) correspond au lieu de résidence habituel du marié.
[38] Excluding Åland Islands. Urban and rural distribution refers to the usual residence of the bride. - Non compris les Îles d'Åland. La répartition entre résidence urbaine et résidence rurale fait référence au lieu de résidence habituel de la mariée.
[39] Data for urban and rural exclude events corresponding to nationals residing outside the country, which may be included in the total. - Les données relatives à les categories urbaine et rurale n'englobent pas les faits d'état civil qui concernent les nationaux se trouvant à l'étranger, lesquels faits peuvent être inclus au total.
[40] The urban and rural categories do not include the data of foreigners, persons of unknown residence and the homeless, whereas the total category includes them. - Les chiffres portant sur la population urbaine et rurale n' incluent pas les données relatives aux étrangers, aux personnes dont la résidence n'est pas connue et aux personnes sans domicile fixe, à l'inverse, le total les inclut.
[41] Including same-sex marriages. Data refer to marriages where one or both partners are residents. - Y compris les mariages entre personnes du même sexe. Les données portent sur les mariages pour lesquels l'un des deux partenaires ou les deux sont résidents.
[42] Data exclude registered partnerships. Including same-sex marriages. Marriages of couples of which at least one partner is recorded in a Dutch municipal register, irrespective of the country where the marriage was performed. - Les données ne comprennent pas les partenariats d'un pacte civil enregistrés. Y compris les mariages entre personnes du même sexe. Correspond aux mariages pour lesquels au moins l'un des partenaires est inscrit sur un registre municipal néerlandais, quel que soit le pays dans lequel le mariage est célébré.
[43] Including same-sex marriages. Marriages registered by place of occurrence of marriage. - Y compris les mariages entre personnes du même sexe. Mariages enregistrés en fonction du lieu de l'événement.
[44] Includes civil and religious marriages as well as not specified. - Englobe les mariages civils et religieux et ceux pour lesquels rien n'a été indiqué.
[45] If either the groom or the bride (or both) is (are) resident in San Marino, their marriage is included in these data, independently of the place of occurrence of marriage. - Si l'un ou les deux époux résident à Saint-Marin, leur mariage est compris dans ces données, quel que soit le lieu où a été conclu le mariage.
[46] Data refer to marriages registered by residence of groom. Excludes data for Kosovo and Metohia. - Les données concernent les mariages enregistrés selon la résidence du marié. Sans les données pour le Kosovo et Metohie.
[47] Data refer to residence of groom or bride before marriage. - Données relatives au lieu de résidence du marié ou de la mariée avant le mariage.
[48] Data refer to usual residence of groom and bride. - Les données se rapportent à la résidence habituelle des époux.
[49] Data based on the residence of groom if he has permanent address in the country, otherwise, based on the residence of bride. If neither partner is a permanent resident, the marriage is not included in the official statistics. - Les données sont fondées sur la résidence du marié si celui-ci a une adresse permanente dans le pays, sinon elles sont fondées sur la résidence de la mariée.

Si aucun des deux partenaires n'est un résident permanent, le mariage n'apparaît pas dans les statistiques officielles.

50 The Government of Ukraine has informed the United Nations that it is not in a position to provide statistical data concerning the Autonomous Republic of Crimea and the city of Sevastopol. - Le gouvernement Ukrainien a informé l'ONU qu'il n'est pas en mesure de fournir des données statistiques concernant la République autonome de Crimée et la ville de Sébastopol.

51 Excluding Channel Islands (Guernsey and Jersey) and Isle of Man, shown separately, if available. Data tabulated by date of occurrence for England and Wales, and by date of registration for Northern Ireland and Scotland. - Non compris les îles Anglo-Normandes (Guernesey et Jersey) et l'île de Man, qui font l'objet de rubriques distinctes, si disponible. Données exploitées selon la date de l'événement pour l'Angleterre et le pays de Galles, et selon la date de l'enregistrement pour l'Irlande du Nord et l'Ecosse.

52 Including United States military personnel, their dependants and contract employees. Including same-sex marriages. - Y compris les militaires des Etats-Unis, les membres de leur famille les accompagnant et les agents contractuels des Etats-Unis. Y compris les mariages entre personnes du même sexe.

53 Including same-sex marriages. Data refer to marriages and civil unions by residence of 'partner 2'. Random rounding to base 3 is applied in this table as a confidentiality measure. - Y compris les mariages entre personnes du même sexe. Les données concernent les mariages et les unions civiles selon la résidence du « partenaire 2 ». Les chiffres sont arrondis à la base 3 de manière aléatoire, pour des raisons de confidentialité.

54 Data cover the period from 1 July of the previous year to 30 June of the present year. - Pour la période allant du 1er juillet de l'année précédente au 30 juin de l'année en cours.

55 Source: Births, Deaths, and Marriages Registration Division, Samoa Bureau of Statistics. - Source : Division de l'enregistrement des naissances, des décès et des mariages du Bureau de statistique du Samoa.

Table 24 - *Demographic Yearbook 2019*

Table 24 presents the marriages cross-classified by age of groom and age of bride for the latest available year between 2010 and 2019.

Description of variables: Marriage is defined as the act, ceremony or process by which the legal relationship of spouses is constituted. The legality of the union may be established by civil, religious or other means as recognized by the laws of each country[1].

Marriage statistics in this table, therefore, include both first marriages and remarriages after divorce, widowhood or annulment. They do not, unless otherwise noted, include resumption of marriage ties after legal separation. These statistics refer to the number of marriages performed, and not to the number of persons marrying.

Age is defined as age at last birthday, that is, the difference between the date of birth and the date of the occurrence of the event, expressed in completed solar years. The age classification used for brides in this table is the following: under 15 years, 5-year age groups through 90-94, and 95 years and over, depending on the availability of data. Age classification for grooms is restricted to: under 15 years, 5-year age groups from 15 to 59, and 60 years and over.

In an effort to provide interpretation of these statistics, countries or areas providing data on marriages by age of groom and bride have been requested to specify "the minimum legal age at which marriage can take place with and without parental consent". This information is presented in the table 24-1 below.

Reliability of data: Data from civil registers of marriages that are reported as incomplete (less than 90 per cent completeness) or of unknown completeness are considered unreliable and are set in *italics* rather than in roman type. Table 23 and the technical notes for that table provide more detailed information on the completeness of marriage registration. For more information about the quality of vital statistics data in general, see Section 4.2 of the Technical Notes.

Limitations: Statistics on marriages by age of groom and age of bride are subject to the same qualifications as have been set forth for vital statistics in general and marriage statistics in particular as discussed in Section 4 of the Technical Notes.

The fact that marriage is a legal event, unlike birth and death that are biological events, has implications for international comparability of data. Marriage has been defined, for statistical purposes, in terms of the laws of individual countries or areas. These laws vary throughout the world. In addition, comparability is further limited because some countries or areas compile statistics only for civil marriages although religious marriages may also be legally recognized; in other countries or areas, the only available records are church registers and, therefore, the statistics may not reflect marriages that are civil marriages only.

Because in many countries or areas marriage is a civil legal contract which, to establish its legality, must be celebrated before a civil officer, it follows that for these countries or areas registration would tend to be almost automatic at the time of, or immediately following, the marriage ceremony. This factor should be kept in mind when considering the reliability of data, described above.

Because these statistics are classified according to age, they are subject to the limitations with respect to accuracy of age reporting similar to those already discussed in connection with Section 3.1.3 of the Technical Notes. It is probable that biases are less pronounced in marriage statistics, because information is obtained from the persons concerned and since marriage is a legal act, the participants are likely to give correct information. However, in some countries or areas, there appears to be a concentration of marriages at the legal minimum age for marriage and at the age at which valid marriage may be contracted without parental consent, indicating perhaps an overstatement in some cases to comply with the law.

Aside from the possibility of age misreporting, it should be noted that marriage patterns at younger ages, that is, for ages up to 24 years, are influenced to a large extent by laws regarding the minimum age for marriage.

Factors that may influence age reporting, particularly at older ages include an inclination to understate the age of the bride in order that it may be equal to or less than that of the groom.

The absence of data in the unknown age group does not necessarily indicate completely accurate reporting and tabulation of the age item. It is sometimes an indication that the unknowns have been eliminated by assigning ages to them before tabulation, or by proportionate distribution after tabulation.

Another age-reporting factor that must be kept in mind in using these data is the variation that may result from calculating age at marriage from year of birth rather than from day, month and year of birth. Information on this factor is given in footnotes when known.

Earlier data: Marriages by age of groom and age of bride have been shown for the latest available year in most issues of the *Demographic Yearbook*. Data cross-classified by age of groom and bride have been presented in previous issues featuring marriage and divorce statistics. For information on the specific topics and the years covered, readers should consult the Historical Index.

24-1 Minimum legal age at which marriage can take place

Country or area	*With parental consent*		*Without parental consent*	
	Groom	*Bride*	*Groom*	*Bride*
Africa				
Botswana	18	18	21	21
Burkina Faso[2]	18	15	20	17
Burundi[5]			21	18
Cameroon[3]	18	15	21	18
Congo			21	18
Egypt	18	18		
Eswatini	18	18	21	21
Ghana			18	18
Guinea	18	18	21	21
Liberia	16	16	21	18
Libya[4]	18	18		
Malawi[5]			18	18
Mauritius	16	16	18	18
Morocco[5]			18	18
Namibia	18	18	21	21
Saint Helena ex. Dep.	16	16	21	21
Senegal	Under 18	Under 18	18	18
Seychelles	16	16	18	18
Sierra Leone[5]			18	18
South Africa[6]	Under 21	Under 21	21	21
Tunisia	15	15	18	18
Uganda[5, 7]			18	18
Zimbabwe	16	16	18	18
America, North				
Anguilla	16	16	18	18
Aruba[8]	16	16	18	18
Bermuda	16	16	18	18
Canada[9]	16	16	18	18
Cayman Islands	16	16	18	18

Country or area	*With parental consent*		*Without parental consent*	
	Groom	*Bride*	*Groom*	*Bride*
Costa Rica	15	15	18	18
Cuba	16	14	18	16
Curaçao	16	16	18	18
Dominican Republic	16	15	18	18
El Salvador	Under 18	Under 18	18	18
Greenland[5]			18	18
Jamaica	16	16	18	18
Mexico[10]	16	14	18	18
Montserrat[11]	16	16	18	18
Nicaragua	16	16	21	21
Panama			18	18
Puerto Rico	17	17	21	21
Saint Helena	16	16	21	21
Saint Vincent and the Grenadines			18	18
Trinidad and Tobago[12]	Under 18	Under 18	18	18
America, South				
Argentina	18	16	21	21
Bolivia (Plurinational State of)[13]	16	14	18	18
Brazil	16	16	18	18
Chile	16	16	18	18
Colombia	14	14	18	18
Ecuador			18	18
Suriname	17	15	21	21
Uruguay	16	16	18	18
Venezuela (Bolivarian Republic of)	16	14	18	18
Asia				
Armenia			18	17
Azerbaijan	18	17		
Bahrain			15	
Cambodia			18	18
China, Hong Kong SAR	16	16	21	21
China, Macao SAR	16	16	18	18
Cyprus	16	16	18	18
Georgia	16	16	18	18
Indonesia			19	16
Iran (Islamic Republic of)	18	15		
Israel[5]			18	18
Japan	18	16	20	20

Country or area	With parental consent		Without parental consent	
	Groom	Bride	Groom	Bride
Jordan	18	18		
Kazakhstan	16	16	18	18
Kyrgyzstan[5]			16	16
Malaysia[14]	18	16 or 18	18 aor21	18 or 21
Mongolia			18	18
Nepal	18	18	20	20
Oman[5]			18	18
Pakistan	18	14		
Philippines	18	18	21	21
Republic of Korea	18	18	19	19
Singapore[15]	Under 21	Under 21	21	21
State of Palestine[16]		14.5	15.5	
Tajikistan	17	17	18	18
Turkey	16	16	18	18
United Arab Emirates[17]	Under 18	Under 18	18	18
Uzbekistan	18	18		
Europe				
Åland Islands[20]			18	18
Albania	Under 18	Under 18	18	18
Andorra	14	14	16	16
Austria[18]	16	16	18	18
Belarus	15	15	18	18
Belgium[5]			18	18
Bosnia and Herzegovina			18	18
Bulgaria	16	16	18	18
Croatia	16	16	18	18
Czechia[19]	16	16	18	18
Denmark	15	15	18	18
Estonia	15	15	18	18
Faeroe Islands[5]			18	18
Finland[20]			18	18
France[5]			18	18
Germany[21]	16	16	18	18
Gibraltar	16	16	18	18
Greece[22]			18	18
Hungary	16	16	18	18
Iceland	No limit	No limit	18	18
Ireland[5, 23]			18	18
Isle of Man	16	16	18	18
Italy	16	16	18	18

Country or area	With parental consent		Without parental consent	
	Groom	Bride	Groom	Bride
Jersey	16	16	18	18
Latvia	16	16	18	18
Liechtenstein[18]			18	18
Lithuania[24]	15	15	18	18
Luxembourg			18	18
Malta			16	16
Montenegro	16	16	18	18
Netherlands	16	16	18	18
North Macedonia	16	16	18	18
Norway	16	16	18	18
Poland[25]			18	18
Portugal	16	16	18	18
Republic of Moldova			18	16
Romania[26]	16	16	18	18
Russian Federation	16	16	18	18
San Marino[27]	16	14	18	18
Serbia[28]	16	16	18	18
Slovakia			16	16
Slovenia	15	15	18	18
Spain	16	16	18	18
Sweden[29]			18	18
Switzerland			18	18
Ukraine[18]	16	16	18	18
United Kingdom of Great Britain and Northern Ireland	16	16	18	18
Oceania				
Australia[30]	16	16	18	18
Cook Islands	16	16	21	21
Guam[31]	17	17	18	18
New Caledonia			18	18
New Zealand	16	16	18	18

NOTES

[1] *Principles and Recommendations for a Vital Statistics System Revision 3,* Sales No. E.13.XVII.10, United Nations, New York, 2014.

[2] In addition, an age waiver may be granted by a civil court for a serious reason from 15 years for women and 18 years for men.

[3] Marriages can be exceptionally authorised by the President of the Republic for brides who are at least 13 years old without parental consent.

[4] According to the Islamic law, marriage requires parental consent. Consent of the bride herself, as well as the guardian's consent are fundamental in the marriage contract. Young men usually choose the consent of the parents. Minimum age at marriage is usually 18 years. According to the law, marriage is not restricted to individuals over the age of 18 years.

[5] The minimum legal age at which marriage can take place is the same with or without parental consent.

[6] Marriages under the age of 18 can be performed with parental consent or with judicial permission if parental consent has been unreasonably refused. Additionally, boys under the age of 18 and girls under the age of 16 may also be required to seek the consent of the Minister of Home Affairs.

[7] As reported by Uganda Bureau of Statistics, marriages with or without parental consent may occur much earlier than 18 years of age.

[8] The legal minimum marriage age is 18, with two exceptions: if the persons concerned are older than 16 and the woman is pregnant or has given birth or the Minister of Security and Justice grants a dispensation based on their request.

[9] Marriage is under provincial and territory legislations. Without parental consent, the minimum legal age at which marriage can take place is 18 years of age in all provinces and territories in Canada except in British Columbia, Newfoundland and Labrador, Nova Scotia, Nunavut, and Yukon where the minimum legal age is 19 years. With parental consent, the minimum legal age is 16 years in all provinces except in Northwest Territories, Nunavut, and Yukon. With parental consent, in Northwest Territories and Yukon, the minimum legal age is 15 years whereas in Nunavut, the minimum legal age is 18 years.

[10] Each of the 31 Federal States and the Federal District has its own civil code for marriage. Marriages under 18 require parental consent. Additionally, in the Federal District and in the states of Guanajuato, Morelos, Puebla and San Luis Potosí the minimum age with parental consent is 16 for both bride and groom and in the states of Michoacán, Nayarit, Sinaloa and Sonora the minimum age with parental consent is 14 for the bride and 16 for the groom.

[11] Consent can be given by a guardian or a person who has custody of the child wishing to marry. Also, the Governor has discretion to permit persons as young as 15 years and 1 day old to marry, if he thinks that getting married is in the best interest of the persons who are intending to marry and the persons in this instance must have also received the necessary consent.

[12] With parental consent, age for marriage is 14 years for males and 12 years for females in a civil marriage; 16 years for males and 12 years for females in a Muslim marriage; 18 years for males and 14 years for females in a Hindu marriage; and 18 years for males and 16 for females in Orisa marriage.

[13] Grooms younger than 16 and brides younger than 14 need court authorization.

[14] For marriage with parental consent, it is 18 years of age for males whereas it is 18 years of age for non-Muslim females and 16 years of age for Muslim females. Without parental consent, it is 21 years of age for non-Muslims and 18 years of age for Muslims.

[15] Specified minimum legal marriage age refers to marriages contracted under the Women's Charter. For Muslim marriages under the Administration of Muslim Law Act, no marriage shall be solemnised when either party is below the age of 18 years. Notwithstanding that, Muslim women below the age of 18 years who have attained the age of puberty may be married under the Administration of the Muslim Law Act.

[16] The legal marriage age for females is 14 years, 6 months and 22 days. There must be parental consent (father or brother if the father is dead). The legal marriage age for males is 15 years, 6 months and 21 days. Parental consent is not required.

[17] People under 18 years old require judge approval for marriage.

[18] Persons less than 18 years old need a decision of the court.

[19] The court may, for important reasons, allow the marriage of a minor over 16 years.

[20] Persons less than 18 years old need the permission of the Ministry of Justice.

[21] Marriage at 16-17 years of age requires that the other spouse be an adult (18 years or older) and an exemption from the requirement of majority by a competent family court.

[22] Under some conditions (e.g. pregnancy) the marriage can take place without age restrictions.

[23] An exemption on the minimum age can be granted by court order if granting of such an exemption is in the best interests of the parties to the intended marriage and good reasons for the application can be demonstrated.

[24] In addition to parental consent, persons less than 18 years old need judicial approval. In case of pregnancy, marriage can be allowed below 15 years of age.

[25] Females can marry at the age of 16 or 17 years with parental and court consent.

[26] Marriage for persons under 18 years requires parental consent, a medical certificate and the agreement by the local family court.

[27] The heads of the State of San Marino can allow marriages of males of 14 years and older and females of 12 years and older.

[28] Marriage is not allowed for persons below the age of 18; only the court may, for good cause, permit marriage to a minor who has attained the age of 16 years of age, and attained physical and mental maturity to exercise the rights and responsibilities of marriage. Parental consent is not required.

[29] With parental consent, no limit but authorities must approve; without parental consent, 18 years of age for Swedish citizens.

[30] Persons 16 or 17 years old need the court approval.

[31] Under 18, both a court order and parent or legal guardian consent are needed.

Tableau 24 – *Annuaire démographique 2019*

Le tableau 24 présente des statistiques concernant les mariages classés selon l'âge de l'époux et selon l'âge de l'épouse pour les années où les données sont disponibles entre 2010 et 2019.

Description des variables : le mariage désigne l'acte, la cérémonie ou la procédure qui établit un rapport légal entre les époux. L'union peut être rendue légale par une procédure civile ou religieuse, ou par toute autre procédure, conformément à la législation du pays[1].

Les statistiques de la nuptialité présentées dans ce tableau comprennent donc les premiers mariages et les remariages faisant suite à un divorce, un veuvage ou une annulation. Toutefois, sauf indication contraire, elles ne comprennent pas les unions reconstituées après une séparation légale. Ces statistiques se rapportent au nombre de mariages célébrés, non au nombre de personnes qui se marient.

L'âge désigne l'âge au dernier anniversaire, c'est-à-dire la différence entre la date de naissance et la date de l'événement, exprimée en années solaires révolues. Le classement par âge pour l'épouse utilisé dans ce tableau comprend les groupes suivants : moins de 15 ans, groupes quinquennaux jusqu'à 90-94 ans, et 95 ans et plus, selon la disponibilité des données. Le classement par âge pour l'époux est : moins de 15 ans, groupes quinquennal de 15 jusqu' à 59 ans et 60 ans et plus.

Dans un effort de fournir l'interprétation de ces statistiques, les pays ou les zones fournissant des données sur les mariages par l'âge de l'épouse et de par l'âge de l'époux ont été demandés d'indiquer « l'âge légal minimum avec auquel le mariage peut avoir lieu avec et sans consentement parental ». Cette information est présentée dans le tableau 24-1 ci-dessous.

Fiabilité des données : les données sur les mariages issues des registres de l'état civil qui sont déclarées incomplètes (degré de complétude inférieur à 90 p. 100) ou dont le degré de complétude n'est pas connu sont jugées douteuses et apparaissent en italique et non en caractères romains. Le tableau 23 et les notes techniques s'y rapportant présentent des renseignements plus détaillés sur le degré de complétude de l'enregistrement des mariages. Pour plus de précisions sur la qualité des données reposant sur les statistiques de l'état civil en général, voir la section 4.2 des notes techniques.

Insuffisance des données : les statistiques des mariages selon l'âge de l'époux et selon l'âge de l'épouse appellent les mêmes réserves que celles formulées à propos des statistiques de l'état civil en général et des statistiques de la nuptialité en particulier (voir la section 4 des Notes techniques).

Le fait que le mariage soit un acte juridique, à la différence de la naissance et du décès, qui sont des faits biologiques, a des répercussions sur la comparabilité internationale des données. Aux fins de la statistique, le mariage est défini par la législation de chaque pays ou zone. Cette législation varie d'un pays à l'autre. La comparabilité est limitée en outre du fait que certains pays et zones ne réunissent des statistiques que pour les mariages civils, bien que les mariages religieux y soient également reconnus par la loi ; dans d'autres, les seuls relevés disponibles sont les registres des églises et, en conséquence, les statistiques peuvent ne pas rendre compte des mariages exclusivement civils.

Le mariage étant, dans de nombreux pays ou zones, un contrat juridique civil qui, pour être légal, doit être conclu devant un officier d'état civil, il s'ensuit que, dans ces pays ou zones, l'enregistrement se fait à peu près systématiquement au moment de la cérémonie ou immédiatement après. Il faut tenir compte de cet élément lorsque l'on évalue la fiabilité des données, dont il est question plus haut.

Étant donné que ces statistiques sont classées selon l'âge, elles appellent les mêmes réserves concernant l'exactitude des déclarations d'âge que celles dont il a déjà été question à la section 3.1.3 des Notes techniques. Il est probable que les statistiques de la nuptialité sont moins faussées par ce genre d'erreur, car les renseignements sont donnés par les intéressés eux-mêmes, et, comme le mariage est un acte juridique, il y a toutes chances que leurs déclarations soient exactes. Toutefois, dans certains pays ou zones, il semble y avoir une concentration de mariages à l'âge minimal légal de nubilité ainsi qu'à l'âge auquel le mariage peut être valablement contracté sans le consentement des parents, ce qui peut indiquer que certains déclarants se vieillissent pour se conformer à la loi.

Outre la possibilité d'erreurs dans les déclarations d'âge, il convient de noter que la législation fixant l'âge minimal de nubilité influe notablement sur les caractéristiques de la nuptialité pour les premiers âges, c'est-à-dire jusqu'à 24 ans.

Parmi les facteurs pouvant exercer une influence sur les déclarations d'âge, en particulier celles qui sont faites par des personnes plus âgées, il faut citer la tendance à diminuer l'âge de l'épouse de façon qu'il soit égal ou inférieur à celui de l'époux.

Si aucun nombre ne figure dans la rangée réservée aux âges inconnus, cela ne signifie pas nécessairement que les déclarations d'âge et l'exploitation des données par âge aient été tout à fait exactes. C'est parfois une indication que l'on a attribué un âge aux personnes d'âge inconnu avant l'exploitation des données ou qu'elles ont été réparties proportionnellement entre les différents groupes après cette opération.

Il importe de ne pas oublier non plus, lorsque l'on utilisera ces données, que l'on calcule parfois l'âge des conjoints au moment du mariage sur la base de l'année de naissance seulement et non d'après la date exacte (jour, mois et année) de naissance. Des renseignements à ce sujet sont donnés en note chaque fois que possible.

Donnés publiées antérieurement : on trouve dans la plupart des éditions de l'*Annuaire démographique* des statistiques concernant les mariages selon l'âge de l'époux et selon l'âge de l'épouse qui ont été établies à partir des données les plus récentes dont on disposait à l'époque. Des données croisant l'âge des époux ont été présentées dans des éditions antérieurs, plus particulièrement consacrées aux statistiques de la nuptialité et de la divortialité. Pour plus de précisions concernant les années et les sujets pour lesquels des données ont été publiées, se reporter à l'index historique.

24-1 L'âge légal minimum auquel le mariage peut avoir lieu

Pays ou zone	*Avec consentement parental*		*Sans consentement parental*	
	Epoux	*Epouse*	*Epoux*	*Epouse*
Afrique				
Afrique du Sud[2]	Moins de 21	Moins de 21	21	21
Botswana	18	18	21	21
Burkina Faso[3]	18	15	20	17
Burundi[6]			21	18
Cameroun[4]	18	15	21	18
Congo			18	18
Egypte	18	18		
Eswatini	18	18	21	21
Ghana			18	18
Guinée	18	18	21	21
Libéria	16	16	21	18
Libye[5]	18	18		
Malawi[6]			18	18
Maurice	16	16	18	18
Maroc[6]			18	18
Namibie	18	18	21	21
Ouganda[6, 7]			18	18
Sainte-Hélène sans dép.	16	16	21	21
Sénégal	Moins de 18	Moins de 18	18	18
Seychelles	16	16	18	18
Sierra Leone[6]			18	18
Tunisie	15	15	18	18
Zimbabwe	16	16	18	18

Pays ou zone	Avec consentement parental		Sans consentement parental	
	Epoux	Epouse	Epoux	Epouse
Amérique du Nord				
Anguilla	16	16	18	18
Aruba[8]	16	16	18	18
Bermudes	16	16	18	18
Canada[9]	16	16	18	18
Costa Rica	15	15	18	18
Cuba	16	14	18	16
Curaçao	16	16	18	18
El Salvador	Moins de 18	Moins de 18	18	18
Groenland[6]			18	18
Îles Caïmanes	16	16	18	18
Jamaïque	16	16	18	18
Mexique[10]	Moins de 18	Moins de 18	18	18
Montserrat[11]	16	16	18	18
Nicaragua	16	16	21	21
Panama			18	18
Porto Rico	17	17	21	21
République dominicaine	16	15	18	18
Sainte-Hélène	16	16	21	21
Saint-Vincent-et-les Grenadines			18	18
Trinité-et-Tobago[12]	Moins de 18	Moins de 18	18	18
Amérique du Sud				
Argentine	18	16	21	21
Bolivie (État plurinational de)[13]	16	14	18	18
Brésil	16	16	18	18
Chili	16	16	18	18
Colombie	14	14	18	18
Equateur			18	18
Suriname	17	15	21	21
Uruguay	16	16	18	18
Venezuela (République bolivarienne du)	16	14	18	18
Asie				
Arménie			18	17
Azerbaïdjan	18	17		
Bahreïn			15	
Cambodge			18	18

Pays ou zone	*Avec consentement parental*		*Sans consentement parental*	
	Epoux	*Epouse*	*Epoux*	*Epouse*
Chine, Hong Kong RAS	16	16	21	21
Chine, Macao RAS	16	16	18	18
Chypre	16	16	18	18
État de Palestine[14]		14.5	15.5	
Géorgie	16	16	18	18
Indonésie			19	16
Iran (République islamique d')	18	15		
Israël[6]			18	18
Japon	18	16	20	20
Jordanie	18	18		
Kazakhstan	16	16	18	18
Kirghizistan[6]			16	16
Malaisie[15]	18	16 et 18	18 et 21	18 et 21
Mongolie			18	18
Népal	18	18	20	20
Oman[6]			18	18
Ouzbékistan	18	17		
Philippines	18	18	21	21
République de Corée	18	18	19	19
Singapour[16]	Moins de 21	Moins de 21	21	21
Tadjikistan	17	17	18	18
Turquie	16	16	18	18
Europe				
Albanie	Under 18	Under 18	18	18
Allemagne[17]	16	16	18	18
Andorre	14	14	16	16
Autriche[18]	16	16	18	18
Bélarus	15	15	18	18
Belgique[Error! Bookmark not defined.]			18	18
Bosnie-Herzégovine			18	18
Bulgarie	16	16	18	18
Croatie	16	16	18	18
Danemark	15	15	18	18
Espagne	16	16	18	18
Estonie	15	15	18	18
Fédération de Russie	16	16	18	18
Finlande[19]			18	18

Pays ou zone	Avec consentement parental		Sans consentement parental	
	Epoux	Epouse	Epoux	Epouse
France[6]			18	18
Gibraltar	16	16	18	18
Grèce[20]			18	18
Hongrie	16	16	18	18
Île de Man	16	16	18	18
Îles d'Åland[19]			18	18
Îles Féroé[6]			18	18
Irlande[6, 21]			18	18
Islande	Pas de limites	Pas de limites	18	18
Italie	16	16	18	18
Jersey	16	16	18	18
Lettonie	16	16	18	18
Liechtenstein[18]			18	18
Lituanie[22]	15	15	18	18
Luxembourg			18	18
Macédoine du Nord	16	16	18	18
Malte			16	16
Monténégro	16	16	18	18
Norvège	16	16	18	18
Pays-Bas	16	16	18	18
Pologne[23]			18	18
Portugal	16	16	18	18
République de Moldova			18	16
Roumanie[24]	16	16	18	18
Royaume-Uni de Grande-Bretagne et d'Irlande du Nord	16	16	18	18
San Marino[25]	16	14	18	18
Serbie[26]	16	16	18	18
Slovaquie			16	16
Slovénie	15	15	18	18
Suède[27]			18	18
Suisse			18	18
Tchéquie[28]	16	16	18	18
Ukraine[18]	16	16	18	18
Océanie				
Australie[29]	16	16	18	18
Guam[30]	17	17	18	18
Îles Cook	16	16	21	21
Nouvelle-Calédonie			18	18

Pays ou zone	Avec consentement parental		Sans consentement parental	
	Epoux	Epouse	Epoux	Epouse
Nouvelle-Zélande	16	16	18	18

NOTES

[1] *Principes et recommandations pour un système de statistique de l'état civil, troisième révision,* numéro de vente : E.13.XVII.10, publication des Nations Unies, New York, 2014.

[2] Il est possible de se marier avant 18 ans avec consentement parental, ou autorisation judiciaire si le consentement parental a été refusé sans motif raisonnable. De plus, les garçons âgés de moins de 18 ans et les filles âgées de moins de 16 ans peuvent être également tenus de demander le consentement du Ministère de l'intérieur.

[3] De plus, une dispense d'âge peut être accordée par un tribunal civil pour motif grave à partir de 15 ans pour les femmes et de 18 ans pour les hommes.

[4] Par ailleurs, à défaut d'avoir l'âge requis pour se marier avec l'aval des parents, la jeune fille peut exceptionnellement être autorisée par le Président de la République à se marier à 13 ans.

[5] Conformément à la loi islamique, le mariage requiert le consentement parental. Le consentement de la mariée, elle-même ainsi que le consentement du tuteur sont fondamentaux dans le contrat de mariage. Les jeunes hommes choisissent habituellement le consentement des parents. L'âge minimum du mariage est généralement 18 ans. Conformément à la loi, le mariage n'est pas limité aux individus âgés de plus de 18 ans.

[6] L'âge minimum légal du mariage est le même avec ou sans le consentement parental.

[7] Tel que le signale l'"Uganda Bureau of Statistics", les mariages avec ou sans le consentement parental peuvent se produire beaucoup plus tôt que 18 ans.

[8] L'âge minimum légal du mariage est 18 ans, avec deux exceptions : si les personnes en cause ont plus de 16 ans et la femme est enceinte ou a accouché, ou si le Ministre de la sécurité et de la justice leur a accordé une dispense sur leur demande.

[9] Le mariage est en vertu des législations provinciales et territoriales. Sans le consentement des parents, l'âge minimum légal du mariage est de 18 ans dans toutes les provinces et territoires du Canada sauf en Colombie-Britannique, Terre-Neuve-et-Labrador, la Nouvelle-Écosse, du Nunavut et du Yukon, où l'âge minimum légal est de 19 ans. Avec le consentement des parents, l'âge minimum légal est de 16 ans dans toutes les provinces sauf dans les Territoires du Nord-Ouest, Nunavut et Yukon. Avec le consentement des parents, dans les Territoires du Nord-Ouest et le Yukon l'âge minimum légal est de 15 ans alors que dans le Nunavut, l'âge minimum légal est de 18 ans.

[10] Chacun des 31 Etats fédéraux et du District fédéral a son propre code civil pour le mariage. Avant 18 ans, il faut le consentement parental pour pouvoir se marier. De plus, dans le District fédéral et les États de Guanajuato, Morelos, Puebla et San Luis Potosí l'âge minimum, avec consentement parental, est de 16 ans pour le fiancé et la fiancée, et dans les États de Michoacán, Nayarit, Sinaloa et Sonora, l'âge minimum avec consentement parental est de 14 ans pour la fiancée et 16 ans pour le fiancé.

[11] Le consentement peut être donné par un tuteur ou une personne qui a la garde de l'enfant qui souhaitent se marier. En outre, le gouverneur a la faculté de permettre aux personnes âgées d'au moins 15 ans et 1 jour de se marier, s'il pense que le mariage est dans le meilleur intérêt des personnes qui ont l'intention de s'unir et que les personnes concernées aient également reçu le consentement nécessaire.

[12] Avec l'âge du le consentement parental, l'âge minimum du mariage pour se marier est de 14 ans pour les hommes et de 12 ans pour les femmes pour un mariage civil ; de 16 ans pour les hommes et de 12 ans pour les femmes pour un mariage musulman ; de 18 ans pour les hommes et de 14 ans pour les femmes pour un mariage hindou, et de18 ans pour les hommes et de 16 pour les femmes pour un mariage orisa.

[13] Il est nécessaire d'avoir une autorisation judiciaire pour se marier avant 16 ans pour les hommes et avant 14 ans pour les femmes.

[14] L'âge légal du mariage pour les femmes est de 14 ans, 6 mois et 22 jours. Le consentement parental (du père ou du frère si le père est mort) est requis. L'âge légal du mariage pour les hommes est de 15 ans, 6 mois et 21 jours. Le consentement parental n'est pas nécessaire.

[15] Pour le mariage avec le consentement parental, il est de 18 ans pour les hommes alors qu'il est de 18 ans pour les femmes non-musulmanes et il est de 16 ans pour les femmes musulmanes. Sans le consentement parental, il est de 21 ans pour les non-musulmans et de 18 ans pour les musulmans.

[16] L'âge minimum légal du mariage spécifié correspond à des mariages contractés en vertu de la Charte des femmes. Pour les mariages musulmans sous l'administration de la « Loi sur le Droit Musulman », aucun mariage ne doit être célébré lorsque l'une des parties est en dessous de l'âge de 18 ans. Néanmoins, les femmes musulmanes en dessous de l'âge de 18 ans qui ont atteint l'âge de la puberté peuvent être mariées dans le cadre de l'administration de la « Loi sur le Droit Musulman ».

[17] Le mariage à 16-17 ans exige que l'autre conjoint soit un adulte (18 ans ou plus) ainsi qu'une exemption de l'obligation de la majorité par un juge aux affaires familiales.

[18] Les personnes âgées de moins de 18 ans doivent obtenir l'autorisation de la justice.

[19] Les personnes âgées de moins de 18 ans doivent obtenir l'autorisation du ministère de la justice.

[20] Dans certaines conditions (par exemple la grossesse), le mariage peut avoir lieu sans restriction d'âge.

[21] Une exemption sur l'âge minimum peut être accordée par ordonnance du tribunal si l'octroi d'une telle exemption est dans le meilleur intérêt des parties ayant l'intention de se marier et si la demande est appuyée par de bonnes raisons.

[22] En plus du consentement parental, les personnes de moins de 18 ans doivent obtenir l'approbation judiciaire. En cas de grossesse, le mariage peut être autorisé en dessous de 15 ans.

[23] Les femmes peuvent se marier à l'âge de 16 ou 17 ans avec les autorisations des parents et du tribunal.

[24] Le mariage avant 18 ans exige le consentement parental, un certificat médical et l'autorisation du tribunal local de famille.

[25] Les chefs de l'État de Saint-Marin peuvent autoriser le mariage d'hommes de 14 ans et plus et de femmes de 12 ans et plus.

[26] Il n'est pas permis de se marier avant 18 ans ; seul le tribunal peut, pour un motif valable, y autoriser une personne mineure ayant atteint l'âge de 16 ans et parvenue à la maturité physique et mentale voulue pour exercer les droits et les responsabilités du mariage. Le consentement parental n'est pas requis.

[27] Avec le consentement des parents, aucune limite mais les autorités doivent approuver. Sans le consentement parental, l'âge minimum légal du mariage est de 18 ans pour les citoyens suédois.

[28] Il est possible de se marier de 16 ans par autorisation judiciaire pour des raisons importantes.

[29] Les personnes âgées 16 ou 17 ans doivent obtenir l'autorisation du tribunal.

[30] Le mariage avant 18 ans exige le consentement parental ou de personne qui a la garde de mineur, et l'autorisation du tribunal.

24. Marriages by age of groom and by age of bride: latest available year, 2010 - 2019
Mariages selon l'âge de l'époux et selon l'âge de l'épouse : dernière année disponible, 2010 - 2019

Continent, country or area, year, code[a] and age of bride / Continent, pays ou zone, date, code[a] et âge de l'épouse	Age of groom - - âge de l'époux												
	Total	0-14	15-19	20-24	25-29	30-34	35-39	40-44	45-49	50-54	55-59	60+	Unknown Inconnu
AFRICA - AFRIQUE													
Botswana[1]													
2018 (+U)													
Total	5 489	-	-	46	523	1 115	1 277	907	573	402	244	402	...
0 - 14	-	-	-	-	-	-	-	-	-	-	-	-	...
15 - 19	11	-	-	3	2	4	1	-	-	1	-	-	...
20 - 24	330	-	-	31	141	103	40	11	3	1	-	-	...
25 - 29	1 234	-	-	11	301	468	310	87	39	10	4	4	...
30 - 34	1 424	-	-	-	65	449	510	253	85	46	12	4	...
35 - 39	1 081	-	-	1	10	79	351	353	177	70	25	15	...
40 - 44	604	-	-	-	3	8	55	167	175	119	49	28	...
45 - 49	338	-	-	-	1	2	7	33	77	96	61	61	...
50 - 54	210	-	-	-	-	1	2	3	15	51	64	74	...
55 - 59	124	-	-	-	-	1	1	-	2	8	26	86	...
60 - 64	76	-	-	-	-	-	-	-	-	-	2	74	...
65 +	57	-	-	-	-	-	-	-	-	-	1	56	...
Cabo Verde[2]													
2018* (+C)													
Total	2 337	...	55[h]	337	471	451	363	229	164	118	73	76	...
16 - 19	5	...	2[h]	2	1	-	-	-	-	-	-	-	...
20 - 24	167	...	21[h]	77	39	18	8	2	-	2	-	-	...
25 - 29	429	...	17[h]	146	130	72	40	12	8	3	1	-	...
30 - 34	453	...	7[h]	61	155	132	59	22	11	5	1	-	...
35 - 39	332	...	3[h]	26	65	110	77	33	8	6	2	2	...
40 - 44	262	...	3[h]	9	35	49	87	47	19	6	7	-	...
45 - 49	215	...	2[h]	7	19	32	38	62	41	10	1	3	...
50 - 54	181	...	-[h]	5	14	16	33	33	38	27	7	8	...
55 - 59	137	...	-[h]	1	7	12	10	11	22	38	25	11	...
60 - 64	75	...	-[h]	1	4	5	6	5	9	13	18	14	...
65 - 69	34	...	-[h]	1	2	2	2	1	5	4	5	12	...
70 - 74	18	...	-[h]	-	-	2	1	1	1	2	3	8	...
75 +	29	...	-[h]	1	-	1	2	-	2	2	3	18	...
Congo													
2014 (+U)													
Total	3 625	...	5	32	275	581	647	512	427	1 146[s]	...	...	...
15 - 19	58	...	...	...	...	...	...	...	...	...	...	...	...
20 - 24	352	...	...	...	...	...	...	...	...	...	...	...	...
25 - 29	677	...	...	...	...	...	...	...	...	...	...	...	...
30 - 34	690	...	...	...	...	...	...	...	...	...	...	...	...
35 - 39	593	...	...	...	...	...	...	...	...	...	...	...	...
40 - 44	482	...	...	...	...	...	...	...	...	...	...	...	...
45 - 49	389	...	...	...	...	...	...	...	...	...	...	...	...
50 +	384	...	...	...	...	...	...	...	...	...	...	...	...
Egypt - Égypte													
2017 (+C)													
Total	912 606	11 898	168 833	380 721	191 823	63 605	30 354	19 854	14 851	11 035	7 302	12 330	...
0 - 14	270 030	7 319	85 729	129 287	41 233	4 958	785	289	163	97	49	121	...
15 - 19	343 095	3 485	72 733	175 825	72 642	13 020	2 806	1 056	643	401	196	288	...
20 - 24	146 595	738	7 721	63 589	48 305	15 988	5 207	2 330	1 228	735	370	384	...
25 - 29	68 241	198	1 561	8 620	22 751	17 646	8 038	4 026	2 436	1 425	836	704	...
30 - 34	36 485	66	491	1 976	4 842	8 909	7 908	5 021	3 169	1 958	1 091	1 054	...
35 - 39	20 915	21	202	586	1 231	2 143	4 222	4 529	3 142	2 162	1 293	1 384	...
40 - 44	11 455	33	126	288	411	602	946	1 958	2 557	1 839	1 233	1 462	...
45 - 49	6 585	6	80	169	163	186	299	454	1 173	1 616	1 115	1 324	...
50 - 54	2 916	4	28	71	56	52	70	119	243	636	714	923	...
55 - 59	1 352	6	15	43	35	29	27	22	56	111	332	676	...
60 - 64	508	3	12	16	12	5	10	17	13	22	53	345	...
65 - 69	222	3	6	6	4	3	3	5	-	11	9	172	...
70 - 74	624	4	55	118	76	37	22	19	23	16	6	248	...
75 +	3 583	12	74	127	62	27	11	9	5	6	5	3 245	...
Lesotho													
2013 (+U)													
Total	4 552	...	11	370	1 402	1 133	635	325	225	175	99	162	15
15 - 19	188	...	9	101	56	15	7	-	-	-	-	-	-
20 - 24	1 230	...	2	235	673	237	55	10	6	8	2	1	1
25 - 29	1 502	...	-	28	611	597	165	55	21	11	7	7	-

24. Marriages by age of groom and by age of bride: latest available year, 2010 - 2019
Mariages selon l'âge de l'époux et selon l'âge de l'épouse : dernière année disponible, 2010 - 2019 (continued - suite)

Continent, country or area, year, code[a] and age of bride / Continent, pays ou zone, date, code[a] et âge de l'épouse	Age of groom - - âge de l'époux												
	Total	0-14	15-19	20-24	25-29	30-34	35-39	40-44	45-49	50-54	55-59	60+	Unknown Inconnu
AFRICA - AFRIQUE													
Lesotho													
2013													
30 - 34	792	...	-	6	51	246	289	109	49	24	9	9	-
35 - 39	370	...	-	-	3	28	103	106	65	34	19	11	1
40 - 44	173	...	-	-	1	1	8	38	57	39	14	15	-
45 - 49	116	...	-	-	-	2	2	6	24	50	22	10	-
50 - 54	40	...	-	-	-	-	1	-	2	8	17	12	-
55 - 59	23	...	-	-	-	-	-	-	1	-	7	15	-
60 - 64	11	...	-	-	-	-	-	-	-	1	2	8	-
65 +	91	...	-	-	6	7	3	1	-	-	-	74	-
Unknown - Inconnu	16	...	-	-	1	-	2	-	-	-	-	-	13
2016 (+U)													
Total	2 640	...	6	149	666	689	473	290	131	236[s]	...	...	...
15 - 19	53	...	...	...	...	...	...	...	...	...	...	...	...
20 - 24	571	...	...	...	...	...	...	...	...	...	...	...	...
25 - 29	840	...	...	...	...	...	...	...	...	...	...	...	...
30 - 34	595	...	...	...	...	...	...	...	...	...	...	...	...
35 - 39	297	...	...	...	...	...	...	...	...	...	...	...	...
40 - 44	144	...	...	...	...	...	...	...	...	...	...	...	...
45 - 49	68	...	...	...	...	...	...	...	...	...	...	...	...
50 +	72	...	...	...	...	...	...	...	...	...	...	...	...
Mauritius - Maurice[3]													
2019 (+C)													
Total	9 709	-	111	910	2 989	2 279	1 341	749	454	369	247	256	4
0 - 14	-	-	-	-	-	-	-	-	-	-	-	-	-
15 - 19	557	-	84	252	147	44	20	5	-	4	-	1	-
20 - 24	1 967	-	24	493	972	346	94	30	5	2	-	1	-
25 - 29	3 337	-	3	140	1 585	1 107	363	83	34	14	4	4	-
30 - 34	1 562	-	-	18	219	605	431	202	53	22	5	6	1
35 - 39	918	-	-	3	45	135	324	231	106	48	13	13	-
40 - 44	533	-	-	3	16	32	82	146	121	81	34	18	-
45 - 49	374	-	-	1	5	10	24	41	89	109	65	30	-
50 - 54	228	-	-	-	-	-	2	8	40	60	74	44	-
55 - 59	142	-	-	-	-	-	1	2	5	25	37	72	-
60 - 64	55	-	-	-	-	-	-	1	1	3	12	38	-
65 - 69	27	-	-	-	-	-	-	-	-	1	3	23	-
70 - 74	5	-	-	-	-	-	-	-	-	-	-	5	-
75 +	1	-	-	-	-	-	-	-	-	-	-	1	-
Unknown - Inconnu	3	-	-	-	-	-	-	-	-	-	-	-	3
Mayotte													
2018 (C)													
Total	345	...	1[f]	21	79	77	65	61[n]	...	30[o]	...	11	...
0 - 19	9	...	...	...	...	...	...	...	...	...	...	...	...
20 - 24	73	...	...	...	...	...	...	...	...	...	...	...	...
25 - 29	91	...	...	...	...	...	...	...	...	...	...	...	...
30 - 34	74	...	...	...	...	...	...	...	...	...	...	...	...
35 - 39	40	...	...	...	...	...	...	...	...	...	...	...	...
40 - 49	36	...	...	...	...	...	...	...	...	...	...	...	...
50 - 59	15	...	...	...	...	...	...	...	...	...	...	...	...
60 +	7	...	...	...	...	...	...	...	...	...	...	...	...
Reunion - Réunion													
2018 (C)													
Total	2 922	...	2[f]	151	594	614	447	569[n]	...	359[o]	...	186	...
0 - 19	19	...	...	...	...	...	...	...	...	...	...	...	...
20 - 24	318	...	...	...	...	...	...	...	...	...	...	...	...
25 - 29	750	...	...	...	...	...	...	...	...	...	...	...	...
30 - 34	606	...	...	...	...	...	...	...	...	...	...	...	...
35 - 39	384	...	...	...	...	...	...	...	...	...	...	...	...
40 - 49	497	...	...	...	...	...	...	...	...	...	...	...	...
50 - 59	272	...	...	...	...	...	...	...	...	...	...	...	...
60 +	76	...	...	...	...	...	...	...	...	...	...	...	...
Saint Helena ex. dep. - Sainte-Hélène sans dép.													
2018 (C)													
Total	10	-	-	1	1	4	1	-	1	1	-	1	...
0 - 14	-	-	-	-	-	-	-	-	-	-	-	-	...

24. Marriages by age of groom and by age of bride: latest available year, 2010 - 2019
Mariages selon l'âge de l'époux et selon l'âge de l'épouse : dernière année disponible, 2010 - 2019 (continued - suite)

Continent, country or area, year, code[a] and age of bride / Continent, pays ou zone, date, code[a] et âge de l'épouse	Age of groom - - âge de l'époux												
	Total	0-14	15-19	20-24	25-29	30-34	35-39	40-44	45-49	50-54	55-59	60+	Unknown Inconnu
AFRICA - AFRIQUE													
Saint Helena ex. dep. - Sainte-Hélène sans dép.													
2018													
15 - 19	-	-	-	-	-	-	-	-	-	-	-	-	...
20 - 24	-	-	-	-	-	-	-	-	-	-	-	-	...
25 - 29	3	-	-	1	1	1	-	-	-	-	-	-	...
30 - 34	1	-	-	-	-	1	-	-	-	-	-	-	...
35 - 39	2	-	-	-	-	2	-	-	-	-	-	-	...
40 - 44	-	-	-	-	-	-	-	-	-	-	-	-	...
45 - 49	-	-	-	-	-	-	-	-	-	-	-	-	...
50 - 54	1	-	-	-	-	-	1	-	-	-	-	-	...
55 - 59	2	-	-	-	-	-	-	-	1	1	-	-	...
60 - 64	1	-	-	-	-	-	-	-	-	-	-	1	...
65 - 69	-	-	-	-	-	-	-	-	-	-	-	-	...
70 - 74	-	-	-	-	-	-	-	-	-	-	-	-	...
75 +	-	-	-	-	-	-	-	-	-	-	-	-	...
Seychelles[4]													
2019 (+C)													
Total	3 078	...	2	83	512	875	605	358	248	179	216[t]	...	...
15 - 19	15	...	1	4	6	4	-	-	-	-	-[t]	...	...
20 - 24	162	...	1	36	58	38	15	5	5	2	2[t]	...	...
25 - 29	782	...	-	19	270	303	116	37	16	12	9[t]	...	...
30 - 34	970	...	-	12	117	388	260	104	54	18	17[t]	...	...
35 - 39	537	...	-	7	36	96	166	114	60	33	25[t]	...	...
40 - 44	259	...	-	2	14	31	32	72	47	33	28[t]	...	...
45 - 49	158	...	-	2	8	9	11	13	46	37	32[t]	...	...
50 - 54	111	...	-	-	3	4	4	8	15	31	46[t]	...	...
55 +	84	...	-	1	-	2	1	5	5	13	57[t]	...	...
South Africa - Afrique du Sud													
2017 (...)													
Total	135 458	...	81	5 022	23 165	29 976	24 941	18 492	12 714	8 347	5 476	7 244	...
15 - 19	886	...	34	423	279	97	31	9	9	2	1	1	...
20 - 24	14 155	...	32	3 286	6 702	2 761	895	269	123	58	17	12	...
25 - 29	35 237	...	10	1 002	13 062	13 199	5 245	1 769	624	191	75	60	...
30 - 34	31 619	...	5	221	2 447	11 061	10 540	4 659	1 680	602	267	137	...
35 - 39	20 708	...	-	69	488	2 223	6 434	6 555	3 001	1 176	451	311	...
40 - 44	13 388	...	-	15	129	493	1 340	3 985	4 080	1 944	880	522	...
45 - 49	8 688	...	-	6	52	103	356	962	2 479	2 430	1 333	967	...
50 - 54	5 088	...	-	-	5	32	83	216	573	1 476	1 390	1 313	...
55 - 59	2 910	...	-	-	-	5	12	53	116	370	802	1 552	...
60 - 64	1 538	...	-	-	1	1	4	12	21	80	211	1 208	...
65 - 69	723	...	-	-	-	1	1	2	5	11	37	666	...
70 +	518	...	-	-	-	-	-	1	3	7	12	495	...
Tunisia - Tunisie													
2017 (...)													
Total	95 336	...	236[f]	4 258	23 220	32 204	17 803	7 518	3 403	2 177	1 439	3 078	...
0 - 19	5 001	...	...	...	...	...	...	...	...	...	...	...	...
20 - 24	23 486	...	...	...	...	...	...	...	...	...	...	...	...
25 - 29	32 524	...	...	...	...	...	...	...	...	...	...	...	...
30 - 34	17 227	...	...	...	...	...	...	...	...	...	...	...	...
35 - 39	8 196	...	...	...	...	...	...	...	...	...	...	...	...
40 - 44	4 326	...	...	...	...	...	...	...	...	...	...	...	...
45 - 49	2 381	...	...	...	...	...	...	...	...	...	...	...	...
50 +	2 195	...	...	...	...	...	...	...	...	...	...	...	...
AMERICA, NORTH - AMÉRIQUE DU NORD													
Anguilla[5]													
2013 (C)													
Total	42	4	9	9	4	4	4	1	-	1	...	...	6
0 - 14	5	2	2	-	-	-	1	-	-	-	...	...	-
15 - 19	12	1	5	3	3	-	-	-	-	-	...	...	-
20 - 24	9	-	1	5	1	1	1	-	-	-	...	...	-
25 - 29	5	1	1	1	-	2	-	-	-	-	...	...	-

24. Marriages by age of groom and by age of bride: latest available year, 2010 - 2019
Mariages selon l'âge de l'époux et selon l'âge de l'épouse : dernière année disponible, 2010 - 2019 (continued - suite)

Continent, country or area, year, code[a] and age of bride / Continent, pays ou zone, date, code[a] et âge de l'épouse	Age of groom - - âge de l'époux												
	Total	0-14	15-19	20-24	25-29	30-34	35-39	40-44	45-49	50-54	55-59	60+	Unknown Inconnu
AMERICA, NORTH - AMÉRIQUE DU NORD													
Anguilla[5]													
2013													
30 - 34	3	-	-	-	-	-	2	1	-	-	...	...	-
35 - 39	2	-	-	-	-	1	-	-	-	1	...	...	-
40 - 44	-	-	-	-	-	-	-	-	-	-	...	...	-
45 - 49	-	-	-	-	-	-	-	-	-	-	...	...	-
50 - 54	-	-	-	-	-	-	-	-	-	-	...	...	-
Unknown - Inconnu	6	-	-	-	-	-	-	-	-	-	...	...	6
Aruba													
2017 (C)													
Total	537	-	11	58	126	100	72	50	52	32	16	19	1
0 - 14	-	-	-	-	-	-	-	-	-	-	-	-	-
15 - 19	3	-	1	2	-	-	-	-	-	-	-	-	-
20 - 24	45	-	6	19	9	6	2	3	-	-	-	-	-
25 - 29	94	-	3	23	47	11	7	3	-	-	-	-	-
30 - 34	80	-	1	6	33	24	9	3	1	3	-	-	-
35 - 39	85	-	-	4	18	30	20	6	5	1	-	-	1
40 - 44	71	-	-	2	9	13	21	12	12	1	-	1	-
45 - 49	54	-	-	1	7	9	7	7	15	6	1	1	-
50 - 54	48	-	-	1	2	4	4	10	13	9	3	2	-
55 - 59	21	-	-	-	1	1	-	3	5	7	4	-	-
60 - 64	21	-	-	-	-	2	2	3	1	2	5	6	-
65 - 69	10	-	-	-	-	-	-	-	-	3	2	5	-
70 - 74	4	-	-	-	-	-	-	-	-	-	1	3	-
75 +	1	-	-	-	-	-	-	-	-	-	-	1	-
Bahamas													
2013 (+C)													
Total	2 122	...	...	...	104	472	498	325	223	163	106	226	5
25 - 29	171	...	...	...	24	64	39	16	3	5	-	20	-
30 - 34	543	...	...	...	27	202	161	62	42	13	12	24	-
35 - 39	391	...	...	...	9	61	131	87	48	24	12	18	1
40 - 44	249	...	...	...	5	21	53	70	50	28	9	13	-
45 - 49	219	...	...	...	5	24	33	28	38	44	23	24	-
50 - 54	192	...	...	...	6	21	28	26	22	38	21	30	-
55 - 59	133	...	...	...	6	17	20	17	9	6	18	39	1
60 +	216	...	...	...	22	62	33	17	10	4	11	56	1
Unknown - Inconnu	8	...	...	...	-	-	-	2	1	1	-	2	2
Bermuda - Bermudes													
2018 (C)													
Total	467	-	1	13	66	130	71	43	38	43	24	38	-
0 - 14	-	-	-	-	-	-	-	-	-	-	-	-	-
15 - 19	1	-	-	1	-	-	-	-	-	-	-	-	-
20 - 24	15	-	-	5	8	2	-	-	-	-	-	-	-
25 - 29	89	-	1	5	43	29	8	1	1	-	-	1	-
30 - 34	135	-	-	2	7	75	36	9	4	-	2	-	-
35 - 39	79	-	-	-	6	21	20	10	12	4	4	2	-
40 - 44	44	-	-	-	1	-	6	19	8	7	2	1	-
45 - 49	36	-	-	-	1	2	-	3	10	12	5	3	-
50 - 54	31	-	-	-	-	1	1	1	3	16	5	4	-
55 - 59	16	-	-	-	-	-	-	-	-	4	4	8	-
60 - 64	15	-	-	-	-	-	-	-	-	-	2	13	-
65 - 69	4	-	-	-	-	-	-	-	-	-	-	4	-
70 - 74	1	-	-	-	-	-	-	-	-	-	-	1	-
75 +	1	-	-	-	-	-	-	-	-	-	-	1	-
Unknown - Inconnu	-	-	-	-	-	-	-	-	-	-	-	-	-
Costa Rica[6]													
2019* (C)													
Total	22 680	-	141	1 984	4 833	5 085	3 364	2 198	1 508	1 132	873	1 534	28
0 - 14	-	-	-	-	-	-	-	-	-	-	-	-	-
15 - 19	681	-	70	364	153	60	18	4	3	2	3	2	2
20 - 24	3 531	-	55	1 047	1 411	639	194	93	38	19	19	14	2
25 - 29	5 689	-	9	378	2 239	1 874	721	242	108	57	28	26	7
30 - 34	4 639	-	4	117	715	1 724	1 151	490	216	117	52	50	3
35 - 39	2 839	-	1	52	207	512	801	625	294	170	79	95	3
40 - 44	1 876	-	1	13	70	192	316	452	358	219	131	122	2
45 - 49	1 285	-	1	8	24	62	108	200	295	248	159	180	-

24. Marriages by age of groom and by age of bride: latest available year, 2010 - 2019
Mariages selon l'âge de l'époux et selon l'âge de l'épouse : dernière année disponible, 2010 - 2019 (continued - suite)

Continent, country or area, year, code[a] and age of bride / Continent, pays ou zone, date, code[a] et âge de l'épouse	Age of groom - - âge de l'époux												
	Total	0-14	15-19	20-24	25-29	30-34	35-39	40-44	45-49	50-54	55-59	60+	Unknown Inconnu
AMERICA, NORTH - AMÉRIQUE DU NORD													
Costa Rica[6]													
2019*													
50 - 54	884	-	-	1	7	13	34	58	124	189	202	253	3
55 - 59	544	-	-	-	1	6	15	24	42	74	128	254	-
60 - 64	347	-	-	-	2	-	1	9	18	24	46	247	-
65 - 69	197	-	-	-	-	1	2	-	8	9	18	159	-
70 - 74	74	-	-	-	1	-	-	-	-	3	5	65	-
75 +	70	-	-	-	-	-	-	-	2	-	2	66	-
Unknown - Inconnu	24	-	-	4	3	2	3	1	2	1	1	1	6
Cuba[7]													
2018 (C)													
Total	58 070	1	909	5 836	9 902	9 430	6 466	5 995	5 900	4 967	3 257	5 394	13
0 - 14	35	-	9	19	5	-	-	1	1	-	-	-	-
15 - 19	3 707	-	526	1 596	927	381	125	57	35	23	15	22	-
20 - 24	9 146	-	246	2 632	3 203	1 634	639	327	189	133	66	76	1
25 - 29	10 882	1	66	931	3 439	3 132	1 426	851	516	260	141	117	2
30 - 34	8 578	-	27	318	1 280	2 349	1 862	1 269	785	397	149	142	-
35 - 39	5 574	-	15	150	503	938	1 155	1 225	822	432	180	151	3
40 - 44	5 092	-	9	73	216	464	629	1 089	1 235	794	325	257	1
45 - 49	5 257	-	8	40	150	282	334	723	1 339	1 241	630	509	1
50 - 54	4 219	-	-	35	78	139	175	283	631	1 080	859	939	-
55 - 59	2 564	-	3	19	46	59	64	93	227	418	584	1 051	-
60 - 64	1 433	-	-	7	20	27	27	42	71	115	207	915	2
65 - 69	830	-	-	7	10	4	6	15	27	41	69	651	-
70 - 74	421	-	-	5	6	4	11	8	9	19	20	339	-
75 +	322	-	-	4	17	17	12	11	13	12	11	225	-
Unknown - Inconnu	10	-	-	-	2	-	1	1	-	2	1	-	3
Curaçao[8]													
2016 (C)													
Total	695	-	1	35	104	108	116	73	70	63	55	59	11
0 - 14	-	-	-	-	-	-	-	-	-	-	-	-	-
15 - 19	9	-	1	5	1	-	1	1	-	-	-	-	-
20 - 24	82	-	-	20	36	9	9	5	3	-	-	-	-
25 - 29	141	-	-	9	46	35	33	8	6	2	2	-	-
30 - 34	133	-	-	1	18	50	23	16	16	2	4	3	-
35 - 39	75	-	-	-	2	9	26	15	10	8	3	2	-
40 - 44	70	-	-	-	1	3	12	21	13	13	5	2	-
45 - 49	57	-	-	-	-	2	9	5	14	13	8	6	-
50 - 54	60	-	-	-	-	-	1	1	8	19	21	10	-
55 - 59	31	-	-	-	-	-	2	1	-	3	10	15	-
60 - 64	11	-	-	-	-	-	-	-	-	2	1	8	-
65 - 69	10	-	-	-	-	-	-	-	-	1	1	8	-
70 - 74	3	-	-	-	-	-	-	-	-	-	-	3	-
75 +	2	-	-	-	-	-	-	-	-	-	-	2	-
Unknown - Inconnu	11	-	-	-	-	-	-	-	-	-	-	-	11
Dominican Republic - République dominicaine													
2019 (+C)													
Total	51 938	-	427	5 887	10 188	8 245	6 687	5 403	4 495	3 754	2 726	4 031	95
0 - 14	-	-	-	-	-	-	-	-	-	-	-	-	-
15 - 19	2 232	-	177	1 097	601	199	72	44	19	10	7	6	-
20 - 24	9 394	-	172	3 081	3 509	1 338	583	283	190	95	57	83	3
25 - 29	10 646	-	53	999	3 701	2 766	1 380	668	421	294	161	193	10
30 - 34	7 896	-	16	364	1 183	2 056	1 860	998	584	355	257	211	12
35 - 39	6 237	-	7	170	560	912	1 352	1 312	792	518	280	323	11
40 - 44	5 075	-	1	85	295	444	718	1 068	1 025	657	384	395	3
45 - 49	4 031	-	-	45	163	280	351	529	821	859	490	492	1
50 - 54	2 832	-	1	19	83	145	212	271	374	549	548	626	4
55 - 59	1 780	-	-	12	39	61	92	133	151	270	359	662	1
60 - 64	934	-	-	4	15	20	33	55	73	98	127	509	-
65 - 69	475	-	-	1	4	6	21	27	28	33	42	313	-
70 - 74	190	-	-	2	2	3	4	2	8	8	12	149	-
75 +	80	-	-	-	-	-	-	2	3	3	1	68	3
Unknown - Inconnu	136	-	-	8	33	15	9	11	6	5	1	1	47

24. Marriages by age of groom and by age of bride: latest available year, 2010 - 2019
Mariages selon l'âge de l'époux et selon l'âge de l'épouse : dernière année disponible, 2010 - 2019 (continued - suite)

Continent, country or area, year, code[a] and age of bride / Continent, pays ou zone, date, code[a] et âge de l'épouse	Age of groom - - âge de l'époux												
	Total	0-14	15-19	20-24	25-29	30-34	35-39	40-44	45-49	50-54	55-59	60+	Unknown Inconnu
AMERICA, NORTH - AMÉRIQUE DU NORD													
El Salvador[9]													
2012 (...)													
Total	*29 267*	-	*1 098*	*6 586*	*6 762*	*5 101*	*3 026*	*2 078*	*1 528*	*989*	*671*	*1 294*	*134*
0 - 14	*37*	-	*10*	*16*	*6*	*3*	*2*	-	-	-	-	-	-
15 - 19	*3 670*	-	*544*	*1 856*	*787*	*250*	*113*	*53*	*25*	*12*	*5*	*9*	*16*
20 - 24	*8 329*	-	*414*	*3 407*	*2 652*	*1 113*	*374*	*176*	*90*	*37*	*12*	*19*	*35*
25 - 29	*6 227*	-	*80*	*933*	*2 304*	*1 713*	*647*	*264*	*153*	*70*	*27*	*23*	*13*
30 - 34	*4 049*	-	*16*	*230*	*704*	*1 360*	*902*	*414*	*223*	*82*	*47*	*53*	*18*
35 - 39	*2 433*	-	*14*	*69*	*179*	*436*	*654*	*509*	*272*	*134*	*74*	*84*	*8*
40 - 44	*1 604*	-	*4*	*25*	*58*	*118*	*208*	*410*	*348*	*175*	*107*	*149*	*2*
45 - 49	*1 144*	-	*2*	*6*	*18*	*54*	*80*	*174*	*290*	*234*	*125*	*157*	*4*
50 - 54	*633*	-	-	*3*	*6*	*15*	*16*	*43*	*84*	*162*	*140*	*164*	-
55 - 59	*403*	-	*1*	*1*	*1*	*6*	*5*	*10*	*23*	*61*	*89*	*206*	-
60 - 64	*242*	-	*1*	-	*1*	*2*	*2*	*10*	*10*	*12*	*26*	*177*	*1*
65 +	*279*	-	*2*	*1*	-	*2*	*3*	*3*	*3*	*7*	*13*	*245*	-
Unknown - Inconnu	*217*	-	*10*	*39*	*46*	*29*	*20*	*12*	*7*	*3*	*6*	*8*	*37*
Grenada - Grenade													
2014 (+C)													
Total	618	...	-	33	119	128	114	65	48	50	34	26	1
15 - 19	3	...	-	3	-	-	-	-	-	-	-	-	-
20 - 24	82	...	-	18	32	23	6	2	-	1	-	-	-
25 - 29	150	...	-	8	63	46	18	5	3	4	1	2	-
30 - 34	135	...	-	3	17	39	40	20	6	5	4	1	-
35 - 39	87	...	-	1	6	12	31	18	8	5	5	1	-
40 - 44	59	...	-	-	1	5	12	15	16	7	2	1	-
45 - 49	42	...	-	-	-	2	5	3	9	13	7	3	-
50 - 54	31	...	-	-	-	-	1	2	5	14	7	2	-
55 - 59	11	...	-	-	-	-	1	-	-	-	4	6	-
60 - 64	8	...	-	-	-	1	-	-	-	1	2	4	-
65 +	9	...	-	-	-	-	-	-	1	-	2	6	-
Unknown - Inconnu	1	...	-	-	-	-	-	-	-	-	-	-	1
Guadeloupe													
2018 (C)													
Total	1 183	...	1[f]	31	140	216	156	291[n]	...	210[o]	...	138	...
0 - 19	4	...	...	...	...	...	...	...	...	...	...	...	...
20 - 24	64	...	...	...	...	...	...	...	...	...	...	...	...
25 - 29	182	...	...	...	...	...	...	...	...	...	...	...	...
30 - 34	234	...	...	...	...	...	...	...	...	...	...	...	...
35 - 39	197	...	...	...	...	...	...	...	...	...	...	...	...
40 - 49	256	...	...	...	...	...	...	...	...	...	...	...	...
50 - 59	170	...	...	...	...	...	...	...	...	...	...	...	...
60 +	76	...	...	...	...	...	...	...	...	...	...	...	...
Guatemala													
2018 (C)													
Total	74 777	...	4 034	23 944	19 351	10 756	5 820	3 199	2 100	1 506	1 274	2 793	...
15 - 19	12 043	...	2 103	6 996	2 235	478	146	44	16	11	5	9	...
20 - 24	26 573	...	1 663	13 281	8 380	2 256	630	200	79	30	26	28	...
25 - 29	15 892	...	207	2 980	6 626	4 092	1 279	386	166	75	44	37	...
30 - 34	8 285	...	48	527	1 640	2 926	1 913	668	274	124	65	100	...
35 - 39	4 352	...	7	117	355	745	1 346	965	384	177	128	128	...
40 - 44	2 594	...	6	32	75	199	389	683	579	298	148	185	...
45 - 49	1 666	...	-	4	27	47	83	184	424	413	207	277	...
50 - 54	1 189	...	-	7	10	13	25	53	133	251	355	342	...
55 - 59	841	...	-	-	2	-	3	14	39	83	213	487	...
60 - 64	550	...	-	-	1	-	3	2	4	31	62	447	...
65 +	792	...	-	-	-	-	3	-	2	13	21	753	...
Mexico - Mexique[10]													
2018 (+C)													
Total	501 298	-	18 078	112 554	134 495	86 853	49 232	30 415	20 942	14 639	11 432	21 999	659
0 - 14	4	-	2	2	-	-	-	-	-	-	-	-	-
15 - 19	51 412	-	11 413	28 736	8 317	1 936	592	209	102	56	23	23	5
20 - 24	134 883	-	5 659	63 832	46 358	12 704	3 889	1 394	561	225	120	125	16
25 - 29	129 675	-	760	15 926	62 350	33 675	10 729	3 555	1 433	626	302	291	28
30 - 34	72 440	-	171	2 897	13 227	28 721	16 062	6 410	2 673	1 150	563	551	15
35 - 39	39 654	-	45	802	3 070	7 105	12 541	8 320	3 917	1 905	995	947	7
40 - 44	25 561	-	12	223	802	1 910	3 857	7 192	5 428	2 814	1 584	1 723	16

24. Marriages by age of groom and by age of bride: latest available year, 2010 - 2019
Mariages selon l'âge de l'époux et selon l'âge de l'épouse : dernière année disponible, 2010 - 2019 (continued - suite)

Continent, country or area, year, code[a] and age of bride / Continent, pays ou zone, date, code[a] et âge de l'épouse	Age of groom - - âge de l'époux												
	Total	0-14	15-19	20-24	25-29	30-34	35-39	40-44	45-49	50-54	55-59	60+	Unknown Inconnu
AMERICA, NORTH - AMÉRIQUE DU NORD													
Mexico - Mexique[10]													
2018													
45 - 49	18 062	-	6	75	244	576	1 121	2 382	4 814	3 772	2 283	2 784	5
50 - 54	11 981	-	3	18	71	139	293	649	1 410	2 924	2 675	3 797	2
55 - 59	8 011	-	1	9	18	33	95	195	414	853	2 019	4 374	-
60 - 64	4 705	-	-	2	8	17	25	60	128	210	637	3 618	-
65 - 69	2 321	-	-	3	2	6	3	14	35	66	171	2 020	1
70 - 74	1 095	-	-	-	-	1	4	11	9	17	39	1 014	-
75 +	763	-	-	2	1	1	2	5	3	10	15	723	1
Unknown - Inconnu	731	-	6	27	27	29	19	19	15	11	6	9	563
Montserrat													
2016 (C)													
Total	10	-	-	1	3	2	1	-	-	-	2	1	...
0 - 14	-	-	-	-	-	-	-	-	-	-	-	-	...
15 - 19	-	-	-	-	-	-	-	-	-	-	-	-	...
20 - 24	2	-	-	1	1	-	-	-	-	-	-	-	...
25 - 29	2	-	-	-	1	-	-	-	-	-	1	-	...
30 - 34	3	-	-	-	1	1	1	-	-	-	-	-	...
35 - 39	1	-	-	-	-	1	-	-	-	-	-	-	...
40 - 44	-	-	-	-	-	-	-	-	-	-	-	-	...
45 - 49	-	-	-	-	-	-	-	-	-	-	-	-	...
50 - 54	-	-	-	-	-	-	-	-	-	-	-	-	...
55 - 59	-	-	-	-	-	-	-	-	-	-	-	-	...
60 - 64	2	-	-	-	-	-	-	-	-	-	1	1	...
65 - 69	-	-	-	-	-	-	-	-	-	-	-	-	...
70 - 74	-	-	-	-	-	-	-	-	-	-	-	-	...
75 +	-	-	-	-	-	-	-	-	-	-	-	-	...
Panama[6]													
2018 (C)													
Total	11 112	-	62	1 078	2 306	2 075	1 523	2 012[n]	...	1 179[o]	...	872	5
0 - 14	-	-	-	-	-	-	-	-[n]	...	-[o]	...	-	-
15 - 19	303	-	33	163	66	26	8	6[n]	...	1[o]	...	-	-
20 - 24	1 740	-	26	629	693	237	80	61[n]	...	9[o]	...	5	-
25 - 29	2 583	-	3	198	1 109	761	275	189[n]	...	36[o]	...	11	1
30 - 34	2 022	-	-	56	305	735	497	354[n]	...	59[o]	...	16	-
35 - 39	1 482	-	-	25	99	243	439	500[n]	...	139[o]	...	37	-
40 - 49	1 728	-	-	7	32	67	209	753[n]	...	485[o]	...	174	1
50 - 59	886	-	-	-	1	5	14	140[n]	...	391[o]	...	335	-
60 - 69	298	-	-	-	-	1	1	8[n]	...	54[o]	...	234	-
70 +	64	-	-	-	-	-	-	-[n]	...	5[o]	...	59	-
Unknown - Inconnu	6	-	-	-	1	-	-	1[n]	...	-[o]	...	1	3
Puerto Rico - Porto Rico													
2019 (C)													
Total	12 511	1	170	1 691	2 546	1 821	1 436	1 189	1 000	868	593	1 196	...
0 - 14	-	-	-	-	-	-	-	-	-	-	-	-	...
15 - 19	217	-	66	126	15	6	-	2	1	1	-	-	...
20 - 24	1 760	-	84	1 022	465	116	37	22	8	4	1	1	...
25 - 29	2 647	-	13	418	1 388	553	172	66	24	7	4	2	...
30 - 34	1 800	-	3	84	451	641	366	135	67	33	13	7	...
35 - 39	1 430	-	3	28	141	319	457	262	119	53	26	22	...
40 - 44	1 207	-	-	11	53	124	253	344	230	126	41	25	...
45 - 49	991	-	1	2	23	38	89	203	290	187	80	78	...
50 - 54	784	-	-	-	4	14	34	100	139	216	134	143	...
55 - 59	652	-	-	-	4	5	22	27	75	147	135	237	...
60 - 64	485	-	-	-	2	3	2	20	33	59	92	274	...
65 - 69	277	-	-	-	-	1	4	6	10	22	42	192	...
70 - 74	145	-	-	-	-	1	-	2	3	8	16	115	...
75 +	116	1	-	-	-	-	-	-	1	5	9	100	...
Saint Vincent and the Grenadines - Saint-Vincent-et-les Grenadines													
2017 (C)													
Total	536	...	3	30	92	89	83	70	57	36	36	39	1
15 - 19	9	...	2	2	4	1	-	-	-	-	-	-	-

24. Marriages by age of groom and by age of bride: latest available year, 2010 - 2019
Mariages selon l'âge de l'époux et selon l'âge de l'épouse : dernière année disponible, 2010 - 2019 (continued - suite)

Continent, country or area, year, code[a] and age of bride — Continent, pays ou zone, date, code[a] et âge de l'épouse	Age of groom - - âge de l'époux												
	Total	0-14	15-19	20-24	25-29	30-34	35-39	40-44	45-49	50-54	55-59	60+	Unknown Inconnu
AMERICA, NORTH - AMÉRIQUE DU NORD													
Saint Vincent and the Grenadines - Saint-Vincent-et-les Grenadines													
2017													
20 - 24	63	...	1	17	22	14	4	2	2	1	-	-	-
25 - 29	104	...	-	4	47	28	15	5	3	2	-	-	-
30 - 34	94	...	-	-	9	26	26	16	10	5	2	-	-
35 - 39	75	...	-	3	3	9	22	19	12	3	1	3	-
40 - 44	65	...	-	1	5	8	12	13	11	6	4	5	-
45 - 49	48	...	-	2	2	2	2	7	11	9	8	5	-
50 - 54	38	...	-	-	-	1	1	6	6	6	11	7	-
55 - 59	26	...	-	1	-	-	1	2	2	2	7	11	-
60 - 64	9	...	-	-	-	-	-	-	-	2	1	6	-
65 +	4	...	-	-	-	-	-	-	-	-	2	2	-
Unknown - Inconnu	1	...	-	-	-	-	-	-	-	-	-	-	1
Trinidad and Tobago - Trinité-et-Tobago[11]													
2014* (C)													
Total	7 682	-	61	779	2 067	1 733	1 027	685	467	333	246	284	-
0 - 14	6	-	6	-	-	-	-	-	-	-	-	-	-
15 - 19	325	-	25	155	93	35	6	8	3	-	-	-	-
20 - 24	1 375	-	22	400	608	217	79	20	15	10	3	1	-
25 - 29	2 315	-	5	145	1 000	715	257	114	50	18	6	5	-
30 - 34	1 451	-	1	53	261	552	304	167	66	24	15	8	-
35 - 39	858	-	1	15	73	141	248	186	99	44	30	21	-
40 - 44	493	-	-	5	19	49	79	101	110	73	34	23	-
45 - 49	388	-	1	5	9	18	40	60	86	81	51	37	-
50 - 54	265	-	-	1	3	4	11	22	36	63	61	64	-
55 - 59	102	-	-	-	1	2	3	7	-	15	30	44	-
60 - 64	57	-	-	-	-	-	-	-	2	3	11	41	-
65 +	47	-	-	-	-	-	-	-	-	2	5	40	-
Unknown - Inconnu	-	-	-	-	-	-	-	-	-	-	-	-	...
Turks and Caicos Islands - Îles Turques et Caïques													
2018 (C)													
Total	464	...	-	18	75	87	63	69	52	41	28	30	1
15 - 19	-	...	-	-	-	-	-	-	-	-	-	-	-
20 - 24	41	...	-	12	15	8	4	1	1	-	-	-	-
25 - 29	83	...	-	5	38	24	10	4	1	1	-	-	-
30 - 34	109	...	-	1	18	40	19	20	5	4	2	-	-
35 - 39	76	...	-	-	3	9	21	22	16	3	1	1	-
40 - 44	57	...	-	-	-	4	7	19	11	10	4	2	-
45 - 49	46	...	-	-	1	1	2	2	15	13	6	6	-
50 - 54	22	...	-	-	-	1	-	-	2	6	8	5	-
55 - 59	18	...	-	-	-	-	-	1	1	1	6	9	-
60 - 64	8	...	-	-	-	-	-	-	-	3	1	4	-
65 +	3	...	-	-	-	-	-	-	-	-	-	3	-
Unknown - Inconnu	1	...	-	-	-	-	-	-	-	-	-	-	1
AMERICA, SOUTH - AMÉRIQUE DU SUD													
Bolivia (Plurinational State of) - Bolivie (État plurinational de)													
2018* (+U)													
Total	*48 502*	*1*	...	...	...	...	...	...	...	...	*2 393*[t]	...	*70*
0 - 14	*3*	...	...	...	...	...	...	...	...	...	...	...	...
15 - 24	*13 160*	...	...	...	...	...	...	...	...	...	...	...	...
25 - 34	*23 867*	...	...	...	...	...	...	...	...	...	...	...	...
35 - 44	*7 766*	...	...	...	...	...	...	...	...	...	...	...	...
45 - 54	*3 281*	...	...	...	...	...	...	...	...	...	...	...	...
55 +	*369*	...	...	...	...	...	...	...	...	...	...	...	...
Unknown - Inconnu	*56*	...	...	...	...	...	...	...	...	...	...	...	...

24. Marriages by age of groom and by age of bride: latest available year, 2010 - 2019
Mariages selon l'âge de l'époux et selon l'âge de l'épouse : dernière année disponible, 2010 - 2019 (continued - suite)

Continent, country or area, year, code[a] and age of bride / Continent, pays ou zone, date, code[a] et âge de l'épouse	Total	0-14	15-19	20-24	25-29	30-34	35-39	40-44	45-49	50-54	55-59	60+	Unknown Inconnu
	Age of groom - - âge de l'époux												
AMERICA, SOUTH - AMÉRIQUE DU SUD													
Brazil - Brésil													
2017 (+U)													
Total	*1064489*	*8*	*25 373*	*181 714*	*248 167*	*210 566*	*142 883*	*87 932*	*58 988*	*41 247*	*26 871*	*40 474*	*266*
0 - 14	*209*	*4*	*104*	*68*	*18*	*7*	*4*	*1*	*3*	-	-	-	-
15 - 19	*97 883*	*4*	*16 421*	*53 647*	*19 184*	*5 700*	*1 897*	*607*	*247*	*112*	*30*	*32*	*2*
20 - 24	*231 097*	-	*6 827*	*90 142*	*86 094*	*31 593*	*10 817*	*3 500*	*1 242*	*504*	*194*	*179*	*5*
25 - 29	*242 917*	-	*1 370*	*26 248*	*96 818*	*74 599*	*28 400*	*9 371*	*3 555*	*1 491*	*607*	*454*	*4*
30 - 34	*182 136*	-	*422*	*7 664*	*31 981*	*64 797*	*46 067*	*18 081*	*7 381*	*3 269*	*1 373*	*1 091*	*10*
35 - 39	*121 654*	-	*155*	*2 714*	*9 976*	*23 380*	*35 997*	*25 826*	*12 671*	*6 145*	*2 620*	*2 170*	-
40 - 44	*73 661*	-	*49*	*817*	*2 809*	*7 124*	*12 996*	*18 472*	*15 161*	*8 333*	*4 111*	*3 786*	*3*
45 - 49	*49 572*	-	*17*	*280*	*849*	*2 382*	*4 557*	*8 007*	*11 591*	*10 224*	*5 845*	*5 818*	*2*
50 - 54	*31 828*	-	*4*	*87*	*302*	*709*	*1 546*	*2 811*	*4 870*	*7 248*	*6 373*	*7 875*	*3*
55 - 59	*16 923*	-	-	*25*	*85*	*175*	*417*	*824*	*1 600*	*2 664*	*3 694*	*7 439*	-
60 - 64	*8 974*	-	*3*	*7*	*24*	*60*	*118*	*286*	*437*	*880*	*1 375*	*5 783*	*1*
65 +	*7 356*	-	*1*	*9*	*16*	*33*	*60*	*140*	*229*	*375*	*649*	*5 844*	-
Unknown - Inconnu	*279*	-	-	*6*	*11*	*7*	*7*	*6*	*1*	*2*	-	*3*	*236*
Chile - Chili													
2018* (+C)													
Total	63 187	-	275	4 775	13 790	14 158	9 136	5 691	3 936	3 085	2 447	4 410	1 484
0 - 14	-	-	-	-	-	-	-	-	-	-	-	-	-
15 - 19	901	-	140	457	206	60	23	9	1	2	2	1	-
20 - 24	7 635	-	107	2 743	3 226	1 105	292	88	50	14	5	5	-
25 - 29	16 449	-	17	1 199	7 785	5 290	1 472	456	134	60	17	19	-
30 - 34	13 060	-	7	251	1 937	5 758	3 349	1 121	406	142	57	32	-
35 - 39	7 716	-	1	79	476	1 411	2 725	1 734	737	329	146	78	-
40 - 44	4 889	-	2	28	113	382	875	1 414	1 024	570	278	203	-
45 - 49	3 750	-	1	12	36	117	287	590	1 007	819	475	406	-
50 - 54	2 812	-	-	3	7	25	90	201	379	731	629	747	-
55 - 59	2 043	-	-	2	3	7	15	59	137	303	518	999	-
60 - 64	1 218	-	-	1	1	1	5	11	42	78	205	874	-
65 - 69	649	-	-	-	-	2	3	8	12	23	73	528	-
70 - 74	354	-	-	-	-	-	-	-	4	10	30	310	-
75 +	228	-	-	-	-	-	-	-	3	4	12	208	1
Unknown - Inconnu	1 483	-	-	-	-	-	-	-	-	-	-	-	1 483
Ecuador - Équateur[12]													
2018 (U)													
Total	*60 849*	-	*1 518*	*11 583*	*16 393*	*11 407*	*6 726*	*3 991*	*2 817*	*2 019*	*1 487*	*2 892*	*16*
0 - 14	-	-	-	-	-	-	-	-	-	-	-	-	-
15 - 19	*5 036*	-	*939*	*2 782*	*938*	*262*	*72*	*16*	*10*	*4*	*4*	*6*	*3*
20 - 24	*15 539*	-	*508*	*6 864*	*5 803*	*1 643*	*470*	*153*	*52*	*24*	*10*	*11*	*1*
25 - 29	*16 048*	-	*59*	*1 589*	*7 542*	*4 689*	*1 425*	*460*	*171*	*70*	*23*	*18*	*2*
30 - 34	*9 155*	-	*10*	*277*	*1 642*	*3 546*	*2 278*	*829*	*313*	*143*	*69*	*46*	*2*
35 - 39	*5 357*	-	*2*	*43*	*345*	*937*	*1 714*	*1 205*	*607*	*268*	*115*	*119*	*2*
40 - 44	*3 376*	-	-	*24*	*84*	*244*	*548*	*896*	*758*	*432*	*226*	*162*	*2*
45 - 49	*2 376*	-	-	*2*	*27*	*70*	*162*	*292*	*616*	*565*	*319*	*323*	-
50 - 54	*1 629*	-	-	*2*	*7*	*11*	*38*	*106*	*215*	*369*	*401*	*477*	*3*
55 - 59	*990*	-	-	-	*1*	*3*	*14*	*26*	*54*	*94*	*236*	*561*	*1*
60 - 64	*607*	-	-	-	*3*	*1*	*4*	*6*	*17*	*38*	*61*	*477*	-
65 - 69	*402*	-	-	-	*1*	-	*1*	*2*	*3*	*10*	*18*	*367*	-
70 - 74	*185*	-	-	-	-	*1*	-	-	-	*2*	*2*	*180*	-
75 +	*149*	-	-	-	-	-	-	-	*1*	-	*3*	*145*	-
Unknown - Inconnu	-	-	-	-	-	-	-	-	-	-	-	-	-
Paraguay													
2018 (U)													
Total	*19 660*	-	*455*	*3 424*	*5 352*	*4 132*	*2 528*	*1 313*	*824*	*570*	*376*	*677*	*9*
0 - 14	-	-	-	-	-	-	-	-	-	-	-	-	-
15 - 19	*2 041*	-	*301*	*1 027*	*473*	*155*	*50*	*23*	*7*	*2*	*2*	*1*	-
20 - 24	*4 621*	-	*118*	*1 749*	*1 838*	*622*	*198*	*57*	*16*	*13*	*3*	*7*	-
25 - 29	*5 306*	-	*28*	*483*	*2 299*	*1 638*	*559*	*165*	*64*	*32*	*20*	*18*	-
30 - 34	*3 196*	-	*6*	*108*	*536*	*1 187*	*810*	*285*	*129*	*71*	*31*	*32*	*1*
35 - 39	*1 923*	-	*2*	*30*	*142*	*371*	*617*	*402*	*181*	*83*	*44*	*51*	-
40 - 44	*976*	-	-	*12*	*37*	*98*	*195*	*225*	*198*	*98*	*63*	*50*	-
45 - 49	*621*	-	-	*10*	*14*	*36*	*65*	*97*	*143*	*128*	*53*	*75*	-
50 - 54	*374*	-	-	*3*	*6*	*14*	*16*	*29*	*55*	*94*	*76*	*81*	-
55 - 59	*244*	-	-	-	*2*	*6*	*6*	*15*	*16*	*28*	*60*	*111*	-
60 - 64	*147*	-	-	-	*1*	*1*	*6*	*8*	*6*	*11*	*10*	*104*	-

24. Marriages by age of groom and by age of bride: latest available year, 2010 - 2019
Mariages selon l'âge de l'époux et selon l'âge de l'épouse : dernière année disponible, 2010 - 2019 (continued - suite)

Continent, country or area, year, code[a] and age of bride / Continent, pays ou zone, date, code[a] et âge de l'épouse	Age of groom - - âge de l'époux: Total	0-14	15-19	20-24	25-29	30-34	35-39	40-44	45-49	50-54	55-59	60+	Unknown Inconnu
AMERICA, SOUTH - AMÉRIQUE DU SUD													
Paraguay													
2018													
65 - 69	*95*	-	-	*1*	-	-	*2*	*4*	*5*	*5*	*8*	*70*	-
70 - 74	*62*	-	-	-	-	-	*1*	*3*	*2*	*2*	*6*	*48*	-
75 +	*31*	-	-	-	-	-	*1*	-	*2*	*1*	-	*27*	-
Unknown - Inconnu	*23*	-	-	*1*	*4*	*4*	*2*	-	-	*2*	-	*2*	*8*
Peru - Pérou[13,14]													
2018 (+C)													
Total	79 740	-	617	7 664	16 967	18 218	13 021	8 480	5 089	3 403	2 331	3 950	...
0 - 14	11	-	3	3	3	1	1	-	-	-	-	-	...
15 - 19	2 650	-	376	1 403	561	213	65	20	6	2	1	3	...
20 - 24	12 184	-	198	4 449	4 943	1 782	552	174	55	12	8	11	...
25 - 29	20 173	-	30	1 424	8 503	6 898	2 266	709	205	77	35	26	...
30 - 34	17 462	-	7	289	2 330	7 164	4 937	1 772	586	215	95	67	...
35 - 39	10 931	-	1	65	482	1 718	3 973	2 867	1 103	421	174	127	...
40 - 44	6 396	-	-	20	105	337	966	2 187	1 535	704	297	245	...
45 - 49	4 015	-	1	6	34	78	199	591	1 211	1 008	480	407	...
50 - 54	2 500	-	-	2	4	19	43	134	305	718	671	604	...
55 - 59	1 506	-	-	1	1	4	15	19	60	182	430	794	...
60 - 64	938	-	-	-	-	2	1	4	17	52	111	751	...
65 - 69	502	-	1	1	-	2	-	2	5	7	21	463	...
70 - 74	268	-	-	-	-	-	-	-	1	3	6	258	...
75 +	204	-	-	1	1	-	3	1	-	2	2	194	...
Venezuela (Bolivarian Republic of) - Venezuela (République bolivarienne du)													
2016 (C)													
Total	84 349	2	1 718	15 084	22 936	16 410	10 357	6 625	4 328	2 720	1 791	2 378	...
0 - 14	72	-	25	33	8	2	3	-	1	-	-	-	...
15 - 19	6 605	1	1 040	3 454	1 403	433	158	53	27	17	9	10	...
20 - 24	20 630	-	459	8 472	7 872	2 441	825	309	157	46	25	24	...
25 - 29	22 412	1	114	2 333	10 214	6 150	2 204	803	352	134	55	52	...
30 - 34	13 919	-	44	533	2 475	5 155	3 193	1 447	603	261	115	93	...
35 - 39	8 483	-	21	154	648	1 538	2 657	1 805	927	418	171	144	...
40 - 44	5 044	-	7	49	200	464	895	1 425	1 000	537	253	214	...
45 - 49	3 227	-	4	24	71	152	295	514	848	629	380	310	...
50 - 54	1 855	-	2	9	20	39	86	192	291	448	389	379	...
55 - 59	1 035	-	1	8	10	16	18	47	77	160	252	446	...
60 - 64	606	-	-	6	5	5	8	17	31	49	104	381	...
65 - 69	252	-	1	3	2	4	7	8	7	11	30	179	...
70 - 74	120	-	-	4	5	1	3	1	6	5	5	90	...
75 +	89	-	-	2	3	10	5	4	1	5	3	56	...
ASIA - ASIE													
Armenia - Arménie													
2018 (+C)													
Total	14 822	...	35	2 159	5 600	3 642	1 563	721	406	219	182	295	...
15 - 19	735	...	25	296	337	73	3	1	-	-	-	-	...
20 - 24	5 452	...	10	1 604	2 817	947	69	3	2	-	-	-	...
25 - 29	4 552	...	-	225	2 166	1 637	444	64	14	2	-	-	...
30 - 34	1 981	...	-	23	217	828	657	189	53	9	3	2	...
35 - 39	940	...	-	6	46	118	309	285	129	26	16	5	...
40 - 44	527	...	-	3	13	21	55	151	139	91	39	15	...
45 - 49	218	...	-	-	3	9	21	20	55	46	43	21	...
50 - 54	129	...	...	1	-	8	5	4	6	27	44	34	...
55 - 59	114	...	-	-	1	1	-	3	7	9	30	63	...
60 +	174	...	-	1	-	-	-	1	1	9	7	155	...
Azerbaijan - Azerbaïdjan													
2018 (+C)													
Total	62 484	...	275	14 309	28 283	11 431	3 637	1 700	987	645	510	707	...
15 - 19	14 133	...	163	5 104	7 329	1 423	99	11	2	1	1	-	...
20 - 24	26 888	...	95	7 866	13 803	4 450	585	73	11	3	-	2	...
25 - 29	12 351	...	10	1 163	6 206	3 519	1 098	278	51	12	7	7	...
30 - 34	4 302	...	5	144	768	1 597	1 082	472	159	43	27	5	...

24. Marriages by age of groom and by age of bride: latest available year, 2010 - 2019
Mariages selon l'âge de l'époux et selon l'âge de l'épouse : dernière année disponible, 2010 - 2019 (continued - suite)

Continent, country or area, year, code[a] and age of bride — Continent, pays ou zone, date, code[a] et âge de l'épouse	Age of groom - - âge de l'époux												
	Total	0-14	15-19	20-24	25-29	30-34	35-39	40-44	45-49	50-54	55-59	60+	Unknown Inconnu
ASIA - ASIE													
Azerbaijan - Azerbaïdjan													
2018													
35 - 39	2 127	...	1	21	141	359	577	533	300	129	50	16	...
40 - 44	1 053	...	1	5	26	58	143	246	255	168	103	48	...
45 - 49	683	...	-	4	5	20	35	64	150	174	121	110	...
50 - 54	458	...	-	1	1	4	12	14	50	92	125	159	...
55 - 59	279	...	-	1	2	1	5	6	5	19	62	178	...
60 +	210	...	-	-	2	-	1	3	4	4	14	182	...
Bahrain - Bahreïn													
2019 (...)													
Total	*5 524*	-	*55*	*1 167*	*2 161*	*1 053*	*436*	*230*	*129*	*293*[s]	...	...	...
0 - 14	*4*	-	*4*	-	-	-	-	-	-	-[s]	...	...	...
15 - 19	*483*	-	*38*	*280*	*126*	*25*	*10*	*2*	-	*2*[s]	...	...	...
20 - 24	*2 101*	-	*13*	*778*	*1 045*	*193*	*46*	*15*	*5*	*6*[s]	...	...	...
25 - 29	*1 643*	-	-	*89*	*873*	*510*	*110*	*32*	*13*	*16*[s]	...	...	...
30 - 34	*625*	-	-	*15*	*96*	*257*	*154*	*52*	*27*	*24*[s]	...	...	...
35 - 39	*312*	-	-	*5*	*14*	*53*	*83*	*73*	*37*	*47*[s]	...	...	...
40 - 44	*150*	-	-	-	*4*	*9*	*27*	*38*	*27*	*45*[s]	...	...	...
45 - 49	*98*	-	-	-	*2*	*3*	*3*	*13*	*15*	*62*[s]	...	...	...
50 +	*108*	-	-	-	*1*	*3*	*3*	*5*	*5*	*91*[s]	...	...	...
Brunei Darussalam - Brunéi Darussalam													
2018 (+C)													
Total	2 653	-	68	541	1 040	511	204	105	70	42	30	41	1
0 - 14	1	...	...	...	...	...	...	...	...	...	...	...	...
15 - 19	167	...	...	...	...	...	...	...	...	...	...	...	...
20 - 24	737	...	...	...	...	...	...	...	...	...	...	...	...
25 - 29	1 032	...	...	...	...	...	...	...	...	...	...	...	...
30 - 34	369	...	...	...	...	...	...	...	...	...	...	...	...
35 - 39	138	...	...	...	...	...	...	...	...	...	...	...	...
40 - 44	92	...	...	...	...	...	...	...	...	...	...	...	...
45 - 49	64	...	...	...	...	...	...	...	...	...	...	...	...
50 - 54	27	...	...	...	...	...	...	...	...	...	...	...	...
55 - 59	16	...	...	...	...	...	...	...	...	...	...	...	...
60 - 64	4	...	...	...	...	...	...	...	...	...	...	...	...
65 - 69	4	...	...	...	...	...	...	...	...	...	...	...	...
70 - 74	2	...	...	...	...	...	...	...	...	...	...	...	...
75 +	-	...	...	...	...	...	...	...	...	...	...	...	...
Unknown - Inconnu	-	...	...	...	...	...	...	...	...	...	...	...	...
China, Hong Kong SAR - Chine, Hong Kong RAS													
2019 (C)													
Total	44 247	-	73	2 242	9 640	12 194	6 807	3 854	2 801	2 131	1 787	2 718	-
0 - 14	-	-	-	-	-	-	-	-	-	-	-	-	-
15 - 19	248	-	29	128	62	20	6	-	1	1	1	-	-
20 - 24	3 866	-	38	1 420	1 547	557	177	61	25	16	11	14	-
25 - 29	13 432	-	2	531	6 321	4 593	1 244	405	149	89	56	42	-
30 - 34	11 865	-	3	114	1 388	5 790	2 814	900	381	231	135	109	-
35 - 39	5 709	-	1	31	211	927	1 916	1 194	643	322	237	227	-
40 - 44	3 294	-	-	11	68	190	430	823	688	401	315	368	-
45 - 49	2 755	-	-	5	30	83	172	339	630	534	379	583	-
50 - 54	1 667	-	-	-	7	27	35	98	209	410	354	527	-
55 - 59	837	-	-	-	3	5	8	26	58	100	244	393	-
60 - 64	319	-	-	1	2	-	4	7	11	20	43	231	-
65 - 69	158	-	-	-	-	2	1	1	6	5	10	133	-
70 - 74	54	-	-	1	-	-	-	-	-	1	2	50	-
75 +	43	-	-	-	1	-	-	-	-	1	-	41	-
Unknown - Inconnu	-	-	-	-	-	-	-	-	-	-	-	-	-
China, Macao SAR - Chine, Macao RAS													
2019 (+C)													
Total	3 724	...	...	245[g]	...	...	...	...	532[r]	...	...	...	...
0 - 24	534	...	...	...	...	...	...	...	...	...	...	...	...
25 - 34	2 435	...	...	...	...	...	...	...	...	...	...	...	...
35 - 44	472	...	...	...	...	...	...	...	...	...	...	...	...
45 +	283	...	...	...	...	...	...	...	...	...	...	...	...

24. Marriages by age of groom and by age of bride: latest available year, 2010 - 2019
Mariages selon l'âge de l'époux et selon l'âge de l'épouse : dernière année disponible, 2010 - 2019 (continued - suite)

Continent, country or area, year, code[a] and age of bride / Continent, pays ou zone, date, code[a] et âge de l'épouse	Age of groom - - âge de l'époux: Total	0-14	15-19	20-24	25-29	30-34	35-39	40-44	45-49	50-54	55-59	60+	Unknown Inconnu
ASIA - ASIE													
Cyprus - Chypre[15,16]													
2016 (C)													
Total	6 375	-	59	687	1 952	1 933	792	322	199	142	106	164	19
0 - 14	-	-	-	-	-	-	-	-	-	-	-	-	-
15 - 19	168	-	15	87	48	12	5	1	-	-	-	-	-
20 - 24	838	-	20	298	371	111	31	5	1	1	-	-	-
25 - 29	2 376	-	13	150	1 147	822	188	29	13	8	3	3	-
30 - 34	1 651	-	7	74	287	791	322	88	36	29	9	8	-
35 - 39	692	-	3	47	67	153	186	125	55	23	13	20	-
40 - 44	310	-	-	24	24	31	41	58	47	34	22	29	-
45 - 49	153	-	-	3	7	7	14	14	34	27	21	26	-
50 - 54	78	-	-	2	1	3	3	2	8	14	22	23	-
55 - 59	46	-	1	-	-	-	1	-	4	6	11	23	-
60 +	41	-	-	1	-	2	-	-	1	-	5	32	-
Unknown - Inconnu	22	...	-	1	-	1	1	-	-	-	-	-	19
Georgia - Géorgie													
2016 (C)													
Total	25 101	...	458[h]	5 695	7 174	4 533	2 919	1 848	1 040	592	386	456	...
16 - 19	2 545	...	...	...	...	...	...	...	...	...	...	...	...
20 - 24	7 978	...	...	...	...	...	...	...	...	...	...	...	...
25 - 29	6 096	...	...	...	...	...	...	...	...	...	...	...	...
30 - 34	3 514	...	...	...	...	...	...	...	...	...	...	...	...
35 - 39	2 204	...	...	...	...	...	...	...	...	...	...	...	...
40 - 44	1 237	...	...	...	...	...	...	...	...	...	...	...	...
45 - 49	673	...	...	...	...	...	...	...	...	...	...	...	...
50 - 54	423	...	...	...	...	...	...	...	...	...	...	...	...
55 - 59	234	...	...	...	...	...	...	...	...	...	...	...	...
60 +	197	...	...	...	...	...	...	...	...	...	...	...	...
Iran (Islamic Republic of) - Iran (République islamique d')[17]													
2018 (+C)													
Total	550 565	23	19 748	148 635	193 813	105 125	39 074	15 348	8 570	5 413	4 185	10 631	...
0 - 14	30 304	8	4 120	17 024	8 189	888	57	14	3	1	-	-	...
15 - 19	150 141	14	12 919	72 276	53 751	10 070	894	136	54	19	4	4	...
20 - 24	146 559	1	2 243	47 374	68 469	24 237	3 469	509	141	65	24	27	...
25 - 29	107 975	-	343	9 515	49 143	36 798	9 249	1 943	567	208	85	124	...
30 - 34	60 442	-	95	1 877	11 330	25 291	14 290	4 489	1 688	635	338	409	...
35 - 39	29 307	-	23	454	2 385	6 525	8 719	5 249	2 793	1 384	759	1 016	...
40 - 44	12 854	-	4	88	440	1 085	1 988	2 408	2 228	1 589	1 097	1 927	...
45 - 49	6 478	-	1	19	85	198	349	504	881	1 044	976	2 421	...
50 - 54	3 217	-	-	3	15	25	46	76	170	382	618	1 882	...
55 - 59	1 732	-	-	2	4	4	9	16	35	74	236	1 352	...
60 - 64	919	-	-	2	1	3	3	1	6	7	44	852	...
65 - 69	387	-	-	1	-	1	1	1	2	3	3	375	...
70 - 74	171	-	-	-	1	-	-	2	-	-	1	167	...
75 +	79	-	-	-	-	-	-	-	2	2	-	75	...
Israel - Israël[18]													
2017 (C)													
Total	50 029	...	2 076	12 824	17 802	9 225	3 265	1 528	740	453	337	663	1 116
15 - 19	6 555	...	1 428	3 382	1 276	163	23	2	1	-	-	1	279
20 - 24	18 396	...	599	8 620	6 968	1 481	232	43	7	7	-	-	439
25 - 29	15 018	...	8	580	8 577	4 453	905	228	39	16	3	1	208
30 - 34	5 184	...	1	29	697	2 622	1 212	407	105	31	6	1	73
35 - 39	1 907	...	-	3	71	314	673	486	191	66	26	13	64
40 - 44	830	...	-	-	6	35	106	234	211	114	43	54	27
45 - 49	462	...	-	-	3	7	13	55	118	108	73	72	13
50 - 54	285	...	-	-	-	1	3	6	28	62	92	84	9
55 - 59	211	...	-	-	-	1	-	2	4	17	58	126	3
60 - 64	134	...	-	-	-	-	-	-	2	3	8	121	-
65 - 69	97	...	-	-	-	-	-	-	-	-	4	92	1
70 - 74	32	...	-	-	-	-	-	-	-	1	-	31	-
75 +	21	...	-	-	-	-	-	-	-	-	-	21	-
Unknown - Inconnu	897	...	40	210	204	148	98	65	34	28	24	46	-

24. Marriages by age of groom and by age of bride: latest available year, 2010 - 2019
Mariages selon l'âge de l'époux et selon l'âge de l'épouse : dernière année disponible, 2010 - 2019 (continued - suite)

Continent, country or area, year, code[a] and age of bride / Continent, pays ou zone, date, code[a] et âge de l'épouse	Age of groom - - âge de l'époux												
	Total	0-14	15-19	20-24	25-29	30-34	35-39	40-44	45-49	50-54	55-59	60+	Unknown Inconnu
ASIA - ASIE													
Japan - Japon[19]													
2018 (+C)													
Total	456 148	-	3 901	49 503	144 666	106 964	64 098	38 768	21 397	10 882	6 349	9 620	...
0 - 14	-	-	-	-	-	-	-	-	-	-	-	-	...
15 - 19	7 157	-	2 807	3 015	736	292	158	74	34	22	9	10	...
20 - 24	71 305	-	975	34 040	23 245	7 879	3 196	1 117	481	178	104	90	...
25 - 29	169 284	-	85	9 925	98 668	40 944	13 173	4 241	1 443	451	187	167	...
30 - 34	101 393	-	24	1 856	18 008	45 897	22 760	8 489	2 880	870	353	256	...
35 - 39	53 667	-	6	501	3 277	9 813	19 815	12 963	4 856	1 474	528	434	...
40 - 44	25 043	-	3	132	591	1 685	3 984	9 210	5 843	2 189	803	603	...
45 - 49	13 007	-	1	22	109	381	813	2 121	4 508	2 746	1 312	994	...
50 - 54	7 077	-	-	10	21	64	163	457	1 092	2 338	1 580	1 352	...
55 - 59	3 582	-	-	2	7	7	30	75	214	503	1 188	1 556	...
60 - 64	1 960	-	-	-	3	-	4	19	37	85	207	1 605	...
65 - 69	1 311	-	-	-	-	1	1	1	8	23	64	1 213	...
70 - 74	814	-	-	-	1	1	1	1	1	2	7	800	...
75 +	548	-	-	-	-	-	-	-	-	1	7	540	...
Jordan - Jordanie[20]													
2010 (+C)													
Total	62 107	...	16 151	25 559	12 760	4 002	1 795	1 151	437	252[s]	...	...	...
18 - 19	1 262	...	1 017	191	40	11	1	2	-	-[s]	...	...	...
20 - 24	14 272	...	6 768	6 453	835	139	42	20	7	8[s]	...	...	...
25 - 29	25 434	...	6 276	12 608	5 720	633	120	45	16	16[s]	...	...	...
30 - 34	11 523	...	1 603	4 782	3 679	1 153	197	70	25	14[s]	...	...	...
35 - 39	4 064	...	299	1 043	1 434	819	350	92	19	8[s]	...	...	...
40 - 44	2 365	...	99	321	681	647	358	217	35	7[s]	...	...	...
45 - 49	1 139	...	35	81	220	283	249	196	57	18[s]	...	...	...
50 - 54	639	...	14	37	73	152	169	121	53	20[s]	...	...	...
55 - 59	425	...	12	18	35	80	95	107	56	22[s]	...	...	...
60 - 64	318	...	11	7	21	40	66	97	39	37[s]	...	...	...
65 +	666	...	17	18	22	45	148	184	130	102[s]	...	...	...
Kazakhstan													
2019 (+C)													
Total	139 504	-	2 254	39 824	49 714	22 588	10 448	6 041	3 477	2 065	1 440	1 653	...
0 - 14	-	-	-	-	-	-	-	-	-	-	-	-	...
15 - 19	16 075	-	1 662	9 340	4 324	652	84	10	2	1	-	-	...
20 - 24	59 908	-	525	27 252	26 342	4 975	660	103	33	11	6	1	...
25 - 29	30 320	-	59	2 756	15 926	8 734	2 149	517	121	42	5	11	...
30 - 34	15 089	-	6	377	2 530	6 402	3 853	1 338	393	118	48	24	...
35 - 39	8 117	-	1	80	466	1 459	2 814	2 066	849	248	89	45	...
40 - 44	4 533	-	-	13	100	299	719	1 555	1 067	485	204	91	...
45 - 49	2 463	-	1	3	15	58	139	358	790	569	350	180	...
50 - 54	1 370	-	-	3	10	7	23	78	169	446	353	281	...
55 - 59	878	-	-	-	-	2	4	11	40	122	302	397	...
60 - 64	437	-	-	-	1	-	2	3	12	19	62	338	...
65 - 69	212	-	-	-	-	-	1	2	1	4	19	185	...
70 - 74	70	-	-	-	-	-	-	-	-	-	1	69	...
75 +	32	-	-	-	-	-	-	-	-	-	1	31	...
Kuwait - Koweït													
2018 (C)													
Total	14 400	-	144	3 248	4 957	2 663	1 318	767	1 303[r]	...	...	...	...
0 - 14	-	-	-	-	-	-	-	-	-[r]	...	...	...	...
15 - 19	1 726	-	109	1 061	458	77	11	3	7[r]	...	...	...	...
20 - 24	5 009	-	34	1 905	2 371	548	100	27	24[r]	...	...	...	...
25 - 29	3 631	-	1	231	1 750	1 125	327	103	94[r]	...	...	...	...
30 - 34	1 839	-	-	34	269	648	467	217	204[r]	...	...	...	...
35 - 39	1 071	-	-	12	71	195	278	228	287[r]	...	...	...	...
40 - 44	612	-	-	4	27	44	101	132	304[r]	...	...	...	...
45 +	512	-	-	1	11	26	34	57	383[r]	...	...	...	...
Kyrgyzstan - Kirghizstan													
2018 (C)													
Total	49 579	-	431	14 139	21 372	7 173	2 841	1 582	893	521	316	311	-
0 - 14	-	-	-	-	-	-	-	-	-	-	-	-	-
15 - 19	9 147	-	332	5 199	3 334	256	16	8	1	-	-	1	-
20 - 24	23 941	-	93	8 426	12 948	2 193	220	38	17	4	1	1	-

24. Marriages by age of groom and by age of bride: latest available year, 2010 - 2019
Mariages selon l'âge de l'époux et selon l'âge de l'épouse : dernière année disponible, 2010 - 2019 (continued - suite)

Continent, country or area, year, code[a] and age of bride / Continent, pays ou zone, date, code[a] et âge de l'épouse	Age of groom - - âge de l'époux: Total	0-14	15-19	20-24	25-29	30-34	35-39	40-44	45-49	50-54	55-59	60+	Unknown Inconnu
ASIA - ASIE													
Kyrgyzstan - Kirghizstan													
2018													
25 - 29	9 132	-	5	460	4 639	2 990	810	167	46	12	2	1	-
30 - 34	3 767	-	1	48	401	1 509	1 120	481	149	41	9	8	-
35 - 39	1 825	-	-	5	41	189	597	580	258	110	33	12	-
40 - 44	837	-	-	1	6	30	67	267	261	125	52	28	-
45 - 49	417	-	-	-	3	4	7	35	125	127	70	46	-
50 - 54	266	-	-	-	-	2	2	4	27	80	89	62	-
55 - 59	150	-	-	-	-	-	2	2	7	19	44	76	-
60 - 64	57	-	-	-	-	-	-	-	2	3	13	39	-
65 - 69	30	-	-	-	-	-	-	-	-	-	3	27	-
70 - 74	4	-	-	-	-	-	-	-	-	-	-	4	-
75 +	6	-	-	-	-	-	-	-	-	-	-	6	-
Unknown - Inconnu	-	-	-	-	-	-	-	-	-	-	-	-	-
Malaysia - Malaisie													
2018 (+C)													
Total	206 253	...	2 835[f]	36 593	85 847	42 319	16 799	8 191	4 714	3 175	2 347	3 433	...
0 - 19	9 629	...	1 700[f]	4 727	2 068	683	227	103	48	34	22	17	...
20 - 24	58 474	...	773[f]	24 522	24 591	6 094	1 558	537	209	90	57	43	...
25 - 29	81 863	...	220[f]	5 698	51 984	18 035	4 022	1 154	424	186	85	55	...
30 - 34	29 936	...	69[f]	1 051	5 466	14 377	5 729	1 908	769	329	156	82	...
35 - 39	12 202	...	34[f]	349	1 181	2 339	4 087	2 277	1 005	507	261	162	...
40 - 44	5 885	...	17[f]	138	337	530	834	1 625	1 103	627	382	292	...
45 - 49	3 713	...	13[f]	70	144	192	242	411	889	733	540	479	...
50 - 54	2 301	...	5[f]	25	50	53	66	127	205	521	502	747	...
55 - 59	1 233	...	2[f]	7	14	10	26	35	52	116	274	697	...
60 - 64	617	...	1[f]	6	9	4	7	11	7	22	52	498	...
65 +	400	...	1[f]	-	3	2	1	3	3	10	16	361	...
Mongolia - Mongolie													
2019 (+C)													
Total	20 043	...	221	4 511	7 481	4 076	1 612	866	627	649[s]	...	...	...
15 - 19	641	...	...	...	...	...	...	...	...	...	...	...	...
20 - 24	6 279	...	...	...	...	...	...	...	...	...	...	...	...
25 - 29	6 827	...	...	...	...	...	...	...	...	...	...	...	...
30 - 34	3 229	...	...	...	...	...	...	...	...	...	...	...	...
35 - 39	1 367	...	...	...	...	...	...	...	...	...	...	...	...
40 - 44	747	...	...	...	...	...	...	...	...	...	...	...	...
45 - 49	499	...	...	...	...	...	...	...	...	...	...	...	...
50 +	454	...	...	...	...	...	...	...	...	...	...	...	...
Philippines[21]													
2018 (U)													
Total	*448 729*	*4*	*6 314*	*88 932*	*162 703*	*103 090*	*43 982*	*17 901*	*9 578*	*5 768*	*4 132*	*6 315*	*10*
0 - 14	*43*	*3*	*11*	*22*	*6*	-	*1*	-	-	-	-	-	-
15 - 19	*27 163*	*1*	*3 545*	*15 529*	*5 898*	*1 466*	*396*	*153*	*78*	*47*	*24*	*26*	-
20 - 24	*132 498*	-	*2 391*	*56 667*	*53 614*	*14 103*	*3 462*	*1 065*	*487*	*272*	*193*	*242*	*2*
25 - 29	*159 760*	-	*277*	*14 151*	*84 553*	*44 519*	*10 964*	*2 850*	*1 121*	*571*	*336*	*415*	*3*
30 - 34	*76 004*	-	*63*	*1 999*	*15 564*	*35 119*	*15 662*	*4 279*	*1 515*	*767*	*464*	*570*	*2*
35 - 39	*28 480*	-	*20*	*401*	*2 392*	*6 323*	*10 415*	*5 008*	*2 026*	*857*	*488*	*549*	*1*
40 - 44	*11 239*	-	*5*	*108*	*475*	*1 141*	*2 249*	*3 235*	*2 045*	*914*	*500*	*567*	-
45 - 49	*6 026*	-	*1*	*27*	*135*	*302*	*591*	*939*	*1 575*	*1 105*	*646*	*705*	-
50 - 54	*3 370*	-	*1*	*12*	*42*	*77*	*170*	*256*	*506*	*849*	*671*	*786*	-
55 - 59	*2 119*	-	-	*5*	*10*	*23*	*40*	*79*	*170*	*279*	*575*	*938*	-
60 - 64	*1 184*	-	-	*6*	*6*	*5*	*18*	*21*	*38*	*80*	*181*	*829*	-
65 - 69	*544*	-	-	*2*	*5*	*3*	*12*	*10*	*13*	*18*	*44*	*437*	-
70 - 74	*192*	-	-	*2*	-	*4*	*2*	*4*	*1*	*7*	*7*	*165*	-
75 +	*99*	-	-	-	*1*	*3*	-	*1*	*3*	*2*	*3*	*86*	-
Unknown - Inconnu	*8*	-	-	*1*	*2*	*2*	-	*1*	-	-	-	-	*2*
Qatar													
2018 (C)													
Total	3 758	...	52[f]	831	1 328	730	341	198	140	86	34	18	...
0 - 19	407	...	28[f]	220	128	21	5	3	1	-	-	1	...
20 - 24	1 328	...	21[f]	497	619	157	21	8	1	3	-	1	...
25 - 29	1 007	...	2[f]	99	474	305	78	24	14	6	5	-	...
30 - 34	520	...	-[f]	11	75	167	133	69	37	18	5	5	...
35 - 39	272	...	-[f]	2	22	46	72	57	35	29	8	1	...

24. Marriages by age of groom and by age of bride: latest available year, 2010 - 2019
Mariages selon l'âge de l'époux et selon l'âge de l'épouse : dernière année disponible, 2010 - 2019 (continued - suite)

Continent, country or area, year, code[a] and age of bride / Continent, pays ou zone, date, code[a] et âge de l'épouse	Age of groom - - âge de l'époux												
	Total	0-14	15-19	20-24	25-29	30-34	35-39	40-44	45-49	50-54	55-59	60+	Unknown Inconnu
ASIA - ASIE													
Qatar													
2018													
40 - 44	116	...	1[f]	-	4	20	21	24	26	11	6	3	...
45 - 49	75	...	-[f]	1	4	10	11	10	20	14	4	1	...
50 - 54	20	...	-[f]	1	-	3	-	1	5	5	4	1	...
55 - 59	9	...	-[f]	-	2	1	-	1	1	-	2	2	...
60 +	4	...	-[f]	-	-	-	-	1	-	-	-	3	...
Republic of Korea - République de Corée[22]													
2019 (+C)													
Total	239 159	-	382	5 890	50 303	83 232	46 262	19 218	12 361	8 297	6 470	6 743	1
0 - 14	-	-	-	-	-	-	-	-	-	-	-	-	-
15 - 19	2 674	-	255	465	275	214	582	597	244	36	5	1	-
20 - 24	16 182	-	109	3 633	6 149	2 806	1 564	1 091	640	145	32	13	-
25 - 29	81 675	-	13	1 448	35 525	34 985	7 106	1 482	745	275	73	23	-
30 - 34	71 431	-	3	263	7 528	40 027	19 095	2 857	1 050	401	145	62	-
35 - 39	30 446	-	-	59	721	4 655	15 497	6 831	1 829	547	203	104	-
40 - 44	11 978	-	1	16	81	466	2 010	4 872	3 012	1 021	360	139	-
45 - 49	9 048	-	1	5	16	68	345	1 224	3 625	2 465	943	355	1
50 - 54	6 991	-	-	1	7	8	58	223	985	2 610	2 206	893	-
55 - 59	4 806	-	-	-	-	2	5	37	196	662	2 011	1 893	-
60 - 64	2 317	-	-	-	1	-	-	2	32	121	435	1 726	-
65 - 69	879	-	-	-	-	1	-	1	3	12	49	813	-
70 - 74	430	-	-	-	-	-	-	-	-	1	7	422	-
75 +	302	-	-	-	-	-	-	1	-	1	1	299	-
Unknown - Inconnu	-	-	-	-	-	-	-	-	-	-	-	-	-
Singapore - Singapour[23,24]													
2019 (+C)													
Total	25 434	-	53	1 129	8 623	7 795	3 471	1 665	1 033	659	492	514	-
0 - 14	-	-	-	-	-	-	-	-	-	-	-	-	-
15 - 19	146	-	31	77	24	7	4	2	-	-	-	1	-
20 - 24	2 611	-	18	700	1 359	326	121	51	22	8	5	1	-
25 - 29	11 143	-	4	281	6 199	3 534	760	214	94	34	8	15	-
30 - 34	6 573	-	-	52	856	3 359	1 466	451	220	94	50	25	-
35 - 39	2 540	-	-	11	140	458	884	541	252	118	87	49	-
40 - 44	1 123	-	-	4	22	77	180	305	236	138	88	73	-
45 - 49	661	-	-	3	15	26	35	75	154	150	106	97	-
50 - 54	343	-	-	1	7	6	14	20	40	82	85	88	-
55 - 59	170	-	-	-	-	2	5	3	12	30	50	68	-
60 +	124	-	-	-	1	-	2	3	3	5	13	97	-
Unknown - Inconnu	-	-	-	-	-	-	-	-	-	-	-	-	-
Sri Lanka													
2014 (+C)													
Total	177 792	-[b]	...	...	...	...	...	...	...	...	...	...	...
0 - 15	90	-[b]	...	...	...	...	...	...	...	...	...	...	...
16 - 20	44 451	-[b]	...	...	...	...	...	...	...	...	...	...	...
21 - 25	63 336	-[b]	...	...	...	...	...	...	...	...	...	...	...
26 - 30	42 964	-[b]	...	...	...	...	...	...	...	...	...	...	...
31 - 35	14 842	-[b]	...	...	...	...	...	...	...	...	...	...	...
36 - 40	6 022	-[b]	...	...	...	...	...	...	...	...	...	...	...
41 - 45	3 081	-[b]	...	...	...	...	...	...	...	...	...	...	...
46 - 50	1 535	-[b]	...	...	...	...	...	...	...	...	...	...	...
51 - 55	786	-[b]	...	...	...	...	...	...	...	...	...	...	...
56 - 60	418	-[b]	...	...	...	...	...	...	...	...	...	...	...
61 - 65	177	-[b]	...	...	...	...	...	...	...	...	...	...	...
66 - 70	68	-[b]	...	...	...	...	...	...	...	...	...	...	...
71 - 75	18	-[b]	...	...	...	...	...	...	...	...	...	...	...
76 +	4	-[b]	...	...	...	...	...	...	...	...	...	...	...
State of Palestine - État de Palestine													
2018 (C)													
Total	43 515	-	2 153	16 284	16 445	4 387	1 498	862	591	396	304	595	...
0 - 14	675	-	171	391	112	1	-	-	-	-	-	-	...
15 - 19	16 966	-	1 770	9 295	5 253	530	80	19	7	6	1	5	...
20 - 24	17 157	-	200	6 119	8 425	1 910	334	98	38	17	11	5	...

24. Marriages by age of groom and by age of bride: latest available year, 2010 - 2019
Mariages selon l'âge de l'époux et selon l'âge de l'épouse : dernière année disponible, 2010 - 2019 (continued - suite)

Continent, country or area, year, code[a] and age of bride / Continent, pays ou zone, date, code[a] et âge de l'épouse	Age of groom - - âge de l'époux											
	Total	0-14	15-19	20-24	25-29	30-34	35-39	40-44	45-49	50-54	55-59	60+	Unknown Inconnu
ASIA - ASIE													
State of Palestine - État de Palestine													
2018													
25 - 29	5 436	-	9	427	2 420	1 474	588	287	126	54	27	24	...
30 - 34	1 649	-	2	37	180	385	347	244	186	130	71	67	...
35 - 39	831	-	-	8	37	69	112	138	131	97	91	148	...
40 - 44	461	-	1	2	12	16	32	57	74	52	55	160	...
45 - 49	193	-	-	3	3	2	3	15	20	25	26	96	...
50 - 54	95	-	-	-	2	-	2	3	4	11	12	61	...
55 - 59	43	-	-	2	-	-	-	1	4	4	8	24	...
60 - 64	6	-	-	-	-	-	-	-	1	-	1	4	...
65 +	3	-	-	-	1	-	-	-	-	-	1	1	...
Tajikistan - Tadjikistan													
2017 (+C)													
Total	78 638	-	2 274	39 639	25 734	5 120	2 262	1 568	933	457	294	269	88
0 - 14	-	-	-	-	-	-	-	-	-	-	-	-	-
15 - 19	34 438	-	2 029	23 068	9 136	183	-	-	-	-	-	-	22
20 - 24	30 941	-	243	16 092	12 927	1 608	42	-	-	-	-	-	29
25 - 29	6 704	-	-	438	3 454	2 132	562	99	10	-	-	-	9
30 - 34	3 269	-	-	-	180	1 149	1 177	478	170	79	28	4	4
35 - 39	1 807	-	-	-	-	41	475	709	309	142	86	45	-
40 - 44	860	-	-	-	-	-	3	278	328	111	68	72	-
45 - 49	309	-	-	-	-	-	-	2	114	91	57	44	1
50 - 54	114	-	-	-	-	-	-	-	-	33	36	45	-
55 - 59	54	-	-	-	-	-	-	-	-	-	18	36	-
60 - 64	17	-	-	-	-	-	-	-	-	-	-	17	-
65 - 69	4	-	-	-	-	-	-	-	-	-	-	4	-
70 - 74	1	-	-	-	-	-	-	-	-	-	-	1	-
75 +	1	-	-	-	-	-	-	-	-	-	-	1	-
Unknown - Inconnu	119	-	2	41	37	7	3	2	2	1	1	-	23
Turkey - Turquie[25]													
2018 (C)													
Total	553 202	-[b]	9 343[h]	127 090	220 361	100 004	42 140	19 857	11 749	7 905	5 595	9 158	...
0 - 15	-	-[b]	-[h]	-	-	-	-	-	-	-	-	-	...
16 - 19	82 756	-[b]	6 998[h]	41 537	27 902	5 321	843	116	26	7	4	2	...
20 - 24	191 601	-[b]	2 015[h]	70 387	91 514	22 930	3 858	677	160	34	14	12	...
25 - 29	151 037	-[b]	170[h]	12 172	85 471	40 412	9 982	2 060	510	178	42	40	...
30 - 34	50 956	-[b]	36[h]	1 123	9 659	21 384	12 498	4 200	1 299	456	186	115	...
35 - 39	27 104	-[b]	16[h]	318	1 751	5 181	9 153	6 009	2 788	1 095	475	318	...
40 - 44	14 230	-[b]	-[h]	68	346	958	2 333	3 894	3 283	1 775	814	759	...
45 - 49	8 540	-[b]	1[h]	17	59	187	481	1 001	2 009	2 116	1 339	1 330	...
50 - 54	4 793	-[b]	-[h]	4	7	24	91	152	409	1 139	1 308	1 659	...
55 - 59	2 706	-[b]	-[h]	1	1	7	20	31	66	242	715	1 623	...
60 - 64	1 420	-[b]	-[h]	-	-	1	2	8	20	38	120	1 231	...
65 - 69	612	-[b]	-[h]	-	-	-	2	2	3	6	25	574	...
70 - 74	293	-[b]	-[h]	-	-	-	1	-	-	1	6	285	...
75 +	129	-[b]	-[h]	-	-	-	-	-	-	2	-	127	...
Unknown - Inconnu	17 025	-[b]	107[h]	1 463	3 651	3 599	2 876	1 707	1 176	816	547	1 083	...
United Arab Emirates - Émirats arabes unis													
2018 (...)													
Total	14 804	-	1 256	4 907	4 106	2 321	1 274	587	222	86	33	10	2
0 - 14	-	-	-	-	-	-	-	-	-	-	-	-	-
15 - 19	103	-	51	38	10	-	4	-	-	-	-	-	-
20 - 24	2 867	-	607	1 777	365	72	33	8	2	2	-	-	1
25 - 29	5 071	-	459	2 181	1 832	422	127	34	10	4	-	2	-
30 - 34	3 091	-	89	643	1 187	810	258	74	20	7	2	-	1
35 - 39	1 690	-	22	162	427	545	372	119	32	7	4	-	-
40 - 44	873	-	9	63	151	251	220	122	43	13	1	-	-
45 - 49	457	-	8	22	73	100	103	102	39	9	-	1	-
50 - 54	305	-	6	11	34	58	89	53	31	16	5	2	-
55 - 59	161	-	1	3	15	34	30	36	26	9	6	1	-
60 - 64	96	-	1	7	4	13	24	22	11	7	6	1	-
65 - 69	49	-	1	-	4	13	8	9	3	4	6	1	-

Continent, country or area, year, code[a] and age of bride / Continent, pays ou zone, date, code[a] et âge de l'épouse	Age of groom - - âge de l'époux												
	Total	0-14	15-19	20-24	25-29	30-34	35-39	40-44	45-49	50-54	55-59	60+	Unknown Inconnu
ASIA - ASIE													
United Arab Emirates - Émirats arabes unis													
2018													
70 - 74	*16*	-	*1*	-	*1*	*1*	*3*	*3*	*1*	*4*	*1*	*1*	-
75 +	*25*	-	*1*	-	*3*	*2*	*3*	*5*	*4*	*4*	*2*	*1*	-
Uzbekistan - Ouzbékistan													
2018 (+C)													
Total	311 379	-	71 711	167 974	43 132	15 925	7 078	2 922	1 234	833	340	230	...
0 - 14	-	-	-	-	-	-	-	-	-	-	-	-	...
15 - 19	2 493	-	1 971	481	35	5	1	-	-	-	-	-	...
20 - 24	105 622	-	37 703	65 308	2 392	187	27	4	-	1	-	-	...
25 - 29	150 050	-	30 641	92 457	25 339	1 445	132	22	9	4	-	1	...
30 - 34	28 741	-	1 293	8 851	11 848	6 152	516	66	12	3	-	-	...
35 - 39	9 898	-	81	655	2 417	4 519	1 995	194	25	11	1	-	...
40 - 44	5 837	-	14	145	707	1 942	2 092	828	81	18	9	1	...
45 - 49	3 485	-	4	51	238	869	1 069	844	341	50	14	5	...
50 - 54	2 184	-	3	14	84	420	605	419	351	244	32	12	...
55 - 59	1 481	-	-	7	40	217	372	278	186	254	108	19	...
60 - 64	820	-	-	2	16	90	171	154	128	120	87	52	...
65 - 69	441	-	-	2	10	56	57	74	70	69	40	63	...
70 - 74	180	-	1	1	3	16	29	19	20	23	26	42	...
75 +	147	-	-	-	3	7	12	20	11	36	23	35	...
EUROPE													
Åland Islands - Îles d'Åland													
2018 (C)													
Total	107	-	-	2	13	27	16	12	16	5	8	8	...
0 - 14	-	-	-	-	-	-	-	-	-	-	-	-	...
15 - 19	-	-	-	-	-	-	-	-	-	-	-	-	...
20 - 24	8	-	-	2	3	2	1	-	-	-	-	-	...
25 - 29	22	-	-	-	7	13	2	-	-	-	-	-	...
30 - 34	19	-	-	-	2	7	6	3	1	-	-	-	...
35 - 39	15	-	-	-	-	4	5	4	2	-	-	-	...
40 - 44	13	-	-	-	1	1	1	5	4	1	-	-	...
45 - 49	11	-	-	-	-	-	1	-	7	1	2	-	...
50 - 54	8	-	-	-	-	-	-	-	2	2	1	3	...
55 - 59	6	-	-	-	-	-	-	-	-	1	3	2	...
60 - 64	4	-	-	-	-	-	-	-	-	-	2	2	...
65 - 69	-	-	-	-	-	-	-	-	-	-	-	-	...
70 - 74	1	-	-	-	-	-	-	-	-	-	-	1	...
75 +	-	-	-	-	-	-	-	-	-	-	-	-	...
Albania - Albanie													
2018 (C)													
Total	23 104	-	165	3 399	9 057	6 422	2 250	879	446	240	122	124	...
0 - 14	1	-	-	1	-	-	-	-	-	-	-	-	...
15 - 19	3 655	-	97	1 056	1 845	594	56	5	1	1	-	-	...
20 - 24	8 734	-	42	1 810	4 056	2 357	409	47	11	1	1	-	...
25 - 29	6 219	-	11	271	2 607	2 329	775	182	31	7	5	1	...
30 - 34	2 343	-	6	93	311	873	659	279	90	20	6	6	...
35 - 39	1 029	-	3	57	90	141	277	251	130	54	18	8	...
40 - 44	530	-	1	44	65	53	49	81	113	79	27	18	...
45 - 49	299	-	3	31	34	34	13	23	57	52	29	23	...
50 - 54	158	-	2	20	29	21	8	9	11	18	20	20	...
55 - 59	86	-	-	10	9	15	2	1	2	5	12	30	...
60 - 64	36	-	-	5	7	5	2	1	-	3	2	11	...
65 - 69	9	-	-	1	1	-	-	-	-	-	2	5	...
70 - 74	2	-	-	-	1	-	-	-	-	-	-	1	...
75 +	3	-	-	-	2	-	-	-	-	-	-	1	...
Andorra - Andorre													
2016 (C)													
Total	295	-	-	18	50	58	62	41	29	20	10	7	...
0 - 14	-	-	-	-	-	-	-	-	-	-	-	-	...
15 - 19	3	-	-	3	-	-	-	-	-	-	-	-	...
20 - 24	30	-	-	11	15	1	2	1	-	-	-	-	...

24. Marriages by age of groom and by age of bride: latest available year, 2010 - 2019
Mariages selon l'âge de l'époux et selon l'âge de l'épouse : dernière année disponible, 2010 - 2019 (continued - suite)

Continent, country or area, year, code[a] and age of bride / Continent, pays ou zone, date, code[a] et âge de l'épouse	Age of groom - - âge de l'époux												
	Total	0-14	15-19	20-24	25-29	30-34	35-39	40-44	45-49	50-54	55-59	60+	Unknown Inconnu
EUROPE													
Andorra - Andorre													
2016													
25 - 29	48	-	-	3	20	17	6	1	1	-	-	-	...
30 - 34	66	-	-	-	10	25	22	3	5	1	-	-	...
35 - 39	63	-	-	1	5	10	23	17	4	2	-	1	...
40 - 44	40	-	-	-	-	3	7	14	8	7	1	-	...
45 - 49	19	-	-	-	-	1	1	4	4	3	5	1	...
50 - 54	17	-	-	-	-	1	1	-	7	5	2	1	...
55 - 59	7	-	-	-	-	-	-	1	-	1	2	3	...
60 - 64	2	-	-	-	-	-	-	-	-	1	-	1	...
65 - 69	-	-	-	-	-	-	-	-	-	-	-	-	...
70 - 74	-	-	-	-	-	-	-	-	-	-	-	-	...
75 +	-	-	-	-	-	-	-	-	-	-	-	-	...
Austria - Autriche[26]													
2018 (C)													
Total	46 465	-	109	2 926	8 999	11 004	7 431	4 426	3 569	3 270	2 308	2 423	...
0 - 14	-	-	-	-	-	-	-	-	-	-	-	-	...
15 - 19	525	-	55	302	130	29	5	3	-	-	1	-	...
20 - 24	5 177	-	43	1 948	2 321	624	146	46	25	11	9	4	...
25 - 29	11 745	-	10	519	5 089	4 437	1 190	283	129	56	19	13	...
30 - 34	10 470	-	-	104	1 150	4 649	3 100	887	348	155	47	30	...
35 - 39	6 375	-	1	28	203	1 018	2 321	1 606	700	314	123	61	...
40 - 44	3 728	-	-	14	69	162	499	1 101	948	552	260	123	...
45 - 49	3 063	-	-	7	16	59	130	345	887	922	447	250	...
50 - 54	2 669	-	-	4	11	17	31	116	409	877	719	485	...
55 - 59	1 614	-	-	-	6	5	3	26	100	294	523	657	...
60 - 64	658	-	-	-	4	3	2	8	19	68	125	429	...
65 - 69	239	-	-	-	-	-	3	4	4	17	20	191	...
70 - 74	130	-	-	-	-	1	1	1	-	4	8	115	...
75 +	72	-	-	-	-	-	-	-	-	-	7	65	...
Belarus - Bélarus													
2018 (C)													
Total	60 714	62[d]	748[j]	13 345	18 832	11 107	5 972	3 608	2 443	1 739	1 378	1 480	...
0 - 17	443	45[d]	113[j]	214	53	15	3	-	-	-	-	-	...
18 - 19	2 989	7[d]	361[j]	1 842	641	104	29	4	-	1	-	-	...
20 - 24	19 490	8[d]	214[j]	9 026	8 059	1 733	359	64	18	7	2	-	...
25 - 29	15 327	2[d]	42[j]	1 812	7 666	4 272	1 140	280	80	15	11	7	...
30 - 34	8 967	-[d]	14[j]	350	1 898	3 515	2 020	771	262	85	40	12	...
35 - 39	5 181	-[d]	2[j]	72	423	1 126	1 671	1 133	487	171	75	21	...
40 - 44	3 034	-[d]	1[j]	22	73	265	562	901	683	335	135	57	...
45 - 49	2 012	-[d]	1[j]	6	14	58	152	335	633	477	234	102	...
50 - 54	1 359	-[d]	-[j]	-	2	12	27	93	206	466	368	185	...
55 - 59	973	-[d]	-[j]	1	3	7	8	21	53	139	384	357	...
60 +	939	-[d]	-[j]	-	-	-	1	6	21	43	129	739	...
Belgium - Belgique[27,28]													
2018 (C)													
Total	45 059	-	503	5 338	13 226	8 626	5 527	3 652	2 947	2 368	1 588	1 279	5
0 - 14	-	-	-	-	-	-	-	-	-	-	-	-	-
15 - 19	76	-	46	27	2	1	-	-	-	-	-	-	-
20 - 24	2 403	-	250	1 652	422	58	12	6	3	-	-	-	-
25 - 29	10 885	-	143	2 601	6 946	956	162	42	21	10	4	-	-
30 - 34	9 703	-	42	713	4 194	3 834	671	169	59	14	4	2	1
35 - 39	6 497	-	13	221	1 083	2 395	2 129	508	111	24	9	4	-
40 - 44	4 331	-	8	71	326	804	1 450	1 180	363	96	27	5	1
45 - 49	3 434	-	1	28	147	336	648	904	956	319	81	14	-
50 - 54	2 941	-	-	13	57	153	286	503	814	791	262	62	-
55 - 59	2 148	-	-	8	29	52	110	220	377	627	545	179	1
60 - 64	1 356	-	-	3	10	25	40	87	155	298	385	353	-
65 - 69	708	-	-	1	5	11	11	22	65	119	176	297	1
70 - 74	335	-	-	-	5	-	3	9	15	46	65	191	1
75 +	236	-	-	-	-	-	2	2	7	24	29	172	-
Unknown - Inconnu	6	-	-	-	-	1	3	-	1	-	1	-	-

24. Marriages by age of groom and by age of bride: latest available year, 2010 - 2019
Mariages selon l'âge de l'époux et selon l'âge de l'épouse : dernière année disponible, 2010 - 2019 (continued - suite)

Continent, country or area, year, code[a] and age of bride / Continent, pays ou zone, date, code[a] et âge de l'épouse	Age of groom - - âge de l'époux												
	Total	0-14	15-19	20-24	25-29	30-34	35-39	40-44	45-49	50-54	55-59	60+	Unknown Inconnu
EUROPE													
Bosnia and Herzegovina - Bosnie-Herzégovine													
2018 (C)													
Total	19 911	-	1 420	6 702	6 011	2 758	1 221	737	456	277	164	161	4
0 - 14	-	-	-	-	-	-	-	-	-	-	-	-	-
15 - 19	182	-	113	60	7	2	-	-	-	-	-	-	-
20 - 24	3 995	-	822	2 649	426	74	12	8	3	-	-	-	1
25 - 29	6 744	-	376	2 846	2 918	495	83	18	5	1	1	-	1
30 - 34	4 538	-	81	917	2 015	1 222	232	49	13	6	2	-	1
35 - 39	1 967	-	18	175	507	687	405	132	34	5	1	3	-
40 - 44	924	-	8	38	99	192	305	200	63	15	3	1	-
45 - 49	564	-	2	9	27	50	120	189	119	36	8	4	-
50 - 54	335	-	-	3	7	26	32	67	103	66	21	10	-
55 - 59	251	-	-	1	2	5	17	42	62	74	34	13	1
60 - 64	165	-	-	-	2	4	5	19	27	32	44	32	-
65 - 69	119	-	-	4	1	1	5	7	14	23	28	36	-
70 - 74	63	-	-	-	-	-	4	3	5	6	12	33	-
75 +	64	-	-	-	-	-	1	3	8	13	10	29	-
Bulgaria - Bulgarie[29]													
2018 (C)													
Total	28 961	-	450	3 358	8 230	7 075	3 899	2 496	1 495	719	500	739	...
0 - 14	-	-	-	-	-	-	-	-	-	-	-	-	...
15 - 19	2 122	-	372	1 155	485	80	25	3	-	2	-	-	...
20 - 24	5 647	-	62	1 600	2 786	938	179	68	6	6	-	2	...
25 - 29	9 036	-	9	484	4 120	3 240	887	220	52	15	7	2	...
30 - 34	5 269	-	3	87	688	2 245	1 509	513	153	47	16	8	...
35 - 39	2 805	-	4	22	100	423	982	852	295	85	27	15	...
40 - 44	1 876	-	-	6	33	123	255	620	541	179	64	55	...
45 - 49	1 039	-	-	2	15	19	51	183	344	219	128	78	...
50 - 54	527	-	-	2	3	5	9	32	76	121	143	136	...
55 - 59	309	-	-	-	-	2	2	4	26	31	93	151	...
60 - 64	168	-	-	-	-	-	-	-	2	11	21	134	...
65 - 69	102	-	-	-	-	-	-	1	-	3	1	97	...
70 - 74	45	-	-	-	-	-	-	-	-	-	-	45	...
75 +	16	-	-	-	-	-	-	-	-	-	-	16	...
Croatia - Croatie[6]													
2018 (C)													
Total	19 921	-	112	1 968	6 356	5 629	2 688	1 203	663	466	284	552	...
0 - 14	-	-	-	-	-	-	-	-	-	-	-	-	...
15 - 19	502	-	74	276	111	27	7	3	1	1	1	1	...
20 - 24	4 021	-	32	1 243	1 873	653	169	38	4	4	1	4	...
25 - 29	7 441	-	4	378	3 599	2 574	660	156	49	17	1	3	...
30 - 34	4 111	-	2	59	635	1 936	1 048	292	92	30	10	7	...
35 - 39	1 737	-	-	12	117	363	622	372	159	55	24	13	...
40 - 44	799	-	-	-	17	61	147	250	174	80	37	33	...
45 - 49	469	-	-	-	4	11	25	69	129	121	62	48	...
50 - 54	335	-	-	-	-	4	5	17	42	108	78	81	...
55 - 59	220	-	-	-	-	-	2	4	7	33	55	119	...
60 - 64	140	-	-	-	-	-	1	1	6	10	11	111	...
65 - 69	73	-	-	-	-	-	-	-	-	5	2	66	...
70 - 74	40	-	-	-	-	-	-	-	-	1	1	38	...
75 +	30	-	-	-	-	-	-	-	-	1	1	28	...
Unknown - Inconnu	3	-	-	-	-	-	2	1	-	-	-	-	...
Czechia - Tchéquie[6]													
2018 (C)													
Total	54 470	-	63	2 826	13 741	13 881	8 808	5 839	3 267	2 362	1 461	2 222	...
0 - 14	-	-	-	-	-	-	-	-	-	-	-	-	...
15 - 19	365	-	34	180	100	29	13	6	3	-	-	-	...
20 - 24	6 269	-	19	1 691	3 019	1 064	330	87	39	10	6	4	...
25 - 29	18 225	-	5	714	8 472	6 126	1 942	679	185	63	24	15	...
30 - 34	12 403	-	2	162	1 687	5 174	3 416	1 356	399	153	34	20	...
35 - 39	6 383	-	3	53	353	1 108	2 188	1 659	611	273	81	54	...
40 - 44	4 194	-	-	19	82	294	688	1 410	920	456	195	130	...
45 - 49	2 661	-	-	5	23	60	170	494	780	647	286	196	...
50 - 54	1 737	-	-	2	5	22	49	117	258	548	397	339	...
55 - 59	1 039	-	-	-	-	2	8	21	60	155	299	494	...

24. Marriages by age of groom and by age of bride: latest available year, 2010 - 2019
Mariages selon l'âge de l'époux et selon l'âge de l'épouse : dernière année disponible, 2010 - 2019 (continued - suite)

Continent, country or area, year, code[a] and age of bride Continent, pays ou zone, date, code[a] et âge de l'épouse	Age of groom - - âge de l'époux												
	Total	0-14	15-19	20-24	25-29	30-34	35-39	40-44	45-49	50-54	55-59	60+	Unknown Inconnu
EUROPE													
Czechia - Tchéquie[6]													
2018													
60 - 64	664	-	-	-	-	1	2	8	11	45	111	486	...
65 - 69	338	-	-	-	-	1	-	1	1	11	21	303	...
70 - 74	156	-	-	-	-	-	1	1	-	1	6	147	...
75 +	36	-	-	-	-	-	1	-	-	-	1	34	...
Denmark - Danemark[30]													
2018 (C)													
Total	32 525	-	34	1 406	6 948	7 435	4 610	3 066	2 393	2 182	1 572	2 171	708
0 - 14	-	-	-	-	-	-	-	-	-	-	-	-	-
15 - 19	168	-	16	77	39	4	2	-	2	1	-	-	27
20 - 24	2 733	-	17	925	1 281	296	68	18	5	2	-	-	121
25 - 29	9 003	-	-	288	4 566	2 975	680	170	84	21	9	7	203
30 - 34	6 859	-	-	33	725	3 367	1 796	527	172	72	22	11	134
35 - 39	3 756	-	-	14	106	495	1 492	959	382	154	58	19	77
40 - 44	2 432	-	-	1	21	76	321	872	669	285	86	50	51
45 - 49	1 904	-	-	-	5	17	61	244	637	589	222	96	33
50 - 54	1 779	-	-	2	2	6	20	75	235	676	483	243	37
55 - 59	1 178	-	-	-	-	1	2	18	38	169	447	492	11
60 - 64	703	-	-	-	-	1	2	3	11	47	108	524	7
65 - 69	331	-	-	-	-	-	-	-	-	4	19	303	5
70 - 74	200	-	-	-	-	-	-	-	-	1	2	196	1
75 +	116	-	-	-	-	-	1	-	-	2	-	112	1
Unknown - Inconnu	1 363	-	1	66	203	197	165	180	158	159	116	118	-
Estonia - Estonie													
2018 (C)													
Total	6 573	-	25	412	1 457	1 646	989	653	459	291	183	223	235
0 - 14	-	-	-	-	-	-	-	-	-	-	-	-	-
15 - 19	109	-	19	44	27	11	3	-	-	-	1	-	4
20 - 24	837	-	6	271	353	119	31	11	5	4	-	-	37
25 - 29	1 784	-	-	68	782	657	150	49	16	7	2	-	53
30 - 34	1 440	-	-	17	213	618	359	120	56	10	2	-	45
35 - 39	877	-	-	2	33	156	294	217	98	30	8	5	34
40 - 44	560	-	-	3	14	33	96	171	145	58	16	6	18
45 - 49	369	-	-	-	2	13	30	51	102	93	36	24	18
50 - 54	219	-	-	-	-	2	7	16	25	61	52	44	12
55 - 59	135	-	-	-	-	-	-	1	5	18	49	53	9
60 - 64	55	-	-	-	-	-	-	-	1	5	14	33	2
65 - 69	36	-	-	-	-	-	-	-	1	-	1	33	1
70 - 74	13	-	-	-	-	-	-	-	-	-	-	12	1
75 +	9	-	-	-	-	-	-	-	-	-	-	8	1
Unknown - Inconnu	130	-	-	7	33	37	19	17	5	5	2	5	-
Faroe Islands - Îles Féroé													
2019 (C)													
Total	244	-	-	17	46	53	41	34	22	15	4	12	...
0 - 14	-	-	-	-	-	-	-	-	-	-	-	-	...
15 - 19	1	-	-	1	-	-	-	-	-	-	-	-	...
20 - 24	36	-	-	13	16	5	2	-	-	-	-	-	...
25 - 29	65	-	-	3	28	18	7	5	3	-	1	-	...
30 - 34	48	-	-	-	2	23	14	6	3	-	-	-	...
35 - 39	36	-	-	-	-	5	13	14	2	2	-	-	...
40 - 44	20	-	-	-	-	2	4	8	3	3	-	-	...
45 - 49	18	-	-	-	-	-	-	-	7	5	2	4	...
50 - 54	8	-	-	-	-	-	1	1	3	2	-	1	...
55 - 59	6	-	-	-	-	-	-	-	1	3	1	1	...
60 - 64	4	-	-	-	-	-	-	-	-	-	-	4	...
65 - 69	1	-	-	-	-	-	-	-	-	-	-	1	...
70 - 74	-	-	-	-	-	-	-	-	-	-	-	-	...
75 +	1	-	-	-	-	-	-	-	-	-	-	1	...
Finland - Finlande[31]													
2018 (C)													
Total	21 921	-	145	1 565	4 978	4 970	3 156	2 080	1 989	1 204	855	979	...
0 - 14	-	-	-	-	-	-	-	-	-	-	-	-	...
15 - 19	338	-	83	193	47	8	5	-	1	-	1	-	...
20 - 24	2 465	-	51	1 035	1 026	258	58	29	5	1	1	1	...
25 - 29	6 042	-	3	235	3 125	1 938	535	140	41	17	6	2	...

24. Marriages by age of groom and by age of bride: latest available year, 2010 - 2019
Mariages selon l'âge de l'époux et selon l'âge de l'épouse : dernière année disponible, 2010 - 2019 (continued - suite)

Continent, country or area, year, code[a] and age of bride — Continent, pays ou zone, date, code[a] et âge de l'épouse	Age of groom - - âge de l'époux												
	Total	0-14	15-19	20-24	25-29	30-34	35-39	40-44	45-49	50-54	55-59	60+	Unknown Inconnu
EUROPE													
Finland - Finlande[31]													
2018													
30 - 34	4 513	-	5	54	555	2 138	1 210	399	100	31	11	10	...
35 - 39	2 635	-	2	23	127	477	976	656	263	75	19	17	...
40 - 44	1 801	-	-	9	51	90	275	592	505	195	59	25	...
45 - 49	1 937	-	1	12	27	37	71	202	879	423	201	84	...
50 - 54	899	-	-	2	14	15	18	47	134	324	244	101	...
55 - 59	611	-	-	-	5	7	2	10	44	100	235	208	...
60 - 64	338	-	-	-	-	2	2	4	13	29	65	223	...
65 - 69	205	-	-	2	1	-	3	1	3	7	11	177	...
70 - 74	94	-	-	-	-	-	1	-	1	1	2	89	...
75 +	43	-	-	-	-	-	-	-	-	1	-	42	...
France[32]													
2016 (C)													
Total	219 549	-	166	9 004	46 926	52 709	33 649	22 808	16 263	13 868	10 339	13 817	...
0 - 14	-	-	-	-	-	-	-	-	-	-	-	-	...
15 - 19	1 366	-	77	623	467	144	42	9	1	2	-	1	...
20 - 24	19 743	-	66	6 083	9 710	2 798	695	228	90	38	16	19	...
25 - 29	57 737	-	17	1 818	29 958	19 397	4 537	1 224	458	191	84	53	...
30 - 34	48 860	-	2	317	5 381	24 038	12 962	3 843	1 435	552	210	120	...
35 - 39	29 564	-	3	111	927	4 647	11 525	7 650	2 860	1 132	435	274	...
40 - 44	19 963	-	-	34	304	1 104	2 823	7 051	4 809	2 350	949	539	...
45 - 49	14 373	-	-	14	115	383	770	2 054	4 379	3 817	1 708	1 133	...
50 - 54	12 179	-	-	3	47	137	207	559	1 729	4 011	3 190	2 296	...
55 - 59	7 843	-	-	1	10	39	60	150	366	1 333	2 631	3 253	...
60 - 64	4 415	-	1	-	4	12	20	32	111	339	836	3 060	...
65 +	3 506	-	-	-	3	10	8	8	25	103	280	3 069	...
Germany - Allemagne													
2018 (C)													
Total	416 562	...	...	18 213[9]	88 516	106 996	63 333	33 281	28 377	30 443	22 840	24 563	...
0 - 24	41 460	...	...	13 709[9]	20 069	5 758	1 280	349	159	87	30	19	...
25 - 29	116 974	...	...	3 509[9]	54 502	44 223	10 726	2 496	923	377	142	76	...
30 - 34	98 393	...	...	674[9]	11 510	46 989	27 202	7 633	2 670	1 176	352	187	...
35 - 39	50 947	...	...	192[9]	1 788	8 353	19 555	12 069	5 449	2 379	785	377	...
40 - 44	25 662	...	...	59[9]	365	1 163	3 412	7 497	7 021	3 955	1 488	702	...
45 - 49	25 187	...	...	32[9]	173	316	804	2 271	7 620	8 287	3 858	1 826	...
50 - 54	26 673	...	...	22[9]	69	123	257	725	3 458	9 953	7 608	4 458	...
55 - 59	17 500	...	...	12[9]	29	55	78	181	863	3 296	6 412	6 574	...
60 - 64	8 226	...	...	-[9]	8	12	13	44	176	737	1 722	5 514	...
65 +	5 540	...	...	4[9]	3	4	6	16	38	196	443	4 830	...
Greece - Grèce													
2018 (C)													
Total	47 428	-	190	1 608	8 674	15 490	10 903	5 158	2 453	1 357	760	835	-
0 - 14	7	-	5	2	-	-	-	-	-	-	-	-	-
15 - 19	757	-	153	322	194	62	20	2	4	-	-	-	-
20 - 24	4 468	-	25	879	1 893	1 153	387	95	23	9	2	2	-
25 - 29	14 356	-	7	321	4 853	6 044	2 394	561	130	38	8	-	-
30 - 34	14 733	-	-	62	1 453	6 690	4 501	1 489	367	127	32	12	-
35 - 39	7 280	-	-	16	234	1 323	2 903	1 794	685	228	68	29	-
40 - 44	2 971	-	-	3	36	181	581	932	711	330	128	69	-
45 - 49	1 415	-	-	2	8	33	101	233	398	337	176	127	-
50 - 54	752	-	-	-	3	4	13	43	109	208	190	182	-
55 - 59	411	-	-	1	-	-	2	7	22	66	120	193	-
60 - 64	168	-	-	-	-	-	1	2	2	11	29	123	-
65 - 69	74	-	-	-	-	-	-	-	-	1	6	67	-
70 - 74	24	-	-	-	-	-	-	-	1	2	-	21	-
75 +	12	-	-	-	-	-	-	-	1	-	1	10	-
Unknown - Inconnu	-	-	-	-	-	-	-	-	-	-	-	-	-
Hungary - Hongrie[7]													
2018 (C)													
Total	50 828	-	316	3 285	11 572	12 550	8 296	5 838	3 090	2 073	1 351	2 457	-
0 - 14	-	-	-	-	-	-	-	-	-	-	-	-	-
15 - 19	1 091	-	230	573	188	57	24	14	4	1	-	-	-
20 - 24	6 558	-	71	1 934	2 842	1 147	344	148	51	13	5	3	-
25 - 29	15 665	-	12	596	6 773	5 502	1 848	674	166	58	23	13	-

24. Marriages by age of groom and by age of bride: latest available year, 2010 - 2019
Mariages selon l'âge de l'époux et selon l'âge de l'épouse : dernière année disponible, 2010 - 2019 (continued - suite)

Continent, country or area, year, code[a] and age of bride Continent, pays ou zone, date, code[a] et âge de l'épouse	Total	0-14	15-19	20-24	25-29	30-34	35-39	40-44	45-49	50-54	55-59	60+	Unknown Inconnu
	Age of groom - - âge de l'époux												
EUROPE													
Hungary - Hongrie[7]													
2018													
30 - 34	10 927	-	-	122	1 365	4 510	3 096	1 309	333	132	39	21	-
35 - 39	6 092	-	3	42	311	989	2 081	1 701	626	211	78	50	-
40 - 44	4 092	-	-	11	78	279	716	1 428	881	398	168	133	-
45 - 49	2 368	-	-	6	12	52	149	421	673	568	266	221	-
50 - 54	1 637	-	-	-	3	12	25	111	261	519	374	332	-
55 - 59	991	-	-	-	-	2	10	25	73	123	269	489	-
60 - 64	813	-	-	-	-	-	1	5	17	36	94	660	-
65 - 69	405	-	-	1	-	-	-	2	4	14	27	357	-
70 - 74	134	-	-	-	-	-	2	-	1	-	8	123	-
75 +	55	-	-	-	-	-	-	-	-	-	-	55	-
Unknown - Inconnu	-	-	-	-	-	-	-	-	-	-	-	-	-
Iceland - Islande[33,34]													
2011 (C)													
Total	1 458	-	3	77	302	334	272	161	111	74	64	55	5
0 - 14	-	-	-	-	-	-	-	-	-	-	-	-	-
15 - 19	6	-	-	2	4	-	-	-	-	-	-	-	-
20 - 24	152	-	3	52	69	21	1	3	1	1	-	-	1
25 - 29	371	-	-	19	173	115	44	9	5	3	1	1	1
30 - 34	350	-	-	3	43	157	104	25	9	3	4	1	1
35 - 39	243	-	-	1	7	33	101	62	22	9	6	1	1
40 - 44	113	-	-	-	3	6	14	44	28	11	3	4	-
45 - 49	94	-	-	-	1	-	6	15	36	24	7	4	1
50 - 54	68	-	-	-	-	1	1	2	9	18	25	12	-
55 - 59	30	-	-	-	-	-	1	-	1	4	15	9	-
60 - 64	18	-	-	-	-	-	-	1	-	1	2	14	-
65 - 69	7	-	-	-	-	-	-	-	-	-	1	6	-
70 - 74	2	-	-	-	-	-	-	-	-	-	-	2	-
75 +	1	-	-	-	-	-	-	-	-	-	-	1	-
Unknown - Inconnu	3	-	-	-	2	1	-	-	-	-	-	-	-
Ireland - Irlande													
2012 (+C)													
Total	20 713	...	102	516	4 523	8 245	3 896	1 585	766	452	258	370	...
15 - 19	237	...	80	91	43	17	5	-	-	-	1	-	...
20 - 24	968	...	22	258	457	168	40	13	7	3	-	-	...
25 - 29	6 485	...	-	136	2 944	2 670	578	110	33	10	-	4	...
30 - 34	8 016	...	-	25	930	4 640	1 858	419	102	28	11	3	...
35 - 39	2 827	...	-	5	120	673	1 149	588	200	67	15	10	...
40 - 44	995	...	-	1	20	54	228	331	198	99	40	24	...
45 - 49	542	...	-	-	8	18	29	97	157	120	71	42	...
50 - 54	340	...	-	-	-	3	6	21	53	97	81	79	...
55 - 59	168	...	-	-	1	2	2	4	12	25	33	89	...
60 - 64	89	...	-	-	-	-	1	2	2	3	6	75	...
65 - 69	26	...	-	-	-	-	-	-	1	-	-	25	...
70 - 74	17	...	-	-	-	-	-	-	1	-	-	16	...
75 +	3	...	-	-	-	-	-	-	-	-	-	3	...
Italy - Italie													
2018 (C)													
Total	195 778	...	176	5 174	33 675	54 800	36 040	21 457	14 396	10 755	7 497	11 808	...
15 - 19	1 189	...	79	618	340	103	29	9	5	1	3	2	...
20 - 24	13 197	...	62	2 961	6 593	2 570	632	213	87	35	22	22	...
25 - 29	52 397	...	17	1 144	20 698	21 615	6 389	1 654	520	212	84	64	...
30 - 34	53 589	...	12	275	4 856	25 160	15 752	4 945	1 626	558	231	174	...
35 - 39	27 082	...	5	74	818	4 252	10 025	6 947	2 890	1 204	505	362	...
40 - 44	17 441	...	1	50	200	756	2 427	5 434	4 420	2 314	1 024	815	...
45 - 49	12 351	...	-	27	106	221	585	1 723	3 368	3 114	1 676	1 531	...
50 - 54	8 974	...	-	17	44	81	147	423	1 208	2 434	2 130	2 490	...
55 - 59	5 093	...	-	4	13	25	38	81	220	682	1 348	2 682	...
60 - 64	2 669	...	-	4	4	12	12	22	43	156	372	2 044	...
65 - 69	1 051	...	-	-	2	3	2	5	7	38	70	924	...
70 - 74	458	...	-	-	-	1	1	-	1	7	23	425	...
75 +	287	...	-	-	1	1	1	1	1	-	9	273	...

24. Marriages by age of groom and by age of bride: latest available year, 2010 - 2019
Mariages selon l'âge de l'époux et selon l'âge de l'épouse : dernière année disponible, 2010 - 2019 (continued - suite)

Continent, country or area, year, code[a] and age of bride / Continent, pays ou zone, date, code[a] et âge de l'épouse	Age of groom - - âge de l'époux: Total	0-14	15-19	20-24	25-29	30-34	35-39	40-44	45-49	50-54	55-59	60+	Unknown Inconnu
EUROPE													
Latvia - Lettonie[6]													
2018 (C)													
Total	13 058	-	41	786	3 038	3 094	1 848	1 071	891	722	513	1 054	-
0 - 14	-	-	-	-	-	-	-	-	-	-	-	-	-
15 - 19	163	-	23	86	41	12	1	-	-	-	-	-	-
20 - 24	1 477	-	14	486	679	215	59	16	5	-	1	2	-
25 - 29	3 647	-	4	172	1 832	1 221	305	60	35	12	2	4	-
30 - 34	2 679	-	-	28	375	1 251	687	215	78	33	9	3	-
35 - 39	1 539	-	-	8	83	304	560	330	164	52	21	17	-
40 - 44	982	-	-	4	20	74	174	288	243	118	34	27	-
45 - 49	773	-	-	2	5	15	46	115	238	201	84	67	-
50 - 54	598	-	-	-	3	1	10	28	99	207	139	111	-
55 - 59	409	-	-	-	-	1	4	17	20	72	137	158	-
60 - 64	306	-	-	-	-	-	1	1	4	21	64	215	-
65 - 69	239	-	-	-	-	-	1	1	5	5	13	214	-
70 - 74	135	-	-	-	-	-	-	-	-	-	7	128	-
75 +	111	-	-	-	-	-	-	-	-	1	2	108	-
Unknown - Inconnu	-	-	-	-	-	-	-	-	-	-	-	-	-
Liechtenstein[6]													
2018 (C)													
Total	242	...	...	8	55	52	46	26	19	14	12	10	...
Lithuania - Lituanie													
2018 (C)													
Total	19 734	-	75	1 711	6 586	4 862	2 308	1 326	984	763	533	586	-
0 - 14	-	-	-	-	-	-	-	-	-	-	-	-	-
15 - 19	363	-	48	185	93	24	9	3	1	-	-	-	-
20 - 24	3 626	-	25	1 137	1 838	494	94	24	10	3	-	1	-
25 - 29	7 105	-	2	328	3 888	2 214	479	137	38	13	3	3	-
30 - 34	3 611	-	-	39	632	1 645	881	268	99	35	6	6	-
35 - 39	1 760	-	-	14	99	373	576	387	200	73	22	16	-
40 - 44	1 108	-	-	6	29	82	214	343	241	112	58	23	-
45 - 49	848	-	-	1	4	22	45	126	277	217	115	41	-
50 - 54	600	-	-	1	2	8	8	26	88	204	168	95	-
55 - 59	367	-	-	-	1	-	2	10	26	81	116	131	-
60 - 64	210	-	-	-	-	-	-	1	3	22	33	151	-
65 - 69	83	-	-	-	-	-	-	1	1	3	10	68	-
70 - 74	37	-	-	-	-	-	-	-	-	-	2	35	-
75 +	16	-	-	-	-	-	-	-	-	-	-	16	-
Unknown - Inconnu	-	-	-	-	-	-	-	-	-	-	-	-	-
Luxembourg[10,35]													
2018 (C)													
Total	1 898	-	3	89	343	492	310	206	157	116	82	99	1
0 - 14	-	-	-	-	-	-	-	-	-	-	-	-	-
15 - 19	16	-	2	10	3	1	-	-	-	-	-	-	-
20 - 24	140	-	1	49	60	17	8	3	2	-	-	-	-
25 - 29	481	-	-	21	213	180	45	10	5	3	3	1	-
30 - 34	464	-	-	5	52	229	107	38	20	6	2	5	-
35 - 39	318	-	-	1	11	44	111	84	36	21	5	5	-
40 - 44	183	-	-	3	1	13	31	53	45	21	12	4	-
45 - 49	117	-	-	-	1	6	6	12	24	36	21	11	-
50 - 54	103	-	-	-	2	1	2	5	22	25	22	24	-
55 - 59	44	-	-	-	-	1	-	-	2	3	15	23	-
60 - 64	22	-	-	-	-	-	-	1	1	1	2	17	-
65 - 69	5	-	-	-	-	-	-	-	-	-	-	5	-
70 - 74	2	-	-	-	-	-	-	-	-	-	-	2	-
75 +	2	-	-	-	-	-	-	-	-	-	-	2	-
Unknown - Inconnu	1	-	-	-	-	-	-	-	-	-	-	-	1
Malta - Malte													
2016 (C)													
Total	3 034	...	3[h]	134	925	907	447	197	156	103	65	96	1
16 - 19	9	...	1[h]	4	3	1	-	-	-	-	-	-	-
20 - 24	362	...	2[h]	76	200	64	14	3	2	-	-	1	-
25 - 29	1 177	...	-[h]	42	603	396	106	20	7	2	-	1	-
30 - 34	725	...	-[h]	8	91	372	178	46	23	5	-	2	-
35 - 39	327	...	-[h]	2	24	62	112	75	31	9	6	5	1
40 - 44	152	...	-[h]	1	2	8	24	36	45	22	9	5	-

24. Marriages by age of groom and by age of bride: latest available year, 2010 - 2019
Mariages selon l'âge de l'époux et selon l'âge de l'épouse : dernière année disponible, 2010 - 2019 (continued - suite)

Continent, country or area, year, code[a] and age of bride / Continent, pays ou zone, date, code[a] et âge de l'épouse	Age of groom - - âge de l'époux												
	Total	0-14	15-19	20-24	25-29	30-34	35-39	40-44	45-49	50-54	55-59	60+	Unknown Inconnu
EUROPE													
Malta - Malte													
2016													
45 - 49	116	...	-[h]	1	1	2	8	12	36	29	13	14	-
50 - 54	85	...	-[h]	-	1	-	5	4	11	26	21	17	-
55 - 59	43	...	-[h]	-	-	-	-	-	1	8	14	20	-
60 - 64	18	...	-[h]	-	-	-	-	-	-	1	2	15	-
65 +	17	...	-[h]	-	-	1	-	-	-	-	-	16	-
Unknown - Inconnu	3	...	-[h]	-	-	1	-	1	-	1	-	-	-
Netherlands - Pays-Bas[10,36]													
2014 (C)													
Total	75 696	...	93	5 415	18 406	18 053	10 388	7 078	5 065	4 156	2 989	4 053	...
15 - 19	707	...	53	359	202	57	17	12	4	2	1	-	...
20 - 24	11 835	...	30	4 051	5 752	1 433	345	130	62	21	3	8	...
25 - 29	22 426	...	7	856	10 426	8 207	1 966	609	201	95	36	23	...
30 - 34	15 494	...	3	105	1 726	7 034	4 306	1 512	478	202	73	55	...
35 - 39	7 942	...	-	24	214	1 050	2 925	2 245	929	329	136	90	...
40 - 44	5 397	...	-	9	53	205	641	1 840	1 499	730	259	161	...
45 - 49	4 147	...	-	8	26	54	137	529	1 325	1 229	503	336	...
50 - 54	3 524	...	-	3	7	8	42	162	427	1 163	1 036	676	...
55 - 59	2 113	...	-	-	-	3	8	31	107	302	702	960	...
60 - 64	1 153	...	-	-	-	2	1	5	27	60	189	869	...
65 - 69	569	...	-	-	-	-	-	2	4	18	44	501	...
70 - 74	251	...	-	-	-	-	-	1	1	4	5	240	...
75 +	138	...	-	-	-	-	-	-	1	1	2	134	...
North Macedonia - Macédoine du Nord[6]													
2018 (C)													
Total	13 494	-	165	2 522	4 999	3 150	1 263	571	351	222	98	153	-
0 - 14	-	-	-	-	-	-	-	-	-	-	-	-	-
15 - 19	1 038	-	129	595	262	40	7	4	-	-	-	1	-
20 - 24	4 371	-	34	1 669	2 060	517	72	12	6	1	-	-	-
25 - 29	4 446	-	2	218	2 364	1 493	292	55	15	5	2	-	-
30 - 34	1 859	-	-	31	264	934	478	112	31	3	3	3	-
35 - 39	831	-	-	6	40	126	344	207	64	33	3	8	-
40 - 44	437	-	-	2	6	29	56	150	128	38	13	15	-
45 - 49	241	-	-	1	3	9	11	25	85	67	23	17	-
50 - 54	144	-	-	-	-	2	3	3	20	57	31	28	-
55 - 59	69	-	-	-	-	-	-	1	2	16	21	29	-
60 - 64	34	-	-	-	-	-	-	1	-	1	2	30	-
65 - 69	21	-	-	-	-	-	-	1	-	1	-	19	-
70 - 74	1	-	-	-	-	-	-	-	-	-	-	1	-
75 +	2	-	-	-	-	-	-	-	-	-	-	2	-
Unknown - Inconnu	-	-	-	-	-	-	-	-	-	-	-	-	-
Norway - Norvège													
2012 (C)													
Total	24 077	-	38	1 503	5 000	5 362	3 852	2 786	1 989	1 440	1 018	1 089	...
0 - 14	-	-	-	-	-	-	-	-	-	-	-	-	...
15 - 19	352	-	19	164	105	35	14	10	3	1	-	1	...
20 - 24	3 246	-	15	1 069	1 372	457	164	79	51	21	7	11	...
25 - 29	6 632	-	3	226	2 933	2 215	721	289	140	61	25	19	...
30 - 34	5 312	-	-	29	486	2 197	1 503	614	245	129	64	45	...
35 - 39	3 099	-	1	13	82	386	1 128	840	352	154	79	64	...
40 - 44	2 083	-	-	1	19	55	259	718	553	270	128	80	...
45 - 49	1 463	-	-	1	2	10	51	180	477	416	201	125	...
50 - 54	981	-	-	-	1	4	9	48	137	301	291	190	...
55 - 59	505	-	-	-	-	1	2	6	24	74	177	221	...
60 - 64	231	-	-	-	-	1	1	2	5	13	37	172	...
65 - 69	129	-	-	-	-	-	-	-	2	-	8	119	...
70 - 74	28	-	-	-	-	-	-	-	-	-	1	27	...
75 +	15	-	-	-	-	-	-	-	-	-	-	15	...
Unknown - Inconnu	1	-	-	-	-	1	-	-	-	-	-	-	...
Poland - Pologne													
2018 (C)													
Total	192 443	-	377	20 871	75 457	46 385	20 732	10 341	5 722	3 680	2 958	5 920	-
0 - 14	-	-	-	-	-	-	-	-	-	-	-	-	-
15 - 19	2 395	-	227	1 446	566	109	35	9	2	-	-	1	-

24. Marriages by age of groom and by age of bride: latest available year, 2010 - 2019
Mariages selon l'âge de l'époux et selon l'âge de l'épouse : dernière année disponible, 2010 - 2019 (continued - suite)

Continent, country or area, year, code[a] and age of bride Continent, pays ou zone, date, code[a] et âge de l'épouse	Age of groom - - âge de l'époux Total	0-14	15-19	20-24	25-29	30-34	35-39	40-44	45-49	50-54	55-59	60+	Unknown Inconnu
EUROPE													
Poland - Pologne													
2018													
20 - 24	44 627	-	129	15 312	23 785	4 392	752	184	51	9	8	5	-
25 - 29	76 997	-	10	3 640	45 256	22 307	4 445	975	245	66	33	20	-
30 - 34	32 788	-	6	365	4 971	15 981	8 177	2 267	663	215	86	57	-
35 - 39	14 419	-	4	87	691	2 865	5 509	3 396	1 125	434	177	131	-
40 - 44	7 779	-	1	16	149	570	1 398	2 520	1 725	778	344	278	-
45 - 49	4 858	-	-	3	31	132	340	764	1 373	1 072	632	511	-
50 - 54	3 046	-	-	2	7	22	56	175	410	751	758	865	-
55 - 59	2 097	-	-	-	-	5	17	36	87	241	587	1 124	-
60 - 64	1 770	-	-	-	1	1	2	11	34	84	228	1 409	-
65 - 69	1 050	-	-	-	-	1	1	4	4	26	77	937	-
70 - 74	435	-	-	-	-	-	-	-	1	2	22	410	-
75 +	182	-	-	-	-	-	-	-	2	2	6	172	-
Unknown - Inconnu	-	-	-	-	-	-	-	-	-	-	-	-	-
Portugal[10,37,38]													
2018 (C)													
Total	34 637	-	135	1 669	7 422	8 608	5 489	3 739	2 386	1 711	1 173	2 305	-
0 - 14	-	-	-	-	-	-	-	-	-	-	-	-	-
15 - 19	340	-	101	155	58	16	7	1	1	-	1	-	-
20 - 24	2 995	-	25	976	1 406	410	110	37	19	10	-	2	-
25 - 29	9 425	-	3	421	4 618	3 226	783	243	84	30	10	7	-
30 - 34	8 058	-	3	83	1 051	3 759	2 092	692	246	73	31	28	-
35 - 39	4 810	-	2	21	220	903	1 740	1 182	427	173	79	63	-
40 - 44	3 214	-	1	7	51	207	567	1 045	721	337	149	129	-
45 - 49	2 111	-	-	3	14	68	138	389	593	476	189	241	-
50 - 54	1 521	-	-	1	4	14	42	122	209	418	337	374	-
55 - 59	1 026	-	-	1	-	4	7	19	64	142	281	508	-
60 - 64	571	-	-	-	-	-	2	8	16	44	70	431	-
65 - 69	325	-	-	1	-	-	-	1	4	5	14	300	-
70 - 74	156	-	-	-	-	-	1	-	2	1	8	144	-
75 +	85	-	-	-	-	1	-	-	-	2	4	78	-
Unknown - Inconnu	-	-	-	-	-	-	-	-	-	-	-	-	-
Republic of Moldova - République de Moldova													
2012[39] (C)													
Total	18 565	-	308	7 229	7 959	2 219	583	143	61	37	12	13	1
0 - 14	-	-	-	-	-	-	-	-	-	-	-	-	-
15 - 19	2 706	-	189	1 743	675	83	11	3	1	1	-	-	-
20 - 24	10 091	-	108	4 720	4 452	710	92	5	2	-	2	-	-
25 - 29	4 470	-	9	714	2 535	975	188	39	7	2	-	1	-
30 - 34	938	-	1	41	274	384	191	33	9	4	1	-	-
35 - 39	241	-	-	8	19	64	79	44	17	9	-	1	-
40 - 44	66	-	-	3	4	1	20	17	15	5	1	-	-
45 - 49	25	-	1	-	-	1	1	1	9	10	1	1	-
50 - 54	11	-	-	-	-	-	1	1	1	2	3	3	-
55 - 59	10	-	-	-	-	-	-	-	-	3	3	4	-
60 - 64	5	-	-	-	-	1	-	-	-	1	1	2	-
65 - 69	-	-	-	-	-	-	-	-	-	-	-	-	-
70 - 74	1	-	-	-	-	-	-	-	-	-	-	1	-
75 +	-	-	-	-	-	-	-	-	-	-	-	-	-
Unknown - Inconnu	1	-	-	-	-	-	-	-	-	-	-	-	1
2018 (C)													
Total	20 399	...	107[f]	3 932	7 740	4 211	1 729	1 643[n]	...	702[o]	...	335	...
0 - 19	1 408	...	...	...	...	...	...	...	...	...	...	...	...
20 - 24	7 452	...	...	...	...	...	...	...	...	...	...	...	...
25 - 29	5 644	...	...	...	...	...	...	...	...	...	...	...	...
30 - 34	2 678	...	...	...	...	...	...	...	...	...	...	...	...
35 - 39	1 300	...	...	...	...	...	...	...	...	...	...	...	...
40 - 49	1 238	...	...	...	...	...	...	...	...	...	...	...	...
50 - 59	511	...	...	...	...	...	...	...	...	...	...	...	...
60 +	168	...	...	...	...	...	...	...	...	...	...	...	...
Romania - Roumanie													
2018 (C)													
Total	143 292	-	667	14 702	45 301	36 526	18 033	11 208	6 734	4 232	2 690	3 199	...
0 - 14	-	-	-	-	-	-	-	-	-	-	-	-	...

24. Marriages by age of groom and by age of bride: latest available year, 2010 - 2019
Mariages selon l'âge de l'époux et selon l'âge de l'épouse : dernière année disponible, 2010 - 2019 (continued - suite)

Continent, country or area, year, code[a] and age of bride / Continent, pays ou zone, date, code[a] et âge de l'épouse	Age of groom - - âge de l'époux												
	Total	0-14	15-19	20-24	25-29	30-34	35-39	40-44	45-49	50-54	55-59	60+	Unknown Inconnu
EUROPE													
Romania - Roumanie													
2018													
15 - 19	7 251	-	412	3 480	2 433	730	152	30	9	-	4	1	...
20 - 24	33 953	-	217	8 666	17 528	6 042	1 167	242	57	22	7	5	...
25 - 29	43 737	-	24	2 110	20 635	15 595	3 979	1 041	248	73	21	11	...
30 - 34	25 111	-	7	347	3 892	11 202	6 495	2 349	560	153	66	40	...
35 - 39	12 500	-	4	65	636	2 272	4 418	3 403	1 133	351	130	88	...
40 - 44	8 568	-	1	23	137	558	1 416	3 010	2 210	782	260	171	...
45 - 49	5 645	-	2	7	35	101	337	911	1 893	1 490	518	351	...
50 - 54	3 294	-	-	3	5	23	58	194	515	1 084	888	524	...
55 - 59	1 763	-	-	1	-	-	5	20	82	207	642	806	...
60 - 64	949	-	-	-	-	1	5	8	21	58	125	731	...
65 - 69	343	-	-	-	-	2	1	-	6	8	23	303	...
70 - 74	116	-	-	-	-	-	-	-	-	2	6	108	...
75 +	62	-	-	-	-	-	-	-	-	2	-	60	...
Russian Federation - Fédération de Russie													
2012[40] (C)													
Total	1213598	...	15 848	312 104	402 995	191 131	105 357	63 778	43 196	34 745	21 315	23 078	51
15 - 19	81 342	...	9 599	50 495	18 055	2 523	468	130	38	20	7	6	1
20 - 24	425 562	...	5 186	200 558	173 664	35 196	7 918	2 062	620	221	80	54	3
25 - 29	337 474	...	802	50 809	166 737	80 206	26 188	8 444	2 758	1 022	326	182	-
30 - 34	154 765	...	189	8 034	34 743	52 674	34 829	15 241	5 645	2 339	749	318	4
35 - 39	83 803	...	50	1 683	7 769	15 610	25 204	18 450	9 030	4 074	1 366	564	3
40 - 44	45 822	...	17	377	1 571	3 745	7 817	13 055	10 391	5 807	2 044	996	2
45 - 49	31 345	...	1	94	327	880	2 159	4 456	9 684	8 528	3 435	1 778	3
50 - 54	25 096	...	1	37	89	230	606	1 487	3 793	9 098	6 198	3 553	4
55 - 59	14 880	...	1	7	22	46	121	360	985	2 837	5 299	5 202	-
60 +	13 481	...	2	8	16	20	47	91	252	798	1 811	10 424	12
Unknown - Inconnu	28	...	-	2	2	1	-	2	-	1	-	1	19
San Marino - Saint-Marin[41]													
2016 (C)													
Total	181	-	-	3	35	49	38	16	6	3	1	4	26
0 - 14	-	-	-	-	-	-	-	-	-	-	-	-	-
15 - 19	-	-	-	-	-	-	-	-	-	-	-	-	-
20 - 24	9	-	-	2	5	1	-	-	-	-	-	-	1
25 - 29	57	-	-	1	23	22	6	3	-	-	-	-	2
30 - 34	44	-	-	-	6	15	15	3	1	-	-	1	3
35 - 39	30	-	-	-	-	7	13	3	2	-	-	-	5
40 - 44	13	-	-	-	1	2	-	2	2	1	-	-	5
45 - 49	4	-	-	-	-	-	-	1	-	1	-	1	1
50 - 54	5	-	-	-	-	-	-	-	-	-	-	-	5
55 - 59	-	-	-	-	-	-	-	-	-	-	-	-	-
60 - 64	-	-	-	-	-	-	-	-	-	-	-	-	-
65 - 69	1	-	-	-	-	-	-	-	-	-	-	1	-
70 - 74	-	-	-	-	-	-	-	-	-	-	-	-	-
75 +	-	-	-	-	-	-	-	-	-	-	-	-	-
Unknown - Inconnu	18	-	-	-	-	2	4	4	1	1	1	1	4
Serbia - Serbie[6,42]													
2018 (+C)													
Total	36 321	-	204	3 547	10 626	10 056	4 819	2 513	1 473	946	747	1 288	102
0 - 14	-	-	-	-	-	-	-	-	-	-	-	-	-
15 - 19	1 215	-	108	581	370	108	30	10	4	1	1	-	2
20 - 24	7 568	-	76	2 130	3 464	1 442	318	91	22	9	1	3	12
25 - 29	11 938	-	12	642	5 425	4 314	1 132	271	79	17	14	9	23
30 - 34	7 189	-	5	131	1 117	3 327	1 797	551	161	59	20	11	10
35 - 39	3 328	-	-	35	152	671	1 161	807	313	97	58	23	11
40 - 44	1 776	-	1	6	41	117	261	566	427	202	83	65	7
45 - 49	1 229	-	-	6	14	26	77	136	334	286	184	161	5
50 - 54	831	-	-	-	4	11	24	45	85	194	213	253	2
55 - 59	540	-	-	-	2	2	4	13	25	52	129	311	2
60 - 64	279	-	-	1	2	2	4	2	7	13	30	217	1
65 - 69	164	-	-	-	-	3	1	3	3	6	5	142	1
70 - 74	64	-	-	-	1	1	1	-	2	3	4	52	-
75 +	40	-	-	-	-	-	2	-	-	2	1	35	-
Unknown - Inconnu	160	-	2	15	34	32	7	18	11	5	4	6	26

24. Marriages by age of groom and by age of bride: latest available year, 2010 - 2019
Mariages selon l'âge de l'époux et selon l'âge de l'épouse : dernière année disponible, 2010 - 2019 (continued - suite)

Continent, country or area, year, code[a] and age of bride / Continent, pays ou zone, date, code[a] et âge de l'épouse	Age of groom - - âge de l'époux												
	Total	0-14	15-19	20-24	25-29	30-34	35-39	40-44	45-49	50-54	55-59	60+	Unknown Inconnu
EUROPE													
Slovakia - Slovaquie[6]													
2018 (C)													
Total	31 177	-	375	2 398	8 907	8 573	4 814	2 620	1 283	825	574	808	...
0 - 14	-	-	-	-	-	-	-	-	-	-	-	-	...
15 - 19	873	-	307	423	103	23	9	5	2	-	1	-	...
20 - 24	4 779	-	60	1 444	2 253	757	189	57	11	5	2	1	...
25 - 29	11 220	-	6	441	5 382	3 861	1 137	293	68	12	14	6	...
30 - 34	7 058	-	2	56	969	3 170	1 905	678	180	57	23	18	...
35 - 39	3 299	-	-	25	138	588	1 207	823	295	130	48	45	...
40 - 44	1 762	-	-	7	45	142	280	568	382	190	90	58	...
45 - 49	892	-	-	1	12	24	71	159	234	200	108	83	...
50 - 54	589	-	-	-	4	5	12	32	98	167	137	134	...
55 - 59	326	-	-	1	1	1	4	3	8	48	101	159	...
60 - 64	204	-	-	-	-	1	-	2	3	14	40	144	...
65 - 69	119	-	-	-	-	1	-	-	2	2	9	105	...
70 - 74	45	-	-	-	-	-	-	-	-	-	1	44	...
75 +	11	-	-	-	-	-	-	-	-	-	-	11	...
Slovenia - Slovénie[43]													
2018 (C)													
Total	7 256	-	14	384	1 618	1 893	1 342	795	405	319	183	303	...
0 - 14	-	-	-	-	-	-	-	-	-	-	-	-	...
15 - 19	65	-	5	40	14	3	-	3	-	-	-	-	...
20 - 24	806	-	8	239	375	140	27	10	2	2	1	2	...
25 - 29	2 078	-	1	66	957	778	202	52	11	3	2	6	...
30 - 34	1 705	-	-	27	198	765	497	150	42	18	5	3	...
35 - 39	1 176	-	-	8	62	163	489	314	99	28	10	3	...
40 - 44	565	-	-	2	7	35	95	198	129	63	20	16	...
45 - 49	324	-	-	2	3	4	28	50	82	92	39	24	...
50 - 54	242	-	-	-	2	4	2	13	32	78	53	58	...
55 - 59	134	-	-	-	-	-	1	3	4	27	34	65	...
60 - 64	82	-	-	-	-	-	1	2	4	5	10	60	...
65 - 69	50	-	-	-	-	1	-	-	-	2	6	41	...
70 - 74	14	-	-	-	-	-	-	-	-	-	2	12	...
75 +	15	-	-	-	-	-	-	-	-	1	1	13	...
Spain - Espagne													
2018 (C)													
Total	160 699	-	119	2 577	19 600	42 642	36 134	23 671	13 525	8 666	5 765	8 000	...
0 - 14	-	-	-	-	-	-	-	-	-	-	-	-	...
15 - 19	652	-	50	273	203	88	31	4	1	2	-	-	...
20 - 24	5 831	-	43	1 346	2 652	1 188	395	129	43	13	10	12	...
25 - 29	31 652	-	19	664	12 073	13 588	3 804	972	319	121	55	37	...
30 - 34	45 336	-	4	188	3 772	22 212	13 878	3 675	1 052	305	144	106	...
35 - 39	31 190	-	1	70	678	4 553	13 715	8 245	2 478	899	339	212	...
40 - 44	19 971	-	2	20	143	751	3 507	8 140	4 535	1 714	666	493	...
45 - 49	11 401	-	-	13	52	186	622	1 982	3 749	2 582	1 199	1 016	...
50 - 54	7 301	-	-	1	14	48	138	426	1 077	2 254	1 745	1 598	...
55 - 59	4 126	-	-	1	8	23	37	76	211	609	1 197	1 964	...
60 - 64	2 055	-	-	1	4	4	6	14	51	140	340	1 495	...
65 - 69	753	-	-	-	1	1	1	7	7	23	55	658	...
70 - 74	296	-	-	-	-	-	-	-	2	3	13	278	...
75 +	135	-	-	-	-	-	-	1	-	1	2	131	...
Sweden - Suède													
2012 (C)													
Total	50 044	-	69	1 803	7 703	10 419	8 284	5 587	4 328	2 880	2 142	2 688	4 141
0 - 14	-	-	-	-	-	-	-	-	-	-	-	-	-
15 - 19	668	-	33	130	81	26	7	1	1	-	-	1	388
20 - 24	4 680	-	27	1 194	1 729	551	164	63	30	7	4	2	909
25 - 29	11 233	-	5	378	4 640	3 898	1 046	288	123	41	15	12	787
30 - 34	10 932	-	2	71	1 004	4 783	3 106	858	319	104	37	30	618
35 - 39	7 543	-	1	12	183	930	3 005	1 924	666	218	81	54	469
40 - 44	5 154	-	1	10	43	175	732	1 768	1 317	434	192	87	395
45 - 49	3 922	-	-	5	19	42	178	525	1 383	905	407	180	278
50 - 54	2 665	-	-	2	2	7	36	127	395	863	690	383	160
55 - 59	1 595	-	-	1	2	6	5	28	75	242	526	647	63
60 - 64	934	-	-	-	-	1	5	4	16	58	150	657	43
65 - 69	468	-	-	-	-	-	-	1	2	8	36	396	25

24. Marriages by age of groom and by age of bride: latest available year, 2010 - 2019
Mariages selon l'âge de l'époux et selon l'âge de l'épouse : dernière année disponible, 2010 - 2019 (continued - suite)

Continent, country or area, year, code[a] and age of bride / Continent, pays ou zone, date, code[a] et âge de l'épouse	Age of groom - - âge de l'époux												
	Total	0-14	15-19	20-24	25-29	30-34	35-39	40-44	45-49	50-54	55-59	60+	Unknown Inconnu
EUROPE													
Sweden - Suède													
2012													
70 - 74	160	-	-	-	-	-	-	-	-	-	4	153	3
75 +	90	-	-	-	-	-	-	-	1	-	-	86	3
Switzerland - Suisse[44]													
2018 (C)													
Total	40 716	-	43	2 039	8 573	11 632	7 280	3 580	2 316	1 949	1 407	1 897	...
0 - 14	-	-	-	-	-	-	-	-	-	-	-	-	...
15 - 19	355	-	15	195	99	27	13	2	3	1	-	-	...
20 - 24	4 319	-	22	1 327	2 060	625	175	49	34	9	9	9	...
25 - 29	11 187	-	3	387	4 844	4 268	1 112	294	144	69	42	24	...
30 - 34	11 449	-	2	83	1 267	5 432	3 187	898	310	138	66	66	...
35 - 39	5 793	-	-	30	200	1 006	2 251	1 279	552	258	131	86	...
40 - 44	2 663	-	1	8	53	168	390	745	564	395	190	149	...
45 - 49	1 861	-	-	4	25	61	105	209	474	485	264	234	...
50 - 54	1 484	-	-	3	16	26	35	83	173	418	342	388	...
55 - 59	882	-	-	2	5	9	7	17	49	131	283	379	...
60 - 64	389	-	-	-	1	5	3	2	10	36	61	271	...
65 - 69	159	-	-	-	1	4	1	2	2	4	14	131	...
70 - 74	94	-	-	-	1	1	-	-	1	2	2	87	...
75 +	81	-	-	-	1	-	1	-	-	3	3	73	...
Ukraine[45]													
2017 (+C)													
Total	249 522	-	3 789	56 884	78 608	45 607	22 588	14 412	9 638	6 731	4 941	6 324	...
0 - 14	8	-	4	4	-	-	-	-	-	-	-	-	...
15 - 19	20 728	-	2 168	12 144	5 205	938	181	51	26	10	3	2	...
20 - 24	82 691	-	1 312	35 807	34 284	8 793	1 735	487	171	63	28	11	...
25 - 29	63 072	-	220	7 128	30 287	17 879	5 259	1 529	486	165	80	39	...
30 - 34	34 565	-	37	1 296	6 995	13 115	7 823	3 372	1 223	455	173	76	...
35 - 39	18 038	-	30	350	1 367	3 664	5 213	4 161	1 962	810	335	146	...
40 - 44	11 273	-	10	87	338	935	1 778	3 210	2 650	1 337	592	336	...
45 - 49	7 427	-	4	45	85	201	469	1 191	2 122	1 766	984	560	...
50 - 54	4 918	-	4	15	28	61	97	304	726	1 473	1 270	940	...
55 - 59	3 222	-	-	6	13	16	24	78	218	480	1 084	1 303	...
60 +	3 580	-	-	2	6	5	9	29	54	172	392	2 911	...
United Kingdom of Great Britain and Northern Ireland - Royaume-Uni de Grande-Bretagne et d'Irlande du Nord[46,47]													
2016 (C)													
Total	287 328	-	628	14 573	67 607	69 874	39 998	25 438	22 168	17 853	12 310	16 855	24
0 - 14	-	-	-	-	-	-	-	-	-	-	-	-	-
15 - 19	1 624	-	408	829	287	59	20	5	6	6	3	1	-
20 - 24	26 380	-	177	9 579	12 226	3 137	833	234	104	50	23	17	-
25 - 29	83 685	-	25	3 235	44 021	26 827	6 647	1 801	682	293	100	53	1
30 - 34	65 325	-	11	631	9 086	31 833	15 817	5 080	1 836	669	232	128	2
35 - 39	33 387	-	3	195	1 457	6 260	12 186	7 699	3 556	1 302	476	253	-
40 - 44	21 240	-	4	63	349	1 253	3 190	6 725	5 601	2 587	975	493	-
45 - 49	19 889	-	-	25	121	356	962	2 827	6 781	5 274	2 253	1 290	-
50 - 54	15 845	-	-	8	40	111	269	807	2 752	5 345	3 939	2 574	-
55 - 59	9 523	-	-	3	8	23	55	190	646	1 783	3 067	3 748	-
60 - 64	5 108	-	-	3	4	6	10	51	156	407	930	3 541	-
65 - 69	3 005	-	-	1	1	5	2	14	36	107	241	2 598	-
70 - 74	1 417	-	-	1	2	-	1	2	8	25	48	1 330	-
75 +	858	-	-	-	-	-	-	-	3	5	23	827	-
Unknown - Inconnu	42	-	-	-	5	4	6	3	1	-	-	2	21
OCEANIA - OCÉANIE													
Australia - Australie[48]													
2018 (+C)													
Total	119 188	-	315	9 821	33 069	30 172	15 296	8 288	6 831	5 307	4 230	5 855	...
0 - 14	-	-	-	-	-	-	-	-	-	-	-	-	...
15 - 19	1 134	-	165	627	258	58	15	4	3	3	3	-	...

24. Marriages by age of groom and by age of bride: latest available year, 2010 - 2019
Mariages selon l'âge de l'époux et selon l'âge de l'épouse : dernière année disponible, 2010 - 2019 (continued - suite)

Continent, country or area, year, code[a] and age of bride / Continent, pays ou zone, date, code[a] et âge de l'épouse	Age of groom - - âge de l'époux												
	Total	0-14	15-19	20-24	25-29	30-34	35-39	40-44	45-49	50-54	55-59	60+	Unknown Inconnu
OCEANIA - OCÉANIE													
Australia - Australie[48]													
2018													
20 - 24	15 699	-	123	6 756	6 597	1 538	388	127	79	32	27	21	...
25 - 29	39 519	-	24	2 024	21 404	12 102	2 647	691	312	164	89	59	...
30 - 34	27 196	-	-	294	4 005	13 536	6 212	1 852	648	312	167	157	...
35 - 39	12 316	-	3	78	593	2 351	4 545	2 552	1 226	504	246	209	...
40 - 44	7 025	-	-	29	150	405	1 070	2 051	1 744	802	433	333	...
45 - 49	5 945	-	-	12	40	124	303	768	1 895	1 507	811	498	...
50 - 54	4 317	-	-	7	12	30	78	183	669	1 383	1 132	822	...
55 - 59	2 862	-	-	7	3	12	27	46	179	466	942	1 171	...
60 - 64	1 561	-	-	-	4	3	12	5	53	96	275	1 106	...
65 - 69	882	-	-	-	-	-	3	5	13	22	76	760	...
70 - 74	448	-	-	-	3	-	-	-	3	4	15	423	...
75 +	292	-	-	-	4	-	-	-	-	-	5	280	...
French Polynesia - Polynésie française[49]													
2018 (C)													
Total	1 369	-	16	180	217	220	194	150	136	83	85	87	1
0 - 14	-	-	-	-	-	-	-	-	-	-	-	-	-
15 - 19	54	-	8	34	8	3	-	1	-	-	-	-	-
20 - 24	205	-	7	105	56	22	8	5	2	-	-	-	-
25 - 29	259	-	1	29	106	68	28	10	7	2	7	1	-
30 - 34	264	-	-	10	28	92	71	25	19	10	6	3	-
35 - 39	186	-	-	1	11	30	57	48	22	9	4	4	-
40 - 44	156	-	-	-	7	4	24	45	41	19	9	7	-
45 - 49	94	-	-	1	1	1	5	11	29	18	11	17	-
50 - 54	70	-	-	-	-	-	1	4	9	14	27	15	-
55 - 59	44	-	-	-	-	-	-	1	6	8	13	16	-
60 - 64	25	-	-	-	-	-	-	-	-	2	6	17	-
65 - 69	5	-	-	-	-	-	-	-	1	-	1	3	-
70 - 74	5	-	-	-	-	-	-	-	-	1	1	3	-
75 +	1	-	-	-	-	-	-	-	-	-	-	1	-
Unknown - Inconnu	1	-	-	-	-	-	-	-	-	-	-	-	1
New Caledonia - Nouvelle-Calédonie													
2010 (C)													
Total	908	...	2[f]	62	149	200	171	169[n]	...	90[o]	...	65	-
0 - 19	13	...	1[f]	6	2	2	1	1[n]	...	-[o]	...	-	-
20 - 24	118	...	-[f]	36	51	18	10	2[n]	...	1[o]	...	-	-
25 - 29	194	...	1[f]	16	77	63	20	13[n]	...	3[o]	...	1	-
30 - 34	205	...	-[f]	4	14	94	62	27[n]	...	4[o]	...	-	-
35 - 39	139	...	-[f]	-	3	19	55	52[n]	...	7[o]	...	3	-
40 - 49	150	...	-[f]	-	2	4	22	65[n]	...	41[o]	...	16	-
50 - 59	59	...	-[f]	-	-	-	1	9[n]	...	30[o]	...	19	-
60 +	30	...	-[f]	-	-	-	-	-[n]	...	4[o]	...	26	-
New Zealand - Nouvelle-Zélande[10,50,51,52]													
2019 (+C)													
Total	19 071	-[b]	39[h]	1 248	4 785	4 782	2 529	1 449	1 173	1 008	837	1 227	...
0 - 15	-	-[b]	-[h]	-	-	-	-	-	-	-	-	-	...
16 - 19	207	-[b]	39[h]	123	30	9	3		-	-	-	-	...
20 - 24	2 820	-[b]	-[h]	1 122	1 332	267	60	21	9	6	3	3	...
25 - 29	6 519	-[b]	-[h]	-	3 420	2 436	456	126	45	21	9	3	...
30 - 34	3 864	-[b]	-[h]	-	-	2 076	1 302	297	120	33	21	18	...
35 - 39	1 680	-[b]	-[h]	-	-	-	705	615	213	90	27	30	...
40 - 44	1 191	-[b]	-[h]	-	-	-	-	387	462	216	78	48	...
45 - 49	1 005	-[b]	-[h]	-	-	-	-	-	324	399	186	99	...
50 - 54	765	-[b]	-[h]	-	-	-	-	-	-	243	312	213	...
55 - 59	528	-[b]	-[h]	-	-	-	-	-	-	-	204	327	...
60 - 64	231	-[b]	-[h]	-	-	-	-	-	-	-	-	234	...
65 - 69	132	-[b]	-[h]	-	-	-	-	-	-	-	-	129	...
70 - 74	87	-[b]	-[h]	-	-	-	-	-	-	-	-	84	...
75 +	42	-[b]	-[h]	-	-	-	-	-	-	-	-	42	...

FOOTNOTES - NOTES

Italics: data from civil registers which are incomplete or of unknown completeness. - Italiques : données incomplètes ou dont le degré d'exactitude n'est pas connu, provenant des registres de l'état civil.

[*] Provisional. - Données provisoires.

[a] 'Code' indicates the source of data, as follows:
C - Civil registration, estimated over 90% complete
U - Civil registration, estimated less than 90% complete
| - Other source, estimated reliable
+ - Data tabulated by date of registration rather than occurence
... - Information not available

Le 'Code' indique la source des données, comme suit :
C - Registres de l'état civil considérés complèts à 90 p. 100 au moins
U - Registres de l'état civil qui ne sont pas considérés complèts à 90 p. 100 au moins
| - Autre source, considérée pas douteuses
+ - Données exploitées selon la date de l'enregistrement et non la date de l'événement
... - Information pas disponible

[b] Refers to 0-15 years of age. - Données se raportent au groupe d'âges 0-15.
[c] Refers to 0-16 years of age. - Données se raportent au groupe d'âges 0-16.
[d] Refers to 0-17 years of age. - Données se raportent au groupe d'âges 0-17.
[e] Refers to 0-18 years of age. - Données se raportent au groupe d'âges 0-18.
[f] Refers to 0-19 years of age. - Données se raportent au groupe d'âges 0-19.
[g] Refers to 0-24 years of age. - Données se raportent au groupe d'âges 0-24.
[h] Refers to 16-19 years of age. - Données se raportent au groupe d'âges 16-19.
[i] Refers to 17-19 years of age. - Données se raportent au groupe d'âges 17-19.
[j] Refers to 18-19 years of age. - Données se raportent au groupe d'âges 18-19.
[k] Refers to 19-24 years of age. - Données se raportent au groupe d'âges 19-24.
[l] Refers to 20-29 years of age. - Données se raportent au groupe d'âges 20-29.
[m] Refers to 30-39 years of age. - Données se raportent au groupe d'âges 30-39.
[n] Refers to 40-49 years of age. - Données se raportent au groupe d'âges 40-49.
[o] Refers to 50-59 years of age. - Données se raportent au groupe d'âges 50-59.
[p] Refers to 35+ years of age. - Données se raportent au groupe d'âges 35+.
[q] Refers to 40+ years of age. - Données se raportent au groupe d'âges 40+.
[r] Refers to 45+ years of age. - Données se raportent au groupe d'âges 45+.
[s] Refers to 50+ years of age. - Données se raportent au groupe d'âges 50+.
[t] Refers to 55+ years of age. - Données se raportent au groupe d'âges 55+.

[1] Source: Vital Statistics Report. - Source: Vital Statistics Report.
[2] Source: Vital Statistics Report, National Statistics Institute. - Source: Rapport sur les statistiques de l'état civil, Institut national de la statistique.
[3] Excludes the islands of St. Brandon and Agalega. - Non compris les îles St. Brandon et Agalega.
[4] Including visitors. - Y compris les visiteurs.
[5] Excluding visitors. - Ne comprend pas les visiteurs.
[6] Data refer to marriages registered by residence of groom. - Les données concernent les mariages enregistrés selon la résidence du marié.
[7] Data refer to marriages registered by residence of bride. - Les données concernent les mariages enregistrés selon le lieu de résidence de la mariée.
[8] Data refers to the number of marriages of which at least one of the partners is a resident of Curacao. - Les données concernent le nombre de mariages dont au moins l'un des partenaires est un résident de Curaçao.
[9] Including marriages where bride/groom are non-residents. - Y compris les mariages pour lesquels le marié et la mariée sont des non-résidents.
[10] Including same-sex marriages. - Y compris les mariages entre personnes du même sexe.
[11] Source: Ministry of Legal Affairs. - Source : Ministère des affaires juridiques.
[12] Excludes nomadic Indian tribes. - Non compris les tribus d'Indiens nomades.
[13] Data are compiled from the National Registers of Identification and Civil Status (RENIEC). - Les données sont rédigées à partir des Registres Nationaux d'Identification et d'État Civil (RENIEC).
[14] Data extracted from online system representing only 86.0% of the total marriages. - Données extraites du système en ligne, qui ne représentent que 86,0 % du nombre total de mariages.
[15] Data refer to marriages of residents only. - Les données ne portent que sur les mariages de résidents.
[16] Data refer to government controlled areas. - Les données se rapportent aux zones contrôlées par le Gouvernement.
[17] Data refer to the Iranian Year which begins on 21 March and ends on 20 March of the following year. - Les données concernent l'année iranienne, qui commence le 21 mars et se termine le 20 mars de l'année suivante.
[18] Includes data for East Jerusalem and Israeli residents in certain other territories under occupation by Israeli military forces since June 1967. - Y compris les données pour Jérusalem-Est et les résidents israéliens dans certains autres territoires occupés depuis 1967 par les forces armées israéliennes.
[19] Data refer to Japanese nationals in Japan only; and to grooms and brides whose marriages occurred and were registered in the same year. - Les données se raportent aux nationaux japonais au Japon seulement; et aux époux et épouses dont le mariage a été célébré et enregistré la même année.
[20] Excluding data for Jordanian territory under occupation since June 1967 by Israeli military forces. Excluding foreigners, including registered Palestinian refugees. - Non compris les données pour le territoire jordanien occupé depuis juin 1967 par les forces armées israéliennes. Non compris les étrangers, mais y compris les réfugiés de Palestine enregistrés.
[21] Excluding marriages by groom and bride that are under "Married" status. - Sauf mariages entre personnes qui ont le statut de « marié(e) ».
[22] Excluding alien armed forces, civilian aliens employed by armed forces, and foreign diplomatic personnel and their dependants. - Non compris les militaires étrangers, les civils étrangers employés par les forces armées ni le personnel diplomatique étranger et les membres de leur famille les accompagnant.
[23] Data comprise civil marriages registered under the Women's Charter and Muslim marriages registered under the Administration of Muslim Law Act. - Les données comprennent les mariages civils enregistrés en vertu de la Charte des droits de la femme, ainsi que les mariages musulmans enregistrés en vertu de la loi sur l'administration du droit islamique.
[24] Excluding marriages previously officiated outside Singapore or under religious and customary rites. - Ne comprend pas les mariages prononcés ailleurs qu'à Singapour ni les mariages religieux ou coutumiers.
[25] Data from MERNIS (Central Population Administrative System). - Données de MERNIS (Système central de données démographiques).
[26] Excluding marriages of aliens temporarily in the area, but including marriages abroad of persons with residence in Austria. - Non compris les mariages d'étrangers temporairement dans la région, mais y compris des mariages à l'étranger de personnes ayant leur résidence en Autriche.
[27] Since 2003, marriage between persons of the same sex is authorized in Belgium, but the sex of spouses is not revealed. In this table, husband is used for first spouse, whereas wife is used for second spouse. - Depuis 2003, le mariage entre personnes de même sexe est autorisé en Belgique, mais le sexe des conjoints n'est pas indiqué. Dans ce tableau, la mention "époux" est utilisée pour le premier conjoint et la mention "épouse" pour le second conjoint.
[28] Including armed forces stationed outside the country and alien armed forces in the area, if the marriage is performed by local authority. - Y compris les militaires nationaux hors du pays et les militaires étrangers en garnison sur le territoire, si le mariage a été célébré par l'autorité locale.
[29] Including nationals outside the country, but excluding foreigners in the country. - Y compris les nationaux à l'étranger, mais non compris les étrangers sur le territoire.
[30] Excluding Faeroe Islands and Greenland shown separately, if available. - Non compris les Iles Féroé et le Groenland, qui font l'objet de rubriques distinctes, si disponible.
[31] Excluding Åland Islands. - Non compris les Îles d'Åland.
[32] Data refer to marriages between persons of different sex. - Les données se rapportent aux mariages entre personnes de sexe différent.
[33] Data for residence abroad are excluded. - Les données relatives aux résidents à l'étranger sont exclues.
[34] Data refer to common residence after marriage. - Données se rapportant à la résidence commune après le mariage.
[35] Data refer to marriages where one or both partners are residents. - Les données portent sur les mariages pour lesquels l'un des deux partenaires ou les deux sont résidents.
[36] Marriages of couples of which at least one partner is recorded in a Dutch municipal register, irrespective of the country where the marriage was performed. - Correspond aux mariages pour lesquels au moins l'un des partenaires est inscrit sur un registre municipal néerlandais, quel que soit le pays dans lequel le mariage est célébré.
[37] Marriages registered by place of occurrence of marriage. - Mariages enregistrés en fonction du lieu de l'événement.
[38] Groom refers to the man for opposite sex marriages, and to spouse 1 as specified in the Civil Register for same sex marriages. Bride refers to the woman for opposite sex marriages, and to spouse 2 as specified in the Civil Register for same sex marriages. - Marié se réfère à l'homme en cas de mariage entre personnes de sexe différent et à l'époux 1 inscrit sur le Registre d'état civil en cas de mariage entre personnes du même sexe. Mariée se réfère à la femme en cas de mariage entre personnes de sexe différent et à l'époux 2 inscrit sur le Registre d'état civil en cas de mariage entre personnes du même sexe.
[39] Data refer to first marriages only. - Données se rapportent aux premiers mariages seulement.

[40] Data refer to population 15 years of age or more. - Les données concernent la population âgée de 15 ans ou plus.
[41] Includes civil and religious marriages as well as not specified. - Englobe les mariages civils et religieux et ceux pour lesquels rien n'a été indiqué.
[42] Excludes data for Kosovo and Metohia. - Sans les données pour le Kosovo et Metohie.
[43] Data refer to usual residence of groom and bride. - Les données se rapportent à la résidence habituelle des époux.
[44] Data based on the residence of groom if he has permanent address in the country, otherwise, based on the residence of bride. If neither partner is a permanent resident, the marriage is not included in the official statistics. - Les données sont fondées sur la résidence du marié si celui-ci a une adresse permanente dans le pays, sinon elles sont fondées sur la résidence de la mariée. Si aucun des deux partenaires n'est un résident permanent, le mariage n'apparaît pas dans les statistiques officielles.
[45] The Government of Ukraine has informed the United Nations that it is not in a position to provide statistical data concerning the Autonomous Republic of Crimea and the city of Sevastopol. - Le gouvernement Ukrainien a informé l'ONU qu'il n'est pas en mesure de fournir des données statistiques concernant la République autonome de Crimée et la ville de Sébastopol.
[46] Data tabulated by date of occurrence for England and Wales, and by date of registration for Northern Ireland and Scotland. - Données exploitées selon la date de l'événement pour l'Angleterre et le pays de Galles, et selon la date de l'enregistrement pour l'Irlande du Nord et l'Ecosse.
[47] Excluding Channel Islands (Guernsey and Jersey) and Isle of Man, shown separately, if available. - Non compris les îles Anglo-Normandes (Guernesey et Jersey) et l'île de Man, qui font l'objet de rubriques distinctes, si disponible.
[48] 1. With the legalisation of same-sex marriages in December 2017, concept of 'Groom' and 'Bride' no longer applied. These have been replaced with 'Person 1' and 'Person 2' respectively. 'Person 1' is mainly comprised of males and 'Person 2' is mainly comprised of females. 2. For confidentiality purposes, perturbation has been applied to data. As a result, component cells may not add to totals. Some totals may also differ between tables, where cross-tabulations of different variables are presented. - 1. Depuis la légalisation du mariage homosexuel en décembre 2017, les catégories « Époux » et « Épouse » ont été remplacées respectivement par « Personne 1 » et « Personne 2 ». La catégorie « Personne 1 » comprend principalement des hommes, « Personne 2 » principalement des femmes. 2. Pour des raisons de confidentialité, les données ont été perturbées. Par conséquent, la somme des différentes cellules peut ne pas correspondre aux totaux. Certains totaux peuvent également différer d'un tableau à un autre lorsque différentes variables sont croisées.
[49] Excluding same-sex marriages. - À l'exclusion des mariages entre personnes du même sexe.
[50] Data refer to marriages and civil unions by residence of 'partner 2'. - Les données concernent les mariages et les unions civiles selon la résidence du « partenaire 2 ».
[51] Random rounding to base 3 is applied in this table as a confidentiality measure. - Les chiffres sont arrondis à la base 3 de manière aléatoire, pour des raisons de confidentialité.
[52] Data are classified by "younger partner" and "older partner" and not by "bride" and "groom". - Les données sont classées selon les catégories « Partenaire plus jeune » et « Partenaire plus âgé » et non pas selon les catégories « Épouse » et « Époux ».

Table 25 - *Demographic Yearbook 2019*

Table 25 presents the number of divorces and crude divorce rates for as many years as possible between 2015 and 2019.

Description of variables: Divorce is defined as a final legal dissolution of a marriage, that is, the separation of husband and wife which confers on the parties the right to remarriage under civil, religious and/or other provisions, according to the laws of each country[1].

Unless otherwise noted, divorce statistics exclude legal separations that do not allow remarriage. These statistics refer to the number of divorces granted, and not to the number of persons divorcing.

Divorce statistics are obtained from court records and/or civil registers according to national practice. The actual compilation of these statistics may be the responsibility of the civil registrar, the national statistical office or other government offices.

The urban/rural classification of divorces is that provided by each country or area; it is presumed to be based on the national census definitions of urban population, which have been set forth at the end of the technical notes for table 6.

Rate computation: Crude divorce rates by urban/rural residence are the annual number of divorces per 1 000 mid-year population. Rates presented in this table have been limited to those countries or areas having at least a total of 30 divorces in a given year. These rates are calculated by the Statistics Division of the United Nations based on the appropriate reference population (for example: total population, nationals only etc.) if known and available. If the reference population is not known or unavailable, the total population is used to calculate the rates. Therefore, if the population that is used to calculate the rates is different from the correct reference population, the rates presented might under- or overstate the true situation in a country or area.

Reliability of data: Each country or area has been asked to indicate the estimated completeness of the divorces recorded in its civil register. These national assessments are indicated by the quality codes "C" and "U" that appear in the first column of this table.

"C" indicates that the data are estimated to be virtually complete, that is, representing at least 90 per cent of the divorces that occur each year, while "U" indicates that data are estimated to be incomplete, that is, representing less than 90 per cent of the divorces occurring each year. The code "..." indicates that no information was provided regarding completeness.

Data from civil registers that are reported as incomplete or of unknown completeness (coded "U" or "...") are considered unreliable. They appear in *italics* in this table and the rates were not computed on data so coded. These quality codes apply only to data from civil registers. For more information about the quality of vital statistics data in general, see section 4.2 of the Technical Notes.

Limitations: Statistics on divorces are subject to the same qualifications as have been set forth for vital statistics in general and divorce statistics in particular as discussed in section 4 of the Technical Notes.

Divorce, like marriage, is a legal event, and this has implications for international comparability of data. Divorce has been defined, for statistical purposes, in terms of the laws of individual countries or areas. The laws pertaining to divorce vary considerably from one country or area to another. This variation in the legal provision for divorce also affects the incidence of divorce, which is relatively low in countries or areas where divorce decrees are difficult to obtain.

Since divorces are granted by courts and statistics on divorce refer to the actual divorce decree, effective as of the date of the decree, marked year-to-year fluctuations may reflect court delays and clearances rather than trends in the incidence of divorce. The comparability of divorce statistics may also be affected by tabulation procedures. In some countries or areas annulments and/or legal separations may be included. This practice is more common for countries or areas in which the number of divorces is small. Information on this practice is given in the footnotes when known.

The registration of a divorce in many countries or areas is the responsibility solely of the court or the authority which granted it. Since the registration recording such cases is part of the records of the court proceedings, divorces are likely to be registered soon after the decree is granted. For this reason the practice of tabulating data by date of registration does not generally pose serious problems of comparability as it does in the case of birth and death statistics.

As noted briefly above, the incidence of divorce is affected by the relative ease or difficulty of obtaining a divorce according to the laws of individual countries or areas. The incidence of divorce is also affected by the ability of individuals to meet financial and other costs of the court procedures. Connected with this aspect is the influence of certain religious faiths on the incidence of divorce. For all these reasons, divorce statistics are not strictly comparable as measures of family dissolution by legal means. Furthermore, family dissolution by other than legal means, such as separation, is not measured in statistics for divorce.

For certain countries or areas there is or was no legal provision for divorce in the sense used here, and therefore no data for these countries or areas appear in this table.

In addition, it should be noted that rates are affected also by the quality and limitations of the population estimates that are used in their computation. The problems of under-enumeration or over-enumeration, and to some extent, the differences in definition of total population, have been discussed in section 3 of the Technical Notes dealing with population data in general, and specific information pertaining to individual countries or areas is given in the footnotes to table 3.

As will be seen from the footnotes, strict correspondence between the numerator of the rate and the denominator is not always obtained; for example, divorces among civilian plus military segments of the population may be related to civilian population only. The effect of this may be to increase the rates but, in most cases, the effect is negligible.

As mentioned above, data for some countries or areas may include annulments and/or legal separations. This practice affects the comparability of the crude divorce rates. For example, inclusion of annulments in the numerator of the rates produces a negligible effect on the rates, but inclusion of legal separations may have a measurable effect on the level.

It should be emphasized that crude divorce rates like crude birth, death and marriage rates may be seriously affected by age-sex structure of the populations to which they relate. Like crude marriage rates, they are also affected by the existing distribution of the population by marital status. Nevertheless, crude divorce rates provide a simple measure of the level and changes in divorces.

The comparability of data by urban/rural residence is affected by the national definitions of urban and rural used in tabulating these data. It is assumed, in the absence of specific information to the contrary, that the definitions of urban and rural used in connection with the national population census were also used in the compilation of the vital statistics for each country or area. However, it cannot be excluded that, for a given country or area, different definitions of urban and rural are used for the vital statistics data and the population census data respectively. When known, the definitions of urban in national population censuses are presented at the end of the technical notes for table 6. As discussed in detail in the notes, these definitions vary considerably from one country or area to another.

In addition to problems of comparability, divorce rates classified by urban/rural residence are also subject to certain special types of bias. If, when calculating divorce rates, different definitions of urban are used in connection with the vital events and the population data, and if this results in a net difference between the numerator and denominator of the rate in the population at risk, then the divorce rates would be biased. Urban/rural differentials in divorce rates may also be affected by whether the vital events have been tabulated in terms of place of occurrence or place of usual residence. This problem is discussed in more detail in section 4.1.4.1 of the Technical Notes.

Earlier data: Divorces have been shown in previous issues of the *Demographic Yearbook*. The earliest data, which were for 1935, appeared in the 1951 issue. For more information on specific topics and years for which data are reported, readers should consult the Historical Index.

NOTES

[1] For definition, please see section 4.1.1 of the Technical Notes.

Tableau 25 – *Annuaire démographique 2019*

Le tableau 25 présente des statistiques concernant les divorces et les taux bruts de divortialité, pour le plus grand nombre d'années possible entre 2015 et 2019.

Description des variables : le divorce est la dissolution légale et définitive des liens du mariage, c'est-à-dire la séparation de l'époux et de l'épouse qui confère aux parties le droit de se remarier civilement ou religieusement, ou selon toute autre procédure, conformément à la législation du pays[1].

Sauf indication contraire, les statistiques de la divortialité n'englobent pas les séparations légales qui excluent un remariage. Ces statistiques se rapportent aux jugements de divorce prononcés, non aux personnes divorcées.

Les statistiques de la divortialité proviennent, selon la pratique suivie par chaque pays, des actes des tribunaux et/ou des registres de l'état civil. L'officier d'état civil, les services nationaux de statistique ou d'autres services gouvernementaux peuvent être chargés d'établir ces statistiques.

La classification des divorces selon le lieu de résidence (zone urbaine ou rurale) est celle qui a été communiquée par chaque pays ou zone ; on part du principe qu'elle repose sur les définitions de la population urbaine utilisées pour les recensements nationaux, qui sont reproduites à la fin des notes techniques du tableau 6.

Calcul des taux : les taux bruts de divortialité selon le lieu de résidence (zone urbaine ou rurale) représentent le nombre annuel de divorces enregistrés pour 1 000 habitants au milieu de l'année. Les taux de ce tableau ne se rapportent qu'aux pays ou zones où l'on a enregistré un total d'au moins 30 divorces pendant une année donnée. Ces taux sont calculés par la division de statistique des Nations Unies sur la base de la population de référence adéquate (par exemple : population totale, nationaux seulement, etc.) si connue et disponible. Si la population de référence n'est pas connue ou n'est pas disponible, la population totale est utilisée pour calculer les taux. Par conséquent, si la population utilisée pour calculer les taux est différente de la population de référence adéquate, les taux présentés sont susceptibles de sous ou sur estimer la situation réelle d'un pays ou d'un territoire.

Fiabilité des données : il a été demandé à chaque pays ou zone d'indiquer le degré estimatif de complétude des données sur les divorces figurant dans ses registres d'état civil. Ces évaluations nationales sont désignées par les codes de qualité "C" et "U" qui apparaissent dans la deuxième colonne du tableau.

La lettre "C" indique que les données sont jugées à peu près complètes, c'est-à-dire qu'elles représentent au moins 90 p. 100 des divorces survenus chaque année ; la lettre "U" signale que les données sont jugées incomplètes, c'est-à-dire qu'elles représentent moins de 90 p. 100 des divorces survenus chaque année. Le code "..." indique qu'aucun renseignement n'a été communiqué quant à la complétude des données.

Les données issues des registres de l'état civil qui sont déclarées incomplètes ou dont le degré de complétude n'est pas connu (code "U" ou "...") sont jugées douteuses. Elles apparaissent en italique dans le tableau et les taux correspondants n'ont pas été calculés. Les codes de qualité ne s'appliquent qu'aux données extraites des registres de l'état civil. Pour plus de précisions sur la qualité des données reposant sur les statistiques de l'état civil en général, voir la section 4.2 des notes techniques.

Insuffisance des données : les statistiques des divorces appellent les mêmes réserves que celles formulées à propos des statistiques de l'état civil en général et des statistiques de divortialité en particulier (voir la section 4 des notes techniques).

Le divorce est, comme le mariage, un acte juridique, et ce fait influe sur la comparabilité internationale des données. Aux fins de la statistique, le divorce est défini par la législation de chaque pays ou zone. La législation sur le divorce varie considérablement d'un pays ou d'une zone à l'autre, ce qui influe aussi sur la fréquence des divorces, laquelle est relativement faible dans les pays ou zones où le jugement de divorce est difficile à obtenir.

Du fait que les divorces sont prononcés par les tribunaux et que les statistiques de la divortialité se rapportent aux jugements de divorce proprement dits, qui prennent effet à la date où ces jugements sont rendus, il se peut que des fluctuations annuelles accusées traduisent le rythme plus ou moins rapide auquel les affaires sont jugées plutôt que l'évolution de la fréquence des divorces. Les méthodes d'exploitation des données peuvent aussi influer sur la comparabilité des statistiques de la divortialité. Dans certains pays ou zones, ces statistiques peuvent comprendre les annulations et/ou les séparations légales. C'est notamment le cas dans les pays ou zones où les divorces sont peu nombreux. Lorsqu'ils sont connus, des renseignements à ce propos sont donnés en note à la fin du tableau.

Étant donné que dans de nombreux pays ou zones, le tribunal ou l'autorité qui a prononcé le divorce est seul habilité à enregistrer cet acte, et, comme l'acte d'enregistrement figure alors sur les registres du tribunal, l'enregistrement suit généralement de peu le jugement. C'est pourquoi la pratique consistant à exploiter les données selon la date de l'enregistrement ne pose généralement pas les graves problèmes de comparabilité auxquels on se heurte dans le cas des statistiques des naissances et des décès.

Comme on l'a brièvement mentionné ci-dessus, la fréquence des divorces est fonction notamment de la facilité relative avec laquelle la législation de chaque pays ou zone permet d'obtenir le divorce. Elle dépend également de la capacité des intéressés à supporter les frais de procédure. Il faut aussi citer l'influence de certaines religions sur la fréquence des divorces. Pour toutes ces raisons, les statistiques de divortialité ne sont pas rigoureusement comparables et ne permettent pas de mesurer exactement la fréquence des dissolutions légales des mariages. De plus, elles ne rendent pas compte des cas de dissolution extrajudiciaire du mariage, comme la séparation.

Dans certains pays ou zones, il n'existe ou il n'existait pas de législation sur le divorce selon l'acception retenue aux fins de ce tableau, si bien que l'on ne dispose pas de données les concernant.

De surcroît, il convient de noter que l'exactitude des taux dépend également de la qualité et des insuffisances des estimations de population qui sont utilisées pour leur calcul. Le problème des erreurs par excès ou par défaut commises lors du dénombrement et, dans une certaine mesure, le problème de l'hétérogénéité des définitions de la population totale ont été examinés à la section 3 des notes techniques, relative à la population en général ; des explications concernant les différents pays ou zones sont données en note à la fin du tableau 3.

Comme on le verra dans les notes, il n'a pas toujours été possible d'obtenir une correspondance rigoureuse entre le numérateur et le dénominateur pour le calcul des taux. Par exemple, les divorces parmi la population civile et les militaires sont parfois rapportés à la population civile seulement. Cela peut avoir pour effet d'accroître les taux, mais, dans la plupart des cas, il est probable que la différence sera négligeable.

Comme indiqué plus haut, les données concernant certains pays ou zones peuvent comprendre les annulations et/ou les séparations légales. Cette pratique influe sur la comparabilité des taux bruts de divortialité. Par exemple, l'inclusion des annulations dans le numérateur a une influence négligeable, mais l'inclusion des séparations légales peut avoir un effet appréciable.

Il faut souligner que les taux bruts de divortialité, de même que les taux bruts de natalité, de mortalité et de nuptialité, peuvent varier sensiblement selon la structure par âge et par sexe. Comme les taux bruts de nuptialité, ils peuvent également varier en raison de la répartition de la population selon l'état matrimonial. Les taux bruts de divortialité offrent néanmoins un moyen simple de mesurer la fréquence et l'évolution des divorces.

La comparabilité des données selon le lieu de résidence (zone urbaine ou rurale) peut être limitée par les définitions nationales des termes « urbain » et « rural » utilisées pour la mise en tableaux de ces données. En l'absence d'indications contraires, on a supposé que les mêmes définitions avaient servi pour le recensement national de la population et pour l'établissement des statistiques de l'état civil pour chaque pays ou zone. Toutefois, il n'est pas exclu que, pour une zone ou un pays donné, des définitions différentes aient été retenues. Les définitions du terme « urbain » utilisées pour les recensements nationaux de population ont été présentées à la fin des notes techniques du tableau 6 lorsqu'elles étaient connues. Comme on l'a précisé dans les notes techniques relatives au tableau 6, ces définitions varient considérablement d'un pays ou d'une zone à l'autre.

Outre les problèmes de comparabilité, les taux de divortialité classés selon le lieu de résidence (zone urbaine ou rurale) sont également sujets à des distorsions particulières. Si l'on utilise des définitions différentes du terme « urbain » pour classer les faits d'état civil et les données relatives à la population lors du calcul des taux et qu'il en résulte une différence nette entre le numérateur et le dénominateur pour le taux de la population exposée au risque, les taux de divortialité s'en trouveront faussés. La différence entre ces taux pour les zones urbaines et rurales pourra aussi être faussée selon que les faits d'état civil auront été classés d'après le lieu de l'événement ou d'après le lieu de résidence habituel. Ce problème est examiné plus en détail à la section 4.1.4.1 des notes techniques.

Données publiées antérieurement : des statistiques concernant les divorces ont déjà été présentées dans des éditions antérieures de l'*Annuaire démographique*. Les plus anciennes, qui portaient sur 1935, ont été publiées dans l'édition de 1951. Pour plus de précisions concernant les années et les sujets pour lesquels des données ont été publiées, se reporter à l'index historique.

NOTE

[1] Pour la définition, voir la section 4.1.1 des Notes techniques.

25. Divorces and crude divorce rates by urban/rural residence: 2015 - 2019
Divorces et taux bruts de divortialité selon la résidence, urbaine/rurale : 2015 - 2019

Continent, country or area, and urban/rural residence Continent, pays ou zone et résidence, urbaine/rurale	Code[a]	Number - Nombre					Rate - Taux				
		2015	2016	2017	2018	2019	2015	2016	2017	2018	2019
AFRICA - AFRIQUE											
Algeria - Algérie[1]											
Total	+U	*59 909*	*62 128*	*65 637*	*65 690*	*65 967*	...	...	...	...	...
Côte d'Ivoire											
Total	+U	...	*1 285*	*1 317*	*1 431*	...	...	...	...	...	...
Egypt - Égypte[2]											
Total	+C	199 867	192 079	198 269	...	...	2.2	2.1	2.1	...	...
Urban - Urbaine	+C	114 780	105 200	108 224	...	...	3.0	2.7	2.7	...	...
Rural - Rurale	+C	85 087	86 879	90 045	...	...	1.7	1.7	1.6	...	...
Lesotho											
Total	+U	...	*169*	*197*	...	...	...	...	...	...	...
Urban - Urbaine	+U	...	*82*	...	...	...	...	...	...	...	...
Rural - Rurale	+U	...	*87*	...	...	...	...	...	...	...	...
Mauritius - Maurice[3]											
Total	+C	2 161	1 910	1 996	2 425	2 174	1.7	1.5	1.6	1.9	1.7
Mayotte											
Total	C	139	...	...	...	...	0.6	...	...	...	...
Reunion - Réunion											
Total	C	1 561	1 482	...	...	...	1.8	1.7	...	...	...
Saint Helena ex. dep. - Sainte-Hélène sans dép.											
Total	C	3	-	-	...	...	...	...	...	...	...
Seychelles											
Total	+C	149	185	207	166	189	1.6	2.0	2.2	1.7	1.9
South Africa - Afrique du Sud											
Total	...	*25 260*	*25 326*	*25 390*	*25 284*	...	...	...	...	...	...
Sudan - Soudan											
Total	U	*43 926*	...	...	...	...	...	...	...	...	...
Tunisia - Tunisie											
Total	...	*14 982*	*15 632*	*16 452*	*16 750*	...	...	...	...	...	...
AMERICA, NORTH - AMÉRIQUE DU NORD											
Aruba											
Total	C	366	382	378	365	361	3.4	3.5	3.4	3.3	3.2
Bermuda - Bermudes[4]											
Total	C	116	120	173	110	...	1.9	1.9	2.7	1.7	...
British Virgin Islands - Îles Vierges britanniques											
Total	C	71	68	49	...	...	2.4	...	...	...	...
Costa Rica											
Total	+C	10 111	13 155	12 661	11 003	*14 009	2.1	2.7	2.6	2.2	*2.8
Cuba											
Total	C	33 174	31 598	32 183	30 443	...	3.0	2.8	2.9	2.7	...
Urban - Urbaine	C	30 990[5]	29 309[5]	29 951[5]	28 143	...	3.6	3.4	3.5	3.3	...
Rural - Rurale	C	2 081[5]	2 125[5]	2 043[5]	2 300	...	0.8	0.8	0.8	0.9	...
Curaçao											
Total	C	375	365	415	374	409	2.4	2.3	2.6	2.3	2.6
Dominica - Dominique											
Total	+C	85	81	67	...	...	1.2	1.1	1.0	...	...
Dominican Republic - République dominicaine											
Total	+C	20 352	21 873	24 218	24 772	26 115	2.0	2.2	2.4	2.4	2.5
Grenada - Grenade											
Total	+C	221	203	...	...	...	2.0	1.8	...	...	...
Guadeloupe											
Total	C	659	...	...	...	...	1.7	...	...	...	...
Guatemala											
Total	C	5 726	5 665	5 808	6 255	...	0.4	0.3	0.3	0.4	...
Jamaica - Jamaïque											
Total	+C	1 734	2 146	2 882	3 402	...	0.6	0.8	1.1	1.2	...
Martinique											
Total	C	369	...	...	...	...	1.0	...	...	...	...

25. Divorces and crude divorce rates by urban/rural residence: 2015 - 2019
Divorces et taux bruts de divortialité selon la résidence, urbaine/rurale : 2015 - 2019 (continued - suite)

Continent, country or area, and urban/rural residence Continent, pays ou zone et résidence, urbaine/rurale	Code[a]	Number - Nombre 2015	2016	2017	2018	2019	Rate - Taux 2015	2016	2017	2018	2019
AMERICA, NORTH - AMÉRIQUE DU NORD											
Mexico - Mexique[6]											
Total	+C	123 883	139 807	147 581	156 556	...	1.0	1.1	1.2	1.2	...
Urban - Urbaine[7]	+C	108 804	119 819	122 052	131 384	...	1.2	1.4	1.4	1.4	...
Rural - Rurale[7]	+C	6 305	6 725	7 793	8 445	...	0.2	0.2	0.2	0.3	...
Nicaragua											
Total	+U	*7 461*	*6 363*	*8 305*	*7 769*	...	...	...	...	...	...
Panama											
Total	C	4 479	4 360	4 470	4 558	*3 081	1.1	1.1	1.1	1.1	*0.7
Urban - Urbaine	C	3 806	3 730	3 778	3 766	*2 571	1.4	1.3	1.3	1.3	*0.9
Rural - Rurale	C	673	630	692	792	*510	0.5	0.5	0.5	0.6	*0.4
Puerto Rico - Porto Rico											
Total	C	11 877	10 998	8 515	9 644	8 453	3.4	3.2	2.6	3.0	2.6
Saint Vincent and the Grenadines - Saint-Vincent-et-les Grenadines											
Total	C	69	72	41	...	...	0.6	0.7	0.4	...	...
Sint Maarten (Dutch part) - Saint-Martin (partie néerlandaise)											
Total	+C	117	89	91	...	...	3.1	2.3	2.2	...	...
Trinidad and Tobago - Trinité-et-Tobago											
Total	C	*2 088	*2 737	...	...	...	*1.5	*2.0	...	...	...
Turks and Caicos Islands - Îles Turques et Caïques											
Total	C	47	36	18	...	...	1.3	0.9	...	...	...
United States of America - États-Unis d'Amérique[8]											
Total	C	800 909	...	...	...	...	2.5	...	...	...	...
AMERICA, SOUTH - AMÉRIQUE DU SUD											
Brazil - Brésil											
Total	...	*328 960*	*344 526*	*295 108*	...	...	...	...	...	...	...
Ecuador - Équateur[9]											
Total	U	*25 692*	*25 648*	*28 771*	*25 670*	...	...	...	...	...	...
Urban - Urbaine[10]	U	*24 021*	*23 180*	*25 685*	*21 827*	...	...	...	...	...	...
Rural - Rurale[10]	U	*1 671*	*2 468*	*3 086*	*3 843*	...	...	...	...	...	...
French Guiana - Guyane française											
Total	C	209	...	...	...	...	0.8	...	...	...	...
Peru - Pérou[11]											
Total	+C	13 757	15 109	15 931	16 742	16 588	0.5	0.5	0.5	0.5	0.5
Suriname[12]											
Total	C	733	636	855	904	...	1.3	1.1	1.5	1.5	...
Uruguay											
Total	C	...	3 623	3 219	3 216	...	...	1.0	0.9	0.9	...
Venezuela (Bolivarian Republic of) - Venezuela (République bolivarienne du)											
Total	C	24 126	21 966	22 673	...	...	0.8	0.7	0.7	...	...
ASIA - ASIE											
Armenia - Arménie											
Total	+C	3 670	3 648	3 940	3 820	...	1.2	1.2	1.3	1.3	...
Urban - Urbaine	+C	2 801	2 923	3 130	3 130	...	1.5	1.5	1.6	1.7	...
Rural - Rurale	+C	869	725	810	690	...	0.8	0.7	0.7	0.6	...
Azerbaijan - Azerbaïdjan											
Total	+C	12 764	13 114	14 514	14 857	...	1.3	1.3	1.5	1.5	...
Urban - Urbaine	+C	8 658	9 173	9 780	9 849	...	1.7	1.8	1.9	1.9	...
Rural - Rurale	+C	4 106	3 941	4 734	5 008	...	0.9	0.9	1.0	1.1	...

25. Divorces and crude divorce rates by urban/rural residence: 2015 - 2019
Divorces et taux bruts de divortialité selon la résidence, urbaine/rurale : 2015 - 2019 (continued - suite)

Continent, country or area, and urban/rural residence Continent, pays ou zone et résidence, urbaine/rurale	Code[a]	Number - Nombre 2015	2016	2017	2018	2019	Rate - Taux 2015	2016	2017	2018	2019
ASIA - ASIE											
Bahrain - Bahreïn											
Total	...	*1 745*	*1 749*	*1 890*	*1 929*	*2 023*	...	...	...	...	...
Bangladesh											
Total	...	...	...	...	*148 140*	*166 500*	...	...	...	...	...
Urban - Urbaine	...	...	...	...	*44 812*	*50 366*	...	...	...	...	...
Rural - Rurale	...	...	...	...	*103 328*	*116 134*	...	...	...	...	...
Brunei Darussalam - Brunéi Darussalam											
Total	+C	545	566	632	552	...	1.3	1.4	1.5	1.2	...
China, Hong Kong SAR - Chine, Hong Kong RAS											
Total	...	*20 075*	*17 196*	*19 394*	*20 321*	*21 157*	...	...	...	...	...
China, Macao SAR - Chine, Macao RAS											
Total	+C	1 168	1 245	1 479	1 544	1 435	1.8	1.9	2.3	2.3	2.1
Cyprus - Chypre[13]											
Total	C	1 807	1 948	1 932	...	...	2.1	2.3	2.2	...	...
Georgia - Géorgie											
Total	C	9 112	9 539	10 222	10 288	...	2.5	2.6	2.7	2.8	...
Urban - Urbaine	C	6 320	6 565	...	...	...	3.0	3.1	...	...	...
Rural - Rurale	C	2 792	2 974	...	...	...	1.8	1.9	...	...	...
Indonesia - Indonésie											
Total	U	*347 256*	...	...	...	...	...	...	...	...	...
Iran (Islamic Republic of) - Iran (République islamique d')[14]											
Total	+C	163 765	174 392	174 578	175 614	...	2.1	2.2	2.2	2.1	...
Urban - Urbaine	+C	146 714	162 668	163 466	164 124	...	2.6	2.7	2.7	2.7	...
Rural - Rurale	+C	17 051	11 724	11 112	11 490	...	0.8	0.6	0.5	0.6	...
Israel - Israël[15]											
Total	C	14 487	14 819	14 741	...	...	1.7	1.7	1.7	...	...
Urban - Urbaine[16]	C	13 095	13 385	13 268	...	...	1.7	1.7	1.7	...	...
Rural - Rurale[16]	C	1 070	1 042	1 097	...	...	1.5	1.4	1.4	...	...
Japan - Japon[17]											
Total	+C	226 215	216 798	212 262	208 333	...	1.8	1.7	1.7	1.6	...
Urban - Urbaine	+C	208 181	199 561	195 520	191 941	...	...	...	...	...	...
Rural - Rurale	+C	18 034	17 237	16 742	16 392	...	...	...	...	...	...
Jordan - Jordanie[18]											
Total	+C	22 070	21 969	21 210	...	...	2.3	2.2	2.1	...	...
Kazakhstan											
Total	+C	53 293	51 993	54 626	54 797	59 796	3.0	2.9	3.0	3.0	3.2
Urban - Urbaine	+C	39 846	38 716	40 774	41 122	44 081	4.0	3.8	3.9	3.9	4.1
Rural - Rurale	+C	13 447	13 277	13 852	13 675	15 715	1.8	1.7	1.8	1.8	2.0
Kuwait - Koweït											
Total	C	7 201	7 223	7 433	7 869	...	1.8	1.8	1.8	1.9	...
Kyrgyzstan - Kirghizstan											
Total	C	8 588	9 102	9 588	10 434	...	1.4	1.5	1.5	1.7	...
Urban - Urbaine	C	4 797	5 297	5 302	5 626	...	2.4	2.6	2.5	2.6	...
Rural - Rurale	C	3 791	3 805	4 286	4 808	...	1.0	0.9	1.0	1.2	...
Malaysia - Malaisie											
Total	+C	...	51 642	50 314	50 356	...	...	1.6	1.6	1.6	...
Maldives											
Total	...	*3 358*	*3 417*	...	...	...	...	...	...	...	...
Urban - Urbaine	...	*1 455*	*1 496*	...	...	...	...	...	...	...	...
Rural - Rurale	...	*1 903*	*1 921*	...	...	...	...	...	...	...	...
Mongolia - Mongolie											
Total	+C	3 873	4 003	3 945	4 201	4 262	1.3	1.3	1.3	1.3	1.3
Urban - Urbaine	+C	3 455	3 501	3 384	3 615	3 781	1.7	1.6	1.6	1.7	1.7
Rural - Rurale	+C	418	502	561	586	481	0.4	0.5	0.6	0.6	0.5
Oman											
Total	U	*3 619*	*3 736*	*3 867*	*3 662*	*3 728*	...	...	...	...	...
Qatar											
Total	C	1 307	1 151	1 206	1 182	...	0.5	0.4	0.4	0.4	...
Urban - Urbaine	C	1 307	1 151	1 206	1 182	...	0.5	0.4	0.4	0.4	...

25. Divorces and crude divorce rates by urban/rural residence: 2015 - 2019
Divorces et taux bruts de divortialité selon la résidence, urbaine/rurale : 2015 - 2019 (continued - suite)

Continent, country or area, and urban/rural residence / Continent, pays ou zone et résidence, urbaine/rurale	Code[a]	Number - Nombre 2015	2016	2017	2018	2019	Rate - Taux 2015	2016	2017	2018	2019
ASIA - ASIE											
Republic of Korea - République de Corée[19]											
Total	+C	109 153	107 328	106 032	108 684	110 831	2.1	2.1	2.1	2.1	2.2
Urban - Urbaine[16]	+C	84 958	83 872	82 470	84 098	85 526	2.0	2.0	2.0	2.0	2.1
Rural - Rurale[16]	+C	21 384	21 504	21 744	22 692	23 509	2.3	2.3	2.3	2.3	2.4
Singapore - Singapour											
Total	+C	7 117	7 207	7 207	6 990	7 330	1.8	1.8	1.8	1.8	1.8
State of Palestine - État de Palestine											
Total	C	8 179	8 510	8 568	8 509	...	1.8	1.8	1.8	1.8	...
Tajikistan - Tadjikistan											
Total	+C	8 346	8 845	10 053	10 976	...	1.0	1.0	1.1	1.2	...
Urban - Urbaine	+C	3 366	3 557	3 870	...	...	1.5	1.6	1.7	...	...
Rural - Rurale	+C	4 980	5 288	6 183	...	...	0.8	0.8	0.9	...	...
Thailand - Thaïlande[20]											
Total	...	*117 880*	*118 539*	*121 617*	*127 265*	*128 514*	...	...	...	...	...
Turkey - Turquie[21]											
Total	C	131 830	126 164	128 411	142 448	...	1.7	1.6	1.6	1.8	...
United Arab Emirates - Émirats arabes unis											
Total	...	*4 913*	*4 599*	*4 403*	*4 506*	*4 554*	...	...	...	...	...
Uzbekistan - Ouzbékistan											
Total	+C	29 647	29 340	31 929	32 326	31 389	0.9	0.9	1.0	1.0	0.9
Urban - Urbaine	+C	19 480	18 605	19 618	19 699	19 475	1.2	1.2	1.2	1.2	1.2
Rural - Rurale	+C	10 167	10 735	12 311	12 627	11 914	0.7	0.7	0.8	0.8	0.7
Viet Nam											
Total	C	24 101	24 308	27 948	28 076	25 702	0.3	0.3	0.3	0.3	0.3
EUROPE											
Åland Islands - Îles d'Åland											
Total	C	77	62	44	54	*59	2.7	2.1	1.5	1.8	*2.0
Urban - Urbaine	C	44	35	29	31	...	3.8	3.0	...	2.6	...
Rural - Rurale	C	33	27	15	23	...	1.9	...	...	...	...
Albania - Albanie											
Total	C	3 761	4 345	4 508	4 846	...	1.3	1.5	1.6	1.7	...
Austria - Autriche[22]											
Total	C	16 351	15 919	16 180	16 304	...	1.9	1.8	1.8	1.8	...
Belarus - Bélarus											
Total	C	32 984	32 628	32 006	33 152	...	3.5	3.4	3.4	3.5	...
Urban - Urbaine	C	28 419	28 326	27 977	29 164	...	3.9	3.8	3.8	3.9	...
Rural - Rurale	C	4 565	4 302	4 029	3 988	...	2.1	2.0	1.9	1.9	...
Belgium - Belgique[23]											
Total	C	24 414	23 583	23 068	...	...	2.2	2.1	2.0	...	...
Urban - Urbaine	C	24 132	...	...	...	...	...	...	...	...	...
Rural - Rurale	C	282	...	...	...	...	...	...	...	...	...
Bosnia and Herzegovina - Bosnie-Herzégovine											
Total	C	2 963	2 773	3 022	3 091	...	0.8	0.8	0.9	0.9	...
Bulgaria - Bulgarie[24]											
Total	C	10 483	10 603	10 411	10 596	...	1.5	1.5	1.5	1.5	...
Urban - Urbaine	C	8 629	8 603	8 438	8 517	...	1.6	1.6	1.6	1.6	...
Rural - Rurale	C	1 854	2 000	1 973	2 079	...	1.0	1.0	1.0	1.1	...
Croatia - Croatie											
Total	C	6 010	7 036	6 265	6 125	...	1.4	1.7	1.5	1.5	...
Urban - Urbaine	C	4 170	4 955	4 408	4 217	...	...	...	...	...	...
Rural - Rurale	C	1 840	2 081	1 857	1 908	...	...	...	...	...	...
Czechia - Tchéquie											
Total	C	26 083	24 996	25 755	24 313	...	2.5	2.4	2.4	2.3	...
Urban - Urbaine	C	19 646	18 569	19 060	17 889	...	2.6	2.4	2.5	2.3	...
Rural - Rurale	C	6 437	6 427	6 695	6 424	...	2.3	2.3	2.4	2.2	...
Denmark - Danemark[25]											
Total	C	16 343	17 222	15 265	15 034	...	2.9	3.0	2.6	2.6	...

25. Divorces and crude divorce rates by urban/rural residence: 2015 - 2019
Divorces et taux bruts de divortialité selon la résidence, urbaine/rurale : 2015 - 2019 (continued - suite)

Continent, country or area, and urban/rural residence Continent, pays ou zone et résidence, urbaine/rurale	Code[a]	Number - Nombre					Rate - Taux				
		2015	2016	2017	2018	2019	2015	2016	2017	2018	2019
EUROPE											
Estonia - Estonie											
Total	C	3 382	3 262	3 323	3 199	...	2.6	2.5	2.5	2.4	...
Urban - Urbaine[26]	C	2 226	2 143	2 283	2 209	...	2.5	2.4	2.5	2.4	...
Rural - Rurale[26]	C	985	908	863	828	...	2.4	2.2	2.1	2.1	...
Faroe Islands - Îles Féroé											
Total	C	78	52	65	59	72	1.6	1.1	1.3	1.2	1.4
Finland - Finlande[27]											
Total	C	13 862	13 479	13 188	12 945	...	2.5	2.5	2.4	2.4	...
Urban - Urbaine	C	10 521	10 254	10 013	9 971	...	2.7	2.6	2.6	2.5	...
Rural - Rurale	C	3 341	3 225	3 175	2 974	...	2.1	2.0	2.0	1.9	...
France											
Total	C	120 731	124 768	...	...	...	1.9	1.9	...	...	...
Germany - Allemagne											
Total	C	163 335	162 397	153 501	148 066	...	2.0	2.0	1.9	1.8	...
Gibraltar											
Total	+C	61	85	...	...	...	1.8	2.5	...	...	...
Greece - Grèce											
Total	C	15 600	11 013	19 190	...	...	1.4	1.0	1.8	...	...
Hungary - Hongrie[12]											
Total	C	20 315	19 552	18 495	16 952	...	2.1	2.0	1.9	1.7	...
Urban - Urbaine[28]	C	15 168	14 741	13 737	12 592	...	2.2	2.1	2.0	1.8	...
Rural - Rurale[28]	C	4 893	4 540	4 426	4 094	...	1.7	1.6	1.5	1.4	...
Ireland - Irlande											
Total	+C	3 289	3 255	3 412	...	...	0.7	0.7	0.7	...	...
Italy - Italie											
Total	C	82 469	99 071	91 629	88 458	...	1.4	1.6	1.5	1.5	...
Latvia - Lettonie											
Total	C	5 151	6 061	5 943	5 967	...	2.6	3.1	3.1	3.1	...
Liechtenstein[29]											
Total	C	98	81	90	74	...	2.6	2.1	2.4	1.9	...
Lithuania - Lituanie											
Total	C	9 371	8 879	8 518	8 640	...	3.2	3.1	3.0	3.1	...
Urban - Urbaine	C	6 394	6 037	5 897	5 900	...	3.3	3.1	3.1	3.1	...
Rural - Rurale	C	2 977	2 842	2 621	2 740	...	3.1	3.0	2.8	3.0	...
Luxembourg											
Total	C	1 345	1 241	1 192	1 230	...	2.4	2.1	2.0	2.0	...
Malta - Malte											
Total	C	372	371	312	349	...	0.8	0.8	0.7	0.7	...
Monaco											
Total	C	74	89	69	78[30]	...	2.0	2.3	1.8	2.0	...
Montenegro - Monténégro											
Total	C	577	703	765	849	841	0.9	1.1	1.2	1.4	1.4
Netherlands - Pays-Bas[6]											
Total	C	34 232[31]	33 414[32]	32 768[32]	30 729[32]	...	2.0	2.0	1.9	1.8	...
North Macedonia - Macédoine du Nord											
Total	C	2 200	1 985	1 994	1 620	...	1.1	1.0	1.0	0.8	...
Urban - Urbaine	C	1 420	1 315	1 309	1 075	...	...	...	...	...	...
Rural - Rurale	C	780	670	685	545	...	...	...	...	...	...
Norway - Norvège[6]											
Total	C	9 793	9 944	10 567	10 162	...	1.9	1.9	2.0	1.9	...
Poland - Pologne											
Total	C	67 296	63 497	65 257	62 843	...	1.8	1.7	1.7	1.7	...
Urban - Urbaine[33]	C	48 896	45 904	46 840	45 153	...	2.1	2.0	2.0	2.0	...
Rural - Rurale[33]	C	17 587	16 690	17 472	16 654	...	1.2	1.1	1.2	1.1	...
Portugal[34]											
Total	C	23 377	22 649	21 577	20 345[6]	...	2.3	2.2	2.1	2.0	...
Republic of Moldova - République de Moldova											
Total	C	11 199	10 605	9 312	10 721	...	4.0	3.8	3.4	4.0	...
Urban - Urbaine	C	10 915	10 112	8 954	10 338	...	...	...	...	...	...
Rural - Rurale	C	284	493	358	383	...	...	...	...	...	...
Romania - Roumanie											
Total	C	31 527	30 497	31 147	30 857	...	1.6	1.5	1.6	1.6	...
Urban - Urbaine	C	21 496	20 485	20 625	19 833	...	2.0	1.9	2.0	1.9	...
Rural - Rurale	C	10 031	10 012	10 522	11 024	...	1.1	1.1	1.2	1.2	...

25. Divorces and crude divorce rates by urban/rural residence: 2015 - 2019
Divorces et taux bruts de divortialité selon la résidence, urbaine/rurale : 2015 - 2019 (continued - suite)

Continent, country or area, and urban/rural residence — Continent, pays ou zone et résidence, urbaine/rurale	Code[a]	Number - Nombre 2015	2016	2017	2018	2019	Rate - Taux 2015	2016	2017	2018	2019
EUROPE											
San Marino - Saint-Marin											
Total	C	65	83	90	...	...	1.9	2.4	2.6	...	...
Serbia - Serbie[35]											
Total	+C	9 381	9 046	9 262	9 995	...	1.3	1.3	1.3	1.4	...
Urban - Urbaine	+C	6 833	6 532	6 714	7 158	...	1.6	1.5	1.6	1.7	...
Rural - Rurale	+C	2 548	2 514	2 548	2 837	...	0.9	0.9	0.9	1.0	...
Slovakia - Slovaquie											
Total	C	9 786	9 286	9 618	9 560	...	1.8	1.7	1.8	1.8	...
Urban - Urbaine	C	5 945	5 664	5 824	5 788	...	2.0	1.9	2.0	2.0	...
Rural - Rurale	C	3 841	3 622	3 794	3 772	...	1.5	1.4	1.5	1.5	...
Slovenia - Slovénie											
Total	C	2 432	2 531	2 387	2 347	...	1.2	1.2	1.2	1.1	...
Urban - Urbaine	C	1 484	1 545	1 483	1 453	...	1.3	1.4	1.3	1.3	...
Rural - Rurale	C	948	986	904	894	...	1.0	1.0	1.0	1.0	...
Spain - Espagne											
Total	C	96 562	96 824	97 960	95 254	...	2.1	2.1	2.1	2.0	...
Sweden - Suède[6]											
Total	C	24 876	24 258	24 210	24 958	...	2.5	2.4	2.4	2.5	...
Switzerland - Suisse											
Total	C	16 982	17 028	15 906	16 542	...	2.1	2.0	1.9	1.9	...
Urban - Urbaine	C	...	14 638	13 729	14 185	...	...	2.1	...	2.0	...
Rural - Rurale	C	...	2 390	2 177	2 357	...	...	1.8	...	1.8	...
Ukraine[36]											
Total	+C	129 373	129 997	128 734	...	...	3.0	3.0	3.0	...	...
United Kingdom of Great Britain and Northern Ireland - Royaume-Uni de Grande-Bretagne et d'Irlande du Nord[37]											
Total	C	112 412	118 158	110 862[38]	...	...	1.7	1.8	1.7	...	...
OCEANIA - OCÉANIE											
American Samoa - Samoas américaines											
Total	C	43	80	89	...	...	0.7	1.3	1.5	...	...
Australia - Australie											
Total	+C	48 517	46 604	49 032	49 404	...	2.0	1.9	2.0	2.0	...
Guam[39]											
Total	C	657	647	683	572	...	4.1	4.0	4.2	3.4	...
New Zealand - Nouvelle-Zélande[40]											
Total	+C	8 523	8 169[41]	8 004[41]	7 455[41]	8 388[41]	1.9	1.7	1.7	1.5	1.7
Pitcairn											
Total	C	...	...	...	...	-	...	...	...	...	...

FOOTNOTES - NOTES

Italics: data from civil registers which are incomplete or of unknown completeness. - Italiques : données incomplètes ou dont le degré d'exactitude n'est pas connu, provenant des registres de l'état civil.

* Provisional. - Données provisoires.

a 'Code' indicates the source of data, as follows:
C - Civil registration, estimated over 90% complete
U - Civil registration, estimated less than 90% complete
| - Other source, estimated reliable
+ - Data tabulated by date of registration rather than occurence
... - Information not available

Le 'Code' indique la source des données, comme suit :
C - Registres de l'état civil considérés complèts à 90 p. 100 au moins
U - Registres de l'état civil qui ne sont pas considérés complèts à 90 p. 100 au moins
| - Autre source, considérée pas douteuses
+ - Données exploitées selon la date de l'enregistrement et non la date de l'événement
... - Information pas disponible

1 Data refer to Algerian population only. - Les données ne concernent que la population algérienne.
2 Including 'revocable divorces' (among Muslim population), which approximate legal separations. - Y compris les 'divorces révocables' (parmi la population musulmane), qui sont plus au moins l'équivalent des séparations légales.
3 Excludes the islands of St. Brandon and Agalega. - Non compris les îles St. Brandon et Agalega.
4 Bermuda is 100 per cent urban. - 100 pour cent de la population des Bermudes est urbaine.
5 The sum of urban and rural doesn't correspond to the total because of unknown residence of divorces of foreigner spouses. - La somme des zones urbaines et rurales ne correspond pas au total en raison de la résidence inconnue des divorces des conjoints étrangers.

[6] Including same sex divorces. - Y compris les divorces entre conjoints du même sexe.
[7] The total number may include 'Unknown residence', but the categories urban and rural do not. - Le nombre total peut inclure les personnes dont la résidence n'est pas connue, à l'inverse des catégories de population urbaine et rurale.
[8] Excluding data for California, Georgia, Hawaii, Indiana, and Minnesota. - À l'exclusion des données pour la Californie, la Géorgie, Hawaï, l'Indiana et le Minnesota.
[9] Excludes nomadic Indian tribes. - Non compris les tribus d'Indiens nomades.
[10] Urban and rural residence refers to the place of usual residence of husband. - Le lieu de résidence (zone urbaine ou zone rurale) correspond au lieu de résidence habituel du mari.
[11] Data are compiled from the National Registers of Identification and Civil Status (RENIEC). - Les données sont rédigées à partir des Registres Nationaux d'Identification et d'État Civil (RENIEC).
[12] Including annulments. - Y compris les annulations.
[13] Data refer to government controlled areas. - Les données se rapportent aux zones contrôlées par le Gouvernement.
[14] Data refer to the Iranian Year which begins on 21 March and ends on 20 March of the following year. - Les données concernent l'année iranienne, qui commence le 21 mars et se termine le 20 mars de l'année suivante.
[15] Includes data for East Jerusalem and Israeli residents in certain other territories under occupation by Israeli military forces since June 1967. - Y compris les données pour Jérusalem-Est et les résidents israéliens dans certains autres territoires occupés depuis 1967 par les forces armées israéliennes.
[16] The total number may include 'Unknown residence', but the categories urban and rural do not. Urban and rural residence refers to the place of usual residence of husband. - Le nombre total peut inclure les personnes dont la résidence n'est pas connue, à l'inverse des catégories de population urbaine et rurale. Le lieu de résidence (zone urbaine ou zone rurale) correspond au lieu de résidence habituel du mari.
[17] Data refer to Japanese nationals in Japan only. - Les données se raportent aux nationaux japonais au Japon seulement.
[18] Excluding data for Jordanian territory under occupation since June 1967 by Israeli military forces. Excluding foreigners, including registered Palestinian refugees. - Non compris les données pour le territoire jordanien occupé depuis juin 1967 par les forces armées israéliennes. Non compris les étrangers, mais y compris les réfugiés de Palestine enregistrés.
[19] Excluding alien armed forces, civilian aliens employed by armed forces, and foreign diplomatic personnel and their dependants. - Non compris les militaires étrangers, les civils étrangers employés par les forces armées ni le personnel diplomatique étranger et les membres de leur famille les accompagnant.
[20] Source: Department of Local Administration, Ministry of Interior. - Source : Département de l'administration locale, Ministère de l'intérieur.
[21] Data from MERNIS (Central Population Administrative System). - Données de MERNIS (Système central de données démographiques).
[22] Excluding divorces of aliens temporarily in the area. - Non compris les divorces d'étrangers temporairement dans la région.
[23] Including divorces among armed forces stationed outside the country and alien armed forces in the area. - Y compris les divorces de militaires nationaux hors du pays et les militaires étrangers en garnison sur le territoire.
[24] Including nationals outside the country, but excluding foreigners in the country. Including annulments. - Y compris les nationaux à l'étranger, mais non compris les étrangers sur le territoire. Y compris les annulations.
[25] Excluding Faeroe Islands and Greenland shown separately, if available. - Non compris les Iles Féroé et le Groenland, qui font l'objet de rubriques distinctes, si disponible.
[26] Urban and rural residence refers to the place of usual residence of husband. The difference between 'Total' and the sum of urban and rural is due to the unknown place of residence of husbands and to husbands living outside the country. - Le lieu de résidence (zone urbaine ou zone rurale) correspond au lieu de résidence habituel du mari. La différence entre le « Total » et la somme des chiffres urbains et ruraux s'explique par le fait que la résidence du mari n'est pas toujours connue ou est située à l'étranger.
[27] Excluding Åland Islands. Including annulments. - Non compris les Îles d'Åland. Y compris les annulations.
[28] The urban and rural categories do not include the data of foreigners, persons of unknown residence and the homeless, whereas the total category includes them. - Les chiffres portant sur la population urbaine et rurale n' incluent pas les données relatives aux étrangers, aux personnes dont la résidence n'est pas connue et aux personnes sans domicile fixe, à l'inverse, le total les inclut.
[29] Data refer to divorces by residence of the husband. - Les données concernent les divorces selon la résidence du mari.
[30] Data include separated. - Y compris les séparés.
[31] Based on the general office for civil registration. - Données provenant des services généraux d'état civil.
[32] Including residents outside the country if listed in a Netherlands population register. - Englobe les résidents se trouvant à l'étranger à condition qu'ils soient inscrits sur le registre de population des Pays-Bas.
[33] Data for urban and rural exclude divorces if both persons live abroad. - Les données pour les zones urbaines et rurales excluent le divorce si les deux personnes vivent à l'étranger.
[34] Data refer to resident spouses only. - Les données concernent uniquement les conjoints résidents.
[35] Excludes data for Kosovo and Metohia. Including annulments. - Sans les données pour le Kosovo et Metohie. Y compris les annulations.
[36] The Government of Ukraine has informed the United Nations that it is not in a position to provide statistical data concerning the Autonomous Republic of Crimea and the city of Sevastopol. - Le gouvernement Ukrainien a informé l'ONU qu'il n'est pas en mesure de fournir des données statistiques concernant la République autonome de Crimée et la ville de Sébastopol.
[37] Excluding Channel Islands (Guernsey and Jersey) and Isle of Man, shown separately, if available. Including annulments. Data tabulated by date of occurrence for England and Wales, and by date of registration for Northern Ireland and Scotland. - Non compris les îles Anglo-Normandes (Guernesey et Jersey) et l'île de Man, qui font l'objet de rubriques distinctes, si disponible. Y compris les annulations. Données exploitées selon la date de l'événement pour l'Angleterre et le pays de Galles, et selon la date de l'enregistrement pour l'Irlande du Nord et l'Ecosse.
[38] Scottish data are provisional. - Les données concernant l'Écosse sont provisoires.
[39] Including United States military personnel, their dependants and contract employees. - Y compris les militaires des Etats-Unis, les membres de leur famille les accompagnant et les agents contractuels des Etats-Unis.
[40] Random rounding to base 3 is applied in this table as a confidentiality measure. - Les chiffres sont arrondis à la base 3 de manière aléatoire, pour des raisons de confidentialité.
[41] Including civil unions and same sex divorces. - Y compris les dissolutions d'unions civiles et de mariages homosexuels.

Annex I: Mid-year population, United Nations estimates: 2010 - 2019
Annexe I : Population au milieu de l'année, estimations des Nations Unies : 2010 - 2019

Continent and country or area Continent et pays ou zone	Population estimates (in thousands) - Estimations de population (en milliers)									
	2010	**2011**	**2012**	**2013**	**2014**	**2015**	**2016**	**2017**	**2018**	**2019**
AFRICA - AFRIQUE										
Algeria - Algérie	35 977	36 661	37 384	38 140	38 924	39 728	40 551	41 389	42 228	43 053
Angola	23 356	24 221	25 108	26 016	26 942	27 884	28 842	29 817	30 810	31 825
Benin - Bénin	9 199	9 461	9 729	10 005	10 287	10 576	10 872	11 175	11 485	11 801
Botswana	1 987	2 015	2 040	2 063	2 089	2 121	2 160	2 205	2 254	2 304
Burkina Faso	15 605	16 082	16 571	17 073	17 586	18 111	18 646	19 193	19 751	20 321
Burundi	8 676	8 958	9 246	9 540	9 844	10 160	10 488	10 827	11 175	11 531
Cabo Verde	493	499	505	512	518	525	531	537	544	550
Cameroon - Cameroun	20 341	20 906	21 485	22 077	22 682	23 298	23 927	24 566	25 216	25 876
Central African Republic - République centrafricaine	4 387	4 419	4 436	4 448	4 464	4 493	4 538	4 596	4 666	4 745
Chad - Tchad	11 952	12 361	12 785	13 220	13 664	14 111	14 562	15 017	15 478	15 947
Comoros - Comores	690	707	724	742	759	777	796	814	832	851
Congo	4 274	4 395	4 510	4 623	4 737	4 856	4 981	5 111	5 244	5 381
Côte d'Ivoire	20 533	21 029	21 547	22 088	22 648	23 226	23 823	24 437	25 069	25 717
Democratic Republic of the Congo - République démocratique du Congo	64 564	66 755	69 021	71 359	73 767	76 245	78 789	81 399	84 068	86 791
Djibouti	840	854	868	883	899	914	929	944	959	974
Egypt - Égypte	82 761	84 529	86 422	88 405	90 425	92 443	94 447	96 443	98 424	100 388
Equatorial Guinea - Guinée équatoriale	944	987	1 031	1 076	1 122	1 169	1 215	1 262	1 309	1 356
Eritrea - Érythrée	3 170	3 214	3 250	3 281	3 311	3 343	3 377	3 413	3 453	3 497
Eswatini	1 065	1 072	1 079	1 087	1 095	1 104	1 114	1 125	1 136	1 148
Ethiopia - Éthiopie	87 640	90 140	92 727	95 386	98 094	100 835	103 603	106 400	109 224	112 079
Gabon	1 624	1 685	1 750	1 817	1 884	1 948	2 008	2 065	2 119	2 173
Gambia - Gambie	1 793	1 848	1 905	1 964	2 024	2 086	2 149	2 214	2 280	2 348
Ghana	24 780	25 388	25 996	26 608	27 224	27 849	28 482	29 121	29 767	30 418
Guinea - Guinée	10 192	10 420	10 652	10 893	11 151	11 432	11 738	12 068	12 414	12 771
Guinea-Bissau - Guinée-Bissau	1 523	1 563	1 605	1 648	1 692	1 737	1 782	1 828	1 874	1 921
Kenya	42 031	43 178	44 343	45 520	46 700	47 878	49 052	50 221	51 393	52 574
Lesotho	1 996	2 004	2 015	2 029	2 043	2 059	2 075	2 092	2 108	2 125
Liberia - Libéria	3 891	4 017	4 136	4 248	4 360	4 472	4 587	4 702	4 819	4 937
Libya - Libye	6 198	6 247	6 286	6 320	6 362	6 418	6 492	6 581	6 679	6 777
Madagascar	21 152	21 744	22 347	22 961	23 590	24 234	24 894	25 571	26 262	26 969
Malawi	14 540	14 962	15 396	15 839	16 290	16 745	17 205	17 670	18 143	18 629
Mali	15 049	15 515	15 979	16 450	16 934	17 439	17 965	18 512	19 078	19 658
Mauritania - Mauritanie	3 494	3 599	3 707	3 817	3 931	4 046	4 164	4 283	4 403	4 526
Mauritius - Maurice[1]	1 248	1 251	1 253	1 255	1 257	1 259	1 262	1 264	1 267	1 270
Mayotte	209	215	221	227	234	240	246	253	260	266
Morocco - Maroc	32 343	32 782	33 242	33 716	34 192	34 664	35 126	35 581	36 029	36 472
Mozambique	23 532	24 188	24 863	25 561	26 286	27 042	27 830	28 649	29 496	30 366
Namibia - Namibie	2 119	2 157	2 195	2 234	2 273	2 315	2 358	2 403	2 448	2 495
Niger	16 464	17 115	17 795	18 504	19 240	20 002	20 789	21 602	22 443	23 311
Nigeria - Nigéria	158 503	162 805	167 229	171 766	176 405	181 137	185 960	190 873	195 875	200 964
Republic of South Sudan - République de Soudan du Sud	9 508	9 831	10 114	10 355	10 555	10 716	10 833	10 911	10 976	11 062
Reunion - Réunion	831	837	844	851	857	863	870	876	883	889
Rwanda	10 039	10 293	10 550	10 812	11 084	11 369	11 669	11 981	12 302	12 627
Sao Tome and Principe - Sao Tomé-et-Principe	180	185	188	192	196	199	203	207	211	215
Senegal - Sénégal	12 678	13 034	13 402	13 782	14 175	14 578	14 994	15 419	15 854	16 296
Seychelles	91	92	93	93	94	95	96	96	97	98
Sierra Leone	6 416	6 563	6 713	6 864	7 017	7 172	7 329	7 488	7 650	7 813
Somalia - Somalie	12 044	12 376	12 715	13 064	13 424	13 797	14 186	14 589	15 008	15 443
South Africa - Afrique du Sud	51 217	52 004	52 833	53 687	54 544	55 386	56 208	57 010	57 793	58 558
Sudan - Soudan	34 545	35 350	36 194	37 073	37 978	38 903	39 847	40 813	41 802	42 813
Togo	6 422	6 596	6 774	6 955	7 138	7 323	7 510	7 698	7 889	8 082
Tunisia - Tunisie	10 635	10 742	10 847	10 953	11 063	11 180	11 304	11 433	11 565	11 695
Uganda - Ouganda	32 428	33 477	34 559	35 695	36 912	38 225	39 649	41 167	42 729	44 270
United Republic of Tanzania - République Unie de Tanzanie[2]	44 347	45 674	47 053	48 483	49 961	51 483	53 049	54 660	56 313	58 005
Western Sahara - Sahara occidental	480	488	496	505	515	526	539	553	567	582
Zambia - Zambie	13 606	14 023	14 465	14 927	15 400	15 879	16 363	16 854	17 352	17 861
Zimbabwe	12 698	12 894	13 115	13 350	13 587	13 815	14 030	14 237	14 439	14 645
AMERICA, NORTH - AMÉRIQUE DU NORD										
Anguilla	13	14	14	14	14	14	14	15	15	15
Antigua and Barbuda - Antigua-et-Barbuda	88	89	90	92	93	94	95	95	96	97
Aruba	102	102	103	103	104	104	105	105	106	106
Bahamas	355	360	364	367	371	374	378	382	386	389
Barbados - Barbade	282	283	284	284	285	285	286	286	287	287

Annex I: Mid-year population, United Nations estimates: 2010 - 2019
Annexe I : Population au milieu de l'année, estimations des Nations Unies : 2010 - 2019 (continued - suite)

Continent and country or area	Population estimates (in thousands) - Estimations de population (en milliers)									
Continent et pays ou zone	2010	2011	2012	2013	2014	2015	2016	2017	2018	2019
AMERICA, NORTH - AMÉRIQUE DU NORD										
Belize	322	330	338	346	353	361	368	376	383	390
Bermuda - Bermudes	65	65	65	64	64	64	63	63	63	63
Bonaire, Saba and Sint Eustatius - Bonaire, Saba et Saint-Eustache	21	22	23	24	24	25	25	25	26	26
British Virgin Islands - Îles Vierges britanniques	28	28	29	29	29	29	29	30	30	30
Canada	34 148	34 539	34 922	35 297	35 664	36 027	36 383	36 732	37 075	37 411
Cayman Islands - Îles Caïmanes	57	58	59	60	61	62	63	63	64	65
Costa Rica	4 577	4 633	4 688	4 742	4 795	4 848	4 899	4 950	4 999	5 048
Cuba	11 226	11 237	11 257	11 283	11 307	11 325	11 335	11 339	11 338	11 333
Curaçao	149	152	155	157	158	160	161	162	163	163
Dominica - Dominique	71	71	71	71	71	71	71	71	72	72
Dominican Republic - République dominicaine	9 695	9 813	9 931	10 048	10 165	10 282	10 398	10 513	10 627	10 739
El Salvador	6 184	6 211	6 238	6 266	6 295	6 325	6 356	6 388	6 421	6 454
Greenland - Groenland	57	57	56	56	56	56	56	56	57	57
Grenada - Grenade	106	107	107	108	109	110	110	111	111	112
Guadeloupe	406	406	404	403	401	400	400	400	400	400
Guatemala	14 630	14 949	15 271	15 596	15 923	16 252	16 583	16 915	17 248	17 581
Haiti - Haïti	9 949	10 100	10 251	10 401	10 549	10 696	10 840	10 982	11 123	11 263
Honduras	8 317	8 481	8 641	8 799	8 956	9 113	9 271	9 429	9 588	9 746
Jamaica - Jamaïque	2 810	2 826	2 842	2 859	2 875	2 891	2 906	2 921	2 935	2 948
Martinique	395	392	388	385	381	378	377	376	376	376
Mexico - Mexique	114 093	115 695	117 274	118 827	120 355	121 858	123 333	124 777	126 191	127 576
Montserrat	5	5	5	5	5	5	5	5	5	5
Nicaragua	5 824	5 903	5 983	6 062	6 143	6 223	6 304	6 385	6 466	6 546
Panama	3 643	3 706	3 771	3 835	3 901	3 968	4 037	4 107	4 177	4 246
Puerto Rico - Porto Rico	3 580	3 560	3 537	3 504	3 454	3 382	3 283	3 164	3 040	2 933
Saint Kitts and Nevis - Saint-Kitts-et-Nevis	49	49	50	50	51	51	52	52	52	53
Saint Lucia - Sainte-Lucie	174	176	177	178	178	179	180	181	182	183
Saint Pierre and Miquelon - Saint Pierre-et-Miquelon	6	6	6	6	6	6	6	6	6	6
Saint Vincent and the Grenadines - Saint-Vincent-et-les Grenadines	108	108	108	109	109	109	109	110	110	111
Sint Maarten (Dutch part) - Saint-Martin (partie néerlandaise)	34	35	36	38	39	40	41	41	42	42
Trinidad and Tobago - Trinité-et-Tobago	1 328	1 336	1 345	1 354	1 362	1 370	1 378	1 384	1 390	1 395
Turks and Caicos Islands - Îles Turques et Caïques	33	33	34	35	35	36	37	37	38	38
United States of America - États-Unis d'Amérique	309 011	311 584	314 044	316 401	318 673	320 878	323 016	325 085	327 096	329 065
United States Virgin Islands - Îles Vierges américaines	106	106	106	105	105	105	105	105	105	105
AMERICA, SOUTH - AMÉRIQUE DU SUD										
Argentina - Argentine	40 896	41 320	41 755	42 196	42 638	43 075	43 508	43 937	44 361	44 781
Bolivia (Plurinational State of) - Bolivie (État plurinational de)	10 049	10 213	10 378	10 542	10 707	10 870	11 032	11 193	11 353	11 513
Brazil - Brésil	195 714	197 515	199 287	201 036	202 764	204 472	206 163	207 834	209 469	211 050
Chile - Chili	17 063	17 234	17 400	17 572	17 759	17 969	18 209	18 470	18 729	18 952
Colombia - Colombie	45 223	45 663	46 076	46 495	46 968	47 521	48 175	48 910	49 661	50 339
Ecuador - Équateur	15 011	15 244	15 474	15 707	15 952	16 212	16 491	16 785	17 084	17 374
Falkland Islands (Malvinas) - Îles Falkland (Malvinas)	3	3	3	3	3	3	3	3	3	3
French Guiana - Guyane française	233	238	244	249	255	261	268	275	283	291
Guyana	749	752	755	759	763	767	771	775	779	783
Paraguay	6 248	6 334	6 422	6 510	6 600	6 689	6 778	6 867	6 956	7 045
Peru - Pérou	29 028	29 264	29 507	29 774	30 090	30 471	30 926	31 444	31 989	32 510
Suriname	529	535	541	547	553	559	565	571	576	581
Uruguay	3 359	3 369	3 379	3 389	3 400	3 412	3 424	3 437	3 449	3 462
Venezuela (Bolivarian Republic of) - Venezuela (République bolivarienne du)	28 440	28 888	29 361	29 781	30 043	30 082	29 851	29 402	28 887	28 516
ASIA - ASIE										
Afghanistan	29 186	30 117	31 161	32 270	33 371	34 414	35 383	36 296	37 172	38 042
Armenia - Arménie	2 877	2 877	2 884	2 898	2 912	2 926	2 936	2 945	2 952	2 958
Azerbaijan - Azerbaïdjan[3]	9 032	9 146	9 265	9 385	9 506	9 623	9 736	9 845	9 950	10 048
Bahrain - Bahreïn	1 241	1 278	1 300	1 315	1 336	1 372	1 426	1 494	1 569	1 641
Bangladesh	147 575	149 273	151 006	152 761	154 517	156 256	157 977	159 685	161 377	163 046
Bhutan - Bhoutan	686	693	702	710	719	728	737	746	754	763
Brunei Darussalam - Brunéi Darussalam	389	394	399	404	410	415	420	424	429	433

Continent and country or area Continent et pays ou zone	2010	2011	2012	2013	2014	2015	2016	2017	2018	2019
	Population estimates (in thousands) - Estimations de population (en milliers)									
ASIA - ASIE										
Cambodia - Cambodge	14 312	14 541	14 780	15 026	15 275	15 521	15 766	16 009	16 250	16 487
China - Chine[4]	1 368 811	1 376 498	1 384 206	1 391 883	1 399 454	1 406 848	1 414 049	1 421 022	1 427 648	1 433 784
China, Hong Kong SAR - Chine, Hong Kong RAS	6 966	7 007	7 047	7 089	7 135	7 186	7 244	7 306	7 372	7 436
China, Macao SAR - Chine, Macao RAS	538	551	564	577	590	602	613	623	632	640
Cyprus - Chypre[5]	1 113	1 125	1 135	1 144	1 152	1 161	1 170	1 180	1 189	1 199
Democratic People's Republic of Korea - République populaire démocratique de Corée	24 549	24 673	24 801	24 930	25 058	25 184	25 308	25 430	25 550	25 666
Georgia - Géorgie[6]	4 099	4 081	4 064	4 049	4 035	4 024	4 015	4 009	4 003	3 997
India - Inde	1 234 281	1 250 288	1 265 780	1 280 842	1 295 601	1 310 152	1 324 517	1 338 677	1 352 642	1 366 418
Indonesia - Indonésie	241 834	245 116	248 452	251 805	255 128	258 383	261 556	264 651	267 671	270 626
Iran (Islamic Republic of) - Iran (République islamique d')	73 763	74 635	75 540	76 482	77 466	78 492	79 564	80 674	81 800	82 914
Iraq	29 742	30 725	31 890	33 157	34 412	35 572	36 611	37 553	38 434	39 310
Israel - Israël	7 346	7 487	7 615	7 735	7 854	7 978	8 109	8 244	8 382	8 519
Japan - Japon	128 542	128 499	128 424	128 314	128 169	127 985	127 763	127 503	127 202	126 860
Jordan - Jordanie	7 262	7 663	8 090	8 519	8 919	9 267	9 554	9 786	9 965	10 102
Kazakhstan	16 252	16 491	16 752	17 026	17 303	17 572	17 831	18 080	18 320	18 551
Kuwait - Koweït	2 992	3 168	3 349	3 526	3 691	3 836	3 957	4 056	4 137	4 207
Kyrgyzstan - Kirghizstan	5 422	5 518	5 622	5 731	5 845	5 959	6 074	6 190	6 304	6 416
Lao People's Democratic Republic - République démocratique populaire lao	6 249	6 348	6 445	6 541	6 640	6 741	6 846	6 953	7 061	7 169
Lebanon - Liban	4 953	5 202	5 538	5 913	6 261	6 533	6 714	6 819	6 859	6 856
Malaysia - Malaisie[7]	28 208	28 651	29 068	29 469	29 867	30 271	30 685	31 105	31 528	31 950
Maldives	366	380	397	416	435	455	476	496	516	531
Mongolia - Mongolie	2 720	2 770	2 825	2 882	2 940	2 998	3 056	3 114	3 170	3 225
Myanmar	50 601	50 991	51 414	51 852	52 281	52 681	53 045	53 383	53 708	54 045
Nepal - Népal	27 013	27 041	26 989	26 917	26 906	27 015	27 263	27 633	28 096	28 609
Oman	3 041	3 251	3 498	3 765	4 027	4 267	4 479	4 666	4 829	4 975
Pakistan	179 425	183 340	187 280	191 261	195 305	199 427	203 631	207 906	212 228	216 565
Philippines	93 967	95 570	97 213	98 872	100 513	102 113	103 664	105 173	106 651	108 117
Qatar	1 856	2 036	2 196	2 337	2 459	2 566	2 654	2 725	2 782	2 832
Republic of Korea - République de Corée	49 546	49 786	50 061	50 346	50 608	50 823	50 983	51 096	51 172	51 225
Saudi Arabia - Arabie saoudite	27 421	28 268	29 155	30 052	30 917	31 718	32 443	33 101	33 703	34 269
Singapore - Singapour	5 131	5 264	5 369	5 454	5 526	5 592	5 654	5 708	5 758	5 804
Sri Lanka	20 262	20 398	20 533	20 663	20 789	20 908	21 021	21 128	21 229	21 324
State of Palestine - État de Palestine[8]	4 056	4 150	4 242	4 334	4 429	4 529	4 636	4 747	4 863	4 981
Syrian Arab Republic - République arabe syrienne	21 363	21 082	20 439	19 578	18 711	17 997	17 466	17 096	16 945	17 070
Tajikistan - Tadjikistan	7 527	7 698	7 875	8 060	8 253	8 454	8 664	8 880	9 101	9 321
Thailand - Thaïlande	67 195	67 518	67 836	68 145	68 439	68 715	68 971	69 210	69 428	69 626
Timor-Leste	1 094	1 113	1 133	1 153	1 174	1 196	1 219	1 243	1 268	1 293
Turkey - Turquie	72 327	73 443	74 651	75 925	77 229	78 529	79 828	81 116	82 340	83 430
Turkmenistan - Turkménistan	5 087	5 174	5 268	5 366	5 466	5 565	5 662	5 758	5 851	5 942
United Arab Emirates - Émirats arabes unis	8 550	8 947	9 142	9 198	9 214	9 263	9 361	9 487	9 631	9 771
Uzbekistan - Ouzbékistan	28 516	28 977	29 449	29 933	30 426	30 930	31 442	31 960	32 476	32 982
Viet Nam	87 968	88 871	89 802	90 753	91 714	92 677	93 640	94 601	95 546	96 462
Yemen - Yémen	23 155	23 808	24 473	25 147	25 823	26 498	27 168	27 835	28 499	29 162
EUROPE										
Albania - Albanie	2 948	2 929	2 914	2 904	2 896	2 891	2 886	2 884	2 883	2 881
Andorra - Andorre	84	84	82	81	79	78	77	77	77	77
Austria - Autriche	8 410	8 454	8 502	8 556	8 615	8 679	8 747	8 820	8 891	8 955
Belarus - Bélarus	9 421	9 415	9 417	9 424	9 432	9 439	9 446	9 450	9 453	9 452
Belgium - Belgique	10 939	11 014	11 085	11 154	11 221	11 288	11 354	11 420	11 482	11 539
Bosnia and Herzegovina - Bosnie-Herzégovine	3 705	3 661	3 605	3 543	3 482	3 429	3 386	3 352	3 324	3 301
Bulgaria - Bulgarie	7 425	7 379	7 334	7 290	7 246	7 200	7 152	7 102	7 052	7 000
Croatia - Croatie	4 328	4 313	4 296	4 277	4 256	4 233	4 209	4 183	4 156	4 130
Czechia - Tchéquie	10 537	10 567	10 581	10 587	10 591	10 601	10 619	10 641	10 666	10 689
Denmark - Danemark	5 555	5 583	5 611	5 638	5 664	5 689	5 711	5 732	5 752	5 772
Estonia - Estonie	1 332	1 328	1 323	1 319	1 316	1 315	1 317	1 319	1 323	1 326
Faroe Islands - Îles Féroé	48	48	48	48	48	48	48	48	48	49
Finland - Finlande[9]	5 366	5 390	5 415	5 439	5 461	5 481	5 498	5 511	5 523	5 532
France	62 880	63 222	63 564	63 894	64 194	64 453	64 668	64 843	64 991	65 130
Germany - Allemagne	80 827	80 856	80 973	81 174	81 450	81 787	82 194	82 658	83 124	83 517
Gibraltar	34	34	34	34	34	34	34	34	34	34
Greece - Grèce	10 888	10 829	10 781	10 741	10 701	10 660	10 615	10 569	10 522	10 473
Holy See - Saint-Siège	1	1	1	1	1	1	1	1	1	1
Hungary - Hongrie	9 927	9 896	9 864	9 834	9 805	9 778	9 753	9 730	9 708	9 685

Annex I: Mid-year population, United Nations estimates: 2010 - 2019
Annexe I : Population au milieu de l'année, estimations des Nations Unies : 2010 - 2019 (continued - suite)

Continent and country or area Continent et pays ou zone	Population estimates (in thousands) - Estimations de population (en milliers)									
	2010	**2011**	**2012**	**2013**	**2014**	**2015**	**2016**	**2017**	**2018**	**2019**
EUROPE										
Iceland - Islande	320	323	326	327	329	330	332	334	337	339
Ireland - Irlande	4 554	4 591	4 608	4 615	4 627	4 652	4 696	4 753	4 819	4 882
Isle of Man - Île de Man	85	85	85	84	83	83	83	84	84	85
Italy - Italie	59 325	59 589	59 879	60 167	60 410	60 578	60 663	60 674	60 627	60 550
Latvia - Lettonie	2 119	2 094	2 069	2 045	2 021	1 998	1 974	1 951	1 928	1 907
Liechtenstein	36	36	37	37	37	37	38	38	38	38
Lithuania - Lituanie	3 124	3 083	3 046	3 009	2 971	2 932	2 890	2 845	2 801	2 760
Luxembourg	508	519	531	543	555	567	579	592	604	616
Malta - Malte	414	418	422	426	430	434	436	438	439	440
Monaco	36	36	36	37	37	38	38	38	39	39
Montenegro - Monténégro	624	625	626	626	627	627	627	628	628	628
Netherlands - Pays-Bas	16 683	16 738	16 792	16 844	16 893	16 938	16 981	17 021	17 060	17 097
North Macedonia - Macédoine du Nord	2 071	2 072	2 074	2 076	2 078	2 079	2 081	2 082	2 083	2 083
Norway - Norvège[10]	4 886	4 948	5 014	5 079	5 142	5 200	5 251	5 296	5 338	5 379
Poland - Pologne	38 330	38 287	38 227	38 158	38 091	38 034	37 989	37 953	37 922	37 888
Portugal	10 596	10 569	10 526	10 473	10 418	10 368	10 326	10 289	10 256	10 226
Republic of Moldova - République de Moldova[11]	4 086	4 079	4 076	4 075	4 073	4 071	4 066	4 060	4 052	4 043
Romania - Roumanie	20 472	20 337	20 227	20 133	20 036	19 925	19 796	19 654	19 506	19 365
Russian Federation - Fédération de Russie	143 479	143 703	143 994	144 325	144 665	144 985	145 275	145 530	145 734	145 872
San Marino - Saint-Marin	31	32	32	33	33	33	34	34	34	34
Serbia - Serbie[12]	8 991	8 964	8 940	8 919	8 898	8 877	8 854	8 830	8 803	8 772
Slovakia - Slovaquie	5 404	5 409	5 415	5 422	5 429	5 436	5 442	5 448	5 453	5 457
Slovenia - Slovénie	2 043	2 051	2 058	2 063	2 067	2 071	2 074	2 076	2 078	2 079
Spain - Espagne[13]	46 931	47 084	47 063	46 931	46 778	46 672	46 634	46 647	46 693	46 737
Sweden - Suède	9 390	9 467	9 543	9 618	9 692	9 765	9 836	9 905	9 972	10 036
Switzerland - Suisse	7 809	7 907	8 008	8 109	8 206	8 297	8 380	8 456	8 526	8 591
Ukraine[14]	45 792	45 620	45 454	45 287	45 112	44 922	44 714	44 488	44 246	43 994
United Kingdom of Great Britain and Northern Ireland - Royaume-Uni de Grande-Bretagne et d'Irlande du Nord	63 460	64 022	64 525	64 984	65 423	65 860	66 298	66 727	67 142	67 530
OCEANIA - OCÉANIE										
American Samoa - Samoas américaines	56	56	56	56	56	56	56	56	55	55
Australia - Australie[15]	22 155	22 538	22 904	23 255	23 596	23 932	24 263	24 585	24 898	25 203
Cook Islands - Îles Cook	18	18	18	18	18	18	18	18	18	18
Fiji - Fidji	860	863	865	866	866	869	872	877	883	890
French Polynesia - Polynésie française	266	268	269	270	272	273	275	276	278	279
Guam	159	160	160	160	161	162	163	164	166	167
Kiribati	103	105	106	108	109	111	113	114	116	118
Marshall Islands - Îles Marshall	56	57	57	57	57	57	58	58	58	59
Micronesia (Federated States of) - Micronésie (États fédérés de)	103	103	105	106	107	109	110	111	113	114
Nauru	10	10	10	10	10	10	10	11	11	11
New Caledonia - Nouvelle-Calédonie	254	257	261	264	268	271	274	277	280	283
New Zealand - Nouvelle-Zélande	4 370	4 419	4 468	4 519	4 568	4 615	4 659	4 702	4 743	4 783
Niue - Nioué	2	2	2	2	2	2	2	2	2	2
Northern Mariana Islands - Îles Mariannes septentrionales	54	54	54	55	55	56	56	57	57	57
Palau - Palaos	18	18	18	18	18	18	18	18	18	18
Papua New Guinea - Papouasie-Nouvelle-Guinée	7 311	7 472	7 631	7 788	7 947	8 108	8 272	8 438	8 606	8 776
Samoa	186	187	189	191	192	194	195	195	196	197
Solomon Islands - Îles Salomon	528	542	556	571	587	603	619	636	653	670
Tokelau - Tokélaou	1	1	1	1	1	1	1	1	1	1
Tonga	104	104	103	102	101	101	101	102	103	104
Tuvalu	11	11	11	11	11	11	11	11	12	12
Vanuatu	236	243	250	257	264	271	278	285	293	300
Wallis and Futuna Islands - Îles Wallis et Futuna	13	12	12	12	12	12	12	12	12	11

SOURCE

United Nations, Department of Economic and Social Affairs, Population Division (2019). 2019 Revision of World Population Prospects - Organisation des Nations Unies, Département des affaires économiques et sociales, Division de la population (2019). Perspectives de la population mondiale : La révision de 2019

FOOTNOTES - NOTES

1 Including Agalega, Rodrigues and Saint Brandon. - Y compris Agalega, Rodrigues et Saint Brandon.
2 Including Zanzibar. - Y compris le Zanzibar.
3 Including Nagorno-Karabakh. - Y compris le Haut-Karabakh.
4 For statistical purposes, the data for China do not include Hong Kong and Macao Special Administrative Regions (SAR) of China. - A des fins statistiques, les données pour la Chine ne comprennent pas les Régions Administratives Spéciales (SAR) de Hong Kong et Macao.
5 Refers to the whole country. - Les données se rapportent au pays en entier.
6 Including Abkhazia and South Ossetia. - Y compris l'Abkhazie et l'Ossétie du Sud.
7 Including Sabah and Sarawak. - Y compris le Sabah et le Sarawak.
8 Including East Jerusalem. - Y compris Jérusalem-Est.
9 Including Åland Islands. - Y compris les îles Åland.
10 Including Svalbard and Jan Mayen Islands. - Y compris Svalbard et l'île Jan Mayen.
11 Including Transnistria. - Y compris la Transnistrie.
12 Including Kosovo. - Y compris le Kosovo.
13 Including Canary Islands, Ceuta and Melilla. - Y compris les îles Canaries, Ceuta et Melilla.
14 Including Crimea. - Y compris la Crimée.
15 Including Christmas Island, Cocos (Keeling) Islands and Norfolk Island. - Y compris les îles Christmas, Cocos (Keeling) et Norfolk.

Annex II: Vital statistics summary, United Nations estimates: 2015-2020
Annexe II: Aperçu des statistiques de l'état civil, estimations des Nations Unies : 2015-2020

Continent and country or area Continent et pays ou zone	Crude birth rate - Taux bruts de natalité	Crude death rate - Taux bruts de mortalité	Infant mortality rate - Décès d'enfants de moins d'un an	Life expectancy at birth - Espérance de vie à la naissance: Male - Masculin	Life expectancy at birth - Espérance de vie à la naissance: Female - Féminin	Total fertility rate - Indice synthétique de fécondité	Natural increase - Accroissement naturel
AFRICA - AFRIQUE							
Algeria - Algérie	24.7	4.7	21.2	75.4	77.8	3.05	20.0
Angola	40.9	8.3	61.5	57.8	63.4	5.55	32.6
Benin - Bénin	36.4	9.0	61.1	59.8	62.8	4.87	27.4
Botswana	25.1	5.8	30.2	66.0	71.9	2.89	19.3
Burkina Faso	38.2	8.3	54.2	60.1	61.6	5.23	29.9
Burundi	39.3	8.0	42.4	59.2	62.8	5.45	31.2
Cabo Verde	19.7	5.6	16.9	69.2	75.9	2.29	14.0
Cameroon - Cameroun	35.6	9.4	61.2	57.5	60.0	4.60	26.3
Central African Republic - République centrafricaine	35.4	12.4	81.9	50.5	54.9	4.75	23.0
Chad - Tchad	42.4	12.2	74.5	52.4	55.2	5.80	30.2
Comoros - Comores	32.1	7.3	53.1	62.3	65.8	4.24	24.8
Congo	33.1	6.8	35.3	62.7	65.6	4.45	26.3
Côte d'Ivoire	35.9	10.2	60.4	56.1	58.6	4.68	25.7
Democratic Republic of the Congo - République démocratique du Congo	41.4	9.6	64.9	58.7	61.7	5.96	31.8
Djibouti	21.7	7.1	33.4	64.6	68.7	2.76	14.6
Egypt - Égypte	26.5	5.8	15.6	69.5	74.1	3.33	20.7
Equatorial Guinea - Guinée équatoriale	33.5	9.4	66.1	57.3	59.4	4.55	24.0
Eritrea - Érythrée	30.6	7.2	34.7	63.6	68.0	4.10	23.4
Eswatini	26.7	9.4	41.4	55.2	63.9	3.03	17.3
Ethiopia - Éthiopie	32.6	6.7	37.0	64.1	67.9	4.30	25.9
Gabon	32.0	6.9	35.3	64.0	68.2	4.00	25.1
Gambia - Gambie	38.8	8.0	44.8	60.2	63.0	5.25	30.8
Ghana	29.6	7.3	35.6	62.6	64.7	3.89	22.2
Guinea - Guinée	36.6	8.5	51.6	60.3	61.5	4.74	28.0
Guinea-Bissau - Guinée-Bissau	35.4	9.7	57.1	55.8	59.7	4.51	25.7
Kenya	28.9	5.5	36.3	63.8	68.5	3.52	23.4
Lesotho	27.0	14.3	62.3	50.4	56.8	3.16	12.7
Liberia - Libéria	33.2	7.6	54.1	62.2	65.0	4.35	25.6
Libya - Libye	19.0	5.1	10.5	69.9	75.7	2.25	13.9
Madagascar	32.8	6.1	29.0	64.9	68.1	4.11	26.7
Malawi	34.3	6.8	41.3	60.3	66.6	4.25	27.5
Mali	41.8	9.8	65.8	58.0	59.5	5.92	32.0
Mauritania - Mauritanie	33.9	7.3	53.4	63.0	66.2	4.59	26.6
Mauritius - Maurice[1]	10.2	8.3	11.2	71.4	78.3	1.39	1.9
Mayotte	28.3	2.7	4.2	76.0	82.9	3.73	25.6
Morocco - Maroc	19.1	5.1	19.9	75.1	77.5	2.42	14.0
Mozambique	37.7	8.6	53.9	57.0	62.9	4.89	29.1
Namibia - Namibie	28.8	8.2	33.4	60.0	65.8	3.42	20.6
Niger	46.3	8.4	46.3	60.7	63.0	6.95	37.9
Nigeria - Nigéria	38.1	12.0	62.1	53.3	55.1	5.42	26.1
Republic of South Sudan - République de Soudan du Sud	35.2	10.6	64.4	56.0	58.9	4.74	24.6
Reunion - Réunion	14.9	6.2	2.7	77.3	83.8	2.27	8.7
Rwanda	32.1	5.3	29.2	66.3	70.5	4.10	26.8
Sao Tome and Principe - Sao Tomé-et-Principe	31.8	4.9	26.4	67.7	72.5	4.35	26.9
Senegal - Sénégal	34.7	5.8	32.7	65.3	69.4	4.65	28.9
Seychelles	16.8	7.8	10.9	69.8	77.3	2.46	9.0
Sierra Leone	33.7	11.9	80.8	53.2	54.9	4.32	21.8
Somalia - Somalie	41.9	10.9	69.3	55.3	58.7	6.12	30.9
South Africa - Afrique du Sud	20.7	9.5	27.2	60.2	67.1	2.41	11.1
Sudan - Soudan	32.4	7.2	42.9	63.1	66.8	4.43	25.1
Togo	33.3	8.6	49.7	59.7	61.4	4.35	24.8
Tunisia - Tunisie	17.7	6.3	12.7	74.4	78.5	2.20	11.5
Uganda - Ouganda	38.4	6.7	46.1	60.4	65.0	5.01	31.8
United Republic of Tanzania - République Unie de Tanzanie[2]	36.9	6.5	41.2	63.0	66.6	4.92	30.4
Western Sahara - Sahara occidental	20.3	4.9	28.8	68.2	71.9	2.42	15.4
Zambia - Zambie	36.3	6.6	45.6	60.3	66.2	4.66	29.7
Zimbabwe	30.8	8.1	38.7	59.2	62.2	3.63	22.8
AMERICA, NORTH - AMÉRIQUE DU NORD							
Antigua and Barbuda - Antigua-et-Barbuda	15.5	6.3	5.2	75.7	77.9	2.00	9.1
Aruba	11.7	9.0	13.6	73.6	78.4	1.90	2.7
Bahamas	14.0	6.7	5.9	71.5	75.9	1.76	7.3
Barbados - Barbade	10.7	9.0	10.0	77.6	80.4	1.62	1.7

Annex II: Vital statistics summary, United Nations estimates: 2015-2020
Annexe II: Aperçu des statistiques de l'état civil, estimations des Nations Unies : 2015-2020 (continued - suite)

Continent and country or area Continent et pays ou zone	Crude birth rate - Taux bruts de natalité	Crude death rate - Taux bruts de mortalité	Infant mortality rate - Décès d'enfants de moins d'un an	Life expectancy at birth - Espérance de vie à la naissance: Male - Masculin	Life expectancy at birth - Espérance de vie à la naissance: Female - Féminin	Total fertility rate - Indice synthétique de fécondité	Natural increase - Accroissement naturel
AMERICA, NORTH - AMÉRIQUE DU NORD							
Belize	20.9	4.7	12.8	71.4	77.6	2.32	16.2
Canada	10.5	7.7	4.5	80.2	84.3	1.53	2.7
Costa Rica	14.1	5.0	7.3	77.4	82.7	1.76	9.1
Cuba	10.2	8.9	4.5	76.7	80.7	1.62	1.3
Curaçao	10.8	8.8	9.1	75.5	81.4	1.76	2.1
Dominican Republic - République dominicaine	19.7	6.1	25.9	70.7	77.1	2.36	13.6
El Salvador	18.4	7.0	14.6	68.1	77.5	2.05	11.4
Grenada - Grenade	16.6	9.5	15.0	70.1	75.0	2.07	7.1
Guadeloupe	11.7	8.2	4.6	78.1	85.2	2.17	3.5
Guatemala	24.8	4.8	20.7	71.0	76.8	2.90	20.0
Haiti - Haïti	24.5	8.6	54.3	61.4	65.7	2.96	16.0
Honduras	21.8	4.4	15.0	72.7	77.3	2.49	17.4
Jamaica - Jamaïque	16.2	7.6	11.8	72.8	75.9	1.99	8.7
Martinique	9.9	9.1	5.6	78.9	85.4	1.88	0.8
Mexico - Mexique	17.7	6.0	13.5	72.1	77.8	2.14	11.8
Nicaragua	20.9	5.1	16.8	70.6	77.7	2.42	15.8
Panama	19.1	5.1	14.1	75.1	81.5	2.47	14.0
Puerto Rico - Porto Rico	7.4	9.3	5.5	76.2	83.3	1.22	-2.0
Saint Lucia - Sainte-Lucie	12.1	7.1	12.5	74.7	77.4	1.44	5.0
Saint Vincent and the Grenadines - Saint-Vincent-et-les Grenadines	14.3	9.2	14.6	70.1	74.9	1.90	5.1
Trinidad and Tobago - Trinité-et-Tobago	13.1	8.3	22.0	70.7	76.0	1.73	4.8
United States of America - États-Unis d'Amérique	12.0	8.7	5.8	76.3	81.3	1.78	3.3
United States Virgin Islands - Îles Vierges américaines	11.8	8.5	8.2	77.7	82.9	2.05	3.3
AMERICA, SOUTH - AMÉRIQUE DU SUD							
Argentina - Argentine	17.1	7.6	10.2	73.0	79.8	2.27	9.5
Bolivia (Plurinational State of) - Bolivie (État plurinational de)	21.9	6.8	29.7	68.3	74.1	2.75	15.1
Brazil - Brésil	14.1	6.4	13.0	71.9	79.3	1.74	7.7
Chile - Chili	12.5	6.1	6.7	77.4	82.3	1.65	6.3
Colombia - Colombie	15.0	5.5	12.6	74.2	79.8	1.82	9.5
Ecuador - Équateur	19.9	5.1	13.6	74.0	79.6	2.44	14.8
French Guiana - Guyane française	25.6	2.9	8.7	76.7	83.0	3.36	22.6
Guyana	20.1	7.4	26.8	66.7	72.9	2.47	12.6
Paraguay	20.7	5.5	19.0	72.1	76.2	2.45	15.2
Peru - Pérou	18.1	5.5	12.8	73.7	79.2	2.27	12.6
Suriname	18.7	7.3	17.5	68.3	74.9	2.43	11.3
Uruguay	13.9	9.5	8.7	73.9	81.3	1.98	4.5
Venezuela (Bolivarian Republic of) - Venezuela (République bolivarienne du)	18.0	7.0	25.7	68.4	76.1	2.28	11.1
ASIA - ASIE							
Afghanistan	32.9	6.5	51.7	62.9	65.8	4.56	26.3
Armenia - Arménie	14.2	9.9	10.8	71.1	78.3	1.76	4.3
Azerbaijan - Azerbaïdjan[3]	17.1	6.8	20.8	70.3	75.3	2.08	10.3
Bahrain - Bahreïn	14.2	2.4	6.0	76.3	78.2	2.00	11.8
Bangladesh	18.4	5.5	26.8	70.5	74.1	2.05	12.8
Bhutan - Bhoutan	17.5	6.3	24.1	71.0	71.6	2.00	11.2
Brunei Darussalam - Brunéi Darussalam	15.0	4.4	7.9	74.5	76.9	1.85	10.6
Cambodia - Cambodge	22.7	6.0	23.7	67.2	71.5	2.52	16.7
China - Chine[4]	11.9	7.1	9.9	74.5	79.0	1.69	4.8
China, Hong Kong SAR - Chine, Hong Kong RAS	11.1	6.6	1.3	81.8	87.5	1.33	4.5
China, Macao SAR - Chine, Macao RAS	11.0	3.9	2.6	81.1	87.0	1.20	7.1
Cyprus - Chypre[5]	10.6	7.0	3.5	78.7	82.8	1.34	3.6
Democratic People's Republic of Korea - République populaire démocratique de Corée	13.9	9.1	13.9	68.3	75.4	1.91	4.9
Georgia - Géorgie[6]	13.6	12.8	9.4	69.1	77.9	2.06	0.7
India - Inde	18.0	7.2	32.0	68.1	70.5	2.24	10.8
Indonesia - Indonésie	18.2	6.4	18.9	69.3	73.6	2.32	11.8
Iran (Islamic Republic of) - Iran (République islamique d')	19.1	4.9	12.8	75.3	77.6	2.15	14.2
Iraq	29.1	4.8	24.1	68.3	72.4	3.68	24.3
Israel - Israël	20.4	5.3	2.7	81.0	84.3	3.04	15.1

Annex II: Vital statistics summary, United Nations estimates: 2015-2020
Annexe II: Aperçu des statistiques de l'état civil, estimations des Nations Unies : 2015-2020 (continued - suite)

Continent and country or area Continent et pays ou zone	Crude birth rate - Taux bruts de natalité	Crude death rate - Taux bruts de mortalité	Infant mortality rate - Décès d'enfants de moins d'un an	Life expectancy at birth - Espérance de vie à la naissance		Total fertility rate - Indice synthétique de fécondité	Natural increase - Accroissement naturel
				Male - Masculin	Female - Féminin		
ASIA - ASIE							
Japan - Japon	7.5	10.4	1.8	81.3	87.5	1.37	-2.9
Jordan - Jordanie	22.0	3.9	14.6	72.7	76.1	2.77	18.2
Kazakhstan	21.4	7.1	7.7	68.8	77.4	2.76	14.2
Kuwait - Koweït	14.4	2.7	7.1	74.6	76.4	2.10	11.7
Kyrgyzstan - Kirghizstan	24.8	6.1	15.5	67.2	75.4	3.00	18.7
Lao People's Democratic Republic - République démocratique populaire lao	23.8	6.5	38.8	65.7	69.2	2.70	17.3
Lebanon - Liban	17.6	4.3	9.4	77.0	80.8	2.09	13.3
Malaysia - Malaisie[7]	16.8	5.1	5.9	74.0	78.1	2.01	11.8
Maldives	14.4	2.8	6.8	77.1	80.4	1.88	11.6
Mongolia - Mongolie	24.4	6.3	18.1	65.5	73.8	2.90	18.1
Myanmar	17.7	8.2	38.4	63.7	69.8	2.17	9.5
Nepal - Népal	20.0	6.4	27.9	68.8	71.7	1.93	13.6
Oman	19.6	2.4	7.3	75.8	80.1	2.93	17.2
Pakistan	28.5	7.0	61.3	66.1	68.0	3.55	21.5
Philippines	20.6	5.8	19.7	67.1	75.3	2.58	14.7
Qatar	9.7	1.2	6.3	78.9	81.8	1.88	8.5
Republic of Korea - République de Corée	7.4	5.9	2.1	79.6	85.7	1.11	1.5
Saudi Arabia - Arabie saoudite	18.0	3.5	6.3	73.7	76.5	2.34	14.6
Singapore - Singapour	8.8	4.4	1.6	81.3	85.5	1.21	4.3
Sri Lanka	16.0	6.6	7.6	73.3	80.1	2.21	9.4
State of Palestine - État de Palestine[8]	29.4	3.5	17.5	72.2	75.5	3.67	26.0
Syrian Arab Republic - République arabe syrienne	24.0	5.5	15.5	65.9	77.7	2.84	18.5
Tajikistan - Tadjikistan	31.2	4.9	29.3	68.6	73.1	3.61	26.3
Thailand - Thaïlande	10.5	7.6	7.8	73.1	80.6	1.54	2.9
Timor-Leste	29.7	6.0	37.3	67.2	71.3	4.10	23.7
Turkey - Turquie	16.2	5.4	8.9	74.3	80.2	2.08	10.8
Turkmenistan - Turkménistan	24.0	7.1	43.3	64.5	71.5	2.79	16.9
United Arab Emirates - Émirats arabes unis	10.4	1.5	5.5	77.1	79.1	1.42	8.9
Uzbekistan - Ouzbékistan	21.8	5.8	20.8	69.4	73.6	2.43	16.0
Viet Nam	16.9	6.3	16.7	71.2	79.4	2.06	10.7
Yemen - Yémen	30.7	6.0	43.2	64.4	67.7	3.84	24.7
EUROPE							
Albania - Albanie	11.8	7.8	8.0	76.7	80.1	1.62	4.0
Austria - Autriche	9.9	9.9	3.2	78.9	83.8	1.53	0.1
Belarus - Bélarus	11.8	12.6	3.0	69.3	79.3	1.71	-0.7
Belgium - Belgique	10.9	9.8	2.8	79.0	83.7	1.72	1.1
Bosnia and Herzegovina - Bosnie-Herzégovine	8.2	10.6	6.0	74.7	79.7	1.27	-2.4
Bulgaria - Bulgarie	9.0	15.4	6.3	71.3	78.5	1.56	-6.4
Croatia - Croatie	8.9	13.1	4.0	75.0	81.4	1.45	-4.2
Czechia - Tchéquie	10.5	10.5	2.3	76.5	81.8	1.64	0.0
Denmark - Danemark	10.7	9.7	3.1	78.7	82.7	1.76	1.0
Estonia - Estonie	10.4	11.6	2.0	74.0	82.5	1.59	-1.3
Finland - Finlande[9]	9.4	9.7	1.7	78.8	84.5	1.53	-0.4
France	11.2	9.3	3.0	79.4	85.4	1.85	2.0
Germany - Allemagne	9.4	11.2	3.2	78.7	83.6	1.59	-1.7
Greece - Grèce	7.8	10.8	2.8	79.5	84.5	1.30	-3.0
Hungary - Hongrie	9.5	12.5	4.1	73.0	80.1	1.49	-3.0
Iceland - Islande	12.1	6.7	1.3	81.2	84.3	1.77	5.4
Ireland - Irlande	13.0	6.0	2.7	80.4	83.7	1.84	7.0
Italy - Italie	7.6	10.5	2.6	81.0	85.4	1.33	-2.8
Latvia - Lettonie	10.8	14.6	3.3	69.9	79.8	1.72	-3.8
Lithuania - Lituanie	10.3	13.6	4.0	70.0	81.1	1.67	-3.2
Luxembourg	10.7	7.1	2.9	79.8	84.2	1.45	3.5
Malta - Malte	9.8	8.2	5.0	80.4	84.1	1.45	1.6
Montenegro - Monténégro	11.8	10.7	2.8	74.2	79.1	1.75	1.1
Netherlands - Pays-Bas	10.1	8.7	2.5	80.3	83.8	1.66	1.4
North Macedonia - Macédoine du Nord	10.9	10.0	10.7	73.6	77.7	1.50	0.9
Norway - Norvège[10]	11.1	8.0	2.1	80.2	84.2	1.68	3.1
Poland - Pologne	9.9	10.1	3.3	74.5	82.4	1.42	-0.2
Portugal	7.8	10.6	3.0	78.7	84.6	1.29	-2.8
Republic of Moldova - République de Moldova[11]	10.2	11.6	12.4	67.4	75.9	1.26	-1.5
Romania - Roumanie	9.8	13.0	6.7	72.4	79.3	1.62	-3.2
Russian Federation - Fédération de Russie	12.8	12.7	5.8	66.8	77.5	1.82	0.1

Annex II: Vital statistics summary, United Nations estimates: 2015-2020
Annexe II: Aperçu des statistiques de l'état civil, estimations des Nations Unies : 2015-2020 (continued - suite)

Continent and country or area Continent et pays ou zone	Crude birth rate - Taux bruts de natalité	Crude death rate - Taux bruts de mortalité	Infant mortality rate - Décès d'enfants de moins d'un an	Life expectancy at birth - Espérance de vie à la naissance: Male - Masculin	Life expectancy at birth - Espérance de vie à la naissance: Female - Féminin	Total fertility rate - Indice synthétique de fécondité	Natural increase - Accroissement naturel
EUROPE							
Serbia - Serbie[12]	9.6	13.2	4.9	73.2	78.4	1.46	-3.6
Slovakia - Slovaquie	10.5	9.9	4.8	73.7	80.8	1.50	0.6
Slovenia - Slovénie	9.7	9.9	1.9	78.3	83.9	1.60	-0.2
Spain - Espagne[13]	8.5	9.0	2.3	80.6	86.1	1.33	-0.5
Sweden - Suède	11.9	9.2	2.0	80.8	84.4	1.85	2.7
Switzerland - Suisse	10.3	8.0	3.4	81.6	85.4	1.54	2.3
Ukraine[14]	9.6	15.2	7.2	66.8	76.6	1.44	-5.6
United Kingdom of Great Britain and Northern Ireland - Royaume-Uni de Grande-Bretagne et d'Irlande du Nord	11.5	9.4	3.8	79.4	82.9	1.75	2.2
OCEANIA - OCÉANIE							
Australia - Australie[15]	12.9	6.6	3.1	81.2	85.2	1.83	6.3
Fiji - Fidji	21.5	8.1	20.3	65.6	69.1	2.79	13.3
French Polynesia - Polynésie française	14.8	5.6	6.7	75.3	79.7	1.95	9.2
Guam	16.6	5.2	8.7	76.5	83.3	2.32	11.4
Kiribati	28.1	6.3	43.0	63.9	72.0	3.58	21.7
Micronesia (Federated States of) - Micronésie (États fédérés de)	22.9	6.6	23.5	66.1	69.4	3.08	16.3
New Caledonia - Nouvelle-Calédonie	14.3	5.7	11.5	74.7	80.2	1.97	8.6
New Zealand - Nouvelle-Zélande	12.6	7.0	3.8	80.3	83.8	1.90	5.7
Papua New Guinea - Papouasie-Nouvelle-Guinée	27.2	7.5	41.9	62.9	65.5	3.59	19.8
Samoa	24.5	5.2	13.4	71.1	75.2	3.90	19.3
Solomon Islands - Îles Salomon	32.7	4.3	15.5	71.1	74.6	4.44	28.5
Tonga	24.5	7.2	12.5	68.8	72.7	3.58	17.3
Vanuatu	29.8	5.3	22.4	68.8	71.9	3.80	24.5

SOURCE

United Nations, Department of Economic and Social Affairs, Population Division (2019). 2019 Revision of World Population Prospects - Organisation des Nations Unies, Département des affaires économiques et sociales, Division de la population (2019). Perspectives de la population mondiale : La révision de 2019

FOOTNOTES - NOTES

1 Including Agalega, Rodrigues and Saint Brandon. - Y compris Agalega, Rodrigues et Saint Brandon.
2 Including Zanzibar. - Y compris le Zanzibar.
3 Including Nagorno-Karabakh. - Y compris le Haut-Karabakh.
4 For statistical purposes, the data for China do not include Hong Kong and Macao Special Administrative Regions (SAR) of China. - A des fins statistiques, les données pour la Chine ne comprennent pas les Régions Administratives Spéciales (SAR) de Hong Kong et Macao.
5 Refers to the whole country. - Les données se rapportent au pays en entier.
6 Including Abkhazia and South Ossetia. - Y compris l'Abkhazie et l'Ossétie du Sud.
7 Including Sabah and Sarawak. - Y compris le Sabah et le Sarawak.
8 Including East Jerusalem. - Y compris Jérusalem-Est.
9 Including Åland Islands. - Y compris les îles Åland.
10 Including Svalbard and Jan Mayen Islands. - Y compris Svalbard et l'île Jan Mayen.
11 Including Transnistria. - Y compris la Transnistrie.
12 Including Kosovo. - Y compris le Kosovo.
13 Including Canary Islands, Ceuta and Melilla. - Y compris les îles Canaries, Ceuta et Melilla.
14 Including Crimea. - Y compris la Crimée.
15 Including Christmas Island, Cocos (Keeling) Islands and Norfolk Island. - Y compris les îles Christmas, Cocos (Keeling) et Norfolk.

Historical index

(See notes at end of index)

Historical index

(See notes at end of index)

Subject-matter	Year of issue	Time coverage
	1979	1975-79
	1980	1976-80
	1981	1962-81
	1982	1978-82
	1983	1979-83
	1984	1980-84
	1985	1981-85
	1986	1967-86
	1987	1983-87
	1988	1984-88
	1989	1985-89
	1990	1986-90
	1991	1987-91
	1992	1983-92
	1993	1989-93
	1994	1990-94
	1995	1991-95
	1996	1992-96
	1997	1993-97
	1997HS[iii]	1948-97
	1998	1994-98
	1999	1995-99
	1999CD[iv]	1980-99
	2000	1996-00
	2001	1997-01
	2002	1998-02
	2003	1999-03
	2004	2000-04
	2005	2001-05
	2006	2002-06
	2007	2003-07
	2008	2004-08
	2009-2010	2006-10
	2011	2007-11
	2012	2008-12
	2013	2009-13
	2014	2010-14
	2015	2011-15
	2016	2012-16
	2017	2013-17
	2018	2014-18
	2019	2015-19
Births	1949-50	1942-49
by age of father	1954	1936-53
	1959	1949-58
	1965	1955-64
	1969	1963-68
	1975	1966-74
	1981	1972-80
	1999CD[iv]	1990-98
	2007-2019	Latest

Subject-matter	Year of issue	Time coverage
Births	1948	1936-47
by age of mother	1949-50	1936-49
	1954	1936-53
	1955-1956	Latest
	1958	Latest
	1959	1949-58
	1960-1964	Latest
	1965	1955-64
	1966-1968	Latest
	1969	1963-68
	1970-1974	Latest
	1975	1966-74
	1976-1978	Latest
	1978HS[ii]	1948-77
	1979-1980	Latest
	1981	1972-80
	1982-1985	Latest
	1986	1977-85
	1987-1991	Latest
	1992	1983-92
	1993-1997	Latest
	1997HS[iii]	1948-96
	1998-99	Latest
	1999CD[iv]	1990-98
	2000-2019	Latest
Births	1949-50	1936-47
by age of mother and birth order	1954	Latest
	1959	1949-58
	1965	1955-64
	1969	1963-68
	1975	1966-74
	1981	1972-80
	1986	1977-85
	1999CD[iv]	1990-98
Births	1965-1968	Latest
by age of mother and sex of child	1969	1963-68
	1970-1974	Latest
	1975	1966-74
	1976-1978	Latest
	1978HS[ii]	1948-77
	1979-1980	Latest
	1981	1972-80
	1982-1985	Latest
	1986	1977-85
	1987-1991	Latest
	1992	1983-92
	1993-1997	Latest
	1997HS[iii]	1948-96
	1998-99	Latest
	1999CD[iv]	1990-98
	2000-2019	Latest

Historical index

(See notes at end of index)

Subject-matter	Year of issue	Time coverage
Births	*see "Births by urban/rural residence* and age of mother*"*	
by age of mother and urban/rural residence		
Births	1948	1936-47
by birth order	1949-50	1936-49
	1954	1936-53
	1955	Latest
	1959	1949-58
	1965	1955-64
	1969	1963-68
	1975	1966-74
	1981	1972-80
	1986	1977-85
	1999CD[iv]	1990-98
Births	1975	Latest
by birth weight	1981	1972-80
	1986	1977-85
	1999CD[iv]	1990-98
Births	1975	Latest
by gestational age	1981	1972-80
	1986	1977-85
	1999CD[iv]	1990-98
Births	1959	1949-58
by legitimacy status	1965	1955-64
	1969	1963-68
	1975	1966-74
	1981	1972-80
	1986	1977-85
	1999CD[iv]	1990-98
Births	2002	1980-02
by month of birth		
Births	1965	Latest
by occupation of father	1969	Latest
Births	1959	1949-58
by sex of child	1965	1955-64
	1967-1968	Latest
	1969	1963-68
	1970-1974	Latest
	1975	1956-75
	1976-1980	Latest
	1981	1962-81
	1982-1985	Latest
	1986	1967-86
	1987-1991	Latest
	1992	1983-92
	1993-1999	Latest
	1999CD[iv]	1990-98
	2000-2019	Latest
Births	1965	Latest
by plurality	1969	Latest
	1975	Latest
	1981	1972-80
	1986	1977-85
	1999CD[iv]	1990-98
Births	1965	Latest
by urban/rural residence	1967	Latest
	1968	1964-68
	1969	1964-68
	1970	1966-70
	1971	1967-71
	1972	1968-72
	1973	1969-73
	1974	1970-74
	1975	1956-75
	1976	1972-76
	1977	1973-77
	1978	1974-78
	1979	1975-79
	1980	1976-80
	1981	1962-81
	1982	1978-82
	1983	1979-83
	1984	1980-84
	1985	1981-85
	1986	1967-86
	1987	1983-87
	1988	1984-88
	1989	1985-89
	1990	1986-90
	1991	1987-91
	1992	1983-92
	1993	1989-93
	1994	1990-94
	1995	1991-95
	1996	1992-96
	1997	1993-97
	1998	1994-98
	1999	1995-99
	1999CD[iv]	1980-99
	2000	1996-00
	2001	1997-01
	2002	1998-02
	2003	1999-03
	2004	2000-04
	2005	2001-05
	2006	2002-06
	2007	2003-07
	2008	2004-08
	2009-2010	2006-10

Historical index

(See notes at end of index)

Historical index

(See notes at end of index)

Historical index

(See notes at end of index)

Historical index

(See notes at end of index)

Subject-matter	Year of issue	Time coverage
	1985	1976-84
	2001	1985-00
	2005	2001-05
Deaths	1957	Latest
by occupation and age, males	1961	1957-60
	1967	1962-66
Deaths	1957	Latest
by type of certification and cause (numbers)	1974	1965-73
	1980	1971-79
	1985	1976-84
Deaths	1957	Latest
by type of certification and cause (percent)	1961	1955-60
	1966	1960-65
	1974	1965-73
	1980	1971-79
	1985	1976-84
Deaths	1967	Latest
by urban/rural residence	1968	1964-68
	1969	1965-69
	1970	1966-70
	1971	1967-71
	1972	1968-72
	1973	1969-73
	1974	1965-74
	1975	1971-75
	1976	1972-76
	1977	1973-77
	1978	1974-78
	1979	1975-79
	1980	1971-80
	1981	1977-81
	1982	1978-82
	1983	1979-83
	1984	1980-84
	1985	1976-85
	1986	1982-86
	1987	1983-87
	1988	1984-88
	1989	1985-89
	1990	1986-90
	1991	1987-91
	1992	1983-92
	1993	1989-93
	1994	1990-94
	1995	1991-95
	1996	1987-96
	1997	1993-97
	1998	1994-98
	1999	1995-99
	2000	1996-00

Subject-matter	Year of issue	Time coverage
	2001	1997-01
	2002	1998-02
	2003	1999-03
	2004	2000-04
	2006	2002-06
	2007	2003-07
	2008	2004-08
	2009-2010	2006-10
	2011	2007-11
	2012	2008-12
	2013	2009-13
	2014	2010-14
	2015	2011-15
	2016	2012-16
	2017	2013-17
	2018	2014-18
	2019	2015-19
Deaths		
of infants (see infant deaths)		
Death rates	1948	1932-47
	1949-50	1932-49
	1951	1905-30[v]
		1930-50
	1952	1920-34[v]
		1934-51
	1953	1920-39[v]
		1940-52
	1954	1920-39[v]
		1946-53
	1955	1920-34[v]
		1946-54
	1956	1947-55
	1957	1930-56
	1958	1948-57
	1959	1949-58
	1960	1950-59
	1961	1945-59[v]
		1952-61
	1962	1945-54[v]
		1952-62
	1963	1945-59[v]
		1954-63
	1964	1960-64
	1965	1961-65
	1966	1920-64[v]
		1951-66
	1967	1963-67
	1968	1964-68
	1969	1965-69
	1970	1966-70
	1971	1967-71

Historical index

(See notes at end of index)

Subject-matter	Year of issue	Time coverage
	1972	1968-72
	1973	1969-73
	1974	1965-74
	1975	1971-75
	1976	1972-76
	1977	1973-77
	1978	1974-78
	1978HS[ii]	1948-78
	1979	1975-79
	1980	1971-80
	1981	1977-81
	1982	1978-82
	1983	1979-83
	1984	1980-84
	1985	1976-85
	1986	1982-86
	1987	1983-87
	1988	1984-88
	1989	1985-89
	1990	1986-90
	1991	1987-91
	1992	1983-92
	1993	1989-93
	1994	1990-94
	1995	1991-95
	1996	1987-96
	1997	1993-97
	1997HS[iii]	1948-97
	1998	1994-98
	1999	1995-99
	2000	1996-00
	2001	1997-01
	2002	1998-02
	2003	1999-03
	2004	2000-04
	2005	2001-05
	2006	2002-06
	2007	2003-07
	2008	2004-08
	2009-2010	2006-10
	2011	2007-11
	2012	2008-12
	2013	2009-13
	2014	2010-14
	2015	2011-15
	2016	2012-16
	2017	2013-17
	2018	2014-18
	2019	2015-19
Death rates	1948	1935-47
by age and sex	1949-50	1936-49
	1951	1936-50
	1952	1936-51
	1953	1940-52
	1954	1946-53
	1955-1956	Latest
	1957	1948-56
	1961	1952-60
	1966	1950-65
	1972	Latest
	1974	1965-73
	1975-1979	Latest
	1978HS[ii]	1948-77
	1980	1971-79
	1981-1984	Latest
	1985	1976-84
	1986-1991	Latest
	1991PA[vii]	1950-1990
	1992	1983-1992
	1993-1995	Latest
	1996	1987-95
	1997	Latest
	1997HS[iii]	1948-96
	1998-2018	Latest
Death rates	1967	Latest
by age, sex and urban/rural residence	1972	Latest
	1974	1965-73
	1975-1979	Latest
	1980	1971-79
	1981-1984	Latest
	1985	1976-84
	1986-1991	Latest
	1991PA[vii]	1950-1990
	1992	1983-1992
	1993-1995	Latest
	1996	1987-95
	1997	Latest
	1997HS[iii]	1948-96
	1998-2006	Latest
Death rates	1951	1947-49
by cause	1952	1947-51[vi]
	1953	1947-52
	1954	1945-53
	1955-1956	Latest
	1957	1952-56
	1958-1960	Latest
	1961	1955-60
	1962-1965	Latest
	1966	1960-65
	1967-1973	Latest
	1974	1965-73
	1975-1979	Latest
	1980	1971-79
	1981-1984	Latest
	1985	1976-84

Historical index

(See notes at end of index)

Subject-matter	Year of issue	Time coverage
	1986-1991	Latest
	1991PA[vii]	1960-90
	1992-1995	Latest
	1996	1987-95
	1997-2000	Latest
	2002	1995-02
	2004	1995-04
	2006	2002-06
	2008	2004-08
	2011	2006-10
	2013	2008-12
	2015	2010-14
	2017	2012-16
	2019	2014-18
Death rates .... by cause, age and sex	1957	Latest
	1961	Latest
	1991PA[vii]	1960-90
Death rates .... by cause and sex	1967	Latest
	1974	Latest
	1980	Latest
	1985	Latest
	1996	Latest
	2006	2002-06
	2008	2004-08
	2011	2006-10
	2013	2008-12
	2015	2010-14
	2017	2012-16
	2019	2014-18
Death rates .... by marital status, age and sex	1961	Latest
	1967	Latest
	1974	Latest
	1980	Latest
	1985	Latest
	1996	Latest
	2003	Latest
Death rates .... by occupation, age and sex	1957	Latest
Death rates .... by occupation and age, males	1961	Latest
	1967	Latest
Death rates .... by urban/rural residence	1967	Latest
	1968	1964-68
	1969	1965-69
	1970	1966-70
	1971	1967-71
	1972	1968-72

Subject-matter	Year of issue	Time coverage
	1973	1969-73
	1974	1965-74
	1975	1971-75
	1976	1972-76
	1977	1973-77
	1978	1974-78
	1979	1975-79
	1980	1971-80
	1981	1977-81
	1982	1978-82
	1983	1979-83
	1984	1980-84
	1985	1976-85
	1986	1982-86
	1987	1983-87
	1988	1984-88
	1989	1985-89
	1990	1986-90
	1991	1987-91
	1992	1983-92
	1993	1989-93
	1994	1990-94
	1995	1991-95
	1996	1987-96
	1997	1993-97
	1998	1994-98
	1999	1995-99
	1987	1983-87
	1988	1984-88
	1989	1985-89
	1990	1986-90
	1991	1987-91
	1992	1983-92
	1993	1989-93
	1994	1990-94
	1995	1991-95
	1996	1987-96
	1997	1993-97
	1998	1994-98
	1999	1995-99
	2000	1996-00
	2001	1997-01
	2002	1998-02
	2003	1999-03
	2004	2000-04
	2005	2001-05
	2006	2002-06
	2007	2003-07
	2008	2004-08
	2009-2010	2006-10
	2011	2007-11
	2012	2008-12
	2013	2009-13
	2014	2010-14

Historical index

(See notes at end of index)

Subject-matter	Year of issue	Time coverage
	2015	2011-15
	2016	2012-16
	2017	2013-17
	2018	2014-18
	2019	2015-19
Death rates	1949-50	1947
estimated (for continents)	1956-1977	Latest
	1978-1979	1970-75
	1980-1983	1975-80
	1984-1986	1980-85
	1984-1986	1980-85
	1987-1992	1985-90
	1993-1997	1990-95
	1998-2000	1995-00
	2001-2005	2000-05
	2006-2010	2005-10
	2011-2015	2010-15
	2016-2019	2015-20
Death rates	1964-1977	Latest
estimated (for macro regions)	1978-1979	1970-75
	1980-1983	1975-80
	1984-1986	1980-85
	1987-1992	1985-90
	1993-1997	1990-95
	1998-2000	1995-00
	2001-2005	2000-05
	2006-2010	2005-10
	2011-2015	2010-15
	2016-2019	2015-20
Death rates	1949-50	1947
estimated (for regions)	1956-1977	Latest
	1978-1979	1970-75
	1980-1983	1975-80
	1984-1986	1980-85
	1987-1992	1985-90
	1993-1997	1990-95
	1998-2000	1995-00
	2001-2005	2000-05
	2006-2010	2005-10
	2011-2015	2010-15
	2016-2019	2015-20
Death rates	1949-50	1947
estimated (for the world)	1956-1977	Latest
	1978-1979	1970-75
	1980-1983	1975-80
	1984-1986	1980-85
	1987-1992	1985-90
	1993-1997	1990-95
	1998-2000	1995-00
	2001-2005	2000-05

Subject-matter	Year of issue	Time coverage
	2006-2010	2005-10
	2011-2015	2010-15
	2016-2019	2015-20
Death rates		
of infants (see infant deaths)		
Density of population	1949-50	1920-49
of continents	1951-1999	Latest
	2000	2000
	2001	2001
	2002	2002
	2003	2003
	2004	2004
	2005	2005
	2006	2006
	2007	2007
	2008	2008
	2009-2010	2010
	2011	2011
	2012	2012
	2013	2013
	2014	2014
	2015	2015
	2016	2016
	2017	2017
	2018	2018
	2019	2019
Density of population	1948-1999	Latest
of countries	2000	2000
	2001	2001
	2002	2002
	2003	2003
	2004	2004
	2005	2005
	2006	2006
	2007	2007
	2008	2008
	2009-2010	2010
	2011	2011
	2012	2012
	2013	2013
	2014	2014
	2015	2015
	2016	2016
	2017	2017
	2018	2018
	2019	2019
Density of population	1964-1999	Latest
of major areas	2000	2000
	2001	2001

Historical index

(See notes at end of index)

Subject-matter	Year of issue	Time coverage
	2002	2002
	2003	2003
	2004	2004
	2005	2005
	2006	2006
	2007	2007
	2008	2008
	2009-2010	2010
	2011	2011
	2012	2012
	2013	2013
	2014	2014
	2015	2015
	2016	2016
	2017	2017
	2018	2018
	2019	2019
Density of population.........	1949-50	1920-49
of regions	1952-1999	Latest
	2000	2000
	2001	2001
	2002	2002
	2003	2003
	2004	2004
	2005	2005
	2006	2006
	2007	2007
	2008	2008
	2009-2010	2010
	2011	2011
	2012	2012
	2013	2013
	2014	2014
	2015	2015
	2016	2016
	2017	2017
	2018	2018
	2019	2019
Density of population.........	1949-50	1920-49
of the world	1952-1999	Latest
	2000	2000
	2001	2001
	2002	2002
	2003	2003
	2004	2004
	2005	2005
	2006	2006
	2007	2007
	2008	2008
	2009-2010	2010
	2011	2011
	2012	2012

Subject-matter	Year of issue	Time coverage
	2013	2013
	2014	2014
	2015	2015
	2016	2016
	2017	2017
	2018	2018
	2019	2019
Disability	*see "Population disabled"*	
Divorces	1951	1935-50
	1952	1936-51
	1953	1950-52
	1954	1946-53
	1955	1946-54
	1956	1947-55
	1957	1948-56
	1958	1940-57
	1959	1949-58
	1960	1950-59
	1961	1952-61
	1962	1953-62
	1963	1954-63
	1964	1960-64
	1965	1961-65
	1966	1962-66
	1967	1963-67
	1968	1949-68
	1969	1965-69
	1970	1966-70
	1971	1967-71
	1972	1968-72
	1973	1969-73
	1974	1970-74
	1975	1971-75
	1976	1957-76
	1977	1973-77
	1978	1974-78
	1979	1975-79
	1980	1976-80
	1981	1977-81
	1982	1963-82
	1983	1979-83
	1984	1980-84
	1985	1981-85
	1986	1982-86
	1987	1983-87
	1988	1984-88
	1989	1985-89
	1990	1971-90
	1991	1987-91
	1992	1988-92
	1993	1989-93
	1994	1990-94

Historical index

(See notes at end of index)

Subject-matter	Year of issue	Time coverage
	1995	1991-95
	1996	1992-96
	1997	1993-97
	1998	1994-98
	1999	1995-99
	2000	1996-00
	2001	1997-01
	2002	1998-02
	2003	1999-03
	2004	2000-04
	2005	2001-05
	2006	2002-06
	2007	2003-07
	2008	2004-08
	2009-2010	2006-10
	2011	2007-11
	2012	2008-12
	2013	2009-13
	2014	2010-14
	2015	2011-15
	2016	2012-16
	2017	2013-17
	2018	2014-18
	2019	2015-19
Divorces	1968	1958-67
by age of husband	1976	1966-75
	1982	1972-81
	1987	1975-86
	1990	1980-89
Divorces	1968	1958-67
by age of wife	1976	1966-75
	1982	1972-81
	1987	1975-86
	1990	1980-89
Divorces	1958	1946-57
by age of wife classified by age of husband	1968	Latest
	1976	Latest
	1982	Latest
	1990	Latest
Divorces	1958	1948-57
by duration of marriage	1968	1958-67
	1976	1966-75
	1982	1972-81
	1990	1980-89
	2007	Latest
	2009-2010	Latest
	2012	Latest
	2014	Latest
	2016	Latest
	2018	Latest

Subject-matter	Year of issue	Time coverage
Divorces	1958	1946-57
by duration of marriage and age of husband, wife	1968	Latest
	1976	Latest
	1982	Latest
	1990	Latest
Divorces	1958	1948-57
by number of children involved	1968	1958-67
	1976	1966-75
	1982	1972-81
	1990	1980-89
	2007	Latest
Divorces	2002	1998-02
by urban/rural residence	2003	1999-03
	2004	2000-04
	2005	2001-05
	2006	2002-06
	2007	2003-07
	2008	2004-08
	2009-2010	2006-10
	2011	2007-11
	2012	2008-12
	2013	2009-13
	2014	2010-14
	2015	2011-15
	2016	2012-16
	2017	2013-17
	2018	2014-18
	2019	2015-19
Divorce, percentage distribution	2007	Latest
by duration of marriage	2009-2010	Latest
	2012	Latest
	2014	Latest
	2016	Latest
	2018	Latest
Divorce, percentage distribution	2007	Latest
by number of children involved		
Divorce rates	1952	1935-51
	1953	1936-52
	1954	1946-53
	1955	1946-54
	1956	1947-55
	1957	1948-56
	1958	1930-57
	1959	1949-58
	1960	1950-59

Subject-matter	Year of issue	Time coverage
	1961	1952-61
	1962	1953-62
	1963	1954-63
	1964	1960-64
	1965	1961-65
	1966	1962-66
	1967	1963-67
	1968	1920-64[v]
		1953-68
	1969	1965-69
	1970	1966-70
	1971	1967-71
	1972	1968-72
	1973	1969-73
	1974	1970-74
	1975	1971-75
	1976	1957-76
	1977	1973-77
	1978	1974-78
	1979	1975-79
	1980	1976-80
	1969	1965-69
	1970	1966-70
	1971	1967-71
	1972	1968-72
	1973	1969-73
	1974	1970-74
	1975	1971-75
	1976	1957-76
	1977	1973-77
	1978	1974-78
	1979	1975-79
	1980	1976-80
	1969	1965-69
	1970	1966-70
	1971	1967-71
	1972	1968-72
	1973	1969-73
	1974	1970-74
	1975	1971-75
	1976	1957-76
	1977	1973-77
	1978	1974-78
	1979	1975-79
	1980	1976-80
	1981	1977-81
	1982	1963-82
	1983	1979-83
	1984	1980-84
	1985	1981-85
	1986	1982-86
	1987	1983-87
	1988	1984-88
	1989	1985-89

Subject-matter	Year of issue	Time coverage
	1990	1971-90
	1991	1987-91
	1992	1988-92
	1993	1989-93
	1994	1990-94
	1995	1991-95
	1996	1992-96
	1997	1993-97
	1998	1994-98
	1999	1995-99
	2000	1996-00
	2001	1997-01
	2002	1998-02
	2003	1999-03
	2004	2000-04
	2005	2001-05
	2006	2002-06
	2007	2003-07
	2008	2004-08
	2009-2010	2006-10
	2011	2007-11
	2012	2008-12
	2013	2009-13
	2014	2010-14
	2015	2011-15
	2016	2012-16
	2017	2013-17
	2018	2014-18
	2019	2015-19
Divorce rates	1968	Latest
by age of husband	1976	Latest
	1982	Latest
	1987	1975-86
	1990	Latest
Divorce rates	1968	Latest
by age of wife	1976	Latest
	1982	Latest
	1987	1975-86
	1990	Latest
Divorce rates	1953	1935-52
for married couples	1954	1935-53
	1958	1935-56
	1968	1935-67
	1976	1966-75
	1978HS[ii]	1948-77
	1982	1972-81
	1990	1980-89
Divorce rates	2002	1998-02
by urban/rural residence	2003	1999-03

Historical index

(See notes at end of index)

Historical index

(See notes at end of index)

Historical index
(See notes at end of index)

Historical index

(See notes at end of index)

Subject-matter	Year of issue	Time coverage
	1957	1948-56
	1958	1948-57
	1959	1920-54[v]
		1953-58
	1960	1950-59
	1961	1945-49[v]
		1952-60
	1962	1945-54[v]
		1952-61
	1963	1945-59[v]
		1953-62
	1964	1959-63
	1965	1950-64[v]
		1955-64
	1966	1950-64[v]
		1956-65
	1967	1962-66
	1968	1963-67
	1969	1950-64[v]
		1959-68
	1970	1965-69
	1971	1966-70
	1972	1967-71
	1973	1968-72
	1974	1965-73
	1975	1966-74
	1976	1971-75
	1977	1972-76
	1978	1973-77
	1979	1974-78
	1980	1971-79
	1981	1972-80
	1982	1977-81
	1983	1978-82
	1984	1979-83
	1985	1975-84
	1986	1977-85
	1987	1982-86
	1988	1983-87
	1989	1984-88
	1990	1985-89
	1991	1986-90
	1992	1987-91
	1993	1988-92
	1994	1989-93
	1995	1990-94
	1996	1987-95
	1997	1992-96
	1998	1993-97
	1999	1994-98
	1999CD[iv]	1990-98
	2000	1995-99
	2001	1997-01
	2002	1998-02

Subject-matter	Year of issue	Time coverage
	2003	1999-03
	2004	2000-04
	2005	2001-05
	2006	2002-06
	2007	2003-07
	2008	2004-08
	2009-2010	2006-10
	2011	2007-11
	2012	2008-12
	2013	2009-13
	2014	2010-14
	2015	2011-15
	2016	2012-16
	2017	2013-17
	2018	2014-18
	2019	2015-19
Foetal death ratios, late	1954	1936-53
by age of mother	1959	1949-58
	1965	1955-64
	1969	1963-68
	1975	1966-74
	1981	1972-80
	1986	1977-85
	1996	1987-95
	1999CD[iv]	1990-98
Foetal death ratios, late	1954	Latest
by age of mother and birth order	1959	1949-58
	1965	3-Latest
	1969	1963-68
	1975	1966-74
	1981	1972-80
	1986	1977-85
	1999CD[iv]	1990-98
Foetal death ratios, late	1957	1950-56
by period of gestation	1959	1949-58
	1961	1952-60
	1965	5-Latest
	1966	1956-65
	1967-1968	Latest
	1969	1963-68
	1974	1965-73
	1975	1966-74
	1980	1971-79
	1981	1972-80
	1985	1976-84
	1986	1977-85
Foetal death ratios, late	1971	1966-70
by urban/rural residence	1972	1967-71
	1973	1968-72
	1974	1965-73

Historical index

(See notes at end of index)

I

Historical index

(See notes at end of index)

Subject-matter	Year of issue	Time coverage
Illiteracy rates....................	*see "Population,* illiteracy rates *"*	
Immigrants........................	*see "Migration ((international)"*	
Infant deaths	1948	1932-47
	1949-50	1934-49
	1951	1935-50
	1952	1936-51
	1953	1950-52
	1954	1946-53
	1955	1946-54
	1956	1947-55
	1957	1948-56
	1958	1948-57
	1959	1949-58
	1960	1950-59
	1961	1952-61
	1962	1953-62
	1963	1954-63
	1964	1960-64
	1965	1961-65
	1966	1947-66
	1967	1963-67
	1968	1964-68
	1969	1965-69
	1970	1966-70
	1971	1967-71
	1972	1968-72
	1973	1969-73
	1974	1965-74
	1975	1971-75
	1976	1972-76
	1977	1973-77
	1978	1974-78
	1978HS[ii]	1948-78
	1979	1975-79
	1980	1971-80
	1981	1977-81
	1982	1978-82
	1983	1979-83
	1984	1980-84
	1985	1976-85
	1986	1982-86
	1987	1983-87
	1988	1984-88
	1989	1985-89
	1990	1986-90
	1991	1987-91
	1992	1983-92
	1993	1989-93
	1994	1990-94
	1995	1991-95

Subject-matter	Year of issue	Time coverage
	1996	1987-96
	1997	1993-97
	1997HS[iii]	1948-97
	1998	1994-98
	1999	1995-99
	2000	1996-00
	2001	1997-01
	2002	1998-02
	2003	1999-03
	2004	2000-04
	2005	2001-05
	2006	2002-06
	2007	2003-07
	2008	2004-08
	2009-2010	2006-10
	2011	2007-11
	2012	2008-12
	2013	2009-13
	2014	2010-14
	2015	2011-15
	2016	2012-16
	2017	2013-17
	2018	2014-18
	2019	2015-19
Infant deaths .... by age and sex	1948	1936-47
	1951	1936-49
	1957	1948-56
	1961	1952-60
	1962-1965	Latest
	1966	1956-65
	1967-1973	Latest
	1974	1965-73
	1975-1979	Latest
	1980	1971-79
	1981-1984	Latest
	1985	1976-84
	1986-1991	Latest
	1992	1983-92
	1993-1995	Latest
	1996	1987-95
	1997-2004	Latest
	2005	1996-05
	2006-2019	Latest
Infant deaths .... by age and sex and urban/rural residence	1967-1973	Latest
	1974	1965-73
	1975-1979	Latest
	1980	1971-79
	1981-1984	Latest
	1985	1976-84
	1986-1991	Latest
	1992	1983-92
	1993-1995	Latest

Historical index

(See notes at end of index)

Historical index
(See notes at end of index)

Subject-matter	Year of issue	Time coverage
	1987	1983-87
	1988	1984-88
	1989	1985-89
	1990	1986-90
	1991	1987-91
	1992	1983-92
	1993	1989-93
	1994	1990-94
	1995	1991-95
	1996	1987-96
	1997	1993-97
	1997HS[iii]	1948-97
	1998	1994-98
	1999	1995-99
	2000	1996-00
	2001	1997-01
	2002	1998-02
	2003	1999-03
	2004	2000-04
	2005	2001-05
	2006	2002-06
	2007	2003-07
	2008	2004-08
	2009-2010	2006-10
	2011	2007-11
	2012	2008-12
	2013	2009-13
	2014	2010-14
	2015	2011-15
	2016	2012-16
	2017	2013-17
	2018	2014-18
	2019	2015-19
Infant mortality rates .... by age and sex	1948	1936-47
	1951	1936-49
	1957	1948-56
	1961	1952-60
	1966	1956-65
	1967	1962-66
	1971-1973	Latest
	1974	1965-73
	1975-1979	Latest
	1980	1971-79
	1981-1984	Latest
	1985	1976-84
	1986-1991	Latest
	1992	1983-92
	1993-1995	Latest
	1996	1987-95
	1997-2019	Latest
Infant mortality rates	1971-1973	Latest
	1974	1965-73
by age and sex and urban/rural residence	1975-1979	Latest
	1980	1971-79
	1981-1984	Latest
	1985	1976-84
	1986-1991	Latest
	1992	1983-92
	1993-1995	Latest
	1996	1987-95
	1997-1999	Latest
Infant mortality rates.......... by urban/rural residence	1967	Latest
	1968	1964-68
	1969	1965-69
	1970	1966-70
	1971	1967-71
	1972	1968-72
	1973	1969-73
	1974	1965-74
	1975	1971-75
	1976	1972-76
	1977	1973-77
	1978	1974-78
	1979	1975-79
	1980	1971-80
	1981	1977-81
	1982	1978-82
	1983	1979-83
	1984	1980-84
	1985	1976-85
	1986	1982-86
	1987	1983-87
	1988	1984-88
	1989	1985-89
	1990	1986-90
	1991	1987-91
	1992	1983-92
	1993	1989-93
	1994	1990-94
	1995	1991-95
	1996	1987-96
	1997	1993-97
	1998	1994-98
	1999	1995-99
	2000	1996-00
	2001	1997-01
	2002	1998-02
	2003	1999-03
	2004	2000-04
	2005	2001-05
	2006	2002-06
	2007	2003-07
	2008	2004-08
	2009-2010	2006-10

Historical index

(See notes at end of index)

Subject-matter	Year of issue	Time coverage
	2011	2007-11
	2012	2008-12
	2013	2009-13
	2014	2010-14
	2015	2011-15
	2016	2012-16
	2017	2013-17
	2018	2014-18
	2019	2015-19
Intercensal rates of population increase	1948	1900-48
	1949-50	1900-50
	1951	1900-51
	1952	1850-1952
	1953	1850-1953
	1955	1850-1954
	1960	1900-61
	1962	1900-62
	1964	1955-64
	1970	1900-70
	1978HS[ii]	1948-78
	1997HS[iii]	1948-97
International migration	*see "Migration"*	

L

Subject-matter	Year of issue	Time coverage
Late foetal deaths	*see "Foetal deaths, late"*	
Life tables .... life expectancy at birth, by sex	1959-1973	Latest
	1974	2 latest
	1975-1978	Latest
	1978HS[ii]	1948-77
	1979	Latest
	1980	2 latest
	1981-1984	Latest
	1985	2 latest
	1986-1991	Latest
	1991PA[vii]	1950-90
	1992-1995	Latest
	1996	2 latest
	1997	Latest
	1997HS[iii]	1948-96
	1998	1995-98
	1999	1995-99
	2000	1995-00
	2001	1997-01
	2002	1998-02
	2003	1999-03
	2004	2000-04
	2005	2001-05
	2006	2002-06
	2007	2003-07
	2008	2004-08

Subject-matter	Year of issue	Time coverage
	2009-10	2006-10
	2011	2007-11
	2012	2008-12
	2013	2009-13
	2014	2010-14
	2015	2011-15
	2016	2012-16
	2017	2013-17
	2018	2014-18
	2019	2015-19
Life tables .... life expectancy at specified ages, by sex	1948	1891-1945
	1951	1891-1950
	1952	1891-1951[vi]
	1953	1891-1952
	1954	1891-1953[vi]
	1955-1956	Latest
	1957	1900-56
	1958-1960	Latest
	1961	1940-60
	1962-1964	Latest
	1966	2 latest
	1967	1900-66
	1968-1973	Latest
	1974	2 latest
	1975-1978	Latest
	1978HS[ii]	1948-77
	1979	Latest
	1980	2 latest
	1981-1984	Latest
	1985	2 latest
	1986-1991	Latest
	1991PA[vii]	1950-90
	1992-1995	Latest
	1996	2 latest
	1997	Latest
	1997HS[iii]	1948-96
	1998-2019	Latest
Life tables .... probabilities of dying at specified ages, by sex	1948	1891-1945
	1951	1891-1950
	1952	1891-1951[vi]
	1953	1891-1952
	1954	1891-1953[vi]
	1957	1900-56
	1961	1940-60
	1966	2 latest
	1974	2 latest
	1980	2 latest
	1985	2 latest
	1996	2 latest
	2008-2019	Latest

Historical index

(See notes at end of index)

Subject-matter	Year of issue	Time coverage
Life tables	1948	1891-1945
survivors at specified	1951	1891-1950
ages, by sex	1952	1891-1951[vi]
	1953	1891-1952
	1954	1891-1953[vi]
	1957	1900-56
	1961	1940-60
	1966	2 latest
	1974	2 latest
	1980	2 latest
	1985	2 latest
	1996	2 latest
Literacy	*see "Population by literacy"*	
Localities..............................	*see "Population in localities"*	

M

Subject-matter	Year of issue	Time coverage
Major civil divisions...........	*see "Population by major civil divisions"*	
Marriages.............................	1948	1932-47
	1949-50	1934-49
	1951	1935-50
	1952	1936-51
	1953	1950-52
	1954	1946-53
	1955	1946-54
	1956	1947-55
	1957	1948-56
	1958	1940-57
	1959	1949-58
	1960	1950-59
	1961	1952-61
	1962	1953-62
	1963	1954-63
	1964	1960-64
	1965	1956-65
	1966	1962-66
	1967	1963-67
	1968	1949-68
	1969	1965-69
	1970	1966-70
	1971	1967-71
	1972	1968-72
	1973	1969-73
	1974	1970-74
	1975	1971-75
	1976	1957-76
	1977	1973-77
	1978	1974-78
	1979	1975-79
	1980	1976-80
	1981	1977-81
	1982	1963-82
	1983	1979-83
	1984	1980-84
	1985	1981-85
	1986	1982-86
	1987	1983-87
	1988	1984-88
	1989	1985-89
	1990	1971-90
	1991	1987-91
	1992	1988-92
	1993	1989-93
	1994	1990-94
	1995	1991-95
	1996	1992-96
	1997	1993-97
	1998	1994-98
	1999	1995-99
	2000	1996-00
	2001	1997-01
	2002	1998-02
	2003	1999-03
	2004	2000-04
	2005	2001-05
	2006	2002-06
	2007	2003-07
	2008	2004-08
	2009-2010	2006-10
	2011	2007-11
	2012	2008-12
	2013	2009-13
	2014	2010-14
	2015	2011-15
	2016	2012-16
	2017	2013-17
	2018	2014-18
	2019	2015-19
Marriages.............................	1948	1936-47
by age of bride	1949-50	1936-49
	1958	1948-57
	1959-1967	Latest
	1968	1958-67
	1969-1975	Latest
	1976	1966-75
	1977-1981	Latest
	1982	1972-81
	1983-1986	Latest
	1987	1975-86
	1988-1989	Latest
	1990	1980-1989

Historical index

(See notes at end of index)

Subject-matter	Year of issue	Time coverage
	1991-1997	Latest
	1998	1993-97
	1999	1994-98
	2000	1995-99
	2001	1997-01
	2002	1998-02
	2003	1999-03
	2004	2000-04
	2005	2001-05
	2006-2019	Latest
Marriages............................	1958	1948-57
by age of bride and age of groom	1968	Latest
	1976	Latest
	1982	Latest
	1990	Latest
	2006-2019	Latest
Marriages............................	1958	1948-57
by age of bride and previous marital status	1968	Latest
	1976	Latest
	1982	Latest
	1990	Latest
Marriages............................	1948	1936-47
by age of groom	1949-50	1936-49
	1958	1948-57
	1959-1967	Latest
	1968	1958-67
	1969-1975	Latest
	1976	1966-75
	1977-1981	Latest
	1982	1972-81
	1983-1986	Latest
	1987	1975-86
	1988-1989	Latest
	1990	1980-1989
	1990-1997	Latest
	1998	1993-97
	1999	1994-98
	2000	1995-99
	2001	1997-01
	2002	1998-02
	2003	1999-03
	2004	2000-04
	2005	2001-05
	2006-2019	Latest
Marriages............................	1958	1948-57
by age of groom and previous marital status	1968	Latest
	1976	Latest
	1982	Latest
	1990	Latest

Subject-matter	Year of issue	Time coverage
Marriages............................	1968	1963-67
by month		
Marriages............................	1958	1946-57
by previous marital status of bride and age	1968	Latest
	1976	Latest
	1982	Latest
	1990	Latest
Marriages............................	1949-50	Latest
by previous marital status of bride and groom	1958	1948-57
	1968	1958-67
	1976	1966-75
	1982	1972-81
	1990	1980-89
Marriages............................	1958	1946-57
by previous marital status of groom and age	1968	Latest
	1976	Latest
	1982	Latest
	1990	Latest
Marriages............................	1968	Latest
by urban/rural residence	1969	1965-69
	1970	1966-70
	1971	1967-71
	1972	1968-72
	1973	1969-73
	1974	1970-74
	1975	1971-75
	1976	1957-76
	1977	1973-77
	1978	1974-78
	1979	1975-79
	1980	1976-80
	1981	1977-81
	1982	1963-82
	1983	1979-83
	1984	1980-84
	1985	1981-85
	1986	1982-86
	1987	1983-87
	1988	1984-88
	1989	1985-89
	1990	1971-90
	1991	1987-91
	1992	1988-92
	1993	1989-93
	1994	1990-94
	1995	1991-95
	1996	1992-96
	1997	1993-97
	1998	1994-98
	1999	1995-99

Historical index

(See notes at end of index)

Historical index

(See notes at end of index)

Subject-matter	Year of issue	Time coverage
	2007	1997-06
	2008	1999-08
	2009-2010	1999-08
	2011-2012	2001-10
	2013-2014	2003-12
	2015-2016	2005-14
	2017-2018	2007-16
	2019	2009-18
Maternal deaths................. by age	1951	Latest
	1952	Latest[vi]
	1957	Latest
	1961	Latest
	1967	Latest
	1974	Latest
	1980	Latest
	1985	Latest
Maternal mortality rates....	1951	1947-50
	1952	1947-51
	1953	Latest
	1954	1945-53
	1955-1956	Latest
	1957	1952-62
	1958-1960	Latest
	1961	1955-60
	1962-1965	Latest
	1966	1960-65
	1967-1973	Latest
	1974	1965-73
	1975	1966-74
	1976	1966-75
	1977	1967-76
	1978	1968-77
	1979	1969-78
	1980	1971-79
	1981	1972-80
	1982	1972-81
	1983	1973-82
	1984	1974-83
	1985	1975-84
	1986	1976-85
	1987	1977-86
	1988	1978-87
	1989	1979-88
	1990	1980-89
	1991	1981-90
	1992	1982-91
	1993	1983-92
	1994	1984-93
	1995	1985-94
	1996	1986-95
	1997	1987-96
	1998	1988-97
	1999	1989-98
	2000	1991-00
	2001	1991-00
	2002	1995-02
	2003	1995-02
	2004	1995-04
	2006	1997-06
	2007	1997-06
	2008	1999-08
	2009-2010	1999-08
	2011-2012	2001-10
	2013-2014	2003-12
	2015-2016	2005-14
	2017-2018	2007-16
	2019	2009-18
Migration (international) ... arrivals	1970	1963-69
	1972	1965-71
	1974	1967-73
	1976	1969-75
	1977	1967-76
	1985	1975-84
	1989	1979-88
	1996	1986-95
Migration (international) ... arrivals, by major categories	1949-50	1945-49
	1951	1946-50
	1952	1947-51
	1954	1948-53
	1957	1951-56
	1959	1953-58
	1962	1956-61
	1966	1960-65
	1968	1966-67
	1977	1967-76
	1985	1975-84
	1989	1979-88
	1996	1986-95
Migration (international) ... continental and inter-continental	1948	1936-47
	1977	1967-76
Migration (international) ... departures	1970	1963-69
	1972	1965-71
	1974	1967-73
	1976	1969-75
	1977	1967-76
	1985	1975-84
	1989	1979-88
	1996	1986-95
Migration (international) ...	1949-50	1945-49
	1951	1946-50

Historical index
(See notes at end of index)

Historical index
(See notes at end of index)

Subject-matter	Year of issue	Time coverage
Population	1948	Latest
by localities of 100 000+ inhabitants	1952	Latest
	1955	1945-54
	1960	1920-61
	1962	1955-62
	1963	1955-63[vi]
	1970	1950-70
	1971	1962-71
	1973	1965-73[vi]
	1979	1970-79[vi]
	1983	1974-83
	1988	1980-88[vi]
	1993	1985-93
	see also "Population of cities of 100 000+ inhabitants"	
Population	1948	Latest
by localities of 20 000+ inhabitants	1952	Latest
	1955	1945-54
	1960	1920-61
	1962	1955-62
	1963	1955-63[vi]
	1970	1950-70
	1971	1962-71
	1973	1965-73[vi]
	1979	1970-79[vi]
	1983	1974-83
	1988	1980-88[vi]
	1993	1985-93
Population	1948	Latest
by locality size-classes and sex	1952	Latest
	1955	1945-54
	1962	1955-62
	1963	1955-63[vi]
	1971	1962-71
	1973	1965-73[vi]
	1979	1970-79[vi]
	1983	1974-83
	1988	1980-88[vi]
	1993	1985-93
Population	1952	Latest
by major civil divisions	1955	1945-54
	1962	1955-62
	1963	1955-63[vi]
	1971	1962-71
	1973	1965-73[vi]
	1979	1970-79[vi]
	1983	1974-83
	1988	1980-88[vi]
	1993	1985-93

Subject-matter	Year of issue	Time coverage
Population	1948	Latest
by marital status, age and sex	1949/50	1926-48
	1955	1945-54
	1958	1945-57
	1962	1955-62[vi]
	1963	1955-63[vi]
	1965	1955-65
	1968	1955-67
	1971	1962-71
	1973	1965-73[vi]
	1976	1966-75
	1978HS[ii]	1948-77
	1982	1972-81
	1987	1975-86
	1990	1980-89
	1997HS[iii]	1948-96
	see also "Population, married" and "Population, single"	
Population	1991PA[vii]	Latest
for persons 60+ and urban/rural		
Population	1948	Latest
for persons 60+ and urban/rural (percentage distribution)		
Population	1956	1945-55
by religion and sex	1963	1955-63
	1964	1955-64[vi]
	1971	1962-71
	1973	1965-73[vi]
	1979	1970-79[vi]
	1983	1974-83
	1988	1980-88[vi]
	1993	1985-93
Population	1956	1945-55
by school attendance, age and sex	1963	1955-63
	1964	1955-64[vi]
	1971	1962-71
	1973	1965-73[vi]
	1979	1970-79
	1983	1974-83
	1988	1980-88[vi]
	1993	1985-93
Population	1948-1952	Latest
by sex (enumerated)	1953	1950-52
	1954-1959	Latest
	1960	1900-61

Historical index

(See notes at end of index)

Subject-matter	Year of issue	Time coverage
	1961	Latest
	1962	1900-62
	1963	1955-63
	1964	1955-64
	1965-1969	Latest
	1970	1950-70
	1971	1962-71
	1972	Latest
	1973	1965-73
	1974-1978	Latest
	1978HS[ii]	1948-78
	1979-1982	Latest
	1983	1974-83
	1984-1997	Latest
	1997HS[iii]	1948-97
	1998-2019	Latest
Population .... by sex (estimated)	1948	1945 & latest
	1949-50-1959	Latest
	1960	1940-60
	1961-1969	Latest
	1970	1950-70
	1971	1962-71
	1972	Latest
	1973	1965-73
	1974-1997	Latest
	1997HS[iii]	1948-97
	1998-1999	Latest
	2000	1991-00
	2001	1992-01
	2002	1993-02
	2003	1994-03
	2004	1995-04
	2005	1996-05
	2006	1997-06
	2007	1998-07
	2008	1999-08
	2009-2010	2001-10
	2011	2002-11
	2012	2003-12
	2013	2004-13
	2014	2005-14
	2015	2006-15
	2016	2007-16
	2017	2008-17
	2018	2009-18
	2019	2010-19
Population .... by single years of age and sex	1955	1945-54
	1962	1955-62
	1963	1955-63[vi]
	1971	1962-71
	1973	1965-73[vi]
	1979	1970-79[vi]

Subject-matter	Year of issue	Time coverage
	1983	1974-83
	1988	1980-88[vi]
	1993	1985-93
Population .... cities	*see "Population of cities"*	
Population .... civil division	*see "Population by major civil divisions"*	
Population .... density	*see "Density of population"*	
Population .... disabled	1991PA[vii]	Latest
Population .... economically active: - by age and sex	1945	1945-54
	1956	1945-55
	1964	1955-64
	1972	1962-72
- by age and sex and urban/rural residence	1973	1965-73[vi]
	1979	1970-79[vi]
	1984	1974-84
	1988	1980-88[vi]
	1994	1985-94
- by age and sex (per cent)	1949-50	1930-48
	1954	Latest
	1955	1945-54
	1956	1945-55
	1964	1955-64
	1972	1962-72
- by age and sex, and urban/rural residence (per cent)	1973	1965-73[vi]
	1979	1970-79[vi]
	1984	1974-84
	1988	1980-88[vi]
	1994	1985-94
- by industry, age and sex	1956	1945-55
	1964	1955-64
	1972	1962-72
- by industry, age, sex and urban/rural residence	1973	1965-74[vi]
	1979	1970-79[vi]
	1984	1974-84
	1988	1980-88[vi]
	1994	1985-94
- by industry, status in employment and sex	1948	Latest
	1949-50	Latest
	1955	1945-54
	1964	1955-64

Historical index

(See notes at end of index)

Subject-matter	Year of issue	Time coverage
	1972	1962-72
- by industry, status in employment and sex and urban/rural residence	1973	1965-73[vi]
	1979	1970-79[vi]
	1984	1974-84
	1988	1980-88[vi]
	1994	1985-94
- by living arrangements, age, sex and urban/rural residence	1987	1975-86
	1995	1985-95
- by occupation, age and sex	1956	1945-55
	1964	1955-64
	1972	1962-72
- by occupation, age, sex, and urban/rural residence	1973	1965-73[vi]
	1979	1970-79[vi]
	1984	1974-84
	1988	1980-88[vi]
	1994	1985-94
- by occupation, status in employment and sex	1956	1945-55
	1964	1955-64
	1972	1962-72
- by occupation, status in employment and sex and urban/rural residence	1973	1965-73[vi]
	1979	1970-7vi[vi]
	1984	1974-84
	1988	1980-88[vi]
	1994	1985-94
- by sex	1948	Latest
	1949-50	1926-48
	1955	1945-54
	1956	1945-55
	1960	1920-60
	1963	1955-63
	1964	1955-64
	1970	1950-70
	1972	1962-72
	1973	1965-73[vi]
	1979	1970-79[vi]
	1984	1974-84
	1994	1985-94
- by status in employment, age and sex	1956	1945-55
	1964	1955-64
	1972	1962-72
- by status in employment, age	1973	1965-73[vi]
	1979	1970-79[vi]

Subject-matter	Year of issue	Time coverage
and sex and urban/rural residence	1984	1974-84
	1988	1980-88[vi]
	1994	1985-94
- female, by marital status and age	1956	1945-55
	1964	1955-64
	1968	Latest
	1972	1962-72
- female, by marital status and age and urban/rural residence	1973	1965-73[vi]
	1979	1970-79[vi]
	1984	1974-84
	1988	1980-88[vi]
	1994	1985-94
- foreign-born by occupation, age and sex	1984	1974-84
	1988	1980-88[vi]
	1994	1985-94
- foreign-born, by occupation and sex	1977	Latest
	see also "Population, foreign-born by occupation, age and sex"	
- unemployed, by age and sex	1949-50	1946-49
Population .... economically inactive by sub-groups and sex	1956	1945-54
	1964	1955-64
	1972	1962-72
	1973	1965-73[vi]
	1979	1970-79[vi]
	1984	1974-84[vi]
	1988	1980-88[vi]
	1994	1985-94
Population .... elderly, by economic, characteristics and urban/rural residence	1991PA[vii]	1950-90
Population .... elderly, by socio-demographic characteristics and urban/rural residence	1991PA[vii]	1950-90
Population .... female, by age and duration of marriage	1968	Latest
Population	1949-50	Latest
	1954	1930-53
	1955	1945-54

Historical index

(See notes at end of index)

Historical index

(See notes at end of index)

Subject-matter	Year of issue	Time coverage
(continents) and regions)	1961	1950-60
	1962	1950-61
	1963	1958-62
		1960-62
	1964	1958-63
		1960-63
	1965	1958-64
		1960-64
	1966	1958-66
		1960-66
	1967	1960-67
		1963-67
	1968	1960-68
		1963-68
	1969	1960-69
		1963-69
	1970	1963-70
		1965-70
	1971	1963-71
		1965-71
	1972	1963-72
		1965-72
	1973	1965-73
		1970-73
	1974	1965-74
		1970-74
	1975	1965-75
		1970-75
	1976	1965-76
		1970-76
	1977	1965-77
		1970-77
	1978-1979	1970-75
	1980-1983	1975-80
	1984-1986	1980-85
	1987-1992	1985-90
	1993-1997	1990-95
	1998-2000	1995-00
	2001-2005	2000-05
	2006-2010	2005-10
	2011-2015	2010-15
	2016-2019	2015-20
Population .... homeless by age and sex	1991PA[vii]	Latest
Population .... illiteracy rates by sex	1948	Latest
	1955	1945-54
	1960	1920-60
	1963	1955-63[vi]
	1964	1955-64[vi]
	1970	1950-70

Subject-matter	Year of issue	Time coverage
Population .... illiteracy rates by sex and urban/rural residence	1973	1965-73
	1979	1970-79[vi]
	1983	1974-83
	1988	1980-88[vi]
	1993	1985-93
Population .... illiterate, by sex	1948	Latest
	1955	1945-54
	1960	1920-60
	1963	1955-63
	1964	1955-64
	1970	1950-70
Population .... illiterate, by sex and age	1948	Latest
	1955	1945-54
	1963	1955-63
	1964	1955-64[vi]
	1970	1950-70
Population .... illiterate, by sex and age and urban/rural residence	1973	1965-73
	1979	1970-79[vi]
	1983	1974-83
	1988	1980-88[vi]
	1993	1985-93
Population .... illiterate, by sex and urban/rural residence	1973	1965-73
	1979	1970-79[vi]
	1983	1974-83
	1988	1980-88[vi]
	1993	1985-93
Population .... in collective living quarters and homeless	1991PA[vii]	Latest
Population .... in households	*see "Population by type of household" and "Households"*	
Population .... in localities	*see "Population by localities" and "Population by locality size-classes"*	
Population .... increase rates	*see "Population growth rates"*	
Population .... literacy rates by sex	1955	1945-54
	see also "Population illiteracy rates"	
Population .... literacy rates by sex and age	1955	1945-54

Historical index

(See notes at end of index)

Subject-matter	Year of issue	Time coverage
	1960	1920-60
	1961	1941-61
	1962	1942-62
	1963	1943-63
	1964	1955-64
	1965	1946-65
	1966	1947-66
	1967	1958-67
	1968	1959-68
	1969	1960-69
	1970	1950-70
	1971	1962-71
	1972	1963-72
	1973	1964-73
	1974	1965-74
	1975	1966-75
	1976	1967-76
	1977	1968-77
	1978	1969-78
	1978HS[ii]	1948-78
	1979	1970-79
	1980	1971-80
	1981	1972-81
	1982	1973-82
	1983	1974-83
	1984	1975-84
	1985	1976-85
	1986	1977-86
	1987	1978-87
	1988	1979-88
	1989	1980-89
	1990	1981-90
	1991	1982-91
	1992	1983-92
	1993	1984-93
	1994	1985-94
	1995	1986-95
	1996	1987-96
	1997	1988-97
	1997HS[iii]	1948-97
	1998	1989-98
	1999	1990-99
	2000	1991-00
	2001	1992-01
	2002	1993-02
	2003	1994-03
	2004	1995-04
	2005	1996-05
	2006	1997-06
	2007	1998-07
	2008	1999-08
	2009-2010	2001-10
	2011	2002-11
	2012	2003-12

Subject-matter	Year of issue	Time coverage
	2013	2004-13
	2014	2005-14
	2015	2006-15
	2016	2007-16
	2017	2008-17
	2018	2009-18
	2019	2010-19
Population	1949-50	1920-49
- of major regions	1951	1950
	1952	1920-51
	1953	1920-52
	1954	1920-53
	1955	1920-54
	1956	1920-55
	1957	1920-56
	1958	1920-57
	1959	1920-58
	1960	1920-59
	1961	1920-60
	1962	1920-61
	1963	1930-62
	1964	1930-63
	1965	1930-65
	1966	1930-66
	1967	1930-67
	1968	1930-68
	1969	1930-69
	1970	1950-70
	1971	1950-71
	1972	1950-72
	1973	1950-73
	1974	1950-74
	1975	1950-75
	1976	1950-76
	1977	1950-77
	1978	1950-78
	1979	1950-79
	1980	1950-80
	1981	1950-81
	1982	1950-82
	1983	1950-83
	1984	1950-84
	1985	1950-85
	1986	1950-86
	1987	1950-87
	1988	1950-88
	1989	1950-89
	1990	1950-90
	1991	1950-91
	1992	1950-92
	1993	1950-93
	1994	1950-94
	1995	1950-95

Historical index

(See notes at end of index)

Subject-matter	Year of issue	Time coverage
	1996	1950-96
	1997	1950-97
	1998-1999	1950-00
	2000	1950-00
	2001	1950-01
	2002	1950-02
	2003	1950-03
	2004	1950-04
	2005	1950-05
	2006	1950-06
	2007	1950-07
	2008	1950-08
	2009-2010	1950-10
	2011	1960-11
	2012	1960-12
	2013	1960-13
	2014	1960-14
	2015	1960-15
	2016	1960-16
	2017	1960-17
	2018	1960-18
	2019	1960-19
Population	1949-50	1920-49
- of regions	1952	1920-51
	1953	1920-52
	1954	1920-53
	1955	1920-54
	1956	1920-55
	1957	1920-56
	1958	1920-57
	1959	1920-58
	1960	1920-59
	1961	1920-60
	1962	1920-61
	1963	1930-62
	1964	1930-63
	1965	1930-65
	1966	1930-66
	1967	1930-67
	1968	1930-68
	1969	1930-69
	1970	1950-70
	1971	1950-71
	1972	1950-72
	1973	1950-73
	1974	1950-74
	1975	1950-75
	1976	1950-76
	1977	1950-77
	1978	1950-78
	1979	1950-79
	1980	1950-80
	1981	1950-81

Subject-matter	Year of issue	Time coverage
	1982	1950-82
	1983	1950-83
	1984	1950-84
	1985	1950-85
	1986	1950-86
	1987	1950-87
	1988	1950-88
	1989	1950-89
	1990	1950-90
	1991	1950-91
	1992	1950-92
	1993	1950-93
	1994	1950-94
	1995	1950-95
	1996	1950-96
	1997	1950-97
	1998-1999	1950-00
	2000	1950-00
	2001	1950-01
	2002	1950-02
	2003	1950-03
	2004	1950-04
	2005	1950-05
	2006	1950-06
	2007	1950-07
	2008	1950-08
	2009-2010	1950-10
	2011	1960-11
	2012	1960-12
	2013	1960-13
	2014	1960-14
	2015	1960-15
	2016	1960-16
	2017	1960-17
	2018	1960-18
	2019	1960-19
Population	1949-50	1920-49
- of the world	1951	1950
	1952	1920-51
	1953	1920-52
	1954	1920-53
	1955	1920-54
	1956	1920-55
	1957	1920-56
	1958	1920-57
	1959	1920-58
	1960	1920-59
	1961	1920-60
	1962	1920-61
	1963	1930-62
	1964	1930-63
	1965	1930-65
	1966	1930-66

Historical index
(See notes at end of index)

Historical index
(See notes at end of index)

Subject-matter	Year of issue	Time coverage
	2014	2005-14
	2015	2006-15
	2016	2007-16
	2017	2008-17
	2018	2009-18
	2019	2010-19
- by age and sex (enumerated)	1963	1955-63
	1964	1955-64[vi]
	1967	Latest
	1970	1950-70
	1971	1962-71
	1972	Latest
	1973	1965-73
	1974-1978	Latest
	1978HS[ii]	1948-77
	1979-1996	Latest
	1979-1997	Latest
	1997HS[iii]	1948-96
	1998-2019	Latest
- by age and sex (estimated)	1963	Latest
	1967	Latest
	1970	1950-70
	1971-1997	Latest
	1997HS[iii]	1948-96
	1998-2019	Latest
- by country or area of birth and sex	1971	1962-71
	1973	1965-73[vi]
- by country or area of birth and sex and age	1977	Latest
- by citizenship and sex	1971	1962-71
	1973	1965-73[vi]
- by citizenship and sex and age	1977	Latest
	1983	1974-83
	1989	1980-88
- by ethnic composition and sex	1971	Latest
	1973	1965-73[vi]
	1979	1970-79[vi]
	1983	1974-83
	1988	1980-88[vi]
	1993	1985-93
- by households, number and size	1968	Latest
	1971	1962-71
	1973	1965-73[vi]
	1976	Latest
	1982	Latest

Subject-matter	Year of issue	Time coverage
	1987	1975-86
	1990	1980-89
	1995	1985-95
	see also "Households"	
- by language and sex	1971	1962-71
	1973	1965-73[vi]
	1979	1970-79[vi]
	1983	1974-83
	1988	1980-88[vi]
	1993	1985-93
- by level of education, age and sex	1971	1962-71
	1973	1965-73[vi]
	1979	1970-79[vi]
	1983	1974-83
	1988	1980-88[vi]
	1993	1985-93
- by literacy, age and sex	1971	1962-71
	1973	1965-73[vi]
	1979	1970-79[vi]
	1983	1974-83
	1988	1980-88[vi]
	1993	1985-93
- by major civil divisions	1971	1962-71
	1973	1965-73[vi]
	1979	1970-79[vi]
	1983	1974-83
	1988	1980-88[vi]
	1993	1985-93
- by marital status, age and sex	1971	1962-71
	1973	1965-73[vi]
- by religion and sex	1971	1962-71
	1973	1965-73[vi]
	1979	1970-79[vi]
	1983	1974-83
	1988	1980-88[vi]
	1993	1985-93
- by school attendance, age and sex	1971	1962-71
	1973	1965-73[vi]
	1979	1970-79[vi]
	1983	1974-83
	1988	1980-88[vi]
	1993	1985-93
- by sex (numbers)	1948	Latest
	1952	1900-51
	1955	1945-54

Subject-matter	Year of issue	Time coverage
	1960	1920-60
	1962	1955-62
	1963	1955-63
	1964	1955-64[vi]
	1967	Latest
	1970	1950-70
	1971	1962-71
	1972	Latest
	1973	1965-73
	1974	1966-74
	1975	1967-75
	1976	1967-76
	1977	1968-77
	1978	1969-78
	1979	1970-79
	1980	1971-80
	1981	1972-81
	1982	1973-82
	1983	1974-83
	1984	1975-84
	1985	1976-85
	1986	1977-86
	1987	1978-87
	1988	1979-88
	1989	1980-89
	1990	1981-90
	1991	1982-91
	1992	1983-92
	1993	1984-93
	1994	1985-94
	1995	1986-95
	1996	1987-96
	1997	1988-97
	1998	1989-98
	1999	1990-99
	2000	1991-00
	2001	1992-01
	2002	1993-02
	2003	1994-03
	2004	1995-04
	2005	1996-05
	2006	1997-06
	2007	1998-07
	2008	1999-08
	2009-2010	2001-10
	2011	2002-11
	2012	2003-12
	2013	2004-13
	2014	2005-14
	2015	2006-15
	2016	2007-16
	2017	2008-17
	2018	2009-18
	2019	2010-19

Subject-matter	Year of issue	Time coverage
- by sex (percent)	1948	Latest
	1952	1900-51
	1955	1945-54
	1960	1920-60
	1962	1955-62
	1970	1950-70
	1971	1962-71
	1973	1965-73
	1974	1966-74
	1975	1967-75
	1976	1967-76
	1977	1968-77
	1978	1969-78
	1979	1970-79
	1980	1971-80
	1981	1972-81
	1982	1973-82
	1983	1974-83
	1984	1975-84
	1985	1976-85
	1986	1977-86
	1987	1978-87
	1988	1979-88
	1989	1980-89
	1990	1981-90
	1991	1982-91
	1992	1983-92
	1993	1984-93
	1994	1985-94
	1995	1986-95
	1996	1987-96
	1997	1988-97
	1998	1989-98
	1999	1990-99
	2000	1991-00
	2001	1992-01
	2002	1993-02
	2003	1994-03
	2004	1995-04
	2005	1996-05
	2006	1997-06
	2007	1998-07
	2008	1999-08
	2009-2010	2001-10
	2011	2002-11
	2012	2003-12
	2013	2004-13
	2014	2005-14
	2015	2006-15
	2016	2007-16
	2017	2008-17
	2018	2009-18
	2019	2010-19

Subject-matter	Year of issue	Time coverage
- by single years of age and sex	1971	1962-71
	1973	1965-73[vi]
	1979	1970-79[vi]
	1983	1974-83
	1993	1985-93
- female, by number of children born alive and age	1971	1962-71
	1973	1965-73[vi]
	1975	1965-74
	1978HS[ii]	1948-77
	1981	1972-80
	1986	1977-85
	1997HS[iii]	1948-96
- female, by number of children living and age	1971	1962-71
	1973	1965-73[vi]
	1975	1965-74
	1978HS[ii]	1948-77
	1981	1972-80
	1986	1977-85
	1997HS[iii]	1948-96
Post-neonatal deaths .... by sex	1948	1936-47
	1951	1936-50
	1957	1948-56
	1961	1952-60
	1963-1965	Latest
	1966	1961-65
	1967	1962-66
	1968-1973	Latest
	1974	1965-73
	1975-1979	Latest
	1980	1971-79
	1981-1984	Latest
	1985	1976-84
	1986-1991	Latest
	1992	1983-92
	1993-1995	Latest
	1996	1987-95
	1997	Latest
	1997HS[ii]	1948-96
	1998-2019	Latest
Post-neonatal deaths .... by urban/rural residence	1971-1973	Latest
	1974	1965-73
	1975-1979	Latest
	1980	1971-79
	1981-1984	Latest
	1985	1976-84
	1986-1991	Latest
	1992	1983-92
	1993-1995	Latest
	1996	1987-95

Subject-matter	Year of issue	Time coverage
	1997	Latest
	1997HS[ii]	1948-96
	1998-1999	Latest
Post-neonatal mortality rates .... by sex	1948	1936-47
	1951	1936-50
	1957	1948-56
	1961	1952-60
	1966	1956-65
	1967	1962-66
	1968-1973	Latest
	1974	1965-73
	1975-1979	Latest
	1980	1971-79
	1981-1984	Latest
	1985	1976-84
	1986-1991	Latest
	1992	1983-92
	1993-1995	Latest
	1996	1987-95
	1997	Latest
	1997HS[ii]	1948-96
	1998-2019	Latest
Post-neonatal mortality rates .... by urban/rural residence	1971-1973	Latest
	1974	1965-73
	1975-1979	Latest
	1980	1971-79
	1981-1984	Latest
	1985	1976-84
	1986-1991	Latest
	1992	1983-92
	1993-1995	Latest
	1996	1987-95
	1997	Latest
	1997HS[ii]	1948-96
	1998-1999	Latest

Historical index

(See notes at end of index)

Subject-matter	Year of issue	Time coverage
R		
Rates	*see "Annulments", "Births", "Deaths", "Divorces", "Fertility", "Illiteracy", "Infant Mortality", "Intercensal", "Life Tables", "Literacy", "Marriages", "Maternal mortality", "Natural increase", "Neo natal mortality", "Population growth", "Post neo natal mortality" and "Reproduction"*	
Ratios	*see "Births", "Child-woman", "Fertility", "Foetal deaths" and "Perinatal mortality"*	
Refugees, by country or area of destination repatriated by the International Refugee Organization	1952	1947-51
Refugees, by country or area of destination resettled by the International Refugee Organization	1952	1947-51
Religion	*see "Population by religion"*	
Reproduction rates, gross and net	1948	1920-47
	1949-50	1900-48
	1954	1920-53
	1965	1930-64
	1969	1963-68
	1975	1966-74
	1978HS[ii]	1948-77
	1981	1962-80
	1986	1967-85
	1997HS[iii]	1948-96
	1999CD[iv]	1980-99
Rural/urban births	*see "Births"*	
Rural/urban population	*see "Population, urban/rural residence"*	

Subject-matter	Year of issue	Time coverage
S		
Sex	*see appropriate subject entry, e.g., "Births", "Death rates", "Migration", "Population", etc.*	
Size of (living) family	1949-50	Latest
female population by age	1954	1930-53
	1955	1945-54
	1959	1949-58
	1963	1955-63
	1965	1955-65
	1968	1955-67
	1969	Latest
	1971	1962-71
	1973	1965-73[vi]
	1975	1965-74
	1978HS[ii]	1948-77
	1981	1972-80
	1986	1977-85
	1997HS[iii]	1948-96
	see also "Children"	
Special text	*see separate listing in Appendix to this Index*	
Special topic	*see "Topic of each Demographic Yearbook"*	
Still births	*see "Foetal deaths, late"*	
Surface area	1949-50-1999	Latest
of continents	2000	2000
	2001	2001
	2002	2002
	2003	2003
	2004	2004
	2005	2005
	2006	2006
	2007	2007
	2008	2008
	2009-2010	2010
	2011	2011
	2012	2012
	2013	2013
	2014	2014
	2015	2015
	2016	2016
	2017	2017
	2018	2018
	2019	2019

Historical index

(See notes at end of index)

Subject-matter	Year of issue	Time coverage
	1969	1925-69
	1975	1956-75
	1981	1962-81
	1986	1967-86
	1992	1983-92
	1999CD[iv]	1980-99
- Nuptiality	*see Topic "Marriage and Divorce" above*	
- Population Ageing and the Situation of Elderly Persons	1991PA[vii]	1950-90
- Population Census:		
· Economic characteristics	1956	1945-55
	1964	1955-64
	1972	1962-72
	1973	1965-73[vi]
	1979	1970-79[vi]
	1984	1974-84
	1988	1980-88[vi]
	1994	1985-94
	2014[viii]	1995-2014
· Educational characteristics	1955	1945-54
	1956	1945-55
	1963	1955-63
	1964	1955-64[vi]
	1971	1962-71
	1973	1965-73[vi]
	1979	1970-79[vi]
	1983	1974-83
	1988	1980-88[vi]
	1993	1985-93
· Ethnic characteristics	1956	1945-55
	1963	1955-63
	1964	1955-64[vi]
	1971	1962-71
	1973	1965-73[vi]
	1979	1970-79[vi]
	1983	1974-83
	1988	1980-88[vi]
	1993	1985-93
· Fertility characteristics	1940/50	1900-50
	1954	1900-53
	1955	1945-54
	1959	1935-59
	1963	1955-63
	1965	1955-65
	1969	Latest
	1971	1962-71

Subject-matter	Year of issue	Time coverage
	1973	1965-73[vi]
	1975	1965-75
	1981	1972-81
	1986	1977-86
	1992	1983-92
· Geographic characteristics	1952	1900-51
	1955	1945-54
	1962	1955-62
	1964	1955-64[vi]
	1971	1962-71
	1973	1965-73[vi]
	1979	1970-79[vi]
	1983	1974-83
	1988	1980-88[vi]
	1993	1985-93
· Household characteristics	1955	1945-54
	1962	1955-62
	1963	1955-63[vi]
	1971	1962-71
	1973	1965-73[vi]
	1976	1966-75
	1983	1974-83
	1987	1975-86
	1995	1985-95
	2013[viii]	1995-2013
· Personal characteristics	1955	1945-54
	1962	1955-62
	1971	1962-71
	1973	1965-73[vi]
	1979	1970-79[vi]
	1983	1974-83
	1988	1980-88[vi]
	1993	1985-93
- Population trends	1960	1920-60
	1970	1950-70

APPENDIX

Special text of each Demographic Yearbook

Divorce:

'Uses of Marriage and Divorce Statistics', 1958.

Marriage:

'Uses of Marriage and Divorce Statistics', 1958.

Households:

'Concepts and definitions of households, householder and institutional population', 1987.

Migration:

'Statistics of International Migration', 1977.

Mortality:

'Recent Mortality Trends', 1951.
'Development of Statistics of Causes of Death', 1951.
'Factors in Declining Mortality', 1957.
'Notes on Methods of Evaluating the Reliability of Conventional Mortality Statistics', 1961.
'Recent Trends of Mortality', 1966.
'Mortality Trends among Elderly Persons', 1991PA[vii].

Natality:

'Graphic Presentation of Trends in Fertility', 1959.
'Recent Trends in Birth Rates', 1965.
'Recent Changes in World Fertility', 1969.

Population

'World Population Trends, 1920-1949', 1949-50.
'Urban Trends and Characteristics', 1952.
'Background to the1950 Censuses of Population', 1955.
'The World Demographic Situation', 1956.
'How Well Do We Know the Present Size and Trend of the World's Population?', 1960.
'Notes on Availability of National Population Census Data and Methods of Estimating their Reliability', 1962.
'Availability and Adequacy of Selected Data Obtained from Population Censuses Taken 1955-1963', 1963.
'Availability of Selected Population Census Statistics: 1955-1964', 1964.
'Statistical Concepts and Definitions of Urban and Rural Population', 1967.
'Statistical Concepts and Definitions of Household', 1968.
'How Well Do We Know the Present Size and Trend of the World's Population?', 1970.
'United Nations Recommendations on Topics to be Investigated in a Population Census Compared with Country Practice in National Censuses taken 1965-1971', 1971.
'Statistical Definitions of Urban Population and their Use in Applied Demography', 1972.
'Dates of National Population and Housing Census carried out during the decade1965-1974', 1974.
'Dates of National Population and/or Housing Censuses taken or anticipated during the decade 1975-1984', 1979.
'Dates of National Population and/or Housing Censuses taken during the decade1965-1974 and taken or anticipated during the decade 1975-1984', 1983.
'Dates of National Population and/or Housing Censuses taken during the decade1975-1984 and taken or anticipated during the decade 1985-1994', 1988 and 1993.
'Statistics Concerning the Economically Active Population: An Overview', 1984.
'Disability', 1991PA[vii].
'Population Ageing', 1991PA[vii].
'Special Needs for the Study of Population Ageing and Elderly Persons', 1991PA[vii].

Historical index

(See notes at end of index)

GENERAL NOTES

This cumulative index covers the contents of each of the 70 issues of the Demographic Yearbook. 'Year of issue' stands for the particular issue in which the indicated subject-matter appears. Unless otherwise specified, 'Time coverage' designates the years for which annual statistics are shown in the Demographic Yearbook referred to in 'Year of issue' column. 'Latest' or '2 latest' indicates that data are for latest available year(s) only.

[i] Only titles not available for preceding bibliography.
[ii] Historical Supplement to the 30th DYB published in a separate volume in year 1979.
[iii] Historical Supplement to the 49th DYB published in a separate volume (CD-ROM) in year 2000.
[iv] Supplement to the 51st DYB focusing on natality published in a separate volume (CD-ROM) in year 2002.
[v] Five year average rates.
[vi] Only data not available for preceding issue.
[vii] Population ageing published in separate volume.
[viii] Tables published online.

Sujet	Année de l'édition	Période considérée
	1953	1920-39 [vi]
		1940-52
	1954	1920-39 [vi]
		1946-53
	1955	1920-34 [vi]
		1946-54
	1956	1947-55
	1957	1930-56
	1958	1948-57
	1959	1949-58
	1960	1950-59
	1961	1945-59 [vi]
		1952-61
	1962	1945-54 [vi]
		1952-62
	1963	1945-59 [vi]
		1954-63
	1964	1960-64
	1965	1961-65
	1966	1920-64 [vi]
		1951-66
	1967	1963-67
	1968	1964-68
	1969	1965-69
	1970	1966-70
	1971	1967-71
	1972	1968-72
	1973	1969-73
	1974	1965-74
	1975	1971-75
	1976	1972-76
	1977	1973-77
	1978	1974-78
	1978SR [i]	1948-78
	1979	1975-79
	1980	1971-80
	1981	1977-81
	1982	1978-82
	1983	1979-83
	1984	1980-84
	1985	1976-85
	1986	1982-86
	1987	1983-87
	1988	1984-88
	1989	1985-89
	1990	1986-90
	1991	1987-91
	1992	1983-92
	1993	1989-93
	1994	1990-94
	1995	1991-95
	1996	1987-96

Sujet	Année de l'édition	Période considérée
	1997	1993-97
	1997SR [ii]	1948-97
	1998	1994-98
	1999	1995-99
	2000	1996-00
	2001	1997-01
	2002	1998-02
	2003	1999-03
	2004	2000-04
	2005	2001-05
	2006	2002-06
	2007	2003-07
	2008	2004-08
	2009-2010	2006-10
	2011	2007-11
	2012	2008-12
	2013	2009-13
	2014	2010-14
	2015	2011-15
	2016	2012-16
	2017	2013-17
	2018	2014-18
	2019	2015-19
Décès, taux de .... d'enfants de moins d'un an	*voir: Mortalités infantile*	
Décès, taux de .... estimatifs, pour les continents	1949-50	1947
	1956-1977	Dernière
	1978-1979	1970-75
	1980-1983	1975-80
	1984-1986	1980-85
	1987-1992	1985-90
	1993-1997	1990-95
	1998-2000	1995-00
	2001-2005	2000-05
	2006-2010	2005-10
	2011-2015	2010-15
	2016-2019	2015-20
Décès, taux de .... estimatifs, pour les grandes régions (continentales)	1964-1977	Dernière
	1978-1979	1970-75
	1980-1983	1975-80
	1984-1986	1980-85
	1987-1992	1985-90
	1993-1997	1990-95
	1998-2000	1995-00
	2001-2005	2000-05
	2006-2010	2005-10
	2011-2015	2010-15
	2016-2019	2015-20

Sujet	Année de l'édition	Période considérée
Décès, taux de.....................	1949-50	1947
estimatifs, pour les régions	1956-1977	Dernière
	1978-1979	1970-75
	1980-1983	1975-80
	1984-1986	1980-85
	1987-1992	1985-90
	1993-1997	1990-95
	1998-2000	1995-00
	2001-2005	2000-05
	2006-2010	2005-10
	2011-2015	2010-15
	2016-2019	2015-20
Décès, taux de.....................	1949-50	1947
estimatifs, pour l'ensemble du monde	1956-1977	Dernière
	1978-1979	1970-75
	1980-1983	1975-80
	1984-1986	1980-85
	1987-1992	1985-90
	1993-1997	1990-95
	1998-2000	1995-00
	2001-2005	2000-05
	2006-2010	2005-10
	2011-2015	2010-15
	2016-2019	2015-20
Décès, taux de.....................	1948	1935-47
selon l'âge et le sexe	1949-50	1936-49
	1951	1936-50
	1952	1936-51
	1953	1940-52
	1954	1946-53
	1955-1956	Dernière
	1957	1948-56
	1961	1952-60
	1966	1950-65
	1967	Dernière
	1972	Dernière
	1974	1965-73
	1975-1978	Dernière
	1978SR [i]	1948-77
	1979	Dernière
	1980	1971-79
	1981-1984	Dernière
	1985	1976-84
	1986-1991	Dernière
	1991 VP [v]	1950-90
	1992	1983-92
	1993-1995	Dernière
	1996	1987-95
	1997	Dernière
	1997SR [ii]	1948-96
	1998-2019	Dernière
Décès, taux de.....................	1967	Dernière
selon l'âge, le sexe et la résidence (urbaine/rurale)	1972	Dernière
	1974	1965-73
	1975-1978	Dernière
	1979	Dernière
	1980	1971-79
	1981-1984	Dernière
	1985	1976-84
	1986-1991	Dernière
	1991 VP [v]	1950-90
	1992	1983-92
	1993-1995	Dernière
	1996	1987-95
	1997	Dernière
	1997SR [ii]	1948-96
	1998-2006	Dernière
Décès, taux de.....................	1951	1947-49
selon la cause	1952	1947-51
	1953	1947-52
	1954	1945-53
	1955-1956	Dernière
	1957	1952-56
	1958-1960	Dernière
	1961	1955-60
	1962-1965	Dernière
	1966	1960-65
	1967-1973	Dernière
	1974	1965-73
	1975-1979	Dernière
	1980	1971-79 [vi]
	1981-1984	Dernière
	1985	1976-84
	1986-1995	Dernière
	1996	1987-95
	1997-2000	Dernière
	2002	1985-02
	2004	1995-04
	2006	2002-06
	2008	2004-08
	2011	2006-10
	2013	2008-12
	2015	2010-14
	2017	2012-16
	2019	2014-18
Décès, taux de.....................	1957	Dernière
selon la cause, l'âge et le sexe	1961	Dernière
	1991 VP [v]	1960-90

Sujet	Année de l'édition	Période considérée
Décès, taux de...................... selon la cause et le sexe	1967	Dernière
	1974	Dernière
	1980	Dernière
	1985	Dernière
	1991 VP [v]	1960-90
	1996	Dernière
	2006	2002-06
	2008	2004-08
	2011	2006-10
	2013	2008-12
	2015	2010-14
	2017	2012-16
	2019	2014-18
Décès, taux de...................... selon l'état matrimonial, l'âge et le sexe	1961	Dernière
	1967	Dernière
	1974	Dernière
	1980	Dernière
	1985	Dernière
	1996	Dernière
	2003	Dernière
Décès, taux de...................... selon la profession, l'âge et le sexe	1957	Dernière
Décès, taux de...................... selon la profession et l'âge (sexe masculin)	1961	Dernière
	1967	Dernière
Décès, taux de...................... selon la résidence (urbaine/rurale)	1967	Dernière
	1968	1964-68
	1969	1965-69
	1970	1966-70
	1971	1967-71
	1972	1968-72
	1973	1969-73
	1974	1965-74
	1975	1971-75
	1976	1972-76
	1977	1973-77
	1978	1974-78
	1979	1975-79
	1980	1971-80
	1981	1977-81
	1982	1978-82
	1983	1979-83
	1984	1980-84
	1985	1976-85
	1986	1982-86
	1987	1983-87
	1988	1984-88
	1989	1985-89
	1990	1986-90
	1991	1987-91
	1992	1983-92
	1993	1989-93
	1994	1990-94
	1995	1991-95
	1996	1987-96
	1997	1993-97
	1998	1994-98
	1999	1995-99
	2000	1996-00
	2001	1997-01
	2002	1998-02
	2003	1999-03
	2004	2000-04
	2005	2001-05
	2006	2002-06
	2007	2003-07
	2008	2004-08
	2009-2010	2006-10
	2011	2007-11
	2012	2008-12
	2013	2009-13
	2014	2010-14
	2015	2011-15
	2016	2012-16
	2017	2013-17
	2018	2014-18
	2019	2015-19
Densité de population .... des continents	1949-50	1920-49
	1951-1999	Dernière
	2001	2001
	2002	2002
	2003	2003
	2004	2004
	2005	2005
	2006	2006
	2007	2007
	2008	2008
	2009-2010	2010
	2011	2011
	2012	2012
	2013	2013
	2014	2014
	2015	2015
	2016	2016
	2017	2017

Sujet	Année de l'édition	Période considérée
Enfants, nombre	1971	1962-71
nés vivants, selon l'âge	1973	1965-73 [iii]
de la mère et la	1975	1965-74
résidence	1981	1972-80
(urbaine/rurale)	1986	1977-85
	1997SR [ii]	1948-96
Espérance de vie	*voir: Mortalité, tables de*	
Etat matrimonial	*voir la rubrique appropriée par sujet, p.ex., Décès, Population, etc.*	

F

Sujet	Année de l'édition	Période considérée
Fécondité, indice synthétique de	1986	1967-1985
	1987-1997	Dernière
	1997SR [ii]	1948-96
	1998	1995-98
	1999	1996-99
	1999CD [vii]	1980-99
	2000	1995-00
	2001	1997-01
	2002	1998-02
	2003	1999-03
	2004	2000-04
	2005	2001-05
	2006	2002-06
	2007	2003-07
	2008	2004-08
	2009-2010	2006-10
	2011	2007-11
	2012	2008-12
	2013	2009-13
	2014	2010-14
	2015	2011-15
	2016	2012-16
	2017	2013-17
	2018	2014-18
	2019	2015-19
Fécondité proportionnelle .	1949-50	1900-50
	1954	1900-52
	1955	1945-54
	1959	1935-59
	1963	1955-63
	1965	1955-65
	1969	Dernière
	1975	1966-74
	1978SR [i]	1948-77
	1981	1962-80
	1986	1967-85
	1997SR [ii]	1948-96
	1999CD [vii]	1980-99
Fécondité, taux global de...	1948	1936-47
	1949-50	1936-49
	1951	1936-50
	1952	1936-50
	1953	1936-52
	1954	1936-53
	1955-1956	Dernière
	1959	1949-58
	1960-1964	Dernière
	1965	1955-64
	1966-1974	Dernière
	1975	1966-74
	1976-1978	Dernière
	1978SR [i]	1948-77
	1979-1980	Dernière
	1981	1962-80
	1982-1985	Dernière
	1986	1977-85
	1987-1991	Dernière
	1992	1983-92
	1993-1997	Dernière
	1997SR [ii]	1948-96
	1998-2019	Dernière

I

Sujet	Année de l'édition	Période considérée
Illégitime	1961	1952-60
morts fœtales tardives	1965	5-Dernières
	1969	1963-68
	1975	1966-74
	1981	1972-80
	1986	1977-85
	voir également: morts fœtales tardives	
Illégitime	1961	1952-60
morts fœtales tardives,	1965	5-Dernières
rapports de	1969	1963-68
	1975	1966-74
	1981	1972-80
	1986	1977-85
Illégitime	1959	1949-58
naissances	1965	1955-64
	1969	1963-68
	1975	1966-74
	1981	1972-80
	1986	1977-85
	1999CD [vii]	1990-98
	voir également: Naissances	

Index historique

(Voir notes à la fin de l'index)

Sujet	Année de l'édition	Période considérée
population dans chaque catégorie de	1963	1955-63 [iii]
	1968	Dernière
	1971	1962-71
	1973	1965-73 [iii]
	1976	Dernière
	1982	Dernière
	1987	1975-86
	1990	1980-89
	1995	1985-95
Ménages .... répartition des chefs, âge, sexe et résidence urbaine/rurale	1987	1975-86
	1995	1985-95
Ménages .... selon la dimension et la résidence (urbaine/rurale	1955	1945-54
	1962	1955-62
	1963	1955-63 [iii]
	1971	1962-71
	1973	1965-73 [iii]
	1976	Dernière
	1982	Dernière
	1987	1975-86
	1990	1980-89
	1995	1985-95
Ménages .... selon le sexe et personnes 60+	1991 VP [v]	Dernière
Ménages .... selon l'âge et le sexe du chef de ménage, la dimension et la résidence urbaine/rurale	1987	1976-86
	1995	1985-95
Ménages .... selon la situation matrimoniale et la résidence urbaine/rurale	1987	1975-86
	1995	1985-95
Ménages .... selon le type de famille et la résidence urbaine/rurale	1987	1975-86
	1995	1985-95
Ménages .... selon le type et la résidence urbaine/rurale	1987	1975-86
	1995	1985-95

Sujet	Année de l'édition	Période considérée
Migration internationale	1948	1936-47
continentale et intercontinentale	1977	1967-76
Migration internationale	1948	1945-47
émigrants (à long terme) selon l'âge et le sexe	1949-50	1946-48
	1951	1948-50
	1952	1949-51
	1954	1950-53
	1957	1953-56
	1959	1955-58
	1962	1958-61
	1966	1960-65
	1970	1962-69
	1977	1967-76
	1989	1975-88
Migration internationale	1948	1945-47
	1949-50	1945-48
	1951	1948-50
	1952	1949-51
	1954	1950-53
	1957	1953-56
	1959	1956-58
	1977	1958-76
	1989	1975-88
Migration internationale	1970	1963-69
entrées	1972	1965-71
	1974	1967-73
	1976	1969-75
	1977	1967-76
	1985	1975-84
	1989	1979-88
	1996	1986-95
Migration internationale	1949-50	1945-49
entrées, par catégories principales	1951	1946-50
	1952	1947-51
	1954	1948-53
	1957	1951-56
	1959	1953-58
	1962	1956-61
	1966	1960-65
	1968	1966-67
	1977	1967-76
	1985	1975-84
	1989	1979-88
	1996	1986-95
Migration internationale	1948	1945-47
	1949-50	1946-48
	1951	1948-50

Sujet	Année de l'édition	Période considérée
Mortalité fœtale tardive, rapports de .... selon la période de gestation	1957	1950-56
	1959	1949-58
	1961	1952-60
	1965	5-Dernières
	1966	1956-65
	1967-1968	Dernière
	1969	1963-68
	1974	1965-73
	1975	1966-74
	1980	1971-79
	1981	1972-80
	1985	1976-84
	1986	1977-85
	1996	1987-95
Mortalité fœtale tardive, rapports de .... selon la résidence (urbaine/rurale)	1971	1966-70
	1972	1967-71
	1973	1968-72
	1974	1965-73
	1975	1966-74
	1976	1971-75
	1977	1972-76
	1978	1973-77
	1979	1974-78
	1980	1971-79
	1981	1972-80
	1982	1977-81
	1983	1978-82
	1984	1979-83
	1985	1975-84
	1986	1977-85
	1987	1982-86
	1988	1983-87
	1989	1984-88
	1990	1985-89
	1991	1986-90
	1992	1987-91
	1993	1988-92
	1994	1989-93
	1995	1990-94
	1996	1987-95
	1997	1992-96
	1998	1993-97
	1999	1994-98
	1999CD [vii]	1990-98
	2000	1995-99
	2001	1997-01
	2002	1998-02
	2003	1999-03
	2004	2000-04
	2005	2001-05
	2006	2002-06
	2007	2003-07
	2008	2004-08
	2009-2010	2006-10
	2011	2007-11
	2012	2008-12
	2013	2009-13
	2014	2010-14
	2015	2011-15
	2016	2012-16
	2017	2013-17
	2018	2014-18
	2019	2015-19
Mortalité infantile (nombres)	1948	1932-47
	1949-50	1934-49
	1951	1935-50
	1952	1936-51
	1953	1950-52
	1954	1946-53
	1955	1946-54
	1956	1947-55
	1957	1948-56
	1958	1948-57
	1959	1949-58
	1960	1950-59
	1961	1952-61
	1962	1953-62
	1963	1954-63
	1964	1960-64
	1965	1961-65
	1966	1947-66
	1967	1963-67
	1968	1964-68
	1969	1965-69
	1970	1966-70
	1971	1967-71
	1972	1968-72
	1973	1969-73
	1974	1965-74
	1975	1971-75
	1976	1972-76
	1977	1973-77
	1978	1974-78
	1978SR [i]	1948-78
	1979	1975-79
	1980	1971-80
	1981	1977-81
	1982	1978-82
	1983	1979-83
	1984	1980-84
	1985	1976-85

Sujet	Année de l'édition	Période considérée
	1957	1948-56
	1961	1952-60
	1966	1956-65
	1967	1962-66
	1971-1973	Dernière
	1974	1965-73
	1975-1979	Dernière
	1980	1971-79
	1981-1984	Dernière
	1985	1976-84
	1986-1991	Dernière
	1992	1983-92
	1993-1995	Dernière
	1996	1987-95
	1997-2019	Dernière
Mortalité infantile, taux de selon l'âge et le sexe et la résidence (urbaine/rurale)	1971-1973	Dernière
	1974	1965-73
	1975-1979	Dernière
	1980	1971-79
	1981-1984	Dernière
	1985	1976-84
	1986-1991	Dernière
	1992	1983-92
	1993-1995	Dernière
	1996	1987-95
	1997-1999	Dernière
Mortalité infantile, taux de selon la résidence (urbaine/rurale)	1967	Dernière
	1968	1964-68
	1969	1965-69
	1970	1966-70
	1971	1967-71
	1972	1968-72
	1973	1969-73
	1974	1965-74
	1975	1971-75
	1976	1972-76
	1977	1973-77
	1978	1974-78
	1979	1975-79
	1980	1971-80
	1981	1977-81
	1982	1978-82
	1983	1979-83
	1984	1980-84
	1985	1976-85
	1986	1982-86
	1987	1983-87
	1988	1984-88
	1989	1985-89
	1990	1986-90
	1991	1987-91

Sujet	Année de l'édition	Période considérée
	1992	1983-92
	1993	1989-93
	1994	1990-94
	1995	1991-95
	1996	1987-96
	1997	1993-97
	1998	1994-98
	1999	1995-99
	2000	1996-00
	2001	1997-01
	2002	1998-02
	2003	1999-03
	2004	2000-04
	2005	2001-05
	2006	2002-06
	2007	2003-07
	2008	2004-08
	2009-2010	2006-10
	2011	2007-11
	2012	2008-12
	2013	2009-13
	2014	2010-14
	2015	2011-15
	2016	2012-16
	2017	2013-17
	2018	2014-18
	2019	2015-19
Mortalité maternelle (nombres)	1951	1947-50
	1952	1947-51
	1953	Dernière
	1954	1945-53
	1955-1956	Dernière
	1957	1952-56
	1958-1960	Dernière
	1961	1955-60
	1962-1965	Dernière
	1966	1960-65
	1967-1973	Dernière
	1974	1965-73
	1975-1979	Dernière
	1980	1971-79
	1981	1972-80
	1982	1972-81
	1983	1973-82
	1984	1974-83
	1985	1975-84
	1986	1976-85
	1987	1977-86
	1988	1978-87
	1989	1979-88
	1990	1980-89

(Voir notes à la fin de l'index)

P

Index historique
(Voir notes à la fin de l'index)

Sujet	Année de l'édition	Période considérée
	1966	1947-66
	1967	1958-67
	1968	1959-68
	1969	1960-69
	1970	1950-70
	1971	1962-71
	1972	1963-72
	1973	1964-73
	1974	1965-74
	1975	1966-75
	1976	1967-76
	1977	1968-77
	1978	1969-78
	1978SR [i]	1948-78
	1979	1970-79
	1980	1971-80
	1981	1972-81
	1982	1973-82
	1983	1974-83
	1984	1975-84
	1985	1976-85
	1986	1977-86
	1987	1978-87
	1988	1979-88
	1989	1980-89
	1990	1981-90
	1991	1982-91
	1992	1983-92
	1993	1984-93
	1994	1985-94
	1995	1986-95
	1996	1987-96
	1997	1988-97
	1997SR [ii]	1948-97
	1998	1989-98
	1999	1990-99
	2000	1991-00
	2001	1992-01
	2002	1993-02
	2003	1994-03
	2004	1995-04
	2005	1996-05
	2006	1997-06
	2007	1998-07
	2008	1999-08
	2009-2010	2001-10
	2011	2002-11
	2012	2003-12
	2013	2004-13
	2014	2005-14
	2015	2006-15
	2016	2007-16
	2017	2008-17

Sujet	Année de l'édition	Période considérée
	2018	2009-18
	2019	2010-19
Population .... des principales divisions administratives	1952	Dernière
	1955	1945-54
	1962	1955-62
	1963	1955-63 [iii]
	1971	1962-71
	1973	1965-73 [iii]
	1979	1970-79 [iii]
	1983	1974-83
	1988	1980-88 [iii]
	1993	1985-93
Population .... des régions	1949-50	1920-49
	1952	1920-51
	1953	1920-52
	1954	1920-53
	1955	1920-54
	1956	1920-55
	1957	1920-56
	1958	1920-57
	1959	1920-58
	1960	1920-59
	1961	1920-60
	1962	1920-61
	1963	1930-62
	1964	1930-63
	1965	1930-65
	1966	1930-66
	1967	1930-67
	1968	1930-68
	1969	1930-69
	1970	1950-70
	1971	1950-71
	1972	1950-72
	1973	1950-73
	1974	1950-74
	1975	1950-75
	1976	1950-76
	1977	1950-77
	1978	1950-78
	1979	1950-79
	1980	1950-80
	1981	1950-81
	1982	1950-82
	1983	1950-83
	1984	1950-84
	1985	1950-85
	1986	1950-86
	1987	1950-87
	1988	1950-88
	1989	1950-89

Index historique

(Voir notes à la fin de l'index)

Sujet	Année de l'édition	Période considérée
	2008	1999-08
	2009-2010	2001-10
	2011	2002-11
	2012	2003-12
	2013	2004-13
	2014	2005-14
	2015	2006-15
	2016	2007-16
	2017	2008-17
	201	2009-18
	2019	2010-19
Population .... selon les principales divisions administratives	*voir: des principales divisions administratives, ci-dessus*	
Population .... selon la religion et le sexe	1956	1945-55
	1963	1955-63
	1964	1955-64 [iii]
	1971	1962-71
	1973	1965-73 [iii]
	1979	1970-79 [iii]
	1983	1974-83
	1988	1980-88 [iii]
	1993	1985-93
Population .... selon la résidence (urbaine/rurale)	1968	1964-68
	1969	1965-69
	1970	1950-70
	1971	1962-71
	1972	1968-72
	1973	1965-73
	1974	1966-74
	1975	1967-75
	1976	1967-76
	1977	1968-77
	1978	1969-78
	1979	1970-79
	1980	1971-80
	1981	1972-81
	1982	1973-82
	1983	1974-83
	1984	1975-84
	1985	1976-85
	1986	1977-86
	1987	1978-87
	1988	1979-88
	1989	1980-89
	1990	1981-90
	1991	1982-91
	1992	1983-92
	1993	1984-93

Sujet	Année de l'édition	Période considérée
	1994	1985-94
	1995	1986-95
	1996	1987-96
	1997	1988-97
	1998	1989-98
	1999	1990-99
	2000	1991-00
	2001	1992-01
	2002	1993-02
	2003	1994-03
	2004	1995-04
	2005	1996-05
	2006	1997-06
	2007	1998-07
	2008	1999-08
	2009-2010	2001-10
	2011	2002-11
	2012	2003-12
	2013	2004-13
	2014	2005-14
	2015	2006-15
	2016	2007-16
	2017	2008-17
	2018	2009-18
	2019	2010-19
Population .... selon la résidence (urbaine/rurale) et :	1948-1952	Dernière
	1953	1950-52
	1954-1959	Dernière
-féminine: selon le nombre total d'enfants nés vivants et l'âge	1971	1962-71
	1973	1965-73 [iii]
	1975	1965-74
	1978SR [i]	1948-77
	1981	1972-80
	1986	1977-85
	1997SR [ii]	1948-96
-féminine: selon le nombre total d'enfants vivants et l'âge	1971	1962-71
	1973	1965-73 [iii]
	1975	1965-74
	1978SR [i]	1948-77
	1981	1972-80
	1986	1977-85
	1997SR [ii]	1948-96
-fréquentant l'école selon l'âge et le sexe	1971	1962-71
	1973	1965-73 [iii]
	1979	1970-79 [iii]
	1983	1974-83
	1988	1980-88 [iii]
	1993	1985-93
-selon l'âge et le sexe: dénombrée	1963	1955-63
	1964	1955-64 [iii]

R

Index historique

(Voir notes à la fin de l'index)

APPENDICE

Texte spécial de chaque Annuaire démographique

Divorce:

"Application des statistiques de la nuptialité et de la divortialité", 1958.

Mariage:

"Application des statistiques de la nuptialité et de la divortialité", 1958.

Ménages:

"Concepts et définitions des ménages, du chef de ménage et de la population des collectivités", 1987.

Migration:

'"Statistiques des migrations internationales",1977.

Mortalité:

"Tendances récentes de la mortalité", 1951.
"Développement des statistiques des causes de décès",1951.
"Les facteurs du fléchissement de la mortalité",1957.
"Notes sur les méthodes d'évaluation de la fiabilité des statistiques classiques de la mortalité",1961.
"Mortalité: Tendances récentes",1966.
"Tendances de la mortalité chez les personnes âgées",1991VP [v].

Natalité:

"Présentation graphiques des tendances de la fécondité",1959.

"Taux de natalité: Tendances récentes",1965.

Population:

"Tendances démo-graphiques mondiales,1920-1949",1949-50.
"Mouvements d'urbanisation et ses caractéristiques",1952.
"Les recensements de population de 1950",1955.
"Situation démographique mondiale",1956.
"Ce que nous savons de l'état et de l'évolution de la population mondiale",1960.
"Notes sur les statistiques disponibles des recensements nationaux de population et méthodes d'évaluation de leur exactitude",1962.
"Disponibilité et qualité de certaines données statistiques fondées sur les recensements de population effectués entre 1955 et 1963",1963.
"Disponibilité de certaines statistiques fondées sur les recensements de population: 1955-1964",1964.

"Définitions et concepts statistiques de la population urbaine et de la population rurale",1967.
"Application des statistiques de la nuptialité et de la divortialité",1958.
"Ce que nous savons de l'état et de l'évolution de la population mondiale",1970.
"Recommandations de l'Organisation des Nations Unies quant aux sujets sur lesquels doit porter un recensement de population, en regard de la pratique adoptée par les différents pays dans les recensements nationaux effectués de 1965 à 1971",1971.
"Les définitions statistiques de la population urbaine et leurs usages en démographie appliquée",1972.

"Evolution récente de la fécondité dans le monde",1969.
"Dates des recensements nationaux de la population et de l'habitation effectués au cours de la décennie 1965-1974", 1974.

"Dates des recensements nationaux de la population et de l'habitation effectués ou prévus, au cours de la décennie 1975-1984",1979.
"Dates des recensements nationaux de la population et/ou de l'habitation effectués au cours de la décennie 1965-1974 et effectués ou prévus au cours de la décennie1975-1984",1983.
"Définitions et concepts statistiques du ménage",1968.
"Dates des recensements nationaux de la population et/ou de l'habitation effectués au cours de la décennie 1975-1984 et effectués ou prévus au cours de la décennie1985-1994", 1988, 1993.
"Statistiques concernant la population active: un aperçu",1984.
"'Etude du vieillissement et de la situation des personnes âgées: Besoins particuliers",1991VP [v].
"Les incapacités", 1991VP [v].
"Le vieillissement", 1991VP [v].

Notes générales

Cet index alphabétique donne la liste des sujets traités dans chacune de 70 éditions de l'Annuaire démographique. La colonne "Année de l'édition" indique l'édition spécifique dans laquelle le sujet a été traité. Sauf indication contraire, la colonne "Période considérée" désigne les années pour lesquelles les statistiques annuelles apparaissant dans l'Annuaire démographique sont indiquées sous la colonne "Année de l'édition". La rubrique "Dernière" ou " 2-Dernières" indique que les données représentent la ou les dernières années disponibles seulement.

[i] Le Supplément rétrospectif du 30ème Annuaire Démographique fait l'objet d'un tirage spécial publié en 1979.
[ii] Le Supplément rétrospectif du 49ème Annuaire Démographique fait l'objet d'un tirage spécial (CD-ROM) publié en 2000.
[iii] Données non disponibles dans l'édition précédente seulement.
[iv] Titres non disponibles dans la bibliographie précédente seulement.
[v] Vieillissement de la population.
[vi] Taux moyens pour 5 ans.
[vii] Le Supplément du 51 Annuaire Démographique, ayant comme suject la natalité, fait l'objet d'un tirage spécial (CD-ROM) publié en 2002.
[viii] Les tableaux sont publiés en ligne.

SUPPLEMENTAL INDEX OF DATASETS PUBLISHED ONLINE[1]

In recent years, additionally to publishing annually the United Nations *Demographic Yearbook*, several demographic and social datasets are published online via the UNdata portal. UNdata portal is an internet based data service maintained by the Statistics Division of the Department of Economic and Social Affairs of the United Nations. Below is an alphabetical order list of datasets published online as of August 2020 . These datasets can be accessed at http://data.un.org/Explorer.aspx?d=POP.

- City population by sex, city and city type
- Deaths by age, sex and urban/rural residence
- Deaths by cause of death, age and sex
- Deaths by month of death
- Deaths by sex and urban/rural residence
- Divorces by urban/rural residence
- Economically active foreign-born population by occupation, age, sex and urban/rural residence
- Employed population by age, sex and industry
- Employed population by age, sex and marital status
- Employed population by occupation, age and sex
- Employed population by status in employment, age and sex
- Employed population by status in employment, industry and sex
- Employed population by status in employment, occupation and sex
- Female population by age, number of children ever born and urban/rural residence
- Female population by age, number of children living and urban/rural residence
- First marriages by age of groom and bride
- Foetal deaths by gestational age
- Foreign population (non-citizens) 15 years of age or over by country of citizenship, educational attainment and sex
- Foreign population (non-citizens) by country of citizenship, age and sex
- Foreign-born population 15 years of age or over by country/area of birth, educational attainment and sex
- Foreign-born population by country/area of birth, age and sex
- Households by age and sex of reference person and by size of household
- Households by broad types of living quarters/number of roofless by urban/rural location
- Households by broad types of living quarters/number of roofless for selected cities
- Households by type of household and sex and marital status of head of household or other reference member
- Households by type of household, age and sex of head of household or other reference member
- Households in housing units by type of housing unit and availability of communication technology devices/access to Internet for selected cities
- Households in housing units by type of housing unit and tenure of household for selected cities
- Households in housing units by type of housing unit and urban/rural residence
- Households in housing units by type of housing unit for selected cities
- Households in housing units by type of housing unit, availability of communication technology devices/access to Internet by urban/rural location
- Households in housing units by type of housing unit, tenure of household and urban/rural residence
- Infant deaths by sex and urban/rural residence
- Inflows by purpose of staying abroad and sex
- Inflows by reason for admission and sex
- Late foetal deaths by age of woman
- Late foetal deaths by sex and urban/rural residence
- Legally induced abortions by urban/rural residence of woman
- Live births by age of father
- Live births by age of mother and sex of child
- Live births by birth order and age of mother
- Live births by birth order and sex of child
- Live births by birth weight and sex of child
- Live births by gestational age
- Live births by marital status of mother

[1] This supplemental index is available only in English.

- Live births by month of birth
- Live births by plurality
- Live births by sex and urban/rural residence
- Live births in wedlock by duration of marriage
- Living quarters by broad types and urban/rural location
- Living quarters by broad types for selected cities
- Marriages by urban/rural residence
- Marriages cross-classified by previous marital status of husband and wife
- Native and foreign-born population by age, sex and urban/rural residence
- Number of departing international migrants by citizenship status, age and sex
- Number of emigrating citizens by future country of usual residence and sex
- Number of incoming foreign migrants by country of citizenship and sex
- Number of incoming international migrants by previous country of usual residence and sex
- Number of incoming migrants by citizenship status, age and sex
- Occupants of housing units by type of housing unit and number of rooms for selected cities
- Occupants of housing units by type of housing unit and urban/rural residence
- Occupants of housing units by type of housing unit for selected cities
- Occupants of housing units by type of housing unit, number of rooms and urban/rural residence
- Occupied housing units by type of housing unit and availability of kitchen for selected cities
- Occupied housing units by type of housing unit and construction material of outer walls for selected cities
- Occupied housing units by type of housing unit and main source of drinking water for selected cities
- Occupied housing units by type of housing unit and main type of fuel used for cooking for selected cities
- Occupied housing units by type of housing unit and main type of solid waste disposal for selected cities
- Occupied housing units by type of housing unit and number of rooms for selected cities
- Occupied housing units by type of housing unit and type of bathing facilities for selected cities
- Occupied housing units by type of housing unit and type of lighting for selected cities
- Occupied housing units by type of housing unit and type of toilet for selected cities
- Occupied housing units by type of housing unit and type of water supply system for selected cities
- Occupied housing units by type of housing unit and urban/rural location
- Occupied housing units by type of housing unit for selected cities
- Occupied housing units by type of housing unit, availability of kitchen and urban/rural location
- Occupied housing units by type of housing unit, construction material of outer walls and urban/rural residence
- Occupied housing units by type of housing unit, main source of drinking water and urban/rural location
- Occupied housing units by type of housing unit, main type of fuel used for cooking and urban/rural location
- Occupied housing units by type of housing unit, main type of solid waste disposal and urban/rural location
- Occupied housing units by type of housing unit, number of rooms and urban/rural location
- Occupied housing units by type of housing unit, type of bathing facilities and urban/rural location
- Occupied housing units by type of housing unit, type of lighting and urban/rural location
- Occupied housing units by type of housing unit, type of toilet and urban/rural location
- Occupied housing units by type of housing unit, type of water supply system and urban/rural location
- Outflows by purpose of going abroad and sex
- Outflows by status at time of departure and sex
- Population 15 years of age and over, by educational attainment, age and sex
- Population 5 to 24 years of age by school attendance, sex and urban/rural residence
- Population by activity status, age, sex and urban/rural residence
- Population by age, sex and urban/rural residence
- Population by broad types of living quarters/number of roofless and sex for selected cities
- Population by broad types of living quarters/number of roofless, sex and urban/rural residence
- Population by citizenship status, age and sex
- Population by language, sex and urban/rural residence
- Population by literacy, age, sex and urban/rural residence
- Population by marital status, age, sex and urban/rural residence
- Population by national and/or ethnic group, sex and urban/rural residence
- Population by religion, sex and urban/rural residence
- Population by sex and urban/rural residence
- Population by type of living quarters, age and sex
- Population in collective living quarters by type of living quarters and sex for selected cities
- Population in collective living quarters by type of living quarters, sex and urban/rural residence

- Population in households by relation to head of household or other reference member and by age and sex
- Population in households by type of household, age and sex
- Population in households by type of household, age and sex of head of household or other reference member
- Population not economically active by functional category, age, sex and urban/rural residence